AF673452

MPP MASTER PROBLEM PACKAGE

New Pattern JEE Problems

Chemistry

for JEE Main & Advanced

Dr. RK Gupta

arihant

ARIHANT PRAKASHAN (Series), MEERUT

arihant

Arihant Prakashan (Series), Meerut

All Rights Reserved

- **© Author**

No part of this publication may be re-produced, stored in a retrieval system or by any means, electronic, mechanical, photocopying, recording, scanning, web or otherwise without the written permission of the publisher. Arihant has obtained all the information in this book from the sources believed to be reliable and true. However, Arihant or its editors or authors or illustrators don't take any responsibility for the absolute accuracy of any information published and the damage or loss suffered thereupon.

All disputes subject to Meerut (UP) jurisdiction only.

- **Administrative & Production Offices**

Regd. Office
'Ramchhaya' 4577/15, Agarwal Road, Darya Ganj, New Delhi -110002
Tele: 011- 47630600, 43518550

Head Office
Kalindi, TP Nagar, Meerut (UP) - 250002, Tel: 0121-7156203, 7156204

- **Sales & Support Offices**
Agra, Ahmedabad, Bengaluru, Bareilly, Chennai, Delhi, Guwahati, Hyderabad, Jaipur, Jhansi, Kolkata, Lucknow, Nagpur & Pune.

- **ISBN** 978-93-26191-68-5
- **PRICE** ₹845.00

Published by Arihant Publications (India) Ltd.

For further information about the books published by Arihant, log on to www.arihantbooks.com or e-mail at info@arihantbooks.com

Follow us on

CONTENTS

INORGANIC CHEMISTRY

PHYSICAL CHEMISTRY

ORGANIC CHEMISTRY

Inorganic Chemistry

01

Mole Concept

Objective Questions Type I [Only one correct option]

In each of the questions below, four choices are given of which only one is correct.

1. A sample of $CaCO_3$ is 50% pure. On heating 1.12 L of CO_2 (at STP) is obtained. Residue left (assuming non-volatile impurity) is

(a) 7.8 g (b) 3.8 g
(c) 2.8 g (d) 8.9 g

2. In the decomposition of 10 g of $MgCO_3$, 0.1 mole CO_2 and 4.0 g MgO are obtained. Hence, percentage purity of $MgCO_3$ is

(a) 50% (b) 60%
(c) 40% (d) 84%

3. Consider the following pairs,

I. CH_4, C_2H_6 II. CO, CO_2
III. NO, NO_2 IV. H_2O, H_2O_2

In which cases, law of multiple proportion is followed?

(a) I, II (b) I, II, III
(c) I, III, IV (d) I, II, III, IV

4. Two substances I and II of carbon and oxygen have respectively 72.73% and 47.06% oxygen. Hence, they follow

(a) law of multiple proportion
(b) law of reciprocal proportion
(c) law of definite proportion
(d) law of conservation of mass

5. In which case purity of the substance is 100%?

(a) 1 mole of $CaCO_3$ gave 11.2 L CO_2 (at STP)
(b) 1 mole of $MgCO_3$ gave 40.0 g MgO
(c) 1 mole of $NaHCO_3$ gave 4 g H_2O
(d) 1 mole of $Ca(HCO_3)_2$ gave 1 mole CO_2

6. Consider the following laws of chemical combination with examples

I. Law of multiple proportion : N_2O, NO, NO_2
II. Law of reciprocal proportion : H_2O, SO_2, H_2S

Which is correct with examples?

(a) I and II
(b) I only
(c) II only
(d) None of the above

7. H_2S contains 94.11% sulphur; SO_2 contains 50% oxygen and H_2O contains 11.11% hydrogen. Thus,

(a) law of multiple proportion is followed
(b) law of reciprocal proportion is followed
(c) law of conservation of mass is followed
(d) All of the above

8. Sodium combines with $^{35}_{17}Cl$ and $^{37}_{17}Cl$ to give two samples of sodium chloride. Their formation follows the law of

(a) gaseous diffusion (b) conservation of mass
(c) reciprocal proportion (d) None of these

9. Among the following statements, one which was not proposed by Dalton was **[JEE Main 2020]**

(a) chemical reactions involve reorganisation of atoms. These are neither created nor destroyed in a chemical reaction.
(b) when gases combine or reproduced in a chemical reaction they do so in a simple ratio by volume provided all gases are at the same T and P.
(c) all the atoms of a given element have identical properties including identical mass. Atoms of different elements differ in mass.
(d) matter consists of indivisible atoms.

10. The ammonia (NH_3) released on quantitative reaction of 0.6 g urea (NH_2CONH_2) with sodium hydroxide (NaOH) can be neutralised by **[JEE Main 2020]**

(a) 100 mL of 0.2 N HCl
(b) 200 mL of 0.4 N HCl
(c) 200 mL of 0.2 N HCl
(d) 100 mL of 0.1 NHCl

11. $^{35}_{17}Cl$ and $^{37}_{17}Cl$ are two isotopes of chlorine. If average atomic mass is 35.5 then ratio of these two isotopes is
(a) 35 : 37 (b) 1 : 3 (c) 3 : 1 (d) 2 : 1

12. Ionic mass of X^{3-} is 17. If it has 10 electrons, then number of neutrons are
(a) 10 (b) 13 (c) 7 (d) 17

13. M^{2+} ion is isoelectronic of SO_2 and has $(Z+2)$ neutrons (Z is atomic number of M). Thus, ionic mass of M^{2+} is
(a) 70 (b) 66 (c) 68 (d) 64

14. X^+, Y^{2+} and Z^- are isoelectronic of CO_2. Increasing order of protons in X^+, Y^{2+} and Z^- is
(a) $X^+ = Y^{2+} = Z^-$ (b) $X^+ < Y^{2+} < Z^-$
(c) $Z^- < X^+ < Y^{2+}$ (d) $Y^{2+} < X^+ < Z^-$

15. X^-, Y^{2-} and Z^{3-} are isotonic and isoelectronic. Thus, increasing order of atomic number of X, Y and Z is
(a) $X < Y < Z$ (b) $Z < Y < X$
(c) $X = Y = Z$ (d) $Z < X < Y$

16. Number of atoms in increasing order in 1.6 g CH_4, 1.7 g NH_3 and 1.8 g H_2O is
(a) $H_2O = NH_3 = CH_4$ (b) $H_2O < NH_3 < CH_4$
(c) $CH_4 < NH_3 < H_2O$ (d) $CH_4 = NH_3 < H_2O$

17. Which has maximum number of H-atoms per gram of the substance?
(a) CH_4 (b) $CuSO_4 \cdot 5H_2O$
(c) H_2O_2 (d) H_2O

18. If each O-atom has two equivalents, volume of one equivalent of O_2 gas at STP is
(a) 22.4 L (b) 11.2 L
(c) 5.6 L (d) 44.8 L

19. Each drop of H_2O has 0.018 mL at room temperature. Number of H_2O molecules in one drop is
(a) 1×10^{-3} (b) 6.02×10^{20}
(c) 22.4×10^{-3} (d) $6.02 \times 3 \times 10^2$

20. 1 g CH_4 and 4 g of compound X have equal number of moles. Thus, molar mass of X is
(a) 16 g mol^{-1} (b) 32 g mol^{-1}
(c) 4 g mol^{-1} (d) 64 g mol^{-1}

21. Mass of one atom of an element is 6.64×10^{-23} g. This is equal to
(a) 6.64×10^{-23} u (b) 40.0 u
(c) $\frac{1}{40}$ u (d) 6.64 u

22. If Avogadro's number would have been 1×10^{-10}, instead of 6.02×10^{23} then mass of one atom of H would be
(a) 1 u (b) 1×10^{10} u
(c) 6 u (d) 6×10^{13} u

23. Mass of one atom of X is 2.66×10^{-23} g, then its 32 g is equal to
(a) $32 \times 2.66 \times 10^{-23}$ mol
(b) $\frac{32}{2.66 \times 10^{-23} \times 6.02 \times 10^{23}}$ mol
(c) $\frac{32 \times 2.66 \times 10^{-23}}{6.02 \times 10^{23}}$ mol
(d) None of the above

24. Number of mole of $^{12}_{6}C$ in 1 amu is
(a) $\frac{1}{N_0}$ (b) N_0
(c) N_0^2 (d) $\frac{1}{N_0 \times 12}$

25. Mass of one $^{14}_{7}N$-atom is
(a) 14 u (b) 7 u (c) 14 g (d) 7 g

26. If two compounds have same empirical formula but different molecular formula, they must have
(a) same viscosity
(b) same vapour density (VD)
(c) different molecular weight
(d) different percentage composition

27. If the equivalent weight of an element is 32, then the percentage of oxygen in its oxide is
(a) 16 (b) 40 (c) 32 (d) 20

28. A hydrocarbon has 3 g carbon per gram of hydrogen, hence, simplest formula is
(a) CH_4 (b) C_6H_6
(c) C_3H_8 (d) CH_2

29. Molar ratio of Na_2SO_3 and H_2O is 1 : 7 in $Na_2SO_3 \cdot xH_2O$. Hence, their mass percentage is
(a) 12.5 : 87.5 (b) 87.5 : 12.5
(c) 50 : 50 (d) 75 : 25

30. Which has the maximum percentage of chlorine?
(a) $C_6H_6Cl_6$ (b) C_6H_5Cl
(c) CH_3Cl (d) CCl_4

31. In which of the following pairs do the two species resemble each other most closely in chemical properties?
(a) $^{1}_{1}H$ and $^{2}_{1}H$ (b) $^{16}_{8}O$ and $^{16}_{8}O^{2-}$
(c) $^{24}_{12}Mg$ and $^{24}_{12}Mg^{2+}$ (d) $^{14}_{7}N$ and $^{14}_{7}N^{3-}$

32. One isotope of a non-metallic element has mass number 127 and 74 neutrons in the nucleus. The anion derived from the isotope has 54 electrons. Hence, symbol for the anion is
(a) $^{127}_{54}X^-$ (b) $^{127}_{53}X^-$
(c) $^{128}_{53}X^-$ (d) $^{128}_{54}X^-$

33. Which of the following is the richest source of ammonia on a mass percentage basis?
(a) NH_4NO_3 (b) NH_2CONH_2
(c) NH_4Cl (d) $HNC(NH_2)_2$

34. Which of the following substances contains greatest mass of chlorine?
(a) 5.0 g Cl_2 (b) 0.5 mol Cl_2
(c) 0.10 mol KCl (d) 30.0 g $MgCl_2$

35. When 0.273 g of Mg is heated strongly in a nitrogen (N_2) atmosphere, 0.378 g of the compound is formed. Hence, compound formed is
(a) Mg_3N_2 (b) Mg_3N
(c) Mg_2N_3 (d) MgN

36. A certain metal sulphide, MS_2, is used extensively as a high temperature lubricant. If MS_2 has 40.06% sulphur by mass sulphur, metal M has atomic mass
(a) 160 u (b) 64 u (c) 40 u (d) 96 u

37. The molar mass of a compound if 0.372 mole of it has a mass of 186 g, is
(a) 200 g (b) 372 g
(c) 500 g (d) 186 g

38. The most abundant elements by mass in the body of a healthy human adult are oxygen (61.4%); carbon (22.9%), hydrogen (10.0 %); and nitrogen (2.6%). The weight which a 75 kg person would gain if all ^1H atoms are replaced by ^2H atoms is **[JEE Main 2017]**
(a) 15 kg (b) 37.5 kg
(c) 7.5 kg (d) 10 kg

39. Mg_2C_3 (X) is decomposed by H_2O forming a gaseous hydrocarbon (Y). 8.4 g of X gives .... mol of Y.
(a) 0.1 (b) 0.2 (c) 0.3 (d) 0.4

40. Number of atoms in 20 g Ca is equal to number of atoms in
(a) 20 g Mg (b) 1.6 g CH_4
(c) 1.8 g H_2O (b) 1.7 g NH_3

41. $Na_2SO_3 \cdot xH_2O$ has 50% H_2O by mass. Hence, x is
(a) 4 (b) 5
(c) 6 (d) 7

42. Mass of one atom of X is 6.66×10^{-23} g. Hence, number of moles of atom X in 40 kg is
(a) 10^3 mol (b) 10^{-3} mol
(c) $\dfrac{40 \times 10^3}{6.66 \times 10^{-23}}$ mol (d) $\dfrac{40 \times 10^3}{6.022 \times 10^{23}}$ mol

43. To make 0.01 mole which of the following has maximum mass?
(a) $NaHCO_3$ (b) Na_2CO_3
(c) Na_2SO_4 (d) $Na_2C_2O_4$

44. In a glass-tube, there are 18 g of glucose. 0.08 mole of glucose is taken. Glucose left in the glass-tube is
(a) 0.10 g (b) 17.92 g
(c) 3.60 mol (d) 3.60 g

45. Rest mass of an electron is 9.11×10^{-31} kg. Molar mass of the electron is
(a) 1.50×10^{-31} kg mol^{-1} (b) 9.11×10^{-31} kg mol^{-1}
(c) 5.5×10^{-7} kg mol^{-1} (d) 6.02×10^{23} kg mol^{-1}

46. A sample of ammonium phosphate $(NH_4)_3PO_4$ contains 3.18 moles of H-atoms. The number of moles of oxygen atom in the sample is
(a) 0.265 (b) 0.795
(c) 1.06 (d) 3.18

47. A sample of $CuSO_4 \cdot 5H_2O$ contains 3.782 g of Cu. How many grams of oxygen are in this sample? (Cu = 63.5)
(a) 0.952 g (b) 3.80 g
(c) 4.761 g (d) 8.576 g

48. Cortisone is a molecular substance containing 21 atoms of carbon per molecule. The mass percentage of carbon in cortisone is 69.98%. Its molar mass is
(a) 176.5 (b) 252.2 (c) 287.6 (d) 360.1

49. If the dot under a question mark has a mass of 1×10^{-6} g, how many atoms are required to make such a dot? (of carbon)
(a) 5×10^{16} (b) 12×10^{-6}
(c) $\dfrac{10^{-6}}{12}$ (d) $\dfrac{1 \times 10^{-6}}{N_0}$

50. One equivalent of magnesium oxide weighs 20 g then one equivalent of magnesium chloride weighs
(a) 29.75 g (b) 47.5 g (c) 95.0 g (d) 20.0 g

51. A spherical ball of radius 7 cm contains 56% iron. If density is 1.4 g/cm^3, number of moles of Fe present approximately is
(a) 10 (b) 15 (c) 20 (d) 25

52. In the following final result is ...0.1 mole $CH_4 + 3.01 \times 10^{23}$ molecules $CH_4 - 9.6$ g $CH_4 = x$ mole H-atoms
(a) 0 mol H atom (b) 0.2 mol H atom
(c) 0.3 mol H atom (d) 0.4 mol H atom

53. CO, CO_2, C_2O_3 follow
(a) law of definite proportion
(b) law of multiple proportion
(c) law of conservation of mass
(d) All of the above

54. In a gas S and O are 50% by mass, hence, their mole ratio is
(a) 1 : 1 (b) 1 : 2 (c) 2 : 1 (d) 3 : 1

55. Which element has maximum percentage in iron (III) sulphate (IV)?
(a) Iron (b) Sulphur
(c) Oxygen (d) Equal

56. How many moles of oxygen are contained in one litre of air if its volume content is 21% in standard conditions?
(a) 0.21 mol (b) 0.045 mol
(c) 0.067 mol (d) 0.0094 mol

57. The percentage composition of carbon by mole in methane is [JEE Main 2019]
(a) 75% (b) 20% (c) 25% (d) 80%

58. Mass of one atom of the element A is 3.9854×10^{-23} g. How many atoms are contained in 1 g of the element A?
(a) 2.5092×10^{22} (b) 6.022×10^{23}
(c) 3.9854×10^{23} (d) 1.66×10^{-23}

59. Analysis of chlorophyll shows that it contains 2.40 per cent magnesium. Thus, number of atoms in 1 g chlorophyll is
(a) 0.001 (b) 1.00
(c) 6.02×10^{20} (d) 1.445×10^{19}

60. Radius of water molecule is (assuming it spherical)
(a) 19.27 nm (b) 19.27 Å
(c) 192.7 pm (d) 19.27 μm

61. Atoms of the element X are spherical. Each atom of the element (atomic mass 23) is at the corner of the cube and is in contact along the edge length, then edge length is (density $= 6.2 \text{ g cm}^{-3}$)
(a) 2.274 Å (b) 1.137 Å (c) 4.548 Å (d) 1.183 Å

62. A sample of ammonium dihydrogen phosphate (I) contains 3.18 moles of hydrogen atom. The number of moles of oxygen atoms in the sample is
(a) 0.265 (b) 0.795 (c) 1.06 (d) 3.18

63. A sample of copper sulphate pentahydrate contains 3.782 g of Cu. How many grams of oxygen are in the sample?
(a) 0.952 g (b) 3.809 g
(c) 4.761 g (d) 8.576 g

64. The ratio of mass per cent of C and H of an organic compound ($C_xH_yO_z$) is 6 : 1. If one molecule of the above compound ($C_xH_yO_z$) contains half as much oxygen as required to burn one molecule of compound C_xH_y completely to CO_2 and H_2O. The empirical formula of compound $C_xH_yO_z$ is [JEE Main 2018]
(a) $C_3H_6O_3$ (b) C_2H_4O
(c) $C_3H_4O_2$ (d) $C_2H_4O_3$

65. Consider the following cases
I. 60 g CH_3COOH II. 30 g HCHO
III. 60 g NH_2CONH_2 IV. 180 g $C_6H_{12}O_6$
Percentage of carbon is identical in
(a) I, II (b) I, III
(c) I, II, III (d) I, II, IV

66. Ethanol-water mixture has 46 g ethanol in 100 g mixture. By a suitable technique volatile component goes off. Thus,
(a) 3 moles of non-volatile component are left
(b) 9 N_0 atoms of non-volatile component are left
(c) 9 N_0 atoms of volatile component are separated
(d) All the above statements are correct

Objective Questions Type II [One or more than one correct option(s)]

In each of the questions below, four choices are given, of which one or more than one are correct.

1. Which is/are correct about 4.25 g NH_3?
(a) It contains 0.25 mole of NH_3
(b) It contains 0.75 mole of H-atoms
(c) It contains total of 1.0 mole of N and H atoms
(d) It contains 1.5×10^{23} molecules of NH_3

2. Which of the following are isoelectronic of O^{2-}?
(a) N^{3-} (b) F^- (c) Ti^+ (d) Na^+

3. Among the following groupings which represents the collection of isoelectronic species?
(a) NO, CN^-, N_2, O_2^- (b) NO^+, C_2^{2-}, O_2^-, CO
(c) N_2, C_2^{2-}, CO, NO (d) CO, NO^+, CN^-, C_2^{2-}

4. The atomic number of an element is always equal to
(a) number of neutrons in the nucleus
(b) half of the atomic weight
(c) electrical charge of the nucleus
(d) number of protons

5. A bivalent metal ion has equivalent mass of 12. Then
(a) equivalent mass of its oxide is 28
(b) molar mass of its oxide is 40
(c) equivalent mass of its hydride is 13
(d) molar mass of its hydride is 14

6. Volume of a gas at NTP is 1.12×10^{-7} cc. The number of molecules is thus equal to
(a) 3.01×10^{12} (b) 3.01×10^{18}
(c) 3.01×10^{24} (d) 3.01×10^{30}

7. Which of the following may contain one proton and one neutron?
(a) H_2^+ (b) ${}^4_2He$
(c) ${}^2_1D$ (d) ${}^3_1T$

8. ${}^{35}_{17}Cl$ and ${}^{37}_{17}Cl$ differ in
(a) atomic number (b) number of neutrons
(c) number of electrons (d) atomic mass

9. Isoelectronic species are represented by pairs
(a) N^{3-}, O^{2-} (b) CO, CN^-
(c) O_2^{2-}, F_2 (d) O_2^-, CN^-

10. X^- is isoelectronic of CO and has $(Z + 2)$ neutrons (Z = atomic number of X^-). Thus,
(a) ionic mass of X^- is 28
(b) ionic mass of X^- is 30
(c) atomic number of X^- is 13
(d) atomic number of X^- is 14

Numerical Value Questions

All these questions have a Numerical value as their answer, solve the questions and write your answer.

1. If the numeric value has more than two decimal places round off the value to two decimal places. 10^{21} molecules are removed from 200 mg of CO_2. Thus, number of moles of CO_2 left is ...... $\times 10^{-3}$.
2. $Al_2(SO_4)_3 \cdot xH_2O$ has 8.20 per cent Al by mass. The value of x is
3. In addition to carbon monoxide (CO) and carbon dioxide (CO_2), there is a third compound of carbon called carbon suboxide. If a 2.500 g sample of carbon suboxide contains 1.32 g of C and 1.18 g of O, such that the law of multiple proportions is followed. O : C = 1 : =
4. $XHCO_3$ and YCO_3 are two pure substances of equal molar masses decomposing as shown

$$2XHCO_3 \xrightarrow{\Delta} H_2O + CO_2 + X_2CO_3$$
$$YCO_3 \xrightarrow{\Delta} YO + CO_2$$

16.8 g of $XHCO_3$ gave 6.2 g of mixture of H_2O and CO_2. Molecular masses of ...... (i) X = ... (ii) Y = ...

5. Cesium atoms are the largest naturally occurring atoms. The radius of cesium atom is 2.62 Å. How many cesium atoms would have to be laid side by side in 10^7 to give a row of cesium atoms 2.50 cm long? Assume that the atoms are spherical.
6. Calculate the volume occupied at NTP in L by
   (i) 2.5 mole of carbon dioxide
   (ii) 14 g of nitrogen gas
7. Calculate the (i) number of ions, in 10^{22} (ii) number of oxygen atom and (iii) total charge in coulomb in 3 g CO_3^{2-}.
8. A 0.534 g of a sample of haemoglobin on analysis was found to contain 0.34% Fe. If each haemoglobin molecule has four Fe^{2+} ions, what is the molecular mass of haemoglobin in amu? (Fe = 56 amu)
9. The aluminium sulphate hydrate $Al_2(SO_4)_3 \cdot yH_2O$ contains 8.20 per cent Al by mass. The value of y is...... (Al = 27, S = 32, O = 16)
10. The mole fraction of glucose ($C_6H_{12}O_6$) in an aqueous binary solution is 0.1. The mass percentage of water in it, to the nearest integer, is .... **[JEE Main 2020, Sep.]**
11. 6.023×10^{22} molecules are present in 10 g of a substance 'x'. The molarity of a solution containing 5 g of substance 'x' in 2 L solution is ...... $\times 10^{-3}$. **[JEE Main 2020, Sep.]**
12. Complete combustion of 3 g of ethane gives $x \times 10^{22}$ molecules of water. The value of x is .... (Round off to the Nearest Integer). [Use : $N_A = 6.023 \times 10^{23}$; Atomic masses in u : C : 12.0 ; O : 16.0 ; H : 1.0] **[JEE Main 2020, Sep.]**

Comprehension Based Questions

In these questions, a passage has been given followed by questions based on it. You have to answer the questions based on the passage given.

***Passage* 1** *Study the following observations and answer the questions at the end of it.*

The following is a crude but effective method for estimating the order of magnitude of Avogadro's number using stearic acid ($C_{18}H_{36}O_2$). When stearic acid is added to water, its molecules collect at the surface and form a monolayer; that is, the layer is only one molecule thick. The cross-sectional area of each stearic acid molecule has been measured to be 0.21 nm^2.

In one experiment it is found that 1.4×10^{-4} g of stearic acid is needed to form a monolayer over water in a dish of diameter 20 cm. (The area of a circle of radius r is πr^2.)

1. Based on these measurements value of Avogadro's number is
   (a) 3×10^{23} (b) 6×10^{23}
   (c) 4×10^{23} (d) 1×10^{23}
2. What is the equivalent of 1g H in amu for this value of Avogadro's number?
   (a) 1.66×10^{-24} (b) 3.33×10^{-24}
   (c) 2.5×10^{-24} (d) 1×10^{-23}

***Passage* 2** *Read the following passage regarding fertilizer K_2O and answer the questions at the end of it.*

Potash is only potassium mineral that is used for its potassium content. Most of the potash produced in the United States goes into fertilizer. The major sources of potash are potassium chloride (KCl) and potassium sulphate (K_2SO_4). Potash production is often reported as the potassium oxide (K_2O) equivalent or the amount of K_2O that could be made from a given mineral. KCl costs ₹ 50 per kg.

1. What is the cost of K per mole of the KCl sample?
   (a) ₹ 13.42 mol^{-1} (b) ₹ 3.73 mol^{-1}
   (c) ₹ 1.00 mol^{-1} (d) ₹ 2.00 mol^{-1}
2. For what price must K_2SO_4 be sold in order to supply the same amount of potassium as in KCl?
   (a) ₹ 58.40 kg^{-1} (b) ₹ 50.00 kg^{-1}
   (c) ₹ 42.82 kg^{-1} (d) ₹ 25.00 kg^{-1}
3. What mass (in kg) of K_2O contains the same number of moles of K atoms as 1.00 kg KCl?
   (a) 0.158 kg (b) 0.315 kg
   (c) 1.262 kg (d) 0.631 kg

***Passage* 3** The mass spectrum (given below) of magnesium has three peaks, which indicates that magnesium has three isotopes. Questions given below are based on this mass spectrum.

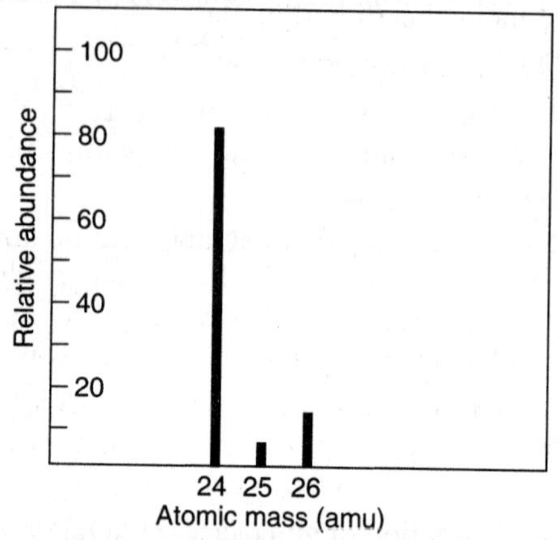

1. Which isotope has maximum number of atoms per gram of each?
   (a) Mg-24 (b) Mg-25
   (c) Mg-26 (d) Equal
2. Number of atoms in one mole of each isotope is placed in increasing order
   (a) $^{25}Mg < ^{26}Mg < ^{26}Mg$ (b) $^{25}Mg < ^{26}Mg < ^{24}Mg$
   (c) $^{26}Mg = ^{25}Mg = ^{24}Mg$ (d) given data is insufficient
3. Average atomic mass of Mg is approximately
   (a) 25.0 (b) 24.3 (c) 25.2 (d) 25.8

***Passage* 4** The equivalent volume is defined as the volume occupied by one equivalent of a substance in the given condition. The equivalent volume of a gaseous substance can be derived from the molar volume.

1. Equivalent volume of O_2 gas at STP is
   (a) 5.6 L (b) 11.2 L (c) 16.8 L (d) 22.4 L
2. Number of hydrogen atoms in H_2 gas in terms of Avogadro's number at STP is
   (a) $2N_0$ (b) $\frac{N_0}{2}$ (c) $\frac{N_0}{4}$ (d) N_0
3. A certain amount of a metal whose equivalent mass is 28 g mol^{-1} displaces 0.7 L of H_2 gas in standard conditions. Thus, mass of the metal is
   (a) 0.07 g (b) 0.70 g (c) 1.75 g (d) 0.875 g

Matrix-Match Type

Given below are Matching Type Questions, with two columns (each having some items) each . Each item of Column I has to be matched with the items of Column II.

1. Match the properties in Column I with the compounds in Column II.

Column I	Column II
A. Identical % of C	1. HCHO
B. Identical % of H	2. $C_6H_{12}O_6$
C. Identical % of O	3. CH_3COOH
D. Same molar mass	4. NH_2CONH_2

2. Match the gases in Column I with their corresponding properties in Column II.

Column I	Column II
A. H_2 gas	1. $2N_0$ atoms per mole
B. O_2 gas	2. Specific heat ratio : 1.40
C. N_2 gas	3. 0.8 L g^{-1} at STP
D. CO gas	4. Lightest gas
E. HCl gas	5. Heaviest gas

3. Match percentage of carbon (in Column I) with the compound (in Column II).

Column I	Column II
A. 20%	1. CH_4
B. 52.2%	2. CO_2
C. 75%	3. C_2H_6O
D. 27.3%	4. CN_2OH_4
E. 12%	5. $CaCO_3$

4. Match the compounds in Column I (1 mole of each) with corresponding properties in Column II.

Column I (1 mole of each)	Column II
A. H_2SO_4	1. 60 g
B. H_3PO_4	2. 98 g
C. H_3PO_3	3. N_0 ionisable H
D. H_3PO_2	4. $2N_0$ ionisable H
E. CH_3COOH	5. $3N_0$ ionisable H
F. N_2H_4CO	6. $4N_0$ H

Single Integer Answer Questions

Answer of these questions is a single digit lying between 0 to 9.

1. Disilane (Si_2H_x) is analysed and found to contain 90.28% silicon by weight. The value of x is ...... (Si = 28)
2. $Na_2SO_3 \cdot zH_2O$ has 50% H_2O by mass. The value of z is ......(Na = 23)
3. In Japan, during earth-quake on April 4, 2011, 0.060 kg of radioactive water leaked into sea from nuclear reactors. How many moles of radioactive water leaked into sea?
4. When 2.495 g of $CuSO_4 \cdot xH_2O$ is heated, 0.05 mole of H_2O is lost forming $CuSO_4$. What is the value of x?
5. Mass of one atom of an element is 6.66×10^{-23} g. How many moles of element are there in 0.320 kg?
6. X^{2-} is isoelectronic of $_{10}Ne$. 1.6 g of X^{2-} has 0.1 mole. The number of neutrons in 1 atoms of X^{2-} is ....
7. Haemoglobin (molar mass 67200) contains 0.33% iron by weight. How many iron atoms are present in one molecule of haemoglobin?
8. The ratio of the mass percentages of 'C' and 'H' and 'C' and 'O' of a saturated acyclic organic compound 'X' are 4 : 1 and 3 : 4 respectively. Then, the moles of oxygen gas required for complete combustion of two moles of organic compound 'X' is .... **[JEE Main 2020, Sep.]**

Answers

Objective Questions Type I [Only one correct option]

1. (a)	2. (d)	3. (d)	4. (a)	5. (b)	6. (a)	7. (b)	8. (d)	9. (b)	10. (a)
11. (c)	12. (a)	13. (a)	14. (c)	15. (b)	16. (b)	17. (a)	18. (c)	19. (b)	20. (d)
21. (b)	22. (a)	23. (b)	24. (d)	25. (a)	26. (c)	27. (d)	28. (a)	29. (c)	30. (d)
31. (a)	32. (b)	33. (d)	34. (b)	35. (a)	36. (d)	37. (c)	38. (c)	39. (a)	40. (b)
41. (d)	42. (a)	43. (c)	44. (d)	45. (c)	46. (c)	47. (d)	48. (d)	49. (a)	50. (b)
51. (c)	52. (a)	53. (b)	54. (b)	55. (c)	56. (d)	57. (b)	58. (a)	59. (c)	60. (c)
61. (a)	62. (c)	63. (d)	64. (d)	65. (d)	66. (d)				

Objective Questions Type II [One or more than one correct option(s)]

1. (a, b, c, d)	2. (a, b, d)	3. (c)	4. (c, d)	5. (b, c)
6. (a)	7. (c)	8. (b, d)	9. (a, b, c)	10. (a, c)

Numerical Value Questions

1. 2.88	2. 18	3. 1.50	4. (i) 23, (ii) 24	5. 4.77
6. (i) 56, (ii) 11.2	7. 3.01	8. 65882.40	9. 18	10. 47
11. 25	12. 18			

Comprehension Based Questions

Passage 1 – 1. (a) 2. (b)
Passage 2 – 1. (b) 2. (c) 3. (d)
Passage 3 – 1. (a) 2. (b) 3. (b)
Passage 4 – 1. (a) 2. (a) 3. (c)

Matrix-Match Type

1. A→ (1,2,3,4); B→ (1,2,3,4); C→ (1,2,3); D→ (3,4)
2. A→ (1,2,4); B→ (1,2,3); C→(1,2,3); D→ (1,2,3); E→ (2,5)
3. A→ (4); B→ (3); C→ (1); D→ (1); E→ (5)
4. A→ (2,4); B→ (2,5); C→ (4); D→ (3); E→ (1,3,6); F→ (6)

Single Integer Answer Questions

1. (6) 2. (7) 3. (3) 4. (5) 5. (8) 6. (8) 7. (4) 8. (5)

Solutions

Objective Questions Type I [Only one correct option]

1. (*a*) $CaCO_3(s) \xrightarrow{\Delta} CaO(s)\downarrow + CO_2(g)\uparrow$

1 mol = 100 g	1 mol = 56 g	22.4 L at STP
0.05 mol = 5 g pure	0.05 mol = 2.8 g	1.12 L at STP

Impure $CaCO_3$ taken = 10 g (5 g pure $CaCO_3$ + 5 g impurity)

CaO(s) left = 2.8 g

Impurity = 5.0 g

Total residue = 7.8 g

2. (*d*) $MgCO_3(s) \xrightarrow{\Delta} MgO(s) + CO_2(g)$

1 mol = 84 g	40 g	1 mol
8.4 g (pure)	4.0 g	0.1 mol
in 10 g sample		

Thus, % of pure $MgCO_3$ = 84%

3. (*d*) I. $\dfrac{\text{C : H mass ratio in } CH_4}{\text{C : H mass ratio in } C_2H_6} = \dfrac{3\text{ g C / gH}}{4\text{ g C / g H}} = 3:4$

II. $\dfrac{\text{C : O mass ratio in CO}}{\text{C : O mass ratio in } CO_2} = \dfrac{6\text{ g C / 16g O}}{6\text{ g C / 32g O}} = 2:1$

III. $\dfrac{\text{N : O mass ratio in NO}}{\text{N : O mass ratio in } NO_2} = \dfrac{14\text{ g N / 10g O}}{14\text{ g N/32g O}} = 2:1$

IV. $\dfrac{\text{H : O mass ratio in } H_2O}{\text{H : O mass ratio in } H_2O_2} = \dfrac{2\text{ g H / 10g O}}{2\text{g H / 32g O}} = 2:1$

Thus, in all cases law of multiple proportion is followed.

4. (*a*)

Substance I	C	O
	27.27	72.73
Mole :	2.2725	4.5456
Ratio :	1 : 2	
Substance II	52.94	47.06
Mole :	4.411	2.94
Ratio :	1.5	1.0
	3 : 1	

5. (*b*) (a) $CaCO_3 \xrightarrow{\Delta} CaO + CO_2$
1 mol → 22.4 L

Actual = 11.2 L

Thus, 50%

(b) $MgCO_3 \xrightarrow{\Delta} MgO + CO_2$
1 mol → 40 g

Thus, 100%

(c) $2NaHCO_3 \xrightarrow{\Delta} Na_2CO_3 + H_2O + CO_2$
2 mol → 18 g
1 mol → 9 g

Actual = 4 g

Thus, 44.4%

(d) $Ca(HCO_3)_2 \xrightarrow{\Delta} CaO + H_2O + 2CO_2$
1 mol → 2 mol

Actual = 1 mol

Thus, 50%

6. (*a*) I. N_2O : NO : NO_2

28 g N/16 g O : 14 g N/16 g O : 14 g N/32 g O

14 g N/8 g O : 14 g N/16 g O : 14 g N/32 g O

4 : 2 : 1

II.

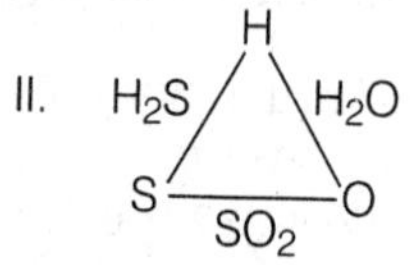

Ratio of H and S in H_2S : 2 g H/32 g S

Ratio of H and O in H_2O : 2 g H/16 g O

Ratio of S and O in SO_2 : 32 g S/32 g O

Thus, law of reciprocal proportion is followed.

Thus, I and II both.

7. (*b*) $\mathbf{H_2S}$ 5.89 g H combines with = 94.11 g S

Hence, 1 g H combines with = 16 g S

$\mathbf{SO_2}$ 50 g O combine with = 50 g S

Hence, 1 g O combines with = 1 g S

$\mathbf{H_2O}$ 11.11 g H combines with = 88.89 g O

1 g H combine with = 8 g O

Thus, law of reciprocal proportion is followed.

8. (*d*) There are two types of NaCl formed. They differ in molar masses due to different isotopes of Cl.

9. (*b*) The postulates given in options (a), (c) and (d) are proposec ⅽy Dalton.

Option (b) is defining the Gay-Lussac's law of combining volumes of gases.

10. (*a*) $\underset{(M=60)}{NH_2CONH_2} + 2\,NaOH \longrightarrow 2\,NH_3 + Na_2CO_3$

No. of moles of urea = Given mass/molar mass

$= \dfrac{0.6}{60} = 0.01\text{ mol } NH_2CONH_2$

∴ It gives 0.02 mol NH_3 as per the equation.

To neutralise it, 0.02 equivalents of HCl needed.

As we know, no. of equivalents of HCl = Normality × Volume

Therefore,

(a) $100 \times 10^{-3} \times 0.2 = 0.02$. (b) $200 \times 10^{-3} \times 0.4 = 0.08$

(c) $200 \times 10^{-3} \times 0.2 = 0.04$ (d) $100 \times 10^{-3} \times 0.1 = 0.01$

Thus, option (a) is correct.

11. (*c*) Average atomic mass $\bar{A} = \dfrac{A_1X_1 + A_2X_2}{X_1 + X_2}$

$35.5 = \dfrac{35X_1 + 37X_2}{X_1 + X_2}$

On solving $\dfrac{X_1}{X_2} = \dfrac{3}{1}$

12. (*a*) X^{3-} has 10 electrons.

Thus, protons (= atomic number) in X^{3-} = 7

neutron + proton = ionic mass = 17

Thus, neutrons = 17 − 7 = 10

13. (*a*) M^{2+} has electrons = 32 (isoelectronic of SO_2)

protons = 34 = Z

neutrons = 36

Thus, ionic mass = 70

14. (*c*) Number of electrons in $CO_2 = 6 + 16 = 22$

	Electrons	Electrons in neutral species = proton
X^+	22	23
Y^{2+}	22	24
Z^-	22	21

Thus, increasing order of proton is $Z^- < X^+ < Y^{2+}$.

15. (*b*) Number of neutrons = number of electrons in X^-, Y^{2-} and Z^{3-}

	Electrons	Z (atomic number)
X^-	E	(E − 1)
Y^{2-}	E	(E − 2)
Z^{3-}	E	(E − 3)

Thus, increasing order of atomic number is $Z < Y < X$.

16. (*b*)

Compound	Number of moles	Molecules	Atoms
CH_4	0.1	$0.1 N_0$	$0.5 N_0$
NH_3	0.1	$0.1 N_0$	$0.4 N_0$
H_2O	0.1	$0.1 N_0$	$0.3 N_0$

17. (*a*)

		H-atoms per gram
(a)	CH_4	$\frac{4N_0}{16} = \frac{N_0}{4} = 0.25 N_0$
(b)	$CuSO_4 \cdot 5H_2O$	$\frac{10N_0}{249.5} = 0.04 N_0$
(c)	H_2O_2	$\frac{2N_0}{34} = 0.0588 N_0$
(d)	H_2O	$\frac{2N_0}{17} = 0.1176 N_0$

18. (*c*) 1 mole O_2 = 2 O-atoms = 4 equivalents oxygen

Volume of 1 mole = 22.4 L at STP

Volume of 1 equivalent = 5.6 L at STP

19. (*b*) 0.018 mL = 0.018 g (density of water = 1g/mL)

$$= \frac{0.018}{18}$$

= 0.001 mol

$= 6.02 \times 10^{20}$ molecules

20. (*d*) $\frac{1\text{g}}{16} CH_4 = \frac{4\text{g}X}{m}$

$m = 64 \text{ g mol}^{-1}$

21. (*b*) Mass of one atom $= 6.64 \times 10^{-23}$ g

Thus, atomic mass $= 6.64 \times 10^{-23} \times 6.02 \times 10^{23} = 40$

22. (*a*) A new Avogadro's number = X

Mass of one H-atom $= \frac{1}{x} = 1$ amu

23. (*b*) Mass of one atom $= 2.66 \times 10^{-23}$ g

Mass of N_0 atoms $= 2.66 \times 10^{-23} \times 6.02 \times 10^{23}$ g mol^{-1}

= atomic mass

Thus, number of moles in 32 g $= \frac{32}{2.66 \times 10^{-23} \times 6.02 \times 10^{23}}$

24. (*d*) 1 mol $^{12}_{6}C$ = 12 g or 1 amu $= \frac{1}{N_0}$

Number of moles in amu $= \frac{1}{12 N_0}$

25. (*a*) N_0 atoms = 14 g or 1 atom $= \frac{14}{N_0} = 14$ amu

26. (*c*) Same empirical formula, it means ratio of atoms is identical. Hence, they differ in molecular weight.

27. (*d*) Equivalent weight of element = 32 g

and that of oxygen = 8 g

Thus, one equivalent of oxide = 40 g

Percentage of oxygen in oxide $= \frac{8}{40} \times 100 = 20\%$

28. (*a*)

Amount	Moles	Ratio
C 3g	$\frac{3}{12} = 0.25$	1
H 1g	$\frac{1}{1} = 1.0$	4

Thus, simplest formula is CH_4.

29. (*c*)

	Na_2SO_3	:	H_2O
Moles	1	:	7
Mass	126		126
Per cent	50		50

30. (*d*) (a) $\text{Cl\%} = \frac{35.5}{35.5 + 12 + 1} = \frac{35.5}{48.5} = \frac{X}{Y}$

(b) $= \frac{35.5}{72 + 5 + 35.5} = \frac{35.5}{112.5}$

(c) $= \frac{35.5}{15 + 35.5} = \frac{35.5}{50.5}$

(d) $= \frac{35.5 \times 4}{12 + 35.5 \times 4} = \frac{35.5}{3 + 35.5} = \frac{35.5}{38.5}$

In all cases value of X = 35.5

Smaller the value of Y, larger the percentage of Cl.

31. (*a*) ^1_1H and ^2_1H are isotopes. Thus, they resemble very closely in their chemical properties.

32. (*b*) $^A_ZX = {}^{A}_{A-N}X = {}^{127}_{127-74}X = {}^{127}_{53}X$

There are 54 electrons. Hence, ionic species is $^{127}_{53}X^-$

33. (*d*) (a) NH_3 in $NH_4NO_3 = \frac{17}{80} = 0.2125$

(b) NH_3 is $NH_2CONH_2 = \frac{34}{62} = 0.5484$

(c) NH_3 in $NH_4Cl = \frac{17}{53.5} = 0.3178$

(d) NH_3 in $HNC(NH_2)_2 = \frac{51}{59 + 4} = 0.8095$

$(NH_2CONH_2 \equiv 2NH_3 - 2H)$

$\therefore$ $NH_2CONH_2 + 2H \equiv 2NH_3$

Similarly, $NHC(NH_2)_2 = 3NH_3 - 4H$

$\therefore$ $NHC(NH_2)_2 + 4H \equiv 3NH_3$

34. (*b*) (a) 5.0 g Cl_2

(b) 0.5 mol $Cl_2 = 0.5 \times 71$ g $= 35.5$ g Cl_2

(c) 0.10 mol KCl = 0.1 mol Cl = 3.55 g Cl

(d) 30.0 g $MgCl_2 = \frac{30.0}{95}$ mol $= 0.2526$ mol $= 17.49$ g Cl_2

35. (*a*) Mass of Mg = 0.273 g

Mass of magnesium and nitrogen compound = 0.378 g

Thus, nitrogen combined = 0.105 g

	Mass	Mole	Mole ratio
Mg	0.273 g	0.011375	1.51 = 3
N	0.105 g	0.0075	1.00 = 2

Thus, Mg_3N_2

36. (*d*) $MS_2 = M + 32 \times 2 = M + 64$

% of sulphur $= \left(\frac{64}{M+64}\right) \times 100 = 40.06$

$\therefore$ $M + 64 = \frac{6400}{40.06}$

$M + 64 = 160 \Rightarrow M = 160 - 64 = 96$

37. (*c*) 0.372 mol = 186 g

1 mol $= \frac{186}{0.372} = 500$ g

38. (*c*) Given, abundance of elements by mass oxygen = 61.4%, carbon = 22.9%, hydrogen = 10% and nitrogen = 2.6%

Total weight of person = 75 kg

Mass due to $^1H = \frac{75 \times 10}{100} = 7.5$ kg

^1H atoms are replaced by ^2H atoms,

Mass due to $^2H = (7.5 \times 2)$ kg

$\therefore$ Mass gain by person = 7.5 kg

39. (*a*) $\underset{(X)}{Mg_2C_3} + H_2O \longrightarrow Mg(OH)_2 + \underset{\substack{(Y) \\ \text{Propyne}}}{CH_3C \equiv CH}$

1 mol — 1 mol

8.4 g

$\frac{8.4}{84} = 0.1$ mol — 0.1 mol

40. (*b*) 20 g Ca $= \frac{20}{40}$ mol $= 0.5$ mol Ca $= 0.5\, N_0$ atoms

(a) 20 g Mg $= \frac{20}{24}$ mol $= 0.833$ mol Mg $= 0.833\, N_0$ atoms

(b) 1.6 g $CH_4 = \frac{1.6}{16}$ mol $= 0.1$ mol $CH_4 = 0.5\, N_0$ atoms

(c) 1.8 g $H_2O = \frac{1.8}{18}$ mol $= 0.1$ mol $H_2O = 0.3\, N_0$ atoms

(d) 1.7 g $NH_3 = \frac{1.7}{17}$ mol $= 0.1$ mol $NH_3 = 0.4\, N_0$ atoms

41. (*d*)

	Mass	Moles	Ratio
Na_2SO_3	= 50	0.3968	1
H_2O	= 50	2.7778	7

Thus, $x = 7$

42. (*a*) Mass of one atom of $X = 6.66 \times 10^{-23}$ g

If atomic mass = A

then mass of one atom $= \frac{A}{N_0}$

$\therefore$ $\frac{A}{N_0} = 6.66 \times 10^{-23}$ g

$A = 6.66 \times 10^{-23} \times N_0$

$= 6.66 \times 10^{-23} \times 6.02 \times 10^{23}$

$= 40$ g mol^{-1}

Hence, 40 kg $X = 40000\, gX = \frac{40000}{40} = 1000$ mol

43. (*c*)

	Molar mass	0.01 mol
(a) $NaHCO_3$	= 84 g	0.84 g
(b) Na_2CO_3	= 106 g	1.06 g
(c) Na_2SO_4	= 142 g	1.42 g
(d) $Na_2C_2O_4$	= 134 g	1.34 g

44. (*d*) 18 g glucose = 0.10 mol glucose

withdrawn = 0.08 mol

left = 0.10 − 0.08 = 0.02 mol = 3.6 g

45. (*c*) Rest mass of electron $= 9.11 \times 10^{-31}$ kg

mass of one mole of electrons $= 9.11 \times 10^{-31} \times 6.02 \times 10^{23}$

$= 5.48 \times 10^{-7}$ kg mol^{-1}

46. (*c*) x mol $(NH_4)_3PO_4 \equiv 12x$ mol H atoms = 3.18 mol

$\therefore$ $x = \frac{3.18}{12} = 0.265$ mol

Thus, O-atoms $= 4x$ mol $= 0.265 \times 4 = 1.06$ mol

47. (*d*) x mol $CuSO_4 \cdot 5H_2O$

$= 249.5x$ g $CuSO_4 \cdot 5H_2O$

$= 63.5\,x$ g Cu $= 3.782$ g Cu

$\therefore$ $63.5\,x = 3.782$

$x = 0.05956$ mol

Every 1 mole of salt has = 9 moles O-atoms

$\therefore$ O-atoms $= 0.05956 \times 9$ mol

$= 0.05956 \times 9 \times 16$ g

$= 8.576$ g O-atoms

48. (*d*) If carbon content is 69.98 g then molar mass = 100 g

If carbon content is 21×12 g then molar mass is

$= \frac{100}{69.98} \times 21 \times 12 = 360.1$ g mol^{-1}

49. (*a*) $\frac{1 \times 10^{-6}}{12} \times N_0 = 5 \times 10^{16}$ atoms

50. (*b*) One equivalent magnesium oxide = 20 g

Since, equivalent mass of O = 8
hence, equivalent mass of Mg = 20 − 8 = 12
Also, equivalent mass of chlorine = 35.5
hence equivalent mass of magnesium chloride = 35.5 + 12
= 47.5

51. (*c*) $\frac{\text{Mass}}{\text{Volume}} = \text{Density}$

$\therefore$ Mass of spherical ball $= V \times d$

$= \frac{4}{3}\pi r^3 \times d$

$= \frac{4}{3} \times \frac{22}{7} \times (7)^3 \times 1.4$

$= 2012.27$ g

Pure Fe content (56%) $= 2012.27 \times \frac{56}{100}$ g $= 1126.87$ g

Thus, moles of Fe = 20.12

52. (*a*) I. 0.1 mol CH_4 = 0.4 mol H-atoms
II. 3.01×10^{23} CH_4 molecules = 0.5 mol CH_4
= 2.0 mol H-atoms
III. 9.6 g CH_4 = 0.6 mol CH_4 = 2.4 mol H-atoms
Thus, I + II − III = 0

53. (*b*) $CO : CO_2 : C_2O_3\ (CO_{1.5})$
1 mol C = 12 g C in CO = 16 g O
= 12 g C in CO_2 = 32 g O
= 12 g C in C_2O_3 = 24 g O
Thus, ratio of O that combines with 12 g C = 2 : 4 : 3

54. (*b*)

	Mass	Moles	Ratio
S	50 g	$\frac{50}{32} = 1.5625$	1
O	50 g	$\frac{50}{16} = 3.125$	2

55. (*c*) Iron (III) Sulphate (IV) is
Fe^{3+} SO_3^{2-} (oxidation of sulphur is = + 4 in SO_3^{2-})
$Fe_2(SO_3)_3$
Fe = 56 × 2 = 112 g
S = 32 × 3 = 96 g
O = 16 × 9 = 144 g

Thus, percentage of O is maximum out of total molar mass of $Fe_2(SO_3)_2$ = 352.

56. (*d*) Oxygen content in 1 L at STP $= \frac{1 \times 21}{100} = 0.21$ L
22.4 L at STP = 1 mol
hence 0.21 L at STP $= \frac{1 \times 0.21}{22.4} = 0.009375$ mol

57. (*b*) The percentage composition of a compound is given by the formula.
% composition = [Composition of a substance in a compound / Total composition total of compound] ×100
In CH_4, mole of carbon = 1
mole of hydrogen = 4

$\therefore$ % of carbon by mole in $CH_4 = \frac{1}{1+4} \times 100 = 20\%$

58. (*a*) 3.9854×10^{-23} g = 1 atom

Thus, $1\text{ g} = \frac{1}{3.9854 \times 10^{-23}}$ atoms

$= 2.5092 \times 10^{23}$ atoms

59. (*c*) Mg in 1 g chlorophyll $= \frac{1 \times 2.4}{100}\text{ g} = \frac{1 \times 2.4}{100 \times 24}$ mol

$= \frac{1 \times 2.4 \times 6.02 \times 10^{23}}{100 \times 24}$ atoms

$= 6.02 \times 10^{20}$ atoms

60. (*c*) Density of water molecule = 1 g/mL
1 g = 1 mL

Thus, $\frac{1}{18}$ mol = 1 mL

$\frac{1}{18} \times 6.02 \times 10^{23}$ molecules = 1 mL

Thus, volume of 1 molecule $= \frac{18}{6.02 \times 10^{23}}$

$= 3 \times 10^{-23}$ mL

Volume of one spherical molecule $= \frac{4}{3}\pi r^3$

$\frac{4}{3}\pi r^3 = 3 \times 10^{-23}$ cm^3

$\therefore$ $r^3 = \frac{3 \times 3 \times 10^{-23}}{4\pi}$ cm^3

$r^3 = 7.162 \times 10^{-23}$ cm^3

$r = 1.927 \times 10^{-8}$ cm

$= 1.927 \times 10^{-10}$ m = 1.927 Å

$= \frac{1.927 \times 10 \times 10^{-10}}{10}$ m

= 0.1927 nm

$= \frac{1.927 \times 100 \times 10^{-10}}{100}$ m

$= 192.7 \times 10^{-12}$ m = 192.7 pm

61. (*a*) Edge length = $AB = 2r$

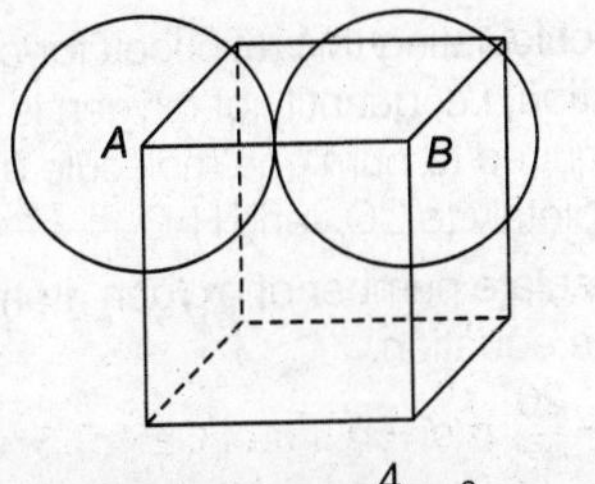

Volume of the spherical atom $= \frac{4}{3}\pi r^3$

$\frac{\text{Mass}}{\text{Volume}} = \text{Density}$

$\text{Volume} = \frac{\text{Mass}}{\text{Density}}$

Mass of one atom $= \frac{m}{N_0} = \frac{23}{6.02 \times 10^{23}}$

$$\therefore \quad \text{Volume} = \frac{23}{6.023 \times 10^{23} \times 6.20}$$

$$\frac{4}{3}\pi r^3 = \frac{23}{6.02 \times 10^{23} \times 6.2}$$

$$r^3 = \frac{3 \times 23}{4\pi \times 6.02 \times 10^{23} \times 6.2}$$

$$r^3 = 1.47 \times 10^{-24} \text{ cm}^3$$

$$r = 1.137 \times 10^{-8} \text{ cm}$$

$$2r = 2.274 \times 10^{-8} \text{ cm} = 2.274 \text{ Å}$$

62. (**c**) Oxidation number of P in phosphate (I) = +1

Thus, anion is : $H_2PO_2^-$

Thus, salt is $NH_4H_2PO_2$

(Ammonium hypophosphite)

$$6 \text{ mol H} \equiv 1 \text{ mol } NH_4H_2PO_2 = 2 \text{ mol (O)}$$

Thus, $\quad 3.18 \text{ mol H} = \frac{2 \times 3.18}{6} \text{ mol (O)} = 1.06 \text{ mol (O)}$

63. (**d**) $CuSO_4 \cdot 5H_2O$

1 mol solute ≡ 1 mol (Cu) ≡ 10 mol (H) ≡ 9 mol (O)

$$63.5 \text{ g (Cu)} = 9 \times 16 \text{ g (O)}$$

Thus, $\quad 3.782 \text{ g (Cu)} = \frac{9 \times 16 \times 3.782}{63.5} \text{ g (O)}$

$$= 8.5765 \text{ g}$$

64. (**d**) We can calculate the simplest whole number ratio of C and H from the data given, as

Element	Relative mass	Molar mass	Relative mole	Simplest whole number ratio
C	6	12	$\frac{6}{12} = 0.5$	$\frac{0.5}{0.5} = 1$
H	1	1	$\frac{1}{1} = 1$	$\frac{1}{0.5} = 2$

Alternatively this ratio can also be calculated directly in the terms of x and y as

$$\frac{12x}{y} = \frac{6}{1} \text{ (given and molar mass of C = 12, H = 1)}$$

Now, after calculating this ratio look for condition 2 given in the question, i.e. quantity of oxygen is half of the quantity required to burn one molecule of compound C_xH_y completely to CO_2 and H_2O.

We can calculate number of oxygen atoms from this as consider the equation.

$$C_xH_y + \left[x + \frac{y}{4}\right]O_2 \longrightarrow xCO_2 + \frac{y}{2}H_2O$$

Number of oxygen atoms required $= 2 \times \left[x + \frac{y}{4}\right] = \left[2x + \frac{y}{2}\right]$

Now given, $z = \frac{1}{2}\left[2x + \frac{y}{2}\right] = \left[x + \frac{y}{4}\right]$

Here we consider x and y as simplest ratios for C and H so now putting the values of x and y in the above equation.

$$z = \left[x + \frac{y}{4}\right] = \left[1 + \frac{2}{4}\right] = 1.5$$

Thus, the simplest ratio figures for x, y and z are $x = 1$, $y = 2$ and $z = 1.5$

Now, put these values in the formula given

i.e. $\quad C_xH_yO_z = C_1H_2O_{1.5}$

So, empirical formula will be $[C_1H_2O_{1.5}] \times 2 = C_2H_4O_3$

65. (**d**) Percentage is irrespective of amount given

I. $\quad CH_3COOH \equiv 2C$

60 g $\quad$ 24 g

$$C_{\%} = \frac{24 \times 100}{60} = 40$$

II. $\quad HCHO \equiv 1\ C$

30 g $\quad$ 12 g

$$C_{\%} = \frac{12 \times 100}{30} = 40$$

III. $\quad NH_2CONH_2 \equiv 1C$

60 g $\quad$ 12 C

$$C\% = \frac{12 \times 100}{60} = 20$$

IV. $\quad C_6H_{12}O_6 \equiv 6\ C$

180 g $\quad$ 72 g

$$C_{\%} = \frac{72 \times 100}{180} = 40$$

Thus, I, II and IV.

66. (**d**) Volatile component is $CH_3CH_2OH = 46 \text{ g} = \frac{46}{46} = 1 \text{ mol}$

1 mole = N_0 molecules

$= 9N_0$ atoms thus, (c) is correct.

Non-volatile component is $H_2O = 54 \text{ g} = \frac{54}{18} = 3$ moles

Thus, (a) is correct $= 3N_0$ atoms

Thus, (b) is correct.

02

Chemical Equations *and* Reaction Stoichiometry

Objective Questions Type I [Only one correct option]

In each of the questions below, four choices are given of which only one is correct.

1. Number of moles of NH_3 formed when 0.535 g of NH_4Cl is completely decomposed by NaOH, is

$$NH_4Cl + NaOH \longrightarrow NH_3 + NaCl + H_2O$$

(a) 0.01 mol (b) 5.35 mol
(c) 1.7 g (d) 0.17 mol

2. 44.8 L of CO_2 at NTP is obtained by heating x g of pure $CaCO_3 \cdot x$ is

(a) 100 g (b) 200 g
(c) 50 g (d) 44.8 g

3. 10 L of hard water with temporary hardness [of $Ca(HCO_3)_2$] required 0.56 g of lime

$$Ca(HCO_3)_2 + CaO \longrightarrow 2CaCO_3 + H_2O$$

Temporary hardness in terms of ppm of $CaCO_3$ is

(a) 56 (b) 1/2 (c) 100 (d) 200

4. $2KClO_3 \longrightarrow 2KCl + 3O_2$. 5.0 g of $KClO_3$ gave 0.03 mole of O_2. Hence, percentage purity of $KClO_3$ is

(a) 49% (b) 50%
(c) 95% (d) 98%

5. $CaCO_3$ is decomposed by HCl (density 1.825 g/cc)

$$CaCO_3 + 2HCl \longrightarrow CaCl_2 + H_2O + CO_2$$

Volume of HCl required to decompose 10 g of 50% pure $CaCO_3$ is

(a) 1.825 mL (b) 3.65 mL
(c) 0.9125 mL (d) 2 mL

6. 100 mL of 20.8% $BaCl_2$ solution and 50 mL of 9.8% H_2SO_4 solution will form $BaSO_4$

(Ba = 137, Cl = 35.5, S = 32, H = 1, O = 16)

$$BaCl_2 + H_2SO_4 \longrightarrow BaSO_4 + 2HCl$$

(a) 23.3 g (b) 11.65 g
(c) 30.6 g (d) None of these

7. 1.70 g $AgNO_3(aq)$ reacts with 5.85 g $NaCl(aq)$ to form AgCl (white ppt.) [Ag = 108 u]

(a) 14.35 g (b) 0.1435 g
(c) 1.435 g (d) 5.85 g

8. When 10 g $CaCO_3$ reacts with 20 g $BaCl_2$

$$BaCl_2 + CaCO_3 \longrightarrow BaCO_3 + CaCl_2$$

then limiting reactant is

(a) $CaCO_3$ (b) $BaCl_2$
(c) $CaCl_2$ (d) None of these

9. In the following reaction,

$$3Ba(NO_3)_2 + 2Na_3PO_4 \longrightarrow Ba_3(PO_4)_2 + 6NaNO_3$$

2 moles each of $Ba(NO_3)_2$ and Na_3PO_4 form $Ba_3(PO_4)_2$

(a) 1 mol (b) 1/3 mol
(c) 2/3 mol (d) 4 mol

10. For complete reaction in (Q. 9) above which reactant is further required?

(a) 1 mol $Ba(NO_3)_2$ (b) 1 mol Na_3PO_4
(c) 2 mol $Ba(NO_3)_2$ (d) 2 mol Na_3PO_4

11. In the following reaction,

$$MnO_2 + 4HCl \longrightarrow MnCl_2 + 2H_2O + Cl_2$$

2 moles MnO_2 react with 4 moles of HCl to form 11.2 L Cl_2 at STP. Thus, per cent yield of Cl_2 is

(a) 25% (b) 50%
(c) 100% (d) 75%

12.

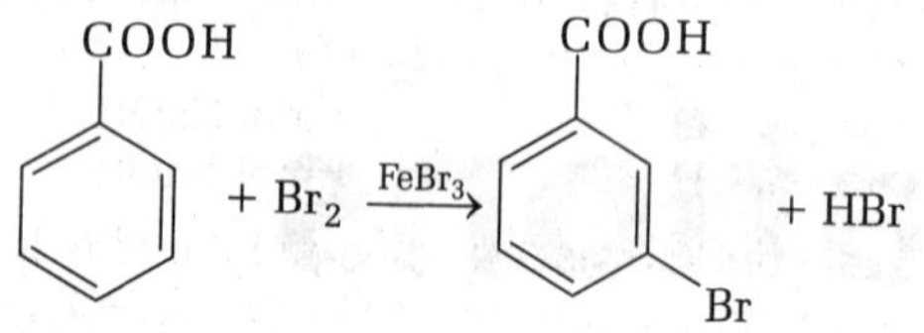

Consider the above reaction where 6.1 g of benzoic acid is used to get 7.8 g of *m*-bromo benzoic acid. The percentage yield of the product is .... (Round off to the Nearest Integer) [Given, Atomic masses : C = 12.0 u, H : 1.0 u, O : 16.0 u, Br = 80.0 u]

(a) 78 (b) 80 **[JEE Main 2019, March]**
(c) 87 (d) 60

13. For the following reaction, the mass of water produced from 445 g of $C_{57}H_{110}O_6$ is

$$2C_{57}H_{110}O_6(s) + 163O_2(g) \longrightarrow 114CO_2(g) + 110\ H_2O(l)$$

(a) 490 g (b) 495 g **[JEE Main 2019, Jan.]**
(c) 445 g (d) 890 g

14. Per cent yield of NH_3 in the following reaction is 80%

$$NH_2CONH_2 + 2NaOH \xrightarrow{\Delta} Na_2CO_3 + 2NH_3$$

6 g NH_2CONH_2 reacts with 8 g NaOH to form NH_3

(a) 3.4 g (b) 2.72 g
(c) 4.25 g (d) 11.2 g

15. 100 mL solution of NaOH (containing 4 g NaOH per litre) and 50 mL of HCl (containing 7.3 g HCl per litre) react as

$$NaOH(aq) + HCl(aq) \longrightarrow NaCl(aq) + H_2O(l)$$

0.5 g of NaCl is formed. Thus, unreacted NaOH is

(a) 0.058 g (b) 3.66 g
(c) 10.8 g (d) 0.63 g

16. Al and $KClO_3$ react together to form Al_2O_3 according to

$$2KClO_3 \longrightarrow 2KCl + 3O_2$$
$$4Al + 3O_2 \longrightarrow 2Al_2O_3$$

4 moles of $KClO_3$ (50% pure) on reaction with excess of Al form how many moles of Al_2O_3?

(a) 2 mol (b) 4 mol
(c) 6 mol (d) 8 mol

17. NaOH is formed according to reaction

$$2Na + \frac{1}{2}O_2 \longrightarrow Na_2O$$
$$Na_2O + H_2O \longrightarrow 2NaOH$$

To make 4 g NaOH, Na required is

(a) 4.6 g (b) 4.0 g
(c) 2.3 g (d) 0.23 g

18. NH_3 is formed in the following steps

I. $Ca + 2C \longrightarrow CaC_2$ 50% yield
II. $CaC_2 + N_2 \longrightarrow CaCN_2 + C$ 100% yield
III. $CaCN_2 + 3H_2O \longrightarrow 2NH_3 + CaCO_3$ 50% yield

To obtain 2 moles NH_3, calcium required is

(a) 1 mol (b) 2 mol
(c) 3 mol (d) 4 mol

19. $MnO_2 + 2KClO_3 \longrightarrow K_2MnO_4 + Cl_2 + 2O_2$
$Cl_2 + K_2MnO_4 \longrightarrow 2KCl + MnO_2 + O_2$

Each reaction takes place to the extent of 50%. 11.2 L of O_2 at STP is obtained from $KClO_3$ using

(a) 0.67 mol (b) 1.12 mol
(c) 1.33 mol (d) 2.66 mol

20. NaOH can be prepared by two methods each with two steps having 100% extent.

I. $2Na + 2H_2O \longrightarrow 2NaOH + H_2$
$2H_2 + O_2 \longrightarrow 2H_2O$

II. $2Na + \frac{1}{2}O_2 \longrightarrow Na_2O$
$Na_2O + H_2O \longrightarrow 2NaOH$

Which gives the better yield?

(a) Only I (b) Only II
(c) Both equal (d) None is suitable

21. Sulphur forms the chlorides S_2Cl_2 and SCl_2. The equivalent mass of S in SCl_2 is 16 g mol^{-1}. Thus, equivalent mass of S in S_2Cl_2 is

(a) 8 g (b) 32 g (c) 16 g (d) 64 g

22. 36.6 g of the crystal hydrate of barium chloride when roasted lose 5.4 g in mass. Thus, salt is [Ba = 137]

(a) $BaCl_2 \cdot 5H_2O$ (b) $BaCl_2 \cdot 4H_2O$
(c) $BaCl_2 \cdot 3H_2O$ (d) $BaCl_2 \cdot 2H_2O$

23. When a mixture consisting of 10 moles of SO_2 and 15 moles of O_2 was passed over a catalyst, 8 moles of SO_3 were formed. Thus, percentage yield of SO_3 w.r.t. SO_2 is

(a) 80% (b) 100% (c) 50% (d) 25%

24. 3.9 g of a mixture of aluminium and its oxide on reaction with aqueous solution of sodium hydroxide, gave 840 mL of a gas under standard conditions. Thus, aluminium content in the mixture is

(a) 3.225 g (b) 0.675 g
(c) 1.35 g (d) 2.70 g

25. Water gas consisting of equal volumes of CO and H_2 is produced when water vapour is passed over red hot coal. Volume of water gas produced under standard state when 3.0 kg of coal is treated for water gas is

(a) 5.6×10^2 L (b) 11.2×10^3 L
(c) 2.8×10^2 L (d) 22.4×10^3 L

26. The decomposition of $CaCO_3$ yielded 11.2 L of CO_2. The mass of KOH required to combine with CO_2 to form carbonate is
(a) 56 g (b) 112 g
(c) 28 g (d) 11.2 g

27. A metal displaced 16.8 mL of H_2 (in standard conditions) from an acid. Volume of N_2 needed to combine with this amount of H_2 into NH_3 is
(a) 11.2 mL (b) 5.6 mL
(c) 8.4 mL (d) 22.4 mL

28. The empirical formula of a compound of carbon with hydrogen is CH_2. 1 L of this gaseous compound has mass equal to that of 1 L N_2 under standard state. Thus, molecular formula of the compound is
(a) C_3H_6 (b) C_2H_4
(c) C_4H_8 (d) C_5H_{10}

29. 1.056 g of the Sn was treated with 1.947 g of I_2. After reaction was over, 0.601 g of Sn was recovered. Thus, empirical formula of the compound formed is (Sn = 119, I = 127)
(a) SnI_2 (b) SnI
(c) SnI_3 (d) SnI_4

30. A mixture of $CuSO_4$ and $CuSO_4 \cdot 5H_2O$ has a mass of 1.245 g. After heating to drive off the water, the mass is only 0.882 g. Thus, mass per cent of $CuSO_4$ is
(a) 19.2% (b) 80.8%
(c) 38.4% (d) 71.6%

31. What mass of CO_2 could be formed by the reaction of 16 g CH_4 with 48 g of O_2?

$$CH_4 + 2O_2 \longrightarrow CO_2 + 2H_2O$$

(a) 44 g (b) 33 g
(c) 16 g (d) 24 g

32. For the formation of 5.00 moles of water, which reaction uses the most nitric acid?
(a) $3Cu + 8HNO_3 \longrightarrow 3Cu(NO_3)_2 + 2NO + 4H_2O$
(b) $Al_2O_3 + 6HNO_3 \longrightarrow 2Al(NO_3)_3 + 3H_2O$
(c) $4Zn + 10HNO_3 \longrightarrow 4Zn(NO_3)_2 + NH_4NO_3 + 3H_2O$
(d) $Cu + 4HNO_3 \longrightarrow Cu(NO_3)_2 + 2NO_2 + 2H_2O$

33. 1 mole of SO_2Cl_2 is dissolved in water and $Ca(OH)_2$ is added to neutralise acidic solution. Moles of $Ca(OH)_2$ required are
(a) 2 (b) 3 (c) 4 (d) 5

34. 0.5 mole of $BaCl_2$ is mixed with 0.2 mole of $(NH_4)_3PO_4$. Maximum number of moles of barium phosphate formed in this reaction is
(a) 0.1 (b) 0.2
(c) 0.3 (d) 0.5

35. 1 g of a carbonate (M_2CO_3) on treatment with excess HCl produces 0.01186 mole of CO_2. The molar mass of M_2CO_3 in g mol^{-1} is **[JEE Main 2017 (Offline)]**
(a) 1186 (b) 84.3
(c) 118.63 (d) 11.86

36. In the following reaction,

$$2H_2S + SO_2 \longrightarrow 2H_2O + 3S$$

1 mole each of SO_2 and H_2S will give sulphur
(a) 1 mol (b) 3 mol
(c) 1.5 mol (d) 2 mol

37. 1 mole BaF_2 is treated with 2 moles of H_2SO_4. To make the resulting mixture neutral, NaOH is added. NaOH required in this process is
(a) 4 mol NaOH (b) 2 mol NaOH
(c) 3 mol NaOH (d) 1 mol NaOH

38. If 0.5 mol of $CaBr_2$ is mixed with 0.2 mol of K_3PO_4, the maximum number of moles of $Ca_3(PO_4)_2$ that can be formed is
(a) 0.1 (b) 0.2 (c) 0.5 (d) 0.7

39. When 35 mL of 0.15 M lead nitrate solution is mixed with 20 mL of 0.12 M chromic sulphate solution, ... $\times 10^{-5}$ moles of lead sulphate precipitate out. (Round off to the Nearest Integer).
(a) 525 (b) 5.25
(c) 675 (d) 675

40. Permanent hardness is due to SO_4^{2-} and Cl^- of Ca^{2+} and Mg^{2+} and is removed by the addition of Na_2CO_3

$$CaSO_4 + Na_2CO_3 \longrightarrow CaCO_3 + Na_2SO_4$$

$$CaCl_2 + Na_2CO_3 \longrightarrow CaCO_3 + 2NaCl$$

If hardness is 100 ppm $CaCO_3$, amount of Na_2CO_3 required to soften 10 L of hard water is
(a) 2.12 g (b) 0.106 g
(c) 10.6 g (d) 1.06 g

41. All the oxygen in a 0.5434 g sample of a pure oxide of iron is removed by reduction in a stream of H_2. The loss in weight is 0.1210 g. Hence, formula of the iron oxide is (Fe = 56)
(a) FeO (b) Fe_2O_3
(c) Fe_3O_4 (d) FeO_2

42. A certain sample of phosphate rock contains 26.26% P_2O_5. A 0.5428 g sample is analysed by precipitating $MgNH_4PO_4 \cdot 6H_2O$ and igniting the precipitate to $Mg_2P_2O_7$. Thus, $Mg_2P_2O_7$ obtained is
(a) 0.8486 g (b) 0.1424 g
(c) 0.3648 g (d) 0.2228 g

43. The calcium in a 0.8432 g sample is precipitated as CaC_2O_4. The precipitate is washed, ignited to $CaCO_3$ and found to weigh 0.3462 g. Percentage of CaO in the sample is
(a) 11.5% (b) 23%
(c) 18% (d) 46%

44. Number of millilitres of a 1.6% $BaCl_2$ (*w*/*V*) solution which is required to precipitate the sulphur as $BaSO_4$ in a 0.60 g sample that contains 12% S is
(a) 58.50 mL (b) 14.63 mL
(c) 29.25 mL (d) 21.00 mL

45. An iron sample contains 18% Fe_3O_4. What is the amount so that it is precipitated as Fe_2O_3 which weighs 0.40 g?
(a) 2.15 g (b) 1.075 g
(c) 4.30 g (d) 2.01 g

46. An aqueous solution of glucose is 10%. The volume in which 1 mol of it is dissolved will be
(a) 0.9 L (b) 9 L (c) 1.8 L (d) 18 L

47. In diammonium phosphate $(NH_4)_2HPO_4$, the percentage of P_2O_5 is
(a) 35.87 (b) 46.44
(c) 51.99 (d) 53.78

48. The oxide of an element contains 67.67% of oxygen. Equivalent weight of the element is
(a) 2.46 (b) 3.82
(c) 4.36 (d) 4.96

49. Which pair has same percentage of carbon?
(a) CH_3COOH and $C_6H_{12}O_6$
(b) CH_3COOH and $C_{12}H_{22}O_{11}$
(c) CH_3COOH and C_2H_5OH
(d) $C_6H_{12}O_6$ and $C_{12}H_{22}O_{11}$

50. The mass of 70% H_2SO_4 required for neutralisation of 1 mole of NaOH is
(a) 70 g (b) 35 g
(c) 30 g (d) 95 g

51. 1000 g $CaCO_3$ solution contains 10 g carbonate. The concentration of solution as carbonate is
(a) 10 ppm (b) 100 ppm
(c) 1000 ppm (d) 10000 ppm

52. 800 g of a 40% solution by weight was cooled. 100 g of solute precipitated. The percentage composition of remaining solution is
(a) 31.4% (b) 20.0%
(c) 23.0% (d) 24%

53. The hydrogen phosphate of certain metal has $MHPO_4$ formula. The formula of metal chloride is
(a) MCl (b) M_2Cl
(c) MCl_3 (d) MCl_2

54. A bivalent metal has 37.2 equivalent weight. The molecular weight of its chloride is
(a) 216.6 (b) 148.8
(c) 145.4 (d) 172.8

55. A boy drinks 500 mL of 9% glucose solution. The number of glucose molecules he has consumed is [mol. wt. of glucose = 180]
(a) 0.5×10^{23} (b) 1.0×10^{23}
(c) 1.5×10^{23} (d) 2.0×10^{23}

56. An aqueous solution of NaCl is 5.85%. The volume in which 1 mole of it is dissolved will be
(a) 1 L (b) 10 L
(c) 5.85 L (d) 58.5 L

57. A 500 g toothpaste contains 0.2 g fluoride. The concentration of fluoride in terms of ppm is
(a) 100 (b) 250 (c) 400 (d) 450

58. The amount of zinc (atomic weight = 65) necessary to produce 224 mL of H_2 by the reaction with an acid will be
(a) 0.65 g (b) 6.5 g
(c) 0.065 g (d) 65 g

59. Mixture containing 1 mole each of $NaHCO_3$, Li_2CO_3 and Na_2CO_3 is heated strongly. CO_2 formed in this process will be
(a) 3.0 mol (b) 2.5 mol
(c) 1.0 mol (d) 1.5 mol

60. $2C + O_2 \longrightarrow 2CO$. In this reaction the mass of carbon will be used up in forming 11.2 L of CO at NTP is
(a) 0.6 g (b) 6 g (c) 12 g (d) 24 g

61. When 8.3 g copper sulphate (249.5) reacts with excess of potassium iodide then the amount of iodine liberated is
(a) 42.3 g (b) 24.3 g
(c) 4.23 g (d) 2.43 g

62. From the complete decomposition of 20 g $CaCO_3$ at STP, the volume of CO_2 obtained is
(a) 2.24 L (b) 4.48 L
(c) 20 L (d) 22.4 L

63. The weight of lime obtained by heating 200 kg of 95% pure lime stone is
(a) 98.4 kg (b) 106.4 kg
(c) 112.8 kg (d) 122.6 kg

64. The percentage of chlorine in $KClO_2$ is
(a) 15.5 (b) 33.3 (c) 17.7 (d) 47.7

65. In the chemical reaction between stoichiometric quantities of $KMnO_4$ and KI in weakly basic solution, what is the number of moles of I_2 released for 4 moles of $KMnO_4$ consumed?
(a) 7 (b) 4 (c) 5 (d) 6

66. Silver metal reacts with chlorine (Cl_2) to yield silver chloride. If 2.00 g of Ag react completely with 0.657 g of Cl_2, empirical formula of silver chloride formed is
(a) $AgCl_2$ (b) Ag_2Cl
(c) $AgCl$ (d) $AgCl_3$

67. If 5.0 g of Al react with 4.45 g of oxygen empirical formula of aluminium oxide is
(a) Al_2O_3 (b) AlO_2
(c) Al_2O (d) AlO_3

68. .... grams of 3-hydroxy propanal ($M_W = 74$) must be dehydrated to produce 7.8 g of acrolein ($M_W = 56$) (C_3H_4O) if the percentage yield is 64. (Round off to the Nearest Integer). [Given : Atomic masses : C : 12.0 u, H : 1.0 u, O : 16.0 u] **[JEE Main 2021, March]**
(a) 12 (b) 13 (c) 14 (d) 16

69. A certain metal sulphide MS_2 is used extensively as a high temperature lubricant. If MS_2 is 40.00% by mass sulphur, atomic mass of M is
(a) 60 (b) 96 (c) 100 (d) 80

70. In the following reaction (B = 11)

$$\underset{6.75\,g}{B_2H_6} + \underset{8.55\,g}{2NaH} \longrightarrow 2NaBH_4$$

	Limiting reactant	Excess reactant
(a)	B_2H_6	NaH = 1.80 g
(b)	NaH	B_2H_6 = 1.76 g
(c)	B_2H_6	NaH = 0.90 g
(d)	Equal	None

71. Assuming fully decomposed, the volume of CO_2 released at STP on heating 9.85 g of $BaCO_3$ (Atomic mass, Ba = 137) will be
(a) 1.12 L (b) 0.84 L (c) 2.24 L (d) 4.06 L

72. Percentage of Se in peroxidase anhydrous enzyme is 0.5% by weight (At. wt. 78.4) then minimum molecular weight of peroxidase anhydrous enzyme is
(a) 1.568×10^4 (b) 1.568×10^3
(c) 15.68 (d) 2.168×10^4

73. The number of moles of oxygen obtained by the electrolytic decomposition of 90 g water is
(a) 2.5 (b) 5 (c) 7.5 (d) 10

74. 4.4 g of CO_2 contains how many litres of CO_2 at STP?
(a) 2.4 L (b) 2.24 L (c) 44 L (d) 22.4 L

75. To prepare a solution of concentration of 0.03 g/mL of $AgNO_3$, what amount of $AgNO_3$ should be added in 60 mL of solution?
(a) 1.8 g (b) 0.8 g
(c) 0.18 g (d) None of these

76. If 30 mL of H_2 and 20 mL of O_2 react to form water, what is left at the end of the reaction?
(a) 10 mL of H_2 (b) 5 mL of H_2
(c) 10 mL of O_2 (d) 5 mL of O_2

77. 11.2 L of CO_2 is absorbed in 1 mole NaOH, Na_2CO_3 formed is $2NaOH + CO_2 \longrightarrow Na_2CO_3 + H_2O$
(a) 5.6 mol (b) 11.2 mol (c) 0.5 mol (d) 1.0 mol

78. The molarity (conc. in mol L^{-1}) of H_2SO_4 solution, which has a density 1.84 g/cc at 35°C and contains 98% by weight is
(a) 1.84 M (b) 18.4 M (c) 20.6 M (d) 24.5 M

79. Complete combustion of 3 g of ethane gives $x \times 10^{22}$ molecules of water. The value of x is .... (Round off to the Nearest Integer). [Use : $N_A = 6.023 \times 10^{23}$; Atomic masses in u ; C : 12.0 ; O : 16.0 ; H : 1.0] **[JEE Main 2021, March]**
(a) 2.88×10^{-3} (b) 28.8×10^{-3}
(c) 288×10^{-3} (d) 18.069×10^{22}

80. The mass of 70% H_2SO_4 required for neutralisation of one mole of NaOH is
(a) 30 g (b) 70 g
(c) 35 g (d) 95 g

81. Concentrated hydrochloric acid contains 37% HCl (by mass). The density of this solution is 1.18 g/mL. The molarity (conc. in mol L^{-1}) of solution is
(a) 10 M (b) 12 M
(c) 13 M (d) 14 M

82. The equivalent weight of phosphoric acid (H_3PO_4) in the reaction

$$NaOH + H_3PO_4 \longrightarrow NaH_2PO_4 + H_2O \text{ is}$$

(a) 59 (b) 49
(c) 25 (d) 98

83. By dissolving 1 mole each of the following acids in 1 L water, the acid which does not give a solution of 1 N strength is
(a) H_3PO_4 (b) $HClO_4$
(c) HNO_3 (d) HCl

84. What maximum amount of $BaSO_4$ gets precipitated if 0.5 mol of $BaCl_2$ is mixed with 1 mole of H_2SO_4?
(a) 0.5 mol (b) 1.0 mol
(c) 1.5 mol (d) 2.0 mol

85. 1 kg of NaOH solution contains 0.04 g of NaOH. The approximate concentration of solution is
(a) 0.04 ppm (b) 0.004 ppm
(c) 40 ppm (d) 400 ppm

86. The volume of oxygen liberated at STP from 0.68 g of H_2O_2 undergoes $2H_2O_2 \longrightarrow 2H_2O + O_2$
(a) 112 mL (b) 224 mL
(c) 56 mL (d) 336 mL

87. $Ca(OH)_2 + H_3PO_4 \longrightarrow CaHPO_4 + 2H_2O$
The equivalent weight of H_3PO_4 in the above reaction is
(a) 21 (b) 27
(c) 38 (d) 49

88. The weight of residue obtained by heating 2.76 g of silver carbonate is
(a) 2.76 g (b) 2.98 g
(c) 2.16 g (d) 2.44 g

89. The number of moles of oxygen present in one litre of air under STP conditions (it contains 21% oxygen) is
(a) 0.246 mol (b) 0.07438 mol
(c) 2.0078 mol (d) 0.0094 mol

90. The concentration of 10% CH_3COOH in mol L^{-1} is
(a) 10 (b) 0.83
(c) 1 (d) 1.67

91. 50 mL of H_2SO_4 require 10 g $CaCO_3$ for complete decomposition percentage of H_2SO_4 is
(a) 9.8% (b) 4.9%
(c) 19.6% (d) 2.45%

92. The minimum amount of $O_2(g)$ consumed per gram of reactant is for the reaction
(Given atomic mass : Fe = 56, O = 16, Mg = 24, P = 31, C = 12, H = 1) **[JEE Main 2019, April]**
(a) $C_3H_8(g) + 5O_2(g) \longrightarrow 3CO_2(g) + 4H_2O(l)$
(b) $P_4(s) + 5O_2(g) \longrightarrow P_4O_{10}(s)$
(c) $4Fe(s) + 3O_2(g) \longrightarrow 2Fe_2O_3(s)$
(d) $2Mg(s) + O_2(g) \longrightarrow 2MgO(s)$

93. For the reaction, $Fe_2O_3 + 3CO \longrightarrow 2Fe + 3CO_2$, the volume of carbon monoxide required at STP to reduce one mole of ferric oxide is
(a) 22.4 dm^3 (b) 44.8 dm^3 (c) 67.2 dm^3 (d) 11.2 dm^3

94. For a reaction,
$N_2(g) + 3H_2(g) \longrightarrow 2NH_3(g)$, identify dihydrogen ($H_2$) as a limiting reagent in the following reaction mixtures. **[JEE Main 2019, April]**
(a) 56 g of N_2 + 10 g of H_2
(b) 35 g of N_2 + 8 g of H_2
(c) 14 g of N_2 + 4 g of H_2
(d) 28 g of N_2 + 6 g of H_2

95. How many 'mL' of perhydrol is required to produce sufficient oxygen which can be used to completely convert 2 L of SO_2 gas to SO_3 gas?
(a) 10 mL (b) 5 mL
(c) 20 mL (d) 30 mL

Objective Questions Type II [One or more than one correct option(s)]

In each of the questions below, four choices are given, of which one or more than one are correct.

1. 11.2 g of mixture of *M*Cl (volatile) and NaCl gave 28.7 g of white ppt with excess of $AgNO_3$ solution. 11.2 g of same mixture on heating gave a gas that on passing into $AgNO_3$ solution gave 14.35 g of white ppt. Hence,
(a) ionic mass of M^+ is 18
(b) mixture has equal mole fraction of *M*Cl and NaCl
(c) *M*Cl and NaCl are in the 1 : 2 molar ratio
(d) ionic mass of M^+ is 10

2. Aqueous solution containing 1 mole of SO_2Cl_2 is neutralised by
(a) 2 moles of $Ca(OH)_2$ (b) 1 mole of $Ca(OH)_2$
(c) 2 moles of KOH (d) 4 moles of KOH

3. Mole fraction of ethanol (C_2H_5OH) in ethanol-water system is 0.25. Thus, it has
(a) 25% ethanol by weight of solution
(b) 75% water by weight of solution
(c) 46% ethanol by weight of solution
(d) 54% water by weight of solution

4. The simplest formula of a compound containing 50% of element *X* (atomic weight 10) and 50% of element *Y* (atomic weight 20) is
(a) XY (b) X_2Y
(c) XY_2 (d) X_2Y_3

5. A certain compound has the molecular formula X_4O_6 having 57.2% *X*. Thus,
(a) atomic mass of *X* is 32
(b) *X* may contain five valence electrons
(c) *X* is an electropositive metal
(d) *X* can be a non-metal

6. An aqueous solution of glucose ($C_6H_{12}O_6$) contains 1 mole of glucose in 1.8 L solution. Thus,
(a) it is 10% aqueous solution
(b) its density is 0.1 g mL^{-1}
(c) solution contains 3.33×10^{20} glucose molecules per mL
(d) solution contains 24 moles of atoms

7. A solution of solute *X* contains 40% *X* by weight of solution. 800 g of this solution was cooled when 100 g of solute is precipitated. Thus, percentage composition of the remaining solution is
(a) 31.4% (b) 20.0%
(c) 23.0% (d) 24.0%

8. In diammonium hydrogen phosphate, $(NH_4)_2HPO_4$, percentage as
(a) P_2O_5 is 53.78% (b) NH_3 is 25.76%
(c) P is maximum (d) N is maximum

9. A sample of metal contains 2.516×10^{23} atoms and has a mass of 82.29 g. Select the correct statements for this case.
(a) Atomic mass of the metal is 197
(b) Number of moles present in the given amount is 0.42
(c) The probable metal is a coin metal
(d) It is natural occurring metal

10. The molar mass of haemoglobin is about 65000 g/mol. Haemoglobin contains 0.35% Fe by mass. Thus, iron atoms present in haemoglobin molecule are
(a) 1 (b) 2 (c) 3 (d) 4

11. Given that the abundance of isotopes $_{54}Fe$, $_{56}Fe$ and $_{57}Fe$ are 5%, 90% and 5% respectively, the atomic mass of Fe is **[IIT JEE 2009]**
(a) 55.85 (b) 55.95 (c) 55.75 (d) 56.05

12. The molar mass of haemoglobin is about 65000 g mol^{-1}. Every haemoglobin contains 4 iron atoms. Thus,
(a) iron content in haemoglobin is 0.35% by mass
(b) 1 mole of haemoglobin contains 56 g iron
(c) 1 mole of haemoglobin contains 224 g iron
(d) if iron content is increased to 0.56%, molar mass of haemoglobin would be higher than 65000 g mol^{-1}.

13. In one process giving below
$2NH_3(g) + CO_2(g) \longrightarrow NH_2CONH_2(aq) + H_2O(l)$
637.2 g of NH_3 are allowed to react with 1142 g of CO_2. In this
(a) NH_3 is the limiting reactant and CO_2 is in excess
(b) NH_3 is in excess and CO_2 is the limiting reactant
(c) 1124 g of urea is formed
(d) 319 g of CO_2 is left unreacted

14. If 0.80 mole of MnO_2 and 146 g of HCl react
$MnO_2 + 4HCl \longrightarrow MnCl_2 + Cl_2 + 2H_2O$
then,
(a) 0.80 mole of Cl_2 is formed
(b) 0.80 mole of HCl remains unreacted
(c) MnO_2 is completely reacts
(d) MnO_2 is the limiting reactant

15. The number of chlorine atoms in 20 mL of chlorine gas at STP is .... $\times 10^{21}$. (Round off to the Nearest Integer).
[Assume chlorine is an ideal gas at STP
$R = 0.083$ L bar mol^{-1} K^{-1}, $N_A = 6.023 \times 10^{23}$]
[JEE Main 2021, March]
(a) 8 (b) 1 (c) 7 (d) 4

16. We have 1.6 g CH_4, 1.7 g NH_3 and 1.8 g H_2O select correct the alternate(s).
(a) There are equal number of moles of each reactant
(b) Total number of atoms in $CH_4 > NH_3 > H_2O$
(c) Total number of H-atoms are in the ratio of 4 : 3 : 2
(d) Total number of C-atoms in CH_4 < that of N-atoms in NH_3 < that of O-atoms in H_2O

17. Density of H_2O is 1 g mL^{-1}. If we have 1 mL H_2O then
(a) it is 55.55 mol L^{-1}
(b) it has 3.33×10^{22} H_2O molecules
(c) it has 3.33×10^{22} H-atoms
(d) it has 6.66×10^{22} O-atoms

Numerical Value Questions

All these questions have a Numerical value as their answer, solve the questions and write your answer.

1. The chief ore of zinc is the sulphide, ZnS. The ore is concentrated by floatation process and then heated in air, which converts the ZnS to ZnO.

$$2ZnS + 3O_2 \xrightarrow{90.6\%} 2ZnO + 2SO_2$$

The ZnO is then treated with dilute H_2SO_4

$$ZnO + H_2SO_4 \xrightarrow{100\%} ZnSO_4 + H_2O$$

to produce $ZnSO_4(aq)$ which produces Zn metal on electrolysis.

$$2ZnSO_4 + 2H_2O \xrightarrow[\text{in kg}]{98.2\%} 2Zn + 2H_2SO_4 + O_2$$

What mass of Zn will be obtained from an ore containing 225 kg of ZnS? Efficiencies of the processes have been indicated above the arrow mark. (Zn = 65, S = 32, O = 16, H = 1)

2. What is the per cent free SO_3 in an oleum ($H_2S_2O_7$) that is labelled "109% H_2SO_4"?

3. A fluorine disposal plant was constructed to carryout the reactions.

$$F_2 + 2NaOH \longrightarrow \frac{1}{2}O_2 + 2NaF + H_2O$$

$$2NaF + CaO + H_2O \longrightarrow CaF_2 + 2NaOH$$

As the plant operated, excess lime was added to bring about complete precipitation of the fluoride as CaF_2. Over a period of operation, 2000 kg of fluorine were fed into a plant and 10000 kg of lime were required. The percentage utilisation of lime was (F = 19, Ca = 40, O = 16)

4. A 0.7160 g of a hydrated metallic sulphate of formula $M_x(SO_4)_y \cdot 18H_2O$ precipitated 0.7002 g of $BaSO_4$. When mixed with K_2SO_4 and crystallised, the metallic sulphate yielded an alum isomorphous with potash alum. The atomic weight of the metal is

5. 50 g of $CaCO_3$ sample, gave 1.12 L CO_2 at STP. The percentage purity of $CaCO_3$ sample.

6. Near room temperature, the density of water is 1.00 g/mL and the density of ethanol (C_2H_6O) is 0.789 g/mL. What volume of ethanol contains the same number of molecules as are present in mL 125 mL H_2O?

7. The minimum number of moles of O_2 required for complete combustion of 1 mole of propane and 2 moles of butane is .... **[JEE Main 2020, Sep.]**

8. $NaClO_3$ is used, even in spacecrafts, to produce O_2. The daily consumption of pure O_2 by a person is 492 L at 1 atm 300 K.

How much amount of $NaClO_3$, in grams, is required to produce O_2 for the daily consumption of a person at 1 atm, 300 K .... in grams ?

$$NaClO_3(s) + Fe(s) \longrightarrow O_2(g) + NaCl(s) + FeO(s)$$

$R = 0.082$ L atm mol^{-1} K^{-1}
[JEE Main 2020, Jan.]

9. The mass of ammonia in grams produced when 2.8 kg of dinitrogen quantitatively reacts with 1 kg of dihydrogen is .... **[JEE Main 2020, Sep.]**

10. The amount of water produced (in g) in the oxidation of 1 mole of rhombic sulphur by conc. HNO_3 to a compound with the highest oxidation state of sulphur is ...... (Given data : Molar mass of water = 18 g mol^{-1}) **[JEE Advanced 2019]**

11. Galena (an ore) is partially oxidised by passing air through it at high temperature. After some time, the passage of air is stopped, but the heating is continued in a closed furnace such that the content undergo self-reduction.

The weight (in kg) of Pb produced per kg of O_2 consumed is ....

(Atomic weights in g mol^{-1} : O = 16, S = 32, Pb = 207) **[JEE Advanced 2018]**

12. The ammonia prepared by treating ammonium sulphate with calcium hydroxide is completely used by $NiCl_2 \cdot 6H_2O$ to form a stable coordination compound. Assume that both the reactions are 100% complete. If 1584 g of ammonium sulphate and 952 g of $NiCl_2 \cdot 6H_2O$ are used in the preparation, the combined weight (in grams) of gypsum and the nickel-ammonia coordination compound thus produced is......... . (Atomic weights in g mol^{-1} : H = 1, N = 14, O = 16, S = 32, Cl = 35.5, Ca = 40, Ni = 59) **[JEE Advanced 2018]**

13. Upon mixing 100.0 mL of 0.1 M potassium sulphate solution and 100.0 mL of 0.05 M barium chloride solution, precipitation of barium sulphate takes place. How many moles of barium sulphate are formed?

Comprehension Based Questions

In these questions, a passage has been given followed by questions based on it. You have to answer the questions based on the passage given.

***Passage* 1** *Questions given below are based on the following stoichiometric equation.*

cis-platin, an anticancer agent used for the treatment of solid tumors, is prepared by the reaction of ammonia with potassium tetrachloroplatinate:

$$\underset{\text{Potassium tetrachloroplatinate (II)}}{K_2PtCl_4} + 2NH_3 \longrightarrow \underset{cis\text{-platin}}{[Pt(NH_3)_2]Cl_2} + 2KCl$$

Assume that 10.0 g of K_2PtCl_4 and 10.0 g of NH_3 are allowed to react. (K = 39, Pt = 195, Cl = 35.5)

1. Which reactant is limiting and which is in excess?

	Limiting	Excess
(a)	K_2PtCl_4	NH_3
(b)	NH_3	K_2PtCl_4

(c) Exact molar ratio

(d) Would be decided by the quantity of the product formed

2. Number of moles of K_2PtCl_6 consumed is

(a) 0.048 (b) 0.024 (c) 0.012 (d) 0.096

3. Number of moles of NH_3 consumed is

(a) 0.048 (b) 0.024 (c) 0.096 (d) 0.192

***Passage* 2** *Questions given below are based on the following sequence of the reactions.*

Phosphoric acid, H_3PO_4, is widely used to make fertilisers, and can be prepared in a two step process.

Step I $P_4 + 5O_2 \longrightarrow P_4O_{10}$

Step II $P_4O_{10} + 6H_2O \longrightarrow 4H_3PO_4$

We allow 310 g of phosphorus to react with excess oxygen, which forms tetraphosphorus decoxide, P_4O_{10}, in 50% yield. In the step II reaction, 25% yield of H_3PO_4 is obtained. (P = 31, H = 1, O = 16)

1. Assume 100% yield then number of moles of H_3PO_4 would be obtained

(a) 1.25 (b) 10.0 (c) 5.0 (d) 2.5

2. Actual number of moles of H_3PO_4 obtained based on experimental conditions is

(a) 5.0 (b) 2.5
(c) 1.25 (d) 0.3125

3. H_3PO_4 thus formed is converted into calcium phosphate by treating with 1 mole of calcium hydroxide. Calcium phosphate obtained is

(a) 2.5 mol (b) 0.33 mol
(c) 0.1563 mol (d) 1.25 mol

***Passage* 3** *Following passage describes the depletion of ozone layer. Read the passage and answer the questions at the end of it.*

The depletion of ozone (O_3) in the stratosphere has been a matter of great concern among scientists in recent years. It believed that ozone can react with nitric oxide (NO) that is discharged from the high altitude jet plane. The reaction is

$$O_3 + NO \longrightarrow O_2 + NO_2$$

1. If 0.740 g of O_3 reacts with 0.670 g of NO, how many gram of NO_2 will be produced?

(a) 0.71 g (b) 0.74 g
(c) 0.68 g (d) 0.81 g

2. Which compound is the limiting reactant?

(a) NO (b) O_3
(c) Both are in equimolar ratio
(d) Both are in stoichiometric ratio

3. Number of moles of the excess reactant remaining at the end of the reaction is

(a) 0.007 mol O_3 (b) 0.014 mol O_3
(c) 0.007 mol NO (d) 0.014 mol NO

***Passage* 4** About half of the world's production of pigments for paints involves the formation of white TiO_2. In the united states, it is made on a large scale by the chloride process, starting with ores containing only small amounts of rutile, TiO_2. The ore is treated with chlorine and carbon (coke). This produces $TiCl_4$ and gaseous products.

$$2TiO_2 + 3C + 4Cl_2 \xrightarrow{70.0\%} 2TiCl_4 + CO_2 + 2CO$$

The $TiCl_4$ is then converted into TiO_2 of high purity.

$$TiCl_4 + O_2 \xrightarrow{93.0\%} TiO_2 + 2Cl_2$$

Efficiencies have been indicated above the arrow mark.
(Ti = 48, Cl = 35.5, O = 16, C = 12)

Answer the following questions.

1. If we start with 100 kg of ore (containing 7.5% rutile), pure TiO_2 obtained is
(a) 4.8825 kg (b) 7.3238 kg
(c) 9.7650 kg (d) 2.4413 kg

2. Cl_2 required in this reaction is
(a) 0.1221 kmol (b) 8.666 kg
(c) 4.333 kg (d) 0.1221 kg

***Passage* 5** A fluorine disposal plant was constructed to carryout the reactions

$$F_2 + 2NaOH \longrightarrow \frac{1}{2}O_2 + 2NaF + H_2O$$

$$2NaF + CaO + H_2O \longrightarrow CaF_2 + 2NaOH$$

As the plant operated, excess lime was added to bring about complete precipitation of the fluoride as CaF_2. Over a period of operation, 2000 kg of fluorine were fed into a plant and 10000 kg of lime were required. (F = 19, Ca = 40, O = 16, H = 1, Na = 23)

Answer the following questions.

1. What was the percentage utilisation of lime (CaO)?
(a) 29.5% (b) 14.75% (c) 59.0% (d) 60.0%

2. CaO used by given quantity of F_2 is
(a) 1475 kg (b) 2947.4 kg (c) 5900 kg (d) 6000 kg

3. CaF_2 precipitated is
(a) 52.64 kmol (b) 263.16 kmol
(c) 35.71 kmol (d) 26.32 kmol

***Passage* 6** 11.2 g of mixture of *M*Cl (volatile) and NaCl gave 28.7 g of white precipitate with excess of $AgNO_3$ solution. 11.2 g of same mixture on heating gave a gas that on passing into $AgNO_3$ solution gave 14.35 g of white precipitate.

Answer the following questions.

1. Ionic mass of M^+ is
(a) 18 (b) 9 (c) 36 (d) 23

2. *M*Cl and NaCl are the molar ratio
(a) 1 : 1 (b) 1 : 2 (c) 2 : 1 (d) 1 : 3

3. In terms of moles, mixture has
(a) 0.2 mol (b) 0.1 mol
(c) 0.15 mol (d) 0.01 mol

Matrix-Match Type

Given below are Matching Type Questions, with two columns (each having some items) each . Each item of Column I has to be matched with the items of Column II.

1. Match the number of moles (in Column I) with the compound (in Column II).

Column I	Column II
A. 0.5 mol	1. 92 g CH_3CH_2OH
B. 1.0 mol	2. 66 g CO_2
C. 1.5 mol	3. 54 g H_2O
D. 2.0 mol	4. 15 g HCHO
E. 3.0 mol	5. 44 g CH_3CHO

2. Match the reaction (in Column I) with the maximum yield of the product (in Column II).

Column I	Column II
A. $\underset{1\,g}{2H_2} + \underset{1\,g}{O_2} \longrightarrow 2H_2O$	1. 1.028 g
B. $\underset{1\,g}{3H_2} + \underset{1\,g}{N_2} \longrightarrow 2NH_3$	2. 1.333 g
C. $\underset{1\,g}{H_2} + \underset{1\,g}{Cl_2} \longrightarrow 2HCl$	3. 1.125 g
D. $\underset{1\,g}{2H_2} + \underset{1\,g}{C} \longrightarrow CH_4$	4. 1.214 g

3. Match Column I (reactant) with the amount in Column II.

Column I	Column II
A. NaOH required to react completely with 1 mole CH_3COOH	1. 1 mol
B. $\underset{84\,g}{MgCO_3} \xrightarrow{\Delta} MgO + CO_2$ residue formed is	2. 1 equivalent
C. $\underset{2\,mol}{2SO_2} + \underset{64\,g}{O_2} \longrightarrow 2SO_3$ Reactant in excess under standard condition	3. 40 g
D. $2H_2 + O_2 \longrightarrow 2H_2O$ O_2 used to form 36 g H_2O	4. 22.4 L at STP
E. $N_2H_4 + O_2 \longrightarrow N_2 + 2H_2O$ N_2 formed from 32 g of each reactant	5. 4 equivalent

Single Integer Answer Questions

Answer of these questions is a single digit lying between 0 to 9.

1. Silicon and hydrogen form a series of compounds with the general formula Si_xH_y. 6.22 g sample of the compound is burnt in oxygen, when 11.64 g SiO_2 and 6.980 g of H_2O are formed. The value of $(x + y)$ in simplest Si_xH_y is.
2. $CaCO_3$ is decomposed by HCl ($d = 1.825$ g/cc). The volume of HCl required to decompose 10 g of $CaCO_3$ of 50% purity is.
3. 2 moles of O_2 are formed in the following reaction with 66.67% yield. $2KClO_3 \longrightarrow 2KCl + 3O_2$ How many moles of $KClO_3$ are taken?
4. What mass of CH_4 (in grams) produces 3.01×10^{23} H_2O molecules when burnt in excess of O_2 ?
5. How many moles of SO_3 are present in 3 moles of oleum?
6. 20.8 g of MCl_x ($M = 137$) on reaction with excess of K_2SO_4 yields 23.3 g of sulphate of metal *M*. Derive the value of *x*.
7. Pure nitrogen is obtained by the decomposition of nitride $M_x(N_3)_y$. What is the value of $(x + y)$?

Answers

Objective Questions Type I [Only one correct option]

1. (a)	2. (b)	3. (d)	4. (a)	5. (d)	6. (b)	7. (c)	8. (b)	9. (c)	10. (a)
11. (b)	12. (a)	13. (b)	14. (b)	15. (a)	16. (a)	17. (c)	18. (d)	19. (a)	20. (c)
21. (b)	22. (d)	23. (a)	24. (b)	25. (b)	26. (a)	27. (b)	28. (b)	29. (d)	30. (a)
31. (b)	32. (c)	33. (a)	34. (a)	35. (b)	36. (c)	37. (a)	38. (a)	39. (a)	40. (d)
41. (a)	42. (d)	43. (b)	44. (c)	45. (a)	46. (c)	47. (d)	48. (b)	49. (a)	50. (a)
51. (d)	52. (a)	53. (d)	54. (c)	55. (c)	56. (a)	57. (c)	58. (a)	59. (d)	60. (b)
61. (c)	62. (b)	63. (b)	64. (b)	65. (d)	66. (c)	67. (a)	68. (d)	69. (b)	70. (b)
71. (a)	72. (a)	73. (a)	74. (b)	75. (a)	76. (d)	77. (c)	78. (b)	79. (d)	80. (b)
81. (b)	82. (d)	83. (a)	84. (a)	85. (c)	86. (b)	87. (d)	88. (c)	89. (d)	90. (d)
91. (c)	92. (c)	93. (c)	94. (a)	95. (a)					

Objective Questions Type II [One or more than one correct option(s)]

1. (a, b)	2. (a, d)	3. (c, d)	4. (b)	5. (a, b, d)
6. (a, b, c, d)	7. (a)	8. (a, b)	9. (a, b, c, d)	10. (d)
11. (b)	12. (a, c, d)	13. (a, c, d)	14. (a, b, c, d)	15. (b)
16. (a, b, c)	17. (a, b)			

Numerical Value Questions

1. 134.14	2. 40	3. 29.5	4. 52	5. 10	6. 405	7. 18	8. 2130	9. 3400	10. 288
11. 6.47	12. 2992	13. 0.005							

Comprehension Based Questions

Passage 1 – 1. (a) 2. (b) 3. (a)

Passage 2 – 1. (b) 2. (c) 3. (b)

Passage 3 – 1. (a) 2. (b) 3. (c)

Passage 4 – 1. (a) 2. (a, b)

Passage 5 – 1. (a) 2. (b) 3. (a)

Passage 6 – 1. (a) 2. (a) 3. (a)

Matrix-Match Types

1. A → (4); B → (5); C → (2); D → (1); E → (3)
2. A → (3); B → (4); C → (1); D → (2)
3. A → (1, 2, 3); B → (1,3); C → (1, 4, 5); D → (1, 4, 5); E → (4, 5)

Integer Type

1. (5) 2. (2) 3. (2) 4. (4) 5. (3) 6. (2) 7. (2)

Solutions

Objective Questions Type I [Only one correct option]

1. (a) $NH_4Cl + NaOH \longrightarrow NH_3 + NaCl + H_2O$

53.2 g — 1 mol = 17 g NH_3

0.535 g — 0.17 g NH_3

2. (b) $CaCO_3 \longrightarrow CaO + CO_2$

100g = 1 mol — 22.4 L at NTP

200 g — 44.8 L at NTP

3. (d) $Ca(HCO_3)_2 + CaO \longrightarrow 2CaCO_3 + H_2O$

56 g — 2×100 g

0.56 g CaO = 2 g $CaCO_3$ in 10 L H_2O

10 L (= 10^4 mL) hard water has $CaCO_3$ = 2 g

$\therefore$ 10^6 mL hard water has $CaCO_3$ = 200 g

Thus, hardness part per million (in ppm) of $CaCO_3$ = 200

4. (a) $2KClO_3 \longrightarrow 2KCl + 3O_2$

2 mol — 3 mol

(2×122.5) g give 3 mol O_2

0.03 mol O_2 is obtained from $= \frac{2\times 122.5}{3}\times 0.03$

= 2.45 g pure $KClO_3$ in 5 g impure sample

Thus, % purity $= \frac{2.45}{5.00}\times 100 = 49\%$

5. (d) $CaCO_3 + 2HCl \longrightarrow CaCl_2 + H_2O + CO_2$

100 g — 73 g

10 g — 7.3 g

(50% pure) 5 g

Eq. of HCl $= \frac{7.3}{2}$ g HCl

$\frac{\text{mass}}{\text{volume}} = \text{density}$

$\therefore$ Volume of HCl $= \frac{\text{mass of HCl}}{\text{density of HCl}} = \frac{7.3}{2\times 1.825} = 2$ mL

6. (b) $BaCl_2 + H_2SO_4 \longrightarrow BaSO_4 + H_2O$

208 g — 98 g — 233 g

100 mL of 20.8% $BaCl_2$ solution = 20.8 g $BaCl_2$ = 0.1 mole of $BaSO_4$

50 mL of 9.8% H_2SO_4 solution = 4.9 g H_2SO_4 = 0.05 mole of $BaSO_4$

Thus, H_2SO_4 is the limiting reagent.

98 g H_2SO_4 gives = 233 g $BaSO_4$

4.9 g H_2SO_4 gives = 11.65 g $BaSO_4$

7. (c) $AgNO_3 + NaCl \longrightarrow AgCl + NaNO_3$

1 mol — 1 mol — 1 mol

170 g — 58.5 g — 143.5 g

1.70 g $AgNO_3$ gives 1.435 g AgCl

5.85 g NaCl gives 14.35 g AgCl

Thus, $AgNO_3$ is the limiting reactant.

AgCl formed = 1.435 g

8. (b) $BaCl_2 + CaCO_3 \longrightarrow BaCO_3 + CaCl_2$

1 mol — 1 mol

208 g — 100 g

10 g $CaCO_3$ reacts with 20.8 g $BaCl_2$

But $BaCl_2$ taken = 20 g

Thus, $BaCl_2$ is the limiting reactant.

9. (c) $3Ba(NO_3)_2 + 2Na_3PO_4 \longrightarrow Ba_3(PO_4)_2 + 6NaNO_3$

3 mol $Ba(NO_3)_2$ give = 1 mol $Ba_3(PO_4)_2$

2 mol $Ba(NO_3)_2$ give $= \frac{2}{3}$ mol $Ba_3(PO_4)_2$

2 mol Na_3PO_4 give = 1 mol $Ba_3(PO_4)_2$

10. (a) 2 mol Na_3PO_4 require = 3 mol $Ba(NO_3)_2$

Thus, 1 mol $Ba(NO_3)_2$ is required further.

11. (b) $MnO_2 + 4HCl \longrightarrow Cl_2$

2 mol — 4 mol — 1 mol = 22.4 L at STP

But Cl_2 formed = 11.2 L at STP.

Thus, % yield $= \frac{11.2}{22.4}\times 100 = 50\%$

12. (a) Moles of benzoic acid $= \frac{6.1}{122}$

= moles of *m*-bromobenzoic acid

So, weight of *m*-bromobenzoic acid

$= \frac{6.1}{122}\times 201$ g

= 10.05 g

% yield $= \frac{\text{Actual weight}}{\text{Theoretical weight}}\times 100$

$= \frac{7.8}{10.05}\times 100 = 77.61\%$

13. (b) $2\,C_{57}H_{110}O_6(s) + 163\,O_2(g) \longrightarrow 110\,H_2O(l) + 114\,CO_2(g)$

Molecular mass of $C_{57}H_{110}O_6$

$= 2\times(12\times 57 + 1\times 110 + 16\times 6)$ g = 1780 g

Molecular mass of 110 H_2O = 110 (2 + 16) = 1980 g

1780 g of $C_{57}H_{110}O_6$ produced = 1980 g of H_2O.

445g of $C_{57}H_{110}O_6$ produced $= \frac{1980}{1780}\times 445$ g of H_2O

= 495 of H_2O

14. (b) $NH_2CONH_2 + 2NaOH \longrightarrow 2NH_3$

60 g — 80 g — $2\times 17 = 34$ g

6 g — 8 g — 3.4 g

If yield is 100% NH_3 formed = 3.4 g

If yield is 80% NH_3 formed $= 3.4\times\frac{80}{100} = 2.72$ g

15. (*a*)
$$\underset{40\text{ g}}{NaOH} + \underset{36.5\text{ g}}{HCl} \longrightarrow \underset{58.5\text{ g}}{NaCl} + H_2O$$

NaOH in 100 mL = 0.4 g

HCl in 50 mL = 0.3675 g

NaCl formed = 0.5 g

58.5 g NaCl is formed from = 40 g NaOH

$$0.5\text{ g NaCl is formed from} = \frac{40}{58.5} \times 0.5 = 0.342\text{ g NaOH}$$

NaOH unreacted = 0.4 − 0.342 = 0.058 g

16. (*a*) From reaction stoichiometry

1 mol $KClO_3$ gives = 1 mol Al_2O_3

Thus, $4 \times \frac{50}{100} = 2$ mol pure $KClO_3$ give = 2 mol Al_2O_3

17. (*c*) Final reaction is
$$\underset{\substack{2\text{ mol}\\46\text{ g}}}{2Na} + H_2O + \frac{1}{2}O_2 \longrightarrow \underset{\substack{2\text{ mol}\\80\text{ g}}}{2NaOH}$$

80 g NaOH is from = 46 g Na

4 g NaOH is from = 2.3 g Na

18. (*d*) **From (III)** 2 mol of NH_3 are formed from = 1 mol pure $CaCN_2$ or 2 mol $CaCN_2$ with 50% yield.

From (II) CaC_2 required by 2 mol $CaCN_2$ = 2 mol

From (I) 2 mol CaC_2 are formed from = 2 mol Ca

= 4 mol Ca if yield is 50%

19. (*a*) Adding reactions,
$$2KClO_3 \longrightarrow 2KCl + 3O_2$$

3 mol O_2 (= 22.4 × 3 L at STP) are formed from = 2 mol $KClO_3$

$$11.2\text{ L }O_2\text{ are formed from} = \frac{2 \times 11.2}{3 \times 22.4}\text{ mol }KClO_3$$
$$= \frac{1}{3}\text{ if yield is 100\%}$$
$$= \frac{2}{3}\text{ mol }KClO_3\text{ if yield is 50\%}$$
$$= 0.67\text{ mol }KClO_3$$

20. (*c*) Both require 2 moles of 2Na for 2 moles of NaOH.

I. $2Na + H_2 + O_2 \longrightarrow 2NaOH$

II. $2Na + \frac{1}{2}O_2 + H_2O \longrightarrow 2NaOH$

Thus, equal yield in both.

21. (*b*) 2Cl ≡ S in SCl_2

$$1\text{ Cl} \equiv \frac{S}{2} = 10\text{ g}$$

Thus, atomic mass of S = 32 g

In S_2Cl_2 2 Cl ≡ 2 S = 64 g

1 Cl ≡ 32 g

22. (*d*) Mass of water in salt = $5.4\text{ g} = \frac{5.4}{18} = 0.3$ mol

Mass of anhydrous salt ($BaCl_2$) = 36.6 − 5.4 = 31.2 g

$$= \frac{31.2}{208} = 0.15\text{ mol}$$

Thus, $BaCl_2 : H_2O = 0.15 : 0.30 = 1 : 2$

Thus, salt is $BaCl_2 \cdot 2H_2O$.

23. (*a*)

	$2SO_2$	$+ O_2$	$\longrightarrow 2SO_3$
	2 mol	1 mol	2 mol
For SO_2	10 mol	5 mol	10 mol
For O_2	30 mol	15 mol	30 mol

If 10 mol SO_2 is taken, O_2 required is 5 mol, forming 10 mol SO_3.

But SO_3 actual formed = 8 mol

Thus, percentage yield of SO_3 w.r.t. $SO_2 = \frac{8}{10} \times 100 = 80\%$

24. (*b*) Since, Al_2O_3 does not react with NaOH so, reaction is represented as :
$$\underset{\substack{1\text{ mol}\\27\text{ g}}}{Al} + NaOH + H_2O \longrightarrow NaAlO_2 + \underset{\substack{1.5\text{ mol}\\33.6\text{ L at STP}}}{1.5H_2}$$

33.6 L H_2 gas are from = 27 g Al

$$0.840\text{ L }H_2\text{ gas are from} = \frac{27 \times 0.840}{33.6}\text{ g Al}$$
$$= 0.675\text{ g Al}$$

25. (*b*)
$$\underset{\substack{1\text{ mol}\\12\text{ g}\\3.0\text{ kg} = 3000\text{ g}}}{C} + H_2O \longrightarrow \underbrace{\underset{1\text{ mol}}{CO} + \underset{1\text{ mol}}{H_2}}_{=44.8\text{ L}}$$

?

12 g coal give = 44.8 L

3000 g coal give = 11200 L

$= 11.2 \times 10^3$ L

26. (*a*)
$$CaCO_3 \longrightarrow CaO + CO_2$$
$$\underset{\substack{2\text{ mol}\\2\text{ mol}\\1\text{ mol}}}{2KOH} + \underset{\substack{1\text{ mol}\\22.4\text{ L}\\11.2\text{ L}}}{CO_2} \longrightarrow K_2CO_3 + H_2O$$

1 mol KOH = 56 g is required

27. (*b*)
$$M + HCl \longrightarrow H_2$$
$$\underset{\substack{1\text{ mol}\\1\text{ volume}\\?}}{N_2} + \underset{\substack{3\text{ mol}\\3\text{ volume}\\16.8\text{ mL}}}{3H_2} \longrightarrow \underset{\substack{2\text{ mol}\\2\text{ volume}}}{2NH_3}$$

3 mL H_2 combine with = 1 mL N_2

16.8 mL combine with = 5.6 mL N_2

28. (*b*) 22.4 L N_2 = 28 g

1 L N_2 = 1.25 g

Thus, mass of 1 L compound = 1.25 g

22.4 L compound has mass = 28 g

Thus, molar mass = 28 g mol

Let molecular formula = $(CH_2)_x$

∴ $14x = 28$

$x = 2$

Thus, C_2H_4

29. (*d*) Sn taken = 1.056 g

Sn unreacted = 0.601 g

Sn reacted = 1.056 − 0.601 = 0.455

$= \frac{0.455}{119}$ mol = 0.004 mol

I_2 reacted = 1.947 g = $\frac{1.947}{254}$ mol = 0.008 mol

Thus, Sn : I_2 = 0.004 : 0.008 = 1 : 2

Thus, empirical formula is $Sn(I_2)_2$ or SnI_4.

30. (*a*) Mass loss is due to H_2O

Let $CuSO_4 \cdot 5H_2O = x$ g

$CuSO_4 = (1.245 - x)$ g

Water = (1.245 − 0.882) = 0.363

$CuSO_4 \cdot 5H_2O \equiv 5H_2O$

1 mol — 5 mol

249.5 g — 90 g

H_2O in x g = $\frac{90x}{249.5}$

$\frac{90x}{249.5} = 0.363$

x = 1.006 g

$CuSO_4$ = (1.245 − 1.006) = 0.239 g

% of $CuSO_4 = \frac{0.239}{1.245} = 19.2\%$

31. (*b*) $CH_4 + 2O_2 \longrightarrow CO_2 + 2H_2O$

1 mol — 2 mol — 44 g

16 g — 64 g

Given 16 g — 48 g = 1.5 mol — ?

Thus, O_2 is the limiting reactant

∴ 2 mol O_2 give = 44 g CO_2

1.5 mol O_2 give = $\frac{44}{2} \times 1.5$ = 33 g CO_2

32. (*c*) Ratio of HNO_3 per mole of H_2O

(a) $\frac{8}{4} = 2$ (b) $\frac{6}{3} = 2$

(c) $\frac{10}{3} = 3.33$ (d) $\frac{4}{2} = 2$

33. (*a*) $SO_2Cl_2 + 2H_2O \longrightarrow H_2SO_4 + 2HCl$

1 mol — 1 mol — 2 mol

$H_2SO_4 + Ca(OH)_2 \longrightarrow CaSO_4 + 2H_2O$

$2HCl + Ca(OH)_2 \longrightarrow CaCl_2 + 2H_2O$

Thus, total $Ca(OH)_2$ required = 2 mol

34. (*a*) $3BaCl_2 + 2(NH_4)_3PO_4 \longrightarrow Ba_3(PO_4)_2 + 6NH_4Cl$

3 mol — 2 mol — 1 mol

Given, 0.5 mol — 0.2 mol — 0.1 mol

Thus, $(NH_4)_3PO_4$ is the limiting reactant giving 0.1 mol $Ba_3(PO_4)_2$.

35. (*b*) $M_2CO_3 + 2HCl \longrightarrow 2MCl + H_2O + CO_2$

1 g — 0.01186 mol

Number of moles of M_2CO_3 reacted

= Number of moles of CO_2 evolved

$\frac{1}{M} = 0.01186$ [M = molar mass of M_2CO_3]

$M = \frac{1}{0.01186} = 84.3$ g mol^{-1}

37. (*a*) $BaF_2 + H_2SO_4 \longrightarrow BaSO_4 + H_2F_2$

1 mol — 1 mol — 1 mol — 1 mol

Given, 1 mol — 2 mol

Thus, unreacted H_2SO_4 = 1 mol

H_2F_2 formed = 1 mol

$H_2SO_4 + 2NaOH \longrightarrow Na_2SO_4 + 2H_2O$

1 mol — 2 mol

$H_2F_2 + 2NaOH \longrightarrow Na_2F_2 + 2H_2O$

1 mol — 2 mol

Thus, total NaOH required by 1 mol H_2F_2 (formed) and 1 mol H_2SO_4 (unreacted) = 4 mol

38. (*a*) $3CaBr_2 + 2K_3PO_4 \longrightarrow 6KBr + Ca_3(PO_4)_2$

3 mol — 2 mol — 6 mol — 1 mol

According to the chemical reaction,

2 mol of K_3PO_4 reacts = 3 mol of $CaBr_2$

0.2 mol of K_3PO_4 reacts = 0.3 mol of $CaBr_2$

Moles of $CaBr_2$ left unreated = 0.5 − 0.3 = 0.2

Hence, K_3PO_4 is the limiting reagent, since it reacts completely and it decides the amount of products, thus formed

2 mol of K_3PO_4 gives 1 mol of $Ca_3(PO_4)_2$.

0.2 mol of K_3PO_4 gives = 0.1 mol of $Ca_3(PO_4)_2$

Thus, the answer is (a).

39. (*a*) $3Pb(NO_3)_2 + Cr_2(SO_4)_3 \longrightarrow 3PbSO_4 + 2Cr(NO_3)_3$

35 mL — 20 mL

0.15 M — 0.12 M

5.25 m.mol = 2.4 m.mol

$= 5.25 \times 10^{-3}$ mol

Therefore, moles of $PbSO_4$ formed = 5.25×10^{-3}

$= 525 \times 10^{-5}$

40. (*d*) $Na_2CO_3 \equiv CaCO_3$

106 g — 100 g

Hardness in 10^6 mL H_2O = 100 g $CaCO_3$

∴ Hardness in 10 L (10^4 mL = 10^4 g) H_2O = 1 g $CaCO_3$

100 g $CaCO_3$ required = 106 g Na_2CO_3

∴ 1 g $CaCO_3$ required = 1.06 g Na_2CO_3

41. (*a*) Iron oxide = 0.5434 g

Oxygen lost as H_2O = 0.1210 g

Iron = 0.5434 − 0.1210 = 0.4224 g

Element	Amount	%	Mole	Ratio
Iron (56)	0.4224 g	77.73	1.39	1
Oxygen (16)	0.1210 g	22.26	1.39	1

Thus, FeO

42. (*d*) $P_2O_5 \longrightarrow Mg_2P_2O_7$

1 mol — 1 mol

142 g — 222 g

P_2O_5 in the mineral = $0.5428 \times \frac{26.26}{100} = 0.1425$ g

Thus, $Mg_2P_2O_7$ obtained = 0.2228 g

43. (*b*) $\underset{\substack{56\text{ g}\\ ?}}{CaO} \longrightarrow CaC_2O_4 \longrightarrow \underset{\substack{100\text{ g}\\ 0.3462\text{ g}}}{CaCO_3}$

Pure CaO in the mineral $= \frac{56}{100} \times 0.3462 = 0.1938$ g

$\therefore$ % of pure CaO $= \frac{0.1938}{0.8432} \times 100 = 23\%$

44. (*c*) $\underset{\substack{32\\ 0.60\times 0.12}}{S} \longrightarrow BaSO_4 \longrightarrow \underset{\substack{208\text{ g}\\ ?}}{BaCl_2}$

$= 0.072$ g

$BaCl_2$ required by 0.072 g sulphur to be precipitated as :

$BaSO_4 = \frac{208}{32} \times 0.072 = 0.468$ g

Thus, volume of $BaCl_2$ solution $= \frac{0.468 \times 100}{1.6}$

$= 29.25$ mL

45. (*a*) $\underset{\substack{1\text{ mol}\\ 232\text{ g}\\ ?}}{Fe_3O_4} \longrightarrow \underset{\substack{1.5\text{ mol}\\ 240\text{ g}\\ 0.40\text{ g}}}{1.5\,Fe_2O_3}$

Fe_3O_4 required by 0.40 g $Fe_2O_3 = \frac{232}{240} \times 0.4$

$= 0.3867$ g (pure)

$= 0.3867 \times \frac{100}{18}$ g

$= 2.15$ g impure Fe_3O_4

46. (*c*) 10 g glucose is in = 100 mL

$\therefore$ 180 g glucose is in $= \frac{100 \times 180}{10}$ mL $= 1800$ mL $= 1.8$ L

47. (*d*) $2(NH_4)_2HPO_4 \equiv P_2O_5$

$2 \times 132\text{ g} \equiv 142\text{ g}$

Thus, % of $P_2O_5 = \frac{142}{264} \times 100 = 53.78$

48. (*b*) Oxygen = 67.67%

Metal = 32.33%

Thus, 67.67 g oxygen combine with = 32.33 g metal

Hence, 8 g oxygen combine with $= \frac{32.33 \times 8}{67.67} = 3.82$

49. (*a*) Same empirical formulae

50. (*a*) $\underset{\substack{2\text{ mol}\\ 1\text{ mol}}}{2NaOH} + \underset{\substack{1\text{ mol}\\ 0.5\text{ mol}}}{H_2SO_4} \longrightarrow Na_2SO_4 + 2H_2O$ $= 49$ g H_2SO_4 (pure)

Thus, 70% H_2SO_4 required $= 49 \times \frac{100}{70} = 70$ g

51. (*d*) ppm $= \frac{10 \times 10^6}{1000} = 10^4$

52. (*a*) Solute present in 800 g solution= $800 \times \frac{40}{100} = 320$ g

Solute precipitated = 100 g

Solute left = 220 g

$\therefore$ Total weight of solution = 800 − 100 = 700 g

700 g solution has solute = 220 g

100 g solution has solute $= \frac{220}{700} \times 100 = 31.43\%$

53. (*d*) $MHPO_4 \rightleftharpoons M^{2+} + HPO_4^{2-}$

Thus, metal is divalent forming MCl_2

54. (*c*) Equivalent weight of $M^{2+} = 37.2$

Thus, molar mass of $M^{2+} = 37.2 \times 2 = 74.4$

Thus, molar mass of $MCl_2 = 74.4 + 71 = 145.4$

55. (*c*) Glucose in 500 mL solution

$= \frac{9 \times 500}{100} = 45$ g

$= \frac{45}{180} = 0.25$ mol

$= 0.25 \times 6.02 \times 10^{23}$ molecules

$= 1.5 \times 10^{23}$

56. (*a*) $\frac{100 \times 58.5}{5.85} = 1000$ mL = 1 L

57. (*c*) $\frac{0.2 \times 10^6}{500} = 400$

58. (*a*) $\underset{\substack{65\text{ g}\\ 0.65\text{ g}}}{Zn} + 2HCl \longrightarrow ZnCl_2 + \underset{\substack{22400\text{ mL}\\ 224\text{ mL}}}{H_2}$

59. (*d*) Carbonates of alkali metal are all state towards heat except Li_2CO_3.

$\underset{1\text{ mol}}{Li_2CO_3} \longrightarrow \underset{1\text{ mol}}{CO_2} + Li_2O$

$Na_2CO_3 \longrightarrow X$

$\underset{\substack{2\text{ mol}\\ 1\text{ mol}}}{2NaHCO_3} \longrightarrow \underset{\substack{1\text{ mol}\\ 0.5\text{ mol}}}{CO_2} + H_2O + Na_2CO_3$

Total $CO_2 = 1.5$ mol

60. (*b*) $\underset{12\text{ g}}{C} \longrightarrow \underset{22.4\text{ L}}{CO}$

22.4 L CO from = 12 g C

11.2 L CO from = 6 g C

61. (*c*) $2CuSO_4 + 4KI \longrightarrow Cu_2I_2 + I_2 + 2K_2SO_4$

2×249.5 g $CaCO_3 \longrightarrow 254$ g I_2

8.3 g $CuSO_4 \longrightarrow \frac{254 \times 8.3}{499}$ g = 4.23 g I_2

62. (*b*) $\underset{\substack{100\text{ g}\\ 20\text{ g}}}{CaCO_3} \longrightarrow CaO + \underset{\substack{22.4\\ \frac{22.4}{5} = 4.48\text{ L}}}{CO_2}$

63. (*b*) $\frac{200 \times 95 \times 56}{100 \times 100} = 106.4$ kg

65. (*d*) In alkaline medium : Iodide is oxidised to iodate

$2MnO_4^- + H_2O + I^- \longrightarrow 2MnO_2 + 2OH^- + IO_3^-$

But, in weakly basic solution :

$K\overset{+7}{Mn}O_4 + K\overset{-1}{I} \longrightarrow \overset{+4}{Mn}O_2 + \overset{0}{I_2}$

Eq. of $KMnO_4$ = Eq. of I_2

$4 \times 3 = n \times 2$

$n = 6$

66. (*c*)

Element	%	Mole	Ratio
Ag	2.00	0.0185	1
Cl	0.657	0.0185	1

Thus, AgCl.

67. (*a*)

		Mol	Mole ratio	
Al	5 g	0.185	1.0	2
O	4.45 g	0.278	1.5	3/1

Thus, Al_2O_3

68. (*d*) $(HO)H_2C-\overset{H_2}{C}-CHO \xrightarrow[64\%]{\Delta} C_3H_4O + H_2O$

$\frac{x}{74}$ mol $\qquad \frac{x}{74} \times 0.64 = \frac{7.8}{56}$

$x = 16.10 \simeq 16.10$

69. (*b*) If atomic weight = M

Then % of $S = \left(\frac{64}{M+64}\right) \times 100 = 40$

$\therefore \quad M = 96$

71. (*a*) On decomposition $BaCO_3$ liberates CO_2 as

$BaCO_3 \longrightarrow BaO + \underset{22.4 \text{ L at STP}}{CO_2 \uparrow}$

197 g of $BaCO_3$ give = 22.4 L of CO_2 at STP

9.85 g $BaCO_3$ will give $= \frac{22.4 \times 9.85}{197} = 1.12$ L

72. (*a*) Suppose molecular weight of enzyme = x

0.5% by weight means in 100 g of enzyme wt. of Se = 0.5 g

In x g of enzyme wt. of Se $= \frac{0.5 \times x}{100}$

Hence, $78.4 = \frac{0.5 \times x}{100}$

$x = 15680 = 1.5680 \times 10^4$

74. (*b*) 4.4 g CO_2 = 0.1 mol = 2.24 L at STP

75. (*a*) Concentration in terms of g/mL is given as

$0.03 = \frac{\text{mass of } AgNO_3}{60}$

Mass of $AgNO_3 = 60 \times 0.03 = 1.8$ g

76. (*d*) $2H_2 + O_2 \longrightarrow 2H_2O$

2 mL 1 mL

30 mL 15 mL

Thus, O_2 left = 5 mL

78. (*b*) 100 g H_2SO_4 solution $= \frac{100}{1.84}$ mL H_2SO_4 solution has

$= 98 \text{ g } H_2SO_4 = 1 \text{ mol } H_2SO_4$

1000 mL H_2SO_4 solution has = 18.4 mol H_2SO_4

79. (*d*) $C_2H_6 \longrightarrow 3H_2O$

0.1 mol 0.3 mol

No. of molecules $= 0.3 \times 6.023 \times 10^{23} = 18.069 \times 10^{22}$

80. (*b*) $2NaOH + H_2SO_4 \longrightarrow Na_2SO_4 + 2H_2O$

81. (*b*) Let mass of solution = 100 g

$\therefore$ Molarity $= \frac{37 \times 1000 \times 1.18}{100 \times 36.5} = 12$ M

82. (*d*) $NaOH + H_3PO_4 \longrightarrow NaH_2PO_4 + H_2O$

40 g 98 g

1 g eq. 1 g eq.

Only 1H is neutralise

Hence, eq. wt. = mol. wt. = 98

83. (*a*) H_3PO_4 is a tribasic acid.

84. (*a*) $BaCl_2 + H_2SO_4 \longrightarrow BaSO_4$

1 mol 1 mol 1 mol

0.5 mol 1 mol 0.5 mol

86. (*b*) $2H_2O_2 \longrightarrow 2H_2O + O_2$

2×34 22400 mL

2×34 g H_2O_2 liberates = 22400 mL of O_2 at STP

0.68 g H_2O_2 liberates $= \frac{0.68 \times 22400}{68} = 224$ mL

87. (*d*) $H_3PO_4 \equiv 2OH^-$, Eq. wt. $= \frac{\text{Molar mass } (H_3PO_4)}{2} = \frac{98}{2} = 49$

88. (*c*) $2Ag_2CO_3 \xrightarrow{\text{Heat}} 4Ag + 2CO_2 + O_2$

2×276(g) 4×108(g)

= 552 = 432

552 g silver carbonate give silver = 432 g

2.76 g of silver carbonate give silver $= \frac{432 \times 2.76}{552}$

= 2.16 g

89. (*d*) Air contains 21% of O_2

Volume of oxygen $= \frac{21}{100} = 0.21$ L

Number of moles of oxygen present in 0.21 L at NTP

$= \frac{0.21}{22.4} = 0.009375$

90. (*d*) 10% acetic acid = 10 g in 100 mL

Conc. in mol $L^{-1} = \frac{10 \times 1000}{60 \times 100} = 1.67$

91. (*c*) $CaCO_3 + H_2SO_4 \longrightarrow CaSO_4 + H_2O + CO_2$

100 g 98 g

10 g 9.8 g

50 mL H_2SO_4 has = 9.8 g

100 mL has = 19.6 g

92. (*c*)

(a) $\underset{44 \text{ g}}{C_3H_8(g)} + \underset{160 \text{ g}}{5O_2(g)} \longrightarrow 3CO_2(g) + 4H_2O(l)$

$\Rightarrow$ 1g of reactant $= \frac{160}{44}$ g of O_2 consumed = 3.64 g

(b) $\underset{124 \text{g}}{P_4(s)} + \underset{160 \text{ g}}{5O_2(g)} \longrightarrow P_4O_{10}(s)$

$\Rightarrow$ 1g of reactant $\frac{160}{124}$ g of O_2 consumed = 129 g

(c) $\underset{244g}{4Fe(s)} + \underset{96g}{3O_2(g)} \longrightarrow 2Fe_2O_3(s)$

$\Rightarrow$ 1 g of reactant $\frac{96}{224}$ g of O_2 consumed = 0.43 g

(d) $\underset{48\,g}{2Mg(s)} + \underset{32\,g}{O_2(g)} \longrightarrow 2MgO(s)$

$\Rightarrow$ 1 g of reactant $\frac{32}{48}$ g of O_2 consumed = 0.67 g

So, minimum amount of O_2 is consumed per gram of reactant (Fe) in reaction (c).

93. (**c**) $\underset{1\,mol}{Fe_2O_3} + \underset{3\,mol}{3CO} \longrightarrow 2Fe + 3CO_2$

Volume of 1 mole carbon monoxide

$= 22.4\,dm^3 (= L)$ (at STP)

1 mole of ferric oxide is reduced by = 3 moles of CO

$= 3 \times 22.4\ dm^3$ (= L) of CO

$= 67.2\ dm^3$ of CO

94. (**a**)

$$\underset{\substack{2\times 14g \\ 28g}}{N_2(g)} + \underset{\substack{3\times 2g \\ 6g}}{3H_2(g)} \longrightarrow \underset{\substack{2(14+3) \\ 34g}}{2NH_3(g)} \quad \ldots(I)$$

28 g N_2 requires 6 g H_2 gas.

(a) 56 g of N_2 requires $\frac{6\ g}{28\ g} \times 56\ g = 12$ g of H_2

12 g of H_2 gas is required for 56 g of N_2 gas but only 10 g of H_2 gas is present in option (a).

Hence, H_2 gas is the limiting reagent.

In option (b), i.e. 35 g of N_2 + 8 g of H_2.

As 28 g N_2 requires 6 g of H_2.

35 g N_2 requires $\frac{6\ g}{28\ g} \times 35$ g $H_2 \Rightarrow 7.5$ g of H_2.

Here, H_2 gas does not act as limiting reagent since 7.5 g of H_2 gas is required for 35 g of N_2 and 8 g of H_2 is present in reaction mixture.

Mass of H_2 left unreacted = 8 − 7.5 g of H_2. = 0.5 g of H_2.

(c) For 14 g of N_2 + 4 g of H_2.

As we know 28 g of N_2 reacts with 6 g of H_2.

14 g of N_2 reacts with $\frac{6}{28} \times 14$g of $H_2 \Rightarrow 3$ g of H_2.

(d) For 28 g of N_2 + 6 g of H_2, i.e. 28 g of N_2 reacts with 6 g of H_2 (by equation I).

95. (**a**) Perhydrol in 30% (*w/V*) H_2O_2, solution

$$\underset{2\,L}{SO_2} + \underset{1\,L}{\frac{1}{2}O_2} \longrightarrow \underset{2\,L}{SO_2}$$

$\therefore$ 1 L O_2 is required

$$\underset{\substack{2\,mol \\ 2\times 34}}{2H_2O_2} \longrightarrow 2H_2O + \underset{\substack{1\,mol \\ 32}}{O_2}$$

Given, moles of perhydrol = 30 g in 100 mL of solution

2 moles of H_2O_2 produces = 1 mole of O_2

$\frac{30}{34}$ moles of H_2O_2 produces = $\frac{30}{2 \times 34}$ moles of O_2

1 mole of O_2 = 22.4 L of O_2

0.44 mole of $O_2 = 22.4 \times 0.44$ L of O_2

= 9.88 L of O_2

$\simeq$ 10 L O_2

100 mL of H_2O_2 solution givens 10 L O_2.

10 mL of H_2O_2 solution gives 1 L O_2.

03

Oxidation-Reduction

Objective Questions Type I [Only one correct option]

In each of the questions below, four choices are given of which only one is correct.

1. Oxidation state of P in $H_4P_2O_5$, $H_4P_2O_6$ and $H_4P_2O_7$ are respectively

(a) +3, +4, +5 (b) +3, +5, +4

(c) +5, +3, +4 (d) +5, +4, +3

2. Which of the following have been arranged in the decreasing order of oxidation number of sulphur?

(a) $S_2O_6^{2-} > S_2O_7^{2-} > S_2O_3^{2-} > S_8$

(b) $H_2SO_4 > SO_2 > H_2S > H_2S_2O_8$

(c) $SO_2^{2+} > SO_4^{2-} > SO_3^{2-} > HSO_4^-$

(d) $H_2SO_5 > H_2SO_3 > SCl_2 > H_2S$

3. Oxidation number of carbonyl carbon in methanal and methanoic acid are respectively

(a) 0, 0 (b) 0, +2

(c) +1, +2 (d) +1, +3

4. Oxidation number of potassium in K_2O, K_2O_2 and KO_2, respectively, is **[JEE Main 2020]**

(a) +1, +4 and +2 (b) +1, + 2 and +4

(c) +1, + 1 and +1 (d) +2, + 1 and $+\frac{1}{2}$

5. Oxidation states of sulphur atoms in $S_4O_6^{2-}$ from left to right respectively are

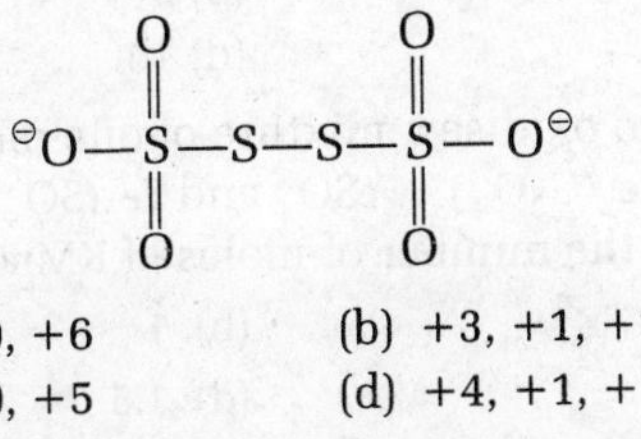

(a) +6, 0, 0, +6 (b) +3, +1, +1, +3

(c) +5, 0, 0, +5 (d) +4, +1, +1, +4

6. Oxidation numbers of Cl atoms in $CaOCl_2$ (bleaching powder) are

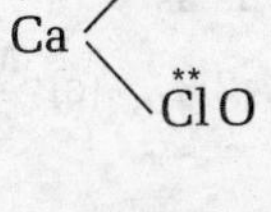

(a) zero on each

(b) − 1 on Cl* and + 1 on Cl**

(c) + 1 on Cl* and − 1 on Cl**

(d) 1 on each

7. In which case oxidation number of Cr has been affected?

(a) $2CrO_4^{2-} + 2H^+ \longrightarrow Cr_2O_7^{2-} + H_2O$

(b) $Cr_2O_7^{2-} + 2OH^- \longrightarrow 2CrO_4^{2-} + H_2O$

(c) $(NH_4)_2Cr_2O_7 \longrightarrow N_2 + Cr_2O_3 + 4H_2O$

(d) $CrO_2Cl_2 + 2OH^- \longrightarrow CrO_4^{2-} + 2HCl$

8. Prussian blue has two types of iron with oxidation number as shown : Fe(III) [Fe(II) $(CN)_6$] What is the net charge on Prussian blue?

(a) − 1 (b) + 1

(c) 0 (d) − 2

9. Select the correct statement in the following reaction

$$NH_4NO_2 \longrightarrow N_2 + 2H_2O$$

(a) Oxidation number of N has changed from − 2 to + 2

(b) Oxidation number of N in NH_4^+ changed from −3 to 0 and that in NO_2^- changed from + 3 to 0

(c) Oxidation number of N in NH_4^+ changed from + 1 to 0 and that in NO_2^- changed from − 1 to 0

(d) No change

10. Which is intramolecular oxidation reduction reaction?

(a) $(NH_4)_2Cr_2O_7 \longrightarrow N_2 + Cr_2O_3 + H_2O$

(b) $NH_4NO_3 \longrightarrow N_2O + 2H_2O$

(c) $2KClO_3 \longrightarrow 2KCl + 3O_2$

(d) All of the above

11. An example of a disproportionation reaction is [JEE Main 2019]

(a) $2MnO_4^- + 10I^- + 16H^+ \longrightarrow 2Mn^{2+} + 5I_2 + 8H_2O$

(b) $2NaBr + Cl_2 \longrightarrow 2NaCl + Br_2$

(c) $2KMnO_4 \longrightarrow K_2MnO_4 + MnO_2 + O_2$

(d) $2CuBr \longrightarrow CuBr_2 + Cu$

12. Which of the following reactions is an example of a redox reaction? [JEE Main 2017]

(a) $XeF_4 + O_2F_2 \longrightarrow XeF_6 + O_2$

(b) $XeF_2 + PF_5 \longrightarrow [XeF]^+PF_6^-$

(c) $XeF_6 + H_2O \longrightarrow XeOF_4 + 2HF$

(d) $XeF_6 + 2H_2O \longrightarrow XeO_2F_2 + 4HF$

13. Consider the following species.
I. $CaOCl_2$ II. $Na_2S_2O_3$ III. Pb_3O_4 IV. $Na_2S_4O_6$
Select the species with different oxidation states of the same element.

(a) I, II (b) I, II, III
(c) II, III, IV (d) I, II, III, IV

14. The oxidation states of Cr, in $[Cr(H_2O)_6]Cl_3$, $[Cr(C_6H_6)_2]$, and $K_2[Cr(CN)_2(O)_2(O_2)(NH_3)]$ respectively are [JEE Main 2018]

(a) +3, +4 and +6 (b) +3, +2 and +4
(c) +3, 0 and +6 (d) +3, 0 and +4

15. In the reaction,
$$Cu + H_2SO_4 \longrightarrow CuSO_4 + H_2O + SO_2$$

(a) H^+ is the oxidising agent
(b) SO_4^{2-} is the oxidising agent
(c) Both (a) and (b) correct
(d) None of the above is correct

16. In the following redox reaction,
$$Cr_2O_7^{2-} + Fe^{2+} \longrightarrow Fe^{3+} + Cr^{3+}$$
1 mole of $Cr_2O_7^{2-}$ oxidises

(a) 1 mole of Fe^{2+} (b) 3 moles of Fe^{2+}
(c) 4 moles of Fe^{2+} (d) 6 moles of Fe^{2+}

17. One mole of ferrous oxalate is oxidised by x mole of MnO_4^- in acidic medium. x is

(a) 0.6 (b) 0.1 (c) 0.3 (d) 1.0

18. Values of p, q, r, s and t are in the following redox reaction
$$pBr_2 + qOH^- \longrightarrow rBr^- + sBrO_3^- + tH_2O$$

	p	q	r	s	t		p	q	r	s	t
(a)	3	6	1	5	3	(b)	3	6	5	3	1
(c)	3	6	5	1	3	(d)	3	5	1	6	3

19. CuS is dissolved in dil. HNO_3. Balanced equation with correct products is

(a) $CuS + 2H^+ + 3NO_3^- \longrightarrow Cu(NO_3)_2 + H_2S + H_2O + NO_2$

(b) $3CuS + 8H^+ + 8NO_3^- \longrightarrow 3Cu(NO_3)_2 + 3S + 4H_2O + 2NO$

(c) $CuS + 4NO_3^- \longrightarrow Cu(NO_3)_2 + H_2S + H_2O$

(d) None of the above is correct

20. In the oxidation of $Fe_2(C_2O_4)_3$ by MnO_4^-/H^+ which species does not appear in final ionic reaction?

(a) Ferric (b) Oxalate
(c) Permanganate (d) All of these

21. If the following is balanced reaction,
$$4O_2^{x-} + 2H_2O \longrightarrow 4OH^- + 3O_2$$
then x is and O_2^{x-} is

(a) -1 and species is superoxide
(b) -2 and species is peroxide
(c) -4 and species is oxide
(d) -1 and species is peroxide

22. O_3 is estimated by I^- in iodometric method. Balanced reaction is

(a) $2H^+ + O_3 + 2I^- \longrightarrow I_2 + O_2 + H_2O$
(b) $2I^- + O_3 + H_2O \longrightarrow I_2 + O_2 + 2OH^-$
(c) Both (a) and (b)
(d) None of the above

23. 0.05 mole of $Ca(OH)_2$ can neutralise H_2SO_4. This H_2SO_4 can be neutralised by

(a) 0.05 mol of NaOH (b) 0.10 mol of NaOH
(c) 0.05 mol of $POH(OH)_2$ (d) None is correct

24. 0.05 equivalent of H_3PO_4 is neutralised by

(a) 0.05 equivalent of NaOH
(b) 0.05 mol of $Al(OH)_3$
(c) Both (a) and (b) correct
(d) None of the above is correct

25. H_3PO_4 can be neutralised by NaOH, $Ca(OH)_2$ and $Al(OH)_3$. 1 equivalent of H_3PO_4 will require mole of each in the ratio

(a) 1 : 1 : 1 (b) 1 : 0.5 : 0.33
(c) 1 : 2 : 3 (d) 2 : 3 : 6

26. In the reaction of oxalate with permanganate in acidic medium, the number of electrons involved in producing one molecule of CO_2 is [JEE Main 2019]

(a) 2 (b) 5
(c) 1 (d) 10

27. In order to oxidise a mixture of one mole of each of FeC_2O_4, $Fe_2(C_2O_4)_3$, $FeSO_4$ and $Fe_2(SO_4)_3$ in acidic medium, the number of moles of $KMnO_4$ required is [JEE Main 2019]

(a) 2 (b) 1
(c) 3 (d) 1.5

28. $NaHC_2O_4$ is neutralised by NaOH and can also be oxidised by $KMnO_4$ (in acidic medium). Equivalent weight is related to molecular weight (M) of $NaHC_2O_4$ in these two reactions as

(a) M, M (b) $2M, 2M$ (c) $\frac{M}{2}, M$ (d) $M, \frac{M}{2}$

29. Equivalent weights of $KMnO_4$ in acidic medium, concentrated alkaline medium and dilute basic medium respectively are $\frac{M}{5}, \frac{M}{1}, \frac{M}{3}$. Reduced products can be
(a) $MnO_2, MnO_4^{2-}, Mn^{2+}$ (b) $MnO_2, Mn^{2+}, MnO_4^{2-}$
(c) $Mn^{2+}, MnO_4^{2-}, MnO_2$ (d) $Mn^{2+}, MnO_2, MnO_4^{2-}$

30. $6CO_2 + 12H_2O \xrightarrow{\text{Sun light}} C_6H_{12}O_6 + 6O_2 + 6H_2O$
Equivalent weights of CO_2 and $C_6H_{12}O_6$ respectively are
(a) 11, 7.5 (b) 44, 180
(c) 22, 15 (d) 44, 90

31. A drunken person was asked to blow a glass tube packed with acidified potassium dichromate. The change in colour of the material from orange to green confirmed the drinking of alcohol. It is due to
I. the oxidation of alcohol with the reduction of dichromate to chromium (III).
II. complex formation of alcohol and dichromate.
III. change in the coordination number of chromium.
Which of the statements given above is/are correct?
(a) I only (b) II only
(c) III only (d) II and III

32. In the following reaction, consider the following statements
$$2Cr(OH)_3 + 3H_2O_2 + 4OH^- \longrightarrow 2CrO_4^{2-} + 8H_2O$$
I. there is colour change from green precipitate to yellow coloured solution.
II. oxidation number of Cr changes from +3 to +6.
III. oxidation number of O in H_2O_2 changes from –2 to –1.
Select the correct statement(s).
(a) I only (b) I and II
(c) II only (d) I and III

33. One way to test for the presence of sugars (say in urine sample) is to treat the sample with silver ions in aqueous ammonia (Tollen's test), with glucose, reaction is
$$C_6H_{12}O_6(aq) + 2Ag^+(aq) + 2OH^-(aq) \longrightarrow$$
In this reaction
(a) glucose is oxidised
(b) silver ion is reduced
(c) a silver-mirror is formed
(d) All of the above are correct

34. A green colour product is formed when acidified $K_2Cr_2O_7$ reacts with
(a) Fe^{2+} (b) SO_2
(c) SO_3^{2-} (d) All of these

35. Which of the following changes requires a reducing agent?
(a) $CrO_4^{2-} \longrightarrow Cr_2O_7^{2-}$
(b) $BrO_3^- \longrightarrow BrO^-$
(c) $H_3AsO_3 \longrightarrow HAsO_4^{2-}$
(d) $Al(OH)_3 \longrightarrow Al(OH)_4^-$

36. In balancing the half-reaction
$$CN^- \longrightarrow CNO^- \text{ (skeletal)}$$
the number of electrons that must be added is
(a) 0 (b) 1 on the right
(c) 1 on the left (d) 2 on the right

37. For the reaction between MnO_4^- and $C_2O_4^{2-}$ in basic solution, the unbalanced equation is
$$MnO_4^- + C_2O_4^{2-} \longrightarrow MnO_2(s) + CO_3^{2-}$$
In a balanced equation, the number of OH^- ions is
(a) 0 (b) 4 on the right
(c) 4 on the left (d) 2 on the left

38. Which of the following is a disproportionation reaction?
(a) $CaCO_3 + 2H^+ \longrightarrow Ca^{2+} + H_2O + CO_2$
(b) $2CrO_4^{2-} + 2H^+ \longrightarrow Cr_2O_7^{2-} + H_2O$
(c) $Cr_2O_7^{2-} + 2OH^- \longrightarrow 2CrO_4^{2-} + H_2O$
(d) $Cu_2O + 2H^+ \longrightarrow Cu + Cu^{2+} + H_2O$

39. When MnO_4^- and I^- react in a strongly basic solution, the products will most likely be
(a) Mn and I_2 (b) MnO_4^{2-}, IO_3^-
(c) MnO_2, O_2, IO^- (d) Mn^{2+}, I_2

40. From the following acids, the one that is strongest is
(a) $HBrO_4$ (b) HOCl
(c) HNO_2 (d) H_3PO_3

41. In an experiment, 20 g of vanadium (V) oxide (molar mass = 182) was reduced by excess of zinc dust in acidic solution to vanadium (II) ions. The required number of moles of iodine to reoxidise vanadium (II) to VO^{2+} is
(a) 0.22 (b) 0.11
(c) 0.30 (d) 0.23

42. For a titration of 100 cm^3 of 0.1 M (0.1 mol L^{-1}) Sn^{2+} to Sn^{4+}, 50 cm^3 of 0.40 M Ce^{4+} solution was required. The oxidation state of cerium in the reduction product is
(a) +1 (b) +2 (c) +3 (d) 0

43. 1 mole of FeC_2O_4 is oxidised by x moles of $Cr_2O_7^{2-}$ in acidic medium, x is
(a) 3 (b) 1.5
(c) 0.5 (d) 1.0

44. In the reaction, 4 moles of electrons are transferred to 1 mole of HNO_3. The possible product obtained due to reduction
(a) 0.4 mole of N_2 (b) 0.5 mole of N_2O
(c) 1 mole of NO_2 (d) 1 mole of NH_3

45. 1 mole of N_2H_4 loses 10 moles of electrons to form a new compound Y. Assuming that all the nitrogen appear in the new compound, what is the oxidation state of nitrogen in Y? (no change in the oxidation state of H)
(a) −1 (b) −3
(c) +3 (d) +5

46. Which combination appears odd *w.r.t.* oxidation number per atom of the underlined?
(a) $H_2\underline{S}O_5, H_2\underline{S}_2O_8, K_2\underline{Cr}_2O_7$ (b) $\underline{Cr}O_5, \underline{Cr}O_4^{2-}, \underline{S}O_4^{2-}$
(c) Both (a) and (b) (d) None of these

47. In $[Cr(O_2)(NH_3)_4(H_2O)]Cl_2$ oxidation number of Cr is +3, then O_2 will be in the form
(a) dioxo (b) peroxo
(c) superoxo (d) oxo

48. Strongest conjugate base is
(a) ClO^- (b) ClO_2^- (c) ClO_3^- (d) ClO_4^-

49. If CO_2 is passed into waste water containing CrO_4^{2-} (yellow) then solution turns
(a) green due to the formation of Cr^{3+}
(b) blue due to the formation of CrO_5
(c) orange due to the formation of $Cr_2O_7^{2-}$
(d) black due to the formation of Cr_2O_3

50. Oxidation number of Cr in the following compounds are *x*, *y*, *z* and *w* respectively
$\underset{x}{K[CrO(O_2)(OH)]}, \underset{y}{K_3[Cr(O_2)_4]}, \underset{z}{(NH_3)_3[Cr(O_2)_2]}, \underset{w}{CrO_2Cl_2}$
These values respectively are
(a) 6, 13, 5, 6 (b) 4, 4, 4, 6
(c) 4, 5, 4, 6 (d) 4, 5, 6, 6

51. If a small amount of $KMnO_4$ is added to conc. H_2SO_4, a green coloured solution with oxidation number of Mn as +7 is formed. Probable compound is
(a) MnO_3HSO_4 (b) K_2MnO_4
(c) MnO_2HSO_4 (d) MnO_2

52. Out of the following redox reactions
I. $NH_4NO_3 \xrightarrow{\Delta} N_2O + 2H_2O$
II. $NH_4NO_2 \xrightarrow{\Delta} N_2 + 2H_2O$
III. $PCl_5 \xrightarrow{\Delta} PCl_3 + Cl_2$
disproportionation is not shown in
(a) I, II (b) II, III (c) I, III (d) I, II and III

53. Bleaching powder ($CaOCl_2$) has two types of chlorine atoms with oxidation number of +1 and −1. It can be represented as
(a) $Ca^{2+}(ClO_2^-)Cl^-$ (b) $Ca^{2+}(ClO_3^-)Cl^-$
(c) $Ca^{2+}(ClO^+)Cl^-$ (d) $Ca^{2+}(ClO^-)Cl^-$

54. In the following redox reaction
$$Zn(s) + NO_3^-(aq) + H^+(aq) \longrightarrow Zn^{2+}(aq) + NH_4^+(aq)$$
$Zn(s)$ and $NO_3^-(aq)$ respectively are
(a) oxidant, reductant (b) reductant, oxidant
(c) both oxidant (d) both reductant

55. Which ordering of compounds is according to the decreasing order of the oxidation state of nitrogen? **[IIT JEE 2012]**
(a) HNO_3, NO, NH_4Cl, N_2 (b) HNO_3, NO, N_2, NH_4Cl
(c) HNO_3, NH_4Cl, NO, N_2 (d) NO, HNO_3, NH_4Cl, N_2

56. Photographic paper is developed with alkaline hydroquinone.

$2AgBr(s) + 2OH^-(aq) +$ 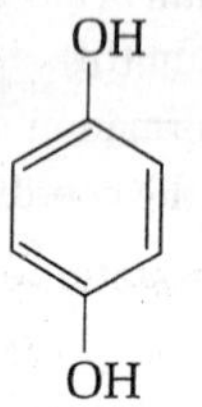 $\longrightarrow$

$2Ag(s) + 2H_2O(l) + 2Br^-(aq) +$ 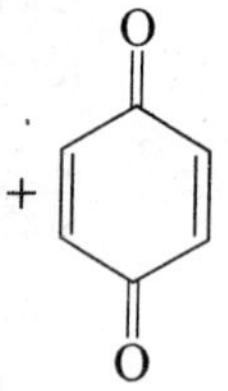

Select the correct statement.
(a) Hydroquinone is the oxidant
(b) Ag^+ is the oxidant
(c) Br^- is the oxidant
(d) Ag^+ is the reductant

57. In the following half-reaction in basic medium
$$Bi^{3+}(aq) \longrightarrow BiO_3^-(aq)$$
one mole of Bi^{3+} have equivalent, equal to
(a) 1 (b) 2 (c) 3 (d) 4

58. The complex $[Fe(H_2O)_5NO]^{2+}$ is formed in the brown ring test for nitrate ion (NO_3^-) when freshly prepared $FeSO_4$ solution is added to aqueous solution of NO_3^- followed by the addition of conc. H_2SO_4. This complex is formed by charge transfer in which
(a) Fe^{2+} changes to Fe^{3+} and NO^+ changes to NO
(b) Fe^{2+} changes to Fe^{3+} and NO changes to NO^+
(c) Fe^{2+} changes to Fe^+ and NO changes to NO^+
(d) no charge transfer takes place

59. When KCN is added to $CuSO_4$ solution there is formation of the stable water soluble complex. This complex is
(a) $K_4[Cu(CN)_6]$ (b) $K_3[Cu(CN)_4]$
(c) $K_2[Cu(CN)_4]$ (d) $K[Cu(CN)_3]$

60. In cyanide method, silver metal is obtained as
$2K[Ag(CN)_2] + Zn \longrightarrow K_2[Zn(CN)_4] + 2Ag$
In this
(a) Ag has been oxidised and Zn has been reduced
(b) Ag has been reduced and Zn has been oxidised
(c) both the metals have been oxidised
(d) both the metals have been reduced

61. In the following unbalanced redox reaction
$$H_2S(g) + SO_2(g) \longrightarrow S(s) + H_2O$$
total number of equivalent of SO_2 is
(a) 4 (b) 3 (c) 2 (d) 1

62. Which has the maximum number of equivalent per mole of the oxidant?
(a) $Zn(s) + VO^{2+}(aq) \longrightarrow Zn^{2+}(aq) + V^{3+}(aq)$
(b) $Ag(s) + NO_3^-(aq) \longrightarrow Ag^+(aq) + NO_2(g)$
(c) $Mg(s) + VO_4^{3-}(aq) \longrightarrow Mg^{2+}(aq) + V^{2+}(aq)$
(d) $I^-(aq) + IO_3^-(aq) \longrightarrow I_3^-(aq)$

63. Which has the least number of equivalent per mole of the reactant?
(a) MnO_4^- changes to MnO_2
(b) MnO_4^- changes to Mn^{2+}
(c) MnO_4^- changes to MnO_4^{2-}
(d) MnO_4^- changes to Mn_2O_3

64. Oxidation number of Cr is +5 in
(a) K_3CrO_8 (b) $(NH_3)_3CrO_4$
(c) K_2CrO_4 (d) $[Cr(NH_3)_5(H_2O)]Cl_3$

65. Sulphur atoms are of two environments in $S_4O_6^{2-}$, difference in oxidation states of two types of sulphur is
(a) 5 (b) 6 (c) 7 (d) 10

66. When Br_2 is passed into hot aqueous solution of Na_2CO_3,
(a) Br^- is formed by reduction
(b) BrO_3^- is formed by oxidation
(c) CO_2 is evolved
(d) All of the above are correct

67. The strength of an aqueous NaOH solution is most accurately determined by titrating : (Note : consider that an appropriate indicator is used) **[JEE Main 2020]**
(a) *Aq.* NaOH in a volumetric flask and concentrated H_2SO_4 in a conical flask
(b) *Aq.* NaOH in a pipette and aqueous oxalic acid in a burette
(c) *Aq.* NaOH in a burette and aqueous oxalic acid in a conical flask
(d) *Aq.* NaOH in a burette and concentrated H_2SO_4 in a conical flask

68. H_2O_2 oxidises MnO_2 to MnO_4^- in basic medium. H_2O_2 and MnO_2 react in the molar ratio of
(a) 1 : 1 (b) 2 : 1
(c) 2 : 3 (d) 3 : 2

69. Equivalent weight of H_3PO_2 in a reaction is found to be half of its molecular weight. It can be due to its
(a) reaction of its two H^+ ions
(b) oxidation to H_3PO_3
(c) Both (a) and (b)
(d) None of the above

70. In the following reaction,
$$VO_3^{2-} + MnO_4^- \longrightarrow Mn^{2+} + VO_4^{3-}$$
1 mole of VO_3^{2-} is oxidised by MnO_4^- using
(a) 0.2 mol
(b) 0.4 mol
(c) 0.8 mol
(d) 1.0 mol

71. Turbunbull's blue has two types of iron with oxidation number as shown $Fe(II)\,[Fe(III)\,CN_6]$
What is the net charge on Turbunbull's blue ?
(a) −1 (b) +1
(c) 0 (d) −2

72. Consider the following redox reactions,
$$xMnO_4^- + yC_2O_4^{2-} + zH^+ \longrightarrow xMn^{2+} + 2yCO_2 + \frac{z}{2}H_2O$$
The values of *x*, *y* and *z* in the reaction are, respectively **[JEE Main 2013]**
(a) 5, 2 and 16 (b) 2, 5 and 8
(c) 2, 5 and 16 (d) 5, 2 and 8

73. $2MnO_4^- + bC_2O_4^{2-} + cH^+ \rightarrow xMn^{2+} + yCO_2 + zH_2O$
If the above equation is balanced with integer coefficients, the value of *c* is .... **[JEE Main 2021, March]**
(a) 15 (b) 16 (c) 4 (d) 10

74. Consider a titration of potassium dichromate solution with acidified Mohr's salt solution using diphenylamine as indicator.
The number of moles of Mohr's salt required per mole of dichromate is **[IIT JEE 2007]**
(a) 3 (b) 4
(c) 5 (d) 6

75. $H_2S_2O_8$ and H_2SO_5 both have +6 oxidation state of sulphur. It is due to
(a) presence of peroxy group
(b) presence of superoxo group
(c) presence of neutral O_2
(d) presence of ozone

Objective Questions Type II [One or more than one correct option(s)]

In each of the questions below, four choices are given, of which one or more than one are correct.

1. If Cl_2 is passed into hot NaOH solution, oxidation number of chlorine changes from
(a) 0 to +5
(b) 0 to −1
(c) 0 to +1
(d) 0 to +7

2. All the following species are strong oxidising agents
I. $S_2O_8^{2-}$ II. $Cr_2O_7^{2-}$
III. MnO_4^-

Their strength as oxidising agents in acidic solution is such that
(a) I > II > III (b) III > II > I
(c) I > III > II (d) III > I > II

3. 0.1 mole of MnO_4^- (in acidic medium) can oxidise
(a) 0.5 mol of Fe^{2+}
(b) 0.25 mol of $C_2O_4^{2-}$
(c) 0.6 mol of $Cr_2O_7^{2-}$
(d) 0.166 mol of FeC_2O_4

4. Which of the following are disproportionation reactions?

(a) 2

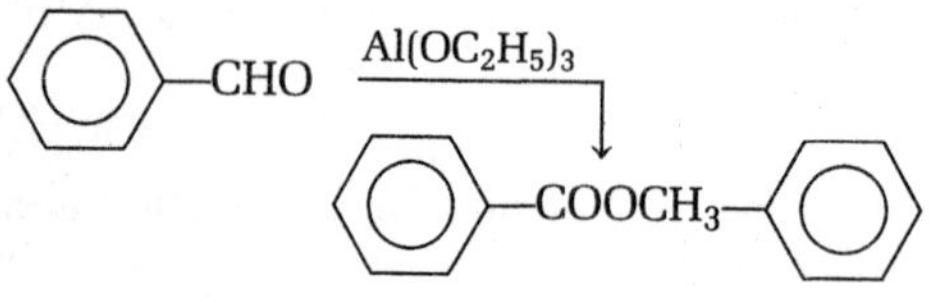

(b) $4H_3PO_3 \xrightarrow{\Delta} 3H_3PO_4 + PH_3$

(c) $NH_4NO_3 \xrightarrow{\Delta} N_2O + 2H_2O$

(d) $PCl_5 \xrightarrow{\Delta} PCl_3 + Cl_2$

5. Which is/are intramolecular disproportionation reaction(s)?

(a) $NH_4NO_2 \xrightarrow{\Delta} N_2 + 2H_2O$

(b) $3H_3PO_2 \xrightarrow{\Delta} 2H_3PO_3 + PH_3$

(c) $\begin{array}{c} CHO \\ | \\ CHO \end{array} + OH^- \longrightarrow \begin{array}{c} COO^- \\ | \\ CH_2OH \end{array}$

(d) $2CH_3CHO \xrightarrow{Al(OC_2H_5)_3} CH_3COOC_2H_5$

6. In the following cases, equivalent weight of the underlined may be equal to molecular weight
(a) $\underline{2CuSO_4} + 4KI \longrightarrow Cu_2I_2 + 2K_2SO_4 + I_2$
(b) $\underline{2Na_2S_2O_3} + I_2 \longrightarrow 2NaI + Na_2S_4O_6$
(c) $\underline{P_4} + 3NaOH + 3H_2O \longrightarrow 3NaH_2PO_2 + PH_3$
(d) $\underline{H_2SO_4} + NaOH \longrightarrow NaHSO_4 + H_2O$

7. The reaction of white phosphorus with aqueous NaOH gives phosphine along with another phosphorus containing compound. The reaction type; the oxidation states of phosphorus in phosphine and the other product are respectively **[IIT JE 2012]**
(a) redox reaction; −3 and −5
(b) redox reaction; 3 and +5
(c) disproportionation reaction; −3 and +5
(d) disproportionation reaction; −3 and +1

8. One mole of ferric oxalate is titrated with acidified potassium permanganate solution. In this
(a) 3 moles of potassium permanganate are required
(b) 1.2 moles of potassium permanganate are required
(c) oxalate ion is oxidised to carbon dioxide
(d) ferric ion is oxidised to ferrate (VI) ion

9. Consider the following reaction,

$$\begin{array}{c} CHO \\ | \\ CHO \end{array} + OH^- \longrightarrow \begin{array}{c} COO^- \\ | \\ CH_2OH \end{array}$$

(a) It is a disproportionation reaction
(b) It is intramolecular redox reaction
(c) OH^- is a reducing as well as oxidising agent
(d) $\begin{array}{c} CHO \\ | \\ CHO \end{array}$ is a reducing as well as oxidising agent

10. The redox reaction among the following is **[JEE Main 2020]**
(a) reaction of H_2SO_4 with NaOH
(b) reaction of $[Co(H_2O)_6]Cl_3$ with $AgNO_3$
(c) combination of dinitrogen with dioxygen at 2000 K
(d) formation of ozone from atmospheric oxygen in the presence of sunlight

11. Select the correct statements.
Equivalent weight of $KMnO_4$ (molar mass = M) is
(a) $\frac{M}{5}$ in acidic medium
(b) $\frac{M}{3}$ in dilute basic medium
(c) M in strongly alkaline medium
(d) $\frac{M}{2}$ in acidic, basic and neutral media

12. Choose the correct statement(s) among the following:
(a) $SnCl_2 \cdot 2H_2O$ is a reducing agent.
(b) SnO_2 reacts with KOH to form $K_2[Sn(OH)_6]$.
(c) A solution of $PbCl_2$ in HCl contains Pb^{2+} and Cl^- ions
(d) The reaction of Pb_3O_4 with hot dilute nitric acid to give PbO_2 is a redox reaction.

13. Out of $\underset{I}{H_2SO_4}, \underset{II}{H_2S_2O_8}, \underset{III}{H_2SO_5}, \underset{IV}{H_2S_2O_3}$ and $\underset{V}{H_2S_2O_7}$

(a) oxidation number of sulphur is +6 in all except IV
(b) peroxy linkage is in I, II and III
(c) peroxy linkage is in II and III
(d) oxidation number of sulphur is −2 in I and V

14. Select the correct statement(s).

(a) Equivalent weight of $Ca(HC_2O_4)_2$ is $M/2$ when it is a reducing agent
(b) Equivalent weight of $Ca(HC_2O_4)_2$ is M when it behaves as an acid
(c) $Ca(HC_2O_4)_2$ can be estimated by MnO_4^- / H^+
(d) $Ca(HC_2O_4)_2$ can be estimated by an acid

Numerical Value Questions

All these questions have a Numerical value as their answer, solve the questions and write your answer.

1. Equivalent mass of Br_2 is 96 g equiv^{-1} in the following disproportionation reaction:

$$Br_2 + OH^- \longrightarrow Br^- + H_2O + \text{oxidised product } (X)$$

Identify the oxidation state of Br in (X)? (Br = 80)

2. HCHO disproportionates to $HCOO^-$ and CH_3OH in the presence of OH^- (Cannizzaro reaction).

$$2HCHO + OH^- \longrightarrow HCOO^- + CH_3OH$$

The equivalent weight of HCHO is …… .

3. A sample of pure $KHC_2O_4 \cdot H_2C_2O_4 \cdot 2H_2O$ (three replaceable hydrogen) requires 4.62 moles of NaOH for titration.

How many moles of $KMnO_4$ will the same sample react with?

4. If 10 g V_2O_5 is dissolved in acid and reduced to V^{2+} by treatment with zinc metal, how many moles of I_2 could be reduced by the resulting V^{2+} solution, as it is oxidised to V^{4+}? (V = 51)

$$V_2O_5 + 10H^+ + 6e^- \longrightarrow 2V^{2+} + 5H_2O$$
$$V^{2+} + I_2 + H_2O \longrightarrow 2I^- + VO^{2+} + 2H^+$$

5. A compound is made of Ba (oxidation number = + 2), Xe (oxidation number = + 8) and oxygen. Xe and O are present in the atomic ratio of 1 : 6. In the 1 mole of compound total moles of each element is ……… .

6. The ion A^{n+} is oxidised to AO_3^- by MnO_4^-, changing to Mn^{2+} in acidic solution. Given that 2.68×10^{-3} moles of A^{n+} requires 1.61×10^{-3} mole of MnO_4^-, the value of n is ……… .

Comprehension Based Questions

In these questions, a passage has been given followed by questions based on it. You have to answer the questions based on the passage given.

Passage 1 Following experiment is given to determine the oxidation state of vanadium at different stages.

When ammonium vanadate is heated with oxalic acid solution, a compound Z is formed. A sample of Z was titrated with $KMnO_4$ solution is hot acidic solution. The resulting liquid was reduced with SO_2, the excess SO_2 boiled off, and the liquid again titrated with $KMnO_4$. The ratio of the volumes of $KMnO_4$ used in the two titrations was 5 : 1. $KMnO_4$ oxidises all oxidation state of vanadium to vanadium (+V) and SO_2 reduces vanadium (+V) to vanadium (+IV).

Read the above experiment and answer the following questions.

1. What is the oxidation state of vanadium in the compound Z?

(a) +2 (b) +1 (c) 0 (d) −1

2. If vanadium exists as VO_4^{3-}, reduced species by SO_2 would be

(a) VO_4^{2-} (b) VO_3^{2-}
(c) VO_2^{2-} (d) VO^{2-}

3. Consider the following redox reaction,

$$VO_3^{2-} + MnO_4^- \longrightarrow Mn^{2+} + VO_4^{3-}$$

1 mole of VO_3^{2-} is oxidised by x mole of MnO_4^-. Thus, x is

(a) 0.2 (b) 0.4 (c) 0.8 (d) 1.0

Passage 2 Read the following experimental facts and answer the questions at the end of it.

"$KMnO_4$ and $K_2Cr_2O_7$ are widely used as volumetric reagents for analytical estimation of iron, hydrogen peroxide, iodide, ozone, sulphite, nitrite, etc. Reaction is carried out in acidic medium."

1. Equivalents of MnO_4^- and $Cr_2O_7^{2-}$ per mole of the ion in acidic medium are in the ratio of

(a) 1 : 1 (b) 1 : 5
(c) 6 : 1 (d) 5 : 6

2. In the determination of Fe^{2+} which reagent is self-indicator?

(a) $KMnO_4$
(b) $K_2Cr_2O_7$
(c) Both (a) and (b)
(d) None of the above

Passage 3 Consider the following Redox Predominance Diagram for iron in different oxidation state.

Oxidation state	Half-reaction	$E°/V$
+6	$FeO_4^{2-} + 8H^+ + 3e^- \rightleftharpoons Fe^{3+} + 4H_2O$	+2.20 V
+3	$Fe^{3+} + e^- \longrightarrow Fe^{2+}$	+0.77 V
+2	$Fe^{2+} + 2e^- \rightleftharpoons Fe$	−0.44 V

Answers the following questions.

1. Select the best oxidising and reducing agent.
(a) Fe, Fe^{2+}
(b) FeO_4^{2-}, Fe^{3+}
(c) FeO_4^{2-}, Fe^{2+}
(d) FeO_4^{2-}, Fe

2. Most thermodynamically stable species is
(a) FeO_4^{2-} (b) Fe^{3+}
(c) Fe^{2+} (d) Fe

3. Least thermodynamically species is
(a) FeO_4^{2-} (b) Fe^{3+}
(c) Fe^{2+} (d) Fe

Passage 4 Every disproportionation reaction is a redox reaction but every redox reaction may not be disproportionation. Disproportionation reaction may be intramolecular if same species is oxidised and reduced. Based on the above statement answer the following questions.

1. A: $2C_6H_5CHO + KOH \longrightarrow C_6H_5COOK + C_6H_5CH_2OH$

B: $3Cl_2 + 6KOH \longrightarrow 5KCl + KClO_3 + 3H_2O$

Select the correct statement.
(a) Both are redox reactions
(b) Both are disproportionation reactions
(c) A is a disproportionation and B is a redox reaction
(d) A is a redox reaction, B is a disproportionation reaction

2. Following reaction is used to produce Br_2

$$5Br^- + BrO_3^- + 6H^+ \longrightarrow 3Br_2 + 3H_2O$$

In this reaction
(a) Br^- disproportionates to Br_2
(b) BrO_3^- disproportionates to Br_2
(c) Br^- has been oxidised and BrO_3^- has been reduced
(d) Br^- has been reduced and BrO_3^- has been oxidised

Matrix-Match Type

Given below are Matching Type Questions, with two columns (each having some items) each . Each item of Column I has to be matched with the items of Column II.

1. Match the different compounds of Mn (in Column I) with oxidation number (in Column II).

	Column I		Column II
A.	MnO_3HSO_4	1.	+4
B.	K_2MnO_4	2.	+7
C.	MnO_2	3.	+6
D.	Mn_2O_3	4.	+2
E.	$Mn(HCO_3)_2$	5.	+3

2. Match the half-reactions (in Column I) with change in oxidation number (in Column II).

Column I	Column II
A. $Cl^- \longrightarrow ClO_4^-$	1. 2
B. $Cr^{3+} \longrightarrow CrO_5$	2. 8
C. $H_2O_2 \longrightarrow O_2$	3. 0
D. $CrO_2^{2+} \longrightarrow CrO_4^{2-}$	4. 3

3. Match the compounds (in Column I) with the matter (in Column II).

Column I	Column II
A. $H_2\underline{S_2}O_8$	1. Peroxy linkage
B. $\underline{Cr}\,O_5$	2. Oxidation number of the underlined atom 6
C. $H_2\underline{S}O_5$	3. H_2O_2 is the hydrolysis product
D. $K_2\underline{Cr}O_4$	4. Caro's acid
E. $(NH_3)_3\overset{IV}{Cr}O_4$	5. Marshall's acid

4. Match the compounds/ions having underlined atoms of different oxidation states (in Column I) with values (in Column II).

	Column I		Column II
A.	$CaO\underline{Cl_2}$	1.	6
B.	$Na_2\underline{S_2}O_3$	2.	3
C.	$\underline{N_2}H_4O_2$	3.	2
D.	$[Fe_2(CN)_6]^-$ (Prussian blue)	4.	−1
E.	$Cr\underline{O_5}$	5.	1
		6.	−2
		7.	−3

Single Integer Answer Questions

Answer of these questions is a single digit lying between 0 to 9.

1. For the following reaction,

$$N_2 + 3H_2 \longrightarrow 2NH_3$$

$$\text{equivalent mass of } N_2 = \frac{\text{molar mass of } N_2}{x}$$

What is the value of x?

2. How many peroxy linkages are present in CrO_5?

3. $S_2O_3^{2-}$ has two types of sulphur. What is the difference in oxidation states of two types of sulphur?

4. What is the oxidation number of Cr in $(NH_3)_3Cr(O_2)_2$?

5. How many of the following underlined atoms have oxidation number of (+6)?

$H_2\underline{S_2}O_3$, $H_2\underline{S}O_5$, $H_2\underline{S_2}O_8$, $H_2\underline{S_2}O_7$, $H_2\underline{Cr_2}O_7$, $K_2\underline{Mn}O_4$, $\underline{Cr}O_3$, $\underline{Cr}O_5$

6. How many of the following underlined atoms have different oxidation number?

$H_2S_2O_3$, $H_2\underline{S_4}O_6$, $CaO\underline{Cl_2}$, $Cr\underline{O_5}$, $Cr\underline{O_3}$, $CrO_2\underline{Cl_2}$

7. Among the following, the number of elements showing only one non-zero oxidation state is O, Cl, F, N, P, Sn, Tl, Na, Ti. **[IIT JEE 2010]**

8. How many of the following species have more than one oxidation state (except zero)?

Cu, Zn, Cr, Mn, Cl, O, P, Sn, Al, Tl

9. In the ring test of NO_3^-, following complex appears as ring $[Fe(H_2O)_5NO]^{2+}$. What is the oxidation state of Fe?

10. Difference in oxidation number of two Cl atoms in bleaching powder is x. What is the value of x?

11. What is the basicity of oxyacid of phosphorus with oxidation number +5?

12. In oxysalt of Mn, equivalent mass is one-fifth of ionic mass of oxysalt. What is the oxidation number of Mn in oxysalt?

13. How many moles of $KMnO_4$ are required to oxidise 10 moles of iron (II) sulphate (IV) in acidic medium?

14. In neutral or faintly alkaline solution, 8 moles of permanganate anion quantitative oxidise thiosulphate anions to produce X moles of a sulphur containing product. The magnitude of X is ... . **[JEE Advanced 2016]**

Answers

Objective Questions Type I [Only one correct option]

1. (a)	2. (d)	3. (b)	4. (c)	5. (c)	6. (b)	7. (c)	8. (a)	9. (b)	10. (d)
11. (d)	12. (a)	13. (d)	14. (c)	15. (b)	16. (d)	17. (a)	18. (c)	19. (b)	20. (a)
21. (a)	22. (c)	23. (b)	24. (a)	25. (b)	26. (c)	27. (a)	28. (d)	29. (c)	30. (a)
31. (a)	32. (b)	33. (d)	34. (d)	35. (b)	36. (d)	37. (c)	38. (d)	39. (b)	40. (a)
41. (a)	42. (c)	43. (c)	44. (b)	45. (c)	46. (d)	47. (c)	48. (a)	49. (c)	50. (c)
51. (a)	52. (d)	53. (d)	54. (b)	55. (b)	56. (b)	57. (b)	58. (c)	59. (b)	60. (b)
61. (a)	62. (d)	63. (c)	64. (a)	65. (a)	66. (d)	67. (c)	68. (d)	69. (b)	70. (a)
71. (a)	72. (a)	73. (b)	74. (d)	75. (a)					

Objective Questions Type II [One or more than one correct option(s)]

1. (a, b)	2. (c)	3. (a, b, d)	4. (a, b)	5. (c)
6. (a, b, d)	7. (c)	8. (b, c)	9. (b, d)	10. (c)
11. (a, b, c)	12. (a, b, c, d)	13. (a, c)	14. (a, b, c)	

Numerical Value Questions

1. 5   2. 30   3. 1.232   4. 0.11   5. 9   6. 2

Comprehension Based Questions

Passage 1 – 1. (c) 2. (c) 3. (d)

Passage 2 – 1. (d) 2. (a)

Passage 3 – 1. (d) 2. (a) 3. (d)

Passage 4 – 1. (a) 2. (c)

Matrix-Match Type

1. A → (2); B → (3); C → (1); D → (5); E → (4)

2. A → (2); B → (4); C → (1); D → (3)

3. A → (1,2,3,5); B → (1,2); C → (1,2,3); D → (2); E → (1)

4. A → (4,5); B → (1,6); C → (2,7); D → (2,3); E → (4,6)

Single Integer Answer Questions

1. (6)	2. (2)	3. (4)	4. (4)	5. (7)	6. (3)	7. (2)	8. (8)	9. (1)	10. (2)
11. (3)	12. (7)	13. (6)	14. (6)						

Solutions

Objective Questions Type I [Only one correct option]

1. (*a*) $H_4P_2O_5$ $\quad 4+2x-10=0$

$x=3$

$H_4P_2O_6$ $\quad 4+2x-12=0$

$x=+4$

$H_4P_2O_7$ $\quad 4+2x-14=0$

$x=+5$

2. (*d*)

$\underset{+5}{S_2O_6^{2-}}$	$\underset{+6}{S_2O_7^{2-}}$	$\underset{+4}{S_2O_3^{2-}}$	$\underset{0}{S_8}$
$\underset{+6}{H_2SO_4}$	$\underset{+4}{SO_2}$	$\underset{-2}{H_2S}$	$\underset{+6}{H_2S_2O_8}$
$\underset{+6}{SO_2^{2+}}$	$\underset{+6}{SO_4^{2-}}$	$\underset{+4}{SO_3^{2-}}$	$\underset{+6}{HSO_4^-}$
$\underset{+6}{H_2SO_5}$	$\underset{+4}{H_2SO_3}$	$\underset{+2}{SCl_2}$	$\underset{-2}{H_2S}$

3. (*b*) 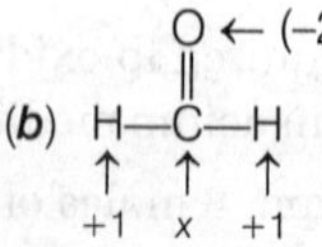

Thus, $x=0$

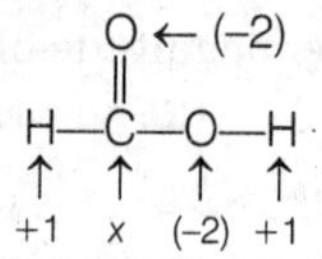

Thus, $x=+2$

4. (*c*) Elements of group 1 (alkali metals) show only one non-zero oxidation number, which is equal to +1.

K_2O consists of K^+ and O^{2-} ions

K_2O_2 (potassium peroxide) consists of K^+ and O_2^{2-} ions. KO_2 (potassium superoxide) consists of K^+ and O_2^- ions.

Thus, in all the given compounds potassium exhibits +1 oxidation state.

5. (*c*) 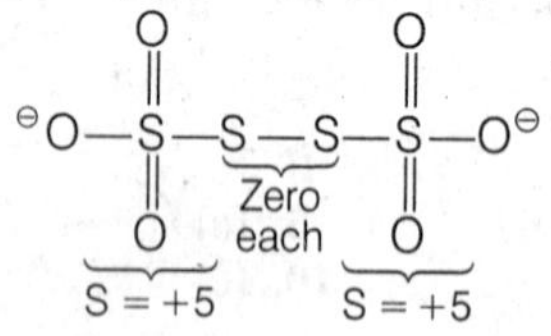

6. (*b*) 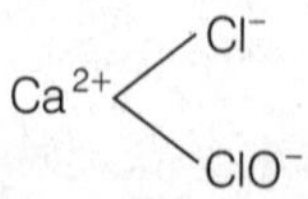

Cl^-, $\quad x=-1$

ClO^- $\quad x-2=-1$

$x=+1$

7. (*c*) $\underset{\uparrow \atop +6}{(NH_4)_2Cr_2O_7} \longrightarrow \underset{\uparrow \atop +3}{Cr_2O_3}$

8. (*a*) $Fe^{III}[Fe^{II}(CN)_6]$

$\uparrow\ \uparrow\ \uparrow$

$+3\ \ +2\ \ -6=-1$

9. (*b*) NH_4^+; $\quad x+4=+1$

$x=-3$

NO_2^-; $\quad x-4=-1$

$x=+3$

N_2; $\quad x=0$

$$\underset{-3}{NH_4^+}+\underset{+3}{NO_2^-}\longrightarrow \underset{0}{N_2}$$

10. (*d*)

Oxidation of	Reduction of
(a) N from −3 (in NH_4^+) to 0 (in N_2)	Cr from +6 (in $Cr_2O_7^{2-}$) to +3 (in Cr_2O_3)
(b) N from −3 (in NH_4^+) to +1 (in N_2O)	N from +5 (in NO_3^-) to +1 (in N_2O)
(c) O from −2 (in ClO_3^-) to 0 (in O_2)	Cl from +5 (in ClO_3^-) to −1 (in Cl^-)

All redox reactions occur within molecule. Hence, all are intramolecular redox reactions.

11. (*d*) In disproportionation reactions, same element undergoes oxidation as well as reduction.

e.g.

$$2\overset{+1}{Cu}Br \longrightarrow \overset{+2}{Cu}Br_2+\overset{0}{Cu}$$

(Reduction: Cu +1 → 0; Oxidation: Cu +1 → +2)

Here, CuBr get oxidised to $CuBr_2$ and also it get reduced to Cu. Other given reactions and their types are given below.

$$2\,\overset{+7}{Mn}O_4^- + 10I^- + 16\,H^+ \longrightarrow 2Mn^{+2}+5I_2+8H_2O$$

(Reduction: Mn; Oxidation: I)

In the given reaction, MnO_4^- get oxidised to Mn^{2+} and I^- get reduced to I_2. It is an example of redox reaction. The reaction takes place in acidic medium.

$$2KMnO_4 \longrightarrow K_2MnO_4+MnO_2+O_2$$

The given reaction is an example of decomposition reaction. Here, one compound split into two or more simpler compounds, atleast one of which must be in elemental form.

$$2NaBr+Cl_2 \longrightarrow 2NaCl+Br_2$$

The given reaction is an example of displacement reaction. In this reaction, an atom (or ion) replaces the ion (or atom) of another element from a compound.

12. (*a*) The reaction in which oxidation and reduction occur simultaneously are termed as redox reaction.

$$\overset{+4}{X}eF_4+\overset{+1}{O_2}F_2 \longrightarrow \overset{+6}{X}eF_6+\overset{0}{O_2}$$

Since, Xe undergoes oxidation while O undergoes reduction. So, it is an example of redox reaction.

13. (*d*) (I) 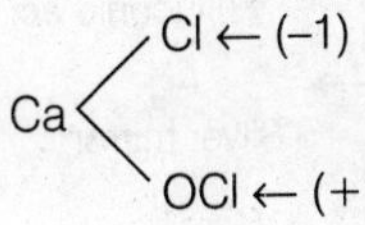 (II) 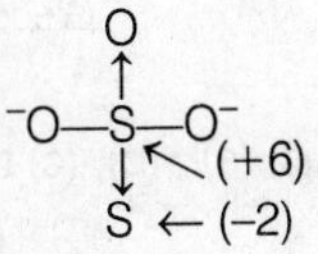

(III) $PbO_2 \cdot 2PbO$
$\uparrow$ +4 $\quad\uparrow$ +2

(IV) 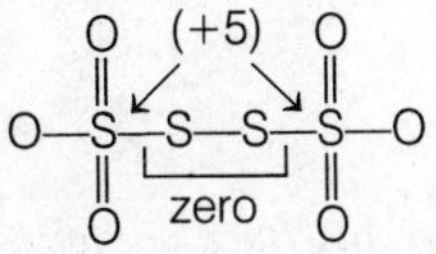

14. (*c*) Let the oxidation state of Cr in all cases is '*x*'

(i) Oxidation state of Cr in $[Cr(H_2O)_6]Cl_3$

$x + (0 \times 6) + (-1 \times 3) = 0$

or $x + 0 - 3 = 0$ or $x = +3$

(ii) Oxidation state of Cr in $[Cr(C_6H_6)_2]$

$x + (2 \times 0) = 0$ or $x = 0$

(iii) Oxidation state of Cr in

$K_2[Cr(CN)_2(O)_2(O_2)(NH_3)]$

$1 \times 2 + x + (-1 \times 2) + (-2 \times 2) + (-2) + 0 = 0$

or $2 + x - 2 - 4 - 2 = 0$ or $x - 6 = 0$ hence, $x = +6$

Thus, +3, 0 and +6 is the answer.

15. (*b*) $\underset{0}{Cu} + \underset{+6}{SO_4^{2-}} \longrightarrow \underset{+2}{Cu^{2+}} + \underset{+4}{SO_2}$

(Oxidation)

Cu is oxidised by SO_4^{2-}.

16. (*d*) $Cr_2O_7^{2-} + Fe^{2+} \longrightarrow Fe^{3+} + Cr^{3+}$

Balance Cr : $Cr_2O_7^{2-} \longrightarrow 2Cr^{3+}$

O.N. of two Cr-atoms $\quad +12 \quad +6$

Change in O.N.] 6 units

$Fe^{2+} \longrightarrow Fe^{3+}$

O.N. of Fe] $\quad +2 \quad +3$

Change in O.N.] 1 unit

by cross-multiplication

$Cr_2O_7^{2-} + 6Fe^{2+} \longrightarrow 6Fe^{3+} + 2Cr^{3+}$

1 mol $Cr_2O_7^{2-} = 6 \text{ mol } Fe^{2+}$

17. (*a*) $MnO_4^- + 5Fe^{2+} \xrightarrow{H^+} 5Fe^{3+} + Mn^{2+}$

$2MnO_4^- + 5C_2O_4^{2-} \xrightarrow{H^+} 10CO_2 + 2Mn^{2+}$

Net : $3MnO_4^- + 5FeC_2O_4 \xrightarrow{H^+} 5Fe^{3+} + 3Mn^{2+} + 10CO_2$

Both Fe^{2+} and $C_2O_4^{2-}$ are oxidised by MnO_4^-

$5\ FeC_2O_4 \equiv 3MnO_4^-$

$1\ FeC_2O_4 \equiv \frac{3}{5} MnO_4^- = 0.6 \text{ mol}$

18. (*c*) $\underset{p}{3Br_2} + \underset{q}{6OH^-} \longrightarrow \underset{r}{5Br^-} + \underset{s}{BrO_3^-} + \underset{t}{3H_2O}$

Br_2 disproportionates to Br^- and BrO_3^- when treated with hot alkali solution.

$[\frac{1}{2}Br_2 + e^- \longrightarrow Br^-] \times 5$

$\frac{1}{2}Br_2 + 6OH^- \longrightarrow BrO_3^- + 3H_2O + 5e^-$

$3Br_2 + 6OH^- \longrightarrow 5Br^- + BrO_3^- + 3H_2O$

19. (*b*) CuS (black ppt.) on boiling with HNO_3 results in the formation of colloidal S and blue coloured solution of $Cu(NO_3)_2$.

20. (*a*) $Fe_2(C_2O_4)_3 \rightleftharpoons 2Fe^{3+} + C_2O_4^{2-}$

MnO_4^- is reduced to Mn^{2+} and $C_2O_4^{2-}$ is oxidised to CO_2.

Fe^{3+} is not affected, hence does not appear in net ionic reaction.

21. (*a*) Reaction is balanced.

Thus, $4x = -4$

$\therefore \quad x = -1$

Thus, O_2^{x-} is O_2^- (Superoxide ion).

22. (*c*) O_3 can be estimated iodometrically in acidic and basic medium both. I^- is oxidised to I_2.

23. (*b*) $\underset{1\text{ mol}}{Ca(OH)_2} + \underset{1\text{ mol}}{H_2SO_4} \longrightarrow CaSO_4 + 2H_2O$

$\underset{1\text{ mol}}{H_2SO_4} + \underset{2\text{ mol}}{2NaOH} \longrightarrow Na_2SO_4 + 2H_2O$

Thus, 0.05 mol $Ca(OH)_2 \equiv 0.05$ mol H_2SO_4

$\equiv 0.10$ mol NaOH

24. (*a*) 1 equivalent of an acid $\equiv$ 1 equivalent of a base

0.05 equivalent of $H_3PO_4 \equiv 0.05$ equivalent of NaOH

(or any base)

25. (*b*) H_3PO_4 (1 equivalent) $\equiv$ 1 equivalent NaOH

$\equiv$ 1 equivalent $Ca(OH)_2$

$\equiv$ 1 equivalent $Al(OH)_3$

In terms of moles

1 equivalent NaOH $\equiv$ 1 mol NaOH

1 equivalent $Ca(OH)_2 = 0.5$ mol $Ca(OH)_2$

1 equivalent $Al(OH)_3 \equiv \frac{1}{3}$ mol $Al(OH)_3$

Thus, molar ratio is $1 : \frac{1}{2} : \frac{1}{3}$.

26. (*c*) Reaction of oxalate with permanganate in acidic medium.

$5C_2O_4^{2-} + 2MnO_4^- \longrightarrow 10CO_2 + 2Mn^{2+} + 8H_2O$

n-factor $(4-3) \times 2 = 2$ $\quad (7-2) = 5$

Number of mole $\quad 5 \quad 2 \quad 10$

$\Rightarrow 5C_2O_4^{2-}$ ions transfer $10e^-$ to produce 10 molecules of CO_2. So, number of electrons involved in producing 10 molecule of CO_2 is 10. Thus, number of electrons involved in producing 1 molecule of CO_2 is 1.

27. (*a*) No. of gram equivalents of *OA* = No. of gm equivalents of *RA*

$(N \times V)_{OA} = (N \times V)_{RA}$

$$(M \times nf \times V)_{OA} = (M \times nf \times V)_{RA}$$
$$(\text{moles} \times nf)_{OA} = (\text{moles} \times nf)_{RA}$$

$KMnO_4$ (In acidic medium)

$$5e^- + 8H^+ + MnO_4^- \longrightarrow Mn^{2+} + H_2O$$

nf = no. of e^- s required for reduction = 5

$Fe(C_2O_4)$

$$Fe^{2+} \longrightarrow Fe^{3+} + e^- \qquad nf = 1$$
$$C_2O_4^{2-} \longrightarrow 2CO_2 + 2e^- \qquad nf = 2 \times 1 = 2$$
$$nf[Fe(C_2O_4)] = 1 + 2 = 3$$

$Fe_2(C_2O_4)_3$

$$Fe^{+3} \Rightarrow nf = 0$$
$$C_2O_4^{2-} \longrightarrow 2CO_2 + 2e^-, nf = 2 \times 3 = 6$$

$nf[Fe_2(C_2O_4)_3] = 0 + 6 = 6$

$FeSO_4$

$$Fe^{+2} \longrightarrow Fe^{+3} \qquad nf = 1$$

$nf\,[FeSO_4] = 1$

28. (*d*) $NaHC_2O_4 + NaOH \longrightarrow Na_2C_2O_4 + H_2O$

$NaHC_2O_4$ behaves as an acid and $1\ H^+ \equiv 1\ OH^-$

Thus, equivalent weight of $NaHC_2O_4 = M$

$$5\,HC_2O_4^- + 2MnO_4^- \longrightarrow 2Mn^{2+} + 10CO_2$$

$HC_2O_4^-$ is oxidised to CO_2 and thus change in oxidation number = + 2 units

$$\text{Equivalent mass} = \frac{M}{2}$$

	Change	Equiv. mass
29. (c) $\underset{+7}{MnO_4^-} \longrightarrow \underset{+2}{Mn^{2+}}$	5	$\frac{M}{5}$
$\underset{+7}{MnO_4^-} \longrightarrow \underset{+6}{MnO_4^{2-}}$	1	M
$\underset{+7}{MnO_4^-} \longrightarrow \underset{+4}{MnO_2}$	3	$\frac{M}{3}$

30. (*a*) $6CO_2 + 12H_2O \xrightarrow{\text{Sunlight}} C_6H_{12}O_6 + 6O_2 + 6H_2O$

$$6CO_2 \equiv C_6H_{12}O_6 \equiv 6O_2 \equiv 192\,g(O)$$

Thus, $8\,g(O) \equiv \frac{6 \times 44 \times 8}{192} CO_2 = 11\,g\ CO_2$

$$\equiv \frac{180 \times 8}{192} g\ C_6H_{12}O_6$$
$$= 7.5\,g\ C_6H_{12}O_6$$

31. (*a*) $\underset{\text{Alcohol}}{CH_3CH_2OH} + \underset{\text{Orange}}{Cr_2O_7^{2-}} + H^+ \longrightarrow \underset{\text{Green}}{Cr^{3+}} + CH_3COOH$

Reduction ($Cr_2O_7^{2-} \to Cr^{3+}$)
Oxidation ($CH_3CH_2OH \to CH_3COOH$)

32. (*b*) $2Cr(OH)_3 + 3H_2O_2 + 4OH^- \longrightarrow 2CrO_4^{2-} + 8H_2O$

O.N.: Cr in $Cr(OH)_3$ (+3) (Green ppt.); O in H_2O_2 (–1); Cr in CrO_4^{2-} +6 (Yellow); O in H_2O (–2)

I. True

II. True

III. False as O.N. of O in H_2O_2 changes from (–1) to (–2)

33. (*d*) It is called silver-mirror test for reducing sugar

$$\underset{\text{Glucose}}{C_5H_{11}O_5CHO} \longrightarrow \underset{\text{Gluconic acid}}{C_5H_{11}O_5 \cdot COOH}$$
$$Ag^+ \longrightarrow \underset{\text{Silver mirror}}{Ag}$$

Thus, (a) , (b), (c) true.

34. (*d*) $Cr_2O_7^{2-} \longrightarrow \underset{\text{Green}}{Cr^{3+}}$

$$Fe^{2+} \longrightarrow Fe^{3+} + e^-$$
$$SO_2 / SO_3^{2-} \longrightarrow SO_4^{2-} + 2e^-$$

$Fe^{2+}, SO_2/SO_3^{2-}$ reduce $Cr_2O_7^{2-}/H^+$ to Cr^{3+} (green)

35. (*b*) (a,d) no change

(b) reduction, (c) oxidation

36. (*d*) $CN^- \longrightarrow CNO^-$

O.N. of nitrogen $4 + x = -1 \qquad 4 + x - 2 = -1$

$x = -5 \qquad x = -3$

CN^- is thus oxidised. Thus, two electrons are lost.

Or

(d) $CN^- \longrightarrow CNO^-$

Balancing O-atom by adding H_2O

$$H_2O + CN^- \longrightarrow CNO^-$$

Balancing H-atom by adding H^+

$$H_2O + CN^- \longrightarrow CNO^- + 2H^+$$

Balancing the charges on both sides,

$$H_2O^{+1} + CN^- \longrightarrow CNO^- + 2H^+ + 2e^-$$

Oxidation

37. (c) $\overset{+7}{Mn}O_4^- + \overset{+3}{C_2}O_4^{2-} \rightarrow \overset{+4}{Mn}O_2(s) + \overset{+4}{C}O_3^{2-}$

Steps involved in balancing the reaction is as follows.

Oxidation half	Reduction half
$C_2O_4^{2-} \longrightarrow CO_3^{2-}$ $C_2O_4^{2-} \longrightarrow 2CO_3^{2-}$ Balancing all atoms	$MnO_4^- \longrightarrow MnO_2$ other than O and H
$2OH^- + C_2O_4^{2-} \longrightarrow 2CO_3^{2-}$ Balancing O-atom	$MnO_4^- \longrightarrow MnO_2$ by adding H_2O
$2OH^- + C_2O_4^{2-} \longrightarrow 2O_3^{2-} + 2H^+$ Balancing H-atom	$MnO_4^- \longrightarrow MnO_2 + 2OH^-$ by adding H^+
$2OH^- + C_2O_4^{2-} \longrightarrow 2CO_3^{2-} + 2H^+ + 2e^-] \times 3$ Balancing charges	$2H^+ + MnO_4^- \longrightarrow MnO_2 + 2OH^-$ by adding e^-
	$3e^- + 2H^+ + MnO_4^- \longrightarrow MnO_2 + 2OH^-$

Making no. of e^- exchange equal and adding both sides

$$3C_2O_4^{2-} + 6e^- + 4H^+ \longrightarrow 6CO_3^{2-} + 6H^+ + 6e^- + 2MnO_2 + 4OH^-$$

38. (*d*) $\underset{+1}{Cu_2O} \longrightarrow \underset{0}{Cu} + \underset{+2}{Cu^{2+}}$

39. (*b*) MnO_4^- oxidises I^- to IO_3^- in strongly basic medium and itself reduced to MnO_4^{2-}.

$$\underset{(+7)}{MnO_4^-} + \underset{(-1)}{I^-} \longrightarrow \underset{+5}{IO_3^-} + \underset{\substack{\text{green}\\+6}}{MnO_4^{2-}}$$

40. (*a*) Strongest acid is that which has maximum value of O.N. of the central atom

$HBrO_4$	O.N. of Br = +7
HOCl	O.N. of Cl = +1
HNO_2	O.N. of N = +3
H_3PO_3	O.N. of P = +3

41. (*a*) $V_2O_5 \longrightarrow V^{2+} \longrightarrow VO^{2+}$

$$\underset{\substack{20\text{ g}\\0.11\text{ mol}}}{V_2O_5} \longrightarrow \underset{0.22\text{ mol}}{2V^{2+}}$$

$$\underset{+2}{V^{2+}} + \underset{0}{I_2} \longrightarrow \underset{+4}{VO^{2+}} + \underset{-2}{2I^-}$$

Thus, $\underset{0.11\text{ mol}}{V_2O_5} \equiv 2V^{2+} = 2VO^{2+} \equiv \underset{0.22\text{ mol}}{2I_2}$

42. (*c*) $Sn^{2+} \longrightarrow Sn^{4+} + 2e^-$ increase in O.N. = 2

$Ce^{4+} + ne^- \longrightarrow Ce^{(4-n)}$ decrease in O.N. = n

To balance

$$nSn^{2+} + 2Ce^{4+} \longrightarrow nSn^{4+} + 2Ce^{(4-n)}$$

Millimoles of $Sn^{2+} = 100 \times 0.1 = 10$

Millimoles of $Ce^{4+} = 50 \times 0.4 = 20$

Thus, $\frac{n}{2} = \frac{10}{20}$

$\therefore$ $n = 1$

Thus, oxidation state of cerium in the reduced product

$= (Ce^{4-1} = Ce^{3+}) = +3$

43. (*c*) $FeC_2O_4 \rightleftharpoons Fe^{2+} + C_2O_4^{2-}$

Fe^{2+} is oxidised to Fe^{3+} and $C_2O_4^{2-}$ to CO_2 by $Cr_2O_7^{2-}$

$$Fe^{2+} \longrightarrow Fe^{3+} + e^-] \times 6$$

$$Cr_2O_7^{2-} + 14H^+ + 6e^- \longrightarrow 2Cr^{3+} + 7H_2O$$

Thus, $6Fe^{2+} \equiv 1\,Cr_2O_7^{2-}$

$$1\,Fe^{2+} \equiv \frac{1}{6} Cr_2O_7^{2-}$$

$$C_2O_4^{2-} \longrightarrow 2CO_2 \times 2e^-] \times 3$$

$$Cr_2O_7^{2-} + 14H^+ + 6e^- \longrightarrow 2Cr^{3+} + 7H_2O$$

$$3C_2O_4^{2-} \longrightarrow Cr_2O_7^{2-}$$

$$1C_2O_4^{2-} \longrightarrow \frac{1}{3} Cr_2O_7^{2-}$$

Thus, total $Cr_2O_7^{2-}$ required $= \frac{1}{6} + \frac{1}{3} = \frac{1}{2} = 0.5$ mol

44. (*b*) $\underset{+5}{HNO_3} + 4e^- \longrightarrow$ Product has O.N. = 1

In N_2O, oxidation number of N = +1. Thus, 0.5 mole of N_2O are formed by reduction of 1 mole of HNO_3 by 4 moles of electrons.

45. (*c*) $N_2H_4 \longrightarrow N_2(---) + 10e^-$

O.N. of two N-atoms = −4 O.N. of two N-atoms in oxidised species

$= -4 + 10 = +6$

Thus, oxidation state of N in new compound = +3.

46. (*d*) H_2SO_5 (peroxy sulphuric acid)

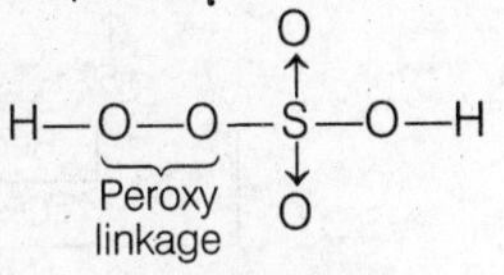

$H_2S_2O_8$ (peroxy disulphuric acid)

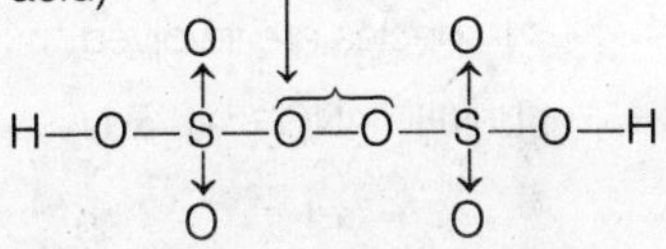

All of the above have O.N. = 6 in sulphur, peroxy linkage (—O—O—) has −1 O.N. for oxygen, CrO_5 has two peroxy linkage, thus O.N. of Cr = +6.

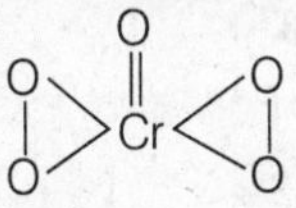

$K_2Cr_2O_7$ and CrO_4^{2-} both has +6 oxidation number for Cr.

47. (*c*) $[Cr(O_2)(NH_3)_4(H_2O)]Cl_2$

$+3 + x + 0 + 0 - 2 = 0$

$\therefore$ $x = -1$

Thus, (O_2) exists as O_2^- (superoxide ion).

48. (*a*) If acid is weak, its conjugate base is strong. Greater the O.N. of Cl, stronger the acid and thus weaker the conjugate base.

	HClO	$HClO_2$	$HClO_3$	$HClO_4$
O.N. of Cl	+1	+3	+5	+7
acid strength	→			
conjugate base	ClO^-	ClO_2^-	ClO_3^-	ClO_4^-
base strength	←			

49. (*c*) $CO_2 + H_2O \rightleftharpoons H_2CO_3 \rightleftharpoons 2H^+$

$$\underset{\text{Yellow}}{2CrO_4^{2-}} + 2H^+ \longrightarrow H_2O + \underset{\text{Orange}}{Cr_2O_7^{2-}}$$

50. (*c*) $K[CrO](O_2)(OH)]$

$+1 + x - 2 - 2 - 1 = 0$

$\therefore$ $x = 4$

$K_3[Cr(O_2)_4]$

$3 + y - 8 = 0, \; y = 5$

$(NH_3)_3[Cr(O_2)_2]$

$0 \quad +z \quad -4 = 0$ thus, $z = 4$

CrO_2Cl_2

$w - 4 - 2 = 0, \quad w = 6$

51. (*a*) MnO_3HSO_4

$x - 6 - 1 = 0$

$x = +7$

52. (*d*) I. $NH_4^+ + NO_3^- \longrightarrow N_2O + 2H_2O$

$-3 \quad +5 \qquad +1$

Reduction (+5 → +1); Oxidation (−3 → +1)

It is a redox but not disproportionation since, different N-species are involved.

II. $NH_4^+ + NO_2^- \longrightarrow N_2$

$-3 \quad +3 \qquad 0$

Same as (I)

III. $PCl_5 \longrightarrow PCl_3 + Cl_2$

$+5\ -1 \qquad +3\ -1 \qquad 0$

P^{5+} is reduced to P^{3+}

Cl^- is oxidised to Cl_2

Thus, different species are involved. Thus, it is also not a disproportionation reaction.

54. (*b*) $Zn \longrightarrow Zn^{2+}$

Zn is oxidised hence, it is a reducing agent (reductant).

$\underset{+5}{NO_3^-} \longrightarrow \underset{-3}{NH_4^+}$

NO_3^- is reduced hence, it is oxidising agent (oxidant).

55. (*b*) $HNO_3 = +5$

$NO = +2$

$N_2 = 0$

$NH_4^+ = -3$

56. (*b*) Ag^+ is reduced hence, it is oxidant. Hydroquinone is oxidised hence, it is reductant.

57. (*b*) $\underset{+3}{Bi^{3+}} \longrightarrow \underset{+5}{BiO_3^-}$

Change in oxidation number = 2 units

Thus, number of equivalents in one mole Bi^{3+} = 2

58. (*c*) $[Fe(H_2O)_5NO]^{+2}$

$x \quad 0 \quad +1 \qquad x + 1 = +2$

$x = +1$

$FeSO_4 \rightleftharpoons Fe^{+2} + SO_4^{2-}$

$Fe^{+2} + e^- \longrightarrow Fe^{+1}$

$\therefore \quad NO \longrightarrow NO^+ + e^-$

61. (*a*) $2H_2S(g) + SO_2(g) \longrightarrow 3S(s) + 2H_2O(l)$

$-2 \qquad +4 \qquad 0$

Change in oxidation number = 4 units

Thus, number of equivalent of SO_2 = 4

62. (*d*)

	Reaction	Change in O.N.	Number of equivalent
(a)	$VO^{2+}(aq) \longrightarrow V^{3+}(aq)$; $x-2 = +2$, $x = +4$ → $+3$	1 unit	1
(b)	$NO_3^-(aq) \longrightarrow NO_2(g)$; $+5$ → $+4$	1 unit	1
(c)	$VO_4^{3-}(aq) \longrightarrow V^{2+}(aq)$; $+5$ → $+2$	3 units	3
(d)	$IO_3^-(aq) \longrightarrow I_3^-(aq)$; $+5$ → $-\frac{1}{3}$	$\frac{16}{3}$	$\frac{16}{3}$

63. (*c*)

	Reaction	Change in O.N.	Equivalent per mol of MnO_4^-
(a)	$\underset{+7}{MnO_4^-} \longrightarrow \underset{+4}{MnO_2}$	3	3
(b)	$\longrightarrow \underset{+2}{Mn^{2+}}$	5	5
(c)	$\longrightarrow \underset{+6}{MnO_4^{2-}}$	1	1
(d)	$\longrightarrow \frac{1}{2}\underset{+3}{Mn_2O_3}$	4	4

64. (*a*) K_3CrO_8 has $[Cr(O_2)_4]^{3-}$ with four peroxy linkage

$[Cr(O_2)_4]^{3-}$

$x - 8 = -3$

$x = +5$

(b) Let $(NH_3)_3CrO_4$

$[Cr(NH_3)_3 \quad (O_2)_2]$

$x + 0 \times 3 + (-2) \times 2 = 0$

$x = +4$

(c) $[Kr_2 \ Cr \ O_4]$

$2 \times 1 + x - 4 \times 2 = 0$

$x = +6$

(d) $[Cr(NH_3)(H_2O)]Cl_3$

$x \quad +0 \quad 0 \quad -3 = 0$

$x = +3$

66. (*d*) $Na_2CO_3 + H_2O \longrightarrow 2NaOH + H_2CO_3$

$H_2CO_3 \longrightarrow H_2O + CO_2$

$6NaOH + Br_2 \longrightarrow \underset{\text{By reduction}}{5NaBr} + \underset{\text{By oxidation}}{NaBrO_3} + 3H_2O$

67. (*c*) The strength of aqueous NaOH solution is most accurately determined by titrating aqueous NaOH in burette and aqueous oxalic acid in conical flask with phenolphthalein as an indicator. (For weak acid-strong base titration, methyl orange cannot be used).
Thus, solution turns colourless to pink at the end point. (Phenolphthalein has pink colour when pH > 10 and it is colourless when pH < 8 (approximately) which is easily to perceive.

If NaOH is taken in conical flask and oxalic acid is added from burette, the end point will be the decolourisation of pink colour which is more difficult to percieve by human eye very quickly.

68. (*d*) $\underset{-2}{H_2O_2} + \underset{+4}{MnO_2} \longrightarrow \underset{+7}{MnO_4^-} + \underset{-4}{2H_2O}$

$-3e^-$ (Mn: +4 → +7); $+2e^-$ (O: −2 → −4)

(oxidation number of two O atoms taken)

Balancing of O.N.

$$3H_2O_2 + 2MnO_2 \longrightarrow MnO_4^- + 6H_2O$$

Thus, $H_2O_2 : MnO_2 = 3 : 2$

69. (*b*) $H_3PO_2 \equiv HPO_2^- + 2H^+$

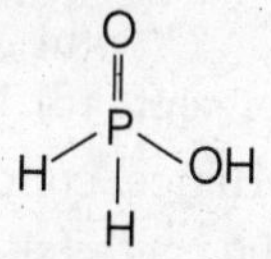

But H_3PO_2 is a monobasic acid, hence, false.

(b) $H_3PO_2 \xrightarrow{[o]} H_3PO_3$

O.N. +1 → +3

$\therefore$ Equivalent weight $= \frac{M}{2}$

70. (*a*) $\underset{+4}{VO_3^{2-}} + \underset{+7}{MnO_4^-} \longrightarrow \underset{+2}{Mn^{2+}} + \underset{+5}{VO_4^{3-}}$

5 unit (Mn: +7 → +2); 1 unit (V: +4 → +5)

Thus, $5VO_3^{2-} + MnO_4^- \longrightarrow Mn^{2+} + 5VO_4^{3-}$

$5 \text{ mol } VO_3^{2-} \equiv 1 \text{ mol } MnO_4^-$

$1 \text{ mol } VO_3^{2-} \equiv 0.2 \text{ mol } MnO_4^-$

71. (*a*) $\overset{II}{Fe}[\overset{III}{Fe}(CN)_6]$

$+2 + 3 - 6 = -1$

73. (*b*) Writting the half reaction oxidation half reaction

$$MnO_4^- \longrightarrow Mn^{2+}$$

Balancing oxygen

$$MnO_4^- \longrightarrow Mn^{2+} + 4H_2O$$

Balancing hydrogen

$$8H^+ + MnO_4^- \longrightarrow Mn^{2+} + 4H_2O$$

Balancing charge

$$5e^- + 8H^+ + MnO_4^- \longrightarrow Mn^{2+} + 4H_2O$$

Reduction half

$$C_2O_4^{2-} \longrightarrow CO_2$$

Balancing carbon

$$C_2O_4^{2-} \longrightarrow 2CO_2$$

Balacing charge

$$C_2O_4^{2-} \longrightarrow 2CO_2 + 2e^-$$

Net equation

$$16H^+ + 2MnO_4^{2-} + 6C_2O_4^{2-} \longrightarrow 10CO_2 + 2Mn^{2+} + 8H_2O$$

So, $c = 16$

74. (*d*) $6Fe^{2+} + Cr_2O_7^{2-} + 14H^+ \longrightarrow 2Cr^{3+} + 6Fe^{3+} + 7H_2O$

75. (*a*) $H_2S_2O_8$,

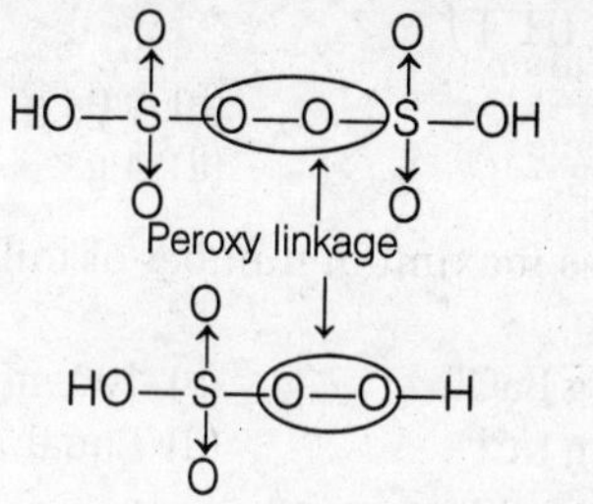

H_2SO_5,

04

Volumetric Methods

Objective Questions Type I [Only one correct option]

In each of the questions below, four choices are given of which only one is correct.

1. Number of millimoles of Cl^- in 100 mL of 1 M $BaCl_2$ solution (assume 100% ionisation) is
(a) 100 (b) 200
(c) 300 (d) 50

2. Volume of $H_2C_2O_4 \cdot 2H_2O$ solution to prepare 0.10 M from 1.575 g of it is
(a) 125 mL (b) 250 mL
(c) 500 mL (d) 1000 mL

3. A sodium hydroxide solution has pH = 12. $\left(pH = \log \frac{1}{(H^+)}\right)$ 100 mL of this solution has NaOH
(a) 0.4 g (b) 0.04 g
(c) 0.004 g (d) 4 g

4. Which has maximum number of millimoles of Cl^- ion?
(a) 0.208 g $BaCl_2$ (b) 100 mL of 0.1 M $BaCl_2$
(c) 0.745 g KCl (d) Equal

5. 100 mL of solution of $CaCl_2$ is evaporated to dryness; residue obtained is 0.111 g. Molarity of $CaCl_2$ solution is
(a) 0.1 M (b) 1.0 M
(c) 0.01 M (d) 0.001 M

6. Hardness in water is 200 ppm $CaCO_3$. Molarity of $CaCO_3$ is
(a) 2×10^{-3} M (b) 1×10^{-3} M
(c) 2×10^{-2} M (d) 2×10^{-4} M

7. Mole fraction of $CaCO_3$ in hard water having hardness 200 ppm $CaCO_3$ is
(a) 0.1 (b) 3.6×10^{-5}
(c) 27.78×10^{-3} (d) 0.035

8. Ethyl alcohol is 46% by weight of solution. Hence, mole fraction of ethyl alcohol is
(a) 0.46 (b) 0.54 (c) 0.75 (d) 0.25

9. Which is temperature independent?
(a) Mass per cent (b) Volume per cent
(c) Mass/volume per cent (d) Molarity

10. HNO_3 is 0.001 M. Hence, concentration in ppm is
(a) 1×10^{-3} (b) 100 (c) 212 (d) 63

11. $NaHC_2O_4$ is 0.1 M when neutralised with NaOH. Hence, it is .... when oxidised with MnO_4^- / H^+.
(a) 0.1 N (b) 0.2 N (c) 0.05 N (d) 0.15 N

12. The molarity of a solution obtained by mixing 750 mL of 0.5 (M) HCl with 250 mL of 2 (M) HCl will be **[JEE Main 2013]**
(a) 0.875 M (b) 1.00 M
(c) 1.75 M (d) 0.0975 M

13. One mole of the salt $NaHC_2O_4 \cdot H_2C_2O_4$ contains
(a) 3 equivalents of H^+ and 4 equivalents of $C_2O_4^{2-}$
(b) 1 equivalent each of H^+ and $C_2O_4^{2-}$
(c) 3 equivalents of H^+ and 2 equivalents of $C_2O_4^{2-}$
(d) None of the above is correct

14. Which has maximum number of milliequivalents?
(a) 100 mL of 0.01 N H_2SO_4 (b) 100 mL of 0.01 N HCl
(c) 100 mL of 0.01 N H_3PO_4 (d) Equal

15. 2.86 g of $Na_2CO_3 \cdot xH_2O$ in 100 mL solution is 0.2 N. Hence, x is
(a) 5 (b) 10 (c) 20 (d) 2

16. Urea solution is one molal. Urea present in 1 kg solution is
(a) 60 g (b) 56.6 g
(c) 10.60 g (d) 10.0 g

17. H_2SO_4 is 98% by weight of solution. Hence, it is
(a) 1 molal (b) 10 molal
(c) 50 molal (d) 500 molal

18. Sucrose solution is 1 molal. Mole fraction of sucrose in the aqueous solution is
(a) 0.018 (b) 0.015 (c) 0.036 (d) 0.009

19. H_3PO_4 ($d = 1.8$ g/mL) is 18 M. Hence, mass percentage and molality are
(a) 18, 32.4 (b) 98, 32.4
(c) 98, 500 (d) 98, 18

20. Mole fraction of glucose in aqueous solution is 0.5. Hence, molality of glucose solution is
(a) 55.55 (b) 1.0 (c) 0.055 (d) 90.0

21. 100 mL of 0.01 M H_2SO_4 is neutralised by
(a) 100 mL of 0.01 M NaOH
(b) 100 mL of 0.01 M $Ca(OH)_2$
(c) 100 mL of 0.01 M $Al(OH)_3$
(d) All the above are correct

22. Resultant molarity of H^+ ion in a mixture of 100 mL of 0.1 M H_2SO_4 and 200 mL of 0.1 M H_3PO_3 is
(a) 0.1 M (b) 0.2 M
(c) 0.267 M (d) 0.133 M

23. 1.575 g of a dibasic acid is neutralised by 25 mL of 1 M NaOH solution. Hence, molar mass of dibasic acid is
(a) 126 g mol^{-1} (b) 63 g mol^{-1}
(c) 12.6 g mol^{-1} (d) None of these

24. 1.06 g Na_2CO_3 is dissolved in 100 mL solution. 10 mL of this solution can be neutralised by
(a) 10 mL of 0.1 N HCl (b) 10 mL of 0.1 M H_3PO_4
(c) 20 mL of 0.1 M H_2SO_4 (d) 20 mL of 0.1 M HCl

25. 100 mL of 1 M BaF_2 solution is mixed with 100 mL of 2 M H_2SO_4. Resulting mixture contains
(a) 0.1 mole of $BaSO_4$ (b) 2 M H^+
(c) Both are correct (d) None is correct

26. Number of moles of $KMnO_4$ required to oxidise 1 L of 1 M iron (II) sulphate (IV) in acidic medium is
(a) 1.0 (b) 0.8 (c) 0.2 (d) 0.6

27. 0.6 g of urea (N_2H_4CO) on reaction with NaOH gave NH_3 which can be neutralised by
(a) 100 mL of 0.1 N HCl (b) 200 mL of 0.2 N HCl
(c) 100 mL of 0.2 N HCl (d) 100 mL of 0.1 N H_2SO_4

28. 0.31 g of N-containing compound on reaction with NaOH gave NH_3 which required 100 mL of 0.1 N HCl. Hence, % of N is
(a) 45.16% (b) 90.32% (c) 22.58% (d) 11.29%

29. 0.6 g NH_2CONH_2 is treated with NaOH and NH_3 formed is passed into 300 mL of 0.1 N H_2SO_4. Unused acid is
(a) 50 mL (b) 25 mL
(c) 100 mL (d) 150 mL

30. A 6.50 molal solution of KOH (*aq.*) has a density of 1.89 g cm^{-3}. The molarity of the solution is .... mol dm^{-3}. (Round off to the Nearest Integer).
[Atomic masses: K : 39.0 u; O :16.0 u; H :1.0 u]
(a) 2.22 (b) 9.00 **[JEE Main 2021, March]**
(c) 4.75 (d) 8.75

31. 1 g of *X* % H_2O_2 required *x* mL of $KMnO_4$ solution in acidic medium. Thus, molarity of $KMnO_4$ solution is
(a) 0.12 M (b) 0.60 M
(c) 0.024 M (d) None of correct

32. 100 mL of $NaHC_2O_4$ required 50 mL of 0.1 M $KMnO_4$ solution in acidic medium. Volume of 0.1 M NaOH required by 100 mL of $NaHC_2O_4$ is
(a) 50 mL (b) 100 mL
(c) 125 mL (d) 150 mL

33. 50 mL of $FeSO_4 \cdot 7H_2O$ solution required 20 mL of 0.1 M $Cr_2O_7^{2-}$ solution in acidic medium. Hence, $FeSO_4 \cdot 7H_2O$ is
(a) 0.24 M (b) 0.24 N
(c) 66.72 g L^{-1} (d) All correct

34. In a titration H_2O_2 is oxidised to O_2 by MnO_4^-. 24 mL of 0.1 M H_2O_2 require 16 mL of 0.1 M MnO_4^- solution. Hence, MnO_4^- changes to
(a) MnO_4^{2-} (b) MnO_2
(c) MnO_4^{2-} (d) Mn_2O_7

35. In the following titrations indicators are
I. Fe^{2+} *vs* $Cr_2O_7^{2-}$ II. Cl^- *vs* Ag^+
III. Fe^{2+} *vs* MnO_4^-

	I	II	III
(a)	self MnO_4^-,	$[Fe(CN)_6]^{4-}$,	CrO_4^{2-}
(b)	$[Fe(CN)_6]^{3-}$,	CrO_4^{2-},	CNS^-
(c)	$[Fe(CN)_6]^{3-}$,	CrO_4^{2-},	self MnO_4^-
(d)	CNS^-,	CrO_4^{2-},	$[Fe(CN)_6]^{3-}$

36. Select the correct statement.
(a) In iodometric titration, hypo is taken in burette
(b) In iodimetric titration, I_2 solution is taken in burette
(c) In iodometric titration I_2 formed exist as I_3^-
(d) All the above are correct statements

37. 100 mL solution of 0.1 N HCl was titrated with 0.2 N NaOH. The nitration was discontinued after adding 30 mL of NaOH. The remaining titration was completed by adding 0.25 N KOH solution. The volume of KOH required from completing the titration is
(a) 70 mL (b) 35 mL
(c) 32 mL (d) 16 mL

38. 1.575 g, of hydrated oxalic acid $(COOH)_2 . nH_2O$ is dissolved in water and the solution is made to 250 mL. On titration, 16.68 mL of this solution is required for neutralisation of 25 mL of *N*/15 NaOH. The value of water crystailisation, i.e. *n*, is
(a) 4 (b) 3 (c) 2 (d) 1

39. Two glucose solutions are mixed. One has a volume of 480 mL and a concentration of 1.50 M and the second has a volume of 520 mL and concentration 1.20 M. The molarity of final solution is
(a) 1.20 M (b) 1.50 M
(c) 1.344 M (d) 2.70 M

40. O_3 oxidises I^- to I_2. Equivalent weight of O_3 is
(a) 48 (b) 32 (c) 8 (d) 4

41. To prepare a solution that is 0.50 M KCl starting with 100 mL of 0.40 M KCl
(a) add 0.75 g KCl (b) add 20 mL of water
(c) add 0.10 mol KCl (d) evaporate 10 mL water

42. How many equivalents are there per mol of H_2S in its oxidation to SO_2?
(a) 2 (b) 4 (c) 6 (d) 8

43. In hot alkaline solution, Br_2 disproportionates to Br^- and BrO_3^-

$$3Br_2 + 6OH^- \longrightarrow 5Br^- + BrO_3^- + 3H_2O$$

Hence, equivalent weight of Br_2 is (molecular weight = M)
(a) $\frac{M}{6}$ (b) $\frac{M}{5}$ (c) $\frac{3M}{5}$ (d) $\frac{5M}{3}$

44. $[Na^+]$ in a solution prepared by mixing 30.00 mL of 0.12 M NaCl with 70 mL of 0.15 M Na_2SO_4 is
(a) 0.135 M (b) 0.141 M
(c) 0.210 M (d) 0.246 M

45. When 80 mL of 0.20 M HCl is mixed with 120 mL of 0.15 M KOH, the resultant solution is the same as a solution of
(a) 0.16 M KCl and 0.02 M HCl
(b) 0.08 M KCl
(c) 0.08 M KCl and 0.01 M KOH
(d) 0.08 M KCl and 0.01 M HCl

46. Moles of KHC_2O_4 (potassium acid oxalate) required to reduce 100 mL of 0.02 M $KMnO_4$ in acidic medium (to Mn^{2+}) is
(a) 0.002 (b) 0.005 (c) 0.001 (d) 0.007

47. $2H_2O_2(l) \longrightarrow 2H_2O(l) + O_2(g)$
100 mL of X molar H_2O_2 gives 3 L of O_2 g under the condition when 1 mole occupies 24 L, value of X is
(a) 2.5 (b) 1.0 (c) 0.5 (d) 0.25

48. The exact volumes of 1 M NaOH solution required to neutralise 50 mL of 1 M H_3PO_3 solution and 100 mL of 2 M H_3PO_2 solution, respectively, are **[JEE Main 2021, March]**
(a) 100 mL and 100 mL (b) 100 mL and 50 mL
(c) 100 mL and 200 mL (d) 50 mL and 50 mL

49. 20 mL of x M HCl neutralises 5 mL of 0.2 M Na_2CO_3 solution to phenolphthalein end-point. The value of x is
(a) 0.167 M (b) 0.133 M
(c) 0.150 M (d) 0.05 M

50. The molality of a H_2SO_4 solution is 9. The weight of the solute in 1 kg H_2SO_4 solution is
(a) 900.0 g (b) 469 g (c) 882.0 g (d) 9.0 g

51. RH_2 (ion exchange resin) can replace Ca^{2+} in hard water

$$RH_2 + Ca^{2+} \longrightarrow RCa + 2H^+$$

1 L of hard water after passing through RH_2 has pH 2. Hence, hardness in ppm of Ca^{2+} is
(a) 200 (b) 100 (c) 50 (d) 125

52. 10 mL of $NaHC_2O_4$ solution is neutralised by 10 mL of 0.1 M NaOH solution. 10 mL of same $NaHC_2O_4$ solution is oxidised by 10 mL of $KMnO_4$ solution in acidic medium. Hence, molarity of $KMnO_4$ is
(a) 0.1 M (b) 0.2 M
(c) 0.04 M (d) 0.02 M

53. For a given mixture of $NaHCO_3$ and Na_2CO_3, volume of a given HCl required is x mL with phenolphthalein indicator and further y mL required with methyl orange indicator. Hence, volume of HCl for complete reaction of $NaHCO_3$ is
(a) $2x$ (b) $\frac{x}{2}$ (c) y (d) $(y - x)$

54. 3 moles of a mixture of $FeSO_4$ and $Fe_2(SO_4)_3$ required 100 mL of 2 M $KMnO_4$ solution in acidic medium. Hence, mole fraction of $FeSO_4$ in the mixture is
(a) $\frac{1}{3}$ (b) $\frac{2}{3}$ (c) $\frac{2}{5}$ (d) $\frac{3}{5}$

55. A mixture of $Na_2C_2O_4(A)$ and $KHC_2O_4 \cdot H_2C_2O_4(B)$ required equal volumes of 0.1 M $KMnO_4$ and 0.1 M NaOH separated. Molar ratio of A and B in the mixture is
(a) 1 : 1 (b) 1 : 5.5
(c) 5.5 : 1 (d) 3.1 : 1

56. 5.3 g of M_2CO_3 is dissolved in 150 mL of 1 N HCl. Unused acid required 100 mL of 0.5 N NaOH. Hence, equivalent weight of M is
(a) 23 (b) 12
(c) 24 (d) 13

57. 1.2 g of Mg is treated with 100 mL of 1 M H_2SO_4. Molar concentration of the H_2SO_4 solution after complete reaction is
(a) 0.5 M (b) 0.005 M
(c) 0.10 M (d) 0.20 M

58. 10 mL of a blood sample (containing calcium oxalate) is dissolved in acid. It required 20 mL of 0.001 M $KMnO_4$ (which oxidises oxalate to carbon dioxide) hence, Ca^{2+} ion in 10 mL blood is
(a) 0.200 g (b) 0.02 g
(c) 2.00 g (d) 0.002 g

59. 1.00 L of 0.15 N NaOH absorbed 11.2 millimoles of CO_2 from air. Hence, new molarity of NaOH is
(a) 0.1276 M (b) 0.1500 M
(c) 0.0224 M (d) 0.0112 M

60. 10 mL of 0.2 N HCl and 30 mL of 0.1 N HCl together exactly neutralise 40 mL of solution of NaOH, which is also exactly neutralised by a solution in water of 0.61 g of an organic acid. What is the equivalent weight of the organic acid ?
(a) 61 (b) 91.5
(c) 122 (d) 183

61. A sample of pure sodium carbonate 0.318 g is dissolved in water and titrated with HCl solution. A volume of 60 mL is required to reach the methyl orange end point. Calculate the molarity of the acid.
(a) 0.1 M (b) 0.2 M
(c) 0.4 M (d) None of these

62. Maximum number of moles of $PbSO_4$ that can be precipitated by mixing 20.00 mL of 0.1 M $Pb(NO_3)_2$ and 30.00 mL of 0.1 M Na_2SO_4 will be
(a) 0.002 (b) 0.003
(c) 0.005 (d) 0.001

63. Equal volumes of 0.200 M HCl and 0.400 M KOH are mixed. The concentration of the principal ions in the resulting solution are
(a) $[K^+] = 0.400$ M, $[Cl^-] = 0.200$ M, $[H^+] = 0.200$ M
(b) $[K^+] = 0.200$ M, $[Cl^-] = 0.200$ M, $[OH^-] = 0.100$ M
(c) $[K^+] = 0.200$ M, $[Cl^-] = 0.100$ M, $[OH^-] = 0.100$ M
(d) $[K^+] = 0.200$ M, $[Cl^-] = 0.100$M, $[OH^-] = 0.200$ M

64. 100 mL of 1 M $KMnO_4$ oxidised 100 mL of H_2O_2 in acidic medium (when MnO_4^- is reduced to Mn^{2+}); volume of same $KMnO_4$ required to oxidise 100 mL of H_2O_2 in basic medium (when MnO_4^- is reduced to MnO_2) will be
(a) $\frac{100}{3}$ mL (b) $\frac{500}{3}$ mL (c) $\frac{300}{5}$ mL (d) 100 mL

65. 10 mL of H_2O_2 solution (volume strength = x) required 10 mL of $\frac{N}{0.56}$ MnO_4^- solution in acidic medium. Hence, x is
(a) 0.56 (b) 5.6
(c) 0.1 (d) 10.0

66. A mixture contains 1 mol each of Fe^{2+} and Fe^{3+} ions. Volume of 1 M MnO_4^- required by the mixture in the oxidation of the given mixture is
(a) 400 mL (b) 200 mL
(c) 100 mL (d) 1000 mL

67. In an experiment, 50 mL of 0.1 M solution of a metallic salt reacted exactly with 25 mL of 0.1 M solution of sodium sulphite. In the reaction SO_3^{2-} is oxidised to SO_4^{2-}. If the original oxidation number of the metal in the salt was 3, what would be the new oxidation number of the metal?
(a) 0 (b) 1 (c) 2 (d) 4

68. Dissolving 120 g of urea (60 g mol^{-1}) in 1000 g of water gave a solution of density 1.15 g/mL. The molarity of solution is **[IIT-JEE 2011]**
(a) 1.78 M (b) 2.00 M
(c) 2.05 M (d) 2.22 M

69. 100 mL of a mixture of NaOH and Na_2SO_4 is neutralised by 10 mL of 0.5 M H_2SO_4. Hence, amount of NaOH in 100 mL mixture is
(a) 0.2 g (b) 0.4 g
(c) 0.6 g (d) 1.0 g

70. 1 mole of ferric oxalate is oxidised by x moles of MnO_4^-. Thus, x is
(a) 1.2 (b) 2.1
(c) 3.1 (d) 1.3

71. 40 mL of 0.05 M solution of Cr^{3+} is oxidised to CrO_4^{2-} by 20 mL of H_2O_2. H_2O_2 is
(a) 0.15 M (b) 0.30 M
(c) 0.10 M (d) 0.20 M

72. The reaction of white phosphorus on boiling with alkali in inert atmosphere resulted in the formation of product 'A'. The reaction 1 mole of 'A' with excess of $AgNO_3$ in aqueous medium gives .... mole(s) of Ag. (Round off to the Nearest Integer). **[JEE Main 2021, March]**
(a) 1 (b) 2 (c) 3 (d) 4

73. I_2 obtained from 0.1 mol of $CuSO_4$ required 100 mL of 1 M hypo solution, hence, mole percentage of pure $CuSO_4$ is
(a) 100 (b) 50 (c) 25 (d) 40

74. 1.2 g of Mg is treated with 100 mL of 1 M H_2SO_4. Molar concentration of the H_2SO_4 solution after complete reaction is
(a) 0.5 M (b) 0.005 M
(c) 0.10 M (d) 0.20 M

75. Stock phosphoric acid solution is 85% H_3PO_4 (by mass of solution) and has a specific gravity of 1.70. Hence, molarity of H_3PO_4 solution is
(a) 8.51 M (b) 1.70 M
(c) 14.74 M (d) 7.37 M

76. 0.116 g of $C_4H_4O_4(A)$ is neutralised by 0.074 g of $Ca(OH)_2$. Hence, protonic hydrogen (H^+) in (A) will be
(a) 1 (b) 2 (c) 3 (d) 4

77. Oxalic acid ($H_2C_2O_4$) forms two series of salt $HC_2O_4^-$ and $C_2O_4^{2-}$. If 0.9 g of oxalic acid is in 100 mL solution, $HC_2O_4^{2-}$ and $C_2O_4^{2-}$ have normality respectively
(a) 0.1 N, 0.1 N (b) 0.1 N, 0.2 N
(c) 0.2 N, 0.2 N (d) 0.2 N, 0.1 N

78. 10 g of MnO_2 on reaction with conc. HCl liberated 0.1 equivalent of Cl_2 (Mn = 55). Hence, per cent purity of MnO_2 is
(a) 87.0 (b) 21.75 (c) 50.0 (d) 43.5

79. 0.106 g of Na_2CO_3 completely neutralises 40.0 mL of H_2SO_4. Hence, normality of H_2SO_4 solution is
(a) 0.05 N (b) 0.025 N
(c) 0.10 N (d) 0.20 N

80. A 20.0 mL solution of Na_2SO_3 required 30 mL of 0.01 M $K_2Cr_2O_7$ solution for the oxidation to Na_2SO_4. Hence, molarity of Na_2SO_3 solution is
(a) 0.015 M (b) 0.045 M
(c) 0.030 M (d) 0.0225 M

81. Normality of a solution that contains 12.64 g of $KMnO_4$ in 500 mL of solution to be used in the reaction that produces K_2MnO_4 ion as the reducing product is
(a) 0.16 N (b) 0.32 N
(c) 0.80 N (d) 0.08 N

82. Iodate ion, IO_3^-, oxidises SO_3^{2-} to SO_4^{2-} in acidic medium. If 100 mL sample of solution containing 2.14 g of KIO_3 reacts with 60 mL of 0.5 M Na_2SO_3 solution, then final oxidation state of iodine is
(a) +5 (b) +3 (c) +1 (d) −1

83. 5.00 mL of 0.10 M oxalic acid solution taken in a conical flask is titrated against NaOH from a burette using phenolphthalein indicator. The volume of NaOH required for the appearance of permanent faint pink colour is tabulated below for five experiments. What is the concentration, in molarity, of the NaOH solution? **[JEE Advanced 2020]**

Exp. No.	Vol. of NaOH (mL)
1	12.5
2	10.5
3	9.0
4	9.0
5	9.0

(a) 0.13 (b) 0.11
(c) 0.16 (d) 0.19

84. The normality of solution obtained by mixing 10 mL of *N*/5 HCl and 30 mL of *N*/10 HCl is
(a) 0.067 N (b) 0.2 N
(c) 0.133 N (d) 0.125 N

85. 0.4 mole of HCl and 0.2 mole of $CaCl_2$ were dissolved in water to have 500 mL of solution, the molarity of Cl^- ion is
(a) 0.8 M (b) 1.6 M
(c) 1.2 M (d) 10.0 M

86. 0.45 g of an acid of molecular weight 90 was neutralised by 20 mL of a 0.5 N caustic potash. The basicity of an acid is
(a) 1 (b) 2 (c) 3 (d) 4

87. In the chemical reaction between stoichiometric quantities of $KMnO_4$ and KI in weakly basic solution, what is the number of moles of I_2 released for 4 moles of $KMnO_4$ consumed? **[JEE Advanced 2020]**
(a) 4 (b) 6
(c) 8 (d) 10

88. A bottle which contains 200 mL of 0.1 M NaOH solution, absorbs 1.00 millimol of CO_2 from the air. This solution is titrated with standard HCl solution using phenolphthalein indicator. Normality of resulting solution is found as
(a) 0.190 N (b) 0.380 N
(c) 0.095 N (d) 0.0475 N

89. Titration of a 0.7439 g sample of impure $Na_2B_4O_7$ (borax) required 31.64 mL of 0.108 M HCl for reaction. In terms of B_2O_3, percentage is

$$B_4O_7^{2-} + 2H_3O^+ + 3H_2O \longrightarrow 4H_3BO_3$$

(a) 46.39% (b) 87.73%
(c) 32.15% (d) 10.11%

90. In the titration of 100 mL of 0.01 M CH_3COOH with 0.01 M NaOH, $[H_3O^+] = K_a$ when
(a) 100 mL of NaOH has been added
(b) 75 mL of NaOH has been added
(c) 50 mL of NaOH has been added
(d) 25 mL of NaOH has been added

Objective Questions Type II [One or more than one correct option(s)]

In each of the questions below, four choices are given, of which one or more than one are correct.

1. 1 g equivalent of a substance is the weight of that amount of a substance which is equivalent to
(a) 0.25 mol O_2
(b) 8 g O_2
(c) 16 g O_2
(d) 0.50 mol O_2

2. 2.84 g of P_4O_{10} is dissolved in 1 L aqueous solution. Thus,
(a) resulting solution is 0.01 M
(b) it is neutralised to Na_3PO_4 by 400 mL of 0.3 M NaOH solution
(c) it is neutralised to $CaHPO_4$ by 400 mL of 0.1 M $Ca(OH)_2$ solution
(d) it cannot be neutralised by basic solution

3. A solution of $KHC_2O_4 \cdot H_2C_2O_4 \cdot 2H_2O$ is 0.2 N as an acid. Then it is
(a) 0.267 N as reducing agent
(b) 0.6 M as an acid
(c) 0.067 M as an acid
(d) 0.067 M a reducing agent

4. A sample of water has a hardness expressed as 77.5 ppm Ca^{2+}. This sample is passed thorugh an ion exchange column and the Ca^{2+} is replaced by H^+. Select the correct statement(s).
(a) pH of the water after it has been so treated is 2.4
(b) Every Ca^{2+} ion is replaced by one H^+ ion
(c) Every Ca^{2+} ion is replaced by two H^+ ions
(d) pH of the solution remains unchanged

5. 10.78 g of H_3PO_4 in 550 mL solution is 0.40 N. Thus, this acid
(a) has been neutralised to HPO_4^{2-}
(b) has been neutralised to PO_4^{3-}
(c) has been reduced to HPO_3^{2-}
(d) has been neutralised to $H_2PO_4^-$

6. Mass of KHC_2O_4 (potassium acid oxalate) required to reduce 100 mL of 0.02 M $KMnO_4$ in acidic medium (to Mn^{2+}) is x g and to neutralise 100 mL of 0.05 M $Ca(OH)_2$ is y g, then
(a) $x = y$ (b) $2x = y$
(c) $x = 2y$ (d) None is correct

7. A solution is 2.00×10^{-4} M in NaCl and 8.0×10^{-4} M in HCl, Thus
(a) pH = 3.1 (b) $p_{Cl^-} = 3.7$ (c) $p_{Na^+} = 3.7$ (d) $p_{Cl^-} = 3.0$

8. $H_2C_2O_4$ and $NaHC_2O_4$ behave as acids as well as reducing agents. Which are correct statements?
(a) Equivalent weight of $H_2C_2O_4$ and $NaHC_2O_4$ are equal to their molecular weights when behaving as reducing agents
(b) 100 mL of 1 M solution of each is neutralised by equal volumes of 1 M $Ca(OH)_2$
(c) 100 mL of 1 N solution of each is neutralised by equal volumes of 1 N $Ca(OH)_2$
(d) 100 mL of 1 M solution of each is oxidised by equal volumes of 1 M $KMnO_4$

9. 100 mL of 1.44% solution of pure FeC_2O_4 in dil. HCl is oxidised by 0.01 M $KMnO_4$. Then volume of $KMnO_4$ required is
(a) 120 mL (b) 600 mL (c) 200 mL (d) 60 mL

10. 25 mL of 0.2 M $AgNO_3$ is mixed with 50.0 mL of 0.08 M Na_2CO_3 solution. Resulting solution has
(a) 0.02 M Na_2CO_3 (b) 0.02 M $AgNO_3$
(c) 0.0025 mol Ag_2CO_3 (d) 0.69 g Ag_2CO_3

Numerical Value Questions

All these questions have a Numerical value as their answer, solve the questions and write your answer.

1. The volume (in mL) of 0.1 N NaOH required to neutralise 10 mL of 0.1 N phosphonic acid is .... **[JEE Main 2020, Sep.]**

2. The SO_2 present in air is mainly responsible for the acid-rain phenomenon. Its concentration can be determined by titration against a standard permanganate solution as follows :

$$5SO_2 + MnO_4^- + 2H_2O \longrightarrow 5SO_4^{2-} + 2Mn^{2+} + 4H^+$$

.... milligrams of SO_2 in a sample of air if 7.37 mL of 0.008 M $KMnO_4$ solution are required for the titration.

3. A sample of pure $KHC_2O_4 \cdot H_2C_2O_4 \cdot 2H_2O$ requires 46.2 mL of 0.1 M NaOH for titration .... millilitres of 0.1 M $KMnO_4$ will the sample react.

4. 100.0 mL sample of hard water is passed through a column of the ion exchange resin H_2R. The water coming off the column requires 15.17 mL of 0.0265 M NaOH for its titration. .... is the hardness of the water expressed as ppm of Ca^{2+}.

5. Two acids, A and B are titrated separately. 25 mL of 1 N Na_2CO_3 solution requires 10 mL of A and 40 mL of B for complete neutralisation. Ratio of volume of A and B would you mix to produce 1 L of 1 N acid solutions = 1 : ......

6. For titrating a certain volume of a reducing substance by 1 M $KMnO_4$, it is found that 20 mL was used in acidic medium, 33.4 mL was used in alkali medium and 100 mL was used in neutral medium. If MnO_4^- is reduced to Mn^{2+} in acidic medium, the ratio of oxidation state MnO_4^- is reduced to in alkaline to neutral medium is ...... : 1.

7. 5.00 mL of 0.10 M oxalic acid solution taken in a conical flask is titrated against NaOH from a burette using phenolphthalein indicator. The volume of NaOH required for the appearance of permanent faint pink colour is tabulated below for five experiments. What is the concentration, in molarity, of the NaOH solution? **[JEE Advanced 2020]**

8. A solution contains 0.1 M of $CuSO_4$ and 0.1 M of $Al_2(SO_4)_3$, what is the total molarity of ions ?

9. For above questions, what is total normality solution ?

10. 12 mg of $MgSO_4$ is present in one kg of water. The degree of hardness of water is .....

11. 10 mL of Na_2CO_3 require 10 mL of 1 M HCl with methyl orange indicator. What is the volume of 1 M HCl (in mL) if phenolphthalein is used as indicator?

12. What is the equivalent weight of ozone if it is estimated iodometrically?

Comprehension Based Questions

In these questions, a passage has been given followed by questions based on it. You have to answer the questions based on the passage given.

Passage 1 *Following experiment is designed to determine calcium content in the blood. Read the experiment and answer the questions at the end of it.*

Calcium oxalate (CaC_2O_4) is insoluble in water. For this reason it can be used to determine the amount of Ca^{2+} ions in fluids such as blood. The calcium oxalate isolated from blood is dissolved in acid and titrated against a standardised $KMnO_4$ solution.

1. In one test it is found that the calcium oxalate isolated from a 10.0 mL sample of blood requires 25 mL of 1×10^{-3} M $KMnO_4$ for titration. Calculate the number of milligrams of calcium per mL of blood
   (a) 0.50 (b) 10.0
   (c) 0.25 (d) 5.0
2. Milliequivalents of $KMnO_4$ used were
   (a) 0.125 (b) 0.025 (c) 0.250 (d) 0.050
3. Calcium content expressed in ppm is
   (a) 250 (b) 200 (c) 150 (d) 100
4. Above titration takes place in acidic medium. Acid chosen is
   (a) H_2SO_4 (b) HCl
   (c) CH_3COOH (d) HCOOH
5. Indicator in the above titration is
   (a) phenolphthalein (b) methylene blue
   (c) methyl orange (d) $KMnO_4$ (self-indicator)

Passage 2 *Following titration method is given to determine total content of the species with variable oxidation states. Answer the questions given at the end of it.*

A quantity of 25.0 mL of solution containing both Fe^{2+} and Fe^{3+} ions is titrated with 25.0 mL of 0.0200 M $KMnO_4$ (in dilute H_2SO_4). As a result, all of the Fe^{2+} ions are oxidised to Fe^{3+} ions. Next 25 mL of the original solution is treated with Zn metal. Finally, the solution requires 40.0 mL of the same $KMnO_4$ solution for oxidation to Fe^{3+}.

$$MnO_4^- + 5Fe^{2+} + 8H^+ \longrightarrow Mn^{2+} + 5Fe^{3+} + 4H_2O$$

1. Molar concentration of Fe^{2+} in the original solution is
   (a) 0.01 M (b) 0.02 M (c) 0.10 M (d) 0.20 M
2. Molar concentration of Fe^{3+} in the original solution is
   (a) 0.06 M (b) 0.16 M
   (c) 0.032 M (d) 0.012 M
3. Zinc added in the second titration will
   (a) oxidise Fe^{2+} to Fe^{3+} (b) reduce Fe^{3+} to Fe^{2+}
   (c) reduce Fe^{3+} to Fe (d) reduce Fe^{2+} to Fe

Passage 3 *Following short write-up describes synthesis of I_2 from natural source chile salt peter.*

Chile salt peter is a natural source of $NaNO_3$ which also contains $NaIO_3$. The $NaIO_3$ can be used as a source of iodine produced in the following reactions:

$$IO_3^- + 3HSO_3^- \longrightarrow I^- + 3H^+ + 3SO_4^{2-} \quad \text{...(i)}$$

$$5I^- + IO_3^- + 6H^+ \longrightarrow 3I_2(s) + 3H_2O \quad \text{...(ii)}$$

1.00 L of the starting solution which contains 5.80 g $NaIO_3$ /L, is treated with stoichiometric quantity of $NaHSO_3$. Then a further quantity of the starting solution is added to the reaction mixture to bring about the second reaction. [I = 127, Na = 23, S = 32]

Answer the following questions.

1. How many grams of $NaHSO_3$ are required in step (i)?
   (a) 5.80 g (b) 17.4 g
   (c) 9.14 g (d) 3.0 g
2. What additional volume of the starting solution must be added in step (ii)?
   (a) 0.2 L (b) 0.4 L
   (c) 0.8 L (d) 1.0 L
3. How many equivalents of IO_3^- are present in one mole of $NaIO_3$ in step (i)?
   (a) 2 (b) 4 (c) 6 (d) 8
4. How many equivalents of IO_3^- are used in step (ii)?
   (a) 6 (b) 5
   (c) 0.06 (d) 0.035

Passage 4 Chromium (III) ion forms many compounds with ammonia. To find the formula of one of these compounds, you titrate the NH_3 in the compound with standarised acid.

$$\underset{(A)}{Cr(NH_3)_xCl_3(aq)} + xHCl \longrightarrow xNH_4^+(aq) + Cr^{3+}(aq) + (x+3)Cl^-(aq)$$

Assume that 40 mL of 1.5 M HCl is used to titrate 2.635 g of (*A*).

Based on the above experiment, answer the following questions.

1. Value of *x* is
   (a) 3 (b) 4
   (c) 5 (d) 6

2. If 1.5 M H_2SO_4 is used instead of 1.5 M HCl, titre value is
(a) 40 mL (b) 20 mL (c) 10 mL (d) 15 mL

3. Probable complex (assume that coordination number of chromium is six) can be
(a) $[Cr(NH_3)_6]Cl_3$
(b) $[Cr(NH_3)_5Cl]Cl_2$
(c) $[Cr(NH_3)_4Cl_2]Cl$
(d) $[CrCl_3]\cdot 6NH_3$

***Passage* 5** Copper containing alloy weighing 0.3175 g is dissolved in an acid, and an excess of KI is added. Estimation of copper in alloy is based on the following reaction..

$$2Cu^{2+}(aq) + 5I^-(aq) \longrightarrow Cu_2I_2(s) + I_3^-(aq)$$
$$I_3^-(aq) + 2S_2O_3^{2-}(aq) \longrightarrow S_4O_6^{2-}(aq) + 3I^-(aq)$$

Answer the following questions based on the above reaction.

1. Oxidising agent (O) and reducing agent (R) in the above reaction :

	O	R
(a)	$Cu^{2+}, S_2O_3^{2-}$	I_3^-, I^-
(b)	$Cu^{2+}, S_2O_3^{2-}$	I_3^-
(c)	Cu^{2+}, I_3^-	$I^-, S_2O_3^{2-}$
(d)	Cu^{2+}, I^-	$I_3^-, S_2O_3^{2-}$

2. Estimation is based on
(a) iodometry
(b) iodimetry
(c) gravimetry
(d) colorimetry

3. If 25 mL of 0.10 M $Na_2S_2O_3$ is required, Cu present in alloy is
(a) 20% (b) 40%
(c) 45% (d) 50%

4. I_2 formed is converted to KI_3 in the given reaction. This shows
(a) I_2 is soluble in H_2O
(b) I_2 is a Lewis acid
(c) I_2 is ionic compound
(d) I^- is a Lewis base

***Passage* 6** Consider the titration of solution *X* of 1 M HCl using 0.1 M NaOH solution with phenolphthalein indicator, by two students *A* and *B*.

Student	Process	Titre volume of NaOH
A	20 mL HCl + 20 mL H_2O + 1 drop phenolphthalein	V_A
B	20 mL HCl + 60 mL H_2O + 1 drop phenolphthalein	V_B

Answer the following questions.

1. What is the relation between V_A and V_B ?
(a) $V_A = V_B$ (b) $2V_A = V_B$
(c) $V_A = 2V_B$ (d) $3V_A = V_B$

2. Before titration, resultant molarity of HCl of the student *A* after addition of H_2O is
(a) same as that of *B*
(b) double as that of *B*
(c) half as that of *B*
(d) one third as that of *B*

3. End-point is
(a) appearance of blue colour
(b) disappearance of blue colour
(c) appearance of pink colour
(d) disappearance of blue colour

***Passage* 7** For titrating a certain volume of a reducing substance by 1 M $KMnO_4$, it is found that 20m L was used in acidic medium, 33.4 mL was used in alkaline medium and 100 mL was used in neutral medium. MnO_4^- is reduced to Mn^{2+} in acidic medium.
Based on this study, answer the following questions.

1. To what state MnO_4^- is reduced to in alkaline medium?
(a) +4 (b) +1
(c) +5 (d) +6

2. To what state MnO_4^- is reduced to in neutral medium?
(a) +4 (b) +5 (c) +6 (d) +7

3. 1 M $KMnO_4$ expressed in terms of normality is in

	Acidic medium	Alkaline medium	Neutral medium
(a)	1 N	1 N	1 N
(b)	5 N	3 N	1 N
(c)	1 N	3 N	5 N
(d)	0.2 N	0.33 N	1 N

***Passage* 8** Bleaching powder and bleach solution are produced on a large scale and used in several house hold products. The effectiveness of bleach solution is often measured by iodometry. **[IIT JEE 2012]**

1. 25 mL of household bleach solution was mixed with 30 mL of 0.50 M KI and 10 mL of 4 N acetic acid. In the titration of the liberated iodine, 48 mL of 0.25 N. $Na_2S_2O_3$ was used to reach the end point. The molarity of the household bleach solution, is
(a) 0.48 M (b) 0.96 M
(c) 0.24 M (d) 0.024 M

2. Bleaching powder contains a salt of an oxoacid as one of its components. The anhydride of that oxoacid, is
(a) Cl_2O (b) Cl_2O_7
(c) ClO_2 (d) Cl_2O_6

Matrix-Match Type

Given below are Matching Type Questions, with two columns (each having some items) each . Each item of Column I has to be matched with the items of Column II.

1. Match the reaction (in Column I) with titration method (in Column II).

Column I	Column II
A. $N_2H_4 + 2I_2 \longrightarrow N_2 + 4H^+ + 4I^-$	1. Iodometric
B. $2CuSO_4 + 4KI \longrightarrow Cu_2I_2 + 2K_2SO_4 + I_2$	2. Redox
C. $MnO_4^- + Fe^{2+} \longrightarrow Mn^{2+} + Fe^{3+}$	3. Kjeldahl
D. $NH_4Cl + NaOH \xrightarrow{\Delta} NH_3$ $2NH_3 + H_2SO_4 \longrightarrow (NH_4)_2SO_4$	4. Iodimetric

2. Match the half-reaction (in Column I) with equivalent mass (molar mass = *M*) (in Column II).

Column I	Column II
A. $Cr_2O_7^{2-} \longrightarrow Cr^{3+}$	1. M
B. $C_2O_4^{2-} \longrightarrow CO_2$	2. $M/2$
C. $MnO_4^- \longrightarrow MnO_2$	3. $M/6$
D. $HC_2O_4^- \longrightarrow C_2O_4^{2-}$	4. $M/3$

3. Match the reactants (in Column I) with the indicator (in Column II).

Column I	Column II
A. $Fe^{2+}/Cr_2O_7^{2-}$	1. Ferric alum
B. $AgNO_3$ / CNS^-	2. MnO_4^- (self)
C. $CuSO_4$/ $KI/S_2O_3^{2-}$	3. $K_3[Fe(CN)_6]$
D. Fe^{2+}/MnO_4^-	4. Starch

4. Match the reaction (in Column I) with the colour at the final stage (in Column II).

Column I	Column II
A. MnO_4^- / H^+ / Fe^{2+}	1. Deep reddish brown
B. MnO_4^-/conc. OH^-/Mn^{2+}	2. Colourless
C. MnO_4^- / H_2O / dil. OH^-	3. Blackish brown
D. $CuSO_4$ / KI	4. Green

5. Match the reactant (in Column I) with the type of titration (in Column II) used for estimation.

Column I	Column II
A. KHC_2O_4	1. Acid-base titration
B. $FeSO_4 \cdot (NH_4)_2SO_4 \cdot 6H_2O$	2. Redox titration
C. $CuSO_4$	3. Iodometric
D. I_2	4. Iodimetric
E. $K_2Cr_2O_7$	

6. Match the half-reaction (oxidation or reduction) (in Column I) with number of electrons exchanged (in Column II).

Column I		Column II
A. $3I^- \longrightarrow I_3^-$	1.	5
B. $Cr_2O_7^{2-} \longrightarrow 2Cr^{3+}$	2.	6
C. $Cl^- \longrightarrow ClO_3^-$	3.	2
D. $N_2 \longrightarrow N_2H_4$	4.	4
E. $MnO_4^- \longrightarrow Mn^{2+}$	5.	3
F. $C_2O_4^{2-} \longrightarrow 2CO_2$	6.	1

Single Integer Answer Questions

Answer of these questions is a single digit lying between 0 to 9.

1. 100 mL of 1 M oxalic acid reduces 100 mL of 1 M MnO_2. What is the change in O.N. of Mn?

2. 100 mL of 1 M H_2SO_4 solution is mixed with 200 mL of 2 M $Ca(OH)_2$ solution. What is the molarity of the resulting solution?

3. KHC_2O_4 solution is 4 N when treated with NaOH. What is the normality of this solution when oxidised by $KMnO_4$?

4. $C_2O_4^{2-}$ can be oxidised to CO_2 by MnO_4^-/H^+ as well as MnO_4^-/OH^-. Ratio of moles of MnO_4^- required per mole of $C_2O_4^{2-}$ in acidic and basic medium is $(x/10)$. What is the value of x?

5. 29.2% (*w/w*) HCl stock solution has density 1.25 g/mL. The volum (mL) of stock solution required to prepare a 200 mL solution of 0.4 M HCl is ...... **[IIT JEE 2012]**

6. How much water (in L) should be added to 100 mL of 1 M $KMnO_4$ solution so that it is 0.5 N in a titration in acidic medium?

7. H_2SO_4 (d = 1.8 g/cc) is 49% by weight of solution. What is the molar concentration of H_2SO_4?

8. A solution of 6 N H_3PO_3 is x M H_3PO_3. What is the value of x?

9. How much urea (in g) is present in 16 g of 10 molal urea solution?

10. 100 mL of 1 M $KMnO_4$ solution is reduced by 150 mL of 1 M $C_2O_4^{2-}$?. What is the oxidation state of manganese salt formed?

11. 1 M MnO_4^- solution is x equiv. L^{-1}. When reduced to Mn^{2+}. Thus, x is ....

12. 6.3 g of an acid (molar mass = 126 g mol^{-1}) reacts completely with 100 mL of 0.5 M $Ca(OH)_2$ solution. Thus, basicity of acid is ....

13. 100 mL of 0.01 M XO_4^- is reduced to X^{n+} by 100 mL of 0.05 M Fe^{2+} in acidic medium. Thus, oxidation state of X in X^{n+} is ....

14. $Cr(NH_3)_xCl_3(aq)$ solution is titrated with $HCl(aq)$ solution.

$$Cr(NH_3)_xCl_3(aq) + xHCl(aq) \longrightarrow xNH_4^+(aq) + Cr^{3+}(aq) + (x+3)Cl^-(aq)$$

Assume that 24.26 mL of 1.5 M HCl is used to titrate 1.580 g of $Cr(NH_3)_xCl_3$. Thus, x is ....

15. We want to prepare 2 L of 0.025 M CH_3COOH solution. Amount of CH_3COOH dissolved is ....

Answers

Objective Questions Type I [Only one correct option]

1. (b)	2. (a)	3. (b)	4. (b)	5. (c)	6. (a)	7. (b)	8. (d)	9. (a)	10. (d)
11. (b)	12. (a)	13. (a)	14. (d)	15. (b)	16. (b)	17. (d)	18. (a)	19. (c)	20. (a)
21. (b)	22. (b)	23. (a)	24. (d)	25. (c)	26. (d)	27. (c)	28. (a)	29. (c)	30. (b)
31. (a)	32. (c)	33. (c)	34. (b)	35. (c)	36. (d)	37. (d)	38. (c)	39. (c)	40. (c)
41. (a)	42. (c)	43. (c)	44. (d)	45. (c)	46. (b)	47. (a)	48. (c)	49. (d)	50. (b)
51. (a)	52. (c)	53. (d)	54. (a)	55. (c)	56. (a)	57. (a)	58. (d)	59. (a)	60. (c)
61. (a)	62. (a)	63. (c)	64. (b)	65. (d)	66. (b)	67. (c)	68. (c)	69. (b)	70. (a)
71. (a)	72. (d)	73. (a)	74. (a)	75. (c)	76. (b)	77. (b)	78. (d)	79. (a)	80. (b)
81. (a)	82. (d)	83. (b)	84. (d)	85. (b)	86. (b)	87. (b)	88. (c)	89. (c)	90. (c)

Objective Questions Type II [One or more than one correct option(s)]

1. (a, b)	2. (b, c)	3. (a, c)	4. (a, c)	5. (a, c)
6. (a)	7. (a, c, d)	8. (c, d)	9. (b)	10. (a, c, d)

Numerical Value Questions

1. 10	2. 9.434	3. 10.42	4. 80.4 ppm	5. 4	6. 1.5	7. 0.11	8. 0.7	9. 1.6.	10. 10
11. 50	12. 48								

Comprehension Based Questions

Passage 1 – 1. (c) 2. (a) 3. (a) 4. (c) 5. (d)

Passage 2 – 1. (c) 2. (a) 3. (c)

Passage 3 – 1. (c) 2. (a) 3. (c) 4. (d)

Passage 4 – 1. (d) 2. (b) 3. (a)

Passage 5 – 1. (c) 2. (a) 3. (d) 4. (b, d)

Passage 6 – 1. (a) 2. (b) 3. (c)

Passage 7 – 1. (a) 2. (c) 3. (b)

Passage 8 – 1. (c) 2. (a)

Matrix-Match Type

1. A → (4); B → (1); C → (2); D → (3)

2. A → (3); B → (2); C → (4); D → (1)

3. A → (4); B → (3); C → (1); D → (2)

4. A → (2); B → (4); C → (3); D → (1)

5. A → (1,2); B → (1,2); C—(2,3); D—(4); E → (2,3)

6. A → (3); B → (2); C—(1); D—(4); E → (1); F → (3)

Single Integer Answer Questions

1. (2)	2. (3)	3. (4)	4. (6)	5. (8)	6. (1)	7. (1)	8. (3)	9. (1)	10. (4)
11. (5)	12. (1)	13. (2)	14. (6)	15. (3)					

Solutions

Objective Questions Type I [Only one correct option]

1. (*b*) $BaCl_2 \rightleftharpoons Ba^{2+} + 2Cl^-$

Millimoles of $Cl^- = 2 \times$ millimoles of $BaCl_2$

$= 2 \times 100 \times 1 = 200$ millimoles

2. (*a*) $H_2C_2O_4 \cdot 2H_2O = 126 \text{ g mol}^{-1}$

$1.575 \text{ g } H_2C_2O_4 \cdot 2H_2O = \frac{1.575}{126} = 0.0125 \text{ mol}$

Let the volume be $= V$ L

$$\therefore \quad \frac{0.0125 \text{ mol}}{V \text{ L}} = 0.10 \text{ M}$$

$$\therefore \quad V = \frac{0.0125}{0.1} = 0.125 \text{ L}$$

$= 125$ mL

3. (*b*) pH $= 12$

$\therefore$ $[H^+] = 10^{-12}$ M

$[OH^-] = 10^{-2} \text{ M} = 10^{-2} \text{ mol L}^{-1}$

$= 10^{-3}$ mol per 100 mL

$= 10^{-3} \times 40$ g NaOH per 100 mL

$= 0.04$ g

4. (*b*) (a) $0.208 \text{ g } BaCl_2 = \frac{0.208}{208}$ mole

$= 1 \times 10^{-3}$ mole

$= 1$ millimole $BaCl_2$

$= 2$ millimoles Cl^-

(b) 100 mL of 0.1 M $BaCl_2 = 100 \times 0.1$ millimoles $BaCl_2$

$= 100 \times 0.2$ millimoles Cl^-

$= 20$ millimoles

(c) $0.745 \text{ g KCl} = \frac{0.745}{74.5}$ mole KCl

$= 0.01$ mole

$= 0.01 \times 1000$ millimoles

$= 10$ millimoles

5. (*c*) $CaCl_2$ (residue) $= 0.111$ g

$= \frac{0.111}{111 \text{ g mol}^{-1}}$

$= 1 \times 10^{-3}$ mol in 100 mL

$= \frac{1 \times 10^{-3} \times 1000}{100}$ mol in 1000 mL

$= 0.01$ M

6. (*a*) $CaCO_3 = 200$ ppm $= 200$ parts per million

$= 200$ g per 10^6 mL

$= 2$ mol per 10^6 mL

$= 2 \times 10^{-3}$ mol per L

$= 2 \times 10^{-3}$ M

7. (*b*) $CaCO_3 = 200 \text{ g} = 2$ mol

$H_2O = 10^6 \text{ g} = \frac{10^6}{18}$ mol

$$\text{Mole fraction of } CaCO_3 = \frac{2}{2 + \frac{10^6}{18}} = 3.6 \times 10^{-5}$$

8. (*d*) Ethanol $= 46 \text{ g} = \frac{46}{46} = 1$ mol

Water $= 54 \text{ g} = \frac{54}{16} = 3$ mol

Total moles $= 1 + 3 = 4$

$$\therefore \quad X_{\text{ethanol}} = \frac{1}{4} = 0.25$$

9. (*a*) Any factor that is volume independent, is temperature independent.

10. (*d*) $HNO_3 = 0.001 \text{ M} = 0.001 \text{ mol L}^{-1} = 0.001 \times 63 \text{ g L}^{-1}$

$= \frac{0.001 \times 63 \times 10^6}{10^3}$ g parts per million $= 63$

11. (*b*) $NaHC_2O_4 \rightleftharpoons Na^+ + H^+ + C_2O_4^{2-}$

NaOH neutralises H^+

MnO_4^-/H^+ oxidises $C_2O_4^{2-}$ to CO_2

Hence, normality $= 2 \times$ Molarity

Thus, Normality $= 2 \times 0.1 \text{ M} = 0.2$ N

12. (*a*) M (HCl) in mixture $= \frac{0.5 \times 750 + 2 \times 250}{750 + 250} = 0.875$ M

13. (*a*) $\underset{1 \text{ mol}}{NaHC_2O_4 \cdot H_2C_2O_4} \rightleftharpoons Na^+ + \underset{3 \text{ mol}}{3H^+} + \underset{2 \text{ mol}}{2C_2O_4^{2-}}$

3 mol $H^+ \equiv 3$ equivalents of H^+

2 mol $C_2O_4^{3-} \equiv 4$ equivalents of $C_2O_4^{2-}$

14. (*d*) Concentration have been taken in normality (g equivalent L^{-1}) hence, 100 mL of 0.01 N H_2SO_4

$= 100$ mL of 0.01 N HCl

$= 100$ mL of 0.01 N H_3PO_4

15. (*b*) Molar mass of $Na_2CO_3 \cdot xH_2O = (106 + 18x)$

$$2.86 \text{ g salt} = \left(\frac{2.86}{106 + 18x} \text{ mole in 100 mL}\right)$$

$$= \left(\frac{28.6}{106 + 18x}\right) \text{ mole in 1000 mL}$$

$$\therefore \quad \text{Molarity} = \left(\frac{28.6}{106 + 18x}\right)$$

Since, $CO_3^{2-} \equiv 2H^+$

Hence, normality $= 2 \times$ molarity $= 0.2$ N

$$\frac{2 \times 28.6}{106 + 18x} = 0.2$$

$x = 10$

16. (*b*) One molal urea solution means 1 kg water has 60 g urea.

Thus, total mass of one molal solution = 1060 g

1060 g solution has urea = 60 g

$$1000 \text{ g solution has urea} = \frac{60 \times 1000}{1060} = 56.6 \text{ g}$$

17. (*d*) 98% by weight of solution means

$$H_2SO_4 = 98 \text{ g} = 1 \text{ mol}$$

$$H_2SO_4 + H_2O \text{ (solution)} = 100 \text{ g}$$

$$\therefore \quad H_2O = 2 \text{ g} = 0.002 \text{ kg}$$

$$\therefore \quad \text{Molality} = \text{conc. in mol kg}^{-1}$$

$$= \frac{1}{0.002} = 500 \text{ molal}$$

18. (*a*) Sucrose = 1 molal = 1 mol in 1000 g H_2O

$$\text{Moles of water} = \frac{1000}{18}$$

Mole of sucrose = 1

$$\text{Total moles} = 1 + \frac{1000}{18}$$

$$\text{Mole fraction of sucrose} = \frac{1}{1+\frac{1000}{18}} = \frac{18}{1018} = 0.018$$

19. (*c*) Density = 1.8 g / mL

Molarity = 18 M = 18 mol H_3PO_4 in 1 L solution

1000 mL solution has H_3PO_4 = 18 mol = 18 × 98 g

1000 mL = (1800 g) solution has H_3PO_4 = 18 × 98 g

$$H_3PO_4 \text{ by mass \% (by weight of solution)} = \frac{18 \times 98}{1800} \times 100 = 98\%$$

or (1800 − 18 × 98) g H_2O (solvent) H_3PO_4 = 18 × 98 g

2 g solvent has H_3PO_4 = 98 g = 1 mol H_3PO_4

1 kg = 1000 g solvent has H_3PO_4 = 500 molal

Thus, 98%, 500 molal

20. (*a*) Mole fraction of glucose = 0.5

Hence, mole fraction of water = 0.5

Thus, moles of water = moles of glucose = *x*

Thus, water = 18 *x* g

$$= \frac{18x}{1000} \text{ kg}$$

$$\text{Molality} = \frac{\text{Moles of glucose}}{\text{kg of } H_2O}$$

$$= \frac{x}{\frac{18x}{1000}} = \frac{1000}{18}$$

$$= 55.55 \text{ mol kg}^{-1}$$

Direct Method

$$\text{Molality} = \frac{1000 x_1 \text{ (glucose)}}{(1 - x_1)\, m_2 \text{ (water)}} = \frac{1000 \times 0.5}{0.5 \times 18} = 55.55$$

21. (*b*) 100 mL of 0.01 M H_2SO_4 (dibasic acid)

Thus, neutralised by 100 mL of 0.01 M

$Ca(OH)_2$ (diacid base)

22. (*b*) H^+ (in H_2SO_4 - a dibasic acid) = 0.2 M

H^+ (in H_3PO_3 - a dibasic acid) = 0.2 M

$$\text{Total } [H^+] = \frac{M_1V_1 + M_2V_2}{V_1 + V_2} = \frac{100 \times 0.2 + 200 \times 0.2}{300} = 0.2 \text{ M}$$

23. (*a*) Milliequivalents of NaOH = 25 × 1

∴ milliequivalent of dibasic acid

(equivalent weight *E*)

$$= \frac{1.575 \times 1000}{E} \text{ g}$$

$$\therefore \quad E = \frac{1.575 \times 1000}{25} = 63$$

$$\therefore \quad \text{Molar mass} = E \times 2 = 126 \text{ g mol}^{-1}$$

24. (*d*) $1.06 \text{ g } Na_2CO_3 = \frac{1.06}{106} \text{ mol} = 0.01 \text{ mol in 100 mL}$

$$\therefore \quad [Na_2CO_3] = \frac{0.01}{\frac{100}{1000} \text{ L}} = 0.1 \text{M}$$

= 0.2 N (being diacid base)

10 mL of 0.2 N Na_2CO_3 = 2 milliequivalent

(a) 10 × 0.1N HCl = 1 milliequivalent

(b) 10 × 0.1M H_3PO_4 = 10 × 0.3N H_3PO_4
= 3 milliequivalent

(c) 20 mL of 0.1 M H_2SO_4 = 20 mL of 0.2 N H_2SO_4
= 4 milliequivalent

(d) 20 mL of 0.1 M HCl = 20 × 0.1N HCl
= 2 millliequivalent

25. (*c*) 100 mL of 1 M BaF_2 = 100 millimoles

100 mL of 2 M H_2SO_4 = 200 millimoles

	BaF_2	+ H_2SO_4	⟶ $BaSO_4$	+ 2HF
	1 mol	1 mol	1 mol	2 mol
Initial	100 millimol	200 millimol		
Final	0	100 millimol	100 millimol	200 millimol

Thus, resulting solution has

= 100 millimoles H_2SO_4 + 200 millimoles HF

= 200 millimoles of H^+ + 200 millimoles of H^+

= 400 millimoles H^+ in 200 mL solution

$$[H^+] = \frac{\frac{400}{1000} \text{ moles}}{\frac{200}{1000} \text{ L}} = 2.0 \text{ M}$$

$$[BaSO_4] = 100 \text{ millimoles } BaSO_4 = 0.1 \text{ mol}$$

Thus, (a) and (b) are true.

26. (*d*) Iron (II) sulphate (IV) is

$$(Fe^{2+})(SO_3^{2-})$$
$$\uparrow \quad\quad \uparrow$$
$$+2 \quad\quad +4$$

Note In IUPAC nomenclature O.N. have been placed after element.

Fe^{2+} is oxidised to Fe^{3+} and SO_3^{2-} is oxidised to SO_4^{2-} by MnO_4^- in acidic medium

1L of 1 M $FeSO_3$ = 1 mole $FeSO_3$

$$5Fe^{2+} + MnO_4^- + 8H^+ \longrightarrow 5Fe^{3+} + Mn^{2+} + 4H_2O$$

$$5SO_3^{2-} + 2MnO_4^- + 6H^+ \longrightarrow 5SO_4^{2-} + 2Mn^{2+} + 3H_2O$$

Thus, $5FeSO_3 \equiv 3MnO_4^-$

$$1FeSO_3 \equiv \frac{3}{5}MnO_4^- = 0.6\,mol$$

27. (*c*) $\underset{1\,mol}{N_2H_4CO} + 2NaOH \longrightarrow Na_2CO_3 + \underset{2\,mol}{2NH_3}$

0.6 g = 0.01 mol   0.02 mol

$$2NH_3 + 2H^+ \longrightarrow 2NH_4^+$$

100 mL of 0.2 N HCl = 20 millimol = 0.02 mol

28. (*a*) $N\,\% = \frac{1.4N_1V_1}{w}$

where, N_1 = normality of acid required to neutralise NH_3

V_1 = volume of acid

$$N\% = \frac{1.4 \times 0.1 \times 100}{0.31} = 45.16\%$$

29. (*c*) $NH_2CONH_2 + 2NaOH \longrightarrow Na_2CO_3 + 2NH_3$

0.6 g = 0.01 mol   0.02 mol

$$\underset{\substack{2\,mol\\0.02\,mol}}{2NH_3} + \underset{\substack{1\,mol\\0.01\,mol}}{H_2SO_4} \longrightarrow (NH_4)_2SO_4$$

= 0.02 equiv.

0.1 N H_2SO_4 = 0.1 equivalent in = 1000 mL

0.02 equivalent in = 200 mL

H_2SO_4 unused = 100 mL

30. (*b*) 6.5 molal KOH = 1000 g solvent has 6.5 moles KOH

so weight of solute = 6.5×56

= 364 g

weight of solution = 1000 + 364 = 1364

Volume of solution = $\frac{1364}{1.89}$ mL

$$\text{Molarity} = \frac{\text{moles of solute}}{V_{solution} \text{ in Litre}} = \frac{6.5 \times 1.89 \times 1000}{1364} = 9.00$$

31. (*a*) 1 g H_2O_2 (impure) = 0.01 *X* g pure H_2O_2

$$H_2O_2 \longrightarrow 2H^+ + O_2 + 2e^-$$

$$MnO_4^- + 8H^+ + 5e^- \longrightarrow Mn^{2+} + 4H_2O$$

1 mol H_2O_2 = 2 equiv. H_2O_2, $E = \frac{\text{molar mass}}{2}$

1 mol MnO_4^- = 5 equiv. MnO_4^- $E = \frac{\text{molar mass}}{5}$

0.01 *X* g pure $H_2O_2 = \frac{0.01\,X}{17}$ equiv. H_2O_2

$= \frac{0.01\,X}{17}$ equiv. of MnO_4^- in *X* mL MnO_4^- solution

$$N\,(MnO_4^-) = \frac{0.01\,X\,1000}{17\,X} = \frac{10}{17}$$

$$M\,(MnO_4^-) = \frac{10}{17 \times 5} = \frac{10}{85} = 0.12\,M$$

32. (*c*) 100 mL of $NaHC_2O_4 \equiv$ 50 mL of 0.1 M MnO_4^-

$$100 \times N_1(C_2O_4^{2-}) \equiv 50 \times 0.5\,N\,MnO_4^-$$

$$N_1 = 0.25\,N\ (\text{as } C_2O_4^{2-})$$

$$M_1(C_2O_4^{2-}) = 0.125\ (\text{as } C_2O_4^{2-})$$

$$\equiv 0.125\,N\ (\text{as } H^+)$$

$\therefore$ $100 \times 0.125\,M\,(H^+) \equiv V \times 0.1$

$\therefore$ $V = 125$ mL

33. (*c*) $Fe^{2+} \longrightarrow Fe^{3+} + e^-$

Molarity = Normality

Equivalent weight = Molar weight

$$Cr_2O_7^{2-} + 6e^- \longrightarrow 2Cr^{3+}$$

Normality = 6 × Molarity

$$\text{Equivalent weight} = \frac{\text{Molecular weight}}{6}$$

20 mL of 0.1 M $Cr_2O_7^{2-} = 20 \times 0.6\,N\,Cr_2O_7^{2-}$

50 mL of N_1 $Fe^{2+} = 20 \times 0.6\,N\,Cr_2O_7^{2-}$

$$N_1 = \frac{20 \times 0.6}{50}$$

$= 0.24\,N\,Fe^{2+}$

$= 0.24\,M\,Fe^{2+}$

$= 0.24 \times 278$

$= 66.72\,gL^{-1}$

$(FeSO_4 \cdot 7H_2O = 278\,g\,mol^{-1})$

34. (*b*) $H_2O_2 \longrightarrow 2H^+ + O_2 + 2e^-$ 0.1 M = 0.2 N

$MnO_4^- \longrightarrow Mn^{x+}$ 0.1 M = 0.1(7 − *x*) N

$$N_1V_1 = N_2V_2$$

$$0.2 \times 24 = 0.1(7 - x)16$$

$$(7 - x) = 3$$

$$x = 4$$

Thus, change in oxidation number of MnO_4^- is 3. Thus, MnO_4^- changes to MnO_2.

35. (*c*) I. $Fe^{2+} \longrightarrow Fe^{3+}$

Fe^{2+}: Blue colour with $[Fe(CN)_6^{3-}]$; Fe^{3+}: No colour with $[Fe(CN)_6]^{3-}$

(Oxidised by $Cr_2O_7^{2-}$)

Thus, when oxidation is complete, there is no blue colour with $[Fe(CN)_6]^{3-}$ used externally.

II. $Ag^+ + Cl^- \longrightarrow AgCl$

Every drop of Ag^+ is converted into white ppt. of AgCl. Any additional drop of Ag^+ gives red ppt. with CrO_4^{2-}

III. $Fe^{2+} \longrightarrow Fe^{3+}$

MnO_4^- oxidises Fe^{2+} to Fe^{3+} and itself reduced to Mn^{2+} (colourless); when oxidation is complete, any additional drop of MnO_4^- imparts its own colour (MnO_4^- is thus self-indicator)

Thus, I. $[Fe(CN)_6]^{3-}$

II. CrO_4^{2-}

III. MnO_4^-

36. (*d*) (a) $CuSO_4 + 4KI \longrightarrow Cu_2I_2 + 2K_2SO_4 + I_2$

$I_2 + 2Na_2S_2O_3 \longrightarrow 2NaI + Na_2S_4O_6$

Liberated I_2 is estimated by $Na_2S_2O_3$ (hypo) taken in burette. Thus, true

(b) I_2 (in burette) + $2N_2S_2O_3 \longrightarrow 2NaI + Na_2S_4O_6$

Thus, true.

(c) $I_2 + KI \rightleftharpoons KI_3$

Thus, true.

38. (*c*) Molecular mass of $(COOH)_2 \cdot nH_2O$

$= 12 \times 2 + 16 \times 4 + 2 + 18n$

$= 90 + 18n$

n-factor = 2

Normality of solution $(N_1) = \dfrac{1.575 \times 2 \times 1000}{(90 + 18n) \times 250}$

$(N_1V_1)_{\text{oxalic acid}} = (N_2V_2)_{\text{NaOH}}$

$$\frac{1.575 \times 2 \times 1000}{(90+18n) \times 250} \times \frac{16.68}{1000} = \frac{1}{15} \times \frac{25}{1000}$$

$$\frac{3 \times 1.575 \times 2 \times 16.68 \times 1000}{5 \times 250} = (90 + 18n)$$

$126 = 90 + 18n$

$36 = 18n$

$n = 2$

40. (*c*) $O_3 + 6I^- + 6H^+ \longrightarrow 3H_2O + 3I_2$

$O_3 \equiv 3I_2 \equiv 6I$

$\therefore \quad I \equiv \dfrac{O_3}{6}$

$\therefore$ Equivalent mass of $O_3 = \dfrac{48}{6} = 8$

41. (*a*) Increase in molar concentration = 0.1 M

= 0.01 mol in 100 mL

= 0.745 g KCl in 100 mL

42. (*c*) $H_2S \longrightarrow SO_2$

$\uparrow$ −2 $\quad \uparrow$ +4

Change in O.N. = 6 units

Thus, 1 mol H_2S = 6 equivalents H_2S

43. (*c*)

	Change in O.N.	*E*
$\frac{1}{2}Br_2 \longrightarrow Br^-$ (0 → −1)	1	$= \frac{M/2}{1}$
$\frac{1}{2}Br_2 \longrightarrow BrO_3^-$ (0 → +5)	5	$= \frac{M/2}{5}$

Net equivalent weight = *E*(in oxidation) + *E*(in reduction)

$$= \frac{M/2}{5} + \frac{M/2}{1} = \frac{3M}{5}$$

44. (*d*) $NaCl \rightleftharpoons Na^+ + Cl^-$

$Na_2SO_4 \rightleftharpoons 2Na^+ + SO_4^{2-}$

$$[Na^+]_{mix} = \frac{30 \times 0.12 + 70 \times 0.15 \times 2}{30 + 70} = 0.246 \text{ M}$$

45. (*c*) 80 mL of 0.20 M HCl = 80 × 0.2

= 16 millimol HCl

120 mL of 0.15 M KOH = 120 × 0.15

= 18 millimol KOH

M_1V_1 (HCl) < M_2V_2 (KOH)

Thus, resulting solution is basic containing KCl and unreacted KOH

$KOH + HCl \longrightarrow KCl + H_2O$

$$[KOH] = \frac{M_2V_2 - M_1V_1}{V_1 + V_2} = \frac{18 - 16}{200} = 0.01 \text{ M}$$

KCl formed = HCl used

= 16 millimoles

= 16×10^{-3} mol in 200 mL or 0.2 L solution

$$\therefore \quad [KCl] = \frac{16 \times 10^{-3}}{0.200 \text{ L}} = 0.08 \text{ M}$$

46. (*b*) $5C_2O_4^{2-} + 2MnO_4^- \longrightarrow Mn^{2+} + 10CO_2$

2 mol of $MnO_4^- \equiv$ 5 mol of $C_2O_4^{2-}$ (KHC_2O_4)

$\dfrac{100 \times 0.02}{1000}$ mol MnO_4^- = 0.005 mol KHC_2O_4

47. (*a*) $2H_2O_2(l) \longrightarrow 2H_2O(l) + O_2(g)$

2 mol

1 mol = 24 L under given condition

24 L O_2 is from = 2 moles H_2O_2

3 L O_2 is from = $\dfrac{2 \times 3}{24}$ = 0.25 mole H_2O_2 in 100 mL solution

Thus, molarity of $H_2O_2 = \dfrac{0.25 \times 1000}{100} = 2.5 \text{ mol L}^{-1}$

48. (*c*) $H_3PO_3 + 2NaOH \longrightarrow Na_2HPO_3 + 2H_2O$

50 mL 1M

1M V = ?

$\Rightarrow \dfrac{n_{NaOH}}{n_{H_3PO_3}} = \dfrac{2}{1}$

$\Rightarrow \dfrac{1 \times V}{50 \times 1} = \dfrac{2}{1} \Rightarrow \boxed{V_{NaOH} = 100 \text{ mL}}$

$H_3PO_2 + 2NaOH \longrightarrow NaH_2PO_3 + H_2O$

100 ml 1M

2M V = ?

$\Rightarrow \dfrac{n_{NaOH}}{n_{H_3PO_3}} = \dfrac{1}{1} \Rightarrow \dfrac{1 \times V}{2 \times 100} = \dfrac{1}{1} \Rightarrow \boxed{V_{NaOH} = 200 \text{ mL}}$

49. (*d*) Phenolphthalein end-point indicates 50% neutralisation of Na_2CO_3 to $NaHCO_3$ stage.

$Na_2CO_3 + HCl \longrightarrow NaHCO_3 + NaCl$

$\therefore$ 0.2 M Na_2CO_3 = 0.2 N Na_2CO_3

$\therefore \quad N_1V_1 = N_2V_2$

(HCl) $\quad (Na_2CO_3)$

$x \times 20 = 0.2 \times 5$

x = 0.05 N = 0.05 M HCl

50. (*b*) 9 molal $H_2SO_4 = 9 \times 98$ g H_2SO_4 in 1000 g H_2O

$= 882$ g H_2SO_4 in 1882 g H_2SO_4 solution

$= \frac{882}{1882} \times 1000$ g H_2SO_4 in 1 kg soiution

$= 469$ g

51. (*a*) $RH_2 + Ca^{2+} \longrightarrow RCa + 2H^+$

Every Ca^{2+} ion is replaced by two H^+ ions

$$pH = 2$$

$$\therefore \quad [H^+] = 10^{-2}\ M$$

$$\therefore \quad [Ca^{2+}] = \frac{10^{-2}}{2}\ M = \frac{10^{-2} \times 40}{2}\ g\ L^{-1}$$

$$\therefore \quad \text{ppm of } Ca^{2+} = \frac{10^{-2} \times 40 \times 10^6}{2 \times 10^3} = 200$$

52. (*c*) $NaHC_2O_4 \rightleftharpoons Na^+ + H^+ + C_2O_4^{2-}$

$$H^+ \equiv OH^-$$

and $\quad C_2O_4^{2-} \equiv MnO_4^-$

$$H^+ + OH^- \longrightarrow H_2O$$

$$C_2O_4^{2-} \longrightarrow 2CO_2 + 2e^-$$

$$MnO_4^- + 8H^+ + 5e^- \longrightarrow Mn^{2+}$$

10 mL of $NaHC_2O_4 \equiv$ 10 mL of 0.1 M NaOH

Thus, $\quad 10 \times M(NaHC_2O_4) = 10 \times 0.1$

$M = 0.1\,M = 0.1\ N$ (since H^+ is neutralised)

$NaHC_2O_4 = 0.1$ N as an acid

$= 0.2$ N as $C_2O_4^{2-}$ oxidised by MnO_4^-

Let $\quad MnO_4^- = x\ M = 5x\ N$

10 mL of 0.2 N $NaHC_2O_4 \equiv$ 10 mL of $5x$ *N* $KMnO_4$

$$10 \times 0.2 = 10 \times 5x$$

$$\therefore \quad x = \frac{0.2}{5} = 0.04\ M$$

53. (*d*) Methyl orange indicates complete neutralisation of Na_2CO_3 and $NaHCO_3$ while phenolphthalein indicates only 50% reaction of Na_2CO_3 to $NaHCO_3$ stage only.

Let volume of given HCl required for complete neutralisation of

$$NaHCO_3 = V_1$$

and for $\quad Na_2CO_3 = V_2$

For phenolphthalein indicator (50% Na_2CO_3) $= \frac{V_2}{2} = x$

For methyl orange (further titration) $= \frac{V_2}{2} + V_1 = y$

$$= x + V_1 = y$$

Volume for $NaHCO_3$, $V_1 = (y - x)$ mL

54. (*a*) Only $FeSO_4$ is oxidised.

$$Fe^{2+} \longrightarrow Fe^{3+} + e^-$$

$$MnO_4^- + 5e^- + 8H^+ \longrightarrow Mn^{2+} + 4H_2O$$

100 mL of 2 M $MnO_4^- = 100 \times 10$ N MnO_4^-

$\equiv 1$ equiv. MnO_4^-

$\equiv 1$ equiv. Fe^{2+}

$\equiv 1$ mol Fe^{2+}

Thus, 1 mole $FeSO_4$ is in mixture of 3 moles of $FeSO_4$ and $Fe_2(SO_4)_3$.

Mole fraction of $FeSO_4 = \frac{1}{3}$

55. (*c*) Let $Na_2C_2O_4(A)$ be $= x$ mol

and $KHC_2O_4 \cdot H_2C_2O_4(B) = y$ mol

Let volume of each titre $= V$ mL

Moles of NaOH used $= \frac{V \times 0.1}{1000} = 10^{-4}\ V$

and equivalent moles of $KMnO_4$ used $= 10^{-4}\ V$

$$\underset{x}{Na_2C_2O_4} \rightleftharpoons \underset{x}{C_2O_4^{2-}} + 2Na^+$$

$$KHC_2O_4 \cdot H_2C_2O_4 \rightleftharpoons \underset{2y}{2C_2O_4^{2-}} + \underset{3y}{3H^+} + K^+$$

Thus, $[H^+]$ in mixture $= 3y =$ NaOH used $= 10^{-4}\ V$

and $[C_2O_4^{2-}]$ in mixture $= (x + 2y)$ moles

Equivalent of $[H^+]$ = Equivalent of NaOH

$$3y = 10^{-4}\ V$$

Equivalent of $C_2O_4^{2-}$ which is oxidised to CO_2 = Equivalent of MnO_4^- which is reduced to Mn^{2+}

$$2(x + 2y) = 5 \times 10^{-4}\ V$$

$$\therefore \quad \frac{(x + 2y)}{3y} = 5$$

$$\frac{x}{3y} + \frac{2}{3} = 2.5$$

$$\frac{x}{y} + 2 = 7.5$$

$$\frac{x}{y} = 7.5 - 2 = 5.5$$

Thus, ratio is $= \frac{x}{y} = \frac{5.5}{1}$

56. (*a*) $M_2CO_3 + 2HCl \longrightarrow 2MCl + H_2O + CO_2$

M is a monovalent cation.

Thus, equivalent weight of

$$M_2CO_3 = \frac{\text{molar mass}}{2} = M + 30$$

Let unused HCl be *V* mL

V mL of 1 N HCl $\equiv$ 100 mL of 0.5 N NaOH

$$\therefore \quad V = 50\ mL$$

1 N HCl used $= 150 - 50 = 100$ mL $= 0.1$ equiv.

$$\text{equiv. of } M_2CO_3 = \frac{5.3}{M + 30} = 0.1$$

$$M = 23$$

57. (*a*) $\underset{24\ g}{Mg} + \underset{98\ g}{H_2SO_4} \longrightarrow MgSO_4 + H_2$

1.2g $\quad \frac{98 \times 1.2}{24} = 4.9$ g

100 mL of 1 M $H_2SO_4 = 0.1$ mol $= 9.8$ g H_2SO_4

H_2SO_4 used $= 4.9$ g

H_2SO_4 left $= 9.8 - 4.9 = 4.9$ g in 100 mL

$= 49\ g\ L^{-1} = \frac{49}{98}\ mol\ L^{-1}$

$= 0.5$ M

58. (*d*) 10 mL Ca^{2+} (as CaC_2O_4)

$$\equiv 20 \text{ mL of } 0.001 \text{ M } MnO_4^-$$
$$= 20 \times 0.005 \text{ N } MnO_4^-$$

$\therefore$ $N(C_2O_4^{2-}) = 2 \times 0.005$ N

$$M(C_2O_4^{2-}) = 0.005 \text{ M}$$
$$M(Ca^{2+}) = 0.005 \text{ M}$$
$$[Ca^{2+}] = 0.005 \times 40 \text{ g L}^{-1}$$
$$= \frac{0.005 \times 40}{100} \text{ g/10 mL}$$
$$= 0.002 \text{ g}$$

59. (*a*) $2NaOH + CO_2 \longrightarrow Na_2CO_3 + H_2O$

1 L of 0.15 N

0.15 mol 0.0112 mol

NaOH required by 0.0112 mol CO_2 = 0.0224 mol

NaOH unreacted = 0.15 − 0.0224

= 0.1276 mol in 1 L

Thus, M (NaOH) = 0.1276 M

62. (*a*) 20.00 mL of 0.1 M $Pb^{2+} = 2 \times 10^{-3}$ mol Pb^{2+}

30.00 mL of 0.1 M $SO_4^{2-} = 3 \times 10^{-3}$ mol SO_4^{2-}

$$Pb^{2+} + SO_4^{2-} \longrightarrow PbSO_4$$

Pb^{2+} is in the limiting a quantity and every 1 mole of Pb^{2+} gives equal moles of $PbSO_4$ hence, $PbSO_4$ formed = 0.002 mol.

63. (*c*) K^+ and Cl^- remain unchanged but due to dilution (in equal volumes), molar concentration of each is halved.

$\therefore$ $[Cl^-] = 0.1$ M

$$[K^+] = 0.2 \text{ M}$$

Also, $[OH^-] > [H^+]$, mixture is basic

$$[OH^-]_{mix} = \frac{0.4 - 0.2}{2} = 0.1 \text{ M}$$

64. (*b*) (I) $H_2O_2 \longrightarrow O_2$, $MnO_4^- \longrightarrow Mn^{2+}$ } O.N. change = 5

(II) $H_2O_2 \longrightarrow O_2$, $MnO_4^- \longrightarrow MnO_2$ } O.N. change = 3

In I (acidic) $N_1V_1 = N_2V_2$ (H_2O_2, MnO_4^-)

$$2M_1 \times 100 = 0.5 \times 100$$
$$M_1(H_2O_2) = 2.5 \text{ M}$$

In II (basic) $N_1V_1 = N_2'V_2'$

$$2M_1 \times 100 = 3 \times M_2 \times V_2'$$
$$2 \times 2.5 \times 100 = 3 \times 1 \times V_2'$$
$$V_2' = \frac{500}{3} \text{ mL}$$

65. (*d*) Equivalent of H_2O_2 = Equivalent of MnO_4^-

$$N_1 \times V_1 = N_2 \times V_2$$
$$N_1(H_2O_2) = \frac{N_2 \times V_2}{V_1}$$
$$= \frac{1}{0.56} \times \frac{10}{10}$$
$$N_1 = \frac{1}{0.56} \text{ N}$$

5.6 vol. strength $\longrightarrow$ 1 N of H_2O_2

1 vol. strength $\longrightarrow \frac{1}{5.6}$ N of H_2O_2

x vol. strength $\longrightarrow \frac{1}{5.6} x$ N of H_2O_2

$$\frac{1}{5.6} x = \frac{1}{0.56} \Rightarrow x = 10$$

66. (*b*) $Fe^{2+} \longrightarrow Fe^{3+} + e^-$
1 mol

$Fe^{3+} \longrightarrow X$
1 mol

Only Fe^{2+} requires MnO_4^-

$$5Fe^{2+} + MnO_4^- + 8H^+ \longrightarrow 5Fe^{3+} + Mn^{2+} + 4H_2O$$

5 mol 1 mol

1 mol $\frac{1}{5}$ mol

Let volume of $KMnO_4 = V$ mL

then moles of $KMnO_4 = \frac{V \times 1}{1000} = \frac{V}{1000}$ mol

$$\frac{1}{5} = \frac{V}{1000} \Rightarrow V = 200 \text{ mL}$$

67. (*c*) SO_3^{2-} is oxidised to SO_4^{2-} (change in O.N. = 2)

25 mL of 0.1 M SO_3^{2-} = 2.5 millimol

= 5.0 milliequivalents of SO_3^{2-}

= 5.0 milliequivalents of M^{3+}

50 mL of 0.1 M M^{3+} = 5 millimol (given)

Thus, decrease in O.N. of M^{3+} should be 1

So that 5 millimol = 5 milliequivalents

Thus, new O.N. of metal = 2

68. (*c*) Total mass of solution = 1120 g

$$\text{Volume} = \frac{1120}{1.15} = 973.91 \text{ mL} = 0.97391 \text{ L}$$
$$\text{Molarity} = \frac{\text{moles}}{\text{litres}} = \frac{120/60}{0.97391} = 2.05 \text{ M}$$

69. (*b*) Na_2SO_4 remains unreacted

$$N_1V_1 = N_2V_2$$
$$N_1 \times 100 = (2 \times 0.5) \times 10$$
$$N_1(\text{NaOH}) = 0.1$$

100 mL of 0.1 N NaOH = 0.01 mol NaOH

= 0.01 × 40 g = 0.4 g

70. (*a*) $Fe_2(C_2O_4)_3 \rightleftharpoons 2Fe^{3+} + 3C_2O_4^{2-}$

1 mol 3 mol

Only $C_2O_4^{2-}$ is oxidised.

$$2MnO_4^- + 5C_2O_4^{2-} \longrightarrow 10CO_2 + 2Mn^{2+}$$

5 mol $C_2O_4^{2-} \equiv 2$ mol MnO_4^-

$\therefore$ 3 mol $C_2O_4^{2-}$ = 1.2 mol MnO_4^-

71. (*a*) 40 mL of 0.05 M Cr^{3+} = 20mL of x *M* H_2O_2

$$40\times 0.05\times 3\ N\ Cr^{3+} = 20\times 2x\ H_2O_2$$

$$x = 0.15\ M$$

Cr^{3+} is oxidised to CrO_4^{2-} by H_2O_2 which is reduced to H_2O.

72. (*d*) $P_4 + 3OH^- + 3H_2O \longrightarrow \underset{(A)}{OH_3} + PO_2^-$

$$\underset{1\ mol}{H_2PO_2^-} + \underset{Excess}{4Ag^+} + 2HO \longrightarrow \underset{4\ mol}{4Ag} + H_3PO_4 + 3H^+$$

73. (*a*)

$$2CuSO_4 + 4KI \longrightarrow CuI_2 + I_2 + 2K_2SO_4$$

$$I_2 + 2Na_2S_2O_3 \longrightarrow 2NaI + Na_2S_4O_6$$

$$2CuSO_4 = 2Na_2S_2O_3$$

$$CuSO_4 = Na_2S_2O_3$$

100 mL of 1 M hypo = 0.1 mol hypo

= 0.1 mol pure $CuSO_4$

Hence, 100% pure

74. (*a*)

$$\underset{24\ g}{Mg} + \underset{(98\ g\ =\ 1\ mol)}{H_2SO_4} \longrightarrow MgSO_4 + H_2$$

1.2 g Mg reacts with = 0.05 mol H_2SO_4

H_2SO_4 taken = 100 mL of 1 M H_2SO_4

= 0.1 mol

∴ H_2SO_4 left = 0.1 − 0.05

= 0.05 mol in 100 mL solution

∴ $[H_2SO_4] = 0.05\times 10 = 0.5\ M$

75. (*c*) 100 g H_3PO_4 solution has = 85 g H_3PO_4

$\frac{100}{1.7}$ mL H_3PO_4 solution has = 85 g H_3PO_4

$$= \frac{85}{98}\ mol$$

∴ $$\text{Molarity} = \frac{85/98\ mol}{\left(\frac{100}{1.7\times 1000}\ L\right)} = 14.74\ M$$

76. (*b*) $0.116\ g\ C_4H_4O_4(A) = \frac{0.116}{116} = 0.001\ mol$

= 0.001 x equivalent

$$0.074\ g\ Ca(OH)_2 = \frac{0.074}{74} = 0.001\ mol$$

= 0.002 equivalent

∴ 0.001 x = 0.002

∴ $x = 2$

77. (*b*) $H_2C_2O_4 \underset{I}{\rightleftharpoons} H^+ + HC_2O_4^- \underset{II}{\rightleftharpoons} H^+ + C_2O_4^{2-}$

Upto stage I—monobasic acid

II—dibasic acid

78. (*d*) $\overset{+4}{MnO_2} + 4HCl \longrightarrow \overset{+2}{Mn}Cl_2 + Cl_2 + 2H_2O$
$(n = 2)$

Eq. of MnO_2 = Eq. of Cl_2 = 0.1

$w = 0.1$

Also, Eq. weight of $MnO_2 = \frac{87}{2}$

So, $$w = \frac{87}{2}\times 0.1$$

⇒ $$w = \frac{8.7}{2}\ 4.35\ g$$

$$\%\ \text{purity} = \frac{4.35}{10}\times 100 = 43.5\%$$

79. (*a*) $0.106\ g\ Na_2CO_3 = \frac{0.106}{106}\ mol = 2\times 10^{-3}$ equivalent

$$H_2SO_4 = \frac{40\ N}{1000}\ \text{equivalents}$$

$$\frac{40\ N}{1000} = 2\times 10^{-3}$$

∴ $N = 0.05\ N\ H_2SO_4$

80. (*b*)

$$SO_3^{2-} + Cr_2O_7^{2-} \longrightarrow 2Cr^{3+} + SO_4^{2-}$$

O.N. = 4, 12, 6, 6 (+6e⁻ for Cr: 12 → 6; −2e⁻ for S: 4 → 6)

$$N_1V_1(SO_3^{2-}) = N_2V_2(Cr_2O_7^{2-})$$

$$2M_1\times 20 = 6\times 0.01\times 30$$

$$M_1 = 0.045\ M$$

81. (*a*)

$$\underset{+7}{MnO_4^-} \longrightarrow \underset{+6}{MnO_4^{2-}}$$

Change in O.N. = 1 unit

∴ Normality = Molarity

12.64 g $KMnO_4$ = 0.08 mol in 0.5 L

= 0.16 M = 0.16 N

82. (*d*) Oxidation state of I in KIO_3 = +5

S in SO_3^{2-} = +4

S in SO_4^{2-} = +6

$$\underset{+5}{IO_3^-} + \underset{+4}{SO_3^{2-}} \longrightarrow \underset{+6}{SO_4^{2-}} + \underset{x<5}{I^x}$$

$$\text{Equivalent of } SO_3^{2-} = \frac{60\times 0.5\times 2}{1000} = 0.06$$

$$\text{Equivalent of } IO_3^- = (5-x)\times\frac{2.14}{214} = (5-x)\ 0.01$$

$$(5-x)\ 0.01 = 0.06$$

$$5 - x = 6$$

$$x = -1$$

83. (*b*) Oxalic acid solution titrated with NaOH solution using phenolphthalein as an indicator.

$$H_2C_2O_4 + 2NaOH \longrightarrow Na_2C_2O_4 + 2H_2O$$

Equivalent of $H_2C_2O_4$ reacted = Equivalent of NaOH reacted

$$= \frac{5\times 2\times 0.1}{1000} = \frac{9\times M_{(NaOH)}\times 1}{1000}$$

$$M_{(NaOH)} = \frac{1}{9} = 0.11$$

84. (*d*) For mixing acidic solutions, resultant normality

$$= \frac{N_1V_1 + N_2V_2}{V_1 + V_2} = \frac{10\times 0.2 + 30\times 0.1}{10 + 3} = 0.125\ N$$

85. (*b*) 0.4 mol HCl ≡ 0.4 mol Cl^-

0.2 mol $CaCl_2$ = 0.4 mol Cl^-

Total moles = 0.8 mol Cl^- in 0.5 L solution

Thus, molarity = 1.6 M

86. (*b*) Equivalents of KOH used $= \frac{20 \times 0.5}{1000} = 0.01$

Moles of acid $= \frac{0.45}{90} = 0.005$ mol

If basicity of acid = x

then equivalents of acid = 0.005 x

∴ $0.005\,x = 0.01$

∴ $x = 2$

87. (*b*) In alkaline medium : Iodide is oxidised to iodate

$$2MnO_4^- + H_2O + I^- \longrightarrow 2MnO_2 + 2OH^- + IO_3^-$$

But, in weakly basic solution :

$$K\overset{+7}{Mn}O_4 + K\overset{-1}{I} \longrightarrow \overset{+4}{Mn}O_2 + \overset{0}{I_2}$$

Eq. of $KMnO_4$ = Eq. of I_2

$4 \times 3 = n \times 2$

$n = 6$

88. (*c*) Moles of NaOH initially $= \frac{200 \times 0.100}{1000} = 0.02$ mol

CO_2 absorbed = 1 millimol = 0.001 mol

$$2NaOH + CO_2 \longrightarrow Na_2CO_3 + H_2O$$

Thus, NaOH reacted = 0.001 × 2 = 0.002 mol

Na_2CO_3 formed = 0.001 mol

NaOH unreacted = 0.02 − 0.002 = 0.018 mol

Thus, HCl required by NaOH for phenolphthalein end-point = 0.018 mol

Equivalent of Na_2CO_3 = 0.002 equivalents

∴ Moles of HCl required by 0.002 equivalents for phenolphthalein end-point $= \frac{0.002}{2} = 0.001$

(50% reaction is indicated upto $NaHCO_3$)

∴ Total HCl = (0.018 + 0.001) mol in 200 mL

≡ (unreacted NaOH + $NaHCO_3$ formed)

∴ $N = \frac{(0.018 + 0.001)}{0.2}$ mol L^{-1}

= 0.095 M = 0.095 N

89. (*c*) $Na_2B_4O_7$ (borax) behaves like a weak base.

Based on reaction :

$$\frac{\text{moles of } Na_2B_4O_7}{\text{moles of HCl}} = \frac{1}{2}$$

Moles of HCl $= \frac{31.64 \times 0.108}{1000}$

$= 3.417 \times 10^{-3}$ mol

∴ Moles of $Na_2B_4O_7 = 1.7085 \times 10^{-3}$ mol

Moles of $B_2O_3 = 2 \times$ moles of $Na_2B_4O_7$

$= 3.417 \times 10^{-3}$ mol

∴ Amount = 0.2392 g

% of $B_2O_3 = \frac{0.2392}{0.7439} \times 100 = 32.15\%$

90. (*c*) This is a special case of buffer

$[H_3O^+] = K_a$

that is pH = pK_a

$$pH = pK_a + \log\frac{[CH_3COO^-]}{[CH_3COOH]}$$

Thus, at this point

$[CH_3COO^-] = [CH_3COOH]$

It means 50% of CH_3COOH is converted into CH_3COO^-

Thus, NaOH required = 50 mL

05

Radioactivity

Objective Questions Type I [Only one correct option]

In each of the questions below, four choices are given of which only one is correct.

1. The term nucleon refers to
(a) electrons belonging to an atom that undergoes nuclear decay
(b) electrons that are emitted from a nucleus in a nuclear reaction
(c) the nuclei of a specific isotope
(d) Both protons and neutrons

2. Which is the best description of an alpha particle?
(a) Charge +2; mass of 4 amu; high penetrating power
(b) Charge +2; mass of 4 amu; low penetrating power
(c) Charge −1; mass of 0 amu; medium penetrating power
(d) Charge 0; mass of 0 amu, no penetrating power

3. Which type of radiation is attracted towards a positive plate?
(a) α (b) β
(c) γ (d) α and β

4. The emission of a particle from an unstable nucleus is called
(a) mutation (b) fission
(c) nuclear decay (d) fusion

5. Which of the following is a natural radioactive element?
(a) Uranium (b) Radium
(c) Thorium (d) All of these

6. Which product is formed by α-emission from ${}^{235}_{92}U$?
(a) ${}^{231}_{90}Th$ (b) ${}^{233}_{90}Th$
(c) ${}^{235}_{93}Np$ (d) ${}^{235}_{92}U$

7. Radioactive disintegration differs from a chemical change in being a/an
(a) nuclear process
(b) exothermic change
(c) spontaneous process
(d) first order kinetics

8. ${}^{238}_{92}U$ (III B, actinide series) emits one α-particle. New element will be a/an
(a) alkali metal (b) alkaline earth metal
(c) actinide (d) chalcogen

9. Which results in the formation of an isotope of the parent element?
(a) Emission of one α-particle
(b) Emission of two β-particles
(c) Emission of one α-and two β-particles
(d) None of the above

10. ${}^{234}_{90}Th$ (IIIB) emits particles such that new element is in IIA. Particles emitted is/are
(a) one α, one β (b) one β, one α
(c) only one β (d) only one α

11. One microcurie of radiation is the quantity of radioactive substance which produces
(a) 3.7×10^{10} disintegration per second (dps)
(b) 6.02×10^{4} dps
(c) 3.7×10^{4} dps
(d) 3.7×10^{7} dps

12. The amount of radiation that produces 2.1×10^{9} units of charge in 1 cm^3 of air is
(a) Curie (b) Roentgen
(c) rem (d) rad

13. A unit used to measure the amount of radiation absorbed per gram of tissue is
(a) Curie (b) Roentgen
(c) rem (d) rad

14. The unit of radiation exposure which allows for the energy and penetrating power of different types of radiation is
(a) Curie (b) Roentgen
(c) rem (d) sievert

15. A Sievert is
(a) the amount of radiation that produces 2.1×10^9 units of charge in one cm^3 of air
(b) a unit used to measure the amount of radiation absorbed per gram of tissue
(c) a unit that allows both for the energy and the penetrating power of different types of radiation
(d) the SI unit for radiation absorbed

16. In a radioactive series, a radioactive isotope decays to stable isotope. $^{232}_{90}Th$ decays by emission of six α- and four β-particles. Stable isotope is
(a) Pu-256 (b) Th-232
(c) Rn-220 (d) Pb-208

17. The half-life of $^{24}_{11}Na$ is 15.0 h. What percentage of it remains after 60 h?
(a) 0.00% (b) 3.13%
(c) 6.25% (d) 12.5%

18. The half-life of nickel-65 is 2.5 days. How much of a 100 g sample has decayed after 7.5 days?
(a) 12.5 g (b) 50.0 g
(c) 75.0 g (d) 87.5 g

19. When a radioactive isotope decays into a nucleus which is also unstable and undergoes decay, and this process is repeated several times, the succession of reaction is called
(a) decay series (b) fission reaction
(c) fusion reaction (d) spallation

20. Which of the following is an artificial man-made series?
(a) Thorium series (b) Neptunium series
(c) Uranium series (d) Actinium series

21. Which equation is true for transient equilibrium?
(λ = disintegration constant; t = half-life)
(a) $N_1\lambda_1 = N_2\lambda_2$ (b) $N_1t_2 = N_2t_1$
(c) Both (a) and (b) (d) None of these

22. For two different disintegration half-lives are equal at equilibrium. This is only when
(a) $N_1 = N_2$ (b) $\lambda_1 = \lambda_2$
(c) $(T_{75})_1 = (T_{75})_2$ (d) All of these

23. At equilibrium, number of atoms disintegrating at two different stages are in the ratio of 1 : 10. If half-life of first stage is 15 minutes, half-life second stage would be
(a) 150 min (b) 15 min
(c) 1.5 min (d) 30 min

24. At two stages of disintegration, disintegration constants are respectively $1 \times 10^{-2}\ s^{-1}$ and $1 \times 10^{-5}\ s^{-1}$. At first stage 2000 atoms are disintegrating. At second stage number of atoms disintegrating would be
(a) 2 (b) 2×10^6
(c) 2×10^{-6} (d) 2×10^9

25. $A \xrightarrow[N_A]{T_{50} = 100\text{ min}} B \xrightarrow[N_B]{T_{75} = 100\text{ min}} C$

At equilibrium N_A/N_B is
(a) 1 (b) 2
(c) 0.5 (d) 20

26. The neutron/proton ratio in an isotope can be decreased by the emission of
(a) an electron (b) a neutron
(c) a gamma ray (d) a positron

27. The unstable nucleus $^{212}_{82}Pb$ decays with β-particle emission, having a half-life of 10 h. From this it follows that the
I. mass number of the product is 212
II. atomic number of the product is 81
III. fraction of the original isotope remaining after 20 h is 1/4
IV. nucleus formed is stable

Select the correct alternate.
(a) I, II and III (b) I and III
(c) II and IV (d) IV

28. The nucleus of an atom is made up of p protons and n neutrons. For the most stable and abundant nuclei
(a) p even, n odd (b) p, n both odd
(c) p odd, n even (d) p, n both even

29. Due to β-emission n/p ratio changes to
(a) $\frac{n+1}{p-1}$ (b) $\frac{n}{p+1}$ (c) $\frac{n-1}{p+1}$ (d) $\frac{n+1}{p+1}$

30. The exchange of particles considered responsible for holding the nucleus together are called
(a) mesons (b) antiprotons
(c) positron (d) neutrons

31. $^{37}_{18}Ar$ captures a K-electron into its nucleus. The product atom formed is
(a) $^{37}_{17}Cl$ (b) $^{38}_{18}Ar$ (c) $^{36}_{18}Ar$ (d) $^{38}_{17}Cl$

32. All of the statements about nuclear reactions are true except
(a) nuclear reactions involve changes in the nucleus of an atom
(b) the rate of a nuclear reaction is increased by the addition of a catalyst
(c) a nuclear reaction is unaffected by the chemical state of the atoms involved
(d) nuclear reactions of the same element vary according to which isotope is involved.

33. Which nuclear reaction is an example of α-emission?
(a) $^{235}_{92}U \longrightarrow {}^{231}_{90}Th + {}^{4}_{2}He$
(b) $^{75}_{34}Se \longrightarrow {}^{75}_{35}Br + {}^{0}_{-1}e$
(c) $^{14}_{7}N + {}^{4}_{2}He \longrightarrow {}^{17}_{8}O + {}^{1}_{1}H$
(d) None of the above

34. Which nuclear reaction is not balanced?

(a) ${}^{10}_{5}B + {}^{4}_{2}He \longrightarrow {}^{13}_{7}N + {}^{1}_{0}n$

(b) ${}^{238}_{92}U + {}^{4}_{2}He \longrightarrow {}^{241}_{95}Am + {}^{1}_{0}n$

(c) ${}^{40}_{18}Ar + {}^{1}_{1}H \longrightarrow {}^{40}_{19}K + {}^{1}_{0}n$

(d) ${}^{14}_{7}N + {}^{4}_{2}He \longrightarrow {}^{17}_{8}O + {}^{1}_{1}H$

35. The nuclear reaction (${}^{10}_{5}B + {}^{1}_{0}n \longrightarrow {}^{7}_{3}Li + {}^{4}_{2}He$) is of the type

(a) n, p (b) n, β (c) n, α (d) α, n

36. Which reaction is an example of chain reaction?

(a) ${}^{235}_{92}U \longrightarrow {}^{4}_{2}He + {}^{231}_{90}Th$

(b) ${}^{75}_{34}Se \longrightarrow {}^{75}_{35}Br + {}^{0}_{-1}e$

(c) ${}^{123}_{53}I \longrightarrow {}^{123}_{53}I$ + energy

(d) ${}^{235}_{92}U + {}^{1}_{0}n \longrightarrow {}^{142}_{56}Ba + {}^{91}_{36}Kr + 3{}^{1}_{0}n$

37. An atom bomb is based on the principle of

(a) nuclear fusion (b) nuclear fission
(c) radioactivity (d) combustion

38. Moderator used in a nuclear reactor is

(a) graphite (b) heavy water
(c) Both (a) and (b) (d) None of these

39. Fuel used in a breeder-reactor is

(a) uranium-235 (b) plutonium-239
(c) uranium-238 (d) All of these

40. Nuclear fission was experimentally observed by

(a) Planck
(b) Rutherford
(c) J.J. Thomson
(d) Hahn and Strassman

41. Which nuclear reaction is an example of fusion emission?

(a) ${}^{238}_{94}Pu + {}^{4}_{2}He \longrightarrow {}^{242}_{96}Cm$

(b) ${}^{22}_{11}Na \longrightarrow {}^{22}_{10}Ne + {}^{0}_{1}\beta$

(c) ${}^{7}_{3}Li + {}^{1}_{1}H \longrightarrow {}^{1}_{0}n + {}^{7}_{4}Be$

(d) ${}^{41}_{18}Ar + {}^{0}_{-1}e \longrightarrow {}^{41}_{17}Cl$

42. The radiant energy from the sun is due to

(a) combustion
(b) nuclear fusion
(c) nuclear fission
(d) chemical reaction

43. Which is based on nuclear fusion reaction?

(a) Hydrogen bomb (b) Atom bomb
(c) RDX (d) REX

44. The high temperature required to initiate nuclear fusion reaction is initially attained through

(a) solar energy
(b) burning of hydrocarbon
(c) nuclear fission
(d) All of the above

45. In which process maximum energy is attained?

(a) $2{}^{2}_{1}H \longrightarrow {}^{3}_{1}H + {}^{1}_{1}H$ (b) ${}^{2}_{1}H + {}^{3}_{1}H \longrightarrow {}^{4}_{2}He + {}^{1}_{0}n$

(c) ${}^{6}_{3}Li + {}^{2}_{1}H \longrightarrow 2{}^{4}_{2}He$ (d) Equal

46. Which reaction shows artificial transmutation by α- bombardment?

(a) ${}^{14}_{7}N + {}^{4}_{2}He \longrightarrow {}^{17}_{8}O + {}^{1}_{1}H$

(b) ${}^{238}_{92}U \longrightarrow {}^{234}_{90}Th + {}^{4}_{2}He$

(c) ${}^{14}_{6}C \longrightarrow {}^{14}_{7}N + {}^{0}_{-1}e$

(d) None of the above

47. In the nuclear reaction, ${}^{27}_{13}Al + {}^{4}_{2}He \longrightarrow {}^{30}_{15}X + {}^{1}_{0}n$, ${}^{30}_{15}X$ is

(a) Si (b) P
(c) S (d) Ar

48. ${}^{30}_{15}X$ changes to ${}^{30}_{14}Si$ by emission of

(a) α-particle (b) β-particle
(c) positron (d) proton

49. ${}^{269}_{110}Ds$ is the recently discovered element IUPAC nomenclature is

(a) Unu (b) Uhe
(c) Uun (d) Nuu

50. Eka-Hg will have IUPAC nomenclature as Uub. Its atomic number is

(a) 80 (b) 110 (c) 111 (d) 112

51. The energy released in nuclear reactions corresponding to 1 amu is about

(a) 940 MeV
(b) 933.21 MeV
(c) 918 MeV
(d) 900 MeV

52. Binding energy due to mass defect of ${}^{4}_{2}He$ is 28 MeV. Thus, binding energy per nucleon is

(a) 14 MeV (b) 28 MeV
(c) 7 MeV (d) 4.67 MeV

53. Select the correct statement.

(a) The more negative the packing fraction of an element, the more stable should be the nucleus

(b) Packing fraction $= \dfrac{\text{mass defect}}{\text{isotopic mass}} \times 10^4$

(c) Fe and Al have positive values of packing fraction

(d) All of the above

54. The maximum binding energy per nucleon is indicated in the mass number range

(a) 40–60 (b) 50–60
(c) 20–30 (d) 55–60

55. 1 amu is equal to

(a) 1.66×10^{-27} kg
(b) 6.02×10^{23} kg
(c) 1 kg
(d) 1×10^{-3} kg

56. Which of the properties of radioisotopes make them useful as tracers in medical or agricultural applications?

I. Their chemical behaviour is the same as non-radioactive isotope.

II. They emit various types of radiation.

III. The nuclear reaction is unaffected by the chemical state of the isotope.

(a) I only (b) I and III
(c) I and II (d) All of these

57. In vivo studies, radioisotope used is
(a) Cr-51 (b) Co-60
(c) Na-24 (d) P-32

58. To trace the flow of blood, radioisotope used is
(a) Co-60 (b) Na-24
(c) P-32 (d) I-123

59. Select the correct statement.
(a) MRI uses radiowaves to stimulate certain nuclei in the presence of magnetic field
(b) P-32 is used for leukemia therapy
(c) I-123 is used in imaging the brain
(d) All of the above

60. Radioactivity can be used in
(a) diagnostic (b) therapeutic
(c) Both (a) and (b) (d) None of these

61. Ionising radiation is dangerous to living things because
(a) it causes nuclear reactions
(b) it causes thermal burns
(c) it alters the chemical structure of atom molecules
(d) it causes electrons to be captured by the nucleus

62. Which of the following is not an example of ionising radiation?
(a) X-rays (b) γ-rays
(c) α-rays (d) UV-rays

63. Ionising radiation is
(a) radiation that only interacts with ions
(b) the same as a proton
(c) a neutron that has acquired a charge, thus forming an ion
(d) high-energy radiation that removes electrons from atom or molecules

64. Select the correct statement.
(a) α- and β-particles can be detected by a Geiger counter
(b) Neutron can be detected by conversion into α-particle by addition of ${}^{10}_{5}B$
(c) Both (a) and (b)
(d) None of the above

65. REM is a unit of
(a) radiation dosage (b) binding energy
(c) packing fraction (d) radioactivity

66. A radioactive element decays by the sequence, and with half-lives, given below

$$X \xrightarrow[30\text{ min}]{\alpha} Y \xrightarrow[2\text{ days}]{2\beta} Z$$

Which of the following statements about this system are correct ?
(a) After two hours, less than 10% of the initial X is left
(b) Maximum amount of Y present at any time before 30 min is less than 50% of the initial amount of X
(c) Atomic numbers of X and Z are same
(d) All of the above are correct statements

67. The most radioactive of the isotopes of an element is the one with the largest value of its
(a) half-life (b) neutron number
(c) atomic number (d) decay constant

68. In uranium mineral, the atomic ratio N_{U-238}/N_{Pb-206} is nearly equal to one. The age (in years) of the mineral is nearly (half-life period of U-238 is 4.5×10^9 yr)
(a) 3.0×10^8 (b) 4.5×10^9
(c) 3.0×10^9 (d) 4.5×10^8

69. For an α-emitting isotope, the value of disintegration constant is 0.49×10^{-10} per year. The amount of the isotope of a given sample will reduce to half its value after a period (in years) of nearly
(a) 0.45×10^{10} (b) 0.9×10^{10}
(c) 1.41×10^{10} (d) 2.82×10^{10}

70. Bombardment of aluminium by α-particle leads to its artificial disintegration in two ways, (i) and (ii) as shown. Products X, Y and Z respectively are

$${}^{27}_{13}Al \xrightarrow{\text{(ii)}} {}^{30}_{15}P + Y$$
$${}^{27}_{13}Al \xrightarrow{\text{(i)}} {}^{30}_{14}Si + X$$
$${}^{30}_{15}P \longrightarrow {}^{30}_{14}Si + Z$$

[IIT JEE 2011]

(a) proton, neutron, positron
(b) neutron, positron, proton
(c) proton, positron, neutron
(d) positron, proton, neutron

71. 1 g of ${}^{200}_{79}Au$ (T_{50} = 13 days) emits a β-particle forming a stable Hg atom. Hg formed at the end of 52 days is
(a) 0.0625 g (b) 0.9375 g
(c) 0.7500 g (d) 0.2500 g

72. Weight of ${}^{14}C$ to have radioactivity 1 curie [λ (disintegration constant) = $4.4\times 10^{-12}\ s^{-1}$] is
(a) 2×10^{-4} kg (b) 0.9×10^{-4} kg
(c) 1.7×10^{-4} kg (d) 3.7×10^{-10} kg

73. If half-life period is 100 years, average life is nearly
(a) 100 yr (b) 70 yr
(c) 144 yr (d) 90 yr

74. There are 0.618 μg of ^{206}Pb and 0.238 μg of ^{238}U in a rock. If T_{50} of ^{238}U is 1.5×10^9 yr, age of the rock is
(a) 1.5×10^9 yr (b) 3.0×10^9 yr
(c) 4.5×10^9 yr (d) 0.75×10^9 yr

75. $A \xrightarrow[T_A]{k_A}$ product, $B \xrightarrow[T_B]{k_B}$ product

A and B are two radioactive elements with half-life periods T_A and T_B (in years) and k_A(year^{-1}) and k_B(atom^{-1} year^{-1}). If half-life periods are equal, disintegration rate at the start of disintegration with same concentration would be
(a) $k_A T_A$ (b) 0.693
(c) Both (a) and (b) (d) None of these

76. The missing fission product in the reaction
$^{235}_{92}U + ^1_0n \longrightarrow ^{146}_{57}La + ... + 3\,^1_0n$ is
(a) $^{86}_{35}Br$ (b) $^{87}_{35}Br$ (c) $^{89}_{35}Br$ (d) $^{89}_{32}Ge$

77. Select the correct alternate.
(a) $^1_1p \longrightarrow ^1_0n$ is positron emission
(b) $^1_1p \longrightarrow ^1_0n$ is K-electron capture
(c) Both (a) and (b)
(d) None of the above

78. Thiosulphate ion, $S_2O_3^{2-}$ on acidification changes to SO_2 along with precipitation of sulphur

$$^{35}S^{32}SO_3^{2-} + 2H^+ \longrightarrow H_2O + SO_2 + S$$

Which is the correct statement?
(a) ^{35}S is in sulphur
(b) ^{35}S is in SO_2
(c) ^{35}S is in both
(d) ^{35}S is in none

79. Which of the following are fissile isotopes?
1. $^{238}_{92}U$ 2. $^{233}_{92}U$ 3. $^{239}_{94}Pu$ 4. $^{232}_{90}U$
Select the correct answer from the following.
(a) 1 and 2 (b) 2 and 3
(c) 1 and 4 (d) All of these

80. Which is the correct combination?

	Emission	Change in Atomic number	Change in Mass number	Change in Neutron number
(a)	α	−2	−2	−2
(b)	β^-	+1	0	−1
(c)	γ	0	0	−1
(d)	β^+	−1	0	0

81. Beta-emission takes place
(a) from the elements above the band of stability
(b) when neutron is converted to proton
(c) with shifting of the new element one group towards right
(d) following all the facts given above

82. Constituents of wine are carbon, hydrogen and oxygen. Half-lives of ^{13}C, ^{15}O and ^3H are respectively 5730 yr, 124 s and 12.5 yr. A bottle of wine was sealed about 6 years ago. To confirm its age, which of the isotopes would you choose to determine its age?
(a) $^{13}_{6}C$ (b) $^{15}_{8}O$
(c) ^3_1H (d) Any of these

83. 'Fat man' relates to
(a) Pu-bomb
(b) U-bomb
(c) Th-bomb
(d) literary word from a book

84. 'Little boy' relates to
(a) Pu-bomb
(b) U-bomb
(c) H-bomb
(d) He-bomb

85. Consider the following statements.
I. 'Carbon-dating' is based on the measurement of activity of ^{14}C.
II. ^{40}K is used to determine age of the objects upto 1 million years old.
III. The uranium-lead method is based on the natural uranium-238 decay series which ends up with the production of stable lead-206.

Select the correct statements.
(a) I, II (b) II, III
(c) I, III (d) I, II, III

86. In the chain reaction,
$$^{238}_{92}U \longrightarrow Ba + Kr + 3\,^1_0n + \text{energy } E$$
neutrons and energy produced at nth step will be
(a) $3n$, nE (b) 3^n, nE
(c) 3^n, $3^{n-1}E$ (d) 3^{n-1}, nE

87. $^{27}_{13}Al$ is a stable isotope. $^{29}_{13}Al$ is expected to disintegrate by
(a) α-emission (b) β-emission
(c) positron emission (d) neutron emission

88. Assuming that only particles emitted from atoms during natural radioactive decay are α and β-particles, which of the following atoms could not possibly result from the natural decay of $^{235}_{92}U$
(a) $^{231}_{89}Ac$ (b) $^{227}_{89}Ac$
(c) $^{225}_{89}Ac$ (d) $^{207}_{82}Pb$

89. Of the following nuclides, the one most likely to be radioactive is
(a) $^{31}_{15}P$ (b) $^{66}_{30}Zn$
(c) $^{14}_{7}N$ (d) $^{14}_{6}C$

90. Of the following nuclides, the one most likely to decay by positron (β^+) emission is
(a) ^{59}Cu (b) ^{63}Cu (c) ^{67}Cu (d) ^{68}Cu

91. Among the following nuclides, the highest binding energy per nucleon is found for

(a) ${}^{3}_{1}H$ (b) ${}^{16}_{8}O$
(c) ${}^{56}_{26}Fe$ (d) ${}^{235}_{92}U$

92. The radiation that produces the greatest number of ions as it passes through matter is

(a) α (b) γ (c) β^- (d) β^+

93. In nuclear reaction,

$${}^{7}_{3}Li + {}^{1}_{1}H \longrightarrow 2{}^{4}_{2}He$$

the mass loss is nearly 0.02 amu. Hence, the energy released (in units of million kcal/mol) in the process is approximately

(a) 430 (b) 220 (c) 120 (d) 50

94. Consider the following nuclear reactions

I. ${}^{14}_{7}N + {}^{4}_{2}He \longrightarrow {}^{17}_{8}O + {}^{1}_{1}H$
II. ${}^{9}_{4}Be + {}^{1}_{1}H \longrightarrow {}^{6}_{3}Li + {}^{4}_{2}He$
III. ${}^{24}_{12}Mg + {}^{4}_{2}He \longrightarrow {}^{27}_{14}Si + {}^{1}_{0}n$
IV. ${}^{10}_{5}B + {}^{4}_{2}He \longrightarrow {}^{13}_{7}N + {}^{1}_{0}n$

Examples of induced radioactivity would include reactions

(a) III and IV (b) I and II
(c) I, III and IV (d) I, II, III and IV

95. Aluminium-25 decays by emitting a positron. The species immediately produced has

(a) $12p, 13n, 13e^-$ (b) $13p, 12n, 13e^-$
(c) $12p, 13n, 12e^-$ (d) $14p, 11n, 14e^-$

96. The half-life of ${}^{99}Tc$ is 6.0 h. Hence, average-life is

(a) 4.17 h (b) 3.0 h
(c) 8.66 h (d) 8.00 h

97. Tritium, ${}^{3}_{1}H$ has a half-life of 12.26 yr. A 5.00 mL sample of tritiated water has an activity of 2.40×10^9 cpm. How many years will it take for the activity to fall to 3.00×10^8 cpm?

(a) 6.13 (b) 12.26 (c) 24.52 (d) 36.78

98. In a series of three steps in radioactive disintegration sequence starting with ${}^{228}_{88}Ra$, the particles emitted are, successively, β^-, β^- and α-particles. The resulting product is an isotope of

(a) ${}_{92}U$ (b) ${}_{90}Th$
(c) ${}_{88}Ra$ (d) ${}_{86}Rn$

99. At radioactive equilibrium, the ratio betweeen the atoms of two radioactive elements A and B was found to be $3.1 \times 10^9 : 1$ respectively. If T_{50} of the element A is 2×10^{10} yr, then T_{50} of the element B is

(a) 6.2×10^9 yr (b) 6.45 yr
(c) 2×10^{10} yr (d) 3.1×10^9 yr

100. A bacterial infection in an internal wound grows as $N'(t) = N_0 \exp(t)$, where the time t is in hours. A dose of antibiotic, taken orally, needs 1 hour to reach the wound. Once it reaches there, the bacterial population goes down as $\frac{dN}{dt} = -5N^2$. What will be the plot of $\frac{N_0}{N}$ vs t after 1 hour? **[JEE Main 2019]**

(a) 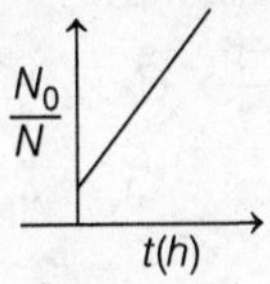

(b) 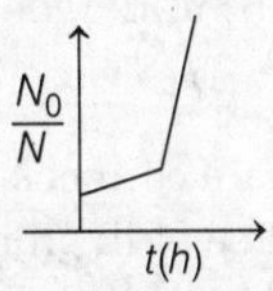

(c) 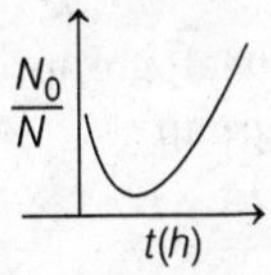

(d) 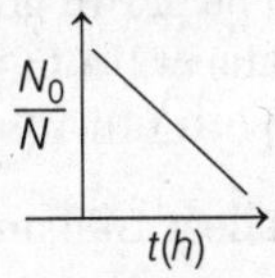

101. Water used as moderator in nuclear reactor is called

(a) heavy water (b) hard water
(c) nuclear water (d) critical water

102. ${}^{14}_{7}N + {}^{1}_{0}n \longrightarrow {}^{14}_{6}C + {}^{1}_{1}H$ is written as

(a) ${}^{14}_{7}N\ (n, e)\ {}^{1}_{1}H$ (b) ${}^{14}_{7}N\ (p, n)\ {}^{14}_{6}C$
(c) ${}^{14}_{7}N\ (n, p)\ {}^{14}_{6}C$ (d) ${}^{14}_{6}C\ (p, n)\ {}^{14}_{7}N$

103. After the emission of a β-particle followed by α-particle from ${}^{214}_{83}Bi$, the number of neutrons in the atom is

(a) 130 (b) 129
(c) 128 (d) 127

Objective Questions Type II [One or more than one correct option(s)]

In each of the questions below, four choices are given, of which one or more than one are correct.

1. Carbon-14 dating method is based on the fact that
(a) carbon-14 fraction is same in all objects
(b) carbon-14 is highly insoluble
(c) ratio of carbon-14 and carbon-12 remains constant during disintegration
(d) carbon-14 is highly soluble

2. Select the correct statement(s).
(a) ^{131}I is used for the treatment of thyroid cancer
(b) ^{59}Co cannot be used for treatment of cancer
(c) ^{33}P is used for treatment of leukemia
(d) Excessive use of radioactive elements cause cancer

3. Radioactive disintegration rate is affected by
(a) temperature (b) pressure
(c) electric field (d) None of these

4. $^{238}_{92}U$ (III B) undergoes follows emissions

$$^{238}_{92}U \xrightarrow{-\alpha} A \xrightarrow{-\alpha} B \xrightarrow{-\beta} C$$

Which is/are correct statements?
(a) A will be of IB group
(b) A will be of IIIB group
(c) B will be of IIA (alkaline earth metal) group
(d) C will be of IIIA (boron family) group

5. In the nuclear transmutation

$$^{9}_{4}Be + X \longrightarrow {}^{8}_{4}Be + Y$$

(X, Y) is are **[JEE Advanced 2013]**
(a) (n, D) (b) (γ, p) (c) (γ, n) (d) (p, D)

6. Mass defect of 1 g gives energy equal to
(a) 9×10^{13} J (b) 5.625×10^{32} eV
(c) 2.15×10^{10} kcal (d) 9×10^{6} ergs

7. Target nucleus A is converted to product nucleus B by (p, n) as: $A(p, n)\, B$
In this case
(a) A and B are isotopes
(b) A and B are isobars
(c) A and B are isotones
(d) B has higher atomic number than that of A

8. In a nuclear reactor, oxides of which of the following metals are used as fuel material?
(a) Uranium (b) Thorium
(c) Actinium (d) Plutonium

9. Two radioactive substances X and Y have disintegration constant in the ratio $2:1$. If half-life of Y is 4 days then after 12 days starting with equal mole fraction of each in mixture of X and Y
(a) mole fraction of X and Y remains unchanged
(b) mole fraction of X is larger than that of Y
(c) mole fraction of X is smaller than that of Y
(d) half-life of X is smaller than that of Y

10. Select the correct statement(s).
(a) Neutron-proton ratio after a nuclide, $^{238}_{92}U$ loses an α-particle is 1.6
(b) $^{27}_{13}Al$ can be converted to $^{30}_{15}P$ by (α, n) reaction
(c) Nuclear fusion reactions are known as thermonuclear reactions
(d) Larger the value of disintegration constant, greater the stability of radioactive element

11. In the decay sequence.

$$^{238}_{92}U \xrightarrow{-x_1} {}^{234}_{90}Th \xrightarrow{-x_2} {}^{234}_{91}Pa \xrightarrow{-x_3} {}^{234}Z \xrightarrow{-x_4} {}^{230}_{90}Th$$

x_1, x_2, x_3 and x_4 are particles/radiation emitted by the respective isotopes. The correct option(s) is(are) **[JEE Advanced 2019]**
(a) Z is an isotope of uranium
(b) x_2 is β^-
(c) x_1 will deflect towards negatively charged plate
(d) x_3 is γ-ray

12. A plot of the number of neutrons (n) against the number of protons (p) of stable nuclei exhibits upward deviation from linearity for atomic number, $Z > 20$. For an unstable nucleus having n/p ratio less than 1, the possible mode(s) of decay is (are) **[JEE Advanced 2016]**
(a) β^--decay (β-emission)
(b) orbital or K-electron capture
(c) neutron emission
(d) β^+-decay (positron emission)

Numerical Value Questions

All these questions have a Numerical value as their answer, solve the questions and write your answer.

1. 1 g of radium produces 0.043 cm^3 of helium gas at STP in one year. The number of α-particles produced in the same period is 11.6×10^{17}. The value of Avogadro's number is 6.023×10^{x}. Find x.

2. The Curie was originally intended to be the activity of one gram of radium-226. [$T_{50} = 1620$ a, here 'a' stands for annum (year) in SI unit]. The actual weight of radium which is equivalent to one Curie is .... in grams (Given: 1 a = 3.1536×10^{7} s)

3. A sample of $^{14}CO_2$ was to be mixed with ordinary CO_2 for a biological tracer experiment. In order that 10 cm^3 of the diluted gas at STP should have

10^4 dis/min, how many μCi of radioactive carbon-14 are needed to prepare 0.06 m^3 of the diluted gas? (in μC)

4. When a positron and an electron collide, they are annihilated and two gamma photons of equal energy are emitted. The wavelength corresponding to this gamma emission is ...... (in pm).

5. A certain radioisotope $^{A}_{Z}X$ (T_{50} = 10 days) decays to give $^{A-4}_{Z-2}Y$. If one gram atom of $^{A}_{Z}X$ is kept in a sealed vessel how much helium will accumulate in 20 days at STP? (in liters)

6. A certain radio isotope $_ZX^A$ (half life = 10 days) decays to give $_{Z-2}Y^{A-4}$. If 1.0 g atom of X is kept in a sealed vessel, find the volume of helium accumulated at STP in 20 days? (in mL)

7. $^{238}_{92}U$ is known to undergo radioactive decay to form $^{206}_{82}Pb$ by emitting alpha and beta particles. A rock initially contained 68×10^{-6} g of $^{238}_{92}U$. If the number of alpha particles that it would emit during its radioactive decay of $^{238}_{92}U$ to $^{206}_{82}Pb$ in three half-lives is $Z \times 10^{18}$, then what is the value of Z? **[JEE Advanced 2020]**

8. During the nuclear explosion, one of the products is ^{90}Sr with half-life of 6.93 years. If 1 μg of ^{90}Sr was absorbed in the bones of a newly born baby in place of Ca, how much time, in years, is required to reduce it by 90% if it is not lost metabolically .... **[JEE Main 2020]**

Comprehension Based Questions

In these questions, a passage has been given followed by questions based on it. You have to answer the questions based on the passage given.

Passage 1 *Read the following passage and answer the questions at the end.*

A person received an anonymous gift of a decorative cube which he placed on his desk. A few months later he became ill and died shortly afterward. After investigation, the cause of his death was linked to the box. The box was air-tight and had no toxic chemicals on it.

1. What might have killed the man?
(a) α-rays emitting material
(b) β-rays emitting material
(c) γ-rays emitting material
(d) KCN

2. Am-241 is used in smoke detectors because it has a long half-life (458 yr). Given the schematic diagram of a smoke detector below, explain how it works?

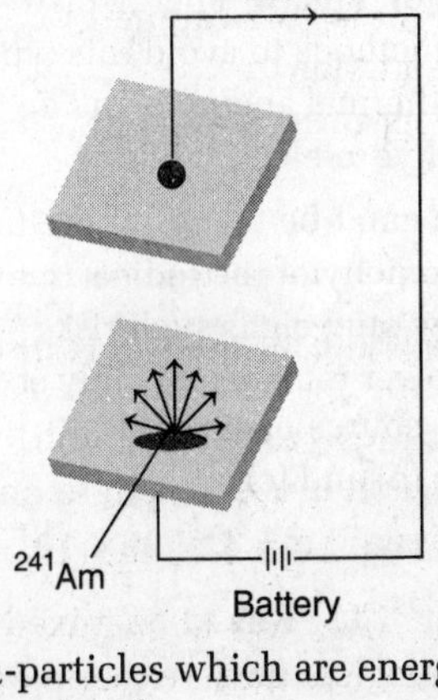

(a) It emits α-particles which are energetic enough to ionise air molecules
(b) It emits β-particle which can complete the circuit
(c) It emits γ-particles which have high penetration
(d) It emits α- and β-particles

Passage 2 *Radiolysis of water yields* H_2 *as given below*

$$2H_2O \longrightarrow H_2O_2 + H_2$$

In the analysis it is found that 1.7 molecules of H_2 are yielded per 100 eV of energy absorbed. A nuclear power reactor of 200 kW capacity has been installed based on this reaction.

Read the above passage and answer the following questions.

1. Above reaction is an Passage of
(a) disproportionation (b) redox
(c) decomposition (d) displacement

2. What mass of heavy water is required to yield 448 kL of heavy hydrogen at STP?
(a) 996 kg (b) 448 kg (c) 800 kg (d) 720 kg

3. Volume of H_2 produced per minute in the above reactor is
(a) 140 L (b) 70 L (c) 35 L (d) 28 L

Passage 3 *Radioactive isotopes find applications in the study of reaction mechanism as well as in the treatment of so many diseases.*

French physician Henri Danlos first used radium in the treatment of tuberculous skin lesion. Now, uses of radioactivity have become a crucial part of modern medical care, both diagnostic and therapeutic.

Various techniques used in medical treatment are grouped into three classes
(i) in vivo procedures
(ii) therapeutic procedures and
(iii) imaging procedures.

Read the above passage and answer the following questions.

1. Consider the following redox reaction
$IO_4^-(aq) + 2I^-(aq) + H_2O(l) \longrightarrow I_2(s) + IO_3^-(aq) + 2OH^-(aq)$
When KIO_4 is added to a solution containing iodide ions labelled with radioactive iodine-128, all the radioactivity appears in I_2 and none in the IO_3^- ion. What can you deduce about the mechanism for the radioactivity appears in I_2 and none in the IO_3^- ion.
(a) I_2 is from I^- only
(b) IO_3^- is from IO_4^- only
(c) IO_3^- is from I^- only
(d) I_2 is from IO_3^- only

2. Radioisotope used in the treatment of diseases
(a) must have short half-life
(b) should give decay product with no radioactivity or very little radioactivity
(c) should be an α- or β-emitter
(d) should have all the characteristics given above

***Passage* 4** To detect bombs that may be smuggled into airplanes, the Federal Aviation Administration (FAA) will soon require all major airports in the United States to install thermal neutron analysers. The thermal neutron analyser will bombard baggage with low-energy neutrons, converting some of the nitrogen-14 nuclei to nitrogen-15, with simultaneous emission of γ rays. Because nitrogen content is usually high in explosives, detection of a high dosage of γ rays will suggest that a bomb may be present.
Read the above passage and answer the following questions.

1. Nuclear process involves reaction
(a) ${}^{14}_{7}N + {}^{1}_{0}n \longrightarrow {}^{15}_{5}N$
(b) ${}^{14}_{7}N + {}^{1}_{0}n \longrightarrow {}^{14}_{6}C + {}^{1}_{1}H$
(c) ${}^{14}_{7}N \longrightarrow {}^{14}_{6}C + {}^{0}_{1}e$
(d) ${}^{14}_{7}N \longrightarrow {}^{15}_{7}N + {}^{-1}_{0}e$

2. The sensitivity of the neutral activation analysis depends on the
(a) neutron flux available for irradiation
(b) availability of nucleus to absorb a neutron
(c) energy of decay process
(d) All of the above are correct

3. Select the correct statement(s).
(a) Photon or particle is ionised and collected by the positive electrode in a Geiger counter
(b) A scintillation counter contains a phosphor, a substance that emits a flash of light when struck by a photon or particle
(c) Both (a) and (b)
(d) None of the above

***Passage* 5** One of the products of radiation fall out from atmospheric bomb testing or nuclear accidents as at Chernobyl is iodine-131. People living in a region where iodine-131 was known to have been deposited were encouraged to use table salt enriched with non-radioactive isotope of iodine.
Read the above short write-up and answer the following questions.

1. Non-radioactive isotope prescribed in the table salt is
(a) I-130 (b) I-127
(c) I-132 (d) I-129

2. The rate of iodine uptake by the thyroid is
(a) dependent upon the iodine concentration
(b) dependent upon pressure of iodine
(c) follows second-order kinetics
(d) independent of iodine concentration

3. By use of non-radioactive iodine isotope in common salt
(a) rate of iodine-131 uptake is sharply reduced compared to uptake of iodine-127
(b) a new non-radioactive isotope is formed
(c) taste of table salt becomes better
(d) iodine-131 being water soluble is eliminated from tissue

***Passage* 6** Don't Press the Panic Button.
Despite the crisis in Japan's Nuclear Plants, India must not take nuclear power off the table.
Answer the following questions.

1. In view of recent nuclear blasts due to Tsunami in Japan countries are
(a) going to stop nuclear-energy plan
(b) devising methods to avoid this type of disaster
(c) stressing thermal energy plan
(d) stressing hydro-electric power

2. Nuclear plan can't be taken off the table because of
(a) unusual toxicity of the radioactive substance
(b) technology outweighs such risks
(c) nuclear power remains the only economically viable renewable source of energy
(d) alternates (b) and (c)

***Passage* 7** G.M. counter is used to count per second (cps) in a decay process. A chemist in a radioactive lab recorded following observation

Reading in cps at different time (in the absence of radioactive substance)

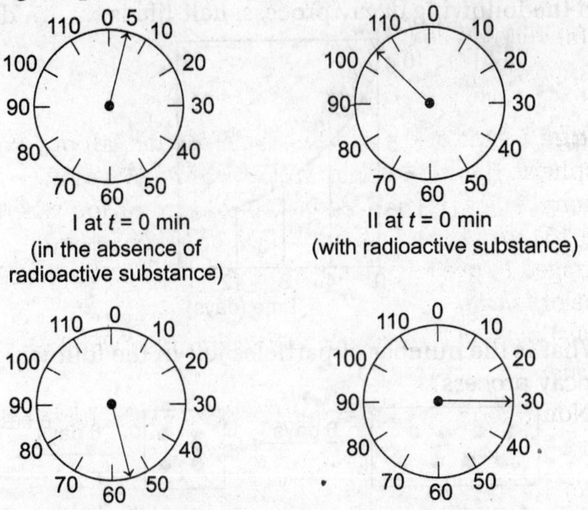

I at t = 0 min (in the absence of radioactive substance)

II at t = 0 min (with radioactive substance)

III at t = 10 min

IV at t = ?

Answer the following questions.

1. CPS as recorded in set IV above will be at time
(a) 10 min
(b) 20 min
(c) 30 min
(d) 40 min

2. What would be CPS at 30 min?
(a) 17.5 cps
(b) 22.5 cps
(c) 12.5 cps
(d) 25.0 cps

3. Decay constant is
(a) 0.693 min^{-1} (b) 0.0693 min^{-1}
(c) 0.00693 min^{-1} (d) 10 min^{-1}

Matrix-Match Type

Given below are Matching Type Questions, with two columns (each having some items) each . Each item of Column I has to be matched with the items of Column II.

1. Match the atomic number of the transuranium element (in Column I) with their IUPAC representation (in Column II).

	Column I		Column II
A.	100	1.	Unp
B.	101	2.	Unh
C.	102	3.	Unq
D.	103	4.	Unt
E.	106	5.	Unu
		6.	Unb
		7.	Unn

2. Match the name of scientist (in Column I) with the discovery or law (in Column II).

	Column I		Column II
A.	Henry-Becquerel	1.	Artificial radioactivity
B.	Soddy-Fajan	2.	Cyclotron
C.	Rutherford	3.	Group displacement law
D.	I. Curie, F. Jolit	4.	Radioactive disintegration
E.	E.O. Lawrence	5.	Radioactivity

3. Match the series (in Column I) with starting element (in Column II) and end element (in Column III).

	Column I	Column II	Column III
A.	$4n$	1. $^{241}_{94}Pu$	I. $^{207}_{87}Pb$
B.	$(4n + 1)$	2. $^{232}_{92}Th$	II. $^{209}_{83}Bi$
C.	$(4n + 2)$	3. $^{235}_{92}U$	III. $^{209}_{83}Pb$
D.	$(4n + 3)$	4. $^{238}_{92}U$	IV. $^{206}_{82}Pb$

4. Match the Column I with the properties (one or more) in Column II.

	Column I		Column II
A.	Determination of age of rock	1.	$N = N_0\left(\frac{1}{2}\right)^y$
B.	Carbon-dating	2.	$\frac{0.693}{\lambda}$
C.	Half-life	3.	$^{238}_{92}U \longrightarrow {}^{206}_{82}Pb$
D.	α-particle	4.	$^{14}_{6}C \longrightarrow {}^{14}_{7}N$
E.	β-particle		

5. Match the Column I giving particles with the reaction involving these particles (one or more) in Column II.

Column I	Column II
A. $^{4}_{2}He$	1. $^{14}_{7}N \longrightarrow {}^{17}_{8}O$
B. $^{1}_{1}H$	2. $^{27}_{13}Al \longrightarrow {}^{30}_{15}P$
C. $^{1}_{0}n$	3. $^{30}_{15}P \longrightarrow {}^{30}_{14}Si$
D. $^{0}_{-1}e$	4. $^{23}_{11}Na \longrightarrow {}^{24}_{11}Na$
E. $^{0}_{1}e$	5. $^{24}_{11}Na \longrightarrow {}^{24}_{12}Mg$

6. Match Column I with Column II and select the correct answer, using the codes given.

	Column I		Column II
A.	^{32}P	1.	Location of tumour in brain
B.	^{24}Na	2.	Location of blood clots and circulatory disorders
C.	^{60}Co	3.	Radio-therapy
D.	^{131}I	4.	Agriculture research

Single Integer Answer Questions

Answer of these questions is a single digit lying between 0 to 9.

1. In the following disintegration

$$^{238}_{92}U \longrightarrow {}^{206}_{82}Pb + \ldots$$

number of β-particles emitted is ....

2. 16 g X changes to 1 g (half-life 1 day) after .... days

3. When $^{7}_{4}Be$ captures one electron, mass number of the element formed is ....

4. 10 g of a radioactive element loses 8.75 g in 9 days. Thus, half-life is .... days.

5. Total number of α and β-particles emitted in nuclear reaction

$^{238}_{92}U \longrightarrow {}^{214}_{82}Pb$ is **[IIT JEE 2009]**

6. The number of neutrons emitted when $^{235}_{92}U$ undergoes nuclear fission to $^{142}_{54}Xe$ and $^{90}_{38}Sr$ is ...... **[IIT JEE 2010]**

7. 1.00 mL solution containing 0.24 μCi of tritium is injected into a dog's blood stream. After a period of time to allow the isotope to be dispersed, a 1.00 mL sample of blood is drawn.
The radioactivity of this sample is found to be 0.04 μCi / mL. What is the total volume of blood in the dog?

8. How many neutrons are contained in A formed by the reaction?

$$^{9}_{4}Be\,(\alpha, n) \longrightarrow A$$

9. How many neutrons are emitted in the reaction?

$$^{236}U \longrightarrow {}^{141}Ba + {}^{92}Kr$$

10. In the following decay process, half-life is .... days

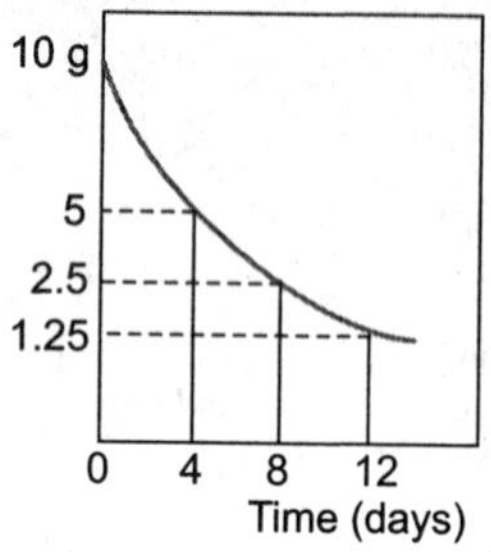

11. What is the number of particles left in the following decay process?

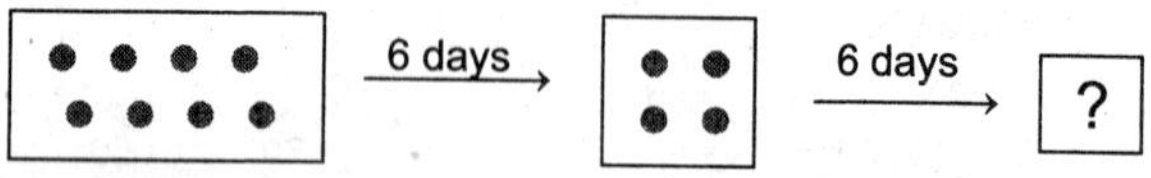

12. In the following reaction,

$$CH_3\overset{O}{\overset{\|}{C}}OH + CH_3CH_2\overset{18}{O}H \longrightarrow CH_3\overset{O}{\overset{\|}{C}}OC_2H_5 + H_2O$$

molar mass difference between water formed in the reaction and ordinary water is .... unit.

13. How many curies are contained in the radioactive change with activity 18.5×10^{10} dps?

14. Carbon-dating uses carbon isotope with number of neutrons ....

15. The periodic table consists of 18 groups. An isotope of copper, on bombadrment with protons, undergoes a nuclear reaction yielding element X as shown below. To which group, element X belongs in the periodic table?

$$^{63}_{29}Cu + {}^{1}_{1}H \longrightarrow 6\,{}^{1}_{0}n + {}^{4}_{2}\alpha + 2\,{}^{1}_{1}H + X$$ **[IIT JEE 2012]**

Answers

Objective Questions Type I [Only one correct option]

1. (d)	2. (b)	3. (b)	4. (c)	5. (d)	6. (a)	7. (a)	8. (c)	9. (c)	10. (d)
11. (c)	12. (b)	13. (c)	14. (c)	15. (d)	16. (d)	17. (c)	18. (d)	19. (a)	20. (b)
21. (c)	22. (d)	23. (a)	24. (b)	25. (b)	26. (a)	27. (b)	28. (d)	29. (c)	30. (a)
31. (a)	32. (b)	33. (a)	34. (b)	35. (c)	36. (d)	37. (b)	38. (c)	39. (d)	40. (d)
41. (c)	42. (b)	43. (a)	44. (c)	45. (c)	46. (a)	47. (b)	48. (c)	49. (c)	50. (d)
51. (b)	52. (c)	53. (d)	54. (b)	55. (a)	56. (d)	57. (a)	58. (b)	59. (d)	60. (c)
61. (c)	62. (d)	63. (d)	64. (c)	65. (a)	66. (d)	67. (d)	68. (b)	69. (c)	70. (c)
71. (b)	72. (a)	73. (c)	74. (b)	75. (c)	76. (b)	77. (c)	78. (a)	79. (c)	80. (b)
81. (d)	82. (c)	83. (a)	84. (b)	85. (d)	86. (d)	87. (d)	88. (c)	89. (d)	90. (a)
91. (a)	92. (a)	93. (a)	94. (d)	95. (c)	96. (c)	97. (d)	98. (c)	99. (b)	100. (a)
101. (a)	102. (c)	103. (c)							

Objective Questions Type II [One or more than one correct option(s)]

1. (c)	2. (a, b, d)	3. (c)	4. (c, d)	5. (c, d)
6. (a, b, c)	7. (b)	8. (a, b, d)	9. (a, b, c)	10. (a, c)
11. (a, b, c)	12. (b, d)			

Numerical Value Questions

1. 23	2. 1.024	3. 27	4. 2.42	5. 16.8
6. 66.40	7. 1.2	8. 23.03		

Comprehension Based Questions

Passage 1 – 1. (c) 2. (a)

Passage 2 – 1. (a) 2. (c) 3. (d)

Passage 3 – 1. (a, b) 2. (d)

Passage 4 – 1. (a) 2. (d) 3. (c)

Passage 5 – 1. (b) 2. (a) 3. (a)

Passage 6 – 1. (b) 2. (d)

Passage 7 – 1. (b) 2. (a) 3. (b)

Matrix-Match Type

1. A → (7); B → (5); C → (6); D → (4); E → (2)
2. A → (5); B → (3); C → (4); D → (1); E → (2)
3. A → (2)–(III); B → (1)–(II); C → (4)–(IV); D → (3)–(I)
4. A → (1,2,3); B → (1,2,4); C → (1,2); D → (3); E → (3,4)
5. A → (1,2); B → (1); C → (2,4); D → (5); E → (3)
6. A → (4); B → (2); C → (3); D → (1)

Single Integer Answer Questions

1. (6)	2. (4)	3. (7)	4. (3)	5. (8)	6. (3)	7. (6)	8. (1)	9. (3)	10. (4)
11. (2)	12. (0)	13. (5)	14. (8)	15. (8)					

Solutions

Objective Questions Type I [Only one correct option]

2. (*b*) $({}_2He^4)^{2+}$

α-particles have low penetrating power. It is positively (+2) charged helium nucleus.

3. (*b*)

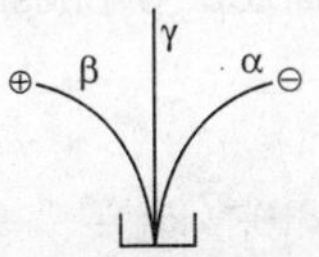

β-particles are negatively charged hence attracted towards positive plate.

6. (*a*) ${}^{235}_{92}U \longrightarrow {}^{b}_{a}X + {}^{4}_{2}He$

$b + 4 = 235$ thus $b = 231$

$a + 2 = 92$ and $a = 90$

Thus, ${}^{b}_{a}X$ is ${}^{231}_{90}Th$.

8. (*c*) ${}^{238}_{92}U \longrightarrow {}^{234}_{90}Th + {}^{4}_{2}He$

IIIB $\quad$ α-particle

Elements with atomic number 90 to 103 form 5*f* series and are called actinides. They are placed in group IIIB.

9. (*c*) ${}^{M}_{Z}A \xrightarrow{-\alpha} {}^{M-4}_{Z-2}X$

$\xrightarrow{-2\beta} {}^{M}_{Z+2}Y$

$\xrightarrow{-\alpha} {}^{M-4}_{Z-2}B \xrightarrow{-2\beta} {}^{M-4}_{Z}C$

A and *C* have same atomic number and are thus isotopes.

Thus, emission of one α- and two β-particles result in the formation of an isotope.

10. (*d*) ${}^{234}_{90}Th \xrightarrow{-\alpha_1} {}^{230}_{88}Rn$

IIIB $\quad$ IIA (alkaline earth elements)

Note Element with atomic number 88 belongs to IIA.

11. (*c*) 1 Curie $= 3.8 \times 10^{10}$ dps

hence, 1 microcurie $= 1 \times 10^{-6}$ Curie

$= 3.7 \times 10^{10} \times 10^{-6}$ dps

$= 3.7 \times 10^{4}$ dps

16. (*d*) ${}^{232}_{90}Th \xrightarrow{-6\alpha} {}^{208}_{78}X$ loss of 12 protons (atomic number) and 24 units atomic mass

$\downarrow -4\beta$

${}^{208}_{82}Y$ increase in 4 units of atomic number

Thus, ${}^{208}_{82}Pb$

17. (*c*) ${}^{24}_{11}Na \longrightarrow {}^{24}_{12}Mg + {}^{0}_{-1}e$ (β)

$y =$ number of half-life $= \dfrac{60}{15} = 4$

$N = N_0 \left(\dfrac{1}{2}\right)^y$

$= 100 \left(\dfrac{1}{2}\right)^4 = \dfrac{100}{16} = 6.25\%$

18. (*d*) $y =$ number of half-life $= \dfrac{7.5}{2.5} = 3$

$N = N_0 \left(\dfrac{1}{2}\right)^y = 100 \left(\dfrac{1}{2}\right)^3$

Amount left $= \dfrac{100}{8} = 12.5\,g$

Amount decayed $= 100 - 12.5 = 87.5\,g$

21. (*c*) For transient equilibrium

$$\left(\frac{dN}{dt}\right)_{\text{parent element}} = \left(\frac{dN}{dt}\right)_{\text{daughter element}}$$

$$\lambda_1 N_1 = \lambda_2 N_2$$

λ_1 and λ_2 are disintegration constant N_1 and N_2 are the number of atoms.

Also, $\lambda_1 \propto \frac{1}{\text{half-life } t_1}$ and $\lambda_2 \propto \frac{1}{t^2}$

Thus, $N_1\lambda_1 = N_2\lambda_2$

$\frac{N_1}{t_1} = \frac{N_2}{t_2}$ or $N_1 t_2 = N_2 t_2$

22. (*d*) $N_1\lambda_1 = N_2\lambda_2$ at equilibrium

$\frac{N_1}{t_1} = \frac{N_2}{t_2}$ t_1 and t_2 are half-lives

If $t_1 = t_2$ then $N_1 = N_2$

If $\lambda_1 = \lambda_2$ then $N_1 = N_2$

Since, $T_{75} = 2T_{50}$

hence, if $(T_{75})_1 = (T_{75})_2$

Then $N_1 = N_2$

23. (*a*) Smaller the half-life, larger the number of atoms thus,

$$\frac{N_1}{t_1} = \frac{N_2}{t_2}$$

$$N_1 t_2 = N_2 t_1$$

$$t_2 = \frac{N_2}{N_1} t_1 - \frac{10}{1} \times 15 = 150 \text{ min}$$

24. (*b*) For disintegration,

$$N_1\lambda_1 = N_2\lambda_2$$

$$N_2 = \frac{\lambda_1}{\lambda_2} N_1 = \frac{1 \times 10^{-2}}{1 \times 10^{-5}} \times 2000$$

$$= 2 \times 10^6$$

25. (*b*) If T_{75} of $B \longrightarrow C$ is 100 min, then $T_{50} = 50$ min

Thus, $N_A T_B = N_B T_A$

$$\frac{N_A}{N_B} = \frac{T_A}{T_B} = \frac{100}{50} = 2$$

26. (*a*) If proton increases, then neutron/proton ratio decreases. When neutron changes to proton, a β-particle (electron) is emitted

$${}_0^1n \longrightarrow {}_1^1H + {}_{-1}^{0}e$$

Thus, *n* (neutron) decreases and *p* (proton) increases. Thus, neutron/proton decreases.

27. (*b*) ${}_{82}^{212}Pb \longrightarrow {}_{83}^{212}Bi + \underset{(\beta)}{{}_{-1}^{0}e}$

$$N = N_0\left(\frac{1}{2}\right)^y = N_0\left(\frac{1}{2}\right)^2 = \frac{N_0}{4}$$

where, $y = \frac{\text{total time}}{\text{half-life}} = \frac{20}{10} = 2$

Thus, I and III are true

29. (*c*) Due to β-emission, neutron changes to proton

$${}_0^1n \longrightarrow {}_1^1H + {}_{-1}^{0}e$$

$${}_Z^MA \longrightarrow {}_{Z+1}^{M}B + {}_{-1}^{0}e$$

neutron $n = M - Z$	neutron $= M - (Z+1) = M - Z - 1$
proton $p = Z$	proton $= Z + 1$

Neutron decreases by 1 unit and proton increases by 1 unit

Thus, new ratio is $\left(\frac{n-1}{p+1}\right)$.

31. (*a*) ${}_{18}^{37}Ar + {}_{-1}^{0}e \longrightarrow {}_{17}^{37}X$

${}_{17}^{37}X$ with atomic number 17 is Cl

Thus, ${}_{17}^{37}Cl$

34. (*b*) ${}_{92}^{238}U + {}_2^4He \longrightarrow {}_{95}^{241}Am + {}_0^1n$

	LHS	RHS	
Mass number	242	242	balanced
Atomic number	94	95	unbalanced

35. (*c*) It capture neutrons and emits α-particle.

Thus, (n, α) ${}_5^{10}B \xrightarrow[n\uparrow \text{ captured}]{\alpha\downarrow \text{ emitted}} {}_3^7Li$

36. (*d*) Three neutrons are released due to attack of one neutron. Additional two electrons further attack U-nucleus and thus a chain reaction starts.

41. (*c*) Smaller nuclei fuse to form heavier nuclei in nuclear fusion reaction.

42. (*b*) ${}_1^1H + {}_1^1H \longrightarrow {}_1^2H$

${}_1^2H + {}_1^1H \longrightarrow {}_2^3He \ldots$

47. (*b*) ${}_{15}^{30}X$ with atomic number-15 is isotope of phosphorus.

48. (*c*) ${}_{15}^{30}X \longrightarrow {}_{14}^{30}Si + \underbrace{{}_1^0e}_{\text{Positron}}$

51. (*b*) 1 amu $= 1.66 \times 10^{-24}$ g $= 1.66 \times 10^{-27}$ kg

$$E = mc^2$$

$$= 1.66 \times 10^{-27} \times (3 \times 10^8)^2$$

$$= 1.4950 \times 10^{-10} \text{ J}$$

$$= \frac{1.4950 \times 10^{-10} \text{ J}}{1.602 \times 10^{-19} \text{ J/eV}}$$

$$= 933.21 \times 10^6 \text{ eV}$$

$$= 933.21 \text{ MeV}$$

52. (*c*) Binding energy per nucleon $= \frac{\text{Total energy}}{\text{Number of nucleon}}$

$$= \frac{28}{4} = 7 \text{ MeV}$$

66. (*d*) ${}_AX \xrightarrow[30 \text{ min}]{-\alpha} {}_{A-2}Y \xrightarrow[2 \text{ days}]{-2\beta} {}_AZ$

A is atomic number of *X*

Half-life period of $X = 30$ min

Total time $= 2$ h $= 120$ min

(y) number of half-lives $= \frac{120}{30} = 4$

X left after 4 half-lives $N = N_0\left(\frac{1}{2}\right)^4 = 100\left(\frac{1}{16}\right) = 6.25\%$

Thus, (a) is true.

Before 30 min (= half-life) amount of X left > 50%
Hence, Y formed < 50%
(since half-life of Y) is 2880 min >> half-life of A)
Thus, (b) is correct.
X and Y are isotopes with same atomic number A, thus, (c) is correct

67. (*d*) $$\frac{-dN}{dt} = \lambda[A]$$

Greater the values of λ (decays constant) greater the activity.

68. (*b*) $$\left(1+\frac{N_{U(238)}}{N_{Pb(206)}}\right) = (2)^n$$

$$(1+1) = (2)^n$$

$$\therefore \quad n = 1 = \frac{t}{T_{50}}$$

$$\therefore \quad t = T_{50} = 4.5\times10^9 \text{ yr}$$

69. (*c*) $$\text{Half-life} = \frac{0.693}{\lambda} = \frac{0.693}{0.49\times10^{-10}} \text{ yr}$$

$$= 1.41\times10^{10} \text{ yr}$$

71. (*b*) $$^{200}_{79}Au \longrightarrow {}^{200}_{80}Hg + {}^{0}_{-1}e \quad (\beta\text{-particle})$$

(Au and Hg: isobars)

$$\text{Number of half-life} = \frac{52}{13} = 4$$

$$\text{Au left after 52 days, } C = C_0\left(\frac{1}{2}\right)^n = 1\left(\frac{1}{2}\right)^4 = \frac{1}{16}$$

$$\text{Hg formed} = 1 - \frac{1}{16} = \frac{15}{16} = 0.9375 \text{ g}$$

72. (*a*) $$1 \text{ curie} = 3.7\times10^{10} \text{ dps}$$

$$-\frac{dN}{dt} = kN$$

$$3.7\times10^{10} = 4.4\times10^{-12}\times\frac{w}{14}\times6.02\times10^{23}$$

$$w = 1.96\times10^{-1} \text{ g} \approx 2\times10^{-4} \text{ kg}$$

74. (*b*) Based on rock-dating

$$\left(1+\frac{[Pb]}{[U]} = (2)^n\right)$$

$$\left(1+\frac{\frac{0.618\times10^{-6}}{206}}{\frac{0.238\times10^{-6}}{238}}\right) = (2)^n$$

$$(2)^2 = (2)^n$$

$$n = 2$$

$$2 = \frac{t}{T_{50}}$$

$$t = 2\times T_{50} = 3\times10^9 \text{ yr}$$

75. (*c*) Based on units of k (disintegration constant) we conclude that disintegration of A follows first-order kinetics and that of B follows second-order kinetics

$$T_{50}(A) = \frac{0.693}{k_A}$$

$$T_{50}(B) = \frac{1}{k_B[B]}$$

Also, $$T_{50}(A) = T_{50}(B) \quad \text{(given)}$$

$$\frac{0.693}{k_A} = \frac{1}{k_B[B]}$$

$$\therefore \quad \frac{k_A}{k_B} = 0.693[B] = 0.693[A] \quad \text{given } [A]=[B]$$

$$(\text{Rate})_A = k_A[A]$$

$$(\text{Rate})_B = k_B[B]^2 = k_B[A]^2$$

$$\frac{(\text{Rate})_A}{(\text{Rate})_B} = \frac{k_A[A]}{k_B[A]^2} = \frac{k_A}{k_B[A]} = 0.693$$

Also, $$k_A T_A = k_A \times \frac{0.693}{k_A} = 0.693$$

Thus, (a) and (b) are true.

76. (*b*) Unknown species is $^{b}_{a}X$.

$$235 + 1 = 146 + b + 3$$

$$b = 87$$

$$92 + 0 = 57 + a$$

$$a = 35$$

Thus, $^{b}_{a}X$ is $^{87}_{35}Br$.

86. (*d*) In the chain reaction,

	Energy	Neutrons
First step	E	3
Second step	$3E$	9
Third step	$9E$	27
nth step	$3^{n-1}E$	3^n

88. (*c*) If α-particles are emitted, difference in atomic mass should be in multiple of 4 units.

(a) 235 − 231 = 4 units Yes
(b) 235 − 227 = 8 units Yes
(c) 235 − 225 = 10 units No
(d) 235 − 207 = 28 units Yes

89. (*d*) $^{14}_{6}C \quad n = 14 - 6 = 8$

$$p = 6$$

$$\frac{n}{p} = \frac{8}{6} = 1.33 > 1$$

Hence, $^{14}_{6}C$ has $\frac{n}{p}$ ratio greater than 1. It emits particles to have $\frac{n}{p} = 1$. Thus, neutron changes to proton by emission of α-particles.

$$^{14}_{6}C \longrightarrow {}^{14}_{7}N + {}^{0}_{-1}e$$

93. (*a*) Mass defect = 0.02 amu

$$= \frac{0.02}{N_0} \text{ g atom}^{-1}$$

$$= \frac{0.02}{N_0} \times N_0 \text{ g mol}^{-1} = 0.02 \text{ g mol}^{-1}$$

$$E = mc^2 = 0.02 \times 9 \times 10^{20} \text{ erg mol}^{-1}$$

$$= \frac{0.02 \times 9 \times 10^{20} \times 0.002}{8.314 \times 10^7 \times 10^6} \text{ million kcal mol}^{-1}$$

$$\approx 430 \quad \begin{pmatrix} 1 \text{ million} = 10^6 \\ 8.314 \times 10^7 \text{ erg} = 0.002 \text{ kcal} \end{pmatrix}$$

94. (*d*) In all cases daughter elements change to stable nuclei.

$$^{17}_{8}O \longrightarrow {}^{16}_{8}O + {}^{1}_{0}n$$

95. (*c*) $^{25}_{13}Al \longrightarrow {}^{0}_{1}e + {}^{25}_{12}Mg$

Proton changes to neutron $^{1}_{1}H \longrightarrow {}^{1}_{0}n + {}^{0}_{1}e$

$^{25}_{12}Mg$ has 12 protons

13 neutrons

12 electrons

96. (*c*) Average life = 1.443 × half-life

= 1.443 × 6.0 = 8.658 h

97. (*d*) $C = C_0 \left(\frac{1}{2}\right)^y$

$$(3.00 \times 10^8) = (2.40 \times 10^9)\left(\frac{1}{2}\right)^y$$

$$\left(\frac{1}{2}\right)^y = \left(\frac{1}{8}\right) = \left(\frac{1}{2}\right)^3$$

$\therefore$ $y = 3$

or $\frac{t}{T_{50}} = 3$

$\therefore$ $t = 3 \times T_{50} = 36.78 \text{ yr}$

99. (*b*) $\frac{N_A}{N_B} = \frac{(T_{50})_A}{(T_{50})_B}$

$$3.1 \times 10^9 = \frac{2 \times 10^{10}}{(T_{50})_B}$$

$$(T_{50})_B = 6.45 \text{ yr}$$

100. (*a*) The expression for bacterial growth is

$$N = N_0 e^t$$

$$\frac{N_0}{N} = e^{-t}$$

From 0 to 1 hour $N'(t) = N_0 e^t$

From 1 hour onwards, $\frac{dN}{dt} = -5N^2$

On differentiating the above equation from N' to N we get.

$$\int_{eN_0}^{N} N^{-2} dN = -5\int_1^t dt \quad [\because \text{At 1 hour, } N' = eN_0]$$

$$\left[\frac{1}{N} - \frac{1}{eN_0}\right] = 5(t-1)$$

Multiply both sides by N_0, we get

$$\frac{N_0}{N} - \frac{1}{e} = 5N_0(t-1)$$

or $$\frac{N_0}{N} = 5N_0(t-1) + \frac{1}{e}$$

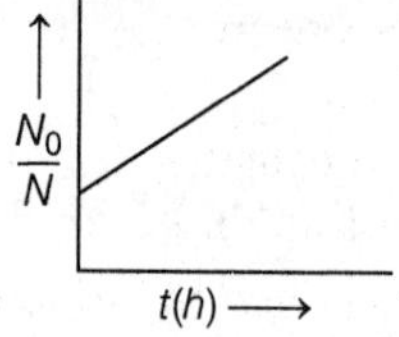

$$\frac{N_0}{N} = 5N_0 t + \left[\frac{1}{e} - 5N_0\right]$$

On comparing the above equation with equation of straight line, $y = mx + c$

We get $m = 5N_0$, $c = \frac{1}{e} - 5N_0$

$\therefore$ Plot of $\frac{N_0}{N}$ *vs* t is shown aside.

102. (*c*) Neutron is absorbed (*n*)

proton is released (*p*)

$^{14}_{7}N\,(n, p)\,^{14}_{6}C$

103. (*c*) $^{214}_{83}Bi \xrightarrow[-\beta]{} {}^{214}_{84}X \xrightarrow[-\alpha]{} {}^{210}_{82}Y$

Neutron = 210 − 82 = 128

06

Chemical Bonding

Objective Questions Type I [Only one correct option]

In each of the questions below, four choices are given of which only one is correct.

1. Formation of anion from a neutral atom *X* is favoured by
(a) high electron affinity
(b) large size of *X*
(c) low ionisation potential
(d) high charge on anion *X*

2. When a chemical bond is formed, there is decrease in
(a) kinetic energy (b) potential energy
(c) repulsive force (d) attractive force

3. Which of the following bonds is the weakest?
(a) Coordinate bond (b) Hydrogen bond
(c) van der Waals' forces (d) Covalent bond

4. An ionic compound A^+B^- is most likely to be formed from *A* and *B* when
(a) ionisation energy of *A* is low
(b) electron affinity of *B* is low
(c) electronegativity of *B* is low
(d) ionisation energy of *B* is low

5. In I_3^-, Lewis base is
(a) I_2 (b) I^- (c) I_2^+ (d) I_2^-

6. Which set contains no ionic species?
(a) NH_4Cl, OF_2, H_2S (b) CO_2, CCl_4, Cl_2
(c) BF_3, AlF_3, TlF_3 (d) I_2, CaO, CH_3Cl

7. Which combination will give the strongest ionic bond?
(a) K^+ and Cl^- (b) K^+ and O^{2-}
(c) Ca^{2+} and Cl^- (d) Ca^{2+} and O^{2-}

8. Ionisation energies (IE) and electron affinities (EA) of F and Cl are given below

Element	IE	EA
F	17.4 eV	3.45 eV
Cl	13.0 eV	3.61 eV

Compound formed between F and Cl is predominantly
(a) F^+Cl^- (b) Cl^+F^-
(c) F—Cl (d) 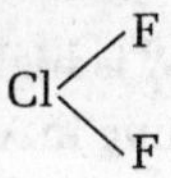

9. Elements *A*, *B* and *C* have respectively 1, 3 and 5 electrons in valence shell. Ionic compound is not formed from
(a) *A* and *C* (b) *A* and *B*
(c) *B* and *B* (d) *B* and *C*

10. $Mg^{2+}O^{2-}$ is formed since
(a) IE of Mg is low
(b) EA of O is low
(c) IE of Mg is high
(d) IE of O is low

11. Solubility of KCl is maximum in
(a) CH_3CH_2OH
(b) CH_3OCH_3
(c) H_2O
(d) CH_3COOH

12. Which pair is not correct order of lattice energy?
(a) KCl > MgO
(b) AlN > MgO
(c) CaO > BaO
(d) $MgCO_3 > CaCO_3$

13. Solubility of NaCl, Na_2SO_4 and Na_3PO_4 in water in increasing order is
(a) $NaCl < Na_2SO_4 < Na_3PO_4$
(b) $Na_3PO_4 < Na_2SO_4 < NaCl$
(c) $NaCl < Na_3PO_4 < Na_2SO_4$
(d) $Na_2SO_4 < NaCl < Na_3PO_4$

14. Select the correct statement.
(a) LiF and MgO are isostructural and also isodimensional, but a crystal of MgO is much harder than one of LiF
(b) The thermal stability of the isomorphous sulphates of Ca^{2+}, Sr^{2+} and Ba^{2+} *w.r.t.* decomposition into metal oxide and sulphur trioxide increases in the order $CaSO_4, SrSO_4, BaSO_4$
(c) Both (a) and (b) are correct
(d) None of the above

15. Select the correct statement.
(a) Both lattice energy and hydration energies decrease with ionic size
(b) Lattice energy can be calculated using Born-Haber cycle
(c) If the anion is large compared to the cation, the lattice energy will remain almost constant within a particular group
(d) All of the above are correct statements

16. Which of the following compounds has both ionic and covalent bonding?
(a) NaBr (b) $Ba(CN)_2$
(c) PCl_5 (d) CH_3CH_2OH

17. Compound *X* is highly volatile and insoluble in water. Bonding in *X* is
(a) ionic
(b) covalent
(c) polar covalent
(d) coordinate

18. The maximum covalency is equal to the number of
(a) paired *p*-electrons
(b) unpaired *s*-electrons
(c) unpaired *s*- and *p*-electrons
(d) *s*- and *p*-electrons in the valence shell

19. Select the incorrect statement.
(a) Double bond is shorter than a single bond
(b) σ-bond is weaker than a π-bond
(c) Double bond is stronger than a single bond
(d) Covalent bond is stronger than a hydrogen bond

20. The As—Cl bond distance in $AsCl_3$ is 2.20 Å. If radius of chlorine atom is 0.99 Å then radius of As atom is
(a) 0.24 Å (b) 3.19 Å (c) 1.21 Å (d) 2.09 Å

21. Covalency of carbon in the CO molecule is three because
(a) an unexcited carbon atom has two unpaired electrons
(b) the carbon atom can be an acceptor of an electron pair
(c) the carbon atom has four valence electrons
(d) maximum covalency of carbon is three

22. Total number of lone pair of electron in I_3^- ion is
(a) 3 (b) 6 **[JEE Main 2018]**
(c) 9 (d) 12

23. If there are five electron pairs in outer shell, then structure and bond angle as predicted by Sidgwick-Powell theory is
(a) octahedron, 90°
(b) trigonal bipyramidal, 120° and 90°
(c) pentagonal bipyramidal, 72° and 90°
(d) tetrahedron, 109° 28′

24. Octet rule is not followed in
(a) CCl_4, N_2O_4 and N_2O_5
(b) $BF_3, BeCl_2$ and NO_2
(c) NaCl, $MgCl_2$, MgO
(d) PCl_3, NH_3, H_2O

25. Which has maximum number of lone-pairs of electrons on the central atom?
(a) XeF_2 (b) H_3O^+
(c) XeF_4 (d) XeF_6

26. Geometrical configuration of BF_3 and NF_3 molecules is
(a) the same because of same covalency of the central atom
(b) different because BF_3 is polar and NF_3 is non-polar
(c) different because BF_3 is non-polar and NF_3 is polar
(d) none is correct

27. Coordinate covalent bond is absent in
(a) $[Fe(CN)_6]^{4-}$
(b) adduct of NH_3 and BH_3
(c) H_3O^+
(d) PCl_3

28. The compound $NH_3—BF_3$ can be easily separated into its compounds because
(a) BF_3 is highly reactive
(b) NH_3 is highly reactive
(c) BF_3 and NH_3 are unstable
(d) BF_3 and NH_3 have their independent existence

29. Consider the following compounds
I. $K_4[Fe(CN)_6]$, II. NH_4Cl, III. H_2SO_4
Ionic, covalent and coordinate bonds are present in
(a) I, II and III
(b) I and III
(c) II and III
(d) I and II

30. The species in which the N-atom is in a state of *sp*-hybridisation is **[JEE Main 2016]**
(a) NO_2^- (b) NO_3^-
(c) NO_2 (d) NO_2^+

31. Which of the following is a positive overlap which leads to bonding?

(a) 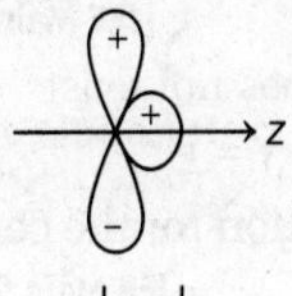

(b) 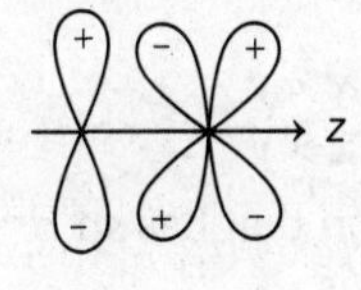

(c) 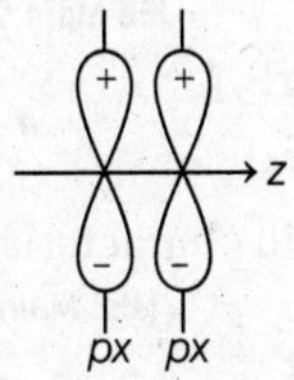

(d) 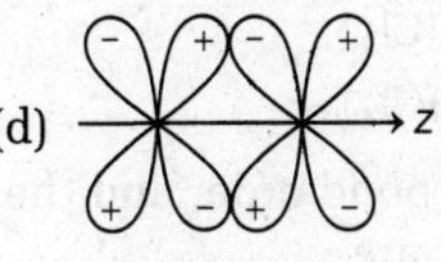

32. The angle between the bonding orbitals of a molecule AX_3 with zero dipole moment is

(a) 120° (b) 109°
(c) 104° (d) 180°

33. Number of bonding pairs (X) and lone pairs (Y) around the central atom in the I_3^- ion are

	X	Y		X	Y
(a)	2	2	(b)	2	3
(c)	3	2	(d)	4	3

34. The nitrogen atoms in NH_3, NH_2^- and NH_4^+ are all surrounded by eight electrons. When these species are arranged in increasing order of H—N—H bond angle, correct order is

(a) NH_3, NH_2^-, NH_4^+ (b) NH_4^+, NH_2^-, NH_3
(c) NH_3, NH_4^+, NH_2^- (d) NH_2^-, NH_3, NH_4^+

35. Which of these molecules have non-bonding electron pairs on the central atom?

I. SF_4 II. ICl_3 III. SO_2

(a) II only (b) I and II only
(c) I and III only (d) I, II and III

36. Which species has the same shape as the NO_3^- ion?

(a) SO_3 (b) SO_3^{2-}
(c) ClF_3 (d) ClO_3^-

37. Which one of the following compounds has the electron-pair geometry as the trigonal bipyramidal with three equatorial positions occupied by lone pairs of electrons?

(a) $AlCl_3$ (b) XeF_2
(c) $[Pt(NH_3)_2Cl_2]$ (d) $CH_3—Mg—Br$

38. Electron pairs occupy localised orbitals. Their orbitals are oriented in such a way that the repulsion between electron clouds becomes

(a) zero (b) minimum
(c) maximum (d) infinite

39. When the number of electron pairs on the central atom is six, then geometry of the molecule is

(a) octahedral (b) trigonal bipyramidal
(c) equilateral triangle (d) linear

40. Arrange the following bonds according to their average bond energies in descending order

C—Cl, C—Br, C—F, C—I

[JEE Main 2020, Jan.]

(a) C—F > C—Cl > C—Br > C—I
(b) C—Br > C—I > C—Cl > C—F
(c) C—I > C—Br > C—Cl > C—F
(d) C—Cl > C—Br > C—I > C—F

41. Lattice enthalpy and enthalpy of solution of NaCl are 788 kJ mol^{-1} and 4 kJ mol^{-1}, respectively. The hydration enthalpy of NaCl is **[JEE Main 2020, Sep.]**

(a) −780 kJ mol^{-1} (b) 780 kJ mol^{-1}
(c) −784 kJ mol^{-1} (d) 784 kJ mol^{-1}

42. Which has a maximum repulsive interaction?

(a) *bp-bp* (b) *lp-lp* (c) *lp-bp* (d) Equal

43. A molecule of the type AX_5 has square pyramidal geometry. Hence, number of lone pairs on A is

(a) 4 (b) 3 (c) 2 (d) 1

44. The bond angle in H_2O is 105° and in H_2S it is 90°. It is due to

(a) the larger size of S-atom as compared to O-atom which minimises repulsion and allows the bonds in H_2S to be purely *p*-type
(b) liquid state of H_2O as compared to gaseous state of SO_2
(c) Both (a) and (b) are correct
(d) None of the above is correct

45. True structure is predicted by

(a) valence-bond approach (b) Sidgwick approach
(c) hybrid formation (d) None of these

46. The hybrid orbital of the central atom in AlF_4^- is

(a) *sp* (b) sp^2 (c) sp^3 (d) dsp^2

47. What hybrid orbitals are employed by carbon atoms 1, 2 and 3, respectively as labelled in the compound shown?

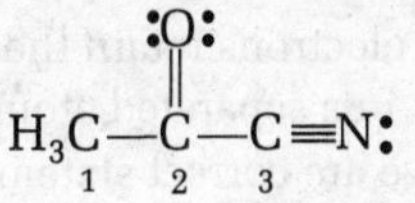

(a) sp^3, *sp*, *sp* (b) sp^3, sp^2, *sp*
(c) sp^3, *sp*, sp^2 (d) sp^3, sp^2, sp^2

48. The geometry of the atoms in the species PCl_4^+ is best described as

(a) tetrahedral
(b) see-saw
(c) square
(d) trigonal bipyramidal

49. In vinyl acetylene $CH{\equiv}C—CH{=}CH_2$, type of overlapping in ($C_2 \sigma C_3$) bond is

(a) sp^2-*sp* (b) *sp* - sp^2
(c) sp^3 - sp^3 (d) sp^3 - sp^2

50. In which case, hybridisation of the central atom is affected when
(a) NH_3 changes to NH_4^+ (b) AlH_3 changes to AlH_4^-
(c) in both cases (d) in none case

51. Hybridisation of the nitrogen atom and electron geometry around nitrogen atom in pyridine is

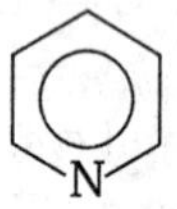

(a) sp^3, pyramidal (b) sp^2, planar trigonal
(c) sp^2, linear (d) sp^3, tetrahedral

52. Which pair of substances will have the most similar geometry?
(a) SO_3, SO_3^{2-} (b) SO_3, SO_4^{2-}
(c) SO_3, CO_3^{2-} (d) SO_4^{2-}, CO_3^{2-}

53. The number of bonds between sulphur and oxygen atoms in $S_2O_8^{2-}$ and the number of bonds between sulphur and sulphur atoms in rhombic sulphur, respectively, are **[JEE Main 2020, Jan.]**
(a) 4 and 6 (b) 8 and 8
(c) 4 and 8 (d) 8 and 6

54. PCl_5 has a shape of trigonal bipyramid whereas IF_5 has the shape of a square pyramid. It is due to
(a) presence of unshared electron pair on I which is oriented so as to minimise repulsion while P in PCl_5 has no unshared pair
(b) octet of P is complete while that of I is incomplete
(c) P and I are of different groups
(d) F and Cl have different extent of repulsion

55. Select the correct statement about valence-bond approach.
(a) Each bond is formed by maximum overlap for its maximum stability
(b) It represents localised electron model of bonding
(c) Most of the electrons retain the same orbital locations as in a separated atoms
(d) All the above are correct statements

56. Among the following molecules/ions,
$$C_2^{2-}, N_2^{2-}, O_2^{2-}, O_2$$
Which one is diamagnetic and has the shortest bond length? **[JEE Main 2019, April]**
(a) C_2^{2-} (b) O_2 (c) O_2^{2-} (d) N_2^{2-}

57. OF and F_2 can be compared in terms of
(a) OF is paramagnetic while F_2 is diamagnetic
(b) OF is more stable towards dissociation into atoms
(c) Both (a) & (b) are correct
(d) None of the above is correct

58. If enthalpy of atomisation for $Br_2(l)$ is x kJ/mol and bond enthalpy for Br_2 is y kJ/mol, the relation between them **[JEE Main 2020, Jan]**
(a) is $x < y$ (b) does not exist
(c) is $x > y$ (d) is $x = y$

59. The ion that has sp^3d^2-hybridisation for the central atom, is **[JEE Main 2019, April]**
(a) $[ICl_2]^-$ (b) $[BrF_2]^-$
(c) $[ICl_4]^-$ (d) $[IF_6]^-$

60. The bond order and the magnetic characteristics of CN^- are **[JEE Main 2020, Jan]**
(a) 3, diamagnetic (b) $2\frac{1}{2}$, paramagnetic
(c) 3, paramagnetic (d) $2\frac{1}{2}$, diamagnetic

61. Which of the following has maximum bond energy?
(a) O_2^- (b) O_2^+
(c) O_2 (d) O_2^{2-}

62. The paramagnetism of oxygen is best explained by
(a) MO theory
(b) Valence bond theory
(c) VSEPR theory
(d) Lewis dot structure

63. In which pair or pairs is the stronger bond found in the first species?
I : O_2^{2-}, O_2; II : N_2, N_2^+; III : NO^+, NO^-
(a) I only
(b) II only
(c) I and III only
(d) II and III only

64. Amongst the following , the linear species is **[JEE Main 2021, March]**
(a) NO_2 (b) Cl_2O
(c) O_3 (d) N_3^-

65. The potential energy curve for the H_2 molecule as a function of internuclear distance is **[JEE Main 2020, Sep.]**

(a)
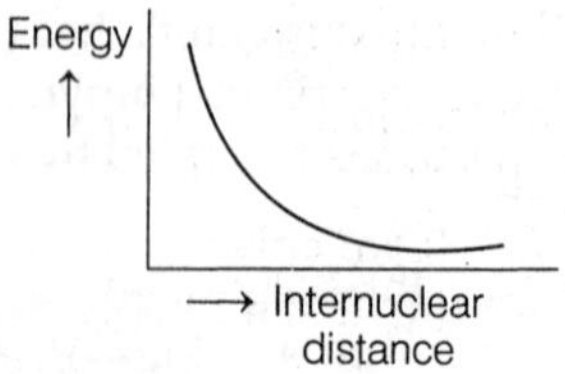

(b)
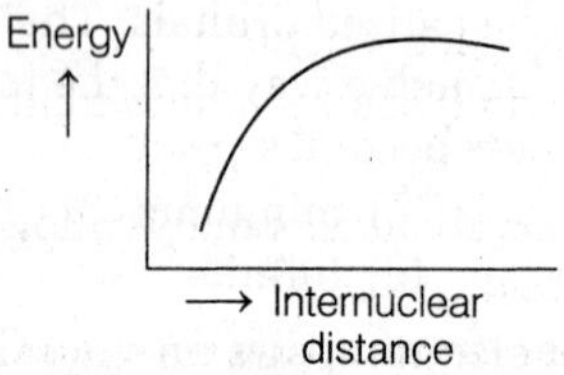

(c)
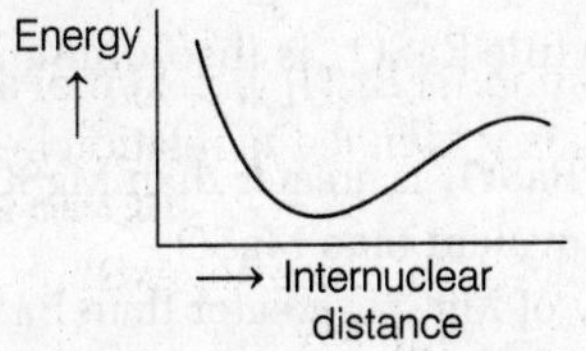

(d)
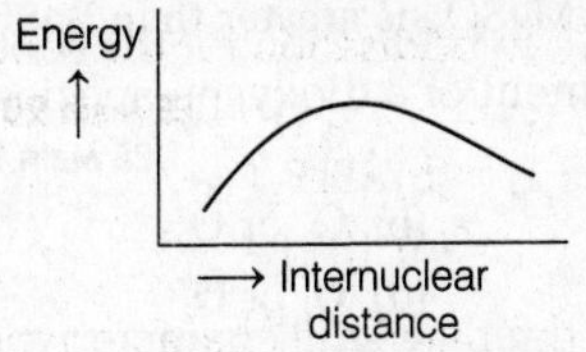

66. The set of elements that differ in mutual relationship from those of the other sets is **[JEE Main 2021, March]**
(a) Li - Mg (b) Be - Al
(c) B - Si (d) Li - Na

67. Compare the first ionisation energy of Mg, Al, Si, P, S. **[JEE Main 2021, Feb.]**
(a) P > S > Si > Mg > Al
(b) P < S < Si < Mg < Al
(c) P > S > Si > Al > Mg
(d) S > P > Si > Al > Mg

68. Assuming that Hund's rule is violated, the bond order and magnetic nature of the diatomic molecule B_2 is **[IIT JEE 2010]**
(a) 1 and diamagnetic
(b) 0 and diamagnetic
(c) 1 and paramagnetic
(d) 0 and paramagnetic

69. The species having pyramidal shape is **[IIT JEE 2010]**
(a) SO_3 (b) BrF_3
(c) SiO_3^{2-} (d) OSF_2

70. A set of inner *d*-complex is
(a) $[Fe(CN)_6]^{4-}, [Ni(CN)_4]^{2-}, [Pt(en)_2]^{2+}$
(b) $[Fe(H_2O)_6]^{3+}, [CoF_6]^{3-}, [Cr(CN)_6]^{3-}$
(c) Both (a) and (b)
(d) None of the above

71. Which of the following has zero dipole moment?
(a) CO (b) SO_2
(c) SO_3 (d) H_2O

72. Which are non-polar molecules?
I. NCl_3 II. SO_3 III. PCl_5
(a) I only (b) II only
(c) I and II only (d) II and III only

73. Which of the following statement is wrong?
(a) A σ-bond is shorter than a π-bond.
(b) Bond energies of σ and σ-bond is allowed but not in case of a π-bond.
(c) Free rotation of atoms about a σ-bond is allowed but not in case of a π-bond.
(d) A σ-bond determines the direction between C-atoms but a π-bond has no primary effect which leads to bonding.

74. Select the correct statement.
(a) BF_3 and NH_3 have same dipole moment
(b) Dipole moment of NH_3 is smaller than that of BF_3
(c) BF_3 molecule has a planar structure, while the NH_3 molecule is tetrahedral
(d) The nitrogen atom has unshared pair of electrons, while the boron atom has a free (vacant) valence orbital.

75. A diatomic molecule has a dipole moment of 1.2 D. If the bond distance is 1.0 Å, fraction of an electronic charge on each atom is
(a) 0.25 (b) 0.33
(c) 0.66 (d) 0.90

76. HCN and HNC molecular have equal number of
(a) lone pair and σ-bonds
(b) σ bonds and π-bonds
(c) π-bonds and lone pairs
(d) lone pairs, σ-bonds and π-bonds

77. Which of the following ions has the maximum polarising power?
(a) Na^+ (b) Ca^{2+}
(c) Mg^{2+} (d) Al^{3+}

78. Consider the following species
I. $S_4O_6^{2-}$ II. S_3O_9 III. $S_2O_5^{2-}$ IV. $P_3O_9^{3-}$
Which of the above species have same number of *X*—O—*X* linkage (*X* = P or S)?
(a) II, III (b) I, III
(c) II, IV (d) I, IV

79. Some ether is added to an aqueous solution mixture of LiCl, NaCl and $AlCl_3$. Which will be extracted into ether?
(a) LiCl, NaCl (b) LiCl, $AlCl_3$
(c) NaCl, $AlCl_3$ (d) LiCl, NaCl, $AlCl_3$

80. Select the correct statement.
(a) Cations with 18 electron shell have greater polarising power than the cations with 8 electron shell
(b) Inner electrons have poor shielding effect on the nucleus and thus electronegativity of the 18 electron shell is increased
(c) CuCl is covalent and NaCl is ionic
(d) All the above are correct statements

81. H-bonding is maximum in
(a) ethanol
(b) methoxy methane
(c) chloroethane
(d) N,N-diethyl amino ethane

82. Which property is not due to H-bonding?
(a) High boiling point of water
(b) High viscosity of glycerol
(c) Solubility of ammonia in water
(d) Polar nature of halogen acid

83. The molecular geometry of SF_6 is octahedral. What is the geometry of SF_4 (including lone pair(s) of electrons, if any)? **[JEE Main 2020, Sep.]**

(a) Tetrahedral (b) Trigonal bipyramidal
(c) Pyramidal (d) Square planar

84. Match the type of interaction in Column *A* with the distance dependence of their interaction energy in Column *B* :

	A		*B*
I.	Ion-ion	(a)	$\frac{1}{r}$
II.	Dipole-dipole	(b)	$\frac{1}{r^2}$
III.	London dispersion	(c)	$\frac{1}{r^3}$
		(d)	$\frac{1}{r^6}$

[JEE Main 2020, Sep.]

(a) I-(b), II-(d), III-(c) (b) I-(a), II-(b), III-(d)
(c) I-(a), II-(b), III-(c) (d) I-(a), II-(c), III-(d)

85. The structure of PCl_5 in the solid state is **[JEE Main 2020, Sep.]**

(a) tetrahedral $[PCl_4]^+$ and octahedral $[PCl_6]^-$
(b) trigonal bipyramidal
(c) square planar $[PCl_4]^+$ and octahedral $[PCl_6]^-$
(d) square pyramidal

86. Arrange the following compounds in increasing dipole moment : toluene (I), *m*-chlorobenzene (II), *o*-dichlorobenzene (III), *p*-dichlorobenzene (IV)

(a) I < IV < II < III (b) IV < I < II < III
(c) IV < I < III < II (d) IV < II < I < III

87. When N_2^+ is formed from N_2 bond-order .... and when O_2^+ is formed from O_2 bond-order ....

(a) increases (b) decreases
(c) increases, decreases (d) decreases, increases

88. Of the species, NO, NO^+, NO^{2+} and NO^-, the one with minimum bond strength is **[JEE Main 2020, Sep.]**

(a) NO^+ (b) NO
(c) NO^{2+} (d) NO^-

89. Among the following, the molecule expected to be stabilised by anion formation is C_2, O_2, NO, F_2.

(a) C_2 (b) F_2 **[JEE Main 2019]**
(c) NO (d) O_2

90. If AB_4 molecule is a polar molecule, a possible geometry of AB_4 is **[JEE Main 2020, Sep.]**

(a) square pyramidal (b) square planar
(c) rectangular planar (d) tetrahedral

91. Among KO_2, AlO_2^-, BaO_2 and NO_2^+, unpaired electron is present in

(a) KO_2 only (b) NO_2^+ and BaO_2
(c) KO_2 and AlO_2^- (d) BaO_2 only

92. $MgSO_4$ is soluble while $BaSO_4$ is insoluble in H_2O. This is because

(a) lattice energy of $BaSO_4$ is greater than $MgSO_4$
(b) $BaSO_4$ is more covalent than $MgSO_4$
(c) hydration energy of Mg^{2+} is greater than Ba^{2+}
(d) lattice energy of $MgSO_4$ is greater than $BaSO_4$

93. If the magnetic moment of a dioxygen species is 1.73 B.M, it may be. **[JEE Main 2020, Jan.]**

(a) O_2, O_2^- or O_2^+ (b) O_2^- or O_2^+
(c) O_2 or O_2^- (d) O_2 or O_2^+

94. Solutions of alkali metals in liquid ammonia at −33°C conduct electricity without chemical reaction at the electrodes. Hence, conductivity should

(a) increase as temperature is lowered
(b) decrease as temperature is lowered
(c) remain constant on changing the temperature
(d) there is always interaction of alkali metal with liquid ammonia

95. Which represents metallic character in an element?

(a) 

(b) 

(c) 

(d) None of these

96. In which of the following molecules would you expect the nitrogen–to–nitrogen bond to be the shortest?

(a) N_2H_4 (b) N_2
(c) N_2O_4 (d) N_2O

97. The formal charge of the O atoms in the ion $[:\ddot{O}=N=\ddot{O}:]^+$ is

(a) −2 (b) −1
(c) 0 (d) +1

98. The hybridisation scheme for the central atom includes a *d*-orbital contribution in

(a) I_3^- (b) PCl_3
(c) NO_3^- (d) H_2Se

99. Delocalised molecular orbitals are found in

(a) H_2 (b) HS^-
(c) CH_4 (d) CO_3^{2-}

100. A substance in which large energy gap separates the valence and conduction band is a/an

(a) metal (b) metalloid
(c) semiconductor (d) insulator

101. Which of the following is an electron-deficient compound?
(a) $NaBH_4$ (b) CO_2 (c) B_2H_6 (d) Al_2Cl_6

102. One of the following is least volatile
(a) HCN (b) HF
(c) H_2O (d) CS_2

103. Which of the following diatomic molecules would be stabilised by the removal of an electron?
(a) C_2 (b) CN
(c) N_2 (d) O_2

104. O_2 molecule is paramagnetic due to presence of
(a) two unpaired electrons in antibonding MO
(b) one unpaired electron in antibonding MO
(c) two unpaired electrons in bonding MO
(d) one unpaired electron in bonding MO

105. Allyl cyanide has
(a) 9 sigma bonds and 4 pi bonds
(b) 9 sigma bonds, 3 pi bonds and 1 lone pair
(c) 8 sigma bonds and 5 pi bonds
(d) 8 sigma bonds, 3 pi bonds

106. The compound that has the largest H—*M*—H bond angle (*M* = N, O, S, C) is **[JEE Main 2020, Sep.]**
(a) H_2O (b) NH_3 (c) H_2S (d) CH_4

107. Which of the following species is not paramagnetic? **[JEE Main 2017]**
(a) NO (b) CO
(c) O_2 (d) B_2

108. Among the following species, identify the isostructural pairs

$$NF_3, NO_3^-, BF_3, H_3O^+, HN_3$$

(a) $[NF_3, NO_3^-]$ and $[BF_3, H_3O^+]$
(b) $[NF_3, HN_3]$ and $[NO_3^-, BF_3]$
(c) $[NF_3, H_3O^+]$ and $[NO_3^-, BF_3]$
(d) $[NF_3, H_3O^+]$ and $[HN_3, BF_3]$

109. Which of the following statements is correct for $CsBr_3$?
(a) It is covalent compound
(b) It contains Cs^{3+} and Br^-
(c) It contains Cs^+ and Br_3^-
(d) It contains Cs^+, Br^- and lattice Br_2 molecule

110. For octahedral Mn (II) and tetrahedral Ni (II) complexes, consider the following statements :
I. Both the complexes can be high spin.
II. Ni(II) complex can very rarely be low spin.
III. With strong field ligands, Mn(II) complexes can be low spin.
IV. Aqueous solution of Mn(II) ions is yellow in colour.

The correct statements is **[JEE Main 2020, Sep.]**
(a) I and II only (b) II, III and IV only
(c) I, II and III only (d) I, III and IV only

111. A central atom in a molecule has two lone pairs of electrons and forms three single bonds. The shape of this moleucle is **[JEE Main 2021, March]**
(a) *see-saw*
(b) T-shaped
(c) planar triangular
(d) trigonal pyramidal

112. Which has maximum dipole moment?

(a) 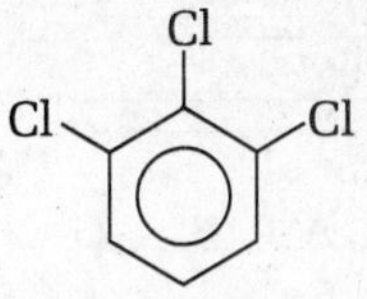

(b) 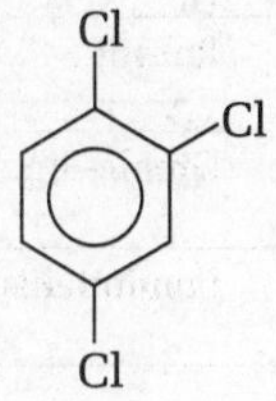

(c) 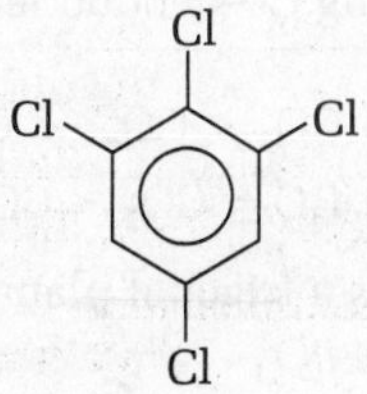

(d) 

113. Bond order of O_2, O_2^+, O_2^- and O_2^{2-} is in order
(a) $O_2^- < O_2^{2-} < O_2 < O_2^+$
(b) $O_2^{2-} < O_2^- < O_2 < O_2^+$
(c) $O_2^+ < O_2 < O_2^- < O_2^{2+}$
(d) $O_2 < O_2^+ < O_2^- < O_2^{2-}$

114. Polarising action of Cd^{2+} on anions is stronger than that of Ca^{2+} because
(a) the charges of the ions are same
(b) their radii are same (Ca^{2+} = 0.104 nm; Cd^{2+} = 0.099 nm)
(c) the Ca^{2+} ion has a noble-gas electron configuration, and the Cd^{2+} ion, an 18-electron configuration of its outer shell
(d) All the above are correct

115. *Ortho*-isomers have dipole moments. In which cases dipole moments are maximum and minimum?

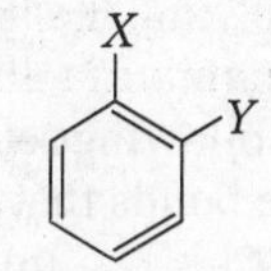

	Maximum		Minimum	
	X	*Y*	*X*	*Y*
(a)	Cl	Cl	CH_3	CH_3
(b)	OH	CH_3	Cl	Cl
(c)	OH	NO_2	CH_3	CH_3
(d)	OH	NO_2	Cl	Cl

116. Match Column I with Column II and select the correct answer.

Column I (Species)	Column II (O—N—O angle)
A. NO_2^+	1. 180°
B. NO_2	2. 132°
C. NO_2^-	3. 120°
D. NO_3^-	4. 115°
	5. 109°

Codes

	A	B	C	D		A	B	C	D
(a)	5	4	3	2	(b)	5	2	4	3
(c)	1	2	4	3	(d)	1	4	3	2

117. The correct order of increasing C—O bond length of CO, CO_3^{2-}, CO_2 is
(a) $CO_3^{2-} < CO_2 < CO$ (b) $CO_2 < CO_3^{2-} < CO$
(c) $CO < CO_3^{2-} < CO_2$ (d) $CO < CO_2 < CO_3^{2-}$

118. One of the following ions has a trigonal planar shape
(a) SO_3^{2-} (b) PO_4^{3-}
(c) CN^- (d) CO_3^{2-}

119. Which of the following molecules or ions is not linear?
(a) $BeCl_2$ (b) I_3^- (c) CS_2 (d) ICl_2^+

120. All the following molecules are linear except one
(a) SO_2 (b) CO_2
(c) HCN (d) NO

121. All the following molecules are polar except one
(a) BCl_3 (b) CH_2Cl_2
(c) NH_3 (d) FNO

122. Correct Lewis structure is
(a) $[:\ddot{O}—C=\ddot{N}:]^-$ (b) $[C\equiv C:]^{2-}$
(c) $[:\ddot{Cl}—\ddot{O}:]^-$ (d) $:\dot{N}=\ddot{O}:$

123. Which of the following has the highest percentage of ionic character in its bonding?
(a) LiI (b) $MgCl_2$
(c) CsF (d) CsI

124. In which of the following sets do all the three compounds have bonds that are mainly ionic?
(a) NaCl, NCl_3, CCl_4 (b) CsBr, $BaBr_2$, SrO
(c) CsF, BF_3, NH_3 (d) Al_2O_3, CaO, SO_2

125. Which of the following is non-polar but contains polar bonds?
(a) HCl (b) CO_2 (c) NH_3 (d) NO_2

126. Which of the following will have the molecular shape of a trigonal bipyramid?
(a) PF_3Cl_2 (b) IF_5
(c) BrF_5 (d) SbF_5^{2-}

127. The expected spin-only magnetic moments (BM) for $[Fe(CN)_6]^{4-}$ and $[FeF_6]^{3-}$ respectively are
(a) 1.73 and 1.73 (b) 1.73 and 5.92
(c) 0 and 1.73 (d) 0 and 5.92

128. Which of the following species/molecules has a planar geometry?
(a) $Ni(CO)_4$ (b) SF_4
(c) $CoCl_4^{2-}$ (d) XeF_4

129. Which of the following can provide an electron pair for the formation of a coordinate covalent bond?
(a) H^+ (b) H^- (c) H_2 (d) He^{2+}

130. The molecules that will have dipole moments are
(a) 1,2-dichloro benzene (b) *cis*-3-hexene
(c) *trans*-2-pentene (d) All of these

131. Which of the following have identical bond order?
I. CN^- II. O_2^-
III. NO^+ IV. CN^+
(a) I, III (b) II, IV
(c) I, II, III (d) I, IV

132. Molecular shapes of SF_4, CF_4 and XeF_4 are
(a) the same, with 2, 0 and 1 lone pair of electrons respectively
(b) the same, with 1, 1 and 1 lone pair of electrons respectively
(c) different with 0, 1 and 2 lone pair of electrons respectively
(d) different with 1, 0 and 2 lone pair of electrons respectively

133. The hybridisation of atomic orbitals of N in NO_2^+, NO_3^- and NH_4^+ are respectively
(a) sp, sp^2, sp^3 (b) sp, sp^3, sp^2
(c) sp^2, sp, sp^3 (d) sp^2, sp^3, sp

134. Which of the following species contain at least one atom that violates the octet rule?
(a) O—Cl—O (b) F—Xe—F
(c) Both (a) and (b) (d) None of these

135. $ZnCO_3$ is thermally more stable than $MgCO_3$, because
(a) $Mg(OH)_2$ exhibits only basic properties while $Zn(OH)_2$ is amphoteric
(b) polarising action of Zn^{2+} with 18 electron configuration on the anion is larger than that of Mg^{2+} with a noble-gas electron configuration and of same size and charge.
(c) Both (a) and (b) are correct
(d) None of the above

136. Stability of the species Li_2, Li_2^- and Li_2^+ increases in the order of **[JEE Main 2013]**
(a) $Li_2 < Li_2^+ < Li_2^-$ (b) $Li_2^- < Li_2^+ < Li_2$
(c) $Li_2 < Li_2^- < Li_2^+$ (d) $Li_2^- < Li_2 < Li_2^+$

137. Which of the following has the smallest bond length?
(a) NO^+ (b) NO
(c) NO^- (d) Equal

138. The percentage of *p*-character in the orbitals forming P—P bonds in P_4 is
(a) 25 (b) 33 (c) 50 (d) 75

139. For the dot structure shown the most likely elements are X = ... and Y = ...

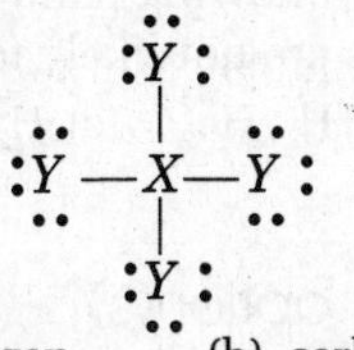

(a) carbon, hydrogen (b) carbon, oxygen
(c) fluorine, carbon (d) carbon, fluorine

140. The common features among the species CN^-, CO and NO^+ are
(a) bond order three and isoelectronic
(b) bond order three and weak field ligands
(c) bond order two and π-acceptors
(d) isoelectronic and weak field ligands

141. Specify the coordination geometry around the hybridisation of N and B atoms in a 1 : 1 complex of BF_3 and NH_3
(a) N : tetrahedral, sp^3; B : tetrahedral, sp^3
(b) N : pyramidal, sp^3; B : pyramidal, sp^3
(c) N : pyramidal, sp^3; B : planar, sp^2
(d) N : pyramidal, sp^3; B : tetrahedral, sp^3

142. Which of the following are isoelectronic and isostructural?
NO_3^-, CO_3^{2-}, ClO_3^-, SO_3
(a) NO_3^-, CO_3^{2-} (b) SO_3, NO_3^-
(c) ClO_3^-, CO_3^{2-} (d) CO_3^{2-}, SO_3

143. Which of the following has —O—O— linkage?
(a) $H_2S_2O_6$ (b) $H_2S_2O_8$
(c) $H_2S_2O_3$ (d) $H_2S_4O_6$

144. Which species has the maximum number of lone pair of electrons on the central atom?
(a) $[ClO_3^-]$ (b) XeF_4
(c) SF_4 (d) $[I_3^-]$

145. According to VSEPR theory, a molecule with three charge clouds including one lone pair would have a shape
(a) bent (b) linear
(c) tetrahedral (d) trigonal planar

146. In a Lewis dot structure, the electrons which complete an octet but are not located between two atoms are referred to as
(a) bonding pairs (b) delta minus electrons
(c) excess electrons (d) lone pairs

147. Elements in period 3 or below don't always "obey" the octet rule because they
(a) can only use *p* orbitals for bonding
(b) can use *s* and *p* orbitals for bonding
(c) can use *s*, *p* and *d* orbitals for bonding
(d) cannot use *d* orbitals for bonding

148. Which set of properties would identify a white solid unknown as a molecular compound?
I. Contains a metal
II. Has a definite crystal structure
III. Dissolves in water, but not in organic liquids
IV. Melts at 80°C
V. Does not conduct electricity in fused state
(a) I, II, III (b) I, III, V (c) II, III, IV (d) II, IV, V

149. The carbon dioxide molecule is linear. The electronegativities of C and O are 2.5 and 3.5 respectively. Based on these values and on consideration of molecular geometry, the C—O bond is .... and the molecule is ....
(a) polar; polar (b) non-polar ; non-polar
(c) polar; non-polar (d) non-polar; polar

150. A molecule in which the central atom forms three single bonds and has one lone pair is said to be have a .... shape.
(a) bent (b) linear
(c) planar (d) pyramidal

151. The water molecule has a .... (X)......... geometry because its central atom has .... (Y) .... bonds and .... (Z) .... lone pairs of electrons.

	X	Y	Z
(a)	bent	2	2
(b)	linear	2	2
(c)	pyramidal	3	1
(d)	tetrahedral	4	0

152. Which of the following molecule does not possess a permanent dipole moment?
(a) H_2S (b) SO_2 (c) CS_2 (d) SO_3

153. The table shown below gives the bond dissociation energies (E_{diss}) for single covalent bonds of carbon (C) atoms with element '*A*', '*B*', '*C*' and '*D*'. Which element has the smallest atoms?

Bond	E_{diss} (kJ mol^{-1})
C—A	240
C—B	328
C—C	276
C—D	485

(a) A (b) B (c) C (d) D

154. AsF_5 molecule is trigonal bipyramidal. The hybrid orbitals used by As atoms for bonding are
(a) $d_{x^2-y^2}, d_{z^2}, s, p_x, p_y$ (b) d_{xy}, s, p_x, p_y, p_z
(c) s, p_x, p_y, p_z, d_{xy} (d) $d_{x^2-y^2}, s, p_x, p_y, p_z$

155. Which one of the following has the highest boiling point?
(a) AsH_3 (b) SbH_3 (c) PH_3 (d) NH_3

156. The shape of XeO_2F_2 molecule is [IIT JEE 2012]
(a) trigonal bipyramidal (b) square planar
(c) tetrahedral (d) *see-saw*

157. In allene (C_3H_4), the type(s) of hybridization of the carbon atoms, is (are) [IIT JEE 2012]
(a) sp and sp^3 (b) sp and sp^2
(c) only sp^3 (d) sp^2 and sp^3

158. Which of the following molecules is expected to exhibit diamagnetic behaviour? [JEE Main 2013]
(a) C_2 (b) N_2 (c) O_2 (d) S_2

159. Which of the following does not obey 18-electron rule?
(a) $Cr(CO)_6$ (b) $Fe(CO)_5$
(c) $V(CO)_6$ (d) $Mn_2(CO)_{10}$

160. In which of the following pairs of molecules/ions both the species are not likely to exist? [JEE Main 2013]
(a) H_2^+, He_2^{2-} (b) H_2^-, He_2^{2-} (c) H_2^{2+}, He_2 (d) H_2^-, He_2^{2+}

Objective Questions Type II [One or more than one correct option(s)]

In each of the questions below, four choices are given, of which one or more than one are correct.

1. Which of the following have identical bond-order?
(a) CN^- (b) O_2^- (c) NO^+ (d) CN^+

2. Select the correct statement(s) about C_3^{4-} ion.
(a) It reacts with H_2O forming C_3H_6
(b) It reacts with H_2O forming C_3H_4
(c) It has two sigma and two pi bonds
(d) It has three sigma and one pi bonds

3. The planar shape of $N(SiH_3)_3$ is explained by the
(a) type of hybrid orbitals of nitrogen
(b) additional $d\pi$-$p\pi$ overlap along the N—Si bond
(c) higher electronegativity of nitrogen
(d) higher electronegativity of silicon

4. Which are the species in which sulphur undergoes sp^3-hybridisation?
(a) SF_4 (b) SCl_2 (c) SO_4^{2-} (d) H_2S

5. Which of the following do not have lone pair?
(a) SiF_4 (b) XeF_4 (c) SF_4 (d) BF_3

6. In which of the following pairs, molecules/ions have similar shape?
(a) CO_2 and H_2O (b) BF_3 and $(CH_3)_3C^{\oplus}$
(c) CCl_4 and $PtCl_4$ (d) NH_3 and BF_3

7. In BrF_3 molecule, the lone pairs occupy equatorial position to minimise
(a) lone pair-bond pair repulsion only
(b) bond pair-bond pair repulsion only
(c) lone pair-lone pair repulsion and lone pair-bond pair repulsion
(d) lone pair-lone pair repulsion only

8. Each of the following op0e option(s) where all four molecules posses permanent dipole moment at room temperature. [JEE Advanced 2019]
(a) SO_2, C_6H_5Cl, H_2Se, BrF_5
(b) $BeCl_2$, CO_2, BCl_3, $CHCl_3$
(c) NO_2, NH_3, $POCl_3$, CH_3Cl
(d) BF_3, O_3, SF_6, XeF_6

9. Among the following the pair in which the two species are isostructural are
(a) SiF_4 and SF_4 (b) IO_3^- and XeO_3
(c) BH_4^- and NH_4^+ (d) PF_6^- and SF_6

10. $PbCl_4$ exists but $PbBr_4$ and PbI_4 do not because of
(a) Br^- and I^- ions are bigger in size
(b) chlorine is a gas
(c) Br_2 and I_2 are more electronegative
(d) inability of bromine and iodine to oxidise Pb^{2+} to Pb^{4+}

11. Which is/are correct statements?
(a) A solute will dissolve in water if hydration energy is greater than lattice energy
(b) If the anion is large compared to the cation, the lattice energy will remain almost constant
(c) Solubility of II A hydroxide is in order.
$Be(OH)_2 < Mg(OH)_2 < Ca(OH)_2 < Sr(OH)_2$
(d) AgF is water soluble

12. In which molecule is the van der Waals force likely to be most important in determining m.p. and b.p.?
(a) ICl (b) Br_2 (c) H_2S (d) CO

13. Which have linear structure?
(a) BeF_2 (b) $Ag[CN]_2^-$
(c) CO_2 (d) XeF_2

14. In I_3^-
(a) I_2 is Lewis acid and I^- as Lewis base
(b) I_2 is Lewis base and I^- as Lewis acid
(c) I_3^- itself behaves as amphoteric anion
(d) I_3^- does not exist

15. In the following case (s), hybridisation of the underlined atom is affected
(a) $\underline{P}Cl_5$ (solid) dissociates into PCl_4^+ and PCl_6^-
(b) LiH reacts with $\underline{Al}H_3$ forming $LiAlH_4$
(c) $\underline{N}H_3$ is protonated
(d) $H_3\underline{P}O_2$ is heated forming PH_3 and H_3PO_3

16. The correct order of the O—O bond length in O_2, H_2O_2 and O_3 is
(a) $H_2O_2 > O_3 > O_2$ (b) $O_2 > O_3 > H_2O_2$
(c) $O_2 > H_2O_2 > O_3$ (d) $O_3 > H_2O_2 > O_2$

17. Which combinations of the compounds and their geometry are correct?
(a) $HgCl_2$—linear (b) ClF_3—V-shaped
(c) ClF_3—T-shaped (d) ICl_4^-—square planar

18. The compound(s) with two lone pairs of electrons on the central atom is(are) **[JEE Advanced 2016]**
(a) BrF_5 (b) ClF_3
(c) XeF_4 (d) SF_4

19. According to Molecular Orbital Theory **[JEE Advanced 2016]**
(a) C_2^{2-} is expected to be diamagnetic
(b) O_2^{2+} expected to be diamagnetic
(c) N_2^{2+} and N_2^- have the same bond order
(d) He_2^+ has the same energy as two isolated He atoms

20. Which of the following is/are electron deficient compounds?
(a) $NaBH_4$ (b) B_2H_6 (c) $AlCl_3$ (d) C_3^{4-}

21. Select the incorrect statements about $[XeF_5]^-$
(a) Xe is sp^3d hybridised
(b) Xe is sp^3d^3 hybridised
(c) It has pentagonal sp^3d^3 structure
(d) It has two lone pairs at the axial position

22. Consider the following compounds
I. $B_3O_3^{3-}$
II. $B_3N_3H_6$
III. $C_5H_5^{\ominus}$
Planar and aromatic character is in
(a) all (b) I and II only
(c) II and III only (d) I and III only

23. The colour of the X_2 molecules of group 17 elements changes gradually from yellow to violet down the group. This is due to **[JEE Advanced 2017]**
(a) the physical state of X_2 at room temperature changes from gas to solid down the group
(b) decreases in HOMO-LUMO gap down the group
(c) decrease in $\pi^* - \sigma^*$ gap down the group
(d) decrease in ionisation energy down the group

24. Which is/are the correct increasing order of the property indicated?
(a) BaO < SrO< CaO < MgO < BeO (lattice energy)
(b) LiF < LiCl < LiBr < LiI (melting point)
(c) $AlF_3 < AlCl_3 < AlBr_3 < AlI_3$ (covalent nature)
(d) NaF< MgO < AlN < SiC (lattice energy)

25. Correct order of thermal stability is/are
(a) $Li_3N > Na_3N > K_3N$
(b) $BeCl_2 > MgCl_2 > CaCl_2$
(c) $K_2CO_3 > Na_2CO_3 > Li_2CO_3$
(d) $BeCO_3 > MgCO_3 < CaCO_3$

Numerical Value Questions

All these questions have a Numerical value as their answer, solve the questions and write your answer.

1. The C—C single-bond distance is 1.54 Å. What is the distance between the terminal carbons in propane? Assume that the four bonds of any carbon atom are pointed towards the corners of a regular tetrahedron (in Å).

2. The dipole moment of HBr is 2.60×10^{-30} C m and the interatomic spacing is 1.41 Å. What is the per cent ionic character of HBr (in %) ?

3. Number of nodal planes present in $p\pi$-$p\pi$ anti-bonding orbital.

4. At 300 K and 1.00 atm, the density of gaseous HF is 3.17 g/L. Number of HF molecule associated will be ....

5. A slightly polar molecule *AB* has dipole moment of 0.24 D. If bond-length is 1 Å, ionic character is ......%

6. In a very ideal imaginary condition, a sample of ice was taken, and its osmotic pressure was found to be 0.274 atm at 300 K (density = 1 g/mL). Thus, number of water units attached to one water unit is ....

7. In O_3, central oxygen atom is hypervalent. It shares .... electron pairs.

8. Total number of orbitals involved in the formation of hybrid orbitals in ClF_2^- is ....

9. The maximum number of hydrogen bonds that a molecule of water can have is ....

10. AX_4 forms square planar type structure. Distance between *A* and *X* atoms is 4 units then distance between two *X* atoms in *trans* position is ....

11. Chlorine reacts with hot and concentrated NaOH and produces compounds (*X*) and (*Y*). Compound (*X*) gives white precipitate with silver nitrate solution. The average bond order between Cl and O atoms in (*Y*) is .... **[JEE Main 2020, Jan.]**

12. The standard heat of formation ($\Delta_f H^0_{298}$) of ethane (in kJ/mol), if the heat of combustion of ethane, hydrogen and graphite are –1560,–393.5 and –286 kJ/ mol, respectively is .... **[JEE Main 2020, Jan.]**

Comprehension Based Questions

In these questions, a passage has been given followed by questions based on it. You have to answer the questions based on the passage given.

***Passage* 1** Boron-containing compounds often have a boron atom with only three bonds (and no lone pairs) two structure have been assigned to BF_3

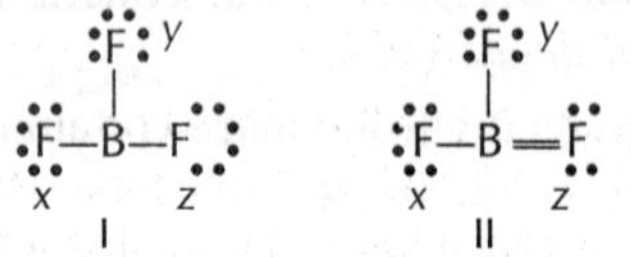

I II

Answer the following questions.

1. Select the correct statements.
   (a) Octet of F is complete in I and II but octet of B is incomplete in I but complete in II
   (b) Octets of F and B are complete in I and II
   (c) Octets of F and B are incomplete in I and II
   (d) Octet of F is complete in I and II but octet of B is complete in I but incomplete in II

2. Formal charge on F atoms designated by x, y and z are

	I			II		
	x	y	z	x	y	z
(a)	−1	−1	−1	0	0	+1
(b)	0	0	0	0	0	1
(c)	0	0	0	−1	+1	−1
(d)	0	0	0	0	0	0

3. Which structure is preferred?
   (a) I (b) II
   (c) Both equally (d) None of these

***Passage* 2** *Consider the following molecules and answer the questions given.*

I. H_2O; II. CO_2; III. NH_3
IV. CCl_4; V. ClF

1. In which compound are the bonds most polar?
   (a) H_2O (b) CO_2 (c) CCl_4 (d) ClF

2. Which compounds are not polar?
   (a) H_2O, CO_2 (b) CO_2, NH_3
   (c) H_2O, CCl_4 (d) CO_2, CCl_4

3. Which atoms in H_2O and ClF are negatively charged?
   (a) O in H_2O and Cl in ClF
   (b) H in H_2O and F in ClF
   (c) O in H_2O and F in ClF
   (d) None of the above is correct

***Passage* 3** The platinum-chlorine distance has been found to be 2.32 Å in several crystalline compounds. This value applies to both of the compounds shown in the figure,

(A) (B)

Based on the above structures, answer the following questions.

1. Cl—Cl distance in structure (*A*) is
   (a) 2.32 Å (b) 4.64 Å
   (c) 1.16 Å (d) 9.28 Å

2. Cl—Cl distance in structure (*B*) is
   (a) 2.32 Å (b) 1.52 Å
   (c) 2.15 Å (d) 3.28 Å

3. *A* is
   (a) *cis*-isomer
   (b) *trans*-isomer
   (c) chiral isomer
   (d) None of the above

***Passage* 4** By the following method you can predict the geometrical shape of species with only one central atom, without first drawing the Lewis structure

1. Total number of electron pairs = (number of valence electrons ± electrons (for ionic charge)/2
2. Number of bond electron pairs = number of atoms −1
3. Number of electron pairs around central atom = total number of electron pairs − 3 [number terminal atoms (except H)]
4. Number lone pair = (number of central electron pairs − number bond pairs)

Read the above method and answer the following questions.

1. If *A* is the central element of the molecule containing *A* and *X* element and *E* the number of electron pairs round it then VSEPR notation AX_3E will be for the molecules
   (a) PCl_5, ICl_4^-
   (b) NH_3, H_2O
   (c) NH_3, ClO_3^-
   (d) ICl_4^-, ClO_3^-

2. VSEPR notation of PCl_5, H_2O and ICl_4^- are

	PCl_5	H_2O	ICl_4^-
(a)	AX_5	AX_2E_2	AX_4E_2
(b)	AX_5	AX_2E	AX_4E
(c)	AX_5	AX_2	AX_4E
(d)	AX_5	AX_2E_2	AX_4E

3. Square planar structure is predicted for
(a) ICl_4^-, ClO_3^- (b) PCl_4^+, PCl_6^-
(c) ICl_4^-, PCl_4^+ (d) $ICl_4^-, [Ni(CN)_4^{2-}]$

Passage 5 *Read the following short write-up and answer the questions at the end of it.*

In certain polar solvents PCl_5 undergoes an ionisation reaction in which Cl^- ion leaves one PCl_5 molecule and attaches itself to another.

$$2PCl_5 \rightleftharpoons PCl_4^+ + PCl_6^-$$

1. Select the **incorrect** statement(s).
(a) Dissociation is a redox reaction
(b) Hybridisation changes from sp^3d to sp^3d^2 (PCl_6^-) and sp^3 (PCl_4^+)
(c) Structure changes from trigonal bipyramidal to tetrahedral (PCl_4^+) and octahedral (PCl_6^-)
(d) None of the above is incorrect

2. Number of lone pairs around phosphorus in PCl_5, PCl_4^+ and PCl_6^- are respectively
(a) 0, 1, 2 (b) 0, 0, 0
(c) 1, 2, 3 (d) 0, 2, 1

Passage 6 *Read the following short write-up and answer the questions at the end of it.*

"Each of the following compounds has a nitrogen-nitrogen bond"

(*A*) N_2, (*B*) N_2H_4 (*C*) N_2F_2

Molecules may be polar or non-polar, that is dependent on the electronegativity difference between two atoms. Their bond-lengths (between N-atoms) have been 1.45 Å, 1.10 Å and 1.22 Å but not in correct order.

1. Compounds have been matched with their bond-length (between N-atoms). Which is not the correct matching?
(a) *A* – 1.10 Å
(b) *B* – 1.45 Å
(c) *C* – 1.22 Å
(d) None of the above

2. Select the incorrect statement(s).
(a) N_2 is an inert gas
(b) N_2F_2 has sp^2-hybridised N-atom
(c) N_2H_4 is an inert solvent
(d) N_2H_4 is used as rocket fuel

Passage 7 *Read the following short-write up and answer the questions at the end of it.*

"Methyl isocyanate is used to make certain pesticides. In December 1984, water leaked into a tank containing this substance at a chemical plant, producing a toxic cloud that killed thousands of people in Bhopal.

1. Which is not the resonance structure of methyl isocyanate?
(a) $CH_3-\ddot{N}=C=\ddot{O}:$ (b) $CH_3-\overset{\ominus}{\ddot{N}}-C\equiv\overset{\oplus}{O}:$
(c) $CH_3-N\equiv\underset{\oplus}{C}-\ddot{O}:^{\ominus}$ (d) $CH_3-\overset{\oplus}{N}\equiv N-\ddot{O}:^{\ominus}$

2. Which of the atoms in CH_3NCO has maximum *s*-character?
(a) N
(b) O
(c) C(in CH_3)
(d) C (bonded to O and N)

3. Total number of lone pairs are
(a) 2 (b) 3 (c) 4 (d) 5

Passage 8 *Assume following structure of* N_2O *and answer the questions.*

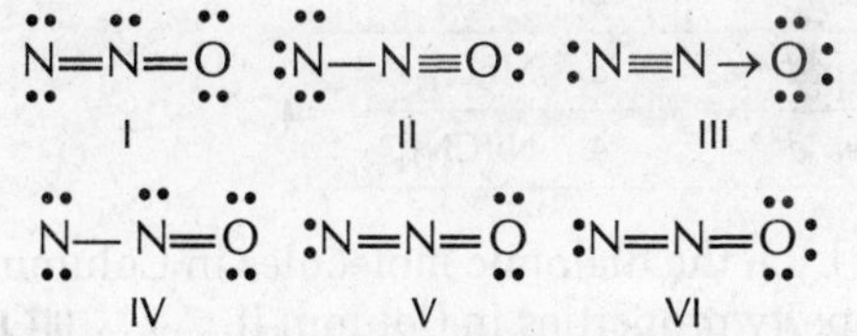

1. Which is the most favourable structure?
(a) I (b) III
(c) V (d) VI

2. Select the correct statement(s).
(a) Structure I is not acceptable as there are 10 electrons on N atom and 18 electrons total
(b) Structure IV is not acceptable as there are only three bonds
(c) Structure VI is not acceptable as there are 10 electrons on oxygen atom
(d) All the above are correct statements

Matrix-Match Type

Given below are Matching Type Questions, with two columns (each having some items) each . Each item of Column I has to be matched with the items of Column II.

1. Match the compounds (in Column I) with the structure (in Column II).

Column I	Column II
A. XeF_4	1. Distorted octahedral
B. XeF_6	2. Tetrahedral
C. XeO_3	3. Square planar
D. XeO_4	4. Pyramidal

2. Match the type of species (in Column I) with the compound (in Column II).

Column I	Column II
A. Ionic species	1. HCl
B. Non-polar covalent	2. $LiCH_3$
C. Polar covalent species having sigma bond only	3. KCH_3
	4. NO

3. Match Column I (hybrid bond orbitals) with Column II (species) and select the correct answer.

Column I	Column II
A. sp^3	1. ICl_4^-
B. dsp^2	2. $TeCl_4$
C. sp^3d	3. MnO_4^-
D. sp^3d^2	4. $Ni(CN)_4^{2-}$

4. Match each the diatomic molecules in Column I with its property/properties in Column II. **[IIT JEE 2009]**

Column I	Column II
A. B_2	1. Paramagnetic
B. N_2	2. Undergoes oxidation
C. O_2^-	3. Undergoes reduction
D. O_2	4. Bond order ≥ 2
	5. Mixing of '*s*' and '*p*' orbitals

5. Match the species (in Column I) with corresponding character(s) (in Column II).

Column I	Column II
A. $\overset{\oplus}{C}H_3$	1. Bond order 3
B. $\overset{\oplus}{C}H_5$	2. Paramagnetic
C. $NO^{\oplus}$	3. sp^2
D. O_2	4. Carbocation
E. N_2	5. Carbonium ion
	6. Octet rule violated

6. Match the species in Column I with the corresponding character(s) in Column II.

Column I	Column II
A. CO_2	1. Zero dipole moment
B. CH_4	2. Expansion of octet
C. $ClF_2^{\oplus}$	3. sp^3-hybridisation
D. PCl_5	4. sp^3d-hybridisation
E. $ClF_2^{\ominus}$	5. Linear

7. Match the species in Column I with their properties in Column II.

Column I	Column II
A. SF_6	1. π bonds are also present
B. O_3	2. σ bonds are only present
C. BeH_2	3. Hypervalent
D. CO	4. Hypovalent
	5. Linear

8. Match the species in Column I with their properties in Column II.

Column I	Column II
A. NH_3	1. Lewis acid
B. $\overset{\ominus}{N}H_2$	2. Lewis base
C. $\overset{\oplus}{N}H_4$	3. Distorted geometery
D. BH_4^-	4. sp^3 hybridised central atom
	5. has two types of H

Single Integer Answer Questions

Answer of these questions is a single digit lying between 0 to 9.

1. In a compound of Xe, F and O

Xe = 60.4% (131.3), F = 17.5% (19.0)

Thus, number of oxygen atom ....

2. Out of $CH_2Cl_2, CH_4, CCl_4, H_2O, CHCl_3$, *d*-dichlorobenzene, *o*-cresol, *p*-xylene, SCl_2, BF_3, IBr and CH_2O, non-zero value of dipole moment is of ....

3. Superoxide ion has .... electrons in antibonding molecular orbitals.

4. Difference of σ and π bonds in $C(CN)_4$ is ....

5. The number of Cl = O bonds in perchloric acid is ".........". **[JEE Main 2020, Sep.]**

6. Among B_2H_6, $B_3N_3H_6$, N_2O, N_2O_4, $H_2S_2O_3$ and $H_2S_2O_8$, the total number of molecules containing covalent bond between two atoms of the same kind is .... **[JEE Advanced 2019]**

7. The sum of the number of lone pairs of electrons on each central atom in the following species is

$[TeBr_6]^{2-}, [BrF_2]^{+}, SNF_3$ and $[XeF_3]^-$

(Atomic numbers : N = 7, F = 9, S = 16, Br = 35, Te = 52, Xe = 54) **[JEE Advanced 2017]**

8. How many maximum number of H atoms are in the same plane in B_2H_6?

9. How many of the following have incomplete duplet or octet on central atom?

$BeCl_2, BH_3, NH_4^+, H^+, H^-, \overset{\oplus}{C}H_3, \overset{\ominus}{C}H_3, CH_2$

10. How many of the following cases hybridisation state of underlined atom changes?

$$\bar{N}H_2 + \underline{S}O_3 \longrightarrow [NH_2SO_3]^-$$
$$\underline{C}H_3COOH \longrightarrow CH_4 + CO_2$$
$$2\underline{P}Cl_5 \longrightarrow \overset{\oplus}{P}Cl_4 + PCl_6^{\ominus}$$
$$CH_3\underline{C}H_2OH \longrightarrow CH_2{=}CH_2 + H_2O$$
$$\underline{Al}H_3 + H^- \longrightarrow AlH_4^-$$
$$2O{=}\underline{O} \rightarrow O \longrightarrow 3O_2$$
$$(CH_3)_3\underline{C}Cl \longrightarrow (CH_3)_3\overset{\oplus}{C} + Cl^-$$

11. Based on VSEPR theory, the number of 90° F—Br—F angles in BrF_5 is .... **[IIT JEE 2010]**

12. The number of species below that have two lone pairs of electrons in their central atom is .... (Round off to the nearest integer) **[JEE Main 2021, March]**

$SF_4, BF_4^-, ClF_3, AsF_3, PCl_5, BrF_5, XeF_4, SF_6$

13. *AX* is a covalent diatomic molecule where *A* and *X* are second row elements of periodic table. Based on molecular orbital theory, the bond order of *AX* is 2.5. The total number of electrons in *AX* is .... **[JEE Main 2021, March]**

Answers

Objective Questions Type I [Only one correct option]

1. (a)	2. (b)	3. (c)	4. (a)	5. (b)	6. (b)	7. (d)	8. (b)	9. (c)	10. (a)
11. (c)	12. (a)	13. (b)	14. (c)	15. (d)	16. (b)	17. (b)	18. (d)	19. (b)	20. (c)
21. (b)	22. (c)	23. (b)	24. (b)	25. (a)	26. (c)	27. (d)	28. (d)	29. (a)	30. (d)
31. (c)	32. (a)	33. (b)	34. (d)	35. (d)	36. (a)	37. (b)	38. (b)	39. (a)	40. (a)
41. (c)	42. (b)	43. (d)	44. (a)	45. (c)	46. (c)	47. (b)	48. (a)	49. (a)	50. (b)
51. (b)	52. (c)	53. (b)	54. (a)	55. (b)	56. (d)	57. (c)	58. (c)	59. (c)	60. (a)
61. (b)	62. (a)	63. (d)	64. (d)	65. (c)	66. (d)	67. (a)	68. (a)	69. (d)	70. (a)
71. (c)	72. (d)	73. (b)	74. (d)	75. (a)	76. (d)	77. (d)	78. (c)	79. (b)	80. (d)
81. (a)	82. (d)	83. (b)	84. (d)	85. (a)	86. (b)	87. (d)	88. (d)	89. (a)	90. (a)
91. (a)	92. (c)	93. (b)	94. (a)	95. (a)	96. (b)	97. (c)	98. (a)	99. (d)	100. (d)
101. (c)	102. (c)	103. (d)	104. (a)	105. (b)	106. (d)	107. (b)	108. (c)	109. (c)	110. (c)
111. (b)	112. (a)	113. (b)	114. (c)	115. (d)	116. (c)	117. (d)	118. (d)	119. (d)	120. (a)
121. (a)	122. (c)	123. (c)	124. (b)	125. (a)	126. (a)	127. (d)	128. (a)	129. (b)	130. (d)
131. (a)	132. (d)	133. (a)	134. (c)	135. (b)	136. (b)	137. (a)	138. (d)	139. (d)	140. (a)
141. (a)	142. (a)	143. (b)	144. (d)	145. (a)	146. (d)	147. (c)	148. (d)	149. (c)	150. (d)
151. (a)	152. (c)	153. (d)	154. (c)	155. (b)	156. (d)	157. (b)	158. (b)	159. (c)	160. (c)

Objective Questions Type II [One or more than one correct option(s)]

1. (a, c)	**2.** (b)	**3.** (a, b)	**4.** (b, c, d)	**5.** (a, d)
6. (b)	**7.** (c)	**8.** (a, c)	**9.** (b, c, d)	**10.** (a)
11. (a, b, c, d)	**12.** (b)	**13.** (a, b, c, d)	**14.** (a)	**15.** (a, b)
16. (a)	**17.** (a, c, d)	**18.** (b, c)	**19.** (a, c)	**20.** (b, c)
21. (b, c, d)	**22.** (a)	**23.** (b, c)	**24.** (a, c, d)	**25.** (a, b, c, d)

Numerical Value Questions

1. 2.52 **2.** 11.5 **3.** 2 **4.** 4 **5.** 5 **6.** 4 **7.** 3 **8.** 5 **9.** 4 **10.** 8 **11.** 1.67 **12.** −193

Comprehension Based Questions

Passage 1 – **1.** (a) **2.** (b) **3.** (a)

Passage 2 – **1.** (a) **2.** (d) **3.** (c)

Passage 3 – **1.** (b) **2.** (d) **3.** (b) **4.** (a)

Passage 4 – **1.** (c) **2.** (a) **3.** (b)

Passage 5 – **1.** (d) **2.** (b)

Passage 6 – **1.** (d) **2.** (c)

Passage 7 – **1.** (c) **2.** (d) **3.** (b)

Passage 8 – **1.** (b) **2.** (d)

Matrix-Match Type

1. A → (3); B → (1); C → (4); D → (2)

2. A → (3); B → (2); C → (1)

3. A → (3); B → (4); C → (2); D → (1)

4. A → (1,2,3,5); B → (2,3,4,5); C → (1,2,3,5); D → (1,3,4,5)

5. A → (3, 4); B → (5, 6); C—(1); D—(2, 3); E → (1)

6. A → (1, 5); B → (1, 3); C → (3); D → (2, 4); E—(3, 5)

7. A → (2,3); B → (1,5); C → (2,4,5); D → (1,2,5)

8. A → (2,3,4); B → (2,3,4); C → (3,5); D—(4,5)

Single Integer Answer Questions

1. (3) **2.** (7) **3.** (7) **4.** (0) **5.** (3) **6.** (4) **7.** (6) **8.** (4) **9.** (5) **10.** (5)
11. (0) **12.** (2) **13.** (15)

Solutions

Objective Questions Type I [Only one correct option]

1. (*a*) $X + e^- \longrightarrow X^-$ $\quad \Delta H = -E$

where E is electron affinity.

X^- is formed when size is small and X has high electron affinity.

2. (*b*) When a chemical bond is formed, potential energy decreases.

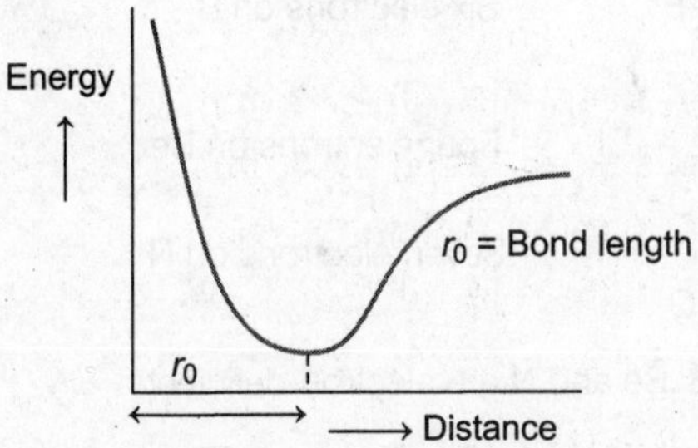

4. (*a*)

$$A \longrightarrow A^+ + e^-$$
$$B + e^- \longrightarrow B^-$$
$$A^+ + B^- \longrightarrow (A^+B^-)$$

A^+ is formed when ionisation energy of A is low.

B^- is formed when electron affinity of B is high.

5. (*b*) $I^- + I_2 \longrightarrow I_3^-$

I^- is electron-pair donor thus is a Lewis-base.

I_2 is electron-pair acceptor thus it is a Lewis-acid [$I^- \rightarrow I_2$]

6. (*b*)

$$NH_4Cl \rightleftharpoons NH_4^+ + Cl^-$$
$$AlF_3 \rightleftharpoons Al^{3+} + 3F^-$$
$$TlF_3 \rightleftharpoons Tl^{3+} + 3F^-$$
$$CaO \rightleftharpoons Ca^{2+} + O_2^-$$

In (a) NH_4Cl is ionic

(b) all are covalent

(c) AlF_3 and TlF_3 are ionic

(d) CaO is ionic

7. (*d*) Force of attraction between cation and anion is

$$F = \frac{kz_1z_2e^2}{r^2}$$

where, k is dielectric constant of the medium.

z_1 and z_2 are charges on cation and anion, and r the internuclear distance.

Size of $Cl^- > O^{2-}$

$K^+ > Ca^{2+}$

Charge on

$Ca^{2+} > K^+$

$O^{2-} > Cl^-$

8. (*b*) IE of Cl < IE of F thus Cl^+ is formed.

EA of Cl > EA of F. It is due to screening effect. F^- is predominantly formed due to greater electronegativity of F.

Thus, Cl^+ F^-

9. (*c*)

Element	Valence electron	Probable group
A	1	Group I (alkali metal)
B	3	Group 13 (boron family)
C	5	Group 15 (nitrogen family)

A can lose electron easily, thus is involved in ionic bond.

B with three valence electrons (as Al) can form ionic compound with element of the type *C* with five electrons (as N) B and B together will not form ionic compound.

10. (*a*) $\quad Mg \longrightarrow Mg^{2+} + 2e^-$

Mg^{2+} is formed by low (IE) of Mg

$$O + 2e^- \longrightarrow O^{2-}$$

O^{2-} is formed by high (EA) of O

11. (*c*) H_2O is polar in nature.

Like dissolves like.

KCl being ionic compound is soluble in polar solvent as H_2O.

12. (*a*) Smaller size of cation

Larger the size of anion

Larger the charge on cation and anion, larger the polarising power and thus larger the covalent nature and such compounds have larger lattice energy.

(a) $K^+ > Mg^{2+}$ size

+1 +2 charge

$Cl^- > O^{2-}$ size

−1 < 2− charge

Thus, MgO is less ionic than KCl thus lattice enrgy of MgO is larger than that of KCl.

Thus, given order is incorrect.

(b) AlN > MgO correct

(c) CaO > BaO correct

(d) $MgCO_3 > CaCO_3$ correct

13. (*b*) Na^+ is identical

Cl^- SO_4^{2-} PO_4^{3-}

$NaCl > Na_2SO_4 > Na_3PO_4$ polar nature

16. (*b*) (a) $NaBr \rightleftharpoons Na^+ + Br^-$ only ionic

(b) $Ba(CN)_2 \rightleftharpoons Ba^{2+} + 2CN^-$

Ba^{2+} and CN^- are joined by ionic bond.

CN^- has covalent bond $^-C\equiv N$

(c) PCl_5 only covalent

(d) CH_3CH_2OH only covalent.

17. (*b*) Compounds which are insoluble in water have covalent bonds. Due to their low boiling points, there are highly volatile.

18. (*d*) Covalency is in covalent compound and is equal to number of valence shell electron in *s*- and *p*- orbitals.

Group	Examples	Valence electrons		Maximum covalency
		s	p	
13	B	2	1	3
14	Si	2	2	4
15	P	2	3	5
16	S	2	4	6
17	Cl	2	5	7

19. (*b*)

Only σ single bond I	One σ, one π double bond II	One σ, two π triple bond III

Bond length I > II > III Thus, (a) is correct.

Bond energy I < II < III Thus, (c) is correct.

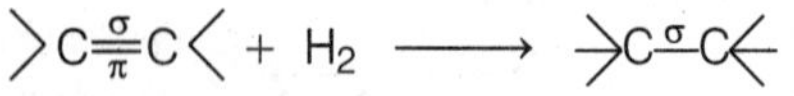

π-bond reacts than π-bond is weaker than σ-bond.

Thus, (b) is incorrect.

H_2O molecules are associated by H-bonding and thus making it liquid

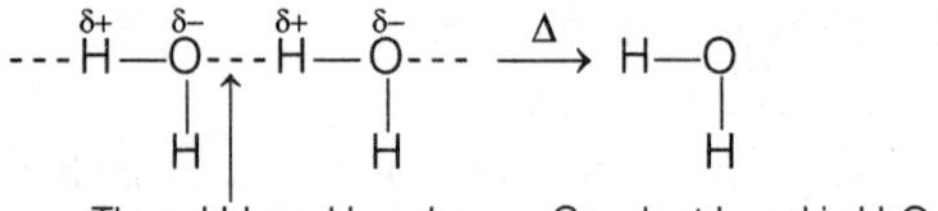

Thus, (d) is correct.

20. (*c*)

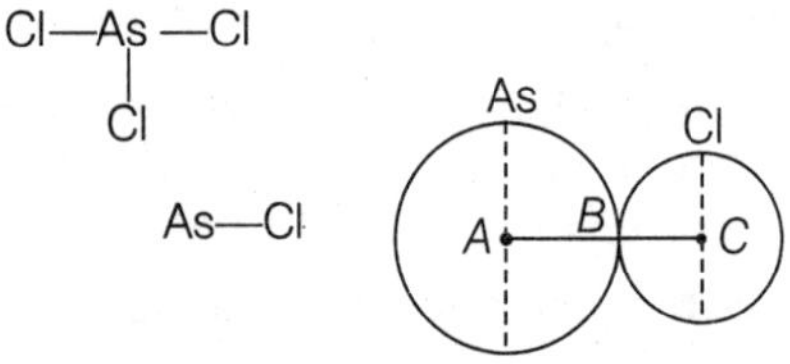

$$AB + BC = AC$$
$$r_{As} + r_{Cl} = AC = 2.20$$
$$r_{As} + 0.99 = 2.20$$
$$r_{As} = 2.20 - 0.99 = 1.21\ \text{Å}$$

21. (*b*)

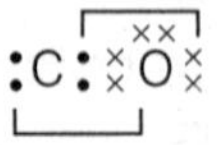

Oxygen can donate one electron pair to carbon, C⇐O

22. (*c*) The structure of I_3^- ion is

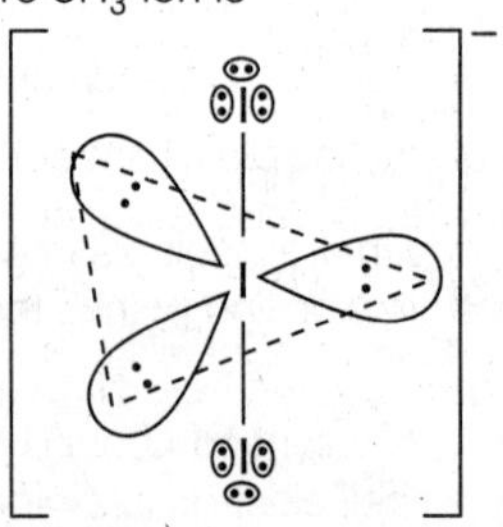

Hence, 9 is the correct answer.

23. (*b*) Three bond pairs are inclined at 120° with one each other, and the other two bond pairs are at 90° with first three, thus structure is : Trigonal bipyramidal (as in PCl_5)

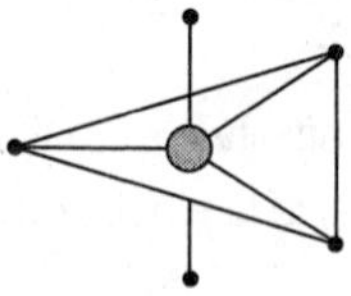

24. (*b*)

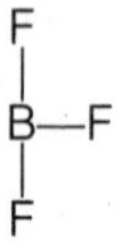

Six electrons on B

Cl — Be — Cl   Four electrons on Be

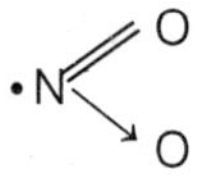

Seven electrons on N

Thus, B, Be and N are electron-deficients.

25. (*a*)

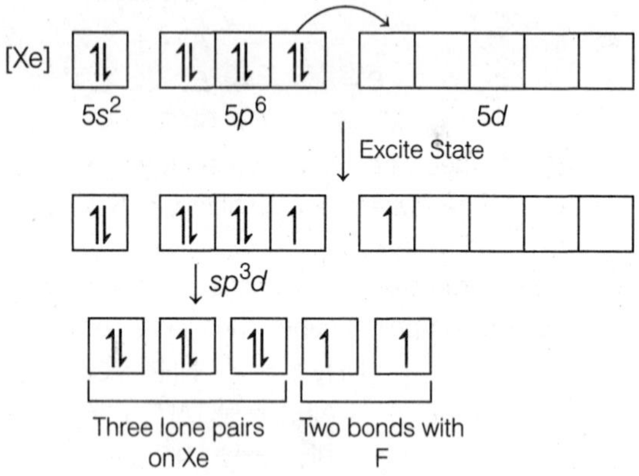

	lone pair	Bond pair
(a) XeF_2	3	2
(b) XeF_4	2	4
(c) H_3O^+	1	3
(d) XeF_6	1	6

26. (*c*)

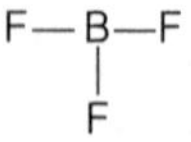

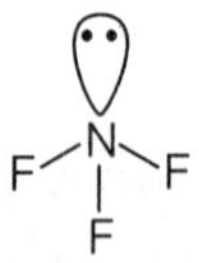

$\mu = 0$
Resultant dipole moment is zero, thus non-polar

$\mu > 0$
Due to lone pair on N, NF_3 is polar

27. (*d*) (a)

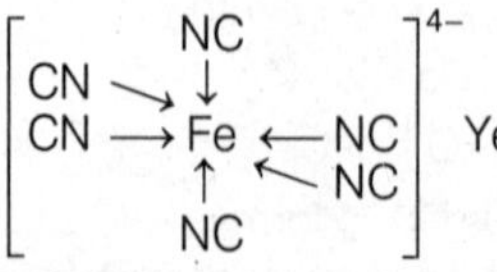

Yes

(b) $[H_3N \rightarrow BH_3]$ Yes

(c) 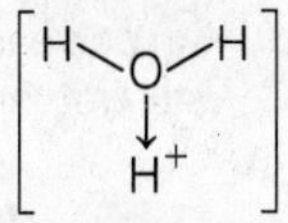 Yes

(d) 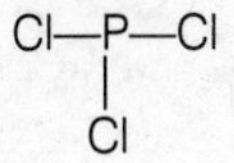 No

28. (*d*) BF_3 and NH_3 are joined by coordinate bond in which NH_3 is a Lewis base and BF_3 is a Lewis acid. They have therefore independent existence and thus separated.

29. (*a*) I. $K_4[Fe(CN)_6] \longrightarrow 4K^+ + [Fe(CN)_6]^{4-}$ (ionic bond)

$[Fe(CN)_6]^{4-}$ has coordinate bonds with Fe^{2+} and CN^-

CN^- has covalent bonding $N \equiv C^{\ominus}$

II. $NH_4Cl \longrightarrow NH_4^+ + Cl^-$ (ionic bond)

NH_4^+ has covalent and coordinate bond

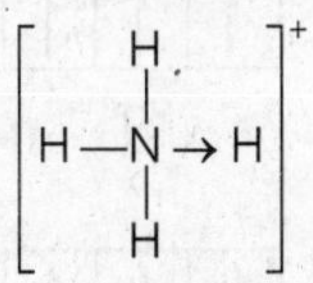

III. $H_2SO_4 \rightleftharpoons 2H^+ + SO_4^{2-}$ (ionic bond)

SO_4^{2-} has covalent and coordinate bond.

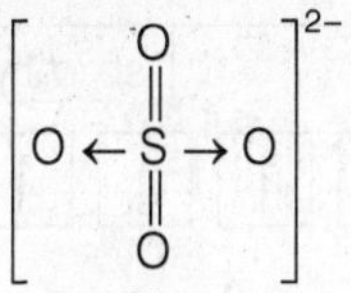

or

Thus, 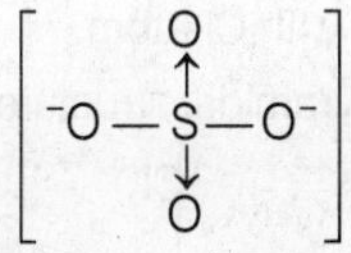

30. (*d*)

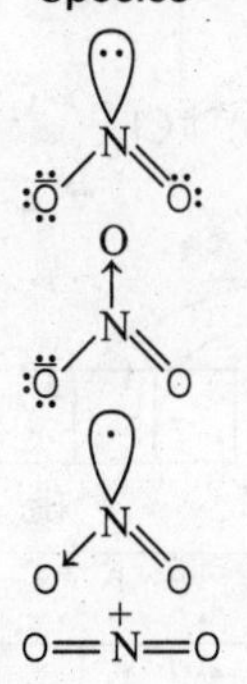

Species	Hybridisation
(1)	sp^2
(2)	sp^2
(3)	sp^2
$O=\overset{+}{N}=O$	sp

32. (*a*) AX_3 has zero dipole moment. Thus, it has no lone pair. Thus, *A* is sp^2-hybridised. Hence

Bond angle = 120°

33. (*b*) I_3^- is formed when I^- (Lewis base) donated one lone pair to I_0 (Lewis acid)

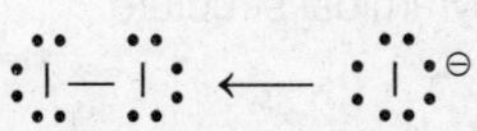

Thus, lone pair on central atom = Three

and bond pair = Two

Thus, $X = 2$ and $Y = 3$

34. (*d*) 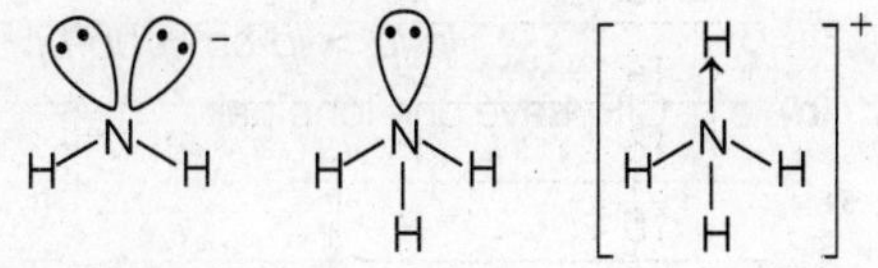

Repulsion $lp-lp$, $lp-bp$, $bp-bp$ > $lp-bp$, $bp-bp$ > $bp-bp$

Due to repulsion, bond angle decreases

Bond angle $NH_2^- < NH_3 < NH_4^+$

35. (*d*)

I. 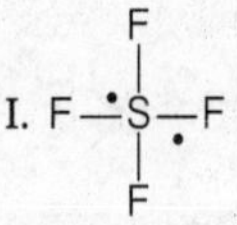

Valence electrons on S = 6

Electrons used in bonding = 4

Non-bonding electrons = 2

II. 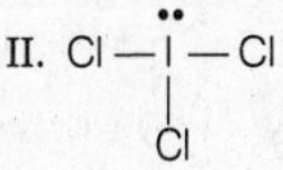

Valence electrons on I = 7

Electrons used in bonding = 3

Non-bonding electrons = 4

III. 

Valence electrons on S = 6

Electrons used in bonding = 4

Non-bonding electrons = 2

36. (*a*)

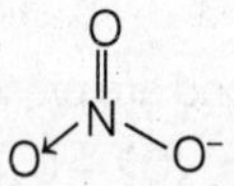

No lone pair on N-atom
sp^2-hybridised N
thus, triangular planar

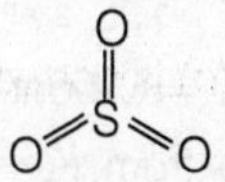

Delocalised π-bonds
and there σ-bonds
thus, triangular planar

37. (*b*) 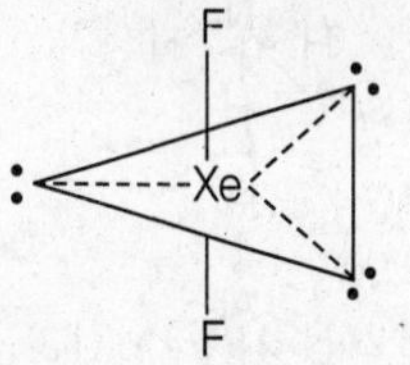

38. (*b*) Minimum repulsion between electrons.

39. (*a*) It is a case of sp^3d^2 or d^2sp^3 hybridisation with octahedral geometry.

40. (*a*) The correct descending order of bonds according to their average bond energies is as follows :

C—F > C—Cl > C—Br > C—I

Bond length is inversely proportional to bond energy.

So, bond length decreases as bond energy increases.

41. (*c*) The enthalpy of solution of an ionic solid is numericlly equal to the sum of its hydration and lattice energies,

i.e. $\Delta H^\circ_{sol} = \Delta H^\circ_{hydration} + \Delta H^\circ_{lattice}$

∴ 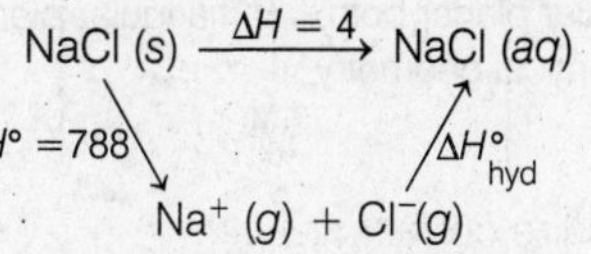

$$\Delta_{sol}H^\circ = \Delta_{lattice}H^\circ + \Delta_{hyd}H^\circ$$

$$4 = 788 + \Delta_{hyd}H°$$
$$\Delta H_{hyd}H° = -784 \text{ kJ/mol}$$

42. (*b*) Repulsion is in order

lp-lp > *lp-bp* > *bp-bp*

43. (*d*) e.g. ClF_5 have one lone pair.

46. (*c*) $AlF_3 + F^- \longrightarrow$

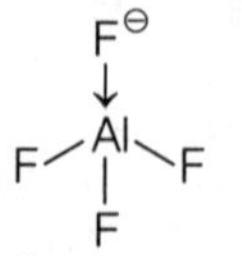

(sp^3 hybridised Al due to four σ-bonds)

47. (*b*).

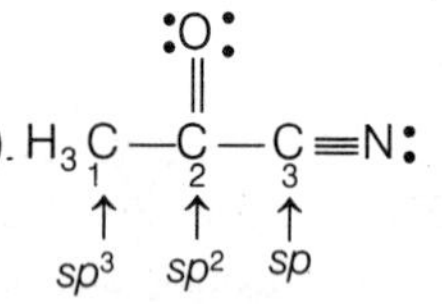

48. (*a*)

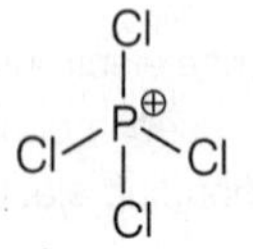

sp^3-hybridised P

49. (*a*)

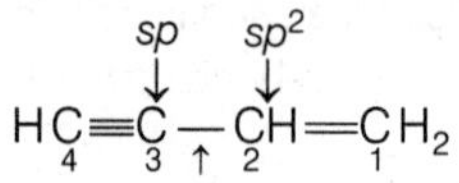

When (C═C) bond and (C≡C) bond are present, numbering is done from (C═C) side. Thus, ($C_2 \overset{\sigma}{—} C_3$) is formed by ($sp^2$-$sp$) overlapping.

50. (*b*)

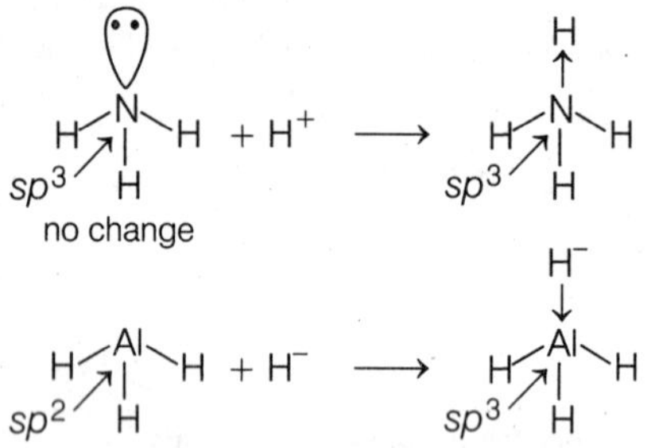

Thus, hybridisation of Al is affected when AlH_3 changes to AlH_4^-, hybridisation of Al changes from sp^2 to sp^3.

51. (*b*)

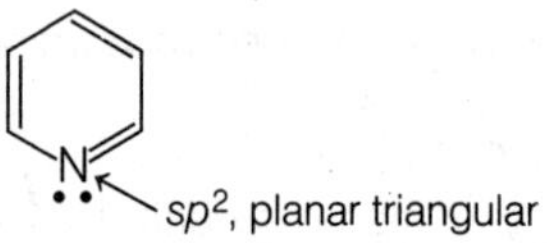

52. (*c*)

Triangular planar both have identical geometry — Triangular planar

53. (*b*) $S_2O_8^{2-}$ is

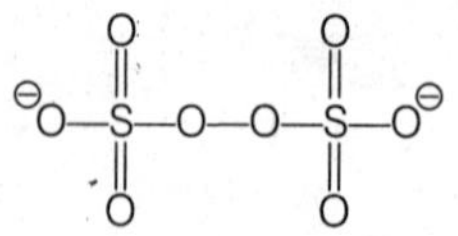

Total number of S—O or S═O bond = 8

Rhombic sulphur is

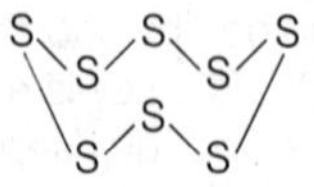

Total number of S—S bond = 8

Thus, the correct answer is (b).

54. (*a*) PCl_5

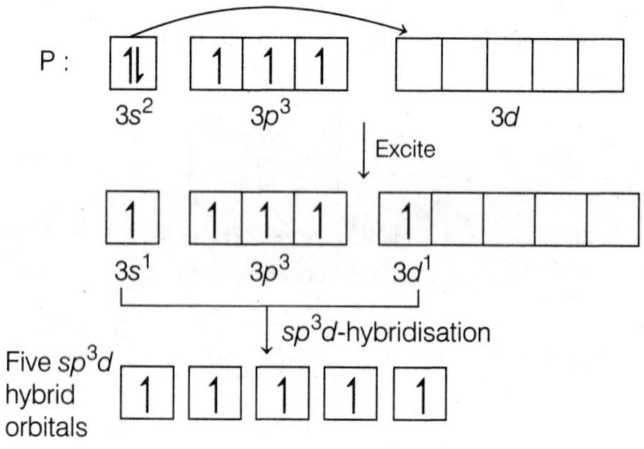

Forming five bonds with Cl-atom

Thus, triangular bipyramidal structure.

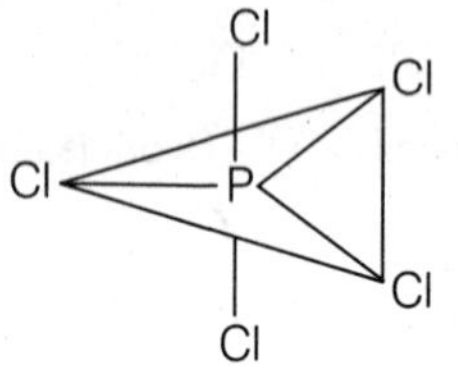

IF_5

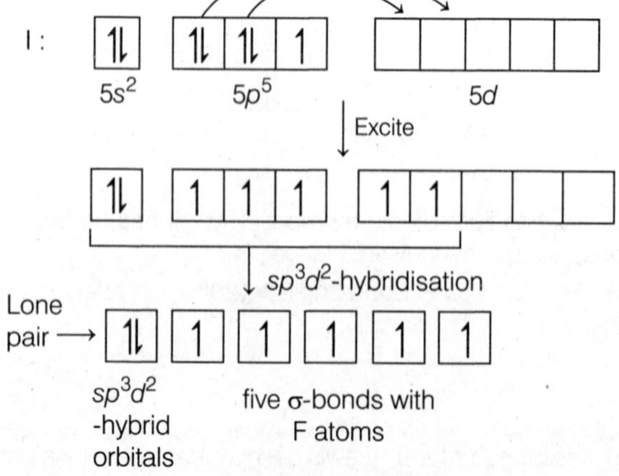

Thus, square pyramidal structure.

56. (*a*)

Species	MO energy order	Bond order (BO)	*n*, no. of unpaired e^-	Magnetic character
$C_2^{2-}(14e^-)$	$[8\bar{e}]\pi_{2p_x^2} = \pi_{2p_y^2}\sigma_{2p_z^2}$	$\frac{6-0}{2}=3$	0	Diamagnetic
$O_2(16e^-)$	$[8\bar{e}]\sigma_{2p_z^2}\pi_{2p_x^2} = \pi_{2p_y^2}\overset{*}{\pi}_{2p_x^1} = \overset{*}{\pi}_{2p_y^1}$	$\frac{6-2}{2}=2$	2	Paramagnetic
$O_2^{2-}(18e^-)$	$[8\bar{e}]\sigma_{2p_z^2}\pi_{2p_x^2} = \pi_{2p_y^2}\overset{*}{\pi}_{2p_x^2} = \overset{*}{\pi}_{2p_y^2}$	$\frac{6-4}{2}=1$	0	Diamagnetic
$N_2^{2-}(16e^-)$	$[8\bar{e}]\pi_{2p_x^2} = \pi_{2p_y^2}\sigma_{2p_z^2}\overset{*}{\pi}_{2p_x^1} = \overset{*}{\pi}_{2p_y^1}$	$\frac{6-2}{2}=2$	2	Paramagnetic

Bond length $\propto \frac{1}{\text{BO (Bond order)}}$

So order of bond length $\underset{(BO=3)}{C_2^{2-}} < \underset{(BO=2)}{O_2} = N_2^{2-} < \underset{(BO=1)}{O_2^{2-}}$

The diamagnetic species with shortest bond length is C_2^{2-} (option-a).

57. (*c*)

Species	Electrons	Bond order	Unpaired electron	
O—F	17	1.5	1	Paramagnetic
F_2	18	1.0	0	Diamagnetic

There is one unpaired electron in (O—F), hence paramagnetic, thus (a) is correct.

Bond order of O—F > F—F

Thus, bond energy of O—F > F—F

Thus, (b) is correct.

58. (*c*) Atomisation of $Br_2(l)$

$$Br_2(l) \longrightarrow 2Br(g);\quad \Delta H = x \text{ kJ mol}^{-1}$$

Which can be considered as sum of following :

$$Br_2(l) \longrightarrow Br_2(g);\ \Delta H = \text{a positive value} \quad ...(i)$$

(endothermic process)

$$Br_2(g) \longrightarrow 2Br(g);\ \Delta H$$

(bond enthalpy of $Br_2) = y$ ..(ii)

$\therefore x = y + $ (positive value), and $x > y$.

59. (*c*) The hybridisation for a central atom in a species can be calculated using formula

$$H = \frac{1}{2}(V + M - C + A)$$

where, H = no. of hybridised orbitals used by central atoms.

V = no. of valence electrons of the central atom.

M = no. of mono-valent atoms (bonded).

C = no. of cationic (positive) charge.

A = No. of anionic (negative) charge.

The hybridisation of given species are as follows :

For $[ICl_2]^-$ and $[BrF_2]^-$

$$H = \frac{1}{2}(7 + 2 - 0 + 1) = 5\,(sp^3d)$$

For $[ICl_4]^-$, $$H = \frac{1}{2}(7 + 4 - 0 + 1) = 6\,(sp^3d^2)$$

For $[IF_6]^-$, $$H = \frac{1}{2}(7 + 6 - 0 + 1) = 7\,(sp^3d^3)$$

60. (*a*) CN^- has 14 electrons (6 from C, 7 from N and 1 for negative charge).

Its MO configuration must be similar to

$$N_2 : \sigma 1s^2\ \sigma^* 1s^2\ \sigma 2s^2\ \sigma^* 2s^2\ \pi 2p_x^2\ \pi 2p_y^2\ \sigma 2p_z^2$$

$$\therefore \text{ Bond order} = \frac{10-4}{2} = 3$$

As there is no unpaired electron in CN^-, thus it is diamagnetic.

61. (*b*) Greater the bond order, greater the bond energy.

		Bond order
(a)	O_2^-	1.5
(b)	O_2^+	2.5
(c)	O_2	2.0
(d)	O_2^{2-}	1.0

62. (*a*) M.O. theory explains filling of electrons in bonding and antibonding M.O. If there are unpaired electrons in these orbitals then paramagnetic.

63. (*d*)

		Bond order	
I.	O_2^{2-}	1	
	O_2	2	Stronger
II.	N_2	3	Stronger
	N_2^+	2.5	
III.	NO^+	3	Stronger
	NO^-	2	

Larger the bond order, greater the bond energy.

64. (*d*)

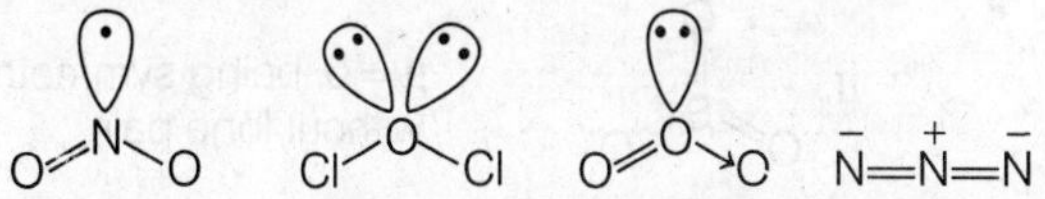

Bent shape Bent shape Bent shape Linear

65. (*c*) When the distance of hydrogen nucleus is decreasing at a particular point, energy is minimum. At this point, potential energy will be least. It is the point when bond formation takes place.

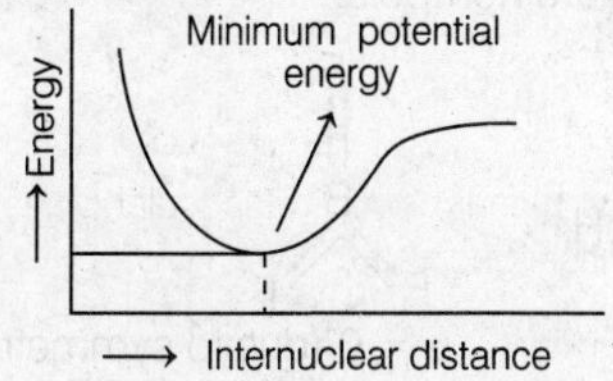

Hence, option (c) is correct.

66. (*d*) Li-Mg, B-Si, Be-Al show diagonal relationship but Li and Na do not show diagonal relationship as both belongs to same group and not placed diagonally.

67. (*a*) I.E. $E \propto$ fully-filled / half-filled configuration

Mg and P have fully-filled and half-filled configuration respectively and I.E. increases along the period.

68. (*a*) $B_2(10)$

$\sigma 1s^2\ \sigma^* 1s^2\ \sigma 2s^2\ \sigma^* 2s^2\ \pi 2p_y^2$

$$N_B = 6$$
$$N_A = 4$$
$$BO = \frac{6-4}{2} = 1$$

It is diamagnetic because all electrons are paired.

69. (*d*) 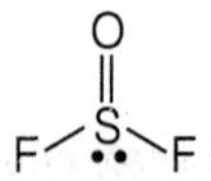

70. (*a*) $[Fe(CN)_6]^{4-}$ d^2sp^3

$[Ni(CN)_4]^{2-}$ dsp^2

$[Pt(en)_2]^{2+}$ dsp^2

Thus, (a) is correct.

(b) $[Fe(H_2O)_6]^{3+}$ sp^3d^2

$[CoF_6]^{3-}$ sp^3d^2

$[Cr(CN)_6]^{3-}$ d^2sp^3

Thus, (b) is not correct.

71. (*c*) 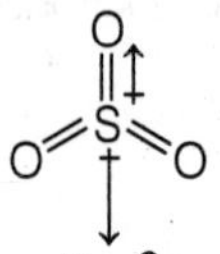

$\mu = 0$

There is no lone pair on SO_3 and also molecule is symmetrical, hence dipole moment is zero.

72. (*d*) I. 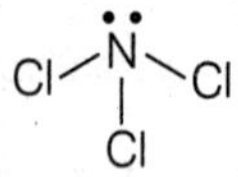 lone pair on N-atoms makes it polar, $\mu > 0$

II. 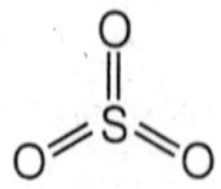 $\mu = 0$, being symmetrical and without lone pair

III. 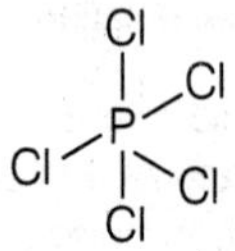 $\mu = 0$, without lone pair

Thus, II and III are non-polar.

74. (*d*) 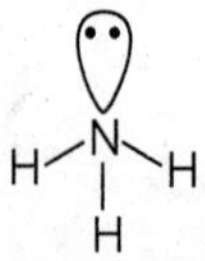 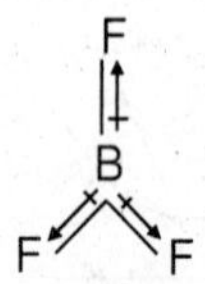

$\mu > 0$ $\mu = 0$ (due to symmetry)

(a) incorrect

(b) $\mu_{NH_3} > \mu_{BF_3}$ thus incorrect.

(c) Due to lone pair of N, NH_3 has pyramidal geometry thus incorrect.

(d) correct

75. (*a*) $\mu = e \times l$

$$e = \frac{\mu}{l} = \frac{1.2\ D}{1.0\ Å} = \frac{1.2 \times 10^{-18}\ \text{esu cm}}{1.0 \times 10^{-8}\ \text{cm}}$$
$$= 1.2 \times 10^{-10}\ \text{esu}$$

Charge on electron = 4.8×10^{-10} esu.

Thus, fraction of charge = $\frac{1.2 \times 10^{-10}}{4.8 \times 10^{-10}} = 0.25$

76. (*d*) $H—C \equiv N:$ has 1 lone pair, 2σ-bonds and two π-bonds

$H—\overset{+}{N} \equiv \overset{-}{C}:$ has 1 lone-pair 2σ-bonds and two π-bonds.

77. (*d*) Smaller the cationic size, larger the charge, larger the polarising power.

Size $Al^{3+} < Mg^{2+} < Na^+ < Ca^{2+}$

and charge $+3 > +2 > +1$

78. (*c*) I. 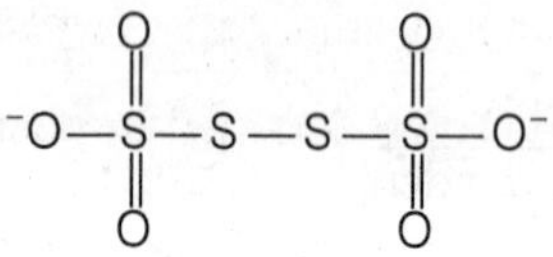

No S—O—S linkage

II. 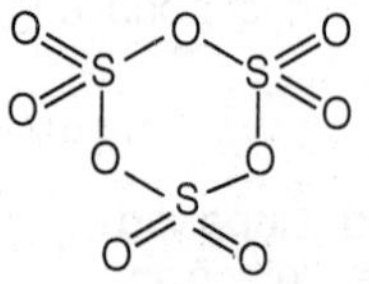

Three (S—O—S) linkages

III. 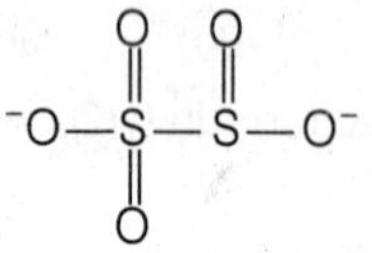

No (S—O—S) linkage

IV. 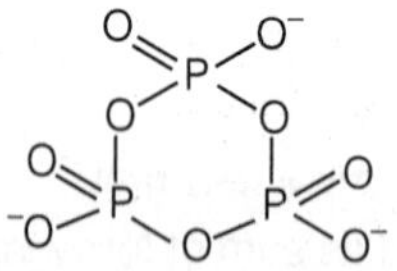

Three, (P—O—P) linkage

Thus, II and IV have *X*—O—*X* (*X* = S, P)

79. (*b*) Ether is a non-polar solvent (covalent) like dissolves likes (covalent)

Smaller the size of cation larger the charge, larger the polarising power and thus larger the covalent nature of the compound with that cation (Cl^- being common)

Size of $Li^+ < Na^+$

Thus, LiCl is predominantly covalent

$Al^{3+} < Na^+$

Charge $+3 > +1$

Thus, $AlCl_3$ is also pedominantly covalent.

LiCl and $AlCl_3$ thus will be extracted into ether.

81. (*a*) (a) $CH_3CH_2-\overset{\delta-}{O}-\overset{\delta+}{H}$ due to polarity there is H-bonding

(b) CH_3-O-CH_3 no polar hydrogen

(c) $Cl-CH_2-CH_3$ no polar hydrogen

(d) $CH_3-CH_2-N(CH_2-CH_3)_2$ no polar hydrogen

Thus, there is H-bonding in ethanol only.

82. (*d*) (a) High boiling point of H_2O is due to intermolecular H-bonding

(b) Glycerol molecules are associated by H-bonding making it viscous.

(c) NH_3 molecules are joined to H_2O molecules by H-bonding, making it water soluble.

(d) Cl-atoms withdraws electron by induction, hence acid is ionised making it polar.

$$Cl \leftarrow CH_2-\overset{O}{\overset{\|}{C}}-O-H \rightleftharpoons ClCH_2\overset{O}{\overset{\|}{C}}O^{\ominus} + H^{\oplus}$$

83. (*b*) The geometry of SF_6 is octahedral and the geometry of SF_4 is trigonal bipyramidal.

SF_6

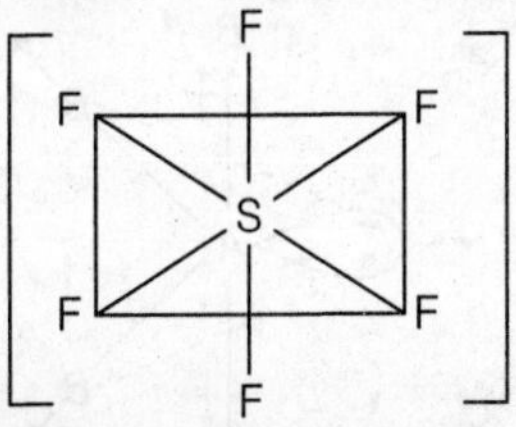

S: sp^3d^2-hybridised
Geometry = shape
= octahedral

SF_4

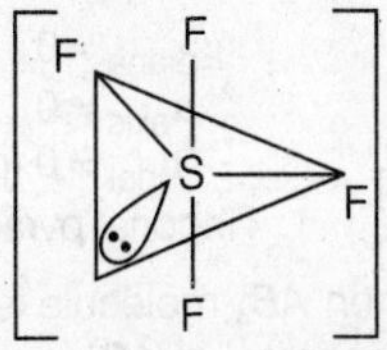

S: sp^3d-hybridised
Geometry = trigonal bipyramidal
Shape = *See-saw*

84. (*d*) When *r* is the inter-nuclear separation,

I. Ion-ion interaction energy $\propto \frac{1}{r}$ [column-*B*(a)]

II. Dipole-dipole interaction energy $\propto \frac{1}{r^3}$ [column-*B* (c)]

(for stationary polar molecules) $\propto \frac{1}{r^6}$ [column-*B* (d)]

(for rotating polar molecules)

III. London dispersion interaction energy $\propto \frac{1}{r^6}$ [column-*B* (d)]

[dipole induced dipole interaction energy $\propto \frac{1}{r^6}$]

So, the matching is, I–(a), II–(c), III–(d)] option (a).

85. (*a*) Phosphorus pentachloride (PCl_5) exist *as* $[PCl_4]^+$ and $[PCl_6]^-$.

Structure of $[PCl_4]^+$

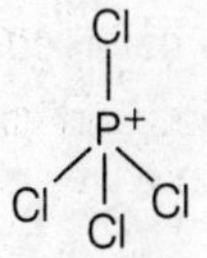

Tetrahedral
(sp^3-hybridisation)

Structure of $[PCl_6]^-$

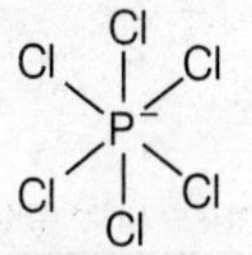

Octahedral
(sp^3d^2-hybridisation)

In solid state PCl_5 prefer to exist as oppositely charged ions like $[PCl_4]^+$ and $[PCl_6]^-$ as the ionic bonding enhances the crystalline nature. These structures $[PCl_4]^+$ and $[PCl_6]^-$. Providing extra stability to solid.

86. (*b*)

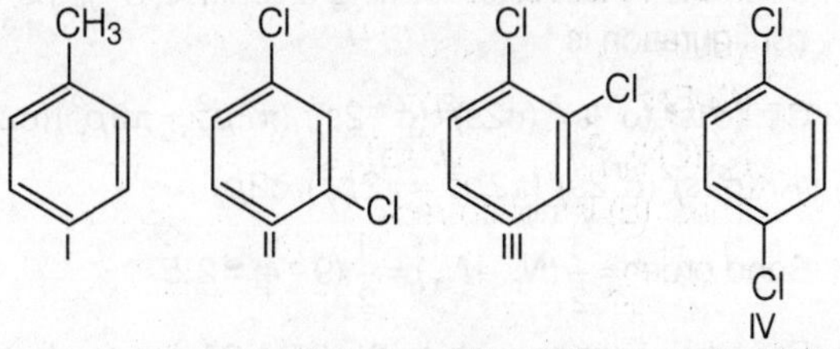

I, II, III, IV

θ = 120° θ = 60° θ = 180°

$$\mu = 2\mu_{C-X}\cos\left(\frac{\theta}{2}\right)$$

$$\mu \propto \cos\left(\frac{\theta}{2}\right)$$

$$\mu \propto \frac{1}{\theta} \quad \text{(since as } \theta \text{ increases, } \cos\theta \text{ decreases)}$$

Thus, $\mu_{IV} = 0\left(\cos\frac{180°}{2} = \cos 90° = 0\right)$

and order being $\mu_{IV} < \underbrace{\mu_I}_{\substack{\text{Single}\\(C-CH_3)}} < \underbrace{\mu_{II} < \mu_{III}}_{\substack{\text{Vvector}\\ \text{summation}}}$

87. (*d*)

	Electrons	Bond order	
N_2	14	3.0	
N_2^+	13	2.5	Decreases
O_2	16	2.0	
O_2^+	15	2.5	Increases

88. (*d*) **Energy order of MOs** **B.O.** $= \frac{N_b - N_a}{2}$

$\sigma_{1s}\sigma^*_{1s}\sigma_{2s}\sigma^*_{2s}\pi_{2p_x} = \pi_{2p_y}\sigma_{2p_z}\pi^*_{2p_x} = \pi^*_{2p_y}$

$NO(15e^-)$:	2	2	2	2	2	2	2	1	0	$\rightarrow \frac{10-5}{2} = 2.5$
$\overset{+}{N}O(14e^-)$:	2	2	2	2	2	2	2	0	0	$\rightarrow \frac{10-4}{2} = 3$
$N\overset{2+}{O}(13e^-)$:	2	2	2	2	2	2	1	0	0	$\rightarrow \frac{9-4}{2} = 2.5$
$N\overset{-}{O}(16e^-)$:	2	2	2	2	2	2	2	1	1	$\rightarrow \frac{10-6}{2} = 2$

We know,

$$\text{Bond length} \propto \frac{1}{\text{B.O. (Bond order)}} \propto \frac{1}{\text{Bond strength}}$$

So,the order of bond strength :

$$NO^+ > NO = NO^{2+} > NO^-$$

So, NO^- has minimum bond strength.

89. (**a**) C_2 will be stabilised after forming anion. The electronic configuration of carbon is $1s^2\,2s^2\,2p^2$. There are twelve electrons in C_2. After forming anion (i. e. C_2^-), the electronic configuration is

C_2^-: $(\sigma 1s)^2(\sigma^* 1s)^2\,(\sigma 2s)^2\,(\sigma * 2s)^2\,(\pi 2p_x^2 = \pi 2p_y^2)(\sigma 2p_z^1)$ or

$KK(\sigma 2s)^2(\sigma^* 2s)^2(\pi 2p_x^2 = \pi 2p_y^2).\,\sigma 2p_z^1$

$$\text{Bond order} = \frac{1}{2}(N_b - N_a) = \frac{1}{2}(9-4) = 2.5$$

For other options such as F_2^-, O_2^-, NO^-, the electronic configurations are as follows :

F_2^- : $(\sigma 1s)^2\,(\sigma^* 1s)^2(\sigma 2s)^2(\sigma^* 2s)^2(\sigma 2p_z)^2$
$(\pi 2p_x^2 = \pi 2p_y^2)\,(\pi^* 2p_x^2 = \pi^* 2p_y^2)(\sigma^* 2p_z^1)$

Bond order $= 1/2(N_b - N_a) = 1/2(10-9) = 0.5$

O_2^- : $(\sigma 1s)^2\,(\sigma^* 1s)^2\,(\sigma 2s)^2\,(\sigma^* 2s)^2\,(\sigma 2p_z)^2$
$(\pi 2p_x^2 = \pi 2p_y^2)\,(\pi^* 2p_x^2 = \pi^* 2p_y^1)$

$$\text{Bond order} = \frac{1}{2}(N_b - N_a) = \frac{1}{2}(10-7) = 1.5$$

NO^- : $(\sigma 1s)^2(\sigma * 1s)^2(\sigma 2s)^2\,(\sigma * 2s)^2\,(\sigma 2p_z)^2$
$(\pi 2p_x^2 = \pi 2p_y^2)\,(\pi^*\,2p_x^1 = \pi^* 2p_y^1)$

$$\text{Bond order} = \frac{1}{2}(N_b - N_a) = \frac{1}{2}(10-6) = 2$$

The value of bond order of C_2^- is highest among the given options.

Bond order between two atoms in a molecule may be taken as an approximate measure of the bond length. The bond length decreases as bond order increases. As a result, stability of a molecule increases.

90. (**a**) If AB_4 molecule is a polar moelcule, a possible geometry of AB_4 is square pyramidal.

All possible structure of AB_4 molecule are as follows:

(i) $AB_4 \Rightarrow L = 0 \Rightarrow A$ is sp^3 (tetrahedral) or
A is dsp^2 (square planar)
$\Rightarrow$ Dipole moment, $\mu = 0$ (Non-polar)

(ii) $AB_4L_2 \Rightarrow L = 2 \Rightarrow A$ is sp^3d^2 (octahedral)
$\Rightarrow \mu = 0$ (Non-polar), because

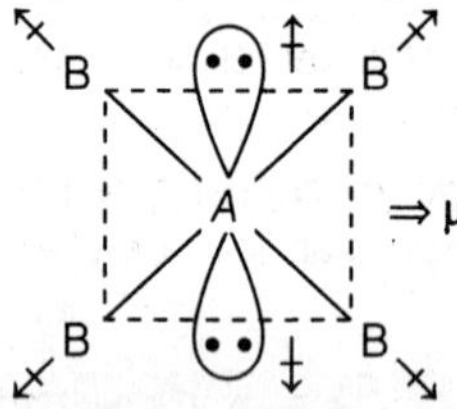

$\Rightarrow \mu_{net} = 0$ (Non-polar)

(Assuming, *B* is more electronegative than *A*)

(iii) $AB_4L \Rightarrow L = 1 \Rightarrow A$ is sp^3d
(square pyramidal or trigonal bipyramidal)
$\Rightarrow \mu \neq 0$ (polar), because

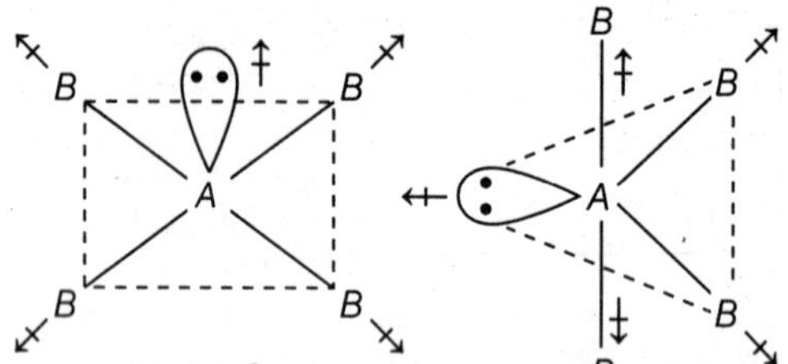

$\mu_{plane} = 0$
$\mu_{axis} \neq 0$
$\mu_{net} \neq 0$ (polar)
[Square pyramidal]

$\mu_{plane} \neq 0$
$\mu_{axis} \neq 0$
$\mu_{net} \neq 0$ (polar)
[Trigonal pyramidal]

So, it can be seen that when AB_4 molecule is a polar molecule then possible geometry of AB_4 is square pyramidal.

91. (**a**) $KO_2 \rightleftharpoons K^+ + O_2^-$ (one unpaired electron)
NO_2^+ (no unpaired electron)
$BaO_2 \rightleftharpoons Ba^{2+} + O_2^{2-}$ (no unpaired electron)
AlO_2^- (no unpaired electron).

92. (**c**) High solubility of $MgSO_4$ is due to high enthalpy of hydration of the smaller Mg^{2+} ion which overcomes the lattice energy factor.

93. (*d*)

Species and number of electrons	Molecular orbital electronic configuration ($\sigma 1s$, $\sigma^* 1s$, $\sigma 2s$, $\sigma^* 2s$, $\sigma 2p_z$, $\pi 2p_x = \pi 2p_y$, $\pi^* 2p_x = \pi^* 2p_y$, $\sigma^* 2p_z$)	Number of unpaired electrons (*n*) and magnetic moment
1. O_2-16 electrons	[⇅] [⇅] [⇅] [⇅] [⇅] [⇅][⇅] [↑][↑] [ ]	$n = 2$, $\mu = \sqrt{n(n+2)}$ $\mu = \sqrt{2 \times 4}$ BM = 2.82 BM
2. O_2^+-15 electrons	[⇅] [⇅] [⇅] [⇅] [⇅] [⇅][⇅] [↑][ ] [ ]	$n = 1$, $\mu = \sqrt{1 \times 3} = 1.73$ BM
3. O_2^--17 electrons	[⇅] [⇅] [⇅] [⇅] [⇅] [⇅][⇅] [⇅][↑] [ ]	$n = 1$, $\mu = 1.73$ BM

1.73 BM is the magnetic moment of O_2^+ and O_2^-.

94. (*a*) The electrical conductivity of a metal decreases as temperature increases.

The increase in temperature causes thermal agitation of the metal ions. This implies the flow of electrons when an electrical field is applied.

95. (*a*) Partially filled bonds or overlapping bonds represent metal.

96. (*b*) Bond order N≡N > N═N > N—N

Bond length Minimum Maximum

(a) 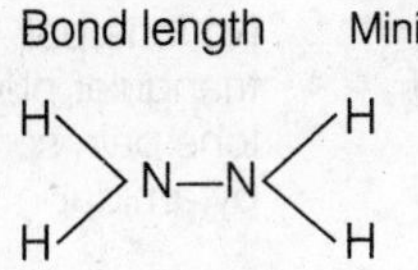

Single bond

(b) N≡N
Triple bond

(c) 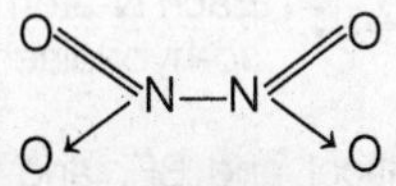

Single bond

(d) :N≡N ⟶ O
triple bond

Bond length is in order (b) < (d) < (a) < (c)

In (d), resonance increases bond length.

In (c), dimer formation is due to unpaired electrons. Hence, dipole-dipole repulsion increases bond length larger than single bond.

97. (*c*) Formal charge $= v - \dfrac{s}{2} - u$

where, v = valence electrons

s = shared electrons (forming bonds)

u = unshared electrons

$[:\ddot{O}{=}N{=}\ddot{O}:]^+$

On oxygen atom: $v = 6$, $s = 4$, $u = 4$

Thus, formal charge $= 6 - \dfrac{4}{2} - 4$

$= 6 - 2 - 4 = 0$

98. (*a*)

I_3^-	$(I_2 \longleftarrow I^-)$	sp^3d	
PCl_3	sp^3		(one lone pair on P)
NO_3^-	sp^2		
H_2Se	sp^3		(two lone pairs on Se)

99. (*d*) 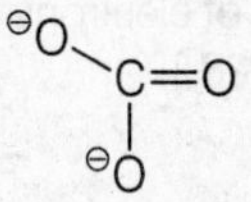

delocalised orbitals cause resonance.

100. (*d*) Energy gap is larger called insulator.

101. (*c*) B_2H_6 has two types of bonding.

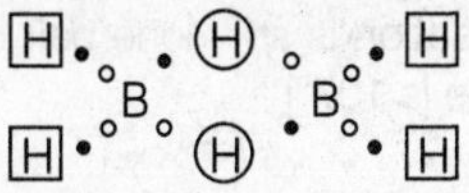

(i) Formed by two electrons between B and [H]

(ii) Formed by one electron between B and (H)

B-atom is thus electron-deficient.

102. (*c*) There is maximum association by intermolecular H-bonding in H_2O thus high boiling point and least volatile.

103. (*d*) A molecule is stabilised if

(a) bond order increases

(b) electron is removed from antibonding M.O. of higher energy

	Electrons	Bond order	
C_2	12	2.0	
C_2^+	11	1.5	
CN	13	2.5	
CN^+	12	2.0	
N_2	14	3.0	
N_2^+	13	2.5	
O_2	16	2.0	(two electrons in antibonding M.O.)
O_2^+	15	2.5	

Thus, O_2^+ is stabilised.

104. (*a*) O_2 (16)

$= (\sigma 1s)^2 (\sigma^* 1s)^2 (\sigma 2s)(\sigma^* 2s)^2 (\sigma 2p_x)^2 (\pi 2p_y)^2 (\pi 2p_z)^2$
$(\pi^* 2p_y)^1 (\pi^* 2p_z)^1$

Anti-bonding M.O. has two unpaired electrons, hence, O_2 is paramagnetic.

105. (*b*) 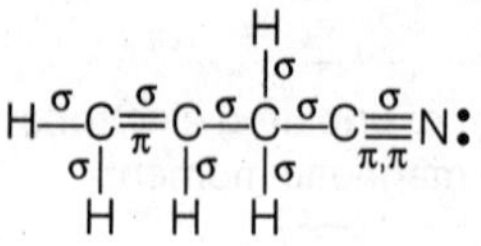

5 (C—H) σ-bonds
3 (C—C) σ-bonds
1 (C—N) σ-bond
1 (C—C) π-bond
2 (C—N) π-bonds
1 lone pair on N

Thus, in all 9σ bonds, 3π bonds and 1 lone pair.

106. (*d*)

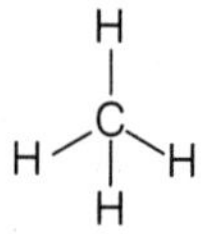

[CH_4 = hybridisation is sp^3, lone pair of electrons is 0, so that bond angle is maximum, i.e., = 109°28]

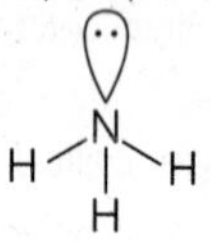

[NH_3= hybridisation is sp^3, lone pair of electron is one, so that bond angle is 107°]

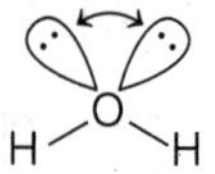

[H_2O = hybridisation is sp^3 lone pair of electrons are two, so that bond angle is 104°5′]

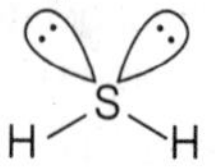

[No hybridisation as according to Drago's rule, so that bond angle is 92°]

According to VSEPR theory.

Lone pair-Lone pair > Lone pair-Bond pair > Bond pair-Bond pair.

107. (*b*) To identify the magnetic nature we need to check the molecular orbital configuration. If all orbitals are fully occupied, species is diamagnetic while when one or more molecular orbitals is/are singly occupied, species is paramagnetic.

(a) NO $(7+8=15)-\sigma 1s^2, \sigma^* 1s^2, \sigma 2s^2, \sigma^* 2s^2,$
$\pi 2p_x^2 = \pi 2p_y^2, \pi 2p_z^2, \pi^* 2p_x^1 = \pi^* 2p_y^0$

One unpaired electron is present.

Hence, it is paramagnetic.

(b) CO $(6+8=14)-\sigma 1s^2, \sigma^* 1s^2, \sigma 2s^2,$
$\sigma^* 2s^2, \pi 2p_x^2 = \pi 2p_y^2, \sigma 2p_z^2$

No unpaired electron is present.
Hence, it is diamagnetic.

(c) O_2 $(8+8=16)-\sigma 1s^2, \sigma^* 1s^2, \sigma 2s^2,$
$\sigma^* 2s^2, \sigma 2p_z^2, \pi 2p_x^2 = \pi 2p_x^2, \pi^* 2p_x^1 = \pi^* 2p_y^1$

Two unpaired electrons are present.
Hence, it is paramagnetic.

(d) B_2 $(5+5)-\sigma 1s^2, \sigma^* 1s^2, \sigma 2s^2, \sigma^* 2s^2 \pi 2p_x^1 = \pi 2p_y^1$

Two unpaired electrons are present.
Hence, it is paramagnetic.

108. (*c*) NF_3 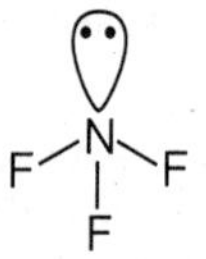 One lone pair, sp^3 three (N—F) bonds (pyramidal)

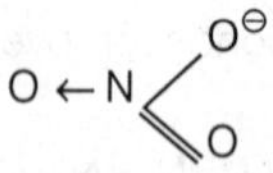 No lone pair, sp^2 (triangular planar)

BF_3 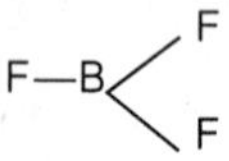 No lone pair, sp^2 triangular planar

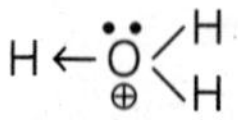 one lone pair, sp^3, pyramidal

HN_3 H—N̈=N≡N: Each N-atom is *sp*-hybridised

Thus, NF_3 and H_3O^+ are identical and BF_3 and NO_3^- are identical.

109. (*c*) $CsBr_3 \longrightarrow Cs^{\oplus} + Br_3^{\ominus}$ (Br_2 with Br^-)

110. (*c*) I. In presence of weak field ligand like Cl^-, both octahedral Mn(II) and tetrahedral Ni(II) complexes can be high spin, like

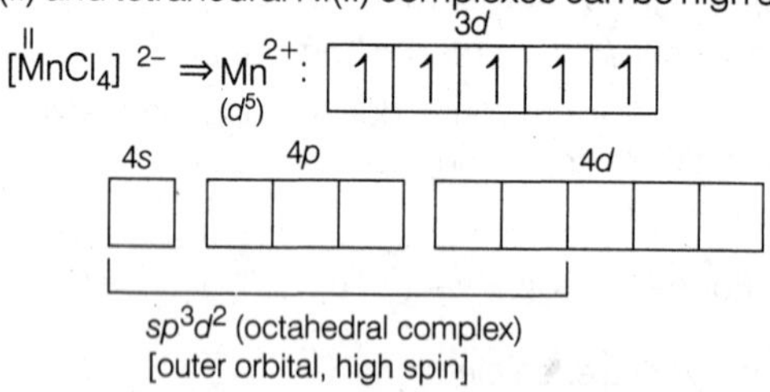

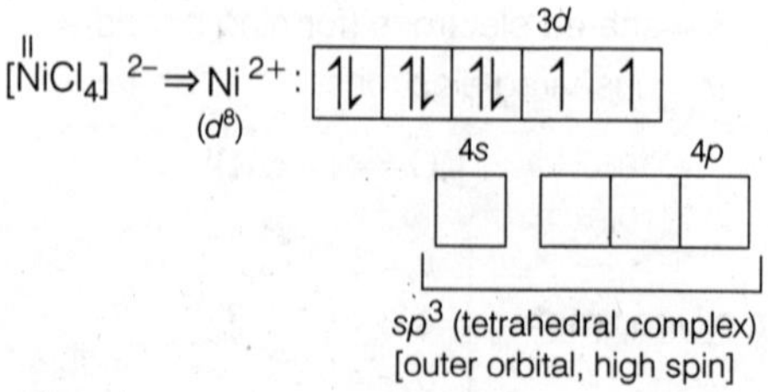

II. In presence of strong field ligand like CN^-, Ni^{2+} can form low spin square planar complex.

||
$[NiCl_4]^{2-}$

$\Rightarrow Ni^{2+}$:
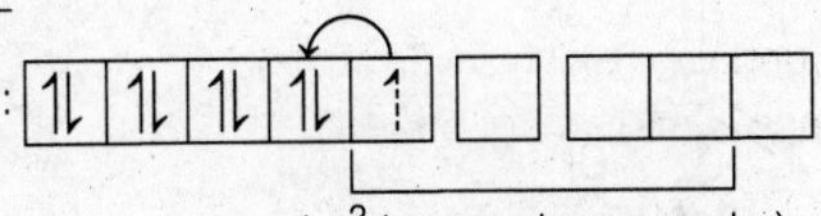

dsp^2 (square planar complex)
[Inner orbital, low spin]

III. With strong field ligands like —CN^-, Mn(II) octahedral complexes can be low spin,

||
$[Mn(CN)_6]^{4-}$

$\Rightarrow Mn^{2+}$:
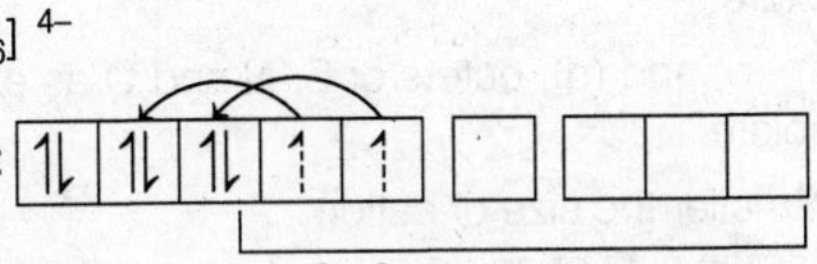

d^2sp^3 (octahedral complex)
[Inner orbital, low spin]

IV. Aqueous solution of Mn(II) ion is pale pink in colour.

Hence, statement I, II and III are correct whereas statement IV is incorrect.

111. (*b*)

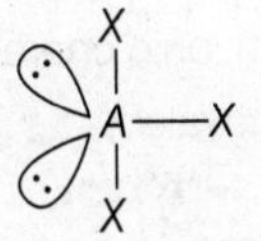

sp^3d-hybridised
T-shaped

112. (*a*) Resultant moment is in one direction in 1,2,3-trichlorobenzene, thus maximum dipole moment.

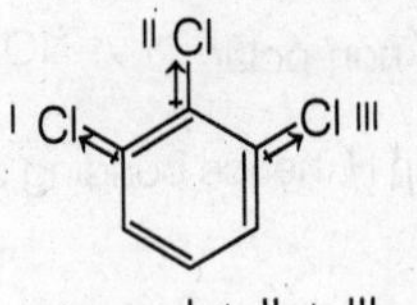

μ_{total} = I + II + III

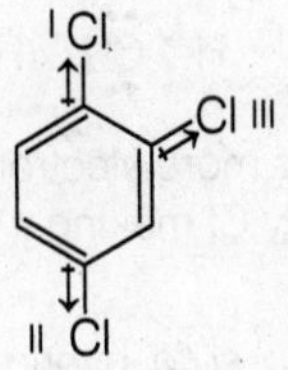

I = –II
Resultant is due to III only

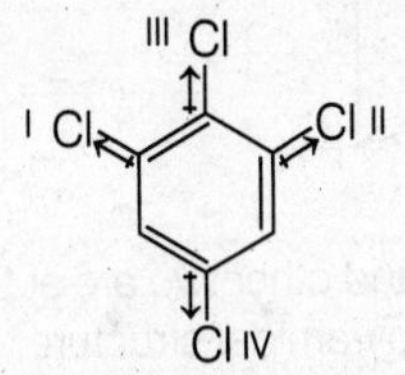

Resultant of I and II is III
and III = – IV
Thus, $\mu = 0$

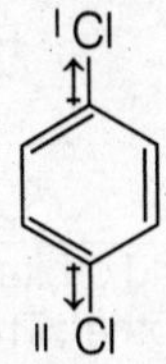

μ = I – II = 0

113. (*b*)

	Electron	Bond order
O_2	16	2.0
O_2^+	15	2.5
O_2^-	17	1.5
O_2^{2-}	18	1.0

Thus, BO is in order

$$O_2^{2-} < O_2^- < O_2 < O_2^+$$

114. (*c*) Ca_{20} : $[Ar]\,4s^2$

Ca^{2+} : [Ar] noble gas configuration

Cd_{48} : $[Kr]_{36}\,5s^2 4d^{10}$

Cd^{2+} : $[[Kr]_{36}\,4d^{10}]\,10 + \underbrace{6+2}_{s^2p^6} = 18$

Electrons 6 configuration of outer shell decreases screening effect, hence polarisation of $Cd^{2+} > Ca^{2+}$.

115. (*d*)

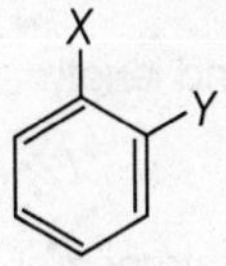

Resultant $\mu = 2\mu' \cos\left(\frac{\theta}{2}\right)$

μ' is the vector moment of the groups *X* and *Y* at ortho position

$$\mu \propto \cos\left(\frac{\theta}{2}\right)$$

$$\mu \propto \frac{1}{\theta}$$

Repulsion increases θ, hence μ decreases attraction decreases θ, hence μ increases.

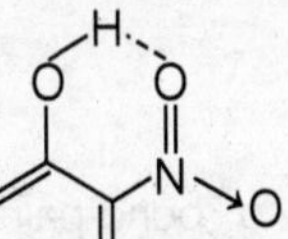

By intramolecular H-bonding in *o*-nitrophenol, θ decreases, hence μ increases.

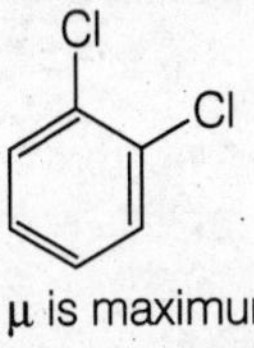

Due to dipole-dipole repulsion of large Cl groups (steric effect) θ increases, hence μ decreases.

Thus, μ is maximum when $X = NO_2$
$Y = OH$
and μ is minimum when $X = Cl$, $Y = Cl$

116. (*c*) (A) 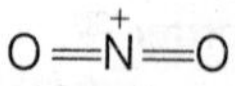 θ = 180°

(B) 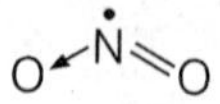 θ = 132°

(C) 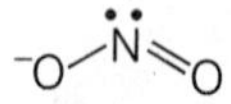 θ = 115°

(D) 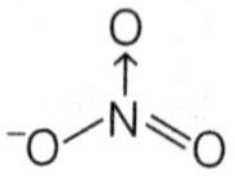 θ = 120°

117. (*d*)

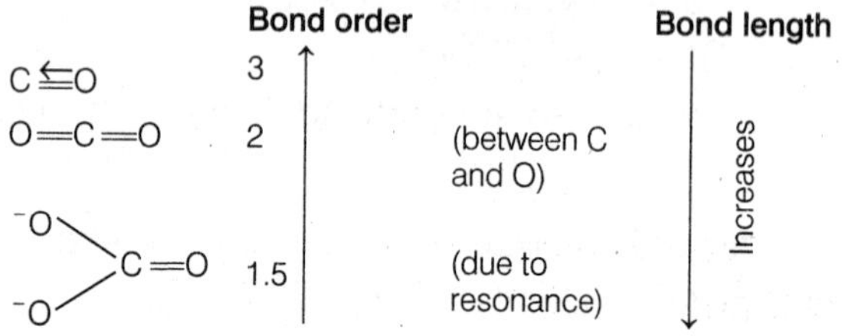

Greater the bond order, smaller the bond length.

118. (*d*) (a) 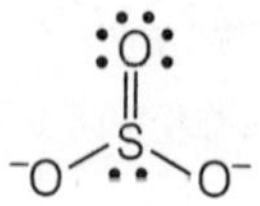 sp^3 distorted tetrahedral

(b) 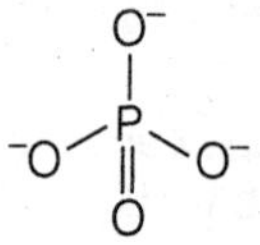 sp^3 tetrahedral

(c) $^-C{\equiv}N$ *sp*-linear

(d) 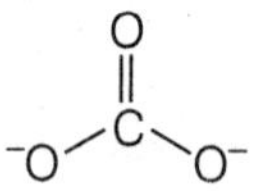 sp^2-triangular planar

119. (*d*) (a) Cl—Be—Cl *sp*-linear

(b) I_2 ⟵ I^-
Lewis acid   Lewis base

There are three lone-pairs and two bond-pairs in the outer-shell of central atom. To minimise repulsive forces, three lone pairs occupy the equatorial position.

Thus, linear bond angle 180°

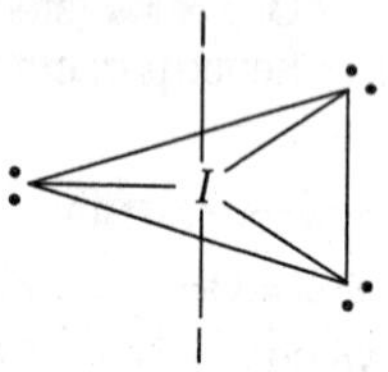

sp-linear
↓
(c) S=C=S

(d) ICl_2

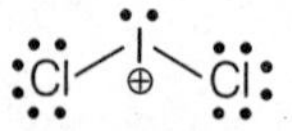 sp^2-hybridised I bent structure

120. (*a*)  sp^2-hybridised S, triangular

HCN, CO_2 and NO are linear.

121. (*a*) 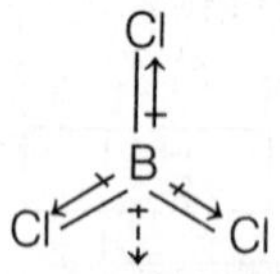

Resultant of two (B—Cl) is compensated by third B—Cl.
Thus $\mu = 0$
Thus, non-polar.

122. (*c*) In (c), octet of Cl and O is completed as for Lewis structure.

In (a), (b) and (d), octets of C, N and O as expected are not complete.

123. (*c*) Smaller the size of cation,
Larger the size of anion,
Larger the charge,
Larger the polarising power and thus smaller the ionic character.

$Li^+ < Mg^{2+} < Cs^+$ size
$+1 < +2$ charge
$F^- < Cl^- < I^-$ size

Thus, (c) has maximum ionic character.

124. (*b*) (a) NCl_3, CCl_4 — covalent
(b) all ionic
(c) BF_3, NH_3 — covalent
(d) SO_2, covalent

125. (*a*) H—Cl is formed by sharing of electron pair between H and Cl

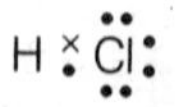 (H—Cl) Thus, non-polar

Since, Cl is more electronegative than H, hence bonding pair is pulled by Cl making it polar.

$\overset{\delta+}{H}—\overset{\delta-}{Cl}$

126. (*a*) PF_3Cl_2 : sp^3d-hybridisation on P.

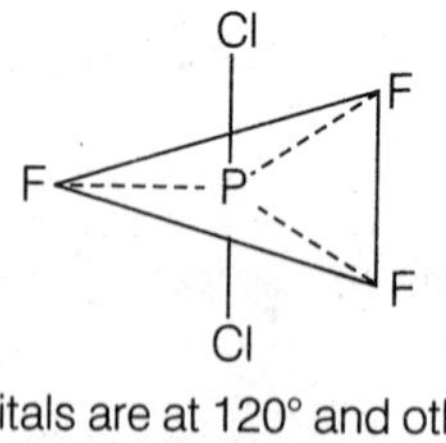

Three hybrid orbitals are at 120° and other two are at 90° with one each other; Thus, trigonal bipyramidal structure.

127. (*d*) $[Fe(CN)_6]^{4-}$

Fe(26) : [Ar] $3d^6\,4s^2$ 

Fe^{2+} with strong ligands (CN^-) : [Ar] $3d^6$ 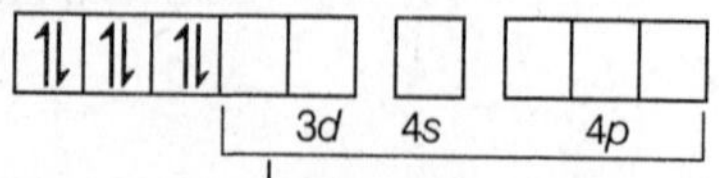

$[Fe(CN)_6]^{4-}$: [Ar] $3d^6$ 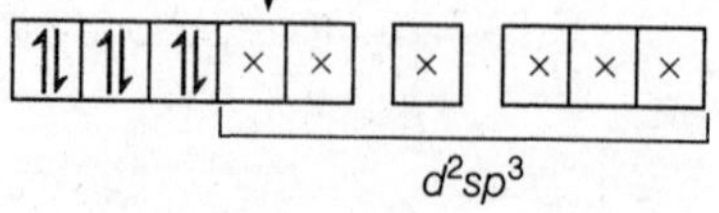

N (unpaired electron) = zero

Thus, magnetic moment = $\sqrt{N(N+2)}$ BM = 0

$[FeF_6]^{3-}$

Fe^{3+} : [Ar] $3d^5$ 

Fe^{3+} with weak ligand (F^-) —no change—

$[FeF_6]^{3-}$: [Ar] $3d^5$ 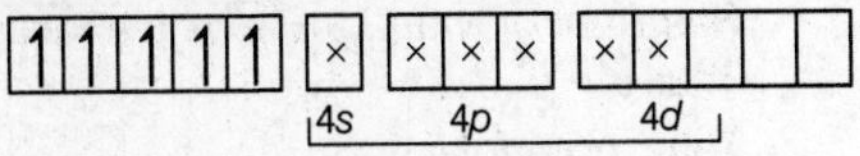

sp^3d^2

N (unpaired electrons) = 5

Magnetic moment = $\sqrt{N(N+2)}$ BM

$= \sqrt{35}$ BM = 5.92 BM

128. (*a*) $Ni(CO)_4$: dsp^2 square planar

SF_4 : sp^3d (one lone pair on S)

$[CoCl_4]^{2-}$: sp^3 tetrahedral

XeF_4 : sp^3d^2 square planar but two lone pairs.

129. (*b*) H^+ : no electron

H^- : one lone pair H^{-}:

H_2 : no lone pair

He^{2+} : no lone pair

130. (*d*) (a) 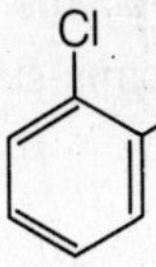 $\mu > 0$ $\mu = 2\mu_{C-X}\cos\left(\frac{\theta}{2}\right) = +ve$

(b) 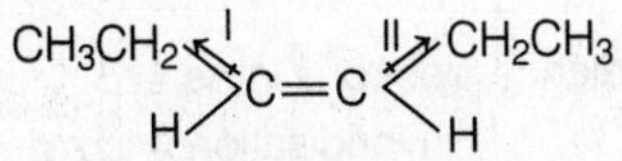 $\mu > 0$ $\mu = I + II$

(c) 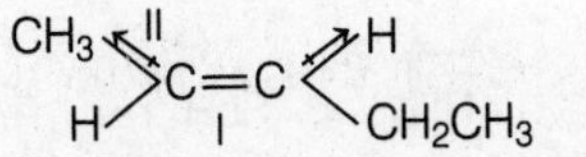 $\mu > 0$ $\mu = I + II = +ve$ $(I > II)$

131. (*a*)

Species	Electrons	Bond order
I. CN^-	14	3.0
II. O_2^-	17	1.5
III. NO^+	14	3.0
IV. CN^+	12	2.0

I and III have same bond-order.

132. (*d*)  One lone-pair, sp^3d

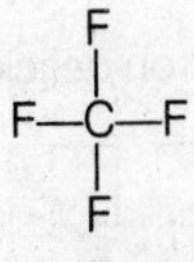 Zero lone-pair, sp^3

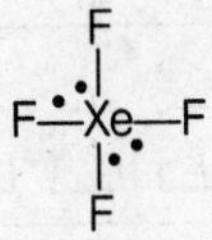 Two lone-pairs, sp^3d^2

133. (*a*) $\overset{\oplus}{N}O_2$ 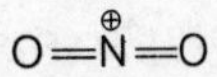 sp

NO_3^- 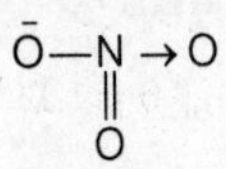 sp^2

NH_4 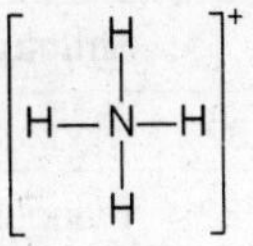 sp^3

134. (*c*) (a) 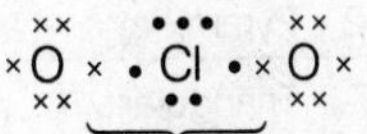

9 electrons

(b) 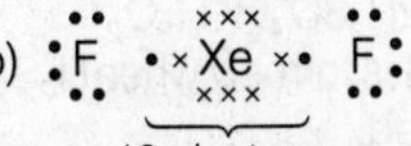

12 electrons

Thus, both violate octet rule.

136. (*b*) For $Li_2 = \sigma 1s^2 \sigma^* 1s^2 \sigma 2s^2$

$$B.O. = \frac{4-2}{2} = 1$$

$$Li_2^+(5) = \sigma 1s^2 * 1s^2 \sigma 2s^1$$

$$B.O = \frac{3-2}{2} = 0.5$$

$$Li_2^-(7) = \sigma 1s^2 \sigma^* 1s^2 \sigma 2s^2 \sigma^* 2s^1$$

$$B.O. = \frac{4-3}{2} = 0.5$$

$$B.O. = Li_2^- < Li_2^+ < Li_2$$

137. (*a*)

Electron	Bond order	Bond length
$NO^{\oplus}$	14	3
NO	15	2.5
$NO^{\ominus}$	16	2.0

Larger the bond order, smaller the bond length.

Thus, $N\overset{\oplus}{O}$.

138. (*d*) P-atom is sp^3-hybridised. Thus, *p*-character in P_4 is 75%.

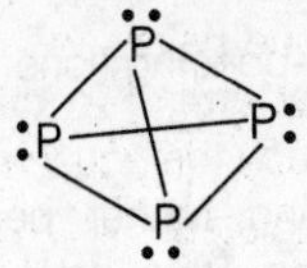

139. (*d*) Atom *X* has complete octet and *Y* has three lone-pair and one (*X*-*Y*) bond. Thus,

X is C and *Y* is F

140. (*a*)

	Electrons	Bond order	Ligand
CN^-	14	3	Strong
CO	14	3	Strong
NO^+	14	3	Weak

141. (*a*) 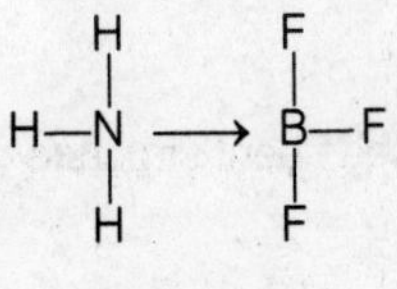

Four bonds on N, no lone pair thus sp^3-tetrahedral	Four bonds on B, no lone pair thus sp^3-tetrahedral

142. (*a*)

	Electrons	Structure
NO_3^-	7 + 24 + 1 = 32	Triangular
CO_3^{2-}	6 + 24 + 2 = 32	Triangular
ClO_3^-	17 + 24 + 1 = 42	Pyramidal
SO_3	16 + 24 = 40	Triangular

143. (*b*) $H_2S_2O_8 + 2H_2O \longrightarrow 2H_2SO_4 + H_2O_2$
H_2O_2 (with ($^-$O—O$^-$) linkage) is formed when $H_2S_2O_8$ (peroxy disulphuric acid) is hydrolysed.

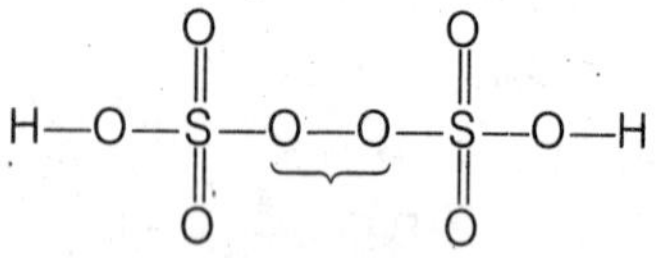

Peroxy linkage

144. (*d*) ClO_3 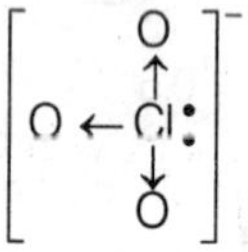 One lone-pair on Cl

XeF_4 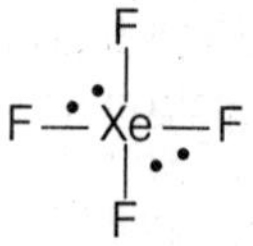 Two lone-pairs on Xe

SF_4 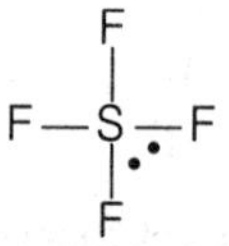 One lone pair on S

I_3^- 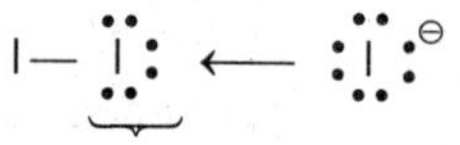 Three lone pairs on I

145. (*a*) Due to presence of lone pair, structure is bent.

146. (*d*) 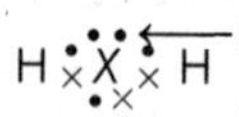

147. (*c*) Third period and further periods involve *s*, *p* and *d*-orbitals for bonding. Thus, octet rule is generally violated.

148. (*d*) Compound is covalent. Thus,

I. Incorrect
II. Correct
III. Incorrect, covalent compound does not dissolve in H_2O
IV. Correct
V. Correct

Thus, II, IV and V

149. (*c*) 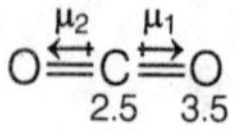

Based on (electronegativity) difference (C—O) bond is polar. But dipole moment of one (C—O) side is compensated by that of other (C—O) side

$$\mu_{Total} = \vec{\mu}_1 + \overleftarrow{\mu}_2 = \vec{\mu}_1 - \vec{\mu}_2 = 0$$

150. (*d*) 

Due to *lp-bp* repulsion, tetrahedral geometry is distorted to pyramidal geometry.

151. (*a*) 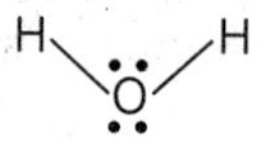

Bent geometry two (O—H) bonds and two lone-pairs.

152. (*c*) S═C═S
Non-polar

153. (*d*) Smaller the size of the atom, greater the force of attraction hence greater the dissociation energy.

Thus, element *D* with smallest size forms strongest (C—*D*) bond.

154. (*c*) AsF_5

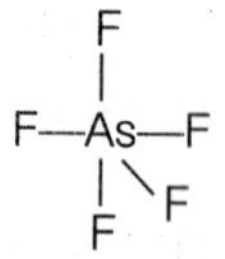

valence electrons in As = 5
hybridisation = sp^3d

155. (*b*) $PH_3 < AsH_3 < NH_3 < SbH_3$
−87.5°C, −62.4°C, −34.5°C, −18.4°C

There is association by H-bonding in NH_3 but molar mass of $SbH_3 >> NH_3$ makes it highest boiling point liquid.

156. (*d*) 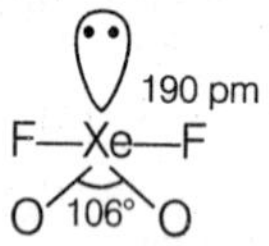

157. (*b*) 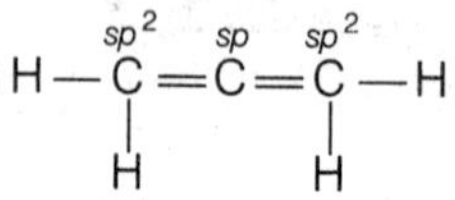

159. (*c*)

(a) $Cr(CO)_6$: 24 + 12 = 36
(b) $Fe(CO)_5$: 26 + 10 = 36
(c) $V(CO)_6$: 23 + 12 = 35 (electron deficient)

160. (*c*) Bond-order = zero

07

Periodic Table and Periodicity

Objective Questions Type I [Only one correct option]

In each of the questions below, four choices are given of which only one is correct.

1. First long period contains .... elements.
(a) 8 (b) 18 (c) 32 (d) 2

2. Recently (in 2003) element with atomic number 110 has been named by IUPAC as
(a) HS (b) Mt (c) Ds (d) Sg

3. Recently (in Aug 2003) two new elements have been discovered with atomic numbers
(a) 113, 114 (b) 114, 115
(c) 115, 116 (d) 113, 115

4. Element 113 is produced *via*
(a) α-decay of element 115 (b) β-decay of element 114
(c) α-decay of element 111 (d) β-decay of element 112

5. Numbering of groups as 1, 2, ... 18 was adopted by IUPAC in
(a) 1986 (b) 1906 (c) 1908 (d) 1988

6. Element with valence shell-electronic configuration as d^5s^1 is placed in
(a) IA, *s*-block (b) VIA, *s*-block
(c) VIB, *s*-block (d) VIB, *d*-block

7. Element of which set does not show correct matching?
(a) $Sc^{3+} \rightarrow [Ne]\,3s^2 3p^6$ zero group
(b) $Fe^{2+} \rightarrow [Ar]\,3d^6$ VIII group
(c) $Cr \rightarrow [Ar]\,3d^5\,4s^1$ VIA group
(d) All of the above

8. Two new elements (discovered in August 2003) with atomic number 113 and 115 are to be placed in
(a) *s*-block (b) *p*-block
(c) *d*-block (d) *f*-block

9. Most stable cation of element 113 will be
(a) M^{3+} (b) M^{2+} (c) M^{+} (d) M_2^{2+}

10. Element with atomic number 115 has configuration as ...... and with most stable cation as ......
(a) $[Rn]\,7s^2 5d^{10} 4f^{14} 7p^3$ M^{3+}
(b) $[Rn]\,7s^2 5d^{10} 4f^{14} 7p^3$ M^{5+}
(c) $[Rn]\,7s^2 5d^{10} 4f^{14} 7p^3$ M^{+}
(d) $[Rn]\,5d^{10} 4f^{14} 7p^5$ M^{5+}

11. The element with $Z = 120$ (not yet discovered) will be an/a **[JEE Main 2019]**
(a) transition metal (b) inner-transition metal
(c) alkaline earth metal (d) alkali metal

12. Elements *X* and *Y* have valence shell electron configuration as
$X: ns^2np^1$; $Y: ns^2np^3$
Which compound is likely formed from *X* and *Y*?
(a) X_3Y_5 (b) Y_3X_5 (c) XY (d) YX

13. Given below are two statements :
Statement I Both $CaCl_2 \cdot 6H_2O$ and $MgCl_2 \cdot 8H_2O$ undergo dehydration on heating.
Statement II BeO is amphoteric whereas the oxides of other elements in the same group are acidic.
In the light of the above statements, choose the correct answer from the options given below :
(a) Statement I is false but statement II is true
(b) Both statement I and statement II are false
(c) Both statement I and statement II are true
(d) Statement I is true but statement II is false

14. Chalcogens are elements of
(a) group 16 (b) *p*-block
(c) ns^2np^4 configuration (d) All are correct

15. M^{3+} has electronic configuration as [Ar] $3d^{10}4s^2$, hence it lies in
(a) *s*-block (b) *p*-block (c) *d*-block (d) *f*-block

16. Transition elements have vacant
(a) *s*-orbitals (b) *p*-orbitals
(c) *d*-orbitals (d) *f*-orbitals

17. Of the following pairs, the one containing examples of metalloid elements in the periodic table is
(a) Na and K (b) F and Cl
(c) Cu and Ag (d) B and Si

18. Pick out the property which is not shown by transition elements.
(a) Show variable oxidation state
(b) Impart colour to flame
(c) Are paramagnetic in nature
(d) Act as catalytic agents

19. Which of the following is a transition element?
(a) Al (b) As (c) Ni (d) Rb

20. Which of the following has the electronic configuration [Ar] $3d^5$?
(a) Cr (b) Fe^{3+} (c) Mn (d) V

21. Which of the following forms a stable +4 oxidation state?
(a) Lanthanum (b) Cerium
(c) Europium (d) Gadolinium

22. The lanthanides have electron configuration with $6s^2$ in common but with variable occupation of the
(a) 6*p*-level (b) 5*p*-level
(c) 5*d*-level (d) 4*f*-level

23. Which group of elements is analogous to the lanthanides?
(a) Halides (b) Actinides
(c) Chalcogenides (b) Borides

24. Electronic configuration of Gd (64) is written as
(a) $[Xe]_{54}\ 4f^7 5d^1 6s^2$
(b) $[Xe]_{54}\ 4f^8 6s^2$
(c) $[Xe]_{54}\ 4f^9 6s^1$
(d) $[Xe]_{54}\ 4f^{10}$

25. Recently discovered element with atomic number 115 is
(a) Uun (b) Uub
(c) Uup (d) Uus

26. In periodic table, metallic elements appear
(a) in the left-hand columns
(b) in the top rows
(c) in the right-hand columns
(d) in the bottom rows

27. The atoms of the elements belonging to the same group of the periodic table will have
(a) the same number of protons
(b) the same number of electrons in the valence-shell
(c) the same number of neutrons
(d) the same number of electrons

28. Which will have graded property similar to electronic configuration $1s^2 2s^2 2p^6 3s^2 3p^6 4s^1$?
(a) [Ar] $3d^{10}4s^1$ (b) [Kr] $4d^{10}5s^1$
(c) [Kr] $5s^1$ (d) All of these

29. Which of the following represents the correct order of increasing first ionisation enthalpy for Ca, Ba, S, Se and Ar? **[JEE Main 2013]**
(a) Ca < S < Ba < Se < Ar (b) S < Se < Ca < Ba < Ar
(c) Ba < Ca < Se < S < Ar (d) Ca < Ba < S < Se < Ar

30. Element with atomic number 113 has been reported in August 2003. Its electronic configuration is similar to that of
(a) Si (b) Ga (c) Bi (d) At

31. Which has maximum stability?
(a) $AsCl_3$ (b) $SbCl_3$
(c) $BiCl_3$ (d) Equal

32. Which reaction has most negative $\Delta G°$ value?
(a) $Ga^{3+} + 2e^- \longrightarrow Ga^+$ (b) $In^{3+} + 2e^- \longrightarrow In^+$
(c) $Tl^{3+} + 2e^- \longrightarrow Tl^+$ (d) Cannot be predicted

33. With respect to oxygen maximum valency is shown by
(a) halogen family (b) oxygen family
(c) nitrogen family (d) boron family

34. Which is best oxidising agent?
(a) Ge^{4+} (b) Pb^{4+} (c) Sn^{4+} (d) Sn^{2+}

35. Valence electrons in the element *A* are 3 and that in element *B* are 6. Most probable compound formed from *A* and *B* is
(a) A_2B (b) AB_2 (c) A_6B_3 (d) A_2B_3

36. The increasing order of atomic radii of the following Group 13 elements is **[JEE Advanced 2016]**
(a) Al < Ga < In < Tl (b) Ga < Al < In < Tl
(c) Al < In < Ga < Tl (d) Al < Ga < Tl < In

37. Screening effect is not observed in
(a) He^+ (b) Li^{2+}
(c) Be^{3+} (d) All of these cases

38. In which case effective nuclear charge is minimum?
(a) Be (b) Be^{2+} (c) Be^{3+} (d) Equal

39. For Be, $Z_{eff} = 1.95$ and for Be^{x+}, $Z_{eff} = 2.30$. Hence, ion is
(a) Be^+ (b) Be^{2+} (c) Be^{3+} (d) Be^0

40. For Cu^+, effective nuclear charge felt by a 3*d*-electron is
(a) 14.25 (b) 13.95 (c) 14.65 (d) 29.0

41. State, which one of the following has the largest atomic radius?
(a) Cs (b) Mg (c) Ba (d) Cr

42. Which one of the following has the smallest atomic radius?
(a) F (b) Cl (c) Cs (d) Mg

43. Covalent radius of nitrogen is 70 pm. Hence, covalent radius of boron is about
(a) 60 pm (b) 110 pm
(c) 50 pm (d) 40 pm

44. In which case bond length is shortened?
(a) When multiplicity occurs between atoms
(b) When electronegativities are different
(c) In both cases
(d) None of the above cases

45. Select the correct statement about radius of an atom.
(a) Values of van der Waals' radii are larger than those of covalent radii because the van der Waals' forces are much weaker than the forces operating between atoms in a covalently bonded molecule
(b) The metallic radii are smaller than the van der Waals' radii, since the bonding forces in the metallic crystal lattice are much stronger than the van der Waals' forces
(c) Both (a) and (b) are correct
(d) None of the above is correct

46. The characteristics of elements *X*, *Y* and *Z* with atomic numbers, respectively, 33, 53 and 83 are
(a) *X* and *Y* are metalloids and *Z* is a metal
(b) *X* is a metalloid, *Y* is a non-metal and *Z* is a metal
(c) *X*, *Y* and *Z* are metals
(d) *X* and *Z* are non-metals and *Y* is a metalloid

47. Select the correct statement(s).
(a) Across a transition series, there is only a small decrease in atomic radius from one element to another due to very small increase in effective nuclear charge
(b) The rate of decrease in the size across the lanthanide series is less than the across the first transition series
(c) Both (a) and (b) are correct statements
(d) None of the above statement is correct

48. Select the incorrect order of size of ions/atoms.
(a) $I^+ < I < I^-$ (b) Fe = Co = Ni
(c) Ni < Cu < Zn (d) None is incorrect

49. Select the correct alternate.
(a) Due to lanthanide contraction Zr and Hf have almost equal size
(b) Due to completion of 3*d*-subshell, the electronic charge density in this subshell becomes very high which increases the inter-electronic repulsion hence, size increases
(c) Both (a) and (b) are correct statements
(d) Both of the above are incorrect statements

50. The lanthanides contraction refers to
(a) ionic radius of the series
(b) valence electrons of the series
(c) the density of the series
(d) electronegativity

51. The second ionisation energy is always higher than the first ionisation energy because the
(a) ion becomes more stable attaining an octet or duplet configurations
(b) electron is more tightly bound to the nucleus in an ion
(c) electron is attracted more by the core electrons
(d) None of the above is the correct

52. Which of the following atoms has the highest first ionisation energy? **[JEE Main 2016]**
(a) Na (b) K
(c) Sc (d) Rb

53. Which has maximum IE?
(a) Mg (b) Mg^+
(c) Mg^{2+} (d) Equal

54. Which pair represents incorrect first IE?
(a) Be > B (b) N > O
(c) Li > Na (d) He > He^+

55. Which represents alkalies metals based on $(IE)_1$ and $(IE)_2$ values?

		$(IE)_1$	$(IE)_2$
(a)	*X*	100	110
(b)	*Y*	95	120
(c)	*Z*	195	500
(d)	*M*	200	250

56. Which element has the highest first IP (Ionisation Potential) ?
(a) N (b) Ne (c) He (d) H

57. IP of an element does not depend on
(a) its nuclear charge
(b) the shielding effect
(c) electron neutrality
(d) penetration effect

58. The dominant factor in determining the IE of the elements on moving down the groups is its
(a) atomic radius
(b) effective nuclear charge
(c) Both (a) and (b)
(d) None of the above

59. Select the correct statement.
(a) $(IE)_1$ of the corresponding elements of 3*d* and 4*d* -series are almost similar
(b) $(IE)_1$ of 5*d*-series elements are smaller than that of 3*d* and 4*d*-series elements
(c) Both (a) and (b) are correct
(d) Both of the above are incorrect

60. Higher values of ionisation energies of the 5*d*-transition elements are consistent with the
(a) relatively smaller effective nuclear charge
(b) relatively smaller size of their atoms
(c) relatively smaller penetration
(d) All of the above are correct

61. The ionisation potential of nitrogen is
(a) same as that of oxygen
(b) less than that of oxygen
(c) greater than that of oxygen
(d) None of the above

62. Nitrogen is found to have higher value of ionisation potential because
(a) it has half-filled *p*-orbitals
(b) it is chemically inert
(c) its shielding effect overcomes the nuclear charge
(d) All of the above are correct

63. Following the transition elements, $(IE)_1$ drops abruptly in Ga, In and Tl. This is due to
(a) decrease in effective nuclear charge
(b) increase in atomic radius
(c) removal of an electron from the singly occupied *np*-orbitals of higher energy than the *ns*-orbitals of Zn, Cd and Hg
(d) None of the above is correct

64. Fex_2 and Fey_3 are known when x and y are **[JEE Main 2021, March]**
(a) x = F, Cl, Br, I and y = F, Cl, Br
(b) x = F, Cl, Br and y = F, Cl, Br, I
(c) x = Cl, Br, I and y = F, Cl, Br, I
(d) x = F, Cl, Br, I and y = F, Cl, Br, I

65. Select the correct order of $(IE)_1$
(a) Cu < Zn < Ga (b) Ag < Cd < In
(c) Hg > Au > Tl (d) None of these

66. The high oxidising power of fluorine is due to
(a) high electron affinity (b) high ionisation energy
(c) Both (a) and (b) (d) None of these

67. Which element has the highest electron affinity?
(a) F (b) Cl (c) Br (d) I

68. Which of the following will have the most negative electron affinity and which the least negative?
(a) F, Cl (b) Cl, F (c) Cl, S (d) Cl, P

69. Select the correct statement.
(a) Electron affinity of nitrogen is much lower than that of its neighbouring elements carbon and oxygen
(b) Electron affinity of F is higher than that of chlorine
(c) Both (a) and (b) are correct
(d) None of the above is correct

70. Which is incorrect statement?
(a) *In solid state* O^{2-} *is stabilised* by neighbouring cations
(b) Formation of O^{2-} from O^- is unfavourable in the gas phase
(c) Electron affinity of O > S
(d) All of the above are incorrect

71. Fluorine is more electronegative than nitrogen. The best explanation is that
(a) the valence electrons in F are on the average, a little closer to the nucleus than in N
(b) the charge on a F nucleus is +9, while that on N nucleus is +7
(c) the valence electrons in F and N are in different shells and thus their energy are greatly different
(d) electronegativity increases from left to right in each of the periods

72. Which of the following sets of elements is arranged in order of increasing electronegativity based on Pauling scale?
(a) S, Si, P (b) P, S, Si (c) S, P, Si (d) P, Si, S

73. The electronegativities of elements A and B are 1.2 and 3.4 units respectively. The type of bond connecting A and B in compound AB is
(a) covalent (b) ionic
(c) coordinate covalent (d) polar covalent

74. Li resembles Mg. This is called diagonal relationship which is attributed to
(a) same value of electronegativity
(b) same value of electron affinity
(c) penetration of sub-shells
(d) identical effective nuclear charge

75. Electronegativity and electron affinity of an element A are X and Y respectively. Hence, ionisation potential of A is
(a) $\frac{X+Y}{2}$ (b) $2X - Y$ (c) $2Y - X$ (d) $2X + Y$

76. Metallic nature increases moving down the group because
(a) nuclear charge increases (b) shielding increases
(c) Both (a) and (b) (c) None of the above

77. Select the correct statement.
(a) More active metals are on the left side of the Periodic Table
(b) Less active metals are on the left side of the Periodic Table
(c) Reducing power decreases moving down the group
(d) All the above are correct statements

78. Out of C, Si, Ge, Sn, Pb metallic nature is in
(a) Ge, Sn, Pb (b) Sn, Pb
(c) Ge, Pb (d) Ge, Sn

79. Out of F_2, Cl_2, Br_2 and I_2, most oxidising agent is
(a) F_2 (b) Cl_2 (c) Br_2 (d) I_2

80. Tendency of I^-, Br^-, Cl^- and F^- to be oxidised is in order
(a) $I^- > Br^- > Cl^- > F^-$ (b) $I^- < Br^- < Cl^- < F^-$
(c) $I^- < Cl^- < F^- < Br^-$ (d) $I^- = Br^- < Cl^- = F^-$

81. The correct option with respect to the Pauling electronegativity values of the elements is **[JEE Main 2019, Jan.]**
(a) P > S (b) Si < Al (c) Te > Se (d) Ga < Ge

82. Which is largest in size in aqueous solution?
(a) Li^+ (b) Na^+ (c) Cs^+ (d) Rb^+

83. Mixture containing aqueous Li^+, Na^+, K^+ ions are electrolysed. Cations are discharged at cathode in the order: (easiest at the end)

$$M^+(aq) + e^- \longrightarrow M$$

(a) Li^+, Na^+, K^+ (b) K^+, Na^+, Li^+
(c) Li^+, K^+, Na^+ (d) Na^+, K^+, Li^+

84. Three elements X, Y and Z are in the 3rd period of the periodic table. The oxides of X, Y and Z, respectively, are basic, amphoteric and acidic. The correct order of the atomic number of X, Y and Z is **[JEE Main 2020, Sep.]**
(a) $Z < Y < X$ (b) $X < Y < Z$
(c) $X < Z < Y$ (d) $Y < X < Z$

85. Extent of hydration of Na^+, Mg^{2+}, Al^{3+} is in order
(a) $Na^+ < Al^{3+} < Mg^{2+}$ (b) $Na^+ < Mg^{2+} < Al^{3+}$
(c) $Al^{3+} < Mg^{2+} < Na^+$ (d) equal

86. An oxide behaves as an acid or a base depending on its
(a) size and charge (b) size only
(c) charge only (d) None of these

87. Which of the following metals forms a amphoteric oxide?
(a) Ca (b) Ni (c) Zn (d) Fe

88. Which of the following oxides is highly basic?
(a) Al_2O_3 (b) Cr_2O_3 (c) Na_2O (d) BaO

89. Point out the oxide which is amphoteric in nature
(a) CO (b) Bi_2O_3 (c) PbO (d) CO_2

90. As we proceed from top to bottom in the periodic table
(a) hydroxides are more basic
(b) oxyacids are less acidic
(c) neither of the above
(d) Both of the above

91. The basic character of hydrides of group 15 (VA)is in which of the following order?
(a) $NH_3 < PH_3 < BiH_3 < SbH_3 < AsH_3$
(b) $NH_3 > PH_3 > AsH_3 > SbH_3 > BiH_3$
(c) $NH_3 < PH_3 < AsH_3 < SbH_3 < BiH_3$
(d) None of the above

92. Ionic hydrides react with water to give
(a) a basic solution (b) an acidic solution
(c) a hydride ion (d) protons

93. Out of BeH_2, CuH_2, CrH_3 and NaH, covalent hydrides are
(a) BeH_2, NaH (b) CuH_2, CrH_3
(c) BeH_2, CuH_2, CrH_3 (d) All of these

94. Reducing action of hydrides is due to
(a) oxidation of H^- to H
(b) oxidation of H to H^+
(c) reduction of H to H^-
(d) reduction of H^+ to H

95. Select the correct statement.
(a) Ionic hydrides are better reducing agents
(b) Covalent nature of hydrides increases across a period and decreases down the group
(c) $LiAlH_4$ can reduce carbonyl compounds to alcohols
(d) All the above are correct statements

96. First, second and third IP values are 100 eV, 150 eV and 1500 eV. Element can be
(a) Be (b) B
(c) F (d) Na

97. $N_0/2$ atoms of $X(g)$ are converted into $X^+(g)$ by energy E_1. $N_0/2$ atoms of $X(g)$ are converted into $X^-(g)$ by energy E_2. Hence, ionisation potential and electron affinity of $X(g)$ are
(a) $\frac{2E_1}{N_0}, \frac{2(E_1 - E_2)}{N_0}$ (b) $\frac{2E_1}{N_0}, \frac{2E_2}{N_0}$
(c) $\frac{(E_1 - E_2)}{N_0}, \frac{2E_2}{N_0}$ (d) None is correct

98. Electron affinity is positive when
(a) O^- is formed from O
(b) O^{2-} is formed from O^-
(c) O^+ is formed from O
(d) electron affinity is always a negative value

99. The oxidation states of nitrogen in NO, NO_2, N_2O and NO_3^- are in the order of **[JEE Main 2021, March]**
(a) $NO_3^- > NO_2 > NO > N_2O$
(b) $NO_2 > NO_3^- > NO > N_2O$
(c) $N_2O > NO_2 > NO > NO_3^-$
(d) $NO > NO_2 > N_2O > NO_3^-$

100. A molecule H—X will be 50% ionic if electronegativity difference of H and X is
(a) 1.2 eV (b) 1.4 eV
(c) 1.5 eV (d) 1.7 eV

101. Melting points of NaCl, NaBr, NaI and NaF will be in order
(a) NaI < NaBr < NaCl < NaF
(b) NaF < NaCl < NaBr < NaI
(c) NaBr < NaF < NaCl < NaI
(d) NaCl < NaI < NaF < NaBr

102. The correct order of increasing ionic character is
(a) $BeCl_2 < MgCl_2 < CaCl_2 < BaCl_2$
(b) $BeCl_2 < CaCl_2 < MgCl_2 < BaCl_2$
(c) $BaCl_2 < CaCl_2 < MgCl_2 < BeCl_2$
(d) $MgCl_2 < CaCl_2 < BeCl_2 < BaCl_2$

103. Fluorine has the highest electronegativity among the $ns^2\ np^5$ group on the Pauling scale, but the electron affinity of fluorine is less than that of chlorine because
(a) the atomic number of fluorine is less than that of chlorine
(b) fluorine being the first member of the family behaves in an unusual manner
(c) chlorine can accommodate an electron better than fluorine by utilising its vacant 3*d*-orbital
(d) small size, high electron density and an increased electron repulsion makes addition of an electron to fluorine less favourable than that in the case of chlorine

104. (*A*), (*B*), (*C*) are elements in the third short period. Oxide of (*A*) is ionic, that of (*B*) is amphoteric and of (*C*) a giant molecule. (*A*), (*B*) and (*C*) will have atomic number in the order
(a) $(A) < (B) < (C)$ (b) $(C) < (B) < (A)$
(c) $(A) < (C) < (B)$ (d) $(B) < (A) < (C)$

105. Going down in a group from F to I, which of the following properties increases
(a) ionic radius (b) ionisation energy
(c) oxidising power (d) electronegativity

106. The sizes of the second and third row transition elements being almost the same. This is due to
(a) *d*-and *f*-orbitals do not shield the nuclear charge very effectively
(b) lanthanide contraction
(c) Both (a) and (b) are true
(d) None of the above is true

107. Following are the values of the electron affinities (in kJ mol^{-1}) of the formation of O^- and O^{2-} from O
(a) −142, −702 (b) −142, 702
(c) 142, 702 (d) −142, −142

108. The statement that is not correct for the periodic classification of elements is
(a) the properties of elements are the periodic functions of their atomic numbers
(b) non-metallic elements are lesser in number than metallic elements
(c) the first ionisation energies of elements along a period do not vary in a regular manner with increase in atomic number
(d) for transition elements the *d*-subshells are filled with electrons monotonically with increase in atomic number

109. The statement is not true for the long form of the periodic table
(a) it reflects the sequence of filling the electrons in the order of the sub-energy shells *s*, *p*, *d* and *f*
(b) it helps to predict the stable valency states of the elements
(c) it reflects trends in physical and chemical properties of the elements
(d) it helps to predict the relative ionicity of the bond between any two elements

110. Following graph shows variation of ionisation potential (IP) with atomic number in second period (Li—Ne). Value of ionisation potential (IP) of Na (11) will be

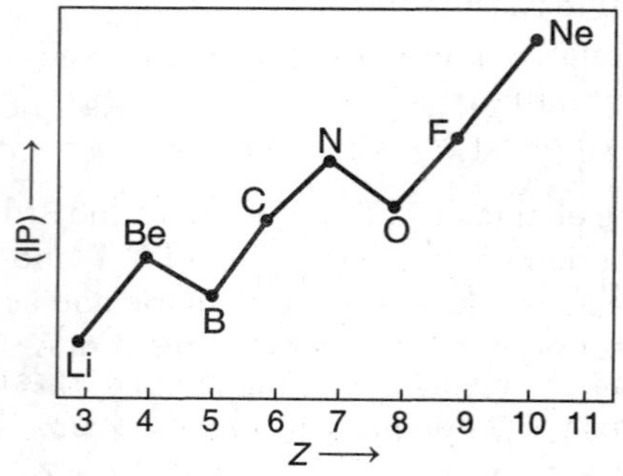

(a) above Ne (b) below Ne but above O
(c) below Li (d) between N and O

111. Based on the fig. in Q. 110, which is the incorrect statements?
(a) I_1 of Be $> I_1$ of B but I_2 of Be $< I_2$ of B
(b) I_1 of Be $< I_1$ of B but I_2 of Be $< I_2$ of B
(c) I_2 of $Be^+ < I_1$ of B^+
(d) I_1 of Be^{2+} is abnormally high

112.
$$M(g) \longrightarrow M^+(g) + e^-, \quad \Delta H = 100 \text{ eV}$$
$$M(g) \longrightarrow M^{2+}(g) + 2e^-, \quad \Delta H = 250 \text{ eV}$$
Which is the incorrect statement?
(a) I_1 of M(g) is 100 eV (b) I_1 *of* M^+(g) is 150 eV
(c) I_2 of M(g) is 250 eV (d) I_2 of M(g) is 150 eV

113. *AB* is predominantly ionic as A^+B^- if
(IP stands for ionisation potential, EA for electron affinity and EN for electronegativity).
(a) $(IP)_A < (IP)_B$ (b) $(EA)_A > (EA)_B$
(c) $(EN)_A < (EN)_B$ (d) $(IP)_B < (IP)_A$

114. Fluorine does not form any polyhalide as other halogens because
(a) it has maximum ionic character
(b) it has low F—F bond energy (38.5 kcal mol^{-1})
(c) of the absence of *d*-orbitals in the valence shell of fluorine
(d) it brings about maximum coordination number in other elements

115. If Aufbau and Hund's rule are not used, then incorrect statement is
(a) K^+ would be coloured ion
(b) Na will be in same *s*-block (if these rules are true)
(c) Cu would be *s*-block element
(d) magnetic moment of Cr(24) would be zero

116. For the element (X), student (A) measured its radius as 102 nm, student (B) as 103 nm and (C) as 100 nm using same apparatus. Their teacher explained that measurements were correct by saying that recorded values by (A), (B) and (C) are
(a) crystal, van der Waals' and covalent radii
(b) covalent, crystal and van der Waals' radii
(c) van der Waals' ionic and covalent
(d) None is correct

117. The relative thermal stabilities of alkali metal halides are such that
(a) CsCl > RbCl > KCl > NaCl > LiCl
(b) LiCl > NaCl > KCl > RbCl > CsCl
(c) CsCl > RbCl < KCl > NaCl < LiCl
(d) CsCl < RbCl > KCl < NaCl > LiCl

118. Within each pair of elements F and Cl, S and Se, and Li and Na, respectively, the elements that release more energy upon an electron gain are **[JEE Main 2020]**
(a) F, Se and Na (b) F, S and Li
(c) Cl, S and Li (d) Cl, Se and Na

119. The heat of hydration of Ca^{2+}, Sr^{2+} and Ba^{2+} in the decreasing order is
(a) $Ca^{2+} > Sr^{2+} > Ba^{2+}$ (b) $Ca^{2+} > Ba^{2+} > Sr^{2+}$
(c) $Sr^{2+} > Ba^{2+} > Ca^{2+}$ (d) $Ba^{2+} > Sr^{2+} > Ca^{2+}$

120. Which of the following have same number of electrons in outermost shell ?
(a) Cr^{2+} and Fe^{+} (b) Sc^{+} and V^{3}
(c) Mn and Cr^{-} (d) Sc^{+} and Ti^{+}

121. If Aufbau rule is not followed, K-19 will be placed in .... block.
(a) *s* (b) *p* (c) *d* (d) *f*

122. Which has maximum ionisation potential?
(a) N (b) O (c) O^{+} (d) Na

123. Which has maximum polarising power in cation ?
(a) Li^{+} (b) Mg^{2+} (c) Al^{3+} (d) O^{2-}

124. Following triads have approximately equal size
(a) Na^{+}, Mg^{2+}, Al^{3+} (*iso*-electronic)
(b) F^{-}, Ne, O^{2-} (*iso*-electronic)
(c) Fe, Co, Ni
(d) Mn^{+}, Fe^{2+}, Cr (*iso*-electronic)

125. Ionic radii of
(a) $Ti^{4+} < Mn^{7+}$ (b) $^{35}Cl^{-} < ^{37}Cl^{-}$
(c) $K^{+} > Cl^{-}$ (d) $P^{3+} > P^{5+}$

126. Which of the following ions has the smallest radius?
(a) Ti^{2+} (b) Pt^{2+} (c) Ni^{2+} (d) Zr^{2+}

127. When the following five anions are arranged in order of decreasing ionic radius, the correct sequence is
(a) $Se^{2-}, I^{-}, Br^{-}, O^{2-}, F^{-}$
(b) $I^{-}, Se^{2-}, O^{2-}, Br^{-}, F^{-}$
(c) $Se^{2-}, I^{-}, Br^{-}, F^{-}, O^{2-}$
(d) $I^{-}, Se^{2-}, Br^{-}, O^{2-}, F^{-}$

128. The ionic radii (in Å) of N^{3-}, O^{2-} and F^{-} respectively are **[JEE Main 2015]**
(a) 1.36, 1.40 and 1.71
(b) 1.36, 1.71 and 1.40
(c) 1.71, 1.40 and 1.36
(d) 1.71, 1.36 and 1.40

129. Which pair is different from the others?
(a) Li—Mg (b) Na—K
(c) Ca—Mg (d) B—Al

130. Which pair is different from the others?
(a) Li—Mg (b) B—Si
(c) Be—Al (d) Li—Na

131. Representative elements belong to
(a) *s*-and *p*-block (b) *d*-block
(c) *d*- and *f*-block (d) *f*-block

132. Covalency is favoured in the following cases
(a) a smaller cation
(b) a larger anion
(c) large charges on cation or anion
(d) in all the above cases

133. The ionisation energy of hydrogen is 13.6 eV and the first ionisation energy of helium is 24.6 eV. Energy evolved in the following electron-gain process is

$$He^{2+} + 2e^{-} \longrightarrow He$$

(a) – 49.2 eV (b) –54.4 eV
(c) – 27.2 eV (d) – 79.0 eV

134. The group number, number of valence electrons and valency of an element with atomic number 15, respectively, are **[JEE Main 2019]**
(a) 16, 5 and 2 (b) 15, 5 and 3
(c) 16, 6 and 3 (d) 15, 6 and 2

135. The electronegativities of N, C, Si and P are such that
(a) P < Si < C < N
(b) Si < P < N < C
(c) Si < P < C < N
(d) P < Si < N < C

136. In general, the properties that decrease and increase down a group in the periodic table, respectively are
(a) electronegativity and atomic radius **[JEE Main 2019]**
(b) electronegativity and electron gain enthalpy
(c) electron gain enthalpy and electronegativity
(d) atomic radius and electronegativity

137. Which of the following will have maximum electron affinity?
(a) $1s^2 2s^2 2p^5$ (b) $1s^2 2s^2 2p^6$
(c) $1s^2 2s^2 2p^6 3s^2 3p^5$ (d) $1s^2 2s^2 2p^6 3s^2 3p^6$

138. Which of the following reactions should be most favoured thermodynamically?
(a) $Na_2O + Cl_2O_7 \longrightarrow 2NaClO_4$
(b) $Na_2O + SO_3 \longrightarrow Na_2SO_4$
(c) $Na_2O + P_2O_5 \longrightarrow 2Na_3PO_4$
(d) $Na_2O + SiO_2 \longrightarrow Na_2SiO_4$

139. The ionic radii of O^{2-}, F^-, Na^+ and Mg^{2+} are 1.35, 1.34, 0.95 and 0.66 Å respectively. The radius of the Ne atom is

(a) 1.39 Å (b) 1.12 Å
(c) 0.85 Å (d) 0.50 Å

140. The following acids have been arranged in the order of decreasing acid strength. Identify the correct order

ClOH (I) BrOH (II) IOH (III)

(a) I > II > III (b) II > I > III
(c) III > II > I (d) I > III > II

141. The atomic radius of Ag is closest to **[JEE Main 2020]**

(a) Hg (b) Au
(c) Ni (d) Cu

142. Which of the following statement is false?

(a) Elements of IB and IIB groups are transition elements
(b) Elements of VB group do not contain metalloids
(c) Elements of IA and IIA groups are normal elements
(d) Elements of IVB group are neither strongly electronegative nor strongly electropositive.

143. The first ionisation energy (in kJ/mol) of Na, Mg, Al and Si respectively, are : **[JEE Main 2020]**

(a) 496, 577, 737, 786 (b) 786, 737, 577, 496
(c) 496, 577, 786, 737 (d) 496, 737, 577, 786

144. Consider the following statements,

I. Cs^+ is more highly hydrated than the other alkali metal ions.
II. Among the alkali metals Li, Na, K and Rb, lithium has the highest melting point.
III. Among the alkali metals only lithium forms a stable nitride by direct combination.

Of these statements

(a) I, II and III are correct
(b) I and II are correct
(c) I and III are correct
(d) II and III are correct

145. Gd (64) has .... unpaired electrons with sum of spin ....

(a) 7, 3.5 (b) 8, 3 (c) 6, 3 (d) 8, 4

146. Which of the following properties shows a clear periodic variation?

(a) First ionisation energy
(b) Molar mass of the element
(c) Number of isotopes of the atom
(d) All of the above

147. Ionisation energy of the element $X(g)$ is I and the electron affinity of $X^+(g)$ is E then

(a) $I = E$ (b) $I = -E$
(c) $I = \frac{E}{2}$ (d) $I = -\frac{E}{2}$

148. For the process

$$X(g) + e^- \longrightarrow X^-(g), \quad \Delta H = x$$

and $$X^-(g) \longrightarrow X(g) + e^-, \quad \Delta H = y$$

Select the correct alternate.

(a) Ionisation energy of $X^-(g)$ is y
(b) Electron affinity of $X(g)$ is x
(c) Electron affinity of $X(g)$ is $-y$
(d) All the above are correct statements

149. The element having greatest difference between its first and second ionisation energy, is **[JEE Main 2019]**

(a) Ca (b) Sc (c) Ba (d) K

150. Which of the following order is wrong?

(a) $NH_3 < PH_3 < AsH_3$ — acidic
(b) Li < Be < B < C — $(IE)_1$
(c) $Al_2O_3 < MgO < Na_2O < K_2O$ — basic
(d) $Li^{2+} < Na^+ < K^+ < Cs^+$ — ionic radius

Objective Questions Type II [One or more than one correct option(s)]

In each of the questions below, four choices are given, of which one or more than one are correct.

1. Stability of ions of Ge, Sn and Pb will be in order

(a) $Ge^{2+} < Sn^{2+} < Pb^{2+}$ (b) $Pb^{4+} < Sn^{4+} < Ge^{4+}$
(c) $Sn^{2+} < Sn^{4+}$ (d) $Pb^{4+} < Pb^{2+}$

2. The first element of a group in many ways differs from the other heavier members of the group. This is due to

(a) the smaller size
(b) the high electronegativity and high ionisation potential
(c) the unavailability of *d*-orbitals
(d) the higher shielding effect

3. The factors that influence the ionisation energies are

(a) the size of the atom
(b) the charge on the nucleus
(c) how effectively the inner electrons screen the nuclear charge
(d) the atomic mass

4. Which is/are correct order of ionic mobility?

(a) $Li^+ < Na^+ < K^+$
(b) $Na^+ < Mg^{2+} < Al^{3+}$
(c) $Al^{3+} < Mg^{2+} < Na^+$
(d) $K^+ < Na^+ < Li^+$

5. The option(s) with only amphoteric oxides is(are) **[JEE Advanced 2017]**

(a) NO, B_2O_3, PbO, SnO_2 (b) Cr_2O_3, CrO, SnO, PbO
(c) Cr_2O_3, BeO, SnO, SnO_2 (d) ZnO, Al_2O_3, PbO, PbO_2

6. An increase in both atomic and ionic radii with atomic number occurs in any group of the Periodic Table and in accordance with this the ionic radii of Ti(IV) and Zr(IV) ions are 0.68 Å and 0.74 Å respectively; but for Hf(IV) ion the ionic radius is 0.75 Å which is almost the same as that for Zr(IV) ion. This is due to
(a) greater degree of covalency in compound of Hf^{4+}
(b) lanthanide contraction
(c) difference in the coordination number of Zr^{4+} and Hf^{4+} in their compounds
(d) actinide contraction

7. When an isotope undergoes K-capture, its mass number
(a) remains the same while the atomic number increases by one
(b) remains the same while the atomic number increases by two
(c) remains the same while the atomic number decreases by one
(d) as well as the atomic number decreases by one

8. The melting point of RbBr is 682°C while that of NaF is 988°C. The principal reason that the melting point of NaF is much higher than that of RbBr is that
(a) the molar mass of NaF is smaller than that of RbBr
(b) the bond in RbBr has more covalent character than the bond in NaF
(c) the difference in electronegativity between Rb and Br is smaller than the difference between Na and F.
(d) the internuclear distance, $r_c + r_a$ is greater for RbBr than for NaF

9. Select the correct statement(s).
(a) Cs^+ is more highly hydrated than the other alkali metal ions
(b) Among the alkali metals Li, Na, K and Rb, lithium has the highest melting point
(c) Ionic mobility of Li^+ is maximum among Li^+, Na^+ and K^+ ions
(d) Ionisation potential of Li is smaller than that of Na

10. Select the correct statements.
(a) Ce, Pr and Nd are *f*-block elements
(b) Cu, Pd and Ni are *d*-block elements
(c) Cu($[Ar]3d^{10}4s^1$) and K($[Ar]4s^1$) have been placed in *s*-block
(d) Si, Ge and As are metalloids

Numerical Value Questions

All these questions have a Numerical value as their answer, solve the questions and write your answer.

1. The energy needed for the following process is 1.96×10^4 kJ mol^{-1}.

$$Li(g) \longrightarrow Li^{3+}(g) + 3e^-$$

If the first ionisation energy of lithium is 520 kJ mol^{-1}, the third ionisation energy of lithium is 11815.05 kJ/mol, then the energy required for the process will be (in kJ/mol)

$$Li^+(g) \longrightarrow Li^{2+}(g) + e^-$$

2. One method for calculating Z_{eff} is to use the equation,

$$Z_{eff} = \sqrt{\frac{(E)(n^2)}{1312\ \text{kJ/mol}}}$$

where, E is the energy necessary to remove an electron from an atom and n is the principal quantum number of the electron. Use this equation to calculate Z_{eff} values for the highest-energy electron in as potassium (E = 418.8 kJ mol^{-1}) and is krypton (E = 1350.7 kJ mol^{-1}).

3. For one-electron species, (IE) is given by

$$(IE) = 13.6\left(\frac{Z^2}{n^2}\right)\text{eV}$$

The (IE) (in eV) of He^+ and Li^{2+} are ......

4. $(IE)_1$ of Cs is 376 kJ mol^{-1}. The maximum number of Cs^+ ions in .... X that can be produced per joule of energy absorbed by a sample of gaseous Cs-atoms?

5. Calculate the electronegativity value of chlorine on Mulliken's scale, given that IP = 13.0 eV and EA = 4.0 eV.

6. From N-atoms of an element A, when half the atoms transform one electron to the another atom. 405 kJ mol^{-1} of energy was found to be consumed. An additional energy of 745 kJ mol^{-1} was further required to convert all the $A^{\ominus}$ ions to $A^{\oplus}$. Calculate the ionisation energy and the electron gain enthalpy of atom in eV (1 eV = 96.48 kJ).

Comprehension Based Questions

In these questions, a passage has been given followed by questions based on it. You have to answer the questions based on the passage given.

***Passage* 1** Following questions are based on Sc($Z = 21$)

1. How many unpaired electron does Sc^{+}, Sc^{2+}, Sc^{3+} have respectively ?
   (a) 0, 1, 0 (b) 1, 2, 3
   (c) 1, 0, 1 (d) 3, 2, 1
2. Z * (effective nuclear charge) is
   (a) 21.0 (b) 20.65 (c) 16.85 (d) 35
3. Effective nuclear charge experienced by $3d$-electron in the formation of Sc^{3+} from Sc^{2+} is
   (a) 4.2 (b) 11.60 (c) 16.85 (d) 9.75

***Passage* 2** Following rule in general, classifies p-block elements into metals, non-metals and metalloids (where, P is the period and N the valence electrons)

$(P + 1) > N$, the element would be metal
$(P + 1) < N$, the element would be non-metal
$(P + 1) = N$, the element would be metalloid

Answer the following questions.

1. Metalloid will be out of elements with atomic number 13, 14, 15, 16
   (a) 13 (b) 14
   (c) 15 (d) 16
2. Metals will be out of 13, 31, 35, 54
   (a) 13, 31 (b) 31, 35
   (c) 35, 54 (d) 13, 54
3. Non-metals will be out of 13, 31, 35, 54
   (a) 13, 31 (b) 31, 35 (c) 35, 54 (d) 13, 54

***Passage* 3** In the following table I_1, I_2 and I_3 of the main group elements in 2nd period have been given.

	Li	Be	B	C	N	O	F	Ne
I_1	513	899	801	1086	1402	1314	1681	2080
I_2	7298	1757	2427	2352	2856	3388	3374	3952
I_3	11815	14848	3660	4620	4578	5300	6050	6122

Answer the following questions based on the above table.

1. There is increase in ionisation energy along a period going Li to Ne, but I_1 of B is less than that of Be. This is due to
   (a) valence electron in B is in $2p$-orbital of higher energy than that of Be in $2s$-orbital of lower energy
   (b) removal of paired electron in Be requires higher energy than that of removal of unpaired electron in B.
   (c) Both (a) and (b) above
   (d) None of the above
2. We observe that I_1 of Be > I_1 of B but I_2 of Be < I_2 of B.
   Select the correct explanation(s).
   (a) Electron in Be is paired while in B, electron is unpaired, hence I_1 of Be > I_1 of B
   (b) Electron in Be^{+} is unpaired while in B^{+}, electron is paired, hence I_2 of Be < I_2 of B.
   (c) Both (a) and (b) above
   (d) None of the above
3. There occurs a fall while going from N to O. It is due to
   (a) stable configuration of N $\boxed{\uparrow}\boxed{\uparrow}\boxed{\uparrow}$
   (b) higher atomic number of O
   (c) stable configuration of O $\boxed{\uparrow\downarrow}\boxed{\uparrow\downarrow}\boxed{\ }$
   (d) lone pairs on O.

***Passage* 4** The sums of first and second ionisation energies and those of third and fourth ionisation energies (in MJ mol^{-1}) of nickel and platinum are

	$(IE)_1 + (IE)_2$	$(IE)_3 + (IE)_4$
Ni	2.49	8.80
Pt	2.66	6.70

Based on this information, answer the following questions.

1. Most common oxidation states of Ni and Pt are respectively
   (a) +2, +2 (b) +4, +2 (c) +2, +4 (d) +4, +4
2. Which is the most stable complex of Ni?
   (a) $[Ni(CN)_4]^{2-}$ (b) $[Ni(CN)_6]^{2-}$
   (c) $[Ni(CN)_3]^{-}$ (d) $[Ni(CO)_6]$
3. Which is the least stable complex of Pt?
   (a) $K_2[PtCl_6]$
   (b) $[Pt(en)_3]Cl_4$
   (c) $K_2[PtCl_4]$
   (d) $K_2[Pt(C_2O_4)_3]$

***Passage* 5** The $(IE)_1$ and the $(IE)_2$ in kJ mol^{-1} of a few elements designated by Roman numerals are shown below.

Element	$(IE)_1$	$(IE)_2$
A	2372	5251
B	520	7300
C	900	1760
D	1680	3380

Based on the above information, answer the following questions.

1. Which of the above elements is likely to be a reactive metal?
(a) A (b) B (c) C (d) D
2. Which of the above elements is likely to a reactive non-metal?
(a) A (b) B
(c) C (d) D
3. Which represents a noble gas?
(a) A (b) B
(c) C (d) D

***Passage* 6** Consider the following table comparing ionic radius

Ion →	N^{3-}	O^{2-}	F^-	Na^+	Mg^{2+}
Number of electron	10	10	10	10	10
Number of nuclear protons	7	8	9	11	12
Ionic radius (pm)	146	140	133	98	79

Answer the following questions.

1. Select the correct alternate(s) in terms of size.
(a) $Na > Na^+$ (b) $Mg > Mg^+ > Mg^{2+}$
(c) $F^- > F$ (d) $O^{2-} > O^- > O$
2. All the above species are isoelectronic but they differ in size. It is due to
(a) increase in number of protons
(b) removal of valence shell
(c) decrease in repulsive force
(d) addition of additional shell

***Passage* 7** The heats of formation (ΔH_f°) of the oxides of the third period, sodium to chlorine, are in kJ mol^{-1}

Na_2O	MgO	Al_2O_3	SiO_2	P_4O_{10}	SO_3	Cl_2O_7
− 416	− 602	− 1676	− 911	− 2984	− 395	+250

Based on these data, answer the following questions.

1. Which oxide has maximum negative heat of formation per oxygen atom?
(a) P_4O_{10} (b) Al_2O_3 (c) Na_2O (d) MgO
2. Most stable and least stable oxides are
(a) P_4O_{10}, Cl_2O_7 (b) Na_2O, Cl_2O_7
(c) MgO, Cl_2O_7 (d) Cl_2O_7, MgO
3. Stability order of the above oxides is
(a) $Cl_2O_7 < SO_3 < P_4O_{10} < SiO_2 < Al_2O_3 < MgO < Na_2O$
(b) $Cl_2O_7 < SO_3 < P_4O_{10} < Na_2O < SiO_2 < Al_2O_3 < MgO$
(c) $Cl_2O_7 < SO_3 < Na_2O < MgO < SiO_2 < Al_2O_3 < P_4O_{10}$
(d) $P_4O_{10} < Al_2O_3 < SiO_2 < MgO < Na_2O < SO_3 < Cl_2O_7$

Matrix-Match Type

Given below are Matching Type Questions, with two columns (each having some items) each . Each item of Column I has to be matched with the items of Column II.

1. Match atomic number of elements (in Column I) with position of elements in the periodic table (in Column II).

Column I		Column II	
A.	19	1.	*p*-block
B.	22	2.	*f*-block
C.	32	3.	*d*-block
D.	64	4.	*s*-block

2. Match the type of elements (in Column I) with the corresponding electronic configuration (in Column II).

Column I		Column II	
A.	Inert gas elements	1.	ns^1 to ns^2np^5
B.	Main group elements	2.	$1s^2$ to ns^2np^6
C.	Transition elements	3.	$(n-2)f^{1-14}$ $(n-1)s^2p^6d^{10}ns^2$
D.	Inner transition elements	4.	$(n-1)d^{1-9}ns^2$
		5.	$(n-1)d^{10}ns^2$

3. Match the atomic number (in Column I) with its IUPAC nomenclature (in Column II).

Column I		Column II	
A.	105	1.	Uuh
B.	107	2.	Uun
C.	109	3.	Uns
D.	110	4.	Unp
E.	116	5.	Une

4. Match the element (in Column I) with its corresponding property (ies) (in Column II).

Column I		Column II	
A.	F	1.	Maximum electron affinity
B.	Cl	2.	Maximum electronegativity
C.	Br	3.	Exists as X_2 in liquid state
D.	I	4.	Exists as X_2 in solid state
E.	At	5.	X_2 sublimates on heating
		6.	X_2 is the best oxidising agent
		7.	Radioactive element

5. Match the oxide in Column II with its corresponding property (ies) in Column II.

	Column I		Column II
A.	Na_2O	1.	Soluble in HCl
B.	MgO	2.	Soluble in NaOH
C.	Al_2O_3	3.	Turns blue litmus red
D.	SiO_2	4.	Turns red litmus blue
E.	P_2O_5	5.	Giant molecule
F.	SO_3	6.	Acid-rain

Single Integer Answer Questions

Answer of these questions is a single digit lying between 0 to 9.

1. Maximum oxidation state shown by Mn is ....
2. Electronegativity $= \frac{(IP) + (EA)}{N}$. This $N =$ ....
3. Stability of Tl is maximum when its valency is ....
4. Catention is maximum for the element with atomic number ....
5. Lanthanides have been placed in period ....
6. Actinides have been placed in period ....
7. Which is maximum hydrated?
8. Which is maximum basic in nature?

Following species have been given. Assign the species (by its number) showing the indicated property.

(1) LiCl (2) $AlCl_3$ (3) Al_2O_3 (4) BaO
(5) LiH (6) Cl_2 (7) F_2 (8) Br_2 (9) $MgCl_2$

9. Number of amphoteric oxides out of Na_2O, MgO, Al_2O_3, SnO_2, BeO_2 and CaO is ....
10. Maximum electron affinity is shown by the species at serial number.
    (1) O (2) F
    (3) Cl^- (4) He (5) N
11. Diatomic molecule is formed by the element at serial number (1) and at serial number ....
    (1) $[Ne]\,3s^2 3p^1$ (2) $[Ne]\,3s^1$
    (3) $[Ne]\,3s^2$ (4) $[He]\,2s^2 2p^3$
    (5) $[Ne]\,3s^2 3p^6$ (6) [Ne]
12. An ionic compound is formed of the type *XY* from *X* with electronic configuration ns^1 and *Y* with valence shell electrons ....
13. Maximum oxidation state shown by chalcogens is ....
14. Ionisation energy of M^{3+} is 217.6 eV compared to that of He^+ (54.4 eV). Thus, atomic number of M^{3+} is ....
15. The 1st, 2nd and 3rd ionisation enthalpies, I_1, I_2, and I_3, of four atoms with atomic numbers $n, n+1, n+2$, and $n+3$, where $n < 10$, are tabulated below. What is the value of n? **[JEE Advanced 2020]**

Atomic number	Ionisation enthalpy (kJ/mol)		
	I_1	I_2	I_3
n	1681	3374	6050
$n+1$	2081	3952	6122
$n+2$	496	4562	6910
$n+3$	738	1451	7733

Answers

Objective Questions Type I [Only one correct option]

1. (b)	2. (c)	3. (d)	4. (a)	5. (d)	6. (d)	7. (a)	8. (b)	9. (c)	10. (a)
11. (c)	12. (c)	13. (b)	14. (d)	15. (b)	16. (c)	17. (d)	18. (b)	19. (c)	20. (b)
21. (b)	22. (d)	23. (b)	24. (a)	25. (c)	26. (a)	27. (b)	28. (c)	29. (c)	30. (b)
31. (c)	32. (c)	33. (a)	34. (b)	35. (d)	36. (b)	37. (d)	38. (a)	39. (d)	40. (a)
41. (a)	42. (a)	43. (b)	44. (c)	45. (c)	46. (b)	47. (c)	48. (b)	49. (c)	50. (a)
51. (b)	52. (c)	53. (c)	54. (d)	55. (c)	56. (c)	57. (c)	58. (a)	59. (a)	60. (b)
61. (c)	62. (a)	63. (c)	64. (a)	65. (c)	66. (a)	67. (b)	68. (d)	69. (a)	70. (c)
71. (a)	72. (b)	73. (b)	74. (a)	75. (b)	76. (c)	77. (a)	78. (b)	79. (a)	80. (a)
81. (d)	82. (a)	83. (a)	84. (b)	85. (b)	86. (a)	87. (c)	88. (d)	89. (c)	90. (d)
91. (b)	92. (a)	93. (c)	94. (a)	95. (d)	96. (a)	97. (b)	98. (b)	99. (a)	100. (d)
101. (a)	102. (a)	103. (d)	104. (a)	105. (a)	106. (c)	107. (b)	108. (c)	109. (d)	110. (c)
111. (a)	112. (c)	113. (d)	114. (c)	115. (a)	116. (a)	117. (b)	118. (c)	119. (a)	120. (c)
121. (c)	122. (c)	123. (c)	124. (c)	125. (d)	126. (c)	127. (d)	128. (c)	129. (a)	130. (d)
131. (a)	132. (d)	133. (d)	134. (b)	135. (c)	136. (a)	137. (c)	138. (a)	139. (a)	140. (a)
141. (b)	142. (d)	143. (d)	144. (d)	145. (d)	146. (a)	147. (b)	148. (d)	149. (d)	150. (b)

Objective Questions Type II [One or more than one correct option(s)]

1. (a, b, c, d)	2. (a, b, c)	3. (a, b, c)	4. (a, c)	5. (c, d)
6. (b)	7. (c)	8. (d)	9. (b)	10. (a, b, d)

Numerical Value Questions

1. 7269	2. (a) 2.26 (b) 4.06 (c) 217.6	3. (a) 54.4 (b) 122.4
4. 1.60	5. 3.03	6. – 3.5

Comprehension Based Questions

Passage 1 – 1. (a) 2. (d) 3. (a)
Passage 2 – 1. (b) 2. (a) 3. (c)
Passage 3 – 1. (c) 2. (c) 3. (a)
Passage 4 – 1. (c) 2. (a) 3. (c)
Passage 5 – 1. (b) 2. (d) 3. (a)
Passage 6 – 1. (a, b, c, d) 2. (a)
Passage 7 – 1. (a) 2. (a) 3. (c)

Matrix-Match Type

1. A → (4); B → (3); C → (1); D → (2)
2. A → (2); B → (1); C → (4,5); D → (3)
3. A → (4); B → (3); C → (5); D → (2); E → (1)
4. A → (2,6); B → (1); C → (3); D → (4,5); E → (7)
5. A → (1,4); B → (1,4); C → (1,2); D → (1,2,5); E → (2,3); F → (2,3,6)

Single Integer Answer Questions

1. (7)	2. (2)	3. (1)	4. (6)	5. (6)	6. (7)	7. (2)	8. (5)	9. (3)	10. (2)
11. (5)	12. (7)	13. (6)	14. (4)	15. (9)					

Solutions

Objective Questions Type I [Only one correct option]

1. (*b*) First long period starts with 4th period [K(19) -- Kr(36)]
Thus, total = 18 elements

4. (*a*) $^{m}_{115}A \longrightarrow {}^{m-4}_{113}B + \alpha\ ({}^{4}_{2}He)$

6. (*d*) Valence shell electronic configuration is d^5s^1
Differentiating electron goes into *d*-orbitals. Thus, *d*-block element. Group VIB.

7. (*a*) Sc^{3+} 18 electrons
Thus, *Z* (atomic number = 21)
$[Ar]\ 4s^2 3d^1$
Thus, III group, thus given matching is incorrect.

8. (*b*) 113 – 32 – 32 – 18 = 31
Thus, 113 and 115 are placed as shown

IIIB		VB	
Ga	31]18	33	As]18
In	49]32	51	Sb]32
Tl	81]32	81	Bi]32
	113 (ns^2np^1)	115 (ns^2np^3)	

Thus, these belong to *p*-block.

9. (*c*) Atomic number 113 belong to *p*-block (Group IIIA).
Probable oxidation states are +1, +3, but due to inert-pair effect

stability of +1 > +3

Thus, M^+

10. (*a*) Atomic number (115) has E.C. has

$$[Rn]_{86}\ 7s^2 5d^{10} 4f^{14} 7p^3$$

Probable oxidation states are +3, + 5.
But due to inert pair effect M^{3+} is the most stable cation.

11. (*c*) The element with $Z = 120$ will be an alkaline earth metal. Recently, oganesson (Og) with atomic number 118 is named by IUPAC is a noble gas and placed just two place before 120. So, the general electronic configuration is represented as [noble gas]ns^2 and element with $Z = 120$ exist as an alkaline earth metal.

12. (*c*) $X : ns^2np^1$
Valency = + 3 (as in Al)
It can lose three electrons to attain stable configuration.
$Y : ns^2np^3$
Valency = – 3 (as in N)
It can gain five electrons to attain stable configuration.
Thus, $X^{3+}Y^{3-}$ or ***XY***

13. (*b*) (a) $CaCl_2 \cdot 6H_2O \xrightarrow{\Delta} \underset{\text{(Anhydrous)}}{CaCl_2} + 6H_2O$

(b) $MgCl_2 \cdot 8H_2O \xrightarrow{\Delta} MgO + 2HCl + 6H_2O$

The dehydration of hydrated chloride of calcium can be achieved. The corresponding hydrated chloride of magnesium on heating suffer hydrolysis.

(c) BeO → Amphoteric
MgO, CaO, SrO, BaO ⇒ All are basic oxide

14. (*d*) Chalcogens are the elements of oxygen family :
Valence shell configuration : ns^2np^4
Group : 16
Block : *p*

15. (*b*) M^{3+} : $[Ar]\ 3d^{10} 4s^2$
M : $[Ar]\ 3d^{10} 4s^2 4p^3$
Three electrons have been removed from 4*p*-subshell.
Thus, *p*-block element.

17. (*d*) (a) Na, K — Metals
(b) F, Cl — Non-metals
(c) Cu, Ag — Metals
(d) B, Si — Metalloids

18. (*b*) Transition metals have very high (IE). They do not emit colour in flame.

19. (*c*) Ni : $[Ar]\ 3d^8 4s^2$
Last electron enters into 3*d*-suborbit.
Thus, *d*-block element.

20. (*b*) Fe(26) : $[Ar]\ 3d^6 4s^2$
Fe^{3+} : $[Ar]\ 3d^5$

21. (*b*) Ce (58) $[Xe]_{54}\ 4f^1 5d^1 6s^2$
Thus, Ce^{4+} has [Xe] configuration.

22. (*d*) Lanthanides form 4*f*-series.

23. (*b*) 5*f*-block elements

24. (*a*) $[Xe]_{54}$ [1|1|1|1|1|1|1] [1| | | |] [1↓]
$4f^7$ — Stable due to half-filled 4*f*-orbits; $5d^1$; $6s^2$

25. (*c*) 1 1 5
↑ ↑ ↑
U u p
Thus, Uup

26. (*a*) Smaller the (IE), greater the metallic nature.

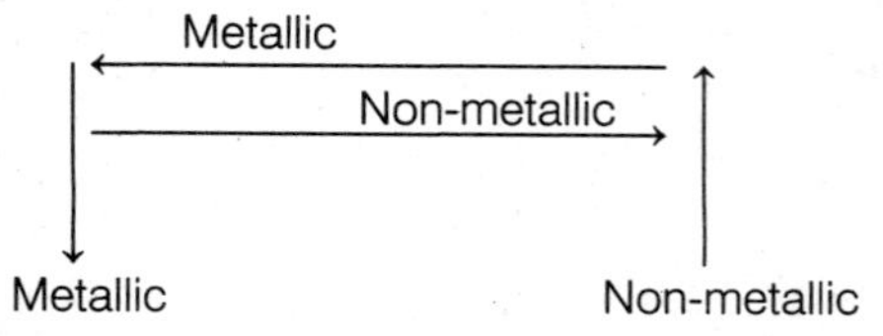

(d) "In bottom row" lanthanides

27. (*b*) Elements in a group have same (EC) in valence shell.

28. (*c*) EC : $1s^2 2s^2 2p^6 3s^3 3p^6 4s^1$

(Total 19 electrons, i.e. $Z = 19$)

It is K (alkali metals of Group 1)

Graded property will be that of same group.

(a) $[Ar]\, 3d^{10} 4s^1$ — Cu group 11

(b) $[Kr]\, 4d^{10} 5s^1$ — Ag group 11

(c) $[Kr]\, 5s^1$ — Rb group 1

30. (*b*) Element with atomic number 113 is placed in group 13 (IIIA) and has EC of valence shell as $ns^2 np^1$.

Si — Group 14

Ga — Group 13

Bi — Group 15

At — Group 17

31. (*c*) As, Sb, Bi are group 15 having oxidation +3 and +5. Stability is in order

$$As^{5+} > Sb^{5+} > Bi^{5+}$$

$$As^{3+} < Sb^{3+} < Bi^{3+} \text{ due to inert-pair effect}$$

Thus, $BiCl_3$ is most stable.

32. (*c*) Due to inert-pair effect, stability of

$$Ga^{3+} > In^{3+} > Tl^{3+}$$

and $\quad Ga^{+} < In^{+} < Tl^{+}$

Thus, $\quad Tl^{3+} + 2e^- \longrightarrow Tl^+$

is most spontaneous. Thus, $\Delta G° < 0$ and is most negative.

33. (*a*) Cl_2O_7 : Cl = +7

34. (*b*) $Pb^{4+} + 2e^- \longrightarrow Pb^{2+}$

Stability of $Pb^{2+} > Pb^{4+}$

Hence, Pb^{4+} is reduced most easily and is thus best oxidising agent.

35. (*d*)

Element	Valence electrons	Possible ion
A	3	A^{3+}
B	6	B^{2-}

$B + 2e^- \longrightarrow B^{2-}$

8 electrons in valence shell (stable)

$A \longrightarrow A^{3+} + 3e^-$
Stable

Thus, $A^{3+}B^{2-}$ A_2B_3

36. (*b*) Due to poor shielding of *d*-orbital in Ga and hence effective nuclear charge the outer e^- experiences more atomic radius of Ga is smaller than that of Al. Thus, Ga < Al < In < Tl.

37. (*d*) He^+, Li^{2+} and Be^{3+} are isoelectronic of H atom (with one electron). Hence, single electron is not screened.

38. (*a*) Effective nuclear charge $Z_{eff} = Z - S$

where, Z = atomic number

and S = screening constant

= 0.35 per electron for electron in *n*th orbit.

= 0.85 per electron for electrons in (*n* – 1)th orbit

= 1.00 per electron for electrons in (*n* – 2)th, (*n* – 3)th, (*n* – 4)th orbit

= 0.30 per electron in 1*s*-orbital (when alone)

Be $1s^2 2s^2$ one valence-electron in 2*s* is screened by one electron in 2*s*-orbital (*n*th orbit) and two electrons in 1*s*-orbital ((*n* – 1) th orbit)

$$\therefore \quad S = 0.35 + 2 \times 0.85 = 2.05$$

$$\therefore \quad Z_{eff} = 4 - 2.05 = 1.95 \text{ (given)}$$

Be^+ $1s^2 2s^1$ 2*s* electron is screened by two electrons in 1*s*-orbital ((*n* – 1) th orbital)

$$S = 2 \times 0.85 = 1.70$$

$$\therefore \quad Z_{eff} = 4 - 1.70 = 2.30$$

Be^{2+} $1s^2$ one electron in 1*s*-orbital (alone exists) is screened by another electron in same orbit. Thus,

$$S = 0.30$$

$$\therefore \quad Z_{eff} = 4 - 0.30 = 3.70$$

Be^{3+} $\quad 1s^1$

no-screening (single electron)

Thus, $\quad Z_{eff} = 4$

Thus, $Z_{effective}$: Be < Be^+ < Be^{2+} < Be^{3+}

40. (*a*) Cu^+

$$\underbrace{1s^2}_{(n-2)} \quad \underbrace{2s^2 2p^6}_{(n-1)} \quad \underbrace{3s^2 3p^6 3d^{10}}_{n}$$

$$S = 2 \times 1 + 8 \times 0.85 + 17 \times 0.35 = 14.75$$

(One *d*-electron is screened by 17 electrons in *n*th, 8 electrons in (*n* – 1) and 2 electrons in (*n* – 2). For values refer Q. 38.)

$$Z_{eff} = 29 - 14.75 = 14.25$$

41. (*a*)

$$r_n = \frac{n^2 a_0}{Z_{eff}}$$

Cs (alkali metal) has largest atomic radius.

42. (*a*) Max ⟵ Size (across); Size ↓ Max (down)

F < Cl < Mg < Cs

43. (*b*) Radius decreases along a period left to right.

B C N O F
⟵ max. 70 pm

Thus, covalent radius of B would be higher than that of N.

44. (*c*) (a) Multiplicity *b/w* atom means multiple of more than atoms well start combining with each other.

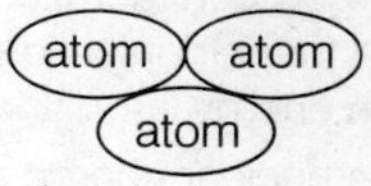

∴ bond length, length decreases.

∴ of is correct

$$\text{Bond length} \propto \frac{1}{\text{Bond strength}}$$

(b) When there is huge difference *b/w* electronegativity *b/w* atoms, atoms forms ionic bond strength of ionic bond > covalent

∴ Bond length decreases.

Hence, (a) and (b) both are correct.

∴ Option (c) is answer.

46. (*b*) $X = {}_{33}As \rightarrow$ Metalloid
$Y = {}_{53}I \rightarrow$ Non-metal
$Z = {}_{83}Bi \rightarrow$ Metal

48. (*b*) Atomic size decreases as we move left to right in *d*-block elements.

50. (*a*) $(IE)_1$ of 5*d*-series are higher, than those of 3*d* and 4*d* -series elements because of presence of 4*f* electrons before 5*d* which poor shielding effective and hence Z_{eff} increases and so $(IE)_1$ also increases.

52. (*c*) Order of first ionisation energy is

$$Sc > Na > K > Rb$$

∵ As we move down group atomic size increases and IE decreases and along period effective nuclear charge increases and IE also increases.

53. (*c*)

$$Mg \longrightarrow Mg^+ + e^- \quad (IE)_1$$
$$Mg^+ \longrightarrow Mg^{2+} + e^- \quad (IE)_2$$
$$Mg^{2+} \longrightarrow Mg^{3+} + e^- \quad (IE)_3$$
$$(IE)_1 < (IE)_2 < (IE)_3$$

54. (*d*) Be

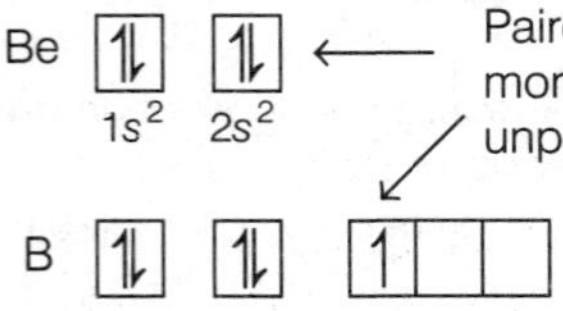

Paired electron requires more energy than unpaired electron in B

Thus, IE of Be > B

N 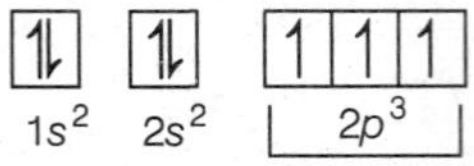

N have higher (IE) than O due to half-filled *p*-orbital

O 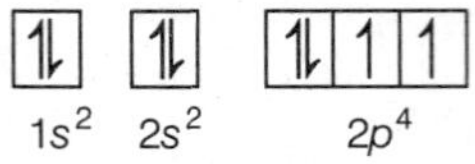

Thus, IE of N > O

$(IE)_{Li > Na}$ due to smaller size of Li

$$He \longrightarrow He^+ + e^- \quad (IE)_1$$
$$He^+ \longrightarrow He^{2+} + e^- \quad (IE)_2$$
$$(IE)_2 > (IE)_1$$

Thus, (IE) of $He^+ > He$
Thus, (d) is incorrect.

55. (*c*) M^+ (alkali metal ion) has inert gas configuration. Thus, after M^+ is formed from *M* (by $(IE)_1$), further ionisation to M^{2+} from M^+ (by $(IE)_2$) requires very high energy.

58. (*a*) Going down the group effective nuclear charge remains almost constant, hence (IE) is dependent on radius of two element.

64. (*a*)

$$\underset{\text{(Unstable)}}{2FeI_3} \longrightarrow \underset{\text{(Stable)}}{2FeI_2} + I_2$$

Due to strong reducing nature of I^-

$$2Fe^{3+} + 2I^- \longrightarrow 2Fe^{3+} + I^-$$

remaining halides of Fe^{2+} and Fe^{3+} are stable.

66. (*a*) $F + e^- \longrightarrow F^-$
Can be reduced easily.

67. (*b*) Chlorine have more electron affinity than fluorine because of very small size of fluorine atom it is difficult for fluorine atom to accommodate an electron in its 2*p*. Whereas in chlorine electron is accommodated in 3*p* and 3*p* > 2*p*.

On Pauling's scale
EN

72. (*b*) Si_{14} [Ne] $3s^2 3p^2$ 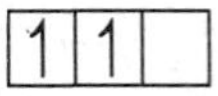 2.8

P_{15} [Ne] $3s^2 3p^3$  2.1

S_{16} [Ne] $3s^2 3p^4$ 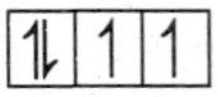 2.5

Thus. $P < S < Si$

73. (*b*) *A* (1.2) is electropositive element
B (3.4) is electronegative element
Thus, ionic bond is formed.

75. (*b*)

$$(EN)_A = \frac{(EA)_A + (IE)_A}{2}$$
$$X = \frac{Y + (IE)_A}{2}$$
$$\therefore \quad (IE)_A = 2X - Y$$

79. (*a*) $F_2 > Cl_2 > Br_2 > I_2$

80. (*a*) I^- is oxidised by Br_2, Cl_2, F_2
Br^- is oxidised by Cl_2, F_2
Cl^- is oxidised by F_2

81. (*d*) The electronegativity values of given elements on the Pauling scale can be shown as follows :

Period No.	Group 13	Group 14	Group 15	Group 16
3	Al (1.5)	Si (1.8)	P (2.1)	S (2.5)
4	Ga (1.6)	Ge (1.8)		Se (2.4)
5				Te (2.01)

On moving from left to right across a period, i.e. from Ga to Se, the effective nuclear charge increases and size decreases.

As a result, the value of electronegativity increases due to increase in the attraction between the outer electrons and the nucleus. Whereas on moving down the group, (i.e. from Se to Te), the atomic size increases.

As a result, the force of attraction between the outer electron and the nucleus decreases. Hence, the electronegativity decreases.

82. (*a*) Size of $Li^+ < Na^+ < Rb^+ < Cs^+$
Hydration $Li^+ > Na^+ > Rb^+ > Cs^+$
Size of hydrated ion $Li^+ > Na^+ > Rb^+ > Cs^+$
smaller the size, $Li^+ < Na^+ < Rb^+ < Cs^+$
larger the hydration, hence larger the size of the hydrated ion (in aqueous solution)
(∵ large number of H_2O molecules are attached)

83. (*a*) Heavier the ion, smaller the ionic mobility.

Size	$Li^+ < Na^+ < K^+$
Hydration	$Li^+ > Na^+ > K^+$
Ionic mobility	$Li^+ < Na^+ < K^+$
Discharged at cathode	$Li^+ < Na^+ < K^+$ (Most easiest)

84. (*b*) While moving across a period, metallic property of elements changes first into metalloids than into non-metallic nature therefore.

⇒ Metal gives basic oxides.
Metalloid produces amphoteric oxides.
Non-metal gives acidic oxides.
So, $X \rightarrow$ metal, $Y \rightarrow$ metalloid and $Z \rightarrow$ non-metal
⇒ Order of atomic number : $X < Y < Z$
⇒ As, X, Y and Z belongs to 3rd period,
X can be Na or Mg
Y can be Al or Si
Z can be P or S or Cl

85. (*b*) Na^+, Mg^{2+} and Al^{3+} are isoelectronic.

Size	$Na^+ > Mg^{2+} > Al^{3+}$		
Charge	+1	+2	+3

Smaller the size of cation,
larger the charge,
Greater the hydration
Thus, $Na^+ < Mg^{2+} < Al^{3+}$

87. (*c*)
$$\underset{\text{Basic oxide}}{ZnO} + 2HCl \longrightarrow ZnCl_2 + H_2O$$
$$\underset{\text{Acidic oxide}}{ZnO} + 2NaOH \longrightarrow Na_2ZnO_2 + H_2O$$

88. (*d*)

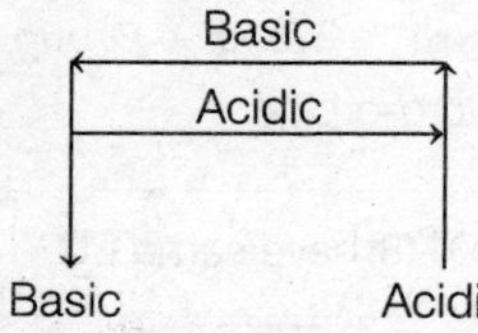

89. (*c*) PbO is soluble in NaOH — an acidic oxide
PbO is soluble in HCl — a basic oxide

91. (*b*) Smaller the size of element, greater the tendency to donate electron-pair. Thus, greater the basic nature.

92. (*a*) $\underset{\text{Ionic hydride}}{2NaH} + 2H_2O \longrightarrow \underset{\text{Basic}}{2NaOH} + 2H_2$

93. (*c*) NaH is an ionic hydride, others are covalent hydrides.

94. (*a*) $H^- \longrightarrow H + e^-$

95. (*d*) (a) $NaH + H_2O \longrightarrow NaOH + \underset{\text{Reducing nature}}{H_2}$

(b)

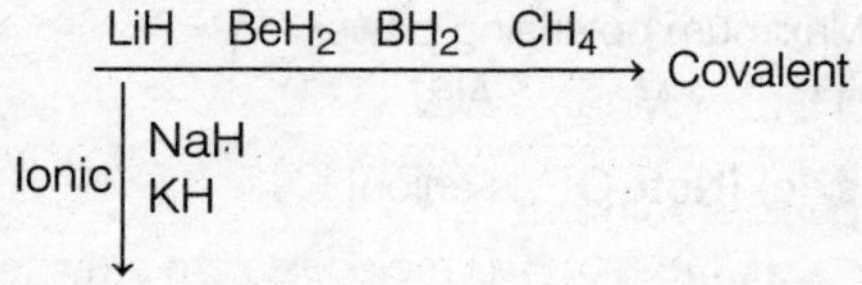

(c) $\rangle C{=}O + LiAlH_4 \longrightarrow \rangle CHOH$

96. (*a*)
$$M \longrightarrow M^+ + e^- \quad (IE)_1 = 100 \text{ eV}$$
$$M \longrightarrow M^{2+} + e^- \quad (IE)_2 = 150 \text{ eV}$$
$$M^{2+} \longrightarrow M^{3+} + e^- \quad (IE)_3 = 1500 \text{ eV}$$

$(IE)_3$ is very high indicating that M^{3+} is not formed easily. Thus, M^{3+} has attained inert gas configuration.

$$\underset{1s^2 2s^2}{Be} \longrightarrow \underset{1s^2 2s^1}{Be^+} + e^-$$
$$\underset{1s^2 2s^1}{Be^+} \longrightarrow \underset{1s^2}{Be^{2+}} + e^-$$

97. (*b*) $X(g) \longrightarrow X^+(g) + e^- \quad E_1$ for $\frac{N_0}{2}$ atoms

$\frac{N_0}{2}$ atoms of $X(g)$ have been ionised, by energy $= E_1$

Thus, ionisation energy $X(g) = \frac{2E_1}{N_0}$ per atom

$X(g) + e^- \longrightarrow X^-(g) \quad E_2$ for $\frac{N_0}{2}$ atoms

Thus, electron affinity of $X(g)$ is $\frac{2E_0}{N_0}$ per atom.

98. (*b*) Electron affinity ⟶ energy change when an electron is added to an isolated gaseous atom.

$$O(g) + e^- \longrightarrow O^-(g); \Delta_{eg}H = -141 \text{kJ}$$
$$O^- + e^- \longrightarrow O^{2-}(g); \Delta_{eg}H = +780 \text{kJ}$$

∵ In order to add 2nd electron the energy has to be supplied to overcome the repulsive force (i.e. electron affinity is positive here).

99. (*a*) The oxidation states of nitrogen in following molecules are as follows:

$$NO_3^- \rightarrow +5$$
$$NO_2 \rightarrow +4$$
$$NO \rightarrow +2$$
$$N_2O \rightarrow +1$$

100. (*d*) $\Delta x \longrightarrow$ E.N. difference
Linus Pauling

$$\text{Ionic character} = 1 - e^{-\left(\frac{\Delta x}{2}\right)^2} \quad \left[50\% = \frac{50}{100} = \frac{1}{2}\right]$$

$$\frac{1}{2} = 1 - e^{-\left(\frac{\Delta x}{2}\right)^2} \Rightarrow \frac{1}{2} = e^{-\left(\frac{\Delta x}{2}\right)^2}$$

$$2^{-1} = e^{-\left(\frac{\Delta x}{2}\right)^2} \Rightarrow \ln 2^{-1} = -\left(\frac{\Delta x}{2}\right)^2$$

$$\ln 2 = -\left(\frac{\Delta x}{2}\right)^2 \Rightarrow \ln 2 = \left(\frac{\Delta x}{2}\right)^2$$

$$4 \ln 2 = (\Delta x)^2$$
$$\Delta x = \sqrt{4 \ln 2} = 1.66$$

101. (*a*) Smaller the size of anion, smaller the polarising power and thus larger the ionic character of NaX. Thus, ionic character

NaI < NaBr < NaCl < NaF

and mp : NaI < NaBr < NaCl < NaF

102. (*a*) Based on Fajan's rule.

104. (*a*)

Ionic	Amphoteric	Giant	
A	*B*	*C* →	Oxide
Na_2O	Al_2O_3	SiO_2	Acidic
↓ Basic			

Thus, atomic number increases in the order $A < B < C$.

105. (*a*)

	Ionic radius	(IE)	Oxidising power	(EN)
F, Cl, Br, I	↓	↑	↑	↑

107. (*b*)
$$O + e^- \longrightarrow O^- \qquad (EA) < 0$$
$$O^- + e^- \longrightarrow O^{2-} \qquad (EA) > 0$$

110. (*c*) (IP) of Na(11) < (IP) of Li(3)

112. (*c*)
$$M(g) \longrightarrow M^+(g) + e^- \qquad I_1(M) = \Delta H_1 = 100 \text{ eV}$$
(a) is correct
$$M^+(g) \longrightarrow M^{2+}(g) + e^- \qquad I_2(M) = 250 - 100 = 150 \text{ eV}$$
or $I_1(M^+) = 150$ eV

(b) is correct

I_2 of $M(g)$ is 150 eV thus (c) is incorrect.

113. (*c*)
$$A \longrightarrow A^+ + e^- \qquad (IP)_A < (IP)_B$$
$$B + e^- \longrightarrow B^- \qquad (EA)_B > (EA)_A$$
$$(EN)_B > (EN)_B$$

115. (*a*) K(19) $1s^2 2s^2 2p^6\ 3s^2 3p^6 3d^1$

K^+(19) $1s^2 2s^2 2p^6\ 3s^2 3p^6$ Colourless ion due to lack of electron in *d*-orbitals

Thus, (a) is incorrect.

116. (*a*)

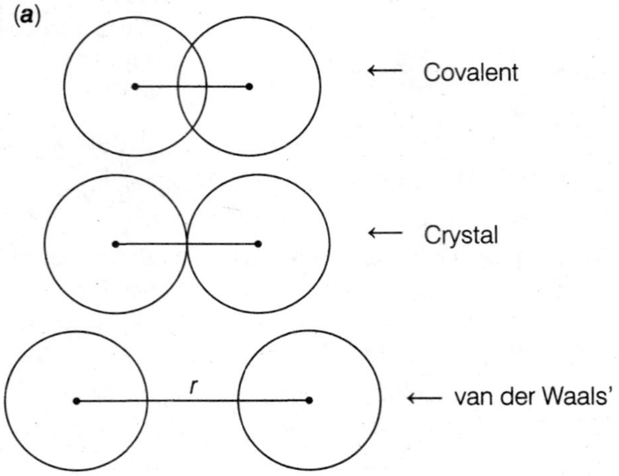

$\Rightarrow R_{\text{van der Waals'}} > R_{\text{crystal}} > R_{\text{covalent}}$

∴ Option (a) .

117. (*b*)

$Li^+ < Na^+ < K^+ < Rb^+ < Cs^+$ (←)	Size
$Li^+ > Na^+ > K^+ > Rb^+ > Cs^+$	Polarising power
Maximum ←	Covalent nature *M*Cl
Maximum ←	Lattice energy of *M*Cl
Maximum ←	Thermal stability

118. (*c*) The first electron gain enthalpy is exothermic (or negative).

Generally, electron gain enthalpy becomes less exothermic (or less negative) when comparing elements of a group from top to bottom. Therefore, electron gain enthalpy of S > Se and Li > Na. But there are some exceptions to this.

One of them is the case of a group 17 elements where electron gain is most negative for Cl instead of F, due to extra small size of fluorine.

∴ Upon an electron gain, energy releases in the order :

Cl > F, S > Se and Li > Na

119. (*a*) **Heat of hydration** The quantity of energy produced when one mole of ions undergo a hydration process (i.e. it is a dissolution energy when solvent used is water).

For group 2 :

$Be^{2+}, Mg^{2+}, Ca^{+2}, Sr^{2+}, Ba^{2+}$ →

Increase in size

Increase in hydration enthalpy ←

120. (*c*) Mn and have $3d^5$ electronic configuration.

121. (*c*) E.C. of K=19 in the absence of Aufbau rule is

$1s^2 2s^2 2p^6\ 3s^2 3p^6\ 3d^1$ ↑

Last-filling electron goes into *d*-orbital.

Thus, *d*-block element.

122. (*c*) Isoelectronic N(7) and O^+(8) have same EC.

N(7), O^+(8)] $1s^2 2s^2 2p^3$ [1|1|1] $2p_x^1\ 2p_y^1\ 2p_z^1$

Most stable due to all unpaired electrons.

O_8] $1s^2 2s^2 2p^4$ [⇅|1|1]

Less stable than O^+ and N

Since, *Z* of O^+ > *Z* of N

Hence, IP of O^+ > N

Na with only one unpaired electron in $3s^1$ has lowest IP.

123. (*c*) Maximum charge density

and Least Size

⇒ Maximum polarising power

$Li^+_{1/r}$ $Mg^{2+}_{2/r}$ $Al^{3+1}_{3/r}$

Thus, (c) [**Note** O^{2-} is anion]

124. (*c*) (a) $r_n \propto \frac{1}{Z}$

$$Na^+ > Mg^{2+} > Al^{3+}$$

(b) $$O^{2-} > F^- < Ne$$

(c) Repulsive forces are balanced by attractive force. Thus, true.

(d) $Mn^+ > Fe^{2+}$

125. (*d*) Ionic radii $\propto \frac{1}{\text{Charge of cation}}$

(a) Ti^{4+} ($Z = 22$, electron = 18) > Mn^{7+} ($Z = 25$ electrons = 18)

(b) $^{37}Cl^- = {}^{35}Cl^-$ ($Z = 17$)

(c) $K^+ < Cl^-$

(d) $P^{3+} > P^{5+}$

Thus, correct.

126. (*c*) $r_n \propto \frac{1}{Z}$

Ti^{2+}(22) > Ni^{2+}(28)
smaller

Pt^{2+} (5*d*-series)
Zr^{2+} (4*d*-series)
have higher number of orbits
hence, larger size.

127. (*d*) Group 16 17

16	17		
O	F	Thus, $F < O$; $F^- < O^{2-}$; $Se > O$; $Se^{2-} > O^{2-}$	$I > Br > F$; $I^- > Br^- > F^-$
S	Cl		
Se	Br		
	I		

$$I > Se$$

$\therefore$ $$I^- > Se^{2-}$$

Thus, $I^- > Se^{2-} > Br^- > O^{2-} > F^-$

128. (*c*) Number of electrons in $N^{3-} = 7 + 3 = 10$

Number of electrons in $O^{2-} = 8 + 2 = 10$

Number of electrons in $F^- = 9 + 1 = 10$

Since, all the three species have each 10 electrons hence they are isoelectronic species.

It is considered that, in case of isoelectronic species as the negative charge increases, ionic radii increases and therefore the value of ionic radii are

$N^{3-} = 1.71$
(highest among the three)
$O^{2-} = 1.40$
$F^- = 1.36$
(lowest among the three)

Time Saving Technique There is no need to mug up the radius values for different ions. This particular question can be solved through following time saving.

Trick *The charges on the ions indicate the size as* $N^{3-} > O^{2-} > F^-$. *Thus, you have to look for the option in which the above trend is followed. Option (c) is the only one in which this trend* is followed. Hence, it is the correct answer.

129. (*a*) (a) Li—Mg diagonal relationship
(b) Na — K
(c) Ca — Mg same group
(d) B — Al

130. (*d*) Except (d) all show diagonal relationship.

Li   Be   B   C
Na   Mg   Al   Si

(Li → Mg, Be → Al, B → Si)

133. (*d*)

$$H(g) \longrightarrow H^+(g) + e^- \quad (IE)_1 = 13.6\,eV$$
$$He(g) \longrightarrow He^+(g) + e^- \quad (IE)_1 = 24.6\,eV$$

$He^+(g)$ is now isoelectronic of $H(g)$.

Thus, $IE\,(He^+) = (IE)_H\,(Z)^2 = 13.6 \times 2^2 = 54.4\,eV$

Thus, $(IE)_1$ of He = 24.6 given

$(IE)_2$ of He = $(IE)_1$ of He^+ = 54.4 eV

Thus, $$He(g) \longrightarrow He^{2+}(g) + 2e^-$$
$$(IE)_1 + (IE)_2 = 24.6 + 54.4 = 79.0\,eV$$

Hence, $He^{2+} + 2e^- \longrightarrow He \qquad \Delta H = -79.0\,eV$

134. (*b*) The group number, number of valence electrons and valency of an element with atomic number 15 are 15, 5 and 3 respectively. Modern periodic table is based on the atomic number. Number of valence electrons present in an atom decides the group number.

Electronic configuration of element having atomic number $15 = 1s^2\,2s^2\,2p^6\,\underbrace{3s^2\,3p^3}_{\text{Valence electrons}}$

As five electrons are present in valence shell, its group number is 15. Valency of element having atomic number 15 is +3 (8 − 5 = 3).

136. (*a*) The summary of variation of periodic properties is given in table below:

S.No.	Periodic property	Variation	
		Along a period	Along a group
1.	Atomic radius	Decreases	Increases
2.	Electron gain enthalpy	Increases	Decreases
3.	Electronegativity	Increases	Decreases

Thus, electronegativity decreases and atomic radius increases down a group in the periodic table.

137. (*c*) (b) and (d) with s^2p^6 configuration has zero values of EA. Cl(c) with empty *d*-orbital has greater EA than F(a).

138. (*a*) Na_2O is basic in nature and other oxides are acidic/basic/amphoteric

	SiO_2	P_2O_5	SO_3	Cl_2O_7
O.N. of element	+4	+5	+6	+7

Acidic nature $\xrightarrow{\text{increases}}$

Thus, greater the acidic nature, greater the tendency of the reaction to occur.

Thus, Cl_2O_7

139. (*a*) In case of Ne van der Waals' radius is taken. Hence, it should have maximum size out of the given option.

140. (*a*) Greater the electronegativity of X(Cl > Br > I) greater the acid strength.
Thus, I > II > III

141. (*b*) The atomic radii of Ag is almost equal to Au due to lanthanide contraction.

142. (*d*) (IV) B contain C, Si, Ge, Sn, Pb
Ge, Sn, Pb are strongly electropositive.

143. (*d*) The first ionisation energy (in kJ/mol) of Na, Mg, Al and Si respectively are

496, 737, 577, 786

All four elements belong to the same period (3rd period) and the general trend in a period from left to right is increase in first ionisation energy, because of increase in nuclear charge and decrease in radii.

Therefore, the expected order of first ionisation enthalpies of given elements should be

Na < Al < Mg < Si

But, first ionisation energies of Mg and Al show anomalous order because Mg has stable [Ne] $3s^2$ configuration and, therefore higher ionisation energy than expected, whereas Al has [Ne]$3s^2 3p^1$ configuration, which on ionisation becomes stable [Ne]$3s^2$.

∴ Its ionisation energy is less than expected.

145. (*d*) Gd : $4f^7 5d^1$

Unpaired electrons = 8

$$\text{Sum of spin} = 8 \times \frac{1}{2} = 4$$

146. (*a*) $(IE)_1$ decreases regularly.

147. (*b*)

$$X(g) \longrightarrow X^+(g) + e^-; \quad \Delta H = I$$
$$X^+(g) + e^- \longrightarrow X(g); \quad \Delta H = -I$$

Thus, $I = -E$

148. (*d*)

$$X(g) + e^- \longrightarrow X^-(g); \quad \Delta H = x \text{ (EA of } X(g))$$
$$X^-(g) \longrightarrow X(g) + e^-; \quad \Delta H = y = \text{IE of } X^-(g)$$
$$= -\text{EA of } X(g)$$

Thus, (a), (b), (c) true.

149. (*d*) The electronic configuration of given elements are as follows :

K(19) = $1s^2 2s^2 2p^6 3s^2 3p^6 4s^1$

Mg(12) = $1s^2 2s^2 2p^6 3s^2$

Sr(38) = $1s^2 2s^2 2p^6 3s^2 3p^6 4s^2 3d^{10} 4p^6 5s^2$

Sc(21) = $1s^2 2s^2 2p^6 3s^2 3p^6 4s^2 3d^1$

First ionisation enthalpy (I.E.) of K is lowest among the given options. Here, the energy required to remove an electron from $4s^1$ is least as only one electron is present in the outermost shell. I.E. (I) is comparatively high for Mg and Sr and two electrons (fully-filled) are placed in *s*-orbital.

Second ionisation enthalpy of K is highest among the given options. Now, removal of an electron occur from p^6 (fully-filled). So, high energy is required to remove the electron. From the above discussion, it can be concluded that ($IE_2 - IE_1$) value is maximum for K (potassium).

150. (*b*) (a) NH_3
PH_3
AsH_3 ↓ Correct
Acidic

(b) Li < B < Be < C (IE)

Be has paired electron hence its (IE) is larger than that of B. Thus, (b) is incorrect.

(c) correct (d) correct.

08

Hydrogen

Objective Questions Type I [Only one correct option]

In each of the questions below, four choices are given of which only one is correct.

1. H_2 gas is liberated at cathode and anode both by electrolysis of the following aqueous solution except in
(a) NaH (b) HCOONa (c) NaCl (d) LiH

2. The set of elements which could form stable, covalent hydrogen bonded hydrides are
(a) nitrogen, oxygen and fluorine
(b) lithium, sodium and potassium
(c) sulphur, selenium and tellurium
(d) chlorine, bromine and iodine

3. The fuel gas obtained by blowing steam over incandescent coal is known as
(a) coal gas (b) water gas
(c) producer gas (d) natural gas

4. Steam is passed over red hot carbon and the gaseous products cooled and passed first through a solution of alkali, then through ammoniacal cuprous chloride and then through water. What is finally collected?
(a) CO_2
(b) A mixture of hydrocarbons
(c) $CO + H_2$
(d) H_2

5. Which among the following is a hydride?
(a) Rongalite (b) Nitrolim
(c) Hydrolith (d) Minium

6. Which of the following easily reacts with water producing hydrogen?
(a) PH_3 (b) B_2H_6 (c) CH_4 (d) H_2S

7. How does H_2O_2 differ from O_3 in its chemical action?
(a) In oxidising PbS to $PbSO_4$
(b) In liberating I_2 from KI
(c) In decolorising acidified $KMnO_4$
(d) In oxidising $K_4[Fe(CN)_6]$ to $K_3[Fe(CN)_6]$

8. Which of the following statements about H_2O_2 is not true?
(a) H_2O_2 is used to clean oil paintings
(b) H_2O_2 acts as oxidising as well as reducing agent
(c) Two hydroxyl groups in H_2O_2 lie in the same plane
(d) It retains same structure in liquid and solid form

9. H_2O_2 is not used as but not as
(a) oxidant, reductant (b) bleaching agent
(c) antiseptic (d) catalyst

10. Which is accepted structure of H_2O_2 in gas phase?
(a) 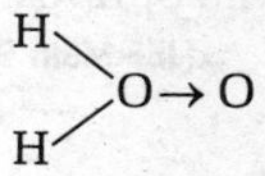
(b) 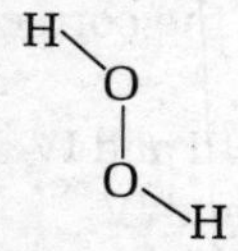
(c) Both (a) and (b) (d) None of these

11. Hydrogen
(a) is placed in I A since it forms monovalent cation H^+
(b) is placed in VII A (halogen family) since it forms monovalent anion H^-
(c) is placed in IV A (carbon family) since both have a half-filled shell of electrons
(d) follows all of the above facts

12. Which is true statement about H_2O?
(a) Hardness can be removed by passing through ion exchange resin
(b) Its presence can be detected by anhydrous $CuSO_4$
(c) It is amphiprotic
(d) All the above are correct statements

13. Bond angles H—O—H and H—O—O— in water and hydrogen peroxide respectively are
(a) 104.5° in both (b) 94.8° in both
(c) 104.5°, 94.8° (d) 94.8° and 104.5°

14. $H_2O_2 \longrightarrow H_2O + O_2$
This represents
(a) oxidation of H_2O_2
(b) reduction of H_2O_2
(c) disproportionation of H_2O_2
(d) acidic nature of H_2O_2

15. Which is a source of nascent hydrogen?
I. Zn + Dil. HCl
II. CH_3OH + Na
III. Electrolysis of H_2O
IV. Silent electric discharge
(a) I, II (b) II, III
(c) I, II, III, IV (d) IV

16. H_2 is adsorbed on palladium surface. It is a case of
(a) occlusion
(b) diffusion
(c) effusion
(d) electroosmosis

17. D_2O (heavy water) and H_2O differ in following except in
(a) freezing point
(b) density
(c) ionic product of water
(d) its reaction with sodium

18. The correct statements about H_2O_2 are
I. used in the treatment of effluents.
II. used as both oxidising and reducing agents.
III. the two hydroxyl groups lie in the same plane.
IV. miscible with water.
Choose the correct answer from the options given below **[JEE Main 2021, March]**
(a) I, II, III and IV
(b) I, II and IV
(c) II, III and IV
(d) I, III and IV

19. Hydrogen peroxide oxidises $[Fe(CN)_6]^{4-}$ to $[Fe(CN)_6]^{3-}$ in acidic medium but reduces $[Fe(CN)_6]^{3-}$ to $[Fe(CN)_6]^{4-}$ in alkaline medium. The other products formed are, respectively. **[JEE Main 2018]**
(a) $(H_2O + O_2)$ and H_2O
(b) $(H_2O + O_2)$ and $(H_2O + OH^-)$
(c) H_2O and $(H_2O + O_2)$
(d) H_2O and $(H_2O + OH^-)$

20. Which is true about different forms of hydrogen?
(a) *Ortho* hydrogen has same spins of two nuclei clockwise or anticlockwise
(b) *Para* hydrogen has different spins of two nuclei
(c) At absolute zero, there is 100% *para* form and at high temperature, there is 75% *ortho* form
(d) All the above are correct

21. Given below are two statements : One is labelled as Assertion (A) and the other labelled as reason (R).
Assertion (A) During the boiling of water having temporary hardness, $Mg(HCO_3)_2$ is converted to $MgCO_3$.
Reason (R) The solubility product of $Mg(OH)_2$ is greater than that of $MgCO_3$.
In the light of the above statements, choose the most appropriate answer from the options given below :
(a) Both (A) and (R) are true but (R) is not the correct explanation of (A)
(b) (A) is true but (R) is false
(c) Both (A) and (R) are true and (R) is the correct explanation of (A)
(d) (A) is false but (R) is true

22. H_2 can be obtained from
(a) water gas (CO + H_2) by liquefaction of CO at low temperature under pressure
(b) water gas by oxidation of CO into CO_2 (by steam) which can be easily removed by dissolving in H_2O
(c) electrolysis of water
(d) All the above methods

23. Out of the following metals which will give H_2 on reaction with NaOH
I. Zn, II. Mg, III. Al, IV. Be
(a) I, II, III, IV (b) I, III, IV
(c) II, IV (d) I, III

24. Choose the correct statement(s).
(a) H_2 is more rapidly adsorbed on to surfaces than D_2
(b) H_2 reacts over 13 times faster with Cl_2 than D_2 because H_2 has a lower energy of activation
(c) Both (a) and (b) are true
(d) None of the above is true

25. Abundance of H_2 in the earth's atmosphere is very small. This is because
(a) the earth's gravitation field is too small to hold so light an element
(b) H_2 exists in *ortho* and *para* form
(c) H_2 is diatomic gas
(d) H_2 is not the metal

26. H_2 reacts much faster with Cl_2 than D_2, because
(a) rate of diffusion of H_2 is greater than D_2
(b) H_2 has lower energy of activation than D_2
(c) Both (a) and (b) are correct
(d) None of the statements is correct

27. Which is true statement about D_2O and H_2O?
(a) D_2O has lower dielectric constant than H_2O
(b) NaCl is more soluble in D_2O than in H_2O
(c) Both (a) and (b) are correct
(d) None of the above is correct

28. Out of LiH, MgH_2 and CuH
(a) all are ionic hydrides
(b) LiH, MgH_2 are ionic and CuH covalent hydride
(c) all are covalent hydrides
(d) LiH is ionic, MgH_2 and CuH are intermediate hydrides

29. The total number of isotopes of hydrogen and number of radioactive isotopes among them, respectively, are **[JEE Main 2019, Jan.]**
(a) 2 and 1 (b) 3 and 2
(c) 2 and 0 (d) 3 and 1

30. In the following compounds H is covalent bonded in case of
(a) BaH_2 (b) CaH_2 (c) SiH_4 (d) NaH

31. Which of the following disproportionates when treated with water?
(a) SO_3 (b) F_2 (c) N_2 (d) Cl_2

32. Hydrogen has three isotopes (*A*), (*B*) and (*C*). If the number of neutron(s) in (*A*), (*B*) and (*C*) respectively, are (*x*), (*y*) and (*z*), the sum of (*x*), (*y*) and (*z*) is **[JEE Main 2020]**
(a) 4 (b) 3
(c) 2 (d) 1

33. H, D and T (isotopes of hydrogen) have nuclear spin quantum number respectively as
(a) $\frac{1}{2}, 1, \frac{1}{2}$ (b) $\frac{1}{2}, \frac{1}{2}, 1$ (c) $\frac{1}{2}, 1, \frac{3}{2}$ (d) $\frac{1}{2}, \frac{1}{2}, \frac{1}{2}$

34. D_2O has maximum density at
(a) 4°C (b) 11.6°C (c) 0°C (d) 0 K

35. H_2O_2 is the hydride of
(a) O_2 (b) H_2O
(c) Both (a) and (b) (d) None of these

36. H_2O_2 can also be obtained by the partial oxidation of 2-propanol.

$$(CH_3)_2CHOH + O_2 \longrightarrow (CH_3)_2CO + H_2O_2$$

Intermediate in this reaction is
(a) 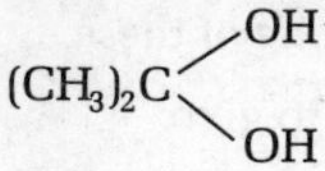 (b) $(CH_3)_3\overset{+}{C}$
(c) 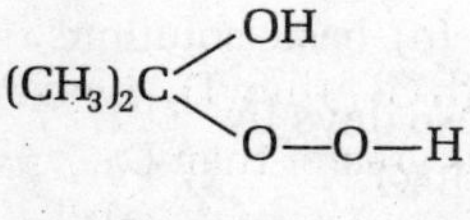 (d) None of these

37. H_2O_2 exists as .... in alkaline medium.
(a) HO_2^- (b) $HO_2^{\oplus}$ (c) O_2^{2-} (d) $H_2O^{\oplus}$

38. In the following reaction using $H_2\overset{18}{O}_2$,

$$2MnO_4^- + 5H_2\overset{18}{O}_2 + 6H^+ \longrightarrow 2Mn^{2+} + 8H_2O + 5O_2$$

^{18}O goes with
(a) H_2O (b) O_2
(c) Both (a) and (b) (d) None of these

39. Water gas is a mixture of
(a) CO and H_2O (b) CO and N_2
(c) CO and H_2 (d) CO and CH_4

40. H^- is a
(a) Lewis base (b) Lowry-Bronsted base
(c) Both (a) and (b) (d) None of these

41. Consider the following reactions

I. $AlH_3 + H^- \longrightarrow AlH_4^-$

II. $H_2O + H^- \longrightarrow H_2 + OH^-$

Select the correct statements based on these reactions.
(a) H^- is a Lewis acid in I and Lewis base in II
(b) H^- is a Lewis base in I and Bronsted base in II
(c) H^- is a Lewis acid in I and Bronsted acid in II
(d) H^- is a Lewis base in I and II

42. Consider the following statements,

I. Rate of transfer of D^+ from D_2O is slower than that of H^- from H_2O

II. K_a for $CH_3COOH \rightleftharpoons CH_3COO^- + H^+$ is smaller than that of K_a for
$$CH_3COOD \rightleftharpoons CH_3COO^- + D^+$$

III. Tritium is a radioactive isotope.

Select the correct statements.
(a) I, II (b) II, III
(c) I, III (d) I, II, III

43. Which is hydrolysis reaction?
(a) $O^{2-}(aq) + H_2O(l) \longrightarrow 2OH^-(aq)$
(b) $O_2^{2-}(aq) + 2H_2O(l) \longrightarrow O_2(g) + 4OH^-(aq)$
(c) $4O_2^-(aq) + 2H_2O(l) \longrightarrow 3O_2(g) + 4OH^-(aq)$
(d) All of the above

44. The hydride ion H^- is stronger base than its hydroxide ion OH^-. Which of the following reactions will occur if sodium hydride (NaH) is dissolved in water?
(a) $2H^-(aq) \longrightarrow H_2 + 2e^-$
(b) $H^-(aq) + H_2O(l) \longrightarrow OH^- + H_2$
(c) $H^- + H_2O(l) \longrightarrow$ No reaction
(d) None of the above

45. Permanent hardness of water can be removed by adding
(a) $NaHCO_3$ (b) Na_2CO_3
(c) $CaOCl_2$ (d) Cl_2

46. Which one of the following statements about water is false? **[JEE Main 2016]**
(a) Water can act both as an acid and as a base
(b) There is extensive intramolecular hydrogen bonding in the condensed phase
(c) Ice formed by heavy water sinks in normal water
(d) Water is oxidised to oxygen during photosynthesis

47. Which statement is not correct for hydrogen?
(a) It has a very high ionisation potential
(b) It is always collected at cathode
(c) It can form bonds in +1 as well as –1 oxidation state
(d) It has same electronegativity as halogens

48. The most stable is
(a) NaH (b) RbH (c) KH (d) LiH

49. H_2O_2 is a reducing agent in the reaction
(a) $Ag_2O + H_2O_2 \longrightarrow 2Ag + H_2O + O_2$
(b) $2KI + H_2O_2 \longrightarrow 2KOH + I_2$
(c) $H_2O_2 + SO_2 \longrightarrow H_2SO_4$
(d) $PbS + 4H_2O_2 \longrightarrow PbSO_4 + 4H_2O$

50. Which cannot be oxidised by H_2O_2?
(a) Na_2SO_3 (b) PbS (c) KI (d) O_3

51. Dil. H_2SO_4 and oxide react to produce hydrogen peroxide. The oxide is
(a) MnO_2 (b) PbO_2 (c) TiO_2 (d) Na_2O_2

52. The temporary hardness of a water sample is due to compound X. Boiling this sample converts X to compound Y. X and Y, respectively, are **[JEE Main 2019, April]**
(a) $Mg(HCO_3)_2$ and $Mg(OH)_2$
(b) $Ca(HCO_3)_2$ and $Ca(OH)_2$
(c) $Mg(HCO_3)_2$ and $MgCO_3$
(d) $Ca(HCO_3)_2$ and CaO

53. Adsorbed hydrogen by palladium is known as
(a) nascent (b) atomic
(c) heavy (d) occluded

54. Pure water can be obtained from sea water by
(a) centrifugation (b) plasmolysis
(c) reverse osmosis (d) sedimentation

55. Zn gives H_2 gas with H_2SO_4 and HCl but not with HNO_3 because
(a) Zn acts as an oxidising agent when reacts with HNO_3
(b) HNO_3 is weaker acid than H_2SO_4 and HCl
(c) in electrochemical series Zn is above hydrogen
(d) NO_3^- is reduced in preference to hydronium ion

56. Mass of one atom is 6.66×10^{-23} g. Its percentage in an hydride is 95.24. Thus, hydride is
(a) MH (b) MH_2 (c) MH_3 (d) MH_4

57. On burning hydrogen in air, the colour of flame is
(a) green (b) light bluish
(c) yellow (d) None of these

58. Triple point of water is
(a) 273.16 K (b) 373.15 K
(c) 203.12 K (d) 193.16 K

59. Hydrogen can be fused to form helium at
(a) high temperature and high pressure
(b) high temperature and low pressure
(c) low temperature and high pressure
(d) low temperature and low pressure

60. Water gas is produced by
(a) passing steam over red hot coke
(b) passing steam and air over red hot coke
(c) burning coke in excess of air
(d) burning coke in limited supply of air

61. Hydrogen is produced by the reaction
(a) $Na_2O_2 + 2HCl$ (b) $Mg + H_2O$
(c) $BaO_2 + HCl$ (d) $H_2S_4O_8 + H_2O$

62. Hydrogen peroxide is prepared in the laboratory by
(a) passing CO_2 into BaO_2
(b) adding MnO_2 to dil. H_2SO_4
(c) adding Na_2O_2 to cold water
(d) adding PbO_2 into $KMnO_4$

63. The hardness of water is estimated by
(a) EDTA method (b) titrimetric method
(c) conductivity method (d) distillation method

64. Hydrogen peroxide is reduced by
(a) ozone
(b) barium peroxide
(c) acidic solution of $KMnO_4$
(d) lead sulphide suspension

65. Hard water is not fit for washing clothes because
(a) it contains impurities
(b) it is acidic in nature
(c) it gives precipitate with soap
(d) it contains Na_2SO_4 and KCl

66. The acid, not suitable for the preparation of hydrogen by the action of metals, is
(a) HCl (b) CH_3COOH
(c) HNO_3 (d) H_2SO_4

67. $Ag_2O + H_2O_2 \longrightarrow 2Ag + H_2O + O_2$
In an above reaction H_2O_2 acts as a/an
(a) oxidising agent (b) reducing agent
(c) bleaching agent (d) None of these

68. Ionic hydride reacts with water to give
(a) hydride ions (b) acidic solution
(c) protons (d) basic solutions

69. H_2O_2 is manufactured these days by
(a) the action of H_2SO_4 on BaO_2
(b) the action of H_2SO_4 on Na_2O_2
(c) electrolysis of 50% Na_2O_2
(d) burning hydrogen in excess oxygen

70. Which of the following is heavy water?
(a) H_2O^{18} (b) H_2O^{16} (c) H_2O_3 (d) D_2O

71. The volume of oxygen liberated at NTP from 15 mL of 20 volume H_2O_2 is
(a) 250 mL (b) 300 mL
(c) 150 mL (d) 200 mL

72. Spin isomerism is shown by
(a) dichloro benzene
(b) hydrogen
(c) dibasic acid
(d) *n*-butane

73. Given below are two statements :
Statement I H_2O_2 can act as both oxidising and reducing agent in basic medium.
Statement II In the hydrogen economy, the energy is transmitted in the form of dihydrogen.
In the light of the above statements, choose the correct answer from the options given below
(a) Both statement I and statement II are false
(b) Both statement I and statement II are true
(c) Statement I is true but statement II is false
(d) Statement I is false but statement II is true

74. The hydride that is not electron deficient is **[JEE Main 2019, Jan.]**
(a) AlH_3 (b) B_2H_6 (c) SiH_4 (d) GaH_3

75. Molar ratio of H_2O_2 oxidised by one mole of MnO_4^- in basic and acidic medium is
(a) 1 : 1 (b) 1 : 2
(c) 3 : 5 (d) 5 : 3

76. Electrolysis of aqueous NaCl and NaH differs in
(a) formation of basic solution at the cathode by NaCl only
(b) formation of basic solution at the cathode by NaH only
(c) formation of H_2 gas at cathode and anode both by NaH only
(d) formation of H_2 gas at cathode and anode both by NaCl only

77. Select the correct statement(s).
(a) Hydride ion is larger than any of the halide ions except iodide
(b) Hydrides ions are reducing agents
(c) Boranes are electron deficient hydrides
(d) All of the above are correct statements

78. Metallic hydrides
(a) are also called interstitial hydrides
(b) are non-stoichiometric, being deficient in hydrogen
(c) are poor conductors of electricity, exhibit less paramagnetism and have hydrogen as atom and not as molecule
(d) have all the properties given above

79. Hydride ion is a
(a) strong conjugate acid of H_2
(b) strong conjugate base of H_2
(c) strong conjugate acid of H^+
(d) strong conjugate base of H^-

80. Select the incorrect statement.
(a) H^+ can exist as $H_9O_4^+$ in water
(b) H_2 is thermally stable
(c) Ionisation of CH_3COOH is slower than that of CH_3COOD
(d) Kinetic isotopic effect is observed when there is retardation in the rate water H_2O is replaced by D_2O.

81. H_2, D_2 and T_2 do not differ in
(a) freezing point (b) boiling point
(c) critical temperature (d) bond energy

82. Industrial source of H_2O_2 is
(a) by oxidation of 2-ethyl anthraquinol in a cyclic process
(b) by partial oxidation of 2-propanol
(c) by both (a) and (b)
(d) None of the above

83. The correct statements among (a) to (d) regarding H_2 as a fuel are : **[JEE Main 2019, Jan.]**
I. It produces less pollutants than petrol.
II. A cylinder of compressed dihydrogen weights ~30 times more than a petrol tank producing the same amount of energy.
III. Dihydrogen is stored in tanks of metal alloys like $NaNi_5$.
IV. On combustion, values of energy released per gram of liquid dihydrogen and LPG are 50 and 142 kJ, respectively.
(a) I, II and III only (b) II, III and IV only
(c) II and IV only (d) I and III only

84. Select the correct statement(s).
(a) H_2O_2 reduces MnO_4^- to Mn^{2+} in acidic medium
(b) H_2O_2 reduces MnO_4^- to MnO_2 in basic medium
(c) H_2O_2 can be used to bleach blackened oil paintings
(d) All the above are correct statements

85. The strength of 11.2 volume solution of H_2O_2 is [Given that molar mass of $H = 1\text{ g mol}^{-1}$ and $O = 16\text{ g mol}^{-1}$] **[JEE Main 2019]**
(a) 1.7% (b) 34% (c) 13.6% (d) 3.4%

86. Perhydrol is
(a) 30% solution of H_2O_2
(b) "100 volume" H_2O_2
(c) Both (a) and (b) are correct
(d) None of the above is correct

87. 10 mL of H_2O_2 solution on treatment with KI and titration of liberated I_2, required 10 mL of 1 N hypo. Thus, H_2O_2 is
(a) 1N
(b) 5.6 volume
(c) 17 gL^{-1}
(d) All are correct

88. In alkaline H_2O_2
(a) Mn^{2+} changes to MnO_2 (b) Cr^{3+} changes to CrO_4^{2-}
(c) Both (a) and (b) are correct
(d) None of the above is correct

89. In basic medium, H_2O_2 exhibits which of the following reactions ?
I. $Mn^{2+} \longrightarrow Mn^{4+}$ II. $I_2 \longrightarrow I^-$
III. $PbS \longrightarrow PbSO_4$
Choose the most appropriate answer from the options given below. **[JEE Main 2021, March]**
(a) I, III only (b) I only (c) II only (d) I, II only

90. Among statements (A) - (D), the correct ones are
(A) decomposition of hydrogen peroxide gives dioxygen.
(B) like hydrogen peroxide, compounds, such as $KClO_3$, $Pb(NO_3)_2$ and $NaNO_3$ when heated liberate dioxygen.
(C) 2-ethylanthraquinone is useful for the industrial preparation of hydrogen peroxide.
(D) hydrogen peroxide is used for the manufacture of sodium perborate. **[JEE Main 2020]**
(a) (A), (B) and (C) only (b) (A), (B), (C) and (D)
(c) (A), (C) and (D) only (d) (A) and (C) only

91. In the following reaction,
$$Cr_2O_7^{2-} + H^+ + H_2O_2 \longrightarrow$$
(a) CrO_5 is formed (b) Cr^{3+} is formed
(c) CrO_4^{2-} is formed (d) no effect of H_2O_2

92. $Na[Cr(OH)_4]$ on reaction with H_2O_2 changes to
(a) Na_2CrO_4 (b) $Na_2Cr_2O_7$
(c) $Cr(OH)_3$ (d) CrO_5

93. Oxidation state of hydrogen is zero in
(a) CaH_2 (b) NaH
(c) PdH_2 (d) NH_3

Objective Questions Type II [One or more than one correct option(s)]

In each of the questions below, four choices are given, of which one or more than one are correct.

1. Select the correct statements:
(a) Boiling point of H_2O, NH_3, HF are maximum in their respective group due to intermolecular H-bonding
(b) Boiling point of CH_4 out of CH_4, SiH_4, GeH_4 and SnH_4 is least due to lack of H-bonding
(c) Benzoic acid forms dimer by H-bonding
(d) H_2O exists as $H_9O_4^+$ in acidic medium

2. H_2O_2 can be obtained when following reacts with H_2SO_4 except with
(a) PbO_2 (b) BaO_2 (c) Na_2O_2 (d) SrO_2

3. How does H_2O_2 differ from O_3 in its chemical action?
(a) In oxidising PbS to $PbSO_4$
(b) In liberating I_2 from KI
(c) In decolourising acidified $KMnO_4$
(d) In oxidising $K_4[Fe(CN)_6]$ to $K_3[Fe(CN)_6]$

4. Which of the following statements about H_2O_2 are true?
(a) H_2O_2 is used to clean oil paintings
(b) H_2O_2 acts as oxidising as well as reducing agent
(c) Two hydroxyl groups in H_2O_2 lie in the same plane
(d) It retains same structure in liquid and solid form

5. H^+, D^+ and T^+ differ in all except in
(a) number of electrons
(b) number of neutrons
(c) ionic mass
(d) electronic configuration

6. Which is a source of nascent hydrogen?
(a) Zn + Dil. HCl, (b) CH_3OH + Na
(c) Electrolysis of H_2O (d) Silent electric discharge

7. Select the correct statement(s) about lime light.
(a) Oxy-hydrogen flame
(b) Used in welding
(c) Temperature of lime light is sufficient to melt even platinum
(d) Produced in an endothermic reaction

8. "10 volume" H_2O_2 means
(a) 1 mL H_2O_2 gives 10 mL O_2 at NTP
(b) 1 g H_2O_2 gives 10 mL O_2 at NTP
(c) 1 mol H_2O_2 gives 10 mL O_2 at NTP
(d) 10 mL gives 1 mol H_2 and 1 mol O_2 at NTP

9. Industrially H_2O_2 is obtained from
(a) 2-ethyl anthraquinol by oxidation and then reduction in a cyclic process
(b) H_2SO_5
(c) $H_2S_2O_8$
(d) BaO_2

10. Temporary hardness and permanent hardness can be removed respectively by addition of
(a) CaO, $CaCO_3$
(b) CaO, Na_2CO_3
(c) Na_2CO_3, CaO
(d) $NaHCO_3$, $CaCl_2$

11. Decomposition of H_2O_2 can be prevented by addition of
(a) ferrous sulphate
(b) oxalic acid
(c) ozone
(d) glycerol

12. Which is/are true statement(s)?
(a) The layer of ice on the surface of river in the winter acts as a thermal insulator between the water below and the air above
(b) The fish and other marine organisms are enabled to survive long periods of freezing weather due to the fact that ice is lighter than water
(c) When ice is formed volume decreases
(d) Density of ice is maximum at 0°C

13. Hydrides of metals are named like
(a) alkane (b) alkene
(c) alkyne (d) None is correct

14. H_2O_2 is "5.6 volume", then
(a) it is 1.7% weight by volume
(b) it is 1 N
(c) it is 1 M
(d) it is 5.6 M

15. H_2 can be obtained from
(a) water gas ($CO + H_2$) by liquefication of CO at low temperature under pressure
(b) water gas by oxidation of CO into CO_2 (by steam) which can be easily removed by dissolving in H_2O
(c) electrolysis of water or NaOH
(d) reaction of NaOH on Zn

16. Out of the following metals which will give H_2 on reaction with NaOH
I. Zn, II. Mg, III. Al, IV. Be
(a) I, II, III, IV (b) I, III, IV
(c) II, IV (d) I, III

17. Which is hydrolysis reaction?
(a) $O^{2-}(aq) + H_2O(l) \longrightarrow 2OH^-(aq)$
(b) $O_2^{2-}(aq) + 2H_2O(l) \longrightarrow O_2(g) + 4OH^-(aq)$
(c) $4O_2^-(aq) + 2H_2O(l) \longrightarrow 3O_2(g) + 4OH^-(aq)$
(d) $Fe^{3+} + 3H_2O \longrightarrow Fe(OH)_3 + 3H^+$

18. Hydrogen and halogen resemble in the
(a) formation of H^+ and X^+
(b) formation of H^- and X^-
(c) formation of H_2 and X_2
(d) following octet rule in H^- and X^-

19. Some of the following properties are similar for metals and their metallic hydrides
(a) hardness (b) metallic lusture
(c) electrical conductivity (d) magnetic property

20. The number of electrons involved when 1 mole of H_2O_2 decomposed as $H_2O_2 \longrightarrow H_2O_2 + O_2$ is
(a) 1 (b) 6 (c) 2 (d) 4

Numerical Value Questions

All these questions have a Numerical value as their answer, solve the questions and write your answer.

1. A 1 g sample of H_2O_2 solution containing x per cent H_2O_2 by weight required x mL of $KMnO_4$ for complete oxidation in acidic medium. Normality of $KMnO_4$ solution is ....

2. A 5.0 mL of H_2O_2 solution liberates 0.508 g of I_2 from an acidified KI solution. The strength of H_2O_2 solution in terms of volume strength at STP is ......

3. H_2O_2 ionises as

$$H_2O_2 \rightleftharpoons H^+ + HO_2^-$$

If pH of H_2O_2 at 20°C is found to be 5.91, than ionic product in 10^{-12} (auto-protolysis constant) of H_2O_2 is ....

4. H_2O_2 is marked "22.4 volume." How much of it (in mL) are required to oxidise 3.4 g H_2S gas?

5. A 'hair-bleach' solution contains H_2O_2. The amount of H_2O_2 in a 12.5 g sample was determined by titration with $KMnO_4$ in acidic solution. If 39.3 mL of 0.5045 N $KMnO_4$ was required, how many equivalents of H_2O_2 are contained in the solution?

6. For above question, what is the mass percentage of H_2O_2 in the bleach solution?

7. A small quantity of manganese dioxide was added to 150 g of an H_2O_2 solution. The oxygen liberated in standard condition occupied a volume of 10^{-3} m^3. The per cent concentration of the initial solution is ....

8. To a 25 mL H_2O_2 solution, excess of acidified solution of potassium iodide was added. The iodine liberated required 20 mL of 0.3 N sodium thiosulphate solution. Calculate the volume strength of H_2O_2 solution.

Comprehension Based Questions

In these questions, a passage has been given followed by questions based on it. You have to answer the questions based on the passage given.

***Passage* 1** *Read the following experiments and answer the questions at the end of it.*

"Research scholar *A* added zinc pieces into aqueous $FeCl_3$ solution and performed some experiments with resultant solution." Research scholar *B* passed H_2 gas into aqueous $FeCl_3$ solution and performed some experiments with resultant solution."

1. Yellow coloured $FeCl_3$ solution changed to light green (appeared as colourless) in the experiment of
   (a) *A* (b) *B*
   (c) Both (a) and (b) (d) None of these
2. Select the correct statements.
   (a) Zn pieces liberate nascent hydrogen on reaction with acidic solution of $FeCl_3$
   (b) $FeCl_3$ solution is reduced to $FeCl_2$ in the experiments of *A* and *B* both
   (c) blue colour complex is formed in both the experiments on reaction with $K_4[Fe(CN)_6]$
   (d) A blood red colour is formed on reaction with KCNS in experiment *B*

***Passage* 2** Depletion of resources of fossil fuels will at some future time make hydrogen, either for use directly by combustion and electrochemically in fuel cells or indirectly *via* hydrogenation of coal, the major alternative to nuclear energy; hence, arises the current interest in the so-called **hydrogen economy**.

A thermochemical cycle for hydrogen production involves at least one element that can exist in two different oxidation states.

$$2H_2O \longrightarrow 2H_2 + O_2$$

Read the above passage and answer the following questions.

1. Production of H_2 from H_2O requires a net input of energy that would come from
   (a) nuclear source (b) solar source
   (c) Both (a) and (b) (d) None of these
2. In the above thermochemical cycle, $FeCl_2$ is one of the catalyst involved and thus regenerated at the end of the reaction, after formed into
   (a) $FeCl_3$, FeO, Fe_2O_3
   (b) $FeCl_3$, Fe_2O_3, Fe_3O_4
   (c) $FeCl_3$, FeO
   (d) $FeCl_3$, Fe_3O_4
3. H_2 is produced in the following thermochemical reaction
   (a) $FeCl_2 + H_2O \longrightarrow$
   (b) $Fe_3O_4 + Cl_2 + HCl \longrightarrow$
   (c) $FeO + H_2O \longrightarrow$
   (d) $FeCl_3 + H_2O \longrightarrow$

***Passage* 3** A hydrogen ion is created when a hydrogen atom loses or group an electron.

Answer the following questions.

1. Which is the correct order of ionisation energy?
   (a) $H < H^+ < H^-$ (b) $H^+ < H < H^-$
   (c) $H^- < H$ (d) $H^- < H < H^+$
2. Hydrogen atom may attain stability by
   (a) forming covalent bond with another hydrogen atom
   (b) forming H^+
   (c) forming H^-
   (d) All of the above facts
3. Number of protons in H, H^+, H^- are
   (a) 1, 0, 2 (b) 1, 1, 1 (c) 0, 0, 0 (d) 1, 0, 1
4. Choose the correct order of lattice energy of hydride.
   (a) LiH < NaH < KH (b) $MgH_2 > CaH_2 > SrH_2$
   (c) LiH < NaH > KH (d) $MgH_2 > CaH_2 > SrH_2$

***Passage* 4** Oxygen forms three types of oxides O^{2-}, O_2^{2-} and O_2^-

Answer the following questions.

1. Which of the following are Bronsted-Lowry bases in aqueous solution?
   (a) O^{2-}, O_2^{2-}, O_2^- (b) O^{2-}, O_2^{2-}
   (c) O_2^-, O_2^{2-} (d) O^{2-}, O_2^-
2. Paramagnetic species is/are
   (a) O^{2-}, O_2^{2-} (b) O_2^-, O_2^{2-} (c) O_2^- (d) O^{2-}
3. In aqueous solution which undergoes disproportionation reaction?
   (a) O^{2-}, O_2^- (b) O^{2-}, O_2^{2-} (c) O_2^-, O_2^{2-} (d) O_2^-

***Passage* 5** $Na[Cr(OH)_4]$, (*A*) green solution changes to yellow coloured solution when boiled with H_2O_2.

Answer the following questions.

1. Yellow coloured solution is due to the formation of
   (a) $Na_2Cr_2O_7$ by oxidation of *A*
   (b) $Na_2Cr_2O_7$ by reduction of *A*
   (c) Na_2CrO_4 by oxidation of *A*
   (d) Na_2CrO_4 by reduction of *A*
2. CO_2 gas is bubbled into yellow coloured solution, then
   (a) Orange-coloured solution of $Na_2Cr_2O_7$ is formed by oxidation
   (b) Orange-coloured solution of $Na_2Cr_2O_7$ is formed by reduction
   (c) Orange-coloured solution of $Na_2Cr_2O_7$ is formed by acidification
   (d) there is no change in colour

***Passage* 6** Two liquids *A* and *B* are made of same atoms, with following properties

	A	*B*
Magnetic property	Diamagnetic	Diamagnetic
KI/H^+/starch	Blue	No colour
Molar mass difference w.r.t. B	16 units	

Answer the following questions.

1. *A* and *B* are respectively
(a) H_2O_2, H_2O
(b) KO_2, K_2O
(c) H_2O, H_2O_2
(d) K_2O, KO_2

2. In alkaline medium, *A* exists as
(a) K_2O_2
(b) KHO_2
(c) K_2O
(d) KO_2

3. A can be used as
(a) oxidising agent
(b) reducing agent
(c) Both (a) and (b)
(d) None of these

Matrix-Match Type

Given below are Matching Type Questions, with two columns (each having some items) each. Each item of Column I has to be matched with the items of Column II.

1. Match the hydrides in Column I with their properties in Column II.

Column I	Column II
A. NaH	1. Conducts electricity in fused state
B. BeH_2	2. Electron deficient
C. CaH_2	3. Liberates H_2 at anode on electrolysis of molten salt
D. OH_2	4. Negative oxidation state of hydrogen atom
	5. Concept of hybridisation is applicable

2. Match order of different properties in Column I with the related property in Column II.

Column I	Column II
A. $HCl < HBr < HI < HF$	1. Boiling point order
B. $H_2S < H_2Se < H_2Te$	2. Melting point order
C. $PH_3 < AsH_3 < SbH_3 < NH_3$	3. Bond polarity order
D. $HF < HCl < HBr < HI$	4. Acidic strength

3. Match the species in Column I with corresponding properties in Column II.

Column I	Column II
A. H_2O	1. Reducing agent
B. H_2O_2	2. Oxidising agent
C. Aqueous Na_2O	3. Paramagnetic
D. Aqueous KO_2	4. Diamagnetic
E. Aqueous CaH_2	5. Turns red litmus blue
	6. Turns blue litmus red

4. Match the species in Column I with the corresponding properties in Column II.

Column I	Column II
A. LiH	1. Reducing agent
B. H_2O	2. Lewis base
C. H_3O^+	3. Conjugate base
D. BH_3	4. Lewis acid
E. H	5. Lowry Bronsted acid
	6. Lowry Bronsted base

Single Integer Answer Questions

Answer of these questions is a single digit lying between 0 to 9.

1. Number of neutrons in the heaviest isotopes of hydrogen is ....

2. Two moles of MnO_4^- reduces *x* mole(s) of H_2O_2 in basic medium. *x* is ....

3. 68 g H_2O_2 will make .... equivalent(s).

4. H_2O_2 is "33.6" volume. Thus, is normality is ....

5. How many moles of H_2O_2 are oxidised by 2 moles of $KMnO_4$ in acidic medium?

5. 5.0 mL of H_2O_2 solution liberates 1.016 g of I_2 from an acidified KI solution. Thus, volume strength (at STP) is approximately ....

7. How many of the following make alkaline solution in water? O^{2-}, O_2^{2-}, O_2^-

8. How many of the following are oxidant?
$H_2O, H_2O_2, KO_2, Na_2O_2, Na_2O, O_3$

9. Ionic product, $[H^+][HO_2^-]$ of H_2O_2 was found to be 1×10^{-12} at a given temperature. Thus, pH of H_2O_2 is ....

10. How many types of water can be formed out of ${}^1_1H, {}^2_1H, {}^3_1H$ and ${}^{16}_8O$?

11. H_2 is formed by electrolysis of aqueous brine solution. In an experiment 0.112 mL of H_2 gas is formed at NTP. What is the pH after electrolysis of brine solution?

12. How many of the following undergo disproportionation when dissolved in water?
$Cl_2, F_2, Na_2O_2, KO_2, K_2O$

Answers

Objective Questions Type I [Only one correct option]

1. (c)	2. (a)	3. (b)	4. (d)	5. (c)	6. (b)	7. (c)	8. (c)	9. (d)	10. (b)
11. (d)	12. (d)	13. (c)	14. (c)	15. (a)	16. (a)	17. (d)	18. (b)	19. (c)	20. (d)
21. (d)	22. (d)	23. (b)	24. (c)	25. (a)	26. (b)	27. (a)	28. (d)	29. (d)	30. (c)
31. (d)	32. (b)	33. (a)	34. (b)	35. (a)	36. (c)	37. (a)	38. (b)	39. (c)	40. (c)
41. (b)	42. (d)	43. (a)	44. (b)	45. (b)	46. (b)	47. (b)	48. (d)	49. (a)	50. (d)
51. (d)	52. (a)	53. (d)	54. (c)	55. (d)	56. (b)	57. (b)	58. (a)	59. (a)	60. (a)
61. (b)	62. (a)	63. (a)	64. (d)	65. (c)	66. (c)	67. (b)	68. (d)	69. (c)	70. (d)
71. (b)	72. (b)	73. (b)	74. (c)	75. (c)	76. (c)	77. (d)	78. (d)	79. (b)	80. (c)
81. (d)	82. (c)	83. (a)	84. (d)	85. (d)	86. (b)	87. (c)	88. (d)	89. (d)	90. (b)
91. (a)	92. (a)	93. (c)							

Objective Questions Type II [One or more than one correct option(s)]

1. (a, c, d)	2. (a)	3. (c)	4. (a, b, d)	5. (a, d)
6. (a, b)	7. (a, b, c)	8. (a)	9. (a)	10. (b)
11. (d)	12. (a, b)	13. (a)	14. (a, b)	15. (a, b, c, d)
16. (b)	17. (a, d)	18. (b, c)	19. (c)	20. (a)

Numerical Value Questions

1. 0.59 N 2. 4.48 3. 1.51 4. 100 mL 5. 0.0198 6. 2.69 7. 1.012 8. 1.344

Comprehension Based Questions

Passage 1 – 1. (a) 2. (a, d)

Passage 2 – 1. (c) 2. (d) 3. (a)

Passage 3 – 1. (c) 2. (d) 3. (b) 4. (d)

Passage 4 – 1. (a) 2. (c) 3. (c)

Passage 5 – 1. (c) 2. (c)

Passage 6 – 1. (a) 2. (b) 3. (c)

Matrix-Match Type

1. A → (1, 3, 4); B → (2, 4, 5); C → (1, 3, 4); D → (3)

2. A → (1, 2); B → (2, 3, 4); C → (1, 2, 3, 4); D → (4)

3. A → (4); B → (1, 2, 4, 5); C → (4, 5); D → (2, 3, 5);

4. A → (1, 2, 3); B → (2, 5, 6); C—(3, 6); D—(1, 4); E → (1)

Single Integer Answer Questions

1. (2)	2. (3)	3. (4)	4. (6)	5. (5)	6. (9)	7. (3)	8. (4)	9. (6)	10. (5)
11. (9)	12. (4)								

Solutions

Objective Questions Type I [Only one correct option]

1. (*c*)

Salt	Ionisation	At cathode	At anode
(a) NaH	$\rightleftharpoons Na^+ + H^-$	$Na^+ + e^- \longrightarrow Na$ $Na + H_2O \longrightarrow NaOH + \frac{1}{2}H_2$	$H^+ + e^- \longrightarrow \frac{1}{2}H_2 + e^-$
(b) HCOONa	$\rightleftharpoons HCOO^- + Na^+$	same	$HCOO^- \longrightarrow \frac{1}{2}H_2 + CO_2 + e^-$
(c) NaCl	$\rightleftharpoons Na^+ + Cl^-$	same	$Cl^- \longrightarrow \frac{1}{2}Cl_2 + e^-$
(d) LiH	$\rightleftharpoons Li^+ + H^-$	$Li^+ + e^- \longrightarrow Li$ $Li + H_2O \longrightarrow LiOH + \frac{1}{2}H_2$	$H^- \longrightarrow \frac{1}{2}H_2 + e^-$

7. (*c*) O_3 does not decolourise $KMnO_4$

14. (*c*)

$$\overset{-1}{H_2O_2} \longrightarrow \overset{-2}{H_2O} + \overset{0}{O_2}$$

Reduction ($-1 \to -2$); Oxidation ($-1 \to 0$)

18. (*b*)

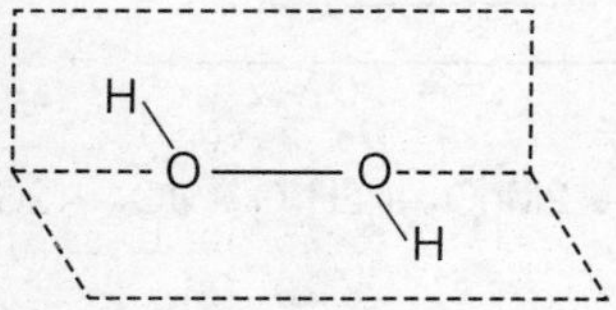

Structure of H_2O_2

(Open book type) → Non-planar

H_2O_2 is used in the treatement of effluents.

$$H_2O_2 \xrightarrow{R.A.} O_2, \quad H_2O_2 \xrightarrow{R.A.} H_2O$$ act as both O.A and R.A.

H_2O_2 is miscible in water due to hydrogen bonding.

19. (*c*)

(i) In acidic medium,

$$[Fe^{2+}(CN)_6]^{4-} + H_2\overset{-1}{O_2} + 2H^+ \longrightarrow [Fe^{3+}(CN)_6]^{3-} + 2H_2\overset{-2}{O}$$

(ii) In alkaline medium,

$$[Fe^{3+}(CN)_6]^{3-} + H_2\overset{-1}{O_2} + 2OH^- \longrightarrow [Fe^{2+}(CN)_6]^{4-} + O_2 + 2H_2O$$

Hence, H_2O (for reaction (i)) and $O_2 + H_2O$ (for reaction (ii)) are produced as by product

21. (*d*) For temporary hardness,

$$Mg(HCO_3)_2 \xrightarrow{\text{Heating}} Mg(OH)_2 \downarrow + 2CO_2 \uparrow$$

Assertion is false.

$MgCO_3$ has high solubility product than $Mg(OH)_2$.

The solubility product of magnesium carbonate is 3.5×10^{-8} and solubility product of $Mg(OH)_2$ is 1.8×10^{-11}. Hence, Reason is correct.

29. (*d*) Hydrogen has three isotopes:

	^1_1H Protium (P)	^2_1H Deuterium (D)	^3_1H Tritium (T)
p	1	1	1
n	0	1	2
$\frac{n}{p}$	0	1	2

Only tritium (T) is radioactive, because of its very high $\frac{n}{p}$ value, $\left(\frac{n}{p} = 2\right)$.

31. (*d*)

$$H_2O + \overset{0}{Cl_2} \longrightarrow \overset{-1}{HCl} + \overset{+1}{HClO}$$

Reduction ($0 \to -1$); Oxidation ($0 \to +1$)

32. (*b*) Number of neutrons in protium (^1_1H) is zero (x).
Number of neutrons in deuterium (^2_1H or ^2_1D) is 1 (y)
Number of neutrons in tritium (^3_1H or ^3_1T) is 2 (z)
So, the sum of x, y and z is $x + y + z = 3$.

44. (*b*) $\underset{\text{Base}}{NaH} + \underset{\text{Acid}}{H_2O} \longrightarrow Na^+ + H^- + H^+ + OH^- \longrightarrow Na^+ + OH^- + H_2\uparrow$

46. (*b*) There is extensive intermolecular H-bonding in the condensed phase.

52. (*a*) The temporary hardness of a water sample is due to compound X [i.e. $Mg(HCO_3)_2$].
Boiling of this sample converts X[i.e. $Mg(HCO_3)_2$] to compound Y[i.e. $Mg(OH)_2$].

Generally, temporary hardness is due to presence of magnesium and calcium hydrogen carbonates. It can be removed by boiling.

During boiling, the soluble $Mg(HCO_3)_2$ is converted into insoluble $Mg(OH)_2$ and $Ca(HCO_3)_2$ changed to insoluble $CaCO_3$.

These precip-itates can be removed by filteration.

$$Mg(HCO_3)_2 \xrightarrow{\text{Heating}} Mg(OH)_2 \downarrow + 2CO_2 \uparrow$$

$$Ca(HCO_3)_2 \xrightarrow{\text{Heating}} CaCO_3 \downarrow + H_2O + CO_2 \uparrow$$

56. (*b*) Mass of one atom $= 6.66 \times 10^{-23}$ g

Mass of N_0 atoms $= 6.66 \times 10^{-23} \times 6.02 \times 10^{23}$ g $= 40$ g

Thus, atomic weight of the element = 40

Element	%	%/at wt.	Ratio
M	95.24	2.381	1
H	4.76	4.76	2

Thus, hydride is MH_2.

61. (*b*) $Mg + H_2O \xrightarrow{\Delta} Mg(OH)_2 + H_2$, other are for H_2O_2

65. (*c*) Hard water does not lather or produce foam easily. Hard water contains bicarbonates, chlorides and sulphates of calcium magnesium which react with the molecules of soap forming insoluble precipitates called scum.

As strength of soap molecules are lost in the chemical reaction, they are not fit for washing clothes.

71. (*b*) "20 volume" means

1 mL H_2O_2 gives = 20 mL O_2 at NTP

thus, 15 mL H_2O_2 gives = 300 mL O_2 at NTP

73. (*b*) (a) H_2O_2 can acts as both oxidising and reducing agent in basic medium.

(i) $2Fe^{3+} + H_2O_2 \longrightarrow 2Fe^{3+} + 2\overset{\cdot\cdot}{O}H^-$

In this reaction, H_2O_2 acts as oxiding agent.

(ii) $2\overset{+7}{Mn}O_4^- + 3H_2O_2 \longrightarrow 2\overset{+4}{Mn}O_2 + 3O_2 + 2H_2O + 2OH^-$

In this reaction, H_2O_2 acts as reducing agent.

(b) The basic principle of hydrogen economy is the transportation and storage of energy in the form of liquids or gaseous dihydrogen.

Advantage of hydrogen economy is that energy is transmitted in the form of dihydrogen and not as electric power.

74. (*a*) GaH_3, AlH_3 and B_2H_6 are the hydrides of group 13 (ns^2np^1), whereas SiH_4 is an hydride of group 14.

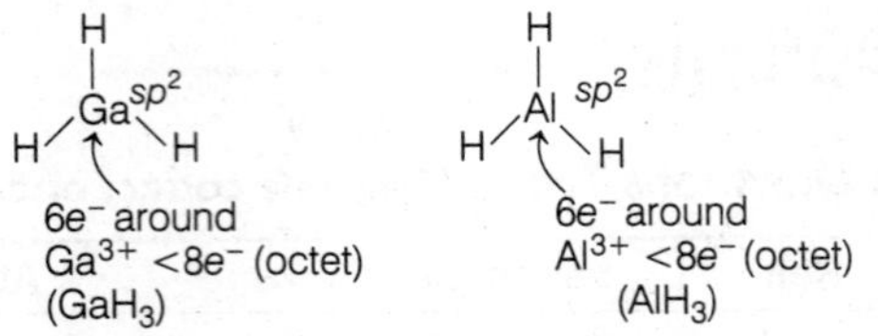

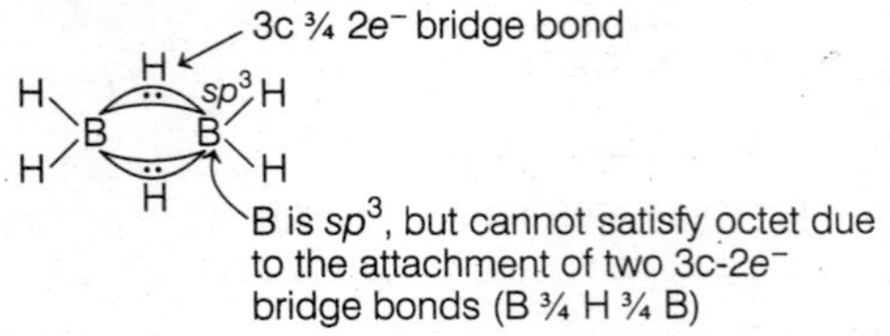

So, B_2H_6, AlH_3 and GaH_3 are electron deficient hydrides.

But, SiH_4 is an electron precise hydride of group-14 (ns^2np^2), i.e. these hydrides can have the required number of electrons to write their conventional Lewis structures.

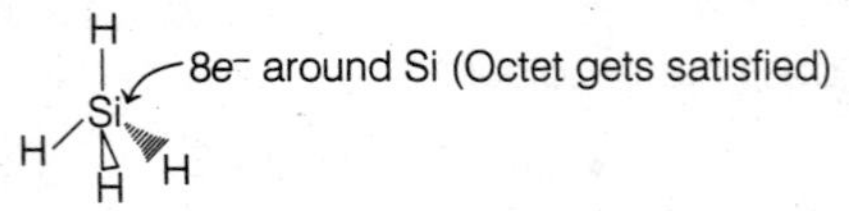

75. (*c*) In basic medium,

$$H_2\overset{-1}{O_2} + \overset{+7}{Mn}O_4 \longrightarrow \overset{+4}{Mn}O_2 + \overset{0}{O_2}$$

(Mn: $+3e^-$; O: $-2e$)

On balancing

$$3H_2O_2 + 2MnO_4^- \longrightarrow 2MnO_2 + 2H_2O + 3O_2 + 2OH^-$$

In acidic medium,

$$H^+ + H_2\overset{-1}{O_2} + \overset{+4}{Mn}O_2 \longrightarrow Mn^{+2} + H_2\overset{-2}{O} + \overset{0}{O_2}$$

On balancing

$$2MnO_4^- + 5H_2O_2 + 6H^+ \longrightarrow 2Mn^{+2} + 8H_2O + 5O_2$$

For 1 mole of MnO_4^-

$$(H_2O_2)_{basic} : (H_2O_2)_{acidic} = \frac{3}{2} : \frac{5}{2} = 3:5$$

83. (*a*) (I) H_2 is a 100% pollution free fuel. So, statement (I) is correct.

(II) Molecular weight of H_2 (2u).

$= \frac{1}{29} \times$ molecular weight of butane,

C_4H_{10} (LPG) [58u].

So, compressed H_2 weighs ~30 times more than a petrol tank and statement (II) is correct.

(III) **NaNi$_5$**, Ti - TiH_2 etc., are used for storage of H_2 in small quantities. Thus, statement (III) is correct.

(IV) On combustion values of energy released per gram of liquid dihydrogen (H_2): 142 kJ g^{-1}, and for LPG: 50 kJ g^{-1}. So, staement (IV) is incorrect.

89. (*d*) In basic medium, oxidising action of H_2O_2.

$$Mn^{2+} + H_2O_2 \longrightarrow Mn^{+4} + 2OH^-$$

In basic medium, reducing action of H_2O_2

$$I_2 + H_2O_2 + 2OH^- \longrightarrow 2I^- + 2H_2O + O_2$$

In acidic medium, oxidising action of H_2O_2.

$$PbS(s) + 4H_2O_2(aq) \longrightarrow PbSO_4(s) + 4H_2O(l)$$

Hence, correct option (d).

90. (*b*) The complete chemical equations for the given reactions are as follows :

(A) $H_2O_2 \xrightarrow{\Delta} H_2O + \frac{1}{2}O_2$

Thus, statement (*A*) is correct.

(B) $KClO_3 \xrightarrow{\Delta} KCl + \frac{3}{2}O_2$

$$Pb(NO_3)_2 \xrightarrow{\Delta} PbO + 2NO_2 + \frac{1}{2}O_2$$

$$NaNO_3 \xrightarrow{\Delta} NaNO_2 + \frac{1}{2}O_2$$

Thus, statement (*B*) is correct.

(C) 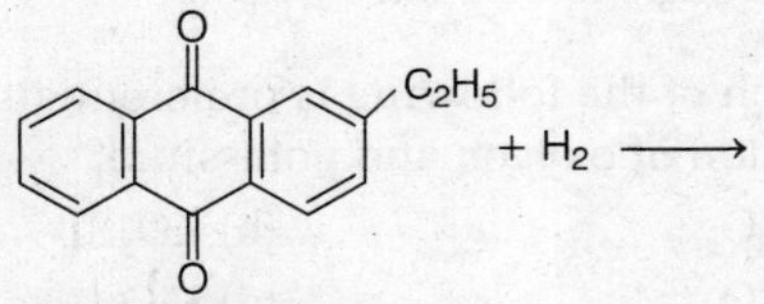

2-ethyl anthraquinone

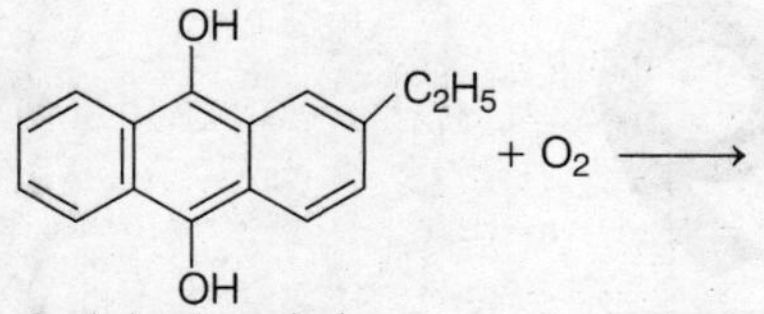

2-ethyl anthraquinol

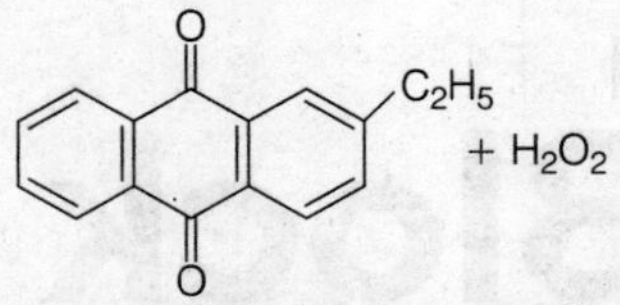

2-ethyl anthraquinone regenerated

Thus, statement (C) is also correct.

(D) $2NaBO_2 + 2H_2O_2 \longrightarrow Na_2B_2O_4(OH)_4$

or $Na_2H_4B_2O_8$ (sodium perborate)

Statement (D) is also correct.

91. (*a*) $Cr_2O_7^{2-} + \underset{\text{conc}}{H^+} \longrightarrow CrO_3$

$$CrO_3 + H_2O_2 \longrightarrow CrO_5$$

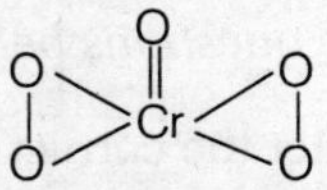

92. (*a*) $Na[Cr(OH)_4] + H_2O_2 \longrightarrow \underset{\text{Yellow}}{Na_2CrO_4}$

93. (*c*) H_2 is adsorbed in Pd-surface. Thus, it is in molecular state with oxidation number of H = 0

09

s-Block Elements

Objective Questions Type I [Only one correct option]

In each of the questions below, four choices are given of which only one is correct.

1. Which is/are not the correct configuration of s-block elements?
(a) $[Ar] 3d^{10} 4s^2$ (b) $[Ar] 3d^{10} 4s^1$
(c) Both (a) and (b) (d) None of these

2. Select the correct statement(s).
(a) Li_2CO_3 decomposes into oxides while other alkali carbonates are thermally stable
(b) LiCl is predominantly covalent
(c) Li_3N is stable
(d) All of the above

3. Alkali metals resemble IB (copper family) in the following respects
(a) +1 valency
(b) sulphates are water soluble
(c) oxides are strong bases
(d) oxides are strong acids

4. Select the incorrect statement.
(a) Na_2CO_3 is thermally stable while Ag_2CO_3 decomposes into Ag, CO_2 and O_2
(b) Ag^+ forms complexes, Na^+ does not
(c) NaCl is water soluble, AgCl is insoluble
(d) NaCl and AgCl both give colour in flame when ignited

5. A colourless solid (*X*) on heating evolved CO_2 and also gave a white residue, soluble in water. Residue also gave CO_2 when treated with dilute acid. (*X*) is
(a) Na_2CO_3 (b) $CaCO_3$
(c) $Ca(HCO_3)_2$ (d) $NaHCO_3$

6. Which of the following is preferentially formed on reaction of oxygen and potassium?
(a) K_2O_2 (b) KO_2
(c) K_2O (d) K_2O_3

7. CO_2 gas along with solid (*Y*) is obtained when sodium salt (*X*) is heated. (*X*) is again obtained when CO_2 gas is passed into aqueous solution (*Y*). (*X*) and (*Y*) are
(a) Na_2CO_3, Na_2O (b) Na_2CO_3, NaOH
(c) $NaHCO_3$, Na_2CO_3 (d) Na_2CO_3, $NaHCO_3$

8. The alkaline earth metal nitrate that does not crystallise with water molecules, is **[JEE Main 2019]**
(a) $Ca(NO_3)_2$ (b) $Sr(NO_3)_2$
(c) $Ba(NO_3)_2$ (d) $Mg(NO_3)_2$

9. The main oxides formed on combustion of Li, Na and K in excess of air respectively are **[JEE Main 2016]**
(a) LiO_2, Na_2O_2 and K_2O (b) Li_2O_2, Na_2O_2 and KO_2
(c) Li_2O, Na_2O_2 and KO_2 (d) Li_2O, Na_2O and KO_2

10. Molten sodium chloride conducts electricity due to the presence of
(a) free electrons (b) ions
(c) Na atom (d) Cl atom

11. Which is the major constituent of gun powder?
(a) Nitre (b) Sulphur
(c) Charcoal (d) Chile saltpetre

12. When SO_2 gas is passed into aqueous Na_2CO_3, product formed is
(a) $NaHSO_4$ (b) Na_2SO_4
(c) $NaHSO_3$ (d) Na_2SO_3

13. CO_2 cannot be obtained by heating
(a) Na_2CO_3 (b) $CaCO_3$
(c) Li_2CO_3 (d) $Ca(HCO_3)_2$

14. Some of alkali metal salts are coloured. Na_2CrO_4—yellow, $KMnO_4$—pink, K_2MnO_4 —green. It is due to
(a) cations are coloured ions
(b) anions are coloured ions
(c) Both (a) and (b) are correct
(d) None of the above is correct

15. Na and Li are placed in dry air. We get
(a) NaOH, Na_2O, Li_2O
(b) Na_2O, Li_2O
(c) Na_2O, Li_2O, Li_3N, NH_3
(d) Na_2O, Li_3N, Li_2O

16. All alkali metals form following compound except
(a) amide, MNH_2
(b) superoxide like KO_2
(c) ionic 'salt-like' hydride MH
(d) basic oxides

17. When a substance *A* reacts with water it produces a combustible gas *B* and a solution of substance *C* in water. When another substance *D* reacts with this solution of *C*, it also produces the same gas *B* on warming but *D* can produce gas *B* on reaction with dilute sulphuric acid at room temperature. *A* imparts a golden yellow colour to a smokeless flame of Bunsen flame. *A*, *B*, *C* and *D* are respectively.
(a) K, H_2, KOH, Al
(b) Na, H_2, NaOH, Zn
(c) CaC_2, C_2H_2, $Ca(OH)_2$, Fe
(d) Ca, H_2, $Ca(OH)_2$, Sn

18. Which of the following is best CO_2 absorber as well as source of O_2 in submarines?
(a) KO_2 (b) NaOH
(c) KOH (d) LiOH

19. Following are the ionisation potential values of (I_1)899 kJ mol^{-1}, (I_2)1757 kJ mol^{-1}, (I_3)15000 kJ mol^{-1}
(a) Na (b) K (c) Be (d) Ne

20. A compound which can be used in space vehicles both to absorb CO_2 and liberate O_2 is
(a) NaOH (b) Na_2O
(c) Na_2O_2 (d) CaO + NaOH

21. Which of the following changes is not realised in the laboratory?
(a) Absorption of NO by alkaline sodium sulphite to form a compound
(b) Combustion of metallic Mg in CO_2
(c) Heating hydrated magnesium chloride to get the anhydrous salt
(d) 'Displacement' of chlorine from $KClO_3$ by iodine to form KIO_3

22. Which is not the *s*-block element?
(a) $[Ar]\,4s^2\,3d^{10}\,4p^6 5s^1$ (b) $1s^2\,2s^2\,2p^1$
(c) $1s^2 2s^1\,2p^1$ (d) $[Ar]\,4s^1\,4p^1$

23. Which will give N_2O on heating?
(a) NH_4NO_2 (b) NH_4NO_3
(c) $NaNO_3$ (d) $LiNO_3$

24. Nitrate can be converted into metal oxide on heating in case of
(a) Li (b) Na
(c) Both (a) and (b) (d) None of these

25. Automobile grease is obtained from
(a) CH_3COONa (b) $C_{17}H_{35}COONa$
(c) CH_3CH_2COOLi (d) $C_{17}H_{35}COOLi$

26. Li_2CO_3 is
(a) added to bauxite in the electrolytic production of aluminium
(b) used to toughen glass
(c) used as medicine as it affects the balance between Na^+ and K^+, and Mg^{2+} and Ca^{2+}
(d) All of the above are correct

27. Which cannot be used to generate H_2?
(a) Al + NaOH (b) Zn + NaOH
(c) Mg + NaOH (d) LiH + H_2O

28. There is loss in weight when mixture of Li_2CO_3 and $Na_2CO_3 \cdot 10H_2O$ is heated strongly. This loss is due to
(a) Li_2CO_3 (b) $Na_2CO_3 \cdot 10H_2O$
(c) Both (a) and (b) (d) None of these

29. Which disproportionates into M_2O_2 (peroxide) and *M* (metal) on heating?
(a) Li_2O (b) Na_2O
(c) Both (a) & (b) (d) None of these

30. Reagent used as fixer in photography
(a) AgBr (b) $AgNO_3$
(c) $Na_2S_2O_3 \cdot 5H_2O$ (d) Both (a) and (c)

31. Which can dissolve I_2?
(a) KI (b) NaI
(c) Both (a) and (b) (d) None of these

32. Lattice energy (numerical value) of chloride of alkali metals is in order
(a) LiCl > NaCl > KCl > RbCl > CsCl
(b) LiCl < NaCl < KCl < RbCl < CsCl
(c) NaCl < KCl < LiCl < RbCl < CsCl
(d) NaCl < KCl < RbCl < CsCl < LiCl

33. Which is the most stable halide of alkali metal?
(a) Sodium fluoride (b) Sodium bromide
(c) Sodium chloride (d) Sodium iodide

34. Which is a pair of paramagnetic species?
(a) KO_2, NO_2 (b) K_2O_2, KO_2
(c) K_2O, NO_2 (d) NO_2, N_2O_2

35. Following compounds are used in fire-works
(a) $LiNO_3$ (b) $BaCl_2$
(c) $(NH_4)_2Cr_2O_7$ (d) All of these

36. Which has least molar solubility in H_2O?
(a) LiCl (b) NaCl (c) KCl (d) CsCl

37. To an acidified dichromate solution, a pinch of Na_2O_2 and ether is added and shaken. What is observed?
(a) Deep violet colour
(b) Red colour changing to green
(c) Copious evolution of oxygen
(d) Bluish-green precipitate

38. Nitrolim is a
(a) mixture of calcium carbide and nitrogen
(b) mixture of calcium cyanamide and carbon
(c) mixture of calcium cyanide and carbon
(d) mixture of NH_4CN and CaCN

39. The common name, "cream of tartar" refers to
(a) $KHC_4H_4O_6$
(b) $K(SbO)C_4H_4O_6$
(c) $KNaC_4H_4O_6$
(d) $Mg_2(OH)_2(C_4H_4O_6)H_2O$

40. Which of the following mixtures cannot be prepared?
(a) $NaHCO_3 + Na_2CO_3$
(b) $Na_2CO_3 + NaOH$
(c) $NaHCO_3 + NaOH$
(d) $H_2CO_3 + NaHCO_3$

41. Noble gases (like He, Ne, Ar, Kr etc.) are isolated from air. One of the steps is/are
(a) heating air with Li or Mg
(b) bubbling air into NaOH solution
(c) Both (a) and (b) are correct
(d) None of the above is correct

42. Which of the following is not used as food preservatives?
(a) NaCl (b) CH_3COOH
(c) C_6H_5COONa (d) HCHO

43. The set of elements that differ in mutual relationship from those of the other sets is **[JEE Main 2021, March]**
(a) Li – Mg (b) B – Si
(c) Be – Al (d) Li – Na

44. Select the correct statement(s).
(a) $CaCO_3$ is more soluble in a solution of CO_2 than in H_2O
(b) Na_2CO_3 is converted to Na_2O and CO_2 on heating
(c) Li_2CO_3 is thermally stable
(d) Presence of $CaCl_2$ or $CaSO_4$ in water causes temporary hardness

45. The alkalide ion is
(a) diamagnetic (b) represented as $\bar{C}H_3$
(c) paramagnetic (d) represented as $\overset{+}{C}H_3$

46. Select the correct statement(s).
(a) Mg^{2+} ions are necessary for the activation of phosphate transfer enzymes.
(b) Mg is present in chlorophyll used in photosynthesis in green plants.
(c) Operation of $Na^+ - K^+$ pumps is biological.
(d) All of the above are correct statements

47. The alkali metals dissolve in liquid NH_3, it is found that
(a) the dilute solutions are blue but the colour changes to bronze with increasing concentration
(b) the blue colour is due to the presence of solvated electrons
(c) the blue solutions are paramagnetic but the bronze-coloured solutions are diamagnetic
(d) All of the facts given above are found

48. The ionic radius of Na^+ ions is 1.02 Å. The ionic radii (in Å) of Mg^{2+} and Al^{3+}, respectively, are **[JEE Main 2021, March]**
(a) 1.05 and 0.99 (b) 0.72 and 0.54
(c) 0.85 and 0.99 (d) 0.68 and 0.72

49. Which one of the following is correct sequence followed by molar ionic conductance of the ions?
(a) $Li^+ < Na^+ < K^+ < Rb^+$
(b) $Rb^+ < K^+ < Na^+ < Li^+$
(c) $Sr^{2+} < Ca^{2+} < Mg^{2+} < Be^{2+}$
(d) $Na^+ < K^+ < Li^+ < Rb^+$

50. M_2O_3 (sesquoxides) is paramagnetic in nature. It is due to the presence of
(a) peroxide ion (b) superoxide ion
(c) oxide ion (d) All of the above

51. Which is/are coloured and paramagnetic?
(a) KO_2 (b) K_2O_3
(c) Both (a) and (b) (d) None of these

52. Mg and Zn do not resemble in following properties
(a) oxides are amphoteric
(b) carbonates on heating form metal oxides
(c) widely used as electrodes
(d) used to prevent corrosion

53. When Cl_2 is passed into moist slaked lime, compound formed is
(a) CaO_2Cl_2 (b) CaO_2Cl (c) $CaOCl_2$ (d) $CaCl_2O_4$

54. The first ionisation potential of Na is 5.1 eV. The value of electron gain enthalpy of Na^+ will be **[JEE Main 2013]**
(a) – 2.55 eV (b) – 5.1 eV (c) – 10.2 eV (d) + 2.55 eV

55. Be and Al do not resemble in
(a) both become passive on reaction with HNO_3 due to formation of oxide layer
(b) their chlorides are Lewis bases
(c) chlorides exist in polymeric form
(d) hydroxides are soluble in alkali as well as in acid

56. Going down to II A group, following properties increase except
(a) solubility of hydroxides in H_2O
(b) hydration energy
(c) thermal stability of carbonates
(d) ionic radius

57. Following are the ionisation potential values of $(I_1) 899$ kJ mol^{-1}, $(I_2) 1757$ kJ mol^{-1}, $(I_3) 15000$ kJ mol^{-1}
(a) Na (b) K (c) Be (d) Ne

58. Which is most stable out of the following?
(a) $[Be(H_2O)_4]^{2+}$ (b) $[Mg(H_2O)_4]^{2+}$
(c) $[Ca(H_2O)_4]^{2+}$ (d) $[Sr(H_2O)_4]^{2+}$

59. Lattice energy of IIA group compounds (oxides, carbonates, flourides)
(a) decreases as size of the ion increases
(b) increases as size of the ion increases
(c) constant for a given type of anion
(d) All of the above are incorrect

60. Which of the following statements are true about II A group elements?
(a) All form nitrides in air
(b) Be is amphoteric
(c) MH_2 is ionic 'salt-like' hydride
(d) All of the above are correct statements

61. Choose the incorrect statement.
(a) $BeCO_3$ is kept in the atmosphere of CO_2 since it is least thermally stable
(b) Be dissolves in alkali forming $[Be(OH)_4]^{2-}$
(c) BeF_2 forms complex ion with NaF in when Be goes with cation
(d) BeF_2 forms complex ion with NaF in which Be goes with anion

62. Both lithium and magnesium display several similar properties due to the diagonal relationship; however, the one which is incorrect is **[JEE Main 2017]**
(a) Both form basic carbonates
(b) Both form soluble bicarbonates
(c) Both form nitrides
(d) nitrates of both Li and Mg yield NO_2 and O_2 on heating

63. Solubility of alkaline earth metal carbonates in water is follows
(a) $BeCO_3 > MgCO_3 > CaCO_3 > BaCO_3$
(b) $BeCO_3 > CaCO_3 > MgCO_3 > BaCO_3$
(c) $BeCO_3 > MgCO_3 < CaCO_3 < BaCO_3$
(d) $BaCO_3 > BeCO_3 < MgCO_3 < CaCO_3$

64. Setting of cement is
(a) exothermic reaction
(b) endothermic reaction
(c) neither endothermic nor exothermic
(d) None of the above

65. Which is main constituent of egg-shell?
(a) $CaCO_3$ (b) $CaSiO_3$
(c) $CaSO_4 \cdot \frac{1}{2} H_2O$ (d) $CaSO_4 \cdot 2H_2O$

66. The deliquescent among the following is
(a) $CaCl_2$ (b) $FeSO_4 \cdot 7H_2O$
(c) $CuSO_4 \cdot 5H_2O$ (d) $BaCl_2 \cdot 2H_2O$

67. Which is the incorrect statement?
(a) The heats of hydration of the dipositive alkaline earth metal ions decrease with an increase in their ionic size.
(b) $NaNO_3$ forms Na_2O on heating
(c) Hydration of alkali metal ion is less than that of II A.
(d) Alkaline earth metal ions, because of their much larger charge to size ratio, exert a much stronger electrostatic attraction on the oxygen of water molecule surrounding them.

68. 1 mole of a substance (X) was treated with an excess of water. 2 moles of readily combustible gas were produced along with solution which when reacted with CO_2 gas produced a white turbidity. The substance (X) could be
(a) Ca (b) CaH_2
(c) $Ca(OH)_2$ (d) $Ca(NO_3)_2$

69. $Na_2[Be(OH)_4]$ is formed when
(a) BeO reacts with NaOH solution
(b) Be reacts with NaOH solution
(c) Both (a) and (b) correct
(d) None of the above is correct

70. Which is used to treat acid indigestion?
(a) $Be(OH)_2$ (b) KOH
(c) $Mg(OH)_2$ (d) $Ca(OH)_2$

71. Which is not obtained when metal carbides react with H_2O?
(a) $Al_4C_3 + H_2O \longrightarrow CH \equiv CH$
(b) $CaC_2 + H_2O \longrightarrow CH \equiv CH$
(c) $Mg_4C_3 + H_2O \longrightarrow CH_3C \equiv CH$
(d) $Be_2C + H_2O \longrightarrow CH_4$

72. Select the correct statement(s).
(a) $CaCO_3$ is more soluble in a solution of CO_2 than in H_2O
(b) $NaCO_3$ is converted to Na_2O and CO_2 on heating
(c) Li_2CO_3 is thermally stable
(d) Presence of $CaCl_2$ or $CaSO_4$ in water causes temporary hardness

73. A metal M readily forms water soluble MSO_4. It also forms oxide MO which becomes inert on heating. Hydroxide $M(OH)_2$ is insoluble in water but soluble in NaOH solution. What is M?
(a) Mg (b) Ba (c) Ca (d) Be

74. Which one of the following has magnesium?
(a) Vitamin B_{12} (b) Chlorophyll
(c) Haemocyanin (d) Carbonic anhydrase

75. In which of the following the hydration energy is higher than the lattice energy?
(a) $BaSO_4$ (b) $MgSO_4$
(c) $RaSO_4$ (d) $SrSO_4$

76. Epsom salt is
(a) $BaSO_4 \cdot 2H_2O$ (b) $CaSO_4 \cdot H_2O$
(c) $MgSO_4 \cdot 2H_2O$ (d) $MgSO_4 \cdot 7H_2O$

77. Slaked lime and chlorine reacts to produce
(a) quicklime
(b) $CaCl_2$
(c) $CaOCl_2$
(d) mixture of $CaCl_2$ and $Ca(OCl_2)$

78. Mg and Li are similar in their properties due to
(a) same e/m ratio (b) same electron affinity
(c) same group (d) same radius

79. Which one of the following hydroxide is insoluble in water?
(a) $Ca(OH)_2$ (b) $Ba(OH)_2$
(c) $Be(OH)_2$ (d) $Mg(OH)_2$

80. The pair of amphoteric hydroxide is
(a) $Al(OH)_3$, LiOH (b) $Be(OH)_2$, $Mg(OH)_2$
(c) $B(OH)_3$, $Be(OH)_2$ (d) $Be(OH)_2$, $Zn(OH)_2$

81. Alkaline earth metals are
(a) reducing agent (b) dehydrating agent
(c) amphoteric (d) oxidising agent

82. Which of the following is not an ore of magnesium?
(a) Carnallite (b) Magnesite
(c) Dolomite (d) Gypsum

83. Be in $BeCl_2$ undergoes
(a) linear hybridisation (b) trigonal hybridisation
(c) tetrahedral hybridisation (d) no hybridisation

84. The product obtained on fusion of $BaSO_4$ and Na_2CO_3 is
(a) $BaCO_3$ (b) BaO
(c) $Ba(OH)_2$ (d) $BaHSO_4$

85. Bleaching powder loses its power on keeping for a long time because
(a) it changes into calcium hypochlorate
(b) it changes into calcium chloride and calcium hydroxide
(c) it absorbs moisture
(d) it changes into calcium chloride and calcium chlorate

86. Among Na^+, Na, Mg and Mg^{2+} the largest particle is
(a) Mg^{2+} (b) Mg (c) Na (d) Na^+

87. The electron affinity of Be is similar to
(a) He (b) B (c) Li (d) Na

88. Bleaching action of $CaOCl_2$ is due to
(a) nascent oxygen (b) chlorine
(c) HClO (d) HCl

89. Ripening of fruits can be caried out in presence of
(a) Na_2SO_4 (b) NaCl (c) $CaCl_2$ (d) CaC_2

90. The right order of the solubility of sulphates of alkaline earth metals in water
(a) Be > Ca > Mg > Ba > Sr
(b) Mg > Be > Ba > Ca > Sr
(c) Be > Mg > Ca > Sr > Ba
(d) Mg > Ca > Ba > Be > Sr

91. Burning of Mg is extinguished by
(a) throwing N_2 liquid (b) throwing sand
(c) throwing ice (d) throwing water

92. Flame test is not given by
(a) Ca (b) Ba (c) Mg (d) Li

93. Lithium shows similarities with magnesium in its chemical behaviour because
(a) similar size, greater electronegativity and lower polarising power
(b) similar size, same electronegativity and lower polarising power
(c) similar size, same electronegativity and similar high polarising power
(d) None of the above

94. The element whose electronic configuration is $1s^2 2s^2 2p^6 3s^2$ is
(a) non-metal (b) noble gas
(c) metalloid (d) metal

95. On strong heating $MgCl_2 \cdot 6H_2O$ the product obtained is
(a) $MgCl_2$ (b) MgO
(c) $MgCl_2 \cdot 2H_2O$ (d) $MgCl_2 \cdot 4H_2O$

96. Which of the following carbonate decompose most easily on heating?
(a) Rb_2CO_3 (b) K_2CO_3
(c) Na_2CO_3 (d) $MgCO_3$

97. In the following reactions, products (A) and (B), respectively, are
$NaOH + Cl_2 \rightarrow (A) + \text{side products (hot and conc.)}$
$Ca(OH)_2 + Cl_2 \rightarrow (B) + \text{side products (dry)}$ **[JEE Main 2020]**
(a) $NaClO_3$ and $Ca(OCl)_2$ (b) $NaClO_3$ and $Ca(ClO_3)_2$
(c) NaOCl and $Ca(OCl)_2$ (d) NaOCl and $Ca(ClO_3)_2$

98. A metal (A) on heating in nitrogen gas gives compound B. B on treatment with H_2O gives a colourless gas, which when passed through $CuSO_4$ solution gives a dark blue-violet coloured solution. A and B respectively, are **[JEE Main 2020]**
(a) Na and Na_3N
(b) Mg and Mg_3N_2
(c) Mg and $Mg(NO_3)_2$
(d) Na and $NaNO_3$

99. A hydrated solid X on heating initially gives a monohydrated compound Y.
Y upon heating above 373 K leads to an anhydrous white powder Z. X and Z, respectively, are
(a) baking soda and soda ash **[JEE Main 2019]**
(b) washing soda and soda ash
(c) baking soda and dead burnt plaster
(d) washing soda and dead burnt plaster

100. The basic character of the alkaline earth metal hydroxides as follows :
(a) $Mg(OH)_2 > Ba(OH)_2 > Ca(OH)_2 > Sr(OH)_2$
(b) $Ba(OH)_2 > Sr(OH)_2 > Ca(OH)_2 > Mg(OH)_2$
(c) $Sr(OH)_2 > Ca(OH)_2 > Ba(OH)_2 > Mg(OH)_2$
(d) $Mg(OH)_2 > Ba(OH)_2 > Sr(OH)_2 > Ca(OH)_2$

101. Be and Al resemble in the following but not in
(a) both form electron deficient hydrides
(b) both are rendered passive by HNO_3
(c) both form amphoteric oxides
(d) both have *sp*-hybridisation in their compounds

102. Select the incorrect statement.
(a) NaOH can be stored in a vessel made of Al
(b) HNO_3 can be stored in a vessel made of Be/Al alloy
(c) HF can be stored in a vessel made of wax
(d) HF attacks glass

103. Metal carbides on reaction with H_2O form CH_4. Carbide can be
(a) CaC_2 (b) Mg_3C_2
(c) Be_2C (d) SiC

Objective Questions Type II [One or more than one correct option(s)]

In each of the questions below, four choices are given, of which one or more than one are correct.

1. Select the correct statement(s).
(a) MO_2 contains the paramagnetic ion O_2^-
(b) O_2^- is stable only in the presence of large cations as K, Rb and Cs
(c) KO_2 is paramagnetic and has orange colour
(d) K_2O has antifluorite structure

2. The compound(s) which generate (s) N_2 gas upon thermal decomposition below 300° C is (are) **[JEE Advanced 2018]**
(a) NH_4NO_3 (b) $(NH_4)_2Cr_2O_7$
(c) $Ba(N_3)_2$ (d) Mg_3N_2

3. Sesquoxides (M_2O_3) of alkali metals
(a) have been prepared by careful thermal decomposition of MO_2
(b) are dark-coloured paramagnetic substances
(c) are colourless diamagnetic substances
(d) are coloured diamagnetic substances

4. Select the correct statement(s).
(a) Alkali metals-ozonides are coloured and paramagnetic
(b) Alkali metals-ozonides are colourless and diamagnetic
(c) Sesquoxides of alkali metals are peroxides disuperoxides $(M^+)_4(O_2^{2-})(O_2^-)_2$
(d) Sesquoxides are paramagnetic due to presence of superoxide ion O_2^-.

5. Sodium sulphate is soluble in water but barium sulphate is sparingly soluble because
(a) The hydration enthalpy of Na_2SO_4 is more than its lattice enthalpy
(b) The lattice enthalpy of $BaSO_4$ is more than its hydration enthalpy
(c) The lattice enthalpy has no role to play in solubility
(d) The lattice enthalpy of Na_2SO_4 is more than its hydration enthalpy.

6. Which of the following statements are false?
(a) $BeCl_2$ exists as dimer in the vapour state and polymeric in the solid state
(b) Calcium hydride in called hydrolith
(c) The oxides of Be and Ca are amphoteric
(d) Bicarbonates of Na and Sr are insoluble in water

7. Select the correct alternate(s).
(a) Solid $LiNO_3$ and $NaNO_3$ and deliquescent
(b) KNO_3 is used in preference to $NaNO_3$ in gun powder
(c) $NaNO_3$ is used in preference to $NaNO_3$ in gun powder
(d) NH_4HCO_3 exists in solid state

8. Select the correct statements.
(a) Oxide ion, peroxide ion and superoxide ions are related to each other as follows :

$$\underset{\text{Oxide ion}}{O^{2-}} \xrightarrow{\frac{1}{2}O_2} \underset{\text{Peroxide ion}}{O_2^{2-}} \xrightarrow{O_2} \underset{\text{Superoxide ion}}{O_2^-}$$

(b) O_2^{2-} and O_2^- are stable towards water
(c) KO_2 will liberate O_2 when reacts with ice cold water
(d) Alkali metal oxides, peroxides and superoxides acts bronsted acid

9. Select the correct statement(s).
(a) Radius of hydrated Li^+ ion is smaller than that of hydrated Cs^+ ion
(b) Ionic mobility of hydrated Li^+ ion is smaller than that of hydrated Cs^+ ion
(c) Hydrated Cs^+ is more conducting that hydrated Na^+ ion
(d) Ionic mobility of hydrated
$Cs^+ > Rb^+ > K^+ > Na^+ > Li^+$

10. Select the correct statements.
   (a) Sodium peroxide (Na_2O_2) is used to purify the air in submarine because it reacts with O_2 to form sodium superoxide
   (b) Amongst alkali metal chlorides, LiCl has lowest melting point
   (c) Amongst alkali metal fluorides, LiF is least soluble H_2O
   (d) $Na_2CO_3.NaHCO_3.2H_2O$ is a mineral called trona
11. Which is/are true statement(s)?
   (a) The heats of hydration of the dipositive alkaline earth metal ions decrease with an increase in their ionic size
   (b) Hydration of alkali metal ion is less than that of IIA.
   (c) Alkaline earth metal ions, because of their much larger charge to size ratio exert a much stronger electrostatic attraction on the oxygen of water molecule surrounding them
   (d) None of the above statements is correct
12. Which are true statements about *s*-block elements?
   (a) Metals are obtained by the electrolysis of fused chlorides
   (b) Oxides are basic except BeO
   (c) +1 valency by alkali metals and +2 valency by alkaline earth metals is shown
   (d) Carbonates are thermally stable
13. The reagent(s) used for softening the temporary hardness of water is (are) **[IIT JEE 2010]**
   (a) $Ca_3(PO_4)_2$ (b) $Ca(OH)_2$
   (c) Na_2CO_3 (d) NaOCl
14. Which of the following properties show a reverse trend in moving down the group of alkali and alkaline earth metals?
   (a) Solubility fo hydroxides
   (b) Solubility of carbonates
   (c) Solubility of sulphates
   (d) Solubility of oxides
15. Which of the following statement(s) is/are not true about the diagonal relationship of Be and Al?
   (a) Their oxides are basic
   (b) They become passive by conc HNO_3
   (c) Both react with NaOH to liberate hydrogen
   (d) Their carbides give acetylene on hydrolysis

Numerical Value Questions

All these questions have a Numerical value as their answer, solve the questions and write your answer.

1. Calcium carbide reacts with nitrogen and forms an important fertilizer, calcium cyanamide. How much calcium cyanamide is formed when 6.4 g of calcium carbide is completely converted into cyanamide?
2. Magnesium oxide when mixed with a saturated solution of $MgCl_2$,sets to a hard mass known as 'Sorel cement' is formed. The composition of Sorel cement is $MgCl_2.nMgO.xH_2O$. What is the value of n ?
3. On heating 8 moles each of Li_2CO_3 and K_2CO_3, total moles of CO_2 evolved ...... ?
4. How many moles of ammonia are produced, on hydrolysis of five moles of Li_3N ?
5. How many water molecules of crystallisation are present in borax ?
6. What is the +ve oxidation state of Cs in Cs_2O_2 ?
7. What is the –ve oxidation of O in Cs_2O?

Comprehension Based Questions

In these questions, a passage has been given followed by questions based on it. You have to answer the questions based on the passage given.

***Passage* 1** *Read the following passage and answer the questions at the end of it.*

Dilute solutions of alkali metals in liquid NH_3 are blue. It is the ammoniated electron which is responsible for the blue colour of the solution, and the electrical conductivity is due to the ammoniated cation, $[M(NH_3)_x]^+$ as well as the ammoniated electron, $[e(NH_3)_y]^-$, values of x and y depend on the extent of solvation (by NH_3). Dilute solutions are paramagnetic due to free electrons.

1. What happens if alkali metal is allowed to react with concentrated ammonia solution?
   (a) Paramagnetic character of solvated electrons is retained
   (b) Solvated electrons associate to form electron-pairs and paramagnetic character decreases
   (c) Reducing character is increased
   (d) Reducing character is not affected

2. Ammoniated solutions of alkali metals are reducing agents due to the presence of free or solvated electrons and can reduce
   (a) O_2 to O_2^{2-}
   (b) $K_2[Ni(CN)_4]$ to $K_4[Ni(CN)_4]$
   (c) Both (a) and (b)
   (d) None of the above

***Passage* 2** *Questions given below are based on the following values of hydration energy and lattice energy.*

Hydration energy $\Delta H_{hyd.}$ ($kJ\ mol^{-1}$)		Lattice energy ΔH_U ($kJ\ mol^{-1}$)	
Li^+	– 499	LiCl	– 840
Na^+	– 390	NaCl	– 776
K^+	– 305	KCl	– 703
Cl^-	– 382		

1. Which salt has maximum heat of hydration?
   (a) LiCl (b) NaCl
   (c) KCl (d) LiCl and KCl equally
2. Heat of hydration (numerical value) of LiCl, NaCl and KCl in the increasing order is
   (a) LiCl < KCl < NaCl (b) LiCl < NaCl < KCl
   (c) LiCl = KCl < NaCl (d) KCl < NaCl < LiCl
3. Maximum heat is absorbed in the dissolution of one mole of
   (a) LiCl (b) NaCl
   (c) KCl (d) equally

***Passage* 3** *Answer the questions based on the following flow-sheet.*

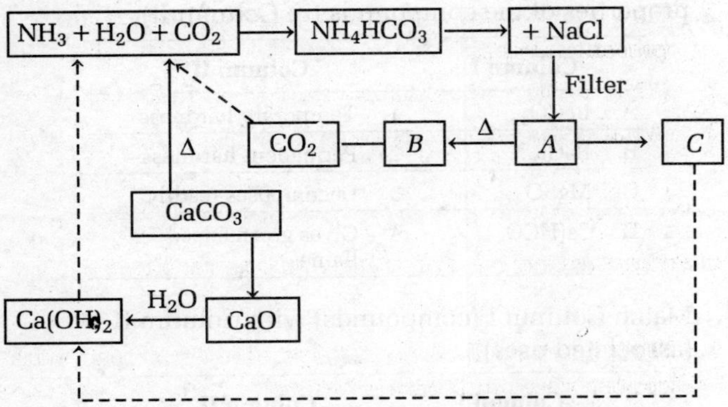

1. This flow-sheet represents
   (a) Solvay process of NaOH
   (b) Solvay process of Na_2CO_3
   (c) Dow process of Na_2CO_3
   (d) None of the above is correct
2. Filtrate *A* contains
   (a) NH_4Cl (b) Na_2CO_3 (c) $NaHCO_3$ (d) $CaCO_3$
3. Species *B* formed is
   (a) NH_3 (b) CO_2 (c) Na_2CO_3 (d) $NaHCO_3$

***Passage* 4** Reduction potentials of group 1 (alkali metals) are given below :

Element	$E°(U)$
$Li^+ + e^- \longrightarrow Li$	–3.045
$Na^+ + e^- \longrightarrow Na$	–2.714
$K^+ + e^- \longrightarrow K$	–2.925
$Rb^+ + e^- \longrightarrow Rb$	–2.925
$Cs^+ + e^- \longrightarrow Cs$	–2.923

Answer the following questions.

1. Which is the best reducing agent?
   (a) Li (b) Na (c) Rb (d) Cs
2. Which is the poorest reducing agent?
   (a) Li (b) Na (c) Rb (d) Cs
3. $E°$ can be related to
   (a) $\Delta G°$ (b) $\Delta H°$
   (c) Both (a) and (b) (d) None of these

***Passage* 5** "Calcium oxide, CaO, is used to remove SO_2 from power plant exhaust."

Based on the above statement, answer the following questions.

1. In what form CaO removes SO_2?
   (a) $CaSO_3$ (b) $CaSO_4$
   (c) $Ca(HSO_3)_2$ (d) $Ca(HSO_4)_2$
2. What mass of SO_2 can be removed using 1.4×10^3 kg CaO ?
   (a) 1.4×10^3 kg (b) 1.6×10^3 kg
   (c) 2.2×10^3 kg (d) 2.4×10^3 kg
3. Presence of SO_2 from power plant exhaust can be detected by
   (a) $Cr_2O_7^{2-}$ which changes to green
   (b) MnO_4^- which changes to colourless
   (c) Both (a) and (b)
   (d) None of the above

***Passage* 6** *Based on the following analytical data, answer the questions.*

A mineral, which can be represented by the formula $Mg_xBa_y(CO_3)_z$, was analysed as described below.

A sample of the mineral was dissolved in excess hydrochloric acid and the solution made up to 100 cm^3 with water. During the process 48 cm^3 of carbon dioxide, measured at 25°C and 1 atmosphere pressure, were evolved.

A 25.0 cm^3 portion of the resulting solution required 25.0 cm^3 of EDTA solution of concentration 0.02 mol dm^3 to reach an end-point. A further 25.0 cm^3 portion gave a precipitate of barium sulphate of mass 0.058 g on treatment with excess dilute sulphuric acid. You may assume that group-2 metal ions form 1 : 1 complexes with EDTA.

Molar volume of any gas at 25°C and 1 atmosphere pressure = 24 dm^3).

1. Formula of the mineral is
(a) $MgBa(CO_3)_4$ (b) $MgBa(CO_3)_2$
(c) $MgBa(CO_3)_3$ (d) $Mg_2Ba(CO_3)_4$
2. In the mineral barium ion can be identified by
(a) green colour in flame
(b) yellow precipitate with CrO_4^{2-} solution
(c) white precipitate with SO_4^{2-}
(d) All of the above
3. Identical mineral of calcium and magnesium ions is
(a) dolomite (b) magnesite (c) epsomite (d) talc

***Passage* 7** *Questions given below are based on the following enthalpy values.*

The standard enthalpy of formation ΔH_f°, of hypothetical CaCl(s) theoretically found to be −188 kJ mol^{-1} and that of $CaCl_2(s)$ −795 kJ mol^{-1}.

1. Which of the following compounds is more stable?
(a) CaCl(s)
(b) $CaCl_2(s)$
(c) Both (a) and (b) are equally stable
(d) Nothing can be said
2. Select the most spontaneous reaction.
(a) $2CaCl(s) \longrightarrow CaCl_2(s) + Ca(s)$
(b) $CaCl_2(s) + Ca(s) \longrightarrow 2CaCl(s)$
(c) $CaCl(s) \longrightarrow Ca(s) + Cl(g)$
(d) $CaCl_2(s) \longrightarrow Ca(s) + Cl_2(g)$

***Passage* 8** ΔG° values (kJ mol^{-1}) for the following cases can given

$$MCO_3 \longrightarrow MO + CO_2$$

	$MgCO_3$	MO	CO_2
			−394.4
Mg	−1028.2	−568.9	
Ca	−1129.2	− 603.4	
Ba	−1134.4	− 520.4	

Answer the following questions.

1. Maximum value of ΔG° is for the reaction when M is
(a) Mg (b) Ca
(c) Ba (d) equal for all cases
2. Thermal stability of the carbonates is in order
(a) $MgCO_3 < CaCO_3 < BaCO_3$
(b) $BaCO_3 < CaCO_3 < MgCO_3$
(c) $MgCO_3 < BaCO_3 < CaCO_3$
(d) $CaCO_3 < BaCO_3 < MgCO_3$
3. Which is decomposed most easily?
(a) $CaCO_3$ (b) $MgCO_3$
(c) $BaCO_3$ (d) Equally

Matrix-Match Type

Given below are Matching Type Questions, with two columns (each having some items) each . Each item of Column I has to be matched with the items of Column II.

1. Match the commercial names (in Column I) with the chemical formulae (in Column II).

Column I	Column II
A. Magnesia	1. BeO
B. Epsom salt	2. $Ca(OH)_2$
C. Anhydrone	3. $MgSO_4 \cdot 7H_2O$
D. Hydrolith	4. CaH_2
E. Beryllia	5. MgO
F. Slaked lime	6. $Mg(ClO_4)_2$

2. Match the mineral names (in Column I) with the chemical formulae (in Column II).

Column I	Column II
A. Magnesite	1. $KCl \cdot MgCl_2 \cdot 6H_2O$
B. Dolomite	2. $MgSO_4 \cdot H_2O$
C. Kieserite	3. $MgCO_3$
D. Carnallite	4. $MgCO_3 \cdot CaCO_3$

3. Match compounds (in Column I) with the specific properties of the compounds (in Column II).

Column I	Column II
A. $BeCO_3$	1. Temporary hardness
B. $BaCl_2$	2. Permanent hardness
C. $MgSO_4$	3. Decomposes readily
D. $Ca(HCO_3)_2$	4. Gives green edged flame

4. Match Column I (compounds) with Column II (associated uses).

Column I (Compounds)	Column II (Associated uses)
A. KO_2	1. Baking
B. $NaHCO_3$	2. Photovoltaic cell
C. LiCl	3. Submarine
D. Cs	4. Humidity control

5. Select the metals (in Column I) with the specific properties of the compounds (in Column II).

Column I	Column II
A. Li	1. Super oxide
B. Na	2. Lewis acid—a chloride
C. K	3. Most negative value of E°_{red}
D. Be	4. Thermally stable carbonate
E. Mg	5. No flame colouration of the chloride

6. Match the commercial names (in Column I) with the chemical formulae (in Column II).

Column I	Column II
A. Caustic potash	1. Na_2CO_3
B. Common salt	2. $Na_2SO_4 \cdot 10H_2O$
C. Soda ash	3. NaCl
D. Lithium oxide	4. KOH
E. Caustic soda	5. $NaHCO_3$
F. Baking soda	6. KNO_3
G. Glaubers' salt	7. Li_2O
H. Salt petre	8. NaOH

7. Match Column I with Column II. **[JEE Main 2021, March]**

Column I	Column II
A. Be	1. Treatment of cancer
B. Mg	2. Extraction of metals
C. Ca	3. Incendiary bombs and signals
D. Ra	4. Windows of X-ray tubes
	5. Bearings for motorengines

8. Match the species in Column I with given property (ies) in Column II.

Column I	Column II
A. Alkalide of halonium	1. Paramagnetic
B. Superoxide of alkali metal	2. Diamagnetic
C. Peroxide of alkali metal	3. Life saving devices
D. Oxide of alkali metal	4. Oxidant
	5. Bleaching agent
	6. Dissolves Zn, Al

Single Integer Answer Questions

Answer of these questions is a single digit lying between 0 to 9.

1. Unpaired electron(s) in superoxide ion ....
2. Potassium sesquoxide has actually .... O-atoms
3. When one mole of Na_2CO_3 is heated, CO_2 obtained is .... mole.
4. Number of HCO_3^- ions joined by H-bonding in $KHCO_3$ is ....
5. When $LiNO_3$ is heated, change in oxidation number of N is ....
6. When $NaNO_3$ is heated, change in oxidation number of N is ....
7. Number of radioactive elements in *s*-block is ....
8. Hydrated sodium sulphite has 50% H_2O. Number of molecules of hydration is ....
9. One mole of lithium nitride is decomposed by H_2O and resultant solution is neutralised by HCl. Number of moles of HCl required is ....
10. Cl_2 disproportionates to NaCl and $NaClO_3$ on passing into hot NaOH solution. In this process each mole of Cl_2 consumes .... mole(s) of NaOH.
11. KO_2 is CO_2 absorber and O_2 producer as shown
$$4KO_2 + CO_2 \longrightarrow K_2CO_3 + xO_2$$
Value of x is ....
12. Na_2CO_3 removes permanent hardness
$$CaSO_4 + Na_2CO_3 \longrightarrow Na_2SO_4 + CaCO_3$$
10 L of hard water required 0.0848 g Na_2CO_3. Thus, hardness in ppm of $CaCO_3$ is ....
13. Magnesium allyide is Mg_2C_x where x is ....
14. Magnesium is coordinated to N-atoms in chlorophyll. Number of rings in chlorophyll is ....
15. 96 g of Mg is burnt in air in a closed chamber. On analysis 25% of Mg is converted into oxide and remaining Mg into other possible product. Residue is dissolving in H_2O and neutralised by H_2SO_4. Number of moles of H_2SO_4 required is ....

Answers

Objective Questions Type I [Only one correct option]

1. (c)	2. (d)	3. (a)	4. (d)	5. (d)	6. (b)	7. (c)	8. (c)	9. (c)	10. (b)
11. (d)	12. (d)	13. (a)	14. (b)	15. (d)	16. (b)	17. (b)	18. (a)	19. (c)	20. (c)
21. (c)	22. (b)	23. (b)	24. (c)	25. (d)	26. (d)	27. (c)	28. (c)	29. (b)	30. (c)
31. (a)	32. (a)	33. (a)	34. (a)	35. (d)	36. (c)	37. (a)	38. (b)	39. (b)	40. (c)
41. (c)	42. (d)	43. (d)	44. (a)	45. (a)	46. (d)	47. (d)	48. (b)	49. (a)	50. (b)
51. (c)	52. (a)	53. (c)	54. (b)	55. (b)	56. (b)	57. (c)	58. (a)	59. (a)	60. (d)
61. (c)	62. (a)	63. (a)	64. (a)	65. (a)	66. (a)	67. (b)	68. (b)	69. (c)	70. (c)
71. (a)	72. (a)	73. (d)	74. (b)	75. (b)	76. (d)	77. (d)	78. (d)	79. (c)	80. (d)
81. (a)	82. (d)	83. (a)	84. (b)	85. (d)	86. (c)	87. (a)	88. (c)	89. (d)	90. (a)
91. (b)	92. (c)	93. (c)	94. (d)	95. (b)	96. (d)	97. (a)	98. (b)	99. (b)	100. (b)
101. (d)	102. (a)	103. (c)							

Objective Questions Type II [One or more than one correct option(s)]

1. (a, b, c, d)	2. (b, c)	3. (a, b)	4. (a, c, d)	5. (a, b)
6. (c, d)	7. (a, b, d)	8. (a, c)	9. (b, c, d)	10. (b, c, d)
11. (a, b, c)	12. (a, b, c)	13. (b, c, d)	14. (b, c)	15. (a, d)

Numerical Value Questionss

1. 8 2. 3 3. 8 4. 5 5. 10 6. 1 7. 1

Comprehension Based Questions

Passage 1 – 1. (b) 2. (c)
Passage 2 – 1. (b) 2. (d) 3. (c)
Passage 3 – 1. (a) 2. (c) 3. (c)
Passage 4 – 1. (a) 2. (b) 3. (c)
Passage 5 – 1. (b) 2. (b) 3. (c)
Passage 6 – 1. (b) 2. (d) 3. (a)
Passage 7 – 1. (b) 2. (a)
Passage 8 – 1. (c) 2. (a) 3. (b)

Matrix-Match Type

1. A→(5); B→(3); C→(6); D→(4); E→(1); F→(2)
2. A→(3); B→(4); C→(2); D→(1)
3. A→(3); B→(4); C→(2); D→(1)
4. A→(3); B→(1); C→(4); D→(2)
5. A→(3); B→(4); C→(1); D→(2); E→(5)
6. A→(4); B→(3); C→(1); D→(7); E→(8); F→(5); G→(2); H→(6)
7. A→(4); B→(3); C→(2); D→(1)
8. A→(2); B→(1,3,4); C→(2,4,5); D→(2,6)

Single Integer Answer Questions

1. (1)	2. (6)	3. (0)	4. (2)	5. (1)	6. (2)	7. (2)	8. (7)	9. (4)	10. (2)
11. (3)	12. (8)	13. (3)	14. (8)	15. (5)					

Solutions

Objective Questions Type I [Only one correct option]

1. (*c*) (a) [Ar] $3d^{10}4s^2$ — Last filling electron is in $3d$ thus it is *d*-block element

(b) [Ar] $3d^{10}4s^1$ — Same as (a)

Thus, both are *d*-block element.

2. (*d*)

(a) $Li_2CO_3 \xrightarrow{\Delta} Li_2O + CO_2$ Thus, (a) is true.	$Na_2CO_3 \xrightarrow{\Delta} \times$
(b) LiCl soluble in ether thus covalent. Thus, (b) is true.	NaCl insoluble in ether but soluble in H_2O thus ionic
(c) Li forms nitride Thus, (c) is true.	Na does not form nitride.

3. (*a*)

IA (Alkali)	IB (Coinage)
(a) NaCl	CuCl +1 valency Thus true.
(b) Na_2SO_4 soluble	$CuSO_4$, Ag_2SO_4 Less soluble
(c) $Na_2O + H_2O \longrightarrow \underset{\text{Strong base}}{2NaOH}$	$Cu_2O + H_2O \longrightarrow \underset{\text{Weak base}}{Cu(OH)_2}$ Thus, false.
(d) Also false	

4. (*d*) NaCl — Golden yellow
AgCl — No flame

5. (*d*) (a) $Na_2CO_3 \xrightarrow{\Delta}$ No CO_2 gas

(b) $CaCO_3 \longrightarrow CaO + CO_2$

CaO $\xrightarrow{H_2O} Ca(OH)_2$

CaO $\xrightarrow{HCl}$ No gas

(c) $Ca(HCO_3)_2 \longrightarrow \underset{\text{Insoluble in } H_2O}{CaCO_3} + H_2O + CO_2$

(d) $2NaHCO_3 \longrightarrow Na_2CO_3 + H_2O + CO_2$

$Na_2CO_3 \xrightarrow{HCl} CO_2 \uparrow$

Na_2CO_3 is water soluble.

6. (*b*) KO_2 is stable due to larger anion O_2^- which polarises K^+.

7. (c) $\underset{(X)}{NaHCO_3} \longrightarrow \underset{(Y)}{Na_2CO_3} + H_2O + CO_2$

$Na_2CO_3 \xrightarrow{CO_2} NaHCO_3$

8. (*c*) A saturated aqueous solution of $\overset{\text{II}}{M}(NO_3)_2$ on crystallisation will produce hydrated crystal, $\overset{\text{II}}{M}(NO_3)_2.nH_2O$ only when hydration enthalpy (ΔH°_{hyd}) of M^{2+} ion will be appreciably more negative.

Hydration of an ion depends on its size. Smaller the size of an ion, higher will be its charge density and as a result it will remain more solvated (hydrated) through ion dipole interaction.

Size of group 2 metal ions increases on going down the group. So, their ability to form hydrated crystals following the order.

$$Ba^{2+} >> Mg^{2++} >> Ca^{2+} >> Sr^{2+} >> Ba^{2+}$$

Thus, $Ba(NO_3)_2$ is slightly or almost insoluble in water.

9. (*c*)

$$2Li + \frac{1}{2}\underset{\text{(Excess)}}{O_2(g)} \longrightarrow Li_2O$$

$$2Na + \underset{\text{(Excess)}}{O_2(g)} \longrightarrow Na_2O_2;$$

$$K + \underset{\text{(Excess)}}{O_2(g)} \longrightarrow KO_2$$

10. (*b*) In molten state $NaCl(l) \rightleftharpoons Na^+ + Cl^-$

12. (*d*) $Na_2CO_3 + SO_2 \longrightarrow Na_2SO_3 + CO_2$

13. (*a*) Na_2CO_3 is thermally stable.

14. (*b*) Alkali salts are colourless

NaCl	colourless	Na_2CrO_4 — yellow since CrO_4^{3-} is yellow
KCl	colourless	K_2CrO_4 — yellow
		$KMnO_4$ — pink since MnO_4^- is pink
		K_2MnO_4 — green since MnO_4^{2-} is green

15. (*d*) $Na + O_2 \longrightarrow Na_2O$

$Li + O_2 \longrightarrow Li_2O$

$Li + Ni \longrightarrow Li_3N$

16. (*b*) Li and Na do not form superoxide MO_2.

17. (*b*) Substance *A* is sodium metal. It reacts with water to produce hydrogen (gas *B*) and sodium hydroxide (compound *C*).

$$2Na + 2H_2O \longrightarrow 2NaOH + H_2 \uparrow.$$

Another substance *D* is zinc.

It reacts with solution of sodium hydroxide, it produces hydrogen has on warming.

$$Zn + 2NaOH \longrightarrow Na_2ZnO_2$$

Zinc also reacts with sulphuric acid at room temperature to produce hydrogen gas.

$$Zn + H_2SO_4 \xrightarrow{\text{Room temperature}} ZnSO_4 + H_2 \uparrow$$

Thus, substance *A*, *B*, *C* and *D*, respectively are Na, H_2, NaOH, Zn.

18. (*a*) $4KO_2 + 2H_2O + 4CO_2 \longrightarrow 4KHCO_3 + 3O_2$

19. (*c*) Third IE (I_3) is very high, thus it represents alkali earth metal (Be)

20. (*c*) $2Na_2O_2 + 2CO_2 \longrightarrow 2Na_2CO_3 + O_2$

22. (*b*) (a) (*s*-block)

(b) (*p*-block)

(c) $1s^2 2s^2$ in ground state — (*s*-block) and $1s^2 2s^1 2p^1$ in excited state.

(d) [Ar] $4s^2$ — ground state
[Ar] $4s^1 4p^1$ — excited state
Thus, *s*-block.

23. (*b*) $NH_4NO_3 \longrightarrow N_2O + 2H_2O$

24. (*c*) $2LiNO_3 \longrightarrow Li_2O + 2NO_2 + \frac{1}{2}O_2$

$Mg(NO_3)_2 \longrightarrow MgO + 2NO_2 + \frac{1}{2}O_2$

27. (*c*) Mg does not react with NaOH.

28. (*c*) $Li_2CO_3 \longrightarrow Li_2O + CO_2\uparrow$

$Na_2CO_3 \cdot 10H_2O \longrightarrow Na_2CO_3 + 10H_2O\uparrow$

29. (*b*) $2Na_2O \longrightarrow Na_2O_2 + 2Na$

30. (*c*) $Na_2S_2O_3$ (as fixer) dissolves unreacted AgBr as

$2Na_2S_2O_3 + AgBr \longrightarrow Na_3[Ag(S_2O_3)_2] + NaBr$

31. (*a*) $KI + I_2 \rightleftharpoons KI_3$

32. (*a*) Smaller cation polarises anion to a greater extent hence larger covalent nature and thus lattice energy.

34. (*a*) KO_2 (O_2^- is paramagnetic due to one unpaired electron)
NO_2 (is paramagnetic due to one unpaired electron on N)

35. (*d*) $LiNO_3$ on ignition imparts crimson red,

$BaCl_2 \longrightarrow$ green

$(NH_4)_2Cr_2O_7 \longrightarrow$ green (due to Cr_2O_3)

36. (*c*) Molar solubility is in mol L^{-1} (Reference Concise Inorganic Chemistry J.D. Lee)

LiCl = 19.6
NaCl = 6.2
KCl = 4.8
RbCl = 7.5
CsCl = 11.0

37. (*a*) $Na_2O_2 + 2H^+Cl^- \longrightarrow H_2O_2 + 2NaCl$

$H_2O_2 + Cr_2O_7^{2-} + 2H^+ \longrightarrow \underset{\text{Deep violet soluble in ether}}{CrO_5}$

38. (*b*) $(CaCN_2 + C)$

39. (*b*) Potassium antimonyl tartrate

40. (*c*) $NaHCO_3$ is acidic and decomposed by NaOH forming Na_2CO_3

$\underset{\text{Acid}}{NaHCO_3} + \underset{\text{Base}}{NaOH} \longrightarrow Na_2CO_3 + H_2O$

41. (*c*) (a) $Li + N_2 \longrightarrow Li_3N$

$Mg + O_2 \longrightarrow MgO$

O_2 and N_2 are removed.

(b) $NaOH + CO_2 \longrightarrow Na_2CO_3$

CO_2 is removed.

42. (*d*) HCHO is used as preservatives of dead biological specimen.

43. (*d*) Li–Mg, B–Si, Be–Al show diagonal relationship but Li and Na do not show diagonal relationship as both belongs to same group and not placed diagonally.

44. (*a*) $CaCO_3 + CO_2 + H_2O \longrightarrow Ca(HCO_3)_2$

$Na_2CO_3 \xrightarrow{\Delta} \times$

$Li_2CO_3 \xrightarrow{\Delta} Li_2O + CO_2$

$CaCl_2/CaSO_4$ make permanent hardness.

45. (*a*) Na^- is alkalide ion

Na $(1s^2 2s^2 2p^6 4s^1)$ ← Paramagnetic due to unpaired electrons

$Na^-(1s^2 2s^2 2p^6 3s^2)$ ← Diamagnetic due to paired electrons

48. (*b*) The ionic radii order is

$Na^+ > Mg^{2+} > Al^{3+}$

49. (*a*) Smaller cation, larger hydration thus smaller molar ionic conductance

Ionic size $Li^+ < Na^+ < K^+ < Rb^+$

Hydration $Li^+ > Na^+ > K^+ > Rb^+$

Size of hydration ion $Li^+ > Na^+ > K^+ > Rb^+$

Molar ionic conductance $Li^+ < Na^+ < K^+ < Rb^+$

50. (*b*) M_2O_3 actually exists as M_4O_6 $[M_4(O_2^{2-})(O_2^-)_2]$ is paramagnetic.

51. (*c*) KO_2 is paramagnetic due to O_2^-.

K_2O_3 is actually K_4O_6.

$K_4(\underset{\text{Peroxide}}{O_2^{2-}})(\underset{\text{Superoxide}}{O_2^-})_2$

Thus, it also paramagnetic.

52. (*a*) MgO basic oxide.

ZnO amphoteric oxide.

Thus, Mg and Zn do not resemble in this behaviour.

53. (*c*) $Ca(OH)_2 + Cl_2 \longrightarrow CaOCl_2 + H_2O$

55. (*b*) Chlorides are Lewis acids.

56. (*b*) Larger the size, smaller the hydration energy.

58. (*a*) Smaller the size of cation, larger the hydration, hence, larger the stability of hydrated ion.

61. (*c*) $2NaF + BeF_2 \longrightarrow Na_2[BeF_4] \rightleftharpoons 2Na^+ + \underset{\text{Anion}}{[BeF_4]^{2-}}$

62. (*a*) Mg can form basic carbonate while Li cannot.

$5Mg^{2+} + 6CO_3^{2-} + 7H_2O \longrightarrow 4MgCO_3 \cdot Mg(OH)_2 \cdot 5H_2O + 2HCO_3^-$

63. (*a*) Solubility of carbonates decreases on moving down the group as hydration energy decreases.

64. (*a*) It involved hydration hence exothermic.

67. (*b*) $2NaNO_3 \xrightarrow{\Delta} 2NaNO_2 + O_2$

68. (*b*) $CaH_2 + 2H_2O \longrightarrow Ca(OH)_2 + 2H_2$

$Ca(OH)_2 \xrightarrow{CO_2} CaCO_3$ (White turbidity)

69. (*c*) $BeO + 2NaOH + H_2O \longrightarrow Na_2[Be(OH)_4]$

$Be + 2NaOH + 2H_2O \longrightarrow Na_2[Be(OH)_4] + H_2$

71. (*a*) $Al_4C_3 + H_2O \longrightarrow CH_4$

72. (*a*) $CaCO_3 + H_2O + CO_2 \longrightarrow \underset{\text{Soluble}}{Ca(HCO_3)_2}$

73. (*d*) $BeSO_4 \longrightarrow \underset{\text{Inert}}{BeO} + SO_3$

$$\downarrow H_2O$$

$$Be(OH)_2 \xrightarrow{NaOH} \underset{\text{Soluble}}{Na_2[Be(OH)_4]}$$

77. (*d*) $Ca(OH)_2 + Cl_2 \longrightarrow CaOCl_2 + CaCl_2$

79. (*c*) In hydroxides of alkaline earth metals, hydration energy does not alter very much while lattice energy decreases down the group due to increase in size.

The overall effects of the two factor is that ΔH solution of the hydroxides

$$(\Delta H_{solution} = \Delta H_{lattice} - \Delta H_{hydration})$$

becomes more negative from Be to Ba and hence solubility increases from top to bottom.

$$Be(OH)_2 < Mg(OH)_2 < Ca(OH)_2 < Sr(OH)_2 < Ba(OH)_2$$

Hence, $Be(OH)_2$ is the least soluble in water.

80. (*d*) $\underset{\text{Basic}}{Be(OH)_2} + 2HCl \longrightarrow BeCl_2 + 2H_2O$

$\underset{\text{Basic}}{Zn(OH)_2} + 2HCl \longrightarrow ZnCl_2 + 2H_2O$

$\underset{\text{Acidic}}{Be(OH)_2} + 2NaOH \longrightarrow Na_2[Be(OH)_4]$

$\underset{\text{Acidic}}{Zn(OH)_2} + 2NaOH \longrightarrow Na_2[Zn(OH)_4]$

81. (*a*) due to low (IE) and most negative $E°$ values

82. (*d*) Gypsum is $CaSO_4 \cdot 2H_2O$.

83. (*a*) *sp*-linear

84. (*b*) $BaSO_4 + Na_2CO_3 \longrightarrow Na_2SO_4 + BaCO_3$

Since, fusion is exothermic process.

$$BaCO_3 \xrightarrow{\Delta} BaO + CO_2 \uparrow$$

85. (*d*) $6CaOCl_2 \longrightarrow 5CaCl_2 + Ca(ClO_3)_2$

86. (*c*) $Mg^{2+} < Na^+$

$Mg < Na$

87. (*a*) Be [⇅] [⇅]
$1s^2$ $2s^2$

He [⇅]

Due to stable electronic configuration tendency to gain electron is minimum.

88. (*c*) $CaOCl_2 + H_2O \longrightarrow Ca(OH)_2 + Cl_2$

$Cl_2 + H_2O \longrightarrow HClO + HCl$

89. (*d*) $CaC_2 + H_2O \longrightarrow Ca(OH)_2 + \underset{\text{Used to ripen fruits}}{CH \equiv CH}$

91. (*b*) Burning of Mg is extinguished by throwing sand fires cannot be extinguished by water. Magnesium continues to burn after oxygen is depleted. It than reacts with nitrogen from air to form magnesium nitride (Mg_3N_2). When attempts are made to extinguish magnesium fires with water, magnesium aggressively reacts with hydrogen gas.

I. $Mg + H_2O(l) \xrightarrow{\Delta} MgO + H_2$

II. $Mg + N_2 \xrightarrow{\Delta} Mg_3N_2$

III. $Mg + \text{Sand} \longrightarrow X$

$Mg + \frac{1}{2}O_2 \longrightarrow MgO$

IV. $Mg + H_2O(s) \xrightarrow{\Delta} MgO + H_2$

95. (*b*) $MgCl_2 \cdot 6H_2O \xrightarrow{\Delta} Mg(OH)_2 \xrightarrow{\Delta} MgO$

96. (*d*) Alkali metal carbonates are not decomposed on heating.

$$MgCO_3 \xrightarrow{\Delta} MgO + CO_2$$

97. (*a*) $\underset{\text{(Hot and conc.)}}{NaOH + 3Cl_2} \longrightarrow \underset{(A)}{NaClO_3} + 5NaCl + 3H_2O \underset{\text{(Dry)}}{2Ca(OH)_2}$

$+ 2Cl_2 \longrightarrow \underset{(B)}{Ca(OCl)_2} + CaCl_2 + 2H_2O$

Thus, A : **$NaClO_3$**, B : **$Ca(OCl)_2$**

98. (*b*) According to the question, $A = Mg$ and $B = Mg_3N_2$

Complete reactions are as follows :

$$6Mg + 2N_2 \longrightarrow 2Mg_3N_2$$

$$Mg_3N_2 + 6H_2O \longrightarrow 3Mg(OH)_2 + 2NH_3$$

$$Cu^{2+} + 4NH_3 \longrightarrow \underset{\text{Dark blue violet colour}}{[Cu(NH_3)_4]^{2+}}$$

99. (*b*) Baking soda ($NaHCO_3$) is not a hydrated solid. Thus, (X) is not baking soda. Thus, option (a) and (c) are incorrect. Dead burnt plaster ($CaSO_4$) is obtained from gypsum *via* the formation of plaster of Paris.

$$\underset{\text{Gypsum}}{CaSO_4 \cdot 2H_2O} \xrightarrow[-1/2\,H_2O]{380\text{-}393\text{ K}} \underset{\text{Plaster of Paris}}{CaSO_4 \cdot \frac{1}{2}H_2O} \xrightarrow[-\frac{1}{2}H_2O]{>393K} \underset{\text{Dead burnt plaster (anhydrous)}}{CaSO_4}$$

Therefore, the reaction takes place as follows :

$$\underset{\substack{\text{Washing soda}\\(X)}}{Na_2CO_3 \cdot 10H_2O} \xrightarrow[-9H_2O]{<373K} \underset{\substack{\text{Monohydrate}\\(Y)}}{Na_2CO_3 \cdot H_2O} \xrightarrow[-H_2O]{>373K} \underset{\substack{\text{Anhydrous white powder}\\\text{(soda ash) }(Z)}}{Na_2CO_3}$$

100. (*b*) All alkaline earth metals except beryllium also react with water to form strongly alkaline hydroxide and moving down the group the heavier alkaline earth metals react more easily with water and are strongest base, e.g. barium hydroxide is the strongest basic hydroxide.

101. (*d*) $BeCl_2$ *sp*

$AlCl_3$ sp^2

102. (*a*) $Al + NaOH + H_2O \longrightarrow NaAlO_2 + 1\frac{1}{2}H_2$

103. (*c*) $Be_2C + H_2O \longrightarrow Be(OH)_2 + CH_4$

10

p-Block Elements I

Objective Questions Type I [Only one correct option]

In each of the questions below, four choices are given of which only one is correct.

1. Select the incorrect statements.
   (a) B_2H_6 has all B—H bond equal
   (b) AlH_3 is colourless solid and is polymeric containing Al—H—Al bridges
   (c) $LiAlH_4$ is ionic compound
   (d) AlX_3(X= Cl, Br, I) have low melting point, are covalent and have the halogen-bridged dimeric structure

2. Select the correct statements.
   (a) Hydrides of B and Si are volatile and catches fire on exposure to air
   (b) Oxides of B and Si(B_2O_3 and SiO_2) are acidic in nature
   (c) Borates and silicates have tetrahedral BO_4 and SiO_4 structural units
   (d) All the above are correct statements

3. NaOH can't be stored in
   (a) Al vessel (b) Zn vessel
   (c) Both (a) and (b) (d) None of these

4. The dipole moments of the given molecules are such that
   (a) $BF_3 > NF_3 > NH_3$
   (b) $NF_3 > BF_3 > NH_3$
   (c) $NH_3 > NF_3 > BF_3$
   (d) $NH_3 > BF_3 > NF_3$

5. Consider the following boron halides
   1. BF_3 2. BCl_3
   3. BBr_3 4. BI_3

   The Lewis acid characters of these halides are such that
   (a) $1 < 2 < 3 < 4$ (b) $1 < 3 < 2 < 4$
   (c) $4 < 3 < 2 < 1$ (d) $4 < 2 < 3 < 1$

6. The correct structural representation of diborane is
   (a) $[BH_2]^+ + [BH_4]^-$
   (b) 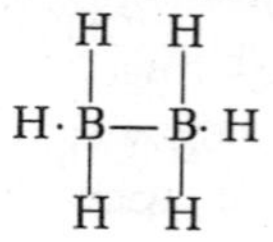
   (c) 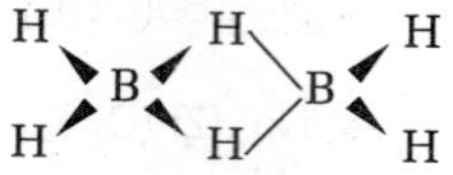
   (d) H_2 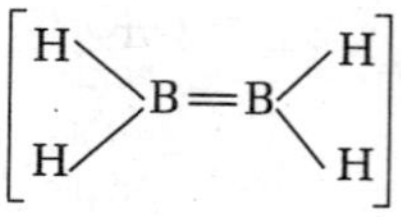

7. Consider the following statements for diborane
   1. Boron is approximately sp^3-hybridised.
   2. B—H—B angle is 180°.
   3. There are two terminal B—H bonds for each boron atom.
   4. There are only 12 bonding electrons available.

   Of these statements
   (a) 1,2 and 4 are correct
   (b) 1,2 and 3 are correct
   (c) 2,3 and 4 are correct
   (d) 1,3 and 4 are correct

8. Molecule(s) possessing three-centre-two electron bonds and three-centre-four electron bonds would include
   (a) B_2H_6 and SiF_4 (b) XeF_6 and BF_6
   (c) B_2H_6 and XeF_6 (d) B_2H_6 alone

9. Which of the following has the regular tetrahedral structure?
   (a) BF_4^- (b) SF_4
   (c) XeF_4 (d) $[Ni(CN)_4]^{2-}$

10. H_3BO_3 and HBO_2 do not differ in
    (a) oxidation number (b) basicity
    (c) melting point (d) structure

11. Light-emitting diodes (LED), laser-diodes and memory chips of computers are made of
(a) gallium
(b) aluminium
(c) arsenic
(d) gallium-arsenide

12. Indium is used
(a) to dope crystals to make *p-n-p* transistors
(b) in thermistors
(c) in low melting point solder
(d) All the above are correct

13. When boron is fused with NaOH, products formed are
(a) $Na_2B_4O_7$ and H_2
(b) $NaBO_2$ and H_2
(c) Na_3BO_3 and H_2
(d) B_2O_3 and H_2

14. Thermite welding uses Al because of
(a) its low melting point
(b) its lightness
(c) its greater affinity for oxygen
(d) All the properties given above

15. Consider the following reactions,
I. $ZnO + C \longrightarrow Zn + CO$
II. $Cr_2O_3 + 2Al \longrightarrow Al_2O_3 + 2Cr$
III. $Al_2O_3 + 2Cr \longrightarrow Cr_2O_3 + 2Al$
In this, possible reactions are
(a) I, III
(b) II, III
(c) I, II
(d) I, II, III

16. Diborane is a Lewis acid forming addition compound $B_2H_6 \cdot 2NH_3$ with NH_3, a Lewis base. This
(a) is ionic and exists as $[BH_2(NH_3)_2]^+$ and $[BH_4]^-$ ions
(b) on heating, is converted into borazine, $B_3N_3H_6$ (called inorganic benzene)
(c) Both (a) and (b) are correct
(d) None of the above is correct

17. $Al_2(SO_4)_3$ is used in the following but not
(a) as a coagulant and precipitant in treating drinking water and sewage
(b) in paper industry
(c) as a mordant in dyeing
(d) in plastic industry

18. General formula of aluminium alums is (M^I is monovalent cation)
(a) $[M^I(H_2O)_6][Al(H_2O)_6](SO_4)_2$
(b) $[M^I(H_2O)_4][Al(H_2O)_6](SO_4)_2$
(c) $[M^I(H_2O)_4][Al(H_2O)_4](SO_4)_4$
(d) $[M^I(H_2O)_6][Al(H_2O)_6](SO_4)_4$

19. Aqueous solution of borax reacts with 2 moles of acids. This is because of
(a) formation of 2 moles of $B(OH)_3$ only
(b) formation of 2 moles of $[B(OH)_4]^-$ only
(c) formation of 1 mole each of $B(OH)_3$ and $[B(OH)_4]^-$
(d) formation of 2 moles each of $[B(OH)_4]^-$ and $B(OH)_3$, of which only $[B(OH)_4]^-$ reacts with acid

20. Borax is used as a buffer since
(a) its aqueous solution contains equal amount of weak acid and its salt
(b) it is easily available
(c) its aqueous solution contains equal amount of strong acid and its salt
(d) statement that borax is a buffer, is wrong

21. While testing BO_3^{3-}, there is green-edged flame on heating the salt with conc. H_2SO_4 and CH_3OH. Green colour is of
(a) $(CH_3)_3B$
(b) $(CH_3O)_3B$
(c) B_2O_3
(d) H_3BO_3

22. Which is insoluble in excess of NH_4OH?
(a) $Al(OH)_3$
(b) $Cu(OH)_2$
(c) $Zn(OH)_2$
(d) $Cd(OH)_2$

23. Borax is converted into B by steps

$$\text{Borax} \xrightarrow{I} H_3BO_3 \xrightarrow{\Delta} B_2O_3 \xrightarrow{II} B$$

I and II reagents are
(a) acid, Al (b) acid, C (c) acid, Fe (d) acid, Mg

24. Boron carbide is used
(a) in nuclear reactor to absorb neutrons
(b) as an abrasive
(c) Both (a) and (b)
(d) None of the above

25. The incorrect statement regarding the structure of C_{60} is: **[JEE Main 2021, March]**
(a) The six-membered rings are fused to both six and five-membered rings.
(b) Each carbon atom forms three sigma bonds.
(c) The five-membered rings are fused only to six-membered rings.
(d) It contains 12 six-membered rings and 24 five-membered rings.

26. Soda free glass fibre are made of
(a) H_3BO_3, B_2O_3 and $Ca_3(BO_3)_2$
(b) H_3BO_3, B_2O_3
(c) H_3BO_3
(d) B_2O_3

27. Na_3AlF_6 is added to Al_2O_3 to
(a) improve the electrical conductivity of the cell
(b) increases rate of production
(c) increase the melting point
(d) decrease the electrical conductivity

28. $Na_2B_4O_7 \cdot 10H_2O \xrightarrow{\Delta} NaBO_2 + (A) + H_2O$

$(A) + MnO \xrightarrow{\Delta} (B)$

(A) and (B) are

(a) Na_3BO_3, $Mn_3(BO_3)_2$
(b) $Na_2(BO_2)_2$, $Mn(BO_2)_2$
(c) B_2O_3, $Mn(BO_2)_2$
(d) None of the above is correct

29. Mixture of $Al(OH)_3$ and $Fe(OH)_3$ can be separated by

(a) HCl (b) NH_4OH
(c) NaOH (d) HNO_3

30. Boric acid is the trivial name for

(a) orthoboric acid (b) metaboric acid
(c) pyroboric acid (d) None of these

31. In H_2O, Ga^+ changes to

(a) Ga^{3+} (b) Ga
(c) Ga and Ga^{3+} (d) Ga^{2+} and Ga^{3+}

32. Al^{3+} of $KAl(SO_4)_2 \cdot 12H_2O$ (alum) can be replaced by

(a) Cr^{3+} (b) Co^{3+}
(c) Fe^{3+} (d) All of these

33. Borax $Na_2B_4O_7 \cdot 10H_2O$ is actually

(a) $Na_2[B_4O_5(OH)_4] \cdot 8H_2O$ (b) $Na_2[B_4O_4(OH)_6] \cdot 7H_2O$
(c) $Na_2[B_4O_3(OH)_8] \cdot 6H_2O$ (d) $Na_2[B_4O_2(OH)_{10}] \cdot 5H_2O$

34. Which reactions can be used to prepare diborane?

I. $NaBH_4 + BF_3$ (in ether) $\longrightarrow$
II. $NaBH_4 + I_2$ —
III. $BF_3 + NaH \longrightarrow$

(a) I, III (b) I, II
(c) II, III (d) I, II and III

35. Which of the following statements about H_3BO_3 is not correct?

(a) It is strong tribasic acid
(b) It is prepared by acidifying an aqueous solution of borax
(c) It has a layer structure in which planar BO_3 units are joined by hydrogen bonds
(d) It does not act as a Lewis acid by accepting hydroxyl ion

36. The type of hybridisation of boron in diborane is

(a) *sp* (b) sp^2
(c) sp^3 (d) sp^3d^2

37. Reactivity of borazole is greater than that of benzene because

(a) borazole is polar compound
(b) borazole is non-polar compound
(c) borazole is electron deficient compound
(d) of localised electrons in it

38. Arsenic drugs are mainly used for the treatment of

(a) cholera (b) typhoid
(c) jaundice (d) syphilis

39. $B(OH)_3 + NaOH \rightleftharpoons NaBO_2 + Na[B(OH)_4] + H_2O$
How can this reaction is made to proceed in forward direction?

(a) Addition of *cis*-1,2-diol
(b) Addition of borax
(c) Addition of *trans*-1,2-diol
(d) Addition of Na_2HPO_4

40. H_3BO_3 is

(a) monobasic acid and weak Lewis acid
(b) monobasic and weak Bronsted acid
(c) monobasic and strong Lewis acid
(d) tribasic and weak Bronsted acid

41. $AlCl_3$ fumes in moist air because it

(a) is covalent (b) is volatile
(c) is hygroscopic (d) forms HCl in moist air

42. The solution of sodium meta aluminate on boiling with ammonium chloride gives a white precipitate of

(a) Al_2O_3 (b) $AlCl_3$
(c) $Al(OH)_3$ (d) $(NH_4)_2SO_4 \cdot Al_2(SO_4)_3$

43. The incorrect statement is

(a) Anhydrous $AlCl_3$ is a covalent substance
(b) Ionic compounds generally have low melting point and boiling point.
(c) A molecule shows a more stable forms as compared to individual atom
(d) CCl_4 is a non-polar solvent

44. Which of the following has the highest first ionisation energy?

(a) Lithium (b) Beryllium (c) Boron (d) Carbon

45. Fusion of borane with NaOH produces

(a) $B_2O_3 + H_2$ (b) $NaBO_2 + H_2$
(c) $Na_2B_4O_7 + H_2$ (d) $Na_3BO_3 + H_2$

46. Radius of Ga is less than that of Al because of

(a) lanthanoid contraction (b) greater screening effect
(c) inert pair effect (d) None of these

47. In the reaction, $B_2O_3 + C + Cl_2 \longrightarrow A + CO$
A is

(a) BCl_2 (b) B_2Cl_2 (c) CCl_2 (d) BCl_3

48. Which of the following compounds is/are possible?

(a) B_2Cl_4, BCl_2, Cl_2B (b) $GaCl_2$, GaS
(c) $Ga[GaCl_4] \cdot Ga_2S_2$ (d) All of these

49. Diamagnetic species can be

(a) B_2Cl_4 (b) $GaCl_2$
(c) GaS (d) All of these

50. Which of the following are used as transition materials and light-emitting devices (LED)?

I. Gallium-phosphides
II. Indium-phosphides
III. Gallium-arsenides
IV. Indium-arsenides

(a) All
(b) Except I all
(c) Except I, II all
(d) Only IV

51. Select the correct statement(s).
(a) Aluminium dissolves in dilute mineral acids but is made passive by concentrated nitric acid
(b) Aluminium vessel can be used as storage of NaOH
(c) Both (a) and (b)
(d) None of the above

52. Thallium and lead are classified as chemically soft because
(a) they have higher affinities for soft anions as I^- and S^{2-} ions
(b) they are soft in reactivity
(c) they are stable in lower oxidation state (Tl^+, Pb^{2+})
(d) they are stable in higher oxidation state (Tl^{3+}, Pb^{4+})

53. The relative stability of the different oxidation state
$Tl^+ > Tl^{3+}, > Ga^{3+} > Ga^+$
$Tl^+ > In^+ > Ga^+$
is an example of
(a) redox potential (b) disproportionation
(c) inert pair effect (d) electron-affinity

54. Thermal stability of boron compounds is in order
(a) $B_2F_4 < B_2Cl_4 < B_2(OR)_4 < B_2(NR_2)_4$
(b) $B_2Cl_4 < B_2F_4 < Br(OR)_4 < B_2(NR_2)_4$
(c) $B_2(NR_2)_4 < B_2(OR)_4 < B_2Cl_4 < B_2F_4$
(d) $B_2(NR_2)_4 < B_2(OR)_4 < B_2F_4 < B_2Cl_4$

55. Anion containing both three-and four-coordinated boron is
(a) $[B(OH)_4]^-$ (b) $B_3O_6^{3-}$
(c) $[B_4O_5(OH)_4]^{2-}$ (d) $B_4O_5[OH_4]^{2-}$

56. Which is the most spontaneous in forward side?
(a) $Al^{3+} + 2e^- \longrightarrow Al^+$ (b) $Ga^{3+} + 2e^- \longrightarrow Ga^+$
(c) $In^{3+} + 2e^- \longrightarrow In^+$ (d) $Tl^{3+} + 2e^- \longrightarrow Tl^+$

57. C_{60} an allotrope of carbon contains **[JEE Main 2019, April]**
(a) 16 hexagons and 16 pentagons
(b) 20 hexagons and 12 pentagons
(c) 12 hexagons and 20 pentagons
(d) 18 hexagons and 14 pentagons

58. The amorphous form of silica is **[JEE Main 2019, April]**
(a) tridymite (b) kieselguhr
(c) cristobalite (d) quartz

59. The correct order of catenation is **[JEE Main 2019, April]**
(a) $C > Sn > Si \approx Ge$
(b) $Si > Sn > C > Ge$
(c) $C > Si > Ge \approx Sn$
(d) $Ge > Sn > Si > C$

60. The one that is extensively used as a piezoelectric material is **[JEE Main 2019, Jan.]**
(a) quartz (b) tridymite
(c) amorphous silica (d) mica

61. The element that shows greater ability to form $p\pi$-$p\pi$ multiple bonds, is **[JEE Main 2019, Jan.]**
(a) Ge (b) Si
(c) Sn (d) C

62. Select the correct statement(s) about group 13 (IIIA) elements.
(a) Stability of hydrides (MH_3) decreases as we move down the group
(b) MX_3 is a strong Lewis acid
(c) $[Al(H_2O)_6]^{3+}$ exists in aqueous solution
(d) All the above are correct statements

63. AlO_2^- is known as
(a) aluminium dioxo ion
(b) meta-aluminate ion
(c) dioxo aluminium ion
(d) aluminium oxide ion

64. In aqueous solution, GaCl disproportionates to
(a) $GaCl_2$ and $GaCl_3$ (b) Ga and $GaCl_3$
(c) $GaCl_2$ and Ga (d) $GaCl_3$ and $GaCl_5$

65. Boron does not form B^{3+} cation easily. It is due to
(a) energy required to form B^{3+} ion is for more than that which would be compensated by lattice energies or hydration energies of such ion
(b) boron is non-metal
(c) boron is semiconductor
(d) None of the above

66. An alloy of boron and aluminium is allowed to react with NH_3. Products formed are
(a) BN, AlN and H_2
(b) $B(NH_2)_3$, $Al(NH_2)_3$ and H_2
(c) BN, $Al(NH_2)_3$ and H_2
(d) $B(NH_2)_3$, AlN and H_2

67. Element $M + N_2 \xrightarrow{\Delta} \xrightarrow{H_2O} NH_3$
Element M belonging to group 13 can be
(a) B or Al (b) Ga or Al
(c) Mg or Al or B (d) Mg or B

68. Reaction of ammonia with excess Cl_2 gives **[JEE Main 2020, Sep.]**
(a) NH_4Cl and N_2 (b) NH_4Cl and HCl
(c) NCl_3 and NH_4Cl (d) NCl_3 and HCl

69. The species in which the N-atom is in a state of sp-hybridisation is **[JEE Main 2016]**
(a) NO_2^- (b) NO_3^- (c) NO_2 (d) NO_2^+

70. Water softener is
(a) borax (b) zeolite
(c) Both (a) and (b) (d) None of these

71. Extra pure N_2 can be obtained by heating [IIT JEE 2011]
(a) NH_3 and CuO (b) NH_4NO_3
(c) $(NH_4)_2Cr_2O_7$ (d) $Ba(N_3)_2$

72. B can be obtained from halide by van Arkel method. This involves reaction
(a) $2BCl_3 + 3H_2 \xrightarrow[\text{filament}]{\text{Red hot W or Ta}} 2B + 6HCl$
(b) $2BI_3 \xrightarrow{\text{Red hot W or Ta}} 2B + 3I_2$
(c) Both (a) and (b)
(d) None of the above

73. Which of the following statements regarding *ortho* boric acid (H_3BO_3) is false?
(a) It acts as a monobasic acid
(b) It is soluble in hot water
(c) It has a planar structure
(d) It acts as a tribasic acid

74. When orthoboric acid is heated to red heat the residue is
(a) boron (b) boric oxide
(c) metaboric acid (d) pyroboric acid

75. Orthoboric acid H_3BO_3 behaves as weak monobasic acid giving H_3O^+ and
(a) $H_2BO_2^+$ (b) $H_2BO_2^-$
(c) $[B(OH)_4]^-$ (d) $[B(OH)_4]^+$

76. Boron sesquioxide is
(a) B_2O_3 (b) BO_3
(c) BO_3^{3-} (d) BO_2^-

77. Select the correct statement(s) about H_3BO_3.
(a) It has triangular BO_3^{3-} units
(b) In solid states, molecules are hydrogen bonded
(c) Both (a) and (b) are correct
(d) None of the above statements is correct

78. The structure of BF_3 is
(a) tetrahedral (b) pyramidal
(c) planar triangular (d) *T*-shaped

79. In BF_3
(a) all the B—F bonds are single covalents in nature
(b) boron-fluorine bond has some double bond character and this bond is delocalised
(c) bond energy and bond length of B—F bond indicate its single bond character
(d) All the bonds are ionic

80. BF_3 behaves as a
(a) Lewis acid and lone pair from the Lewis base is filled into empty $2p_z$ orbital
(b) Lewis base and lone pair on B is donated to empty orbital of the Lewis acid
(c) amphoteric species due to interaction with acid and base both
(d) polymer substance

81. B_2Cl_4
(a) can be formed by passing BCl_3 over Hg at low pressure in an electric discharge
(b) can exist on non-eclipsed and planar structure
(c) decomposes at low temperature
(d) can show all the facts given above

82. BF_3 on hydrolysis forms
(a) H_3BO_3
(b) HBF_4
(c) Both (a) and (b)
(d) None of the sbove

83. Which of the following is false statement?
(a) BH_3 is a Lewis acid
(b) All the B—H distance in diborane (B_2H_6) are equal
(c) Boranes are easily hydrolysed
(d) $LiAlH_4$ reduces BCl_3 to borane

84. In B_2H_6
(a) there is direct boron-boron bond
(b) the B—H bonds are ionic
(c) it is isostructural to C_2H_6
(d) boron atoms are linked through hydrogen bridges

85. From B_2H_6 all the following can be prepared except
(a) H_3BO_3 (b) $NaBH_4$
(c) $B_2(CH_3)_6$ (d) B_2O_3

86. Boron nitride has the structure of the type
(a) both diamond and graphite
(b) graphite
(c) diamond
(d) NaCl

87. Which of the following is the false statement?
(a) Reducing action of $NaBH_4$ and $LiAlH_4$ are specific
(b) B_2H_6 reduces alkene to primary alcohol
(c) Both (a) and (b) are the false statements
(d) None of the above is false statement

88. Beryllium and aluminium have similar properties because
(a) they belong to same group
(b) they have different electronegativity
(c) they have same electronegativity
(d) they have same ionisation energy

89. The solubility of $Al(OH)_3$ in strong NaOH solution is best explained by the formation of
(a) AlO_3^- ion
(b) double salt
(c) a peptised colloidal sol
(d) a complex hydroxyl aluminate ion

90. On passing CO_2 into aqueous solution containing Al^{3+}
(a) $Al_2(CO_3)_3$ is formed
(b) $Al(OH)_3$ is precipitated
(c) $[Al(OH)_4]^-$ is formed
(d) colloidal $Al(OH)_3$ is formed

91. Addition of sodium carbonate to a solution of an oxide in water produces CO_2. This experiment indicates that
(a) the oxide is that of a non-metal
(b) the oxide is basic
(c) the oxide is amphoteric
(d) the oxide is neutral

92. Dimer formation can take place with
(a) BH_3 (b) $AlCl_3$
(c) NO_2 (d) All of these

93. The major constituent in cement is
(a) silica (b) magnesium oxide
(c) calcium carbonate (d) iron oxide

94. Hardening of cement is due to
(a) dehydration
(b) hydrolysis
(c) hydration and hydrolysis
(d) polymerisation

95. Alums are used as mordant in dyeing because
(a) dye is adsorbed on $Al(OH)_3$ which is deposited on fibre in the hydrolysis process
(b) dye is adsorbed on KOH formed due to hydrolysis
(c) Both (a) and (b)
(c) None of the above

96. Alum is found to contain hydrated monovalent cation $[M(H_2O)_6]^+$, trivalent cation $[M'(H_2O)_6]^{3+}$ and SO_4^{2-} in the ratio of
(a) 1 : 1 : 1 (b) 1 : 2 : 3 (c) 1 : 3 : 2 (d) 1 : 1 : 2

97. About 2 to 5% of gypsum ($CaSO_4 \cdot 2H_2O$) is added to Portland cement. It is just to
(a) increase the setting rate of the cement during hydration
(b) slow down the setting rate to increase strength during hydration
(c) Both (a) and (b)are correct
(d) None of the above is correct

98. Stability of hydrides of carbon family is in order
(a) $CH_4 > SiH_4 > GeH_4 > SnH_4 > PbH_4$
(b) $CH_4 < SiH_4 < GeH_4 < SnH_4 < PbH_4$
(c) $CH_4 > SnH_4 > GeH_4 > SiH_4 > PbH_4$
(d) None of the above

99. A group 15 element, which is a metal and forms a hydride with strongest reducing power among group 15 hydrides. The element is **[JEE Main 2021, March]**
(a) Sb (b) P (c) As (d) Bi

100. Dry ice is
(a) $H_2O(s)$ (b) $NH_3(g)$
(c) $CO_2(s)$ (d) $PH_3(g)$

101. Select the correct statements.
(a) Hydrides of B and Si are volatile and catch fire on exposure to air
(b) Oxides of B and Si (B_2O_3 and SiO_2) are acidic in nature
(c) Borates and silicates have tetrahedral BO_4 and SiO_4 structural units
(d) All the above are correct statements

102. Select the correct statements.
(a) Catenation is maximum in carbon
(b) Carbon has pronounced ability to form $p\pi$-$p\pi$ multiple bonds to itself and to other elements like O and N
(c) Both (a) and (b) are correct
(d) None of the above is correct

103. Consider the following statements,
I. In diamond, each carbon atom is linked tetrahedrally to four other carbon atoms by sp^3 bonds.
II. Graphite has planar hexagonal layers of carbon atoms held together by weak van der Waals' forces.
III. Silicon exists only in diamond structure due to its tendency to form $p\pi$-$p\pi$ bonds to itself.

In this
(a) Only I and II are correct
(b) Only I is correct
(c) Only II and III are correct
(d) All the above are correct statements

104. Out of CO_2, SiO_2, GeO_2, SnO_2 and PbO_2
(a) CO_2 and SiO_2 are acidic, SnO_2 is amphoteric and PbO_2 is an oxidising agent
(b) PbO_2 is converted to $Pb(NO_3)_2$ on reaction with HNO_3
(c) Both (a) and (b) are correct
(d) None of the above is correct

105. Which is the incorrect statement about silicones?
(a) They are repeating units (SiO_4) in silicates
(b) They are synthetic polymers containing repeated R_2SiO_2 units
(c) They are formed by hydrolysis of R_2SiCl_2
(d) All the above are incorrect statements

106. Which one of the following bonds has the highest bond energy?
(a) C—C (b) Si—Si
(c) Ge—Ge (d) Sn—Sn

107. Which of the following species have undistorted octahedral structures?
1. SF_6 2. PF_6^-
3. SiF_6^{2-} 4. SeF_6

Select the correct answer using the codes given below.
(a) 2, 3 and 4
(b) 1, 3 and 4
(c) 1, 2 and 3
(d) 1, 2 and 4

108. Which of the following statements are true for zeolites?

1. They are formed by the replacement of some of the silicon atoms of the SiO_2 lattice, by say, aluminium.
2. They have a more closed structure than feldspar.
3. They can absorb CO_2, NH_3 and EtOH.
4. They can separate straight chain hydrocarbons from a mixture containing both straight, chain and branched chain hydrocarbons.

Of these statements

(a) 1, 2 and 3 are correct (b) 1, 3 and 4 are correct
(c) 1, 2 and 4 are correct (d) 2, 3 and 4 are correct

109. Artificial gem used for cutting glass is
(a) graphite (b) diamond (c) SiC (d) $CaCN_2$

110. Red lead used as primer for iron to prevent it from rusting is
(a) Pb_3O_4 (b) PbO (c) PbO_2 (d) Pb_2O

111. Lead as impurity in the extraction of silver is removed by
(a) Parke's process (b) Solvay process
(c) Cyanide process (d) None of these

112. Holme's signals can be given by using
(a) $CaC_2 + CaCN_2$ (b) $CaC_2 + Ca_3P_2$
(c) $CaC_2 + CaCO_3$ (d) $Ca_3P_2 + CaCN_2$

113. Which is/are true statements?
(a) Diamond is unaffected by conc acids but graphite reacts with hot conc. HNO_3 forming mellitic acid, $C_6(COOH)_6$
(b) CO is toxic because it forms a complex with haemoglobin in the blood
(c) C_3O_2, carbon suboxide, is a foul-smelling gas
(d) All the above are true statements

114. Gas that strikes in thundering of light is
(a) CO (b) NO (c) CO_2 (d) H_2

115. NO_2 is not obtained when following is heated
(a) $Pb(NO_3)_2$ (b) $AgNO_3$
(c) $LiNO_3$ (d) KNO_3

116. In which case hydrolysis is faster

(a) 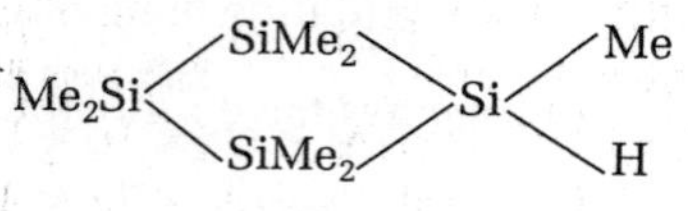

(b) 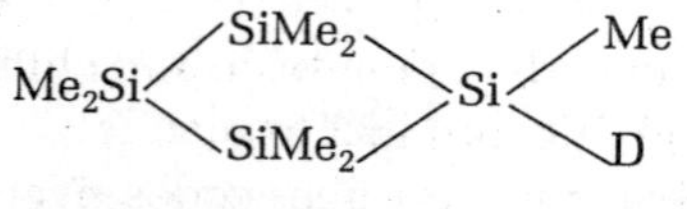

(c) at equal rate
(d) no hydrolysis

117. Which of the following is the ionic carbide?
(a) Fe_3C (b) SiC
(c) CaC_2 (d) Cu_2C

118. The silicate anion in the mineral kinoite is a chain of three SiO_4 tetrahedra that share corners with adjacent tetrahedra. The mineral also contains Ca^{2+} ions, Cu^{2+} ions, and water molecules in a 1 : 1 : 1 ratio. The mineral is
(a) $Ca_2Cu_2Si_3O_{10} \cdot 2H_2O$ (b) $CaCuSi_3O_{10} \cdot H_2O$
(c) $Ca_2Cu_2Si_3O_8 \cdot 2H_2O$ (d) $Ca_2Cu_2Si_3O_6 \cdot 2H_2O$

119. The best oxidising agent of the following oxides is
(a) SnO_2 (b) PbO_2 (c) HgO (d) MgO

120. Dipole moment of CO is very small (0.1 D) (inspite of the larger difference in electronegativity between C and O) and negative end of the dipole lies near the less electronegative C-atom. It is due to
(a) occupation of anti-bonding molecular orbitals
(b) occupation of empty *d*-orbitals
(c) occupation of lone-pairs
(d) occupation of the lone pairs as well as empty *d*-orbitals

121. $B(OH)_3 + NaOH \rightleftharpoons NaBO_2 + Na[B(OH)_4] + H_2O$
How can this reaction is made to proceed in forward direction?
(a) Addition of cis 1, 2-diol (b) Addition of borax
(c) Addition of trans 1, 2-diol (d) Addition of Na_2HPO_4

122. In graphite, additional electrons are
(a) localised on each C-atom
(b) localised on every third C-atom
(c) present in anti-bonding orbital
(d) delocalised forming extended π-bonding system

123. $PbO_2 \longrightarrow PbO \quad \Delta G_{298} < 0$
$SnO_2 \longrightarrow SnO \quad \Delta G_{298} > 0$
Most probable oxidation state of Pb and Sn will be
(a) Pb^{4+}, Sn^{4+} (b) Pb^{4+}, Sn^{2+}
(c) Pb^{2+}, Sn^{2+} (d) Pb^{2+}, Sn^{4+}

124. When vapours of $SiCl_4$ are passed over hot Mg, then the product formed is
(a) $SiCl_2 + MgCl_2$ (b) $MgSi + Cl_2$
(c) $MgSiCl_6$ (d) $Si + MgCl_2$

125. The pair in which phosphorus atoms have a formal oxidation state of +3 is **[JEE Main 2016 (Offline)]**
(a) pyrophosphorous and hypophosphoric acids
(b) orthophosphorous and hypophosphoric acids
(c) pyrophosphorous and pyrophosphoric acids
(d) orthophosphorous and pyrophosphorous acids

126. Carbon and silicon belong to group 14. What is the nature of carbide of silicon?
(a) Covalent (b) Ionic
(c) Interstitial (d) None of these

127. Which of the following shows electrical conduction?
(a) Potassium ion (b) Graphite
(c) Diamond (d) Sodium ion

128. Water glass is
(a) glass made up of water (b) sodium silicate
(c) water gas (d) crystal carbonate

129. Good reducing nature of H_3PO_2 is attributed to the presence of **[JEE Main 2019, Jan.]**
(a) two P—H bonds (b) one P—H bond
(c) two P—OH bonds (d) one P—OH bond

130. The reaction of NO with N_2O_4 at 250 K gives **[JEE Main 2020, Sep.]**
(a) N_2O (b) NO_2 (c) N_2O_3 (d) N_2O_5

131. The correct order of the oxidation states of nitrogen in NO, NO_2, NO_2 and N_2O_3 is **[JEE Main 2019, April]**
(a) $NO_2 < NO < N_2O_3 < N_2O$
(b) $N_2O < NO < N_2O_3 < NO_2$
(c) $O_2 < N_2O_3 < NO < N_2O$
(d) $N_2O < N_2O_3 < NO < NO_2$

132. The gas evolved by heating potassium ferrocyanide crystals with conc. H_2SO_4 is
(a) CO (b) CO_2
(c) SO_2 (d) SO_3

133. Graphite is a good conductor of heat and electricity because it contains
(a) layers of carbon atoms (b) sheet like structure
(c) free electrons (d) $p\pi$-$d\pi$ bonding

134. $(Me_2)_2SiCl_2$ on hydrolysis will produce
(a) $(Me)_2Si(OH)_2$
(b) $(Me)_2Si{=}O$
(c) $[—O—(Me)_2Si—O—]_n$
(d) $Me_2SiCl(OH)$

135. The reaction of P_4 with X leads selectively to P_4O_{10}. The X is **[IIT JEE 2011]**
(a) dry O_2
(b) a mixture of O_2 and N_2
(c) moist O_2
(d) O_2 in the presence of aqueous NaOH

136. Which one of the following statements about the zeolite is false?
(a) They are used as cation exchangers
(b) They have open structure which enables them to take up small molecules
(c) Zeolites are aluminosilicats having three dimensional network
(d) Some of the SiO_4^{4-} units are replaced by AlO_4^{5-} and AlO_6^{9-} ions in zeolites

137. By passing air over red hot coke the gas obtained is
(a) coal gas (b) water gas
(c) oil gas (d) producer gas

138. White lead is
(a) $PbSO_4 \cdot PbO$ (b) $PbCO_3 \cdot PbO$
(c) $PbCO_3$ (d) $Pb(OH)_2 \cdot PbCO_3$

139. Silicon is an important constituent of
(a) rocks (b) amalgams
(c) chlorophyll (d) haemoglobin

140. When chlorine is passed through molten tin, the product obtained is
(a) $SnCl_4$ (b) $[SnCl_6]^{2-}$
(c) $[SnCl_4]^{2-}$ (d) $SnCl_2$

141. In making casting of metal, silicon is used as
(a) oxidiser (b) semiconductor
(c) deoxidiser (d) None of these

142. Sindoor is represented by
(a) $Pb(NO_3)_2$ (b) $PbCO_3 \cdot Pb(OH)_2$
(c) $Pb(OH)_2 \cdot 4PbCO_3$ (d) Pb_3O_4

143. Lead is soluble in
(a) CH_3COOH (b) H_2SO_4
(c) HCl (d) HNO_3

144. Quartz is a crystalline variety of
(a) silicon carbide (b) sodium silicate
(c) silica (d) silicon

145. Percentage of lead in lead pencil is
(a) 30 (b) 20 (c) 10 (d) zero

146. Which of the following halides is least stable and doubtful existence?
(a) CI_4 (b) SnI_4 (c) GeI_4 (d) PbI_4

147. Select the correct statement about stability of cations.
(a) $Ge^{4+} > Sn^{4+} > Pb^{4+}$
(b) $Ge^{2+} < Sn^{2+} < Pb^{2+}$
(c) $Pb^{2+} > Pb^{4+} > Sn^{4+} > Sn^{2+}$
(d) All the above are correct statements

148. The compound that does not produce nitrogen gas by the thermal decomposition is **[JEE Main 2018]**
(a) $Ba(N_3)_2$ (b) $(NH_4)_2Cr_2O_7$
(c) NH_4NO_2 (d) $(NH_4)_2SO_4$

149. The pair that contains two P—H bonds in each of the oxoacids is **[JEE Main 2019, Jan.]**
(a) $H_4P_2O_5$ and $H_4P_2O_6$ (b) H_3PO_3 and H_3PO_2
(c) $H_4P_2O_5$ and H_3PO_3 (d) H_3PO_2 and $H_4P_2O_5$

150. The relative stability of + 1 oxidation state of group 13 elements follows the order **[JEE Main 2019, Jan.]**
(a) Al < Ga < Tl < In (b) Al < Ga < In < Tl
(c) Tl < In < Ga < Al (d) Ga < Al < In < Tl

151. When a mixture of carbon monoxide and chlorine is exposed to sunlight the product formed is
(a) thionyl chloride (b) phosgene
(c) phosphine (d) carbon tetrachloride

152. Stable oxides of carbon are
(a) CO, CO_2, C_3O_2 (b) CO_2, C_3O_2, C_2O
(c) CO, CO_2 (d) C_2O, C_3O_2

153. CO behaves as
(a) Lewis acid (b) Lewis base
(c) amphoteric oxide (d) None of these

154. The correct statement with respect to dinitrogen is **[JEE Main 2020, 6 Sep.]**
(a) N_2 is paramagnetic in nature.
(b) it can combine with dioxygen at 25°C.
(c) liquid dinitrogen is not used in cryosurgery.
(d) it can be used as an inert diluent for reactive chemicals.

155. The reaction in which the hybridisation of the underlined atom is affected is **[JEE Main 2020, 4 Sep.]**
(a) $\underline{Xe}F_4 + SbF_5 \longrightarrow$ (b) $H_2\underline{S}O_4 + NaCl \xrightarrow{420\text{ K}}$
(c) $H_3\underline{P}O_2 \xrightarrow{\text{Disproportionation}}$ (d) $\underline{N}H_3 \xrightarrow{H^+}$

156. When zeolite is treated with hard water, there is exchange reaction between calcium/magnesium ion/and ......
(a) aluminium ion (b) sodium ion
(c) water of hydration (d) sulphate ion

157. Hot conc. HNO_3 converts graphite into
(a) graphite oxide
(b) benzene hexacarboxylic acid
(c) Both (a) and (b)
(d) None of the above

158. Silicon reacts with hot solution of NaOH forming
(a) $Si(OH)_4$ (b) $Si(OH)_2$
(c) SiO_2 (d) Na_4SiO_4

159. Formula of the following silicate anion is

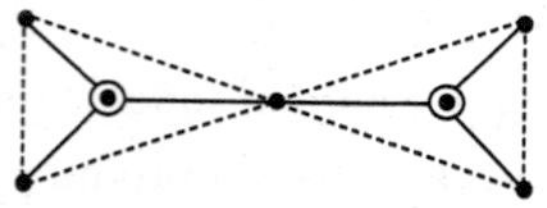

(a) SiO_4^{4-} (b) $Si_2O_7^{6-}$ (c) $Si_2O_8^{6-}$ (d) $Si_3O_9^{6-}$

160. The basic structural unit of feldspar, zeolites, mica and asbestos is **[JEE Main 2019, 12 April]**
(a) $(SiO_3)^{2-}$ (b) SiO_2 (c) $(SiO_4)^{4-}$
(d) $-\!\left(\overset{R}{\underset{R}{Si}}-O\right)_{\!n}\!-$ (R = Me)

161. Select the correct statement(s).
(a) Si uses all of its valence electrons in an sp^3-hybridisation and crystallises in an fcc structure similar to diamond.
(b) Diamond is an electrical insulator, graphite is an electrical conductor but silicon is a semiconductor.
(c) Most common silica is quartz.
(d) All of the above are correct statements.

162. Which among the following statements is false regarding glass?
(a) It absorbs ultra-violet light
(b) It consists of silicates of sodium and alkali
(c) HF causes marking on glass
(d) All the halogen acids (HF, HCl, HBr and HI) are stored in glass bottles

163. Silicones are
(a) synthetic polymers containing repeated R_2SiO units
(b) silicates with common SiO_4 unit
(c) ketones with silyl group (SiH_3) similar to alkyl $(SiH_3)_2CO$
(d) Zircon (neso silicates)

164. Non-oxide ceramics can be
(a) B_4C (b) SiC
(c) Si_3N_4 (d) All of these

165. The correct statement among the following is **[JEE Main 2019, 12 April]**
(a) $(SiH_3)_3N$ is planar and less basic than $(CH_3)_3N$.
(b) $(SiH_3)_3N$ is pyramidal and more basic than $(CH_3)_3N$.
(c) $(SiH_3)_3N$ is pyramidal and less basic than $(CH_3)_3N$.
(d) $(SiH_3)_3N$ is planar and more basic than $(CH_3)_3N$.

166. Amphoteric oxides are
(a) SnO, SnO_2 (b) GeO, GeO_2
(c) Both (a) and (b) (d) None of these

167. Compound used on thermal insulator is
(a) silica gel (b) zeolites
(c) silicones (d) asbestos

168. $SnCl_2$ can be used as
(a) reducing agent
(b) oxidising agent
(c) catalyst in Friedel Crafts reaction
(d) a base

169. The hydrides of the first elements in groups 15-17 namely NH_3, H_2O and HF respectively shows abnormally high values for melting and boiling points. This is due to
(a) small size of N, O and F
(b) the ability to form extensive intermolecular H-bonding
(c) the ability to form extensive intramolecular H-bonding
(d) effective forces of interaction

170. Which silicon compound is used as lubricant?
(a) Asbestos (b) Silicones (c) Zeolite (d) Mica

171. Out of Si, Ge, Sn and Pb which forms stable ionic compounds in divalent state?
(a) Pb (b) Sn (c) Ge (d) Si

172. Pb_3O_4 reacts with HNO_3 forming nitrate and oxide which are
(a) $Pb(NO_3)_4$ from PbO_2, and PbO remains unreacted

(b) $Pb(NO_3)_2$ from PbO, and PbO_2 remains unreacted
(c) $Pb(NO_3)_2$ and $Pb(NO_3)_4$, and PbO remains unreacted
(d) Pb_3O_4 remains insoluble in HNO_3

173. Unstable lead compounds are
(a) $PbCl_4$, $PbBr_4$ and PbI_4 (b) $PbCl_2$, $PbBr_2$ and PbI_2
(c) PbO, PbO_2 and Pb_3O_4 (d) $PbCl_4^{2-}$, $PbCl_6^{2-}$

174. $PbCl_2$ is soluble in
(a) dil. HCl (b) CH_3COOH
(c) hot water (d) dil. H_2SO_4

175. Aqueous solutions of the following are matched according to their properties shown. Select the correct matching.
(a) Cl_2O_7 — acidic
(b) Al_2Cl_6 — white fumes
(c) Al_2O_3 — amphoteric
(d) All of the above are correct matching

176. Borazine $B_3N_3H_6(A)$ is converted into disubstituted product $B_3N_3H_4X_2(B)$. Number of isomers of B would be
(a) 2
(b) 4
(c) 6
(d) No isomer, exists as single product

177. S_3O_9 is a trimer of SO_3. Number of (S—S) bonds in S_3O_9 is
(a) three (b) two
(c) one (d) zero

178. Of the following acids
I : hypo phosphorous acid
II : hydrofluoric acid,
III : oxalic acid
IV : glycine
(a) I, II are monobasic; III dibasic acid and IV amphoteric
(b) II monobasic; I, III dibasic acid; IV amphoteric
(c) I monobasic, II, III dibasic, IV amphoteric
(d) I, II, III dibasic; IV amphoteric

179. Which forms $p\pi$–$p\pi$ multiple bonds with itself and with C and O?
(a) P, As (b) N, As
(c) N, P (d) N

180. In P_4 (tetrahedral)
(a) each P is joined to four P
(b) each P is joined to three P
(c) each P is joined to two P
(d) P_4 does not exist

181. Maximum number of covalent bonds formed by N and P respectively are
(a) 3, 5 (b) 3, 6
(c) 4, 5 (d) 4, 6

182. For the hydrides of nitrogen family going down the group
(a) stability decreases
(b) reducing activity increases
(c) bond angle HMH decreases
(d) All the above variations followed

183. The electronegativities of N, C, Si and P are such that
(a) P < Si < C < N (b) Si < P < N < C
(c) Si < P < C < N (d) P < Si < N < C

184. Glacial phosphoric acid is
(a) HPO_3 (b) H_3PO_3
(c) H_3PO_4 (d) $H_4P_2O_7$

185. Phosgene can be obtained when
(a) white phosphorus reacts with alkali
(b) calcium phosphide reacts with water
(c) chloroform reacts with air
(d) bone comes in contact with water

186. The set of elements that differ in mutual relationship from those of the other sets is
(a) Li – Mg (b) B – Si
(c) Be – Al (d) Li – Na

187. Which of the following statements are true?
(a) Cold and very dilute HNO_3 forms NH_4NO_3 with Zn or Sn
(b) Concentrated HNO_3 forms H_2SnO_3 with Sn
(c) Cold and more concentrated HNO_3 forms NO_2 with Cu
(d) All the above are correct

188. NO_2 is not obtained when following is heated
(a) $Pb(NO_3)_2$ (b) $AgNO_3$ (c) $LiNO_3$ (d) KNO_3

189. Which is least basic?
(a) NF_3 (b) NCl_3 (c) NBr_3 (d) NI_3

190. Which is/are correct statements about P_4O_6 and P_4O_{10}?
(a) Both form oxyacids H_3PO_3 and H_3PO_4 respectively
(b) In P_4O_6 each P is joined to four O and in P_4O_{10} each P is joined to six O atoms
(c) Both (a) and (b)
(d) None of the above

191. Which of the following compounds do not exist?
N_4, P_4, PCl_5, NCl_5, NCl_3, P_2O_5, NO_2, PO_2
(a) N_4, NCl_5, NO_2
(b) N_4, NCl_5, PO_2
(c) PCl_5, NCl_5, PO_2
(d) All of these

192. Which of the following is/are paramagnetic?
NO_2, NO, N_2O_4, N_2O_2, N_2O_5
(a) Only NO_2
(b) NO_2, NO
(c) NO, NO_2, N_2O_5
(d) All are paramagnetic

193. Which of the following dibasic acids shows geometrical isomerism?
(a) Hyponitrous acid $H_2N_2O_2$
(b) Maleic acid $C_4H_4O_4$
(c) Both (a) and (b)
(d) None of the above

194. Red and white phosphorus will differ but not in
(a) smell
(b) solubility in $CHCl_3$
(c) exhibiting phosphorescence
(d) reactions with HNO_3

195. The C—C bond length is maximum in **[JEE Main 2019, April]**
(a) graphite (b) C_{70}
(c) C_{60} (d) diamond

196. N_2O (laughing gas) finds use in the following except
(a) as a propellant for whipped ice-cream
(b) as an anaesthetic
(c) for the preparation of N_3H
(d) as fuel for rockets

197. Which is/are used as an anaesthetic?
(a) N_2O (b) C_2H_4
(c) $CHCl_3$ (d) All of these

198. Which is a set of acid salts and can react with base?
(a) NaH_2PO_2, Na_2HPO_3, NaH_2PO_4
(b) Na_2HPO_3, NaH_2PO_3, Na_2HPO_4
(c) $NaHCO_3$, NaH_2PO_3, Na_2HPO_4
(d) All of the above

199. Which is used as a rocket fuel?
(a) N_2H_4 (b) Polybudiene
(c) Both (a) and (b) (d) None of these

200. NH_3 can't be obtained by
(a) heating of NH_4NO_3 or NH_4NO_2
(b) heating of NH_4Cl or $(NH_4)_2CO_3$
(c) heating of NH_4NO_3 with NaOH
(d) reaction of AlN or Mg_3N_2 or $CaCN_2$ with H_2O

201. The wrong statement about N_2O is
(a) it is nitrous oxide
(b) it is least reactive oxide of nitrogen
(c) it is not a linear molecule
(d) it is known as laughing gas

202. The true statement for the acids of phosphorus. H_3PO_2, H_3PO_3 and H_3PO_4 is
(a) their acidic nature is : $H_3PO_4 < H_3PO_3 < H_3PO_2$
(b) all of them are reducing in nature
(c) all of them are tribasic acids
(d) the geometry of phosphorus is tetrahedral in all the three

203. Which of the following compounds has the greatest ionic character?
(a) PCl_5 (b) $SiCl_4$
(c) CCl_4 (d) BCl_3

204. Fe^{3+} oxidises NH_2OH to
(a) NO_2 (b) N_2O
(c) N_2 (d) NO

205. Fe^{2+} reduces NH_2OH to
(a) NH_3 (b) N_3H
(c) N_2H_4 (d) N_2

206. All of the following are bases except
(a) N_2H_4 (b) NH_2OH
(c) NH_3 (d) N_3H

207. An example of an "*ortho*" acid is
(a) $HAsO_2$ (b) H_3AsO_4
(c) $(HPO_3)_n$ (d) $H_4As_2O_7$

208. Compound used in safety matches is
(a) P_4S_3 (b) P_4 (c) P_2O_5 (d) PCl_3

209. N_2O is formed when
(a) moist Fe reacts with NO
(b) Sn^{2+} reacts with conc. HNO_3 in presence of HCl
(c) cold dil. HNO_3 reacts with Cu and Zn
(d) by all the reactions

210. Arsenic drugs are mainly used for the treatment of
(a) cholera (b) typhoid
(c) jaundice (d) syphilis

211. Aluminium is usually found in +3 oxidation state. In contrast, thallium exists in +1 and +3 oxidation states. This is due to **[JEE Main 2019, Jan.]**
(a) lattice effect
(b) lanthanoid contraction
(c) inert pair effect
(d) diagonal relationship

212. Among the following, the paramagnetic compound is
(a) Na_2O_2 (b) P_2O_5
(c) N_2O (d) KO_2

213. The statement that is incorrect about the interstitial compounds is **[JEE Main 2019, April]**
(a) they are very hard
(b) they have metallic conductivity
(c) they have high melting points
(d) they are chemically reactive

214. Diborane (B_2H_6) reacts independently with O_2 and H_2O to produce, respectively. **[JEE Main 2019, April]**
(a) B_2O_3 and H_3BO_3 (b) B_2O_3 and $[BH_4]^-$
(c) H_3BO_3 and B_2O_3 (d) HBO_2 and H_3BO_3

215. The percentage of *p*-character in the orbitals forming P—P bonds in P_4 is
(a) 25 (b) 33
(c) 50 (d) 75

216. Which blue-liquid is obtained on reacting equimolar amounts of two gases at –30°C?
(a) N_2O (b) N_2O_3 (c) N_2O_4 (d) N_2O_5

217. Calcium cyanamide on treatment with steam produces
(a) $NH_3 + CaO$ (b) $NH_3 + CaHCO_3$
(c) $NH_3 + CaCO_3$ (d) $NH_3 + Ca(OH)_2$

218. Which gas cannot be collected over water?
(a) O_2 (b) PH_3
(c) N_2 (d) SO_2

219. NaOCl reacts with NH_3 to produce
(a) NH_2OH (b) NH_2NH_2
(c) N_2 (d) NO

220. Cold solution of barium nitrite on mixing with sulphuric acid produces
(a) $BaSO_4 + HNO_2$ (b) $BaSO_4 + HNO_3$
(c) $BaSO_4 + NO_2$ (d) $BaSO_4 + N_2 + O_2$

221. On hydrolysis, PCl_3 gives
(a) H_3PO_3 (b) H_3PO_4
(c) $POCl_3$ (d) HPO_3

222. On photochemical decomposition of HNO_3 the products formed are
(a) NO and O_2 (b) NO_2 and O_2
(c) N_2O_4 and NO_2 (d) N_2O_5 and NO_2

223. Nitric oxide is formed by the reaction of
(a) $C + N_2O$ (b) $Cu + HNO_3$
(c) $Cu + N_2O$ (d) $Cu + NO_2$

224. On heating lead nitrate the product formed is
(a) NO (b) NO_2
(c) N_2O (d) N_2O_5

225. The number of P—O—P bonds in cyclic metaphosphoric acid is
(a) zero (b) two (c) three (d) four

226. Polyphosphates are used as water softening agents because they
(a) form soluble complexes with anionic species
(b) precipitate anionic species
(c) form soluble complexes with cationic species
(d) precipitate cationic species

227. Solid crystalline PCl_5 has structure which of the following?
(a) Bi-pyramidal moieties
(b) Octahedral and tetrahedral ions
(c) Square-pyramidal moieties
(d) Pentagonal moieties

228. The structural formula of hypophosphorus acid is

(a) 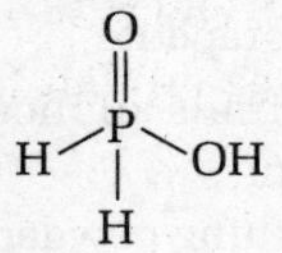
(b) 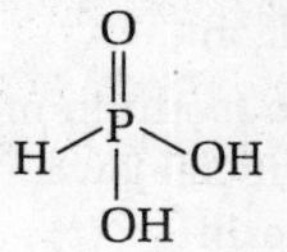
(c) 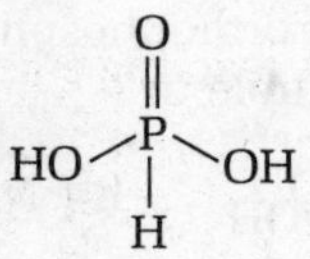
(d) 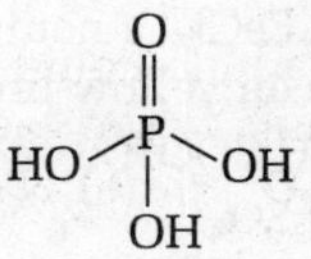

229. $4HNO_3 + P_4O_{10} \longrightarrow 4HPO_3 + X$
In the above reaction, the product X is
(a) NO_2 (b) N_2O_3 (c) N_2O_4 (d) N_2O_5

230. Which of the following oxides of nitrogen is paramagnetic?
(a) N_2O (b) N_2O_5 (c) NO_2 (d) N_2O_3

231. Which of the following is arranged in the increasing order of enthalpy of vaporisation?
(a) NH_3, PH_3, AsH_3 (b) AsH_3, PH_3, NH_3
(c) NH_3, AsH_3, PH_3 (d) PH_3, AsH_3, NH_3

232. The statement true for N_3^- is
(a) It has non-linear structure
(b) It is called pseudohalogen
(c) the formal oxidation state of nitrogen in this anion is +1
(d) It is isoelectronic with N_2O

233. Metallic tin and conc. HNO_3 reacts to form
(a) metastannic acid
(b) stannic nitrate
(c) stannous nitrite
(d) stannous nitrate

234. PI_3 upon hydrolysis gives
(a) monobasic acid and dibasic acid
(b) monobasic acid and tribasic acid
(c) monbasic acid and a salt
(d) dibasic acid and tribasic acid

235. Common name of phosgene is
(a) carbon tetrachloride
(b) phosphoryl chloride
(c) carbonyl chloride
(d) phosphorus trichloride

236. The bond angle in AsH_3 is greater than that in
(a) NH_3
(b) H_2O
(c) BCl_3
(d) None of the above

237. When PCl_3 reacts with sulphuric acid sulphuryl chloride is formed as the final product. This shows that sulphuric acid
(a) has two hydroxyl groups in its structure
(b) is a derivative of sulphur dioxide
(c) is a dibasic acid
(d) has greater affinity for water

238. Pentavalent phosphorus is more stable compared to that of nitrogen even through they belong to same group; it is due to
(a) more reactivity of phosphorus
(b) inert nature of nitrogen
(c) presence of d-orbital
(d) large size of phosphorus atom

239. Which of the following oxides of nitrogen is solid?
(a) NO_2 (b) N_2O (c) N_2O_3 (d) N_2O_5

240. The element which forms oxides in all oxidation states +1 to +5 is
(a) N (b) P
(c) As (d) Sb

241. Among the VA(15) group elements one of them forms a compound sold under the name **'Pearl White'.** The element used is
(a) N (b) P (c) Sb (d) Bi

242. White arsenic has the chemical composition
(a) As_2 (b) As_4
(c) As_2O_5 (d) As_2O_3

243. Both NF_3 and NCl_3 are covalent but they differ in the extent of hydrolysis because
(a) NF_3 is more stable than NCl_3 and hydrolysis product of NF_3, HOF, does not exist
(b) dipole moment of NF_3 is greater than that of NCl_3
(c) electronegativity of F is greater than that of Cl
(d) Cl can expand its octet by using *d*-orbitals

244. Nitrogen differs from P, As, Sb and Bi in the following properties
(a) It forms diatomic molecule
(b) It is not able to extent its coordination number beyond four
(c) Nitrogen does not function as a Lewis acid whereas P, As, Sb and Bi do so
(d) In all the properties given above

245. The element that does not show catenation is **[JEE Main 2019, Jan.]**
(a) Ge (b) Sn (c) Si (d) Pb

246. Hydrazine is not
(a) a reducing agent (b) an oxidising agent
(c) an acid (d) a base

247. What is the role of phosphate ion in a detergent?
(a) It reduces pH of the water
(b) It increase pH of the water
(c) It removes Ca^{2+} and Mg^{2+} ions from water that causes hardness
(d) It increases its solubility in water

248. A gaseous substance dissolves in water giving a pale blue solution which decolourises $KMnO_4$ and oxidises KI to I_2. Gaseous substance is
(a) N_2O_5 (b) NH_3
(c) N_2O_3 (d) HNO_3

249. '*X*' melts at low temperature and is a bad conductor of electricity in both liquid and solid state. *X* is **[JEE Main 2020, Jan.]**
(a) carbon tetrachloride (b) silicon carbide
(c) mercury (d) zinc sulphide

250. $p\pi$-$p\pi$ multiple bonding between nitrogen atoms is present in
(a) hyponitrous acid (b) nitrous acid
(c) nitric acid (d) in all of these

251. The chloride that cannot get hydrolysed is **[JEE Main 2019, Jan.]**
(a) $SnCl_4$ (b) CCl_4 (c) $PbCl_4$ (d) $SiCl_4$

252. Correct statements among (I) to (IV) regarding silicones are:
I. They are polymers with hydrophobic character.
II. They are biocompatible.
III. In general, they have high thermal stability and low dielectric strength.
IV. Usually, they are resistant to oxidation and used as greases. **[JEE Main 2019, Jan.]**
(a) I and II only (b) I, II, III only
(c) I, II, III and IV (d) I, II and IV only

253. A colourless salt gives a white ppt (soluble in ammonium acetate) and a brown coloured pungent gas on reaction with conc. H_2SO_4. Salt is
(a) $Ba(NO_3)_2$ (b) $Pb(NO_3)_2$
(c) $NaNO_3$ (d) NH_4NO_3

254. Nitration of aromatic compounds is done using a mixture of conc. H_2SO_4 and conc. HNO_3. Intermediate formed in the nitration process is
(a) NO_2^+ (nitronium ion) (b) NO_3^- (nitrate ion)
(c) NO^+ (nitrosonium ion) (d) NO_2^- (nitrite ion)

255. $NaNO_2$ and $NaNO_3$ are used as food additives and generally added to meat to
(a) retard oxidation of meat to brown coloured material
(b) prevent growth of botulism bacteria
(c) impart red colour to oxidised meat by NO by reaction of heme in blood
(d) make all of the functions given above effective

256. Nitrites in water may react with amines under acidic conditions in the stomach to
(a) give carcinogenic compounds
(b) give proteins
(c) keep stomach acidity free
(d) produce free amino acids

257. A substance which gives an yellow precipitate when boiled with an excess of nitric acid and ammonium molybdate, and red precipitate with $AgNO_3$ is
(a) orthophosphate (b) pyrophosphate
(c) metaphosphate (d) hypophosphate

258. This salt of oxoacids of phosphorus is used as washing detergent
(a) wavellite (b) microcosmic salt
(c) calgon (d) chlorapatite

259. Calgon (sodium metaphosphate) finds application as
(a) artificial jewel (b) paint
(c) a resin (d) washing powder

260. With $FeCl_3$, a neutral solution of orthophosphate gives an yellow precipitate insoluble in
(a) CH_3COOH (b) HCl
(c) H_2SO_4 (d) NaOH

261. Phosphorus trichloride, PCl_3, undergoes hydrolysis to produce an oxoacid. It has the formula

(a) HPO_3 (b) H_3PO_3
(c) H_3PO_4 (d) H_3PO_2

262. The solid PCl_5 exists as

(a) PCl_3 (b) PCl_4^+
(c) PCl_6^- (d) PCl_4^+ and PCl_6^-

263. $\underset{X}{PCl_5} + \underset{Y}{CH_3}\underset{Z}{CH_2OH} \longrightarrow$

In the above reaction Cl replaces one of the H-atoms in CH_3CH_2OH. This H is of

(a) C (in *X*) (b) C (in *Y*)
(c) O (in *Z*) (d) any of *X*, *Y* and *Z*

264. The high reactivity and low volatility of white phosphorus is due to

(a) tetrahedrally arranged P_4 units
(b) bond angle of 60°
(c) weak van der Waals' force of attraction
(d) increased steric (strain) factor

265. The correct statements among I to III regarding group 13 element oxides are: **[JEE Main 2019, April]**

I. Boron trioxide is acidic.
II. Oxides of aluminium and gallium are amphoteric.
III. Oxides of indium and thallium are basic.

(a) I, II and III (b) I and III only
(c) I and II only (d) II and III only

Objective Questions Type II [One or more than one correct option(s)]

In each of the questions below, four choices are given, of which one or more than one are correct.

1. Which fumes in moist air?

(a) $AlCl_3$ (b) BF_3 (c) $CuSO_4$ (d) NH_3

2. Select the correct statement(s).

(a) BF_3 fumes strongly in moist air and is partially hydrolysed by excess of water
(b) BF_3 is converted into the adducts $BF_3 \cdot H_2O$ and $BF_3 \cdot 2H_2O$ with small amounts of water at low temperature
(c) H_3BO_3 is a weak acid but HBF_4 is a very strong acid
(d) KBF_4 is sparingly soluble in water

3. Select the correct statement(s).

(a) BF_3 forms adducts with NH_3, *R*OH and RNH_2
(b) BCl_3 forms adducts with NH_3, H_2O and RNH_2
(c) BCl_3 reacts with liquid NH_3 and ethanol forming $B(NH_2)_3$ and $B(OEt)_3$
(d) $[BCl_4]^-$, $[BBr_4]^-$ and $[BI_4]^-$ ions can be made only in non-aqueous media

4. Select the correct statement(s).

(a) Boron trimethyl is a weaker Lewis acid than the boron trihalides or monoborane
(b) Lewis acid property when Me_3N is a donor is in order : $BBr_3 > BCl_3 > BF_3 \sim BH_3 > BMe_3$
(c) Lewis acid property when Me_3P is a donor is in order : $BBr_3 > BCl_3 \sim BH_3 > BF_3 \sim BMe_3$
(d) Lewis acid property when CO is a donor : no adduct is formed with halides and Lewis acid property of $BH_3 >> BF_3 \cdot BMe_3$

5. Select the correct statement(s).

(a) A saturated solution of boric acid in water is neutral to the indicator bromocresol green
(b) AlF_3 is insoluble in anhydrous HF
(c) Aqueous solution of KHF_2 is basic to the indicator bromocresol green
(d) Aqueous solution of boric acid and potassium hydrogen difluoride is alkaline to bromocresol indicator

6. Select the correct statement(s).

(a) Diborane is an electron-deficient compound
(b) Diborane is stoichiometrically analogous to ethane (C_2H_6)
(c) Total electrons involved in bonding are 12 in diborane and ethane
(d) Total electrons involved in bonding are 12 in diboroane and 14 in ethane

7. Boric acid is a weak Lewis acid proton comes from

(a) by its ionisation
(b) when it forms complex with H_2O
(c) when it forms borate esters with alcohol
(d) All of the above

8. Select the correct statement(s).

(a) On the basis of Lewis acidity, an oxygen atom is more effective than an fluorine atom as a π-donor towards boron
(b) 1,2-diols have a strong tendency to form borate esters on account of chelate effect
(c) Borate esters are stable due to chelate effect
(d) None of the above is correct statement

9. Actual source of protons in boric acid is based on the following

(a) $B(OH)_3(aq) + 2H_2O(l) \rightleftharpoons H_3O^+(aq) + [B(OH)_4]^-(aq)$
(b) $\underset{\text{in neutral or basic solution}}{3B(OH)_3(aq)} \rightleftharpoons [B_3O_3(OH)_4]^-(aq) + H^+(aq) + 2H_2O(l)$
(c) $B(OH)_3 \rightleftharpoons H_2BO_3^- + H^+$
(d) All of the above

10. Select the correct statement(s).
(a) Aluminium monohalides are formed by the reactions of the trihalides with aluminium at 1300K followed by rapid cooling
(b) Aluminium monochloride (red) is formed when aluminium reacts with HCl at 1200 K
(c) Aluminium monohalides disproportionates at room temperature
(d) Ga_2Cl_4 exists as $Ga^+[GaCl_4]^-$ and is diamagnetic and has crystalline structure.

11. Consider the following statements,
I. Boric acid is a mild antiseptic and is used as a food preservative.
II. Borax and other borates are used in water-treatment, timber preservation, glass manufacture.
III. Sodium peroxoborate is an important constituent of washing powder.

Select the correct statement.
(a) I, II (b) II, III (c) I, III (d) I, II, III

12. Select the correct alternate(s).
(a) The group BN is isoelectronic with C_2
(b) No species with $B \equiv N$ group is formed
(c) Common form of boron nitride has an ordered layer structure closely resembling that of graphite
(d) AlN has the wurtzite structure

13. $SiCl_4$ is hydrolysed but CCl_4 is not hydrolysed because
(a) Si has vacant *d*-orbitals and can accommodate lone-pair of electrons from oxygen of water
(b) Si has relatively large size and can increase its coordination number from four to five
(c) Si has relatively smaller size and thus interaction with H_2O is spontaneous
(d) Si has oxidation number of six while carbon has oxidation number of four in all its compounds.

14. Select the correct statement(s).
(a) In α-graphite, the layers are arranged in the sequence *ABAB* ......
(b) In β-graphite, the layers are arranged in the sequence *ABCABC* ......
(c) In α-graphite, the layers are arranged in the sequence *ABCABC* ......
(d) In β-graphite, the layers are arranged in the sequence *ABAB* ......

15. Select the statement(s).
(a) The enthalpy difference between α- and β-graphite is very large and thus two forms are not interconvertible
(b) The enthalpy difference between α- and β- graphite is very small and two forms are interconvertible
(c) α-graphite changes to β-graphite at about 1300 K.
(d) β-graphite changes to α-graphite at about 1300 K

16. Select ionic carbides.
(a) Al_4C_3, CaC_2, Mg_2C_3 (b) Al_4C_3, SiC, B_4C
(c) CaC_2, Mg_2C_3 (d) CaC_2, SiC, Mg_2C_3

17. Silly putty
(a) is a silicone polymer
(b) has a composition intermediate between silicone oils and silicone rubbers
(c) is an asbestos
(d) is not related to any chemical

18. The great thermal and chemical stability of silicones is attributed to high strength of
(a) silicon-carbon bond (b) silicon-oxygen bond
(c) silicon-silicon bond (d) carbon-carbon bond

19. Correct statement(s) out of the following is
(a) $N(CH_3)_3$ has pyramidal structure
(b) $N(SiH_3)_3$ shows planar arrangement
(c) SiC is highly volatile
(d) SiO_2 is called silane

20. Group 14 (carbon family) elements have the following properties
(a) They are all network solids with octahedral network
(b) Only SiO_2 is a network solid with tetrahedral coordination and is a giant molecule
(c) SnO_2 and PbO_2 are amphoteric oxides
(d) All oxides are acidic

21. Silicones
(a) are synthetic polymer containing repeating (R_2SiO_2) units
(b) are formed by hydrolysis of R_2SiCl_2
(c) are natural occurring repeating (SiO_4) units
(d) single R_2SiO_2 unit

22. Select the correct statement(s).
(a) $COCl_2$ is called phosphine gas
(b) C_3O_2 (carbon suboxide) has sp^2 hybridised carbons
(c) CO is toxic because it forms a complex with haemoglobin in the blood
(d) Diamond is unaffected by concentrated acid but graphite is oxidised to mellitic acid with concentrated HNO_3.

23. Gases responsible for "green-house effect" are
(a) CO_2 (b) H_2O (c) O_3 (d) N_2

24. Select the correct statement(s).
(a) Graphite is composed of planar, two dimensional sheets of sp^2-hybridised carbon atoms
(b) Each sheet is a network of fused, hexagonal rings of carbons
(c) The layers in graphite are held together by relatively weak van der Waals' forces of attraction.
(d) Graphite is thermodynamically the most stable allotropic form of carbon.

25. Select the correct statement(s).
(a) In graphite, only three electrons (out of four) are involved in σ bonding
(b) π-bonding electrons in graphite are delocalised over the whole structure
(c) Conduction of electricity in graphite is due to mobile electrons
(d) Diamond is insulator due to absence of mobile electrons

26. Conc. H_2SO_4 reacts with carbon forming
(a) CO_2 (b) SO_2 (c) H_2CO_3 (d) H_2SO_3

27. Carbon suboxide (C_3O_2) is formed, when
(a) carbon reacts with conc. H_2SO_4
(b) malonic acid reacts with P_4O_{10}
(c) carbon reacts with strong alkali solution
(d) oxalic acid is heated strongly

28. NH_2OH can be used as
(a) an oxidising agent
(b) a reducing agent
(c) an autioxidant in photographic developers
(d) oxime forming reagent (with carbonyl compound)

29. Select the correct statement(s).
NH_2OH forms *syn* and *anti* isomer with
(a) benzaldehyde
(b) acetone
(c) acetaldehyde
(d) benzophenone

30. Nylon-6 is formed from caprolactam which is formed from
(a) cyclohexanone and hydroxyl amine
(b) cyclohexanone and hydrazine
(c) benzophenone and hydrazine
(d) benzophenone and hydroxylamine

31. Select the correct statement(s).
(a) $SbCl_3$ is hydrolysed to orange SbOCl soluble in dil. HCl
(b) $BiCl_3$ is hydrolysed to white BiOCl soluble in dil. HCl
(c) PCl_5 can change to PCl_6^- and PCl_4^+ with no change in hybridisation of P
(d) NCl_5 and PCl_5 are stable compounds

32. N_2H_4 and H_2O_2 show similarity in
(a) hybridisation of central atoms
(b) oxidising nature
(c) reducing nature
(d) molar mass

33. In acidic medium N_2H_4
(a) is oxidised to N_2
(b) loses four electrons
(c) has equivalent mass 8
(d) reduces $AuCl_3$ to AuCl

34. N_2H_4 reduces IO_3^- / H^+
(a) to I^+
(b) with I_2 as an intermediate indicated by violet colour in CCl_4 layer
(c) indicated by blue colour with starch
(d) to I^-

35. N_2H_4
(a) is an endothermic compound
(b) burns in air with evolution of heat in an exothermic compound
(c) is kinetically stable
(d) reduces $FeCl_3$ to $FeCl_2$ in acidic medium

36. Thermodynamic tendency of $PH_3(g)$ to react with $HX(g)$ would be favoured by
(a) low H—X bond energy
(b) high electron affinity of X
(c) high lattice energy of $PH_4X(s)$
(d) high electronegativity of P

37. The following side reaction in the production of N_2H_4

$$N_2H_4 + 2NH_2Cl \longrightarrow N_2 + 2NH_4Cl$$

(a) is catalysed by traces of heavy metals as Cu^{2+}
(b) is suppressed by addition of gelatin or glue
(c) is made reversible by removing N_2
(d) is made reversible by adding NaOH

38. The nitrogen oxide(s) that contain(s) N—N bond(s) is (are) **[IIT JEE 2009]**
(a) N_2O (b) N_2O_3
(c) N_2O_4 (d) N_2O_5

39. With reference to *aqua-regia*, choose the correct option(s). **[JEE Advanced 2019]**
(a) *Aqua-regia* is prepared by mixing conc. HCl and conc. HNO_3 in 3 : 1 (v/v) ratio
(b) The yellow colour of *aqua-regia* is due to the presence of NOCl and Cl_2
(c) eaction of gold with *aqua-regia* produces an anion having Au in +3 oxidation state
(d) Reaction of gold with *aqua regia* produces NO_2 in the absence of air

40. Based on the compounds of group 15 elements, the correct statement(s) is (are) **[JEE Advanced 2018]**
(a) Bi_2O_5 is more basic than N_2O_5
(b) NF_3 is more covalent than BiF_3
(c) PH_3 boils at lower temperature than NH_3
(d) The N—N single bond is stronger than the P—P single bond

41. The crystalline form of borax has **[JEE Advanced 2016]**
(a) tetranuclear $[B_4O_5(OH)_4]^{2-}$ unit
(b) all boron atoms in the same plane
(c) equal number of sp^2 and sp^3-hybridised boron atoms
(d) one terminal hydroxide per boron atom

Numerical Value Questions

All these questions have a Numerical value as their answer, solve the questions and write your answer.

1. How many of the following have two σ and two π-bonds?
$C_3^{4-}, CN_2^{2-}, CO_2, C_2^{2-}, C_2H_4, CN^-$
2. How many of the fuel gases have CO and H_2 both as combustible gases?
LPG, water gas, Producer gas, Coal gas, CNG
3. A mixture contains 3 moles of CO and CO_2. On passing the mixture over heated charcoal, volume increases to 5 moles. Thus, CO_2 in the mixture is .... mole(s).
4. What is the total negative charge on the silicate $[Si_4O_{11}]$?
5. How many of the species are isoelectronic?
$N_2O, CO_2, CN_2^{2-}, N_3^-, NH_2OH, N_3H$
6. In the following, equilibrium partial pressure of NH_3, N_2 and H_2 gases are 4, 1 and 2 atm respectively at 300 K. What is the value of K_p?
$N_2(g) + 3H_2(g) \rightleftharpoons 2NH_3(g)$
7. In the oxidation of N_2H_4 to N_2, equivalent weight of N_2H_4 would be ....
8. How many species out of the following have reducing properties?
$NH_3, PH_3, H_3PO_2, H_3PO_3, H_3PO_4, LiAlH_4, BH_3$
9. In a molecule of pyrophosphoric acid, the number of P—OH, P=O and P—O—P bonds/moiety(ies) respectively are x, y, z. Find $(x + y + z)$? **[JEE Main 2020, Sep.]**
10. The number of 2-centre-2-electron and 3-centre-2-electron bonds in B_2H_6, respectively, are .... **[JEE Main 2019, Jan.]**
11. White phosphorus on reaction with concentrated NaOH solution in an inert atmosphere of CO_2 gives phosphine and compound (*X*). (*X*) on acidification with HCl gives compound (*Y*). The basicity of compound (*Y*) is **[JEE Main 2020, Jan.]**
12. In PCl_5, how many (P—Cl) are inclined at 120° with one each?
13. Among the following the number of compounds that can react with PCl_5 to give $POCl_3$ is $O_2, CO_2, SO_2, H_2O, H_2SO_4, P_4O_{10}$ is .... **[IIT JEE 2011]**
14. Consider the following reactions,

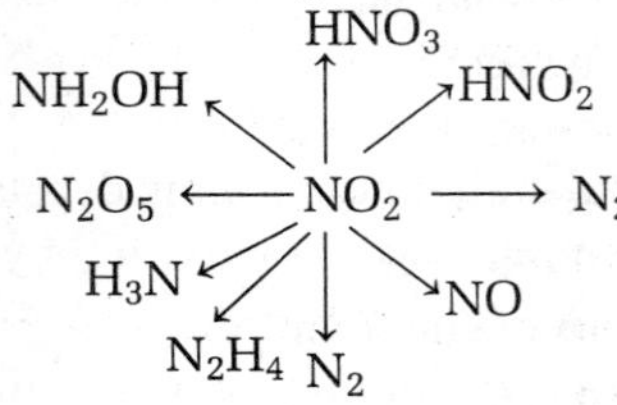

In how many reactions NO_2 has been oxidised?
15. The number of pentagons in C_{60} and trigons (triangles) in white phosphorus, respectively, are .... **[JEE Main 2019, April]**

Comprehension Based Questions

In these questions, a passage has been given followed by questions based on it. You have to answer the questions based on the passage given.

Passage 1 The tetrafluoroborate anion BF_4^-, is a Lewis base. The other tetrahaloborate anions, BCl_4^- and BBr_4^-, can be prepared in non-aqueous solvents.

Based on the above short write-up, answer the following questions.

1. BF_4^- is
(a) F^- donor
(b) a lone-pair acceptor
(c) a lone-pair donor
(d) solvated in aqueous solution
2. BCl_4^- and BBr_4^- are stable in
(a) H_2O (b) alcohol
(c) Both (a) and (b) (d) None of these

Passage 2 Certain aspects of the aqueous chemistry of aluminium compounds derive from the nature of the hydrated aluminium ion-$[Al(H_2O)_6]^{3+}$.

$[Al(H_2O)_6]^{3+} + H_2O \rightleftharpoons [Al(H_2O)_5(OH^-)]^{2+} + H_3O^+$

Read the above write-up and answer the following questions.

1. Above equilibrium indicates that
(a) H_2O is a Lowry-Bronsted acid
(b) H_2O is a Lowry-Bronsted base
(c) H_2O is a Lowry-Bronsted acid as well as a base
(d) H_2O is neither acid nor base
2. Above equilibrium is expressed in
(a) strongly acidic solution
(b) alkaline solution
(c) aqueous solution
(d) All of the above
3. Ionisation of the above equilibrium is favoured in
(a) strongly acidic solution
(b) alkaline solution
(c) aqueous solution
(d) All of the above

Passage 3 Diborane is an electron deficient compound. Stoichiometrically, it is analogous to ethane, C_2H_6. However, the total number of electrons involved in bonding and less in diborane.

Read the above short note and answer the following questions.

1. Bonding electrons involved
   (a) in B_2H_6 is 14 and in C_2H_6 is 16
   (b) in B_2H_6 is 12 and in C_2H_6 is 14
   (c) in B_2H_6 is 10 and in C_2H_6 is 12
   (d) in B_2H_6 is 16 and in C_2H_6 is 18
2. Octet is complete in
   (a) boron in diborane
   (b) carbon in ethane
   (c) boron in diborane and carbon in ethane
   (d) None of the above
3. Consider the following statements for diborane,
   I. Boron is approximately sp^3 hybridised.
   II. B—H—B angle is 180°.
   III. There are two terminal B—H bonds for each boron atom.
   IV. There are only 12 bonding electrons available.
   Of these statements
   (a) I, III and IV are correct
   (b) I, II and III are correct
   (c) II, III and IV are correct
   (d) I, II and IV are correct

Passage 4 Study the following sequence of reactions :

Alkaline $\xleftarrow{H_2O}$ A(white crystalline) $\xrightarrow{\Delta}$ B (transparent bead)

B $\xrightarrow{Cu^{2+}, \Delta}$ C(green-coloured bead)

C $\xrightarrow{\Delta \text{ in reducing flame}}$ D (red-coloured bead)

A $\xrightarrow{H_2SO_4}$ E (white crystalline compound on cooling)

1. *A* is
   (a) $NaBO_2$ (b) $Na_2B_4O_7$
   (c) H_3BO_3 (d) HBO_3
2. *B* is
   (a) $NaBO_2$ (b) B_2O_3
   (c) Na_3BO_3 (d) H_3BO_3
3. *C* and *D* respectively are
   (a) Cu_2BO_2, CuO (b) $Cu(BO_2)_2$, $CuBO_2$
   (c) $Cu_2B_2O_4$, CuO (d) $Cu(BO_2)_2$, $Cu_2B_2O_4$

Passage 5 *Read the following discovery and answer the questions at the end.*

"Elemental carbon appears in many structural forms or allotropes. Three of these forms are crystalline—diamond, graphite and the recently discovered fullerence (buckyball)—while more than 40 others, including coke and carbon black, are amorphous. Now there seems to be set a fourth crystalline allotrope of carbon, reported in 1995 by Richard Lagow at the University of Texas."

1. Newly discovered allotrope of carbon has the form
   (a) polyyne (b) fullerene
   (c) buckyball (d) None of these
2. Structures of different allotropes of carbon have been compared. Which represents incorrect comparison?
   (a) Allotrope discovered in 1995 — *sp*–hybridised carbon
   (b) Buckyball — *sp*–hybridised carbon
   (c) Graphite — sp^2–hybridised carbon
   (d) Diamond — sp^3–hybridised carbon
3. Consider the following statements about buckyball,
   A. It is also called fullerence.
   B. It is also called buckminster fullerence.
   C. Bucky tubes (made of fullerenes) are several times stronger than steel wires.
   D. Buckyball is a plastic polymer.
   Select the correct statement(s).
   (a) *A, C, D* (b) *A, B, C* (d) *A, B, D* (d) *B, C, D*

Passage 6 *Read the following short write-up and answer the questions at the end of it.*

The name '**silica**' covers an entire group of minerals, which have the general formula SiO_2, the most common of which is **quartz**. Quartz is a framework silicate with SiO_4 tetrahedra arranged in spirals. The spirals can turn in a clockwise or anti-clockwise direction—a feature that results in there being two mirror images, optically active, varieties of quartz.

1. The following pictures represent various silicate anions. Their formulae are respectively

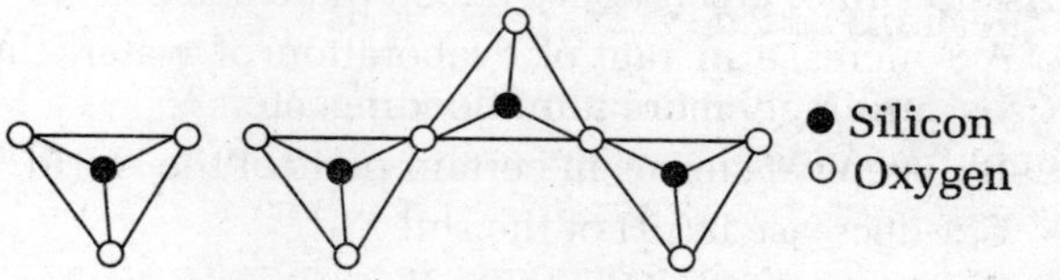

   (a) SiO_3^{2-} $Si_3O_7^{2-}$
   (b) SiO_4^{4-} $Si_3O_{10}^{8-}$
   (c) SiO_4^{2-} $Si_3O_9^{2-}$
   (d) SiO_3^{4-} $Si_3O_7^{8-}$
2. $Si_3O_9^{6-}$ (having three tetrahedra) is represented as

   (a) 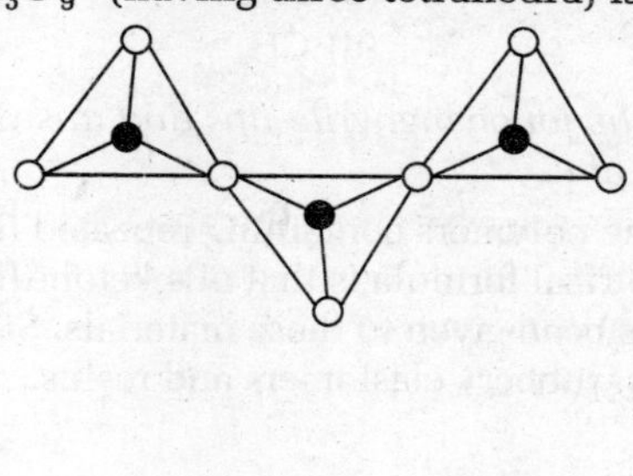

(b) 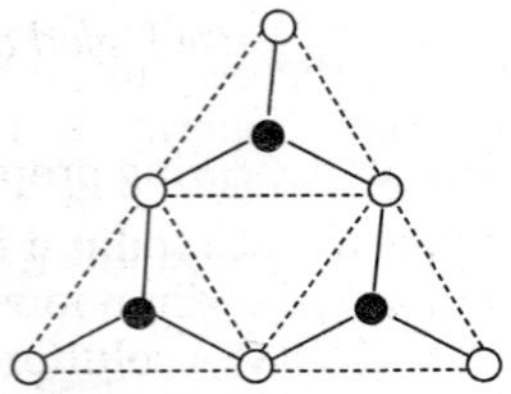

(c) Both (a) and (b)
(d) None of the above

3. The silicate anion in the mineral kinoite is a chain of three SiO_4 tetrahedra that share corners with adjacent tetrahedra. The mineral also contains Ca^{2+} ions, Cu^{2+} ions, and water molecules in a 1 : 1 : 1 ratio mineral is represented as
(a) $CaCuSi_3O_{10} \cdot H_2O$
(b) $CaCuSi_3O_{10} \cdot 2H_2O$
(c) $Ca_2Cu_2Si_3O_{10} \cdot 2H_2O$
(d) None of the above

Passage 7 *Questions given below are based on the following technical report.*

The CO_2 as well as H_2O absorbs strongly in the infrared region, and its presence in the atmosphere decreases the loss of heat from the earth by radiation. This global warming is called the **'green house effect'** (other gases, including the oxides of nitrogen from car exhausts, freons from aerosols and refrigerators and methane from bacteria in the soil and in the rumen of cows, also add to the green house effect). The concentration of atmospheric CO_2 has increased by 10%. This is resulting in the increase in the mean temperature of the earth by 2.5°C, varying from 2°C at the equator to 4°C at the poles. This could have dramatic effects on the climate.

1. As a result of green house effect, there can be
A : increase in rate of evaporation of water, thus, untimely more rain, flooding, etc.
B : tropical storms in certain parts of the world
C : decrease in pH of the soil
D : increase in pH of the soil
Select the correct alternate.
(a) B, C, D (b) A, C, D
(c) A, B, D (d) A, B, C

2. Which of the following is growing at a faster rate than CO_2 thus responsible for the green house effect?
(a) CFC (b) N_2O
(c) O_3 (d) CH_4

Passage 8 *Read the following write-ups and answer the questions at the end of it.*

Silicones are synthetic polymers containing repeated R_2SiO units. Since, the empirical formula is that of a ketone (R_2CO), the name silicone has been given to these materials. Silicones can be made into oils, rubbery elastomers and resins. They find a variety of applications because of their chemical inertness, water repelling nature, heat-resistance and good electrical insulating property.

Commercial silicon polymers are usually methyl derivatives and to a lesser extent phenyl derivatives and are synthesised by the hydrolysis of

R_2SiCl_2[R = methyl (Me) or phenyl (ϕ)]

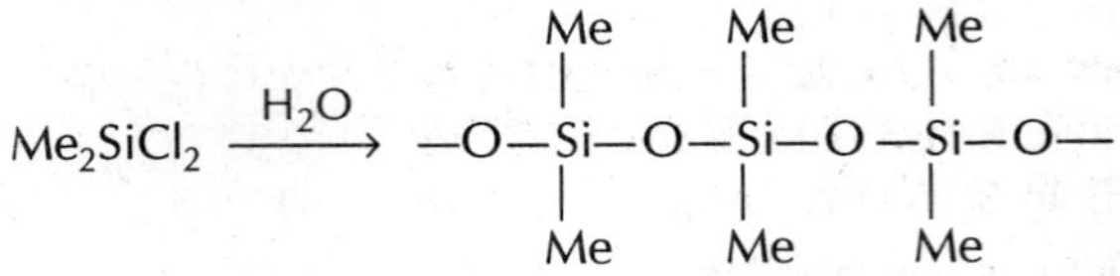

1. If we mix $SiMe_3Cl$ with $SiMe_2Cl_2$, we get silicones of the type

(a) 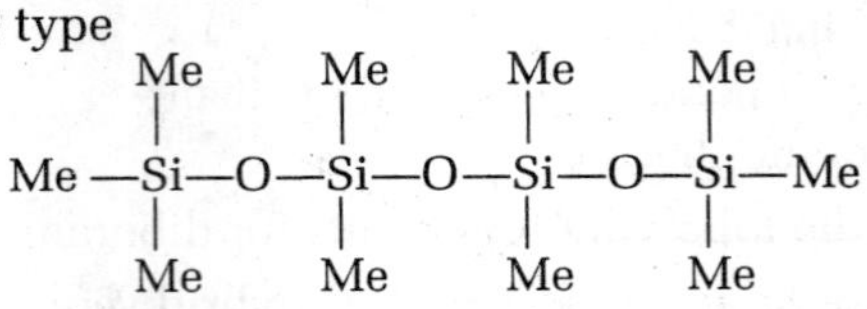

(b) 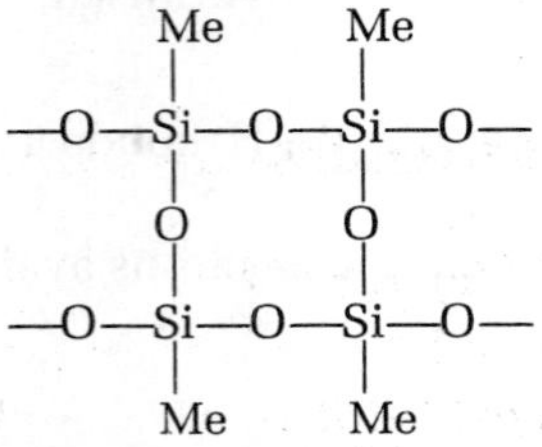

(c) Both (a) and (b)
(d) None of the above

2. If we start with $SiMeCl_3$ as the starting material, silicones formed is

(a) 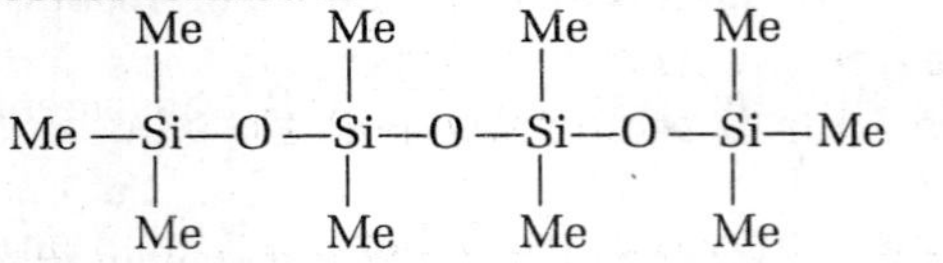

(b) 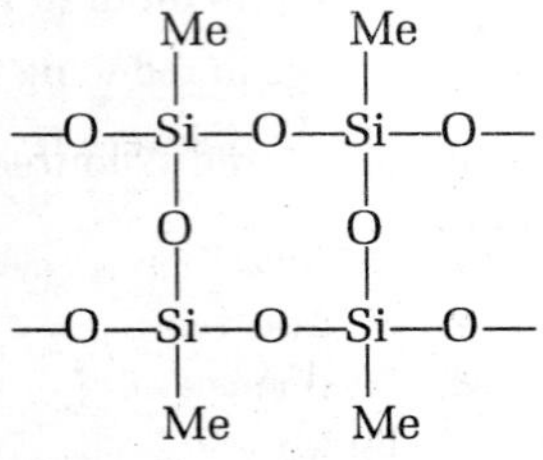

(c) Both (a) and (b)
(d) None of the above

Passage 9 *Question given below is based on the following structures:*

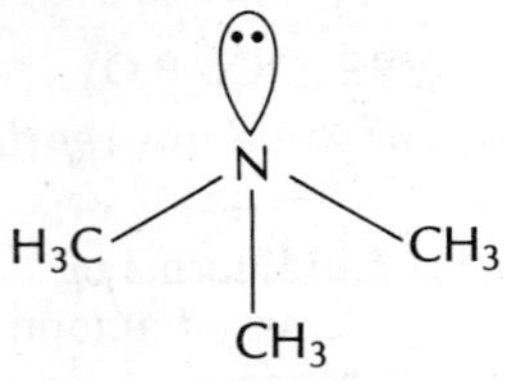

Pyramidal

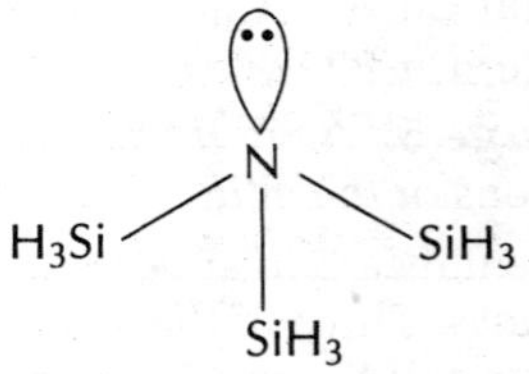

Planar

1. Structures of $N(CH_3)_3$ and $N(SiH_3)_3$ are different. It is due to the fact that
   (a) silicon also uses *d*-orbitals in multiple bonding
   (b) in case of $N(SiH_3)_3$, lone pair of N-atom is transferred to the empty *d*-orbitals of silicon ($p\pi$-$d\pi$ overlapping)
   (c) Both (a) and (b)
   (d) None of the above

***Passage* 10** *Consider the following scheme involving oxides and oxy-acids of nitrogen. Based on this answer the questions given at the end.*

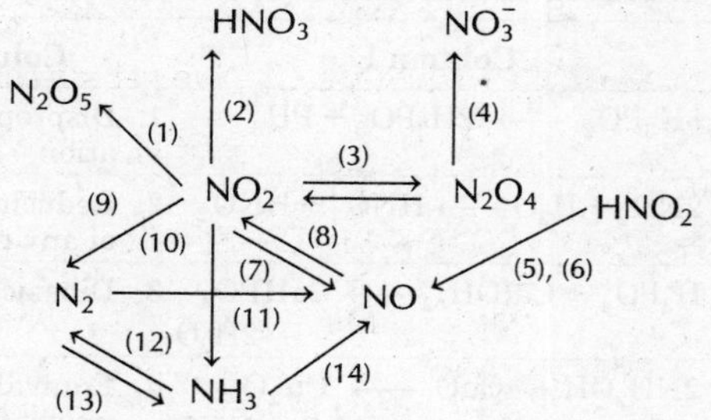

1. Out of the following which reactions are disproportionations?
   (a) 2, 10 (b) 2, 3
   (c) 1, 11 (d) 13, 14
2. In which case change in oxidation number is maximum?
   (a) 1 (b) 10 (c) 5 (d) 11

***Passage* 11** *Questions given below are based on the following experiment.*

An oxyacid of phosphorus has the following properties
Complete neutralisation of the acid with sodium hydroxide solution gives an aqueous solution of sodium ions and oxy-acid anions in the ratio 2 : 1. When a solution of the acid is warmed with silver nitrate solution metallic silver is deposited.

1. What is the structure of the oxy-acid?

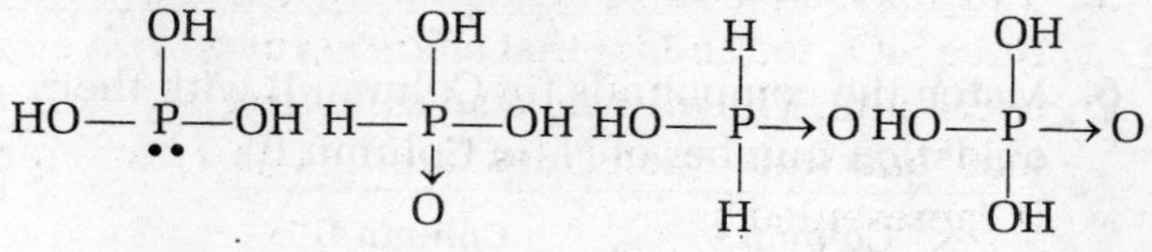

1 2 3 4

   (a) 1 (b) 2
   (c) 3 (d) 4
2. This oxy-acid is converted into .... on reaction with acetic anhydride.
   (a) $(CH_3CO)_2HPO_4$
   (b) $(CH_3CO)_2HPO_3$
   (c) P_2O_3
   (d) P_2O_5
3. pH of 0.01 M solution of the sodium salt of this acid formed (assume $pK_{a_1} = 2x$) is
   (a) $6 + 2x$ (b) $6 - 2x$
   (c) $6 - x$ (d) $6 + x$

Matrix-Match Type

Given below are Matching Type Questions, with two columns (each having some items) each . Each item of Column I has to be matched with the items of Column II.

1. Match the compounds (in Column I) with their use (in Column II).

Column I (Compound)	Column II (Use)
A. Boric acid	1. In Friedel-Craft acylation
B. Borax	2. Mild antiseptic
C. Aluminium chloride	3. Washing powder
D. Sodium peroxoborate	4. Buffer

2. Match the types of borates (in Column I) with their formula (in Column II).

(Column I (Types of borates)	Column II (Formula)
A. Metaborate	1. $NaBO_3 \cdot 4H_2O$
B. Orthoborates	2. $Mg_2B_2O_5$
C. Pyroborates	3. $K_3(BO_2)_3$
D. Perborate	4. $Ca_3(BO_3)_2$

3. Match the items (in Column I) with their formula (in Column II).

Column I (Items)	Column II (Formula)
A. Tetraboric acid	1. $B_3N_3H_6$
B. Borax	2. $Ga(OH)_2$
C. Borazine	3. $H_2B_4O_7$
D. Amphoteric	4. $Na_2B_4O_7 \cdot 10H_2O$

4. Match the acids (in Column I) with number of acid salts formed by them (in Column II).

Column I	Column II
A. Hypophosphorus acid	1. Two
B. Orthophosphorus acid	2. Zero
C. Orthophosphoric acid	3. One
D. Mellitic acid	4. Five

5. Match the reactions of metals with dilute HNO_3 (in Column I) with the nitrogen compounds (obtained by oxidation/reduction (in Column II).

	Column I		Column II
A.	$Mg + \text{Dil. } HNO_3$	1.	NO
B.	$Zn + \text{Dil. } HNO_3$	2.	H_2
C.	$Sn + \text{Dil. } HNO_3$	3.	N_2O
D.	$Pb + \text{Dil. } HNO_3$	4.	NH_4NO_3

6. Match the compounds (in Column I) with their oxidation number of N (in Column II).

	Column I		Column II
A.	N_2H_4	1.	–1
B.	NH_2OH	2.	3
C.	HNO_2	3.	4
D.	NO_2	4.	5
E.	HNO_3	5.	–2

7. Match the compounds in Column I with their corresponding property (ies) in Column II.

	Column I		Column II
A.	Borax	1.	Electron deficient
B.	Ortho boric acid	2.	sp^2-hybridisation
C.	Borane	3.	Coloured beads with CuO
D.	Alums	4.	Mordant in dyeing
E.	Boron nitride	5.	Triangular planar
		6.	Changes $CH_3CH{=}CH_2$ into alcohol by anti-Markownikoff's addition

8. Match the species in Column I with their characteristics in Column II.

	Column I	Column II
A.	Benzene	1. Six-membered ring
B.	Borazine	2. Delocalisation of π electrons
C.	Inorganic graphite	3. sp^2-hybridised
D.	Borane	4. Mole fraction of H 0.5
		5. Mole fraction of N and B equal
		6. Mole fraction of boron 0.5

9. Match the oxide of Column I with their corresponding property (ies) in Column II.

	Column I		Column II
A.	Pb_3O_4	1.	Oxidation state +2
B.	SnO_2	2.	Oxidation state +4
C.	PbO_2	3.	Amphoteric
D.	CO_2	4.	Basic
E.	GeO	5.	Acidic

10. Match the reaction in Column I with their corresponding characteristic(s) in Column II.

Column I	Column II
A. $3H_3PO_2 \longrightarrow 2H_3PO_3 + PH_3$	1. Disproportionation
B. $2NO_2 + H_2O \longrightarrow HNO_3 + HNO_2$	2. Reducing nature of any reactant
C. $H_3PO_4 + Ca(OH)_2 \longrightarrow CaHPO_4 + 2H_2O$	3. Dibasic acid
D. $2NH_2OH + 4CuO \longrightarrow Cu_2O\downarrow + N_2O + 3H_2O$	4. Equivalent weight (reactant) $= \dfrac{\text{mol. wt}}{4}$
	5. Reactant is paramagnetic
	6. Oxidising nature of any reactant

11. Match List-I with List-II. **[JEE Main 2021, March]**

	List I (Industrial process)		List II (Application)
A.	Haber's process	1.	HNO3 synthesis
B.	Ostwald's process	2.	Aluminium extraction
C.	Contact process	3.	NH_3 synthesis
D.	Hall-Heroult process	4.	H_2SO_4 synthesis

12. Name of oxo acid oxidation state of 'P'. **[JEE Main 2021, March]**

	List I (Name of oxo acid)		List II (Oxidation state of 'P')
A.	Hypophosphorus acid	1.	+5
B.	Orthophosphoric acid	2.	+4
C.	Hypophosphoric acid	3.	+3
D.	Orthophosphorus acid	4.	+2
		5.	+1

Single Integer Answer Questions

Answer of these questions is a single digit lying between 0 to 9.

1. In the hydrolysis of borax
$$Na_2B_4O_7 + 7H_2O \longrightarrow 2Na[B(OH)_4] + B(OH)_3$$
products formed are to be neutralised by HCl. Number of moles of HCl required per mole of borax hydrolysed is ....
2. Total number of B and N atom in borazine is ....
3. $B(OH)_3$ can accept ...... hydroxide ion(s) from H_2O.
4. Aluminium methanide contains .... carbon atom(s).
5. Borax is found to have .... tetrahedral unit(s).
6. B_2H_6 has B—H terminal bonds and B—H bridging bonds which is equal to ....
7. Total electrons involved in all the B—H bridging bond is ....
8. A *x*—membered ring is formed in $(BN)_n$ where *x* is ....
9. Al(*s*) is to be converted into $Al^{3+}(aq)$ ion. How many steps are involved? (Assume ionisation in one step)
10. When malonic acid is dehydrated using P_4O_{10} at 150°C, species formed has total number of atoms ....
11. Among B_2H_6, $B_3N_3H_6$, N_2O, N_2O_4, $H_2S_2O_3$ and $H_2S_2O_8$, the total number of molecules containing covalent bond between two atoms of the same kind is ....
12. How many of the following oxides are basic oxides?
CO_2, SnO_2, PbO, PbO_2, Pb_3O_4, Al_2O_3
13. For the half-cell reaction,
$M^{2+} + 2e^- \longrightarrow M$
$E°$ (in volts) are given for different metals

Cu	Zn	Fe	Pb	Sn
0.34	–0.76	–0.48	–0.13	–0.14

How many of these metals can reduce Cu^{2+} to Cu?
14. Out of the elements C, S, Ge, Sn and Pb only +4 oxidation state is shown by how many element(s)?
15. How many elements in group 14 are used as semiconductor?

Answers

Objective Questions Type I [Only one correct option]

1. (a)	2. (d)	3. (c)	4. (c)	5. (c)	6. (c)	7. (d)	8. (d)	9. (a)	10. (a)
11. (d)	12. (d)	13. (c)	14. (c)	15. (c)	16. (c)	17. (d)	18. (a)	19. (d)	20. (a)
21. (b)	22. (a)	23. (d)	24. (c)	25. (d)	26. (a)	27. (a)	28. (c)	29. (c)	30. (a)
31. (c)	32. (d)	33. (a)	34. (d)	35. (a)	36. (c)	37. (d)	38. (a)	39. (a)	40. (a)
41. (c)	42. (c)	43. (b)	44. (d)	45. (c)	46. (b)	47. (d)	48. (d)	49. (d)	50. (a)
51. (a)	52. (a)	53. (c)	54. (b)	55. (d)	56. (d)	57. (b)	58. (b)	59. (c)	60. (a)
61. (d)	62. (d)	63. (b)	64. (b)	65. (a)	66. (c)	67. (a)	68. (d)	69. (d)	70. (c)
71. (d)	72. (b)	73. (d)	74. (b)	75. (c)	76. (a)	77. (c)	78. (c)	79. (b)	80. (a)
81. (d)	82. (c)	83. (b)	84. (d)	85. (c)	86. (b)	87. (d)	88. (c)	89. (d)	90. (b)
91. (a)	92. (d)	93. (d)	94. (c)	95. (a)	96. (d)	97. (b)	98. (a)	99. (d)	100. (c)
101. (d)	102. (c)	103. (d)	104. (c)	105. (a)	106. (a)	107. (d)	108. (b)	109 (c)	110. (a)
111. (a)	112. (b)	113. (d)	114. (b)	115. (d)	116. (c)	117. (c)	118. (a)	119 (b)	120. (a)
121. (a)	122. (b)	123. (d)	124. (b)	125. (d)	126. (b)	127. (b)	128. (b)	129. (a)	130. (c)
131. (b)	132. (b)	133. (c)	134. (b)	135. (b)	136. (d)	137. (d)	138. (d)	139. (a)	140. (a)
141. (c)	142. (d)	143. (d)	144. (c)	145. (b)	146. (d)	147. (d)	148. (d)	149. (d)	150. (b)
151. (b)	152. (c)	153. (b)	154. (d)	155. (a)	156. (a)	157. (b)	158. (d)	159. (b)	160. (c)
161. (d)	162. (d)	163. (a)	164. (d)	165. (d)	166. (c)	167. (d)	168. (a)	169. (b)	170. (b)
171. (a)	172. (c)	173. (a)	174. (c)	175. (d)	176. (b)	177. (b)	178. (c)	179. (d)	180. (b)
181. (a)	182. (d)	183. (c)	184. (c)	185. (c)	186. (d)	187. (d)	188. (d)	189. (a)	190. (c)
191. (d)	192. (c)	193. (c)	194. (d)	195. (d)	196. (d)	197. (d)	198. (c)	199. (c)	200. (a)
201. (c)	202. (d)	203. (b)	204. (b)	205. (b)	206. (d)	207. (b)	208. (a)	209. (d)	210. (d)
211. (c)	212. (d)	213. (d)	214. (a)	215. (d)	216. (b)	217. (c)	218. (d)	219. (b)	220. (a)
221. (a)	222. (b)	223. (b)	224. (b)	225. (c)	226. (c)	227. (b)	228. (a)	229. (d)	230. (c)
231. (d)	232. (d)	233. (a)	234. (a)	235. (c)	236. (d)	237. (a)	238. (c)	239. (c)	240. (a)
241. (c)	242. (d)	243. (a)	244. (d)	245. (d)	246. (c)	247. (d)	248. (c)	249. (a)	250. (a)
251. (b)	252. (d)	253. (b)	254. (a)	255. (d)	256. (a)	257. (a)	258. (d)	259. (c)	260. (a)
261. (b)	262. (d)	263. (c)	264. (d)	265. (a)					

Objective Questions Type II [One or more than one correct option(s)]

1. (a, b) 2. (a, b, c, d) 3. (a, c, d) 4. (a, b, c, d) 5. (a, b, d) 6. (a, b, d) 7. (b)
8. (a, b, c) 9. (a) 10. (a, b, c, d) 11. (d) 12. (a, b, c, d) 13. (a, b)
14. (a, b) 15. (b, d) 16. (a) 17. (a, b) 18. (a, b) 19. (a, b)
20. (b, c) 21. (a, b) 22. (*c*, *d*) 23. (a, b) 24. (a, b, c, d) 25. (a, b, c, d)
26. (a, b, c, d) 27. (b) 28. (a, b, c, d) 29. (a, c) 30. (a) 31. (a, b)
32. (a, b, c) 33. (a, b, c) 34. (a, b, c) 35. (a, b, c, d) 36. (a, b, c) 37. (a, b) 38. (a, b, c)
39. (a, b, c) 40. (a, b, c) 41. (a, c, d)

Numerical Value Questions

1. (4) 2. (2) 3. (2) 4. (6) 5. (5) 6. (2) 7. (8) 8. (6) 9. (7) 10. (6)
11. (2) 12. (3) 13. (4) 14. (2) 15. (16)

Comprehension Based Questions

Passage 1 – 1. (c) 2. (d)
Passage 2 – 1. (c) 2. (a) 3. (b)
Passage 3 – 1. (b) 2. (b) 3. (a)
Passage 4 – 1. (b) 2. (b) 3. (b)
Passage 5 – 1. (a) 2. (b) 3. (b)
Passage 6 – 1. (b) 2. (b) 3. (c)
Passage 7 – 1. (d) 2. (a)
Passage 8 – 1. (a) 2. (b)
Passage 9 – 1. (c)
Passage 10 – 1. (a,c) 2. (d)
Passage 11 – 1. (b) 2. (c) 3. (d)

Matrix-Match Type

1. → A—(2); B—(4); C—(1); D—(3)
2. → A—(3); B—(4); C—(2); D—(2)
3. → A—(3); B—(4); C—(1); D—(2)
4. → A—(2); B—(3); C—(1); D—(4)
5. → A—(2); B—(3); C—(4); D—(1);
6. → A—(5); B—(1); C— (2); D—(3); E — (4);
7. → A—(3); B—(1,2,3,5); C—(2,5,6); D—(4); E—(2)
8. → A—(1,2,3,4); B—(1,2,3,4,5,6); C—(1,2,3,5); D—(3,6)
9. → A—(1,2,3); B—(2,3); C—(2,4); D—(2,5); E—(1,3);
10. → A—(1,2,6); B—(1,2,5,6); C — (3); D — (2,4,6)
11. → A—(3); B—(1); C—(4); D—(2)
12. → A—(5); B—(1); C — (2); D — (3)

Single Integer Answer Questions

1. (2) 2. (6) 3. (6) 4. (1) 5. (2) 6. (8) 7. (8) 8. (6) 9. (3) 10. (5)
11. (3) 12. (4) 13. (4) 14. (1) 15. (2)

Solutions

Objective Questions Type I [Only one correct option]

1. (*a*) B_2H_6 has two types of bonds
α : formed by sharing of one electron between B and H
β : formed by sharing of two electrons between B and H
Bond length $\alpha > \beta$

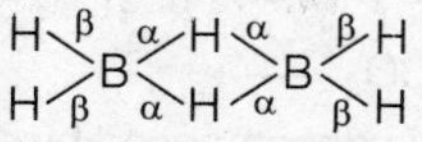

3. (*c*) NaOH reacts with Al and Zn both thus cannot be stored in vessel made of Al or Zn.

$$2Al + 2NaOH + 2H_2O \longrightarrow 2NaAlO_2 + 3H_2$$
$$Zn + 2NaOH \longrightarrow Na_2ZnO_2 + H_2$$

9. (*a*) BF_4^- — tetrahedral
SF_4 : sp^3d (one lone pair)
XeF_4 : sp^3d^2 (two lone pairs)
$[Ni(CN)_4]^{2-}$: dsp^2

10. (*a*)

	ON
H_3PO_3	+3
HBO_2	+3

13. (*c*) $6NaOH + 2B \longrightarrow 2Na_3BO_3 + 3H_2$

21. (*b*) $BO_3^{3-} + H_2SO_4 \longrightarrow H_3BO_3$

$$H_3BO_3 + 3CH_3OH \longrightarrow \underset{\text{Green}}{(CH_3O)_3B} + H_2O$$

22. (*a*) $Al(OH)_3$ is precipitated in NH_4OH medium.

23. (*d*) Borax $\xrightarrow{H^+} H_3BO_3 \xrightarrow{\Delta} B_2O_3 \xrightarrow{Mg} B$

25. (*d*) Structure of C_{60}

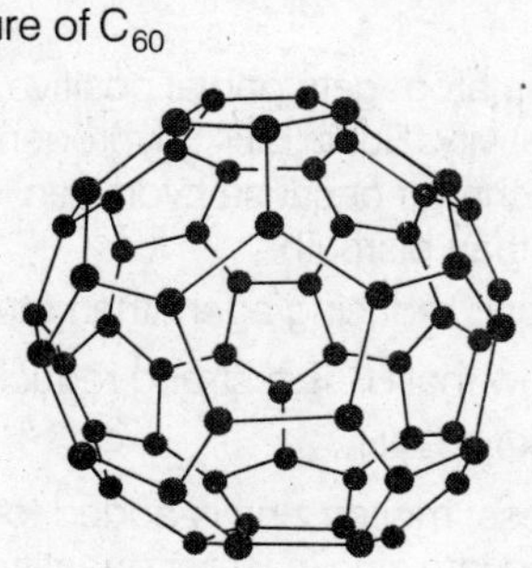

It contain 20 hexagons (20) and 12 pentagons (12) so option (d) is correct.

29. (*c*) NaOH dissolves $Al(OH)_3$; $Fe(OH)_3$ remains insoluble.

$$NaOH + Al(OH)_3 \longrightarrow \underset{\text{Soluble}}{Na[Al(OH)_4]}$$

31. (*c*) $3Ga^+ \longrightarrow 2Ga + Ga^{3+}$ (disproportionation)

32. (*d*) All being trivalent

35. (*a*) It is weak monobasic acid.

41. (*c*) $AlCl_3 + H_2O \longrightarrow Al(OH)_3 + \underset{\text{Fumes}}{3HCl\uparrow}$

42. (*c*) $NH_4Cl + NaAlO_2 + H_2O \longrightarrow NaCl + Al(OH)_3 + NH_3$

43. (*b*) Ionic compounds have high m.p. and high b.p.

45. (*d*) $6NaOH + B_2H_6 \longrightarrow 2Na_3BO_3 + 6H_2$

51. (*a*) $2Al + 6HCl \longrightarrow 2AlCl_3 + 3H_2$

$$2Al + 3[O] \xrightarrow{HNO_3} Al_2O_3$$
$$2Al + 2NaOH + 2H_2O \longrightarrow 2NaAlO_2 + 3H_2$$

55. (*d*)

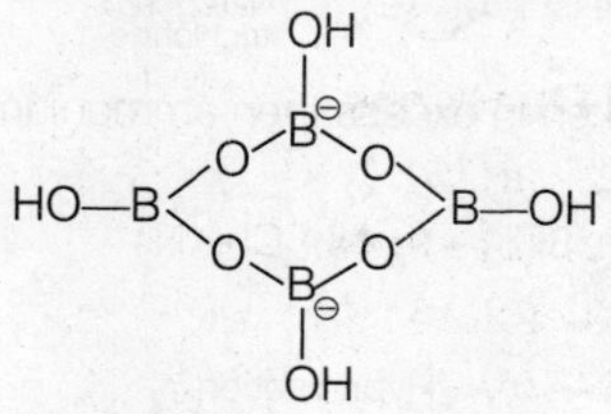

56. (*d*) Stability of $Ga^+ < In^+ < Tl^+$

$$Ga^{3+} > In^{3+} > Tl^{3+}$$

due to inert pair effect.

57. (*b*) C_{60} is aromatic allotrope of carbon containing 12 pentagons and 20 hexagons. It is a fullerene having a shape like soccer ball and called Buckminster fullerene.

58. (*b*) Silica occurs in nature in several amorphous and crystalline forms. Kieselguhr is the amorphous form of silica. Quartz, tridymite and cristobalite are crystalline forms of silica.

59. (*c*) Catenation property is an unique property of group 14 elements. Down the group 14, catenation power decreases as:

$$C > Si > Ge \approx Sn$$

Pb does not show catenation.

60. (*a*) Piezoelectric materials are those materials that produce an electric current when they are placed under mechanical stress. Crystalline solids can be used as piezoelectric material hence, quartz is a correct answer.

61. (*d*) Carbon (C) has greatest ability to form stable $p\pi$-$p\pi$ multiple bonds. $2p$-orbitals of this element participate in the process. The stability of multiple bonds of C is attributed to their closeness with C-nucleus. Thus, the smaller size of C plays a significant role in the process.

62. (*d*) (a) (M—H) bond energy decreases — true
(b) MX_3 is electron-deficient and thus is a Lewis acid — true.
(c) Al^{3+} is hydrated due to +3 charge and smaller cationic size — true.

64. (*b*) $3GaCl \longrightarrow \underset{\text{By reduction}}{\overset{\uparrow}{2Ga}} + \underset{\text{By oxidation}}{\overset{\uparrow}{GaCl_3}}$

66. (*c*)

$$B + NH_3 \longrightarrow BN + H_2$$
$$Al + NH_3 \longrightarrow Al(NH_2)_3 + H_2$$

67. (*a*)

$$B + N_2 \longrightarrow BN \xrightarrow{H_2O} NH_3$$
$$Al + N_2 \longrightarrow AlN \xrightarrow{H_2O} NH_3$$

68. (*d*) A yellow explsive liquid hydrogen trichloride is formed

$$N + \underset{\text{(Excess)}}{3Cl_2} \longrightarrow 3HCl + \underset{\text{Nitrogen trichloride}}{NCl_3}$$

It here ammonia is taken in excess then ammonium chloride is formed.

$$\underset{\text{(Excess)}}{7NH_3} + 3Cl_2 \longrightarrow NH_4Cl + N_2$$

69. (*d*)

Species | Hybridisation

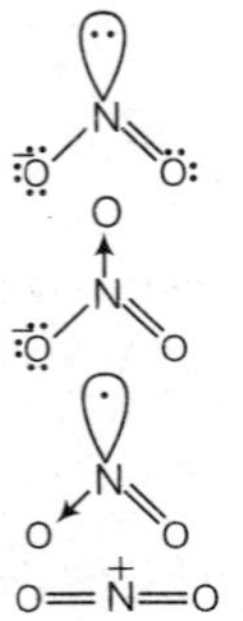

sp^2

sp^2

sp^2

sp

74. (*b*) $2H_3BO_3 \longrightarrow B_2O_3 + 3H_2O$

75. (*c*) $B(OH)_3 + 2H_2O \longrightarrow [B(OH)_4]^- + H_3O^+$

78. (*c*) sp^2 hybridised B

79. (*b*)

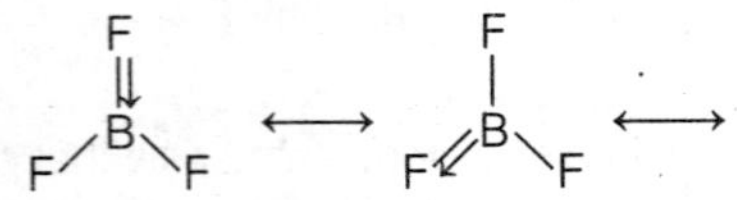

81. (*d*) There is free rotation about (B—B) bond and in liquid and gaseous state B_2Cl_4 exists as non-eclipsed and planar structure.

$$BCl_3 \xrightarrow{Hg} B_2Cl_4 + Hg_2Cl_2$$

82. (*c*)

$$BF_3 + 3H_2O \longrightarrow H_3BO_3 + HF$$
$$HF + BF_3 \longrightarrow HBF_4$$

83. (*b*)

84. (*d*)

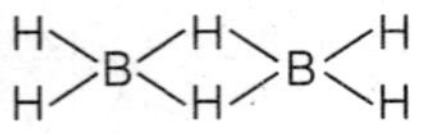

87. (*d*) $CH_3\overset{\overset{O}{\|}}{C}CH_3 \xrightarrow{LiAlH_4} CH_3CH_2OH + CH_3OH$

$$\xrightarrow{NaBH_4} X$$

Tnus, reducing action of $NaBH_4$ and $LiAlH_4$ is specific—true

$$CH_3CH{=}CH_2 \xrightarrow[H_2O_2,\, OH^-]{B_2H_6} \underset{1° \text{ alcohol}}{CH_3CH_2CH_2OH} \text{ true}$$

89. (*d*) $Al(OH)_3 + NaOH \longrightarrow Na[Al(OH)_4]$

90. (*b*) $CO_2 + H_2O \longrightarrow H_2CO_3 \rightleftharpoons CO_3^{2-} + 2H^+$

$$2Al^{3+} + 3CO_3^{2-} + 3H_2O \longrightarrow 2Al(OH)_3 + 3CO_2$$

91. (*a*) Oxide + $Na_2CO_3 \longrightarrow$

Since carbonate is decomposed by oxide, forming CO_2, thus, oxide is acidic in nature, and thus is oxide that of non-metal.

92. (*d*)

$$2BH_3 \longrightarrow B_2H_6$$
$$2AlCl_3 \longrightarrow Al_2Cl_6$$
$$2NO_2 \longrightarrow N_2O_4$$

BH_3, $AlCl_3$ and NO_2, are all electron-deficients, hence dimer formation takes place.

94. (*c*) Hydration is an exothermic process.

99. (*d*) In group 15

N, P] → Non-metal

As, Sb] → Metalloid

Bi] → Metal

Hydrides of group 15 elements are:

NH_3

PH_3

AsH_3

SbH_3

BiH_3

In NH_3, hydrogen atom gets partial positive charge due to less electronegativity. But in BiH_3, hydrogen atom gets partial negative charge because hydrogen is more electronegative than bismuth.

i.e. BiH_3 is a strong reducing agent than others because we know that H^- is a strong reducing agent.

102. (*c*) C=C, C=O, C≡N

111. (*a*) In this process, molten zinc is added to mineral when silver is extracted into zinc in larger quantity than lead.

112. (*b*) Holme's signals are used to guide the ships. Containers with holes and filled with CaC_2 and Ca_3P_2 are thrown into sea water. Water reacts with CaC_2 forming C_2H_2 and Ca_3P_2 forming PH_3.

$$CaC_2 + 2H_2O \longrightarrow Ca(OH)_2 + CH{\equiv}CH$$
$$Ca_3P_2 + 6H_2O \longrightarrow 3Ca(OH)_2 + 2PH_3$$

PH_3 further reacts with H_2O and burns with flame which further ignites C_2H_2 and flame in the form of torch is helpful in guiding the ways to missing ships.

114. (*b*) $N_2 + O_2 \longrightarrow NO$

115. (*d*) $2KNO_3 \xrightarrow{\Delta} 2KNO_2 + O_2$

116. (*c*) Since Si—H and Si—D bonds are not affected, hence hydrolysis takes place at equal rates.

117. (*c*) $CaC_2 \rightleftharpoons Ca^{2+} + C_2^{2-}$

119. (*b*) $Pb^{2+} + 2e^- \longrightarrow Pb^{2+}$

Stability of $Pb^{2+} > Pb^{4+}$, hence Pb^{4+} (PbO_2) is best oxidising agent.

123. (*d*) Due to inert-pair effect

$$Pb^{2+} > Pb^{4+}$$
$$Sn^{4+} > Sn^{2+}$$

124. (*d*) $SiCl_4 + 2Mg \longrightarrow 2MgCl_2 + Si$

125. (*d*) Orthophosphorous acid, H_3PO_3 :

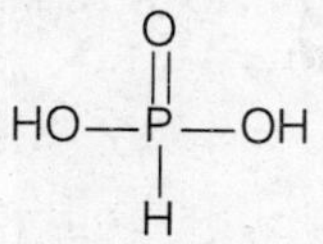

$H_3\overset{x}{P}O_3 = 3 + x + 3(-2) = 0$ or $x = +3$

Pyrophosphorous acid,

$H_4P_2O_5$:

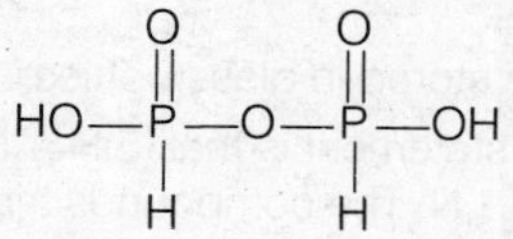

$$H_4\overset{x}{P}_2O_5 = 4 + 2x + 5(-2) = 0$$
$$4 + 2x - 10 = 0 \Rightarrow x = +3$$

126. (*a*) SiC — Covalent

127. (*b*) Due to vacant electrons

128. (*b*) Na_2SiO_3, $CaSiO_3$

129. (*a*) The structure of H_3PO_2 (hypophosphorous) acid is

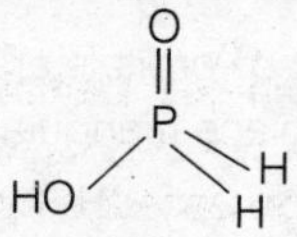

Due to the presence of two P—H bonds, H_3PO_2 acts a strong reducing agent. e.g.

$$4\overset{+1}{Ag}NO_3 + H_3\overset{+1}{P}O_2 + 2H_2O \longrightarrow 4\overset{0}{Ag}\downarrow + H_3\overset{+5}{P}O_4 + 4HNO_3$$

130. (*c*) Nitrogen monoxide react with dinitrogen tetraoxide at 250 K temperature forms blue solid.

$$2NO + N_2O_4 \xrightarrow{250\text{ K}} 2N_2O_3$$

N_2O_3 is acidic in nature. In N_2O_3, N has +3 oxidation state. Generally, oxides with higher oxidation states are more acidic than oxides having lower oxidation state. It is a blue solid because it strongly absorbs in the visible region to appear bright blue in colour.

131. (*b*) The correct increasing order of oxidation state of nitrogen for nitrogen oxides is

$$\overset{+1}{N}_2O < \overset{+2}{N}O < \overset{+3}{N}_2O_3 < \overset{+4}{N}O_2$$

- Oxidation state of N in N_2O is
$$2(x) - 2 = 0;\ x = +\frac{2}{2} = +1$$
- Oxidation state of N in NO is
$$x - 2 = 0;\ x = +2$$
- Oxidation state of N in N_2O_3 is
$$2x + 3(-2) = 0;\ x = \frac{6}{2} = 3$$
- Oxidation state of N in NO_2 is
$$x + 2(-2) = 0;\ x - 4 = 0;\ x = +4$$

132. (*a*) $K_4[Fe(CN)_6] + 6H_2SO_4 + 6H_2O \longrightarrow 2K_2SO_4 + FeSO_4 + 3(NH_4)_2SO_4 + 6CO$

134. (*b*)

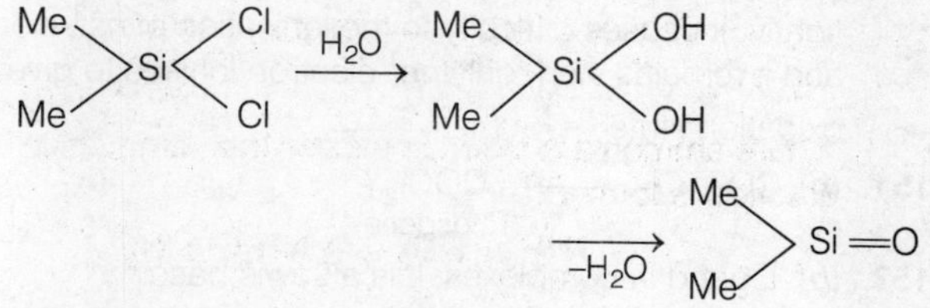

137. (*d*) $(CO + N_2)$

140. (*a*) $Sn + 2Cl_2 \longrightarrow SnCl_4$

143. (*d*) $PbCl_2, PbSO_4$ — Insoluble

CH_3COOH does not react

$Pb(NO_3)_2$ — Soluble

147. (*d*) Due to inert-pair effect stability of +2 oxidation state increases and that of +4 oxidation state decreases along a group 14.

148. (*d*) The thermal decomposition of given compounds is shown below

$$(NH_4)_2Cr_2O_7 \xrightarrow{\Delta} N_2 + 4H_2O + Cr_2O_3$$
$$NH_4NO_2 \xrightarrow{\Delta} N_2 + 2H_2O$$
$$(NH_4)_2SO_4 \xrightarrow{\Delta} 2NH_3 + H_2SO_4$$
$$Ba(N_3)_2 \longrightarrow Ba + 3N_2$$

Thus, only $(NH_4)_2SO_4$ does not gives N_2 on heating (It give NH_3). While rest of the given compounds gives N_2 on their thermal decomposition.

149. (*d*) Let us consider the structure of the phosphorus oxyacids,

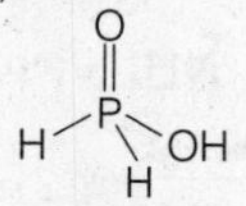

H_3PO_2
Hypophosphorus acid
(P—H bonds=2)

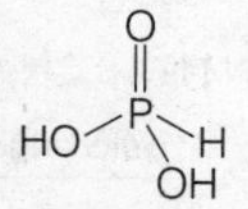

H_3PO_3
Orthophosphorus acid
(P—H bond=1)

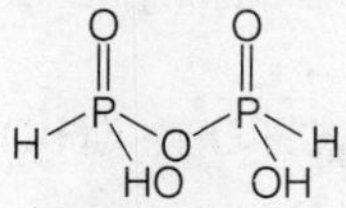

$H_4P_2O_5$
Pyrophosphorus acid
(P—H bonds=2)

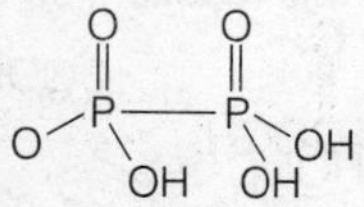

$H_4P_2O_6$
Hypophousphoric acid
(P—H bond=0)

150. (*b*) The stability order of + 3 and + 1 oxidation states of group 13 elements will be:

$B^{3+} > Al^{3+} > Ga^{3+} > In^{3+} >> Tl^{3+}$

(order of + 3 oxidation state)

$B^{+} << Al^{+} < Ga^{+} < In^{+} < Tl^{+}$

(order of + 1 oxidation state)

The presence of two oxidation states in *p*-block elements is due to the inert pair effect.

Because of the presence of poor shielding *d* and *f*-orbitals, as we move from Ga to Tl, effective nuclear charge of these elements increases so as to hold the valence ns^2 electrons tightly. It causes difficulty to the ionisation of ns^2-electrons and it remains inert, only np^1-electron ionises to give + 1 oxidation state.

151. (*b*) $CO + Cl_2 \longrightarrow COCl_2$ (Phosgene)

153. (*b*) Ligand in complexes, it is a Lewis base.

$Ni + 4CO \longrightarrow [Ni(CO)_4]$

154. (*d*)

(a) All electrons in N_2 are paired, thus it is diamagnetic, not paramagnetic.

(b) $N_2 + O_2 \underset{}{\overset{\text{Above } 2000°C}{\rightleftharpoons}} 2NO(g)$

(c) Liquid N_2 gas is used to create extremely cold temperature to distroy diseased tissues located outside the body.

(d) N_2 gas used as a diluent due to it's inert nature.

Hence, the correct option is (d).

155. (*a*) Complete reaction with change in hybridisation is as follows :

(a) $\underline{Xe}F_4 + SbF_5 \longrightarrow [XeF_3]^+[SbF_6]^-$
sp^3d^2 → sp^3d (Change in hybridisation)

(b) $H_2\underline{S}O_4 + 2NaCl \longrightarrow Na_2SO_4 + 2HCl$
sp^3 → sp^3 (No change in hybridisation)

(c) $H_3PO_2 \xrightarrow[\Delta]{\text{Disproportionation}} H_3PO_4 + PH_3$
sp^3 → sp^3 (No change in hybridisation)

(d) $\ddot{N}H_3 \xrightarrow{N^+} \overset{+}{N}H_4$
sp^3 → sp^3 (No change in hybridisation)

In the reaction (a), hybridisation of Xe in XeF_4 is sp^3d^2 converted into $[XeF_3]^+$ and hybridisation of Xe in $[XeF_3]^+$ is sp^3d. In this reaction, sp^3d^2-hybridisation change into sp^3d.

157. (*b*)

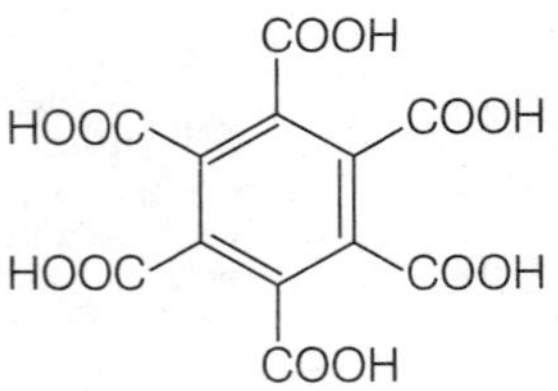

158. (*d*) $4NaOH + Si \longrightarrow Na_4SiO_4 + 2H_2$

159. (*b*)

		Charge
Two	Si^{4+}	+8
Seven	O^{2-}	−14
$Si_2O_7^{6-}$		

160. (*c*) The basic structural unit of feldspar, zeolites, mica and asbestos is $(SiO_4)^{4-}$. These all are silicates. All silicates involve two types of Si—O bonds.

(i) Terminal Si— O bonds in which oxygen is bonded to a silicon and not other atom.

(ii) Bridging Si—O—Si bonds in which oxygen is bonded to two silicon atoms.

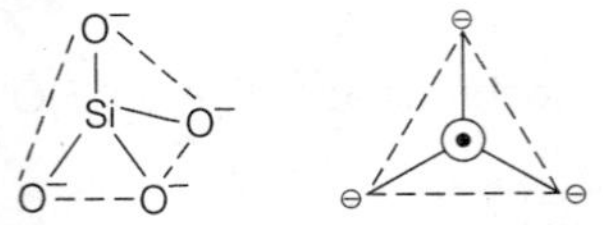

Tetrahedral structure of SiO_4^{2-} anion

In SiO_4^{4-} ion, each Si atom is bonded to four oxygen atoms tetrahedrally.

162. (*d*) HF can't be stored in glass bottles.

165. (*d*) The correct statement is that $(SiH_3)_3N$ is planar and less basic than $(CH_3)_3N$. The compounds trimethylamine $(CH_3)_3N$ and trisilylamine $(SiH_3)_3N$ have similar formulae, but have totally different structures.

In trimethylamine the arrangement of electrons is as follows :

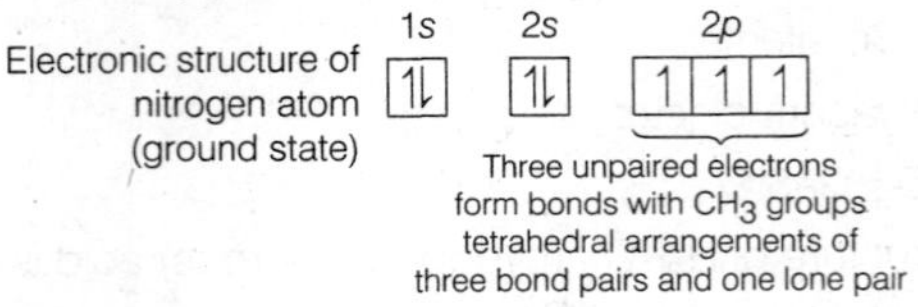

In trisilylamine, three sp^2 orbitals are used for σ-bonding, giving a plane triangular structure.

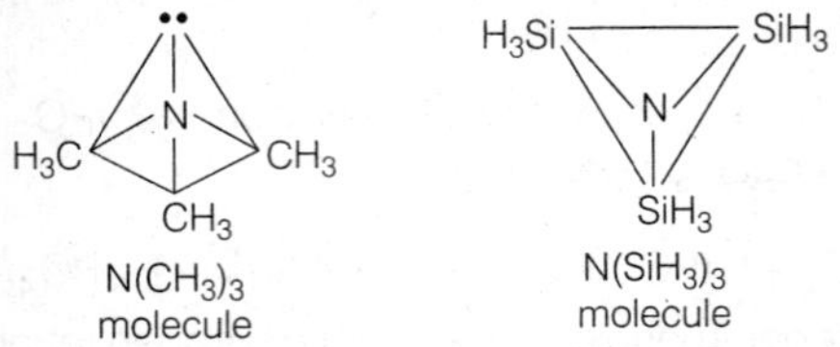

168. (*a*) $SnCl_2 + 2FeCl_3 \longrightarrow 2FeCl_2 + SnCl_4$

172. (*b*) Pb_3O_4 is a double oxide $PbO_2 \cdot 2PbO$.

PbO is not affected by HNO_3.

PbO changes to $Pb(NO_3)_2$.

176. (*b*)

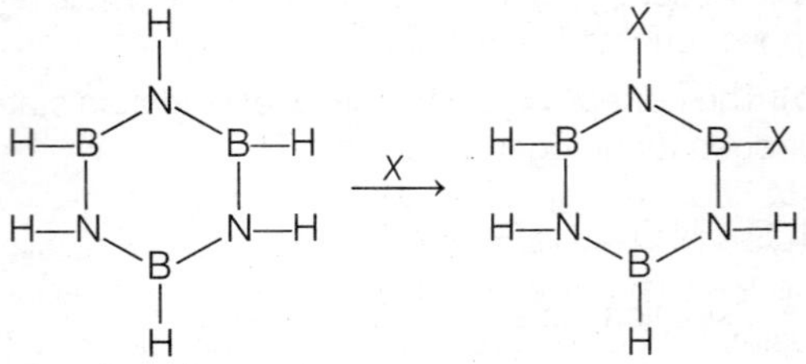

Borazine
(*A*)

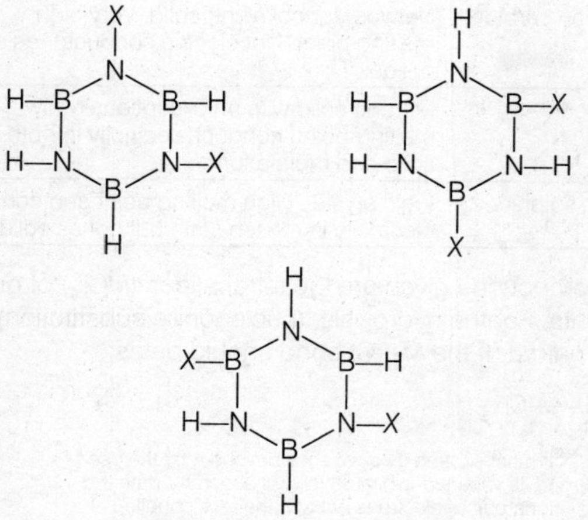

In all four different isomers of *B*.

177. (*b*) $4HNO_3 \longrightarrow 2H_2O + 2NO_2 + 3O_2$

178. (*c*) I. H_3PO_2 is monobasic acid forming NaH_2PO_2

II. H_2F_2 forms two series of salts KHF_2 and K_2F_2 Thus, dibasic acid.

III. $H_2C_2O_4$ is dibasic acid.

IV. CH_2NH_2 ← basic, $COOH$ ← acidic. Thus, amphoteric.

179. (*d*) $C{\equiv}N$, $N{\equiv}N$, $O \leftarrow N{=}O$

180. (*b*)

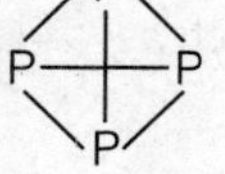

185. (*c*) $CHCl_3 + O_2 \longrightarrow \underset{\text{Phosgene}}{COCl_2} + HCl$

186. (*d*) Li–Mg, B–Si, Be–Al show diagonal relationship but Li and Na do not show diagonal relationship as both belongs to same group and not placed diagonally.

188. (*d*) $2KNO_3 \xrightarrow{\Delta} 2KNO_2 + O_2$

190. (*c*) $P_4O_6 + H_2O \longrightarrow H_3PO_3$ (ON of +3 in both)

$P_4O_{10} + H_2O \longrightarrow H_3PO_4$ (ON of +5 in both)

192. (*b*) NO and NO_2 have unpaired electrons, thus paramagnetic.

193. (*c*)

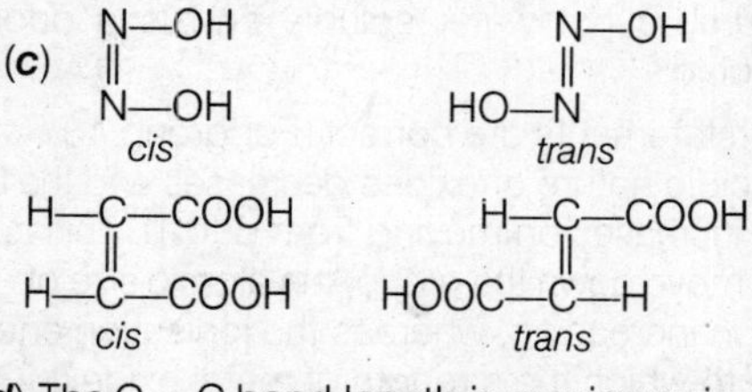

195. (*d*) The C—C bond length is maximum in diamond having value 154 pm. Here, each carbon atom undergoes sp^3-hybridisation and linked to four other carbon atoms by using hybridised orbitals in tetrahedral fashion. It has a rigid three-dimensional network of carbon atoms.

C—C bond length within the layers of graphite is 141.5 pm. In C_{60}, C—C distances between single and double bonds are 143.5 pm and 138.3 pm respectively.

200. (*a*) $NH_4NO_3 \xrightarrow{\Delta} N_2O + 2H_2O$

$NH_4NO_2 \xrightarrow{\Delta} N_2 + 2H_2O$

205. (*b*) $NH_4OH + Fe^{2+} \longrightarrow Fe^{3+} + N_3H$

206. (*d*) $N_3H \rightleftharpoons \underset{\text{Azide}}{N_3^{\ominus}} + H^+$

211. (*c*) Due to inert pair effect, group-13 elements (ns^2np^1) show + 3 and + 1 oxidation states in their compounds. Stability order of these oxidation states will be as,

+ 3 oxidation states

$$B^{3+} > Al^{3+} > Ga^{3+} > In^{3+} > Tl^{3+}$$

B^{3+} does not exist in free states. All B(III) compounds are covalent.

+ 1 oxidation states

$$B^+ < Al^+ < Ga^+ < In^+ < Tl^+$$

B^+ does not exist in ionic as well covalent compounds.

212. (*d*) $KO_2 \rightleftharpoons K^+ + O_2^-$

O_2^- (superoxide) is paramagnetic.

213. (*d*) Interstitial compounds are formed when a neutral atom with a small radius occupies in an interstitial hole (tetrahedral or octahedral voids) in a transition metal's hcp or ccp lattices (host lattice). Examples of small atoms (guest atom) are H, B, C and N.

Interstitial compounds are non-stoichiometric (Birtholide) in composition. They are very hard with very high melting points. The electrical conductivity of interstitial compounds are comparable to that of the pure metal. These are chemically unreactive in nature.

214. (*a*) Diborane (B_2H_6) reacts independently with O_2 and H_2O to produce B_2O_3 and H_3BO_3 respectively. Diborane is a colourless, highly toxic gas, having boiling point 180 K. Because of its inflammable nature, it catches fire spontaneously when exposed to air and burns in oxygen releasing an enormous amount of energy as:

$$B_2H_6 + 3O_2 \longrightarrow B_2O_3 + 3H_2O + 1976\,\text{kJ/mol}$$

It gets hydrolysed readily to give boric acid.

$$\underset{\text{Borane}}{B_2H_6} + 6H_2O \longrightarrow \underset{\text{Orthoboric acid}}{2H_3BO_3} + \underset{\text{Dihydrogen}}{6H_2\uparrow}$$

215. (*d*)

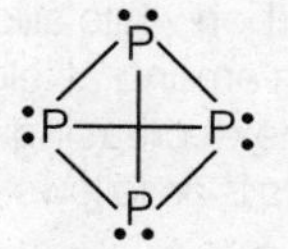

Each P-atom is sp^3 hybridised.

Thus, *p*-character is 75%.

216. (*b*) $NO + NO_2 \longrightarrow N_2O_3$

217. (*c*) $CaCN_2 + 3H_2O \longrightarrow CaCO_3 + 2NH_3$

218. (*d*) SO_2 is soluble in H_2O.

219. (*b*) $NH_3 + NaOCl \longrightarrow NaOH + NH_2Cl$

$NH_2Cl + NH_3 \longrightarrow NH_2NH_2 + HCl$

220. (*a*) $Ba(NO_2)_2 + H_2SO_4 \longrightarrow BaSO_4 + 2HNO_2$

221. (*a*) $PCl_3 + 3H_2O \longrightarrow H_3PO_3 + 3HCl$

224. (*b*) $Pb(NO_3)_2 \xrightarrow{\Delta} 2NO_2 + PbO$

227. (*b*) $2PCl_5 \rightleftharpoons \underset{\text{Octahedral}}{PCl_6^{\ominus}} + \underset{\text{Tetrahedral}}{PCl_4^{\oplus}}$

228. (*a*) Monobasic acid

229. (*d*) N_2O_5, HNO_3 have N-atom with +5 oxidation number.

231. (*d*) $\underset{\text{Most volatile}}{PH_3} < AsH_3 < \underset{\text{Least volatile due to H-bonding}}{NH_3}$

232. (*d*)

	Electrons
N_2O :	$14 + 8 = 22$
N_3^- :	$21 + 1 = 22$

234. (*a*) $PI_3 + 3H_2O \longrightarrow \underset{\text{Dibasic}}{H_3PO_3} + \underset{\text{Monobasic}}{HI}$

237. (*a*) 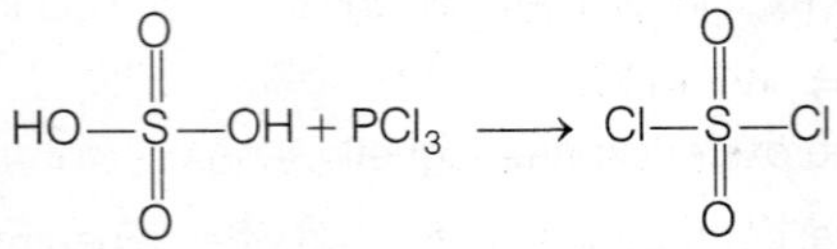

238. (*c*) 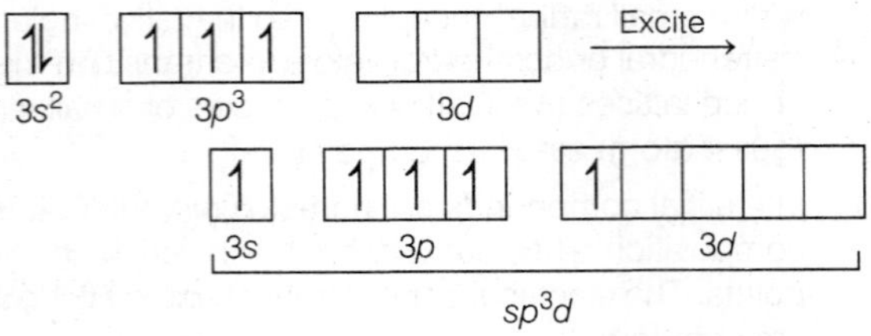

240. (*a*)

N_2O	+1
NO	+2
N_2O_3	+3
NO_2	+4
N_2O_5	+5

245. (*d*) The property of self-linking of atoms of an element through covalent bonds to form straight or branched chains and rings of different sizes is called catenation. Down the group, catenation tendency decreases due to decrease in element bond strength. Carbon (C), silicon (Si), germanium (Ge), tin (Sn), lead (Pb) are group-14 elements.

Catenation tendency is highest in carbon while silicon has second highest tendency of catenation among all elements of family due to higher bond energy. The decreasing tendency of catenation among group 14 elements is as follows:

$$C >> Si > Ge \approx Sn$$

However, Pb does not show catenation.

249. (*a*) '*X*' is carbon tetrachloride. It is a molecular solid. It melts at low temperature and is a bad conductor of electricity in both liquid and solid state.

Other options are explained as follows :

(1)	Silicon carbide	Network (or covalent) solid. Very high melting point. Not electric conductor as solid or liquid.
(2)	Mercury	Metallic solid with an exceptionally low melting point, conduct electricity in both solid and molten forms.
(3)	Zinc sulphide	Ionic crystal. High melting point and conduct electricity in molten state but not as solid.

251. (*b*) The compounds given are the tetrahalides (MCl_4) of group 14 elements. For the hydrolysis, (nucleophilic substitution) of MCl_4 the nature of the *M*—Cl bond should be as:

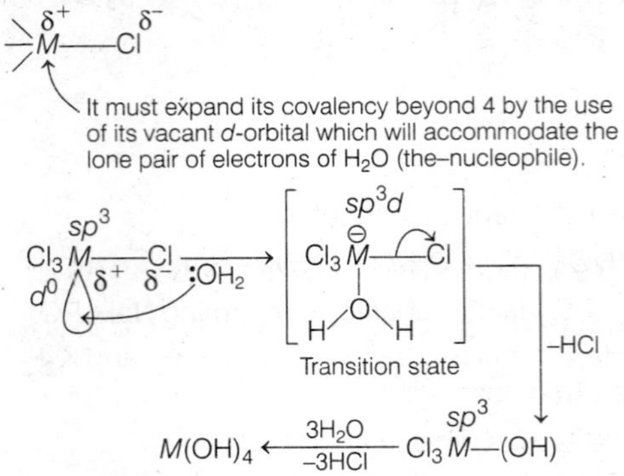

Here, *M* can be Si, Sn and Pb because they have vacant *nd*-orbital. But, carbon is a member of second period ($n = 2$, $l = 0, 1$), it does not have *d*-orbital ($l = 2$). So, CCl_4 will not be hydrolysed and correct option is (b).

252. (*d*) Silicones are polysiloxanes with general chemical formula, $[R_2SiO]_n$, where *R* is an organic group such as: $—CH_3$, $—C_2H_5$, $—C_6H_5$ etc.

Silicones have many useful properties:

(i) They repel water and form watertight seals.

(ii) They are heat resistant because of constancy of properties over a wide range of temperature (– 100° to 250° C).

(iii) Silicones are non-toxic.

(iv) Silicones are biocompatible because these do not support microbiological growth and these have high gas permeability at room temperature.

(v) They are resistant to O_2, O_3 and UV-radiation.

(vi) Silicones are formulated to be electrically insulative.

(vii) Silicone grease is typically used as a lubricant for brake components in automobiles, since it is stable at high temperature, is not water soluble and is a odourless viscous liquid.

265. (*a*) All the given statements are correct. For group 13 elements, the acidic nature of oxides decreases and the basic nature of oxides increases on moving from B to Tl. This is because as we move down the group, the atomic size of elements goes on increasing, whereas the ionisation energy decreases, due to which the strength of metal oxide (MO) bond goes on decreasing. T

hus, boron trioxide or boron oxide is acidic and reacts with basic oxides to give metal borates. Aluminium and gallium oxides are amphoteric while oxides of indium and thallium are basic in nature.

11

p-Block Elements II

Objective Questions Type I [Only one correct option]

In each of the questions below, four choices are given of which only one is correct.

1. Oil of vitriol is
(a) HNO_3 (b) HCl
(c) H_2SO_4 (d) H_3PO_4

2. Which of the following has peroxy linkage?
(a) $H_2S_2O_3$ (b) H_2SO_5
(c) $H_2S_2O_7$ (d) $H_2S_4O_6$

3. Which of the following can be used as dehydrating agents?
(a) Conc. H_2SO_4
(b) $POCl_3$
(c) P_2O_5
(d) All of these

4. The thermal stability of hydrides of oxygen family is in order
(a) $H_2Po < H_2Te < H_2Se < H_2S < H_2O$
(b) $H_2Po < H_2O < H_2Te < H_2Se < H_2S$
(c) $H_2S < H_2O < H_2Te < H_2Se < H_2Po$
(d) $H_2O < H_2S < H_2Te < H_2Se < H_2Po$

5. In case of oxygen family (Group 16).
(a) the tendency for catenation decreases markedly as we go down the group
(b) maximum coordination of oxygen is four due to lack of *d*-orbital but that of other elements is six due to presence of *d*-orbital
(c) the tendency to form multiple bonds with C, N and O decreases as going down the group from S to Te.
(d) All of the above are correct statements

6. Which does not have (S—S) bond?
(a) $H_2S_2O_3$ (b) $H_2S_2O_5$ (c) $H_2S_2O_4$ (d) S_3O_9

7. Which has maximum pK_a value?
(a) H_2O (b) H_2S
(c) H_2Se (d) H_2Te

8. Consider the following species
I. $[O_2]^{2-}$ II. $[CO]^+$ III. $[O_2]^+$
Among these species sigma bond alone is present in
(a) I, II, and III (b) II alone
(c) II and III (d) I alone

9. Which of the following species have undistorted octahedral structures?
I. SF_6 II. PF_6^-
III. SiF_6^{2-} IV. SeF_6
Select the correct answer using the codes given below.
(a) II, III and IV (b) I, III and IV
(c) I, II and III (d) I, II and IV

10. Consider the following compounds
I. Sulphur dioxide
II. Hydrogen peroxide
III. Ozone
Among these compounds, those which can act as bleaching agents would include
(a) I and III (b) II and III
(c) I and II (d) I, II and III

11. A considerable part of the harmful UV rays of the sun does not reach the surface of the earth. This is because high above the earth's atmosphere, there is a layer of
(a) O_3 (b) CO_2 (c) SO_2 (d) NO

12. Hypervalent ion is/are
(a) SO_3^{2-} (b) PO_4^{3-} (c) SO_4^{2-} (d) ClO_4^-

13. Which is/are true statements?
(a) Sulphur trioxide exists as cyclic trimer in solid state, S_3O_9
(b) Selenium trioxide solid is a cyclic tetramer, Se_4O_{12}

(c) TeO_3 is a solid with a network structure in which TeO_6 octahedra share all vertices
(d) All of the above are correct

14. Which is thermocromic?
(a) S_4N_4 (b) $B_3N_3H_6$
(c) S_8 (d) None of these

15. The best reducing agent of the following is
(a) H_2S (b) Cl^-
(c) SO_4^{2-} (d) O_3

16. All of the following have a tetrahedral shape except
(a) SO_4^{2-} (b) XeF_4
(c) ClO_4^- (d) XeO_4

17. The term 'thio' is used in the names of all of the following compounds except
(a) $Na_2S_2O_3$ (b) $NaCS_3$
(c) NaSCN (d) Na_2SO_3

18. Cold solution of barium nitrite on mixing with sulphuric acid produces
(a) $BaSO_4 + HNO_2$
(b) $BaSO_4 + HNO_3$
(c) $BaSO_4 + NO_2$
(d) $BaSO_4 + N_2 + O_2$

19. Which of the following product is formed by the reaction of sulphur dioxide with chlorine in presence of sunlight?
(a) SO_2Cl (b) SO_2Cl_2
(c) $SOCl_2$ (d) SO_3Cl

20. Which of the following bonds has the least energy?
(a) Se—Se (b) Te—Te
(c) S—S (d) O—O

21. Oxalic acid on heating with conc. H_2SO_4 produce
(a) H_2O and CO_2 (b) CO, CO_2 and H_2O
(c) CO_2 and H_2S (d) CO and CO_2

22. Which of the following is not a chalcogen?
(a) Se (b) O
(c) S (d) Na

23. Which of the following gas is insoluble in water?
(a) SO_2 (b) H_2 (c) NH_3 (d) CO_2

24. Which one of the following acid possesses oxidising, reducing and complex forming properties?
(a) HNO_3 (b) HCl
(c) H_2SO_4 (d) HNO_2

25. Na_2CO_3 reacts with SO_2 in alkaline medium to produce
(a) Na_2SO_4 (b) Na_2SO_3
(c) $NaHSO_4$ (d) $NaHSO_3$

26. The number of S—S bonds in sulphur trioxide trimer, (S_3O_9) is
(a) three (b) two
(c) one (d) zero

27. Sulphur dioxide levels in the atmosphere can be reduced by using
(a) catalytic converters in industry
(b) static electricity to attract it in factory chimneys
(c) more efficient car-engines
(d) low-sulphur fuels

28. What does Green Chemisry in terms of environment mean?
(a) Green house effect
(b) Reactions related to depletion of ozone layer
(c) Photosynthetic reactions in plants
(d) Reduction in the use and production of hazardous chemicals

29. Which one of the following compounds is not a protonic acid?
(a) $SO(OH)_2$ (b) $SO_2(OH)_2$
(c) $B(OH)_3$ (d) $Po(OH)_3$

30. Which of the following gas mixture is used by the divers inside the sea?
(a) O_2 + He (b) O_2 + Xe
(c) O_2 + Ar (d) $O_2 + N_2$

31. A group 16 element exists in the monoatomic state in metallic lattice. It also exists in two crystalline forms. The metal is
(a) sulphur (b) polonium
(c) selenium (d) tellurium

32. To a piece of charcoal sulphuric acid is added. Then
(a) there is no reaction
(b) water gas is formed
(c) SO_2 and CO_2 are evolved
(d) CO and SO_2 are evolved

33. The correct order of O—O bond length in O_2, H_2O_2 and O_3 is
(a) $H_2O_2 > O_3 > O_2$ (b) $O_2 > H_2O_2 > O_3$
(c) $O_3 > H_2O_2 > O_2$ (d) $O_2 > O_3 > H_2O_2$

34. Which of the following is used in vulcanization of rubber?
(a) SF_6 (b) CF_4 (c) Cl_2F_2 (d) C_2F_2

35. Aqueous solutions of hydrogen sulphide and sulphur dioxide when mixed together yield
(a) sulphur trioxide and water
(b) sulphur and sulphuric acid
(c) sulphur and water
(d) hydrogen preroxide and sulphur

36. Which of the following have highest melting points?
(a) *p*-block elements (b) *s*-block elements
(c) *d*-block elements (d) None of these

37. Electron affinity is positive, when
(a) O changes into O^-
(b) O^- changes into O^{2-}
(c) O changes into O^+
(d) electron affinity is always negative

38. Consider the following compounds
I. $Na_2S_2O_3$ II. $Na_2S_4O_6$ III. $CaOCl_2$
Among these compounds identify those that have different oxidation states for same type of atoms
(a) I and III (b) I and III
(c) I and II (d) I, II and III

39. Select the correct statement(s).
(a) O_3 molecule is resonance stabilised
(b) There is 3-centre, 4-electron π-bond system in O_3
(c) Ozone layer is being depleted by fluorocarbons
(d) All the above are correct statements

40. Alkali ozonides are
(a) paramagnetic in nature
(b) hydrolytically unstable and decompose to superoxides
(c) decreasing in stability as size of alkali metal decreases
(d) having all the above statements as correct

41. Among CH_4, NH_3 and H_2O, acidicity of H_2O is maximum because
(a) oxygen contains two lone pairs of electrons
(b) bond angle in H_2O is less than 109°28′ due to VSEPR
(c) oxygen is more electronegative than C or N
(d) H_2O is an associated liquid

42. An experiment involving absorption of oxygen and its quantitative estimation would involve use of
(a) caustic soda (b) pyrogallol
(c) conc sulphuric acid (d) turpentine oil

43. Estimation of ozone can be made quantitatively by
(a) decomposition into O_2 and absorption of O_2 into pyrogallol
(b) volumetric method using KI and titration of the liberated iodine using hypo solution
(c) oxidative ozonolysis method
(d) all methods given above

44. Oxidative ozonolysis of 2-butene in the presence of Zn or dimethyl sulphide forms
(a) CH_3CHO (b) CH_3COOH
(c) CO_2 (d) $(CH_3)_2CO$

45. The process of obtaining sulphur by the borehole method is called
(a) the Frasch process
(b) the Lablanc process
(c) the Calcaroni process
(d) the Mannheium process

46. When molten sulphur is suddenly cooled by pouring into water, it takes the form of
(a) milk of sulphur
(b) colloidal sulphur
(c) flower of sulphur
(d) plastic sulphur

47. $FeS + HCl \longrightarrow A + B(g)$
Gas B is passed into aqueous solution of C to form A. Select the correct statements based on the above facts.
(a) Colour of C changes from yellow to very light green
(b) Gas B turns lead acetate paper black
(c) A form deep blue colour with $K_3[Fe(CN)_6]$
(d) All the above facts are true

48. The number of ionisable hydrogens present in the product obtained from a reaction of phosphorus trichloride and phosphonic acid is **[JEE Mains 2021, March]**
(a) 3 (b) 0 (c) 2 (d) 1

49. H_2S precipitates aqueous $ZnCl_2$ solution in
(a) acidic medium (b) neutral medium
(c) Both (a) and (b) (d) None of these

50. In the presence of H_2O, SO_2 acts as
(a) an oxidising agent
(b) a reducing agent
(c) a hydrolysing agent
(d) a redox reagent

51. SO_2 behaves as a reducing agent when
(a) passed over hot CuO
(b) mixed with moist H_2S
(c) passed through acidified $KMnO_4$ solution
(d) passed through $FeSO_4$ solution

52. When an article is bleached by SO_2 it loses its colour. The colour can be restored by
(a) exposure to air (b) heating
(c) dilution (d) None of these

53. Total number of lone pair of electron in I_3^- ion is **[JEE Main 2018]**
(a) 3 (b) 6
(c) 9 (d) 1

54. The compound of sulphur used as a solvent in rubber industry is
(a) $SO_2(OH)Cl$ (b) SO_2 (c) SO_3 (d) S_2Cl_2

55. S—S bond is present in
(a) α-$(SO_3)_n$ (b) γ-(S_3O_9) (c) $H_2S_2O_3$ (d) $H_2S_2O_8$

56. The compound which has no reaction with $KMnO_4$ is
(a) perdisulphuric acid
(b) sulphurous acid
(c) hydrogen sulphide
(d) hydrogen peroxide

57. Which of the following can convert acidified $Cr_2O_7^{2-}$ to green?
(a) $SO_2/H_2SO_3/H_2SO_4$ (b) $SO_3/H_2SO_3/H_2S$
(c) $SO_3^{2-}/H_2S/Fe^{2+}$ (d) $S_2O_3^{2-}/SO_3/Fe^{3+}$

58. $Na_2S_2O_3$ is used in photography for fixing the negative. It removes the AgBr by
(a) complex formation $Na_3[Ag(S_2O_3)_2]$
(b) oxidation of AgBr to Br_2
(c) reduction of AgBr to Ag
(d) formation of double salt

59. Aqueous hypo solution on reaction with aqueous $AgNO_3$ gives
(a) yellow ppt changing to black
(b) white ppt changing to black
(c) orange ppt changing to blue
(d) no ppt

60. $S_2O_3^{2-}$ has
(a) S—S linkage (b) S—O linkage
(c) Both (a) and (b) (d) None of these

61. Of the following acids
I. Hypophosphorous acid
II. Oxalic acid
III. Glycine
(a) I, II are monobasic, III dibasic and amphoteric
(b) II monobasic, I dibasic acid, III amphoteric
(c) I monobasic, II dibasic, III amphoteric
(d) I, II dibasic, III amphoteric

62. The oxidation states of nitrogen in NO, NO_2, N_2O and NO_3^- are in the order of **[JEE main 2021, March]**
(a) $NO_3^- > NO_2 > NO > N_2O$
(b) $NO_2 > NO_3^- > NO > N_2O$
(c) $N_2O > NO_2 > NO > NO_3^-$
(d) $NO > NO_2 > N_2O > NO_3^-$

63. $HClO_4$, HNO_3 and HCl are all very strong acids in aqueous solution. In glacial acetic acid medium, their acid strength is such that
(a) $HClO_4 > HNO_3 > HCl$
(b) $HNO_3 > HClO_4 > HCl$
(c) $HCl > HClO_4 > HNO_3$
(d) $HCl > HClO_4 \sim HNO_3$

64. Bleaching of a fabric cloth is done using A and excess of chlorine is removed using B is
(a) $CaOCl_2, Na_2SO_3$ (b) $Na_2S_2O_3, CaOCl_2$
(c) $CaCl_2, Na_2S_2O_3$ (d) $CaOCl_2, Na_2S_2O_3$

65. In the following reactions, products (A) and (B), respectively, are
$NaOH + Cl_2 \rightarrow (A) +$ side products (hot and conc.)
$Ca(OH)_2 + Cl_2 \rightarrow (B) +$ side products (dry) **[JEE Main 2020]**
(a) $NaClO_3$ and $Ca(OCl)_2$ (b) $NaClO_3$ and $Ca(ClO_3)_2$
(c) NaOCl and $Ca(OCl)_2$ (d) NaOCl and $Ca(ClO_3)_2$

66. Which one of the following is the weakest base as per the Bronsted concept?
(a) $[ClO_4]^-$ (b) $[ClO_3]^-$ (c) $[ClO_2]^-$ (d) $[ClO]^-$

67. Which one of the following is not a true "per acid"?
(a) $HClO_4$ (b) H_2SO_5 (c) $H_2S_2O_8$ (d) H_3PO_5

68. Which is/are true statement(s)?
(a) Basic nature of X^- is in order $F^- > Cl^- > Br^- > I^-$
(b) HI is strongest acid of HF, HCl, HBr and HI
(c) The ionic character of M—X bond decreases in the order M—F > M—Cl > M—Br > M—I
(d) All the above are correct statements

69. The products obtained when chlorine gas reacts with cold and dilute aqueous NaOH are **[JEE Main 2017]**
(a) ClO^- and ClO_3^- (b) ClO_2^- and ClO_3^-
(c) Cl^- and ClO^- (d) Cl^- and ClO_2^-

70. Select the incorrect statement.
(a) ClO_2 and Cl_2O are used as bleaching agents for paper pulp and textiles
(b) OCl^- (hypohalites) salts are used as detergent
(c) OCl^- disproportionates in alkaline medium
(d) BrO_3^- is oxidised to Br_2 by Br^- in acidic medium

71. Consider the following boron halides
I. BF_3 II. BCl_3
II. BBr_3 IV. BI_3
The Lewis acid characters of these halides are such that
(a) I < II < III < IV (b) I < III < II < IV
(c) IV < III < II < I (d) IV < II < III < I

72. Which of the following compounds possesses Lewis acid character?
I. BF_3 II. SiF_4 III. PF_5
Select the correct answer using the codes given below.
Codes
(a) I alone (b) I, II and III
(c) II and III (d) I and III

73. Which of the underlined atoms in oxyacids have sp^3-hybridised atoms?
(a) $H\underline{Cl}O_4, H_2\underline{S}O_4, H\underline{N}O_2$ (b) $H_2\underline{S}O_4, H_3\underline{P}O_4, H\underline{N}O_3$
(c) $H\underline{Cl}O_4, H_2\underline{S}O_4, H_2\underline{S}O_5$ (d) $H\underline{Cl}O_4, H\underline{N}O_3, H\underline{Cl}O_3$

74. Which one of the following arrangements does not truly represent the property indicated against it?
(a) $Br_2 < Cl_2 < F_2$: Oxidising power
(b) Br < Cl < F : Electronegativity
(c) Br < F < Cl : Electron affinity
(d) $Br_2 < Cl_2 < F_2$: Bond energy

75. The mixture of concentrated HCl and HNO_3 made in 3 : 1 ratio contains
(a) ClO_2 (b) NOCl
(c) NCl_3 (d) N_2O_4

76. The formula for calcium chlorite is
(a) $Ca(ClO_4)_2$ (b) $Ca(ClO_3)_2$
(c) $CaClO_2$ (d) $Ca(ClO_2)_2$

77. Which one will liberate Br_2 from KBr?
(a) I_2 (b) SO_2 (c) HI (d) Cl_2

78. An important product in the ozone depletion by chlorofluorocarbons is
(a) Cl_2 (b) OCl
(c) F_2 (d) O_2F_2

79. Which one is the strongest bond?
(a) Br—F (b) F—F
(c) Cl—F (d) Br—Cl

80. Which one of the following oxoacids of chlorine is the least oxidising in nature?
(a) $HClO$ (b) $HClO_2$
(c) $HClO_3$ (d) $HClO_4$

81. Good reducing nature of H_3PO_2 is attributed to the presence of
(a) two P— H bonds (b) one P— H bond
(c) two P— OH bonds (d) one P — OH bond
[JEE Main 2019, Jan.]

82. Which of the following will displace the halogen from the solution of the halide?
(a) Br_2 added to NaI (b) Br_2 added to NaCl
(c) Cl_2 added to KCl (d) Cl_2 added to NaF

83. The high oxidising power of fluorine is due to
(a) high electron affinity
(b) high heat of dissociation and low heat of hydration
(c) low heat of dissociation and high heat of hydration
(d) high heat of dissociation and high heat of hydration

84. When Cl_2 is passed through cold dil. NaOH, the products are
(a) NaCl, NaOCl and H_2O
(b) NaCl, $NaClO_2$ and H_2O
(c) NaCl, $NaClO_3$ and H_2O
(d) NaCl, $NaClO_4$ and H_2O

85. Which is the strongest oxidising agent out of the following?
(a) I_2 (b) Cl_2 (c) Br_2 (d) F_2

86. Chlorine on reaction with hot and oncentrated sodium hydroxide gives **[JEE Main 2019, Jan.]**
(a) Cl^- and ClO^- (b) Cl^- and ClO_3^-
(c) ClO_3^- and ClO_2^- (d) Cl^- and ClO_2^-

87. Select the correct statement(s) regarding behaviour of HF as non-aqueous solvent.
(a) HCl behaves as an acid and HF as a base
(b) $HClO_4$ behaves as a base and HF as an acid
(c) HNO_3 and H_2SO_4 behave as base and HF as an acid
(d) All of the above are correct statements

88. Acid strength of oxoacids of chlorine is in order
(a) $HOCl < HClO_2 < HClO_3 < HClO_4$
(b) $HClO_4 < HClO_3 < HClO_2 < HOCl$
(c) $HClO_3 < HClO_4 < HClO_2 < HOCl$
(d) $HClO_2 < HClO_3 < HOCl < HClO_4$

89. Acid strength of oxoacids of halogen is in order
(a) HOF > HOCl > HOBr > HOI
(b) HOI > HOBr > HOCl > HOF
(c) HOI > HOCl > HOBr > HOF
(d) HOCl > HOBr > HOI > HOF

90. Which has peroxy linkage?
(a) Perchloric acid (b) Hypochloro acid
(c) Para perchloric acid (d) None of these

91. SO_2 can reduce
(a) $HClO_3$ to HCl (b) $Cr_2O_7^{2-}/H^+$ to Cr^{3+}
(c) MnO_4^-/H^+ to Mn^{2+} (d) All of these

92. Bleaching powder is disinfectant for purification of water when water born germs are killed. But disinfectant activity is destroyed. It is due to its disproportionation into
(a) $CaCl_2$ and Cl_2
(b) $CaCl_2$ and $Ca(ClO_3)_2$
(c) CaO and Cl_2
(d) CaO, Cl_2 and $CaCl_2$

93. 10 g of bleaching powder on reaction with KI required 100 mL of 1 N hypo. Thus, % of pure bleaching powder is
(a) 100% (b) 80% (c) 63.5% (d) 35.5%

94. CH_3CH_2OH on reaction with bleaching powder forms
(a) $CHCl_3$ (b) CCl_3CHO
(c) CH_2ClCHO (d) CCl_4

95. The correct statement about ICl_5 and ICl_4^- is **[JEE Main 2019, April]**
(a) ICl_5 is square pyramidal and ICl_4^- is tetrahedral
(b) ICl_5 is square pyramidal and ICl_4^- is square planar
(c) Both are isostructural
(d) ICl_5 is trigonal bipyramidal and ICl_4^- is tetrahedral

96. Cl_2O, Br_2O, I_2O have positive value of ΔG (free energy) indicating that
(a) these oxides are stable
(b) these oxides are unstable and changes to X_2 and O_2
(c) these disproportionate into X^- and XO^-
(d) these oxides can form interhalogen compounds

97. Select the correct statement(s).
(a) Cl_2O and ClO_2 are used as bleaching agents and as germicides
(b) I_2O_5 is used in the quantitative estimation of CO
(c) Bond angle XOX varies in the order
FOF < ClOCl < BrOBr
(d) All of the above are correct statements

98. The bond angle in OF_2 out of OF_2, Cl_2O, Br_2O is minimum. It is because in case of OF_2
(a) electrons are nearer to fluorine due to high electronegativity of F compared to Cl to Br
(b) lone pair-lone pair repulsion decreases bond angle
(c) Both (a) and (b) are correct
(d) None of the above is correct

99. ClO_2 is the anhydride of
(a) HOCl (b) $HClO_2$
(c) $HClO_3$ (d) $HClO_2$ and $HClO_3$

100. ClO_3 is the mixed anhydride of
(a) $HClO_2$ and $HClO_3$ (b) $HClO_3$ and $HClO_4$
(c) $HClO_2$ and $HClO_4$ (d) $HClO_2$ and $HClO_3$

101. Chlorine dioxide
(a) is paramagnetic in nature
(b) has odd-electron bond
(c) is stable
(d) has all the above properties true

102. Select the incorrect statement(s).
(a) Cl_2O_6 is diamagnetic in solid state
(b) ClO_3 is paramagnetic and exists in liquid state
(c) Cl_2O_6 is anhydride of $HClO_3$
(d) ClO_3 forms dimer due to unpaired electron

103. Cl_2 gas is passed into aqueous solution of KBr and KI and $CHCl_3$ added. It is observed that there is
(a) violet colour in $CHCl_3$ layer
(b) yellow colour in $CHCl_3$ layer
(c) yellow colour in aqueous layer
(d) violet colour in $CHCl_3$ layer

104. End-product of the hydrolysis of XeF_6 is
(a) XeF_4O (b) XeF_2O_2
(c) XeO_3 (d) XeO_3^-

105. When water is allowed to freeze in the presence of Ar, Kr or Xe under pressure then
(a) atoms of noble gas (G) trapped in the crystal lattice of ice giving clathrates corresponding to the composition $8G \cdot 26H_2O$
(b) these are called noble gas hydrates
(c) Both (a) and (b) are correct
(d) None of the above is correct

106. Select the correct statements.
(a) Helium has the lowest melting point and boiling point
(b) Helium can diffuse through rubber, PVC and even glass
(c) Ar, Kr and Xe form clathrate
(d) All the above are correct statements

107. Consider the following transformations

I. $XeF_6 + NaF \longrightarrow Na^+[XeF_7]^-$

II. $2PCl_5(s) \longrightarrow [PCl_4]^+ [PCl_6]^-$

III. $[Al(H_2O)_6]^{3+} + H_2O \rightarrow [Al(H_2O)_5OH]^{2+} + H_3O^+$

Possible transformations are
(a) I, II, III (b) I, III
(c) I, II (d) II, III

108. HF has highest boiling point among hydrogen halides, because it has [JEE Main 2019, April]
(a) lowest ionic character
(b) strongest van der Waals' interactions
(c) strongest hydrogen bonding
(d) lowest dissociation enthalpy

109. The type of hybridisation and number of lone pair(s) of electrons of Xe in $XeOF_4$, respectively, are [JEE Main 2019, Jan.]
(a) sp^3d^2 and 1 (b) sp^3d and 2
(c) sp^3d and 1 (d) sp^3d^2 and 2

110. Neon lamps are used in botanical gardens and in green houses as they
(a) provides oxygen
(b) provide better light
(c) stimulate growth of plants
(d) None of the above

111. Which of the following gas mixture is used by the divers inside the sea?
(a) O_2 + He (b) O_2 + Xe
(c) O_2 + Ar (d) $O_2 + N_2$

112. The gas not absorbed by coconut charcoal is
(a) He (b) Ne (c) Ar (d) Kr

113. When the first electron gain enthalpy ($\Delta_{eg} H$) of oxygen is – 141 kJ / mol, its second electron gain enthalpy is [JEE Main 2019, Jan.]
(a) a positive value
(b) a more negative value than the first
(c) almost the same as that of the first
(d) negative, but less negative than the first

114. The oxoacid of sulphur that does not contain bond between sulphur atoms is [JEE Main 2019, April]
(a) $H_2S_2O_3$ (b) $H_2S_2O_4$
(c) $H_2S_2O_7$ (d) $H_2S_4O_6$

115. XeF_2 forms .... with AsF_5.
(a) XeF^+ cation and AsF_4^+
(b) XeF_2^- anion and AsF_4^+
(c) AsF_4^+ cation and AsF_4^-
(d) XeF^+ cation and AsF_6^- anion

116. Molecule(s) possessing two-centre two electron bonds and three centre-four electron bonds would include
(a) B_2H_6 and SiF_4 (b) XeF_6 and BF_6
(c) B_2H_6 and XeF_6 (d) B_2H_6 alone

117. Hydrates of helium and neon have not been prepared because of
(a) low polarisability
(b) small size
(c) low boiling point
(d) All of these

118. Thermal stability of hydrates of group 18 elements
(a) increases down the group
(b) decreases down the group
(c) remains unchanged
(d) first increases up to Ar and then decreases

119. Which have distorted geometry based on VSEPR model?
(a) XeF_2, XeF_4, XeO_3 (b) $XeOF_2, XeO_3, XeF_2$
(c) NH_3, SO_2, H_2O (d) All of these

120. Second most abundant element in the universe (after hydrogen) is
(a) Al (b) Fe
(c) He (d) Ne

121. Helium accumulates in the earth's crust through
(a) α-decay of radioactive element
(b) thermonuclear reactions
(c) β-decay of radioactive element
(d) γ-decay of radioactive element

122. Xenon fluorides acts as fluoride donor with
(a) AsF_5 (b) BF_3
(c) HF (d) All of these

123. Xenon fluoride act as fluoride acceptor with
(a) RbF (b) CsF
(c) Both (a) and (b) (d) None of these

124. XeF_6 is conducting in the presence of
(a) BF_3 (b) RbF
(c) HF (d) All of these

125. Which is most basic fluoride?
(a) XeF_6
(b) XeF_2
(c) XeF_4
(d) None is basic, all are acids

126. Basic character of fluorides increases in the order
(a) $XeF_6 < XeF_4 < XeF_2$ (b) $XeF_2 < XeF_4 < XeF_6$
(c) $XeF_2 = XeF_4 < XeF_6$ (d) $XeF_2 > XeF_4 < XeF_6$

127. Which is the best fluorinating agent?
(a) XeF_2 (b) XeF_4 (c) XeF_6 (d) XeO_2F_2

Objective Questions Type II [One or more than one correct option(s)]

In each of the questions below, four choices are given, of which one or more than one are correct.

1. Which are correct statements?
(a) All halogens form oxoacids
(b) All halogens show −1, +1, +3, +5, +7 oxidation states
(c) Hydrofluoric acid forms KHF_2 and K_2F_2 and attacks glass
(d) Oxidising power is in order $F_2 > Cl_2 > Br_2 > I_2$

2. Select the correct statement(s).
(a) ClO_2 and Cl_2O are used as bleaching agents for paper pulp and textiles
(b) OCl^- salts are used as detergents
(c) OCl^- disproportionates in alkaline medium
(d) BrO_3^- is oxidised to Br_2 by Br^- in acidic medium

3. In the structure of
(a) IF_2^+, bond angle is smaller than the tetrahedral angle because of lone pair-lone pair repulsion
(b) IF_4^+, there is sp^3 hybridisation with bond angle of 109°28′
(c) IF_6^+, there are six bonding electrons and no lone pairs.
(d) IF_4^+, two F-atoms one at equatorial positions and two are inclined at an angle less than 120° due to lone pair-bond pair repulsion

4. In the conversion of Br^- to BrO_2^-
(a) there is anodic oxidation in basic solution
(b) equivalent mass of Br^- is 20 (atomic weight of Br = 80)
(c) there is anodic oxidation in acidic medium
(d) there is cathodic reduction in basic solution

5. In the conversion of BrO_3^- to BrO_4^-
(a) there is no change in oxidation number
(b) reduction takes place in basic solution
(c) reaction also takes place by XeF_2
(d) equivalent mass of BrO_3^- is one-half of ionic mass

6. Select the correct statement(s).
(a) Chile saltpetre ($NaNO_3$) is a main source of I_2
(b) IO_3^- is reduced to I^- and which in turn oxidised to I_2 by IO_3^- in acidic medium
(c) Anhydrous HF is a non-conductor of electricity
(d) F_2 is obtained by electrolysis of molten KHF_2

7. Select the correct statement(s).
(a) Colours of the halogens (F_2, Cl_2, Br_2, I_2) in the gas phase are complimentary colours.
(b) Colour is due to transition of an electron from the highest occupied π* molecular orbital to the lowest unoccupied σ* molecular orbital
(c) ClO_2 is paramagnetic due to unpaired electrons
(d) ClO_2 dimerises to Cl_2O_4 as NO_2 dimerises to N_2O_4

8. Base on the $E°$ values gives

$$\frac{1}{2}F_2 + e^- \longrightarrow F^- \quad E° = 2.87\ V$$
$$\frac{1}{2}Cl_2 + e^- \longrightarrow Cl^- \quad E° = 1.40\ V$$
$$\frac{1}{2}Br_2 + e^- \longrightarrow Br^- \quad E° = 1.09\ V$$
$$\frac{1}{2}I_2 + e^- \longrightarrow I^- \quad E° = 0.62\ V$$

(a) Oxidising power of F_2 is maximum
(b) Oxidising power of I_2 is maximum
(c) Oxidising power is in order $F_2 > Cl_2 > Br_2 > I_2$
(d) Oxidising power is in order $F_2 < Cl_2 < Br_2 < I_2$

9. $CHCl_3$ and H_2O form two separate immiscible layers Br_2 (orange) and I_2 (violet) are soluble in organic layer due to a greater extent. In test tube A ($KI + CHCl_3 + H_2O$) and test tube B ($KI + KBr + CHCl_3 + H_2O$) Cl_2 gas is passed then (based on $E°$ values in Q. 8)
(a) organic layer in A appear violet
(b) organic layer in B appear orange
(c) organic layer in B appear violet
(d) organic layer in B first appears violet then orange

10. Select the correct statement(s).
(a) pK_a value of HI (strongest halogen acid) is most negative
(b) high H—F bond strength makes H—F a weak acid in dilute aqueous solution
(c) Halogen forms clatharates by freezing solution in water
(d) K_a values of HX is in order HF < HCl < HBr < HI

11. Select the correct statement(s).
(a) The noble gases are present to the extent of about 1% in the earth's atmosphere, the chief component being argon
(b) Helium is the second most abundant element in the universe after hydrogen
(c) There are two stable isotopes of helium ^3_2He, ^4_2He
(d) ^4_2He is formed by thermonuclear fusion reaction in stars $4\,^1_1H \longrightarrow \,^4_2He + 2\,_1e^0$

12. With respect to hypochlorite, chlorate and perchlorate ions, choose the correct statement(s). **[JEE Advanced 2020]**
(a) The hypochlorite ion is the strongest conjugate base.
(b) The molecular shape of only chlorate ion is influenced by the lone pair of electrons of Cl.
(c) The hypochlorite and chlorate ions disproportionate to give rise to identical set of ions.
(d) The hypochlorite ion oxidises the sulphite ion.

13. Helium is used
(a) as a refrigerant (in liquid form) in low-temperature physics
(b) as a substituent for nitrogen in the breathing gas for deep-sea divers
(c) in radiation therapy
(d) in fluorescent tubes

14. Select the correct statement(s) about XeF_4.
(a) They are thermodynamically stable
(b) Xe—F bond energy is very high
(c) They are endothermic compounds
(d) They are exothermic compounds

15. The correct statement(s) about O_3 is (are)
(a) O—O bond length are equal
(b) thermal decomposition of O_3 is endothermic
(c) O_3 is diamagnetic in nature
(d) O_3 has a bent structure

16. The correct statement(s) about the oxoacids, $HClO_4$ and HClO, is (are) **[JEE Advanced 2017]**
(a) The central atom in both $HClO_4$ and HClO is sp^3-hybridised
(b) $HClO_4$ is formed in the reaction between Cl_2 and H_2O
(c) The conjugate base of $HClO_4$ is weaker base than H_2O
(d) $HClO_4$ is more acidic than HClO because of the resonance stabilisation of its anion

17. The colour of the X_2 molecules of group 17 elements changes gradually from yellow to violet down the group. This is due to **[JEE Advanced 2017]**
(a) decrease in $\pi^* - \sigma^*$ gap down the group
(b) decrease in ionisation energy down the group
(c) the physical state of X_2 at room temperature changes from gas to solid down the group
(d) decreases in HOMO-LUMO gap down the group

Numerical Value Questions

All these questions have a Numerical value as their answer, solve the questions and write your answer.

1. SO_2 turns lime water milky, 3.2 g of SO_2 gives milkyness ....

2. Number of electrons forming bond between Cl and O in ClO_2 is ....

3. How many of the following have Cl atom in rp^3 hybridised state ? $ClO_2, Cl_2O, Cl_2O_2, Cl_2O_5, ClO_4^-$

4. At 143 K, the reaction of XeF_2 with O_3F_2 produce a xenon compound Y. The total number of lone pair(s) of electrons present on the whole molecule of X is .... **[JEE Advanced 2019]**

5. The amount of water produced (in g) in the oxidation of 1 mole of rhombic sulphur by conc. HNO_3 to a compound with the highest oxidation state of sulphur is .... (Given data : Molar mass of water $= 18 \text{ g mol}^{-1}$).

6. Chlorine reacts with hot and concentrated NaOH and produces compounds (X) and (Y). Compound (X) gives white precipitate with silver nitrate solution. The averate bond order between Cl and O atoms in (Y) is .... **[JEE Main 2020]**

7. The reaction of white phosphorus on boiling with alkali in inert atmosphere resulted in the formation of product '*A*'. The reaction 1 mole of '*A*' with excess of $AgNO_3$ in aqueous medium gives ……… mol(s) of Ag. (Round off to the Nearest Integer). **[JEE Main 2021, March]**

8. A xenon compound '*A*' upon partial hydrolysis gives XeO_2F_2. The number of lone pair of electrons present in compound *A* is ……… (Round off to the Nearest integer). **[JEE Main 2021, March]**

Comprehension Based Questions

In these questions, a passage has been given followed by questions based on it. You have to answer the questions based on the passage given.

***Passage* 1** Peroxydisulphuric acid and its salts are powerful oxidising agents, thus can be used to estimate reducing agents and also to study the kinetics of the reaction.

Answer the following questions.

1. Peroxydisulphuric acid
   (a) is also called Marshall's acid
   (b) has two peroxy linkages
   (c) liberates I_2 with KI in a fast reaction
   (d) has oxidation number of sulphur as +7

2. As compared to H_2SO_5, $H_2S_2O_8$
   (a) has two peroxy linkage
   (b) liberates I_2 from KI slowly and thus kinetics of oxidation of KI by $S_2O_8^{2-}$ can be studied
   (c) has different oxidation number
   (d) reacts with $KMnO_4$

***Passage* 2** Two acids have been derived from H_2O_2 by replacing H by (SO_2OH) group. Both the acids have one peroxy linkage H—O—O—H

$$\underset{H_2SO_5}{H—O—O—SO_2—OH}$$

$$\underset{H_2S_2O_8}{HO—SO_2—O—O—SO_2—OH}$$

Based on the above study, answer the following questions.

1. Which is called Marshall's acid and which is called Caro's acid?
   (a) H_2SO_5, $H_2S_2O_8$
   (b) $H_2S_2O_8$, H_2SO_5
   (c) H_2SO_5, $H_2S_2O_7$
   (d) $H_2S_2O_3$, H_2SO_5

2. $H_2S_2O_8$ is obtained at anode by the electrolysis of ……
   (a) H_2SO_3
   (b) $H_2S_2O_4$
   (c) H_2SO_4
   (d) H_2O_2 and H_2SO_4

3. Which reacts with $KMnO_4$?
   (a) H_2SO_3 (b) H_2SO_5
   (c) H_2SO_4 (d) $H_2S_2O_8$

***Passage* 3** Sodium thiosulphate is the laboratory reagent used in iodometric and iodimetric titration. This also finds used in photography.

Based on the above passage, answer the following questions.

1. If I_2 is the titre in a titration *A* and I_2 is formed *in situ* in a titration *B*, then these are respectively
   (a) iodometric, iodimetric
   (b) iodimetric, iodometric
   (c) both iodimetric
   (d) both iodometric

2. Sodium thiosulphate is called …… (I) and is used as …… (II) and removes unreacted light sensitive AgBr by forming the complex …… (III)

	I	II	III
(a)	hypo	developer	$[AgS_2O_3]^-$
(b)	hypo	fixer	$[Ag(S_2O_3)_2]^{3-}$
(c)	hypo	fixer	$[Ag_2(S_2O_3)]$
(d)	None of the above is correct		

***Passage* 4** When metallic copper is heated with conc. sulphuric acid, various types of products are formed depending on standard reduction potential.

Answer the following questions based on the above study.

1. Which reaction is possible?
   (a) $Cu + 2H^+ \longrightarrow Cu^{2+} + H_2$
   (b) $Cu^{2+} + H_2 \longrightarrow Cu + 2H^+$
   (c) Both (a) and (b)
   (d) None of the above

2. When Cu reacts with conc. H_2SO_4
   (a) Cu is oxidised to Cu^{2+}
   (b) SO_4^{2-} is reduced to SO_2
   (c) Both of the above reactions take place
   (d) None of the above reaction takes place

3. There is also formation of CuS which is formed by
   (a) $SO_4^{2-} + 8H^+ + 8e^- \longrightarrow S^{2-} + H_2O$
   (b) $SO_2 + 6H^+ + 6e^- \longrightarrow H_2S + 2H_2O$
   (c) Both (a) and (b)
   (d) None of the above

Passage 5 This question concerns the elements of Group 17 — fluorine, chlorine, bromine and iodine.

When sodium chloride is treated with concentrated sulphuric acid, a colourless gas, *X*, which fumes in moist air, is formed. When sodium iodide is treated in the same way a coloured vapour, *Y*, is product. If 90% phosphoric(v) acid is used instead of sulphuric acid, a colourless gas is produced in each reaction.

1. Gases *X* and *Y* are respectively
(a) Cl_2, I_2
(b) HCl, I_2
(c) HCl, HI
(d) HClO, I_2

2. With 90% phosphoric acid (H_3PO_4), colourless gases formed are
(a) HCl, HI (b) Cl_2, I_2
(c) HCl, I_2 (d) Cl_2, HI

3. Behaviour of H_2SO_4 and H_3PO_4 is different towards NaI because
(a) H_2SO_4 is stronger acid than H_3PO_4
(b) H_2SO_4 is a strong oxidising agent and oxidises colourless gas to coloured vapour *Y*
(c) H_3PO_4 is tribasic acid
(d) H_2SO_4 is a dibasic acid

Passage 6 Water pollution can be by dissolved gases. Bad smell of water is due to H_2S and can be removed by treatment with bleaching powder.

$$\underset{\text{Bleaching powder}}{CaOCl_2} + H_2O \longrightarrow Ca(OH)_2(aq) + Cl_2(aq)$$

$$H_2S(aq) + Cl_2(aq) \longrightarrow 2HCl(aq) + S(s)$$

Based on the above treatment answer the following questions.

1. If H_2S content of contaminated water is 22 ppm by mass, Cl_2 required to remove all the H_2S from 200 gallons of water (1 gallon = 3.785 L) is
(a) 30.00 g (b) 71.00 g
(c) 17.5 g (d) 35.00 g

2. 25.0 L of a natural gas measured at 25°C and 740 mm Hg is bubbled through $Pb^{2+}(aq)$, a precipitate weighing 0.3938 g is obtained. ‰(ppt—parts per thousand L) of H_2S by volume in the natural gas is, (Pb = 206)
(a) 0.225% (b) 2.25%
(c) 5.25% (d) 0.525%

Passage 7 XeO_3 is an oxidising agent and this can be used to estimate reducing agents.

$$\text{I. } XeO_3 + 6H^+ + 9I^- \longrightarrow Xe + 3H_2O + 3I_3^-$$

$$\text{II. } XeO_3 + 6H^+ + 6Fe^{2+} \longrightarrow Xe + 3H_2O + 6Fe^{3+}$$

Answer the following questions.

1. Reaction can be studied by measuring pressure of the reaction mixture with time variation can be of the type

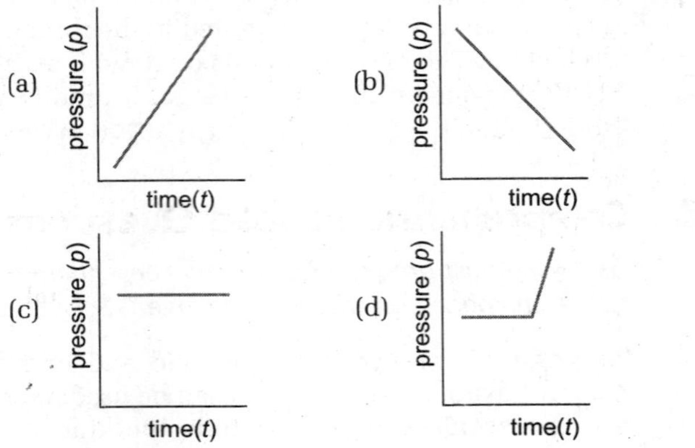

2. Select the correct statement(s).
(a) Equivalent of XeO_3 in I and II is in the ratio 1 : 1
(b) Equivalent mass of $I_2 = \dfrac{\text{molar mass}}{9}$
(c) Equivalent mass of $Fe^{2+} = \dfrac{\text{molar mass}}{6}$
(d) All the above are correct statements

Passage 8 Bleaching powder and bleach solution are produced on a large scale and used in several house hold products. The effectiveness of bleach solution is often measured by iodometry. **[IIT JEE 2012]**

1. 25 mL of household bleach solution was mixed with 30 mL of 0.50 M KI and 10 mL of 4 N acetic acid. In the titration of the liberated iodine, 48 mL of 0.25 N $Na_2S_2O_3$ was used to reach the end point. The molarity of the household bleach solution, is
(a) 0.48 M (b) 0.96 M (c) 0.24 M (d) 0.024 M

2. Bleaching powder contains a salt of an oxoacid as one of its components. The anhydride of that oxoacid, is
(a) Cl_2O (b) Cl_2O_7 (c) ClO_2 (d) Cl_2O_6

Example 9 The reactions of Cl_2 gas with cold-dilute and hot concentrated NaOH in water give sodium salts of two (different) oxoacids of chlorine, *P* and *Q* respectively.
The Cl_2 gas reacts with SO_2 gas, in the presence of charcoal, to give a product *R*. *R* reacts with white phosphorus to give a compound *S*. On hydrolysis, *S* gives an oxoacid of phosphorus *T*. **[JEE Advanced 2013]**

1. *P* and *Q* respectively, are the sodium salts of
(a) hypochlorous and chloric acids
(b) hypochlorous and chlorous acids
(c) chloric and perchloric acid
(d) chloric and hypochlorous acids

2. *R*, *S* and *T*, respectively, are
(a) SO_2Cl_2, PCl_5 and H_3PO_4 (b) SO_2Cl_2, PCl_3 and H_3PO_3
(c) $SOCl_2$, PCl_3 and H_3PO_2 (d) $SOCl_2$, PCl_5 and H_3PO_4

Matrix-Match Type

Given below are Matching Type Questions, with two columns (each having some items) each . Each item of Column I has to be matched with the items of Column II.

1. Match the compounds (in Column I) with the structures (in Column II).

Column I	Column II
A. XeF_4	1. Distorted octahedral
B. XeF_6	2. Tetrahedral
C. XeO_3	3. Square planar
D. XeO_4	4. Pyramidal

2. Match the types of glass (in Column I) with their characteristics (in Column II).

Column I	Column II
A. Alumino-silicate glass	1. Very high transparency
B. Calcium-alkali silicate glass	2. Cheap laboratory glass-wares
C. Lead glass	3. Optical glass
D. Soda glass	4. Domestic glass for window
	5. Low coefficient of expansion

3. Match molecules/ions (in Column I) with their shapes (in Column II).

Column I	Column II
A. ClF_3	1. Square planar
B. $[PCl_4]^+$	2. T-shaped
C. XeF_4	3. Tetrahedral
D. XeO_3	4. Pyramidal

4. Match the acids in Column I with their corresponding properties in Column II.

Column I	Column II
A. H_2SO_5	1. Hydrolysed to give H_2O_2
B. H_2SO_4	2. Hydrolysed to give H_2SO_4
C. $H_2S_2O_7$	3. S—S bond present
D. $H_2S_2O_3$	4. Peroxy linkage present
E. $H_2S_2O_8$	5. S in different oxidation state
	6. O in different oxidation state
	7. Hygroscopic

5. Match the species in Column I with the corresponding properties in Column II.

Column I	Column II
A. SO_2	1. Turns lime water milky
B. CO_2	2. Turns $Cr_2O_7^{2-}/H^+$ solution green
C. Cl_2	3. Turns KI/starch blue
D. Br_2	4. Disinfectant for drinking water
E. O_3	5. Green house effect
	6. Acid rain
	7. Controls pH of blood

6. Match the species in Column I with their corresponding properties in Column II.

Column I	Column II
A. XeO_3	1. Hydrolysis product of XeF_6
B. $XeOF_4$	2. sp^3
C. XeO_2F_4	3. sp^3d^2
D. XeO_3F_2	4. Tetrahedral
E. XeO_4	5. Trigonal pyramidal
	6. Square pyramidal
	7. Trigonal bipyramidal

7. All the compounds listed in Column I react with water. Match the result of the respective reactions with the appropriate option listed in Column II. **[IIT JEE 2010]**

Column I	Column II
A. $(CH_3)_2SiCl_2$	1. Hydrogen halide formation
B. XeF_4	2. Redox reaction
C. Cl_2	3. Reacts with glass
D. VCl_5	4. Polymerization
	5. O_2 formation

8. Match the species in Column I (Process) with the corresponding properties in Column II (Catalyst).

Column I (Process)	Column II (Catalyst)
A. Deacron's process	1. ZSM-5
B. Contact process	2. $CuCl_2$
C. Cracking of hydrocarbons	3. Particles 'Ni'
D. Hydrogenation of vegetable oils	4. V_2O_5

[JEE Mains 2021, March]

Single Integer Answer Questions

Answer of these questions is a single digit lying between 0 to 9.

1. O_2 is paramagnetic due to .... unpaired electrons.
2. SO_2 reduces $Cr_2O_7^{2-}$ to Cr^{3+}; change in oxidation number of Cr is ....
3. Maximum oxidation state shown by sulphur in its compounds is ....
4. There are equal number of sulphur atoms in thiosulphuric acid, Marshall's acid and oleum. This number is ....
5. How many S—S bonds are there in S_3O_9?
6. How many SOS angles are there in S_3O_9?
7. How many of the following have peroxy linkages? $H_2S_2O_3, H_2S_2O_8, H_2SO_5, CrO_5, BaO_2, KO_2$
8. How many of the following can be the oxidising agent?
$$H_2S, H_2SO_4, H_2SO_3, H_2S_2O_3$$
9. ${}^{35}_{17}Cl$ and ${}^{37}_{17}Cl$ are two isotopes of chlorine in mass ratio of $3 : x$ where $x =$ ....
10. Maximum acidic character is shown by the oxyacids of halogens with oxidation number of halogens as ....
11. $3Cl_2 + xNaOH \longrightarrow NaCl + NaClO_3$. x is ....
12. ClO_2 has odd-electron bonds. How many electrons are involved in (Cl—O) bond?
13. How many of the following have underlined atoms in different oxidation states?
$K_2Hg\underline{I_4}, CaO\underline{Cl_2}, Na_2\underline{S_2}O_3, Na_2\underline{S_4}O_6, H_2\underline{S}O_5, H_2S_2\underline{O_8}, Cr\underline{O_5}, \underline{I_3^-}$
14. How many of them are water insoluble? AgF, AgCl, AgBr, AgI, CaF_2, $BaSO_4$
15. XeF_4 disproportionates in aqueous solution to Xe(0) and Xe(VI). Xe(VI) is formed from which oxidation state (...........)
16. Bond-order of He_2^{2+} is ....
17. XeF_6 reacts with quartz forming XeO_3
$$2XeF_6 + xSiO_2 \longrightarrow$$
What is the value of x?
18. Out of F, Cl, Br, I, Xe, He, Ne, O, how many forms compounds with positive oxidation state?
19. Out of the following how many have Xe in sp^3d hybridisation? XeF_2, XeF_4, XeF_6, $XeOF_2$, XeO_3.
20. Reaction of Br_2 with Na_2CO_3 in hot aqueous solution gives sodium bromide and sodium bromate with the evolution of CO_2 gas. The number of sodium bromide molecules involved in the balanced chemical equation is ...... **[IIT JEE 2011]**

Answers

Objective Questions Type I [Only one correct option]

1. (c)	2. (b)	3. (d)	4. (a)	5. (d)	6. (a)	7. (a)	8. (d)	9. (d)	10. (c)
11. (a)	12. (d)	13. (d)	14. (a)	15. (a)	16. (b)	17. (d)	18. (a)	19. (b)	20. (b)
21. (b)	22. (d)	23. (b)	24. (a)	25. (b)	26. (d)	27. (d)	28. (d)	29. (c)	30. (a)
31. (b)	32. (c)	33. (a)	34. (a)	35. (c)	36. (a)	37. (b)	38. (d)	39. (d)	40. (d)
41. (c)	42. (b)	43. (b)	44. (a)	45. (a)	46. (d)	47. (d)	48. (c)	49. (b)	50. (b)
51. (c)	52. (a)	53. (c)	54. (d)	55. (c)	56. (a)	57. (c)	58. (a)	59. (b)	60. (c)
61. (c)	62. (a)	63. (a)	64. (d)	65. (a)	66. (a)	67. (a)	68. (d)	69. (c)	70. (a)
71. (a)	72. (a)	73. (c)	74. (d)	75. (b)	76. (d)	77. (d)	78. (b)	79. (c)	80. (d)
81. (a)	82. (a)	83. (c)	84. (a)	85. (d)	86. (b)	87. (c)	88. (a)	89. (b)	90. (d)
91. (d)	92. (b)	93. (c)	94. (a)	95. (d)	96. (b)	97. (d)	98. (a)	99. (d)	100. (b)
101. (d)	102. (c)	103. (a)	104. (c)	105. (c)	106. (d)	107. (a)	108. (c)	109. (a)	110. (c)
111. (a)	112. (a)	113. (a)	114. (c)	115. (d)	116. (d)	117. (d)	118. (a)	119. (d)	120. (c)
121. (a)	122. (d)	123. (c)	124. (d)	125. (b)	126. (a)	127. (c)			

Objective Questions Type II [One or more than one correct option(s)]

1. (c, d)	2. (a, c, d)	3. (a, c, d)	4. (a, b)	5. (a, b, c, d)
6. (a, b, c, d)	7. (a, b, c)	8. (a, c)	9. (a, c)	10. (a, b, c, d)
11. (a, b, d)	12, (a, b, d)	13. (a, b)	14. (a, b, d)	15. (a, c, d)
16. (a, c, d)	17. (a, d)			

Numerical Value Questions

1. 6	2. 7	3. 4	4. 19	5. 288
6. 1.67	7. 4	8. 19		

Comprehension Type

Passage 1 – 1. (a) 2. (b)
Passage 3 – 1. (b) 2. (b)
Passage 5 – 1. (b) 2. (a) 3. (b)
Passage 7 – 1. (c) 2. (b)
Passage 9 – 1. (c) 2. (a)
Passage 2 – 1. (b) 2. (c) 3. (a)
Passage 4 – 1. (b) 2. (c) 3. (a)
Passage 6 – 1. (a) 2. (a)
Passage 8 – 1. (c) 2. (a)
Passage 10 – 1. (a) 2. (a)

Matrix-Match Type

1. A → (3); B → (1); C → (4); D → (2)
2. A → (5); B → (4); C → (3); D → (2)
3. A → (2); B → (3); C → (1); D → (4)
4. A → (1,2,4,6); B → (7); C → (2,7); D → (3,5); E → (1,2,4,6)
5. A → (1,2,6); B → (1,5,7); C → (3,4); D → (3); E → (3,4)
6. A → (1,2,5); B → (1,3,6); C → (1,3); D → (2,4); E → (7)
7. A → (1,4); B → (1,2,3,4); C → (1,2,5); D → (1)
8. A → (2); B → (4); C → (1); D → (3)

Single Integer Answer Questions

1. (2)	2. (6)	3. (6)	4. (2)	5. (0)	6. (3)	7. (4)	8. (2)	9. (1)	10. (7)
11. (6)	12. (3)	13. (5)	14. (5)	15. (8)	16. (1)	17. (3)	18. (5)	19. (2)	20. (5)

Solutions

Objective Questions Type I [Only one correct option]

1. (*c*) H_2SO_4 is the side produced in the extraction of Cu from $CuSO_4$ called **blue-vitriol**.

2. (*b*) $H_2SO_5 + H_2O \longrightarrow H_2SO_4 + H_2O_2$

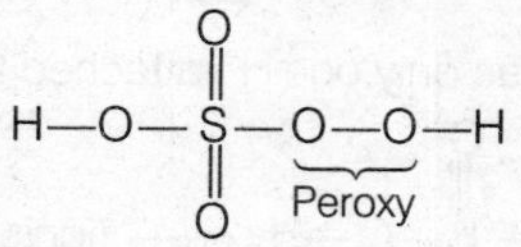

6. (*a*)

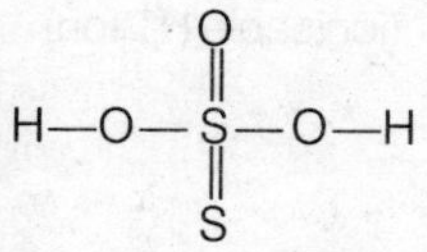

7. (*a*) Acidic nature increases down the group

$H_2O < H_2S < H_2Se < H_2Te$

K_a ⟶ max.

pK_a ⟵

8. (*d*) $\overset{\ominus}{O} \overset{\sigma}{—} \overset{\ominus}{O}$

10. (*c*) H_2O_2 and SO_2 are bleaching agent.

$\underset{\text{Black}}{PbS} + 4H_2O_2 \longrightarrow \underset{\text{White}}{PbSO_4} + 4H_2O$

$SO_2 + 2H_2O \longrightarrow H_2SO_3 + \underset{\text{Bleaching property}}{2H}$

12. (*d*) Oxidation number of Cl = +7
Thus, maximum value.

16. (*b*) SO_4^{2-}, ClO_4^-, XeO_4 — tetrahedral
XeF_4 — sp^3d^2 (square planar)

18. (*a*) $Ba(NO_2)_2 + H_2SO_4 \longrightarrow BaSO_4 + 2HNO_2$

19. (*b*) $SO_2 + Cl_2 \xrightarrow{\text{Sunlight}} SO_2Cl_2$

20. (*b*) Bond-energy decreases going down the group
Te—Te < Se—Se < S—S < O—O

21. (*b*) H_2SO_4 is dehydrating agent.

$\begin{matrix} COOH \\ | \\ COOH \end{matrix} \xrightarrow{\text{Conc. } H_2SO_4} CO + CO_2 + H_2O$

22. (*d*) Oxygen family elements (O, S, Se, Te, Po) are called chalcogen.

25. (*b*) $Na_2CO_3 + 2H_2O \longrightarrow 2NaOH + H_2CO_3$
$2NaOH + SO_2 \longrightarrow Na_2SO_3 + H_2O$

26. (*d*)

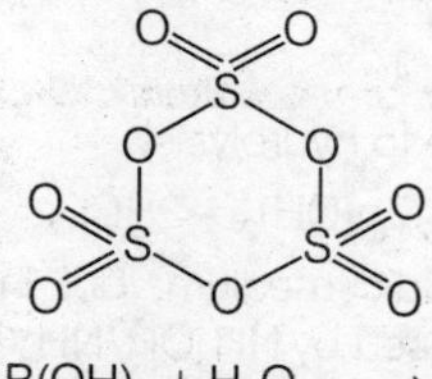

29. (*c*) $B(OH)_3 + H_2O \longrightarrow B(OH)_4^- + H^+$
H^+ ion is released by H_2O.

32. (*c*) $C + H_2SO_4 \longrightarrow CO_2 + H_2O + SO_2$

33. (*a*) $O{=}O$ Double bond
$H{-}O{-}O{-}H$ Single bond
$O{=}O \rightarrow O$ Between double bond and single bond

$$\text{Bond length} \propto \frac{1}{\text{Number of bonds}}$$

35. (*c*) $2H_2S + SO_2 \longrightarrow 2H_2O + 3S$

37. (*b*) $O^- + e^- \longrightarrow O^{2-}$
$\Delta H > 0$

38. (*d*)

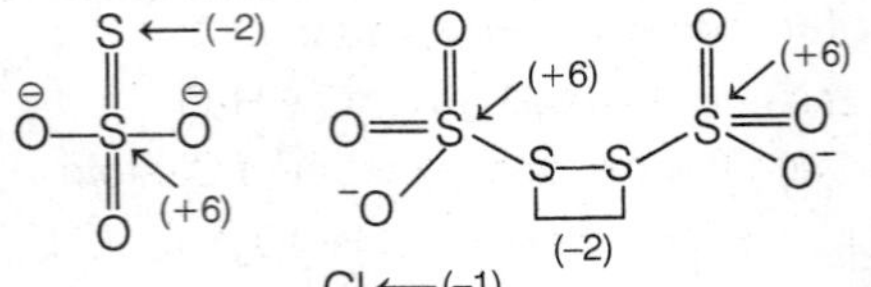

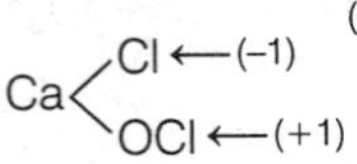

40. (*d*) O_3^- (ozonide) is paramagnetic.

$$2O_3^- \longrightarrow \underset{\text{Superoxide}}{2O_2^-} + O_2$$

Stability decreases as size of M^+ (alkali metal ion) decreases.

41. (*c*) $H{-}\ddot{O}{-}H \longrightarrow HO^{\ominus} + H^+$

42. (*b*) Pyrogallol dissolves O_2.

43. (*b*)
$$KI + H_2O + O_3 \longrightarrow I_2 + KOH + O_2$$
$$I_2 + 2Na_2S_2O_3 \longrightarrow 2NaI + Na_2S_4O_6$$

44. (*a*)
$$CH_3CH{=}CHCH_3 \xrightarrow[H_2O]{O_3/Zn} 2CH_3CHO$$

H_2O_2 is formed as side product when reacts with Zn or DMS and thus further oxidation of CH_3CHO to CH_3COOH is prevented.

45. (*a*) $S{=}C{=}S$
d-orbital is present in sulphur (in excited state).

47. (*d*)
$$FeS + 2HCl \longrightarrow \underset{A}{FeCl_2} + \underset{B}{H_2S}$$
$$\underset{\text{Yellow}}{2FeCl_3} + H_2S \longrightarrow \underset{\text{Light green}}{2FeCl_2} + 2HCl + S$$
$$(CH_3COO)_2Pb + H_2S \longrightarrow \underset{\text{Black}}{PbS} + 2CH_3COOH$$
$$FeCl_2 + K_3[Fe(CN)_6] \longrightarrow \underset{\text{Turnbull's blue}}{KFe[Fe(CN)_6]} + 2KCl$$

48. (*c*) $PCl_3 + H_3PO_3 \longrightarrow H_4P_2O_5$

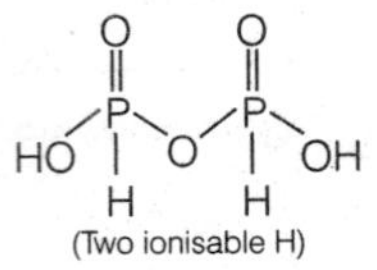

(Two ionisable H)

49. (*b*) $ZnCl_2$ solution is acidic due to hydrolysis.
$$ZnCl_2 + H_2O \longrightarrow Zn(OH)_2 + 2HCl$$
ZnS is not precipitated in acidic medium, but in neutral medium. HCl formed is neutralised by NH_4OH/NH_4Cl.

50. (*b*)
$$SO_2 + 2H_2O \longrightarrow H_2SO_4 + 2H$$
H acts as reducing agent.

51. (*c*) $2MnO_4^- + 5SO_2 + 2H_2O \longrightarrow 5SO_4^{2-} + 2Mn^{2+} + 4H^+$

52. (*a*)
$$\text{Colour} \underset{\text{Air/oxidation}}{\overset{SO_2/\text{reduction}}{\rightleftarrows}} \text{Colourless}$$

53. (*c*) The structure of I_3^- ion is

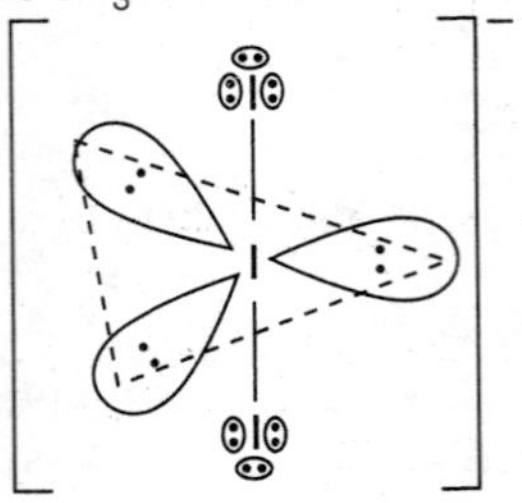

Hence, 9 is the correct answer.

55. (*c*)

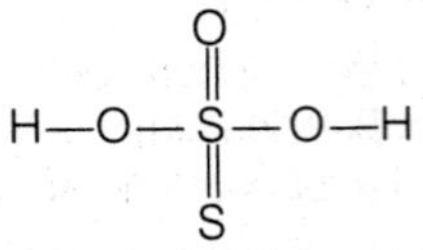

56. (*a*) $H_2S_2O_8$ has maximum oxidation state of sulphur and thus cannot be further oxidised by $KMnO_4$.

57. (*c*)
$$Cr_2O_7^{2-} + SO_3^{2-} \longrightarrow SO_4^{2+} + \underset{\text{Green}}{Cr^{3+}}$$
$$Cr_2O_7^{2-} + H_2S \longrightarrow S + \underset{\text{Green}}{Cr^{3+}}$$
$$Cr_2O_7^{2-} + Fe^{2+} \longrightarrow \underset{\text{Green}}{Cr^{3+}} + Fe^{3+}$$

58. (*a*) $AgBr + 2Na_2S_2O_3 \longrightarrow Na_3[Ag(S_2O_3)_2] + NaBr$

59. (*b*) $2AgNO_3 + Na_2S_2O_3 \longrightarrow \underset{\text{White}}{Ag_2S_2O_3} + 2NaNO_3$
$$Ag_2S_2O_3 + H_2O \longrightarrow \underset{\text{Black}}{Ag_2S} + H_2SO_4$$

61. (*c*)
$$H_3PO_2 \rightleftharpoons H^+ + H_2PO_2^-$$
Monobasic, as only one H^+ attached to O-atom.

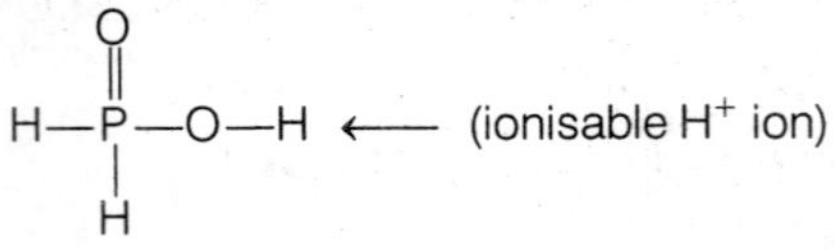

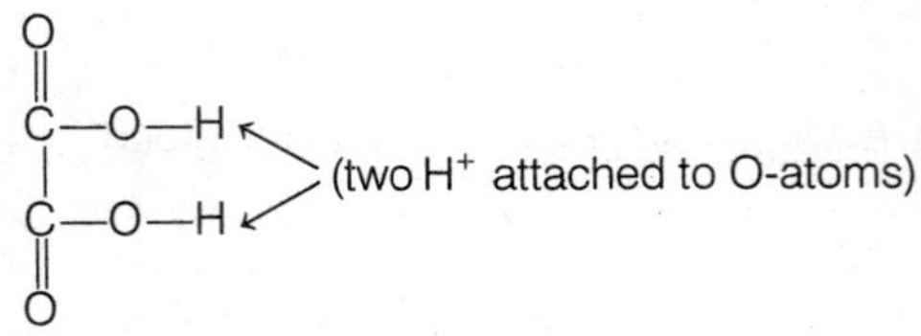

Dibasic

$CH_2{-}NH_2$] basic
|
COOH] acidic

Thus, amphoteric.

62. (*a*) The oxidation states of nitrogen in following molecules are as follows :
$NO_3^- \rightarrow 3$, $NO_2 \rightarrow +4$, $NO \rightarrow +2$ and $N_2O \rightarrow +1$

64. (*d*) $CaOCl_2 + H_2O \longrightarrow Ca(OH)_2 + Cl_2$

$Cl_2 + 2Na_2S_2O_3 \longrightarrow 2NaCl + Na_2S_4O_6$

65. (*a*) $\underset{\text{(Hot and conc.)}}{6\,NaOH + 3Cl_2} \longrightarrow \underset{(A)}{NaClO_3} + 5NaCl + 3H_2O$

$\underset{\text{(Dry)}}{2Ca(OH)_2} + 2Cl_2 \longrightarrow \underset{(B)}{Ca(OCl)_2} + CaCl_2 + 2H_2O$

Thus, $A : NaClO_3$

$B : Ca(OCl)_2$

66. (*a*) If acid is weak, its conjugate base is strong and *vice-versa*.

$HClO < HClO_2 < HClO_3 < HClO_4$

$\xrightarrow{\hspace{4cm}}$ Acid strength

$ClO^- > ClO_2^- > ClO_3^- > ClO_4^-$

$\xrightarrow{\hspace{4cm}}$ Conjugate base strength

ClO_4^- is the weakest base.

67. (*a*) H_2SO_5 perxoy sulphuric acid ⎤
$H_2S_2O_8$ peroxy disulphuric acid ⎥ have peroxy linkage
H_3PO_5 peroxyphosphoric acid ⎦
$HClO_4$ perchloric acid] no peroxy linkage

69. (*c*) Cl_2, Br_2 and I_2 form a mixture of halide and hypohalites when react with cold dilute alkalies while a mixture of halides and haloate when react with concentrated cold alkalies.

$Cl_2 + 2NaOH \longrightarrow NaCl + NaClO + H_2O$ (Cold and dilute)

$\therefore$ Cl^- and ClO^- are obtained as products when chlorine gas reacts with cold and dilute aqueous NaOH.

72. (*a*) Boron is electron-deficient in BF_3.

73. (*c*) 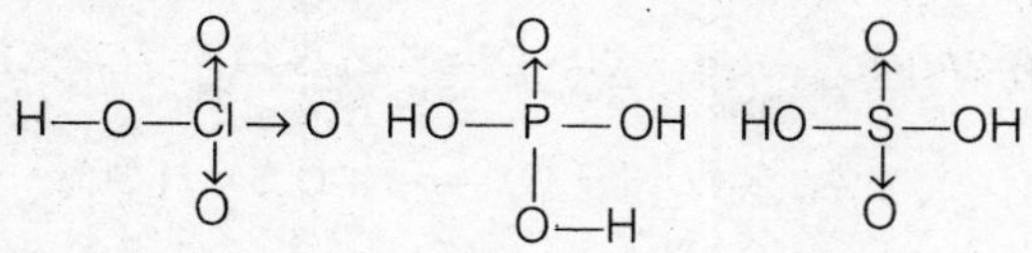

74. (*d*) $F_2 < Br_2 < Cl_2$

75. (*b*) Mixture is called *aqua-regia*.

$HNO_3 + 3HCl \longrightarrow NOCl + 2H_2O + 2Cl$

76. (*d*) ClO_2^- is chlorite.

77. (*d*) $2KBr + Cl_2 \longrightarrow 2KCl + Br_2$

80. (*d*) $\underset{\substack{\uparrow \\ +7}}{HClO_4}$ (least oxidiable)

81. (*a*) The structure of H_3PO_2 (hypophosphorous) acid is

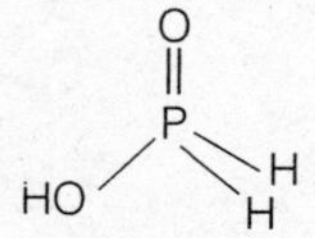

Due to the presence of two P—H bonds, H_3PO_2 acts a strong reducing agent. e.g.

$4\overset{+1}{Ag}NO_3 + H_3\overset{+1}{P}O_2 + 2H_2O \longrightarrow 4\overset{0}{Ag}\downarrow + H_3\overset{+5}{P}O_4 + 4HNO_3$

82. (*a*) Oxidising power of X_2

$F_2 > Cl_2 > Br_2 > I_2$

84. (*a*) $2NaOH + Cl_2 \longrightarrow NaCl + NaClO + H_2O$

86. (*b*) Halogens form halates and halides with hot and concentrated solution of NaOH as :

$3X_2 + 6NaOH \longrightarrow 5NaX + NaXO_3 + 3H_2O$

So, Cl_2 will also give Cl^- (as NaCl) and ClO_3^- (as $NaClO_3$) in the above reaction.

Thus, option (b) is correct.

Note When halogens react with cold and dilute solution of NaOH, hypohalites and halides are produced as:

$X_2 + 2NaOH \longrightarrow NaX + NaXO + H_2O$

88. (*a*) Acid strength $\propto$ oxidation number of Cl-atom

$\underset{+1}{HClO} < \underset{+3}{HClO_2} < \underset{+5}{HClO_3} < \underset{+7}{HClO_4}$

91. (*d*)

$HClO_3 + e^- \xrightarrow{H^+} HCl$

$Cr_2O_7^{2-} + e^- \xrightarrow{H^+} Cr^{3+}$

$MnO_4^- + e^- \xrightarrow{H^+} Mn^{2+}$

92. (*b*) $3ClO^- \longrightarrow 2Cl^- + ClO_3^-$

93. (*c*) $CaOCl_2 + H_2O \longrightarrow Ca(OH)_2 + Cl_2$

$Cl_2 + 2KI \longrightarrow 2KCl + I_2$

$2Na_2S_2O_3 + I_2 \longrightarrow 2NaI + Na_2S_4O_6$

$CaOCl_2 \equiv Cl_2 \equiv I_2 \equiv 2Na_2S_2O_3$

Hypo $= 100 \times 10$ milliequivalent

$= 0.1$ equivalent

Thus, $CaOCl_2 \equiv 0.1$ equivalent

$= \frac{12.7}{2}$ g $= 6.35$ g in 10 g sample

Thus, % purity $= 63.5\%$

94. (*a*)

$CaOCl_2 + H_2O \longrightarrow Ca(OH)_2 + Cl_2$

$Cl_2 + H_2O \longrightarrow 2HCl + O$

$CH_3CH_2OH \xrightarrow{\text{O (oxidn)}} CH_3CHO$

$CH_3CHO + 3Cl_2 \longrightarrow CCl_3CHO + HCl$

$CCl_3CHO + Ca(OH)_2 \longrightarrow CHCl_3 + (HCOO)_2Ca$

95. (*d*) For $\ddot{I}Cl_5$

$H = \frac{1}{2}(7 + 5 - 0 + 0) = 6\,(sp^3d^2)$

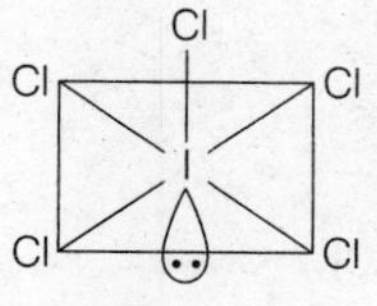

sp^3d^2-hybridised
Geometry : Octahedral
Shape / Structure : Square pyramidal

For $\ddot{I}Cl_4^-$

$H = \frac{1}{2}(7 + 4 - 0 + 1) = 6\,(sp^3d^2)$

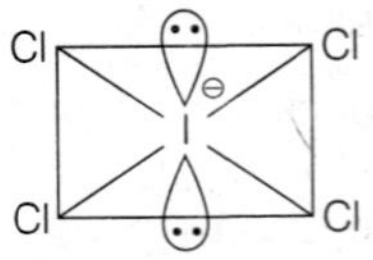

sp^3d^2-hybridised
Geometry : Octahedral
Shape/Structure : Square planar

So, ICl_5 and ICl_4^- are isolobal but not isostructural.

96. (*b*) $2X_2O \longrightarrow 2X_2 + O_2$

99. (*d*) $HClO_2 + HClO_3 \longrightarrow 2ClO_2 + H_2O$

100. (*b*) $HClO_3 + HClO_4 \longrightarrow 2ClO_3 + H_2O$

103. (*a*) $2KBr + Cl_2 \longrightarrow 2KCl + Br_2$

Br_2 also oxidises KI to I_2 forming violet layer in $CHCl_3$

$$2KI + Br_2 \longrightarrow 2KBr + \underset{\text{Violet}}{I_2}$$

104. (*c*) $XeF_6 \longrightarrow XeOF_4 \longrightarrow XeO_2F_2 \longrightarrow XeO_3$

108. (*c*) HF has highest boiling point among hydrogen halides because it has strongest hydrogen bonding. Here, the hydrogen bond exists between hydrogen of one molecule and fluorine atom of another molecule as shown below.

$$\ldots\overset{\delta+}{H}—\overset{\delta-}{F}\ldots\overset{\delta+}{H}—\overset{\delta-}{F}\ldots\overset{\delta+}{H}—\overset{\delta-}{F}$$

In this molecule, hydrogen bond behaves like a bridge between two atoms that holds one atom by covalent bond and the other by hydrogen bond.

109. (*a*) In $XeOF_4$, Xe is sp^3d^2-hybridised. Geometry of the molecule is octahedral, but shape of the molecule is square pyramidal.

According to VSEPR, theory it has one π bond. Remaining six electron pairs form an octahedron with one position occupied by a lone pair.

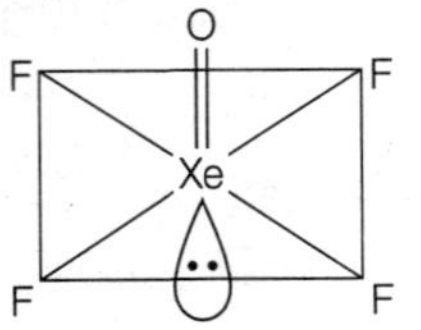

[Number of bp = 5
Number of lp = 1]

Here, Xe contains one lone pair of electrons.

113. (*a*) As given, the first electron gain enthalpy of oxygen can be shown as,

$$O(g) + e^- \longrightarrow O^-(g), \quad \Delta_{eg}H_1 = -141\ \text{kJ/mol}$$

The expression of second electron gain enthalpy of oxygen will be,

$$O^-(g) + e^- \longrightarrow O^{2-}(g), \quad \Delta_{eg}H_2 = +\text{ve}$$

$\Delta_{eg}H_2$ of oxygen is positive, i.e. endothermic, because a strong electrostatic repulsion will be observed between highy negative O^- and the incoming electron (e^-). A very high amount of energy will be consumed (endothermic) by the system to overcome the electrostatic repulsion.

114. (*c*) S—S bond is not present in $H_2S_2O_7$ (pyrosulphuric acid or oleum).

$H_2S_2O_7 \Rightarrow$ 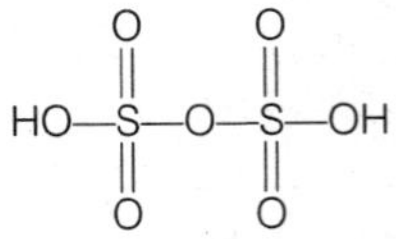

While the other given oxoacids of sulphur, i.e. $H_2S_2O_3$ (thiosulphuric acid), $H_2S_2O_4$ (hyposulphurous or dithionous acid) and $H_2S_4O_6$ (tetrathionic acid) contains S—S bonds.

$H_2S_2O_3 \Rightarrow$ 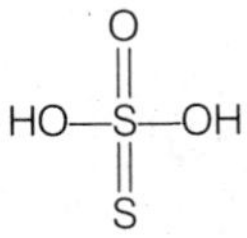

$H_2S_2O_4 \Rightarrow$ 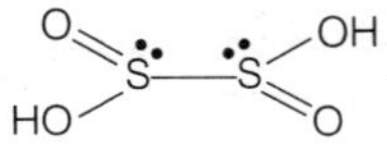

$H_2S_4O_6 \Rightarrow$ 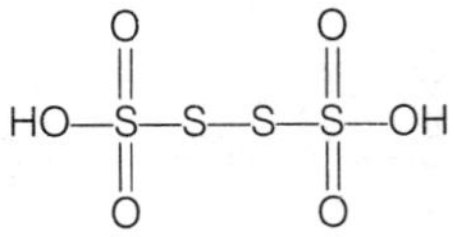

115. (*d*) $XeF_2 + AsF_5 \longrightarrow [XeF]^+[AsF_6]^-$

121. (*a*) ${}^{226}_{88}Ra \longrightarrow {}^{222}_{86}Rn + {}^{4}_{2}He$

122. (*d*)

$$AsF_5 + XeF_4 \longrightarrow [XeF_3]^+[AsF_6]^-$$
$$BF_3 + XeF_4 \longrightarrow [XeF_3]^+[BF_4^-]$$
$$HF + XeF_4 \longrightarrow [XeF_3]^+[HF_2]^-$$

123. (*c*) RbF or CsF + $XeF_4 \longrightarrow [Rb]^+[XeF_5]^-$

124. (*d*) Ions are formed, hence conducting.

12

d-and f-Block Elements (The Transition and Inner-Transition Elements)

Objective Questions Type I [Only one correct option]

In each of the questions below, four choices are given of which only one is correct.

1. Out of $AgNO_3$, AgF and $AgClO_4$, water soluble salts are
(a) AgF (b) AgF, $AgNO_3$
(c) AgF, $AgNO_3$, $AgClO_4$ (d) None of these

2. Four successive members of the first row transition elements listed below with atomic numbers. Which one of them is expected to have the highest $E^\circ_{M^{3+}/M^{2+}}$ value? **[JEE Main 2013]**
(a) Cr ($Z = 24$) (b) Mn ($Z = 25$)
(c) Fe ($Z = 26$) (d) Co ($Z = 27$)

3. Stability of Cu^+ and Ag^+ halide complexes are in the order
(a) I > Br > Cl > F (b) F > Cl > Br > I
(c) Cl > F > I > Br (d) Br > I > Cl > F

4. Which of the following exists as white salt in anhydrous state?
(a) CuF_2 (b) $CuSO_4$
(c) Both (a) and (b) (d) None of these

5. Which oxides will not give metal on heating?
(a) HgO (b) ZnO (c) Ag_2O (c) All of these

6. When KI (excess) is added to
I. $CuSO_4$ II. $HgCl_2$
III. $Pb(NO_3)_2$
(a) a white ppt. of CuI in I, a orange ppt. HgI_2 in II and a yellow ppt PbI_2 in III
(b) a white ppt. of CuI in I, an orange ppt. dissolving to HgI_4^{2-} in II, and a yellow ppt of PbI_2 in III
(c) a white ppt. of CuI, HgI_2 and PbI_2 in each case
(d) None of the above is correct

7. Most common oxidation state of lanthanides is
(a) +2 (b) +3 (c) +4 (d) +5

8. The purest form of Fe is
(a) stainless steel (b) steel
(c) cast iron (d) wrought iron

9. In $Na_2[Fe(CN)_5NO]$, sodium nitroprusside,
(a) oxidation state of Fe is +2
(b) this has NO^+ as ligand
(c) Both (a) and (b)
(d) None of the above is correct

10. $FeSO_4$ solution gives brown colour ring in testing nitrates or nitrites. This is
(a) $[Fe(H_2O)_5NO]^{2+}$ (b) $[Fe(H_2O)_5NO_2]^{2+}$
(c) $[Fe(H_2O)_4(NO)_2]^{2+}$ (d) $[Fe(H_2O)_4NO]^{2+}$

11. $FeCl_3 \cdot 6H_2O$ is actually
(a) $[Fe(H_2O)_6]Cl_3$ (b) $[Fe(H_2O_5Cl]Cl_2 \cdot H_2O$
(c) $[Fe(H_2O)_4Cl_2]Cl \cdot 2H_2O$ (d) $[Fe(H_2O)_3Cl_3] \cdot 3H_2O$

12. Ni^{2+}, in traces, can be tested using
(a) sodium nitroprusside
(b) dimethyl glyoxime
(c) ammonium sulphocyanide
(d) potassium ferrocyanide

13. $CuSO_4$ can be estimated volumetrically
(a) by reaction with KI followed by reaction with $Na_2S_2O_3$
(b) by reaction with $BaCl_2$
(c) by reaction with $K_4Fe(CN)_6$
(d) None of the above is correct

14. Which is the correct statement?
(a) Ammoniacal CuCl is used to measure the amount of CO in gas samples
(b) Ammoniacal CuCl gives red ppt with CH≡CH
(c) Both (a) and (b) are correct
(d) None of the above is correct

15. Which is not the true statement about FeO?
(a) It is non-stoichiometric and is metal deficient
(b) It is basic oxide
(c) Its aqueous solution changes to $Fe(OH)_3$ and then to $Fe_2O_3 \cdot (H_2O)_n$ by atmospheric oxygen
(d) It gives red colour with KCNS

16. Match Column I with Column II and select the correct answer using the codes given below the Columns.

Column I (Metals)		Column II (Ores)	
A.	Zinc	1.	Azurite
B.	Tin	2.	Carnallite
C.	Copper	3.	Calamine
D.	Magnesium	4.	Cassiterite

Codes

	A	B	C	D
(a)	3	4	2	1
(b)	3	4	1	2
(c)	4	1	3	2
(d)	4	3	2	1

17. Haemoglobin and chlorophyll contain respectively
(a) Fe, Co (b) Fe, Mn (c) Mg, Fe (d) Fe, Mg

18. Due to lanthanide contraction
(a) Fe, Co, Ni have equal size
(b) Zr and Hf have equal size
(c) all *f*-block ions have equal size
(d) all isoelectronic ions have equal size

19. In $Cr_2O_7^{2-}$ every Cr is linked to
(a) two O atoms (b) three O atoms
(c) four O atoms (d) five O atoms

20. For Ni and Pt different IP in MJ mol^{-1} are given below

	$(IP)_1 + (IP)_2$	$(IP)_3 + (IP)_4$
Ni	2.49	8.80
Pt	2.60	6.70

Hence
(a) nickel (II) compounds tend to be thermodynamically more stable than platinum (II)
(b) platinum (IV) compounds tend to be more stable than nickel (IV)
(c) Both (a) and (b) are correct
(d) None of the above is correct

21. Paramagnetism is given by the relation $\mu = 2\sqrt{s(s+1)}$ magnetons where '*s*' is the total spin. On this basis, the paramagnetism of Cu^+ ion is
(a) 3.88 magnetons (b) 2.83 magnetons
(c) 1.41 magnetons (d) zero

22. The oxygen carrying pigment, oxy-haemocyanin, containing two copper ions is diamagnetic, because
(a) the two copper ions are in +1 oxidation state
(b) one of the copper ions is in +1 oxidation state and the other is in +2 oxidation state
(c) there are strong anti-ferromagnetic interactions between the two copper ions
(d) there are ferromagnetic interactions between the two copper ions

23. Match Column I with Column II and select the correct answer using the codes given below the Columns.

Column I (Alloys)		Column II (Constituents)	
A.	Gun metal	1.	Lead + tin
B.	German silver	2.	Copper + tin + zinc
C.	Brass	3.	Copper + zinc
D.	Solder	4.	Copper + zinc + nickel

Codes

	A	B	C	D
(a)	1	3	4	2
(b)	4	2	1	3
(c)	2	4	3	1
(d)	3	1	2	4

24. Ferromagnetism is shown by
(a) Zn, Cu, Cd (b) Fe, Co, Ni
(c) Zn, Hg, Se (d) All of these

25. Ti^{2+} is purple while Ti^{4+} is colourless, because
(a) there is no crystal field effect in Ti^{4+}
(b) Ti^{2+} has $3d^2$ configuration
(c) Ti^{4+} has $3d^2$ configuration
(d) Ti^{4+} is a very small cation when compared to Ti^{2+} and hence, does not absorb any radiation

26. Silver ornaments turn black by atmospheric
(a) O_2 (b) N_2
(c) Cl_2 (d) H_2S

27. $Cr_2O_7^{2-} \xrightarrow{pH = x} CrO_4^{2-} \xrightarrow{pH = y} Cr_2O_7^{2-}$
pH values *x* and *y* can be
(a) 4 and 5 (b) 4 and 8
(c) 8 and 4 (d) 8 and 9

28. In dilute alkaline solution MnO_4^- changes to
(a) MnO_4^{2-} (b) MnO_2
(c) Mn_2O_3 (d) MnO

29. Cl_2 gas is obtained by various reactions but not by
(a) $KMnO_4$ + conc. HCl $\xrightarrow{\Delta}$
(b) KCl + $K_2Cr_2O_7$ + conc. H_2SO_4 $\xrightarrow{\Delta}$
(c) MnO_2 + conc. HCl $\xrightarrow{\Delta}$
(d) KCl + F_2 $\longrightarrow$

30. Which is not the true statement about $KMnO_4$?
(a) Its solution is unstable in acidic medium
(b) Its small quantity added to conc. H_2SO_4, a green coloured solution containing MnO_3^+ ions is formed
(c) MnO_4^- changes to Mn^{2+} in basic solution
(d) It is a self-indicator in Fe^{2+} or $C_2O_4^{2-}$ titration

31. Pyrolusite in MnO_2 is used to prepare $KMnO_4$. Steps are

$$MnO_2 \xrightarrow{I} MnO_4^{2-} \xrightarrow{II} MnO_4^-$$

I and II are
(a) fuse with KOH/air, electrolytic oxidation
(b) fuse with KOH/air, electrolytic reduction
(c) fuse with conc HNO_3/air, electrolytic reduction
(d) All the above are correct

32. Fe is made passive by
(a) dil. H_2SO_4 (b) dil. HCl
(c) aqua-regia (d) conc. H_2SO_4

33. Maximum magnetic moment is shown by
(a) d^5 (b) d^6
(c) d^7 (d) d^8

34. Magnetic moment of Cr (Z =24), Mn^+ (Z =25) and Fe^{2+} (Z = 26) are x, y, z. They are in order
(a) $x < y < z$ (b) $x = y < z$
(c) $z < x = y$ (d) $x = y = z$

35. Interstitial compound is formed by
(a) Fe, Co (b) Co, Ni
(c) Fe, Ni (d) All of these

36. A jeweller is selling 22-carat gold articles with 95% purity, it is approximately
(a) exact (b) 3.5% higher
(c) 3.5% lower (d) 5% lower

37. Which is not the true statement?
(a) Ions of *d*-block elements are coloured due to *d-d* transition
(b) Ions of *f*-block elements are coloured due to *f-f* transition
(c) $[Sc(H_2O)_6]^{3+}$, $[Ti(H_2O)_6]^{4+}$ are coloured complexes
(d) Cu^+ is colourless ion

38. Match the catalysts in Column I with their uses in Column II.

Column I		Column II	
A.	$TiCl_4$	1.	Adams catalyst in reduction
B.	$PdCl_2$	2.	in preparation of $(CH_3)_2SiCl_2$
C.	Pt/PtO	3.	Reppe synthesis
D.	Cu	4.	used as the Ziegler-Natta catalyst in polythene production
E.	Ni-complexes	5.	Wacker process for converting C_2H_4 to CH_3CHO

Codes

	A	B	C	D	E
(a)	4	5	1	2	3
(b)	4	5	2	1	3
(c)	5	4	1	3	2
(d)	2	1	3	5	4

39. When (*A*) NH_4VO_3 is heated.
(*B*) $(NH_4)_2Cr_2O_7$ is heated
(a) in both cases N_2 is formed
(b) in both cases NH_3 is formed
(c) in (*A*) NH_3 and in (*B*) N_2 are formed
(d) in (*A*) N_2 and in (*B*) NH_3 are formed

40. $FeCr_2O_4$ (chromite) is converted to Cr by following steps

$$\text{Chromite} \xrightarrow{I} Na_2CrO_4 \xrightarrow{II} Cr_2O_3 \xrightarrow{III} Cr$$

I, II and III are

	I	II	III
(a)	Na_2CO_3/air, Δ	C	C
(b)	NaOH/air, Δ	C, Δ	Al, Δ
(c)	NaOH/air, Δ	C, Δ	Mg, Δ
(d)	conc. H_2SO_4, Δ	NH_4Cl, Δ	C, Δ

41. When H_2O_2 is added to an acidified solution of $K_2Cr_2O_7$
(a) solution turns green due to formation of Cr_2O_3
(b) solution turns yellow due to formation of K_2CrO_4
(c) a deep blue-violet coloured compound $CrO(O_2)_2$ is formed
(d) solution gives green ppt. of $Cr(OH)_3$

42. Out of $SiCl_4$, $TiCl_4$, PO_4^{3-}, SO_4^{2-}, CrO_4^{2-}, CCl_4 isostructural are
(a) $SiCl_4$, $TiCl_4$ (b) SO_4^{2-}, CrO_4^{2-}
(c) Both (a) and (b) (d) None of these

43. Maximum oxidation state is shown by
(a) Os (b) Mn (c) Cr (d) Co

44. Following elements do not show the properties characteristic of *d*-block elements
(a) Cu, Ag, Au (b) Zn, Hg, Cd
(c) Sc, Ti, V (d) Fe, Co, Ni

45. The ability of *d*-block elements to form complexes is due to
(a) small and highly charged ions
(b) vacant low energy orbitals to accept lone pair of electrons from ligands
(c) Both (a) and (b) are correct
(d) None of the above is correct

46. AgCl and NaCl are colourless. NaBr and NaI are also colourless but AgBr and AgI are coloured. This is due to
(a) Ag^+ polarises Br^- and I^-
(b) Ag^+ has unpaired *d*-orbital
(c) Ag^+ depolarises Br^- and I^-
(d) None of the above is correct

47. Which is the correct statement?

(a) In less acidic solution $K_2Cr_2O_7$ and H_2O_2 give violet coloured diamagnetic $[CrO(O_2)(OH)]^-$ ion

(b) In alkaline H_2O_2, K_3CrO_8 (with tetraperoxo species) $[Cr(O_2)_4]^{3-}$ is formed

(c) In ammoniacal solution, $K_2Cr_2O_7$ gives $(NH_3)_3CrO_4$

(d) All of the above are correct statements

48. $\underline{A} \xrightarrow{4\,KOH,\,O_2} 2\underset{(Green)}{\underline{B}} + 2H_2O$

$3\underline{B} \xrightarrow{4\,HCl} 2\underset{(Purple)}{\underline{C}} + MnO_2 + 2H_2O$

$2\underline{C} \xrightarrow{H_2O,\,KI} 2\underline{A} + 2KOH + \underline{D}$

In the above sequence of reactions, $\underline{A}$ and $\underline{D}$, respectively, are **[JEE Mains 2019, Jan.]**

(a) KI and $KMnO_4$ (b) MnO_2 and KIO_3

(c) KI and K_2MnO_4 (d) KIO_3 and MnO_2

49. For CrO_3 following is not true statement.

(a) It is called chromic acid

(b) It is colourless due to $3d^{10}$ configuration

(c) It is bright orange solid and colour arises due to charge transfer

(d) It is toxic and corrosive

50. Only +2, +3, +4 oxidation states are shown by

(a) Sc, Ti (b) Fe, Ni

(c) Ti, Ni (d) Zn, Ni

51. Coagulation of blood takes place by

(a) ferric alum (b) potash alum

(c) Both (a) and (b) (d) None of these

52. When KCN comes in contact with blood, one dies immediately, it is due to

(a) CN^- forms stable complex with iron of haemoglobin of blood

(b) CN^- combines with H_2O of blood causing it poison

(c) Both (a) and (b) are correct

(d) None of the above is correct

53. MnO_4^- is of intense pink colour, though Mn is in (+7) oxidation state. It is due to

(a) oxygen gives colour to it

(b) charge transfer when Mn gives its electron to oxygen

(c) charge transfer when oxygen gives its electron to Mn making it Mn (+VI) hence, coloured

(d) None of the above is correct

54. The common positive oxidation states for an element with atomic number 24 are **[JEE Main 2021, March]**

(a) + 2 to + 6 (b) + 1 and + 3 to + 6

(c) + 1 and + 3 (d) + 1 to + 6

55. In $[Fe(CN)_5(NO^+)]^{2-}$, Fe has +3 state. It can be decided by

(a) magnetic measurement

(b) colligative property

(c) colour

(d) hybridisation

56. In 3*d* transition series, if nuclear charge increases, the screening effect

(a) increases

(b) decreases

(c) first decreases and then increases

(d) first increases and then decreases

57. Reason of passivity of iron is

(a) Fe_2O_3 (b) Fe_3O_4

(c) FeO (d) $Fe_2O_3 \cdot 3H_2O$

58. Which forms interstitial compound?

(a) Fe (b) Co

(c) Ni (d) All of these

59. Which shows maximum magnetic moment among the bivalent ions of the first transition series?

(a) Fe^{2+} (b) Co^{2+}

(c) Ni^{2+} (d) Mn^{2+}

60. Select the incorrect statement(s).

(a) Ionisation energies of 5*d*-elements are greater than those of 3*d* and 4*d* elements

(b) Cu(I) is diamagnetic while Cu(II) is paramagnetic

(c) $[Ti(H_2O)_6]^{3+}$ is coloured while $[Sc(H_2O)_6]^{3+}$ is colourless

(d) Transition elements cannot form complexes

61. Guigret's green is

(a) $NiO \cdot 2H_2O$ (b) $Cr_2O_3 \cdot 2H_2O$

(c) $CuSO_4 \cdot 2H_2O$ (d) $CrO \cdot 2H_2O$

62. Which is wrongly matched?

(a) Duralumin — Al + Cu + Mg + Mn

(b) Alnico — Fe + Al + Ni + Cu

(c) German silver — Cu + Zn + Ni

(d) Monel metal — Cu + Zn + Sn

63. Formula of green vitriol oil is

(a) $FeSO_4 \cdot 7H_2O$ (b) $MgSO_4 \cdot 7H_2O$

(c) $ZnSO_4 \cdot 7H_2O$ (d) $CuSO_4 \cdot 5H_2O$

64. Which of the following compounds is amphoteric?

(a) $Cr(OH)_2$ (b) $Fe(OH)_2$

(c) $Cr(OH)_3$ (d) $Fe(OH)_3$

65. Increasing basic properties of TiO_2, ZrO_2 and HfO_2 are in order

(a) $TiO_2 < ZrO_2 < HfO_2$

(b) $HfO_2 < ZrO_2 < TiO_2$

(c) $HfO_2 < TiO_2 < ZrO_2$

(d) $ZrO_2 < TiO_2 < HfO_2$

66. Which is called chromic acid?

(a) CrO (b) Cr_2O_3

(c) CrO_3 (d) CrO_2

67. What are the species *A* and *B* in the following

$$CrO_3 + H_2O \longrightarrow A \xrightarrow{OH^-} B?$$

(a) $H_2CrO_4, H_2Cr_2O_7$ (b) $H_2Cr_2O_7, Cr_2O_3$

(c) $CrO_4^{2-}, Cr_2O_7^{2-}$ (d) $H_2Cr_2O_7, CrO_4^{2-}$

68. Which of the following arrangements does not represent the correct order of the property stated against it? **[JEE Main 2013]**
(a) $V^{2+} < Cr^{2+} < Mn^{2+} < Fe^{2+}$: paramagnetic behaviour
(b) $Ni^{2+} < Co^{2+} < Fe^{2+} < Mn^{2+}$: ionic size
(c) $Co^{3+} < Fe^{3+} < Cr^{3+} < Sc^{3+}$: stability in aqueous solution
(d) Sc < Ti < Cr < Mn : number of oxidation states

69. The element Ds lies in
(a) *s*-block (b) *p*-block
(c) *d*-block (d) *f*-block

70. Which of the following is called white vitriol?
(a) $ZnCl_2$ (b) $MgSO_4 \cdot 7H_2O$
(c) $ZnSO_4 \cdot 7H_2O$ (d) $Al_2(SO_4)_3$

71. Which one of the following statements is not correct?
(a) Zinc dissolves in sodium hydroxide solution
(b) Carbon monoxide reduces iron (III) oxide to iron
(c) Mercury (II) iodide dissolves in excess of potassium iodide solution
(d) Tin(IV) chloride is made by dissolving tin solution in concentrated hydrochloric acid

72. Which of the following statements concerning lanthanides elements is false?
(a) Lanthanides are separated from one another by ion-exchange method
(b) Ionic radii of trivalent lanthanides steadily increase with increase in the atomic number
(c) All lanthanides are highly dense metals
(d) More characteristic oxidation state of lanthanides elements is +3

73. The mercury is the only metal which is liquid at 0°C. This is due to its
(a) weak metallic bond
(b) high ionisation energy
(c) high vapour pressure
(d) Both (a) and (b)

74. A transition element *X* has a configuration [Ar] $3d^4$, in its +3 oxidation state. Its atomic number is
(a) 25 (b) 26 (c) 22 (d) 19

75. Which of the following elements is responsible for oxidation of water to O_2 is biological processes?
(a) Fe (b) Cu (c) Mn (d) Mo

76. Which one of the following ionic species will impart colour to an aqueous solution?
(a) Ti^{4+} (b) Cu^+
(c) Zn^{2+} (d) Cr^{3+}

77. Which of the following statements is not correct?
(a) $La(OH)_3$ is less basic than $Lu(OH)_3$
(b) In lanthanide series ionic radius of Ln^{3+} ion decreases
(c) La is actually an element of transition series rather lanthanide
(d) Atomic radius of Zr and Hf are same because of lanthanide contraction

78. The correct order of ionic radii of Y^{3+}, La^{3+}, Eu^{3+} and Lu^{3+} is
(Atomic number of Y = 39, La = 57, Eu = 63, Lu = 71)
(a) $Lu^{3+} < Eu^{3+} < La^{3+} < Y^{3+}$
(b) $La^{3+} < Eu^{3+} < Lu^{3+} < Y^{3+}$
(c) $Y^{3+} < La^{3+} < Eu^{3+} < Lu^{3+}$
(d) $Y^{3+} < Lu^{3+} < Eu^{3+} < La^{3+}$

79. The atomic radius of Ag is closest to **[JEE Main 2020]**
(a) Hg (b) Au (c) Ni (d) Cu

80. The basic character of the transition metal monoxides follows the order
(Atomic number Ti = 22, V = 23, Cr = 24, Fe = 26)
(a) TiO > FeO > VO > CrO
(b) TiO > VO > CrO > FeO
(c) TiO > CrO > TiO > FeO
(d) CrO > VO > FeO > TiO

81. The colour of light absorbed by an aqueous solution of $CuSO_4$ is **[JEE Advanced 2013]**
(a) orange-red (b) blue-green
(c) yellow (d) violet

82. Among K, Ca, Fe and Zn, the element which can form more than one binary compound with chlorine is
(a) Fe (b) Zn (c) K (d) Ca

83. Philospher's wool on treatment with cobalt nitrate, produces
(a) $CoBaO_2$ (b) $CoZnO_2$
(c) $CoSrO_2$ (d) $CoMgO_2$

84. Which of the following does not react with AgCl?
(a) NH_4OH (b) $NaNO_3$
(c) $Na_2S_2O_3$ (d) Na_2CO_3

85. Which of the following is used as purgative?
(a) HgS (b) Hg_2Cl_2
(c) $HgCl_2$ (d) $ZnSO_4$

86. The reactivity of transition elements decreases with
(a) the decrease in the atomic number
(b) the increase in the atomic number
(c) low heat of hydration
(d) None of the above

87. Fulminating gold is
(a) $AuCl_3$ (b) Au_2S
(c) $Au(NH_2)=NH$ (d) $H[Au(Cl)_4]$

88. An extremely hot copper wire reacts with steam to produce
(a) Cu_2O (b) CuO_2 (c) Cu_2O_2 (d) CuO

89. Ag is obtained from $AgNO_3$ with
(a) NH_3 (b) PH_3 (c) AsH_3 (d) Na_2CO_3

90. The incorrect statement for *d*-block element is
(a) it shows magnetic property
(b) it has variable valency
(c) it has tendency of formation of coloured ions
(d) it has complete *d*-orbitals

91. Which of the following transition element shows the highest oxidation state?
(a) Mn (b) Fe (c) V (d) Cr

92. To protect iron against corrosion, the most durable metal plating on it, is
(a) nickel plating (b) tin plating
(c) copper plating (d) zinc plating

93. $K_2Cr_2O_7$ on heating with aqueous NaOH, gives
(a) CrO_4^{2-} (b) $Cr(OH)_3$ (c) $Cr_2O_7^{2-}$ (d) $Cr(OH)_2$

94. The lanthanide contraction is responsible for the fact that
(a) Zn and Y have about the same radii
(b) Zr and Nb have similar oxidation state
(c) Zr ahd Hf have about the same radii
(d) Zr and Zn have the same oxidation state

95. The electronic configuration of (Gd) (At. no. 64) is
(a) [Xe] $4f^8, 5d^9, 6s^2$ (b) [Xe] $4f^7, 5d^1, 6s^2$
(c) [Xe] $4f^6, 5d^2, 6s^2$ (d) [Xe] $4f^3, 5d^3, 6s^2$

96. Which one of the following elements shows maximum number of different oxidation states in its compounds?
(a) Eu (b) La
(c) Gd (d) Am

97. Oxidation state of Fe in Fe_3O_4 is
(a) $\frac{3}{2}$ (b) $\frac{4}{5}$ (c) $\frac{5}{4}$ (d) $\frac{8}{3}$

98. Bell-metal is an alloy of
(a) Cu + Pb (b) Cu + Sn
(c) Cu + Zn (d) Cu + Ni

99. Of the following transition metals, the maximum number of oxidation states are exhibited by
(a) chromium ($Z = 24$) (b) manganese ($Z = 25$)
(c) iron ($Z = 26$) (d) titanium ($Z = 22$)

100. Which of the following is not an actinide?
(a) Curium (b) Californium
(c) Uranium (d) Terbium

101. The nature of Fe_2O_3 is
(a) acidic (b) basic
(c) amphoteric (d) None of these

102. The metal present in vitamin B_{12} is
(a) cobalt (b) iron
(c) manganese (d) magnesium

103. Which among the following is consumed by humans in the elemental form?
(a) Cu (b) Pb (c) Ag (d) Hg

104. Anhydrous ferric chloride is prepared by
(a) heating hydrated ferric chloride at a high temperature in a stream of air
(b) heating metallic iron in a stream of dry chlorine gas
(c) reaction of feric oxide with HCl
(d) reaction of metallic iron with HCl

105. When MnO_2 is fused with KOH and KNO_2, a coloured compound is formed, the product and its colour is
(a) K_2MnO_4, green (b) $KMnO_4$, purple
(c) Mn_2O_3, brown (d) Mn_3O_4, black

106. $(NH_4)_2Cr_2O_7$ on heating gives a gas which is also given by
(a) heating NH_4NO_2 (b) heating NH_4NO_3
(c) $Mg_3N_2 + H_2O$ (d) $Na + H_2O_2$

107. The pair of compounds having metals in their highest oxidation state is
(a) $MnO_2, FeCl_3$ (b) $[MnO_4]^-, CrO_2Cl_2$
(c) $[Fe(CN)_6]^{3-}, [Co(CN)_3]$ (d) $[NiCl_4]^{2-}, [CoCl_4]^-$

108. Europium is
(a) *s*-block element (b) *p*-block element
(c) *d*-block element (d) *f*-block element

109. Spin only magnetic moment of the compound $Hg[Co(SCN)_4]$ is
(a) $\sqrt{3}$ (b) $\sqrt{15}$ (c) $\sqrt{24}$ (d) $\sqrt{8}$

110. Which pair of compounds is expected to show similar colour in aqueous medium?
(a) $FeCl_3$ and $CuCl_2$ (b) $VOCl_2$ and $CuCl_2$
(c) $VOCl_2$ and $FeCl_2$ (d) $FeCl_2$ and $MnCl_2$

111. A solution of a metal ion when treated with KI gives a red precipitate which dissolves in excess KI to give a colourless solution. Moreover, the solution of metal ion on treatment with a solution of cobalt(II) thiocyanate gives rise to a deep blue crystalline precipitate. The metal ion is
(a) Pb^{2+} (b) Hg^{2+} (c) Cu^{2+} (d) Co^{2+}

112. Consider a titration of potassium dichromate solution with acidified Mohr's salt solution using diphenylamine as indicator. The number of moles of Mohr's salt required per mole of dichromate is
(a) 3 (b) 4 (c) 5 (d) 6

113. Consider the following statements,
I. The size of the lanthanide M^{3+} ions decreases as the atomic number of *M* increases.
II. Electronic spectra of lanthanides show very broad bands.
III. As with transition metals, coordination number six is very common in lanthanide complexes.
Which of the statements given above is/are correct?
(a) I only (b) I and II (c) I and III (d) III only

114. A red solid is insoluble in water. However, it becomes soluble if some KI is added to water. Heating the red solid in a test tube results in liberation of some violet coloured fumes and droplets of a metal appear on the cooler parts of the test tube. The red solid is
(a) $(NH_4)_2Cr_2O_7$ (b) HgI_2
(c) HgO (d) Pb_3O_4

115. What would happen when as solution of potassium chromate is treated with an excess of dilute nitric acid?
(a) Cr^{3+} and $Cr_2O_7^{2-}$ are formed
(b) $Cr_2O_7^{2-}$ and H_2O are formed
(c) CrO_4^{2-} is reduced to +3 state of Cr
(d) None of the above

116. Which one of the following nitrates will leave behind a metal on strong heating?
(a) Ferric nitrate (b) Copper nitrate
(c) Manganese nitrate (d) Silver nitrate

117. Cerium ($Z = 58$) is an important member of lanthanides. Which of the following statements about cerium is incorrect?
(a) The common oxidation states of cerium are +3 and +4
(b) The +3 oxidation states of cerium is more stable than the +4 state
(c) The +4 oxidation state of cerium is not known in solutions
(d) Cerium (IV) acts as an oxidising agent

118. Calomel (Hg_2Cl_2) on reaction with ammonium hydroxide gives
(a) HgO (b) Hg_2O
(c) $NH_2—Hg—Hg—Cl$ (d) $HgNH_2Cl$

119. Which of the following factors may be regarded as the main cause of lanthanide contraction?
(a) Greater shielding of 5*d*-electron by 4*f*-electrons
(b) Poorer shielding of 5*d*-electron by 4*f*-electrons
(c) Effective shielding of one 4*f*-electrons by another in the subshell
(d) Poor shielding of one of 4*f*-electrons by another in the subshell

120. Amongst the following, identify the species with an atom in +6 oxidation state
(a) MnO_4^- (b) $Cr(CN)_6^{3-}$ (c) NiF_6^{2-} (d) CrO_2Cl_2

121. Second ionisation energies of chromium and copper are larger than those of their neighbouring elements (V, Mn, Ni, Zn). It is due to the fact that
(a) second electron in each case is removed from 4*s* orbital
(b) second electron is removed from stable half-filled 3*d* sub-orbit in case of chromium and from stable completely filled 3*d* sub-robit in case of copper
(c) electrode potential of these elements (Cr and Cu) are higher than those of their neighbouring elements
(d) their atomic radii are different due to screening effect.

122. CrO_2Cl_2 is formed while testing
(a) NO_3^- (b) Cl^- (c) Cr^{3+} (d) Fe^{3+}

123. The most abundant element is
(a) Cu (b) Hg (c) Cd (d) Fe

124. Which represents correct comparison of the stability of ions?
(a) $MnO_4^- < Mn^{2+}$ (b) $Cr^{2+} < Cr^{3+}$
(c) $CrO_4^{2-} < Cr^{3+}$ (d) All of these

125. Select the coloured and paramagnetic ions
(a) Cu^+, Zn^{2+}, Cd^{2+}
(b) Sc^{3+}, Ti^{4+}, V^{5+}
(c) Cu^{2+}, Cr^+, Mn^{2+}
(d) Ni^{2+}, Cu^+, Hg^{2+}

126. Different (variable) oxidation state is shown by transition elements. It is due to the fact
(a) $(n-1)d$ electrons may be excited to *ns* orbital
(b) *ns* electrons may be excited to $(n-1)d$ orbitals
(c) $(n-1)d$-electron may get involved along with *ns* electrons in bonding
(d) None of the above facts is correct

127. In the following reactions, ZnO is respectively acting as a/an **[JEE Main 2017]**
(i) $ZnO + Na_2O \longrightarrow Na_2ZnO_2$
(ii) $ZnO + CO_2 \longrightarrow ZnCO_3$
(a) base and acid (b) base and base
(c) acid and acid (d) acid and base

128. In which case(s) there is change in oxidation number
(a) Aqueous solution of CrO_4^{2-} is acidified
(b) SO_2 gas is passed into $Cr_2O_7^{2-}/H^+$
(c) $Cr_2O_7^{2-}$ solution is made alkaline
(d) CrO_2Cl_2 is dissolved in NaOH

129. Factors which affect the stability of the compounds are
(a) the energy of sublimation
(b) the lattice energy
(c) the solvation energy
(d) All of the above

130. Which forms protective and non-corrosive oxide layer?
(a) Cr (b) Ni
(c) Zn (d) Cu

131. First IE of 5*d*-elements are higher than those of 3*d* and 4*d*-elements. This is due to
(a) greater effective nuclear charge acting on outer valence electrons
(b) greater effective nuclear charge is experienced because of the weak shielding of the nucleus by 4*f*-electrons
(c) Both (a) and (b)
(d) None of the above

132. NH_4Cl is used to clear metal surfaces because
(a) it dissociates into NH_3 and HCl on heating
(b) NH_3 forms soluble complexes with the metal
(c) HCl forms a volatile
(d) None of the above

133. Most transition metals
I. forms sets of compounds which display different oxidation states of the metal.
II. form coloured ions in solution.
III. burn vigorously in oxygen.
IV. replace H_2 from dilute acids.
Of these
(a) I, II, III are correct (b) II, III, IV and correct
(c) I, II are correct (d) All are correct

134. A blue solution of copper sulphate becomes darker when treated with excess of ammonia. This is because
(a) ammonia molecules replace water molecules in the solution
(b) ammonia is stronger ligand than water
(c) ammonia forms a stable complex ion $[Cu(NH_3)_4]^{2+}$ with Cu^{2+} ions.
(d) All of the above are correct

135. Effective atomic number (EAN) of Fe in brown ring complex $[Fe(H_2O)_5NO]^{2+}$
(a) 36 (b) 37 (c) 38 (d) 39

136. Select the correct relative stability.
(a) $[Cu(CN)_4]^{3-} > [Cd(CN)_4]^{3-}$
(b) $PtCl_4^{2-} > NiCl_4^{2-}$
(c) $[NiCl_6]^{2-} > [PtCl_6]^{2-}$
(d) $[Cd(CN)_4]^{2-} > [Cu(CN)_4]^{3-}$

137. Magnetic moment of $[Ni(CN)_4]^{2-}$ is zero but that of $[Ni(H_2O)_4]^{2+}$ is 2.83 BM.
It is because of
(a) different oxidation state of Ni in two complexes
(b) CN^- is a strong ligand making two unpaired electrons in Ni^{2+} paired while in $[Ni(H_2O)_4]^{2+}$, two electrons remain unpaired H_2O being weak ligand
(c) Both (a) and (b)
(d) None of the above

138. There are three electrons unpaired in $[Co(H_2O)_6]^{2+}$ and calculated value of magnetic moment is 3.87 BM which is quite different from the experimental value of 4.40 BM. This is because of
(a) increase in number of unpaired electrons
(b) some contribution of the orbital motion of the electron to the magnetic moment
(c) change in orbital spin of the electron
(d) *d-d** transition

139. Cu^{2+} has a stronger polarising power than that of Ca^{2+} because
(a) Cu^{2+} ion is smaller than Ca^{2+} ion
(b) Ca^{2+} has inert gas configuration whereas Cu^{2+} ion does not
(c) copper shows variable valency, calcium does not
(d) Cu^{2+} is smaller than Ca^{2+} ion and the *d*-electrons in Cu^{2+} ion shield the nucleus poorly

140. Atoms of the transition elements are smaller than those of the *s*-block elements. This is because of
(a) usual contraction in size across a horizontal period
(b) orbital electrons added to the penultimate *d*-shell rather than to the outer shell of the atom
(c) Both (a) and (b)
(d) None of the above

141. Select the correct order of sizes of different species.
(a) Zr = Hf; Nb = Ta; Fe = Co = Ni
(b) $Zr^{4+} < Zr$; $Nb^{3+} < Ta^{3+}$, $Fe^{3+} < Fe^{2+} < Fe$
(c) $Zr^{4+} = Hf^{4+}$; $Nb^{3+} = Ta^{3+}$; Fe < Co < Ni
(d) $Zr^{4+} < Hf^{4+}$ $Nb^{3+} = Ta^{3+}$, Ni < Cu < Co

142. The radii of the elements from chromium ($Z = 24$) to copper ($Z = 29$) are very close to one another. This is due to
(a) lanthanide contraction
(b) the fact that successive addition of *d*-electrons screen the outer electrons (4*s*) from the inward pull of the nucleus
(c) increase in radii due to increase in *n* is compensated by decrease in radii due to increase in *Z*
(d) atomic radii do not remain constant but decrease in a normal gradation

143. The lanthanoid contraction is due to
(a) filling of 4*f* before 4*d*
(b) filling of 4*d* before 4*f*
(c) filling of 4*f* before 5*d*
(d) filling of 5*d* before 4*f*

144. Magnetic moment of $[Ti(H_2O)_6]^{3+}$ is
(a) 1.73 BM (b) 2.83 BM
(c) 3.87 BM (d) 4.90 BM

145. Magnetic moment of Fe is similar to that of
(a) $[Fe(H_2O)_6]^{2+}$ (b) $[Cr(H_2O)_6]^{2+}$
(c) Both (a) and (b) (d) None of these

146. The atomic numbers of vanadium (V), chromium (Cr), manganese (Mn) and iron are respectively 23, 24, 25 and 26. Which one of these may be expected to have the highest second ionization enthalpy?
(a) V (b) Cr (c) Mn (d) Fe

147. Arrange the following metal complex/compounds in the increasing order of spin only magnetic moment. Presume all the three, high spin system.
(Atomic numbers of Ce = 58, Gd = 64 and Eu = 63)
I. $(NH_4)_2[Ce(NO_3)_6]$ II. $Gd(NO_3)_3$ II. $Eu(NO_3)_3$
[JEE main 2021, March]
(a) II < I < III (b) III < I < II
(c) I < II < III (d) I < III < II

148. Increasing value of magnetic moments of
I. $Ni(CO)_4$, II. $[Ti(H_2O)_6]^{2+}$, III. $[V(H_2O)_6]^{3+}$, IV. $[V(H_2O)_6]^{2+}$ is
(a) I < II < III < IV (b) IV < III < II < I
(c) II < III < I < IV (d) II < I < III < IV

149. Which of the following is colourless?

(a) $[Zn(H_2O)_6]^{2+}$ (b) $[V(H_2O)_6]^{2+}$
(c) $[Mn(H_2O)_6]^{3+}$ (d) $[Fe(H_2O)_6]^{2+}$

150. Which is the coloured ion?

(a) $[Cu(CN)_4]^{3-}$ (b) $[Sc(H_2O)_6]^{3+}$
(c) $[Mn(H_2O)_6]^{3+}$ (d) All of these

151. Which of the following is not an actinoid?

(a) Am (b) Cm
(c) Fm (d) Tm

152. Which of the following is paramagnetic as well as coloured ion?

(a) Cu^+ (b) Cu^{2+}
(c) Sc^{3+} (d) Ti^{4+}

153. Select the correct statement(s).

(a) Colour of the ion arises due to *d-d** transition
(b) Colour we observe is the complimentary colour absorbed by the compound
(c) Both (a) and (b) are correct
(d) None of the above is correct

154. Non-stoichiometry is shown

(a) due to variable valency of transition elements
(b) due to defects in solid structures
(c) due to both (a) and (b)
(d) due to none of the above

155. Cementite is

(a) interstitial compound of iron and carbon
(b) an alloy of Fe and Cr
(c) a compound resembling cement
(d) an ore of iron

156. Which catalyst is matched according to its name and function?

	Catalyst	Name	Function
(a)	$TiCl_4$	Fenton's reagent	Oxidation of alcohols
(b)	$FeSO_4/H_2O_2$	Ziegler-Natta	Polythene preparation
(c)	Pd/C	Lindlar	Hydrogen to give *cis*-alkene
(d)	Pt/PtO	Adam	Synthesis of CH_3OH

157. Select the correct statement.

(a) Fe and Mo atoms are present in nitrogen fixing enzymes
(b) A cobalt atom lies at the centre of the vitamin B_{12} coenzyme
(c) Fe atoms are involved in the ferrodoxins of photosynthetic process
(d) All of the above are correct statements

158. Which is the set of non-stoichiometric compounds?

(a) NaCl, FeO, $MgCl_2$ (b) FeO, CuS, VSe
(c) Fe_3O_4, NaCl, CuS (d) CuCl, CuS, MgO

159. Arrange VO_2^+, $Cr_2O_7^{2-}$ and MnO_4^- in increasing oxidising power

(a) $MnO_4^- < Cr_2O_7^{2-} < VO_2^+$
(b) $VO_2^+ < Cr_2O_7^{2-} < MnO_4^-$
(c) $VO_2^+ < MnO_4^- < Cr_2O_7^{2-}$
(d) $Cr_2O_7^{2-} < MnO_4^- < VO_2^+$

160. $KMnO_4$ is the oxosalt of

(a) MnO_2 (b) Mn_2O_7 (c) MnO_3 (d) Mn_2O_3

161. In the following reaction sequence in aqueous solution, the species *X*, *Y* and *Z*, respectively, are

$$S_2O_3^{2-} \xrightarrow{Ag^+} \underset{\text{(Clear solution)}}{X} \xrightarrow{Ag^+} \underset{\text{(White ppt.)}}{Y} \xrightarrow{\text{With time}} \underset{\text{(Black ppt.)}}{Z}$$

[JEE Advanced 2016]

(a) $[Ag(S_2O_3)_2]^{3-}$, $Ag_2S_2O_3$, Ag_2S
(b) $[Ag(S_2O_3)_3]^{5-}$, Ag_2SO_3, Ag_2S
(c) $[Ag(SO_3)_2]^{3-}$, $Ag_2S_2O_3$, Ag
(d) $[Ag(SO_3)_3]^{3-}$, Ag_2SO_4, Ag

162. VO_2 is an amphoteric oxide and in acidic medium it forms

(a) VO^{2+} (b) VO_2^+ (c) V^{3+} (d) VO_2^{2+}

163. CrO_2^{2+} is the cation formed from

(a) CrO (b) Cr_2O_3 (c) CrO_5 (d) CrO_3

164. The oxide Cr_2O_3 is

(a) acidic (b) amphoteric
(c) basic (d) ozonide

165. At pH = 4, $Cr_2O_4^{2-}$ exists as

(a) CrO_4^{2-} (b) CrO_3 (c) CrO_2^{2+} (d) $Cr_2O_7^{2-}$

166. At pH = 12, $Cr_2O_7^{2-}$ changes to

(a) CrO_3 (b) CrO_2^{2+}
(c) CrO_4^{2-} (d) no change

167. In acidic medium H_2O_2 changes $K_2Cr_2O_7$ to CrO_5 (deep violet solution in ether) having two peroxy linkage. Oxidation number of Cr in CrO_5 is

(a) +10 (b) −10 (c) +4 (d) +6

168. In alkaline H_2O_2, $Cr_2O_7^{2-}$ changes to tetraperoxo species ... having oxidation number of Cr as ...

(a) CrO_4^{2-} 6
(b) CrO_5 6
(c) CrO_8^{3-} 5
(d) CrO_8^{3-} 11

169. MnO_4^{2-} can be converted to MnO_4^-

(a) by oxidation with Cl_2
(b) by electrochemical oxidation at anode
(c) by both (a) and (b) methods
(d) by none of the above methods

170. In acidic medium MnO_4^{2-}
(a) disproportionates to MnO_2 and MnO_4^-
(b) is oxidised to MnO_4^-
(c) is reduced to MnO_2
(d) is reduced to Mn^{2+}

171. Alkaline $KMnO_4$ (Baeyer's reagent) can be used to test unsaturation in (*A*).

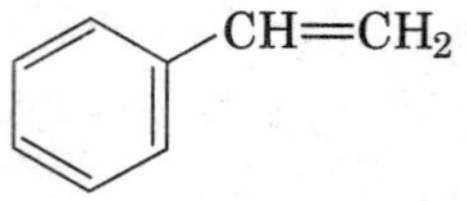

(*A*)

In this case
(a) unsaturation in side-chain is affected
(b) unsaturation in benzene nucleus is affected
(c) unsaturation in both is affected
(d) Baeyer's reagent cannot be used

172. $KMnO_4$ spot can be bleached by
(a) H_2O_2/H^+ (b) SO_2/H^+
(c) $C_2O_4^{2-}/H^+$ (d) All of these

173. Traces of MnO_4^- in conc. H_2SO_4 may change to
(a) Mn_2O_7 (b) MnO_3^+
(c) MnO_2 (d) MnO_4^{2-}

174. A white solid *Y*, on heating gives off a gas which turns lime water milky; the residue is yellow when hot; white when cold. The solid *Y* is probably
(a) $ZnCO_3$ (b) $PbCO_3$
(c) $ZnSO_4$ (d) $Zn(NO_3)_2$

175. Aqueous ZnO can neutralise HCl as well as NaOH solution. Thus, ZnO is an
(a) acidic oxide
(b) basic oxide
(c) amphoteric oxide
(d) amphiprotic oxide

176. Which is not blackened by atmosphere H_2S?
(a) $Pb(CH_3COO)_2$ (b) $Zn(CH_3COO)_2$
(c) $Cu(CH_3COO)_2$ (d) $Hg(CH_3COO)_2$

177. ZnO in CH_3COOH gives bluish white ppt with *X*. *X* is
(a) $K_4[Fe(CN)_6]$ (b) $K_3[Fe(CN)_6]$
(c) $Na_2[Fe(CN)_5NO]$ (d) $Fe(CO)_5$

178. Select the correct statement.
(a) $ZnSO_4 \cdot 7H_2O$ is called epsom salt
(b) $ZnSO_4 \cdot 7H_2O$ is isomorphous with Glauber's salt
(c) $ZnSO_4 \cdot 7H_2O$ with BaS is called lithopone
(d) All the above are correct statements

179. Silver nitrate solution is kept in brown bottles in the laboratory because
(a) it reacts with ordinary bottles
(b) ordinary bottles catalyst the decomposition
(c) the materials of brown bottles do not react with it
(d) brown bottles cut the passage of light through it

180. On addition of $AgNO_3$ to four different test tubes containing different solutions, one of them gave a white precipitate. It may be
(a) $CHCl_3$ (b) $CaCl_2$
(c) KNO_3 (d) CCl_4

181. Select the correct statement.
(a) PH_3 reduces $AgNO_3$ to metallic Ag
(b) Organic tissues turn $AgNO_3$ black by reducing it to Ag
(c) AgCN is soluble in KCN
(d) All of the above are correct statements

182. Hypo ($Na_2S_2O_3$)
(a) dissolves AgBr in photographic plate
(b) gives white precipitate with $AgNO_3$; white precipitate changes to black on dilution
(c) gives both reactions
(d) gives none of the above reactions

183. Sugar in urine sample can be detected by
I. Fehling's solution
II. Benedict's solution
III. Tollen's solution.
Select the correct alternate.
(a) I, II, III (b) I, III
(c) I, II (d) II, III

184. If a person is asked to prepare the blue print of a building plan, he can use
(a) $FeCl_3 + K_4[Fe(CN)_6]$
(b) $FeCl_2 + K_3[Fe(CN)_6]$
(c) $FeCl_2 + K_4[Fe(CN)_6]$
(d) Fe(Ct) + $K_3[Fe(CN)_6]$ Ct is citrate

185. If $FeCl_3 \cdot 6H_2O$ would exist as a complex, one mole of it in aqueous solution on reaction with excess of $AgNO_3$ forms
(a) 1 mole of AgCl (white precipitate)
(b) 2 moles of AgCl
(c) 3 moles of AgCl
(d) no reaction

186. $K_3[Fe(CN)_6]$ is used as an external indicator in the dichromate estimation of Fe^{2+}. Following change is observed
(a) colourless to blue (b) blue to red
(c) colourless to red (d) blue to colourless

187. If zinc pieces are added yellow $FeCl_3$ solution, it turns to very light green. It is because
(a) $FeCl_3$ solution is acidic due to hydrolysis and zinc added produces nascent hydrogen causing reduction of $FeCl_3$ to $FeCl_2$
(b) $FeCl_3$ solution is basic and zinc added produces H_2 which reduces $FeCl_3$ to $FeCl_2$
(c) Zinc reduces $FeCl_3$ to $FeCl_2$
(d) None of the above is correct

188. At 300°C, $FeCl_3$
(a) decomposes into $FeCl_2$ and Cl_2
(b) decomposes into Fe and Cl_2
(c) sublimes to give liquid $FeCl_3$
(d) sublimes to give gaseous dimer $(FeCl_3)_2$

189. The compound that get oxidised even on exposure to air is
(a) Fe_2O_3 (b) $FeCl_2$ (c) $FeCl_3$ (d) $Fe_2(SO_4)_3$

190. Rust contains $Fe_2O_3 \cdot H_2O$. Rust spots can be removed by
(a) $Na_2S_2O_3$ (hypo) (b) SO_2
(c) $H_2C_2O_4$ (oxalic acid) (d) $KMnO_4$

191. Which of the following combination will produce H_2 gas? **[JEE Advanced 2017]**
(a) Fe metal and conc. HNO_3
(b) Cu metal and conc. HNO_3
(c) Au metal and NaCN (*aq*) in the presence of air
(d) Zn metal and NaOH (*aq*)

192. On passing Cl_2 gas into alkaline hydrated Fe_2O_3 solution
(a) red purple solution of Na_2FeO_4 is formed
(b) colourless $NaFeO_2$ is formed due to dissolution of Fe_2O_3 into NaOH
(c) $Fe(OH)_3$ is formed
(d) no reaction takes place

193. Fe_3O_4 is called
(a) haematite (b) magnetite
(c) casserite (d) dolomite

194. Isomorphous salts are
(a) green vitriol, blue vitriol and Epsom salt
(b) green, vitriol, white vitriol and blue vitriol
(c) green vitriol, white vitriol and Epsom salt
(d) blue vitriol, white vitriol and Epsom salt

195. $[Fe(H_2O)_5NO]^{2+}$ is brown-ring complex in NO_3^-. In this complex
(a) NO transfers its electron to Fe^{2+} so that there are three electrons unpaired making iron as Fe(I) and nitrosyl as NO^+
(b) magnetic moment of Fe is 3.87 BM
(c) the colour is due to charge transfer
(d) All of the above are correct statements

196. $K_2Cr_2O_7/H^+$ changes to green by
(a) Fe^{2+} (b) SO_3^{2-}
(c) Both (a) and (b) (d) None of these

197. Some of the following reagents are used as **primary standard.**
I. $KMnO_4$ II. NaOH III. $K_2Cr_2O_7$;
IV. $FeSO_4 \cdot (NH_4)_2SO_4 \cdot 6H_2O$ V. $H_2C_2O_4 \cdot 2H_2O$
Select the primary standard
(a) all except II, IV (b) all except I, II
(c) all except I, II, III (d) only IV

198. Most oxidising agent is
(a) $[WO_4]^{2-}$ (b) $[CrO_4]^{2-}$ (c) $[CeO_4]^{2-}$ (d) $[MnO_4]^{2-}$

199. Fehling's solution consists of two separate alkaline solutions. One solution contains $CuSO_4$. The other solution contains.
(a) $NaHCO_3$ (b) $KNaC_4H_4O_6$
(c) $KHCO_3$ (d) K_2CO_3

200. If H_2S gas is passed into a solution of Cu^{2+}, Cd^{2+} having excess of KCN
(a) CuS and CdS both are precipitated
(b) soluble complex $[Cu(CN)_4]^{3-}$ and $[Cd(CN)_4]^{2-}$ are formed and no effect of passing H_2S gas
(c) soluble complex $[Cu(CN)_4]^{3-}$ and $[Cd(CN)_4]^{2-}$ as are formed, of which CdS is precipitated as yellow ppt.
(d) soluble complex $[Cu(CN)_4]^{3-}$ and $[Cd(CN)_4]^{2-}$ are formed of which CuS is precipitated as black ppt.

201. When K_2CrO_4 is added to $CuSO_4$ solution, there is formation of $CuCrO_4$ as well as $CuCr_2O_7$. Formation of $CuCr_2O_7$ is due to
(a) basic nature of $CuSO_4$ solution which converts CrO_4^{2-} to $Cr_2O_7^{2-}$
(b) acidic nature of $CuSO_4$ solution which converts CrO_4^{2-} to $Cr_2O_7^{2-}$
(c) $CuSO_4$ has the typical property of converting $CuCrO_4$ is formed to $CuCr_2O_7$
(d) no $CuCr_2O_7$ is formed

202. In an atmosphere with industrial smog, Cu corrodes to
(a) basic sulphate $Cu_2(OH)_2SO_4$
(b) basic carbonate $Cu_2(OH)_2CO_3$
(c) Both (a) and (b)
(d) None of the above

203. $Na_2S_2O_3$
(a) reduces Cu^{2+} to Cu^+
(b) reduces I_2 to I^-
(c) complexes AgBr as $[Ag(S_2O_3)_2]^{3-}$
(d) undergoes all the above are correct

204. The element which forms ions in dimeric state is
(a) iron (b) mercury
(c) cadmium (d) nickel

205. Mixture is supposed to contain nitrates of Pb^{2+} and Hg_2^{2+}. On adding dil. HCl both are precipitated as white precipitate
Select the correct statement(s).
(a) $PbCl_2$ (white precipitate) is soluble in hot water and formation of yellow precipitate on adding KI to hot solution confirms Pb^{2+}
(b) Hg_2Cl_2 is blackened by NH_3, and changes to $HgCl_2$ by aqua-regia. $HgCl_2$ can be detected by KI when orange precipitate soluble in excess of KI is formed.
(c) both tests are conclusive
(d) none of the tests is conclusive

206. Hg_2Cl_2 ionises as .... and cation has .... unpaired electron(s).

(a) $2Hg^+$ and $2Cl^-$, two (b) Hg_2^{2+} and $2Cl^-$, two
(c) Hg_2^{2+} and $2Cl^-$, one (d) Hg_2^{2+} and $2Cl^-$, no

207. The basic and amphoteric oxides of transition metals are

(a) soluble in oxidising acids forming hexa-aquo ions $[MH_2O_6]^{n+}$
(b) insoluble in oxidising acids forming hexa-aquo ions $[M(H_2O)_6]^{n+}$
(c) soluble in non-oxidising acids forming hexa-aquo ions $[M(H_2O)_6]^{n+}$
(d) insoluble in non-oxidising acids forming hexa-aquo ions $[M(H_2O)_6]^{n+}$

208. A colourless aqueous solution contains nitrates of two metals, X and Y. When it was added to an aqueous solution of NaCl, a white precipitate was formed. This precipitate was found to be partly soluble in hot water to give a residue P and a solution Q. The residue P was soluble in aqueous NH_3 and also in excess sodium thiosulphate.The hot solution Q gave a yellow precipitate with KI. The metals X and Y, respectively, are

(a) Ag and Pb (b) Ag and Cd
(c) Cd and Pb (d) Cd and Zn

209. In the following reaction

$$nCH_2{=}CH_2 \longrightarrow \text{+}CH_2{-}CH_2\text{+}_n$$

Catalyst is

(a) Adam (b) Ziegler-Natta
(c) Ni/Pd (d) Fe/Mo

210. $TiCl_4$ is a

(a) Bronsted-Lowry acid
(b) Bronsted-Lowry base
(c) Lewis acid
(d) Lewis base

211. Which of the following are sets of diamagnetic species?

(a) $TiCl_4, O_2, [Ni(CN)_4]^{2-}, [Ni(H_2O)_4]^{2+}$
(b) $TiCl_4, [Ni(CN)_4]^{2-}, CO, [Ni(H_2O)_4]^{2+}$
(c) $TiCl_4, [Ni(CN)_4^{2-}]$, CO
(d) $TiCl_4$, $[Ni(CN)_4]^{2-}$, O_2

212. Which are not blackend by atmospheric H_2S?

(a) TiO_2 (b) ZnO
(c) $ZnSO_4$ + BaS (d) All of these

213. Elements after atomic number 92 are called

(a) lanthanoids
(b) actinoids
(c) inner-transition elements
(d) transuranium elements

214. Ln^{3+} (trivalent lanthanides ions) have EC

(a) [Xe] $4f^1$ to [Xe] $4f^{14}$
(b) [Xe] $4d^1 4f^1$ to [Xe] $4d^1 4f^{14}$
(c) [Xe] $4d^2 4f^0$ to [Xe] $4d^1 4f^{14}$
(d) [Xe] $4f^0$ to [Xe] $4f^{14}$

215. A certain metal will liberate hydrogen from dilute acids. It will react with water to form hydrogen only when the metal is heated and the water is in the form of steam. The metal is probably

(a) iron (b) potassium
(c) copper (d) mercury

216. The magnetic moment μ, of transition metals is related to the number of unpaired electrons, n as

(a) $\mu = n(n+2)^2$ (b) $\mu = n^2(n+2)$
(c) $\mu = \dfrac{n}{(n+2)}$ (d) $\mu = \sqrt{n(n+2)}$

217. Misch metal is

(a) an alloy of lathanide and copper
(b) an alloy of lanthanide and nickel
(c) an alloy of lanthanide, iron and carbon
(d) an alloy of calcium and copper

218. Which of the following mixture is chromic acid?

(a) $K_2Cr_2O_7$ + HCl
(b) K_2SO_4 + conc. H_2SO_4
(c) $K_2Cr_2O_7$ + conc. H_2SO_4
(d) H_2SO_4 + HCl

219. An^{3+} (trivalent actinoid ions) have configuration

(a) $5f^0$ to $5f^{14}$ (b) $5f^1$ to $5f^{14}$
(c) $5f^2$ to $5f^{14}$ (d) $5f^0$ to $5f^{13}$

220. In reduction of dichromate by Fe(II), the number of electrons involved per chromium atom is

(a) 2 (b) 3 (c) 4 (d) 1

221. Select the correct statement(s).

(a) Pu^{4+} disproportionates to Pu^{3+} and PuO_2^{2+} in strongly acidic solution
(b) Maximum oxidation state of Np is +7
(c) UO_2^{2+} is stable
(d) All of the above are correct statements

222. Uranium reacts with conc. HNO_3

(a) to give $U(NO_3)_4$ and H_2
(b) to give $U(NO_3)_2$ and NO_2
(c) $UO_2(NO_3)_2$ and H_2
(d) to make metal passive

223. What is the spin-only magnetic moment value (BM) of a divalent metal ion with atomic number 25, in it's aqueous solution ? **[JEE Main 2021, March]**

(a) 5.92 (b) 5.0
(c) zero (d) 5.26

224. The electronic configuration of bivalent europium and trivalent cerium are
(atomic number : Xe = 54, Ce = 58 Eu = 63) **[JEE Main 2020]**
(a) [Xe] $4f^7$ and [Xe] $4f^1$
(b) [Xe] $4f^7 6s^2$ and [Xe] $4f^2 6s^2$
(c) [Xe] $4f^2$ and [Xe] $4f^7$
(d) [Xe] $4f^4$ and [Xe] $4f^9$

225. Four successive members of the first row transition elements are listed below with their atomic numbers. Which one of them is expected to have the highest third ionization enthalpy?
(a) Vanadium ($Z = 23$) (b) Chromium ($Z = 24$)
(c) Iron ($Z = 26$) (d) Manganese ($Z = 25$)

226. The number of moles of $KMnO_4$ reduced by one mole of KI in alkaline medium is
(a) one fifth (b) five (c) one (d) two

227. Thermal decomposition of a Mn compound (X) at 513 K results in compound (Y), MnO_2 and a gaseous product. MnO_2 reacts with NaCl and concentrated H_2SO_4 to give a pungent gas Z. X, Y and Z, respectively, are **[JEE Main 2019, April]**
(a) K_2MnO_4, K_2MnO_4 and Cl_2
(b) K_2MnO_4, $KMnO_4$ and SO_2
(c) $KMnO_4$, K_2MnO_4 and Cl_2
(d) K_2MnO_4, $KMnO_4$ and Cl_2

228. The common oxidation state of the elements of lanthanide series is
(a) +1 (b) +3 (c) +4 (d) +6

229. Which alloy contains Cu, Sn and Zn?
(a) Gun metal (b) Solder
(c) Type metal (d) Bronze

230. Finely divided iron combines with CO to give
(a) $Fe(CO)_5$ (b) $Fe_2(CO)_9$
(c) $Fe_3(CO)_{12}$ (d) $Fe(CO)_6$

231. Green vitriol is formed by
(a) $FeS_2 + H_2O + O_2$ (b) $FeS_2 + H_2O + CO_2$
(c) $FeS_2 + CO + CO_2$ (d) $FeS_2 + CO$

232. Lanthanide and actinides resemble in
(a) electronic configuration
(b) oxidation state
(c) ionisation energy
(d) formation of complexes

233. Stainless steel is an alloy of
(a) Cu (b) Ni and Cr
(c) Mn (d) Zn

234. Solder is an alloy of
(a) 70% lead, 30% tin (b) 30% lead, 70% tin
(c) 80% lead, 20% tin (d) 90% copper, 10% tin

235. Which of the following is a highly corrosive salt?
(a) $FeCl_2$ (b) $PbCl_2$ (c) Hg_2Cl_2 (d) $HgCl_2$

236. Based on the following equilibria

$$Fe^{2+} \rightleftharpoons Fe^{3+} + e^-; \quad E° = -0.771\ V$$
$$[Fe(CN)_6]^{4-} \rightleftharpoons [Fe(CN)_6]^{3-} + e^-; \quad E° = -0.36\ V$$

Select the correct statements.
(a) Iron in +2 state is more stable than in +3 state
(b) Unstable ion can be stabilised by complexing it with a suitable ligand.
(c) Both (a) and (b)
(d) None of the above are correct statements

237. The transition element having least enthalpy of atomisation is **[JEE Main 2019]**
(a) Zn (b) V (c) Fe (d) Cu

238. The Mohr's salt is shown by
(a) $FeSO_4(NH_4)_2SO_4 \cdot 6H_2O$
(b) $FeSO_4(NH_3)_2SO_4 \cdot 6H_2O$
(c) $K_2SO_4Al_2(SO_4)_3 \cdot 24H_2O$
(d) $FeSO_2(NH_2)_4SO_4 \cdot 6H_2O$

239. The composition of duralumin is
(a) Al 94%, Mg 6%
(b) Cu 56%, Zn 24%, Ni 20%
(c) Cu 95, Al 5%
(d) Al 95%, Cu 4%, Mn 0.5%, Mg 0.5%

240. Lanthanide for which +II and +III oxidation states are common is
(a) La (b) Nd (c) Ce (d) Eu

241. The colourless species is
(a) VCl_3 (b) $VOSO_4$
(c) Na_3VO_4 (d) $[V(H_2O)_6]SO_4 \cdot H_2O$

242. MnO_4^{2-} (1 mol) in neutral aqueous medium disproportionates to
(a) $\frac{2}{3}$ mol of MnO_4^- and $\frac{1}{3}$ mol of MnO_2
(b) $\frac{1}{3}$ mol of MnO_4^- and $\frac{2}{3}$ mol of MnO_2
(c) $\frac{1}{3}$ mol of Mn_2O_7 and $\frac{1}{7}$ mol of MnO_2
(d) $\frac{2}{3}$ mol of Mn_2O_7 and $\frac{1}{3}$ mol of MnO_2

243. An aqueous solution of $CoCl_2$ on addition of excess of concentrated HCl turn blue due to formation of
(a) $[Co(H_2O)_4Cl_2]$ (b) $[Co(H_2O)_2Cl_4]^{2-}$
(c) $[CoCl_4]^{2-}$ (d) $[Co(H_2O)_2Cl_2]$

244. The diamagnetic species is
(a) $[Ni(CN)_4]^{2-}$ (b) $[NiCl_4]^{2-}$
(c) $[CoCl_4]^{2-}$ (d) $[CoF_6]^{2-}$

245. Among the following pairs of ions, the lower oxidation state in aqueous solutions is more stable than the other in
(a) Ti^+, Ti^{3+} (b) Cu^+, Cu^{2+}
(c) Cr^{2+}, Cr^{3+} (d) V^{2+}, VO^{2+}

246. The colour imparted by Co(II) compounds to glass is
(a) green (b) deep blue
(c) yellow (d) red

247. Given below, catalyst and corresponding process/reaction are matched. The mismatch is
(a) $[RhCl(PPh_3)_2]$: Hydrogenation
(b) $TiCl_4 + Al(C_2H_5)_3$: Polymerisation
(c) V_2O_5 : Haber-Bosch process
(d) Nickel : Hydrogenation

248. KI and $CuSO_4$ solutions on mixing produce
(a) $Cu_2I_2 + K_2SO_4$
(b) $Cu_2I_2 + KI_3 + K_2SO_4$
(c) $CuI_2 + K_2SO_4$
(d) $CuI_2 + KI_3 + K_2SO_4$

249. The reactivity of transition elements decreases with
(a) the decrease in the atomic number
(b) the increase in the atomic number
(c) low heat of hydration
(d) None of the above

250. Catalyst used in making H_2SO_4 in contact process is
(a) V_2O_5 (b) Fe_2O_3
(c) Cr_2O_3 (d) CrO_3

251. The incorrect configuration is
(a) K = [Ar] $4s^1$
(b) Cr = [Ar] $3d^5, 4s^1$
(c) Cr = [Ar] $3d^4, 4s^2$
(d) Cu = [Ar] $3d^{10}, 4s^1$

252. By annealing, steel
(a) becomes soft
(b) becomes liquid
(c) becomes hard and brittle
(d) is covered with a thin film of Fe_3O_4

253. Transition metals show paramagnetism due to
(a) characteristic configuration
(b) high lattice energy
(c) variable oxidation states
(d) unpaired electrons

254. The oxides, CrO_3, MoO_3 and WO_3 are strongly
(a) neutral (b) acidic
(c) basic (d) None of these

255. The outer electronic configuration of transitional elements is
(a) $(n-1)\,s^2nd^{1-2}$
(b) $(n+1)s^2nd^{1-5}$
(c) $(n-1)s^2p^6(n-1)d^{1\text{-}10}, ns^{1,2}$
(d) $ns^2(n+1)d^{1-10}$

256. The highest magnetic moment will be shown by
(a) Ni (b) Co (c) Fe (d) Sc

257. Which of the following is not a member of 3*d*-transition series?
(a) Fe (b) Co (c) Au (d) Cu

258. Which is most soluble in water?
(a) AgBr (b) AgCl
(c) AgF (d) AgI

259. Addition of $SnCl_2$ to $HgCl_2$ give precipitate
(a) white turning to red
(b) white turning to grey
(c) black turning to white
(d) None of the above

260. The stability of ferric ion is due to
(a) half filled *f*-orbitals
(b) half filled *d*-orbitals
(c) completely filled *f*-orbitals
(d) completely filled *d*-orbitals

261. Which of the following lanthanide is commonly used?
(a) Lanthanium (b) Nobelium
(c) Thorium (d) Cerium

262. $4K_2Cr_2O_7 \xrightarrow{\text{Heat}} 4K_2CrO_4 + 3O_2 + X$; in the above reaction X is
(a) CrO_3 (b) Cr_2O_7 (c) Cr_2O_3 (d) CrO_5

263. Cr^{2+} and Mn^{3+} both have d^4 configuration. Thus
(a) both are reducing agents
(b) both are oxidising agents
(c) Cr^{2+} is an oxidising agent while Mn^{3+} is a reducing agent
(d) Mn^{3+} is an oxidising agent while Cr^{2+} is a reducing agent

264. Which of the following is most stable among Cu^+, Fe^+, Fe^{2+} and Fe^{3+}?
(a) Cu^+ (b) Fe^+
(c) Fe^{2+} (d) Fe^{3+}

265. Brown glass and cement have, which element common in them?
(a) Fe (b) Al
(c) Na (d) All of these

266. The atomic size of cerium and promethium is quite close, due to
(a) they are in same period in Periodic Table
(b) their electronic configuration is same
(c) *f*-electrons have poor shielding effect
(d) nuclear charge is higher on cerium than promethium

267. The trivalent ion having largest size is
(a) Ti (b) Zr
(c) Hf (d) La

268. The transition metal used as a catalyst is
(a) nickel (b) platinum
(c) cobalt (d) All of these

269. Transition elements does not show
(a) paramagnetism
(b) colour
(c) fixed valency
(d) All of these

270. Aluminium appears like gold when mixed with
(a) 90% Cu
(b) 75% Ni
(c) 80% Sn
(d) 80% Co

271. Iron is dropped in very dil. HNO_3, it gives
(a) ferric nitrate
(b) ferric nitrate and NO_2
(c) ferrous nitrate and ammonium nitrate
(d) ferrous nitrate and nitric oxide

272. Stainless steel contains
(a) Fe + Cr + Cu (b) Fe + C + Ni
(c) Fe + Cr + Ni (d) Fe + Ni + Cu

273. Which of the following alloys is used for making magnets for hearing aids?
(a) Alnico (b) German silver
(c) Invar (d) Monel metal

274. Cuprous ion is colourless while cupric ion is coloured because
(a) both have half-filled *p*- and *d*-orbitals
(b) both have unpaired electrons in *d*-orbitals
(c) cuprous ion has incomplete *d*-orbital and cupric ion has a complete *d*-orbital
(d) cuprous ion as a complete *d*-orbital and cupric ion has an incomplete *d*-orbital

Objective Questions Type II [One or more than one correct option(s)]

In each of the questions below, four choices are given, of which one or more than one are correct.

1. When KCN is added to $CuSO_4$ solution
(a) KCN acts as a reducing agent
(b) KCN acts as a complexing agent
(c) complex $K_3[Cu(CN)_4]$ is formed
(d) complex $K_2[Cu(CN)_4]$ is formed

2. Which will not give metal on heating?
(a) Ag_2CO_3 (b) $ZnCO_3$ (c) HgO (d) CuO

3. Electron transfer from $Fe(H_2O)_6^{2+}$ to $Fe(H_2O)_6^{3+}$ is likely to occur *via*
(a) *d*-*d* transition
(b) inner sphere electron transfer
(c) S_N1 mechanism
(d) outer sphere electron transfer

4. Which of the following are coloured due to charge transfer?
(a) $KMnO_4$ (b) CrO_3
(c) $CuSO_4$ (d) $FeCl_3$

5. Reduction of the metal centre in aqueous permanganate ion involves **[IIT JEE 2011]**
(a) three electrons in neutral medium
(b) five electrons in neutral medium
(c) three electrons in alkaline medium
(d) five electrons in acidic medium

6. N_2 gas can be obtained by heating
(a) $(NH_4)_2Cr_2O_7$
(b) NH_4NO_2
(c) NH_4VO_3
(d) NH_4NO_3

7. Which are correct statements about $KMnO_4$?
(a) Its solution is unstable in acidic medium
(b) Its small quantity added to conc. H_2SO_4, a green coloured solution containing MnO_3^+ ions is formed
(c) MnO_4^- changes to Mn^{2+} in basic solution
(d) It is self-indicator in Fe^{2+} or $C_2O_4^{2-}$ titration

8. Which are correct statements?
(a) In less acidic solution $K_2Cr_2O_7$ and H_2O_2 gives violet coloured diamagnetic $[CrO(O_2)(OH)]^-$ ion
(b) In alkaline H_2O_2, K_3CrO_8 (with tetraperoxo species $[Cr(O_2)_4]^{3-}$) is formed
(c) In ammoniacal solution, $(NH_3)_3CrO_4$ is formed
(d) CrO_4^{2-} changes to $Cr_2O_7^{2-}$ by oxidation

9. For CrO_3 following is not true statement.
(a) It is called chromic acid
(b) It is colourless due to $3d^0$ configuration
(c) It is bright orange solid and colour arises due to charge transfer
(d) It is toxic and corrosive

10. Lanthanoids are
(a) 14 elements in the sixth period (atomic no. = 90 to 103) that are filling 4*f*-sublevel
(b) 14 elements in the seventh period (atomic no. = 90 to 103) that are filling 5*f*-sublevel
(c) 14 elements in the sixth period (atomic no. = 58 to 71) that are filling 4*f*-sublevel
(d) 14 elements in the seventh period (atomic no. = 58 to 71) that are filling 4*f*-sublevel

11. When CO_2 is passed into aqueous
(a) Na_2CrO_4 solution, its yellow colour changes to orange
(b) K_2MnO_4 solution, it disproportionates to $KMnO_4$ and MnO_2
(c) $Na_2Cr_2O_7$ solution, its orange colour changes to green
(d) $KMnO_4$ solution, its pink colour changes to green

12. Which of the following halides react(s) with $AgNO_3(aq)$ to give a precipitate that dissolves in $Na_2S_2O_3(aq)$? **[IIT JEE 2012]**
(a) HCl
(b) FF
(c) HBr
(d) HI

13. Standard reduction electrode potential at Zn^{2+}/Zn is –0.76 V. This means
(a) ZnO is reduced to Zn by H_2
(b) Zn liberates H_2 with conc. acids
(c) Zn is generally the anode in an electrochemical cell
(d) Zn is generally the cathode in an electrochemical cell

14. Select the correct statement(s) about $[CoCl_6]^{4-}$ complex.
(a) It is paramagnetic
(b) It is a low-spin complex
(c) Oxidation number of cobalt is –4
(d) The coordination number of cobalt is 6

15. Why does aqueous Fe(III) ion develop intense red colour when it reacts with SCN^- ion while Fe(II) ion does not?
(a) Fe(III) ion forms a charge transfer complex with SCN^- ions
(b) Fe(III) is reduced to Fe(I) which is deep red in colour
(c) SCN^- ion is oxidised to CN^- which forms red coloured complex with Fe(III) ion
(d) SCN^- does not form any complex with Fe(III) ion

16. Select the correct statement(s).
(a) Stabilities of variable oxidation states can be explained by standard electrode potential
(b) Cr^{2+} is unstable and Cr^{3+} is stable in aqueous solution
(c) Fe^{2+} is stable and Fe^{3+} is unstable in aerated water
(d) All of the above are correct statements

17. Select the correct statement(s).
(a) When $FeCl_3$ solution is added to $K_4[Fe(CN)_6]$ solution, in addition to $Fe^{III}[Fe^{II}(CN)_6]^-$, $Fe^{II}[Fe^{III}(CN)_6]^-$ is also formed due to side redox reaction
(b) When $FeCl_2$ solution is added to $K_3[Fe(CN)_6]$ solution, in addition to $Fe^{II}[Fe^{II}(CN)_6]^-$ $Fe^{III}[Fe^{II}(CN)_6]^-$ is also formed due to side redox reaction
(c) $Fe^{III}[Fe^{II}(CN)_6]^-$ is paramagnetic while $Fe^{II}[Fe^{III}(CN)_6]^-$ is diamagnetic
(d) $Fe^{III}[Fe^{II}(CN)_6]^-$ is diamagnetic while $Fe^{II}[Fe^{III}(CN)_6]^-$ is paramagnetic

18. Select the correct statement(s) about oxides of *d*-block elements.
(a) *M*O type oxides have NaCl-type structure
(b) All oxides are thermodynamically stable, their heats of formation being negative ($\Delta H_f^\circ < 0$)
(c) Oxides of the same metal in different oxidation state have different stabilities
(d) The oxides are basic in low oxidation states and acidic in high oxidation states

19. With reference to *aqua-regia*, choose the correct option(s). **[JEE Advanced 2019]**
(a) The yellow colour of *aqua-regia* is due to the presence of NOCl and Cl_2.
(b) *Aqua-regia* is prepared by mixing conc. HCl and conc. HNO_3 in 3 : 1 (v/v) ratio
(c) Reaction of gold with *aqua-regia* produces an anion having Au in +3 oxidation state
(d) Reaction of gold with *aqua-regia* produces NO_2 in the absence of air

20. The correct statement(s) about Cr^{2+} and Mn^{3+} is/are [atomic number of Cr = 24 and Mn = 25] **[JEE Advanced 2015]**
(a) Cr^{2+} is a reducing agent
(b) Mn^{3+} is an oxidising agent
(c) both Cr^{2+} and Mn^{3+} exhibit d^4 electronic configuration
(d) when Cr^{2+} is used as a reducing agent, the chromium ion attains d^5 electronic configuration

21. Fe^{3+} is reduced to Fe^{2+} by using **[JEE Advanced 2015]**
(a) H_2O_2 in presence of NaOH
(b) Na_2O_2 in water
(c) H_2O_2 in presence of H_2SO_4
(d) Na_2O_2 in presence of H_2SO_4

22. Fusion of MnO_2 with KOH in presence of O_2 produces a salt *W*. Alkaline solution of *W* upon electrolytic oxidation yields another salt *X*. The manganese containing ions present in *W* and *X*, respectively, are *Y* and *Z*. Correct statement(s) is (are) **[JEE Advanced 2019]**
(a) Both *Y* and *Z* are coloured and have tetrahedral shape.
(b) *Y* is diamagnetic in nature while *Z* is paramagnetic.
(c) In both *Y* and *Z*, π-bonding occurs between *p*-orbitals of oxygen and *d*-orbitals of manganese.
(d) In aqueous acidic solution, *Y* undergoes disproportionation reaction to give *Z* and MnO_2

23. Consider the following reactions (unbalanced).

$Zn + \text{Hot conc. } H_2SO_4 \longrightarrow G + R + X$

$Zn + \text{conc. NaOH} \longrightarrow T + Q$

$G + H_2S + NH_4OH \longrightarrow Z \text{ (a precipitate)} + X + Y$

Choose the correct option(s). [JEE Advanced 2019]

(a) The oxidation state of Zn in T is +1
(b) R is a V-shaped molecule
(c) Bond order of Q is 1 in its ground state
(d) Z is dirty white in colour

24. The correct statement (s) regarding the binary transition metal carbonyl compounds is (are) (Atomic numbers : Fe = 26, Ni = 28) [JEE Advanced 2018]

(a) Total number of valence shell electrons at metal centre in $Fe(CO)_5$ or $Ni(CO)_4$ is 16
(b) These are predominantly low spin in nature
(c) Metal-carbon bond strengthens when the oxidation state of the metal is lowered
(d) The carbonyl C—O bond weakens when the oxidation state of the metal is increased

Comprehension Based Questions

In these questions, a passage has been given followed by questions based on it. You have to answer the questions based on the passage given.

Passage 1 *From the data given in the table, answer the following questions*

Covalent Radii of the Transition Elements (pm)

K	Ca	Sc	Ti	V	Cr	Mn	Fe	Co	Ni	Cu	Zn
203	174	144	132	122	117	117	117	116	115	117	125
			Zr	Nb							
			145	134							
			Hf	Ta							
			144	134							

1. Atoms of the transition elements are smaller than those of the *s*-block elements. This is because of

(a) usual contraction in size across a horizontal period
(b) orbital electrons added to the penultimate *d*-shell rather than to the outer shell of the atom
(c) Both (a) and (b)
(d) None of the above

2. The radii of the elements from chromium ($Z = 24$) to copper ($Z = 29$) are very close to one another. This is due to

(a) lanthanide contraction
(b) the fact that successive addition of *d*-electrons screen the outer electrons (4*s*) from the inward pull of the nucleus
(c) increase in radii due to increase in n is compensated by decrease in radii due to increase in Z
(d) All of the above

3. From the table, atomic radii of Zr and Hf and those of Nb and Ta are same. It is due to

(a) lanthanide contraction
(b) the fact that increase in size due to increase in n is compensated by decrease in size due to increase in Z based on equation $r_n = \dfrac{n^2 a_0}{Z}$
(c) Both (a) and (b)
(d) None of the above

Passage 2 *Read the following short write-up and answer the questions given.*

"The transition elements have an unparalleled tendency to form coordination compounds with Lewis bases that is with groups which are able to donate an electron pair (called ligands)."

1. The tendency to form complexes by transition metal compared to *s* and *p*-block elements is due to

(a) their smaller size
(b) higher nuclear charge
(c) presence of low energy vacant orbitals to accept lone pair of electrons donated by ligands
(d) All of the above

2. Out of $[Fe(CN)_6]^{4-}$, $[Ni(CN)_4]^{2-}$ and $[Ni(CO)_4]$

(a) all have identical geometry
(b) all are paramagnetic
(c) all are diamagnetic
(d) $[Fe(CN)_6]^{4-}$ is diamagnetic but $[Ni(CN)_4]^{2-}$ and $[Ni(CO)_4]$ are paramagnetic

Passage 3 *Taking into account the following experimental fact answer the questions given at the end.*

"When metallic copper is heated with concentrated sulphuric acid, in addition to copper(II) sulphate and sulphur dioxide, some copper (II) sulphide is also formed."

1. In which reaction, SO_2 is formed?

(a) $SO_4^{2-} + 2e^- \longrightarrow$
(b) $SO_4^{2-} + 8e^- \longrightarrow$
(c) $SO_4^{2-} + 6e^- \longrightarrow$
(d) All of these

2. Copper (II) sulphide is formed because following side reaction is favourable due to its low solubility in acidic medium

(a) $SO_4^{2-} + 4H^+ + 2e^- \longrightarrow$
(b) $SO_4^{2-} + 8H^+ + 8e^- \longrightarrow$
(c) Both (a) and (b)
(d) None of the above

***Passage* 4** *Read the following short write-up and answer the questions given at the end.*

Recent X-ray work, IR and other spectroscopic methods have proved that Turnbull's blue is identical to Prussian blue.

1. What is the common formula of Turnbull's blue and Prussian blue?
   (a) $Fe_3[Fe(CN)_6]_2$ (b) $Fe_4[Fe(CN)_6]_3$
   (c) $KFe[Fe(CN)_6]$ (d) $KFe_2[Fe(CN)_6]$
2. Intense blue colour arises as a result of
   (a) electron transfer between Fe(II) and Fe(I)
   (b) electron transfer between Fe(II) and Fe(III)
   (c) *d-d** transition
   (d) spin magnetic moment

***Passage* 5** *Based on the following statements answer the questions given at the end.*

Statement The mercurous ion is written as Hg_2^{2+} while the cuprous ion is written as Cu^+.

Statement Cu^+ is d^{10} ion and colourless but Cu_2O is red and Cu_2S is black.

1. Mercurous ion is written as Hg_2^{2+} because
   (a) magnetic moment of mercurous ion is zero and thus, 6*s* unpaired electron has been used in bonding to make Hg_2^{2+}
   (b) in aqueous solution two Hg^+ ions are solvated forming Hg_2^{2+}
   (c) $HgCl_2$ disproportionates to Hg_2Cl_2 and Hg
   (d) None of the above is correct
2. There is no *d-d** transition in Cu^+(I) ion, but Cu_2O(I) and Cu_2S(I) are coloured because of
   (a) presence of electronegative ions O^{2-}, S^{2-}
   (b) presence of divalent anions
   (c) charge transfer of electrons from O^{2-} or S^{2-} to the vacant orbitals of Cu^+
   (d) All of the above

***Passage* 6** *Based on the following experimental facts answer the questions given at the end.*

"Green solution of potassium manganate (VI), turns purple and a brown solid is precipitated when CO_2 is bubbled into the solution".

1. Above change is observed when CO_2 is passed into aqueous solution of the given ion. Function of CO_2 is
   (a) it makes solution acidic due to formation of H_2CO_3
   (b) it makes the solution basic due to formation of CO_3^{2-}
   (c) it is simply the medium of the reaction
   (d) None of the above is correct
2. Given experiment involves
   (a) acid-base reaction
   (b) a redox reaction
   (c) disproportionation reaction
   (d) decomposition reaction
3. What happens when CO_2 is passed into aqueous chromate (VI) solution?
   (a) CrO_3 is formed (b) CrO_5 is formed
   (c) Cr^{3+} is formed (d) $Cr_2O_7^{2-}$ is formed

***Passage* 7** *Read the following passage and answer the questions at the end of it.*

When a piece of iron is dipped in conc. HNO_3, a slight reaction takes place which then ceases completely. There is no change in the appearance of the iron, but this does not displace Cu from $CuSO_4$ solution which is however a common property of Fe. This behaviour is also observed with Cr and Al when in contact with HNO_3.

1. Above phenomenon is called
   (a) corrosion (b) rusting (c) passivity (d) reduction
2. When exposed to air and moisture, iron gets rapidly oxidised to
   (a) FeO (b) $Fe_2O_3 \cdot xH_2O$
   (c) Fe_3O_4 (d) $FeO \cdot Fe_2O_3$
3. Select some facts about passivity and corrosion (rusting) of iron.
   I. Rusting is an electrochemical phenomenon
   II. Passivity of iron prevents it from rusting
   III. Passivity and rusting are reversible processes

   Select the correct statements.
   (a) I, II (b) II, III
   (c) I, III (d) I, II, III

***Passage* 8** *Based on the following qualitative test of chromium, answer the questions given at the end of it.*

In qualitative analysis, a confirmatory test for chromium involves the formation of a blue transient peroxo species, CrO_5. It is formed when H_2O_2 is added to on acidic solution containing $Cr_2O_7^{2-}$.

1. Select the correct statement about CrO_5.
   (a) It has two types of oxygen-peroxide and oxide
   (b) Oxidation number of Cr is + 10
   (c) It is formed by oxidation of $Cr_2O_7^{2-}$
   (d) All of the above are correct statements
2. CrO_5 can be represented as

(a) 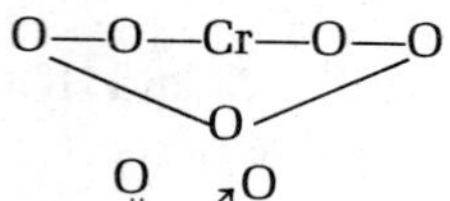
(b) 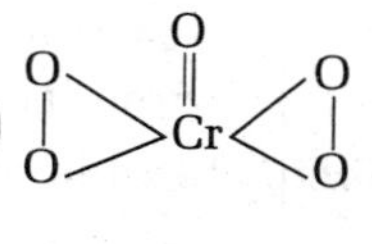
(c) 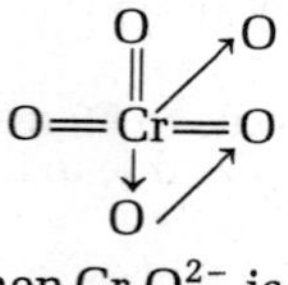
(d) 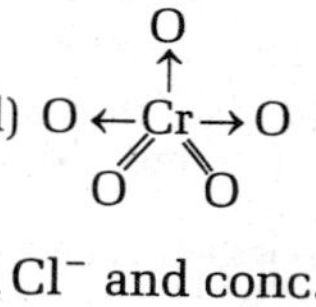

3. When $Cr_2O_7^{2-}$ is heated with Cl^- and conc. H_2SO_4 deep red vapours of chromyl chloride are formed. Deep red vapours have formula
   (a) $CrOCl_2$ (b) $(CrO)_2Cl_2$
   (c) CrO_2Cl_2 (d) CrO_3Cl

Passage 9 *Read the following observation and answer the questions given at the end.*

In an atmosphere with industrial smog, Cu corrodes to a basic sulphate $Cu_2(OH)_2SO_4$ and basic carbonate $Cu_2(OH)_2CO_3$.

1. Basic sulphate is generally formed during acid rain with a reaction

(a) $2Cu + 2H_2O + SO_3 \longrightarrow Cu_2(OH)_2SO_4$

(b) $2Cu + H_2O + SO_3 + O_2 \longrightarrow Cu_2(OH)_2SO_4$

(c) $2Cu + H_2O + SO_2 + O_2 \longrightarrow Cu_2(OH)_2SO_4$

(d) All of the above

2. Formation of basic carbonate and basic sulphate involves some of the steps

I. a redox reaction

II. acid-base neutralisation reaction

III. precipitation reaction

IV. decomposition

Select the steps actually taking place.

(a) I, III, IV (b) II, III, IV

(c) I, II, IV (d) I, II, III

3. This type of corrosion

(a) forms a tough adherent coating that protects the underlying metal

(b) causes loss of copper and thus the articles made of copper

(c) causes poisoning of the atmosphere

(d) gives a direct method of preparing basic copper carbonate and basic copper sulphate

Matrix-Match Type

Given below are Matching Type Questions, with two columns (each having some items) each . Each item of Column I has to be matched with the items of Column II.

1. Match the alloys (in Column I) with the constituents metal (in Column II).

	Column I		Column II
A.	Gun metal	1.	Pb, Sn
B.	German silver	2.	Cu, Sn, Zn
C.	Brass	3.	Cu, Zn
D.	Solder	4.	Cu, Zn, Ni

2. Match the natural coordination compounds (in Column I) with metals therein (in Column II).

	Column I		Column II
A.	Nitrogenases	1.	Cu
B.	Cytochrome oxidase	2.	Mo
C.	Cytochrome C	3.	Zn
D.	Carboxy peptidase	4.	Fe

3. Match the lanthanide ions (Ln^{3+}, in Column I) with their calculated magnetic moments (in Column II).

	Column I		Column II
A.	Ce^{3+}	1.	7.94 BM
B.	Nd^{3+}	2.	4.90 BM
C.	Gd^{3+}	3.	1.73 BM
D.	Pm^{3+}	4.	3.87 BM

4. Match the catalysts in Column I with their uses in Column II.

	Column I		Column II
A.	$TiCl_4$	1.	Adams catalyst in reduction
B.	$PdCl_2$	2.	In preparation of $(CH_3)_2SiCl_2$
C.	Pt/PtO	3.	Reppe synthesis
D.	Cu	4.	Used as the *Natta* catalyst in polythene production
E.	Ni	5.	Wake process for converting C_2H_4 to CH_3CHO

5. Match the alloys (in Column I) with their constituents (in Column II).

	Column I		Column II
A.	Invar	1.	70% Cu + 30% Zn
B.	Brass	2.	66% Ni + 33% Cu
C.	Monel	3.	36% Ni
D.	Coinage metal	4.	60% Ni + 20% Fe + 20% Cr
E.	Nichrome	5.	75% Cu + 25% Ni

6. Match the compounds in Column I with their uses in Column II.

	Column I		Column II
A.	Hg_2Cl_2	1.	Metallurgial extraction of Ag
B.	ZnO	2.	Electrode
C.	$ZnSO_4$	3.	Luminous paints
D.	Zn	4.	Lithopone

7. Match the underlined atoms in Column I with oxidation number in Column II.

	Column I		Column II
A.	$\underline{Mn}O_4^-$	1.	1
B.	$\underline{Cr}O_4^{2-}$	2.	2
C.	$\underline{Fe}\,[Fe^{II}(CN)_6]^-$	3.	3
D.	$\underline{Zn}O_2^{2-}$	4.	6
E.	$[\underline{Ag}(CN)_2]^-$	5.	7

8. Match catalyst is (Column I) according to its name and funtion.

Column I (Catalyst)		Column II (Name)		Column III (Function)
A. $TiCl_4$	1.	Fenton's reagent	P.	Oxidation of alcohol
B. $FeSO_4/H_2O_2$	2.	Ziegler-Natta	Q.	Polythene preparation
C. Pd/C	3.	Lindlar	R.	Hydrogenation of alkynes to give *cis*-alkene
D. Pt/PtO	4.	Adam	S.	Synthesis of CH_3OH

9. Match the complex ion (Column I) with its spin-only spin-only magnetic moment (Column II).

	Column I		Column II
A.	$[Co(NH_3)_6]^{3+}$	1.	1.73 BM
B.	$[Fe(CN)_6]^{3-}$	2.	5.92 BM
C.	$[Mn(H_2O)_6]^{2+}$	3.	0.0 BM
D.	$[Ni(H_2O)_6]^{2+}$	4.	2.83 BM

10. Match the species in Column I that can react (oxidise, reduce, give ppt) species in Column II.

	Column I		Column II
A.	Fe^{2+}	1.	$Cr_2O_7^{2-}$
B.	$C_2O_4^{2-}$	2.	CrO_4^{2-}
C.	Pb^{2+}	3.	$[Fe(CN)_6]^{3-}$
D.	Ag^+	4.	MnO_4^-
E.	SO_2	5.	$S_2O_3^{2-}$

11. Match the compounds in Column I with their properties in Column II.

	Column I		Column II
A.	$FeSO_4$	1.	Paramagnetic
B.	$CuSO_4$	2.	Quantitative estimation by $K_2Cr_2O_7$
C.	$FeCl_3$	3.	Colour with $K_4[Fe(CN)_6]$
D.	$ZnCl_2$	4.	Colour with $K_3[Fe(CN)_6]$
		5.	Gives ppt when H_2S gas is passed into aqueous solution
		6.	Aqueous solution turns blue litmus red.

Single Integer Answer Questions

Answer of these questions is a single digit lying between 0 to 9.

1. Magnetic moment of Mn in $MnSO_4$ is 5.91 BM. Thus, it has .... electrons in 3*d*-orbitals.
2. 2.674 g of $CoCl_3 \cdot 6NH_3$ (molar mass = 267.4 g mol^{-1}) in aqueous solution gave 4.305 g of white precipitate of AgCl (molar mass = 143.5 g mol^{-1}). On reaction with excess of $AgNO_3$ solution. Thus, Cl atoms in outer sphere of the complex is ....
3. Number of oxygen atom(s) between two chromium atoms in $Cr_2O_7^{2-}$ is ....
4. When CrO_5 is treated with H_2O_2 and KOH, a red-brown compound $K_3[Cr(O)_x]$ is formed. *x* is ....
5. 2.78 g of $FeSO_4 \cdot xH_2O$ on treatment with excess of $BaCl_2$ solution gives 2.33 g of white precipitate of $BaSO_4$. What is value of *x*? (Ba = 137, S = 32, Fe = 56, O = 16)
6. How many of the following also forms dimer?
NO_2, $AlCl_3$, $FeCl_3$, N_2O_5, $CuSO_4$, PCl_3
7. How many of the following are paramagnetic as well as coloured species?
O_2, NO_2, Cu^{2+}, Hg_2^{2+}, Fe^{2+}, Fe^{3+}, $[Fe(CN)_6]^{4-}$, $[Fe(CN)_6]^{3-}$, $[Ni(H_2O)_6]^{2+}$, $[Ni(CN)_4]^{2-}$
8. What is van't Hoff factor of $Hg_2(NO_2)_2$ if it is 100% ionised in aqueous solution?
9. How many of the following have underlined atoms in different oxidation states?
$Hg\underline{I}_4^{2-}$, $\underline{S}_2O_3^{2-}$, $\underline{S}_4O_6^{2-}$, $\underline{Cr}O_5$, $\underline{Fe}_3O_4$, $\underline{Pb}_3O_4$
10. How many of the following pairs have approximately equal radii
(Zr, Hf), (Nb, Ta), (Cr, Mn), (Mn, Fe), (Nb^{3+}, Ta^{3+}), (Zr^{4+}, Hf^{4+})
11. How many of the following are amphoteric?
ZnO, Al_2O_3, VO_2, V_2O_5, P_2O_5, Cr_2O_3, CrO_3
12. How many H_2O molecules are in coordination sphere in $FeCl_3 \cdot 6H_2O$?
13. In the chemical reaction between stoichiometric quantities of $KMnO_4$ and KI in weakly basic solution, what is the number of moles of I_2 released for 4 moles of $KMnO_4$ consumed?
14. How many of the following use outer *d*-orbital in complex formation?
$[Ni(H_2O)_4]^{2+}$, $Ni(CO)_4$, $[Ni(CN)_4]^{2-}$, $[Fe(CN)_6]^{4-}$, $[Fe(H_2O)_6]^{2+}$, $[Cr(NH_3)_6]^{3+}$

15. An acidified solution of potassium chromate was layered with an equal volume of amyl alcohol. When it was shaken after the addition of 1 mL of 3% H_2O_2, a blue alcohol layer was obtained. The blue colour is due to the formation of a chromium (VI) compound '*X*'. What is the numbner of oxygen atoms bonded to chromium through only single bond in a molecule of *X*? **[JEE Advanced 2020]**

16. There are 24 electrons in $Mn^+, Cr, Co^{3+}, Fe^{2+}, Ni^{4+}$ How many of these have d^5 configuration?

17. When CrO_5 is treated with H_2O_2 and KOH, a red-brown compound $K_3[Cr(O_2)_x]$ is formed.

18. What is the sum of oxidation number of iron in Prussian blue?

19. Among the species given below, the total number of diamagnetic species is ...... H atom, NO_2 monomer, O_2^- (superoxide), dimeric sulphur in vapur phase, Mn_3O_4, $(NH_4)_2[FeCl_4]$, $(NH_4)_2[NiCl_4]$, K_2MnO_4, K_2CrO_4 **[JEE Advanced 2018]**

Answers

Objective Questions Type I [Only one correct option]

1. (c)	**2.** (d)	**3.** (a)	**4.** (c)	**5.** (b)	**6.** (b)	**7.** (b)	**8.** (d)	**9.** (c)	**10.** (a)
11. (c)	**12.** (b)	**13.** (a)	**14.** (c)	**15.** (d)	**16.** (b)	**17.** (d)	**18.** (b)	**19.** (c)	**20.** (c)
21. (d)	**22.** (a)	**23.** (c)	**24.** (b)	**25.** (b)	**26.** (d)	**27.** (c)	**28.** (a)	**29.** (b)	**30.** (c)
31. (a)	**32.** (c)	**33.** (a)	**34.** (c)	**35.** (d)	**36.** (b)	**37.** (c)	**38.** (a)	**39.** (c)	**40.** (b)
41. (c)	**42.** (c)	**43.** (a)	**44.** (b)	**45.** (c)	**46.** (a)	**47.** (d)	**48.** (b)	**49.** (b)	**50.** (c)
51. (c)	**52.** (a)	**53.** (c)	**54.** (a)	**55.** (a)	**56.** (a)	**57.** (b)	**58.** (a)	**59.** (d)	**60.** (d)
61. (b)	**62.** (d)	**63.** (a)	**64.** (c)	**65.** (a)	**66.** (c)	**67.** (d)	**68.** (a)	**69.** (c)	**70.** (c)
71. (d)	**72.** (b)	**73.** (a)	**74.** (a)	**75.** (c)	**76.** (d)	**77.** (a)	**78.** (d)	**79.** (b)	**80.** (b)
81. (a)	**82.** (a)	**83.** (b)	**84.** (c)	**85.** (b)	**86.** (b)	**87.** (c)	**88.** (d)	**89.** (b)	**90.** (d)
91. (a)	**92.** (d)	**93.** (a)	**94.** (c)	**95.** (b)	**96.** (d)	**97.** (d)	**98.** (b)	**99.** (b)	**100.** (d)
101. (b)	**102.** (a)	**103.** (c)	**104.** (b)	**105.** (a)	**106.** (a)	**107.** (b)	**108.** (d)	**109** (b)	**110.** (b)
111. (b)	**112.** (d)	**113.** (b)	**114.** (b)	**115.** (b)	**116.** (d)	**117.** (c)	**118.** (d)	**119** (d)	**120.** (d)
121. (b)	**122.** (a)	**123.** (b)	**124.** (d)	**125.** (c)	**126.** (c)	**127.** (d)	**128.** (b)	**129.** (d)	**130.** (a)
131. (b)	**132.** (b)	**133.** (c)	**134.** (d)	**135.** (b)	**136.** (a)	**137.** (b)	**138.** (b)	**139.** (d)	**140.** (c)
141. (a)	**142.** (b)	**143.** (c)	**144.** (a)	**145.** (c)	**146.** (b)	**147.** (d)	**148.** (a)	**149.** (a)	**150.** (c)
151. (d)	**152.** (b)	**153.** (c)	**154.** (c)	**155.** (a)	**156.** (c)	**157.** (d)	**158.** (b)	**159.** (b)	**160.** (b)
161. (a)	**162.** (a)	**163.** (d)	**164.** (b)	**165.** (d)	**166.** (c)	**167.** (d)	**168.** (c)	**169.** (c)	**170.** (a)
171. (a)	**172.** (d)	**173.** (b)	**174.** (a)	**175.** (c)	**176.** (b)	**177.** (a)	**178.** (c)	**179.** (d)	**180.** (b)
181. (d)	**182.** (c)	**183.** (a)	**184.** (a)	**185.** (a)	**186.** (d)	**187.** (a)	**188.** (d)	**189.** (b)	**190.** (c)
191. (d)	**192.** (a)	**193.** (b)	**194.** (c)	**195.** (d)	**196.** (c)	**197.** (b)	**198.** (b)	**199.** (b)	**200.** (c)
201. (b)	**202.** (c)	**203.** (d)	**204.** (b)	**205.** (c)	**206.** (d)	**207.** (c)	**208.** (a)	**209.** (b)	**210.** (c)
211. (c)	**212.** (d)	**213.** (d)	**214.** (a)	**215.** (a)	**216.** (d)	**217.** (c)	**218.** (c)	**219.** (b)	**220.** (b)
221. (d)	**222.** (d)	**223.** (a)	**224.** (a)	**225.** (d)	**226.** (d)	**227.** (a)	**228.** (b)	**229.** (a)	**230.** (a)
231. (a)	**232.** (b)	**233.** (b)	**234.** (b)	**235.** (d)	**236.** (c)	**237.** (a)	**238.** (a)	**239.** (d)	**240.** (d)
241. (c)	**242.** (a)	**243.** (c)	**244.** (a)	**245.** (b)	**246.** (b)	**247.** (c)	**248.** (b)	**249.** (b)	**250.** (a)
251. (c)	**252.** (a)	**253.** (d)	**254.** (b)	**255.** (c)	**256.** (c)	**257.** (c)	**258.** (c)	**259.** (b)	**260.** (b)
261. (d)	**262.** (c)	**263.** (d)	**264.** (d)	**265.** (a)	**266.** (c)	**267.** (d)	**268.** (d)	**269.** (c)	**270.** (a)
271. (c)	**272.** (c)	**273.** (a)	**274.** (d)						

Objective Questions Type II [One or more than one correct option(s)]

1. (a, b, c)	**2.** (b, d)	**3.** (b)	**4.** (a, b)	**5.** (c, d)
6. (a, b)	**7.** (a, b, d)	**8.** (a, b, c)	**9.** (b)	**10.** (c)
11. (a, b)	**12.** (a, c, d)	**13.** (c)	**14.** (a, d)	**15.** (a)
16. (a, b)	**17.** (a, b, d)	**18.** (a, b, c, d)	**19.** (a, c)	**20.** (a, b, c)
21. (a, b)	**22.** (a, c, d)	**23.** (b, c, d)	**24.** (b, c)	

Comprehension Based Questions

Passage 1 – **1.** (c) **2.** (b) **3.** (a)
Passage 2 – **1.** (d) **2.** (c)
Passage 3 – **1.** (a) **2.** (b)
Passage 4 – **1.** (c) **2.** (b)
Passage 5 – **1.** (a) **2.** (c)
Passage 6 – **1.** (a) **2.** (c) **3.** (d)
Passage 7 – **1.** (c) **2.** (b) **3.** (a)
Passage 8 – **1.** (a) **2.** (b) **3.** (c)
Passage 9 – **1.** (d) **2.** (a) **3.** (b)

Matrix-Match Type

1. A→ (2); B→ (4); C→ (3); D→ (1)
2. A→ (2); B→ (1); C→(4); D→ (3)
3. A→ (3); B→ (1); C→ (1); D→ (2)
4. A→ (4); B→ (5); C→ (1); D→ (2); E→ (3)
5. A→ (3); B→ (1); C→ (2); D→ (5); E→ (4)
6. A→ (2); B→ (3); C→ (4); D→ (1)
7. A→ (5); B→ (4); C→ (3); D→ (2); E→ (1)
8. A→ (2-Q); B→ (1-P); C→ (3-R); D→ (4-S)
9. A→ (3); B→ (1); C→ (2); D→ (4)
10. A→ (1,3,4); B→ (1,4); C→ (2); D→ (2,5); E→ (1,4)
11. A→(1, 2, 4, 6); B→ (1, 3, 5, 6); C→ (1, 3, 6); D→ (3, 6)

Single Interger Answer Questions

1. (5)	**2.** (3)	**3.** (1)	**4.** (8)	**5.** (7)	**6.** (3)	**7.** (7)	**8.** (3)	**9.** (5)	**10.** (6)
11. (5)	**12.** (4)	**13.** (6)	**14.** (2)	**15.** (4)	**16.** (2)	**17.** (4)	**18.** (5)	**19.** (1)	

Solutions

Objective Questions Type I [Only one correct option]

1. (*c*) Most silver salts are insoluble in water except $AgNO_3$, $AgClO_4$, AgF, $Ag(C_3H_3O_2)$, AgF is soluble in water due to higher electronegativity of fluorine.

2. (*d*) E°_{red} increases left to right.

3. (*a*) Larger anion stabilises to a greater extent.

5. (*b*) Metals lying above H in electrochemical series are not obtained from their oxides by heating.

$$HgO \longrightarrow Hg + O_2$$
$$ZnO \longrightarrow \text{no reaction}$$
$$Ag_2O \longrightarrow Ag + O_2$$

6. (*b*) I. $2CuSO_4 + 4KI \longrightarrow \underset{\text{White ppt.}}{Cu_2I_2\downarrow} + I_2 + K_2SO_4$

II. $HgCl_2 + 2KI \longrightarrow 2KCl + \underset{\text{Orange ppt.}}{HgI_2\downarrow}$

$HgI_2 + 2KI \longrightarrow \underset{\text{Soluble}}{K_2HgI_4}$

III. $Pb(NO_3)_2 + 2KI \longrightarrow \underset{\text{Yellow ppt.}}{PbI_2\downarrow} + 2KNO_3$

9. (*c*)

$$NO \longrightarrow NO^+ + e^-$$
$$Fe^{3+} + e^- \longrightarrow Fe^{2+}$$

Oxidation state of Fe is +2 and NO^+ is ligand.

10. (*a*) Ring is formed by charge transfer.

$$NO \longrightarrow NO^+ + e^-$$
$$Fe^{2+} + e^- \longrightarrow Fe^{2+}$$

12. (*b*) $Ni^{2+} + DMG \longrightarrow \underset{\text{Cherry red ppt.}}{[Ni(DMG)_2]^{2+}}$

13. (*a*) $2CuSO_4 + 4KI \longrightarrow K_2SO_4 + Cu_2I_2 + I_2$

$$I_2 + 2Na_2S_2O_3 \longrightarrow 2NaI + Na_2S_4O_6$$

15. (*d*) Fe(III) gives red colour with KCNS.

17. (*d*) Haemoglobin → Heme group → Iron (Fe)
Chlorophyll → Magnesium (Mg)

19. (*c*) In $Cr_2O_7^{2-}$, every Cr is linked to four O atoms.

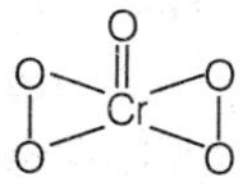

21. (*d*) Cu^+ : $[Ar]\,3d^{10}$
No unpaired electron, thus $s = 0$

24. (*b*) Ferromagnetism is permanent magnetism in the atom/ion. It is due to unpaired electrons.

Fe(26) = $[Ar]\,3d^6\,4s^2$;

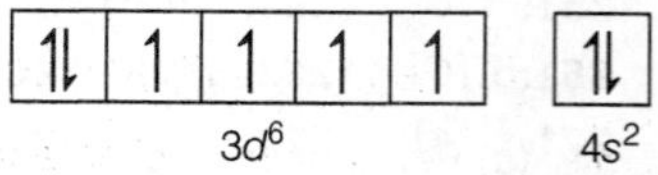

Co(27) = $[Ar]\,3d^7\,4s^2$;

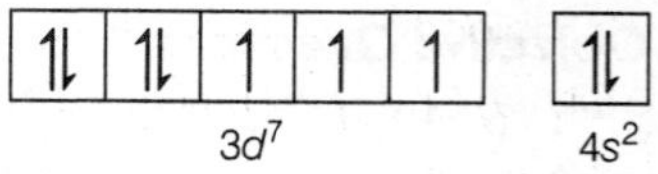

Ni(28) = $[Ar]\,3d^8\,4s^2$;

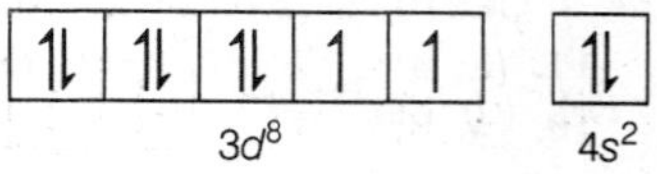

25. (*b*) Ti(22) : [Ar] $4s^2\ 3d^2$

Ti^{2+} : [Ar] $3d^2$ = [1 | 1 | | |]

Ti^{4+} : [Ar] $3d^0$

Ti^{2+} has two unpaired electrons in $3d$ and thus *d*-*d* * transition is possible due to absorption of light in visible region.

26. (*d*) $2Ag^+ + H_2S \longrightarrow Ag_2S$ (black)

27. (*c*) $Cr_2O_7^{2-} + 2OH^- \longrightarrow 2CrO_4^{2-} + H_2O$

pH > 7 (x > 7)

$2CrO_4^{2-} + 2H^+ \longrightarrow Cr_2O_7^{2-} + H_2O$

pH < 7 (y < 7)

30. (*c*) MnO_4^- charges to MnO_4^{2-} or MnO_2 in basic medium.

31. (*a*) $MnO_2 \xrightarrow{\text{Fused with KOH/air}} MnO_4^{2-} \xrightarrow[\text{oxidation}]{\text{Electrolytic}} MnO_4^-$

33. (*a*) Maximum unpaired electrons [1 | 1 | 1 | 1 | 1] d^5

34. (*c*) Magnetic moment $\mu = \sqrt{N(N+2)}$ BM.

where, N = unpaired electrons

Cr(24) [Ar] $3d^5 4s^1$ $N = 6$, $\mu = \sqrt{48}$ BM $= x$

Mn^+ [Ar] $3d^5 4s^1$ $N = 6$, $\mu = \sqrt{48}$ BM $= y$

Fe^{2+} [Ar] $3d^6$ $N = 4$, $\mu = \sqrt{24}$ BM $= z$

[⥮ | 1 | 1 | 1 | 1]

$N = 4$

Thus, $z < x = y$

36. (*b*) 24 carat gold is 100%

Thus, 22-carat gold is 91.67%

Thus, 3.5% higher

39. (*c*) $NH_4VO_3 \xrightarrow{\Delta} NH_3$

$(NH_4)_2Cr_2O_7 \xrightarrow{\Delta} N_2$

42. (*c*) Isostructural $SiCl_4$, $TiCl_4 \rightarrow$ Square planar

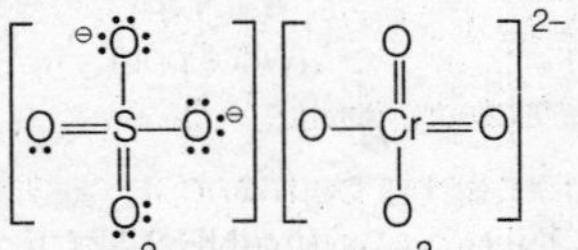

(SO_4^{2-}) (CrO_4^{2-})

44. (*b*) Generally salts are colourless due to d^{10}-configuration.

51. (*c*) Ferric alum and potash alum used for coagulation of blood.

54. (*a*) Cr(Z = 24) [Ar] $4s^1 3d^5$

Cr shows common oxidation states starting from + 2 to + 6.

59. (*d*) Mn^{2+} (d^5) [1 | 1 | 1 | 1 | 1]

61. (*b*) Guigret's green is $Cr_2O_3 \cdot 2H_2O$

65. (*a*) Greater the series $5d > 4d > 3d$, greater will be the basic properties.

$TiO_2 < ZrO_2 < HfO_2$

67. (*d*) $CrO_3 + H_2O \longrightarrow \underset{(A)}{H_2Cr_2O_7} \xrightarrow{OH^-} \underset{(B)}{CrO_4^{2-}}$

68. (*a*) $V^{2+} < Cr^{2+} < Mn^{2+} < Fe^{2+}$

↓ $3d^3$ ↓ $3d^4$ ↓ $3d^5$ ↓ $3d^6$

Greater the number of unpaired electrons, greater will be paramagnetic behaviour.

74. (*a*) $X = [Ar]3d^4$

$X^{3+} = [Ar]3d^7$

Total atomic number = 18 + 4 + 3 = 25.

78. (*d*) Ionic radii : $Y^{3+} < Lu^{3+} < Eu^{3+} < La^{3+}$.

79. (*b*) The atomic radii of Ag is almost equal to Au due to lanthanide contraction.

93. (*a*) $K_2Cr_2O_7 + NaOH \xrightarrow{\Delta} CrO_4^{2-} + KOH$

106. (*a*) $(NH_4)_2Cr_2O_7 \xrightarrow{\Delta} Cr_2O_3 + N_2 + 4H_2O$

$NH_4NO_2 \xrightarrow{\Delta} N_2 + 2H_2O$

109. (*b*) $[Co(SCN)_4]^{2-}$, cobalt is +2 with three unpaired electrons in $3d$. Thus, $\mu = \sqrt{15}$ BM.

112. (*d*) $6Fe^{2+} + Cr_2O_7^{2-} \longrightarrow 6Fe^{3+} + 2Cr^{3+}$

114. (*b*) $HgI_2 + 2KI \longrightarrow K_2HgI_4$

$HgI_2 \longrightarrow Hg + I_2$ (Violet)

115. (*b*) $CrO_4^{2-} + 2H^+ \longrightarrow Cr_2O_7^{2-} + H_2O$

116. (*d*) $AgNO_3 \xrightarrow{\Delta} Ag_2O \xrightarrow{\Delta} 2Ag + O_2$

118. (*d*) $Hg_2Cl_2 + 2NH_3 \longrightarrow \underset{\text{White}}{HgNH_2Cl} + \underset{\text{Black}}{Hg} + NH_4Cl$

121. (*b*) Cr(24) = [Ar] [1 | 1 | 1 | 1 | 1] $3d^5$ [1] $4s^1$

Cr^+ = [Ar] [1 | 1 | 1 | 1 | 1] $3d^5$ ⟵ Completely half-filled $3d$-subshell configuration

Cu(29) = [Ar] [⥮ | ⥮ | ⥮ | ⥮ | ⥮] $3d^{10}$ [1] $4s^1$

Cu^+(28) = [Ar] [⥮ | ⥮ | ⥮ | ⥮ | ⥮] $3d^{10}$ ⟵ Completely filled $3d$-subshell configuration

Both are stable configuration and removal of next electron requires very high energy. Thus, second IE is very high.

V^+ [Ar] $3d^3 4s^1$) Second electron is removed for

Mn^+ [Ar] $3d^5 4s^1$) $4s$ subshell, thus, second IE is

Ni^+ [Ar] $3d^8 4s^1$) low.

Zn^+ [Ar] $3d^{10} 4s^1$)

125. (*c*) Ion is coloured if there are unpaired electrons in *d*-suborbit.

Paramagnetic nature is also due to unpaired electrons.

Thus, every coloured ion is also paramagnetic.

$Cu^{2+} = [Ar]\,3d^9$ one unpaired electron in $3d$.

$Cr^{+} = [Ar]\,3d^5$; five unpaired

$Mn^{2+} = [Ar]\,3d^5$ electrons in $3d$

127. (*d*) Zinc oxide (ZnO) when react with Na_2O it act as acid while with CO_2 it act as base. Therefore, it is an amphoteric oxide.

$$\underset{\text{Acid}}{ZnO} + \underset{\text{Base}}{Na_2O} \longrightarrow \underset{\text{Salt}}{Na_2ZnO_2}$$

$$\underset{\text{Base}}{ZnO} + \underset{\text{Acid}}{CO_2} \longrightarrow \underset{\text{Salt}}{ZnCO_3}$$

128. (*b*) $\underset{+6}{Cr_2O_7^{2-}} + \underset{+4}{SO_2} \longrightarrow \underset{+6}{SO_4^{2-}} + \underset{+3}{Cr^{3+}}$

135. (*b*) $NO \longrightarrow NO^+ + e^-$ $\quad 25 + 12 \longrightarrow 37$

$Fe^{2+} + e^- \longrightarrow Fe^+ (25e)$

141. (*a*) Zr = Hf, Nb = Ta (Similar due to lanthanide contraction)

144. (*a*) $[Ti(H_2O)_6]^{3+} \Rightarrow Ti^{3+} \Rightarrow d^1$

$$n = 1 = \sqrt{n(n+2)}$$
$$= \sqrt{3} = 1.73\text{BM}$$

146. (*b*) Cr^{3+} : $[Ar]\,3d^5$ stable

147. (*d*) I. ${}_{58}Ce \longrightarrow [Xe]\,4f^2, 5d^0 6s^2$

In complex $Ce^{4+} \longrightarrow [Xe]\,4f^0, 5d^0 6s^2$

there is no unpaired electron so, $\mu_m = 0$.

II. ${}_{64}Gd^{3+} \longrightarrow [Xe]\,4f^7, 5d^0 6s^0$

contain seven unpaired electrons so,

$\mu_m = \sqrt{7(7+2)} = \sqrt{63}$ B.M.

III. ${}_{63}Eu^{3+} \longrightarrow [{}_{54}Xe]\,4f^6, 5d^0 6s^0$

contain six unpaired electron

so, $\mu_m = \sqrt{6(6+2)} = \sqrt{48}$ B.M.

Hence, order of spin only magnetic movement II > III > I.

148. (*a*) Magnetic moment

$$[V(H_2O)_6]^{2+} > [V(H_2O)_6]^{3+} > [Ti(H_2O)_6]^{2+} > Ni(CO)_4$$

$$\underset{3d^3}{V^{2+}} \qquad \underset{3d^2}{V^{3+}} \qquad \underset{3d^2}{Ti^{2+}} \qquad \underset{3d^{10}}{Ni^0}$$

159. (*b*) This is due to increasing stability of the lower species to which they are reduced.

$$VO_2^+ < Cr_2O_7^{2-} < MnO_4^-$$

Oxidation state $\quad +5 \quad +6 \quad +7$

161. (*a*) $2S_2O_3^{2-} + Ag^+ \longrightarrow \underset{\text{(Clear solution)}}{[Ag(S_2O_3)_2]^{3-}}$

$$[Ag(S_2O_3)_2]^{3-} + 3Ag^+ \longrightarrow \underset{\text{(White ppt.)}}{2Ag_2S_2O_3}$$

$$Ag_2S_2O_3 + H_2O \longrightarrow \underset{\text{(Black ppt.)}}{Ag_2S} + H_2SO_4$$

163. (*d*) $CrO_3 + 2H^+ \longrightarrow CrO_2^{2+} + H_2O$

165. (*d*) $2CrO_4^{2-} + 2H^+ \longrightarrow Cr_2O_7^{2-} + H_2O$

166. (*c*) $Cr_2O_7^{2-} + 2OH^- \longrightarrow 2CrO_4^- + H_2O$

170. (*a*) $2MnO_4^{2-} \xrightarrow{H^+} MnO_2 + MnO_4^-$

176. (*b*) ZnS is white.

185. (*a*) $[Fe(H_2O)_4Cl_2]Cl \cdot 2H_2O$

186. (*d*) $Fe^{2+} + [Fe(CN)_6]^{3-} \longrightarrow$ Blue

$\xrightarrow[\text{(By oxidation)}]{Fe^{3+}}$ No colour

190. (*c*) Fe^{3+} forms soluble complex with oxalic acid.

191. (*d*) $\underset{\text{Amphoteric}}{Zn} + 2NaOH \longrightarrow Na_2ZnO_2 + H_2$

192. (*a*) $Fe_2O_3 + OH^- + Cl_2 \longrightarrow [FeO_4]^{2-}$

195. (*d*) $NO \longrightarrow NO^+ + e^-$,

$\underset{3d^6}{Fe^{2+}} + e^- \longrightarrow \underset{3d^7}{Fe^+}$ (three unpaired electrons)

⥮	1	1	1	1

⥮	⥮	1	1	1

Magnetic moment $= \sqrt{N(N+2)}$
$= \sqrt{15}$ BM

201. (*b*) $CuSO_4 + 2H_2O \rightleftharpoons Cu(OH)_2 + H_2SO_4$

$2CrO_4^{2-} + 2H^+ \rightleftharpoons Cr_2O_7^{2-} + H_2O$

207. (*c*) Non-oxidising acids (as HCl) dissolve basic and amphoteric oxides, e.g. Cr_2O_3.

$$Cr_2O_3 + 6HCl \longrightarrow 2CrCl_3 + 3H_2O$$

$CrCl_3$ is hydrated in aqueous solution existing as $[Cr(H_2O)_6]^{3+}$.

208. (*a*) *X* : Ag *Y* : Pb *P* : AgCl *Q* : $PbCl_2$

$$AgNO_3 + Pb(NO_3)_2 \xrightarrow{NaCl} \underset{(P)}{AgCl\,(\downarrow)} + \underset{(Q)}{PbCl_2}$$

Heat followed by filteration

AgCl (*P*) (White ppt.) $\quad$ $PbCl_2$ (*Q*) (Hot solution) $\xrightarrow{KI}$ PbI_2 (Yellew ppt.)

$$\underset{(P)}{AgCl(s)} + \underset{\text{(Excess)}}{2NH_3} \longrightarrow [Ag(NH_3)_2]^+Cl^-$$

$\downarrow 2N_2S_2O_3$

$Na_3[Ag(S_2O_3)_2] + NaCl$
Soluble complex salt

Hence, the correct option is (a).

220. (*b*) $Cr_2O_7^{2-} \xrightarrow{6e^-} 2Cr^{3+}$

6 electrons for two Cr

3 electrons per Cr

223. (*a*) Electronic configuration of divalent metal ion having atomic number 25 is

	$1s^2$	$2s^2$	$2p^6$	$3s^2$	$3p^6$	$3d^5$
$Mn(aq)^{+2}$	⇅	⇅	⇅ ⇅ ⇅	⇅	⇅ ⇅ ⇅	↑ ↑ ↑ ↑ ↑

Total number of unpaired electrons = 5

μ (Magnetic moment) $= \sqrt{n(n+2)}$ BM

where, n = number of unpaired e^-

$\therefore \quad \mu = \sqrt{5(5+2)} = \sqrt{35}$ BM = 5.92 BM

224. (*a*) The electronic configuration of bivalent europium and trivalent cerium are as follows:

$${}_{63}Eu = [Xe]\,4f^7 5d^0 6s^2 \Rightarrow Eu^{2+} = [Xe]\,4f^7$$

$${}_{58}Ce = [Xe]\,4f^1 5d^1 6s^2 \Rightarrow Ce^{3+} = [Xe]\,4f^1$$

225. (*d*) Third electron which is removed in third ionisation potential enthalpy belongs to $3d^3$ subshell in V.

$$\text{In } {}_{23}V = 1s^2 2s^2 2p^6\, 3s^2 3p^6 3d^3 4s^2$$

Third electron which is removed in third ionisation potential enthalpy belongs to $3d^4$ subshell.

$${}_{24}Cr = 1s^2 2s^2 2p^6 3s^2 3p^6 3d^5 4s^1$$

Third electron which is removed in third ionisation potential enthalpy belongs to $3d^6$ subshell.

$${}_{26}Fe = 1s^2 2s^2 2p^6 3s^2 3p^6 3d^6 4s^2$$

Third electron which is removed in third ionisation potential belongs to $3d^5$ subshell. In all elements shell and subshells are same.

Required amount of energy is based upon the stability of *d*-subshell. Hence, Mn shows highest third ionisation potential or enthalpy.

$${}_{25}Mn = 1s^2 2s^2 2p^6 3s^2 3p^6 3d^5 4s^2$$

226. (*d*) In alkaline solution, $KMnO_4$ is reduced to MnO_2 (black).

$$2KMnO_4 + 2H_2O \longrightarrow 2MnO_2 + 2KOH + 3[O]$$

$$KI + 3[O] \longrightarrow KIO_3$$

$$\overline{2KMnO_4 + 2H_2O + KI \longrightarrow 2MnO_2 + 2KOH + KIO_3}$$

Hence, 2 moles of $KMnO_4$ are reduced to MnO_2 by 1 mole of KI.

227. (*a*) Thermal decomposition of Mn compound (*X*), i.e. $KMnO_4$ at 513 K results in compound *Y* (i.e. K_2MnO_4), MnO_2 and a gaseous product. MnO_2 reacts with NaCl and concentrated H_2SO_4 to give a pungent gas *Z*(i.e. Cl_2). The reactions involved are as follows :

$$\underset{(X)}{2KMnO_4} \xrightarrow[\Delta]{513K} \underset{(Y)}{K_2MnO_{4}}{}_4 + MnO_2 + O_2(g)$$

$$MnO_2 + 4NaCl + 4H_2SO_4 \longrightarrow \underset{\substack{(Z)\\ \text{Pungent gas.}}}{MnCl_2} + 4NaHSO_4 + 2H_2O + Cl_2(g)$$

236. (*c*) $E° < 0$, it means forward equilibria are not spontaneous. Thus, Fe^{2+} is more stable than Fe^{3+}.

In $[Fe(CN)_6]^{4-}$ oxidation number of Fe = + 2.

and in $[Fe(CN)_6]^{3-}$ oxidation number of Fe = + 3.

Due to complex ion, $E°$ decreases, thus stability can be increased by complexing ion.

237. (*a*) For transition metals,

$\Delta H°_{\text{Atomisation}} \propto$ Strength of metallic bonding

$\propto$ Number of unpaired electrons in the metal atom

For the given 3*d*-transition metals,

V	Fe	Cu	Zn
$3d^3 4s^2$	$3d^6 4s^2$	$3d^{10} 4s^1$	$3d^{10} 4s^0$
$n = 3$	$n = 4$	$n = 0$	$n = 0$

[$\because n$ = no. of unpaired electrons]

$\Delta° H_{\text{Atomisation}}$ (kJ mol^{-1}) = 515 418 339 130

So, absence of unpaired *d*-electrons and larger size of Zn atoms, make the crystal lattice of Zn less closely packed.

245. (*b*) Cu^+ : $[Ar]\,3d^{10}$ all electrons paired.

248. (*b*) $2CuSO_4 + 4KI \longrightarrow Cu_2I_2 + K_2SO_4 + I_2$

$$I_2 + KI \longrightarrow KI_3$$

251. (*c*) $[Ar]\,4s^1 3d^5$

254. (*b*) $CrO_3 + H_2O \longrightarrow H_2CrO_4$ (acidic)

256. (*c*) Fe has 4 unpaired electrons.

259. (*b*) $SnCl_2 + HgCl_2 \longrightarrow \underset{\text{White}}{Hg_2Cl_2} \xrightarrow{SnCl_2} \underset{\text{Grey}}{Hg}$

263. (*d*) $Mn^{3+} + e^- \longrightarrow Mn^{2+}$

$3d^4$	$3d^5$
↑ ↑ ↑ ↑ ☐	↑ ↑ ↑ ↑ ↑

Extra stability is gained when Mn^{3+} is reduced to Mn^{2+} and is thus an oxidising agent.

$$Cr^{2+} \longrightarrow Cr^{3+} + e^-$$

$3d^4$	
↑ ↑ ↑ ↑ ☐	↑ ↑ ↑ ☐ ☐] has half-filled t_{2g} level

264. (*a*) Fe^{3+} : $[Ar]\,3d^5$; Cu^+ : $[Ar]\,3d^{10}$

271. (*c*) Nascent H reduces NO to NH_3 which changes to NH_4NO_3.

13

Coordination Compounds

Objective Questions Type I [Only one correct option]

In each of the questions below, four choices are given of which only one is correct.

1. A compound has the empirical formula $CoCl_3 \cdot 5NH_3$. When an aqueous solution of this compound is mixed with excess silver nitrate, 2 moles of AgCl precipitate per mol of compound. On reaction with excess HCl, no NH_4^+ is detected. Hence, it is

(a) $[Co(NH_3)_5Cl_2]Cl$

(b) $[Co(NH_3)_5Cl]Cl_2$

(c) $[Co(NH_3)_5Cl_3]$

(d) $[Co(NH_3)_4Cl_2]Cl \cdot NH_3$

2. In the above compound in (Q. 1),

(a) all the Cl show primary valency (PV)

(b) two Cl show (PV) and one Cl secondary valency (SV)

(c) two Cl show (PV) and one Cl (PV) as well as (SV)

(d) all the Cl show (SV)

3. The theory that can completely/ properly explain the nature of bonding in $[Ni(CO)_4]$ is : **[JEE Main 2020]**

(a) Werner's theory

(b) Crystal field theory

(c) Valence bond theory

(d) Molecular orbital theory

4. Why is $[Ni(en)_3]^{2+}$, nearly 10^{10} times more stable than $[Ni(NH_3)_6]^{2+}$?

(a) NH_3 evaporates easily and causes instability to $[Ni(NH_3)_6]^{2+}$ complex

(b) Six NH_3 ligands cause steric hindrance around the Ni^{2+} centre

(c) 'en' is a chelating ligand and forms thermodynamically more stable complexes

(d) NH_3 is the weakest ligand known

5. Which of the following complexes is diamagnetic?

(a) $[Fe(CN)_6]^{4-}$ (b) $[Cu(NH_3)_4]^{2+}$

(c) $[Ti(H_2O)_6]^{3+}$ (d) $[Ni(en)_2]^{2+}$

6. $[Co(NO_2)(NH_3)_5]^{2+}$ is yellow in colour, then its linkage isomer is

(a) yellow (b) red (c) blue (d) orange

7. Which of the following complexes is not a chelate?

(a) bis (dimethylglyoximato) nickel (II)

(b) potassium ethylenediaminetetrathiocyanato chromate (III)

(c) tetrammine carbonatocobalt (III) nitrate

(d) *trans*-diglycinatoplatinum (II)

8. Which of the following complexes exhibit optical isomerism?

(a) *trans*-tetramminedithiocyanatochromium(III) ion

(b) *cis*-diamminedicarbonatocobaltate (III) ion

(c) *trans*-diamminedicarbonatocobaltate (III) ion

(d) *cis*-glycinatoplatinum (II)

9. The one that will show optical activity is (en = ethane-1, 2-diamine) **[JEE Main 2019]**

(a) 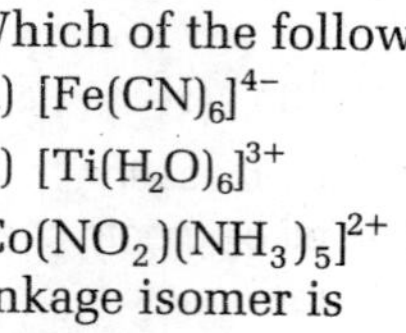

(b) 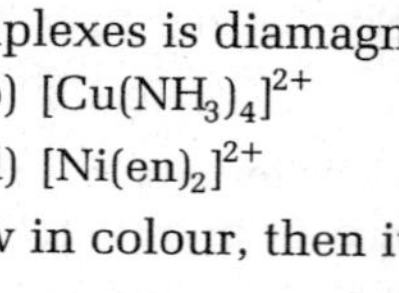

(c) 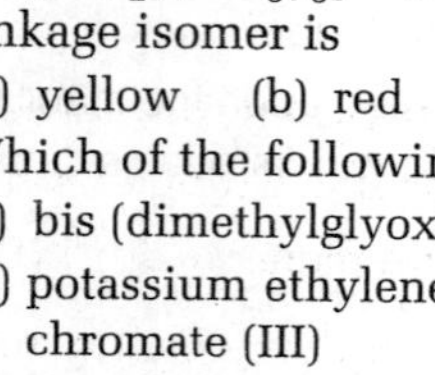

(d) 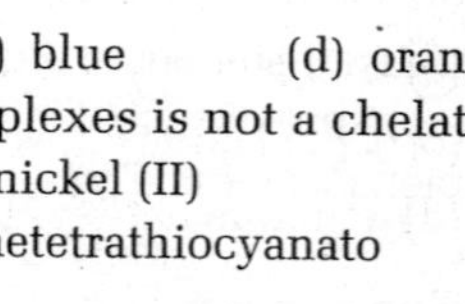

10. Which one of the following complexes shows optical isomerism? **[JEE Main 2016]**
(a) *cis* $[Co(en)_2Cl_2]Cl$ (b) *trans* $[Co(en)_2Cl_2]Cl$
(c) $[Co(NH_3)_4Cl_2]Cl$ (d) $[Co(NH_3)_3Cl_3]$

11. Among $[Ni(CO)_4]$, $NiCl_4^{2-}$, $[Co(NH_3)_4Cl_2]Cl$, $Na_3[CoF_6]$, Na_2O_2 and CsO_2, the total number of paramagnetic compounds is **[JEE Advanced 2016]**
(a) 2 (b) 3
(c) 4 (d) 5

12. Among $Ni(CO)_4$, $[Ni(CN)_4]^{2-}$ and $NiCl_4^{2-}$
(a) $Ni(CO)_4$ and $[Ni(CN)_4]^{2-}$ are diamagnetic and $NiCl_4^{2-}$ is paramagnetic
(b) $Ni(CO)_4$ and $NiCl_4^{2-}$ are diamagnetic and $[Ni(CN)_4]^{2-}$ is paramagnetic
(c) $Ni(CO)_4$ is diamagnetic and $[Ni(CN)_4]^{2-}$ and $NiCl_4^{2-}$ are paramagnetic
(d) $NiCl_4^{2-}$ and $[Ni(CN)_4]^{2-}$ are diamagnetic and $Ni(CO)_4$ is paramagnetic

13. The pair having the same magnetic moment is [at. no. Cr = 24, Mn = 25, Fe = 26 and Co = 27] **[JEE Main 2016]**
(a) $[Cr(H_2O)_6]^{2+}$ and $[Fe(H_2O)_6]^{2+}$
(b) $[Mn(H_2O)_6]^{2+}$ and $[Cr(H_2O)_6]^{2+}$
(c) $[CoCl_4]^{2-}$ and $[Fe(H_2O)_6]^{2+}$
(d) $[Cr(H_2O)_6]^{2+}$ and $[CoCl_4]^{2-}$

14. Which is true for $[Ni(en)_2]^{2+}$, $Z(Ni) = 28$?
(a) Paramagnetism, dsp^2, square planar, CN of Ni = 2
(b) Diamagnetism, dsp^2, square planar, CN of Ni = 4
(c) Diamagnetism, sp^3, tetrahedral, CN of Ni = 4
(d) Paramagnetism, sp^3, square planar, CN of Ni = 4

15. The correct order of the spin only magnetic moment of metal ions in the following low spin complexes, $[V(CN)_6]^{4-}$, $[Fe(CN)_6]^{4-}$, $[Ru(NH_3)_6]^{3+}$, and $[Cr(NH_3)_6]^{2+}$, is **[JEE Main 2019]**
(a) $Cr^{2+} > Ru^{3+} > Fe^{2+} > V^{2+}$ (b) $V^{2+} > Cr^{2+} > Ru^{3+} > Fe^{2+}$
(c) $V^{2+} > Ru^{3+} > Cr^{2+} > Fe^{2+}$ (d) $Cr^{2+} > V^{2+} > Ru^{3+} > Fe^{2+}$

16. The correct order of the spin only magnetic moments of the following complexes is
I. $[Cr(H_2O)_6]Br_2$
II. $Na_4[Fe(CN)_6]$
III. $Na_3[Fe(C_2O_4)_3]$ $(\Delta_0 > P)$
IV. $(Et_4N)_2[CoCl_4]$
(a) II ≈ I > IV > III (b) I > IV > III > II
(c) III > I > IV > II (d) III > I > III > IV

17. Which has maximum EAN of the underlined atoms? (Cr = 24, Co = 27, Fe = 26, Ni = 28)
(a) $[\underline{Cr}(EDTA)]^-$ (b) $[\underline{Co}(en)_3]^{3+}$
(c) $[\underline{Fe}(C_2O_4)_3]^{3-}$ (d) $[\underline{Ni}(CN)_4]^{2-}$

18. Which has maximum coordinating (donor) points?
(a) DMG (b) EDTA
(c) en (d) py

19. Following ligands can show linkage isomerism
(a) CNS (b) NO_2
(c) CN (d) All of these

20. $[Fe^{II}(O_2)(CN)_4Cl]^{4-}$ is named as
(a) chlorotetracyanodioxoferrate (II) ion
(b) chlorotetracyanoperoxoferrate (II) ion
(c) chlorotetracyanosuperoxoferrate (II) ion
(d) None of the above is correct

21. Which of the following complex species is not expected to exhibit optical isomerism? **[JEE Main 2013]**
(a) $[Co(en)_3]^{3+}$ (b) $[Co(en)_2Cl_2]^+$
(c) $[Co(NH_3)_3Cl_3]$ (d) $[Co(en)(NH_3)Cl_2]^+$

22. Consider the following reaction and statements :
$[Co(NH_3)_4Br_2]^+ + Br^- \longrightarrow [Co(NH_3)_3Br_3] + NH_3$
I. Two isomers are produces if the reactant complex ion is a *cis*-isomer.
II. Two isomers are produced if the reactant complex ion is a *trans*-isomer.
III. Only one isomer is produced if the reactant complex ion is a *trans*-isomer.
IV. Only one isomer is produced if the reactant complex ion is a *cis*-isomer.

The correct statements are **[JEE Main 2018]**
(a) I and II (b) I and III
(c) III and IV (d) II and IV

23. Which one of the following complex species does not obey the EAN rule?
(a) $[Cu(CN)_4]^{3-}$ (b) $[Cr(NH_3)_6]^{3+}$
(c) $[Fe(CN)_6]^{4-}$ (d) $[Ni(CO)_4]$

24. Which has aromatic ring in complex?
(a) DMG in dimethyl glyoximate
(b) Cyclopenta-dienyl anion in ferrocene
(c) Both (a) and (b)
(d) None of the above

25. Extraction of Ag from sulphide ore and removal of unreacted silver from photographic plate involve complexes
(a) $[Ag(S_2O_3)_2]^{3-}$ in both
(b) $[Ag(CN)_2]^-$ in both
(c) $[Ag(S_2O_3)_2]^{3-}$, $[Ag(CN)_2]^-$
(d) $[Ag(CN)_2]^-$, $[Ag(S_2O_3)_2]^{3-}$

26. $[Co(NH_3)_5(NO_2)]^{2+}$ and $[Co(NH_3)_5(ONO)]^{2+}$ will differ in
(a) colour (b) structure
(c) hybridisation (d) magnetic moment

27. In which case racemic mixture is obtained on mixing its mirror images in 1 : 1 molar ratio?
(a) $[Cr(en)_3]^{3+}$ (b) $[Ni(DMG)_2]$
(c) *Cis*-$[Cu(Gly)_2]$ (d) In all cases

28. EAN of the elements (*) are equal in
(a) $\overset{*}{Ni}(CO)_4$, $[\overset{*}{Fe}(CN)_6]^{4-}$ (b) $[\overset{*}{Ni}(en)_2]^{2+}$, $[\overset{*}{Fe}(H_2O)_6]^{2+}$
(c) $[\overset{*}{Co}(CN)_6]^{3-}$, $[\overset{*}{Fe}(CN)_6]^{3-}$ (d) $[\overset{*}{Ni}(en)_2]^{2+}$, $[\overset{*}{Sc}(H_2O)_6]^{3+}$

29. Which one of the following is an example of coordination isomerism?
(a) $[Co(NH_3)_5Br]SO_4$ and $[Co(NH_3)_5SO_4]Br$
(b) $[Co(NH_3)_5NO_2]Cl_2$ and $[Co(NH_3)_5ONO]Cl_2$
(c) $[Cr(H_2O)_6]Cl_3$ and $[Cr(H_2O)_5Cl]Cl_2 \cdot H_2O$
(d) $[Cr(NH_3)_6][Co(CN)_6]$ and $[Co(NH_3)_6][Cr(CN)_6]$

30. Which of the following compounds show optical isomerism?
I. *Cis*-$[Co(NH_3)_4Cl_2]^+$ II. *Trans*-$[Co(en)_2Cl_2]^+$
III. *Cis*-$[Co(en)_2Cl_2]^+$ IV. $[Co(en)_3]^{3+}$

Select the correct answer using the codes given below.
(a) I and II (b) II and III
(c) III and IV (d) I, III and IV

31. Lead poisoning in the body can be removed by
(a) EDTA in the form of calcium dihydrogen salt
(b) *cis*-platin
(c) Zeise's salt
(d) DMG

32. Of the following complex ions, one exhibits optical isomerism. That one is
(a) *cis*-$[Co(en)_2Cl_2]^+$ (b) $[Co(NH_3)_4Cl_2]^+$
(c) $[Co(NH_3)_2Cl_4]^-$ (d) *trans*-$[Co(en)_2Cl_2]^+$

33. Of the following complex ions, one exhibits isomerism. That is
(a) $[Ag(NH_3)_2]^+$ (b) $[Co(NH_3)_5NO_2]^{2+}$
(c) $[Pt(en)Cl_2]$ (d) $[Co(NH_3)_5Cl]^{2+}$

34. Of the following complex ions, one is a Bronsted-Lowry acid. That one is
(a) $[Cu(NH_3)_4]^{2+}$ (b) $[FeCl_4]^-$
(c) $[Fe(H_2O)_6]^{3+}$ (d) $[Zn(OH)_4]^{2-}$

35. Of the following complex ions, the one that probably has the largest overall formation constant, K_f, is
(a) $[Co(NH_3)_6]^{3+}$ (b) $[Co(H_2O)_6]^{3+}$
(c) $[Co(H_2O)_4(NH_3)_2]^{3+}$ (d) $[Co(en)_3]^{3+}$

36. When concentrated HCl is added to a, solution of $[Co(H_2O)_6]^{2+}$ ion, an intense blue colour develops due to the formation which one of the following?
(a) $[CoCl_6]^{4-}$ (b) $[CoCl_4]^{2-}$
(c) $[CoCl_2(H_2O)_4]$ (d) $[CoCl(H_2O)_5]^+$

37. Select the correct statement.
(a) Complex ion $[MoCl_6]^{3-}$ is paramagnetic
(b) Complex ion $[Co(en)_3]^{3+}$ is diamagnetic
(c) Both (a) and (b) are correct
(d) None of the above is correct

38. The geometrics of the ammonia complexes of NI^{2+}, Pt^{2+} and Zn^{2+}, respectively are **[JEE Advanced 2016]**
(a) Octahedral square planar and tetrahedral
(b) Square planar, octahedral and tetrahedral
(c) Tetrahedral square planar and octahedral
(d) Octahedral tetrahedral and square planar

39. The complex $[Fe(H_2O)_5NO]^{2+}$ is formed in the brown ring test for nitrates when freshly prepared $FeSO_4$ solution is added to aqueous solution of NO_3^- followed by addition of conc. H_2SO_4. Select correct statement about this complex.
(a) Colour change is due to charge transfer
(b) It has iron in +1 oxidate state and nitrosyl as NO^+
(c) It has magnetic moment of 3.87 BM confirming three unpaired electrons in Fe
(d) All the above are correct statements

40. While Ti^{3+}, V^{3+}, Fe^{3+} and Co^{2+} afford a large number of tetrahedral complexes, Cr^{3+} never does this, the reason being
(a) Cr^{3+} forces high crystal field splitting with a varieties of ligands
(b) crystal field stabilisation energy in octahedral *vis-a-vis* tetrahedral Cr^{3+} system plays the deciding role
(c) the ionic radius of Cr^{3+} is the largest among the other M^{3+} ions mentioned
(d) electronegativity of Cr^{3+} is the largest among these trivalent 3*d*-metals and so chromium prefers to be associated with as many ligands as its ionic radius permits

41. Isomerisms exhibited by $[Cr(NH_3)_2(H_2O)_2Cl_2]^+$ are
(a) ionisation, optical
(b) hydrate, optical
(c) geometrical, optical
(d) coordinate, geometrical

42. The crystal field-splitting for Cr^{3+} ion in octahedral field increases for ligands I^-, H_2O, NH_3, CN^- and the order is
(a) $I^- < H_2O < NH_3 < CN^-$
(b) $CN^- < I^- < H_2O < NH_3$
(c) $CN^- < NH_3 < H_2O < I^-$
(d) $NH_3 < H_2O < I^- < CN^-$

43. Which of the following types of bonds are present in $CuSO_4 \cdot 5H_2O$?
I. Electrovalent II. Covalent III. Coordinate

Select the correct answer out of
(a) I, II (b) II, III (c) I, III (d) I, II, III

44. Arrange the following in order of decreasing number of unpaired electrons

I. $[Fe(H_2O)_6]^{2+}$ II. $[Fe(CN)_6]^{3-}$
III. $[Fe(CN)_6]^{4-}$ IV. $[Fe(H_2O)_6]^{3+}$

(a) IV, I, II, III (b) I, II, III, IV
(c) III, II, I, IV (d) II, III, I, IV

45. In an octahedral complex, if ligands on one axis are displaced little away from their ideal positions, the crystal field splitting of *d*-orbitals for this complex is as given below

$d_{x^2-y^2}$ d_{z^2} d_{xy} d_{yz} d_{xz}

The ligands are displaced on which axis/ axes

(a) *x*- and *y* (b) *y*-only
(c) *x*-only (d) *z*-only

46. On treatment of 100 mL of 0.1 M solution of $CoCl_3 \cdot 6H_2O$ with excess of $AgNO_3$; 1.2×10^{22} ions are precipitated. The complex is **[JEE Main 2017]**

(a) $[Co(H_2O)_4Cl_2]Cl \cdot 2H_2O$
(b) $[Co(H_2O)_3Cl_3] \cdot 3H_2O$
(c) $[Co(H_2O)_6]Cl_3$
(d) $[Co(H_2O)_5Cl]Cl_2 \cdot H_2O$

47. Aqueous Fe(III) ion develops intense red colour with SCN^- while Fe(II) does not. It is due to

(a) Fe(III) ion forms a charge transfer complex with SCN^- ions
(b) Fe(III) is reduced to Fe(I) which is deep red in colour
(c) SCN^- ion oxidises to CN^- ion that forms red complex with Fe(III) ion
(d) SCN^- ion does not form any complex with Fe(II) ion

48. The intense blue colour of Prussian blue salts arises from which one of the following?

(a) *d-d* transition
(b) inter valence electron transfer
(c) ligand to metal charge transfer
(d) metal to ligand charge transfer

49. Which one of the following is the correct order of the wavelengths of absorption for complexes?

I. $[Ni(H_2O)_6]^{2+}$ II. $[Ni(NH_3)_6]^{2+}$
III. $[Ni(NO_2)_6]^{4-}$

(a) I > II > III
(b) II > I > III
(c) III > II > I
(d) III > I > II

50. What are the spin-only magnetic moments (in BM) for Ni(II) ion in square-planar and octahedral geometry, respectively?

(a) 0, 2.83 (b) 2.83, 2.83
(c) 2.83, 0 (d) 0, 0

51. Which one of the following complexes is expected to have lowest Δ_o values?

(a) $[Co(NH_3)_6]^{3+}$ (b) $[CoF_6]^{3-}$
(c) $[Rh(NH_3)_5]^{3+}$ (d) $[Ir(NH_3)_6]^{3+}$

52. If Δ_o and Δ_t represent crystal field splitting energies for *d*-orbitals for octahedral and tetrahedral geometries respectively, then for d^6 (high spin in both cases), what are CFSE (ignore the pairing energy) respectively?

(a) $0.6\,\Delta_o$ and $0.6\,\Delta_t$ (b) $0.4\,\Delta_o$ and $0.4\,\Delta_t$
(c) $0.4\,\Delta_o$ and $0.6\,\Delta_t$ (d) $0.6\,\Delta_o$ and $0.4\,\Delta_t$

53. The complex $[Co(NH_3)_5(NO_2)]^{2+}$ and $[Co(NH_3)_5(ONO)]^{2+}$ are called

(a) ionisation isomer (b) linkage isomers
(c) coordination isomer (d) geometrical isomer

54. The complex

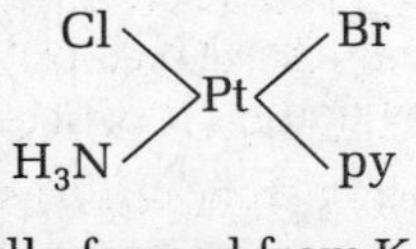

can be formally formed from $K_2[PtCl_4]$ by which one of the following sequences of substitution of the chloride ions?

(a) Py, Br^-, NH_3 (b) Br^-, Py, NH_3
(c) Br^-, NH_3, Py (d) NH_3, Br^-, Py

55. Consider the following statements in respect of $[CoCl_6]^{4-}$ complex ion

I. It is paramagnate
II. It is low-spin complex
III. Oxidation number of cobalt is –4
IV. The coordination number of cobalt is 6

Select the correct statements.

(a) All of the above (b) III and IV only
(c) I and IV only (d) I and II only

56. The reaction between metallic silver and aqueous NaCN forming a soluble complex occurs in the presence of

(a) nitrogen (b) helium
(c) argon (d) oxygen

57. What type of isomerism is present in the pair of complexes $[Co(NH_3)_5Br]SO_4$ and $[Co(NH_3)_5SO_4]Br$?

(a) Linkage isomerism
(b) Ligand isomerism
(c) Ionisation isomerism
(d) Coordination isomerism

58. Which of the following is an example of coordination compound?

(a) $CoCl_3 \cdot 6NH_3$
(b) $KCl \cdot MgCl_2 \cdot 6H_2O$
(c) $FeSO_4 \cdot 6H_2O$
(d) $FeSO_4 \cdot (NH_4)_2SO_4 \cdot 6H_2O$

59. $FeSO_4$ on treatment with excess of KCN gives a product that does not give test of Fe^{2+}, the product formed is

(a) $[Fe(CN)_2]SO_4$ (b) $K_3[Fe(CN)_6]$
(c) $K_4[Fe(CN)_6]$ (d) $KFe[Fe(CN)_6]$

60. The correct structures of trans-$[NiBr_2(PPh_3)_2]$ and meridonial-$[Co(NH_3)_3(NO_2)_3]$, respectively, are **[JEE Main 2021, March]**

(a) 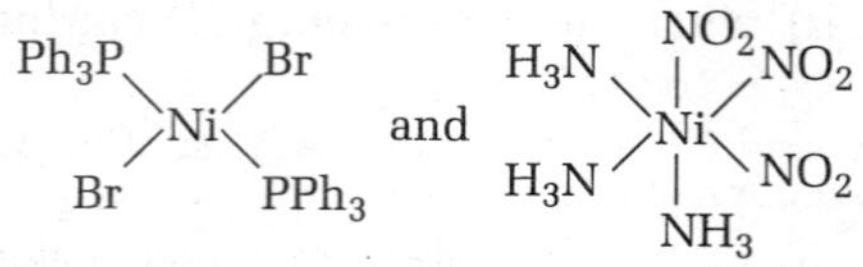

(b) 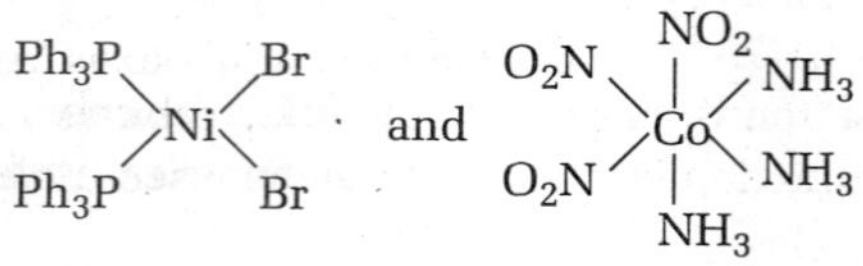

(c) 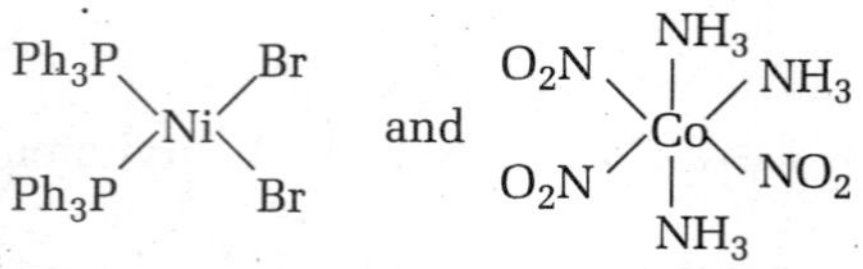

(d) 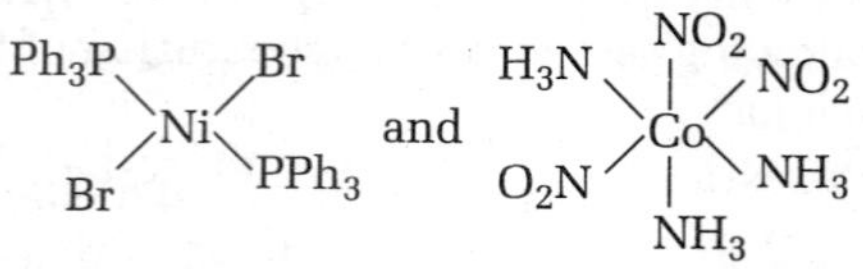

61. Ink contains Fe^{3+}. Spot of ink can be removed by addition of $C_2O_4^{2-}$. Complex formed is
(a) $|Fe(C_2O_4)_6]^{3-}$ (b) $[Fe(C_2O_4)_3]^{3-}$
(c) $[Fe(C_2O_4)_3]^{2-}$ (d) $[Fe(C_2O_4)_3]^{4-}$

62. The ions or molecules attached to the central metal atom or ion in a complex are called
(a) ligands (b) chelates
(c) ambident (d) Lewis acid

63. In the complex $[Fe(NH_3)_6]^{3+}$
(a) Fe^{3+} is a Lewis acid (b) NH_3 is a Lewis base
(c) Both (a) & (b) correct (d) None is correct

64. The closed ring compounds formed by bidentate ligands, on binding to a metal or metal ions, are called
(a) ligands (b) chelates (c) complexes (d) ambident

65. Coordination number of calcium is six in
(a) $[Ca(EDTA)]^{2-}$ (b) CaC_2O_4
(c) $[Ca(C_2O_4)_2]^{2-}$ (d) $CaSO_4 \cdot 4H_2O$

66. In the complex $[Pt(O_2)(en)_2(Br)]^{2+}$, coordination number and oxidation number of platinum are
(a) 4, 3 (b) 4, 5 (c) 4, 6 (d) 6, 4

67. Coordination number of Cr is six. A complex with $C_2O_4^{2-}$, en and superoxide O_2^- will be in the ratio to make complex $[Cr(C_2O_4)_x(en)_y(O_2)_z]^-$

	x	y	z		x	y	z
(a)	1	1	1	(b)	1	1	2
(c)	1	2	2	(d)	2	1	1

68. The isomer(s) of $[Co(NH_3)_4Cl_2]$ that has/have a Cl—Co—Cl angle of 90°, is/are
(a) *cis* and *trans* (b) meridional and *trans*
(c) *cis* only (d) *trans* only

69. IUPAC name of $K_4[Fe(CN)_6]$ is
(a) potassium hexacyano iron (II)
(b) potassium iron (II) hexacyano
(c) tetrapotassium iron (II) hexacyano
(d) potassium hexacyanoferrate (II)

70. Potassium diamminedicyanosulphatosuperoxo platinate (IV) is
(a) $K[Pt(CN)_2(O_2)(SO_4)(NH_3)_2]$
(b) $K_4[Pt(NH_3)_2(CN)_2(SO_4)(O_2)]$
(c) $K_2[Pt(NH_3)_2(CN)_2(SO_4)(O_2)]$
(d) $K_3[Pt(NH_3)_2(CN)_2(SO_4)(O_2)]$

71. Pentamminechloroplatinum (IV) chloride ionises to give
(a) two ions (b) three ions (c) four ions (d) five ions

72. Potassium trisoxalatochromate (III) is
(a) $K_3[Cr(C_2O_4)_3]$ (b) $K[Cr(C_2O_4)_3]$
(c) $K_2[Cr(C_2O_4)_3]$ (d) $K_4[Cr(C_2O_4)_3]$

73. Hexammine platinum (IV) tetrachloroplatinate (II) is
(a) $[Pt(NH_3)_6][PtCl_4]$ (b) $[Pt(NH_3)_6]_2[PtCl_4]$
(c) $[Pt(NH_3)_6][PtCl_4]_2$ (d) $[Pt(NH_3)_6]_3[PtCl_4]_2$

74. The complex that can show *fac*-and *mer*-isomers is
(a) $[Pt(NH_3)_2Cl_2]$ (b) $[Co(NH_3)_3(NO_2)_3]$
(c) $[Co(NH_3)_4Cl_2]^+$ (d) $[CoCl_2(en)_2]$

75. In which case geometrical isomers is possible with M as metal ion?
(a) MX_2Y_2 (b) MX_2Y_4 (c) $MX_2Y_2Z_2$ (d) In all cases

76. Dipole moment will be zero in complexes
I. $[Ni(CN)_4]^{2-}$ II. *cis*-$Pt[(NH_3)_2Cl_2]$
III. *trans*-$[Pt(NH_3)_2Cl_2]$
(a) I and II (b) I and III (c) II and III (d) I, II and III

77. Select the correct statement.
(a) Geometrical isomer may differ in dipole moment and visible/UV spectra
(b) Complexes of the type $[Ma_3b_3]$ can also have facial (fac) and meridional (mer) isomer
(c) No optical isomer exists for the complex *trans*-$[Co(en)_2Cl_2]^+$
(d) All the above are correct

78. Complex $[Co(en)_2Cl_2]^+$ can
(a) exist as *cis*- and *trans*-isomer
(b) enantiomorphic pair *d* and *l* are formed if the isomer in which two unidentate ligands (Cl^-) have to be *cis-cis* to each other
(c) Both (a) and (b) correct
(d) None of the above is correct

79. Optical isomers are
I. enantiomers
II. non-superimposable
III. have the property of chirality
IV. form racemic mixture if present in 1 : 1 ratio
Select the correct alternate.
(a) I, II, IV are correct (b) I, II, III are correct
(c) All are correct (d) All are incorrect

80. The complex

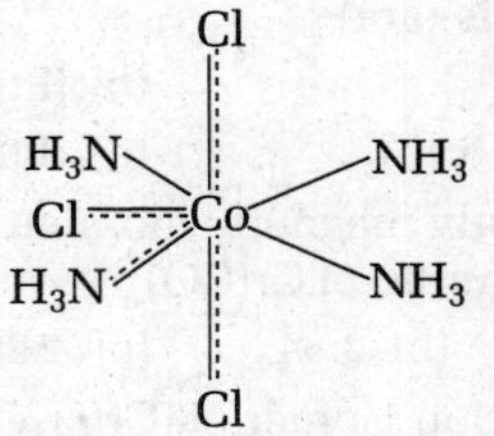

(a) is the molecular complex
(b) has four ions in the aqueous solution
(c) primary valency of cobalt is six
(d) All the above are correct

81. Which contains monovalent cationic complex?
(a) $CoCl_3 \cdot 6NH_3$ (b) $CoCl_3 \cdot 5NH_3$
(c) $CoCl_3 \cdot 4NH_3$ (d) $CoCl_3 \cdot 3NH_3$

82. Which complex gives three chloride ions per formula unit?
(a) $CrCl_3 \cdot 6H_2O$ (b) $CrCl_3 \cdot 5H_2O$
(c) $CrCl_3 \cdot 4H_2O$ (d) All of these

83. In the complex $PtCl_4 \cdot 4NH_3$
(a) two Cl^- ligands satisfy primary as well as secondary valencies
(b) four NH_3 ligands satisfy secondary valency
(c) ions are $[Pt(NH_3)_4Cl_2]^{2+}$ and $2Cl^-$
(d) All the above are correct statements

84. In the complex $CoCl_3 \cdot 4NH_3$
(a) coordination entity is $[Co(NH_3)_4Cl_2]^+$
(b) counter ion is Cl^-
(c) Both (a) & (b) correct
(d) None of the above is correct

85. Which has maximum number of unpaired electrons?
(a) $[Cr(NH_3)_6]^{3+}$ (b) $[CoF_6]^{3-}$
(c) $[Co(NH_3)_6]^{3+}$ (d) $Ni(CO)_4$

86 Select the correct statement.
(a) $[Fe(CN)_6]^{4-}$ and $[Fe(H_2O)_6]^{2+}$ can be distinguished by magnetic moment
(b) $[Ni(CN)_4]^{2-}$ and $[Ni(CO)_4]$ both are diamagnetic
(c) $[Fe(CN)_6]^{3-}$ and $[Co(NH_3)_6]^{2+}$ have equal magnetic moment
(d) All the above are correct statements

87. $[Ni(CN)_4]^{2-}$ and $[Ni(CO)_4]$ have
(a) sp^3 hybridised Ni in both cases
(b) sp^3 and sp^2d-hybridised Ni
(c) dsp^2 and sp^3 hybridised Ni
(d) dsp^2 in both cases

88. $[Fe(H_2O)_6]^{2+}$ and $[Fe(CN)_6]^{4-}$ differ in
(a) geometry, magnetic moment
(b) magnetic moment and colour
(c) geometry and hybridisation
(d) None of the above

89. The crystal field splitting energy for octahedral (Δ_0) and tetrahedral (Δ_t) complexes is related as
(a) $\Delta_t = -\frac{4}{9}\Delta_o$ (b) $\Delta_t = \frac{1}{2}\Delta_o$
(c) $\Delta_o = -2\Delta_t$ (d) $\Delta_o = -\frac{4}{9}\Delta_t$

90. Select the correct statement.
(a) The $d_{x^2-y^2}$ and d_{z^2} orbitals are directed along a set of mutually perpendicular x, y and z-axes. As a group, these orbitals are called, e_g orbitals
(b) The d_{xy}, d_{yz} and d_{xz} orbitals lie between the axes and collectively called t_{2g} orbitals
(c) Both (a) & (b) are correct
(d) None of the above is correct

91. Which pair is not associated with complimentary colour?
(a) Orange — blue (b) Yellow — purple
(c) Green — red (d) Red — yellow

92. Which is the incorrect observation?
(a) For the complex, $[CoF_6]^{3-}$, F^- is a weak-field ligand, so that $\Delta_{oct} < P$ (electron-pairing energy) and is thus high spin complex
(b) For the complex, $[Co(NH_3)_6]^{3+}$, NH_3 is a strong-field ligand, so that $\Delta_{oct} > P$ and thus low spin complex
(c) $\Delta_t = +\frac{4}{9}\Delta_{oct}$
(d) Greater the ionic charge on the central metal ion, the greater the value of Δ

93. For the complex ML_2, stepwise formation constants for

$$M + L \rightleftharpoons ML$$
$$ML + L \rightleftharpoons ML_2$$

are 4 and 3. Hence, overall stability constant for

$$M + 2L \rightleftharpoons ML_2 \text{ is}$$

(a) 12 (b) 7
(c) 1.33 (d) 0.75

94. Select the correct statement.
(a) Chelation effect is maximum for five or six-membered rings
(b) Complex ions in which ligands can be interchanged rapidly are said to be labile
(c) Both (a) and (b) are correct
(d) None of the above is correct

95. One mole of the complex compound $Co(NH_3)_5Cl_3$, gives 3 moles of ion on dissolution in water. One mole of the same complex reacts with 2 moles of $AgNO_3$ solution to yield 2 moles of AgCl(s)
The structure of the complex is
(a) $[Co(NH_3)_5Cl]Cl_2$
(b) $[Co(NH_3)_3Cl_2] \cdot 2NH_3$
(c) $[Co(NH_3)_4Cl_2]Cl \cdot NH_3$
(d) $[Co(NH_3)_4Cl]Cl_2 \cdot NH_3$

96. Which of the following reactions are kinetically favourable?

I. $[Cu(H_2O)_4]^{2+} + 4NH_3 \longrightarrow [Cu(NH_3)_4]^{2+} + 4H_2O$

II. $[Cu(H_2O)_4]^{2+} + 4Cl^- \longrightarrow [CuCl_4]^{2-} + 4H_2O$

III. $[Co(H_2O)_6]^{3+} + 6Cl^- \longrightarrow [CoCl_6]^{3-} + 4H_2O$

(a) I, III (b) II, III (c) I, II (d) I, II, III

97. Select the incorrect statement.

(a) $[Ni(en)_3]^{2+}$ is less stable than $[Ni(NH_3)_6]^{2+}$

(b) Increase in stability of the complexes due to presence of multidentate cyclic ligand is called macrocyclic effect

(c) A complex ion that exchanges ligands slowly is said to be non-labile or inert

(d) For a given ion and ligand, greater the charge on the metal ion, greater the stability

98. Extraction of metals or other processes is through the complex formation

I. Cyanide process;

II. Monds process

III. Photographic fixing process

Complexes formed in these methods are

	I	II	III
(a)	$[Ag(NH_3)_2]Cl$	$Ni(CO)_4$	$[Ag(CN)_2]^-$
(b)	$[Ag(CN)_2]^-$	$Ni(CO)_4$	$[Ag(S_2O_3)_2]^{3-}$
(c)	$[Ag(CN)_2]^-$	$[Ag(S_2O_3)_2]^{3-}$	$Ni(CO)_4$
(d)	$[Cd(CN)_4]^{2-}$	$Ni(CO)_4$	$[Ag(S_2O_3)_2]^{3-}$

99. Cu^{2+} and Cd^{2+} are distinguished through formation of complex $[Cu(CN)_4]^{3-}$ and $[Cd(CN)_4]^{2-}$, when H_2S gas is passed

(a) there is yellow precipitate due to CdS

(b) there is black precipitate due to CuS

(c) there is blue precipitate due to CuS

(d) there is precipitation of CuS and CdS together

100. As per IUPAC nomenclature, the name of the complex $[Co(H_2O)_4(NH_3)_2]Cl_3$ is **[IIT JEE 2012]**

(a) tetraaquadiaminecobalt (III) chloride

(b) tetraaquadiamminecobalt (III) chloride

(c) diaminetetraquacobalt (III) chloride

(d) diamminetetraaquacobalt (III) chloride

101. $NiCl_2\{P(C_2H_5)_2(C_6H_5)\}_2$ exhibits temperature dependent magnetic behaviour (paramagnetic/diamagnetic) the coordination geometries of Ni^{2+} in the paramagnetic and diamagnetic states are respectively **[IIT JEE 2012]**

(a) tetrahedral and tetrahedral

(b) square planar and square planar

(c) tetrahedral and square planar

(d) square planar and tetrahedral

102. Zeisse's salt is

(a) $[Pt(NH_3)_2Cl_2]$ (b) $K[PtCl_3(C_2H_4)]$

(c) $Fe(C_5H_5)_2$ (d) None of these

103. The compound(s) that exhibit(s) geometrical isomerism is (are) **[IIT JEE 2009]**

(a) $[Pt(en)Cl_2]$ (b) $[Pt(en)_2]Cl_2$

(c) $[Pt(en)_2Cl_2]Cl_2$ (d) $[Pt(NH_3)_4]Cl_2$

104. The spin only magnetic moment value (in Bohr magneton units) of $Cr(CO)_6$ is **[IIT JEE 2009]**

(a) 0 (b) 2.84 (c) 4.90 (d) 5.92

105. The ionization isomer of $[Cr(H_2O)_4Cl(NO_2)]Cl$ is **[IIT JEE 2010]**

(a) $[Cr(H_2O)_4(O_2N)]Cl_2$ (b) $[Cr(H_2O)_4Cl_2](NO_2)$

(c) $[Cr(H_2O)_4Cl(ONO)]Cl$ (d) $[Cr(H_2O)_4Cl_2(NO_2)]\cdot H_2O$

106. The correct structure of ethylenediaminetetraacetic acid (EDTA) is **[IIT JEE 2010]**

(a) 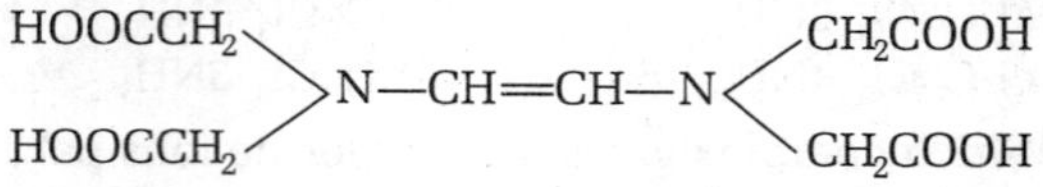

(b) 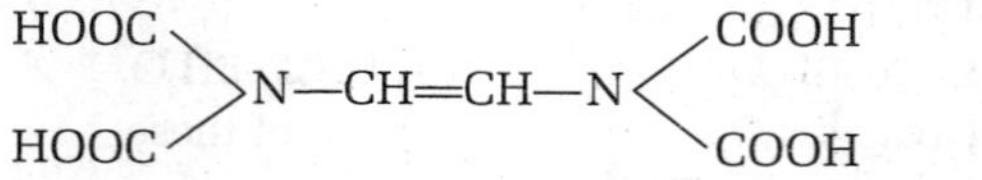

(c) 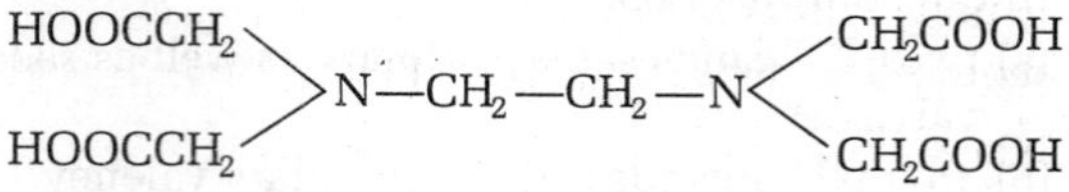

(d) 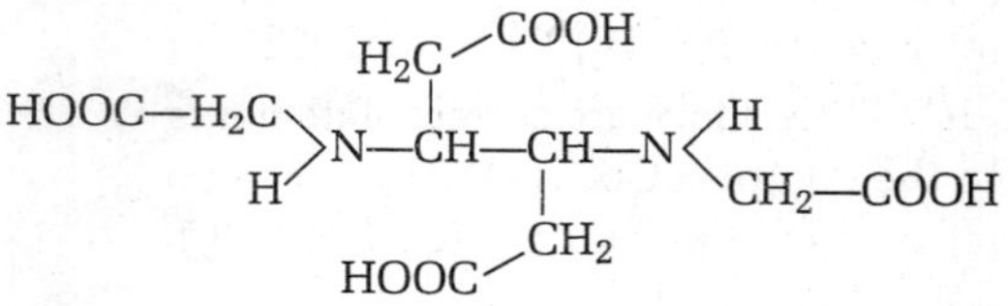

107. The complex showing a spin-only magnetic moment of 2.82 BM is **[IIT JEE 2010]**

(a) $Ni(CO)_4$ (b) $[NiCl_4]^{2-}$

(c) $Ni(PPh_3)_4$ (d) $[Ni(CN)_4]^{2-}$

108. Geometrical shapes of the complexes formed by the reaction of Ni^{2+} with Cl^-.CN^- and H_2O, respectively, are **[IIT JEE 2011]**

(a) octahedral, tetrahedral and square planar

(b) tetrahedral, square planar and octahedral

(c) square planar, tetrahedral and octahedral

(d) octahedral, square planar and octahedral

109. Among the following complexes (*K-P*) $K_3[Fe(CN)_6](K)$, $[Co(NH_3)_6]Cl_3(L)$, $Na_3[Co(ox)_3](M)$, $[Ni(H_2O)_6]Cl_2(N)$, $K_2[Pt(CN)_4](O)$ and $[Zn(H_2O)_6](NO_3)_2(P)$ the diamagnetic complexes are

(a) *K, L, M, N* (b) *K, M, O, P* **[IIT JEE 2011]**

(c) *L, M, O, P* (d) *L, M, N, O*

110. Consider the following complex, ions, *P*, *Q* and *R* $P = [FeF_6]^{3-}$, $Q = [V(H_2O)_6]^{2+}$ and $R = [Fe(H_2O)_6]^{2+}$. The correct order of the complex ions, according to their spin-only magnetic moment values (in BM) is **[JEE Advanced 2013]**

(a) $R < Q < P$ (b) $Q < R < P$

(c) $R < P < Q$ (d) $Q < P < R$

Objective Questions Type II [One or more than one correct option(s)]

In each of the questions below, four choices are given, of which one or more than one are correct.

1. Which are correct statements?
(a) $[Ag(NH_3)_2]^+$ is linear with *sp* hybridised Ag^+ ion
(b) $NiCl_4^{2-}$, VO_4^{3-} and MnO_4^- have tetrahedral geometry
(c) $[Cu(NH_3)_4]^{2+}$, $[Pt(NH_3)_4]^{2+}$ and $[Ni(CN)_4]^{2-}$ have dsp^2 hybridisation of the metal ion
(d) $Fe(CO)_5$ have bipyramidal structure with dsp^3 hybridised iron

2. Which of the following are paramagnetic?
(a) $[Ni(CN)_4]^{2-}$ (b) $[NiCl_4]^{2-}$
(c) $[CoF_6]^{3-}$ (d) $[Co(NH_3)_6]^{3+}$

3. Which of the following can show coordination isomerism?
(a) $[Cu(NH_3)_4][PtCl_4]$ (b) $[Fe(NH_3)_6]_2[Pt(CN)_6]_3$
(c) $[Co(NH_3)_6][Cr(C_2O_4)_3]$ (d) $[Pt(en)_3](SO_4)_2$

4. 0.0012 mol of $CrCl_3 \cdot 6H_2O$ was passed through a cation exchange resin and acid coming out of it required 28.5 mL of 0.125 M NaOH. Hence, complex is
(a) $[Cr(H_2O)_5Cl]Cl_2 \cdot H_2O$ (b) $[Cr(H_2O)_4Cl_2] \cdot 2H_2O$
(c) $[Cr(H_2O)_6]Cl_3$ (d) $[Cr(H_2O)_3Cl_3] \cdot 3H_2O$

5. The correct option(s) regarding the complex $[Co(en)(NH_3)_3(H_2O)]^{3+}$ ($en = H_2NCH_2CH_2NH_2$) is (are) **[JEE Advanced 2018]**
(a) It has two geometrical isomers
(b) It will have three geometrical isomers, if bidentate 'en' is replaced by two cyanide ligands
(c) It is paramagnetic
(d) It absorbs light at longer wavelength as compared to $[Co(en)(NH_3)_4]^{3+}$

6. Identify the complexes which is/are expected to be coloured
(a) $Ti(NO_3)_4$ (b) $[Cu(NCCH_3)]^+ BF_4^-$
(c) $[Cr(NH_3)_6]Cl_3$ (d) $K_3[VF_6]$

7. Nitroprusside ion is
A : $[Fe^{II}(CN)_5NO^+]^{2-}$ and not
B : $[Fe^{III}(CN)_5NO]^{2-}$. A and B can be differentiated by
(a) estimating the concentration of iron
(b) measuring the concentration of CN^-
(c) measuring the magnetic moment
(d) thermally decomposing the compound

8. Choose the correct statement(s) among the following:
(a) $[FeCl_4]^-$ has tetrahedral geometry. **[JEE Advanced 2020[**
(b) $[Co(en)(NH_3)_2Cl_2]^+$ has 2 geometrical isomers.
(c) $[FeCl_4]^-$ has higher spin-only magnetic moment than $[Co(en)(NH_3)_2Cl_2]^+$.
(d) The cobalt ion in $[Co(en)(NH_3)_2Cl_2]^+$ has sp^3d^2 hybridisation.

9. Bidentate ligands are
(a) $C_2O_4^{2-}$ (oxalate)
(b) en (ethylenediamine)
(c) DMG (dimethyl glyoxime)
(d) Gly (glycine)

10. Which of the following complexes are chelates?
(a) *bis*-(dimethyl glyoximato) nickel (II)
(b) potassium ethylenediaminetetracyanato chromate (III)
(c) tetraamminedicyanocobalt (III) nitrate
(d) *trans*-diglycinatopalladium (II)

11. CN^- is a strong field ligand. This is due to the fact that
(a) it carries negative charge
(b) it is a conjugate base of weak acid
(c) it can accept electrons from metal species
(d) it forms high spin complexes with metal species

12. The pair (s) of coordination complexes/ions exhibiting the same kind of isomerism is/are **[IIT JEE Advanced 2013]**
(a) $[Cr(NH_3)_5Cl]Cl_2$ and $[Cr(NH_3)_4Cl_2]Cl$
(b) $[Co(NH_3)_4Cl_2]^+$ and $[Pt(NH_3)_2(H_2O)Cl]^+$
(c) $[CoBr_2Cl_2]^{2-}$ and $[PtBr_2Cl_2]^{2-}$
(d) $[Pt(NH_3)_3(NO_3)]Cl$ and $[Pt(NH_3)_3Cl]Br$

13. Which of the following coordination compounds would exhibit optical isomerism?
(a) Pentaamminenitrocobalt(III) iodide
(b) Diamminedichloroplatinum(II)
(c) *Trans*-dicyanobis (ethylenediamine) chromium(III) chloride
(d) *Tris*-(ethylenediamine) cobalt(III) bromide

14. In which of the following compounds transition metal may have zero oxidation state?
(a) $[Fe(CO)_5]$ (b) $[Ni(CN)_4]^{2-}$ (c) Fe_2O_3 (d) CrO_5

15. Addition of excess aqueous ammonia to a pink coloured aqueous solution of $MCl_2 \cdot 6H_2O(X)$ and NH_4Cl gives an octahedral complex Y in the presence of air. In aqueous solution, complex Y behaves as 1 : 3 electrolyte. The reaction of X with excess HCl at room temperature results in the formation of a blue coloured complex Z. The calculated spin only magnetic moment of X and Z is 3.87 B.M., whersas it is zero for complex Y. **[JEE Advanced 2017]**
Among the following options, which statement(s) is (are) correct?
(a) The hybridisation of the central metal ion in Y is d^2sp^3.
(b) Addition of silver nitrate to Y given only two equivalents of silver chloride.
(c) When X and Y are in equilibrium at 0°C, the colour of the solution is pink.
(d) Z is a tetrahedral complex.

Numerical Value Questions

All these questions have a Numerical value as their answer, solve the questions and write your answer.

1. What is the ratio of uncomplexed to complexed Zn^{2+} ion in a solution that is 10 M in NH_3, if the stability constant of $[Zn(NH_3)_4]^{2+}$ is 3×10^9 ? Ratio is 3.3×10^{-x}, find x.
2. If excess of $AgNO_3$ solution is added to 100 mL of a 0.024 M solution of dichlorobis (ethylenediamine) cobalt (III) chloride, how many moles of AgCl be precipitated?
3. Oxidation number of Cr in the following complex is

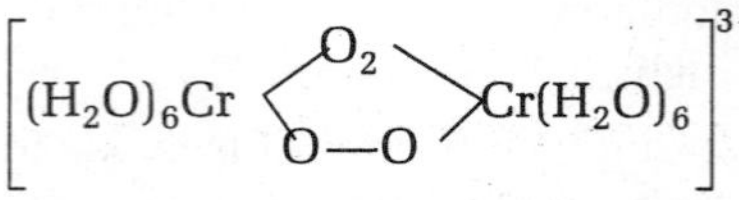

4. Secondary valency of Pt in $[Pt(en)_2Cl_2]Cl_2$ are
5. Consider the following complexes:

   I. K_2PtCl_6 II. $PtCl_4 \cdot 2NH_3$
   III. $PtCl_4 \cdot 3NH_3$ IV. $PtCl_4 \cdot 5NH_3$

   The electrical conductances in aqueous solutions of how many complexes are greater than 100 are
6. $[Pt(NH_3)(NO_2)Py(NH_2OH)]^+$ will form geometrical isomers
7. The coordination number of Pt in the complex ion $[Pt(en)_2Cl_2]^{2+}$ is
8. The number of unpaired electrons expected for the complex ion $[Cr(NH_3)_6]^{2+}$ is
9. What is CFSE of a free Co(II) ion on forming the tetrahedral chloro complex $[CoCl_4]^{2-}$ (in the units of Δ_o)?
10. Total number of *cis* N—Mn—Cl bond angles (that is Mn—N and Mn—Cl bonds in *cis* positions) present in a molecule of *cis* $[Mn(en)_2Cl_2]$ complex is ....
    (en = $NH_2CH_2CH_2NH_2$) **[JEE Advance 2019]**
11. The ammonia prepared by treating ammonium sulphate with calcium hydroxide is completely used by $NaCl_2.6H_2O$ to form a stable coordination compound. Assume that both the reactions are 100% complete. If 1584 g of ammonium sulphate and 952 g of $NiCl_2.6H_2O$ are used in the preparation the combined weight (Atomic weights in g mol^{-1} H = 1, N = 14, O = 16, S = 32, Cl = 35.5, Ca = 40, Ni = 59) **[JEE Advance 2018]**

Comprehension Based Questions

In these questions, a passage has been given followed by questions based on it. You have to answer the questions based on the passage given.

Passage 1 Three different compounds (*A*, *B* and *C*) are known to have the empirical formula $CrCl_3 \cdot 6H_2O(X)$

When exposed to a dehydrating agent *A* loses 2 moles of water per mole of the compound (*X*),

B loses 1 mole of water and compounds *C* loses no water.

Answer the following questions.

1. Thus, *A*, *B* and *C* are

	A	*B*	*C*
(a)	$[Cr(H_2O)_4Cl_2]Cl \cdot 2H_2O$;	$[Cr(H_2O)_5Cl]Cl_2 \cdot H_2O$;	$[Cr(H_2O)_6]Cl_3$
(b)	$[Cr(H_2O)_2Cl_3] \cdot 4H_2O$;	$[Cr(H_2O)Cl_3] \cdot 5H_2O$;	$[CrCl_3] \cdot 6H_2O$
(c)	$[Cr(H_2O)_3Cl_3] \cdot 3H_2O$;	$[Cr(H_2O)_4Cl_2] \cdot 2H_2O$;	$[Cr(H_2O)_6]Cl_3$
(d)	$[Cr(H_2O)_6]Cl_3$;	$[Cr(H_2O)_5Cl]Cl_2 \cdot H_2O$;	$[Cr(H_2O)_4Cl_2]Cl \cdot 2H_2O$

2. Which is most conducting in aqueous solution?
   (a) *A* (b) *B* (c) *C* (d) Equal
3. One mole each of *A*, *B* and *C* is treated with excess of $AgNO_3$. There is formation of white precipitate of AgCl.

   Moles of white precipitates are

	A	*B*	*C*		*A*	*B*	*C*
(a)	1	2	3	(b)	3	2	1
(c)	1	3	2	(d)	3	1	2

Passage 2 The octahedral complex ions $[FeCl_6]^{3-}$ and $[Fe(CN)_6]^{3-}$ are both paramagnetic but the former is high spin and the latter is low spin.

Based on the above study, answer the following questions.

1. High spin complex $[FeCl_6]^{3-}$ has the *d*-configuration as
   (a) $t_{2g}^3 e_g^2$ (b) t_{2g}^5 (c) $t_{2g}^2 e_g^3$ (d) e_g^5
2. Low spin complex $[Fe(CN)_6]^{3-}$ has the *d*-configuration as
   (a) $t_{2g}^3 e_g^2$ (b) t_{2g}^5 (c) $t_{2g}^2 e_g^3$ (d) e_g^5
3. Unpaired electrons in $[FeCl_6]^{3-}$ and $[Fe(CN)_6]^{3-}$ are respectively
   (a) 5, 2 (b) 5, 1 (c) 3, 2 (d) 2, 3

Passage 3 The Alsatian-Swiss chemist Alfred Werner pioneered the field of coordination chemistry in the late nineenth century. At that time, a number of compounds of cobalt (III) chloride with ammonia were known, with general formulae $CoCl_3 \cdot xNH_3$ $x = 3$ to 6

Treatment of these compounds with aqueous HCl acid did not remove the ammonia. However treatment of the compounds with excess of $AgNO_3$ at 273 K gave white precipitate of AgCl in varying ratio depending on the structure. Also each complex had electrical conductivity of varying nature. Based on the above study, answer the following questions.

1. Which complex has the maximum electrical conductivity?
   (a) $CoCl_3 \cdot 3NH_3$ (b) $CoCl_3 \cdot 4NH_3$
   (c) $CoCl_3 \cdot 5NH_3$ (d) $CoCl_3 \cdot 6NH_3$

2. There is no reaction of the compound with aqueous HCl indicating that there is no free NH_3. Thus, NH_3 ligand is bonded to cobalt (III) by
(a) primary valency
(b) secondary valency
(c) Both (a) and (b)
(d) None of the above

3. One mole of the compound gave three moles of white precipitate of AgCl, on reaction with aqueous $AgNO_3$. Thus, complex is
(a) $CoCl_3 \cdot 4NH_3$
(b) $CoCl_3 \cdot 5NH_3$
(c) $CoCl_3 \cdot 6NH_3$
(d) All of these

***Passage* 4** Consider the following reactions

I. $[Co(NH_3)_6]^{3+}(aq) + 6H_3O^+(aq) \rightleftharpoons [Co(H_2O)_6]^{3+}(aq) + 6NH_4^+(aq)$

The products are favoured in the above reaction

II. $[Co(NH_3)_6]^{2+}(aq) + 6H_3O^+(aq) \longrightarrow [Co(H_2O)_6]^{2+}(aq) + 6NH_4^+(aq)$

This, reactions (II) takes place with H_2O in a matter of seconds

Based on the above reactions, answer the following questions.

1. Select the correct statement.
(a) $[Co(NH_3)_6]^{3+}$ is thermodynamically and kinetically stable relative to $[Co(H_2O)_6]^{3+}$
(b) $[Co(NH_3)_6]^{3+}$ is thermodynamically unstable but kinetically stable relative to $[Co(H_2O)_6]^{3+}$
(c) $[Co(NH_3)_6]^{3+}$ is thermodynamically and kinetically unstable relative to $[Co(H_2O)_6]^{3+}$
(d) $[Co(NH_3)_6]^{3+}$ is thermodynamically stable but kinetically unstable relative to $[Co(H_2O)_6]^{3+}$

2. Which is true in terms of $\Delta G°$?
(a) ΔG_I° is more negative than that of II
(b) ΔG_I° is less negative than that of II
(c) $\Delta G_I^\circ = \Delta G_{II}^\circ < 0$
(d) $\Delta G_I^\circ = \Delta G_{II}^\circ > 0$

3. Which is thermodynamically unstable and also kinetically labile?
(a) $[Co(H_2O)_6]^{3+}$
(b) $[Co(H_2O)_6]^{2+}$
(c) $[Co(NH_3)_6]^{3+}$
(d) $[Co(NH_3)_6]^{2+}$

***Passage* 5** The octahedral complex ion $[FeCl_6]^{3-}$ and $[Fe(CN)_6]^{3-}$ are both paramagnetic.

Answer the following questions.

1. Select the correct statements.
(a) $[FeCl_6]^{3-}$ and $[Fe(CN)_6]^{3-}$ both are high-spin complex
(b) $[FeCl_6]^{3-}$ is high-spin and $[Fe(CN)_6]^{3-}$ is low-spin complex
(c) $[FeCl_6]^{3-}$ is low-spin and $[Fe(CN)_6]^{3-}$ is high-spin complex
(d) $[FeCl_6]^{3-}$ and $[Fe(CN)_6]^{3-}$ both are low-spin complexes

2. $[FeCl_6]^{3-}$ has
(a) five unpaired electrons ($t_{2g}^3 e_g^2$)
(b) one unpaired electron (t_{2g}^1)
(c) three unpaired electrons ($t_{2g}^1 e_g^2$)
(d) all the above electrons paired

3. Select the correct statement.
The CFSE for
(a) $[FeCl_6]^{3-}$ is zero
(b) $[Fe(CN)_6]^{3-}$ is $-2\Delta_o$
(c) Both (a) and (b) are correct
(d) None of the above is correct

***Passage* 6** *Read the following experiment and answer the questions at the end of it.*

"A student in 1895 prepared three coordination compounds containing chromium with the following properties.

	Formula	Colour	Cl^- ions in solution per formula units
(*A*)	$CrCl_3 \cdot 6H_2O$	Violet	3
(*B*)	$CrCl_3 \cdot 6H_2O$	Light green	2
(*C*)	$CrCl_3 \cdot 6H_2O$	Dark green	1

1. Which complex has maximum molecules of hydration?
(a) *A* (b) *B* (c) *C* (d) Equally

2. Complexes *A*, *B*, *C* are represented as
(a) *A* : $[Cr(H_2O)_6]Cl_3$
B : $[Cr(H_2O)_5Cl]Cl_2 \cdot H_2O$
C : $[Cr(H_2O)_4Cl_2]Cl \cdot 2H_2O$
(b) *A* : $[Cr(H_2O)_3Cl_3] \cdot 3H_2O$
B : $[Cr(H_2O)_4Cl_2]Cl \cdot 2H_2O$
C : $[Cr(H_2O)_5Cl]Cl_2 \cdot H_2O$
(c) *A* : $[Cr(H_2O)_6]Cl_3$
B : $[Cr(H_2O)_6]Cl_3$
C : $[Cr(H_2O)_6]Cl_3$
(d) None of the above

3. Structural formula of B indicating primary and secondary valencies both is

(a) 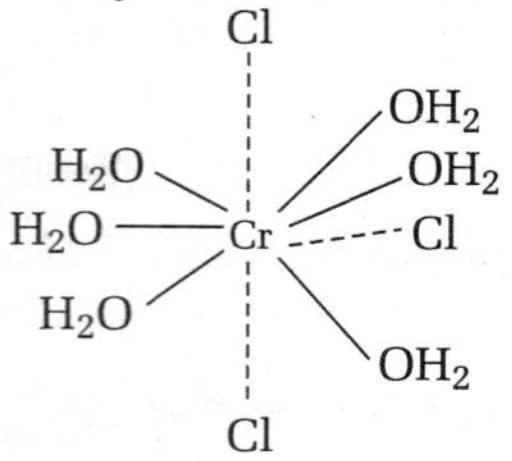

(b) 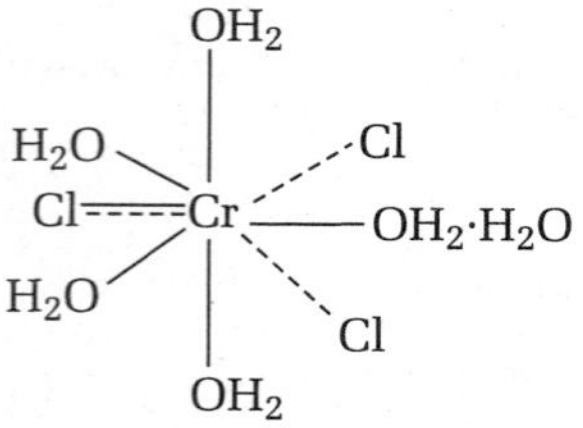

(c) 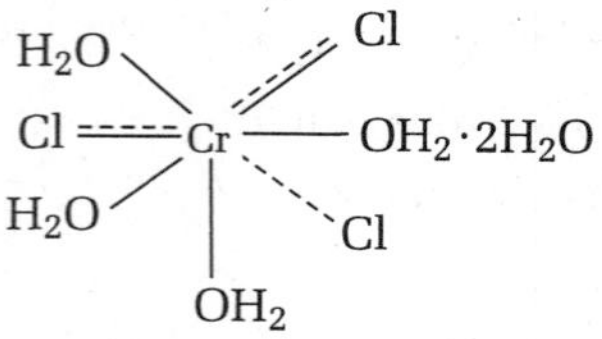

(d) None of the above

***Passage* 7** *Read the following experimental method and answer the questions at the end of it.*

A rose-coloured compound has the empirical formula $CoCl_3 \cdot 5NH_3 \cdot H_2O$. Two moles of this compound react with concentrated sulphuric acid to form HCl(g) and one mole of a new compound with empirical formula $Co_2(SO_4)_3 \cdot 10NH_3 \cdot 5H_2O$. When this new compound is dried at room temperature, it loses three moles of water per mol of $Co_2(SO_4)_3 \cdot 10NH_3 \cdot 5H_2O$.

1. What is the formula of the rose-coloured compound?
(a) $[Co(NH_3)_5Cl]Cl_2 \cdot H_2O$ (b) $[Co(NH_3)_5H_2O]Cl_2$
(c) $[Co(NH_3)_3(H_2O) \cdot Cl_2]Cl$ (d) None of these

2. What is the structure of the new complex formed?
(a) $[Co—(NH_3)_5—Co—(NH_3)_5](SO_4)_3 \cdot 5H_2O$
(b) $[Co—(NH_3)_5—Co—(NH_3)_5(SO_4)](SO_4)_2 \cdot 5H_2O$
(c) 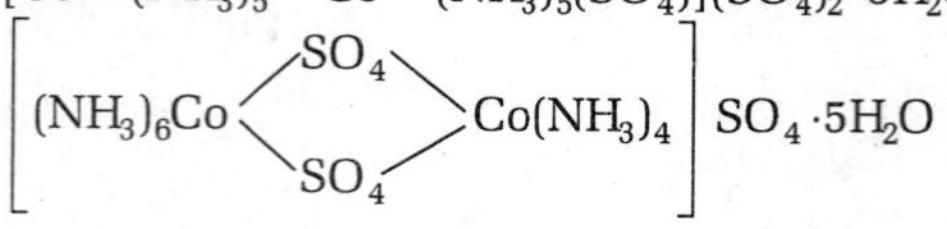
(d) None of the above

***Passage* 8** Mr. William isolated two complexes and in Chemical Absract, he reported.

"A metal complex having composition $Cr(NH_3)_4Cl_2Br$ has been isolated in two forms (A) and (B). The form (A) reacts with $AgNO_3$ to give a white precipitate readily soluble in dilute aqueous ammonia, whereas (B) gives a pale yellow precipitate soluble in concentrated ammonia.

Read the above report from Chemical Abstract and answer the questions at the end of it.

1. Complex A and B are respectively
(a) $[Cr(NH_3)_4Cl_2]Br, [Cr(NH_3)_4Br]Cl_2$
(b) $[Cr(NH_3)_4Br]Cl_2, [Cr(NH_3)_4Cl_2]Br$
(c) $[Cr(NH_3)_4ClBr]Cl, [Cr(NH_3)_4Cl_2]Br$
(d) $[Cr(NH_3)_4Cl_2]Br, [Cr(NH_3)_4ClBr]Cl$

2. Cr atom is .... hybridised.
(a) sp^3d^2 in both complexes
(b) d^2sp^3 in both complexes
(c) sp^3d^2 in A and d^2sp^3 in B
(d) d^2sp^3 in A and sp^3d^2 in B

3. EAN and magnetic moment of Cr in A and B are
(a) 33, $\sqrt{15}$ BM (b) 36, $\sqrt{15}$ BM
(c) 33, $\sqrt{24}$ BM (d) 36, $\sqrt{24}$ BM

***Passage* 9** *Study the following short write up and answer the questions at the end of it.*

A, B and C are three complexes of chromium (III) with the empirical formula $H_{12}O_6Cl_3Cr$. All the three complexes have water and chloride ions as ligands. Complex A does not react with concentrated H_2SO_4, whereas complexes B and C lose 6.75% and 13.5% of their original weight respectively, on treatment with concentrated H_2SO_4.

1. Complex A is
(a) $[Cr(H_2O)_6]Cl_3$
(b) $[Cr(H_2O)_5Cl]Cl_2 \cdot H_2O$
(c) $[Cr(H_2O)_4Cl_2]Cl \cdot 2H_2O$
(d) None of these

2. Loss in weight on treatment with concentrated H_2SO_4 is due to
(a) Cl^- is lost as HCl
(b) Cr^{3+} is lost as $Cr_2(SO_4)_3$
(c) H_2O is lost due to absorption
(d) Cl^- is lost as Cl_2

3. Select the correct statement(s).
(a) Conductance in these complexes is in order $C < B < A$
(b) EAN and nuclear spin of chromium are identical in each complex
(c) Non-reactivity of A with conc. H_2SO_4 is due to absence of water molecules outside coordinated sphere
(d) All of the above are correct

Matrix-Match Type

Given below are Matching Type Questions, with two columns (each having some items) each . Each item of Column I has to be matched with the items of Column II.

1. Match the complex (in Column I) with the hybridisation of the central ion (in Column II).

Column I		Column II	
A.	$Ni(CO)_4$	1.	sp^3d^2
B.	$[Ni(CN)_4]^{2-}$	2.	sp^3
C.	$[Fe(CN)_6]^{4-}$	3.	d^2sp^3
D.	$[MnF_6]^{4-}$	4.	dsp^2

2. Match the complex (in Column I) with the geometry (in Column II).

Column I		Column II	
A.	$[Ni(CN)_4]^{2-}$	1.	Tetrahedral
B.	$[ZnCl_4]^{2-}$	2.	Trigonal bipyramidal
C.	$[Fe(CO)_5]$	3.	Square planar
D.	$[Co(NO_2)_6]^{4-}$	4.	Square pyramid
		5.	Octahedral

3. Match the complex (in Column I) with the equivalent conductance (in Column II).

Column I		Column II	
A.	$[Pt(NH_3)_5Cl]Cl_3$	1.	229
B.	$[Pt(NH_3)_4Cl_2]Cl_2$	2.	97
C.	$[Pt(NH_3)_3Cl_3]Cl$	3.	404
D.	$[Pt(NH_3)_6]Cl_4$	4.	523

4. Match the complex (in Column I) with the oxidation number of Co (in Column II).

Column I		Column II	
A.	$[Co(NCS)(NH_3)_5]SO_3$	1.	−1
B.	$Na[Co(CO)_4]$	2.	0
C.	$Na_4[Co(S_2O_3)_3]$	3.	+1
D.	$Co_2(CO)_5$	4.	+2
		5.	+3

5. Match the complex (in Column I) with the type of isomerism (in Column II).

Column I		Column II	
A.	$[Co(NH_3)_4Cl_2]$	1.	Optical
B.	*cis*-$[Co(en)_2Cl_2]$	2.	Ionisation
C.	$[Co(en)_2(NO_2)Cl]SCN$	3.	Coordination
D.	$[Co(NH_3)_6][Cr(CN)_6]$	4.	Geometrical

6. Match complex ion (in Column I) with number of unpaired electrons (in Column II).

Column I		Column II	
A.	$[Fe(H_2O)_6]^{2+}$	1.	0
B.	$[Fe(H_2O)_6]^{3+}$	2.	1
C.	$[Fe(CN)_6]^{4-}$	3.	2
D.	$[Fe(CN)_6]^{3-}$	4.	3
E.	$[Ni(H_2O)_4]^{2+}$	5.	4
		6.	5

7. Match the complex (in Column I) with its corresponding property (ies) (given in Column II).

Column I		Column II	
A.	$[Ni(DMG)_2]$	1.	Chelation
B.	$Na_3[Fe(C_2O_4)_3]$	2.	Paramagnetic
C.	$[Ni(en)_2]Cl_2$	3.	Diamagnetic
D.	$Ni(Co)_4$	4.	Conducting
		5.	H-bonding

8. Match the complex (in Column I) with its corresponding property (ies) (in Column II).

Column I		Column II	
A.	$[Co(NH_3)_6][Cr(CN)_6]$	1.	Linkage isomerism
B.	$[Cr(NH_3)_3(NO_2)_3]$	2.	Solvate isomerism
C.	$[Cr(H_2O)_6]Cl_3$	3.	Coordinate isomerism
D.	*cis*-$[CrCl_2(ox)_2]^{3-}$	4.	Optical isomerism

[JEE Main 2021, March]

Single Integer Answer Questions

Answer of these questions is a single digit lying between 0 to 9.

1. $[Co(NH_3)_6]^{3+}$ has .... unpaired electron(s) in t_{2g} orbitals.

2. In the high spin complexes of Cr^{3+} number of unpaired electron in t_{2g} orbitals is ....

3. Total number of ions due to ionisation of the complex $CoCl_3 \cdot 6H_2O$ is ....

4. Total number of orbitals used in hybridisation of octahedral complex $[Fe(CN)_6]^{3-}$ is ....

5. Square-planar $[Ni(CN)_4]^{2-}$ uses .... *d*-orbital(s) in hybridisation.

6. CFSE of high-spin d^5-Mn^{2+} complex is ....

7. Total number of geometrical isomers for the complex $[RhCl(CO)(PPh_3)(NH_3)]$ is .... **[IIT JEE 2010]**

8. The volume (in mL) of 0.1 M $AgNO_3$ for complete precipitation of chloride ions present in 30 mL of 0.01 M solution of $[Cr(H_2O)_5Cl]Cl_2$ as silver chloride is .... **[IIT JEE 2011]**

9. Magnetic moment of a complex is 4.9 BM. Thus, unpaired electron(s) may be ....

10. Nickel dimethylglyoximate is stable due to chelation. Chelate ring(s) is/are ....

11. Ethylenediamine displaces H_2O in the complex $[Fe(H_2O)_6]^{3+}$ in three steps

$$[Fe(H_2O)_6]^{3+} + 3\text{ en} \longrightarrow [Fe(en)_3]^{3+} + 6H_2O$$

Stepwise formation constants are

$$\log k_1 = 4.34$$
$$\log k_2 = 3.31$$
$$\log k_3 = 2.05$$

Overall formation constant is $A \times 10^B$ A is ....

12. EDTA is a multidentate ligand. Its deniticity (multicity) is ....

13. $CrCl_3H_{12}O_6$ loses 13.5% water on treatment with conc. H_2SO_4. Number of water molecules lost is ......

14. Total number of *cis* NN—Mn—Cl bond angles (that is Mn—N and Mn—Cl bonds in *cis* positions) present in a molecule of *cis*-$[Mn(en)_2Cl_2]$ complex is ...... (en = $NH_2CH_2CH_2NH_2$) **[JEE Advanced 2019]**

15. $EDTA^{4-}$ is ethylenediamine tetraacetate ion. The total number of N—Co—O bond angles in $[Co(EDTA)]^-$ complex ion is .... **[JEE Advanced 2013]**

16. The number of geometric isomers possible for the complex $[CoL_2Cl_2]^-$ ($L = H_2NCH_2CH_2O^-$) is **[JEE Advanced 2016]**

17. The equivalents of ethylene diamine required to replace the neutral ligands from the coordination sphere of the *trans*-complex of $CaCl_3.4NH_3$ is .... **[JEE Main 2021, March]**

Answers

Objective Questions Type I [Only one correct option]

1. (b)	2. (c)	3. (d)	4. (c)	5. (a)	6. (b)	7. (c)	8. (b)	9. (c)	10. (a)
11. (b)	12. (a)	13. (a)	14. (b)	15. (b)	16. (b)	17. (b)	18. (b)	19. (d)	20. (c)
21. (c)	22. (b)	23. (b)	24. (b)	25. (d)	26. (a)	27. (a)	28. (a)	29. (d)	30. (d)
31. (a)	32. (a)	33. (b)	34. (c)	35. (d)	36. (a)	37. (c)	38. (a)	39. (d)	40. (b)
41. (c)	42. (a)	43. (d)	44. (a)	45. (a)	46. (d)	47. (a)	48. (b)	49. (a)	50. (a)
51. (d)	52. (c)	53. (b)	54. (d)	55. (c)	56. (d)	57. (c)	58. (a)	59. (c)	60. (d)
61. (b)	62. (a)	63. (c)	64. (b)	65. (a)	66. (c)	67. (b)	68. (c)	69. (d)	70. (a)
71. (c)	72. (a)	73. (c)	74. (b)	75. (d)	76. (b)	77. (d)	78. (c)	79. (c)	80. (a)
81. (c)	82. (a)	83. (d)	84. (c)	85. (b)	86. (d)	87. (c)	88. (b)	89. (a)	90. (c)
91. (d)	92. (c)	93. (a)	94. (c)	95. (a)	96. (c)	97. (a)	98. (b)	99. (a)	100. (c)
101. (c)	102. (b)	103. (c)	104. (a)	105. (b)	106. (c)	107. (b)	108. (b)	109. (c)	110. (b)

Objective Questions Type II [One or more than one correct option(s)]

1. (a, b, c, d)	2. (b, c)	3. (a, c)	4. (c)	5. (a, b, d)
6. (c)	7. (c)	8. (a, c)	9. (a, b, c, d)	10. (a, b, d)
11. (b)	12. (b, d)	13. (d)	14. (a)	15. (a, c, d)

Numerical Value Questions

1. (14)	2. (0.0024)	3. (3)	4. (6)	5. (3)
6. (3)	7. (6)	8. (4)	9. (1.2)	10. (6)
11. (2992)				

Comprehension Based Qeustions

Passage 1 – 1. (a) 2. (c) 3. (a)
Passage 2 – 1. (a) 2. (b) 3. (b)
Passage 3 – 1. (d) 2. (b) 3. (d)
Passage 4 – 1. (b) 2. (b) 3. (d)
Passage 5 – 1. (b) 2. (a) 3. (c)
Passage 6 – 1. (c) 2. (a) 3. (b)
Passage 7 – 1. (b) 2. (d)
Passage 8 – 1. (c) 2. (b) 3. (a)
Passage 9 – 1. (a) 2. (c) 3. (d)

Matrix-Match Type

1. A → (2); B → (4); C → (3); D → (1)
2. A → (3); B → (1); C → (2); D → (4)
3. A → (3); B → (1); C → (2); D → (4)
4. A → (5); B → (1); C → (4); D → (2)
5. A → (4); B → (1); C → (2); D → (3)
6. A → (5); B → (6); C → (1); D → (2); E → (3)
7. A → (1,3,5); B → (1,2,4); C → (1,3,4); D → (3)
8. A → (3); B → (1); C → (2); D → (4)

Single Integer Answer Questions

1. (0)	2. (3)	3. (4)	4. (6)	5. (1)	6. (0)	7. (3)	8. (6)	9. (4)	10. (4)
11. (5)	12. (6)	13. (2)	14. (2)	15. (8)	16. (5)	17. (2)			

Solutions

Objective Questions Type I [Only one correct option]

1. (*b*) $\underset{1\text{ mol}}{CoCl_3 \cdot 5NH_3} \xrightarrow{AgNO_3} 2\text{ mol AgCl}$

Thus, 2 Cl are outside coordinate sphere

$\downarrow$ HCl

No NH_4^+

Thus, NH_3 are inside coordinate sphere.
Thus, complex is $[Co(NH_3)_5Cl]Cl_2$.

2. (*c*) Given complex is shown as

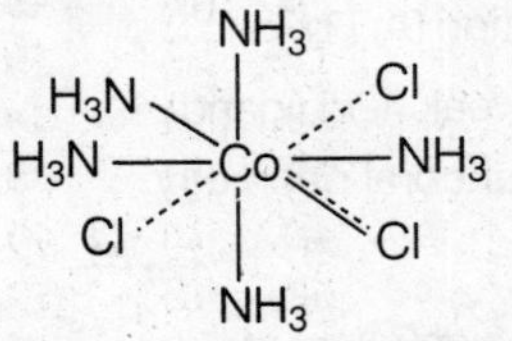

---- PV, —— SV, ==== dual

3. (*d*) Bonding in metal carbonyls like $[Ni(CO)_4]$ can't be properly explained by Werner's theory, valence bond theory or crystal field theory. The concept of synergic bonding based on molecular orbital theory is used to explain their bonding. In $Ni(CO)_4$, backbonding involves filled *d*-orbitals of Ni and antibonding π^* orbitals of carbon monoxide is part of synergic bonding.

4. (*c*) 'en' is a chelating ligand and forms the thermodynamically most stable complex.

5. (*a*) Species with all paired electrons is diamagnetic.

$Fe^{2+} = [Ar]\, 3d^6$

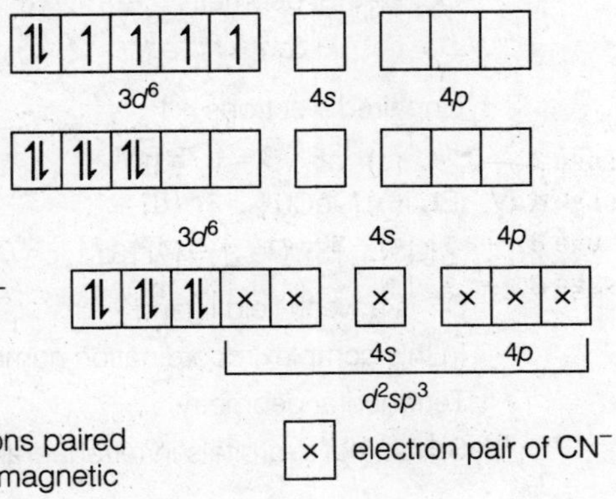

All electrons paired
Thus, diamagnetic

☒ electron pair of CN^-

6. (*b*) $[Co(NO_2)(NH_3)_5]^{2+}$ is yellow in colour but $[Co(ONO)(NH_3)_5]^{2+}$ gives red colour.

7. (*c*) $[Co(NH_3)_4(CO_3)]NO_3$
no chelation

8. (*b*)

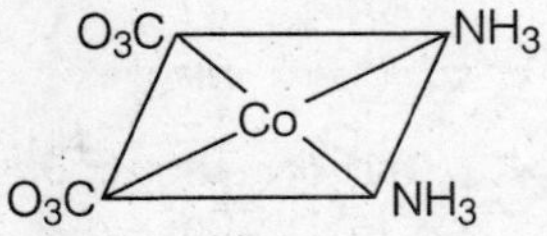

cis

Mirror-images are not superimposable.

9. (*c*) Optical activity is the ability of a chiral molecule to rotate the plane of polarised light, measured by a polarimeter. A chiral molecule does not have any plane of symmetry.

If a molecule possess any plane of symmetry, then it is an achiral molecule. Given options (a), (b) and (d) possess plane of symmetry.

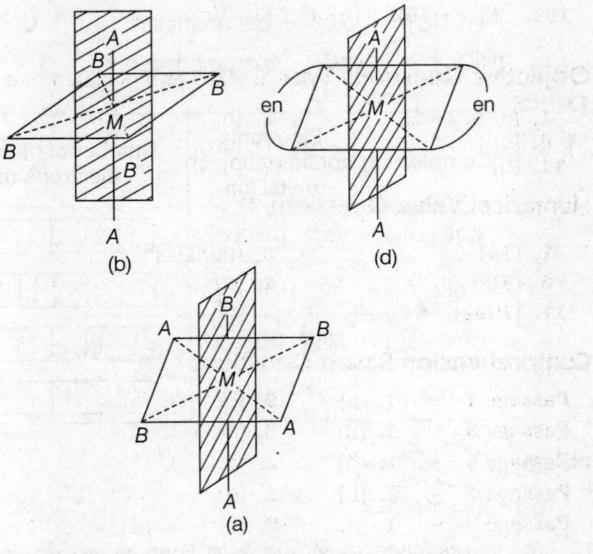

Only molecule (c) does not possess any plane of symmetry. Hence, it is a chiral molecule and shows optical activity.

10. (*a*)

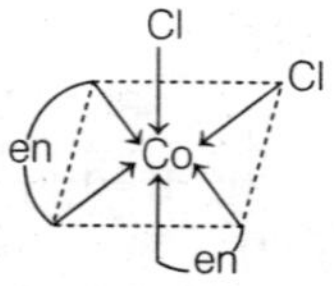

cis-$[Co(en)_2Cl_2]Cl$
(optically active)

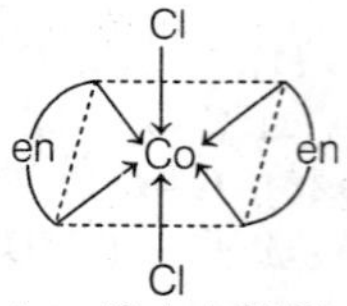

trans-$[Co(en)_2Cl_2]Cl$
(optically inactive due to plane of symmetry)

$[Co(NH_3)_4Cl_2]Cl$ can exist in both *cis* and *trans* forms that are given below:

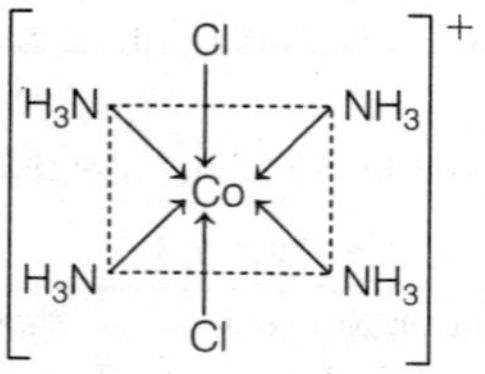

trans-$[Co(NH_3)_4Cl_2]Cl$
(optically inactive)

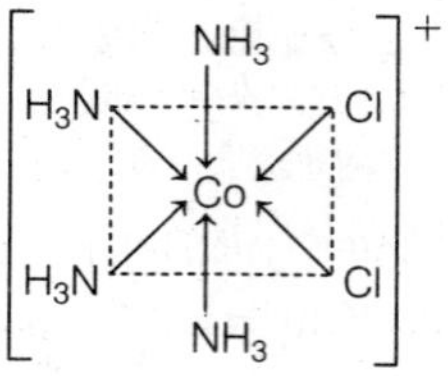

cis-$[Co(NH_3)_4Cl_2]Cl$
(optically inactive)

$[Co(NH_3)_3Cl_3]$ exists in *fac* and *mer*-isomeric forms and both are optically inactive.

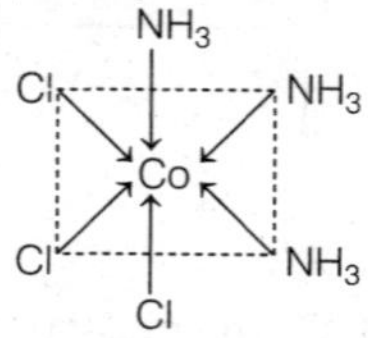

fac-isomer
(optically inactive)

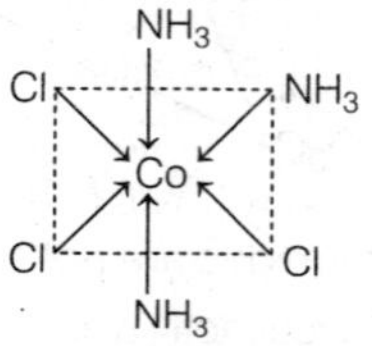

mer-isomer
(optically inactive)

11. (*b*) Number of paramagnetic compounds are 3.
Following compounds are paramagnetic.

$$[NiCl_4]^{2-}, Na_3[CoF_6], CsO_2$$

12. (*a*)

$Ni(CO)_4$	sp^3	diamagnetic
$[Ni(CN)_4]^{2-}$	dsp^2	diamagnetic
$[NiCl_4]^{2-}$	sp^3	paramagnetic

13. (*a*)

Complex ion	Electronic configuration of metal ion	Number of unpaired electrons (*n*)
$[Cr(H_2O)_6]^{2+}$	Cr^{2+}; $[Ar]\,3d^4$	↑ ↑ ↑ ↑ ☐ ; 4
$[Fe(H_2O)_6]^{2+}$	Fe^{2+}; $[Ar]\,3d^6$	↑↓ ↑ ↑ ↑ ↑ ; 4
$[Mn(H_2O)_6]^{2+}$	Mn^{2+}; $[Ar]\,3d^5$	↑ ↑ ↑ ↑ ↑ ; 5
$[CoCl_4]^{2-}$	Co^{2+}; $[Ar]\,3d^7$	↑↓ ↑↓ ↑ ↑ ↑ ; 3

14. (*b*) $[en\ Ni\ en]^{2+}$

dsp^2, CN of Ni = 4

15. (*b*) In presence of strong field ligands, $\Delta_0 > p$, for fourth electron it is more energetically favourable to occupy t_{2g} orbital with configuration $t_{2g}^4 e_g^0$ and form low spin complexes.

The correct order of the spin only magnetic moment of metal ions in the given low-spin complexes is $V^{2+} > Cr^{2+} > Ru^{3+} > Fe^{2+}$.

All the given complexes possess strong field ligands (CN, NH_3). Hence, readily form low spin complexes.

Complex	Oxidation state	Configuration	Orbital splitting	No. of unpaired electrons
$[V(CN)_6]^{4-}$	V^{2+}	$t_{2g}^3 e_g^0$	e_g: ☐ ☐; t_{2g}: ↑ ↑ ↑	3
$[Cr(NH_3)_6]^{2+}$	Cr^{2+}	$t_{2g}^4 e_g^0$	e_g: ☐ ☐; t_{2g}: ↑↓ ↑ ↑	2
$[Ru(NH_3)_6]^{3+}$	Ru^{3+}	$t_{2g}^5 e_g^0$	e_g: ☐ ☐; t_{2g}: ↑↓ ↑↓ ↑	1
$[Fe(CN)_6]^{4-}$	Fe^{2+}	$t_{2g}^6 e_g^0$	e_g: ☐ ☐; t_{2g}: ↑↓ ↑↓ ↑↓	0

16. (*b*) I. In $[Cr(H_2O)_6]Br_2$, chromium is in Cr^{2+} having electronic configuration $[Ar]3d^4$.

H_2O is a weak field ligand.

It has octahedral geometry

$\therefore \quad 3d^4 = t_{2g}^3 e_g^1$

Unpaired electrons = 4

$\mu_s = \sqrt{4 \times 6} = \sqrt{24}$ BM

II. $Na_4[Fe(CN)_6] \longrightarrow Fe^{2+} = [Ar]3d^6$

CN^- is a strong field ligand

Octahedral geometry

$\therefore \quad 3d^6 = t_{2g}^6 e_g^0$

Unpaired electrons = 0

$\mu_s = 0$

III. $Na_3[Fe(C_2O_4)] \longrightarrow Fe^{3+} = [Ar]3d_5$

$\Delta_o > p$ (Given)

Octahedral geometry

$\therefore \quad 3d^5 = t_{2g}^5 e_g^0$

Unpaired electrons = 1

$\mu_s = \sqrt{3} = 1.73$ BM

IV. $(Et_4N)_2[CoCl_4]$

$[CoCl_4]^{2-} : Co_{2+} = [Ar]3d^7$

Cl^- is a weak field ligand.

In this complex, coordination number is 4

Tetrahedral geometry

Splitting of *d*-orbitals in tetrahedral field is

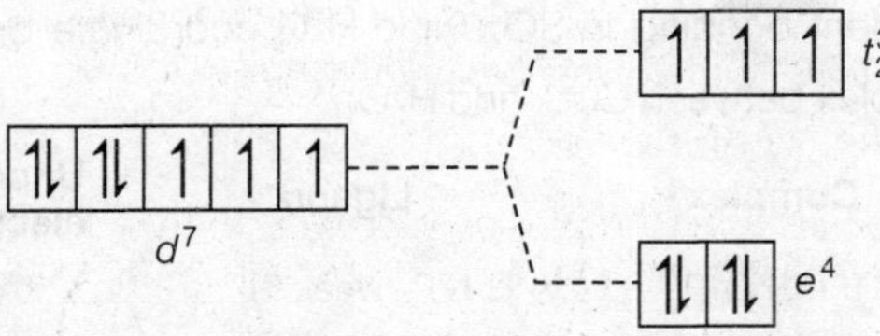

Unpaired electrons = 3

$\mu_s = \sqrt{15}$ BM

$\therefore$ Spin only magnetic moment order is :

I > IV > III > II

17. (*b*) $[Cr(EDTA)]^-$

EDTA = Hexadentate

$Z = 24$

ON of Cr = + 3

Thus, (EAN) of Cr $= 24 - 3 + 2 \times 6 = 33$

$[Co(en)_3]^{3+}$

en = bidenate

$Z = 27$

ON of Co = + 3

EAN of Co $= 27 - 3 + 12 = 36$

$[Fe(C_2O_4)_3^{3-}]$

$C_2O_4^{2-}$ = bidentate

$Z = 26$

ON of Fe = + 3

EAN of Fe $= 26 - 3 + 12 = 35$

$[Ni(CN)_4]^{2-}$ CN^- = monodentate

$Z = 28$

ON of Ni = + 2

EAN of Ni $= 28 - 2 + 8 = 34$

18. (*b*) DMG, en : Bidentate

EDTA : Hexadentate

py : Unidentate

19. (*b*) Linkage isomerism can be shown hy CNS, NO_2 and CN.

$CNS \rightleftharpoons NCS$; $NO_2 \rightleftharpoons ONO$; $C{\equiv}N{\equiv}N{\equiv}C$

20. (*c*) $[Fe(O_2)(CN)_4(Cl)]^{4-}$

$\uparrow \; \downarrow \; \downarrow \; \downarrow$

$+2 \; -2x \; -4 \; -1 = -4$

$2x = -1$

Thus, oxygen is as superoxo.

21. (*c*) It does not lack symmetry.

22. (*b*) If the reactant is *cis* isomer than following reaction takes place.

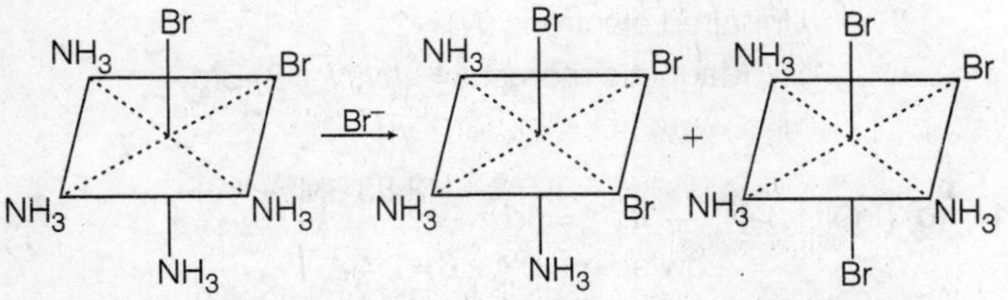

cis-isomer *facial* *meridonial*

i.e. two isomers are produced. If the reactant is *trans* isomer than following reaction takes place.

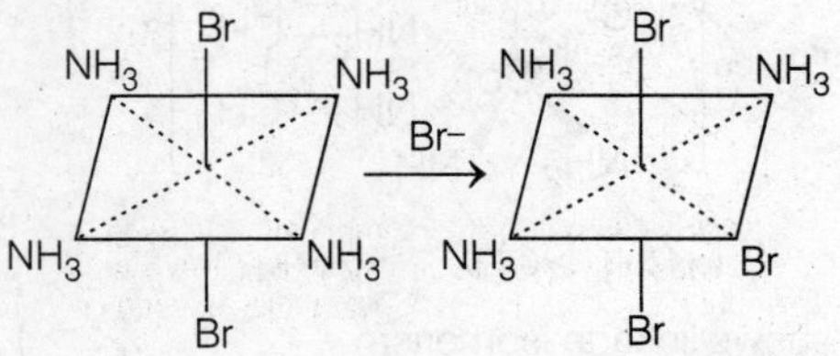

trans *meridonial*

i.e. only 1 isomer is produced.

Thus, statement (I) and (III) are correct resulting to option (b) as the correct answer.

23. (*b*) EAN rule is not followed in which EAN of metal ≠ EC of nearest inert gas

Complex	Z	ON	Electrode from ligand (*L*)	EAN $= Z - (ON) + L$
(a)	29	+1	8	36
(b)	24	+3	12	33
(c)	26	+2	12	36
(d)	28	0	8	36

$[Cr(NH_3)_6]^{3+}$ does not follow EAN rule.

24. (*b*)  is aromatic.

25. (*d*) $Ag_2S + CN^- \longrightarrow [Ag(CN)_2]^-$

AgBr (In photographic plate) $+ 2S_2O_3^{2-} \longrightarrow [Ag(S_2O_3)_2]^{3-} + Br^-$

26. (*a*) Due to different in linkage of NO_2 (metal linked to Co) and ONO (metal linked to Co) they differ in colour.

27. (*a*) $[Cr(en)_3]^{3+}$ exists as enantiomer and thus 1 : 1 mixture of two optically active forms results in the formation of racemic mixture.

28. (*a*)

	Z	ON	Electron from ligand (*L*)	EAN $Z - (ON) + L$
$Ni(CO)_4$	28	0	8	36
$[Fe(CN)_6]^{4-}$	26	2	12	36
$[Ni(en)_2]^{2+}$	28	2	8	34
$[Fe(H_2O)_6]^{2+}$	26	2	12	36
$[Co(CN)_6]^{3-}$	27	3	12	36
$[Fe(CN)_6^{3-}]$	26	3	12	35
$[Sc(H_2O)_6]^{3+}$	21	3	12	30

29. (*d*) In which cation and anion both are complexes.

30. (*d*) II does not form enantiomers.

31. (*a*) EDTA (in the form of dihydrogen salt) forms insoluble compound with Pb^{2+} and is thus drained out.

32. (*a*)

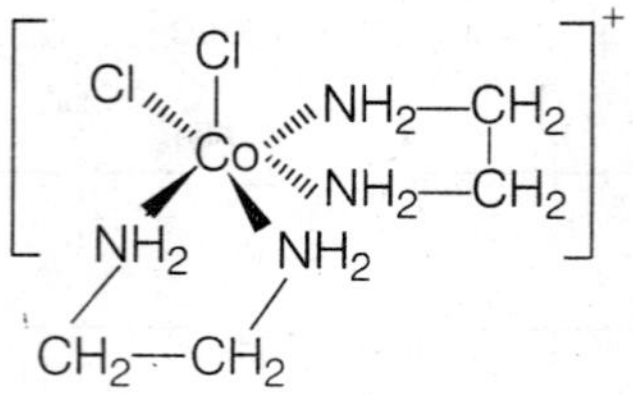

33. (*b*) It shows linkage isomerism.

34. (*c*) $[Fe(H_2O)_6]^{3+} \rightleftharpoons [Fe(H_2O)_6(OH^-)]^{2+} + H^+$
H^+ ion donor thus, Bronsted-Lowry acid.

35. (*d*) $[Co(en)_3]^{3+}$ is most stable due to chelate formation. Thus, highest K_f value.

36. (*a*) $[Co(H_2O)_6]^{2+} + 6Cl^- \longrightarrow [CoCl_6]^{4-} + 6H_2O$
Cl^- replaces H_2O ligands and intense blue colour is developed.

37. (*c*) Cl^- is a weak ligand hence $[MoCl_6]^{3-}$ — sp^3d^2 hybridisation and with unpaired electrons is paramagnetic.
(en) is a strong ligand hence $[Co(en)_3]^{3+}$ — d^2sp^3 hybridisation and with all paired electrons is diamagnetic.

38. (*a*) $\underset{\text{Octahedral}}{[Ni(NH_3)_6]^{2+}}$; $\underset{\text{Square planar}}{[Pt(NH_3)_4]^{2+}}$; $\underset{\text{Tetrahedral}}{[Zn(NH_3)_4]^{2+}}$

39. (*d*) Fe^{2+} changes to brown-coloured ring complex

(b) $NO \longrightarrow NO^+ + e^-$

$Fe^{2+} + e^- \longrightarrow Fe^+$

(c) Fe^{2+} [Ar] $3d^6$ | ⥮ | 1 | 1 | 1 | 1 |

Fe^+ [Ar] $3d^7$ | ⥮ | ⥮ | 1 | 1 | 1 |

Three unpaired electrons

Magnetic moment $= \sqrt{N(N+2)} = \sqrt{15} = 3.87$ BM

Thus, (a), (b) and (c) are true.

40. (*b*) Crystal field stabilisation energy in octahedral *Vis-a-vis* tetrahedral Cr^{3+} system plays the deciding role.

41. (*c*)

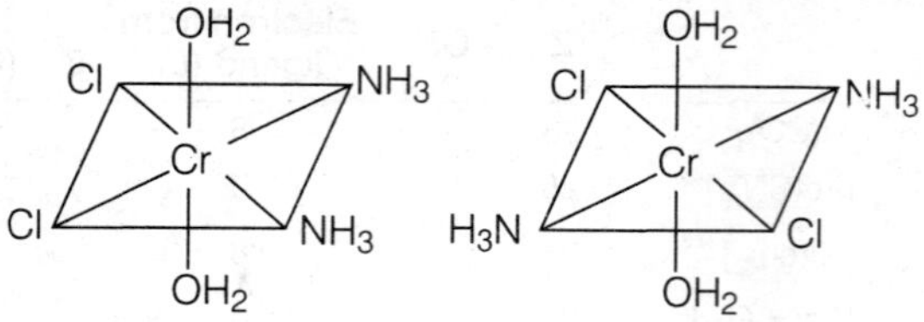

cis w.r.t. NH_3 and Cl   *trans* w.r.t. NH_3 Cl, H_2O

Enantiomers are non-superimposable.
Thus, it exhibit geometrical and optical isomer.

42. (*a*) If acid is weak, its conjugate base is strong ligand.

HI > HCN	acid strength
$I^- < CN^-$	ligand strength
$NH_3 > H_2O$	ligand strength

43. (*d*) $CuSO_4 \cdot 5H_2O$ exists as $[Cu(H_2O)_4]SO_4 \cdot H_2O$
Ionic bonding between $[Cu(H_2O)_4]^{2+}$ and SO_4^{2-}
Covalent bonding in SO_4^{2-} and H_2O coordinate bonding in complex between Cu^{2+} and H_2O.

44. (*a*)

Complex	Ligand	Unpaired electrons
I. $[Fe(H_2O)_6]^{2+}$	H_2O — weak	4
II. $[Fe(CN)_6]^{3-}$	CN^- — strong	1
III. $[Fe(CN)_6]^{4-}$	CN^- — strong	0
IV. $[Fe(H_2O)_6]^{3+}$	H_2O — weak	5

Thus, IV > I > II > III

45. (*a*) Ligand are displace on *x* and *y* axis in octahedral complex.

46. (*d*) Molarity $(M) = \dfrac{\text{Number of moles of solute}}{\text{Volume of solution (in L)}}$

$\therefore$ Number of moles of complex

$$= \frac{\text{molarity} \times \text{volume (in mL)}}{1000} = \frac{0.1 \times 100}{1000} = 0.01 \text{ mole}$$

$$\text{Number of moles of ions precipitate} = \frac{1.2 \times 10^{22}}{6.02 \times 10^{23}}$$

$$= 0.02 \text{ moles}$$

$\therefore$ Number of Cl^- present in ionisation sphere

$$= \frac{\text{Number of moles of ions precipitated}}{\text{Number of moles of complex}} = \frac{0.02}{0.01} = 2$$

$\therefore$ 2 Cl^- are present outside the square brackets, i.e. in ionisation sphere. Thus, the formula of complex is $[Co(H_2O)_5Cl]Cl_2 \cdot H_2O$

47. (*a*) Fe (III) ion forms a charge transfer complex with SCN^- ions.

48. (*b*) $Fe^{3+} + [Fe^{II}(CN)_6]^{4-} \longrightarrow Fe^{2+} + [Fe^{III}(CN)_6]^{3-}$

49. (*a*) $E = h\nu = \dfrac{hc}{\lambda}$

$\therefore \quad \lambda = \dfrac{hc}{E}$

Weaker the ligands, smaller the energy difference, hence larger the value of λ.

50. (*a*) $H_2O < NH_3 < NO_2$ ligand strength and energy. In square planar as in $[Ni(CN)_4^{2-}]$, hybridisation is dsp^2 thus all electrons are paired,

Magnetic moment $= 0$

In octahedral geometry as in $[NiCl_6]^{4-}$, hybridisation is sp^3d^2,

Unpaired electrons $(N) = 2$

Magnetic moment $= \sqrt{N(N+2)}$ BM

$= \sqrt{8}$

$= 2.83$ BM

51. (*d*) $[Ir(NH_3)_6]^{3+} \rightarrow Ir^{3+} = 5d^6$

Low spin $= 0.4 \times 6 = 2.4\,\Delta_o$

53. (*b*) ligands are
—NO_2, metal linked to N
—ONO, metal linked to O

54. (*d*) Ligand strength is in order , Py < Br^- < NH_3

Thus, replacement of Cl^- ligands by above ligands is in same order.

55. (*c*) $[CoCl_6]^{4-}$
Oxidation number of cobalt = +2
CN of cobalt = 6

Co^{2+} = [Ar] $3d^7$

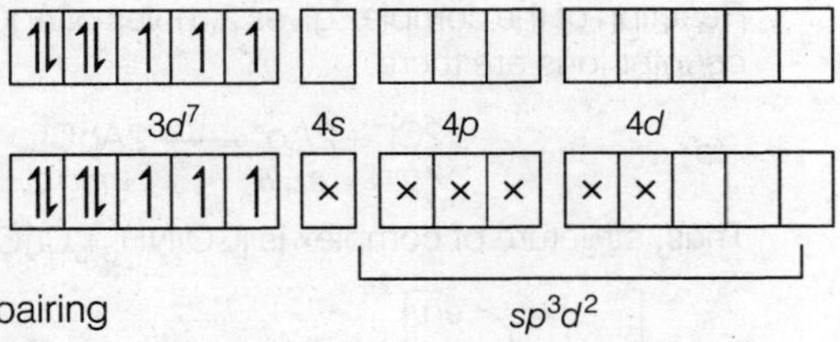

Cl^- a weak ligand

hence, no pairing

It is thus paramagnetic and high spin complex.
Thus, (I) and (IV) are correct.

57. (*c*) Ionisation isomerism :

$$[Co(NH_3)_5Br]SO_4 \rightleftharpoons [Co(NH_3)_5SO_4]Br$$

58. (*a*) (a) $[Co(NH_3)_6]Cl_3$
(b) double salt
(c) simple salt
(d) double salt

59. (*c*) $FeSO_4 + 6KCN \longrightarrow K_2SO_4 + K_4[Fe(CN)_6]$

60. (*d*) *trans*-$[NiBr_2(PPh_3)_2]$ is

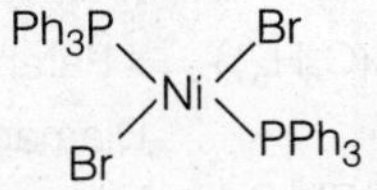

meridional-$[Co(NH_3)_3(NO_2)_3]$ is

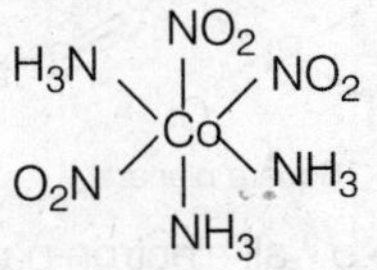

61. (*b*) $Fe^{3+} + 3C_2O_4^{2-} \longrightarrow [Fe(C_2O_4)_3]^{3-}$ Soluble

62. (*a*) The ions or molecules attached to the central metal atom or ion in a complex formed is called ligand (*L*)

63. (*c*) Fe^{3+} (Lewis acid) + $6NH_3$ (Lewis base) $\longrightarrow [Fe(NH_3)_6]^{3+}$

64. (*b*) The closed ring compounds formed by bidentate ligands on binding to a metal or metal ions are called chelates.

65. (*a*) EDTA is hexadentate.

66. (*c*) $[Pt(O_2)(en)_2(Br)]^{2+}$ (O_2: Superoxide (−1); en: Bidentate)

Thus, ON = + 4 and CN = 6

67. (*b*) $[Cr(C_2O_4),(en),(O_2)_2]^-$

68. (*c*) The isomers of $[Co(NH_3)_4Cl_2]$ that have a Cl—Co—Cl angle of 90° is *cis* only.

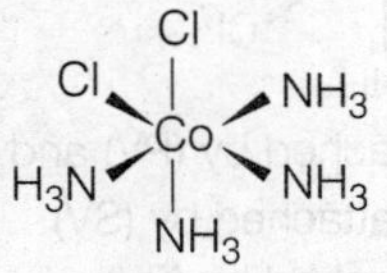

trans isomer has Cl—Co—Cl angle of 180°.

69. (*d*) K_4 $[\overset{+2}{Fe}(CN)_6]$
Cation Anion

70. (*a*) Anion is $[\underset{+4}{Pt}\,\underset{+0}{(NH_3)_2}\,\underset{-2}{(CN)_2}\,\underset{-2}{(SO_4)}\,\underset{-1=-1}{(O_2)}]$

Cation is K^+

$$K[Pt(CN)_2(O_2)(SO_4)(NH_3)_2]$$

71. (*c*) $[\underset{+4}{Pt}(NH_3)_5\underset{-1}{Cl}]^{3+}Cl^-$

Thus, complex is

$$[Pt(NH_3)_5Cl]Cl_3 \rightleftharpoons \underbrace{[Pt(NH_3)_5Cl]^{3+} + 3Cl^-}_{\text{four ions}}$$

72. (*a*) $Cr^{3+} + 3(C_2O_4)^{2-} \longrightarrow K^+[Cr(C_2O_4)_3]^{3-}$

Thus, complex is $K_3[Cr(C_2O_4)_3]$.

73. (*c*) $[\overset{IV}{Pt}(NH_3)_6]^{4+}$ $[\overset{II}{Pt}Cl_4]^{2-}$

Thus, complex is $[Pt(NH_3)_6][PtCl_4]_2$

74. (*b*) Octahedral coordination entities of the type $[Ma_3b_3]$ shows geometrical isomers : *fac* and *mer* isomers. Among the given complexes, the complex withgeneral formula $[Ma_3b_3]$ is $[Co(NH_3)_3(NO_2)_3]$. Thus, it can show *fac* and *mer* isomers as follows:

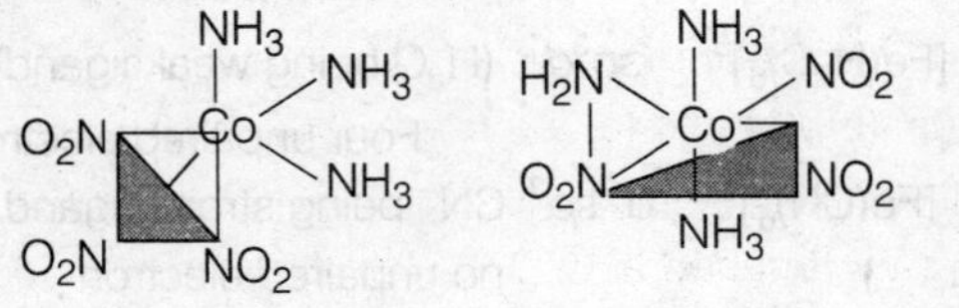

(*fac*) (*mer*)

75. (*d*) Geometrical isomers with *M* metal ion is

$$MX_2Y_2,\ MX_2Y_4,\ MX_2Y_2Z_2$$

76. (*b*) $[Ni(CN)_4]^{2-}$. ⇒ *D.M* = 0

trans-$[Pt(NH_3)_2Cl_2]$ ⇒ D.M = 0

80. (*a*) $[Co(NH_3)_3Cl_3] \rightleftharpoons$ no ionisation

Thus, is the molecular complex.

81. (*c*) ON of Co = + 3 and CN of Co = 6

(a) $[Co(NH_3)_6]Cl_3 \rightleftharpoons [Co(NH_3)_6]^{3+} + 3Cl^-$

(b) $[Co(NH_3)_5Cl]Cl_2 \rightleftharpoons [Co(NH_3)_5Cl]^{2+} + 2Cl^-$

(c) $[Co(NH_3)_4Cl_2]Cl \rightleftharpoons [Co(NH_3)_4Cl_2]^+ + Cl^-$
Monovalent cation

(d) $[Co(NH_3)_3Cl_3] \rightleftharpoons$ no ionisation

82. (*a*) $[Cr(H_2O)_6]Cl_3 \rightleftharpoons [Cr(H_2O)_6]^{3+} + 3Cl^-$

83. (*d*)

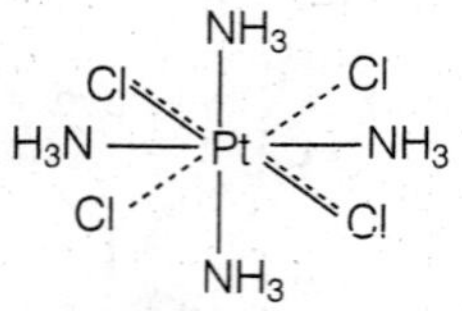

==== two Cl attached by (PV) and (SV)

—— four NH_3 attached by (SV)

----- two Cl attached by (PV)

84. (*c*) Complex is

$$[Co(NH_3)_4Cl_2]Cl \rightleftharpoons [Co(NH_3)_4Cl_2]^+ + Cl^-$$

85. (*b*)

		Unpaired electron
(a) $[Cr(NH_3)_6]^{3+}$	(d^2sp^3)	3
(b) $[CoF_6]^{3-}$	(sp^3d^2)	4
(c) $[Co(NH_3)_6]^{3+}$	d^2sp^3	0
(d) $Ni(CO)_4$	sp^3	0

86. (*d*) Unpaired electrons

(a) $[Fe(CN)_6]^{4-}$ 0

$[Fe(H_2O)_6]^{2+}$ 4

Thus, they differ in magnetic moment.

(b) $[Ni(CN)_4]^{2-}$ dsp^2 diamagnetic

$Ni(CO)_4$ sp^3 diamagnetic

Thus, true

(c) Unpaired electron

$[Fe(CN)_6]^{4-}$ 4 d^2sp^3

$[Co(NH_3)_6]^{3+}$ 4 d^2sp^3

Thus, true

87. (*c*) $[Ni(CN)_4]^{2-}$: dsp^2 square planar

$Ni(CO)_4$: sp^3 tetrahedral

88. (*b*) $[Fe(H_2O)_6]^{3+}$ sp^3d^2 (H_2O being weak ligand)

Four unpaired electrons

$[Fe(CN)_6]^4$ d^2sp^3 CN^- being strong ligand

no unpaired electron

Both have octahedral geometrical but differ in colour.

89. (*a*) $\Delta t = \frac{-4}{9}\Delta_0$ and $\Delta_0 > \Delta t$

91. (*d*) Complementary colour of red is green.

93. (*a*)

$$M + L \rightleftharpoons ML, \quad K_1 = \frac{[ML]}{[M][L]} = 4$$

$$M + L \rightleftharpoons ML_2, \quad K_2 = \frac{[ML_2]}{[ML][L]} = 3$$

$$M + 2L \rightleftharpoons ML_2 \quad K_3 = \frac{[ML_2]}{[M][L]^2}$$

$$K_1 = K_1K_2 = 12$$

95. (*a*) One mole of the complex compound $Co(NH_3)_5Cl_3$ gives 3 moles of ions on dissolution in water.

Thus, its dissociation can be shown as.

$$[Co(NH_3)_5Cl]Cl_2 \rightleftharpoons \underbrace{[Co(NH_3)_5Cl]^{2+} + 2Cl^-}_{3\text{ ions}}$$

Reaction of the complex gives 2 moles of AgCl suggest that 2 counter ions are there.

$$\underset{2\text{ mol}}{2Cl^-} + \underset{2\text{ mol}}{2Ag^+} \longrightarrow \underset{2\text{ mol}}{2AgCl}$$

Thus, structure of complex is $[CO(NH_3)_5Cl]Cl_2$.

97. (*a*)

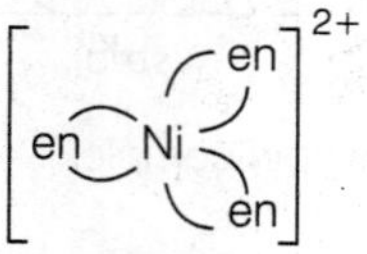

Chelate complex thus more stable than $[Ni(NH_3)_6]^{2+}$.

98. (*b*) I. $Ag_2S + CN^- \longrightarrow [Ag(CN)_2]^-$

II.` $Ni + 4CO \longrightarrow [Ni(CO)_4]$

III. $AgBr + 2S_2O_3^{2-} \longrightarrow [Ag(S_2O_3)_2]^{3-}$

99. (*a*) $[Cu(CN)_4]^{3-}$ is stable, does not ionise

$[Cd(CN)_4]^{2-}$ is unstable, ionises to form Cd^{2+}, thus CdS is precipitated.

100. (*c*) $[Co(H_2O)_4(NH_3)_2]Cl_3 \Rightarrow$ diaminetetra aquacobalt (III) chloride

101. (*c*) $NiCl_2\{P(C_2H_5)_2(C_6H_5)\}_2 \Rightarrow$ Paramagnetic in tetrahedral.

Diamagnetic in square planar.

102. (*b*) Zeisse' salt $K[PtCl_3(C_2H_4)]$

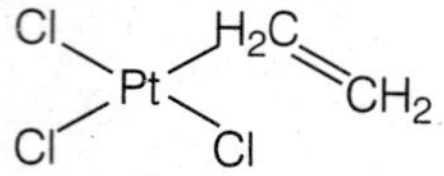

Square planar

104. (*a*) $Cr(CO)_6 - Cr^0 \rightarrow d^6$ all electron paired spin only magnetic moment is 0.

107. (*b*) $[NiCl_4]^{2-} \Rightarrow Ni^{2+} \rightarrow d^8 \rightarrow$ 2 unpaired election

$$\sqrt{n(n+2)} = \sqrt{2(2+2)} = \sqrt{8} = 2.82$$

14

General Principles and Processes of Isolation of Metals

Objective Questions Type I [Only one correct option]

In each of the questions below, four choices are given of which only one is correct.

1. Si of high purity to be used in semiconductor can be prepared by the following methods.

I. $SiO_2 + 2C \longrightarrow Si + 2CO$

II. $Si + 2Cl_2 \longrightarrow SiCl_4$

$SiCl_4 + 2Mg \longrightarrow Si + 2MgCl_2$

Better method is

(a) I (b) II
(c) Both (a) and (b) (d) None of these

2. Main source of lead is PbS. It is converted to Pb by

I. $PbS \xrightarrow[\Delta]{air} PbO + SO_2$

$PbO \xrightarrow{C} Pb + CO_2$

II. $PbS \xrightarrow[\Delta]{air} PbO + PbS$

$PbO + PbS \xrightarrow{PbS} Pb + SO_2$

Self-reduction process is

(a) I (b) II
(c) Both (a) and (b) (d) None of these

3. Oxidation states of the metal in the minerals given are **[IIT JEE 2011]**

	Haematite	Magnesite
(a)	II, III	III
(b)	II, III	II
(c)	II	II, III
(d)	III	II, III

4. In the cyanide extraction process of silver from argentite ore, the oxidising and reducing agents used are respectively **[IIT JEE 2012]**

(a) O_2 and CO (b) O_2 and Zn
(c) HNO_3 and Zn dust (d) HNO_3 and CO

5. Formation of $Ni(CO)_4$ and subsequent its decomposition into Ni and CO (recycled) makes the basis of Mond's process

$$Ni + 4CO \xrightarrow{T_1} Ni(CO)_4 \xrightarrow{T_2} Ni + 4CO$$

T_1 and T_2 are

(a) 100°C, 50°C (b) 50°C, 100°C
(c) 50°C, 230°C (d) 230°C, 50°C

6. Oxides of the various metals are converted into metal by heating but not in

(a) Ag_2O (b) CuO
(c) HgO (d) All are correct

7. When $FeCr_2O_4$ (chromite) is reduced with C in an electric-arc furnace

(a) Cr and Fe_2O_3 are formed
(b) Fe and Cr_2O_3 are formed
(c) Fe and Cr (ferrochrome) are formed
(d) $FeCrO_4$ is formed

8. In the extraction of chlorine by electrolysis of brine

(a) oxidation of Cl^- ion to chlorine gas occurs at cathode
(b) reduction of Cl^- ion to chlorine gas occurs at anode
(c) for overall reaction $\Delta G°$ has a negative value
(d) a displacement reaction takes place

9. Extraction of gold and silver involves leaching the metal with CN^- ion. The metal is recovered by
   (a) displaccement of metal by some other metal from the complex
   (b) roasting of metal complex
   (c) calcination followed by roasting
   (d) thermal decomposition of metal complex

10. Example of autoreduction is
   (a) $2FeS + 3O_2 \longrightarrow 2FeO + 2SO_2$
   (b) $FeO + SiO_2 \longrightarrow FeSiO_3$
   (c) $2Cu_2S + 3O_2 \longrightarrow 2Cu_2O + 2SO_2$
   (d) $2Cu_2O + Cu_2S \longrightarrow 6Cu + SO_2$

11. Copper matter is converted into blister copper by taking it into a silica lined convertor. Blistered appearance is due to which reaction?
   (a) $2Cu_2S + 3O_2 \longrightarrow 2Cu_2O + 2SO_2$
   (b) $Cu_2O + C \longrightarrow 2Cu + CO$
   (c) $2Cu_2O + Cu_2S \longrightarrow 6Cu + CO$
   (d) $Cu^{2+} + Zn \longrightarrow Zn^{2+} + Cu$

12. The froth floatation process is applied for sulphide ores and sodium ethyl xanthate acts as a collector of sulphide ore. In this process
   (a) the hydrophobic end prefers to stay in air and the hydrophilic end prefers to stay in water
   (b) the hydrophobic end prefers to stay in water and the hydrophilic end prefers to stay in air
   (c) both ends prefer to stay in water
   (d) both ends prefer to stay in air

13. The process that involves the removal of sulphur from the ores is **[JEE Main 2021]**
   (a) smelting (b) roasting
   (c) leaching (d) refining

14. Sulphide ores are common for the metals **[JEE Advanced 2013]**
   (a) Ag, Cu, Pb (b) Ag, Cu, Sn
   (c) Ag, Mg, Pb (d) Al, Cu, Pb

15. In the extraction of nickel by Mond's process, the metal is obtained by
   (a) electrochemical reduction
   (b) thermal decomposition
   (c) chemical reduction by aluminium
   (d) reduction by carbon

16. The purest form of commercial iron is **[JEE Main 2020]**
   (a) cast iron
   (b) scrap iron and pig iron
   (c) wrought iron
   (d) pig iron

17. In the metallurgy of iron, when $CaCO_3$ is added to blast furnace, calcium ion appears as
   (a) CaO (b) metallic Ca
   (c) gangue (d) slag

18. Iron obtained from blast furnace is
   (a) wrought iron (b) cast iron
   (c) pig iron (d) steel

19. Four metals and their methods of refinement are given
   (i) Ni, Cu, Zr, Ga
   (ii) Electrolysis, van-Arkel process, Zone refining, Mond's process
   Choose the right method for each.
   (a) Ni : Electrolysis, Cu : van-Arkel process, Zr : Zone refining, Ga : Mond's process
   (b) Ni : Mond's process, Cu : Electrolysis, Zr : van-Arkel process, Ga : Zone refining
   (c) Ni : Mond's process, Cu : van-Arkel process, Zr : Zone refining, Ga : Electrolysis
   (d) Ni : Electrolysis, Cu : Zone refining, Zr : van-Arkel process, Ga : Mond's process

20. On igniting Fe_2O_3 at 1400°C, the product obtained is
   (a) Fe_2O_3 melt (b) FeO
   (c) Fe_3O_4 (d) metallic iron

21. Consider the following metallurgical processes.
   I. Heating impure metal with CO and distilling the resulting volatile carbonyl (b.p. 43°C) and finally decomposing at 150° to 200°C to get the pure metal.
   II. Heating the sulphide ore in air until a part is converted to oxide and then further heating in the absence of air to let the oxide react with unchanged sulphide.
   III. Electrolysing the molten electrolyte containing approximately equal amounts of the metal chloride and $CaCl_2$ to obtain the metal.
   The processes used for obtaining sodium, nickel and copper are respectively
   (a) I, II and III (b) II, III and I
   (c) III, I and II (d) II, I and III

22. Extraction of aluminium from aluminium oxide (Al_2O_3) is best done by
   (a) electrolytic reduction of Al_2O_3
   (b) reduction of Al_2O_3 with carbon
   (c) reduction of Al_2O_3 with sodium
   (d) reduction of Al_2O_3 with CO

23. Consider the following statements.
   Roasting is carried out to
   I. convert sulphide to oxide and sulphate
   II. remove water of hydration
   III. melt the ore
   IV. remove arsenic and sulphur impurities
   Of these statements
   (a) I, II and III are correct (b) I and IV are correct
   (c) I, II and IV are correct (d) II, III and IV are correct

24. The element which could be extracted by electrolytic reduction of its oxide dissolved in a high temperature melt is
(a) sodium (b) magnesium
(c) fluorine (d) aluminium

25. Chemical leaching is useful in the concentration of
(a) copper pyrites (b) bauxite
(c) galena (d) cassiterite

26. Which one of the following is not a method of concentration of metals?
(a) Gravity separation
(b) Froth floatation process
(c) Electromagnetic separation
(d) Smelting

27. Blister Cu is about
(a) 60% Cu (b) 90% Cu
(c) 98% Cu (d) 100% Cu

28. There are following extraction process of silver but not
(a) as a side product in electrolytic refining of copper
(b) Parke's process in which Zn is used to extract silver by solvent extraction from molten lead
(c) by reaction of silver sulphide with KCN and then reaction of soluble complex with Zn.
(d) by heating $Na[Ag(CN)_2]$

29. $Ag_2S + NaCN \longrightarrow (A)$
$(A) + Zn \longrightarrow (B)$
(B) is a metal. Hence, (A) and (B) are
(a) $Na_2[Zn(CN)_4]$, Zn (b) $Na[Ag(CN)_2]$, Ag
(c) $Na_2[Ag(CN)_4]$, Ag (d) $Na_3[Ag(CN)_4]$, Ag

30. Carbon reduction cannot be applied for the extraction of Al from Al_2O_3. This is based on the following facts.
Fact-I The temperature requirement is very high about 2000°C.
Fact II Based on Ellingham diagram.
Fact III Al obtained in the vapour state is difficult to handle.
Fact IV Al gets converted into Al_4C_3 (carbide).
Select the correct fats.
(a) All except I (b) All except II
(c) All except III (d) All are correct facts

31. Which of the following does not contain Mg?
(a) Magnetite (b) Magnesite
(c) Asbestos (d) Carnallite

32. Calcination is the process of heating the ore
(a) in inert gas
(b) in the presence of air
(c) in the absence of air
(d) in the presence of CaO and MgO

33. $Ag_2S + NaCN + Zn \longrightarrow Ag$
This method of extraction of Ag by complex formation and then its displacement is called
(a) Parke's method
(b) Mac Arthur-Forrest method
(c) Serpeck method
(d) Hall's method

34. Calamine malachite magnetite and cryolite respectively, are **[JEE Advanced 2019]**
(a) $ZnCO_3, CuCO_3, Fe_2O_3, Na_3AlF_6$
(b) $ZnSO_4, CuCO_3, Fe_2O_3, AlF_3$
(c) $ZnSO_4, Cu(OH)_2, Fe_2O_4, Na_3AlF_6$
(d) $ZnCO_3, CuCO_3, Cu(OH)_2, Fe_3O_4, Na_3AlF_6$

35. Formation of metallic copper from the sulphide ore in the normal thermo-metallurgical process essentially involves which one of the following reaction?
(a) $CuS + \frac{3}{2}O_2 \longrightarrow CuO + SO_2$
(b) $CuS + \frac{3}{2}O_2 \longrightarrow CuO + SO_2$
$2CuO + CuS \longrightarrow 3Cu + SO_2$
(c) $CuS + 2O_2 \longrightarrow CuSO_4$
(d) $CuS + \frac{3}{2}O_2 \longrightarrow CuO + SO_2$
$CuSO_4 + CuS \longrightarrow 2Cu + 2SO_2$
$CuO + CO \longrightarrow Cu + CO_2$

36. Annealing of steel is the process of heating steel
(a) to a bright red hot and then cooling it slowly
(b) to a bright red hot and then cooling it suddenly
(c) to a temperature much below redness and cooling it slowly
(d) None of the above

37. Out of Cu_2S, HgS, Ag_2S and ZnS, roasting will convert the minerals into metal in case of
(a) Cu_2S, ZnS (b) HgS, ZnS
(c) Cu_2S, Ag_2S (d) HgS, Ag_2S

38. The method of zone refining of metals is based on the principle of
(a) greater noble character of the solid metal than that of the impurity
(b) greater solubility of the impurity in the molten state than in the solid
(c) greater mobility of the pure metal than that of impurity
(d) higher melting point of the impurity than that of the pure metal

39. Splitting of silver is
(a) reduction of ammoniacal silver nitrate solution by tartarate
(b) extraction of silver from its ore Ag_2S, by hydrometallurgy
(c) making of silver amalgam during filling of teeth
(d) cooling of molten silver with the evolution of oxygen causing violent spurting

40. In the extraction of Cu, the reaction takes place in bessemer converter is
(a) $2Cu_2O + Cu_2S \longrightarrow 6Cu + SO_2$
(b) $2CuFeS_2 + O_2 \longrightarrow Cu_2S + FeS + SO_2$
(c) $2Cu_2S + 3O_2 \longrightarrow 2Cu_2O + 2SO_2$
(d) $2FeS + 3O_2 \longrightarrow 2FeO + 2SO_2$

41. Sodium is made by the electrolysis of molten mixture of about 40% NaCl and 60% $CaCl_2$ because
(a) $CaCl_2$ helps in conduction of electricity
(b) Ca^{2+} can reduce NaCl to Na
(c) Ca^{2+} can displace Na from NaCl
(d) this mixture has a lower melting point than NaCl

42. Calcium is obtained by the
(a) roasting of limestone
(b) electrolysis of solution of calcium chloride in H_2O
(c) electrolysis of molten anhydrous calcium chloride
(d) reduction of calcium chloride with carbon

43. Which one of the following elements constitutes a major impurity in pig iron?
(a) Silicon (b) Oxygen
(c) Sulphur (d) Graphite

44. Purification of aluminium by electrolytic refining, is known as
(a) Hall's process (b) Baeyer's process
(c) Hoope's process (d) Serpeck's process

45. Cassiterite is an ore of
(a) Mn (b) Ni
(c) Sb (d) Sn

46. The process used for purification $Al_2O_3 \cdot 2H_2O$ is
(a) magnetic separation
(b) froth floatation
(c) leaching
(d) liquation

47. Froth floatation is a process of
(a) oxidation
(b) reduction
(c) refining
(d) concentration

48. Which one of the following ores is best concentrated by froth floatation method? **[JEE Main 2016]**
(a) Siderite (b) Galena
(c) Malachite (d) Magnetitde

49. Malachite is an ore of
(a) silver (b) mercury
(c) magnesium (d) copper

50. Flux is used to remove
(a) basic impurities
(b) acidic impurities
(c) all types of impurities
(d) acidic and basic both impurities

51. Mac Arthur process is used for the extraction of
(a) Al (b) Ag
(c) Cu (d) Zn

52. The chemical process in the production of steel from haematite ore involves
(a) reduction
(b) oxidation
(c) reduction followed by oxidation
(d) oxidation followed by reduction

53. Which of the following ore is concentrated by both, magnetic and gravimetric separation?
(a) Dolomite (b) Tinstone
(c) Galena (d) Bauxite

54. Which of the following processes is used in extractive metallurgy of magnesium?
(a) Fused salt electrolysis
(b) Self reduction
(c) Aqueous solution electrolysis
(d) Thermite reduction

55. The methods chiefly used for the extraction of lead and tin from their ores are respectively
(a) self reduction and carbon reduction
(b) self reduction and electrolytic reduction
(c) carbon reduction and self reduction
(d) cyanide process and carbon reduction

56. Extraction of zinc from zinc blende is achieved by
(a) electrolytic reduction
(b) roasting followed by reduction with carbon
(c) roasting followed by reduction with another metal
(d) roasting followed by self-reduction

57. Which one of the following statements is correct? In the metallurgy of sodium by electrolysis, excess of calcium chloride is mixed with sodium chloride to
(a) make the latter a good conductor
(b) make the latter soft
(c) generate more energy for the electrolytic cell
(d) assist liquefication of the latter at a much lower temperature

58. Consider the following statements.
I. Pig iron is malleable and ductile.
II. Pig iron can be melted to produce cast iron of desired shapes.
III. Wrought iron is obtained by heating pig iron with iron oxide in a furnace.

Which of the statement(s) given above is/are correct?
(a) I only (b) I and II
(c) II and III (d) III only

59. Main process for extracting nickel in the pure form uses which one of the following?
(a) Vapour phase refining (b) Zone refining
(c) Electrolysis (d) Solvent extraction

60. Which is not the correct statement?
(a) Cassiterite, chromite and pitchblende are concentrated by hydraulic washing (Tabling).
(b) Pure Al_2O_3 is obtained from the bauxite ore by leaching in the Baeyer's process.
(c) Sulphide ore is concentrated by calcination method.
(d) Roasting can convert sulphide into oxide or sulphate and part of sulphide may also act as a reducing agent.

61. NaCN is sometimes added in the froth floatation process as a depressant when ZnS and PbS minerals are expected because
(a) $Pb(CN)_2$ is precipitated while no effect as ZnS
(b) ZnS forms soluble complex $Na_2[Zn(CN)_4]$ while PbS forms froth
(c) PbS forms soluble complex $Na_2[Pb(CN)_4]$ while ZnS forms froth
(d) NaCN is never added in froth floatation process

62. Which method is not correct given for the refining of crude metals?
(a) **Distillation** zinc and mercury
(b) **Liquation** tin
(c) **van-Arkel** Zirconium
(d) **Mond process** lead

63. Self-reduction of CuS to Cu can be carried out in
(a) Bessemer converter (b) Pierce-Smith converter
(c) Both (a) and (b) (d) None of these

64. Select the incorrect reduction process.
(a) $2[Ag(CN)_2]^- + Zn \longrightarrow [Zn(CN)_4]^{2-} + 2Ag$
(b) $CuO + H_2 \longrightarrow Cu + H_2O$
(c) $ZnO + H_2 \longrightarrow Zn + H_2O$
(d) $MgO + C \longrightarrow Mg + CO$

65. Ellingham diagram represents
(a) change of ΔG with temperature
(b) change of ΔH with temperature
(c) change of ΔG with pressure
(d) change of $(\Delta G - T\Delta S)$ with temperature

66. Selection of temperature to carry out a reduction process depends so as to make
(a) ΔG negative (b) ΔG positive
(c) ΔH negative (d) ΔH positive

67. The reduction of an oxide by aluminium is called
(a) Ellingham process
(b) Goldschmidt's aluminothermite process
(c) Kroll's process
(d) van-Arkel process

68. Select the correct statement.
(a) In the decomposition of an oxide, into oxygen and gaseous metal, entropy increases.
(b) Decomposition of an oxide is an endothermic change.
(c) To make $\Delta G°$ negative, temperature should be high enough so that $T\ \Delta S° > \Delta H°$.
(d) All of the above are correct statements

69. The compound that does not produce nitrogen gas by the thermal decomposition is **[JEE Main 2018]**
(a) $Ba(N_3)_2$
(b) $(NH_4)_2Cr_2O_7$
(c) NH_4NO_2
(d) $(NH_4)_2SO_4$

70. Calamine, malachite, magnetite and cryolite, respectively, are **[JEE Advanced 2019]**
(a) $ZnCO_3$, $CuCO_3$, Fe_2O_3, Na_3AlF_6
(b) $ZnSO_4$, $CuCO_3$, Fe_2O_3, AlF_3
(c) $ZnSO_4$, $Cu(OH)_2$, Fe_3O_4, Na_3AlF_6
(d) $ZnCO_3$, $CuCO_3 \cdot Cu(OH)_2$, Fe_3O_4, Na_3AlF_6

71. The most important method of making steel is
(a) BOP process (b) BOD process
(c) pudding process (d) smelting

72. Cementite is
(a) predominant content of cement
(b) a mineral of calcium
(c) a carbide of iron in steel
(d) None of the above

73. Phosphorus separates, in the extraction of iron, as
(a) slag, $Ca_3(PO_4)_2$ (b) volatile, P_2O_5
(c) slag, $Mg_3(PO_4)_2$ (d) Ca_3P_2

74. Tempering of steel
(a) is the heating the steel to appropriate temperature and then cooling it rapidly
(b) increases mechanical strength
(c) changes ratio of carbon in cementite
(d) All of the above.

75. C_{60} an allotrope of carbon contains **[JEE Main 2019]**
(a) 16 hexagons and 16 pentagons
(b) 20 hexagons and 12 pentagons
(c) 12 hexagons and 20 pentagons
(d) 18 hexagons and 14 pentagons

76. In the following reactions, ZnO is respectively acting as a/an **[JEE Main 2017]**

$$ZnO + Na_2O \longrightarrow Na_2ZnO_2$$
$$ZnO + CO_2 \longrightarrow ZnCO_3$$

(a) base and acid (b) base and base
(c) acid and acid (d) acid and base

77. In the leaching of Ag_2S with NaCN, a stream of air is also passed. It is because of
(a) reversible nature of reaction between Ag_2S and NaCN
(b) to oxide Na_2S formed into $Na_2S_2O_3$ and sulphur
(c) Both (a) and (b)
(d) None of the above

78. $(Ag + Pb)\text{ alloy} \xrightarrow[\text{is added}]{\text{melt and zinc}} (Ag + Pb + Zn)\text{ melt}$

$\xrightarrow{\text{cool}} \boxed{\begin{array}{c}\text{Layer } X \\ \hline \text{Layer } Y\end{array}}$

Select the correct statement(s) based on the above scheme.

(a) Larger *X* contains zinc and silver
(b) Larger *Y* contains lead and silver but amount of silver in this layer is smaller than in the layer *X*.
(c) *X* and *Y* are immiscible layers
(d) All of the above are correct statements

79. During the electrolysis of carnallite, $MgCl_2$ is decomposed and not KCl. This is because of
(a) lower decomposition voltage of $MgCl_2$ than that of KCl
(b) reverse reaction, $MgCl_2 + 2K \longrightarrow Mg + 2KCl$ if KCl is decomposed under other experimental condition
(c) Both (a) and (b)
(d) None of the above

80. NaCl and $CaCl_2$ are also added to fused $MgCl_2$ in the electrolysis of $MgCl_2$ since
(a) melting point is decreased and conductivity is increased
(b) melting point is increased and conductivity is decreased
(c) melting point and conductivity both are decreased
(d) melting point and conductivity both are increased

81. Which is the sulphate ore of Mg?
(a) Dolomite (b) Carnallite (c) Magnesite (d) Kieserite

82. Poling process
(a) reduced SnO_2 to Sn
(b) oxidises impurities like iron and removes as scum
(c) uses green poles
(d) involves all of the above

83. Softening of lead means
(a) melting pure lead at high temperature
(b) removal of impurities, except silver, present in commercial lead
(c) formation of lead alloy
(d) formation of 100% pure lead

84. Softened lead is desilverised by
(a) Parke's method (b) Pattinson' method
(c) Both (a) and (b) (d) None of these

85. Select the incorrect statement.
(a) When the lead-silver alloy is rich in silver, lead is removed by the cupellation process
(b) When the lead-silver alloy is rich in lead, lead is removed by Parke's or Pattinson's process
(c) Zinc forms an alloy with lead from which lead is separated
(d) Zinc forms an alloy with silver, from which zinc is separated by distillation

86. In the **Baeyer's process**
(a) Al_2O_3 goes into solution as soluble $Al(OH)_4^-$ while other basic oxides as TiO_2 and Fe_2O_3 remain insoluble.
(b) Al_2O_3 changes to AlN which in turn decomposed by H_2O
(c) Al_2O_3 changes to $Al_2(CO_3)_3$ which changes to $AlCl_3$
(d) None of the above is correct

87. In electrolysis of Al_2O_3 by Hall-Heroult process
(a) Cryolite $Na_3[AlF_6]$ lowers the m.p. of Al_2O_3 and increases its electrical conductivity.
(b) Al is obtained at cathode and probably CO_2 at anode
(c) both (a) and (b) are correct
(d) None of the above is correct

88. $\boxed{\text{Bauxite}} \xrightarrow[\uparrow N_2]{+C} \boxed{AlN}\ (\uparrow CO) \xrightarrow{H_2O} Al(OH)_3 \xrightarrow{\Delta} Al_2O_3$

This flow-sheet is for
(a) Baeyer's process
(b) Serpeck's process
(c) Hall's process
(d) Kroll's process

89. Corundum is .... mineral of Al.
(a) silicate (b) oxide
(c) double salt (d) sulphate

90. Which mineral has been named incorrectly?
(a) Bauxite : $Al_2O_3 \cdot 2H_2O$
(b) Corundum : Al_2O_3
(c) Cryolite : $3NaF \cdot AlF_3$
(d) Feldspar : $Be_3Al_2Si_6O_{18}$

91. Which ore contains both iron and copper?
(a) Cuprite
(b) Chalcocite
(c) Chalcopyrite
(d) Malachite

92. Extraction of zinc from zinc blende is achieved by
(a) electrolytic reduction
(b) roasting followed by reduction with carbon
(c) roasting followed by reduction with another metal
(d) roasting followed by self-reduction

93. The method of zone refining of metals is based on the principle of
(a) greater noble character of the solid metal than that of the impurity
(b) greater solubility of the impurity in the molten state than in the solid
(c) greater mobility of the pure metal than that of impurity
(d) higher melting point of the impurity than that of the pure metal

94. The minimum voltage required to electrolyse alumina in the Hall-Heroult process is
Given, $\Delta G_f^\circ(Al_2O_3) = -1520$ kJ mol^{-1}
$\Delta G_f^\circ(CO_2) = -394$ kJ mol^{-1}
(a) 1.575 V (b) 1.60 V (c) 1.312 V (d) −2.62 V

95. Wolframite ore is separated from tin stone ore by the process of
(b) roasting (b) electromagnetic
(c) smelting (d) calcination

96. Chalcopyrites is an ore of
(a) gallium (b) copper
(c) calcium (d) magnesium

97. Thomas slag is
(a) $Ca_3(PO_4)_2 \cdot 2H_2O$ (b) $Ca_3(PO_4)_2 \cdot CaSiO_3$
(c) $MgSiO_3$ (d) $CaSiO_3$

98. Among the following statements, the incorrect one is
(a) zinc blende and iron pyrites are sulphides
(b) calamine and siderite are carbonates
(c) malachite and chalcocite are the copper ore
(d) argentite and cuprite are oxides

99. The silver is extracted by Parke's process. The basis of this method is
(a) silver is immiscible in molten Zn
(b) Ag is miscible in NaCN
(c) Ag is more miscible in molten zinc than in molten Pb
(d) Ag is more miscible in molten Pb in comparison to molten zinc

100. Railway wagon axles are made by heating iron rods embedded in charcoal powder. This process is known as
(a) tempering (b) annealing
(c) sherar dising (d) case hardening

101. Electro refining is used for refining of
(a) Cu (b) Fe (c) Pb (d) Al

102. To dissolve argentite ore which of the following is used
(a) $Na[Ag(CN)_2]$ (b) NaCN (c) NaCl (d) HCl

103. In aluminothermic process, Al acts as a
(a) flux (b) oxidising agent
(c) reducing agent (d) solder

104. The ore carnallite is represented by structure
(a) $Na_2Al_2O_3$ (b) Na_3AlF_6
(c) $KClMgCl_2 \cdot 6H_2O$ (d) Fe_3O_4

105. Which of the following statement is incorrect?
(a) Pure aluminium oxide is obtained by heating aluminium hydroxide.
(b) Cryolite lowers down the melting point of bauxite in electrolytic cell for extraction of aluminium.
(c) Carbonate ores are converted into oxides by roasting ore in air.
(d) Mercury cannot be produced by roasting the cinnabar ore in air.

106. Select some statements about metallurgical extraction of Al.
I. Cryolite and fluorspar are added to molten alumina.
II. Aqueous solution of Al^{3+} salts cannot be taken as electrolyte.
III. Molten $AlCl_3$ can be taken instead by molten alumina.
IV. Hall's process is adopted for the beneficiation of low grade red beauxite.

Select the correct statements.
(a) All except III (b) All except II
(c) I and II only (d) I and IV only

107. Extraction of Al from bauxite is carried out by various stages in Hall's process which involves
I. Removal of sand and heavier impurities by gravity separation method.
II. Removal of magnetic impurities by magnetic separator.
III. Fusing the concentrated finely divided ore with Na_2CO_3 and $CaCO_3$ and then extracting with H_2O.
IV. Ignition at 1100°C.
V. Passing CO_2.

Correct order of these steps are
(a) I, II, III, V, IV (b) II, I, III, V, IV
(c) V, IV, III, I, II (d) I, III, V, IV, II

108. Which of the following is not the by-product obtained in the extraction of copper?
(a) SO_2 which is further used in the manufacture of H_2SO_4 by the contact process
(b) Gold, silver and platinum obtained as anode mud
(c) $FeSO_4$ which is used to prepare green vitriol
(d) $FeSiO_3$ obtained as slag, used in road making

109. Out of the following reactions which does not indicate slag formation?
(a) $Fe_2O_3 + P_2O_5 \longrightarrow 2FePO_4$
(b) $PbO + SiO_2 \longrightarrow PbSiO_3$
(c) $3MgO + P_2O_5 \longrightarrow Mg_3(PO_4)_2$
(d) None of the above

110. Metal can be obtained by the carbon reduction method
$$ZnO + C \longrightarrow Zn + CO$$
Which of the following curves can be taken that the metal obtained is in vapour state by this method?

(a)
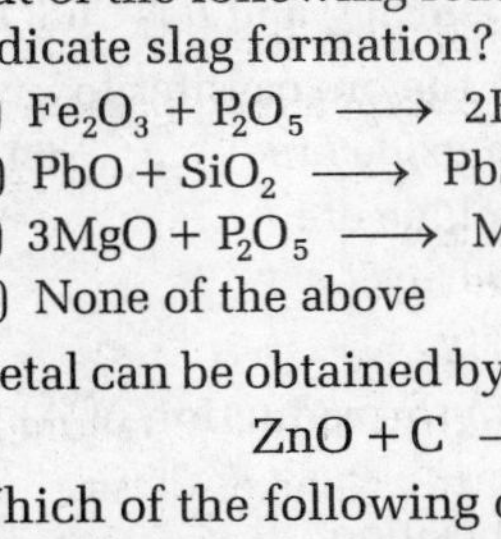

(b) 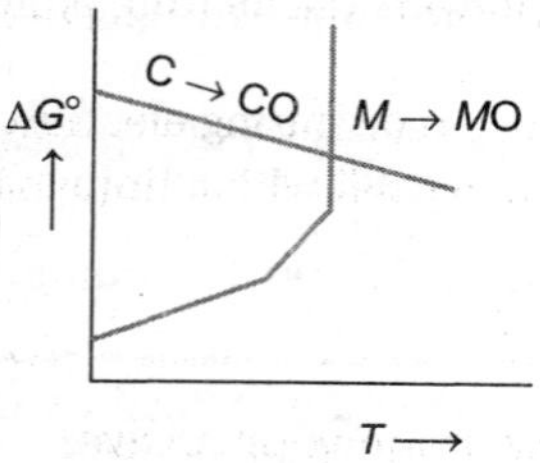

(c) 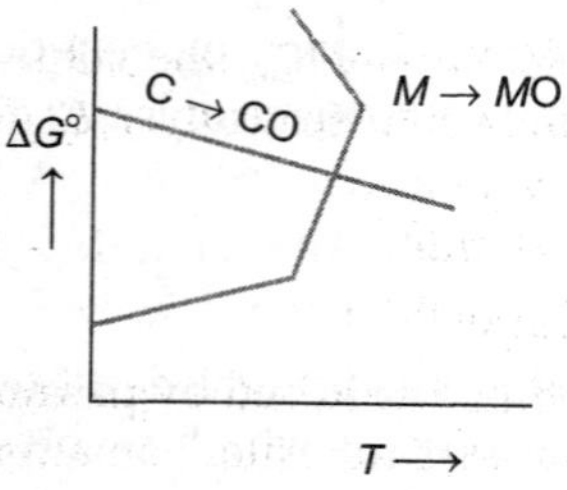

(d) 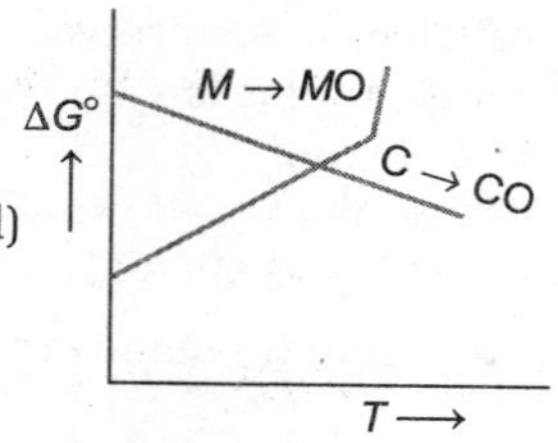

111. The reaction, $Cr_2O_3 + 2Al \longrightarrow Al_2O_3 + 2Cr$ $(\Delta G^\circ = -421\,kJ)$ is thermodynamically feasible as a apparent from the Gibbs energy value. But it does not take place at room temperature, because
(a) at room temperature activation energy requried for the reduction is not attained.
(b) reaction is exothermic
(c) reaction is endothermic
(d) reverse reaction is spontaneous

Objective Questions Type II [One or more than one correct option(s)]

In each of the questions below, four choices are given, of which one or more than one are correct.

1. Following reaction(s) is/are not involved in thermite process
(a) $3Mn_3O_4 + 8Al \longrightarrow 9Mn + 4Al_2O_3$
(b) $Cr_2O_3 + 2Al \longrightarrow Al_2O_3 + 2Cr$
(c) $2Fe + Al_2O_3 \longrightarrow 2Al + Fe_2O_3$
(d) $B_2O_3 + 2Al \longrightarrow 2B + Al_2O_3$

2. Consider the following steps

$$CuS \xrightarrow{\text{Roast in air}} (A) \xrightarrow{\text{Roast without air}} (B)$$

Which are the correct statements?
(a) It is self-reduction
(b) It involves disproportionation
$Cu_2S \longrightarrow Cu + CuS$
(c) (A) is a mixture of CuO and CuS and (B) is a mixture of Cu and SO_2
(d) (A) is a mixture of Cu and SO_2 and B is $CuSO_4$

3. Extraction of metal from the ore cassiterite involves **[IIT JEE 2011]**
(a) carbon reduction of an oxide ore
(b) self-reduction of a sulphide ore
(c) removal of copper impurity
(d) removal of iron impurity

4. Carbon cannot be used in the reduction of Al_2O_3 because
(a) it is an expensive proposition
(b) the enthalpy of formation of CO_2 is more than that of Al_2O_3
(c) pure carbon is not easily available
(d) the enthalpy of formation of Al_2O_3 is too high

5. In which of the following isolations no reducing agent is required?
(a) Iron from haematite
(b) Aluminium from bauxite
(c) Mercury from cinnabar
(d) Zinc from zinc blende

6. Extraction of copper from copper pyrite $(CuFeS_2)$ involves (One or More Than One Option Correct) **[JEE Advanced 2016]**
(a) crushing followed by concentration of the ore by froth-floatation
(b) removal of iron as slag
(c) self reduction step to produce 'blister copper' following evolution of SO_2
(d) refining of 'blister copper' by carbon reduction

7. The carbon-based reduction method is not used for the extraction of **[JEE Advanced 2013]**
(a) tin from SnO_2
(b) iron from Fe_2O_3
(c) aluminium from Al_2O_3
(d) magnesium from $MgCO_3$–$CaCO_3$

8. Boron can be obtained by various methods but not by
(a) thermal decomposition of B_2H_6
(b) pyrolysis of BI_3 (van-Arkel)
(c) reducing BCl_3 with H_2
(d) electrolysis of fused BCl_3

9. The cyanide process of gold extraction involves leaching out gold from its ore with CN^- in the presence of Q in water to form R. Subsequently, R is treated with T to obtain Au and Z. Choose the correct option(s). **[JEE Advanced 2019]**
(a) Q is O_2
(b) Z is $[Zn(CN)_4]^{2-}$
(c) T is Zn
(d) R is $[Au(CN)_4]^-$

10. Following method is not used for extraction of Al
(a) van-Arkel
(b) Serpeck
(c) Bayer
(d) Hall-Heroult

11. Which among the following statement(s) is(are) true for the extraction of aluminium from bauxite?
(a) Hydrated Al_2O_3 precipitates, when CO_2 is bubbled through a solution of sodium aluminate.
(b) Addition of Na_3AlF_6 lowers the melting point of alumina.
(c) CO_2 is evolved at the anode during electrolysis.
(d) The cathode is a steel vessel with a lining of carbon.

Numerical Value Questions

All these questions have a Numerical value as their answer, solve the questions and write your answer.

1. Following method of extracting Zn is based on thermodynamics
(A) $2ZnS + 3O_2 \longrightarrow 2ZnO + 2SO_2$
(B) $ZnO + C \longrightarrow Zn + CO$
ΔG_f° (standard free energies of formation, in kJ mol^{-1}) of
ZnS = −205.4; ZnO = −318.2
SO_2 = −300.4; CO = −137.3
The free energy changes of the above reactions *B* is ....

2. From these two statements estimate the quantity of Mg that has been produced since the metal was discovered.
   - All the Mg produced in the world could have been made from as little as 4 km^3 of sea water.
   - The quantity of Mg^{2+} in sea water is 1272 g $Mg^{2+}/10^6$ kg sea water (the density of sea water is 1.03 g cm^{-3}, 1 $km^3 = 10^{15}$ cm^3). The quantity is 5.24×10^6 kg.

3. Use the relationship $\Delta G^\circ = -nFE^\circ_{cell}$ the value of minimum voltage required to electrolyse Al_2O_3 in the Hall-Heroult process is ....
ΔG_f° $(Al_2O_3) = -1520$ kJ mol^{-1}
ΔG_f° $(CO_2) = -394$ kJ mol^{-1}

4. Galena (an ore) is partially oxidised by passing air through it at high temperature. After some time, the passage of air is stopped, but the heating is continued in a closed furnace such that the contents undergo self-reduction. The weight (in kg) of Pb produced per kg of O_2 consumed is .... (Atomic weights in g mol^{-1}: O = 16, S = 32, Pb = 207)

5. In Duma's method of estimation of nitrogen, 0.1840 g of an organic compound gave 30 mL of nitrogen collected at 287 K and 758 mm of Hg pressure.
The percentage composition of nitrogen in the compound is .... (Round off to the Nearest Integer). [Given : Aqueous tension at 287 K = 14 mm of Hg]

Comprehension Based Questions

In these questions, a passage has been given followed by questions based on it. You have to answer the questions based on the passage given.

Passage 1 *Following passage describes extraction of zinc from zinc sulphide. Answer the questions at the end of it.*

The chief ore of zinc is the sulphide, ZnS. The ore is concentrated by floatation process and then heated in air, which converts the ZnS to ZnO.

$$2ZnS + 3O_2 \xrightarrow{90.6\%} 2ZnO + 2SO_2 \quad ...(i)$$

The ZnO is then treated with dilute H_2SO_4

$$ZnO + H_2SO_4 \xrightarrow{100\%} ZnSO_4 + H_2O \quad ...(ii)$$

to produce $ZnSO_4$(aq.) which produces Zn metal on electrolysis.

$$2ZnSO_4 + 2H_2O \xrightarrow{98.2\%} 2Zn + 2H_2SO_4 + O_2 ...(iii)$$

1. What mass of Zn will be obtained from an ore containing 225 kg of ZnS? Efficiencies of the process have been indicated above the arrow mark. (Zn = 65, S = 32, O = 16, H = 1)
(a) 134 kg (b) 112 kg
(c) 102 kg (d) 130 kg

2. What amount of current is required (with 100% efficiency) in step (iii) if it takes one month?
(a) 10.2 A (b) 15.4 A
(c) 17.0 A (d) 154.0 A

3. ZnO in step (i) can also be dissolved in NaOH forming
(a) $Zn(OH)_2$ (b) Na_2ZnO_2
(c) Zn_2O_3 (d) $NaZn(OH)_4$

***Passage* 2** *Questions given below are based on the following sequence of reactions.*

At high temperature carbon reacts with water to produce a mixture of carbon monoxide, CO and hydrogen, H_2.

$$C + H_2O \xrightarrow{\text{Red heat}} CO + H_2$$

CO is separated from H_2 and then used to separate nickel from cobalt by forming a volatile compound, nickel tetracarbonyl, $Ni(CO)_4$.

$$Ni + 4CO \longrightarrow Ni(CO)_4$$

1. How many moles of $Ni(CO)_4$ could be obtained from the CO produced by the reaction of 75.0 g of carbon? Assume 100% reaction and 100% recovery in both steps.
(a) 6.25 (b) 1.563 (c) 3.125 (d) 25.0

2. Formation of volatile $Ni(CO)_4$ and its subsequent heating gives pure Ni. This process is called
(a) Hall (b) Dow (c) Serpeck (d) Mond

***Passage* 3** $FeCr_2O_4$ (chromite) is a good source of chromium and its compounds like Na_2CrO_4, $Na_2Cr_2O_7$. *Questions are based on the following reactions.*

P. $FeCr_2O_4 + NaOH + Air \longrightarrow A + Fe_2O_3$

Q. $A + B \longrightarrow Na_2Cr_2O_7$

R. $Na_2Cr_2O_7 + X \xrightarrow{\Delta} Cr_2O_3$

S. $Cr_2O_3 + Y \longrightarrow Cr$

1. Compounds (*A*) and (*B*) are
(a) Na_2CrO_4, H_2SO_4
(b) $Na_2Cr_2O_7, HCl$
(c) Na_2CrO_5, H_2SO_4
(d) $Na_4[Fe(OH)_6], H_2SO_4$

2. (*X*) and (*Y*) are
(a) Al and C (b) C and Al
(c) C in both (d) Al in both

3. Na_2CrO_4 and Fe_2O_3 are separated by
(a) dissolving in conc. H_2SO_4
(b) dissolving in NH_3
(c) dissolving in H_2O
(d) dissolving in dil. HCl

***Passage* 4** Copper is the most noble of the first row transition metals and occurs in small deposits in several countries. Ores of copper include chalcanthite ($CuSO_4 \cdot 5H_2O$), atacamite ($Cu_2Cl(OH)_3$), cuprite (Cu_2O), copper glance (Cu_2S) and malachite ($Cu_2(OH_2CO_3)$). However, 80% of the world copper production comes from the ore chalcopyrite ($CuFeS_2$). The extraction of copper from chalcopyrite involves partial roasting, removal of iron and self-reduction. **[IIT JEE 2011]**

1. Partial roasting of chalcopyrite produces
(a) Cu_2S and FeO
(b) Cu_2O and FeO
(c) CuS and Fe_2O_3
(d) Cu_2O and Fe_2O_3

2. Iron is removed from chalcopyrite as
(a) FeO (b) FeS
(c) Fe_2O_3 (d) $FeSiO_3$

3. In self-reduction, the reducing species is
(a) S (b) O^{2-}
(c) S^{2-} (d) SO_2

***Passage* 5** *Read the following cyclic process of recovery of copper from a copper wire and answer the questions at the end of it.*

The following "cycle of copper" experiment is performed in some general chemistry laboratories. The series of reactions starts with copper and ends with metallic copper. The steps are as follows:

1. A piece of copper wire of known mass is allowed to react with concentrated nitric acid [the products are copper(II) nitrate, nitrogen dioxide, and water].
2. The copper (II) nitrate is treated with a sodium hydroxide solution to form copper (II) hydroxide precipitate.
3. On heating copper (II) hydroxide decomposes to yield copper (II) oxide.
4. The copper (II) oxide is reacted with concentrated sulphuric acid to yield copper (II) sulphate.
5. Copper(II) sulphate is treated with an excess of zinc metal to form metallic copper.
6. The remaining zinc metal is removed by treatment with hydrochloric acid and metallic copper is filtered, dried, and weighted.

1. Assuming that a student started with 65.6 g of copper, calculate the theoretical yield of copper sulphate.
(a) 165 g (b) 82.4 g
(c) 90 g (d) 100.2 g

2. Copper obtained at the end of the cycle is .... amount originally taken.
(a) less than
(b) greater than
(c) nearly equal
(d) only copper salts are obtained

3. $CuSO_4$ solution thus formed is subjected to electrolysis. To deposit all the copper formed at the end, a current of 50 A will have to be used for approximately.
(a) 10 h (b) 1 h
(c) 5 h (d) 0.5 h

***Example* 6** *Questions given below are based on the given diagram for extractive metallurgy.*

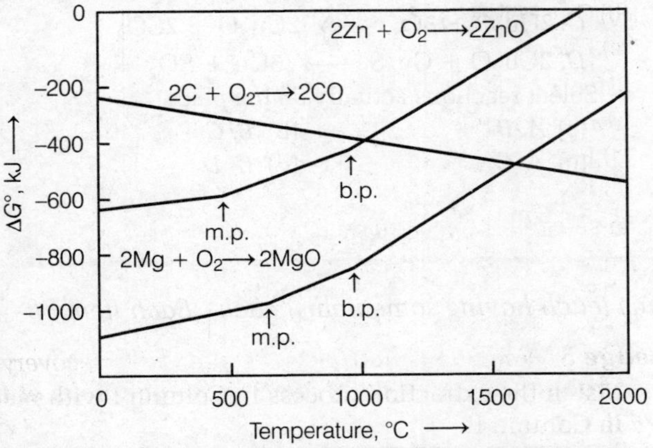

The points noted by arrows are the melting and boiling points of the metals zinc and magnesium. ΔG° as a function of temperature for some reactions of extractive metallurgy.

1. At what approximate temperature, zinc and carbon have equal affinity for oxygen?

(a) 1000°C (b) 1500°C
(c) 500°C (d) 1200°C

2. To make the following reduction process spontaneous, temperature should be

$$ZnO + C \longrightarrow Zn + CO$$

(a) < 1000°C
(b) > 1100°C
(c) < 500°C
(d) > 500°C but < 1000°C

3. At 1100°C, which reaction is spontaneous to a maximum extent?

(a) $MgO + C \longrightarrow Mg + CO$
(b) $ZnO + C \longrightarrow Zn + CO$
(c) $MgO + Zn \longrightarrow Mg + ZnO$
(d) $ZnO + Mg \longrightarrow MgO + Zn$

***Example* 7** The Ellingham diagram for a number of metallic sulphides is reproduced below.

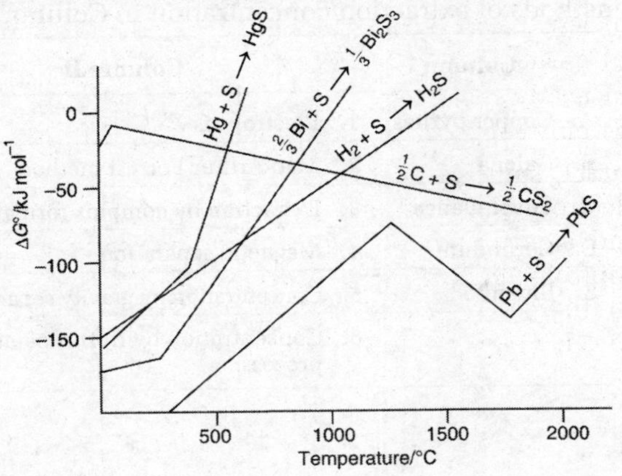

Answer the questions given.

1. Formation of which of the sulphides is most spontaneous?

(a) HgS (b) Bi_2S_3 (c) PbS (d) CS_2

2. Which occurs to minimum extent in nature?

(a) HgS (b) H_2S (c) Bi_2S_3 (d) CS_2

3. Which of the following sulphides can be reduced to metal by H_2 at about 1000 K?

(a) HgS (b) PbS
(c) Bi_2S_3 (d) None of these

Example* 8** ***From the following flow-sheet for the extraction of pure metal, answer the questions at the end of it.

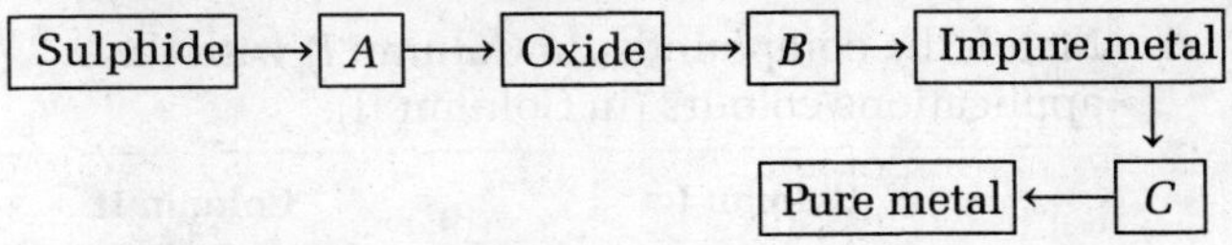

1. Step *A* is

(a) roasting
(b) smelting
(c) calcination
(d) bessemerisation

2. Step *B* (reduction) can be carried out using

(a) carbon
(b) more electropositive element
(c) Both (a) and (b)
(d) None of the above

3. Some of the following metals are obtained by electrolysis of their fused salts
Al, Na, Cu, Ag, Mg, Ca. These metals are

(a) Cu, Ag (b) Al, Na, Cu
(c) Ag, Mg, Ca (d) Al, Na, Mg, Ca

***Example* 9** *Given flow-sheet is for the extraction of copper. Based on this, answer the questions given at the end.*

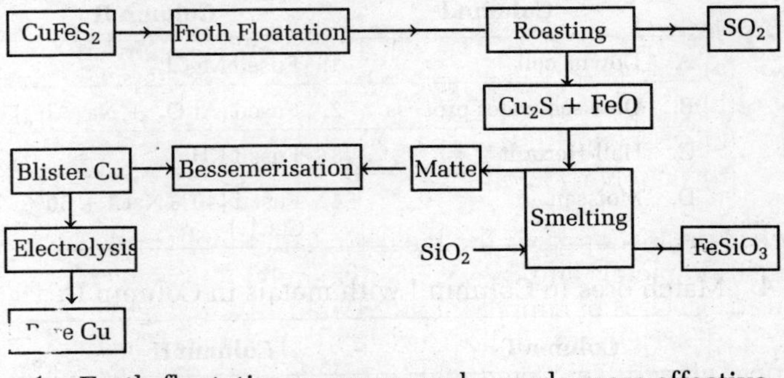

1. Froth-floatation process can be made more effective by

(a) use of pine oil which produces stable froth
(b) use of sodium ethyl xanthate as a collector that coats the particles of ore
(c) Both (a) and (b)
(d) None of the above

2. Smelting process is carried at about 1400°C. Two layers are formed
(a) bottom layer contains copper-matte
(b) upper layer contains copper-matte
(c) copper-matte remains in both the layers
(d) copper-matte is not present in any of the layers

3. Some of the reactions taking place during bessemerisation are

A. $FeO + SiO_2 \longrightarrow FeSiO_3$
B. $2FeS + 3O_2 \longrightarrow 2FeO + 2SO_2$
C. $2Cu_2S + 3O_2 \longrightarrow 2Cu_2O + 2SO_2$
D. $2Cu_2O + Cu_2S \longrightarrow 6Cu + SO_2$

Select reactions actually taking place
(a) *A, B* (b) *B, C*
(c) *A, C* (d) *C, D*

Matrix-Match Type

Given below are Matching Type Questions, with two columns (each having some items) each . Each item of Column I has to be matched with the items of Column II.

1. Match the compounds (in Column I) with their applications/colours (in Column II).

Column I	Column II
A. Pb_3O_4	1. White lead
B. $(PbCO_3)_2 \cdot Pb(OH)_2$	2. Rust proofing sheets
C. Ca_2PbO_4	3. Road signs and markings
D. $PbCrO_4$	4. Red lead

2. Match the reactions taking place in blast furnace (in Column I) with temperature-range of operations (in Column II).

Column I	Column II
A. $Fe_2O_3 + CO \longrightarrow CO_2 + Fe$	1. 1200°C
B. $C + CO_2 \longrightarrow CO$	2. 900°C
C. $C + H_2O \longrightarrow CO + H_2$	3. 600°C
D. $CaO + SiO_2 \longrightarrow CaSiO_3$	4. 1100°C

3. Match process (in Column I) with electrolytes (in Column II).

Column I	Column II
A. Downs cell	1. Fused $MgCl_2$
B. Dow sea-water process	2. Fused $(Al_2O_3 + Na_3AlF_6)$
C. Hall-Heroult	3. Fused KHF_2
D. Moissan	4. Fused (40% NaCl + 60% $CaCl_2$)

4. Match ores in Column I with metals in Column II.

Column I	Column II
A. Carnallite	1. Zinc
B. Calamine	2. Titanium
C. Ilmenite	3. Magnesium
D. Chalcopyrite	4. Copper

5. Match the extraction process in Column I with metals in Column II.

Column I	Column II
A. Self reduction	1. Zirconium
B. Carbon reduction	2. Silver
C. Complex formation and displacement by metal	3. Copper
D. Decomposition of iodide	4. Boron

6. Match the method in Column I with related reaction in Column II.

Column I	Column II
A. Mond's process	1. $Cr_2O_3 + 2Al \longrightarrow Al_2O_3 + 2Cr$
B. van-Arkel-de-Broglie process	2. $TiCl_4 + Mg \xrightarrow{1000-1150°C} Ti + 2MgCl_2$
C. Thermite process	3. $Ni(CO)_4 \xrightarrow{230°C} Ni + 4CO$
D. Kroll process	4. $2CuO + CuS \longrightarrow 3Cu + SO_2$
E. Self reduction	5. $ZrI_4 \xrightarrow{\Delta} Zr + 2I_2$

7. Match the species in Column I with then corresponding methods of extraction/concentration in Column II.

Column I	Column II
A. Copper pyrites	1. Electrolysis
B. Galena	2. Mac-Arthur Forrest method
C. Silver glance	3. Extraction by complex formation
D. Corundum	4. Magnetic separation
E. Ilmenite	5. Concentration by gravity separation
	6. Concentration by froth-floatation process

8. Match the elements in Column I with their corresponding mineral formation in Column II.

Column I	Column II
A. Calcium	1. Oxide
B. Copper	2. Sulphide
C. Magnesium	3. Phosphate
D. Silver	4. Carbonate
E. Aluminium	5. Chloride
	6. Fluoride
	7. Sulphate

9. Match Column I and Column II.

Column I	Column II
A. Haematite	1. $Al_2O_3 . xH_2O$
B. Bauxite	2. Fe_2O_3
C. Magnetite	3. $CuCO_3 . Cu(OH)_2$
D. Malachite	4. Fe_3O_4

[JEE Main 2021, March]

10. Match Column I and Column II.

Column I	Column II
A. Mercury	1. Vapour phase refining
B. Copper	2. Distillation refining
C. Silicon	3. Electrolytic refining
D. Nickel	4. Zone refining

[JEE Main 2021, March]

Single Integer Answer Questions

Answer of these questions is a single digit lying between 0 to 9.

1. Epsomite is $MgSO_4 \cdot xH_2O$, where y = ...

2. When one mole of Ag_2CO_3 is strongly heated, residue is .... mole(s).

3. In the following reaction slag $CaSiO_3$ is formed

$$Ca_3(PO_4)_2 + C + SiO_2 \longrightarrow P_4 + CaSiO_3 + CO$$

If one mole of P_4 is formed, then $CaSiO_3$ formed is .... moles.

4. Total number of atoms in one unit of chalcopyrites are ....

5. One unit of corundum has .... oxygen atoms.

6. E°_{red} values are

	E°
$Ag^+ + e^- \longrightarrow Ag$	+ 0.80 V
$Zn^{2+} + 2e^- \longrightarrow Zn$	– 0.76 V
$Fe^{2+} + 2e^- \longrightarrow Fe$	– 0.44 V
$Cu^{2+} + 2e^- \longrightarrow Cu$	+ 0.34 V
$Hg^{2+} + 2e^- \longrightarrow Hg$	+ 0.79 V
$Mg^{2+} + 2e^- \longrightarrow Mg$	– 2.37 V
$Al^{3+} + 3e^- \longrightarrow Al$	– 1.66 V

How many of the metals can displace Cu from $CuSO_4$ solution?

7. If reduction of Cu^{2+} by Al is possible then E°_{cell} will be ...... volt.

$$3Cu^{2+} + 2Al \longrightarrow 2Al^{3+} + 3Cu$$

8. How many of the following ores can be enriched by FFP?

dolomite, cerussite, argentite, pyrites, anhydrite, cinnabar, chalcopyrite, galena, greenockite, chalcocite

9. Phosphate rock is represented as $Pb_{10}(PO_4)_xCl_2$ what is the value of x?

10. In the electrolysis of $AgNO_3$ solution, 97.2 g of Ag is deposited on passing current for 9650 s. What is the value of current in amperes?

11. Al_2O_3 is converted to AlN on heating with carbon in the atmosphere of N_2. How much carbon is required to convert 23 g of Al_2O_3 into AlN?

12. $Al(OH)_3$ is soluble in alkaline solution of pH 8.3010. Thus, $[NaOH] = y \times 10^{-6}$ what is the value of y?

Answers

Objective Questions Type I [Only one correct option]

1. (b)	2. (b)	3. (d)	4. (b)	5. (c)	6. (b)	7. (c)	8. (c)	9. (a)	10. (d)
11. (c)	12. (a)	13. (b)	14. (a)	15. (b)	16. (c)	17. (d)	18. (c)	19. (b)	20. (d)
21. (c)	22. (a)	23. (c)	24. (d)	25. (b)	26. (d)	27. (c)	28. (d)	29. (b)	30. (b)
31. (a)	32. (c)	33. (b)	34. (d)	35. (b)	36. (a)	37. (d)	38. (b)	39. (d)	40. (a)
41. (d)	42. (c)	43. (d)	44. (a)	45. (d)	46. (c)	47. (d)	48. (b)	49. (d)	50. (d)
51. (b)	52. (d)	53. (b)	54. (a)	55. (a)	56. (b)	57. (a)	58. (b)	59. (a)	60. (c)
61. (b)	62. (d)	63. (c)	64. (c)	65. (a)	66. (a)	67. (b)	68. (d)	69. (d)	70. (d)
71. (c)	72. (c)	73. (a)	74. (b)	75. (b)	76. (d)	77. (c)	78. (d)	79. (b)	80. (a)
81. (d)	82. (c)	83. (b)	84. (c)	85. (c)	86. (a)	87. (c)	88. (b)	89. (b)	90. (d)
91. (c)	92. (b)	93. (b)	94. (b)	95. (b)	96. (b)	97. (b)	98. (d)	99. (c)	100. (d)
101. (a)	102. (b)	103. (c)	104. (c)	105. (c)	106. (a)	107. (b)	108. (c)	109 (d)	110. (b)
111. (c)									

Objective Questions Type II [One or more than one correct option(s)]

1. (c)	2. (a, c, d)	3. (a, c, d)	4. (d)	5. (c)
6. (a, b, c)	7. (d)	8. (d)	9. (a, b, c)	10. (a)
11. (a, b, c, d)				

Numerical Value Questions

1. + 180.9 2. 5.24 3. 1.60 4. 6.47 5. 19

Comprehension Based Questions

Passage 1 – 1. (a) 2. (d) 3. (d)
Passage 2 – 1. (b) 2. (d)
Passage 3 – 1. (a) 2. (b) 3. (a)
Passage 4 – 1. (b) 2. (a) 3. (c)
Passage 5 – 1. (a) 2. (c) 3. (b)
Passage 6 – 1. (a) 2. (b) 3. (d)
Passage 7 – 1. (c) 2. (d) 3. (a, c)
Passage 8 – 1. (a) 2. (c) 3. (d)
Example 9 – 1. (c) 2. (a) 3. (d)

Matrix-Match Type

1. $A \to (4); B \to (1); C \to (2); D \to (3)$
2. $A \to (2); B \to (4); C \to (3); D \to (1)$
3. $A \to (4); B \to (1); C \to (2); D \to (3)$
4. $A \to (3); B \to (1); C \to (2); D \to (4)$
5. $A \to (3); B \to (4); C \to (2); D \to (1)$
6. $A \to (3); B \to (5); C \to (1); D \to (2); E \to (4)$
7. $A \to (1,6); B \to (6); C \to (1,2,3,6); D \to (1,5); E \to (4,5)$
8. $A \to (3,4,6,7); B \to (1,2,4); C \to (1,5); D \to (2,5)$ $E \to (1,6)$
9. $A \to (2); B \to (1); C \to (4); D \to (3)$
10. $A \to (2); B \to (3); C \to (4); D \to (1)$

Single Interger Answer Questions

1. (7)	2. (2)	3. (6)	4. (4)	5. (3)	6. (4)	7. (2)	8. (7)	9. (6)	10. (9)
11. (9)	12. (2)								

Solutions

Objective Questions Type I [Only one correct option]

1. (*b*) Method II is better than I as I emits CO which causes pollution.
2. (*b*) PbS changes to PbO which is further reduced to Pb by PbS itself in self reduction process.
6. (*b*) Oxides of the metal are converted into metal if they are above Hg in activity series

Cu, Hg Ag

$$Ag_2O \xrightarrow{\Delta} Ag$$

$$HgO \xrightarrow{\Delta} Hg$$

$$CuO \xrightarrow{\Delta} \text{No effect}$$

7. (*c*) $FeO \cdot CrO_3 + C \longrightarrow \underbrace{Fe + Cr}_{\text{Ferrochrome}} + CO$

8. (*c*) $NaCl(aq) \longrightarrow Na^+(aq) + Cl^-(aq)$

Oxidation at anode $2Cl^-(aq) \longrightarrow Cl_2(g) + 2e^-$

Reduction at cathode $2Na^+(aq) + 2e^- \longrightarrow 2Na$

$$2Na + 2H_2O \longrightarrow 2NaOH + H_2$$

Thus, (a) is incorrect (b) is incorrect only (c) is correct since $\Delta G° < 0$ implies reaction is spontaneous.

10. (*d*) Auto-reduction involves roasting and then reduction in a convertor.
Sulphide ore is roasted by oxide ore and also reduction takes place.
11. (*c*) Copper obtained has blistered appearance due to evolution of SO_2 thus, called blister copper.
12. (*a*) Ethyl part is hydrophobic and it prefers to stay in air. Xanthate part is hydrophilic and it prefers to stay in water.

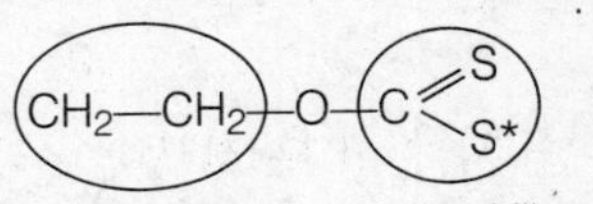

Hydrophobic Hydrophilic

13. (*b*) In roasting process, metal sulphide (MS) ore are converted into metal oxide and sulphur is remove in the form of SO_2 gas.

$$2\,MS + 3O_2 \xrightarrow{\Delta} 2\,MO + 2\,SO_2 \uparrow$$

17. (*d*) $CaCO_3 \xrightarrow{\Delta} CaO + CO_2$

$$CaO + P_2O_5 \longrightarrow Ca_3(PO_4)_2$$

18. (*c*) Pig iron : 95% Fe
4% C and varying quantities of other impurities.
19. (*b*) Ni — Mond's process; Cu — Electrolysis
Zr — van-Arkel process; Ga — Zone refining.
21. (*c*) I. Mond's process for Ni
II. Self-reduction process for Cu
III. Electrolysis of fused NaCl for Na

Thus, III — Na, I — Ni, II — Cu

27. (*c*) After bessemerisation of the concentrated ore, Cu obtained is 98% pure. It is called blister Cu.
29. (*b*) $Ag_2S + 4NaCN \longrightarrow \underset{(A)}{2Na[Ag(CN)_2]} + Na_2S$

$$Na[Ag(CN)_2] + Zn \longrightarrow \underset{(B)}{Ag}$$

34. (*d*) $ZnCO_3$-Calamine (zinc ore)
$CuCO_3 \cdot Cu(OH)_2$-Malachite (copper ore)
Fe_3O_4-Magnetite (iron ore)
Na_3AlF_6-Cryolite (aluminium ore)
Thus, option (d) is correct.
35. (*b*) Self-reduction process taking place in a bessemer converter. Copper obtained is 98% and is called **blister copper**.
37. (*d*) $HgS \xrightarrow{\Delta} HgO \xrightarrow{\Delta} Hg$

$$Ag_2S \xrightarrow{\Delta} Ag_2O \longrightarrow Ag$$

48. (*b*) Sulphide ores are concentrated by froth floatation method. e.g. Galena (PbS).
54. (*a*) $MgCl_2(\text{fused}) \xrightarrow{\text{Current}} Mg^{2+} + 2Cl^-$

At cathode: $Mg^{2+} + 2e^- \longrightarrow Mg$

At anode: $2Cl^- \longrightarrow Cl_2 + 2e^-$

55. (*a*) $PbS + O_2 \xrightarrow{\Delta} PbO + PbSO_4 + SO_2$

$$PbS + 2PbO \xrightarrow{\Delta} Pb + SO_2$$

$$SnO_2 + C \xrightarrow{\Delta} Sn + CO$$

59. (*a*) $Ni + CO \longrightarrow \underset{\text{Vapour}}{Ni(CO)_4} \xrightarrow{\Delta} Ni + 4CO \uparrow$

68. (*d*) (a) $ZnO(s) \xrightarrow{\Delta} Zn(s) + O_2(g)$

Due to the formation of gaseous products

$$\Delta S > 0$$

(b) It absorbs heat thus $\Delta H > 0$

(c) $\Delta G° = \Delta H° - T\Delta S°$

If $T\Delta S° > \Delta H°$

then, $\Delta G° < 0$

69. (*d*) The thermal decomposition of given compounds is shown below

$$(NH_4)_2Cr_2O_7 \xrightarrow{\Delta} N_2 + 4H_2O + Cr_2O_3$$

$$NH_4NO_2 \xrightarrow{\Delta} N_2 + 2H_2O$$

$$(NH_4)_2SO_4 \xrightarrow{\Delta} 2NH_3 + H_2SO_4$$

$$Ba(N_3)_2 \longrightarrow Ba + 3N_2$$

Thus, only $(NH_4)_2SO_4$ does not gives N_2 on heating (It give NH_3). While rest of the given compounds gives N_2 on their thermal decomposition.

70. (*d*) $ZnCO_3$-Calamine (zinc ore)

$CuCO_3 \cdot Cu(OH)_2$-Malachite (copper ore)

Fe_3O_4-Magnetite (iron ore)

Na_3AlF_6-Cryolite (aluminium ore)

Thus, option (d) is correct.

75. (*b*) C_{60} is aromatic allotrope of carbon containing 12 pentagons and 20 hexagons. It is a fullerene having a shape like soccer ball and called Buckminster fullerene.

76. (*d*) Zinc oxide (ZnO) when react with Na_2O it act as acid while with CO_2 it act as base. Therefore, it is an amphoteric oxide.

$$\underset{\text{Acid}}{ZnO} + \underset{\text{Base}}{Na_2O} \longrightarrow \underset{\text{Salt}}{Na_2ZnO_2}$$

$$\underset{\text{Base}}{ZnO} + \underset{\text{Acid}}{CO_2} \longrightarrow \underset{\text{Salt}}{ZnCO_3}$$

94. (*b*) $2Al_2O_3(s) + 3C \longrightarrow 4Al(s) + 3CO_2$

$$\Delta G^\circ = 3\Delta G_f^\circ(CO_2) - 2\Delta G^\circ(Al_2O_3)$$

$$= -3 \times 394 - 2(-1520)$$

$$= -1182 + 3040 = +1858 \text{ kJ}$$

$$\Delta G^\circ = -nFE^\circ$$

$$1858 \times 1000 = -12 \times 96500 \times E^\circ$$

$$\therefore \quad E^\circ = -1.60 \text{ V}$$

Thus, voltage requires = 1.60 V

102. (*b*) $Ag_2S + NaCN + O_2 \longrightarrow Na[Ag(CN)_2]$

105. (*c*) $CaCO_3 \xrightarrow{\text{Calcination}} CaO + CO_2$

106. (*a*) I. CaF_2 (fluorspar) and Na_3AlF_6 (cryolite) reduce melting point of the mixture CaF_2 improves electrical conductivity of the melting as compared to molten Al_2O_3.

II. Aqueous solution of Al^{3+} cannot be taken since H_2 gas is formed in preference to Al.

III. Molten $AlCl_3$ being covalent is poor conductor. It sublimes at melting point. Hence, cannot be taken.

IV. Hall's process is adopted for the extraction of Al from bauxite.

Thus, III incorrect.

107. (*b*) II. Magnetic impurities should be separated before gravity separation as it involves H_2O.

108. (*c*) (a) SO_2 is formed during roasting and autoreduction.

$$SO_2 \longrightarrow SO_3 \xrightarrow{H_2O} H_2SO_4$$

Thus, correct.

(b) Gold, silver and platinum are recovered from anode mud of electrolytic refining thus, correct.

(c) $FeSO_4$ is never formed thus is not the by-product.

(d) $FeSO_4$ (slag) is also formed.

15

Inorganic Salt Analysis

Objective Questions Type I [Only one correct option]

In each of the questions below, four choices are given of which only one is correct.

1. Yellow coloured solution of $FeCl_3$ changes to light green when
(a) $SnCl_2$ is added (b) Zn is added
(c) H_2S gas is passed (d) All true

2. Fe^{2+} does not give blue colour with $K_4[Fe(CN)_6]$ but on its reaction with (X), blue colour appears. (X) can be
(a) MnO_4^-/H^+ (b) H_2SO_4
(c) NH_3 (d) HCl

3. $Fe(OH)_3$ and $Cr(OH)_3$ ppt are separated by
(a) *aq.* NH_3 (b) HCl
(c) $NaOH/H_2O_2$ (d) H_2SO_4

4. Turnbull's blue and Prussian's blue respectively are
I. $Fe^{II}[Fe^{II}(CN)_6]^{2-}$ II. $Fe^{III}[Fe^{III}(CN)_6]$
III. $Fe^{II}[Fe^{III}(CN)_6]^-$ IV. $Fe^{III}[Fe^{II}(CN)_6]^-$
(a) I, II (b) I, III
(c) III, IV (d) IV, III

5. Which of the following are soluble in excess of NaOH (X) : As_2S_3; (Y) : CuS; (Z) : $AlCl_3$?
(a) X, Y, Z (b) Y, Z
(c) X, Z (d) X, Y

6. A mixture on heating gave a gas used as an anaesthetic, 1.1 g of gas occupies 0.56 L at NTP. Mixture contains
(a) $NaNO_3 + NH_4Cl$ (b) $NaNO_2 + NH_4Cl$
(c) $CaCO_3 + MgCO_3$ (d) $NH_4Cl + Na_2SO_4$

7. Aqueous solution contains $ZnCl_2$, $CdCl_2$ and $CuCl_2$. On passing H_2S gas, there is a precipitation of ...... as sulphide.
(a) Zn^{2+}, Cd^{2+} (b) Cu^{2+}, Cd^{2+}
(c) Zn^{2+}, Cu^{2+} (d) Zn^{2+}, Cu^{2+}, Cd^{2+}

8. Ferric alum gives red colour with NH_4SCN due to formation of
(a) $Al(SCN)_3$ (b) $[Fe(SCN)_3]^-$
(c) $Fe(SCN)_3$ (d) $[Fe(SCN)]^{2+}$

9. Colourless salt (X) $\xrightarrow{\Delta}$ (Y) $\xrightarrow{Cu^{2+}, \Delta}$ coloured bead (Z). (X) can be
(a) borax (b) microcosmic salt
(c) Both (a) and (b) (d) None of these

10. $KCl + \text{conc } H_2SO_4 + K_2Cr_2O_7 \xrightarrow{\Delta} (X) \xrightarrow{NaOH} (Y)$.
(X) is reddish brown coloured gas soluble in NaOH forming (Y). (X) and (Y) are
(a) Cr_2OCl_2, Na_2CrO_3 (b) $Cr_2O_2Cl_2$, Na_2CrO_3
(c) CrO_2Cl, Na_2CrO_4 (d) CrO_2Cl_2, Na_2CrO_4

11. Aqueous solution of $BaBr_2$ gives yellow ppt with
(a) K_2CrO_4 (b) $AgNO_3$
(c) Both (a) and (b) (d) None of these

12. $\underset{\text{Orange}}{Cr_2O_7^{2-}} \underset{pH = y}{\overset{pH = x}{\rightleftharpoons}} \underset{\text{Green}}{CrO_4^{2-}}$. This change is based on change in pH. Probable values of x and y can be
(a) 8, 6
(b) 8, 10
(c) 4, 6
(d) change is independent of pH

13. H_2S would separate the following at pH < 7
(a) Zn^{2+}, Co^{2+} (b) Cu^{2+}, Cd^{2+}
(c) Cu^{2+}, Cr^{3+} (d) Cu^{2+}, As^{3+}

14. Solution of (X) in dil. $HCl + H_2O \longrightarrow$ white turbidity. (X) $\xrightarrow{H_2S/HCl}$ black ppt (Y). (Y) is soluble in
(a) H_2SO_4 (b) YAS
(c) HNO_3 (d) HCl

15. $K_2Cr_2O_7$ + conc. H_2SO_4 + H_2O_2 + ether $\longrightarrow$ blue perchromic anhydride (in ethereal layer). Blue colour is due to
(a) CrO_3 (b) H_2CrO_4
(c) $H_2Cr_2O_3$ (d) CrO_5

16. There is foul smell in presence of moisture with
(a) $AlCl_3$ (b) $Al_2(SO_4)_3$
(c) FeS (d) $FeSO_4$

17. $AgNO_3$ gives white ppt with hypo changing to black after sometime. Black ppt is of
(a) $Ag_2S_2O_3$ (b) Ag_2SO_4
(c) $Ag_2S_4O_6$ (d) Ag_2S

18. SO_2 and CO_2 both turn lime water (*A*) milky, SO_2 also turns $K_2Cr_2O_7/H^+$ (*B*) green while O_2 is soluble in pyrogallol (*C*) turning it black. These gases are to be detected in order by using these reagents in a mixture. The order is
(a) (*A*), (*B*), (*C*) (b) (*B*), (*C*), (*A*)
(c) (*B*), (*A*), (*C*) (d) (*A*), (*C*), (*B*)

19. Aluminium sulphate (*X*) is slightly insoluble in water. It is converted into soluble sodium sulphate by using Na_2CO_3 in the preparation of sodium carbonate extract. Moles of (*Y*), required for complete conversion of 1 mole of (*X*) into soluble sulphate, is
(a) 1 (b) 2 (c) 3 (d) 4

20. $CoCl_2$ gives blue colour with NH_4SCN in ethereal layer due to formation of
(a) $(NH_4)_2[Co(SCN)_4]$ (b) $(NH_4)_4[Co(SCN)_6]$
(c) $(NH_4)_3[Co(SCN)_6]$ (d) $(NH_4)[Co(SCN)_4]$

21. $HgCl_2$ + excess of KI $\longrightarrow$ (*A*) $\xrightarrow{NH_3/NaOH}$ (*B*).
(*A*) and (*B*) respectively are
(a) K_2HgI_4 (Nessler's reagent), 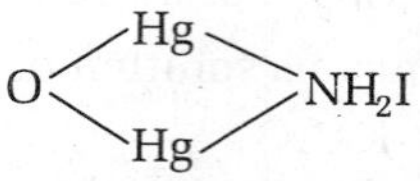
(*A*) (Iodide of Millon's base) (*B*)
(b) (*B*), (*A*)
(c) Both (*A*)
(d) Both (*B*)

22. NH_4SCN can be used to test one or more out of Fe^{3+}, Co^{2+}, Cu^{2+}
(a) Fe^{3+} only
(b) Co^{2+}, Cu^{2+}
(c) Fe^{3+}, Cu^{2+}
(d) All of the above

23. $K_4[Fe(CN)_6]$ can be used to detect one or more out of Fe^{2+}, Fe^{3+}, Zn^{2+}, Cu^{2+}, Cd^{2+}
(a) Fe^{2+}, Fe^{3+} (b) Fe^{3+}, Zn^{2+}, Cu^{2+}
(c) All but Fe^{3+} (d) All but Fe^{2+}

24. Aqueous solution containing one mole borax reacts with two moles of acids. This is because of
(a) formation of 2 moles of $B(OH)_3$ only
(b) formation of 2 moles of $[B(OH)_4]^-$ only
(c) formation of 1 mole each of $[B(OH)_3]$ and $[B(OH)_4]^-$
(d) formation of 2 mol each of $[B(OH)_4]^-$ and $B(OH)_3$, of which only $[B(OH)_4]^-$ reacts with acid.

25. Kjeldahl's method cannot be used to estimate nitrogen for which of the following compounds? **[JEE Main 2020]**
(a) $C_6H_5NO_2$ (b) $NH_2-\overset{\overset{\large O}{\|}}{C}-NH_2$
(c) $CH_3CH_2-C\equiv N$ (d) $C_6H_5NH_2$

26. In sodium carbonate bead test, chromium salts (green) change to coloured bead
(a) yellow, $PbCrO_4$ (b) yellow, $BaCrO_4$
(c) yellow, Na_2CrO_4 (d) orange, $Na_2Cr_2O_7$

27. Cu^{2+} and Ag^+ are both present in the same solution. To precipitate one of the ions and leave the other in solution, add
(a) H_2S (*aq*) (b) HCl(*aq*)
(c) HNO_3(*aq*) (d) NH_4NO_3(*aq*)

28. The addition of K_2CO_3(*aq*) to the following solutions is expected to produce a precipitate in every case but one. That one is
(a) $BaCl_2$(*aq*) (b) $CaBr_2$(*aq*)
(c) Na_2SO_4(*aq*) (d) $Pb(NO_3)_2$(*aq*)

29. Upon treatment with ammoniacal H_2S, the metal ion that precipitates as a sulphide is **[JEE Advanced 2013]**
(a) Fe (III) (b) Al (III)
(c) Mg (II) (d) Zn (II)

30. Magnesium powder burns in air to give **[JEE Main 2019]**
(a) MgO and Mg_3N_2
(b) $Mg(NO_3)_2$ and Mg_3N_2
(c) MgO only
(d) MgO and $Mg(NO_3)_2$

31. $Cu(OH)_2$ is highly soluble in all of the following except one. The exception is
(a) H_2O (b) NH_3(*aq*)
(c) HCl(*aq*) (d) HNO_3(*aq*)

32. To increase significantly the concentration of free Zn^{2+} ion is a solution of the complex ion $[Zn(NH_3)_4]^{2+}$,
$Zn^{2+}(aq) + 4NH_3(aq) \rightleftharpoons [Zn(NH_3)_4]^{2+}(aq)$
add to the solution some
(a) H_2O (b) HCl(*aq*)
(c) NH_3(*aq*) (d) NH_4Cl(*aq*)

33. The best way to ensure complete precipitation from saturated $H_2S(aq)$ of a metal ion M^{2+}, as its sulphide, $MS(s)$, is to

(a) add an acid (b) increase $[H_2S]$ in solution
(c) raise the pH (d) heat the solution

34. Of the following solutions the one that is acidic is

(a) $ZnSO_4(aq)$ (b) $NaAl(OH)_4(aq)$
(c) $NaHCO_3(aq)$ (d) $KNO_3(aq)$

35. Of the following oxides, all are soluble in $NaOH(aq)$ except

(a) ZnO (b) Al_2O_3 (c) Fe_2O_3 (d) SnO_2

36. Colourless salt (A) + dil. H_2SO_4 + KI $\xrightarrow{\text{Starch}}$ blue colour. (A) can be

(a) $K_2Cr_2O_7$ (b) MnO_2
(c) NH_4NO_2 (d) NH_4Cl

37. Three test tubes A, B, C contain Pb^{2+}, Hg_2^{2+} and Ag^+ (but unknown). To each aqueous solution NaOH is added in excess. Following changes occur.

A. Black ppt.
B. Brown ppt.
C. White ppt but dissolves in excess of NaOH

A, B and C contain respectively

(a) Pb^{2+}, Hg_2^{2+} and Ag^+ (b) Hg_2^{2+}, Ag^+, Pb^{2+}
(c) Ag^+, Pb^{2+}, Hg_2^{2+} (d) Ag^+, Hg_2^{2+}, Pb^{2+}

38. Consider the following equilibrium

$$AgCl\downarrow + 2NH_3 \rightleftharpoons \underset{\text{Soluble}}{[Ag(NH_3)_2]^+} + Cl^-$$

White ppt. of AgCl appears on adding

(a) NH_3 (b) aq. NaCl
(c) aq. HNO_3 (d) aq. NH_4Cl

39. Ag_2CrO_4 ppt. is soluble in

(a) dil. HNO_3 (b) aq. NH_3
(c) Both (a) and (b) (d) None of these

40. A mixture contains Cu^{2+}, Al^{3+} and Ni^{2+}. Following steps have been adopted but written in disorder

I. Filter, boil of H_2S gas and add NH_4Cl, heat and add NH_4OH.
II. Filter, add NH_4OH and pass H_2S gas.
III. Pass H_2S gas into acidified solution of mixture.

Steps will be used in the following order

(a) I, II, III (b) III, I, II (c) III, II, I (d) I, III, II

41. Aqueous solution of salt

$$(A) + K_2CrO_4 \longrightarrow \underset{\text{(Red ppt.)}}{(B)} \xrightarrow{Aq.\ NH_3} \underset{\text{(Black)}}{(C)}$$. A is

(a) $AgNO_3$ (b) $Pb(NO_3)_2$
(c) $Hg_2(NO_3)_2$ (d) $Ca(NO_3)_2$

42. A is a colourless substance. Aqueous solution of A gives reddish-orange ppt. with KI; ppt. dissolves in excess of KI forming a colourless solution. If NH_4Cl and NaOH solution is added to this colourless solution reddish brown ppt is formed. Substance A is

(a) Epsom salt (b) Mohr's salt
(c) Calomel (d) Corrosive sublimate

43. CoS (black) obtained in group IV of salt analysis is dissolved in aqua regia, treated with an excess of $NaHCO_3$ and then Br_2 water is added. An apple green coloured stable complex is formed. It is

(a) sodium cobaltocarbonate
(b) sodium cobaltibromide
(c) sodium cobalticarbonate
(d) sodium cobaltobromide

44. Conc. HNO_3 is added before proceeding to test for group III. This is to

(a) Convert Fe^{+2} ion into Fe^{+3} ion
(b) Oxidise any remaining H_2S
(c) Form nitrates which give granular precipitates
(d) Increase ionisation of NH_4OH

45. Borax on heating strongly above its melting point melts to a liquid, which then solidifies to a transparent mass commonly known as borax-bead. The transparent glassy mass consists of

(a) sodium pyroborate
(b) boric anhydride
(c) sodium metaborate
(d) boric anhydride and sodium metaborate

46. If CO_2 gas is passed into aq. Na_2CrO_4 yellow solution

(a) aq. $Na_2Cr_2O_7$ (orange) solution is formed
(b) aq. $Cr_2(CO_3)_2$ is formed
(c) $Cr(OH)_3$ is precipitated
(d) no action

47. A mixture of two colourless substances was dissolved in water. When gaseous Cl_2 was passed through the solution, a deep brown colour developed. Addition of $BaCl_2$ or NaOH to the original solution give a white precipitate. The mixture contained

(a) $NaNO_3$ and $AlCl_3$ (b) NaBr and KCl
(c) MgI_2 and $MgSO_4$ (d) $BaSO_4$ and $PbCl_2$

48. A suspension containing insoluble substances ZnS, CuS, HgS, Ag_2S, and FeS, is treated with 2N HCl. On filtering, the filtrate contained appreciable amounts of which one of the following groups?

(a) Zinc and mercury (b) Silver and iron
(c) Copper and mercury (d) Zinc, copper and iron

49. A yellow solid known to be a single compound is completely insoluble in hot water but dissolves in hot dilute HCl to give an orange solution. When this solution is cooled, a white crystalline ppt is formed.

This white ppt redissolves on heating the solution. The compound is

(a) $Fe(OH)_3$ (b) $PbCrO_4$
(c) K_2CrO_4 (d) $Co(OH)_2$

50. '*X*' is a colourless salt giving following reactions

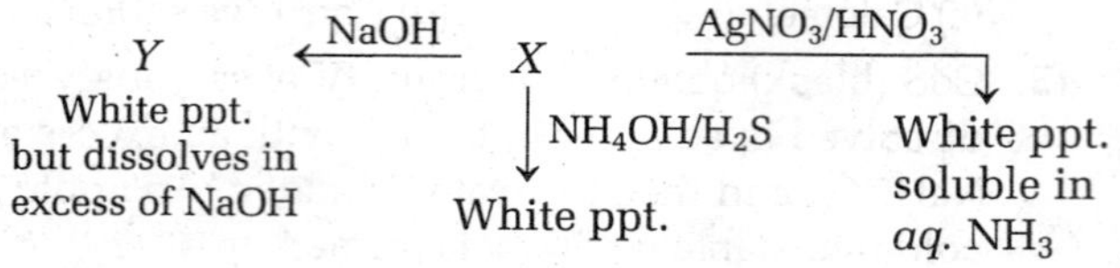

X can be

(a) $AlCl_3$ (b) $ZnCl_2$
(c) $Zn(CH_3COO)_2$ (d) $ZnBr_2$

51. A mixture upon adding conc. H_2SO_4 gives orange red fumes. It may contain the anion pair

(a) $CrO_4^{2-} + Cl^-$ (b) $Br^- + Cl^-$
(c) $NO_3^- + Cl^-$ (d) $CrO_4^{2-} + NO_3^-$

52. When calomel reacts with NH_4OH, we get

(a) $Hg(NH_2)Cl + Hg$ (b) $NH_2—Hg—Hg—Cl$
(c) Hg_2O (d) HgO

53. When metal '*M*' is treated with NaOH, a white gelatinous precipitate '*X*' is obtained, which is soluble in excess of NaOH. Compound '*X*' when heated strongly gives an oxide which is used in chromatography as an adsorbent. The metal '*M*' is **[JEE Main 2018]**

(a) Zn (b) Ca
(c) Al (d) Fe

54. Sodium salt of an organic acid '*X*' produces effervescence with conc. H_2SO_4. '*X*' reacts with the acidified aqueous $CaCl_2$ solution to give a white precipitate which decolourises acidic solution of $KMnO_4$. '*X*' is **[JEE Main 2017]**

(a) C_6H_5COONa (b) $HCOONa$
(c) CH_3COONa (d) $Na_2C_2O_4$

55. In the following reaction sequence in aqueous solution, the species *X*, *Y* and *Z*, respectively, are

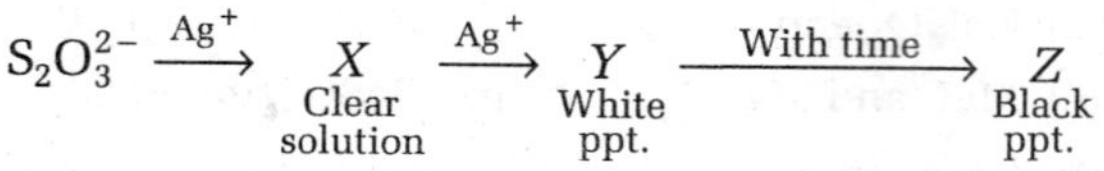

[JEE Advanced 2016]

(a) $[Ag(S_2O_3)_2]^{3-}, Ag_2S_2O_3, Ag_2S$
(b) $[Ag(S_2O_3)_3]^{5-}, Ag_2SO_3, Ag_2S$
(c) $[Ag(SO_3)_2]^{3-}, Ag_2S_2O_3, Ag$
(d) $[Ag(SO_3)_3]^{3-}, Ag_2SO_4, Ag$

56. The reagent(s) that can selectively precipitate S^{2-} from a mixture of S^{2-} and SO_4^{2-} in aqueous solution is/are **[JEE Advanced 2016]**

(a) $CuCl_2$ (b) $BaCl_2$
(c) $Pb(OOCCH_3)_2$ (d) $Na_2[Fe(CN)_5NO]$

57. Passing H_2S gas into a mixture of $Mn^{2+}, Ni^{2+}, Cu^{2+}$ and Hg^{2+} ions in an acidified aqueous solution precipitates **[IIT JEE 2011]**

(a) CuS and HgS (b) MnS and CuS
(c) MnS and NiS (d) NiS and HgS

58. The solution of sodium meta aluminate on boiling with ammonium chloride gives a white precipitate of

(a) Al_2O_3 (b) $AlCl_3$
(c) $Al(OH)_3$ (d) $NaAl(OH)_4$

59. Nitrite (NO_2^-) interferes in the **'ring-test'** of nitrate (NO_3^-). Some of the following reagents can be used for the removal of nitrite.

I. NH_4Cl
II. $(NH_2)_2CS$ (thiourea)
III. NH_2SO_3H (sulphamic acid)
IV. Sulphanilic acid

Correct choice is

(a) I, II (b) I, II, IV (c) I, II, III (d) I, III, IV

60. Consider the following reaction,

$$\text{Nitrite} + \text{acetic acid} + \text{thiourea} \longrightarrow N_2 + SCN^- + 2H_2O$$

Formation of the product in the above reaction can be identified by

(a) $FeCl_3$/dil. HCl when blood red colour appears
(b) $FeCl_3$/dil. HCl when blue colour appears
(c) $K_2Cr_2O_7$ / HCl when green colour appears
(d) $KMnO_4$/HCl when colourless solution is formed

61. Zinc pieces are added to acidified solution of SO_3^{2-}. Gas liberated can

(a) turn lead acetate paper black
(b) turn lime water milky
(c) give both of the above tests
(d) give none of the above tests

62. DMG gives a rosy red crystalline ppt. with

(a) Zn^{2+} (b) Ni^{2+} (c) Co^{2+} (d) Mn^{2+}

63. Select the correct statement(s).

(a) $Ag_2S_2O_3$ appears as white precipitate when $Na_2S_2O_3$ reacts with $AgNO_3$
(b) $Ag_2S_2O_3$ is unstable turning black on standing due to formation of Ag_2S
(c) $S_2O_3^{2-}$ can form soluble complex $[Ag(S_2O_3)_2]^{3-}$ with Ag^+
(d) All of the above are correct statements

64. A gas *X* is passed through water to form a saturated solution. The aqueous solution on treatment with silver nitrate gives a white precipitate. The saturated aqueous solution also dissolves magnesium ribbon with evolution of a colourless gas *Y*. Identify *X* and *Y*.

(a) $X = CO_2, Y = Cl_2$ (b) $X = Cl_2, Y = CO_2$
(c) $X = Cl_2, Y = H_2$ (d) $X = H_2, Y = Cl_2$

65. An aqueous solution of a substance gives a white precipitate on treatment with dilute hydrochloric acid, which dissolves on heating. When hydrogen sulphide is passed through the hot acidic solution, a black precipitate is obtained. The substance is a

(a) Hg^{2+} salt (b) Cr^{2+} salt (c) Ag^{+} salt (d) Pb^{2+} salt

66. $[X] + H_2SO_4 \longrightarrow [Y]$ a colourless gas with irritating smell

$[Y] + K_2Cr_2O_7 + H_2SO_4 \longrightarrow$ green solution

$[X]$ and $[Y]$ are

(a) SO_3^{2-}, SO_2 (b) Cl^-, HCl (c) S^{2-}, H_2S (d) CO_3^{2-}, CO_2

67. The green colour produced in the borax bead test of a chromium(III) salt is due to **[JEE Advanced 2019]**

(a) CrB (b) Cr_2O_3 (c) $Cr_2(B_4O_7)_3$ (d) $Cr(BO_2)_3$

68. A sodium salt of an unknown anion when treated with $MgCl_2$ gives white precipitate only boiling. The anion is

(a) SO_4^{2-} (b) HCO_3^- (c) CO_3^{2-} (d) NO_3^-

69. A metal nitrate reacts with KI to give a black precipitate which on addition of excess of KI converts into orange colour solution. The cation of metal nitrate is

(a) Hg^{2+} (b) Bi^{3+} (c) Pb^{2+} (d) Cu^+

70. A solution of a metal ion when treated with KI gives a red precipitate which dissolves in excess KI to give a colourless solution. Moreover, the solution of metal ion on treatment with a solution of cobalt(III) thiocyanate gives rise to a deep blue crystalline precipitate. The metal ion is

(a) Pb^{2+} (b) Hg^{2+} (c) Cu^{2+} (d) Co^{2+}

71. Sodium fusion extract, obtained from aniline, on treatment with iron (II) sulphate and H_2SO_4, in presence of air gives a Prussian blue precipitate. The blue colour is due to the formation of

(a) $Fe_4[Fe(CN)_6]_3$ (b) $Fe_3[Fe(CN)_6]_2$ (c) $Fe_4[Fe(CN)_6]_2$ (d) $Fe[Fe(CN)_6]_3$

72. A dark violet colour mixture in presence of dil. HCl changes to pale yellow solution. Mixture may contain

(a) MnO_4^-, Fe^{2+} (b) $MnO_4^-, C_2O_4^{2-}$ (c) $I^-, Cr_2O_7^{2-}$ (d) None is correct

73. Mixture is initially orange in colour. When solution is prepared in dil. acid, it changes to dark brown colour. Mixture contains

(a) $HgI_2, Cr_2O_7^{2-}$ (b) $I^-, Cr_2O_7^{2-}$ (c) I^-, Cu^{2+} (d) I^-, SO_3^{2-}

74. A salt contains cation A^{2+} and anion B^{2-}. Both decolourise MnO_4^- in acidic medium. Salt is

(a) ferrous oxalate (b) ferric oxalate (c) Both (a) and (b) (d) None of these

75. A on reaction with dil. H_2SO_4 gives a colourless pungent gas that can turn $Cr_2O_7^{2-}/H^+$ green. Green colour is due to formation of

(a) CrO_4^{2-} (b) Cr^{3+} (c) CrO_3 (d) CrO_2Cl_2

76. Aqueous solution of A can dissolve AgBr forming a soluble complex B. A also reacts with aqueous $AgNO_3$ solution giving white ppt. C changing to black ppt D. A, B, C and D are

	A	*B*	*C*	*D*
(a)	$Na_2S_2O_3$	$Na_3[Ag(S_2O_3)_2]$	$Ag_2S_2O_3$	Ag_2S
(b)	$Na_2S_2O_3$	$Ag_2S_2O_3$	Ag_2S	$Na_3[Ag(S_2O_3)_2]$
(c)	NH_3	$[Ag(NH_3)_2]Br$	$Ag(OH)$	Ag_2O
(d)	NH_3	$Na[Ag(OH)_2]$	Ag_2O	$[Ag(NH_3)_2]Br$

77. S^{2-} and SO_3^{2-} can be distinguished using

(a) $(CH_3COO)_2Pb$
(b) $Na_2[Fe(CN)_5NO]$
(c) Both (a) and (b)
(d) None of the above

78. A mixture contains NO_2^- and SO_3^{2-}. On adding dilute H_2SO_4 and KI and then starch, blue colour appears. This is due to

(a) NO_2^- (b) SO_3^{2-} (c) Both (a) and (b) (d) None of these

79. Aqueous solution of a mixture contains Br^- and I^-. On passing Cl_2 gas and adding $CHCl_3$, then organic layer will be

(a) violet (b) reddish brown (c) colourless (d) blue

80. $[Fe(H_2O)_5NO]^{2+}$ is formed as brown ring in NO_3^- test. Fe in this complex has ...... unpaired electrons.

(a) one (b) two (c) three (d) four

81. Which is the volatile compound burning with green flame?

(a) $(C_2H_5)_3B$ (b) $(C_2H_5)_3BO_3$ (c) $Ba(NO_3)_2$ (d) $BaCl_2$

82. Test of this anion is not performed in glass test tubes. This anion is

(a) F^- (b) AsO_4^{3-} (c) PO_4^{3-} (d) BO_3^{3-}

83. HF attacks glass (Na_2SiO_3) forming

(a) Na_2SiF_4 (b) Na_2SiF_3 (c) Na_2SiF_6 (d) H_4SiO_4

84. SiF_4 is hydrolysed by H_2O forming

(a) H_2SiF_6, H_4SiO_4 (b) H_2SiF_4, H_2SiF_6 (c) H_2SiF_6, H_2SiO_3 (d) H_2SiF_6, SiO_2

85. Water soluble mixture $\xrightarrow[\text{(ii) Filter}]{\text{(i) BaCl}_2}$ White ppt.

Filtrate + Br_2 water + $BaCl_2$ $\longrightarrow$ White ppt.

Mixture contains

(a) SO_3^{2-} only (b) SO_4^{2-} only

(c) Both (a) and (b) (d) None of these

86. White ppt of AgCl and $PbCl_2$ can be separated using

(a) *aq.* NH_3

(b) hot water

(c) Both (a) and (b)

(d) None of these

87. White ppt of *A* on reaction with *aq.* NH_3 are blackened. Select correct statement about *A*.

(a) *A* is also called calomel

(b) *A* reacts with *aq.* NH_3 forming $HgNH_2Cl$

(c) *A* changes to grey on reaction with $SnCl_2$

(d) All of the above are correct statements

88. Aqueous solution of *A* gives yellow ppt with *aq.* K_2CrO_4. *A* may contain

(a) Pb^{2+} or Ag^+ or Ba^{2+} (b) Pb^{2+} or Ba^{2+}

(c) Ag^+ or Ba^{2+} (d) Pb^{2+} or Ag^+

89. Ag_2CrO_4 (brick red ppt.) is soluble in

(a) dil. HNO_3 or *aq.* NH_3 (b) dil. HCl or *aq.* NH_3

(c) dil. HNO_3 or dil. HCl (d) H_2O or dil. HNO_3

90. Ag_2CrO_4 + $H^+NO_3^-$ $\longrightarrow$ Soluble *A*, *A* is

(a) Ag_2CrO_4 (b) $AgNO_3$

(c) $Ag_2Cr_2O_7$ (d) Ag_2O

91. A colourless salt gives white ppt with $CaCl_2$ solution and can also decolourise MnO_4^- / H^+. Salt is decomposed by conc. H_2SO_4 forming gases

(a) CO_2, SO_2 (b) CO, CO_2

(c) CO, SO_2 (d) N_2, CO, CO_2

92. The green colour produced in the borax bead test a chromium (III) salt is due to

(a) Cr_2O_3 (b) CrB

(c) $Cr(BO_2)_3$ (d) $Cr_2(B_4O_2)_3$

93. By H_2O_2/OH^-, $Cr(OH)_3$ changes to

(a) CrO_3 (b) $Cr_2O_7^{2-}$

(c) CrO_4^{2-} (d) $[Cr(OH)_4]^-$

94. On adding KNO_2 and CH_3COOH solution to the neutral solution of $CoCl_2$, there is formation of yellowish orange precipitate of

(a) $K_3[Co(NO_2)_6]$

(b) $K_4[Co(NO_2)_6]$

(c) $K_3[Co(NO_2)_4(CH_3COO)_2]$

(d) $K_2[Co(NO_2)_4]$

95. A colourless aqueous solution contains nitrates of two metals, *X* and *Y*. When it was added to an aqueous solution of NaCl, a white precipitate was formed. This precipitate was found to be partly soluble in hot water to give a residue *P* and a solution *Q*. The residue *P* was soluble in aqueous NH_3 and also in excess sodium thiosulphate. The hot solution *Q* gave a yellow precipitate with KI. The metals *X* and *Y*, respectively are **[JEE Advanced 2020]**

(a) Ag and Pb (b) Ag and Cd

(c) Cd and Pb (d) Cd and Zn

96. PbO_2 oxidises MnO_2 (black) to

(a) MnO_4^{2-} (b) MnO_4^-

(c) Mn^{2+} (d) Mn_2O_7

97. Test tube *A* contains $ZnCl_2$ aqueous solution while test tube *B* contains *aq* $CdCl_2$ solution. On passing H_2S gas

(a) ZnS is precipitated

(b) CdS is precipitated

(c) Both (a) and (b) are precipitated

(d) None of the above is precipitated

98. Dimethyl glyoxime and $NaHSO_3/NH_4CNS$ are used to distinguish and separate Cu^{2+} and Ni^{2+}. These are used in order

(a) HSO_3^- /CNS^- then DMG

(b) DMG then HSO_3^-/CNS^-

(c) at random

(d) given reagents are not suitable

99. Which cation cannot be identified by flame test?

(a) Na^+ (b) K^+

(c) Ba^{2+} (d) Mg^{2+}

100. When microcosmic salt is heated, transparent bead is of

(a) $NaPO_3$ (b) $Na(NH_4)HPO_4$

(c) $NaBO_2$ (d) B_2O_3

101. In borax-bead test there is formation of transparent bead of

(a) $NaPO_3$ and $NaBO_2$ (b) $NaBO_2$ and $Na_2B_4O_7$

(c) $NaBO_2$ and B_2O_3 (d) $NaPO_3$ and B_2O_3

Objective Questions Type II [One or more than one correct option(s)]

In each of the questions below, four choices are given, of which one or more than one are correct.

1. $K_4[Fe(CN)_6]$ can be used to test
(a) Fe^{3+} (b) Fe^{2+} (c) Zn^{2+} (d) Cd^{2+}

2. NaOH can dissolve
(a) $Cr(OH)_3$ (b) $Al(OH)_3$
(c) $Zn(OH)_2$ (d) $Fe(OH)_3$

3. Ag^+ and Pb^{2+} ions are precipitated together by addition of
(a) *aq.* NH_3 (b) $K_2C_2O_4$ solution
(c) dil. HNO_3 (d) KI solution

4. An inorganic mixture gives yellow precipitate on boiling with conc. HNO_3 and ammonium molybdate $((NH_4)_2MoO_4)$. Thus, inorganic mixture can be
(a) $(NH_4)_3PO_4$ (b) $(NH_4)_3AsO_4$
(c) $Pb(NO_3)_2$ (d) $(NH_4)_2C_2O_4$

5. Consider the following reaction
Nitrite + acetic acid + thiourea $\longrightarrow N_2 + SC\overset{\ominus}{N} + 2H_2O$
Formation of the product in the above reaction cannot be identified by
(a) $FeCl_3$ /dil.HCl wen blood-red colour appears
(b) $FeCl_3$/dil. HCl when blue colour appears
(c) $K_2Cr_2O_7$ /HCl when green colour appears
(d) $KMnO_4$/HCl when colourless solution is formed

6. The correct option(s) to distinguish nitrate salts to Mn^{2+} and Cu^{2+} taken separately is (are) **[JEE Advanced 2018]**
(a) Mn^{2+} shows the characteristic green colour in the flame test
(b) Only Cu^{2+} shows the formation of precipitate by passing H_2S in acidic medium
(c) Only Mn^{2+} shows the formation of precipitate by passing H_2S in faintly basic medium
(d) Cu^{2+} / Cu has higher reduction potential than Mn^{2+} /Mn (measured under similar conditions)

7. Each of these solutions is added to a mixture of aqueous solutions of iodide and chloroform $(CHCl_3)$ separately. Which will gave a positive test for iodine when the solutions are vigorously mixed?
(a) NaCl solution (b) NaBr solution
(c) Chlorine water (d) Bromine water

8. Zinc oxalate can be tested by
(a) NaOH when white precipitate is formed which dissolves in excess of NaOH
(b) $KMnO_4$ which is decolourised
(c) $CaCl_2$ which gives white precipitate
(d) $K_4[Fe(CN)_6]$ which gives yellowish white precipitate

9. Select the correct statement(s).
(a) CdS and As_2S_3 can be separated using NaOH or yellow ammonium sulphide
(b) $FeCl_3$ gives blue precipitate with $K_4[Fe(CN)_6]$
(c) $FeCl_3$ gives blood red colour with KCNS
(d) *Aq* $FeCl_3$ is reduced to $FeCl_2$ when Zn pieces are added

10. Which of the following statement(s) is/are correct?
(a) In $S_2O_3^{2-}$, both sulphur are different in nature.
(b) Sodium acetate and lead acetate on heating giving same type of product, whereas Mn, Sn, Fe oxalate salt giving different type of products.
(c) Aqueous solution of $OCl^{\ominus}$, S^{2-} and CO_3^{2-} are basic in nature.
(d) $NO_2^{\ominus}$ oxidises $I^{\ominus}$ whereas Br_2 and Cl_2 oxidise $NO_2^{\ominus}$.

11. When a substance *A* reacts with water it produces a combustible gas *B* and a solution of substance *C* in water. When another substance *D* reacts with this solution of *C*, it also produces the same gas *B* on warming but *D* can produce gas *B* on reaction with dilute sulphuric acid at room temperature. *A* imparts a deep golden yellow colour to a smokeless flame of Bunsen burner. *A, B, C,* and *D,* respectively are
(a) Na, H_2, NaOH, Zn (b) K, H_2, KOH, Al
(c) CaH_2, $Ca(OH)_2$, Sn (d) CaC_2, C_2H_2, $Ca(OH)_2$, Fe

12. In the separation of Cu^{2+} and Cd^{2+} in 2nd group of qualitative analysis of cations tetrammine copper (II) sulphate and tetrammine cadmium(II) sulphate react with KCN to form the corresponding cyanide complexes, which one of the following pairs of the complexes and their relative stabilities enables the separation of Cu^{2+} and Cd^{2+}?
(a) $K_3[Cu(CN)_4]$: less stable and
$K_2[Cd(CN)_4]$: more stable
(b) $K_3[Cu(CN)_4]$: more stable and
$K_2[Cd(CN)_4]$: less stable
(c) $K_2[Cu(CN)_4]$: less stable and
$K_2[Cd(CN)_4]$: more stable
(d) $K_2[Cu(CN)_4]$: more stable and
$K_2[Cd(CN)_4]$: less stable

13. Nessler's reagent is used for the test of
(a) CrO_4^{2-} (b) MnO_4^- (c) NH_4^+ (d) PO_4^{3-}

14. A colourless salt is precipitated as hydroxide on adding. *aq.* NaOH precipitate dissolves in excess *aq.* NaOH and precipitation occurs on adding *aq.* NH_4Cl. Colourless salt may be
(a) $AlCl_3$ (b) $ZnCrO_4$ (c) $ZnCl_2$ (d) $AlPO_4$

15. For the given aqueous reaction which of the statement(s) is (are) true?

$$\text{(Excess) KI} + K_3[Fe(CN)_6] \xrightarrow{\text{Dil. } H_2SO_4} \text{Brownish-yellow solution}$$

$$\downarrow ZnSO_4$$

(White precipitate + Brownish-yellow filtrate)

$$\downarrow Na_2S_2O_3$$

Colourless solution **[IIT JEE 2012]**

(a) The first reaction is a redox reaction
(b) White precipitate is $Zn_3[Fe(CN)_6]_2$
(c) Addition of filtrate to starch solution gives blue colour
(d) White precipitate is solution in NaOH solution

Comprehension Based Questions

In these questions, a passage has been given followed by questions based on it. You have to answer the questions based on the passage given.

***Passage* 1** Silver nitrate gives a white precipitate (*A*) with aqueous sodium thiosulphate (*B*); the precipitate dissolves in excess of thiosulphate. If the precipitate is heated with water, it turns black (*C*), and the supernant liquid then gives a white precipitate (*D*) with acidified barium nitrate solution.
Read the above analysis-report and answer the questions given below.

1. Species *A* and *B* are respectively

	A	*B*
(a)	$Ag_2S_2O_3$	$Ag(S_2O_3)_2^{3-}$
(b)	AgS_2O_3	$Ag(S_2O_3)_2^{2-}$
(c)	AgS_2O_3	$Ag(S_2O_3)_2^{3-}$
(d)	$Ag(S_2O_3)_2^{3-}$	$Ag_2S_2O_3$

2. Select the correct explanation for the formation of *C* and *D*
(a) When (*B*) is heated with H_2O, H_2S is formed which gives black ppt. of Ag_2S.
(b) Ag_2S (black *C*) is precipitated alongwith H_2SO_4 (in supernant layer) which gives white ppt. with $Ba(NO_3)_2$ solution
(c) Ag_2SO_4 (black *C*) is precipitated alongwith H_2S which gives white ppt. with $Ba(NO_3)_2$ solution
(d) None of the above is correct explanation

***Passage* 2** *Questions given below are based on the following analysis.*

A coloured solution known to contain two metal ions, was treated with excess cold sodium hydroxide solution. When filtered a whitish solid, slowly changing to brown, was retained on the filter paper and a colourless solution collected as the filtrate. Dropwise addition of hydrochloric acid to the filtrate produced a white precipitate which dissolved in excess acid. Treatment of the residue from the filter paper with a solution of a strong oxidiser produced a reddish-violet solution.

1. Indicate any pairs of ions which on testing as above leads to the observed changes
(a) Zn^{2+} and Mn^{2+} ions (b) Mg^{2+} and Zn^{2+} ions
(c) Mn^{2+} and Mg^{2+} ions (d) Fe^{2+} and Zn^{2+} ions

2. Filtrate obtained after separation of white solid contains
(a) ZnO (b) Na_2ZnO_2
(c) MnO (d) Na_2MnO_2

3. Reddish-violet solution is decolourised by
(a) SO_3^{2-}, $C_2O_4^{2-}$, Fe^{2+} (b) SO_4^{2-}, HCO_3^-, Fe^{3+}
(c) NO_2^-, SO_4^{2-}, Fe^{2+} (d) H_2O_2, $C_2O_4^{2-}$, CO_3^{2-}

***Passage* 3** You have a mixture of CO_2, SO_2 and O_2 gas. You have been provided the following reagents for testing
(*A*) lime water
(*B*) acidified potassium dichromate solution
(*C*) pyrogallol

1. If order is *A*, *B*, *C*, then which gas remains unchecked
(a) CO_2 (b) SO_2
(c) O_2 (d) None of these

2. Acidified $K_2Cr_2O_7$ solution has been used to test
(a) SO_2
(b) CO_2
(c) O_2
(d) mixture of SO_2 and CO_2

3. Gas responsible for green-house effect is
(a) O_2 (b) SO_2
(c) CO_2 (d) CO_2 and O_2

***Passage* 4** A colourless mixture of two salts (*A*) and (*B*) (excess) is soluble in H_2O. Separately (*A*) turns blue litmus red and (*B*) turns red litmus blue. (*A*) gives white ppt. with (*B*), which dissolves in excess of (*B*) forming (*C*). (*A*) when placed in moist air gives fumes and can form dimer. (*A*) gives white ppt. with NH_4Cl and NH_4OH soluble in (*B*). A also gives white ppt. with $AgNO_3$ soluble in NH_4OH.

Read the above analysis report and answer the following questions.

1. *A* turns blue litmus red. It is due to acidic solution because of
(a) hydrolysis of cation of *A*
(b) hydrolysis of anion of *A*
(c) hydrolysis of both cation and anion
(d) None of the above is correct

2. NH_4Cl and NH_4OH acts as a buffer for precipitation of *A* as white ppt. If pK_b of $NH_3(aq)$ is 4.74, pH of equimolar $[NH_4^+]$ and $[NH_3]$ will be
(a) 4.74 (b) 9.26 (c) 7.00 (d) 14.00

3. If ppt. formed by addition of NH_4Cl and NH_4OH is of the form $M(OH)_3$ then pH at which 2×10^{-12} M M^{3+} ion is precipitated is (K_{sp} of $M(OH)_3 = 2 \times 10^{-33}$)
(a) 7 (b) 5 (c) 6 (d) 8

Passage 5 Presence of Fe^{3+} in an aqueous solution can be made by addition of sodium acetate (in excess) when a reddish-brown colour is formed".

*Read the above short **write-up** and answer the following questions.*

1. Reddish-brown colour is due to formation of
(a) $[Fe(H_2O)_4(CH_3COO)_2]^+$
(b) $[Fe(CH_3CO_4)_6]^{3-}$
(c) $[Fe_3(OH)_2(CH_3COO)_6]^+$
(d) $[Fe_2(H_2O)_4(CH_3COO)_4]^{2+}$

2. Excess of sodium acetate is added in the above test. It is because
(a) it acts as a buffer to control pH of the reaction otherwise reaction is made reversible
(b) it makes the solution alkaline which destroys acidic effect if any
(c) sodium acetate has low K_{sp} value
(d) sodium acetate has high K_{sp} values

3. Presence of Fe^{3+} can also be detected by .... when .... is formed.
(a) KCNS, $Fe(CNS)_3$ ... blood red
(b) KCNS, $[Fe(CNS)]Cl_2$ ... blood red colour
(c) KCNS, $[Fe(CNS)_2Cl$ ... blood red colour
(d) KCN, $K_3[Fe(CN)_6]$ ... blue precipitate

Passage 6 "Sometimes it happens that when H_2S gas is passed into a solution in dil. HCl (in qualitative analysis of cations), yellowish white turbidity appears."

Read the above short write-up and answer the following questions.

1. Yellowish white turbidity is of
(a) SO_3^{2-} formed by oxidation of H_2S by HCl
(b) colloidal sulphur formed by oxidation of H_2S by certain oxidising agent
(c) SO_4^{2-} formed by oxidation of H_2S by H_2O
(d) None of the above is correct

2. A colourless salt on reaction with dil. HCl gives a colourless pungent gas that turns $K_2Cr_2O_7$ solution green. A student passed H_2S gas immediately after adding dil. HCl and got colloidal yellowish suspension before any precipitation occurs. This is due to
(a) SO_3^{2-} which is decomposed to SO_2 forming S with H_2S
(b) NO_2^- which oxidises H_2S to colloidal sulphur
(c) Both of the above
(d) None of the above

Passage 7 When a KI solution was added to a solution of mercury (II) chloride, a precipitate [mercury (II) iodide] formed. A student plotted the mass of the precipitate *versus* the volume of the KI solution added and obtained the following graph.

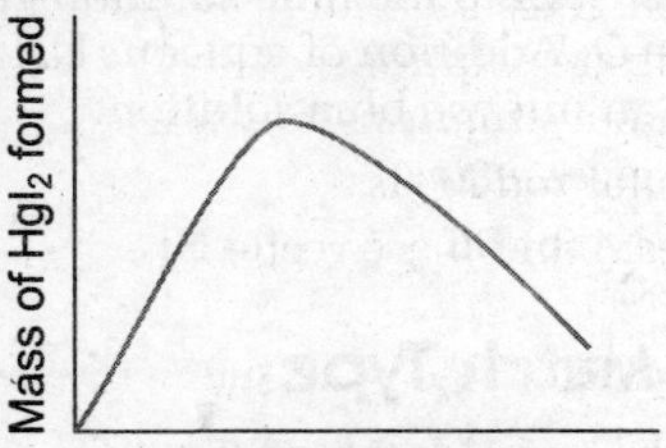

Based on the above graph, answer the following question.

1. As KI is added to $HgCl_2$ solution, there is increase in the mass of HgI_2 but after a maximum point is reached, mass of HgI_2 decreases. It is due to
(a) formation of soluble K_3HgI_5
(b) formation of soluble K_2HgI_4
(c) decomposition of HgI_2 into Hg_2I_2 and I_2
(d) decomposition of HgI_2 into Hg and I_2

2. Species formed after maximum is attained is called
(a) Nessler's reagent (b) Tollen's reagent
(c) iodide of Millon's base
(d) None of the above is correct

3. (Refer Q. 2). Species formed in Q. 2 is added to hot NH_4Cl solution containing some NaOH, then there is formation of
(a) brown precipitate of iodide Millon's base
(b) yellow colouration of K_2HgI_4
(c) blue precipitate of $(NH_4)_2HgI_2Cl_2$
(d) None of the above

Passage 8 *p*-amino-N,N-dimethylaniline is added to a strongly acidic solution of *X*. The resulting solution is treated with a few drops of aqueous solution of *Y* to yield blue colouration due to the formation of methylene blue. Treatment of the aqueous solution of *Y* with the reagent potassium hexacyanoferrate (II) leads to the formation of an intense blue precipitate. The precipitate dissolves on excess addition of the reagent. Similarly, treatment of the solution of Y with the solution of potassium hexacyanoferrate (III) leads to a brown colouration due to the formation of Z. **[IIT JEE 2009]**

1. The compound X, is
(a) $NaNO_3$ (b) $NaCl$
(c) Na_2SO_4 (d) Na_2S
2. The compound Y, is
(a) $MgCl_2$ (b) $FeCl_2$
(c) $FeCl_3$ (d) $ZnCl_2$
3. The compound Z, is
(a) $Mg_2[Fe(CN)_6]$ (b) $Fe[Fe(CN)_6]^+$
(c) $Fe[Fe(CN)_6]^-$ (d) $K_2Zn_3[Fe(CN)_6]_2$

***Passage* 9** When a metal rod M is dipped into an aqueous colourless concentrated solution of compound N, the solution turns light blue. Addition of aqueous NaCl to the blue solution gives a white precipitate O. Addition of aqueous NH_3 dissolves O and gives an intense blue solution. **[IIT JEE 2011]**

1. The metal rod M, is
(a) Fe (b) Cu (c) Ni (d) Co
2. The compound N, is
(a) $AgNO_3$ (b) $Zn(NO_3)_2$
(c) $Al(NO_3)_3$ (d) $Pb(NO_3)_2$
3. The final solution contains
(a) $[Pb(NH_3)_4]^{2+}$ and $[CoCl_4]^{2-}$
(b) $[Al(NH_3)_4]^{3+}$ and $[Cu(NH_3)_4]^{2+}$
(c) $[Ag(NH_3)_2]^+$ and $[Cu(NH_3)_4]^{2+}$
(d) $[Ag(NH_3)_2]^+$ and $[Ni(NH_3)_6]^{2+}$

***Passage* 10** An aqueous solution of a mixture of two inorganic salts, when treated with dilute HCl, gave a precipitate (P) and filtrate (Q). The precipitate (P) was found to dissolve in hot water. The filtrate (Q) remained unchanged when treated with H_2S in a dilute mineral acid medium. However, it gave a precipitate (R) with H_2S in an ammoniacal medium. The precipitate (R) gave a coloured solution (S) when treated with H_2O_2 in an aqueous NaOH medium.

1. The precipitate (P) contains
(a) Pb^{2+} (b) Hg_2^{2+} (c) Ag^+ (d) Hg^{2+}
2. The coloured solution (S) contains **[JEE Advanced 2013]**
(a) $Fe_2(SO_4)_3$ (b) $CuSO_4$ (c) $ZnSO_4$ (d) Na_2CrO_4

Matrix-Match Type

Given below are Matching Type Questions, with two columns (each having some items) each . Each item of Column I has to be matched with the items of Column II.

1. Match the set of ion and reagent (in Column I) with colour obtained (in Column II).

	Column I		Column II
A.	$Fe^{3+} + [Fe(CN)_6]^{4-}$	1.	Cherry red
B.	$Fe^{3+} + CNS^-$	2.	Pink
C.	Ni^{2+} + DMG	3.	Blood red
D.	$CrO_4^{2-} + Pb^{2+}$	4.	Blue
E.	$Mn^{2+} + PbO_2 + H^+$	5.	Yellow ppt.

2. Match the reactions in Column I with the substances in Column II.

	Column I		Column II
A.	A white, waxy solid, normally stored under water because it spontaneously inflames in air.	1.	HNO_3
B.	A viscous liquid that reacts with table sugar, giving a charred mass.	2.	Cl_2
C.	An acid that reacts with copper metal, releasing brown fumes.	3.	P
D.	A pale greenish yellow gas that dissolves in aqueous NaOH to give a solution used as a bleach.	4.	H_2SO_4

3. Match the cations in Column I with the colour of bead in Column II (in borax-bead test).

	Column I		Column II
A.	Cu^{2+}	1.	Violet
B.	Fe^{3+}	2.	Blue
C.	Cr^{3+}	3.	Yellow
D.	Mn^{2+}	4.	Green
E.	Co^{2+}	5.	Yellowish brown

4. Match the cation (in Column I) with the reagent (in Column II) used to identify the cation.

	Column I		Column II
A.	Cu^{2+}	1.	KCNS
B.	Ni^{2+}	2.	K_2CrO_4
C.	Fe^{3+}	3.	$NH_3(aq)$
D.	Ca^{2+}	4.	DMG
E.	Ba^{2+}	5.	$(NH_4)_2C_2O_4$

5. Match the qualitative analysis group (in Column I) with the group reagent (in Column II).

	Column I		Column II
A.	Group I	1.	NH_4OH / NH_4Cl
B.	Group II	2.	H_2S / NH_4OH
C.	Group III	3.	Dil. HCl
D.	Group IV	4.	H_2S / HCl

6. Match the reagents (in Column I) with the cations (in Column II) which can be identified.

	Column I		Column II
A.	$K_4[Fe(CN)_6]$	1.	Zn^{2+}
B.	NH_4CNS	2.	Fe^{3+}
C.	CH_3COONa	3.	Cu^{2+}
D.	H_2S / H^+	4.	Cd^{2+}
E.	H_2S/NH_2OH - NH_4Cl	5.	Ni^{2+}

7. Match the reagents (in Column I) with the cations (in Column II) which can be identified.

	Column I		Column II
A.	$AgNO_3$	1.	Cl^-
B.	$FeCl_3$	2.	Br^-
C.	$BaCl_2$	3.	I^-
D.	$(CH_3COO)_2Pb$	4.	CH_3COO^-
E.	Cl_2 water	5.	CrO_4^{2-}

Single Integer Answer Questions

Answer of these questions is a single digit lying between 0 to 9.

1. SO_2 turns acidified $K_2Cr_2O_7$ solution green. Oxidation number of the green-coloured ion is …………

2. Brown coloured ring formed in the nitrate test has formula $[Fe(H_2O)_5NO]SO_4$. Unpaired electrons in Fe is …………

3. Ferrous sulphate heptahydrate is used to fortify foods with iron. The amount (in grams) of the salt required to achieve 10 ppm of iron in 100 kg of wheat is ……… . **[JEE Main 2020]**

(Atomic weight : Fe = 55.85; S = 32.00; O = 16.00)

4. Aqueous neutral solution of $FeCl_3$ reacts and acetate to form a reddish brown colour compound $[Fe_3(OH)_2(CH_3COO)_x]^+$, where, x is ………..

5. $FeCl_3$ gives blood red colour of formula $[Fe(CNS)(H_2O)_y]^{2+}$ with KCNS. Here, y = ………..

6. Copper metaborate is formed in the test of copper ion in borax-bead test. Number of boron atoms in copper metaborate is ………..

7. AgBr dissolved in $Na_2S_2O_3$, 1 mole of AgBr is dissolved in x mole of $Na_2S_2O_3$. Where, x is …… .

8. Blue coloured precipitate of Prussian blue has total of iron atom(s) ………

9. In neutral or faintly alkaline solution, 8 moles of permanganate anion quantitatively oxidise thiosulphate anions to produce X moles of a sulphur containing product. The magnitude of X is **[JEE Advanced 2016]**

10. When 35 mL of 0.15 M lead nitrate solution is mixed with 20 mL of 0.12 M chromic sulphate solution, ……… $\times 10^{-5}$ moles of lead sulphate precipitate out. (Round off to the Nearest Integer). **[JEE Main 2021, March]**

Answers

Objective Questions Type I [Only one correct option]

1. (d)	**2.** (a)	**3.** (c)	**4.** (c)	**5.** (c)	**6.** (b)	**7.** (b)	**8.** (d)	**9.** (c)	**10.** (d)
11. (c)	**12.** (a)	**13.** (c)	**14.** (c)	**15.** (d)	**16.** (c)	**17.** (d)	**18.** (c)	**19.** (c)	**20.** (a)
21. (a)	**22.** (d)	**23.** (d)	**24.** (d)	**25.** (a)	**26.** (c)	**27.** (b)	**28.** (c)	**29.** (d)	**30.** (a)
31. (a)	**32.** (b)	**33.** (c)	**34.** (a)	**35.** (c)	**36.** (c)	**37.** (b)	**38.** (c)	**39.** (c)	**40.** (b)
41. (c)	**42.** (d)	**43.** (c)	**44.** (b)	**45.** (d)	**46.** (a)	**47.** (c)	**48.** (d)	**49.** (b)	**50.** (b)
51. (a)	**52.** (a)	**53.** (c)	**54.** (d)	**55.** (a)	**56.** (a)	**57.** (a)	**58.** (c)	**59.** (c)	**60.** (a)
61. (a)	**62.** (b)	**63.** (d)	**64.** (c)	**65.** (d)	**66.** (a)	**67.** (d)	**68.** (b)	**69.** (b)	**70.** (b)
71. (a)	**72.** (a)	**73.** (b)	**74.** (a)	**75.** (b)	**76.** (a)	**77.** (c)	**78.** (a)	**79.** (a)	**80.** (c)
81. (b)	**82.** (a)	**83.** (c)	**84.** (a)	**85.** (c)	**86.** (c)	**87.** (d)	**88.** (b)	**89.** (a)	**90.** (c)
91. (b)	**92.** (c)	**93.** (c)	**94.** (a)	**95.** (a)	**96.** (b)	**97.** (b)	**98.** (a)	**99.** (d)	**100.** (a)
101. (c)									

Objective Questions Type II [One or more than one correct option(s)]

1. (a, c, d)	**2.** (b, c)	**3.** (b, d)	**4.** (a, b)	**5.** (b, c, d)
6. (b, d)	**7.** (c, d)	**8.** (a, b, c, d)	**9.** (a, b, c)	**10.** (a, c, d)
11. (a)	**12.** (b)	**13.** (c)	**14.** (a, c)	**15.** (a, c, d)

Comprehension Based Qeustions

Passage 1 – **1.** (a) **2.** (b)

Passage 2 – **1.** (a) **2.** (b) **3.** (a)

Passage 3 – **1.** (b) **2.** (a) **3.** (c)

Passage 4 – **1.** (a) **2.** (b) **3.** (a)

Passage 5 – **1.** (c) **2.** (a) **3.** (b)

Passage 6 – **1.** (b) **2.** (a)

Passage 7 – **1.** (b) **2.** (a) **3.** (a)

Passage 8 – **1.** (d) **2.** (c) **3.** (c)

Passage 9 – **1.** (b) **2.** (a) **3.** (c)

Passage 10 – **1.** (a) **2.** (d)

Matrix-Match Type

1. A→(4); B→(3); C→(1); D→(5); E→(2)
2. A→(3); B—(4); C→(1); D→(2)
3. A→(4); B—(5); C→(3); D→(1); E→(2)
4. A→(3); B—(4); C→(1); D→(5); E→(2)
5. A→(3); B—(4); C→(1); D→(2)
6. A→(1,2,3,4); B→(2,3); C→(2); D→(3,4) E→(1,5)
7. A→(1,2,3,5); B→(4); C→(5); D→(3,5); E→(2,3)

Single Integer Answer Questions

1. (3)	**2.** (3)	**3.** (5)	**4.** (6)	**5.** (5)	**6.** (2)	**7.** (2)	**8.** (4)	**9.** (6)	**10.** (5)

Solutions

Objective Questions Type I [Only one correct answer]

1. (*d*) (a) $2FeCl_3 + SnCl_2 \longrightarrow \underset{\text{Light green}}{2FeCl_2} + SnCl_4$

(b) $FeCl_3$ solution is acidic due to hydrolysis.

$$FeCl_3 + 3H_2O \longrightarrow Fe(OH)_3 + 3HCl$$

Zinc pieces added liberate H (nascent) *in situ* and reduces $FeCl_3$ to $FeCl_2$.

$$FeCl_3 + 2H \longrightarrow FeCl_2 + HCl$$

(c) $2FeCl_3 + H_2S \longrightarrow 2FeCl_2 + 2HCl + S$

2. (*a*) Fe^{2+} is oxidised to Fe^{3+} by MnO_4^- / H^+

Fe^{3+} gives blue colour with $K_4[Fe(CN)_6]$

$$Fe^{2+} + MnO_4^- + H^+ \longrightarrow Fe^{3+} + Mn^{2+} + H_2O$$

$$Fe^{3+} + [Fe(CN)_6]^{4-} \longrightarrow \underset{\text{Prussian blue}}{Fe[Fe(CN)_6]^-}$$

3. (*c*) $Cr(OH)_3$ is oxidised to CrO_4^{2-} (soluble) by $NaOH / H_2O_2$. $Fe(OH)_3$ is not affected.

$$Cr(OH)_3 + OH^- + H_2O_2 \longrightarrow \underset{\text{Soluble (yellow)}}{CrO_4^{2-}}$$

4. (*c*) $Fe^{2+} + [Fe^{III}(CN)_6]^{3-} \longrightarrow \underset{\text{Turnbull's blue}}{Fe^{II}[Fe^{III}(CN)_6]^-}$

$$Fe^{3+} + [Fe^{II}(CN)_6]^{4-} \longrightarrow \underset{\text{Prussian's blue}}{Fe^{III}[Fe^{II}(CN)_6]^-}$$

5. (*c*) $As_2S_3 + 6NaOH \longrightarrow \underbrace{Na_3AsO_3 + Na_3AsS_3}_{\text{Soluble}} + 3H_2O$

$$AlCl_3 + 3NaOH \longrightarrow Al(OH)_3 + 3NaCl$$
$$Al(OH)_3 + NaOH \longrightarrow \underset{\text{Soluble}}{Na[Al(OH)_4]}$$

6. (*b*) Gas is N_2O (laughing gas)

$$NaNO_2 + NH_4Cl \longrightarrow NH_4NO_2 + NaCl$$
$$NH_4NO_2 \longrightarrow \underset{\text{Molar mass = 44}}{N_2O} + 2H_2O$$
$$0.56\ L\ N_2O \equiv 1.1\ g$$
$$22.4\ L\ N_2O \equiv 44\ g$$

Thus, gas is N_2O.

7. (*b*)
$$ZnCl_2 + 2H_2O \longrightarrow Zn(OH)_2 + 2HCl$$
$$CdCl_2 + 2H_2O \longrightarrow Cd(OH)_2 + 2HCl$$
$$CuCl_2 + 2H_2O \longrightarrow Cu(OH)_2 + 2HCl$$

Cd^{2+} and Cu^{2+} ions are precipitated as CdS and CuS in acidic medium when H_2S gas is passed. This medium is provided by hydrolysis of their chlorides.

Zn^{2+} as ZnS is not precipitated in HCl medium on passing H_2S gas.

8. (*d*) $Fe^{3+} + SCN^- \longrightarrow [Fe(SCN)]^{2+}$

9. (*c*) $\underset{\text{Borax}}{Na_2B_4O_7} \xrightarrow{\Delta} NaBO_2 + \underbrace{B_2O_3}_{\text{Transparent bead}}$

$$B_2O_3 + CuO \longrightarrow \underset{\text{Coloured bead}}{Cu(BO_2)_2}$$
$$\underset{\text{Microcosmic salt}}{Na(NH_4)HPO_4} \xrightarrow{\Delta} \underset{\text{Transparent bead}}{NaPO_3} + H_2O + NH_3$$
$$NaPO_3 + CuO \longrightarrow \underset{\text{Coloured bead}}{Na[CuPO_4]}$$

10. (*d*) $KCl + \underset{\text{Conc.}}{H_2SO_4} \longrightarrow KHSO_4 + HCl$

$$K_2Cr_2O_7 + 2H_2SO_4 \longrightarrow 2KHSO_4 + 2CrO_3 + H_2O$$
$$CrO_3 + 2HCl \longrightarrow CrO_2Cl_2 + H_2O$$
$$CrO_2Cl_2 + 2NaOH \longrightarrow \underset{\text{Yellow }(Y)}{Na_2CrO_4} + HCl$$

11. (*c*) $BaBr_2 + K_2CrO_4 \longrightarrow \underset{\text{Yellow ppt.}}{BaCrO_4\downarrow}$

$$BaBr_2 \xrightarrow{AgNO_3} \underset{\text{Yellow ppt.}}{AgBr\downarrow}$$

12. (*a*) $Cr_2O_7^{2-} + 2OH^- \longrightarrow 2CrO_4^{2-} + H_2O \quad pH > 7$

$$2CrO_4^{2-} + 2H^+ \longrightarrow Cr_2O_7^{2-} + H_2O \quad pH < 7$$

13. (*c*) Zn^{2+}, Co^{2+} precipitated by $H_2S/NH_4OH, NH_4Cl$

Cu^{2+}, Cd^{2+}	precipitated by H_2S/HCl	
Cu^{2+}, As^{3+}	only Cu^{2+} is precipitated	
Cu^{2+}, Cr^{3+}	by H_2S/HCl ($pH < 7$)	

14. (*c*) *X* is $BiCl_3$.

$$BiCl_3 + H_2O \longrightarrow \underbrace{BiOCl}_{\text{White turbidity}} + 2HCl$$
$$BiOCl + 2HCl \longrightarrow BiCl_3 + H_2O$$
$$\downarrow H_2S$$
$$Bi_2S_3 \text{ (black ppt. soluble in } HNO_3)$$

15. (*d*) $K_2Cr_2O_7 + 2H_2SO_4 \longrightarrow 2KHSO_4 + 2CrO_3 + H_2O$

$$CrO_3 \xrightarrow{H_2O_2} CrO_5$$

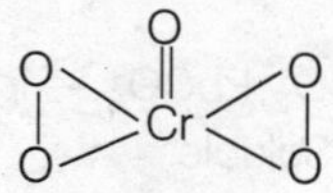

Blue in ethereal layer.

16. (*c*) $FeS + 2H_2O \longrightarrow Fe(OH)_2 + \underset{\text{Foul smell}}{H_2S}$

17. (*d*) $2AgNO_3 + Na_2S_2O_3 \longrightarrow 2NaNO_3 + Ag_2S_2O_3$

$$Ag_2S_2O_3 + H_2O \longrightarrow \underset{\text{Black}}{Ag_2S} + H_2SO_4$$

18. (*c*) SO_2, O_2, CO_2

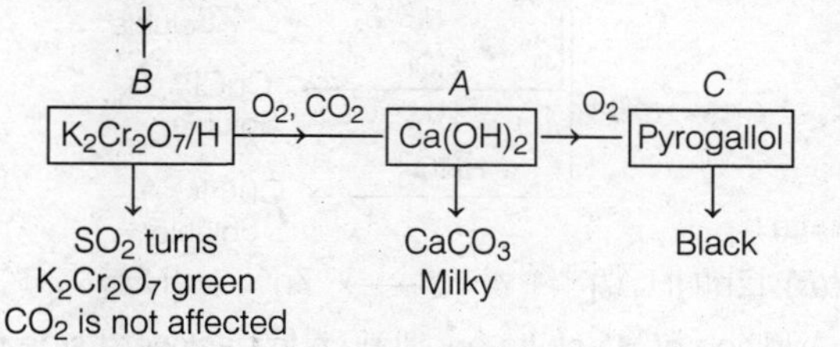

Thus, order is *B*, *A*, *C*.

19. (*c*) $\underset{\text{Insoluble 1}}{Al_2(SO_4)_3} + \underset{3}{3Na_2CO_3} \longrightarrow \underset{\text{Soluble}}{3Na_2SO_4} + Al_2(CO_3)_3$

21. (*a*) $HgCl_2 + 2KI \longrightarrow HgI_2 \xrightarrow[\text{excess}]{2KI} \underset{(A)}{K_2HgI_4}$

$$K_2HgI_4 + NH_3/NaOH \longrightarrow$$

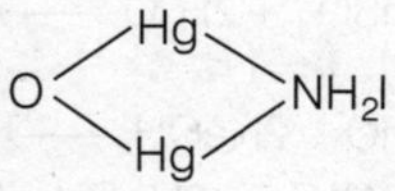

(*B*)

22. (*d*) $Cu^{2+} + 2SCN^- \longrightarrow \underset{\text{Black}}{Cu(SCN)_2\downarrow} \xrightarrow{\Delta} \underset{\text{White}}{CuSCN\downarrow} + (SCN)_2$

$$Fe^{3+} + SCN^- \longrightarrow \underset{\text{Red}}{[Fe(SCN)]^{2+}}$$
$$Co^{2+} + SCN^- \longrightarrow \underset{\text{Blue}}{[Co(SCN)_4]^{2-}}$$

23. (*d*) $Fe^{2+} + \underset{A}{[Fe(CN)_6]^{4-}} \longrightarrow$ no colour

$$Fe^{3+} + A \longrightarrow \underset{\text{Prussian blue}}{Fe^{III}[Fe^{II}(CN)_6]^-}$$
$$Zn^{2+} + [Fe(CN)_6]^{4-} \longrightarrow \underset{\text{Bluish white ppt.}}{Zn_2[Fe(CN)_6]\downarrow}$$
$$Cu^{2+} + [Fe(CN)_6]^{4-} \longrightarrow \underset{\text{Reddish brown}}{Cu_2[Fe(CN)_6]\downarrow}$$
$$Cd^{2+} + [Fe(CN)_6]^{4-} \longrightarrow \underset{\text{Bluish white.}}{Cd_2[Fe(CN)_6]\downarrow}$$

24. (*d*) $[B_4O_5(OH)_4]^{2-} + 5H_2O \longrightarrow 2B(OH)_3 + 2[B(OH)_4]^-$

$$2[B(OH)_4]^- + 2HCl \longrightarrow B(OH)_3 + 2H_2O + 2Cl^-$$

Each $[B(OH)_4]^-$ has one neutralisable OH^-.

25. (*a*) Kjeldahl's method cannot be used for nitro compounds, diazo compounds and compounds with nitrogen in a ring, because these on reaction with H_2SO_4 do not give ammonium ion.

27. (*b*)
$$Ag^+ + Cl^- \longrightarrow \underset{\text{White ppt.}}{AgCl\downarrow}$$
$$Cu^{2+} + Cl^- \longrightarrow \underset{\text{Soluble}}{CuCl_2}$$

28. (*c*) $BaCO_3, CaCO_3, PbCO_3$ — Insoluble
Na_2CO_3 — Soluble

30. (*a*) Magnesium powder burns in air to give MgO and Mg_3N_2. MgO does not combine with excess oxygen to give any superoxide. Mg reacts with nitrogen to form magnesium nitride (Mg_3N_2).
$$Mg + O_2 \longrightarrow MgO$$
$$3Mg + N_2 \longrightarrow Mg_3N_2$$

31. (*a*)
$$Cu(OH)_2 + NH_3 \longrightarrow \underset{\text{Soluble}}{[Cu(NH_3)_4]^{2+}}$$
$$Cu(OH)_2 \xrightarrow{HCl} \underset{\text{Soluble}}{CuCl_2}$$
$$Cu(OH)_2 \xrightarrow{HNO_3} \underset{\text{Soluble}}{Cu(NO_3)_2}$$

32. (*b*) $[Zn(NH_3)_4]^{2+} + 4H^+ \longrightarrow Zn^{2+} + 4NH_4^+$
Addition of H^+ shifts equilibrium in backward side releasing Zn^{2+} ions.

33. (*c*) $H_2S \rightleftharpoons 2H^+ + S^{2-}$
On increasing pH, $[H^+]$ decreases, hence $[S^{2-}]$ increases making precipitation of M^{2+} as MS.

34. (*a*) $ZnSO_4 + 2H_2O \longrightarrow Zn(OH)_2\downarrow + \underset{\text{Acidic}}{2H_2SO_4}$

35. (*c*) $ZnO + 2NaOH \longrightarrow Na_2[ZnO_2] + H_2O$
$Al_2O_3 + 2NaOH \longrightarrow 2Na[AlO_2] + H_2O$
$SnO_2 + 2NaOH \longrightarrow Na_2[SnO_3] + H_2O$
$Fe_2O_3 + NaOH \longrightarrow$ Insoluble

36. (*c*) $NH_4NO_2 + H^+ \longrightarrow HNO_2$
$$HNO_2 \xrightarrow[\text{Starch}]{KI} \text{blue}$$

40. (*b*)

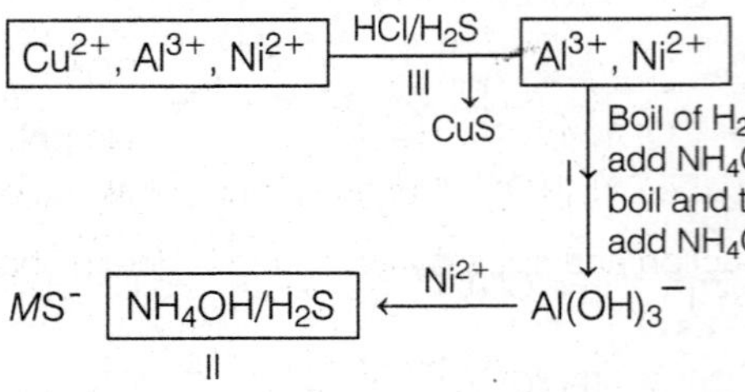

41. (*c*) $Hg_2(NO_3)_2 \xrightarrow{K_2CrO_4} \underset{\text{Red}}{Hg_2CrO_4} \xrightarrow{NH_3}$ Black (Hg)

42. (*d*) $HgCl_2 \xrightarrow{KI} HgI_2 \xrightarrow{KI} K_2HgI_4 \xrightarrow{NH_4Cl/NaOH}$
Reddish brown

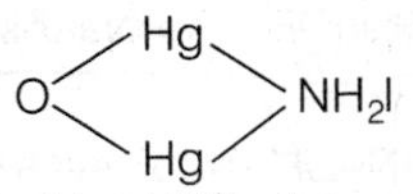

Iodide of Million's base

45. (*d*) $Na_2B_4O_7 \xrightarrow{\Delta} \underbrace{2NaBO_2 + B_2O_3}_{\text{Bead}}$

46. (*a*) $CO_2 + H_2O \longrightarrow H_2CO_3 \rightleftharpoons H^+ + HCO_3^-$
$$2CrO_4^{2-} + 2H^+ \longrightarrow \underset{\text{Orange}}{Cr_2O_7^{2-}} + H_2O$$

47. (*c*) $MgI_2 + Cl_2 \longrightarrow MgCl_2 + \underset{\text{Deep brown}}{I_2}$
$$MgSO_4 + BaCl_2 \longrightarrow \underset{\text{White ppt.}}{BaSO_4\downarrow}$$

48. (*d*) On adding 2NHCl, AgCl and $HgCl_2$ are precipitated. Filtrate will contain Zn^{2+}, Cu^{2+} and Fe^{2+}.

49. (*b*) $PbCrO_4 + HCl \longrightarrow PbCl_2 + H_2CrO_4$
$$2CrO_4^{2-} + 2H^+ \longrightarrow \underset{\text{Orange}}{Cr_2O_7^{2-}} + H_2O$$

50. (*b*) $\underset{X}{ZnCl_2} + NaOH \longrightarrow \underset{Y}{Zn(OH)_2} \xrightarrow{NaOH} Na_2ZnO_2$
$$ZnCl_2 \xrightarrow{NH_4OH/H_2S} \text{White ppt.}$$
$$ZnCl_2 \xrightarrow{AgNO_3} \underset{\text{White ppt.}}{AgCl\downarrow} \xrightarrow{NH_3} \underset{\text{Soluble}}{[Ag(NH_3)_2]Cl}$$

51. (*a*) $2CrO_4^{2-} + \underset{\text{From } H_2SO_4}{2H^+} \longrightarrow Cr_2O_7^{2-} + H_2O$
$$Cr_2O_7^{2-} + \underset{\text{Conc.}}{H_2SO_4} \longrightarrow CrO_3$$
$$Cl^- + H_2SO_4 \longrightarrow HCl + HSO_4^-$$
$$CrO_3 + 2HCl \longrightarrow \underset{\text{Orange red fumes}}{CrO_2Cl_2} + H_2O$$

52. (*a*) $\underset{\text{Calomel}}{Hg_2Cl_2} + NH_3 \longrightarrow \underbrace{HgNH_2Cl + Hg}$

53. (*c*) Among the given metals Al forms white gelatinous ppt. with NaOH.
Hence, the probable metal can be Al. This ppt. is dissolved in excess of NaOH due to the formation of sodium metal Aluminate. Both the reactions are shown below.
$$Al^{3+} \xrightarrow{NaOH} \underset{\text{White gelatinous ppt. }(X)\text{ of aluminium hydroxide}}{Al(OH)_3} \xrightarrow{\text{Excess of NaOH}} \underset{\text{Sodium metaaluminate) soluble}}{NaAlO_2}$$
Aluminium hydroxide on strong heating gives alumina (Al_2O_3) which is used as an adsorbent in chromatography. This reaction can be seen as :
$$2Al(OH)_3 \xrightarrow{\Delta} Al_2O_3 + 3H_2O$$
Thus, metal M is Al.
Ca, being below sodium in electrochemical reactivity series, cannot displaces Na from its aqueous solution.

Zn reacts with NaOH to form sodium zincate which is a soluble compound.

Fe reacts with sodium hydroxide to form tetrahydroferrate (II) sodium which is again a soluble complex.

54. (*d*) The reaction takes place as follows

$$\underset{(X)}{Na_2C_2O_4} + \underset{\text{(Conc.)}}{H_2SO_4} \longrightarrow Na_2SO_4 + H_2O + \underset{\text{Effervescence}}{CO\uparrow + CO_2\uparrow}$$

$$\underset{(X)}{Na_2C_2O_4} + CaCl_2 \longrightarrow \underset{\text{White ppt.}}{CaC_2O_4} + 2NaCl$$

$$5CaC_2O_4 + \underset{\text{Purple}}{2KMnO_4} + 8H_2SO_4 \longrightarrow K_2SO_4 + 5CaSO_4 + \underset{\text{Colourless}}{2MnSO_4} + 10CO_2 + 8H_2O$$

Hence, *X* is $Na_2C_2O_4$.

55. (*a*) $$Ag^+ + 2S_2O_3^{2-} \rightarrow \underset{\text{(Clear solution)}}{\underset{X}{[Ag(S_2O_3)_2]^{3-}}} \xrightarrow{Ag^+} \underset{\text{(White)}}{\underset{Y}{Ag_2S_2O_3}} \xrightarrow{\text{With time}} \underset{\text{Black}}{\underset{Z}{Ag_2S}}$$

$$Ag_2S_2O_3 + H_2O \longrightarrow Ag_2S + H_2SO_4$$

56. (*a*) The reagent that can selectively precipitate S^{2-} and SO_4^{2-} in aqueous solution is $CuCl_2$.

$$S^{2-} + CuCl_2 \longrightarrow CuS\downarrow + 2Cl^-$$

57. (*a*) Cu^{2+} and Hg^{2+} are precipitated in acidic medium.

58. (*c*) $NaAlO_2 + NH_4Cl + H_2O \longrightarrow NaCl + Al(OH)_3\downarrow + NH_3$

59. (*c*) $NH_4Cl, (NH_2)_2CS, NH_2SO_3H$ decompose NO_2^- to N_2.

60. (*a*) $SCN^- + FeCl_3 \longrightarrow \underset{\text{Blood red}}{[Fe(SCN)]Cl_2} + Cl^-$

61. (*a*) $SO_3^{2-} + 2H^+ \longrightarrow SO_2 + H_2O$

$$Zn + 2H^+ \longrightarrow Zn^{2+} + 2H$$

$$SO_2 + 4H \longrightarrow H_2S + 2H_2O$$

$$(CH_3COO)_2Pb + H_2S \longrightarrow \underset{\text{Black}}{PbS\downarrow}$$

63. (*d*) $2AgNO_3 + Na_2S_2O_3 \longrightarrow \underset{\text{White}}{Ag_2S_2O_3} + 2NaNO_3$

$$Ag_2S_2O_3 + H_2O \longrightarrow H_2SO_4 + \underset{\text{Black}}{Ag_2S\downarrow}$$

$$AgNO_3 + \underset{\text{Excess}}{2Na_2S_2O_3} \longrightarrow Na_3[Ag(S_2O_3)_2] + NaNO_3$$

64. (*c*) $\underset{(X)}{Cl_2} + H_2O \longrightarrow HCl + HClO$

$$Mg + 2HCl \longrightarrow MgCl_2 + \underset{(Y)}{H_2}$$

65. (*d*) $Pb^{2+} + 2HCl \longrightarrow \underset{\text{White ppt.}}{PbCl_2\downarrow} \xrightarrow{H_2S} \underset{\text{Black ppt.}}{PbS}$

soluble in hot water

66. (*a*) $\underset{(X)}{SO_3^{2-}} + 2H^+ \longrightarrow \underset{(Y)}{SO_2}$

$$Cr_2O_7^{2-} + SO_2 + H^+ \longrightarrow \underset{\text{Green}}{Cr^{3+}} + SO_4^{2-}$$

67. (*d*) $Na_2B_4O_7 \cdot 10H_2O \xrightarrow{\Delta} Na_2B_4O_7 \xrightarrow{\Delta} NaBO_2 + B_2O_3$

$$Cr_2O_3 + B_2O_3 \longrightarrow \underset{\text{(Green colour bead)}}{Cr(BO_2)_3}$$

68. (*b*) $MgCl_2 + 2HCO_3^- \longrightarrow Mg(HCO_3)_2$

$$Mg(HCO_3)_2 \xrightarrow{\Delta} MgCO_3 + H_2O + CO_2$$

69. (*b*) $Bi^{3+} + 3I^- \longrightarrow \underset{\text{Black ppt.}}{BiI_3\downarrow}$

$$BiI_3 + KI \longrightarrow \underset{\text{Orange solution}}{K[BiI_4]}$$

70. (*b*) $Hg^{2+} + 2I^- \longrightarrow \underset{\text{Red ppt.}}{HgI_2\downarrow}$

$$HgI_2 + 2I^- \longrightarrow \underset{\text{Soluble}}{HgI_4^{2-}}$$

$$Co(SCN)_3 + Hg^{2+} \longrightarrow \text{Deep blue crystalline ppt.}$$

71. (*a*) $[Fe(CN)_6]^{4-}$ is formed which forms Prussian blue with Fe^{3+}

$$Fe^{3+} + [Fe(CN)_6]^{4-} \longrightarrow \underset{\text{Prussian blue}}{Fe_4[Fe(CN)_6]_3}$$

72. (*a*) MnO_4^- is reduced to Mn^{2+} by Fe^{2+} which is oxidised to Fe^{3+}.

$$5Fe^{2+} + MnO_4^- + 8H^+ \longrightarrow Mn^{2+} + 5Fe^{3+} + 4H_2O$$

73. (*b*) $I^- + Cr_2O_7^{2-}$ (orange)

$$I^- + Cr_2O_7^{2-} + H^+ \longrightarrow Cr^{3+} + I_2$$

$$I_2 + KI \longrightarrow \underset{\text{Dark brown}}{KI_3}$$

74. (*a*) $\left.\begin{matrix} Fe^{2+} \\ C_2O_4^{2-} \end{matrix}\right]$ decolourise MnO_4^-/H^+

76. (*a*) $AgBr + \underset{(A)}{2Na_2S_2O_3} \longrightarrow \underset{(B)}{Na_3[Ag(S_2O_3)_2]} + NaBr$

$$2AgNO_3 + Na_2S_2O_3 \longrightarrow \underset{(C)}{Ag_2S_2O_3} + 2NaNO_3$$

$$\underset{\text{Black ppt.}}{Ag_2S\downarrow} \xleftarrow{H_2O} Ag_2S_2O_3$$

77. (*c*)

	S^{2-}	SO_3^{2-}
$(CH_3COO)_2Pb$	Black ppt.	No ppt.
$Na_2[Fe(CN)_5NO]$	Purple colour	No colour

80. (*c*) Reaction and appearance of ring is due to charge transfer.

$$NO \longrightarrow NO^+ + e^-$$

$$Fe^{2+} + e^- \longrightarrow Fe^+$$

⇅	1	1	1	1

⇅	⇅	1	1	1

Three unpaired electrons

$$[Fe^+(H_2O)_5NO^+] \equiv [Fe(H_2O)_5NO]^{2+}$$

Note Presence of three unpaired electrons is confirmed by magnetic moment of Fe which is $\sqrt{15}$ BM.

83. (*c*) $6HF + Na_2SiO_3 \longrightarrow Na_2SiF_6 + 3H_2O$
Glass

84. (*a*) $SiF_4 + 4H_2O \longrightarrow H_4SiO_4 + 4HF$

$2HF + SiF_4 \longrightarrow H_2SiF_6$

86. (*c*) $\underset{\text{Insoluble in hot water } PbCl_2}{AgCl} + 2NH_3 \longrightarrow \underset{\text{Soluble}}{[Ag(NH_3)_2]Cl}$

Soluble in hot water

87. (*d*) $\underset{\text{Calomel}}{Hg_2Cl_2} + NH_3 \longrightarrow \underbrace{HgNH_2Cl + Hg}_{\text{Black}}$

$\xrightarrow{SnCl_2} SnCl_4 + \underset{\text{Grey}}{Hg}$

88. (*b*) $PbCrO_4, BaCrO_4$ both are yellow.

90. (*c*) $2Ag_2CrO_4 + 2HNO_3 \longrightarrow \underset{\text{Soluble}}{Ag_2Cr_2O_7} + 2AgNO_3 + H_2O$

91. (*b*) Salt contains $C_2O_4^{2-}$.

$$CaCl_2 + C_2O_4 \longrightarrow \underset{\text{White ppt.}}{CaC_2O_4 \downarrow}$$

$C_2O_4^{2-}$ decolourises MnO_4^-/H^+

$$CaC_2O_4 \longrightarrow CaO + CO + CO_2$$

92. (*c*) Borax bead test is performed only for coloured salt. Borax (sodium pyroborate), $Na_2B_4O_7 \cdot 10H_2O$ on heating gets fused and lose water of crystallisation. It swells up into fluffy white porous mass which melts into a colourless liquid which later form a clear transparent glassy bead consisting of boric anhydride and sodium metaborate.

$$Na_2B_4O_7 \cdot 10H_2O \xrightarrow{\Delta} Na_2B_4O_7 + 10H_2O \uparrow$$

$$Na_2B_4O_7 \xrightarrow{\Delta} \underbrace{\underset{\text{Boric anhydride}}{B_2O_3} + \underset{\text{Sodium metaborate}}{2NaBO_2}}_{\text{Glassy bead}}$$

Boric anhydride is non-volalite. When it react with Cr(III) salt then deep green complex is formed.

$$2Cr^{3+} + 3B_2O_3 \longrightarrow \underset{\text{Deep green}}{2Cr(BO_2)_3}$$

Hence, option (c) is correct.

94. (*a*) $CH_3COOH + KNO_2 \longrightarrow CH_3COOK + HNO_2$

$CoCl_2 + 2KNO_2 \longrightarrow Co(NO_2)_2$

$3KNO_2 + Co^{II}(NO_2)_2 + 2HNO_2 \longrightarrow \underset{\substack{\text{Potassium} \\ \text{cobaltinitrite} \\ \text{(yellowish orange pH)}}}{K_3[Co^{III}(NO_2)_6]} + H_2O + NO \uparrow$

95. (*a*)

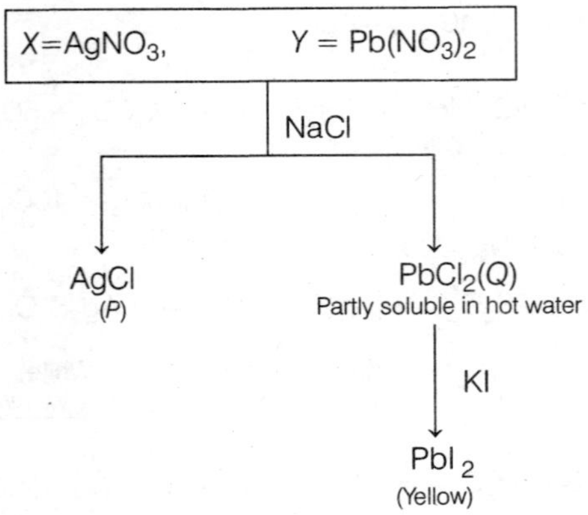

$$AgCl + 2NH_3 \longrightarrow [Ag(NH_3)_2]Cl$$

$$AgCl + 2Na_2S_2O_3 \longrightarrow Na_3[Ag(S_2O_3)_2] + 2NaCl$$

96. (*b*) $PbO_2 + MnO_2 + H^+ \longrightarrow \underset{\text{Purple/violet}}{MnO_4^-}$

97. (*b*) $ZnCl_2 + H_2S \longrightarrow ZnS + 2HCl$

$CdCl_2 + H_2S \longrightarrow CdS + 2HCl$

ZnS is soluble in HCl hence not precipitated.

98. (*a*) $Cu^{2+} \xrightarrow{NaHSO_3} Cu^+$

$Cu^+ + CNS^- \longrightarrow \underset{\text{White ppt.}}{CuCNS \downarrow}$

Filtrate contains Ni^{2+} and gives cherry red ppt with DMG.

100. (*a*) $Na(NH_4)HPO_4 \xrightarrow{\Delta} \underset{\text{Bead}}{NaPO_3} + H_2O + NH_3$

Physical Chemistry

01

Units and Measurements

Objective Questions Type I [Only one correct option]

In each of the questions below, four choices are given of which only one is correct.

1. The number of significant figures in 0.00210 is
(a) five (b) six
(c) four (d) three

2. The decimal equivalent of $\frac{1}{0.6}$ up to four significant figures may be written as
(a) 1.666 (b) 1.6666
(c) 1.667 (d) 01.666

3. 0.00167 is written in three significant figures with scientific notation as
(a) 1.67×10^{-3} (b) 167.0×10^{-5}
(c) 16.7×10^{-4} (d) 1.670×10^{-3}

4. 17.675 is rounded off to four significant figures as
(a) 17.68 (b 17.67
(c) 17.6750 (d) 17.7

5. 20.665 is rounded off to four significant figures as
(a) 20.67 (b) 20.66
(c) 20.6650 (d) 22.665

6. In which of the following numbers, all the zeros are not significant?
(a) 0.002 (b) 0.0020
(c) 0.00200 (d) 0.002000

7. $1 + 2\,(17 - 15.1) = x$. Hence, x is equal to
(a) 4.8 (b) 19.9 (c) 5 (d) 5.0

8. Number of significant figures in the answer of the following will be

$$\frac{(29.2 - 20.2)\,(1.79 \times 105)}{1.39}$$

(a) 4 (b) 3 (c) 2 (d) 1

9. Which has maximum number of significant figures?
(a) 0.000010 (b) 0.216
(c) 2.1×10^{6} (d) 0.021

10. If $\frac{1.40 \times 2.67 \times 1.93}{2.800 \times 5.340 \times 1.93} = x$, then x is
(a) 0.2500 (b) 0.0025×10^{-2}
(c) 0.25 (d) 0.250

11. Average velocity $\left(= \sqrt{\frac{8\,RT}{\pi M}}\right)$ of O_2 gas at 10°C in ms^{-1} is
(a) $\sqrt{\frac{8 \times 0.0821 \times 10}{32\pi}}$ (b) $\sqrt{\frac{8 \times 8.314 \times 10}{32\pi}}$
(c) $\sqrt{\frac{8 \times 8.314 \times 283}{32\pi}}$ (d) $\sqrt{\frac{8 \times 8314 \times 283}{32\pi}}$

12. Electromotive force (EMF), E of a cell is related to standard EMF, $E°$ by the equation

$$E = E° - \frac{0.0591}{n} \log K$$

where, K is reaction quotient and n the number of electrons. Which is correct graphical representation?

(a)
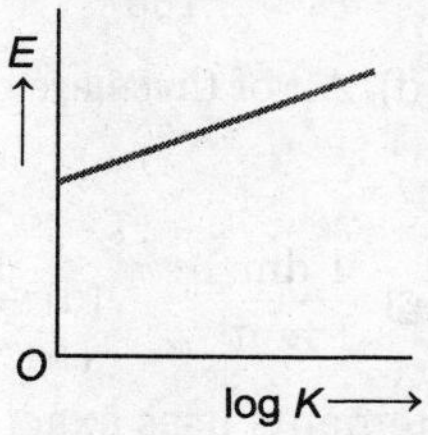

(b)
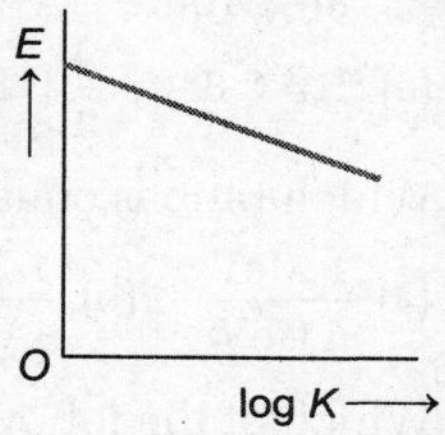

(c)
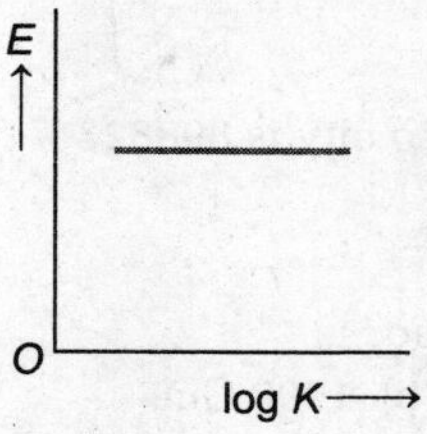

(d)
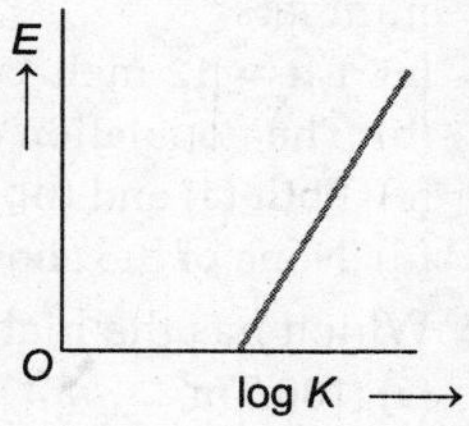

13. If x is the slope of the line of the graph in Q. (12) (above) then

(a) $n = 0.0591\ x$ (b) $n = \frac{x}{0.0591}$

(c) $n = \frac{0.0591}{x}$ (d) None is correct

14. Variation of concentration (in mol L^{-1}) with time (in second) is given by

$$\left(\frac{dx}{dt}\right) = k\ [A]^n$$

where, k is rate constant and n the order of the reaction. If $n = 2$ then, k is expressed in the unit of

(a) L mol^{-1} s^{-1} (b) mol L^{-1} s^{-1}

(c) L^2 mol^{-2} s^{-1} (d) s^{-1}

15. $x°$ is the same in °F and °C. $x°$ is

(a) 180° (b) – 273°

(c) – 40° (d) – 32°

16. The density of silver is 10.5 g/cm^3. This value in kg/m^3 would be

(a) 1.05×10^4 kg / m^3 (b) 10.5×10^4 kg / m^3

(c) 1.05×10^3 kg / m^3 (d) 10.5×10^2 kg / m^3

17. The distance between two hydrogen atoms in a hydrogen molecule is 74 pm. This distance is also equal to

(a) 7.4×10^{-11} m

(b) 0.074 nm

(c) 0.74 Å

(d) All are correct

18. Helium has the lowest boiling point of all the element at – 452°F. This value in degree celsius is

(a) – 219°C (b) – 189°C

(c) – 269°C (d) – 226°C

19. On the Reaumur scale, water freezes at 0°R and boils at 80°R. Hence,

(a) $\frac{°R}{80} = \frac{°C}{100}$ (b) $\frac{°R}{80} = \frac{°F - 32}{180}$

(c) $°R = 0.8°C = \frac{4}{9}(°F - 32)$ (d) All of these are correct

20. Which ratio is equal to 100?

(a) $\frac{1\ \text{MeV}}{1\ \text{GeV}}$ (b) $\frac{1\ \text{Tm}}{1\ \text{Gm}}$ (c) $\frac{1\ \text{dm}}{1\ \text{mm}}$ (d) $\frac{1\ \mu\text{L}}{1\ \text{nL}}$

21. Which of the following statements uses exact numbers?

(a) 1 ft = 12 inch

(b) The population of Mexico city is 8988230

(c) Both (a) and (b)

(d) None of the above

22. Which has the highest value?

(a) 100 Tm (b) 1000 Gm

(c) 10^4 Mm (d) 10^6 nm

23. Increasing order of prefix : micro, nano, pico and femto is

(a) micro < nano < pico < femto

(b) nano < micro < pico < femto

(c) pico < nano < micro < femto

(d) femto < pico < nano < micro

24. Multiplication by 10^3 will convert

(a) pico into nano

(b) nano into micro

(c) femto into pico

(d) All of the above

25. 1 Ts in terms of the SI base unit is equal to

(a) 1×10^3 s (b) 1×10^9 s

(c) 1×10^{12} s (d) 1×10^{-12} s

26. Name and symbol of the prefixes used with SI units to indicate multiplication by the following exact quantities 10^3, 10^{-2}, 0.1 and 10^{-3} respectively are

(a) k, c, d, m (b) m, d, c, k

(c) d, k, c, m (d) k, m, d, c

27. EMF value is obtained in volt by the following operation

[**Hint :** JC^{-1} is volt]

(a) $\frac{8.314\ \text{J mol}^{-1}\ \text{K}^{-1} \times 298\ \text{K}}{96500\ \text{C mol}^{-1}}$

(b) $\frac{8.314 \times 10^7\ \text{erg mol}^{-1}\ \text{K}^{-1} \times 298\ \text{K}}{1\ \text{F}}$

(c) $\frac{0.0821\ \text{L atm mol}^{-1}\ \text{K}^{-1}}{96500\ \text{C mol}^{-1}}$

(d) $\frac{2\ \text{cal mol}^{-1}\ \text{K}^{-1}}{96500\ \text{C mol}^{-1}}$

28. How many significant figures should be used for the answer to the following calculation?

$$\frac{(0.082056)\ (298.15)\ (0.379)}{(0.9480)}$$

(a) 2 (b) 3 (c) 4 (d) 5

29. How many significant figures are there in the answer to the following calculation?

$$0.0325 + 0.0812 + 0.0631$$

(a) 2 (b) 3 (c) 4 (d) 5

30. If $\frac{29.837 - 29.241}{32.064} = x$

then x (with correct significant figures) is

(a) 0.00186 (b) 0.01860

(c) 0.0186 (d) 1.86×10^{-2}

31. $\frac{732.11 + 6.3}{760.00} = x$

x is equal to (with correct number of SF)

(a) 0.9716 (b) 0.972

(c) 0.97 (d) 9.7×10^{-2}

32. 57.675 is rounded off to in four significant figures as

(a) 5.768×10^1 (b) 57.68
(c) 5.767 (d) 0.5767×10^2

33. 917.65 is rounded off to in four significant figures as

(a) 917.6 (b) 917.7
(c) 917.65 (d) 9.176×10^1

34. Of the following masses, that which is expressed to the nearest milligrams is

(a) 32.7 g (b) 32.71 g
(c) 32.707 g (d) 32.7068 g

35. The greatest length of the following group is

(a) 4.0 m (b) 140 inch
(c) 12 ft (d) 0.001 km

36. Of the following numbers, the one with three significant figures is

(a) 22.03 (b) 0.0260
(c) 0.070 (d) 2000

37. The highest temperature of the following group is

(a) 217 K (b) 273 K
(c) 217°F (d) 105°C

38. The largest volume of the following group is that of

(a) 445 g of water at 4°C (density $= 1 g/cm^3$)
(b) 600 g of chloroform at 20°C (density $= 1.5 g/cm^3$)
(c) 155 cm^3 of steel
(d) 0.50 L milk

39. Of the following substances, the greatest density is that of

(a) 1000 g of water at 4°C
(b) 100.0 cm^3 of chloroform weighing 198.9 g
(c) a 10.0 cm^3 piece of wood weighing 7.72 g
(d) an ethyl alcohol-water mixture of density 0.83 g/cm^3

40. SI unit of pressure is

(a) pascal (b) atmosphere
(c) metre (d) $dyne/cm^2$

41. SI unit of EMF is

(a) joule (b) millivolt
(c) volt (d) ampere

42. SI unit of radioactivity is

(a) Curie (b) Becquerel
(c) Rutherford (d) Gray

43. For the reaction $A \longrightarrow$ Product

$$k = \frac{1}{t}\left[\frac{1}{a-x} - \frac{1}{a}\right]$$

where, k is rate constant (in $mol^{-1}s^{-1}$) and a and $(a-x)$ are the concentration of A at the start and after time interval t sec. A graph between $(a-x)^{-1}$ and time t is of the type

(a)
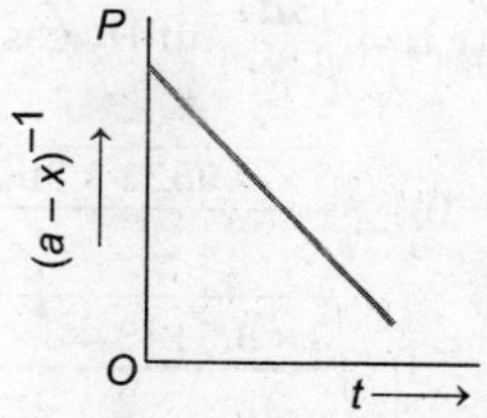

(b)
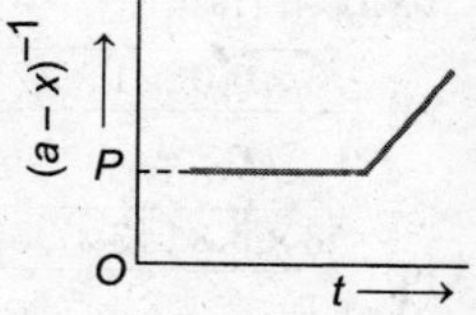

(c)
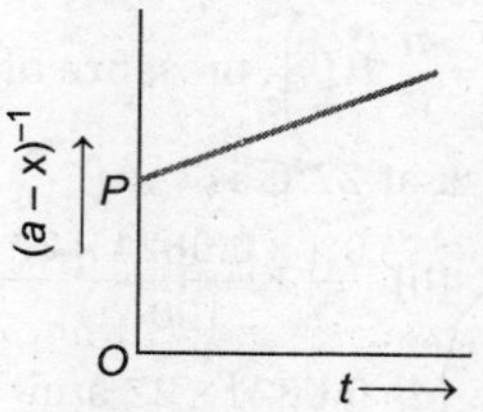

(d)
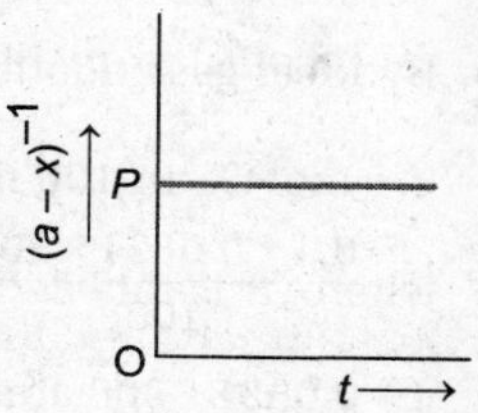

44. If $OP = 0.01$ mol^{-1} then initial concentration a is (in the above question)

(a) 0.01 mol
(b) 10 mol
(c) 0.1 mol
(d) 100 mol

45. Following equation gives variation of equilibrium constant K with temperature T

$$\log K = \log A - \frac{\Delta H}{2.303\, RT}$$

Graphically this variation is represented as

(a)
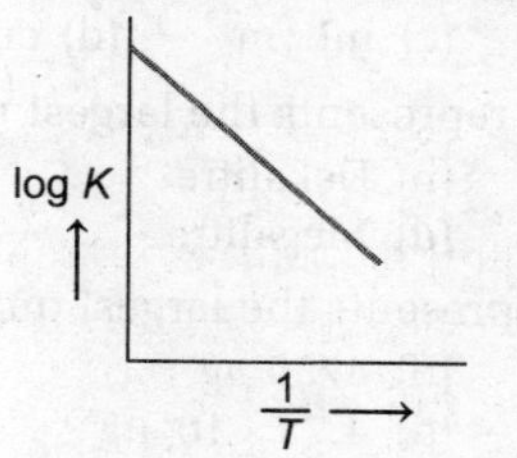

(b)
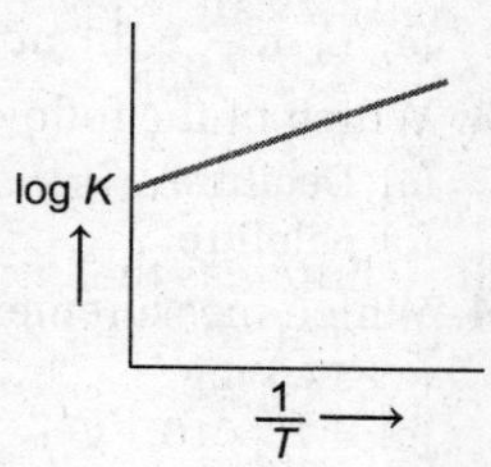

(c)
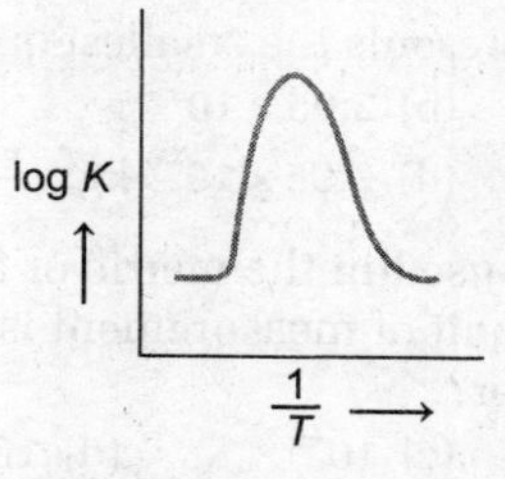

(d)
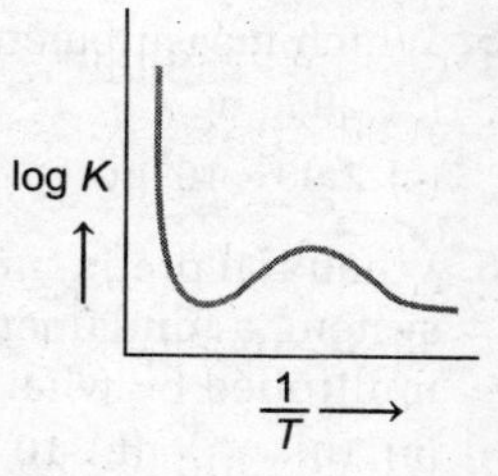

46. Rate law of a given equation of n th order

$A \longrightarrow$ Product

is given by $\left(\frac{dx}{dt}\right) = k\,[A]^n$

A straight line is inclined at 45° when a graph between $\log\left(\frac{dx}{dt}\right)$ and $\log [A]$ is plotted. Hence, n is

(a) 0 (b) 1
(c) 2 (d) 0.5

47. Root mean square velocity $u = \sqrt{\frac{3RT}{M}}$ of H_2 gas at 27°C in m s^{-1} is

(a) $\sqrt{\frac{3 \times 0.0821 \times 27}{2}}$ (b) $\sqrt{\frac{3 \times 0.0821 \times 300}{2}}$

(c) $\sqrt{\frac{3 \times 8.3143 \times 300}{2}}$ (d) $\sqrt{\frac{3 \times 8.3143 \times 3 \times 10^5}{2}}$

48. By ideal gas equation $\left(p = \frac{n}{V} RT\right)$, pressure of 0.1 mol O_2 in 100 mL flask at 27°C is

(a) $\frac{0.1 \times 0.0821 \times 300}{100}$ atm (b) $\frac{0.1 \times 0.0821 \times 27}{100}$ atm

(c) 0.0821×300 atm (d) 0.0821×27 atm

49. Consider the following unit values of energy

A : 1 L atm B : 1 erg C : 1 J D : 1 kcal

Increasing order of these values is

(a) $A = B = C = D$ (b) A < B < C < D

(c) B < C < A < D (d) D < A < C < B

50. The metric unit to measure volume is

(a) litre (b) mL (c) m^3 (d) cm^3

51. The abbreviation for the metric unit used to measure mass is

(a) k (b) m (c) g (d) s

52. The SI unit for volume is ... and the metric unit for volume is ...

(a) L, m^3 (b) m^3, L (c) mL, m^3 (d) cm^3, m^3

53. Which of the following represents the largest unit?

(a) Decilitre (b) Dekalitre

(c) Kilolitre (d) Megalitre

54. Which measurement represents the largest quantity?

(a) 47.3 mg (b) 4730 ng

(c) 4.73×10^{-4} g (d) 4.73×10^3 μg

55. Which measurement represents the smallest quantity?

(a) 2950 ng (b) 2.95×10^{-4} g

(c) 2.95×10^3 μg (d) 2.95×10^{-6} kg

56. When the prefix *milli* is used in the metric or SI system, a fundamental unit of measurement is multiplied by what factor?

(a) 10^3 (b) 10^{-3} (c) 10^{-6} (d) 10^{-2}

57. When the prefix *centi* is used in the metric system a fundamental unit of measurement is multiplied by what factor?

(a) 10^2 (b) 10^{-3} (c) 10^{-2} (d) 10^3

58. Which choice best describes the degree of uncertainty in the measurement of 16.30 g?

(a) The uncertainty cannot be determined without additional information

(b) The quantity is exact

(c) ± 0.10 g

(d) ± 0.01 g

59. Which choice best describes the degree of uncertainty in the measurement of 4.0032 g?

(a) The uncertainty cannot be determined with additional information3

(b) The quantity is exact

(c) The measurement is between 4.002 and 4.004 g

(d) The measurement is between 4.0031 and 4.0033 g

60. What is 0.0970 written in scientific notation?

(a) 970×10^{-4} (b) 97×10^{-3}

(c) 9.70×10^{-2} (d) 97.0×10^{-2}

61. How many ng are there in 5.2 mg?

(a) 5.2×10^3 ng (b) 5.2×10^6 ng

(c) 5.2×10^9 ng (d) 5.2×10^{-9} ng

62. What temperature is 75°F on the Kelvin scale?

(a) 24 K (b) 348 K (c) 297 K (d) 215 K

63. Least count of an analytical balance is 0.0002 g. Which of the following is the correct recorded value?

[**Hint** Result should be reported upto four decimal places such that fourth decimal digit should be even number (including zero; i.e. 0, 2, 4, 6, 8)]

(a) 9.3171 g (b) 9.317 g

(c) 9.3175 g (d) 9.3170 g

64. The SI unit of electrical resistance is ohm which is defined as

(a) 1 ohm = 1 VA (b) 1 ohm = 1 VA^{-1}

(c) 1 ohm = 1 WA (d) 1 ohm = 1 WA^{-1}

65. The SI unit of voltage is volt (V) which is defined as

(a) 1 V = 1 WA^{-1} (b) 1 V = 1 WA

(c) 1 V = 1 ohm A (d) 1 V = 1 ohm A^{-1}

66. Joule can have the dimension of

(a) kg m^{-1} s^{-1} (b) m kg^{-1} s^{-1}

(c) kg m^2 s^{-2} (d) kg m^2 s^2

67. $\left(\frac{3RT}{M}\right)^{1/2}$ represents

(a) velocity (b) momentum

(c) energy (d) pressure

68. 1 mmHg is equal to

(a) 7.502×10^{-3} N m^{-2} (b) 133.3 N m^{-2}

(c) 7.502×10^3 N m^{-2} (d) 0.1333 N m^{-2}

69. Area is expressed in the unit of barn. One barn is equal to

(a) 10^{-12} m^2 (b) 10^{-19} m^2 (c) 10^{-22} m^2 (d) 10^{-23} m^2

70. One horse power (HP) is equal to 7.457×10^2 W. Which represent incorrect relation?

(a) 1 HP = 745.7 J s^{-1}

(b) 1 W = 1.341×10^{-3} HP

(c) 1 J s^{-1} = 1.341 kg HP

(d) 1 J s^{-1} = 1.341 milli HP

Objective Questions Type II [One or more than one correct option(s)]

In each of the questions below, four choices are given, of which one or more than one are correct.

1. Which of the following numbers consists of four significant figures?
(a) 319.1 (b) 8.000×10^{-4}
(c) 70×10^{-5} (d) 6.600×10

2. Which of the following is true about 5 calorie.
(a) 21 J (b) 1.3×10^{20} eV
(c) 2.6×10^{22} eV (d) 18 J

3. 100 Kelvin is equal to
(a) – 173°C (b) – 279.7°F
(c) – 167.2°F (d) 173°C

4. Which of the following quantities is expressed in its SI unit?
(a) 100°C (b) 250 kg
(c) 100 metre (d) 10 mol

5. Energy can be represented in
(a) Joule (b) electron volt
(c) units (d) Watt

6. Which of the following is not a correct relation?
(a) 1 litre = 10^{-3} cm^3 (b) 1 litre = 10^{-3} dm^3
(c) 1 litre = 10^{-3} m^3 (d) 1 litre = 1 dm^3

7. Which of the statements is true about new STP?
(a) Pressure = 1 bar
(b) Pressure = 1 atm
(c) 1 mol = 22.4 L
(d) 1 mol = 22.7 L

8. Standard melting point of water is
(a) 0°C (b) –273 K
(c) 32 F (d) 273 K

Numerical Value Questions

All these questions have a Numerical value as their answer, solve the questions and write your answer.

1. The radius of a hydrogen atom is about 0.37 Å, and the average radius of the earth's orbit around the sun is about 1.5×10^8 km. The ratio of the average radius of the earth's orbit to the radius of hydrogen atom is ...... $\times 10^{21}$.

2. van't Hoff isochore equation showing variation of log K_p with temperature T is

$$\log_{10} K_p = -\frac{\Delta H^\circ}{2.303\,RT} + \text{constant}$$

If graph between $\log_{10} K_p$ and T^{-1} gives a straight line of slope 6.04×10^3 K, than ΔH° is ....

3. The density of the lightest metal, lithium (Li), is 5.34×10^2 kg / m^3. The density in g/cm^3 is ....

4. Cesium atoms are the largest naturally occurring atoms. The radius of a cesium atom is 2.62 Å. ...... $\times 10^7$ cesium atoms would have to be laid side by side to give a row of cesium atoms 1.00 inch long? Assume that the atoms are spherical ......

5. On the Reaumur scale, water freezes at 0°R and boils at 80°R. What is the boiling point of mercury on this scale if it boils at 356.6°C?

6. What is the value of x

Given, $\log x = -\dfrac{(3.762 + 0.012)}{(8 \times 10^4)}$

7. An average adult has 5.2 L of blood. The volume is ...... $\times 10^{-3}$ m^3.

8. How many calories are present in 5 joule?

Comprehension Based Questions

In these questions, a passage has been given followed by questions based on it. You have to answer the questions based on the passage given.

***Passage* 1** One cubic millimeter of oil is spread on the surface of water so that the oil film has an area of 1 square metre.

Answer the following questions.

1. Thickness of the film in Å unit is
(a) 1 Å (b) 10 Å (c) 100 Å (d) 0.1 Å

2. How much area in square meters will one litre of point cover of it is brushed out to a uniform thickness of 100 microns?
(a) 10 m^2 (b) 1 m^2 (c) 0.1 m^2 (d) 0.01 m^2

***Passage* 2** *Read the following passage and answer the questions at the end of it.*

It is inconvenient to be limited to decimal representations of numbers. In chemistry, very large and very small numbers are commonly used.

The number of atoms is about 12 grams (g) of carbon is represented by 6 followed by 23 zeros. Atoms typically have dimensions of parts of nanometers, *i.e.*, 10 decimal places. A far more practical method of representation is called *scientific* or *exponential notation.*

A number expressed in scientific notation is a number between 1 and 10 which is then multiplied by 10 raised to a whole number power.

1. The number of atom in 12 g of carbon is equal to

(a) $12\,N_0$ (b) $\frac{12}{N_0}$

(c) N_0 (d) $\frac{N_0}{12}$

2. The number between 1 and 10 indicated above is called

(a) coefficient (b) exponential factor

(c) logarithm (d) linear function

3. The factor of 10 raised to a whole number power is called

(a) coefficient (b) linear function

(c) logarithm (d) exponential

Matrix-Match Type

Given below are Matching Type Questions, with two columns (each having some items) each . Each item of Column I has to be matched with the items of Column II.

1. Match the physical quantity in Column I with SI unit in Column II.

	Column I (Physical quantity)		Column II (SI unit)
A.	Force	1.	$N\,m^{-2}$
B.	Energy	2.	$kg\,m^2s^{-3}$
C.	Pressure	3.	$J\,A^{-1}s^{-1}$
D.	Electric potential difference	4.	$kg\,m\,s^{-2}$
		5.	A s
		6.	$kg\,m^2s^{-2}$

2. Match the different unit value of energy in Column I with corresponding values in cals in Column II.

	Column I (Energy unit)	Column II (Equivalent value in cal)
A.	1 erg	1. 0.24
B.	1 L atm	2. 2.4×10^{-8}
C.	1 J	3. 24.4
D.	1 eV	4. 3.85×10^{-20}

3. Match the physical quantity in Column I with SI unit in Column II.

Column I (Physical quantity)		Column II (SI unit)
A. Frequency	1.	VA^{-1}
B. Power	2.	$N\,m^{-2}$
C. Electric charge	3.	$JA^{-1}s^{-1}$
D. Electric resistance	4.	s^{-1}
	5.	A s
	6.	$kg\,m^2s^{-3}$

4. Match the concentration form in Column I with unit in Column II.

	Column I		Column II
A.	Molality	1.	$mol\,dm^{-3}$
B.	Molarity	2.	$mol\,kg^{-1}$
C.	Mole fraction	3.	$kg\,dm^{-3}$
D.	Density	4.	unitless

5. Second order rate constant k is given by

$$k = \frac{1}{t}\left[\frac{1}{a-x} - \frac{1}{a}\right]$$

Graphically

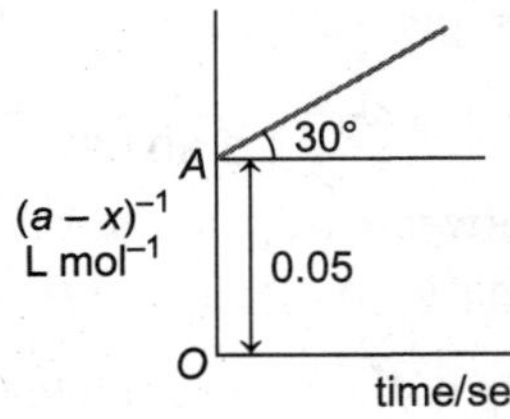

Match the kinetic parameter in Column I with the values obtained from graph in Column II.

	Column I		Column II
A.	k ($L\,mol^{-1}\,s^{-1}$)	1.	230.92
B.	a ($mol\,L^{-1}$)	2.	0.0866
C.	rate at start ($mol\,L^{-1}\,s^{-1}$)	3.	0.5773
D.	half-life (sec)	4.	20.0

Single Integer Answer Questions

Answer of these questions is a single digit lying between 0 to 9.

1. Prefix tera X prefix nano $= 10^x$
   The value of x is ....
2. How many significant figures are there in 0.00409100?
3. $5 \text{ pm} = 5 \times 10^{-x}$ nm
   The value of x is ....
4. Density of alcohol is 0.8 g/mL. The weight of 5 mL of alcohol is ....
5. In how many significant figures, answer of the following calculation will be expressed? 0.58×324.65
6. How many kJ are in 2.58×10^{-3} kW hour?
7. How many watts are contained in 5.362×10^{-3} horse power?
8. Radioactivity is measured in the unit of curie, Rutherford. (Ru)
   $$1 \text{ Ru} = 1 \times 10^x \text{ dps.}$$
   What is the value of x?

Answers

Objective Questions Type I [Only one correct option]

1. (d)	2. (c)	3. (a)	4. (a)	5. (b)	6. (a)	7. (c)	8. (b)	9. (b)	10. (d)
11. (d)	12. (b)	13. (c)	14. (a)	15. (c)	16. (a)	17. (d)	18. (c)	19. (d)	20. (a)
21. (c)	22. (a)	23. (d)	24. (d)	25. (c)	26. (a)	27. (a)	28. (b)	29. (c)	30. (d)
31. (c)	32. (b)	33. (a)	34. (c)	35. (a)	36. (b)	37. (d)	38. (d)	39. (b)	40. (a)
41. (c)	42. (b)	43. (c)	44. (d)	45. (a)	46. (b)	47. (d)	48. (c)	49. (c)	50. (a)
51. (c)	52. (b)	53. (d)	54. (a)	55. (a)	56. (b)	57. (c)	58. (d)	59. (d)	60. (c)
61. (b)	62. (c)	63. (d)	64. (b)	65. (b)	66. (c)	67. (a)	68. (b)	69. (d)	70. (c)

Objective Questions Type II [One or more than one correct option(s)]

1. (a, b, d)	2. (a, b)	3. (a, b)	4. (b, c, d)	5. (a, b, c)
6. (a, b)	7. (a, d)	8. (a, c, d)		

Numerical Value Questions

1. 4.054	2. 115.65 kJ mol^{-1}	3. 0.534 g/cm^3	4. $n = 4.85$	5. 285.28 R
6. 0.99989	7. 5.2	8. 1.2		

Comprehension Based Questions

Example 1 – 1. (a) 2. (a)
Example 3 – 1. (c) 2. (a) 3. (d)

Matrix-Match Type

1. A → (4); B → (6); C → (1); D → (3);
2. A → (2); B → (3); C → (1); D → (4)
3. A → (4); B → (6); C → (5); D → (1);
4. A → (2); B → (1); C → (4); D → (3)
5. A → (3); B → (4); C → (1); D → (2);

Single Integer Answer Questions

1. (2)	2. (6)	3. (3)	4. (4)	5. (2)	6. (9)	7. (4)	8. (6)

Solutions

Objective Questions Type I [Only one correct option]

4. (*a*) 17.675 ← This is last digit. ↑ This is odd number thus 7 rounded off to 8

5. (*b*) 20.665 ← This is last digit ↑ This is even number thus no change in 6

7. (*c*) Least value of SF is one, thus final result is reported in one SF.

11. (*d*) Result is to be reported in $m\ s^{-1}$ (SI unit)

$R = 8.3143\ J\ mol^{-}\ K^{-1},\ T = 283\ K$

$m = 32\ g\ mol^{-1} = 32 \times 10^{-3}\ kg\ mol^{-1}$

12. (*b*)

$$E = E° - \frac{0.0591}{n} \log K$$

$$y = c - mx \quad \text{(equation for a straight line)}$$

Thus, given equation can be compared with standard equation.

When, $x = 0, y = c$ (+ve intercept on *y*-axis)

and when $y = 0, x = \frac{c}{m}$ (+ve intercept on *x*-axis)

As *x* increases, *mx* increases, thus $(c - mx)$ or *y* decreases.

Thus, on increasing $\log K$, *E* decreases

13. (*c*)

$$\text{Slope} = -m = -\frac{0.0591}{n}$$

$\therefore$ $$m = \frac{0.0591}{n}$$

Given, $$\text{slope} = x = \frac{0.0591}{n}$$

Thus, $$n = \frac{0.0591}{x}$$

14. (*a*)

$$\frac{dx}{dt} = k[A]^2$$

$$\frac{\text{conc (mol L}^{-1})}{\text{time (s)}} = k\ (\text{mol L}^{-1})^2$$

$$k = \text{L mol}^{-1}\ s^{-1}$$

15. (*c*)

$$\frac{x - 32}{180} = \frac{x}{100}$$

$$5(x - 32) = 9x$$

$$x = -40°$$

16. (*a*)

$$\frac{10.5\ g}{cm^3} = \frac{10.5 \times 10^{-3}\ kg}{10^{-6}\ m^3} = 10.5 \times 10^3\ kg\ m^{-3}$$

$$= 1.05 \times 10^4\ kg\ m^{-3}$$

17. (*d*) $74\ pm = 74 \times 10^{-12}\ m = 7.4 \times 10^{-11}\ m$

Thus, (a) is true.

$$= 74 \times 10^{-3} \times 10^{-9}\ m$$

$$= 0.074 \times 10^{-9}\ m = 0.074\ nm$$

Thus, (b) is true

$$= 74 \times 10^{-2} \times 10^{-10}\ m$$

$$= 0.74 \times 10^{-10}\ m = 0.74Å$$

Thus, (c) is true.

18. (c)

$$\frac{F - 32}{180} = \frac{C}{100}$$

or $$\frac{-452 - 32}{9} = \frac{C}{5}$$

$$C = -268.888 = -269°C$$

20. (*a*) (a) $\frac{1\ MeV}{1\ GeV} = \frac{10^6\ eV}{10^9\ eV} = 10^{-3}$. Thus, false

(*b*) $\frac{1\ Tm}{1\ Gm} = \frac{10^{12}\ m}{10^9\ m} = 10^3$. Thus, false

(*c*) $\frac{1\ dm}{1\ mm} = \frac{10^{-1}\ m}{10^{-3}\ m} = 10^2$. Thus, true

22. (*a*) (a) $100\ Tm = 10^{14}\ m$ (*b*) $1000\ Gm = 10^{12}\ m$

(*c*) $10^4\ Mm = 10^{10}\ m$ (*d*) $10^6\ nm = 10^{-3}\ m$

25. (*d*) (a) pico $(10^{-12}) \times 10^3 = 10^{-9}$ (nano)

(*b*) nano $(10^{-9}) \times 10^3 = 10^{-6}$ (micro)

(*c*) femto $(10^{-15}) \times 10^3 = 10^{-12}$ (pico)

44. (*d*) Since, $OP = 0.01\ mol^{-1}$, hence

$$\frac{1}{a} = 0.01\ mol^{-1}$$

$\therefore$ $$a = 100\ mol$$

45. (*a*) This represents a straight line $y = c - mx$

46. (*b*)

$$\left(\frac{dx}{dt}\right) = k\ [A]^n$$

$\therefore$ $$\log\left(\frac{dx}{dt}\right) = n \log [A] + \log k$$

$$y = mx + c$$

Hence, $m\ (\text{slope}) = n = \tan 45° = 1$

$\therefore$ $n = 1$

47. (*d*) Take the values in SI (MKS) unit

$$R = 8.314\ J\ mol^{-1}\ K^{-1}$$

$$M(H_2) = 2\ g\ mol^{-1}$$

$$= 2 \times 10^{-3}\ kg\ mol^{-1}$$

49. (*c*)

$$R = 0.0821\ L\ atm\ mol^{-1}\ K^{-1}$$

$$= 8.314 \times 10^7\ ergs\ mol^{-1}\ K^{-1}$$

$$= 8.314\ J\ mol^{-1}\ K^{-1}$$

$$= 0.002\ kcal\ mol^{-1}\ K^{-1}$$

$$= x\ \text{(assume)}$$

$\therefore$ $$1\ L\ atm = \frac{x}{0.0821} = A$$

$$1\ erg = \frac{x}{8.314 \times 10^7} = B$$

$$1\ J = \frac{x}{8.314} = C$$

$$1\ kcal = \frac{x}{0.002} = D$$

Thus, $B < C < A < D$,

02

Atomic Structure

Objective Questions Type I [Only one correct option]

In each of the questions below, four choices are given of which only one is correct.

1. If m_n is the mass of the neutron and m_e that of the electron then $\frac{m_n}{m_e}$ is

(a) 1836 (b) 1839 (c) 1 (d) ∞

2. The wave number of the spectral line in the emission spectrum of hydrogen will be equal to 8/9 times the Rydberg's constant if the electron jumps from

(a) $n = 3$ to $n = 1$ (b) $n = 10$ to $n = 1$
(c) $n = 9$ to $n = 1$ (d) $n = 2$ to $n = 1$

3. Some sub-nuclear particles are
I. antiproton; II. μ-meson; III. π-meson; IV. neutrino; V. positron.
Increasing order of year of discovery is (starting from the earliest)

(a) V < II < III < I < IV (b) V < IV < III < II < I
(c) I < II < III < IV < V (d) V < III < IV < II < I

4. Mass of proton is

(a) 1.0000 amu (b) 1.0073 amu
(c) 1.0087 amu (d) 5.486×10^{-4} amu

5. Select the correct statement based on Rutherford's model.

(a) Most of the space in an atom between the nucleus and the revolving electron is empty
(b) Electrons are called planetary electrons
(c) Protons give positive charge on the nucleus but nuclear mass is determined by proton and neutron both
(d) All of the above are correct statements

6. Which has maximum spin?

(a) Electron (b) Proton
(c) Neutron (d) Equal spin

7. Which is heaviest compared to that of electron?

(a) π-meson (b) μ-meson
(c) Neutrino (d) Positron

8. Ratio of radius of atom to that of nucleus is of the order of

(a) 10^{-10} (b) 10^{-15}
(c) 10^{5} (d) 10^{-5}

9. The application of electric and magnetic fields deflected certain rays in the discharge tube towards cathode. This proved that

(a) electrons are negatively charged particles
(b) protons are positively charged particles
(c) neutrons are neutral particles
(d) None of the above statements is true

10. Mass of the proton is equal to that of

(a) positron (b) neutrino
(c) pion (d) anti-proton

11. A near UV photon of 300 nm is absorbed by a gas and then re-emitted as two photons. One photon is red with the wavelength 760 nm. Hence, wavelength of the second photon is

(a) 460 nm (b) 1060 nm
(c) 496 nm (d) 300 nm

12. Arrange the following metal complex / compounds in the increasing order of spin only magnetic moment. Presume all the three, high spin system.

(Atomic numbers Ce = 58, Gd = 64 and Eu = 63.)

(*A*) $(NH_4)_2[Ce(NO_3)_6]$ (*B*) $Gd(NO_3)_3$
(*C*) $Eu(NO_3)_3$

[JEE Main 2021, March]

(a) (*B*) < (*A*) < (*C*) (b) (*C*) < (*A*) < (*B*)
(c) (*A*) < (*B*) < (*C*) (d) (*A*) < (*C*) < (*B*)

13. Select the correct statement.
(a) Visible light consists of electromagnetic waves of oscillating electric and magnetic fields
(b) In vacuum, types of all electromagnetic radiation travel at the same speed
(c) Both (a) and (b) are correct statements
(d) None of the above is correct statement

14. Select the correct statement.
(a) The ideal body, which emits and absorbs all frequencies, is called a black body
(b) The exact frequency distribution of the emitted radiation from a black body depends upon its temperature
(c) The radiation emitted goes from a lower frequency to a higher frequency as the temperature increases
(d) All of the above are correct statements

15. A wavelength of 400 nm corresponds to
(a) frequency $(\nu) = 7.5 \times 10^{14}$ Hz
(b) wave number $(\bar{\nu}) = 2.5 \times 10^{6}\ m^{-1}$
(c) momentum $(mv) = 1.66 \times 10^{-27}\ kg\ m\ s^{-1}$
(d) All of the above are correct values

16. Threshold energy is also called
(a) work function (b) potential energy (PE)
(c) kinetic energy (KE) (d) sum of (PE) and (KE)

17. If in Moseley's equation, given constants $a = b = 1$, then for the frequency $\nu = 400\ s^{-1}$, element will be
(a) K (b) Na (c) Rb (d) Cs

18. Frequency of matter wave is equal to
(a) (KE)/2 h (b) 2 (KE)/h (c) (KE)/h (d) λ

19. There is a transition from $n = 1$ to $n = 2$ and then $n = 2$ to $n = 3$, then
(a) ΔE values as well as frequency are additive
(b) wavelength as well as frequency are additive
(c) ΔE values as well as wavelength are additive
(d) all of the parameters, (ΔE, frequency and wavelength) are additive.

20. Number of waves made by a Bohr electron in one complete revolution in its fourth orbit is
(a) 2 (b) 3 (c) 4 (d) ∞

21. An electron in H-atom in its ground state absorbs 1.50 times as much as energy as the minimum required for its escape (13.6 eV) from the atom. Thus KE given to emitted electron is
(a) 13.6 eV (b) 20.4 eV
(c) 34.0 eV (d) 6.8 eV

22. Which of the following electronic transitions requires that the greatest quantity of energy be absorbed by a hydrogen atom?
(a) $n = 1$ to $n = 2$ (b) $n = 2$ to $n = 4$
(c) $n = 3$ to $n = 6$ (d) $n = 1$ to $n = \infty$

23. Wave number of a spectral line for a given transition is $x\ cm^{-1}$ for He^{+}, then its value for Be^{3+} (isoelectronic of He^{+}) for same transition is
(a) $x\ cm^{-1}$ (b) $4x\ cm^{-1}$
(c) $\frac{x}{4}\ cm^{-1}$ (d) $2x\ cm^{-1}$

24. Electron falls from seventh energy level and lower energy level to give bands in Paschen series. Total number of bands obtained are
(a) 4 (b) 3
(c) 2 (d) 1

25. The potential energy of an electron in the first Bohr orbit in the He^{+} ion is
(a) −13.6 eV (b) −27.2 eV
(c) −54.4 eV (d) − 108.8 eV

26. **'Hartree'** is the atomic unit of energy and is equal to
(a) − 13.6 eV $atom^{-1}$
(b) − 27.12 eV $atom^{-1}$
(c) + 13.6 eV $atom^{-1}$
(d) + 27.12 eV $atom^{-1}$

27. R_H (Rydberg constant) is $x\ m^{-1}$ for H-atom. For He^{+} ion corresponding value for this constant is
(a) $100\ x\ cm^{-1}$ (b) $400\ x\ cm^{-1}$
(c) $4x\ cm^{-1}$ (d) $0.04\ x\ cm^{-1}$

28. A **continuum** in spectrum is observed due to the following.
(a) once an electron is completely free from the nucleus, it is no longer restricted to quantised discrete energy states
(b) electron takes up continuously the ordinary kinetic energy corresponding to its speed in free space
(c) Both the reasons are correct
(d) None of the two reasons are correct.

29. Which of the pair of orbitals have electronic density along the axis?
(a) d_{xz}, d_{yz} (b) $d_{x^2-y^2}, d_{z^2}$
(c) d_{xy}, d_{yz} (d) d_{xy}, d_{z^2}

30. Given this set of quantum numbers for a multi-electron atom 2, 0, 0, $\frac{1}{2}$ and 2, 0, 0, $-\frac{1}{2}$. What is the next higher allowed set of n and l quantum numbers for this atom in its ground state?
(a) $n = 2, l = 0$ (b) $n = 2, l = 1$
(c) $n = 3, l = 0$ (d) $n = 3, l = 1$

31. The number of subshells associated with $n = 4$ and $m = -2$ quantum numbers is **[JEE Main 2020, Sep.]**
(a) 8 (b) 2
(c) 16 (d) 4

32. In a suborbit, there are three radial nodes. This suborbit can be
(a) $4s$ or $5p$
(b) $4d$ or $5p$
(c) $4s$ or $4p$
(d) $3s$ or $3p$

33. Number of nodal planes in $4p$ suborbit will be
(a) 0
(b) 1
(c) 2
(d) 3

34. Consider the hypothetical situation where the azimuthal quantum number, l takes values 0, 1, 2, ... $n+1$, where n is the principle quantum number. Then, the element with atomic number **[JEE Main 2020, Sep.]**
(a) 8 is the first noble gas
(b) 13 has a half-filled valence subshell
(c) 9 is the first alkali metal
(d) 6 has a $2p$-valence subshell

35. Which of the quantum numbers determines orientation of the orbital?
(a) n
(b) l
(c) m_l
(d) m_s

36. Consider the following statements.
I. The spin angular momentum of the electron is constant and cannot be changed.
II. For spin $= +\frac{1}{2}$, spin angular momentum is $\frac{\sqrt{3}h}{4\pi}$.
III. Spin angular momentum is a vector quantity and can have only two orientations relative to a chosen axis.

Of these the correct statements are
(a) I, II
(b) II, III
(c) I, III
(d) I, II, III

37. Select the correct statement.
(a) m_s determines orientation of the spin of the electron
(b) An electron spin angular momentum vector of length $\frac{\sqrt{3}}{2}$ units can take only two orientations with respect to a specified axis
(c) Both the statements are correct
(d) None of the above statements is correct

38. If angular momentum quantum number can take value of n also (in addition to other possible values) then total number of electrons in first orbit would have been
(a) 2
(b) 6
(c) 8
(d) 10

39. Electrons in various degenerate orbitals of a sub-shell can be filled (by changing spins etc.) by following arrangements,

$$\frac{x!}{(x-y)!\,y!}$$

where, $x = 2 \times$ number of orbitals
$y =$ number of electrons
A p^2-configuration can be written as many as
(a) 15 ways
(b) 6 ways
(c) 45 ways
(d) 10 ways

40. The number of orbitals associated with quantum numbers $n = 5$, $m_s = +\frac{1}{2}$ is **[JEE Main 2020, Jan.]**
(a) 25
(b) 50
(c) 15
(d) 11

41. If azimuthal quantum number could have value of n also (in addition to normal value), then EC of V($Z = 23$) would have been
(a) $1s^2, 2s^2, 2p^6, 3s^2, 3p^6, 4s^2, 3d^3$
(b) $1s^2, 1p^6, 2s^2, 2p^6, 2d^7$
(c) $1s^2, 1p^6, 2s^2, 2p^6, 3s^2, 2d^5$
(d) $1s^2, 1p^6, 2s^2, 2p^6, 3s^1, 2d^6$

42. Under the condition given above, magnetic moment of Ti ($Z = 22$) would have been
(a) $\sqrt{24}$ BM
(b) $\sqrt{48}$ BM
(c) $\sqrt{35}$ BM
(d) 0

43. $1s^2\,2s^2\,2p^6$ represents
(a) macroscopic property of an element
(b) microscopic property of an element
(c) Both (a) and (b)
(d) None of the above

44. Which of the following species contains only three electrons in valence shell?

Li, B, N, F, Al

(a) Li, B
(b) B, N
(c) B, Al
(d) N

45. The following elements are in the fourth period of the periodic table

Ca V Co Zn As

of those listed the ones that have unpaired electrons in the ground state electronic configuration are
(a) Ca, V and Co
(b) V, Co and Zn
(c) Ca, Zn and As
(d) V, Co and As

46. I. $n = 3, l = 2, m_l = -2$
II. $n = 3, l = 1, m_l = 0$
III. $n = 3, l = 0, m_l = -1$
IV. $n = 3, l = 2, m_l = 0$
V. $n = 3, l = 3, m_l = -2$

Of these quantum state designations which does not describe an allowed state for an electron in an atom?
(a) I and IV
(b) III and V
(c) II and V
(d) IV and V

47. What is the spin-only magnetic moment value (BM) of a divalent metal ion with atomic number 25, in it's aqueous solution? **[JEE Main 2021, March]**

(a) 5.92 (b) 5.0
(c) Zero (d) 5.26

48. In some regions of space around nucleus $\psi^2 = 0$; this region is called

(a) nucleus (b) spherical nodes
(c) orbital (d) orbit

49. Highest electron probability in 1*s* orbital exists at a point in the vicinity of

(a) spherical nodes (b) circumference
(c) nucleus (d) plane

50. Consider the following figures *A* and *B* indicating distribution of charge density (electron probability ψ^2) with distance *r*.

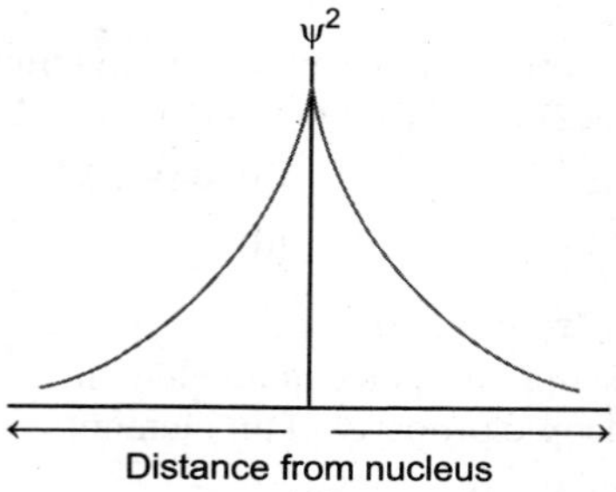

(*A*)

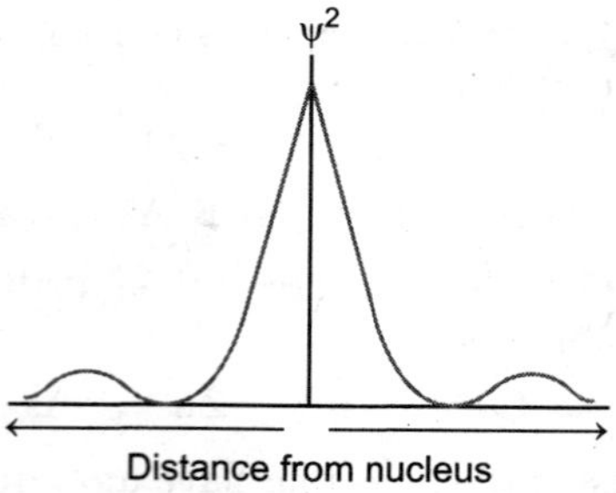

(*B*)

Select the correct statement (*s*).

(a) *A* and *B* both are for 1 *s* (b) *A* and *B* both are for 2*s*
(c) *A* is for 2 *s*, *B* is for 1 *s* (d) *A* is for 1*s*, *B* is for 2*s*

51. If there are total of $(n+1)$ nodes in a string of length l, then correct relationship is

(a) $l = \frac{n\lambda}{2}$ (b) $l = (n+1)\frac{\lambda}{2}$
(c) $l = \frac{(n-1)\lambda}{2}$ (d) $l = 2n\lambda$

52. Select the correct statement.

(a) $|\psi|^2$ measures the electron probability density at a point in an atom
(b) ψ and $|\psi|^2$ vary as a function of the three coordinates *r* (radial part), θ and ϕ (angular part)
(c) Both (a) and (b) are correct
(d) None of the above is correct

53. The plot of the radial wave function *R* as a function of distance *r* of the electron from the nucleus for 2*p*-orbital is

(a) 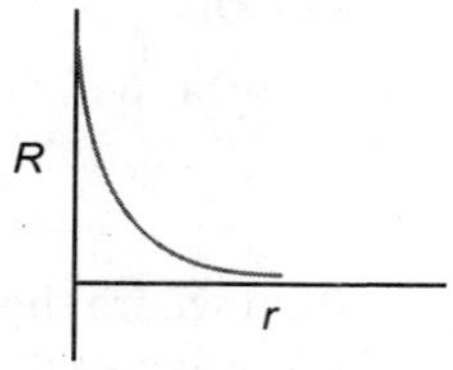

(b) 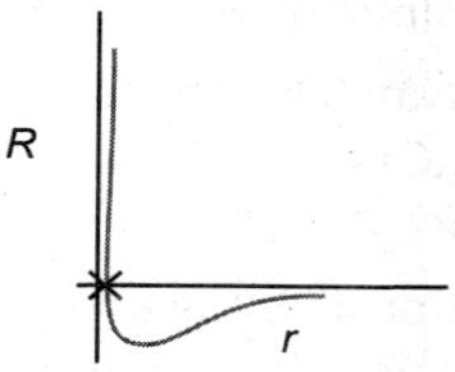

(c) 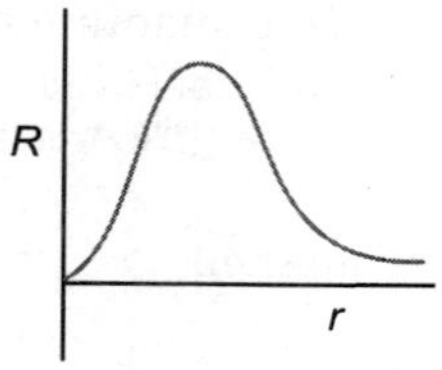

(d) 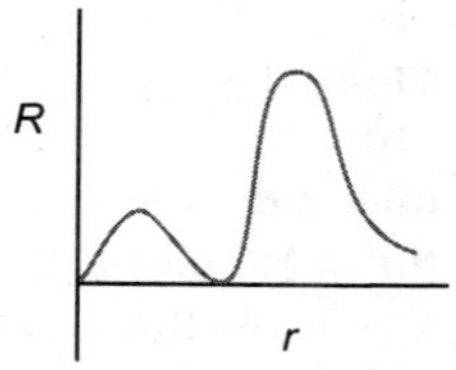

54. The plot of the radial density function $4\pi^2 R^2$ as a function of distance *r* of the electron from the nucleus for 2*s*-orbital is [given in questions (53) above]

55. The plot of the radial probability density R^2 as a function *r* for 1*s*-orbital is [given in question (53) above]

56. Select the correct alternate.

(a) Radial probability function gives the probability of finding the electron at a distance *r* from the nucleus
(b) The maximum in the curve corresponds to the distance at which the probability of finding the electron is maximum
(c) This distance is called the radius of maximum probability (52.9 pm for hydrogen)
(d) All the above statements are correct statements

57. A certain orbital has no angular nodes and two radial nodes. The orbital is

(a) 2 s (b) 3 s (c) 3 *p* (d) 2 *p*

58. The ratio of the energy of the electron in ground state of hydrogen to the electron in first excited state of Be^{3+} is **[JEE Main 2021, March]**

(a) 1 : 4 (b) 1 : 8 (c) 1 : 16 (d) 16 : 1

59. The number of *d*-electrons in Fe^{2+} $(Z = 26)$ is not equal to that of

(a) *p*-electrons in Ne $(Z = 10)$
(b) *s*-electrons in Mg $(Z = 12)$
(c) *d*-electrons in Fe $(Z = 26)$
(d) *p*-electrons in Cl $(Z = 17)$

60. The orbital angular momentum of an electron in 2*s* orbital is

(a) $+\frac{1}{2}\frac{h}{2\pi}$ (b) zero
(c) $\frac{h}{2\pi}$ (d) $\sqrt{2}\frac{h}{2\pi}$

61. Bohr model can explain the spectrum of
(a) the hydrogen atom only
(b) an atom or ion having one electron only
(c) the hydrogen molecule only
(d) the sodium atom only

62. Of the following, radiation with maximum wavelength is
(a) UV (b) Radiowave
(c) X-ray (d) IR

63. Magnetic moment of X^{n+} $(Z = 26)$ is $\sqrt{24}$ BM. Hence, number of unpaired electrons and value of n respectively are
(a) 4, 2 (b) 2, 4 (c) 3, 1 (d) 0, 2

64. Zeeman effect explains splitting of lines in
(a) magnetic field (b) electric field
(c) Both (a) and (b) (d) None of these

65. In the presence of magnetic field d-sub-orbit is
(a) 5-fold degenerate (b) 3-fold degenerate
(c) 7-fold degenerate (d) non-degenerate

66. $\frac{e}{m}$ ratio was determined by
(a) J.J. Thomson (b) Dalton
(c) Chadwick (d) Goldstein

67. Size of the nucleus is
(a) 10^{-13} cm (b) 10^{-10} m
(c) 10^{-1} nm (d) All are correct

68. Visible spectrum extends from 400 nm (violet) to red (750 nm). Hence, frequency ratio is
(a) 4/15 (b) 8/15
(c) 15/8 (d) None of these

69. Which of the following arrangements of electrons is mostly likely to be stable?

	3d	4s
(a)	↑ ↑ ↑ ↑ ↑	↑
(b)	⇅ ↑ ↑ ↑ ↑	
(c)	↑ ↑ ↑ ↑ ↑	↑
(d)	↑ ↑ ↑ ↑	⇅

70. Which of the following orbitals has/have zero probability of finding the electron in xy plane?
(a) p_z (b) d_{yz} (c) d_{zx} (d) p_x

71. How fast is an electron moving if it has a wavelength equal to the distance it travels in one second?
(a) $\sqrt{\frac{h}{m}}$ (b) $\sqrt{\frac{m}{h}}$ (c) $\sqrt{\frac{h}{p}}$ (d) $\sqrt{\frac{h}{2\,(KE)}}$

72. Each orbital has a nodal plane. Which of the following statements about nodal planes is not true?
(a) A plane on which there is zero probability that the electron will be found
(b) A plane on which there is maximum probability that the electron will be found
(c) Both (a) and (b)
(d) None of the above

73. The figure that is not a direct manifestation of the quantum nature of atoms is **[JEE Main 2020, Sep.]**

(a)
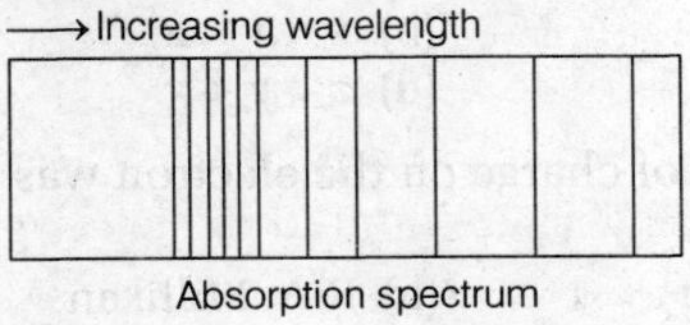

(b)
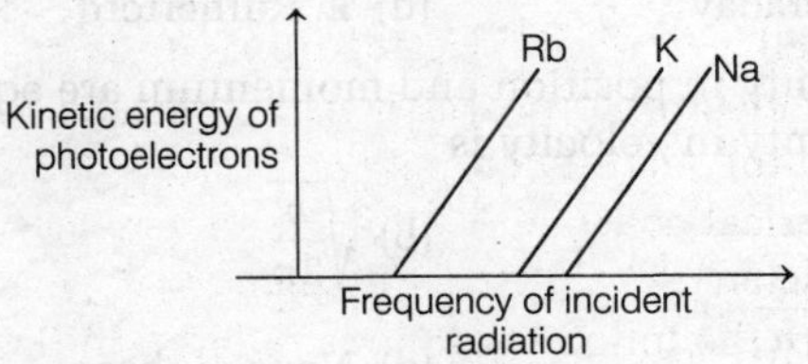

(c)
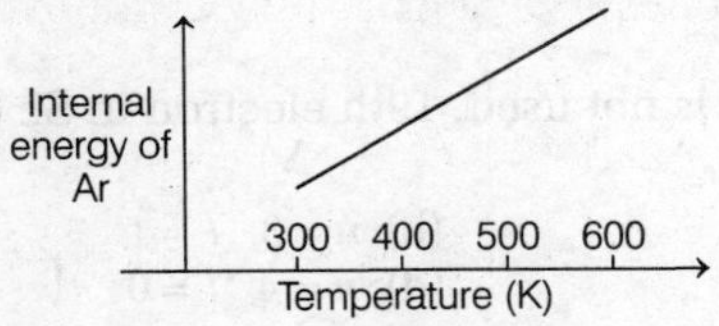

(d)
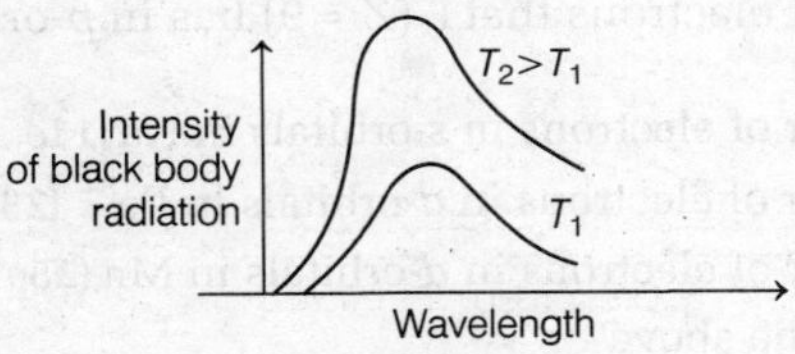

74. Energy of an electron is given by
$$E = -2.178 \times 10^{-18}\ \text{J}\left(\frac{Z^2}{n^2}\right).$$
Wavelength of light required to excite an electron in an hydrogen atom from level $n = 1$ to $n = 2$ will be ($h = 6.62 \times 10^{-34}$ Js and $c = 3.0 \times 10^8\ \text{ms}^{-1}$) **[JEE Main 2013]**
(a) 1.214×10^{-7} m (b) 2.816×10^{-7} m
(c) 6.500×10^{-7} m (d) 8.500×10^{-7} m

75. Which has [Ar] $3d^5 4s^1$ configuration each having 24 e?
(a) Cr (b) Mn^+
(c) Both (a) and (b) (d) None of these

76. Millikan's oil drop experiment and diffraction effect showed respectively
(a) wave nature and particle nature
(b) particle and wave nature
(c) Millikan showed both the nature
(d) diffraction showed both the nature

77. To whom was awarded Nobel Prize in the field of quantum mechanics?
(a) Einstein
(b) Planck
(c) Heisenberg
(d) Schrödinger

78. Magnetic moments of V ($Z = 23$), Cr ($Z = 24$) and Mn ($Z = 25$) are x, y, z. Hence,
(a) $x = y = z$ (b) $x < y < z$
(c) $x < z < y$ (d) $z < y < x$

79. Absolute value of charge on the electron was determined by
(a) J.J. Thomson (b) R.A. Millikan
(c) M. Faraday (d) E. Rutherford

80. Uncertainty in position and momentum are equal. Uncertainty in velocity is
(a) $\sqrt{\frac{h}{\pi}}$ (b) $\sqrt{\frac{h}{2\pi}}$
(c) $\frac{1}{2m}\sqrt{\frac{h}{\pi}}$ (d) None of these

81. If Aufbau rule is not used, 19th electron in Sc ($Z = 21$) will have
(a) $n = 3,\ l = 0$ (b) $n = 3,\ l = 1$
(c) $n = 3,\ l = 2$ (d) $n = 4,\ l = 0$

82. Number of electrons that F ($Z = 9$) has in p-orbitals is equal to
(a) number of electrons in s-orbitals in Na ($11e^-$)
(b) number of electrons in d-orbitals in Fe^{3+} ($23e^-$)
(c) number of electrons in d-orbitals in Mn ($25e^-$)
(d) All of the above

83. The kinetic energy of an electron in the second Bohr orbit of a hydrogen atom is [a_0 is Bohr's radius] **[IIT JEE 2012]**
(a) $\frac{h^2}{4\pi^2 m a_0^2}$ (b) $\frac{h^2}{16\pi^2 m a_0^2}$
(c) $\frac{h^2}{32\pi^2 m a_0^2}$ (d) $\frac{h^2}{64\pi^2 m a_0^2}$

84. The first use of quantum theory to explain the structure of atom was made by
(a) Heisenberg (b) Bohr
(c) Planck (d) Einstein

85. If each orbital can hold a maximum of 3 electrons, the number of elements in 4th period of periodic table (long form) is
(a) 48 (b) 54 (c) 27 (d) 36

86. If the radius of first Bohr orbit is x, then de-Broglie wavelength of electron in 3rd orbit is nearly
(a) $2\pi x$ (b) $6\pi x$ (c) $9x$ (d) $\frac{x}{3}$

87. If the shortest wavelength of H atom in Lyman series is x, then longest wavelength in Balmer series of He^+ is
(a) $\frac{9x}{5}$ (b) $\frac{36x}{5}$
(c) $\frac{x}{4}$ (d) $\frac{5x}{9}$

88. The shortest wavelength of H atom in the Lyman series is λ_1. The longest wavelength in the Balmer series of He^+ is **[JEE Main 2020, Sep.]**
(a) $\frac{36\lambda_1}{5}$ (b) $\frac{5\lambda_1}{9}$ (c) $\frac{9\lambda_1}{5}$ (d) $\frac{27\lambda_1}{5}$

89. The difference between the radii of 3rd and 4th orbits of Li^{2+} is ΔR_1. The difference between the radii of 3rd and 4th orbits of He^+ is ΔR_2. Ratio $\Delta R_1 : \Delta R_2$ is **[JEE Main 2020, Sep.]**
(a) 3 : 2 (b) 8 : 3 (c) 2 : 3 (d) 3 : 8

90. The allowed energies of a hydrogenic atom are determined solely by the principal quantum number. 'n', $E = \frac{-hcR}{n^2}$, $n = 1, 2, \ldots$, R Rydberg constant. Which of the following statements about R is/are true?
(a) Its numerical value is $1.09 \times 10^5\ \text{cm}^{-1}$
(b) It depends on Planck's constant (h)
(c) It depends on permittivity of open space (ε_0)
(d) All of the above

91. For the Balmer series in the spectrum of H atom, $\bar{v} = R_H \left\{\frac{1}{n_1^2} - \frac{1}{n_2^2}\right\}$, the correct statements among (I) to (IV) are
(I) As wavelength decreases, the lines in the series converge
(II) The integer n_1 is equal to 2
(III) The lines of longest wavelength corresponds to $n_2 = 3$
(IV) The ionisation energy of hydrogen can be calculated from wave number of these lines
[JEE Main 2020, Jan.]
(a) I, II, IV (b) II, III, IV (c) I, III, IV (d) I, II, III

92. Hund's rule deals with the distribution of electrons in
(a) a quantum shell (b) an orbit
(c) an orbital (d) degenerate orbitals

93. Which describes orbital?
(a) ψ (b) ψ^2
(c) $|\psi^2|\ \psi$ (d) None of these

94. s-orbital is spherically symmetrical hence
(a) it is directional independent
(b) angular dependent
(c) Both (a) and (b)
(d) None of the above

95. In centro-symmetrical system, the orbital angular momentum, a measure of the momentum of a particle travelling around the nucleus, is quantised. Its magnitude is
(a) $\sqrt{l(l+1)}\,\frac{h}{2\pi}$ (b) $\sqrt{l(l-1)}\,\frac{h}{2\pi}$
(c) $\sqrt{S(S+1)}\,\frac{h}{2\pi}$ (d) $\sqrt{S(S-1)}\,\frac{h}{2\pi}$

96. The correct set of four quantum numbers for the valence electron of rubidium ($Z = 37$) is
(a) $n = 5, l = 0, m = 0, m_s = +\frac{1}{2}$
(b) $n = 5, l = 1, m = 0, m_s = +\frac{1}{2}$
(c) $n = 5, l = 1, m = 1, m_s = +\frac{1}{2}$
(d) $n = 6, l = 0, m = 0, m_s = +\frac{1}{2}$

97. If n and l are respectively the principal and azimuthal quantum numbers, then the expression for calculating the total number of electrons in any energy level is
(a) $\sum_{l=1}^{l=n} 2(2l+1)$ (b) $\sum_{l=1}^{l=n-1} 2(2l+1)$
(c) $\sum_{l=0}^{l=n+1} 2(2l+1)$ (d) $\sum_{l=0}^{l=n-1} 2(2l+1)$

98. Which one of the following orbitals is nearest to the nucleus?
(a) $4f$ (b) $5d$ (c) $6s$ (d) $7p$

99. Energy equivalent of 10.00 cm^{-1} is
(a) 2.0×10^{-22} J per photon
(b) 28.6×10^{-3} kcal mol^{-1} photon
(c) 12.0×10^{-2} kJ mol^{-1} photon
(d) All of the above are correct

100. Which of the following relates to light as wave motion?
(a) Diffraction (b) Interference
(c) Both (a) and (b) (d) None of these

101. When a certain metal was irradiated with light of frequency 3.2×10^{16} Hz, photoelectrons emitted had twice the kinetic energy as did photoelectrons emitted when the same metal was irradiated with light of frequency 2.0×10^{16} Hz. Hence, threshold frequency is
(a) 0.8×10^{15} Hz (b) 8.0×10^{15} Hz
(c) 0.8×10^{14} Hz (d) 6.4×10^{16} Hz

102. An orbital for which the electron probability distribution is spherically symmetric about the nucleus is
(a) $2p$ (b) $3s$ (c) $3p$ (d) $3d$

103. If travelling at equal speeds, the longest wavelength of the following matter waves is that for
(a) an electron (b) a proton
(c) a neutron (d) an alpha particle (He^{2+})

104. The ground state electronic configuration of Fe^{3+} is
(a) $[Ar] 3d^3 4s^2$ (b) $[Ar] 3d^6 4s^2$
(c) $[Ar] 3d^5$ (d) $[Ar] 3d^4 4s^1$

105. The atom with lowest atomic number that has a ground state electronic configuration of $(n-1)d^6 ns^2$ is in the
(a) 2nd period (b) 3rd period
(c) 4th period (d) 5th period

106. If there were three possibilities of electron spin, K (19) would be placed in
(a) s-block (b) p-block
(c) d-block (d) f-block

107. A particular electromagnetic radiation with wavelength 200 nm
(a) has a higher frequency than radiation with wavelength 400 nm
(b) is in the visible region of the electromagnetic spectrum
(c) has a greater speed in vacuum than does radiation of wavelength 400 nm
(d) has a greater energy content per photon than does radiation with wavelength 100 nm

108. Which of the following best describes the emission spectrum of atomic hydrogen?
(a) A discrete series of lines of equal intensity and equally spaced with respect to wavelength
(b) A series of only four lines
(c) A continuous emission of radiation of all frequencies
(d) Several discrete series of lines with both intensity and spacings between lines decreasing as the wavelength number increases within each series

109. Atomic emission spectra of an element cannot be used to
(a) identify the element
(b) determine the mass number of the nucleus of the atom
(c) measure the difference in energy between pairs of stationary states of the atom
(d) calculate the ionisation energy of the atom

110. The ionisation energy of gaseous Na atoms is 495.80 kJ mol^{-1}. The lowest possible frequency of light that can ionise a Na atom is
(a) 4.76×10^{14} s^{-1}
(b) 7.50×10^{14} s^{-1}
(c) 1.24×10^{15} s^{-1}
(d) 3.15×10^{15} s^{-1}

111. The cathode-ray experiments carried out J.J. Thomson demonstrated that
(a) α-particles are the nuclei of He atoms
(b) the ratio of charge to mass for the particles of the cathode rays is constant if different gases are placed in the tube
(c) the mass of an atom is essentially all contained in its very small nucleus
(d) cathode rays are streams of negatively charged ions

112. If the electron in a hydrogen atom drops from the $n = 6$ to the $n = 4$ level, the radiation emitted is in which series of lines in the spectrum of atomic hydrogen?

(a) Lyman (b) Balmer
(c) Paschen (d) Brackett

113. A line with wave number 1.028×10^{-2} nm^{-1} is emitted in the spectrum of atomic hydrogen. In what region of the electromagnetic spectrum does this line occur?

(a) Far UV (b) Near UV
(c) Visible (d) Near IR

114. Which of the following statements about Millikan's oil drop experiment is true?

(a) When the electric field is turned on, all the oil-drops move towards the positively charged plate
(b) The charge on each oil-drop is the electronic charge
(c) In the absence of the electric field, the speed with which the drop falls depends only upon the acceleration of gravity
(d) Some oil-drops become positively charged and some become negatively charged after colliding with gaseous ions

115. The radius of the second Bohr orbit for hydrogen atom is (Planck's constant $(h) = 6.6262 \times 10^{-34}$ Js; mass of electron $= 9.1091 \times 10^{-31}$ kg ; charge of electron $(e) = 1.60210 \times 10^{-19}$ C; permitivity of vacuum $(\epsilon_0) = 8.854185 \times 10^{-12} kg^{-1} m^{-3} A^2$)

[JEE Main 2017 (Offline)]

(a) 1.65 Å (b) 4.76 Å (c) 0.529 Å (d) 2.12 Å

116. To move the electron in one H atom from the ground state to the second excited state, 12.084 eV are needed. How much energy is needed to cause 1 mole of H atoms to undergo this transition?

(a) 728 kJ (b) 984 kJ
(c) 1036 kJ (d) 1164 kJ

117. Which of the graphs shown below does not represent the relationship between incident light and the electron ejected from metal surface?

[JEE Main 2019, Jan.]

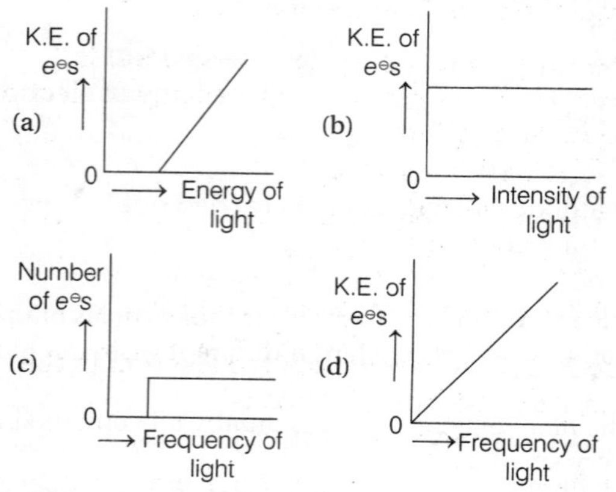

118. The amount of energy required to remove the electron from a Li^{2+} ion its ground state is how many times greater than the amount of energy needed to remove the electron from an H atom in its ground state?

(a) 2 (b) 9
(c) 4 (d) 6

119. A typical golf ball weighs 40.0 g. If it is moving with a velocity of 20.0 ms^{-1}, its de-Broglie wavelength is

(a) 1.66×10^{-34} nm (b) 8.28×10^{-32} nm
(c) 8.28×10^{-25} nm (d) 1.66×10^{-24} nm

120. What is the energy, in joules, of a photon of IR light with wavelength 4.0×10^3 nm?

(a) 5.0×10^{-20} (b) 7.5×10^{-20}
(c) 4.0×10^{-16} (d) 2.5×10^{-14}

121. The most intense line in the Brackett series of the spectrum of atomic hydrogen is the transition

(a) $n_2 = \infty \rightarrow n_1 = 1$
(b) $n_2 = 8 \rightarrow n_1 = 4$
(c) $n_2 = \infty \rightarrow n_1 = 4$
(d) $n_2 = 4 \rightarrow n_1 = 3$

122. Atomic unit of length is called ...... and denoted by ......

(a) Bohr, Å (b) Bohr, a_0
(c) Bohr, l (d) Einstein, a_0

123. Hamiltonia operator $\hat{\mathbf{H}}$ is the sum of two energy operators. These are

(a) mechanical and potential
(b) kinetic and mechanical
(c) kinetic and potential
(d) thermal and potential

124. Select the correct statement.

(a) Radial part is dependent on r and angular part is dependent on θ and ϕ
(b) Angular wave function '$\theta\phi$' depends only on l and m_l independent on n for a given type of orbital
(c) Both (a) and (b) are correct
(d) None of the above is correct

125. Energy for 7.25×10^{15} photons of 5.37×10^{14} s^{-1} frequency in Einstein unit is

(a) 1.20×10^{-8} (b) 2.58×10^{-3}
(c) 3.56×10^{-19} (d) 8.33×10^{7}

126. A black body is an object which is capable of

(a) emitting all frequencies of radiation uniformly
(b) absorbing all frequencies of radiation uniformly
(c) emitting and absorbing all frequencies of radiation uniformly
(d) emitting and absorbing all frequencies of radiation at random

127. Number of photons emitted by a 100 W (Js^{-1}) yellow lamp in 1.0 s is (λ of yellow light is 560 nm)
(a) 2.8×10^{20} (b) 2.8×10^{18}
(c) 1.1×10^{20} (d) 2.2×10^{20}

128. Time taken to produce 1 mole of the photons in above case is
(a) 40 min (b) 36 min
(c) 12 min (d) 340 min

129. The wavelength of a neutron with a translatory kinetic energy equal to kT at 300 K is
(a) 178 pm (b) 200 pm
(c) 17.8 pm (d) 20.0 pm

130. Speed of an electron of wavelength 3.0 cm is
(a) 2.43 m s^{-1} (b) 0.0243 m s^{-1}
(c) 24.3 m s^{-1} (d) 0.243 m s^{-1}

131. A laser used to read CDs emits red light of wavelength 700 nm. How many photons does it emit each second if its power is 1.0 W?
(a) $1.76 \times 10^{18} \text{ s}^{-1}$ (b) $7.04 \times 10^{18} \text{ s}^{-1}$
(c) $6.0 \times 10^{23} \text{ s}^{-1}$ (d) $3.52 \times 10^{18} \text{ s}^{-1}$

132. Consider the following statements.
I. $|\psi|^2$ is a measure of electron density at a point in an atom.
II. Radial probability function ($= 4\pi r^2 R^2$) gives the probability of finding the electron at a distance r (atomic radius) from the nucleus regardless of direction.
III. The shape of an orbital is defined as a surface of constant probability density that encloses some large fraction of the probability of finding the electron.

Select the correct statement(s).
(a) I, II (b) II, III
(c) I, III (d) I, II, III

133. The radius of hydrogen atom in the ground state is 0.53 Å. The radius of Li^{2+} ion (atomic number = 3) in a similar state is
(a) 0.17 Å (b) 0.265 Å
(c) 0.53 Å (d) 1.06 Å

134. Uncertainty in position of an electron (mass $= 9.1 \times 10^{-28}$ g) moving with a velocity of 3×10^4 cm/s accurate up to 0.001% will be
(a) 1.93 cm (b) 3.84 cm
(c) 5.76 cm (d) 7.68 cm

135. In a Bohr's model of atom when an electron in H-atom jumps from $n = 1$ to $n = 3$, how much energy will be emitted or absorbed?
(a) 2.15×10^{-11} erg /atom
(b) 0.1936×10^{-10} erg /atom
(c) 2.389×10^{-12} erg /atom
(d) 0.239×10^{-10} erg /atom

136. What will be the longest wavelength line in Balmer's series of spectrum?
(a) 566 nm (b) 556 nm
(c) 546 nm (d) 656 nm

137. Bohr radius for the hydrogen atom ($n = 1$) is approximately 0.530 Å. The radius for the first excited state ($n = 2$) orbit is (in Å)
(a) 0.13 (b) 1.06 (c) 4.77 (d) 2.12

138. The position of both, an electron and a helium atom is known within 1.0 mm. Further the momentum of the electron is known within $5.0 \times 10^{-26} \text{ kg m s}^{-1}$. The minimum uncertainty in the measurement of the momentum of the helium atom is
(a) 50 kg m s^{-1}
(b) 80 kg m s^{-1}
(c) $80 \times 10^{-26} \text{ kg m s}^{-1}$
(d) $5.0 \times 10^{-26} \text{ kg m s}^{-1}$

139. Which of the following configurations is correct for iron?
(a) $1s^2, 2s^2 2p^6, 3s^2 3p^6 3d^5$
(b) $1s^2, 2s^2 2p^6, 3s^2 3p^6, 4s^2 3d^5$
(c) $1s^2, 2s^2 2p^6, 3s^2 3p^6, 4s^2 3d^7$
(d) $1s^2, 2s^2 2p^6, 3s^2 3p^6, 4s^2 3d^6$

140. The uncertainty in momentum of an electron is 1×10^{-5} m/s. The uncertainty in its position will be ($h = 6.62 \times 10^{-34} \text{ kg m}^2 / \text{s}$)
(a) 1.05×10^{-28} m (b) 1.05×10^{-26} m
(c) 5.27×10^{-30} m (d) 5.25×10^{-28} m

141. Who modified Bohr's theory by introducing elliptical orbits for electron path?
(a) Hund (b) Thomson
(c) Rutherford (d) Sommerfeld

142. The configuration $1s^2, 2s^2 2p^5, 3s^1$ shows
(a) excited state of O_2^-
(b) excited state of neon atom
(c) excited state of fluorine atom
(d) ground state of fluorine atom

143. The energy of electron in first energy level is -21.79×10^{-12} erg per atom. The energy of electron in second energy level is
(a) -54.47×10^{-12} erg atom^{-1}
(b) -5.447×10^{-12} erg atom^{-1}
(c) -0.5447×10^{-12} erg atom^{-1}
(d) -0.05447×10^{-12} erg atom^{-1}

144. The de-Broglie wavelength of the electron in the ground state of hydrogen atom is [KE = 13.6 eV]; $1 \text{ eV} = 1.6 \times 10^{-19}$ J
(a) 33.29 nm (b) 3.329 nm
(c) 0.3329 nm (d) 0.0332 nm

145. The atomic numbe of an element is 17. The number of orbitals containing electron pairs in its valence shell are

(a) 2 (b) 3
(c) 4 (d) 5

146. Rutherford's experiment, which established the nuclear model of the atom used a beam of

(a) β-particles, which impinged on a metal foil and got absorbed
(b) γ-rays, which impinged on a metal foil and ejected electrons
(c) helium atoms, which impinged on a metal foil and got scattered
(d) helium nuclei, which impinged on a metal foil and got scattered

147. The shortest wavelength transition in the Paschen series in hydrogen occurs at 821 nm; at what wavelength does it occur in Li^{2+} (isoelectronic of hydrogen)?

(a) 91.2 nm (b) 273.6 nm
(c) 821.0 nm (d) 7389.0 nm

148. Sum of spin of **three** α-electrons and two β-electrons is

(a) $\frac{5}{2}$ (b) $\frac{1}{2}$ (c) $-\frac{1}{2}$ (d) $-\frac{5}{2}$

149. P is the probability of finding the 1s electron of hydrogen atom in a spherical shell of infinitesimal thickness, dr, at a distance r from the nucleus. The volume of this shell is $4\pi r^2 dr$. The qualitative sketch of the dependence of P on r is **[JEE Advanced 2016]**

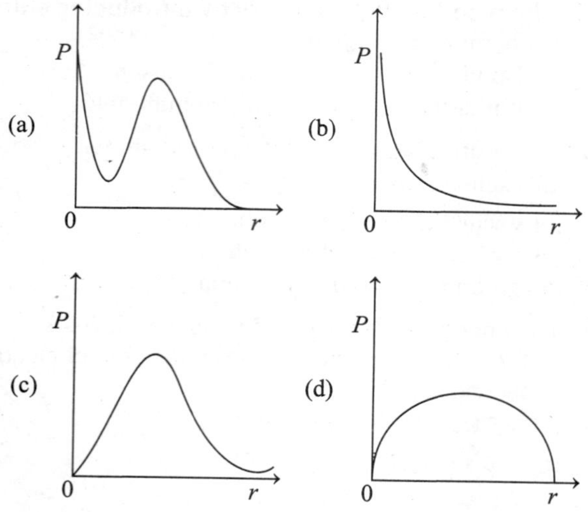

150. Select the correct matching for **3d-orbital.**

	n	l	Angular nodes	Radial nodes
(a)	3	2	2	1
(b)	3	2	2	0
(c)	3	2	1	1
(d)	3	2	1	0

151. The electronic configuration of an element is $1s^2 2s^2 2p^6 3s^2 3p^6 3d^5 4s^1$. This represents its

(a) excited state
(b) ground state
(c) cationic form
(d) anionic form

152. The number of nodal planes in a p_x orbital is

(a) one (b) two
(c) three (d) zero

153. The quantum numbers $+\frac{1}{2}$ and $-\frac{1}{2}$ for the electron spin represent

(a) rotation of the electron in clockwise and anti-clockwise direction respectively
(b) rotation of the electron in anti-clockwise and clockwise direction respectively
(c) magnetic moment of the electron pointing up and down respectively
(d) two quantum mechanical spin states which have no classical analogue

154. Which one of the following about an electron occupying the 1s-orbital in a hydrogen atom is incorrect? (The Bohr radius is represented by a_0) **[JEE Main 2019, April]**

(a) The electron can be found at a distance $2a_0$ from the nucleus.
(b) The magnitude of the potential energy is double that of its kinetic energy on an average.
(c) The probability density of finding the electron is maximum at the nucleus.
(d) The total energy of the electron is maximum when it is at a distance a_0 from the nucleus.

155. The graph between $|\psi|^2$ and r (radial distance) is shown below. This represents **[JEE Main 2019, April]**

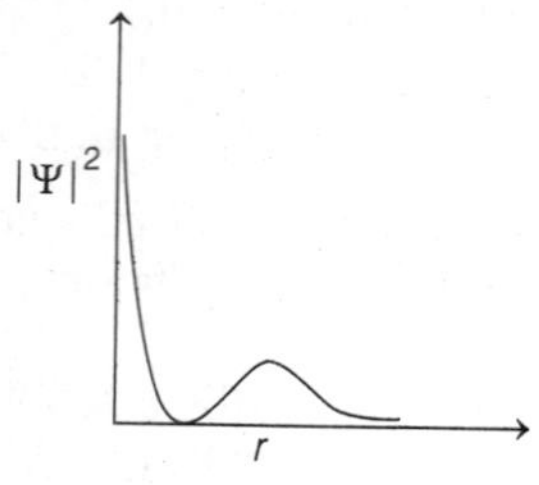

(a) 1s-orbital (b) 2p-orbital
(c) 3s-orbital (d) 2s-orbital

156. What is the work function of the metal, if the light of wavelength 4000 Å generates photoelectron of velocity 6×10^5 ms^{-1} from it? **[JEE Main 2019, Jan.]**

(Mass of electron $= 9 \times 10^{-31}$ kg
Velocity of light $= 3 \times 10^8$ ms^{-1}
Planck's constant $= 6.626 \times 10^{-34}$ Js
Charge of electron $= 1.6 \times 10^{-19}$ JeV^{-1})

(a) 4.0 eV (b) 2.1 eV
(c) 0.9 eV (d) 3.1 eV

157. Calculate the wavelength (in nanometer) associated with a proton moving at 1.0×10^3 m s^{-1} (Mass of proton $= 1.67 \times 10^{-27}$ kg and $h = 6.63 \times 10^{-34}$ Js)

(a) 0.032 nm (b) 0.40 nm
(c) 2.5 nm (d) 14.0 nm

158. Which of the following is the energy of a possible excited state of hydrogen? **[JEE Main 2015]**

(a) + 13.6 eV (b) − 6.8 eV (c) − 3.4 eV (d) + 6.8 eV

159. Which of the following sets of quantum numbers represents the highest energy of an atom?

(a) $n = 3, l = 1, m = 1, s = +1/2$
(b) $n = 3, l = 2, m = 1, s = +1/2$
(c) $n = 4, l = 0, m = 0, s = +1/2$
(d) $n = 3, l = 0, m = 0, s = +1/2$

160. The ratio of the shortest wavelength of two spectral series of hydrogen spectrum is found to be about 9. The spectral series are **[JEE Main 2019, April]**

(a) Lyman and Paschen (b) Brackett and Pfund
(c) Paschen and Pfund (d) Balmer and Brackett

161. Uncertainty in the position of an electron (mass $= 9.1 \times 10^{-31}$ kg) moving with a velocity 300 m s^{-1}, accurate upon 0.001% will be ($h = 6.63 \times 10^{-34}$ Js)

(a) 19.2×10^{-2} m (b) 5.76×10^{-2} m
(c) 1.92×10^{-2} m (d) 3.84×10^{-2} m

162. The frequency of light emitted for the transition $n = 4$ to $n = 2$ of He^+ is equal to the transition in H atom corresponding to which of the following?

(a) $n = 3$ to $n = 1$ (b) $n = 2$ to $n = 1$
(c) $n = 3$ to $n = 2$ (d) $n = 4$ to $n = 3$

163. For any given series of spectral lines of atomic hydrogen, let $\Delta\bar{v} = \bar{v}_{max} - \bar{v}_{min}$ be the difference in maximum and minimum frequencies in cm^{-1}. The ratio $\Delta\bar{v}_{Lyman} / \Delta\bar{v}_{Balmer}$ is **[JEE Main 2019, April]**

(a) 27 : 5 (b) 5 : 4 (c) 9 : 4 (d) 4 : 1

164. Ionisation energy of He^+ is 19.6×10^{-18} J atom^{-1}. The energy of the first stationary state ($n = 1$) of Li^{2+} is

(a) 4.41×10^{-16} J atom^{-1} (b) -4.41×10^{-17} J atom^{-1}
(c) -2.2×10^{-15} J atom^{-1} (d) 8.82×10^{-17} J atom^{-1}

165. In an atom, an electron is moving with a speed of 600 m/s with an accuracy of 0.005%. Certainty with which the position of the electron can be located is ($h = 6.6 \times 10^{-34}$ kg m^2 s^{-1}, mass of electron $e_m = 9.1 \times 10^{-31}$ kg).

(a) 1.52×10^{-4} m (b) 5.10×10^{-3} m
(c) 1.92×10^{-3} m (d) 3.84×10^{-3} m

166. The energies, E_1 and E_2 of two radiations are 25 eV and 50 eV respectively. The relation between their wavelengths *i.e.*, λ_1 and λ_2 will be

(a) $\lambda_1 = \frac{1}{2}\lambda_2$ (b) $\lambda_1 = \lambda_2$
(c) $\lambda_1 = 2\lambda_2$ (d) $\lambda_1 = 4\lambda_2$

167. According to Bohr's theory, the angular momentum of an electron in 5th orbit is

(a) $25\frac{h}{\pi}$ (b) $1.0\frac{h}{\pi}$ (c) $10\frac{h}{\pi}$ (d) $2.5\frac{h}{\pi}$

168. If p is the momentum of the fastest electron ejected from a metal surface after the irradiation of light having wavelength λ, then for 1.5 p momentum of the photoelectron, the wavelength of the light should be (Assume kinetic energy of ejected photoelectron to be very high in comparison to work function) **[JEE Main 2019, April]**

(a) $\frac{4}{9}\lambda$ (b) $\frac{3}{4}\lambda$ (c) $\frac{2}{3}\lambda$ (d) $\frac{1}{2}\lambda$

169. A gas absorbed photon of 355 nm and emits at two wavelengths. If one of the emission is at 680 nm, the other is at

(a) 1035 nm (b) 325 nm
(c) 743 nm (d) 518 nm

Objective Questions Type II [One or more than one correct option(s)]

In each of the questions below, four choices are given, of which one or more than one are correct.

1. Which of the following each with 24 electrons can have $[Ar]3d^5 4s^1$ electronic configuration?

(a) Fe^{2+} (b) Mn^+
(c) Cr (d) Co^{3+}

2. Many elements have non-integral atom masses because

(a) they have isotopes
(b) there isotopes have non-integral masses
(c) their isotopes have different masses
(d) the constituents, neutrons, protons and electrons combine to give fractional masses

3. Energy equivalent of 10.00 cm^{-1} is

(a) 2×10^{-22} J per photon
(b) 2.9×10^{-2} kcal mol^{-1} photon
(c) 1.2×10^{-1} kJ mol^{-1} photon
(d) 2×10^{-15} ergs per photon

4. The electronic configuration of a given species (M) is $1s^2 2s^2 2p^6 3s^2 3p^6 3d^5 4s^1$. This can be its

(a) excited state (b) ground state
(c) cationic form M^+ (d) anionic form M^-

5. If the quantum number l could have the value n also then

(a) Sc ($Z = 21$) would have configuration as $1s^2 1p^6 2s^2 2p^6 2d^3\ 3s^2$

(b) Fe ($Z = 26$) would have two unpaired electrons

(c) Fe^{2+} and Fe^{3+} would be coloured ions

(d) Cu^{2+} would be coloured and paramagnetic

6. If Aufbau rule and Hund's rule are not considered, which of the following statements are correct?

(a) Fe^{2+} will have configuration as

[Ar]

⇅	⇅	⇅		

$3d^6$

(b) Cu^{2+} is colourless ion

(c) Mn has magnetic moment of $\sqrt{3}$ BM

(d) K^+ belongs to d-block

7. Decrease in atomic number is observed during

(a) α-emission
(b) β-emission
(c) positron emission
(d) electron capture

8. Electron in He^+ ion falls from seventh level and subsequent lower levels to first level, then

(a) total of six emission lines are obtained

(b) spectrum belongs to Lyman series

(c) total of five emission lines are obtained

(d) spectrum belongs to Balmer series

9. Which of the following statement is correct?

(a) The electronic configuration of Cr is $[Ar]3d^5 4s^1$.

(b) The magnetic quantum number may have negative value

(c) In silver atom, 23 electrons have a spin of one type and 24 of the opposite type

(d) The oxidation state of nitrogen in HN_3 is -3

10. Consider the following observations

$$He^{2+} + 2e^- \longrightarrow He; \quad \Delta H° = -79.0 \text{ eV}$$

$$He^+ + e^- \longrightarrow He; \quad \Delta H° = x \text{ eV}$$

$$He^{2+} + e^- \longrightarrow He^+; \quad \Delta H° = -54.4 \text{ eV}$$

Select the correct statements.

(a) First ionisation energy of He^+ is 54.5 eV

(b) First ionisation energy of He is 24.6 eV

(c) Second ionisation energy of He is 54.4 eV

(d) α-particle gains two electrons by losing energy of 79.0 eV

11. Consider only transition involving the $n = 1$ through $n = 6$ energy levels for H-atom. Then,

(a) total of 15 lines are emitted

(b) photons of highest frequency are emitted from the level $n = 6$ to $n = 2$

(c) photons of longest wavelength are emitted from the level $n = 6$ to $n = 2$

(d) Spectral lines lie in visible, ultraviolet and infra-red region.

12. A possible excited state of the H-atom has the electron in a $4p$-orbital. Thus,

	n	l	m	s
(a)	4	1	0	+ 1/2
(b)	4	1	−1	− 1/2
(c)	4	1	+1	+ 1/2
(d)	4	0	0	− 1/2

13. Place the following types of radiation in the order of increasing energy per photon.

I. yellow light from sodium lamp.

II. X-rays from a X-ray room.

III. microwave from microwave oven.

IV. FM music station of 91.7 MHz.

(a) IV < III < I < II

(b) IV < III < II < I

(c) I < II < IV < III

(d) III < IV < II < I

14. The sum of the number of neutrons and protons in the isotope of hydrogen is

(a) 6
(b) 2
(c) 4
(d) 3

15. The ground state energy of hydrogen atom is −13.6 eV. Consider an electronic state Ψ of He^+ whose energy, azimuthal quantum number and magnetic quantum number are −3.4 eV, 2 and 0, respectively. Which of the following statement(s) is(are) true for the state Ψ? **[JEE Advanced 2019]**

(a) It is a $4d$ state

(b) The nuclear charge experienced by the electron in this state is less than $2e$, where e is the magnitude of the electronic charge

(c) It has 2 angular nodes

(d) It has 3 radial nodes

Numerical Value Questions

All these questions have a Numerical value as their answer, solve the questions and write your answer.

1. The Lyman series of the hydrogen spectrum can be represented by the equation in terms of wave number

$$\bar{\nu} = 1.09603 \times 10^7 \text{ m}^{-1}\left[\frac{1}{1^2} - \frac{1}{n^2}\right]$$

(where, $n = 2, 3, \ldots$)

Calculate the maximum and minimum wavelength of lines in this series.

2. Energy of the electron in H-atom is 1.50 times as much as energy as the minimum required for its escape (13.6 eV) from the atom. The wavelength of the emitted electrons is ....

3. The accelerating potential needed to produce an electron beam with an effective wavelength of 0.090 Å is ...... $\times 10^4$ eV.

4. One mole of He^+ ion is excited. Spectral analysis showed the existence of 50% ions in 3rd level, 25% in 2nd level and remaining 25% in ground state. Ionisation energy of He^+ is 54.4 eV; The total energy evolved when all the ions return to ground state is ...... $\times 10^6$ J.

5. The maximum precision with which the momentum may be known if the position of an electron is determined to within ± 0.001 Å is ......× 10^{22} Ns.

6. A near ultraviolet photon of 300 nm is absorbed by a gas and then re-emitted as two photons. One photon is red with wavelength 760 nm. The wavelength of the second photon would be ......

7. Not considering the electronic spin, the degeneracy of the second exited state ($n = 3$) of H-atom is a while the degeneracy of the second exited state of its is **[JEE Advanced 2015]**

8. When light of wavelength 248 nm falls on a metal of threshold energy 3.0 eV, the de-Broglie wavelength of emitted electrons is .... Å.

[Use : $\sqrt{3}$ = 1.73, h = 6.63 × 10–34 Js

$m_e = 9.1 \times 10^{-31}$ kg ; c = 3.0 × 108 ms^{-1};

1eV = 1.6×10^{-19}J] **[JEE Main 2021, March]**

9. The number of orbitals with $n = 5$, $m_l = +2$ is .... **[JEE Main 2021, Marth]**

10. In the ground state of atomic Fe(Z = 26), the spin-only magnetic moment is .... $\times 10^{-1}$ BM.

[Given : $\sqrt{3}$ = 1.73, $\sqrt{2}$ = 1.41] **[JEE Main 2021 March]**

Comprehension Based Questions

In these questions, a passage has been given followed by questions based on it. You have to answer the questions based on the passage given.

***Passage* 1** *Read the following passage and answer the questions at the end of it.* **[IIT JEE 2010]**

The hydrogen-like species Li^{2+} is in a spherically symmetric state S_1 with one radial node. Upon absorbing light the ion undergoes transition to a state S_2. The state S_2 has one radial node and its energy is equal to the ground state energy of the hydrogen atom.

1. The state S_1 is

(a) 1 *s* (b) 2 *s* (c) 2 *p* (d) 3 *s*

2. Energy of the state S_1 in unit of the hydrogen atom ground state energy is

(a) 0.75 (b) 1.50 (c) 2.25 (d) 4.50

3. The orbital angular momentum quantum number of the state S_2 is **[IIT JEE 2010]**

(a) 0 (b) 1 (c) 2 (d) 3

***Passage* 2** *Read the following sentence and answer the questions at the end of it.*

It is not possible to determine precisely both the position and the momentum (or velocity) of a small moving particle (*e.g.*, electron, proton, etc.)

1. Above statement is known as

(a) de-Broglie principle

(b) Pauli's exclusion principle

(c) Heisenberg's principle of indeterminacy

(d) Aufbau principle

2. Equation(s) related to above statement is/are

(a) $\Delta x \cdot \Delta p \geq \frac{\hbar}{2}$

(b) $\Delta x \cdot \Delta v \geq \frac{\hbar}{2\text{ m}}$

(c) $\Delta E \cdot \Delta t \geq \frac{h}{4\pi}$

(d) All of these

3. If uncertainties in the measurement of position and momentum of an electron are equal, then uncertainty in the measurement of its velocity is approximately

(a) 8.0×10^{12} m s^{-1}

(b) 6.0×10^{12} m s^{-1}

(c) 4.0×10^{12} m s^{-1}

(d) 2.0×10^{12} m s^{-1}

***Passage* 3** *Read the following passage and answer the questions at the end of it.*

The behaviour of an electron in an atom is described mathematically by a wave function, or orbital. It turns out that each wave function contains three variables, called **quantum numbers,** which are represented as n, l and m_l. These quantum numbers describe the energy level of an orbital and define the shape and orientation of the region in space where the electron will be found.

1. Which quantum number determines orientation of the electron?
(a) Principal (b) Secondary
(c) Magnetic (d) Spin

2. Orbital angular momentum is quantised and is given by
(a) $\sqrt{l(l+1)}\,\hbar$ (b) $\sqrt{n(n+2)}\,\hbar$
(c) $\sqrt{m(m+1)}\,\hbar$ (d) $\sqrt{s(s+1)}\,\hbar$

3. Radial nodes are maximum in
(a) $4s$ (b) $4p$
(c) $3d$ (d) $5f$

***Passage* 4** *Read the following rules and answer the questions at the end of it.*

1. Electrons in various suborbits of an orbit are filled in increasing order of their energies.
II. Pairing of electrons in various orbitals of a suborbit takes place only after each orbital is half-filled.
III. No two electrons in an atom can have the same set of quantum numbers.

1. Cr $(Z=24)$, $Mn^+(Z=25)$, $Fe^{2+}(Z=26)$ and $Co^{3+}(Z=27)$ are isoelectronic each having 24 electrons. Thus,
(a) all have configurations as [Ar] $4s^1 3d^5$
(b) Cr and Mn^+ have configurations as [Ar] $4s^1 3d^5$ while Fe^{2+} and Co^{3+} have configuration as [Ar] $3d^6$
(c) all have configurations as [Ar] $3d^6$
(d) all have configurations as [Ar] $4s^2\, 3d^6$

2. A compound of vanadium has a magnetic moment of 1.73 BM. Electronic configuration of the vanadium ion in the compound is
(a) [Ar] $4s^0 3d^1$ (b) [Ar] $4s^2 3d^3$
(c) [Ar] $4s^1 3d^0$ (d) [Ar] $4s^0\, 3d^5$

3. Which of these ions are expected to be paramagnetic and coloured in aqueous solution?
(a) $Fe^{3+}, Ti^{3+}, Co^{3+}$
(b) Cu^+, Ti^{4+}, Sc^{3+}
(c) Fe^{3+}, Ni^{2+}, V^{5+}
(d) Cu^+, Cu^{2+}, Fe^{2+}

***Passage* 5** *Read the following assumption and answer the questions at the end of it.*

Imagine a universe in which the four quantum numbers can have the same possible values as in our universe except that angular-momentum quantum number l can have integral values of 0, 1, 2, ... $(n+1)$; (instead of 0, 1, 2, ... $(n-1)$).

1. Electronic configuration of the element with atomic number 12, based on the above assumption is
(a) $1s^2 2s^2 2p^6 3s^2$ (b) $1s^2 2s^2 2p^8$
(c) $1s^2 1p^6 2s^2 1d^2$ (d) $1s^2 1p^6 2s^2 2p^2$

2. Based on above assumption magnetic moment of the element with atomic number 15 is
(a) $\sqrt{35}$ BM (b) $\sqrt{15}$ BM (c) $\sqrt{24}$ BM (d) $\sqrt{8}$ BM

***Passage* 6** Energy of the electron in H-atom is 1.50 times as much as energy as the minimum required for its escape (13.6 eV) from the atom.

Answer the following questions.

1. Energy difference of two energy levels is
(a) 13.6 eV (b) 20.4 eV
(c) 6.8 eV (d) 9.07 eV

2. Wavelength of the emitted radiation is
(a) 471 pm (b) 1228 pm (c) 4529 pm (d) 236 pm

***Passage* 7** Consider only transition involving the $n=1$ through $n=5$ energy levels for the H-atom.

Answer the following questions.

1. How many emission lines are possible considering only the five quantum numbers?
(a) 5 (b) 9 (c) 10 (d) 11

2. Photons of the highest frequency are emitted in a transition from the
(a) $n=5$ to $n=1$ (b) $n=5$ to $n=2$
(c) $n=5$ to $n=3$ (d) $n=5$ to $n=4$

3. The emission line having the longest wavelength corresponds to a transition from the level $n=5$ to
(a) level $n=1$ (b) level $n=2$
(c) level $n=3$ (d) level $n=4$

***Passage* 8** The ionisation energy of hydrogen is 13.6 eV and the first ionisation energy of helium is 24.6 eV.

Answer the following questions.

1. What is first ionisation energy of He^+ (isoelectronic of H atom)?
(a) 13.6 eV (b) 24.6 eV
(c) 38.2 eV (d) 54.4 eV

2. What is enthalpy change of the following process?

$$He^{2+}(g) + 2e^- \longrightarrow He(g)$$

(a) – 13.6 eV (b) – 24.6 eV
(c) – 79.0 eV (d) – 38.2 eV

***Passage* 9** The wave function, ψ_{n, l, m_l} is a mathematical function whose value depends upon spherical polar coordinates (r, θ, ϕ) of the electron and characterised by the quantum number n, l and m_l. Here r is distance from nucleus, θ is colatitude and ϕ is azimuth. In the mathematical functions given in the Table, Z is atomic number and a_0 is Bohr radius. **[JEE Advanced 2017]**

Column 1	Column 2	Column 3
(I) 1s-orbital	(i) $\psi_{n, l, m_l} \propto \left(\frac{Z}{a_0}\right)^{\frac{3}{2}} e^{-\left(\frac{Zr}{a_0}\right)}$	(P) 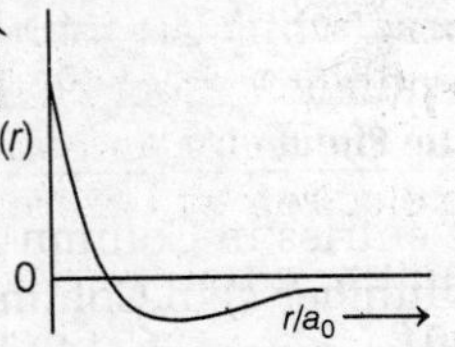
(II) 2s-orbital	(ii) One radial node	(Q) Probability density at nucleus $\propto \frac{1}{a_0^3}$
(III) $2p_z$-orbital	(iii) $\psi_{n, l, m_l} \propto \left(\frac{Z}{a_0}\right)^{\frac{5}{2}} re^{-\left(\frac{Zr}{a_0}\right)} \cos\theta$	(R) Probability density is maximum at nucleus
(IV) $3d_z^2$-orbital	(iv) xy-plane is a nodal plane	(S) Energy needed to excite electron from $n = 2$ state to $n = 4$ state is $\frac{27}{32}$ times the energy needed to excite electron from $n = 2$ state to $n = 6$ state

1. For He^+ ion, the only incorrect combination is
(a) (I) (i) (S) (b) (II) (ii) (Q) (c) (I) (iii) (R) (d) (I) (i) (R)

2. For the given orbital in column 1, the only correct combination for any hydrogen-like species is
(a) (II) (ii) (P) (b) (I) (ii) (S) (c) (IV) (iv) (R) (d) (III) (iii) (P)

3. For hydrogen atom, the only correct combination is
(a) (I) (i) (P) (b) (I) (iv) (R) (c) (II) (i) (Q) (d) (I) (i) (S)

Matrix-Match Type

Given below are Matching Type Questions, with two columns (each having some items) each. Each item of Column I has to be matched with the items of Column II.

1. Match the equation in Column I with the name/type in Column II.

Column I	Column II
A. $\Delta x \cdot \Delta p \geq \frac{h}{4\pi}$	1. Photoelectric effect
B. $mvr = \frac{nh}{2\pi}$	2. de-Broglie equation
C. $r_1 = \frac{h^2}{4\pi^2 me^2}$	3. Ritz combination principle
D. $\bar{\nu} = R_H \left[\frac{1}{n_1^2} - \frac{1}{n_2^2}\right]$	4. Heisenberg uncertainty rule
E. $h\Delta\nu = \frac{1}{2}mv^2$	5. Bohr's radius of H-atom
F. $\lambda = \frac{h}{\sqrt{2m\ (KE)}}$	6. Angular momentum is quantised.

2. Match the rule given in Column I with the statement given in Column II.

Column I	Column II
A. Pauli's exclusion principle	1. Transition from the higher shell to K shell
B. Zeeman effect	2. In orbitals of equivalent energy electron spins remain unpaired if possible.
C. Uncertainty principle	3. No two electrons may have all the four quantum numbers identical.
D. Lyman series	4. Square of the wave function.
E. Schrodinger equation	5. $\Delta p \cdot \Delta x = h/4\pi$
F. Photoelectric effect	6. The effect of magnetic field on the atomic spectra.
G. Hund's rule	7. Energy required to remove an electron
H. Ionisation potential	8. Emission of electrons caused by indirect light of sufficient energy.

3. Match the spectral line in Column I with corresponding lowest energy transition in Column II.

Column I (Line)	Column II (Transition)
A. Lyman	1. $n = 6$ to $n = 5$
B. Paschen	2. $n = 5$ to $n = 4$
C. Brackett	3. $n = 7$ to $n = 6$
D. Balmer	4. $n = 4$ to $n = 3$
E. Pfund	5. $n = 3$ to $n = 2$
F. Humphries	6. $n = 2$ to $n = 1$

4. Match the type of series given in Column I with the wavelength range given in Column II.

Column I	Column II
A. Lyman	1. Ultraviolet
B. Paschen	2. Near infrared
C. Balmer	3. Far infrared
D. Pfund	4. Visible

5. Match the entries in Column I with the correctly related quantum number(s) in Column II. Indicate your answer by darkening the appropriate bubbles of the 4 × 4 matrix given in the ORS.

Column I	Column II
A. Orbital angular momentum of the electron in a hydrogen-like atomic orbital	1. Principal quantum number
B. A hydrogen-like one-electron wave function obeying Pauli principle	2. Azimuthal quantum number
C. Shape, size and orientation of hydrogen-like atomic orbitals	3. Magnetic quantum number
D. Probability density of electron at the nucleus in hydrogen-like atom	4. Electron spin quantum number

6. According to Bohr's theory

E_n = Total energy, K_n = Kinetic energy, V_n = Potential energy, r_n = Radius of nth orbit.

Match the following.

Column I	Column II
A. $V_n/K_n = ?$	1. 0
B. If radius of n th orbit $\propto E_n^x$, $x = ?$	2. −1
C. Angular momentum in lowest orbital	3. −2
D. $\frac{1}{r^n} \propto Z^y$, $y = ?$	4. 1

7. Match the (E.C) of the species with the rules violated in writing them as given in Column II.

Column I	Column II
A. K(19) $1s^2 2s^2 2p^6, 3s^2 3p^6 3d^1$	1. Aufbau rule
B. N(7) $1s^2\ 2s^2$ [↑↓ | ↑ |]	2. Hund's rule
C. Cr(24) | Ar | $3d^4 4s^2$	3. Pauli's exclusion principle
D. O(8) $1s^2\ 2s^2$ [↑↓ | ↑ | ↑]	
E. F(9) $1s^2\ 2s^2\ 2p^4\ 3s^1$ [↑↓ | ↑ | ↑] [↑]	

8. Match the species in Column I with their related properties in Column II.

Column I	Column II
A. N(7)	1. Paramagnetic
B. Co^{2+}(27)	2. Sum of spin 1.5
C. Mn^{4+}(25)	3. Coloured ion
D. Fe^{2+}(26)	4. Magnetic moment $\sqrt{24}$ BM

9. Wave number of the spectral line of the H-like species (atmic number Z) is given by

$$\bar{\nu} = \bar{R}_H Z^2 \left[\frac{1}{n_1^2} - \frac{1}{n_2^2}\right]$$

Match the given parameter in Column I with the related equations in Column II.

Column I	Column II
A. Frequency of α-line in Balmer series in Li^{2+}	1. $0.36\ \bar{R}_H$
B. Maximum wavelength of spectral line in Brackett series of Be^{3+}	2. $8\ \bar{R}_H$
C. Minimum wavelength of spectral line in P-fund series of B^{4+}	3. $\bar{R}_H$
D. Wave number of β-line in Lyman series of Li^{2+}	4. $1.25\ \bar{R}_H C$

10. Consider the Bohr's model of a one-electron atom where the electron moves around the nucleus. In the following Column I contains some quantities for the nth orbit of the atom and Column II contains options showing how they depend on n.

Column I	Column II
A. Radius of the n th orbit	1. $\propto n^{-2}$
B. Angular momentum of the electron in the nth orbit	2. $\propto n^{-1}$
C. Kinetic energy of the electron in the nth orbit	3. $\propto n^0$
D. Potential energy of the electron in the nth orbit	4. $\propto n^1$
	5. $\propto n^2$
	6. $\propto n^{1/2}$

Single Integer Answer Questions

Answer of these questions is a single digit lying between 0 to 9.

1. How many of the following have d^5 arrangement in their electronic configuration?
$Fe^{3+}(Z=26), Fe^{2+}(Z=26)$, Mn $(Z=25)$, Cr $(Z=24)$, V^{2-} $(Z=23)$
2. How many of the following are paramagnetic?
N(7), O(8), N_2, O_2, $Fe^{2+}(26)$, $Sc^{3+}(21)$, $V^{3+}(23)$, $V^{5+}(23)$
3. How many of the following elements have ns^1 configuration?
Li(3), K(19), Cr(24), Cu(29), Rb(37), Ag(47), $Cs^+(55)$ Mo(42)
4. Total nodes in 7*d* suborbit are …… .
5. How many electrons in Si(14) will have same spins (↑, clockwise) if one starts with this spin?
6. The value of '*l*' if a new azimuthal quantum number called '*g*' also is in use after *f*-suborbit is …… .
7. The maximum number of electrons that can have principal quantum number, $n=3$, and spin quantum number, $m_s=-1/2$ is …….. **[IIT JEE 2011]**
8. The work function (ϕ) of some metals is listed below. The number of metals which will show photoelectric effect when light of 300 nm falls on the metal is

Metal	Li	Mg	Na	K	Cu	Ag	Fe	Pt	W
ϕ (eV)	2.4	3.7	2.3	2.2	4.8	4.3	4.7	6.3	4.75

[IIT JEE 2011]

9. The atomic masses of He and Ne are 4 and 20 amu, respectively. The value of the de-Broglie wavelength of He gas at –73°C is "*M*" times that of the de-Broglie wavelength of Ne at 727°C. "*M*" is … **[JEE Advanced 2013]**
10. At what minimum atomic number, would a transition from $n=2$ to $n=1$ level result in the emission of X-rays with $\lambda = 3 \times 10^{-8}$ m?
$(\bar{R}_H = 1.097 \times 10^7 \text{ m}^{-1})$
11. 2×10^8 atoms of carbon are arranged side by side. Calculate the radius of carbon (in pm) atom of the length of this arrangement is 0.24 cm.
12. Magnetic moment of $M^{x+}(Z=26)$ is 5.916 BM. What is the value of *x*?
13. For a given transition from n_2 – level to n_1 level
$$\bar{v} = \bar{R}_H Z^2 \left[\frac{1}{n_1^2} - \frac{1}{n_2^2}\right]$$
What is the value of n_2 for γ-liner in Brackett series?
14. Spectral line of maximum wavelength in *p*-fund series is obtained at what value of n_2?
$$\bar{v} = R_H Z^2 \left[\frac{1}{n_1^2} - \frac{1}{n_2^2}\right]$$
15. Given, $Cs(g) \longrightarrow Cs^+(g) + e^-$ $\Delta H° = 3.89$ eV
How many electrons can be removed from gaseous Cs by the energy of red eight of wavelength 700 nm?

Answers

Objective Questions Type I [Only one correct option]

1. (b)	**2.** (a)	**3.** (a)	**4.** (b)	**5.** (d)	**6.** (d)	**7.** (a)	**8.** (c)	**9.** (a)	**10.** (d)
11. (c)	**12.** (d)	**13.** (c)	**14.** (d)	**15.** (d)	**16.** (a)	**17.** (b)	**18.** (b)	**19.** (a)	**20.** (c)
21. (b)	**22.** (d)	**23.** (b)	**24.** (a)	**25.** (d)	**26.** (b)	**27.** (d)	**28.** (c)	**29.** (b)	**30.** (b)
31. (b)	**32.** (a)	**33.** (b)	**34.** (b)	**35.** (c)	**36.** (d)	**37.** (c)	**38.** (c)	**39.** (a)	**40.** (a)
41. (c)	**42.** (b)	**43.** (b)	**44.** (c)	**45.** (d)	**46.** (b)	**47.** (a)	**48.** (b)	**49.** (c)	**50.** (d)
51. (a)	**52.** (c)	**53.** (c)	**54.** (d)	**55.** (a)	**56.** (d)	**57.** (b)	**58.** (a)	**59.** (d)	**60.** (b)
61. (b)	**62.** (b)	**63.** (a)	**64.** (a)	**65.** (a)	**66.** (a)	**67.** (a)	**68.** (c)	**69.** (a)	**70.** (a)
71. (a)	**72.** (b)	**73.** (c)	**74.** (a)	**75.** (c)	**76.** (b)	**77.** (b)	**78.** (c)	**79.** (c)	**80.** (c)
81. (c)	**82.** (d)	**83.** (c)	**84.** (b)	**85.** (c)	**86.** (b)	**87.** (a)	**88.** (c)	**89.** (c)	**90.** (d)
91. (d)	**92.** (d)	**93.** (a)	**94.** (a)	**95.** (a)	**96.** (a)	**97.** (d)	**98.** (c)	**99.** (d)	**100.** (c)
101. (b)	**102.** (b)	**103.** (a)	**104.** (c)	**105.** (c)	**106.** (b)	**107.** (a)	**108.** (d)	**109.** (b)	**110.** (c)
111. (b)	**112.** (d)	**113.** (b)	**114.** (d)	**115.** (d)	**116.** (d)	**117.** (d)	**118.** (b)	**119.** (c)	**120.** (a)
121. (c)	**122.** (b)	**123.** (c)	**124.** (c)	**125.** (a)	**126.** (c)	**127.** (a)	**128.** (b)	**129.** (a)	**130.** (b)
131. (d)	**132.** (d)	**133.** (a)	**134.** (a)	**135.** (b)	**136.** (d)	**137.** (d)	**138.** (d)	**139.** (d)	**140.** (c)
141. (d)	**142.** (b)	**143.** (c)	**144.** (c)	**145.** (b)	**146.** (d)	**147.** (b)	**148.** (b)	**149.** (c)	**150.** (b)
151. (b)	**152.** (a)	**153.** (d)	**154.** (d)	**155.** (d)	**156.** (b)	**157.** (b)	**158.** (c)	**159.** (b)	**160.** (a)
161. (c)	**162.** (b)	**163.** (c)	**164.** (c)	**165.** (c)	**166.** (c)	**167.** (d)	**168.** (a)	**169.** (c)	

Objective Questions Type II [One or more than one correct option(s)]

1. (b, c) **2.** (a, c) **3.** (a, b, c, d) **4.** (b, c) **5.** (a, b, c)
6. (a, c, d) **7.** (a, c, d) **8.** (a, b) **9.** (a, b, c) **10.** (a, b, c, d)
11. (a, b, c, d) **12.** (a, b, c) **13.** (a) **14.** (b, d) **15.** (a, c)

Numerical Value Questions

1. $\lambda_{max} = 121.65$ nm and $\lambda_{min} = 91.24$ nm **2.** 4.71 Å **3.** 1.86 **4.** 3.31
5. 0.02 **6.** 496 nm **7.** 1 **8.** 9.00 **9.** 3.00 **10.** 49.00

Comprehension Based Questions

Passage 1 – **1.** (b) **2.** (c) **3.** (b)
Passage 2 – **1.** (c) **2.** (d) **3.** (a)
Passage 3 – **1.** (c) **2.** (a) **3.** (a)
Passage 4 – **1.** (b) **2.** (a) **3.** (a)
Passage 5 – **1.** (c) **2.** (a)
Passage 6 – **1.** (c) **2.** (a)
Passage 7 – **1.** (c) **2.** (a) **3.** (d)
Passage 8 – **1.** (d) **2.** (c)
Passage 9 – **1.** (c) **2.** (a) 3. (d)

Matrix-Match Type

1. A → (4); B → (6); C → (5); D → (3); E → (1); F → –(2).
2. A → (3); B → (6); C → (5); D → (1); E → (4); F → (8); G → (2); H → (7).
3. A → (6); B → (4); C → (2); D → (5); E → (1); F → (3).
4. A → (1); B → (2); C → (4); D → (3).
5. A → (2); B → (1),(2),(3),(4) C → (1),(2),(3); D–(1),(2),(3)
6. A → (3); B → (2); C → (1); D → (4)
7. A → (1); B → (2,3) C → (1,2,3); D → (2,3); E → (1,2,3)
8. A → (1,2); B → (1,2,3); C → (1,2,3); D → (1,3,4)
9. A → (4); B → (1); C → (3); D → (2)
10. A → (5); B → (5); C → (1); D → (1)

Single Integer Answer Questions

1. (4) **2.** (5) **3.** (7) **4.** (6) **5.** (8) **6.** (4) **7.** (9) **8.** (4) **9.** (5) **10.** (2)
11. (6) **12.** (3) **13.** (7) **14.** (6) **15.** (2)

Solutions

Objective Questions Type I [Only one correct option]

1. (*b*) $\frac{m_n}{m_e} = \frac{1.67495 \times 10^{-27} \text{ kg}}{9.1091 \times 10^{-31} \text{ kg}} = 1839$

8. (*c*) $\frac{\text{radius of atom}}{\text{radius of nucleus}} = \frac{10^{-10} \text{ m}}{10^{-15} \text{ m}} = 10^5$

11. (*c*) Energy values are additives

$$E = E_1 + E_2$$

$$\frac{hc}{\lambda} = \frac{hc}{\lambda_1} + \frac{hc}{\lambda_2}$$

$$\frac{1}{\lambda} = \frac{1}{\lambda_1} + \frac{1}{\lambda_2}$$

$$\lambda = 300 \text{ nm}, \quad \lambda_1 = 760 \text{ nm}$$

$$\therefore \quad \lambda_2 = 495.6 \text{ nm}, \approx 496 \text{ nm}$$

12. (*d*) (*A*) $^{58}Ce \rightarrow [Xe]4f^2\, 5d^0\, 6s^2$

In complex $Ce^{2+} \rightarrow [Xe]\, 4f^0 5d^0 6s^0$

there is no unpaired electron so $\mu_m = 0$

(*B*) $_{64}Gd^{3+} \rightarrow [Xe]4f^7 5d^0 6s^0$

contain seven unpaired electrons so,

$$\mu_m = \sqrt{7(7+2)} = \sqrt{63} \text{ B.M.}$$

(*C*) $_{63}Eu^{3+} \rightarrow [54Xe]4f^5 5d^0 6s^0$

contain six unpaired electron

so, $\mu_m = \sqrt{6(6+2)} = \sqrt{48}$ B.M.

Hence, order of spin only magnetic movement

$$B > C > A$$

15. (*d*) $\lambda = 400 \text{ nm} = 400 \times 10^{-9} \text{ m}$

(a) $\nu = \frac{c}{\lambda} = \frac{3 \times 10^8 \text{ m s}^{-1}}{400 \times 10^{-9} \text{ m}} = 7.5 \times 10^{14} \text{ s}^{-1}$ (Hz)

Thus, true

(b) $\bar{\nu} = \frac{1}{\lambda} = \frac{1}{400 \times 10^{-9}} = 2.5 \times 10^6 \text{ m}^{-1}$

Thus, true

(c) $\lambda = \frac{h}{m\upsilon}$

$\therefore \quad m\nu = \frac{h}{\lambda} = \frac{6.626 \times 10^{-34} \text{ J s}}{400 \times 10^{-9} \text{ m}}$

$= 1.66 \times 10^{-27} \text{ kg ms}^{-1}$

Thus, true

17. (*b*) Moseley's equation is

$$\sqrt{\nu} = a(Z - b)$$

$$\sqrt{400} = 1(Z - 1)$$

$Z = 21$ (atomic number of sodium)

18. (*b*) $\nu \text{(matter wave)} = \frac{\text{velocity } \nu}{\lambda} = \frac{\nu}{h/m\upsilon} = \frac{mv^2}{h}$

$$= \left(\frac{2\text{KE}}{h}\right)$$

20. (*c*) The number of waves made by a Bohr electron in an orbit is equal to its principal quantum number (or number of orbit).

21. (*b*) Energy in ground state = 13.6 eV

Energy absorbed = 1.5 × 13.6 eV = 20.4 eV

Energy in higher level = 34.0 eV

∴ Energy emitted = 34.0 − 13.6 = 20.4 eV

∴ KE to the emitted electron = 20.4 eV

22. (*d*) $\Delta E = \text{constant}\left[\frac{1}{n_1^2} - \frac{1}{n_2^2}\right]$

Transition with maximum value of n_2 and least value of n_1 will absorb greatest quantity of energy.

23. (*b*) $\bar{\nu} \text{ (wave number)} = \bar{R}_H Z^2 \left[\frac{1}{n_1^2} - \frac{1}{n_2^2}\right]$

$$\bar{\nu}_1 (He^+, Z = 2) = \bar{R}_H (2)^2 \left[\frac{1}{n_1^2} - \frac{1}{n_2^2}\right]$$

$$\bar{\nu}_2 (Be^{3+}, Z = 4) = \bar{R}_H (4)^2 \left[\frac{1}{n_1^2} - \frac{1}{n_2^2}\right]$$

$$\frac{\bar{\nu}_2}{\bar{\nu}_1} = 4 \quad \therefore \quad \bar{\nu}_2 = 4\bar{\nu}_1 = 4x$$

24. (*a*) For Paschen series $n_1 = 3$

Thus, following λ emissions are possible

n_2		n_1
7	→	3
6	→	3
5	→	3
4	→	3

Thus, total four emissions.

25. (*d*) PE = 2 × total energy $= -2 \times \left(\frac{13.6 Z^2}{n^2}\right)$

For helium $Z = 2$, and $n = 1$ in first Bohr orbit

Thus, $\quad \text{PE} = -2 \times \frac{13.6 \times (2)^2}{1^2} = -108.8 \text{ eV}$

27. (*d*) $R_H = \frac{2\pi^2 me^4 k^2}{ch^3}$ for H-atom

$R_Z = \frac{2\pi^2 me^4 k^2 (Z^2)}{ch^3}$ for an atom/ion with atomic number Z

$$\therefore \quad \frac{R_Z}{R_H} = Z^2$$

$\therefore \quad R_Z(He^+) = R_H Z^2$

$= x \times 4 = 4x\ m^{-1}$

$= \frac{4x}{100}\ cm^{-1} = 0.04\ x\ cm^{-1}$

31. (*b*) Principal quantum number (n) signifies the shell or orbit number.

From the number of values of azimuthal quantum number (l), we can calculate number of subshells present in a shell as,

$l = 0 \ldots. (n-1)$

So, when $n = 4$

The permissible values of l and subshells are

$l = 0 \rightarrow s$-subshell

$= 1 \rightarrow p$-subshell

$= 2 \rightarrow d$-subshell

$= 3 \rightarrow f$-subshell

But, here values of l are restricted by the value of magnetic quantum number, $m = -2$, where, m depends on l as

$m = -l \ldots. 0 \ldots. +l$

So, $m = -2$ value is possible for two subshells, *viz.*, $l = 3$ (f-subshell) and $l = 2$ (d-subshell) only.

$l = 3 \Rightarrow m = -3, -2 - 1, 0, +1, +2, +3$

$l = 2 \Rightarrow m = -2, -1, 0, +1, +2$

32. (*a*) Number of radial nodes $= (n - l - 1) = 3$

	n	l	$n-l-1$
4s	4	0	3
5p	5	1	3

33. (*b*) Number of nodal planes $= l$

Thus, for $4p$, $l = 1$, hence nodal plane $= 1$

34. (*b*) Hypothetical situation :

Azimuthal quantum number (l) $= 0 - (n - 1)$

n = Principal quantum number

For, $n = 1$ $\quad l = 0,\ 1,\ 2$

$\downarrow \quad \downarrow \quad \downarrow$

$1s \quad 1p \quad 1d$

$1s^2 \quad 1p^6 \quad 1d^{10}$

Number of electrons in s-orbital $= 2$

Number of electrons in p-orbital $= 6$

Number of electrons in d-orbital $= 10$

$Z = 13$ (Half-filled valence sub-shell)

For $n = 1$, $1s^2 1p^6 1d^5$ ($Z = 13$)

Number of electrons in $1d$-orbital are 5. (It is half-filled).

Element with atomic number 9 is not first alkali metal but a halogen $1s^2 2s^2 2p^5$.

First noble gas has atomic number 2 not 8.

38. (*c*) $l = 0, 1, 2, \ldots, n$ instead of $0, 1, 2, \ldots, (n-1)$

For $n = 1$,	Orbitals	Electrons
$l = 0\ m = 0$	one	2
$l = 1\ m = -1, 0, +1$	three	6

Total electrons $= 8$

39. (*a*) For p-orbital $l = 1$, thus orbitals $= 3$

$\therefore x = 6, y = 2$

$\therefore$ Thus, number of arrangements $= \frac{x!}{(x-y)!\,y!}$

$= \frac{6!}{4!2!} = \frac{6 \cdot 5 \cdot 4!}{4!2!} = 15$ ways

40. (*a*) According to quantum mechanical atom model, for each value of n (principal quantum number), there are 'n' different values of l (azimuthal quantum number), i.e. $l = 0, 1, 2, \ldots, (n-1)$.

And, for each value of l, there are $2l + 1$ different values of m_l (magnetic quantum number), i.e. $m_l = 0, \pm 1, \pm 2 \ldots \pm l$.

$\therefore$ Total number of possible combinations of n, l and m_l, for a given value of n is n^2, and each such combination is associated with an orbital.

Each orbital can occupy a maximum of two electrons, having a different value of spin quantum number (m_s), which are $+\frac{1}{2}$ or $-\frac{1}{2}$.

$\therefore$ Number of orbitals associated with $n = 5$ is $n^2 = 25$. Each of those orbitals can be associated with $m_s = +\frac{1}{2}$ as well as $m_s = -\frac{1}{2}$.

$\therefore$ Answer $= 25$

41. (*c*)

n	l	Notation	Orbital	Electron	
1	0	1s	1	2	$1s^2$
	1	1p	3	6	$1p^6$
2	0	2s	1	2	$2s^2$
	1	2p	3	6	$2p^6$
	2	2d	5	10	$2d^{10}$
3	0	3s	1	2	$3s^2$
	1	3p	3	6	$3p^6$
	2	3d	5	10	$3d^{10}$
	3	3f	7	14	$3f^{14}$

By Aufbau rule, electron will be filled in increasing order of energy, i.e. $(n + l)$ rule. (minimum the value of $(n + l)$, smaller the energy thus earlier the filling of orbitals).

$1s < 1p < 2s < 2p < 3s < 2d \ldots.$

V($Z = 23$) will have electronic configuration as

$1s^2 1p^6 2s^2 2p^6 3s^2 2d^5$

42. (*b*) Ti ($Z = 22$) has EC under the given condition as $1s^2 1p^6 2s^2 2p^6 3s^2 2d^4$ which changes to stable configurations as

$1s^2\ 1p^6\ 2s^2\ 2p^6\ 3s^1\ 2d^5$ [1] [1|1|1|1|1]
$3s^1$ $2d^5$

Thus, unpaired electrons $= N = 6$

Magnetic moment $= \sqrt{N(N+2)}$ BM $= \sqrt{48}$ BM

47. (*a*) Electronic configuration of divalent metal ion having atomic number 25 is [Ar] $3d^5 4s^2$

For $Mn^{+2}_{(aq)} \Rightarrow$

$1s^2$ $2s^2$ $2p^6$ $3s^2$ $3p^6$ $3d^5$
[⇅] [⇅] [⇅|⇅|⇅] [⇅] [⇅|⇅|⇅] [1|1|1|1|1]

Total number of unpaired electrons = 5

μ (Magnetic moment) $= \sqrt{n(n+2)}$ BM

where, n = number of unpaired e^-

$\therefore \quad \mu = \sqrt{5(5+2)} = \sqrt{35}$ BM $= 5.92$ BM

57. (*b*) $1 = 0 \Rightarrow$'s' orbital

$$n - l - 1 = 2$$
$$n - 1 = 2 \Rightarrow n = 3$$

58. (*a*) $E_n = -13.6\left(\frac{Z^2}{n^2}\right)$ eV

for H-atom, $Z = 1$

$E_1(\text{H}) = -13.6$ eV in ground state $n = 1$,

Be^{3+}, $n = 2$ for $Z = 4$

$$E_2(Be^{3+}) = \left[\frac{-13.6 \times (4)^2}{(2)^2}\right] \text{ in first excited state,}$$

$$\therefore \quad E_1 = E_2 = 1 : 4$$

60. (*b*) Orbital angular momentum $= \sqrt{l(l+1)}\frac{h}{2\pi} = 0$

Since ($l = 0$) for 2*s*-electron

63. (*a*) Magnetic moment with N unpaired electrons

$$= \sqrt{N(N+2)} \text{ BM}$$
$$\therefore \quad \sqrt{N(N+2)} = \sqrt{24}$$
$$N(N+2) = 24$$

This gives $N = 4$ (and $N = -6$, which is invalid.)

$N = 4$ (unpaired electrons)

$\therefore N = 4$ and $n = 2$

X ($Z = 26$) [Ar] $3d^6 4s^2$ — $3d^6$: [⇅|1|1|1|1] $4s^2$: [⇅]

X^{2+} [Ar] $3d^6$ — $3d^6$: [⇅|1|1|1|1] $4s^0$: [ ]

N = 4 (unpaired electrons)

71. (*a*) $\lambda = \frac{h}{mv}$ but $v = \lambda$

$$\therefore \quad \lambda v = v^2 = \frac{h}{m}$$
$$\therefore \quad v = \sqrt{\frac{h}{m}}$$

73. (*c*) Quantum nature of atoms are associated with following phenomena or processes :

(i) Absorption spectrum
(ii) Emission spectrum
(iii) Black body radiation
(iv) Photo-electricity

Internal energy (U) of particles like atoms depends upon the thermodynamic variables (p, V, T) of the system. Thus, $U = f(p, T)$

or $\quad U = f_1(T, V)$

or $\quad U = f_2(p, V)$

So, quantum nature of atom is not associated with its internal energy.

Graph (c) is not a direct manifestation of the quantum nature of atoms.

83. (*c*)
$$mvr = \frac{nh}{2\pi}$$
$$m^2v^2 = \frac{n^2h^2}{4\pi^2r^2}$$
$$\text{KE} = \frac{1}{2}mv^2 = \frac{1}{2}\frac{m^2v^2}{m} = \frac{n^2h^2}{8\pi^2r^2m}$$
$$r_n = \frac{n^2a_0}{Z} = \frac{n^2a_0}{1}$$
$$\therefore \quad \text{KE} = \frac{n^2h^2}{8\pi^2(n^2a_0)^2\,m}$$
$$= \frac{h^2}{8\pi^2n^2a_0^2m} = \frac{h^2}{32\pi^2a_0^2m} \quad (\text{if } n = 2)$$

86. (*b*)
$$m\upsilon r_n = \frac{nh}{2\pi}$$
$$m\upsilon\left(\frac{n^2a_0}{Z}\right) = \frac{nh}{2\pi}\Bigg];$$

$a_0 = x$ = Bohr's radius of H-atom

$n = 3, Z = 1$

$$mv\left(\frac{9x}{1}\right) = \frac{3h}{2\pi}$$
$$mv = \frac{h}{6\pi x}$$
$$\therefore \quad \lambda = \frac{h}{m\upsilon} = 6\pi x$$

87. (*a*) $\frac{1}{\lambda} = \bar{R}_H Z^2 \left[\frac{1}{n_1^2} - \frac{1}{n_2^2}\right]$

For Lyman series $n_1 = 1$, λ is shortest if $n_2 = \infty$

$\therefore \quad \bar{R}_H = \frac{1}{x}$ for H-atom ($Z = 1$)

For Balmer series, $n_1 = 2$, λ is longest if $n_2 = 3$

$$\frac{1}{\lambda_{max}} = \left(\frac{1}{x}\right)(2)^2\left[\frac{1}{2^2} - \frac{1}{3^2}\right] \text{ for He}^+ \text{ ion } (Z = 2)$$
$$\therefore \quad \lambda_{max} = \frac{9x}{5}$$

88. (*c*) As we know that, $\Delta E = \frac{hc}{\lambda}$

Hence, λ will be, $\lambda = \frac{hc}{\Delta E}$

For, λ = minimum, i.e. shortest, ΔE = maximum

For Lyman series, $n = 1$ and for ΔE_{max} transition must be form $n = \infty$ to $n = 1$.

So, $\frac{1}{\lambda} = R_H Z^2 \left(\frac{1}{n_1^2} - \frac{1}{n_2^2}\right)$ $(\because n_1 = 1 \text{ and } n_2 = \infty)$

$$\frac{1}{\lambda} = R_H \left(\frac{1}{1^2} - \frac{1}{\infty^2}\right) \times (1)^2$$

$$\frac{1}{\lambda} = R_H (1 - 0) \Rightarrow \frac{1}{\lambda} = R \times (1)^2 \Rightarrow \lambda_1 = \frac{1}{R}$$

For longest wavelength, ΔE = minimum for Balmer series, $n = 3$ to $n = 2$ will have ΔE minimum.

For He^+, $Z = 2$

So, $\frac{1}{\lambda_2} = R_H \times 2^2 \left(\frac{1}{n_1^2} - \frac{1}{n_2^2}\right)$

$$\frac{1}{\lambda_2} = R_H \times 4\left(\frac{1}{4} - \frac{1}{9}\right), \frac{1}{\lambda_2} = R_H \times 4 \times \frac{5}{36}$$

$$\frac{1}{\lambda_2} = R_H \times \frac{5}{9} \Rightarrow \lambda_2 = \lambda_1 \times \frac{9}{5}$$

89. (*c*) We know that, $r = 0.529 \frac{n^2}{Z}$ Å

For Li^{2+} $(r_{Li^{2+}})_{n=4} - (r_{Li^{2+}})_{n=3}$

$\Rightarrow$ $\frac{0.529}{3}(16 - 9) = \Delta R_1$ ...(i)

For He^+ $(r_{He^+})_{n=4} - (r_{He^+})_{n=3}$

$\Rightarrow$ $\frac{0.529}{3}(16 - 9) = \Delta R_2$ ...(ii)

$$\frac{\Delta R_1}{\Delta R_2} = \frac{\frac{0.529}{3}(16-9)}{\frac{0.529}{2}(16-9)} = \frac{2}{3}$$

Hence, the ratio of $\Delta R_1 : \Delta R_2$ is 2 : 3.

91. (*d*) Statements I, II and III are correct. The explanations of these statements are as follows :

(I) In each series of hydrogen spectrum, lines converge at the higher frequency or lower wavelength limit.

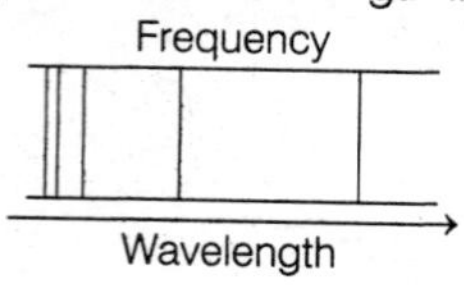

$\therefore$ This is correct.

(II) For Balmer series, $n_1 = 2$

$\therefore$ This is correct.

(III) Longest wavelength represents the smallest wave number

$$\bar{\nu} = R_H\left(\frac{1}{n_1^2} - \frac{1}{n_2^2}\right). (n_2 > n_1)$$

When $n_1 = 2$, smallest value of $\bar{\nu}$ is for $n_2 = 3$

$\therefore$ This is a correct statement.

(IV) This statement is not correct. It's corrected form is as follows: Ionisation energy of hydrogen can be calculated from Lyman series lines ($n = 1$) only by using the following formula,

$$\bar{\nu} = R_H\left[\frac{1}{(1)^2} - \frac{1}{\infty^2}\right]$$

101. (*b*) $h\nu = h\nu_0 + (KE)$

$$KE = h(\nu - \nu_0)$$
$$(KE)_1 = h(3.2 \times 10^{16} - \nu_0)$$
$$(KE)_2 = h(2.0 \times 10^{16} - \nu_0)$$

Given, $(KE)_1 = 2(KE)_2$

$$h(3.2 \times 10^{16} - \nu_0) = 2h(2.0 \times 10^{16} - \nu_0)$$

$\therefore$ $\nu_0 = 8.0 \times 10^{15}$ Hz

106. (*b*) K-19 would have been represented as : $1s^3 2s^3 2p^9 3s^3 3p^1$

Last electrons occupies *p*-orbital, hence *p*-block element,

115. (*d*) Bohr radius $(r_n) = \epsilon_0 n^2 h^2$

$$r_n = \frac{n^2h^2}{4\pi^2 me^2 kZ} \Rightarrow k = \frac{1}{4\pi \epsilon_0}$$

$\therefore$ $r_n = \frac{n^2h^2 \epsilon_0}{\pi me^2 Z} = n^2 \frac{a_0}{Z}$

where, m = mass of electron, e = charge of electron

h = Planck's constant, k = Coulomb constant

$$r_n = \frac{n^2 \times 0.53}{Z} \text{ Å}$$

Radius of nth Bohr orbit for H-atom

$= 0.53 n^2$ Å

[$Z = 1$ for H-atom]

$\therefore$ Radius of 2nd Bohr orbit for H-atom

$= 0.53 \times (2)^2 = 2.12$ Å

116. (*d*) $\Delta E = 12.084$ eV

$= 12.084 \times 1.6 \times 10^{-19}$ J per atom

$= 12.084 \times 1.6 \times 10^{-19} \times 6.02 \times 10^{23}$ J mol^{-1}

$= 1164$ kJ

117. (*d*) For photoelectric effect,

(i) $KE = E - E_0$

where, KE = Kinetic energy of ejected electrons.

E = Energy of incident light = $h\nu$

E_0 = Threshold energy = $h\nu_0$

ν = Frequency of incident light

ν_0 = Threshold frequency

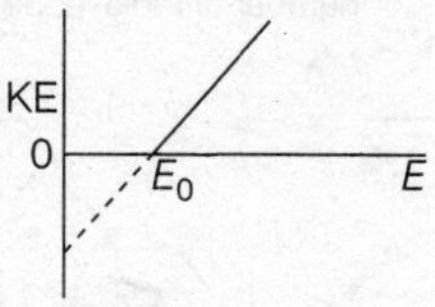

Slope = ± 1, intercept = – E_0

So, option (a) is correct.

(ii) KE of ejected electrons does not depend on the intensity of incident light.

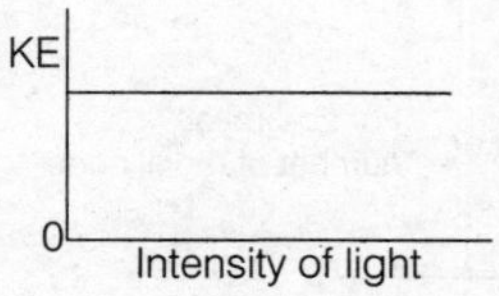

So, option (b) is correct.

(iii) When, number of ejected electrons is plotted with frequency of light, we get

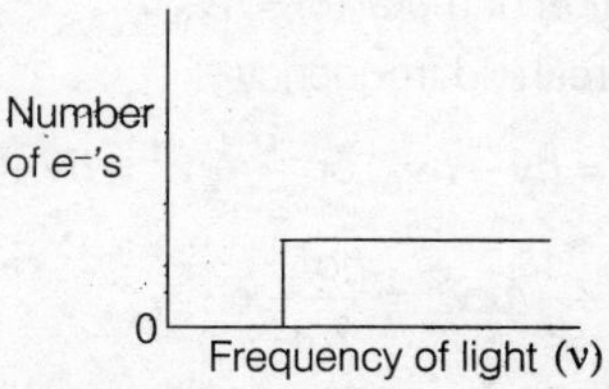

Slope = + h, intercept = – $h\nu_0$

So, option (d) is not correct.

127. (*a*) $E = Nh\nu = N\dfrac{hc}{\lambda}$

$$E = 100\ \text{W}(\text{Js}^{-1}) \times 1\ \text{s} = 100\ \text{J}$$

$$\therefore \quad N = \frac{E\lambda}{hc} = \frac{100 \times 560 \times 10^{-9}}{6.626 \times 10^{-34} \times 3 \times 10^{8}} = 2.82 \times 10^{20}$$

128. (*b*) 2.82×10^{20} photons are produced in = 1s

$$\therefore \ 6.02 \times 10^{23} \text{ photons are produced in} = \frac{6.02 \times 10^{23}}{2.82 \times 10^{20}}\ \text{s} = 2135\ \text{s} = 35.58 = 36\ \text{min}$$

129. (*a*) $\text{KE} = kT = \dfrac{RT}{N_0} = \dfrac{8.3143 \times 300}{6.02 \times 10^{23}}\ \text{J} = 4.143 \times 10^{-21}\ \text{J}$

m(neutron) = 1.67495×10^{-27} kg

$$\lambda = \frac{h}{m\upsilon} = \frac{h}{\sqrt{2m(\text{KE})}}$$

$$= \frac{6.626 \times 10^{-34}}{\sqrt{2 \times 1.67495 \times 10^{-27} \times 4.143 \times 10^{-21}}}$$

$$= 1.778 \times 10^{-10}\ \text{m} = 177.8\ \text{pm}$$

130. (*b*) $\lambda = \dfrac{h}{m\upsilon}$

$$\therefore \quad \upsilon = \frac{h}{m\lambda} = \frac{6.626 \times 10^{-34}}{9.1 \times 10^{-31} \times 3 \times 10^{-2}} = 0.0243\ \text{ms}^{-1}$$

131. (*d*) Power = 1 W = 1 J s^{-1}

$$\therefore \quad E \text{ per second} = 1\ \text{J s}^{-1} \times 1 = 1\ \text{J}$$

$$E = Nh\nu = \frac{Nhc}{\lambda}$$

$$\therefore \quad N = \frac{E\lambda}{hc} = \frac{1 \times 700 \times 10^{-9}}{6.626 \times 10^{-34} \times 3 \times 10^{8}} = 3.52 \times 10^{18}\ \text{s}^{-1}$$

133. (*a*) $r_n = \dfrac{n^2 a_0}{Z}$

$$r_1(\text{H}) = \frac{a_0}{1} = a_0 = 0.53\ \text{Å}$$

$$r_1(\text{Li}^{2+}) = \frac{a_0}{3} = \frac{0.53}{3} = 0.17\ \text{Å}$$

134. (*a*) $\Delta x \cdot \Delta\upsilon \approx \dfrac{h}{4\pi m}$

$$\Delta x \approx \frac{h}{4\pi m \Delta\upsilon}$$

$$\approx \frac{6.626 \times 10^{-27}}{4\pi \times 9.1 \times 10^{-28} \times 3 \times 10^{4} \times \dfrac{0.001}{100}} = 1.93\ \text{cm}$$

135. (*b*) $\Delta E = 13.6\left[\dfrac{1}{n_1^2} - \dfrac{1}{n_2^2}\right]\text{eV} = 13.6\left[\dfrac{1}{1^2} - \dfrac{1}{3^2}\right]$

$$= 13.6 \times \frac{8}{9}\ \text{eV} = 13.6 \times \frac{8}{9} \times 1.6 \times 10^{-19}\ \text{J}$$

$$= 1.936 \times 10^{-18}\ \text{J atom}^{-1}$$

$$= 1.936 \times 10^{-18} \times 10^{7}\ \text{erg atom}^{-1}$$

$$= 0.1936 \times 10^{-10}\ \text{erg atom}^{-1}$$

136. (*d*) $\bar{\nu}_{min} = \dfrac{1}{\lambda_{max}} = \bar{R}_H\left[\dfrac{1}{n_1^2} - \dfrac{1}{n_2^2}\right]$

where, $n_2 = (n_1 + 1)$

For Balmer series $n_1 = 2$

$$\therefore \quad \frac{1}{\lambda_{max}} = \bar{R}_H\left[\frac{1}{2^2} - \frac{1}{3^2}\right] = 10967900 \times \frac{5}{36}\ \text{m}^{-1}$$

$$\lambda_{max} = 6.56 \times 10^{-7}\ \text{m} = 656 \times 10^{-9}\ \text{nm} = 656\ \text{nm}$$

144. (*c*) $\lambda = \dfrac{h}{\sqrt{2m(\text{KE})}} = \dfrac{6.626 \times 10^{-34}}{\sqrt{2 \times 9.1 \times 10^{-31} \times 13.6 \times 1.6 \times 10^{-19}}}$

$$= 3.329 \times 10^{-10}\ \text{m} = 0.3329 \times 10^{-9}\ \text{m}$$

$$= 0.3329\ \text{nm}$$

149. (*c*) This graph shows the probability of finding the electron within shell at various distances from the nucleus (radial probability).

The curve shows the maximum, which means that the radial probability is greatest for a given distance from the nucleus. This distance is equal to Bohr's radius = a_0

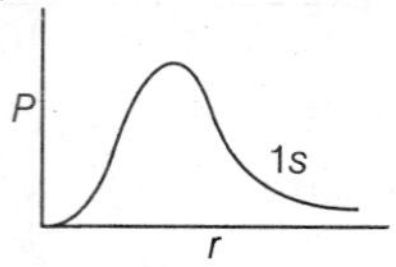

(a) It is for 2s-orbital.

(b) It is radial wave function for 1s.

(c) Correct

(d) Probability cannot be zero at a certain distance from nucleus.

150. (*b*) Angular nodes = l

Radial nodes = $(n - l - 1)$

151. (*b*) It is stable configuration of Cr in ground state

152. (*a*) Nodal planes = l (numerical value) = 1 (for p_x)

154. (*d*) Statement (d) is incorrect. For 1s-orbital radial probability density (R^2) against r is given as:

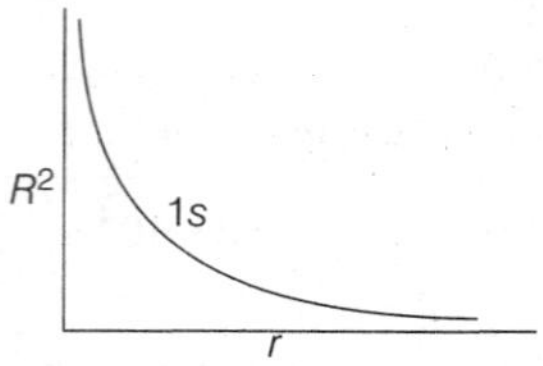

For 1s-orbital, probability density decreases sharply as we move away from the nucleus.

The radial distribution curves obtained by plotting radial probability functions *vs* r for 1s-orbital is

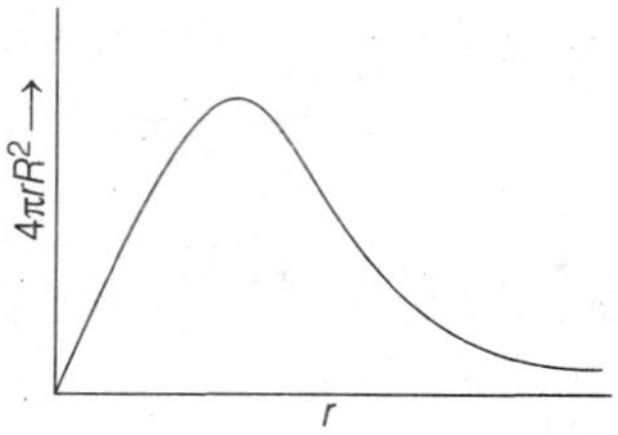

The graph initially increases and then decreases. It reaches a maximum at a distance very close to the nucleus and then decreases. The maximum in the curve corresponds to the distance at which the probability of finding the electron in maximum.

155. (*d*) The graphs between $|\psi|^2$ and r are radial density plots having $(n - l - 1)$ number of radial nodes. For 1s, 2s, 3s and 2 p-orbitals these are respectively.

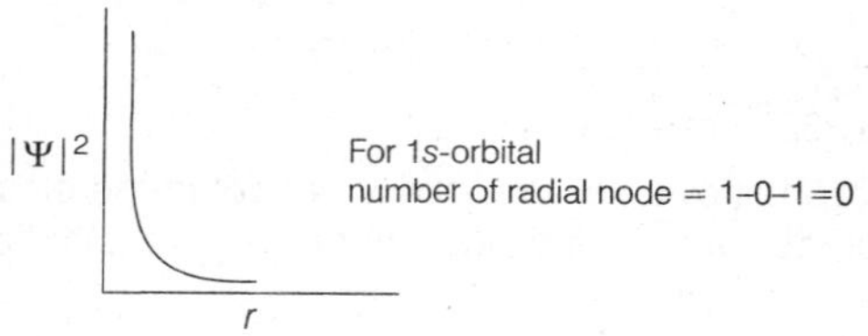

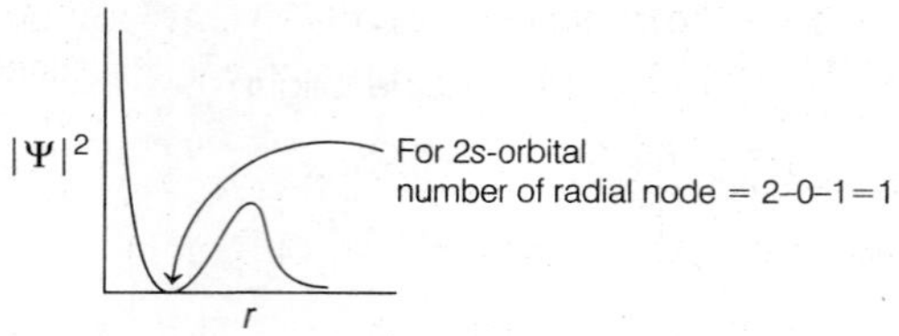

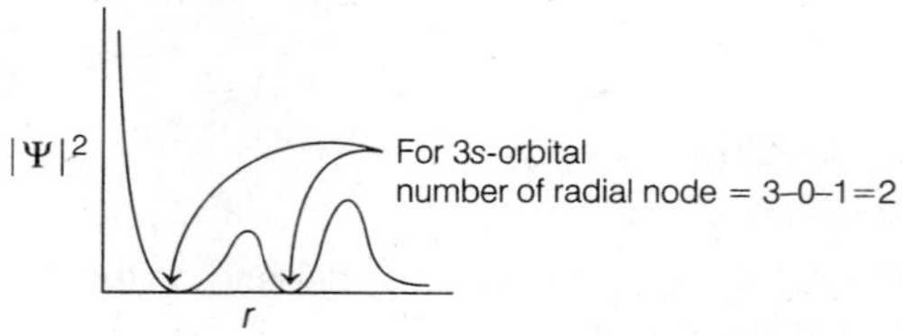

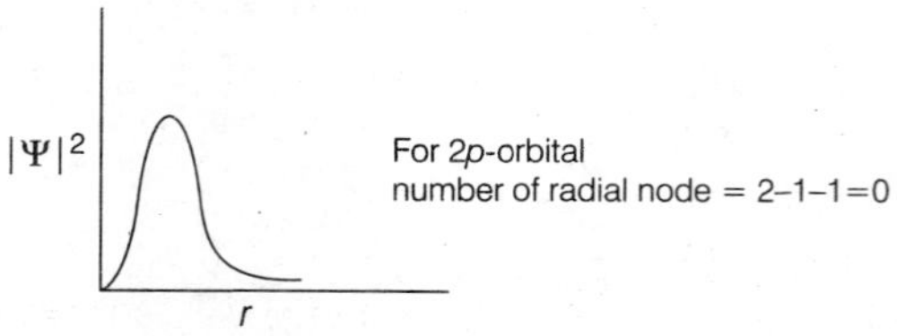

Thus, the given graph between $|\psi|^2$ and r represents 2s-orbital.

156. (*b*) Work function of metal $(\phi) = h\nu_0$

where, ν_0 = threshold frequency

Also, $\frac{1}{2}m_e v^2 = h\nu - h\nu_0$ or $\frac{1}{2}m_e v^2 = h\nu - \phi$ ...(i)

$$\frac{1}{2}m_e v^2 = \frac{hc}{\lambda} - \phi \quad \text{...(ii)}$$

Given : $\lambda = 4000$ Å $= 4000 \times 10^{-10}$m

$v = 6 \times 10^5$ ms^{-1},

$m_e = 9 \times 10^{-31}$ kg, $c = 3 \times 10^8$ ms^{-1}

$h = 6.626 \times 10^{-34}$ Js

Thus, on substituting all the given values in Eq. (i), we get

$$\frac{1}{2} \times 9 \times 10^{-31} \text{ kg} \times (6 \times 10^5 \text{ ms}^{-1})^2$$

$$= \frac{6.626 \times 10^{-34} \text{ J s} \times 3 \times 10^8 \text{ ms}^{-1}}{4000 \times 10^{-10}\text{m}} - \phi$$

$\therefore \phi = 1.62 \times 10^{-21}$ kgm^{2}s^{-2} $- 4.96 \times 10^{-19}$ J

$= 3.36 \times 10^{-19}$ J [1 kg m^{2}s^{-2} = 1J]

$= 2.1$ eV

157. (*b*) According to de-Broglie relationship.

$$\lambda = \frac{h}{mv} = \frac{6.63 \times 10^{-34}}{1.67 \times 10^{-27} \times 1 \times 10^3}$$

$= 3.97 \times 10^{-10}$ m ~ 0.40 nm

158. (*c*)

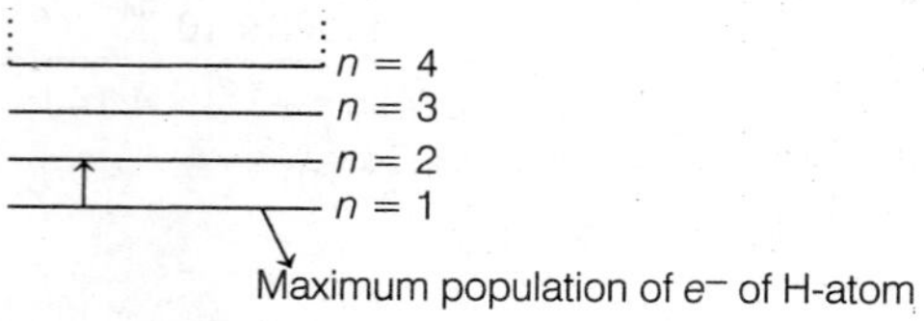

Since, at $n = 1$, the population of electrons is maximum *i.e.* at ground state. So, maximum excitation will take place from $n = 1$ to $n = 2$.

Hence, $n = 2$ is the possible excited state.

Now, we have the formula for energy of H-atom

$$(E_n)_H = -13.6 \frac{Z^2}{n^2} \text{ eV}$$

where, Z = atomic number

Z for H-atom = 1

$$\therefore \quad (E_n)_H = -13.6 \times \frac{1}{2^2} \text{eV}$$

$$= -\frac{13.6}{4} \text{eV} = -3.4 \text{ eV}$$

159. (*b*)

	$n+l$	
(a) $3p$	4	$\therefore$ Energy order = $3s < 3p < 4s < 3d$
(b) $3d$	5	
(c) $4s$	4	
(d) $3s$	3	

160. (*a*) According to Rydberg's equation,

$$\frac{1}{\lambda} = \frac{R_H}{hc}\left(\frac{1}{n_1^2} - \frac{1}{n_2^2}\right) \quad \text{or} \quad \frac{1}{\lambda} \propto \left(\frac{1}{n_1^2} - \frac{1}{n_2^2}\right)$$

For shortest wavelength, i.e. highest energy spectral line, n_2 will be (∞).

For the given spectral series, ratio of the shortest wavelength of two spectral series can be calculated as follows :

$$\text{(a)} \quad \frac{\lambda_L}{\lambda_P} = \frac{\frac{1}{3^2} - \frac{1}{\infty^2}}{\frac{1}{1^2} - \frac{1}{\infty^2}} = \frac{\frac{1}{9} - 0}{1 - 0} = \frac{1}{9}$$

$$\text{(b)} \quad \frac{\lambda_{Bk}}{\lambda_{Pf}} = \frac{\frac{1}{5^2} - \frac{1}{\infty^2}}{\frac{1}{4^2} - \frac{1}{\infty^2}} = \frac{1}{25} \times \frac{16}{1} = \frac{16}{25}$$

$$\text{(c)} \quad \frac{\lambda_P}{\lambda_{Pf}} = \frac{\frac{1}{5^2} - \frac{1}{\infty^2}}{\frac{1}{3^2} - \frac{1}{\infty^2}} = \frac{1}{25} \times \frac{9}{1} = \frac{9}{25}$$

$$\text{(d)} \quad \frac{\lambda_B}{\lambda_{Bk}} = \frac{\frac{1}{4^2} - \frac{1}{\infty^2}}{\frac{1}{2^2} - \frac{1}{\infty^2}} = \frac{1}{16} \times \frac{4}{1} = \frac{1}{4}$$

Note *Lyman* = L ($n_1 = 1$), *Balmer* = B ($n_1 = 2$)

Paschen = P ($n_1 = 3$), Brackett = Bk ($n_1 = 4$)

Pfund = Pf ($n_1 = 5$)

161. (*c*) By Heisenberg's uncertainty principle

$$\Delta x \cdot m\Delta \upsilon \geq \frac{h}{4\pi}$$

or

$$\Delta x \cdot \Delta \upsilon \geq \frac{h}{4\pi m}$$

$$\Delta x = \frac{6.63 \times 10^{-34}}{4 \times 3.14 \times 9.1 \times 10^{-31} \times 300 \times 0.001 \times 10^{-2}}$$

$$= 0.01933 = 1.93 \times 10^{-2} \text{ m}$$

162. (*b*)

$$\nu = \frac{\Delta E}{h}$$

$$\Delta E = 2.18 \times 10^{-18} Z^2 \left[\frac{1}{n_1^2} - \frac{1}{n_2^2}\right] \text{J}$$

$$\therefore \quad \nu = \frac{2.18 \times 10^{-18}}{h} Z^2 \left[\frac{1}{n_1^2} - \frac{1}{n_2^2}\right]$$

$$\nu(\text{He}^+) = \frac{2.18 \times 10^{-18}}{h} (Z^2) \left[\frac{1}{2^2} - \frac{1}{4^2}\right]$$

$$= \frac{2.18 \times 10^{-18}}{h} \left[\frac{1}{1^2} - \frac{1}{2^2}\right] = \nu \text{ (H)}$$

Thus, $n_1 = 1$ and $n_2 = 2$

163. (*c*) For any given series of spectral lines of atomic hydrogen.

Let $\Delta\bar{\nu} = \bar{\nu}_{max} - \bar{\nu}_{min}$ be the difference in maximum and minimum frequencies in cm^{-1}.

For Lyman series,

$$\Delta\bar{\nu} = \bar{\nu}_{max} - \bar{\nu}_{min}$$

General formula: $\bar{\nu} = 109677 \left[\frac{1}{n_i^2} - \frac{1}{n_f^2}\right]$

For Lyman $n_1 = 1$, $n_2 = 2, 3, \ldots$

$$\bar{\nu}_{max} = 109{,}677\left(\frac{1}{1} - \frac{1}{\infty}\right) = 109{,}677\left(\frac{1}{1} - 0\right) = 109{,}677$$

$$\bar{\nu}_{min} = 109{,}677\left(\frac{1}{1} - \frac{1}{(2)^2}\right)$$

$$\Delta\bar{\nu}_{\text{Lyman}} = \bar{\nu}_{max} - \bar{\nu}_{min}$$

$$= 109{,}677 - \left[\frac{109{,}677 \times 3}{4}\right] = \frac{109{,}677}{4}$$

For Balmer series,

$$\bar{\nu}_{max} = 109{,}677\left(\frac{1}{(2)^2} - \frac{1}{\infty}\right) \Rightarrow \frac{109677}{4}$$

$$\bar{\nu}_{min} = 109{,}677\left(\frac{1}{(2)^2} - \frac{1}{(3)^2}\right) \Rightarrow \frac{109677 \times 5}{36}$$

$$\Delta\bar{\nu} = \bar{\nu}_{max} - \bar{\nu}_{min}$$

$$\Delta\bar{\nu}_{\text{Balmer}} = \frac{109{,}677}{4} - \left[\frac{109{,}677}{36} \times 5\right] = 109{,}677\left(\frac{1}{9}\right)$$

$$\frac{\Delta\bar{\nu}_{\text{Lyman}}}{\Delta\bar{\nu}_{\text{Balmer}}} = \frac{109{,}677/4}{109{,}677/9} \Rightarrow \frac{\Delta\bar{\nu}_{\text{Lyman}}}{\Delta\bar{\nu}_{\text{Balmer}}} = \frac{9}{4}$$

$\therefore$ The ratio of $\frac{\Delta\bar{\nu}_{\text{Lyman}}}{\Delta\bar{\nu}_{\text{Balmer}}}$ is 9 : 4.

164. (*b*)
$$(\text{IE})_Z = (\text{IE})_H \left(\frac{Z^2}{n^2}\right)$$
$$(\text{IE})_{He^+} = (\text{IE})_H \left(\frac{4}{1}\right)$$
$$(\text{IE})_{Li^{2+}} = (\text{IE})_H \left(\frac{9}{1}\right)$$
$$\therefore \quad \frac{(\text{IE})_{Li}^{2+}}{(\text{IE})_{He^+}} = \frac{9}{4}$$
$$(\text{IE})_{Li^{2+}} = \frac{9}{4} \times 19.6 \times 10^{-18} \text{ J atom}^{-1}$$
$$= 4.41 \times 10^{-17}$$

Thus, energy of Li^{2+} 1*s* is -4.41×10^{-17}.

165. (*c*) By Heisenberg's uncertainty principle
$$\Delta x \cdot m\Delta V \geq \frac{h}{4\pi}$$
$$\Delta V = 0.005\%$$
or
$$600 \text{ m s}^{-1} = \frac{600 \times 0.005}{100} = 0.03 \text{ m s}^{-1}$$
$$\Delta x \times 9.1 \times 10^{-31} \times 0.03 = \frac{6.6 \times 10^{-34}}{4 \times 3.14}$$
Hence,
$$\Delta x = \frac{6.6 \times 10^{-34}}{4 \times 3.14 \times 0.03 \times 9.1 \times 10^{-31}}$$
$$= 1.92 \times 10^{-3} \text{ m}$$

166. (*c*) $\frac{E_1}{E_2} = \frac{\lambda_2}{\lambda_1} \Rightarrow \frac{25}{50} = \frac{\lambda_2}{\lambda_1}$

or
$$\lambda_1 = 2\lambda_2$$

167. (*d*) Angular momentum of an electron
$$= m\upsilon r = \frac{nh}{2\pi} \text{ (} n \text{ is orbit number)}$$
$$\text{in 5th orbit} = \frac{5h}{2\pi} = \frac{2.5h}{\pi}$$

168. (*a*) The expression of kinetic energy of photo electrons,
$$\text{KE} = \frac{1}{2}mv^2 = E - E_0$$

When, KE >> E_0, the equation becomes,
$$\text{KE} = \frac{1}{2}mv^2 = E$$
$$\Rightarrow \quad \frac{1}{2}mv^2 = \frac{hc}{\lambda} \Rightarrow \frac{p^2}{2m^2} = \frac{hc}{\lambda}$$
$$\Rightarrow \quad \lambda = hc \times 2m^2 \times \frac{1}{p^2}$$
$$\Rightarrow \quad \lambda \propto \frac{1}{p^2}$$

$E = \frac{hc}{\lambda}$ = energy of incident light.

E_0 = threshold energy or work functions,
$$\frac{1}{2}mv^2 = \frac{1}{2} \times \frac{(mv)^2}{m^2} = \frac{1}{2} \times \frac{p^2}{m^2}$$

$\because p$ = momentum = mv

As per the given condition,
$$\frac{\lambda_2}{\lambda_1} = \left(\frac{p_1}{p_2}\right)^2$$
$$\Rightarrow \quad \frac{\lambda_2}{\lambda} = \left(\frac{p}{1.5 \times p}\right)^2 = \left(\frac{2}{3}\right)^2 = \frac{4}{9}$$
$$\Rightarrow \quad \lambda_2 = \frac{4}{9}\lambda \qquad \left[\begin{array}{l}\because \lambda_1 = \lambda \\ p_1 = p\end{array}\right]$$

169. (*c*) Energy values are always additive.
$$E_{\text{total}} = E_1 + E_2$$
$$\frac{hc}{\lambda} = \frac{hc}{\lambda_1} = \frac{hc}{\lambda_2}$$

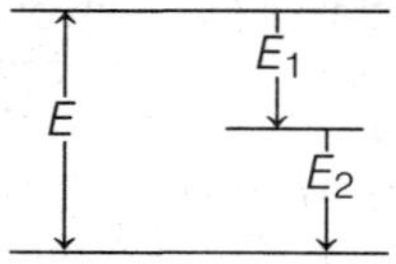

$$\therefore \quad \frac{1}{\lambda} = \frac{1}{\lambda_1} + \frac{1}{\lambda_2},$$
$$\frac{1}{355} = \frac{1}{680} = \frac{1}{\lambda_2}$$
$$\lambda_2 = 742.77 \text{ nm} \approx 743 \text{ nm}$$

03

States of Matter

Gaseous State

Objective Questions Type I [Only one correct option]

In each of the questions below, four choices are given of which only one is correct.

1. Which represents the largest pressure?
(a) One atmosphere
(b) Five pounds per square inch
(c) One mm of Hg
(d) One hundred pascal

2. Which pair of molecules has the strongest dipole-dipole interactions?
(a) NH_3 and CH_4 (b) NH_3 and NH_3
(c) CH_4 and CH_4 (d) CO_2 and CO_2

3. Which of the assumptions of the kinetic-molecular theory best explains the observations that a gas can be compressed?
(a) Gas molecules move at random with no attractive forces between them
(b) The velocity of gas molecules is proportional to their kelvin temperature
(c) The amount of space occupied by a gas is much greater than the space occupied by the actual gas molecules
(d) In collisions with the walls of the container or with other molecules, energy is conserved

4. What weight of hydrogen at STP could be contained in a vessel that holds 3.36 L O_2 gas at STP?
(a) 0.21 g (b) 4.8 g (c) 0.30 g (d) 3.36 g

5. The relative strength of interionic/intermolecular forces in decreasing order is **[JEE Main 2020]**
(a) dipole-dipole > ion-dipole > ion-ion
(b) ion-ion > ion-dipole > dipole-dipole
(c) ion-dipole > ion-ion > dipole-dipole
(d) ion-dipole > dipole-dipole > ion-ion

6. Weight of 112 mL of oxygen gas at NTP on liquefaction would be
(a) 0.32 g (b) 0.64 g
(c) 0.16 g (d) 0.96 g

7. The volume of gas A is twice than that of gas B. The compressibility factor of gas A is thrice than that of gas B at same temperature. The pressures of the gases for equal number of moles are **[2019 Main Jan.]**
(a) $p_A = 2p_B$
(b) $2p_A = 3p_B$
(c) $p_A = 3p_B$
(d) $3p_A = 2p_B$

8. Atmospheric pressure is 76 cm Hg and pressure of the gas is 77 cm Hg. Hence, height h of the mercury column in open arm is
(a) 1 cm
(b) $\frac{1}{13.6 \times 980}$ cm
(c) 153 cm
(d) $1 \times 13.6 \times 980$ cm

9. A flask of gaseous CCl_4 was weighed at measured temperature and pressure. CCl_4 was replaced by O_2 at the same temperature and pressure. The mass of the CCl_4 vapour will be
(a) five times as heavy as O_2
(b) one fifth heavy as compared to O_2
(c) same as that of O_2
(d) twice as heavy as O_2

10. Which is not a correct representation of Boyle's law?

(a) 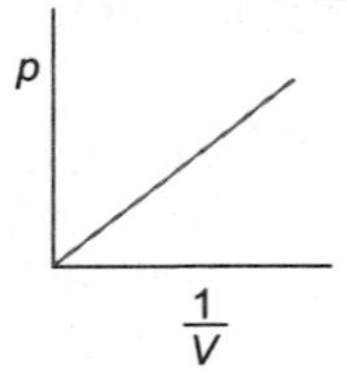

(b) 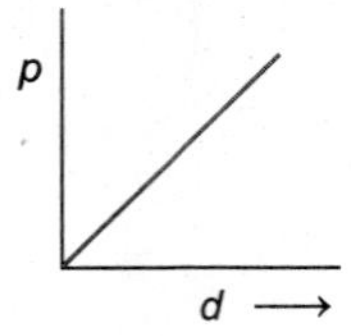

(c) 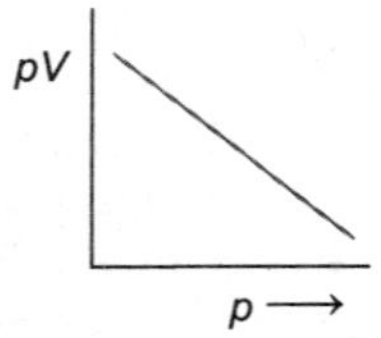

(d) 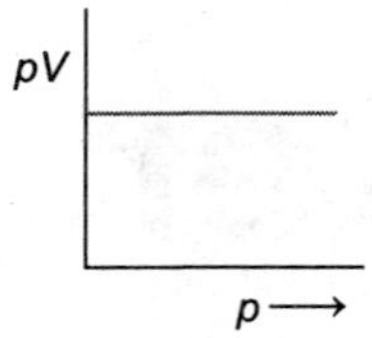

11. Which does not represent isobar given by Charles' law?

(a) 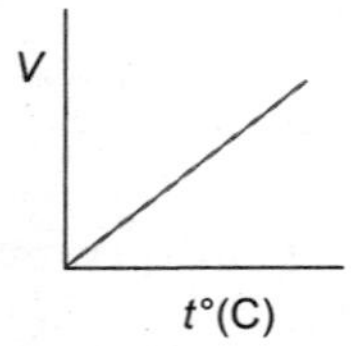

(b) 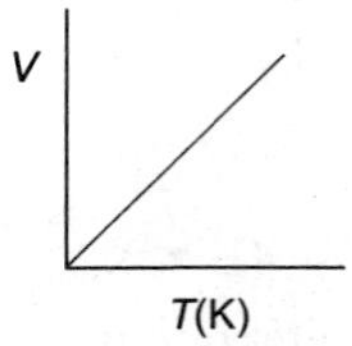

(c) Both (a) and (b)   (d) None of these

12. When the volume of a gas is plotted *versus* the Celsius temperature with pressure and number of moles held constant, the X-intercept is at what temperature?
(a) 0°C   (b) – 273°C
(c) The b.p. of the gas   (d) The m.p. of the gas

13. Which is a correct statement of Gay-Lussac's law describing the behaviour of a fixed amount of gas?
(a) As pressure increases, volume increases at constant temperature
(b) As pressure increases, volume decreases at constant temperature
(c) As temperature increases, pressure decreases at constant volume
(d) As temperature increases, pressure increases at constant volume

14. According to Avogadro's law, the volume of a gas will ... as ... if ... are held constant.
(a) increase; number of moles; pressure and temperature
(b) decrease; number of moles; pressure and temperature
(c) increase; temperature, pressure and number of moles
(d) decrease; pressure; temperature and number of moles

15. A balloon has maximum capacity of 20 L. At one atmospheric pressure 10 L of air is filled in the balloon. It will burst when pressure is (assuming isothermal condition)
(a) 0.5 atm   (b) 0.4 atm
(c) 0.7 atm   (d) 0.8 atm

16. A sealed container with gas at 2.00 atm is heated from 20.0 K to 40.0 K. The new pressure is .
(a) 0.50 atm   (b) 1.00 atm
(c) 4.00 atm   (d) 2.14 atm

17. At 27°C, which set is not for Boyle's law?

(a)	$p =$ 380 mm Hg $V =$ 100 mL	(b)	$p =$ 1 atm $V =$ 0.050 L
(c)	$p =$ 190 mm Hg $V =$ 0.200 L	(d)	$p =$ 1 atm $V =$ 150 mL

18. If the density of a certain gas at 30°C and 768 Torr is 1.35 kg/m^3, then density at STP is
(a) 1.48 kg/m^3 (b) 1.27 kg/m^3
(c) 1.35 kg/m^3 (d) 1.00 kg/m^3

19. The relative rate of diffusion of a gas (molar mass = 128) as compared to oxygen is
(a) 2 times   (b) 1/4   (c) 1/8   (d) 1/2

20. If 4 g of oxygen diffuse through a very narrow hole, how much hydrogen would have diffused under identical conditions?
(a) 16 g   (b) 1 g   (c) 1/4 g   (d) 64 g

21. A quantity of gas is collected in a graduated tube over the mercury. The volume of gas at 18°C is 50.0 mL and the level of mercury in the tube is 100 mm above the outside mercury level. The barometer reads 750 Torr. Hence, volume at STP is approximately
(a) 22 mL   (b) 40 mL
(c) 20 mL   (d) 44 mL

22. A gas at a pressure of 5.0 atm is heated from 0° to 546°C and is simultaneously compressed to one-third of its original volume. Hence, final pressure is
(a) 15.0 atm   (b) 30.0 atm
(c) 45.0 atm   (d) $\frac{5}{9}$ atm

23. For gaseous state, if most probable speed is denoted by C^*, average speed by $\overline{C}$ and mean square speed by C, then for a large number of molecules, the ratios of these speeds are **[JEE Main 2013]**
(a) $C^* : \overline{C} : C = 1.225 : 1.128 : 1$
(b) $C^* : \overline{C} : C = 1.228 : 1.225 : 1$
(c) $C^* : \overline{C} : C = 1 : 1.128 : 1.225$
(d) $C^* : \overline{C} : C = 1 : 1.225 : 1.128$

24. A mixture of Ar (40) and N_2 gases have a density of 1.40 g L^{-1} at STP. Hence, weight fraction of N_2 approximately in the mixture is
(a) 0.3   (b) 0.7   (c) 0.4   (d) 0.5

25. A 34.0 L cylinder contains 212 g O_2 gas at 27°C. What mass of $O_2(g)$ must be released to reduce the pressure to 2.463 atm?
(a) 103.2 g   (b) 108.8 g
(c) 100.0 g   (d) 32.0 g

26. A quantity of hydrogen gas occupies a volume of 30.0 mL at a certain temperature and pressure. What volume would half this mass of hydrogen occupy at triple the absolute temperature and the pressure were one-ninth that of the original gas?
(a) 405 mL (b) 810 mL
(c) 81 mL (d) None of these

27. What per cent of a sample of nitrogen must be allowed to escape if its temperature, pressure and volume are to be changed as given?

273°C, 3.00 atm 1.65 L	→	0°C, 0.75 atm 0.55 L

(a) 16.67% (b) 83.33% (c) 75.00% (d) 25.00%

28. A 1.00 L vessel containing 1.00 g H_2 gas at 27°C is connected to a 2.00 L vessel containing 88.0 g CO_2 gas, at also 27°C. When the gases are completely mixed, total pressure is
(a) 20.525 atm (b) 4.105 atm
(c) 16.420 atm (d) 730.69 atm

29. In a gaseous mixture at 20°C the partial pressure of the components are,
H_2 : 150 Torr CH_4 : 300 Torr
CO_2 : 200 Torr C_2H_4 : 100 Torr
Volume per cent of H_2 is
(a) 26.67 (b) 73.33 (c) 80.00 (d) 20

30. 1 g H_2, 2 g He and 3 g NO are contained in 1.1 L flask at 300 K. Total pressure exerted by the mixture is
(a) 5.45 atm (b) 6.0 atm
(c) 24.63 atm (d) 134.34 atm

31. Which of the assumptions of the kinetic-molecular theory best explains the observation that a balloon collapses when exposed to liquid nitrogen (which is much colder than a cold winter day)?
(a) Gas molecules move at random with no attractive forces between them
(b) The velocity of gas molecules is proportional to their Kelvin temperature
(c) The amount of space occupied by a gas is much greater than the space occupied by the actual gas molecules
(d) Collisions with the walls of the container or with other molecules are elastic

32. Which of the assumption of the kinetic-molecular theory best explains Daltons law of partial pressure?
(a) Gas molecules move at random with no attractive forces between them
(b) The velocity of gas molecules is proportional to their Kelvin temperature
(c) The amount of space occupied by a gas is much greater than the space occupied by the actual gas molecules
(d) Collisions with the walls of the container or with other molecules are elastic

33. At the same temperature and pressure which of the following gas will have highest KE per mol?
(a) H_2 (b) O_2
(c) CH_4 (d) Equal

34. At what temperature will the total KE of 0.30 mole of He be the same as the total KE of 0.40 mole Ar at 400 K?
(a) 533 K (b) 400 K
(c) 346 K (d) 300 K

35. The molecular velocities of two gases at same temperature are u_1 and u_2, their molar masses are m_1 and m_2 respectively. Which of the following expression is correct?
(a) $\frac{m_1}{u_1^2} = \frac{m_2}{u_2^2}$ (b) $m_1u_1 = m_2u_2$
(c) $\frac{m_1}{u_1} = \frac{m_2}{u_2}$ (d) $m_1u_1^2 = m_2u_2^2$

36. 50 mL of H_2 gas diffuses through a small hole from a vessel in 20 min. Time taken by 40 mL of O_2 gas to diffuse under similar conditions will be
(a) 12 min (b) 64 min
(c) 8 min (d) 32 min

37. The average molecular speed is greatest in which of the following gas samples?
(a) 1.0 mol of O_2 at 560 K
(b) 0.50 mol of Ne at 500 K
(c) 0.20 mol of CO_2 at 440 K
(d) 2.0 mol of He at 140 K

38. It takes 26 s for 10 mL of H_2 to effuse through a porous membrane. It takes 130 s for 10 mL of an unknown gas under identical condition to effuse. Hence, molecular weight of the unknown gas is (in g mol^{-1})
(a) 100 (b) 80 (c) 50 (d) 40

39. The average kinetic energy of an ideal gas per molecule in SI unit at 25°C will be
(a) 6.17×10^{-21} kJ (b) 6.17×10^{-21} J
(c) 6.17×10^{-20} J (d) 6.17×10^{-20} kJ

40. A comparison is made at standard temperature and pressure (STP) of 0.50 mol $H_2(g)$ and 1.0 mol He (g). The two gases will
(a) have equal average molecular kinetic energies
(b) have equal molecular speed
(c) occupy equal volumes
(d) have equal effusion rates

41. Which of the following equations involve microscopic properties?
(a) $pV = nRT$ (b) $U = \sqrt{(u^2)}$
(c) $KE = \frac{1}{2}mu^2$ (d) $\frac{R_1}{R_2} = \sqrt{\frac{M_2}{M_1}}$

42. Consider the following properties,

I. $pV = nRT$; II. $p_{total} = p_1 + p_2 + p_3$

III. $\frac{R_1}{R_2} = \sqrt{\frac{M_2}{M_1}}$; IV. $U = \sqrt{(u^2)}$

Which represent macroscopic properties?

(a) I, II, III and IV (b) I, II and III
(c) I and II (d) I and III

43. KE per unit volume is

(a) $\frac{3}{2}P$ (b) $\frac{3}{2}RT$ (c) $\frac{3}{2}\frac{RN}{N_0}$ (d) $\frac{3}{2}\frac{RT}{n}$

44. Select the correct statement(s).

(a) The velocity at which distribution of molecules is maximum is called most probable velocity
(b) Most probable velocity of a gas is larger than root mean square velocity
(c) Both (a) and (b)
(d) None of the above is correct

45. Select the correct statement (s).

(a) Kinetic energy is zero at 0°C.
(b) rms velocity of O_2 at 27°C is $= \sqrt{\frac{3 \times 8.314 \times 300}{32}}$ ms^{-1}
(c) Distribution of molecules is very small when $u \to 0$ or $u \to \infty$
(d) All the above statements are correct

46. One molecule is moving at a speed of 1 m s^{-1} and two molecules are moving at 2 m s^{-1}. Hence, root mean square velocity is

(a) 1 m s^{-1} (b) 1.67 m s^{-1}
(c) 3 m s^{-1} (d) 1.73 m s^{-1}

47. Select the correct order of molecular velocities

(a) $u_{rms} < u_{av} < u_{mp}$ (b) $u_{av} < u_{mp} < u_{rms}$
(c) $u_{mp} < u_{av} < u_{rms}$ (d) $u_{mp} < u_{rms} < u_{av}$

48. Which of the following gases follows non-ideal behaviour?

(a) N_2 gas having density 1.25 g L^{-1} at STP
(b) 2.8 g CO gas in 0.1 L flask exerting a pressure of 24.63 atm at 300 K
(c) 1.6 g CH_4 in 0.5 L flask at 273 K exerting a pressure of 4 atm
(d) 0.1 g H_2 gas at STP occupies volume of 1.12 L

49. The ratio of van der Waals' constants a and b, $\left(\frac{a}{b}\right)$ has the dimension of

(a) atm L^{-1} (b) L atm mol^{-1}
(c) L mol^{-1} (d) atm L mol^{-2}

50. Gas deviates from ideal gas nature because molecules

(a) are colourless
(b) attract each other
(c) contain covalent bond
(d) show Brownian motion

51. The van der Waals' equation of state reduces itself to the ideal gas equation at

(a) high pressure and low temperature
(b) low pressure and low temperature
(c) low pressure and high temperature
(d) high pressure and high temperature

52. For CO, isotherm is of the type as shown. Near the point A, compressibility factor Z is

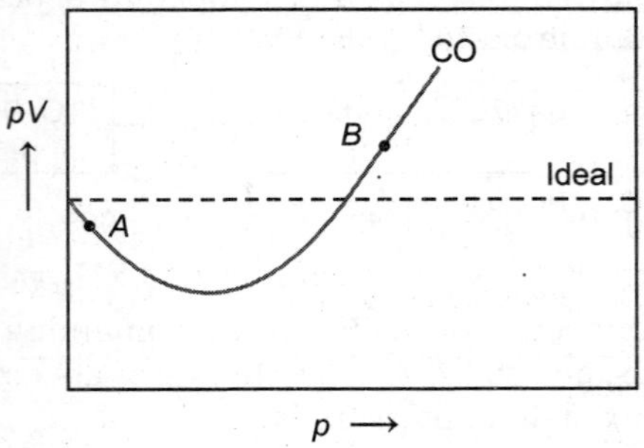

(a) $\left(1 + \frac{b}{V}\right)$ (b) $\left(1 - \frac{b}{V}\right)$
(c) $\left(1 + \frac{a}{RTV}\right)$ (d) $\left(1 - \frac{a}{RTV}\right)$

53. In the above Q. (52), near the point B, compressibility factor Z is about

(a) $\left(1 - \frac{b}{V}\right)$ (b) 1 (c) $\left(1 + \frac{b}{V}\right)$ (d) $\left(1 - \frac{a}{RTV}\right)$

54. If $\left(\frac{ab}{V^2}\right)$ is negligible, then second virial coefficient B in virial equation is

(a) $\left(b - \frac{a}{RT}\right)$ (b) $\left(b + \frac{a}{RT}\right)$
(c) $\left(b + \frac{a}{RTV}\right)$ (d) $\left(b - \frac{a}{RTV}\right)$

55. Consider isotherms I, II and III

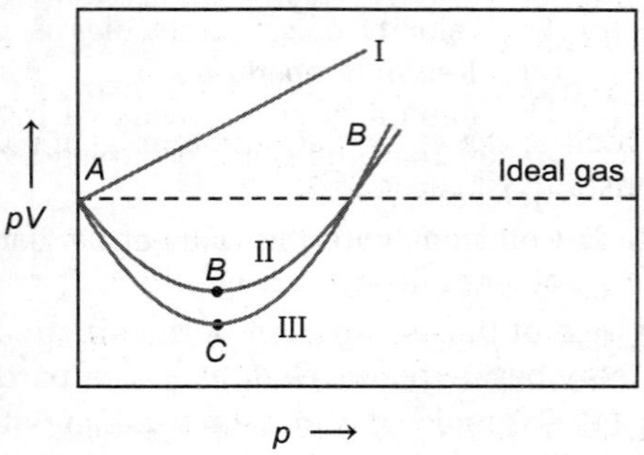

Select the correct statement.

(a) For light gases (like H_2), isotherm I is obtained
(b) When force of attraction is negligible, isotherms II and III are followed after point B or C
(c) When co-volume is neglected, isotherms II and III are followed A to B or A to C
(d) All the above are correct statements

56. In terms of critical constants, compressibility factor is

(a) 1 (b) $\frac{3}{4}$

(c) $\frac{3}{7}$ (d) $\frac{3}{8}$

57. Match Column I with Column II and select the correct answers.

	Column I		Column II
A.	Critical temperature	1.	$\frac{a}{Rb}$
B.	Boyle's temperature	2.	$\frac{2a}{Rb}$
C.	Inversion temperature	3.	$\frac{T}{T_c}$
D.	Reduced temperature	4.	$\frac{8a}{27Rb}$

Codes

	A	B	C	D		A	B	C	D
(a)	2	1	4	3	(b)	4	3	2	1
(c)	2	3	4	1	(d)	4	1	2	3

58. An ideal gas obeying kinetic gas equation can be liquefied if

(a) its temperature is more than critical temperature
(b) its pressure is more than critical pressure
(c) its pressure is more than critical pressure but temperature is less than critical temperature
(d) it cannot be liquefied at any value of p and T

59. Consider the following statements.
The coefficient B in the virial equation of state

$$pV_m = RT\left(1 + \frac{B}{V_m} + \frac{B}{V_m^2} + \dots\right)$$

I. is independent of temperature
II. is equal to zero at Boyle's temperature
III. has the dimension of molar volume

Which of the above statements are correct?

(a) I and II (b) I and III
(c) II and III (d) I, II and III

60. Which of the following statements on critical constants of gases are correct?

I. Larger the T_c / p_c value of a gas, larger would be the excluded volume.
II. Critical temperature (T_c) of a gas is greater than its Boyle's temperature (T_b).
III. At the critical point in the van der Waals' gas isotherm.

$$\left(\frac{\partial p}{\partial V_m}\right) T_c = 0$$

Select the correct answer using the codes given below.

(a) I and II (b) I and III
(c) II and III (d) I, II and III

61. Consider the following statements.
If the van der Waals' parameters of two gases are given as

	a (atm L^2 mol^{-2})	b (L^2 mol^{-1})
Gas X :	6.5	0.056
Gas Y :	8.0	0.011

then A : V_c $(X) < V_c$ (Y)
B : p_c $(X) < p_c$ (Y)
C : T_c $(X) < T_c$ (Y)

Select the correct alternate.

(a) A alone (b) A and B
(c) A, B and C (d) B and C

62. To liquefy gaseous substances whose critical temperatures are below room temperature requires

(a) high pressure and lowering of temperature (below T_c)
(b) low pressure and raising of temperature (above T_c)
(c) high pressure and raising of temperature (above T_c)
(d) low pressure and lowering of temperature (below T_c)

63. T_c of CO_2 gas is 31°C. CO_2 is

(a) a gas at 35°C and vapour at 25°C
(b) a gas at 35°C as well as at 25°C
(c) vapour at 35°C as well as at 25°C
(d) a gas at 35°C and liquid at 25°C

64. Phenomenon of critical constants was first given by

(a) van't Hoff (b) Thomas Andrew
(c) Avogadro (d) Gay Lussac

65. Select the correct statements.

(a) Fluids above the critical temperature are known as supercritical fluids
(b) Supercritical fluids can dissolve many organic substances
(c) CO_2 above 31°C and above 600 bar pressure is used to remove coffeine from coffee beans, instead of using chlorofluoro carbons
(d) All the above are correct statements

66. By what factor does the average velocity of a gaseous molecule increases, when the temperature (in Kelvin) is doubled?

(a) 1.4 (b) 2.0
(c) 2.8 (d) 4.0

67. A gaseous mixture was prepared by taking equal moles of CO and N_2. If the total pressure of the mixture was found 1 atm, the partial pressure of the nitrogen (N_2) in the mixture is

(a) 1 atm (b) 0.5 atm
(c) 0.8 atm (d) 0.9 atm

68. Equal weights of CH_4 and H_2 are mixed in a container at 25°C. Fraction of total pressure exerted by methane is

(a) $\frac{1}{2}$ (b) $\frac{1}{3}$ (c) $\frac{1}{9}$ (d) $\frac{8}{9}$

69. A bubble of gas released at the bottom of a lake increases to eight times its original volume when it reaches the surface. Assuming that atmospheric pressure is equivalent to the pressure exerted by a column of water, 10 m height, the depth of the lake is

(a) 80 m (b) 90 m (c) 70 m (d) 10 m

70. A quantity of gas is confined in a chamber of constant volume. When the chamber is immersed in a bath of melting ice, the pressure of the gas is 1000 Torr. Final temperature when the pressure manometer indicates an absolute pressure of 400 Torr, is

(a) 109 K (b) 273 K
(c) 373 K (d) 0 K

71. At the top of the mountain the thermometer reads 0°C and the barometer reads 710 mmHg. At the bottom of the mountain the temperature is 30°C and pressure is 760 mmHg. Density of air at the top with that at the bottom is

(a) 1 : 1 (b) 1.04 : 1
(c) 1 : 1.04 (d) 1 : 1.5

72. 0.5 moles of gas A and x moles of gas B exert a pressure of 200 Pa in a container of volume $10\,m^3$ at 1000 K. Given R is the gas constant in $JK^{-1}\,mol^{-1}$, x is **[JEE Main 2019, Jan.]**

(a) $\frac{2R}{4-R}$ (b) $\frac{4-R}{2R}$ (c) $\frac{4+R}{2R}$ (d) $\frac{2R}{4+R}$

73. What weight of hydrogen at STP could be contained in a vessel that holds 4.8 g oxygen at STP?

(a) 4.8 g (b) 3.0 g (c) 0.6 g (d) 0.3 g

74. Ideal gas equation in terms of KE per unit volume, E, is

(a) $\frac{3}{2}RT$ (b) $\frac{2}{3}E$ (c) $\frac{2}{3}RT$ (d) $\frac{3}{2}E$

75. The compressibility factor of gas is less than unity at STP, therefore

(a) V_m (molar volume) > 22.4 L
(b) $V_m < 22.4$ L
(c) $V_m = 22.4$ L
(d) $V_m = 44.8$ L

76. I, II, III are three isotherms respectively at T_1, T_2 and T_3. Temperature will be in order

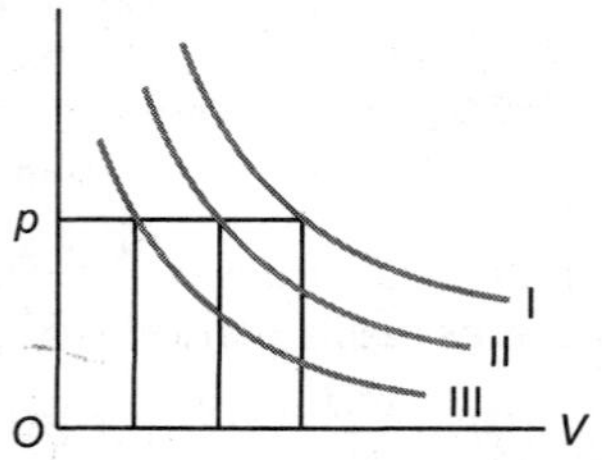

(a) $T_1 = T_2 = T_3$ (b) $T_1 < T_2 < T_3$
(c) $T_1 > T_2 > T_3$ (d) $T_1 > T_2 = T_3$

77. NH_3 gas is liquefied more easily than N_2. Hence,

(a) van der Waals' constants a and b of $NH_3 >$ that of N_2
(b) van der Waals' constant a and b of $NH_3 <$ that of N_2
(c) $a\,(NH_3) > a\,(N_2)$ but $b\,(NH_3) < b\,(N_2)$
(d) $a\,(NH_3) < a\,(N_2)$ but $b\,(NH_3) > b\,(N_2)$

78. van der Waals' equation for one mole of CO_2 gas at low pressure will be

(a) $\left(p + \frac{a}{V^2}\right)V = RT$ (b) $p(V-b) = RT - \frac{a}{V^2}$
(c) $p = \frac{RT}{V-b}$ (d) $p = \left(\frac{RT}{V-b} - \frac{a}{V^2}\right)$

79. In an auto engine with no pollution controls, about 5% of the fuel (C_8H_{18}) is unburned. Molar ratio of CO and C_8H_{18} emitted in the exhaust gas is

(a) 100 (b) 152
(c) 50 (d) 5

80. If v is the volume of one molecule of a gas under given conditions then van der Waals' constant b is

(a) $4v$ (b) $\frac{4v}{N_0}$
(c) $\frac{N_0}{4v}$ (d) $4vN_0$

81. $N_2 + 3H_2 \longrightarrow 2NH_3$. 1 mole N_2 and 4 moles H_2 are taken in 15 L flask at 27°C. After complete conversion of N_2 into NH_3, 5 L of H_2O is added. Pressure set up in the flask is

(a) $\frac{3 \times 0.0821 \times 300}{15}$ atm (b) $\frac{2 \times 0.0821 \times 300}{10}$ atm
(c) $\frac{1 \times 0.0821 \times 300}{15}$ atm (d) $\frac{1 \times 0.0821 \times 300}{10}$ atm

82. Which has maximum value of mean free path?

(a) CO_2 (b) H_2 (c) O_2 (d) N_2

83. Spark plugs are not necessary in a diesel engine because

(a) compression of the gases heats them above the ignition temperature of the fuel
(b) diesel is more volatile than petrol
(c) there is deposition of carbon in the spark plug which is difficult to remove
(d) diesel is easily ignited

84. A gas in an open container is heated from 27°C to 127°C. The fraction of the original amount of the gas remaining in the container will be

(a) 3/4 (b) 1/2 (c) 1/4 (d) 1/8

85. When an ideal gas undergoes unrestrained expansion, no cooling occurs because the molecules

(a) are above the inversion temperature
(b) exert no attractive force on the other
(c) do work equal to the loss in KE
(d) collide without loss of energy

86. When CO_2 under high pressure is released from a fire extinguisher, particles of solid CO_2 are formed, despite the low sublimation temperature (−77° C) of CO_2 at 1.0 atm. It is due to
(a) the gas does work pushing back the atmosphere using KE of molecules and thus lowering the temperature
(b) volume of the gas is decreased rapidly hence, temperature is lowered
(c) Both (a) and (b)
(d) None of the above

87. X mL of H_2 gas effuse through a hole in a container in 5 s. The time taken for the effusion of the same volume of the gas specified below under ideal conditions is
(a) 10 s : He (b) 20 s : O_2
(c) 25 s : CO (d) 55 s : CO_2

88. The temperature at which a real gas obeys the ideal gas laws over a fairly wide range of pressure is
(a) critical temperature (b) inversion temperature
(c) Boyle's temperature (d) reduced temperature

89. The pressure of real gas is less than the pressure of an ideal gas because of
(a) increase in collisions
(b) increase in intermolecular forces
(c) finite size of molecules
(d) statement is incorrect

90. O_2 gas at STP contained in a flask was replaced by SO_2 under same conditions. The weight of SO_2 will be
(a) equal to that of O_2 (b) half that of O_2
(c) twice that of O_2 (d) one-fourth of O_2

91. At what temperature will hydrogen molecules have the same KE per mol as nitrogen molecules at 280 K?
(a) 280 K (b) 40 K (c) 400 K (d) 50 K

92. Which of the following is an intensive variable for an ideal gas?
(a) V (b) p (c) n (d) T

93. See the figure

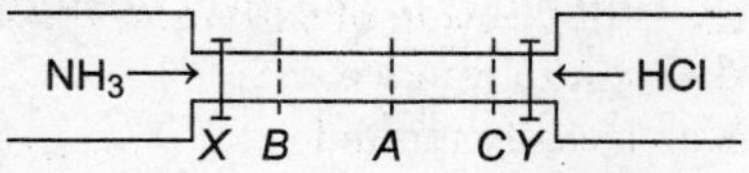

The valves of X and Y are opened simultaneously. The white fumes of NH_4Cl will first form at
(a) A (b) B
(c) C (d) A, B and C simultaneously

94. The temperature to which a gas must be cooled before it can be liquefied by compression is called
(a) Boyle's temperature
(b) critical temperature
(c) liquefaction temperature
(d) inversion temperature

95. Distribution of molecules with velocity is represented by the curve as shown; velocity at point A is

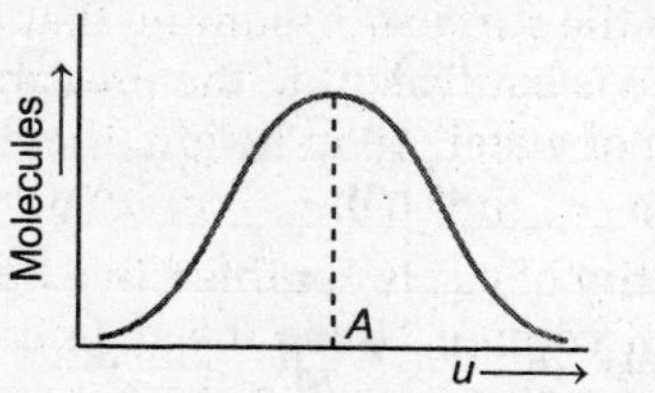

(a) $\sqrt{\frac{3RT}{M}}$ (b) $\sqrt{\frac{2RT}{M}}$ (c) $\sqrt{\frac{8RT}{\pi M}}$ (d) $\sqrt{\frac{RT}{M}}$

96. The volume of helium gas is 44.8 L at
(a) 100°C and 1 atm (b) 0°C and 1 atm
(c) 0°C and 0.5 atm (d) 100°C and 0.5 atm

97. Which gas shows a real behaviour?
(a) 8 g O_2 at STP occupies 5.6 L
(b) 1 g H_2 in 0.5 L flask exerts a pressure of 24.63 atm at 300 K
(c) 1 mol NH_3 at 300 K and 1 atm occupies volume 22.4 L
(d) 5.6 L of CO_2 at STP is equal to 11 g

98. For the non-zero volume of the molecules, real gas equation for n moles of the gas will be
(a) $\left(p + \frac{a}{V^2}\right)V = RT$ (b) $pV = nRT + nbP$
(c) $p(V - nb) = nRT$ (d) (b) and (c) true

99. Actual graph for the given parameters in (Q. 98) will be
(a) I, III
(b) I, II
(c) III
(d) I

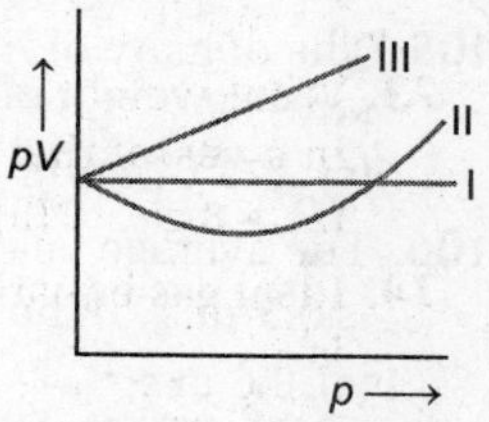

100. One mole of a monoatomic real gas satisfies the equation $p(V - b) = RT$ where, b is a constant. The relationship of interatomic potential $V(r)$ and interatomic distance r for gas is given by

[JEE Advanced 2015]

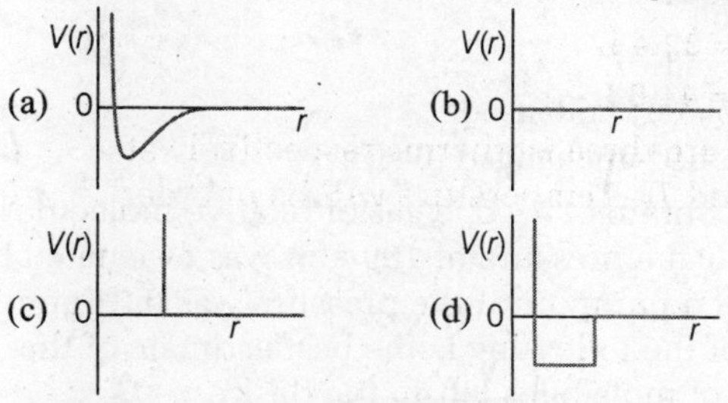

101. For the non-zero values of force of attraction between gas molecules, gas equation will be
(a) $pV = nRT - \frac{n^2a}{V}$ (b) $pV = nRT + nbP$
(c) $pV = nRT$ (d) $p = \frac{nRT}{V - b}$

102. Consider the following table.

Gas	$a/(\text{k Pa dm}^6\text{mol}^{-1})$	$b/(\text{dm}^3\text{mol}^{-1})$
A	642.32	0.05196
B	155.21	0.04136
C	431.91	0.05196
D	155.21	0.4382

a and b are van der Waals' constants. The correct statement about the gases is **[2019 Main April]**

(a) gas C will occupy lesser volume than gas A; gas B will be lesser compressible than gas D
(b) gas C will occupy more volume than gas A; gas B will be more compressible than gas D
(c) gas C will occupy more volume than gas A; gas B will be lesser compressible than gas D
(d) gas C will occupy more volume than gas A; gas B will be lesser compressible than gas D

103. The rms velocity of hydrogen is $\sqrt{7}$ times the rms velocity of nitrogen. If T is the temperature of the gas then

(a) $T(H_2) = T(N_2)$ (b) $T(H_2) > T(N_2)$
(c) $T(H_2) < T(N_2)$ (d) $T(H_2) = \sqrt{7}T(N_2)$

104. A gas in an open container is heated from 27°C to 127°C. The fraction of the original amount of gas escaped from the container will be

(a) 3/4 (b) 1/2 (c) 1/4 (d) 1/8

105. The density of neon will be minimum at

(a) STP (b) 0°C, 2 atm
(c) 273°C, 1 atm (d) 273°C, 2 atm

106. The average velocity of an ideal gas molecule at 27°C is 0.3 m s^{-1}. The average velocity at 927°C will be

(a) 0.6 m s^{-1} (b) 0.3 m s^{-1}
(c) 0.9 m s^{-1} (d) 3 m s^{-1}

107. A balloon filled with ethyne is pricked with a sharp point and quickly dropped in a tank of H_2 gas under identical conditions. After a while the balloon will have

(a) shrunk
(b) enlarged
(c) completely collapsed
(d) remained unchanged in size

108. A flask contains 12 g of a gas of relative molecular mass 120 at a pressure of 100 atm was evacuated by means of a pump until the pressure was 0.01 atm. Which of the following is the best estimate of the number of molecules left in the flask?
($N_0 = 6\times 10^{23}$ mol^{-1})

(a) 6×10^{19} (b) 6×10^{18} (c) 6×10^{17} (d) 6×10^{13}

109. Energy of sublimation of solid helium is much lower than that of ice because

(a) large part of sublimation energy of ice is used to overcome hydrogen bonding
(b) ice melts at much higher temperature
(c) in solid helium, there is van der Waals' force of attraction between helium atoms
(d) All of the above statements are correct

110.

Gas	O_2	N_2	NH_3	CH_4
a	1.360	1.390	4.170	2.253

The table indicates the value of van der Waals' constant a. (in L^2 atm mol^{-2}). The gas which can most easily be liquefied is

(a) O_2 (b) N_2 (c) NH_3 (d) CH_4

111. Which of the following is/are correct statement(s)?

(a) van der Waals' constant a is a measure of attractive force
(b) van der Waals' constant b is also called co-volume or excluded volume
(c) b is expressed in L mol^{-1}
(d) All of the above

112. At what temperature will the total KE of 0.3 mole of He be the same as the total KE of 0.40 mole of Ar at 400 K?

(a) 533 K (b) 400 K (c) 346 K (d) 300 K

113. Consider the following statements,

I. Atmospheric pressure is less at the top of a mountain than at sea level.
II. Gases are much more compressible than solids or liquids.
III. When the atmospheric pressure increases, the height of the mercury column rises.

Select the correct statement(s).

(a) I and II (b) II and III
(c) I and III (d) I, II and III

114. Where is the pressure less than 1 atm?

(a) At a place where water boils at 110°C
(b) At a place where water boils at 90°C
(c) At a place below sea level
(d) At a place where water boils at 100°C

115. Given J-tube has 2.4 mL of air at a pressure of 1 atm. On adding mercury, volume of air is reduced to 1.9 mL as shown. Difference in the level of mercury in two columns is

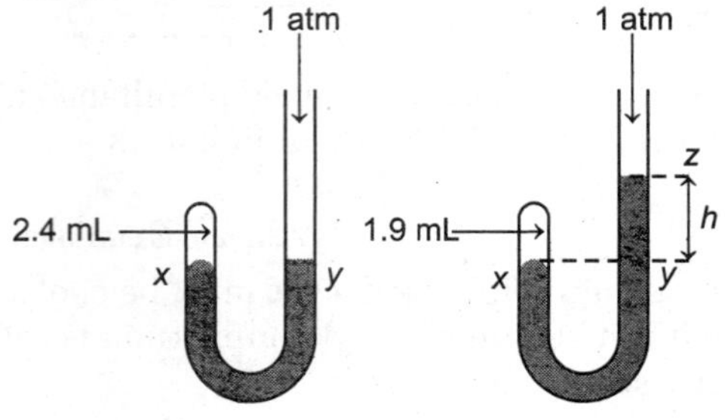

(a) 700 mm (b) 200 mm
(c) 900 mm (d) 760 mm

116. Which of the following is not the correct set of pressure and volume at constant temperature?

	p	V
(a)	1 atm	200 mL
(b)	760 mm	0.2 L
(c)	0.5 atm	100 L
(d)	2 atm	100 mL

117. Assume that for every increase in height of 1 m, pressure decreases by 10 mmHg. Initially an experimental air balloon of maximum 200 L capacity has 150 L air at 1 atm at sea-level. At what height, the balloon is expected to burst?

(a) 15 m above sea-level (b) 19 m above sea-level
(c) 10 m above sea-level (d) 20 m above sea-level

118. A 10.0 cm column of air is trapped by a column of Hg 4.00 cm long in capillary tube of uniform bore when the tube is held horizontally in a room at 1 atm.

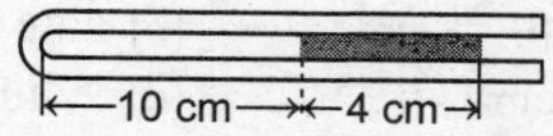

Length of the air column when the tube is held vertically with the open end up is

(a) 9.50 cm (b) 10.52 cm
(c) 3.53 cm (d) 4.61 cm

119. A sample of gas at 0°C and 1.00 atm pressure occupies 3.00 L. What change in temperature is necessary to adjust the pressure of that gas to 1.5 atm after it has been transferred to a 2.00 L container?

(a) 273° (b) 0°
(c) 5° (d) 10°

120. Just below this temperature, gases would theoretically have a negative volume (which is however not possible)

(a) absolute zero (b) −100°C
(c) 100°C (d) 100 K

121. Which must be the lowest temperature possible?

(a) 0°C (b) 100°C
(c) 373°C (d) −273.15°C

122. Select the correct statement(s).

(a) Absolute zero (0 K) is the temperature reached when all possible thermal energy has been removed from a substance
(b) A substance cannot be cooled any further after all thermal energy has been removed
(c) Both (a) and (b)
(d) None of the above

123. A quantity of hydrogen is confined in a chamber of constant volume. When the chamber is immersed in a bath of melting ice, the pressure of the gas is 1000 Torr. What is the temperature when the pressure is 400 Torr?

(a) 109.2°C (b) 109.2 K
(c) 273 K (d) 100 K

124. Boyle's law and Avogadro's law are applicable under limiting condition. This limiting condition is

(a) $p \to 0$ (b) $T \to 0$
(c) $V \to 0$ (d) $p \to \infty$

125. By Avogadro's law,

$$V = kn$$

If volume occupied by 1 mole of a gas at STP is 22.4 L, then k is ... if we take 0.5 mole of gas under same condition of temperature and pressure

(a) 22.4 L mol^{-1} (b) 11.2 L mol^{-1}
(c) 44.8 mol^{-1} (d) 5.6 L mol^{-1}

126. The combination of plots which does not represent isothermal expansion of an ideal gas is **[2019 Main, Jan.]**

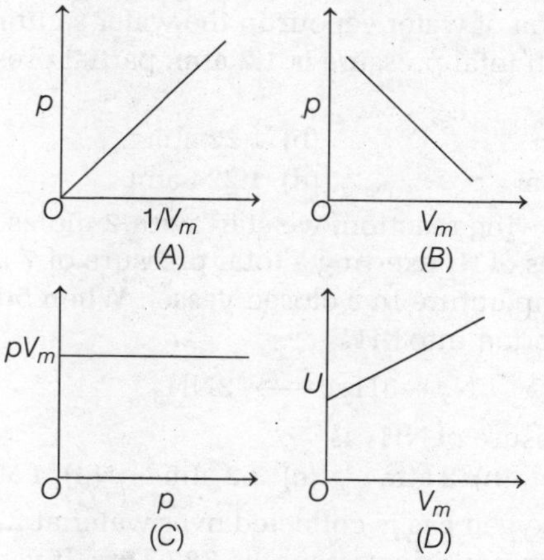

(a) (A) and (C) (b) (B) and (C)
(c) (B) and (D) (d) (A) and (D)

127. Certain amount of gas occupies 1 L at STP. In which case number of molecules will change?

(a) Temperature is changed (b) Pressure is changed
(c) Both (a) and (b) (d) None of these

128. Following is not the gas law

(a) $V \propto n$ at constant p and T
(b) $p \propto T$ at constant V
(c) $d \propto T^{-1}$ at constant p
(d) All the above represent gas laws

129. If X_m, X_p and X_v represent mole fraction, pressure fraction and volume fraction respectively then

(a) $X_m = X_p = X_v$ (b) $X_m = \frac{1}{X_p} = \frac{1}{X_v}$
(c) $X_m = X_p = \frac{1}{X_v}$ (d) $\frac{1}{X_m} = \frac{1}{X_p} = X_v$

130. A 1 L flask contains 32 g O_2 gas at 27°C. What mass of O_2 must be released to reduce the pressure in the flask to 12.315 atm?

(a) 8 g (b) 16 g
(c) 24 g (d) 0 g

131. The density of phosphorus vapour at STP is 5.54 gL^{-1}. Hence, molecular formula of phosphorus is
(a) P_2 (b) P_3 (c) P_4 (d) P_8

132. A 100 mL flask contained H_2 at 200 Torr, and a 200 mL flask contained He at100 Torr. The two flask were then connected so that each gas filled their combined volume. Assuming no change in temperature, total pressure is
(a) 300 Torr (b) 66.66 Torr
(c) 150 Torr (d) 133.33 Torr

133. 1 g H_2 and x g O_2 gas exert a total pressure of 5 atm. At a given temperature partial pressure of O_2 gas is 4 atm, O_2 in the mixture is
(a) 1 mol (b) 2 mol (c) 3 mol (d) 4 mol

134. Mole fraction of water vapour in the water saturated air is 0.02. If total pressure is 1.2 atm, partial pressure of dry air is
(a) 1.18 atm (b) 1.22 atm
(c) 1.176 atm (d) 1.224 atm

135. In the following reaction, we start with 2 moles of N_2 and 5 moles of H_2 exerting a total pressure of 7 atm at a given temperature in a closed vessel. When 50% of N_2 is converted into NH_3

$$N_2 + 3H_2 \longrightarrow 2NH_3$$

partial pressure of NH_3 is
(a) 2.8 atm (b) 2 atm (c) 3.2 atm (d) 4 atm

136. A 3.00 L oxygen gas is collected over water at 27°C when the baromteric pressure is 787 Torr. If vapour pressure of water is 27 Torr at 27°C, moles of O_2 gas will be
(a) 0.122 (b) 0.126 (c) 0.004 (d) 0.152

137. Consider the following pairs of gases A and B.

	A	B
I.	CO_2	N_2O
II.	CO	N_2
III.	O_2	O_3
IV.	H_2O	D_2O
V.	$^{235}UF_6$	$^{238}UF_6$

Relative rates of effusion of gases A and B is in the order
(a) I = II < V < IV < III (b) I = II < III < IV < V
(c) I = II < IV < III < V (d) I < II < III < IV < V

138. A large cylinder of helium filled at 1000 pascal had a small thin orfice through which helium escaped into an evacuated space at the rate of 6.4 mmol/h. How long will it take for 10 mmol SO_2 to leak through a similar orfice if the SO_2 were confined at the same pressure?
(a) 6.25 h (b) 0.39 h
(c) 4.42 h (d) 1.00 h

139. Rate of effusion of LPG (a mixture of *n*-butane and propane) is 1.25 times that of SO_3. Hence, mass fraction of *n*-butane in LPG is
(a) 0.75 (b) 0.25 (c) 0.50 (d) 0.67

140. 100 mL of H_2 gas diffuses in 10 s. X mL of O_2 gas diffuses in t s. X and t cannot be
(a) 100 mL, 40 s (b) 25 mL, 10 s
(c) 100 mL, 10 s (d) 5 mL, 2 s

141. A mixture of C_3H_8 and CH_4 exerts a pressure of 320 mmHg at temperature T K in a V litre flask. On complete combustion, gaseous mixture contains CO_2 only and exerts a pressure of 448 mmHg under identical conditions. Hence, mole fraction of C_3H_8 in the mixture is
(a) 0.2 (b) 0.8 (c) 0.25 (d) 0.75

142. Average volume available to a molecule in a sample of ideal gas at STP is
(a) 3.72×10^{-20} cm^3 (b) 2.69×10^{19} cm^3
(c) 22400 cm^3 (d) $22400 \times 6.02 \times 10^{23}$ cm^3

143. Ratio of the rate of diffusion of He to H_2 at 0°C is same to the case
(a) when temperature is changed to 100°C
(b) when O_2 and CH_4 are taken instead of He and H_2
(c) when volume of the flask is doubled
(d) All the above are correct

144. A 1 L sample of CO initially at STP is heated to 546°C and its volume is increased to 2L. Which of the following is affected to a maximum extent?
(a) RMS velocity (b) KE
(c) Ideal behaviour (d) None is affected

145. If excluded volume is taken zero, compressibility factor Z is
(a) $\left(1 - \frac{a}{RTV}\right)$ (b) $\left(1 + \frac{pb}{RT}\right)$
(c) $\frac{pV}{RT}$ (d) $\frac{RT}{pV}$

146. Compressibility factor for H_2 behaving as real gas is
(a) 1 (b) $\left(1 - \frac{a}{RTV}\right)$ (c) $\left(1 + \frac{pb}{RT}\right)$ (d) $\frac{RTV}{(1-a)}$

147. If $\overline{V}$ is the observed molar volume of real gas and $\overline{V}_{id}$ is the molar volume of an ideal gas then Z is
(a) $\overline{V}\,\overline{V}_{id}$ (b) $\frac{\overline{V}}{\overline{V}_{id}}$ (c) $\frac{\overline{V}_{id}}{\overline{V}}$ (d) $\frac{\overline{V}^2}{\overline{V}_{id}}$

148. Select the correct statements.
(a) Gases tend to behave non-ideally at low temperatures and high pressures
(b) Gases tend to behave ideally at high temperatures and low pressures
(c) The extent to which Z deviates from 1 is a measure of the non-ideality of a gas
(d) All of the above are correct statements

149. Volume of a molecule is related to van der Waals' constant b and N_0 by equation

(a) $V = \frac{b}{N_0}$ (b) $V = 4bN_0$

(c) $V = \frac{4b}{N_0}$ (d) $V = \frac{b}{4N_0}$

150. N_2 (T_c = 126 K) is to be called ...... at 100 K.

(a) gas (b) vapour

(c) liquid (d) metastable

151. NH_3 (T_c = 132.2° C) is to be called ...... at a temperature at which water boils (at 1 atmospheric pressure)

(a) vapour (b) gas

(c) liquid (d) super gas

152. Consider the following statements.

I. Gaseous substances whose critical temperatures are above room temperatures can be liquefied by applying sufficient pressure to the gas.

II. Gaseous substances whose critical temperatures are below room temperature can be liquefied by the application of pressure and lowering of temperature below T_c.

Select the correct alternate.

(a) I (b) II

(c) Both (a) and (b) (d) None of these

153. Select the correct statement(s).

(a) We can condense vapour simply by applying pressure

(b) To liquefy a gas one must lower the temperature below T_c and also apply pressure

(c) At T_c, there is no distinction between liquid and vapour state, hence density of the liquid is nearly equal to density of the vapour

(d) All of the above statements are correct statements

154. Arrange T_i, T_b and T_c in increasing order

(a) $T_i < T_c < T_b$ (b) $T_b < T_c < T_i$

(c) $T_c < T_b < T_i$ (d) $T_i < T_b < T_c$

155. For a given gas T_c = 40 K hence, T_i is

(a) 40 K (b) 270K (c) 135 K (d) 540 K

156. Boyle's temperature of various gases are given below.

Gas	T_B, K
H_2	117
He	23
CH_4	498
O_2	406

Which can be liquefied most easily?

(a) H_2 (b) He

(c) CH_4 (d) O_2

157. Which has least value?

(a) $\frac{T_i}{T_b}$ (b) $\frac{T_i}{T_c}$

(c) $\frac{T_b}{T_c}$ (d) $\frac{T_c}{T_b}$

158. Mean free path is largest for the gas

(a) H_2 (b) Cl_2 (c) N_2 (d) O_2

159. In which case mean free path is not affected?

(a) H_2 gas at 100°C and 1 atm is transferred into a vessel at 50°C and 0.5 atm

(b) O_2 gas at 200 K and 2 atm is transferred into a vessel at 400 K and 1 atm

(c) O_2 gas is replaced by H_2 gas keeping other variables constant

(d) Medium is made more viscous

160. Collision diameter is least in case of

(a) H_2 (b) He

(c) CO_2 (d) N_2

161. Mean free path increases if

(a) H_2 is replaced by He

(b) He is replaced by H_2

(c) He is replaced by O_2

(d) O_2 is replaced by CO_2

162. Out of H_2, CO, N_2 and CO_2, the gas which has least mean free path

(a) has maximum value of a (van der Waals' constant)

(b) is easily liquefied

(c) has maximum value of T_b (Boyle's temperature)

(d) for all of the above cases

163. One litre of gas A at two atmospheric pressure and two litres of gas B at three atmospheric pressure are mixed in a four litre flask to form an ideal gas mixture. What will be the final pressure of the gaseous mixture if the gases initially and finally were at the same temperature?

(a) 1.0 atm (b) 1.5 atm

(c) 2.0 atm (d) 2.5 atm

164. A mixture of nitrogen and oxygen has a density of 1.00 g L^{-1} and the average molecular weight of 31.2 g mol^{-1} at 27°C and 600 mmHg pressure. The mole fraction of nitrogen, assuming ideal gas behaviour, is

(a) 0.78 (b) 0.60

(c) 0.40 (d) 0.22

165. At what temperature will oxygen molecules (molar mass : 32 g mol^{-1}) have the same average kinetic energy as helium atoms (atomic mass : 4 g mol^{-1}) at 320 K ?

(a) 40 K (b) 160 K

(c) 320 K (d) 640 K

166. A gas obeys the equation of state $p(V-b)=RT$ where b is constant. The slope for an isochore will be
(a) negative (b) zero
(c) $\frac{R}{(V-b)}$ (d) $\frac{R}{p}$

167. If the mean free path of gaseous molecules is 60 cm at a pressure of 1×10^{-4} mm Hg, what will be its mean free-path when the pressure is increased by 100 times at constant temperature?
(a) 6.0×10^{-1} cm (b) 6.0 cm
(c) 6.0×10^{1} cm (d) 6.0×10^{2} cm

168. The van der Waals' constants (a and b) of two gases A and B are

	a/dm^6 atm mol^{-2}	b/dm^3 mol^{-1}
A:	1.360	0.318
B:	3.592	0.0426

The critical parameters p_c, V_c and T_c are related as
(1) $p_c(A) < p_c(B)$
(2) $V_c(A) < V_c(B)$
(3) $T_c(A) < T_c(B)$
Select the correct answer using the codes given below.
(a) 1 alone (b) 2 and 3
(c) 1 and 2 (d) 1 and 3

169. An open-ended mercury manometer is used to measure the pressure exerted by a trapped gas as shown in the figure. Atmospheric pressure is 749 mmHg. What is the pressure of the trapped gas?

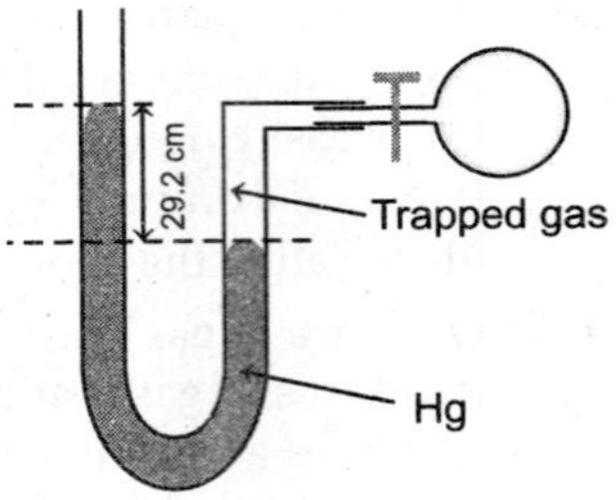

(a) 292 mmHg (b) 457 mmHg
(c) 749 mmHg (d) 1041 mmHg

170. Which gas will have the greatest density at 25°C and 1 atm pressure?
(a) O_3 (b) SiH_4
(c) PH_3 (d) C_3H_8

171. By what ratio will the average velocity of the molecules in a gas change when the temperature is raised from 50°C to 200°C?
(a) 1.21/1 (b) 1.46/1
(c) 2/1 (d) 4/1

172. The pressure on a sample of water at its triple point is reduced while the temperature is held constant. Which phase changes are favoured?
I. Fusion; II. Sublimation; III. Vaporisation
(a) Only I (b) II and III
(c) I and II (d) II and III

173. The triple point of CO_2 occurs at 5.1 atm and –56°C. Its critical temperature is 31°C and solid CO_2 is more dense than liquid CO_2. Under which suitable condition is liquid CO_2 stable at equilibrium?
(a) 10 atm, –25°C (b) 5.1 atm, –25°C
(c) 10 atm, 33°C (d) 5.1 atm, –100°C

174. One mole $N_2O_4(g)$ at 300 K is kept in a closed container under one atmosphere. It is heated to 600 K when 20% of $N_2O_4(g)$ decomposes to $NO_2(g)$. The resultant pressure is
(a) 1.2 atm (b) 2.4 atm
(c) 2.0 atm (d) 1.0 atm

175. Equal weights of HF, HCl, HBr and HI at 87°C and 750 mm Hg pressure are taken. The correct sequence of these gases in the increasing order of their volume is
(a) HF < HCl < HBr < HI
(b) HI < HBr < HCl < HF
(c) HBr < HI < HF < HCl
(d) HCl < HBr < HI < HF

176. Under isobaric condition, volume becomes 1.5 times when temperature changes from
(a) 40°C to 60°C
(b) 273°C to 546°C
(c) Both (a) and (b)
(d) None of the above

177. Consider a sample of helium and a sample of neon, both at 30°C and 1.5 atm. Both samples have a volume of 5.0 L. Which statement concerning these samples is not true?
(a) Each sample contains the same number of atoms of gas
(b) Each sample weighs the same amount
(c) Each sample contains the same number of moles of gas
(d) The density of the neon is greater than the density of the helium

178. Which combination of characteristics is most likely to be associated with molecules having strong dipole-dipole interactions?
I. Polar bond
II. Asymmetric shape
III. Relatively low boiling point
IV. Large surface area
(a) I and III (b) II and IV
(c) I and II (d) III and IV

179. At a high altitude water boils at 95°C instead of 100°C as at sea level because
(a) the atmospheric pressure is greater
(b) the atmospheric pressure is less
(c) the climate is cooler
(d) the vapour pressure of water is greater

180. Collision frequency of a gas at 1 atm pressure is Z; its value at 0.5 atm will be
(a) $0.25Z$ (b) $2Z$
(c) $0.50Z$ (d) Z

181. Under isothermal and isochroic conditions, the rates of diffusion r_1 and r_2 of gases (1) and (2) having densities d_1 and d_2 are related by the expression
(a) $r_1 = \sqrt{\frac{r_2 d_1}{d_2}}$ (b) $r_1 = \sqrt{\frac{r_2 d_2}{d_1}}$
(c) $r_1 = r_2\sqrt{\frac{d_1}{d_2}}$ (d) $r = r_2\sqrt{\frac{d_2}{d_1}}$

182. The volume of 0.0168 mole of O_2 obtained by thermal decomposition of $KClO_3$ and collected by displacement of water is 428 mL at a pressure of 754 mmHg at 25°C. The pressure of water vapour at 25°C is
(a) 18 mmHg (b) 20 mmHg
(c) 24 mmHg (d) 30 mmHg

183. The ratio between the root mean square velocity of H_2 at 50 K and that of O_2 at 800 K is
(a) 4 (b) 2 (c) 1 (d) 0.25

184. The vapour pressure of water at 300 K in a closed container is 0.4 atm. If the volume of the container is doubled, its vapour pressure at 300 K will be
(a) 0.8 atm (b) 0.2 atm
(c) 0.4 atm (d) 0.6 atm

185. The density of air at STP is 0.00130 g/mL. Thus, vapour density of air will be
(a) 14.56 (b) 0.0013
(c) 0.0026 (d) 7.69

186. Densities of CO and N_2 are in the ratio of 1 : 2 and their temperatures are in the ratio of 2 : 1, thus the ratio of their pressure is
(a) 1 : 1 (b) 1 : 2 (c) 2 : 1 (d) 4 : 1

187. If the four tubes of a car are filled to the same pressure with N_2, O_2, H_2 and Ne separately, then which one will be filled first?
(a) N_2 (b) O_2
(c) Ne (d) H_2

188. Root mean square velocity of a gas is x m s^{-1} at a pressure p atm and temperature T K. If pressure is made $2p$ under isothermal condition, root mean square speed becomes
(a) $2x$ (b) $4x$ (c) $\frac{x}{2}$ (d) x

189. A vessel contains 0.5 mol each of SO_2, H_2 and CH_4. Its outlet was made open and closed after sometime. Thus, order of partial pressure will be
(a) $p_{SO_2} > p_{CH_4} > p_{H_2}$ (b) $p_{H_2} > p_{CH_4} > p_{SO_2}$
(c) $p_{H_2} > p_{SO_2} > p_{CH_4}$ (d) $p_{H_2} = p_{SO_2} = p_{CH_4}$

190. The root mean square velocity of a monoatomic gas (molar mass m g mol^{-1}) is u. Its kinetic energy per mol (E) is related to u by equation
(a) $u = \sqrt{\frac{3E}{m}}$ (b) $u = \sqrt{\frac{2E}{3m}}$
(c) $u = \sqrt{\frac{2E}{m}}$ (d) $u = \sqrt{\frac{E}{3m}}$

191. Molar volume of CO_2 is maximum at
(a) STP (b) 400 K and 1 atm
(c) 273 K and 2 atm (d) 546 K and 2 atm

192. Which of the following statements is not true about the effect of an increase in temperature on the distribution of molecular velocities in a gas?
(a) The most probable velocity increases
(b) The fraction of the molecules with the most probable speed increases
(c) The distribution becomes broader
(d) The area under the curve remains unaffected

193. Boyle's law is represented by the equation
(a) $\frac{d^2p}{dV} = -\frac{p}{dT}$ (b) $\frac{dp}{dV} = \frac{p}{V}$
(c) $\frac{d^2p}{dV} = \frac{p}{dT}$ (d) $\frac{dp}{dV} = -\frac{p}{V}$

194. Consider the following equations
I. $\left(\frac{dp}{dV}\right)_T = \frac{k}{V}$ II. $\left(\frac{dp}{dV}\right)_T = \frac{-k}{V^2}$
III. $\left(\frac{dp}{dV}\right)_T = \frac{-k}{V}$ IV. $V \propto \frac{1}{p}$
Boyle's law is represented by
(a) II, IV (b) II, III
(c) I, II (d) I, III, IV

195. Select the correct statements.
(a) $\left(\frac{dV}{dT}\right)_p = k$ for Charles' law
(b) $\left(\frac{dp}{dV}\right)_T = \frac{-k}{V^2}$ for Boyle's law
(c) $\left(\frac{dp}{dV}\right) = -\frac{p}{V}$ for Boyle's law
(d) All the above are correct statements

196. One way of writing the equation of state for real gas is
$$Z = \left[1 + \frac{B}{V} + \ldots\right]$$
where B is constant. B in terms of van der Waals' constant a and b is
(a) $\left(b - \frac{a}{RT}\right)$ (b) $\left(b + \frac{a}{RT}\right)$
(c) $\left(a - \frac{b}{RT}\right)$ (d) $\left(a + \frac{b}{RT}\right)$

197. 0.24 g of a volatile substance on vaporisation gave 45 mL vapours at NTP. Thus, vapour density of substance is (VD of $H_2 = 1$)
(a) 119.5 (b) 11.95 (c) 59.75 (d) 5.975

198. A gas cylinder containing cooling gas can withstand a pressure of 14.9 atm. The pressure gauge of cylinder indicates 12 atm at 27°C. Cylinder will explode at a temperature
(a) 87.5°C (b) 99.5°C
(c) 115.5°C (d) 135.5°C

199. Consider the following statements,
I. A boundary is **diathermic** if a change of state is observed when two objects at different temperatures are brought into contact.
II. A boundary is **adiabatic** if no change occurs even though the two objects have different temperatures.
III. Thermal equilibrium is established if no change of state occurs when two objects *A* and *B* are in contact through a diathermic boundary.

Select the correct statements.
(a) I and II (b) II and III
(c) I and III (d) I, II and III

200. Consider the following statements,
I. Repulsive forces are significant when the molecules are close together on average.
II. Attractive intermolecular forces are important when the molecules are fairly close together but not necessarily touching.
III. Attractive forces are ineffective when the molecules are far apart.

Select the correct statements.
(a) I, II and III (b) I and II
(c) I and III (d) II and III

201. A vessel is filled with a mixture of oxygen and nitrogen. At what ratio of the partial pressures will the masses of the gases be identical?
(a) $p_{O_2} = p_{N_2}$ (b) $p_{O_2} = 0.875\, p_{N_2}$
(c) $p_{O_2} = 1.14\, p_{N_2}$ (d) $p_{O_2} = 2p_{N_2}$

202. The partial pressure of oxygen in air is 22 kPa. What is the oxygen content in per cent volume?
(a) 42% (b) 21.7%
(c) 11% (d) 5.5%

203. Hydrogen was collected in one case over water, and in another over mercury in the same conditions. In both cases, the volume of the gas was the same. Amounts of hydrogen collected over
(a) both liquids were identical
(b) the water was greater
(c) the mercury was greater
(d) nothing can be predicted from the given data

204. Points I, II and III in the following plot respectively correspond to (V_{mp} : most probable velocity) **[JEE Main 2019]**

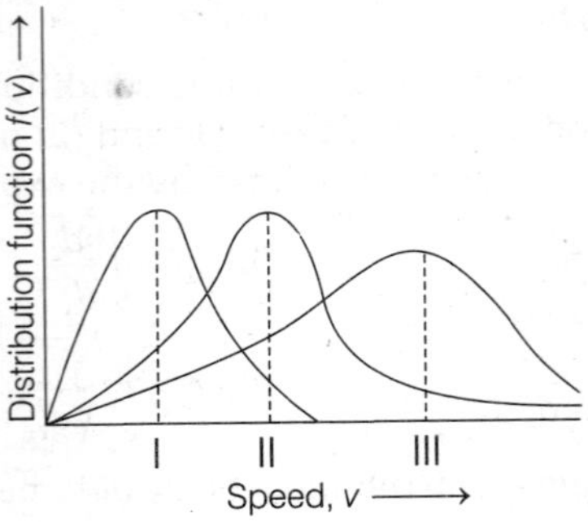

(a) v_{mp} of H_2(300 K); v_{mp} of N_2(300 K); v_{mp} of O_2(400 K)
(b) v_{mp} of O_2(400 K); v_{mp} of N_2(300 K); v_{mp} of H_2(300 K)
(c) v_{mp} of N_2(300 K); v_{mp} of O_2(400 K); v_{mp} of H_2(300 K)
(d) v_{mp} of N_2(300 K) ; v_{mp} of H_2(300 K); v_{mp} of O_2(400 K)

205. Two closed bulbs of equal volume (V) containing an ideal gas initially at pressure p_i and temperature T_1 are connected through a narrow tube of negligible volume as shown in the figure below. The temperature of one of the bulbs is then raised to T_2. The final pressure p_f is **[JEE Main 2016]**

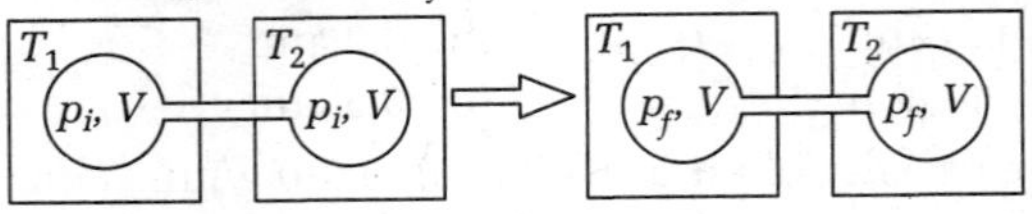

(a) $2p_i\left(\frac{T_1}{T_1 + T_2}\right)$ (b) $2p_i\left(\frac{T_2}{T_1 + T_2}\right)$
(c) $2p_i\left(\frac{T_1T_2}{T_1 + T_2}\right)$ (d) $p_i\left(\frac{T_1T_2}{T_1 + T_2}\right)$

206. Compressibility factor for CO_2 at 400 K and 71.0 bars is 0.8697. Molar volume of CO_2 under these conditions is
(a) 22.4 L (b) 2.24 L
(c) 0.41 L (d) 19.5 L

207. Potassium hydroxide solutions are used to absorb CO_2. How many litres of CO_2 at 1.00 atm and 22°C would be absorbed by an aqueous solution containing 15.0 g of KOH?

$$2KOH + CO_2 \longrightarrow K_2CO_3 + H_2O$$

(a) 3.24 L (b) 1.62 L
(c) 6.48 L (d) 0.324 L

208. If the intermolecular forces vanish away, what is the volume occupied by molecules contained in 4.5 kg of water at NTP?
(a) 5.6 m^3 (b) 4.5 m^3
(c) 11.2 m^3 (d) 11.2 L

209. Consider the following statements,

I. At the limit of vanishing pressure, where all gases behave ideally, the volume tends to infinity and intermolecular distances become enormously large.

II. Gases with weak intermolecular forces obey the ideal gas law at relatively high pressures.

III. Gases with strong intermolecular forces obey the ideal gas law at relatively low pressures.

Select the correct statement(s).

(a) Only I (b) Only II (c) I and II (d) I, II and III

210. The volume of a gas increases by a factor of 2 while the pressure decreases by a factor of 3. Given that the number of moles is unaffected, the factor by which the temperature changes is

(a) 3/2 (b) 3×2 (c) 2/3 (d) 1/6

211. The number of molecules inside a soap bubble 1.0 cm in diameter at atmospheric pressure and 25°C is

(a) 1.29×10^{22} (b) 1.29×10^{19}
(c) 1.03×10^{23} (d) 1.03×10^{20}

212. A gas cylinder containing colling gas can withstand a pressure of 14.9 atm. The pressure gauge of cylinder indicates 12 atm at 27°C. Due to sudden fire in the building the temperature starts rising. The temperature at which cylinder explode is

(a) 87.5°C (b) 99.5°C
(c) 115.5°C (d) 135.5°C

213. At a constant volume the specific heat of a gas is 0.075 cal/g and its molecular weight is 40. The gas is

(a) monoatomic (b) diatomic
(c) triatomic (d) None of these

214. 8 L of H_2 react with 6 L of Cl_2. The final volume of reaction mixture is [when p and T are constants]

(a) 12 (b) 14
(c) 2 (d) 8

215. Which is not the correct value of R (gas constant)?

(a) 8.314 $dm^3 \ K^{-1} \ mol^{-1}$
(b) 8.314 dm^3 kPa $K^{-1} \ mol^{-1}$
(c) 62.364 dm^3 Torr $K^{-1} \ mol^{-1}$
(d) 1.987 cal $K^{-1} \ mol^{-1}$

Objective Questions Type II [One or more than one correct option(s)]

In each of the questions below, four choices are given, of which one or more than one are correct.

1. Which of the following statements are incorrect?

(a) Molar volume of every gas at STP is 22.4 L
(b) Under critical states compressibility factor is 1
(c) All gases will have equal value of average KE at a given temperature
(d) At absolute zero, KE is $\frac{3}{2}R$

2. Select the correct statements.

(a) Gases tend to behave nonideally at low temperatures and high pressures
(b) Gases tend to behave ideally at high temperatures and low pressures
(c) The extent to which Z deviates from 1 is a measure of the nonideality of a gas
(d) $Z = 1$ under critical states

3. Select the correct statement(s).

(a) Absolute zero (0 K) is the temperature reached when all possible thermal energy has been removed from a substance
(b) A substance cannot be cooled any further after all thermal energy has been removed
(c) Volume occupied by 1 mol of a real gas at STP is 22.4 L
(d) At absolute zero, vibrational energy is zero

4. Consider following statements,

I. Atmospheric pressure is less at the top of a mountain than at sea level.

II. Gases are much more compressible than solids or liquids.

III. When the atmospheric pressure increases, the height of the mercury column rises.

Select the correct statement(s).

(a) I and II (b) II and III
(c) I and III (d) I, II and III

5. In which case(s) dimer formation changes the physical state?

(a) $AlCl_3$ (b) NO_2
(c) NO (d) N_2O

6. Select the correct statements.

(a) Vapour may be condensed to liquid by the application of pressure
(b) To liquefy a gas one must lower the temperature below T_c and apply pressure
(c) At T_c there is no distinction between liquid and vapour state
(d) At T_c, density of liquid is very high as compared to its gaseous state

7. Mean free path increases if

(a) H_2 is replaced by He (b) He is replaced by H_2
(c) He is replaced by O_2 (d) O_2 is replaced by CO_2

8. Out of H_2, CO, N_2 and CO_2, the gas which has least mean free path.

(a) has a maximum value of a (van der Waals constant)
(b) is easily liquefied
(c) has maximum value of T_b
(d) has maximum value of T_c

9. The critical temperature of water is higher than that of O_2 because H_2O molecule has
(a) fewer electrons than O_2
(b) two covalent bonds
(c) V-shape
(d) dipole moment

10. Which of the following are correct statements?
(a) van der Waals' constant a is a measure of attractive force
(b) van der Waals' constant b is also called co-volume or excluded volume
(c) b is expressed in L mol^{-1}
(d) b is one-third of critical volume

11. At 47°C and 16.0 atm, the molar volume of NH_3 gas is about 10% less than the molar volume of an ideal gas. This is due to
(a) NH_3 decomposes to N_2 and H_2 at 47°C
(b) the force of attraction between NH_3 molecules is significant at this temperature and pressure
(c) the volume occupies by NH_3 molecules themselves is a significant fraction of the volume of the container at this temperature and pressure
(d) at 16 atm, NH_3 molecules no longer move randomly

12. We have column of Hg of 76 cm high and 1.00 cm^2 in cross-sectional area at 0°C. In which case, pressure will change?
(a) Column height is changed
(b) Cross-sectional area is changed
(c) In both cases
(d) In none of the cases.

13. When a gas is expanded at constant temperature
(a) the pressure decreases
(b) the kinetic energy of the molecules remains the same
(c) the kinetic energy of the molecules decreases
(d) the number of molecules of the gas decreases

14. According to kinetic theory of gases **[IIT JEE 2011]**
(a) collisions the always elastic
(b) heavier molecules transfer more momentum to the wall of the container
(c) only a small number of molecules have very high velocity
(d) between collisions, the molecules move in a straight line with constant velocities

15. The van der Waal's equation for n mole of real gas is $\left(p + \frac{n^2 a}{V}\right)(V - nb) = nRT$ where a and b are van der Waals' constant. Which of the following statements are true about a and b when the temperature of the state is too low?
(a) Both remains same
(b) a remains same, b varies
(c) a varies, b remains same
(d) Both varies

16. At which pressure and temperature conditions is the behaviour of a real gas closest to that of an ideal gas?
(a) 15 atm and 200 K
(b) 1 atm and 273 K
(c) 0.5 atm and 500 K
(d) 380 mmHg and 227°C

17. Which of the following statement(s) is(are) correct regarding the root mean square speed (U_{rms}) and average translational kinetic energy (E_{av}) of a molecule in a gas at equilibrium? **[JEE Advanced 2019]**
(a) U_{rms} is inversely proportional to the square root of its molecular mass
(b) U_{rms} is doubled when its temperature is increased four times
(c) E_{av} is doubled when its temperature is increased four times
(d) E_{av} at a given temperature does not depend on its molecular mass

18. For an ideal gas under isobaric condition a graph between log V and log T
(a) is linear with unit slope
(b) represents Boyle's law
(c) represents Charles' law
(d) represents Gay Lussac law

19. Which of the following statements is wrong for gases?
(a) Gases do not have a definite shape and volume
(b) Volume of the gas is equal to volume of container confining the gas
(c) Confirmed gas exerts uniform pressure on the walls of its container in all directions
(d) Mass of gas cannot be determined by weighing a container in which it is enclosed

20. An ideal gas, obeying kinetic theory of gases cannot be liquefied, because
(a) its critical temperature is above 0°C
(b) its molecules are relatively small in size
(c) it solidifies before becoming a liquid
(d) forces acting between its molecules are negligible

21. An ideal gas is expanded form (p_1, V_1, T_1) to (p_2, V_2, T_2) under different conditions. The correct statement(s) among the following is (are) **[JEE Advanced 2017]**
(a) The work done by the gas is less when it is expanded reversibly from V_1 to V_2 under adiabatic conditions as compared to that when expanded reversibly form V_1 to V_2 under isothermal conditions.
(b) The change in internal energy of the gas is (i) zero, if it is expanded reversibly with $T_1 = T_2$, and (ii) positive, if it is expanded reversibly under adiabatic conditions with $T_1 \neq T_2$.
(c) If the expansion is carried out freely, it is simultaneously both isothermal as well as adiabatic
(d) The work done on the gas is maximum when it is compressed irrversibly from (p_2, V_2) to (p_1, V_1) against constant pressure p_1.

Numerical Value Questions

All these questions have a Numerical value as their answer, solve the questions and write your answer.

1. The diffusion coefficient of an ideal gas is proportional to its mean free path and mean speed. The absolute temperature of an ideal gas is increased 4 times and its pressure is increased 2 times. As a result, the diffusion coefficient of this gas increases x times. The value of x is....... **[JEE Advanced 2016]**

2. An open vessel at 27°C is heated until three fifths of the air in it has been expelled. Assuming that the volume of the vessel remains constant, find the temperature to which the vessel has been heated.

3. A vessel of capacity 1 dm^3 contains 1.03×10^{23} H_2 molecules exerting pressure of 101.325 kPa. The RMS and average speed are ......

4. The pressure exerted by a non-reactive gaseous mixture of 6.4 g of methane and 8.8 g of carbon dioxide in a 10 L vessel at 27°C is .... kPa. **[JEE Main 2021, March]**
[Assume gases are ideal, $R = 8.314$ J mol^{-1} K^{-1}
Atomic masses : C : 12.0 u, H : 1.0 u, O : 16.0 u]

5. The temperature at which the average translational energy of a molecule is equal to the kinetic energy of the electron in the first Bohr orbit is ...... $\times 10^5$ K.
$\left[\text{translation energy} = \dfrac{3RT}{2} \text{ per mol}\right]$

6. The critical temperature, T_c and critical pressure for methane are 191 K and 46.4×10^5 Nm^{-2} respectively. The radius of a methane molecule is ......

7. A 0.02 mole sample of N_2O_4 is placed in a 0.5 L container at 27°C. The pressure of the sample is 1.2 atm. Find the fraction of N_2O_4 that undergoes dissociation to form NO_2.

8. The density of steam at 100.0°C and 1×10^5 pascal is 0.6 kg m^{-3}. Calculate the compressibility factor (Z) from these data.

9. The number of chlorine atoms in 20 mL of chlorine gas at STP is______10^{21}. **[JEE Main 2021, March]**
[Assume chlorine is an ideal gas at STP
$R = 0.083$ L bar mol^{-1} K^{-1}, $N_A = 6.023 \times 10^{23}$]

10. Two flasks of equal volumes have been joined by a narrow tube of negligible volume. Initially both flasks are at 300 K containing 0.60 mole of O_2 gas at 0.5 atm pressure. One of the flasks is then placed in a thermostat of 600 K. Calculate number of moles of O_2 gas in each flask.

11. A closed tank has two compartments A and B, both filled with oxygen (assumed to be ideal gas). The partition separating the two compartments is fixed and is a perfect heat insulator (Fig. 1). If the old partition is replaced by a new partition which can slide and conduct heat but does not allow the gas to leak across (Fig. 2), the volume (in m^3) of the compartment A after the system attains equilibrium is .... **[JEE Advanced 2018]**

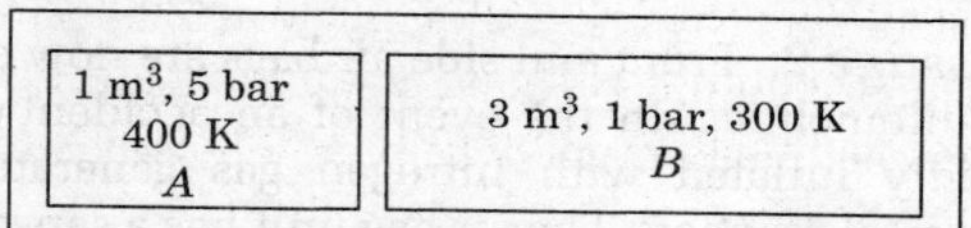

Fig. 1

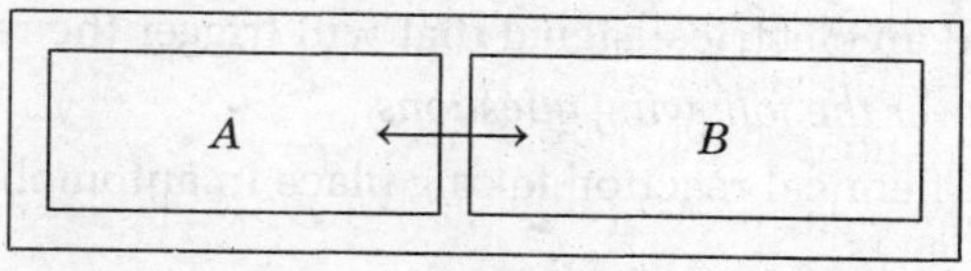

Fig. 2

12. At 20°C, two balloons of equal volume and porosity are filled to a pressure of 2 atm, one with 14 kg N_2 and other with 1 kg of H_2. The N_2 balloon leaks to a pressure of 1/2 atm in 1 hr. How long will it take for H_2 balloon to reach a pressure of 1/2 atm?

Comprehension Based Questions

In these questions, a passage has been given followed by questions based on it. You have to answer the questions based on the passage given.

***Passage* 1** A technician is working with dry ice (solid CO_2) in a closed 6000 L fume hood maintained at a constant pressure of 1.00 atm and a constant temperature of 27°C. He will succumb to CO_2 poisoning when the concentration rises to 10% by volume of the atmosphere, in case he has not been conditioned to tolerate CO_2.

Answer the following questions.

1. In case of ventilation stops, minimum weight of dry ice that can sublimate is
(a) 1.07 kg (b) 2.14 kg
(c) 0.55 kg (d) no sublimation

2. As compared to normal ice (solid H_2O) solid CO_2
(a) can be transported easily
(b) occupies less volume
(c) does not melt
(d) All of the above are correct statements

***Passage* 2** Front and side air bags are now common in automobiles. In the event of an accident a bag is rapidly inflated with nitrogen gas generated by a chemical reaction. The air bag unit has a sensor that is sensitive to sudden deceleration of the vehicle and will send an electrical signal that will trigger the reaction.

Answer the following questions.

1. Chemical reaction taking place in automobile air bag is
(a) $2NH_3 \longrightarrow N_2 + 3H_2$
(b) $NH_4NO_2 \longrightarrow N_2 + 2H_2O$
(c) $NaN_3 \longrightarrow 2Na + 3N_2$
(d) None of the above

2. The nitrogen gas in an automobile air bag, with a volume of 65 L, exerts a pressure of 829 mm Hg at 25°C. Amount of N_2 gas in the air bag is
(a) 2.9 mol (b) 1.9 mol
(c) 1.45 mol (d) 0.95 mol

3. Mass of sodium azide required to provide N_2 gas needed to inflate a 75.0 L bag to a pressure of 1.3 atm at 25°C is
(a) 173 g (b) 85 g
(c) 42.5 g (d) 340 g

***Passage* 3** A closed bulb contains 0.01 mole of inert helium gas and a sample of solid white NH_4Cl. Assume that the volume of the solid NH_4Cl is negligible compared to the volume of the bulb. The pressure of the He gas at 27°C is found to be 114 mm Hg. The bulb is then heated to 327°C. All the NH_4Cl decomposed and final pressure recorded was 908 mm Hg. Assume all the gases are ideal.

Answer the following questions,

1. What is the partial pressure of HCl(*g*) in the bulb at 327°C, when reaction is complete?
(a) 340 mm Hg (b) 3.97 mm Hg
(c) 797 mm Hg (d) 170 mm Hg

2. How many moles of $NH_4Cl(s)$ were in the bulb at 27°C?
(a) 0.030 mol
(c) 0.0150 mol
(c) 0.060 mol
(d) None of the above is correct

***Passage* 4** A 100 dm^3 flask contains 10 moles each of N_2 and H_2 at 777 K. After equilibrium was reached, partial pressure of H_2 was 1 atm. At this point 5 L of $H_2O(l)$ was added and gas mixture was cooled to 298 K.

Answer the following questions.

1. How many moles of N_2, H_2 and NH_3 are at equilibrium?

	N_2	H_2	NH_3
(a)	5	2.5	5
(b)	7.19	1.57	5.62
(c)	1.57	7.19	5.62
(d)	5.02	1.57	7.19

2. How much pressure is exerted at 298 K?
(a) 2.26 atm (b) 3.52 atm
(c) 2.14 atm (d) 4.12 atm

***Passage* 5** *Read the following passage and answer the questions at the end of it.*

The apparatus shown consists of three temperature-jacketed 1.000 L bulbs connected by stopcocks. Bulb *A* contains a mixture of $H_2O(g)$, $CO_2(g)$ and $N_2(g)$ at 25°C and a total pressure of 564 mm Hg. Bulb *B* is empty and is held at a temperature of –70°C. Bulb *C* is also empty and is held at a temperature of –190°C. The stopcocks are closed, and the volume of the lines connecting the bulbs is zero. CO_2 sublimes at –78°C, and N_2 boils at –196°C.

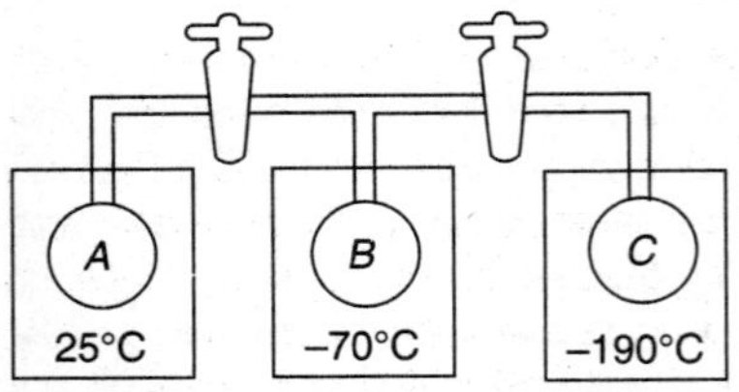

1. The stopcock between A and B is opened and the system is allowed to come to equilibrium. The pressure in A and B is now 219 mmHg. Select correct alternate:
   (a) A contains $CO_2(g)$ and $N_2(g)$ and B contains $CO_2(g)$, $N_2(g)$ and $H_2O(s)$
   (b) A contains $CO_2(g)$ and B contains $N_2(g)$ and $H_2O(l)$
   (c) A contains $CO_2(g)$, $N_2(g)$ and $H_2O(s)$ and B contains $CO_2(g)$ and $N_2(g)$
   (d) A contains $H_2O(g)$ and B contains $H_2O(g)$, $N_2(g)$ and $CO_2(g)$
2. How many moles of H_2O are in the system?
   (a) 0.026 mol (b) 0.0013 mol
   (c) 0.013 mol (d) 0.13 mol

Passage 6 *Read the following passage and answer the questions at the end of it.*

This mixing of different gases by random molecular motion and with frequent collisions is called **diffusion.** A similar process in which gas molecules escape without collisions through a tiny hole into a vacuum is called **effusion.**

1. Select correct alternate(s).
   (a) All gases spontaneously diffuse into one another when they are brought into contact
   (b) Diffusion into a vacuum will take place much more rapidly than diffusion into another gas
   (c) Both the rate of diffusion of a gas and its rate of effusion depend on its molar mass
   (d) All of the above statements are correct
2. The stopcock of the bulbs X (containing NH_3) and Y (containing HCl) are opened simultaneously, white fumes of NH_4Cl are formed at point B. If $AB = 36.5$ cm, then BC is approximately

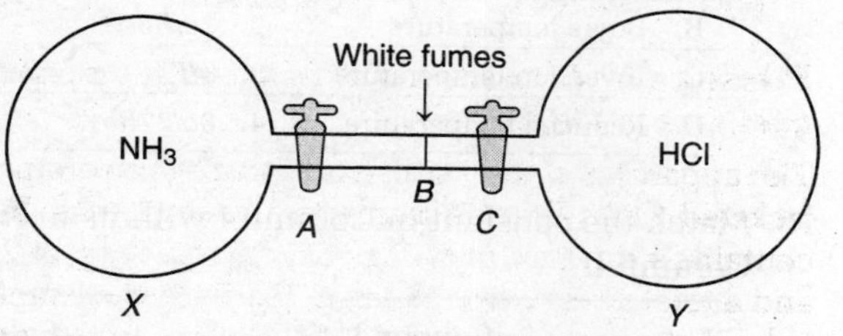

(a) 18.0 cm (b) 25.0 cm (c) 20.0 cm (d) 36.5 cm

Passage 7 *Read the following passage and answer the questions at the end of it.*

Homogeneous mixing and compressibility both result from the fact that the molecules are far apart in gases. Mixing occurs because individual gaseous molecules have little interaction with their neighbours and, assuming that no reaction takes place, the chemical identities of those neighbours are irrelevant. Compressibility is possible in gases because only about 0.1% of the volume of a typical gas is taken up by the molecules themselves under normal circumstances; the remaining 99.9% is empty space.

1. Compressibility factor of a gas is given by
   (a) $\frac{pV}{R}$ (b) $\frac{pV}{R^2}$
   (c) $\frac{R}{pV}$ (d) $\frac{pV}{nRT}$
2. Assume molecules are spherical of radius 1 Å, volume occupied by molecules in one mole of a gas at NTP is
   (a) 2.52 m^3
   (b) 2.52×10^{-4} m^3
   (c) 2.52×10^{-6} m^3
   (d) 2.52×10^{-2} m^3

Passage 8 *Read the following passage and answer the questions at the end of it.*

Variation of volume with temperature was first studied by French chemist, Jacques Charles, in 1787 and then extended by another French chemist Joseph Gay-Lussac in 1802. For a fixed mass of a gas under isobaric condition, variation of volume V with temperature t°C is given by

$$V = V_0[1 + \alpha t]$$

where V_0 is the volume at 0°C, at constant pressure.

1. For every 1° change in temperature, the volume of the gas changes by .... of the volume at 0°C
   (a) $\frac{1}{273}$ unit (b) 1 unit
   (c) 273 unit (d) 22.4 unit
2. Select the incorrect statement
   (a) α (given above) is called volume coefficient
   (b) Value of α is 3.66×10^{-3} °C^{-1} for all gases
   (c) 273 K is the lowest possible temperature attained
   (d) Absolute zero is the temperature reached when all possible thermal energy has been removed from a substance
3. Under isochoric condition, graphs between p and T are shown below. Volume order is

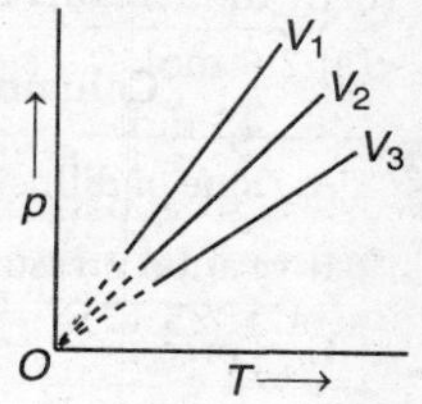

   (a) $V_1 = V_2 = V_3$
   (b) $V_1 > V_2 > V_3$
   (c) $V_1 < V_2 < V_3$
   (d) $V_2 < V_1 < V_3$

Passage 9 *Read the following passage and answer the questions at the end of it.*

Gases tend to behave non-ideally at low temperatures and high pressures, and to explain deviation from ideal behaviour two types of corrections-volume correction and pressure correction are introduced.

1. Application of pressure and volume correction gives van der Waals' equation, and other related equations. Which of the following is not the correct equation for the given name?

(a) van der Waals' : $\left[p^2 + \frac{n^2a}{V^2}\right][V - nb] = nRT$

(b) Virial : $pV = RT\left[1 + \frac{B}{V} + \frac{C}{V^2} + \dots\right]$

(c) Clausius : $\left[p + \frac{a}{TV^2}\right][V - b] = RT$

(d) Dieterici : $p(V - b) = RTe^{-a/RTV}$

2. Following represents equation of state for n moles of real gas $\left[p + \frac{n^2a}{V^2}\right][V - nb] = nRT$

Select the correct statements.

(a) Constant a is a measure of force of attraction between gas molecules and $\frac{n^2a}{V^2}$ is also called internal pressure

(b) a is expressed in atm L^2 mol^{-2}, b is expressed in L mol^{-1}

(c) At high pressure, compression factor is $\left(1 + \frac{pb}{RT}\right)$

(d) All of the above are correct statements

Matrix-Match Type

Given below are Matching Type Questions, with two columns (each having some items) each. Each item of Column I has to be matched with the items of Column II.

1. Match the experimental facts in Column I with the explanation according to kinetic theory in Column II.

Column I	Column II
A. Compressibility of gases	1. Molecules attract each other at close range.
B. Diffusibility of gases	2. Molecules strike each other and the walls of the container without loss of energy.
C. Expansion of gases on heating	3. The speed of molecules increases as the temperature increases.
D. Gases exert pressure	4. Molecules are in rapid, haphazard motion.
E. Gases may be liquefied	5. Molecules are widely separated, can be forced together.

2. Match the term in Column I with its proportional term in Column II.

Column I	Column II
A. Rate of diffusion	1. Mole fraction
B. Partial pressure	2. $time^{-1}$
C. Force	3. Temperature
D. Kinetic energy	4. Rate of change of momentum
E. Pressure under isothermal condition	5. Density

3. Match the term in Column I with its expression in Column II.

Column I	Column II
A. RMS velocity	1. $\sqrt{8RT/\pi M}$
B. Average velocity	2. $\frac{1}{3}\frac{mNu^2}{V}$
C. Most probable velocity	3. $\sqrt{3RT/M}$
D. Pressure by kinetic theory of gases	4. $\sqrt{2RT/M}$

4. Match the temperature in Column I with its value in Column II.

Column I	Column II
A. Critical temperature	1. a/Rb
B. Boyle temperature	2. $2a/Rb$
C. Inversion temperature	3. T/T_c
D. Reduced temperature	4. $8a/27Rb$

5. Match the constant in Column I with its unit in Column II.

Column I	Column II
A. Gas constant	1. JK^{-1}
B. van der Waals' constant 'a'	2. dm^3 mol^{-1}
C. Boltzmann constant k	3. atm L^2 mol^{-2}
D. van der Waals' constant 'b'	4. JK^{-1} mol^{-1}

6. Match the compression factor (Z) under different condition in Column I with its value in Column II.

Column I	Column II
A. Z for ideal gas	1. $\frac{3}{8}$
B. Z for real gas at low p	2. $(1 + pb/RT)$
C. Z for real gas at high p	3. 1
D. Z for critical state	4. $(1 - a/RTV)$

7. Match the properties/amount of given in Column I with related parameters/relation in Column II.

Column I	Column II
A. $pV = \left(RT + \frac{p}{b}\right)$	1. Real gas equation at low p
B. $pV = \left(RT - \frac{a}{V}\right)$	2. Real gas equation for H_2
C. $pV = RT$	3. Real gas equation at high p
D. $\frac{pV}{RT} = \left(1 + \frac{b}{V}\right)$	4. Real gas equation under high temperature
	5. Ideal gas equation per mole

8. van der Waals' equation for n moles of a gas is

$$\left[p + \frac{n^2 a}{V^2}\right][V - nb] = nRT$$

Match various parameters given in Column I with their values in terms of 'a', 'b', T etc., in Column II.

Column I	Column II
A. Compressibility factor for He for any pressure range	1. $\left(1 - \frac{a}{RTV}\right)$
B. Compressibility factor for N_2 in lower pressure range	2. $\left(1 + \frac{Pb}{RT}\right)$
C. Compressibility factor for CO_2 in higher pressure range	3. 3/8
D. Compressibility factor for a real gas at very high temperature	4. $\left(\frac{a}{Rb}\right)$
E. Boyle's temperature	5. 1
F. Compressibility factor for critical states	6. $3b$

Single Integer Answer Questions

Answer of these questions is a single digit lying between 0 to 9.

1. Consider the following data,

Gas	Volume of container	Temperature	Pressure
N_2	5 L	27°C	3 atm
H_2	2 L	127°C	5 atm

Moles of N_2 occupied under given conditions are n-times that of H_2. What is the value of n?

2. It has been estimated that each square meter of the earth's surface supports 1×10^7 g of air above it. O_2 content in it is 19.2% by weight and it occupies $x \times 10^4$ moles. The value of x is

3. What is the height of a column of water that exerts the same pressure as column of mercury 0.662 m high?

4. What is the mass of 1.07 L of cyclopropane (C_3H_6) gas (used as an anesthetic) when measured at STP?

5. 1.0 g H_2 and 5.00 g He are confined to a volume of 5.0 L at 20°C. The partial pressure of He is (in atm)?

6. 0.142 g sample of $Fe_x(CO)_y$ is oxidised to CO_2 exerting a pressure of 44.9 mm Hg at 298 K in 1.50-L flask. The value of y in the simplest formula of the carbonyl per unit of Fe is

7. A spherical ballon of 21 cm diameter is to be filled up with nitrogen at NTP from a cylinder containing the gas at 20 atmospheres at 27°C. If the cylinder can hold 2.82 litres of water, calculate the number of ballons that can be filled up.

8. 34.05 mL of phosphorus vapours (P_x) weighs 0.062 g at 820 K and 1 atm. What is the value of x?

9. Rate of diffusion of H_2 is n-times that of O_2. What is value of n?

10. Temperature of CO (behaving ideally) is increased from 27°C to 927°C. By what factor its average velocity affected?

11. Which gas (by S.N.) has the highest value of van der Waals' constant 'a'?

(1) H_2 (2) He (3) N_2 (4) CO_2
(5) CH_4 (6) NH_3 (7) CO (8) HCl
(9) PCl_5

12. To an evacuated vessel with movable piston under external pressure of 1 atm, 0.1 mole of He and 1.0 mole of an unknown compound (vapour pressure 0.68 atm at 0°C) are introduced. Considering the ideal gas behaviour, the total volume (in litre) of the gases at 0°C is close to **[IIT JEE 2011]**

13. A spherical balloon of 21 cm diameter is to be filled with H_2 at NTP from a cylinder containing the gas at 20 atm at 27°C. If the cylinder can hold 2.80 L of water, calculate the number of balloons that can be filled up using pumping.

Answers

Objective Questions Type I [Only one correct option]

1.	(a)	**2.**	(b)	**3.**	(c)	**4.**	(c)	**5.**	(b)	**6.**	(c)	**7.**	(b)	**8.**	(a)	**9.**	(a)	**10.**	(c)
11.	(a)	**12.**	(b)	**13.**	(d)	**14.**	(a)	**15.**	(b)	**16.**	(c)	**17.**	(d)	**18.**	(a)	**19.**	(d)	**20.**	(b)
21.	(b)	**22.**	(c)	**23.**	(c)	**24.**	(b)	**25.**	(a)	**26.**	(a)	**27.**	(b)	**28.**	(a)	**29.**	(d)	**30.**	(c)
31.	(c)	**32.**	(a)	**33.**	(d)	**34.**	(a)	**35.**	(d)	**36.**	(b)	**37.**	(d)	**38.**	(c)	**39.**	(b)	**40.**	(a)
41.	(b)	**42.**	(b)	**43.**	(a)	**44.**	(a)	**45.**	(a)	**46.**	(d)	**47.**	(c)	**48.**	(c)	**49.**	(b)	**50.**	(b)
51.	(a)	**52.**	(d)	**53.**	(c)	**54.**	(a)	**55.**	(d)	**56.**	(d)	**57.**	(d)	**58.**	(d)	**59.**	(c)	**60.**	(d)
61.	(d)	**62.**	(a)	**63.**	(a)	**64.**	(b)	**65.**	(d)	**66.**	(a)	**67.**	(b)	**68.**	(c)	**69.**	(c)	**70.**	(a)
71.	(b)	**72.**	(b)	**73.**	(d)	**74.**	(b)	**75.**	(b)	**76.**	(c)	**77.**	(a)	**78.**	(a)	**79.**	(b)	**80.**	(d)
81.	(d)	**82.**	(b)	**83.**	(a)	**84.**	(a)	**85.**	(b)	**86.**	(a)	**87.**	(b)	**88.**	(c)	**89.**	(b)	**90.**	(c)
91.	(a)	**92.**	(d)	**93.**	(c)	**94.**	(d)	**95.**	(b)	**96.**	(c)	**97.**	(c)	**98.**	(d)	**99.**	(c)	**100.**	(c)
101.	(a)	**102.**	(b)	**103.**	(c)	**104.**	(c)	**105.**	(c)	**106.**	(a)	**107.**	(b)	**108.**	(b)	**109**	(d)	**110.**	(c)
111.	(d)	**112.**	(a)	**113.**	(d)	**114.**	(b)	**115.**	(b)	**116.**	(c)	**117.**	(b)	**118.**	(a)	**119**	(b)	**120.**	(a)
121.	(d)	**122.**	(c)	**123.**	(b)	**124.**	(a)	**125.**	(a)	**126.**	(c)	**127.**	(d)	**128.**	(d)	**129.**	(a)	**130.**	(b)
131.	(c)	**132.**	(d)	**133.**	(b)	**134.**	(c)	**135.**	(b)	**136.**	(a)	**137.**	(a)	**138.**	(a)	**139.**	(c)	**140.**	(c)
141.	(a)	**142.**	(a)	**143.**	(d)	**144.**	(b)	**145.**	(a)	**146.**	(c)	**147.**	(b)	**148.**	(d)	**149.**	(d)	**150.**	(b)
151.	(a)	**152.**	(c)	**153.**	(d)	**154.**	(c)	**155.**	(b)	**156.**	(a)	**157.**	(d)	**158.**	(a)	**159.**	(a)	**160.**	(b)
161.	(a)	**162.**	(d)	**163.**	(c)	**164.**	(d)	**165.**	(d)	**166.**	(c)	**167.**	(a)	**168.**	(d)	**169.**	(d)	**170.**	(a)
171.	(a)	**172.**	(d)	**173.**	(a)	**174.**	(b)	**175.**	(b)	**176.**	(b)	**177.**	(b)	**178.**	(c)	**179.**	(b)	**180.**	(c)
181.	(d)	**182.**	(c)	**183.**	(c)	**184.**	(c)	**185.**	(a)	**186.**	(a)	**187.**	(d)	**188.**	(d)	**189.**	(a)	**190.**	(c)
191.	(b)	**192.**	(b)	**193.**	(d)	**194.**	(a)	**195.**	(d)	**196.**	(a)	**197.**	(c)	**198.**	(b)	**199.**	(d)	**200.**	(a)
201.	(b)	**202.**	(b)	**203.**	(c)	**204.**	(c)	**205.**	(b)	**206.**	(c)	**207.**	(a)	**208.**	(a)	**209.**	(d)	**210.**	(c)
211.	(b)	**212.**	(b)	**213.**	(a)	**214.**	(b)	**215.**	(a)										

Objective Questions Type II [One or more than one correct option(s)]

1. (*b, d*)	**2.** (*a, b, c*)	**3.** (*b, d*)	**4.** (*d*)	**5.** (*b*)
6. (*a, b, c*)	**7.** (*a*)	**8.** (*a, b, c*)	**9.** (*d*)	**10.** (*a, b, c, d*)
11. (*b*)	**12.** (*a*)	**13.** (*a, b*)	**14.** (*a, c, d*)	**15.** (*a*)
16. (*c, d*)	**17.** (*a, b, d*)	**18.** (*a, c*)	**19.** (*d*)	**20.** (*a, c, d*)

Numerical Value Questions

1. 4 **2.** 477°C **3.** 868.35 ms^{-1} **4.** 150 **5.** 1.0504 **6.** radius = 0.162 nm **7.** 0.22 **8.** 0.97 **9.** (1)

10. n_1 = 0.4 mole at 300 K, n_2 = 0.2 mole at 600 K **11.** 2.22 **12.** 16.04 min

Comprehension Based Questions

Passage 1 – **1.** (a) **2.** (d)

Passage 2 – **1.** (c) **2.** (a) **3.** (a)

Passage 3 – **1.** (a) **2.** (b)

Passage 4 – **1.** (b) **2.** (a)

Passage 5 – **1.** (a) **2.** (b)

Passage 6 – **1.** (d) **2.** (b)

Passage 7 – **1.** (d) **2.** (b)

Passage 8 – **1.** (a) **2.** (c) **3.** (c)

Passage 9 – **1.** (c) **2.** (d)

Matrix-Match Type

1. A → (2); B → (1); C → (3); D → (1); E → (5)

2. A → (2); B → (1); C → (4); D → (3); E → (5)

3. A → (3); B → (1); C → (4); D → (2)

4. A → (4); B → (1); C → (2); D → (3)

5. A → (4); B → (3); C → (1); D → (2)

6. A → (3); B → (4); C → (2); D → (1)

7. A → (2,3); B → (1); C → (4); D → (2,3)

8. A → (2); B → (1); C → (2); D → (5); E → (4); F → (3)

Single Integer Answer Questions

1.	(2)	**2.**	(6)	**3.**	(9)	**4.**	(2)	**5.**	(6)	**6.**	(5)	**7.**	(10)	**8.**	(4)	**9.**	(4)	**10.**	(2)
11.	(6)	**12.**	(7)	**13.**	(10)														

Solutions

Objective Questions Type I [Only one correct option]

4. (*c*) 22.4 L O_2 at STP = 1 mol O_2

$$3.36 \text{ L } O_2 \text{ at STP} = \frac{3.36}{22.4} \text{ mol } O_2 = 0.15 \text{ mol } O_2$$

$$= 0.15 \text{ mol } H_2 = 0.30 \text{ g } H_2$$

5. (*b*) Interionic (ion-ion) forces are stronger than ion-dipole, which in turn are stronger than intermolecular forces like dipole-dipole interaction.

This is because in case of ion-ion interactions there is complete transfer of electrostatic charges from one atom to another. Whereas in dipole-dipole interactions, there is involvement of only partial charges.

The strength of ion-dipole interactions lies intermediate to that of ion-ion and dipole-dipole interactions.

Thus, the correct decreasing order of relative strength is :

Ion-ion > ion-dipole > dipole-dipole.

7. (*b*) Given, $Z_A = 3Z_B$

Compressibility factor $(Z) = \frac{pV}{nRT}$ [for real gases]

On substituting in equation (i), we get

$$\frac{p_A V_A}{n_A R T_A} = \frac{3 p_B V_B}{n_B R T_B} \quad \ldots\text{(ii)}$$

Also, it is given that

$$V_A = 2V_B,\ n_A = n_B \text{ and } T_A = T_B$$

∴ Eq. (ii) becomes

$$\frac{p_A \times 2V_B}{n_B R T_B} = \frac{3 p_B V_B}{n_B R T_B}$$

$$\Rightarrow \quad 2p_A = 3p_B$$

8. (*a*) $p_{gas} = p_{atm} + hdg$

$$\therefore \quad hdg = p_{gas} - p_{atm}$$

$$\therefore \quad = 77 - 76 = 1 \text{ cmHg} = 1 \times d \times g$$

$$\therefore \quad h = 1 \text{ cm}$$

15. (*b*) It will burst when volume is just larger than 20 L

$$p_1V_1 = 10 \text{ L atm},\ V_2 > 20 \text{ L}$$

	p_2	V_2
(a)	0.5 atm	20 L
(b)	0.4 atm	25 L (> 20 L)
(c)	0.7 atm	14.28 L
(d)	0.8 atm	12.5 L

16. (*c*) Since volume is constant.

$$\frac{p_2}{p_1} = \frac{T_2}{T_1} \text{ and } p_2 = 2 \times \frac{40}{20} = 4 \text{ atm}$$

17. (*d*)

	p/atm	*V*/L	*pV*/L-atm
(a)	380 mmHg = 0.5 atm	100 mL = 0.1	0.05
(b)	1 atm	0.05 L	0.05
(c)	190 mm Hg = 0.25 atm	0.200 L	0.05
(d)	1 atm	150 mL = 0.150 L	0.15 L

$(p_1V_1 \neq p_2V_2)$

18. (*a*)

$$pV = nRT$$

$$p = \frac{n}{V} RT = \frac{w}{mV} RT = \frac{dRT}{m}$$

(where, $d = \frac{w}{V}$ density in g L^{-1})

$$d = \frac{pm}{RT}$$

$$\therefore \quad \frac{d_2}{d_1} = \frac{p_2 m_2 T_1}{p_1 m_1 T_2} = \frac{p_2 T_1}{p_1 T_2} \quad \text{(for a given gas)}$$

$$d_2 = \frac{1.35 \times 760 \times 303}{768 \times 273}$$

$$= 1.48 \text{ kg/m}^3$$

19. (*d*) $\frac{r_X}{r_{O_2}} = \sqrt{\frac{M(O_2)}{M(X)}} = \sqrt{\frac{32}{128}} = \frac{1}{2}$

20. (*b*) $\frac{r_{H_2}}{r_{O_2}} = \sqrt{\frac{32}{2}} = 4$

$$r_{H_2} = 4r_{O_2} = 4 \times \frac{4}{32} \text{ mol } H_2$$

$$= \frac{4 \times 4 \times 2}{32} \text{ g } H_2 = 1 \text{ g}$$

21. (*b*) Under given condition, pressure

$$= 750 - 100 = 650 \text{ Torr}$$

$$\frac{p_1V_1}{T_1} = \frac{p_2V_2}{T_2}$$

$$\frac{650 \times 50}{291} = \frac{760 \times V_2}{273}$$

$$\therefore \quad V_2 = 40.1 \text{ mL}$$

22. (*c*)

$$\frac{p_1V_1}{T_1} = \frac{p_2V_2}{T_2}$$

$$\frac{5 \times V_1}{273} = \frac{p_2 \times \frac{V_1}{3}}{819}$$

$$p_2 = 45 \text{ atm}$$

24. (*b*) $p = \frac{n}{V} RT = \frac{w}{mV} RT = \frac{dRT}{m}$

$$\therefore \ m \text{ (molar mass of mixture)} = \frac{dRT}{p}$$

$$= \frac{1.40 \times 0.0821 \times 273}{1}$$

$$= 31.38 \text{ g mol}^{-1}$$

Let, mixture contains x part N_2 and $(1 - x)$ part Ar.

$$\therefore \quad 31.38 = \frac{m_1 x + m_2(1 - x)}{x + (1 - x)}$$

$$31.38 = \frac{28 + 40(1 - x)}{1}$$

$$\therefore \quad x = 0.72$$

25. (*a*)
$$p = \frac{n}{V}RT = \frac{w}{mV}RT$$
$$w = \frac{pmV}{RT} = \frac{2.463 \times 32 \times 34}{0.0821 \times 300} = 108.8 \text{ g}$$
O_2 already present = 212 g

Thus, O_2 to be released = 212 − 108.8 = 103.2 g

26. (*a*)
$$\frac{p_1V_1}{n_1T_1} = \frac{p_2V_2}{n_2T_2}$$
$$\frac{p_1 \times 30}{\frac{w_1}{m_1} \times T_1} = \frac{\frac{p_1}{9} \times V_2}{\frac{w_1}{2m_1} \times 3T_1}$$
$$V_2 = \frac{30 \times 9 \times 3}{2} = 405 \text{ mL}$$

27. (*b*)
$$\frac{p_1V_1}{T_1} = \frac{3 \times 1.65}{546} = 9.066 \times 10^{-3}$$
$$\frac{p_2V_2}{T_2} = \frac{0.75 \times 0.55}{273} = 1.51 \times 10^{-3} < \frac{p_1V_1}{T_1}$$
Hence, N_2 gas in LHS should escape to make
$$\frac{p_1V_1}{T_1} = \frac{p_2V_2}{T_2}$$
$$\therefore \quad V_1 = \frac{p_2V_2 \times T_1}{T_2 \times p_1} = \frac{0.75 \times 0.55 \times 546}{273 \times 3} = 0.275 \text{ L}$$
Volume of N_2 escaped = 1.65 − 0.275 = 1.375 L

Hence, fraction of N_2 escaped $= \frac{1.375}{1.65} = 0.8333$

28. (*a*) $p = \frac{n_1 + n_2}{V_1 + V_2} RT = \frac{0.5 + 2}{1 + 2} \times 0.0821 \times 300$
$$= 20.525 \text{ atm}$$

29. (*d*) Total pressure = 750 Torr

p_{H_2} pressure = 150 Torr

$\therefore$ mole fraction of $H_2 = \frac{150}{750} = 0.2$

$\therefore$ Volume per cent = 20

30. (*c*)
$$p = \frac{n(\text{Total})}{V} RT$$
$$n_{\text{Total}} = n(H_2) + n(\text{He}) + n(\text{NO})$$
$$= \frac{1}{2} + \frac{2}{4} + \frac{3}{30} = 1.1 \text{ mol}$$
$$\therefore \quad p = \frac{1.1 \times 0.0821 \times 300}{1.1} = 24.63 \text{ atm}$$

34. (*a*)
$$\text{KE of } n \text{ moles} = \frac{3}{2} nRT$$
$$(\text{KE})_{\text{He}} = (\text{KE})_{\text{Ar}}$$
$$\frac{3 \times 0.3 \times R \times T}{2} = \frac{3 \times 0.4 \times R \times 400}{2}$$
$$T = 533.3 \text{ K}$$

35. (*d*) If molecular velocities are root mean square type at temperature *T* K then
$$u_1 = \sqrt{\frac{3RT}{m_1}}$$
$$u_2 = \sqrt{\frac{3RT}{m_2}}$$
$$\frac{u_1^2}{u_2^2} = \frac{m_2}{m_1}$$
$$\therefore \quad m_1u_1^2 = m_2u_2^2$$

36. (*b*)
$$r(H_2) = \frac{50}{20} = 2.5$$
$$r(O_2) = \frac{40}{t}$$
$$\frac{r(H_2)}{r(O_2)} = \frac{2.5}{40/t} = \sqrt{\frac{M(O_2)}{M(H_2)}} = \sqrt{\frac{32}{2}} = 4$$
$$2.5t = 160$$
$$\therefore \quad t = 64 \text{ min}$$

37. (*d*)
$$u(\text{av}) = \sqrt{\frac{8RT}{\pi M}}$$
$$u(\text{av}) \propto \sqrt{\frac{T}{M}}$$
but independent of number of moles
$$u(O_2) \propto \sqrt{\frac{560}{32}} = 4.18$$
$$u(\text{Ne}) \propto \sqrt{\frac{500}{20}} = 5.0$$
$$u(CO_2) \propto \sqrt{\frac{440}{44}} = 3.16$$
$$u(\text{He}) \propto \sqrt{\frac{140}{4}} = 5.92$$

38. (*c*)
$$r_{H_2} = \frac{10}{26} \text{ mL s}^{-1}$$
$$r_X = \frac{10}{130} \text{ mL s}^{-1}$$
$$\frac{r_{H_2}}{r_X} = \frac{10}{26} \Big/ \frac{10}{130} = \sqrt{\frac{m(X)}{m(H_2)}} = \sqrt{\frac{m(X)}{2}}$$
$$5 = \sqrt{\frac{m(X)}{2}}$$
$$\therefore \quad m(X) = 50 \text{ g mol}^{-1}$$

39. (*b*) $\overline{\text{KE}} = \frac{3RT}{2N_0} = \frac{3 \times 8.3143 \times 298}{2 \times 6.02 \times 10^{23}} = 6.17 \times 10^{-21}$ J

43. (*a*)
$$\text{KE} = \frac{3}{2} nRT = \frac{3}{2} pV$$
$$\therefore \quad \text{KE per unit volume} = \frac{\text{KE}}{V} = \frac{3}{2} p$$

45. (*c*) $KE = \frac{3}{2}nRT = \frac{3}{2}nR(0+273) = \frac{3}{2}nR \times 273$

Thus, (a) is incorrect.

(b) $\text{rms}(O_2) = \sqrt{\frac{3RT}{M}} = \sqrt{\frac{3 \times 8.3143 \times 300}{32 \times 10^{-3}}}$

Thus, (b) is incorrect

(molar mass of O_2 in SI unit is 32×10^{-3} kg mol^{-1})

(c) is correct.

46. (*d*) $u(\text{rms}) = \sqrt{\frac{\Sigma u^2}{\Sigma n}} = \sqrt{\frac{N_1 u_1^2 + N_2 u_2^2}{N_1 + N_2}} = \sqrt{\frac{1 + 2 \times 4}{1+2}}$

$= 1.73 \text{ m s}^{-1}$

48. (*c*) Non-ideal behaviour is followed if

$pV \neq nRT$

(a) $p = \frac{n}{V}RT = \frac{w}{mV}RT = \frac{dRT}{m}$

LHS $p = 1$ atm

RHS $\frac{dRT}{m} = \frac{1.25 \text{ g L}^{-1} \times 0.0821 \text{ L atm mol}^{-1} \text{ K}^{-1} \times 273 \text{ K}}{28 \text{ g mol}^{-1}}$

$= 1$

Thus, $p = \frac{dRT}{m}$ Thus, ideal behaviour

(b) $pV = nRT$

$24.63 \times 0.1 = \frac{2.8}{28} \times 0.0821 \times 300$

$2.463 = 2.463$

Thus, ideal behaviour.

(c) $pV = nRT$

$4 \times 0.5 = \frac{1.6}{16} \times 0.0821 \times 273$

$2 = 2.24$

Thus, $pV \neq nRT$

Thus, non-ideal behaviour.

52. (*d*) At point *A* near low pressure region, volume is very high thus

$(V - b) \approx V$

$\therefore \left(p + \frac{a}{V^2}\right)V = RT$

$pV + \frac{a}{V} = RT$

$Z = \frac{pV}{RT} = \left(1 - \frac{a}{RTV}\right)$

53. (*c*) At point *B* at high pressure, volume is low

$\therefore \left(p + \frac{a}{V^2}\right) \approx p$

$\therefore p(V - b) = RT$

By approximation $pV = RT$

$\frac{p}{RT} = \frac{1}{V}$

$Z = \frac{pV}{RT} = 1 + \frac{pb}{RT} = \left(1 + \frac{b}{V}\right)$

54. (*a*) $\left(p + \frac{a}{V^2}\right)(V - b) = RT$

$pV + \frac{a}{V} - \frac{ab}{V^2} - pb = RT$

$pV = RT + pb - \frac{a}{V} = RT + \frac{RT}{V}b - \frac{a}{V}$

$= RT\left[1 + \frac{1}{V}\left(b - \frac{a}{RT}\right) + \dots\right]$

On comparison with

$pV = RT\left(1 + \frac{B}{V} + \dots\right)$

$B = \left(b - \frac{a}{RT}\right)$

66. (*a*) Average velocity, $v_{av} = \sqrt{\frac{8RT}{\pi M}}$

$\therefore v_{av} \propto \sqrt{T}$

$\Rightarrow \frac{v_1}{v_2} = \sqrt{\frac{T}{2T}} \Rightarrow v_2 = \sqrt{2}v_1 = 1.4\, v_1$

67. (*b*) Equal number of moles exert same partial pressure at same temperature and pressure. Therefore, partial pressure of N_2 in the mixture is 0.5 atm.

($p_{total} = p_1 + p_2$; 1 atm $= 2p_1$; $p_1 = 0.5$ atm)

68. (*c*) Suppose *w* kg of each is taken

$n_{CH_4} = \frac{w}{16}$

$n_{H_2} = \frac{w}{2}$

$p_{CH_4} = p_{total} \times$ mole fraction

$= p_{total} \times \frac{\frac{w}{16}}{\frac{w}{2} + \frac{w}{16}} = p_{total} \times \frac{1}{9}$

69. (*c*) $p_1V_1 = p_2V_2$
(at bottom) (at surface)

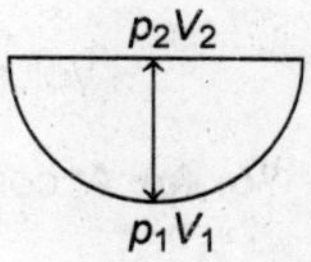

$p = h \cdot d \cdot g$

$p_1V_1 = (p + p_1)V$

$= (hdg + 10g)V$

$= (hg + 10g)V$

$p_1V_2 = 10g \times 8V$

$\Rightarrow (hg + 10g)V = 10g \times 8V$

$h + 10 = 80$

$h = 70$ m

70. (*a*) Initial temperature (of melting ice) $= 0°C = 273$ K

At constant volume $p \propto T$

$\therefore T_2 = \frac{p_2 T_1}{p_1} = \frac{400 \times 273}{1000} = 109.2$ K

71. (*b*) Density $(d) = \frac{pm}{RT}$

$$d \propto \frac{p}{T} \quad \text{(if } m \text{ is same)}$$

$$\frac{(d)_{top}}{(d)_{bottom}} = \left(\frac{p_{top}}{T_{top}}\right)\left(\frac{T_{bottom}}{p_{bottom}}\right) = \left(\frac{710}{273}\right)\left(\frac{303}{760}\right) = 1.04$$

72. (*b*) From the ideal gas equation,

$$pV = \Sigma nRT \quad \text{...(i)}$$

Given: $p = 200$ Pa, $V = 10\,m^3$, $T = 1000$ K

$n_A = 0.5$ moles, $n_B = x$ moles

On substituting the given values in equation (i), we get

$$200 \times 10 = (n_A + n_B) \times R \times 1000$$

$$0.5 + x = \frac{200 \times 10}{R \times 1000}$$

$$\frac{1}{2} + x = \frac{2}{R} = \frac{2}{R} - \frac{1}{2} = \frac{4-R}{2R}$$

73. (*d*) Moles of O_2 = Moles of H_2

$$4.8 \text{ g } O_2 = \frac{4.8}{32} = 0.15 \text{ mol } O_2$$

$$= 0.15 \text{ mol } H_2 = 0.30 \text{ g } H_2$$

74. (*b*) $pV = RT$

Kinetic energy per unit volume $E = \frac{3}{2}RT$

$\therefore \quad RT = \frac{2}{3}E$

$\therefore \quad p$ (per unit volume) $= RT = \frac{2}{3}E$

75. (*b*) $\frac{pV}{RT} = z, \quad z < 1$

$\therefore \quad \frac{pV}{RT} < 1$

at STP $\quad \frac{p}{RT} = \frac{1}{0.0821 \times 273} = \frac{1}{22.4}$

$$\frac{V_m}{22.4} < 1$$

$\therefore \quad V_m < 22.4$ L

76. (*c*) At constant pressure (parallel to *V*-axis)

$$V_1 > V_2 > V_3$$

Since, $V \propto T$, hence $T_1 > T_2 > T_3$

77. (*a*) If a gas is liquefied, it means volume is decreased and attractive force exists. *a* is a measure of attractive force and *b* the co-volume, hence

$$a(NH_3) > a(N_2)$$

and $\quad b(NH_3) > b(N_2)$

78. (*a*) At low pressure, *V* is high, hence $(V - b) \approx V$

79. (*b*) $\underset{\substack{1\text{ mol}\\0.95\text{ mol}}}{C_8H_{18}} + 8.5O_2 \longrightarrow \underset{\substack{8\text{ mol}\\7.6\text{ mol}}}{8CO} + 9H_2O$

Emitted gas contains 0.05 mol C_8H_{18} and 7.6 mol of CO if 1 mol of C_8H_{18} is the fuel.

$\therefore \quad \frac{CO}{C_8H_{18}} = \frac{7.6}{0.05} = 152$

80. (*d*) $b = 4V$ where, *V* is the volume of molecules in one mole of the gas

$\therefore \quad v \times N_0 = V$

$\therefore \quad b = 4N_0 v$

81. (*d*)

	N_2	+ $3H_2$	$\longrightarrow$ $2NH_3$
Taken	1	4	0
Reacts	1	3	

$$H_2 \text{ left} = 1 \text{ mol}$$

$$NH_3 \text{ formed} = 2 \text{ mol}$$

but $NH_3(g)$ dissolves in water forming NH_4OH. Residual gas is only H_2 which exerts pressure.

Volume = 15 – 5 = 10 L (5 L is occupied by H_2O added)

$\therefore \quad p = \frac{n}{V}RT = \frac{1 \times 0.0821 \times 300}{10}$ atm

82. (*b*) λ(Mean free path) $= \frac{1}{\sqrt{2}\pi\sigma^2 N}$

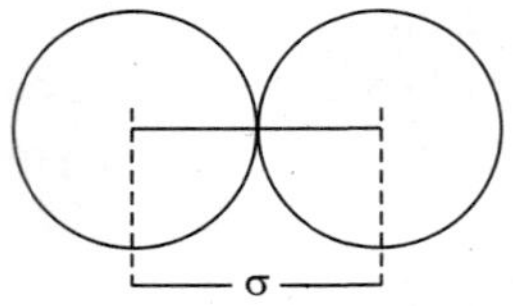

where, σ is the collision diameter.

$\therefore \quad \lambda \propto \frac{1}{\sigma^2}$

H_2 is smallest in size

84. (*a*) $pV = nRT$

$$n \propto T^{-1}$$

$$\frac{n_2}{n_1} = \frac{T_1}{T_2} = \frac{300}{400} = \frac{3}{4}$$

87. (*b*) $\frac{R_1}{R_2} = \frac{V/t_1}{V/t_2} = \frac{t_2}{t_1} = \sqrt{\frac{M_2}{M_1}}$

(a) $\quad \frac{10}{5} = \sqrt{\frac{4}{2}} = \sqrt{2}$: false

(b) $\quad \frac{20}{5} = \sqrt{\frac{32}{2}} = 4$, true

90. (*c*) Number of moles remains unchanged. One mole SO_2 replaces one mole of O_2, hence

$$32 \text{ g } O_2 = 64 \text{ g } SO_2$$

91. (*a*) KE $= \frac{3}{2}RT$ per mol

This does not contain molar mass, hence KE remains constant for every gas.

93. (*c*) Rate of diffusion of NH_3 (molar mass = 17) is larger than that of HCl (molar mass of HCl = 36.5), hence NH_3 covers more distance than HCl. NH_3 and HCl react to form white fumes of NH_4Cl.

96. (*c*) $V = \frac{n}{p}RT = \frac{1 \times 0.0821 \times 273}{0.5} = 44.8$ L

97. (*c*) Gas is real if $\frac{pV}{nRT} \neq 1$

98. (*d*) For non-zero volume, *b* cannot be neglected

$\therefore \quad p(V - nb) = nRT$

99. (*c*) As given above $pV = nRT + npb$

On increasing *p*, *npb* increases, hence *pV* increases, hence isotherm III.

100. (*c*) Equation of state $p(V - b) = RT$ indicates absence of intermolecular attraction or repulsion, hence interatomic potential remains constant on increasing 'π' in the beginning. As the molecules come very close, their electronic and nuclear repulsion increases abruptly.

101. (*a*) $\left(p + \frac{n^2a}{V^2}\right) \quad (V - nb) \quad = nRT$

not neglected   can be neglected

$$\therefore \quad \left(p + \frac{n^2a}{V^2}\right) V = nRT$$

$$pV + \frac{n^2a}{V} = nRT$$

$$\therefore \quad pV = \left(nRT - \frac{n^2a}{V}\right)$$

102. (*b*) For 1 mole of a real gas, the van der Waals' equation is

$$\left(p + \frac{a}{V^2}\right)(V - b) = RT$$

The constant '*a*' measures the intermolecular force of attraction of gas molecules and the constant '*b*' measures the volume correction by gas molecules after a perfectly inelastic binary collision of gas molecules.

For gas *A* and gas *C* given value of '*b*' is 0.05196 dm^3 mol^{-1}. Here,

$a \propto$ intermolecular force of attraction

$\propto$ compressibility $\propto$ real nature

$\propto \frac{1}{\text{volume occupied}}$

Value of a/(kPa dm^6 mol^{-1}) for gas *A* (642.32) > gas *C* (431.91) So, gas *C* will occupy more volume than gas *A*.

Similarly, for a given value of *a* say 155.21 kPa dm^6 mol^{-1} for gas *B* and gas *D*

$\frac{1}{b} \propto$ intermolecular force of attraction

$\propto$ compressibility $\propto$ real nature

$\propto \frac{1}{\text{volume accupied}}$

b/(dm^3 mol^{-1}) for gas *B* (0.04136) < Gas *D* (0.4382)

So, gas *B* will be more compressible than gas *D*.

103. (*c*)

$$\text{rms }(H_2) = \sqrt{\frac{3RT(H_2)}{2}}$$

$$\text{rms }(N_2) = \sqrt{\frac{3RT(N_2)}{28}}$$

$$\text{rms }(H_2) = \sqrt{7}\text{rms }(N_2)$$

$$\sqrt{\frac{3RT(H_2)}{2}} = \sqrt{7} \cdot \sqrt{\frac{3RT(N_2)}{28}}$$

$$\therefore \quad \frac{T(H_2)}{2} = \frac{T(N_2)}{4}$$

$$T(H_2) = \frac{T(N_2)}{2}$$

105. (*c*) $d = \frac{pm}{RT}, \quad d \propto \frac{p}{T}$

(a) $d \propto \frac{1}{273}$

(b) $d \propto \frac{2}{273}$

(c) $d \propto \frac{1}{546}$ (least)

(d) $d \propto \frac{2}{546}$

106. (*a*) $u_{av} \propto \sqrt{T}$

$$\frac{u_2}{u_1} = \sqrt{\frac{T_2}{T_1}} = \sqrt{\frac{1200}{300}} = 2.0$$

$$\therefore \quad u_2 = 0.6 \text{ m s}^{-1}$$

107. (*b*) Rate of diffusion of $H_2 > C_2H_2$ (ethyne)

Hence, H_2 diffuses into balloon, enlarging its size.

108. (*b*) $pV = nRT$

$$p \propto n$$

$$n_2 = n_1 \frac{p_2}{p_1} = 0.1 \times \frac{0.01}{100} \text{ mol} = 10^{-5}$$

$$\therefore \quad \text{molecules} = N_0 \times 10^{-5}$$

$$= 6.02 \times 10^{18}$$

110. (*c*) ***a*** van der Waals' constant is a measure of attractive force. Larger the value of ***a*** greater the liquefaction,

112. (*a*) $\text{KE} = \frac{3}{2}nRT$

$\text{KE} \propto nT$ (independent of gas)

$$(\text{KE})_{Ar} = (\text{KE})_{He}$$

$$0.4 \times 400 = 0.3 \times (T)_{He}$$

$$(T)_{He} = \frac{1600}{3} = 533 \text{ K}$$

115. (*b*) Atmospheric pressure = 760 mmHg

$$p_1V_1 = p_2V_2$$

$$p_2 = \frac{p_1V_1}{V_2} = \frac{760 \times 2.4}{1.9} = 960 \text{ mmHg}$$

$\therefore$ Difference in column = 960 − 760 = 200 mm

116. (*c*) At constant temperature

pV = constant

(a) $pV = 1 \times 0.2 = 0.2$ atm L

(b) $pV = \frac{760}{760} \times 0.2 = 0.2$ atm L

(c) $pV = 0.5 \times 0.1 = 0.05$ atm L

(d) $pV = 2 \times 0.1 = 0.2$ atm L

117. (*b*) Balloon will burst when volume > 200 L

At this point $p_2 = \frac{p_1V_1}{V} = \frac{1 \times 150}{200} = 0.75$ atm = 570 mm

Decrease in pressure = 760 − 570 = 190 mm

Height up to which it can resist bursting

$$= \frac{190 \text{ mm}}{10 \text{ mm / m}} = 19 \text{ m}$$

Thus, at a height above 19 m, balloon will burst.

118. (*a*) When open end up, the weight of mercury represents an increase in the pressure on the gas of 4.00 cmHg = 40 mmHg

∴ Final pressure = 760 + 40 = 800 mmHg

$$p_1V_1 = p_2V_2$$
$$p_1 \times A \times l_1 = p_2 \times A \times l_2$$

where, A is the area of cross-section (which is constant) and l_1, l_2 length

$$\therefore \quad p_1 \times l_1 = p_2 \times l_2$$
$$760 \times 10 = 800 \times l_2$$
$$l_2 = 9.50 \text{ cm}$$

119. (*b*)
$$\frac{p_1V_1}{T_1} = \frac{p_2V_2}{T_2}$$
$$\frac{1 \times 3}{273} = \frac{1.5 \times 2}{T_2}$$
$$T_2 = 273 \text{ K}$$

Hence, no change is required, *i.e.,* 0°.

123. (*b*) $p \propto T$ (at constant volume)

$T_2 = T_1 \frac{p_2}{p_1} = 273$ (temperature of melting ice) $\times \frac{400}{1000}$

$= 109.2$ K

125. (*a*) $k = \frac{V}{n} = \frac{22.4}{1}$ mol L^{-1}

when $n = 0.5$ mol, $V = 11.2$ L, hence $k = 22.4$ mol L^{-1} (again constant)

126. (*c*) In isothermal expansion, $pV_m = K$ (constant)

This relation is plotted in graph 'C'

Likewise, $$p = \frac{K}{V_m}$$

This relation is plotted in graph "*A*".

Thus, graph *B* and *D* are incorrect.

For them the correct graphs are:

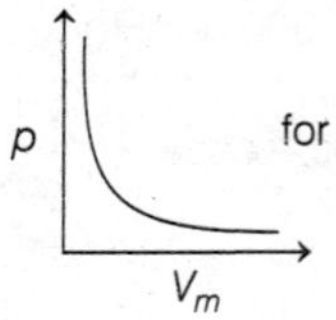

for graph *B* and

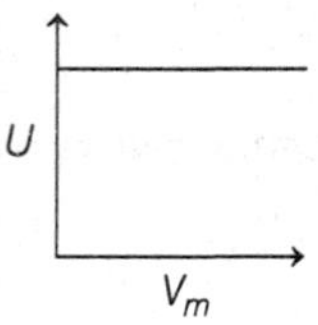

for graph *D* at constant temp.

127. (*d*) Number of molecules = $n \times N_0$

n remains constant.

129. (*a*) n_1 = moles of component I = $\frac{p_1V_1}{RT_1} = \frac{p_1V_1}{RT}$

n_2 = moles of component II = $\frac{p_2V_2}{RT_2} = \frac{p_2V_2}{RT}$

$$X_m \text{ (of component I)} = \frac{n_1}{n_1 + n_2} = \frac{p_1V_1}{p_1V_1 + p_2V_2}$$
$$= \frac{V_1}{V_1 + V_2} = X_V \text{ at constant } p$$
$$= \frac{p_1}{p_1 + p_2} = X_p \text{ at constant } V$$

Hence, $X_m = X_v = X_p$

130. (*b*) $pV = nRT = \frac{w}{m}RT$

$$\therefore \quad w = \frac{pVm}{RT} = \frac{12.315 \times 1 \times 32}{0.0821 \times 300} = 16 \text{ g}$$

∴ O_2 to be released = 32 − 16 = 16 g

131. (*c*)
$$d = \frac{pm}{RT}$$
$$m \text{ (phosphorus)} = \frac{dRT}{p}$$
$$= \frac{5.54 \times 0.0821 \times 273}{1}$$
$$= 124.1 \text{ g mol}^{-1}$$

∴ If molecular formula is $(p)_x$ then $32x = 124.1$

$x = 4$

Hence, P_4.

132. (*d*)
$$n_{H_2} = \frac{pV}{RT} = \frac{20000}{RT}$$
$$n_{He} = \frac{pV}{RT} = \frac{20000}{RT}$$
$$\therefore \quad n_{H_2} + n_{He} = \frac{40000}{RT}$$

Total volume = 300 mL

$$p = \frac{n}{V}RT = \frac{40000\,RT}{RT \times 300}$$
$$= \frac{400}{3} = 133.33 \text{ Torr}$$

133. (*b*)
$$p_{H_2} + p_{O_2} = 5 \text{ atm}$$

Partial pressure = $p_{total} \cdot$ mole fraction

$$p_{O_2} = p_{total} X_{O_2}$$
$$4 = 5\left(\frac{\frac{x}{32}}{\frac{x}{32} + \frac{1}{2}}\right)$$
$$x = 64 \text{ g} = 2 \text{ mol } O_2$$

134. (*c*) X (dry air) = 1 − 0.02 = 0.98

∴ Partial pressure (dry air) = 0.98 × 1.2 = 1.176

135. (*b*)

	N_2 +	$3H_2$ ⟶	$2NH_3$
Taken	2	5	0
Reacted (50% of N_2)	1	3	
Left	1	2	2

Total moles of N_2, H_2 and NH_3 = 5 mol

initial mole = 7

pressure at start = 7 atm

hence, pressure at equilibrium = 5 atm

$\therefore$ partial pressure of $NH_3 = \frac{2}{5} \times 5 = 2$ atm

136. (*a*) $p(O_2) = 787 - 27 = 760$ Torr = 1 atm

$$p = \frac{n}{V} RT$$

$\therefore$ $1 = \frac{n}{3} \times 0.0821 \times 300$, $n = 0.122$ mol

137. (*a*) $\frac{r_A}{r_B} = \sqrt{\frac{M_B}{M_A}}$

I. $= \sqrt{\frac{44}{44}} = 1$

II. $= \sqrt{\frac{28}{28}} = 1$

III. $= \sqrt{\frac{48}{32}} = 1.225$

IV. $= \sqrt{\frac{20}{18}} = 1.054$

V. $= \sqrt{\frac{352}{349}} = 1.004$

$\therefore$ I = II < V < IV < III

138. (*a*) $\frac{r_{SO_2}}{r_{He}} = \sqrt{\frac{4}{64}} = \frac{1}{4}$

$\therefore$ $r_{SO_2} = \frac{1}{4}(r_{He}) = 1.6$ mmol / h

$\therefore$ Time taken by 10 mmol $SO_2 = \frac{10}{1.6} = 6.25$ h

139. (*c*) $\frac{r_{LPG}}{r_{SO_3}} = \sqrt{\frac{80}{M(LPG)}} = 1.25$

$\therefore$ $\frac{80}{M} = (1.25)^2$

$\therefore$ $M(LPG) = 51.2$

$$M = \frac{M_1(\text{butane})\, X_1 + M_2\,(\text{propane})\, X_2}{X_1 + X_2}$$

$$51.2 = \frac{58X_1 + 44(1 - X_1)}{1}$$

$X_1 \approx 0.50$

140. (*c*) $r_{H_2} = \frac{100}{10} = 10$ mL/s

$$r_{O_2} = \frac{X}{t}$$

but $\frac{r_{H_2}}{r_{O_2}} = \sqrt{\frac{32}{2}} = \sqrt{16} = 4$

$\therefore$ $r_{O_2} = \frac{1}{4}(r_{H_2}) = 2.5$ mL/s

$\therefore$ $\frac{X}{t} = 2.5$ mL/s = (a), (b) and (d) $\neq$ (c)

141. (*a*) $C_3H_8 = n_1$ mol

$CH_4 = n_2$ mol

Total mol = $(n_1 + n_2)$

$\therefore$ Mole fraction of $C_3H_8 = \left(\frac{n_1}{n_1 + n_2}\right)$

$$p = \frac{n}{V} RT$$

$$320 = \frac{(n_1 + n_2)}{V} RT$$

$$\underset{n_1}{C_3H_8} \xrightarrow{\text{air oxidation}} \underset{3n_1}{3CO_2}$$

$$\underset{n_2}{CH_4} \xrightarrow{\text{air oxidation}} \underset{n_2}{CO_2}$$

$\therefore$ $448 = \frac{(3n_1 + n_2)RT}{V}$

$\therefore$ $\frac{448}{320} = \frac{3n_1 + n_2}{n_1 + n_2}$

$1.4(n_1 + n_2) = 3n_1 + n_2$

$n_1 = 0.25 n_2$

$\therefore$ Mole fraction of $C_3H_8 = \frac{0.25 n_2}{0.25 n_2 + n_2} = 0.2$

142. (*a*) One mole gas = N_0 molecules = 22400 mL at STP

$\therefore$ Average volume per molecule = $\frac{22400}{N_0}$

$= 3.72 \times 10^{-20}$ cm^3

144. (*b*) RMS velocity $= \sqrt{\frac{3RT}{M}} \propto \sqrt{T}$

$$KE = \frac{3}{2} RT$$

$$KE \propto T$$

Hence, KE is affected to maximum extent.

145. (*a*) $\left(p + \frac{a}{V^2}\right) V = RT, \quad b = 0$

$$pV + \frac{a}{V} = RT$$

$$\frac{pV}{RT} + \frac{a}{RTV} = 1$$

$\therefore$ $\frac{pV}{RT} = \left(1 - \frac{a}{RTV}\right) = z$

146. (*c*) For H_2, attractive forces are neglected, hence

$$\frac{a}{V^2} = 0$$

$\therefore$ $p(v - b) = RT$

$$pV = RT + pb$$

$\therefore$ $\frac{pV}{RT} = \left(1 + \frac{pb}{RT}\right) = z$

147. (*b*) For ideal gas $\frac{p\bar{V}_{id}}{RT} = 1$

$\therefore \quad \bar{V}_{id} = \frac{RT}{p}$

For real gas, $p\bar{V} = RT$

$$\frac{p\bar{V}}{RT} = Z$$

$$\frac{\bar{V}}{\bar{V}_{id}} = Z$$

149. (*d*) $b = 4 \times$ volume of molecules in one mole gas

$= 4 \times N_0 \times V$ (volume of one molecule)

$\therefore \quad V = \frac{b}{4N_0}$

155. (*b*) $T_c = \frac{8a}{27Rb}$

$$T_i = \frac{2a}{Rb}$$

$\therefore \quad \frac{T_i}{T_c} = \frac{27}{4}$

$\therefore \quad T_i = \frac{27}{4} \times 40 = 270 \text{ K}$

163. (*c*) $pV = nRT$

$$n_1 = \frac{p_1V_1}{RT_1}$$

$$n_2 = \frac{p_2V_2}{RT_2}$$

$$p_{\text{total}} = (n_1 + n_2)\frac{RT}{V}$$

$$= \frac{(p_1V_1 + p_2V_2)}{RT}\frac{RT}{V} \quad (T_1 = T_2 = T)$$

$$= \frac{p_1V_1 + p_2V_2}{V}$$

$$= \frac{1 \times 2 + 2 \times 3}{4} = 2 \text{ atm}$$

164. (*d*) $p = \frac{nRT}{V} = \frac{w}{mV}RT = \frac{dRT}{m}$

Let N_2 be $= w_1$ g with x %

O_2 be $= w_2$ g with $(100 - x)$%

$\therefore \quad \bar{M} = \frac{m_1x + m_2(100 - x)}{x + (100 - x)}$

$$31.2 = \frac{28x + 32(100 - x)}{100}$$

$\therefore \quad x = 20$

$\therefore \quad N_2 = 20 \text{ g} = \frac{20}{28} \text{ mol} = 0.71 \text{ mol}$

Thus, $O_2 = 80 = \frac{80}{32} \text{ mol} = 2.50 \text{ mol}$

$\therefore$ Mole fraction of $N_2 = \frac{0.71}{3.21} = 0.22$

165. (*c*) Average KE $= \frac{\frac{3}{2}RT}{N_0}$ Independent of molar mass

166. (*c*) $p(V - b) = RT$

$$p = \frac{RT}{(V - b)} \quad \text{(compare with } y = mx\text{)}$$

A graph between p and T at constant volume (isochoric) is a straight line of slope $= \frac{R}{(V - b)}$

167. (*a*) Mean free path $\lambda \propto \frac{T}{p}$

$\therefore \quad \frac{\lambda_2}{\lambda_1} = \frac{p_1}{p_2}$ at constant temperature

$$\lambda_2 = 60 \times \frac{1 \times 10^{-4}}{1 \times 10^{-2}} = 0.60$$

168. (*d*)

	Gas A	***Gas B***
$p_c = \frac{a}{27b^2}$	$p_c(A) = 0.498$	$p_c(B) = 73.3$
$T_c = \frac{8a}{27Rb}$	$T_c(A) = 15.43$	$T_c(B) = 84.7$
$V_c = 3b$	$V_c(A) = 0.954$	$V_c(B) = 0.1278$

Thus, $p_c(A) < P_c(B)$

$T_c(A) < T_c(B)$

$V_c(A) > V_c(B)$

169. (*d*) $p_{\text{total}} = p_{\text{atmospheric}} + p_{\text{gas}}$

$= (749 + 29.2 \times 10)$ mmHg

$= 1041$ mmHg

170. (*a*) $p = \frac{dRT}{m}, \quad d = \frac{pm}{RT}$

$\therefore \quad d \propto m$ under given condition

171. (*a*) $u = \sqrt{\frac{8RT}{\pi M}}$

$$u \propto \sqrt{T}$$

$$\frac{u_2}{u_1} = \sqrt{\frac{T_2}{T_1}}$$

$$= \sqrt{\frac{473}{323}} = 1.21$$

174. (*b*) $N_2O_4 \rightleftharpoons 2NO_2$

	N_2O_4	$2NO_2$
Initial	1	0
At equilibrium	$(1 - x)$	$2x$

Total moles at equilibrium $= (1 + x) = 1.2$

$$pV = nRT$$

$$\frac{p_2V_2}{p_1V_1} = \frac{n_2RT_2}{n_1RT_1}$$

$$\frac{p_2 \times V}{1 \times V} = \frac{1.2 \times R \times 600}{1 \times R \times 300}$$

$$p_2 = 2.4 \text{ atm}$$

176. (*b*)
$$pV = nRT$$
$$\frac{V_2}{V_1} = \frac{T_2}{T_1} = 1.5$$
(a) $\frac{T_2}{T_1} = \frac{333}{313} = 1.064$ false

(b) $\frac{T_2}{T_1} = \frac{819}{546} = 1.5$ true

180. (*c*) Collision frequency $Z = \frac{\pi\sigma^2 u_{av} p}{kT}$

(σ = collision diameter)

u_{av} = average velocity

$k = \frac{R}{N_0}$ = Boltzmann constant

T = temperature)
$$Z \propto p$$

182. (*c*)
$$pV = nRT$$
$$p_{atm} = \frac{n}{V}RT = \frac{0.0168 \times 0.0821 \times 298}{0.428}$$
$$= 0.9603 \text{ atm}$$
$$p_{atm} = 730 \text{ mmHg}$$
$$\therefore \quad p_{total} = p_{atm} + p_{vapour}$$
$$754 = 730 + p_{vapour}$$
$$V_{vapour} = 24 \text{ mmHg}$$

183. (*c*)
$$u \propto \sqrt{\frac{T}{M}}$$
$$\frac{u(H_2)}{u(O_2)} = \sqrt{\frac{50}{2} \times \frac{32}{800}} = 1$$

185. (*a*)
$$p = \frac{dRT}{m}$$
$$\therefore \quad m = \frac{dRT}{p}$$
$$d = 0.0013 \text{ g/mL} = 1.3 \text{ g/L}$$
$$\therefore \quad m = \frac{1.3 \times 0.0821 \times 273}{1} = 29.12 \text{ g mol}^{-1}$$
$$\therefore \text{ Vapour density} = \frac{\text{molar mass}}{2} = \frac{29.12}{2} = 14.56$$

186. (*a*)
$$p = \frac{dRT}{m}$$
$$\frac{p_1}{p_2} = \frac{d_1T_1m_2}{d_2T_2m_1} = \frac{1 \times 2 \times 28}{2 \times 1 \times 28} = 1:1$$

190. (*c*)
$$u = \sqrt{\frac{3RT}{M}}, \ E = \frac{3}{2}RT$$
$$\therefore \quad u = \sqrt{3 \times \frac{2E}{3M}} = \sqrt{\frac{2E}{M}}$$

191. (*b*)
$$pV = RT$$
$$V = \frac{RT}{p}, \quad V \propto \frac{T}{p}$$

Greater the value of $\left(\frac{T}{p}\right)$, greater the molar volume.

193. (*d*)
$$p = \frac{k}{V}$$
$$\frac{dp}{dV} = -\frac{k}{V^2} = -\frac{pV}{V^2} = -\frac{p}{V}$$

194. (*a*) By Boyle's law,
$$p = \frac{k}{V}\left(p \propto \frac{1}{V}\right)$$
$$\therefore \quad \frac{dp}{dV} = -\frac{k}{V^2} = -\frac{pV}{V^2} = -\frac{p}{V}$$

198. (*b*)
$$\frac{T_2}{T_1} = \frac{p_2}{p_1}$$
$$T_2 = 300 \times \frac{14.9}{12} = 372.5 \text{ K} = 99.5°\text{C}$$

204. (*c*) From kinetic gas equation,

Most probable velocity $(v_{mp}) = \sqrt{\frac{2RT}{M}}$

where, R = gas constant, T = temperature,

M = molecular mass
$$v_{mp} = \sqrt{\frac{2RT}{M}}, \text{ i.e. } v_{mp} \propto \sqrt{\frac{T}{M}}$$

Gas	M	T(K)	$\sqrt{T/M}$
H_2	2	300	$\sqrt{300/2} = \sqrt{150}$ ...III (Highest)
N_2	28	300	$\sqrt{300/28} = \sqrt{10.71}$ ...I (Lowest)
O_2	32	400	$\sqrt{400/32} = \sqrt{12.5}$ ... II

So,

I corresponds to v_{mp} of N_2 (300 K)

II corresponds to v_{mp} of O_2 (400 K)

III corresponds to v_{mp} of H_2 (300 K)

206. (*c*)
$$Z = \frac{pV}{nRT} = 0.8697$$
$$\therefore \quad V_m = \frac{0.8697 \times nRT}{p} = \frac{0.8697 \times 1 \times 0.083 \times 400}{71}$$
$$= 0.41 \text{ L } (R = 0.083 \text{ bar dm}^3 \text{ K}^{-1}\text{mol}^{-1})$$

210. (*c*)
$$\frac{p_1V_1}{n_1RT_1} = \frac{p_2V_2}{nRT_2}$$
$$\frac{p_1V_1}{T_1} = \frac{p_1 \times 2V_1}{3 \times T_2}$$
$$\therefore \quad T_2 = \frac{2}{3}T_1$$

211. (*b*) Volume $= \frac{4}{3}\pi r^3 = \frac{4}{3} \times \frac{22}{7} \times (0.5)^3 \text{ cm}^3$
$$= 0.5236 \text{ cm}^3 = 0.5236 \times 10^{-3} \text{ L}$$
$$\text{Moles of bubbles} = \frac{pV}{RT} = \frac{1 \times 0.5236 \times 10^{-3}}{0.0821 \times 298}$$
$$n = 2.14 \times 10^{-5}$$
$$\text{Molecules} = nN_0 = 1.29 \times 10^{19}$$

04

Liquid State

Objective Questions Type I [Only one correct option]

In each of the questions below, four choices are given of which only one is correct.

1. One of the following properties increases with rise in temperature
(a) viscosity (b) surface tension
(c) vapour pressure (d) density

2. Phase change from gas to solid is called
(a) sublimation (b) deposition
(c) fusion (d) vaporisation

3. There are some phase changes for which $\Delta H > 0$, $\Delta S > 0$
I. sublimation II. deposition
III. freezing IV. condensation
V. fusion VI. vaporisation
These phase changes can be
(a) I, II and III (b) IV, V and VI
(c) I, II, V and VI (d) I, V and VI

4. Randomness (disorder) increases in the order
(a) gas $\rightarrow$ liquid $\rightarrow$ solid (b) gas $\rightarrow$ solid $\rightarrow$ liquid
(c) solid $\rightarrow$ liquid $\rightarrow$ gas (d) solid $\rightarrow$ gas $\rightarrow$ liquid

5. When a phase-change takes place
(a) $\Delta H_{\text{sublimation}} = -\Delta H_{\text{deposition}}$
(b) $\Delta H_{\text{sublimation}} = \Delta H_{\text{fusion}} + \Delta H_{\text{vaporisation}}$
(c) $-\Delta H_{\text{sublimation}} = \Delta H_{\text{condensation}} + \Delta H_{\text{freezing}}$
(d) All of the above are correct

6. Some of the following properties of liquids arise because of the molecular interaction and thermal energy
I. vapour pressure II. surface tension
III. viscosity
They are
(a) I and II (b) I and III
(c) II and III (d) I, II and III

7. Molecular interactions between molecules is in order
(a) solid < liquid < gas (b) solid < gas < liquid
(c) gas < liquid < solid (d) liquid < solid < gas

8. Which is compressible fluid?
(a) Gas (b) Liquid
(c) Solid (d) All of these

9. Which has negligible translatory motion?
(a) Gas (b) Liquid
(c) Solid (d) All of these

10. Select the incorrect statement.
(a) Gases are compressible fluids
(b) The molecular interaction energy practically overpowers the thermal energy in solid state
(c) Molecular interactions between molecules are identical in steam, water and ice
(d) Liquid is incompressible fluid

11. Select the correct statement(s).
(a) When evaporation takes place, cooling takes place
(b) Evaporation takes place at all temperatures, boiling takes place only at the boiling point
(c) Evaporation is a surface phenomenon
(d) All of the above

12. Clausius-Clapeyron equation is
(a) $\dfrac{d\log_{10} p}{dT} = \dfrac{\Delta H}{2.303\,RT^2}$
(b) $\dfrac{d\log_{10} p}{dT} = -\dfrac{\Delta H}{2.303\,RT}$
(c) $\dfrac{d\log_{10} p}{dT} = -\dfrac{\Delta H}{2.303\,RT^2}$
(d) $\dfrac{d\log_{10} p}{dT} = \dfrac{\Delta H}{2.303\,RT}$

13. Boiling point of water at a place is found to be 110°C. At this place
(a) external pressure is less than 1 atm
(b) external pressure is greater than 1 atm
(c) external pressure is equal to 1 atm
(d) cooking takes longer time

14. Graphically variation of $\log_{10} p$ with $\frac{1}{T}$ is shown. If $\tan \theta$ (slope of the line) $= -2\,K$, latent heat of vaporisation of the given liquid is

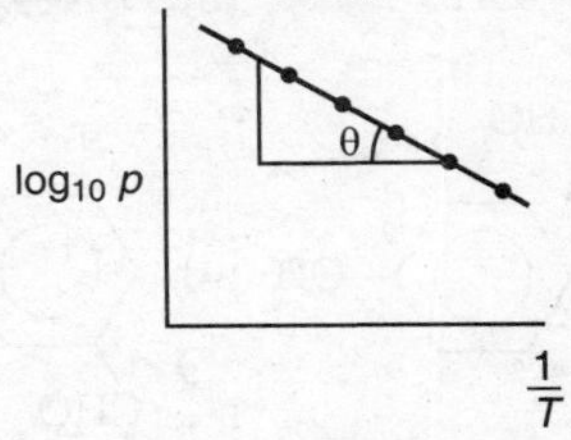

(a) 2.303 cal mol^{-1} (b) 4.606 cal mol^{-1}
(c) 9.212 cal mol^{-1} (d) 4.00 cal mol^{-1}

15. Clausius-Clapeyron equation can also be written as $p = Ae^{-\Delta H/RT}$ where, A is called pre-exponential factor. If

$$\log_{10} p(\text{mm}) = -\frac{4000\ (\text{K})}{T} + 10$$

then A and ΔH (in terms of R) respectively are
(a) $10, -4000 \times 2.303 \times R$
(b) $10, 4000 \times 2.303 \times R$
(c) $10^{10}, 4000 \times 2.303 \times R$
(d) $10^{10}, 4000 \times R$

16. Two bubbles of different radii are connected by a hollow tube, then
(a) smaller bubble gets smaller, larger gets larger
(b) smaller bubble gets larger and larger gets smaller
(c) both get smaller
(d) both get larger and ultimately burst

17. Downward force due to gravity when liquid (density d) is in a column of radius r set-up at height h is balanced by upward thrust due to surface tension. Hence,
(a) $2\pi r \gamma = r^2 hdg$ (b) $2 r \gamma = hdg$
(c) $2 r \gamma = \pi hdg$ (d) $2\gamma = rhdg$

18. When one end of the fine capillary which is open at both ends is immersed in water, water would completely fill in it. It is due to
(a) surface tension which pulls the water into the capillary
(b) the surface tension which is great enough to overcome the attraction of gravity in water in fine capillary
(c) Both (a) and (b)
(d) None of the above

19. Some of the following statements are correct.
I. The water drop in vacuum is perfectly spherical.
II. The shape of water drop is distorted due to action of gravity.
III. Soaps and detergents drastically decrease the surface tension of water.
IV. As temperature increases, surface tension also increases and becomes maximum at critical temperature.
Select the correct statements.
(a) I, II, III and IV (b) II, III and IV
(c) I, II and III (d) I and III

20. Some of the following decrease surface tension of a liquid
I. increase in temperature of the liquid
II. mixing of detergent in the liquid
III. decrease in temperature
These can be
(a) II, III (b) I, II (c) II only (d) I only

21. The qualitative sketches I, II and III given below show the variation of surface tension with molar concentration of three different aqueous solutions of KCl, CH_3OH and $CH_3(CH_2)_{11}OSO_3^-Na^+$ at room temperature. **[JEE Advanced 2016]**

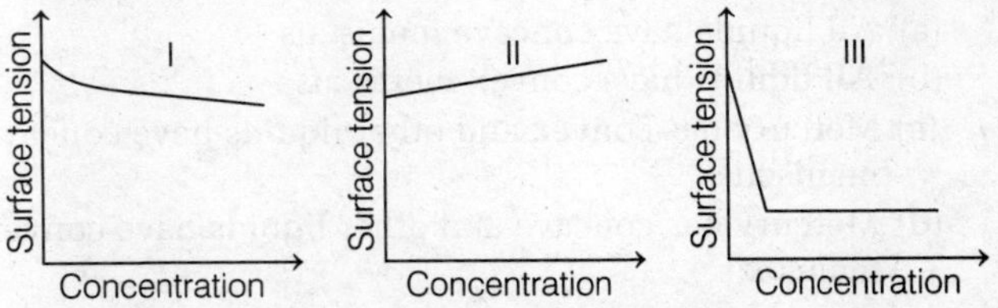

The correct assignment of the sketches is

	I	II	III
(a)	KCl	CH_3OH	$CH_3(CH_2)_{11}OSO_3^-Na^+$
(b)	$CH_3(CH_2)_{11}OSO_3^-Na^+$	CH_3OH	KCl
(c)	KCl	$CH_3(CH_2)_{11}OSO_3^-Na^+$	CH_3OH
(d)	CH_3OH	KCl	$CH_3(CH_2)_{11}OSO_3^-Na^+$

22. Some of the following properties are transport properties
I. viscosity II. surface tension
III. thermal conductance IV. diffusion
Select the correct alternate of transport properties.
(a) I, II, III and IV
(b) I, III and IV
(c) I and III
(d) III and IV

23. This property increases with increase in temperature
(a) viscosity of liquid
(b) viscosity of gas
(c) Both (a) and (b)
(d) None of the above

24. Which among of the following has least surface tension?
(a) Benzene (b) Acetic acid
(c) Diethyl ether (d) Chlorobenzene

25. Effect of temperature on viscosity is given by
(a) hole theory (b) Arrhenius theory
(c) adsorption theory (d) collision theory

26. Which has maximum vapour pressure at a given temperature?
(a) $CH_3CH_2CH_2OH$ (b) 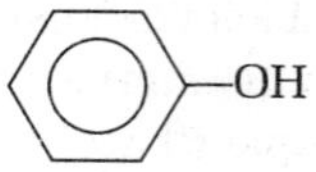
(c) $CH_3—O—CH_3$ (d) CH_3COOH

27. Following properties will decrease with increase in temperature except
(a) surface tension (b) viscosity
(c) density (d) vapour pressure

28. At critical temperature of a liquid, surface tension is
(a) zero (b) infinite
(c) varies liquid to liquid (d) can't be measured

29. Unit of viscosity is
(a) poise (b) dyne/cm
(c) joule/m^2 (d) joule

30. Which is true statement?
(a) All liquids have concave meniscus
(b) All liquids have convex meniscus
(c) Mercury has convex and other liquids have concave meniscus
(d) Mercury has concave and other liquids have convex meniscus

31. One poise is equal to
(a) 100 centipoise (b) 0.1 kg m^{-1} s^{-1}
(c) Both (a) and (b) (d) None of these

32. Which is not a surface phenomenon?
(a) Surface tension (b) Viscosity
(c) Evaporation (d) All of these

33. Clausius-Clapeyron equation is
(a) $\frac{d \log p}{dT} = \frac{\Delta H_{vap}}{2.303 RT^2}$
(b) $\log p = \log A - \frac{\Delta H_{vap}}{2.303 RT}$
(c) Both (a) and (b)
(d) None of the above

34. Surface tension of water is 73 dyne cm^{-1} at 20°C. If surface area is increased by 0.10 m^2, work done is
(a) 7.3 erg (b) 7.3×10^4 erg
(c) 73 J (d) 0.73 J

35. $H_2O(l) \xrightleftharpoons{1\ atm} H_2O(g), \Delta H_{vap} = 10$ kcal mol^{-1}.
If pressure is increased
(a) steam is liquefied (b) b.p. of H_2O is elevated
(c) Both (a) and (b) (d) None of these

36. The predominant intermolecular forces present in ethyl acetate, a liquid, are **[JEE Main 2020]**
(a) London dispersion and dipole-dipole
(b) London dispersion, dipole-dipole and hydrogen bonding
(c) dipole-dipole and hydrogen bonding
(d) hydrogen bonding and London dispersion

37. Which is maximum volatile?
(a) 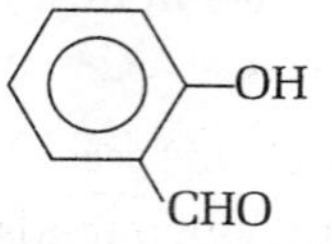
(b) 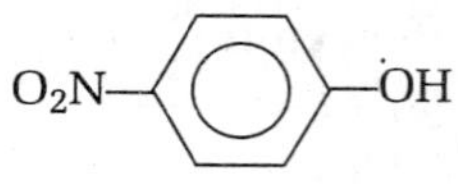
(c) 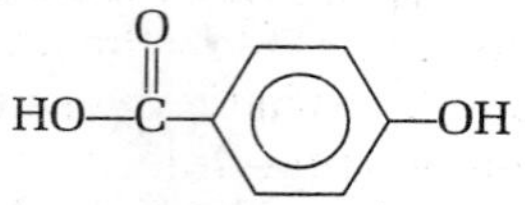
(d) 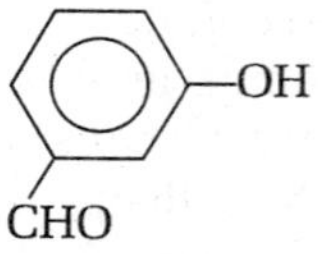

38. HF has highest boiling point among hydrogen halides, because it has **[JEE Main 2019]**
(a) lowest ionic character
(b) strongest van der Waals' interactions
(c) strongest hydrogen bonding
(d) lowest dissociation enthalpy

39. If detergent is added
(a) surface tension decreases
(b) surface tension increases
(c) surface tension can increase or decrease
(d) No effect

40. Types of forces that can be present in ethanol giving it a liquid state
(a) dipole-dipole interaction
(b) London forces
(c) hydrogen bonding
(d) All of the above

41. Of these quantities, the one that we expect to be largest
(a) molar heat capacity of liquid
(d) heat of fusion
(c) heat of vaporisation
(d) heat of sublimation

42. Of the compounds HF, CH_4, CH_3OH and N_2H_4, hydrogen bonding as important intermolecular force is expected in
(a) None of these
(b) Two of these
(c) All but one of these
(d) All of the above

43. The intermolecular force of attraction between non-polar molecules is called
(a) H-bonding
(b) dispersion forces
(c) interionic attraction
(d) adhesive forces

44. Evaporation and boiling differs
(a) evaporation is spontaneous at all temperatures while boiling is at constant temperature
(b) boiling is spontaneous at all temperatures while evaporation takes place at constant temperature
(c) both are spontaneous at all temperatures
(d) evaporation is exothermic while boiling is endothermic

45. If latent heat of vaporisation is L at boiling point T(K) then entropy of vaporisation is
(a) LT (b) LT^{-1}
(c) TL^{-1} (d) None of these

46. As heat is removed from a liquid which tends to supercool, its temperature drops below the freezing point and then rises suddenly. What is the source of heat which causes the temperature rise?
(a) The enthalpy of fusion
(b) The enthalpy of vaporisation
(c) The enthalpy of sublimation
(d) The enthalpy of deposition

47. As supercooled water freezes spontaneously, its temperature rises to 0°C, ΔH for the spontaneous process is equal to

$$H_2O(l) \text{ at } -10°C \longrightarrow H_2O(l) \text{ at } 0°C$$

(a) enthalpy of fusion (b) enthalpy of vaporisation
(c) enthalpy of sublimation (d) zero

48. 1 g of I_2 is in 10 mL $CHCl_3$. When 400 mL H_2O is added into it, concentration of I_2 in $CHCl_3$ falls to 0.80 g. Hence, partition coefficient of I_2 in $CHCl_3$ and H_2O is
(a) 400 (b) 200 (c) 300 (d) 160

49. Partition coefficient of I_2 in CCl_4 and H_2O is 400. 10 mL of CCl_4 solution containing 1 g I_2 is shaken with 0.4 L H_2O. I_2 extracted into water when equilibrium is attained will be
(a) $\frac{1}{11}$ g (b) $\frac{10}{11}$ g (c) $\frac{1}{10}$ g (d) $\frac{1}{9}$ g

50. Benzoic acid is distributed between water and benzene. Concentration of benzoic acid in two layers are

Conc.	I	II	III
C (in H_2O)	0.1 M	0.2 M	0.3 M
C (in benzene)	0.01 M	0.04 M	0.09 M

Hence, benzoic acid is
(a) monomer in both layers
(b) dimer in both layers
(c) monomer in water and dimer in benzene
(d) monomer in benzene and dimer in water

51. Distribution coefficient of solute X between ether and water is 2. 1 g of solute X is in 100 g water. If X is extracted into ether by 100 mL of it then
(a) 0.667 g of X is extracted into ether if it is used in one part of 100 mL
(b) 0.75 g of X is extracted into ether if it is used in two parts of 50 mL each
(c) Both (a) and (b)
(d) None of the above

52. Select the correct statement(s).
(a) The standard boiling temperature is the temperature at which the vapour pressure of the substance is 1 bar
(b) The normal boiling temperature is the temperature at which the vapour pressure of the substance is 1 atm
(c) Substances for which $T > T_c$ and $p > p_c$ are called super critical fluids
(d) All the above are correct statements

53. Phase rule is given by $F = C - P + 2$ where, F is degrees of freedom, C the number of components and P the number of phases. At triple point in the following equilibria,

$$H_2O(s) \rightleftharpoons H_2O(l) \rightleftharpoons H_2O(g)$$

F is equal to
(a) 0 (b) 1 (c) 2 (d) 3

54. Number of phases in the following equilibrium is

$$CaCO_3(s) \rightleftharpoons CaO(s) + CO_2(g)$$

(a) 1 (b) 2
(c) 3 (d) can't be predicted

55. Select the incorrect statement.
(a) The properties of liquid crystals are intermediate between liquids and solids
(b) Surface tension of a liquid is maximum at critical temperature
(c) Viscosity decreases with increase in temperature
(d) CO_2 and H_2O show the unusual properties of supercritical fluids

56. Which of following correctly represents the relation between capillary rise h and capillary radius r?

(a)
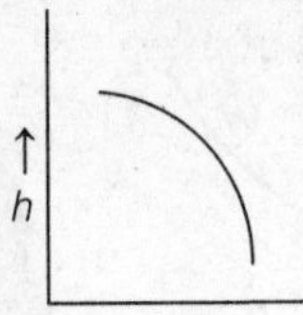

(b)
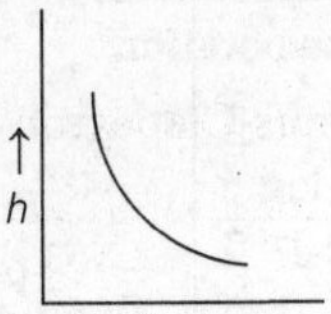

(c)
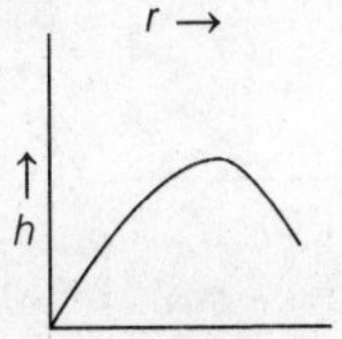

(d)
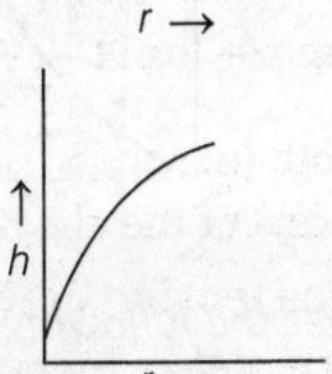

57. The best scientific method to test the presence of water in a liquid is
(a) use of litmus paper (b) taste
(c) use of anhydrous $CuSO_4$ (d) smell

58. The nature of intermolecular forces among benzene molecule is
(a) hydrogen bonding
(b) dispersion forces
(c) dipole-dipole attraction
(d) ion-dipole attraction

59. Distribution law cannot be applicable for a system in which I_2 is distributed in between
(a) water and alcohol (b) water and benzene
(c) water and chloroform (d) water and acetone

60. Mixture of aniline and water can be separated by
(a) vacuum distillation (b) chromatography
(c) separating funnel (d) steam distillation

61. Consider the following statements.
I. Density of water is maximum at 277 K
II. Density of water increases from 273 to 277 K and beyond this decreases as expansion predominates
III. Due to extensive hydrogen bonding, water has a very high heat capacity

Select the correct statements.
(a) I, II (b) II, III
(c) I, III (d) I, II, III

62. Supercritical CO_2 ($ScCO_2$) is ideally suited in
(a) food processing
(b) production of pharmaceuticals
(c) Both (a) and (b)
(d) None of the above

63. Supercritical fluid chromatography (SFC) uses mobile phase which is
(a) supercritical CO_2
(b) supercritical H_2O
(c) supercritical NH_3
(d) supercritical $CHCl_3$

64. Select the correct statement(s).
(a) A great advantage of $ScCO_2$ is that there are no noxious residues once the solvent has been allowed to evaporate
(b) $ScCO_2$ is being used for dry cleaning which avoids the use of carcinogenic and environmentally deleterious chlorinated hydrocarbons
(c) Supercritical water (ScH_2O) also exists
(d) All the above are correct statements

65. Select the correct statement(s).
(a) Liquid lead does not wet a solid iron surface since the interfacial tension between these two phases is quite large
(b) Alloys of tin and lead are used in soldering because the interfacial tension between the liquid and solid is reduced and the liquid flows over the solid surface
(c) Both (a) and (b)
(d) None of the above

Comprehension Based Questions

In these questions, a passage has been given followed by questions based on it. You have to answer the questions based on the passage given.

***Passage* 1** The phase diagram for a pure substance is shown below. Use this diagram and your knowledge about changes of phase

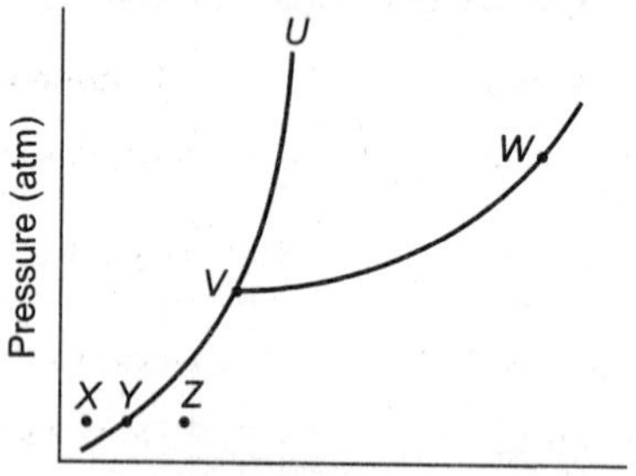

Answer the following questions.

1. What characteristics are specific to the system only at point V?
(a) Liquid $\rightleftharpoons$ Solid
(b) Solid $\rightleftharpoons$ Vapour
(c) Liquid $\rightleftharpoons$ Vapour
(d) Solid $\rightleftharpoons$ Liquid $\rightleftharpoons$ Vapour

2. What happens if temperature is increased from X to Y at 1.0 atm?
(a) Solid is completely vaporised
(b) Solid and vapour are in equilibrium
(c) Solid and liquid are in equilibrium
(d) Liquid and vapour are in equilibrium

3. In a phase change (say solid to liquid or liquid to solid) $\Delta G = \Delta H - T\Delta S$ where
(a) ΔH is the enthalpy change associated with making or breaking the intermolecular attractions that hold solid and liquid together and ΔS is associated with change in disorder between the various phases
(b) ΔH is associated with change in disorder while ΔS is associated with energy change
(c) both are associated with change in disorder
(d) both are associated with change in energy

***Passage* 2** Following passage explains effect of temperature on the vapour pressure of liquid.

Answer the questions given at the end.

Effect of Temperature on Vapour Pressure

The quantity of heat required to evaporate a given liquid at constant temperature is defined as the heat of vaporisation.

Variation of vapour pressure with temperature is given by **Clausius-Clapeyron equation.**

$$\log_e p = -\frac{\Delta H_{vap}}{RT} + \log_e A$$

A liquid is said to be at its boiling temperature if its vapour pressure is equal to external pressure. Therefore, the boiling point of water in particular and of liquids in general decreases as altitude of a place increases where the external pressure is less than 1 atmosphere (normal b.p. of water is 373.15 K at 1 atmosphere).

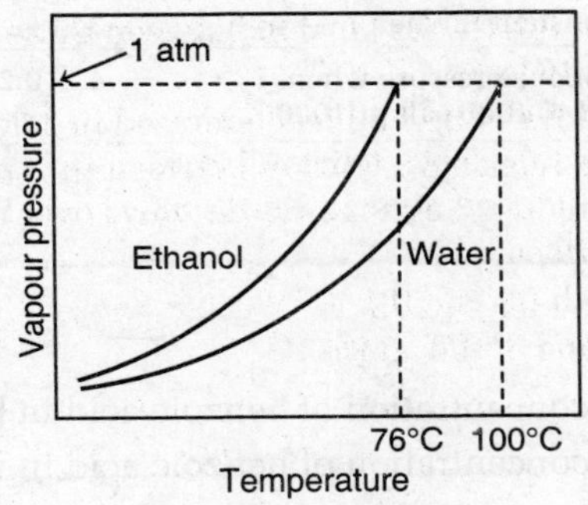

On top of Mount Everest, e.g., where the atmospheric pressure is only about 260 mmHg, water boils at approximately 71°C. Conversely, if the external pressure on a liquid is greater than 1 atm., the vapour pressure necessary for boiling is reached later, and the liquid boils at a temperature greater than normal boiling point.

1. Clausius-Clapeyron can be written in the following form

(a) $p = Ae^{-\Delta H_{vap}/RT}$

(b) $\dfrac{d \log_{10} p}{dT} = \dfrac{\Delta H_{vap}}{2.303\, RT^2}$

(c) $\dfrac{d \log_e p}{dT} = -\dfrac{\Delta H_{vap}}{RT^2}$

(d) $p = Ae^{\Delta H_{vap}/RT}$

2. For a given liquid at a given temperature vapour pressure is given by

$$\log_{10} p(\text{mm}) = -\frac{400\ (\text{K})}{T} + 10$$

Vapour pressure of the liquid at 400 K is

(a) 9 mm (b) –9 mm

(c) 10^9 mm (d) 10^{-9} mm

3. Latent heat of vaporisation of the above case in the given temperature range is

(a) –400 R

(b) 400 R

(c) –400 × 2.303 R

(d) 400 × 2.303 R

Matrix-Match Type

Given below are Matching Type Questions, with two columns (each having some items) each . Each item of Column I has to be matched with the items of Column II.

1. Match the Column I with Column II.

Column I (Measurement)	Column II (Property studied)
A. Vapour pressure of a liquid at different temperatures	1. Molecular weight
B. Volumes of a gas at different pressures at constant temperature	2. Enthalpy of vaporisation
C. Limiting density of a gas when $p \to 0$ at a constant temperature	3. Virial coefficients
D. Surface tension of aqueous solution	4. Critical micelle concentration

2. Match the term in Column I with its definition in Column II.

	Column I		Column II
A.	Sublimation	1.	The change of solid to a liquid
B.	Deposition	2.	The change of a liquid to a solid
C.	Condensation	3.	The change of a liquid to a gas
D.	Vaporisation	4.	The change of a gas to a liquid
E.	Fusion	5.	The change of a solid to a gas
		6.	The change of a gas to a solid

3. Match the liquids in Column I with viscosity in Column II at a given temperature.

Column I	Column II
A. Water	1. 9.0
B. Glycerol	2. 0.2
C. Benzene	3. 2.0
D. Tar-coal	4. 1.0

4. Match the physical property in Column I with unit in Column II.

Column I	Column II
A. Viscosity	1. $J\ mol^{-1}\ K^{-1}$
B. Surface tension	2. $J\ m^{-2}$
C. Latent-heat	3. $N\ m^{-1}$
D. Surface energy	4. $kg\ m^{-1}\ s^{-1}$

5. Match the type of forces in Column I with the substances having them in Column II.

Column I	Column II
A. H-bonding	1. Water
B. Dipole-dipole interaction	2. Glycerol
C. Cohesive forces	3. *o*-nitrophenol
D. Adhesive forces	4. Water and oil

6. Variation of vapour pressure with temperature is given by $p = Ae^{-\Delta H/RT}$ Graphically, $\log_{10} p$ against $\frac{1}{T}$ is a straight line

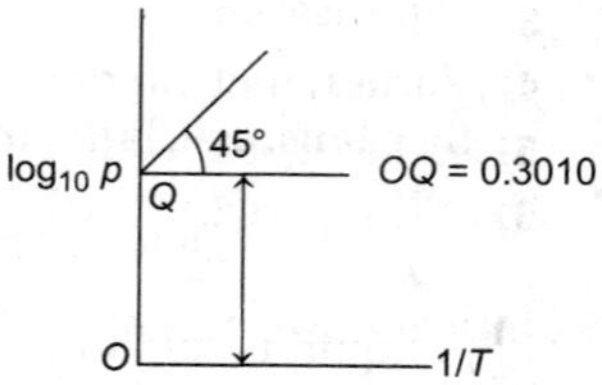

Match the parameters in Column I with their values in Column II.

Column I	Column II
A. Latent heat (ΔH_{vap}) in cals	1. 2.0
B. Vapour pressure when $T \to \infty$	2. 4.606
C. Constant A when $T \to \infty$	3. ∞
D. Vapour pressure when ΔH = 4606 cals at 1000 K	4. 0.20

Integer Type

Solve the following Problem and write your answer.

1. The number of phases present in the following equilibrium are $CaCO_3(s) \rightleftharpoons CaO(s) + CO_2(g)$

2. The number of water molecules coordinated directly to one water molecule in liquid state are ....

3. How much energy (in ~ kJ) is required to vaporise 900 kJ of water at 100°C?
ΔH°_{vap} = 40.0 kJ mol^{-1} at 100°C.

4. How many of the following solids undergo sublimation on heating?

Iodine, water, carbon dioxide, ammonium chloride, naphthalene, *p*-dichlorobenzene, camphor.

5. Benzoic acid is distributed between benzene and water.

C_1 = concentration of benzoic acid in benzene
C_2 = concentration of benzoic acid in water.

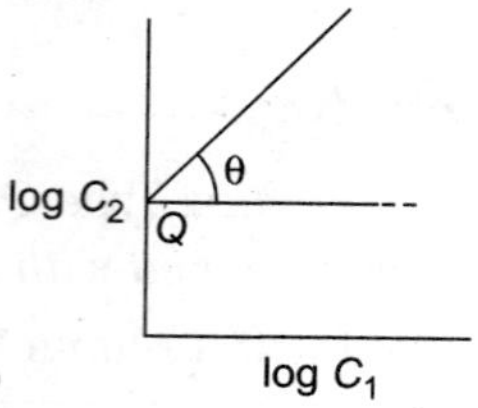

$$\theta = \tan^{-1}(0.5)$$

The number of molecules of benzoic acid associated in benzene based on this study are

Answers

Objective Questions Type I [Only one correct option]

1. (a)	**2.** (b)	**3.** (d)	**4.** (c)	**5.** (d)	**6.** (d)	**7.** (c)	**8.** (a)	**9.** (c)	**10.** (c)
11. (d)	**12.** (a)	**13.** (b)	**14.** (c)	**15.** (c)	**16.** (b)	**17.** (d)	**18.** (c)	**19.** (c)	**20.** (b)
21. (d)	**22.** (b)	**23.** (b)	**24.** (c)	**25.** (a)	**26.** (c)	**27.** (d)	**28.** (a)	**29.** (a)	**30.** (c)
31. (c)	**32.** (b)	**33.** (c)	**34.** (b)	**35.** (c)	**36.** (a)	**37.** (a)	**38.** (c)	**39.** (a)	**40.** (d)
41. (d)	**42.** (c)	**43.** (b)	**44.** (a)	**45.** (b)	**46.** (a)	**47.** (d)	**48.** (d)	**49.** (a)	**50.** (c)
51. (c)	**52.** (d)	**53.** (a)	**54.** (c)	**55.** (b)	**56.** (b)	**57.** (c)	**58.** (b)	**59.** (a)	**60.** (d)
61. (d)	**62.** (c)	**63.** (a)	**64.** (d)	**65.** (c)					

Comprehension Based Questions

Passage 1 – **1.** (d) **2.** (b) **3.** (a)

Passage 2 – **1.** (a) **2.** (c) **3.** (d)

Matrix-Match Type

1. A→(2); B→(3); C→(1); D→(4)

2. A→(5); B→(6); C→(4); D→(3); E→(1)

3. A→(4); B→(3); C→(2); D→(1)

4. A→(4); B→(3); C→(1); D→(2)

5. A→(1,2,3); B→(1,2,3); C→(1,2,3); D→(4)

6. A→(2); B→(1); C→(1); D→(4)

Single Integer Answer Questions

1. (3) **2.** (4) **3.** (2) **4.** (2) **5.** (2)

Solutions

Objective Questions Type I [Only one correct option]

14. (*c*) Variation of $\log_{10} p$ with $\frac{1}{T}$ is given by Clausius-Clapeyron equation (linear equation)

$$\log_{10} p = -\frac{\Delta H}{2.303RT} + A$$

$$\text{slope} - \frac{\Delta H}{2.303R} = -2 \text{ (given)}$$

$\therefore$
$$\Delta H = 2.303\, R \times 2 = 2.303 \times 2 \times 2 = 9.212 \text{ cal mol}^{-1}$$

15. (*c*)
$$p = Ae^{-\Delta H/RT}$$

$$\log_e p = \log_e \cdot e^{-\Delta H/RT} + \log_e A$$

$$\log_e p = -\frac{\Delta H}{RT} + \log_e A$$

$$2.303 \log_{10} p = -\frac{\Delta H}{RT} + 2.303 \log_{10} A$$

$$\log_{10} p = -\frac{\Delta H}{2.303\, RT} + \log_{10} A$$

$$\log_{10} p \text{ (mm)} = \frac{-4000 \text{ (K)}}{T} + 10$$

Thus,
$$\frac{\Delta H}{2.303R} = 4000$$

$\therefore$
$$\Delta H = 2.303 \times R \times 4000$$

and
$$\log_{10} A = 10$$

$\therefore$
$$A = 10^{10}$$

21. (*d*) I (CH_3OH) : Surface tension decreases as concentration increases.

II (KCl) : Surface tension increases with concentration for ionic salt.

III [$CH_3(CH_2)_{11}OSO_3^- Na^+$] : It is an anionic detergent.

There is decrease in surface tension before micelle formation, and after CMC (Critical Micelle Concentration) is attained, no change in surface tension.

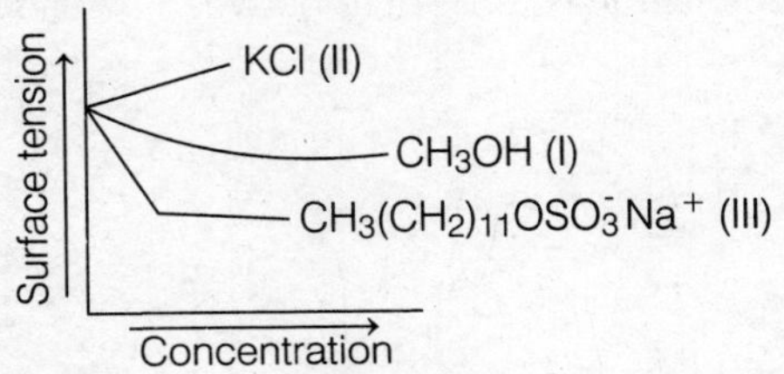

26. (*c*) CH_3OCH_3 lacks H-bonding hence most volatile, hence, maximum vapour pressure.

27. (*d*) On increasing temperature, vaporisation increases. Hence, vapour pressure increases.

34. (*b*) Work done = surface tension × increase in area

$$= 73 \text{ dyne cm}^{-1} \times 0.10 \text{ m}^2$$
$$= 73 \text{ dyne cm}^{-1} \times 0.10 \times 10^4 \text{ cm}^2$$
$$= 7.3 \times 10^4 \text{ erg}$$

35. (*c*) $H_2O(l) \rightleftharpoons H_2O(g)$. This is endothermic process, taking place with increase in pressure. If pressure is increased, equilibrium is displaced in backward side (Le-Chatelier) hence, steam is liquefied. To boil the liquid again, boiling point increases.

36. (*a*) Ethyl acetate ($CH_3—\overset{\overset{\displaystyle O}{||}}{C}—O—CH_2—CH_3$) molecules are polar. So, dipole-dipole interaction is present between its molecules. There are no such groups such as hydroxyl (—OH) which are capable of forming hydrogen bond. London dispersion forces are present in all substances involving ethyl acetate also.

Thus, in ethyl acetate, the predominant intermolecular forces are London dispersion and dipole-dipole forces.

37. (*a*) In case of *o*-hydroxy benzaldehyde (a), there is intramolecular H-bonding due to which it has minimum boiling point out of (a), (b), (c) and (d).

38. (*c*) HF has highest boiling point among hydrogen halides because it has strongest hydrogen bonding. Here, the hydrogen bond exists between hydrogen of one molecule and fluorine atom of another molecule as shown below.

$$\ldots \overset{\delta+}{H}—\overset{\delta-}{F}\ldots\overset{\delta+}{H}—\overset{\delta-}{F}\ldots\overset{\delta+}{H}—\overset{\delta-}{F}$$

In this molecule, hydrogen bond behaves like a bridge between two atoms that holds one atom by covalent bond and the other by hydrogen bond.

45. (*b*) $\Delta S = \frac{L}{T} = LT^{-1}$

48. (*d*) I_2 present in 10 mL $CHCl_3$ = 0.8 g

I_2 extracted into 400 mL H_2O = 0.2 g

$$\therefore \quad C_{I_2}(CHCl_3) = \frac{0.8}{10} \text{ g mL}^{-1}$$

$$C_{I_2}(H_2O) = \frac{0.2}{400} \text{ g mL}^{-1}$$

$$\therefore \quad \frac{C_{I_2}(CHCl_3)}{C_{I_2}(H_2O)} = \frac{\frac{0.8}{10}}{\frac{0.2}{400}} = 160$$

49. (*a*) Let I_2 extracted into water = *x* g

I_2 left in $CCl_4 = (1 - x)$ g

$$\therefore \quad C_{I_2}(CCl_4) = \frac{1-x}{10} \text{ g mL}^{-1}$$

$$C_{I_2}(H_2O) = \frac{x}{400} \text{ g mL}^{-1}$$

$$\frac{C_{I_2}(CCl_4)}{C_{I_2}(H_2O)} = 400 = \frac{\frac{1-x}{10}}{\frac{x}{400}}$$

$$\therefore \quad x = \frac{1}{11} \text{ g}$$

51. (*c*) If w_n = solute extracted into solvent II by *n* extractions

w = solute initially in solvent I

V_1 = volume of solvent I

V_2 = volume of solvent II to be used in *n* parts

$$\frac{C_2}{C_1} = K \text{ (Partition coefficient)}$$

then $$w_n = w - w\left(\frac{nV_1}{nV_1 + KV_2}\right)^n$$

(I) If $n = 1, V_1 = 100$ mL, $V_2 = 100$ mL, $w = 1$ g, $K = 2$

then $$w_1 = 1 - 1\left(\frac{1}{3}\right) = \frac{2}{3} = 0.667$$

Thus, (a) is true.

(II) If $n = 2, V_1 = 100$ mL, $V_2 = 100$ mL, $w = 1$ g, $K = 2$

then $$w_2 = 1 - 1\left(\frac{1}{2}\right)^2 = \frac{3}{4} = 0.75 \text{ g}$$

Thus, (b) is true also.

05

Solid State

Objective Questions Type I [Only one correct option]

In each of the questions below, four choices are given of which only one is correct.

1. Dipole-dipole forces exist in

(a) $CHCl_3$ (b) O_2

(c) C_2H_6 (d) All of these

2. Consider the following compounds.

I. Cl_2O II. XeF_4

III. BF_3 IV. CH_3CH_2Cl

Which of the above example(s) will have non-zero value of dipole moment?

(a) I, II, III (b) II, III, IV (c) I, IV (d) II

3. Silica (SiO_2) can be crystalline as well as amorphous, with following properties.

I. Crystalline

II. The SiO_4^{4-} tetrahedra are randomly joined giving rise to polymeric chains or three-dimensional sheets.

III. Have high and sharp melting point.

Which of I, II and III are matched with amorphous solids?

(a) I, II (b) I, III (c) II, III (d) II

4. Consider the bcc unit cells of the solids 1 and 2 with the position of atoms as shown below. The radius of atom B is twice that of atom A. The unit cell edge length is 50% more is solid 2 than in 1. What is the approximate packing efficiency in solid 2? **[JEE Main 2019, April]**

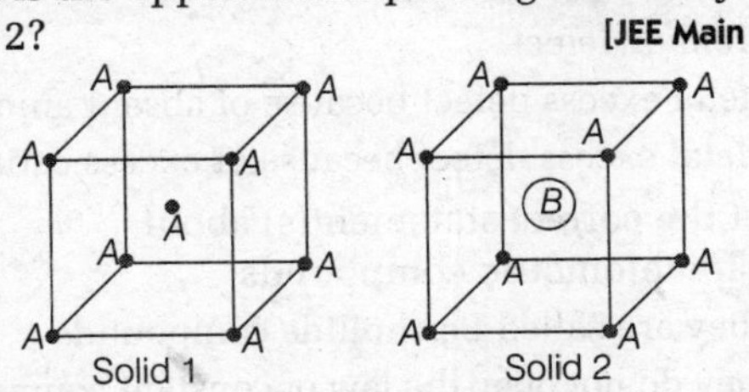

Solid 1 Solid 2

(a) 65% (b) 90%

(c) 75% (d) 45%

5. Select the correct statement(s).

(a) Crystalline solids are anisotropic

(b) Amorphous solids are isotropic

(c) Both (a) and (b)

(d) None of the above

6. A salt AB crystallises in the CsCl structure. The anions at the corners touch each other and the cation in the centre. Hence, radius ratio r_+/r_- is

(a) 0.225 (b) 0.441 (c) 0.625 (d) 0.732

7. In the following NaCl type structure.

Salt	Anion-anion distance	Cation-anion distance
MT	2.40 Å	1.70 Å
MQ	1.63 Å	1.15 Å
RT	2.66 Å	1.88 Å
RQ	2.09 Å	1.48 Å

MT is represented as

(a)

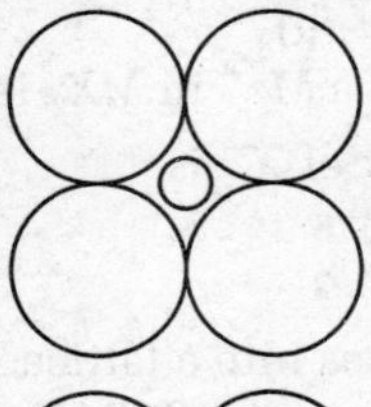

(b)

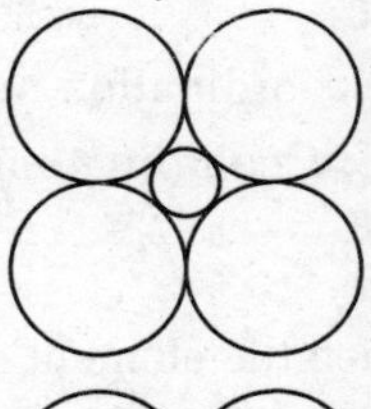

(c)

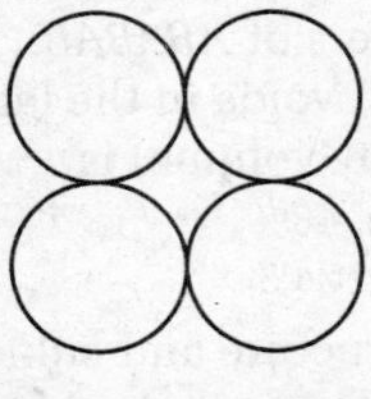

(d)

8. Based on internuclear distances given in Q. (7) above, radius of M^+ is

(a) 0.68 Å (b) 0.35 Å

(c) 0.80 Å (d) 1.20 Å

9. Adjoining structure decided based on the values in Q.(7) above, is of

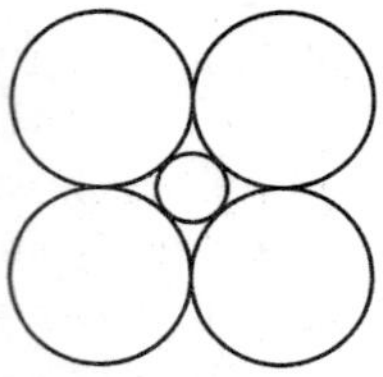

(a) *MQ*
(b) *RT*
(c) KCl
(d) All of the above

10. A solid has a structure in which W atoms are located at the cube corners of the unit cell, O atoms are located at the cube edges and the Na atoms at the cube centres. Lattice is of the type with formula
(a) simple cubic, $NaWO_3$
(b) simple cubic, Na_2WO_3
(c) tetrahedral, $NaWO_3$
(d) body-centred, $NaWO_3$

11. At what angles for the first order diffraction, spacing between two planes respectively are λ and $\frac{\lambda}{2}$?
(a) $0°, 90°$ (b) $90°, 0°$
(c) $30°, 90°$ (d) $90°, 30°$

12. Which primitive unit cell has unequal edge lengths ($a \neq b \neq c$) and all axial angles different from 90°? **[JEE Main 2019, Jan.]**
(a) Hexagonal (b) Monoclinic
(c) Tetragonal (d) Triclinic

13. A solid having density of 9×10^3 kg m^{-3} forms face centred cubic crystals of edge length $200\sqrt{2}$ pm. What is the molar mass of the solid? [Avogadro constant $= 6 \times 10^{23}$ mol^{-1}, $\pi = 3$] **[JEE Main 2019, Jan.]**
(a) 0.03050 kg mol^{-1} (b) 0.4320 kg mol^{-1}
(c) 0.0432 kg mol^{-1} (d) 0.0216 kg mol^{-1}

14. Ice crystallises in a hexagonal lattice having volume of the unit cell as 132×10^{-24} cm^3. If density is 0.92 g cm^{-3} at a given temperature, then number of H_2O molecules per unit cell is
(a) 1 (b) 2
(c) 3 (d) 4

15. The coordination number of a M^{2+} in MX_2 is 8. Hence, coordination number of X^- is
(a) 8 (b) 6
(c) 4 (d) 2

16. A metallic element crystallises into a lattice containing a sequence of layers of *ABABAB*....... Any packing of spheres leaves out voids in the lattice. Percentage of empty space (by volume) is
(a) 52% (b) 48%
(c) 50% (d) 74%

17. Hexagonal closest packed structure and cubic closest packed structure for a given element would be expected to have the same density because of
(a) same molar mass
(b) same coordination number and packing fraction
(c) Both (a) and (b)
(d) None of the above

18. The edge length of the NaCl unit cell is ... if radius of Na^+ is 97 pm and radius of Cl^- is 181 pm.
(a) 556 pm (b) 278 pm
(c) 139 pm (d) 120 pm

19. If the edge length of an NaH unit cell is 488 pm, what is the length of an Na—H bond if it crystallises as fcc structure?
(a) 488 pm (b) 122 pm
(c) 244 pm (d) 976 pm

20. Which has maximum per cent volume occupied by the spheres?
(a) Simple cubic
(b) Body-centred cubic
(c) Hexagonal closest packed
(d) Cubic closest packed

21. Structure shown here represents

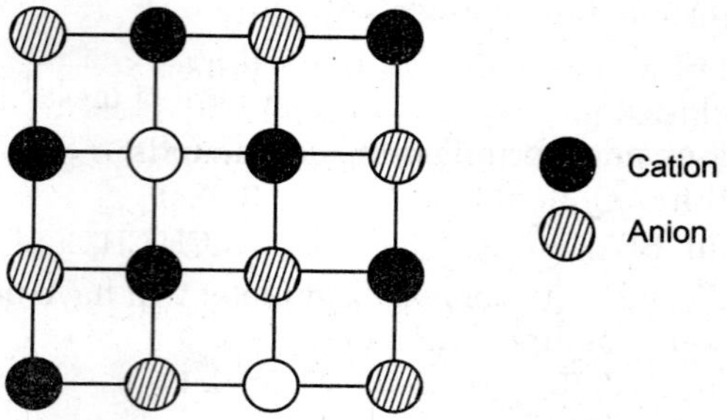

(a) Schottky defect (b) Frenkel defect
(c) Metal excess defect (d) None of these

22. Structure shown here represents

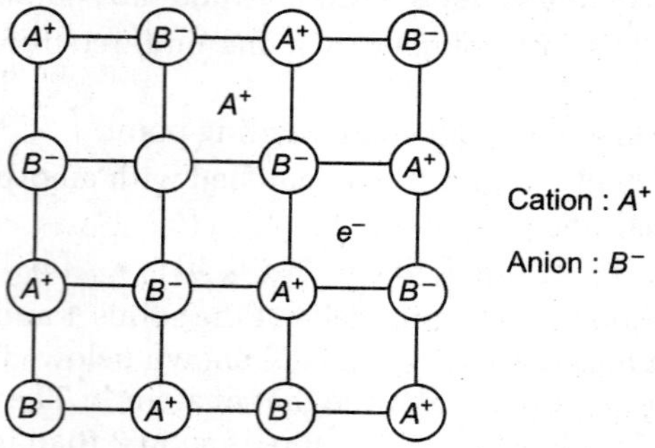

(a) Schottky defect
(b) Frenkel defect
(c) Metal excess defect because of absent anion
(d) Metal excess defect because of excess cation

23. Select the correct statement(s) about non-stoichiometric compounds.
(a) They are called Berthollide compounds
(b) They do not obey the law of constant composition
(c) Electrical neutrality is maintained either by having extra electrons in the structure or changing the charge on some of the metal ions
(d) All of the above statements

24. Select the correct statement(s).
(a) The non-stoichiometric form of NaCl is yellow and that of KCl is blue-lilac
(b) Solids containing *F*-centres (Farbe) are paramagnetic
(c) Conduction by electrons is called *n*-type semiconduction
(d) All of the above

25. Consider the following statements.
I. If an Fe^{2+} is missing from its lattice site in FeO, then there must be two Fe^{3+} ions somewhere in the lattice to balance the electrical charges.
II. Crystals with metal deficiency defects are called super-conductors.
III. Crystals with metal deficiency defects are called semiconductors.

Select the correct alternate.
(a) I, II (b) I, III
(c) II only (d) I only

26. Lithium selenide can be described as a closest-packed array of selenide ions with lithium ions in all of the tetrahedral holes. Formula of lithium selenide is
(a) Li_2Se (b) LiSe (c) $LiSe_2$ (d) Li_3Se

27. Edge length of M^+X^- (fcc structure) is 7.2 Å. Assuming $M^+—X^-$ contact along the cell edge, radius of X^- ion is (r_{M^+} = 1.6 Å)
(a) 2.0 Å (b) 5.6 Å (c) 2.8 Å (d) 3.8 Å

28. An element has a face-centred cubic (fcc) structure with a cell edge of *a*. The distance between the centres of two nearest tetrahedral voids in the lattice is **[JEE Main 2019, April]**
(a) $\sqrt{2}a$ (b) a (c) $\frac{a}{2}$ (d) $\frac{3}{2}a$

29. At very low temperature, oxygen O_2, freezes and forms a crystalline solid. Which term best describes the solid?
(a) Covalent network (b) Molecular crystals
(c) Metallic (d) Ionic

30. The mass of a unit cell of NaCl corresponds to
(a) 1 Na^+ and 6 Cl^- (b) 1 Cl^- and 6 Na^+
(c) 1 Na^+ and 1 Cl^- (d) 4 Cl^- and 4 Na^+

31. If the unit cell of a mineral has cubic close packed (ccp) array of oxygen atoms with *m* fraction of octahedral holes occupied by aluminium ions and *n* fraction of tetrahedral holes occupied by magnesium ions, *m* and *n* respectively, are **[JEE Advanced 2015]**
(a) $\frac{1}{2}, \frac{1}{8}$ (b) $1, \frac{1}{4}$ (c) $\frac{1}{2}, \frac{1}{2}$ (d) $\frac{1}{4}, \frac{1}{8}$

32. A group of 13 element if added in small amounts to Ge, ... is formed.
(a) *n*-type semiconductor (b) *p*-type semiconductor
(c) insulator (d) rectifier

33. The substance whose resistance gets reduced to virtually zero at very low temperature is called
(a) electrical conductor (b) hyper conductor
(c) semiconductor (d) super conductor

34. The presence of *F*-centres in a crystal makes it
(a) conducting (b) colourless
(c) coloured (d) non-conducting

35. The basic unit of all silicates is
(a) SiO_3^{2-} (b) SiO_2 (c) SiO_4^{2-} (d) SiO_4^{4-}

36. Amorphous materials are infact considered as
(a) supercooled liquids (b) supercooled solids
(c) covalent network (d) molecular crystals

37. The nature of cohesive forces in water is
(a) van der Waals' (b) covalent network
(c) H-bonding (d) None of these

38. The two types of holes which occur in any close-packed structures are
(a) tetrahedral, octahedral (b) trigonal, octahedral
(c) trigonal, tetrahedral (d) only octahedral

39. The point defect which lowers the density of the material is
(a) Schottky (b) Frenkel
(c) Both (a) and (b) (d) None of these

40. An electron trapped in an anion vacancy within the crystal is called
(a) *n*-type conductor (b) *p*-type conductor
(c) *F*-centre (d) insulator

41. The *n*-type semiconductor is obtained when Si is doped with
(a) Al (b) Ge
(c) B (d) As

42. The *p*-type semiconductor is obtained when Si is doped with
(a) Al (b) Ge
(c) Ga (d) As

43. BCC type structure is for
(a) NaCl (b) CsCl
(c) Both (a) and (b) (d) None of these

44. FCC type structure is for
(a) CsCl (b) AgCl
(c) MgO (d) Both (b) and (c)

45. 6 : 6 of NaCl coordination changes to 8 : 8 coordination on
(a) applying high *p* (b) increase in temperature
(c) Both (a) and (b) (d) no effect on coordination

46. In octahedral void and tetrahedral void, radius ratio is (in closest packing)

(a) $\frac{0.414}{0.225}$ (b) $\frac{0.225}{0.414}$

(c) 0.225×0.414 (d) None of these

47. Density of a crystal is

(where, a is the edge length, z the number of atoms in the unit cell and M is the molecular weight).

(a) $\frac{a^3 \times N_0}{z \times M}$ (b) $\frac{z \times M}{a^3 \times N_0}$

(c) $\frac{z \times M}{a^3}$ (d) $\frac{M}{a^3 N_0}$

48. A compound is formed by elements A and B and is cubic. A atoms are at the corners and B atoms are at the face centre. What is the formula?

(a) AB (b) AB_2

(c) AB_3 (d) A_3B

49. Schottky defect is due to

(a) missing of electron from normal lattice site

(b) missing of an atom from normal lattice site

(c) Both (a) and (b)

(d) None of the above

50. Frenkel defect is the

(a) Schottky defect

(b) interstitial defect

(c) combination of (a) and (b)

(d) None of the above

51. Ferrimagnetism is in

(a) ↑↑↑↑↑ (b) ↑↓↑↓

(c) ↑↑↑↓↓ (d) None of these

52. Ferromagnetism is in

(a) ↑↑↑↑↑ (b) ↑↓↑↓

(c) ↑↑↑↓↓ (d) None of these

53. Antiferromagnetism is in

(a) ↑↑↑↑↑ (b) ↑↓↑↓

(c) Both (a) and (b) (d) None of these

54. Ferrimagnetic is converted into ferromagnetic at

(a) 300 K (b) 400 K

(c) 600 K (d) 850 K

55. Of the following crystal lattices, the one that has the largest packing fraction

(a) bcc

(b) fcc

(c) simple cubic

(d) simple tetragonal

56. If the radius of an octahedral void is r and radius of the atom in close packing is R, then

(a) $r = 0.732\,R$ (b) $R = 0.414\,r$

(c) $r = 0.414\,R$ (d) $R = 0.732\,r$

57. $ABCABC$ type of arrangement of different layers, in a closest packed structure is called

(a) hcp

(b) bcc

(c) fcc

(d) cubic closest packed (ccp)

58. The hcp arrangement of ions is described by

(a) $ABAB$ (b) $ABABA$

(c) $ABCABC$ (d) $ABCABCABC$

59. The coordination number of ccp structure is

(a) 16 (b) 12 (c) 8 (d) 4

60. Zinc blende structure is obtained when Zn^{2+} occupies

(a) all tetrahedral sites

(b) half tetrahedral sites

(c) all octahedral sites

(d) half octahedral sites

61. In a solid AB having the NaCl structure, 'A' atom occupies the corners of the cubic unit cell. If all the face-centred atom along one of the axes are removed, then the resultant stoichiometry of the solid is

(a) AB_2 (b) A_2B (c) A_4B_3 (d) A_3B_4

62. Element 'B' forms ccp structure and 'A' occupies half of the octahedral voids, while oxygen atoms occupy all the tetrahedral voids. The structure of bimetallic oxide is **[JEE Main 2019, April]**

(a) A_2BO_4 (b) AB_2O_4

(c) A_2B_2O (d) A_4B_2O

63. If the three interaxial angles defining the unit cell are all equal in magnitude, the crystal cannot belong to the

(a) orthorhombic system (b) cubic system

(c) hexagonal system (d) tetragonal system

64. A crystal is made of particles A and B . A froms FCC packing and B occupies all the octahedral voids. If all the particles along the plane as shown in figure are removed then the formula of the crystal would be

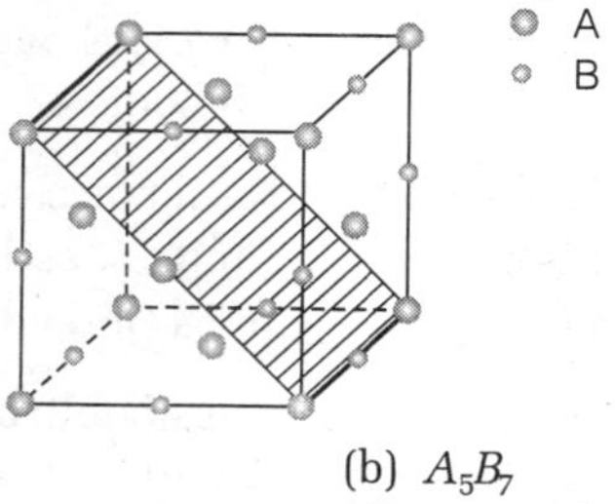

(a) AB (b) A_5B_7

(c) A_7B_5 (d) None of these

65. A compound contains two types of atoms, X and Y. Its crystal structure is a cubic lattice with X atoms at the corners of the unit cells and Y atoms at the body centres. The simplest formula is

(a) X_2Y (b) XY (c) XY_2 (d) XY_3

66. A compound of formula A_2B_3 has the hcp lattice. Which atom forms the hcp lattice and what fraction of tetrahedral voids is occupied by the other atoms ? **[JEE Main 2019, Jan.]**

(a) hcp lattice- A, $\frac{2}{3}$ tetrahedral voids-B

(b) hcp lattice-A, $\frac{1}{3}$ tetrahedral voids-B

(c) hcp lattice-B, $\frac{1}{3}$ tetrahedral voids-A

(d) hcp lattice-B, $\frac{2}{3}$ tetrahedral voids-A

67. For which of the following ionic crystalline solids, does the cation-anion bond have the largest amount of covalent character?

(a) CdS (b) NaBr
(c) BaO (d) LiF

68. The packing efficiency of the two-dimensional square unit cell shown below is **[IIT JEE 2010]**

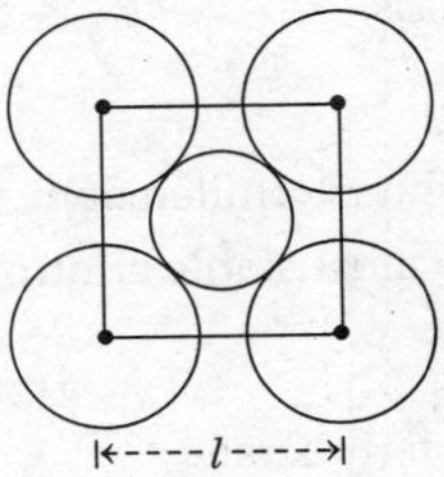

(a) 39.27% (b) 68.02%
(c) 74.05% (d) 78.54%

69. A compound M_pX_q has cubic close packing (ccp) arrangement of X. Its unit cell structure is shown below. The empirical formula of the compound, is **[IIT JEE 2012]**

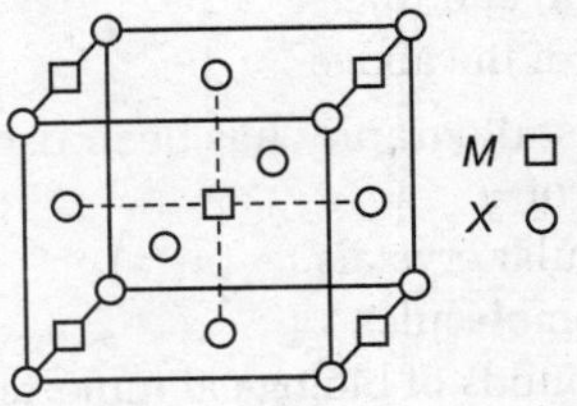

(a) MX (b) MX_2 (c) M_2X (d) M_5X_{14}

70. Which of the following crystals has the largest lattice energy?

(a) KCl (b) RbI
(c) MgO (d) NaF

71. Each rubidium halide crystallising in the NaCl-type lattice has a unit cell length 0.30 Å greater than that for corresponding potassium salt ($r_{(K^+)} = 1.33$ Å) of the same halogen. Hence, ionic radius of Rb^+ is

(a) 1.18 Å (b) 1.48 Å
(c) 1.63 Å (d) 1.03 Å

72. An element crystallises in a face-centred cubic (fcc) unit cell with cell edge a. The distance between the centres of two nearest octahedral voids in the crystal lattice is **[JEE Main 2020, Sep.]**

(a) $\frac{a}{\sqrt{2}}$ (b) a (c) $\sqrt{2}a$ (d) $\frac{a}{2}$

73. It is stated that ZnS does not crystallise in the NaCl structure. It is due to

(a) the $\frac{r_+}{r_-}$ ratio is 0.402, too low to avoid anion-anion contact in the NaCl structure

(b) ZnS is water insoluble, NaCl is water soluble

(c) ZnS is water soluble, NaCl is water insoluble

(d) Zn belongs to d-block, Na belongs to s-block

74. A compound alloy of gold and copper crystallises in a cubic lattice in which the gold atoms occupy the lattice points at the corners of a cube and the copper atoms occupy the centres of each of the cube faces. Hence, compound alloy has formula

(a) AuCu (b) Au_3Cu
(c) Au_2Cu (d) $AuCu_3$

75. Each NH_3 molecule has six other NH_3 molecules as nearest neighbours in solid state; ΔH of sublimation of NH_3 molecule at the m.p. is 30.8 kJ mol^{-1}, and in the absence of H-bonding estimated ΔH of sublimation is 14.4 kJ mol^{-1}. Hence, strength of H-bond in solid NH_3 is

(a) 5.47 kJ mol^{-1} (b) 10.93 kJ mol^{-1}
(c) 16.40 kJ mol^{-1} (d) −16.4 kJ mol^{-1}

76. A diatomic molecule X_2 has a body-centred cubic (bcc) structure with a cell edge of 300 pm. The density of the molecule is 6.17 g cm^{-3}. The number of molecules present in 200 g of X_2 is (Avogadro constant $(N_A) = 6 \times 10^{23}$ mol^{-1}) **[JEE Main 2020, Sep.]**

(a) $40N_A$ (b) $2N_A$ (c) $8N_A$ (d) $4N_A$

77. The intermediate compound LiAg crystallises in a cubic lattice in which both Li and Ag atoms have coordination number of 8. To what crystal class does the unit cell belong?

(a) NaCl (b) CsCl
(c) ZnS (d) CsF_2

78. A mineral having the formula AB_2 crystallises in the cubic close-packed lattice, with the A atoms occupying the lattice points. Hence, coordination numbers of A and B atoms are

(a) 4, 8 (b) 4, 4 (c) 8, 8 (d) 8, 4

79. Fraction of the tetrahedral sites occupied by B atoms in above case is about

(a) 50% (b) 75%
(c) 100% (d) 67%

80. AgI crystallises in the cubic close-packed zinc blended structure. Assuming that the iodide ions occupy the lattice points, fraction of the tetrahedral sites occupied by silver ions is about
(a) 50% (b) 75%
(c) 100% (d) 33%

81. A metallic element has a cubic lattice. Each edge of the unit cell 2 Å. The density of the metal is 2.5 g cm^{-3}. The unit cells in 200 g of the metal are
(a) 1×10^{24} (b) 1×10^{20}
(c) 1×10^{22} (d) 1×10^{25}

82. Schottky defect in crystals is observed when
(a) equal number of cations and anions are missing from the lattice
(b) density of crystals is increased
(c) an ion leaves its normal site and occupies an interstitial site
(d) unequal number of cations and anions are missing from the lattice

83. An fcc crystal contains how many atoms in each unit cell?
(a) 4 (b) 6 (c) 3 (d) 8

84. If we mix a pentavalent impurity in a crystal lattice of germanium, what type of semiconductor formation will occur?
(a) *p*-type semiconductor
(b) *n*-type semiconductor
(c) Both (a) and (b)
(d) None of these

85. An element (atomic mass $= 100$) having bcc structure has unit cell edge 400 pm. Then, density of the element is
(a) 10.376 g/cc (b) 5.191 g/cc
(c) 7.289 g/cc (d) 2.144 g/cc

86. The intermetallic compound LiAg crystallises in cubic lattice in which both lithium and silver have coordination number of eight. The crystal class is
(a) simple cube
(b) body-centred cube
(c) face-centred cube
(d) None of these

87. The edge length of face centred unit cubic cell is 508 pm. If the radius of the cation is 110 pm, the radius of the anion is
(a) 288 pm (b) 398 pm
(c) 144 pm (d) 618 pm

88. The second order Bragg diffraction of X-rays with $\lambda = 1.0$ Å from a set of parallel planes in a metal occurs at an angle 60°. The distance between the scattering planes in the crystal is
(a) 1.155 Å (b) 1.00 Å
(c) 2.00 Å (d) 1.7 Å

89. In crystals of which of the following ionic compounds would you expect maximum distance between centres of cations and anions?
(a) LiF (b) CsF (c) CsI (d) LiI

90. Which has maximum energy band-gap?
(a) ZnSe (b) GaAs (c) Ge (d) Equal

91. Select the correct statement(s).
(a) Highest filled bonding orbitals are called valence band
(b) Lowest unfilled antibonding orbitals are called the conduction band
(c) Both (a) and (b)
(d) None of the above

92. Which has least energy gap between conduction band and valence band?
(a) Carbon (diamond) (b) Silicon
(c) Germanium (d) Tin

93. Nano-test tube or nanorope are made of
(a) silicate glass
(b) diamond
(c) graphite
(d) C_{60} (buckminsterfullerene)

94. Which is the most stable allotropic form of carbon?
(a) Diamond
(b) Graphite
(c) Buckminsterfullerene
(d) None of these

95. Select the correct statement(s).
(a) Helium forms an hcp crystal above 25 atm at about zero Kelvin
(b) Nitrogen forms on fcc crystal at 63K, N_2 molecules being oriented in T-shaped pairs
(c) Both (a) and (b)
(d) None of the above

96. X-ray crystallography has been used to decide structure of
(a) molecular crystals
(b) macromolecules
(c) compounds of biological importance
(d) All of the above

97. A crystal is a repetition of a pattern called
(a) motif (b) basis
(c) Both (a) and (b) (d) None of these

98. Which set forms covalent crystals involving sp^3 hybrid orbitals?
(a) C, Si, Ge, Sn (b) B, Al, Ga, In
(c) C, B, N, P (d) Li, Na, K, Rb

99. In a binary compound, atoms of element *A* form a hcp structure and those of element *M* occupy 2/3 of the tetrahedral voids of the hcp structure. The formula of the binary compound is **[JEE Main 2021, March]**
(a) M_2A_3 (b) M_4A_3 (3) M_4A (4) MA_3

100. A crystal is made up of metal ions M_1 and M_2 and oxide ions. Oxide ions form a ccp lattice structure. The cation M_1 occupies 50% of octahedral voids and the cation M_2 occupies 12.5% of tetrahedral voids of oxide lattice. The oxidation numbers of M_1 and M_2 are, respectively **[JEE Main 2020, Sep.]**
(a) +2, + 4 (b) +1, + 3 (c) +3, + 1 (d) +4, + 2

101. A solid is formed by two elements P and Q. The element Q forms cubic close packing and atoms of P occupy one-third of tetrahedral voids. The formula of the compound is
(a) PQ_3 (b) P_3Q (c) P_2Q_3 (d) P_3Q_2

102. The arrangement of X^- ions around A^+ ion in solid AX is given in the figure. If the radius of X^- is 250 pm, the radius of A^+ is **[JEE Advanced 2013]**

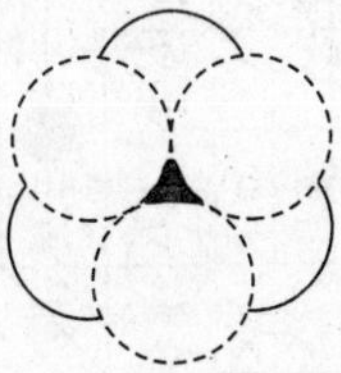

(a) 104 pm (b) 125 pm
(c) 183 pm (d) 57 pm

103. The radius of the largest sphere which fits properly at the centre of the edge of a body centred cubic unit cell is (Edge length is represented by 'a')
(a) $0.134a$ (b) $0.027a$ **[JEE Main 2019, Jan.]**
(c) $0.047a$ (d) $0.067a$

104. Crystals can be classified into basic crystal habits equal to
(a) 7
(b) 4
(c) 14
(d) 2

105. Sodium metal crystallises in body-centred cubic lattice with cell edge, 4.29 Å. What is the radius of sodium atom?
(a) 2.86 Å
(b) 6.81 Å
(c) 1.68 Å
(d) 1.86 Å

Objective Questions Type II [One or more than one correct option(s)]

In each of the questions below, four choices are given, of which one or more than one are correct.

1. bcc type structure is for
(a) NaCl (b) CsCl (c) MgO (d) AgCl

2. fcc type structure is for
(a) CsCl (b) AgCl
(c) MgO (d) KCl

3. 8 : 8 coordination of CsCl is found to change into 6 : 6 on
(a) applying high pressure
(b) increase in temperature
(c) applying low pressure
(d) decrease in KCl temperature

4. Antiflourite structure is for
(a) ThO_2 (b) Na_2O
(c) NaCl (d) None of these

5. Which is true of radius ratio of $\frac{r^+}{r^-}$?
(a) is 0.732 to 0.414, coordination number is 6 and is octahedral
(b) is above 0.732, coordination number is 8, and is cubic
(c) is 0.225 to 0.155, coordination number is 3, and is triangular
(d) is 0.732 to 0.878, coordination number is 8 and cubic

6. Number of atoms in different cubic unit cells of monoatomic substance is
(a) simple cubic-1 (b) bcc-2
(c) fcc-4 (d) fcc-6

7. Which is true?
(a) Piezoelectricity is due to net dipole moment
(b) Some electric current is produced on heating polar crystals, this is pyroelectricity
(c) Ferroelectricity is due to alignment of dipole in same direction
(d) Ferrielectricity is due to alignment of dipole in same direction

8. Which is true?
(a) Rochelle's salt is ferroelectric while lead zirconate is antiferroelectric
(b) Rochelle's salt is antiferroelectric and lead zirconate ferroelectric
(c) Both are ferroelectric
(d) Both are antiferroelectric

9. Superconductivity was first found by
(a) Debye-Huckel (b) Kammerling Onnes
(c) Newton (d) Stephene

10. Silica in amorphous form is used in
(a) photovolatic cell
(b) conductivity cell
(c) standard hydrogen electrode
(d) glass electrode

11. For which of the following crystals would you expect the assumption of anion-anion contact to be invalid?
(a) CsBr (b) NaI (c) NaF (d) KCl

12. If the three interaxial angles defining the unit cell are all equal in magnitude, the crystal cannot belong to the
(a) orthorhombic system (b) cubic system
(c) hexagonal system (d) tetragonal system

13. Amorphous solids
(a) do not have sharp melting points
(b) are isotropic
(c) have same mechanical strength, electrical and optical properties in all directions
(d) are semiliquids

14. Glasses and plastics are
(a) amorphous solids (b) supercooled liquids
(c) isotropic (d) ferromagnetic

15. Hexagonal closest-packed structure and a cubic closest-packed structure for a given element would be expected to have
(a) the same coordination number (CN)
(b) the same packing fraction
(c) different coordination number
(d) different packing fraction

16. With respect to graphite and diamond, which of the statement(s) given below is (are) correct? **[IIT JEE 2012]**
(a) Graphite is harder than diamond.
(b) Graphite has higher electrical conductivity than diamond
(c) Graphite has higher themal conductivity than diamond
(d) Graphite has higher C—C bond order than diamond

17. Which of the following cannot be regarded as molecular solids?
(a) SiC (b) AlN (c) Diamond (d) I_2

18. In which of the following arrangement octahedral voids are formed?
(a) hcp (b) bcc
(c) Simple cubic (d) fcc

19. Which of the following defects decrease density?
(a) Interstitial (b) Vacancy
(c) Frenkel (d) Schottky

20. Antiferromagnetic substances have zero value of magnetic moment, because the domains
(a) get oriented in the direction of the applied magnetic field
(b) get oriented opposite to the direction of the applied magnetic field
(c) are oppositely oriented with respect to each other without the application of the magnetic field
(d) Cancel out each other's magnetic moment

21. The cubic unit cell structure of a compound containing cation M and anion X is shown below. When compared to the anion, the cation has smaller ionic radius. Choose the correct statement(s).

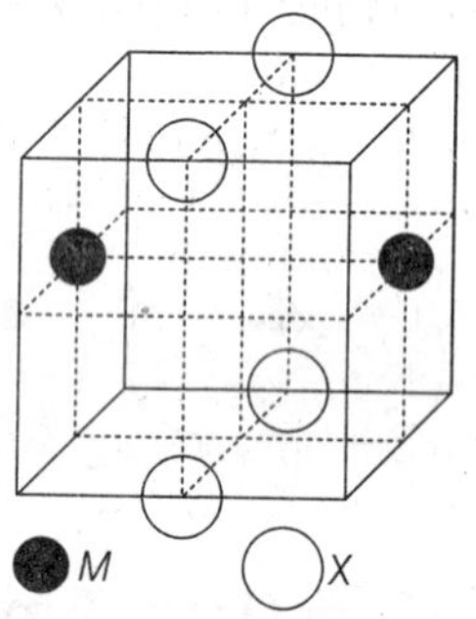

(a) The empirical formula of the compound is MX.
(b) The cation M and anion X have different coordination geometries.
(c) The ratio of $M—X$ bond length of the cubic unit cell edge length is 0.866.
(d) The ratio of the ionic radii of cation M to anion X is 0.414.

22. The correct statement(s) for cubic close packed (ccp) three dimensional structure is (are) **[JEE Advanced 2016]**
(a) The number of the nearest neighbours of an atom present in the topmost layer is 12
(b) The packing efficiency of atom is 74%
(c) The number of octahedral and tetrahedral voids per atom are 1 and 2, respectively
(d) The unit cell edge length is $2\sqrt{2}$ times the radius of the atom

Numerical Value Questions

All these questions have a Numerical value as their answer, solve the questions and write your answer.

1. The limiting radius ratio $\frac{r_+}{r_-}$ for a square planar crystal structure in which B^- ions are at the corners of the square and A^+ ions are at the centre.

2. The C.N. of Cs^+ ($r_+ = 1.6$ Å, $r_- = 1.81$ Å) in CsCl is.....

3. A fcc cell contains $8X$ atoms at the corners of the cell and $6Y$ atoms at the faces. How many atoms are present in empirical formula of the solid?

4. A crystalline solid of a pure substance has a face-centred cubic structure with a cell edge of 400 pm. If the density of the substance in the crystal is 8 g cm^{-3}, then the number of atoms present in 256 g of the crystal is $N \times 10^{24}$. The value of N is .... **[JEE Advanced 2017]**

5. A certain element crystallises in a bcc lattice of unit cell edge length 27 Å. If the same element under the same conditions crystallises in the fcc lattice, the edge length of the unit cell in Å will be .... **[JEE Main 2021, March]**

[Assume each lattice point has a single atom]
[Assume $\sqrt{3} = 1.73$, $\sqrt{2} = 1.41$]

6. The density of solid argon is 1.65 g per cc at −233°C. If the argon atom is assumed to be a sphere of radius 1.54×10^{-8} cm, what percentage of solid argon is apparently empty space? (Ar = 40)

7. When an electron in an excited molybdenum atom falls from the *L* to the *K* shell, an X-ray is emitted. These X-rays are diffracted at angle of 7.75° by planes with a separation of 2.64 Å. The difference in energy between the *K* shell and *L* shell in molybdenum, assuming a first order diffraction is ...... $\times 10^{-16}$ J

8. Find the critical radius ratio for body-centered coordination.

9. The distance between layers in a NaCl crystal is 282 pm. X-rays are diffracted from these layers at an angle of 23.0°. Assuming that $n = 1$, the wavelength of the X-rays in nm is ......

10. Sodium metal crystallises in body-centred cubic lattice with the cell edge $a = 4.29$ Å. The radius of sodium atom is ......

11. The fraction of the unit cell shown is ......

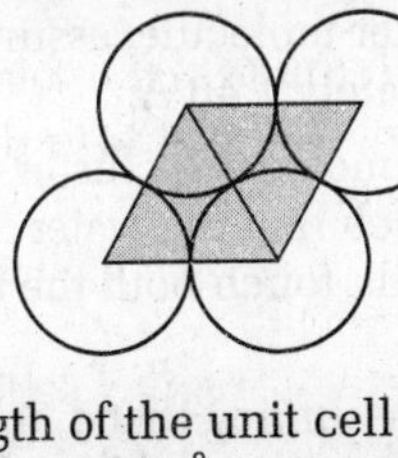

12. The edge length of the unit cell of LiCl (NaCl-like structure, fcc) is 5.14 Å. Assuming that the lithium ion is small enough that the chloride ions are in contact. The ionic radius for the chloride ion is ......

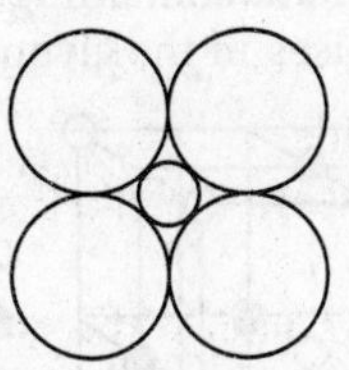

13. The unit cell length of a NaF crystal is 4.634 Å. If the ionic radius of Na^+ is 95 pm. The ionic radius of F^-, assuming anion-cation contact and a face-centred cubic is ......

14. Calculate the *c*/*a* ratio for an ideally close packed HCP crystal is ......

15. Look at the sodium chloride structure in figure and use it to calculate $\frac{r_+}{r_-}$.

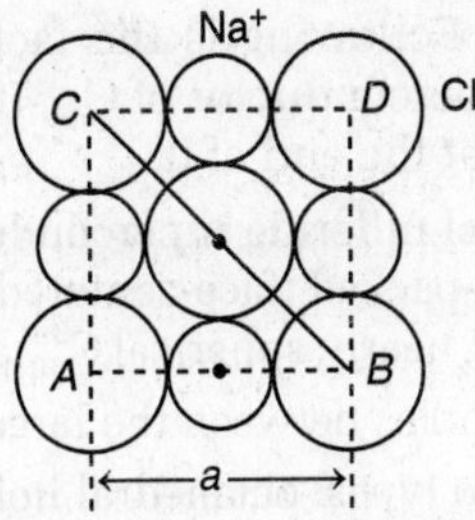

16. Ga (atomic mass 70 u) crystallises in a hexagonal close packed structure. The total number of voids in 0.581 g of Ga is .... $\times 10^{21}$. **[JEE Main 2021, March]**

Comprehension Based Questions

In these questions, a passage has been given followed by questions based on it. You have to answer the questions based on the passage given.

***Example* 1** Read the following passage and answer the questions at the end of it.

Doping a silicon crystal with a group-13 element (with three valence electrons) such as B, Al, Ga or In produces a semiconductor with three electrons in dopant.

The place where fourth electron is missing is called an **electron vacancy or hole.**

1. Silicon that has been doped with group-15 elements is called
(a) *p*-type semiconductor
(b) *n*-type semiconductor
(c) electron vacancy or hole
(d) *e*-type semiconductor

2. If NaCl is doped with 10^{-3} mol % $SrCl_2$, then concentration of cation vacancies is
(a) 6.02×10^{23}
(b) 6.02×10^{20}
(c) 6.02×10^{18}
(d) 6.02×10^{15}

3. What are the types of the following semiconductors I and II?

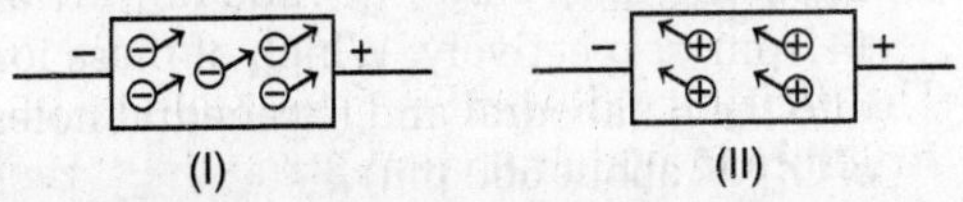

(I) (II)

(a) I *p*-type, II *n*-type
(b) I *n*-type, II *p*-type
(c) Both *n*-type
(d) Both *p*-type

***Example* 2** Following statement is given to decide the structure of the given lattice.

Perovskite, a mineral containing calcium, oxygen and titanium crystallises in the given cubic unit cell.

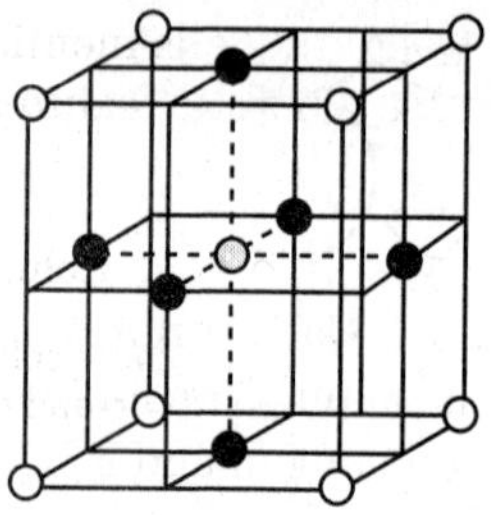

1. What is the formula of perovskite?
   (a) $CaTiO_2$ (b) $CaTiO_3$
   (c) Ca_2TiO_3 (d) $Ca(TiO_2)_2$
2. Oxidation state of titanium in the given lattice is
   (a) +2 (b) +3 (c) +4 (d) –4

***Example* 3** Following is the fact about the newly discovered superconductor of C_{60} (fullerene). Answer the questions at the end of it.

The alkali metal fulleride superconductors M_3C_{60} have a cubic closest-packed (face-centered cubic) arrangement of nearly spherical C_{60}^{3-} anions with M^+ cations in the holes between the larger C_{60}^{3-} ions. The holes are of two types: octahedral holes, which are surrounded octahedrally by six C_{60}^{3-} ions, and tetrahedral holes, which are surrounded tetrahedrally by four C_{60}^{3-} ions.

1. How many C_{60}^{3-} ions, octahedral holes, and tetrahedral holes are present per unit cell?
   (a) 5, 4, 4 (b) 3, 8, 4 (c) 4, 4, 4 (d) 2, 1, 2
2. Specify fractional coordinates for all the octahedral and tetrahedral holes.
   (Fractional coordinates are fractions of the unit cell edge lengths. For example, a hole at the centre of the cell has fractional coordinates $\frac{1}{2}, \frac{1}{2}, \frac{1}{2}$.)
   (a) $\frac{1}{2}, \frac{1}{2}, \frac{1}{2}$ (b) $\frac{1}{3}, \frac{1}{3}, \frac{1}{3}$ (c) $\frac{1}{4}, \frac{1}{4}, \frac{1}{4}$ (d) $\frac{1}{2}, \frac{1}{2}, \frac{1}{4}$
3. The ionic radii of Na^+, K^+ and Rb^+ are 97, 133 and 147 pm, respectively. Which of these ions will fit into the octahedral and tetrahedral holes? (radius of C_{60}^{3-} is about 500 pm)
   (a) Na^+ (b) K^+
   (c) Rb^+ (d) All of these

***Example* 4** By taking three-dimensional view of a crystal, one can evaluate number of nearest neighbours and also the shortest distance between them.

In the simple cubic form of manganese there are Mn atoms at the corners of a simple cubic unit cell that is 6.30 Å on edge.

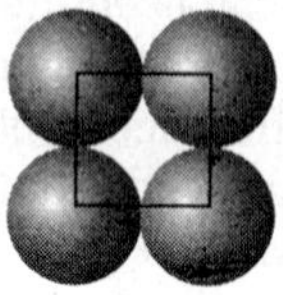

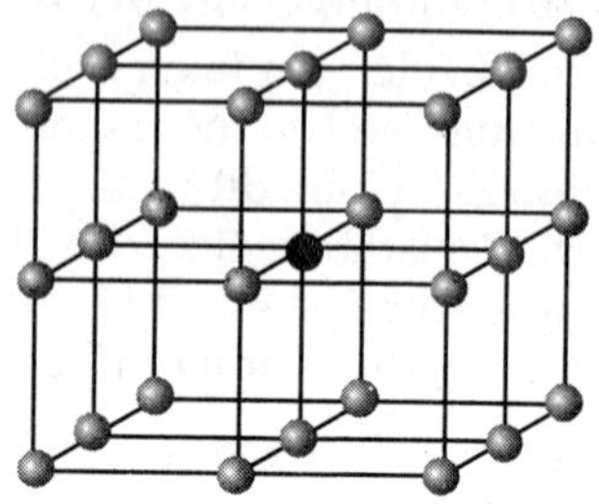

1. What is shortest distance between neighbouring Mn atoms?
   (a) 6.30 Å (b) 3.15 Å
   (c) 12.60 Å (d) 8.91 Å
2. How many nearest neighbours does each atom have?
   (a) 2 (b) 4 (c) 6 (d) 8

***Example* 5** Electrolytes are hydrated to different extent; size of the ion is the deciding factor.

The radius of a water molecule, assuming a spherical shape, is approximately 1.40 Å.

Assume that water molecules cluster around each metal ion in a solution such that the water molecules essentially touch both the metal ion and each other.

On this basis, and assuming that 4, 6, 8 and 12 are the only possible coordination numbers, and size of cations as

Mg^{2+} (radius 0.65 Å)Al^{3+} (radius 0.50 Å)
Rb^+ (radius 1.48 Å) Sr^{2+} (radius 1.13 Å)

Answer the following questions.

1. Maximum number of water molecules that can hydrate Mg^{2+} ion is
   (a) 4 (b) 6
   (c) 12 (d) 8
2. Which of the following ions is hydrated to maximum extent?
   (a) Mg^{2+} (b) Al^{3+}
   (c) Rb^+ (d) Sr^{2+}
3. Which fumes in moist air?
   (a) $AlCl_3$ (b) $MgSO_4$
   (c) NaCl (d) KCl

Matrix-Match Type

Given below are Matching Type Questions, with two columns (each having some items) each . Each item of Column I has to be matched with the items of Column II.

1. Match the limiting radius ratio in Column I with the shape of the crystal in Column II.

	Column I		Column II
A.	< 0.155	1.	Octahedral
B.	0.155–0.225	2.	Body-centred cubic
C.	0.225–0.414	3.	Planar triangle
D.	0.414–0.732	4.	Linear
E.	0.732–0.999	5.	Tetrahedral

2. Match the shape of the molecule in Column I with coordination number in Column II.

Column I	Column II
A. Linear	1. 6
B. Planar triangle	2. 4
C. Square planar	3. 8
D. Octahedral	4. 2
E. Body-centred cubic	5. 3

3. Match the cubic unit cell in Column I with the number of atoms in unit cell in Column II.

Column I	Column II
A. Simple cubic	1. 4
B. Body-centred cubic	2. 1
C. Face-centred cubic	3. 2

4. Match the elements in Column I with the shape of the crystal in Column II.

Column I	Column II
A. Be	1. Body-centred cubic
B. Ca	2. Simple cubic
C. Ba	3. Face-centred cubic
D. Mn	4. Hexagonal close-packed

5. Match the cubic structure in Column I with packing density in Column II.

Column I	Column II
A. Simple cubic	1. 0.68
B. FCC	2. 0.52
C. BCC	3. 0.74

6. Match the crystal system/unit cells mentioned in Column I with their characteristic features mentioned in Column II.

Column I	Column II
A. Simple cubic and face-centred cubic	1. have these cell parameters $a = b = c$ and $\alpha = \beta = \gamma$
B. Cubic and rhombohedral	2. are two crystal systems
C. Cubic and tetragonal	3. have only two crystallographic angles of 90°
D. Hexagonal and monoclinic	4. belong to same crystal system

7. Match the defects in Column I with the statements in given Column II.

Column I	Column II
A. Frenkel defect	1. shown by non-ionic solids and density of solids decreases
B. Schottky defect	2. shown by ionic solids and decreases density of solid.
C. Simple vacancy defect	3. shown by non-ionic solids and increases density of the solid
D. Simple interstitial defect	4. shown by ionic solids and density of the solid remains the same

8. Match the items in Column I with their properties in Column II.

	Column I		Column II
A.	Cu metal	1.	Electrolytic conductor
B.	NaCl in fused state	2.	*p*-type semiconductor
C.	Silicon with phosphorus	3.	*n*-type semiconductor
D.	Germanium with boron	4.	Electronic conductor

9. Match the compounds in Column I with their parameters in Column II.

	Column I		Column II
A.	CsBr	1.	Formula units per unit cell 4
B.	NaCl	2.	Face-centred
C.	ZnS	3.	Body-centred
D.	CaF_2	4.	CN : 8 : 8
		5.	CN : 6 : 6

10. Match the type of unit cell given in Column I with the features given in Column II.

Column I	Column II
A. Body centred cubic unit cell	1. Edge length of the three perpendicular sides $a = b = c$
B. Face centred cubic unit cell	2. $a \neq b \neq c$
C. Primitive cubic cell	3. Number of atoms per unit cell is one
D. End centred orthorhombic unit cell	4. Number of atoms per unit cell is one in addition to the contribution from the corner atoms
	5. Number of atoms per unit cell is three in addition to the contribution from the corner atoms

11. Bragg's equation is given by

$n\lambda = 2d \sin \theta$ (d = edge length)

Match the angle θ in Column I with edge length (d) in Column II for different values of n.

Column I		Column II
A. $\theta = 30°$	$n = 1$	1. $d = 2\lambda$
B. $\theta = 45°$	$n = 2$	2. $d = \lambda$
C. $\theta = 60°$	$n = 3$	3. $d = \sqrt{2}\lambda$
D. $\theta = 90°$	$n = 4$	4. $d = \sqrt{3}\lambda$

12. Interionic distances (bond length) of some compounds are given below

RbI = 3.67 Å KCl = 3.14 Å

RbBr = 3.44 Å NaCl = 2.79 Å

KBr = 3.29 Å NaF = 2.31 Å

Ionic radius of iodide (I^-) ion

Match the ion in Column I with the ionic radius in Column II.

Column I	Column II
A. Rb^+	1. 1.96 Å
B. K^+	2. 1.81 Å
C. Na^+	3. 1.33Å
D. Cl^-	4. 0.98 Å
E. Br^-	5. 1.48 Å
F. F^-	6. 2.19 Å

Single Integer Answer Questions

Answer of these questions is a single digit lying between 0 to 9.

1. How many Na^+ and Cl^- ions are present in one unit cell of NaCl?
2. How many total atoms are in unit cell of body-centred cubic structure?
3. How many nearest neighbours are there in body-centred cubic structure?
4. How many nearest neighbours are there in a simple cubic?
5. How many steps are involved in the formation of $Na^+(g)Cl^-(g)$ lattice from $Na(s)$ and $Cl_2(g)$?
6. For $\theta = 30°$, Bragg's equation is found to be d(edge length) $= 4\lambda$. The order of diffraction is ....
7. Ratio of ionic radius of cation to anion is in the range 0.15 – 0.22. What is permitted coordination number of cation by anion?
8. A solid has a structure in which W atoms are located at the cube corners of the unit cell, O atoms are located at the cube edges and the Na atoms at the cube centres. Total atoms in one formula unit are ... .
9. Silver (atomic weight = 108 g mol^{-1}) has a density of 10.5 g cm^{-3}. The number of silver atoms on a surface of area 10^{-12} m^2 can be expressed in scientific notation as $y \times 10^x$. The value of x is .... **[IIT JEE 2010]**
10. The number of hexagonal faces that are present in a truncated octahedron is .... **[IIT JEE 2011]**
11. Consider an ionic solid MX with NaCl structure. Construct a new structure (Z) whose unit cell is constructed from the unit cell of MX following the sequential instruction given below. Neglect the charge balance. **[JEE Advanced 2018]**
    (a) Remove all the anions (X) except the central one
    (b) Replace all the face centered cations (M) by anions (X)
    (c) Remove all the corner cations (M)
    (d) Replace the central anion (X) with cation (M)
    The value of $\left(\dfrac{\text{Number of anions}}{\text{Number of cations}}\right)$ in Z is .....

Answers

Objective Questions Type I [Only one correct option]

1. (a)	**2.** (c)	**3.** (d)	**4.** (b)	**5.** (c)	**6.** (d)	**7.** (a)	**8.** (b)	**9.** (d)	**10.** (a)
11. (c)	**12.** (d)	**13.** (a)	**14.** (d)	**15.** (c)	**16.** (b)	**17.** (b)	**18.** (a)	**19.** (c)	**20.** (b)
21. (a)	**22.** (d)	**23.** (d)	**24.** (d)	**25.** (d)	**26.** (a)	**27.** (a)	**28.** (c)	**29.** (b)	**30.** (d)
31. (a)	**32.** (b)	**33.** (d)	**34.** (c)	**35.** (d)	**36.** (a)	**37.** (c)	**38.** (a)	**39.** (a)	**40.** (c)
41. (d)	**42.** (c)	**43.** (b)	**44.** (d)	**45.** (a)	**46.** (a)	**47.** (b)	**48.** (c)	**49.** (a)	**50.** (c)
51. (c)	**52.** (a)	**53.** (b)	**54.** (d)	**55.** (b)	**56.** (c)	**57.** (d)	**58.** (b)	**59.** (b)	**60.** (b)
61. (a)	**62.** (b)	**63.** (c)	**64.** (a)	**65.** (b)	**66.** (c)	**67.** (a)	**68.** (d)	**69.** (b)	**70.** (c)
71. (b)	**72.** (a)	**73.** (a)	**74.** (d)	**75.** (a)	**76.** (d)	**77.** (b)	**78.** (d)	**79.** (c)	**80.** (a)
81. (d)	**82.** (a)	**83.** (a)	**84.** (b)	**85.** (b)	**86.** (b)	**87.** (c)	**88.** (a)	**89.** (c)	**90.** (a)
91. (c)	**92.** (d)	**93.** (d)	**94.** (b)	**95.** (c)	**96.** (d)	**97.** (c)	**98.** (a)	**99.** (b)	**100.** (a)
101. (c)	**102.** (a)	**103.** (d)	**104.** (a)	**105.** (d)					

Objective Questions Type II [One or more than one correct option(s)]

1. (d)	**2.** (a, b, c)	**3.** (b, d)	**4.** (b, d)	**5.** (b)
6. (a, b, c)	**7.** (a)	**8.** (a, b, c)	**9.** (d)	**10.** (a, b, c, d)
11. (b)	**12.** (a)	**13.** (a, b)	**14.** (a, c, d)	**15.** (a)
16. (c, d)	**17.** (a, b, d)	**18.** (a, c)	**19.** (d)	**20.** (a, c, d)
21. (a, c)	**22.** (b, c, d)			

Numerical Value Questions

1. $\frac{r_+}{r_-} = 0.414$, **2.** $\frac{r_+}{r_-} = \frac{1.6}{1.81} = 0.8840$, Thus, structure is bcc with C.N. = 8.

3. Hint. 4 Number of atoms of X in crystal at the corner $= \frac{8}{8} = 1$, Number of atoms of Y in crystal $= \frac{6}{2} = 3$, Thus, XY_3

4. 2 **5.** 33 **6.** Empty space $= 1 - 0.380 = 0.620$ % $= 62\%$

7. 27.89 **8.** 0.732 **9.** 0.2204 nm **10.** Radius $r = \frac{\sqrt{3}a}{4} = \frac{\sqrt{3} \times 4.29 \text{ Å}}{4} = 1.86$ Å

11. Packing fraction $= \frac{\pi R^2}{2\sqrt{3}R^2} = 0.907$ **12.** $r_{Cl^-} = \frac{b}{2} = 1.8173$ Å **13.** $r\,(F^-) = 231.7 - 95 = 136.7$ pm

14. 1.633 **15.** $\frac{r_+}{r_-} = 0.414$ **16.** 15

Comprehension Based Questions

Example 1 – 1. (b) 2. (c) 3. (b)
Example 2 – 1. (b) 2. (c)
Example 3 – 1. (a) 2. (c) 3. (b)
Example 4 – 1. (a) 2. (c)
Example 5 – 1. (c) 2. (b) 3. (a)

Matrix-Match Type

1. A → (4); B → (3); C → (5); D → (1); E → (2)
2. A → (4); B → (5); C → (2); D → (1); E → (3)
3. A → (2); B → (3); C → (1)
4. A → (4); B → (3); C → (1); D → (2)
5. A → (2); B → (3); C → (1)
6. A → (1,4); B → (1,2); C → (2); D → (3)
7. A → (4); B → (2); C → (1); D → (3)
8. A → (4); B → (1); C → (3); D → (2)
9. A → (3,4); B → (1,2,5); C → (1,2); D → (1,2)
10. A → (1,4); B → (1,5); C → (1,3); D → (1,2,4)
11. A → (2); B → (3); C → (4); D → (1)
12. A → (5); B → (3); C → (4); D → (2); E → (1); F → (3)

Single Integer Answer Questions

1. (8)	**2.** (2)	**3.** (8)	**4.** (6)	**5.** (5)	**6.** (4)	**7.** (3)	**8.** (5)	**9.** (7)	**10.** (8)
11. (3)									

Solutions

Objective Questions Type I [Only one correct option]

4. (*b*) **Key Idea** Packing efficiency

$$= \frac{\text{Volume occupied by sphere}}{\text{Volume of cube}} \times 100$$

Given, $r_B = 2r_A$; $a_2 = a_1 + \frac{50}{100} a_1 = 1.5\, a_1$

For bcc lattice

$$4r_A = \sqrt{3}\, a_1 \Rightarrow r_A = \frac{\sqrt{3}\, a_1}{4} \Rightarrow a_1 = \frac{4r_A}{\sqrt{3}}$$

$$\therefore \quad a_2 = 1.5\left(\frac{4r_A}{\sqrt{3}}\right) = \frac{3}{2}\left(\frac{4r_A}{\sqrt{3}}\right)$$

$$a_2 = 2\sqrt{3}\, r_A$$

$$\text{Packing efficiency} = \frac{\frac{4}{3}\pi r_A^3 \times z_A + \frac{4}{3}\pi r_B^3 \times z_B}{a_2^3}$$

[As the atoms A are present at the edges only $z_A = \frac{1}{8} \times 8 = 1$, atom B is present only at the body centre $z_B = 1$]

$$\therefore \quad PE_2 = \frac{\left(\frac{4}{3}\pi r_A^3 \times 1\right) + \left(\frac{4}{3}\pi r_B^3 \times 1\right)}{a_2^3}$$

$$= \frac{\frac{4}{3}\pi r_A^3 + \frac{4}{3}\pi (2r_A)^3}{(2\sqrt{3} r_A)^3}$$

$$= \frac{\frac{4}{3}\pi r_A^3 \times 9}{8 \times 3\sqrt{3}\, r_A^3} = \frac{\pi}{2\sqrt{3}}$$

$$= 90.72\% \approx 90\%$$

10. (*a*) W atoms are at the cube corner.

Thus, number of W atoms $= \frac{8}{8} = 1$

O atoms are at the edges.

Thus, number of O atoms $= \frac{6}{2} = 3$

Thus, anion is WO_3^-.

Thus, lattice is $NaWO_3$.

11. (*c*) $2a \sin\theta = n\lambda$ (Bragg's equation)

For, $n = 1$

$2a \sin\theta = \lambda$

(i) If $\theta = 30°$, $2a \sin 30° = \lambda$

$\therefore \quad a = \lambda$

(ii) If $\theta = 90°$, $2a \sin 90° = \lambda$

$\therefore \quad a = \frac{\lambda}{2}$

12. (*d*) Triclinic primitive unit cell has dimensions as, $a \neq b \neq c$ and $\alpha \neq \beta \neq \gamma \neq 90°$.

Among the seven basic or primitive crystalline systems, the triclinic system is most unsymmetrical. In other cases, edge length and axial angles are given as follows :

Hexagonal : $a = b \neq c$ and $\alpha = \beta = 90°, \gamma = 120°$

Monoclinic : $a \neq b \neq c$ and $\alpha = \gamma = 90°, \beta \neq 90°$

Tetragonal : $a \neq b \neq c$ and $\alpha = \beta = \gamma = 90°$

13. (*a*) Density of a crystal

$$d = \frac{M \times Z}{N_A \times a^3} \Rightarrow M = \frac{d \times N_A \times a^3}{Z}$$

Given, $d = 9 \times 10^3$ kg m^{-3}

M = Molar mass of the solid

$Z = 4$ (for fcc crystal)

N_A = Avogadro's constant $= 6 \times 10^{23}$ mol^{-1}

a = Edge length of the unit cell

$= 200\sqrt{2}$ pm $= 200\sqrt{2} \times 10^{-12}$ m

On substituting all the given values, we get

$$= \frac{(9 \times 10^3)\text{ kg m}^{-3} \times (6 \times 10^{23})\text{ mol}^{-1} \times (200\sqrt{2} \times 10^{-12})^3 \text{m}^3}{4}$$

$$= 0.0305 \text{ kg mol}^{-1}$$

14. (*d*) Density, $d = \frac{Mz}{N_0 a^3}$

where, M = molar mass $= 18$ g mol^{-1}

N_0 = Avogadro's number $= 6.02 \times 10^{23}$

Volume $= a^3 = 132 \times 10^{-24}$ cm^3

$$\therefore \quad 0.92 = \frac{18 \times z}{6.02 \times 10^{23} \times 132 \times 10^{-24}}$$

$$\therefore \quad z = 4$$

18. (*a*)

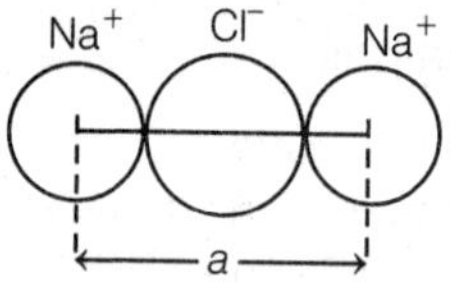

$$a = 2r_{Na^+} + 2r_{Cl^-} = 2(97 + 181) = 556 \text{ pm}$$

19. (*c*) As in Q. (18)

27. (*a*)

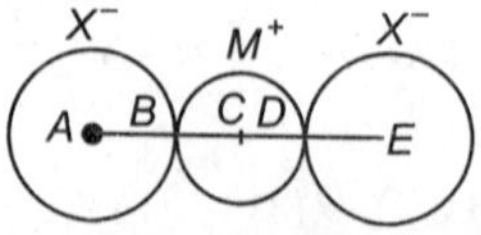

$$AE = 7.2 \text{ Å} = AB + BC + CD + DE$$

$$= r_{X^-} + r_{M^+} + r_{M^+} + r_{X^-} = 2(r_{X^-} + r_{M^+})$$

$$\therefore \quad r_{X^-} = 2.0 \text{ Å}$$

28. (*c*) In fcc unit cell, two tetrahedral voids are formed on each of the four non-parallel body diagonals of the cube at a distance of $\sqrt{3}a/4$ from every corner along the body diagonal.

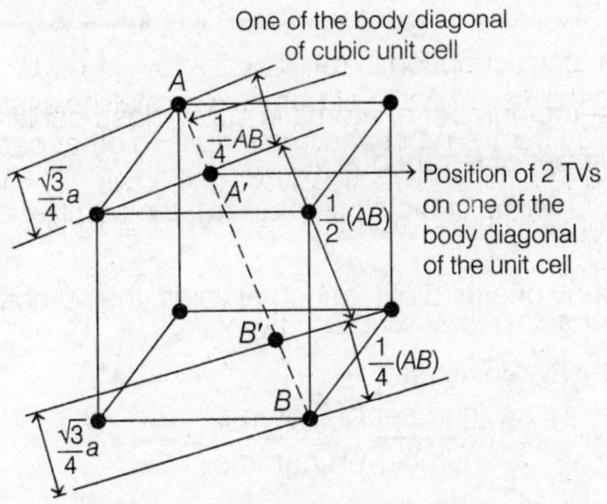

The angle between body diagonal and an edge is $\cos^{-1}(1/\sqrt{3})$. So, the projection of the line on an edge is $a/4$.

Similarly, other tetrahedral void also will be $a/4$ away.

So, the distance between these two is

$$\left[a-\frac{a}{4}\right]-\frac{a}{4}=\frac{a}{2}.$$

30. (*d*) Every unit cell of NaCl has $4Cl^-$ and $4Na^+$ ions.

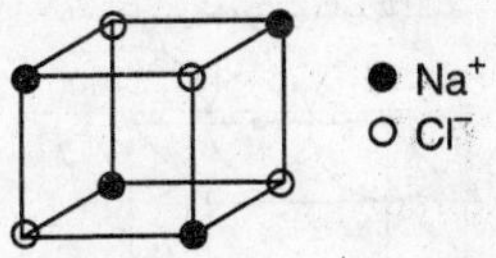

31. (*a*) Oxide ions are at ccp positions, hence $4O^{2-}$ ions. Also, there are four octahedral voids and eight tetrahedral voids. Since '*m*' fraction of octahedral voids contain Al^{3+} and '*n*' fraction of tetrahedral voids contain Mg^{2+} ions, to maintain electroneutrality $2(2Al^{3+} = +6$ charge) and ($Mg^{2+} = +2$ charge), will make unit cell neutral

Hence: $m=\frac{2}{4}=\frac{1}{2}, n=\frac{1}{8}$

32. (*b*) Ge is tetravalent while group-13 element has three electrons in valence shell, thus there is positive charge (*p*), hence *p*-type semiconductor.

41. (*d*) *n*-type semiconductor (negative) is formed when there is extra electron available for conduction. Si has four electrons in valence shell, while As has five. Thus, extra one electron makes *n*-type semiconductor on doping Si with As.

62. (*b*) The number of element '*B*' inthe crystal structure = $4N$

Number of tetrahedral voids = $2N$

Number of octahedral voids = N

$\therefore$ Number of '*A*' in the crystal $=\frac{N}{2}=\frac{4}{2}=2$

Number of oxygen (O) atoms $= 2N = 2\times 4 = 8$

$\therefore$ The structure of bimetallic oxide $= A_2B_4O_8$

$= AB_2O_4$

64. (*a*) No. of *A* atoms left $= 4-\underbrace{\left(\frac{1}{8}\times 4\right)}_{\text{Corner atoms}}-\underbrace{\left(\frac{1}{2}\times 2\right)}_{\text{Face corner atoms}}=\frac{5}{2}$

No. of *B* atoms left $= 4-\underbrace{\left(\frac{1}{4}\times 2\right)}_{\text{Edge center atoms}}-\underbrace{(1\times 1)}_{\text{Body center atoms}}=\frac{5}{2}$

The simplest formula of crystal is *AB*.

65. (*b*) Cubic lattice is bcc type.

Number of *X* atoms at the corner $=\frac{8}{8}=1$

Number of *Y* atoms at the centre $=\frac{1}{1}=1$

Thus, ratio of $X:Y=1:1$

Thus, formula is *XY*.

66. (*c*) Total effective number of atoms in hcp unit lattice = Number of octahedral voids in hcp = 6

$\therefore$ Number of tetrahedral voids (TV) in hcp

= 2 × Number of atoms in hcp lattice

$= 2\times 6 = 12$

As, formula of the lattice is A_2B_3.

	A	*B*
Suppose,	$\left(\frac{1}{3}\times TV\right)$	(hcp)
⇒	$\frac{1}{3}\times 12$	6
⇒	$\frac{2}{3}$	1
⇒	2	3

So, $A=\frac{1}{3}$ tetrahedral voids, B = hcp lattice

71. (*b*) There is increase in 0.30 Å unit length. This is due to two atoms at the corners.

Thus, $r_{Rb^+} = 1.33\ \text{Å} + \frac{0.30\ \text{Å}}{2} = 1.48\ \text{Å}$

72. (*a*)

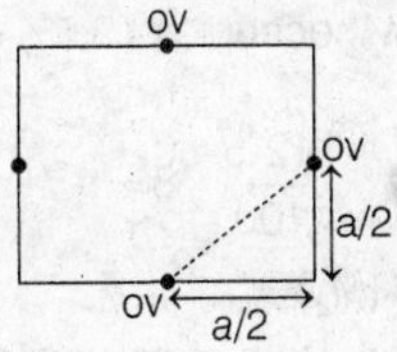

In fcc octahedral voids are present at the edge centers at body center.

Minimum distance between centers of two octahedral voids.

$$x=\sqrt{\left(\frac{a}{2}\right)^2+\left(\frac{a}{2}\right)^2}=\sqrt{\frac{a^2}{4}+\frac{a^2}{4}}=\frac{a}{\sqrt{2}}$$

74. (*d*) Number of Au atoms at the corners $=\frac{8}{8}=1$

Number of Cu atoms at the faces $=\frac{6}{2}=3$

Hence, formula is $AuCu_3$.

75. (*a*) Total strength of all H-bonds = 30.8 − 14.4

= 16.4 kJ mol^{-1}

There are six nearest neighbours, but each hydrogen bond involves 2 molecules. Hence, effective neighbours = 3

Hence, strength of H-bond $= \frac{16.4}{3} = 5.47$ kJ mol^{-1}

76. (*d*) We know that, $d = \frac{Z \times M}{a^3 \times N_A}$

Given, density $d = 6.17$ g,

edge length $a = 300$ pm $= 3 \times 10^{-8}$ cm,

$$N_A = 6 \times 10^{23} \text{ mol}^{-1}$$

$$\therefore \quad 6.17 = \frac{2 \times M}{(3 \times 10^{-8})^3 \times 6 \times 10^{23}} \quad \text{(For bcc, } Z = 2)$$

$$\Rightarrow \quad M = 50 \text{ g/mol}$$

Hence, number of molecules present in 200 g of X_2 is

$$N = \frac{w}{M} \times N_A = \frac{200}{50} \times N_A = 4N_A$$

99. (*b*) Given : Element A form hcp structure. Element M occupy $\frac{2}{3}$ of tetrahedral voids of the hcp structure. So, formula of the compound is

$$M_{12 \times \frac{2}{2}} A_6$$

$$M_8 A_6$$

$$M_4 A_3$$

100. (*a*) Number of O^{2-} ions in ccp = 4

Total charge on oxide = − 8

Number of tetrahedral voids = 8

Number of voids = 4

Number of cation M_1 occupies 50% of octahedral voids,

$$\frac{50}{100} \times 4 = 2$$

Number of cation M_2 occupies 12.5% of tetrahedral voids of oxide lattice,

$$\frac{12.5}{100} \times 8 = 1$$

So, formula is $(M_1)_2(M_2)O_4$.

This must be neutral. Both metals must have + 8 charge on total.

From given options : $\begin{cases} \text{Oxidaion number of } M_1 = +2 \\ \text{Oxidaion number of } M_2 = +4 \end{cases}$

$$\therefore \quad (2 \times +2) + (1 \times +4) = +8$$

Hence, correct option is (a).

101. (*c*) Let the number of atoms in cubic close packing be x.

$\therefore$ Number of tetrahedral voids $= 2x$

Since, Q forms cubic close packing, the number of Q atoms $= x$

P occupy one third of tetrahedral voids, the number of P atoms $= \frac{2}{3}x$

$$\frac{\text{number of } P \text{ atoms}}{\text{number of } Q \text{ atoms}} = \frac{2x}{3x} = \frac{2}{3}$$

Therefore, the formula of the compound is P_2Q_3.

103. (*d*) For body centred cubic bcc structure,

$$\text{radius } (R) = \frac{\sqrt{3}}{4} a \quad \text{...(i)}$$

Where, a = edge length

According to question, the structure of cubic unit cell can be shown as follows:

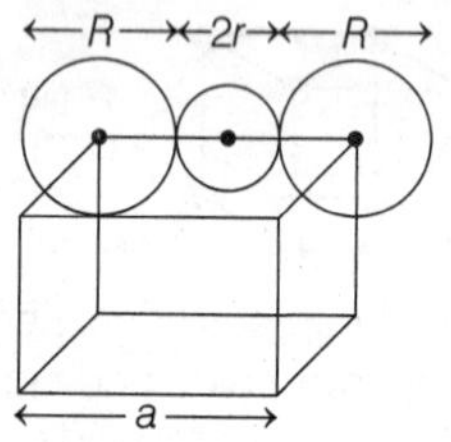

$$\therefore \quad a = 2(R + r) \quad \text{...(ii)}$$

On substituting the value of R from Eq. (i) to Eq. (ii), we get

$$\frac{a}{2} = \frac{\sqrt{3}}{4} a + r \Rightarrow r = \frac{a}{2} - \frac{\sqrt{3}}{4} a = \frac{2a - \sqrt{3}a}{4}$$

$$r = \frac{a(2 - \sqrt{3})}{4} \Rightarrow r = 0.067a$$

104. (*a*) There are seven crystal systems and 14 Bravais lattices.

105. (*d*) For a body-centred cubic lattice, the radius of atom is

$$r = \frac{\sqrt{3}}{4} \cdot a$$

$$a = 4.29 \text{ Å}$$

$$\therefore \quad r = \frac{1.732 \times 4.29}{4} = 1.86 \text{ Å}$$

06

Chemical Equilibrium

Objective Questions Type I [Only one correct option]

In each of the questions below, four choices are given of which only one is correct.

1. Naphthalene, a white solid used to make mothballs, has a vapour pressure of 0.10 mmHg at 27°C. Hence, K_p and K_C for the equilibrium are

$$C_{10}H_8(s) \rightleftharpoons C_{10}H_8(g)$$

(a) 0.10, 0.10
(b) 0.10, 4.1×10^{-3}
(c) 1.32×10^{-4}, 5.36×10^{-6}
(d) 5.36×10^{-6}, 1.32×10^{-4}

2. For the following equilibrium,

$$N_2O_4(g) \rightleftharpoons 2NO_2(g)$$

K_p is found to be equal to K_C. This is attained when
(a) $T = 1$ K (b) $T = 12.18$ K
(c) $T = 27.3$ K (d) $T = 273$ K

3. For the following gaseous equilibria X, Y and Z at 300 K

X. $2SO_2 + O_2 \rightleftharpoons 2SO_3$

Y. $PCl_5 \rightleftharpoons PCl_3 + Cl_2$

Z. $2HI \rightleftharpoons H_2 + I_2$

ratio of K_p and K_c in the increasing order is
(a) $X = Y = Z$ (b) $X < Y < Z$
(c) $X < Z < Y$ (d) $Z < Y < X$

4. For the following equilibrium,

$$PCl_5(g) \rightleftharpoons PCl_3(g) + Cl_2(g)$$

K_p is found to be equal to K_X. This is attained at
(a) 1 atm (b) 0.5 atm (c) 2 atm (d) 4 atm

5. $N_2 + 3H_2 \rightleftharpoons 2NH_3$ is a gaseous phase equilibrium reaction taking place in a 5 L flask at 400 K. For this
(a) $K_C = K_X$ (b) $K_C = 25K_X$
(c) $K_X = 25K_C$ (d) $K_C = 5K_X$

6. A reaction has a forward rate constant 2.3×10^6 s^{-1} and an equilibrium constant of 4.0×10^8. What is the rate constant for the reverse reaction?

(a) 1.1×10^{-15} s^{-1}
(b) 5.8×10^{-3} s^{-1}
(c) 1.7×10^{2} s^{-1}
(d) 9.2×10^{14} s^{-1}

7. For the reaction, $N_2O_4(g) \rightleftharpoons 2NO_2(g)$, K_C is 6.10×10^{-3} at 25°C. Hence, K_C for the equilibrium reaction

$$NO_2(g) \rightleftharpoons \frac{1}{2}N_2O_4(g) \text{ is}$$

(a) 1.64×10^2 (b) 81.97
(c) 3.14 (d) 12.80

8. $CH_3OH(g)$ can be prepared using equation

$$CO(g) + 2H_2(g) \rightleftharpoons CH_3OH(g), \quad K_C = 4 \times 10^2$$

At equilibrium, a 5 L flask contains equal moles of $CO(g)$ and $CH_3OH(g)$. Hence, number of moles of H_2 at equilibrium is
(a) 0.25 mol
(b) 0.10 mol
(c) 0.50 mol
(d) 0.125 mol

9. At a given temperature, equilibrium is attained when 50% of each reactant is converted into the products

$$A(g) + B(g) \rightleftharpoons C(g) + D(g)$$

If amount (in mol) of $B(g)$ is doubled, percentage of B converted into products will be
(a) 100% (b) 50%
(c) 66.67% (d) 33.33%

10. The position of the equilibrium for a system when $K_C = 4.6 \times 10^{-15}$ can be described as being favoured to ...., the concentration of products is relatively ...
(a) the right, larger (b) the left, small
(c) the left, larger (d) the right, small

11. For the reactions,

$$CaCO_3(s) \longrightarrow CaO(s) + CO_2(g), p_{CO_2} = 2 \text{ atm}$$

$$CO_2(g) + C(s) \longrightarrow 2CO(g), \quad K = 6 \text{ atm}$$

Hence, equilibrium constant for the reaction

$$CaCO_3(s) + C(s) \rightleftharpoons CaO(s) + 2CO(g) \text{ is}$$

(a) 8 atm (b) 4 atm (c) 12 atm (d) 3 atm

12. For the equilibrium,

I. $C_6H_5COOH + H_2O \rightleftharpoons C_6H_5COO^- + H_3O^+$; $K_1 = 6.30 \times 10^{-5}$

II. $C_6H_5COOH + OH^- \rightleftharpoons C_6H_5COO^- + H_2O$; $K_2 = 6.30 \times 10^9$

III. $H_2O + H_2O \rightleftharpoons H_3O^+ + OH^-$; $K_3 = ?$

K_3 using the above equilibria is

(a) $(6.30)^2 \times 10^4$ (b) 1.0×10^{-14}

(c) 1×10^{14} (d) $(6.30)^{-2} \times 10^{-4}$

13. If β_1, β_2 and β_3 are stepwise formation constants of MCl, MCl_2, MCl_3 and K is the overall formation constant of MCl_3, then (charges omitted)

(a) $K = \beta_1 + \beta_2 + \beta_3$

(b) $\frac{1}{K} = \frac{1}{\beta_1} + \frac{1}{\beta_2} + \frac{1}{\beta_3}$

(c) $\log K = \log \beta_1 + \log \beta_2 + \log \beta_3$

(d) $p_K = \log \beta_1 + \log \beta_2 + \log \beta_3$ $(p_K = -\log K)$

14. The rate of the elementary reaction $H_2(g) + I_2(g) \longrightarrow 2HI(g)$ at 25°C is given by

$$\text{Rate} = 1.7 \times 10^{-18} [H_2][I_2]$$

The rate of decomposition of gaseous HI to $H_2(g)$ and $I_2(g)$ at 25°C is rate $= 2.4 \times 10^{-21} [HI]^2$. Equilibrium constant for the formation of one mole of gaseous HI from the $H_2(g)$ and $I_2(g)$ is

(a) 708 (b) 354

(c) 0.0014 (d) 26.6

15. In the following equilibria,

I. $A + 2B \rightleftharpoons C$; $K_{eq} = K_1$

II. $C + D \rightleftharpoons 3A$; $K_{eq} = K_2$

III. $6B + D \rightleftharpoons 2C$; $K_{eq} = K_3$

Hence,

(a) $3K_1 : K_2 = K_3$ (b) $K_1^3 : K_2^2 = K_3$

(c) $3K_1 : K_2^2 = K_3$ (d) $K_1^3 : K_2 = K_3$

16. For the reactions,

$$NH_4^+ + 2H_2O \rightleftharpoons NH_4OH + H_3O^+; K_1 = 5.56 \times 10^{-10}$$

$$H_2O + H_2O \rightleftharpoons H_3O^+ + OH^-; \quad K_2 = 1 \times 10^{-14}$$

hence, K_3 of the reaction,

$$NH_4OH \rightleftharpoons NH_4^+ + OH^- \text{ is}$$

(a) 1.8×10^5 (b) 1.8×10^{-5}

(c) 5.56×10^4 (d) 5.56×10^{-4}

17. For the equilibrium,

$$NH_2COONH_4(s) \rightleftharpoons 2NH_3(g) + CO_2(g)$$

$p_{CO_2} = 1$ atm at 100°C. Hence, equilibrium constant is

(a) 1 atm^3 (b) 2 atm^3

(c) 4 atm^3 (d) 3 atm^3

18. In the following reaction,

$$A(g) \underset{k_2}{\overset{k_1}{\rightleftharpoons}} B(g)$$

$$\frac{-d[A]}{dt} = k_1[A] \text{ for the forward reaction}$$

$$\frac{-d[B]}{dt} = k_2[B] \text{ for the backward reaction}$$

Half-life period of the forward reaction is 10 min and that of backward reaction is 1 min. Thus, equilibrium constant is **[JEE Main 2012]**

(a) 0.693 (b) 0.0693

(c) 0.10 (d) 10.0

19. Mercurous chloride, $Hg_2Cl_2(s)$, in saturated solution exists as mercurous ion and chloride ion. Hence, equilibrium constant is

(a) $[Hg^+]^2[Cl^-]^2$

(b) $[Hg_2^{2+}][Cl^-]^2$

(c) $[Hg^+][Cl^-]$

(d) None of the above

20. For the following equilibrium,

$$2Fe(s) + 3H_2O(g) \rightleftharpoons Fe_2O_3(s) + 3H_2(g)$$

$K_C = 27$. Hence, ratio of molar concentration of $H_2(g)$ and $H_2O(g)$ is

(a) 3 (b) 1 (c) 9 (d) 27

21. The value of K_C for the dissociation reaction

$$H_2(g) \rightleftharpoons 2H(g) \text{ is } 1.2 \times 10^{-42}$$

This equilibrium mixture contains mainly

(a) $H_2(g)$

(b) H(g) atoms

(c) 1 : 1 molar mixture of H_2 and H

(d) 1 : 2 molar mixture of H_2 and H

22. Consider the following reactions in equilibrium with equilibrium concentration 0.01 M of every species

I. $PCl_5 \rightleftharpoons PCl_3 + Cl_2$ II. $H_2 + I_2 \rightleftharpoons 2HI$

III. $N_2 + 3H_2 \rightleftharpoons 2NH_3$

Extent of the reactions taking place is

(a) I = II = III

(b) I < II < III

(c) III < II < I

(d) II < I < III

23. The equilibrium constant K_C for the reaction of H_2 with I_2 is 57.0 at 700 K

$$H_2(g) + I_2(g) \underset{k_b}{\overset{k_f}{\rightleftharpoons}} 2HI; \quad K_C = 57 \text{ at } 700\text{ K}$$

Select the correct statement.
(a) Rate constant k_f for the formation of HI is smaller than that of rate constant k_b of the dissociation of HI
(b) $k_f > k_b$
(c) Addition of catalyst increases value of K_C
(d) Addition of catalyst decreases value of K_C

24. For which of the following reactions will the equilibrium mixture contain an appreciable concentration of both reactants and products ?
(a) $Cl_2(g) \rightleftharpoons 2Cl(g), K_C = 6.4 \times 10^{-39}$
(b) $Cl_2(g) + 2NO(g) \rightleftharpoons 2NOCl(g), \quad K_C = 3.7 \times 10^8$
(c) $Cl_2(g) + 2NO_2(g) \rightleftharpoons 2NO_2Cl(g), K_C = 1.8$
(d) All of the above

25. $N_2O_4 \rightleftharpoons 2NO_2, K_C = 4$. This reversible reaction is studied graphically as shown in the given figure. Select the correct statements out of I, II and III.
I. Reaction quotient has maximum value at point A.
II. Reaction proceeds left to right at a point when. $[N_2O_4] = [NO_2] = 0.1$ M.
III. $K_C = Q$ when point D or F is reached.

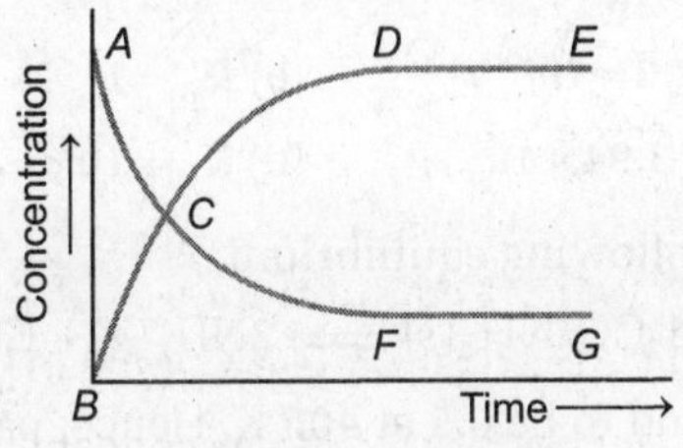

(a) I, II (b) II, III (c) I, III (d) I, II, III

26. For the reversible reaction net rate is,

$$2NO(g) + O_2(g) \rightleftharpoons 2NO_2(g)$$

$$\left(\frac{dx}{dt}\right)_{net} = 2.6 \times 10^3 [NO]^2 [O_2] - 4.1 [NO_2]^2$$

If a reaction mixture contains 0.01 mole each of NO and O_2 and 0.1 mole of NO_2 in 1 L closed flask, then above reaction is
(a) shifted in forward direction
(b) shifted in backward direction
(c) in equilibrium
(d) given values are incomplete

27. Without knowing the value of reaction quotient which of the following reaction can be predicted to go to completion at 25°C?
(a) $CH_3OCH_3(l) \rightleftharpoons CH_3OCH_3(g)$
(b) $H_2O(l) \rightleftharpoons H_2O(g)$
(c) $H_2(g) \rightleftharpoons 2H(g)$
(d) Sulphur $(s) \rightleftharpoons$ Sulphur (g)

28. For the following equilibrium reaction,

$$N_2O_4(g) \rightleftharpoons 2NO_2(g),$$

NO_2 is 50% of the total volume at a given temperature. Hence, vapour density of the equilibrium mixture is
(a) 34.5 (b) 25.0 (c) 23.0 (d) 20.0

29. Abnormal vapour density of the mixture of PCl_5, PCl_3 and Cl_2 in the following equilibrium **[JEE Main 2014]**

$$PCl_5(g) \rightleftharpoons PCl_3(g) + Cl_2(g)$$

is found to be 80 (P = 31, Cl = 35.5). Extent of dissociation of $PCl_5(g)$ is approximately
(a) 80% (b) 50% (c) 40% (d) 30%

30. In the dissociation of N_2O_4 into NO_2, $(1 + x)$ varies with the vapour densities ratio $\left(\frac{D}{d}\right)$ as given by

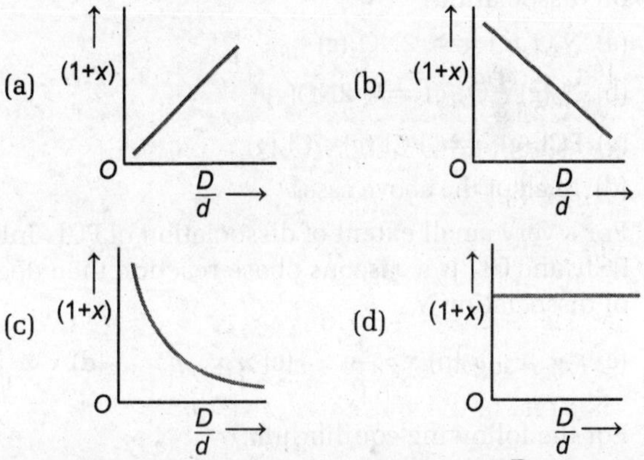

31. In the above question (30), x varies with $\frac{D}{d}$ according to

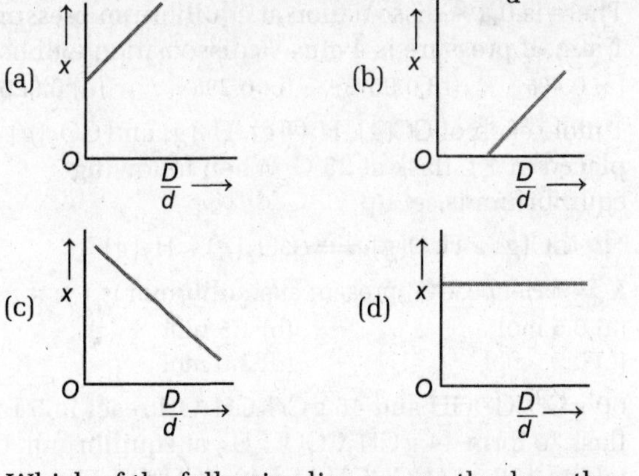

32. Which of the following lines correctly show the temperature dependence of equilibrium constant, K, for an exothermic reaction? **[JEE Main 2018]**

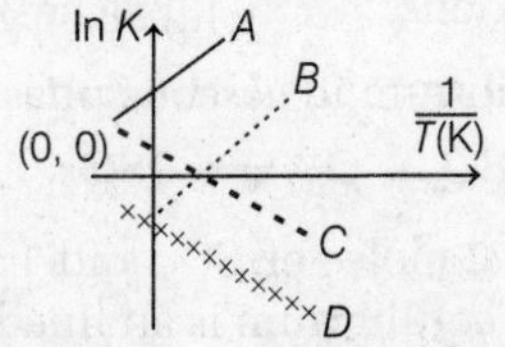

(a) A and B (b) B and C
(c) C and D (d) A and D

33. For the following equilibrium, ratio of theoretical and experimental vapour density is 1.5.

$$N_2O_4(g) \rightleftharpoons 2NO_2(g)$$

Thus, NO_2 in the total mixture is .... % by volume.
(a) 50% (b) 100% (c) 67% (d) 33%

34. For the following equilibrium, van't Hoff factor is 0.80

$$2A(g) \rightleftharpoons A_2(g)$$

Hence, volume per cent of $A_2(g)$ in the total mixture is
(a) 25% (b) 50% (c) 80% (d) 40%

35. In the equilibrium, $PCl_5 \rightleftharpoons PCl_3 + Cl_2$ starting with 2 moles of PCl_5 in 5 L flask at 350 K, there is 80% dissociation. Hence, equilibrium pressure is
(a) 11.50 atm (b) 32.2 atm
(c) 20.7 atm (d) 13.8 atm

36. In which case(s), vapour density remains unchanged on dissociation?
(a) $N_2O_4(g) \rightleftharpoons 2NO_2(g)$
(b) $N_2(g) + O_2(g) \rightleftharpoons 2NO(g)$
(c) $PCl_5(g) \rightleftharpoons PCl_3(g) + Cl_2(g)$
(d) In all of the above cases

37. For a very small extent of dissociation of PCl_5 into PCl_3 and Cl_2 is a gaseous phase reaction then degree of dissociation x
(a) $x \propto p$ (b) $x \propto \frac{1}{p}$ (c) $x \propto \sqrt{p}$ (d) $x \propto \sqrt{\frac{1}{p}}$

38. For the following equilibrium,

$$H_2(g) \rightleftharpoons 2H(g)$$

There is 0.1% dissociation at equilibrium pressure of 1 atm. If pressure is 4 atm, % dissociation will be
(a) 0.4% (b) 0.05% (c) 0.2% (d) 0.025%

39. 1 mole each of $CO(g)$, $H_2O(g)$, $H_2(g)$ and $CO_2(g)$ are placed in 1 L flask at 25°C. When following equilibrium is set up

$$CO(g) + H_2O(g) \rightleftharpoons CO_2(g) + H_2(g)$$

$K_p = 9$. Hence, CO_2 present at equilibrium is
(a) 0.5 mol (b) 1.5 mol
(c) 0.25 mol (d) 3.0 mol

40. 60 g CH_3COOH and 46 g CH_3CH_2OH react in 5 L flask to form 44 g $CH_3COOC_2H_5$ at equilibrium. On taking 120 g CH_3COOH and 46 g CH_3CH_2OH, $CH_3COOC_2H_5$ formed at equilibrium is
(a) 44 g (b) 20.33 g
(c) 22 g (d) 58.66 g

41. For the equilibrium in gaseous phase

$$2SO_2 + O_2 \rightleftharpoons 2SO_3$$

we start with 2 moles of SO_2 and 1 mole of O_2 at 3 atm. When equilibrium is attained, pressure change to 2.5 atm. Hence, K_p is
(a) 3 atm^{-1} (b) 2.5 atm^{-1} (c) 2 atm^{-1} (d) 0.5 atm^{-1}

42. Sulphide ion (S^{2-}) reacts with solid sulphur forming S_2^{2-} and S_3^{2-} with formation constants 12 and 132. Formation constant of S_3^{2-} from sulphur and S_2^{2-} is
(a) 12 (b) 132 (c) 132 × 12 (d) 11

43. The equilibrium constants for the reaction H_3BO_3 + glycerine $\rightleftharpoons$ ($H_3BO_3 \cdot$ glycerine) is 0.90. Glycerine present per litre of 0.1 M H_3BO_3 to convert 60% of H_3BO_3 into ($H_3BO_3 \cdot$ glycerine) is
(a) 0.167 M (b) 1.67 M
(c) 0.0167 M (d) 10.67 M

44. 1 mole of PCl_5 taken at 5 atm, dissociates into PCl_3 and Cl_2 to the extent of 50%

$$PCl_5(g) \rightleftharpoons PCl_3(g) + Cl_2(g)$$

Thus, K_p is
(a) 2.5 (b) 1.67 (c) 0.5 (d) 2.0

45. For the following equilibrium $N_2O_4 \rightleftharpoons 2NO_2$; $K_C = 0.67$. If we start with 3 moles of NO_2 and 1 mole of N_2O_4 in 1 L flask, then NO_2 present at equilibrium is
(a) 1.5 mol (b) 2.0 mol (c) 0.5 mol (d) 1.0 mol

46. $CaCO_3(s) \rightleftharpoons CaO(s) + CO_2(g)$
For this equilibrium it is found that

$$\log K_p = 8 - \frac{6400}{T(K)}$$

At $T = 527°C$
(a) $K_p = 7.2 \times 10^{-5}$ (b) $K_p = 1$
(c) $K_p = 13.94 \times 10^3$ (d) $K_p = 10$

47. For the following equilibrium,

$$NH_2CO_2NH_4(s) \rightleftharpoons 2NH_3(g) + CO_2(g)$$

K_p is found to be 0.5 at 400 K. Hence, partial pressure of NH_3 and CO_2 are respectively
(a) 2.0, 1.0 atm (b) 1.0, 2.0 atm
(c) 1.0, 0.5 atm (d) 0.5, 1.0 atm

48. In each of the following total pressure setup at equilibrium is assumed to be equal and is 1 atm with equilibrium constants K_p given
I. $CaCO_3(s) \rightleftharpoons CaO(s) + CO_2(g); K_1$
II. $NH_4HS(s) \rightleftharpoons NH_3(g) + H_2S(g); K_2$
III. $NH_2CO_2NH_4(s) \rightleftharpoons 2NH_3(g) + CO_2(g); K_3$
In the increasing order
(a) $K_1 = K_2 = K_3$ (b) $K_1 < K_2 < K_3$
(c) $K_3 < K_2 < K_1$ (d) None of these

49. Which of the following on the addition will cause deep red colour to disappear?

$Fe^{3+}(aq)$	+	SCN^-	$\rightleftharpoons$	$Fe(SCN)^{2+}(aq)$
Pale yellow		Colourless		Deep red

I. $AgNO_3$ II. $HgCl_2$
III. $H_2C_2O_4$ (oxalic acid)
(a) I, II (b) II, III (c) I, III (d) I, II, III

50. Following equilibrium is disturbed by

$$CaCO_3(s) \rightleftharpoons CaO(s) + CO_2(g)$$

(a) addition of $CaCO_3$ (b) addition of CaO
(c) addition of CO_2 (d) All of these

51. Which factor will shift the following equilibrium in forward direction?

$$AgCl(s) \rightleftharpoons Ag^+(aq) + Cl^-(aq)$$

(a) Addition of $NH_3(aq)$
(b) Addition of $AgNO_3(aq)$
(c) Addition of NaCl(*aq*)
(d) Addition of AgCl(*s*)

52. In the manufacturing of H_2SO_4 with the following equilibrium

$$2SO_2(g) + O_2(g) \rightleftharpoons 2SO_3(g)$$

reaction proceeds in the forward direction if
(a) some H_2O is added (b) some SO_3 is added
(c) some SO_2 is removed (d) some O_2 is removed

53. The binding of oxygen by haemoglobin (Hb), giving oxyhaemoglobin (HbO_2), is partially regulated by the concentration of H_3O^+ and dissolved CO_2 in blood.

$$HbO_2 + H_3O^+ + CO_2 \rightleftharpoons H^+\text{–}Hb\text{–}CO_2 + O_2 + H_2O$$

Release of O_2 is favoured when there is
(a) production of lactic acid during excertion
(b) production of CO_2 during excertion
(c) Both (a) and (b)
(d) None of the above

54. In the following equilibrium amount of CO(*g*) can be decreased by

$$2CO(g) + O_2(g) \rightleftharpoons 2CO_2(g)$$

(a) decreasing volume at constant temperature
(b) adding argon gas
(c) adding O_2 gas
(d) All of the above

55. Pressure is doubled in each of the following equilibria. In which case yield is maximum?
(a) $C(s) + H_2O(g) \rightleftharpoons CO(g) + H_2(g)$
(b) $2H_2(g) + O_2(g) \rightleftharpoons 2H_2O(g)$
(c) $2Fe(s) + 3H_2O(g) \rightleftharpoons Fe_2O_3(s) + 3H_2(g)$
(d) $N_2O_4(g) \rightleftharpoons 2NO_2(g)$

56. Increase in the pressure for the following equilibrium

$$H_2O(l) \rightleftharpoons H_2O(g)$$

result in the
I. formation of more $H_2O(l)$
II. formation of more $H_2O(g)$
III. increase in boiling point of $H_2O(l)$
IV. decrease in boiling point of $H_2O(l)$
Hence, correct statements are
(a) I, II (b) II, III
(c) I, III (d) I, IV

57. $CO_2(g)$ can be dissolved in H_2O as given by

$$CO_2(g) + H_2O(l) \rightleftharpoons CO_2(aq)$$

Solubility of CO_2 in H_2O can be increased by
(a) increasing pressure
(b) decreasing pressure
(c) decreasing volume of H_2O
(d) increasing $CO_2(g)$

58. For the following equilibrium,
$Si(s) + 2Cl_2(g) \rightleftharpoons SiCl_4(g)$, formation of product (*x*) is
(a) $x \propto P$ (b) $x \propto \frac{1}{P}$
(c) $x \propto \sqrt{P}$ (d) $x \propto \sqrt{\frac{1}{P}}$

59. Consider the following gas phase reaction

$$2A(g) + B(g) \rightleftharpoons C(g) + D(g); \quad \Delta H^\circ = +\text{ ve}$$

which affects neither the composition nor the value of K_C?
(a) Addition of reactants (b) Addition of helium
(c) Addition of catalyst (d) Increase in temperature

60. Variation of $\log_{10} K$ with $\frac{1}{T}$ is shown by the following graph in which straight line is at 45°, hence ΔH° is

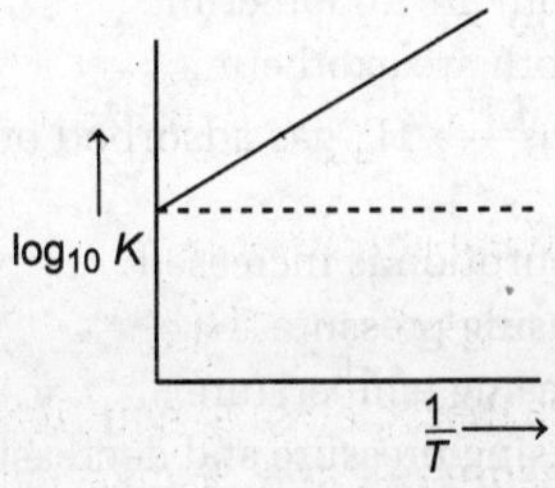

(a) +4.606 cal (b) −4.606 cal
(c) 2 cal (d) −2 cal

61. Formation of acetone (*A*) is favoured for the following equilibrium if

$$(CH_3)_2CHOH(g) \rightleftharpoons \underset{(A)}{(CH_3)_2CO(g)} + H_2(g); \quad \Delta H = +57.3 \text{ kJ}$$

(a) the temperature is increased
(b) the volume is increased at constant temperature
(c) $H_2(g)$ is withdrawn
(d) under all the conditions given above

62. When a sample of NO_2 is placed in a container, this equilibrium is rapidly established.

$$2NO_2(g) \rightleftharpoons N_2O_4(g)$$

Equilibrium mixture is darker in colour at high temperature and low pressure. This indicates that
(a) ΔH is +ve and NO_2 is darker in colour than N_2O_4
(b) ΔH is +ve and N_2O_4 is darker in colour than NO_2
(c) ΔH is −ve and NO_2 is darker in colour than N_2O_4
(d) ΔH is −ve and N_2O_4 is darker in colour than NO_2

63. In which case increase in temperature will increase the quantity of the product?

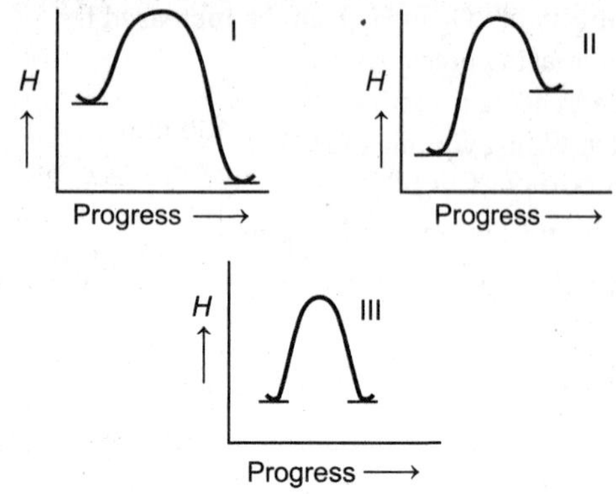

(a) I, II (b) I, III (c) II, III (d) II

64. Consider the following equilibria at 300 K and 400 K with their equilibrium constants

		300 K	400 K
I.	$A(g) \rightleftharpoons 2B(g)$	$K_{eq} = 10$	$K_{eq} = 5$
II.	$C(g) \rightleftharpoons D(g)$	$K_{eq} = 2$	$K_{eq} = 5$

Thus,

(a) I is endothermic, II is exothermic
(b) I is exothermic, II is endothermic
(c) I and II both are endothermic
(d) I and II both are exothermic

65. $H_2(g) + Ni(s) \longrightarrow H_2$ gas adsorbed on nickel surface + Heat.

Extent of adsorption is increased

(a) on increasing pressure
(b) on decreasing temperature
(c) on increasing pressure and decreasing temperature
(d) on increasing both pressure and temperature

66. When NH_3 is heated in a 0.50 L flask at 700 K and 100 atm pressure, it decomposes into N_2 and H_2 and their equilibrium moles are given below

$$\underset{0.30}{2NH_3(g)} \rightleftharpoons \underset{0.30}{N_2(g)} + \underset{0.90}{3H_2(g)}$$

Which of the pairs given represents correct value?

	Initial moles of NH_3	**for NH_3 formation**
(a)	0.80	9.72
(b)	0.90	9.72
(c)	0.80	0.103
(d)	0.90	0.103

67. For the reaction,

$2SO_2(g) + O_2(g) \longrightarrow 2SO_3(g)$, $\Delta H = -57.2$ kJ mol^{-1} and $K_C = 1.7 \times 10^{16}$. Which of the following statement is incorrect? **[JEE Main 2019, April]**

(a) The equilibrium constant decreases as the temperature increases
(b) The addition of inert gas at constant volume will not affect the equilibrium constant
(c) The equilibrium will shift in forward direction as the pressure increases
(d) The equilibrium constant is large suggestive of reaction going to completion and so no catalyst is required

68. When equilibrium is attained

(a) $\Delta G° = 0$ (b) $E° = 0$
(c) $K = 0$ (d) None of these

69. A cell reaction is spontaneous if

(a) $E_{cell} > 0$ (b) $\Delta G < 0$
(c) $K > 1$ (d) All of these

70. van't Hoff isochore equation is

(a) $\log_{10} K = -\dfrac{\Delta H°}{2.303\,RT} + \dfrac{\Delta S°}{R}$

(b) $\dfrac{d \log_{10} K}{dt} = \dfrac{\Delta H°}{2.303RT^2}$

(c) Both (a) and (b)
(d) None of the above

71. If ΔH and ΔG are negative and ΔS is positive then reaction is

(a) spontaneous at all temperatures
(b) non-spontaneous at all temperatures
(c) spontaneous at low temperature and non-spontaneous at high temperature
(d) in equilibrium

72. $\Delta G°$ at 25°C for the reaction,

$$\frac{1}{2}N_2(g) + \frac{3}{2}H_2 \rightleftharpoons NH_3(g)$$

is -16.5 kJ mol^{-1}. Hence, thermodynamic equilibrium constant is

(a) 1.08 (b) 7.80×10^2
(c) 4.57×10^6 (d) 7.98×10^{34}

73. Two solids dissociate as follows:

$A(s) \rightleftharpoons B(g) + C(g)$; $K_{p_1} = x$ atm^2
$D(s) \rightleftharpoons C(g) + E(g)$; $K_{p_2} = y$ atm^2

The total pressure when both the solids dissociate simultaneously is **[JEE Main 2019, Jan.]**

(a) $\sqrt{x+y}$ atm (b) $x^2 + y^2$ atm
(c) $(x+y)$ atm (d) $2(\sqrt{x+y})$ atm

74. Consider the reaction,

$$N_2(g) + 3H_2(g) \rightleftharpoons 2NH_3(g)$$

The equilibrium constant of the above reaction is K_p. If pure ammonia is left to dissociate, the partial pressure of ammonia at equilibrium is given by (Assume that $p_{NH_3} << p_{total}$ at equilibrium) **[JEE Main 2019, Jan.]**

(a) $\dfrac{3^{3/2} K_p^{1/2} P^2}{4}$ (b) $\dfrac{3^{3/2} K_p^{1/2} P^2}{16}$

(c) $\dfrac{K_p^{1/2} P^2}{16}$ (d) $\dfrac{K_p^{1/2} P^2}{4}$

75. For an isomerisation reaction $A \rightleftharpoons B$, the temperature dependence of equilibrium constant is given by

$$\log_e K = 4.0 - \frac{2000}{T}$$

The value of ΔS° at 400 K is, therefore

(a) $4R$ (b) $5R$
(c) $400\ R$ (d) $2000\ R$

76. For the reactions, $I_2(aq) \rightleftharpoons I_2(\text{oil})$. Equilibrium constant is K_1.

$I_2(\text{oil}) \rightleftharpoons I_2(\text{ether})$ Equilibrium constant is K_2 for reaction.

$I_2(aq) \rightleftharpoons I_2(\text{ether})$ Equilibrium constant $= K_3$.

The relation between K_1, K_2, K_3 is

(a) $K_3 = K_1 + K_2$ (b) $K_3 = K_1K_2$
(c) $K_3 = K_1/K_2$ (d) $K_3 = K_2/K_1$

77. Which statement is not correct?

(a) Rate of an exothermic reaction increases with temperature
(b) Solubility of NaOH increases with temperature
(c) K_p for $N_2(g) + 3H_2(g) \rightleftharpoons 2NH_3(g)$ increases with increase in pressure
(d) For gaseous reaction, $2B \rightarrow A$ K_p is smaller than K_C

78. Which represents variation of K_{eq} with temperature?

(a) $\log_e K_{eq} = \text{constant} - \frac{\Delta H}{RT}$

(b) $\log_{10} K_{eq} = \text{constant} - \frac{\Delta H}{RT}$

(c) $\frac{d \log_{10} K_{eq}}{dT} = \frac{\Delta H}{RT^2}$

(d) $\frac{d \log_e K_{eq}}{dT} = -\frac{\Delta H}{RT^2}$

79. For the reaction, $C(s) + CO_2(g) \longrightarrow 2CO(g)$, $K_p = 63$ atm at 1000 K. If at equilibrium $p_{CO} = 10\ p_{CO_2}$, then the total pressure of the gases at equilibrium is

(a) 6.3 atm (b) 6.93 atm
(c) 0.63 atm (d) 0.63 atm

80. In the reaction, $AB(g) \rightleftharpoons A(g) + B(g)$ at 30°C, K_p for the dissociation equilibrium is 2.56×10^{-2} atm. If the total pressure at equilibrium is 1 atm, then the percentage dissociation of AB is

(a) 87% (b) 13% (c) 43.5% (d) 16%

81. Final pressure is higher than initial pressure of a container filled with an ideal gas at constant temperature. What will be the value of equilibrium constant?

(a) $K = 1.0$ (b) $K = 10.0$ (c) $K > 1.0$ (d) $K < 1.0$

82. $CH_3COCH_3(g) \rightleftharpoons CH_3CH_3(g) + CO(g)$

Initial pressure CH_3COCH_3 is 100 mm. When equilibrium is set up mole fraction of $CO(g)$ is $\frac{1}{3}$, hence K_p is

(a) 100 mm (b) 50 mm
(c) 25 mm (d) 150 mm

83. For the following equilibrium $N_2O_4 \rightleftharpoons 2NO_2$ in gaseous phase, NO_2 is 50% of the total volume when equilibrium is setup. Hence, per cent of dissociation of N_2O_4 is

(a) 50% (b) 25%
(c) 66.66% (d) 33.33%

84. PCl_5 is 40% dissociated when pressure is 2 atm. It will be 80% dissociated when pressure is approximately

(a) 0.2 atm (b) 0.5 atm
(c) 0.3 atm (d) 0.6 atm

85. 2 moles PCl_5, 1 mole Cl_2 and 1 mole PCl_3 are taken in 1 L flask. When equilibrium is setup, PCl_5 is found to 50% dissociated into the products. Hence, K_C is

(a) 4 mol L^{-1} (b) 1.5 mol L^{-1}
(c) 1 mol L^{-1} (d) 0.17 mol L^{-1}

86. $N_2 + 3H_2 \rightleftharpoons 2NH_3$. This is gaseous phase reaction taking place in 1 L flask at 127°C. Starting with 1 mole N_2 and 3 moles H_2, equilibrium mixture required 500 mL of 1 M HCl. Hence, K_C is approximately

(a) 0.006 (b) 0.08
(c) 0.03 (d) 2.05

87. Equilibrium constant for the reaction,

$$NH_4OH + H^+ \rightleftharpoons NH_4^+ + H_2O$$

is 1.8×10^9. Hence, equilibrium constant for

$$NH_3(aq) + H_2O \rightleftharpoons NH_4^+ + OH^- \text{ is}$$

(a) 1.8×10^{-5} (b) 1.8×10^5
(c) 1.8×10^{-9} (d) 5.55×10^{-10}

88. For the reaction, $A + B \rightleftharpoons C + D$, equilibrium concentration of $[C] = [D] = 0.5$ M, if we start with 1 mole each of A and B. Percentage of A converted into C if we start with 2 moles of A and 1 mole of B, is

(a) 25 % (b) 40 %
(c) 66.66% (d) 33.33%

89. Consider the following reversible chemical reactions,

$$A_2(g) + B_2(g) \overset{K_1}{\rightleftharpoons} 2AB(g) \quad \text{...(i)}$$

$$6AB(g) \overset{K_2}{\rightleftharpoons} 3A_2(g) + 3B_2(g) \quad \text{...(ii)}$$

The relation between K_1 and K_2 is **[JEE Main 2019, Jan.]**

(a) $K_2 = K_1^3$ (b) $K_1K_2 = 3$
(c) $K_2 = K_1^{-3}$ (d) $K_1K_2 = \frac{1}{3}$

90. For the reaction,

$$NH_2COONH_4(s) \rightleftharpoons 2NH_3(g) + CO_2(g)$$

the equilibrium constant $K_p = 2.92 \times 10^{-5}$ atm^3. The total pressure of the gaseous products when 1 mole of reactant is heated, will be

(a) 0.0194 atm
(b) 0.0388 atm
(c) 0.0582 atm
(d) 0.0667 atm

91. The equilibrium constant at 298 K for a reaction, $A + B \rightleftharpoons C + D$ is 100. If the initial concentrations of all the four species were 1 M each, then equilibrium concentration of D (in mol L^{-1}) will be **[JEE Main 2016]**

(a) 0.818 (b) 1.818
(c) 1.182 (d) 0.182

92. Volume of the flask in which species are transferred is double of the earlier flask. In which of the following cases, equilibrium constant is affected?

I. $N_2(g) + 3H_2(g) \rightleftharpoons 2NH_3(g)$

II. $N_2(g) + O_2(g) \rightleftharpoons 2NO(g)$

III. $PCl_5(g) \rightleftharpoons PCl_3(g) + Cl_2(g)$

IV. $2NO(g) \rightleftharpoons N_2(g) + O_2(g)$

(a) I, II (b) II, III
(c) I, III (d) III, IV

93. 1 mole each of A and B and 3 moles each of C and D are placed in 1 L flask, if equilibrium constant is 2.25 for $A + B \rightleftharpoons C + D$, equilibrium concentrations of A and C will be in the ratio

(a) 2 : 3 (b) 3 : 2
(c) 1 : 2 (d) 2 : 1

94. $2SO_2 + O_2 \rightleftharpoons 2SO_3$. Starting with 2 mole SO_2 and 1 mole O_2 in 1 L flask, mixture required 0.4 mole MnO_4^- in acidic medium. Hence, K_C is

(a) 2 (b) 0.4
(c) 1.6 (d) 2.6

95. For the reaction, $PCl_5 \rightleftharpoons PCl_3 + Cl_2$ in gaseous phase, $K_C = 4$. In a 2 L flask, there are 2 moles each of PCl_3 and Cl_2 and 0.5 mole of PCl_5. Equilibrium concentration of PCl_5 is

(a) 0.25 mol L^{-1} (b) 0.125 mol L^{-1}
(c) 0.75 mol L^{-1} (d) 1.00 mol L^{-1}

96. For $N_2 + 3H_2 \rightleftharpoons 2NH_3$, 1 mole N_2 and 3 moles H_2 are at 4 atm. Equilibrium pressure is found to be 3 atm. Hence, K_p is

(a) $\frac{1}{(0.5)(0.15)^3}$ (b) $\frac{1}{(0.5)(1.5)^3}$

(c) $\frac{3 \times 3}{(0.5)(1.5)^3}$ (d) None of these

97. Solubility(S) of a solute in a solvent (say H_2O) is dependent on temperature as given by $S = A\,e^{-\Delta H/RT}$, where ΔH is heat of reaction.

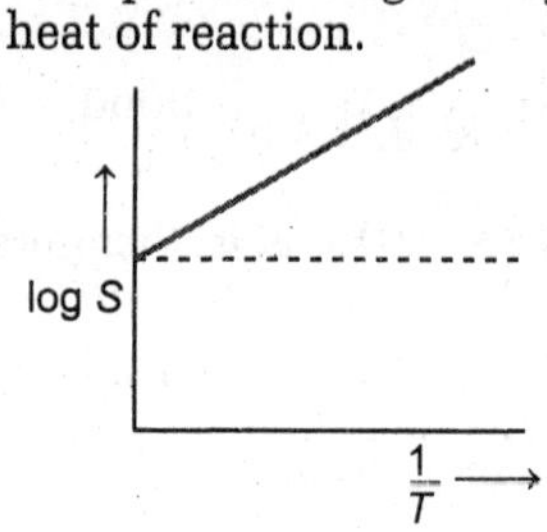

$$\text{Solute} + H_2O \rightleftharpoons \text{Solution}$$
$$\Delta H = \pm x$$

For a given solution variation of log S with temperature is shown graphically. Hence, solute is

(a) $CuSO_4 \cdot 5H_2O$ (b) NaCl
(c) sucrose (d) CaO

98. Boiling point of H_2O (l) increases when

(a) pressure is increased
(b) pressure is decreased
(c) when studied at a mountain
(d) Both (a) and (c)

99. Consider the following reactions (in gaseous phase) in equilibrium with equilibrium concentrations 0.1 M of every species

I. $2SO_2 + O_2 \rightleftharpoons 2SO_3$;

II. $N_2 + 3H_2 \rightleftharpoons 2NH_3$;

III. $N_2O_4 \rightleftharpoons 2NO_2$;

IV. $4NO + 6H_2O \rightleftharpoons 4NH_3 + 5O_2$;

Extent of reaction will be in the order

(a) I = II = III = IV (b) I = II = III < IV
(c) III < I = IV < II (d) IV < III < I < II

100. For the equilibrium,

$$Ag^+ + 2NH_3 \rightleftharpoons Ag(NH_3)_2^+; \quad K_1 = 1.8 \times 10^7$$

and $Ag^+ + Cl^- \rightleftharpoons AgCl$; $K_2 = 5.6 \times 10^9$

hence, for the equilibrium

$$AgCl + 2NH_3 \rightleftharpoons Ag(NH_3)_2^+ + Cl^-$$

equilibrium constant is

(a) 0.32×10^{-2} (b) 0.31×10^{-21}
(c) 1.01×10^{17} (d) 1.01×10^{-17}

101. For the reversible reaction in equilibrium,

$$N_2(g) + O_2(g) \underset{k_2}{\overset{k_1}{\rightleftharpoons}} 2NO(g)$$

$C_0 = Ce^{-2.1 \times 10^{-3} t}$ for the forward reaction and $C'_0 = C'e^{-4.2 \times 10^{-4} t}$ for the backward reaction, hence, K_C for the above equilibrium is

(a) 5.0 (b) 2.0
(c) 0.5 (d) 2

102. The standard Gibbs energy change at 300 K for the reaction, $2A \rightleftharpoons B + C$ is 2494. 2J. At a given time, the composition of the reaction mixture is $[A] = \frac{1}{2}$, $[B] = 2$ and $[C] = \frac{1}{2}$. The reaction proceeds in the

$(R = 8.314 JK / mol, e = 2.718)$ **[JEE Main 2015]**

(a) forward direction because $Q > K_C$
(b) reverse direction because $Q > K_C$
(c) forward direction because $Q < K_C$
(d) reverse direction because $Q < K_C$

103. For the following equilibria relation between K_c and K_x is

$$2SO_2(g) + O_2(g) \rightleftharpoons 2SO_3(g)$$

(a) $K_C = K_x (RT)^{-1}$ (b) $K_C = K_x (RT)$
(c) $K_C = K_x \left(\frac{1}{V}\right)$ (d) $K_C = K_x (V)$

104. For the equilibrium, $2H_2O(g) \rightleftharpoons 2H_2(g) + O_2(g)$ equilibrium constant is K_1.
For the equilibrium, $2CO_2 \rightleftharpoons 2CO(g) + O_2(g)$, equilibrium constant is K_2.
The equilibrium constant for

$$CO_2(g) + H_2(g) \rightleftharpoons CO(s) + H_2O(g) \text{ is}$$

(a) K_1K_2 (b) $\frac{K_1}{K_2}$ (c) $\sqrt{\frac{K_1}{K_2}}$ (d) $\sqrt{\frac{K_2}{K_1}}$

105. K_p/K_C for the reaction,

$$CO(g) + \frac{1}{2}O_2(g) \rightleftharpoons CO_2(g) \text{ will be}$$

(a) 1 (b) $\sqrt{RT}$ (c) $\frac{1}{\sqrt{RT}}$ (d) RT

106. Consider the following statements regarding the potential energy (PE) diagram for the reaction $A \longrightarrow B$ shown in the figure.

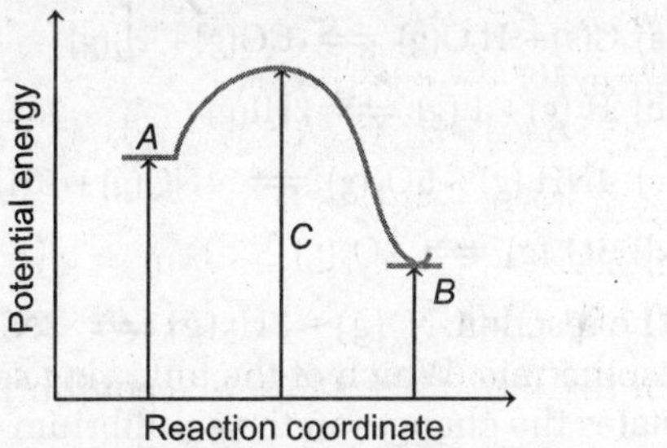

I. PE of the activated complex is greater for the forward reaction than for the reverse reaction.
II. ΔE of the forward reaction $(B - A)$.
III. Activation energy (reverse) > activation energy (forward).

Which of the above statements are correct?

(a) I alone (b) Both I and II
(c) Both II and III (d) III alone

107. The rate of the elementary gaseous phase reaction $2NO + O_2 \rightleftharpoons 2NO_2$ at 380°C is given by

$$\text{Rate} = 2.6 \times 10^3 [NO_2]^2 [O_2]$$

The rate of the reverse reaction at 380°C is given by

$$\text{Rate} = 4.1 [NO_2]^2$$

Hence, equilibrium constant for the formation of NO_2 by chemical equation

$$NO + \frac{1}{2}O_2 \rightleftharpoons NO_2 \text{ is}$$

(a) 6.34×10^2 (b) 1.577×10^{-3}
(c) 25.18 (d) 3.97×10^{-2}

108. In the following reaction, $PCl_5 \rightleftharpoons PCl_3 + Cl_2$ study is made graphically till equilibrium is attained. Following graphs were taken

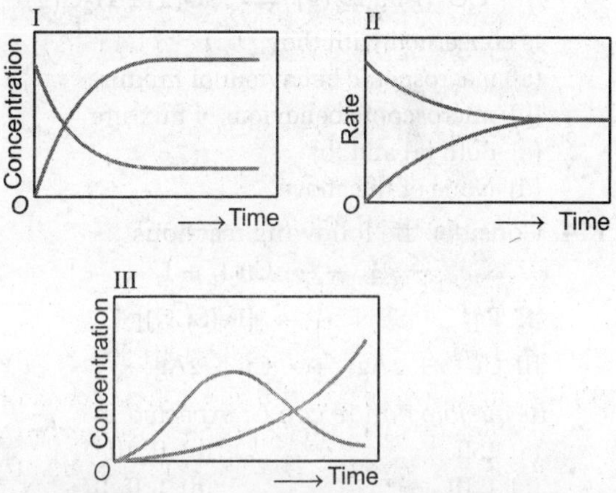

Correct graphs are

(a) I, II, III (b) II, III
(c) I, III (d) I, II

109. NO_2 (brown colour gas) exists in equilibrium with N_2O_4 (colourless gas) as given by chemical equation

$$2NO_2 \rightleftharpoons N_2O_4$$

Mixture is slightly brown due to existence of NO_2. If pressure is increased

(a) colour intensity is increased
(b) colour intensity is decreased
(c) colour intensity first increases and then decreases
(d) no change in colour intensity

110. In the presence of a catalyst, what happens to the chemical equilibrium?

(a) Energy of activation of the forward and backward reactions are lowered by same amount
(b) Equilibrium amount is not disturbed
(c) Rates of forward and reverse reactions increase by the same factor
(d) All of the above

111. A system in equilibrium is described by the gaseous phase equation

$$\text{Heat} + SO_2Cl_2 \rightleftharpoons SO_2 + Cl_2$$

Which of the following statements is true?

(a) Addition of Cl_2 will shift the equilibrium towards right and temperature is raised
(b) Addition of Cl_2 will shift the equilibrium towards left and temperature is raised
(c) Withdrawl of Cl_2 and SO_2 will shift the equilibrium towards left and temperature is raised
(d) Withdrawl of SO_2 and Cl_2 will shift the equilibrium towards left and temperature is lowered

112. If reaction quotient $Q = 1$ for a reaction then

(a) $\Delta G = 0$ (b) $\Delta G° = 0$ (c) $\Delta G° = 0$ (d) $\Delta G = \Delta G°$

113. Study of the equilibrium of the type

$$CO_2(g) + H_2(g) \rightleftharpoons CO(g) + H_2O(g)$$

is concerned with the

(a) macroscopic behaviour of mixture
(b) microscopic behaviour of mixture
(c) Both (a) and (b)
(d) None of the above

114. Consider the following reactions

I. $2Cu^{2+} + 4I^- \longrightarrow Cu_2I_2 + I_2$

II. $Fe^{3+} + SCN^- \longrightarrow [Fe(SCN)]^{2+}$

III. $Cu^{2+} + 2Ag \longrightarrow Cu + 2Ag^+$

Reversible nature can be expected in

(a) I, II (b) II, III
(c) I, III (d) I, II, III

115. When a burner on a gas stove is operating at one setting, the size of the flame does not change.

$$CH_4 + 2O_2 \longrightarrow CO_2 + 2H_2O$$

It is due to

(a) that on equilibrium among CH_4, O_2, CO_2 and H_2O is established
(b) that products escape continuously as well as reactants are added continuously
(c) that CO_2, CH_4 and O_2 are gases
(d) that pressure is decreased

116. Select the incorrect statement.

(a) There is no change in the concentration of the reactants and products at equilibrium
(b) Equilibrium is always dynamic
(c) Equilibrium can be approached from either of the sides
(d) Catalyst can alter the state of equilibrium

117. For the following reaction, $A \longrightarrow B + C$, given that

(A)	$-\dfrac{d[A]}{dt}$
0.10 M	1×10^{-2} mol L^{-1} s^{-1}
0.20 M	2×10^{-2} mol L^{-1} s^{-1}

If this sets in equilibrium and $K_C = 10$ mol L^{-1}, then rate constant of the backward reaction is

(a) 1×10^{-2} L mol^{-1} s^{-1} (b) 1×10^{-3} L mol^{-1} s^{-1}
(c) 1×10^{2} L mol^{-1} s^{-1} (d) 1×10^{3} L mol^{-1} s^{-1}

118. The approach of the following equilibrium was observed kinetically from both directions

$$PtCl_4^{2-} + H_2O \rightleftharpoons Pt(H_2O)Cl_3^- + Cl^-$$

At 25°C, it is found

$$\frac{-d[PtCl_4^{2-}]}{dt} = (3.9\times 10^{-5}\ s^{-1})[PtCl_4^{2-}] - (2.1\times 10^{-3}\ L\ mol^{-1}\ s^{-1})[Pt(H_2O)Cl_3^-][Cl^-]$$

value of K_C when fourth Cl^- is complexed in the reaction,

$$Pt(H_2O)Cl_3^- + Cl^- \rightleftharpoons PtCl_4^{2-} + H_2O \text{ is}$$

(a) 1.85×10^{-2} mol L^{-1} (b) 1.86×2 mol L^{-1}
(c) 53.85 mol L^{-1} (d) 8.19×10^{-8} L mol^{-1} s^{-1}

119. For the reaction, $2A(g) + 2B(g) \rightleftharpoons 3C(g)$ at a certain temperature, K_C is 2.5×10^{-2}. For which conditions will the reaction proceed to the right at the same temperature?

	$[A]$	$[B]$	$[C]$
(a)	0.01 M	0.10 M	0.10 M
(b)	1.0 M	1.0 M	1.0 M
(c)	1.0 M	0.10 M	0.10 M
(d)	1.0 M	1.0 M	0.10 M

120. The equilibrium constant for the reaction

$$OCl^-(aq) + H_2O(l) \rightleftharpoons HOCl(aq) + OH^-(aq)$$

is 3.6×10^{-7}. Hence, K_a for HOCl is

(a) 2.8×10^{-8} (b) 3.6×10^{-7}
(c) 6.0×10^{-1} (d) 2.8×10^{6}

121. In which reaction will an increase in the volume of the container favour the formation of products?

(a) $C(s) + H_2O(g) \rightleftharpoons CO(g) + H_2(g)$
(b) $H_2(g) + I_2(g) \rightleftharpoons 2HI(g)$
(c) $4NH_3(g) + 5O_2(g) \rightleftharpoons 4NO(g) + 6H_2O(l)$
(d) $3O_2(g) \rightleftharpoons 2O_3(g)$

122. The reaction, $N_2(g) + 3H_2(g) \rightleftharpoons 2NH_3(g)$ is exothermic. Which of the following sets correctly states the changes in the equilibrium yield of NH_3 when the reaction conditions are altered as indicated ?

	Increase in temperature	Increase in pressure	Use of catalyst
(a)	more NH_3	less NH_3	no change
(b)	less NH_3	more v	no change
(c)	more NH_3	less NH_3	more NH_3
(d)	less NH_3	more NH_3	more NH_3

123. Starting with 2 moles of HI, at equilibrium total number of moles for the reaction $2HI \rightleftharpoons H_2 + I_2$, if α is degree of dissociation, is
(a) 2 (b) $2-\alpha$
(c) 1 (d) $1-\alpha$

124. If K_1 and K_2 are the respective equilibrium constants for the two reactions

I. $XeF_6(g) + H_2O(g) \rightleftharpoons XeOF_4(g) + 2HF(g)$

II. $XeO_4(g) + XeF_6(g) \rightleftharpoons XeOF_4(g) + XeO_3F_2(g)$

then equilibrium constant of the reaction

III. $XeO_4(g) + 2HF(g) \rightleftharpoons XeO_3F_2(g) + H_2O(g)$

will be
(a) $K_1/(K_2)^2$ (b) $K_1 \cdot K_2$ (c) K_1/K_2 (d) K_2/K_1

125. 1 mole of HI was heated in a sealed tube at 440°C till the equilibrium was reached. HI was found to be 22% decomposed. The equilibrium constant for dissociation reaction: $2HI \rightleftharpoons H_2 + I_2$ is
(a) 1.99 (b) 0.282
(c) 0.01988 (d) 0.0796

126. The equilibrium constant of a reaction, $A + B \rightleftharpoons C + D$ is 300. If the volume of reaction flask is trippled, the equilibrium constant is
(a) 300 (b) 600
(c) 900 (d) 100

127. 1 mole of CH_3COOH and 1 mole of C_2H_5OH reacts to produce $\frac{2}{3}$ mole of $CH_3COOC_2H_5$, the equilibrium constant is
(a) 2 (b) +2 (c) −4 (d) +4

128. $A + 2B \rightleftharpoons 2C + D$, initial concentration of B was 1.5 times that of A, but the equilibrium concentration of A and B are found to be equal. The equilibrium constant for the reaction is
(a) 4 (b) 8 (c) 12 (d) 16

129. In the following reaction,

$$A + B + Q \rightleftharpoons C + D$$

the temperature is increased then concentration of the product will
(a) remain constant
(b) decrease
(c) increase
(d) first increase then decrease

130. $2HCl(g) \rightleftharpoons H_2(g) + Cl_2(g)$
For the above reaction, the equilibrium constant is 1.0×10^{-5}. If the equilibrium concentrations of H_2 and Cl_2 are 1.2×10^{-3} M and 1.2×10^{-4} M, respectively, then the concentration of HCl is
(a) 12×10^{-4} M (b) 12×10^{-3} M
(c) 12×10^{-2} M (d) 12×10^{-1} M

131. For the reaction $A + B \rightleftharpoons 2C$, 2 moles of A and 3 moles of B are allowed to react. If the equilibrium constant is 4 at 400°C, then the moles of C at equilibrium
(a) 1 (b) 2.4
(c) 3.6 (d) 4

132. 5.1 g NH_4SH is introduced in 3.0 L evacuated flask at 327° C. 30% of the solid NH_4SH decomposed to NH_3 and H_2S as gases. The K_p of the reaction at 327° C is ($R = 0.082$ atm mol^{-1}K^{-1}, molar mass of S = 32 g mol^{-1}, molar mass of N = 14 g mol^{-1}) **[JEE Main 2019, Jan.]**
(a) 0.242×10^{-4} atm^2 (b) 0.242 atm^2
(c) 4.9×10^{-3} atm^2 (d) 1×10^{-4} atm^2

133. At high altitude the boiling point of water lowers because
(a) atmospheric pressure is high
(b) atmospheric pressure is low
(c) temperature is low
(d) None of the above

134. The equilibrium constant (K_c) for the following reaction at 298 K is

$$3Sn^{4+} + 2Cr \longrightarrow 3Sn^{2+} + 2Cr^{3+}$$

$(E^\circ_{cell} = 0.887\text{ V}, n = 6)$
(a) 1×10^{90} (b) 1×10^{19} (c) 1×10^{20} (d) 1×10^{39}

135. At 300 K,

$A \rightleftharpoons$ Product ; $\Delta G^\circ_T = -200$ kJ mol^{-1}

$B \rightleftharpoons$ Product ; $\Delta G^\circ_T = -100$ kJ mol^{-1}

Thus, ratio of equilibrium constant at 300 K is
(a) 2 (b) 100 (c) 0.5 (d) 0.01

136. A graph between $\log_e K$ and $\frac{1}{T}$ is of the type

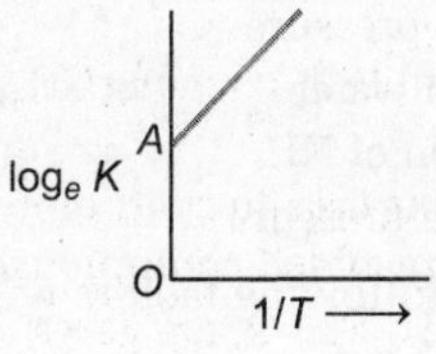

Thus,
(a) $\Delta H^\circ > 0$ and $\Delta A^\circ = \frac{\Delta S^\circ}{R}$
(b) $\Delta H^\circ < 0$ and $\Delta A^\circ = \frac{\Delta S^\circ}{R}$
(c) $\Delta H^\circ > 0$ and $\Delta A^\circ = -\frac{\Delta S^\circ}{R}$
(d) $\Delta H^\circ < 0$ and $\Delta A^\circ = -\frac{\Delta S^\circ}{R}$

137. For the equilibrium with equilibrium constant K_p and α

$$A(g) \rightleftharpoons 2B(g)$$

then, the fraction of $A(g)$ molecules dissociated

(a) $\alpha = \sqrt{\dfrac{K_p}{K_p + 4p}}$ (b) $\alpha = \sqrt{\dfrac{K_p + 4p}{K_p}}$

(c) $\alpha = \left(\dfrac{K_p}{K_p + 4p}\right)^2$ (d) $\alpha = \left(\dfrac{K_p}{K_p + 4p}\right)$

138. $Ca(HCO_3)_2(s)$ decomposes as

$$Ca(HCO_3)_2(s) \longrightarrow CaCO_3(s) + H_2O(g) + CO_2(g)$$

Total pressure at equilibrium is found to be 0.12 bar. Thus, K_p is

(a) 0.24 (b) 0.06 (c) 0.0036 (d) 0.0144

139. In the above equilibrium vessel also contained 0.20 bar $H_2O(g)$. Then partial pressure of $CO_2(g)$ is

(a) 0.20 bar (b) 0.018 bar
(c) 0.04 bar (d) 0.10 bar

140. The value of ΔH for the reaction,

$X_2(g) + 4Y_2(g) \rightleftharpoons 2XY_4(g)$ is less than zero.
Formation of $XY_4(g)$ will be favoured at

(a) high pressure and low temperature
(b) high temperature and high pressure
(c) low pressure and low temperature
(d) high temperature and low pressure

Objective Questions Type II [One or more than one correct option(s)]

In each of the questions below, four choices are given, of which one or more than one are correct.

1. For which of the following reactions is the equilibrium constant called an acidity constant?

(a) $2H_2O \rightleftharpoons H_3O^+ + OH^-$
(b) $H_2S + H_2O \rightleftharpoons H_3O^+ + HS^-$
(c) $HONO + H_2O \rightleftharpoons ONO^- + H_3O^+$
(d) $H_3O^+ + CH_3NH_2 \rightleftharpoons CH_3NH_3^+ + H_2O$

2. Which of the following statements about the reaction quotient Q, are correct?

(a) The reaction quotient Q, and the equilibrium constant always have the same numerical value
(b) Q may be $> < = K_{eq}$
(c) Q (numerical value) varies as reaction proceeds
(d) $Q = 1$ at equilibrium

3. Which of the following factors will increase solubility of $NH_3(g)$ in H_2O?

$$NH_3(g) + H_2O(aq) \rightleftharpoons NH_4OH(aq)$$

(a) Increase in pressure
(b) Addition of water
(c) Liquefaction of NH_3
(d) Decrease in pressure

4. Which of the following factors will affect solubility of CaO in H_2O?

(a) Pressure
(b) Temperature
(c) Addition of water
(d) Volume

5. For the following equilibrium

$$NH_4HS(s) \rightleftharpoons NH_3(g) + H_2S(g)$$

partial pressure of NH_3 will increase

(a) if NH_3 is added after equilibrium is established
(b) if H_2S is added after equilibrium is established
(c) temperature is increased
(d) volume of the flask is decreased

6. Formation of Y from X is through the graph. It can be concluded:

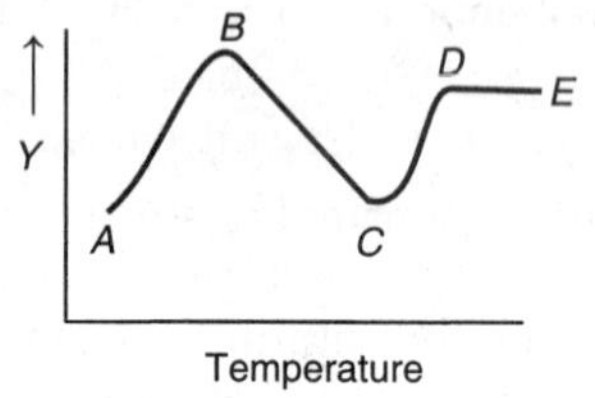

(a) reaction A to B is endothermic
(b) reaction A to B as well as C to D is exothermic
(c) reaction B to C is exothermic
(d) $\Delta H = 0$ for the stage D to E

7. For a reaction taking place in a container in equilibrium with its surroundings, the effect of temperature on its equilibrium constant K in terms of change in entropy is described by **[JEE Advanced 2017]**

(a) With increase in temperature, the value of K for endothermic reaction increases because unfavourable change in entropy of the surroundings decreases
(b) With increase in temperature, the value of K for exothermic reaction decreases because favourable change in entropy of the surrounding decreases
(c) With increase in temperature, the value of K for endothermic reaction increases because the entropy change of the system is negative
(d) With increase in temperature, the value of K for exothermic reaction decreases because the entropy change of the system is positive

8. Which are true statements for the following equilibrium?

$$H_2O(l) \rightleftharpoons H_2O(g)$$

(a) Increase in pressure will result in the formation of more liquid water
(b) Increase in pressure will increase boiling point
(c) Decrease in pressure will vaporise $H_2O(l)$ to a greater extent
(d) Increase in pressure will liquefy steam

9. Which is/are correct relation(s) for thermodynamic equilibrium constant?
(a) $\Delta G° = -2.303\, RT \log K$
(b) $\Delta G = \Delta G° + 2.303\, RT \log K$
(c) $E°_{cell} = \frac{0.0591}{n} \log K$
(d) $E = E° - \frac{0.0591}{n} \log K$

10. Which is/are correct relation(s) for equilibrium constant K?
(a) $\Delta G° = -2.303\, RT \log K$
(b) $E_{cell}° = \frac{2.303\, RT \log K}{nF}$
(c) $K = \frac{\Sigma[\text{product}]}{\Sigma[\text{reactant}]}$
(d) $\log K = \log A - \frac{\Delta H}{2.303\, RT}$

11. Volume of the flask in which species are transferred is double of the earlier flask. In which of the following cases, equilibrium constant is affected?
(a) $N_2(g) + 3H_2(g) \rightleftharpoons 2NH_3(g)$
(b) $N_2(g) + O_2(g) \rightleftharpoons 2NO(g)$
(c) $PCl_5(g) \rightleftharpoons PCl_3(g) + Cl_2(g)$
(d) $2NOBr(g) \rightleftharpoons N_2(g) + O_2(g)$

12. In the presence of a catalyst, what happens to the chemical equilibrium?
(a) Energy of activation of the forward and backwards reactions are lowered by same amount
(b) Equilibrium amount is not disturbed
(c) Rates of forward and reverse reactions increase by the same factor
(d) More product is formed

13. A system in equilibrium is described by the gaseous phase equation

$$\text{Heat} + SO_2Cl_2 \rightleftharpoons SO_2 + Cl_2$$

Which of the following statements is true?
(a) Addition of Cl_2 will shift the equilibrium towards right and temperature is raised
(b) Addition of Cl_2 will shift the equilibrium towards left and temperature is raised
(c) Withdrawl of Cl_2 and SO_2 will shift the equilibrium towards left and temperature is raised
(d) Withdrawl of SO_2 and Cl_2 will shift the equilibrium towards left and temperature is lowered

14. Study of the equilibrium of the type

$$CO_2(g) + H_2(g) \rightleftharpoons CO(g) + H_2O(g)$$

is concerned with the
(a) macroscopic behaviour of mixture
(b) microscopic behaviour of mixture
(c) gaseous phase reaction
(d) None of the above

15. Consider the following reactions
I. $2Cu^{2+} + 4I^- \longrightarrow Cu_2I_2 + I_2$
II. $Fe^{3+} + SCN^- \longrightarrow [Fe(SCN)]^{2+}$
III. $Cu^{2+} + 2Ag \longrightarrow Cu + 2Ag^+$
Reversible nature can be expected in
(a) I, II (b) II, III
(c) I, III (d) I, II, III

16. When a burner on a gas stove is operating at one setting, the size of the flame does not change.

$$CH_4 + 2O_2 \longrightarrow CO_2 + 2H_2O$$

It is due to
(a) that on equilibrium among CH_4, O_2, CO_2 and H_2O is established
(b) that products escape continuously as well as reactants are added continuously
(c) that CO_2, CH_4 and O_2 are gases
(d) that pressure is decreased

17. Select the correct statements.
(a) There is no change in the concentration of the reactants and products at equilibrium
(b) Equilibrium is always dynamic
(c) Equilibrium can be approached from either of the sides
(d) Catalyst can alter the state of equilibrium.

18. The equilibrium $2Cu^{I} \rightleftharpoons Cu^{0} + Cu^{II}$ in aqueous medium at 25°C shifts towards the left in the presence of **[IIT JEE 2011]**
(a) NO_3^- (b) Cl^- (c) SCN^- (d) CN^-

19. The thermal dissociation of equilibrium of $CaCO_3(s)$ is studied under different conditions.

$$CaCO_3(s) \rightleftharpoons CaO(s) + CO_2(g)$$

For this equilibrium, the correct statement(s) is are **[JEE Advanced 2013]**
(a) ΔH is dependent on T
(b) K is independent of the initial amount of $CaCO_3$
(c) K is dependent on the pressure of CO_2 at a given T
(d) ΔH is independent of the catalyst, if any

Numerical Value Questions

All these questions have a Numerical value as their answer, solve the questions and write your answer.

1. Consider the following heterogeneous equilibrium at 295 K

$$NH_4HS(s) \rightleftharpoons NH_3(g) + H_2S(g)$$

The partial pressure of each gas is 0.265 atm than K_p and K_C for the reaction are .... .

2. For the reaction $A(g) \rightleftharpoons B(g)$ at 495 K,

$$\Delta_r G° = -9.478 \text{ kJ mol}^{-1}.$$

If we start the reaction in a closed container at 495 K with 22 millimoles of A, the amount of B is the equilibrium mixture is .... millimoles.

$[R = 8.314 \text{ J mol}^{-1} \text{ K}^{-1}; \ln 10 = 2.303]$

[JEE Main 2021, March]

3. Variation of equilibrium constant K with temperature T is given by van't Hoff equation

$$\log K = \log A - \frac{\Delta H°}{2.303 RT}$$

A graph between $\log K$ and T^{-1} was a straight line as shown in the figure and having

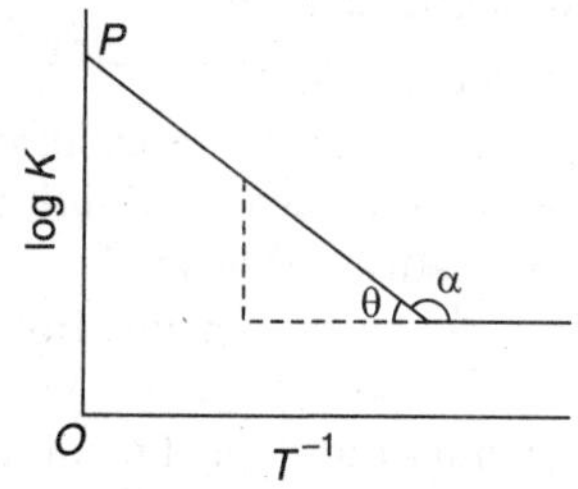

$$\theta = \tan^{-1}(0.5) \quad \text{and} \quad OP = 10.$$

Calculate equilibrium constant K at 298 K.

4. Consider the reaction, $N_2O_4(g) \rightleftharpoons 2NO_2(g)$.

The temperature at which $K_C = 20.4$ and $K_p = 600.1$, is ... K.

[Assume all gases are ideal and $R = 0.0831 \text{ L bar K}^{-1} \text{ mol}^{-1}$]

[JEE Main 2021, March]

5. $PCl_5(g)$ dissociates according to the reaction

$$PCl_5(g) \rightleftharpoons PCl_3(g) + Cl_2(g)$$

at 523 K, $K_p = 1.78$ atm. Compute the density of the equilibrium mixture in g dm^{-3} at 1 atm pressure.

6. The decomposition reaction

$2N_2O_5(g) \xrightarrow{\Delta} 2N_2O_4(g) + O_2(g)$ is started in a closed cylinder under isothermal isochoric condition at an initial pressure of 1 atm. After $Y \times 10^3$ s, the pressure inside the cylinder is found to be 1.45 atm. If the rate constant of the reaction is $5 \times 10^{-4} \text{ s}^{-1}$, assuming ideal gas behaviour, the value of Y is ....

7. At a certain temperature and a total pressure of 1.2 atm, the partial pressure of an equilibrium mixture

$$2A(g) \rightleftharpoons B(g)$$

are $p_A = 0.60$ atm and $p_B = 0.60$ atm

If the total pressure were increased to 1.5 atm, what would be the partial pressure of A and B at equilibrium?

8. A quantity of PCl_5 was heated in a 12 dm^3 flask at 523 K.

$$PCl_5(g) \rightleftharpoons PCl_3(g) + Cl_2(g)$$

At equilibrium, the flask contains 0.20 mol PCl_5 and 0.32 mol each of PCl_3 and Cl_2 than K_C and $\Delta G°$ are

9. At 300 K and 1 atm pressure, dinitrogen tetroxide is 20 per cent dissociated into nitrogen dioxide. The equilibrium constant and standard free energy change for the reaction

$$N_2O_4 \rightleftharpoons 2NO_2$$

at this temperature are ....

10. The equilibrium constant K_p for the reaction $A + B \rightleftharpoons C + D$ is 1.34 at 60°C and 6.64 at 100°C. The free energy change of this reaction at each temperature, and the mean heat content (enthalpy) change over the temperature range are ....

11. For the following reaction, the equilibrium constant K_C at 298 K is 1.6×10^{17}.

$$Fe^{2+}(aq) + S^{2-}(aq) \rightleftharpoons FeS(s)$$

When equal volumes of 0.06 M $Fe^{2+}(aq)$ and 0.2 M $S^{2-}(aq)$ solutions are mixed, the equilibrium concentration of $Fe^{2+}(aq)$ is found by $Y \times 10^{-17}$ M. The value of Y is .... **[JEE Advanced 2019]**

12. K_p for the reaction $PCl_5(g) \rightleftharpoons PCl_3(g) + Cl_2(g)$ at 250°C is 0.82.

Calculate the degree of dissociation a temperature under a total pressure of 5 atm.

13. Ammonia under a pressure of 13 atm. at 27°C is heated to 327°C is a closed vessel in the presence of catalyst. Under these conditions, NH_3 partially decomposes to H_2 and N_2. The vessel is such that the volume remains effectively constant, whereas the pressure increases to 50 atm. Calculate the % age of NH_3 usually decom posed.

Comprehension Based Questions

In these questions, a passage has been given followed by questions based on it. You have to answer the questions based on the passage given.

***Passage* 1** *Answer the questions based on the following experiment.*

Consider the reaction in aqueous solution of iron (III) and thiocyanate ($S\bar{C}N$) ions to give an equilibrium mixture that contains the Fe—N bonded red complex ion $[Fe(NCS)]^{2+}$

$$\underset{\text{Pale yellow}}{Fe^{3+}(aq)} + \underset{\text{Colourless}}{SCN^-(aq)} \rightleftharpoons \underset{\text{Red}}{[Fe(NCS)^{2+}](aq)}$$

1. What happens if we add aqueous $FeCl_3$?
(a) Red colour gets darker
(b) Solution becomes colourless
(c) Solution turns pale yellow
(d) Solution turns blue

2. What happens if we add oxalic acid?
(a) Solution turns yellow because of $Fe^{3+}(aq)$
(b) Solution turns yellow because of the formation of $[Fe(C_2O_4)_3^{3-}]$
(c) Fe^{3+} is precipitated as $Fe_2(C_2O_4)_3$
(d) Solution remains deep red

3. What happens if we add aqueous $HgCl_2$?
(a) Solution turns yellow because of $Fe^{3+}(aq)$
(b) Solution turns yellow because of formation of $[Hg(SCN)_4^{2-}]$
(c) Precipitate of $Hg(SCN)_2$ is formed
(d) No effect

***Passage* 2** *Study the following experiment and answer the question at the end of it.*

The complexation of Fe^{2+} with the chelating agent dipyridyl (abbreviated dipy) has been studied kinetically in both the forward and reverse direction. For the complexation reaction

$$Fe^{2+} + 3\,\text{dipy} \longrightarrow Fe(\text{dipy})_3^{2+}$$

The rate of the formation of the complex at 25°C is given by

$$\text{Rate} = (1.45 \times 10^{13}\ L^3\ mol^{-3}\ s^{-1})\ [Fe^{2+}]\ [\text{dipy}]^3$$

and for the reverse reaction, the rate of disappearance of the complex is

$$\text{Rate} = (1.22 \times 10^{-4}\ s^{-1})\ [Fe(\text{dipy})_3^{2+}]$$

1. What is the stability constant of the complex? (It is simply equilibrium constant at the stage when rate of forward reaction is equal to that of the backward reaction).
(a) 1.8×10^9 (b) 3.3×10^{-6}
(c) 8.4×10^{-18} (d) 1.2×10^{17}

***Passage* 3** *Questions given below are based on the following graphical study.*

The progress of the reaction $A \rightleftharpoons nB$ with time is shown.

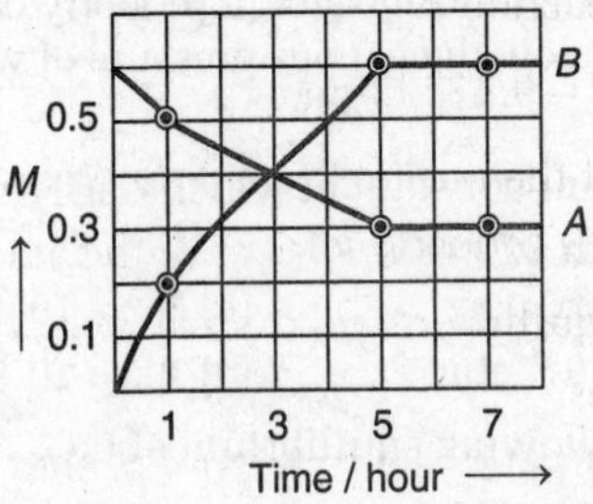

1. Stoichiometric coefficient of the product B is
(a) 1 (b) 2
(c) 3 (d) 4

2. Equilibrium constant K_C of the above graphical study is
(a) 2 (b) 0.83
(c) 0.5 (d) 1.2

3. Initial rate of conversion of A into products is
(a) $0.1\ M\ h^{-1}$
(b) $0.2\ M\ h^{-1}$
(c) $0.3\ M\ h^{-1}$
(d) $0.00\ M\ h^{-1}$

***Passage* 4** *Answer the question based on the following experiment.*

In the preparation of MgO, the reaction is

$$MgCO_3(s) \rightleftharpoons MgO(s) + CO_2(g)$$

Experiments carried out between 850°C and 950°C led to a set of K_p values fitting an empirical equation

$$\log K_p = 7.310 - \frac{8500}{T}$$

1. If the reaction is carried out in quiet air, what temperature would be predicted from the equation for the complete decomposition of the $MgCO_3$?
(a) 1163°C
(b) 890°C
(c) 1650°C
(d) 1373°C

***Passage* 5** *Read the following passage and answer the questions at the end of it.*

The moisture content of a gas is often expressed in terms of the **dew point** which is the temperature to which a gas must be cooled before it becomes saturated with water vapours. At this temperature, water or ice (depending on the temperature) will be deposited on a solid surface. Dew point of H_2O is 43°C at which vapour pressure of ice formed is 0.07 Torr.

$$CaCl_2 \cdot 2H_2O(s) \rightleftharpoons CaCl_2(s) + 2H_2O(g)$$

$CaCl_2(s)$ has its desiccating properties due to the formation of $CaCl_2 \cdot 2H_2O(s)$

A substance is the most effective drying agent, if it has the lowest vapour pressure of water in equilibrium with it.

A hydrated salt will lose water (a property called **efflorescent**) below the vapour pressure of water at that temperature.

1. Equilibrium constant at which $CaCl_2(s)$ has desiccating property is
   (a) 0.07 torr (b) 9.2×10^{-5} atm
   (c) 4.9×10^{-3} atm^2 (d) 8.5×10^{-9} atm^2
2. For the following equilibrium at 0°C,

$$Na_2SO_4 \cdot 10H_2O(s) \rightleftharpoons Na_2SO_4(s) + 10H_2O(g)$$
$$K_p = 4.08 \times 10^{-25}$$

   $Na_2SO_4 \cdot 10H_2O(s)$ will lose water at 0°C at
   (a) 4×10^{-3} atm (b) 4×10^{-4} atm
   (c) 4×10^{-2} atm (d) 4×10^{-1} atm

Passage 6 *Questions are based on the manufacture of* Na_2CO_3 *by Solvay process.*

In the manufacture of $Na_2CO_3(s)$ by Solvay process, $NaHCO_3(s)$ is decomposed by heating.

$$2NaHCO_3(s) \rightleftharpoons Na_2CO_3(s) + CO_2(g) + H_2O(g)$$
$$K_p = 0.23 \text{ at } 100°C \quad \Delta H° = +136 \text{ kJ}$$

1. If a sample of $NaHCO_3(s)$ is brought to a temperature of 100°C in a closed container total gas pressure at equilibrium is
   (a) 0.96 atm (b) 0.23 atm
   (c) 0.48 atm (d) 0.46 atm
2. A mixture of 1.00 mole each of $NaHCO_3(s)$ and $Na_2CO_3(s)$ is introduced into a 2.5 L flask in which $p_{CO_2} = 2.10$ atm and $p_{H_2O} = 0.94$ atm. When equilibrium is established at 100°C, then partial pressure of
   (a) $CO_2(g)$ and $H_2O(g)$ will be greater than their initial pressure
   (b) $CO_2(g)$ and $H_2O(g)$ will be less than their initial pressure
   (c) $CO_2(g)$ will be larger and that of $H_2O(g)$ will be less than their initial pressure
   (d) $H_2O(g)$ will be larger and that of $CO_2(g)$ will be less than their initial pressure

Passage 7 Following passage illustrates the role of O_2 supply to the tissues which in turn can affect body functioning. Answer the questions given below:

The combination of oxygen with haemoglobin (Hb) molecule, which carries oxygen through the blood, is a complex reaction but can be represented in a simplified way as

$$Hb(aq) + O_2(aq) \rightleftharpoons HbO_2(aq)$$

where HbO_2 is oxyhaemoglobin and is a source of oxygen for tissues.

Answer the following questions.

1. What happens if source of $O_2(aq)$ is cut off?
   (a) Equilibrium proceeds in backward side
   (b) Supply of oxyhaemoglobin is depleted
   (c) Both (a) and (b)
   (d) None of the above
2. What happens to the human body system at high altitude (where partial pressure of O_2 is only about 0.14 atm, compared with 0.2 atm at sea level)?
   I. Supply of oxyhaemoglobin is depleted.
   II. Supply of oxyhaemoglobin is increased.
   III. It can cause hypoxia.
   IV. Victim may slip into coma.
   Select the correct alternates.
   (a) I, II
   (b) I, II, III
   (c) II, III, IV
   (d) I, III, IV

Passage 8. Thermal decomposition of gaseous X_2 to gaseous X at 298 K takes place according to the following equation:

$$X_2(g) \rightleftharpoons 2X(g)$$

The standard reaction Gibbs energy, $\Delta_r G°$, of this reaction is positive. At the start of the reaction, there is one mole of X_2 and no X. As the reaction proceeds, the number of moles of X formed is given by β. Thus, $\beta_{equilibrium}$ is the number of moles of X formed at equilibrium. The reaction is carried out at a constant total pressure of 2 bar. Consider the gases to behave ideally. **[JEE Advanced 2016]**

1. The equilibrium constant K_p for this reaction at 298 K, in terms of $\beta_{equilibrium}$ is
   (a) $\dfrac{8\beta^2_{equilibrium}}{2-\beta_{equilibrium}}$ (b) $\dfrac{8\beta^2_{equilibrium}}{4-\beta^2_{equilibrium}}$
   (c) $\dfrac{4\beta^2_{equilibrium}}{2-\beta_{equilibrium}}$ (d) $\dfrac{4\beta^2_{equilibrium}}{4-\beta^2_{equilibrium}}$
2. The incorrect statement among the following for this reaction, is
   (a) Decrease in the total pressure will result in the formation of more moles of gaseous X
   (b) At the start of the reaction, dissociation of gaseous X_2 takes place spontaneously
   (c) $\beta_{equilibrium} = 0.7$ (d) $K_C < 1$

Matrix-Match Type

Given below are Matching Type Questions, with two columns (each having some items) each . Each item of Column I has to be matched with the items of Column II.

1. Match the chemical reaction in equilibrium (in Column I) with the pressure dependent of degree of dissociation of the reaction (in Column II).

Column I	Column II
A. $N_2(g) + 3H_2(g) \rightleftharpoons 2NH_3(g)$	1. $x \propto \sqrt{p}$
B. $2SO_2(g) + O_2(g) \rightleftharpoons 2SO_3(g)$	2. $x \propto \sqrt{\frac{1}{p}}$
C. $PCl_5(g) \rightleftharpoons PCl_3(g) + Cl_2(g)$	3. $x \propto p$
D. $N_2(g) + O_2(g) \rightleftharpoons 2NO\ (g)$	4. $x \times p^0$

2. Match the change of pressure and temperature in Column I with the direction in Column II.

Column I	Column II
A. p is increased	1. Solubility of KCl in H_2O is increased.
B. p is decreased	2. Solubility of gas in H_2O is increased.
C. T is increased	3. Dissociation of PCl_5 is increased.
D. T is decreased	4. Exothermic reaction is in forward side.

3. $\ln k = -\frac{\Delta H^\circ}{RT} + \frac{\Delta S^\circ}{R}$

Match the given function in Column I with its relation given in Column II.

Column I	Column II
A. ΔG°	1. $\Delta G^\circ + 2.303\,RT \log Q$
B. ΔH°	2. $\Delta H^\circ - T\Delta S^\circ$
C. ΔG	3. $-2.303\,RT \log K$
D. $-nFE^\circ_{cell}$	4. $\frac{2.303RT_1T_2}{(T_2 - T_1)} \log \frac{k_2}{k_1}$

4. Match chemical reactions in Column I with relation between K_p and K_c in Column II.

Column I	Column II
A. $N_2(g) + 3H_2(g) \rightleftharpoons 2NH_3(g)$	1. $K_p = K_C$
B. $2SO_2(g)+O_2(g) \rightleftharpoons 2SO_3(g)$	2. $K_p = K_C/(RT)^2$
C. $PCl_5(g) \rightleftharpoons PCl_3(g) + Cl_2(g)$	3. $K_p = K_C/(RT)$
D. $NH_4HS(g) \rightleftharpoons NH_3(g) + H_2S(g)$	4. $K_p = K_C(RT)^2$
E. $H_2(g) + I_2(g) \rightleftharpoons 2HI(g)$	5. $K_p = K_C(RT)$

5. Match the effect of variables (T, p, etc) in Column I on the equilibrium in Column II.

Column I	Column II
A. Increase in pressure, boiling point is elevated	1. $H_2O(l) \rightleftharpoons H_2O(g)$ $\Delta H^\circ > 0$
B. Increase in pressure more gas is liquefied	2. $CO_2(g) + H_2O(l) \rightleftharpoons H_2CO_3(aq)$ $\Delta H^\circ < 0$
C. Solubility of a gas increases with increase in pressure	3. $N_2(g) + 3H_2(g) \rightleftharpoons 2NH_3(g)$ $\Delta H^\circ < 0$
D. More product is formed on lowering temperature	4. $PCl_5(g) \rightleftharpoons PCl_3(g) + Cl_2(g)$ $\Delta H^\circ > 0$
E. More reactant is formed on lowering temperature.	5. $NH_3(g) + H_2O(l) \rightleftharpoons NH_4OH\ (aq)$ $\Delta H^\circ < 0$

6. Given,

$$AgCl(s) \rightleftharpoons Ag^+(aq) + Cl^-(aq), \quad K_1 = 1.8 \times 10^{-10}$$
$$Ag^+(aq) + 2NH_3(aq) \rightleftharpoons [Ag(NH_3)_2]^+(aq), \quad K_2 = 1.6 \times 10^7$$

Match the required values for Column I with their calculated values in Column II.

Column I	Column II
A. Equilibrium constant when AgCl(s) is dissolved in aqueous NH_3	1. 1.6×10^7
B. Solubilily of AgCl (s)	2. 2.88×10^{-3}
C. Formation constant of $[Ag(NH_3)_2]^+$	3. 1.34×10^{-5}
D. Ratio of complexed Ag^+ to uncomplexed Ag^+ when $(NH_3) = 0.01$ M	4. 1.6×10^3

7. In the following reaction, $A(g) \underset{k_2}{\overset{k_1}{\rightleftharpoons}} B(g)$

$$-\frac{d[A]}{dt} = k_1[A], \quad -\frac{d[B]}{dt} = k_2[B]$$
$$t_{50} = 10 \text{ min} \quad t_{50} = 1 \text{ min}$$

Match the parameters in Column I with their related values in Column II.

Column I	Column II
A. Rate constant k_1	1. 10
B. Rate constant k_2	2. 0.1
C. Equilibrium constant	3. 0.693
D. Time of 99.9% reaction of B	4. 0.0693

Single Integer Answer Questions

Answer of these questions is a single digit lying between 0 to 9.

1. Equilibrium $A \rightleftharpoons nB$ is represented graphically as

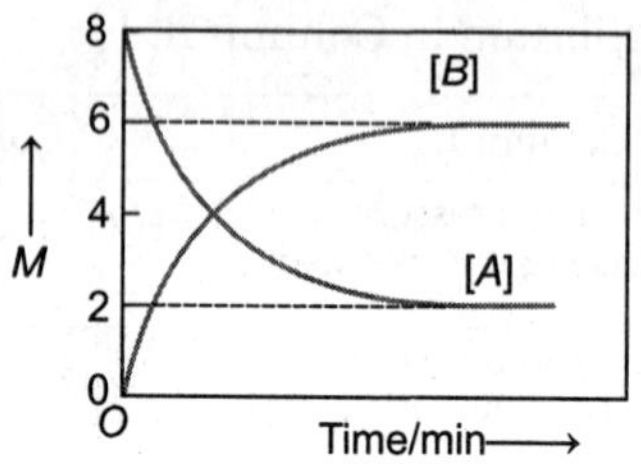

The value of n is ....

2. Following equilibrium is set up at 25°C after heating.

$Ca(HCO_3)_2(s) \rightleftharpoons CaO(s) + 2CO_2(g) + H_2O(l); K_p = 36$

The partial pressure of CO_2 is ....

3. Consider the following equilibrium

$$A + B \rightleftharpoons C + D$$

On taking 1 mole A and 1 mole B, 50% of A is converted into C. On taking $(1 + x)$ mole of A and 1 mole B, 75% of B is converted into C. The value of x is ....

4. In the following equilibrium in 5 L flask $K_C = 1$

$$2SO_2(g) + O_2(g) \rightleftharpoons 2SO_3(g);\ K_C = 1$$

At equilibrium, moles of SO_2 and SO_3 are equal. How many moles of O_2 are present in flask at equilibrium?

5. Consider the following equilibrium

$$2A + 5B \rightleftharpoons 3C + D$$

One starts with 3 moles of A and 4 moles of B. At equilibrium, moles of A and C are equal? How many moles of B are present at equilibrium?

6. In the following equilibrium, moles concentration were determined by $KMnO_4$ in acidic medium

$$2SO_2(g) + O_2(g) \rightleftharpoons 2SO_3(g)$$

Starting with 2 moles SO_2 and 1 mole O_2 in 1 L flask, mixture required 0.4 mole of $KMnO_4$ at equilibrium. The value of equilibrium constant is

7. For isomerisation of

$$n\text{-butane} \rightleftharpoons \text{Isobutane}$$

$$\log_e K = 4.0 - \frac{2000}{T}$$

What is the value of $\Delta S°$ at 400 K (in cals)?

8. For the equilibrium

$2A \rightleftharpoons A_2 \qquad K_{eq} = 16$

and for, $A \rightleftharpoons \frac{1}{2}A_2 \qquad K_{eq} = K_1$

The value of K_1 is ....

9. Starting with 1 mole H_2 and 1 mole I_2, 1 mole of HI is formed at equilibrium. How many moles of $Na_2S_2O_3$ are required to decolourise unreacted I_2?

10. For the following equilibrium,

$$PCl_5(g) \rightleftharpoons PCl_3(g) + Cl_2(g)$$

4 moles of PCl_5 are placed in 5 L flask. At a given temperature, 50% of PCl_5 is dissociated. What is the partial pressure of Cl_2 if equilibrium pressure is 18 atm?

11. Starting with 5 moles each of N_2 and H_2, 2 moles of NH_3 are formed at equilibrium.

$$N_2(g) + 3H_2(g) \rightleftharpoons 2NH_3(g)$$

Determine the total moles of reactants and products.

Answers

Objective Questions Type I [Only one correct option]

1. (c)	2. (b)	3. (c)	4. (a)	5. (b)	6. (b)	7. (d)	8. (a)	9. (d)	10. (b)
11. (c)	12. (b)	13. (c)	14. (d)	15. (d)	16. (b)	17. (c)	18. (c)	19. (b)	20. (a)
21. (a)	22. (b)	23. (b)	24. (c)	25. (b)	26. (b)	27. (a)	28. (a)	29. (d)	30. (c)
31. (b)	32. (a)	33. (c)	34. (a)	35. (c)	36. (b)	37. (d)	38. (b)	39. (b)	40. (d)
41. (c)	42. (d)	43. (b)	44. (a)	45. (b)	46. (b)	47. (c)	48. (c)	49. (d)	50. (c)
51. (a)	52. (a)	53. (c)	54. (d)	55. (b)	56. (c)	57. (a)	58. (c)	59. (c)	60. (b)
61. (d)	62. (c)	63. (d)	64. (b)	65. (c)	66. (d)	67. (d)	68. (d)	69. (d)	70. (c)
71. (a)	72. (b)	73. (d)	74. (b)	75. (a)	76. (b)	77. (c)	78. (a)	79. (b)	80. (d)
81. (d)	82. (b)	83. (d)	84. (a)	85. (a)	86. (c)	87. (a)	88. (d)	89. (c)	90. (c)
91. (b)	92. (c)	93. (a)	94. (a)	95. (a)	96. (b)	97. (d)	98. (a)	99. (c)	100. (a)
101. (a)	102. (b)	103. (d)	104. (d)	105. (c)	106. (c)	107. (c)	108. (d)	109 (b)	110. (d)
111. (b)	112. (d)	113. (a)	114. (b)	115. (b)	116. (a)	117. (a)	118. (c)	119 (d)	120. (a)
121. (a)	122. (b)	123. (a)	124. (d)	125. (c)	126. (a)	127. (d)	128. (a)	129. (c)	130. (c)
131. (b)	132. (b)	133. (b)	134. (a)	135. (b)	136. (b)	137. (a)	138. (c)	139. (b)	140. (a)

Objective Questions Type II [One or more than one correct option(s)]

1. (b, c) 2. (b, c) 3. (a, b) 4. (b, c) 5. (a, c, d)
6. (a, c, d) 7. (a, b) 8. (a, b, c, d) 9. (a, c) 10. (a, b, d)
11. (a, c) 12. (a, b, c) 13. (b) 14. (a, c) 15. (b)
16. (b) 17. (a, b, c) 18. (b, c, d) 19. (a, b, c, d)

Numerical Value Questions

1. 1.2×10^{-4} 2. 20 3. $K = 9.96\times 10^{9}$ 4. 354 5. 2.7 g dm^{-3} 6. 2.3

7. $p_B = \frac{1.5x}{(1-x)} = 0.81$ atm 8. 13.7187 kJ mol^{-1} 9. 4.470 kJ mol^{-1} 10. 1.24 kJ 11. 8.9

12. 0.375 13. 66.7%

Comprehension Based Questions

Passage 1 – 1. (b) 2. (b) 3. (b) Passage 2 – 1. (d)
Passage 3 – 1. (b) 2. (d) 3. (a) Passage 4 – 1. (b) Passage 5 – 1. (d) 2. (a)
Passage 6 – 1. (a) 2. (b) Passage 7 – 1. (c) 2. (d) Passage 8 – 1. (b) 2. (c)

Matrix-Match Type

1. A→(3); B→(1); C→(2); D→(4)
2. A→(2); B→(3); C→(1); D→(4)
3. A→(2); B→(4); C→(1); D→(3)
4. A→(2); B→(3); C→(5); D→(4); E→(1)
5. A→(1); B→(1); C→(2,5); D→(2,3,5); E→(1,4)
6. A→(2); B→(3); C→(1); D→(4)
7. A→(3); B→(1); C→(1); D→(4)

Single Integer Answer Questions

1. (1) 2. (6) 3. (2) 4. (5) 5. (1) 6. (2) 7. (8) 8. (4) 9. (1) 10. (6)
11. (8)

Solutions

Objective Questions Type I [Only one correct option]

1. (*c*) $K_p = p_{C_{10}H_8(g)} = 0.10 \text{ mm} = \frac{0.10}{760} \text{ atm} = 1.32 \times 10^{-4}$

$$K_C = \frac{K_p}{(RT)^{\Delta n}} = \frac{K_p}{RT} = \frac{1.32 \times 10^{-4}}{0.0821 \times 300} = 5.36 \times 10^{-6}$$

2. (*b*)

$$K_p = K_C (RT)^{\Delta n}$$
$$K_p = K_C (RT)$$
$$K_p = K_C \quad \text{when} \quad (RT) = 1$$
$$T = \frac{1}{R} = \frac{1}{0.0821} = 12.18$$

4. (*a*) $K_p = K_x (p)^{\Delta n_g}$

K_x is the equilibrium constant when concentrations are taken in terms of mole fractions.

$$K_p = K_x (p)$$
$$K_p = K_x \quad \text{when} \quad p = 1 \text{ atm}$$

9. (*d*)

$$\begin{array}{lcccc} & A(g) + & B(g) \rightleftharpoons & C(g) + & D(g) \\ t = 0 & 1 & 1 & 0 & 0 \\ \text{At equil.} & (1-x) & (1-x) & x & x \end{array}$$

$$x = 0.5$$

$\therefore$ $$K_C = \frac{[C][D]}{[A][B]} = 1$$

$$\begin{array}{cccc} A(g) + & B(g) \rightleftharpoons & C(g) + & D(g) \\ 1 & 2 & 0 & 0 \\ (1-y) & (2-y) & y & y \end{array}$$

$\therefore$ $$K_C = 1 = \frac{y^2}{(1-y)(2-y)}$$

$\therefore$ $$y = \frac{2}{3}$$

$\therefore$ % of B converted into products $= \frac{y}{2} \times 100 = 33.33\%$

11. (*c*) I. $$(K_p)_I = p_{CO_2} = 2$$

II. $$(K_p)_{II} = \frac{p_{CO}^2}{p_{CO_2}} = 6$$

$$CaCO_3(s) + C(s) \rightleftharpoons CaO(s) + 2CO(g)$$
$$(K_p)_{III} = p_{CO}^2 = (K_p)_1 (K_p)_2 = 12$$

(Only gaseous species are taken in the expression of K_p.)

12. (*b*) (I) – (II) gives (III)

$\therefore$ $$K_3 = \frac{K_1}{K_2} = 1 \times 10^{-14}$$

13. (*c*)

$$M + Cl \longrightarrow MCl$$
$$MCl + Cl \longrightarrow MCl_2$$
$$MCl_2 + Cl \longrightarrow MCl_3$$
$$\overline{M + 3\,Cl \longrightarrow MCl_3}$$

$$\beta_1 = \frac{[MCl]}{[M][Cl]}; \quad \beta_2 = \frac{[MCl_2]}{[MCl][Cl]}; \quad \beta_3 = \frac{[MCl_3]}{[MCl_2][Cl]}$$

$\therefore$ $$K = \frac{[MCl_3]}{[M][Cl]^3} = \beta_1 \beta_2 \beta_3$$

$$\log K = \log \beta_1 + \log \beta_2 + \log \beta_3$$

16. (*b*) $NH_4OH + H_3O^+ \rightleftharpoons NH_4^+ + 2H_2O \quad K_1' = \frac{1}{K_1} = \frac{10^{10}}{5.56}$

$$2H_2O \rightleftharpoons H_3O^+ + OH^- \quad K_2 = 1 \times 10^{-14}$$

$\therefore$ $$NH_4OH \rightleftharpoons NH_4^+ + OH^- \quad K_3 = \frac{K_2}{K_1} = 1.8 \times 10^{-5}$$

17. (*c*) Only gaseous reactants are considered.

$$\underset{}{NH_2COONH_4(s)} \rightleftharpoons \underset{2x}{2NH_3(g)} + \underset{x}{CO_2(g)}$$

$\therefore$ $$p_{CO_2} = \frac{p_{\text{total}}}{3} = 1 \text{ atm}$$

$$p_{NH_3} = \frac{2p_{\text{total}}}{3} = 2 \text{ atm}$$

$\therefore$ $$K_p = p_{NH_3}^2 \cdot p_{CO_2} = 4 \text{ atm}^3$$

18. (*c*) T_{50} of first order reaction $= \frac{0.693}{k}$

$\therefore$ $$T_{50} \propto \frac{1}{k}$$

$\therefore$ $$K_C = \frac{k_1}{k_2} = \frac{(T_{50})_2}{(T_{50})_1} = \frac{1}{10} = 0.1$$

20. (*a*) $$K_C = \frac{[H_2]^3}{[H_2O]^3} = 27$$

$\therefore$ $$\frac{[H_2]}{[H_2O]} = (27)^{1/3} = 3$$

21. (*a*) Since, K_C is very small, hence $[H_2]$ is predominant.

22. (*b*)

Equilibrium	K_c
I	10^{-2}
II	1
III	10^4

Thus, extent of reaction is I < II < III.

23. (*b*) Since, $K_C > 1$

hence $k_f > k_b$

25. (*b*) I. $$Q = \frac{[NO_2]^2}{[N_2O_4]}$$

Since, $[NO_2]$ is maximum and $[N_2O_4]$ is minimum at point *A*, hence *Q* is minimum at this point. Thus, false.

II. $$Q = \frac{(0.1)^2}{(0.1)} = 0.1 < K_C$$

Thus, reaction proceeds left to right.

Thus, true

III. $K_C = Q$ when equilibrium is reached at point D or F

Thus, true

26. (*b*) $K_C = \dfrac{k_f}{k_b} = \dfrac{2.6 \times 10^3}{4.1} = 6.34 \times 10^2$

and $Q = \dfrac{[NO_2]^2}{[NO]^2\,[O_2]} = \dfrac{(0.1/1)^2}{[0.01]^2\,[0.01]} = 10^4$

$$Q >> K_C$$

Thus, reaction shifts in backward direction so that Q (reaction quotient) approaches K_C.

28. (*a*)

$$N_2O_4(g) \rightleftharpoons 2NO_2(g)$$

	N_2O_4	$2NO_2$
	1	0
	$(1-x)$	$2x$

Total moles $= 1 - x + 2x = (1 + x)$

Since, $pV = nRT$

$\therefore$ $V \propto n$

$$\% \text{ of } NO_2 = \left(\frac{2x}{1+x}\right) \times 100 = 50$$

$\therefore$ $x = \dfrac{1}{3}$

$$(1+x) = \frac{D}{d} = \frac{\text{theoretical VD}}{\text{experimental VD}}$$

$$(1+x) = \frac{4}{3} = \frac{46}{d}$$

$\therefore$ $d = \dfrac{46 \times 3}{4} = 34.5$

30. (*c*) $x = \dfrac{D-d}{d} = \dfrac{D}{d} - 1$

$\therefore$ $(1+x) = \dfrac{D}{d}$

As $\dfrac{D}{d}$ increases (due to decrease in d)

$(1+x)$ remains constant

31. (*b*) At $x = 0$, $\dfrac{D}{d} = 1$

and if x increases, $\dfrac{D}{d}$ also increases

32. (*a*) From thermodynamics,

$$\ln k = \frac{-\Delta H^\circ}{RT} + \frac{\Delta S^\circ}{R} \quad \ldots\text{(i)}$$

Mathematically, the equation of straight line is

$$y = c + mx \quad \ldots\text{(ii)}$$

After comparing Eq. (ii) with (i) we get,

slope $= \dfrac{-\Delta H^\circ}{R}$ and intercept $= \dfrac{\Delta S^\circ}{R}$

Now, we know for exothermic reaction ΔH is negative (–)ve.

But here, Slope $= \dfrac{-\Delta H^\circ}{R}$ is positive

So, lines A and B in the graph represent temperature dependence of equilibrium constant K for an exothermic reaction as shown below

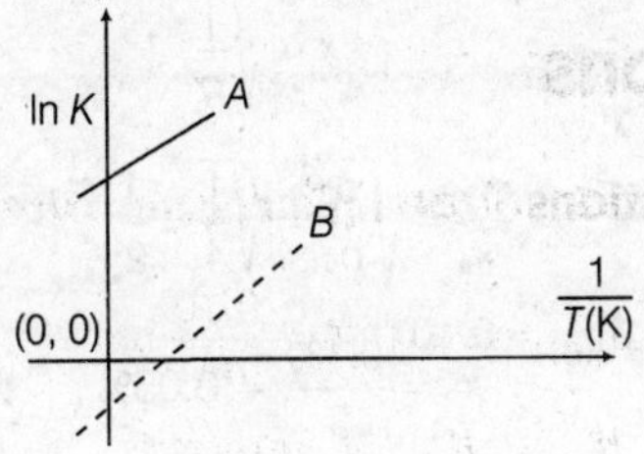

33. (*c*) $\dfrac{D}{d} = 1.5 = 1 + x$

$\therefore$ $x = 0.5$

	N_2O_4	$\rightleftharpoons$ $2NO_2$
Initially	1	0
equilibrium	$(1-x)$	$2x$

Total moles at equilibrium $= 1 - x + 2x = 1 + x$

$$\% \text{ of } NO_2 = \frac{2x \times 100}{1+x} = \frac{2 \times 0.5 \times 100}{1.5} = 66.67\%$$

34. (*a*) $2A(g) \rightleftharpoons A_2(g)$

	$2A(g)$	$A_2(g)$
Initially	1	0
equilbrium	$(1-2x)$	x

Total moles at equilibrium $= (1 - 2x + x) = (1 - x)$

$\therefore$ van't Hoff factor $(i) = 1 - x = 0.80$

$\therefore$ $x = 0.2$

Mole fraction or volume fraction of $A_2(g)$ in mixture

$$= \frac{x}{1-x} = \frac{0.2}{0.8} = \frac{1}{4}$$

$\therefore$ $\% = 25\%$

35. (*c*)

$$PCl_5 \rightleftharpoons PCl_3 + Cl_2$$

PCl_5	PCl_3	Cl_2
2	0	0
$(2-x)$	x	x

$x = 2 \times 0.8 = 1.6$

$\therefore$ Total moles at equilibrium $= 2 + x = 3.6$

$$p_{equal} = \frac{n}{V}RT = \frac{3.6}{5} \times 0.0821 \times 350 = 20.7 \text{ atm}$$

37. (*d*) $PCl_5(g) \rightleftharpoons PCl_3(g) + Cl_2(g)$

$$\Delta n_g = 1$$

$$x \text{ (degree of dissociation)} \propto \left(\frac{1}{p}\right)^{\Delta n_g/2}$$

$$x \propto \left(\frac{1}{p}\right)^{1/2}$$

or $K_p = \dfrac{px^2}{1-x^2} \approx px^2$

$$x^2 = \frac{K_p}{p}$$

$\therefore$ $x \propto \sqrt{\dfrac{1}{p}}$

38. (*b*) $H_2(g) \rightleftharpoons 2H(g)$

$$\Delta n_g = +1$$

$\therefore \quad x \propto \sqrt{\frac{1}{p}}$

$\therefore \quad \frac{x_2}{x_1} = \sqrt{\frac{p_1}{p_2}} = \sqrt{\frac{1}{4}} = \frac{1}{2}$

$x_2 = \frac{0.1\%}{2} = 0.05\%$

39. (*b*) $CO(g) + H_2O(g) \rightleftharpoons CO_2(g) + H_2(g)$

Initially	1	1	1	1
equilibrium	$(1-x)$	$(1-x)$	$(1+x)$	$(1+x)$

$K_C = \frac{[CO_2][H_2]}{[CO][H_2O]}$

$9 = \frac{(1+x)^2}{(1-x)^2}$

$\therefore \quad \frac{1+x}{1-x} = 3$

$x = 0.5$

$\therefore \quad [CO_2] = 1 + x = 1 + 0.5 = 1.5 \text{ mol}$

40. (*d*) $CH_3COOH + C_2H_5OH \rightleftharpoons CH_3COOC_2H_5 + H_2O$

Case I Initially	60 g = 1 mol	46 g = 1 mol	0	0
Equilibrium	$(1-x)$	$(1-x)$	x	x

$x = 44\text{g} = 0.5 \text{ mol}$

Case II Initially	120 g = 2 mol	40 g = 1 mol	0 0	0 0
Equilibrium	$(2-y)$	$(1-y)$	y	y

Since, temperature is constant, K_C remains same in both cases

$\therefore \quad K_C = \frac{[CH_3COOC_2H_5][H_2O]}{[CH_3COOH][C_2H_5OH]}$

$$= \frac{\frac{x}{5} \times \frac{x}{5}}{\left(\frac{1-x}{5}\right)\left(\frac{1-x}{5}\right)} = \frac{\frac{y}{5} \times \frac{y}{5}}{\left(\frac{2-y}{5}\right)\left(\frac{1-y}{5}\right)}$$

$$\frac{x^2}{(1-x)^2} = \frac{y^2}{(2-y)(1-y)}$$

$$\frac{(0.5)^2}{(0.5)^2} = \frac{y^2}{(2-y)(1-y)}$$

$$y = \frac{2}{3} \text{ mol} = \frac{2}{3} \times 88 \text{ g} = 58.66 \text{ g}$$

41. (*c*) $2SO_2(g) + O_2(g) \rightleftharpoons 2SO_3(g)$

Initially	2	1	0
Equilibrium	$(2-2x)$	$(1-x)$	$2x$

Total moles at equilibrium $= (3-x)$

$\frac{p_2}{p_1} = \frac{n_2}{n_1} \quad \left[\begin{array}{l} pV = nRT \\ p \propto n \text{ under given condition} \end{array}\right]$

$\frac{2.5}{3} = \frac{3-x}{3}$

$\therefore \quad x = 0.5$

$$K_p = \frac{p^2_{SO_3}}{p^2_{SO_2} p_{O_2}} = \frac{\left[2.5\left(\frac{2x}{3-x}\right)\right]^2}{\left[2.5\left(\frac{2-2x}{3-x}\right)\right]^2\left[2.5\left(\frac{1-x}{3-x}\right)\right]}$$

$$K_p = \frac{(3-x)x^2}{(1-x)^3 2.5} = \frac{(2.5)(0.5)^2}{(0.5)^3(2.5)} = 2 \text{ atm}^{-1}$$

43. (*b*) H_3BO_3 + glycerine $\rightleftharpoons$ (H_3BO_3. glycerine)

$[H_3BO_3]$ taken = 0.1 M

60% of $[H_3BO_3]$ is converted into product

$\therefore \quad [H_3BO_3]_{equil} = 0.1 - 0.1 \times 0.6 = 0.04 \text{ M}$

and $\quad [H_3BO_3 \cdot \text{glycerine}] = 0.1 \times 0.6 = 0.06 \text{ M}$

$$K = 0.90 = \frac{[H_3BO_3 \cdot \text{glycerine}]}{[H_3BO_3][\text{glycerine}]} = \frac{0.06}{0.04 \times [\text{glycerine}]}$$

$[\text{glycerine}] = 1.67 \text{ M}$

44. (*a*) $PCl_5(g) \rightleftharpoons PCl_3(g) + Cl_2(g)$

Initially	1	0	0
Equilibrium	$(1-x)$	x	x

$x = 0.5$

Total moles at equilibrium $= 1 + x = 1.5$ mol

Pressure due to 1 mole of PCl_5 = 5 atm

$\therefore$ Equilibrium pressure due to 1.5 moles of gaseous species = 7.5 atm

$(p \propto n)$

$\therefore \quad K_p = \frac{p_{eq}\, x^2}{(1-x^2)} = \frac{7.5 \times (0.5)^2}{[1-(0.5)^2]} = 2.5$

45. (*b*) $N_2O_4(g) \rightleftharpoons 2NO_2(g)$

$Q = \frac{[NO_2]^2}{[N_2O_4]} = 9 > K_C$

Thus, equilibrium is displaced in backward side.

$2NO_2 \rightleftharpoons N_2O_4(g)$

3	1
$(3-2x)$	$(1+x)$

$K_C' = \frac{1}{K_C} = \frac{1}{0.67} = \frac{(1+x)}{(3-2x)^2} = 1.5$

Only permissible value of x that satisfies above equation is $x = 0.5$

Thus, NO_2 at equilibrium $= 3 - 2x = 2$ mol

46. (*b*) $\log K_p = 8 - \frac{6400}{T} = 8 - \frac{6400}{800} = 0$

$\therefore \quad K_p = 1$

47. (*c*) $NH_2CO_2NH_4(s) \rightleftharpoons 2NH_3(g) + CO_2(g)$

$2x \qquad x$

$p_{NH_3} = \frac{2p}{3}, \quad p_{CO_2} = \frac{p}{3}$

where, p is the total pressure at equilibrium

$K_p = p^2_{NH_3} \cdot p_{CO_2} = \frac{4p^3}{27} = 0.5$

$\therefore \quad p = 1.5 \text{ atm}$

$\therefore \quad p_{NH_3} = 1 \text{ atm}, \quad p_{CO_2} = 0.5 \text{ atm}$

Note Only gaseous species have been taken in the equation for K_p.

48. (*c*) I. $CaCO_3(s) \rightleftharpoons CaO(s) + CO_2(g)$
$\qquad\qquad\qquad\qquad\qquad\qquad x$

$$p_{CO_2} = p\frac{x}{x} = p$$

$\therefore$ $K_p = p = K_1$

$\therefore$ $K_1 = 1$

II. $NH_4HS(s) \rightleftharpoons NH_3(g) + H_2S(g)$
$\qquad\qquad\qquad\qquad x \qquad x$

$$p_{NH_3} = \frac{px}{2x} = \frac{p}{2}$$

$$p_{H_2S} = \frac{px}{2x} = \frac{p}{2}$$

$\therefore$ $K_p = p_{NH_3} \cdot p_{H_2S} = \frac{p^2}{4} = K_2$

$\therefore$ $K_2 = 0.25$

III. $NH_2CO_2NH_4(s) \rightleftharpoons 2NH_3(g) + CO_2(g)$
$\qquad\qquad\qquad\qquad 2x \qquad x$

$$p_{NH_3} = \frac{2xp}{3x} = \frac{2}{3}p$$

$$p_{H_2S} = \frac{xp}{3x} = \frac{p}{3}$$

$$K_p = p_{NH_3}^2 p_{H_2S} = \frac{4p^3}{27} = K_3$$

$\therefore$ $K_3 = 0.148$

Thus, $K_3 < K_2 < K_1$

49. (*d*) Which removes reactants

$$Ag^+ + SCN^- \longrightarrow AgCNS\downarrow$$

$$Hg^{2+} + SCN^- \longrightarrow Hg(CNS)_2\downarrow$$

$$Fe^{3+} + 3C_2O_4^{2-} \longrightarrow \underset{\text{Soluble}}{[Fe(C_2O_4)_3]^{3-}}$$

58. (*c*) $x \propto \left(\frac{1}{p}\right)^{\Delta n/2}$

Δn = moles of gaseous products – moles of gaseous reactants

$= -1$

$\therefore$ $x \propto \sqrt{p}$

60. (*b*) $\log_{10} K = \log_{10} A - \frac{\Delta H°}{2.303\,RT}$

$$\text{Slope} = -\frac{\Delta H°}{2.303\,R} = \tan 45° = 1$$

$\therefore$ $\Delta H° = -2.303\,R \times \text{slope} = -4.606$ cal

66. (*d*)

	$2NH_3$	$\rightleftharpoons$	$N_2(g)$	+	$3H_2(g)$
Initially	a		0		0
equilibrium	$(a-2x)$		x		$3x$

$x = 0.30$

$\therefore$ $a - 2x = 0.30$

$\therefore$ $a = 0.90$

Thus, initial moles of NH_3 = 0.90 mol

$$K_C = \frac{[N_2][H_2]^3}{[NH_3]^2} = \frac{\left(\frac{0.30}{0.50}\right)\left(\frac{0.90}{0.50}\right)^3}{\left(\frac{0.30}{0.50}\right)^2} = 9.72$$

Thus, K_C for NH_3 formation $= \frac{1}{9.72} = 0.103$

67. (*d*) The explanation of given statements are as follows:

(a) For the given equilibrium, ΔH is negative, so the equilibrium constant will decrease with increase in temperature and the equilibrium will shift in the backward direction.

Thus, statement (a) is correct.

(b) When inert gas is added at constant volume and constant temperature, an equilibrium remains undisturbed.

Thus, statement (b) is correct.

(c) For the equilibrium,

$\Delta n_g = 2 - (2+1) = -1$, i.e. (–ve)

So, increase in pressure will shift the equilibrium in the forward direction.

Thus, statement (c) is correct.

(d) The reaction takes place in the presence of a catalyst which is $V_2O_5(s)$ in contact process or $NO(g)$ in chamber process.

Thus, statement (d) is incorrect.

72. (*b*) $\Delta G = -2.303\,RT \log K$

$$-16.5 = -2.303 \times 8.3143 \times 10^{-3} \times 298 \log K$$

$\therefore$ $\log K = 2.89$

$\therefore$ $K = 7.80 \times 10^2$

73. (*d*) The equilibrium reaction for the dissociation of two solids is given as:

$$A(s) \rightleftharpoons B(g) + C(g)$$

At equilibrium $\qquad p_1 \qquad p_1 + p_2$

$$K_{p_1} = x = p_B \cdot p_C = p_1(p_1 + p_2) \quad \text{...(i)}$$

Similarly, $D(s) \rightleftharpoons C(g) + E(g)$

At equilibrium $\qquad p_1 + p_2 \cdot p_2$

$$K_{p_2} = y = p_C \cdot p_E = (p_1 + p_2)p_2 \quad \text{...(ii)}$$

On adding Eq. (i) and (ii), we get.

$$K_{p_1} + K_{p_2} = x + y = p_1(p_1 + p_2) + p_2(p_1 + p_2)$$

$$= (p_1 + p_2)^2$$

or $\sqrt{x+y} = p_1 + p_2$ ...(iii)

Now, total pressure is given as

$$p_T = p_B + p_C + p_E$$

$$= p_1 + (p_1 + p_2) + p_2$$

$$= 2(p_1 + p_2) \quad \text{...(iv)}$$

On substituting the value of $p_1 + p_2$ from Eq. (iii) to Eq. (iv), we get

$$p_T = 2\sqrt{x+y}$$

74. (*b*) $N_2(g) + 3H_2(g) \rightleftharpoons 2NH_3(g)$

At equilibrium: $p_{N_2} = P,\quad p_{H_2} = 3P,\quad p_{NH_3} = 2P$

$\Rightarrow\quad p_{(total)} = p_{N_2} + p_{H_2} + p_{NH_3} \simeq p_{N_2} + p_{H_2}$

$[\because P_{(total)} >> p_{NH_3}]$

$= p + 3p = 4p$

Now, $$K_p = \frac{p^2_{NH_3}}{p_{N_2} \times p^3_{H_2}} = \frac{p^2_{NH_3}}{p \times (3p)^3}$$

$$= \frac{p^2_{NH_3}}{27 \times p^4} = \frac{p^2_{NH_3}}{27 \times \left(\frac{P}{4}\right)^4} \qquad [\because P = 4p]$$

$$K_p = \frac{p^2_{NH_3} \times 4^4}{3^2 \times 3 \times P^4}$$

$$\Rightarrow\quad p^2_{NH_3} = \frac{3^2 \times 3 \times P^4 \times K_p}{4^4}$$

$$\Rightarrow\quad p_{NH_3} = \frac{3 \times 3^{1/2} \times P^2 \times K_p^{1/2}}{4^2} = \frac{3^{3/2} \times P^2 \times K_p^{1/2}}{16}$$

75. (*a*) van't Hoff equation giving variation of equilibrium constant, K with temperature T is

$$\log_e K = -\frac{\Delta H°}{RT} + \frac{\Delta S°}{R}$$

Given, $$\log_e K = -\frac{2000}{T} + 4.0$$

$\therefore$ $$\frac{\Delta S°}{R} = 4$$

$\therefore$ $$\Delta S° = 4R$$

76. (*b*) If the equation is obtained by adding two equations, equilibrium constants are multiplied. So, (b)

77. (*c*) $\because K_p$ is a function of temperature and stoichiometric coefficient only.

79. (*b*) $$K_p = \frac{p^2_{CO}}{p_{CO_2}}$$

Let $p_{CO_2} = x,\quad p_{CO} = 10x$

$63 = 100x$ or $x = 0.63$

$\therefore\ p_{CO_2} = 0.63,\quad p_{CO_2} = 6.3$

Total equilibrium pressure $= 6.3 + 0.63 = 6.93$ atm

80. (*d*) $AB(g) \longrightarrow A(g) + B(g)$

$$K_p = \frac{\alpha^2 p}{1-\alpha^2} = 2.56 \times 10^{-2} \text{ atm}$$

$$\frac{\alpha^2 \times 1\text{atm}}{1-\alpha^2} = 2.56 \times 10^{-2} \text{ atm}$$

$$\alpha = 0.16 = 16\%$$

81. (*d*) $K < 1.0$

82. (*b*) $CH_3COCH_3(g) \rightleftharpoons CH_3CH_3(g) + CO(g)$

	$CH_3COCH_3(g)$	$CH_3CH_3(g)$	$CO(g)$
Initial mole	1	0	0
At equilibrium	$(1-x)$	x	x

Total moles at equilibrium : $(1 + x)$

$$X_{CO} = \frac{x}{1+x} = \frac{1}{3} \quad \therefore\ x = 0.5$$

$\therefore$ Total moles at equilibrium $= 1.5$

$\because$ Initial pressure $= 100$ mm

$\therefore$ Equilibrium pressure $= 150$ mm

$\therefore$ $p_{CO} = 50$ mm

$p_{CH_3CH_3} = 50$ mm

$p_{CH_3COCH_3} = 50$ mm

$\therefore$ $$K_p = \frac{p_{CH_3CH_3} \cdot p_{CO}}{p_{CH_3COCH_3}} = 50 \text{ mm}$$

83. (*d*) $N_2O_4 \rightleftharpoons 2NO_2$

N_2O_4	$2NO_2$
1	0
$(1-x)$	$2x$

Number of moles $\propto$ volume(Since, $pV = nRT\ \therefore V \propto n$)

Total moles $= (1 + x)$

$\therefore$ $$\% \text{ of } NO_2 \text{ by volume} = \frac{2x}{1+x} \times 100 = 50$$

$\therefore$ $$x = \frac{1}{3} = 0.33$$

84. (*a*) $PCl_5 \rightleftharpoons PCl_3 + Cl_2$

$$K_p = \frac{px^2}{(1-x^2)}$$

$$\frac{p_1 x_1^2}{(1-x_1^2)} = \frac{p_2 x_2^2}{(1-x_2^2)}$$

$$\frac{2 \times (0.40)^2}{[1-(0.40)^2]} = \frac{p_2(0.80)^2}{[1-(0.80)^2]}$$

$\therefore$ $$p_2 = 0.21 \text{ atm}$$

85. (*a*) $PCl_5 \rightleftharpoons PCl_3 + Cl_2$

PCl_5	PCl_3	Cl_2
2	1	1
$(2-x)$	$(1+x)$	$(1+x)$

$x = 2 \times 0.50 = 1$

$\therefore$ $$K_C = \frac{[PCl_3][Cl_2]}{[PCl_5]} = \frac{\left(\frac{2}{1}\right)\left(\frac{2}{1}\right)}{\left(\frac{1}{1}\right)} = 4 \text{ mol L}^{-1}$$

86. (*c*) $N_2 + 3H_2 \rightleftharpoons 2NH_3$

N_2	$3H_2$	$2NH_3$
1	3	0
$(1-x)$	$(3-3x)$	$2x$

$2x \equiv 500$ mL of 1 M HCl $= 0.5$ mol

$\therefore$ $x = 0.25$

$\therefore$ $$[N_2] = \frac{1-x}{1} = (1-0.25) = 0.75 \text{ M}$$

$$[H_2] = \left(\frac{3-3x}{1}\right) = \frac{3-0.75}{1} = 2.25 \text{ M}$$

$$[NH_3] = \frac{2x}{1} = 0.50 \text{ M}$$

$\therefore \quad K_C = \frac{[NH_3]^2}{[N_2][H_2]^3} = \frac{(0.50)^2}{(0.75)(2.25)^3} = 0.03$

87. (*a*) $NH_4OH + H^+ \rightleftharpoons NH_4^+ + H_2O$

$$K = \frac{[NH_4^+][H_2O]}{[NH_4OH][H^+]} = 1.8 \times 10^9$$

$$NH_3 + H_2O \longrightarrow NH_4OH \rightleftharpoons NH_4^+ + OH^-$$

$\therefore \quad K' = \frac{[NH_4^+][OH^-]}{[NH_4OH]}$

$\therefore \quad \frac{K'}{K} = [H^+][OH^-] = K_w$ (ionic product of water)

$= 1 \times 10^{-14}$

$\therefore \quad K' = 1.8 \times 10^{-5}$

88. (*d*)

A	+ B	$\rightleftharpoons C$	+ D	
1	1	0	0	Set I
$(1-x)$	$(1-x)$	x	x	
2	1	0	0	Set II
$(2-y)$	$(1-y)$	y	y	

$$K_C = \frac{x^2}{(1-x)^2} = \frac{y^2}{(2-y)(1-y)} = 1 \quad \text{Since, } x = 0.5$$

$\therefore \quad y = 2/3$

Fraction of A converted into products $= \frac{2/3}{2} = \frac{1}{3} = 0.33$

89. (*c*) (i) $A_2(g) + B_2(g) \rightleftharpoons 2AB(g) \quad K_1 = \frac{[AB]^2}{[A_2][B_2]}$

(ii) $6AB(g) \rightleftharpoons 3A_2(g) + 3B_2(g)$

$$K_2 = \frac{[A_2]^3[B_2]^3}{[AB]^6} = \frac{1}{\left(\frac{[AB]^2}{[A_2][B_2]}\right)^3} = \frac{1}{K_1^3},$$

$\Rightarrow \quad K_2 = K_1^{-3}$

90. (*c*) $NH_2COONH_4(s) \rightleftharpoons 2NH_3(g) + CO_2(g)$

$(1-x) \qquad 2x \qquad x$

Only gaseous substances are NH_3 and CO_2

$\therefore$ Total moles of gaseous substances = 3x

$\therefore \quad p_{NH_3} = p_{eq} \cdot \frac{2x}{3x} = \frac{2}{3} p_{eq}$

$p_{CO_2} = \frac{1}{3} p_{eq}$

$\therefore \quad K_p = (p_{NH_3})^2 (p_{CO_2})$

$$= \left(\frac{2}{3} p_{eq}\right)^2 \left(\frac{1}{3} p_{eq}\right) = 2.92 \times 10^{-5}$$

$\therefore \quad p_{eq} = 0.0582$ atm

91. (*b*)

	A	+ B	$\rightleftharpoons C$	+ D
Initially at $t = 0$	1	1	1	1
At equilibrium	$1-x$	$1-x$	$1+x$	$1+x$

$$K_{eq} = \frac{[C][D]}{[A][B]} = \frac{(1+x)(1+x)}{(1-x)(1-x)} = \frac{(1+x)^2}{(1-x)^2}$$

or $\quad 100 = \left(\frac{1+x}{1-x}\right)^2$ or $10 = \frac{1+x}{1-x}$

or $\quad 10 - 10x = 1 + x$ or $10 - 1 = x + 10x$

$9 = 11x \Rightarrow x = \frac{9}{11} = 0.818$

$\therefore \quad [D] = 1 + x = 1 + 0.818 = 1.818$

92. (*c*) In which case $\Delta n_g \neq 0$, equilibrium constant is affected thus, I and III.

93. (*a*) $A + B \rightleftharpoons C + D$

Initially $\quad 1 \quad 1 \quad 3 \quad 3$

Reaction quotient before equilibrium is attained

$$= \frac{[C][D]}{[A][B]} = 9 > K_c \ (2.25)$$

Thus, reaction shifts in backward side

$\therefore$	C	+ D	$\rightleftharpoons A$	+ B
Initially	3	3	1	1
Equilibrium	$(3-x)$	$(3-x)$	$(1+x)$	$(1+x)$

$\therefore \quad K_C' = \frac{1}{K_C} = \frac{1}{2.25} = \frac{(1+x)^2}{(3-x)^2}$

$$\left(\frac{1+x}{3-x}\right) = \frac{1}{1.5}$$

$\therefore \quad x = 0.6$

$\therefore \quad \frac{[A]}{[C]} = \frac{1+x}{(3-x)} = \frac{1.6}{2.4} = \frac{2}{3}$

94. (*a*) SO_2 is oxidised by MnO_4^- in acidic medium.

$$5SO_2 + 2MnO_4^- \longrightarrow 2Mn^{2+} + 5SO_4^{2-}$$

$2 \text{ mol } MnO_4^- \equiv 5 \text{ mol } SO_2$

hence, $\quad 0.4 \text{ mol } MnO_4^- \equiv 1 \text{ mol } SO_2$

$$2SO_2 + O_2 \rightleftharpoons 2SO_3$$

$2 \qquad 1 \qquad 0$

$(2-2x) \quad (1-x) \quad 2x$

$(2-2x) = 1$ mol (as determined by MnO_4^-)

$\therefore \quad x = 0.5$

$\therefore \quad [SO_3] = \frac{2x}{V} = 1$ M

$[SO_2] = \frac{2-2x}{V} = 1$ M

$[O_2] = \frac{1-x}{V} = 0.5$ M

$\therefore \quad K_C = \frac{[SO_3]^2}{[SO_2]^2[O_2]} = 2$

95. (*a*) $PCl_5 \rightleftharpoons PCl_3 + Cl_2$

$0.5 \qquad 2 \qquad 2$ mol

$$Q \text{ (reaction quotient)} = \frac{[PCl_3][Cl_2]}{[PCl_5]} = \frac{\frac{2}{2} \times \frac{2}{2}}{\frac{0.5}{2}} = 4$$

Thus, $Q = K_C$, reaction mixture is in equilibrium.

$\therefore \quad [PCl_5] = \frac{0.5}{2} = 0.25 \text{ mol L}^{-1}$

96. (*b*)

$$N_2 + 3H_2 \rightleftharpoons 2NH_3$$

Initially 1 3 0

At equilibrium $(1-x)$ $(3-3x)$ $2x$

Initial mol $(n_1) = 4$

Pressure $(p_1) = 4 \text{ atm}$

Equilibrium mol $(n_2) = (4-2x)$

Equilibrium pressure $(p_2) = 3 \text{ atm}$

$$\frac{n_2}{n_1} = \frac{p_2}{p_1}$$

$$\frac{(4-2x)}{4} = \frac{3}{4}$$

$$\therefore \quad 4 - 2x = 3$$

$$x = 0.5$$

$$X_{N_2} = \frac{1-x}{4-2x} = \left(\frac{0.5}{3}\right)$$

$$X_{H_2} = \frac{3-3x}{4-2x} = \frac{1.5}{3}$$

$$X_{NH_3} = \frac{2x}{4-2x} = \frac{1}{3}$$

$$\therefore \quad p_{N_2} = 3 \times \frac{0.5}{3} = 0.5 \text{ atm}$$

$$p_{H_2} = 1.5 \text{ atm}$$

$$p_{NH_3} = 1 \text{ atm}$$

$$\therefore \quad K_p = \frac{(p_{NH_3})^2}{(p_{N_2})(p_{H_2})^3} = \frac{1}{(0.5)(1.5)^3}$$

97. (*d*) Solubility increases as $\left(\frac{1}{T}\right)$ increases or T decreases.

Thus, $\Delta H = -\text{ve}$, hydration takes place. Hence, solute is CaO.

99. (*c*) Equilibrium concentration is 0.1 M in each case. Calculate K_C in each case. Greater the value of K_C, greater the extent of reaction.

100. (*a*) $Ag^+ + 2NH_3 \rightleftharpoons Ag(NH_3)_2^+ \quad K_1 = 1.8 \times 10^7$

$$AgCl \rightleftharpoons Ag^+ + Cl^- \quad K_2' = \frac{1}{K_2} = \frac{1}{5.6 \times 10^9}$$

$$\therefore \quad AgCl + 2NH_3 \rightleftharpoons Ag(NH_3)_2^+ + Cl^-$$

$$K = K_1 K_2' = \frac{K_1}{K_2} = \frac{1.8 \times 10^7}{5.6 \times 10^9} = 3.21 \times 10^{-3}$$

101. (*a*)

$$C = C_0 e^{-kt}$$

$$\therefore \quad k_f = 2.1 \times 10^{-3}$$

$$k_b = 4.2 \times 10^{-4}$$

$$K_C = \frac{k_f}{k_b} = 5.0$$

102. (*b*) Given, $\Delta G° = 24942 \text{ J}$

$$Q = \frac{[B][C]}{[A]^2} = \frac{2 \times \frac{1}{2}}{\left(\frac{1}{2}\right)^2} = 4$$

$\therefore$ We know, $\Delta G = \Delta G° + RT \ln Q$

$$= 2494.2 + 8.314 \times 300 \ln 4$$

$$= 28747.27 \text{ J } (+\text{ ve value})$$

Also, we have $\Delta G = RT \ln \frac{Q}{K}$

If ΔG is positive, $Q > K$

Therefore, reaction shifts in reverse direction.

103. (*d*)

$$K_p = K_C (RT)^{\Delta n}$$

$$K_p = K_x (p)^{\Delta n}$$

$$\therefore \quad K_C (RT)^{\Delta n} = K_x (p)^{\Delta n}$$

$$K_C = K_x \left(\frac{p}{RT}\right)^{\Delta n} = K_x \left(\frac{1}{V}\right)^{\Delta n} = K_x \left(\frac{1}{V}\right)^{-1} = K_x (V)$$

105. (*c*)

$$\Delta n = -\frac{1}{2}$$

$$\therefore \quad K_p = K_C (RT)^{-(1/2)}$$

$$\therefore \quad \frac{K_p}{K_C} = \frac{1}{\sqrt{RT}}$$

107. (*c*)

$$(\text{Rate})_f = k_f [NO]^2 [O_2]$$

$$(\text{Rate})_b = k_b [NO_2]^2$$

$\therefore$ At equilibrium

$$\frac{k_f}{k_b} = \frac{[NO_2]^2}{[NO]^2[O_2]} = \frac{2.6 \times 10^3}{4.1} = K_C$$

$\therefore$ For $NO + \frac{1}{2} O_2 \rightleftharpoons NO_2$

$$K_C' = \sqrt{K_C} = 25.18$$

109. (*b*) By Le-Chatelier's principle, due to increase in pressure equilibrium shifts in the direction of low pressure (in which number of mol decreases), i.e. forward side.

112. (*d*) $\Delta G = \Delta G° + 2.303 RT \log Q$

if $Q = 1$, $\quad \therefore \Delta G = \Delta G°$

114. (*b*) I is not reversible due to formation of insoluble Cu_2I_2.

117. (*a*)

$$\frac{-d[A]}{dt} = k[A]^n$$

On doubling $[A]$, rate is doubled. Hence, $n = 1$

$$\therefore \quad k_f = \frac{-d[A]/dt}{[A]} = \frac{1 \times 10^{-2}}{0.1} = 0.1 \text{ mol L}^{-1} \text{ s}^{-1}$$

$$K_C = \frac{k_f}{k_b}$$

$\therefore \quad k_b = \frac{k_f}{K_C} = \frac{0.1}{10} = 1 \times 10^{-2}$ L mol^{-1} s^{-1}

118. (*c*) For the given reaction

$$k_f = 3.9 \times 10^{-5}\ s^{-1}$$

$$k_b = 2.1 \times 10^{-3}\ L\ mol^{-1}\ s^{-1}$$

$$\therefore K_C = \frac{k_f}{k_b} = \frac{3.9 \times 10^{-5}}{2.1 \times 10^{-3}}\ mol\ L^{-1} = 0.0186\ mol\ L^{-1}$$

$$\therefore K_C'\text{ of the required reaction} = \frac{1}{K_C} = 53.85\ L\ mol^{-1}$$

119. (*d*)

$$Q = \frac{[C]^3}{[A]^2[B]^2}$$

(a) $= 1000 >> K_C$
(b) $= 1 > K_C$
(c) $= 0.1 > K_C$
(d) $= 1 \times 10^{-3} < K_C$

Reaction proceeds to right in which $Q < K_C$

120. (*a*) $HOCl \rightleftharpoons H^+ + OCl^-$

$$K_a = \frac{[H^+][OCl^-]}{[HOCl]} \quad \text{...(i)}$$

$$OCl^- + H_2O \rightleftharpoons HOCl + OH^-$$

$$K_{eq} = \frac{[HOCl][OH^-]}{[OCl^-]} \quad \text{...(ii)}$$

$$K_a K_{eq} = [H^+][OH^-] = K_w = 1 \times 10^{-14}$$

$$\therefore \quad K_a = \frac{K_w}{K_{eq}} = \frac{1.0 \times 10^{-14}}{3.6 \times 10^{-7}} = 2.8 \times 10^{-8}$$

121. (*a*) $x(\text{product}) \propto \left(\frac{1}{p}\right)^{\Delta n_g/2} \propto (V)^{\Delta n_g/2}$

	Δn_g	x
(a)	1	$\alpha\sqrt{V}$
(b)	0	no effect
(c)	-5	$\alpha(V)^{-5/2}$
(d)	-1	$\alpha(V)^{-1/2}$

123. (*a*)

	$2HI \rightleftharpoons$	H_2 +	I_2
Initially:	2	0	0
At equilibrium	$2 - 2\alpha$	α	α

$\therefore$ Total moles at equilibrium $= 2 - 2\alpha + \alpha + \alpha = 2$

124. (*d*) (II) − (I) = (III)

Thus, equilibrium constant of III $= \frac{K_2}{K_1}$

125. (*c*)

$2HI \rightleftharpoons$	H_2 +	I_2
1	0	0
$(1 - x)$	$\frac{x}{2}$	$\frac{x}{2}$

$$x = 0.22$$

$$K_C = \frac{x^2}{4(1-x)^2} = \frac{(0.22)^2}{4\ (1 - 0.22)^2} = 0.01988$$

126. (*a*) $A + B \rightleftharpoons C + D$

Δn = moles of products − moles of reactants
$= 0$

Thus, K_p or K_C is independent of pressure or volume.

127. (*d*)

CH_3COOH +	$C_2H_5OH \rightleftharpoons$	$CH_3COC_2H_5$ +	H_2O
1	1	0	0
$(1 - x)$	$(1 - x)$	x	x

$$x = 2/3$$

$$K_C = \frac{[CH_3COOC_2H_5][H_2O]}{[CH_3COOH][C_2H_5OH]} = \frac{x^2}{(1-x)^2} = \frac{\left(\frac{2}{3}\right)^2}{\left(\frac{1}{3}\right)^2} = 4$$

128. (*a*)

	A +	$2B \rightleftharpoons$	$2C$ +	D
Initially	1 M	1.5 M	0	0
Equilibrium	$(1 - x)$ M	$(1.5 - 2x)$ M	$2x$ M	x M

Given, $1 - x = 1.5 - 2x$

$$x = 0.5$$

$\therefore \quad [A] = 0.5$ M, $[C] = 1$ M

$[B] = 0.5$ M, $[D] = 0.5$ M

$$K_C = \frac{[C]^2[D]}{[A][B]^2} = \frac{(1)^2(0.5)}{(0.5)(0.5)^2} = 4$$

130. (*c*)

$$K_C = \frac{[H_2][Cl_2]}{[HCl]^2}$$

$$1 \times 10^{-5} = \frac{(1.2 \times 10^{-3})(1.2 \times 10^{-4})}{[HCl]^2}$$

$\therefore \quad [HCl]^2 = 0.0144\ M^2$

$\therefore \quad [HCl] = 0.12$ M

131. (*b*)

A +	$B \rightleftharpoons$	$2C$
2	3	0
$(2 - x)$	$(3 - x)$	$2x$

Active mass $[A] = \frac{2-x}{V}$,

$$[B] = \frac{3-x}{V}, [C] = \frac{2x}{V}$$

$$K_C = \frac{[C]^2}{[A][B]} = \frac{\left(\frac{2x}{V}\right)^2}{\left(\frac{2-x}{V}\right)\left(\frac{3-x}{V}\right)}$$

$$4 = \frac{4x^2}{(2-x)(3-x)}$$

$$x^2 = x^2 - 5x + 6$$

$\therefore \quad x = 1.2$

$\therefore$ Moles of C at equilibrium $= 2x = 2.4$

132. (*b*) Molar mass of $NH_4SH = 18 + 33 = 51$ g mol^{-1}

Number of moles of NH_4SH introduced in the vessel

$$= \frac{\text{Weight}}{\text{Molar mass}} = \frac{5.1}{51} = 0.1\text{mol}$$

	$NH_4SH(s) \rightleftharpoons$	$NH_3(g)$ +	$H_2S(g)$
Number of moles at $t = 0$	0.1	0	0
At $t = t_{eq}$	0.1(1 − 0.03)	30% of 0.1 = 0.03	30% of 0.1 = 0.03
Active mass (mol L^{-1})		$\frac{0.03}{3} = 0.01$	$\frac{0.03}{3} = 0.01$

$$K_C = \frac{[NH_3]\,[H_2S]}{[NH_4HS(s)]} = \frac{0.01 \times 0.01}{1} = 10^{-4}\ (\text{molL}^{-1})^2$$

$$\Rightarrow K_p = K_C (RT)^{\Delta n_g}$$

[where, $\Delta n_g = \Sigma n_{\text{product}} - \Sigma n_{\text{reactant}}] = 2 - 0 = 2$

$$\therefore \quad K_p = K_C (RT)^2$$

$$= 10^{-4} \times [0.082 \times (273 + 327)]^2\ \text{atm}^2$$

$$= 0.242\ \text{atm}^2$$

134. (*a*)

$$\Delta G° = -nFE°$$

Also

$$\Delta G° = -2.303\, RT \log K$$

$$\therefore \log K = \frac{nFE°}{2.303\, RT} = \frac{6 \times 96500 \times 0.887}{2.303 \times 8.3143 \times 298} = 90$$

$$\therefore \quad K = 10^{90}$$

135. (*b*)

$$\Delta G_A^\circ = -2.303\, RT \log_{10} K_A$$

$$\Delta G_B^\circ = -2.303\, RT \log_{10} K_B$$

$$\therefore \quad \frac{\Delta G_A^\circ}{\Delta G_B^\circ} = \log_{10} \frac{K_A}{K_B}$$

$$2 = \log_{10} \frac{K_A}{K_B}$$

$$\therefore \quad \frac{K_A}{K_B} = 10^2 = 100$$

136. (*b*) As $\frac{1}{T}$ increase (T decreases) log K or K increases. Thus, given reaction is exothermic, i.e. $\Delta H° A < 0$

$$\log_e K = \frac{\Delta H°}{RT} + \frac{\Delta S°}{R}$$

Thus, slope is $\frac{\Delta H°}{R}$ and $\Delta A° = \frac{\Delta S°}{R}$

138. (*c*) $Ca(HCO_3)_2(s) \longrightarrow CaO(s) + CO_2(g) + H_2O(g)$

Total pressure is due to $CO_2(g)$ one $H_2O(g)$ molar ratio being equal.

Thus, $\quad p_{CO_2} = p_{H_2O}$

and $\quad p_{CO_2} + p_{H_2O} = 0.12$

$\therefore \quad p_{CO_2} = p_{H_2O} = 0.06$ bar

$\therefore \quad K_p = p_{CO_2} \cdot p_{H_2O} = 0.0036$

139. (*b*) When $\quad p_{H_2O} = 0.20$ bar

then $\quad K_p = p_{H_2O} \cdot p_{CO_2}$

$$0.0036 = 0.2 \times p_{CO_2}$$

$\therefore \quad p_{CO_2} = 0.018$ bar

140. (*a*) According to Le-Chatelier's principle the reaction (in forward direction) is favourable at high pressure and low temperature because Δn_g = negative and reaction is exothermic in forward direction.

07

Ionic Equilibrium

Objective Questions Type I [Only one correct option]

In each of the questions below, four choices are given of which only one is correct.

1. C_2H_5OH ionises as

(a) $C_2H_5OH \rightleftharpoons C_2H_5O^- + H^+$

(b) $2C_2H_5OH \rightleftharpoons C_2H_5OH_2^+ + C_2H_5O^-$

(c) $C_2H_5OH \rightleftharpoons C_2H_5^+ + OH^-$

(d) $C_2H_5OH + H_2O \rightleftharpoons C_2H_5O^- + H_3O^+$

2. C_2H_5ONa is a .... in C_2H_5OH.

(a) strong base (b) strong acid

(c) weak acid (d) weak base

3. NH_4NO_3 is a

(a) strong base in NH_3 (b) weak base in NH_3

(c) strong acid in NH_3 (d) weak acid in NH_3

4. Select the correct statement(s).

(a) Arrhenius theory is restricted to aqueous solution

(b) Franklin's theory is applicable also to other ionisable systems

(c) Both (a) and (b)

(d) None of the above

5. In the following equilibrium,

$$B + H_2O \rightleftharpoons BH^+ + OH^-$$

(a) Arrhenius acid-base concept is observed

(b) Franklin's acid-base concept is observed

(c) Both (a) and (b)

(d) None of the above

6. Consider the following reactions,

I. $H_2CO_3(aq) + HSO_4^-(aq) \rightleftharpoons H_2SO_4(aq) + HCO_3^-(aq)$

II. $HF(aq) + Cl^-(aq) \rightleftharpoons HCl(aq) + F^-(aq)$

III. $HF(aq) + NH_3(aq) \rightleftharpoons NH_4^+ + F^-(aq)$

IV. $HSO_4^-(aq) + CN^-(aq) \rightleftharpoons HCN(aq) + SO_4^{2-}(aq)$

Reactions proceeding to the right are

(a) I and II (b) III and IV (c) I and III (d) II and IV

7. Conjugate base of H_2 is

(a) H^+ (b) H_2^+ (c) H^- (d) H_3^-

8. Conjugate base of HO_2^- is

(a) O_2^- (superoxide ion) (b) H_2O_2

(c) O_2^{2-} (peroxide ion) (d) O_2^+

9. In the following

$$\underset{(A)}{[Al(H_2O)_6]^{3+}} + \underset{(B)}{HCO_3^-} \rightleftharpoons \underset{(C)}{[Al(H_2O)_5OH]^{2+}} + \underset{(D)}{H_2CO_3}$$

Species behaving as Bronsted-Lowry acids are

(a) $(A), (D)$ (b) $(B), (C)$

(c) $(B), (D)$ (d) $(A), (C)$

10. Which is Bronsted-Lowry acid as well as Arrhenius acid?

(a) H_2 (b) HCO_3^- (c) NH_3 (d) NH_2^-

11. Following reaction,

$$NH_4^+(aq) + CN^-(aq) \rightleftharpoons HCN(aq) + NH_3(aq)$$

proceeds in

(a) forward direction (b) backward direction

(c) in both sides equally (d) can't be predicted

12. Out of the following, amphiprotic species are

I. $H_2PO_2^-$ II. HPO_3^{2-}

III. HCO_3^- IV. $CH_3CO_2^-$

V. HPO_4^{2-}

(a) I, II, III and V (b) I and V

(c) III and V (d) II, III and V

13. What are correct statement(s) about H^- (hydride)?

(a) It is Bronsted-Lowry base of H_2

(b) It resembles halide

(c) It is isoelectronic of He

(d) All the above are correct statements

14. Consider the following reactions

I : $[Al(OH)_3(H_2O)_3] + OH^- \rightleftharpoons [Al(OH)_4(H_2O)_2^-] + H_2O$
X

II : $[Al(OH)_3(H_2O)_3] + H_3O^+ \rightleftharpoons [Al(OH)_2(H_2O)_4^+] + H_2O$
X

Select the correct statement.
(a) *X* is an acid in I and base in II
(b) *X* is a base in I and acid in II
(c) *X* is a base in I and II both
(d) *X* is an acid in I and II both

15. If following proceed in forward side

$$HNO_2 + HF \rightleftharpoons H_2F^+ + NO_2^-$$
$$CH_3COOH + HF \rightleftharpoons F^- + CH_3COOH_2^+$$
$$H_2O + CH_3COOH \rightleftharpoons H_3O^+ + CH_3COO^-$$

then increasing order of acid strength is
(a) $H_2O < CH_3COOH < HF < HNO_2$
(b) $HNO_2 < HF < CH_3COOH < H_2O$
(c) $HNO_2 < HF < H_2O < CH_3COOH$
(d) $HNO_2 < CH_3COOH < HF < H_2O$

16. Select the correct statement(s) about $H_2PO_4^-$ and NH_4^+.
(a) Both behave as Bronsted-Lowry acid
(b) $H_2PO_4^-$ is a Lewis-base as well as Bronsted-Lowry base
(c) $H_2PO_4^-$ is amphiprotic
(d) All the above are correct statements

17. In the interaction of $B(CH_3)_3$ with $N(CH_3)_3$
(a) $B(CH_3)_3$ is a Lewis base and $N(CH_3)_3$ is a Lewis acid
(b) $B(CH_3)_3$ is a Lewis acid and $N(CH_3)_3$ is a Lewis base
(c) Both are Lewis acids
(d) Both are Lewis bases

18. A carbocation (as $\overset{\oplus}{C}H_3$) is
(a) a Lewis acid (b) an electrophilic reagent
(c) Both (a) and (b) (d) None of these

19. Which is/are Lewis acids out of $\overset{\ominus}{C}H_3$ (carbanion), $\overset{\oplus}{C}H_5$ (carbonium ion), $\overset{\oplus}{C}H_3$ (carbenium ion)?
(a) $\overset{\oplus}{C}H_5, \overset{\oplus}{C}H_3$ (b) $\overset{\oplus}{C}H_3, \overset{\ominus}{C}H_3$
(c) $\overset{\oplus}{C}H_3$ (d) $\overset{\oplus}{C}H_5$

20. Which behaves as a Lewis base as well as Bronsted-Lowry base?
(a) Carbonium ion (b) Carbenium ion
(c) Carbanion (d) All of these

21. Relative strength cannot be compared in aqueous solution of the following pair
(a) $HClO_4$ and HBr (b) $HClO_4$ and HNO_3
(c) H_2SO_4 and HNO_3 (d) All of these

22. Select the correct acid-base equilibrium
(a) $HNO_3 + HF \rightleftharpoons H_2NO_3^+ + F^-$
(b) $HNO_3 + HF \rightleftharpoons H_2F^+ + NO_3^-$
(c) $CH_3COOH + NH_3 \rightleftharpoons CH_3COOH_2^+ + NH_2^-$
(d) $HF + H_2O \rightleftharpoons H_2F^+ + OH^-$

23. Consider the following statements.
I. CH_3COOH (a weak acid) behaves as a strong acid in NH_3.
II. HNO_3 (a strong acid) behaves as a base in HF.
III. H_2SO_4 dissociates to a very small extent in glacial CH_3COOH.
Select correct alternate for these statements.
(a) I and III (b) II and III
(c) I and II (d) I, II and III

24. HCl exists as
(a) Cl^- (b) H_3O^+ (c) HCl (d) $H_3O^+Cl^-$

25. Select aprotic solvents out of
water, benzene, trimethyl amine, carbon tetrachloride
I II III IV
(a) Only I (b) II and IV
(c) II, III and IV (d) I, III and IV

26. Strongest acid and strongest base pair is
(a) H_3O^+, H_2O (b) H_3O^+, OH^-
(c) H_2O, H_3O^+ (d) OH^-, H_3O^+

27. Autoprotolysis constant of NH_3 is
(a) $[NH_4^+][NH_3]$ (b) $[NH_2^-][NH_3]$
(c) $[NH_4^+][NH_2^-]$ (d) $\frac{[NH_4^+]}{[NH_2^-]}$

28. Autoprotolysis constant of a weak acid *HA* is 4×10^{-8}. Hence, $[A^-]$ is
(a) 2×10^{-4} M (b) 0.25×10^{-6} M
(c) 16×10^{-16} M (d) 4×10^{-8} M

29. At –50°C autoprotolysis of NH_3 gives $[NH_4^+] = 1 \times 10^{-15}$ M hence, autoprotolysis constant of NH_3 is
(a) $\sqrt{1 \times 10^{-15}}$ (b) 1×10^{-30}
(c) 1×10^{-15} (d) 2×10^{-15}

30. pH of 10^{-8} N NaOH is
(a) 8.0 (b) 6.0 (c) 6.98 (d) 7.02

31. Milliequivalent of $Ba(OH)_2$ present in 100 mL solution to have pH = 13, is
(a) 10^{-2} (b) 10 (c) 0.1 (d) 0.01

32. At a temperature under high pressure,
$$K_w(H_2O) = 1 \times 10^{-10}$$
A solution of pH 5.4 under these conditions is said to be
(a) acidic (b) basic
(c) neutral (d) amphoteric

33. A weak monobasic acid is 0.1% ionised at 0.1 M. Hence, its pH is

(a) 2 (b) 3 (c) 4 (d) 5

34. Which has maximum pH?

(a) 0.01 M H_2SO_4 (b) 0.01 M HCl
(c) 0.01 M $Ca(OH)_2$ (d) 0.01 M NaOH

35. In which case change in pH is maximum?

(a) 1 mL of pH = 2 is diluted to 100 mL
(b) 0.01 mol of NaOH is added into 100 mL of 0.01 M NaOH solution
(c) 100 mL of H_2O is added into 900 mL of 10^{-6} M HCl
(d) 100 mL of pH = 2 solution is mixed with 100 mL of pH = 12

36. A weak monoacid base has pH = 10 at 0.01 M. % ionisation of base is

(a) 0.01% (b) 0.001%
(c) 0.0001% (d) 1.0%

37. 100 mL solution of pH = 6 is diluted to 1000 mL. Resulting solution has pH

(a) 7.0 (b) 6.7 (c) 7.3 (d) 6.4

38. In a basic solution pH is 12.3. Hence, $[OH^-]$ is

(a) 2×10^{-2} M (b) 5×10^{-13} M
(c) 3×10^{-12} M (d) 4×10^{-10} M

39. When you calculate pH of a solution, $[H_3O^+]$ from H_2O is required in the following

(a) 10^{-5} M HCl (b) 10^{-5} M NaOH
(c) 10^{-8} M NaOH (d) 10^{-6} M $Ca(OH)_2$

40. The K_a value for the acid HA is 1.0×10^{-6}. What is the value of K for the reaction?

$$A^- + H_3O^+ \rightleftharpoons HA + H_2O$$

(a) 1.0×10^{-8} (b) 1.0×10^{8}
(c) 1.0×10^{-3} (d) 1.0×10^{6}

41. pK_b of *aq*. NH_3 is 4.74, hence pH of 0.01 M NH_3 solution is

(a) 3.37 (b) 10.63 (c) 2.00 (d) 12.00

42. CH_3COOH is 2.0% ionised ($K_a = 1.8\times10^{-5}$), hence its molar concentration is

(a) 0.045 M (b) 0.02 M
(c) 3.6×10^{-5} M (d) 0.090 M

43. A weak monobasic acid is 0.01% ionised when its concentration is 1 M. Hence, $[OH^-]$ is

(a) 1×10^{-4} M (b) 1×10^{-10} M
(c) 1×10^{4} M (d) 1×10^{10} M

44. % ionisation of a weak acid is 1% at 1 M, hence % ionisation is ... at 4 M.

(a) 4% (b) 5%
(c) 0.5% (d) 0.2%

45. A mixture of weak acid is 0.1 M in HCOOH ($K_a = 1.8\times10^{-4}$) and 0.1 M in HOCN ($K_a = 3.3\times10^{-4}$). Hence, $[H_3O^+]$ is

(a) 7.14×10^{-3} M (b) 4.1×10^{-4} M
(c) 0.20 M (d) 4.1×10^{-3} M

46. At 25°C, $[H_3O^+] = 1\times10^{-7}$ M in water, hence, K_a is

(a) 1×10^{-14} (b) 5.55×10^{-15}
(c) 1.8×10^{-16} (d) 55.5×10^{-10}

47. What is the value of K_w in 0.01 M NaOH?

(a) 1×10^{-15} (b) 1×10^{-13}
(c) 1×10^{-16} (d) 1×10^{-14}

48. 0.1 M solution of CH_3COOH should be diluted to .... times so that pH is doubled.

(a) four times (b) 5.55×10^{4} times
(c) 5.55×10^{6} times (d) 10^{-2} times

49. $[H_3O^+]$ in 0.1 M H_2SO_4 at two stages

$$H_2SO_4 \rightleftharpoons H^+ + HSO_4^-$$
$$HSO_4^- \rightleftharpoons H^+ + SO_4^{2-}$$ are

(a) 0.1 M, 0.1 M (b) 0.1 M, > 0.01 M
(c) > 0.1 M, > 0.1 M (d) 0.1 M, < 0.1 M

50. The pH of blood is 7.40. What is the ratio of $\frac{[HPO_4^{2-}]}{[H_2PO_4^-]}$ in the blood? ($pK_a(H_2PO_4^-) = 7.10$)

(a) 2 : 1 (b) 1 : 2 (c) 3 : 1 (d) 1 : 3

51. pK_a of a weak acid (*HA*) and pK_b of a weak base (*BOH*) are 3.2 and 3.4, respectively. The pH of their salt (*AB*) solution is **[JEE Main 2017]**

(a) 7.2 (b) 6.9
(c) 7.0 (d) 1.0

52. The K_{sp} for the following dissociation is 1.6×10^{-5}

$$PbCl_2(s) \rightleftharpoons Pb^{2+}(aq) + 2Cl^-(aq)$$

Which of the following choices is correct for a mixture of 300 mL 0.134 M $Pb(NO_3)_2$ and 100 mL 0.4 M NaCl ? **[JEE Main 2020, Jan.]**

(a) $Q < K_{sp}$ (b) $Q > K_{sp}$
(c) $Q = K_{sp}$ (d) Not enough data provided

53. Amongst the following, the form of water with the lowest ionic conductance at 298 K is **[JEE Main 2020, Jan.]**

(a) saline water used for intravenous injection
(b) distilled water
(c) water from a well
(d) sea water

54. The solubility product of $Cr(OH)_3$ at 298 K is 6.0×10^{-31}. The concentration of hydroxide ions in a saturated solution of $Cr(OH)_3$ will be **[JEE Main 2020, Jan.]**

(a) $(2.22\times10^{-31})^{1/4}$ (b) $(18\times10^{-31})^{1/4}$
(c) $(4.86\times10^{-29})^{1/4}$ (d) $(18\times10^{-31})^{1/2}$

55. We have acidic buffer of CH_3COONa and CH_3COOH. One or more of the following operations will not change pH
I. diluting the mixture ten times
II. adding some HCl
III. adding some NaOH
IV. adding equal moles of CH_3COONa and CH_3COOH into the buffer
Select correct alternate.
(a) I, II, III and IV (b) II and III
(c) I and IV (d) II and IV

56. Which buffer solution has maximum pH?
(a) Mixture which is 0.1 M in CH_3COOH and 0.1 M in CH_3COONa [$pK_a(CH_3COOH) = 4.74$]
(b) Mixture which is 0.2 M in CH_3COOH and 0.2 M in CH_3COONa
(c) Mixture which is 0.1 M in NH_4Cl and 0.1 M in NH_4OH [$pK_a(NH_4^+) = 9.26$]
(d) All the solutions have equal pH which is 4.74

57. The stoichiometry and solubility product of a salt with the solubility curve given below is, respectively: **[JEE Main 2020, Jan.]**

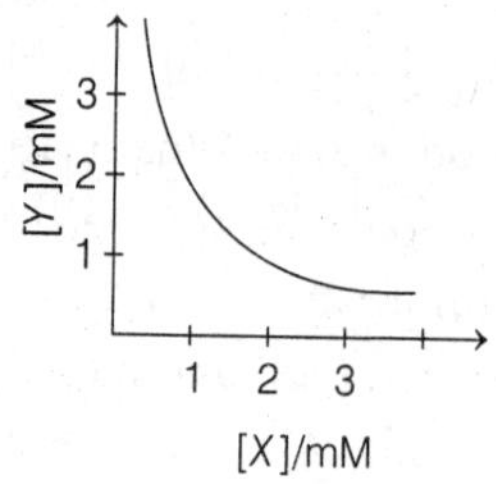

(a) $X_2Y, 2\times10^{-9}$ M^3 (b) $XY, 2\times10^{-6}$ M^3
(c) $XY_2, 1\times10^{-9}$ M^3 (d) $XY_2, 4\times10^{-9}$ M^3

58. The strength of an aqueous NaOH solution is most accurately determined by titrating : (Note : consider that an appropriate indicator is used) **[JEE Main 2020, Jan.]**
(a) *Aq.* NaOH in a volumetric flask and concentrated H_2SO_4 in a conical flask
(b) *Aq.* NaOH in a pipette and aqueous oxalic acid in a burette
(c) *Aq.* NaOH in a burette and aqueous oxalic acid in a conical flask
(d) *Aq.* NaOH in a burette and concentrated H_2SO_4 in a conical flask

59. A weak acid *HA* has degree of dissociation *x*. Thus $(pH - pK_a)$ is
(a) p_x (b) p_{1-x} (c) $p_{1-x} + p_x$ (d) $p_{1-x} - p_x$

60. pK_{a_1} of carbonic acid in blood at body temperature (37°C) is 6.1. Hence, ratio $[HCO_3^-]/[H_2CO_3]$ is approximately
(a) 1.3 : 1 (b) 1 : 1.3
(c) 20 : 1 (d) 1 : 20

61. For the following Assertion and Reason, the correct option is
Assertion The pH of water increases with increase in temperature.
Reason The dissociation of water into H^+ and OH^- is an exothermic reaction. **[JEE Main 2020, Jan.]**
(a) Assertion is not true, but Reason is true.
(b) Both assertion and Reason are true and the Reason is the correct explanation for the Assertion.
(c) Both Assertion and Reason are false.
(d) Both Assertion and Reason are true, but the Reason is not the correct explanation for the Assertion.

62. If solubility product of $Zr_3(PO_4)_4$ is denoted by K_{sp} and its molar solubility is denoted by *S*, then which of the following relation between *S* and K_{sp} is correct? **[JEE Main 2019]**
(a) $S = \left(\frac{K_{sp}}{144}\right)^{1/6}$ (b) $S = \left(\frac{K_{sp}}{6912}\right)^{1/7}$
(c) $S = \left(\frac{K_{sp}}{929}\right)^{1/9}$ (d) $S = \left(\frac{K_{sp}}{216}\right)^{1/7}$

63. Oxygen from inhaled air combines with haemoglobin, and oxygenated haemoglobin ionises releasing a proton which is removed in the following reactions
(a) $H^+ + CO_2 \rightleftharpoons HCO_3^-$
(b) $HCO_3^- + H_2O \rightleftharpoons H_3O^+ + CO_3^{2-}$
(c) $HCO_3^- + H^+ \rightleftharpoons H_2CO_3$
(d) in all of the above

64. Which of the following reagents affect per cent dissociation of $C_6H_5\overset{O}{\overset{\|}{C}}OH$?
(a) NaOH (b) NH_4OH
(c) HBr (d) All of these

65. Ionisation of NaOH is decreased in presence of
(a) AcOH (b) MeOH
(c) EtOH (d) None of these

66. K_a of AcOH is 1.8×10^{-5}. What is $[H_3O^+]$ in a solution which is 0.01 M AcOH and 0.005 M calcium acetate?
(a) 1.8×10^{-5} M (b) 3.6×10^{-5} M
(c) 0.9×10^{-5} M (d) 0.005 M

67. pK_b of NH_3 is 4.74; moles of ammonium sulphate to be added to 0.5 L of 0.01 M *aq* NH_3 to have pH of 9.26 is
(a) 0.005 (b) 0.0025
(c) 0.01 (d) 0.002

68. $[Ag^+]$ in saturated AgCl in presence of 1 M KCl [$K(AgCl) = 1\times10^{-10}$] is
(a) 1×10^{-5} M (b) 1×10^{-20} M
(c) 1×10^{-10} M (d) 2×10^{-10} M

69. Degree of ionisation of 1 M HCOOH is decreased to a maximum extent in presence of
(a) 1 M HCHO (b) 1 M NaOH
(c) 1 M HCOONa (d) equally in all

70. Solubility of Ag_2CrO_4 is decreased in presence of
(a) $AgNO_3$ (b) AgCl
(c) $BaCrO_4$ (d) $PbCrO_4$

71. Blood pH is controlled by concentration of H_2CO_3 and HCO_3^-. In presence of $NaHCO_3$, pH of blood is
(a) increased (b) decreased
(c) no change (d) statement is wrong

72. A weak acid (*HA*) is 4% ionised at 1 M. Per cent ionisation is 1% in presence of A^- of
(a) 0.04 M (b) 0.16 M
(c) 0.02 M (d) 0.10 M

73. $[OH^-]$ in a solution prepared by mixing equal volumes of 0.3 M methyl amine (CH_3NH_2, $K_b = 3.7\times 10^{-4}$) and 0.60 M $CH_3NH_3^+Cl^-$
(a) 3.7×10^{-4} M (b) 7.4×10^{-4} M
(c) 3.7×10^{-2} M (d) 1.85×10^{-4} M

74. An aqueous solution contains an unknown concentration of Ba^{2+}. When 50 mL of a 1 M solution of Na_2SO_4 is added, $BaSO_4$ just begins to precipitate. The final volume is 500 mL. The solubility product of $BaSO_4$ is 1×10^{-10}. What is the original concentration of Ba^{2+}? **[JEE Main 2018]**
(a) 5×10^{-9} M (b) 2×10^{-9} M
(c) 1.1×10^{-9} M (d) 1.0×10^{-10} M

75. Solubility of $BaSO_4$ in aqueous solution is 1×10^{-5} M. Hence, solubility in 0.1 M $BaCl_2$ is
(a) 1×10^{-10} M (b) 1×10^{-9} M
(c) 1×10^{-4} M (d) 1×10^{-5} M

76. Molar solubility of $Al(OH)_3$ is increased in presence of
(a) NaOH (b) HCl
(c) Both (a) and (b) (d) None of these

77. A saturated solution prepared by dissolving Ag_2CO_3 in water has $[Ag^+] = 2.56\times 10^{-4}$ M. Hence, its K_{sp} is
(a) 8.4×10^{-12} (b) 1.68×10^{-13}
(c) 6.6×10^{-8} (d) 1.6×10^{-2}

78. $K_{sp}(BaSO_4)$ is 1.1×10^{-10}. In which case is $BaSO_4$ precipitated?
(a) 100 mL of 4×10^{-3} M $BaCl_2$ + 300 mL of 6.0×10^{-4} M Na_2SO_4
(b) 100 mL of 4×10^{-4}M $BaCl_2$ + 300 mL of 6.0×10^{-8} M Na_2SO_4
(c) 300 mL of 4×10^{-4} M $BaCl_2$ + 100 mL of 6.0×10^{-8} M Na_2SO_4
(d) In all cases

79. K_{sp} of $Al(OH)_3$ is 1.0×10^{-15}. pH of the saturated solution is about
(a) 5.0 (b) 9.0
(c) 4.1 (d) 10.4

80. K_{sp} of H_2S is 1×10^{-22}. $[S^{2-}]$ in a buffer of pH 6 is
(a) 1×10^{-16} M (b) 1×10^{-12} M
(c) 1×10^{-10} M (d) 1×10^{-8} M

81. K_{sp} of CdS is 8.0×10^{-27} and that of H_2S is 1×10^{-22}. 1×10^{-14} M, $CdCl_2$ solution is precipitated on passing H_2S when pH is about
(a) 4 (b) 6
(c) 5 (d) 7

82. K_{sp} of $Mg(OH)_2$ is 1.8×10^{-11} at 30°C. Its molar solubility is ... at pH = 12.
(a) 1.8×10^{-11} M (b) 1.8×10^{-9} M
(c) 1.34×10^{-54} M (d) 1.8×10^{-7} M

83. In group III analysis, buffer used to precipitate cations as hydroxide is
(a) $NH_4Cl + NH_4OH$
(b) $HCO_3^- + CO_2$
(c) $CH_3COOH + CH_3COONa$
(d) $C_6H_5COOH + C_6H_5COONa$

84. 100 mL of 0.02 M benzoic acid ($pK_a = 4.2$) is titrated using 0.02 M NaOH. pH after 50 mL and 100 mL of NaOH have been added are
(a) 3.50, 7 (b) 4.2, 7
(c) 4.2, 8.1 (d) 4.2, 8.25

85. pH of 0.01 M aqueous solution of Na*X*, Na*Y* and Na*Z* are 8, 9 and 10 respectively. Strongest acid of H*X*, H*Y* and H*Z* is
(a) H*X* (b) H*Y*
(c) H*Z* (d) Can't be predicted

86. 40 mL of 0.025 M solution of the protonated form of the amino acid phenyl alanine (H_2A^+) is treated with 10 mL of 0.1 M NaOH. pH at this stage is ($pK_{a_1} = 1.82$, $pK_{a_2} = 9.13$ of H_2A^+)
(a) 5.48 (b) 7.00 (c) 1.82 (d) 9.13

87. Henry's constant (in kbar) for four gases α, β, γ and δ in water at 298 K is given below :

	α	β	γ	δ
K_H	50	2	2×10^{-5}	0.5

(density of water = 10^3 kg m^{-3} at 298 K)
This table implies that **[JEE Main 2020, Sep.]**
(a) α has the highest solubility in water at a given pressure
(b) solubility of γ at 308 K is lower than at 298 K
(c) The pressure of a 55.5 molal solution of γ is 1 bar
(d) The pressure of a 55.5 molal solution of δ is 250 bar

88. Consider the following statements. **[JEE Main 2019]**

I. The pH of a mixture containing 400 mL of 0.1 M H_2SO_4 and 400 mL of 0.1 M NaOH will be approximately 1.3.

II. Ionic product of water is temperature dependent.

III. A monobasic acid with $K_a = 10^{-5}$ has a pH = 5. The degree of dissociation of this acid is 50%.

IV. The Le-Chatelier's principle is not applicable to common-ion effect.

The correct statements are

(a) I, II and IV (b) II and III

(c) I and II (d) I, II and III

89. pK_{a_1}, pK_{a_2} and pK_{a_3} of H_3PO_4 are respectively x, y and z. pH of 0.01 M Na_2HPO_4 solution is

(a) 2 (b) $\left(\frac{x+y}{2}\right)$

(c) $\left(\frac{y+z}{2}\right)$ (d) $\left(\frac{x+y+z}{2}\right)$

90. pK_b of NH_3 is 4.74 and pK_b of A^-, B^- and C^- are 4, 5 and 6 respectively. Aqueous solution of 0.01 M has pH in the increasing order

(a) $NH_4A < NH_4B < NH_4C$

(b) $NH_4C < NH_4B < NH_4A$

(c) $NH_4C < NH_4A < NH_4B = 7$

(d) all have equal pH being salt of weak acid and weak base

91. Arrange the following solutions in the decreasing order of pOH.

I. 0.01 M HCl II. 0.01 M NaOH

III. 0.01 M CH_3COONa IV. 0.01 M NaCl

[JEE Main 2020, Sep.]

(a) (I) > (III) > (IV) > (II) (b) (I) > (IV) > (III) > (II)

(c) (II) > (III) > (D) > (I) (d) (II) > (IV) > (III) > (I)

92. Degree of hydrolysis of the following is independent of concentration

I. NH_4CN II. NH_4HCO_3

III. NaHS IV. CH_3NH_3Cl

(a) I, II, III and IV (b) I and IV

(c) I, III and IV (d) I, II and III

93. Following are some of the certain facts of Ostwald's theory of acid-base indicators.

I. Ionised and unionised forms have different colours

II. Colour change is indicated at the end point when unionised form changes to ionised form due to change in pH

III. Benzenoid form changes to quinonoid form and *vice-versa* due to change in pH

Select the correct facts.

(a) I, II and III (b) I and III

(c) I and II (d) II and III

94. Select the correct statement(s).

(a) Methyl orange is red in alkali solution and yellow in acid solution

(b) Phenolphthalein is pink in alkali solution and colourless in acid solution

(c) Both (a) and (b)

(d) None of the above

95. Indicator can exist in two forms depending on the medium

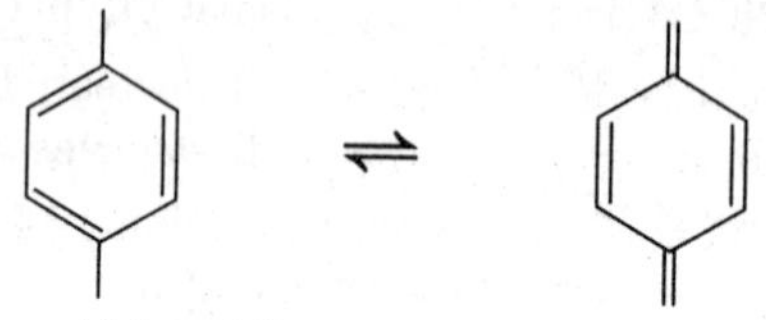

benzenoid form (*A*) quinonoid form (*B*)

Select the correct statement(s).

(a) Methyl orange assumes form (*A*) in alkali solution and form (*B*) in acid solution

(b) Phenolphthalein assumes form (*A*) in acid solution and form (*B*) in alkaline solution

(c) Thymophthalein assumes form (*A*) in acid solution and form (*B*) in alkali solution

(d) All of the above

96. For any weak acid indicator HIn ionising as

$$HIn \rightleftharpoons H^+ + In^-$$

colour of the unionised form (HIn) is observed when

(a) $\frac{[In^-]}{[HIn]} = \frac{1}{10}$ (b) $pH = pK_a - 1$

(c) Both (a) and (b) (d) None of these

97. In the above case colour of the ionised form (In^-) is observed when

(a) $\frac{[In^-]}{[HIn]} = 10$ (b) $pH = pK_a + 1$

(c) Both (a) and (b) (d) None of these

98. Select the correct statements about indicators.

(a) Near the equivalence point $pH = pK_a$ for weak acid indicator and $pH = (14 - pK_b)$ for weak base indicator

(b) Most indicators have a transition range of two pH units

(c) Methyl orange assumes quinonoid form in acid solution

(d) All the above statements are correct

99. pK_{In} of the indicator is 10. At the equivalence point pH is

(a) 5 (b) 10

(c) 7.5 (d) 7.0

100. An indicator is a weak acid and pH range of its colour is 3 to 5. If the neutral points of the indicator lies in the centre of the hydrogen ion concentration corresponding to given pH range then pH at the equivalence points is

(a) 3.3 (b) 4.0 (c) 7.0 (d) 5.0

101. In the titration of weak acid with strong base which indicator can't be used
(a) methyl orange
(b) phenolphthalein
(c) Both (a) and (b)
(d) None of these

102. In the titration of weak base with strong acid which indicator can't be used
(a) methyl orange (b) phenolphthalein
(c) Both (a) and (b) (d) None of these

103. Titration curve if a strong base is titrated with strong acid is

(a) 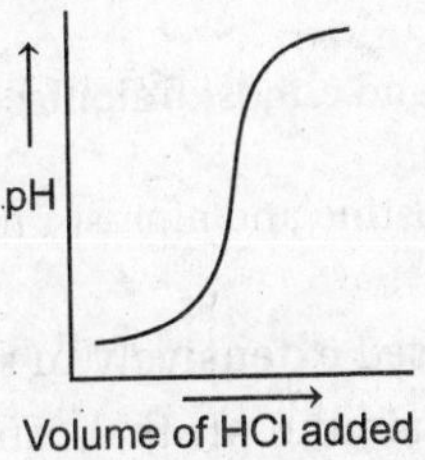

(b) 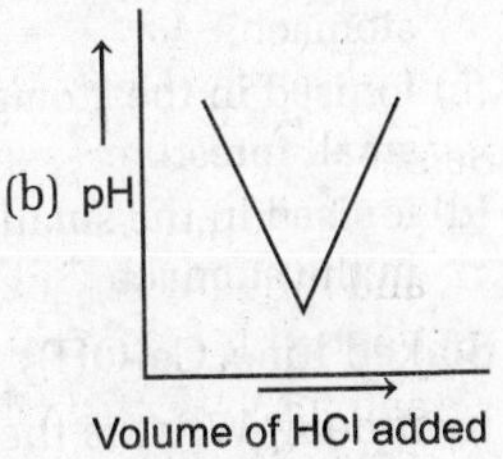

(c) 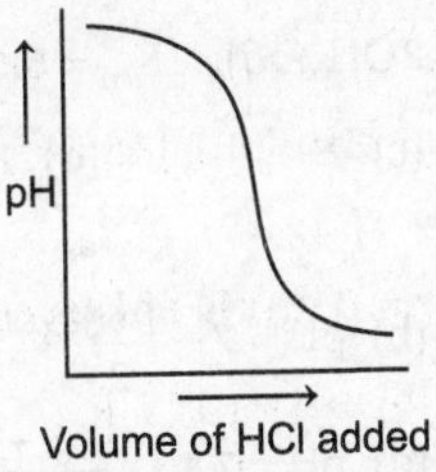

(d) 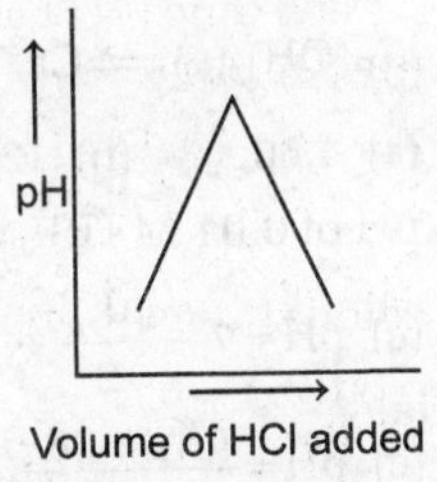

104. 100 mL of 0.1 M HCl is titrated using 0.1 M NaOH, using phenolphthalein indicator. pH after 50 mL of NaOH has been added is
(a) 7.0 (b) − 1.48
(c) 6.0 (d) 1.48

105. Which of the following reagents listed below could be added to water to make 0.10 M solution of NH_4^+?
(a) NH_3 (b) NH_4Cl
(c) NH_2Cl (d) CH_3CONH_2

106. In the reaction,
$$[Al(H_2O)_6^{3+}] + H_2O \rightleftharpoons [Al(H_2O)_5(OH)^{2+}] + H_3O^+$$
(a) $Al(H_2O)_6^{3+}$ is a base (b) $Al(H_2O)_6^{3+}$ is an acid
(c) Both (a) and (b) (d) None of these

107. Which is true about Zwitter ion $\overset{+}{N}H_3CH_2COO^-$?
(a) $NH_2CH_2COO^-$ is its conjugate base
(b) $H_3\overset{+}{N}CH_2COOH$ is its conjugate acid
(c) Both (a) and (b)
(d) None of the above

108. Autoionisation of liquid NH_3 is
$$2NH_3 \rightleftharpoons NH_4^+ + NH_2^-$$
with $K_{NH_3} = [NH_4^+][NH_2^-] = 10^{-30}$ at −50°C

Number of amide ions NH_2^-, present per mm^3 of pure liquid NH_3 is
(a) 602 (b) 300
(c) 200 (d) 100

109. *B*OH is a weak base. Molar concentration of *B*OH that provides a $[OH^-]$ of 1.5×10^{-3} M $[K_b(BOH) = 1.5 \times 10^{-5} M]$ is
(a) 0.15 M (b) 0.1515 M
(c) 0.0015 M (d) 1.5×10^{-5} M

110. pH of the solution containing 50.0 mL of 0.3 M HCl and 50.0 mL of 0.4 M NH_3 is
$$[pK_a(NH_4^+) = 9.26]$$
(a) 4.74 (b) 9.26
(c) 8.78 (d) 4.63

111. Which of the following solutions will have pH of 4.74?
(a) 100 mL of 1 M CH_3COOH ($pK_a = 4.74$) at the equivalent point using NaOH
(b) 50 mL of 1 M CH_3COONa + 25 mL of 1 M HCl
(c) 50 mL of 1 M of CH_3COOH + 25 mL of 1 M NaOH
(d) Both (b) and (c)

112. pH at which an acid indicator with $K_a = 1 \times 10^{-5}$ changes colour when the indicator is 1×10^{-3} M, is
(a) 5 (b) 3 (c) 8 (d) 4

113. A weak base *B*, has basicity constant $K_b = 2 \times 10^{-5}$. The pH of any solution in which $[B] = [BH^+]$ is
(a) 4.7 (b) 7.0 (c) 9.3 (d) 9.7

114. The correctly balanced net ionic equation for the reaction that occurs when a solution of acetic acid is mixed with a solution of sodium carbonate is
(a) $CH_3COOH(aq) + CO_3^{2-}(aq) \rightleftharpoons CH_3COO^-(aq) + HCO_3^-(aq)$
(b) $H_3O^+(aq) + CO_3^{2-}(aq) \rightleftharpoons HCO_3^-(aq) + H_2O$
(c) $CH_3COOH(aq) + Na_2CO_3(aq) \rightleftharpoons CH_3COO^-(aq) + NaHCO_3(aq) + Na^+(aq)$
(d) $CH_3COOH(aq) + OH^-(aq) \rightleftharpoons CH_3COO^-(aq) + H_2O$

115. pH of a mixture containing 0.10 M X^- (base) and 0.20 M *HX* with $pK_b(X^-) = 4$ is
(a) 4 + log 2 (b) 4 − log 2
(c) 10 + log 2 (d) 10 − log 2

116. Assuming 100% ionisation which will have maximum pH?
(a) 0.01 M NH_4Cl (b) 0.01 M $(NH_4)_2SO_4$
(c) 0.01 M $(NH_4)_3PO_4$ (d) Equal

117. $H_2O + H_3PO_4 \rightleftharpoons H_3O^+ + H_2PO_4^-$, $pK_1 = 2.15$
$H_2O + H_2PO_4^- \rightleftharpoons H_3O^+ + HPO_4^{2-}$, $pK_2 = 7.20$
Hence, pH of 0.01 M NaH_2PO_4 is
(a) 9.35 (b) 4.675 (c) 2.675 (d) 7.350

118. Per cent ionisation of a weak acid can be calculated using the formula

(a) $100\sqrt{\dfrac{K_a}{C}}$ (b) $\dfrac{100}{1+10^{(pK_a - pH)}}$

(c) Both (a) and (b) (d) None of these

119. pH of a mixture of 1 M benzoic acid ($pK_a = 4.20$) and 1 M sodium benzoate is 4.5. In 300 mL buffer, benzoic acid is

(a) 200 mL (b) 150 mL

(c) 100 mL (d) 50 mL

120. The solubility of A_2X_3 is S mol L^{-1}. Its solubility product is

(a) $6S^4$ (b) $64S^4$ (c) $36S^5$ (d) $108S^5$

121. If the freezing point of 0.1 molal $HA(aq)$ is $-0.2046°C$, then pH of the solution is $[K_f(H_2O) = 1.86° mol^{-1}\ kg]$

(a) 1 (b) 2 (c) 1.3 (d) 1.7

122. If the equilibrium constant of the reaction of weak acid HA with strong base is 10^9, then pH of 0.1 M Na*A* is

(a) 5 (b) 9

(c) 7 (d) 8

123. pH of mixture of HA and A^- buffer is 5. K_b of $A^- = 10^{-10}$. Hence, $[HA]/[A^-]$ will be

(a) 1 (b) 10

(c) 0.1 (d) 100

124. 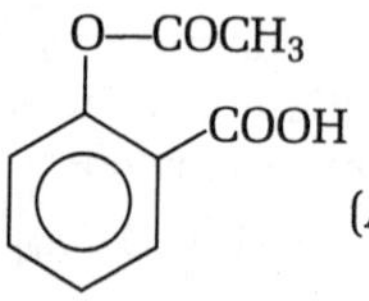

(Aspirin) is a pain reliever with $pK_a = 2$. Two tablets each containing 0.09 g of aspirin are dissolved in 100 mL solution. pH will be

(a) 0.5 (b) 1.0

(c) 0.0 (d) 2.0

125. Number of $(OH)^-$ in 1 mL solution of pH = 13 is

(a) 1×10^{-13} (b) 6.00×10^7

(c) 6.00×10^{13} (d) 6.02×10^{19}

126. 1 M NH_4OH and 1 M HCl are mixed to make total volume of 300 mL. If pH of the mixture is 9.26 and $pK_a(NH_4^+) = 9.26$ then volume ratio of NH_4OH and HCl will be

(a) 1 : 1 (b) 1 : 2 (c) 2 : 1 (d) 3 : 1

127. pK_a (CH_3COOH) is 4.74. *x* moles of lead acetate and 0.1 mole of acetic acid in 1 L solution make a solution of pH = 5.04. Hence, *x* is

(a) 0.2 (b) 0.05 (c) 0.1 (d) 0.02

128. A solution is a mixture of 0.05 M NaCl and 0.05 M NaI. The concentration of iodide ion in the solution when AgCl just starts precipitating is equal to (K_{sp} AgCl $= 1 \times 10^{-10}\ M^2$; K_{sp} AgI $= 4 \times 10^{-16}\ M^2$)

(a) 4×10^{-6} M (b) 2×10^{-8} M

(c) 2×10^{-7} M (d) 8×10^{-15} M

129. The pK_a of acetylsalicylic acid (aspirin) is 3.5. The pH of gastric juice in human stomach is about 2.3 and the pH in the small intestine is about 8. Aspirin will be

(a) unionised in the small intestine and in the stomach

(b) completely ionised in the small intestine and in the stomach

(c) ionised in the stomach and almost unionised in the small intestine

(d) ionised in the small intestine and almost unionised in the stomach

130. Slaked lime, $Ca(OH)_2$ is used extensively in sewage treatment. What is the maximum pH that can be established in $Ca(OH)_2(aq)$?

$$Ca(OH)_2(s) \rightleftharpoons Ca^{2+}(aq) + 2OH^-(aq), \quad K_{sp} = 5.5 \times 10^{-6}$$

(a) 1.66 (b) 12.35 (c) 7 (d) 14

131. pH of 0.01 M HS^- will be

(a) $pH = 7 + \dfrac{pK_a}{2} + \dfrac{\log C}{2}$ (b) $pH = 7 - \dfrac{pK_b}{2} + \dfrac{\log C}{2}$

(c) $pH = \dfrac{pK_1 + pK_2}{2}$ (d) $pH = 7 + \left(\dfrac{pK_a - pK_b}{2}\right)$

132. Solution of aniline hydrochloride is *X* due to hydrolysis of *Y*. *X* and *Y* are

(a) basic $C_6H_5NH_3^+$ (b) acidic $C_6H_5NH_3^+$

(c) basic Cl^- (d) acidic Cl^-

133. pH of the solution after NaCl solution is electrolysed will

(a) remain constant (b) increase

(c) decrease (d) can't be determined

134. $FeCl_3$ solution is acidic due to hydrolysis of

(a) $FeCl_3$ (b) Fe^{3+}

(c) Cl^- (d) None of these

135. Silver iodide is used in cloud seeding to produce rain

$$AgI \rightleftharpoons Ag^+(aq) + I^-(aq); \quad K_{sp} = 8.5 \times 10^{-7}$$

$AgNO_3$ and KI are mixed to give $[Ag^+] = 0.010$ M; $[I^-] = 0.015$ M. Will AgI precipitate?

(a) Yes

(b) No

(c) Can't say

(d) This depends on $[NO_3^-]$ and $[K^+]$

136. pK_a of lactic acid $\left(CH_3—\underset{\displaystyle OH}{\underset{|}{C}}—COOH\right)$ is 5. pH of 0.005 M calcium lactate solution is
(a) 10.5 (b) 8.5
(c) 5.0 (d) 9.7

137. Lemon juice normally has a pH of 2. If all the acid in the lemon juice is citric acid and there are no citrate salts present, then what will be the citric acid concentration [HCit] in the lemon juice ? (Assume that only the first hydrogen of citric acid is important)
$HCit \rightleftharpoons H^+ + Cit^-$, $K_a = 8.4 \times 10^{-4}$ mol L^{-1}
(a) 8.4×10^{-4} M (b) 4.2×10^{-4} M
(c) 16.8×10^{-4} M (d) 12.0×10^{-2} M

138. The solubility products of *MA*, *MB*, *MC* and *MD* are 1.8×10^{-10}, 4×10^{-3}, 4×10^{-8} and 6×10^{-5} respectively. If a 0.01 M solution of *MX* is added dropwise to a mixture containing *A*, *B*, *C* and *D* ions then the one to be precipitated first will be
(a) *MA* (b) *MB*
(c) *MC* (d) *MD*

139. Amphoteric behaviour is shown by
(a) H_2CO_3 and Al_2O_3 (b) HCO_3^- and H_2O
(c) HCO_3^- and H_3O^+ (d) H_2CO_3 and H_2O

140. A 50.00 mL sample of acetic acid was titrated with 0.1200 M KOH and 38.62 mL of base were required to reach the equivalence point. What was the pH of the titration mixture, when 19.31 mL of base has been added? [pK_a (acetic acid) = 4.74]
(a) 2.94 (b) 3.54
(c) 4.74 (d) 5.74

141. Which of the hydrated species can exist?
I. $H_5O_2^+$ II. H_3O^+
III. $H_3O_2^-$ IV. $H_5O_3^-$
Select the correct alternate.
(a) Only II (b) I and II
(c) I, II and III (d) I, II, III and IV

142. What is $[NH_4^+]$ in a solution that is 0.02 M NH_3 and 0.01 M KOH? [$K_b(NH_3) = 1.8 \times 10^{-5}$]
(a) 3.6×10^{-5} M (b) 1.8×10^{-5} M
(c) 0.9×10^{-5} M (d) 7.2×10^{-5} M

143. The pH of a solution resulting when 50 mL of 0.2 M HCl is mixed with 50 mL of 0.20 M AcOH ($K_a = 1.8 \times 10^{-5}$) is
(a) 0.70 (b) 0.30 (c) 1.00 (d) 2.00

144. pK_{a_1} and pK_{a_2} of H_2SO_3 are 1.82 and 7.20. pH after 20 mL of 0.160 M NaOH is added to 40 mL of 0.080 M H_2SO_3 is
(a) 7.00 (b) 1.82
(c) 8.80 (d) 4.51

145. The acid ionisation (hydrolysis) constant of Zn^{2+} is 1.0×10^{-9}. Hence, pH of 0.001 M solution of $ZnCl_2$ is
(a) 9.0 (b) 3.0 (c) 6.0 (d) 7.0

146. 0.2 M AcOH is ... % dissociation in 0.1 M HCl (K_a of AcOH = 1.8×10^{-5}).
(a) 0.018% (b) 0.036%
(c) 1.8% (d) 3.6%

147. Basic dissociation constant of $Zn(OH)^+$ is ... if acid ionisation constant of Zn^{2+} is 1.0×10^{-9}.
(a) 1×10^{-9} (b) 1×10^{9}
(c) 1×10^{5} (d) 1×10^{-5}

148. At what pH will a 1.0×10^{-3} M solution of an indicator with $K_b = 1.0 \times 10^{-10}$ change colour
(a) 3.0 (b) 4.0 (c) 10.0 (d) 7.0

149. An acid indicator is ... % in its basic form at a pH of 5 ($K_a = 1 \times 10^{-5}$)
(a) 20% (b) 40%
(c) 50% (d) 100%

150. Which one of the following is most soluble?
(a) CuS ($K_{sp} = 8 \times 10^{-37}$)
(b) MnS ($K_{sp} = 7 \times 10^{-16}$)
(c) Bi_2S_3 ($K_{sp} = 1 \times 10^{-70}$)
(d) Ag_2S ($K_{sp} = 6 \times 10^{-51}$)

151. The solubility of AgCl will be minimum in
(a) 0.001 M $AgNO_3$ (b) 0.01 M NaCl
(c) 0.01 M $CaCl_2$ (d) pure water

152. Conjugate base of Zn^{2+} is
(a) $Zn(OH)^+$ (b) $Zn(OH)_2$
(c) ZnO (d) $Zn(H_2O)^{2+}$

153. An acid solution of 0.005 M has a pH of 5. The degree of ionisation of acid is
(a) 0.1×10^{-2} (b) 0.2×10^{-2}
(c) 0.5×10^{-4} (d) 0.6×10^{-6}

154. The solubility product of CuS, CdS and HgS are $10^{-31}, 10^{-44}, 10^{-54}$, respectively. The solubility of these sulphides are in the order
(a) CdS > HgS > CuS
(b) HgS > CdS > CuS
(c) CdS > CuS > HgS
(d) CuS > CdS > HgS

155. The solubility product of $BaCl_2$ is 4×10^{-9}. Its solubility in mol L^{-1} is
(a) 4×10^{-3} (b) 4×10^{-9}
(c) 1×10^{-3} (d) 1×10^{-9}

156. The solubility of a saturated solution of calcium fluoride is 2×10^{-4} mol L^{-1}. Its solubility product is
(a) 12×10^{-2} (b) 14×10^{-4}
(c) 22×10^{-11} (d) 32×10^{-12}

157. The ionisation constant of phenol is higher than that of ethanol because
(a) phenoxide ion is bulkier than ethoxide
(b) phenoxide ion is stronger base than ethoxide
(c) phenoxide ion is stabilised through delocalisation
(d) phenoxide ion is less stable than ethoxide

158. A solution having pH = 13 contained H^+ ions in 1 mL of solution which is
(a) 6.02×10^7 (b) 4.54×10^5
(c) 8.42×10^8 (d) 6.15×10^7

159. How many times a solution of pH = 2 has higher acidity than the solution of pH = 6?
(a) 400 (b) 800
(c) 1200 (d) 10000

160. The K_a for formic acid is 2.0×10^{-4} mol L^{-1}, then K_h for $HCOO^-$ is
(a) 2×10^{-5} mol L^{-1}
(b) 4×10^{-7} mol L^{-1}
(c) 5×10^{-11} mol L^{-1}
(d) 5×10^{-5} mol L^{-1}

161. A solution having hydronium ion concentration is 6.2×10^{-9} mol/L, its pH is
(a) 6.42 (b) 7.34
(c) 8.21 (d) 8.94

162. On dissolving CO_2 in water the following equilibrium is established

$$CO_2 + 2H_2O \rightleftharpoons H_3O^+ + HCO_3^-$$

For which the value of equilibrium constant is 3.8×10^{-7} and pH = 6.0. The $\frac{[HCO_3^-]}{[CO_2]}$ ratio is
(a) 3.8 (b) 0.38
(c) 13.8 (d) 1.38

163. The solubility product of $PbBr_2$ is 10.8×10^{-5}. It is 70% dissociated in saturated solution. The solubility of salt is
(a) 4.285×10^{-2} (b) 6.756×10^{-3}
(c) 3.399×10^{-4} (d) 5.435×10^{-2}

164. The silver ion in a solution is precipitated by addition of chloride ion. The final volume of solution is 500 mL. What should be the concentration of Cl^- ion if not more than 0.10 mg of Ag^+ ion remains unprecipitated?
($K_{sp}(AgCl) = 1.0 \times 10^{-10}$)
(a) 5.4×10^{-5} M (b) 1.9×10^{-6} M
(c) 5.4×10^{-4} M (d) 1.9×10^{-7} M

165. For the reaction,

$$Hg^{2+} + 2Cl^- \rightleftharpoons HgCl_2; \quad K = 1.65 \times 10^{13}$$

concentration of Hg^{2+} at the equivalence point in the titration of 2.0 mmol of Hg^{2+} with Cl^- when final volume is 100 mL, is
(a) 8.25×10^{14} M (b) 1.65×10^{13} M
(c) 2.87×10^6 M (d) 6.72×10^{-6} M

166. 0.1 mol of CH_3NH_2 ($K_b = 5 \times 10^{-4}$) is mixed with 0.08 mol of HCl and diluted to 1 L. What will be the H^+ concentration in the solution?
(a) 8×10^{-2} M (b) 8×10^{-11} M
(c) 1.6×10^{-11} M (d) 8×10^{-5} M

167. At the equivalence point in the titration of CrO_4^{2-} with Ag^+

$$2Ag^+ + CrO_4^{2-} \rightleftharpoons Ag_2CrO_4(s)$$

(a) $p_{Ag} + 2p_{CrO_4} = pK_{sp}$
(b) $3p_{CrO_4} = pK_{sp} + 2\log 2$
(c) $3p_{Ag} + 2\log 2 = pK_{sp}$
(d) All of these are true

168. Internal proton transfer can take place in one or more of the following acids
I. Glycine II. Anthranilic acid
III. Sulphanilic acid IV. Salicylic acid
Select such acids
(a) I, II and III (b) I, III and IV
(c) II, III and IV (d) All of these

169. Select the correct statement(s).
(a) When we add NH_4Cl to water, solution becomes acidic due to weak acid NH_4^+.
(b) When we add CH_3COONa, solution becomes basic due to Na^+.
(c) At 100°C, pH = 6 in water thus, it is basic solution.
(d) pH of 1×10^{-7} M HCl is 7.

170. pK_{In} of bromocresol green is 4.7. Thus, ratio of its yellow and blue forms at pH 3.7 is
(a) 1:10 (b) 10:1 (c) 1:1 (d) 1:3

171. Select the correct statement(s).
(a) When pH of blood rises above about 7.45, alkalosis occurs.
(b) When pH of blood falls below about 7.35, acidosis occurs.
(c) Respiratory alkalosis is caused by hyperventilation, or excessive respiration.
(d) All of the above

172. Following is the titration curve of CH_3COOH against NaOH added with phenolphthalein as the indicator.

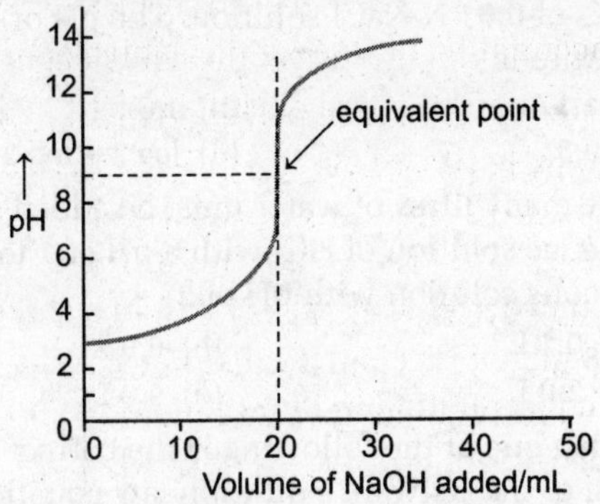

K_{In} value of phenolphthalein is 4.0×10^{-10}. Thus, incorrect statement is
(a) it begins to change colour from the pH 9.4
(b) it begins to change colour from acid colourless at pH 8.4 to the base form (reddish pink) at pH 10.4
(c) phenolphthalein is suitable indicator for CH_3COOH — NaOH titration
(d) phenolphthalein is a weak acid

173. $Ag^+ + NH_3 \rightleftharpoons [Ag(NH_3)]^+$; $k_1 = 3.5 \times 10^{-3}$
$[Ag(NH_3)]^+ + NH_3 \rightleftharpoons [Ag(NH_3)_2]^+$; $k_2 = 1.7 \times 10^{-3}$
then the formation constant of $[Ag(NH_3)_2]^+$ is
(a) 6.00×10^{-6} (b) 6.00×10^{6}
(c) 6.00×10^{-9} (d) None of these

174. Select the correct statement(s).
(a) Red colour of methyl red is due to the structure

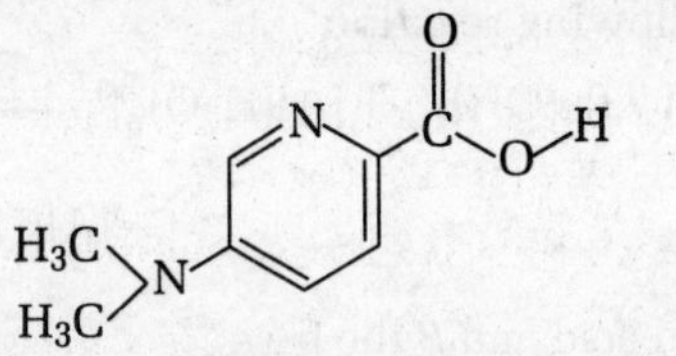

(b) Yellow colour of methyl red is due to the structure

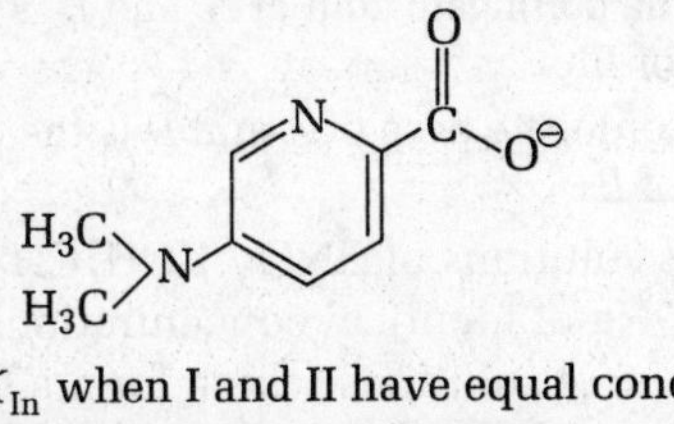

(c) pH = pK_{In} when I and II have equal concentrations
(d) All the above are correct statements

175. Adding 0.25 mL of a strong monoprotic acid solution to 500 mL of water produced a pH of 2.00. Thus, concentration of the strong acid is
(a) 10 M (b) 20 M (c) 5 N (d) 2 M

176. A solution is 0.1 M with respect to Ag^+, Ca^{2+}, Mg^{2+} and Al^{3+} which will precipitate at lowest concentration of $[PO_4^{3-}]$ when solution of Na_3PO_4 is added?
(a) Ag_3PO_4 ($K_{sp} = 1 \times 10^{-6}$)
(b) $Ca_3(PO_4)_2$ ($K_{sp} = 1 \times 10^{-33}$)
(c) $Mg_3(PO_4)_2$ ($K_{sp} = 1 \times 10^{-24}$)
(d) $AlPO_4$ ($K_{sp} = 1 \times 10^{-20}$)

177. Which is not example of common ion effect?
(a) NaCl + AgCl
(b) H_2S + HCl
(c) CH_3COOH + NaOH
(d) $NH_4OH + NH_4Cl$

178. 1 dm^3 solution containing 10^{-5} moles each of Cl^- ions and CrO_4^{2-} ions is treated with 10^{-4} moles of silver nitrate. Which one of the following observations is made?

$[K_{sp}\ Ag_2CrO_4 = 4 \times 10^{-12}]$
$[K_{sp}\ AgCl = 1 \times 10^{-10}]$

(a) Precipitation does not occur.
(b) Silver chromate gets precipitated first.
(c) Silver chloride gets precipitated first.
(d) Both silver chromate and silver chloride start precipitating simultaneously.

179. The K_{sp} of Ag_2CrO_4 is 1.1×10^{-12} at 298 K. The solubility (in mol/L) of Ag_2CrO_4 in a 0.1 M $AgNO_3$ solution is **[JEE Advanced 2013]**
(a) 1.1×10^{-11} (b) 1.1×10^{-10}
(c) 1.1×10^{-12} (d) 1.1×10^{-9}

180. For preparaing a buffer solution of pH = 7.0, which buffer system you will choose?
(a) $H_3PO_4, H_2PO_4^-$ (b) $H_2PO_4^-, HPO_4^{2-}$
(c) HPO_4^{2-}, PO_4^{3-} (d) H_3PO_4, PO_4^{3-}

181. The charge balance equation of species in 0.100 M acetic acid solution is given by
(a) $[H^+] = [OH^-]$
(b) $[H^+] = [CH_3COO^-]$
(c) $[H^+] = [OH^-] + [CH_3COO^-]$
(d) $2[H^+] = [OH^-] + [CH_3COO^-]$

182. Two acids A and B have pK_a 4 and 6, then
(a) A is 4/6 times stronger than B.
(b) A is 10 times stronger than B.
(c) A is 6/4 times stronger than B.
(d) B is 10 times stronger than A.

183. Both HCOOH and CH_3COOH solutions have equal pH. If $\frac{K_1}{K_2}$ (ratio of acid ionisation constants) of these acids is 4, their molar concentration ratio will be
(a) 2 (b) 0.5 (c) 4 (d) 0.25

184. The dissociation constant for acetic acid and HCN at 25°C are 1.5×10^{-5} and 4.5×10^{-10} respectively. The equilibrium constant for the equilibrium,

$CN^- + CH_3COOH \rightleftharpoons HCN + CH_3COO^-$ would be

(a) 3.0×10^{5} (b) 3.0×10^{-5}
(c) 3.0×10^{-4} (d) 3.0×10^{4}

185. 30 cc of $\frac{M}{3}$ HCl, 20 cc of $\frac{M}{2}$ HNO_3 and 40 cc of $\frac{M}{4}$ NaOH solutions are mixed and the volume was made up to 1 dm^3. The pH of the resulting solution is

(a) 2 (b) 1 (c) 3 (d) 8

186. pH value of which one of the following is not equal to one?

(a) 0.1 M HNO_3
(b) 0.05 M H_2SO_4
(c) 0.1 M CH_3COOH
(d) 50 cm^3 of 0.4 M HCl + 50 cm^3 of 0.2 M NaOH

187. Calculate the normality of 250 mL aqueous solution of H_2SO_4 having pH = 0.00.

(a) 0.25 N (b) 0.50 N
(c) 1 N (d) 2 N

188. 0.1 M HCl and 0.1 M H_2SO_4 each of volume 2 mL are mixed and the volume is made upto 6 mL by adding 2 mL of 0.01 N NaCl solution. The pH of the resulting mixture is

(a) 1.17 (b) 1.0
(c) 0.3 (d) log 2 − log 3

189. How many litres of water must be added to 1 L of an aqueous solution of HCl with a pH of 1 to create an aqueous solution with pH of 2? **[JEE Main 2013]**

(a) 0.1 L (b) 0.9 L
(c) 2.0 L (d) 9.0 L

190. Which one of the following is the correct quadratic form of the Ostwald's dilution law equation?

(a) $\alpha^2C + \alpha K - K = 0$ (b) $\alpha^2C - \alpha K - K = 0$
(c) $\alpha^2C - \alpha K + K = 0$ (d) $\alpha^2C + \alpha K + K = 0$

191. The solubility product of a salt having formula M_2X_3 is 2.2×10^{-20}. If the solubility of an another salt having formula M_2X is twice the molar solubility of M_2X_3, the solubility product of M_2X is

(a) 3×10^{-12} (b) 9.16×10^{-5}
(c) 4.58×10^{-5} (d) 2.76×10^{-18}

Objective Questions Type II [One or more than one correct option(s)]

In each of the questions below, four choices are given, of which one or more than one are correct.

1. An acid-base indicator has a K_a of 3.0×10^{-5}. The acid form of the indicator is red and the basic form is blue. Then

(a) pH is 4.05 when indicator is 75% red
(b) pH is 5.00 when indicator is 75% blue
(c) pH is 5.00 when indicator is 75% red
(d) pH is 4.05 when indicator is 75% blue

2. The equilibrium constant for the reaction

$HONO(aq) + CN^-(aq) \rightleftharpoons HCN(aq) + ONO^-(aq)$ is 1.1×10^{6}. From the magnitude of this K_{eq} one can conclude that

(a) CN^- is stronger base than ONO^-
(b) HCN is a stronger acid than HONO
(c) the conjugate base of HONO is ONO^-
(d) the conjugate acid of CN^- is HCN

3. The pH of a solution of 0.10 M CH_3COOH increases when which of the following substances is added?

(a) $NaHSO_4$ (b) $HClO_4$ (c) NH_4NO_3 (d) K_2CO_3

4. All of the following are acid-base conjugate pairs

(a) HONO, NO_2^- (b) H_3O^+, OH^-
(c) $CH_3NH_3^+, CH_3NH_2$ (d) HS^-, S^{2-}

5. Consider the following examples

I. blood II. saline solution
III. benzoic acid + sodium benzoate

Solution(s) with no buffer capacity is/are

(a) I and II (b) Only II
(c) II and III (d) I and III

6. In the following reaction

$$\underset{A}{[Cu(H_2O)_3(OH)]^+} + \underset{B}{[Al(H_2O)_6]^{3+}} \longrightarrow \underset{C}{[Cu(H_2O)_4]^{2+}} + \underset{D}{[Al(H_2O)_5(OH)]^{2+}}$$

(a) A is an acid and B the base
(b) A is a base and B the acid
(c) C is the conjugate acid of A, and D is the conjugate base of B
(d) C is conjugate base of A and D is the conjugate acid of B.

7. Aqueous solutions of HNO_3, KOH, CH_3COOH, and CH_3COONa of identical concentrations are provided. The pair(s) of solutions which form a buffer upon mixing is (are) **[IIT JEE 2010]**

(a) HNO_3 and CH_3COOH (b) KOH and CH_3COONa
(c) HNO_3 and CH_3COONa (d) CH_3COOH and CH_3COONa

8. Which is true about Zwitter ion $\overset{+}{N}H_3CH_2COO^-$?

(a) $NH_2CH_2COO^-$ is its conjugate base
(b) $H_3\overset{+}{N}CH_2COOH$ is its conjugate acid
(c) It migrates to cathode in acidic solution
(d) It migrates to anode in basic solution

9. Which is the set of amphiprotic species?
(a) H_3O^+, HPO_4^{2-}, HCO_3^-
(b) H_2O, HPO_3^{2-}, $H_2PO_2^-$
(c) HSO_4^-, $H_2PO_4^-$, $H_2PO_3^-$
(d) HCO_3^-, HPO_3^{2-}, HPO_4^{2-}

10. H_2O is Lewis acid and Lowry-Bronsted acid in
(a) $H_2O + H_2O \rightleftharpoons H_3O^+ + HO^-$
(b) $NH_3 + H_2O \rightleftharpoons NH_4^+ + OH^-$
(c) $CaO + H_2O \rightleftharpoons Ca(OH)_2$
(d) $CH_3COO^- + H_2O \rightleftharpoons CH_3COOH + OH^-$

11. The following reaction occurs in the body
$$CO_2 + H_2O \rightleftharpoons H_2CO_3 \rightleftharpoons H^+ + HCO_3^-$$
If CO_2 escapes from the system
(a) pH will decrease
(b) hydrogen ion concentration will decrease
(c) H_2CO_3 concentration remains unaltered
(d) forward reaction will be promoted

12. The following equilibrium is established when hydrogen chloride is dissolved in acetic acid.
$$HCl + CH_3COOH \rightleftharpoons Cl^- + CH_3COOH_2^+$$
The set that characterises the conjugate acid-base pair is
(a) (HCl, CH_3COOH) and ($CH_3COOH_2^+$, Cl^-)
(b) (HCl, $CH_3COOH_2^+$) and (CH_3COOH, Cl^-)
(c) ($CH_3COOH_2^+$, HCl) and (Cl^-, CH_3COOH)
(d) (HCl, Cl^-) and ($CH_3COOH_2^+$, CH_3COOH)

13. Which of the following will not function as buffer solution?
(a) $NaCl + NaOH$ (b) Borax + Boric acid
(c) $NaH_2PO_4 + Na_2HPO_4$ (d) $NH_4Cl + NH_4OH$

14. The pH of a solution of 0.10 M CH_3COOH increases, when which of the following substances is added?
(a) $NaHSO_4$ (b) $HClO_4$
(c) NH_4NO_3 (d) K_2CO_3

15. Select the correct statement(s).
(a) NH_4Cl is a strong acid in liquid NH_3.
(b) $NaNH_2$ is a strong base in liquid NH_3.
(c) CH_3COOH is a base in H_2SO_4.
(d) H_3O^+ is the strongest acid that can exist in aqueous solution.

Numerical Value Questions

All these questions have a Numerical value as their answer, solve the questions and write your answer.

1. Ionic product of water at 100°C is 55 times than that at 25°C.
Calculate the value of pH of water at 100°C

2. The ion product of D_2O is 1.35×10^{-15} at 25°C.
For what values of pD will a solution be acidic in D_2O ?

3. The value of hydrolysis constant K_h is .... $\times 10^{-5}$ pH of the following solution at 25°C. 0.1 M ammonium acetate, $K_a = K_b = 1.8 \times 10^{-5}$

4. The equilibrium constants for glycine (α-amino acetic acid) are given in terms of K_1 and K_2 of the protonated form
$$HOOC—CH_2—NH_3^+ \rightleftharpoons HOOC—CH_2—NH_2 + H^+ \quad K_1 = 4.5 \times 10^{-3}$$
$$HOOC—CH_2—NH_2 \rightleftharpoons {}^-OOC—CH_2—NH_2 + H^+ \quad K_2 = 1.7 \times 10^{-10}$$
Calculate the pH of 0.01 M glycine in pure water

5. Calculate the pH of 1 M NaH_2PO_4 and 1 M Na_2HPO_4 for H_3PO_4, $pK_{a_1} = 2.15$, $pK_{a_2} = 7.20$, $pK_{a_3} = 12.37$

6. The "fixing" of photographic films involves dissolving of unexposed silver bromide in hypo solution (sodium thiosulphate).
$$AgBr(s) + 2S_2O_3^{2-}(aq) \rightleftharpoons [Ag(S_2O_3)_2]^{3-}(aq) + Br^-(aq)$$
The molar solubility of $AgBr(s)$ in 0.10 M. $Na_2S_2O_3$. is .... $\times 10^{-2}$ M
$$K_{sp}(AgBr) = 5.4 \times 10^{-13},$$
$$K_f[Ag(S_2O_3)_2]^{3-} = 2.9 \times 10^{13}$$

7. Two solutions, A and B, each of 100 L was made by dissolving 4 g of NaOH and 9.8 g of H_2SO_4 in water, respectively. The pH of the resultant solution obtained from mixing 40 L of solution A and 10 L of solution B is......... **[JEE Main 2020]**

8. The solubility of a salt of weak acid (AB) at pH 3 is $Y \times 10^{-3}$ mol L^{-1}. The value of Y is......... .
(Given that, the value of solubility product of AB $(K_{sp}) = 2 \times 10^{-10}$ and the value of ionisation constant of HB $(K_a) = 1 \times 10^{-8}$ **[JEE Advanced 2018]**

9. Two salts A_2X and MX have the same value of solubility product of 4.0×10^{-12}. The ratio of their molar solubilities, i.e. $\frac{S(A_2X)}{S(MX)}$ = ... **[JEE Main 2021, March]**
(Round off to the nearest integer).

10. 0.01 moles of a weak acid $HA(K_a = 2.0 \times 10^{-6})$ is dissolved in 1.0 L of 0.1 M HCl solution. The degree of dissociation of HA is .... $\times 10^{-5}$ (Round off to the nearest integer). **[JEE Main 2021, March]**
[Neglect volume change on adding HA. Assume degree of dissociation <<1]

11. In order to prepare a buffer solution of pH 5.74, sodium acetate is added to acetic acid. If the concentration of acetic acid in the buffer is 1.0 M, the concentration of sodium acetate in the buffer is .... M. (Round off to the nearest integer).
[Given : pK_a (acetic acid) = 4.74] **[JEE Main 2021, March]**

12. Sulphurous acid (H_2SO_3) has $K_{a_1} = 1.7 \times 10^{-2}$ and $K_{a_2} = 6.4 \times 10^{-8}$. The pH of 0.588 M H_2SO_3 is .... (Round off to the Nearest Integer)

13. The solubility of $CdSO_4$ in water is 8.0×10^{-4} mol L^{-1}. Its solubility in 0.01 M H_2SO_4 solution is .... $\times 10^{-6}$ mol L^{-1}. (Round off to the nearest integer) (Assume that solubility is much less than 0.01 M) **[JEE Main 2021, March]**

Comprehension Based Questions

In these questions, a passage has been given followed by questions based on it. You have to answer the questions based on the passage given.

***Passage* 1** *Read the following passage and answer the questions at the end of it.*
Acid rain is an environmental concern all over the world. In assessing the acidity of rainfall, it is important to have an idea of the acidity of natural rainwater. Assuming that natural rain water (that is, rainwater uncontaminated with nitric acid or sulphuric acid) is in equilibrium with 3.6×10^{-4} atmCO_2 (the Henry's law constant is 1.25×10^6 Torr).

$$K_{a_1}(H_2CO_3) = 4.3 \times 10^{-7}$$

1. What is the pH of natural rain water?
(a) 5.64 (b) 5.70 (c) 7.00 (d) 7.40

2. pH of natural rain water would have been in pre-industrial times when the partial pressure of CO_2 was about 2.8×10^{-4} atm.
(a) 7.0 (b) 5.64
(c) 7.4 (d) 5.70

3. If SO_2 content in the atmosphere is 0.12 ppm by volume, pH of rain water (assume 100% ionisation of acid rain as monobasic acid.)
(a) 5.7 (b) 5.6 (c) 5.4 (d) 2.0

***Passage* 2** *Following titration method is taken to compute stepwise ionisation constant of a weak dibasic acid.*

A has two ionisation proton and there can be stepwise neutralisation by NaOH

A : 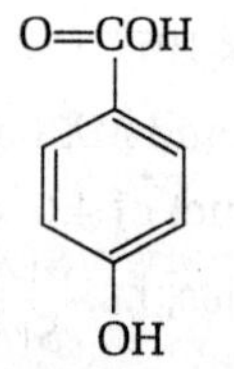

p-hydroxybenzoic acid

25 mL of a dilute aqueous solution of *A* is titration with 0.02 M NaOH (*aq*) and pH measured.

Step	Volume of NaOH added	pH
I	8.12 mL	4.57
II	16.24 mL	7.02 (at equivalence point)

1. Which H^+ is removed in step I ?

(a) 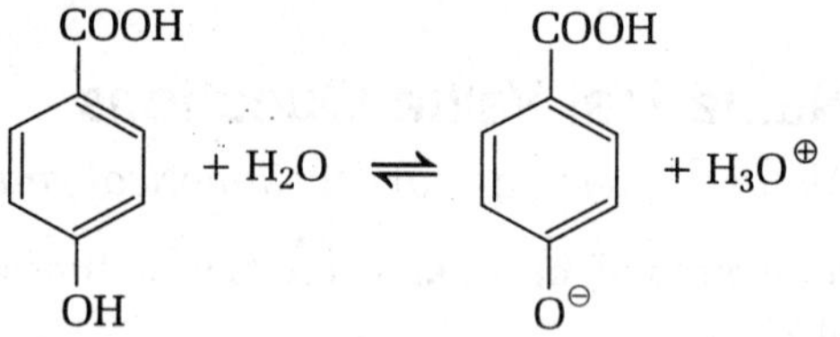

(b) 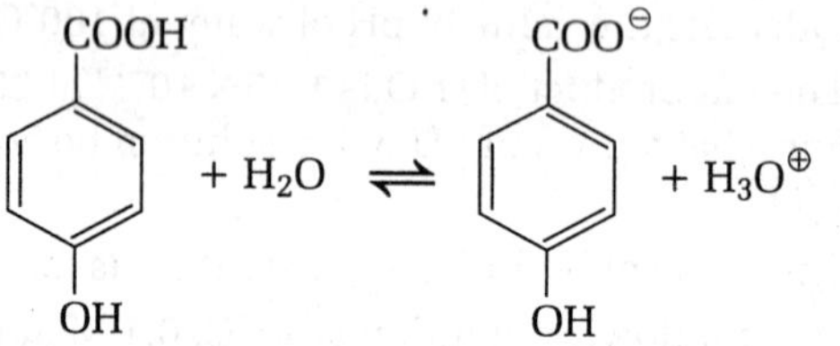

(c) Both 50% in each part
(d) $H_2O + H_2O \rightleftharpoons H_3O^{\oplus} + OH^{\ominus}$
(autoprotolysis of H_2O)

2. $pK_{a_1}(= -\log K_{a_1})$ of *p*-hydroxybenzoic acids is
(a) 4.57 (b) 9.47 (c) 4.90 (d) 7.00

3. $pK_{a_2}(= -\log K_{a_2})$ of *p*-hydroxy benzoic acid is
(a) 4.57 (b) 7.00 (c) 9.47 (d) 4.90

***Passage* 3** *Read the following passage about amino acid.*
Methionine is an essential amino acid. Its protonated form given below behaves as a dibasic acid.

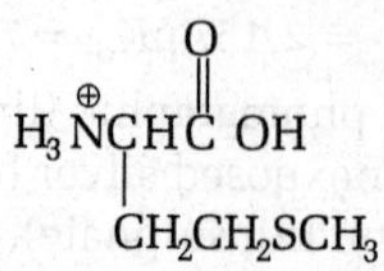

$pK_{a_1} = 2.28$ and $pK_{a_2} = 9.20$

1. Zwitter ionic form of methionine is

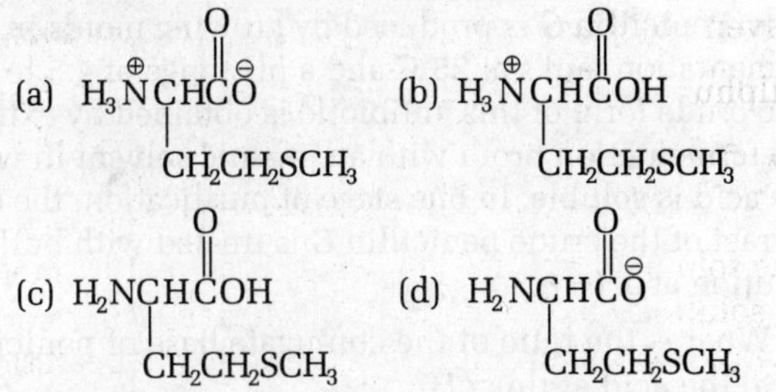

2. 30.0 mL of 0.06 M solution of the protonated form of this amino acid is treated with 0.09 M NaOH. pH after addition of 20 mL of NaOH is
(a) 2.28 (b) 9.20
(c) 5.75 (d) 456

Passage 4 *Read the following passage giving the role of CO_2 buffer in controlling pH of blood.*

Several factors are involved in the control of the pH of blood. A particularly important one is the ratio of dissolved HCO_3^- to H_2CO_3. $CO_2(g)$ is moderately soluble in water and in aqueous solution reacts only to a limited extent to produce H_2CO_3.

$$CO_2 + H_2O \rightleftharpoons H_2CO_3(aq)$$

$$H_2CO_3 + H_2O \rightleftharpoons HCO_3^- + H_3O^+, pK_{a_1} = 6.11$$

$$HCO_3^- + H_2O \rightleftharpoons CO_3^{2-} + H_3O^+; pK_{a_2} = 10.25$$

In the H_2CO_3, HCO_3^- buffer system we deal only with the first ionisation step (K_{a_1}): H_2CO_3 is a weak acid and HCO_3^- is the conjugate base (salt). CO_2 enters the blood from tissues as the by-product of metabolic reaction. In lungs, $CO_2(g)$ is exchanged for $O_2(g)$, which is transported throughout the body by the blood.

1. The pH of blood stream is maintained by a proper balance of H_2CO_3 and $NaHCO_3$ concentration. What volume of 5 M $NaHCO_3$ solution should be mixed with a 10 mL sample of blood which is 2 M in H_2CO_3 in order to maintain its pH?
(a) 40 mL (b) 38 mL
(c) 50 mL (d) 78 mL

2. Important diagonostic analysis in the blood is
(a) $[H_2PO_4^-]/[HPO_4^-]$ (b) $[HCO_3^-]/[CO_2]$
(c) $[CO_3^{2-}]/[HCO_3^{2-}]$ (d) $[PO_4^{3-}]/[HPO_4^{2-}]$

3. Following reaction occurs in the body

$$CO_2 + H_2O \rightleftharpoons H_2CO_3 \rightleftharpoons H^+ + HCO_3^-$$

If CO_2 escapes from the system
(a) pH will decreases
(b) pH will increase
(c) $[H_2CO_3]$ remains unchanged
(d) forward reaction is promoted

Passage 5 *Following experiment is taken to determine solubility of a sparingly soluble salt. Answer the questions given at the end.*

Aqueous calcium chloride solution is mixed with sodium oxalate and precipitate of calcium oxalate formed filtered and dried. Its saturated solution was prepared and 250 mL of this solution was titrated with 0.001 M $KMnO_4$ solution, when 6.0 mL of this was required.

1. Which is the indicator in the above titration?
(a) Methyl orange (b) Phenolphthalein
(c) Sulphuric acid (d) $KMnO_4$ itself

2. Number of moles of $KMnO_4$ required in this titration is
(a) 6×10^{-3} (b) 6×10^{-6}
(c) 250 (d) 2.5×10^{-1}

3. Number of moles of oxalate present in given saturated solution of calcium oxalate is
(a) 6×10^{-6} (b) 3×10^{-6}
(c) 1.5×10^{-6} (d) 1.5×10^{-5}

Passage 6 *Read the following experiment and answer the questions given at the end of it.*

An experiment to measure the solubility product constant of $CaSO_4$ involve passing a saturated solution of $CaSO_4(aq)$ through an ion exchange column pictured here, Ca^{2+} ion is retained on the column and two H_3O^+ ions appear in the solution leaving the column for every Ca^{2+} ion retained. A 25.00 mL sample of saturated $CaSO_4(aq)$ is passed through the column, followed by a small volume of water. The solution collected is then diluted to 100.0 mL in a volumetric flask. Finally, 10.00 mL of the solution from the volumetric flask is titrated with 8.25 mL of 0.0105 M NaOH.

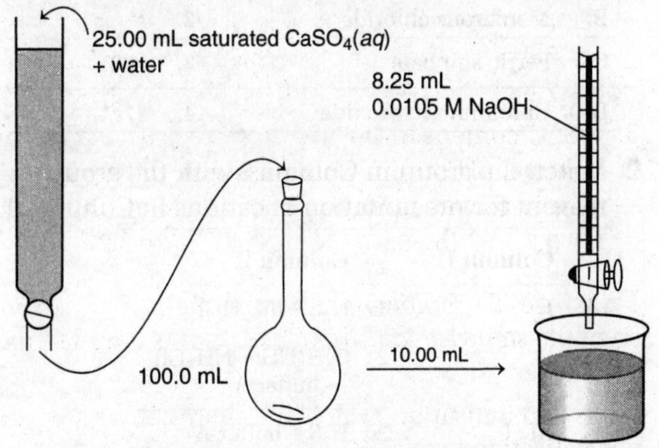

1. $[Ca^{2+}]$ in the original solution is
(a) 2.16×10^{-3} M (b) 6.93×10^{-2} M
(c) 4.33×10^{-4} M (d) 1.90×10^{-5} M

2. $[SO_4^{2-}]$ in the diluted solution is
(a) 8.66×10^{-3} M (b) 7.5×10^{-5} M
(c) 1.73×10^{-3} M (d) 1.9×10^{-5} M

3. pH of the solution coming out of column is
(a) 2.36 (b) 4.16
(c) 5.00 (d) 2.06

Passage 7 *Following passage is based on the study of effect of buffer solution on the pH of antibiotics.*

One of the most common antibiotics is penicillin G (benzylpenicillinic acid), which has the following structure

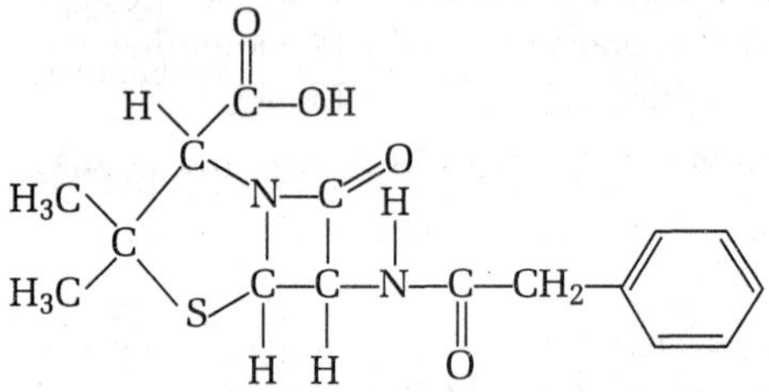

It is a weak monoprotic acid

$$HP \rightleftharpoons H^+ + P^- \quad K_a = 1.64 \times 10^{-3}$$

where HP denotes the parent acid and P^- the conjugate base. Penicillin *G* is produced by growing molds in fermentation tanks at 25°C and a pH range of 4.5 to 5.0. The crude form of this antibiotic is obtained by extracting the fermentation broth with an organic solvent in which the acid is soluble. In one stage of purification, the organic extract of the crude penicillin *G* is treated with buffer solution at pH = 6.50.

1. What is the ratio of the conjugate base of penicillin G to the acid at this pH?
(a) 5.2×10^3 (b) 3.2×10^6
(c) 1.8×10^3 (d) 5.6×10^4

2. Penicillin G is not suitable for oral administration, but the sodium salt (NaP) is because it is soluble. Calculate the pH of a 0.12 M NaP solution formed when a tablet containing the salt is dissolved in a glass of water
(a) 6.07 (b) 7.93 (c) 0.44 (d) 13.56

3. Which hydrogen is acidic?
(a) H attached to N (b) H attached to C
(c) H attached to O (d) all H are acidic

Matrix-Match Type

Given below are Matching Type Questions, with two columns (each having some items) each. Each item of Column I has to be matched with the items of Column II.

1. Match the salt in Column I with its relation for K_{sp} in Column II in terms of solubility *s* mol L^{-1}.

	Column I (salt)		Column II (K_{sp})
A.	Aluminium phosphate	1.	$4s^3$
B.	Mercurous chloride	2.	s^2
C.	Ferric sulphate	3.	$108s^5$
D.	Chromium hydroxide	4.	$27s^4$

2. Match the group in Column I with the group reagent for precipitation of cations in Column II.

Column I	Column II
A. I	1. H_2S + dil. HCl
B. II	2. ($NH_4OH + NH_4Cl$) — buffer A
C. III	3. H_2S + buffer A
D. IV	4. dil. HCl

3. Match compound in Column I with its use in Column II.

	Column I		Column II
A.	Boron trifluoride	1.	Redox indicator
B.	Phenolphthalein	2.	Lewis base
C.	Water	3.	Acid base indicator
		4.	Fluoro borane
		5.	Lewis acid
		6.	Amphiprotic

4. Match the constant in Column I with its unit in Column II.

Column I	Column II
A. Gas constant (*R*)	1. mol dm^{-3}
B. Ionic product of water	2. mol^2 dm^{-6}
C. Ionisation constant (HA)	3. dm^3 atm mol^{-1} K^{-1}
D. van der Waals' constant '*a*'	4. constant (unitless)
E. (pH − pK_a)	5. dm^6 atm mol^{-2}

5. Match the salt in Column I with its equation of pH in Column II.

Column I (Salt)	Column II (pH)
A. Weak acid and strong base	1. $\frac{1}{2}\,pK_w$
B. Strong acid and weak base	2. $\frac{1}{2}[pK_w + pK_a - pK_b]$
C. Weak acid and weak base	3. $\frac{1}{2}[pK_w - pK_b - \log C]$
D. Strong acid and strong base	4. $\frac{1}{2}[pK_w + pK_a + \log C]$

6. Match the following.

	Column I	Column II
A.	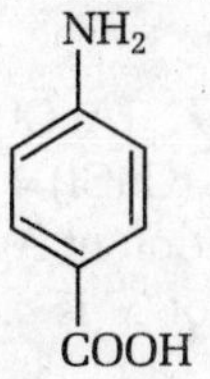	1. Lewis acid
B.	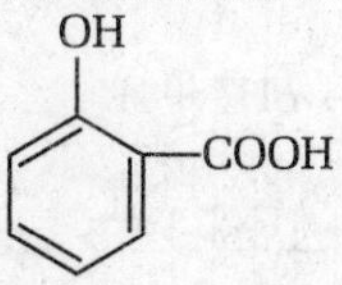	2. Lewis base
C.	$H_2PO_4^-$	3. Lowry-Bronsted acid
D.	HPO_4^{2-}	4. Lowry-Bronsted base
E.	HPO_3^{2-}	5. Zwitter ion
F.	$H_2PO_2^-$	6. Amphiprotic

7. Match the species in Column I with their behaviour in aqueous solution given in Column II.

Column I	Column II
A. CH_3COONa	1. Acidic
B. $CuSO_4$	2. Basic
C. NaCl	3. Neutral
D. NaH_2PO_3	4. Turns blue litmus red
	5. Turns red litmus blue
	6. Amphiprotic

Single Integer Answer Questions

Answer of these questions is a single digit lying between 0 to 9.

1. How many of the following behave as dibasic acids in aqueous solution?
H_3PO_2, H_3PO_3, H_3PO_4, H_2SO_4, $H_2C_2O_4$ (oxalic acid) $H_6C_4O_4$ (succinic acid), $H_4C_2O_4$ (ethanoic acid) H_2CO_3 (carbonic acid), H_6C_6O (carbolic acid)

2. How many of the following will have pH less than 7 in aqueous solution?
1×10^{-7} M HCl, 1×10^{-7} M NaOH, 1×10^{-2} M CH_3COONa, 1×10^{-2} M NH_4Cl, 1×10^{-2} M CH_3COONH_4?

3. pH of 1 mL of a strong monobasic acid increases by 1 unit on mixing *x* mL H_2O. What is the value of *x*?

4. Ionisation constant of weak monobasic acid is 1×10^{-6}. What is pK_b of the conjugate base?

5. How many of the following behave as Lewis base as well as Lowry-Bronsted base?
NH_3, H_2O, $AlCl_3$, glycine, HCO_3^-, $H_2PO_2^-$, $H_2PO_3^{2-}$

6. Ionisation constant of weak monobasic acid is 1×10^{-6}. What is the pH of a mixture of 0.01 M this acid and its 0.005 M calcium salt?

7. Solubility product of H_2S is 1×10^{-21} M^3. At what pH can it give $[S^{2-}] = 1\times10^{-7}$ M?

8. Ionisation constant of weak monobasic acid is 1×10^{-4}. What is pH when 100 mL of 0.01 M this acid is 50% neutralised by 0.01 M NaOH?

9. The dissociation constant of a substituted benzoic acid at 25°C is 1.0×10^{-4}. The pH of 0.01 M solution of its sodium salt is **[IIT JEE 2009]**

10. Amongst the following, the total number of compounds whose aqueous solution turns red litmus paper blue is
KCN K_2SO_4 $(NH_4)_2C_2O_4$ NaCl
$Zn(NO_3)_2$ $FeCl_3$ K_2CO_3 NH_4NO_3
LiCN **[IIT JEE 2010]**

11. If the solubility product of AB_2 is 3.20×10^{-11} M^3, then the solubility of AB_2 in pure water is .... $\times 10^4$ mol L^{-1}. [Assuming that neither kind of ion reacts with water] **[JEE Main 2020, Sep.]**

12. A solution of 0.1 M weak base (*B*) is titrated with 0.1 M of a strong acid (*HA*). The variation of pH of the solution with the volume of *HA* added is shown in the figure below.

What is the pK_b of the base? The neutralisation reaction is given by

$$B + HA \longrightarrow BH^+ + A^-.$$

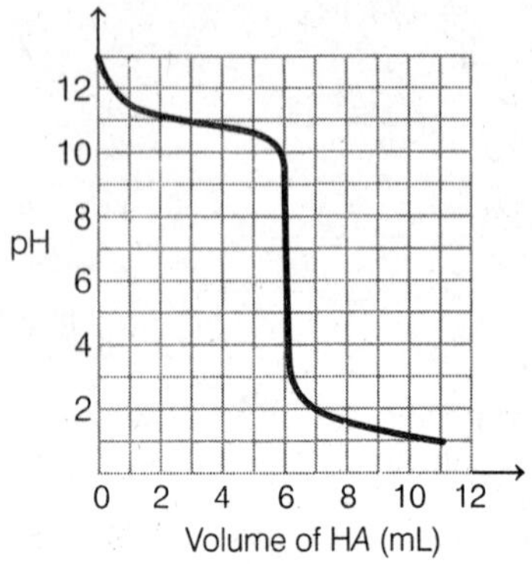

13. Solubility product of Hg_2Cl_2 in 32×10^{-18} and solubility is $y \times 10^{-6}$ M. What is the value of y?

14. What is the mass of NaOH is 1 L solution to prepare a solution of pH 13?

15. 10 mL of 0.1 N HCl is neutralised by a mixture of 1 mL of 0.1N KOH and x mL of 0.1N NaOH. What is the value of x?

16. HCOOH and CH_3COOH solution have equal pH at the ratio of molar concentration of 0.25. What is the ratio of their ionisation constants?

17. Solubility product of Al_xB is s and solubility of the salt is $\sqrt{s}$. What is the value of x?

18. Which salt (S.N.) has solubility equal to K_{sp} in presence of 1 M cation?
(1) Hg_2Cl_2 (2) $Ag_2C_2O_4$ (3) $Al_2(SO_4)_3$ (4) $FeCl_3$
(5) $Mg(OH)_2$ (6) $Fe(OH)_3$

19. pK_b of X^- is 6. What is pH of a solution containing 0.1 M X^- and 0.1 M of HX?

20. In 1 L saturated solution of AgCl [$K_{sp}(AgCl) = 1.6 \times 10^{-10}$ 0.01 mole of CuCl [$K_{sp}(CuCl) = 1.0 \times 10^{-6}$] is added. The resultant concentration of Ag^+ in the solution is 1.6×10^{-x}. The value of 'x' is .... **[IIT JEE 2011]**

Answers

Objective Questions Type I [Only one correct option]

1. (b)	2. (a)	3. (c)	4. (c)	5. (a)	6. (b)	7. (c)	8. (c)	9. (a)	10. (b)
11. (b)	12. (c)	13. (d)	14. (c)	15. (a)	16. (d)	17. (b)	18. (c)	19. (c)	20. (c)
21. (d)	22. (a)	23. (d)	24. (d)	25. (c)	26. (b)	27. (c)	28. (a)	29. (c)	30. (d)
31. (b)	32. (b)	33. (c)	34. (c)	35. (d)	36. (d)	37. (b)	38. (a)	39. (c)	40. (d)
41. (b)	42. (c)	43. (b)	44. (c)	45. (a)	46. (c)	47. (d)	48. (b)	49. (d)	50. (d)
51. (b)	52. (b)	53. (b)	54. (d)	55. (c)	56. (a)	57. (d)	58. (c)	59. (d)	60. (c)
61. (c)	62. (b)	63. (c)	64. (d)	65. (d)	66. (a)	67. (b)	68. (c)	69. (c)	70. (a)
71. (a)	72. (b)	73. (d)	74. (c)	75. (c)	76. (c)	77. (a)	78. (a)	79. (d)	80. (c)
81. (c)	82. (d)	83. (a)	84. (c)	85. (a)	86. (a)	87. (d)	88. (d)	89. (c)	90. (b)
91. (b)	92. (d)	93. (c)	94. (b)	95. (d)	96. (c)	97. (c)	98. (a)	99. (b)	100. (a)
101. (a)	102. (b)	103. (c)	104. (d)	105. (b)	106. (b)	107. (c)	108. (a)	109 (a)	110. (c)
111. (d)	112. (a)	113. (c)	114. (d)	115. (d)	116. (c)	117. (b)	118. (c)	119 (c)	120. (d)
121. (b)	122. (b)	123. (c)	124. (d)	125. (d)	126. (c)	127. (c)	128. (c)	129. (d)	130. (b)
131. (c)	132. (b)	133. (b)	134. (b)	135. (a)	136. (b)	137. (d)	138. (a)	139. (b)	140. (c)
141. (d)	142. (a)	143. (c)	144. (d)	145. (c)	146. (a)	147. (d)	148. (b)	149. (c)	150. (b)
151. (c)	152. (a)	153. (b)	154. (d)	155. (c)	156. (d)	157. (c)	158. (a)	159. (d)	160. (c)
161. (c)	162. (b)	163. (a)	164. (a)	165. (d)	166. (b)	167. (b)	168. (a)	169. (a)	170. (b)
171. (d)	172. (a)	173. (a)	174. (d)	175. (b)	176. (d)	177. (c)	178. (c)	179. (b)	180. (b)
181. (d)	182. (b)	183. (d)	184. (d)	185. (a)	186. (c)	187. (c)	188. (b)	189. (d)	190. (a)
191. (c)									

Objective Questions Type II [One or more than one correct option(s)]

1. (a, b)	2. (a, c, d)	3. (d)	4. (a, c, d)	5. (b)
6. (b, c)	7. (c, d)	8. (a, b, c, d)	9. (c)	10. (a)
11. (b)	12. (d)	13. (a)	14. (d)	15. (a, b, c, d)

Numerical Value Questions

1. pH = 6.13
2. A solution having $p_D < 7.45$ will be acidic.
3. 3.08
4. 2.17 M,
5. 4.675, 9.785
6. Molar solubility of 4.44
7. 10.6
8. 4.47
9. 50
10. 2
11. 10
12. 1
13. 64

Comprehension Based Questions

Passage 1 – 1. (a) 2. (d) 3. (a)

Passage 2 – 1. (b) 2. (a) 3. (c)

Passage 3 – 1. (a) 2. (c)

Passage 4 – 1. (d) 2. (b) 3. (b)

Passage 5 – 1. (d) 2. (b) 3. (d)

Passage 6 – 1. (b) 2. (c) 3. (d) 4. (d)

Passage 7 – 1. (a) 2. (b) 3. (c)

Matrix-Match Type

1. A → (2); B → (1); C → (3); D → (4)
2. A → (4); B → (1); C → (2); D → (3)
3. A → (5); B → (1); C → (6)
4. A → (3); B → (2); C → (1); D → (5); E → (4)
5. A → (4); B → (3); C → (2); D → (1)
6. A → (2,3,4,5,6); B → (1,3); C → (3,4,6); D → (3,4,6); E → (4); F → (4)
7. A → (2,5); B → (1,4); C → (3); D → (2,5,6)

Single Integer Answer Questions

1. (5)	2. (2)	3. (9)	4. (8)	5. (4)	6. (6)	7. (7)	8. (4)	9. (8)	10. (3)
11. (2)	12. (3)	13. (2)	14. (4)	15. (9)	16. (4)	17. (1)	18. (2)	19. (8)	20. (7)

Solutions

Objective Questions Type I [Only one correct option]

9. (*a*) H_2O in $[Al(H_2O)_6]^{3+}$ is a source of H^+ thus, proton is accepted by HCO_3^-

Thus, $[Al(H_2O)_6^{3+}]$ is proton donor and HCO_3^- is proton-acceptor which is converted into H_2CO_3(acid)

Thus, Bronsted-Lowry acids are $[Al(H_2O)_6]^{3+}$ and H_2CO_3.

12. (*c*) H_3PO_2 is a monobasic acid

$$H_3PO_2 \rightleftharpoons H_2PO_2^- + H^+$$
$$H_2PO_2^- \rightleftharpoons \text{No ionisation}$$

Thus, $H_2PO_2^-$ is proton acceptor but not proton donor.

H_3PO_3 is a dibasic acid

$$H_3PO_3 \rightleftharpoons H_2PO_3^- + H^+$$
$$H_2PO_3^- \rightleftharpoons HPO_3^{2-} + H^+$$
$$HPO_3^{2-} \rightleftharpoons \text{No ionisation}$$

$H_2PO_3^-$ is proton acceptor as well as proton-donor but HPO_3^{2-} is only proton-acceptor.

H_3PO_4 is a tribasic acid

$$H_3PO_4 \rightleftharpoons H_2PO_4^- + H^+$$
$$H_2PO_4^- \rightleftharpoons HPO_4^{2-} + H^+$$
$$HPO_4^{2-} \rightleftharpoons PO_4^{3-} + H^+$$

$H_2PO_4^-$ and HPO_4^{2-} both are proton-donor as well as proton-acceptor.

H_2CO_3 is a dibasic acid

$$H_2CO_3 \rightleftharpoons H^+ + HCO_3^-$$
$$HCO_3^- \rightleftharpoons H^+ + CO_3^{2-}$$

HCO_3^- is proton donor as well as proton-acceptor.

Thus, $H_2PO_3^-, HPO_4^{2-}, H_2PO_4^-, HCO_3^-$ are amphiprotic.

15. (*a*) HNO_2 is proton-donor and is thus stronger acid than HF. HF is proton-donor and is thus stronger acid than CH_3COOH. CH_3COOH is proton-donor and is thus stronger acid than H_2O.

$$HNO_2 > HF$$
$$HF > CH_3COOH$$
$$CH_3COOH > H_2O$$

17. (*b*) $N(CH_3)_3$ has vacant lone-pair on N-atom which can be donated to electron-deficient B-atom of $B(CH_3)_3$.

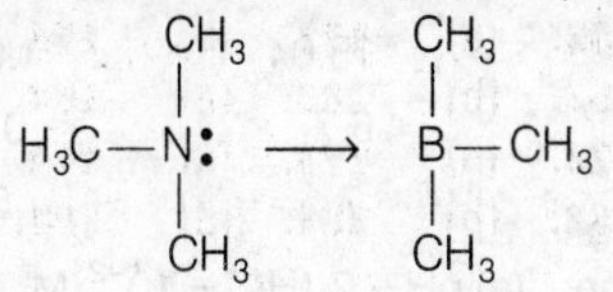

19. (*c*) Electron-deficient species is only $\overset{\oplus}{C}H_3$ (carbenium ion) and is thus Lewis acid.

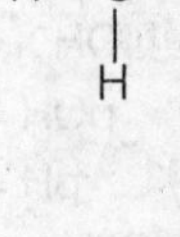

20. (*c*) $\overset{\ominus}{C}H_3 + \overset{\oplus}{H} \longrightarrow CH_4$

$\overset{\ominus}{C}H_3$ (carbanion) is $\overset{\oplus}{H}$ ion acceptor thus Bronsted-Lowry base.

$\overset{\ominus}{C}H_3$ has lone-pair and can be donated thus it is a Lewis-base.

28. (*a*) $HA + HA \rightleftharpoons H_2A^- + A^-$

$$[H_2A^-] = [A^-]$$
$$K = [H_2A^-][A^-] = 4 \times 10^{-8}$$
$$[H_2A^-]^2 = [A^-]^2 = 4 \times 10^{-8}$$
$$\therefore \quad [A^-] = 2 \times 10^{-4}\text{ M}$$

30. (*d*) $[NaOH] = 10^{-8}$ M

$$[OH^-] = 10^{-8}\text{ M}$$
$$[H^+] = 10^{-6}\text{ M}$$

pH ≠ 6 since solution is basic

$[OH^-]$ of water in this dilute solution should be added

$$\therefore \quad [OH^-]_{Total} = \underbrace{1 \times 10^{-7}\text{ M}}_{H_2O} + \underbrace{1 \times 10^{-8}\text{ M}}_{NaOH} = 11 \times 10^{-8}$$
$$\therefore \quad pOH = 8 - \log 11$$
$$pH = 14 - pOH = 6 + \log 11 = 7.02$$

31. (*b*) $pH = 13$

$$\therefore \quad [H^+] = 10^{-13}\text{ M}$$
$$[OH^-] = 10^{-1}\text{ M} = 0.1\text{ mol L}^{-1}$$
$$[Ba(OH)_2] = 0.1\text{ N}$$
$$= 0.1 \times 100 = 10\text{ milliequivalents}$$

32. (*b*) $K_w = 1 \times 10^{-10}$

$$\therefore \quad [H^+] = [OH^-] = 10^{-5}\text{ M}$$

pH = 5 for neutral solution.

pH < 5 acidic, pH > 5 basic

33. (*c*) $[H^+] = 0.1 \times \dfrac{0.1}{100} = 10^{-4}$ M

$$\therefore \quad pH = -\log [H^+] = 4$$

35. (*d*)

	pH before	pH after	Changes
(a)	2	4	2
(b)	12	13.04	1.04
(c)	6	6.7	0.7
(d)	2	7	5

Explanation (a) pH = 2, $[H^+] = 10^{-2}$ M

$$M_1V_1 = M_2V_2$$
$$10^{-2} \times 1 = M_2 \times 100$$
$$M_2 = 10^{-4}$$
$$\therefore \quad pH = 4$$

(b) $[OH^-] = 10^{-2}$

$$pOH = 2$$
$$pH = 12$$

100 mL of 0.01 M NaOH contains = 0.001 mol

NaOH added = 0.01 mol

Total moles = 0.011 mol

$$\therefore \quad [OH^-]_{final} = 0.011 \times 10 = 0.11\text{ M}$$
$$pOH = 0.96$$
$$pH = 13.04$$

(c) $[HCl] = 10^{-6}$ M

$$[H^+] = 10^{-6}\text{ M}$$
$$pH = 6$$

after dilution $[HCl] = 10^{-7}\text{ M} = [H^+]$

$[H^+]$ in $H_2O = 10^{-7}$ M

$$\text{Total } [H^+] = 10^{-7} + 10^{-7} = 2 \times 10^{-7}$$
$$\therefore \quad pH = 7 - \log 2 = 6.7$$

(d) pH = 2, $[H^+] = 10^{-2}$ M

pH = 12, $[H^+] = 10^{-12}$ M

$$\therefore \quad [OH^-] = 10^{-2}\text{ M}$$

Thus, on mixing solution becomes neutral thus, pH = 7

36. (*d*) $BOH \rightleftharpoons B^+ + OH^-$

$$pH = 10$$
$$\therefore \quad pOH = 4$$
$$\therefore \quad [OH^-] = 10^{-4} = Cx$$
$$\therefore \quad x = \frac{10^{-4}}{0.01} = 10^{-2}$$

% ionisation = $10^{-2} \times 100 = 1$

37. (*b*) pH = 6

$$\therefore \quad [H^+] = 10^{-6}\text{ M}$$

Also solution is acidic (pH < 7) and dilution will not change its acidic nature

$$[H^+]_{diluted} = \frac{100 \times 10^{-6}}{1000} = 1 \times 10^{-7}\text{ M}$$

$[H^+]$ from H_2O is also required while calculating resultant concentration.

$$\text{Total } [H^+] = [H^+]_{diluted} + [H^+]_{H_2O}$$
$$= 1 \times 10^{-7} + 1 \times 10^{-7}$$
$$= 2 \times 10^{-7}\text{ M}$$
$$pH = -\log 2 \times 10^{-7} = 6.7$$

40. (*d*) $HA + H_2O \rightleftharpoons H_3O^+ + A^-$

$$K_a = 1 \times 10^{-6}$$

Given reaction is reverse of ionisation of HA, thus,

$$K = \frac{1}{K_a} = 1 \times 10^6$$

41. (*b*) $[OH^-] = \sqrt{K_b C}$

$$\therefore \quad pOH = \frac{1}{2}[pK_b - \log C] = 3.37$$
$$\therefore \quad pH = 14 - pK_b = 10.63$$

43. (*b*) $[H^+] = Cx = 1 \times \frac{0.01}{100} = 1 \times 10^{-4}$ M

$\therefore$ $[OH^-] = \frac{K_w}{[H^+]} = \frac{1 \times 10^{-14}}{1 \times 10^{-4}} = 1 \times 10^{-10}$ M

44. (*c*) $x_1 = \sqrt{\frac{K_a}{C_1}}$

$x_2 = \sqrt{\frac{K_a}{C_2}}$

$\therefore$ $\frac{x_2}{x_1} = \sqrt{\frac{C_1}{C_2}}$

$x_2 = x_1 \sqrt{\frac{C_1}{C_2}} = 1 \times \frac{1}{2} = 0.5\%$

45. (*a*) $[H_3O^+] = \sqrt{K_1C_1 + K_2C_2}$

$= \sqrt{1.8 \times 10^{-4} \times 0.1 + 3.3 \times 10^{-4} \times 0.1}$

$= 7.14 \times 10^{-3}$ M

46. (*c*) $[H_3O^+] = 1 \times 10^{-7}\ M = \sqrt{K_aC}$

For H_2O, $[H_2O] = 1$ g / mL $= 1000$ g / L $= \frac{1000}{18}$ M

$\therefore$ $\sqrt{\frac{1000K_a}{18}} = 1 \times 10^{-7}$

$\therefore$ $K_a = 1.8 \times 10^{-16}$

48. (*b*) $pH = \frac{1}{2}[pK_a - \log 1] = \frac{pK_a}{2}$

pH′ (twice of pH) $= pK_a$

$\therefore$ $pK_a = \frac{1}{2}[pK_a - \log C]$

$-\log C = pK_a = -\log K_a$

$C = K_a = 1.8 \times 10^{-5}$ M

$\therefore$ dilution $= \frac{1}{C} = 5.55 \times 10^4$ times

51. (*b*) For a salt of weak acid and weak base,

$pH = 7 + \frac{1}{2}pK_a - \frac{1}{2}pK_b$

Given, $pK_a(HA) = 3.2$, $pK_a(BOH) = 3.4$

$\therefore$ $pH = 7 + \frac{1}{2}(3.2) - \frac{1}{2}(3.4)$

$= 7 + 1.6 - 1.7 = 6.9$

52. (*b*) $PbCl_2(s) \rightleftharpoons Pb^{2+}(aq) + 2Cl^-(aq)$; $K_{sp} = 1.6 \times 10^{-5}$

For mixture, 300 mL 0.134 M $Pb(NO_3)_2$ and 100 mL 0.4 M NaCl

After mixing, total volume = 400 mL

$[Pb^{2+}]$ after mixing (before any precipitate forms)

$= \frac{300 \times 0.134}{400} = \frac{3 \times 0.134}{4} \approx \frac{1}{10}$

$[Cl^-]$ after mixing (before any precipitate forms)

$= \frac{100 \times 0.4}{400} = 0.1$

As we know,

$Q = [Pb^{2+}][Cl^-]^2 = \frac{3 \times 0.134}{4} \times 10^{-2} \approx 10^{-3}$

53. (*b*) Among the given options, distilled water has the lowest ionic conductance at 298 K.

Water from well or sea contains mineral ions,

So, they have ionic conductance.

Saline water is an electrolyte and contain ions.

$\therefore$ It also has ionic conductance.

54. (*d*) K_{sp} of $Cr(OH)_3$ at 298 K is 6.0×10^{-31}.

$[OH^-]$ in saturated solution of $Cr(OH)_3 = ?$

$$Cr(OH)_3 \rightleftharpoons \underset{S}{Cr^{3+}} + \underset{S}{3OH^-}$$

In a saturated solution, $K_{sp} = [Cr^{3+}][OH^-]^3$

$= S(3S)^3 = 27S^4 = 6.0 \times 10^{-31}$

$\therefore$ $S^4 = \frac{6.0 \times 10^{-31}}{27} \Rightarrow S = \left(\frac{6.0 \times 10^{-31}}{27}\right)^{\frac{1}{4}}$

$[OH^-] = 3S = 3\left(\frac{6.0 \times 10^{-31}}{27}\right)^{\frac{1}{4}}$

$= \left(\frac{6.0 \times 3^4}{3^3} \times 10^{-31}\right)^{\frac{1}{4}} = (18 \times 10^{-31})^{\frac{1}{4}}$

56. (*a*) pH = 4.74

(*b*) pH = 4.74

(c) $pOH = pK_b = 14 - pK_a = 4.74$

$\therefore$ pH = 9.26

57. (*d*) Units given for all options is M^3, or $(mol\ L^{-1})^3$, which implies that, the equilibrium has three ions. Therefore,

$XY_2 \rightleftharpoons X^{2+}(aq) + 2Y^-(aq)$, $K_{sp} = [X^{2+}][Y^-]^2$

or $X_2Y \rightleftharpoons 2X^+(aq) + Y^{2-}(aq)$, $K_{sp} = [X^+]^2[Y^{2-}]$

(i) K_{sp} in case of XY_2,

$K_{sp} = (1 \times 10^{-3})(2 \times 10^{-3})^2 = 4 \times 10^{-9}\ M^3$

(ii) K_{sp} in case of X_2Y,

$K_{sp} = (1 \times 10^{-3})^2(2 \times 10^{-3}) = 2 \times 10^{-9}$ M

The only matching value of K_{sp} from options that satisfies the concentration values from graph is

$[X^{2+}] = 1\ mM = 1 \times 10^{-3}$ M and $[Y^-] = 2 \times 10^{-3}$ M

Thus, salt is XY_2 and

$K_{sp} = (10^{-3})(2 \times 10^{-3})^2 = 4 \times 10^{-9}\ M^3$

58. (*c*) The strength of aqueous NaOH solution is most accurately determined by titrating aqueous NaOH in burette and aqueous oxalic acid in conical flask with phenolphthalein as an indicator. (For weak acid-strong base titration, methyl orange cannot be used).

Thus, solution turns colourless to pink at the end point. (Phenolphthalein has pink colour when pH > 10 and it is colourless when pH < 8 (approximately) which is easily to perceive.

If NaOH is taken in conical flask and oxalic acid is added from burette, the end point will be the decolourisation of pink colour which is more difficult to percieve by human eye very quickly.

59. (*d*) $HA \rightleftharpoons H^+ + A^-$

Initial	C	0	0
After ionisation	$C - Cx$	?	Cx

$$K_a = \frac{[H^+][A^-]}{[HA]}$$

$$[H^+] = K_a \frac{[HA]}{[A^-]} = K_a \frac{C(1-x)}{Cx} = K_a \left(\frac{1-x}{x}\right)$$

$$\log [H^+] = \log K_a + \log (1-x) - \log x$$

$$-\log [H^+] = -\log K_a - \log (1-x) - (-\log x)$$

$$pH = pK_a + p_{(1-x)} - p_x$$

$$pH - pK_a = p_{1-x} - p_x$$

61. (*c*) The dissociation of water into H^+ and OH^- is an endothermic reaction.

∴ As temperature increases, its equilibrium constant also increases.

∴ $[H^+]$ and $[OH^-]$ in water at equilibrium increases with increase in temperature.

∴ $pH = -\log[H^+]$ decreases, as temperature increases.

So, both Assertion and Reason are false.

62. (*b*) The concentration of a substance in a saturated solution is defined as its solubility(*S*).

For $A_xB_y \rightleftharpoons xA^{y+} + yB^{x-}$; $K_{sp} = [A^{y+}]^x [B^{x-}]^y$

For, $Zr_3(PO_4)_4$,

$$\underset{}{Zr_3(PO_4)_4(s)} \rightleftharpoons \underset{3S\,M}{3Zr^{4+}(aq)} + \underset{4\,SM}{4PO_4^{3-}(aq)}$$

$$K_{sp} = [Zr^{4+}]^3 [PO_4^{3-}]^4$$

$$K_{sp} = (3S)^3(4S)^4 = 6912\, S^7$$

or $$S = \left(\frac{K_{sp}}{6912}\right)^{\frac{1}{7}}$$

Thus, the relation between molar solubility(*S*) and solubility product (K_{sp}) will be

$$S = \left(\frac{K_{sp}}{6912}\right)^{1/7}$$

66. (*a*) $\underset{0.005\,M}{(CH_3COO)_2Ca} \rightleftharpoons Ca^{2+} + \underset{\text{Acetate}}{2CH_3COO^-}$

$$2 \times 0.005 = 0.01\ M$$

$$CH_3COOH + H_2O \rightleftharpoons CH_3COO^- + H_3O^+$$

$$K_a = \frac{[CH_3COO^-]\,[H_3O^+]}{[CH_3COOH]}$$

$$1.8 \times 10^{-5} = \frac{(0.01)\,[H_3O^+]}{(0.01)}$$

∴ $[H_3O^+] = 1.8 \times 10^{-5}$ M

67. (*b*) $\underset{x\,mol}{(NH_4)_2SO_4} \rightleftharpoons \underset{2x\,mol}{2NH_4^+} + SO_4^{2-}$

$$[NH_4^+] = \frac{2x}{0.5}\ mol\ L^{-1} = 4x\ M$$

$$[NH_3] = 0.01\ M$$

$$pH = 9.26,\ pOH = 4.74$$

$$pOH = pK_b + \log\frac{[NH_4^+]}{[NH_3]}$$

$$4.74 = 4.74 + \log\frac{(4x)}{(0.01)}$$

$$\frac{4x}{0.01} = 1$$

$$4x = 0.01$$

$$x = \frac{0.01}{4}\ mol = 0.0025\ mol$$

68. (*c*) $AgCl \rightleftharpoons Ag^+ + Cl^-$

$$K = [Ag^+]\,[Cl^-]$$

$$1 \times 10^{-10} = [Ag^+](1)$$

$$[Ag^+] = 1 \times 10^{-10}\ M$$

70. (*a*) AgCl, $BaCrO_4$, $PbCrO_4$ are sparingly soluble salts hence, are not effective in decreasing solubility of Ag_2CrO_4.

72. (*b*) $HA \rightleftharpoons H^+ + A^-$

$$K_a = Cx^2 = 1 \times \left(\frac{4}{100}\right)^2 = 1.6 \times 10^{-3}$$

$$K_a = \frac{[H^+][A^-]}{[HA]},$$

$$[H^+] = Cx = 1 \times 0.01 = 0.01\ M$$

∴ $$1.6 \times 10^{-3} = \frac{0.01\,[A^-]}{1}$$

$$[A^-] = 0.16\ M$$

73. (*d*) $CH_3NH_2 + H_2O \rightleftharpoons CH_3NH_3^+ + OH^-$

$$K_b = \frac{[CH_3NH_3^+][OH^-]}{[CH_3NH_2]}$$

$$3.7 \times 10^{-4} = \frac{0.60\,[OH^-]}{0.3}$$

∴ $[OH^-] = 1.85 \times 10^{-4}$ M

74. (*c*) Its given that the final volume is 500 mL and this final volume was arrived when 50 mL of 1 M Na_2SO_4 was added to unknown Ba^{2+} solution.

So, we can interpret the volume of unknown Ba^{2+} solution as 450 mL i.e.

$$\underset{\text{solution}}{\underset{Ba^{2+}}{450\text{mL}}} + \underset{\text{solution}}{\underset{Na_2SO_4}{50\text{mL}}} \longrightarrow \underset{\text{solution}}{\underset{BaSO_4}{500\text{mL}}}$$

From this we can calculate the concentration of SO_4^{2-} ion in the solution *via*

$$M_1V_1 = M_2V_2$$
$$1 \times 50 = M_2 \times 500$$

(as 1M Na_2SO_4 is taken into consideration)

$$M_2 = \frac{1}{10} = 0.1\text{M}$$

Now for just precipitation,

Ionic product = Solubility product (K_{sp})

i.e. $[Ba^{2+}][SO_4^{2-}] = K_{sp}$ of $BaSO_4$

Given, K_{sp} of $BaSO_4 = 1 \times 10^{-10}$

So, $[Ba^{2+}][0.1] = 1 \times 10^{-10}$

or $[Ba^{2+}] = 1 \times 10^{-9}$ M

Remember This is the concentration of Ba^{2+} ions in final solution. Hence, for calculating the $[Ba^{2+}]$ in original solution we have to use, $M_1V_1 = M_2V_2$

as $M_1 \times 450 = 10^{-9} \times 500$

so, $M_1 = 1.1 \times 10^{-9}$M

75. (*c*)
$$BaSO_4 \rightleftharpoons Ba^{2+} + SO_4^{2-}$$
$$[Ba^{2+}][SO_4^{2-}] = K_{sp}$$
$$(0.1)[SO_4^{2-}] = 1 \times 10^{-5}$$
$$[SO_4^{2-}] = 1 \times 10^{-4} \text{ M}$$

77. (*a*)
$$Ag_2CO_3 \rightleftharpoons 2Ag^+ + CO_3^{2-}$$
$$[Ag^+] = 2.56 \times 10^{-4} \text{ M}$$
$$\therefore \quad [CO_3^{2-}] = \frac{[Ag^+]}{2} = 1.28 \times 10^{-4} \text{ M}$$
$$K_{sp} = [Ag^+]^2 [CO_3^{2-}]$$
$$= (2.56 \times 10^{-4})^2 (1.28 \times 10^{-4}) = 8.4 \times 10^{-12}$$

78. (*a*) Consider dilution factor due to mixing. $BaSO_4$ is precipitated if

$$[Ba^{2+}][SO_4^{2-}] > K_{sp}$$

(a)
$$[Ba^{2+}]_{mix} = \frac{4 \times 10^{-3}}{4} = 10^{-3} \text{ M}$$
$$[SO_4^{2-}]_{mix} = \frac{3 \times 6 \times 10^{-4}}{4} = 4.5 \times 10^{-4} \text{ M}$$
$$[Ba^{2+}][SO_4^{2-}] = 4.5 \times 10^{-7} > K_{sp}$$

79. (*d*)
$$Al(OH)_3 \rightleftharpoons \underset{s}{Al^{3+}} + \underset{3s}{3OH^-}$$
$$\therefore \quad K_{sp} = [Al^{3+}][OH^-]^3$$
$$1 \times 10^{-15} = 27s^4$$
$$s = \left(\frac{1 \times 10^{-15}}{27}\right)^{1/4} = 7.8 \times 10^{-5}$$
$$\therefore \quad [OH^-] = 3s = 2.34 \times 10^{-4}$$
$$\therefore \quad pOH = -\log[OH^-] = 3.63$$
$$\therefore \quad pH = 10.37$$

80. (*c*)
$$H_2S \rightleftharpoons 2H^+ + S^{2-}$$
$$\therefore \quad K_{sp} = [H^+]^2[S^{2-}]$$
$$1 \times 10^{-22} = 10^{-12}[S^{2-}]$$
$$\therefore \quad [S^{2-}] = 1 \times 10^{-10} \text{ M}$$

81. (*c*)
$$H_2S \rightleftharpoons 2H^+ + S^{2-}$$
$$CdS \rightleftharpoons Cd^{2+} + S^{2-}$$
$$K_{sp}(CdS) = [Cd^{2+}][S^{2-}]$$
$$8 \times 10^{-27} = (1 \times 10^{-14})[S^{2-}]$$
$$\therefore \quad [S^{2-}] = 8 \times 10^{-13} \text{ M}$$

Also, $[H^+]^2[S^{2-}] = K_{sp}(H_2S)$

$$[H^+]^2(8 \times 10^{-13}) = 1 \times 10^{-22}$$
$$[H^+]^2 = 1.25 \times 10^{-10}$$
$$\therefore \quad [H^+] = 1.11 \times 10^{-5}$$
$$\therefore \quad pH \approx 5$$

82. (*d*)
$$Mg(OH)_2 \rightleftharpoons \underset{s}{Mg^{2+}} + 2OH^-$$
$$pH = 12$$
$$pOH = 2$$
$$\therefore \quad [OH^-] = 10^{-2} \text{ M}$$
$$K_{sp} = [Mg^{2+}][OH^-]^2$$
$$1.8 \times 10^{-11} = (s)(10^{-2})^2$$
$$\therefore \quad s = 1.8 \times 10^{-7} \text{ M}$$

84. (*c*) Millimol of benzoic acid = 2

Millimol of NaOH in first addition = 1

Millimol of NaOH in second addition = 2

	C_6H_5COOH +	$NaOH \rightleftharpoons$	C_6H_5COONa +	H_2O
Initial	2	0	0	0
After first addition of NaOH	(2 − 1) = 1	(1 − 1) = 0	1	1
After second addition of NaOH	(2 − 2) = 0	(2 − 2) = 0	2	

After first addition mixture is a buffer containing 1 millimol each of C_6H_5COONa and C_6H_5COOH

$$\therefore \quad pH = pK_a + \log\frac{[C_6H_5COONa]}{[C_6H_5COOH]} = pK_a = 4.2$$

After second addition, there are only 2 millimol C_6H_5COONa in 200 mL solution and due to hydrolysis solution is basic.

$$[C_6H_5COO^-] = \frac{2 \times 10^{-3}}{0.2} = 1 \times 10^{-2} \text{ M}$$
$$C_6H_5COO^- + H_2O \rightleftharpoons C_6H_5COOH + OH^-$$
$$\therefore \quad pH = 7 + \frac{pK_a}{2} + \frac{\log C}{2} = 7 + 2.1 - 1 = 8.1$$

86. (*a*) For amphiprotic salt

$$pH = \frac{pK_{a_1} + pK_{a_2}}{2} = \frac{1.82 + 9.13}{2} = 5.48$$

87. (*d*) Henry's equation for solubility (S) of a gas (β) in a liquid is expressed in terms of mole-fraction of the gas (χ_B) at a given temperature,

$$p = K_H \times \chi_B = K_H \times S$$

So, solubility of gas, $S \propto \frac{1}{K_H}$ at T(K) and given pressure.

Order of solubility of the gases (high the value of K_H, lower is the solubility) : $\gamma > \delta > \beta > \alpha$

So, option (a) is not correct.

Again, $K_H \propto$ temperature, i.e. solubility of the gas will decrease with increase in temperature also.

But this conclusion cannot be drawn from table.

So, option (b) is not correct.

We know, mole-fraction of a solute (B) in a binary aqueous solution,

$$\chi_B = \frac{18m}{1000 + 18m} \quad [\because m = \text{molality}]$$

For γ at $m = 55.5$ molal

$$p = K_H^{\gamma} \times m = (2 \times 10^{-5}) \times \left(\frac{18 \times 55.5}{1000 + 18 \times 55.5}\right)$$

$$= 1.81 \times 10^{-5} \text{ K bar} = 1.8 \times 10^{-2} \text{ bar}$$

So, option (c) is not correct.

For δ at $m = 55.5$ molal

$$p = K_H^{\delta} = (0.5) \times \left(\frac{18 \times 55.5}{1000 + 18 \times 55.5}\right)$$

$$= 0.2498 \text{ k bar} \simeq 250 \text{ bar}$$

So, option (d) is correct.

88. (*d*) The explanation of given statements are as follows:

In statement (I), millimoles of H^+

$$= 400 \times 0.1 \times 2 = 80$$

Millimoles of $OH^- = 400 \times 0.1 = 40$ (Limiting reagent).

$\therefore$ Millimoles of H^+ left $= 80 - 40 = 40$

$$[H^+] = \frac{40}{400 + 400} = \frac{40}{800} M = \frac{1}{20} M$$

$$\Rightarrow \quad pH = -\log[H^+] = -\log\left(\frac{1}{20}\right)$$

$$= -\log 1 + \log 2 + \log 10$$

$$= -0 + 0.301 + 1$$

$\Rightarrow 1.30$

Hence, the option (a) is correct.

In statement (II), ionic product of H_2O is temperature dependent.

$K_w = [H^+][OH^-] \approx 10^{-14} (\text{mol/L})^2$ at 25°C

With increase in temperature, dissociation of H_2O units into H^+ and OH^- ions will also increase. As a result, the value of ionic product, $[H^+] \times [OH^-]$ will be increased. e.g.

Temperature	K_w (mol/L²)
5°C	0.186×10^{-14}
25°C	1.008×10^{-14}
45°C	4.074×10^{-14}

Hence, the option (b) is correct.

In statement (III), for a weak monobasic acid HA.

$$HA \rightleftharpoons H^{\oplus} + A^{\ominus}$$

$$(1-\alpha)C\,M \quad \alpha C\,M \quad \alpha C\,M$$

$\Rightarrow$ pH of the solution is 5, i.e.

$$[H^+] = 10^{-5} M = \alpha C$$

$$\Rightarrow \quad K_a = \frac{\alpha C \times \alpha C}{(1-\alpha)C} = \frac{10^{-5} \times \alpha}{1-\alpha}$$

$$\Rightarrow \quad 10^{-5} = \frac{10^{-5} \times \alpha}{1-\alpha} \Rightarrow \alpha = 0.5$$

$$\Rightarrow \quad \alpha\% = 50$$

Hence, the option (c) is correct.

In statement (IV), Le-Chatelier's principle is applicable to common ion effect. Because, in presence of common ion (given) by strong electrolyte (say, $Na^+ \bar{A}$), the product of the concentration terms in RHS increases. For the weaker electrolyte, HA (say) the equilibrium shifts to the LHS, $HA \rightleftharpoons H^{\oplus} + A^{\ominus}$.

As a result dissociation of HA gets suppressed. Hence, the option (d) is incorrect

89. (*c*) HPO_4^{2-} is amphiprotic and it involves pK_{a_2} and pK_{a_3}

$$HPO_4^{2-} \rightleftharpoons H^+ + PO_4^{3-} \qquad K_{a_3}$$

$$HPO_4^{2-} + H^+ \rightleftharpoons H_2PO_4^- \qquad \frac{1}{K_{a_2}}$$

For such cases

$$pH = \frac{pK_{a_2} + pK_{a_3}}{2} = \left(\frac{y + z}{2}\right)$$

90. (*b*) Salts (NH_4A, NH_4B, NH_4C) are of weak acid and weak base.

$$pH = 7 + \frac{pK_a}{2} - \frac{pK_b}{2}$$

Thus, greater the value of pK_a of HA, greater the pH.

$$pK_b(A^-, B^-, C^-) \mid \underset{4}{A^-} < \underset{5}{B^-} < \underset{6}{C^-}$$

$$pK_a(HA, HB, HC) \mid \underset{8}{HC} < \underset{9}{HB} < \underset{10}{HA}$$

Thus, pH ($NH_4C < NH_4B < NH_4A$)

91. (*b*) (I) pOH of 0.01 M HCl :

$$\underset{(0.01M)}{HCl} \longrightarrow \underset{(0.01M)}{H^+} + \underset{(0.01M)}{OH^-}$$

$$[H^+] = (0.01M) \quad pH = -\log[H^+]$$

$$\Rightarrow -\log(10^{-2}) \Rightarrow 2$$

$$\therefore \quad pOH = 14 - pH \Rightarrow 14 - 2 = 12$$

(II) pOH of 0.01 M NaOH :

$$\underset{(0.01M)}{NaOH} \longrightarrow \underset{(0.01M)}{Na^+} + \underset{(0.01M)}{OH^-}$$

$$[OH^-] = 10^{-2}$$

$$\therefore \quad pOH = -\log[OH^-]$$

$$\Rightarrow \quad -\log(10^{-2}) = 2$$

(III) pOH of 0.01 M $CH_3CO\overset{-}{O}\overset{+}{Na}$: (salt of weak acid + strong base)

$$pH = 7 + \frac{1}{2}[pK_a + \log(10^{-2})]$$

$\therefore$ pH > 7, thus pOH < 7

(IV) pOH of 0.01 M NaCl :

(It is a salt of strong acid + strong base)

$\therefore$ $pH = pOH \Rightarrow 7$

Thus, order of pOH value : (I) > (IV) > (III) > (II)

Hence, the correct option is (b).

96. (*c*) $HIn \rightleftharpoons H^+ + In^-$

$$pH = pK_a + \log\frac{[In^-]}{[HIn]}$$

When colour of unionised form is seen

$$\frac{[In^-]}{[HIn]} = \frac{1}{10}$$

$\therefore$ $pH = pK_a - 1$

97. (*c*) When colour of ionised form is seen

$$\frac{[In^-]}{[HIn]} = 10$$

$\therefore$ $pH = pK_a + 1$

100. (*a*) pH range 3 to 5

$\therefore$ $[H^+]$ between 10^{-3} to 10^{-5}

$$[H^+] \text{ at the equivalence point} = \frac{10^{-3} + 10^{-5}}{2}$$

$$= 5.05 \times 10^{-4}\ M$$

$\therefore$ $pH = 3.3$

104. (*d*) 0.1 MHCl = 100 mL $\therefore$ $N_1V_1(\text{acid}) = 10$

0.1 M NaOH = 50 mL $N_2V_2(\text{base}) = 5$

Thus, $N_1V_1 > N_2V_2$

Resultant mixture is acidic

$$\text{Resultant } [H^+] = \frac{N_1V_1 - N_2V_2}{V_1 + V_2} = \frac{1}{30}$$

$$\therefore \quad pH = -\log[H^+] = -\log\left(\frac{1}{30}\right) = 1.48$$

106. (*b*) $[Al(H_2O)_6]^{3+} \rightleftharpoons [Al(H_2O)_5OH]^{2+} + H^+$

↑

H^+ ion donor, hence acid.

107. (*c*) $\overset{\oplus}{N}H_3CH_2COOH \overset{-H^+}{\rightleftharpoons} \overset{\oplus}{N}H_3CH_2COO^- \overset{-H^+}{\rightleftharpoons} NH_2CH_2COO^-$

Conjugate acid Conjugate base

108. (*a*) $[NH_2^-] = [NH_4^+] = \sqrt{K_{NH_3}} = 10^{-15}\ M = 10^{-15}\ mol\ L^{-1}$

$$10^{-15}\ mol\ L^{-1} = \frac{10^{-15}\ mol}{1000\ cm^3} = \frac{10^{-15}\ mol}{10^6\ mm^3}$$

$$= \frac{10^{-15} \times 6.02 \times 10^{23}}{10^6}\ NH_2^- \text{ ion / mm}^3 = 602$$

109. (*a*) $BOH \rightleftharpoons B^+ + OH^-$

By Ostwald's dilution law

$$[OH^-] = \sqrt{K_bC}$$

$$1.5 \times 10^{-3} = \sqrt{1.5 \times 10^{-5} \times C}$$

$\therefore$ $C = 0.15\ M$

110. (*c*) Milliequivalents of HCl = $50 \times 0.3 = 15$

Milliequivalents of $NH_3 = 50 \times 0.4 = 20$

$$NH_3 + HCl \rightleftharpoons NH_4Cl$$

NH_3 neutralised by HCl = 15 milliequivalents

$NH_4^+Cl^-$ formed = 15 milliequivalents

NH_3 unreacted = 5 milliequivalents

$$pK_a(NH_4^+) = 9.26$$

$$pK_b(NH_3) = 14 - 9.26 = 4.74$$

$$pOH = pK_b + \log\frac{[NH_4^+]}{[NH_3]} = 4.74 + \log\frac{15}{5} = 5.22$$

$\therefore$ $pH = 14 - 5.22 = 8.78$

111. (*d*) Due to hydrolysis of CH_3COONa (formed at equivalence point) solution is alkaline pH > 7, hence (a) is not true.

In (b) and (c) $[CH_3COOH] = [CH_3COONa]$

$$pH = pK_a + \log\frac{[CH_3COONa]}{[CH_3COOH]} = pK_a$$

112. (*a*) Acid indicator is HIn

$$HIn \rightleftharpoons H^+ + In^-$$

It changes colour when $[In^-] = [HIn]$

$$K_a = \frac{[H^+][In^-]}{[HIn]} = [H^+] = 1 \times 10^{-5}$$

$\therefore$ $pH = 5$

113. (*c*) $\underset{B}{NH_4OH} \rightleftharpoons \underset{BH^+}{NH_4^+} + OH^-$

$$K_b = \frac{[BH^+]}{[B]}[OH^-] = [OH^-] = 2 \times 10^{-5}$$

$\therefore$ $pOH = 5 - \log 2$

$\therefore$ $pH = 14 - pOH = 9 + \log 2 = 9.3$

114. (*d*) Na_2CO_3 solution is alkaline due to hydrolysis

$$CO_3^{2-} + 2H_2O \rightleftharpoons H_2CO_3 + 2OH^-$$

OH^- neutralises CH_3COOH

115. (*d*) By Henderson's equation,

$$pOH = pK_b + \log\frac{[HX]}{[X^-]} = 4 + \log 2$$

$\therefore$ $pH = 14 - pOH = 10 - \log 2$

117. (*b*) $H_2PO_4^-$ is amphiprotic.

$$pH = (pK_1 + pK_2)/2 = \frac{2.15 + 7.20}{2} = 4.675$$

119. (*c*) If benzoic acid = x mL = x millimol

sodium benzoate = (300 – x) mL = (300 – x) millimol

$$pH = pK_a + \log\frac{[\text{sodium benzoate}]}{[\text{benzoic acid}]}$$

$$4.5 = 4.2 + \log\left(\frac{300 - x}{x}\right)$$

$$\frac{300 - x}{x} = 2, \quad x = 100\ mL$$

121. (*b*) $\Delta T_f = K_f(\text{molarity}) \times i$

$$0.2046 = 1.86° \times 0.1(1+x)$$

$$(1+x) = \frac{0.2046}{0.186} = 1.1$$

$$x = 0.1$$

$\therefore$ $[H^+] = Cx = 0.1 \times 0.1 = 0.01$

$\therefore$ pH = 2

i is van't Hoff factor = $(1+x)$ in binary salt like HA

122. (*b*) $HA + OH^- \rightleftharpoons H_2O + A^-$

$$K = \frac{[A^-]}{[HA][OH^-]}$$

$$HA \rightleftharpoons H^+ + A^-$$

$$K_a = \frac{[H^+][A^-]}{[HA]}$$

$\therefore$ $\frac{K_a}{K} = [H^+][OH^-] = K_w$

$$K_a = K_w K = 10^{-14} \times 10^9 = 10^{-5}$$

$\therefore$ $pK_a = 5$

A^- solution is alkaline due to hydrolysis

$\therefore$ $\text{pH} = 7 + \frac{pK_a}{2} + \frac{\log C}{2} = 7 + \frac{5}{2} + \frac{\log 0.1}{2} = 9$

123. (*c*) $K_b(A^-) = 10^{-10}$

$$pK_b = 10$$

$\therefore$ $pK_a(HA) = 14 - 10 = 4$

$$\text{pH} = pK_a + \log\frac{[A^-]}{[HA]}$$

$$5 = 4 + \log\frac{[A^-]}{[HA]}$$

$\therefore$ $1 = \log\frac{[A^-]}{[HA]}$

$$\frac{[A^-]}{[HA]} = 10$$

$$\frac{[HA]}{[A^-]} = \frac{1}{10} = 0.1$$

124. (*d*) Aspirin is a weak acid = 0.09×2 g / 100 mL = 1.8 g L^{-1}

$$= \frac{1.8}{180} \text{ mol L}^{-1} = 0.01 \text{ M}$$

$$\text{pH (weak acid)} = \frac{1}{2}[pK_a - \log C] = \frac{1}{2}[2+2] = 2$$

125. (*d*) pH = 13, pOH = 1

$[OH^-] = 10^{-1}$ M = 0.1 mol / L = 0.0001 mol /mL

$= 1 \times 10^{-4} \times 6.02 \times 10^{23}$ OH^- ions per mL

$= 6.02 \times 10^{19}$

126. (*c*) pH = 9.26 indicates $[NH_4OH] > [HCl]$ and thus mixture is a buffer since HCl will react with equivalent amount of NH_4OH forming NH_4Cl

Let HCl = x mL = x millimol

$NH_4OH = (300 - x)$ mL $= (300 - x)$ millimol

NH_4Cl formed = x millimol

NH_4OH unreacted = $300 - x - x = (300 - 2x)$ millimol

$$\text{pOH} = 14 - 9.26 = 4.74$$

$$pK_b = 14 - 9.26 = 4.74$$

$$\text{pOH} = pK_b + \log\frac{[NH_4^+]}{[NH_4OH]}$$

$$4.74 = 4.74 + \log\frac{x}{(300-2x)}$$

$$\frac{x}{300-2x} = 1$$

$\therefore$ $x = 100$ mL = volume of HCl

$(300 - x) = 200$ mL = volume of NH_4OH

Hence, 2 : 1.

127. (*c*) x mol $(CH_3COO)_2Pb = 2x$ mol CH_3COO^-

$\therefore$ $[CH_3COOH] = 0.1$ M

$[CH_3COO^-] = 2x$ M

$\therefore$ $\text{pH} = pK_a + \log\frac{[CH_3COO^-]}{[CH_3COOH]}$

$$5.04 = 4.74 + \log 20x$$

$$20x = 2$$

$$x = 0.1 \text{ mol}$$

128. (*c*) $K_{sp}(AgCl) > K_{sp}(AgI)$

hence, AgI is precipitated before AgCl

$$[Ag^+] \text{ to precipitated } Cl^- = \frac{1 \times 10^{-10}}{0.05} = 2 \times 10^{-9} \text{ M}$$

$$[I^-] \text{ at this stage} = \frac{K_{sp}(AgI)}{[Ag^+]} = \frac{4 \times 10^{-16}}{2 \times 10^{-9}} = 2 \times 10^{-7} \text{ M}$$

130. (*b*) $K_{sp} = 5.5 \times 10^{-6}$

$$Ca(OH)_2 \rightleftharpoons Ca^{2+} + 2OH^-$$

$$[Ca^{2+}][OH^-]^2 = 5.5 \times 10^{-6}$$

$$4S^3 = 5.5 \times 10^{-6}$$

$$S = 0.0111$$

$\therefore$ $[OH^-] = 2S = 0.0111 \times 2 = 0.0222$

$\therefore$ pOH = 1.65

pH = 12.35

136. (*b*) 0.005 M calcium lactate $(La)_2Ca$

$\therefore$ [lactate] = 0.01 M

$$\text{pH} = 7 + \frac{pK_a}{2} + \frac{\log C}{2} = 7 + 2.5 - 1 = 8.5$$

137. (*d*) $[H^+] = \sqrt{K_a C}$, pH = 2, $\therefore [H^+] = 10^{-2}$ M

$$10^{-2} = \sqrt{K_a C}$$

$$10^{-4} = 8.4 \times 10^{-4} \times C$$

$\therefore$ $C = 11.9 \times 10^{-2} \approx 12.0 \times 10^{-2}$M

140. (*c*) For equivalent point KOH required = 38.62 mL when half of this volume (19.31 mL) has been added, 50% acid is neutralised and at this stage

$[CH_3COOK] = [CH_3COOH]$

$\therefore \quad pH = pK_a = 4.74$

142. (*a*) $NH_4OH \rightleftharpoons NH_4^+ + OH^-$

$$K_b = \frac{[NH_4^+][OH^-]}{[NH_4OH]}$$

$$1.8 \times 10^{-5} = \frac{[NH_4^+][0.01]}{(0.02)}$$

$\therefore \quad [NH_4^+] = 3.6 \times 10^{-5}$ M

143. (*c*) In a mixture of weak acid (resultant concentration C_1 mol L^{-1} and ionisation constant K_1) and a strong acid (resultant concentration C_2 mol L^{-1}) total $[H_3O^+]$ is

$$[H_3O^+] = \frac{C_2 + \sqrt{C_2^2 + 4K_1C_1}}{2}$$

Due to dilution by one another

$$C_1(AcOH) = \frac{0.2}{2} = 0.1 \text{ M}$$

$$C_2(HCl) = \frac{0.2}{2} = 0.1 \text{ M}$$

$$\therefore [H_3O^+] = \frac{(0.1) + \sqrt{(0.1)^2 + 4 \times 1.8 \times 10^{-5} \times 0.1}}{2} = 0.1 \text{ M}$$

$\therefore \quad pH = -\log [H_3O^+] = 1$

Alternately AcOH is a weak acid. Its $[H_3O^+] <<< 0.2$ M. It simply caused dilution of HCl.

$$\text{Resultant due to dilution} [HCl] = \frac{0.2 \times 50}{100} = 0.1 \text{ M}$$

$\therefore \quad pH = 1$

144. (*d*) $H_2SO_3 + NaOH \rightleftharpoons NaHSO_3 + H_2O$

20 mL of 0.100 M NaOH ≡ 3.2 millimol NaOH

40 mL of 0.080 M H_2SO_3 = 3.2 millimol H_2SO_3

Thus, H_2SO_3 is converted into $NaHSO_3$, HSO_3^- is amphiprotic (H^+ ion donor as well as acceptor)

$$\underset{\text{Acid}}{HSO_3^-} \rightleftharpoons H^+ + SO_3^{2-}$$

$$\underset{\text{Base}}{HSO_3^-} + H^+ \rightleftharpoons H_2SO_4$$

$$pH = \frac{pK_{a_1} + pK_{a_2}}{2}$$

$$= \frac{1.82 + 7.20}{2} = 4.51$$

145. (*c*) $Zn^{2+} + H_2O \rightleftharpoons Zn(OH)^+ + H^+$

$$K_h = 1 \times 10^{-9}$$

$$K_h = \frac{K_w}{K_b(Zn(OH)_2)}$$

$$\therefore \quad K_b = \frac{K_w}{K_h} = 1 \times 10^{-5}$$

$$pK_b = 5$$

$$\therefore \quad pH = 7 - \left(\frac{pK_b + \log C}{2}\right) = 7 - \frac{(5-3)}{2} = 6$$

146. (*a*) $\underset{\substack{C \\ (C - Cx)}}{AcOH} \rightleftharpoons \underset{\substack{0 \\ Cx}}{AcO^-} + \underset{\substack{0 \\ Cx}}{H^+}$ (weak acid)

$HCl \rightleftharpoons Cl^- + H^+$ (strong acid)

Total $\quad [H^+] = Cx + 0.1 \approx 0.1$ M

$$K_a = \frac{[AcO^-][H^+]}{[AcOH]}$$

$$1.8 \times 10^{-5} = \frac{Cx \times 0.1}{C(1-x)} \approx 0.1x$$

$\therefore \quad x = 1.8 \times 10^{-4}$

% dissociation $= 1.8 \times 10^{-4} \times 100 = 0.018\%$

147. (*d*) $Zn^{2+} + H_2O \rightleftharpoons Zn(OH)^+ + H^+$

Due to hydrolysis $K_h = \frac{K_w}{K_b}$

$$\therefore \quad K_b = \frac{K_w}{K_h} = \frac{1 \times 10^{-14}}{1 \times 10^{-9}} = 1 \times 10^{-5}$$

148. (*b*) For weak base indicator, at equivalence point

$$[InOH] = [In^+]$$

$$InOH \rightleftharpoons In^+ + OH^-$$

$$\therefore \quad pOH = pK_b + \log \frac{[In^+]}{[InOH]} = pK_b = 10$$

$\therefore \quad pH = 14 - 10 = 4$

149. (*c*) $HIn \rightleftharpoons In^- + H^+$

$$pH = pK_a + \log \frac{[In^-]}{[HIn]}$$

$$5 = 5 + \log \frac{[In^-]}{[HIn]}$$

$$\therefore \quad \frac{[In^-]}{[HIn]} = 1$$

Thus, 50% of $[In^-]$ and $[HIn]$ exist so that $\frac{[HI^-]}{[HIn]} = 1$

150.

(*b*) Compound	K_{sp}	Related K_{sp} to solubility (*S*)	*S*
CuS	8×10^{-37}	$K_{sp} = S^2$	8.94×10^{-19} M
MnS	7×10^{-16}	$K_{sp} = S^2$	2.64×10^{-8} M
Bi_2S_3	1×10^{-70}	$K_{sp} = 108S^5$	3.92×10^{-15} M
Ag_2S	6×10^{-51}	$K_{sp} = 4S^3$	1.14×10^{-17} M

Thus, MnS is most soluble.

151. (*c*) Due to common ion effect, solubility of sparingly soluble salt is decreased. Larger the concentration of common ion, greater the effect.

153. (*b*) $pH = 5$

$\therefore \quad [H_3O^+] = 10^{-5}$ M $= Cx = 0.005 \times x$

$\therefore \quad x = 2 \times 10^{-3}$

155. (*c*) $BaCl_2 \rightleftharpoons \underset{S}{Ba^{2+}} + \underset{2S}{2Cl^-}$

$$K_{sp} = [Ba^{2+}][Cl^-]^2 = (S)(2S)^2 = 4S^3$$

$$S = \left(\frac{K_{sp}}{4}\right)^{1/3} = 1 \times 10^{-3}\ M$$

156. (*d*) $CaF_2 \rightleftharpoons \underset{S}{Ca^{2+}}(aq) + \underset{2S}{2F^-}(aq)$

$$K_{sp} = [Ca^{2+}][F^-]^2 = (S)(2S)^2 = 4S^3$$

$$= 4(2 \times 10^{-4})^3 = 32 \times 10^{-12}\ m^3$$

158. (*a*) $pH = 13$

$$[H^+] = 10^{-13}\ M = 10^{-13}\ mol\ L^{-1}$$

$$[H^+]\text{ in 1 mL} = \frac{10^{-13}}{1000} = 10^{-16}\ mol$$

$$= 10^{-16} \times 6.02 \times 10^{23}$$

$$= 6.02 \times 10^7\ H^+\text{ ions}$$

159. (*d*) $pH = 2,\ [H^+]_1 = 10^{-2}\ M$

$pH = 6\ \ [H^+]_2 = 10^{-6}\ M$

$$\therefore \frac{[H^+]_1}{[H^+]_2} = \frac{10^{-2}}{10^{-6}} = 10^4\text{ times}$$

160. (*c*) $HCOO^- + H_2O \rightleftharpoons HCOOH + OH^-$

$$K_h = \frac{K_w}{K_a} = \frac{1 \times 10^{-14}}{2 \times 10^{-4}} = 5 \times 10^{-11}$$

162. (*b*) $pH = pK_a + \log \frac{[HCO_3^-]}{[CO_2]}$

$$6.0 = -\log 3.8 \times 10^{-7} + \log \frac{[HCO_3^-]}{[CO_2]}$$

$$6.0 = +6.42 + \log \frac{[HCO_3^-]}{[CO_2]}$$

$$\therefore \log \frac{[HCO_3^-]}{[CO_2]} = -0.42$$

$$\therefore \frac{[HCO_3^-]}{[CO_2]} = 0.38$$

163. (*a*) $PbBr_2 \rightleftharpoons \underset{0.7S}{Pb^{2+}} + \underset{2 \times 0.7S}{2Br^-}$

$$K_{sp} = [Pb^{2+}][Br^-]^2 = (0.7S)(2 \times 0.7\,S)^2$$

$$10.8 \times 10^{-5} = (0.7)^3 \times 4S^3$$

$$\therefore S = 4.285 \times 10^{-2}\ M$$

164. (*a*) $[Ag^+] = 0.1\ mg = (0.1 \times 10^{-3}\ g)$ in 500 mL H_2O

$$= \frac{0.1 \times 10^{-3}}{108}\text{ mol in 500 mL } H_2O$$

$$= \frac{0.1 \times 10^{-3} \times 2}{108}\text{ mol in 1 L } H_2O = 1.85 \times 10^{-6}\ M$$

$$[Ag^+]\ [Cl^-] = 1.0 \times 10^{-10}$$

$$\therefore [Cl^-] = \frac{1.0 \times 10^{-10}}{1.85 \times 10^{-6}} = 5.4 \times 10^{-5}\ M$$

165. (*d*) $[Hg^{2+}] = 2.0$ millimol in 100 mL solution

$$= \frac{2 \times 10^{-3}\ mol}{0.1\ L} = 2 \times 10^{-2}\ M = 0.02\ M$$

Since, stability constant of $HgCl_2$ is large (1.65×10^{13}) the value of $[Hg^{2+}]$ should be small.

At the end point

$$[Cl^-] = 2\ [Hg^{2+}]$$

$$[HgCl_2] = 0.020 - [Hg^{2+}]$$

$$\approx 0.02\ M$$

$$\therefore \frac{[HgCl_2]}{[Hg^{2+}]\ [Cl^-]^2} = 1.65 \times 10^{13}$$

$$\frac{0.02}{[Hg^{2+}]\ (2[Hg^{2+}])^2} = 1.65 \times 10^{13}$$

$$\therefore 4\ [Hg^{2+}]^3 = \frac{0.02}{1.65 \times 10^{13}}$$

$$\therefore [Hg^{2+}] = 6.72 \times 10^{-6}\ M$$

166. (*b*) $CH_3NH_2 + H^+Cl^- \rightleftharpoons CH_3NH_3^+Cl^-$

Initial	0.1	0.08	
Final	0.02	—	0.08 M

$$CH_3NH_2 + H_2O \rightleftharpoons CH_3NH_3^+ + OH^-$$

$$K_b = \frac{[CH_3NH_3^+][OH^-]}{[CH_3NH_2]}$$

$$5 \times 10^{-4} = \frac{(0.08)[OH^-]}{(0.02)}$$

$$[OH^-] = 1.25 \times 10^{-4}\ M$$

$$[H^+] = \frac{K_w}{[OH^-]} = \frac{1 \times 10^{-14}}{1.25 \times 10^{-4}}$$

$$= 8 \times 10^{-11}\ M$$

167. (*b*) $Ag_2CrO_4 \rightleftharpoons 2Ag^+ + CrO_4^{2-}$

$$[Ag^+] = 2\ [CrO_4^{2-}]$$

$$[Ag^+]^2\ [CrO_4^{2-}] = K_{sp}$$

$$[2CrO_4^{2-}]^2\ [CrO_4^{2-}] = K_{sp}$$

$$[CrO_4^{2-}]^3 = \frac{K_{sp}}{4}$$

$$3\log[CrO_4^{2-}] = \log K_{sp} - \log 4$$

$$-3\log[CrO_4^{2-}] = -\log K_{sp} + 2\log 2$$

$$3p_{CrO_4} = pK_{sp} + 2\log 2$$

168. (**a**) Internal proton transfer can take place in compounds which can donate proton (*i.e.*, Lowry-Bronsted acid) as well as can accept proton (Lowry-Bronsted base).

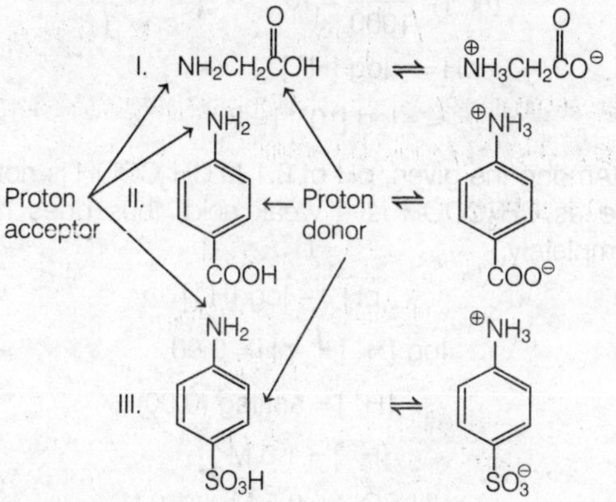

Thus, I, II, III

169. (*a*) $NH_4Cl + H_2O \rightleftharpoons NH_4OH + HCl$

$$NH_4^+ + Cl^- + H_2O \rightleftharpoons NH_4OH + H^+ + Cl^-$$

$$NH_4^+ + H_2O \rightleftharpoons NH_4OH + H^+$$

acidic (H^+) due to NH_4^+ thus correct.

(b) $CH_3COO^- + H_2O \rightleftharpoons CH_3COOH + OH^-$

basic (OH^-) due to CH_3COO^- thus incorrect

(c) At 100°C, $K_w = [H^+][OH^-] = 1 \times 10^{-12}$

$\therefore$ $[H^+] = [OH^-] = 10^{-6}$

pH = pOH = 6 thus neutral

Thus, incorrect

(d) HCl is an acid pH < 7 thus, incorrect.

170. (**b**)

$$pH = pK_{In} + \log\frac{[blue]}{[yellow]}$$

$$3.7 = 4.7 + \log\frac{[blue]}{[yellow]}$$

$$-1 = \log\frac{[blue]}{[yellow]}$$

$$1 = \log\frac{[yellow]}{[blue]}$$

$\therefore$ [yellow] : [blue] = 10 : 1

172. (*a*) $pK_{In} = -\log K_{In} = 10 - \log 4 = 9.4$

Thus, it is the equivalent point. pH colour change starts from ($pK_{In} - 1$) and completes at ($pK_{In} + 1$).

Thus, (a) is incorrect

173. (*a*) Adding,

$$Ag^+ + 2NH_3 \rightleftharpoons [Ag(NH_3)_2^+]$$

$$K = K_1K_2 = 3.5 \times 10^{-3} \times 1.7 \times 10^{-3}$$

$$= 5.95 \times 10^{-6} \approx 6.00 \times 10^{-6}$$

175. (*b*) pH = 2, $\therefore$ $M(H^+) = 10^{-2}$ M

$$M_1V_1 = M_2V_2$$

$$M_1 \times 0.25 = 10^{-2} \times 500 \quad : \quad M_2 = 20\text{ M}$$

176. (*d*) (a) $Ag_3PO_4 \rightleftharpoons 3Ag^+ + PO_4^{3-}$

$$K_{sp} = [Ag^+]^3[PO_4^{3-}]$$

$$[PO_4^{3-}] = \frac{K_{sp}}{(0.1)^3} = \frac{1 \times 10^{-6}}{10^{-3}} = 10^{-3}$$

(b) $Ca_3(PO_4)_2 \rightleftharpoons 3Ca^{2+} + 2PO_4^{3-}$

$$K_{sp} = [Ca^{2+}]^3[PO_4^{3-}]^2$$

$$10^{-33} = (0.1)^3[PO_4^{3-}]^2$$

$$[PO_4^{3-}]^2 = \frac{10^{-33}}{10^{-3}}$$

$$[PO_4^{3-}] = 10^{-15}\text{ M}$$

$$PO_4^{3-} = 5 \times 10^{-16}$$

(c) $Mg_3(PO_4)_2 \rightleftharpoons \underset{0.1}{3Mg^{2+}} + \underset{2x}{2PO_4^{3-}}$

as in (b) $[PO_4^{3-}]^2 = \dfrac{10}{10^{-3}}$

$$[PO_4^{3-}] = 3.16 \times 10^{-11}\text{ M}$$

$(pK_b = -\log K_b = 1.8 \times 10^{-5} = 4.74)$

Thus, $\alpha = \dfrac{[H^+]}{C} = \dfrac{10^{-5}}{0.005} = 2 \times 10^{-3}$

Thus, 0.2%

(d) $AlPO_4 \rightleftharpoons \underset{0.1}{Al^{3+}} + \underset{x}{PO_4^{3-}}$

$$PO_4^{3-} = \frac{K_{sp}}{0.1} = \frac{10^{-20}}{0.1} = 10^{-19}\text{ M}$$

177. (*c*) Common ion effect is the suppression of degree of dissociation of a weak electrolyte in the presence of a strong electrolyte having common ion.

Among the given, CH_3COOH + NaOH has no common ion, thus does not exhibit common ion effect.

178. (*c*) For precipitation,

ionic product > solubility product (K_{sp})

For Ag_2CrO_4

ionic product = $[Ag^+]^2[CrO_4^-] = (10^{-4})^2(10^{-5}) = 10^{-13}$

K_{sp} of $Ag_2CrO_4 = 4 \times 10^{-12}$

Here, K_{sp} > ionic product

Thus, no precipitate is obtained.

For AgCl,

ionic product = $[Ag^+][Cl^-] = [10^{-4}][10^{-5}] = 10^{-9}$

K_{sp} (AgCl) = 1×10^{10}

Here, ionic product > K_{sp}

So, precipitate will form.

Thus, silver chloride gets precipitated first.

179. (*b*)
$$K_{sp} = [Ag^+]^2[CrO_4^{2-}]$$
$$1\times10^{-12} = (0.1)^2[CrO_4^{2-}]$$
$$\therefore \quad s = [CrO_4^{2-}] = 1\times10^{-10}\text{ M}$$

180. (*b*) A weak acid and its conjugate base HPO_4^{2-}.

181. (*d*)
$$CH_3COOH \rightleftharpoons CH_3COO^- + H^+$$
$$[CH_3COO^-] = [H^+] \quad \ldots(i)$$
$$H_2O \rightleftharpoons H^+ + OH^-$$
$$[H^+] = [OH^-] \quad \ldots(ii)$$

From Eqs. (i) and (ii), we get
$$[H^+] + [H^+] = [CH_3COO^-] + [OH^-]$$
$$2[H^+] = [CH_3COO^-] + [OH^-]$$

182. (*b*)
$$pK_a = -\log K_a$$
$$\therefore \quad (pK_a)_A = -\log (K_a)_A$$
$$(K_a)_A = \text{antilog}(-4) = 10^{-4}$$

Similarly, $(K_a)_B = \text{antilog}(-6) = 10^{-6}$
$$\frac{\text{Strength of } A}{\text{Strength of } B} = \sqrt{\frac{K_a}{K_b}} = \sqrt{\frac{10^{-4}}{10^{-6}}} = 10$$

$\therefore$ Strength of $A = 10 \times$ strength of B.

183. (*d*) As pH of HCOOH sol. = pH of CH_3COOH sol. $[H^+]$ in HCOOH sol. = $[H^+]$ in CH_3COOH sol.
$$K_1 = \frac{[HCOO^-][H^+]}{[HCOOH]} = \frac{[H^+]^2}{[HCOOH]}$$
$$K_2 = \frac{[CH_3COO^-][H^+]}{[CH_3COOH]} = \frac{[H^+]^2}{[CH_3COOH]}$$
$$\Rightarrow \quad K_1[HCOOH] = K_2[CH_3COOH]$$
$$\therefore \quad \frac{[HCOOH]}{[CH_3COOH]} = \frac{K_2}{K_1} = \frac{1}{4} = 0.25$$

184. (*d*)
$$CH_3COOH \rightleftharpoons CH_3COO^- + H^+$$
$$K_{\text{acetic acid}} = 1.5\times10^{-5} = \frac{[CH_3COO^-][H^+]}{[CH_3COOH]}$$
$$HCN \rightleftharpoons H^+ + CN^-$$
$$K_{HCN} = 4.5\times10^{-10} = \frac{[H^+][CN^-]}{[HCN]}$$

For equilibrium :
$$CN^- + CH_3COOH \rightleftharpoons HCN + CH_3COO^-$$
$$K = \frac{[CH_3COO^-][HCN]}{[CN^-][CH_3COOH]} = \frac{K_{\text{acetic acid}}}{K_{HCN}}$$
$$= \frac{1.5\times10^{-5}}{4.5\times10^{-10}} = 3.3\times10^4 \approx 3.0\times10^4$$

185. (*a*) Total milliequivalents of $H^+ = 20\times\frac{1}{2} + 30\times\frac{1}{3} = 20$

Total milliequivalents of $OH^- = 40\times\frac{1}{4} = 10$

Thus, milliequivalents of H^+ left $= 20 - 10 = 10$

Total volume of solution $= 1\text{ dm}^3 = 1000$ mL
$$\therefore \quad [H^+] = \frac{10}{1000} = 10^{-2}$$
$$\Rightarrow \quad pH = -\log[H^+]$$
$$= -\log[10^{-2}] = 2$$

186. (*c*) Among the given, pH of 0.1 M CH_3COOH is not equal to one as CH_3COOH is a weak acid, thus does not ionise completely.

187. (*c*)
$$pH = -\log[H^+]$$
$$\log[H^+] = -pH = 0.00$$
$$[H^+] = \text{antilog}(0.00)$$
$$[H^+] = 1.0\text{ M}$$
$$(H_2SO_4) = 0.5\text{ M} = 1.0\text{ N}$$

Normality is an intensive property whether one takes 1 L or 250 mL it is same.

188. (*b*) Millimoles of $H^+ = 0.1\times2 + 0.1\times2\times2 = 0.6$

Total volume in mL = 6
$$pH = -\log[H^+] = -\log\left(\frac{0.6}{6}\right)$$
$$= -\log 0.1 = 1$$

189. (*d*)
$$pH = 1;\ N_1 = 1\times10^{-1}\text{ M}$$
$$pH = 2;\ N_2 = 1\times10^{-2}\text{ M}$$
$$N_1V_1 = N_2V_2$$
$$1\times10^{-1}\times1 = 1\times10^{-2}\times V_2$$
$$V_2 = 10\text{ L, Water added} = 10 - 1 = 9\text{ L}$$

190. (*a*) According to Ostwald's dilution law
$$K = \frac{C\alpha^2}{1-\alpha}$$
or
$$K - K\alpha = C\alpha^2$$
or
$$C\alpha^2 + K\alpha - K = 0.$$

191. (*c*)
$$\underset{}{M_2X_3} \rightleftharpoons \underset{2S}{2M^{3+}} + \underset{3S}{3X^{2-}} \text{ (where, } s = \text{solubility)}$$
$$K_{sp} = (2S)^2\cdot(3S)^3 = 108S^5$$
or
$$2.2\times10^{-20} = 108S^5$$
$$\therefore \quad S = 4.59\times10^{-5}$$

08

Chemical Kinetics

Objective Questions Type I [Only one correct option]

In each of the questions below, four choices are given of which only one is correct.

1. Rate of formation of SO_3 in the following reaction

$$2SO_2 + O_2 \longrightarrow 2SO_3$$

is 100 g min^{-1}. Hence, rate of disappearance of O_2 is

(a) 50 g min^{-1} (b) 100 g min^{-1}

(c) 200 g min^{-1} (d) 20 g min^{-1}

2. For $xA + yB \rightarrow zC$, $-\frac{d[A]}{dt} = -\frac{d[B]}{dt} = 1.5\frac{d[C]}{dt}$ then x, y and z are

(a) 1, 1, 1 (b) 3, 2, 3 (c) 3, 3, 2 (d) 2, 2, 3

3. For a gaseous reaction, the rate is often expressed in terms of $\left(\frac{dp}{dt}\right)$ instead of $\left(\frac{dC}{dt}\right)$ or $\left(\frac{dn}{dt}\right)$, where, C is the concentration and n is the number of moles. Hence, relation between three expressions is

(a) $\frac{dC}{dt} = \frac{1}{V}\left(\frac{dn}{dt}\right) = \frac{1}{RT}\left(\frac{dp}{dt}\right)$

(b) $\frac{dC}{dt} = \left(\frac{dn}{dt}\right) = \left(\frac{dp}{dt}\right)$

(c) $\frac{dC}{dt} = \left(\frac{dn}{dt}\right) = \frac{V}{RT}\left(\frac{dp}{dt}\right)$

(d) None of the above

4. For the reaction, $2NH_3 \longrightarrow N_2 + 3H_2$

$$-\frac{d[NH_3]}{dt} = k_1[NH_3], \quad \frac{d[N_2]}{dt} = k_2[NH_3],$$

$$\frac{d[H_2]}{dt} = k_3[NH_3]$$

Then relation between k_1, k_2 and k_3 is

(a) $1.5k_1 = 3k_2 = k_3$ (b) $2k_1 = k_2 = 3k_3$

(c) $k_1 = k_2 = k_3$ (d) $k_1 = 3k_2 = 2k_3$

5. In the following reaction,

$$xA \longrightarrow yB$$

$$\log\left[-\frac{d[A]}{dt}\right] = \log\left[\frac{d[B]}{dt}\right] + 0.3$$

where, negative sign indicates rate of disappearance of the reactant.

Thus, $x : y$ is

(a) 1 : 2

(b) 2 : 1

(c) 3 : 1

(d) 3 : 10

6. Reaction rates are determined by all of the following factors except

(a) the number of collisions between molecules

(b) the force of collisions between molecules

(c) the orientation of collisions between molecules

(d) the spontaneity of the reaction

7. A rapid reaction is distinguished by

(a) being unaffected by catalysts

(b) having a large heat of reaction

(c) having a small heat of reaction

(d) having a small value of activation energy

8. For a chemical reaction to occur, all of the following must happen except

(a) a large enough number of collisions must occur

(b) chemical bonds in the reactants must break

(c) reactant particles must collide with enough energy for change to occur

(d) reactant particles must collide with correct orientation

9. Higher order (>3) reactions are rare due to **[JEE Main 2015]**

(a) low probability of simultaneous collision of all the reacting species
(b) increase in entropy and activation energy as more molecules are involved
(c) shifting of equilibrium towards reactants due to elastic collisions
(d) loss of active species on collision

10. A reaction follows the given concentration-time graph. The rate for this reaction at 20 s will be

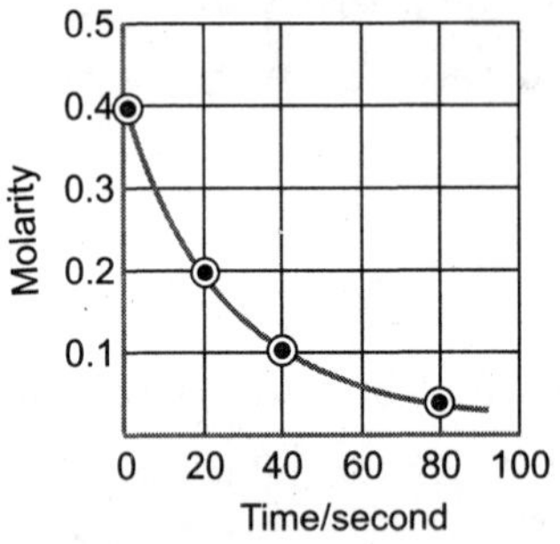

(a) 4×10^{-3} M s^{-1}
(b) 8×10^{-3} M s^{-1}
(c) 2×10^{-2} M s^{-1}
(d) 1×10^{-2} M s^{-1}

11. For the complex,

$$Ag^+ + 2NH_3 \rightleftharpoons [Ag(NH_3)_2^+]$$

$$\left(\frac{dx}{dt}\right) = 2\times 10^7 \text{ L}^2 \text{ mol}^{-2}\text{s}^{-1} [Ag^+][NH_3]^2 - 1\times 10^{-2} \text{ s}^{-1} [Ag(NH_3)_2^+]$$

Hence, ratio of rate constants of the forward and backward reaction is

(a) 2×10^7 L^2 mol^{-2} (b) 2×10^9 L^2 mol^{-2}
(c) 1×10^{-2} L^2 mol^{-2} (d) 0.5×10^{-9} L^2 mol^2

12. In the reaction,

$$N_2 + 3H_2 \rightleftharpoons 2NH_3$$

$$\left(\frac{dx}{dt}\right) = 1\times 10^2 M^{-3} [N_2][H_2]^3 - 1\times 10^{-3} M^{-1} [NH_3]^2$$

$$\frac{[N_2][H_2]^3}{[NH_3]^2} = 10^{-5} M^2 \quad \text{if} \left(\frac{dx}{dt}\right) \text{is}$$

(a) 0 (b) 1×10^5 (c) 1×10^{-5} (d) 1×10^{-3}

13. In the following graphical representation for the reaction $A \longrightarrow B$ there are two types of regions

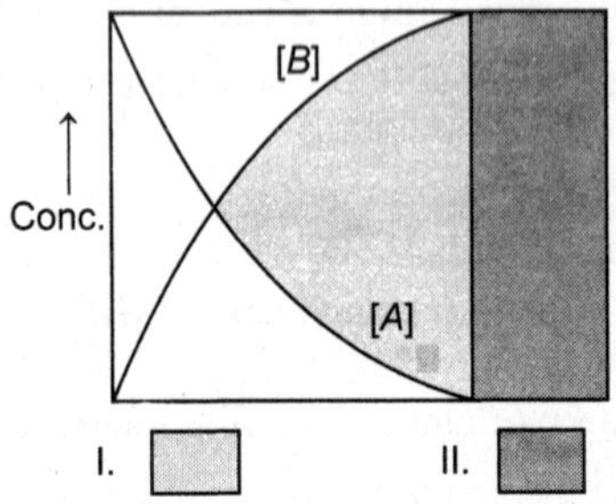

(a) I and II both represent kinetic region at different time interval
(b) I and II both represent equilibrium region at different time interval
(c) I represents kinetic while II represents equilibrium region
(d) I represents equilibrium while II represents kinetic region

14. For a reaction of reversible nature, net rate is

$$\left(\frac{dx}{dt}\right) = k_1 [A]^2 [B]^{-1} - k_2[C]$$

hence, given reaction is

(a) $2A + \frac{1}{B} \rightleftharpoons C$ (b) $2A - B \rightleftharpoons C$
(c) $2A \rightleftharpoons C + B^{-1}$ (d) None of these

15. For a reaction, net rate is

$$\left(\frac{dx}{dt}\right) = k[A]^2[B]^{-2} - k'[C]$$

then, select the correct statement.

(a) $-\frac{d[A]^2}{dt} = \frac{d[B]^2}{dt} = \frac{d[C]}{dt}$ is the relation among different rates
(b) $2A \rightleftharpoons 2B + C$ is the required reaction
(c) Both (a) and (b) are correct
(d) None of the above is correct

16. The reaction of ozone with oxygen atom in the presence of chlorine atom can occur by the two-step process shown here with the rate constant for each step

$$O_3(g) + Cl(g) \longrightarrow O_2(g) + ClO(g), \quad k_1 = 5.2\times 10^9 \text{ L mol}^{-1} \text{ s}^{-1}$$

$$ClO(g) + O(g) \longrightarrow O_2(g) + Cl(g), \quad k_2 = 2.6\times 10^{10} \text{ L mol}^{-1} \text{ s}^{-1}$$

Which of the values below is the closest to the rate constant of the overall net reaction, given by the equation

$$O_3(g) + O(g) \longrightarrow 2O_2(g)?$$

(a) 5.2×10^9 L mol^{-1} s^{-1} (b) 2.6×10^{10} L mol^{-1} s^{-1}
(c) 3.1×10^{10} L mol^{-1} s^{-1} (d) 1.4×10^{20} L mol^{-1} s^{-1}

17. Rate law of the reaction $A \rightarrow$ Product is, rate = $k[A]$. Graphically it is represented as

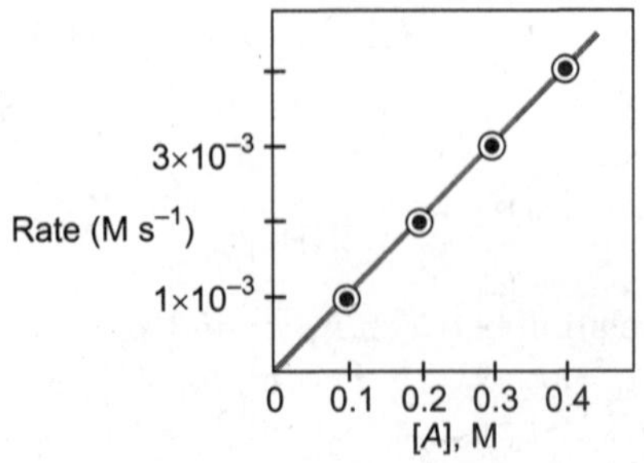

Hence, rate constant is

(a) 3×10^{-4} s^{-1} (b) 1×10^{-2} s^{-1}
(c) 3×10^{-2} s^{-1} (d) 1×10^{-4} s^{-1}

18. For a given reaction, $A \rightarrow$ Product, rate is 1×10^{-4} M s^{-1} when $[A] = 0.01$ M and rate is 1.41×10^{-4} M s^{-1} when $[A] = 0.02$ M. Hence, rate law is

(a) $-\frac{d[A]}{dt} = k[A]^2$ (b) $\frac{-d[A]}{dt} = k[A]$

(c) $\frac{-d[A]}{dt} = \frac{k}{4}[A]$ (d) $\frac{-d[A]}{dt} = k[A]^{1/2}$

19. Following reaction can take place in both direction $A \underset{k_2}{\overset{k_1}{\rightleftharpoons}} B$. For the forward reaction

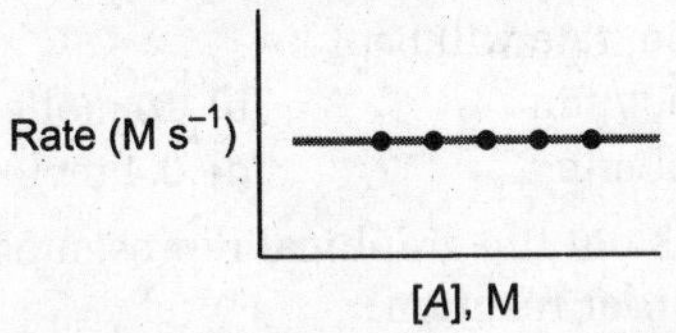

and for the backward reaction

$[B]$	Rate
0.01 M	1×10^{-2} M s^{-1}
0.02 M	2×10^{-2} M s^{-1}

Hence, net reaction rate is

(a) $= k_1[A] - k_2[B]$

(b) $= k_1 - k_2[B]$

(c) $= k_1[A] - k_2$

(d) $= k_1 - k_2$

20. At a given temperature, $k_1 = k_2$ for the reaction

$$A + B \rightleftharpoons C + D$$

If $\left[\frac{dx}{dt}\right] = k_1[A][B] - k_2[C][D]$

in which set of the concentration reaction ceases?

	$[A]$	$[B]$	$[C]$	$[D]$
(a)	0.1 M	0.2 M	0.3 M	0.4 M
(b)	0.4 M	0.25 M	0.2 M	0.5 M
(c)	0.2 M	0.2 M	0.3 M	0.2 M
(d)	0.2 M	0.2 M	0.4 M	0.2 M

21. The following reaction is first-order in A and first-order in B

$A + B \longrightarrow$ Product, Rate $= k[A][B]$

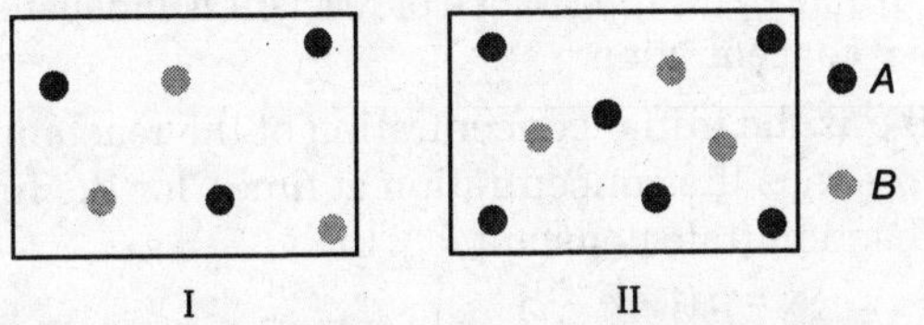

I II

Relative rate of this reaction in vessels I and II of equal volume is

(a) 1 : 1 (b) 1 : 2 (c) 2 : 1 (d) 1 : 4

22. Relative value of rate constants (k) in I and II of question (21) is

(a) 1 : 1 (b) 1 : 2 (c) 2 : 1 (d) 1 : 3

23. The rate of the reaction, $A + B_2 \longrightarrow AB + B$ is directly proportional to the concentration of A and independent of concentration of B_2, hence, rate law is

(a) $k[A][B_2]$ (b) $k[A]^2[B_2]$

(c) $k[A]$ (d) $k[B_2]$

24. For the following reaction,

$$(CH_3)_3CCl + H_2O \longrightarrow (CH_3)_3COH + HCl$$

$\left(\frac{dx}{dt}\right) = k[(CH_3)_3CCl]$, hence, rate determining step is

(a) $(CH_3)_3CCl \longrightarrow (CH_3)_3C^{\oplus} + Cl^{\ominus}$

(b) $(CH_3)_3CCl + H_2O \longrightarrow (CH_3)_3COH + HCl$

(c) $(CH_3)_3C^{\oplus} + H_2O \longrightarrow (CH_3)_3COH + H^+$

(d) $H^+ + Cl^- \longrightarrow HCl$

25. Which of the following plots is(are) correct for the given reaction? **[JEE Advanced 2020]**

($[P]_0$ is the initial concentration of P)

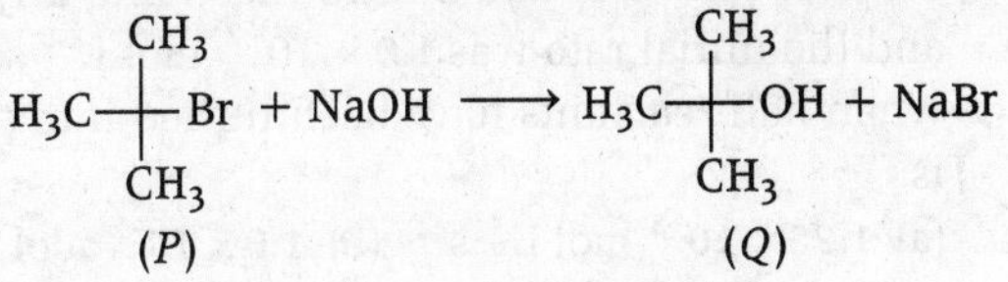

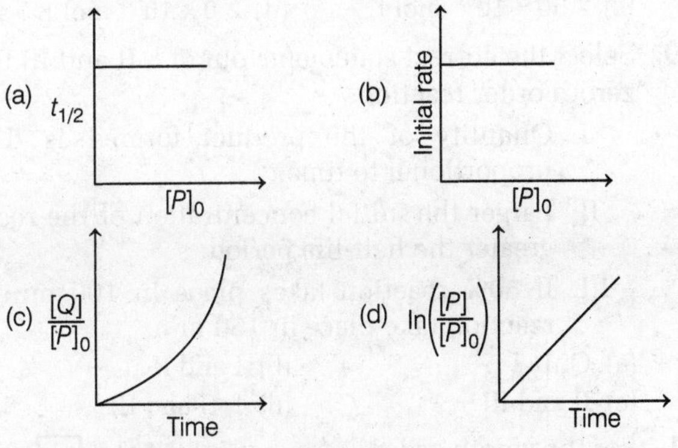

26. If for the reaction, $A \rightarrow B$

$$-\frac{d[A]}{dt} = 2\frac{d[B]}{dt}$$

then rate law is

(a) $-\frac{d[A]}{dt} = k[A]^2$ (b) $\frac{d[B]}{dt} = k[A]$

(c) $\frac{d[A]}{dt} = k[A]^2$ (d) $-\frac{d[B]}{dt} = k[B]^2$

27. For the reaction, $2A + 3B \longrightarrow$ product, A is in excess and on changing the concentration of B from 0.1 M to 0.4 M, rate becomes doubled. Thus, rate law is

(a) $\frac{dx}{dt} = k[A]^2[B]^3$ (b) $\frac{dx}{dt} = k[A][B]$

(c) $\frac{dx}{dt} = k[A]^0[B]^2$ (d) $\frac{dx}{dt} = k[B]^{1/2}$

28. The reaction of hydrogen and iodine monochloride is represented by the equation,

$$H_2(g) + 2ICl(g) \longrightarrow 2HCl(g) + I_2(g)$$

This reaction is first-order in $H_2(g)$ and also first order in $ICl(g)$. Which of these proposed mechanism can be consistent with the given information about this reaction?

Mechanism I

$$H_2(g) + 2ICl(g) \longrightarrow 2HCl(g) + I_2(g)$$

Mechanism II

$$H_2(g) + ICl(g) \xrightarrow{\text{Slow}} HCl(g) + HI(g)$$

$$HI(g) + ICl(g) \xrightarrow{\text{Fast}} HCl(g) + I_2(g)$$

(a) Only I (b) Only II
(c) Both I and II (d) Neither I nor II

29. For the non-equilibrium process, $A + B \rightarrow$ products, the rate is first order *wrt* A and second order wrt B. If 1.0 mol each of A and B introduced into a 1.0 L vessel and the initial rate was 1.0×10^{-2} mol L^{-1} s^{-1}, rate when half reactants have been turned into products is

(a) 1.25×10^{-3} mol L^{-1} s^{-1} (b) 1.0×10^{-2} mol L^{-1} s^{-1}
(c) 2.50×10^{-3} mol L^{-1} s^{-1} (d) 2.0×10^{-2} mol L^{-1} s^{-1}

30. Select the correct statements out of I, II and III for zeroth order reaction.

I. Quantity of the product formed is directly proportional to time.
II. Larger the initial concentration of the reactant, greater the half-life period.
III. If 50% reaction takes place in 100 min, 75% reaction take place in 150 min.

(a) Only I (b) I and II
(c) II and III (d) I, II and III

31. For the zeroth order reaction, sets I and II are given, hence, x is

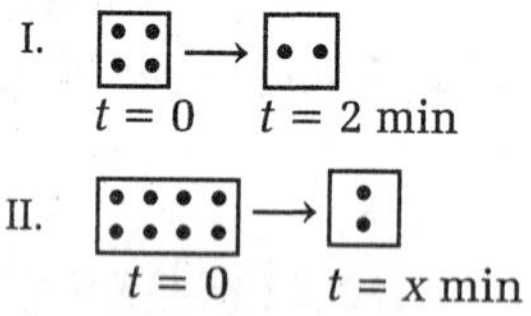

(a) 2 min (b) 3 min
(c) 4 min (d) 6 min

32. In the question (31), in set II final stage as shown is attained after

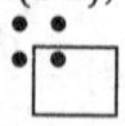

(a) 4 min (b) 3 min
(c) 2 min (d) 1 min

33. Out of the following which is zeroth order reaction?

(a) $H_2 + Cl_2 \longrightarrow 2HCl$
(b) $C_6H_5N_2Cl \longrightarrow C_6H_5Cl + N_2$
(c) $2H_2O_2 \longrightarrow 2H_2O + O_2$
(d) None of the above

34. Rate constant of the zeroth order can be expressed as

(a) min^{-1} atm (b) s^{-1} mol
(c) h^{-1} L^{-1} mol (d) All are correct

35. A certain zeroth order reaction has $k = 0.025$ M s^{-1} for the disappearance of A. What will be the concentration of A after 15 s if the initial concentration is 0.50 M?

(a) 0.50 M (b) 0.375 M (c) 0.125 M (d) 0.060 M

36. For the reaction, $A \longrightarrow$ Products, $-\frac{d[A]}{dt} = k$ and at different time interval, $[A]$ values are

Time	0	5 min	10 min	15 min
$[A]$	20 mol	18 mol	16 mol	14 mol

At 20 min, rate will be

(a) 12 mol/min (b) 10 mol/min
(c) 8 mol/min (d) 0.4 mol/min

37. Which is not the graphical representation for the zeroth order reaction?

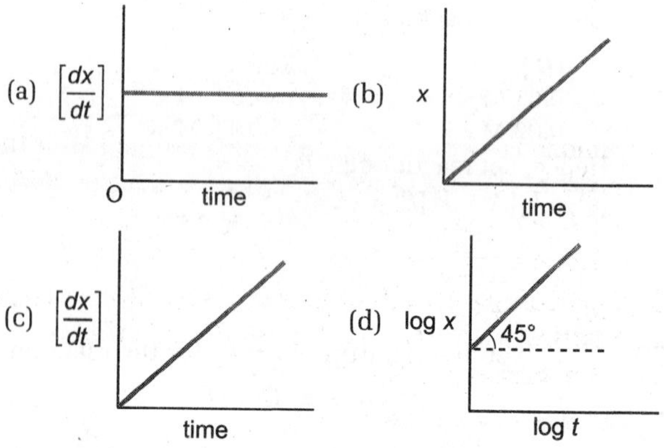

38. Which is not the correct statement for zeroth order reaction?

(a) $\left(\frac{dx}{dt}\right) = k[A]^0$ (b) $x = kt$
(c) $\log x = \log t + \log k$ (d) $\frac{1}{x} = \frac{1}{t} + \frac{1}{k}$

39. For zeroth order reaction

(a) E_a (energy of activation) is zero
(b) heat of reaction is zero
(c) rate of disappearance is zero
(d) rate of disappearance of reactant is independent of concentration

40. If a is the initial concentration of the reactant and $(a - x)$ is the concentration at time t for the first order reaction (rate constant k_1), then

I : $x = a(1 - e^{-k_1 t})$

II : $(a - x) = a\left(\frac{1}{2}\right)^y$ where, $y = \frac{t}{T_{50}}$

III : $k_1 = \frac{2.303}{t} \log_{10}\left(\frac{a}{a - x}\right)$

Correct statements are

(a) I and II (b) II and III
(c) I and III (d) I, II and III

41. A reaction of first order completed 90% in 90 min, hence, it is completed 50% in approximately
(a) 50 min
(b) 54 min
(c) 27 min
(d) 62 min

42. Consider the following reactions

$$A \rightarrow P1;\ B \rightarrow P2;\ C \rightarrow P3;\ D \rightarrow P4,$$

The order of the above reactions are a, b, c and d, respectively. The following graph is obtained when log[rate] *vs* log[conc.] are plotted:

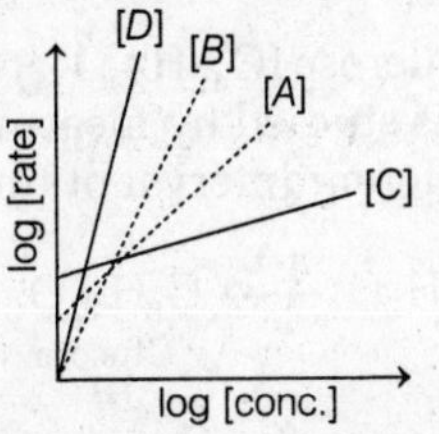

Among the following, the correct sequence for the order of the reactions is **[JEE Main 2020, Sept.]**
(a) $D > A > B > C$ (b) $A > B > C > D$
(c) $C > A > B > D$ (d) $D > B > A > C$

43. T_{50} (half-life period) of first order reaction is 10 min. Starting with 10 mol L^{-1}, rate after 20 min is
(a) 0.0693 mol L^{-1} min^{-1}
(b) 0.0693×2.5 mol L^{-1} min^{-1}
(c) 0.0693×5 mol L^{-2} min^{-1}
(d) 0.0693×10 mol L^{-1} min^{-1}

44. For the first order reaction T_{av} (average life), T_{50} and T_{75} in the increasing order are
(a) $T_{50} < T_{av} < T_{75}$ (b) $T_{50} < T_{75} < T_{av}$
(c) $T_{av} < T_{50} < T_{75}$ (d) $T_{av} = T_{50} < T_{75}$

45. The rate constant for the reaction,

$$2N_2O_5 \longrightarrow 4NO_2 + O_2$$

is $3 \times 0 \times 10^{-5}$ s^{-1}. If the rate at a given time is 2.40×10^{-5} mol L^{-1} s^{-1}, then concentration of N_2O_5 at that time is
(a) 1.4 (b) 1.2
(c) 0.04 (d) 0.8

46. In the following reaction, $A \longrightarrow$ Product, I and II are two different sets of first order reaction

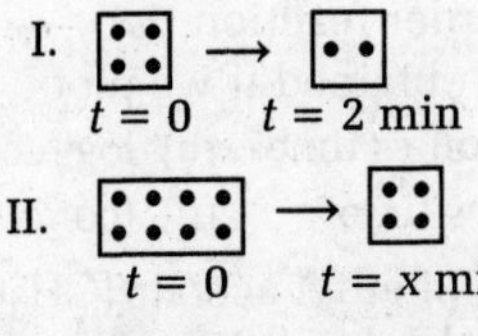

x is equal to
(a) 10 min (b) 5 min
(c) 2.5 min (d) 2 min

47. Rate constant of a first order reaction is 0.0693 min^{-1}. If we start with 20 mol L^{-1}, it is reduced to 2.5 mol L^{-1} in
(a) 10 min (b) 20 min
(c) 30 min (d) 40 min

48. One of the following reaction is not of first order
(a) $2H_2O_2 \longrightarrow 2H_2O + O_2$
(b) 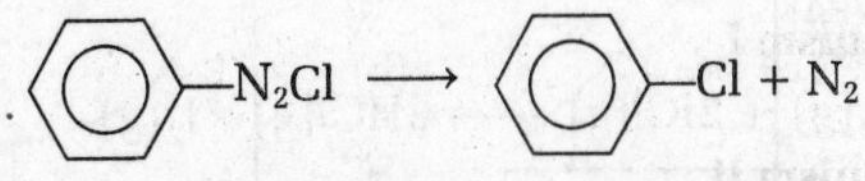

(c) $CH_3COOC_2H_5 + H_2O \longrightarrow CH_3COOH + C_2H_5OH$
(d) $CH_3COOC_2H_5 + NaOH \longrightarrow CH_3COONa + C_2H_5OH$

49. Half-lifes of first order and zeroth order reactions are same. Ratio of rates at the start of reaction is
(a) 0.693 (b) $\frac{1}{0.693}$
(c) 2×0.693 (d) $\frac{2}{0.693}$

50. In the following second order reaction

$$A + B \longrightarrow \text{Product}$$

$$\text{rate constant } k = \frac{2.303}{t(a-b)} \log_{10} \frac{b(a-x)}{a(b-x)}$$

(where, a and b are the initial concentrations of A and B). This changes to first order rate constant when
(a) $a >> b$ (b) $t \rightarrow \infty$
(c) $t \rightarrow 0$ (d) $x \rightarrow a$

51. For the given reaction, $A \longrightarrow$ Product

$$\frac{dx}{dt} = k[A]^2$$

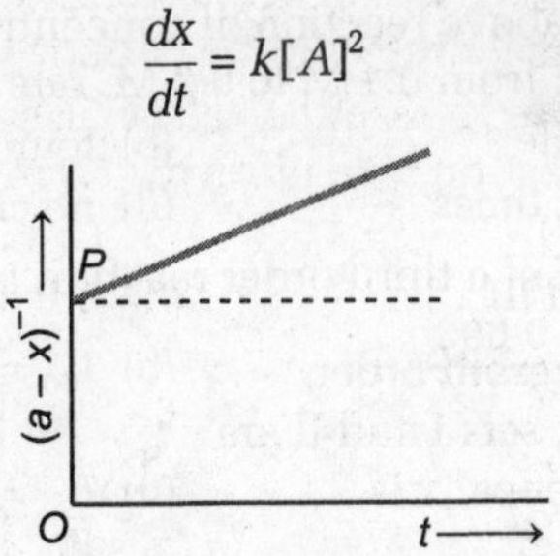

If $k = 1.0 \times 10^{-2}$ L mol^{-1} min^{-1} and $OP = 0.10$ L mol^{-1} then rate at the start of the reaction is
(a) 1.0×10^{-2} mol L^{-1} min^{-1}
(b) 1.0 mol L^{-1} min^{-1}
(c) 1.0×10^{2} mol L^{-1} min^{-1}
(d) 1.0×10^{-4} mol L^{-1} min^{-1}

52. Which is not true for a second order reaction?
(a) It can have rate constant 1×10^{-2} L mol^{-1} s^{-1}
(b) Its half-life is inversely proportional to its initial concentration
(c) Time to complete 75% reaction is twice of half-life
(d) $T_{50} = \frac{1}{k_a}$

53. $A \rightarrow$ Product and $\left(\frac{dx}{dt}\right) = k[A]^2$

If $\log\left(\frac{dx}{dt}\right)$ is plotted against $\log [A]$, then graph is of the type

(a) 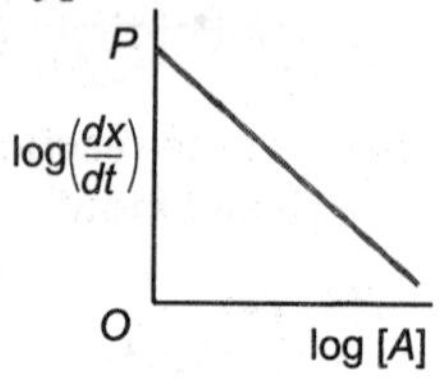

(b) 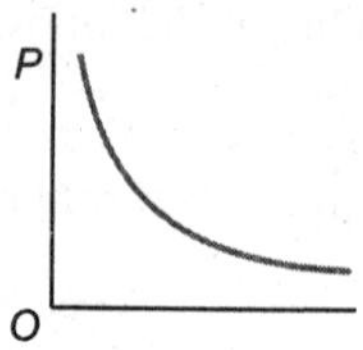

(c) 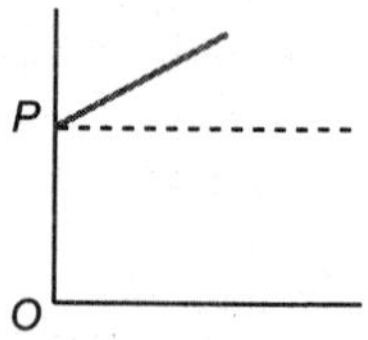

(d) 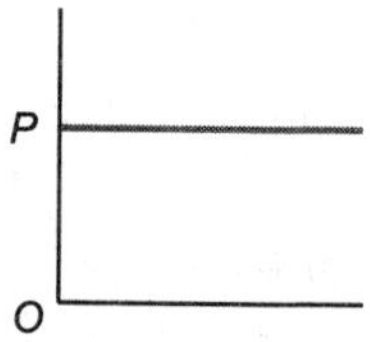

54. Slope of the line of the above question is

(a) 1 (b) 2 (c) 3 (d) 4

55. $A \rightarrow$Product, $\frac{dx}{dt} = k[A]^3$

If a is the initial concentration and $(a - x)$ is the concentration of A after time t, then rate constant is given by

(a) $k = \frac{1}{t}\left[\frac{1}{(a-x)} - \frac{1}{a}\right]$ (b) $k = \frac{1}{2t}\left[\frac{1}{(a-x)^2} - \frac{1}{a^2}\right]$

(c) $k = \frac{2.303}{t}\log\left(\frac{a}{a-x}\right)$ (d) $k = \frac{x}{t}$

56. For the above reaction, if concentration of A is changed from 0.1 M to 0.2 M, rate becomes

(a) double (b) four times

(c) eight times (d) no change

57. Half-life of a third order reaction is

(a) $T_{50} = \frac{0.693}{k}$ (b) $T_{50} = \frac{1}{ka}$

(c) $T_{50} = \frac{a}{2k}$ (d) $T_{50} = \frac{1.5}{ka^2}$

58. Half-lives of second and third order reactions are equal. Ratio of rates of second and third order reactions at the start of the reaction is

(a) $\frac{2}{3}$ (b) $\frac{3}{2}$ (c) 0.693 (d) 3

59. For an elementary chemical reaction, $A_2 \underset{k_{-1}}{\overset{k_1}{\rightleftharpoons}} 2A$, the expression for $\frac{d[A]}{dt}$ is

[JEE Main 2019, Jan.]

(a) $2k_1[A_2] - k_{-1}[A]^2$ (b) $k_1[A_2] - k_{-1}[A]^2$

(c) $2k_1[A_2] - 2k_{-1}[A]^2$ (d) $k_1[A_2] + k_{-1}[A]^2$

60. Acid hydrolysis of ester is first order reaction and rate constant is given by

$$k = \frac{2.303}{t}\log\frac{V_\infty - V_0}{V_\infty - V_t}$$

where, V_0, V_t and V_∞ are the volume of standard NaOH required to neutralise acid present at a given time, if ester is 50% neutralised then

(a) $V_\infty = V_t$ (b) $V_\infty = (V_t - V_0)$

(c) $V_\infty = 2V_t - V_0$ (d) $V_\infty = 2V_t + V_0$

61. If no catalyst (H^+) is present in acid hydrolysis of ester (in question (60) above) then rate constant k is

(a) $\frac{2.303}{t}\log\frac{V_0}{(V_t - V_\infty)}$ (b) $\frac{2.303}{t}\log\frac{V_\infty}{(V_\infty - V_t)}$

(c) $\frac{2.303}{t}\log\frac{V_0}{V_t}$ (d) $\frac{2.303}{t}\log\frac{V_\infty}{(V_t - V_\infty)}$

62. Inversion of sucrose $(C_{12}H_{22}O_{11})$ is first-order reaction and is studied by measuring angle of rotation at different interval of time

$$\underset{\substack{\text{Sucrose}\\ d}}{C_{12}H_{22}O_{11}} + H_2O \xrightarrow{H^+} \underset{\substack{\text{Glucose}\\ d}}{C_6H_{12}O_6} + \underset{\substack{\text{Fructose}\\ l}}{C_6H_{12}O_6}$$

If $(r_\infty - r_0) \equiv a$ and $(r_\infty - r_t) \equiv (a - x)$, (where, r_0, r_t and r_∞ are the angle of rotation at the start, at the time t and at the end of the reaction respectively), then there is 50% inversion when

(a) $r_0 = 2r_t - r_\infty$ (b) $r_0 = r_t - r_\infty$

(c) $r_0 = r_t - 2r_\infty$ (d) $r_0 = r_t + r_\infty$

63. In the above question (62), solution is optically inactive when

(a) $r_t = a$ (b) $r_t = 0$

(c) $r_t = x$ (d) $r_t = (a + x)$

64. ${}^{M}_{Z}A(g) \longrightarrow {}^{M-8}_{Z-4}B(g) + \alpha$-particles

The radioactive disintegration follows first order kinetics. Starting with 1 mole of A in a 1 L closed flask at 27°C, pressure set up after two half-life is approximately

(a) 25 atm (b) 12 atm (c) 37 atm (d) 40 atm

65. A G.M. counter is used to study the radioactive process of first order. In the absence of radioactive substance A, it counts 3 disintegration per second (dps). When A is placed in the G.M. counter, it records 23 dps at the start and 13 dps after 10 min. It records x dps after next 10 min and A has half-life period y min. x and y are

(a) 8 dps, 10 min (b) 5 dps, 10 min

(c) 5 dps, 20 min (d) 5 dps, 5 min

66. For a second order reaction, $2A \longrightarrow$ Product, a straight line is obtained if we plot

(a) concentration *vs* time (b) log (conc.) *vs* time

(c) log (conc.) *vs* time^{-1} (d) (conc.)$^{-1}$ *vs* time

67. Saponification of ethyl acetate $(CH_3COOC_2H_5)$ by NaOH is studied by titration of the reaction mixture have 1 : 1 molar ratio of the reactants. If 10 mL of 1 N HCl is required by 5 mL of the solution at the start and 8 mL of 1 N HCl is required by another 5 mL after 10 min, then rate constant is

(a) $k = \frac{2.303}{10} \log \frac{10}{8}$ (b) $k = \frac{2.303}{10} \log \frac{10}{2}$

(c) $k = \frac{1}{10}\left[\frac{1}{8} - \frac{1}{10}\right]$ (d) $k = \frac{1}{10}\left[\frac{1}{2} - \frac{1}{10}\right]$

68. For the reaction, $A(g) \longrightarrow B(g) + C(g)$

rate law is $-\frac{d[A]}{dt} = k[A]$

At the start pressure is 100 mm and after 10 min, pressure is 120 mm, hence, rate constant (min^{-1}) is

(a) $\frac{2.303}{10} \log \frac{6}{5}$ (b) $\frac{2.303}{10} \log 5$

(c) $\frac{2.303}{10} \log \frac{5}{4}$ (d) $\frac{2.303}{10} \log \frac{5}{6}$

69. For the reaction, $A(g) + 2B(g) \longrightarrow C(g) + D(g)$

$$\frac{dx}{dt} = k[A][B]^2$$

Initial pressure of A and B are respectively 0.60 atm and 0.80 atm. At a time when pressure of C is 0.20 atm, rate of the reaction, relative to the initial value is

(a) $\frac{1}{6}$ (b) $\frac{1}{48}$ (c) $\frac{1}{4}$ (d) $\frac{1}{24}$

70. For a reaction, $2A + B \longrightarrow$ Product, rate law is.

$$-\frac{d[A]}{dt} = k[A]$$

At a time when $t = \frac{1}{k}$, concentration of the reactant is (C_0 = initial concentration)

(a) $\frac{C_0}{e}$ (b) $C_0 e$ (c) $\frac{C_0}{e^2}$ (d) $\frac{1}{C_0}$

71. Rate constant k for the above case in question (73) is

(a) $k = \frac{2.303}{t} \log_{10} \frac{C_0}{C}$ (b) $k = \sqrt{2.303 \log_{10} e}$

(c) $k = \sqrt{2.303 \log_{10} C_0}$ (d) None of these

72. If in the fermentation of sugar in an enzymatic solution that is initially 0.12 M the concentration of the sugar is reduced to 0.06 M in 10 h and to 0.03 M in 20 h, then, order of the reaction is

(a) 0 (b) 1 (c) 2 (d) 3

73. For the reaction of the zeroth order, variation of $\log T_{50}$ with $\log a$ (where, T_{50} is half-life period and a is the initial concentration) is given by

(a) 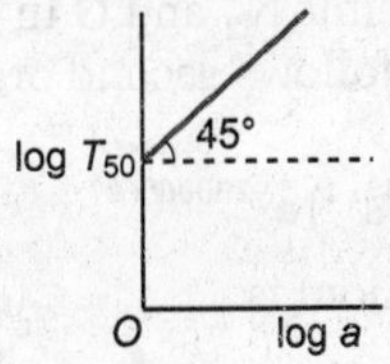

(b) 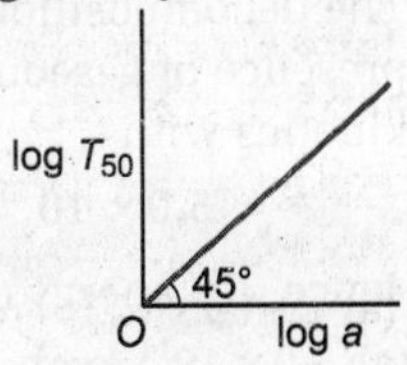

(c) 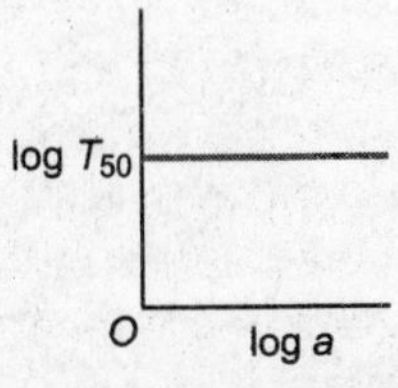

(d) 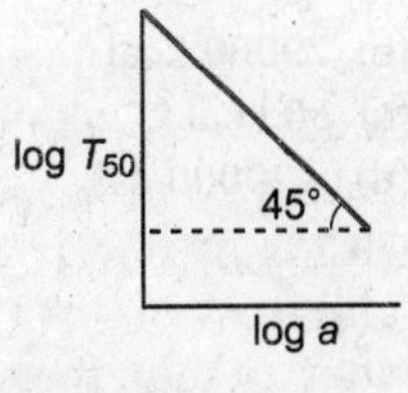

74. For a reaction, graph between $\log T_{50}$ (y-axis) and $\log a$ (x-axis) is a straight line parallel to x-axis. Hence, order is

(a) 0 (b) 1 (c) 2 (d) 3

75. Time of 75% reaction is thrice of time of 50% reaction. Hence, order is

(a) 0 (b) 1 (c) 2 (d) 3

76. Concentration of the reactant A in the reaction ($A \rightarrow B$) at different times are given below.

Time (minutes)	[A]
0	0.069 M
17	0.052 M
34	0.035 M
51	0.018 M

Hence, order is with rate constant

(a) zero, 0.001 M min^{-1} (b) 1, 0.001 min^{-1}

(c) 2, 0.001 M^{-1} min^{-1} (d) 1, 0.01 min^{-1}

77. For the reaction, $aA + bB \longrightarrow$ Product

$$\frac{dx}{dt} = k[A]^a[B]^b$$

If concentration of A is doubled, rate is four times. If concentration of B is made four times, rate is doubled. Hence,

(a) $-\frac{d[A]}{dt} = -\frac{d[B]}{dt}$ (b) $-\frac{d[A]}{dt} = -4\frac{d[B]}{dt}$

(c) $-4\frac{d[A]}{dt} = -\frac{d[B]}{dt}$ (d) None of these

78. The results given in the below table were obtained during kinetic studies of the following reaction :

$$2A + B \rightarrow C + D$$

Experi-ment	[A]/mol L^{-1}	[B]/mol L^{-1}	Initial rate/mol L^{-1} min^{-1}
I	0.1	0.1	6.00×10^{-3}
II	0.1	0.2	2.40×10^{-2}
III	0.2	0.1	1.20×10^{-2}
IV	X	0.2	7.20×10^{-2}
V	0.3	Y	2.88×10^{-1}

X and Y in the given table are respectively

[JEE Main 2020, Sep.]

(a) 0.4, 0.4 (b) 0.4, 0.3 (c) 0.3, 0.4 (d) 0.3, 0.3

79. If $\left(\frac{dx}{dt}\right) = k[H^+]^n$ and rate becomes 100 times when pH changes from 2 to 1. Hence, order is

(a) 1 (b) 2 (c) 3 (d) 0

80. Consider the following reaction,

$$Zn + 2H^+ \longrightarrow Zn^{2+} + H_2$$

Half-life period is independent of concentration of Zn at constant pH. At constant Zn concentration, half-life is 10 min at pH = 2 and half-life is 100 min at pH = 3. Hence, rate law is

(a) $k[Zn][H^+]$ (b) $k[Zn][H^+]^2$
(c) $k[Zn]^0[H^+]$ (d) $k[Zn]^0[H^+]^2$

81. Following are the values of E_a and ΔH for three reactions carried out at the same temperature

$I : E_a = 20 \text{ kJ mol}^{-1}, \ \Delta H = -60 \text{ kJ mol}^{-1}$

$II : E_a = 10 \text{ kJ mol}^{-1}, \ \Delta H = -20 \text{ kJ mol}^{-1}$

$III : E_a = 40 \text{ kJ mol}^{-1}, \Delta H = +15 \text{ kJ mol}^{-1}$

If all the three reactions have same frequency factor then fastest and slowest reactions are

	Fastest	Slowest
(a)	I	II
(b)	II	III
(c)	I	III

(d) can't be predicted.

82. For a reaction, $A \longrightarrow B, E_a = 10 \text{ kJ mol}^{-1}$ and $\Delta H = 5 \text{ kJ mol}^{-1}$. Thus, potential-energy profile for this reaction is

(a)
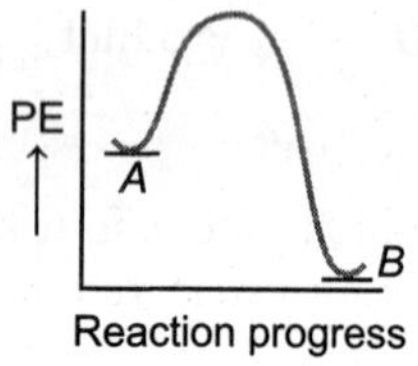

(b)
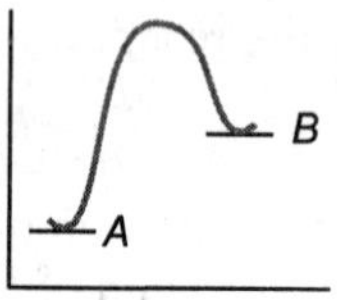

(c)
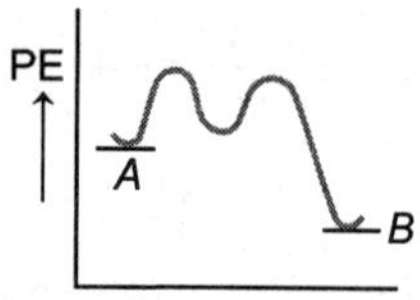

(d)
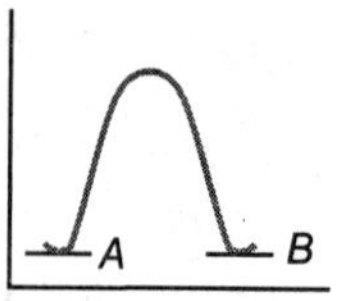

83. Energy of activation of $B \longrightarrow A$ in Q. 82 above is
(a) 25 kJ mol^{-1} (b) 10 kJ mol^{-1}
(c) 5 kJ mol^{-1} (d) -25 kJ mol^{-1}

84. Milk turns sour at 40°C three times as faster as 0°C. Hence, E_a in cal of turning of milk sour is

(a) $\dfrac{2.303 \times 2 \times 313 \times 273}{40} \log 3$

(b) $\dfrac{2.303 \times 2 \times 313 \times 273}{40} \log\left(\dfrac{1}{3}\right)$

(c) $\dfrac{2.303 \times 2 \times 40}{273 \times 313} \log 3$

(d) None of the above

85. Graph between $\log k$ and $\frac{1}{T}$ (k is rate constant in s^{-1} and T is the temperature in K) is a straight line. If $OX = 5$ and slope of the line $= -\frac{1}{2.303}$ then E_a is

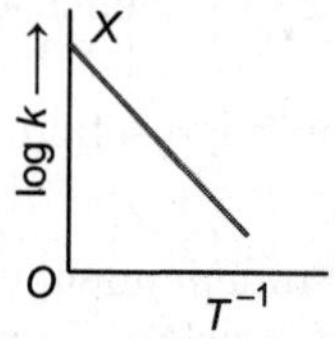

(a) 2.303×2 cal (b) $\dfrac{2}{2.303}$ cal
(c) 2 cal (d) None of these

86. Which one of the following statements for the order of a reaction is incorrect?
(a) Order of reaction is always whole number
(b) Order can be determined only experimentally
(c) Order is not influenced by stoichiometric coefficient of the reactants
(d) Order of reaction is sum of power to the concentration terms of reactants to express the rate of reaction

87. A chemical reaction proceeds into the following steps

Step I $\quad 2A \rightleftharpoons X$ fast

Step II $\quad X + B \rightleftharpoons Y$ slow

Step III $\quad Y + B \rightleftharpoons$ Product fast

The law for the overall reaction is
(a) rate $= k[A]^2$ (b) rate $= k[B]^2$
(c) rate $= k[A][B]$ (d) rate $= k[A]^2[B]$

88. The time required for 100% completion of a zero order reaction is
(a) ak (b) $\dfrac{a}{2k}$ (c) $\dfrac{a}{k}$ (d) $\dfrac{2k}{a}$

89. The following data were obtained during the first order decomposition of $2A(g) \longrightarrow B(g) + C(s)$ at a constant volume and at a particular temperature.

S.No.	Time	Total pressure in Pascal
1	At the end of 10 min	300
2	After completion	200

The rate constant in min^{-1} is
(a) 0.0693 (b) 69.3
(c) 6.93 (d) 6.93×10^{-4}

90. Rate constant of a reaction with a virus is $3.3 \times 10^{-4} \text{ s}^{-1}$. Time required for the virus to become 75% inactivated is
(a) 35 min (b) 70 min
(c) 105 min (d) 17.5 min

91. The decomposition of N_2O into N_2 and O in the presence of gaseous argon follows second order kinetics with

$$k = (5.0 \times 10^{11} \text{ L mol}^{-1}\text{s}^{-1}) e^{-29000(K)/T}$$

Hence, E_a (energy of activation) is
(a) 5.0×10^{11} kcal
(b) 29000 kcal
(c) 58 kcal
(d) -29000 cal

92. For the reaction,

$$2NO + Br_2 \longrightarrow 2NOBr,$$

the following mechanism has been given

$$NO + Br_2 \xrightarrow{\text{Fast}} NOBr_2$$

$$NOBr_2 + NO \xrightarrow{\text{Slow}} 2NOBr$$

Hence, rate law is

(a) $k[NO]^2[Br_2]$ (b) $k[NO][Br_2]$

(c) $k[NOBr_2][NO]$ (d) $k[NO][Br_2]^2$

93. There is formation of H_2O_2 in the upper atmosphere

$$H_2O + O \longrightarrow 2OH \longrightarrow H_2O_2$$

$$\Delta H = 72 \text{ kJ mol}^{-1}; \quad E_a = 77 \text{ kJ mol}^{-1}$$

E_a for the bimolecular recombination of two OH radicals to form H_2O and O is

(a) 149 kJ mol^{-1} (b) – 149 kJ mol^{-1}

(c) 5 kJ mol^{-1} (d) –5 kJ mol^{-1}

94. Consider the given plot of enthalpy of the following reaction between *A* and *B*.

$$A + B \longrightarrow C + D$$

Identify the incorrect statement. **[JEE Main 2019, April]**

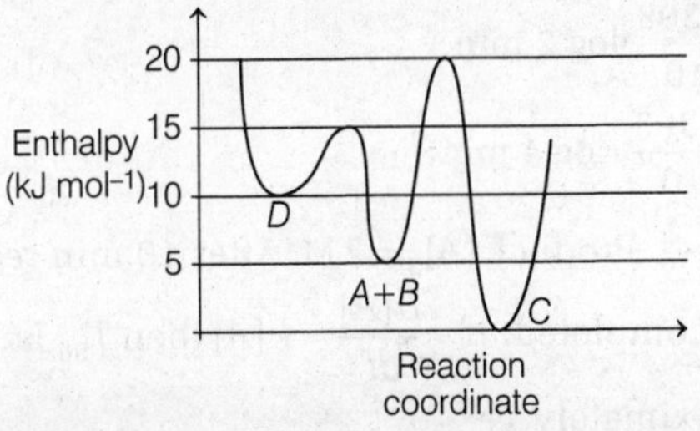

(a) *D* is kinetically stable product.

(b) Formation of *A* and *B* from *C* has highest enthalpy of activation.

(c) *C* is the thermodynamically stable product.

(d) Activation enthalpy to form *C* is 5 kJ mol^{-1} less than that to form *D*.

95. $A \longrightarrow B, \Delta H = -10 \text{ kJ mol}^{-1}, E_a = 50 \text{ kJ mol}^{-1}$ then E_a of $B \longrightarrow A$ will be

(a) 40 kJ mol^{-1} (b) 50 kJ mol^{-1}

(c) –50 kJ mol^{-1} (d) 60 kJ mol^{-1}

96. Rate constant $k = 1.2 \times 10^3 \text{ mol}^{-1}\text{L s}^{-1}$ and $E_a = 2.0 \times 10^2 \text{ kJ mol}^{-1}$. When $T \to \infty$

(a) $A = 2.0 \times 10^2 \text{ kJ mol}^{-1}$

(b) $A = 1.2 \times 10^3 \text{ mol}^{-1} \text{ L s}^{-1}$

(c) $A = 1.2 \times 10^3 \text{ mol L}^{-1} \text{ s}^{-1}$

(d) $A = 2.4 \times 10^3 \text{ kJ mol}^{-1} \text{ s}^{-1}$

97. For a reaction for which the activation energies of the forward and reverse directions are equal in value

(a) the stoichiometry is the mechanism

(b) $\Delta H = 0$

(c) $\Delta S = 0$

(d) the order is zero

98. The rate of a chemical reaction generally increases rapidly even for small temperature increase because of rapid increase in the

(a) collision frequency

(b) fraction of molecules with energies in excess of the activation energy

(c) activation energy

(d) average kinetic energy of molecules

99. Select the correct statement.

(a) A collision between reactant molecules must occur with a certain minimum energy before it is effective in yielding product molecules

(b) $\dfrac{d(\log_{10} k)}{dt} = \dfrac{E_a}{2.303 \, RT^2}$ is called Arrhenius equation

(c) Both (a) and (b)

(d) None of the above

100. Graph between concentration *x* of the product and time of the reaction, $A \longrightarrow B$ is of the type I.

Hence, graph between $-\dfrac{d[A]}{dt}$ and time will be of the type

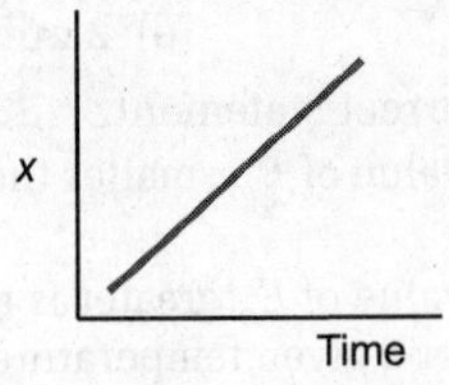

(a)
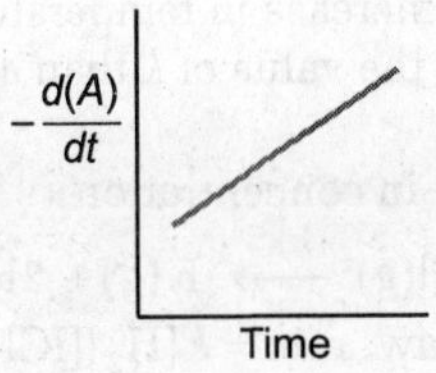

(b)
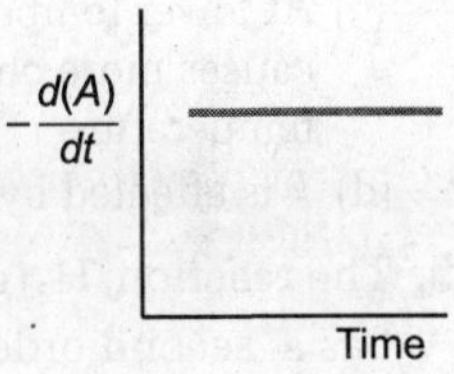

(c)
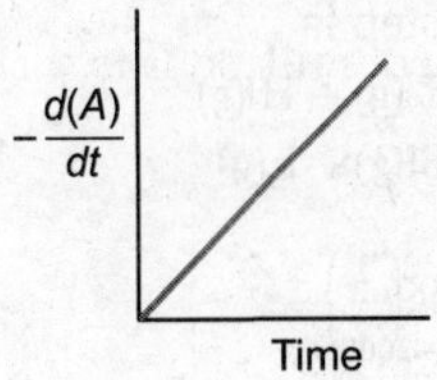

(d)
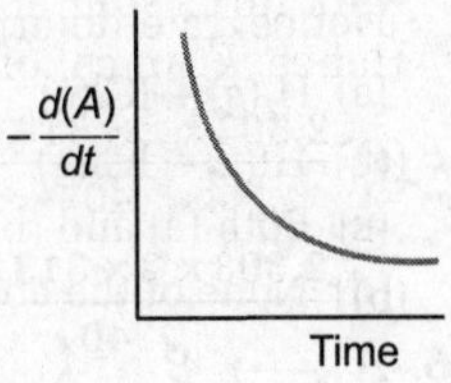

101. Following is the graph between $\log T_{50}$ and $\log a$ (a = initial concentration) for a given reaction at 27°C. Hence, order is

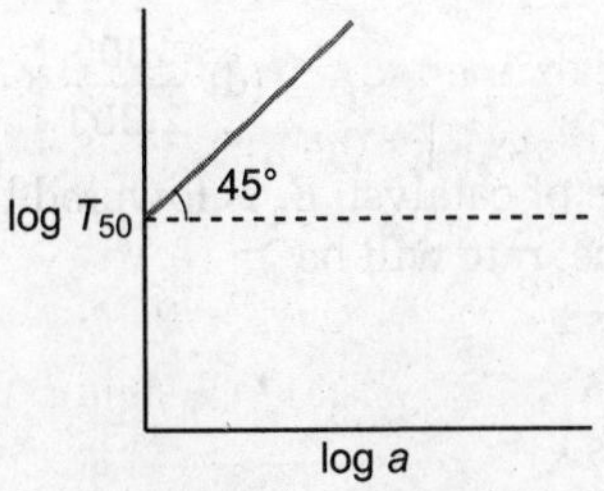

(a) 0 (b) 1 (c) 2 (d) 3

102. Following is the graph between $(a-x)^{-1}$ and time t for a second order reaction

$$\theta = \tan^{-1}(0.5)$$
$$OA = 2\text{L mol}^{-1}$$

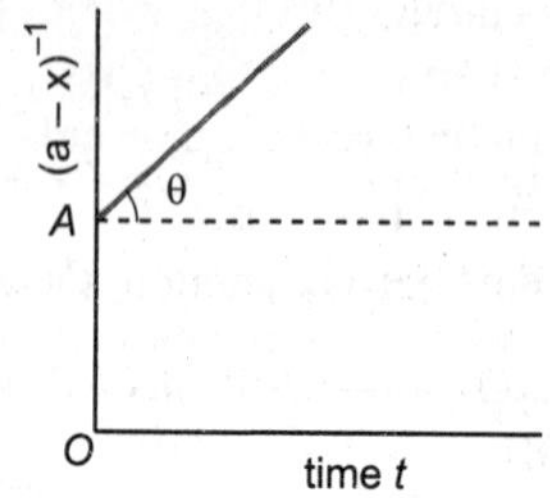

Hence, rate at the start of the reaction is
(a) 1.25 $\text{mol}^{-1}\ \text{min}^{-1}$
(b) 0.5 $\text{mol L}^{-1}\ \text{min}^{-1}$
(c) 0.125 $\text{mol L}^{-1}\ \text{min}^{-1}$
(d) 1.25 $\text{mol L}^{-1}\ \text{min}^{-1}$

103. Half-life period of the reaction in Q. (102) is
(a) 1.386 min (b) 4 min
(c) 16 min (d) 2 min

104. Select the incorrect statement.
(a) Larger the value of E_a, smaller the value of rate constant (k)
(b) Larger the value of E_a, greater is the effect on the value of k for a given temperature change
(c) At lower temperature, increase in temperature causes more change in the value of k than at higher temperature
(d) k is affected by change in concentration

105. The reaction, $H_2(g) + 2ICl(g) \longrightarrow I_2(g) + 2HCl(g)$ has a second order rate law, rate $= k[H_2][ICl]$.
Hence, rate-determining step is
(a) $H_2(g) + ICl(g) \longrightarrow HCl(g) + HI(g)$
(b) $HI(g) + ICl(g) \longrightarrow HCl(g) + I_2(g)$
(c) Both (a) and (b)
(d) None of the above

106. $A \longrightarrow B \quad k_A = 10^{15}\, e^{-2000/T}$
$C \longrightarrow D \quad k_C = 10^{14}\, e^{-1000/T}$
Temperature T/K at which ($k_A = k_C$) is
(a) 1000 K (b) 2000 K
(c) $\frac{2000}{2.303}$ K (d) $\frac{1000}{2.303}$ K

107. In presence of catalyst, E_a is lowered by 2 kcal at 27°C. Hence, rate will be
(a) 20 times
(b) 14 times
(c) 28 times
(d) 2 times

108.

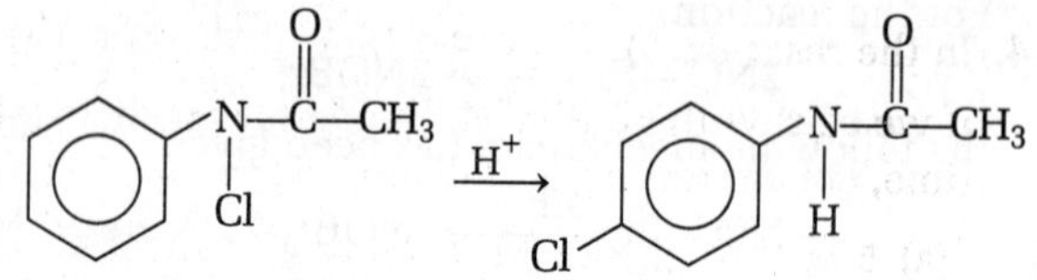

Reaction kinetics can be studied by
(a) measurement of pH
(b) titration with hypo after adding KI
(c) Both (a) and (b) are correct
(d) None of the above is correct

109.

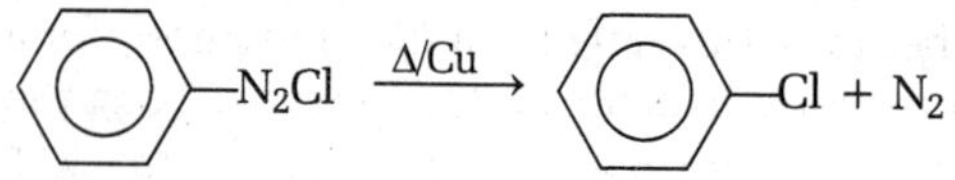

(A)

Half-life is independent of concentration of A. After 10 min volume of N_2 gas is 10 L and after complete reaction 50 L. Hence, rate constant is
(a) $\frac{2.303}{10} \log 5\ \text{min}^{-1}$
(b) $\frac{2.303}{10} \log 1.25\ \text{min}^{-1}$
(c) $\frac{2.303}{10} \log 2\ \text{min}^{-1}$
(d) $\frac{2.303}{10} \log 4\ \text{min}^{-1}$

110. $A \longrightarrow$ Product, $[A]_0 = 2$ M. After 10 min reaction is 10% completed. If $-\frac{d[A]}{dt} = k[A]$ then T_{50} is approximately
(a) 0.693 min (b) 69.3 min
(c) 66.0 min (d) 0.0693 min

111. $2N_2O_5 \longrightarrow 4NO_2 + O_2$
If $-\frac{\Delta[N_2O_5]}{\Delta t} = k_1[N_2O_5]$, $\frac{\Delta[NO_2]}{\Delta t} = k_2[N_2O_5]$,
$\frac{\Delta[O_2]}{\Delta t} = k_3[N_2O_5]$
then
(a) $k_1 = k_2 = k_3$ (b) $2k_1 = k_2 = 4k_3$
(c) $2k_1 = 4k_2 = k_3$ (d) None of these

112. A reaction is catalysed by H^+ ion; in presence of HA rate constant is $2 \times 10^{-3}\ \text{min}^{-1}$ and in presence of HB rate constant is $1 \times 10^{-3}\ \text{min}^{-1}$. HA and HB (both strong acids) have relative strength as
(a) 0.5 (b) 0.002 (c) 0.001 (d) 2

113. For the first order reaction ($C = C_0 e^{-k_1 t}$) and $T_{av} = k_1^{-1}$. After two average lives, concentration of the reactant is reduced to
(a) 25% (b) 75%
(c) $\frac{100}{e}$% (d) $\frac{100}{e^2}$%

114. In the reaction, $A \longrightarrow$ Product, $-\frac{d[A]}{dt} = k_1[A]$
If we start with 10 M of A, then after one natural-life time, concentration of A decreased to

(a) 5 M (b) 2.5 M (c) $\frac{10\text{ M}}{e}$ (d) $\frac{10\text{ M}}{e^2}$

115. Half-life period of the first order reaction is 100 days. After 144.3 days, concentration of the reactant is reduced to ... of the original value

(a) $\frac{1}{e}$ (b) $\frac{1}{e^2}$ (c) 10% (d) 20%

116. Number of natural life times (T_{av}) required for a first order reaction to achieve 99.9% level of completion is

(a) 2.3 (b) 6.9 (c) 9.2 (d) 0.105

117. The rate law for the dimerisation of NO_2 into N_2O_4 is

$$-\frac{d[NO_2]}{dt} = k[NO_2]^2$$

Which of the following changes will change the value of the specific rate constant k?

(a) Doubling the total pressure
(b) Decreasing the pressure
(c) Changing the volume of the flask
(d) Changing the temperature

118. Rate constant k varies with temperature as given by equation

$$\log k\ (\text{min}^{-1}) = 5 - \frac{2000\text{ K}}{T}$$

Consider the following about this equation.

I. Pre-exponential factor is 10^5
II. E_a is 9.212 kcal
III. Variation of $\log k$ with $\frac{1}{T}$ is linear.

Select the correct statement.

(a) I, II and III (b) I and III
(c) II and III (d) I and II

119. When temperature of a reaction is changed from T_1 and T_2, half-life is found to decrease. Thus,

(a) $T_1 > T_2$ and reaction is endothermic
(b) $T_2 > T_1$ and reaction is exothermic
(c) $T_1 > T_2$ and reaction is exothermic
(d) $T_2 > T_1$ and reaction can be exothermic or endothermic

120. In the following simultaneous reaction,

$$\text{methyl cyclopropane} \xleftarrow{3.8\times10^{-4}\ s^{-1}} \text{bicyclohexane} \xrightarrow{1.20\times10^{-4}\ s^{-1}} \text{cyclohexane}$$

cyclohexane formed is

(a) 12% (b) 38% (c) 50% (d) 24%

121. Following reaction takes place by mechanism

$$NO_2 + CO \longrightarrow NO + CO_2$$

Step I $NO_2 + NO_2 \xrightarrow{k_1,\text{ slow}} NO_3 + NO$

Step II $NO_3 + CO \xrightarrow{k_2,\text{ fast}} NO_2 + CO_2$

Hence, $\left(\frac{dx}{dt}\right)$ for the given reaction is

(a) $k_1[NO_2]^2 - k_2[NO_3][CO]$ (b) $k_1[NO_2]^2 + k_2[NO_3][CO]$
(c) $k_1[NO_2]^2$ (d) $k_1[NO_2] + k_2[CO]$

122. For the reaction, $2Fe^{2+} + H_2O_2 \longrightarrow 2Fe^{3+} + 2OH^-$, $\frac{d[Fe^{3+}]}{dt} = k[Fe^{2+}][H_2O_2]$, hence, slow step is

(a) $Fe^{2+} + H_2O_2 \longrightarrow Fe^{3+} + OH^- + OH$
(b) $Fe^{2+} + OH \longrightarrow Fe^{3+} + OH^-$
(c) $2Fe^{2+} + H_2O_2 \longrightarrow 2Fe^{3+} + 2OH^-$
(d) $Fe^{2+} \longrightarrow Fe^{3+} + e^-$

123. For the following reaction, $A \rightleftharpoons B + 10$ kcal increase in temperature

(a) increases rate of the forward as well as backward reaction
(b) increases rate of the forward reaction but decreases that of backward reaction
(c) decreases rate of the forward reaction but increases that of the backward reaction
(d) decreases rate of forward as well as backward reaction.

124. For the second order reaction,

$$2A \longrightarrow \text{Product}$$

the initial concentration of A is 0.1 M and rate constant is $2\times10^{-3}\ \text{dm}^3\ \text{mol}^{-1}\ \text{s}^{-1}$. The half-life period of the reaction is

(a) 5 s (b) 50 s (c) 500 s (d) 5000 s

125. The activation energy of a reaction is zero. At 280 K rate constant is $1.6\times10^{-6}\ s^{-1}$. The rate constant at 300 K is

(a) zero (b) $3.2\times10^{-6}\ s^{-1}$
(c) $1.6\times10^{-5}\ s^{-1}$ (d) $1.6\times10^{-6}\ s^{-1}$

126. For the reaction,

$2H_2(g) + 2NO(g) \longrightarrow N_2(g) + 2H_2O(g)$ rate law is rate $= k[NO]^2[H_2]$. Mechanism is given by

Step I $2NO \longrightarrow N_2O_2$
Step II $N_2O_2 + H_2 \longrightarrow N_2O + H_2O$
Step III $N_2O + H_2 \longrightarrow N_2 + H_2O$

Rate law is true if

(a) step I is the slow step
(b) step II is the slow step
(c) step III is the slow step
(d) step I and II are slow steps

127. Rate constant k of a reaction is dependent on temperature

$$k = Ae^{-E_a/RT}$$

k has the least value at

(a) high T and high E_a (b) high T and small E_a
(c) low T and low E_a (d) low T and high E_a

128. Which of the these factors affect the value of the specific rate constant for the reaction?

$$2A(g) \longrightarrow B(g)$$

(a) Temperature only
(b) Temperature and concentration
(c) Pressure only
(d) Pressure and concentration

129. Which of the reactions represented in these diagrams will show the greatest increase in rate for a given increase in temperature?

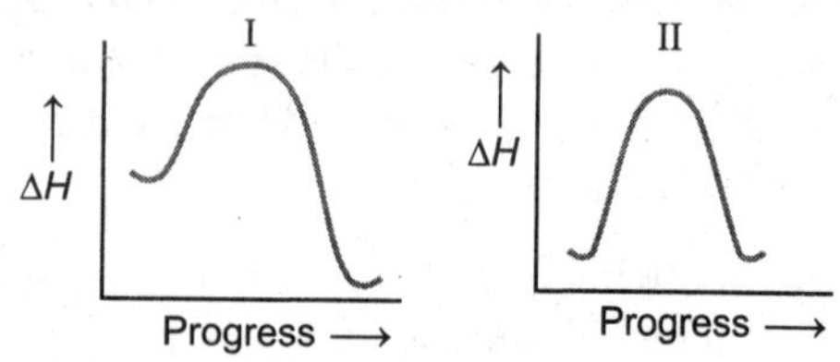

(a) I forward (b) I reversed
(c) II forward (d) II reversed

130. For the following reaction,

$$A \xrightarrow{500\text{ K}} \text{Products}$$

$$A \xrightarrow{400\text{K/catalyst}} \text{Product}$$

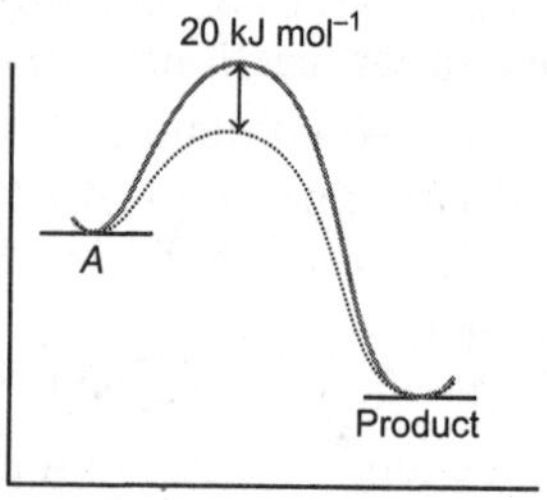

___ no catalyst
---- in presence of catalyst

$$\text{If}\left(\frac{-d[A]}{dt}\right)_{500\text{ K}} = -\left(\frac{d[A]}{dt}\right)_{400\text{ K}}$$

then E_a is approximately

(a) 200 kJ mol^{-1} (b) 100 kJ mol^{-1}
(c) 20 kJ mol^{-1} (d) 120 kJ mol^{-1}

131. A particular reaction increases by a factor of 2 when the temperature is increased from 27°C to 37°C. Hence, activation energy of the reaction is

(a) 12.9 kcal (b) 0.14 kcal
(c) 1.1 kcal (d) None is correct

132. A chemical reaction is said to take place through the various stages with $\Delta G°$ values indicated by the graph.

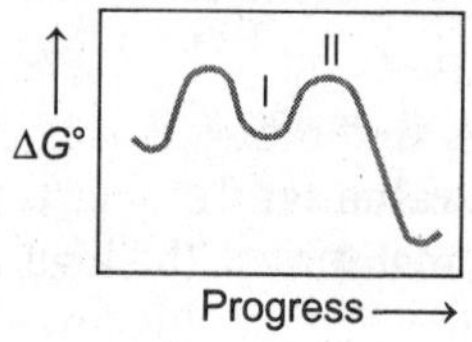

Stages I and II represent respectively

	I	II
(a)	activated complex	activated complex
(b)	reaction intermediate	activated complex
(c)	activated complex	reaction intermediate
(d)	reaction intermediate	reaction intermediate

133. The reaction of $NO_2(g)$ and $O_3(g)$ is first order in $NO_2(g)$ and $O_3(g)$

$$2NO_2(g) + O_3(g) \longrightarrow N_2O_5(g) + O_2(g)$$

The reaction can take place by mechanism

I. $NO_2 + O_3 \xrightarrow{\text{Slow}} NO_3 + O_2$

$NO_3 + NO_2 \xrightarrow{\text{Fast}} N_2O_5$

II. $O_3 \xrightarrow{\text{Fast}} O_2 + O$

$NO_2 + O \xrightarrow{\text{Slow}} NO_3$

$NO_3 + NO_2 \xrightarrow{\text{Fast}} N_2O_5$

Select the correct mechanism.

(a) Only I (b) Only II
(c) Both I and II (d) None of I and II

134. What function of $[x]$, plotted against time, will give a straight line for a second-order reaction?

(a) $[x]$ (b) $[x]^2$ (c) $\log [x]$ (d) $\frac{1}{[x]}$

135. Two reactions with different activation energies have the same rate at room temperature. Which statement correctly describes the rates of these two reactions at the same higher temperature?

(a) The reaction with the greater activation energy will be faster
(b) The reaction will the smaller activation energy will be faster
(c) The two reactions will have the same rate
(d) Temperature range is also required

136. Match the graphical study with their order of the reactions

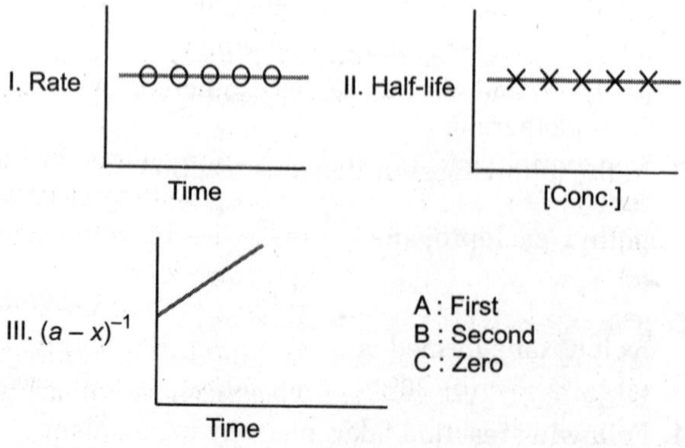

A : First
B : Second
C : Zero

	I	II	III		I	II	III
(a)	A	B	C	(b)	B	C	A
(c)	C	B	A	(d)	C	A	B

137. The rates of many chemical reactions double for a ten degree rise in temperature. Which of these factors does not contribute to this change in the rate with increasing temperature?
(a) The average kinetic energy of the reactant species
(b) The number of collisions in a given time
(c) The number of very energetic spector
(d) The activation energy

138. The bromination of acetone that occurs in acid solution is represented by

$$CH_3COCH_3(aq) + Br_2(aq) \longrightarrow CH_3COCH_2Br_2(aq) + HBr(aq)$$

Given

Initial concentrations, M			Initial rate, Disappearance of Br_2, Ms^{-1}
$[Br_2]$	$[CH_3COCH_3]$	$[H^+]$	
0.050	0.30	0.050	5.7×10^{-5}
0.10	0.30	0.050	5.7×10^{-5}
0.10	0.30	0.10	1.2×10^{-4}
0.050	0.40	0.20	3.1×10^{-4}

Based on the above data, rate law is
(a) $\left(\frac{dx}{dt}\right) = k[CH_3COCH_3][Br_2][H^+]$
(b) $\left(\frac{dx}{dt}\right) = k[CH_3COCH_3][H^+]$
(c) $\left(\frac{dx}{dt}\right) = k[CH_3COCH_3][Br_2]$
(d) $\left(\frac{dx}{dt}\right) = k[CH_3COCH_3][Br_2][H^+]^2$

139. Given the following diagram for the reaction
$A + B \longrightarrow C + D$

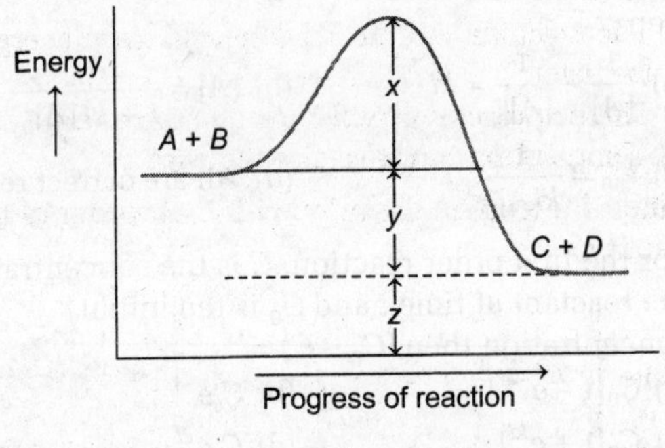

The enthalpy change and activation energy for the reverse reaction, $C + D \longrightarrow A + B$ are respectively
(a) x, y
(b) $x, x + y$
(c) $y, x + y$
(d) $y, y + z$

140. The rate constant for the reaction,
$2N_2O_5 \longrightarrow 4NO_2 + O_2$ is $3.0 \times 10^{-5}\ s^{-1}$. If the rate is $2.40 \times 10^{-5}\ M\ s^{-1}$, then the concentration of N_2O_5 (in mol L^{-1}) is
(a) 1.4
(b) 1.2
(c) 0.04
(d) 0.8

141. If I is the intensity of absorbed light and C is the concentration of AB for the photochemical process.
$AB + h\nu \longrightarrow AB^*$, the rate of formation of AB^* is directly proportional to
(a) C
(b) I
(c) I^2
(d) $C \cdot I$

142. In a first order reaction the concentration of reactant decreases from 800 mol/dm^3 to 50 mol/dm^3 in 2×10^4 s. The rate constant of reaction is
(a) $2 \times 10^4\ s^{-1}$
(b) $3.45 \times 10^{-5}\ s^{-1}$
(c) $1.386 \times 10^{-4}\ s^{-1}$
(d) $3 \times 10^{-4}\ s^{-1}$

143. (A) follows first order reaction. $(A) \longrightarrow$ Product
Concentration of A, changes from 0.1 M to 0.025 M in 40 min. Find the rate of reaction of A when concentration of A is 0.01 M
(a) 3.47×10^{-4} M min^{-1}
(b) 3.47×10^{-5} M min^{-1}
(c) 1.73×10^{-4} M min^{-1}
(d) 1.73×10^{-5} M min^{-1}

144. Consider a reaction, $aG + bH \longrightarrow$ Products. When concentration of both the reactants G and H is doubled, the rate increases by eight times. However, when concentration of G is doubled keeping the concentration of H fixed, the rate is doubled. The overall order of the reaction is
(a) 0
(b) 1
(c) 2
(d) 3

145. Rate of the reaction in terms of the pressure of the reactant (assume rate as an extensive property) is

$$CH_3CHO \longrightarrow CO + CH_4$$

(a) $-\frac{V}{RT}\frac{dp_{CH_3CHO}}{dt}$
(b) $-\frac{1}{RT}\frac{dp_{CH_3CHO}}{dt}$
(c) $-\frac{1}{RTV}\frac{dp_{CH_3CHO}}{dt}$
(d) $\frac{n_{CH_3CHO}}{V}\frac{dp_{CH_3CHO}}{dt}$

146. Consider the following parallel reactions with rate constants

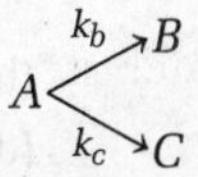

k_b and k_c. Select the correct statement(s).
(a) At any time point, the ratio $\frac{[B]}{[C]}$ is identical
(b) $\frac{[B]}{[C]} = \frac{k_b}{k_c}$
(c) As the rate constant for one of the parallel reactions increases relative to the other, the greater the final concentration of the corresponding product
(d) All of the above are correct statements

147. Consider the following reaction,

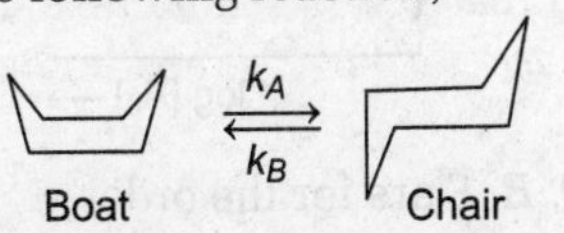

The reaction is first order in each direction, with an equilibrium constant of 10^4. For the conversion of chair form to boat form $e^{-Ea/RT} = 4.35 \times 10^{-8}$ at 298 K

with pre-exponential factor of 10^{12} s^{-1}. Apparent rate constant ($= k_A + k_B$) at 298 K is

(a) 4.35×10^4 s^{-1}
(b) 4.35×10^8 s^{-1}
(c) 4.35×10^{-8} s^{-1}
(d) 4.35×10^{12} s^{-1}

148. In a first order reaction, $A \longrightarrow P$, the ratio of $a/(a-x)$ was found to be 8 after 60 min. If the concentration is 0.1 M then the rate of reaction is

(a) 2.226×10^{-3} mol L^{-1} min^{-1}
(b) 3.466×10^{-3} mol L^{-1} min^{-1}
(c) 4.455×10^{-3} mol L^{-1} min^{-1}
(d) 5.532×10^{-3} mol L^{-1} min^{-1}

149. A proposed mechanism for the formation of N_2O_5 from NO_2 and O_3 is

$$NO_2 + O_3 \xrightarrow{k_1} NO_3 + O_2$$

$$NO_2 + NO_3 + M \xrightarrow{k_2} N_2O_5 + M$$

Rate law expression for the production of N_2O_5 based on this mechanism is

(a) $k_2[NO_2][NO_3]$ (b) $k_2[NO_2][O_3]$
(c) $k_1k_2[NO_2][O_3]$ (d) $k_1[NO_2][O_3]$

150. For a given reaction.

$$2H_2O_2 \longrightarrow 2H_2O + O_2$$

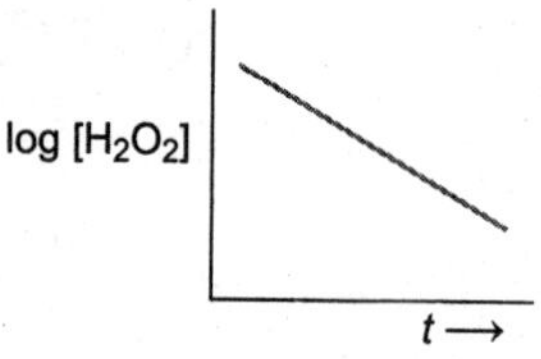

Graph between log $[H_2O_2]$ and time t is of the type Thus, rate law is

(a) $k[H_2O_2]^2$ (b) $k[H_2O_2]$
(c) $k[H_2O_2]^0$ (d) $k[H_2O_2]^{-1}$

151. For n^{th} order reaction.

$$\left(\frac{dx}{dt}\right) = \text{Rate} = k[A]_0^n$$

Graph between log (rate) against log $[A]_0$ is of the type

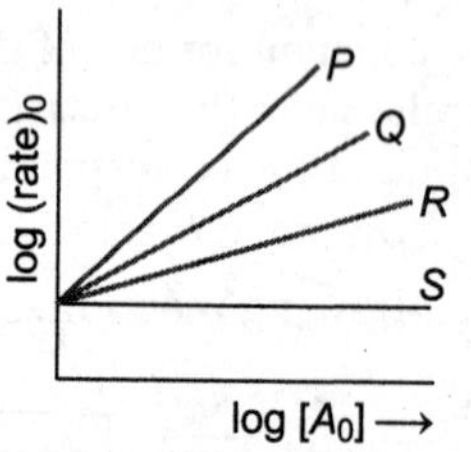

Lines P, Q, R, S are for the order

	P	Q	R	S		P	Q	R	S
(a)	0	1	2	3	(b)	3	2	1	0
(c)	1	2	3	0	(d)	0	3	2	1

152. For nth order reaction.

$$C_t = C_0 - kt$$

(where, C_0 is initial concentration, C_t is the concentration after time t). This shows that n is

(a) zero (b) one
(c) two (d) three

153. The acid catalysed bromination of acetone in aqueous solution

$$CH_3COCH_3 + Br_2 \xrightarrow{H^+} CH_3COCH_2Br + H^+ + Br^-$$

is found to obey the following rate law

$$\text{rate} = k[CH_3COCH_3][H^+][Br_2]^0$$

Thus, rate determing step is

(a) $CH_3COCH_3 + H^+ \longrightarrow CH_3C(OH)CH_3^{\oplus}$
(b) $CH_3COHCH_3^{\oplus} + Br_2 \longrightarrow CH_3COCH_2Br + 2H^+ + Br^-$
(c) Both (a) and (b)
(d) None of the above

154. If $-\left(\frac{dN}{dt}\right)_0$ is the initial activity and $-\left(\frac{dN}{dt}\right)$ is the activity at time t in a radioactive disintegration then

(a) $-\left(\frac{dN}{dt}\right)_0 = -\left(\frac{dN}{dt}\right)e^{-kt}$ (b) $-\left(\frac{dN}{dt}\right) = -\left(\frac{dN}{dt}\right)_0 e^{-kt}$
(c) $-\left(\frac{dN}{dt}\right) = \left(\frac{dN}{dt}\right)_0 e^{-kt}$ (d) $-\left(\frac{dN}{dt}\right)_0 = \left(\frac{dN}{dt}\right)e^{-kt}$

155. For the second order reaction $A \longrightarrow$ Product

$[A]_0$ = concentration of the reactant A at $t = 0$
$[A]$ = concentration of the reactant at time t
then

(a) $\frac{1}{[A]} - \frac{1}{[A]_0} = kt$ (b) $[A] = \frac{[A]_0}{1 + kt[A]_0}$
(c) $t_{50} = \frac{1}{k[A]_0}$ (d) All are correct relations

156. For the first order reaction, C is the concentration of the reactant at time t and C_0 is the initial concentration then $(C_0 - C) =$

(a) $C_0[1 - e^{-kt}]$ (b) C_0e^{-kt}
(c) $C_0[1 + e^{kt}]$ (d) C_0e^{kt}

157. The rate constant for the reaction in gaseous phase

$$O + O_3 \longrightarrow 2O_2$$

is 8.0×10^{-15} cm^3 $molecule^{-1}$ s^{-1} at 298 K. Corresponding value in dm^3 mol^{-1} s^{-1} is

(a) 4.8×10^6 dm^3 mol^{-1} s^{-1}
(b) 1.33×10^{-6} dm^3 mol^{-1} s^{-1}
(c) 4.8×10^8 dm^3 mol^{-1} s^{-1}
(d) 1.33×10^6 dm^3 mol^{-1} s^{-1}

158. For the second order reaction, concentration (x) of the product at time t starting with initial concentration $[A_0]$ is

(a) $\frac{kt\,[A_0]^2}{1+kt[A_0]}$ (b) $\frac{k+[A_0]^2}{1+kt}$

(c) $\frac{1+kt[A_0]^2}{k+[A_0]^2}$ (d) None of these

159. A bacterial infection in an internal wound grows as $N'(t) = N_0 \exp(t)$, where the time t is in hours. A dose of antibiotic, taken orally, needs 1 hour to reach the wound. Once it reaches there, the bacterial population goes down as $\frac{dN}{dt} = -5N^2$. What will be the plot of $\frac{N_0}{N}$ vs t after 1 hour ?

[JEE Main 2019, April]

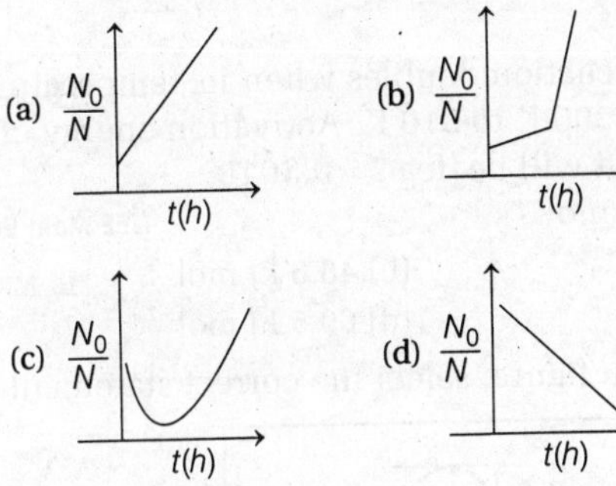

160. For a first order reaction, the time taken to reduce the initial concentration by a factor of 1/4 is 20 min. The time required to reduce initial concentration by a factor of 1/16 is

(a) 20 min (b) 10 min

(c) 80 min (d) 40 min

161. Give the relation between half reaction time ($t_{1/2}$) and initial concentration of reactant for ($n-1$) order reaction

(a) $t_{1/2} \propto [R]_0$ (b) $t_{1/2} \propto [R]_0^{2-n}$

(c) $t_{1/2} \propto [R]_0^{n+1}$ (d) $t_{1/2} \propto [R]_0^{n-2}$

162. The activation energy of a reaction at a given temperature is found to be 2.303 RT J mol^{-1}. The ratio of rate constant to the Arrhenius factor is

(a) 0.01 (b) 0.1

(c) 0.02 (d) 0.001

163. For the reaction, $N_2O_5(g) \longrightarrow 2NO_2(g) + \frac{1}{2}O_2(g)$ the value of the rate of disappearance of N_2O_5 is given as 6.25×10^{-3} mol L^{-1} s^{-1}. The rate of formation of NO_2 and O_2 is given respectively as

(a) 1.25×10^{-2} mol L^{-1} s^{-1} and 6.25×10^{-3} mol L^{-1} s^{-1}

(b) 6.25×10^{-3} mol L^{-1}s^{-1} and 6.25×10^{-3} mol L^{-1} s^{-1}

(c) 1.25×10^{-2} mol L^{-1} s^{-1} and 3.125×10^{-3} mol L^{-1} s^{-1}

(d) 6.25×10^{-3} mol L^{-1}s^{-1} and 3.125×10^{-3} mol L^{-1} s^{-1}

164. For a reaction between gaseous compounds,

$$2A + B \longrightarrow C + D$$

the reaction rate $= k[A][B]$. If the volume of the container is made $\frac{1}{4}$ of the initial, then what will be the rate of reaction as compared to the initial rate?

(a) 16 times (b) 4 times

(c) $\frac{1}{8}$ times (d) $\frac{1}{16}$ times

165. In the hydrolysis of an organic chloride in presence of large excess of water,

$$RCl + H_2O \longrightarrow ROH + HCl$$

(a) moleculartiy and order of reaction both are 2.

(b) molecularity is 2 but order of reaction is 1.

(c) molecularity is 1 but order of reaction is 2.

(d) molecularity is 1 and order of reaction is also 1.

166. By increase in temperature by 10 K, the rate of reaction becomes double. How many times the rate of reaction will be if the temperature is increased from 303 K to 353 K?

(a) 4 (b) 8

(c) 16 (d) 32

167. The first order rate constant for the decomposition of ethyl iodide by the reaction,

$$C_2H_5I(g) \longrightarrow C_2H_4(g) + HI(g)$$

at 600 K is 1.60×10^{-5} s^{-1}. Its energy of activation is 209 kJ mol^{-1}. What is the rate constant of the reaction at 700 K?

(a) 6.36×10^{3} s^{-1} (b) 6.36×10^{-3} s^{-1}

(c) 6.36×10^{3} s (d) 6.36×10^{-3} s

168. The following graph shows how $t_{1/2}$ (half-life) of a reactant R changes with the initial reactant concentration a_0. The order of the reaction will be

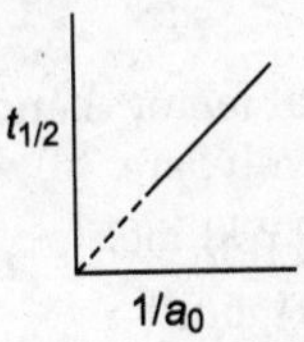

(a) 0 (b) 1 (c) 2 (d) 3

169. Pick the appropriate choice about collision theory of reaction rates.

I. It explains the effect of temperature on rate of reaction.

II. It assumes that the reactants must be in correct orientation to react.

III. It says rate depends upon the frequency at which reactants collide.

IV. The collisions having energy higher than the threshold value will give successful reactions.

The correct points are

(a) I, III, IV (b) II, IV

(c) I, IV (d) I, II, III, IV

170. In the reaction, $P + Q \longrightarrow R + S$ the time taken for 75% reaction of P is twice the time taken for 50% reaction of P. The concentration of Q varies with reaction time as shown in the figure. The overall order of the reaction is **[JEE Advanced 2013]**

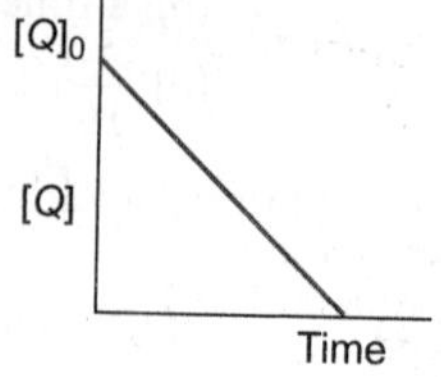

(a) 2 (b) 3 (c) 0 (d) 1

171. For the reaction in alkaline aqueous solution,

$$3BrO^- \longrightarrow BrO_3^- + 2Br^-$$

the value of the second order (in BrO^-) rate constant at 350 K in the rate law for $-\dfrac{\Delta[BrO^-]}{\Delta t}$ was found to be $0.056 \text{ L mol}^{-1} \text{ s}^{-1}$. Then

(a) rate constant is $0.019 \text{ L mol}^{-1} \text{ s}^{-1}$ when rate law is $+\dfrac{\Delta[BrO_3^-]}{\Delta t}$

(b) rate constant is $0.037 \text{ L mol}^{-1} \text{ s}^{-1}$ when rate law is $+\dfrac{\Delta[Br^-]}{\Delta t}$

(c) rate of the reaction is $0.056 \text{ mol L}^{-1} \text{ s}^{-1}$ when $[BrO^-] = 1$ M

(d) All of the above are correct statements

172. For a first order reaction $A \rightarrow P$, the temperature (T) dependent rate constant (k) was found to follow the equation

$$\log k = \frac{2000}{T} + 6.0$$

The pre-exponential factor A and the activation energy E_a, respectively, are **[IIT JEE 2009]**

(a) $1.0 \times 10^6 \text{ s}^{-1}$ and 9.2 kJ mol^{-1}

(b) 6.0 s^{-1} and 16.6 kJ mol^{-1}

(c) $1.0 \times 10^6 \text{ s}^{-1}$ and 16.6 kJ mol^{-1}

(d) $1.0 \times 10^6 \text{ s}^{-1}$ and 38.3 kJ mol^{-1}

173. Plots showing the variation of the rate constant (k) with temperature (T) are given below. The plot that follows Arrhenius equation is **[IIT JEE 2010]**

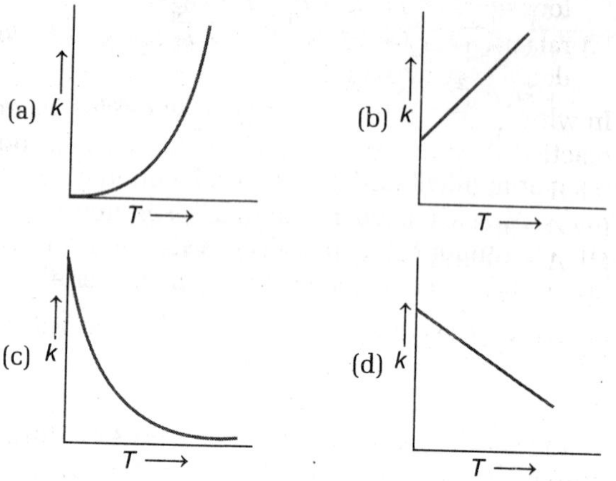

174. The rate of a reaction doubles when its temperature changes from 300 K to 310 K. Activation energy of such a reaction will be ($\log 2 = 0.3010$; $R = 8.314 \text{ JK}^{-1} \text{ mol}^{-1}$). **[JEE Main 2013]**

(a) 53.6 kJ mol^{-1} (b) 48.6 kJ mol^{-1}

(c) 58.5 kJ mol^{-1} (d) 60.5 kJ mol^{-1}

175. From the given figure, select the correct statement.

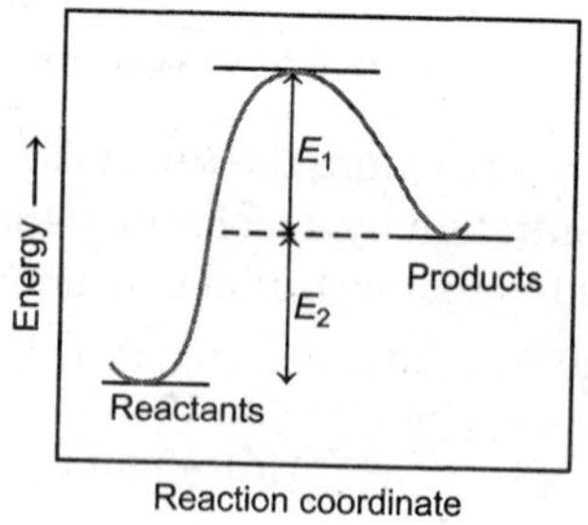

(a) Activation energy of forward reaction is $(E_1 + E_2)$ and product is less stable than reactant

(b) Activation energy of forward reaction is $(E_1 + E_2)$ and product is more stable than reactant

(c) Activation energy of backward reaction is E_2 and that of forward reaction is E_1

(d) Activation energy of backward reaction is E_1 and product is more stable than reactant

Objective Questions Type II [One or more than one correct option(s)]

In each of the questions below, four choices are given, of which one or more than one are correct.

1. Which of the following statements are correct about half-life period?

(a) It is proportional to initial concentration for zeroth order

(b) Average life = 1.44 half-life for first order reaction

(c) Time of 75% reaction is thrice of half-life period in second order reaction

(d) 99.9% reaction takes place in 100 minutes for the case when rate constant is 0.0693 min^{-1}

2. $Zn + 2H^+ \longrightarrow Zn^{2+} + H_2$

Half-life period is independent of concentration of zinc at constant pH. For the constant concentration of Zn, rate becomes 100 times when pH is decreased from 3 to 2. Hence,

(a) $\frac{dx}{dt} = k[Zn]^0[H^+]^2$ (b) $\left(\frac{dx}{dt}\right) = k[Zn][H^+]^2$

(c) rate is not affected if concentration of zinc is made four times and that of H^+ ion is halved

(d) rate becomes four times if concentration of H^+ ion is doubled at constant Zn concentration

3. In which of the following case, E_a of the backward reaction is greater than that of the forward reaction?

(a) $A + 10\text{ kcal} \longrightarrow B,\ E_a = 50\text{ kcal}$

(b) $A + 20\text{ kcal} \longrightarrow B,\ E_a = 40\text{ kcal}$

(c) $A + 40\text{ kcal} \longrightarrow B,\ E_a = 10\text{ kcal}$

(d) $A - 40\text{ kcal} \longrightarrow B,\ E_a = 20\text{ kcal}$

4. $\underset{(g)}{A} \longrightarrow \underset{(g)}{B} + \underset{(g)}{C} \quad \frac{-d[A]}{dt} = k[A]$

At the start pressure is 100 mm and after 10 min, pressure is 120 mm. Hence, rate constant (min^{-1}) is

(a) $\frac{2.303}{10}\log\frac{120}{100}$ (b) $\frac{2.303}{10}\log\frac{100}{20}$

(c) $\frac{2.303}{10}\log\frac{100}{80}$ (d) $\frac{2.303}{10}\log\frac{100}{120}$

5. 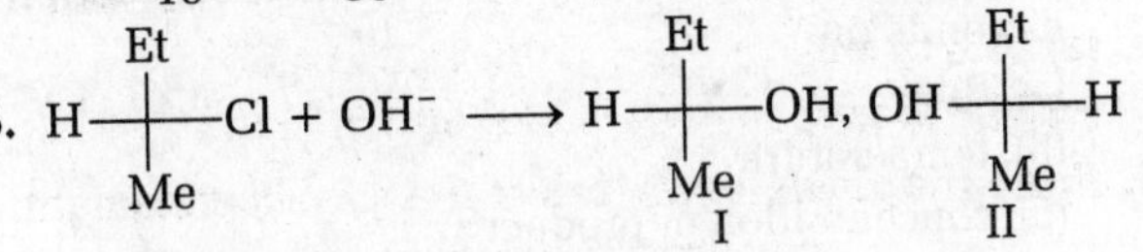

Which of the following statements are correct?

(a) It is unimolecular nucleophilic substitution reaction S_N1 if I or II is formed

(b) It is biomolecular nucleophilic substitution reaction S_N2 if I or II is formed

(c) It is S_N1 if I and its enantiomer are formed so that mixture is racemic

(d) It is S_N2 if II is formed

6. The reaction,

$$A(g) + 2B(g) \longrightarrow C(g) + D(g)$$

Initial pressure of A and B are respectively $p_A = 0.60$ atm, $p_B = 0.80$ atm. When $p_C = 0.20$ atm, the rate of the reaction relative to the initial rate, is

(a) $\frac{1}{48}$ (b) $\frac{1}{24}$ (c) $\frac{1}{6}$ (d) $\frac{1}{4}$

7. Rate constant k varies with temperature by equation, $\log k\ (\text{min}^{-1}) = 5 - \frac{2000\text{ K}}{T}$. We can conclude

(a) pre-exponential factor A is 5

(b) E_a is 2000 kcal

(c) pre-exponential factor A is 10^5

(d) E_a is 9.212 kcal

8. In the nuclear transmutation,

$^9_4\text{Be} + X \rightarrow {}^8_4\text{Be} + Y, (X, Y)$ is/are

(a) (γ, n) (b) (P, D) (c) (n, D) (d) (γ, P)

9. For a reaction for which activation energies of the forward and reverse directions are equal in value:

(a) the stoichiometry is the mechanism

(b) $\Delta H = 0$

(c) $\Delta S = 0$

(d) the order is zero

10. A reaction is catalysed by H^+ ion. In presence of HA, rate constant is $2 \times 10^{-3}\ \text{min}^{-1}$ and in presence of HB rate constant is $1 \times 10^{-3}\ \text{min}^{-1}$, HA and HB both being strong acids, we may conclude

(a) equilibrium constant is 2

(b) HA is stronger than HB

(c) relative strength of HA and HB is 2

(d) HA is weaker than HB and relative strength is 0.5

11. Activation energy of a chemical reaction can be determined by

(a) evaluating rate constant at standard temperature

(b) evaluating velocities of reaction at two different temperatures

(c) evaluating rate constants at two different temperatures

(d) changing concentration of reactants

12. A plot of the number of neutrons (N) against the number of protons(P) of stable nucler exhibits upward deviation from linearity for atomic number $Z > 20$. For an unstable nucleus having N/P ratio less than 1, the possible mode(s) of decay is/are **[JEE Advanced 2016]**

(a) β-decay (β-emission)

(b) orbital or K-electron catpture

(c) neutron emission

(d) β^+-decay (position emission)

13. In the following reaction, how is the rate of appearance of the underlined product related to the rate of disappearance of the underlined reactant?

$$BrO_3^-(aq) + 5\underline{Br^-}(aq) + 6H^+(aq) \longrightarrow 3\underline{Br_2}(l) + 3H_2O(l)$$

(a) $\frac{d[Br_2]}{dt} = -\frac{5}{3}\frac{d[Br^-]}{dt}$ (b) $\frac{d[Br_2]}{dt} = -\frac{d[Br^-]}{dt}$

(c) $\frac{d[Br_2]}{dt} = -\frac{d[Br^-]}{dt}$ (d) $\frac{d[Br_2]}{dt} = -\frac{3}{5}\frac{d[Br^-]}{dt}$

14. $3A \longrightarrow B + C$

It would be a zero order reaction when

(a) the rate of reaction is proportional to square of concentration of A

(b) the rate of reaction remains same at any concentration of A

(c) the rate remains unchanged at any concentration of B and C

(d) the rate of reaction doubles if concentration of B is increased to double

15. The potential energy diagram for a reaction $R \longrightarrow P$ is given below

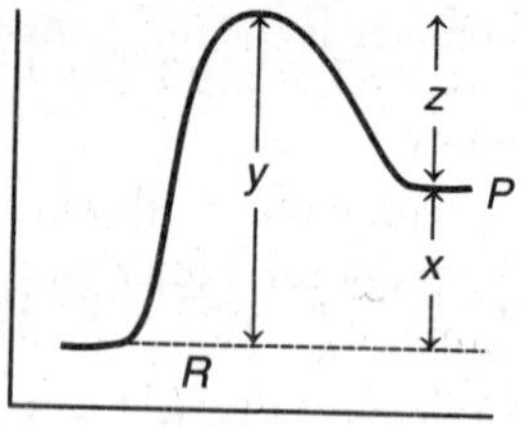

$\Delta H°$ of the reaction corresponds to the energy.
(a) x (b) y (c) z (d) $(x + y)$

16. For the first order reaction,
$2N_2O_5(s) \longrightarrow 4NO_2(g) + O_2(g)$ [IIT JEE 2011]
(a) the concentration of the reactant decreases exponentially with time.
(b) the half-life of the reaction decreases with increasing temperature.
(c) the half-life of the reaction depends on the initial concentration of the reactant.
(d) the reaction proceeds of 99.6% completion in eight half-life duration.

17. The initial rate of hydrolysis of methyl acetate (1 M) by a weak acid (HA, 1 M) is 1/100th of that of a strong acid (HX, 1 M) at 25°C. The K_a (HA) is [JEE Advanced 2013]
(a) 1×10^{-4} (b) 1×10^{-5} (c) 1×10^{-6} (d) 1×10^{-3}

18. For a first order reaction $A(g) \longrightarrow 2B(g) + C(g)$ at constant volume and 300 K, the total pressure at the beginning $(t = 0)$ and at time t are p_0 and p_t, respectively. Initially, only A is present with concentration $[A]_0$, and $t_{1/3}$ is the time required for the partial pressure of A to reach $1/3^{rd}$ of its initial value. The correct option(s) is (are) (Assume that all these gases behave as ideal gases) [JEE Advanced 2018]

(a)
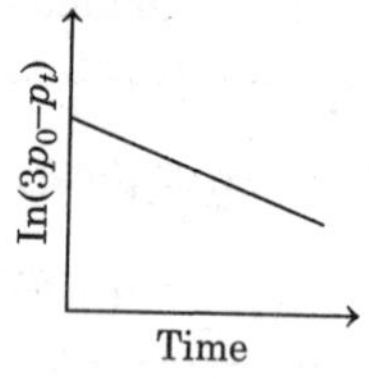

(b)
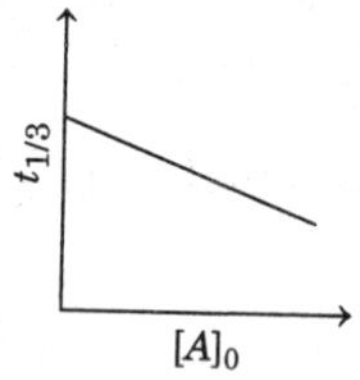

(c)
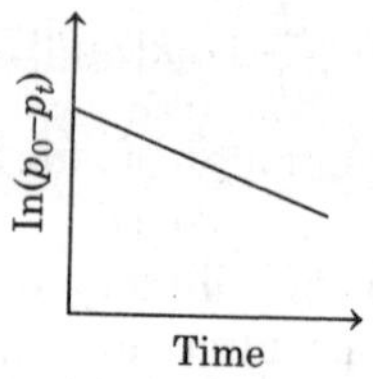

(d)
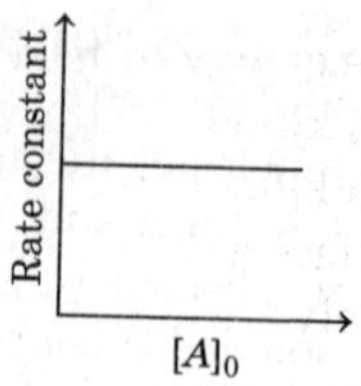

19. In a bimolecular reaction, the steric factor P was experimentally determined to be 4.5. the correct option(s) among the following is(are) [JEE Advanced 2017]
(a) The activation energy of the reaction is unaffected by the value of the steric factor
(b) Experimentally determined value of frequency factor is higher than that predicted by Arrhenius equation
(c) The value of frequency factor predicted by Arrhenius equation is higher than that determined experimentally
(d) Since $P = 4.5$, the reaction will not proceed unless an effective catalyst is used

20. The specific rate constant of a first order reaction depends on
(a) time
(b) temperature
(c) concentration of product
(d) concentration of the reactants

21. According to the Arrhenius equation, [JEE Advanced 2016]
(a) a high activation energy usually implies a fast reaction
(b) rate constant increases with increase in temperature. This is due to a greater number of collisions whose energy exceeds the activation energy
(c) higher the magnitude of activation energy, stronger is the temperature dependence of the rate constant
(d) the pre-exponential factor is a measure of the rate at which collisions occur, irrespective of their energy

Numerical Value Questions

All these questions have a Numerical value as their answer, solve the questions and write your answer.

1. The rate of the gaseous reaction,
$A(g) + B(g) \longrightarrow$ Product
is given by expression $\frac{dx}{dt} = k[A][B]$
If the volume of the reaction vessel is suddenly reduced to one-fourth of the initial volume. The ratio of the final rate to initial rate is

2. What will be the initial rate of a reaction if its rate constant is 10^{-3} min^{-1} and the concentration of the reactant is 0.2 mol dm^{-3}? How much of the reactant will be converted into the products in 200 min?

3. Decomposition of CH_3COCH_3 into C_2H_6 and CO follows first order kinetics with $T_{50} = 810$ s. Time takes for acetone vapour pressure to drop to 0.30 atm from 2 atm is

4. The decomposition of N_2O into N_2 and O_2 in presence of gaseous argon follows second order kinetics, with $k = (5.0\times 10^{11}\ L\ mol^{-1}\ s^{-1})e^{\frac{-29000\ K}{T}}$
Arrhenius parameters are
[**Hint** Compare it with $k = Ae^{-E_a/RT}$]

5. The energy of activation for a hypothetical reaction is 285 kJ/mol for the uncatalysed reaction and 135 kJ/mol for the reaction catalysed on the metal surface at 27°C. The effect on the rate in presence of catalyst is ...... $\times 10^6$ times.

6. A hydrogenation reaction is carried out at 500 K. If the same reaction is carried out in the presence of a catalyst at the same rate, the temperature required is 400 K. The activation energy of the reaction if the catalyst lowers the activation barrier by 20 kJ mol^{-1} is ......

7. The rate constant at 25°C for the reaction of NH_4^+ and OH^- to form $NH_4OH\,(aq.NH_3)$ is $4.0\times 10^{10}\ M^{-1}s^{-1}$. The rate constant for proton transfer to NH_3 is ...... $\times 10^{-5}$ (Ionisation constant of $aq.NH_3$ is 1.8×10^{-5}).

8. The Arrhenius equations for the rate constant of decomposition of methyl nitrite and ethyl nitrite are

$$k_1(s^{-1}) = 10^{13} \exp\left(\frac{-152300\ \text{J mol}^{-1}}{RT}\right)$$

$$\text{and } k_2(s^{-1}) = 10^{14} \exp\left(\frac{-157700\ \text{J mol}^{-1}}{RT}\right)$$

respectively. The temperature at which the rate constant are equal is ....

9. Consider the following reversible reaction,

$$A(g) + B(g) \rightleftharpoons AB(g)$$

The activation energy of the backward reaction exceeds that of the forward reaction by $2RT$ (in J mol^{-1}). If the pre-exponential factor of the forward reaction is 4 times that of the reverse reaction, the absolute value of $\Delta G^\ominus$ (in J mol^{-1}) for the reaction at 300 K is ....

(Given ; $\ln(2) = 0.7$ $RT = 2500$ J mol^{-1} at 300 K and G is the Gibbs energy) **[JEE Advanced 2018]**

10. The number of molecules with energy greater than the threshold energy for a reaction increases five fold by a rise of temperature from 27 °C to 42 °C. Its energy of activation in J/mol is ....
(Take $\ln 5 = 1.6094$; $R = 8.314$ J mol^{-1} K^{-1}) **[JEE Main 2020, Sept.]**

11. The decomposition of formic acid on gold surface follows first order kinetics. If the rate constant at 300 K is $1.0 \times 10^{-3}\ s^{-1}$ and the activation energy $E_a = 11.488$ kJ mol^{-1}, the rate constant at 200 K is .... $\times 10^{-5}\ s^{-1}$. **[JEE Main 2021, March]**
(Given : $R = 8.314$ J mol^{-1} K^{-1})

12. A and B decompose via first order kinetics with half-lives 54.0 min and 18.0 min respectively. Starting from an equimolar non-reactive mixture of A and B, the time taken for the concentration of A to become 16 times that of B is .... min. **[JEE Main 2021, March]**

13. The reaction $2A + B_2 \rightarrow 2AB$ is an elementary reaction. For a certain quantity of reactants, if the volume of the reaction vessel is reduced by a factor of 3, the rate of the reaction increases by a factor of .... **[JEE Main 2021, March]**

14. A reaction has a half life of 1 min. The time required for 99.9% completion of the reaction is .... min. (Round off to the nearest integer)
[Use : ln 2= 0.69, ln 10 = 2.3] **[JEE Main 2021, March]**

Comprehension Based Questions

In these questions, a passage has been given followed by questions based on it. You have to answer the questions based on the passage given.

Passage 1 *Read the following experiments and answer the questions at the end of it.*

Peroxyacetyl nitrate (PAN) is an air pollutant produced in photochemical smog by the reaction of hydrocarbons, oxides of nitrogen and sunlight. It dissociates as

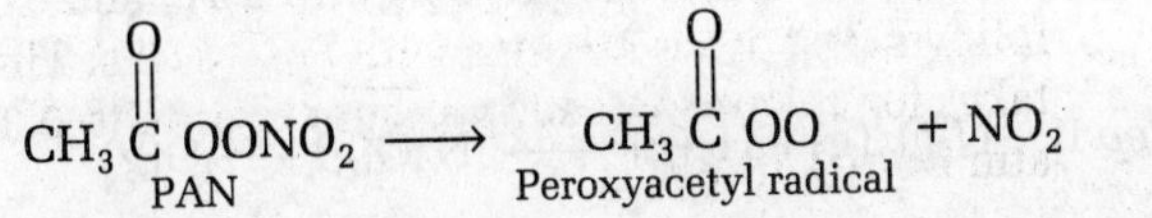

A sample of polluted air is analysed for its PAN content which is reported as molecules PAN per litre of air at 25°C.

Time (min)	Molecules $\times 10^{-14}$ / L air
0.0	5.0
10.0	4.0
20.0	3.2
30.0	2.6
40.0	2.1
50.0	1.7
60.0	1.3

1. Determine the order of the PAN decomposition reaction
(a) 0 (b) 1 (c) 2 (d) 3

2. Rate constant of the reaction is
(a) 0.0231 min^{-1} (b) 0.009 $min^{-1}2$
(c) 0.0231 L mol^{-1} min^{-1} (d) 0.009 L mol^{-1} min^{-1}

3. Half-life of the reaction is
(a) 10 min (b) 20 min
(c) 30 min (d) 60 min

Passage 2 *Study the following experiment and answer the questions at the end of it.*

The following reaction was studied at 25°C in benzene solution containing 0.1 M pyridine

$$\underset{A}{CH_3OH} + \underset{B}{(C_6H_5)_3CCl} \longrightarrow \underset{C}{(C_6H_5)_3C \cdot OCH_3} + HCl$$

The following sets of data were observed

Set	Initial concentration		Time Δt	Final concentration $[C]$
	$[A]_0$	$[B]_0$		
I	0.10 M	0.05 M	25 min	0.0033 M
II	0.10 M	0.10 M	15 min	0.0039 M
III	0.20 M	0.10 M	7.5 min	0.0077 M

1. Rates $\frac{d[C]}{dt}$ in sets I, II and III are respectively (in M min^{-1})

	I	II	III
(a)	1.30×10^{-4}	2.6×10^{-4}	1.02×10^{-3}
(b)	0.033	0.0039	0.0077
(c)	0.02×10^{-4}	0.04×10^{-4}	0.017

(d) None of the above

2. Rate law of the above experiment is
(a) $k[A][B]$ (b) $k[A]^2[B]$
(c) $k[A][B]^2$ (d) $k[A]^2[B]^0$

3. Rate constant of the above experiment is (in L^2 M^{-2} min^{-1})
(a) 1.3×10^{-1} (b) 2.6×10^{-2}
(c) $2\ 6 \times 10^{-1}$ (d) 1.3×10^{-2}

Passage 3 *Study the two photochemical reactions and answer the questions at the end.*

For the overall reaction between A and B to yield C and D, two mechanisms are proposed

I. $A + B \longrightarrow AB^* \longrightarrow C + D, k_1' = 1 \times 10^{-5}\ M^{-1}\ s^{-1}$

II. $A \longrightarrow A^* \longrightarrow E,\ k_1 = 1 \times 10^{-4}\ s^{-1}$

$E + B \longrightarrow C + D,\ k_2 = 1 \times 10^{10}\ M^{-1}\ s^{-1}$

(species with * are short-lived)

1. Rate law for mechanism I when concentration of each is 0.1 M, is
(a) 1×10^{-7} M s^{-1} (b) 1×10^{-6} M s^{-1}
(c) 1×10^{-5} M s^{-1} (d) 1×10^{-4} M s^{-1}

2. Rate law for mechanism II when concentration of each 1 M is
(a) 1×10^{-4} M s^{-1}
(b) 1×10^{10} M s^{-1}
(c) 1×10^{-6} M s^{-1}
(d) 1×10^{-10} M s^{-1}

3. At what concentration of B, rates of two mechanism are equal?
(a) 1 M (b) 5 M
(c) 7 M (d) 10 M

Passage 4 *Read the following industrial methods of* H_2SO_4 *and answer the question at the end.*

Professor Molina of the Massachusetts Institute of Technology won the 1995 Nobel Prize in Chemistry for his work on atmospheric chemistry. One reaction that he has studied in detail is the acid rain reaction which produces H_2SO_4 in the atmosphere. He has proposed two possible stoichiometric reactions.

Proposal A : $H_2O(g) + SO_3(g) \longrightarrow H_2SO_4(g)$

Proposal B : $2H_2O(g) + SO_3(g) \longrightarrow H_2SO_4(g) + H_2O(g)$

1. Using simple collision theory, what reaction orders would be expected for proposal B ?

Proposal B is thought to proceed by the following two-step process

$$SO_3 + 2H_2O \underset{k_{-1}}{\overset{k_1}{\rightleftharpoons}} SO_3 \cdot 2H_2O \text{ (Fast)}$$

$$SO_3 \cdot 2H_2O \xrightarrow{k_2} H_2SO_4 + H_2O \text{ (Slow)}$$

($SO_3 \cdot 2H_2O$ is a complex which is stabilized by hydrogen bonds and $k_2 << k_1$ or k_{-1})
(a) $k[H_2O][SO_3]$
(b) $k[H_2O]^2[SO_3]$
(c) $k[SO_3]$
(d) $k[H_2O]$

Passage 5 *Question given at the end is based on the following mechanism.*

Reaction between nitric oxide and hydrogen takes place by the following mechanism

Step I $\quad 2NO(g) \underset{k_{-1}}{\overset{k_1}{\rightleftharpoons}} N_2O_2(g)$ (Fast)

Step II $\quad N_2O_2(g) + H_2(g) \xrightarrow{k_2} N_2O(g) + H_2O(g)$ (Slow, rate determining)

Step III $\quad N_2O(g) + H_2(g) \xrightarrow{k_3} N_2(g) + H_2O(g)$ (Fast)

The first step, which is reversible, has a rate constant k_1 for the forward reaction and k_{-1} for the reverse reaction. The forward and reverse reactions of step I occur at the same rate, and both are fast compared with step II.

1. Rate of the overall reaction in terms of the concentration of the reactants is

(a) $\frac{k_1k_2}{k_{-1}}[NO]^2[H_2]$ (b) $\frac{k_1k_2}{k_{-1}}[NO][H_2]^2$

(c) $k_1k_2[NO]^2[H_2]$ (d) $\frac{k_2}{k_1}[NO]^2[H_2]$

***Passage* 6** A group of mountain climbers set up a camp at 3 km altitude and experience a barometric pressure of 0.69 atm. They discover that pure water boils at 90°C and it takes 300 min of cooking to make a "three-minute" egg.

Answer the following questions.

1. What is the ratio of rate constants at 100°C to 90°C?
   (a) 300
   (b) 100
   (c) 3
   (d) 0.01
2. What is the activation energy for this change?
   (a) 62.4 kcal
   (b) 2.60 kcal
   (c) 25.9 kcal
   (d) None of the above is correct

***Passage* 7** N_2O_5 decompose according to the following equation.

$$N_2O_5 \xrightarrow{k} 2NO_2 + \frac{1}{2}O_2$$

The following mechanism has been followed

$$N_2O_5 \overset{K_{eq}}{\rightleftharpoons} NO_2 + NO_3$$

$$NO_2 + NO_3 \xrightarrow{k_1} NO_2 + O_2 + NO$$

$$NO + NO_3 \xrightarrow{k_2} 2NO_2$$

Answer the following questions.

1. Select the correct alternate.

(a) $\frac{d[O_2]}{dt} = k_1K_{eq}[N_2O_5]$ (b) $\frac{d[O_2]}{dt} = k_1k_2[NO_2][NO_3]$

(c) $\frac{d[O_2]}{dt} = k_1[N_2O_5]$ (d) None of these

2. A half-life is independent of the concentration of N_2O_5 then

(a) $\frac{-d[N_2O_5]}{dt} = k$ (b) $\frac{-d[N_2O_5]}{dt} = k[N_2O_5]$

(c) $\frac{-d[N_2O_5]}{dt} = K_{eq}[N_2O_5]$ (d) $\frac{-d[N_2O_5]}{dt} = K_{eq}[NO_2][NO_3]$

***Passage* 8** You have the general reaction

$$A + 2B + C \longrightarrow AB + BC$$

Kinetics is studied based on the following observations.

	[A]	[B]	[C]	$-\frac{d[A]}{dt}$
		mol L^{-1}		mol L^{-1} s^{-1}
1.	1.00	1.00	2.00	1.00
2.	2.00	1.00	2.00	2.00
3.	2.00	2.00	2.00	8.00
4.	2.00	2.00	4.00	8.00

Answer the following questions.

1. Half-life period is independent of
   (a) (*A*) (b) (*B*) (c) (*C*) (d) (*A*) and (*C*)
2. For over all reaction, half-life is 100 minute when concentration of each reactant is 1 M. What is the half-life if concentration is 2 M?
   (a) 200 min (b) 100 min (c) 50 min (d) 25 min
3. Rate controlling step is
   (a) $A + C \rightarrow AC$ (b) $2B + C \rightarrow B_2C$
   (c) $A + 2B \rightarrow AB_2$ (d) $2C \rightarrow C_2$

Matrix-Match Type

Given below are Matching Type Questions, with two columns (each having some items) each . Each item of Column I has to be matched with the items of Column II.

1. Match order of the reaction (in Column I) with the corresponding rate constant (in Column II).

Column I (Order)	Column II (Rate constant)
A. Zeroth	1. $k = \frac{1}{2t}\left[\frac{1}{(a-x)^2} - \frac{1}{a^2}\right]$
B. First	2. $k = \frac{1}{t}\left[\frac{1}{(a-x)} - \frac{1}{a}\right]$
C. Second	3. $k = \frac{x}{t}$
D. Third	4. $k = \frac{1}{t}\log_e\left(\frac{a}{a-x}\right)$

2. Match the order of reaction (in Column I) with its property (in Column II).

Column I (Order)	Column II (Property)
A. Zeroth	1. Half-life $\propto \frac{1}{a^2}$
B. First	2. Half-life $\propto \frac{1}{a}$
C. Second	3. Half-life is doubled on doubling the initial concentration.
D. Third	4. 50% reaction takes same time even if concentration is halved or doubled.

3. Match order of the reaction (in Column I) with the unit of rate constant (in Column II).

Column I (Order)	Column II (Unit)
A. Zeroth	1. $L^2\ mol^{-2}\ s^{-1}$
B. First	2. $L\ mol^{-1}\ s^{-1}$
C. Second	3. $mol\ L^{-1}\ s^{-1}$
D. Third	4. s^{-1}

4. Match the order of reaction in Column I with their related properties in Column II

Column I	Column II
A. Zero	1. $\left(\frac{dx}{dt}\right) = k$ when $(A)_0 = 1\ M$
B. First	2. 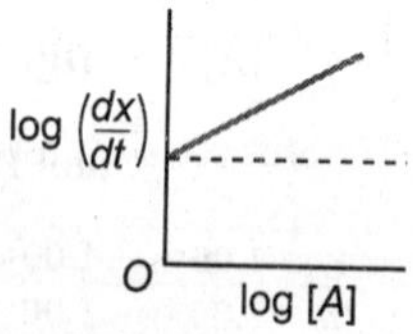
C. Second	3. $T_{50} = 2 \times T_{75}$
D. Third	4. Rate becomes 8 times on doubling concentration of A.

5. Match the graphs in Column I with their, related properties in Column II.

Column I	Column II
A. 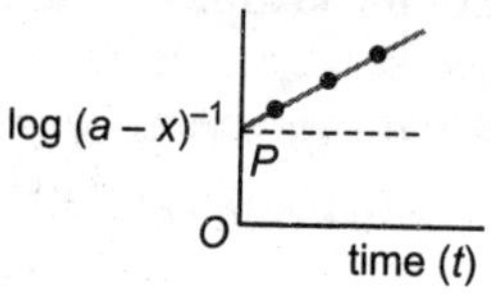	1. Rate constant is equal to rate of reaction
B. 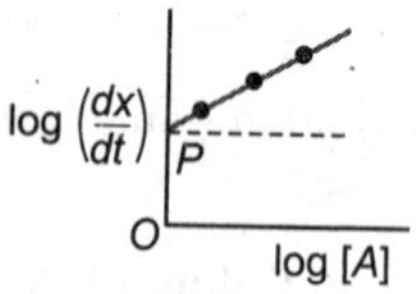	2. If $OP = 0.5$ rate $= 4k$
C. 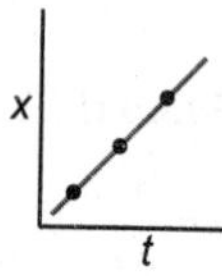	3. If $OP = 0.3010$ half-life $= 1$ at $[A]_0 = 0.5$ M
D. log (a – x) 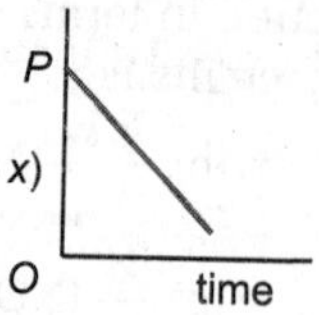	4. If $OP = 0.3010$ rate $= 2\ k$
	5. Half-life is independent of initial concentration
	6. Rate becomes 4 times on doubling $[A]$

6. Rate constant (k) of a reaction is given by

$$\log_{10} k(\text{min}^{-1}) = 5 - \frac{2 \times 10^3 k}{T}$$

Match the given property in Column I with its related value in Column II.

Column I	Column II
A. Arrhenius constant in (min^{-1})	1. 1.0
B. Order of reaction	2. 2.0
C. Rate of the reaction at initial concentration of 0.2 M at 500 K	3. 10^5
D. Energy of activation (in kcal)	4. 9.2

7. Rate law of the nth order reaction is given by

$$\left(\frac{dx}{dt}\right) = k[A]^n$$

Match different properties in Column I with their related values of half-life Column II.

Column I	Column II
A. Straight line of graph between $\log\left(\frac{dx}{dt}\right)$ and $\log [A]$ is inclined at 45°.	1. Half-life period increases as $[A]$ increase.
B. Graph between $\log\left(\frac{dx}{dt}\right)$ and $\log [A]$ is a straight line parallel to $\log [A]$ axis.	2. Half-life period is independent of concentration.
C. If $[A] = [H^+]$ and pH decreases by 1 unit, rate becomes 100 times.	3. Half-life is 100 min at 1 M and 25 min at 2 M
D. On doubling $[A]$, rate become eight times.	4. Half-life $\propto \frac{1}{[H^+]}$

Single Integer Answer Questions

Answer of these questions is a single digit lying between 0 to 9.

1. For the following reaction,

$$Fe(s) + 2H^+(aq) \longrightarrow Fe^{2+}(aq) + H_2(aq)$$

rate law is $\frac{dx}{dt} = k[Fe][H^+]^2$

If pH is decreased by x units at constant [Fe] rate becomes 100 times. What is the value of x?

2. For a certain first order reaction 32% of the reactant is left after 570 s. The rate constant of this reaction is ______ $\times 10^{-3}\ s^{-1}$.

[Given : $\log_{10}^2 = 0.301$, $\ln 10 = 2.303$] **[JEE Main 2021, March]**

3. For a reaction $E_a = 7.06 \times 10^4\ J\ mol^{-1}$.

If temperature is increased from 273 K to 283 K, how much rate is multiplied?

4. What is the relation between t_{75} and t_{50} for second-order reaction?

5. Enthalpy change $(A \rightarrow B)$ is -3 kcal mol^{-1} and energy of activation of this process is 5 kcal mol^{-1}. What is the energy of activation of $(B - A)$ in kcal mol^{-1}?

6. $2\ NO(g) + Cl_2(g) \rightleftharpoons 2\ NOCl(s)$

This reaction was studied at $-10°C$ and the following data was obtained **[JEE Main 2021, March]**

run	$[NO]_0$	$[Cl2]_0$	r_0
1	0.10	0.10	0.18
2	0.10	0.20	0.35
3	0.20	0.20	1.40

$[NO]_0$ and $[Cl_2]_0$ are the initial concentrations and r_0 is the initial reaction rate.

The overall order of the reaction is ....

7. In the following reaction,

$$2N_2O_5 \longrightarrow 4NO_2 + O_2$$

$$-\frac{d[N_2O_5]}{dt} = k_1[N_2O_5]$$

$$+\frac{d[NO_2]}{dt} = k_2[N_2O_5]$$

$$+\frac{d[O_2]}{dt} = k_3[N_2O_5]$$

If $k_3 = 1$ (in given unit), what is the value of $(k_1 + k_2 + k_3)$?

8. Following is the presentation of first-order reaction

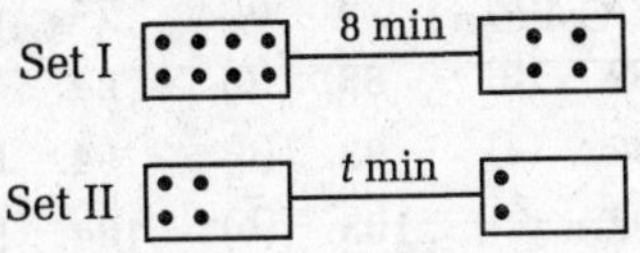

What is the value of t?

9. Rate constant of a reaction $\left(\frac{dx}{dt}\right) = k[A]^n$ is $1.2 \times 10^{-5}\ M^{-1}s^{-1}$. Graphical study between $(a - x)^{-1}$ and t is a straight line cutting $(a - x)^{-1}$axis at $0.2\ M^{-1}$. What is initial concentration of A?

10. The concentration of R in the reaction $R \rightarrow P$ was measured as a function of time and the following data is obtained

[R] (molar)	1.0	0.75	0.40	0.10
t (min)	0.0	0.05	0.12	0.18

The order of the reaction is **[IIT JEE 2010]**

11. An organic compound undergoes first order decomposition. The time taken for its decomposition to 1/8 and 1/10 of its initial concentration are $t_{1/8}$ and $t_{1/10}$ respectively. What is the value of $\frac{[t_{1/8}]}{[t_{1/10}]} \times 10$?

$(\log_{10} 2 = 0.3)$ **[IIT JEE 2012]]**

Answers

Objective Questions Type I [Only one correct option]

1. (d)	**2.** (c)	**3.** (a)	**4.** (a)	**5.** (b)	**6.** (d)	**7.** (d)	**8.** (a)	**9.** (a)	**10.** (d)
11. (b)	**12.** (a)	**13.** (c)	**14.** (b)	**15.** (b)	**16.** (a)	**17.** (b)	**18.** (d)	**19.** (b)	**20.** (b)
21. (b)	**22.** (a)	**23.** (c)	**24.** (a)	**25.** (a)	**26.** (a)	**27.** (d)	**28.** (b)	**29.** (a)	**30.** (d)
31. (d)	**32.** (a)	**33.** (a)	**34.** (d)	**35.** (c)	**36.** (d)	**37.** (c)	**38.** (d)	**39.** (d)	**40.** (d)
41. (c)	**42.** (d)	**43.** (b)	**44.** (a)	**45.** (d)	**46.** (d)	**47.** (c)	**48.** (c)	**49.** (c)	**50.** (a)
51. (b)	**52.** (c)	**53.** (c)	**54.** (b)	**55.** (b)	**56.** (c)	**57.** (d)	**58.** (a)	**59.** (c)	**60.** (c)
61. (b)	**62.** (a)	**63.** (b)	**64.** (c)	**65.** (a)	**66.** (d)	**67.** (c)	**68.** (c)	**69.** (a)	**70.** (a)
71. (d)	**72.** (b)	**73.** (a)	**74.** (b)	**75.** (c)	**76.** (a)	**77.** (b)	**78.** (c)	**79.** (b)	**80.** (b)
81. (c)	**82.** (b)	**83.** (c)	**84.** (a)	**85.** (c)	**86.** (a)	**87.** (d)	**88.** (c)	**89.** (a)	**90.** (a)
91. (c)	**92.** (a)	**93.** (c)	**94.** (d)	**95.** (d)	**96.** (b)	**97.** (b)	**98.** (b)	**99.** (c)	**100.** (b)
101. (a)	**102.** (c)	**103.** (b)	**104.** (d)	**105.** (a)	**106.** (d)	**107.** (c)	**108.** (b)	**109.** (b)	**110.** (c)
111. (b)	**112.** (d)	**113.** (d)	**114.** (c)	**115.** (a)	**116.** (b)	**117.** (d)	**118.** (a)	**119** (d)	**120.** (d)
121. (c)	**122.** (a)	**123.** (a)	**124.** (d)	**125.** (d)	**126.** (b)	**127.** (d)	**128.** (a)	**129.** (c)	**130.** (b)
131. (a)	**132.** (b)	**133.** (c)	**134.** (d)	**135.** (d)	**136.** (d)	**137.** (d)	**138.** (b)	**139.** (c)	**140.** (d)
141. (b)	**142.** (c)	**143.** (a)	**144.** (d)	**145.** (b)	**146.** (d)	**147.** (b)	**148.** (b)	**149.** (d)	**150.** (b)
151. (b)	**152.** (a)	**153.** (a)	**154.** (b)	**155.** (b)	**156.** (a)	**157.** (a)	**158.** (a)	**159.** (a)	**160.** (d)
161. (b)	**162.** (b)	**163.** (c)	**164.** (a)	**165.** (b)	**166.** (d)	**167.** (b)	**168.** (c)	**169.** (d)	**170.** (a)
171. (d)	**172.** (d)	**173.** (a)	**174.** (a)	**175.** (d)					

Objective Questions Type II [One or more than one correct option(s)]

1. (a, b, c, d)	**2.** (b, c, d)	**3.** (d)	**4.** (c)	**5.** (c, d)
6. (c)	**7.** (c, d)	**8.** (b)	**9.** (b)	**10.** (bc)
11. (c)	**12.** (a)	**13.** (d)	**14.** (b)	**15.** (a)
16. (a, b, d)	**17.** (a)	**18.** (a, d)	**19.** (a)	**20.** (b)
21. (b, c, d)				

Numerical Value Questionns

1. 16 : 1

2. $x = 18.12\%$

3. 2218 s

4. 241.11 kJ mol^{-1}

5. 1.31

6. $E_a = 100$ kJ mol^{-1}

7. $K_b = \dfrac{[NH_4^+][OH^-]}{[NH_3]} = 1.8$

= ionisation constant of $aq. NH_3$

8. $T = 282$ K

9. 8500 J/mol

10. – 84297.5 J/mol

11. 10

12. 108

13. 27

14. 10

Comprehension Based Questions

Passage 1 – **1.** (b) **2.** (a) **3.** (c)

Passage 2 – **1.** (a) **2.** (b) **3.** (c)

Passage 3 – **1.** (a) **2.** (a) **3.** (d)

Passage 4 – **1.** (a)

Passage 5 – **1.** (a)

Passage 6 – **1.** (b) **2.** (a)

Passage 7 – **1.** (a) **2.** (b)

Passage 8 – **1.** (a) **2.** (d) **3.** (c)

Matrix-Match Type

1. A→ (3); B→ (4); C→ (2); D→ (1)
2. A→ (3); B→ (4); C→ (2); D→ (1)
3. A→ (3); B→ (4); C→ (2); D→ (1)
4. A→ (1,2); B→ (1,2,3); C→ (1,2); D→ (1,2)
5. A→ (2,3,6); B→ (3); C→ (1); D→ (4,5)
6. A→ (3); B→ (1); C→ (2); D→ (4)
7. A→ (2); B→ (1); C→ (4); D→ (3)

Single Integer Answer Questions

1. (1) 2. (2) 3. (3) 4. (3) 5. (8) 6. (3) 7. (8) 8. (8) 9. (5) 10. (0)
11. (9)

Solutions

Objective Questions Type I [Only one correct option]

1. (*d*) $-\frac{1}{2}\frac{d[SO_2]}{dt}=\frac{-d[O_2]}{dt}=+\frac{1}{2}\frac{d[SO_3]}{dt}$

$\because$ given $\frac{d[SO_3]}{dt}=100 \text{ g min}^{-1}=1.25 \text{ mol min}^{-1}$

$$\therefore \quad \frac{-d[O_2]}{dt}=\frac{1}{2}\frac{d[SO_3]}{dt}=\frac{1.25}{2}\text{ mol min}^{-1}$$

$$=\frac{1.25}{2}\times 32 \text{ g min}^{-1}=20 \text{ g min}^{-1}$$

3. (*a*)

$$pV=nRT$$

$$\left(\frac{dp}{dt}\right)V=\left(\frac{dn}{dt}\right)RT$$

$$\left(\frac{dp}{dt}\right)=\left(\frac{dn}{dt}\right)\frac{RT}{V}$$

Also, $p=\frac{n}{V}RT=CRT$

$$\left(\frac{dp}{dt}\right)=\left(\frac{dC}{dt}\right)RT$$

$$\therefore \quad \left(\frac{dp}{dt}\right)=\left(\frac{dn}{dt}\right)\frac{RT}{V}=\left(\frac{dC}{dt}\right)RT$$

$$\therefore \quad \left(\frac{dp}{dt}\right)\frac{1}{RT}=\left(\frac{dn}{dt}\right)\frac{1}{V}=\left(\frac{dC}{dt}\right)$$

4. (*a*) $2NH_3 \longrightarrow N_2+3H_2$

$$\frac{-d[NH_3]}{2dt}=\frac{+d[N_2]}{dt}=\frac{1}{3}\frac{d[H_2]}{dt}$$

$$\frac{k_1[NH_3]}{2}=k_2[NH_3]=\frac{k_3[NH_3]}{3}$$

$$\therefore \quad 1.5k_1=3k_2=k_3$$

5. (*b*)

$$xA \longrightarrow yB$$

$$-\frac{1}{x}\frac{d[A]}{dt}=\frac{1}{y}\frac{d[B]}{dt}$$

$$\frac{-d[A]}{dt}=\frac{x}{y}\frac{d[B]}{dt}$$

$$\log\left[\frac{-d[A]}{dt}\right]=\log\left[\frac{d[B]}{dt}\right]+\log\left(\frac{x}{y}\right)$$

On comparison,

$$\log\left(\frac{x}{y}\right)=0.3$$

$$\therefore \quad \frac{x}{y}=2$$

9. (*a*) The main conditions for the occurrence of a reaction is proper orientation and effective collision of the reactants. Since the chances of simultaneous collision with proper orientation between more than 3 species is very rare, so reaction with order greater than 3 are rare)

10. (*d*) Rate $\frac{\Delta x}{\Delta t}=\frac{0.2-0}{20-0}$

$$=\frac{0.2}{20}=\frac{1}{100}=1\times10^{-2}\text{ M s}^{-1}$$

11. (*b*)

$$Ag^+ + 2NH_3 \underset{k_b}{\overset{k_f}{\rightleftharpoons}} Ag[NH_3]_2^+$$

$$\left(\frac{dx}{dt}\right)_{net}=k_f[Ag][NH_3]^2-k_b[Ag[NH_3]_2^+]$$

On comparison $k_f=2\times10^7 \text{ L}^2 \text{ m}^{-2}\text{s}^{-1}$

$$k_b=1\times10^{-2}\text{ s}^{-1}$$

$$\therefore \quad \frac{k_f}{k_b}=\frac{2\times10^7 \text{ L}^2 \text{ mol}^{-2}\text{ s}^{-1}}{1\times10^{-2}\text{ s}^{-1}}$$

$$=2\times10^9 \text{ L}^2 \text{ mol}^{-2}$$

12. (*a*)

$$N_2+3H_2 \underset{k_b}{\overset{k_f}{\rightleftharpoons}} 2NH_3$$

$$\left(\frac{dx}{dt}\right)_{net}=k_f[N_2][H_2]^3-k_b[NH_3]^2$$

Also, $\frac{[NH_3]^2}{[N_2][H_2]^3}=\frac{k_f}{k_b}$

or $\frac{[N_2][H_2]^3}{[NH_3]^2}=\frac{k_b}{k_b}=\frac{1\times10^{-3}}{1\times10^{2}}=1\times10^{-5}$

Thus, $\left(\frac{dx}{dt}\right)=0$

18. (*d*)
$$\frac{-d[A]}{dt} = k[A]^n$$
$$1 \times 10^{-4} = k[0.01]^n$$
$$1.41 \times 10^{-4} = k[0.02]^n$$
$$(1.41) = (2)^n$$
$$(2)^{1/2} = (2)^n$$
$$\therefore \quad n = \frac{1}{2}$$
$$\therefore \quad \frac{-d[A]}{dt} = k[A]^{1/2}$$

19. (*b*) Based on (A), rate is independent of (A) and when (B) is doubled, rate is also doubled.

Thus, for forward reaction rate law $= k_1[A]^0 = k_1$

and for backward reaction rate law $= k_2[B]$

Thus, net rate $= k_1 - k_2[B]$

20. (*b*) Reaction ceases if
$$k_1[A][B] = k_2[C][D]$$
$$[A][B] = [C][D]$$

27. (*d*) A is in excess, hence, rate is not affected by change in concentration of A.
$$R = k[0.1]^b$$
$$2k = k(0.4)^b$$
$$2 = (4)^b$$
$$(4)^{1/2} = (4)^b$$
$$\therefore \quad b = \frac{1}{2}$$

31. (*d*) By set I, half-life is 2 min. In set II number of moles have been doubled thus, half-life is also doubled, i.e. now it is 4 min. Thus,

8 mol change to 4 mol in = 4 min

and 4 mol change to 2 mol in = 2 min

Thus, total time = 6 min

35. (*c*)
$$\frac{dx}{dt} = k = 0.025 \text{ M s}^{-1}$$
or
$$\frac{x}{t} = k = 0.025 \text{ M s}^{-1}$$
$$x = 15 \times 0.025 = 0.375 \text{ M}$$
Thus, $[A] = 0.50 - 0.375 = 0.125$ M

36. (*d*) $\frac{dx}{dt} = k$

Rate is constant but concentration of the reactant decreases linearly. At 20 min $[A] = 12$ mol

Thus,
$$\Delta x = 20 - 12 = 8 \text{ mol}$$
$$\Delta t = 20.0 = 20 \text{ min}$$
$$\therefore \quad \frac{\Delta x}{\Delta t} = \frac{8}{20} = 0.4 \text{ mol/min}$$

41. (*c*)
$$k = \frac{2.303}{t}\log\left(\frac{a}{a-x}\right)$$
$$k = \frac{2.303}{90}\log\left(\frac{100}{100-90}\right)$$
$$= \frac{2.303}{90}\log 10 = \frac{2.303}{90} \text{ min}^{-1}$$
Also,
$$k = \frac{2.303}{t_{50}}\log\frac{100}{100-50} = \frac{2.303}{t_{50}}\log 2$$
$$\therefore \quad \frac{2.303 \log 2}{t_{50}} = \frac{2.303}{90}$$
$$\therefore \quad t_{50} = \log 2 \times 90$$
$$= 0.3 \times 90 = 27 \text{ min}$$

42. (*d*) We know that,
$$\text{Rate} = k\,(\text{concentration})^n$$
[n = order of reaction and k = rate constant]

Taking log both side,
$$\log(\text{Rate}) = \log k + n \log[\text{concentration}]$$
Slope of graph is the order of reaction greater the slope, greater is the order of reaction.

∴ Correct sequence for the order of reaction is
$$D > B > A > C.$$
Hence, the correct option is (d).

43. (*b*)
$$T_{50} = 10 \text{ min}$$
$$\therefore \quad k = \frac{0.693}{10} = 0.0693 \text{ min}^{-1}$$
Conc. at start = 10 M

Conc. after 20 min (two half-lives) = 2.5 M
$$\therefore \quad \left(\frac{dx}{dt}\right) = k[A]$$
$$= 0.0693 \times 2.5 \text{ M min}^{-1}$$

46. (*d*) In both sets, 50% of the reactant is converted into products, hence, takes equal time, half-life period being independent of concentration.

47. (*c*)
$$T_{50} = \frac{0.693}{0.0693} = 10 \text{ min}$$
$$2.5 = 20\left(\frac{1}{2}\right)^y$$
$$\therefore \quad \left(\frac{1}{8}\right) = \left(\frac{1}{2}\right)^y$$
$$\left(\frac{1}{2}\right)^3 = \left(\frac{1}{2}\right)^y$$
$$\therefore \quad y = 3 = \frac{t}{t_{50}}$$
$$\therefore \quad t = 30 \text{ min}$$

49. (*c*)
$$T_{50}(\text{zeroth}) = \frac{a}{2k_0}$$
$$T_{50}(\text{first}) = \frac{0.693}{k_1}$$

$$\frac{a}{2k_0} = \frac{0.693}{k_1}$$

$$\therefore \quad \frac{k_1}{k_0} = \frac{2 \times 0.693}{a}$$

$$\frac{\left(\frac{dx}{dt}\right)_1}{\left(\frac{dx}{dt}\right)_0} = \frac{k_1 a}{k_0} = 2 \times 0.693$$

51. (*b*) $\left(\frac{dx}{dt}\right) = k[A]^2$

It represents second order reaction

$$k = \frac{1}{t}\left[\frac{1}{a-x} - \frac{1}{a}\right]$$

$$\frac{1}{(a-x)} = kt + \frac{1}{a}$$

Thus, graph between $(a-x)^{-1}$ and time t is a straight line $(y = mx + c)$

$$\therefore \quad OP = \frac{1}{a} = 0.10 \text{ L mol}^{-1}$$

$$\therefore \quad a = 10 \text{ mol L}^{-1}$$

$$\therefore \quad \left(\frac{dx}{dt}\right) = 1 \times 10^{-2} \text{ L mol}^{-1} \text{ min}^{-1} \times (10 \text{ mol L}^{-1})^2$$

$$= 1.0 \text{ mol L}^{-1} \text{ min}^{-1}$$

58. (*a*) T_{50} (second order) $= T_{50}$ (third order)

$$\frac{1}{k_2 a} = \frac{3}{2k_3 a^2}$$

$$\therefore \quad \frac{k_2}{k_3} = \frac{2a}{3}$$

$$R_2 = \left(\frac{dx}{dt}\right)_2 = k_2(a)^2$$

$$R_3 = \left(\frac{dx}{dt}\right)_3 = k_3(a)^3$$

$$\therefore \quad \frac{R_2}{R_3} = \frac{k_2}{k_3 a} = \frac{2}{3}$$

59. (*c*) The elementary reaction, $A_2 \underset{k_{-1}}{\overset{k_1}{\rightleftharpoons}} 2A$

follows opposing or reversible kinetics,

(i) Rate of the reaction,

$$r = r_{\text{forward}} - r_{\text{backward}}$$
$$= k_1[A_2] - k_{-1}[A]^2 \quad \text{... (i)}$$

(ii) Again, rate of the reaction can be expressed as,

$$r = -\frac{d[A_2]}{dt} = +\frac{1}{2}\frac{d[A]}{dt}$$

So, the rate of appearance of A,

i.e. $\frac{d[A]}{dt} = 2r = 2k_1[A_2] - 2k_{-1}[A]^2$ [From Eq. (i)]

60. (*c*) $RCOOR' + H_2O \xrightarrow{H^+} RCOOH + R'OH$

At $t = 0$:	a	0	0
At time t :	$(a-x)$	x	x
At time ∞ :	$(a-a)$	a	a

At $t = 0, V_0 =$ volume of NaOH due to H^+ (catalyst)

$$V_t = x + V_0$$
$$V_\infty = a + V_0$$

If ester is 50% hydrolysed then $x = \frac{a}{2}$

$$V_t = \frac{a}{2} + V_0$$
$$a = 2V_t - 2V_0$$

$$\therefore \quad V_\infty = 2V_t - 2V_0 + V_0 = 2V_t - V_0$$

61. (*b*) If no acid is present as catalyst then

$$V_0 = 0$$

$$\therefore \quad k = \frac{2.303}{t}\log\frac{V_\infty}{(V_\infty - V_t)}$$

62. (*a*) When 50% inversion has taken place then

$$(a-x) = \frac{a}{2}$$
$$2(a-x) = a$$
$$2(r_\infty - r_t) = r_\infty - r_0$$
$$2r_\infty - 2r_t = r_\infty - r_0$$
$$r_0 = 2r_t - r_\infty$$

64. (*c*) Reaction decay shows emission of two helium atoms. Thus, in two half-lives A decomposed $= \frac{3}{4}$ mol

and helium formed $= \frac{3}{4} \times 2 = 1.5$ mol

$$\therefore \quad p = \frac{n}{V}RT$$
$$= 1.5 \times 0.0821 \times 300$$
$$= 36.94 \text{ atm}$$

65. (*a*) There is an error of 3 dps

$\therefore \quad C_0 = 20$ dps, $C_t = 10$ dps

Thus, half-life = 10 min

In next 10 min $C_t = 5$ dps

$\therefore$ recorded value with error = 8 dps

67. (*c*) $CH_3COOC_2H_5 + NaOH \longrightarrow CH_3COONa + C_2H_5OH$

1 : 1

It follows second order rate law

$$k = \frac{1}{t}\left[\frac{1}{a-x} - \frac{1}{a}\right]$$

At start 5 mL of NaOH ≡ 10 mL of 1 N HCl

$\therefore a =$ millimoles of NaOH at start $= 10 \times 1 = 10$

After 10 min, $(a-x) =$ millimoles of NaOH $= 8 \times 1 = 8$

$$\therefore \quad k = \frac{1}{10}\left[\frac{1}{8} - \frac{1}{10}\right]$$

68. (**c**) Reactants and products are in gaseous state thus,

$$A(g) \longrightarrow B(g) + C(g)$$

	$A(g)$	$B(g)$	$C(g)$
At $t = 0$	p_i	0	0
At $t = t$	$(p_i - x)$	x	x

total pressure at time $t = p_t = p_i - x + x + x = p_i + x$

$\therefore \quad x = (p_t - p_i)$

and $\quad (a - x) = p_i - (p_t - p_i) = 2p_i - p_t$

Given, $\quad p_i = a = 100$ mm

$p_t = 120$ mm

$\therefore \quad (a - x) = 2p_i - p_t = 80$ mm

$$\therefore \quad k = \frac{2.303}{10} \log \frac{100}{80}$$

$$k = \frac{2.303}{10} \log \frac{5}{4}$$

69. (**a**) $\left(\frac{dx}{dt}\right)_0 = k(0.60)(0.80)^2 = 0.384\,k$

$$A(g) + 2B(g) \longrightarrow C(g) + D(g)$$

$A(g)$	$2B(g)$	$C(g)$	$D(g)$
0.60	0.80	0	0
$(0.60 - x)$	$(0.80 - 2x)$	x	x

$x = 0.2$ atm

$\therefore \quad [A] = 0.4$ atm

$[B] = 0.4$

$$\therefore \quad \left(\frac{dx}{dt}\right)_t = k(0.4)(0.4)^2 = 0.064\,k$$

$$\therefore \quad \left(\frac{dx}{dt}\right)_t \bigg/ \left(\frac{dx}{dt}\right)_0 = \frac{0.064k}{0.384k} = \frac{1}{6}$$

70. (**a**) $k = \frac{1}{t} \log_e \frac{C_0}{C} = k \log_e \left(\frac{C_0}{C}\right)$

$$\therefore \quad \log_e \left(\frac{C_0}{C}\right) = 1$$

$$\frac{C_0}{C} = e$$

$$\therefore \quad C = \frac{C_0}{e}$$

71. (**d**) $C = \frac{C_0}{e}$ under given condition

$$\therefore \quad k = \frac{2.303}{t} \log \frac{C_0}{C} = \frac{2.303}{t} \log_{10} e$$

$$k = \frac{2.303}{1/k} \log_{10} e$$

$$\therefore \quad 2.303 \log_{10} e = 1$$

Thus, none (d)

72. (**b**) 0.12 M $\longrightarrow$ 0.06 M 10 h (50% reaction)

0.12 M $\longrightarrow$ 0.03 M 20 h (75% reaction)

Time of 75% reaction $= 2 \times$ time of 50% reaction

Which is property of first order reaction.

73. (**a**) $T_{50} \propto \left(\frac{1}{a}\right)^{n-1}$

$T_{50} \propto a \qquad n = 0$

$T_{50} = ka$

$\log T_{50} = \log a + \log k$

Thus, a graph between $\log T_{50}$ and $\log a$ is a straight line of slope 45°.

74. (**b**) As in Q. 73

$T_{50} = k(a)^{1-n}$

$\log T_{50} = (1 - n) \log a + \log k$

$(1 - n) = 0$

$\therefore \quad n = 1$

75. (**c**)

Order	t_{50}	t_{75}	t_{75} / t_{50}
0	$a/2k_0$	$\frac{3a}{4k_0}$	1.5
1	$0.693/k_1$	$2 \times 0.693/k_1$	2
2	$\frac{1}{k_2 a}$	$\frac{3}{k_2 a}$	3

76. (**a**) We can apply **hit** and **trial** method. First we use integration equation of zeroth order.

t	$[A]$		x	$k_0 = \frac{x}{t}$
0	0.069 M = a		0	
17	0.052 M	$(a - x)$	0.017 M	$\frac{0.017}{17} = 1 \times 10^{-3}$ M min^{-1}
34	0.035 M	$(a - x)$	0.034 M	$\frac{0.034}{34} = 1 \times 10^{-3}$ M min^{-1}
51	0.018 M	$(a - x)$	0.051 M	$\frac{0.051}{51} = 1 \times 10^{-3}$ M min^{-1}

Since, for every set of values k_0 comes out to be constant hence, zeroth order reaction.

$$k_0 = 1 \times 10^{-3} \text{ M min}^{-1}$$

77. (**b**) $\left(\frac{dx}{dt}\right) = k\,[A]^a [B]^b$

$$4\left(\frac{dx}{dt}\right) = k\,[2A]^a [B]^b$$

$$2\left(\frac{dx}{dt}\right) = k\,[A]^a [4B]^b$$

$\therefore \quad 4 = (2)^a \Rightarrow a = 2$

$2 = (4)^b$

or $\quad (4)^{1/2} = (4)^b \Rightarrow b = \frac{1}{2}$

$$\therefore \quad 2A + \frac{1}{2}B \longrightarrow \text{product}$$

$\therefore \qquad -\frac{1}{2}\frac{d[A]}{dt} = -2\frac{d[B]}{dt}$

$$-\frac{d[A]}{dt} = -4\frac{d[B]}{dt}$$

78. (*c*) Let, the rate law is : $r \propto [A]^a[B]^b$

$\therefore$ a and b are the order of reaction w.r.t A and B respectively.

$\Rightarrow$ Comparing first three (I, II, III) experiments :

$$\frac{r_{II}}{r_I} = \left(\frac{0.1}{0.1}\right)^a \times \left(\frac{0.2}{0.1}\right)^b \Rightarrow \frac{2.4\times10^{-2}}{6\times10^{-3}} = 1\times2^b$$

$\Rightarrow \qquad 2^b = 4 \Rightarrow b = 2$

$$\frac{r_{III}}{r_I} = \left(\frac{0.2}{0.1}\right)^a \times \left(\frac{0.1}{0.1}\right)^2$$

$\Rightarrow \qquad \frac{12\times10^{-2}}{6\times10^{-3}} = 2^a \times 1$

$\Rightarrow \qquad 2^a \times 2 \Rightarrow a = 1$

$\Rightarrow r_I = k\times(0.1)^1(0.1)^2 \Rightarrow 6\times10^{-3} = k\times10^{-3}$

$\Rightarrow k = 6\,L^2\,mol^{-2}\,min^{-1}$

$\Rightarrow$ Expt. IV : $r_{II} = 6\times(X)^1\times(0.2)^2$

$\Rightarrow 72\times10^{-2} = 6\times(X)\times(4\times10^{-2}) \Rightarrow X = 0.3\,mol\,L^{-1}$

$\Rightarrow$ Expt. V : $r_V = 6\times(0.3)^1\times(Y)^2$

$\Rightarrow 2.88\times10^{-1} = 6\times0.3\times(Y)^2 \Rightarrow Y = 0.4\,mol\,L^{-1}$

79. (*b*)

pH	$[H^+]$
2	10^{-2} M
1	10^{-1} M

$$\left(\frac{dx}{dt}\right) = k\,(10^{-2})^n$$

$$100\left(\frac{dx}{dt}\right) = k\,(10^{-1})^n$$

$\therefore \qquad 100 = (10)^n$

$$(10)^2 = (10)^n$$

$\therefore \qquad n = 2$

80. (*b*) Half-life period is independent of concentration of zinc thus, order wrt Zn = 1

pH	$[H^+]$	t_{50}
2	10^{-2} M	10 min
3	10^{-3} M	100 min

$$\frac{(t_{50})_2}{(t_{50})_1} = \left(\frac{[H^+]_1}{[H^+]_2}\right)^{n-1}$$

$$\left(\frac{100}{10}\right) = \left(\frac{10^{-2}}{10^{-3}}\right)^{n-1}$$

$$(10) = (10)^{n-1}$$

$\therefore \qquad n - 1 = 1$

$\therefore \qquad n = 2$

Thus, rate law $= k\,[Zn]\,[H^+]^2$

82. (*b*) Reaction is endothermic.

83. (*c*) If $E_a = 10\,kJ\,mol^{-1}$ for $A \rightarrow B$

and $\Delta H = 5\,kJ\,mol^{-1}$ for $A \rightarrow B$

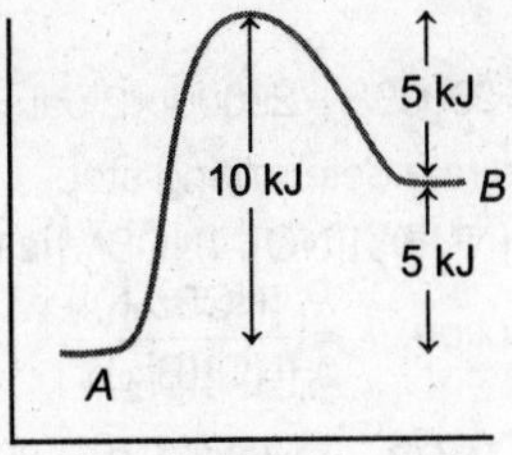

Then, $E_a = 5\,kJ\,mol^{-1}$ for $B \rightarrow A$

85. (*c*) $\log_{10} = \log_{10} A - \frac{E_a}{2.303\,RT}$

$$\text{slope} = -\frac{E_a}{2.303\,R} = -\frac{1}{2.303}$$

$\therefore \qquad E_a = R = 2\,cal$

86. (*a*) Order of reaction can be 0, 1, 2, 3 or even a fractional number.

87. (*d*) Taking slow step

$$\frac{dx}{dt} = k'[X][B]$$

From step I $\quad K_{eq} = \frac{[X]}{[A]^2} \Rightarrow [X] = K_{eq}[A]^2$

$$\frac{dx}{dt} = k'\cdot K_{eq}[A]^2[B] = k[A]^2[B]$$

88. (*c*) For a zero order reaction, $\frac{dx}{dt} = k$,

or $\qquad dx = kdt \qquad [\int dx = \int k\,dt]$

$$x = dt$$

For 100% completion of the reaction, $x = a$

therefore, $\qquad a = kt$ or $t = \frac{a}{k}$

89. (*a*)

	$2A(g)$ $\longrightarrow$	$B(g)$ +	$C(s)$
initial pressure at $t = 0$	p_i	0	solid does not give pressure
after time $t = 10$ min	$p_c - 2x$	x	
after complete reaction	$pi - p_i$	$\frac{p_i}{2}$	

$$p_t = p_c - 2x + x = p_i - x = 300\,P$$

$$p_\infty = p_i - p_c + \frac{p_c}{2} = \frac{p_i}{2} = 200\,P$$

Thus, $\quad p_C = 400\,P = a$ and $x = 100\,P$

Thus, $\quad p_i - x = 300 - 100 = 200\,P$

$\therefore \qquad k = \frac{2.303}{t}\log\frac{p_i}{p_c - x}$

$$= \frac{2.303}{10}\log\frac{400}{200} = 0.0693\,min^{-1}$$

90. (*a*) $k = 3.3\times10^{-4}\,s^{-1}$

unit indicates first order reaction

$\therefore \qquad T_{50} = \frac{0.693}{k} = 2100\,s = 35\,min$

91. (*c*) $k = (5.0 \times 10^{11}\ \text{L mol}^{-1}\ \text{s}^{-1})e^{-29000(\text{K})/T}$

Compare it with $k = Ae^{-E_a/RT}$

$\therefore \quad \dfrac{E_a}{R} = 29000$

$\therefore \quad E_a = 29000R = 29000 \times 2\ \text{cal} = 58\ \text{kcal}$

92. (*a*) Slow step is rate determining step

$\therefore$ Rate law $= k\,[NOBr_2][NO]$, $[NOBr_2]$ is the intermediate

For the fast reaction, $k = \dfrac{[NOBr_2]}{[NO][Br_2]}$

$\therefore \quad [NOBr_2] = k[NO][Br_2]$

$\therefore \quad$ Rate law $= k[NO]^2[Br_2] = k'\,[NO]^2[Br_2]$

93. (*c*)

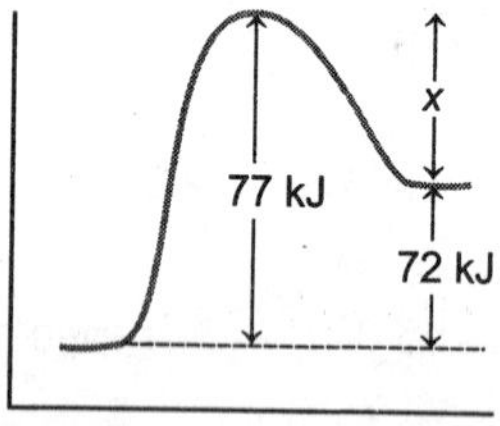

$x(H_2O_2 \longrightarrow H_2O + O) = 77 - 72 = 5\ \text{kJ mol}^{-1}$

94. (*d*) Only statement (d) is incorrect. Corrected statement is "Activation enthalpy to form *C* is 15 kg mol^{-1} more than 5 kg mol^{-1} that is required to form *D*." It can be easily explained by following graph.

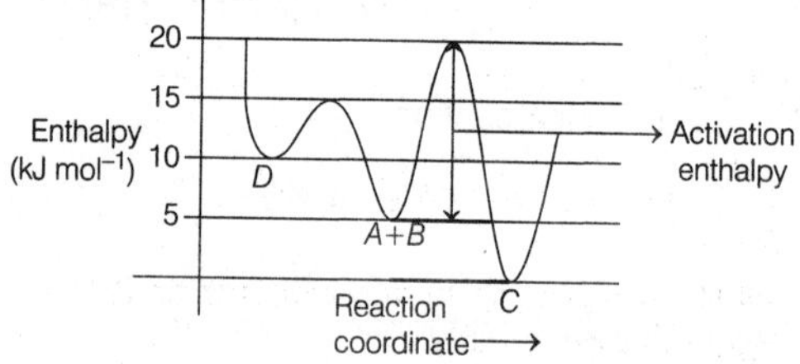

Activation enthalpy (or energy) is the extra energy required by the reactant molecules that result into effective collision between them to form the products.

95. (*d*) $\Delta H(A \rightarrow B) = -10$ kJ (exothermic reaction)

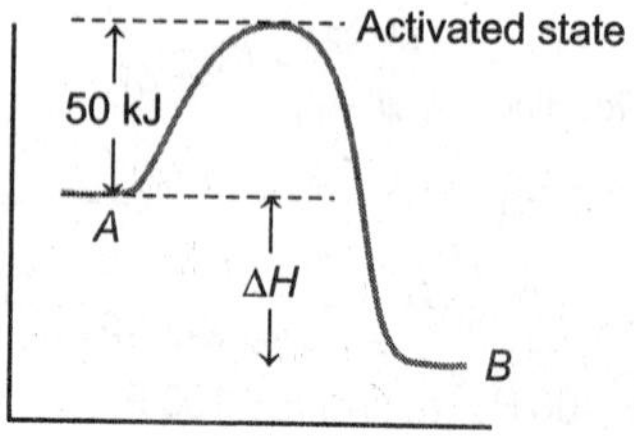

$\therefore \quad \Delta H(B \rightarrow A) = 10\ \text{kJ}$

$E_a(A \rightarrow \text{activated state}) = 50\ \text{kJ}$

$\therefore \quad E_a\ (B \rightarrow \text{activated state}) = 50 + 10 = 60\ \text{kJ mol}^{-1}$

96. (*b*) $k = Ae^{-E_a/RT}$

when, $T \rightarrow \infty$

$\therefore \quad k = Ae^0 = A$

$\therefore \quad A = k = 1.2 \times 10^3\ \text{mol}^{-1}\ \text{L s}^{-1}$

100. (*b*) Graph I indicates zeroth order reaction.

Hence, $\quad -\dfrac{d[A]}{dt} = k$

101. (*a*) $T_{50} \propto \left(\dfrac{1}{a}\right)^{n-1}$ for *n*th order reaction

$$T_{50} = k(a)^{1-n}$$

$$\log T_{50} = (1-n)\log a + \log k$$

Thus, graph between $\log T_{50}$ and $\log a$ is linear of slope

$$(1-n) = \tan 45\ (\text{given}) = 1$$

$\therefore \quad n = 0$

102. (*c*) $k = \dfrac{1}{t}\left[\dfrac{1}{a-x} - \dfrac{1}{a}\right]$ for second order reaction

$\therefore \quad \dfrac{1}{a-x} = kt + \dfrac{1}{a}$

Graph between $(a-x)^{-1}$ and time *t* is linear.

$\therefore \quad \text{slope} = k = \tan\theta = 0.5\ \text{L mol}^{-1}\ \text{min}^{-1}$

$$OA = \frac{1}{a} = 2\ \text{L mol}^{-1}$$

$\therefore \quad a = 0.5\ \text{mol L}^{-1}$

Rate $= k(a)^2 = 0.5 \times 0.5 \times 0.5 = 0.125\ \text{mol L}^{-1}\ \text{min}^{-1}$

103. (*b*) $T_{50} = \dfrac{1}{ka} = \dfrac{1}{0.5 \times 0.5} = 4$ min

106. (*d*)

$$k_A = k_C$$

$$10^{15}\,e^{-2000/T} = 10^{14}e^{-1000/T}$$

$$10 = e^{1000/T}$$

$\therefore \quad \log_e 10 = \dfrac{1000}{T}$

$\therefore \quad T = \dfrac{1000}{\log_e 10} = \dfrac{1000}{2.303}$ K

107. (*c*) $k(\text{no catalyst}) = Ae^{-E_a/RT}$

$k'(\text{catalyst present}) = Ae^{-(E_a - 2)/RT}$

$\therefore \quad \dfrac{k'}{k} = e^{2/RT} = e^{2/0.002 \times 300} = e^{3.33} = 28$

$\therefore \quad k' = 28k$

108. (*b*) Cl attached to N-atom in the reactant is an oxidising agent and can oxidise KI to I_2 thus, iodometric method is used.

109. (*b*) T_{50} is independent of concentration of *A*. Hence, first order reaction.

	A	$\longrightarrow$	$N_2(g)$	
At $t = 0$,	a		0	
At time t,	$(a-x)$		$x = 10$ L	(after 10 min)
At complete reaction,	$(a-a)$		$a = 50$ L	

$\therefore \quad (a-x) = 40$ L

$\therefore \quad k = \dfrac{2.303}{10}\log\dfrac{50}{40} = \dfrac{2.303}{10}\log 1.25\ \text{min}^{-1}$

110. (c) $k = \frac{2.303}{10}\log\frac{100}{90} = 0.0105\ \text{min}^{-1}$

$\therefore \quad T_{50} = \frac{0.693}{0.0105} = 65.7\ \text{min}$

111. (b) Based on the given reaction

$$-\frac{1}{2}\frac{\Delta[N_2O_5]}{\Delta t} = \frac{1}{4}\frac{\Delta[NO_2]}{\Delta t} = \frac{\Delta[O_2]}{\Delta t}$$

$$\frac{k_1}{2}[N_2O_5] = \frac{k_2}{4}[N_2O_5] = k_3[N_2O_5]$$

$\therefore \quad 2k_1 = k_2 = 4k_3$

112. (d) Relative strength = ratio of rate constants $= \frac{2}{1}$

113. (d) $C = C_0 e^{-k_1 t}$

After $t = \frac{2}{k_1}$ ($\frac{1}{k_1}$ is called average life)

$$C = C_0 e^{-2} = \frac{C_0}{e^2} = \frac{100}{e^2}\ \%$$

114. (c) Reaction is of first order

$\therefore \quad C = C_0 e^{-k_1 t} = 10e^{-1} = \frac{10}{e}$ at $t = \frac{1}{k_1}$

115. (a) $T_{50} = 100$ days

$\therefore \quad k\ (\text{first order}) = \frac{0.693}{T_{50}} = \frac{0.693}{100}\ \text{day}^{-1}$

$$C = C_0 e^{-kt}$$

$$= C_0\left(e^{-\frac{0.693}{100}\times 144.3}\right) = C_0 e^{-1} = \frac{C_0}{e},$$

116. (b) Natural life times $= \frac{1}{k} = T_{av}$

$$T_{99.9} = 10 \times T_{50} = \frac{10 \times 0.693}{k} = \frac{6.93}{k}$$

$\therefore$ number of natural life times $= \frac{6.93}{k} \Big/ \frac{1}{k} = 6.93$

118. (a) $\log k\ (\text{min}^{-1}) = 5 - \frac{2000\ K}{T}$

$$\log_{10} k = \log_{10} A - \frac{E_a}{2.303\,RT}$$

I : $\log A = 5$, $A = 10^5$, true

$$\frac{E_a}{2.303\,R} = 2000$$

II : $E_a = 2000 \times 2.303 \times 0.002$ kcal

$= 9.212$ kcal, true

III : Equation represents straight line, hence true,

120. (d) $C \xleftarrow{k_2} A \xrightarrow{k_1} B$

$$\%\ \text{of}\ B = \left(\frac{k_1}{k_1 + k_2}\right) \times 100$$

121. (c) Slow step is rate determining step.

124. (d) T_{50} (second order) $= \frac{1}{ka} = \frac{1}{2 \times 10^{-3} \times 0.1} = 5000$ s

125. (d) $E_a = \frac{2.303\,RT_1T_2}{(T_2 - T_1)}\log\frac{k_2}{k_1}$

If $E_a = 0$, then $\log\frac{k_2}{k_1} = 0$

$\therefore \quad \frac{k_2}{k_1} = 1$

$\therefore \quad k_1 = k_2$

127. (d) $k = Ae^{-E_a/RT} = Ae^{RT/E_a}$

k is least when T is low and E_a high

130. (b) $k_{500} = Ae^{-E_a/500R}$

$$k_{400} = Ae^{-(E_a - 20)/400R}$$

$$e^{-E_a/500R} = e^{-(E_a - 20)/400R}$$

$$E_a/500 = E_a - \frac{20}{400}$$

$$E_a = 100\ \text{kJ mol}^{-1}$$

131. (a) $\frac{k_2}{k_1} = 2$

$\therefore \quad E_a = \frac{2.303 \times 0.002 \times 300 \times 310}{10}\log 2$

$= 12.8898 \approx 12.9$ kcal

134. (d) For second order reaction :

$$k = \frac{1}{t}\left(\frac{1}{a - x} - \frac{1}{a}\right)$$

$\therefore \quad \left(\frac{1}{a - x}\right) = kt + \frac{1}{a}$

Graph between $\frac{1}{a - x}$ and t is a straight line.

136. (d) I. $\left(\frac{dx}{dt}\right) = k$ for zeroth order reaction, i.e. C.

II. Half-life is independent of concentration for the first order reaction, i.e. A.

III. Graph between $(a - x)^{-1}$ and time is linear for second order reaction hence B.

140. (d) $k = 3.0 \times 10^{-5}\ \text{s}^{-1}$

unit of k indicates that it is first order reaction. Thus, rate law is

$$\left(\frac{dx}{dt}\right) = k\,[N_2O_5]$$

$$2.4 \times 10^{-5}\ \text{M s}^{-1} = 3.0 \times 10^{-5}\ \text{s}^{-1}\ [N_2O_5]$$

$\therefore \quad [N_2O_5] = 0.8$ M

142. (c) $k = \frac{2.303}{2 \times 10^4}\log\frac{800}{50} = 1.386 \times 10^{-4}\ \text{s}^{-1}$

143. (a) $k = \frac{2.303}{40}\log\frac{0.1}{0.025} = 0.03466\ \text{min}^{-1}$

$$\frac{dx}{dt} = k\,[A] = 0.03466 \times 0.01$$

$$= 3.47 \times 10^{-4}\ \text{M min}^{-1}$$

144. (d) $\left(\frac{dx}{dt}\right) = k\,[G]^a[H]^b$

$$8\left(\frac{dx}{dt}\right) = k\,[2G]^a[2H]^b$$

$$2\left(\frac{dx}{dt}\right) = k\,[2G]^a[H]^b$$

$\therefore$ $2 = (2)^a \Rightarrow a = 1$

$8 = (2)^a(2)^b$

$4 = (2)^b \Rightarrow b = 2$

Thus, overall order $= 1 + 2 = 3$

145. (*b*) $pV = nRT$

$\therefore$ $p = \frac{n}{V}RT$

$p_{CH_3CHO} = [CH_3CHO]RT$

$\therefore$ $[CH_3CHO] = \frac{p_{CH_3CHO}}{RT}$

$\therefore$ $\frac{-d\,[CH_3CHO]}{dt} = -\frac{1}{RT}\frac{dp_{CH_3CHO}}{dt}$

147. (*b*) $k_B = Ae^{-E_a/RT} = 10^{12} \times 4.35 \times 10^{-8}$

$= 4.35 \times 10^4\ s^{-1}$

Also equilibrium constant $= \frac{k_A}{k_b} = 10^4$

$\therefore$ $k_A = k_B \times 10^4 = 4.35 \times 10^8\ s^{-1}$

148. (*b*) $k = \frac{2.303}{t}\log\left(\frac{a}{a-x}\right) = \frac{2.303}{60}\log 8 = 0.03466\ min^{-1}$

$\left(\frac{dx}{dt}\right) = k\,[A] = 0.03466 \times 0.1 = 3.466 \times 10^{-3}\ M\ min^{-1}$

150. (*b*) Logarithm function is linear which is for first order reaction.

$$\frac{kt}{2.303} = \log a - \log(a-x)$$

$\therefore$ $\log(a-x) = -\frac{kt}{2.303} + \log a$

$\log[H_2O_2]_t = -\frac{kt}{2.303} + \log[H_2O_2]_0$ (constant)

Graph between $\log[H_2O_2]_t$ and t is a straight line.

151. (*b*) $\left(\frac{dx}{dt}\right) = k[A]_0^4$

$\log\left(\frac{dx}{dt}\right) = n\log[A_0] + \log k$

Thus, $n = \text{slope} = \text{order}$

Greater the order, larger the slope.

Thus, $P = 3,\ Q = 2,\ R = 1,\ S = 0$

152. (*a*) For zeroth order, $k = \frac{x}{t}$

$\therefore$ $x = kt$

$a = C_0 =$ initial concentration

$(a-x) = C_t =$ initial concentration

$\therefore$ $x = C_0 - C_t$

$\therefore$ $kt = C_0 - C_t$

$\therefore$ $C_t = C_0 - kt$

153. (*a*) By rate law, reaction is first order in acetone, first order in H^+.

154. (*b*) $-\left(\frac{dN}{dt}\right)_0 = kN_0$

$-\left(\frac{dN}{dt}\right) = kN$

and $N = N_0e^{-kt}$

$\therefore$ $-\left(\frac{dN}{dt}\right) = kN_0e^{-kT} = -\left(\frac{dN}{dt}\right)_0 e^{-kT}$

155. (*b*) For second order reaction

$$k = \frac{1}{t}\left[\frac{1}{[A]} - \frac{1}{[A]_0}\right]$$

$\therefore$ $kt = \frac{1}{[A]} - \frac{1}{[A]_0}$

$kt + \frac{1}{[A]_0} = \frac{1}{[A]}$

$\frac{kt[A]_0 + 1}{[A]_0} = \frac{1}{[A]}$

$\therefore$ $[A] = \frac{[A]_0}{kt[A]_0 + 1}$

157. (*a*) $k = 8.0 \times 10^{-15}\ cm^3\ molecule^{-1}\ s^{-1}$

$= \frac{8.0 \times 10^{-15}}{1000}\ dm^3\ molecule^{-1}\ s^{-1}$

$= \frac{8.0 \times 10^{-15}}{1000}\ dm^3\ molecule^{-1}\ s^{-1}$

$= 4.8 \times 10^6\ dm^3\ mol^{-1}\ s^{-1}$

$$\left(\begin{array}{l} 1\ cm = \frac{1}{10}\ dm \\ 1\ molecule = \frac{1}{N_0}\ mol = \frac{1}{6.0 \times 10^{23}}\ mol \\ \therefore \frac{1}{molecule} = \frac{6.0 \times 10^{23}}{mol} \end{array}\right)$$

158. (*a*) $k = \frac{1}{t}\left[\frac{1}{a-x} - \frac{1}{a}\right] = \frac{1}{t}\frac{x}{(a-x)(a)}$

$k = \frac{1}{t}\frac{x}{[A][A_0]}$

$\therefore$ $x = kt[A][A_0]$

Also, $k = \frac{1}{t}\left[\frac{1}{[A]} - \frac{1}{[A_0]}\right]$

$kt = \frac{1}{[A]} - \frac{1}{[A_0]}$

$kt + \frac{1}{[A_0]} = \frac{1}{[A]} \Rightarrow \frac{kt[A_0] + 1}{[A_0]} = \frac{1}{[A]}$

$\therefore$ $[A] = \frac{[A_0]}{kt[A_0 + 1]}$

$\therefore$ $x = \frac{kt[A_0]^2}{kt[A_0] + 1}$

159. (*a*) The expression for bacterial growth is $N = N_0 e^t$

$$\Rightarrow \quad \frac{N_0}{N} = e^{-t}$$

From 0 to 1 hour $N'(t) = N_0 e^t$

From 1 hour onwards, $\frac{dN}{dt} = -5N^2$

On differentiating the above equation from N' to N we get.

$$\int_{eN_0}^{N} N^{-2} dN = -5\int_1^t dt \qquad [\because \text{At 1 hour, } N' = eN_0]$$

$$\left[\frac{1}{N} - \frac{1}{eN_0}\right] = 5(t-1)$$

Multiply both sides by N_0, we get

$$\frac{N_0}{N} - \frac{1}{e} = 5N_0(t-1)$$

$$\frac{N_0}{N} = 5N_0(t-1) + \frac{1}{e}$$

$$\frac{N_0}{N} = 5N_0 t + \left[\frac{1}{e} - 5N_0\right]$$

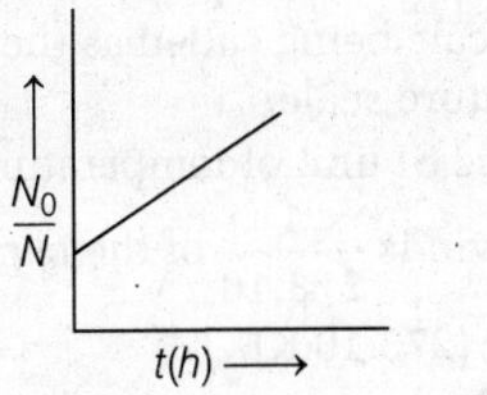

On comparing the above equation with equation of straight line, $y = mx + c$

We get $\quad m = 5N_0$

$$c = \frac{1}{e} - 5N_0$$

$\therefore$ Plot of $\frac{N_0}{N}$ vs t is shown aside.

160. (*d*) $\quad C = C_0 \left(\frac{1}{2}\right)^y$

$$y = \frac{\text{total time}}{T_{50}} = \frac{t}{T_{50}}$$

Case I $\quad C = \frac{40}{4}$

$$\frac{C_0}{4} = C_0\left(\frac{1}{2}\right)^y$$

$$y = 2 = \frac{20}{T_{50}}$$

$\therefore \quad T_{50} = 10 \text{ min}$

Case II $\quad C = \frac{C_0}{16}$

$$\therefore \quad \frac{C_0}{16} = C_0\left(\frac{1}{2}\right)^y \Rightarrow \left(\frac{1}{16}\right) = \left(\frac{1}{2}\right)^y$$

$$\left(\frac{1}{2}\right)^4 = \left(\frac{1}{2}\right)^y$$

$$y = 4$$

$$t = T_{50} \times 4 = 40 \text{ min}$$

161. (*b*) $T_{50} \propto \left(\frac{1}{R_0}\right)^{x-1}$ of order $= x$

If $\quad x = n - 1$

$$T_{50} \propto \left(\frac{1}{R_0}\right)^{n-2}$$

$$T_{50} \propto (R_0)^{2-x}$$

162. (*b*) $\quad \log k = \log A - \frac{E_a}{2.303\,RT}$

$$\log k - \log A = -\frac{E_a}{2.303\,RT}$$

$$\log\left(\frac{k}{A}\right) = -\frac{2.303RT}{2.303RT} = -1$$

$$\frac{k}{A} = \text{antilog } (-1.0) = 1 \times 10^{-1} = 0.1$$

167. (*b*) $E_0 = 209 \text{ kJ mol}^{-1} = 209 \times 10^3 \text{ J mol}^{-1}$

$$k_1 = 1.60 \times 10^{-5} \text{ s}^{-1}, T_1 = 600 \text{ K}$$

$$k_2 = ? \quad T_2 = 700 \text{ K}$$

$$E_a = \frac{2.303\,RT_1T_2}{(T_2 - T_1)} \log \frac{k_2}{k_1}$$

$$209 \times 10^3 = \frac{2.303 \times 8.314 \times 600 \times 700 \log}{(700 - 600)} \frac{k_2}{1.60 \times 10^{-5}}$$

$$\log \frac{k_2}{1.60 \times 10^{-5}} = 2.599$$

$$\frac{k_2}{1.60 \times 10^{-5}} = 397.12$$

$$\therefore \quad k_2 = 397.12 \times 1.60 \times 10^{-5}$$

$$= 6.36 \times 10^{-3} \text{ s}^{-1}$$

168. (*c*) $\quad t_{1/2} \propto \frac{1}{a_0^{n-1}}$;

$$a_0^{n-1} = a_0 \text{ (given)}$$

$$\therefore \quad n - 1 = 1 \Rightarrow n = 2.$$

171. (*d*) For the given reaction

$$-\frac{1}{3}\frac{\Delta[\text{BrO}^-]}{\Delta t} = \frac{\Delta[\text{BrO}_3^-]}{\Delta t} = +\frac{1}{2}\frac{\Delta[\text{Br}^-]}{\Delta t}$$

Given, $\frac{\Delta[\text{BrO}^-]}{\Delta t} = 0.056 \text{ L mol}^{-1}\text{s}^{-1}[\text{BrO}^-]^2$

(being second order reaction)

(a) $\frac{\Delta[\text{BrO}_3^-]}{\Delta t} = -\frac{1}{3}\frac{\Delta[\text{BrO}^-]}{\Delta t} = \frac{0.056}{3} = 0.019 \text{ L mol}^{-1} \text{ s}^{-1}$

Thus, true.

(b) $\frac{\Delta[\text{Br}^-]}{\Delta t} = \frac{2}{3}\left[-\frac{\Delta[\text{BrO}^-]}{\Delta t}\right] = \frac{2}{3} \times 0.056 = 0.037 \text{ mol L}^{-1} \text{ s}^{-1}$

Thus, true.

(c) $-\frac{\Delta[\text{BrO}^-]}{\Delta t} = k[\text{BrO}^-]^2 = 0.056(5)^2 = 0.056 \text{ mol L}^{-1}\text{s}^{-1}$

Thus, true.

09

Thermodynamics

Objective Questions Type I [Only one correct option]

In each of the questions below, four choices are given of which only one is correct.

1. Out of p, V and T

(a) p and V are independent variables and T is dependent variable
(b) p and T are independent variables and V is dependent variable
(c) V and T are independent variables and p is dependent variable
(d) All are dependent as well as independent variables

2. Out of boiling point (I), entropy (II), pH (III) and emf of a cell (IV), extensive properties are

(a) I, II (b) I, II, III
(c) I, III, IV (d) All of these

3. Out of internal energy (*A*), temperature (*B*), pressure (*C*), volume (*D*), work (*E*) and enthalpy (*F*), state functions are

(a) *A, B, C, D* (b) *A, B, C, E, F*
(c) *A, E, F* (d) *A, C, E*

4. Out of following statements : I, II, and III

I. A system may be a complex as a human body or as simple as a mixture consisting of a drop of water.
II. A system is said to be macroscopic when it consists of large number of molecules, atoms or ions.
III. Pressure, volume, temperature and surface area are some macroscopic properties.

Select the correct statements.

(a) I, II, III (b) I, II (c) I, III (d) II, III

5. Out of the following which is not the set of intensive properties?

(a) Boiling point, pH, molarity
(b) Volume, area, length
(c) Freezing point, elevation in boiling point, volume
(d) Refractive index, molality, density

6. Select the correct statements.

(a) The kelvin scale of temperature is based on the absolute zero of temperature and triple point of water, scale being called as thermodynamic temperature scale.
(b) The basic SI unit of temperature is kelvin.
(c) One kelvin is $\frac{1}{273.16}$ of the triple point temperature of water (273.16 K)
(d) All of the above are correct statements

7. Triple point of water corresponds to

(a) 1 atm, 0°C (b) 1 atm, 0 K
(c) 4.58 torr, 0.01°C (d) 1 atm, 0.01°C

8. 1 mole of $Al_4C_3(s)$ reacts with H_2O in a closed vessel at 27°C against atmospheric pressure. Work done is

(a) − 1800 cal (b) − 600 cal
(c) + 1800 cal (d) zero

9. If the above system is in an open vessel then work done is

(a) −1800 cal (b) − 600 cal
(c) + 1800 cal (d) + 600 cal

10. Consider the following chemical changes,

I. $CaC_2(s) + 2H_2O(l) \longrightarrow Ca(OH)_2(s) + C_2H_2(g)$
II. $2SO_2(g) + O_2(g) \longrightarrow 2SO_3(g)$
III. $2Fe(s) + 3H_2O(g) \longrightarrow Fe_2O_3(s) + 3H_2(g)$

Work is done by the system in the cases of

(a) I, II (b) II, III
(c) I only (d) None of these

11. In question (14) above, work is done on the system in the case of

(a) I, II, III (b) I, II (c) I only (d) Only II

12. Consider the following statements,

I. When the system returns to its original condition, the overall change in a state function is zero.

II. When a gas expands, work energy is released, hence work done is negative and is done by the system.

III. $C(s) + CO_2(g) \longrightarrow 2CO(g)$

In this Δn_g = zero, hence no work is done.

Select the correct statement(s)

(a) I, II, III (b) I, II (c) II, III (d) I, III

13. Numerical value of work done is maximum in case of

(a) $C_3H_8(g) + 5O_2(g) \longrightarrow 3CO_2(g) + 4H_2O(l)$

(b) $C(s) + CO_2(g) \longrightarrow 2CO(g)$

(c) $3Fe(s) + 4H_2O(g) \longrightarrow Fe_3O_4(s) + 4H_2(g)$

(d) $NH_4Cl(s) \longrightarrow NH_3(g) + HCl(g)$

14. If $W = -20$ kJ the negative sign indicates that the

(a) expanding system gains work energy and does work on the surroundings

(b) expanding system loses work energy and does work on the surroundings

(c) expanding system gains work energy and does work on the system

(d) expanding system loses work energy and does work by the surroundings

15. 1 mole each of CaC_2, Al_4C_3, Mg_2C_3 reacts with H_2O in separate open flask. Numerical value of work done by the system is in order

(a) $CaC_2 < Al_4C_3 = Mg_2C_3$

(b) $CaC_2 < Al_4C_3 < Mg_2C_3$

(c) $CaC_2 = Mg_2C_3 < Al_4C_3$

(d) $CaC_2 = Mg_2C_3 = Al_4C_3$

16. Select the correct statement(s).

(a) When energy is transferred to the system from the surroundings as work, the surroundings do work on the system and the value of work (W) positive.

(b) When energy is transferred from the system to the surroundings as work, work is done on the surroundings and the value of W is negative.

(c) Both (a) and (b)

(d) None of the above

17. If bond energy of N—H bond is x cal mol^{-1}, change in internal energy in the following chemical process is

$$NH_3(g) \longrightarrow N(g) + 3H(g)$$

(a) x cal (b) $4x$ cal

(c) $3x$ cal (d) $2x$ cal

18. Select the correct statement(s).

(a) When work is done on the system, internal energy of the system increases

(b) When work is done by the system, internal energy of the system decreases

(c) Both (a) and (b)

(d) None of the above

19. Temperature of one mole of helium gas is increased by 1°C, hence increase in internal energy is

(a) 7 cal (b) 5 cal

(c) 3.5 cal (d) 3 cal

20. Which has maximum internal energy?

(a) Helium gas (b) Oxygen gas

(c) Ozone gas (d) Equal

21. Consider the reaction shown

$$2CO(g) + O_2(g) \longrightarrow CO_2(g) + 135.2 \text{ kcal } (\Delta E)$$

This reaction is ... because the sign of ΔE is ...

(a) endothermic, positive

(b) exothermic, positive

(c) endothermic, negative

(d) exothermic, negative

22. The value of ΔE is positive when energy is transferred from the

(a) surroundings to the system

(b) system to the surroundings

(c) system to system

(d) surroundings to surroundings

23. In the following changes A to B, ΔE_1 (change in internal energy of path I) and ΔE_2 (change in internal energy of path II) are related to one each other by

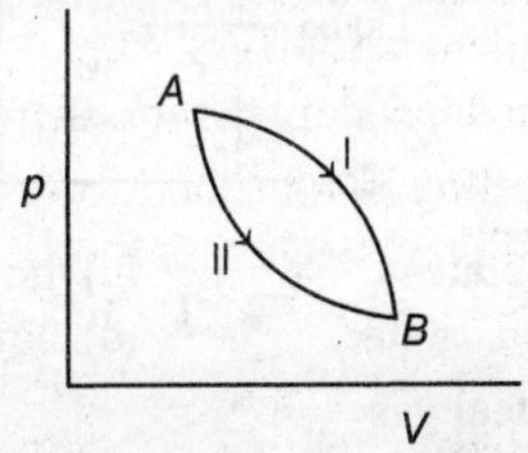

(a) $\Delta E_1 > \Delta E_2$

(b) $\Delta E_2 > \Delta E_1$

(c) $\Delta E_1 = \Delta E_2$

(d) temperature is also required to corelate them

24. During which of the following processes, does entropy decrease ?

I. Freezing of water to ice at 0°C

II. Freezing of water to ice at –10°C

III. $N_2(g) + 3H_2(g) \longrightarrow 2NH_3(g)$

IV. Adsorption of CO(g) and lead surface

V. Dissolution of NaCl in water

(a) I, II, III and IV only

(b) II and III only

(c) I and V only

(d) I, III and V only

25. $\Delta H = \Delta E$ is for the case

(a) $C_2H_4(g) + H_2(g) \longrightarrow C_2H_6(g)$

(b) $C(s) + CO_2(g) \longrightarrow 2CO(g)$

(c) $NH_4HS(s) \longrightarrow NH_3(g) + H_2S(g)$

(d) $CH_4(g) + 2O_2(g) \longrightarrow CO_2(g) + 2H_2O(g)$

26. A gas is cooled and loses 50 J of heat. The gas contracts as it cools and work done on the system equal to 20 J is exchanged with the surroundings. Hence, ΔE is

(a) 70 J (b) −30 J (c) 30 J (d) −70 J

27. For all gases, $C_p - C_V = R$. This R is the

(a) change in kinetic energy when temperature of 1 mole of a gas is increased by 1°C
(b) mechanical work when the temperature of 1 mole of a gas is increased by 1°C
(c) change in potential energy when gas is allowed to fall
(d) None of the above

28. When an ideal gas expands in vacuum work done is

(a) R (b) $\frac{3}{2}R$ (c) $4R$ (d) 0

29. From the figure representing enthalpy change of various transition as indicated, a substance has maximum enthalpy when present in

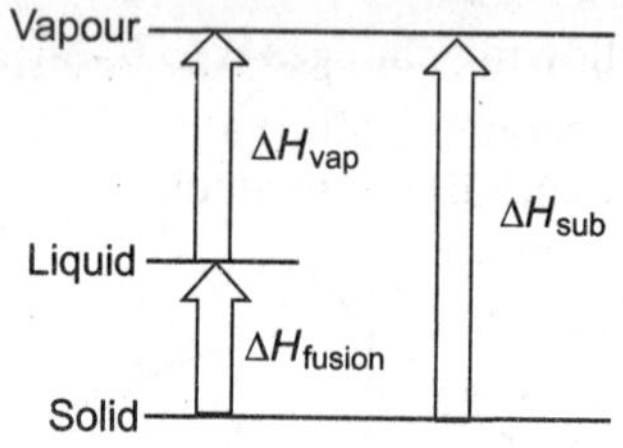

(a) solid state (b) liquid state
(c) gaseous state (d) equal in all states

30. For an ideal gas

(a) pV = constant under isothermal condition
(b) $\left(\frac{\partial E}{\partial V}\right)_T = 0$
(c) Both (a) and (b)
(d) None of the above

31. When 1 mole of $CO_2(g)$ occupying volume 10 L at 27°C is expanded under adiabatic condition, temperature falls to 150 K. Hence, final volume is

(a) 20 L (b) 5 L (c) 80 L (d) 40 L

32. For silver, $C_p(\text{J K}^{-1}\text{mol}^{-1}) = 23 + 0.01\,T$. If the temperature ($T$) of 3 moles of silver is raised from 300 K to 1000 K at 1 atm pressure, the value of ΔH will be close to **[JEE Main 2019]**

(a) 62 kJ (b) 16 kJ (c) 21 kJ (d) 13 kJ

33. Among the following the set of parameters that represents path functions, is **[JEE Main 2019]**

(A) $q + W$ (B) q
(C) W (D) $H - TS$

(a) (A) and (D) (b) (A), (B) and (C)
(c) (B), (C) and (D) (d) (B) and (C)

34. ΔU is equal to **[JEE Main 2017]**

(a) isochoric work (b) isobaric work
(c) adiabatic work (d) isothermal work

35. Given, $\text{C(graphite)} + O_2(g) \longrightarrow CO_2(g)$; $\Delta_r H° = -393.5 \text{ kJ mol}^{-1}$

$H_2(g) + \frac{1}{2}O_2(g) \longrightarrow H_2O(l)$; $\Delta_r H° = -285.8 \text{ kJ mol}^{-1}$

$CO_2(g) + 2H_2O(l) \longrightarrow CH_4(g) + 2O_2(g)$; $\Delta_r H° = +890.3 \text{ kJ mol}^{-1}$

Based on the above thermochemical equations, the value of $\Delta_r H°$ at 298 K for the reaction,

$\text{C(graphite)} + 2H_2(g) \longrightarrow CH_4(g)$ will be **[JEE Main 2017]**

(a) $+78.8 \text{ kJ mol}^{-1}$ (b) $+144.0 \text{ kJ mol}^{-1}$
(c) $-74.8 \text{ kJ mol}^{-1}$ (d) $-144.0 \text{ kJ mol}^{-1}$

36. 8 g of O_2 gas at 27°C is compressed to half of the volume under isothermal and reversible condition. Work done (in cal) on the system is

(a) $W = 0$
(b) $W = 2.303 \times 150 \log 2$
(c) $W = -2.303 \times 150 \log 2$
(d) $W = -2.303 \times 300 \times 8 \times 2 \log 2$

37. Efficiency of a Carnot's engine is 100% when

(a) sink is placed at 0°C
(b) sink is placed at 0 K
(c) source is placed at 100°C
(d) source is placed at 400°C

38. The heats of combustion of carbon and carbon monoxide are − 393.5 and − 283.5 kJ mol^{-1}, respectively. The heat of formation (in kJ) of carbon monoxide per mole is **[JEE Main 2016]**

(a) 676.5 (b) −676.5 (c) −110.5 (d) 110.5

39. One mole of an ideal gas at 300 K in thermal contact with surroundings expands isothermally from 1.0 L to 2.0 L against a constant pressure of 3.0 atm. In this process, the change in entropy of surroundings (ΔS_{surr}) in JK^{-1} is (1 L atm = 101.3 J) **[JEE Advanced 2016]**

(a) 5.763 (b) 1.013
(c) − 1.013 (d) − 5.763

40. Select the correct statement(s).

(a) At absolute zero of the sink work obtained is maximum.
(b) Kinetic energy of a molecule is zero at 0°C
(c) Volume of one mole of gas is 22.4 L at 0 K
(d) All of the above

41. Heat obtained due to expansion of 1 mol of H_2 gas at 1000 K from 10 L to 100 L under isothermal reversible condition is absorbed by an engine having a sink at 300 K. Useful work obtained is

(a) −1382 cal (b) −3224 cal
(c) 1382 cal (d) 3224 cal

42. Which has the maximum entropy of vaporisation?
(a) Ethanol (l) (b) Benzene (l)
(c) Toluene (l) (d) $CO_2(g)$

43. Select the correct statement(s) about entropy S.
(a) $S_{(vapour)} > S_{(solid)} > S_{(liquid)}$
(b) $S_{(vapour)} > S_{(liquid)} > S_{(solid)}$
(c) $S_{(vapour)} < S_{(liquid)} < S_{(solid)}$
(d) $S_{(vapour)} = S_{(liquid)} > S_{(solid)}$

44. Water and alcohols have unusually large entropies of vaporisation. This is because of
(a) larger molecular weight
(b) larger density
(c) extensive hydrogen bonding
(d) lower free energy

45. Select the correct alternate for the endothermic change.
(a) $\Delta H < 0,\ \Delta S_{(system)} < 0$
(b) $\Delta H > 0,\ \Delta S_{(system)} < 0$
(c) $\Delta H < 0,\ \Delta S_{(surroundings)} < 0$
(d) $\Delta H > 0, \Delta S_{(surroundings)} < 0$

46. The combustion of benzene (l) gives $CO_2(g)$ and $H_2O(l)$. Given that heat of combustion of benzene at constant volume is -3263.9 kJ mol^{-1} at 25° C; heat of combustion (in kJ mol^{-1}) of benzene at constant pressure will be ($R = 8.314$ JK^{-1}mol^{-1}) **[JEE Main 2018]**
(a) 4152.6 (b) −452.46
(c) 3260 (d) −3267.6

47. Select the correct alternate about entropy.
(a) $\lim_{T \to \infty} S = 0$
(b) $\lim_{T \to 0} S = \infty$
(c) $\lim_{T \to 0} S = 0$
(d) $S_{(liquid)} > S_{(vapour)}$

48. Which of the following processes is spontaneous?
(a) Diffusion of perfume molecules from one side of the room to the other
(b) Decomposition of solid $CaCO_3$
(c) Heat flow from a cold object to a hot object
(d) Climbing up a mountain

49. Select the correct statement(s).
(a) By Trouton's rule, entropy of vaporisation of most liquids is 88 ± 5 J mol^{-1} K^{-1} at normal b.p.
(b) Due to extensive H-bonding $H_2O(l)$ is most ordered, hence, its entropy of vaporisation is usually high
(c) Entropy of $CaCO_3(s)$ is zero at −273°C
(d) All of the above

50. The true statement amongst the following is **[JEE Main 2020, Jan.]**
(a) S is not a function of temperature but ΔS is a function of temperature.
(b) Both ΔS and S are functions of temperature.
(c) Both S and ΔS are not functions of temperature.
(d) S is a function of temperature but ΔS is not a function of temperature.

51. For silver, C_p(J K^{-1}mol^{-1}) $= 23 + 0.01$T. If the temperature (T) of 3 moles of silver is raised from 300 K to 1000 K at 1 atm pressure, the value of ΔH will be close to **[JEE Main 2019, April]**
(a) 62 kJ (b) 16 kJ (c) 21 kJ (d) 13 kJ

52. Which is not true about G?
(a) G is a state function
(b) Decrease in G, ($-\Delta G$) is equal to net work done
(c) If ΔG is positive, reaction is spontaneous
(d) $\Delta G = \Delta G°$ if $K = 1$

53. Which one of the following equations does not correctly represent the first law of thermodynamics for the given processes involving an ideal gas? (Assume non- expansion work is zero) **[JEE Main 2019, April]**
(a) Cyclic process : $q = -W$
(b) Adiabatic process : $\Delta U = -W$
(c) Isochoric process : $\Delta U = q$
(d) Isothermal process : $q = -W$

54. $H_2O_{ice}(s) \rightleftharpoons H_2O(l)$, $\Delta H° = +6.01$ kJ mol^{-1},
$\Delta S° = 22.0$ J K^{-1} mol^{-1}
Formation of ice is favoured at a temperature
(a) above 0°C (b) below 0°C
(c) at 0°C (d) above 10°C

55. For the reaction, at 298 K
$$CaCO_3(s) \longrightarrow CaO(s) + CO_2(g),$$
$$\Delta H° = 178.3 \text{ kJ}, \Delta S° = 160 \text{ J K}^{-1}$$
Select the correct statement(s).
(a) The reaction is spontaneous at this temperature (298 K)
(b) If temperature is decreased forward reaction is favoured
(c) The reaction is spontaneous in forward direction only at temperature above 1000 K
(d) The reaction is spontaneous in forward direction only at temperature above 1114 K

56. 5 moles of an ideal gas at 100 K are allowed to undergo reversible compression till its temperature becomes 200 K. If $C_V = 28$ JK^{-1} mol^{-1}, calculate ΔU and ΔpV for this process. ($R = 8.0$ JK^{-1} mol^{-1}) **[JEE Main 2019, April]**
(a) $\Delta U = 2.8$ kJ; $\Delta(pV) = 0.8$ kJ
(b) $\Delta U = 14$ J; $\Delta(pV) = 0.8$ J
(c) $\Delta U = 14$ kJ; $\Delta(pV) = 4$ kJ
(d) $\Delta U = 14$ kJ; $\Delta(pV) = 18$ kJ

57. For the reaction, $A \longrightarrow B, \Delta H = +\text{ ve}, \ \Delta S = -\text{ ve}$
This reaction is
(a) non-spontaneous at all temperatures
(b) non-spontaneous at low temperature
(c) non-spontaneous at high temperature
(d) spontaneous at high temperature

58. $H_2O(g) \rightleftharpoons H_2O(l), \Delta H = -10 \text{ kcal mol}^{-1}$. For this transition, vapour pressure change with temperature as given

(a)
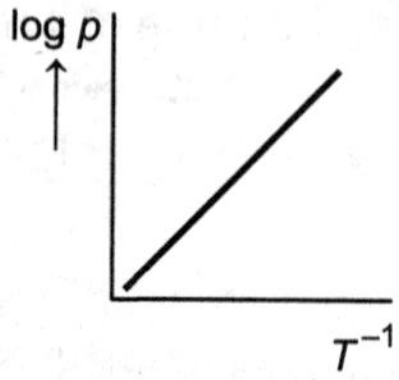

(b)
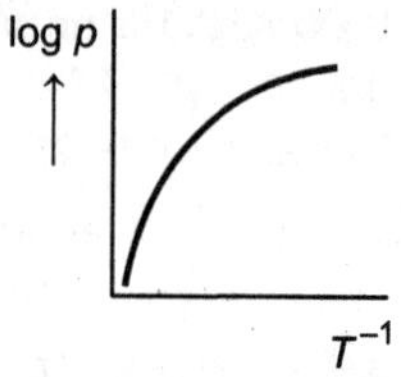

(c)
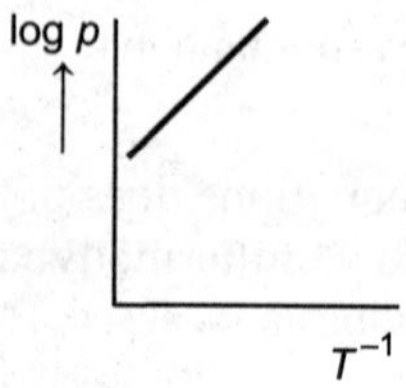

(d)
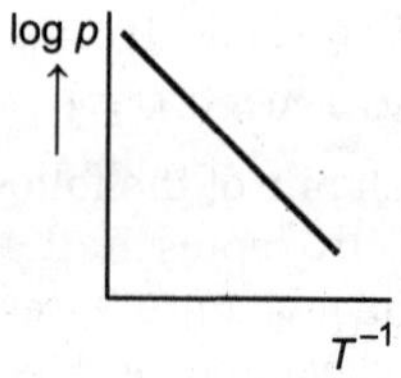

59. For the equilibrium, liquid $\rightleftharpoons$ gas, Clapeyron-Clausius equation(s) is
(a) $P = Ae^{-\Delta H/RT}$
(b) $\log_{10} P = -\dfrac{\Delta H}{2.303\, RT} + \text{constant}$
(c) $\dfrac{d \log_{10} P}{dT} = \dfrac{\Delta H}{2.303\, RT^2}$
(d) All of the above

60. Which is equal to the total work done?
(a) $-\Delta A$ (b) $-\Delta G$
(c) $-\Delta H$ (d) $-\Delta E$

61. For the equilibrium at 298 K

$$2H_2O \rightleftharpoons H_3O^+ + OH^- \qquad K = 1 \times 10^{-14}$$

$\Delta G°$ is approximately
(a) 100 kJ (b) – 80 kJ
(c) 80 kJ (d) –100 kJ

62. If $\Delta G = \Delta H - T\Delta S$ and $\Delta G = \Delta H + T\left[\dfrac{d(\Delta G)}{dT}\right]_P$
then variation of emf of a cell E, with temperature, T, is given by
(a) $\dfrac{\Delta H}{nF}$ (b) $\dfrac{\Delta G}{nF}$ (c) $\dfrac{\Delta S}{nF}$ (d) $-\dfrac{\Delta S}{nF}$

63. 1 g H_2 gas at STP is expanded so that volume is doubled. Hence, work done is
(a) 22.4 L atm (b) 5.6 L atm
(c) 11.2 L atm (d) 44.8 L atm

64. All the natural processes in the universe produce
(a) a decrease in entropy of the universe
(b) an increase in entropy of the universe
(c) no change in entropy
(d) sometimes increase or sometimes decrease in entropy

65. Following reaction occurs at 25°C

$$2NO\,(g, 1\times 10^{-5}\text{ atm}) + Cl_2(g, 1\times 10^{-2}\text{ atm}) \rightleftharpoons 2NOCl\,(g, 1\times 10^{-2}\text{ atm})$$

$\Delta G°$ is
(a) –45.65 kJ (b) – 28.53 kJ
(c) –22.82 kJ (d) –57.06 kJ

66. 1 mole of NH_3 ($\gamma = 1.33$) gas at 27°C is expanded under adiabatic condition to make volume 8 times. Final temperature and work done respectively are
(a) 150 K, 900 cal (b) 150 K, 400 cal
(c) 250 K, 1000 cal (d) 200 K, 800 cal

67. Temperature of 1 mole of a gas is increased by 1° at constant pressure. Work done is
(a) R (b) $2R$
(c) $\dfrac{R}{2}$ (d) $3R$

68. Carnot cycle is said to have 25% efficiency when it operates between T (source) and 300 K (sink). Temperature T is
(a) 300 K (b) 350 K
(c) 375 K (d) 400 K

69. Which is equal to the total work done?
(a) Decrease in G
(b) Decrease in A
(c) Decrease in H
(d) Decrease in E

70. Molar heat capacity of water (liquid) in equilibrium with water vapour at constant pressure is
(a) zero
(b) 40.45 kJ $\text{mol}^{-1}\ \text{K}^{-1}$
(c) 75.48 J $\text{mol}^{-1}\ \text{K}^{-1}$
(d) ∞

71. For a reaction,

$$4M(s) + nO_2(g) \longrightarrow 2M_2O_n(s)$$

The free energy change is plotted as a function of temperature. The temperature below which the oxide is stable could be inferred from the plot as the point at which **[JEE Main 2020, Sep.]**
(a) the slope changes from negative to positive
(b) the free energy change shows a change from negative to positive value
(c) the slope changes from positive to negative
(d) the slope changes from positive to zero

72. The enthalpy of neutralisation of a weak monoprotic acid (*HA*) in 1M solution with a strong base is -56 kJ mol^{-1}. If the unionised acid required 1.5 kJ/mol heat for its complete ionisation and enthalpy of neutralisation of the strong monobasic acid with a strong monobasic base is -57.0 kJ mol. What is the % ionisation of the weak acid in molar solution?
(a) 33.33 % (b) 66.66 %
(c) 35.5 % (d) 71 %

73. A calorimeter initially contains 100 g of water, at a temperature of 24.9 °C. 10 g of ammonium nitrate (NH_4NO_3), also at 24.0°C, is added to the water, and the final temperature is 18.0°C. What is the heat of solution of ammonium nitrate in kJ/mol ? The specific heat capacity of the solution is 4.0 J/°C g.
(a) 422.4 kJ/mol (b) 42.24 kJ/mol
(c) 211.2 kJ/mol (d) 21.12 kJ/mol

74. For an ideal gas Joule-Thomson coefficient is
(a) positive
(b) negative
(c) zero
(d) dependent on molecular weight

75. For $A \longrightarrow B, \Delta H = 4\,\text{kcal mol}^{-1}$, $\Delta S = 10$ cal mol^{-1} K^{-1}. Reaction is spontaneous when temperature can be
(a) 400 K (b) 300 K
(c) 500 K (d) None of these

76. If a process is both endothermic and spontaneous, then
(a) $\Delta S > 0$ (b) $\Delta S < 0$
(c) $\Delta H < 0$ (d) $\Delta G > 0$

77. For the gas-phase decomposition,
$$PCl_5(g) \rightleftharpoons PCl_3(g) + Cl_2(g)$$
(a) $\Delta H < 0, \Delta S < 0$ (b) $\Delta H > 0, \Delta S > 0$
(c) $\Delta H > 0, \Delta S < 0$ (d) $\Delta H < 0, \Delta S > 0$

78. When the reaction mixture is mostly reactants then
(a) $Q << 1$ (b) $RT \log_{10} Q << 0$
(c) $\Delta G > 0$ (d) All of these

79. Under what conditions $\Delta G = \Delta G°$?
(a) $Q = 1$ (b) $Q > 1$
(c) $Q < 1$ (d) $Q = 0$

80. When equilibrium is attained
(a) $Q = 1$ (b) $\Delta G = 0$
(c) $\Delta G° = 0$ (d) $\Delta G = -\,2.303\,RT \log K$

81. $A \longrightarrow B, \Delta H =$+ve. Graph between $\log_{10} p$ and $\frac{1}{T}$ is a straight line of slope $\frac{1}{4.606}$. Hence, ΔH is
(a) 1 cal (b) 2 cal
(c) 4 cal (d) $-$ 1 cal

82. A 0.05 L sample of 0.2 M aqueous HCl acid is added to 0.05 L of 0.2 M aqueous NH_3 in a calorimeter. Heat capacity of entire calorimeter system is 500 J/K. The temperature increase in 1.0 K. Calculate $\Delta_r H°$ in kJ/mol for the following reaction:
$$HCl(aq.) + NH_3(aq) \longrightarrow N_4Cl(aq.)$$
(a) $-$ 50 (b) $-$ 60
(c) $-$55 (d) $-$ 58

83. $T\,\Delta S$ represents
(a) change in free energy
(b) change in internal energy
(c) quantitative measure of the randomness of a system
(d) work done on the system

84. If the inversion temperature of a gas is -80°C, then it will produce cooling under Joule-Thomson effect at
(a) 298 K (b) 273 K
(c) 193 K (d) 173 K

85. Sign of ΔG for the melting of ice is negative at
(a) 265 K (b) 270 K (c) 271 K (d) 274 K

86. Driving force of a reaction is the
(a) resultant of enthalpy and entropy change
(b) resultant of enthalpy and internal energy change
(c) resultant of entropy and internal energy change
(d) term concerned with driving of a car

87. For the reaction,
$$2Cl(g) \longrightarrow Cl_2(g)$$
(a) $\Delta H = +$ ve, $\Delta S = +$ ve
(b) $\Delta H = +$ ve, $\Delta S = -$ ve
(c) $\Delta H = -$ ve, $\Delta S = +$ ve
(d) $\Delta H = -$ ve, $\Delta S = -$ ve

88. $H_2(g) + \frac{1}{2}O_2(g) \longrightarrow H_2O(l)$
BE(H—H) $= x_1$; BE(O=O) $= x_2$
BE(O—H) $= x_3$;
Latent heat of vaporisation of water liquid into water vapour $= x_4$, then $\Delta_f H$ (heat of formation of liquid water) is
(a) $x_1 + \frac{x_2}{2} - x_3 + x_4$ (b) $2x_3 - x_1 - \frac{x_2}{2} - x_4$
(c) $x_1 + \frac{x_2}{2} - 2x_3 - x_4$ (d) $x_1 + \frac{x_2}{2} - 2x_3 + x_4$

89. When one mole of an ideal gas is compressed to half its initial volume and simultaneously heated to twice its initial temperature, the change in entropy (ΔS) is
(a) $C_V \ln 2$ (b) $C_p \ln 2$
(c) $R \ln 2$ (d) $(C_V - R) \ln 2$

90. The third law of thermodynamics states that in the limit $T \to 0$
(a) $G = 0$ (b) $H = 0$ (c) $E = 0$ (d) $S = 0$

91. Select the correct statement(s).
(a) Kinetic energy is the energy of motion
(b) Potential energy is stored energy
(c) Fuel gases (as LPG) contain potential energy in their chemical bonds
(d) All of the above

92. Kinetic energy of an article of 20 g is 4 J while that of another article of same mass is 16 J. Hence, velocity ratio of their motion is
(a) 1 : 4 (b) 4 : 1
(c) 1 : 2 (d) 2 : 1

93. A substance mass of 10 kg at height of 10 m is allowed to fall. A place where kinetic energy is 200 J, potential energy is
(a) 1000 J (b) 800 J
(c) 200 J (d) –800 J

94. For the reaction at 1000°C,

$$CaCO_3(s) \longrightarrow CaO(s) + CO_2(g),$$
$$\Delta G° = -27 \text{ kJ}, p_{CO_2} = 0.0033 \text{ atm}$$

hence, ΔG at this temperature is
(a) –60.5 kJ (b) –87.5 kJ (c) –33.5 kJ (d) +33.5 kJ

95. One mole of an ideal gas ($C_V = 20 \text{ J K}^{-1} \text{ mol}^{-1}$) initially at STP is heated at constant volume to twice the initial temperature. For the process, W and q will be
(a) $W = 0$; $q = 5.46$ kJ
(b) $W = 0$; $q = 0$
(c) $W = -5.46$ kJ; $q = 5.46$ kJ
(d) $W = 5.46$ kJ; $q = 5.46$ kJ

96. For an isomerisation reaction $A \rightleftharpoons B$, the temperature dependence of equilibrium constant is given by

$$\log_e K = 4.0 - \frac{2000}{T}$$

The value of $\Delta S°$ at 300 K is therefore
(a) $4R$ (b) $5R$
(c) $400R$ (d) $2000R$

97. A reaction that is spontaneous can be described as
(a) proceeding in both the forward and reverse directions
(b) having the same rate in both the forward and reverse directions
(c) releasing heat to the surroundings
(d) proceeding without external influence once it has begun

98. In thermodynamics a process is called reversible when **[IIT JEE 2001]**
(a) surroundings and system change into each other
(b) there is no boundary between system and surroundings
(c) the surroundings are always in equilibrium with the system
(d) the system changes into surroundings spontaneously

99. A process which is unfavourable with respect to enthalpy, but favourable with respect to entropy
(a) could occur at low temperature, but not at high temperatures
(b) could occur at high temperatures, but not at low temperatures
(c) could not occur regardless of temperature
(d) could occur at any temperature

100. How much energy must be supplied to change 36 g of ice at 0°C to water at room temperature, 25°C?

$$\Delta H°_{\text{fusion}} = 6.01 \text{ kJ mol}^{-1}$$
$$C_{p, \text{liquid}} = 4.18 \text{ JK}^{-1}\text{g}^{-1}$$

(a) 12 kJ (b) 16 kJ (c) 19 kJ (d) 22 kJ

101. For a particular reaction, $\Delta H° = -38.3$ kJ and $\Delta S° = -113 \text{ JK}^{-1}$. This reaction is
(a) spontaneous at all temperatures
(b) non-spontaneous at all temperatures
(c) spontaneous at a temperature below 338 K
(d) spontaneous at a temperature above 339 K

102. $2Al_2O_3(s) \longrightarrow 4Al(s) + 3O_2(g), \Delta G = +138$ kcal
Considering the contribution of entropy to the spontaneity of this reaction, the reaction is ... and entropy of the system ...
(a) spontaneous, increases
(b) spontaneous, decreases
(c) non-spontaneous, increases
(d) non-spontaneous, decreases

103. All of the statements regarding the symbol ΔG are true except
(a) it refers to the free energy of the reaction
(b) it allows us to predict the spontaneity of a reaction
(c) it allows us to identify an exothermic reaction
(d) it allows us to identify an endergonic reaction

104. When solid melts, there is
(a) decrease in enthalpy (b) increase in enthalpy
(c) decrease in entropy (d) no change in enthalpy

105. Following reaction is occurring in an automobile

$$2C_8H_{18}(g) + 25O_2(g) \longrightarrow 16CO_2(g) + 18H_2O(g)$$

The sign of $\Delta H, \Delta S$ and ΔG would be
(a) +, –, + (b) –, +, –
(c) –, +, + (d) +, +, –

106. Standard state Gibbs' free energy change for isomerization reaction,

$$cis\text{-2-pentene} \rightleftharpoons trans\text{-2-pentene}$$

is – 3.67 kJ/mol at 400 K. If more *trans*-2-pentene is added to the reaction vessel, then
(a) more *cis*-2-pentene is formed
(b) additional *trans*-2-pentene is formed
(c) equilibrium remains unaffected
(d) equilibrium is shifted in the forward direction

107. The factor of ΔG values is important in metallurgy. The ΔG values for the following reactions at 800°C are given as

I. $S_2(s) + 2O_2(g) \longrightarrow 2SO_2(g)$; $\Delta G = -544$ kJ
II. $2Zn(s) + S_2(s) \longrightarrow 2ZnS(s)$; $\Delta G = -293$ kJ
III. $2Zn(s) + O_2(g) \longrightarrow 2ZnO(s)$; $\Delta G = -480$ kJ

The ΔG for the reaction,

$$2ZnS(s) + 3O_2(g) \longrightarrow 2ZnO(s) + 2SO_2(g)$$

will be

(a) – 357 kJ (b) – 731 kJ
(c) – 773 kJ (d) – 229 kJ

108. A gas placed in a cylinder fitted with a frictionless piston expands against a constant external pressure of 1 atm from a volume of 5 L to 10 L by absorbing 400 J heat. The change in internal energy is

(a) 88.76 J (b) –102.22 J
(c) –106.35 J (d) –122.22 J

109. $2H_2(g) + O_2(g) \longrightarrow 2H_2O(l)$. At 300 K, if the entropies of $H_2(g)$, $O_2(g)$ and $H_2O(l)$ are 126.6, 201.20 and 68.0 JK^{-1} mol^{-1} respectively; the entropy change for this reaction is

(a) 22.4 (b) –22.4
(c) –318.4 (d) 318.4

110. A gas expands isothermally against a constant external pressure of 1 atm from a volume of 10 dm^3 to a volume of 20 dm^3. It absorbs 800 J of thermal energy from its surroundings. The ΔU is

(a) – 312 J (b) + 123 J
(c) – 213 J (d) + 231 J

111. 1 mole of an ideal gas for which $C_V = 3/2\,R$ is heated reversibly at a constant pressure of 1 atm from 25°C to 100°C.

The ΔH is

(a) 3.725 (b) 37.5 (c) 375 (d) 3750

112. When 1 mole of water at 100°C is converted into steam at 100°C at a constant pressure of 1 atm., the entropy change (in cal $K^{-1}mol^{-1}$) is: [Heat of vaporisation of water at 100°C = 540 cal/g]

(a) 6.66 (b) 12.44 (c) 20.22 (d) 26.06

113. $NH_3(g) + HCl(g) \longrightarrow NH_4Cl(s)$

For the above reaction

(a) ΔH is –ve and ΔS is +ve
(b) ΔS is –ve and ΔH is +ve
(c) both ΔH and ΔS are –ve
(d) both ΔS and ΔH are +ve

114. 1 mole of an ideal gas is allowed to expand reversibly and adiabatically from a temperature of 27°C. The work done is 3 kJ. The final temperature of the gas is equal to ($C_V = 20$ J $mol^{-1}K^{-1}$)

(a) 75 K (b) 150 K
(c) 225 K (d) 300 K

115. Consider the following statements about thermodynamics.

I. It is macroscopic science concerning such properties as pressure, temperature, and volume.
II. Unlike quantum mechanics, it is not based on a specific molecular model.
III. It helps us to predict the direction and extent of chemical reactions, it tells us nothing about the rate of a process.

Select the correct statements.

(a) I and II (b) II and III
(c) I and III (d) I, II and III

116. Supercooled water is liquid water that has been cooled below its normal freezing point. This state is thermodynamically

(a) stable and tends to freeze into ice spontaneously
(b) unstable and tends to freeze into ice spontaneously
(c) stable and tends to fuse into liquid spontaneously
(d) unstable and tends to fuse into liquid spontaneously

117. Which one of the following statements is false ?

(a) Work is a state function
(b) Temperature is a state function
(c) Change in the state is completely defined when the initial and final states are specified
(d) Work appears at the boundary of the system

118. One mole of a gas undergoes a change of state (2.0 atm, 3.0 L, 95 K) → (4.0 atm, 5.0 L, 245 K) with a change in internal energy, $\Delta U = 30.0$ L-atm. The change in enthalpy (ΔH) of the process in L-atm is

(a) 40.0 (b) 42.3
(c) 44.0
(d) not defined as P is not constant

119. A quantity of 0.50 mole of an ideal gas at 20°C expands isothermally against a constant pressure of 2.0 atm from 1.0 L to 5.0 L. Entropy change of the system is

(a) 6.7 J K^{-1} (b) – 2.8 J K^{-1}
(c) 3.9 J K^{-1} (d) None is correct

120. A quantity of 0.850 mol of an ideal gas initially at a pressure of 15.0 atm and 300 K is allowed to expand isothermally until its final pressure is 1.00 atm. Work done if the expansion is carried out against a constant external pressure of 1.00 atm is (1 L atm = 101.3 J)

(a) – 5.74×10^3 J (b) – 1.98×10^3 J
(c) 5.74×10^3 J (d) 0.00 J

121. When one mole of a monoatomic ideal gas at T K undergoes adiabatic change under a constant external pressure of 1atm, volume changes from 1 L to 2 L. The final temperature in kelvin would be

(a) $\dfrac{T}{2^{2/3}}$ (b) $T + \dfrac{2}{3 \times 0.0821}$
(c) T (d) $T - \dfrac{2}{3 \times 0.0821}$

122. A monoatomic ideal gas undergoes a process in which the ratio of p to V at any instant is constant and equals to 1. What is the molar heat capacity of the gas?

(a) $\frac{4R}{2}$ (b) $\frac{3R}{2}$

(c) $\frac{5R}{2}$ (d) 0

123. $\Delta H_{vap} = 30 \text{ kJ mol}^{-1}$ and $\Delta S_{vap} = 75 \text{ J mol}^{-1} \text{ K}^{-1}$.

Thus, temperature of vapour at one atmosphere is

(a) 400 K (b) 350 K

(c) 298 K (d) 250 K

124. Consider the following figure representing the increase in entropy of a substance from absolute zero to its gaseous state at some temperature.

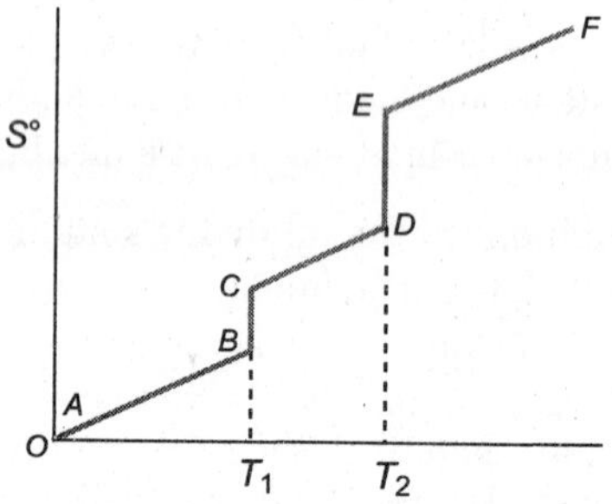

$\Delta S°$ (fusion) and $\Delta S°$ (vaporisation) are respectively indicated by

(a) *AB, BC* (b) *BC, CD*

(c) *BC, DE* (d) *CD, DE*

125. Consider the following cyclic process

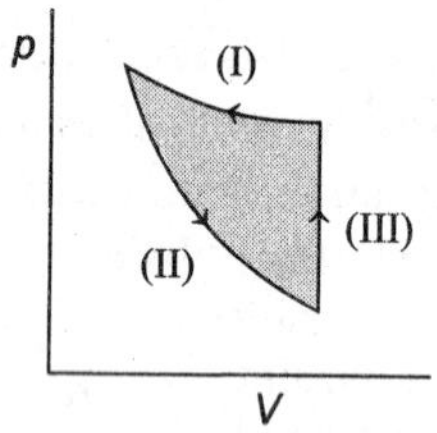

I. Isothermal II. Adiabatic

III. Constant-volume process

Sum of the work and heat in the above is

(a) Zero (b) pV (c) R (d) $-pV$

126. For adiabatic change, some relations are:

I. $w = \int C_V dT$ II. $\frac{V_1}{V_2} = \left(\frac{T_2}{T_1}\right)^{C_V/R}$

III. $pV^{\gamma} = \text{constant}$

IV. $\frac{p_1}{p_2} = \left(\frac{V_2}{V_1}\right)^{C_p/C_V}$

Select the correct statement(s).

(a) All except II (b) All except II, IV

(c) All except I (d) All of these

127. For an isothermal process

I. $\Delta E = 0$ II. $\left(\frac{\partial E}{\partial V}\right)_T = 0$

III. $q + W = 0$

Select the correct statement(s).

(a) I, II (b) I, III (c) II, III (d) I, II, III

128. The direct conversion of A to B is difficult, hence it is carried out by the following shown path

$$\begin{array}{ccc} C & \longrightarrow & D \\ \uparrow & & \downarrow \\ A & & B \end{array}$$

Given, $\Delta S_{(A \to C)} = 50$ eu

$\Delta S_{(C \to D)} = 30$ eu

$\Delta S_{(B \to D)} = 20$ eu

where, eu is entropy unit, then $\Delta S_{(A \to B)}$ is

(a) + 100 eu (b) + 60 eu

(c) − 100 eu (d) − 60 eu

129. If external pressure is held at 5.00 atm in (q–118) above until the expansion stops and then further reduced to 1.00 atm, then work done is

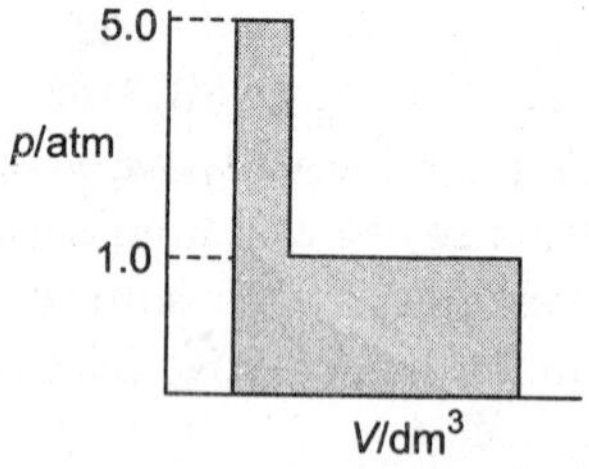

(a) −476 J (b) −4.70 J

(c) −476 kJ (d) −4.70 kJ

130. One of the earliest uses of steam engine was for lifting weights. Estimate the number of moles of superheated steam at 398 K needed to lift a woman of 60 kg mass by 5.0 m

(a) 8.9 mol (b) 0.89 mol

(c) 89 mol (d) 0.089 mol

131. Standard entropy of X_2, Y_2 and XY_3 are 60, 40 and 50 $\text{JK}^{-1} \text{ mol}^{-1}$, respectively. For the reaction,

$\frac{1}{2}X_2 + \frac{3}{2}Y_2 \longrightarrow XY_3, \Delta H = -30$ kJ, to be at equilibrium, the temperature will be

(a) 1250 K (b) 500 K (c) 750 K (d) 1000 K

132. Identify the correct statement regarding a spontaneous process.

(a) For a spontaneous process is an isolated system, the change in entropy is positive

(b) Endothermic processes are never spontaneous

(c) Exothermic process are always spontaneous

(d) Lowering of energy in the reaction process is the only criterion for spontaneity

133. The following diagram represents the $(p-V)$ changes of a gas. Thus, total work done is

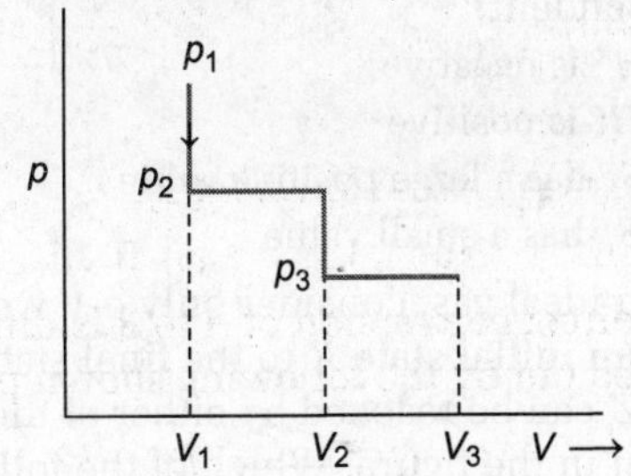

(a) $p_2(V_2-V_1)+p_3(V_3-V_2)$ (b) $p_1(V_2-V_1)+p_3(V_3-V_2)$
(c) $p_2(V_3-V_1)+p_3(V_2-V_1)$ (d) $p_2(V_3-V_2)+p_3(V_2-V_1)$

134. An ideal gas is allowed to expand both reversibly and irreversibly in an isolated system. If T_i is the initial temperature and T_f is the final temperature, which of the following statements is correct?

(a) $(T_f)_{irrev} > (T_f)_{rev}$
(b) $T_f > T_i$ for reversible process but $T_f = T_i$ for irreversible process
(c) $(T_f)_{rev} = (T_f)_{irrev}$
(d) $T_f = T_i$ for both reversible and irreversible processes

135. A piston filled with 0.04 mole of an ideal gas expands reversibly from 50.0 mL to 375 mL at constant temperature of 37.0°C. As it does so, it absorbs 208 J of heat.

The values of q and W for the process will be ($R = 8.314$ J/mol K, ln 7.5 = 2.01) **[JEE Main 2013]**

(a) $q = +208$ J, $W = -208$ J
(b) $q = -208$ J, $W = -208$ J
(c) $q = -208$ J, $W = +208$ J
(d) $q = +208$ J, $W = +208$ J

Objective Questions Type II [One or more than one correct option(s)]

In each of the questions below, four choices are given, of which one or more than one are correct.

1. $C_p - C_V = R$. This R is not equal to
(a) change in KE
(b) change in rotational energy
(c) work done which system can do on expanding the gas per mol per degree increase in temperature
(d) change in PE

2. Which is equal to the total work done?
(a) Decrease in G (b) Decrease in A
(c) Decrease in H (d) Decrease in E

3. Which of the following does not have zero entropy even at absolute zero?

$CO, CO_2, NaCl, NO$

(a) CO, CO_2 (b) CO, NO (c) $CO_2, NaCl$ (d) $NaCl$

4. Although dissolution of NH_4Cl in water is endothermic yet it dissolves because
(a) ΔG is positive (b) ΔH is positive
(c) ΔS is positive (d) ΔA is positive

5. Driving force of a reaction is the
(a) resultant of enthalpy and entropy change
(b) resultant of enthalpy and internal energy change
(c) resultant of entropy and internal energy change
(d) term concerned with driving of a car

6. Sign of ΔG is positive at low temperature when
(a) ΔH is positive and ΔS is positive
(b) ΔH is negative and ΔS is negative
(c) ΔH is negative and ΔS is positive
(d) ΔH is negative and ΔS is zero

7. Given the following reactions

I. $N_2(g) + 2O_2(g) \longrightarrow 2NO_2(g)$, $\Delta H_I = 16.18$ kcal
II. $N_2(g) + 2O_2(g) \longrightarrow N_2O_4(g)$, $\Delta H_{II} = 2.31$ kcal

Based on the above facts
(a) NO_2 is more stable than N_2O_4 at low temperature
(b) N_2O_4 is more stable than NO_2 at low temperature
(c) both are equally stable at low temperature
(d) None of the above

8. In a chemical reaction the values of ΔH and $T\Delta S$ are of the following types

I. ΔH is negative and $T\Delta S$ is positive
II. ΔH is negative and $T\Delta S$ is negative but $|\Delta H| > |T\Delta S|$
III. ΔH is positive and $T\Delta S$ is negative but $|\Delta H| < |T\Delta S|$
IV. ΔH is positive and $T\Delta S$ is negative but $|\Delta H| > |T\Delta S|$

The given reaction is feasible if
(a) I and II are valid
(b) II and III are valid
(c) I and IV are valid
(d) I and III are valid

9. Choose the reaction(s) from the following options, for which the standard enthalpy of reaction is equal to the standard enthalpy of formation. **[JEE Advanced 2019]**
(a) $2C(g) + 3H_2(g) \longrightarrow C_2H_6(g)$
(b) $2H_2(g) + O_2(g) \longrightarrow 2H_2O(l)$
(c) $\frac{3}{2}O_2(g) \longrightarrow O_3(g)$
(d) $\frac{1}{8}S_8(s) + O_2(g) \longrightarrow SO_2(g)$

10. Select the correct statement(s).
(a) Kinetic energy is the energy of motion
(b) Potential energy is stored energy
(c) Fuel gases (as LPG) contain potential energy in their chemical bonds
(d) Potential energy is always zero

11. Consider the following statements,

I. Spontaneous processes involving macroscopic objects proceed with a decrease in potential energy.

II. Expansion of an ideal gas is a spontaneous process in which there is no change of energy at all.

III. For a spontaneous process in an isolated system, the change in entropy is positive.

Select the correct statements.

(a) I, II (b) I, III
(c) II, III (d) I, II, III

12. What are the signs of the entropy charge (+ or –) in the following?

I. A liquid crystallises into a solid

II. Temperature of a crystalline solid is raised from 0 K to 115 K

III. $2NaHCO_3(s) \longrightarrow Na_2CO_3(s) + CO_2(g) + H_2O(g)$

IV. $H_2(g) \longrightarrow 2H(g)$

	I	II	III	IV		I	II	III	IV
(a)	–	+	+	+	(b)	–	–	–	+
(c)	–	–	–	+	(d)	+	–	–	–

13. A reversible cyclic process for an ideal gas is shown below. Here, p, V and T are pressure, volume and temperature, respectively. The thermodynamic parameters q, w, H and U are heat, work, enthalpy and internal energy, respectively. **[JEE Advanced 2018]**

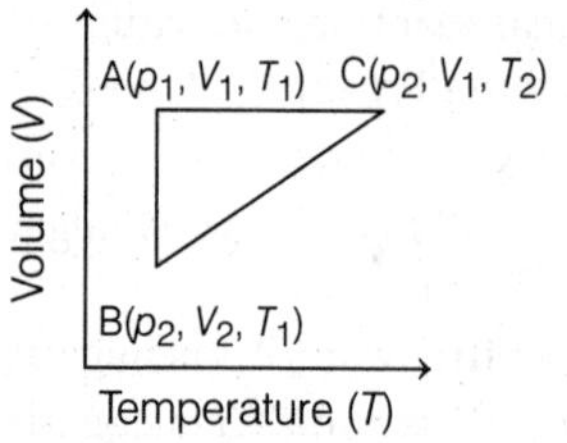

The correct options is (are)

(a) $q_{AC} = \Delta U_{BC}$ and $w_{AB} = p_2(V_2 - V_1)$

(b) $w_{BC} = p_2(V_2 - V_1)$ and $q_{BC} = \Delta H_{AC}$

(c) $\Delta H_{CA} < \Delta U_{CA}$ and $q_{AC} = \Delta U_{BC}$

(d) $q_{BC} = \Delta H_{AC}$ and $\Delta H_{CA} > \Delta U_{CA}$

14. Out of following properties, state functions are **[IIT JEE 2009]**

(a) irreversible expansion work

(b) reversible expansion work

(c) internal energy, E

(d) enthalpy, H

15. Consider the following statement.

I. $S°$ values for all elements in their standard states are positive

II. $S°$ values for all aqueous ions are positive

III. $\Delta S°$ values for all spontaneous reactions are positive

Select the correct statements.

(a) I only (b) I and II only
(c) II and III only (d) I, II and III

16. Under which circumstances would the free energy change for a reaction be relatively temperature independent?

(a) $\Delta H°$ is negative

(b) $\Delta H°$ is positive

(c) $\Delta S°$ has a large positive value

(d) $\Delta S°$ has a small value

17. For an ideal gas, consider only p-V work in going from an initial state X to the final state Z. The final state Z can be reached by either of the two paths shown in the figure. Which of the following choice(s) is (are) correct? [Take ΔS as change in entropy and W as work done].

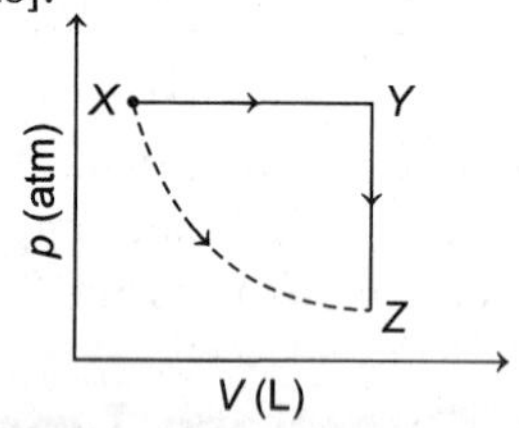

[IIT JEE 2012]

(a) $\Delta S_{X \to Z} = \Delta S_{X \to Y} + \Delta S_{Y \to Z}$

(b) $W_{x \to Z} = W_{X \to Y} + W_{Y \to Z}$

(c) $W_{x \to Z \to Z} = W_{X \to Y}$

(d) $\Delta S_{X \to Y \to Z} = \Delta S_{X \to Y}$

18. In the process of dissolving sugar in water, the entropy increases. This means that the signs of ΔS is ..., and that the randomness of the system ...

(a) undetermined, increases (b) positive, decreases
(c) positive, increases (d) negative, decreases

19. The reversible expansion of an ideal gas under adiabatic and isothermal conditions is shown in the figure. Which of the following statement(s) is (are) correct? **[IIT JEE 2012]**

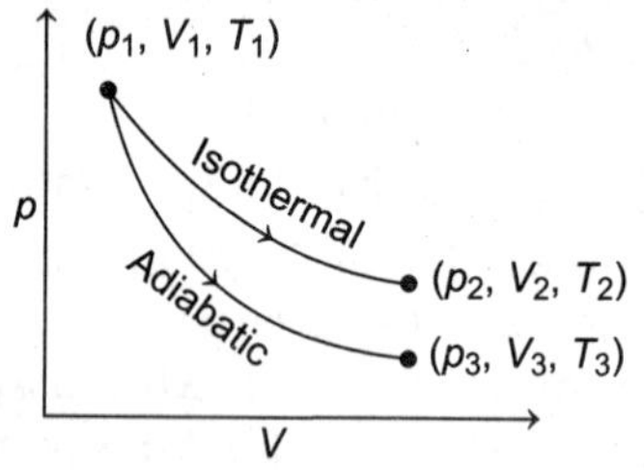

(a) $T_1 = T_2$

(b) $T_3 > T_1$

(c) $W_{isothermal} > W_{adiabatic}$

(d) $\Delta U_{isothermal} > \Delta U_{adiabatic}$

20. Which one of the following are correct statements?

(a) The net increase in entropy of the system is zero in any reversible cyclic process

(b) The isothermally available energy present in a system is called its free energy

(c) The change of free energy with pressure for one mole of a perfect gas at constant pressure is

$$\Delta G = RT \log_e \frac{p_2}{p_1}$$

(d) For a spontaneous change $(\Delta G)_{T,p} > 0$

Numerical Value Questions

All these questions have a Numerical value as their answer, solve the questions and write your answer.

1. The work done when a gas is compressed in a cylinder is 462 J. During this process, there is a heat transfer of 128 J from the gas to the surroundings. .... is the change in internal energy of the process.

2. A certain electric motor produced 15 kJ of energy each second as mechanical work and lost 2 kJ as heat to the surroundings. ...... is the change in the internal energy of the motor and its power supply each second?

3. Consider a system consisting of 1 mole of a diatomic gas contained in a piston. What is the temperature change of the gas if $q = 50.0$ J and $W = -100.0$ J?

4. A gas originally at 1.10 atm and 298 K underwent a reversible adiabatic expansion to 1.00 atm and 287 K. .... is the molar heat capacity of the gas.

5. One mole of an ideal diatomic gas underwent an adiabatic expansion from 298 K, 15.00 atm, and 5.25 L to 2.5 atm against a constant external pressure of 1.00 atm. ... is the final temperature of the system?

6. A strip of magnesium of mass 15 g is dropped into a beaker of dilute HCl. Calculate the work done by the system as a result of the reaction. The atmospheric pressure is 1.0 atm and the temperature 25°C.

7. A gas expands and does p-V work on the surroundings equal to 300 J. At the same time, it absorbs 200 J of heat from the surroundings. What is the change in energy of the system?

8. A sample consisting of 1.00 mole of a perfect gas, for which $C_{V,m} = 3/2\,R$, initially at $p_1 = 1.00$ atm and $T_1 = 300$ K, is heated reversibly to 400 K at constant volume. Calculate the final pressure.

9. For a dimerisation reaction

$$2A(g) \longrightarrow A_2(g),$$

at 298 K, $\Delta U^{\ominus} = -20$ kJ mol^{-1},
$\Delta S^{\ominus} = -30$ JK^{-1} mol^{-1}, then the $\Delta G^{\ominus}$ will be .... J. **[JEE Main 2020, Sep.]**

10. At ...... temperature will the following reaction have $\Delta G = -777.8$ kJ, if $\Delta H = -843.7$ kJ and $\Delta S = -165$ JK^{-1}?

$$2Pb(s) + 3O_2(g) \longrightarrow 2PbO(s) + 2O_2(g)$$

11. .... is the normal boiling point of $Br_2(l)$ if
$\Delta H^{\circ}_{f,\,Br_2(g)} = 30.91$ kJ mol^{-1} and
$S^{\circ}_{Br_2(g)} = 152.2$ J mol^{-1} K^{-1} and
$S^{\circ}_{Br_2(g)} = 245.4$ J mol^{-1} K^{-1}?
Assume that ΔH and ΔS do not change with temperature.

12. The internal energy change (in J) when 90 g of water undergoes complete evaporation at 100°C is ...., (Given : ΔH_{vap} for water at 373 K = 41kJ/mol, $R = 8.314$ JK^{-1}mol^{-1}) **[JEE Main 2020, Sep.]**

13. The Gibbs energy change (inJ) for the given reaction at $[Cu^{2+}] = [Sn^{2+}] = 1$M and 298 K is

$$Cu(s) + Sn^{2+}(aq) \longrightarrow Cu^{2+}(aq) + Sn(s);$$

$(E^{\circ}_{Sn^{2+}/Sn} = -0.16\ 0.16$ V, $E^{\circ}_{Cu^{2+}/Cu} = 0.34$ V,
Take, $F = 96500$ C mol^{-1}) **[JEE Main 2020, Sep.]**

14. Consider a 70% efficient hydrogen-oxygen fuel cell working under standard conditions at 1 bar and 298 K. Its cell reaction is

$$H_2(g) + \frac{1}{2}O_2(g) \longrightarrow H_2O(l)$$

The work derived from the cell on the consumption of 1.0×10^{-3} mole of $H_2(g)$ is used to compress 1.00 mole of a monoatomic ideal gas in a thermally insulated container. What is the change in the temperature (in K) of the ideal gas?

15. A cylinder containing an ideal gas (0.1 mol of 1.0 dm^3) is in thermal equilibrium with a large volume of 0.5 molal aqueous solution of ethylene glycol at its freezing point. If the stoppers S_1 and S_2 (as shown in the figure) are suddenly withdrawn, the volume of the gas in litres after equilibrium is achieved will be ..... (Given, K_f (water) = 2.0 K kg mol^{-1}, $R = 0.08$ dm^3 atm K^{-1}mol^{-1}) **[JEE Main 2020, Jan.]**

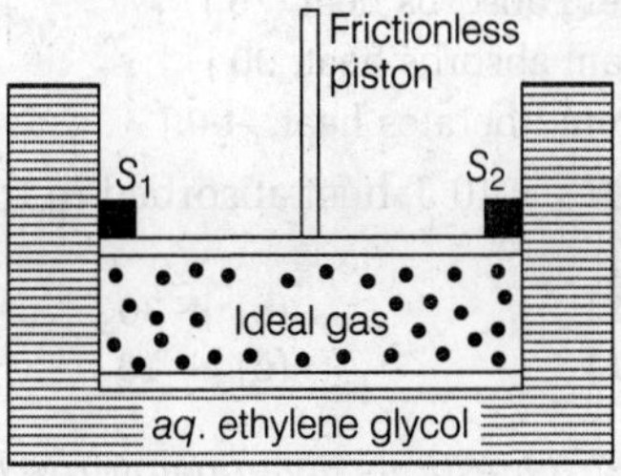

16. For the reaction; $A(l) \longrightarrow 2B(g)$
$\Delta U = 2.1$ kcal, $\Delta S = 20$ cal K^{-1} at 300 K.
Hence, ΔG in kcal is .... **[JEE Main 2020, Jan.]**

17. At constant volume, 4 mol of an ideal gas when heated from 300 K to 500 K changes its internal energy by 5000 J. The molar heat capacity at constant volume is .... **[JEE Main 2020, Jan.]**

18. The magnitude of work done by a gas that undergoes a reversible expansion along the path ABC shown in the figure is .... **[JEE Main 2020, 8 Jan.]**

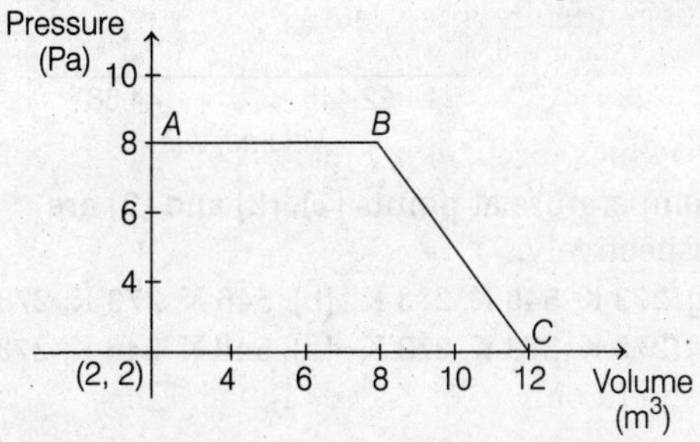

Comprehension Based Questions

In these questions, a passage has been given followed by questions based on it. You have to answer the questions based on the passage given.

***Passage* 1** *Study the following experiment and answer the questions at the end of it.*

When a system is taken from state A to state B along the path ACB as shown, 80 J of heat flows into the system and the system does 30 J of work.

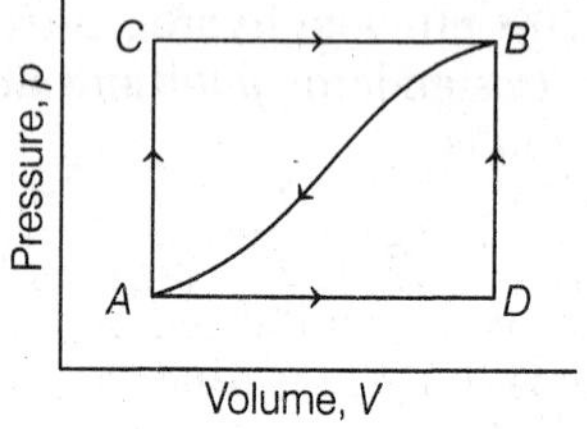

1. How much heat flows into the system along path ADB if the work done is 10 J?
   (a) 80 J (b) –50 J
   (c) 50 J (d) 30 J
2. When the system is returned from state B to A along the curved path, workdone on the system is 20 J. Does the system absorb or liberate heat, and how much?
   (a) System liberates heat, –70 J
   (b) System absorbs heat, 70 J
   (c) System absorbs heat, 90 J
   (d) System liberates heat, –90 J
3. If $H_D - H_A = 40$ J, heat absorbed in the process DB is
   (a) + 50 J (b) + 30 J
   (c) + 60 J (d) + 10 J

***Passage* 2** *Questions given below are based on the following experiment.*

A sample consisting of 1 mole of a monoatomic perfect gas $\left(C_V = \frac{3}{2}R\right)$ is taken through the cycle as shown.

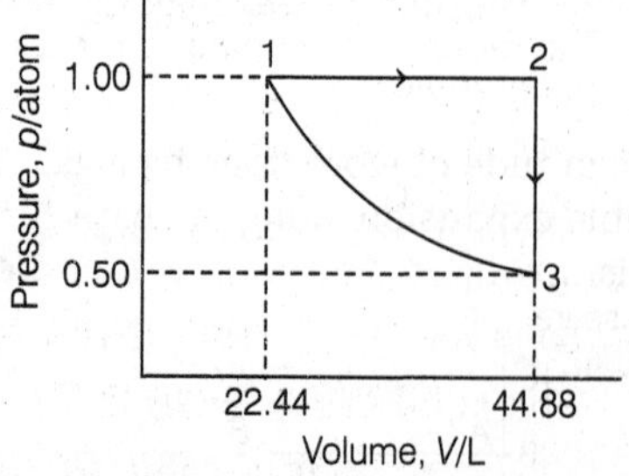

1. Temperature at points (1), (2) and (3) are respectively.
   (a) 273 K, 546 K, 273 K (b) 546 K, 273 K, 273 K
   (c) 273 K, 273 K, 273 K (d) 546 K, 546 K, 273 K
2. ΔH for the overall cycle is
   (a) $+ 5.67 \times 10^3$ J (b) $- 5.67 \times 10^3$ J
   (c) $- 11.34 \times 10^3$ J (d) zero
3. ΔE for the process $(1 \rightarrow 2)$ is
   (a) 0.00 J (b) $+ 3.40 \times 10^3$ J
   (c) – 3.40 J (d) $- 3.40 \times 10^3$ J

***Passage* 3** *Questions given below are based on the following isotherm.*

Assume perfect gas behaviour in the following isotherm. Take $C_V = \frac{3}{2}R, T = 313$ K

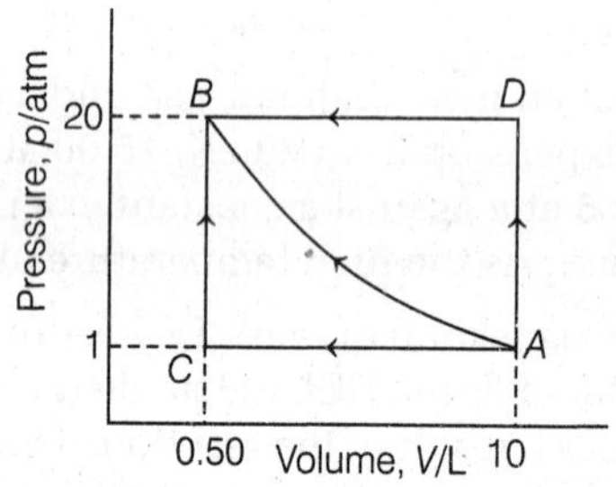

1. Number of moles of gas in this system at the start is
   (a) 0.39 mol (b) 0.17 mol
   (c) 0.78 mol (d) 0.34 mol
2. Work done on the gas along the path ACB is
   (a) 17 kJ (b) 19 kJ (c) 29.5 kJ (d) 10 kJ
3. Work done on the gas along the path ADB is
   (a) 15.2 kJ (b) 17.7 kJ (c) 18.0 kJ (d) 19 kJ

***Passage* 4** *Read the following passage and answer the questions at the end.*

A fixed mass m of a gas is subjected to transformation of states from K to L to M to N and back to K as shown in the figure.

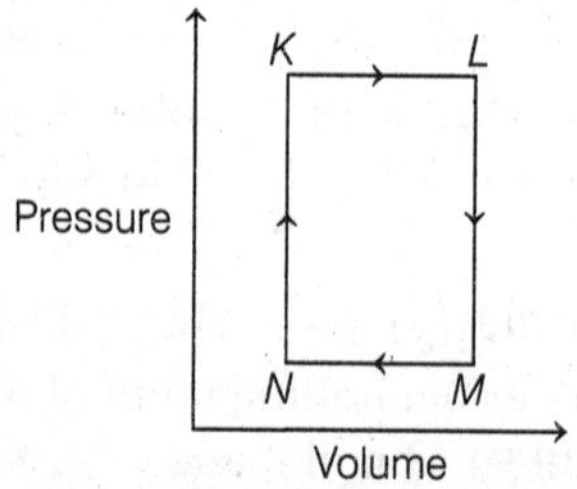

1. The succeeding operations that enable this transformation of states are
   (a) heating, cooling, heating, cooling
   (b) cooling, heating, cooling, heating
   (c) heating, cooling, cooling, heating
   (d) cooling, heating, heating, cooling

2. The pair of isochoric processes among the transformation of states is **[JEE Advanced 2013]**
(a) K to L and L to M (b) L to M and N to K
(c) L to M and M to N (d) M to N and N to K

***Passage* 5** *Following problem is based on thermodynamic law. Answer the questions given at the end of it.*

The second law of thermodynamics is a fundamental law of science. In this problem we consider the thermodynamics of an ideal gas, phase transition and chemical equilibrium.

Three moles of CO_2 gas expands isothermally (in thermal contact with the surroundings; temperature = 15.0°C) against a fixed external pressure of 1.00 bar. The initial and final volumes of the gas are 10.0 L and 30.0 L, respectively.

1. Select the correct order of the entropy change
(a) $\Delta S_{sys} > 0, \Delta S_{surr} = 0$ (b) $\Delta S_{sys} < 0, \Delta S_{surr} > 0$
(c) $\Delta S_{sys} > 0, \Delta S_{surr} < 0$ (d) $\Delta S_{sys} = 0, \Delta S_{surr} = 0$

2. Assuming CO_2 to be an ideal gas ΔS_{system} is
(a) 27.4 J K^{-1} (b) 9.1 J K^{-1}
(c) –27.4 J K^{-1} (d) – 9.1 J K^{-1}

3. $\Delta S_{surrounding}$ is
(a) 27.4 J K^{-1} (b) + 6.94 J K^{-1}
(c) 0.00 J K^{-1} (d) –6.94 J K^{-1}

***Passage* 6** *Answer the questions based on the synthesis of isooctane, an additive for petrol to enhance its octane number.*

The following is an Passage of an alkylation reaction that is important in the production of isooctane (2,2,4-trimethylpentane) from two components of crude oil, isobutane and isobutene. *Iso*-octane is an antiknock additive for gasoline.

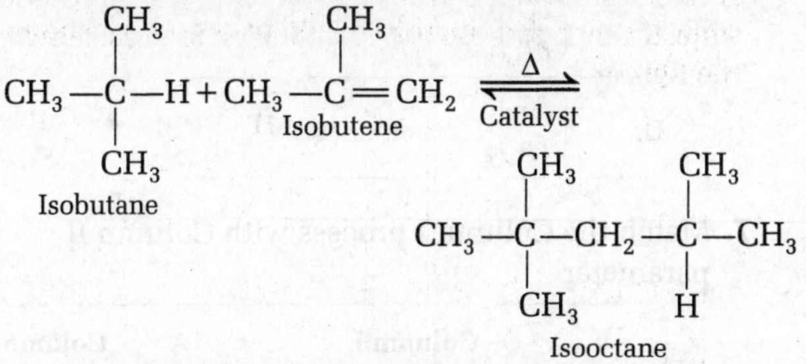

The thermodynamic equilibrium constant, K, for this reaction at 25°C is 4.3×10^6, and $\Delta H°$ is –78.58 kJ/mol.

1. $\Delta G°$ of the above reaction at 25°C is
(a) –16.44 kJ mol^{-1}
(b) +16.44 kJ mol^{-1}
(c) –37.85 kJ mol^{-1}
(d) +37.85 kJ mol^{-1}

2. Select the correct statements.
(a) Increase in temperature displaces the reaction in forward side
(b) Reaction becomes more spontaneous in backward side at 800°C
(c) Catalyst decreases activation energy and thus rate of formation of isooctane is increased
(d) Thermodynamic equilibrium constant is independent of temperature

***Passage* 7** *Consider the following reaction,*

$$2NO(g) + O_2(g) \rightleftharpoons 2NO_2(g); \quad K_p = 1.6 \times 10^{12}$$

and ΔG_f° (NO) at 298 K = 86.6 RT mol^{-1}.

Answer the following questions.

1. What is the value of $\Delta G_f^\circ (NO_2)$ at 298K?
(a) 51.8 kJ mol^{-1}
(b) 103.6 kJ mol^{-1}
(c) – 51.8 kJ mol^{-1}
(d) – 103.6 kJ mol^{-1}

2. What is ΔG_f° for the reaction
$$NO_2(g) \rightleftharpoons NO(g) + \frac{1}{2}O_2(g)?$$
(a) 34.82 kJ mol^{-1}
(b) – 34.82 kJ mol^{-1}
(c) – 69.6 kJ mol^{-1}
(d) +69.6 kJ mol^{-1}

3. If $\Delta G°$ for $N_2O_4(g) \rightleftharpoons 2NO_2$ is 1161 cal at 298K, what is ΔG at this temperature?
(a) 406 cal
(b) – 212 cal
(c) + 203 cal
(d) – 406 cal

***Passage* 8** In the human body, the enzyme phospho glucose mutase catalyses the conversion of

$$A \rightleftharpoons B$$

glucose - 1 - phosphate $\rightleftharpoons$ glucose - 6 - phosphate

K_{eq} = 20 at 300K.

Answer the following questions.

1. $\Delta G°$ at 300K is
(a) – 1.8 kcal (b) + 18.0 kcal
(c) – 1800 kcal (d) – 0.18 kcal

2. If any non-equilibrium exists at
$$(A) = 0.001 \text{ M and } (B) = 0.05 \text{ M}$$
then ΔG is
(a) – 0.55 kcal (b) + 0.55 kcal
(c) + 5.5 kcal (d) – 5.5 kcal

Matrix-Match Type

Given below are Matching Type Questions, with two columns (each having some items) each . Each item of Column I has to be matched with the items of Column II.

1. Match the Column I statement with Column II single term of the statement.

Column I	Column II
A. The amount of energy which must be invested in a reaction to get it started.	1. Endergonic
B. A process or reaction that has a negative value of ΔG.	2. Chemical equilibrium
C. A state in which the rate of forward reaction is exactly equal to the rate of the reverse reaction.	3. Activation energy
D. A process or reaction which consumes heat.	4. Endothermic
E. A process or reaction that has a positive value of ΔG.	5. Exothermic
F. A process or reaction that releases heat.	6. Exergonic

2. Match equation's name in Column I with equation in Column II.

Column I	Column II
A. van't Hoff isochore	1. $\log_e \frac{p_2}{p_1} = \frac{\Delta H_V}{R}\left[\frac{1}{T_1} - \frac{1}{T_2}\right]$
B. Kirchhoff's equation	2. $\Delta G = \Delta H + T\left[\frac{d\,\Delta G}{dT}\right]_p$
C. Clausius-Clapeyron equation	3. $\frac{d \log_e K_p}{dT} = \frac{\Delta H^\circ}{RT^2}$
D. Gibbs-Helmholtz equation	4. $\left[\frac{\partial\,\Delta H}{\partial T}\right]_p = \Delta C_p$

3. Match equation's name in Column I with its presentation in Column II.

Column I (Equation)	Column II (Variation of quantity)
A. Clausius-Clapeyron	1. EMF with concentration
B. Gibbs-Helmholtz	2. Equilibrium constant with temperature
C. Nernst	3. Free energy with temperature
D. van't Hoff	4. Pressure with temperature in phase equilibria.

4. Match the Column I thermodynamic properties with Column II equation.

Column I (Thermodynamic properties)	Column II (Equation)
A. Free energy change of a reaction (ΔG).	1. $-RT \log K$
B. Enthalpy change of a reaction in a standard state (ΔH°).	2. $RT^2\left(\frac{d \ln K}{dT}\right)_P$
C. Entropy change (ΔS°).	3. $-nFE$
D. Free energy change of a reaction in a standard state (ΔG°).	4. $-\left(\frac{d\Delta G}{dT}\right)_P$

5. Match the physical properties in Column I with their relation in Column II.

Column I		Column II
A. ΔG	1.	$(\Delta E + p\Delta V)$
B. ΔH	2.	$-nFE$
C. ΔS°	3.	$-RT \log K$
D. ΔG°	4.	$nR \log\left(\frac{V_2}{V_1}\right)$

6. Match the Column I relation with Column II state functions.

Column I	Column II
A. $\left(\frac{\partial T}{\partial p}\right)_H$	1. $-\frac{H}{T^2}$
B. $\frac{\partial}{\partial T}\left(\frac{G}{T}\right)_P$	2. $-S$
C. $\left(\frac{\partial G}{\partial T}\right)_P$	3. V
D. $\left(\frac{\partial G}{\partial p}\right)_T$	4. $\mu\, JT$

7. Match the Column I process with Column II parameter.

Column I	Column II
A. Reversible adiabatic expansion	1. $\Delta H = 0$
B. Joule-Thomson expansion	2. $\Delta E = 0$
C. Reversible evaporation of a liquid at its normal boiling point	3. $\Delta G = 0$
D. Adiabatic free expansion	4. $\Delta S = 0$

Single Integer Answer Questions

Answer of these questions is a single digit lying between 0 to 9.

1. 1 L of NH_3 at 27°C is expanded adiabatically to x litres and final temperature is – 123°C. What is the value of x?
2. 1 mole of an ideal gas is expanded by increasing its temperature by 1° at constant pressure. How much mechanical work (in cal) does it do?
3. Calculate the work done by the reaction (in Litre-atm)

$$Fe(s) + H_2SO_4(aq) \longrightarrow FeSO_4(aq) + H_2(g)$$

When 0.3125 mole of H_2 gas is collected at 273 K at 1.0 atm.

4. A quantity of 4.0 moles of an ideal gas at 20°C expands isothermally against a constant pressure of 2.0 atm from 1.0 L to 10.0 L. What is the entropy change of the system (in cals)?
5. In a constant volume calorimeter, 3.5 g of a gas with molecular weight 28 was burnt in excess oxygen at 298.0 K. The temperature of the calorimeter was found to increases from 298.0 K to 298.45 K due to the combustion process. Given that the heat capacity of the calorimeter is 2.5 kJ K^{-1}, the numerical value for the enthalpy of combustion of the gas in kJ mol^{-1} is **[IIT JEE 2009]**
6. One mole of an ideal gas is taken from a to b along two paths denoted by the solid and the dashed lines as shown in the graph below. If the work done along the solid line path is W_s and that along the dotted line path is W_d, then the integer closest to the ratio $\frac{W_d}{W_s}$ is

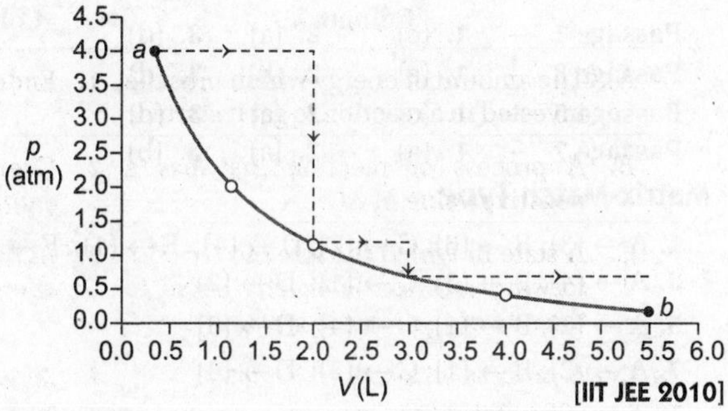

[IIT JEE 2010]

7. In a constant volume, calorimeter, 3.5 g of a gas with molecular weight 28 was burnt in excess oxygen at 298.0 K. The temperature of the calorimeter was found to increase from 298.0 K to 298.45 K due to the combust process. Given that the heat capacity of the calorimeter is 2.5 kJ K^{-1}, the numerical value for the enthalpy of combustion of the gas in kJ mol^{-1} is **[JEE Advaced 2009]**
8. C_V value of H_2 at high temperature is $\frac{x}{2}R$. Find x.

Answers

Objective Questions Type I [Only one correct option]

1. (b)	2. (c)	3. (a)	4. (a)	5. (b)	6. (d)	7. (c)	8. (d)	9. (a)	10. (c)
11. (d)	12. (b)	13. (a)	14. (b)	15. (c)	16. (c)	17. (c)	18. (c)	19. (d)	20. (c)
21. (d)	22. (a)	23. (c)	24. (a)	25. (d)	26. (b)	27. (b)	28. (d)	29. (c)	30. (c)
31. (c)	32. (a)	33. (d)	34. (c)	35. (c)	36. (c)	37. (b)	38. (c)	39. (c)	40. (a)
41. (d)	42. (a)	43. (b)	44. (c)	45. (d)	46. (d)	47. (c)	48. (a)	49. (d)	50. (b)
51. (a)	52. (c)	53. (b)	54. (b)	55. (d)	56. (c)	57. (d)	58. (d)	59. (d)	60. (a)
61. (c)	62. (c)	63. (c)	64. (b)	65. (a)	66. (a)	67. (a)	68. (d)	69. (b)	70. (d)
71. (b)	72. (a)	73. (d)	74. (c)	75. (c)	76. (a)	77. (b)	78. (d)	79. (a)	80. (b)
81. (a)	82. (a)	83. (c)	84. (c)	85. (d)	86. (a)	87. (d)	88. (c)	89. (d)	90. (d)
91. (d)	92. (c)	93. (b)	94. (b)	95. (a)	96. (a)	97. (d)	98. (c)	99. (b)	100. (b)
101. (c)	102. (c)	103. (c)	104. (b)	105. (b)	106. (a)	107. (b)	108. (c)	109. (c)	110. (c)
111. (c)	112. (d)	113. (c)	114. (b)	115. (d)	116. (b)	117. (a)	118. (b)	119. (a)	120. (b)
121. (a)	122. (a)	123. (a)	124. (c)	125. (a)	126. (d)	127. (d)	128. (b)	129. (a)	130. (b)
131. (c)	132. (a)	133. (a)	134. (a)	135. (a)					

Objective Questions Type II [One or more than one correct option(s)]

1. (a, b, d)	2. (b)	3. (b)	4. (c)	5. (a)
6. (a)	7. (b)	8. (a)	9. (c, d)	10. (a, b, c)
11. (d)	12. (a)	13. (b, c)	14. (a, c, d)	15. (d)
16. (d)	17. (a, c)	18. (c)	19. (a, c, d)	20. (a, b, c)

Numerical Value Questions

1. + 334 J 2. $\Delta E = q + W = -2 - 15 = -17$ kJ 3. The gas will cool by 2.4 K. 4. $C_p = 5$ cal mol^{-1}
5. $T_2 = 264$ K 6. -1.55 kJ mol^{-1} 7. -100 J 8. $q = \Delta E - W = 1.25$ kJ
9. -13537.7 10. 399.4 K 11. 331.65 K 12. 189494 13. 96500 14. 13.32 15. 2.18
16. -2.7 17. 6.25 18. 48

Comprehension Based Questions

Passage 1 – 1. (c) 2. (a) 3. (d)
Passage 2 – 1. (a) 2. (d) 3. (b)
Passage 3 – 1. (a) 2. (b) 3. (d)
Passage 4 – 1. (c) 2. (b)
Passage 5 – 1. (c) 2. (a) 3. (d)
Passage 6 – 1. (c) 2. (b)
Passage 7 – 1. (a) 2. (a) 3. (b)
Passage 8 – 1. (a) 2. (b)

Matrix-Match Type

1. A → (3); B → (6); C → (2); D → (4); E → (1); F → (5)
2. A → (3); B → (4); C → (1); D → (2)
3. A → (4); B → (3); C → (1); D → (2)
4. A → (3); B → (2); C → (4); D → (1)
5. A → (2); B → (1); C → (4); D → (3)
6. A → (4); B → (1); C → (2); D → (3)
7. A → (2); B → (1); C → (3); D → (4)

Single Integer Answer Questions

1. (8) 2. (2) 3. (6) 4. (8) 5. (9) 6. (2) 7. (9) 8. (5)

Solutions

Objective Questions Type I [Only one correct option]

8. (*d*) $W = -p\Delta V$
Since, vessel is closed hence, volume = constant
$\therefore \quad \Delta V = 0$
$\therefore \quad W = -p\Delta V = 0$

9.(*a*) $\underset{1\text{ mol}}{Al_4C_3(s)} + 12H_2O(l) \longrightarrow 4Al(OH)_3 + \underset{3\text{ mol}}{3CH_4}$
Initial volume $V_1 = 0$
Final volume $= V_2$ due to 3 mol CH_4

$$W = -p(V_2 - V_1)$$
$$= -p \times V_2 = -\frac{pnRT}{p} = -nRT$$
$$= -3 \times 2 \times 300 = -1800 \text{ cal}$$

10. (*c*)

Reaction	Δn_g	$W = -p\Delta V$	Nature
I	+1	–ve	by the system
II	–1	+ve	on the system
III	0	0	—

11. (*d*) (I) only, (II) only.

15. (*c*) $\underset{1\text{ mol}}{CaC_2(s)} + 2H_2O \longrightarrow Ca(OH)_2 + \underset{1\text{ mol}}{C_2H_2(g)}$

$Al_4C_3(s) + 12H_2O \longrightarrow 4Al(OH)_3 + \underset{3\text{ mol}}{3CH_4(g)}$

$\underset{1\text{ mol}}{Mg_2C_3(s)} + 4H_2O \longrightarrow 2Mg(OH)_2 + \underset{1\text{ mol}}{C_3H_4(g)}$

Thus, $CaC_2 = Mg_2C_3 < Al_4C_3$

17. (*c*) There are three N—H bonds in NH_3 hence, change in internal energy = 3*x*.

19. (*d*) $C_V = \left(\frac{\Delta E}{\Delta T}\right)_V$

$\therefore \quad \Delta E = C_V \,\Delta T = \frac{3}{2} R \times 1$

$= \frac{3}{2} \times 2 = 3$ cal (For monoatomic gas $C_V = \frac{3}{2} R$)

24. (*a*) I. Water $\xrightarrow{0°C}$ ice; ΔS = –ve
II Water $\xrightarrow{-10°C}$ ice; ΔS = –ve
III. $N_2(g) + 3H_2(g) \longrightarrow 2NH_3(g)$; ΔS = –ve
IV. Adsorption; ΔS = –ve
V. $NaCl(s) \longrightarrow Na^+(aq) + Cl^-(aq)$; ΔS = +ve

26. (*b*) System loses heat, hence $q = -50$ J
Also gas contracts due to cooling, hence $W = 20$ J
$\therefore \quad \Delta E = q + W = -50 + 20 = -30$ J

27. (*b*) Mechanical work = $p\Delta V$
For one mole of a gas at temperature *T*
$$pV = RT$$
At constant pressure when temperature is increased by 1° volume increases (say by ΔV) then
$$p(V + \Delta V) = R(T + 1)$$
$\therefore \quad pV + p\Delta V = RT + R$
$\therefore \quad p\Delta V = R$

31. (*c*) For adiabatic expansion
$$\frac{T_2}{T_1} = \left(\frac{V_1}{V_2}\right)^{\gamma - 1}$$
$\gamma = 1.33$ for CO_2 (triatomic gas)

$$\left(\frac{150}{300}\right) = \left(\frac{10}{V_2}\right)^{0.33}$$

$$\left(\frac{1}{2}\right) = \left(\frac{10}{V_2}\right)^{1/3}$$

$$\frac{10}{V_2} = \frac{1}{8}$$

$$\therefore \quad V_2 = 80\text{ L}$$

32. (*a*) According to Kirchoff's relation,

$$\Delta H = n\int_{T_1}^{T_2} C_p dT \quad \ldots(i)$$

where, ΔH = Change in enthalpy.

C_p = Heat capacity at constant pressure.

Given, $n = 3$ moles, $T_1 = 300$ K, $T_2 = 1000$ K, $C_p = 23 + 0.01T$

On substituting the given values in Eq. (i), we get

$$\Delta H = 3\int_{300}^{1000}(23 + 0.01T)dT = 3\int_{300}^{1000} 23dT + 0.01T\,dT$$

$$= 3\left[23T + \frac{0.01T^2}{2}\right]_{300}^{1000}$$

$$= 3\left[23(1000 - 300) + \frac{0.01}{2}(1000^2 - 300^2)\right]$$

$$= 3[16100 + 4550] = 61950 \text{ J} \approx 62 \text{ kJ}$$

33. (*d*) q (heat) and W (work) represents path functions. These variables are path dependent and their values depends upon the path followed by the system in attaining that state. They are inexact differentials whose integration gives a total quantity depending upon the path.

Option (a), i.e. $q + W$ and option (d), i.e. $H\text{–}TS$ are state functions. The value of state functions is independent to the way in which the state is attained. All the state functions are exact differentials and cyclic integration involving a state functions is zero.

34. (*c*) According to first law of thermodynamics,

$$\Delta U = q + W = q - p\Delta V$$

In isochoric process ($\Delta V = 0$), $\Delta U = q$

In isobaric process ($\Delta p = 0$), $\Delta U = q$

In adiabatic process ($q = 0$) $\Delta U = W$

In isothermal process ($\Delta T = 0$) and $\Delta U = 0$

$\therefore$ ΔU is equal to adiabatic work.

35. (*c*) Based on given $\Delta_f H^\circ$

$$\Delta_f H^\circ = H^\circ_{CO_2} = -393.5 \text{ kJ mol}^{-1} \quad \ldots(i)$$

$$\Delta_f H^\circ = H^\circ_{H_2O} = -285.8 \text{ kJ mol}^{-1} \quad \ldots(ii)$$

$$\Delta_f H^\circ = H^\circ_{O_2} = 0.00 \text{ (elements)} \quad \ldots(iii)$$

Required thermal reaction is for $\Delta_f H^\circ$ of CH_4.

Thus, from III

$$890.3 = [\Delta_f H^\circ(CH_4) + 2\Delta_f H^\circ(O_2)] - [\Delta_f H^\circ(CO_2) + 2\Delta_f H^\circ(H_2O)]$$

$$= \Delta_f H^\circ(CH_4) + 0] - [-393.5 - 2 \times 285.5]$$

$$\therefore \quad \Delta_f H^\circ(CH_4) = -74.8 \text{ kJ/mol}$$

36. (*c*) Work done $= 2.303\,nRT \log \frac{V_2}{V_1}$

$$= 2.303 \times \frac{1}{4} \times 2 \times 300 \log \frac{1}{2}$$

$$= -2.303 \times 150 \log 2 \text{ cal}$$

37. (*b*) η (Carnot's cycle) $= \frac{T_2(\text{source}) - T_1(\text{sink})}{T_2}$

$$1 = 1 - \frac{T_1}{T_2}$$

$$\eta = 1 \text{ when } T_1 = 0 \text{ K}$$

38. (*c*) $C(s) + O_2(g) \longrightarrow CO_2(g)$;

$$\Delta H = -393.5 \text{ kJ mol}^{-1} \quad \ldots(i)$$

$$CO + \frac{1}{2}O_2 \longrightarrow CO_2(g);$$

$$\Delta H = -283.5 \text{ kJ mol}^{-1} \quad \ldots(ii)$$

On subtracting Eq. (ii) from Eq. (i), we get

$$C(s) + \frac{1}{2}O_2(g) \longrightarrow CO(g);$$

$$\Delta H = (-393.5 + 283.5) \text{ kJ mol}^{-1} = -110 \text{ kJmol}^{-1} \text{ (approx.)}$$

39. (*c*) By first law, $\Delta E = Q + W$

For isothermal expansion, $\Delta E = 0$

$$\therefore \quad Q = -W$$

$$-Q_{irrev} = W_{irrev} = p\Delta V = 3(2 - 1) = 3 \text{ L atm}$$

Also, $\Delta S_{surr} = \frac{Q_{irrev}}{T} = \frac{(-3 \times 101.3) \text{ J}}{300 \text{ K}}$

$$= -\frac{303.9}{300} = -1.013 \text{ JK}^{-1}$$

40. (*a*) $\eta = 1 - \frac{T_1}{T_2}$

When $T_1 = 0$ K

$\therefore$ $\eta = 1$

Thus, (a) true.

(b) $KE = \frac{3}{2}RT = \frac{3}{2}R(0 + 273)$

Thus, (b) false.

(c) $V = kT = 0$ at 0 K

Thus, false.

41. (*d*) $W = q = 2.303\,nRT \log \frac{V_2}{V_1}$

$$= 2.303 \times 1 \times 2 \times 1000 \log \frac{100}{10} = 4606 \text{ cal}$$

$$\eta = \frac{T_2 - T_1}{T_2} = \frac{q_2 - q_1}{q_2} = 1 - \frac{q_1}{q_2}$$

$$\therefore \quad \frac{T_1}{T_2} = \frac{q_1}{q_2}$$

$$\frac{300}{1000} = \frac{q_1}{4606}$$

$$q_1 = 1381.8 \text{ cal}$$

$\therefore$ Thus, useful work obtained

$$= 4606 - 1381.8 = 3224.2 \text{ cal}$$

46. (***d***) Calculate the heat of combustion with the help of following formula

$$\Delta H_p = \Delta U + \Delta n_g RT$$

where, ΔH_p = Heat of combustion at constant pressure

ΔU = Heat at constant volume (It is also called ΔE)

Δn_g = *Change in number of moles (In gaseous state).*

R = Gas constant; T = Temperature.

From the equation,

$$C_6H_6(l) + \frac{15}{2}O_2(g) \longrightarrow 6CO_2(g) + 3H_2O(l)$$

Change in the number of gaseous moles i.e.

$$\Delta n_g = 6 - \frac{15}{2} = -\frac{3}{2} \text{ or } -1.5$$

Now we have Δn_g and other values given in the question are

$$\Delta U = -3263.9 \text{ kJ/mol}$$

$$T = 25° \text{ C} = 273 + 25 = 298 \text{ K}$$

$$R = 8.314 \text{ JK}^{-1}\text{mol}^{-1}$$

So, $\quad \Delta H_p = (-3263.9) + (-1.5) \times 8.314 \times 10^{-3} \times 298$

$$= -3267.6 \text{ kJ mol}^{-1}$$

50. (***b***) Statement (b) is a true statement whereas all other statements are incorrect.

By definition,

$$dS = \frac{dQ}{T} \text{ and } \Delta S = \frac{\int dQ}{T}$$

$\therefore$ ΔS is a function of temperature.

S is also a function of temperature.

51. (***a***) According to Kirchoff's relation,

$$\Delta H = n\int_{T_1}^{T_2} C_p dT \quad \ldots\text{(i)}$$

where, ΔH = Change in enthalpy.

C_p = Heat capacity at constant pressure.

Given, $n = 3$ moles, $T_1 = 300$ K, $T_2 = 1000$ K,

$C_p = 23 + 0.01T$

On substituting the given values in Eq. (i), we get

$$\Delta H = 3\int_{300}^{1000}(23 + 0.01T)dT = 3\int_{300}^{1000} 23dT + 0.01T\,dT$$

$$= 3\left[23T + \frac{0.01T^2}{2}\right]_{300}^{1000}$$

$$= 3\left[23(1000-300) + \frac{0.01}{2}(1000^2 - 300^2)\right]$$

$$= 3[16100 + 4550] = 61950 \text{ J} \approx 62 \text{ kJ}$$

53. (***b***) From the 1st law of thermodynamics,

$$\Delta U = q + W$$

where, ΔU = change in internal energy

q = heat, W = work done

The above equation can be represented for the given processes involving ideal gas as follows:

(a) **Cyclic process** For cyclic process, $\Delta U = 0$

$$\therefore \quad q = -W$$

Thus, option (a) is correct.

(b) **Adiabatic process** For adiabatic process,

$$q = 0 \Rightarrow \Delta U = W$$

Thus, option (b) is incorrect.

(c) **Isochoric process** For isochoric process, $\Delta V = 0$. Thus, $W = 0$ ($\because W = p\Delta V$).

$$\therefore \quad \Delta V = q$$

Thus, option (c) is correct.

(d) **Isothermal process** For isothermal process,

$$\Delta U = 0$$

$$\therefore \quad q = -W$$

Thus, option (d) is correct.

56. (***c***) Given, $n = 5$ mol, $T_2 = 200$ K, $T_1 = 100$ K

$$C_V = 28 \text{ JK}^{-1}\text{mol}^{-1}$$

$$\Delta U = nC_V\Delta T = nC_V(T_2 - T_1)$$

$$= 5 \text{ mol} \times 28 \text{ JK}^{-1}\text{mol}^{-1} \times (200-100) \text{ K}$$

$$= 14{,}000 \text{ J} = 14 \text{ kJ}$$

$$\Delta pV = nR\Delta T = nR(T_2 - T_1)$$

$$= 5 \text{ mol} \times 8 \text{ JK}^{-1}\text{ mol}^{-1} \times (200-100) \text{ K}$$

$$= 4000 \text{ J} = 4 \text{ kJ}$$

61. (***c***) $\Delta G° = -2.303 RT \log K$

$$= -2.303 \times 8.3143 \times 10^{-3} \times 298 \log 1 \times 10^{-14}$$

$$= 80 \text{ kJ}$$

62. (***c***) On comparison

$$\Delta S = -\left(\frac{d(\Delta G)}{dT}\right)_p = nF\left(\frac{dE_{cell}}{dT}\right)_p$$

$$\therefore \quad \left(\frac{dE_{cell}}{d}\right)_p = \frac{\Delta S}{nF}$$

63. (***c***) $\quad$ 1 g H_2 at STP = 0.5 mol = 11.2 L = V_1

$$W = p(V_2 - V_1) = p(2V_1 - V_1) = pV_1 = 1 \times 11.2 \text{ L atm}$$

65. (***a***) $2NO(g) + Cl_2(g) \rightleftharpoons 2NOCl(g)$

$$K_p = \frac{p^2_{NOCl}}{p^2_{NO}\, p_{Cl_2}} = 1 \times 10^8$$

K_p is thermodynamic equilibrium constant (relative to 1 atm) and is considered as unitless quantity.

$$\Delta G° = -2.303RT \log K_p$$

$$= -2.303 \times 8.314 \times 10^{-3} \times 298 \log 10^8 \text{ kJ}$$

$$= -45.65 \text{ kJ}$$

66. (*a*) For adiabatic change

$$T_2 = T_1\left(\frac{V_1}{V_2}\right)^{\gamma-1} = 300\left(\frac{1}{8}\right)^{1.33-1}$$

$$= 300\left(\frac{1}{8}\right)^{1/2} = 150\,K$$

$$W = -nC_V(T_2 - T_1)$$

$$= -1\times 3\times 2\,(150-300) = 900 \text{ cal}$$

67. (*a*) $pV = RT$ at temperature T K

$p(V+\Delta V) = R(T+1)$ at temperature $(T+1)$ K

$\therefore \quad pV + p\Delta V = RT + R$

$\therefore \quad p\Delta V = R$

68. (*d*) $$\eta = \frac{T_2\,(\text{source}) - T_1\,(\text{sink})}{T_2}$$

$$0.25 = \frac{T_2 - 300}{T_2} = 1 - \frac{300}{T_2}$$

$\therefore \quad T_2 = 400$ K

70. (*d*) When two phases are in equilibrium, temperature is constant, hence, $\Delta T = 0, C_p = \infty$

74. (*c*) If gas is ideal, there is no force of attraction between molecules, hence, expansion takes place without loss of energy.

75. (*c*) $$\Delta G = \Delta H - T\,\Delta S$$

For spontaneous reaction, $\Delta G = -$ ve

i.e. $\quad T\,\Delta S > \Delta H$

or $\quad T > \dfrac{\Delta H}{\Delta S} > \dfrac{4\times 1000}{10} > 400$ K

77. (*b*) This is endothermic reaction $\Delta H > 0$.

Also number of moles of gaseous substances increases, hence randomness increases.

Thus, $\quad \Delta S > 0$

81. (*a*) By Clapeyron-Clausius equation

$$\log p = -\frac{\Delta H}{2.303\,RT} + \text{constant}$$

$$\frac{\Delta H}{2.303\,R} = \frac{1}{4.606}$$

$$\Delta H = \frac{2.303\times 2}{4.606} = 1 \text{ cal}$$

85. (*d*) $$H_2O(s) \rightleftharpoons H_2O(l)$$

This is spontaneous at a temperature above 0°C.

89. (*d*) When there is simultaneously change in temperature and volume (or pressure).

$$\Delta S = nC_V \log_e\left(\frac{T_2}{T_1}\right) + nR\log_e\left(\frac{V_2}{V_1}\right)$$

$$= C_V\log_e\left(\frac{2}{1}\right) + R\log_e\frac{1}{2}$$

$$= C_V\log_e 2 - R\log_e 2$$

$$= (C_V - R)\log_e 2$$

92. (*c*) $$\text{KE} = \frac{1}{2}mv^2$$

$$\therefore \quad \frac{E_1}{E_2} = \frac{v_1^2}{v_2^2}$$

$$\therefore \quad \frac{v_1}{v_2} = \sqrt{\frac{E_1}{E_2}} = 1:2$$

93. (*b*) PE $= mgh = 10\times 10\times 10 = 1000$ J at the height of 10 m.

When body falls potential energy decreases and kinetic energy increases such that

KE + PE = total energy

$\therefore \quad$ PE $= 1000 - 200 = 800$ J

94. (*b*) $\Delta G = \Delta G° + 2.303\,RT\log K$

$K = p_{CO_2} = 0.0033$

$\therefore\ \Delta G = -27 + 2.303\times 8.314\times 10^{-3}\times 1273\log p_{CO_2}$

$= -87.5$ kJ

95. (*a*) $W = p\Delta V = p\times 0 = 0$

$q = C_V(\Delta T) = 20\times 273 = 5460$ J

96. (*a*) Variation of K with temperature is given by

$$\log_e K = \frac{\Delta S°}{R} - \frac{\Delta H°}{RT}$$

On comparison with $\log K = 4.0 - \dfrac{2000}{T}$

$\therefore \quad \dfrac{\Delta S°}{R} = 4 \quad \therefore \quad \Delta S° = 4R$

106. (*a*) $\Delta G° = -$ ve

If we add *trans*-2-pentene, equilibrium is displaced in the direction of less *trans*-2-pentene (Le-Chatelier principle).

107. (*b*) Operate I + III – II

we set the required reaction

$\therefore \quad \Delta G = -544 - 480 - (-293) = -731$ kJ

108. (*c*) $W = -p\Delta V = -p(V_2 - V_1) = -1(10-5) = -5$ L atm

$= -5\times 101.27$ J $= -506.35$ J

$q = 400$ J

$\Delta U = q + W = 400 - 506.35 = -106.35$ J

110. (*c*) $W = -p\Delta V = -p(V_2 - V_1) = -1(20-10) = -10$ L dm^3

$= -10\times 101.27$ J $= -1012.7$ J

$\Delta U = q + W = 800 - 1012.7 = -212.7$ J

111. (*c*) $C_p - C_V = R$

$$C_p = C_V + R = \frac{5}{2}R$$

$$\left(\frac{\Delta H}{\Delta T}\right)_p = C_p$$

$$\Delta H = C_p\,\Delta T = \frac{5}{2}R\,(373-298)$$

$$= \frac{5}{2}\times 2\times 75 \text{ cal}$$

$$= 375 \text{ cal}$$

112. (*d*) ΔH (vap) = 540 cal g^{-1} = 540 × 18 cal mol^{-1}

$$\therefore \Delta S \text{ (vap)} = \frac{\Delta H(\text{vap})}{\text{b.p.}} = \frac{540 \times 18}{373} = 26.06 \text{ cal K}^{-1}\text{ mol}^{-1}$$

114. (*b*) For an adiabatic expansion

$$W = -nC_V (T_2 - T_1)$$

$$3 = -1 \times \frac{20}{1000} [T_2 - 300]$$

$$T_2 = 150 \text{ K}$$

118. (*b*) $\Delta H = \Delta U + \Delta nR(T_2 - T_1)$

$$= 30 + 1 \times 0.0821 \times (245 - 95)$$

$$= 30 + 12.3 = 42.3 \text{ L atm}$$

119. (*a*) $\Delta S_{system} = 2.303\, nR \log \frac{V_2}{V_1}$

$$= 2.303 \times 0.5 \times 8.3143 \log \frac{5}{1}$$

$$= 6.69 \text{ K}^{-1}\text{ J} \approx 6.7 \text{ JK}^{-1}$$

120. (*b*) $W = -np\Delta V = -np(V_2 - V_1) = -np\left[\frac{RT}{p_2} - \frac{RT}{p_1}\right]$

$$= -nRTp\left[\frac{1}{p_2} - \frac{1}{p_1}\right]$$

$$= -0.85 \times 0.0821 \times 300 \times 1\left[\frac{1}{1} - \frac{1}{15}\right]$$

$$= -19.54 \text{ L atm} = -19.54 \times 101.27 \text{ J}$$

$$= -1.98 \times 10^3 \text{ J}$$

121. (*a*) For an adiabatic change

$$T_2 = T_1\left(\frac{V_1}{V_2}\right)^{\gamma - 1} = T\left(\frac{1}{2}\right)^{0.66}, \gamma = 1.66 \text{ for monatomic gas}$$

$$= \frac{T}{2^{2/3}}$$

124. (*c*) Fusion (fusion temperature T_1) and vaporisation (vaporisation temperature T_2) take place at constant temperature.

Thus, $\Delta S°$ (fusion) = BC

$\Delta S°$ (vaporisation) = DE

125. (*a*) Net work done = 0

127. (*d*) I. For isothermal change, $\Delta U = 0$ true

II. $\left(\frac{\partial U}{\partial V}\right)_T = 0$ true

III. $\Delta U = q + W$ by first law

$0 = q + W$ true

130. (*b*) Potential energy = mgh = 60 × 9.8 × 5 = 2940 J

Work done by machine = −2940 J

$$pV = nRT$$

$$\therefore \quad n = \frac{pV}{RT} = \frac{W}{RT} = \frac{2940}{8.3143 \times 398} = 0.89 \text{ mol}$$

131. (*c*) $\Delta S = S\,(XY_3) - \frac{1}{2} S\,(X_2) - \frac{3}{2} S\,(Y_2)$

$$= 50 - 30 - 60 = -40 \text{ J mol}^{-1}\text{ K}^{-1}$$

$$\Delta H = -30 \text{ kJ} = -30000 \text{ J}$$

$$\Delta G = \Delta H - T\Delta S$$

At equilibrium, $\Delta G = 0$

$$T = \frac{\Delta H}{\Delta S} = \frac{-30000}{-40} = 750 \text{ K}$$

10

Thermochemistry

Objective Questions Type I [Only one correct option]

In each of the questions below, four choices are given of which only one is correct.

1. $A + B + 40$ cal $\rightarrow C + D$. In this reaction

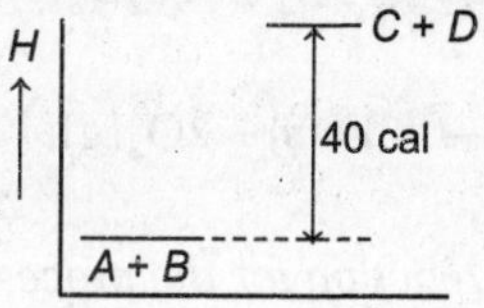

(a) heat is absorbed
(b) temperature of the surrounding falls
(c) can be represented as in figure
(d) All of the above

2. $N_2 + 3H_2 \longrightarrow 2NH_3 + 22$ kcal
Select the correct alternate about this reaction.
(a) It is an endothermic reaction
(b) It is an exothermic reaction
(c) System gets heated
(d) None of the above

3. $2SO_2 + O_2 \longrightarrow 2SO_3$
In this reaction some of the following facts are observed
I. Surroundings get heated.
II. Increase in temperature favours dissociation of SO_3.
(a) This is an endothermic reaction
(b) This is an exothermic reaction
(c) Pressure has no effect on this reaction
(d) Concentration has no effect on this reaction

4. Dissolution of NH_4Cl in H_2O is
(a) an exothermic reaction
(b) an endothermic reaction
(c) a reaction with $\Delta H = 0$
(d) a reaction with $\Delta S = 0$

5. $N_2 + O_2 \longrightarrow 2NO, \Delta H = 43.2$ kcal
Based on the reaction shown, which statement is true?
(a) 43.2 kcal are consumed when 1.00 g of N_2 reacts
(b) 43.2 kcal are consumed when 1.00 g of O_2 reacts
(c) 43.2 kcal are consumed when 1.00 mole of O_2 reacts
(d) 43.2 kcal are released when 2.00 moles of NO are formed

6. Consider the following changes,

I. adsorption	III. freezing
II. fusion	IV. vaporisation

Exothermic changes are

(a) I, II	(b) I, III
(c) I, IV	(d) II, IV

7. Consider the following reactions.
I. C (graphite) + $O_2(g) \longrightarrow CO_2(g)$; $\Delta H° = -x_1$ cal
II. $CO(g) + \frac{1}{2}O_2(g) \longrightarrow CO_2(g)$; $\Delta H° = -x_2$ cal
Based on the above data, $\Delta H°_f(CO_2)$ is

(a) $-x_1$ cal	(b) $-x_2$ cal
(c) $(x_2 - x_1)$ cal	(d) $(x_1 - x_2)$ cal

8. From Q. (7) above, $\Delta H°_f(CO)$ is

(a) $-x_1$	(b) $-x_2$
(c) $x_2 - x_1$	(d) $x_1 - x_2$

9. $\Delta H_f°$ [$H_2O(g)$] is -58 kcal mol^{-1} and $\Delta H°_f$[$H_2O(l)$] is -68 kcal mol^{-1}
Hence, $\Delta S°$ (vaporisation) of $H_2O(l)$ to $H_2O(g)$ at 1 atm pressure (100°C) is

(a) 10 cal mol^{-1} K^{-1}	(b) 10 kcal mol^{-1} K^{-1}
(c) 126 kcal mol^{-1} K^{-1}	(d) 27 cal mol^{-1} K^{-1}

10. The process with negative entropy change is [JEE Main 2019, Jan]
(a) synthesis of ammonia from N_2 and H_2
(b) dissociation of $CaSO_4(s)$ to $CaO(s)$ and $SO_3(g)$
(c) dissolution of iodine in water
(d) sublimation of dry ice

11. For the following gaseous phase reaction at 298 K
$$F_2 + 2HCl \longrightarrow 2HF + Cl_2 \quad \Delta H° = -84.4 \text{ kcal}$$
If $\Delta H_f^\circ(HF) = -64.2$ kcal mol^{-1} then $\Delta H°$ (HCl) is
(a) 20.2 kcal mol^{-1} (b) -22.0 kcal mol^{-1}
(c) -20.2 kcal mol^{-1} (d) $+22.0$ kcal mol^{-1}

12. For the reaction,
$$3N_2O(g) + 2NH_3(g) \longrightarrow + 4N_2(g) + + 3H_2O(g)$$
$$\Delta H° = -879.6 \text{ kJ}$$
If ΔH_f° of $NH_3(g) = -45.9$ kJ mol^{-1}, $H_2O(g) = -241.8$ kJ mol^{-1} then ΔH_f° of $N_2O(g)$ is (in kJ mol^{-1})
(a) +246 (b) +82
(c) −82 (d) −246

13. The diagram below shows the enthalpy change for the chemical reactions between N_2, O_2, NO and NO_2

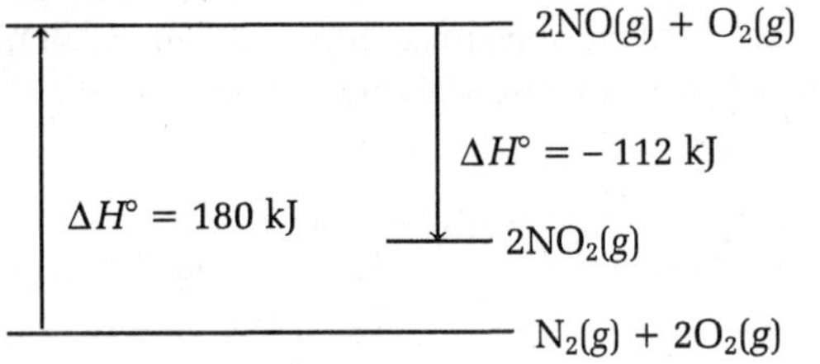

Select the correct statement.
(a) The standard heat of formation of NO_2 is 68 kJ mol^{-1}
(b) The oxidation reaction of N_2 to NO_2 is endothermic
(c) The standard heat of formation of NO is 90 kJ mol^{-1}
(d) The oxidation reaction of NO to NO_2 is endothermic

14. Given,

	ΔH_f°, kJ mol^{-1}
$B_2O_3(s)$	− 1272.8
$COCl_2(g)$	− 218.8
$BCl_3(g)$	− 403.8
$CO_2(g)$	− 393.5

Thus, $\Delta H°$ of the reaction
$$B_2O_3(s) + 3COCl_2(g) \longrightarrow 2BCl_3(g) + 3CO_2(g) \text{ is}$$
(a) 694.3 kJ (b) −3917.3 kJ
(c) −59.7 kJ (d) 354.9 kJ

15. In the explosion of two moles of TNT with a volume of approximately 274 mL produces gases with a volume of 448 L at room temperature and at 1 atm
$$\underset{\text{TNT}}{2C_7H_5N_3O_6(s)} \longrightarrow 12CO(g) + 5H_2(g) + 3N_2(g) + 2C(s)$$
Hence, pV work done during explosion is
(a) 45.34 kJ (b) 0.45 kJ
(c) 8.314×10^{-3} kJ (d) 8.314 kJ

16. Heat of vaporisation of $A(l)$ is x_1 cal and heat of fusion of A s) is x_2 cal. Hence, heat of sublimation of $A(s)$ is
(a) $x_1 - x_2$ (b) $x_2 - x_1$
(c) $x_1 + x_2$ (d) $-(x_1 + x_2)$

17. Consider the following reactions,
I. $NH_4HS(s) \rightleftharpoons NH_3(g) + H_2S(g)$
II. $CaCO_3(s) \rightleftharpoons CaO(s) + CO_2(g)$
III. $PCl_5(g) \rightleftharpoons PCl_3(g) + Cl_2(g)$
In which case(s), $\Delta H - \Delta E = RT$?
(a) I, II, III (b) I, II
(c) II, III (d) I, III

18. Given,
I. $2Fe(s) + O_2(g) \longrightarrow 2FeO(s)$; $\Delta H° = -544.0$ kJ
II. $4Fe(s) + 3O_2(g) \longrightarrow 2Fe_2O_3(s)$; $\Delta H° = -1648.4$ kJ
III. $Fe_3O_4 \longrightarrow 3Fe(s) + 2O_2(g)$; $\Delta H° = +1118.4$ kJ
Hence, heat of reaction for the process is
$$FeO(s) + Fe_2O_3(s) \longrightarrow Fe_3O_4(s)$$
(a) − 1074.0 kJ (b) − 22.2 kJ
(c) + 249.8 kJ (d) +2214.6 kJ

19. Heat of reaction $A(s) + B(g) \longrightarrow 2C(g)$ is 40 kJ at 300 K and constant volume. Hence, heat of reaction at constant pressure and at 300 K is,
(a) 42.5 kJ (b) 37.5 kJ (c) 40.0 kJ (d) 30.0 kJ

20. Heat of reaction varies with temperature as given by
(a) $\Delta H_2 = \Delta H_1 + \Delta C_P \int_{T_1}^{T_2} dT$
(b) $\Delta H_2 = \Delta H_1 + \Delta C_V \int_{T_1}^{T_2} dT$
(c) $\Delta E_2 = \Delta E_1 + \Delta C_P \int_{T_1}^{T_2} dT$
(d) All of the above are correct

21. Heat of combustion of CH_4, C_2H_6 and C_3H_8 are respectively − 210, − 368.4 and − 526.3 kcal mol^{-1}. Hence, heat of combustion of C_8H_{16} is approximately
(a) −1270 kcal mol^{-1} (b) −684 kcal mol^{-1}
(c) −840 kcal mol^{-1} (d) −1000 kcal mol^{-1}

22. Heat of combustion of CH_4 at 25°C and 1 atm constant pressure is −210 kcal mol^{-1}
$$CH_4(g) + 2O_2(g) \longrightarrow CO_2(g) + 2H_2O(l)$$
Hence, heat of combustion at constant volume is
(a) −210 kcal mol^{-1} (b) −198 kcal mol^{-1}
(c) −208.8 kcal mol^{-1} (d) −211.2 kcal mol^{-1}

23. Heat of combustion of $C_6H_6(l)$ is, if heat of formation of $C_6H_6(l)$, $H_2O(l)$ and $CO_2(g)$ are $-x_1, -x_2$ and $-x_3$ cal respectively
(a) $x_1 - x_2 - x_3$ (b) $x_1 - 6x_2 - 3x_3$
(c) $x_1 + x_2 + x_3$ (d) $x_1 - 3x_2 - 6x_3$

24. Heat of combustion of CH_4, C_2H_6 and C_3H_8 are respectively −210, − 368.4 and −526.3 kcal mol^{-1}. Hence, maximum calorific value is of
(a) C_3H_8 (b) C_2H_6
(c) CH_4 (d) equal

25. Calorific value of H_2 is −143 kJ g^{-1}. Hence, ΔH_f° of H_2O is
(a) −143 kJ mol^{-1} (b) −286 kJ mol^{-1}
(c) +143 kJ mol^{-1} (d) +286 kJ mol^{-1}

26. Heat of combustion of $H_2(g) = -241.8$ kJ mol^{-1}
$C(s) = -393.5$ kJ mol^{-1}
$C_2H_5OH(l) = -1234.7$ kJ mol^{-1}
Hence, heat of formation of $C_2H_5OH(l)$ is
(a) − 2747.1 kJ mol^{-1} (b) − 277.7 kJ mol^{-1}
(c) 277.7 kJ mol^{-1} (d) 2747.1 kJ mol^{-1}

27. Consider the following reactions,

I. $C(s) + \frac{1}{2}O_2(g) \longrightarrow CO(g), \quad \Delta H_1 = x_1$

II. $CO(g) + \frac{1}{2}O_2(g) \longrightarrow CO_2(g), \quad \Delta H_2 = x_2$

III. $C(s) + CO_2(g) \longrightarrow 2CO(g), \quad \Delta H_3 = x_3$

Select the correct statements.
(a) Heat of formation of CO_2 is $(x_1 + x_2)$
(b) Heat of combustion of C is $(x_1 + x_2)$
(c) $\Delta H_3 = \Delta H_1 - \Delta H_2$
(d) All of the above are correct statements

28. Which represents enthalpy of combustion?
(a) $C_6H_6(l) + 4.5O_2(g) \longrightarrow 6CO(g) + 3H_2O(l)$, $\Delta H = -200$ kcal
(b) $C(g) + O_2(g) \longrightarrow CO_2(g)$, $\Delta H = +94$ kcal
(c) $CH_4(g) + 2O_2(g) \longrightarrow CO_2(g) + 2H_2O(l)$, $\Delta H = -210$ kcal
(d) $2C(s) + O_2(g) \longrightarrow 2CO(g)$, $\Delta H = -52$ kcal

29. Heat of combustion of $C(s)$, $H_2(g)$ and $CH_4(g)$ are $-x_1$, $-x_2$ and $-x_3$. Hence, heat of formation of $CH_4(g)$ is
(a) $-x_1 - x_2 + x_3$ (b) $-x_1 - 2x_2 - x_3$
(c) $-x_1 - x_2 + 2x_3$ (d) $-x_1 - 2x_2 + x_3$

30. In the complete combustion of C_2H_6, 54 g of H_2O is formed and 370 kcal of heat is evolved.
Hence, heat of combustion of C_2H_6 is
(a) 370 kcal mol^{-1} (b) −370 kcal mol^{-1}
(c) −6.61 kcal mol^{-1} (d) 6.61 kcal mol^{-1}

31. The heat released on neutralisation of CsOH with all strong acids is 13.4 kcal mol^{-1}. The heat released on neutralisation of CsOH with HF (weak acid) is 16.4 kcal mol^{-1}. ΔH° of ionisation of HF in water is
(a) 39.8 kcal (b) − 39.8 kcal
(c) − 3.0 kcal (d) + 3.0 kcal

32. For the reactions,

I. $HS^- \longrightarrow H^+ + S^{2-}, \quad \Delta H = 14.22$ kcal

II. $OH^- + HS^- \longrightarrow S^{2-} + H_2O, \quad \Delta H = 0.86$ kcal

Hence, Δ of the reaction, $H^+ + OH^- \longrightarrow H_2O$ is
(a) 15.08 kcal (b) −15.08 kcal
(c) 13.36 kcal (d) −13.36 kcal

33. If $\Delta H_f^\circ(H_2O)$ is −286.20 kJ mol^{-1} then $\Delta H_f^\circ(OH^-)$ is
(a) −228.88 kJ mol^{-1} (b) +228.88 kJ mol^{-1}
(c) −343.52 kJ mol^{-1} (d) +343.52 kJ mol^{-1}

34. In the following reaction, involving neutralisation of HF (a weak acid) with NaOH (a strong base).
$HF(aq) + NaOH(aq) \longrightarrow NaF(aq) + H_2O(l)$
$\Delta\ ^\circ = -68.6$ kJ mol^{-1}
This values is much higher than the heat of neutralisation of strong acid with strong base (=−57.3 kJ mol^{-1}). This is due to
(a) in aqueous solution, HF behaves as a strong acid
(b) there is hydration of F^- ion in aqueous solution, and the process is exothermic
(c) Both (a) and (b)
(d) None of the above

35. Enthalpy change when 1 mole of H_2SO_4 is completely neutralised by NaOH is
(a) −13.7 kcal (b) −27.4 kcal
(c) −6.85 kcal (d) +27.4 kcal

36. 30 mL of 0.10 M $Ba(OH)_2(aq)$ is added to 30 mL of 0.10 M $H_2SO_4(aq)$. The rise in temperature is ΔT_1. If experiment is repeated by taking 90 mL of each solution, the rise in temperature is ΔT_2. Hence
(a) $\Delta T_2 = 3\Delta T_1$ (b) $\Delta T_1 = \Delta T_2$
(c) $\Delta T_1 = 3\Delta T_2$ (d) $\Delta T_1 = 2\Delta T_2$

37. Heat of dissociation of CH_3COOH is 0.005 kcal g^{-1}, hence enthalpy change when 1 mole of $Ca(OH)_2$ is completely neutralised by CH_3COOH is
(a) − 27.4 kcal (b) − 13.6 kcal
(c) − 26.8 kcal (d) − 27.1 kcal

38. When 30 mL of 0.10 M NaOH reacts with 10 mL of 0.10 M HCl, enthalpy charge is −13.7 cal, when 20 mL of 0.10 M HCl, is further added, enthalpy change would be
(a) −13.7 cal (b) −27.4 cal
(c) 13.7 cal (d) 27.4 cal

39. What is enthalpy change when 100 mL of 1 M H_2SO_4 is completely neutralised by 100 mL of 1 M $Ca(OH)_2$?
(a) −13.7 kcal (b) − 27.4 kcal
(c) −1.37 kcal (d) − 2.74 kcal

40. $Ca(OH)_2 + HCl \longrightarrow Ca(OH)Cl + H_2O, \; \Delta H_1$

$Ca(OH)Cl + HCl \longrightarrow CaCl_2 + H_2O, \; \Delta H_2$

ΔH_1 and ΔH_2 for 1 : 1 molar ratio of each reactant are

(a) −6.85 kcal, − 6.85 kcal
(b) −13.7 kcal, −13.7 kcal
(c) −27.4 kcal, −27.4 kcal
(d) −6.85 kcal, −13.7 kcal

41. $\Delta H_f°$ for chloride ion from the following data is

$\frac{1}{2}H_2(g) + \frac{1}{2}Cl_2(g) \longrightarrow HCl(g), \quad \Delta H_f^\circ = -22.1$ kcal

$HCl(g) + nH_2O \longrightarrow H^+(aq) + Cl^-(aq),$

$\Delta H°_{298\,K} = -17.9$ kcal

(a) −40.0 kcal (b) +40.0 kcal
(c) +17.9 kcal (d) +22.1 kcal

42. $\Delta H°_f\,[K^+(aq)], \Delta H°_f\,[Cl^-(aq)]$ and $\Delta H_f^\circ(KCl)$ are respectively −60.04, −40.0 and −104.18 kcal. Hence, $\Delta H°$ for the process at 25°C of dissolving 1.00 mol of KCl in large excess of water

$KCl(s) \longrightarrow K^+(aq) + Cl^-(aq)$ is

(a) −4.14 kcal (b) +4.14 kcal
(c) +20.04 kcal (d) −20.04 kcal

43. For the process : $H_2O(l) \longrightarrow H_2O(g)$ at $T = 100°C$ and 1 atmosphere pressure, the correct choice is

(a) $\Delta S_{system} > 0$ and $\Delta S_{surrounding} > 0$ **[JEE Advanced 2014]**
(b) $\Delta S_{system} > 0$ and $\Delta S_{surrounding} < 0$
(c) $\Delta S_{system} < 0$ and $\Delta S_{surrounding} > 0$
(d) $\Delta S_{system} < 0$ and $\Delta S_{surrounding} < 0$

44. The dissolution of $CaCl_2 \cdot 6H_2O$ in large volume of water is endothermic to the extent of 3.5 kcal mol^{-1}. For the reaction

$CaCl_2(s) + 6H_2O(l) \longrightarrow CaCl_2 \cdot 6H_2O(s)$

$\Delta H = -$ 23.2 kcal. Hence, heat of solution of $CaCl_2$ (anhydrous) in a large volume of water is

(a) 26.7 kcal (b) −26.7 kcal
(c) 19.7 kcal (d) −19.7 kcal

45. $\Delta H°_f\,[HCl(g)] = -22.1$ kcal mol^{-1} and $\Delta H_f^\circ\,[Cl^-(aq)] = -40$ kcal mol^{-1}, then enthalpy change in the standard state when HCl(g) is dissolved in excess of H_2O is

(a) −17.9 kcal mol^{-1} (b) −62.1 kcal mol^{-1}
(c) +62.1 kcal mol^{-1} (d) +17.9 kcal mol^{-1}

46. Instant cold packs used to treat athletic injuries contain water and

(a) solid NH_4Cl (b) soild NH_4NO_3
(c) solid NH_4HCO_3 (d) solid $(NH_4)_2C_2O_4$

47. Lattice energy of NaCl(s) is 788 kJ mol^{-1} and enthalpy of hydration is − 784 kJ mol^{-1}. Hence, heat of solution of NaCl(s) is

(a) 4 kJ mol^{-1} (b) − 4 kJ mol^{-1}
(c) − 1572 kJ mol^{-1} (d) 1572 kJ mol^{-1}

48. If a certain solution process is endothermic and the solution is subsequently diluted

(a) more heat will be absorbed by the same solution from the surroundings
(b) more heat will be liberated to the surroundings
(c) no heat will be absorbed or liberated
(d) enthalpy data is also required

49. $LiCl(s) + H_2O(l) \rightleftharpoons Li^+(aq) + Cl^-(aq)$

$\Delta H = -$ 37.1 kJ mol^{-1}

Variation of solubility S with temperature T is given by

(a)
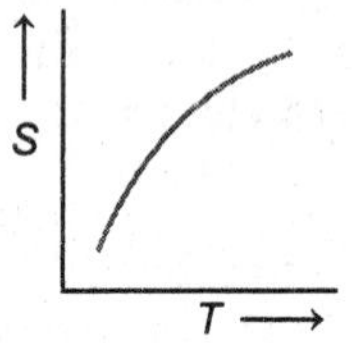

(b)
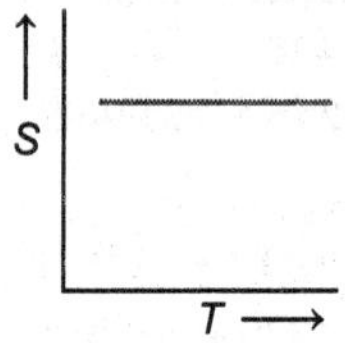

(c)
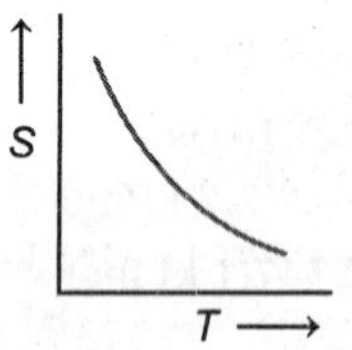

(d)
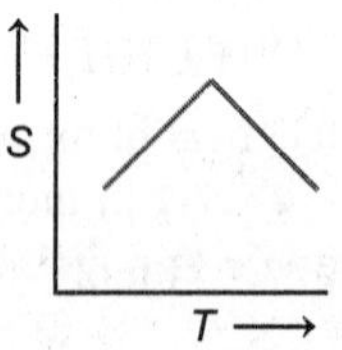

50. Bond energies of N≡N bond, H—H bond and N—H bond are respectively x_1, x_2 and x_3 kJ mol^{-1}. Hence, $\Delta H°_f(NH_3)$ is

(a) $x_1 + 3x_2 - x_3$ (b) $x_1 + x_2 - x_3$
(c) $\frac{x_1}{2} + \frac{3}{2}x_2 - 3x_3$ (d) $x_1 + 3x_2 - 6x_3$

51. For the reactions,

I. $CH_4(g) \longrightarrow C(g) + 4H(g), \quad \Delta H = x_1$
II. $C_2H_6(g) \longrightarrow 2C(g) + 6H(g), \quad \Delta H = x_2$

From I and II, bond energy of C—C bond is

(a) $x_1 - x_2$ (b) $x_2 - x_1$ (c) $x_2 + 1.5\,x_1$ (d) $x_2 - 1.5\,x_1$

52. ΔH of the following reaction,

$2H_2(g) + O_2(g) \longrightarrow 2H_2O(l)$, is determined by

(a) BE of H—H, BE of O=O and BE of H—O bond
(b) all the values is (a) and heat of vaporisation of $H_2O(l)$
(c) $\Delta H_f^\circ(H_2), \Delta H_f^\circ(O_2)$ and $\Delta H_f^\circ(H_2O)$
(d) alternates (b) and (c) are correct

53. C(graphite) + $\frac{1}{2}O_2(g) + 2H_2(g) \longrightarrow CH_3OH(l)$; for this reaction ΔH is to be calculated. Some of the values given below can be taken

I. Heat of atomisation of C (graphite)
II. BE of O=O bond
III. BE of H—H bond
IV. BE of C—H bond
V. BE of O—H bond
VI. BE of C—O bond
VII. Heat of vaporisation of $CH_3OH(l)$

Hence, correct alternates are

(a) I to VII all (b) all except I and VII
(c) all except VII (d) all except I, VI and VII

54. $H_2O(g) \longrightarrow H(g) + OH(g), \Delta H = x_1$
$OH(g) \longrightarrow H(g) + O(g), \Delta H = x_2$
Based on these value, BE of O—H bond is
(a) $x_1 + x_2$ (b) $\frac{x_1 + x_2}{2}$
(c) $\frac{x_1 - x_2}{2}$ (d) $2(x_1 + x_2)$

55. Bond energies of H—H and Cl—Cl bonds are 430 kJ mol^{-1} and 242 kJ mol^{-1} respectively. If heat of formation of HCl is – 91 kJ mol^{-1}, the bond energy of HCl (in kJ mol^{-1}) is
(a) 430 + 242 – 91 (b) 430 + 242 + 91
(c) 215 + 121 – 91 (d) 215 + 121 + 91

56. The enthalpy of hydrogenation of 1-pentene is + 126 kJ mol^{-1}. The enthalpy of hydrogenation of 1,3-pentadiene is +230 kJ mol^{-1}. Hence, resonance (delocalisation) energy of 1,3-pentadiene is
(a) 22 kJ (b) 104 kJ
(c) 252 kJ (d) 11 kJ

57. Based on the values of BE given, ΔH°_f of $N_2H_4(g)$ is

N—N	159 kJ mol^{-1}	H—H	436 kJ mol^{-1}
N=N	418 kJ mol^{-1}	H—N	389 kJ mol^{-1}
N≡N	941 kJ mol^{-1}		

(a) + 711 kJ mol^{-1} (b) + 98 kJ mol^{-1}
(c) – 98 kJ mol^{-1} (d) – 711 kJ mol^{-1}

58. For the reaction,
$$O(g) + O_2(g) \longrightarrow O_3(g), \quad \Delta H^\circ = -107.2 \text{ kJ}$$
Hence, the average bond energy in O_3 is (assume O=O bond energy 498.8 kJ mol^{-1})
(a) 606.0 kJ mol^{-1} (b) 107.2 kJ mol^{-1}
(c) 391.6 kJ mol^{-1} (d) 303.0 kJ mol^{-1}

59. For the chemical reaction, $X \rightleftharpoons Y$, the standard reaction Gibbs energy depends on temperature T (in K) as
$$\Delta_r G^\circ \text{ (in kJ mol}^{-1}) = 120 - \frac{3}{8}T$$
The major component of the reaction mixture at T is **[JEE Main 2019, Jan.]**
(a) Y if T = 280 K (b) X if T = 350 K
(c) X if T = 315 K (d) Y if T = 300 K

60. If $\Delta H_f^\circ(C_2H_4)$, $\Delta H_f^\circ(C_2H_6)$ are x_1 and x_2 kcal mol^{-1}, then heat of hydrogenation of C_2H_4 is
(a) $x_1 + x_2$ (b) $x_1 - x_2$
(c) $-(x_1 - x_2)$ (d) $x_1 + 2x_2$

61. $\Delta H^\circ_f(NO_2) = 33.84$ kJ mol^{-1}
$\Delta H^\circ_f(N_2O_4) = 9.66$ kJ mol^{-1}
hence, dimerisation of NO_2 forming N_2O_4 is
(a) endothermic (b) isothermic
(c) exothermic (d) isochoric

62. From the following data, calculate, bond energy of the F_2^- ion
$$F_2(g) \longrightarrow 2F(g) \quad \Delta H^\circ = 156.9 \text{ kJ}$$
$$F^-(g) \longrightarrow F(g) + e^- \quad \Delta H^\circ = 333 \text{ kJ}$$
$$F_2^-(g) \longrightarrow F_2(g) + e^- \quad \Delta H^\circ = 290 \text{ kJ}$$
(a) 446.9 kJ (b) 113.9 kJ
(c) 779.9 kJ (d) 623.0 kJ

63. For the reactions,
$$C(\text{graphite}) + O_2(g) \longrightarrow CO_2(g)\ \Delta H^\circ = x_1$$
$$H_2(g) + \frac{1}{2}O_2(g) \longrightarrow H_2O(l)\ \Delta H = x_2$$
$$2C_2H_2(g) + 5O_2(g) \longrightarrow 4CO_2(g) + 2H_2O(l), \Delta H = x_3$$
Hence, heat of formation of $C_2H_2(g)$ is
(a) $x_1 + x_2 - x_3$ (b) $2x_1 + x_2 - \frac{x_3}{2}$
(c) $-x_1 - x_2 + x_3$ (d) $-x_1 - x_2 + \frac{x_3}{2}$

64. Consider the following chemical change, ΔH/ kcal
I. $2Na(s) + 2H_2O(l) \longrightarrow 2NaOH(aq) + H_2(g)$, –88
$H_2(g) + \frac{1}{2}O_2(g) \longrightarrow H_2O(l)$, – 68
II. $2Na(s) + \frac{1}{2}O_2(g) \longrightarrow Na_2O(s)$, – 100
$Na_2O(s) + H_2O(l) \longrightarrow 2NaOH(aq)$ x
Value of x is
(a) – 68 kcal (b) – 88 kcal
(c) – 100 kcal (d) – 56 kcal

65. If F—F bond energy is x, then heat of formation of F(g) is :
(a) $\frac{x}{2}$ (b) $-\frac{x}{2}$
(c) x (d) $-x$

66. Enthalpy change in the formation of Cl^+Cl^- (imaginary) lattice from Cl_2 based on following data is Cl—Cl bond energy = x_1, ionisation energy of Cl = x_2
electron affinity of Cl = x_3, lattice energy of Cl^+Cl^- = x_4
(a) $x_1 + x_2 + x_3 + x_4$
(b) $x_1 + x_2 - x_3 - x_4$
(c) $-x_1 + x_2 - x_3 + x_4$
(d) $-(x_1 + x_2 + x_3 + x_4)$

67. A bomb calorimeter has a heat capacity of 783 JC^{-1}, and contains 254 g of water which has a specific heat of 4.184 $g^{-1}°C^{-1}$. Heat absorbed/evolved by a reaction when the temperature changes from 23.73°C to 26.01°C is
(a) 1.78 kJ absorbed
(b) 2.42 kJ absorbed
(c) 1.78 kJ evolved
(d) 4.21 kJ absorbed

68. Latent heat of fusion of ice is 6.02 kJ mol^{-1}. The heat capacity of water is 4.18 J g^{-1} °C^{-1}. 500 g of liquid water is to be cooled from 20°C to 0°C. Number of ice cubes (each of one mole) required are

(a) 1 (b) 7
(c) 14 (d) 125

69. Specific heat water is 4.184 J/g°C. Hence, molar heat capacity of water is

(a) $\frac{4.184}{18}$ J/mol °C (b) 4.184×18 J/mol °C
(c) 4.184 J/mol °C (d) $\frac{18}{4.184}$ J/mol °C

70. The heats of combustion of carbon and carbon monoxide are – 393.5 and – 283.5 kJ mol^{-1}, respectively. The heat of formation (in kJ) of carbon monoxide per mole is **[JEE Main 2016]**

(a) 676.5 (b) –676.5
(c) –110.5 (d) 110.5

71. Temperature of 12 g of substances is raised from 20°C to 30°C by absorption of 240 kJ of heat. Hence, specific heat of the substance is

(a) 2 kJ/g°C (b) 24 kJ/g°C
(c) 20 kJ/g°C (d) 240 kJ/g°C

72. Specific heat of N_2 at constant pressure is 0.25 cal/g°C. Hence, specific heat at constant volume is

(a) 1.72 cal/g°C (b) 0.25 cal/g°C
(c) 5.00 cal/g°C (d) 0.18 cal/g°C

73. Specific heat of water is 1 cal/g°C. If 25 g of water absorbs 100 cal of heat, final temperature becomes 44°C. Thus, initial temperature is

(a) 48°C (b) 40°C
(c) 36°C (d) 25°C

74. Consider the following change

1 kg water liquid at 25°C $\xrightarrow{\Delta H_1}$ 1 kg water liquid at 100°C $\xrightarrow{\Delta H_2}$ 1 kg water steam at 100°C

Specific heat of water = 1 cal/g°C

Latent heat of vaporisation of water = 10 kcal/mol

ΔH_1 is

(a) 75 kcal (b) 556 kcal
(c) 750 kcal (d) 75 cal

75. ΔH_2 in the above question is

(a) 75 cal (b) 750 kcal
(c) 556 kcal (d) None of these

76. Enthalpy change for the reaction, $4H(g) \longrightarrow 2H_2(g)$ is –869.5 kJ. The dissociation energy of H—H bond is

(a) + 217.4 kJ (b) – 434.8 kJ
(c) – 869.6 kJ (d) + 434.8 kJ

77. The enthalpy of solution of sodium chloride is 4 kJ mol^{-1} and its enthalpy of hydration of ions is –784 kJ mol^{-1}. Then the lattice enthalpy of NaCl (in kJ mol^{-1}) is

(a) + 788 (b) + 4
(c) +398 (d) + 780

78. Four grams of graphite is burnt in a bomb calorimeter of heat capacity 30 kJ K^{-1} in excess of oxygen at 1 atm pressure. The temperature rises from 300 to 304 K. What is the enthalpy of combustion of graphite (in kJ mol^{-1})?

(a) 360 (b) 1440
(c) –360 (d) –1440

79. Given,

(1) $NH_3(g) + 3Cl_2(g) \rightleftharpoons NCl_3(g) + 3HCl(g);\quad -\Delta H_1$

(2) $N_2(g) + 3H_2(g) \rightleftharpoons 2NH_3(g);\quad -\Delta H_2$

(3) $H_2(g) + Cl_2(g) \rightleftharpoons 2HCl(g);\quad \Delta H_3$

The heat of formation of $NCl_3(g)$ in terms of $\Delta H_1, \Delta H_2$ and ΔH_3 is

(a) $\Delta H_f = -\Delta H_1 - \frac{\Delta H_2}{2} - \frac{3}{2}\Delta H_3$

(b) $\Delta H_f = \Delta H_1 + \frac{\Delta H_2}{2} - \frac{3}{2}\Delta H_3$

(c) $\Delta H_f = \Delta H_1 + \frac{\Delta H_2}{2} - \frac{3}{2}\Delta H_3$

(d) None of the above

80. The heat liberated when 1.89 g of benzoic acid is burnt in a bomb calorimeter at 25°C increases the temperature of 18.94 kg of water by 0.632°C. If the specific heat of water at 25°C is 0.998 cal/ g-deg, the value of the heat of combustion of benzoic acid at constant pressure is

(a) 881.1 kcal (b) 771.2 kcal
(c) 981.1 kcal (d) 871.2 kcal

81. The heats of neutralisation of four acids *A*, *B*, *C* and *D* when neutralised against a common base are 13.7, 9.4, 11.2 and 12.4 kcal respectively. The weakest among these acids is

(a) *A* (b) *B*
(c) *C* (d) *D*

82. Enthalpy of combustion of methane and ethane are –210 kcal/mol and –368 kcal/mol respectively. The enthalpy of combustion of decane is

(a) –158 kcal (b) –1632 kcal
(c) –1700 kcal (d) Data is incomplete

83. The heats of atomisation of $PH_3(g)$ and $P_2H_4(g)$ are 953 kJ mol^{-1} and 1485 kJ mol^{-1} respectively. The P—P bond energy in kJ mol^{-1} is

(a) 213 (b) 426
(c) 318 (d) 1272

84. Calculate $\Delta H°$ for the reaction,
$Na_2O(s) + SO_3(g) \longrightarrow Na_2SO_4(s)$ given the following:
$Na(s) + H_2O(l) \longrightarrow NaOH(s) + \frac{1}{2}H_2(g), \ \Delta H° = -146$ kJ
$Na_2SO_4(s) + H_2O(l) \longrightarrow 2NaOH(s) + SO_3(g),$
$\Delta H° = +418$ kJ
$2Na_2O(s) + 2H_2(g) \longrightarrow 4Na(s) + 2H_2O(l),$
$\Delta H° = +259$ kJ
(a) +823 kJ (b) −581 kJ (c) −435 kJ (d) +531 kJ

85. For which of the following equations is the enthalpy change at 25°C and 1 atm equal to $\Delta H_f^\circ(CH_3OH, l)$?
(a) $CO(g) + 2H_2(g) \longrightarrow CH_3OH(l)$
(b) $C(g) + 4H(g) + O(g) \longrightarrow CH_3OH(l)$
(c) $C(g) + 2H_2(g) + O(g) \longrightarrow CH_3OH(l)$
(d) $C(\text{graphite}) + 2H_2(g) + \frac{1}{2}O_2(g) \longrightarrow CH_3OH(l)$

86. The standard heat of combustion of propane is − 2220.1 kJ mol^{-1}. The standard heat of vaporisation of liquid water is 44.0 kJ mol^{-1}. What is $\Delta H°$ of
$C_3H_8(g) + 5O_2(g) \longrightarrow 3CO_2(g) + 4H_2O(g)$?
(a) −2220.1 kJ (b) −2044.1 kJ
(c) −2396.1 kJ (d) −2176.1 kJ

87. The standard heat of combustion of Al is − 837.8 kJ mol^{-1} at 25°C. If Al reacts with O_2 at 25°C, which of the following releases 250 kcal of heat?
(a) The reaction of 0.624 mol of Al
(b) The formation of 0.624 mol of Al_2O_3
(c) The reaction of 0.312 mol of Al
(d) The formation of 0.150 mol of Al_2O_3

88. Given, $C_{(\text{graphite})} + O_2(g) \longrightarrow CO_2(g);$
$\Delta_r H° = -393.5$ kJ mol^{-1}
$H_2(g) + \frac{1}{2}O_2(g) \longrightarrow H_2O(l); \ \Delta_r H° = -285.8$ kJ mol^{-1}
$CO_2(g) + 2H_2O(l) \longrightarrow CH_4(g) + 2O_2(g);$
$\Delta_r H° = +890.3$ kJ mol^{-1}
Based on the above thermochemical equations, the value of $\Delta_r H°$ at 298 K for the reaction,
$C_{(\text{graphite})} + 2H_2(g) \longrightarrow CH_4(g)$ will be
[JEE Main 2017]
(a) + 78.8 kJ mol^{-1} (b) + 144.0 kJ mol^{-1}
(c) − 74.8 kJ mol^{-1} (d) − 144.0 kJ mol^{-1}

89. $(\Delta H - \Delta E)$ for the formation of NH_3 from N_2 and H_2 is
(a) RT (b) $2RT$
(c) $-RT$ (d) $-2RT$

90. Heat of neutralisation of $H_2C_2O_4$ (oxalic acid) is − 26 kcal mol^{-1}. Hence, dissociation energy of
$H_2C_2O_4 \rightleftharpoons 2H^+ + C_2O_4^{2-}$ is
(a) 12.3 kcal mol^{-1} (b) 1.4 kcal mol^{-1}
(c) −13.7 kcal mol^{-1} (d) −1.4 kcal mol^{-1}

91. $A(l) \xrightleftharpoons{1\text{ atm}} A(g), \Delta H_{\text{vap}} = 460.6$ cal mol^{-1}, b.p. = 50 K. What is boiling point at 10 atm?
(a) 150 K
(b) 75 K
(c) 100 K
(d) None of these is correct

92. $H_2(g) + \frac{1}{2}O_2(g) \longrightarrow H_2O(l)$
BE (H—H) = x_1; BE(O=O) = x_2; BE(O—H) = x_3
Latent heat of vaporisation of water liquid into water vapour = x_4 then ΔH_f (heat of formation of liquid water) is
(a) $x_1 + \frac{x_2}{2} - x_3 + x_4$ (b) $2x_3 - x_1 - \frac{x_2}{2} - x_4$
(c) $x_1 + \frac{x_2}{2} - 2x_3 - x_4$ (d) $x_1 + \frac{x_2}{2} - 2x_3 + x_4$

93. If ΔH of a reaction is 100 kJ mol^{-1}, then the activation energy must be
(a) greater than 100 kJ mol^{-1}
(b) less than 100 kJ mol^{-1}
(c) equal to 100 kJ mol^{-1}
(d) None of the above

94. Variation of heat of reaction with temperature is given by Kirchhoff's equation, which is
(a) $\Delta H_2 = \Delta H_1 + \Delta C_p(T_2 - T_1)$
(b) $\frac{\Delta H_2 - \Delta H_1}{\Delta T} = \Delta C_p$
(c) $\frac{d(\Delta H)}{\Delta T} = \Delta C_p$
(d) All of the above

95. Given, $Na(s) \xrightarrow{S} Na(g)$
$Na(g) \xrightarrow{I} Na^+(g) + e^-$
$Cl_2(g) \xrightarrow{D} 2Cl(g)$
$Cl(g) + e^- \xrightarrow{-E} Cl^-(g)$
$Na^+(g) + Cl^-(g) \xrightarrow{-U} NaCl(s)$
[letters above arrow (⟶) are energy parameters], ΔH_f of NaCl is
(a) $S + I + D - E - U$ (b) $S + I + \frac{D}{2} + E + U$
(c) $S + I + \frac{D}{2} - E - U$ (d) $S + I + \frac{D}{2} - E + U$

96. C(diamond) ⟶ C(graphite), $\Delta S_{300\text{ K}} = 10$ cal K^{-1}
$C(\text{diamond}) + O_2 \longrightarrow CO_2, \ \Delta H_{300} = -91$ kcal mol^{-1}
$C(\text{graphite}) + O_2 \longrightarrow CO_2, \ \Delta H = x$ at 300 K, x is
(a) − 81 kcal (b) 101 kcal
(c) −94 kcal (d) 88 kcal

97. For $N_2 + 3H_2 \longrightarrow 2NH_3 + 22$ kcal, E_a (energy of activation) is 70 kcal. Hence, E_a of

$2NH_3 \longrightarrow N_2 + 3H_2$ is

(a) 92 kcal (b) 70 kcal
(c) –70 kcal (d) –92 kcal

98. Heat of hydrogenation of ethene is x_1 and that of benzene is x_2. Hence, resonance energy of benzene is

(a) $x_1 - x_2$ (b) $x_1 + x_2$
(c) $3x_1 - x_2$ (d) $x_1 - 3x_2$

99. $C_2H_6(g) + 3.5\, O_2(g) \longrightarrow 2CO_2(g) + 3H_2O(g)$

$\Delta S_{vap}(H_2O, l) = x_1$ cal K^{-1} (b.p.T_1)

$\Delta H_f(H_2O, l) = x_2, \Delta H_f(CO_2) = x_3, \quad \Delta H_f(C_2H_6) = x_4$

Hence, ΔH of the reaction is

(a) $2x_3 + 3x_2 - x_4$ (b) $2x_3 + 3x_2 - x_4 + 3x_1T_1$
(c) $2x_3 + 3x_2 - x_4 - 3x_1T_1$ (d) $x_1T_1 + x_2 + x_3 - x_4$

100. The C—Cl bond energy can be calculated from

(a) ΔH_f° (CCl_4, l) only
(b) $\Delta H_f^\circ(CCl_4, l)$ and BE (Cl_2)
(c) $\Delta H_f^\circ(CCl_4, l)$, BE (Cl_2)
(d) $\Delta H_f^\circ(CCl_4, l)$ BE (Cl_2), $\Delta H_f^\circ(C, g)$ and ΔH°_{vap} (CCl_4)

101. Given the standard enthalpies at 25°C, in kJ mol^{-1}, for the following two reactions

$Fe_2O_3(s) + \frac{3}{2}C(s) \longrightarrow \frac{3}{2}CO_2(g) + 2Fe(s),$ $\Delta H^\circ = +234.1$

$C(s) + O_2(g) \longrightarrow CO_2(g),$ $\Delta H^\circ = -393.5$

The ΔH° value for $4Fe(s) + 3O_2(g) \longrightarrow 2Fe_2O_3(s)$ is calculated as

(a) $\frac{3}{2}(-393.5) - 234.1$ (b) $\frac{3}{2}(-393.5) + 234.1$
(c) $-393.5 - 234.1$ (d) $3(-393.5) - 2(234.1)$

102. The enthalpy change for which of the following processes represents the enthalpy of formation of AgCl?

(a) $Ag^+(aq) + Cl^-(aq) \longrightarrow AgCl(s)$
(b) $Ag(s) + AuCl(s) \longrightarrow Au(s) + AgCl(s)$
(c) $Ag(s) + \frac{1}{2}Cl_2(g) \longrightarrow AgCl(s)$
(d) $AgCl(s) \longrightarrow Ag(s) + \frac{1}{2}Cl_2(s)$

103. Which combination of the following equations have enthalpy changes equal to ΔH_{comb} (C)?

I. $C + O_2 \longrightarrow CO_2$

II. $C + \frac{1}{2}O_2 \longrightarrow CO$

III. $CO + \frac{1}{2}O_2 \longrightarrow CO_2$

(a) I, II (b) I, II, III
(c) I, III (d) I

104. In the reactions,

I. $H_2 \longrightarrow 2H, \quad \Delta H = 436$ kJ

II. $H_2 + \frac{1}{2}O_2 \longrightarrow H_2O, \quad \Delta H = -241.81$ kJ

III. $2H + \frac{1}{2}O_2 \longrightarrow H_2O, \quad \Delta H = ?$

H_2O can be formed either by II or III. Ratio of enthalpy change in III to II is

(a) 2.8 (b) 0.36
(c) 1.2 (d) 0.82

105. Specific heat of aluminium is 0.214 cal/g°C. Heat required to raise the temperature of 40.0 g of Al from 20° to 30°C is

(a) 85.6 cal (b) 3.2 cal
(c) 171.2 cal (d) 342.4 cal

106. Enthalpy of sublimation of iodine is 24 cal g^{-1} at 200°C. If specific heat of $I_2(s)$ and I_2 (vap.) are 0.055 and 0.031 cal g^{-1} K^{-1} respectively, then enthalpy of sublimation of iodine at 250°C in cal g^{-1} is **[JEE Main 2019, April]**

(a) 2.85 (b) 5.7
(c) 22.8 (d) 11.4

107. At 25°C and 1 atm, which one of the following has non-zero ΔH_f° ?

(a) Fe (b) O (c) C(*s*) (d) Ne

108. The heat of formation of MgO, Al_2O_3 and SiO_2 are – 602, –1676, – 911 kJ mol^{-1}. Most stable oxide is,

(a) MgO (b) Al_2O_3
(c) SiO_2 (d) can't be predicted

109. Stability order of oxides given in Q. 108 is

(a) $MgO < SiO_2 < Al_2O_3$
(b) $SiO_2 < Al_2O_3 < MgO$
(c) $Al_2O_3 < SiO_2 < MgO$
(d) $MgO < Al_2O_3 < SiO_2$

110. Hydration energies of Li^+ and Cl^- are – 499 and – 382 kJ mol^{-1}. If lattice energy of LiCl is –840 kJ mol^{-1}, heat of solution of LiCl is

(a) +41 kJ mol^{-1} (b) –1222 kJ mol^{-1}
(c) –1621 kJ mol^{-1} (d) – 41 kJ mol^{-1}

111. Heat of neutralisation of NaOH with equivalent amount of acid is maximum in case of

(a) HCl (b) HNO_3
(c) HF (d) CH_3COOH

112. The combustion of glucose takes place as per reaction,

$C_6H_{12}O_6 + 6O_2 \longrightarrow 6CO_2 + 6H_2O,$
$\Delta H = -72$ kcal mol^{-1}

The energy released by the combustion of 1.6 g of glucose is

(a) – 0.72 kcal (b) – 0.27 kcal
(c) – 0.46 kcal (d) – 0.64 kcal

113. The reaction, $MgO(s) + C(s) \rightarrow Mg(s) + CO(g)$, for which $\Delta_r H° = + 491.1$ kJ mol^{-1} and $\Delta_r S° = 198.0$ JK^{-1}mol^{-1}, is not feasible at 298 K. Temperature above which reaction will be feasible is **[JEE Main 2019, Jan]**

(a) 2040.5 K (b) 1890.0 K
(c) 2380.5 K (d) 2480.3 K

114. On burning 4.0 g of iron to ferric oxide at constant pressure, the heat evolved is 29.28 kJ. The enthalpy of formation of ferric oxide is (At. wt. of Fe = 56)

(a) 81.98 kJ mol^{-1} (b) –81.98 kJ mol^{-1}
(c) 819.8 kJ mol^{-1} (d) –819.8 kJ mol^{-1}

115. 2.0 g of CH_4 on combustion produce 25 kcal. Heat of combustion of CH_4 would be

(a) – 200 kcal (b) – 400 kcal
(c) – 500 kcal (d) – 600 kcal

116. The heat of formation of CO_2 is –95 kcal. The amount of carbon which on burning will evolve 1000 kcal is

(a) 12.63 g (b) 17.95 g
(c) 126.3 g (d) 179.5 g

117. The heat of combustion of benzoic acid is –2546 kJ mol^{-1} at 25°C and 1 atm. The ΔE is

(a) –1555.6 kJ (b) –2244.76 kJ
(c) –2544.76 kJ (d) –2868.66 kJ

118. The enthalpy of combustion of C_6H_6 is –3250 kJ mol^{-1}. When 0.39 g of benzene is burnt in excess of oxygen in an open vessel, the amount of heat liberated is

(a) –16.25 J (b) –16.25 kJ
(c) –32.5 J (d) –32.5 kJ

119. The heat of formation of $C_{12}H_{22}O_{11}(s), CO_2(g)$ and $H_2O(l)$ are – 530, – 94.3 and – 68.3 kcal/mol respectively. The amount of $C_{12}H_{22}O_{11}$ to supply 2700 kcal of energy is

(a) 382.70 g (b) 832.74 g
(c) 463.9 g (d) 684 g

120. The standard enthalpies of combustion of fumaric acid and maleic acid (to four CO_2 and H_2O) are –1336.0 kJ mol^{-1} and –1359.2 kJ mol^{-1}, respectively. Thus, enthalpy of the following isomerisation process is

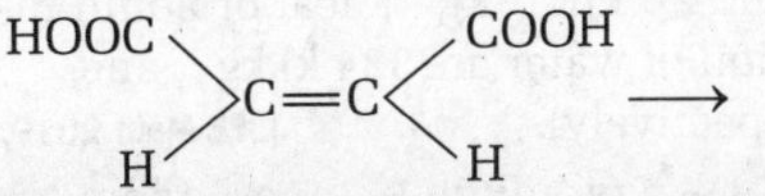

Maleic acid

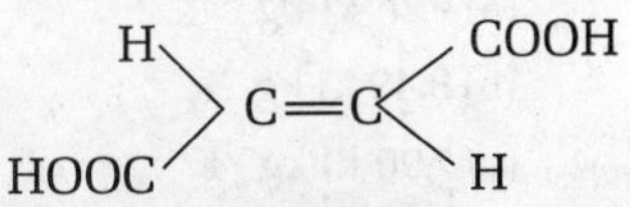

Fumaric acid

(a) 23.2 kJ mol^{-1} (b) –23.2 kJ mol^{-1}
(c) –2695.2 kJ mol^{-1} (d) +2695.2 kJ mol^{-1}

121. The standard molar enthalpy of formation of molecular oxygen at 298 K is zero. Thus, its value at 315 K is ($C_p^\circ(O_2)$ is 29.4 JK mol^{-1})

(a) zero (b) 0.5 kJ mol^{-1}
(c) –0.5 kJ mol^{-1} (d) can't be predicted

122. The bond energy (in kcal mol^{-1}) of C—C single bond is approximately **[IIT JEE 2010]**

(a) 1 (b) 10 (c) 100 (d) 1000

123. The species which by definition has zero standard molar enthalpy of formation at 298 K is **[IIT JEE 2010]**

(a) $Br_2(g)$ (b) $Cl_2(g)$
(c) $H_2O(g)$ (d) $CH_4(g)$

124. The following reaction is performed at 298K

$$2NO(g) + O_2(g) \rightleftharpoons 2NO_2(g)$$

The standard free energy of formation of NO (g) is 86.6 kJ/mol at 298 K. What is the standard free energy of formation of $NO_2(g)$ at 298 K? ($K_p = 1.6 \times 10^{12}$) **[JEE Main 2015]**

(a) $R(298)\ \text{In}\ (1.6 \times 10^{12}) - 86600$

(b) $86600 + R(298)\ \text{In}\ (1.6 \times 10^{12})$

(c) $86600 - \dfrac{\text{In}\ (1.6 \times 10^{12})}{R(298)}$

(d) $0.5\ [2 \times 86600 - R(298)\ \text{In}\ (1.6 \times 10^{12})]$

125. In a constant volume calorimeter, 3.5 g of a gas with molecular weight 28 was burnt in excess oxygen at 298.0 K. The temperature of the calorimeter was found to increases from 298.0 K to 298.45 K due to the combustion process. Given, that the heat capacity of the calorimeter is 2.5 kJ K^{-1}, the numerical value for the enthalpy of combustion of the gas in kJ mol^{-1} is

(a) 9 (b) 6
(c) 8 (d) 4

126. On the basis of the following thermochemical data: [$\Delta G_f^\circ H^+(aq) = 0$]

$$H_2O(l) \longrightarrow H^+(aq) + OH^-(aq); \quad \Delta H° = 57.32 \text{ kJ}$$

$$H_2(g) + \frac{1}{2} O_2(g) \longrightarrow H_2O(l); \quad \Delta H° = -286.02 \text{ kJ}$$

the value of the enthalpy of formation of OH^- ion at 25°C is

(a) –22.88 kJ (b) –228.88 kJ
(c) +228.88 kJ (d) –343.52 kJ

127. Oxidising power of chlorine in aqueous solution can be determined by the parameters indicated below

$$\frac{1}{2} Cl_2(g) \xrightarrow{\frac{1}{2} \Delta_{diss} H^\ominus} Cl(g) \xrightarrow{\Delta_{EA} H^\ominus} Cl^-(g) \xrightarrow{\Delta_{hyd} H^\ominus} Cl^-(aq)$$

The energy involved in the conversion of $\frac{1}{2}Cl_2(g)$ to $Cl^-(aq)$ (using the data, $\Delta_{diss}H^{\ominus}_{Cl_2} = 240$ kJ mol^{-1}, $\Delta_{EA}H^{\ominus}_{Cl} = -349$ kJ mol^{-1}, $\Delta_{hyd}H^{\ominus}_{Cl} = -381$ kJ mol^{-1}) will be

(a) + 152 kJ mol^{-1} (b) −610 kJ mol^{-1}
(c) −850 kJ mol^{-1} (d) +120 kJ mol^{-1}

128. Assuming that water vapour is an ideal gas, internal energy change (ΔU) when 1 mole water is vaporised at 1 bar pressure at 100°C, (Given, molar enthalpy of vaporisation of water at 1 bar and 373 K = 41 kJ mol^{-1} and $R = 8.3$ J mol^{-1} K^{-1}) will be

(a) 4.100 kJ mol^{-1}
(b) 3.7904 kJ mol^{-1}
(c) 37.904 kJ mol^{-1}
(d) 41.00 kJ mol^{-1}

129. The standard enthalpy of formation (ΔH_f°) at 298 K for methane, $CH_4(g)$, is −74.8 kJ mol^{-1}. The additional information required to determine the average energy for C—H bond formation would be

(a) the dissociation energy of H_2 and enthalpy of sublimation of carbon
(b) latent heat of vaporization of methane
(c) the first four ionization energies of carbon and electron gain enthalpy of hydrogen
(d) the dissociation energy of hydrogen molecule, H_2

130. The enthalpy changes for the following processes are listed below

$Cl_2(g) = 2Cl(g)$,	242.3 kJ mol^{-1}
$I_2(g) = 2I(g)$,	151.0 kJ mol^{-1-1}
$ICl(g) = I(g) + Cl(g)$,	211.3 kJ mol^{-1}
$I_2(s) = I_2(g)$,	62.76 kJ mol^{-1}

Given that the standard states for iodine and chlorine are $I_2(s)$ and $Cl_2(g)$, the standard enthalpy of formation of ICl (g) is

(a) −14.6 kJ mol^{-1} (b) −16.8 kJ mol^{-1}
(c) +16.8 kJ mol^{-1} (d) +244.8 kJ mol^{-1}

131. The standard enthalpy of formation of NH_3 is −46.0 kJ mol^{-1}. If the enthalpy of formation of H_2 from its atoms is −436 kJ mol^{-1} and that of N_2 is −712 kJ mol^{-1}, the average bond enthalpy of N—H bond in NH_3 is

(a) − 964 kJ mol^{-1}
(b) + 352 kJ mol^{-1}
(c) + 1056 kJ mol^{-1}
(d) − 1102 kJ mol^{-1}

132. Consider the reaction,

$4NO_2(g) + O_2(g) \longrightarrow 2N_2O_5(g), \Delta_r H = -111$ kJ. If $N_2O_5(s)$ is formed instead of $N_2O_5(g)$ in the above reaction, the $\Delta_r H$ value will be
(Given, ΔH of sublimation for N_2O_5 is 54 kJ mol^{-1})

(a) − 165 kJ (b) + 54 kJ (c) + 219 kJ (d) − 219 kJ

133. Given, $\Delta_{diss}\ H^\circ(Cl_2) = 240$ kJ mol^{-1}

$\Delta_{eg}\ H^\circ(Cl) = -349$ kJ mol^{-1}

$\Delta_{hyd}\ H^\circ(Cl^-) = -381$ kJ mol^{-1}

Energy involved in the conversion of 1 mole of $Cl_2(g)$ into $Cl^-(aq)$ is

(a) + 152 kJ mol^{-1} (b) − 610 kJ mol^{-1}
(c) − 1220 kJ mol^{-1} (d) − 850 kJ mol^{-1}

134. The enthalpy of neutralisation for the first proton of $H_2S(aq)$ is − 33.7 kJ mol^{-1}. Thus, enthalpy change for the following step is

$$H_2S(aq) \longrightarrow HS^-(aq) + H^+(aq)$$

(a) 23.6 kJ mol^{-1} (b) − 23.6 kJ mol^{-1}
(c) 57.3 kJ mol^{-1} (d) − 57.3 kJ mol^{-1}

135. Using the data provided, calculate the multiple bond energy (kJ mol^{-1}) of a C≡C bond in C_2H_2. That energy is (take the bond energy of a C—H bond as 350 kJ mol^{-1}) **[IIT JEE 2012]**

$2C(s) + H_2(g) \longrightarrow C_2H_2(g)$; $\Delta H = 225$ kJ mol^{-1}

$2C(s) \longrightarrow 2C(g)$; $\Delta H = 1410$ kJ mol^{-1}

$H_2(g) \longrightarrow 2H(g)$; $\Delta H = 330$ kJ mol^{-1}

(a) 1165 (b) 837
(c) 865 (d) 815

136. The combustion of benzene (l) gives $CO_2(g)$ and $H_2O(l)$. Given that heat of combustion of benzene at constant volume is −3263.9 kJ mol^{-1} at 25° C; heat of combustion (in kJ mol^{-1}) of benzene at constant pressure will be ($R = 8.314$ JK^{-1}mol^{-1}) **[JEE Main 2018]**

(a) 4152.6 (b) −452.46
(c) 3260 (d) −3267.6

137. The entropy change associated with the conversion of 1 kg of ice at 273 K to water vapours at 383 K is (Specific heat of water liquid and water vapour are 4.2 kJK^{-1}kg^{-1} and 2.0 kJK^{-1} kg^{-1}; heat of liquid fusion and vapourisation of water are 334 kJ kg^{-1} and 2491 kJkg^{-1} respectively). **[JEE Main 2019, Jan.]**

(log 273 = 2.436, log 373 = 2.572, log 383 = 2.583)

(a) 9.26 kJ kg^{-1} K^{-1}
(b) 8.49 kJ kg^{-1}K^{-1}
(c) 7.90 kJ kg^{-1}K^{-1}
(d) 2.64 kJ kg^{-1}K^{-1}

Objective Questions Type II [One or more than one correct option(s)]

In each of the questions below, four choices are given, of which one or more than one are correct.

1. In the following

I. $H_2O(s) \longrightarrow H_2O(l)$;

II. $CH_4(g) + 2O_2(g) \longrightarrow CO_2(g) + 2H_2O(g)$

III. $H_2(g) \longrightarrow 2H(g)$;

IV. $Na(s) + \frac{1}{2}Cl_2(s) \longrightarrow NaCl(s)$

equations representing formation of the compound used to determine ΔH_f° are

(a) I, III, IV (b) I, III
(c) II, IV (d) IV

2. Standard molar enthalpy of CO_2 is not equal to

(a) zero
(b) the standard molar enthalpy of combustion of gaseous carbon
(c) the sum of standard molar enthalpies of CO and O_2
(d) the standard molar enthalpy of combustion of carbon(s)

3. Factors that influence the heat of reaction are

(a) the physical state of reactants and products
(b) the temperature
(c) the pressure or volume
(d) the method by which the final products are obtained

4. Select the correct relations.

(a) $\Delta E_{T_2} = \Delta E_{T_1} + \Delta C_V (T_2 - T_1)$
(b) $\Delta H_T = \Delta E_T + \Delta n_g\ RT$
(c) $\log T + (\gamma - 1) \log V = \text{constant}$
(d) $\log p + \gamma \log V = \text{constant}$

5. Select the correct statements.

(a) Alcohol-flames tend to be cooler than hydrocarbon flames
(b) If bond energies of N≡N, H—H, and N—H bonds are q_1, q_2 and q_3 respectively then heat of formation of NH_3 is $q_3 - q_1 - q_2$
(c) Heat of reaction is independent of physical states
(d) Heat of combustion of CO is $-q$ kcal then heat of formation of CO_2 is $-q$ kcal.

6. Which signifies standard states?

(a) Ideal gas at 1 bar and the given temperature
(b) Pure liquid at 1 bar and the given temperature
(c) Stable crystalline form at 1 bar and given temperature
(d) Any physical state of a substance at 1 bar and at 273 K

7. Select the correct statement(s).

(a) The standard state of a gaseous species is ideal gas at 1 atm and 298 K
(b) Combustion process is always exothermic
(c) Dissolution of a solute in water is always endothermic
(d) The bond energy and bond dissociation energy are same

8. Consider the following statements.

I. The standard heat of formation of liquid chlorine, $Cl_2(l)$, at 298 K is taken is zero.
II. Heat of reaction involving ideal gases increases with increase of pressure.
III. ΔH_f° for $O_2(g)$ is zero by convention.
IV. ΔH_f° for HCl(g) is different from ΔH_f° for HCl(aq).

Select the corect statements.

(a) I, II, III (b) I, III, IV
(c) II, III (d) III, IV

9. Select the correct statements.

(a) From the following reaction

$$CO(g) + O_2(g) \longrightarrow CO_2(g), \quad \Delta H = q_1$$

Heat of formation of $CO_2(g)$ is q_1.

(b) From the following reaction

$$C(\text{graphite}) + \frac{1}{2}O_2(g) \longrightarrow CO(g) \quad \Delta H = q_2$$

Heat of combustion of carbon is q_2.

(c) From the above reactions, heat of formation of CO_2 is $q_1 + q_2$
(d) From th above reactions, heat of combustion of CO(g) is q_1 and that of carbon is $q_1 + q_2$

10. Select the correct thermodynamic equations.

(a) $dE = \left(\frac{\partial E}{\partial T}\right)_V dT + \left(\frac{\partial E}{\partial V}\right)_T dV$

(b) $dH = \left(\frac{\partial H}{\partial T}\right)_p dT + \left(\frac{\partial H}{\partial P}\right)_T dp$

(c) $\left(\frac{\partial H}{\partial p}\right)_T = V - T\left(\frac{\partial V}{\partial T}\right)_p$

(d) $\Delta H_{T_2} = \Delta H_{T_1} + \Delta C_V (T_2 - T_1)$

11. Consider the following thermochemical changes

I. $PbO(s) + S(s) + \frac{3}{2}O_2(g) \longrightarrow PbSO_4(s) \quad \Delta H = q_1$

II. $PbO(s) + H_2SO_4 \cdot 5H_2O(l) \longrightarrow PbSO_4(s) + 6H_2O(l) \quad \Delta H = q_2$

III. $SO_3(g) + 6H_2O(l) \longrightarrow H_2SO_4 \cdot 5H_2O(l) \quad \Delta H = q_3$

Heat of formation of SO_3 can be evaluated by following algebraic summation.

(a) I – II – III (b) II + III – I
(c) I + II – III (d) II – III – I

12. From the following graph we conclude

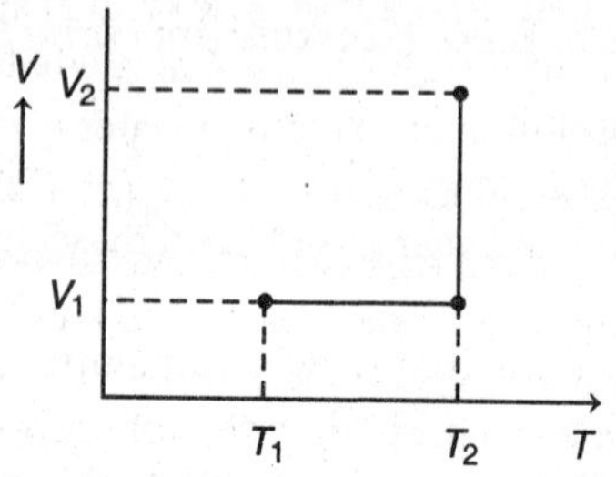

(a) there is change from initial state p_1, V_1, T_1 to final state p_2, V_2, T_2

(b) $dE = \left(\frac{\partial E}{\partial T}\right)_V dT + \left(\frac{\partial E}{\partial V}\right)_T dV$

(c) $dH = \left(\frac{\partial E}{\partial T}\right)_V dT + \left(\frac{\partial E}{\partial V}\right)_T dV$

(d) $dG = dH + TdS$

13. Choose the reaction(s) from the following options, for which the standard enthalpy of reaction is equal to the standard enthalpy of formation. **[JEE Advanced 2019]**

(a) $2C(g) + 3\ H_2(g) \longrightarrow C_2H_6(g)$

(b) $2H_2(g) + O_2(g) \longrightarrow 2H_2O(l)$

(c) $\frac{3}{2}O_2(g) \longrightarrow O_3(g)$

(d) $\frac{1}{8}S_8(s) + O_2(g) \longrightarrow SO_2(g)$

Numerical Value Questions

All these questions have a Numerical value as their answer, solve the questions and write your answer.

1. From the following heats of reaction,

(a) $CaCO_3(s) \longrightarrow CaO(s) + CO_2(g)$, $\Delta H = 178.1$ kJ

(b) $CaO(s) + H_2O(l) \longrightarrow Ca(OH)_2(s)$, $\Delta H = -64.8$ kJ

(c) $Ca(OH)_2(s) \longrightarrow Ca^{2+}(aq) + 2OH^-(aq)$,

$\Delta H = -16.2$ kJ

ΔH for below reaction is …… .

$Ca^{2+}(aq) + 2OH^-(aq) + CO_2(g) \longrightarrow CaCO_3(s) + H_2O(l)$

2. Calculate the enthalpy of formation of gaseous 3-methyl-1-butene $[CH_3—\underset{\displaystyle CH_3}{\underset{|}{C}H}—CH{=}CH_2]$ from the following bond enthalpy data at 298 K

Bond	C—H	C—C	C=C	H—H
Enthalpy (kJ mol^{-1})	413.4	347.7	615.0	436.6

and heat of sublimation of carbon(s) is 718.4 kJ mol^{-1}.

3. Standard enthalpies of combustion of $C_2H_4(g)$, $C_2H_6(g)$ and $H_2(g)$ are – 1410.8, –1559.8 and – 285.9 kJ mol^{-1} at constant pressure and 298 K respectively. The enthalpy of hydrogenation of $C_2H_4(g)$ at constant volume and at 298 K is

4. The heat liberated on complete combustion of 7.8 g of benzene is 327 kJ. This heat has been measured at constant volume and at 27°C. The heat of combustion of benzene at constant pressure is ($R = 8.3$ J mol^{-1} K^{-1})

5. The polymerisation of ethylene to linear polyethylene is represented by the reaction

$$nCH_2{=}CH_2 \longrightarrow {+}CH_2—CH_2{+}_n$$

where n is large integral value. Calculate the enthalpy of polymerisation per mol of ethylene at 298 K. The average enthalpies of bond dissociation for (C=C) and (C—C) at 298 K are 590 and 331 kJ mol^{-1}.

6. Calculate the standard heat of formation of $H_2O_2(l)$ if
BE of H—H bond = 435 kJ mol^{-1},
BE of O=O bond = 498 kJ mol^{-1}
BE of O—H bond = 464 kJ mol^{-1},
BE of O—O bond = 142 kJ mol^{-1}
Enthalpy of vaporisation of $H_2O_2(l)$ at 25°C= 51.47 kJ mol^{-1}

7. Calculate ΔH_f° for chloride ion from the following data.

$\frac{1}{2}H_2(g) + \frac{1}{2}Cl_2(g) \longrightarrow HCl(g)$, $\Delta H_f^\circ = -92.4$ kJ

$HCl(g) + nH_2O \longrightarrow H^+(aq) + Cl^-(aq)$, $\Delta H_{298\text{ K}} = -74.8$ kJ

$\Delta H_f^\circ(H^+)(aq) = 0.0$ kJ

8. A 0.1 mole sample of solid NH_4Cl was dissolved in 50.0 mole of water, the temperature of the solution decreased. A small electrical immersion heater restored the temperature of the system by passing 0.1246 A from a 15.03 V power supply for a period of 809 s. Determine ΔH° for

$$NH_4Cl(s) \xrightarrow{500\text{ mol } H_2O} NH_4Cl \quad (\text{in } 500 \text{ mol } H_2O)$$

9. Ethanol can undergo decomposition to form two sets of products.

$$\Delta H^\circ\ C_2H_5OH(g) \rightarrow \begin{cases} \text{I} & C_2H_4(g) + H_2O(g), \quad 45.54 \text{ kJ} \\ \text{II} & CH_3CHO(g) + H_2(g), \quad 68.91 \text{ kJ} \end{cases}$$

If the molar ratio of C_2H_4 to CH_3CHO is 8 :1 in a set of product gases, determine the energy involved in the decomposition process.

10. Tin is obtained from cassiterite by reduction with coke. Use the data given below to determine the minimum temperature (in K) at which the reduction of cassiterite by coke would take place.

At 298 K : $\Delta_f H°[SnO_2(s)] = -581.0$ kJ mol^{-1},

$\Delta_f H°[(CO_2)(g)] = -394.0$ kJ mol^{-1}

$S°[SnO_2(s)] = 56.0$ J K^{-1}mol^{-1}

$S°[Sn(s)] = 52.0$ JK^{-1} mol^{-1}

$S°[C(s)] = 6.0$ J K^{-1} mol^{-1}

$S°[CO_2(g)] = 210.0$ JK^{-1}mol^{-1}

Assume that, the enthalpies and the entropies are temperature independent. **[JEE Advanced 2020]**

11. For the reaction; $A(l) \longrightarrow 2B(g)$

$\Delta U = 2.1$ kcal, $\Delta S = 20$ cal K^{-1} at 300 K.

Hence, ΔG in kcal is .... **[JEE Main 2020]**

12. For a dimerisation reaction, $2A(g) \longrightarrow A_2(g)$, at 298 K, $\Delta U^{\ominus} = -20$ kJ mol^{-1}, $\Delta S^{\ominus} = -30$ JK^{-1} mol^{-1}, then the $\Delta G^{\ominus}$ will be .... J. **[JEE Main 2020, Sep.]**

13. The standard head of formation at 298 K for $CCl_4(l), H_2O(l), CO_2(g)$ and $HCl(g)$ are –106.7, –241.8. –393.7 and –92.5 kJ/mol. Calculate the standard heat of reaction :

$CCl_4(l) + 2H_2O(l)\ 0 \longrightarrow CO_2(g) + 4HCl(g)$.

14. The standard enthalpy of combustion at 25°C of hydrogen, cyclohexene (C_6H_{10}) and cyclohexane (C_6H_{10}) are –241, –3800 and –3920 kJ/mol respectively. Calculate the enthalpy of hydrogenation of cyclohexene.

15. The heat of combustion of ehene gas is 330 kcal mol^{-1}. Calculate C=C bond energy (in kcal/mol). Bond energy of C—H bond is 93.6 kcal/mol, $\Delta_f H^{\ominus}$ for CO_2 (g) and $H_2O(l)$ are –942. kcal/mol and –61 kcal/mol respectively.

Heat of atomisation of carbon and hydrogen are 150 and 104 kcal/mol respectively.

Comprehension Based Questions

In these questions, a passage has been given followed by questions based on it. You have to answer the questions based on the passage given.

Passage 1 A common rocket propellant is a mixture of one part liquid hydrazine (N_2H_4) as fuel and two parts liquid hydrogen peroxide (H_2O_2) as oxidiser .

$$N_2H_4(l) + 2H_2O_2(l) \longrightarrow N_2(g) + 4H_2O(g)$$

ΔH_f° of $N_2H_4(l) = +12.0$ kcal mol^{-1}

$H_2O(g) = -58.0$ kcal mol^{-1}

$H_2O_2(l) = -46.0$ kcal mol^{-1}

Answer the following questions.

1. Select the endothermic compound(s).
(a) N_2H_4
(b) H_2O, H_2O_2
(c) N_2H_4, H_2O_2
(d) N_2H_4, H_2O

2. Hypergolic reactants are
(a) N_2H_4, H_2O
(b) N_2H_4, H_2O_2
(c) H_2O, H_2O_2
(d) None of the above

3. Enthalpy change when 1 g of $N_2H_4(l)$ is ignited by H_2O_2 is (in kcal)
(a) – 152.0 (b) – 4.75
(c) + 152.0 (d) + 4.75

Passage 2 The hydrogen-filled dirigible "Hindenberg" had a gas volume of 1.4×10^8 L. Assume that it was filled to a pressure of 1 atm at 273 K.

Assume ΔH_f° (H_2O) at 298 K = – 57.8 kcal mol^{-1}

Answer the following questions.

1. How many moles of H_2 are used?
(a) 6.25×10^6 mol (b) 1.4×10^8 mol
(c) 22.4 mol (d) 6.25×10^3 mol

2. How much energy is released when all the H_2 is completely burnt to gaseous products at 298 K?
(a) -7.2×10^8 kcal
(b) -3.26×10^8 kcal
(c) -3.6×10^4 kcal
(d) -7.2×10^5 kcal

Passage 3 In a hydrogen bomb, deuterium nuclei fuse to produce a helium nucleus. In the process, 5 MeV of energy is released per deuterium.

Assume that

– 1 / 7000 of natural hydrogen is D

– ΔH_{comb}° of gasoline (C_8H_{18}) = – 5100 kJ mol^{-1}

– density of gasoline = 0.703 g/cm^3

Answer the following questions.

1. How much energy is released from 1L of H_2O?
   (a) -7.64×10^6 kJ L^{-1}
   (b) -7.64×10^3 kJ L^{-1}
   (c) -3.82×10^6 kJ L^{-1}
   (d) -3.82×10^3 kJ L^{-1}
2. How much gasoline (in litres) are required to produce same energy as from 1L of H_2O?
   (a) 171.5 L
   (b) 244 L
   (c) 486 L
   (d) None of the above

***Passage* 4** *Read the following passage and answer the questions at the end.*

I. A student heated a sample of a metal weighing 32.6 g to 99.83°C and put it into 100.0 g of water at 23.62°C in a calorimeter. The final temperature was 24.41°C. The student calculated the specific heat of the metal, but neglected to use the heat capacity of the calorimeter. The specific heat of water is 4.184 J/g.°C. What was his answer? The metal was known to be chromium, molybdenum, or tungsten.

By comparing the value of the specific heat to those of the metals (Cr, 0.460; Mo, 0.250; W, 0.135 J/g.°C), the student identified the metal.

II. A student at the next laboratory bench did the same experiment, obtained the same data, and used the heat capacity of the calorimeter in his calculations. The heat capacity of the calorimeter was 410 J/°C.

1. Metal identified by first student was
   (a) Cr
   (b) Mo
   (c) W
   (d) None of the above
2. Metal identified by the student in the next laboratory was
   (a) Cr
   (b) Mo
   (c) W
   (d) None of the above

***Passage* 5** Born-Haber cycle. We will illustrate the method by calculating the lattice energy of NaCl.

Figure shows the Born-Haber cycle for NaCl. The several interesting reactions in this cycle are as follows.

Ionisation $\quad Na \longrightarrow Na^+ + e^-$.

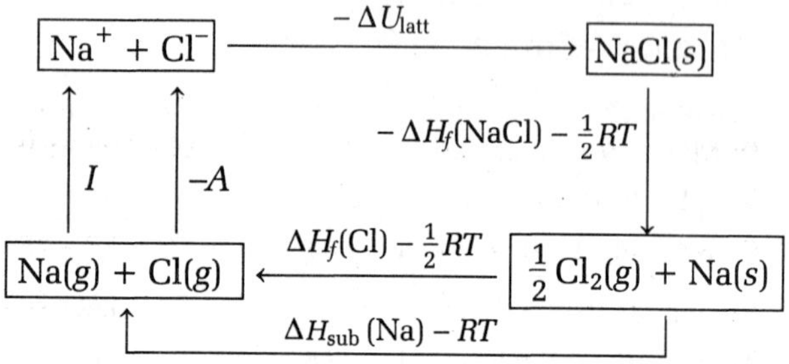

The energy for this reaction (I) is called the ionization potential or ionisation energy. It is measured by spectroscopic and electron impact techniques.

Sublimation $\quad Na(s) \longrightarrow Na(g)$.

Electron capture $\quad Cl + e^- \longrightarrow Cl^-$.

The energy for the attachment of an electron to an atom, molecule, or ion is given the symbol $-A$, where A is called the **electron affinity.**

Bond dissociation $\quad \frac{1}{2}Cl_2(g) \longrightarrow Cl(g)$.

The enthalpy of this reaction is the enthalpy of formation of chlorine atoms from the molecules.

Formation of NaCl

$$Na(s) + \frac{1}{2}Cl_2(g) \longrightarrow NaCl\ (s).$$

This is the formation reaction for NaCl from the elements in their stable form.

Answer the following questions.

1. Thus, lattice energy of NaCl(s) is
   (a) $-\Delta H_f(NaCl) + \Delta H_f(Cl) + \Delta H_{sub}(Na) + A + I + 2RT$
   (b) $\Delta H_f(NaCl) + \Delta H_f(Cl) + \Delta H_{sub}(Na) - A - I - 2RT$
   (c) $-\Delta H_f(NaCl) + \Delta H_f(Cl) + \Delta H_{sub}(Na) - A + I - 2RT$
   (d) None of the above
2. Which is the most stable compound?
   (a) NaCl (b) $MgCl_2$ (c) KCl (d) RbCl
3. Which is the most stable compound?
   (a) LiF (b) LiCl (c) LiBr (d) LiI

Matrix-Match Type

Given below are Matching Type Questions, with two columns (each having some items) each . Each item of Column I has to be matched with the items of Column II.

1. Match the reaction in Column I with relation between ΔH and ΔE in Column II.

Column I	Column II
A. $C(s) + O_2(g) \longrightarrow CO_2(g)$	1. $\Delta H = \Delta E + RT$
B. $N_2(g) + 3H_2(g) \longrightarrow 2NH_3(g)$	2. $\Delta H = \Delta E$
C. $NH_4HS(s) \longrightarrow NH_3(g) + H_2S(g)$	3. $\Delta H = \Delta E - 2RT$
D. $PCl_5(g) \longrightarrow PCl_3(g) + Cl_2(g)$	4. $\Delta H = \Delta E + 2RT$
E. $2SO_2(g) + O_2(g) \longrightarrow 2SO_3(g)$	5. $\Delta H = \Delta E - RT$

2. Match the reaction in Column I with their terms in Column II.

Column I	Column II
A. $CO(g) + \frac{1}{2}O_2(g) \longrightarrow CO_2(g)$	1. Heat of neutralisation
B. $2H_2(g) + O_2(g) \longrightarrow 2H_2O(l)$	2. Heat of combustion
C. $C(s) + O_2(g) \longrightarrow CO_2(g)$	3. Heat of formation
D. $NaOH(aq) + HCl(aq) \longrightarrow NaCl(aq) + H_2O(l)$	4. Fuel cell

3. Column equation/law in Column I with statement in Column II.

Column I	Column II
A. Arrhenius equation	1. Variation of enthalpy of a reaction with temperature.
B. Kirchhoff equation	2. Variation of rate constant with temperature.
C. Second law of thermodynamics	3. Entropy of an isolated system tends to increase and reach a maximum value.
D. Hess's law of constant heat summation	4. Enthalpy change in a reaction is always constant and independent of the manner in which the reaction occurs.

4. Match the reaction in Column I with the enthalpy charge associated with it in Column II.

Column I	Column II
A. $H_2 + \frac{1}{2}O_2 \longrightarrow H_2O$	1. Heat of combustion
B. $CH_4 + O_2 \longrightarrow CO_2 + H_2O$	2. Heat of formation
C. $H^+ + OH^- \longrightarrow H_2O$	3. Heat of solution
D. $SO_2 + \frac{1}{2}O_2 \longrightarrow SO_3$	4. Heat of neutralisation
E. $\frac{1}{2}N_2 + \frac{1}{2}O_2 \longrightarrow NO$	5. Lattice energy

5. Bond energies (kcal mol^{-1}) are given below

Bond	B.E.
H—H	104
H—Cl	103
H—C	87
H—O	111
Cl—Cl	58
Cl—C	79
O=O	118
C—C	83

Match the reaction in Column I with their $\Delta H°$ (based on B.E. values) in Column II.

Column I	Column II
A. $2H_2(g) + O_2(g) \longrightarrow 2H_2O(g)$	1. −216
B. $CH_4(g) + 2O_2(g) \longrightarrow CO_2(g) + 2H_2O(g)$	2. +37
C. $CH_4(g) + Cl_2(g) \longrightarrow CH_3Cl\ (g) + HCl(g)$	3. −118
D. $C_2H_6(g) + Cl_2(g) \longrightarrow C_2H_5Cl\ (g) + HCl(g)$	4. −37

Single Integer Answer Questions

Answer of these questions is a single digit lying between 0 to 9.

1. Heat of combustion of C (diamond) = −7.583 kcal/g
Heat of combustion of C (graphite) = −7.833
Value of $\Delta H°$ when 12 g diamond is converted to graphite is ....

2. ΔC_p of the following is $-x$ (R).
The value of x is

$$N_2(g) + 3H_2(g) \longrightarrow 2NH_3(g)$$

3. Heat of combustion of $A(s)$ is − 10 kcal mol^{-1} and that of $B(s)$ is − 15 kcal mol^{-1}.
Mixture containing 3 moles $A(s)$ and x moles $B(s)$ on combustion released 105 kcal of heat. The value of x is ....

4. Heat of neutralisation of HA (weak acid) by strong base is − 9.7 kcal per equivalent. The dissociation energy of HA (in kcal) is ....

5. A sample gives off 5230 cal when burnt in a bomb calorimeter.
The temperature of the calorimeter assembly increased by 4.385°C.
What is heat capacity of the calorimeter in kJ per degree celsius?

6. Heat of neutralisation of a polybasic acid by strong base is – 54.8 kcal mol^{-1}. What is basicity of the acid?

7. In the following reaction,
$$2H_2(g) + O_2(g) \longrightarrow 2H_2O(l),\ \Delta H^\circ = -136\ \text{kcal mol}^{-1}$$
30.222 kcal of heat is released.
How much water (in grams) is formed?

8. The standard enthalpy of combustion at 25°C of hydrogen, cyclohexne (C_6H_{10}) and cyclohexane (C_6H_{12}) are −241, – 3800 and −3920 kJ/mol respectively. If the heat of hydrogenation of cyclohexene is $-xyz$ kJ/mol. Find the value of $(x + y + z)$?

Answers

Objective Questions Type I [Only one correct option]

1. (d)	2. (b)	3. (b)	4. (b)	5. (c)	6. (b)	7. (a)	8. (c)	9. (d)	10. (a)
11. (b)	12. (b)	13. (b)	14. (c)	15. (a)	16. (c)	17. (c)	18. (b)	19. (a)	20. (a)
21. (a)	22. (c)	23. (d)	24. (c)	25. (b)	26. (b)	27. (d)	28. (a)	29. (d)	30. (b)
31. (c)	32. (d)	33. (a)	34. (b)	35. (b)	36. (b)	37. (c)	38. (b)	39. (d)	40. (b)
41. (a)	42. (b)	43. (b)	44. (d)	45. (a)	46. (b)	47. (a)	48. (a)	49. (c)	50. (c)
51. (d)	52. (d)	53. (a)	54. (b)	55. (d)	56. (a)	57. (b)	58. (d)	59. (c)	60. (c)
61. (c)	62. (b)	63. (b)	64. (d)	65. (a)	66. (a)	67. (d)	68. (b)	69. (b)	70. (c)
71. (a)	72. (d)	73. (b)	74. (a)	75. (c)	76. (d)	77. (a)	78. (a)	79. (a)	80. (b)
81. (b)	82. (b)	83. (a)	84. (b)	85. (d)	86. (b)	87. (b)	88. (c)	89. (c)	90. (b)
91. (c)	92. (c)	93. (a)	94. (d)	95. (c)	96. (c)	97. (a)	98. (c)	99. (b)	100. (d)
101. (d)	102. (c)	103. (d)	104. (a)	105. (a)	106. (c)	107. (b)	108. (a)	109. (b)	110. (d)
111. (c)	112. (d)	113. (d)	114. (d)	115. (a)	116. (c)	117. (c)	118. (b)	119. (d)	120. (a)
121. (b)	122. (c)	123. (b)	124. (d)	125. (a)	126. (b)	127. (b)	128. (c)	129. (a)	130. (c)
131. (b)	132. (d)	133. (c)	134. (a)	135. (d)	136. (d)	137. (a)			

Objective Questions Type II [One or more than one correct option(s)]

1. (d)	2. (b, c, d)	3. (d)	4. (c)	5. (c, d)
6. (a, b, c)	7. (b)	8. (d)	9. (c, d)	10. (a, b, c)
11. (a)	12. (a, b)	13. (c, d)		

Numerical Value Questions

1. $Ca^{2+}(aq) + 2OH^-(aq) + CO_2(g) \longrightarrow CaCO_3(s) + H_2O(l)\ \Delta H = -97\text{kJ}$
2. -17.1 kJ mol^{-1}
3. $\Delta E^\circ = -134.42$ kJ mol^{-1}
4. $\Delta H^\circ = -3273.74$ kJ mol^{-1}
5. $\Delta H = (BE)_{C=C} - 2(BE)_{C-C} = 590 - 2 \times 331 = -72$ kJ
6. -188.47 kJ mol^{-1}
7. $\Delta H_f^\circ(Cl^-) = -74.8 - 92.4 = -167.2$ kJ
8. 15.15 kJ
9. 48.137 kJ
10. 935 K
11. – 2.70
12. −135375 J
13. – 173.4 kJ/mol
14. – 121 kJ/mol
15. −153.2 kcal/mol

Comprehension Based Questions

Passage 1 → 1. (a) 2. (b) 3. (b)
Passage 2 → 1. (a) 2. (b)
Passage 3 → 1. (a) 2. (b)
Passage 4 → 1. (c) 2. (b)
Passage 5 → 1. (c) 2. (b) 3. (a)

Matrix-Match Type

1. A→(2); B→(3); C→(4); D→(1); E→(5)
2. A→(2); B→(4); C→(3); D→(1).
3. A→(2); B→(1); C→(3); D→(4).
4. A→(1,2); B→(1); C→(4); D→(1); E→(1,2)
5. A→(3); B→(1); C→(4); D→(4)

Single Integer Answer Questions

1. (3) 2. (6) 3. (5) 4. (4) 5. (5) 6. (4) 7. (8) 8. (4)

Solutions

Objective Questions Type I [Only one correct option]

7. (*a*) ΔH_f° is the enthalpy change when one mole of the substance is formed from its elements.

CO_2 is formed in step I directly.

8. (*c*) CO is formed as

$$C(\text{graphite}) + \frac{1}{2}O_2(g) \longrightarrow CO(g)$$

(I – II) gives above equation

Thus, $\Delta H^\circ = (x_2 - x_1)$

9. (*d*) I. $H_2(g) + \frac{1}{2}O_2(g) \longrightarrow H_2O(g), \Delta H_f^\circ = -58\,\text{kcal mol}^{-1}$

II. $H_2(g) + \frac{1}{2}O_2(g) \longrightarrow H_2O(l), \Delta H_f^\circ = -68\,\text{kcal mol}^{-1}$

(I – II) gives $H_2O(l) \longrightarrow H_2O(g),\ \Delta H^\circ_{vap} = 10\text{ kcal mol}^{-1}$

$$\therefore\ \Delta S^\circ_{vap} = \frac{\Delta H^\circ_{vap}}{T} = \frac{10 \times 1000\text{ cal mol}^{-1}}{373\text{ K}} = 26.8$$

$$\approx 27\text{ cal mol}^{-1}\text{ K}^{-1}$$

10. (*a*) The explanation of all the options are as follows :

(a) $N_2(g) + 3H_2(g) \longrightarrow 2NH_3(g), \Delta n_g = 2 - (1+3) = -2$

So, ΔS is also negative (entropy decreases)

(b) $CaSO_4(s) \xrightarrow{\Delta} CaO(s) + SO_3(g), \Delta n_g = (1+0) - 0 = +1$

So, $\Delta S = +\text{ve}$

(c) In dissolution, $\Delta S = +$ ve because molecules/ions of the solid solute (here, iodine) become free to move in solvated/dissolved state of the solution,

$$I_2(s) \xrightarrow[\text{(KI)}]{\text{Water}} I_2(aq)$$

(d) In sublimation process, molecules of solid becomes quite free when they become gas,

$$\underset{\text{Dry ice}}{CO_2(s)} \longrightarrow CO_2(g)$$

So, ΔS will be positive.

11. (*b*) ΔH_f = enthalpy of that substance and enthalpy of element = zero

Thus, $H(\text{HF}) = -64.2\text{ kcal mol}^{-1}$

Thus, $\Delta H^\circ = (2H_{HF} + H_{Cl_2}) - (2H_{HCl} + H_{F_2})$

$-84.4 = 2 \times (-64.2) + 0 - 2H_{HCl} - 0$

$\therefore\ H_{HCl} = -22.0\text{ kcal}$

12. (*b*) $\Delta H^\circ = [4\Delta H_f(N_2) + 3\Delta H_f(H_2O(g))] - [3\Delta H_f(N_2O) + 2\Delta H_f(NH_3)]$

$-879.6 = [0 + 3(-241.8) - 3\Delta H_f(N_2O) - 2(-45.9)]$

$\Delta H_f^\circ(N_2O) = 82.0\text{ kJ mol}^{-1}$

15. (*a*) Mechanical work (*p-V* work) $= p\Delta V = p(V_2 - V_1)$

$= 1(448 - 0.274)$ L atm

$= 447.726$ L atm

$$= \frac{447.726 \times 8.3143 \times 10^{-3}}{0.0821}\text{ kJ} = 45.34\text{ kJ}$$

16. (*c*)

$A(l) \longrightarrow A(g)$ $\quad \Delta H\ x_1$

$A(s) \longrightarrow A(l)$ $\quad x_2$

Thus, $A(s) \longrightarrow A(g)$ $\quad (x_1 + x_2)$

18. (*b*) Operate $-\left(\frac{I}{2} + \frac{II}{2} + III\right)$

$\Delta H^\circ = -22.2$ kJ

19. (*a*) Δn_g (gaseous species) $= 2 - 1 = 1$

$\Delta H = \Delta E + \Delta n_g RT$

$= 40 + 1 \times 8.3143 \times 10^{-3} \times 300 = 42.5$ kJ

21. (*a*) By difference heat of combustion of

$CH_2 = -158.4\text{ kcal mol}^{-1}$

Thus, heat of combustion of C_8H_{16} (two H-atoms less than C_8H_{18}) $= -1267.2\text{ kcal mol}^{-1}$

22. (*c*) $\Delta n_g = -2$

Using $\Delta H = \Delta E + \Delta n_g RT$

$-210 = \Delta E - 2 \times 0.002 \times 298$

$\therefore\ \Delta E = -208.81$ kcal

23. (*d*) $C_6H_6(l) + 7.5\,O_2(g) \longrightarrow 6CO_2(g) + 3H_2O(l)$

Since, $\Delta H_f(X) = H(X)$

$\therefore\ \Delta H = 6\Delta H_f(CO_2) + 3\Delta H_f(H_2O) - \Delta H_f(C_6H_6)$

$= -6x_3 - 3x_2 + x_1$

24. (*c*) Calorific values are expressed in cal/g of the substance

Substance	Heat of combustion (kcal/mol)	Calorific value kcal/g
CH_4	–210	13.125
C_2H_6	–368.4	12.28
C_3H_8	–526.3	11.96

25. (*b*) Calorific value of $H_2 = -143\text{ kJ g}^{-1} = -286\text{ kJ mol}^{-1}$

Thus, heat of combustion of $H_2 = -286\text{ kJ mol}^{-1}$

26. (*b*) $H_2(g) + \frac{1}{2}O_2(g) \longrightarrow H_2O(l)\ \Delta H^\circ = -241.8\text{ kJ mol}^{-1}$

$\therefore\ \Delta H_f^\circ(H_2O) = -241.8\text{ kJ mol}^{-1}$

$C(s) + O_2(g) \longrightarrow CO_2(g)$

$\Delta H^\circ = -393.5\text{ kJ mol}^{-1}$

$\therefore\ \Delta H_f^\circ(CO_2) = -393.5\text{ kJ mol}^{-1}$

$C_2H_5OH(l) + 3O_2(g) \longrightarrow 2CO_2(g) + 3H_2O(l)$

$\Delta H = -1234.7\text{ kJ mol}^{-1}$

$\Delta H^\circ = 2\Delta H_f^\circ(CO_2) + 3\Delta H_f^\circ(H_2O) - \Delta H_f^\circ(C_2H_5OH)$

$-1234.7 = -2 \times 393.5 - 3 \times 241.8 - \Delta H_f^\circ(C_2H_5OH)$

$\therefore\ \Delta H_f^\circ(C_2H_5OH) = -277.7\text{ kJ mol}^{-1}$

28. (*a*) does not give complete oxidation of C_6H_6 since, CO can be further oxidised to CO_2.

(*b*) C(*g*) is in gaseous state.

(*c*) represents complete oxidation of CH_4.

(*d*) gives incomplete oxidation of C(*s*).

30. (*b*) $\underset{1\text{ mol}}{C_2H_6} + 3.5O_2 \longrightarrow 2CO_2 + \underset{3\text{ mol} = 54\text{ g}}{3H_2O}$

Since, 54 g of H_2O is formed, 1 mol of C_2H_6 has been combusted

$\therefore$ Heat of combustion of C_2H_6 = – 370 kcal mol^{-1}

31. (*c*) (A) $\underset{\text{Strong base}}{CsOH} + \underset{\text{Strong acid}}{HX} \rightleftharpoons CsX + H_2O$ – 13.4 kcal mol^{-1}

$$OH^- + H^+ \rightleftharpoons H_2O \quad -13.4\text{ kcal mol}^{-1}$$

(B) $CsOH + HF \rightleftharpoons CsF + H_2O$ – 16.4 kcal mol^{-1}

Reaction (B) consists of $\quad \Delta H$

I. $HF \rightleftharpoons H^+ + F^- \quad x$

II. $CsOH + H^+ \rightleftharpoons Cs^+ + H_2O \quad -13.4$

$$x - 13.4 = -16.4$$

$\therefore$ $x = -3.0$ kcal mol^{-1}

32. (*d*) (II – I) gives required equation

$$H^+ + OH^- \longrightarrow H_2O$$

$\therefore$ $\Delta H = 0.86 - 14.22 = -13.36$ kcal

33. (*a*) $H^+ + OH^- \longrightarrow H_2O$

$\Delta H = -57.3$ kJ mol^{-1} (standard value)

$$\Delta H = -57.3 = \Delta H_f^\circ(H_2O) - \Delta H_f^\circ(H^+) - \Delta H_f^\circ(OH^-)$$

$$= -286.2 - 0 - \Delta H_f^\circ(OH^-)$$

$\therefore$ $\Delta H_f^\circ(OH^-) = -228.9$ kJ mol^{-1}

35. (*b*) 1 mol H_2SO_4 = 2 equivalents of H_2SO_4

$\therefore$ ΔH° (neutralisation) = – 13.7 × 2 = – 27.4 kcal

37. (*c*) $CH_3COOH \rightleftharpoons CH_3COO^- + H^+, \Delta H = 0.005$ kcal g^{-1}

= 0.30 kcal mol^{-1}

$\therefore$ $2CH_3COOH \rightleftharpoons 2CH_3COO^- + 2H^+, \Delta H = 0.60$ kcal mol^{-1}

$\underset{\text{Strong base}}{Ca(OH)_2} \rightleftharpoons Ca^{2+} + 2OH^-, \quad \Delta H = 0$

$2H^+ + 2OH^- \rightleftharpoons 2H_2O, \quad \Delta H = -13.7 \times 2 = -27.4$

$\therefore$ $2CH_3COOH + Ca(OH)_2 \rightleftharpoons (CH_3COO)_2Ca + 2H_2O$

$\Delta H = -27.40 + 0.60 = -26.80$ kcal

38. (*b*) NaOH = 30 mL of 0.1 M = 3 millimol

HCl = 10 mL of 0.1 M + 20 mL of 0.1 M HCl

= 3 millimol

Thus, NaOH is completely neutralised.

$\therefore$ Heat of neutralisation of 0.003 mol of NaOH by 0.003 mol of HCl = –13.7 × 0.003 kcal = 0.0411 kcal

= – 41.1 cal

Thus, additional heat in second stage = – 41.4 – 13.7

= – 27.4 cal

39. (*d*) 100 mL of 1 M H_2SO_4 = 100 millimol = 0.1 mol

= 0.2 equivalent

100 mL of 1 M $Ca(OH)_2$ = 0.2 equivalent

Thus, H_2SO_4 is completely neutralised.

$\therefore$ Heat of neutralisation = – 0.2 × 13.7 = – 2.74 kcal

40. (*b*) $Ca(OH)_2 + HCl \longrightarrow Ca(OH)Cl + H_2O$

One equivalent of $Ca(OH)_2$ is neutralised.

Thus, $\Delta H = -13.7$ kcal

Similarly in step II

41. (*a*) I. $\frac{1}{2}H_2(g) + \frac{1}{2}Cl_2(g) \longrightarrow HCl(g), \ \Delta H_f^\circ = -22.1$ kcal

II. $HCl(g) + nH_2O \longrightarrow H^+(aq) + Cl^-(aq)$

$\Delta H_f^\circ = -17.9$ kcal

Adding $\frac{1}{2}H_2(g) + \frac{1}{2}Cl_2(g) + nH_2O \longrightarrow H^+(aq) + Cl^-(aq)$

$\Delta H_f^\circ = -40.0$ kcal

$\therefore$ $\Delta H = -40.0 = [\Delta H_f^\circ(H^+) + \Delta H_f^\circ(Cl^-)] - \frac{1}{2}[\Delta H_f^\circ(H_2) + \Delta H_f^\circ(Cl_2)]$

$$-40.0 = 0 + \Delta H_f^\circ(Cl^-)$$

$\therefore$ $\Delta H_f^\circ(Cl^-) = -40$ kcal

42. (*b*) $\Delta H^\circ_{\text{solution}} = \Delta H_f^\circ(K^+) + \Delta H_f^\circ(Cl^-) - \Delta H_f^\circ(KCl)$

$= -60.04 - 40.0 - (-104.18) = +4.14$ kcal

44. (*d*) $CaCl_2(s) + 6H_2O \longrightarrow CaCl_2 \cdot 6H_2O(s) - 23.2$ kcal

$CaCl_2 \cdot 6H_2O(s) + aq \longrightarrow CaCl_2 \cdot 6H_2O(aq) + 3.5$ kcal

Thus, $CaCl_2(s) + aq$ (excess) $\longrightarrow CaCl_2 \cdot 6H_2O(aq)$

–19.7 kcal

50. (*c*) $N_2(g) + 3H_2(g) \longrightarrow 2NH_3(g)$

$\Delta H^\circ = [3(BE)_{H—H} + (BE)_{N\equiv N}] - 6(BE)_{N—H}$

$= 3x_2 + x_1 - 6x_3$

$\therefore$ $\Delta H_f^\circ(NH_3) = \frac{x_1}{2} + \frac{3x_2}{2} - 3x_3$

51. (*d*) I. $CH_4(g) \longrightarrow C(g) + 4H(g) \Delta H = x$, for four C—H bonds

$\therefore$ BE of (C—H) bond $= \frac{x_1}{4}$

II. $C_2H_6(g) \longrightarrow 2C(g) + 6H(g)$

$\Delta H = x_2 = (BE)_{C—C} + 6(BE)_{C—H}$

$= (BE)_{C—C} + 6 \times \frac{x_1}{4}$

$\therefore$ $(BE)_{C—C} = x_2 - 1.5x_1$

54. (*b*) In all two O—H bonds are broken, thus

$$(BE)_{O—H} = \frac{x_1 + x_2}{2}$$

55. (*d*) $\frac{1}{2}H_2(g) + \frac{1}{2}Cl_2(g) \longrightarrow HCl(g)$

$$\Delta H = -91 = \frac{1}{2}(BE)_{H—H} + \frac{1}{2}(BE)_{Cl—Cl} - (BE)_{HCl}$$

$$-91 = \frac{1}{2} \times 430 + \frac{1}{2} \times 242 - (BE)_{HCl}$$

$\therefore$ $(BE)_{HCl} = (215 + 121 + 91)$ kJ mol^{-1}

56. (*a*) Hydrogenation of 1-pentene causes reduction of one (C=C) bond.

Theoretical heat of hydrogenation of 1,3-pentadiene

$$= 252 \text{ kJ mol}^{-1}$$

Experimental value $= 230$ kJ mol^{-1}

$\therefore$ Resonance energy $= 252 - 230 = 22$ kJ

57. (*b*) $N{\equiv}N + 2H{-}H \longrightarrow H{-}\underset{H}{\underset{|}{N}}{-}\underset{H}{\underset{|}{N}}{-}H$

$$\Delta H_f^\circ = [(BE)_{N\equiv N} + 2(BE)_{H-H}] - [(BE)_{N-N} + 4(BE)_{N-H}]$$

$$= [941 + 2 \times 436] - [159 + 4 \times 389]$$

$$= +\ 98 \text{ kJ mol}^{-1}$$

59. (*c*) For a given value of T,

(i) If $\Delta_r G^\circ$ becomes < 0, the forward direction will be spontaneous and then the major and minor components will be Y and X respectively.

(ii) If $\Delta_r G^\circ$ becomes > 0, the forward direction will be non-spontaneous and then the major and minor components will be X and Y respectively.

(a) $\Delta_r G^\circ = 120 - \frac{3}{8} \times 280 = 15$

i.e. $\Delta_r G^\circ > 0$, major component $= X$;

(b) $\Delta_r G^\circ = 120 - \frac{3}{8} \times 350 = -11.25$

i.e. $\Delta_r G^\circ < 0$, major component $= Y$

(c) $\Delta_r G^\circ = 120 - \frac{3}{8} \times 315 = 1.875$

i.e. $\Delta_r G^\circ > 0$, major component $= X$

(d) $\Delta_r G^\circ = 120 - \frac{3}{8} \times 300 = 7.5$

i.e. $\Delta_r G^\circ > 0$, major component $= X$

60. (*c*) $C_2H_4 + H_2 \longrightarrow C_2H_6$

$$\Delta H = \Delta H_f^\circ(C_2H_6) - \Delta H_f^\circ(C_2H_4) - \Delta H_f^\circ(H_2)$$

$$= x_2 - x_1 - 0 = (x_2 - x_1)$$

61. (*c*) $2NO_2 \longrightarrow N_2O_4$

$$\Delta H^\circ = 9.66 - 2 \times 33.84 = -\ 58.02 \text{ kJ}$$

Thus, exothermic (c)

62. (*b*) $F_2^-(g) \longrightarrow F(g) + F^-(g)$

I + III − II gives required equation

$\therefore$ $\Delta H^\circ = 113.9$ kJ

63. (*b*) Based on given values, $\Delta H_f^\circ(CO_2) = x_1$ or $\Delta H_f^\circ(H_2O) = x_2$

$$x_3 = 4x_1 + 2x_2 - 2\Delta H_f^\circ(C_2H_2)$$

$\therefore$ $\Delta H_f^\circ(C_2H_2) = 2x_1 + x_2 - \frac{x_3}{2}$

64. (*d*) $\Delta H_I^\circ = -\ 156$ kcal, $\Delta H_{II}^\circ = -\ 100 + x$

Both I and II represent same chemical change

$$2Na + \frac{1}{2}O_2 + H_2O \longrightarrow 2NaOH$$

Thus, $-156 = -100 + x$

$\therefore$ $x = -\ 56$ kcal

66. (*a*)

	ΔH
$Cl_2 \longrightarrow Cl + Cl$	x_1
$Cl \longrightarrow Cl^+ + e^-$	x_2
$Cl + e^- \longrightarrow Cl^-$	x_3
$Cl^+ + Cl^- \longrightarrow Cl^+Cl^-$	x_4
$Cl_2 \longrightarrow Cl^+Cl^-$,	$\Delta H = x_1 + x_2 + x_3 + x_4$

67. (*d*) $\Delta t = (273 + 26.01) - (273 + 23.73) = 2.28°$

$$q_{bomb} = C\,\Delta t = 783 \times 2.28 \text{ J} = 1785.24 \text{ J}$$

$q_{water} = m$(water) s(specific heat) Δt(increase in temperature)

$$= 254 \times 4.184 \times 2.28 = 2423.04 \text{ J}$$

$\therefore$ Heat absorbed $= 4208.28$ J $= 4.21$ kJ

68. (*b*) Total heat lost $= -\ ms\Delta t = -\ 500 \times 4.18 \times 20$

$$= -41800 \text{ J} = -41.8 \text{ kJ}$$

Latent heat of fusion of ice $= 6.02$ kJ mol^{-1}

$\therefore$ Number of cubes each of one mole required $= \frac{41.8}{6.02} \approx 7$

69. (*b*) Convert value per gram into per mol by multiplying by molar mass (18 g mol^{-1}).

70. (*c*) $C(s) + O_2(g) \longrightarrow CO_2(g)$; $\Delta H = -\ 393.5$ kJ mol^{-1} ...(i)

$CO + \frac{1}{2}O_2 \longrightarrow CO_2(g)$; $\Delta H = -\ 283.5$ kJ mol^{-1} ...(ii)

On subtracting Eq. (ii) from Eq. (i), we get

$$C(s) + \frac{1}{2}O_2(g) \longrightarrow CO(g);$$

$\Delta H = (-\ 393.5 + 283.5)$ kJ mol^{-1} $= -\ 110$ kJ mol^{-1} (approx.)

71. (*a*) $\Delta H = ms\Delta t$

$$240 \times 1000 \text{ J} = 12 \times s \times 10$$

$$s = 2000 \text{ J} = 2 \text{ kJ/g°C}$$

73. (*b*) $\Delta H = ms\Delta t = ms(t_2 - t_1)$

$$100 = 25 \times 1 \times [(273 + 44) - t_1]$$

$$t_1 = 313 \text{ K} = 40°\text{C}$$

74. (*a*) $\Delta H_1 = ms\Delta t$ (change in temperature only)

$$= 1000 \times 1 \times 75 = 75000 \text{ cal} = 75 \text{ kcal}$$

75. (*c*) $\Delta H_2 = m \times L$ (physical state changes only, latent heat is involved)

$$= \frac{1000}{18} \times 10 = 556 \text{ kcal}$$

76. (*d*) The dissociation energy of H—H bond is

$$= \frac{869.6}{2} = 434.8 \text{ kJ}$$

77. (*a*) (i) $NaCl(s) + (aq) \longrightarrow Na^+(aq) + Cl^-(aq)$;

$\Delta H_1 = 4$ kJ mol^{-1}

(ii) $Na^+(g) + Cl^-(g) + aq \longrightarrow Na^+(aq) + Cl^-(aq)$;

$\Delta H_2 = -784$ kJ mol^{-1}

Eq. (i) − (ii)

$NaCl(s) \longrightarrow Na^+(g) + Cl^-(g) = 788$ kJ mol^{-1}

78. (*a*) $C(s) + O_2(g) \longrightarrow CO_2(g)$

Moles of graphite $= \frac{4}{12}$

$\Delta H = 30 \times 4 \times 3$ kJ mol^{-1} = 360 kJ mol^{-1}

Combustion reactions are exothermic in nature.

79. (*a*) Formation of $NCl_3(g)$ is shown by

$$\frac{1}{2}N_2(g) + \frac{3}{2}Cl_2(g) \longrightarrow NCl_3(g), \quad \Delta H_4 = ?$$

Operate Eqs. (2) $\times \frac{1}{2}$ − (3) $\times \frac{3}{2}$ + (1)

Thus, $\Delta H_4 = \frac{-\Delta H_2}{2} = \frac{3\Delta H_3}{2} - \Delta H_1 = -\left[\Delta H_1 + \frac{\Delta H_2}{2} + \frac{3\Delta H_3}{2}\right]$

80. (*b*) Heat capacity, $C_V = 18.94 \times 0.998 \times 10^3$

$= 18.902 \times 10^3$ cal/deg

Moles of benzoic acid $= \frac{1.89}{122}$

$C_p = C_V + R = 18.902 \times 10^3 + 2$

$= 18.904 \times 10^3$ cal / deg

Heat of combustion $= \frac{C_p \times \Delta t}{\text{moles}}$

$= \frac{18.904 \times 10^3 \times 0.632 \times 122}{1.89}$

$= 771.2 \times 10^3$ cal

= 771.2 kcal

81. (*b*) In case of weak acids, some of the heat evolved during neutralisation reaction is utilised to ionise the weak acid. Thus, less heat is evolved. Hence, lower the value of heat of neutralisation, weaker is the acid. Thus, *B* is the weakest acid.

82. (*b*) Given, $CH_4 + 2O_2 \longrightarrow CO_2 + 2H_2O$;

$\Delta H = -210$ kcal / mol ...(i)

$C_2H_6 + \frac{7}{2}O_2 \longrightarrow 2CO_2 + 3H_2O$;

$\Delta H = -368$ kcal/mol ...(ii)

On substracting Eq. (i) from Eq. (ii), we get

$CH_2 + \frac{3}{2}O_2 \longrightarrow CO_2 + H_2O$;

$\Delta H = -158$ kcal / mol ...(iii)

∴ Enthalpy of combustion of one CH_2 unit

= −158 kcal / mol

$\Delta H_{comb}(C_{10}H_{22}) = \Delta H_{comb}(CH_4) + 9 \times \Delta H_{comb}(CH_2)$

$= -210 + (9 \times -158) = -1632$ kcal

83. (*a*) For PH_3, P—H bond energy

$= \frac{\text{heat of atomisation of } PH_3}{3}$

$= \frac{953 \text{ kJ mol}^{-1}}{3} = 317.67$ kJ mol^{-1}

For P_2H_4,

Heat of atomisation = P — P bond energy + 4 × P — H bond energy

∴ P—P bond energy = 1485 − (4 × 317.67)

= 214.3 kJ mol^{-1} ≈ 213 kJ mol^{-1}

84. (*b*) By '$2A + \frac{C}{2} - B$', we get

$Na_2O + SO_3 \longrightarrow Na_2SO_4$;

$\Delta H = -2 \times 146 + \frac{259}{2} - 418$

or $\Delta H = -580.5 \approx -581$ kJ

85. (*d*) ΔH_f° is the enthalpy change when one mole of the substance is formed from its elements but gases should be in the molecular state or $H_2(g)$, $O_2(g)$.

86. (*b*) $H_2O(l)$ formed has been converted into $H_2O(g)$, i.e.

$H_2O(l) \longrightarrow H_2O(g)$

by absorbing heat 44.0 kJ mol^{-1}. Hence, heat absorbed by 4 mol $H_2O(l) = 4 \times 44 = 176$

ΔH(Net) = − 2220.1 + 176

= − 2044.1 kJ

87. (*b*) $2Al + \frac{3}{2}O_2 \longrightarrow Al_2O_3$

2 mol   1.5 mol O_2 1 mol Al_2O_3

1 mol   0.75 mol O_2 0.5 mol Al_2O_3

$\Delta H^\circ = -837.8$ kJ mol^{-1}

837.8 kJ mol^{-1} ≡ combustion of 1 mol Al or formation of 0.5 mol Al_2O_3

∴ 250 kcal $= \frac{250 \times 8.314^*}{2}$ kJ ≡ 1.24 mol Al

or 0.62 mol of Al_2O_3

(*Values of *R* (gas constant) have been used as energy conversion factor)

88. (*c*) Based on given $\Delta_r H^\circ$

$\Delta_f H^\circ = H^\circ_{CO_2} = -393.5$ kJ mol^{-1} ...(i)

$\Delta_f H^\circ = H^\circ_{H_2O} = -285.8$ kJ mol^{-1} ...(ii)

$\Delta_f H^\circ = H^\circ_{O_2} = 0.00$ (elements) ...(iii)

Required thermal reaction is for $\Delta_f H^\circ$ of CH_4.

Thus, from III

$890.3 = [\Delta_f H^\circ(CH_4) + 2\Delta_f H^\circ(O_2)]$

$- [\Delta_f H^\circ(CO_2) + 2\Delta_f H^\circ(H_2O)]$

$= \Delta_f H^\circ(CH_4) + 0] - [-393.5 - 2 \times 285.5]$

∴ $\Delta_f H^\circ(CH_4) = -74.8$ kJ / mol

89. (*c*) $\frac{1}{2}N_2(g) + \frac{3}{2}H_2(g) \longrightarrow NH_3(g); \Delta n_g = -1$

∴ $(\Delta H - \Delta E) = -RT$

90. (*b*) $H_2C_2O_4$ is a weak (dibasic acid).

$H_2C_2O_4 \rightleftharpoons 2H^+ + C_2O_4^{2-}, \quad \Delta H = q$

$2H^+ + 2OH^- \rightleftharpoons 2H_2O, \quad \Delta H = -27.4$ kcal

$H_2C_2O_4 + 2OH^- \rightleftharpoons C_2O_4^{2-} + 2H_2O, \Delta H = -q + 27.4$

∴ $(q - 27.4) = -26.0$

∴ $q = 1.4$ kcal mol^{-1}

91. (*c*) Use Clapeyron-Clausius equation

$$\Delta H = \frac{2.303\,RT_1T_2}{(T_2 - T_1)} \log \frac{p_2}{p_1}$$

$$\left(\frac{1}{T_1} - \frac{1}{T_2}\right) = \frac{2.303\,R}{\Delta H} \log \frac{p_2}{p_1}$$

$$\left(\frac{1}{50} - \frac{1}{T_2}\right) = \frac{2.303 \times 2}{460.6} \log \frac{10}{1}$$

$$T_2 = 100\text{ K}$$

92. (*c*)

$$H_2(g) + \frac{1}{2}O_2(g) \longrightarrow H_2O(g)$$

$$x_1 \qquad \frac{x_2}{2} \qquad 2x_3$$

$$\Delta H = \left(x_1 + \frac{x_2}{2} - 2x_3\right) \quad \text{based on (BE) values}$$

$$H_2O(g) \longrightarrow H_2O(l)$$

$$\Delta H = -x_4$$

$$\therefore \quad \Delta H(\text{net}) = \left(x_1 + \frac{x_2}{2} - 2x_3 - x_4\right)$$

93. (*a*) $E_a > \Delta H$ (for endothermic reaction)

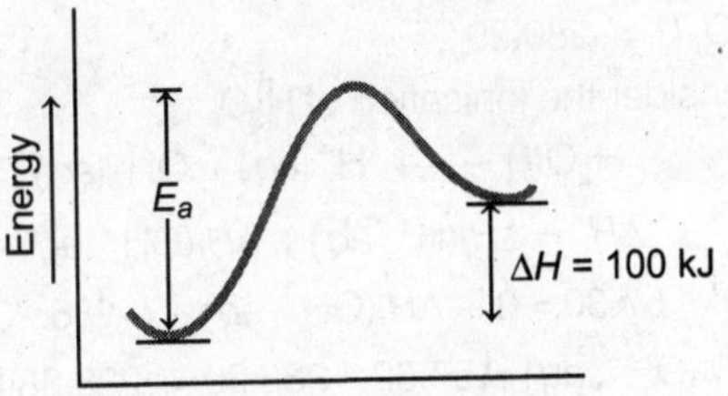

$$E_a > 100\text{ kJ}$$

95. (*c*) $Na(s) + \frac{1}{2}Cl_2(g) \longrightarrow NaCl(s)$

This is obtained when all the given reactions are added, after dividing Eq. (iii) by 2

$$\therefore \quad \Delta H = S + I + \frac{D}{2} - E - U$$

96. (*c*)

$$C(\text{diamond}) \longrightarrow C(\text{graphite})$$

$$\Delta S = \frac{q}{T}$$

$$\therefore \quad q = T \times \Delta S = 300 \times 10\text{ cal} = 3\text{ kcal}$$

$C(\text{diamond}) + O_2 \longrightarrow CO_2$, $\quad \Delta H = -91$ kcal mol^{-1}

$C(\text{graphite}) \longrightarrow C(\text{diamond})$, $\quad \Delta H = -3$ kcal

$C(\text{graphite}) + O_2 \longrightarrow CO_2$, $\quad \Delta H = -94$ kcal

97. (*a*) $E_a(\text{backward}) = 70 + 22 = 92$ kcal

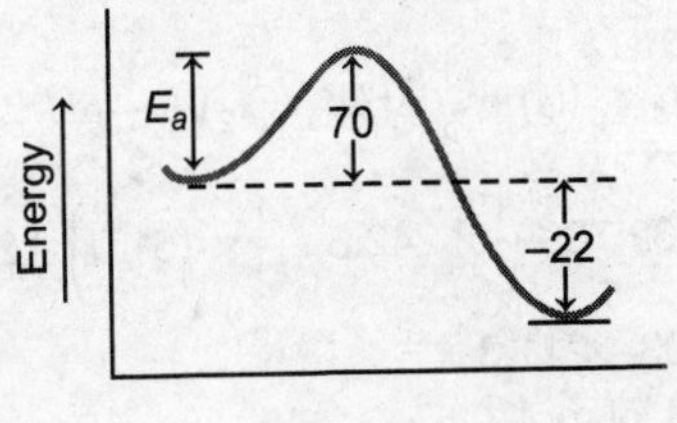

98. (*c*)

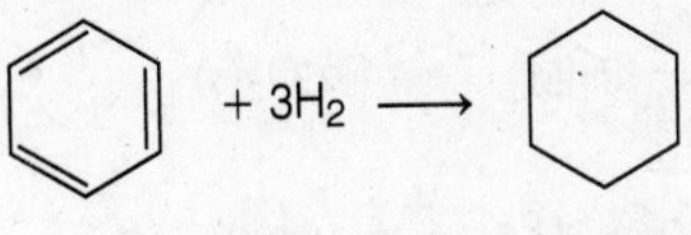

$\Delta H = x_2$

$$CH_2{=}CH_2 + H_2 \longrightarrow C_2H_6, \quad \Delta H = x_1$$

Benzene has three (C=C) bonds.

Based on hydrogenation of ethene,

$$\Delta H \text{ (hydrogenation of benzene)} = 3x_1$$

$$\therefore \quad \text{Resonance energy} = (3x_1 - x_2)$$

99. (*b*)

$$\Delta S = \frac{\Delta H}{T}$$

$$\therefore \quad \Delta H_{vap} = T\Delta S = T_1 x_1$$

$\therefore$ Heat required to vaporise 3 moles of $H_2O(l) = 3x_1T_1$

$$\therefore \quad \Delta H = 2x_3 + 3x_2 + 3x_1T_1 - x_4$$

104. (*a*) $\Delta H(\text{III}) = \Delta H(\text{II}) - \Delta H(\text{I})$

$$= -241.81 - 436.00 = -677.81\text{ kJ}$$

$$\frac{\Delta H(\text{III})}{\Delta H(\text{II})} = 2.8$$

105. (*a*) $\Delta H = ms\theta = 40 \times 0.214 \times 10\text{ cal} = 85.6\text{ cal}$

106. (*c*) When q is the amount of heat involved in a system then at constant pressure

$$q = q_p \text{ and } C_p\Delta T = \Delta H$$

Given reaction : $I_2(s) \longrightarrow I_2(g)$

Specific heat of $I_2(s) = 0.055$ cal g^{-1} K^{-1}.

Specific heat of $I_2(\text{vap}) = 0.031$ cal g^{-1}K^{-1}.

Enthalpy (H_1) of sublimation of iodine = 24 cal g^{-1}

If q is the amount of heat involved in a system then at constant pressure $q = q_p$ and $\Delta H = C_p\Delta T$

$$H_2 - H_1 = C_p(T_2 - T_1)$$

$$H_2 = H_1 + \Delta C_p(T_2 - T_1)$$

$$H_2 = 24 + (0.031 - 0.055)(250 - 200)$$

$$H_2 = 24 + (-0.024)(50) = 24 - 1.2 = 22.8\text{ cal/g}$$

Thus, the enthalpy of sublimation of iodine at 250 is 22.8 cal/g.

112. (*d*) Moles of glucose $= \frac{1.6}{180}$ mol

Thus, heat released $= -72 \times \frac{1.6}{180}$ kcal $= -0.64$ kcal

113. (*d*) According to Gibbs-Helmholtz equation,

$$\Delta_r G° = \Delta_r H° - T\Delta_r S°$$

For a reaction to be feasible (spontaneous)

$$\Delta_r G° < 0$$

$$\Delta_r H° - T\Delta_r S° < 0$$

Given, $\Delta_r H° = +491.1$ kJ mol^{-1},

$$\Delta_r S° = 198\text{ JK}^{-1}\text{mol}^{-1}$$

$$\therefore \quad 491.1 \times 10^3 - T \times 198 < 0$$

$$T > \frac{491.1 \times 10^3}{198} = 2480.3\text{ K}$$

$\therefore$ Above 2480.3 K reaction will become spontaneous.

114. (*d*) $$\underset{2\text{ mol}}{2Fe(s)} + \underset{2}{\frac{3}{2}}O_2(g) \longrightarrow \underset{1\text{ mol}}{Fe_2O_3(s)}$$

$$\text{Moles of Fe} = \frac{4}{56} = \frac{1}{14}\text{ mol}$$

$$\text{Moles of } Fe_2O_3 \text{ formed} = \frac{1}{28}\text{ mol}$$

$$\text{Heat released} = 29.28\text{ kJ}$$

$$\therefore\ \Delta H_f^\circ (Fe_2O_3) = -\frac{29.28}{1/28}\text{ kJ mol}^{-1} = -819.84\text{ kJ mol}^{-1}$$

115. (*a*) $\text{Moles of } CH_4 = \frac{2}{16} = \frac{1}{8}\text{ mol}$

$$\therefore\ \Delta H^\circ\text{ (combustion)} = -\frac{25}{1/8} = -200\text{ kcal mol}^{-1}$$

116. (*c*) $$C(s) + O_2(g) \longrightarrow CO_2(g)$$

$$\Delta H_f^\circ (CO_2) = -95\text{ kcal mol}^{-1}$$

$$= -95\text{ kcal / 12g of carbon}$$

Thus, carbon required for 1000 kcal of heat $= \frac{12}{95} \times 1000$

$$= 126.3\text{ g}$$

117. (*c*) $C_6H_5COOH(s) + 7.5O_2(g) \longrightarrow 7CO_2(g) + 3H_2O(l)$

$$\Delta n_g = -0.5$$

$$\therefore\ \Delta H = \Delta E + \Delta n_g RT$$

$$-2546 = \Delta E - 0.5 \times 8.3143 \times 10^{-3} \times 298$$

$$\Delta E = -2544.76\text{ kJ mol}^{-1}$$

118. (*b*) Moles of benzene $= \frac{0.39}{78} = 5 \times 10^{-3}$ mol

Thus, heat released $= -3250 \times 5 \times 10^{-3}$ kJ

$$= -16.25\text{ kJ}$$

119. (*d*) $C_{12}H_{22}O_{11}(s) + 12O_2(g) \longrightarrow 12CO_2(g) + 11H_2O(l)$

$$\Delta H^\circ_{comb} = [12\,\Delta H_f^\circ(CO_2) + 11\,\Delta H_f^\circ(H_2O)] - [\Delta H_f^\circ (C_{12}H_{22}O_{11})]$$

$$= -1352.9\text{ kcal}$$

Thus, number of moles of $C_{12}H_{22}O_{11}$ for getting 2700 kcal of heat

$$= \frac{2700}{1352.9} \approx 2\text{ mol} = 684\text{ g}$$

120. (*a*) $\Delta H^\circ = \Delta H_c^\circ$ (fumaric acid) $- \Delta H_c^\circ$ (maleic acid)

$$= -1336.0 - (-1359.2) = +23.2\text{ kJ}$$

121. (*b*) $\Delta H_2^\circ = \Delta H_1^\circ + \Delta C_p (T_2 - T_1)$

$$= 0 + 29.4\ (315 - 298)\text{ J} = 499.8\text{ J mol}^{-1}$$

$$= 0.5\text{ kJ mol}^{-1}$$

124. (*d*) For the given reaction,

$$2NO(g) + O_2(g) \rightleftharpoons 2NO_2(g)$$

Given, ΔG_f° (NO) = 86.6 kJ / mol

$\Delta G_f^\circ (NO_2) = ?\quad K_p = 1.6 \times 10^{12}$

Now, we have,

$$\Delta G_f^\circ = 2\Delta G^\circ_{f(NO_2)} - [2\Delta G^\circ_{f(NO)} + \Delta G^\circ_{f(O_2)}]$$

$$= -RT\ln K_p = 2\Delta G^\circ_{f(NO_2)} - [2 \times 86{,}600 + 0]$$

$$\Delta G^\circ_{f(NO_2)} = \frac{1}{2}[2 \times 86{,}600 - R \times 298 \ln\ (1.6 \times 10^{12})]$$

$$\Delta G^\circ_{f(NO_2)} = 0.5\,[2 \times 86{,}600 - R \times (298) \ln\ (1.6 \times 10^{12})]$$

125. (*a*) The temperature rise is

$$\Delta T = T_2 - T_1 = 298.45 - 298 = 0.45\text{ K}$$

This indicates that heat produced from combustion of 3.5 g of compound rises temperature of calorimeter by 0.45 K.

Heat produced $= 0.45\text{ K} \times 2.5\text{ k JK}^{-1} = 1.125$ kJ

⇒ Heat produced from 28 g of compound (1.0 mol)

$$= \frac{1.125}{3.5} \times 28 = 9\text{ kJ}$$

126. (*b*) Consider the heat of formation of H_2O

$$H_2(g) + \frac{1}{2}O_2(g) \longrightarrow H_2O(l);\ \Delta H = -286.20\text{ kJ}$$

$$\Delta H_r = \Delta H_f(H_2O, l) - \Delta H_f(H_2, g) - \frac{1}{2}\Delta H_f(O_2, g)$$

$$-286.20 = \Delta H_f(H_2O, l) - 0 - 0$$

$$\Delta H_f(H_2O, l) = -286.20$$

Now, consider the ionisation of H_2O

$$H_2O(l) \longrightarrow H^+(aq) + OH^-(aq)\quad \Delta H = 57.32\text{ kJ}$$

$$\Delta H_r = \Delta H_f(H^+, aq) + \Delta H_f(OH^-, aq) - \Delta H_f(H_2O, l)$$

$$57.30 = 0 + \Delta H_f(OH^-, aq) - (-286.20)$$

Thus, $\Delta H_f(OH^-, aq) = 57.32 - 286.20 = -228.88$ kJ

127. (*b*) $$\frac{1}{2}Cl_2(g) \longrightarrow Cl^-(aq)$$

$$\Delta H = \frac{1}{2}\Delta H_{diss}\ (Cl_2) + \Delta H_{EA}Cl + \Delta H_{hyd}\ (Cl^-)$$

$$= \frac{240}{2} - 349 - 381 = -610\text{ kJ mol}^{-1}$$

128. (*c*) $$H_2O(l) \longrightarrow H_2O(g)$$

$$\Delta n = 1 - 0 = 1$$

$$\Delta E = \Delta H - \Delta nRT$$

$$= 41 - 1 \times 8.3 \times 373 \times 10^{-3} (R = 8.3 \times 10^{-3})$$

$$= 37.9\text{ kJ mol}^{-1}$$

129. (*a*) Carbon is found in solid state. The state of substance affects the enthalpy change.

$$C(s) \longrightarrow C(g)\text{ sublimation}$$

and $$H_2(g) \longrightarrow 2H(g)\text{ dissociation}$$

are required for C—H bond.

130. (*c*) $$\frac{1}{2}I_2(s) + \frac{1}{2}Cl_2(g) \longrightarrow ICl(g)$$

$$\Delta H = \left[\frac{1}{2}\Delta H_{s \to g}(I_2) + \frac{1}{2}\Delta H_{diss.}(Cl_2) + \frac{1}{2}\Delta H_{diss.}\ (I_2)\right] - \Delta H\,ICl$$

$$= \left(\frac{1}{2} \times 62.76 + \frac{1}{2} \times 242.3 + \frac{1}{2} \times 151.0\right) - 211.3$$

$$= 228.03 - 211.3$$

$$\Delta H = 16.73\text{ kJ mol}^{-1}$$

131. (*b*) Given, $2H \longrightarrow H_2, \quad \Delta H^\circ = -436\ \text{kJ mol}^{-1}$

$2N \longrightarrow N_2, \quad \Delta H^\circ = -712\ \text{kJ mol}^{-1}$

$\frac{3}{2}H_2 + \frac{1}{2}N_2 \longrightarrow NH_3, \quad \Delta H_f^\circ = -46\ \text{kJ mol}^{-1}$

Thus, $(BE)_{(H-H)} = 436\ \text{kJ mol}^{-1}$

$(BE)_{(N-N)} = 712\ \text{kJ mol}^{-1}$

$(BE)_{(N-H)} = ?$

Based on (BE) values ΔH_f°

$$\frac{3}{2}(BE)_{H-H} + \frac{1}{2}(BE)_{N-N} - 3(BE)_{N-H}$$

$$436 \times \frac{3}{2} + 712 \times \frac{1}{2} - 3x = -46$$

$$\therefore \quad x(BE_{N-H}) = 352\ \text{kJ mol}^{-1}$$

132. (*d*) $4NO_2(g) + O_2(g) \longrightarrow 2N_2O_5(g), \ \Delta_r H = -111\ \text{kJ}$

$2N_2O_5(g) \longrightarrow 2N_2O_5(s), \ \Delta_s H = (-54 \times 2)\ \text{kJ}$

$4NO_2(g) + O_2(g) \longrightarrow 2N_2O_5(s), \ \Delta_r H = -219\ \text{kJ}$

Note : ΔH of sublimation of $N_2O_5(s)$ is $+ 54\ \text{kJ mol}^{-1}$.
Thus, for reverse process, it is $- 54\ \text{kJ mol}^{-1}$.

133. (c) Hydration involves

	ΔH°
$Cl_2(g) \longrightarrow 2Cl(g);$	$240\ \text{kJ mol}^{-1}$
$2Cl(g) + 2e^- \longrightarrow 2Cl^-(g);$	$-349 \times 2\ \text{kJ}$
$2Cl^-(g) + aq \longrightarrow 2Cl^-(aq)\ ;$	-381×2

$Cl_2(g) + aq \longrightarrow 2Cl^-(aq)\ \Delta H = 240 - 698 - 762$

$= -1220\ \text{kJ mol}^{-1}$

134. (*a*) Let enthalpy change of the following step be q

$H_2S\ (aq) \longrightarrow HS^-\ (aq) + H^+(aq); \quad \Delta H = q$

$H^+\ (aq) + OH^-\ (aq) \longrightarrow H_2O(l); \quad \Delta H = -57.3\ \text{kJ mol}^{-1}$

$H_2S\ (aq) + OH^-\ (aq) \longrightarrow HS^-\ (aq) + H_2O\ (l);$

$\Delta H = -33.7\ \text{kJ mol}^{-1}$

Thus, $q - 57.3 = -33.7$

$\therefore \quad q = 57.3 - 33.7 = 23.6\ \text{kJ mol}^{-1}$

136. (*d*) Calculate the heat of combustion with the help of following formula

$$\Delta H_p = \Delta U + \Delta n_g RT$$

where, ΔH_p = Heat of combustion at constant pressure
ΔU = Heat at constant volume (It is also called ΔE)
Δn_g = Change in number of moles (In gaseous state).
R = Gas constant; T = Temperature.

From the equation,

$$C_6H_6(l) + \frac{15}{2}O_2(g) \longrightarrow 6CO_2(g) + 3H_2O(l)$$

Change in the number of gaseous moles i.e.

$$\Delta n_g = 6 - \frac{15}{2} = -\frac{3}{2} \text{ or } -1.5$$

Now we have Δn_g and other values given in the question are

$\Delta U = -3263.9\ \text{kJ/mol}$

$T = 25^\circ\text{C} = 273 + 25 = 298\ \text{K}$

$R = 8.314\ \text{JK}^{-1}\text{mol}^{-1}$

So, $\Delta H_p = (-3263.9) + (-1.5) \times 8.314 \times 10^{-3} \times 298$

$= -3267.6\ \text{kJ mol}^{-1}$

137. (*a*) The conversion of 1 kg of ice at 273 K into water vapours at 383 K takes place as follows:

$$\underset{273\text{K}}{H_2O(s)} \xrightarrow{\Delta S_1} \underset{273\text{K}}{H_2O(l)} \xrightarrow{\Delta S_2} \underset{373\text{K}}{H_2O(l)}$$

$$\underset{373\text{K}}{H_2O(l)} \xrightarrow{\Delta S_3} \underset{373\text{K}}{H_2O(g)}$$

$$\underset{383\text{K}}{H_2O(g)} \xleftarrow{\Delta S_4} \underset{373\text{K}}{H_2O(g)}$$

$$\Delta S_1 = \frac{\Delta H_{\text{fusion}}}{\Delta T_{\text{fusion}}} = \frac{334\ \text{kJ kg}^{-1}}{273\ \text{K}} = 1.22\ \text{kJ kg}^{-1}\text{K}^{-1}$$

$$\Delta S_2 = C \ln \frac{T_2}{T_1} = 4.2\ \text{kJ K}^{-1}\text{kg}^{-1} \ln\left(\frac{373\ \text{K}}{273\ \text{K}}\right)$$

$= 4.2 \times 2.303\ (\log 373 - \log 273)\ \text{kJ K}^{-1}\text{kg}^{-1}$

$= 4.2 \times 2.303\ (2.572 - 2.436)$

$= 1.31\ \text{kJ K}^{-1}\text{kg}^{-1}$

$$\Delta S_3 = \frac{\Delta H_{\text{vap.}}}{\Delta T_{\text{vap.}}} = \frac{2491\ \text{kJ kg}^{-1}}{373\ \text{K}} = 6.67\ \text{kJ kg}^{-1}\text{K}^{-1}$$

$$\Delta S_4 = C \ln \frac{T_2}{T_1} = 2\ \text{kJ K}^{-1}\text{kg}^{-1} \ln\left(\frac{383\ \text{K}}{373\ \text{K}}\right)$$

$= 2 \times 2.303\ (\log 383 - \log 373)\ \text{kJ K}^{-1}\ \text{kg}^{-1}$

$= 2 \times 2.303\ (2.583 - 2.572)\ \ \text{kJ K}^{-1}\ \text{kg}^{-1}$

$= 0.05\ \text{kJ K}^{-1}\ \text{kg}^{-1}$

$\Delta S_{\text{total}} = \Delta S_1 + \Delta S_2 + \Delta S_3 + \Delta S_4$

$= 1.22 + 1.31 + 6.67 + 0.05$

$= 9.26\ \text{kJ kg}^{-1}\ \text{K}^{-1}$

11

Solution and Its Colligative Properties

Objective Questions Type I [Only one correct option]

In each of the questions below, four choices are given of which only one is correct.

1. There are some of the characteristics of the supersaturated solution

I. Equilibrium exists between solutions and solute

II. If a crystal of solute is added to supersaturated solution, crystallisation occurs rapidly

III. Supersaturated solutions contain more solute than they should at a particular temperature

Correct characteristics of supersaturated solutions are

(a) I, II, III (b) II, III
(c) I, III (d) I, II

2. When KCl dissolves in water

(a) $\Delta H = +\text{ ve}, \Delta S = +\text{ ve}, \Delta G = +\text{ ve}$
(b) $\Delta H = +\text{ ve}, \Delta S = -\text{ve}, \Delta G = -\text{ve}$
(c) $\Delta H = +\text{ ve}, \Delta S = +\text{ ve}, \Delta G = -\text{ve}$
(d) $\Delta H = -\text{ ve}, \Delta S = -\text{ve}, \Delta G = +\text{ve}$

3. Naphthalene dissolves in ether or benzene due to

(a) similar dipole-dipole attraction
(b) similar London dispersion forces
(c) H-bonding
(d) ion-ion attractions

4. During dissolution of a solute in a solvent, following, are the three operative interactions

I. solvent – solvent
II. solute – solvent
III. solute –solute

Which of the following takes place with the absorption heat?

(a) I, II
(b) II, III
(c) I, II, III
(d) I, III

5. Which statement best explains the meaning of the phrases "like dissolves like"?

(a) A solute will easily dissolve a solute of similar mass
(b) A solvent and solute with similar intermolecular forces will readily form a solution
(c) The only true solutions are formed when water dissolves a non-polar solute
(d) The only true solutions are formed when water dissolves a polar solute

6. The dissolving process is exothermic when

(a) the energy released in solvation exceeds the energy used in breaking up solute-solute and solvent-solvent interactions
(b) the energy used in solvation exceeds the energy released in breaking up solute-solute and solvent-solvent interactions
(c) the energy released in solvation is about the same as the energy used in breaking up solute-solute and solvent-solvent interactions
(d) the energy used in solvation is about the same as the energy used in breaking up solute-solute and solvent-solvent interactions

7. Consider the following four liquids.

1. **Water** highly polar; H-bonding
2. **Hexanol** slightly polar; some H-bonding
3. **Chloroform** slightly polar; no H-bonding
4. **Octane** non-polar; no H-bonding

Which pair of liquids is immiscible?

(a) Water and octane
(b) Water and hexanol
(c) Hexanol and chloroform
(d) Chloroform and octane

8. An ionic compound that attracts atmospheric water so strongly that a hydrate is formed is said to be
(a) dilute (b) hygroscopic
(c) immiscible (d) miscible

9. The solubility of gases in liquids
(a) increases with increase in pressure and temperature
(b) decreases with increase in pressure and temperature
(c) increases with increase in pressure and decrease in temperature
(d) decreases with increase in pressure and increase in temperature

10. The solubility of $N_2(g)$ in water exposed to the atmosphere, when the partial pressure is 593 mm, is 5.3×10^{-4} M. Its solubility at 760 mm and at the same temperature is
(a) 4.1×10^{-4} M (b) 6.8×10^{-4} M
(c) 1500 M (d) 2400 M

11. Persons are medically considered to have lead poisoning if they have a concentration of greater than 10 micrograms of lead per decilitre of blood. Concentration in parts per billion is
(a) 1000 (b) 100
(c) 10 (d) 1

12. Glucose solution is 25% by weight of solution. Its percent concentration by weight of solvent is
(a) 20% (b) 25%
(c) 33.3% (d) 16.66%

13. What mass of solution of 0.50 molal glucose solution is required to obtain 0.15 mole glucose?
(a) 327 g (b) 300 g
(c) 273 g (d) None is correct

14. 8 g of NaOH is dissolved in 18 g of H_2O. Mole fraction of NaOH in solution and molality (in mol kg^{-1}) of the solution respectively are **[JEE Main 2019, Jan.]**
(a) 0.2, 11.11 (b) 0.167, 22.20
(c) 0.2, 22.20 (d) 0.167, 11.11

15. We have 100 mL of 0.1 M KCl solution. To make it 0.2 M,
(a) evaporate 50 mL water
(b) evaporate 50 mL solution
(c) add 0.1 mol KCl
(d) add 0.01 mol KCl

16. Colligative properties have many practical uses, some of them may be
I. melting of snow by salt
II. desalination of sea water
III. determination of molar mass
IV. determination of melting point and boiling point of solvent
Actual practical uses are
(a) I, II (b) III, IV
(c) I, II, III (d) II, III, IV

17. Select the correct statement(s).
(a) When solid $CaCl_2$ is added to liquid water, the temperature rises
(b) When solid $CaCl_2$ is added to ice at 0°C, the temperature falls
(c) Both (a) and (b)
(d) None of the above

18. Acetic acid in benzene solution forms dimer due to intermolecular H-bonding. For this case van't Hoff factor is
(a) $i = 1$ (b) $i > 1$
(c) $i < 1$ (d) inclusive

19. A complex containing K^+, Pt (IV) and Cl^- is 100% ionised giving $i = 3$. Thus, complex is
(a) $K_2[PtCl_4]$ (b) $K_2[PtCl_6]$
(c) $K_3[PtCl_5]$ (d) $K[PtCl_3]$

20. In which case, van't Hoff factor i remains unchanged
(a) $PtCl_4$ reacts with KCl
(b) *aq.* $ZnCl_2$ reacts with *aq.* NH_3
(c) *aq.* $FeCl_3$ reacts with *aq.* $K_4[Fe(CN)_6]$
(d) $KMnO_4$ reduced to MnO_2 in alkaline medium

21. van't Hoff factors are x, y, z in the case of association, ionisation and no change respectively. Increasing order is
(a) $x < y < z$ (b) $x = y = z$
(c) $y < x < z$ (d) $x < z < y$

22. If $pK_a = -\log K_a = 4$, and $K_a = Cx^2$ then van't Hoff factor for weak monobasic acid when $C = 0.01$ M is
(a) 1.01 (b) 1.02
(c) 1.10 (d) 1.20

23. An aqueous solution of 0.01 M CH_3COOH has van't Hoff factor of 1.01. If pH = $-\log [H^+]$, pH of 0.01 M CH_3COOH solution would be
(a) 2 (b) 3
(c) 4 (d) 5

24. pH of 1 M HA (weak acid) is 2. Hence, van't Hoff factor is
(a) 1.2 (b) 1.02
(c) 1.1 (d) 1.01

25. In which case van't Hoff factor is maximum?
(a) KCl, 50% ionised (b) K_2SO_4, 40% ionised
(c) $FeCl_3$, 30% ionised (d) $SnCl_4$, 20% ionised

26. Consider the following terms,
I. mK_b II. mK_f
III. $\frac{\Delta T_b}{i}$ IV. K_b
Terms which can be expressed in degree (temperature) are
(a) III, IV (b) I, II
(c) I, II, III (d) I, III

27. Elevation in boiling point of a molar glucose solution ($d = 1.2$ g mL^{-1}) is

(a) 0.98 K_b (b) K_b
(c) 1.20 K_b (d) 1.02 K_b

28. 1 g of a non-volatile, non-electrolyte solute is dissolved in 100 g of two different solvents A and B, whose ebullisocopic constants are in the ratio of 1 : 5. The ratio of the elevation in their boiling points, $\frac{\Delta T_b(A)}{\Delta T_b(B)}$, is **[JEE Main 2019, April]**

(a) 5 : 1 (b) 10 : 1
(c) 1 : 5 (d) 1 : 0.2

29. Elevation in boiling point of an aqueous urea solution is 0.52°. ($K_b = 0.52°$ mol^{-1} kg). Hence, mole fraction of urea in this solution is

(a) 0.982 (b) 0.0567
(c) 0.943 (d) 0.018

30. A complex of iron and cyanide ions is 100% ionised at 1 m (molal). If its elevation in b.p. is 2.08°. ($K_b = 0.52°$ mol^{-1} kg) then the complex is

(a) $K_3[Fe(CN)_6]$ (b) $Fe(CN)_2$
(c) $K_4[Fe(CN)_6]$ (d) $Fe(CN)_4$

31. Which has the highest boiling point?

(a) 0.1 M Na_2SO_4
(b) 0.1 M $C_6H_{12}O_6$ (glucose)
(c) 0.1 M $MgCl_2$
(d) 0.1 M $Al(NO_3)_3$

32. What is the normal boiling point of the solution represented by the phase diagam?

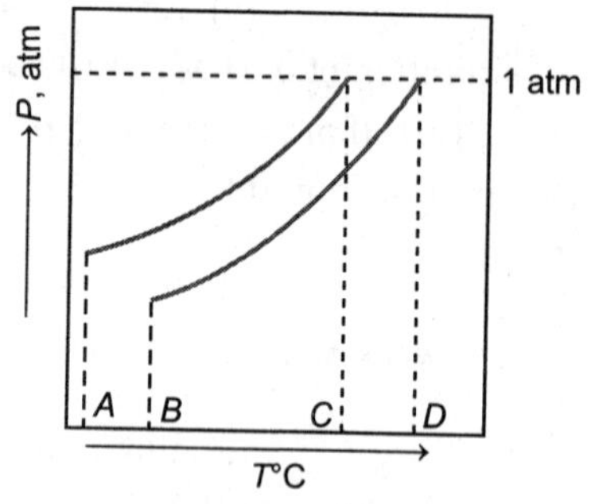

(a) A (b) B
(c) C (d) D

33. A graph of vapour pressure and temperature for three different liquids X, Y and Z is shown below :

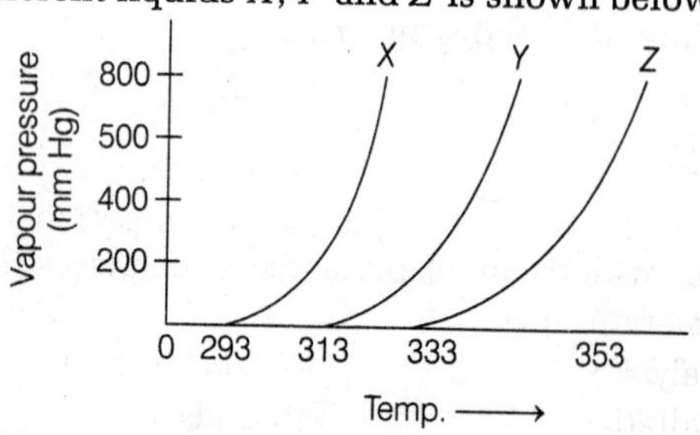

The following inference are made :

A. X has higher intermolecular interactions compared to Y.
B. X has lower intermolecular interactions compared to Y.
C. Z has lower intermolecular interactions compared to Y.

The correct inference(s) is/are **[JEE Main 2020, Jan.]**

(a) (C) (b) (B) (c) (A) (d) (A) and (C)

34. Ratio of $\Delta T_b / K_b$ of 6% AB_2 and 9% A_2B (AB_2 and A_2B both are non-electrolytes) is 1 mol/kg in both cases. Hence, atomic masses of A and B are respectively

(a) 60, 90 (b) 40, 40 (c) 40, 10 (d) 10, 40

35. Which represents correct difference?

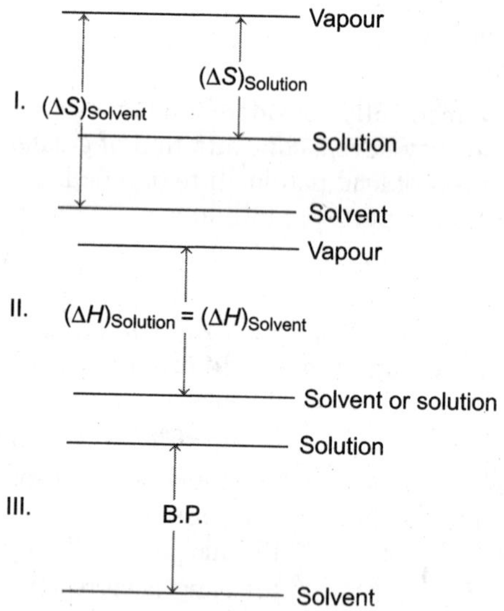

(a) I, II, III (b) I, III (c) II, III (d) I, II

36. If cost per gram were not a concern which of the following substances would be most efficient per unit molar mass for melting snow from side-walls and roads?

(a) Glucose, $C_6H_{12}O_6$ (b) LiCl
(c) NaCl (d) $CaCl_2$

37. An aqueous solution of a solute AB has b.p. of 101.08°C (AB is 100% ionised in boiling point of the solution) and freezes at −1.80°C.

($K_b / K_f = 0.3$) Hence, AB

(a) is 100% ionised at the f.p. of the solution
(b) behaves as non-electrolyte at the f.p. of the solution
(c) forms dimer
(d) None of the above

38. Density of 1 M solution of a non-electrolyte $C_6H_{12}O_6$ is 1.18 g/mL. If $K_f(H_2O)$ is 1.86° mol^{-1} kg, solution freezes at **[JEE Advanced 2011]**

(a) −1.58°C (b) −1.86°C
(c) −3.16°C (d) 1.86°C

39. Mole fraction of a non-electrolyte in aqueous solution is 0.07. If K_f is 1.86° mol^{-1} kg, depression in freezing point ΔT_f, is
(a) 0.26° (b) 1.86° (c) 0.13° (d) 7.78°

40. $K_f m$ is expressed in the unit of
(a) molar mass (b) mass
(c) temperature (degree) (d) molality

41. What is the normal freezing point of the solution represented by the phase diagram?

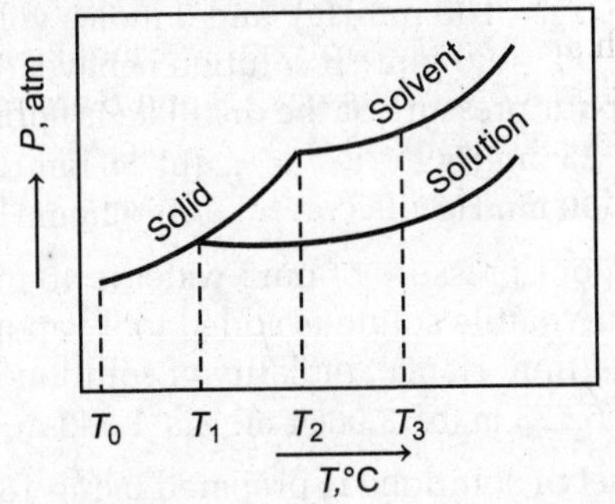

(a) T_1 (b) T_2 (c) T_3 (d) T_0

42. Select the correct statement(s).
(a) Solution has more molecular randomness than a pure solvent has, the entropy change between solution and solid is larger than the entropy change between pure solvent and solid
(b) Heats of fusion of solution and solvent are similar since, similar forces of intermolecular forces are involved
(c) Sugar containing solution freezes at a lower temperature than pure water
(d) All the above are correct statements

43. 60 g of urea is dissolved in 1100 g solution. To keep $\Delta T / K_f$ as 1 mol/kg, water separated in the form of ice is
(a) 40 g (b) 60 g
(c) 100 g (d) 200 g

44. Some entropy change are represented in figure.

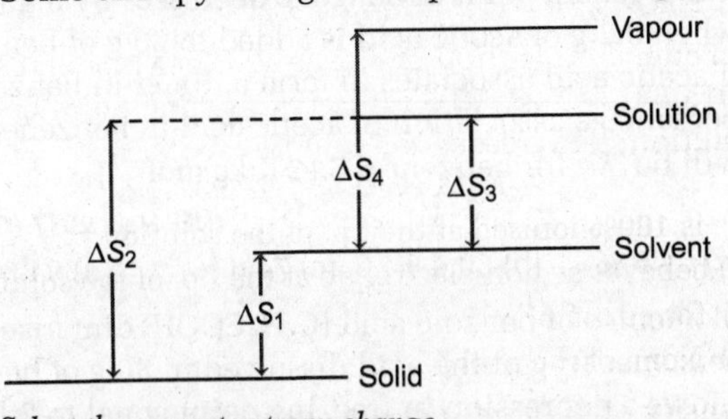

Select the correct entropy change.
(a) $\Delta S_1, \Delta S_2, \Delta S_3$
(b) $\Delta S_1, \Delta S_2, \Delta S_4$
(c) $\Delta S_1, \Delta S_2, \Delta S_3, \Delta S_4$
(d) ΔS_2 and ΔS_4

45. Human blood gives rise to an osmotic pressure of approximately 7.65 atm at body temperature, 37°C. Hence, molarity of an intravenous glucose solution be to have the same osmotic pressure as blood is
(a) 0.30 M (b) 0.20 M
(c) 0.10 M (d) 0.50 M

46. Osmotic pressure of insulin solution at 298 K is found to be 0.0072 atm. Hence, height of water column due to this pressure is
[given d(Hg) = 13.6 g/mL]
(a) 0.76 cm (b) 0.70 cm
(c) 7.4 cm (d) 76 cm

47. Osmosis involved in
(a) excretion of urine
(b) interchange of nutrients and waste products between tissue cells and their surroundings
(c) in both cases
(d) in none of the above cases

48. Desalinating of sea water is now done using
(a) reverse osmosis
(b) osmosis
(c) filtration
(d) evaporation

49. We have 200 mL of 6% urea solution at 27°C. Osmotic pressure due to osmosis is
(R = 0.0821 L atm mol^{-1} K^{-1})
(a) 24.63 atm
(b) 12.315 atm
(c) 4.926 atm
(d) 6.157 atm

50. If "A" contains 2% NaCl and is separated by a semipermeable membrane from "B" which contains 10% NaCl, which event will occur?
(a) NaCl will flow from "A" to "B"
(b) NaCl will flow from "B" to "A"
(c) Water will flow from "A" to "B"
(d) Water will flow from "B" to "A"

51. What is osmolarity of a 0.20 M KCl solution?
(a) 0.10 osmol
(b) 0.20 osmol
(c) 0.30 osmol
(d) 0.40 osmol

52. Red blood cells are placed in a solution and neither haemolysis nor crenation occurs. Therefore, the solution is
(a) hypertonic (b) hypotonic
(c) isotonic (d) isotopic

53. The passage of a solvent across a semipermeable membrane because of concentration differences is called
(a) dialysis (b) haemolysis
(c) hydration (d) osmosis

54. Match the terms with definitions.

	Term	Definition
I.	Haemolysis	A The shrinking of a red blood cell when placed in a solution of greater osmolarity than the cell itself.
II.	Crenation	B. Refers to two solutions of same osmolarity.
III.	Hygroscopic	C. Refers to a solution having a greater osmolarity than 0.30 osmol, the osmolarity of normal red blood cells.
IV.	Hypertonic	D. An ionic compound which attracts water molecules from the atmosphere.
V.	Isotonic	E. The swelling and bursting of a red blood cell when placed in a solution of lower osmolarity than the cell itself.

Codes

	I	II	III	IV	V		I	II	III	IV	V
(a)	A	B	C	D	E	(b)	E	D	C	B	A
(c)	E	D	B	C	A	(d)	E	A	D	C	B

55. At a given temperature, total vapour pressure in torr of a mixture of volatile components A and B is given by

$$p = 120 - 75X_B$$

hence, vapour pressure of pure A and B respectively (in torr) are

(a) 120, 75 (b) 120, 195
(c) 120, 45 (d) 75, 45

56. For the solution of the gases w, x, y and z in water at 298 K, the Henry's law constants (K_H) are 0.5, 2, 35 and 40 K bar, respectively. The correct plot for the given data is **[JEE Main 2019, April]**

(a) 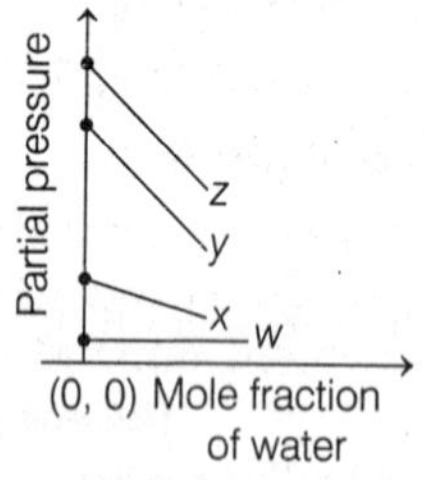

(b) 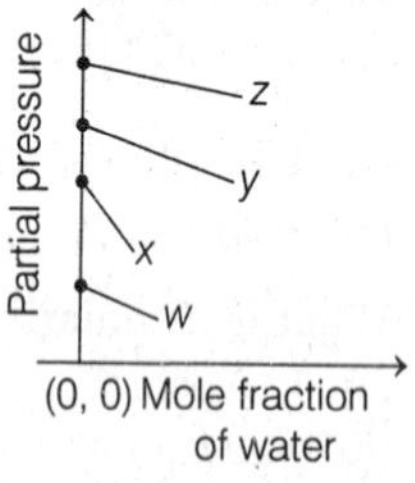

(c) 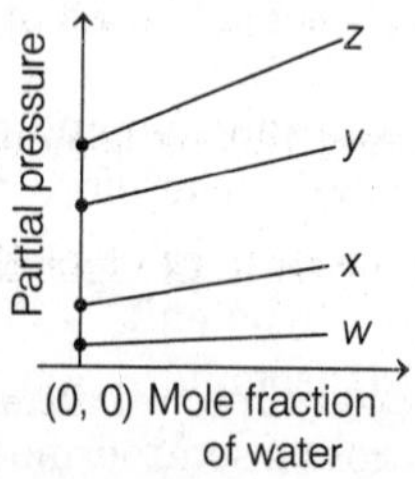

(d) 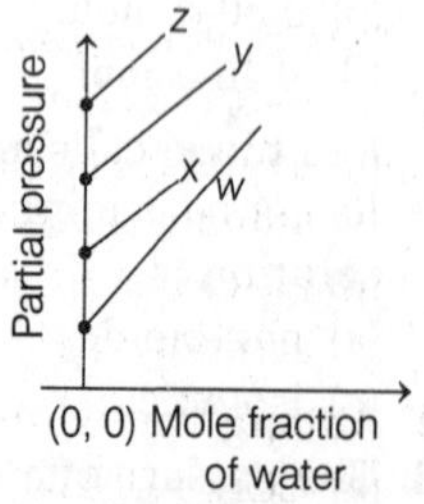

57. Water and chlorobenzene are immisible liquids. Their mixture boils at 90°C under a reduced pressure of 7.82×10^4 Pa. The vapour pressure of pure water at 90°C is 7.03×10^4 Pa. On weight per cent basis, chlorobenzene in the distillate is equal to (mol. wt. of chlorobenzene is 112.5 g mol^{-1})

(a) 50 (b) 60 (c) 70 (d) 80

58. Moles of K_2SO_4 to be dissolved in 12 moles of water to lower its vapour pressure by 10 mmHg at a temperature at which vapour pressure of pure water is 50 mm is

(a) 3 mol (b) 2 mol (c) 1 mol (d) 0.5 mol

59. A mixture contains 1 mole volatile liquid A (p_A° = 100 mmHg) and 3 moles volatile liquid B (p_B° = 80 mm). If solution behave ideally, total vapour pressure of the distillate is approximately

(a) 85 mmHg (b) 86 mmHg
(c) 90 mmHg (d) 92 mmHg

60. Vapour pressure of pure water is 40 mm. If a non-volatile solute is added to it vapour pressure falls by 4 mm. Hence, molality of solution is

(a) 6.173 m (b) 3.0864 m (c) 1.543 m (d) 0.772 m

61. A set of solutions is prepared using 180 g of water as a solvent and 10 g of different non-volatile solutes A, B and C. The relative lowering of vapour pressure in the presence of these solutes are in the order
[Given, molar mass of $A = 100$ g mol^{-1}; $B = 200$ g mol^{-1}; $C = 10{,}000$ g mol^{-1}] **[JEE Main 2020, Sep.]**

(a) $B > C > A$ (b) $C > B > A$
(c) $A > B > C$ (d) $A > C > B$

62. Vapour density of $PCl_5(g)$ dissociating into $PCl_3(g)$ and $Cl_2(g)$ is 100. Hence, van't Hoff factor for the case

$$PCl_5(g) \rightleftharpoons PCl_3(g) + Cl_2(g) \text{ is}$$

(a) 1.85 (b) 3.70 (c) 1.085 (d) 1.0425

63. A solution contain 62 g of ethylene glycol in 250 g of water is cooled upto −10° C. If K_f for water is 1.86 K kg mol^{-1}, then amount of water (in g) separated as ice is **[JEE Main 2019, Jan.]**

(a) 32 (b) 48 (c) 64 (d) 16

64. The freezing point of benzene decreases by 0.45°C when 0.2 g of acetic acid is added to 20 g of benzene. If acetic acid associates to form a dimer in benzene, percentage association of acetic acid in benzene will be (K_f for benzene = 5.12 K kg mol^{-1}) **[JEE Main 2017 (Offline)]**

(a) 64.6 % (b) 80.4 % (c) 74.6 % (d) 94.6 %

65. Molecules of benzoic acid (C_6H_5COOH) dimerise in benzene. 'w' g of the acid dissolved in 30 g of benzene shows a depression in freezing point equal to 2 K. If the percentage association of the acid to form dimer in the solution is 80, then w is
(Given that K_f = 5 K kg mol^{-1}, molar mass of benzoic acid = 122 g mol^{-1}) **[JEE Main 2019, Jan.]**

(a) 1.8 g (b) 1.0 g (c) 2.4 g (d) 1.5 g

66. A colligative property of a solution depends on the
(a) arrangement of atoms in solute molecule
(b) total number of molecules of solute and solvent
(c) number of molecules of solute in solution
(d) mass of the solute molecules

67. Select the correct statement.
(a) Osmosis, like all colligative properties, results from an increase in entropy as pure solvent passes through the membrane and mixes with the solution
(b) Desalination of sea-water is done by reverse osmosis
(c) Both (a) and (b) are correct statements
(d) None of the above is correct statement

68. Which has maximum freezing point?
(a) 6 g urea solution in 100 g H_2O
(b) 6 g acetic solution in 100 g H_2O
(c) 6 g sodium chloride in 100 g H_2O
(d) All have equal freezing point

69. Aluminium phosphate is 100% ionised in 0.01 molal aqueous solution. Hence, $\Delta T_b / K_b$ is
(a) 0.01 (b) 0.015 (c) 0.0175 (d) 0.02

70. Aqueous solution of barium phosphate which is 100% ionised has $\Delta T_f / K_f$ as 0.05. Hence, given solution is
(a) 0.01 molal (b) 0.02 molal
(c) 0.04 molal (d) 0.05 molal

71. van't Hoff factors of aqueous solutions of X, Y, Z are 1.8, 0.8 and 2.5. Hence, their
(a) boiling point : $Z < X < Y$
(b) freezing point : $Z < X < Y$
(c) osmotic pressure : $X = Y = Z$
(d) vapour pressure : $Y < X < Z$

72. Select the correct statement(s).
(a) The fundamental cause of all colligative properties is the higher entropy of the solution relative to that of the pure solvent
(b) The freezing point of hydrofluoride solution is larger than that of equimolal hydrogen chloride solution
(c) 1 M glucose solution and 0.5 M NaCl solution are isotonic at a given temperature
(d) All of the above are correct statements

73. Which has maximum value of van't Hoff factor?
(a) KO_2 (b) NH_2CONH_2
(c) $C_6H_{12}O_6$ (d) $C_{12}H_{22}O_{11}$

74. Decimolar solution of potassium ferricyanide, $K_3[Fe(CN)_6]$ has osmotic pressure of 3.94 atm at 27°C. Hence, percent ionisation of the solute is
(a) 10% (b) 20% (c) 30% (d) 40%

75. Mole fraction of the solute in a 1.00 molal aqueous solution is
(a) 1.7700 (b) 1.7770
(c) 0.0177 (d) 0.0344

76. 0.004 M Na_2SO_4 is isotonic with 0.01 M glucose. Degree of dissociation of Na_2SO_4 is **[JEE Advanced 2004]**
(a) 75% (b) 50%
(c) 25% (d) 85%

77. A solution of two liquids boils at a temperature more than the boiling point of either them. Hence, the binary solution shows
(a) negative deviation from Raoult's law
(b) positive deviation from Raoult's law
(c) no deviation from Raoult's law
(d) positive or negative deviation from Raoult's law depending upon the composition

78. The system that forms maximum boiling azeotrope is
(a) carbon-di-sulphide — acetone
(b) benzene — toluene
(c) acetone — chloroform
(d) *n*-hexane — *n*-heptane

79. The freezing point depression constant for waer is $-1.86° \text{ cm}^{-1}$. If 5.00 g Na_2SO_4 is dissolved in 45.0 g H_2O, the freezing point is changed by −3.82°C. Calculate the van't Hoff factor for Na_2SO_4
(a) 0.381 (b) 2.05
(c) 2.63 (d) 3.11

80. The van't Hoff factor i for a compound which undergoes dissociation in one solvent and association in other solvent is respectively
(a) greater than one and greater than one
(b) less than one and greater than one
(c) less than one and less than one
(d) greater than one and less than one

81. The change of energy of freezing 1.00 kg of liquid water at 0°C and 1 atm is
(a) 236.1 kJ kg^{-1} (b) 333.4 kJ kg^{-1}
(c) −333.4 kJ kg^{-1} (d) −236.7 kJ kg^{-1}

82. At 35°C, the vapour pressure of CS_2 is 512 mm Hg and that of acetone is 344 mm Hg. A solution of CS_2 in acetone has a total vapour pressure of 600 mm Hg. The false statement amongst the following is **[JEE Main 2020, Jan.]**
(a) Raoult's law is not obeyed by this system
(b) CS_2 and acetone are less attracted to each other than to themselves
(c) a mixture of 100 mL CS_2 and 100 mL acetone has a volume < 200 mL
(d) heat must be absorbed in order to produce the solution at 35°C

83. Among the following, the azeotropic mixture is
(a) $CCl_4 + CHCl_3$
(b) $C_6H_{14} + C_7H_{16}$
(c) $C_2H_5Br + C_2H_5Cl$
(d) chlorobenzene + bromobenzene

84. Four solutions of K_2SO_4 with the following concentration 0.1 m, 0.01 m, 0.001 m and 0.0001 m are available. The maximum value of van't Hoff factor, i corresponds to
(a) 0.0001 m solution (b) 0.001 m solution
(c) 0.01 m solution (d) 0.1 m solution

85. Pure benzene freezes at 5.3°C. A solution of 0.223 g of phenylacetic acid ($C_6H_5CH_2COOH$) in 4.4 g of benzene ($K_f = 5.12$ kg mol^{-1}) freezes at 4.47°C. From the observation, one can conclude that
(a) phenylacetic acid exists as such in benzene
(b) phenylacetic acid undergoes partial ionisation in benzene
(c) phenylacetic acid undergoes complete ionisation in benzene
(d) phenylacetic acid dimerises in benzene

86. A 0.0020 molal aqueous solution of an ionic compound $[Co(NH_3)_5(NO_2)]Cl$ freezes at −0.00732°C. Number of moles of ions which one mole of ionic compound produces on being dissolved in water will be ($K_f = 1.86°$ mol^{-1} kg)
(a) 2 (b) 3 (c) 4 (d) 1

87. The concentration (in mol/L) of the solution having osmotic pressure 0.0821 atm at 300 K will be
(a) 0.33 (b) 0.066
(c) 0.3×10^{-2} (d) 3

88. The order of boiling points of four equimolar aqueous solutions is $C < B < A < D$. The correct order of their freezing points is
(a) $D < C < B < A$ (b) $D > C < B < A$
(c) $D < B > A < C$ (d) $D > A > B > C$

89. Which of the following pair of solutions are expected to isotonic at the same temperature?
(a) 0.2 M urea and 0.2 M NaCl
(b) 0.1 M urea and 0.2 M $MgCl_2$
(c) 0.1 M NaCl and 0.1 M Na_2SO_4
(d) 0.1 M $Ca(NO_3)_2$ and 0.1 M Na_2SO_4

90. In countries nearer to polar region, the roads are sprinkled with $CaCl_2$. This is
(a) to minimise the snow fall
(b) to minimise pollution
(c) to minimise the accumulation of dust on the road
(d) to minimise the wear and tear of the roads

91. The vapour pressure of a pure liquid A is 40 mmHg at 310 K. The vapour pressure of this liquid in a solution with liquid B is 32 mmHg. Mole fraction of A in the solution, if it obeys Raoult's law, is
(a) 0.8 (b) 0.5 (c) 0.2 (d) 0.4

92. The vapour pressure of pure liquid solvent A is 0.80 atm. When a non-volatile substance B is added to the solvent, its vapour pressure drops to 0.60 atm; mole fraction of the component B in the solution is
(a) 0.50 (b) 0.25 (c) 0.75 (d) 0.40

93. Mole fraction of the toluene in the vapour phase which is in equilibrium with a solution of benzene ($p° = 120$ torr) and toluene ($p° = 80$ torr) having 2.0 moles of each, is
(a) 0.50 (b) 0.25 (c) 0.60 (d) 0.40

94. Total vapour pressure of mixture of 1 mole A ($p_A^\circ = 150$ torr) and 2 moles B ($p_B^\circ = 240$ torr) is 200 mm. In this case
(a) there is positive deviation from Raoult's law
(b) there is negative deviation from Raoult's law
(c) there is no deviation from Raoult's law
(d) molecular masses of A and B are also required

95. The vapour pressure of pure benzene, C_6H_6 at 50°C is 268 Torr. How many moles of non-volatile solute per mol of benzene is required to prepare a solution of benzene having a vapour pressure of 167 Torr at 50°C?
(a) 0.377 (b) 0.605 (c) 0.623 (d) 0.395

96. 1 mole each of following solutes are taken in 5 moles water,
A. NaCl B. K_2SO_4 C. Na_3PO_4 D. glucose
Assuming 100% ionisation of the electrolyte, relative decrease in vapour pressure will be in the order
(a) A < B < C < D (b) D < C < B < A
(c) D < A < B < C (d) equal

97. Sea water is found to contain NaCl and $MgCl_2$. If NaCl is 80% ionised and $MgCl_2$ is 50% ionised then van't Hoff factor is
(a) 1.3 (b) 5.0 (c) 3.3 (d) 3.8

98. During depression of freezing point in a solution, the following are in equilibrium **[JEE Advanced 2003]**
(a) liquid solvent, solid solvent
(b) liquid solvent, solid solute
(c) liquid solute, solid solute
(d) liquid solute, solid solvent

99. An azeotropic solution of two liquids has a boiling point lower than either of them when it
(a) shows negative deviation from Raoult's law
(b) shows positive deviation from Raoult's law
(c) shows ideal behaviour
(d) is saturated

100. At 25°C, the vapour pressure of pure methyl alcohol is 92.0 torr. Mole fraction of CH_3OH in a solution in which vapour pressure of CH_3OH is 23.0 torr at 25°C, is
(a) 0.25 (b) 0.75 (c) 0.50 (d) 0.66

101. Depression of freezing point of 0.01 molal *aq.* CH_3COOH solution is 0.02046°. 1 molal urea solution freezes at −1.86°C. Assuming molality equal to molarity, pH of CH_3COOH solution is
(a) 2 (b) 3 (c) 3.2 (d) 4.2

102. pH of a 0.1 M monobasic acid is found to be 2. Hence, its osmotic pressure at a given temperature T (K) is
(a) 0.1 RT (b) 0.11 RT
(c) 1.1 RT (d) 0.01 RT

103. Lowering of vapour pressure due to a solute in 1 molal aqueous solution at 100°C is
(a) 13.44 torr (b) 14.12 torr
(c) 312 torr (d) 352 torr

104. The most likely of the following mixtures to be an ideal solution is
(a) NaCl—H_2O (b) C_2H_5OH—C_6H_6
(c) $C_6H_{16}(l)-H_2O$ (d) C_6H_5OH—H_2O

105. Mole fraction of the component A in vapour phase is X_1 and mole fraction of component A in liquid mixture is X_2 ($p°_A$ = vapour pressure of pure A; $p°_B$ = vapour pressure of pure B), then total vapour pressure of the liquid mixture is
(a) $\frac{p_A^\circ X_2}{X_1}$ (b) $\frac{p_A^\circ X_1}{X_2}$ (c) $\frac{p_B^\circ X_1}{X_2}$ (d) $\frac{p_B^\circ X_2}{X_1}$

106. Which is true about enthalpy of solution containing benzene and toluene?
(a) $\Delta H_{soln.} < 0$
(b) $\Delta H_{soln.} = 0$
(c) $\Delta H_{soln.} > 0$
(d) $\Delta H_{soln.}$ may be zero or greater than zero

107. 2.56 g of sulphur in 100 g of CS_2 has depression in freezing popint of 0.010°, K_f = 0.1° (molal)$^{-1}$. Hence, atomicity of sulphur in CS_2 is
(a) 2 (b) 4 (c) 6 (d) 8

108. Mole fraction of A vapours above the solution in mixture of A and B (X_A = 0.4) will be [$p°_A$ = 100 mm, $p°_B$ = 200 mm]
(a) 0.4 (b) 0.8
(c) 0.25 (d) None of these

109. If relative decrease in vapour pressure is 0.4 for a solution containing 1 mole NaCl in 3 moles H_2O, NaCl is ... % ionised.
(a) 60% (b) 50% (c) 100% (d) 40%

110. Relative decrease in vapour pressure of an aqueous glucose dilute solution is found to be 0.018. Hence, elevation in boiling point is : (It is given 1 molal aq. urea solution boils at 100.54°C at 1 atm pressure)
(a) 0.018° (b) 0.18° (c) 0.54° (d) 0.03°

111. Which has maximum osmotic pressure at temperature T?
(a) 100 mL of 1 M urea solution
(b) 300 mL of 1 M glucose solution
(c) Mixture of 100 mL of 1 M urea solution and 300 mL of 1 M glucose solution
(d) All of the above are isotonic

112. Relative decrease in vapour pressure of an aqueous solution containing 2 moles $[Cu(NH_3)_3Cl]Cl$ in 3 moles H_2O is 0.50. On reaction with $AgNO_3$, this solution will form
(a) 1 mol AgCl (b) 0.25 mol AgCl
(c) 2 mol AgCl (d) 0.40 mol AgCl

113. Vapour pressure of pure A, $p°_A$ = 100 mmHg
Vapour pressure of pure B, $p°_B$ = 150 mmHg
Distillate of vapours of a solution containing 2 moles A and 3 moles B will have total vapour pressure, approximately, on condensation
(a) 135 mm (b) 130 mm
(c) 140 mm (d) 145 mm

114. $FeCl_3$ on reaction with $K_4[Fe(CN)_6]$ in aqueous solution gives blue colour. These are separated by a semipermeable membrane AB as shown. Due to osmosis there is

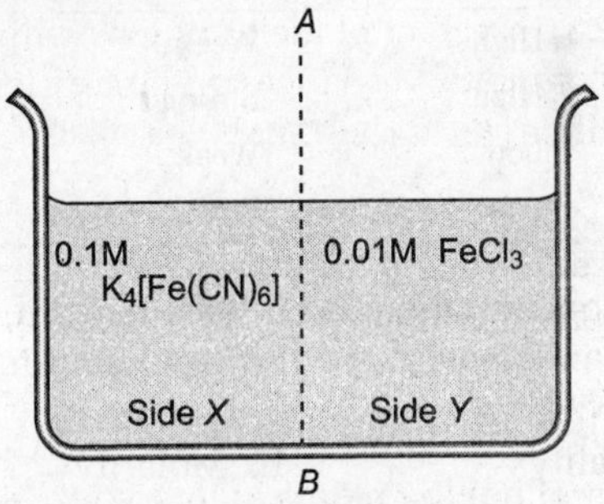

(a) blue colour formation in side X
(b) blue colour formation in side Y
(c) blue colour formation in both of the sides X and Y
(d) no blue colour formation

115. The degree of dissociation 'α' of a weak electrolyte is where, N is the number of ions given by 1 mole of the electrolyte.
(a) $\frac{i-1}{N+1}$ (b) $\frac{i-1}{N-1}$ (c) $\frac{N-1}{i-1}$ (d) $\frac{N+1}{i-1}$

116. Which of the following azeotropic solutions has the boiling point less than boiling point of the constituents A and B?
(a) $CHCl_3$ and CH_3COCH_3
(b) CS_2 and CH_3COCH_3
(c) CH_3CH_2OH and CH_3COCH_3
(d) CH_3CHO and CS_2

117. A solution contains 0.1 mole acetamide in 1 L of glacial acetic acid. When the solution is cooled, the first crystal that appeared at the freezing point contains the molecules of
(a) acetamide only
(b) acetic acid only
(c) both acetamide and acetic acid
(d) either acetamide and acetic acid depending upon the conditions of the experiment

118. 12.2 g of benzoic acid ($M = 122$) in 100 g benzene has depression in freezing point 2.6°; $K_f = 5.2°$ kg/mol. If there is 100% polymerisation, number of molecules of benzoic acid in associated state is
(a) 1 (b) 2 (c) 3 (d) 4

119. 25 mL of an aqueous solution of KCl was found to require 20 mL of 1 M $AgNO_3$ solution when titrated using a K_2CrO_4 as indicator. Depression in freezing point of KCl solution with 100% ionisation will be [$K_f = 2.0°$ mol^{-1} kg and molarity= molality]
(a) 5.0° (b) 3.2°
(c) 1.6° (d) 0.8°

120. Which combination of vapour pressure, intermolecular forces and ΔH_{vap} (latent heat of vaporisation) is matched correctly?

	Vapour pressure	Intermolecular forces	ΔH_{vap}
(a)	High	Weak	Small
(b)	High	Strong	Large
(c)	Low	Weak	Large
(d)	Low	Strong	Small

121. Which concentration can be calculated if the mole fraction and density of an aqueous solution of HCl are known?
I. Molality II. Molarity
III. Per cent by mass
(a) Only I (b) Only III
(c) I and II only (d) I, II and III

122. The Henry's law constant for the solubility of N_2 gas in water at 298 K is 1.0×10^5 atm. The mole fraction of N_2 in air is 0.8. The number of moles of N_2 from air dissolved in 10 moles of water of 298 K and 5 atm pressure is **[IIT JEE 2009]**
(a) 4.0×10^{-4} (b) 4.0×10^{-5}
(c) 5.0×10^{-4} (d) 4.0×10^{-6}

123. The freezing point (in °C) of solution containing 0.1 g of $K_3[Fe(CN)_6]$ (mol. wt. 329) in 100 g of water ($K_f = 1.86$ K kg mol^{-1}) is **[IIT JEE 2011]**
(a) -2.3×10^{-2} (b) -5.7×10^{-2}
(c) -5.7×10^{-3} (d) -1.2×10^{-2}

124. For a dilute solution containing 2.5 g of a non-volatile non-electrolyte solute in 100 g of water, the elevation in boiling point at 1 atm pressure is 2°C. Assuming concentration of solute is much lower than the concentration of solvent, the vapour pressure (mm of Hg) of the solution is (take $K_b = 0.76$ K kg mol^{-1}).
(a) 724 (b) 740 **[IIT JEE 2012]**
(c) 736 (d) 718

125. The boiling point elevation constant for toluene is 3.32 K kg mol^{-1}, the normal boiling point of toluene is 110.7° C. The enthalpy of vaporisation of toluene would be nearly
(a) 17.0 kJ mol^{-1} (b) 34.0 kJ mol^{-1}
(c) 51.0 kJ mol^{-1} (d) 68.0 kJ mol^{-1}

126. Consider the following statements,
I. Isotonic solution have the same molar concentration at a given temperature
II. The molal elevation constant K_b is characteristic of a solvent and is independent of the solute added
III. The freezing point of 0.1 M KCl solution is more than that of 0.1 M aqueous $AlCl_3$ solution
Which of the above statements are correct?
(a) I and II (b) II and III
(c) I and III (d) I, II and III

127. Osmosis results from
(a) an increase in entropy
(b) a decrease in entropy
(c) a decrease in enthalpy
(d) a decrease in internal energy

128. The dissolution of a substance in a solvent is accompanied with
(a) change in enthalpy (b) change in entropy
(c) Both (a) and (b) (d) None of the above

129. Which of the following interactions are endothermic?
(a) NaCl with H_2O (b) CH_3CH_2OH with H_2O
(c) Both (a) and (b) (d) None of the above

130. The phase diagrams for the pure solvent (solid lines) and the solution (non-volatile solute, dashed line) are recorded below

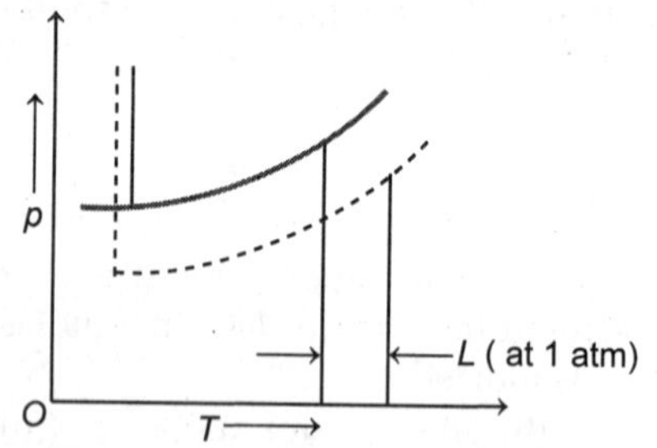

The quantity indicated by L in the figure is (m = molality)
(a) Δp (b) ΔT_f
(c) $K_b m$ (d) $K_f m$

131. The total concentration of dissolved particles inside red blood cells is approximately 0.30 M and the membrane surrounding the cells is semipermeable. What would be the osmotic pressure (in atmosphere) inside the cells become if the cells were removed from the blood plasma and placed in pure water at 298 K?
(a) 7.34 atm (b) 1.78 atm
(c) 2.34 atm (d) 0.74 atm

132. A process analogous of osmosis is
(a) peptisation (b) coagulation
(c) distillation (d) dialysis

133. The fundamental cause of ΔT (depression is)
(a) higher entropy of the solution relative to that of pure solvent
(b) lower entropy of the solution relative to that of pure solvent
(c) higher enthalpy of the solution relative to that of pure solvent
(d) lower enthalpy of the solution relative to that of pure solvent

134. The vapour pressure of water at 20°C is 17.54 mmHg. What will be the vapour pressure of the water in the apparatus shown after the piston is lowered, decreasing the volume of the gas above the liquid to one half of its initial volume? (assume temperature constant)

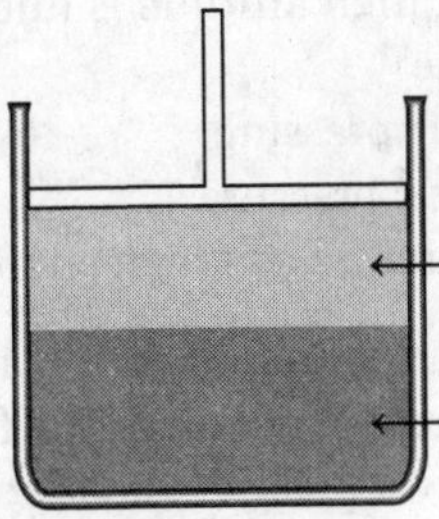

(a) 8.77 mmHg
(b) 17.54 mmHg
(c) 35.08 mmHg
(d) between 8.77 and 17.54 mmHg

135. Cellulose acetate is used as semipermeable membrane in desalination of sea water (reverse osmosis). It is because it is
(a) permeable to water but impermeable to impurities and ions
(b) impermeable to water, but permeable to impurities and ions
(c) permeable to water, impurities and ions
(d) impermeable to water, impurities and ions.

136. Select the incorrect statement.
(a) Na^+ and K^+ ions are responsible for maintaining proper osmotic pressure balance inside and outside of the cells of organism
(b) 200 mL 1 M urea solution and 300 mL 1 M glucose solution are not isotonic
(c) Aquatic species are more comfortable in cold water rather than in warm water
(d) Solubility of a gas in liquid decreases with increase in temperature

137. Which of the following salts has the same value of van't Hoff factor i as that of $K_3[Fe(CN)_6]$?
(a) $Al_2(SO_4)_3$ (b) NaCl
(c) Na_2SO_4 (d) $Al(NO_3)_3$

138. The relationship between osmotic pressure at 273 K when 10 g glucose (p_1), 10 g urea (p_2) and 10g sucrose (p_3) are dissolved in 240 mL of water, is
(a) $p_1 > p_2 > p_3$ (b) $p_3 > p_1 > p_2$
(c) $p_2 > p_1 > p_3$ (d) $p_2 > p_3 > p_1$

139. Vapour pressure of CCl_4 at 25°C is 143 mm Hg. 0.5 g of a non-volatile solute (mol. wt. = 65) is dissolved in 100 mL CCl_4. Find the vapour pressure of the solution (Density of CCl_4 = 1.58 g / cm^3)
(a) 141.9 mm (b) 142.5 mm
(c) 140.0 mm (d) 144.0 mm

140. The vapour pressure of a solvent is decreased by 10 mm of mercury when a non-volatile solute was added to the solvent. The mole fraction of the solute in the solution is 0.2. What should be the mole fraction of the solvent if the decrease in the vapour pressure is to be 20 mm of mercury?
(a) 0.8 (b) 0.6
(c) 0.4 (d) 0.2

141. An aqueous solution containing 1 g of urea boils at 100.25°C. The aqueous solution containing 3 g of glucose in the same volume will boil at
(a) 100°C (b) 100.5°C
(c) 100.25°C (d) 100.75°C

142. Consider the following solution ionisation being 100%, assume molarity = molality
(I) 0.05 M $NaNO_3$ (II) 0.075 M $CuSO_4$
(III) 0.14 M sucrose (IV) 0.04 M $BaCl_2$

The correct order for decreasing freezing point is
(a) I > IV > III > II (b) II > III > IV > I
(c) IV > II > I > III (d) III > II > IV > I

143. Sea water is approximately 0.70 M in NaCl. It can be desalinated by reverse osmosis. For 50% recovery additional osmotic pressure required (on sea-water side) at 298 K is
(a) 30 atm (b) 45 atm
(c) 68 atm (d) 90 atm

144. What will be the ratio of the masses of formalin HCHO and glucose $C_6H_{12}O_6$ contained in equal volumes of solutions having the same osmotic pressure at the given temperature?
(a) 1 : 1 (b) 1 : 2
(c) 1 : 3 (d) 1 : 6

145. At what temperature does an aqueous solution containing 3×10^{23} molecules of a non-electrolyte in 250 g H_2O freeze? (Molal elevation constant of H_2O is 1.86° mol^{-1} kg)
(a) 273 K (b) 269.28 K
(c) 271.14 K (d) 270 K

146. 250 g of an organic solvent contains x g of a non-electrolyte of molar mass m. The cryoscopic constant of the solvent is K_f degree mol^{-1} kg. Thus, ΔT_f (depression in freezing point) is

(a) $\frac{K_f x}{m}$ (b) $\frac{4K_f x}{m}$ (c) $\frac{K_f x}{4m}$ (d) $\frac{K_f x}{250\ m}$

147. An ideal solution is made from 5 moles of benzene and 3.25 moles of toluene. At 298 K, the vapour pressure of pure benzene and pure toluene are 96.4 torr and 28.9 torr. Vapour phase first appears at

(a) 760 torr (b) 96.4 torr
(c) 28.9 torr (d) 69.8 torr

148. At –47°C, the vapour pressure of pure ethyl bromide (C_2H_5Br) is 10.0 torr and that of pure ethyl chloride (C_2H_5Cl) is 40.0 torr. Assuming ideal behaviour, mole fraction of C_2H_5Cl in the vapour phase is 0.80. Hence, mole fraction of C_2H_5Cl in the liquid state is

(a) 0.20 (b) 0.50 (c) 0.75 (d) 0.25

149. Consider the following statemefits.

I. An ideal solution is one in which both components obey Raoult's law.

II. A colligative property is a property that depends on the number of solute particles, not their chemical identity; they arise from the effect of a solute on the entropy of solution.

III. An azeotrope is a mixture that vapourises and condenses without a change of composition.

Select the correct statement(s).

(a) I, II (b) I, III
(c) II, III (d) I, II, III

150. Select the incorrect statement.

(a) An euteitic is a mixture that freezes and melts without change of composition
(b) A regular solution is one in which the entropy of mixing, but not the enthalpy of mixing, is the same as for an ideal solution
(c) Both (a) and (b)
(d) None of the above

151. Partial pressure needed to dissolve 21 mg of CO_2 in 100 g of water at 298 K is (K_H (Henry's law constant for CO_2 is 2.937 kPa m^3 mol^{-1})

(a) 14.0 kPa (b) 7.0 kPa
(c) 121.0 kPa (d) 79.0 kPa

152. The vapour pressure of chloromethane at various mole fraction (X) in a mixture at 298 K was found to be as follows :

X	0.005	0.009	0.019	0.024
p/torr	205	363	756	946

Thus, Henry's law constant is

(a) 4×10^4 torr (b) 2×10^4 torr
(c) 2.5×10^{-5} $torr^{-1}$ (d) 5×10^{-5} $torr^{-1}$

153. Low concentration of oxygen in the blood and tissues of people living at high altitude is due to

(a) low temperature
(b) low atmospheric pressure
(c) high atmospheric pressure
(d) both low temperature and high atmospheric pressure

154. Considering the formation, breaking and strength of hydrogen bond, predict which of the following mixtures will show a positive deviation from Raoult's law?

(a) Methanol and acetone
(b) Chloroform and acetone
(c) Nitric acid and water
(d) Phenol and aniline

155. An unripe mango placed in a concentrated salt solution to prepare pickle, shrivels because

(a) it gains water due to osmosis
(b) it loses water due to reverse osmosis
(c) it gains water due to reverse osmosis
(d) it loses water due to osmosis

Objective Questions Type II [One or more than one correct option(s)]

In each of the questions below, four choices are given, of which one or more than one are correct.

1. Which is/are true about ideal solutions?

(a) The volume of mixing is zero
(b) The enthalpy of mixing is zero
(c) The entropy of mixing is zero
(d) The enthalpy of mixing is negative

2. Freezing point lowering expression is

$$\Delta T_f = K_f\ m\ \text{(molality)}$$

Which of the following assumptions are considered for the validity of above equation?

(a) The solution is dilute
(b) The ΔH_f (latent heat of fusion of solvent) is independent of temperature between the actual and normal freezing point
(c) The solid-phase consists of pure solvent when solution is allowed to cool
(d) ΔT_f is not equal to $3K_f$ for 3 mol L^{-1} solution

3. At 35°C, the vapour pressure of CS_2 is 512 mmHg, and of acetone is 344 mmHg. A solution of CS_2 and acetone in, which the mole fraction of CS_2 is 0.25, has a total vapour pressure of 600 mmHg. Which of the following statements is/are correct?

(a) A mixture of 100 mL of acetone and 100 mL of CS_2 has a volume of 200 mL
(b) When acetone and CS_2 are mixted at 35°C, heat must be absorbed in order to produce a solution at 35°C.
(c) Process of mixing is exothermic
(d) Entropy of mixing is zero

4. Based on the given diagram, which of the following statements regarding the solutions of two miscible volatile liquids are correct?

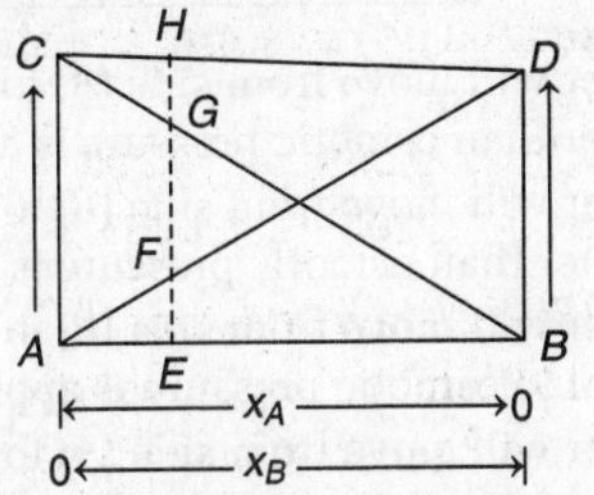

(a) Plots AD and BC show the Raoult's law is obeyed for the solution in which B is a solvent and A is the solute and as well as for that in which A is solvent and B is solute
(b) Plots CD shows that Dalton's law of partial pressures is obeyed by the binary solutions of components A and B
(c) $EF + EG = EH$; and AC and BD correspond to the vapour pressure of the pure solvents A and B respectively
(d) As B is added to the component A, vapour pressure of A as well as of B changes

5. Some of the following gases are soluble in water due to formation of their ions.

I. CO_2 II. NH_3 III. HCl
IV. CH_4 V. H_2

Water-insoluble gases can be
(a) I, IV, V (b) I, V (c) I, II, III (d) IV, V

6. Select the correct statements.
(a) Gases which have high value of van der Waals' constant 'a' are easily liquefied
(b) Easily liquefied gases are water soluble
(c) Ions forming gases in a solvent are soluble in that solvent
(d) When CO_2 gas is dissolved in water, pressure is decreased

7. Select the incorrect statement.
(a) Higher the value of k_H (Henry's law constant) at a given pressure, the lower is the solubility of the gas in the liquid.
(b) Solubility of a gas in a liquid decreases with increase in temperature and pressure.
(c) To minimise the painful effects accompanying the decomposition of deep sea divers, O_2 diluted with less soluble He gas is used as breathing gas.
(d) The solubility of a gas in a liquid is governed by Henry's law.

8. Which of the following concentration factors can be calculated if the mole fraction and density of an aqueous solution of HCl are known?
(a) Molality (b) Molarity
(c) Per cent by mass (d) Normality

9. Consider the following solutions,
I. 1 M aqueous glucose solution
II. 1 M aqueous sodium chloride solution
III. 1 M aqueous ammonium phosphate solution
IV. 1 M benzoic acid in benzene
Select the correct statements for the above solutions.
(a) All are isotonic solutions
(b) III is hypertonic of I, II and IV
(c) IV is hypotonic of I, II and III
(d) II is hypotonic of III but hypertonic of I and IV

10. Which combination of (I) vapour pressure, (II) intermolecular forces and (III) ΔH_{vap} (latent heat of vaporisation) is matched correctly.

	I	II	III
(a)	High	Weak	Small
(b)	High	Strong	Large
(c)	Low	Weak	Large
(d)	Low	Strong	Small

11. When mercuric iodide is added to the aqueous solution of potassium iodide, then
(a) freezing point is raised
(b) freezing point is lowered
(c) freezing point does not change
(d) boiling point does not change

12. Which is/are correct statement(s)?
(a) When mixture is more volatile, there is positive deviation from Raoult's law.
(b) When mixture is less volatile, there is negative deviation from Raoult's law.
(c) Ethanol and water form ideal solution
(d) $CHCl_3$ and water form ideal solution

13. At 40°C, the vapour pressure in torr of methanol and ethanol solution is $P = 119x + 135$ where, x is the mole fraction of methanol. Hence,
(a) vapour pressure of pure methanol is 119 torr
(b) vapour pressure of pure ethanol is 135 torr
(c) vapour pressure of equimolar mixture of each is 127 torr
(d) mixture is completely immiscible

14. Consider the following cases,
I. 2 M CH_3COOH solution in benzene at 27°C where, there is dimer formation to the extent of 100%
II. 0.5 M KCl *aq.* solution at 27°C, which ionises 100%; which is/are true statement(s)?
(a) Both are isotonic (b) I is hypertonic
(c) II is hypertonic (d) None is correct

15. Which one of the statements given below concerning properties of solutions, describes a colligative effect?

(a) Boiling point of pure water decreases by the addition of ethanol

(b) Vapour pressure of pure water decreases by the addition of nitric acid

(c) Vapour pressure of pure benzene decreases by the addition of naphthalene

(d) Boiling point of pure benzene increases by the addition of toluene

16. Which of the following factor(s) affect the solubility of a gaseous solute in the fixed volume of liquid solvent?

I. Nature of solute

II. Temperature

III. Pressure

(a) I and II at constant T

(b) I and II at constant p

(c) II and III only

(d) II only

17. Benzene and naphthalene form an ideal solution at room temperature. For this process, the true statement(s) is (are) **[JEE Advanced 2013]**

(a) $\Delta G > 0$

(b) $(\Delta S)_{\text{system}} > 0$

(c) $(\Delta S)_{\text{surrounding}} > 0$

(d) $\Delta H = 0$

18. We have three aqueous solutions of NaCl labelled as 'A', 'B' and 'C' with concentrations 0.1 M, 0.01 M and 0.001 M and 0.001 M, respectively. The value of vant Hoff factor for these solutions will be in the order ....

(a) $i_A < i_B < i_C$ (b) $i_A > i_B > i_c$

(c) $i_A = i_B = i_C$ (d) $i_A < i_B < i_c$

19. Which of the following statements is/are correct?

(a) Two different solutions of sucrose of same molality prepared in different solvents will have the same depression in freezing point.

(b) The osmotic pressure of a solution is given by the equation $\pi = CRT$ (where, C is the molarity of the solution)

(c) Decreasing order of osmotic pressure for 0.01 M aqueous solutions of barium chloride, potassium chloride, acetic acid and sucrose is

$$BaCl_2 > KCl > CH_3COOH > \text{sucrose}$$

(d) According to Raoult's law, the vapour pressure exerted by a volatile component of a solution is directly proportional to its mole fraction in the solution

20. Consider the figure and mark the correct option(s)

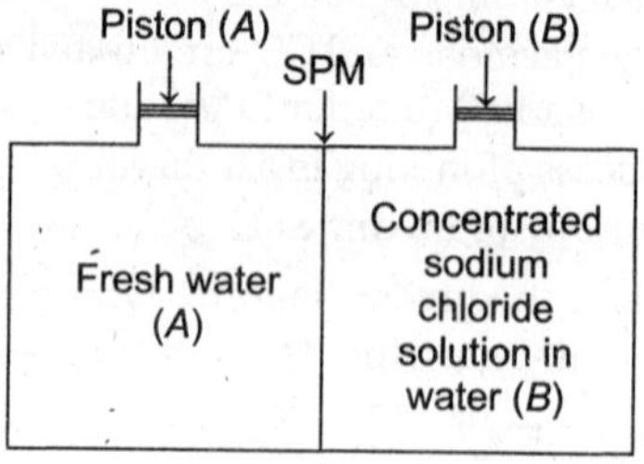

(a) water will move from side (A) to side (B) if a pressure lower than osmotic pressure is applied on piston (B)

(b) water will move from side (B) to side (A) if a pressure greater than osmotic pressure is applied on piston (B)

(c) water will move from side (B) to side (A) if a pressure equal to osmotic pressure is applied on piston (B)

(d) water will move from side (A) to side (B) if pressure equal to osmotic pressure is applied on piston (A)

21. For a solution formed by mixing liquids L and M, the vapour pressure of L plotted against the mole fraction of M in solution is shown in the following figure. Here x_L and x_M represent mole fractions of L and M, respectively, in the solution. The correct statement(s) applicable to this system is (are) **[JEE Advanced 2017]**

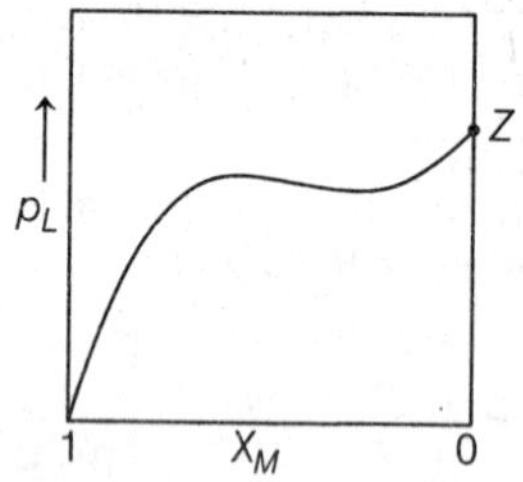

(a) The point Z represents vapour pressure of pure liquid M and Raoult's law is obeyed from $x_L = 0$ to $x_L = 1$

(b) Attractive intermolecular interactions between L - L in pure liquid L and M - M in pure liquid M are stronger than those between L - M when mixed in solution

(c) The point Z represents vapour pressure of pure liquid M and Raoult's law is obeyed when $x_L \to 0$

(d) The point Z represents vapour pressure of pure liquid L and Raoult's law is obeyed when $x_L \to 1$

22. Mixture(s) showing positive deviation from Raoult's law at 35°C is (are) **[JEE Advanced 2016]**

(a) carbon tetrachloride + methanol

(b) carbon disulphide + acetone

(c) benzene + toluene

(d) phenol + aniline

Numerical Value Questions

All these questions have a Numerical value as their answer, solve the questions and write your answer.

1. A handbook gives the concentration of water in a 2.772 M aqueous solution of NaOH as 998.0 gL^{-1}. The molality and mole fraction of NaOH in this solution are ......

2. AB_2 is 10% dissociated in water to A^{2+} and B^-. The boiling point of a 10.0 molal aqueous solution of AB_2 is .... °C. (Round off to the Nearest Integer).
[Given : Molal elevation constant of water $K_b = 0.5$ K kg mol^{-1} Boiling point of pure water = 100° C] **[JEE Main 2021, March]**

3. A decimolar solution of potassium ferrocyanide, $K_4[Fe(CN)_6]$ is 50% dissociated at 300 K. The osmotic pressure of the solution is .... $\times 10^5 Nm^{-2}$
($R = 8.314$ $JK^{-1} mol^{-1}$)

4. A solution containing 0.011 kg barium nitrate in 0.1 kg water boils at 100.46°C. Calculate the degree of ionisation of the salt. $m\,[Ba(NO_3)_2] = 261.0$ g mol^{-1} and $K_b(H_2O) = 0.52$ kg mol^{-1} K.

5. The freezing point of a solution containing 50 cm^3 of ethylene glycol in 50 g of water is found to be −34°C. Assuming ideal behaviour, density of ethylene glycol is ....

6. The amount of ice that will separate out on cooling a solution containing 50 g of ethylene glycol in 200 g water to −9.3°C is ...... [$K_f(H_2O)$ is 1.86° mol^{-1} kg].

7. The freezing point of an aqueous solution of a non electrolyte having an osmotic pressure of 2.0 atm at 300 K is ....
[$K_f(H_2O) = 1.86°$ kg mol^{-1},
$R = 0.0821$ L atm mol^{-1} K^{-1}]

8. A solution of non-volatile olute in water freezes at −0.30°C. The vapour pressure of pure water at 298 K is 23.51 mmHg and K_f for water is 1.86° mol^{-1} kg. Calculate the vapour pressure of this solution.

9. A 1 molal $K_4Fe(CN)_6$ solution has a degree of dissociation of 0.4. Its boiling point is equal to that of another solution which contains 18.1 weight percent of a non-electrolytic solute *A*. The molar mass of *A* is ...... u. (Round off to the Nearest Integer).
[Density of water = 1.0 g cm^{-3}] **[JEE Main 2021, March]**

10. Water boils at 100°C at 1 atmospheric pressure. What is vapour pressure at 40°C? What is vapour pressure lowering of 0.2 molal urea solution at 40°C? Latent heat of vaporisation (ΔH) is 10 kcal mol^{-1} in the given temperature range.

11. If the freezing point of a 0.01 molal aqueous solution of a cobalt (III) chloride-ammonia complex (which behaves as a strong electrolyte) is − 0.0558°C, the number of chloride(s) in the coordination sphere of the complex is ....
[K_f of water = 1.86 K kg mol^{-1}] **[JEE Advanced 2015]**

12. Liquids *A* and *B* form ideal solution over the entire range of composition. At temperature *T*, equimolar binary solution of liquids *A* and *B* has vapour pressure 45 torr. At the same temperature, a new solution of *A* and *B* having mole fractions x_A and x_B, respectively, has vapour pressure of 22.5 torr. The value of x_A / x_B in the new solution is ....
(Given that the vapour pressure of pure liquid *A* is 20 torr at temperature *T*) **[JEE Advanced 2018]**

13. The plot given below shows $p-T$ curves (where p is the pressure and T is the temperature) for two solvents *X* and *Y* and isomolal solution of NaCl in these solvents. NaCl completely dissociates in both the solvents.

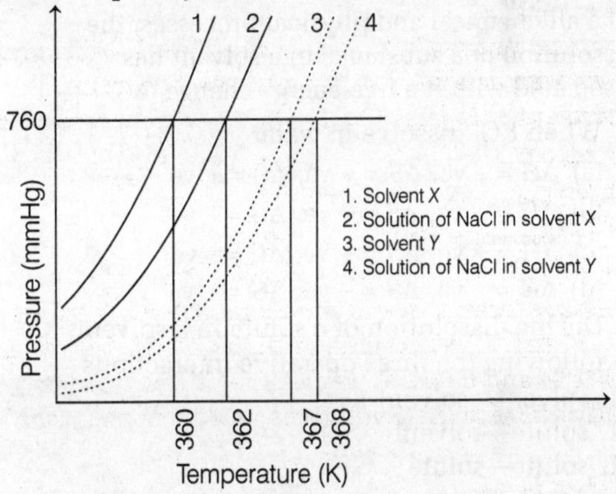

On addition of equal number of moles of a non-volatile solute *S* in equal amount (in kg) of these solvents, the elevation of boiling point of solvent *X* is three times that of solvent *Y*. Solute S is known to undergo dimerisation in these solvents. If the degree of dimerisation is 0.7 in solvent *Y*, the degree of dimerisation in solvent *X* is .... **[JEE Advanced 2018]**

14. On dissolving 0.5 g of a non-volatile non-ionic solute to 39 g of benzene, its vapour pressure decreases from 650 mmHg to 640 mmHg. The depression of freezing point of benzene (in K) upon addition of the solute is .... (Given data : Molar mass and the molal freezing point depression constant of benzene are 78 g mol^{-1} and 5.12 K kg mol^{-1}, respectively). **[JEE Advanced 2019]**

15. Liquids *A* and *B* form ideal solution for all compositions of *A* and *B* at 25°C. Two such solutions with 0.25 and 0.50 mole fractions of *A* have the total vapour pressure of 0.3 and 0.4 bar, respectively. What is the vapour pressure of pure liquid *B* in bar?

16. The mole fraction of urea in an aqueous urea solution containing 900 g of water is 0.05. If the density of the solution is 1.2 g cm^{-3}, then molarity of urea solution is ...... (Given data : Molar masses of urea and water are 60 g mol^{-1} and 18 g mol^{-1}, respectively) **[JEE Advanced 2019]**

17. 2 molal solution of a weak acid HA has a freezing point of 3.885°C. The degree of dissociation of this acid is .... $\times 10^{-3}$. (Round off to the Nearest Integer). [Given : Molal depression constant of water = 185 K kg mol^{-1} Freezing point of pure water = 0°C] **[JEE Main 2021, March]**

18. The osmotic pressure of a solution of NaCl is 0.10 atm and that of a glucose solution is 0.20 atm. The osmotic pressure of a solution formed by mixing 1 L of the sodium chloride solution with 2 L of the glucose solution is $x \times 10^{-3}$ atm. x is .... (nearest integer). **[JEE Main 2020, Sep.]**

19. A solute a dimerises in water. The boiling point of a 2 molar solution of A is 100.52°C. The percentage association of A is. .... (Round off to the Nearest Integer) [Use : K_b for water = 0.52 K kg mol^{-1} Boiling point of water = 100°C]

Comprehension Based Questions

In these questions, a passage has been given followed by questions based on it. You have to answer the questions based on the passage given.

***Passage* 1** *Following is the scientific observation. Answer the questions at the end of it.*

Like all chemical and physical processes, the dissolution of a substance in a solvent has associated with it a free-energy change, ΔG.

1. When KCl dissolve in water
(a) $\Delta H = +$ ve, $\Delta S = +$ ve, $\Delta G = +$ ve
(b) $\Delta H = +$ ve, $\Delta S = -$ ve, $\Delta G = -$ ve
(c) $\Delta H = +$ ve, $\Delta S = +$ ve, $\Delta G = -$ ve
(d) $\Delta H = -$ ve, $\Delta S = -$ ve, $\Delta G = +$ ve

2. During dissolution of a solute in a solvent, following the three operative interactions
I. solvent—solvent
II. solute—solvent
III. solute—solute

Which of the following takes place with the absorption heat?
(a) I, II
(b) II, III
(c) I, II, III
(d) I, III

3. The dissolving process is exothermic when
(a) the energy released in solvation exceed the energy used in breaking up solute-solute and solvent-solvent interactions.
(b) the energy used in solvation exceeds the energy released in breaking up solute-solute and solvent-solvent interactions
(c) the energy released in solvation is about the same as the energy used in breaking up solute-solute and solvent-solvent interactions
(d) the energy used in solvation is about the same as the energy used in breaking up solute-solute and solvent-solvent interactions

***Passage* 2** *Answer the questions (given below) which are based on the following diagram.*

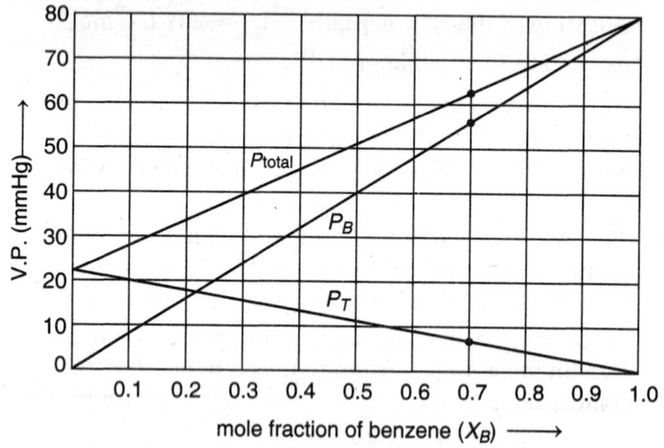

Vapour pressure plots of benzene-toluene mixtures at 20°C. Solutions of benzene and toluene are ideal. Raoult's law is valid for both components over the entire range of concentration.

1. An ideal solution consisting of two components A and B (such as benzene and toluene) is one in which
(a) the intermolecular attractions $A, \ldots A, B, \ldots B$ and $A \ldots B$ are equal.
(b) $\Delta H_{mix} = 0$, $\Delta V_{mix} = 0$
(c) Both of the above conditions are followed
(d) None of the above conditions are followed

2. There is deviation from ideal behaviour if mixture contains
(a) n-hexane and n-heptane
(b) chlorobenzene and bromobenzene
(c) o-xylene and p-xylene
(d) acetone and chloroform

***Passage* 3** *Answer the questions (given below) which are based on the following diagram.*

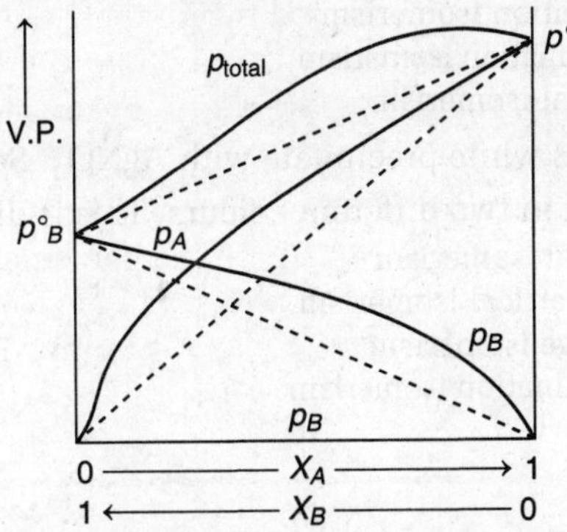

Vapour pressure diagram for real solutions of two liquids A and B that exhibit a positive deviation from Raoult's law. The vapour pressure of both A and B are greater than predicted by Raoult's law. The dashed lines represented the plots for ideal solutions.

1. Consider some facts about the above phase diagram

I. This is observed when $A \dots B$ attractions are greater than average of $A \dots A$ and $B \dots B$ attraction.

II. $\Delta H_{mix} = +$ ve, $\Delta V_{mix} = +$ ve

III. Boiling point is smaller than expected such that vaporisation is increased

IV. Mixture is called azeotropic mixture

Select the correct facts.

(a) I, II, III (b) II, III, IV (c) I, III, IV (d) I, II, III, IV

2. Total vapour pressure of mixture of 1 mol of volatile component A ($p^\circ_A = 100$ mm Hg) and 3 mol of volatile component B ($p^\circ_B = 60$ mmHg) is 75 mm. For such case

(a) there is positive deviation from Raoult's law

(b) boiling point has been lowered

(c) force of attraction between A and B is smaller than that between A and A or between B and B

(d) All the above statements are correct

***Passage* 4** *Read the following sentence and answer the questions at the end of it.*

Benzoic acid dimerises in benzene but ionises in aqueous solution.

1. Equimolal solutions of (A) benzoic acid in benzene and (B) in aqueous solution are taken. Thus,

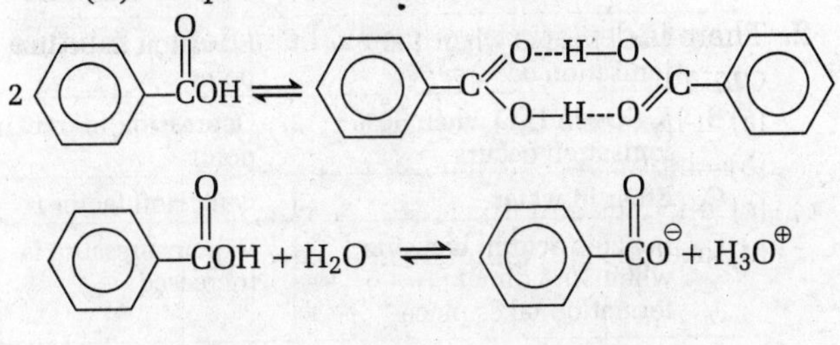

(a) van't Hoff factor of $(A) > (B)$

(b) van't Hoff factor of $(A) < (B)$

(c) van't Hoff factor of $(A) = (B)$

(d) dimer formation or ionisation is not possible

***Passage* 5** Q. 1, 2 *and* 3 *are based on the following activities (A) with observations (O) and results or reason (R).*

If A, O are correct and R is incorrect, write (a)

If A, O are correct and R is also correct, write (b)

If A, O are incorrect and R is also correct, write (c)

If A, correct and O, R are incorrect, write (d)

Activity (A)	**Observation** (O)	**Result/ Reason** (R)
0.01 M $K_3[Fe(CN)_6]$ and 0.1 M $FeCl_3$ solution are separated by a semipermeable membrane	Osmosis takes place from 0.01 M solution to 0.1 M solution but no blue colour formation either of side.	Osmosis takes place from dilute to concentrated solution and it is the only solvent (H_2O) that flows.
1 mole each of benzene and toluene are mixed	$p^\circ_{total} = p^\circ_B X_B + p^\circ_T X_T$	There is positive deviation from Raoult's law
Ether is added to H_2O	Boiling point is elevated	Boiling point is elevated when a volatile solute is added to a solvent.

***Passage* 6** HgI_2 is insoluble in water. This solute is added into KI solution.

Answer the following questions.

1. What happens to HgI_2 solution?

(a) It dissolves forming K_2HgI_2

(b) It does not dissolve but KI combines with it forming KI_2

(c) It undergoes ionisation to Hg^{2+} and I^- ions

(d) Theres is no interaetion

2. Select the correct statement(s).

(a) Freezing point is lowered

(b) Boiling point is elevated

(c) Freezing point is elevated

(d) Boiling point is lowered

3. van't Hoff factor

(a) increases by 1 unit

(b) decreases by 1 unit

(c) increases by 2 unit

(d) decreases by 2 unit

Passage 7 A 0.002 molal aqueous solution of an ionic compound $Co(NH_3)_5(NO_2)Cl$ freezes at $-0.00732°C$. $K_f(H_2O) = 1.86°C\ mol^{-1}\ kg$.

Answer the following questions.

1. How many moles of ions does 1.0 mole of the salt produce on being dissolved in water?
(a) 2
(b) 3
(c) 4
(d) No ionisation (molecular state)

2. Above salt can show
(a) geometrical isomerism
(b) ionisation isomerism
(c) coordination isomerism
(d) optical isomerism

3. Salt gives white precipitate with $AgNO_3$. Salt itself can exist in two different colours. This is due to
(a) optical isomerism
(b) geometrical isomerism
(c) linkage isomerism
(d) coordination isomerism

Matrix-Match Type

Given below are Matching Type Questions, with two columns (each having some items) each . Each item of Column I has to be matched with the items of Column II.

1. Match the system (in Column I) with its type (in Column II).

Column I	Column II
A. Ethyl alcohol-water system	1. Immiscible liquid mixture
B. Phenol-water system	2. Azeotropic mixture
C. Water-nitrobenzene system	3. Partially miscible liquid mixture
	4. Ternary mixture

2. Match the terms (in Column I) with its explanation (in Column II).

Column I	Column II
A. Upper critical solution temperature	1. At which a gas cannot be liquefied
B. Isotonic solutions	2. Solutions have same osmotic pressure
C. Cryoscopic constant	3. Solutions have same vicosity
	4. ΔT produced by 1 g of a solute in a litre
	5. ΔT per mole of solute/1000 g of solvent and above
	6. At and above which two immiscible liquids become miscible

3. Match the laws given in Column I with expressions given in Column II.

Column I	Column II
A. Raoult's law	1. $\Delta T_f = K_f m$
B. Henry's law	2. $\pi = CRT$
C. Elevation of boiling point	3. $p = x_1 p_1^\circ + x_2 p_2^\circ$
D. Depression in freezing point	4. $\Delta T_b = K_b m$
E. Osmotic pressure	5. $p = K_H \cdot x$

4. Match the solutions in Column I with their concentration/ nature in Column II.

Column I	Column II
A. 98% H_2SO_4 solution (by mass of solution) with density = $1.8\ g\ mL^{-1}$	1. 18 M
B. 17.64 g H_3PO_4 in 10 mL solution behaving as strong electrolyte	2. 500 mol kg^{-1}
C. 100 mL of 36 N $Ca(OH)_2$ required exactly 100 mL of .... H_2SO_4	3. Neutral solution
D. 10.8 g urea in 12 g solution ($d = 1.2\ g\ mL^{-1}$)	4. 36 N normality
	5. 54 N normality

5. Match the solutions in Column I with their related properties in Column II.

Column I	Column II
A. Etheral solution in water.	1. Vapour pressure is lowered
B. Urea solution in water	2. Boiling point is increased.
C. $CHCl_3$ solution in acetone	3. Vapour pressure is increased
D. Benzene in toluene	4. Azeotropic

6. Match the solutions in Column I with their related properties in Column II.

Column I	Column II
A. NaCl in H_2O when 100% ionisation occurs.	1. Elevation in boiling point
B. K_2SO_4 in H_2O when 50% ionisation occurs	2. Depression in freezing point
C. Ether in water	3. van't Hoff factor i
D. Benzoic acid in benzene when 50% dimer formation takes place	4. Vapour pressure is increased

7. The following table lists the concentration of the principal ions in sea water at 25°C.

Ion	Conc/ppm	Ion	Conc/ppm
Na^+	1.08×10^4	Cl^-	1.95×10^4
Mg^{2+}	1.29×10^3	SO_4^{2-}	9.05×10^2
Ca^{2+}	4.12×10^2	Br^-	67
K^+	3.80×10^2		

On the basis of this table match the given parameter (f.p., b.p. (in °C) and osmotic pressure (in atm) in Column I with the corresponding values in Column II $k_f(H_2O) = 1.86°\ mol^{-1}\ kg$, $K_b(H_2O) = 0.54°\ mol^{-1}\ kg$

	Column I		Column II
A.	Depression in freezing point of sea water	1.	1.1
B.	Elevation in boiling point of sea water	2.	0.60
C.	Osmotic pressure of sea water at 0°C	3.	2.05
D.	Minimum pressure needed to purify water by reverse osmosis under given condition	4.	26.91
E.	Molality of sea water	5.	0.00
		6.	24.65

Single Integer Answer Questions

Answer of these questions is a single digit lying between 0 to 9.

1. Liquids A and B form an ideal solution. At 45°C, the vapour pressure of pure A and pure B are 66 torr and 88 torr, respectively. Calculate the value of $10\ X'_B$, where X'_B is the composition of the vapour in equilibrium with a solution containing 36 mole per cent A at this temperature.

2. Iron (III) sulphate is 50% ionised in aqueous solution at 298 K. Than van't Hoff factor is ....

3. Phenol (C_6H_5OH) is found to exist as polymer. If there is 100% polymerisation, determine number of phenol molecules polymerised in aqueous solution if 9.4 g of phenol in 100 g water freezes at – 0.93°C. Molal depression constant of water is $1.86°\ mol^{-1}$ kg.

4. A 0.001 molal solution of Pt $(NH_3)_4Cl_4$ in water had a freezing point depression of 0.0054°C. How many ions are obtained due to ionisation? $K_f(H_2O) = 1.86$ kg mol^{-1} K. Assume 100% ionisation

5. x g of a non-electrolyte (molar mass 20) are dissolved in 1.0 L of 0.05 M NaCl aqueous solution. The osmotic pressure of this mixture was found to be 4.92 atm at 27°C. What is value of x? Assume complete dissociation of NaCl and ideal behaviour of this solution. (Solution constant = 0.082 L atm $mol^{-1}\ K^{-1}$).

6. H_2SO_4 is 98% by weight of solution, molality is $M\times 10^2$. The value of M is ......

7. Vapour pressure of pure A is 120 torr and that of B is 150 torr. Vapour pressure of mixture of 1 mole A and x mole B is 140 torr. The value of x is ....

8. What is van't Hoff factor of aqueous aluminum phosphate solution? (assume 100% ionisation).

9. 18.0 g $C_n(H_2O)_n$ in 100 g H_2O lowers the freezing point of water by 1.86 K. Molal depression constant of water is 1.86 K mol^{-1} kg. The value of n is

10. 1 mL of 5 M H_2SO_4 solution is diluted to final 1 N solution by mixing water? The amount of water in mL is added is

11. 25.6 g of sulphur is 100 g benzene shows depression in freezing point of 5.12°. K_f (benzene) = 5.12 K mol^{-1} kg)

How many sulphur atoms are in molecular sulphur formed?

12. On adding w g of non-volatile solute (molar mass 42 g mol^{-1}) in 114 g octane (C_8H_{18}). Vapour pressure is reduced to 84%. What is the value of w?

13. 1×10^{-3} molal solution of $[Pt(NH_3)_4Cl_4]$ in H_2O shows depression in freezing point by 0.0054°C. $K_f(H_2O) = 1.86°\ mol^{-1}kg$. How many ions are formed per formula unit of complex?

Answers

Objective Questions Type I [Only one correct option]

1. (b)	**2.** (c)	**3.** (b)	**4.** (d)	**5.** (b)	**6.** (a)	**7.** (a)	**8.** (b)	**9.** (c)	**10.** (b)
11. (b)	**12.** (c)	**13.** (a)	**14.** (d)	**15.** (d)	**16.** (c)	**17.** (c)	**18.** (c)	**19.** (b)	**20.** (b)
21. (d)	**22.** (c)	**23.** (c)	**24.** (d)	**25.** (c)	**26.** (c)	**27.** (a)	**28.** (c)	**29.** (d)	**30.** (a)
31. (d)	**32.** (d)	**33.** (b)	**34.** (c)	**35.** (a)	**36.** (d)	**37.** (b)	**38.** (b)	**39.** (d)	**40.** (c)
41. (a)	**42.** (d)	**43.** (a)	**44.** (c)	**45.** (a)	**46.** (c)	**47.** (c)	**48.** (a)	**49.** (a)	**50.** (c)
51. (d)	**52.** (c)	**53.** (d)	**54.** (d)	**55.** (c)	**56.** (a)	**57.** (c)	**58.** (c)	**59.** (b)	**60.** (a)
61. (c)	**62.** (d)	**63.** (c)	**64.** (d)	**65.** (c)	**66.** (c)	**67.** (c)	**68.** (a)	**69.** (d)	**70.** (a)
71. (b)	**72.** (d)	**73.** (a)	**74.** (b)	**75.** (c)	**76.** (a)	**77.** (a)	**78.** (c)	**79.** (c)	**80.** (d)
81. (c)	**82.** (c)	**83.** (a)	**84.** (a)	**85.** (d)	**86.** (a)	**87.** (c)	**88.** (c)	**89.** (d)	**90.** (a)
91. (a)	**92.** (b)	**93.** (d)	**94.** (b)	**95.** (b)	**96.** (c)	**97.** (d)	**98.** (a)	**99.** (b)	**100.** (a)
101. (b)	**102.** (b)	**103.** (a)	**104.** (a)	**105.** (a)	**106.** (b)	**107.** (d)	**108.** (c)	**109** (c)	**110.** (c)
111. (d)	**112.** (a)	**113.** (a)	**114.** (d)	**115.** (b)	**116.** (c)	**117.** (b)	**118.** (b)	**119** (b)	**120.** (a)
121. (d)	**122.** (a)	**123.** (a)	**124.** (a)	**125.** (b)	**126.** (d)	**127.** (b)	**128.** (c)	**129.** (c)	**130.** (b)
131. (a)	**132.** (d)	**133.** (a)	**134.** (b)	**135.** (a)	**136.** (b)	**137.** (d)	**138.** (c)	**139.** (a)	**140.** (c)
141. (c)	**142.** (a)	**143.** (c)	**144.** (d)	**145.** (b)	**146.** (b)	**147.** (d)	**148.** (b)	**149.** (d)	**150.** (d)
151. (a)	**152.** (a)	**153.** (b)	**154.** (a)	**155.** (d)					

Objective Questions Type II [One or more than one correct option(s)]

1. (a, b)	**2.** (a, b, d)	**3.** (b)	**4.** (a, c, d)	**5.** (d)
6. (a, b, c, d)	**7.** (b)	**8.** (a, b, c, d)	**9.** (b, c, d)	**10.** (a)
11. (b)	**12.** (a, b)	**13.** (b)	**14.** (a)	**15.** (c)
16. (a, b)	**17.** (b, d)	**18.** (a)	**19.** (b, c, d)	**20.** (b)
21. (b, d)	**22.** (a, b)			

Numerical Value Questions

1. 0.0476 **2.** 106 **3.** 7.4826 **4.** $x = 0.55$ **5.** $d = \frac{56.67}{50} = 1.133 \text{ g / cm}^3$ **6.** 38.7 g **7.** 0.151°C

8. 23.44 mmHg **9.** 85 **10.** 0.2095 torr **11.** 1 **12.** 19 **13.** 0.05 **14.** 0.2 **15.** 1.02 **16.** 2.98 **17.** 50

18. 167 **19.** 100

Comprehension Based Questions

Passage 1 – **1.** (c) **2.** (d) **3.** (a)

Passage 2 – **1.** (c) **2.** (d)

Passage 3 – **1.** (b) **2.** (d)

Passage 4 – **1.** (b)

Passage 5 – **1.** (b) **2.** (a) **3.** (d)

Passage 6 – **1.** (a) **2.** (c,d) **3.** (b)

Passage 7 – **1.** (a) **2.** (b) **3.** (c)

Matrix-Match Type

1. A → (2); B → (3); C → (1)

2. A → (6); B → (2); C → (3)

3. A → (3); B → (5); C → (4); D → (1); E → (2)

4. A → (1,2,4); B → (1,5); C → (1,3,4); D → (1,3)

5. A → (3); B → (1,2); C → (1,4); D → (1)

6. A → (1,2,3); B → (1,2,3); C → (4); D → (1,2)

7. A → (3); B → (2); C → (6); D → (6); E → (1)

Single Integer Answer Questions

1. (7)	**2.** (3)	**3.** (2)	**4.** (3)	**5.** (2)	**6.** (5)	**7.** (2)	**8.** (2)	**9.** (6)	**10.** (9)
11. (8)	**12.** (8)	**13.** (3)							

Solutions

Objective Questions Type I [Only one correct option]

10. *(b)* Solubility ∝ pressure

$$\frac{S_2}{S_1} = \frac{p_2}{p_1}$$

$$S_2 = 5.3 \times 10^{-4} \times \frac{760}{593}$$

$$= 6.8 \times 10^{-4}\ \text{M}$$

12. *(c)*

$$\frac{w_1}{w_1 + w_2} = 0.25 = \frac{1}{4}$$

$$\therefore \quad \frac{w_1}{w_2} = \frac{1}{3} = 0.33$$

13. *(a)* 0.50 molal glucose solution means 1000 g water has

$$= 0.50 \text{ mol glucose}$$

$$= 90 \text{ g glucose}$$

Total mass of solution = 1000 + 90 = 1090 g

90 g glucose is in = 1090 g solution

$$\therefore \quad 0.15 \text{ mol } (= 27 \text{ g}) \text{ is in} = \frac{1090 \times 27}{90}$$

$$= 327 \text{ g}$$

14. *(d)* Mole fraction of solute

$$= \frac{\text{number of moles of solute} + \text{number of moles solvent}}{\text{number of moles of solute}}$$

$$\chi_{\text{Solute}} = \frac{n_{\text{Solute}}}{n_{\text{Solute}} + n_{\text{Solvent}}} = \frac{\dfrac{w_{\text{solute}}}{Mw_{\text{solute}}}}{\dfrac{w_{\text{solute}}}{Mw_{\text{solute}}} + \dfrac{w_{\text{solvent}}}{Mw_{\text{solvent}}}}$$

Given, $w_{\text{solute}} = w_{\text{NaOH}} = 8\,\text{g}$

$Mw_{\text{solute}} = Mw_{\text{NaOH}} = 40\ \text{g mol}^{-1}$

$w_{\text{solvent}} = w_{H_2O} = 18\,\text{g}$

$Mw_{\text{solvent}} = 18\ \text{g mol}^{-1}$

$$\therefore \chi_{\text{Solute}} = \chi_{\text{NaOH}} = \frac{\dfrac{8}{40}}{\dfrac{8}{40} + \dfrac{18}{18}} = \frac{0.2}{0.2 + 1} = \frac{0.2}{1.2} = 0.167$$

Now, molality $(m) = \dfrac{\text{Moles of solute}}{\text{Mass of solvent (in kg)}}$

$$= \frac{\dfrac{w_{\text{solute}}}{Mw_{\text{solute}}}}{w_{\text{solvent}}\text{(in g)}} \times 1000$$

$$= \frac{\dfrac{8}{40}}{18} \times 1000$$

$$= \frac{0.2}{18} \times 1000$$

$$= 11.11\ \text{mol kg}^{-1}$$

Thus, mole fraction of NaOH in solution and molality of the solution respectively are 0.167 and 11.11 mol kg^{-1}.

19. *(b)* i = van't Hoff factor = $1 + (y - 1)x$

(y = number of ions, x = degree of ionisation)

		y	$i = 1 + (y-1)x$
(a) K_2PtCl_4	$2K^+ + PtCl_4^{2-}$	3	$1 + 2 = 3$
(b) K_2PtCl_6	$2K^+ + PtCl_6^{2-}$	3	3

In (a), oxidation number of Pt = 2

In (b), oxidation number of Pt = 4

20. *(b)* i remains unchanged when number of ions before and after complex formation remains constant.

Solute	y	Complex	y
(a) $PtCl_4$	5	$K_2[PtCl_6]$	3
(b) $ZnCl_2$	3	$[Zn(NH_3)_4]Cl_2$	3

22. *(c)*

$$HA \rightleftharpoons H^+ + A^-$$

$$i = [1 + (y-1)x] = 1 + x$$

$$pK_a = 4 = -\log K_a$$

$$\therefore \quad K_a = 10^{-4} = Cx^2$$

$$1 \times 10^{-4} = 0.01 \times x^2$$

$$x = 0.1$$

$$\therefore \quad i = 1 + x = 1.1$$

23. *(c)* As above

$$\underset{\substack{C \\ (C - Cx)}}{CH_3COOH} \rightleftharpoons \underset{\substack{0 \\ Cx}}{CH_3COO^-} + \underset{\substack{0 \\ Cx}}{H^+}$$

$$i = [1 + (y-1)x] = 1 + x = 1.01$$

$$x = 0.01$$

$$[H^+] = Cx = 0.01 \times 0.01 = 1 \times 10^{-4}\ \text{M}$$

$$\therefore \quad \text{pH} = 4$$

24. *(d)* pH = 2

$$\therefore \quad [H^+] = 10^{-2}\ \text{M} = Cx = x$$

$$\therefore \quad i = (1 + x) = 1 + 0.01 = 1.01$$

25. *(c)*

Solute	y	x	$i = [1 + (y-1)x]$
(a) KCl	2	0.5	1.5
(b) K_2SO_4	3	0.4	1.8
(c) $FeCl_3$	4	0.3	1.9
(d) $SnCl_4$	5	0.2	1.8

27. *(a)* 1 molar glucose solution means 1 L solution has solute = 1 mol glucose

1200 g solution has solute = 180 g glucose

(since, $d = 1.2\ \text{g mL}^{-1}$)

1020 g solvent (water) has solute = 180 g glucose

$$\therefore \quad \Delta T_b = \frac{1000 K_b\, w_1}{m_1 w} = \frac{1000 \times K_b \times 180}{180 \times 1020} = 0.98\, K_b$$

28. *(c)* The expression of elevation of boiling point,

$$\Delta T_b = K_b \times m \times i = K_b \times \frac{w_2 \times 1000}{M_2 \times w_1} \times i$$

where, m = molality

i = van't Hoff factor = 1 (for non-electrolyte/non-associable)

w_2 = mass of solute in g = 1g (present in both of the solutions)

M_2 = molar mass of solute in g mol^{-1} (same solute in both of the solutions)

w_1 = mass of solvent in g = 100 g (for both of the solvents A and B)

K_b = ebullioscopic constant

So, the expression becomes,

$$\Delta T_b \propto K_b$$

$$\Rightarrow \frac{\Delta T_b(A)}{\Delta T_b(B)} = \frac{K_b(A)}{K_b(B)} = \frac{1}{5} \qquad \left[\text{Given } \frac{K_b(A)}{K_b(B)} = \frac{1}{5}\right]$$

29. (*d*)
$$\Delta T_b = \text{Molality} \times K_b$$
$$0.52 = m \times 0.52$$
$$\text{Molality} = 1 \text{ mol kg}^{-1}$$
$$\therefore \quad U$$
$$\text{Water} = \frac{1000}{18} = 55.55$$
$$\text{Mole fraction of urea} = \frac{1}{56.55} = 0.018$$

33. (*b*) From given graph it can be seen that , X has higher vapour pressure as compared to Y at lower temperature (or to attain same vapour pressure, Y need higher temperature than X). It means that intermolecular interactions must be weaker in X as compared to Y, which further must be weaker than Z by the same reason also. Hence, option (b) is correct.

34. (*c*)
$$\Delta T = \frac{1000 K_b w_1}{m_1 w_2}$$
$$\frac{\Delta T}{K_b}(AB_2) = \frac{1000 \times 6}{m_1 \times 100} = 1$$
$$\therefore \quad m_1(AB_2) = 60 = A + 2B$$
$$\frac{\Delta T}{K_b}(A_2B) = \frac{1000 \times 9}{m_1 \times 100} = 1$$
$$\therefore \quad m_1(A_2B) = 90 = 2A + B$$
$$\therefore \quad A = 40, \; B = 10$$

38. (*b*) 1 M $C_6H_{12}O_6$(molar mass = 180 g mol^{-1})

1000 mL solution has = 180 g solute

1180 g solution has = 180 g solute

1000 g solvent has = 180 g solute

Thus, molality = 1 molal

$$\therefore \quad \Delta T_f = K_f \text{ molality}$$
$$= 1.86 \times 1 = 1.86°$$
$$\therefore \quad \text{Freezing point} = -1.86°\text{C}$$

43. (*a*) 1100 g solution has 60 g urea

Thus, water = 1040 g

$$\Delta T_f = \frac{1000 K_f w_1}{m_1 w_2}$$
$$\frac{\Delta T_f}{K_f} = \frac{1000 \times 60}{60 \times w_2} = 1$$
$$\therefore \quad w_2 = 1000 \text{ g}$$

Thus, ice formed = 1040 − 1000 = 40 g

45. (*a*)
$$\pi = MST$$
$$7.65 = M \times 0.0821 \times 310$$
$$\therefore \quad M = 0.30 \text{ M}$$

46. (*c*)
$$p = 0.0072 \text{ atm}$$
$$= 0.0072 \times 76 \text{ cm of Hg}$$
$$= 0.0072 \times 76 \times 13.6 \text{ cm of mercury column}$$
Also $\quad p = h \times 1 \text{ cm of water column}$
$$h \times 1 = 0.0072 \times 76 \times 13.6 \text{ cm}$$
$$\therefore \quad h = 0.0072 \times 76 \times 13.6 \text{ cm} = 7.4 \text{ cm}$$

49. (*a*) Osmotic pressure is dependent on concentration only.

51. (*d*) $KCl \rightleftharpoons K^+ + Cl^-$

Osmosis is a colligative property and thus, osmolarity of 0.2 M KCl = 0.4 M

55. (*c*)
$$p = p_A^\circ X_A + p_B^\circ X_B = p_A^\circ(1 - X_B) + p_B^\circ X_B$$
$$= p_A^\circ - (p_A^\circ - p_B^\circ)X_B = 120 - 75X_B$$
Thus, $\quad p_A^\circ = 120$ torr
$$p_A^\circ - p_B^\circ = 75 \text{ torr}$$
$$\therefore \quad p_B^\circ = 45 \text{ torr}$$

56. (*a*) According to Henry's law (at constant temperature)

$p_{gas} = K_H \times \chi_{gas\,(solute)} = K_H \times [1 - \chi_{H_2O\,(solvent)}]$

$p_{gas} = K_H - K_H\,\chi_{H_2O}$

p_{gas} = partial pressure of the gas above its solution with a liquid (solvent) say water.

χ_{gas} = mole fraction of the gas (solute) in the solution.

χ_{H_2O} = mole fraction of water (solvent).

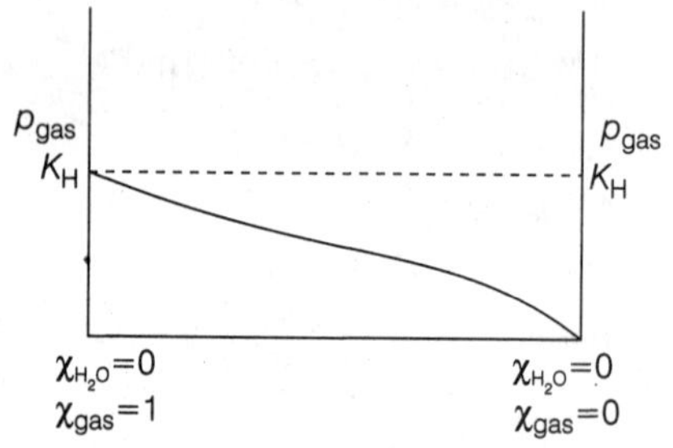

[i.e. $p_{gas} = K_H$] Higher the value of K_H, higher will be the partial pressure of the gas (p_{gas}), at a given temperature. The plot of p_{gas} vs χ_{H_2O} gives a (–ve) slope.

$$p_{gas} = K_H - K_H \times \chi_{H_2O}$$

Comparing the above equation with the equation of straight line $y = mx + c$

Slope = − K_H , intercept = K_H

So, (i) Higher the value of K_H, more (–ve) will be the slope and it is for z (K_H = 40 K bar)

(ii) Higher the value of K_H, higher with the value of intercept, i.e. partial pressure and it is also for z.

57. (*c*) $pV = nRT$

$$p_{mix} = 7.82 \times 10^4 \text{ Pa}$$

$$p_1 + p_2 = 7.82 \times 10^4 \text{ Pa}$$

$$p_1 = 7.03 \times 10^4 \text{ Pa}$$

$$\therefore \quad p_2 = 0.79 \times 10^4 \text{ Pa}$$

$$p \propto n \propto \frac{w}{m}$$

$$\therefore \quad \frac{w_2 m_1}{w_1 m_2} = \frac{p_2}{p_1}$$

$$w_2 = w_1 \frac{p_2 m_2}{p_1 m_1} = \frac{0.79 \times 10^4 \times 112.5}{7.03 \times 10^4 \times 18} = 0.70$$

58. (*c*) Lowering of vapour pressure is colligative property

thus, $\quad i\,(K_2SO_4) = 1 + (y-1)x = 1 + 2x = 3$

$$\therefore \text{ If} \quad \frac{\Delta p}{p^\circ} = \frac{n_1 i}{n_1 i + n_2}$$

$$\frac{10}{50} = \frac{3n_1}{3n_1 + 12} = \frac{n_1}{n_1 + 4}$$

$$n_1 = 1$$

59. (*b*)

$$p_{Total} = p_A^\circ X_A + p_B^\circ X_B$$

$$= 100 \times \frac{1}{4} + 80 \times \frac{3}{4} = 85$$

$$X_A' \text{ (vapours)} = \frac{p_A^\circ X_A}{p_{total}} = \frac{25}{85} = \frac{5}{17}$$

$$X_B' \text{ (vapours)} = \frac{12}{17}$$

$$p_{total\,(distillate)} = p_A^\circ X_A' + p_B^\circ X_B'$$

$$= 100 \times \frac{5}{17} + 80 \times \frac{12}{17} = 86 \text{ mmHg}$$

60. (*a*)

$$\frac{\Delta p}{p^\circ} = X_{solute} = \frac{n_1}{n_1 + n_2}$$

$$\frac{4}{40} = \frac{n_1}{n_1 + n_2}$$

$$n_2 = 9n_1, \quad \frac{w_2}{m_2} = 9n_1$$

$$w_2 = 9n_1 m_2$$

$$\text{Molality} = \frac{1000 w_1}{m_1 w_2} = \frac{1000 n_1}{w_2}$$

$$= \frac{1000 n_1}{9 n_1 m_2} = \frac{1000}{9 \times 18} = 6.173 \text{ molal}$$

61. (*c*) Relative lowering in vapour pressure

(RLVP) $= \dfrac{p^\circ - p_S}{p^\circ} = \chi_{\text{solute}}$ or RLVP $= \dfrac{\Delta p}{p^\circ} = \chi_{\text{solute}}$

$n \rightarrow$ moles of solute $= \dfrac{w}{M}$; $N \rightarrow$ moles of solvent $= \dfrac{W}{M}$

Given, weight of solvent (water) = 180 g

Weight of different non-volatile solute w_A, w_B and $w_C = 10$

Molar mass of $M_A = 100 \text{ g mol}^{-1}$

$M_B = 200 \text{ g mol}^{-1} \Rightarrow M_C = 10{,}000 \text{ g mol}^{-1}$

RLVP for *A*,

$$\left(\frac{\Delta p}{p^\circ}\right)_A = \frac{\frac{10}{100}}{\frac{10}{100} + \frac{180}{18}} = \frac{0.1}{1.1} = 0.091$$

RLVP for *B*,

$$\left(\frac{\Delta p}{p^\circ}\right)_B = \frac{\frac{10}{200}}{\frac{10}{200} + \frac{180}{18}} = \frac{0.05}{10.05} = 0.0049$$

RLVP for *C*,

$$\left(\frac{\Delta p}{p^\circ}\right)_C = \frac{\frac{10}{10{,}000}}{\frac{10}{10{,}000} + \frac{180}{18}} = \frac{0.001}{0.001 + 10} = \frac{0.001}{10.001}$$

$$= 0.000099$$

From the above value the relative lowering of vapour pressure in the presence of there solute are in the following order :

$$\left(\frac{\Delta p}{p^\circ}\right)_A > \left(\frac{\Delta p}{p^\circ}\right)_B > \left(\frac{\Delta p}{p^\circ}\right)_C$$

Hence, option (c) is correct.

62. (*d*)

$$PCl_5 \rightleftharpoons PCl_3 + Cl_2$$

$$i = 1 + (y-1)x = (1 + x)$$

$$x = \frac{D - d}{d} = \frac{104.25 - 100}{100} = \frac{4.25}{100} = 0.0425$$

$$\therefore \quad i = 1 + x = 1.0425$$

where, (D = theoretical V.D. $= \dfrac{\text{molar mass}}{2}$

d = experimental V.D.)

63. (*c*) Considering the expression of the depression in freezing point of a solution,

$$\Delta T_f = K_f \times m \times i$$

$$T_f^\circ - T_f = K_f \times \frac{w_B \times 1000}{M_B \times w_A (\text{in g})} \times i \quad \ldots\text{(i)}$$

Here, $T_f^\circ = 0°C$, $T_f = -10°C$

w_B = mass of ethylene glycol = 62 g

M_B = molar mass of ethylene glycol

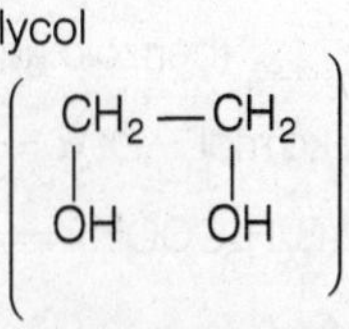

$= 62 \text{ g mol}^{-1}$

w_A = mass of water in g as liquid solvent,

i = van't-Hoff factor = 1, (for ethylene glycol in water)

$K_f = 1.86 \text{ K kg mol}^{-1}$

On substituting in Eq. (i), we get

$$0 - (-10) = 1.86 \times \frac{62 \times 1000}{62 \times w_A} \times 1$$

$$\Rightarrow \quad w_A = \frac{1.86 \times 62 \times 1000}{10 \times 62} = 186\,g$$

So, amount of water separated as ice (solid solvent)

$$= 250 - w_A = (250 - 186)\,g = 64\,g$$

64. **(d)** Let the degree of association of acetic acid (CH_3COOH) in benzene is α, then

$$2CH_3COOH \rightleftharpoons (CH_3COOH)_2$$

Initial moles	1	0
Moles at equilibrium	$1-\alpha$	$\frac{\alpha}{2}$

$\therefore$ Total moles $= 1 - \alpha + \frac{\alpha}{2} = 1 - \frac{\alpha}{2}$ or $i = 1 - \frac{\alpha}{2}$

Now, depression in freezing point (ΔT_f) is given as

$$\Delta T_f = i\,K_f m \quad \text{... (i)}$$

where, K_f = molal depression constant or cryoscopic constant.

m = molality

$$\text{Molality} = \frac{\text{number of moles of solute}}{\text{weight of solvent (in kg)}} = \frac{0.2}{60} \times \frac{1000}{20}$$

Putting the values in Eq. (i)

$$\therefore \quad 0.45 = \left[1 - \frac{\alpha}{2}\right](5.12)\left[\frac{0.2}{60} \times \frac{1000}{20}\right]$$

$$1 - \frac{\alpha}{2} = \frac{0.45 \times 60 \times 20}{5.12 \times 0.2 \times 1000}$$

$$\Rightarrow \quad 1 - \frac{\alpha}{2} = 0.527 \Rightarrow \frac{\alpha}{2} = 1 - 0.527$$

$$\therefore \quad \alpha = 0.946$$

Thus, percentage of association = 94.6%

65. **(c)** Molecules of benzoic acid dimerise in benzene as:

$$2(C_6H_5COOH) \rightleftharpoons (C_6H_5COOH)_2$$

Now, we know that depression in freezing point (ΔT_f) is given by following equation:

$$\Delta T_f = i \times K_f \times m = \frac{i \times K_f \times w_{solute} \times 1000}{Mw_{solute} \times w_{solvent}} \quad \text{...(i)}$$

Given, w_{solute} (benzoic acid) = w g

$w_{solvent}$ (benzene) = 30 g

Mw_{solute} (benzoic acid) = 122 g mol^{-1}, $\Delta T_f = 2$ K

$K_f = 5$ K kg mol^{-1}, %α = 80 or $\alpha = 0.8$

$$2(C_6H_5COOH) \rightleftharpoons (C_6H_5COOH)_2$$

Initial	1	0
Final	$1-\alpha$	$\alpha/2$
	$= 1 - 0.8 = 0.2$	$0.8/2 = 0.4$

Total number of moles at equilibrium

$$= 0.2 + 0.4 = 0.6$$

$$i = \frac{\text{Number of moles at equilibrium}}{\text{Number of moles present initially}}$$

$$i = \frac{0.6}{1} = 0.6$$

On substituting all the given values in Eq. (i), we get

$$2 = \frac{0.6 \times 5 \times w \times 1000}{122 \times 30}, \quad w = 2.44\,g$$

Thus, weight of acid (w) is 2.4 g.Molecules of benzoic acid dimerise in benzene as:

$$2(C_6H_5COOH) \rightleftharpoons (C_6H_5COOH)_2$$

Now, we know that depression in freezing point (ΔT_f) is given by following equation:

$$\Delta T_f = i \times K_f \times m = \frac{i \times K_f \times w_{solute} \times 1000}{Mw_{solute} \times w_{solvent}} \quad \text{...(i)}$$

Given, w_{solute} (benzoic acid) = w g

$w_{solvent}$ (benzene) = 30 g

Mw_{Solute} (benzoic acid) = 122 g mol^{-1}, $\Delta T_f = 2$ K

$K_f = 5$ Kkg mol^{-1}, %α = 80 or $\alpha = 0.8$

$$2(C_6H_5COOH) \rightleftharpoons (C_6H_5COOH)_2$$

Initial	1	0
Final	$1-\alpha$	$\alpha/2$
	$= 1 - 0.8$	$0.8/2 = 0.4$
	$= 0.2$	

Total number of moles at equilibrium

$$= 0.2 + 0.4 = 0.6$$

$$i = \frac{\text{Number of moles at equilibrium}}{\text{Number of moles present initially}}$$

$$i = \frac{0.6}{1} = 0.6$$

On substituting all the given values in Eq. (i), we get

$$2 = \frac{0.6 \times 5 \times w \times 1000}{122 \times 30}, \quad w = 2.44\,g$$

Thus, weight of acid (w) is 2.4 g.

69. **(d)** $$AlPO_4 \rightleftharpoons Al^{3+} + PO_4^{3-}$$

$$i = 1 + x = 2$$

$$\Delta T_b = \text{molality} \times K_b \times i = 0.01 \times K_b \times 2$$

$$\therefore \quad \frac{\Delta T_b}{K_b} = 0.02$$

75. **(c)** Mole of solute = 1

$$\text{Moles of water} \frac{1000}{18} = 55.55$$

$$\text{Mole fraction of solute} = \frac{1}{56.55} = 0.0177$$

77. **(a)** The vapour pressure of the solution is lower than that of either of two liquids. Hence, the solution shows negative deviation from Raoult's law.

78. **(c)** Solutions which show negative deviation form Raoult's law are also called maximum boiling azeotrope. Chloretone molecules are joined by H-bonding.

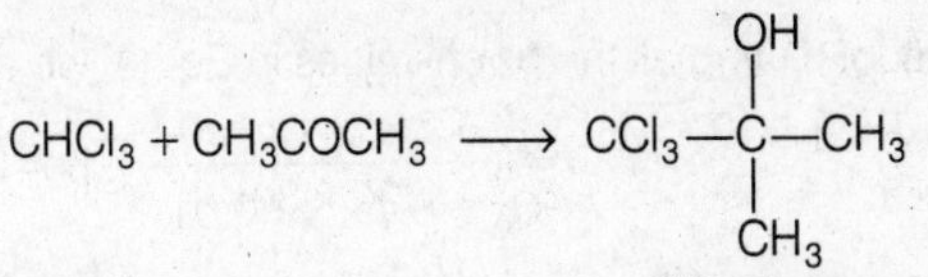

Chloretone

Hence, acetone-chloroform forms maximum boiling azeotrope.

79. **(c)** Using $\Delta T_f = i \times K_f \times m$

$$m = \frac{1000 w_1}{m_1 w_2} = \frac{1000 \times 5}{142 \times 45} = 0.782$$

$$i = \frac{\Delta T_f}{m K_f} = \frac{3.82}{0.782 \times 1.86} = 2.63$$

80. **(d)** In case of dissociation, van't Hoff factor, $i > 1$

In case of association van't Hoff factor, $i < 1$

81. **(c)** $\because H_2O(l) \longrightarrow H_2O(s) \quad \Delta H = -6.0 \text{ kJ mol}^{-1}$

Number of moles in 1 kg water

$$= \frac{1.00 \times 10^3}{18} = 55.5 \text{ mol}$$

$\because$ When 1 mole of water freezes, energy change $= -6.0$ kJ

$\therefore$ When 55.56 mole water freezes, energy changes

$$= \frac{-6.0}{1} \times 55.56 \text{ kJ} = -333.36 \text{ kJ kg}^{-1}$$

$$= -333.3 \text{ kJ kg}^{-1}$$

82. **(c)** The incorrect statement among the given statements is (c) and the explanation of all the statements is as follows :

According to Raoult's law, vapour pressure of the solution p_{id} (ideal vapour pressure) $= p_A{}^\circ + (p_B{}^\circ - p_A{}^\circ) x_B$

(A = solvent : acetone, B = solute : CS_2)

Given; $p_A{}^\circ = 344$ mm Hg.

$p_B{}^\circ = 512$ mm Hg.

$\therefore \quad p_{id} = 3.44 + (512 - 344) x_B$

or $\quad p_{id} = 344 + 168\, x_B$ and so, $0 < x_B < 1$.

Also, total vapour pressure $(p) = 600$ mmHg

$\therefore$ For any value of x_B, $p > p_{id}$.

Since $p \neq p_{id}$, so, option (a) is correct.

Option (b) is also correct. Since $p > p_{id}$, (i.e. positive deviation) therefore attractive force between CS_2 and acetone is weaker than $CS_2 - CS_2$ or acetone-acetone attraction.

Option (c) is incorrect as for positive deviation, $\Delta V > 0$ because final volume of solution must be greater than the sum of volumes of components taken.

Option (d) is correct. Since, in such solution, $\Delta_{mix} H$ is positive because energy is required to break A—A and B—B bonds.

83. **(a)** Only non-ideal solutions form azeotropic mixtures (constant boiling mixtures). Among the given only CCl_4 and $CHCl_3$ form non-ideal solution, thus, they form azeotropic mixture.

84. **(a)** van't Hoff factor, $i \propto \dfrac{1}{\text{concentration, } C}$

Since, $\quad i = [1 + (y - 1)\, x] = (1 + 2x)$

y = number of ions in K_2SO_4

x = degree of ionisation

$x \propto$ dilution.

$\therefore$ 0.0001 m solution has the maximum van't Hoff factor.

85. **(d)** Depression in freezing point, $\Delta T_f = K_f m$ (where, m = molality)

$$= 5.12 \times \frac{0.223 \times 1000}{4.4 \times 136} = 1.91$$

$\therefore$ Theoretical $\Delta T_f = 1.91$

Actual $\Delta T_f = 5.3°C - 4.47°C = 0.83°C$

$\therefore \quad i = \dfrac{0.83}{1.91} = 0.43$

$\because \quad i < 1$

$\therefore$ Association will take place.

Thus, it can be said that phenylacetic acid dimerises in benzene.

86. **(a)** $\Delta T_f = i K_f m$

or $\quad i = \dfrac{\Delta T_f}{K_f \times m} = \dfrac{0.00732}{1.86 \times 0.0020} = 1.9 \simeq 2.$

87. **(c)** $\pi = CRT$

$$C = \frac{\pi}{RT} = \frac{0.0821}{0.0821 \times 300} = 0.33 \times 10^{-2} \text{ mol/L}$$

88. **(c)** Elevation in boiling point and depression in freezing point, both are the colligative properties, i.e. dependent only upon the number of particles. In other words, as the number of particles increases, boiling point increases but freezing point decreases. Since, the order of boiling point is

$$C < B < A < D$$

$\therefore$ The order of freezing point is

$$D < A < B < C \quad \text{or} \quad D < B > A < C$$

89. **(d)** Both will furnish equal number of ions in solution. So, if value of 'i' is same, the solutions will exert equal osmotic pressure.

$$Ca(NO_3)_2 \rightleftharpoons Ca^{2+} + 2NO_3^-; \qquad i = 3$$

$$Na_2SO_4 \rightleftharpoons 2Na^+ + SO_4^{2-}; \qquad i = 3$$

90. **(a)** $CaCl_2$ acts as a non-volatile solute and results in depression in freezing point. Thus, snow fall is reduced and prevents blocking of roads in the polar region.

91. **(a)** $\quad p_A(\text{in mixture}) = p_A^\circ X_A$

$\therefore \quad X_A = \dfrac{p_A}{p_A^\circ} = \dfrac{32}{40} = 0.8$

92. **(b)** By Raoult's law,

relative decrease in v.p. = mole fraction of solute B

$$\frac{0.80 - 0.60}{0.80} = X_B = 0.25$$

93. (*d*) Mole fraction of toluene vapour $= \dfrac{p_T^\circ X_T}{p_T^\circ X_T + p_B^\circ X_B}$

X_T = mole fraction of toluene in solution = 0.5

X_B = mole fraction of benzene = 0.5

p_T° = v.p. of pure toluene = 80 mm

p_T° = v.p. of pure benzene = 120 mm

$$= \frac{80}{80+120} = 0.40$$

94. (*b*) $p_{\text{total}} = p_A^\circ X_A + p_B^\circ X_B$

$$= 150 \times \frac{1}{3} + 240 \times \frac{2}{3}$$

= 210 mm > 200 mm (given)

Observed value of total vapour pressure is decreased hence, there is negative deviation.

95. (*b*) By Raoult's law,

Relative decrease in v.p. = mole fraction of solute

$\therefore \quad \dfrac{268-167}{268} = X_{\text{solute}} = \dfrac{n}{1+n}$ (n = mole of solute)

$\therefore \quad n = 0.605$

96. (*c*) Relative decrease in vapour pressure = mole fraction of water = 5 mol

Solute	Mole in solution	Mole fraction of solute
A(NaCl)	2	$\frac{2}{7} = 0.29$
B(K_2SO_4)	3	$\frac{3}{8} = 0.38$
C(Na_3PO_4)	4	$\frac{4}{9} = 0.44$
D (Glucose)	1	$\frac{1}{6} = 0.17$

Hence, $D < A < B < C$

97. (*d*) van't Hoff factor for NaCl $= 1 + x = 1 + 0.8 = 1.8$

van't Hoff factor for $MgCl_2 = 1 + 2x = 1 + 2 \times 0.5 = 2.0$

$\therefore$ total van't Hoff factor = 3.8

98. (*a*) liquid solvent, solid solvent

99. (*b*) When boiling point is lower, it means vaporisation is increased, hence v.p. is greater than theoretical value, hence, positive deviation.

100. (*a*) $p_{CH_3OH} = p^\circ_{CH_3OH} X_{CH_3OH}$

$\therefore \quad X_{CH_3OH} = \dfrac{23}{92} = \dfrac{1}{4} = 0.25$

101. (*b*) $(\Delta T)_{CH_3COOH} = K_f \times 0.01 \times i = 0.02046$

$(\Delta T)_{\text{urea}} = K_f \times 1 = 1.86$

$\therefore \quad i = 1.1 = (1 + x)$

$\therefore \quad x = 0.1$

$[H^+]$ in $CH_3COOH = Cx = 1 \times 10^{-3}$ M

$\therefore \quad$ pH = 3

102. (*b*) pH = 2

$[H^+] = 10^{-2}$ M

$\therefore \quad Cx = 0.1 \times x = 0.01$

$\therefore \quad x = 0.1$

$\therefore$ i for monobasic acid $= 1 + x = 1.1$

$\therefore \quad \pi = MRT\, i = 0.1(RT)(1.1) = 0.11\,RT$

103. (*a*) 1 molal aqueous solution means 1 mole solute in 1000 g H_2O

$\therefore \quad X_{\text{solute}} = \dfrac{1}{1 + \left(\dfrac{1000}{18}\right)} = \dfrac{18}{1018}$

$\therefore \quad \dfrac{\Delta p}{p^\circ} = \dfrac{18}{1018}$

$\therefore$ Δp (lowering of v.p.) $= p^\circ X_{\text{solute}} = 760 \times \dfrac{18}{1018}$

= 13.44 Torr

105. (*a*) X_1 = mole fraction of *A* in vapour phase $= \dfrac{X_2 p_A^\circ}{p_{\text{total}}}$

$\therefore \quad p_{\text{total}} = \dfrac{X_2\, p_A^\circ}{X_1}$

107. (*d*) Let atomicity be n, then it exists as $(S)_n$

molar mass = (32n)

$$\Delta T_f = \frac{1000 w_1 K_f}{m_1 w_2}$$

$\therefore \quad m_1$ (sulphur) $= \dfrac{1000 \times 2.56 \times 0.1}{0.01 \times 100} = 256$

$\therefore \quad 32n = 256$

$\therefore \quad n = 8$

108. (*c*) Mole fraction of *A* in vapour phase $= \dfrac{p_A^\circ X_A}{p_{\text{total}}}$

$$= \frac{100 \times 0.4}{100 \times 0.4 + 200 \times 0.6}$$

= 0.25

109. (*c*) NaCl is ionised in aqueous solution

$\therefore \quad \dfrac{\Delta p}{p^\circ} = \dfrac{(1+x)\,n_1}{(1+x)\,n_1 + n_2} = \dfrac{1+x}{1+x+3} = 0.4$

$\therefore \quad x = 1$

110. (*c*) $(\Delta T)_b$ for urea solution $= 0.54^\circ = K_f \times$ molality $= K_f \times 1$

$\therefore \quad K_f = 0.54^\circ$ kg mol^{-1}

$$\frac{\Delta p}{p^\circ} = \frac{w_1 m_2}{m_1 w_2}$$

$$\frac{w_1}{m_1 w_2} = \frac{\Delta p}{p^\circ m_2} = \frac{0.018}{18}$$

$$\Delta T_b(\text{glucose}) = \frac{1000 K_f w_1}{m_1 w_2}$$

$$= 1000 \times 0.54 \times \frac{0.018}{18} = 0.54^\circ$$

111. (*d*) $\pi = MST$, osmotic pressure depends on molarity which is constant in all cases.

112. (*a*) $[Cu(NH_3)_3Cl]Cl \rightleftharpoons [Cu(NH_3)_3Cl]^+ + Cl^-$

Complex ionises in aqueous solution and Ag^+ reacts with free Cl^- ion. Degree of ionisation = x

$$i = (1 + x)$$

$$\frac{\Delta p}{p^\circ} = \frac{n_1(1+x)}{n_1(1+x)+n_2}$$

$$= \frac{2(1+x)}{2(1+x)+3} = 0.5$$

$\therefore$ $x = 0.5$ hence, complex is 50% ionised.

$\therefore$ $Cl^- = 2 \times 0.5 = 1$ mol

$$Cl^- + Ag^+ \longrightarrow AgCl\downarrow$$

$\therefore$ $AgCl = 1$ mol

114. (*d*) Osmosis of the solvent (H_2O) and not of ions takes place. Hence, no colour change appears.

115. (*b*) $i = 1 + (N-1)\alpha$

$\therefore$ $\alpha = \frac{i-1}{(N-1)}$

118. (*b*) $\Delta T_f = \frac{1000 K_f w_1}{m_1 w_2}$

$\therefore$ m_1 (benzoic acid in benzene) $= \frac{1000 K_f w_1}{\Delta T_f w_2}$

$$= \frac{1000 \times 5.2 \times 12.2}{2.6 \times 100}$$

$$= 244 \text{ g mol}^{-1}$$

but theoretical value $= 122$ g mol^{-1}

Hence, there is dimer formation (by H-bonding)

119. (*b*) $\frac{M_1 V_1}{KCl} = \frac{M_2 V_2}{AgNO_3}$

$$M_1 (KCl) = \frac{1 \times 20}{25} = 0.8 \text{ M}$$

$$i = (1 + x) = 1 + 1 = 2$$

$\therefore$ $\Delta T_f = \text{molality} \times K_f \times i = 0.8 \times 2 \times 2 = 3.2^\circ$

125. (*b*) $K_b = \frac{RT_0^2}{1000\, \Delta H_V}$

$\therefore$ $\Delta H_V = \frac{RT_0^2}{1000 K_b}$

$$= \frac{8.314 \times 10^{-3} \times (383.7)^2}{1000 \times 3.32}$$

$$= 0.3687 \text{ kJ g}^{-1}$$

$$= 0.3687 \times 92 \text{ kJ mol}^{-1}$$

$$= 33.9 \text{ kJ mol}^{-1}$$

$$\approx 34 \text{ kJ mol}^{-1}$$

137. (*d*) $K_3[Fe(CN)_6] \rightleftharpoons \underbrace{3K^+ + [Fe(CN)_6]^{3-}}_{y=4}$

$$i = 1 + (y-1)x = 1 + 3x$$

		i
$Al_2(SO_4)_3 \rightleftharpoons 2Al^{3+} + 3SO_4^{2-}$	$y = 5$	$(1 + 4x)$
$NaCl \rightleftharpoons Na^+ + Cl^-$	$y = 2$	$(1 + x)$
$Na_2SO_4 \rightleftharpoons 2Na^+ + SO_4^{2-}$	$y = 3$	$(1 + 2x)$
$Al(NO_3)_3 \rightleftharpoons Al^{3+} + 3NO_3^-$	$y = 4$	$(1 + 3x)$

138. (*c*) $p = MST(i) = \frac{w}{mV} ST(i)$

All are non-electrolyte $i = 1$

$$\frac{w}{V} \text{ same}$$

Thus, $p \propto \frac{1}{m \text{ (molar mass)}}$

$$m(\text{urea} = 60) < m\,(\text{glucose} = 180) < m\,(\text{sucrose} = 342)$$

Thus, p_2 (urea) $> p_1$ (glucose) $> p_3$ (sucrose)

139. (*a*) Vapour pressure of solution $= p_0 X_{\text{solvent}}$

$$n_1 \text{ (solute)} = \frac{0.5}{65} = \frac{1}{130}$$

$$n_2 \text{ (solvent)} = \frac{100 \times 1.58}{154} = 1.026$$

$$X_2 = \frac{1.026}{\left(\frac{1}{130} + 1.026\right)} = 0.9926$$

$\therefore$ Vapour pressure of solution $= 141.93$

140. (*b*) By Raoult's law

relative decrease in vapour pressure = mole fraction of solute

$$\frac{\Delta p}{p^\circ} = X_1$$

$$\frac{10}{p^\circ} = 0.2$$

In second case

$$\frac{20}{p^\circ} = X_1'$$

$\therefore$ $\frac{20}{10} = \frac{X_1'}{0.2}$

$$X_1' = 0.4$$

$\therefore$ Mole fraction of solvent $= 1 - 0.4 = 0.6$

141. (*c*) $\Delta T_b = \frac{1000 w_1 K_b}{m_1 w_2}$

$$0.25 = \frac{1000 \times 1 \times K_b}{60 \times w_2}$$

$$\Delta T_b = \frac{1000 \times 3 \times K_b}{180 \times w_2}$$

$\therefore$ $\Delta T_b = 0.25$

$\therefore$ Boiling point $= 100 + 0.25 = 100.25°$C

142. **(a)** F.P. $= 0 - \Delta T_f = -\Delta T_f$

Thus, greater the value of ΔT_f smaller the f.p.

		i	ΔT_f
(I)	0.05 M $NaNO_3$	$1 + x = 2$	$0.05 \times 2 \times K_f = 0.1 K_f$
(II)	0.075 M $CuSO_4$	$1 + x = 2$	$0.075 \times 2 \times K_f = 0.15 K_f$
(III)	0.14 M sucrose	1	$0.14 \times 1 \times K_f = 0.14 K_f$
(IV)	0.04 M $BaCl_2$	$1 + 2x = 3$	$0.04 \times 3 \times K_f = 0.12 K_f$

Thus, decreasing order of f.p. is I > IV > III > II.

143. **(c)** $\pi = MST(i)$

$$= 0.7 \times 0.0821 \times 298 \times 2 = 34.25 \text{ atm}$$

For 50% recovery pressure is just double of required to prevent osmosis.

144. **(d)** Solutions are isotonic, hence, number of moles are equal

$\therefore$ $$n_1 \text{ (HCHO)} = n_2 \, (C_6H_{12}O_6)$$

$$\frac{w_1}{m_1} = \frac{w_2}{m_2}$$

$$\frac{w_1}{w_2} = \frac{m_1}{m_2} = \frac{30}{180} = 1:6$$

145. **(b)** Moles of solute $= \dfrac{3 \times 10^{23}}{6 \times 10^{23}} = 0.5 = \dfrac{w_1}{m_1}$

$$\Delta T_f = \frac{1000 \times w_1 \times K_f}{m_1 \times w_2}$$

$$= \frac{1000 \times 0.5 \times 1.86}{250} = 3.72°$$

$\therefore$ $$\text{F.P.} = 273 - 3.72 = 269.28 \text{ K}$$

147. **(d)** $p_{\text{total}} = p_B^\circ X_B + p_T^\circ X_T$

$$= \frac{96.4 \times 5}{8.25} + \frac{28.9 \times 3.25}{8.25} = 69.8$$

148. **(b)** $p_{\text{total}} = p^\circ_{C_2H_5Br} X_{C_2H_5Br} + p^\circ_{C_2H_5Cl} X_{C_2H_5Cl}$

$$X'_{C_2H_5Cl} \text{ (vapour phase)} = \frac{p^\circ_{C_2H_5Cl} X_{C_2H_5Cl}}{p_{\text{total}}}$$

$$0.80 = \frac{40 X_{C_2H_5Cl} \text{ (liquid phase)}}{40 X_{C_2H_5Cl} + 10(1 - X_{C_2H_5Cl})}$$

$$= \frac{4 X_{C_2H_5Cl}}{4 X_{C_2H_5Cl} + 1 - X_{C_2H_5Cl}}$$

$\therefore$ $$X_{C_2H_5Cl} = 0.50$$

151. **(a)** 21 mg $= 21 \times 10^{-3}$ g CO_2 in 100 g H_2O

$$= \frac{21 \times 10^{-3}}{44} \text{ mole } CO_2 \text{ in 100 mL } H_2O \; (d = 1 \text{g/mL})$$

$$= \frac{21 \times 10^{-3} \times 10}{44} \text{ mol/dm}^3 = \frac{21 \times 10}{44} \text{ mol/m}^3$$

$$p_{CO_2} = K_H \times [CO_2]$$

$$= 2.937 \text{ k Pa m}^3 \text{ mol}^{-1} \times \frac{21 \times 10}{44} \text{ mol m}^{-3}$$

$$= 14.0 \text{ kPa}$$

152. **(a)** $p_{CM} = K_H X_{CM}$

$$K_H = \frac{p_{CM}}{X_{CM}} \text{ (CM = chloromethane)}$$

$$= \frac{205}{0.005} = 4 \times 10^4$$

12

Electrochemistry

Objective Questions Type I [Only one correct option]

In each of the questions below, four choices are given of which only one is correct.

1. In the electrorefining of metals, impure metal is
(a) cathode and oxidation takes place
(b) anode and oxidation takes place
(c) anode and reduction takes place
(d) cathode and reduction takes place

2. For electrosynthesis of a substance
(a) $\Delta G = +ve$ and $E_{cell} = -ve$
(b) $\Delta G = -ve$ and $E_{cell} = +ve$
(c) $\Delta G = -ve$ and $E_{cell} = -ve$
(d) $\Delta G = +ve$ and $E_{cell} = +ve$

3. During discharging of lead-storage acid battery following reaction takes place

$$Pb(s) + PbO_2(s) + 2H_2SO_4 \longrightarrow 2PbSO_4(s) + 2H_2O$$

If 2.5 A of current is drawn for 965 min H_2SO_4 consumed is
(a) 0.75 mol (b) 3.00 mol (c) 1.50 mol (d) 4.50 mol

4. If fully charged battery contains 1.5 L of 5.00 M H_2SO_4 in question (3) above, concentration of H_2SO_4 after current is drawn is
(a) 3.50 M (b) 2.00 M (c) 4.25 M (d) 4.00 M

5. Electrochemical equivalent of Cu in the reaction

$$Cu^{2+} + 2e^- \longrightarrow Cu \text{ is}$$

(a) $\frac{63.5}{96500}$ (b) $\frac{63.5}{96500 \times 2}$
(c) $\frac{63.5 \times 2}{96500}$ (d) $\frac{96500}{63.5 \times 2}$

6. Resistivity of a material is equal to resistance when
(a) cell constant = 1 cm^{-1}
(b) cell constant = 0.1 cm^{-1}
(c) cell constant = 10 cm^{-1}
(d) cell constant = 100 cm^{-1}

7. Cell constant is maximum in case of a
(a) wire of length 100 cm and area 100 cm
(b) wire of length 10 cm and area 10 cm
(c) one centimeter cube of a material
(d) equal in all cases

8. Which quantity is temperature independent?
(a) Resistivity
(b) Conductivity
(c) Cell constant
(d) Cell emf

9. When a certain conductivity cell was filled with 0.01 M solution of KCl, it had a resistance of 160 Ω at 25°C, and when filled with 0.005 M NaOH, it had a resistance of 190 Ω. If specific resistance of KCl solution is, 700 Ω-cm, specific conductance (Ω^{-1} cm^{-1}) of NaOH solution is
(a) 0.00120
(b) 0.00170
(c) 0.00180
(d) 0.00190

10. Variation of resistance with increase in cell constant gives graph of the type

(a) 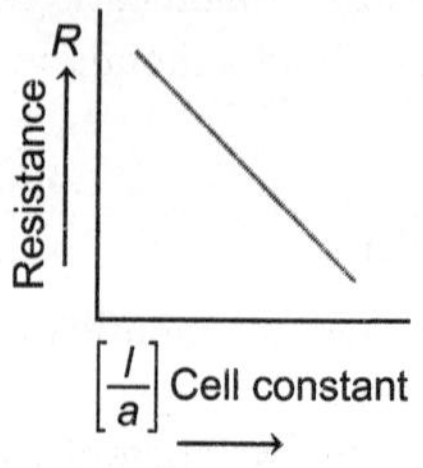

(b) 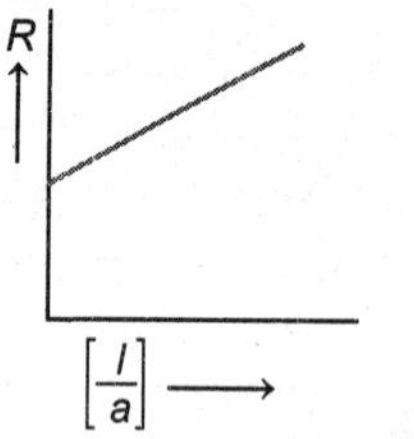

(c) 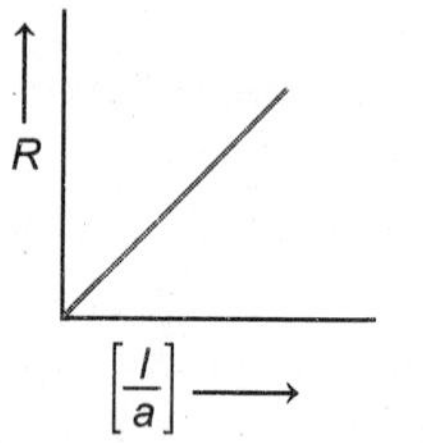

(d) 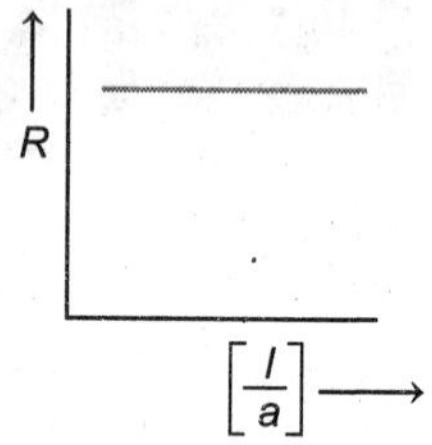

11. 0.1 M H_2SO_4 is diluted to 0.01 M H_2SO_4. Hence, its molar conductance will be

(a) 10 times (b) $\frac{1}{10}$th
(c) 100 times (d) 10000 times

12. In the above case, equivalent conductance will be

(a) 100 times (b) $\frac{1}{10}$th
(c) 1000 times (d) 10 times

13. 0.1 M aqueous solution of a dibasic acid is diluted such that its equivalent conductance is five times. Hence, final concentration is

(a) 0.01 N (b) 0.02 N
(c) 0.04 N (d) 0.055 N

14. 500 mL of an aqueous solution contains 0.1 mole of the solute AB; if its specific conductance is x S cm^{-1}, its molar conductance will be .... S cm^2 mol^{-1}.

(a) $10x$ (b) $5000x$ (c) x (d) $200x$

15. Reciprocal of siemen is

(a) volt (b) ohm
(c) ampere (d) Coulomb

16. In the variation of Λ_m with $\sqrt{C}$,

$\Lambda_m = \Lambda_m^\infty - (A + B\,\Lambda_m^\infty)\sqrt{C}$, A and B are called

(a) van der Waals' constant
(b) Debye-Huckel constants
(c) Onsager constants
(d) critical constants

17. From the above equation in question (16), it is evident that

(a) $\Lambda_m > \Lambda_m^\infty$
(b) $\Lambda_m = \Lambda_m^\infty$ as $\sqrt{C} \to 0$
(c) A and B both are dependent on temperature T and dielectric constant D of the medium
(d) All the above are correct statements

18. Following are some facts about electrolytic conduction.

I. Λ_m decreases with $\sqrt{C}$ due to increase in interionic attraction between ions.
II. For weak electrolytes, there is rapid increase in the degree of ionisation with dilution hence, interionic attraction decreases and Λ_m or Λ_{eq} increases rapidly in lower concentration range.
III. Λ_m^∞ can be obtained by extrapolation to $\sqrt{C} = 0$.

Correct statements are

(a) I, II and III (b) I and III
(c) I and II (d) II and III

19. Which has maximum value of Λ_{eq} at constant temperature assuming 100% ionisation of each electrolyte?

(a) 0.1 M HCl (b) 0.1 M H_2SO_4
(c) 0.1 M H_3PO_4 (d) Equal

20. Which has maximum value of Λ_{eq} at constant temperature assuming 100% ionisation of each electrolyte?

(a) 0.1 M H_2SO_4
(b) 0.1 M H_3PO_3
(c) 0.1 M $H_2PO_4^-$
(d) Equal

21. Λ_{AgCl}^∞ can be obtained

(a) by extrapolation of the graph Λ and $\sqrt{C}$ to zero concentration
(b) by known values of Λ^∞ of $AgNO_3$, HCl and HNO_3
(c) Both (a) and (b)
(d) None of the above

22. Which factor (s) is/are responsible for decrease in electrolytic conduction?

(a) Dilution
(b) Increase in temperature
(c) Interionic attraction in higher concentration range
(d) None of the above

23. The ionic conductance of H^+ and SO_4^{2-} are 350 and 80 S cm^2 equiv^{-1}, hence equivalent conductance (S cm^2 equivalent^{-1}) and molar conductance (S cm^2 mol^{-1}) of H_2SO_4 will be

(a) 430, 430 (b) 860, 430
(c) 215, 430 (d) 430, 860

24. Equivalent conductance of $BaCl_2$, H_2SO_4 and HCl are x_1, x_2 and x_3 S cm^2 equiv^{-1} at infinite dilution. If specific conductance of saturated $BaSO_4$ solution is of y S cm^{-1}, then K_{sp} of $BaSO_4$ is

(a) $\frac{10^3\,y}{2(x_1 + x_2 - 2x_3)}$ (b) $\frac{10^6\,y^2}{(x_1 + x_2 - 2x_3)^2}$

(c) $\frac{10^6\,y^2}{4(x_1 + x_2 - 2x_3)^2}$ (d) $\frac{x_1 + x_2 - 2x_3}{10^6\,y^2}$

25. Benzoic acid solution is titrated with NaOH conductometrically, graphical representation of the titration is

(a) 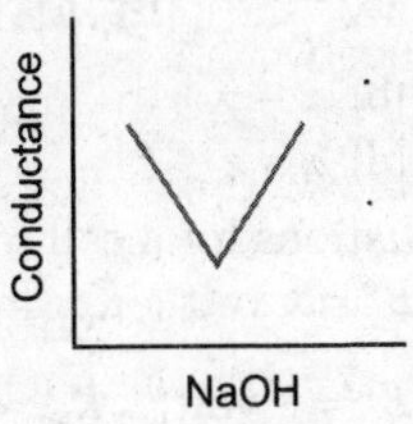

(b) 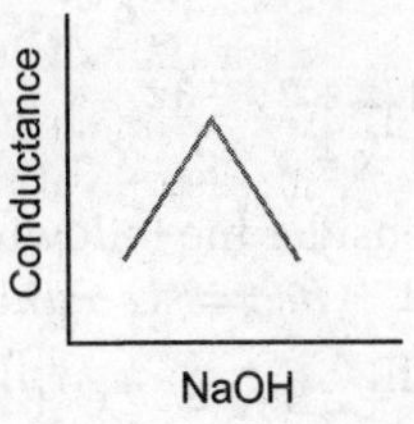

(c) 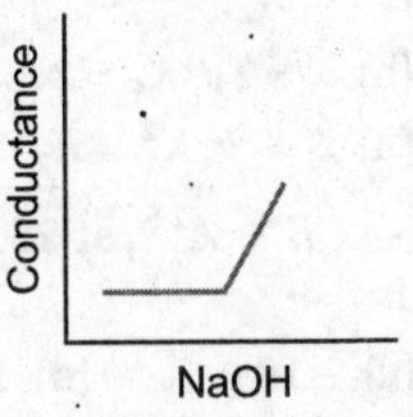

(d) 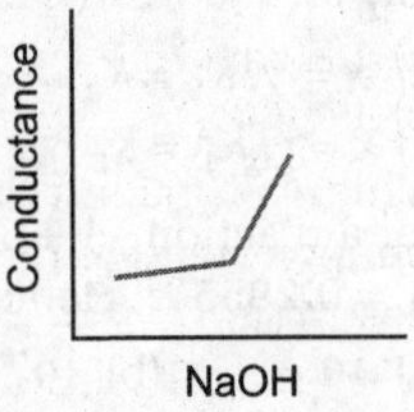

26. Ionisation constant of a weak acid (*HA*) in terms of Λ_m^∞ and Λ_m is

(a) $K_a = \dfrac{C\Lambda_m^\infty}{(\Lambda_m - \Lambda^\infty)}$ (b) $K_a = \dfrac{C\Lambda_m^2}{\Lambda_m^\infty(\Lambda_m^\infty - \Lambda_m)}$

(c) $K_a = \dfrac{C(\Lambda_m^\infty)^2}{\Lambda_m^\infty(\Lambda_m^\infty - \Lambda_m)}$ (d) None of these

27. In a galvanic cell, the salt-bridge [JEE Advanced 2014]

(a) does not participate chemically in the cell reaction
(b) stops the diffusion of ions from one electrode to another
(c) is necessary for the occurrence of the cell reaction
(d) ensures mixing of the two electrolytic solutions

28. The technique of protecting a metal from corrosion by connecting it to a second metal (that is more easily oxidised) is called

(a) cathodic protection (b) anodic protection
(c) galvanisation (d) annealing

29. In corrosion of iron

(a) an electrochemical (galvanic cell) is formed in which Fe acts as anode and cathode where O_2 is reduced
(b) electrons flow from anode to cathode through the metal while ions flow through the water droplets
(c) dissolved O_2 oxidises Fe^{2+} to Fe^{3+} before it is deposited as rust ($Fe_2O_3 \cdot H_2O$).
(d) All of the above take place

30. In an atmosphere with industrial smog, Cu corrodes to a basic sulphate (and also basic carbonate). This basic sulphate is

(a) $Cu_2(OH)_2SO_4$ (b) $Cu(OH)_2(SO_4)_2$
(c) $Cu(OH)SO_4$ (d) $Cu(OH)(SO_4)_2$

31. Silver ornaments turn black in the atmosphere. It is due to formation of

(a) Ag_2O, Ag_2S (b) $AgNO_3$, Ag_2S
(c) $Ag(OH)$, Ag_2CO_3 (d) Ag

32. In anodising

(a) metal ion in the electrolyte is reduced and the metal is coated on the surface of the metal cathode
(b) anode metal is oxidised to yield a metal oxide coat
(c) Both (a) and (b)
(d) None of the above

33. Select the correct statement(s).

(a) In a galvanic cell, a spontaneous chemical reaction generates an electric current
(b) In an electrolytic cell, an electric current drives a non-spontaneous reaction
(c) In a galvanic cell, cell reaction is exothermic
(d) All the above statements are correct

34. Consider the following statements about a galvanic cell.

I. Electrons flow through H_2O (medium) from anode to cathode.
II. Electrons flow through wire from anode to cathode.
III. Salt bridge is necessary to complete the electrical circuit.

Select the correct alternate(s).

(a) I, II and III
(b) I and III
(c) II and III
(d) I and II

35. In the galvanic cell,

$$Fe(s) + 2Fe^{3+}(aq) \longrightarrow 3Fe^{2+}(aq)$$

(a) Fe(*s*) is the cathode because it is in contact with $Fe^{2+}(aq)$
(b) Fe(*s*) is the cathode because it is in contact with $Fe^{3+}(aq)$
(c) Fe(*s*) can't be used as cathode since it would directly react with Fe^{3+}, then short-circuiting the cell
(d) salt-bridge contains Fe^{2+} and Fe^{3+} ions

36. For the cell reaction,

$$Cu(s) + Cl_2(aq) \longrightarrow Cu^{2+}(aq) + 2Cl^-(aq)$$

cell notation is

(a) $Cu(s)|Cu^{2+}(aq)||Cl^-(aq)|Cl_2(g)|C(s)$
(b) $C(s)|Cl^-(aq)|Cl_2(g)||Cu^{2+}(aq)|Cu(s)$
(c) $Cu(s)|Cu^{2+}(aq)||Cl^-(aq)|Cl_2(g)$
(d) $Cu(s)|Cu^{2+}(aq)||Cl_2(aq)|Cl^-(aq)$

37. For the galvanic cell,

$$Pt(s)|Fe^{2+}, Fe^{3+}||Fe^{2+}|Fe$$

cell reaction is

(a) $3Fe^{2+} + Fe \longrightarrow 2Fe^{3+}$
(b) $3Fe^{2+} \longrightarrow Fe + 2Fe^{3+}$
(c) $Fe + 2Fe^{3+} \longrightarrow 3Fe^{2+}$
(d) None of the above

38. Consider the following half-cell reactions.

I. $A + e^- \longrightarrow A^-$; $E° = 0.96$ V

II. $B^- + e^- \longrightarrow B^{2-}$; $E° = -0.12$ V

III. $C^+ + e^- \longrightarrow C$; $E° = +0.18$ V

IV. $D^{2+} + 2e^- \longrightarrow D$; $E° = -1.12$ V

What combination of two half-cells would result in a cell with the largest potential?

(a) I and II (b) I and III (c) I and IV (d) II and IV

39. Let C_{NaCl} and C_{BaSO_4} be the conductances (in S) measured for saturated aqueous solutions of NaCl and $BaSO_4$, respectively, at a temperature T. Which of the following is false? **[JEE Main 2020, Sep.]**

(a) Ionic mobilities of ions from both salts increase with T.

(b) $C_{BaSO_4}(T_2) > C_{BaSO_4}(T_1)$ for $T_2 > T_1$

(c) $C_{NaCl}(T_2) > C_{NaCl}(T_1)$ for $T_2 > T_1$

(d) $C_{NaCl} >> C_{BaSO_4}$ at a given T

40. Given,

$Co^{3+} + e^- \longrightarrow Co^{2+}$; $E° = +1.81$ V

$Pb^{4+} + 2e^- \longrightarrow Pb^{2+}$; $E° = +1.67$ V

$Ce^{4+} + e^- \longrightarrow Ce^{3+}$; $E° = +1.61$ V

$Bi^{3+} + 3e^- \longrightarrow Bi$; $E° = +0.20$ V

Oxidising power of the species will increase in the order **[JEE Main 2019 April]**

(a) $Ce^{4+} < Pb^{4+} < Bi^{3+} < Co^{3+}$ (b) $Bi^{3+} < Ce^{4+} < Pb^{4+} < Co^{3+}$

(c) $Co^{3+} < Ce^{4+} < Bi^{3+} < Pb^{4+}$ (d) $Co^{3+} < Pb^{4+} < Ce^{4+} < Bi^{3+}$

41. For the cell $Zn|\ Zn^{2+}(1M)||\ Cu^{2+}(1M)|\ Cu$, $E°_{cell}$ is 1.10 V, $E^{\ominus}_{Cu^{2+}/Cu} = 0.34$ V and for the cell $Cu|\ Cu^{2+}(1M)||\ Ag^+(1M)|\ Ag$, $E°_{cell} = 0.46$ V hence, $E°_{cell}$ of the cell

$Zn|\ Zn^{2+}\ (1M)||\ Ag^+\ (1M)|\ Ag$ is

(a) -0.04 V (b) $+0.04$ V

(c) $+0.30$ V (d) $+1.56$ V

42. If $Sn^{2+} + 2e^- \longrightarrow Sn$; $E° = -0.14$ V

$Sn^{4+} + 2e^- \longrightarrow Sn^{2+}$; $E° = 0.13$ V

then

(a) Sn^{2+} is unstable and disproportionates to Sn^{4+} and Sn

(b) Sn^{2+} is stable and disproportionation reaction is not spontaneous

(c) Sn^{4+} is easily reduced to Sn

(d) None of the above is correct

43. For the reaction, $2Fe^{3+} + Fe \longrightarrow 3Fe^{2+}$, $E° = 1.21$ V, hence

(a) the reaction occurs even in the absence of a second half-cell or a current

(b) in a complete cell, Fe is anode but Pt is the cathode

(c) Fe can't be used as cathode, because it would directly react with Fe^{3+}, thus short-circuiting the cell

(d) All of the above are correct

44. Calculate the standard cell potential (in V) of the cell in which following reaction takes place

$$Fe^{2+}(aq) + Ag^+(aq) \longrightarrow Fe^{3+}(aq) + Ag(s)$$

Given that, $E°_{Ag^+/Ag} = x$ V

$E°_{Fe^{2+}/Fe} = y$ V

$E°_{Fe^{3+}/Fe} = z$ V **[JEE Main 2019, April]**

(a) $x + 2y - 3z$ (b) $x - y$

(c) $x + y - z$ (d) $x - z$

45. Consider the following equations for a cell reaction

$A + B \rightleftharpoons C + D$ $E° = x$ volt, $K_{eq} = K_1$

$2A + 2B \rightleftharpoons 2C + 2D$ $E° = y$ volt, $K_{eq} = K_2$

then

(a) $x = y, K_1 = K_2$ (b) $x = 2y, K_1 = 2K_2$

(c) $x = y, K_1^2 = K_2$ (d) $x^2 = y, K_1^2 = K_2$

46. For a reaction, $A + B^{2+} \longrightarrow B + A^{2+}$, at 25°C, $E° = 0.2955$ V. Hence, K_{eq} is

(a) 10 (b) 10^{10} (c) -10 (d) 10^{-10}

47. The standard reduction potentials of Cu^{2+}/Cu and Cu^+/Cu are 0.339 V and 0.518 V respectively. The standard electrode potential of Cu^{2+}/Cu^+ half-cell is

(a) 0.16 V (b) -0.179 V

(c) -0.16 V (d) $+0.179$ V

48. $Al^{3+}(aq) + 3e^- \longrightarrow Al(s)$; $E° = -1.66$ V

$Cu^{2+}(aq) + 2e^- \longrightarrow Cu(s)$; $E° = +0.34$ V

What voltage is produced under standard conditions to give a spontaneous reactions by combination of these two half-cells?

(a) 1.32 V (b) -1.32 V

(c) 2.00 V (d) -2.00 V

49. $2Ag^+(aq) + Cu(s) \longrightarrow Cu^{2+}(aq) + 2Ag(s)$

The standard potential for this reaction is 0.46 V. Which change will increase the standard potential the most?

(a) Doubling the $[Ag^+]$

(b) Halving the $[Cu^{2+}]$

(c) Doubling the size of the Cu(s) electrode

(d) Standard potential is considered only for 1 M solutions

50. For the half-cells

Cu^+/Cu $E° = +0.52$ V

Cu^{2+}/Cu^+ $E° = +0.16$ V

hence, $E°$ for the disproportionation reaction

$2Cu^+ \longrightarrow Cu^{2+} + Cu$ would be

(a) 0.36 V (b) 0.78 V (c) 0.84 V (d) -0.36 V

51. Given, that $E^{\ominus}_{O_2/H_2O} = +1.23$ V;

$E^{\ominus}_{S_2O_8^{2-}/SO_4^{2-}} = 2.05$ V;

$E^{\ominus}_{Br_2/Br^{\ominus}} = +1.09$ V, $E^{\ominus}_{Au^{3+}/Au} = +1.4$ V

The strongest oxidising agent is **[JEE Main 2019, April]**

(a) Au^{3+} (b) O_2 (c) $S_2O_8^{2-}$ (d) Br_2

52. For the galvanic cell

$Cu \mid Cu^{2+}(0.01\ M) \| Ag^{+}(0.1\ M) \mid Ag$, E°_{cell} is 0.46 V
$\ominus \qquad\qquad\qquad\qquad \oplus$

at 298 K. Hence, E_{cell} is

(a) 0.460 V (b) 0.519 V (c) 0.401 V (d) 0.430 V

53. For the following electrochemical cell at 298K
$Pt\ (s) \mid H_2(g,\ 1\ bar) \mid H^{+}(aq,\ 1M) \| M^{4+}(aq), M^{+2}(aq) \mid Pt\ (s)$

$E_{cell} = 0.092$ V When $\dfrac{[M^{+2}](aq)]}{[M^{+4}](aq)]} = 10^{x}$

Geven, $E^{\circ}_{M^{4+}|M^{2+}} = 0.151$ V; $2.303\dfrac{RT}{F} = 0.059$ V

The value of x is **[JEE Advanced 2016]**

(a) −2 (b) −1 (c) 1 (d) 2

54. $Zn \mid Zn^{2+}(10^{-4}\ M) \| H_2O \mid Pt(H_2)$, $E^{o}_{cell} = 0.76$ V at 298 K. Hence, E_{cell} is
(1 bar under H_2)

(a) 0.93 V (b) 0.23 V (c) 0.46 V (d) 0.64 V

55. For the following cell $Zn \mid Zn^{2+} \| Cd^{2+} \mid Cd$,

$E_{cell} = 0.30$ V, $E^{\circ}_{cell} = 0.36$ V, then value of $\dfrac{[Cd^{2+}]}{[Zn^{2+}]}$ is

(a) 10 (b) 0.01 (c) 0.1 (d) 100

56. For the cell,

$Hg \mid Hg_2Cl_2 \mid Cl^{-}(0.1\ M) \| Cl^{-}(0.01\ M) \mid Pt(Cl_2)$, E°_{cell} is 1.10 V. hence, E_{cell} is

(a) 1.1591 V (b) − 1.1591 V
(c) 1.0409 V (d) − 1.0409 V

57. If the Pb^{2+} concentration is maintained at 1.0 M. What is the $[Cu^{2+}]$ when the cell potential drops to zero? $E^{\circ}_{cell} = 0.473$ V,

$Pb \mid Pb^{2+}(1.0\ M) \| Cu^{2+}(1.0 \times 10^{-4}\ M) \mid Cu(s)$

(a) 1×10^{-16} M (b) 1×10^{16} M
(c) 1.0×10^{-14} M (d) 1.0×10^{14} M

58. Which has maximum potential (numerical value) for the half-cell reaction?

$$2H^{+} + 2e^{-} \longrightarrow H_2$$

(a) 1.0 M HCl
(b) A solution having pH 4
(c) Pure water
(d) 1.0 M NaOH

59. $Pt(H_2) \mid 0.01\ M\ H^{+} \| 0.1\ M\ H^{+} \mid Pt(H_2)$. If $E_{cell} = 0.00$ V
(x atm under the first $Pt(H_2)$, y atm under the second)

then $\dfrac{x}{y}$ is

(a) 100 (b) 10 (c) 0.01 (d) 0.1

60. pH of the solution in the anode compartment of the following cell at 25°C is x when $E_{cell} - E^{\circ}_{cell} = 0.0591$ V,

$Pt(H_2) \mid pH = x \| Ni^{2+}(1M) \mid Ni$, x is
(1 atm under $Pt(H_2)$)

(a) 4 (b) 3 (c) 2 (d) 1

61. For the half-cell, $Cl^{-}/Pt(Cl_2), (E - E^{\circ})$

(a) increases as $[Cl^{-}]$ increases
(b) decreases as $[Cl^{-}]$ increases
(c) remains constant as $[Cl^{-}]$ increases
(d) can't be predicted

62. Following behaves as SHE at a pressure of
$Pt, H_2 \mid H_2O$

(a) 1 bar (b) 10^{-14} bar (c) 10^{7} bar (d) 10^{14} bar

63. Half-cell reaction for a half-cell,

$$Hg(l) + 2OH^{-}(aq) \longrightarrow HgO(s) + H_2O(l) + 2e^{-}$$

This half-cell is reversible to

(a) $H_2O(l)$ (b) $HgO(s)$
(c) $OH^{-}(aq)$ (d) All are correct

64. For the half-cell given below

$Pt(H_2) \mid pH = 2,$
(1 atm under $Pt(H_2)$)

half-cell potential is

(a) 0.0591 V (b) 0.0295 V (c) 0.1182 V (d) 0.00 V

65. Quinhydrone half-cell is reversible to

(a) H^{+} (b) quinone
(c) quinol (d) None of these

66. For the calomel half-cell, $Hg, Hg_2Cl_2 \mid Cl^{-}(aq)$ values of electrode potentials are plotted at different $\log [Cl^{-}]$. Variation is represented by

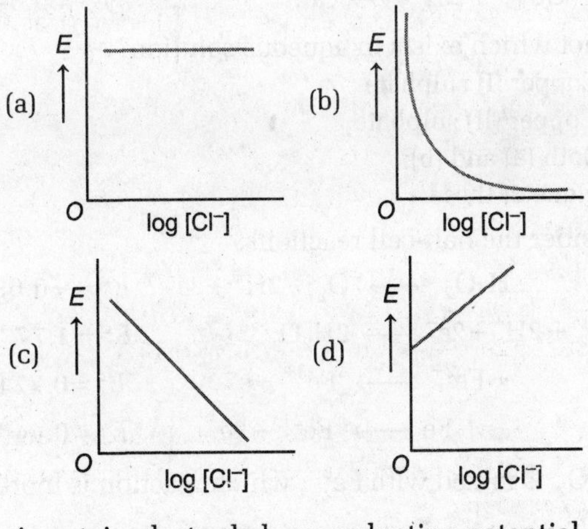

67. A certain electrode has a reduction potential of 0.100 V when measured against a standard calomel electrode (anode); $E^{\circ}_{calomel} = -0.244$ V. Potential *versus* SHE is

(a) − 0.344 V (b) − 0.144 V
(c) + 0.144 V (d) + 0.344 V

68. Following is the concentration cell reversible to anion

$Pt(Cl_2) \mid Cl^{-}(C_1) \| Cl^{-}(C_2) \mid Pt(Cl_2)$
(1 bar under each $Pt(Cl_2)$)

cell reaction is spontaneous if

(a) $C_1 > C_2$ (b) $C_1 < C_2$ (c) $C_1 = C_2$ (d) $C_1 = 0$

69. For the following cell with gas electrodes at p_1 and p_2 as shown

$$\underset{\text{at } p_1}{Pt(Cl_2)} \mid \underset{1\text{ M}}{HCl} \mid \underset{\text{at } p_2}{Pt(Cl_2)}$$

cell reaction is spontaneous if

(a) $p_1 = p_2$ (b) $p_1 > p_2$
(c) $p_1 < p_2$ (d) $p_2 = 0$

70. Select the incorrect statement.

(a) If salt-bridge is removed, potential falls to zero
(b) Liquid-junction potential developed across the boundary of the two solutions of different concentrations is minimised if concentration cells are used
(c) Calomel electrode contains calcium chloride solution in contact with Pt electrode
(d) Quinhydrane electrode is reversible to H^+

71. For the following cell reaction,

$$Pb(s) + Hg_2SO_4(s) \rightleftharpoons PbSO_4(s) + 2Hg(l)$$

$$E^\circ_{cell} = 0.92 \text{ V}$$

$$K_{sp}(PbSO_4) = 2 \times 10^{-8}, \ K_{sp}(Hg_2SO_4) = 1 \times 10^{-6}$$

Hence, E_{cell} is

(a) 0.92 V (b) 0.89 V (c) 1.04 V (d) 0.95 V

72. If for the half-cell reactions E° values are known

$$Cu^{2+} + e^- \longrightarrow Cu^+, \quad E^\circ = 0.15 \text{ V}$$

$$Cu^{2+} + 2e^- \longrightarrow Cu, \quad E^\circ = 0.34 \text{ V}$$

predict which exists in aqueous solution?

(a) Copper (I) sulphate
(b) Copper (II) sulphate
(c) Both (a) and (b)
(d) None of these

73. Consider the half-cell reactions,

$$H_2O_2 \longrightarrow O_2 + 2H^+ + 2e^- \quad E^\circ = -0.69 \text{ V}$$

$$H_2O_2 + 2H^+ + 2e^- \longrightarrow 2H_2O \quad E^\circ = 1.77 \text{ V}$$

$$Fe^{2+} \longrightarrow Fe^{3+} + e^- \quad E^\circ = 0.771 \text{ V}$$

$$Fe \longrightarrow Fe^{2+} + 2e^- \quad E^\circ = 0.44 \text{ V}$$

If H_2O_2 is mixed with Fe^{2+}, which reaction is more likely?

(a) Oxidation of Fe^{2+} to Fe^{3+}
(b) Reduction of Fe^{2+} to Fe
(c) Both (a) and (b) reactions
(d) None of the above reactions

74. For the following half-cell reactions, E° values are also given

$$Mn^{2+} + 2H_2O \longrightarrow MnO_2 + 4H^+ + 2e^-, \quad E^\circ = -1.23 \text{ V}$$

$$MnO_4^- + 4H^+ + 3e^- \longrightarrow MnO_2 + 2H_2O, \ E^\circ = +1.70 \text{ V}$$

Select the correct statement(s).

(a) Mn^{2+} reacts with MnO_4^- in acid solution to form MnO_2
(b) $Mn(MnO_4)_2$ is stable in acid solution
(c) MnO_2 disproportionates to Mn^{2+} and MnO_4^- in acid solution
(d) None of the above is correct

75. Consider the following sets.

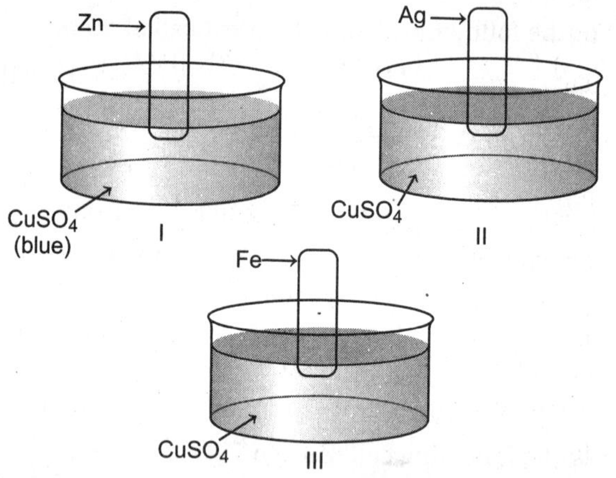

Blue colour solution changes to colourless (or fades) in

(a) I, II and III (b) I and II
(c) II and III (d) I and III

76. Consider the following half-cell reactions

$$Fe^{2+} \longrightarrow Fe^{3+} + e^-; \quad E^\circ = -0.77 \text{ V}$$

$$O_2 + 4H^+ + 4e^- \longrightarrow 2H_2O; \quad E^\circ = 1.229 \text{ V}$$

$$Fe \longrightarrow Fe^{2+} + 2e^-; \quad E^\circ = 0.44 \text{ V}$$

Select the correct statement(s).

(a) Fe^{2+} solutions are not stable in air
(b) Fe nails can prevent oxidation of Fe^{2+} to Fe^{3+} by air
(c) Corrosion of Fe takes place by air
(d) All of the above

77. Consider the following reduction processes:

$$Zn^{2+} + 2e^- \longrightarrow Zn(s); E^\circ = -0.76 \text{ V}$$

$$Ca^{2+} + 2e^- \longrightarrow Ca(s); E^\circ = -2.87 \text{ V}$$

$$Mg^{2+} + 2e^- \longrightarrow Mg(s); E^\circ = -2.36 \text{ V}$$

$$Ni^{2+} + 2e^- \longrightarrow Ni(s); E^\circ = -0.25 \text{ V}$$

The reducing power of the metals increases in the order **[JEE Main 2019, Jan]**

(a) Zn < Mg < Ni < Ca (b) Ni < Zn < Mg < Ca
(c) Ca < Zn < Mg < Ni (d) Ca < Mg < Zn < Ni

78. Consider the following half-cell reactions,

$$Cu^{2+} + 2e^- \longrightarrow Cu \quad E^\circ = 0.34 \text{ V}$$

$$Zn^{2+} + 2e^- \longrightarrow Zn \quad E^\circ = -0.76 \text{ V}$$

$$SO_4^{2-} + 4H^+ + 2e^- \longrightarrow SO_2 + 2H_2O \quad E^\circ = 1.17 \text{ V}$$

Hence, select the correct statement(s).

(a) Cu reacts with dil. H_2SO_4 forming H_2 and SO_2
(b) Cu reacts with concentrated H_2SO_4 forming SO_2
(c) Zn reacts with concentrated H_2SO_4 forming SO_2
(d) Both (b) and (c)

79. For the following cell-reaction, $Cu(s) + 2Ag^+(aq) \longrightarrow 2Ag(s) + Cu^{2+}(aq), E^\circ_{cell}$ is 0.46 V at 300 K and 0.48 V at 310 K. Hence, entropy change is
(a) 193 JK^{-1} (b) 386 JK^{-1}
(c) 579 JK^{-1} (d) −193 JK^{-1}

80. The temperature coefficient of the emf of the cell in question (79) above is
(a) 0.02 VK^{-1} (b) 0.2 VK^{-1}
(c) 0.002 VK^{-1} (d) 2VK^{-1}

81. For the half-cell reaction,
$$2H_2O + 2e^- \longrightarrow H_2 + 2OH^-,$$
$E^\circ = -0.8277$ V at 298 K. Hence, autoprotolysis constant for water is
(a) 1×10^{-10} (b) 1×10^{-12}
(c) 1×10^{-13} (d) 1×10^{-14}

82. $E^\circ_{Al^{3+}/Al} = -1.66$ V and K_{sp} of $Al(OH)_3 = 1.0 \times 10^{-33}$. Reduction potential of the above couple at pH = 14 is
(a) − 2.31 V
(b) + 2.31 V
(c) + 1.01 V
(d) − 1.01 V

83. Which statement is true and about a galvanic cell employing Pb, Cu, Pb^{2+} and Cu^+?
$$E^\circ_{Pb^{2+}/Pb} = -0.127 \text{ V}; E^\circ_{Cu^+/Cu} = +0.518 \text{ V}$$
(a) Spontaneous cell-reaction will be in the cell
$$Pb\,|Pb^{2+}\,||\,Cu^+|Cu$$
(b) $E^\circ_{cell} = 0.645$ V
(c) Both (a) and (b) are correct
(d) None of the above is correct

84. The reduction of oxygen gas in 1 M aqueous acid is represented by the equation.
$$O_2(g) + 4H^+(aq) + 4e^- \longrightarrow 2H_2O(l); \quad E^\circ = 1.23 \text{ V}$$
The potential for this reaction at physiological pH where, $[H^+] = 1 \times 10^{-7}$ M and the partial pressure of O_2 is 1 atm, will be closest to which value?
(a) 0.18 V (b) 0.41 V
(c) 0.82 V (d) 1.64 V

85. Select the correct statement(s).
(a) In lead-storage battery, galvanic cells are linked in series
(b) Cathode and anode compartments are not separated in a battery as oxidising agents and reducing agents both are solids
(c) Recharging of a storage battery is a non-spontaneous process
(d) All the above are correct statements

86. "Maintenance-free" batteries now in use in place of common batteries have
(a) electrodes made of lead-lead oxide
(b) electrodes made of calcium-containing lead alloy
(c) non-aqueous solvents as medium
(d) platinum electrodes

87. If a chemical reaction is carried out in a fuel cell, the maximum amount of useful work that can be obtained from the cell is
(a) ΔG (b) ΔH
(c) $\frac{\Delta G}{\Delta H}$ (d) $T\Delta S$

88. In which reactants are not contained within the cell but are continuously supplied from external source?
(a) Lithium battery
(b) Fuel cell
(c) Dry cell
(d) Lead-storage battery

89. Cathode is made of .... in mercury battery.
(a) Zn
(b) ZnO in contact with steel
(c) steel in contact with HgO
(d) Zn in contact with HgO

90. Some of the batteries are rechargable
I. Dry-cell battery
II. Lead-storage (acid) battery
III. Nickel-cadmium battery
IV. Lithium battery
V. Fuel cell
Select the correct alternate(s).
(a) I, II and III (b) II, III and IV
(c) III, IV and V (d) II, III and V

91. During the electrolysis of aqueous $Zn(NO_3)_2$ solution
(a) Zn plates out at the cathode
(b) Zn plates out at the anode
(c) H_2 gas is evolved at the anode
(d) O_2 gas is evolved at the anode

92. When a dilute aqueous Li_2SO_4 solution is electrolysed, the products formed at the anode and cathode, respectively, are
(a) S and Li (b) O_2 and Li
(c) SO_2 and H_2 (d) O_2 and H_2

93. In the electrolysis of aqueous solution of $Hg(NO_3)_2$, following reactions may occur
I. $Hg^{2+}(aq) + 2e^- \longrightarrow Hg(l);$ $E^\circ = 0.79$ V
II. $2H_2O(l) \longrightarrow O_2(g) + 4e^- + 4H^+(aq)$ $E^\circ = -1.23$ V
III. $2H_2O + 2e^- \longrightarrow H_2(g) + 2OH^-(aq)$ $E^\circ = -0.83$ V
Actual reactions taking place are
(a) I and II (b) I and III
(c) II and III (d) I, II and III

94. Schematic diagram of an electrolytic-cell is

(a)
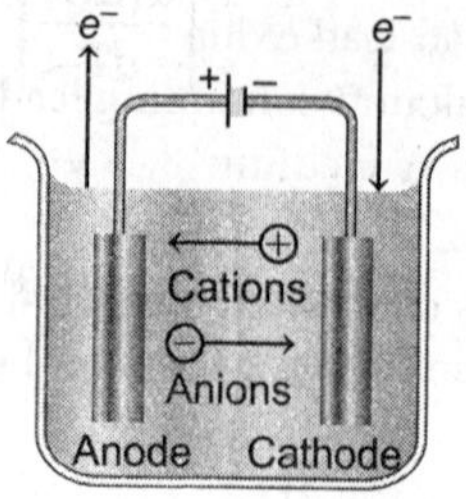

(b)
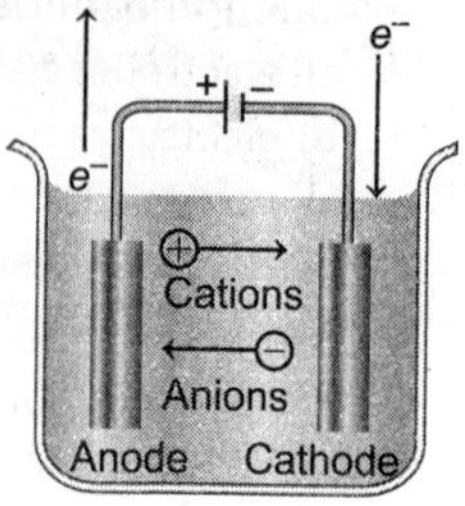

(c)
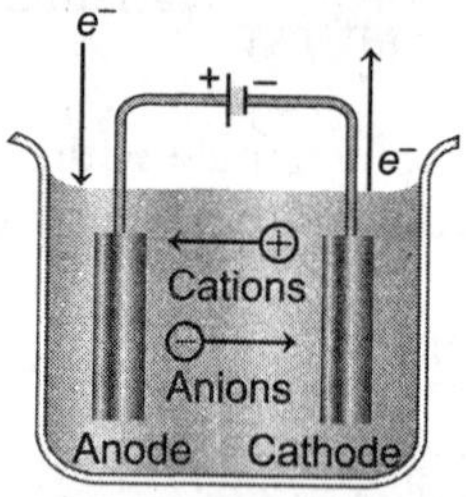

(d) None of the above is the correct presentation

(d) None of the above is the correct presentation

95. Consider certain observations about electrolysis.

I. Electric current is used to drive a non-spontaneous reaction.

II. E_{cell} is positive and ΔG is negative.

III. Cations and anions are discharged at the cathode and anode respectively.

IV. Over-voltage is responsible that a particular reaction takes place.

Correct observations are

(a) I, II and III (b) II, III and IV
(c) I, III and IV (d) I, II and IV

96. If an aqueous NaCl solution is electrolysed, which phenomenon is not observed?

(a) The concentration of Na^+ ion decreases
(b) $Cl_2(g)$ is produced at the anode
(c) The solution become more basic
(d) $H_2(g)$ is produced at the cathode

97. What products are formed during the electrolysis of a concentrated aqueous solution of sodium chloride?

I. $Cl_2(g)$ II. $NaOH(aq)$ III. $H_2(g)$

(a) Only I
(b) I and II
(c) I and III
(d) I, II and III

98. When aqueous solution of KCl is electrolysed, resultant solution

(a) has pH > 7
(b) turns red litmus blue
(c) is basic in nature
(d) satisfies all the condition given above

99. Match the following combinations of electrical unit with their terms as single unit.

Electrical unit	Single unit
I. joule/volt	A. ohm
II. joule/second	B. ampere
III. joule/ampere^2 second	C. coulomb
IV. coulomb/second	D. watt

	I	II	III	IV
(a)	A	B	C	D
(b)	C	D	A	B
(c)	D	C	B	A
(d)	C	D	B	A

100. A current of 5.00 A flowing for 30.00 min deposits 3.048 g of zinc at the cathode. Hence, equivalent weight of zinc is

(a) 65.4 (b) 130.8
(c) 32.7 (d) 16.85

101. 100 g Al is to be deposited on the cathode of the electrolytic cell containing Al_2O_3 in the solvent Na_3AlF_6 by a current of 125 A. If at the cathode, reaction is

$$Al^{3+} + 3e^- \longrightarrow Al$$

then time required for the passage of current is (Al = 27)

(a) 143 min (b) 429 min
(c) 48 min (d) 286 min

102. 96500 coulomb deposits 107.8 g of silver. If electronic charge is 1.6×10^{-19} C, value of Avogadro's number is

(a) 6.02×10^{-23} mol^{-1}
(b) 6.02×10^{23} mol^{-1}
(c) 6.02×10^{19} mol^{-1}
(d) 6.02×10^{-19} mol^{-1}

103. A certain current liberates 0.500 g of H_2 in 2.00 h. How many gram of oxygen can be liberated by the same current in the same time?

(a) 0.500 g (b) 8.00 g
(c) 4.00 g (d) 16.00 g

104. A solution of $Ni(NO_3)_2$ is electrolysed between platinum electrodes using 0.1 Faraday electricity. How many mole of Ni will be deposited at the cathode? **[JEE Main 2019, April]**

(a) 0.20 (b) 0.10
(c) 0.15 (d) 0.05

105. When Al_2O_3 is electrolysed, aluminium is produced at one electrode and oxygen gas at the other electrode. For a given quantity of electricity, ratio of number of moles of aluminium to the number of moles of oxygen gas is

(a) 1 : 1 (b) 2 : 1 (c) 2 : 3 (d) 4 : 3

106. For the following cell,
$Zn(s) | ZnSO_4(aq) || CuSO_4(aq) | Cu(s)$, when the concentration of Zn^{2+} is 10 times the concentration of Cu^{2+}, the expression for ΔG (in J mol^{-1}) is
[F is Faraday constant; R is gas constant; T is temperature; $E°$ (cell) = 1.1 V] **[JEE Advanced 2017]**
(a) 2.303 RT +1.1 F (b) 1.1 F
(c) 2.303 RT − 2.2 F (d) −2.2 F

107. 1 Faraday of electricity is passed through the solutions containing 1 mole each of $CuSO_4$, $AlCl_3$ and $SiCl_4$. Number of moles of Cu, Al and Si formed will be in the ratio
(a) 1 : 1 : 1 (b) 2 : 3 : 4
(c) 6 : 4 : 3 (d) 3 : 4 : 6

108. In a process of electrolysis, MnO_4^- is converted into MnO_2. By 1 Faraday, one mole of MnO_4^- will give
(a) 1 mol of MnO_2 (b) 0.5 mol of MnO_2
(c) 0.66 mol of MnO_2 (d) 0.33 mol of MnO_2

109. 9.65 C of electric current is passed through fused anhydrous $MgCl_2$. The magnesium metal thus obtained is completely converted into a Grignard reagent. The number of moles of Grignard reagent obtained is
(a) 5×10^{-4} (b) 1×10^{-4} (c) 5×10^{-5} (d) 1×10^{-5}

110. Which pair of electrolytes could not be distinguished by the products of electrolysis using inert electrodes?
(a) 1 M $CuSO_4$ solution, 1 M $CuCl_2$ solution
(b) 1 M KCl solution, 1 M KI solution
(c) 1 M $AgNO_3$ solution, 1 M $Cu(NO_3)_2$ solution
(d) 1 M KCl solution, 1 M NaCl solution
(e) 1 M $CuBr_2$ solution, 1 M $CuSO_4$ solution

111. For the following cell reaction,
$$Ag | Ag^+ | AgCl | Cl^{\ominus} | Cl_2, Pt$$
$$\Delta G_f^\circ (AgCl) = -109 \text{ kJ/mol}$$
$$\Delta G_f^\circ (Cl^{\ominus}) = -129 \text{ kJ/mol}$$
$$\Delta G_f^\circ (Ag^+) = 78 \text{ kJ/mol}$$
$E°$ of the cell is
(a) − 0.60 V (b) 0.60 V
(c) 6.0 V (d) None of these

112. For the cell, $Zn(s) | Zn^{2+} || Cu^{2+} | Cu(s)$, the standard cell voltage, E°_{cell} is 1.10 V. When a cell using these reagents was prepared in the lab, the measured cell voltage was 0.98 V. One possible explanation for the observed voltage is
(a) there were 2.00 mol of Cu^{2+} but only 1.00 mol of Zn^{2+}
(b) the Zn electrode had twice the surface of the Cu electrode
(c) the $[Zn^{2+}]$ was larger than the $[Cu^{2+}]$
(d) the volume of the Zn^{2+} solution was larger than the volume of the Cu^{2+} solution

113. $\Delta G = \Delta H - T\Delta S$ and $\Delta G = \Delta H + T\left[\frac{d(\Delta G)}{dT}\right]_p$ then $\left(\frac{dE_{cell}}{dT}\right)$ is
(a) $\frac{\Delta S}{nF}$ (b) $\frac{nE}{\Delta S}$ (c) $-nFE_{cell}$ (d) $+nFE_{cell}$

114. $Zn + Cu^{2+}(aq) \rightleftharpoons Cu + Zn^{2+}(aq)$
Reaction quotient is $Q = \frac{[Zn^{2+}]}{[Cu^{2+}]}$. Variation of E_{cell} with log Q is of the type with OA = 1.10 V. E_{cell} will be 1.1591 V when

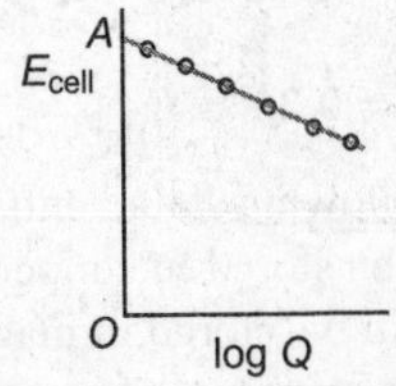

(a) $\frac{[Cu^{2+}]}{[Zn^{2+}]} = 0.01$ (b) $\frac{[Zn^{2+}]}{[Cu^{2+}]} = 0.01$
(c) $\frac{[Zn^{2+}]}{[Cu^{2+}]} = 0.1$ (d) $\frac{[Zn^{2+}]}{[Cu^{2+}]} = 1$

115. For the half-cell

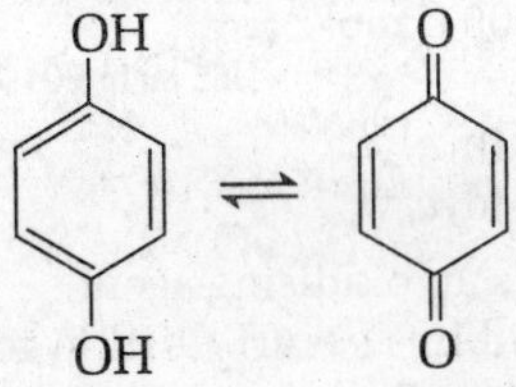

$+ 2H^+ + 2e^-$; $E° = 1.30$ V

At pH = 2, electrode potential is
(a) 1.36 V (b) 1.30 V
(c) 1.42 V (d) 1.20 V

116. For the cell given below $Zn | Zn^{2+} || Cu^{2+} | Cu$, $(E_{cell} - E^\circ_{cell})$ is − 0.12 V. It will be when
(a) $[Zn^{2+}]/[Cu^{2+}] = 10^2$ (b) $[Zn^{2+}]/[Cu^{2+}] = 10^{-2}$
(c) $[Zn^{2+}]/[Cu^{2+}] = 10^4$ (d) $[Zn^{2+}]/[Cu^{2+}] = 10^{-4}$

117. A solution containing one mole per litre each of $Cu(NO_3)_2$, $AgNO_3$, $Hg_2(NO_3)_2$ and $Mg(NO_3)_2$ is being electrolysed by using inert electrodes. The values of the standard oxidation potentials in volts are
$Ag/Ag^+ = -0.8$; $Hg/Hg^{2+} = -0.79$;
$Cu/Cu^{2+} = -0.34$; $Mg/Mg^{2+} = 2.37$.
The order in which metals will be formed at the cathode, will be
(a) Ag, Cu, Hg, Mg (b) Ag, Hg, Cu, Mg
(c) Ag, Hg, Cu (d) Cu, Hg, Ag

118. Ag | Ag^+(1 M) || Ag^+(2M) | Ag, 0.5 F of electricity
1 L solution 1 L solution
in the LHS (anode) and 1 F electricity in the RHS (cathode) is first passed making them independent electrolytic cells at 298 K. EMF of the cell after electrolysis will be
(a) increased (b) decreased
(c) no change (d) time is also required

119. Pt(H_2) | pH = 2 || pH = 3 | Pt(H_2). The cell reaction
1 atm 1 atm
for the given cell is
(a) spontaneous (b) non-spontaneous
(c) equilibrium (d) None of these

120. Given, $E^\circ_{Ag^+/Ag} = 0.80\text{ V}, E^\circ_{Mg^{2+}/Mg} = -2.37\text{ V},$

$$E^\circ_{Cu^{2+}/Cu} = 0.34\text{ V}, E^\circ_{Hg^{2+}/Hg} = 0.79\text{ V}$$

Which of the following statement(s) is/are correct?
(a) $AgNO_3$ can be stored in copper vessel
(b) $Cu(NO_3)_2$ can be stored in magnesium vessel
(c) $CuCl_2$ can be stored in silver vessel
(d) $HgCl_2$ can be stored in copper vessel

121. If the standard electrode potential for a cell is 2V at 300 K, the equilibrium constant (*K*) for the reaction,

$$Zn(s) + Cu^{2+}(aq) \rightleftharpoons Zn^{2+}(aq) + Cu(s)$$

at 300 K is approximately
($R = 8\text{ JK}^{-1}\text{mol}^{-1}, F = 96000\text{ C mol}^{-1}$)
[JEE Main 2019, Jan.]
(a) e^{-160} (b) e^{160}
(c) e^{-80} (d) e^{320}

122. In acidic medium MnO_4^- is an oxidising agent.
$MnO_4^- + 8H^+ + 5e^- \longrightarrow Mn^{2+} + 4H_2O$. If H^+ ion concentration is doubled, electrode potential of the half-cell MnO_4^-, Mn^{2+}/Pt will
(a) increase by 28.46 mV
(b) decrease by 28.46 mV
(c) increase by 14.23 mV
(d) decrease by 142.30 mV

123. Metal can be prevented from rusting by
(a) connecting iron to more electropositive metal—a case of cathodic protection
(b) connecting iron to more electropositive metal—a case of anodic protection
(c) connecting iron to less electropositive metal—a case of anodic protection
(d) connecting iron to less electropositive metal—a case of cathodic protection

124. Number of electrons lost during electrolysis of 0.355 g of Cl^- is
(a) 0.01 (b) 0.01 N_0
(c) 0.02 N_0 (d) $\frac{0.01}{2\,N_0}$

125. 1 mole of electrons passes through each of the solution of $AgNO_3$, $CuSO_4$ and $AlCl_3$ when Ag, Cu and Al are deposited. Their molar ratio will be
(a) 1 : 1 : 1 (b) 6 : 3 : 2
(c) 6 : 3 : 1 (d) 1 : 3 : 6

126. Assume that during electrolysis of $AgNO_3$, only H_2O is electrolysed and O_2 is formed as

$$2H_2O \longrightarrow 4H^+ + O_2 + 4e^-$$

O_2 formed at NTP due to passage of 2 A of current for 965 s is
(a) 0.112 L (b) 0.224 L
(c) 11.2 L (d) 22.4 L

127. During electrolysis of acidified water, O_2 gas is formed at the anode. To produce O_2 gas at the anode at the rate of 0.224 cc per second at STP, current passed is
(a) 0.224 A (b) 2.24 A
(c) 9.64 A (d) 3.86 A

128. For $M^{2+} + 2e^- \longrightarrow M$, 0.275 g of metal *M* is deposited at the cathode due to passage of 1 A of current for 965 s. Hence, atomic weight of the metal *M* is
(a) 27.5 (b) 55.0
(c) 110.0 (d) 13.75

129. A conducting wire carries a current of 0.965 A. Rate of flow of electrons per second at a given point is
(a) $1 \times 10^{-5}\,N_0$ (b) N_0
(c) 0.965 N_0 (d) $\frac{N_0}{0.965}$

130. A quantity of electrical charge that brings about the deposition of 4.5 g Al from Al^{3+} at the cathode will also produce the following volume (STP) of $H_2(g)$ from H^+ at the cathode
(a) 44.8 L (b) 22.4 L (c) 11.2 L (d) 5.6 L

131. How long (approximate) should water be electrolysed by passing through 100 amperes current so that the oxygen released can completely burn 27.66 g of diborane?
(Atomic weight of $B = 10.8\,\mu$) **[JEE Main 2018]**
(a) 6.4 hours (b) 0.8 hours (c) 3.2 hours (d) 1.6 hours

132. 100 mL of a buffer of 1 M $NH_3(aq)$ and 1 M $NH_4^+(aq)$ are placed in two volatic cells separately. A current of 1.5 A is passed through both cells for 20 min. If electrolysis of water only takes place

$$2H_2O + O_2 + 4e^- \longrightarrow 4OH^- \quad \text{(RHS)}$$

$$2H_2O \longrightarrow 4H^+ + O_2 + 4e^- \quad \text{(LHS)}$$

then pH of the
(a) LHS half-cell will increase
(b) RHS half-cell will increase
(c) Both half-cells will increase
(d) Both half-cells will decrease

133. Cost of electricity for the production of x L H_2 at STP at cathode is ₹ x, then cost of electricity for the production of x L O_2 gas at STP at anode will be (assume 1 mol of electrons as one unit electricity)

(a) $2x$ (b) $4x$
(c) $16x$ (d) $32x$

134. Anode mud is a

(a) mixture of impure metals like Fe
(b) SO_2 gas
(c) mixture of Ag, Au, Pt
(d) None of the above

135. Cell constant has unit

(a) cm (b) cm^{-1}
(c) cm^2 (d) mol L^{-1}

136. Which one of the following graphs between molar conductivity (Λ_m) *versus* $\sqrt{C}$ is correct? **[JEE Main 2019, April]**

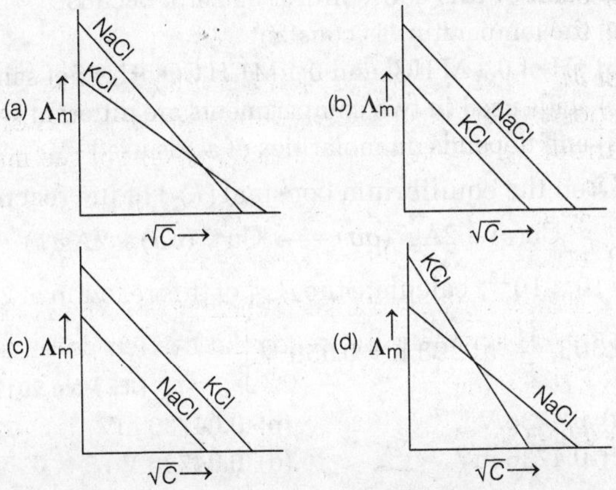

137. Consider the statements S_1 and S_2 :

S_1 : Conductivity always increases with decrease in the concentration of electrolyte.

S_2 : Molar conductivity always increases with decrease in the concentration of electrolyte.

The correct option among the following is **[JEE Main 2019, April]**

(a) S_1 is correct and S_2 is wrong
(b) S_1 is wrong and S_2 is correct
(c) Both S_1 and S_2 are wrong
(d) Both S_1 and S_2 are correct

138. Specific conductance of 0.01 N KCl solution is $x\ \Omega^{-1}\ cm^{-1}$ having conductance $y\ \Omega^{-1}$. Specific conductance of 0.01 N NaCl having conductance $z\ \Omega^{-1}$, is

(a) $\frac{yx}{z}$ (b) $\frac{zx}{y}$
(c) $\frac{z}{yx}$ (d) None of these

139. Equivalent conductance of 1 M CH_3COOH is $10\ \Omega^{-1}\ cm^2\ equiv^{-1}$ and at infinite dilution $200\ \Omega^{-1}\ cm^2\ equiv^{-1}$. Hence, percentage ionisation of CH_3COOH is

(a) 5% (b) 2%
(c) 4% (d) 1%

140. Equivalent conductance of saturated $BaSO_4$ is $400\ \Omega^{-1}\ cm^2\ equiv^{-1}$ and specific conductance is $8 \times 10^{-5}\ \Omega^{-1}\ cm^{-1}$. Hence, K_{sp} of $BaSO_4$ is

(a) $4 \times 10^{-8}\ M^2$
(b) $1 \times 10^{-8}\ M^2$
(c) $2 \times 10^{-4}\ M^2$
(d) $1 \times 10^{-4}\ M^2$

141. CH_3COOH is titrated with NaOH solution. Which is true statement?

(a) Conductance decreases up to equivalence point, after which it increases
(b) Conductance increases up to equivalence point, after which it decreases
(c) Conductance first increases (but not rapidly) up to equivalence point and then increases rapidly after equivalence point
(d) None of the above

142. Reduction potential of half-cell

AgI(aq) saturated | Ag, ($E^\circ_{Ag^+/Ag} = 0.8$ V, K_{sp} of AgI is 10^{-16}) is V

(a) 0.328 (b) 1.272
(c) −0.328 (d) − 0.144

143. 1 L of 1 M $CuSO_4$ solution is electrolysed. After passing 2 F of electricity, molarity of $CuSO_4$ solution will be

(a) $\frac{M}{2}$ (b) $\frac{M}{4}$
(c) M (d) 0

144. Debye Huckel theory predicts

(a) variation of velocity constant with T
(b) variation of equivalent conductance with concentration
(c) variation of equivalent constant with P
(d) None of the above

145. Salt-bridge contains

(a) calomel (b) corrosive sublimate
(c) H_2O (d) *agar-agar* paste

146. $2Hg(l) + 2Cl^-(aq) \longrightarrow Hg_2Cl_2(s) + 2e^-$, half-cell will be

(a) Hg, Hg_2Cl_2 | Cl^-
(b) Cl^- | Hg, Hg_2Cl_2
(c) Hg | Cl^-
(d) None of the above

147. $2Ce^{4+} + Co \longrightarrow 2Ce^{3+} + Co^{2+}$
$E^\circ_{cell} = 1.89$ V, $E^\circ_{Co^{2+}/Co} = -0.28$ V, hence, $E^\circ_{Ce^{4+}/Ce^{3+}}$ is
(a) 0.805 V (b) 1.61 V
(c) – 0.805 V (d) – 1.61 V

148. Consider the half-cell reaction,
$$O_2(g) + 4H^+(aq) + 4e^- \longrightarrow 2H_2O$$
By what factor are *n*, *Q*, *E* and *E*° changed if all the stoichiometric coefficients are multiplied by the factor two?

	n	*Q*	*E*	*E*°
(a)	doubled	Q^2	no change	no change
(b)	doubled	no change	doubled	no change
(c)	doubled	doubled	doubled	no change
(d)	doubled	doubled	doubled	doubled

149. For a Ag–Zn button cell, net reaction
$$Zn(s) + Ag_2O(s) \longrightarrow ZnO(s) + 2Ag(s)$$
$$\Delta G_f^\circ(Ag_2O) = -11.21 \text{ kJ mol}^{-1}$$
$$\Delta G_f^\circ(ZnO) = -318.3 \text{ kJ mol}^{-1}$$
Hence, E°_{cell} of the button cell is
(a) 3.182 V (b) 1.71 V
(c) –1.591 V (d) 1.591 V

150. In Hall process, in the production of Al, carbon is used as the anode material. The reactions are
(a) anode $Al^{3+} + 3e^- \longrightarrow Al$
cathode $C(s) + 2O^{2-} \longrightarrow CO_2(s) + 4e^-$
(b) anode $C(s) + 2O^{2-} \longrightarrow CO_2(g) + 4e^-$
cathode $Al^{3+} + 3e^- \longrightarrow Al$
(c) anode $Al \longrightarrow Al^{3+} + 3e^-$
cathode $CO_2 + 4e^- \longrightarrow C(s) + 2O^{2-}$
(d) None of the above

151. For the reaction,
$$4Al + 3O_2 + 6H_2O + 4OH^- \longrightarrow 4Al(OH)_4^-;$$
$$E^\circ_{cell} = 2.73 \text{ V}$$
and $\Delta G_f^\circ(OH^-) = -57$ kJ mol^{-1}
$\Delta G_f^\circ(H_2O) = -237.2$ kJ mol^{-1}
ΔG° for this reaction is
(a) -3.16×10^3 kJ mol^{-1}
(b) -0.79×10^3 kJ mol^{-1}
(c) -0.263×10^3 kJ mol^{-1}
(d) 0.263×10^3 kJ mol^{-1}

152. $\Delta G_f^\circ[Al(OH)_4^-]$ for the above case is
(a) 5.21×10^3 kJ mol^{-1} (b) 1.303×10^3 kJ mol^{-1}
(c) 3.59×10^3 kJ mol^{-1} (d) 1.438×10^3 kJ mol^{-1}

153. For the cell, $Zn(s)|Zn^{2+}(aq)||M^{x+}(aq)|M(s)$, different half cells and their standard electrode potentials are given below.

$M^{x+}(aq)/M(s)$	$Au^{3+}(aq)/Au(s)$	$Ag^+(aq)/Ag(s)$	$Fe^{3+}(aq)/Fe^{2+}(aq)$	$Fe^{2+}(aq)/Fe(s)$
$E^\circ_{M^{x+}/M}/V$	1.40	0.80	0.77	– 0.44

If $E^\circ_{Zn^{2+}/Zn} = -0.76$ V, which cathode will give a maximum value of E°_{cell} per electron transferred? **[JEE Main 2019, Jan.]**
(a) $\frac{Ag^+}{Ag}$ (b) $\frac{Fe^{2+}}{Fe}$
(c) $\frac{Au^{3+}}{Au}$ (d) $\frac{Fe^{3+}}{Fe^{2+}}$

154. A electrochemical cell is set up as
$Pt(H_2) \mid HCl(0.1 \text{ M}) \mid\mid CH_3COOH(0.1 \text{ M}) \mid Pt(H_2)$
The emf of this cell will not be zero, because
(a) the temperature is constant
(b) pH of 0.1 M HCl and 0.1 M CH_3COOH is not same
(c) acids used in two compartments are different
(d) emf depends on molarities of acids used

155. Given the equilibrium constant (K_C) of the reaction :
$$Cu(s) + 2Ag^+(aq) \longrightarrow Cu^{2+}(aq) + 2Ag(s)$$
is 10×10^{15}, calculate the E°_{cell} of this reaction at 298 K.
$\left[2.303 \frac{RT}{F} \text{ at 298 K} = 0.059 \text{ V}\right]$ **[JEE Main 2019, Jan.]**
(a) 0.4736 V (b) 0.04736 mV
(c) 0.4736 mV (d) 0.04736 V

156. The specific conductance of 0.1 N KCl solution at 23°C is 0.012 Ω^{-1} cm^{-1}. The resistance of cell containing the solution at the same temperature was found to be 55 Ω. The cell constant will be
(a) 0.142 cm^{-1} (b) 0.66 cm^{-1}
(c) 0.918 cm^{-1} (d) 1.12 cm^{-1}

157. $Cu^+(aq)$ is unstable in solution and undergoes simultaneous oxidation and reduction according to the reaction,
$$2Cu^+(aq) \rightleftharpoons Cu^{2+}(aq) + Cu(s)$$
choose the correct *E*° for above reaction if
$E^\circ_{Cu^{2+}/Cu} = 0.34$ V and $E^\circ_{Cu^{2+}/Cu^+} = 0.15$ V
(a) – 0.38 V (b) + 0.49 V
(c) + 0.38 V (d) – 0.19 V

158. Λ°_m for NaCl, HCl and Na*A* are 126.4, 425.9 and 100.5 S cm^2 mol^{-1}, respectively. If the conductivity of 0.001 M H*A* is 5×10^{-5} S cm^{-1}, degree of dissociation of HA is **[JEE Main 2019, Jan.]**
(a) 0.25 (b) 0.50 (c) 0.75 (d) 0.125

159. 0.04 N solution of a weak acid has specific conductance 4.23×10^{-4} mho cm^{-1} and degree of dissociation is 0.0612. The equivalent conductance (ohm^{-1} cm^2 $equiv^{-1}$) of weak acid at infinite dilution is

(a) 1.72 (b) 17.29
(c) 142.27 (d) 172.79

160. The resistance of 0.1 N solution of salt is found to be 2.5×10^3 Ω. The equivalent conductance of solution (cell constant = 1.15 cm^{-1}) in Ω^{-1} cm^2 $equiv^{-1}$ is

(a) 3.8 (b) 4.6 (c) 6.4 (d) 7.6

161. A galvanic cell is with standard oxidation electrode potential of zinc =+ 0.76 V and of copper=− 0.34 V. The emf with $\Delta G°$ negative is

(a) + 076 V (b) + 0.34 V (c) − 1.1 V (d) + 1.1 V

162. For the following half-cell reactions

$$Ox_1 + ae^- \rightleftharpoons Red_1 \qquad E_1^\circ$$

and $$Ox_2 + be^- \rightleftharpoons Red_2 \qquad E_2^\circ$$

Potential at the equivalence point is

(a) $\frac{E_1^\circ + E_2^\circ}{a+b}$ (b) $\frac{bE_1^\circ + aE_2^\circ}{a+b}$

(c) $\frac{aE_1^\circ + bE_2^\circ}{a+b}$ (d) $aE_1^\circ + bE_2^\circ$

163. Potential at the equivalence point in the titration of Fe^{2+} with MnO_4^- is

$$Fe^{3+} + e^- \rightleftharpoons Fe^{2+}; \qquad E_1^\circ$$

$$MnO_4^- + 8H^+ + 5e^- \rightleftharpoons Mn^{2+} + 4H_2O; \qquad E_2^\circ$$

(a) $E = \frac{E_1^\circ + 5E_2^\circ}{6} - 0.08$ pH

(b) $E = \frac{5E_1^\circ + E_2^\circ}{6} + 0.08$ pH

(c) $E = \frac{E_1^\circ + E_2^\circ}{6} + 0.08$ pH

(d) $E = E_1^\circ + E_2^\circ - 0.08$ pH

Objective Questions Type II [One or more than one correct option(s)]

In each of the questions below, four choices are given, of which one or more than one are correct.

1. Electrode potential of the given half cells

$Pt(H_2) \mid H^+(C_1)$; $Pt(Cl_2) \mid Cl^-(C_2)$; $Ag \mid Ag^+(C_3)$
with p_1 (I), p_2 (II), (III)

(a) will increase on increasing C_1, C_2 and C_3
(b) will decrease on increasing C_1, C_2 and C_3
(c) will decrease on increasing C_1 and C_3 and increase on increasing C_2
(d) will remain constant if C_1 and C_2 is doubled and p_1 and p_2 is made four times for half-cells I and II

2. There is blue colour formation if
(a) Cu electrode is placed inside $AgNO_3$ solution
(b) Cu electrode is placed inside $ZnSO_4$ solution
(c) Cu electrode is placed inside dil. HNO_3
(d) Cu electrode is placed inside dil. H_2SO_4

3. The formation of rust on the surface of iron occurs through the reaction
(a) $Fe(s) \longrightarrow Fe^{2+}(aq) + 2e^-$ at anode
(b) $O_2(g) + 4H^+(aq) + 4e^- \longrightarrow 2H_2O(l)$ at cathode
(c) $4Fe^{2+}(aq) + O_2(g) + 4H_2O(l) \longrightarrow 2Fe_2O_3(s) + 8H^+$
(d) $Fe_2O_3(s) + xH_2O(l) \longrightarrow Fe_2O_3 \cdot xH_2O$

4. In which case ($E_{cell} - E_{cell}^\circ$) is zero
(a) Cu | Cu^{2+} (0.01 M) || Ag^+(0.1 M) | Ag
(b) $Pt(H_2)$ | pH = 1 || Zn^{2+} (0.01 M) | Zn
(c) $Pt(H_2)$ pH = 1 || Zn^{2+}(1 M) | Zn
(d) $Pt(H_2)$ | H^+ (0.01 M) || Zn^{2+}(0.01 M) | Zn

5. Reactions taking place in a fuel cell are
(a) $O_2(g) + 2H_2O(l) + 4e^- \longrightarrow 4OH^-(aq)$ at the cathode
(b) reaction in (a) at the anode
(c) $2H_2(g) + 4OH^-(aq) \longrightarrow 4H_2O(l) + 4e^-$ at the anode
(d) reaction in (c) at the cathode

6. It is not advisable to
(a) stir sugar solution with a steel spoon
(b) stir copper sulphate solution with a silver spoon
(c) stir copper sulphate solution with a zinc spoon
(d) stir silver nitrate solution with a copper spoon

7. Which of the following changes will increase the emf of the cell $Co(s) \mid CoCl(M_1) \mid\mid HCl(M_2) \mid H_2(g) \mid Pt(s)$?
(a) Increase the volume of the $CoCl_2$ solution from 100 to 200 mL
(b) Increase M_2 from 0.010 to 0.500 M
(c) Increase the pressure of $H_2(g)$ from 1.00 to 2.00 atm
(d) Increase the mass of the Co electrode from 10.0 to 20.0 g

8. Consider the cell,

$Cd(s) \mid Cd^{2+}(1.0\ M) \mid\mid Cu^{2+}(1.0\ M) \mid Cu(s)$.

If we wanted to made a cell with a more positive voltage using the same substances, we should
(a) increase both the $[Cd^{2+}]$ and $[Cu^{2+}]$ to 2.00 M
(b) increase only the $[Cd^{2+}]$ to 2.00 M
(c) decrease both the $[Cd^{2+}]$ and $[Cu^{2+}]$ to 0.10 M
(d) decrease only the $[Cd^{2+}]$ to 0.100 M

9. What is the value of the reaction quotient, Q, for the cell?

$Ni(s) \mid Ni(NO_3)_2(0.190\ M) \parallel KCl\ (0.40\ M)$
$Pt(s) \mid Cl_2\,(g,\ 1.0\ atm)$

(a) 3.1×10^{-1} (b) 1.3×10^{-1}
(c) 8.0×10^{-2} (d) 3.0×10^{-2}

10. Which of the following is/are function(s) of salt-bridge?
(a) It completes the electrical circuit with electrons flowing from one electrode to other through external wires and a flow of ions between the two compartments through salt-bridge
(b) It prevents the accumulation of the ions
(c) Both (a) and (b) correct
(d) None of the above

11. By passage of 1 F of electricity
(a) 1 mol of Cu is deposited
(b) 0.5 mol of Mg is deposited
(c) 9 g of Al is deposited
(d) 5.6 L of O_2 gas evolved at anode

12. Which is/are correct statement ?
(a) No corrosion takes place in vacuum
(b) Corrosion is protected by electroplating
(c) During rusting $Fe_2O_3 . xH_2O$ is formed
(d) In presence of electrolyte corrosion takes place with greater rate

13. In which of the following cells will the emf be independent of the activity of the chloride ion?
(a) $Zn \mid ZnCl_2\ (aq) \mid Pt(Cl_2)$
(b) $Zn \mid ZnCl_2(aq) \parallel KCl(aq) \mid AgCl(s),\ Ag$
(c) $Ag,\ AgCl\ (s) \mid KCl\ (aq) \mid Pt(Cl_2)$
(d) $Hg,\ Hg_2Cl_2(s) \mid KCl(aq) \parallel AgNO_3(aq) \mid Ag$

14. For the reduction of NO_3^- ion in an aqueous solution $E°$ is $+0.96$ V. Values of $E°$ for some metal ions are given below

$V^{2+}(aq) + 2e^- \longrightarrow V;\quad E° = -1.19\ V$
$Fe^{3+}(aq) + 3e^- \longrightarrow Fe;\quad E° = -0.04\ V$
$Au^{3+}(aq) + 3e^- \longrightarrow Au;\quad E° = +1.40\ V$
$Hg^{2+}(aq) + 3e^- \longrightarrow Hg;\quad E° = +0.86\ V$

The pair(s) of metals that is (are) oxidized by NO_3^- in aqueous solution is (are) **[IIT JEE 2009]**
(a) V and Hg
(b) Hg and Fe
(c) Fe and Au
(d) Fe and V

15. The cell emf is independent of concentration of the species of the cell in
(a) $Fe \mid FeO(s) \mid KOH(aq) \mid NiO(s) \mid Ni_2O_3 \mid Ni$
(b) $Pt \mid (H_2) \mid HCl \mid Pt(Cl_2)$
(c) $Zn \mid Zn^{2+} \parallel Cu^{2+} \mid Cu$
(d) $Hg,\ Hg_2Cl_2 \mid KCl \parallel AgNO_3 \mid Ag$

16. Which of the following graph incorrectly represents the variation of molar conductance (Λ_m) with dilution for a strong electrolyte ?

(a) 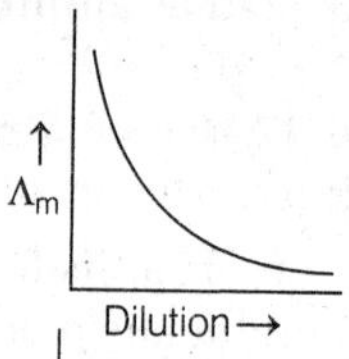

(b) 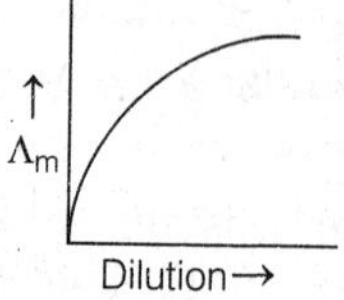

(c) 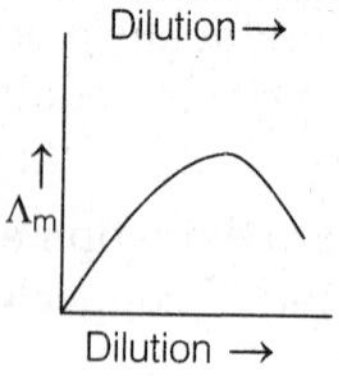

(d) 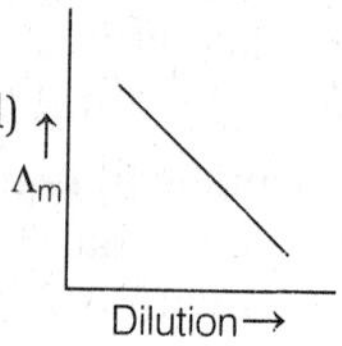

17. The reaction
$Cu^{2+}(aq) + 2Cl^-(aq) \longrightarrow Cu(s) + Cl_2(g)$
has $E°_{cell} = -1.02$ V. This reaction
(a) can be made to produce electricity in a voltaic cell
(b) can be made to occur in an electrolysis cell
(c) occurs whenever Cu^{2+} and Cl^- are brought together in an aqueous solution
(d) can occur in acidic but not in basic solution

18. When $Na_2SO_4(aq)$ is electrolysed between Pt electrodes, the reaction that occurs at cathode is
(a) $Na^+ + e^- \longrightarrow Na$ (b) $H^+ + e^- \longrightarrow \frac{1}{2}H_2$
(c) $2OH^- \longrightarrow \frac{1}{2}O_2 + H_2O + 2e^-$
(d) $2H_2O + 2e^- \longrightarrow H_2 + 2OH^-$

19. Standard electrode potential data are useful for understanding the suitability of an oxidant in a redox titration. Some half-cell reactions and their standard potentials are given below :

$MnO_4^-(aq) + 8H^+(aq) + 5e^- \longrightarrow Mn^{2+}(aq) + 4H_2O(l);\quad E° = 1.51\ V$
$Cr_2O_7^{2-}(aq) + 14H^+(aq) + 6e^- \longrightarrow 2Cr^{3+}(aq) + 7H_2O(l);\quad E° = 1.38\ V$
$Fe^{3+}(aq) + e^- \longrightarrow Fe^{2+}(aq);\ E° = 0.77\ V$
$Cl_2(g) + 2e^- \longrightarrow 2Cl^-(aq);\ E° = 1.40\ V$

Identify the only incorrect statement regarding the estimation of aqueous $Fe(NO_3)_2$.
(a) MnO_4^- can be used in aqueous HCl
(b) $Cr_2O_7^{2-}$ can be used in aqueous HCl
(c) MnO_4^- can be used in aqueous H_2SO_4
(d) $Cr_2O_7^{2-}$ can be used in aqueous H_2SO_4

20. Given, $E^o_{Ag^+/Ag} = 0.80\ V,\ E^o_{Mg^{2+}/Mg} = -2.37\ V$
$E^o_{Cu^{2+}/Cu} = 0.34\ V,\ E^o_{Hg^{2+}/Hg} = 0.79\ V$

Which of the following statements is/are incorrect ?
(a) $AgNO_3$ can be stored in copper vessel
(b) $Cu(NO_3)_2$ can be stored in magnesium vessel
(c) $CuCl_2$ can be stored in silver vessel
(d) $HgCl_2$ can be stored in copper vessel

Numerical Value Questions

All these questions have a Numerical value as their answer, solve the questions and write your answer.

1. Cadmium is usually found in small quantities wherever zinc is found. Unlike zinc, which is an essential element in trace amounts, cadmium is an environmental poison. To measure cadmium ion concentration by potentiometric method, we need to know the standard electrode potential for Cd^{2+}/Cd couple. The following voltaic cell is constructed and its voltage is measured.

$$Cd(s)|Cd^{2+}(1\ M)||Cu^{2+}\ 1\ M\ |\ Cu(s), \quad E^\circ_{cell} = 0.74\ V,$$

$$E^\circ_{Cu^{2+}/Cu} = 0.34\ V$$

The standard potential for Cd^{2+}/Cd electrode is ....

2. A galvanic cell consists of a Mg electrode in a 1.0 M $Mg(NO_3)_2$ solution and a Ag electrode in a 1.0 M $AgNO_3$ solution. The standard emf of this electrochemical cell at 25°C is ....

$$E^\circ_{Mg^{2+}/Mg} = -2.37\ V, \quad E^\circ_{Ag^+/Ag} = 0.80\ V$$

3. Calculate the E° and E of the cell

$$Sn\ |\ Sn^{2+}\ (1M)\ ||\ Pb^{2+}\ (0.001M)\ |\ Pb$$

$$E^\circ_{Sn^{2+}/Sn} = -0.14\ V,\ E^\circ_{Pb^{2+}/Pb} = -0.13\ V$$

What do you infer from the cell emf ?

4. $E^\circ_{Ag^+/Ag} = 0.799$ V and $E^\circ_{Cu^{2+}/Cu} = 0.337$ V respectively. Construct a galvanic cell using these electrodes so that its standard emf is positive. For what concentration of Ag^+ will the emf of the cell be zero at 25°C if $[Cu^{2+}] = 0.01$ M?

5. For a concentration cell,

$$\underset{A}{Cu\ |\ Cu^{2+}(0.75\ M)}\ ||\ \underset{B}{Cu^{2}(?)\ |\ Cu}\ ;\ E_{cell} = -0.045\ V$$

What is $[Cu^{2+}]$ inside B ?

6. An acidic solution of dichromate is electrolysed for 8 minutes using 2A current. As per the following equation

$$Cr_2O_7^{2-} + 14H^+ + 6e^- \longrightarrow 2Cr^{3+} + 7H_2O$$

The amount of Cr^{3+} obtained was 0.104 g. The efficiency of the process(in %) is (Take : $F = 96000$ C, atomic mass of chromium =52) .... **[JEE Main 2020, Sep.]**

7. The equilibrium constant for the reaction at 298 K is .... $\times 10^{26}$.

$$Fe + CuSO_4 \rightleftharpoons FeSO_4 + Cu$$

$$E^\circ_{Fe^{2+}/Fe} = -0.44\ V, \quad E^\circ_{Cu^{2+}/Cu} = 0.34\ V$$

8. (M^{n+}) solution was electrolysed for 75 min by a current of 0.30 A. The weight of the metal deposited was 0.958 g. The value of n if atomic weight of M is 137 is

9. The equivalent conductance of an aqueous solution of 1.0283×10^{-3} g equivalent acetic acid per litre is 48.15 Ω^{-1} cm^2 equiv^{-1} at 25°C. At infinite dilution value is 390.7 Ω^{-1}cm^2 equiv^{-1}. The degree of ionisation and ionisation constant of acetic acid is .... $\times 10^5$.

10. A weak monobasic acid is 5% dissociated in 0.1 mol dm^{-3} solution. The limiting molar conductivity at infinite dilution is 4.00×10^{-2} Ω^{-1} m^2 mol^{-1}. The conductivity of a 0.05 mol dm^{-3} solution of the acid is .... $\times 10^{-2}$.

11. An old hand book lets the equivalent conductance of 0.01 N solution of $CaCl_2$ as 120.36 Ω^{-1}cm^2 equiv^{-1}. Convert this value to the molar conductance a units of Ω^{-1} m^2 mol^{-1}.

12. For the reaction,

$$4Al(s) + 3O_2(g) + 6H_2O + 4OH^- \longrightarrow 4[Al(OH)_4^-];$$

$$E^\circ_{cell} = 2.73\ V$$

If $\Delta G_f^\circ[OH^-] = -157$ kJ mol^{-1},

$\Delta G_f^\circ(H_2O) = -237.2$ kJ mol^{-1},

The value of $\Delta G_f^\circ[Al(OH)_4^-]$ (free energy of formation of $[Al(OH)_4^-]$) is .... $\times 10^3$ kJ mol^{-1}

13. The concentrations of K^+ ions in the interrior (in) and exterior (ex) of a nerve cell are 400 mM and 15 mM respectively. Calculate electrical potential that exists across the membrane.

14. By how much is the oxidising power of the MnO_4^-/Mn^{2+} couple decreased if the H^+ concentration is decreased from 1 M to 10^{-4} M at 25°C? Assume other species have no change in concentration.

15. Knowing that K_{sp} for AgCl is 1.0×10^{-10}, calculate E for Ag^+/Ag electrode immersed in 1.00 M KCl at 25°C.

$$E^\circ_{Ag^+/Ag} = 0.799\ V$$

16. A 300 mL solution of NaCl was electrolysed for 6.00 min. If the pH of the final solution was 12.24, calculate the average current used.

17. Kohlrausch found from conductivity measurement on very pure water that the degree of dissociation of water is 1.9×10^{-9}. The equivalent conductance of water is ..... $\times 10^{-6}$ohm^{-1}cm^2 equie^{-1}.

$$\lambda_0(H^+) = 350 \quad \text{and} \quad \lambda_0(OH^-) = 200$$

18. The photoelectric current from Na (work function, $w_0 = 2.3$ eV) is stopped by the output voltage of the cell Pt(s) | H_2(g, 1 bar) | HCl (aq., pH = 1) | AgCl(s) | Ag (s).

The pH of aqueous HCl required to stop the photoelectric current from $K(w_0 = 2.25\text{ eV})$, all other conditions remaining the same, is .... $\times 10^{-2}$ (to the Nearest Integer).

Given, $2.303\frac{RT}{F} = 0.06\text{ V}; E^\circ_{AgCl|Ag|Cl^-} = 0.22\text{ V}$

[JEE Main 2020, Sep.]

19. For the electrochemical cell,

$Mg(s)|Mg^{2+}(aq, 1\text{ M})||Cu^{2+}(aq, 1\text{ M})|Cu(s)$

The standard emf of the cell is 2.70 V at 300 K. When the concentration of Mg^{2+} is changed to x M, the cell potential changes to 2.67 V at 300 K. The value of x is ....

(Given, $\frac{F}{R} = 11500\text{ K V}^{-1}$, where F is the Faraday constant and R is the gas contant, In (10) = 2.30)

[JEE Advanced 2018]

20. Consider an electrochemical cell : $A(s)|A^{n+}(aq, 2\text{M})||B^{2n+}(aq, 1\text{M})\ B(s)$. The value of $\Delta H^\ominus$ for the cell reaction is twice of $\Delta G^\ominus$ at 300 K. If the emf of the cell is zero, the $\Delta S^\ominus$ (in J K^{-1} mol^{-1}) of the cell reaction per mole of B formed at 300 K is ....

(Given : $\ln(2) = 0.7$, R (universal gas constant) $= 8.3\text{ J K}^{-1}\text{ mol}^{-1}$. H, S and G are enthalpy, entropy and Gibbs energy, respectively.) **[JEE Advanced 2018]**

21. The surface of copper gets tarnished by the formation of copper oxide. N_2 gas was passed to prevent the oxide formation during heating of copper at 1250 K.

However, the N_2 gas contains 1 mole % of water vapour as impurity.

The water vapour oxidises copper as per the reaction given below

$$2Cu(g) + H_2O(g) \longrightarrow Cu_2O(s) + H_2(g)$$

p_{H_2} is the minimum partial pressure of H_2 (in bar) needed to prevent the oxidation at 1250 K. The value of $\ln(p_{H_2})$ is ....

(Given : total pressure = 1 bar, R (universal gas constant) = 8 J K^{-1} mol^{-1}, ln(10) = 2.30 Cu(s) and $Cu_2O(s)$ are mutually immiscible.)

At 1250 K : $2Cu(s) + 1/2\,O_2(g) \longrightarrow Cu_2O(s)$;

$\Delta G^\ominus = -78{,}000\text{ J mol}^{-1}$

$H_2(g) + \frac{1}{2}O_2(g) \longrightarrow H_2O(g)$;

$\Delta G^\ominus = -1{,}78{,}000\text{ J mol}^{-1}$; G is the Gibbs energy

[JEE Advanced 2018]

22. A 5.0 m mol dm^{-3} aqueous solution of KCl has a conductance of 0.55 mS when measured in a cell constant 1.3 cm^{-1}. The molar conductivity of this solution is ...... $mSm^2\ mol^{-1}$. **[JEE Main 2021, March]**

23. A KCl solution of conductivity 0.14 S m^{-1} shows a resistance of 4.19 Ω in a conductivity cell. If the same cell is filled with an HCl solution, the resistance drops to 1.03 Ω. The conductivity of the HCl solution is ... $\times 10^{-2}$ S m^{-1}. **[JEE Main 2021, March]**

24. For the reaction

$2Fe^{3+}(aq) + 2I^-(aq) \longrightarrow 2Fe^{2+}(aq) + I_2(s)$ the magnitude of the standard molar free energy change, $\Delta_r G^\circ_m = -$ ...... kJ

$$\left[\begin{array}{ll} E^\circ_{Fe^{2+}/Fe(s)} = -0.440\text{V}; & E^\circ_{Fe^{3+}/Fe(s)} = -0.036\text{V} \\ E^\circ_{I_2/2I^-} = 0.539\text{V}; & F = 96500\text{C} \end{array}\right]$$

[JEE Main 2021, March]

25. The molar conductivities at infinite dilution of barium chloride, sulphuric acid and hydrochloric acid are 280, 860 and 426 S cm^2 mol^{-1} respectively. The molar conductivity at infinite dilution of barium sulphate is ...... S cm^2 mol^{-1} **[JEE Main 2021, March]**

Comprehension Based Questions

In these questions, a passage has been given followed by questions based on it. You have to answer the questions based on the passage given.

***Passage* 1** The following diagram shows an electrochemical cell in which the respective half-cells contain aqueous 1.0 M solutions of the salts XCl_2 and YCl_3. Given that $3X(s) + 2Y^{3+}(aq) \longrightarrow 3X^{2+}(aq) + 2Y(s)\ e_{cell} > 0$

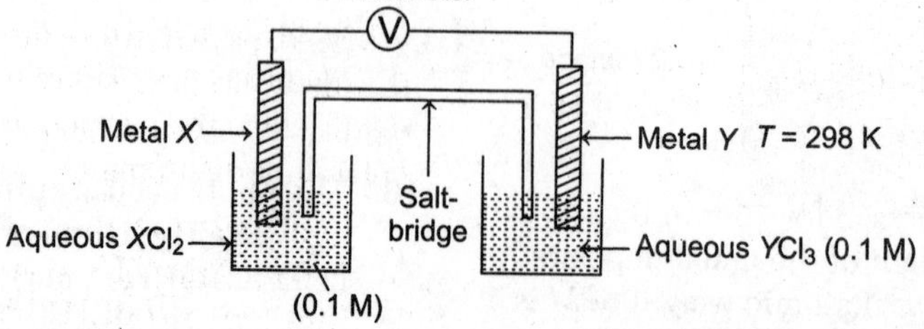

Based on this, answer the given questions.

1. Which of the following statements is correct?

I. The electrode made from metal X has positive polarity

II. Electrode Y is the anode

III. The flow of electrons is from Y to X

IV. The reaction at electrode X is an oxidation

V. The salt bridge would most likely contain silver nitrate

(a) Only I (b) Only IV (c) Only V (d) All except V

2. If salt-bridge is removed

(a) $E°_{X/X^{2+}}$ changes (b) $E°_{Y/Y^{3+}}$ changes

(c) E_{cell} drops to zero (d) E_{cell} increases

3. If $E°_{X/X^{2+}} = 0.20$ V, $E°_{Y/Y^{3+}} = 0.40$ V then $E°_{cell}$ of the above designed cell is

(a) 0.60 V (b) −0.60 V (c) 0.20 V (d) −0.20 V

***Passage* 2** *Following data can be taken to fabricate cells for spontaneous reactions.*

Consider following half-cell reactions and corresponding standard (reduction) electrode potentials

I.	$A + e^- \longrightarrow A^-$	$E° = -0.24$ V
II.	$B^- + e^- \longrightarrow B^{2-}$	$E° = +1.25$ V
III.	$C^- + 2e^- \longrightarrow C^{3-}$	$E° = -1.25$ V
IV.	$D + 2e^- \longrightarrow D^{2-}$	$E° = +0.68$ V
V.	$E + 4e^- \longrightarrow E^{4-}$	$E° = +0.38$ V

1. Which combination of two half-cells would result in a cell with the largest standard potential?

(a) I and III (b) II and III (c) I and II (d) IV and V

2. If every ion has concentration 0.1 M in the cell with largest standard potential then potential of the cell at 298 K is

(a) 2.50 V (b) 1.49 V

(c) 1.06 V (d) 1.91 V

***Passage* 3** *Following is a new car-battery. Answer the questions based on it.*

The zinc-air battery shows much promise for electric cars because it is light weight and rechargeable".

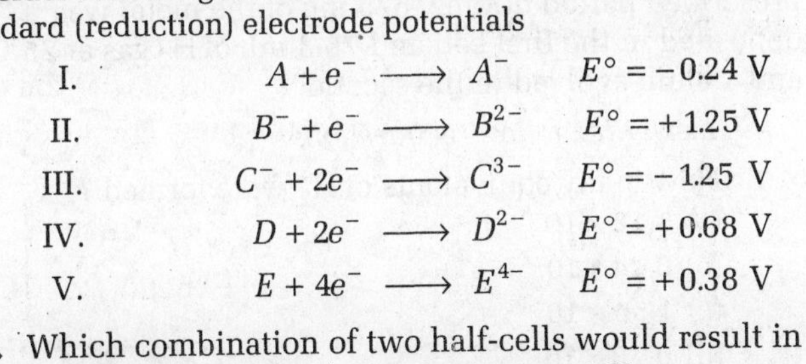

The net transformation is

$$Zn(s) + \frac{1}{2}O_2(g) \longrightarrow ZnO(s)$$

1. Half-cell reaction at the anode is

(a) $Zn \longrightarrow Zn^{2+} + 2e^-$

(b) $Zn + 2OH^- \longrightarrow Zn(OH)_2 + 2e^-$

(c) $O_2 + 2H_2O + 4e^- \longrightarrow 4OH^-$

(d) None of the above

2. Half-cell reaction at the cathode is

(a) $Zn \longrightarrow Zn^{2+} + 2e^-$

(b) $Zn + 2OH^- \longrightarrow Zn(OH)_2 + 2e^-$

(c) $O_2 + 2H_2O + 4e^- \longrightarrow 4OH^-$

(d) $Zn + H_2O \longrightarrow ZnO + H_2$

3. EMF of the cell under operating condition when partial pressure of O_2 gas is 0.21 atm is

(a) 1.64 V (b) 1.65 V (c) −1.64 V (d) 2.07 V

***Passage* 4** *Following passage describes the occurence of corrosion of metals. Give the answers of the questions given at the end.*

Corrosion is the oxidative deterioration of a metal, such as conversion of iron to rust [$Fe_2O_3 \cdot xH_2O$], the tarnishing of silver (due to formation of Ag_2O), development of a green coating on copper and bronze.

Corrosion is basically an electrochemical phenomenon. A metal is oxidised by loss of electrons to oxygen and forms metal oxide. Corrosion of iron (rusting) occurs in presence of water and oxygen (air).

1. Oxidation reaction that initiates corrosion is

(a) $H_2 \longrightarrow 2H^+ + 2e^-$

(b) $Fe \longrightarrow Fe^{2+} + 2e^-$

(c) $2H_2O \longrightarrow O_2 + 4H^+ + 4e^-$

(d) None of the above

2. One of the reactions that take place during corrosion is $O_2(g) + 4H^+(aq) + 4e^- \longrightarrow 2H_2O$

Source of $H^+(aq)$ is

(a) CO_2 (b) acid rain

(c) Both (a) and (b) (d) None of these

3. During rusting of iron, Fe^{2+} is formed which is further oxidised to Fe^{3+} by

(a) atmospheric O_2 (b) CO_2

(c) acid rain (d) All of these

***Passage* 5** *Following technique is adopted to check suspected drunk drivers. Read the passage and answer the questions at the end of it.*

When suspected drunk drivers are tested with a Breathalyzer, the alcohol (ethanol) in the exhaled breath is oxidised to ethanoic acid with an acidic solution of potassium dichromate:

$$\underset{\text{Ethanol}}{3CH_3CH_2OH(aq)} + 2Cr_2O_7^{2-}(aq) + 16H^+(aq) \longrightarrow$$

$$\underset{\text{Ethanoic acid}}{3CH_3COOH(aq)} + 4Cr^{3+}(aq) + 11H_2O(l)$$

The Breathalyzer measures the colour change and produces a meter reading calibrated in terms of blood alcohol content.

1. Colour of the testing solution changes from
   (a) yellow to blue
   (b) colourless to green
   (c) orange to green
   (d) green to orange

2. If the standard half-cell potential for reduction of ethanoic acid to ethanol is 0.06 V and that of reduction of $Cr_2O_7^{2-}$ to Cr^{3+} is 1.33 V, then E°_{cell} of the reaction taking place in alcohol meter is
   (a) 1.39 V (b) 1.27 V
   (c) −1.39 V (d) −1.51 V

3. What is the value of E for the reaction when the concentrations of ethanol, ethanoic acid, $Cr_2O_7^{2-}$, and Cr^{3+} are 1.0 M and the pH is 4.00?
   (a) 0.31 V (b) −1.01 V
   (c) 1.64 V (d) 0.95 V

***Passage* 6** The concentration of potassium ions inside a biological cell is at least twenty times higher than the outside. The resulting potential difference across the cell is important in several processes such as transmission of nerve impulses and maintaining the ion balance. A simple model for such a concentration cell involving a metal M is

$$M(s) \mid M^+(aq; 0.05 \text{ molar}) \mid\mid M^+(aq; 1 \text{ molar}) \mid M(s)$$

For the above electrolytic cell the magnitude of the cell potential $|E_{cell}| = 70$ mV. **[IIT JEE 2010]**

1. For the above cell
   (a) $E_{cell} < 0; \Delta G > 0$ (b) $E_{cell} > 0; \Delta G < 0$
   (c) $E_{cell} < 0; \Delta G^\circ > 0$ (d) $E_{cell} > 0; \Delta G^\circ < 0$

2. If the 0.05 molar solution of M^+ is replaced by a 0.0025 molar M^+ solution, then the magnitude of the cell potential would be
   (a) 35 mV (b) 70 mV
   (c) 140 mV (d) 700 mV

***Passage* 7** *Following passage is concerned with problems for the persons having amalgam filling in their teeth. Read the passage and answer the questions at the end of it.*

Accidentally chewing on a stray fragment of aluminium foil can cause a sharp tooth pain if the aluminium comes in contact with an amalgam filling. The filling, an alloy of silver, tin, and mercury acts as the cathode of a tiny galvanic cell, the aluminium behaves as the anode, and saliva serves as the electrolyte. When the aluminium and the filling come in contact, an electric current passage from the aluminium to the filling, which is sensed by a nerve in the tooth. Aluminium is oxidised at the anode, and O_2 gas is reduced to water at the cathode.

$$E^\circ_{Al^{3+}/Al} = -1.66 \text{ V}, \quad E^\circ_{O_2, H^+/H_2O} = 1.23 \text{ V}$$

1. If a filling makes contact with a gold inlay in a nearby tooth, then
   (a) corrosion of the filling (Sn/Hg/Ag) takes place
   (b) unpleasant metallic taste is released
   (c) Both (a) and (b)
   (d) None of the above

2. Net reaction taking place when amalgam is in contact with aluminium foil
   (a) $Al + O_2 + OH^- \longrightarrow Al(OH)_4^- + H_2O$
   (b) $4Al + 3O_2 + 12H^+ \longrightarrow 4Al^{3+} + 6H_2O$
   (c) $4Al + 3O_2 \longrightarrow 2Al_2O_3$
   (d) $2H_2 + O_2 \longrightarrow 2H_2O$

3. Standard EMF experienced by the person with dental filling is
   (a) 2.89 V (b) −2.89 V
   (c) −0.93 V (d) + 0.43 V

***Passage* 8** Two electrochemical cells were fitted with inert platinum electrodes and connected in series. The first cell contained a solution of metal nitrate and the second cell, the metal sulphate. After operation of the cell for a prescribed period of time, 675 mg of the metal was deposited in the first cell and 76.3 mL of H_2 gas at 25°C and 1 atom evolved in the second.

Answer the follo ıg questions.

1. How many equivalents of H_2 were formed ?
   (a) 3.12×10^{-3}
   (b) 6.24×10^{-3}
   (c) 1.56×10^{-3}
   (d) 0.78×10^{-3}

2. What is the equivalents mass of metal?
   (a) 108.2 (b) 54.1
   (c) 216.4 (d) 27.05

***Passage* 9** The electrochemical cell shown below is a concentration cell. $M \mid M^{2+}$ (saturated solution of a sparingly soluble salt, MX_2) $\mid\mid M^{2+}(0.001 \text{ mol dm}^{-3}) \mid M$.

The emf of the cell depends on the difference in concentration of M^{2+} ions at the two electrodes. The emf of the cell at 298 K is 0.059 V. **[IIT JEE 2012]**

1. The solubility product (K_{sp}; mol^3 dm^{-9}) of MX_2 at 298 K based on the information available the given concentration cell is
   (take $2.303 \times R \times 298 \text{ K}/F = 0.059$ V)
   (a) 1×10^{-15} (b) 4×10^{-15}
   (c) 1×10^{-12} (d) 4×10^{-12}

2. The value of ΔG (kJ mol^{-1}) for the given cell is (take 1 F = 96500 C mol^{-1})
   (a) − 5.7 (b) 5.7
   (c) 11.4 (d) − 11.4

Matrix-Match Type

Given below are Matching Type Questions, with two columns (each having some items) each . Each item of Column I has to be matched with the items of Column II.

1. Match the terms in Column I with the terms in Column II.

	Column I		Column II
A.	Weak electrolyte	1.	Copper
B.	Strong electrolyte	2.	Quinhydrone
C.	Insulator	3.	Sodium chloride
D.	Electronic conductor	4.	Buffer
E.	Indicator electrode	5.	Acetic acid

2. Match the salt in Column I with corresponding use in Column II.

	Column I		Column II
A.	Hg_2Cl_2	1.	Used in salt-bridge
B.	Quinhydrone	2.	Measurement of cell constant
C.	Lead acetate	3.	Redox electrode
D.	NH_4NO_3	4.	Calomel electrode
E.	0.1 N KCl	5.	Used in platinising solution

3. Match electrode in Column I with its presentation in Column II.

	Column I		Column II
A.	Electrode reversible with respect to cation.	1.	$Pt/Fe^{2+}, Fe^{3+}$
B.	Electrode reversible with respect to anion	2.	$\underset{1\text{ bar}}{Pt, H_2} \mid H^+ (a = 1)$
C.	Redox electrode	3.	$Ag \mid AgCl(s), HCl\,(aq)$
D.	Reference electrode	4.	$Ag \mid AgNO_3$

4. Match the electrode in Column I with its general name in Column II.

	Column I		Column II
A.	Calomel	1.	Reference
B.	Glass	2.	Redox
C.	Hydrogen	3.	Membrane
D.	Quinhydrone	4.	Gas

5. Match the physical term in Column I with the unit in Column II.

	Column I		Column II
A.	Conductance	1.	siemen m^2 mol^{-1}
B.	Resistivity	2.	m^{-1}
C.	Conductivity	3.	volt per ampere
D.	Molar conductivity	4.	siemen
E.	Cell constant	5.	siemen m^{-1}
F.	Resistance	6.	ohm metre

6. Match the cell/cell reaction is Column I with their properties/values in Column II.

	Column I		Column II
A.	$\underset{\ominus}{Cu \mid} Cu^{2+}(0.01\,M) \| Ag^+(0.1\,M) \underset{\oplus}{\mid Ag}$	1.	$E_{cell} = E^\circ_{cell}$
B.	$Ag \mid Ag^+ (0.1\,M) \|\mid Zn^{2+}(0.01\,M) \mid Zn$	2.	$E_{cell} > 0$
C.	$Pt(H_2) \mid H^+ (1\,M) \| Cu^{2+} (1\,M) \mid Cu$	3.	$E_{cell} < 0$
D.	$Cu \mid Cu^{2+} (0.1\,M) \| Mg^{2+} (0.01\,M) \mid Mg$	4.	Cell reaction spontaneous

7. The standard reduction potential data at 25°C is given below.

$$E^\circ(Fe^{3+}/Fe^{2+}) = +0.77\text{ V};$$
$$E^\circ(Fe^{2+}/Fe) = -0.44\text{ V};$$
$$E^\circ(Cu^{2+}/Cu) = +0.34\text{ V};$$
$$E^\circ(Cu^{+}/Cu) = +0.52\text{ V};$$
$$E^\circ(O_2(g) + 4H^+ + 4e^- \longrightarrow 2H_2O) + 1.23\text{ V};$$
$$E^\circ(O_2(g) + 2H_2O + 4e^- \longrightarrow 4OH) + 0.40\text{ V}$$
$$E^\circ(Cr^{3+}/Cr) = -0.74\text{ V};$$
$$E^\circ(Cr^{2+}/Cr) = +0.91\text{ V}$$

Match E° of the redox pair in Column I with the values given in Column II.

	Column I		Column II
A.	$E^\circ(Fe^{3+}/Fe)$	1.	− 0.18 V
B.	$E^\circ(4H_2O \rightleftharpoons 4H^+ + 4OH^-)$	2.	0.4 V
C.	$E^\circ(Cu^{2+} + Cu \longrightarrow 2Cu^+)$	3.	0.04 V
D.	$E^\circ(Cr^{3+}, Cr^{2+})$	4.	0.83 V

[JEE Advanced 2013]

8. Match the statements in Column I with the observations is Column II.

Column I	Column II
A. Copper plates dipped in $AgNO_3$ solution	1. Colour of solution fades
B. Copper plates dipped in dil. H_2SO_4	2. Solution turns blue
C. Zinc plate dipped in $CuSO_4$ solution	3. No reaction observed
D. Copper plate dipped in $FeCl_3$ solution	4. Cell reaction spontaneous

9. An aqueous solution of X is added slowly to an aqueous solution of Y as shown in Column I. The variation in conductivity of these reactions is given in Column II. Match Column I with Column II.

Column I	Column II
A. $\underset{X}{(C_2H_5)_3N} + \underset{Y}{CH_3COOH}$	1. Conductivity decreases and then increases
B. $\underset{X}{KI(0.1\,M)} + \underset{Y}{AgNO_3(0.01\,M)}$	2. Conductivity decreases and then does not change much
C. $\underset{X}{CH_3COOH} + \underset{Y}{KOH}$	3. Conductivity increases and then does not change much
D. $\underset{X}{NaOH} + \underset{Y}{HI}$	4. Conductivity does not change much and then increases

[JEE Advanced 2013]

Single Integer Answer Questions

Answer of these questions is a single digit lying between 0 to 9.

1. Number of moles of Faradays required in the reduction of one mole of Al_2O_3 to Al are

2. In the following cell,

$$\underset{\ominus}{Zn} \mid Zn^{2+}(x\,M) \| Cu^{2+}(1\,M) \mid \underset{\oplus}{Cu}$$

$E°_{cell} = 1.10$ V and $E_{cell} = 1.082$ V.
The value of x is

3. For the following half-cell,

$$Pt\,(H_2)\,|\,H^+; \quad E = 0.2364\text{ V}.$$

The pH of the solution is

4. Equivalent conductance of 1 N solution of H_3PO_4 is (Λ_c) and that of 0.2 N is $x\,\Lambda_c$. What is the value of x?

5. How many of the following metals will displace H_2 on reaction with dil HCl?

Fe, Zn, Mg, Ag, Cr, Hg, Al, Cr, Sn, Cd

6. On passing a certain amount of current, 4 g of Mg is formed. How much Al is formed by same current?

7. During the electrolysis of conc H_2SO_4, it was found that $H_2S_2O_8$ and O_2 were liberated in a molar ratio of 3 : 1.

How many moles of H_2 were found in terms of moles of $H_2S_2O_8$? (Express your answer as : 3 × moles of H_2).

8. For the oxidation of ferric oxalate to CO_2. 18 F of electricity is required. how many moles of ferric oxalate is oxidised?

9. For the following cell,

$$\underset{\ominus}{Zn} \mid Zn^{2+}(1\,M) \| Ag^+(x \times 10^{-6}\,M) \mid \underset{\oplus}{Ag}$$

$E_{cell} = 1.250$ V and $E°_{cell} = 1.56$ V
What is the value of x?

10. For the following cell,

$$\underset{\ominus}{Ag} \mid Ag^+ \text{ (saturated } Ag_2CrO_4) \| Ag^+(0.125\,M) \mid \underset{\oplus}{Ag}$$

$$E_{cell} = 0.183\text{ V}.$$

$$K_{sp}(Ag_2CrO_4) = y \times 10^{-12}$$

The value of y is ....

11. Amount Ca deposited when current of 5.36 A is passed for 1 hour through fused $CaCl_2$ is ....

12. For the following cell,

$$\underset{\ominus}{\underset{1\text{ atm}}{Pt(H_2)}} \mid H^+ \| Ag^+ \mid \underset{\oplus}{Ag^+}$$

$(E_{cell} - E°_{cell}) = 0.06$ V.

The value of $\log \dfrac{[Ag^+]}{[H^+]}$ is ....

13. Using $Cr_2O_7^{2-}$ aqueous solution, $E°_{red} = 1.33$ V and $\Delta G° = -770.07$ kJ.

The valency of the ion formed after reduction is ....

14. All the energy released from the reaction $X \rightarrow Y, \Delta_r G° = -193\,kJ\,mol^{-1}$ is used for oxidising M^+ as $M^+ \rightarrow M^{3+} + 2e^-, E° = -0.25$ V.

Under standard conditions, the number of moles of M^+ oxidised when one mole of X is converted to Y is $[F = 96500\text{ C mol}^{-}]$ [JEE Advanced 2015]

15. The conductance of a 0.0015 M aqueous solution of a weak monobasic acid was determined by using a conductivity cell consisting of platinised Pt electrodes. The distance between the electrodes is 120 cm with an area of cross section of 1 cm^2. The conductance of this solution was found to be 5×10^{-7} S. The pH of the solution is 4. The value of limiting molar conductivity (Λ_m°) of this weak monobasic acid in aqueous solution is $Z \times 10^2$ S cm^{-1} mol^{-1}. The value of Z is [JEE Advanced 2017]

Answers

Objective Questions Type I [Only one correct option]

1. (b)	2. (a)	3. (c)	4. (d)	5. (b)	6. (a)	7. (d)	8. (c)	9. (a)	10. (c)
11. (c)	12. (d)	13. (c)	14. (b)	15. (b)	16. (b)	17. (d)	18. (a)	19. (a)	20. (d)
21. (b)	22. (c)	23. (d)	24. (c)	25. (d)	26. (b)	27. (a)	28. (a)	29. (d)	30. (a)
31. (a)	32. (b)	33. (d)	34. (c)	35. (c)	36. (c)	37. (b)	38. (b)	39. (c)	40. (b)
41. (d)	42. (b)	43. (b)	44. (a)	45. (c)	46. (b)	47. (a)	48. (c)	49. (d)	50. (a)
51. (c)	52. (a)	53. (d)	54. (c)	55. (b)	56. (a)	57. (a)	58. (d)	59. (c)	60. (d)
61. (b)	62. (b)	63. (c)	64. (c)	65. (a)	66. (d)	67. (d)	68. (a)	69. (c)	70. (c)
71. (d)	72. (b)	73. (a)	74. (a)	75. (a)	76. (d)	77. (d)	78. (d)	79. (b)	80. (c)
81. (d)	82. (a)	83. (c)	84. (c)	85. (d)	86. (b)	87. (a)	88. (b)	89. (c)	90. (b)
91. (d)	92. (d)	93. (a)	94. (b)	95. (c)	96. (a)	97. (d)	98. (d)	99. (b)	100. (c)
101. (a)	102. (b)	103. (c)	104. (d)	105. (d)	106. (d)	107. (c)	108. (d)	109. (c)	110. (d)
111. (a)	112. (c)	113. (a)	114. (b)	115. (c)	116. (c)	117. (c)	118. (c)	119. (b)	120. (c)
121. (a)	122. (a)	123. (a)	124. (b)	125. (b)	126. (a)	127. (d)	128. (d)	129. (a)	130. (d)
131. (c)	132. (b)	133. (a)	134. (c)	135. (b)	136. (c)	137. (d)	138. (b)	139. (a)	140. (b)
141. (c)	142. (d)	143. (d)	144. (b)	145. (d)	146. (a)	147. (b)	148. (a)	149. (d)	150. (b)
151. (a)	152. (b)	153. (c)	154. (b)	155. (a)	156. (b)	157. (c)	158. (d)	159. (d)	160. (b)
161. (d)	162. (b)	163. (a)							

Objective Questions Type II [One or more than one correct option(s)]

1. (c, d)	2. (a, c)	3. (a, b, c, d)	4. (a, b)	5. (a, c)
6. (c, d)	7. (b)	8. (d)	9. (d)	10. (c)
11. (b, c, d)	12. (a, b, c, d)	13. (c)	14. (a, b, d)	15. (a)
16. (a, c, d)	17. (b)	18. (d)	19. (a)	20. (a, c, d)

Numerical Value Questions

1. $E^\circ_{Cd^{2+}/Cd} = -x = -0.40$ V

2. Mg is more electropositive than Ag hence,

$$Mg \longrightarrow Mg^{2+} + 2e^-; E^\circ_{Mg/Mg^{2+}} = -E^\circ_{Mg^{2+}/Mg} = +2.37 \text{ V}$$

$$2Ag^+ + 2e^- \longrightarrow 2Ag; \quad E^\circ_{Ag^+/Ag} = +0.80 \text{ V}$$

$$\text{Net} \quad 2Ag^+ + Mg \longrightarrow Mg^{2+} + 2Ag; \; E^\circ_{cell} = 3.17 \text{ V}$$

3. -0.07865 V

4. $[Ag^+] = x = 1.523 \times 10^{-9}$ M

5. $x = 0.0225$ M

6. 60

7. $K_{eq} = 2.49$

8. $n = 2$

9. 1.78

10. Conductivity = 4.48

11. 2.4072×10^{-2} W^{-1} m^2 mol^{-1} (1 mol of $CaCl_2$ = 2 equivalents $CaCl_2$)

12. $\Delta G^\circ_f [Al(OH)_4^-] = -1.30$

13. 0.0843 V

14. -0.38 V

15. 0.208 V

16. 1.4 A

17. 1.045

18. 58.3

19. 10

20. -11.62 J / K-mol

21. 14.6

22. 14

23. 57

24. 45

25. 288

Comprehension Based Questions

Passage 1 – 1. (b) 2. (c) 3. (d) 4. (c)

Passage 2 – 1. (b) 2. (a)

Passage 3 – 1. (b) 2. (c) 3. (b)

Passage 4 – 1. (b) 2. (c) 3. (a)

Passage 5 – 1. (c) 2. (b) 3. (d) 4. (d)

Passage 6 – 1. (b) 2. (c)

Passage 7 – 1. (c) 2. (b) 3. (a)

Passage 8 – 1. (b) 2. (a)

Passage 9 – 1. (b) 2. (d)

Matrix-Match Type

1. A → (5); B → (3); C → (4); D → (1); E → (2)
2. A → (4); B → (3); C → (5); D → (1); E → (2)
3. A → (4); B → (3); C → (1); D → (2)
4. A → (1); B → (3); C → (4); D → (2)
5. A → (4); B → (6); C → (5); D → (1); E → (2); F → (3)
6. A → (1,2,4); B → (1,3); C → (1,2,4); D → (3)
7. A → (3); B → (4); C → (1); D → (2)
8. A → (2,4); B → (3); C → (1,4); D → (1,4)
9. A → (3); B → (4); C → (2); D → (1)

Single Integer Answer Questions

1. (6)	2. (4)	3. (4)	4. (5)	5. (7)	6. (3)	7. (5)	8. (3)	9. (6)	10. (4)
11. (4)	12. (1)	13. (3)	14. (4)	15. (6)					

Solutions

Objective Questions Type I [Only one correct option]

3. (c) **Oxidation** $Pb(s) + SO_4^{2-}(aq) \longrightarrow PbSO_4(s) + 2e^-$

Reduction $PbO_2(s) + 4H^+(aq) + SO_4^{2-}(aq) + 2e^- \longrightarrow PbSO_4(s) + 2H_2O(l)$

$$Pb(s) + PbO_2(s) + 2H_2SO_4(aq) \longrightarrow 2PbSO_4(s) + 2H_2O(l)$$

Thus, 2 moles H_2SO_4 are consumed by exchange of 2 moles of electrons. $\therefore$ $z = \frac{\text{moles of } H_2SO_4}{\text{moles of electrons} \times 96500}$

$$= \frac{2 \times 98}{2 \times 96500}$$

$$w = zit$$

$$= \frac{2 \times 98 \times 2.5 \times 965 \times 60}{2 \times 96500} = 147 \text{ g} = 1.5 \text{ mol}$$

4. (d) $H_2SO_4 = 5$ M initially

Thus, 1.5 L H_2SO_4 contains $= 1.5 \times 5 = 7.5$ mol H_2SO_4

H_2SO_4 consumed $= 1.5$ mol (as in Q. 3)

H_2SO_4 left $= 6.0$ mol in 1.5 L

$\therefore$ $[H_2SO_4] = \frac{6.0}{1.5} = 4.0$ M

9. (a) Resistance = specific resistance × cell constant

$$(R)_{KCl} = (S)_{KCl} \times (\text{cell constant})$$

$$(R)_{NaOH} = (S)_{NaOH} \times (\text{cell constant})$$

$$\frac{(R)_{KCl}}{(R)_{NaOH}} = \frac{(S)_{KCl}}{(S)_{NaOH}}$$

$$\frac{160}{190} = \frac{700}{(S)_{NaOH}}$$

$\therefore$ $(S)_{NaOH} = 831.25$ ohm-cm

$\therefore$ specific conductance $(\kappa)_{NaOH} = 1.20 \times 10^{-3}\ \Omega^{-1}\ cm^{-1}$

11. (c) If dilution is made V-times molar and specific conductance becomes V-times

0.1 M H_2SO_4 changes to 0.01 M H_2SO_4

Thus, dilution is 100 times.

13. (c) Equivalence conductance is **five times**, hence, dilution is also **five times**

$\therefore$ $0.1\ M \times V \equiv M' \times 5\ V$

$\therefore$ M' (final) $= 0.02$ M

$= 0.04$ N (due to dibasic acid)

14. (b) Concentration of solute = 0.1 mol in 0.5 L = 0.2 M

$$\text{Molar conductance} = \frac{1000 \times \text{specific conductance}}{\text{molarity}}$$

$$= \frac{1000 \times x}{0.2} = 5000\ x\ S\ cm^2\ mol^{-1}$$

23. (d) $\Lambda_{eq} = \lambda^{\infty}(H^+) + \lambda^{\infty}(SO_4^{2-})$

$= 80 + 350$

$= 430\ S\ cm^2$ equivalent^{-1}

Since, molar mass of $H_2SO_4 = 98 = 2 \times$ equivalent mass

$\therefore$ $\Lambda_m = 2 \times 430$

$= 860\ S\ cm^2\ mol^{-1}$

24. (c) $\Lambda^{\circ}_{BaSO_4} = \Lambda^{\circ}_{BaCl_2} + \Lambda^{\circ}_{H_2SO_4} - 2\Lambda^{\circ}_{HCl} = (x_1 + x_2 - 2x_3)$

$$\Lambda^{\circ}_{BaSO_4} = \frac{1000 \times \text{sp. conductance}}{\text{solubility (in saturated solution)}}$$

$$(x_1 + x_2 - 2x_3) = \frac{1000y}{\text{solubility}}$$

$\therefore$ Solubility $(BaSO_4) = \frac{1000\ y}{(x_1 + x_2 - 2x_3)}$ N

$$= \frac{1000\ y}{2(x_1 + x_2 - 2x_3)} \text{ M}$$

$$BaSO_4 \rightleftharpoons Ba^{2+} + SO_4^{2-}$$

$$K_{sp}(BaSO_4) = [Ba^{2+}][SO_4^{2-}]\ M^2$$

$$= \frac{10^6 y^2}{4(x_1 + x_2 - 2x_3)^2}$$

25. (d) $C_6H_5COOH + OH^- \longrightarrow C_6H_5COO^- + H_2O$

$C_6H_5COO^- + H_2O \longrightarrow C_6H_5COOH + OH^-$

When NaOH (strong base) is added to C_6H_5COOH (weak acid), $C_6H_5COO^-$ is formed but at the same time it is hydrolysed releasing OH^-.

Thus, initially conductance increases slightly. After C_6H_5COOH is completely neutralised further addition causes rapid increase in conductance.

38. (*b*)

Set	Cells	Oxid at	Red at	E°_{cell}
(a)	I and II	II $B^{2-} \rightarrow B^- + e^-$	I $A + e^- \rightarrow A^-$	$0.12 + 0.96 = 1.08$ V
(b)	I and III	III $C \rightarrow C^+ + e^-$	I $A + e^- \rightarrow A^-$	$-0.18 + 0.96 = 0.78$ V
(c)	I and IV	IV $D \rightarrow D^{2+} + 2e^-$	I $A + e^- \rightarrow A^-$	$1.12 + 0.96 = 2.08$ V
(d)	II and IV	IV $D \rightarrow D^{2+} + 2e^-$	II $B^- + e^- \rightarrow B^{2-}$	$1.12 - 0.12 = 1.00$ V

40. (*b*) Negative E° means that redox couple is weaker oxidising agent than H^+/H_2 couple. Positive E° means that redox couple is a stronger oxidising agent than H^+/H_2 couple

Given, $Co^{3+} + e^- \longrightarrow Co^{2+}; E^\circ = +1.81$ V

$Pb^{4+} + 2e^- \longrightarrow Pb^{2+}; E^\circ = +1.67$ V

$Ce^{4+} + e^- \longrightarrow Ce^{3+}; E^\circ = +1.61$ V

$Bi^{3+} + 3e^- \longrightarrow Bi; E^\circ = +0.20$ V

Oxidising power of the species increases in the order of $Bi^{3+} < Ce^{4+} < Pb^{4+} < Co^{3+}$.

Higher the emf value, stronger the oxidising power. The maximum value of emf is possessed by Co^{3+}. Hence, it has maximum oxidising power. Whereas Bi^{3+} possess the lowest emf value. Hence, it has minimum oxidising power.

41. (*d*) $E^\circ_{cell} = E^\circ_{Zn/Zn^{2+}} + E^\circ_{Cu^{2+}/Cu}$ first cell

$$1.10 = E^\circ_{Zn/Zn^{2+}} + 0.34$$

$$\therefore \quad E^\circ_{Zn/Zn^{2+}} = 0.76 \text{ V}$$

$E^\circ_{cell} = E^\circ_{Cu/Cu^{2+}} + E^\circ_{Ag^+/Ag}$ second cell

$$0.46 = -0.34 + E^\circ_{Ag^+/Ag}$$

$$E^\circ_{Ag^+/Ag} = 0.80 \text{ V}$$

For third cell

$$E^\circ_{cell} = E^\circ_{Zn/Zn^{2+}} + E^\circ_{Ag^+/Ag} = 0.76 + 0.80 = 1.56 \text{ V}$$

42. (*b*) A cell reaction is spontaneous if

$$E^\circ_{cell} = + \text{ve}$$

$$Sn^{2+} \longrightarrow Sn^{4+} + 2e^- \quad E^\circ = -0.13 \text{ V}$$

$$Sn^{2+} + 2e^- \longrightarrow Sn \quad E^\circ = -0.14 \text{ V}$$

$$2Sn^{2+} \longrightarrow Sn^{4+} + Sn \quad E^\circ_{cell} = -0.27 \text{ V}$$

Thus, (a) is not possible.

44. (*a*) $Fe^{2+}(aq) + Ag^+(aq) \longrightarrow Fe^{3+}(aq) + Ag(s)$

$$\therefore \quad E^\circ_{cell} = E^\circ_{Ag^+/Ag} - E^\circ_{Fe^{3+}/Fe^{2+}} = xV - E^\circ_{Fe^{3+}/Fe^{2+}} \quad \ldots \text{(i)}$$

Now, for two half-cells

(i) $Fe^{2+} + 2e^- \longrightarrow Fe;\ E^\circ_{Fe^{2+}/Fe} = E^\circ_1 = yV\ \Delta G^\circ_2 = -2FE^\circ_1$

(ii) $Fe^{3+} + 3e^- \longrightarrow Fe;\ E^\circ_{Fe^{3+}/Fe} = E^\circ_2 = zV\ \Delta G^\circ_2 = -3FE^\circ_2$

So, $Fe^{3+} + e^- \longrightarrow Fe^{2+};\ E^\circ_{Fe^{3+}/Fe^{2+}} = E^\circ_3 = ?;$

$$\Delta G^\circ_3 = -1 \times FE^\circ_3$$

Again, $\Delta G^\circ_3 = \Delta G^\circ_2 - \Delta G^\circ_1$

$$\Rightarrow \quad -FE^\circ_3 = -3FE^\circ_2 - (-2FE^\circ_1)$$

$$\Rightarrow \quad -E^\circ_3 = 2E^\circ_1 - 3E^\circ_2 \Rightarrow E^\circ_3 = 3E^\circ_2 - 2E^\circ_1$$

$$\Rightarrow E^\circ_{Fe^{3+}/Fe^{2+}} = (3z - 2y)\text{V}$$

So, from equation (i)

$$E^\circ_{cell} = xV - (3z - 2y)\text{ V} = (x - 3z + 2y)\text{ V}$$

46. (*b*)
$$E^\circ = \frac{2.303\,RT}{nF} \log K_{eq}$$

$$0.2955 = \frac{0.0591}{2} \log K_{eq}$$

$$\therefore \quad K_{eq} = 10^{10}$$

47. (*a*) I. $Cu^{2+} + 2e^- \longrightarrow Cu \quad E^\circ_1 = 0.339$ V, $n_1 = 2$

II. $Cu^+ + e^- \longrightarrow Cu \quad E^\circ_2 = 0.518$ V, $n_2 = 1$

III. $Cu^{2+} + e^- \longrightarrow Cu^+ \quad E^\circ_3 = ? \quad n_3 = 1$

I − II = III

$$\therefore \quad \Delta G^\circ_{III} = \Delta G^\circ_I - \Delta G^\circ_{II}$$

$$-n_3FE^\circ_3 = -n_1FE^\circ_1 + n_2FE^\circ_2$$

$$\therefore \quad E^\circ_3 = \frac{n_1E^\circ_1 - n_2E^\circ_2}{n_3} = \frac{0.678 - 0.518}{1} = 0.160 \text{ V}$$

48. (*c*) Reducing power of Al is larger than that of Cu.

	E°
$Al \longrightarrow Al^{3+} + 3e^-] \times 2$	1.66 V
$Cu^{2+} + 2e^- \longrightarrow Cu \quad] \times 3$	0.34 V
$\therefore \quad 2Al + 3Cu^{2+} \longrightarrow 3Cu + 2Al^{3+}$	2.00 V

50. (*a*) I. $Cu^+ + e^- \longrightarrow Cu \quad E^\circ_1 = 0.52$ V

II. $Cu^{2+} + e^- \longrightarrow Cu^+ \quad E^\circ_2 = 0.16$ V

III. $2Cu^+ \longrightarrow Cu^{2+} + Cu \quad E^\circ_3 = ?$

(I − II) gives III

$$\therefore \quad E^\circ_3 = 0.36 \text{ V}$$

51. (*c*) Higher the standard reduction potential ($E^\circ_{M^{n+}/M}$), better is oxidising agent. Among the given, $E^\circ_{S_2O_8^{2-}/SO_4^{2-}}$ is highest, hence $S_2O_8^{2-}$ is the strongest oxidising agent.

The decreasing order of oxidising agent among the given option is as follows:

$$S_2O_8^{2-} > Au^{3+} > O_2 > Br_2$$

52. (*a*) $Cu + 2Ag^+ \longrightarrow 2Ag + Cu^{2+}$

$$K = \frac{[Cu^{2+}]}{[Ag^+]^2} = \frac{0.01}{(0.1)^2} = 1$$

$$\therefore \quad E = E^\circ - \frac{0.0591}{2} \log K$$

$$= 0.46 - \frac{0.0591}{2} \log 1 = 0.46 \text{ V}$$

54. (*c*)

$$\begin{array}{l} Zn \longrightarrow Zn^{2+} + 2e^- \\ 2H^+ + 2e^- \longrightarrow H_2 \\ \hline Zn + 2H^+ \longrightarrow Zn^{2+} + H_2 \\ \hline \end{array}$$

$$K = \frac{[Zn^{2+}][H_2]}{[Zn][H^+]^2}$$

In H_2O, $[H^+] = 1 \times 10^{-7}$ M under standard condition (298 K, 1 bar)

$$K = \frac{(10^{-4})(1)}{(1)(10^{-7})^2} = 10^{10}$$

$$\therefore \quad E = E^\circ - \frac{0.0591}{2} \log K$$

$$= 0.76 - \frac{0.0591}{2} \log 10^{10} = 0.4645 \text{ V}$$

55. (*b*)

$$E = E^\circ_{cell} - \frac{0.0591}{2} \log \frac{[Zn^{2+}]}{[Cd^{2+}]}$$

$$0.30 = 0.36 - \frac{0.0591}{2} \log \frac{[Zn^{2+}]}{[Cd^{2+}]}$$

$$\log \frac{[Zn^{2+}]}{[Cd^{2+}]} = \frac{0.06 \times 2}{0.0591} \approx 2$$

$$\therefore \quad \frac{[Zn^{2+}]}{[Cd^{2+}]} = 10^2 \Rightarrow \frac{[Zn^{2+}]}{[Cd^{2+}]} = 0.01$$

56. (*a*)

$$\begin{array}{l} 2Hg(l) + 2Cl^-(aq)_{(L)} \longrightarrow Hg_2Cl_2(s) + 2e^- \\ Cl_2(g) + 2e^- \longrightarrow 2Cl^-(aq)_{(R)} \\ \hline 2Cl^-(aq)_{(L)} \longrightarrow 2Cl^-(aq)_{(R)} \end{array}$$

$$K = \frac{[Cl^-]_R^2}{[Cl^-]_L^2} = \frac{(0.01)^2}{(0.1)^2} = 0.01$$

$$E_{cell} = E^\circ_{cell} - \frac{0.0591}{2} \log K$$

$$= 1.10 - \frac{0.0591}{2} \log (0.01) = 1.1591 \text{ V}$$

57. (*a*)

$$\begin{array}{l} Pb(s) \rightleftharpoons Pb^{2+}(aq) + 2e^- \\ Cu^{2+}(aq) + 2e^- \longrightarrow Cu(s) \\ \hline Cu^{2+}(aq) + Pb(s) \rightleftharpoons Pb^{2+}(aq) + Cu(s) \end{array}$$

$$K = \frac{[Pb^{2+}]}{[Cu^{2+}]} = \frac{1}{[Cu^{2+}]}$$

$$\therefore \quad E = E^\circ - \frac{0.0591}{2} \log K$$

$$= E^\circ + \frac{0.0591}{2} \log [Cu^{2+}]$$

$$0 = 0.473 + \frac{0.0591}{2} \log [Cu^{2+}]$$

$$\log [Cu^{2+}] = -16$$

$$\therefore \quad [Cu^{2+}] = 1 \times 10^{-16} \text{ M}$$

58. (*d*)

$$2H^+ + 2e^- \longrightarrow H_2 \quad K = \frac{1}{[H^+]^2}$$

$$E = E^\circ + \frac{0.0591}{2} \log [H^+]^2$$

$$= E^\circ + 0.0591 \log [H^+]$$

$$= E^\circ - 0.0591 \text{ pH}, = -0.0591 \text{ pH}$$

(a) $E = 0.0591 \log 1 = 0$

(b) $E = -0.0591 \times 4 = -0.2364$ V

(c) $E = +0.0591 \times 10^{-7} = -0.4137$ V

(d) 1.0 M NaOH = 1.0 M $[OH^-] = 10^{-14}$ M $[H^+]$

$\therefore \quad E = 0.0591 \log 10^{-14} = -0.8274$ V

59. (*c*) LHS

$$\underset{x \text{ atm}}{H_2(g)} \rightleftharpoons \underset{0.01 \text{ M}}{2H^+(g)} + 2e^-$$

RHS

$$\underset{0.1 \text{ M}}{2H^+(aq)} + 2e^- \longrightarrow \underset{y \text{ atm}}{H_2(g)}$$

$$\underset{x}{H_2(g)} + \underset{0.1 \text{ M}}{2H^+(aq)} \rightleftharpoons \underset{0.01 \text{ M}}{2H^+} + \underset{y \text{ atm}}{H_2(g)}$$

$$K = \frac{(0.01)^2 y}{(0.1)^2 x} = 0.01 \left(\frac{y}{x}\right)$$

$$E_{cell} = E^\circ_{cell} - \frac{0.0591}{2} \log (0.01) \left(\frac{y}{x}\right)$$

$$0 = 0 + 0.0591 \log 10 - \frac{0.0591}{2} \log \frac{y}{x}$$

$$\log 10 = \log \left(\frac{y}{x}\right)^{1/2}$$

$$\therefore \quad 10 = \left(\frac{y}{x}\right)^{1/2} \Rightarrow \left(\frac{x}{y}\right)^{1/2} = \frac{1}{10}$$

$$\therefore \quad \frac{x}{y} = 0.01$$

60. (*d*) $Ni^{2+}(aq) + H_2(g) \rightleftharpoons Ni(s) + 2H^+(aq)$

$$K = \frac{[H^+]^2}{[Ni^{2+}]} = [H^+]^2$$

$$\therefore \quad E_{cell} = E^\circ_{cell} - \frac{0.0591}{2} \log [H^+]^2$$

$$(E_{cell} - E^\circ_{cell}) = 0.0591 \text{ pH}$$

$$0.0591 = 0.0591 \text{ pH}$$

$$\therefore \quad \text{pH} = 1$$

61. (*b*)

$$Cl_2 + 2e^- \longrightarrow 2Cl^-$$

$$K = [Cl^-]^2$$

$$\therefore \quad E = E^\circ - \frac{0.0591}{2} \log [Cl^-]^2$$

$$(E - E^\circ) = -0.0591 \log [Cl^-]$$

$$(E - E^\circ) = 0.0591 \log \left[\frac{1}{Cl^-}\right]$$

Thus, as $[Cl^-]$ increases, $(E - E^\circ)$ decreases.

62. (*b*) Instead of H^+ (1 M), H_2O has been taken

$$\text{Pt}, H_2(g) \underset{\ominus}{|} H_2O\ [H^+] = 10^{-7} \text{ M}$$

Oxidation takes place being anode

$$H_2(g) \longrightarrow 2H^+(aq) + 2e^-$$

$$E = E^\circ - \frac{0.0591}{2} \log \frac{[H^+]^2}{p_{H_2}}$$

$$0 = 0 - \frac{0.0591}{2} \log \frac{(10^{-7})^2}{p_{H_2}}$$

$$\frac{(10^{-7})^2}{(p_{H_2})} = 1$$

$\therefore$ $p_{H_2} = 10^{-14}$ bar

64. (*c*) $Pt(H_2) \mid pH = 2$

$$H_2(g) \rightleftharpoons 2H^+ + 2e^-$$

$$K = [H^+]^2 = (10^{-2})^2 = 10^{-4} \text{ M}$$

$$E = E^\circ - \frac{0.0591}{2} \log 10^{-4} = 0.1182 \text{ V}$$

65. (*a*) Quinhydrone contains quinone (*A*) and quinol(*B*) in 1 : 1 ratio

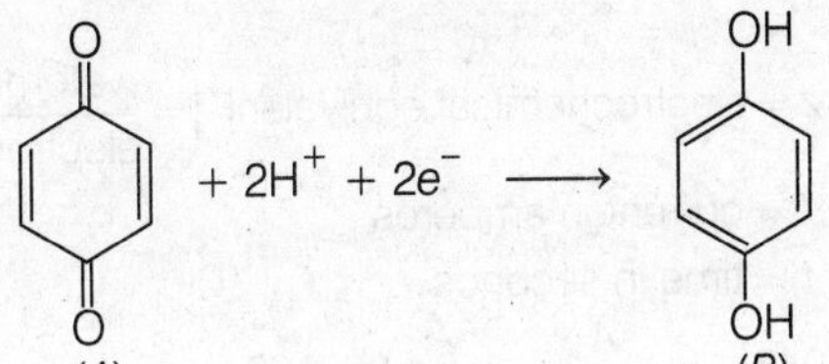

(*A*) (*B*)

Thus, $K = \frac{1}{[H^+]^2}$

Thus, *E* depends on $[H^+]$.

66. (*d*) Half-cell reaction is

$$2Hg(l) + 2Cl^-(aq) \longrightarrow Hg_2Cl_2(s) + 2e^-$$

$$\therefore \quad K = \frac{1}{[Cl^-]^2}$$

$$E = E^\circ - \frac{0.0591}{2} \log \frac{1}{[Cl^-]^2}$$

$$E = E^\circ + 0.0591 \log [Cl^-]$$

Thus, *E* increases as $[Cl^-]$ increases.

67. (*d*) $E^\circ_{calomel} + E^\circ_X = 0.10$

$$E^\circ_X = 0.344 \text{ V}$$

Since, $E^\circ_{SHE} = 0.00$ V

Hence, E°_X (w.r.t) = 0.344 V

68. (*a*) At LHS $\underset{(C_1)}{Cl^-} \longrightarrow \frac{1}{2} Cl_2 + e^-$; $E^\circ = x$

At RHS $\frac{1}{2} Cl_2 + e^- \longrightarrow \underset{(C_2)}{Cl^-}$; $E^\circ = -x$

$$\therefore \quad Cl^-(C_1) \longrightarrow Cl^-(C_2)$$

$$\therefore \quad K = \frac{C_2}{C_1}, \quad E^\circ_{cell} = 0$$

$$\therefore \quad E = 0 - 0.0591 \log \frac{C_2}{C_1} = 0.0591 \log \left(\frac{C_1}{C_2}\right)$$

Cell reaction is spontaneous if $C_1 > C_2$ and thus, $E > 0$.

69. (*c*) At LHS $2Cl^-(aq) \longrightarrow \underset{p_1}{Cl_2(g)} + 2e^-$

At RHS $\underset{p_2}{Cl_2(g)} + 2e^- \longrightarrow 2Cl^-(aq)$

$$\underset{p_2}{Cl_2(g)} \longrightarrow \underset{p_1}{Cl_2(g)}$$

$$K = \frac{p_1}{p_2}$$

$$E = E^\circ_{cell} - \frac{0.0591}{2} \log \frac{p_1}{p_2}$$

$$= 0 + \frac{0.0591}{2} \log \frac{p_2}{p_1}$$

To make $E > 0$, $p_2 > p_1$

71. (*d*) $Pb(s) \rightleftharpoons Pb^{2+}(aq) + 2e^-$

$$Hg_2^{2+}(aq) + 2e^- \longrightarrow 2Hg(l)$$

$$Hg_2^{2+}(aq) + Pb(s) \longrightarrow Pb^{2+}(aq) + 2Hg(l)$$

$$\therefore \quad K = \frac{[Pb^{2+}]}{[Hg_2^{2+}]}$$

$[Pb^{2+}]$ in LHS is from $PbSO_4$

$$\therefore \quad [Pb^{2+}] = \sqrt{K_{sp}\ (PbSO_4)} = \sqrt{2 \times 10^{-8}}$$

$$= 1.41 \times 10^{-4} \text{ M}$$

$[Hg_2^{2+}]$ in RHS is from Hg_2SO_4

$$\therefore \quad [Hg_2^{2+}] = \sqrt{K_{sp}\ (Hg_2SO_4)}$$

$$= \sqrt{1 \times 10^{-6}} = 1 \times 10^{-3} \text{ M}$$

$$\therefore \quad K = \frac{1.41 \times 10^{-4}}{1 \times 10^{-3}} = 1.41 \times 10^{-1} \text{ M}$$

$$\therefore \quad E = E^\circ - \frac{0.0591}{2} \log 1.41 \times 10^{-1}$$

$$= 0.92 + 0.025 = 0.95 \text{ V}$$

72. (*b*)

$\times 2\ [Cu^+ \longrightarrow Cu^{2+} + e^-$ $\quad E^\circ = -0.15$ V

$Cu^{2+} + 2e^- \longrightarrow Cu$ $\quad E^\circ = 0.34$ V

$Cu^+ \longrightarrow Cu^{2+} + Cu$ $\quad E^\circ = 0.19$ V

In aqueous solution, Cu^+ disproportionates to Cu^{2+} and Cu Thus, Cu^+ is not stable but Cu^{2+} is stable.

73. (**a**) $H_2O_2 + 2H^+ + 2Fe^{2+} \longrightarrow 2Fe^{3+} + 2H_2O$

$$E^\circ_{cell} = 1.77 + 0.771 = 2.541 \text{ V}$$

74. (**a**) $2MnO_4^- + 3Mn^{2+} + 2H_2O \longrightarrow 5MnO_2 + 4H^+$;

$$E^\circ = 0.47 \text{ V}$$

Thus, cell reaction in which Mn^{2+} on reaction with MnO_4^- forms MnO_2 in acidic medium.

77. (*b*) Reducing power of an element

$$\propto \frac{1}{\text{Standard reduction potential}}$$

Here, $E^\circ_{M^{2+}/M}$ values of the given metals are as,

Metals	Ni	Zn	Mg	Ca
E° (V)	−0.25	−0.76	−2.36	−2.87

$\longrightarrow$ Reducing power

Thus, the correct order of increasing reducing power of the given metal is, Ni < Zn < Mg < Ca.

78. (*d*) $Cu + 2H^+(\text{dil. } H_2SO_4) \longrightarrow Cu^{2+} + H_2$

$$E^\circ_{cell} = E^\circ_{Cu/Cu^{2+}} + E^\circ_{SHE} = -0.34 \text{ V}$$

Thus, (a) is not feasible

$$Cu + SO_4^{2-} + 4H^+ \longrightarrow Cu^{2+} + SO_2 + 2H_2O$$

$$E^\circ_{cell} = -0.34 + 1.17 = 0.83 \text{ V}$$

$$E^\circ_{cell} > 0$$

Thus, (b) is feasible.

Similarly, (c) is feasible.

79. (*b*) By Gibbs Helmholtz equation

$$\Delta G = \Delta H + T\left[\frac{d(\Delta G)}{dT}\right]$$

also, $\Delta G = \Delta H - T\Delta S$

$$\therefore \quad \Delta S = -\left[\frac{d(\Delta G)}{dT}\right] = \frac{-d(-nFE)}{dT} = nF\left(\frac{dE}{dT}\right)$$

$$= 2 \times 96500 \times \frac{(0.48 - 0.46)}{310 - 300}$$

$$= 386 \text{ JK}^{-1}$$

80. (*c*) Temperature coefficient $= \frac{dE}{dT} = \frac{0.02}{10} = 0.002 \text{ VK}^{-1}$

81. (*d*) $2H_2O + 2e^- \longrightarrow H_2 + 2OH^-; \quad E^\circ = -0.8277 \text{ V}$

$H_2 \longrightarrow 2H^+ + 2e^-; \quad E^\circ = 0.00 \text{ V}$

$\therefore \quad 2H_2O \rightleftharpoons 2H^+ + 2OH^-; \quad E^\circ = -0.8277 \text{ V}$

$$E = E^\circ - \frac{0.0591}{2}\log [H^+]^2 [OH^-]^2$$

At equilibrium $E = 0$

$$\therefore \quad E^\circ = \frac{0.0591}{2}\log [H^+]^2 [OH^-]^2$$

$$-0.8277 = 0.0591 \log [H^+][OH^-]$$

$$-0.8277 = 0.0591 \log K_w$$

$$\therefore \quad K_w = 1 \times 10^{-14}$$

82. (*a*) pH = 14, pOH = 0

$\therefore \quad [OH^-] = 1 \text{ M}$

$$K_{sp}[Al(OH)_3] = 1.0 \times 10^{-33}$$

$$[Al^{3+}][OH^-]^3 = 1 \times 10^{-33}$$

$$\therefore \quad [Al^{3+}] = 1 \times 10^{-33} \text{ M}$$

$$Al^{3+}(aq) + 3e^- \longrightarrow Al(s)$$

$$K = \frac{1}{[Al^{3+}]} = 1 \times 10^{33}$$

$$\therefore \quad E = E^\circ - \frac{0.0591}{3}\log K$$

$$= -1.66 - \frac{0.0591}{3}\log 1 \times 10^{33} = -2.31 \text{ V}$$

83. (*c*)

	E°
$Pb \longrightarrow Pb^{2+} + 2e^-$	+ 0.127 V
$2Cu^+ + 2e^- \longrightarrow Cu$	+ 0.518 V
$2Cu^+ + Pb \longrightarrow Pb^{2+} + Cu$	+ 0.645 V

Thus, (a) and (b) are true.

84. (*c*) $K = \frac{1}{p_{O_2} \cdot [H^+]^4} = \frac{1}{1 \times (10^{-7})^4} = 1 \times 10^{28}$

$$E = E^\circ - \frac{0.0591}{n}\log K$$

$$= 1.23 - \frac{0.0591}{4}\log 10^{28} = 0.8163 \text{ V}$$

100. (*c*) Amount of zinc = 3.048 g

$$Zn^{2+} + 2e^- \longrightarrow Zn$$

$$w = zit$$

where, z = electrochemical equivalent $\left(= \frac{\text{atomic weight}}{\text{electrons} \times 96500}\right)$

i = current in amperes

t = time in seconds

$$3.048 = \frac{A}{2 \times 96500} \times 5 \times 30 \times 60$$

$$A = 65.36 \text{ g mol}^{-1}$$

$\therefore$ Equivalent weight $= \frac{A}{2} = 32.68$ g equivalent^{-1}

101. (*a*) $Al^{3+} + 3e^- \longrightarrow Al$

$$w = zit$$

$$100 = \frac{27 \times 125 \times t}{3 \times 96500}$$

$$t = 8578 \text{ s} = 143 \text{ min}$$

102. (*b*) Number of moles of Ag $= \frac{107.9}{107.9} = 1$

Number of Ag atoms $= 1 \times N_0$ (where, N_0 is the Avogadro's number)

Total charge $= N_0 \times 1.6 \times 10^{-19}$ C

$\therefore N_0 \times 1.6 \times 10^{-19} = 96500$ (charge carried by 1 mole of electrons)

$$\therefore \quad N_0 = \frac{96500}{1.6 \times 10^{-19}} = 6.03 \times 10^{23} \text{ mol}^{-1}$$

103. (*c*) $H_2O(l) \longrightarrow H_2(g) + 1/2\, O_2(g)$

1 mol; 0.5 mol
0.5 g = 0.25 mol; 0.125 mol = 4 g

Alternately $2H^+ + 2e^- \longrightarrow H_2$

Equivalent weight of $H_2 = \frac{2}{2} = 1$

$$2O^{2-} \longrightarrow O_2 + 4e^-$$

Equivalent weight of $O_2 = \frac{32}{4} = 8$

By Faraday's second law of electrolysis

$$\frac{\text{weight of } O_2}{\text{weight of } H_2} = \frac{\text{equivalent weight of } O_2}{\text{equivalent weight of } H_2}$$

$$\text{weight of } O_2 = \frac{8 \times 0.5}{1} = 4 \text{ g}$$

104. (*d*) A solution of $Ni(NO_3)_2$ is electrolysed between platinum electrodes using 0.1 Faraday electricity. It means that 0.1 equivalent of Ni^{2+} will be discharged.

Electrolysis of $Ni(NO_3)_2$ gives

$$Ni^{2+} + 2e^- \longrightarrow Ni (\text{Atomic mass of Ni} = 58.7)$$

Number of equivalents = Number of moles × number of electrons.

$$0.1 = \text{Number of moles} \times 2$$

$$\therefore \text{Number of moles of Ni} = \frac{0.1}{2} = 0.05$$

105. (*d*) $Al_2O_3 \longrightarrow 2Al + \frac{3}{2}O_2$

$$\text{Ratio of Al to } O_2 = 2 : \frac{3}{2} = 4 : 3$$

106. (*d*) The redox reaction is : $Zn(s) + Cu^{2+} \longrightarrow Zn^{2+} + Cu$

The Nernst equation is $E = E° - \frac{2.303RT}{2F}\log 10$

$$= 1.1 - \frac{2.303RT}{2F}$$

Also, $\Delta G = -nEF = -2F\left(1.1 - \frac{2.303RT}{2F}\right)$

$$= -2.2F + 2.303RT = 2.303RT - 2.2F$$

107. (*c*) **Reaction** **Number of moles formed by 1F**

Reaction	Number of moles formed by 1F
$Cu^{2+} + 2e^- \longrightarrow Cu$	$\frac{1}{2}$
$Al^{3+} + 3e^- \longrightarrow Al$	$\frac{1}{3}$
$Si^{4+} + 4e^- \longrightarrow Si$	$\frac{1}{4}$
Ratio	$\frac{1}{2} : \frac{1}{3} : \frac{1}{4}$
	$6 : 4 : 3$

108. (*d*) $\underset{+7}{MnO_4^-} \longrightarrow \underset{+4}{MnO_2}$

Thus, electrons gained = 3

Thus, 1 mole of MnO_4^- gives $= \frac{1}{3}$ mol $MnO_2 = 0.33$

109. (*c*) ∵ 96500 C current produce 12 g Mg

∴ 9.65 C current produce 1.2×10^{-3} g of Mg

$$= \frac{1.2 \times 10^{-3}}{24} = 5 \times 10^{-5} \text{ mol}$$

$$\underset{}{R—X} + \underset{5 \times 10^{-5}\text{ mol}}{Mg} \longrightarrow \underset{5 \times 10^{-5}\text{ mol}}{RMgX}$$

110. (*d*) Electrolysis of both KCl and NaCl liberates H_2 at the cathode and Cl_2 at the anode. The resulting solutions will be different.

111. (*a*) For the given cell,

$$Ag \mid Ag^+ \mid AgCl \mid Cl^{\ominus} \mid Cl_2, Pt$$

the cell reactions are as follows

At anode $Ag \longrightarrow Ag^+ + e^-$

At cathode $AgCl + e^- \longrightarrow Ag(s) + Cl^-$

Net cell reaction $AgCl \longrightarrow Ag^+ + Cl^-$

$$\therefore \quad \Delta G°_{\text{reaction}} = \Sigma\Delta G°_p - \Sigma\Delta G°_R$$

$$= (78 - 129) - (-109)$$

$$= +58 \text{ kJ/mol}$$

$$\Delta G° = -nFE°$$

$$58 \times 10^3 \, J = -1 \times 96500 \times E°_{\text{cell}}$$

$$E°_{\text{cell}} = \frac{-58 \times 1000}{96500}$$

$$= -0.6 \text{ V}$$

112. (*c*) $E_{\text{cell}} < E°_{\text{cell}} - \frac{0.0591}{2}\log\frac{[Zn^{2+}]}{[Cu^{2+}]}$

$$E_{\text{cell}} < E°_{\text{cell}}$$

$$\Rightarrow \quad [Zn^{2+}] > [Cu^{2+}]$$

113. (*a*) On comparison $\frac{d(\Delta G)}{dT} = -\Delta S$

$$-nF\left(\frac{dE_{\text{cell}}}{dT}\right) = -\Delta S$$

$$\frac{dE_{\text{cell}}}{dT} = \frac{\Delta S}{nF}$$

114. (*b*) $E_{\text{cell}} = E°_{\text{cell}} - \frac{0.0591}{2}\log\frac{|Zn^{2+}|}{|Cu^{2+}|}$

from graph $OA = E°_{\text{cell}} = 1.10$ V

If $\frac{[Zn^{2+}]}{[Cu^{2+}]} = 10^{-2}$ M

then $E_{\text{cell}} = 1.1591$ V

115. (*c*) In this electrode

$[A] = [B]$ in quinhydrone electrode

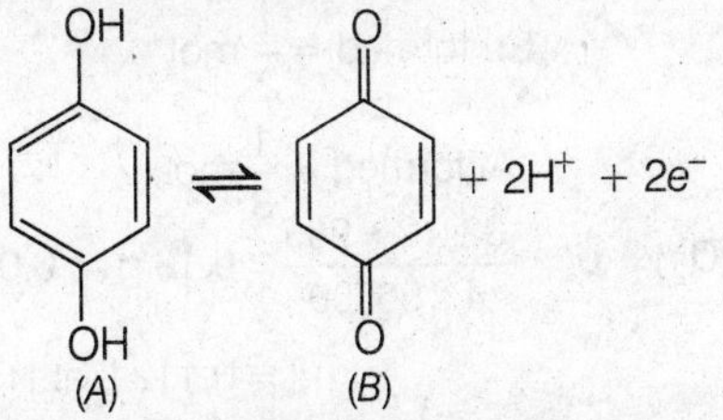

(*A*) (*B*)

Hence, $Q = [H^+]^2$

$$E = E° - \frac{0.0591}{2}\log[H^+]^2$$

$$= E° - 0.0591 \log [H^+]$$

$$= E° + 0.0591 \text{ pH}$$

$$= 1.30 + 0.0591 \times 2 \approx 1.42 \text{ V}$$

116. (c) $E_{cell} - E°_{cell} = -\frac{0.0591}{2}\log\frac{[Zn^{2+}]}{[Cu^{2+}]} = -\frac{0.06}{2}\log 10^4$

$= -0.12$ V

117. (c) Reducing nature of Mg > Cu > Hg > Ag. Thus, order of deposition will be Ag, Hg, Cu, Mg will remain in the ionic state $[Mg^{2+}]$

118. (c) $E = E° + \frac{0.0591}{1}\log\frac{[Ag^+]_R}{[Ag^+]_L}$

$= 0 + 0.0591 \log 2 = 0.0591 \times 0.301$ V

After current is passed $[Ag^+]_R = 1$ M

$[Ag^+]_L = 0.5$ M

Hence, no change in emf

120. (c) Reducing nature of Mg > Cu > Hg > Au

121. (b) The relationship between standard electrode potential ($E°$) and equilibrium constant (K) of the cell reaction,

$$Zn(s) + Cu^{2+}(aq) \rightleftharpoons Zn^{2+}(aq) + Cu(s)$$

can be expressed as, $E° = \frac{RT}{nF}\ln K \Rightarrow K = e^{nFE°/RT}$

Given, $n = 2$, $F = 96000$ C mol^{-1}, $E° = 2$ V, $R = 8$ JK^{-1}mol^{-1}

$T = 300$ K

$\therefore \quad K = e^{\frac{2 \times 96000 \times 2}{8 \times 300}} = e^{160}$

122. (a) $E = E° + \frac{0.0591}{5}\log (2)^8$

$E - E° = \frac{0.0591}{5} \times 8 \log 2 = 0.02846$ V $= 28.46$ mV

124. (b) $Cl^- \longrightarrow \frac{1}{2}Cl_2 + e^-$

0.355 g Cl^- = 0.01 mol of Cl^- = 0.01 N_0

125. (b)

$Ag^+ + e^- \longrightarrow Ag$

$Cu^{2+} + 2e^- \longrightarrow Cu$

$Al^{3+} + 3e^- \longrightarrow Al$

Ag formed = 1 mol

Cu formed $= \frac{1}{2}$ mol

Al formed $= \frac{1}{3}$ mol

126. (a) $w(O_2) = zit = \frac{32 \times 2 \times 965}{4 \times 96500} = 0.16$ g $= 0.005$ mol

$= 0.112$ L at NTP

127. (d) As in Q. (126). 0.224 cc $O_2 = 3.2 \times 10^{-4}$ g

$i = \frac{w}{zt} = \frac{3.2 \times 10^{-4} \times 96500 \times 4}{2 \times 1} = 3.86$ A

128. (b) $w = \frac{\text{Atomic wt.}}{96500 \times \text{Electron}} \times i \times t$

Atomic weight = 55

129. (a) Rate of flow of electrons per second $= \frac{0.965}{96500} N_0$

130. (d)

$2H^+ + 2e^- \longrightarrow H_2$

$Al^{3+} + 3e^- \longrightarrow Al$

$\frac{w(H_2)}{w(Al)} = \frac{E(H_2)}{E(Al)} = \frac{1}{9}$

$w(H_2) = 4.5 \times \frac{1}{9} = 0.5$ g

$= \frac{1}{4}$ mol H_2

$= 5.6$ L H_2 at STP

131. (c) Given that, $i = 100$ amp. also, 27.66 g of diborane (B_2H_6)

Molecular mass of $B_2H_6 = 10.8 \times 2 + 6 = 27.6$

Number of moles of B_2H_6 in 27.66 g

$= \frac{\text{Given mass}}{\text{Molar mass}} = \frac{27.66}{27.6} \approx 1$

Now consider the equation

$$B_2H_6 + 3O_2 \longrightarrow B_2O_3 + 3H_2O$$

From the equation we can interpret that 3 moles of oxygen is required to burn 1 mole (i.e. 27.6 g) B_2H_6 completely.

Also consider the electrolysis reaction of water i.e.

$$H_2O \rightleftharpoons 2H^+ + O^{--}$$

$$2H^+ \xrightarrow[\text{Cathode}]{+2e^-} 2H \longrightarrow H_2\uparrow$$

$$O^{--} \xrightarrow[-2e^{-1}]{\text{Anode}} O \xrightarrow[\text{atoms}]{\text{2 such}} O_2\uparrow$$

From the above equation it can be easily interpreted that in electrolysis of water for the production of 1 mole of oxygen from 1 mole of H_2O at anode 4 moles electrons are required.

Likewise for the production of 3 moles of O_2 12(3 × 4) moles of electrons will be needed.

So, the total amount of charge required to produce 3 moles of oxygen will be 12 × F or 12 × 96500

We know $\quad Q = it$

So, $12 \times 96500 = 100 \times t$ in seconds

or $\frac{12 \times 96500}{100 \times 3600} = t$ in hours = 32 hours

132. (b) At LHS there is formation of H^+ ion and in RHS OH^- ion

LHS $\quad NH_4OH + H^+ \longrightarrow NH_4^+ + H_2O$

RHS $\quad NH_4^+ + OH^- \longrightarrow NH_4OH$

At LHS concentration of NH_4OH decreases and that of NH_4^+ increases and reverse at RHS

$$pOH = pK_b + \log\frac{[NH_4^+]}{[NH_4OH]}$$

Hence, pOH at LHS increase hence pH decreases and that of RHS increases.

133. (a) $2H_2O + 2e^- \longrightarrow H_2 + 2OH^-$ ...(i)

$2H_2O \longrightarrow O_2 + 4H^+ + 4e^-$ ...(ii)

From (i) 1 mol of H_2 = 22.4 L H_2 is obtained by 2 units

$$x \text{ L of } H_2 = \frac{2x}{22.4} \text{ units costing ₹} x$$

Thus, 1 unit costs = ₹ 11.2

From (ii) 22.4 L at NTP costs = 4 units = 4 × 11.2₹

x L costs $= 2x$

136. (*c*) NaCl and KCl are strong electrolytes. So, the study of their molar conductances (λ_m) can be experimentally verified by Debye-Huckel Onsagar equation,

$$\Lambda_m^c = \Lambda_m^0 - B\sqrt{C}$$

Λ_m^c = molar conductance at concentration.

Λ_m^0 = molar conductance at infinite dilution. i.e. $C \to 0$

B = Debye-Huckel Onsagar constant.

For (both NaCl and KCl) a strong binary electrolyte like *AB*, the nature of the plot of Λ_m *vs* $\sqrt{C}$ will be

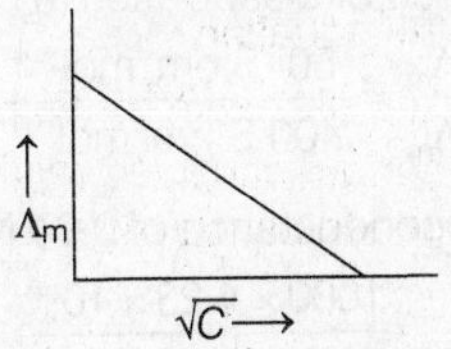

Size of $Na^{\oplus}$ is being smaller than $K^{\oplus}$ and $Na^{\oplus}$ will remain in more hydrated state, i.e. larger sized in aqueous solution. As a result, ionic mobility as well as ionic conductance of $Na^{\oplus}$ (or NaCl as $Cl^{\ominus}$ is common to NaCl and KCl) will be lower than $K^{\oplus}$ (or KCl). Thus, the plot of Λ_m *vs* $\sqrt{C}$ for NaCl and KCl is as follows :

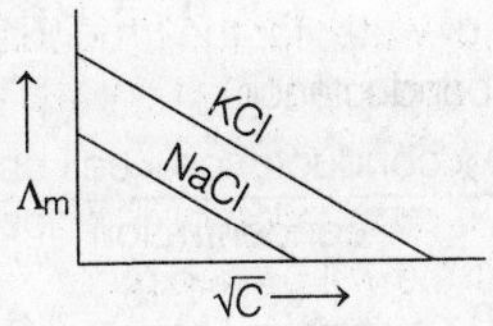

137. (*d*) The explanation of statements (S_1 and S_2) are as follows :

In conductivity cell, conductivity (κ) is equal to the sum of ionic conductances (c), of an electrolytic solution present is unit volume of the solution enclosed by two electrodes of unit area ($a \neq 1$) separated by a unit length ($l = 1$).

$$\kappa = c \times \frac{l}{a} \Rightarrow \kappa = c \text{ when } l = 1, a = 1$$

So, with decrease in the concentration of electrolyte, number of ions in the given unit volume also decreases, i.e. κ [conductivity] also decreases.

Thus, statement S_1 is wrong. S_2 : Molar conductivity (λ_m) is defined as the conducting power of all the ions present in a solution containing 1 mole of an electrolyte.

$$\lambda_m = \kappa \times V_{mL} = \kappa \times \frac{1000}{M}$$

where, V_{mL} = volume in mL containing 1 mole of electrolyte

m = molar concentration (mol/L)

So, in a conductivity cell, $\lambda_m \propto \frac{1}{M}$

i.e. molar conductivity increases with decrease in the concentration (M) of electrolyte.

Thus, statement S_2 is correct.

139. (*a*) $x = \frac{\Lambda_c}{\Lambda_0} = \frac{10}{200} = 0.05$

140. (*b*) $\lambda_0(BaSO_4) = \frac{1000 \times \text{sp. conductance}}{\text{conc. (Normality)}}$

$$\text{Normality} = \frac{1000 \times 8 \times 10^{-5}}{400}$$

$$\therefore \quad \text{Molarity} = \frac{\text{normality}}{2} = 10^{-4} \text{M}$$

$$\therefore \quad K_{sp} = S^2 = 10^{-8} \text{ M}^2$$

Note : In K_{sp}, S is solubility in mol L^{-1} (molarity)

143. (*d*) 1 L of 1 M $CuSO_4$ = 1 mol of Cu^{2+}

$$Cu^{2+} + 2e^- \longrightarrow Cu$$

2 F of electricity will convert dil Cu^{2+} into Cu, hence $[CuSO_4] = 0$

149. (*d*) $\Delta G° = \Delta G_f(ZnO) - \Delta G_f(Ag_2O)$

$= -318.30 + 11.21 = -307.09$ kJ

$= -307.09 \times 10^3$ J

$$\Delta G° = -nFE°_{cell}$$

$$\therefore \quad -307.09 \times 10^3 = -2 \times 96500 \times E°_{cell}$$

$$\therefore \quad E°_{cell} = 1.591 \text{ V}$$

153. (*c*)

Cell: Anode (A) Cathode (C)	$E°_{cell}$ (SRP) = $E°_C - E°_A$	$E°_{cell}$ free $\bar{e}$ transfer
Zn Ag 1. $[Zn + 2Ag^+ \to Zn^{2+} + 2Ag]$	0.80 − (−0.76) = + 1.56 V for $2e^-$	$+\frac{1.56}{2} = +0.78$ V
Zn Fe 2. $[Zn + Fe^{2+} \to Zn^{2+} + Fe]$	− 0.44 − (− 0.76) = + 0.32 V for $2e^-$	$+\frac{0.32}{2} = +0.16$ V
Zn Au 3. $[3Zn + 2Au^{3+} \to 3Zn^{2+} + 2Au]$	1.40 − (−0.76) = + 2.4 V for $6e^-$	$+\frac{2.16}{6} = +0.36$ V
Zn Fe 4. $[3Zn + 2Fe^{3+} \to Zn^{2+} + 2Fe^{2+}]$	0.77 − (−0.76) = + 1.53 V for $2e^-$	$+\frac{1.53}{2} = +0.765$ V

154. (*b*) Since, CH_3COOH is a weak acid and emf is dependent on pH, Also pH of 0.1 M HCl < pH of 0.1 M CH_3COOH.

155. (*a*) According to Nernst equation,

$$E_{cell} = E°_{cell} - \frac{2.303\,RT}{nF}\log Q$$

Given, $\frac{2.303\,RT}{F} = 0.059\,V$

$\therefore$ $$E_{cell} = E°_{cell} - \frac{0.059}{n}\log Q$$

At equilibrium, $E_{cell} = 0$

$$E°_{cell} = \frac{0.059}{n}\log K_C$$

For the given reaction, $n = 2$

Also, $K_C = 10 \times 10^{15}$ [given]

$\therefore$ $$E°_{cell} = \frac{0.059}{2}\log(10 \times 10^{15}) = 0.472\,V \approx 0.473\,V$$

156. (*b*) Specific conductance = conductance × cell constant

$$0.012 = \frac{1}{55} \times \text{cell constant}$$

$\therefore$ Cell constant = $0.66\,cm^{-1}$

157. (*c*) $Cu^+ \longrightarrow Cu^{2+} + Cu$

Oxidation

Reduction

We want $E°_{oxidation}$ $(= E°_{Cu^+/Cu^{2+}})$

and $E°_{reduction}$ $(= E°_{Cu^+/Cu})$

$$E°_{Cu^+/Cu^{2+}} = -E°_{Cu^{2+}/Cu^+} = -0.15\,V \text{ (given)}$$

$$E°_{Cu^{2+}/Cu} = +0.34\,V$$

$Cu^{2+} + 2e^- \longrightarrow Cu$		$E_1° = 0.34\,V$	$n_1 = 2$
$Cu^+ \longrightarrow Cu^{2+} + e^-$		$E_2° = -0.15\,V$	$n_2 = 1$
$Cu^+ + e^- \longrightarrow Cu$		$E_3° = ?$	$n_3 = 1$

$$\Delta G_3° = \Delta G_1° + \Delta G_2°$$

$$-n_3E_3° = -n_1E_1° - n_2E_2°$$

$\therefore$ $$E_3° = \frac{n_1E_1° + n_2E_2°}{n_3}$$

$$= \frac{2 \times 0.34 + 1(-0.15)}{1}$$

$\therefore$ $$E°_{Cu^+/Cu} = 0.53\,V$$

$Cu^+ \longrightarrow Cu^{2+} + e^-$;	$E° = -0.15\,V$
$Cu^+ + e^- \longrightarrow Cu$;	$E° = 0.53\,V$
$2Cu^+ \longrightarrow Cu^{2+} + Cu$	$E° = 0.38\,V$

158. (*d*) According to Kohlrausch's law, the molar conductivity of *HA* at infinite dilution is given as,

$$\Lambda°_m(HA) = [\Lambda°_m(H^+) + \Lambda°_m(Cl^-)] + [\Lambda°_m(Na^+) + \Lambda°_m(A^-)] - [\Lambda°_m(Na^+) + \Lambda°_m(Cl^-)]$$

$$= 425.9 + 100.5 - 126.4$$

$$= 400\,S\,cm^2\,mol^{-1}$$

Also, molar conductivity at given concentration is given as,

$$\Lambda_m = \frac{1000 \times \kappa}{M}$$

Given, κ = conductivity $\Rightarrow 5 \times 10^{-5}\,S\,cm^{-1}$

M = Molarity $\Rightarrow$ 0.001 M

$\therefore$ $$\Lambda_m = \frac{1000 \times 5 \times 10^{-5}\,S\,cm^{-1}}{10^{-3}\,M} = 50\,S\,cm^2\,mol^{-1}$$

Therefore, degree of dissociation (α), of *HA* is,

$$\alpha = \frac{\Lambda_m}{\Lambda°_m} = \frac{50\,S\,cm^2 mol^{-1}}{400\,S\,cm^2 mol^{-1}} = 0.125$$

159. (*d*) Equivalent conductance of 0.04 N weak acid

$$= \frac{1000 \times 4.23 \times 10^{-4}}{0.04}$$

$$= 10.575\,\Omega^{-1}cm^2\,equiv^{-1}$$

Also, x (degree of ionisation) $= \frac{\Lambda_c}{\Lambda_\infty}$

$$0.0512 = \frac{10.575}{\Lambda_\infty}$$

$$\Lambda_\infty = 172.79\,\Omega^{-1}\,cm^2\,equiv^{-1}$$

160. (*b*) Equivalent conductance

$$= \frac{1000 \times \text{conductance} \times \text{cell constant}}{\text{concentration}}$$

$$= 1000 \times \frac{1}{2.5 \times 10^3} \times \frac{1.15}{0.1} = 4.6$$

163. (*a*) $$E_1 = E_1° - \frac{0.0591}{5}\log\frac{[Fe^{2+}]}{[Fe^{3+}]}$$

$$E_2 = E_2° - \frac{0.0591}{5}\log\frac{[Mn^{2+}]}{[MnO_4^-][H^+]^8}$$

$E_1 = E_2 = E_{equiv}$ at equivalent point

$$6E_{equiv} = (E_1° + 5E_2°) - 0.0591\log\frac{[Fe^{2+}][Mn^{2+}]}{[MnO_4^-][Fe^{3+}][H^+]^8}$$

Since $\frac{[Fe^{2+}][Mn^{2+}]}{[MnO_4^-][Fe^{3+}]} = 1$ at equivalent point

$\therefore$ $$E_{equiv} = \left(\frac{E_1° + 5E_2°}{6}\right) - 0.08\,pH$$

13

Surface Chemistry

Objective Questions Type I [Only one correct option]

In each of the questions below, four choices are given of which only one is correct.

1. Ink is adsorbed on the chalk. In this ink and chalk are respectively

(a) adsorbate, adsorbent (b) adsorbent, adsorbate
(c) both adsorbent (d) both adsorbate

2. Which are not purely surface phenomena?

(a) Viscosity, surface tension (b) Adsorption, absorption
(c) Absorption, viscosity (d) Adsorption, viscosity

3. There are certain properties related to adsorption

I. reversible.
II. formation of unimolecular layer.
III. low heat of adsorption.
IV. occurs at low temperature and decreases with increasing temperature.

Which of the above properties are for physical adsorption?

(a) I, II and III (b) I, III and IV
(c) II, III and IV (d) I and III

4. Following is the variation of physical adsorption with temperature

(a)
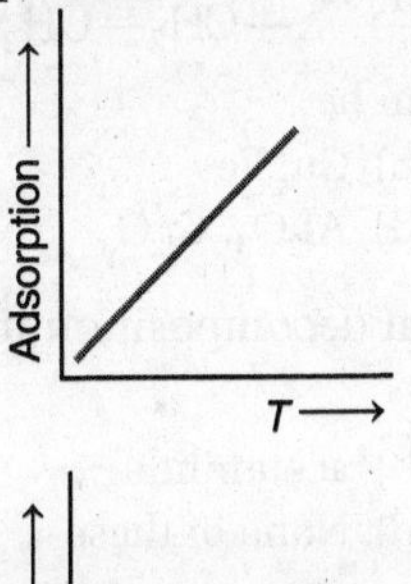

(b)
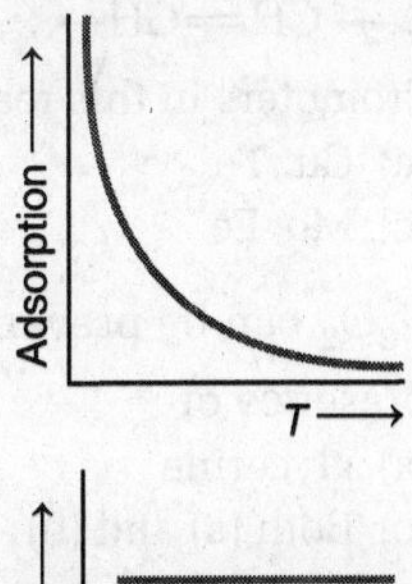

(c)
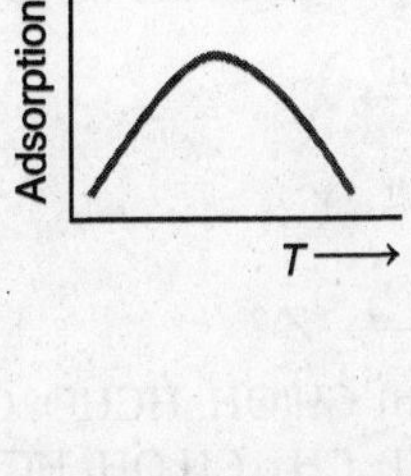

(d)
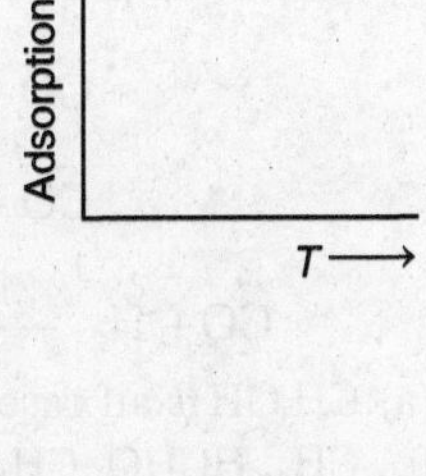

5. Select the correct statement(s).

(a) Residual force-field on a surface is responsible for adsorption
(b) Rate of adsorption is very rapid in the beginning but decreases until equilibrium is attained
(c) Desorption and adsorption are two opposite terms
(d) All of the above are correct statements

6. Which gas is adsorbed to maximum extent on the given surface?

(a) NH_3
(b) H_2
(c) N_2
(d) O_2

7. The incorrect statements below regarding colloidal solutions is **[JEE Main 2021, March]**

(a) a colloidal solution shows colligative properties.
(b) an ordinary filter paper can stop the flow of colloidal particles
(c) the flocculating power of Al^{3+} is more than that of Na^+
(d) a colloidal solution shows Brownian motion of colloidal particles

8. Adsorption is

(a) an exothermic process hence, increase in temperature decreases adsorption in cases where van der Waals' forces exist between adsorbate and adsorbent
(b) an endothermic process hence, increase in temperature increases adsorption
(c) an exothermic process hence, increase in temperature increases adsorption
(d) None of the above

9. Graph between $\log\left(\frac{x}{m}\right)$ and $\log p$ is a straight line at angle 45° with intercept OA as shown. Hence, $\left(\frac{x}{m}\right)$ at a pressure of 0.2 atm is

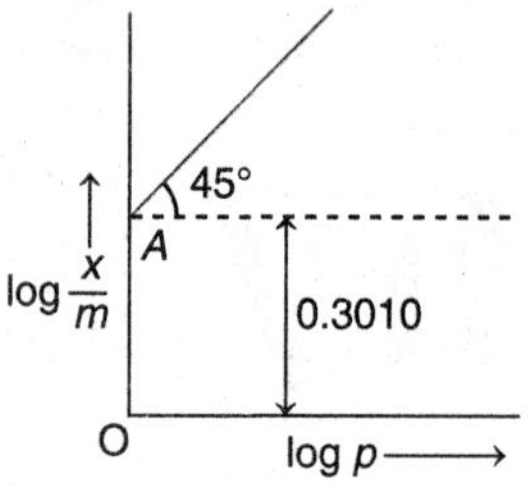

(a) 0.2 (b) 0.4 (c) 0.6 (d) 0.8

10. In the following isotherm

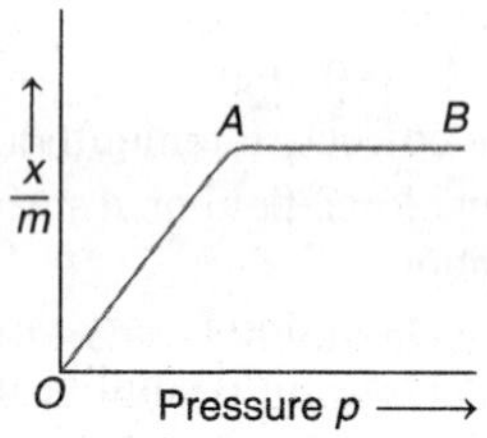

(a) $\frac{x}{m} \propto p^0$ when point A is reached

(b) desorption may start along AB

(c) $\frac{x}{m} \propto p^{1/n}$ along OA

(d) All of the above are correct

11. When saturation is attained in terms of adsorption, variation of $\left(\frac{x}{m}\right)$ and C (concentration) is given by the portion of the isotherm.

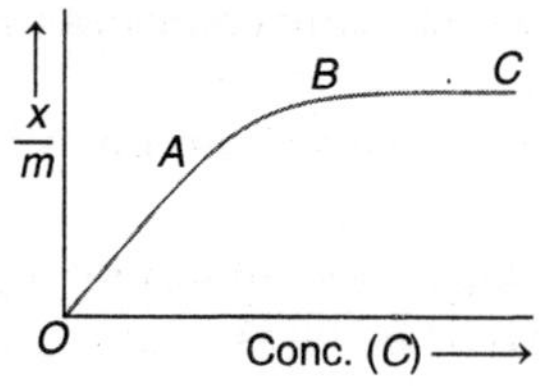

(a) OA (b) OB (c) AB (d) BC

12. Lake test of aluminium ion is based on adsorption of blue litmus on

(a) solid surface of Al (b) solid surface of $Al(OH)_3$

(c) solid surface of Al_2O_3 (d) solid surface of $AlCl_3$

13. When a litmus solution is shaken with a piece of charcoal

(a) it is decolourised (b) it turns red to blue

(c) it turns blue to red (d) None of these

14. 50 mL of 1 M oxalic acid (molar mass = 126) is shaken with 0.5 g of wood charcoal. The final concentration of the solution after adsorption is 0.5 M. What is the amount of oxalic acid adsorbed per gram of carbon?

(a) 3.15 (b) 1.575

(c) 6.30 (d) 12.60

15. For the adsorption of solution on a solid surface $\frac{x}{m} = kC^{1/n}$. Adsorption isotherm of $\log\left(\frac{x}{m}\right)$ and $\log C$ was found of the type

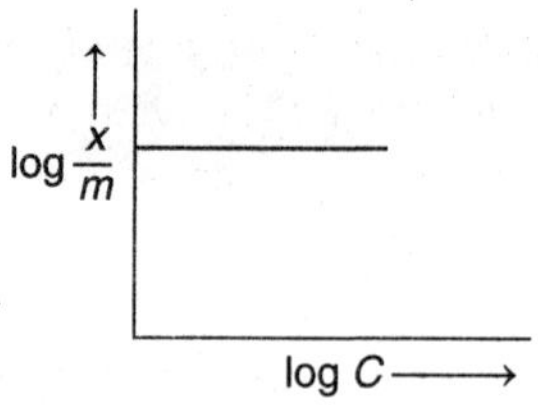

This is when

(a) $C = 0$ (b) $\frac{1}{n} = 0$

(c) $C =$ constant (d) $C = 2$ M

16. In the following reactions, catalysts used have been shown above the arrow. Which are not the suitable catalysts ?

I. $2H_2O_2(aq) \xrightarrow{I^-(aq)} 2H_2O(l) + O_2(g)$

II. $HCl\ (g) + O_2(g) \xrightarrow{NO(g)} 2H_2O(l) + Cl_2(g)$

III. $2H_2(g) + O_2(g) \xrightarrow{MnO_2} 2H_2O(l)$

(a) I and II (b) II and III

(c) I and III (d) I, II and III

17. Hydrolysis of ester ($RCOOR'$) is slow initially but becomes fast as reaction proceeds. It is due to formation of .... which catalyses the reaction.

(a) H_2O (b) $RCOOH$

(c) $R'OH$ (d) $RCOO^-$

18. $\ldots—CH{=}CH—\ldots + H_2 \xrightarrow{Ni} \ldots—CH_2—CH_2—\ldots$

Promoters in this reaction can be

(a) Cu, Te (b) Cu, Fe

(c) Mo, Fe (d) Al_2O_3, Cr_2O_3

19. H_2O_2 can be prevented from decomposition in presence of

(a) glycerine (b) acetanilide

(c) Both (a) and (b) (d) None of these

20. What are the products X, Y, Z (aliphatic class) in

$$CO + H_2 \xrightarrow{Ni} X$$

$$CO + H_2 \xrightarrow{Cu} Y$$

$$CO + H_2 \xrightarrow{ZnO + Cr_2O_3} Z ?$$

(a) CH_3OH is all cases (b) CH_3OH, HCHO, CH_4

(c) CH_4, HCHO, CH_3OH (d) CH_4, CH_3OH, HCHO

21. $RCOCl + H_2 \xrightarrow{\text{S in quinoline}} A$, A is
(a) RCH_2OH (b) $RCHO$
(c) $RCOOH$ (d) $RCOOR$

22. Equilibrium constant changes
(a) if some catalyst is added
(b) if temperature is changed
(c) if pressure is changed
(d) if concentration is changed

23. A catalyst accelerates the rate of reaction by
(a) decreasing energy of activation
(b) increasing Arrhenius constant
(c) increasing both
(d) decreasing both

24. Following reaction is catalysed by $Br^-(aq)$

$$2H_2O_2(aq) \longrightarrow 2H_2O(l) + O_2(g)$$

This is an example of
(a) homogeneous catalysis (b) heterogeneous catalysis
(c) Both (a) and (b) (d) None of the above

25. It is instructed that automobiles with catalytic converter must use unleaded gasolines because
(a) leaded gasolines may give more fumes
(b) surface of the catalyst is rendered ineffective by adsorption of lead
(c) automobiles with catalytic converter cannot run on leaded-gasolines
(d) unleaded-gasoline is cheaper

26. In the human body, enzyme that catalyses the reaction of CO_2 with H_2O is
(a) invertase (b) urease
(c) nitrogenase (d) carbonic anhydrate

27. Sorption is the term used when
(a) adsorption takes place (b) absorption takes place
(c) Both (a) and (b) (d) desorption takes place

28. Following are the events taking place to explain adsorption theory
I : desorption
II : diffusion of the reactants along the surface
III : adsorption of the reactants
IV : formation of the activated surface complex
These events are taking place in the following order
(a) I, II, III and IV (b) III, II, IV and I
(c) III, IV, I and II (d) IV, III, II and I

29. Following reaction is catalysed by MnO_2

$$2KClO_3 \xrightarrow{\Delta} 2KCl + 3O_2$$

If reaction mixture is plunged into water at the intermediate stage, sometime solution appears green. This indicates the formation of the intermediate
(a) KCl (b) $KMnO_4$
(c) K_2MnO_4 (d) Mn_2O_4

30. In the atmosphere, there is formation of ozone from oxygen.

$$3O_2 \longrightarrow 2O_3$$

This is catalysed by
(a) NO (b) N_2 (c) CO (d) sunlight

31. 'Lock-key' fit theory is for
(a) homogeneous catalysis (b) heterogeneous catalysis
(c) enzyme action (d) None of these

32. In lead-chamber process, NO is the catalyst

$$2SO_2 + O_2 \longrightarrow 2SO_3$$

Formation of the intermediate is indicated by
(a) brown coloured vapour
(b) green coloured vapour
(c) light yellow coloured vapour
(d) violet coloured vapour

33. Following are the terms about activity and selectivity.
I. Activity is the ability of catalysts to accelerate chemical reactions and selectivity is the ability of catalysts to direct reaction to yield particular products.
II. Activity is the ability of catalysts to direct reaction to yield particular products and selectivity is the ability of catalysts to accelerate chemical reactions.
Select the correct term.
(a) Only I
(b) Only II
(c) I and II
(d) None of the above

34. With respect to drug-enzyme interaction, identify the wrong statement **[JEE Main 2021, March]**
(a) Non-competitive inhibitor binds to the allosteric site
(b) Allosteric inhibitor changes the enzyme's active site
(c) Allosteric inhibitor competes with the enzyme's active site
(d) Competitive inhibitor binds to the enzyme's active site

35. The void space in zeolites forms more than 50% of the total volume which is occupied by
(a) silicates
(b) aluminates
(c) water molecules
(d) Na^+, Mg^{2+} and Ca^{3+} ions

36. ZSM-5 is one of the zeolite with formula
(a) $H_x[(AlO_2)_x \cdot (SiO_2)_{96-x}] \cdot 16H_2O$
(b) $Na_{56}[(AlO_2)_{56} \cdot (SiO_2)_{36}] \cdot 250H_2O$
(c) $Na_2Ca(AlO_2)_2(SiO_2)_4 \cdot 6H_2O$
(d) None of the above is correct

37. Zeolite can be used to soften water when
(a) Ca^{2+} or Mg^{2+} ions in zeolite are replaced by Na^+ ions in hard water

(b) Ca^{2+} ions in zeolite are replaced by Mg^{2+} ions in hard water
(c) Na^{+} ions in zeolite are replaced by Ca^{2+} and Mg^{2+} ions in hard water
(d) None of the above is correct

38. The aerosol is a kind of colloid in which **[JEE Main 2019, April]**
(a) gas is dispersed in liquid
(b) gas is dispersed in solid
(c) liquid is dispersed in water
(d) solid is dispersed in gas

39. Kraft temperature is the temperature **[JEE Main 2020, Sep.]**
(a) below which the aqueous solution of detergents starts freezing
(b) below which the formation of micelles takes place
(c) above which the aqueous solution of detergents starts boiling
(d) above which the formation of micelles takes place

40. The Tyndall effect is observed only when following conditions are satisfied **[JEE Main 2017]**
1. The diameter of the dispersed particles is much smaller than the wavelength of the light used.
2. The diameter of the dispersed particle is not much smaller than the wavelength of the light used.
3. The refractive indices of the dispersed phase and dispersion medium are almost similar in magnitude.
4. The refractive indices of the dispersed phase and dispersion medium differ greatly in magnitude.

(a) 1 and 4 (b) 2 and 4
(c) 1 and 3 (d) 2 and 3

41. Opal (mineral with liquid inclusion) is a
(a) gel (liquid dispersed in solid phase)
(b) solid sol (solid dispersed in solid phase)
(c) sol (solid dispersed in liquid)
(d) foam (gas dispersed in liquid)

42. Mayonnaise represents
(a) a sol (b) an aerosol
(c) a foam (d) an emulsion

43. Select the correct statement(s).
(a) A hydrophilic colloid is a colloid in which there is a strong attraction between the dispersed phase and water
(b) A hydrophobic colloid is a colloid in which there is a lack of attraction between the dispersed phase and water
(c) Hydrophobic sols are often formed when a solid crystallises rapidly from a chemical reaction or a supersaturated solution
(d) All of the above

44. Protein solutions are
(a) hydrophobic in nature (b) hydrophilic in nature
(c) Both (a) and (b) (d) None of these

45. A colloid of gold particles is
(a) hydrophobic in nature
(b) is a sol (of solid dispersed in water)
(c) Both (a) and (b)
(d) None of the above

46. Some of the properties given below are for colloidal sols.
I. Viscosity same as that of the medium.
II. Extensive hydration takes place.
III. Particles migrate either towards cathode or anode in an electric field.
IV. Particles cannot be detected even under ultra-microscope.

Select the properties which are true for lyophilic colloidal sols.
(a) I and II (b) III and IV (c) I and III (d) II and IV

47. 10 mL of 1 mM surfactant solution forms a monolayer covering 0.24 cm^2 on a polar substrate. If the polar head is approximated as a cube, what is its edge length? **[JEE Main 2019]**
(a) 2.0 pm (b) 0.1 nm (c) 1.0 pm (d) 2.0 nm

48. For a linear plot of $\log(x/m)$ *versus* $\log p$ in a Freundlich adsorption isotherm, which of the following statements is correct?
(k and n are constants) **[JEE Main 2016]**
(a) $1/n$ appears as the intercept
(b) Only $1/n$ appears as the slope
(c) $\log\left(\frac{1}{n}\right)$ appears as the intercept
(d) Both k and $1/n$ appear in the slope term

49. Molar conductivity (Λ_m) of aqueous solution of sodium stearate, which behaves as a strong electrolyte, is recorded at varying concentrations (C) of sodium stearate. Which one of the following plots provides the correct representation of micelle formation in the solution? **[JEE Advanced 2019]**
(critical micelle concentration (CMC) is marked with an arrow in the figures)

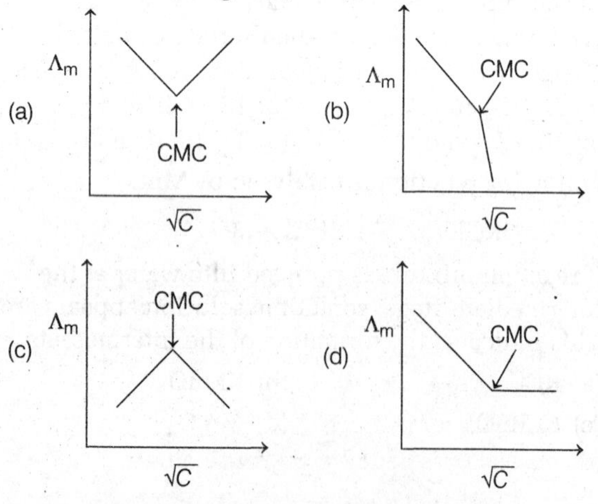

50. For the coagulation of a negative sol, the species below, that has the highest flocculating power is

(a) SO_4^{2-} (b) Ba^{2+} **[JEE Main 2021, March]**

(c) Na^+ (d) PO_4^{3-}

51. Which type of solutions is not filtrable through filter paper and parchment membrane both?

(a) True solutions and colloidal sol
(b) Colloidal sol and suspension
(c) True solution and suspension
(d) Suspension only

52. Select the correct statement(s).

(a) The process of dialysis is similar to osmosis, except that both solvent and small solute particles can pass through the semi-permeable dialysis membrane
(b) Proteins can be purified by dialysis
(c) Haemidialysis is used to cleanse the blood of patients whose kidneys have malfunctioned
(d) All of the above

53. Which is correct in case of van der Waals' adsorption?

(a) High temperature, high pressure
(b) Low temperature, high pressure
(c) Low temperature, low pressure
(d) High temperature, low pressure

54. Peptisation is

(a) conversion of a colloidal into precipitate form
(b) conversion of precipitate into colloidal sol
(c) conversion of metal into colloidal sol by passage of electric current
(d) conversion of colloidal sol into macromolecules

55. A mixture of gases O_2, H_2 and CO are taken in a closed vessel containing charcoal. The graph that represents the correct behaviour of pressure with time is **[JEE Main 2020, Jan.]**

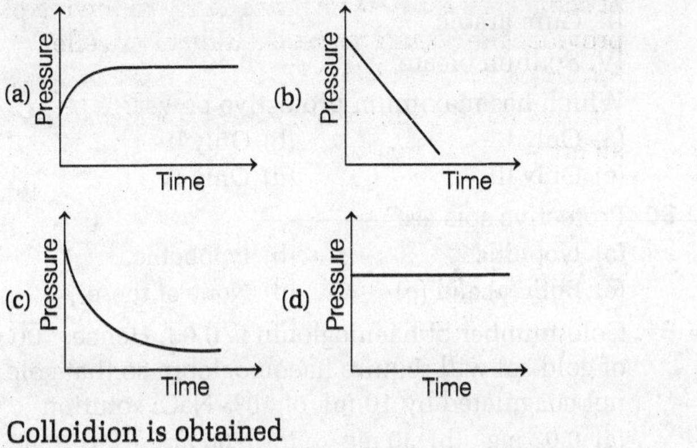

56. Colloidion is obtained

(a) when cellulose nitrate is peptised by organic solvents as ethanol
(b) when high electric current is passed between metal electrodes
(c) colloidal sol is heated
(d) *aq.* NaOH is added to cellulose nitrate

57. Haemidialysis is used to

(a) separate colloidal sol from water
(b) separate charged and uncharged particles
(c) cleanse the blood of patients whose kidneys have malfunctioned
(d) None of the above

58. Select the incorrect statement(s).

(a) Surface active agents like soaps and synthetic detergents are micelles
(b) Soaps are emulsifying agents
(c) $C_{17}H_{35}$ (hydrocarbon part) and —COO^- (carboxylate) part of stearate ion ($C_{17}H_{35}COO^-$) both are hydrophobic
(d) All the above are incorrect statements

59. Which part of the soap ($RCOO^-$) dissolves grease and forms micelle?

(a) *R* part (called tail of the anion)
(b) —COO^- part (called head of the anion)
(c) Both (a) and (b)
(d) None of the above

60. In multimolecular colloidal sols, atoms or molecules are held together by

(a) H-bonding
(b) van der Waals' forces
(c) ionic bonding
(d) polar covalent bonding

61. Select the correct statement(s) about phospholipids.

(a) In aqueous solution, they form micelles
(b) They form bilayers
(c) They are principal components of cell membranes
(d) All of the above are correct statements

62. Cleansing action of soap occurs because

(a) oil and grease can be absorbed into the hydrophobic centres of soap micelles and washed away
(b) oil and grease can be absorbed into hydrophilic centres of soap micelles and washed away
(c) oil and grease can be absorbed into both hydrophilic and hydrophobic centres but not washed away
(d) cleansing action is not related to micelles

63. Intensity of the scattered light depends on the difference between .... of dispersed phase and dispersion medium.

(a) densities (b) refractive indices
(c) viscosity (d) surface tension

64. Electro-osmosis is observed when

(a) dispersion medium begins to move in an electric field
(b) dispersed phase begins to move in an electric field
(c) in both (a) and (b)
(d) None of the above

65. Tyndall effect is not observed in
(a) suspension (b) starch sol
(c) gold sol (d) NaCl solution

66. Adsorption of a gas follows Freundlich adsorption isotherm. x is the mass of the gas adsorbed on mass m of the adsorbent. The plot of $\log \frac{x}{m}$ *versus* $\log p$ is shown in the given graph. $\frac{x}{m}$ is proportional to **[JEE Main 2019, April]**

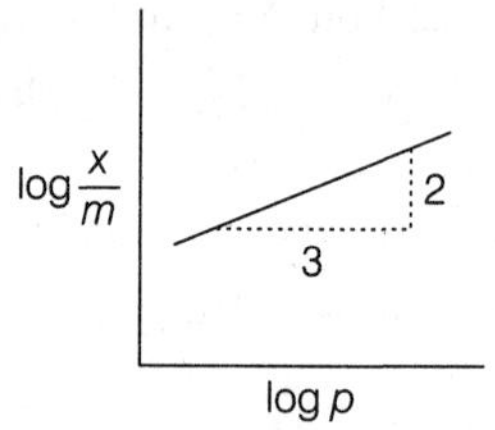

(a) $p^{2/3}$ (b) $p^{3/2}$ (c) p^3 (d) p^2

67. As per Hardy-Schulze formulation, the flocculation values of the following for ferric hydroxide sol are in the order **[JEE Main 2020, Jan.]**
(a) $K_3[Fe(CN)_6] < K_2CrO_4 < AlCl_3 < KBr < KNO_3$
(b) $AlCl_3 > K_3[Fe(CN_6] > K_2CrO_4 > KBr = KNO_3$
(c) $K_3[Fe(CN)_6] < K_2CrO_4 < KBr = KNO_3 = AlCl_3$
(d) $K_3[Fe(CN)_6] > AlCl_3 > K_2CrO_4 > KBr > KNO_3$

68. Potential difference of the electrical double layer formed in a colloidal sol is called
(a) EMF (b) Zeta potential
(c) Brownian potential (d) Nernst potential

69. SnO_2 is taken in basic medium and current is passed. Colloidal sol migrates towards
(a) anode (+ve plate) (b) cathode (–ve plate)
(c) Both (a) and (b) (d) None of these

70. Fixed parts of a colloidal sol of AgI are respectively $[AgI] Ag^+$ and $[AgI] I^-$ in presence of
(a) KI and $AgNO_3$ (b) KI and KI
(c) AgI and KI (d) $AgNO_3$ and KI

71. Peptisation is a **[JEE Main 2019, April]**
(a) process of bringing colloidal molecule into solution
(b) process of converting precipitate into colloidal solution
(c) process of converting a colloidal solution into precipitate
(d) process of converting soluble particles to form colloidal solution

72. Zeta potential or electro-kinetic potential is dependent on
(a) viscosity
(b) dielectric constant
(c) velocity of the colloidal particles when an electric field is applied
(d) All of the above

73. Colloidal sulphur particles are negatively charged with $S_2O_3^{2-}$ and other ions on the surface of sulphur. Hence, most effective electrolyte in coagulating colloidal sulphur is
(a) NaCl (b) $MgCl_2$
(c) $AlCl_3$ (d) Na_2SO_4

74. Aluminium hydroxide forms a positively charged sol. Which of the following ionic substances should be most effective in coagulating the sol?
(a) NaCl (b) $Fe_2(SO_4)_3$
(c) $CaCl_2$ (d) K_3PO_4

75. $[AgI] I^-$ colloidal sol can be coagulated by the addition of a suitable cation. 1 mol of $[AgI] I^-$ requires mol of $AgNO_3$, $Pb(NO_3)_2$ and $Fe(NO_3)_3$ as
(a) 1, 1, 1 (b) 1, 2, 3
(c) 1, $\frac{1}{2}$, $\frac{1}{3}$ (d) 6, 3, 2

76. Flocculation value of a coagulating electrolyte is expressed in
(a) millimol L^{-1}
(b) mol L^{-1}
(c) mg K^{-1}
(d) microgram mL^{-1}

77. The charges on the colloidal CdS sol and TiO_2 sol are, respectively **[JEE Main 2021, March]**
(a) positive and positive (b) positive and negative
(c) negative and negative (d) negative and positive

78. Gold number is maximum for the lyophilic sol
(a) gelatin (b) haemoglobin
(c) sodium oleate (d) potato starch

79. Gold number of some lyophilic sols are
I. Casein – 0.01
II. Haemoglobin – 0.03
III. Gum arabic – 0.15
IV. Sodium oleate – 0.40
Which has maximum protective power?
(a) Only I (b) Only II
(c) Only III (d) Only IV

80. Protective sols are
(a) lyophilic (b) lyophobic
(c) Both (a) and (b) (d) None of these

81. Gold number of haemoglobin is 0.03. Hence, 100 mL of gold sol will require haeomoglobin so that gold is not coagulated by 10 mL of 10% NaCl solution
(a) 0.03 mg (b) 30 mg (c) 0.30 mg (d) 3 mg

82. What happens when gelatin is added to gold sol?
(a) Gold sol is destabilised and peptisation occurs
(b) Gold sol is stabilised and no coagulation takes place
(c) Gold sol is destabilised and coagulation takes place
(d) Gold sol is stabilised and peptisation takes place

83. Adsorption of a gas follows Freundlich adsorption isotherm. If x is the mass of the gas adsorbed on mass m of the adsorbent, the correct plot of $\frac{x}{m}$ *versus* p is **[JEE Main 2020, Sep.]**

(a) 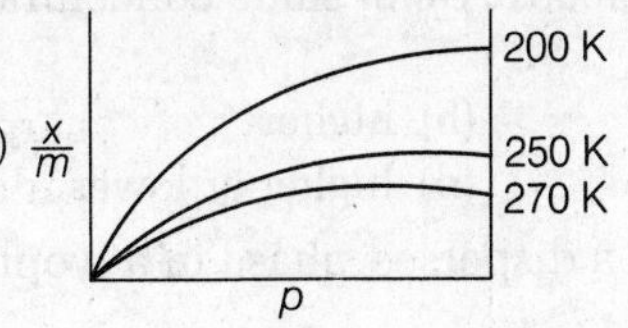

(b) 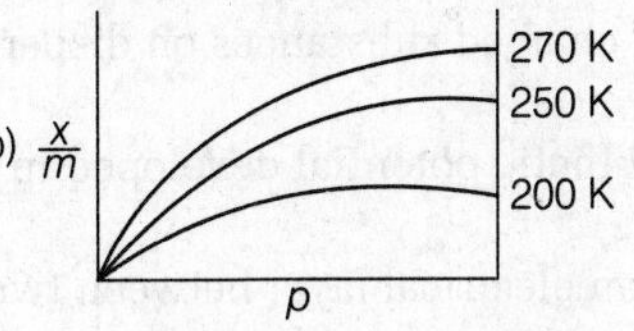

(c) 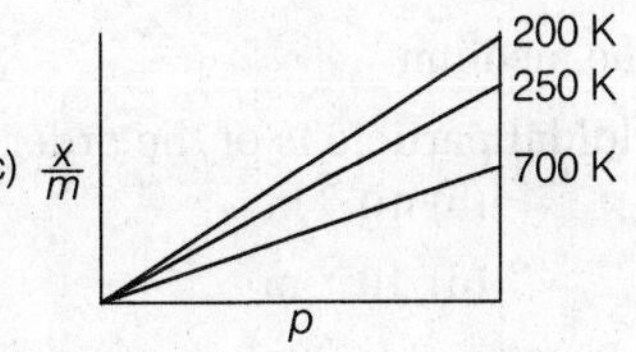

(d) 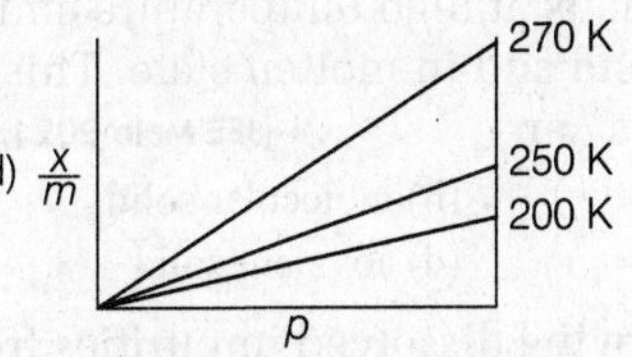

84. Identify the correct molecular picture showing what happens at the critical micellar concentration (CMC) of an aqueous solution of a surfactant (polar head; ~~ non-polar tail; • water). **[JEE Main 2020, Sep.]**

(A) 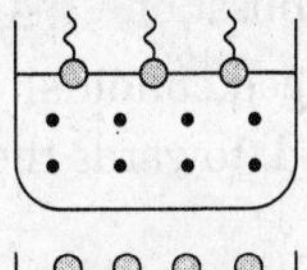

(B) 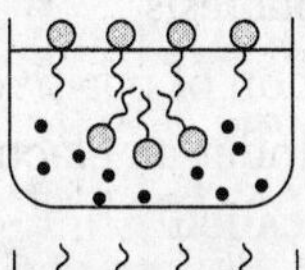

(C) 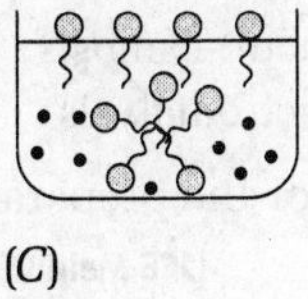

(D) 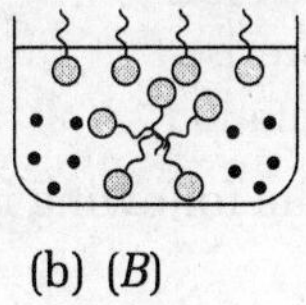

(a) (C) (b) (B)
(c) (D) (d) (A)

85. Some of the properties of emulsions are

I. Emulsions scatter light and thus exhibit Tyndall effect.

II. Oily emulsions are more viscous than the aqueous emulsions.

III. Electrical conductance of aqueous emulsions is higher than that of oily emulsion and increases on the addition of electrolyte.

Select the correct properties.

(a) I and II (b) I and III
(c) II and III (d) I, II and III

86. Select the correct statement(s).

(a) Emulsifiers stabilise the emulsion
(b) Soaps, detergents, long-chain sulphonic acids and lyophilic colloids are emulsifiers
(c) Cleansing action of soap is due to formation of emulsions
(d) All the above are correct statements

87. Coagulation or de-emulsification can be done by some of the methods given below.

I. By addition of a substance which would destroy the emulsifier.

II. By addition of an electrolyte which would destroy the charge.

III. By heating, freezing and centrifuging.

Select the correct methods.

(a) I and II (b) I, II and III
(c) Only II (d) Only III

88. Rubber plating and chrome tanning of leather are based on

(a) electro-osmosis
(b) Tyndall effect
(c) electrophoresis
(d) Brownian motion

89. Water carrying impurities is purified by addition of potash alum. Al^{3+} of the potash alum causes

(a) peptisation of negatively charged turbidity
(b) coagulation of negatively charged turbidity
(c) peptisation of positively charged turbidity
(d) coagulation of positively charged turbidity

90. Artificial rain is caused by spray of

(a) electrified sand or salt
(b) neutral salt or sand
(c) negatively charged sand or salt
(d) positively charged sand or salt

91. Artificial smoke screens are made by

(a) aluminium oxide (b) lead oxide
(c) sodium oxide (d) titanium oxide

92. Milk is an emulsion of fat dispersed in water. It is stabilised by

(a) casein – a lyophilic colloidal sol
(b) casein – a lyophobic colloidal sol
(c) lactose – a lyophilic colloidal sol
(d) lactose – a lyophobic colloidal sol

93. If x is the amount of adsorbate and m is the amount of adsorbent, which of the following relations is not related to adsorption process?

(a) $\frac{x}{m} = p \times T$ (b) $\frac{x}{m} = f(p)$ at constant T

(c) $\frac{x}{m} = f(T)$ at constant p (d) $p = f(T)$ at constant $\left(\frac{x}{m}\right)$

94. Choose the incorrect statement in respect of physisorption.
(a) It is not specific in nature
(b) It arises because of van der Waals' forces
(c) It is reversible in nature
(d) Enthalpy of physisorption is in the range 80-240 kJ mol^{-1}

95. Which one of the following does not involve coagulation?
(a) Clotting of blood by the use of ferric chloride
(b) Formation of delta region
(c) Treatment of drinking water by potash alum
(d) Peptisation

96. Amongst the following statements regarding adsorption, those that are valid are: **[JEE Main 2020, Sep.]**
(A) ΔH becomes less negative as adsorption proceeds.
(B) On a given adsorbent, ammonia is adsorbed more than nitrogen gas.
(C) On adsorption, the residual force acting along the surface of the adsorbent increases.
(D) With increase in temperature, the equilibrium concentration of adsorbate increases.
(a) (D) and (A)
(b) (B) and (C)
(c) (A) and (B)
(d) (C) and (D)

97. Which of the following has maximum coagulation power with ferric hydroxide sol?
(a) Cryolite (b) $K_2C_2O_4$
(c) $K_3[Fe(CN)_6]$ (d) $K_4[Fe(CN)_6]$

98. Example of intrinsic colloid is
(a) As_2S_3 sol (b) S sol
(c) egg albumin (d) $Fe(OH)_3$ sol

99. Of which of the following colloidal systems, fog is an example?
(a) Liquid dispersed in gas
(b) Gas dispersed in gas
(c) Solid dispersed in gas
(d) Solid dispersed in liquid

100. The correct option among the following is **[JEE Main 2019, April]**
(a) colloidal medicines are more effective, because they have small surface area.
(b) brownian motion in colloidal solution is faster if the viscosity of the solution is very high.
(c) addition of alum to water makes it unfit for drinking.
(d) colloidal particles in lyophobic sols can be precipitated by electrophoresis.

101. Arsenic (III) sulphide forms a sol with a negative charge. Which of the following ionic substances should be most effective in coagulating the sol ?
(a) KCl (b) $MgCl_2$
(c) $Al_2(SO_4)_3$ (d) Na_3PO_4

102. Brownian motion is ...... property.
(a) electrical (b) mechanical
(c) optical (d) colligative

103. The colligative property of a colloidal sol compared to solution of non-electrolyte of same concentration will be
(a) same (b) higher
(c) lower (d) higher or lower

104. The stabilisation of a dispersed phase in a lyophobic colloid is due to
(a) the adsorption of charged substances on dispersed phase
(b) the large electro-kinetic potential developed in the colloid
(c) the formation of an electrical layer between two phases
(d) the viscosity of the medium

105. The diameter of colloidal particle is of the order
(a) 10^{-3} m (b) 10^{-6} m
(c) 10^{-15} m (d) 10^{-7} m

106. A hard substance melts at high temperature and is an insulator in both solid and in molten state. This solid is most likely to be a / an **[JEE Main 2021, March]**
(a) ionic solid (b) molecular solid
(c) metallic solid (d) covalent solid

107. The process of removing dissolved impurities from a colloidal system, by means of diffusion through suitable membrane under the influence of an electric field is called
(a) electro-osmosis (b) electrodialysis
(c) electrophoresis (d) peptisation

108. The migration of positively charged colloidal particles, under an electrical field, towards the cathode is called
(a) cataphoresis (b) electro-osmosis
(c) sedimentation (d) electrodialysis

109. Which of the following is used for the preparation of colloids? **[JEE Main 2020, Sep.]**
(a) Bredig's Arc method (b) Ostwald process
(c) Mond process (d) van Arkel method

110. The colloidal sol of As_2S_3 prefers to adsorb
(a) NO_3^- (b) K^+ (c) S^{2-} (d) H^+

111. If a freshly formed ppt. of SnO_2 is peptised by a small amount of NaOH, these colloidal particles may be represented as
(a) $[SnO_2]\ SnO_3^{2-} : 2Na^+$ (b) $[SnO_2]\ Sn^{4+} : O^{2-}$
(c) $[SnO_2]\ Na^+ : OH^-$ (d) $[SnO_2]\ Sn^{4+} : OH^-$

112. Smoke has generally blue tinge. It is due to
(a) scattering (b) coagulation
(c) Brownian motion (d) electro-osmosis

113. Although, nitrogen does not adsorb on a surface at room temperature, it adsorbs on the surface at 83 K. Which one of the following statements is correct?
(a) At 83 K, there is formation of monolayer.
(b) At 83 K, nitrogen is adsorbed as atoms.
(c) At 83 K, nitrogen molecules are held by chemical bonds.
(d) At 83 K, there is formation of multimolecular layers.

114. In adsorption of oxalic acid on activated charcoal, the activated charcoal is called
(a) adsorbent (b) adsorbate
(c) adsorber (d) absorber

115. There is desorption of physical adsorption when
(a) temperature is increased
(b) temperature is decreased
(c) pressure is increased
(d) concentration is increased

116. The rate of chemisorption
(a) decreases with increase of pressure
(b) increases with increase of pressure
(c) is independent of pressure
(d) is independent of temperature

117. Oil soluble dye is mixed with emulsion and emulsion remains colourless. Then it is
(a) O-in-W (b) W-in-O (c) O-in-O (d) W-in-W

118. Amount of gas adsorbed per gram of adsorbent increases with pressure, but after certain limit is reached, adsorption becomes constant. It is where
(a) multilayers are formed
(b) desorption takes place
(c) temperature is increased
(d) absorption also starts

119. 'Silica-garden' is developed by setting of coloured ions in the void of silicates. It is a case of
(a) adsorption (b) absorption
(c) Both (a) and (b) (d) None of these

120. Compared to common colloidal sols micelles have
(a) higher colligative properties
(b) lower colligative properties
(c) same colligative properties
(d) None of the above

121. For the graph below, select **correct** order of temperature?

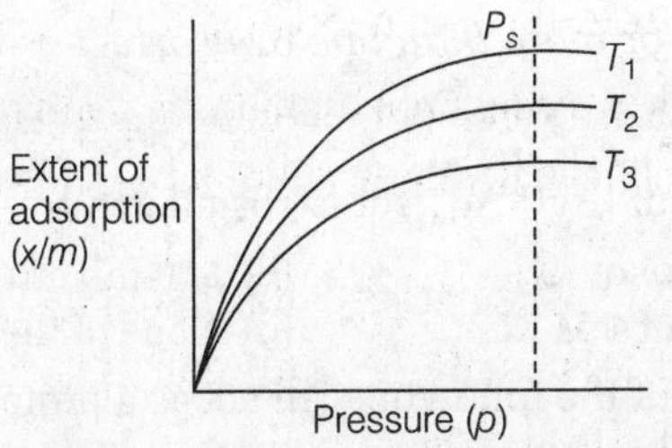

(a) $T_1 > T_2 > T_3$ (b) $T_2 > T_3 > T_1$
(c) $T_3 > T_2 > T_1$ (d) $T_1 = T_2 = T_3$

122. Which of the following is present at the time of cracking of hydrocarbons?
(a) Copper (b) Zeolite
(c) Nickel (d) Molybdenum

123. The ability of the catalyst to direct the reaction to yield particular product is called
(a) reactivity (b) selectivity
(c) activity (d) fugacity

124. Which of the following is an example of zeolite?
(a) ZSM-5 (b) $AgNO_3$
(c) $Mg(OH)_3$ (d) $Co(OH)_3$

125. Which of the following small-sized elements can replace the silicon and aluminium in the frame work at zeolites?
(a) Boron (b) Magnesium
(c) Phosphorus (d) All of these

126. Zeolites are microporous aluminosilicates with general formula
(a) $M[(AlO_2)_x]\cdot m\,H_2O$
(b) $M_x[(AlO_2)_x(SiO_2)_y]$
(c) $M_x[(SiO_2)_y]\cdot m\,H_2O$
(d) $M_{x/n}[(AlO_2)_x(SiO_2)_y]\cdot m\,H_2O$

127. Catalyst used in polymerisation of ethene is
(a) $TiCl_4$ and AlR_3 (b) Fe, Co
(c) H_3PO_4 (d) zeolites

128. Gold number of a lyophilic sol is such property that
(a) the larger its value, the greater is the peptising power
(b) the lower its value, the greater is the peptising power
(c) the lower its value, the greater is the protecting power
(d) the larger its value, the greater is the protecting power

129. Energy of activation of forward and backward reaction are equal in cases (numerical values) where
(a) $\Delta H = 0$
(b) no catalyst present
(c) $\Delta S = 0$
(d) stoichiometry is the mechanism

130. At 400 K, energy of activation of a reaction is decreased by 0.8 kcal in presence of catalyst. Hence, rate will be
(a) increased by 2.72 times
(b) increased by 1.18 times
(c) decreased by 2.72 times
(d) increased by 6.26 times

131. Which of the following sols is hydrophobic?
(a) Starch (b) Gum
(c) Sulphur (d) Gelatin

132. Gold number is associated with
(a) electrophoresis (b) protective colloids
(c) Tyndall effect (d) isotonic solutions

133. The statement not applicable to chemisorption is that it is
(a) highly specific
(b) independent of temperature
(c) irreversible
(d) slow

134. Physical adsorption is inversely proportional to
(a) temperature (b) volume
(c) concentration (d) All of these

135. Which one of the following is most readily adsorbed on activated charcoal?
(a) N_2 (b) H_2 (c) SO_2 (d) O_2

136. When a fresh precipitate is turned back in colloidal form, the process is known as
(a) dialysis (b) coagulation
(c) peptisation (d) electro-osmosis

137. Select suitable catalyst for

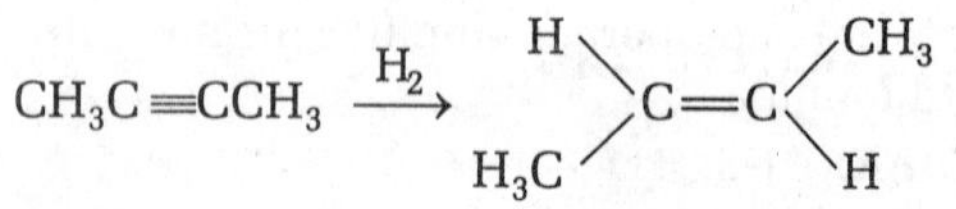

(a) Li / NH_3 (b) Lindlar
(c) Cu (d) Pd/PdO

138. Which is/are correctly matched?
(a) Aerosol — Liquid dispersed in a gas
(b) Smoke — Solid dispersed in a gas
(c) Emulsion — Liquid dispersed in liquid
(d) All of the above are correctly matched

139. Select the correct statement(s).
(a) Milk is an emulsion of water in fats
(b) Clays may be peptised by alkalis, the OH^- ion being the active agent
(c) Both (a) and (b)
(d) None of the above

140. Select the correct statement(s).
(a) A gel is a system in which one component, at least, has a low rigidity and at least one component has a high mobility
(b) A surfactant is an amphipathic substance that is it has both hydrophobic and hydrophilic regions
(c) Both (a) and (b)
(d) None of the above

141. Select the incorrect statement(s).
(a) Micellar system are used as detergents and drug carriers
(b) The enthalpy of formation of micelles is positive thus, it is an endothermic process
(c) Both of these are incorrect
(d) None of the above is correct

142. The extra stability of lyophilic colloids is due to
(a) charge on the particles
(b) a protective film of the dispersion medium on the particles
(c) the smaller size of the particles
(d) the larger size of the particles

143. Among the electrolytes Na_2SO_4, $CaCl_2$, $Al_2(SO_4)_3$ and NH_4Cl, the most effective coagulating agent for Sb_2S_3 sol is **[IIT JEE 2009]**
(a) Na_2SO_4 (b) $CaCl_2$
(c) $Al_2(SO_4)_3$ (d) NH_4Cl

144. The coagulating power of electrolytes having ions Na^+, Al^{3+} and Ba^{2+} for arsenic sulphide sol increases in the order. **[JEE Main 2013]**
(a) $Al^{3+} < Ba^{2+} < Na^+$
(b) $Na^+ < Ba^{2+} < Al^{3+}$
(c) $Ba^{2+} < Na^+ < Al^{3+}$
(d) $Al^{3+} < Na^+ < Ba^{2+}$

145. Methylene blue from its aqueous solution, is adsorbed on activated charcoal at 25°C. For this process, the correct statement is **[JEE Advanced 2013]**
(a) the adsorption requires activation at 25°C
(b) the adsorption is accompanied by a decrease in enthalpy
(c) the adsorption increase with increase of temperature
(d) the adsorption is irreversible

Objective Questions Type II [One or more than one correct option(s)]

In each of the questions below, four choices are given, of which one or more than one are correct.

1. Which of the following statements is/are correct about adsorption?
(a) It is a selective and specific process
(b) It is a reversible process
(c) An increase in the gaseous adsorbate causes increase in adsorption. However, at higher pressure, the adsorption becomes constant
(d) It is an endothermic process

2. 1 mole of [AgI] Ag^+ sol is coagulated by
(a) 1 mol of KI (b) 500 mL of 1 M K_2SO_4
(c) 1 L of 1 M KI (d) None of these

3. Which of the following can act as a protective colloid?
(a) Gelatin (b) Silica gel
(c) Oil-in-water emulsion (d) All of these

4. An emulsifier is an agent which
(a) accelerates the dispersion
(b) homogenises an emulsion
(c) stabilises an emulsion
(d) acids the flocculation of an emulsion

5. On adding $AgNO_3$ solution into KI solution, a negatively charged colloidal sol is obtained when they are in
(a) 100 mL of 0.1 M $AgNO_3$ + 100 mL of 0.1 M KI
(b) 100 mL of 0.1 M $AgNO_3$ + 100 mL of 0.2 M KI
(c) 100 mL of 0.2 M $AgNO_3$ + 100 mL of 0.1 M KI
(d) 100 mL of 0.15 $AgNO_3$ + 100 mL of 0.25 M KI

6. Adsorption is the phenomenon in which a substance
(a) accumulates on the surface of the other substance
(b) goes into the body of the other substances
(c) remains close to the other substance
(d) None of the above

7. Which of the following is/are not characteristic of chemisorption?
(a) It is irreversible
(b) It is specific
(c) It is multilayer phenomenon
(d) Heat of adsorption of about –400 kJ

8. Chromatography is a technique based on
(a) adsorption and then dispersion of solute
(b) absorption of solute
(c) hydration of solute
(d) evaporation of solute

9. Oil soluble dye is mixed with water-in-oil emulsion then
(a) dispersion medium is coloured
(b) dispersed phase is coloured
(c) dispersion medium is colourless
(d) dispersed phase is colourless

10. There is no scum formation when hard water is being used. The washing powder can be
(a) $C_{17}H_{35}COONa$
(b) 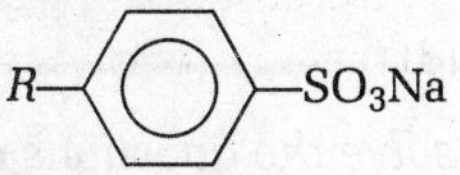
(c) Both (a) and (b)
(d) None of these

11. Softening of hard water is done using sodium aluminium silicate (zeolite). This causes
(a) adsorption of Ca^{2+} and Mg^{2+} ions of hard water replacing Na^+ ions
(b) adsorption of Ca^{2+} and Mg^{2+} of hard water replacing Al^{3+} ions
(c) adsorption of Na^+ of hard water replacing Al^{3+}
(d) adsorption of Al^{3+} of hard water replacing Na^+

12. Which is/are true statements?
(a) Water vapour is absorbed by anhydrous calcium chloride but adsorbed by silica gel
(b) NH_3 is absorbed by water but adsorbed by charcoal
(c) Sugar is decolourised by animal charcoal based on adsorption
(d) H_2O is absorbed by conc. H_2SO_4

13. Anionic surfactants are
(a) $C_{17}H_{35}COONa$
(b) 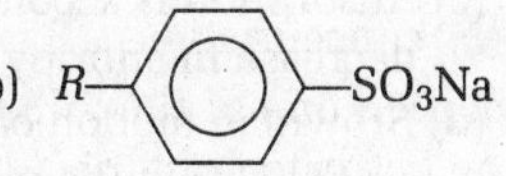
(c) $(CH_2OH)_4\overset{+}{N}$
(d) None of these

14. Non-ionogenic surfactants are
(a) 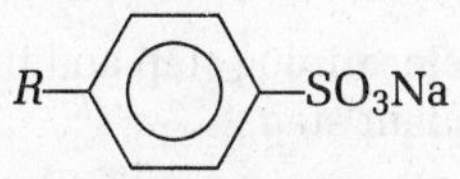
(b) $C_{17}H_{35}COONa$
(c) $C_nH_{2n+1}(OCH_2CH_2)_xOH$
(d) 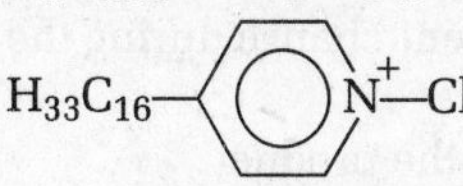

15. Which of the following statements are true for hydrophilic sols?
(a) They do not require electrolytes for stability
(b) Their coagulation is reversible
(c) Their viscosity is of the order of that of water
(d) Their surface tension is usually lower than that of dispersion medium

16. Which one of the following statements are incorrect?
(a) Brownian movement is more pronounced for smaller particles than for bigger ones
(b) Sols of metal sulphides are lyophilic
(c) Schulze-Hardy law states, the bigger the size of the ion, the greater is its coagulating power
(d) One would expect charcoal to adsorb chlorine more strongly than hydrogen sulphide

17. Which are correct statements for a catalyst?
(a) It does not alter E_a
(b) The surface of a catalyst adsorbs reactants
(c) Catalyst may form intermediates with the reactants
(d) Action of enzyme catalyst is always specific

18. Reactions in zeolite catalyst depend on
(a) pores
(b) apertures
(c) size of cavities
(d) pressure

19. The zeolites have shape selectivity depending on
(a) pore structure
(b) atomic structure
(c) molecular structure
(d) None of the above

20. The correct statement(s) about surface properties is(are) **[JEE Advanced 2017]**

(a) The critical temperatures of ethane and nitrogen are 563 K and 126 K, respectively. The adsorption of ethane will be more than that of nitrogen of same amount of activated charcoal at a given temperature
(b) Cloud is an emulsion type of colloid in which liquid is dispersed phase and gas is dispersion medium
(c) Adsorption is accompanied by decrease in enthalpy and decrease in entropy of the system
(d) Brownian motion of colloidal particles does not depend on the size of the particles but depends on viscosity of the solution

21. Which is/are correct statement about the role of a catalyst in a reaction?

(a) It is reactant in a rate-determining step and then a product of some subsequent step
(b) It provides an alternate mechanism with a lower energy of activation
(c) In increases the rate of chemical reaction but does not itself undergo a permanent change during the course of the reaction
(d) It increases quantity of the product

22. Colloidal solutions of gold prepared by different methods are of different colours because of

(a) different diameters of colloidal gold particles
(b) variable valency of gold
(c) different concentration of gold particles
(d) impurities produced by different methods

23. The correct statement(s) pertaining to the adsorption of gas on a solid surface is (are) **[IIT JEE 2011]**

(a) Adsorption is always exothermic
(b) Physisorption may transform into chemisorption at high temperature
(c) Physisorption increases with increasing temperature but chemisorption decreases with increasing temperature
(d) Chemisorption is more exothermic than physisorption, however it is very slow due to higher energy of activation

24. Choose the correct reason(s) for the stability of the lyophobic colloidal particles. **[IIT JEE 2012]**

(a) Preferential adsorption of ions on their surface from the solution
(b) Preferential adsorption of solvent on their surface from the solution
(c) Attraction between different particles having opposite charges on their surface
(d) Potential difference between the fixed layer and the diffused layer of opposite charges around the colloidal particles

25. The given graph/data I, II, III and IV represent general trends observed for different physisorption and chemisorption processes under mild conditions of temperature and pressure.

Which of the following choice(s) about I, II, III and IV is (are) correct?

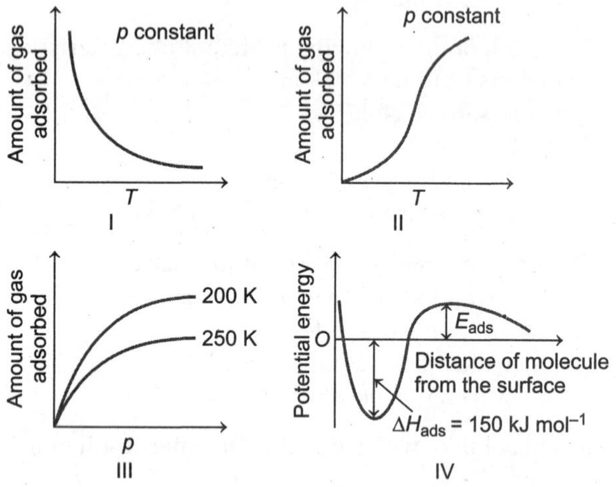

[IIT JEE 2012]

(a) I is physisorption and II is chemisorption
(b) I is physisorption and III is chemisorption
(c) IV is chemisorption and II is chemisorption
(d) IV is chemisorption and III is chemisorption

Numerical Value Questions

All these questions have a Numerical value as their answer, solve the questions and write your answer.

1. Graph between $\log\left(\frac{x}{m}\right)$ and $\log p$ is a straight line at an angle 45° with intercept on y-axis 0.3010. Calculate the amount of the gas adsorbed in gram per gram of the adsorbent when pressure is 0.2 atm.

2. Stearic acid, $C_{17}H_{35}COOH$, has a density of $0.85\ g/cm^3$. The molecule occupies an area of $0.205\ nm^2$ in a closed-packed surface, film. Calculate the length of the molecule.

3. The mass of gas adsorbed, x per unit mass of adsorbate, m was measured at various pressures, p. A graph between $\log \frac{x}{m}$ and $\log p$ gives a straight line with slope equal to 2 and the intercept equal to 0.4771.

The value of $\frac{x}{m}$ at a pressure of 4 atm is

(Given, $\log 3 = 0.4771$) **[JEE Main 2020, Sep.]**

4. For Freundlich adsorption isotherm, a plot of $\log\left(\frac{x}{m}\right)$ (y-axis) and $\log p$ (x-axis) gives a straight line. The intercept and slope for the line is 0.4771 and 2, respectively. The mass of gas, adsorbed per gram of adsorbent if the initial pressure is 0.04 atm, is .... $\times 10^{-4}$g. ($\log 3 = 0.4771$) **[JEE Main 2020, Sep.]**

5. The flocculation value of HCl for arsenic sulphide sol. is 30 m mol L^{-1}. If H_2SO_4 is used for the flocculation of arsenic sulphide, the amount in grams of H_2SO_4 is 250 mL required for the above purpose is .... (Molecular mass of H_2SO_4 = 98 g/mol) **[JEE Main 2020, Jan.]**

Comprehension Based Questions

In these questions, a passage has been given followed by questions based on it. You have to answer the questions based on the passage given.

***Passage* 1** *Following passage describes characteristics of emulsions.*

Emulsions

If a pair of immiscible liquids such as olive oil and water are mixed and shaken vigorously, a dispersion of very fine droplets of one liquid in the other will result. Such a dispersion is termed emulsion.

- One of the components in emulsion is water and the other one an oily substance immiscible in water.
- Emulsion droplets are bigger than sol particles ($\approx 10^{-6}$ m) and can be seen under an ordinary microscope or sometimes even with a magnifying glass.
- Emulsions resemble lyophobic sols in some of the properties.

Emulsion can be identified by dye-test.

1. In the following emulsions

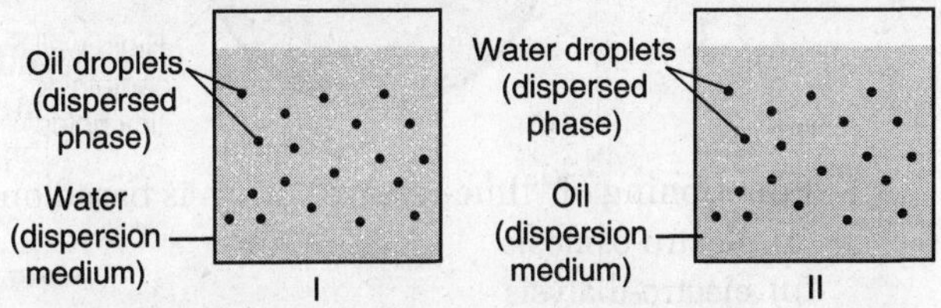

(a) I is of oil-in-water type and II is of water-in-oil type
(b) I is of water-in-oil type and II is of oil-in-water type
(c) Both are of oil-in-water type
(d) Both are of water-in-oil type

2. An oil-soluble dye is shaken with the given emulsion under study. We observe that whole background appears coloured. This indicates that emulsion is
(a) water-in-oil type
(b) oil-in-water type
(c) liquid under study is pure oil
(d) liquid under study is pure water

3. An oil-soluble dye is shaken with the given emulsion under study. We observe coloured drops when seen under microscope. Thus emulsion is
(a) water-in-oil type
(b) oil-in-water
(c) liquid under study is pure oil
(d) liquid under study is pure water

***Passage* 2** *Following passage is on the technical aspect of micelles (associated colloids). Read the passage and answer the questions at the end of it.*

There are certain colloids which behave as normal strong electrolytes at low concentrations, but exhibit colloidal properties at higher concentrations due to the formation of aggregated particles. These are known as **micelles** or **associated colloids**. Surface active agents like soaps and synthetic detergents belong to this class.

1. Select the incorrect statement(s).
(a) Surface active agents like soaps and synthetic detergents are micelles
(b) Soaps are emulsifying agents
(c) $C_{17}H_{35}$ (hydrocarbon part) and —COO^- (carboxylate) part of stearate ion ($C_{17}H_{35}COO^-$) both are hydrophobic
(d) All the above are incorrect statements

2. Which part of the soap ($RCOO^-$) dissolves grease and forms micelle?
(a) R part (called tail of the anion)
(b) —COO^- part (called head of the anion)
(c) Both (a) and (b)
(d) None of the above

3. In multimolecular colloidal sols, atoms or molecules are held together by
(a) H-bonding
(b) van der Waals' forces
(c) ionic bonding
(d) polar covalent bonding

***Passage* 3** *Following passage is about the applications of surfactants. Answer the questions at the end of it.*

Surfactants are the substances which get preferentially adsorbed at the air-water, oil-water and solid-water interfaces, forming an oriented monolayer wherein the hydrophilic groups point towards the aqueous phase and hydrocarbon chains point towards the air or towards the oil phase.

Phosphates were added to commercial detergents but the use of detergents containing phosphates is now discouraged.

1. Phosphates were added to commercial detergents because
   (a) they complexed the metal ions that contribute to water hardness and kept them dissolved
   (b) they controlled acidity and influenced micelle formation
   (c) they caused eutrophication
   (d) they increased BDO (biological dissolved oxygen) in water
2. In detergents/surfactants, use of phosphates is being discouraged because
   (a) there is an overgrowth of vegetation in presence of phosphate which is a plant nutrient
   (b) overgrowth and the subsequent decay of the dead plants lead to decreased dissolved O_2 in water
   (c) Both (a) an (b)
   (d) None of the above
3. Biodegradable detergent is
   (a) ABS-type
   (b) LAS-type
   (c) Both of these
   (d) None of the above

***Passage* 4** *Observe the following figure carefully and answer the questions at the end of it.*

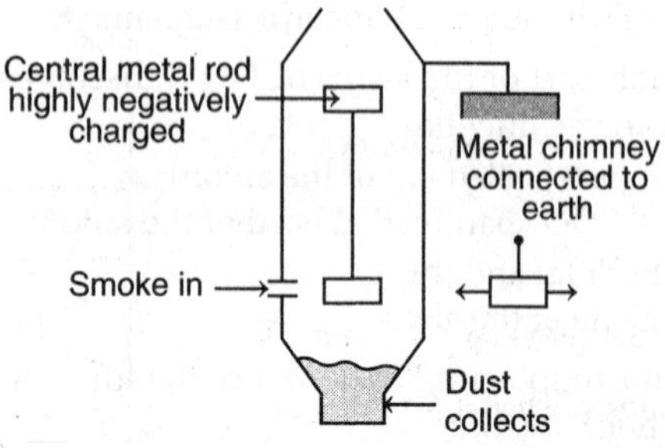

1. Above device is for .... and is based on ....
   (a) using waste gases as source of energy—electrophoresis
   (b) removing dust particles—electroprecipitation
   (c) cutting down pollution—electrophoresis
   (d) cutting down pollution—dialysis
2. Above device is called
   (a) electrodialyses
   (b) electrostatic precipitator
   (c) electroosomiser
   (d) None of the above
3. Rubber plating and chrome tanning of leather are based on
   (a) electro-osmosis
   (b) Tyndall effect
   (c) electrophoresis
   (d) Brownian motion

***Passage* 5** Following passage is about "Time-release" drugs. Answer the questions at the end.

"Time-release" drugs have the advantage of releasing the drug to the body at a constant rate so that the drug concentration at any time is not too high as to have harmful side effects or too low as to be ineffective. A schematic diagram of a pill that works on this basis is shown below.

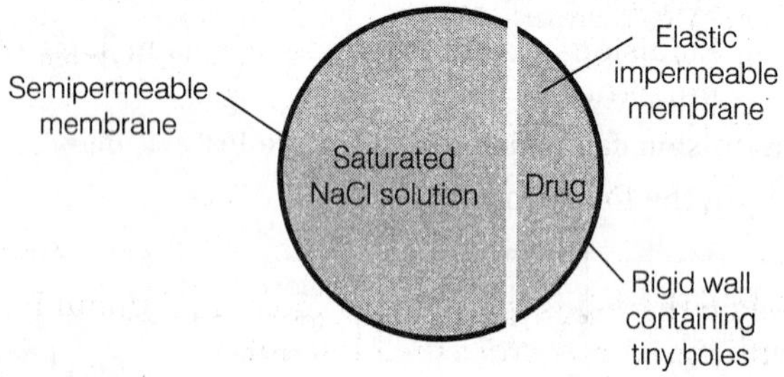

1. Functioning of "time-release" drugs is based on
   (a) electro-osmosis
   (b) electro-dialysis
   (c) osmosis
   (d) dialysis
2. Biochemists use this technique to study the contents of red blood cells which are protected from the external environment by a semipermeable membrane
   (a) dialysis
   (b) haemolysis
   (c) osmosis
   (d) electrophoresis

Matrix-Match Type

Given below are Matching Type Questions, with two columns (each having some items) each . Each item of Column I has to be matched with the items of Column II.

1. Match Column I with Column II.

Column I (Term)	Column II (Related property)
A. Coagulation	1. Scattering of light
B. Lyophilisation	2. Washing of precipitate
C. Peptisation	3. Purification of colloids
D. Tyndall effect	4. Electrolyte

2. Match reaction (in Column I) with catalyst employed (in Column II).

Column I	Column II
A. Hydrogenation of oil	1. Iron
B. Friedel-Crafts' reaction	2. Anhydrous $AlCl_3$
C. Oxidation of SO_2 to SO_3 by contact process	3. Vanadium pentoxide
D. Haber process	4. Nickel
	5. Zinc

3. Match the classification of colloids system in Column I with their example in Column II

Column I	Column II
A. Liquid dispersed in gas	1. Smoke
B. Soild dispersed in gas	2. Whipped cream
C. Gas dispersion liquid	3. Butter
D. Liquid dispersed in soild	4. Volcanic dust
	5. Fogs
	6. Clouds

4. Match the solids (placed at random) in Column I with the correct order in Column II.

Column I	Column II
A. 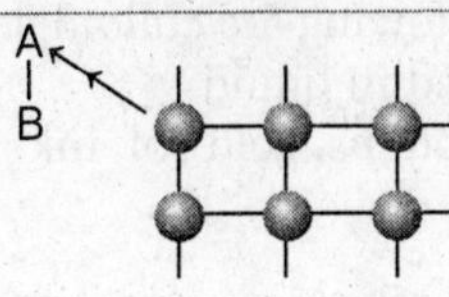 I	1. I
B. 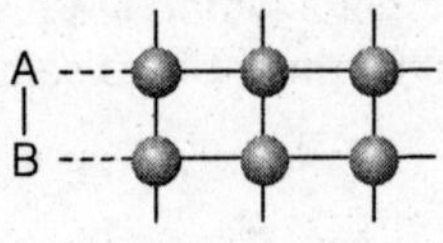 II	2. II
C. 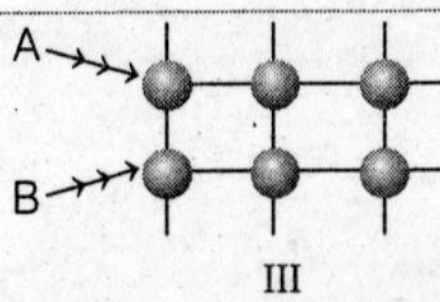 III	3. III
D. 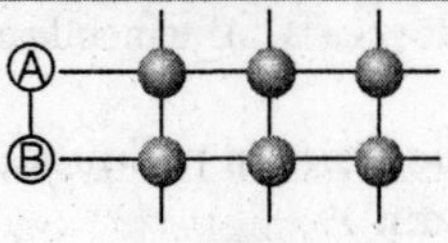 IV	4. IV
E. 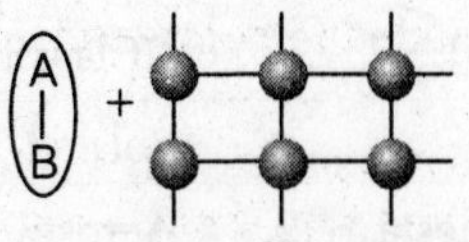 V	5. V

4. Match the colloidal sol formed in Column I with their properties in Column II.

Column I	Column II
A. $FeCl_3 + H_2O$	1. Positive charged colloidal sol
B. $As_2O_3 + H_2S$	2. Negatively charged colloidal sol
C. $AgNO_3$ + KI (excess)	3. Coagulated by Al^{3+}
D. $AgNO_3$ (excess) + KI	4. Coagulated by PO_4^{3-}

6. Frendlich adsorption isothermi is given by equation :

$$\frac{x}{m} = k(p)^{1/n}$$

Match the coordinates (given) in Column I with type of graph in Column II.

Column I	Column II
A. Between $\frac{x}{m}$ and p when $\frac{1}{n} = 0$	1. 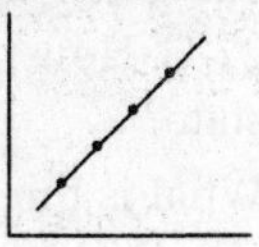
B. Between $\frac{x}{m}$ and p when $n = 1$	2. 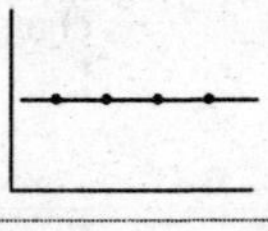
C. Between $\log\left(\frac{x}{m}\right)$ and $\log p$ when $n = 1$	3. 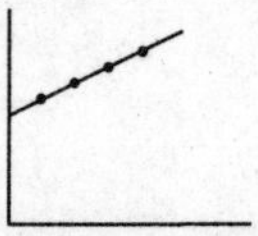
D. Between $\log\left(\frac{x}{m}\right)$ and $\log p$ when $\frac{1}{n} = 0$	4. 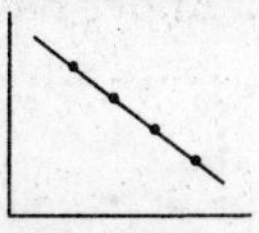

7. Match column A (catalyst) with column B (process).

Column A	Column B
A. SiO_2	1. Cracking of hydrocarbon
B. Pt	2. Alkylation of benzene
C. Zeolites	3. Automobile converter

8. Following are various types of colloids. Match column X with column Y.

X (Colloids)	Y (Classification)
A. Rain cloud	1. Sol
B. Milk of magnesia	2. Aerosol
C. Soap suds	3. Gel
D. Butter	4. Foam

9. Column A is for the names of the processes and Column B is for the catalysts used.

Column A	Column B
A. Ostwald	1. Ni
B. Steam hydrocarbon re-forming	2. NO
C. Fischer-Tropsch	3. Pt
D. Lead-chamber	4. Co/Al_2O_3

10. Match the catalysts Column I with products Column II.

Column I (Catalyst)	Column II (Product)
A. V_2O_5	1. Polyethlyene
B. $TiCl_4$ / $Al(Me)_3$	2. Ethanal
C. $PbCl_2$	3. H_2SO_4
D. Iron oxide	4. NH_3

[JEE Main 2019, April]

Single Integer Answer Questions

Answer of these questions is a single digit lying between 0 to 9.

1. $[AgI]I^-$ is coaguated by $FeCl_3$. How many moles of $[AgI]I^-$ are coagulated by 1 mole of $FeCl_3$?

2. 0.008 g of starch is required to prevent coagulation of 10 mL of gold sol when 1 mL of 10% NaCl solution is present. What is gold number of starch sol?

3. Positively charged colloidal sol is formed by hydrolysis of $FeCl_3$. How many total ions are present in fixed layer and diffused layer.

4. 2.56 g of sulphur (in the form of colloidal sol) in 100 g CS_2 shows osmotic pressure of 2.463 atm at 27°C. How many sulphur atoms are in colloidal state?

5. What is the value of k in question (4)?

6. What is the value of n based on $\left(\frac{x}{m}\right) = k(p)^{1/n}$?

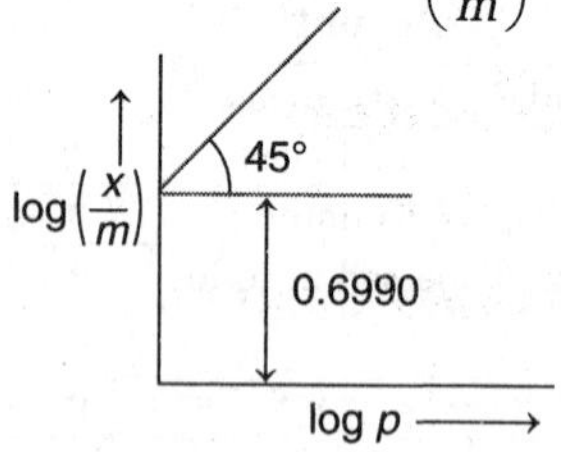

7. $KClO_3$ decomposition is catalysed by MnO_2. A green coloured intermediate of Mn is formed. What is the oxidation number of Mn of this intermediate?

8. How many of the following are colloidal systems having solid dispersed in liquid?
Fog, cloud, foam, proteins, gold sol, ink, paint, arsenic sulphide sol.

Answers

Objective Questions Type I [Only one correct option]

1. (a)	2. (c)	3. (b)	4. (b)	5. (d)	6. (a)	7. (b)	8. (a)	9. (b)	10. (d)
11. (d)	12. (b)	13. (a)	14. (c)	15. (b)	16. (b)	17. (b)	18. (a)	19. (c)	20. (c)
21. (b)	22. (b)	23. (a)	24. (a)	25. (b)	26. (b)	27. (c)	28. (b)	29. (c)	30. (a)
31. (c)	32. (a)	33. (a)	34. (c)	35. (c)	36. (a)	37. (c)	38. (d)	39. (d)	40. (b)
41. (a)	42. (b)	43. (d)	44. (a)	45. (c)	46. (d)	47. (a)	48. (b)	49. (b)	50. (b)
51. (d)	52. (d)	53. (b)	54. (b)	55. (c)	56. (a)	57. (c)	58. (c)	59. (c)	60. (b)
61. (d)	62. (a)	63. (b)	64. (a)	65. (d)	66. (a)	67. (c)	68. (b)	69. (a)	70. (b)
71. (b)	72. (d)	73. (c)	74. (d)	75. (c)	76. (a)	77. (d)	78. (d)	79. (a)	80. (a)
81. (c)	82. (b)	83. (a)	84. (d)	85. (d)	86. (d)	87. (b)	88. (c)	89. (b)	90. (a)
91. (d)	92. (a)	93. (a)	94. (d)	95. (d)	96. (c)	97. (d)	98. (c)	99. (a)	100. (d)
101. (c)	102. (b)	103. (c)	104. (c)	105. (d)	106. (d)	107. (b)	108. (a)	109 (a)	110. (c)
111. (a)	112. (a)	113. (d)	114. (a)	115. (a)	116. (b)	117. (a)	118. (a)	119 (a)	120. (b)
121. (a)	122. (b)	123. (b)	124. (a)	125. (d)	126. (d)	127. (a)	128. (c)	129. (a)	130. (a)
131. (c)	132. (b)	133. (b)	134. (a)	135. (b)	136. (c)	137. (b)	138. (d)	139. (a)	140. (c)
141. (d)	142. (b)	143. (c)	144. (b)	145. (b)					

Objective Questions Type II [One or more than one correct option(s)]

1. (a, b, c)	2. (a, b, c)	3. (a)	4. (b)	5. (b, d)
6. (a)	7. (c)	8. (a)	9. (a)	10. (b)
11. (a)	12. (a, b, c, d)	13. (a, b)	14. (c)	15. (a, b, d)
16. (b, c, d)	17. (b, c, d)	18. (a, b, c)	19. (a)	20. (a, c)
21. (a, b, c)	22. (a)	23. (a, b, d)	24. (a, d)	25. (a, c)

Numerical Value Questions

1. 0.4 g 2. 2.71 nm 3. 6 4. 48 5. 0.37

Comprehension Based Questions

Passage 1 – 1. (a) 2. (d) 3. (b)

Passage 2 – 1. (c) 2. (c) 3. (b)

Passage 3 – 1. (a,b) 2. (c) 3. (b)

Passage 4 – 1. (c) 2. (c) 3. (b)

Passage 5 – 1. (c) 2. (b)

Matrix-Match Type

1. A → (4); B → (3); C → (2); D → (1)
2. A → (4); B → (2); C → (3); D → (1)
3. A → (5,6); B → (1,4); C → (2); D → (3)
4. A → (5); B → (2); C → (3); D → (4); E → (1)
5. A → (1,4); B → (2,3); C → (2,3); D → (1,4)
6. A → (2); B → (1); C → (4); D → (2)
7. A → (4); B → (3); C → (1)
8. A → (2); B → (1); C → (4); D → (3)
9. A → (3); B → (1); C → (4); D → (3)
10. A → (3); B → (1); C → (2); D → (4)

Single Integer Answer Questions

1. (3) 2. (8) 3. (4) 4. (8) 5. (5) 6. (1) 7. (6) 8. (5)

Solutions

Objective Questions Type I [Only one correct option]

7. (**b**) (a) Colloidal solution exhibits colligative properties

(b) An ordinary filter cannot stop the flow of colloidal particles.

(c) Flocculating power increases with increase in the opposite charge of electrolyte.

(d) Colloidal particles show brownian motion.

9. (**b**) $\log\left(\frac{x}{m}\right) = \log k + \frac{1}{n}\log p$

Given $\log k = 0.3010 =$ intercept on y- axis

and $\frac{1}{n} = \tan 45 = 1$ (slope)

$$\log\left(\frac{x}{m}\right) = 0.3010 + 1\log 0.2$$

$$= \log 2 + \log 0.2 = \log 0.4$$

$$\therefore \quad \left(\frac{x}{m}\right) = 0.4$$

34. (**c**) Some drug do not bind to the enzyme's active site. These bind to a different site of enzyme which is called allosteric site. This binding of inhibitor at allosteric site changes the shape of the active site in such a way that substrate cannot recognise it. Such inhibitor is known as non-competitive inhibitor.

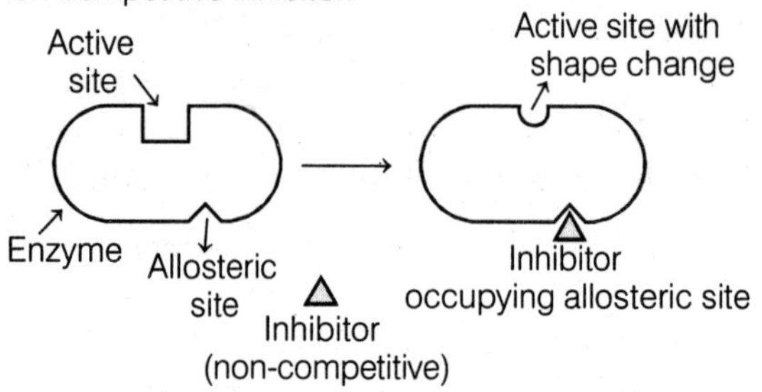

38. (**d**) The aerosol is a kind of colloid in which solid is dispersed in gas. e.g. smoke, dust.

39. (**d**) Micelles formation take place only above a particular temperature called kraft temperature (T_K).

Hence, the correct option is (d).

40. (**b**) Colloidal solutions show Tyndall effect due to scattering of light by colloidal particles in all directions in space. It is observed only under the following conditions.

(i) The diameter of the colloids should not be much smaller than the wavelength of light used.

(ii) The refractive indices of the dispersed phase and dispersion medium should differ greatly in magnitude.

47. (**a**) Given, volume = 10 mL

Molarity = 1 mM = 10^{-3} M

$\therefore$ Number of millimoles = 10 mL $\times 10^{-3}$ M $= 10^{-2}$

Number of moles = 10^{-5}

Now, number of molecules

= Number of moles × Avogadro's number

$= 10^{-5} \times 6 \times 10^{23} = 6 \times 10^{18}$

Surface area occupied by 6×10^{18} molecules

$= 0.24\ \text{cm}^2$

$\therefore$ Surface area occupied by 1 molecule

$$= \frac{0.24}{6 \times 10^{18}} = 0.04 \times 10^{-18}\ \text{cm}^2$$

As it is given that polar head is approximated as cube. Thus, surface area of cube = a^2, where

a = edge length

$\therefore \quad a^2 = 4 \times 10^{-20}\ \text{cm}^2$

$a = 2 \times 10^{-10}\ \text{cm} = 2$ pm

48. (**b**) According to Freundlich adsorption isotherm, $\frac{x}{m} = kp^{1/n}$

On taking logarithm of both sides, we get

$$\log\frac{x}{m} = \log k + \log p^{1/n} \text{ or}$$

$$\log\frac{x}{m} = \log k + \frac{1}{n}\log p \quad y = c + mx$$

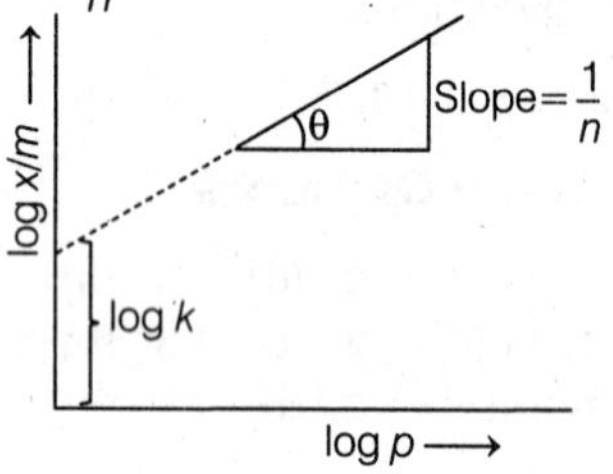

$y = \log\frac{x}{m}$, c = intercept = $\log k$,

m = slope = $\frac{1}{n}$ and $x = \log p$

49. (**b**) The aqueous solution of ionic surfactant, i.e. sodium stearate ($C_{17}H_{35}CO\bar{O}\overset{+}{Na}$) acts as a strong univalent type of electrolyte in the concentration range below the CMC and the linear function of dependence of Λ_m on $\sqrt{C}$ has a small negative slope.

50. (**b**) To coagulate negative sol, cation with higher charge has higher coagulation value.

55. (**c**) Option (c) is the graph that represents correct behaviour of pressure with time. With passage of time, the pressure of the gases decreases and finally reach a constant value.

It is due to adsorption of gases by charcoal. The decrease in pressure is faster in the beginning, but as the adsorbent charcoal gets saturated, pressure attains constancy.

66. (*a*) **Key Idea** According to Freundlich,

$$\frac{x}{m} = Kp^{1/n} \ [n > 1]$$

where, m = mass of adsorbent, x = mass of the gas adsorbed, $\frac{x}{m}$ = amount of gas adsorbed per unit mass of solid adsorbent,
p = pressure, K and n = constants.
The logarithm equation of Freundlich adsorption isotherm is

$$\log \frac{x}{m} = \log K + \frac{1}{n} \log p$$

On comparing the above equation with straight line equation, ($y = mx + c$)
we get

$$m = \text{slope} = \frac{1}{n} \text{ and } c = \log K$$

From the given plot,

$$m = \frac{y_2 - y_1}{x_2 - x_1} = \frac{1}{n} = \frac{2}{3} \Rightarrow \frac{x}{m} = Kp^{2/3}$$

67. (*c*) Ferric hydroxide sol (and other metal oxide and hydroxide sols) is generally positively charged. So, as per Hardy-Schulze rule, the flocculation power is greatest for electrolyte having most highly negatively charged anion.
∴ Flocculation power follow the order

$$\underset{\text{Anionic charge : (-3)}}{K_3[Fe(CN)_6]} > \underset{(-2)}{K_2CrO_4} > \underset{(-1)}{KBr} = KNO_3 = AlCl_3$$

As flocculation power increases, flocculation value decreases. Therefore, order of flocculation values is

$$K_3[Fe(CN)_6] < K_2CrO_4 < KBr = KNO_3 = AlCl_3$$

71. (*b*) Peptisation is a process of converting precipitate into colloidal solution. This process involves the shaking of precipitate with the dispersion medium in the presence of small amount of electrolyte. The electrolyte added is called **peptising agent**.

During peptisation, the precipitate adsorbs one of the ions of the electrolyte on its surface. This causes the development of positive or negative charge on precipitates, which ultimately breakup into smaller particles of the size of a colloid.

75. (*c*) $[AgI]I^-$ can be coagulated by the addition of cation (Ag^+, Pb^{2+}, Fe^{3+}, etc)

$$\underset{1\text{ mol}}{[AgI]I^-} + \underset{1\text{ mol}}{Ag^+} \longrightarrow AgI$$

$$\underset{\substack{2\text{ mol}\\1\text{ mol}}}{2[AgI]I^-} + \underset{\substack{1\text{ mol}\\\frac{1}{2}\text{ mol}}}{Pb^{2+}} \longrightarrow 2AgI + PbI_2$$

$$\underset{\substack{3\text{ mol}\\1\text{ mol}}}{3[AgI]I^-} + \underset{\substack{1\text{ mol}\\\frac{1}{3}\text{ mol}}}{Fe^{3+}} \longrightarrow 3AgI + FeI_3$$

Thus, 1 mole of $[AgI]I^-$ is coagulated by the addition of 1 mole of $AgNO_3$ or $\frac{1}{2}$ mol $Pb(NO_3)_2$ or $\frac{1}{3}$ mol of $Fe(NO_3)_3$

77. (*d*) CdS sol → –ve sol
TiO_2 sol → +ve sol

81. (*c*) By definition of **Gold Number** 10 mL of gold sol is prevented from coagulation in presence of 1 mL of 10% NaCl by = 0.03 mg haemoglobin.
Thus, 100 mL of gold sol is prevented from coagulation in presence of 10 mL of 10% NaCl by = 0.3 mg haemoglobin.

83. (*a*) Freundlich adsorption gives the variation in the quantity of gas adsorbed by a unit mass of solid adsorbent with the change in pressure of the system for a given temperature.

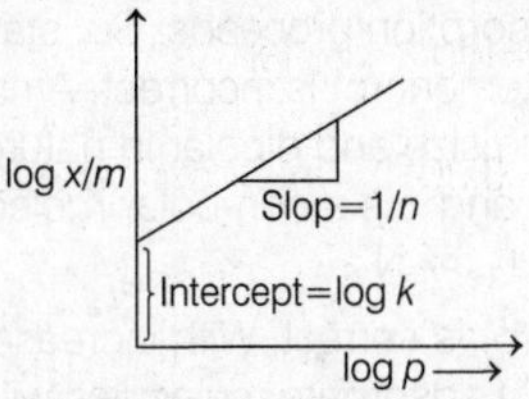

The expression for the Freundlich isotherm can be represented by the following equation.

$$\frac{x}{m} = kp^{1/n}$$

where, $n > 1$
where, x is the mass of gas adsorbed, x is the mass of adsorbent. p is pressure and n is a constant, which depends upon the nature of adsorbent and the gas at a given temperature.
Taking the logarithm on both side of the equation,

$$\log \frac{x}{m} = \log k + \frac{1}{n} \log p$$

$$\frac{x}{m} \propto p \quad \text{(At low pressure)}$$

$$\frac{x}{m} \propto p^{\circ} \quad \text{(At high pressure)}$$

On increasing temperature physical adsorption decreases

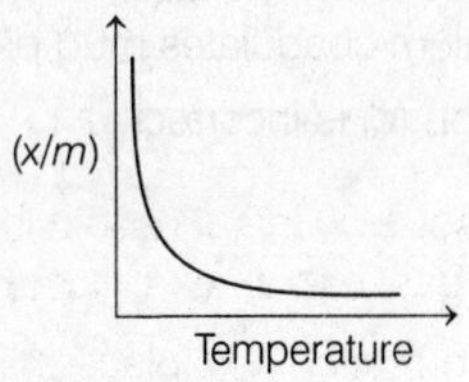

Hence, option (a) is correct.

84. (*d*) CMC (critical micelle concentration) is the concentration of a surfactant in a bulk phase, above which aggregates of surfactant molecules, so called micelles, start to form.

- A micelle is an aggregate of monomer surfactant molecules dispersed in a liquid colloid.
- Hydrophilic 'Head' regions in contact with surrounding solvent, sequestering the hydrophobic ' Tail' regions in the micelle centre.

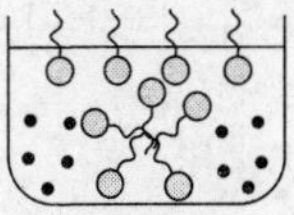

Hence, option (d) is correct.

93. (**a**) $\frac{x}{m} = p \times T$ is the incorrect relation.

94. (**d**) Enthalpy of adsorption is in the range 80 – 240 kJ mol^{-1}. Enthalpy of physisorption is in the range of 20 – 40 kJ mol^{-1}.

95. (**d**) Peptisation is the process of converting a precipitate into collidal sol by shaking it with dispersion medium in the presence of a small amount of electrolyte.

96. (**c**) On adsorption (both physical and chemical), the residual force acting along the surface of absorbent decreases. So, ΔH of the adsorption becomes less negative as adsorption proceeds. So, statement (a) is correct but statement (c) is incorrect. Ammonia molecules (NH_3) is larger in size and dipolar in nature. Nitrogen is smaller in size and it is a non-polar molecule. So, degree of adsorption : $NH_3 > N_2$.

So, statement (b) is correct. With increase in temperature, kinetic energy of adsorbate molecules will increase and hence, its equilibrium concentration will decrease.
So, statement (d) is not correct.

97. (**d**) $K_4[Fe(CN)_6]$

A negative ion causes the precipitation of positively charged sol and *vice versa*. According to Hardy-Schulze rule, in coagulation of a positive sol ferric hydroxide, the flocculating power is maximum for $[Fe(CN)_6]^{4-}$ ion.

100. (**d**) The explanation of the given statements are as follows :

(a) Colloidal medicines are more effective because they (dispersed phase) have larger surface area.

Thus, option (a) is incorrect.

(b) Brownian motion of dispersed phase particles in colloidal solution is faster if the viscosity of the solution is very low. Thus, option (b) is incorrect.

(c) Addition of alum ($K_2SO_4 \cdot Al_2(SO_4)_3 \cdot 24H_2O$), an electrolyte to water makes it fit for drinking purposes because alum coagulates mud particles from water.

Thus, option (c) is incorrect.

(d) Precipitation of lyophobic solution particles by electrophoresis is called cottrell precipitation, Thus, option (d) is correct.

106. (**d**) Covalent or network solid have very high melting point and they are insulators in their solid and molten form.

109. (**a**) Using Bredig's arc method, colloids (metal sols which are lyophobic) can be prepared.

In this method, two electrodes of metal (whose sol is to be prepared) are dipped in concentrated alkali.

The electrodes act as arc for high voltage transmission of current. The metal particles get dispersed in the medium to produce metal sols like Au-sol, Ag-sol, Pt-sol etc.

Ostwald process is an industrial process for manufacturing HNO_3. Reactions are as follows :

(i) $4NH_3 + 5O_2 \xrightarrow[\text{500 K, 9 atm}]{\text{Pt gauge}} 3NO + 6H_2O$

(ii) $2NO + O_2 \longrightarrow 2NO_2$

(iii) $3NO_2 + H_2O \longrightarrow 2HNO_3 + NO$

Mond process is associated with refining of nickel.

$$\underset{\text{Crude}}{Ni} + 4\,O \xrightarrow{80°C} [Ni(CO)_4] \xrightarrow[-4\,CO]{200°C} \underset{\text{Pure}}{Ni}$$

van Arkel method, ultra pure Zr, Hf, Ti metals get refined.

$$\underset{\text{Crude}}{Zr} + 4I_2 \xrightarrow{600°C} ZrI_4(g) \xrightarrow[-2\,I_2]{1800°C} \underset{\text{Pure}}{Zr}$$

111. (**a**) SnO_2 dissolves NaOH forming Na_2SnO_3

$$SnO_2 + 2NaOH \longrightarrow Na_2SnO_3 + H_2O$$

SnO_3^{2-} is adsorbed by SnO_2 forming negatively charged colloidal sol

$$[SnO_2]SnO_3^{2-} : 2Na^+$$

130. (**a**) $k = Ae^{-E_a/RT}$ if no catalyst

$k' = Ae^{-(E_a - 0.8)/RT}$ if catalyst,

$\therefore \quad \frac{k'}{k} = e^{0.8/RT} = e^{0.8/0.002 \times 400} = 2.72$

Organic Chemistry

01

Purification and Elemental Analysis of Organic Compounds

Objective Questions Type I [Only one correct option]

In each of the questions below, four choices are given of which only one is correct.

1. Prussian blue can be represented as

$$\underset{x}{\underset{\uparrow}{Fe}}[\underset{y}{\underset{\uparrow}{Fe}}(CN)_6]^-$$

Oxidation numbers of Fe atoms (indicated by x and y) are

(a) 2, 2 (b) 2, 3
(c) 3, 2 (d) 3, 3

2. In the detection of N and S both in the compound by Lassaigne fusion test, blood red colour is due to the formation of

(a) $[Fe(CNS)]^+$ (b) $[Fe(CNS)_2]^+$
(c) $[Fe(CNS)_3]^-$ (d) $[Fe(CNS)]^{2+}$

3. Sulphur is converted into Na_2S in Lassaigne fusion test. Na_2S can be detected by

I. CH_3COOH; II. $(CH_3COO)_2Pb$,
III. $Na_2[Fe(CN)_5NO]$

Correct codes are

(a) I, II (b) II, III
(c) I, III (d) Only III

4. When CO_2 is passed into lime water, solution turns milky due to formation of I but milkyness disappears due to the formation of II. I and II are

(a) $CaCO_3, Ca(HCO_3)_2$
(b) $Ca(HCO_3)_2, CaCO_3$
(c) $Ca(OH)_2, CaCO_3$
(d) $CaCO_3, Ca(OH)_2$

5. Detection of phosphorus in the compound can be done by its conversion into phosphate. Reagent to identify phosphate ion is

(a) sodium nitroprusside (b) ammonium molybdate
(c) potassium ferrocyanide (d) potassium ferricyanide

6. In Carius method for the estimation of sulphur, precipitate is of

(a) $BaSO_4$ (b) $Ba(HSO_4)_2$
(c) BaS (d) Ag_2S

7. Carius method can be used for the estimation of

(a) sulphur (b) halogen
(c) Both (a) and (b) (d) None of these

8. Automatic estimation of elements in organic compound is done by

(a) ENT—analyser
(b) CHN—analyser
(c) MRI—analyser
(d) X-ray—analyser

9. Phosphorus is estimated as

(a) $Mg_2P_2O_7$ (b) Na_3PO_4 (c) P_2O_3 (d) P_2O_5

10. CH_3NH_2 changes to CH_3OH on reaction with HNO_2. There is

(a) increase in % of carbon
(b) decrease in % of carbon
(c) increase in % of hydrogen
(d) no change in % of carbon

11. Hydrocarbon X contains 3 g carbon per gram of hydrogen. Simplest formula of the hydrocarbon X is
(a) CH (b) CH_2 (c) CH_3 (d) CH_4

12. Which has maximum percentage of chlorine?
(a) $C_6H_6Cl_6$ (b) CH_3Cl
(c) C_6H_5Cl (d) $C_2H_4Cl_2$

13. Which is not related to $C_2H_4O_2$ in any respect?
(a) CH_2O (b) CH_4N_2O
(c) $C_4H_4O_4$ (d) $C_4H_8O_4$

14. Percentage of carbon increases when CH_3CH_2OH changes to
(a) CH_3CHO (b) CH_3COOH
(c) CO_2 (d) In all cases

15. In chromatography technique, the purification of compound is independent of **[JEE Main 2021, March]**
(a) mobility or flow of solvent system
(b) solubility of the compound
(c) length of the column or TLC plate
(d) physical state of the pure compound

16. 0.63 g of a dibasic acid neutralises 100 mL of 0.1 N NaOH solution. Molar mass of dibasic acid is
(a) 63 (b) 126 (c) 31.5 (d) 12.6

17. Which method is not correctly matched to determine molecular weight?
(a) Volatile substance—Victor Meyer
(b) Organic base—platinum salt
(c) Organic acid—silver salt
(d) Non-electrolyte (like sucrose)—Carius

18. Silver salt of a diabasic acid has 27% silver. Molar mass of dibasic acid is
(a) 400 (b) 200
(c) 293 (d) 586

19. Which one of the following is likely to give a precipitate with $AgNO_3$ solution? **[JEE Main 2019, April]**
(a) $CH_2{=}CH{-}Cl$ (b) CCl_4
(c) $CHCl_3$ (d) $(CH_3)_3CCl$

20. Depression in freezing point of 1 molal urea solution is 0.54°. Depression in freezing point when 0.18 g of a non-electrolyte is added to 10 g water is 0.054°. Thus, molar mass of the non-electrolyte is
(a) 180 g mol^{-1} (b) 90 g mol^{-1}
(c) 18 g mol^{-1} (d) 9.0 g mol^{-1}

21. Which of the organic compounds will give red colour in Lassaigne test?
(a) NaCNS (b) $NH_2\overset{\overset{S}{||}}{C}NH_2$
(c) $NH_2\overset{\overset{O}{||}}{C}NH_2$ (d) 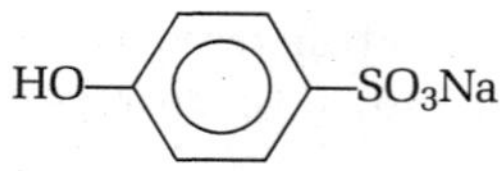

22. Organic compound $A \xrightarrow{HNO_3/AgNO_3}$ white ppt. can be due to
(a) NH_4Cl (b) 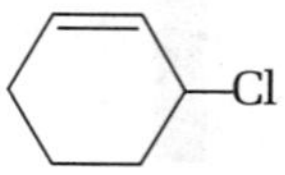
(c) 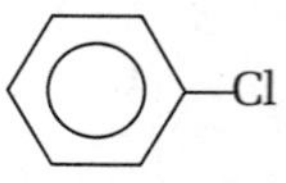 (d) 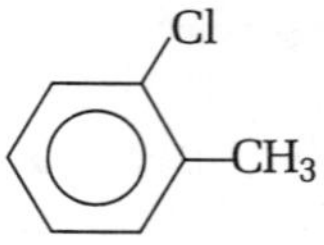

23. In the detection of nitrogen, blue/green colour is due to the formation of Prussian blue. It is
(a) $NaFe^{III}[Fe^{II}(CN)_6]$ (b) $NaFe^{II}[Fe^{III}(CN)_6]$
(c) $Na_4[Fe(CN)_6]$ (d) $Na_3[Fe(CN)_6]$

24. Which factor is most important in determining the chemistry of an organic molecule?
(a) The melting point
(b) The functional group
(c) The number of branches in the carbon chain
(d) The number of carbon-hydrogen bonds

25. 6 g of the organic compound on heating with NaOH gave NH_3 which is neutralised by 200 mL of 1 N HCl. Percentage of nitrogen is
(a) 12% (b) 60%
(c) 46.67% (d) 26.67%

26. Haemoglobin is a chromoprotein having 4 atoms of Fe in each molecule. Analysis showed 0.35% Fe. Hence, its molecular weight is
(a) 64000 D (b) 56000 D (c) 12000 D (d) 1200 D

27. An organic compound A contain 20% C, 46.66% N, 6.66% H. It gave NH_3 gas on heating with NaOH. A can be
(a) CH_3CONH_2 (b) $C_6H_5CONH_2$
(c) NH_2CONH_2 (d) $CH_3NHCONH_2$

28. The sulphur content of cystine is 26.7 per cent. Given that cystine contains two sulphur atoms, molecular weight of cystine is approximately
(a) 120 (b) 240 (c) 100 (d) 60

29. Tyrosine is one of the amino acids present in protein. Its content in protein is 0.22% and its molecular weight is 181 g mol^{-1}. Lowest molecular weight of protein is
(a) 18100 (b) 2200 (c) 82273 (d) 18132

30. The reagents that can selectively precipitate S^{2-} from a mixture of S^{2-} and SO_4^{2-} in aqueous solution is/are **[JEE Advanced 2016]**
(a) $CuCl_2$ (b) $BaCl_2$
(c) $Pb(OOCH_3)_2$ (d($Na_2[Fe(CN)_5NO$

31. R—Mg—Br + $H_2O \longrightarrow RH\,(g)$. Gas occupies 1.4 L per g of RH at STP. Hence, R—Mg—Br is
(a) CH_3CH_2MgBr (b) C_6H_5MgBr
(c) $CH_3CH_2CH_2MgBr$ (d) CH_3MgBr

32. $\underset{A}{RN_2Cl} \xrightarrow[Cu]{\Delta} \underset{B}{RCl} + N_2$, 1 g of A gave 0.2 g of B.
Hence, A is
(a) $CH_3CH_2N_2Cl$ (b) $C_6H_5N_2Cl$
(c) CH_3N_2Cl (d) None is correct

33. Glycerol can be separated from spent-lye in soap industry by
(a) steam distillation
(b) fractional distillation
(c) distillation under reduced pressure
(d) ordinary distillation

34. Aniline (an aromatic base) is separated from water-aniline mixture by
(a) fractional distillation
(b) steam distillation
(c) distillation under reduced pressure
(d) None of the above

35. Steam distillation is based on the fact that vaporisation of organic liquid takes place at
(a) lower temperature than its boiling point
(b) higher temperature than its boiling point
(c) its boiling point
(d) water and organic liquid both undergo distillation

36. Naphthalene has some sand impurity. It can be purified by
(a) sublimation
(b) steam distillation
(c) TLC
(d) column chromatography

37. Mixture of amino acids can be separated by
(a) sublimation
(b) chromatography
(c) distillation under steam
(d) distillation under reduced pressure

38. Sprayer used in the detection of amino acids is
(a) Iodine (b) Benedict's solution
(c) Fehling's solution (d) Ninhydrin solution

39. The relative adsorption of each component of the mixture is expressed in terms of
(a) adsorption factor
(b) retention factor
(c) co-factor
(d) sorption factor

40. Adsorbent is made of ... in TLC.
(a) silica gel (b) alumina
(c) Both (a) and (b) (d) None of these

41. Partition coefficient of an organic compound (A) is 20 between ether and water. 5 g of (A) in 50 mL water is shaken wih 50 mL ether. (A) extracted into ether is
(a) 4.0 g (b) 4.2 g (c) 4.6 g (d) 4.8 g

42. Solubility of an organic compound is 10 g/100 mL water at 20°C and 60 g/100 mL water at 70°C. 30 g of an impure organic compound is dissolved in 50 mL water at 70°C and cooled to 20°C. Crystals formed weigh
(a) 5 g (b) 20 g (c) 25 g (d) 30 g

43. The most suitable method of separation of a 1 : 1 mixture of *ortho*- and *para*-nitrophenol is
(a) sublimation (b) chromatography
(c) crystallisation (d) steam distillation

44. Which of the following techniques is most suitable for the identification of cyclohexanone from a mixture containing benzoic acid, cyclohexane and cyclohexanone?
(a) Crystallisation (b) Infra-red spectroscopy
(c) Sublimation (d) Evaporation

45. Which one of the following is not used for the purification of solid impurities?
(a) Distillation (b) Sublimation
(c) Crystallisation (d) None of these

46. The process of distillation involves all of the following except
(a) change of state (b) boiling
(c) condensation (d) evaporation

47. Steam distillation is useful for the purification of substances which
(a) are insoluble in water
(b) are volatile in steam
(c) are associated with non-steam volatile impurities
(d) have all the above characteristics

48. Chromatography technique is used for the separation of
(a) small samples of mixtures
(b) plant pigments
(c) dyestuffs
(d) All of the above

49. Which of the following is not sublimate?
(a) Naphthalene (b) Camphor
(c) Chlorine (d) Benzoic acid

50. A mixture of camphor and benzoic acid can be easily separated by
(a) sublimation (b) extraction with solvent
(c) fractional crystallisation (d) chemical method

51. A compound is decomposed at its boiling point. It can be purified by
(a) vacuum distillation (b) steam distillation
(c) fractional distillation (d) sublimation

52. Reagent, 1-naphthylamine and sulphanilic acid in acetic acid is used for the detection of
[JEE Main 2021, March]
(a) N_2O (b) NO^+ (c) NO (d) NO^{2-}

53. Absolute alcohol cannot be obtained by simple fractional distillation because
(a) pure C_2H_5OH is unstable
(b) C_2H_5OH forms hydrogen bonds with water
(c) boiling point of C_2H_5OH is very close to that of water
(d) constant boiling azeotropic mixture is formed with water

54. In paper chromatography
(a) mobile phase is liquid and stationary phase is solid
(b) mobile phase is solid and stationary phase is liquid
(c) both phases are liquids
(d) both phases are solids

55. Glycerol is separated in soap industries by [JEE Main 2020, Sep.]
(a) fractional distillation
(b) differential extraction
(c) steam distillation
(d) distillation under reduced pressure

56. Duma's method involves the determination of nitrogen content in the organic coompound in the form of
(a) NH_3 (b) N_2
(c) NaCN (d) $(NH_4)_2SO_4$

57. In which of the following, molar mass determined by crysocopic method is different from the normal value?
(a) Urea (b) Benzoic acid
(c) Glucose (d) Sucrose

58. Middleton's fusion method uses
(a) zinc
(b) sodium carbonate
(c) sodium metal
(d) mixture of zinc and sodium carbonate

59. Adsorption chromatography has

	Absorbent	Eluent
(a)	Solid	Liquid
(b)	Liquid	Solid
(c)	Solid	Solid
(d)	Liquid	Liquid

60. In Duma's method of estimation of nitrogen, 0.35 g of an organic compound gave 55 mL of N_2 collected at 300 K and 715 mm pressure (aqueous tension of water is 15 mm). Percentage of nitrogen in the compound is
(a) 14.45 (b) 15.45
(c) 16.45 (d) 17.45

61. 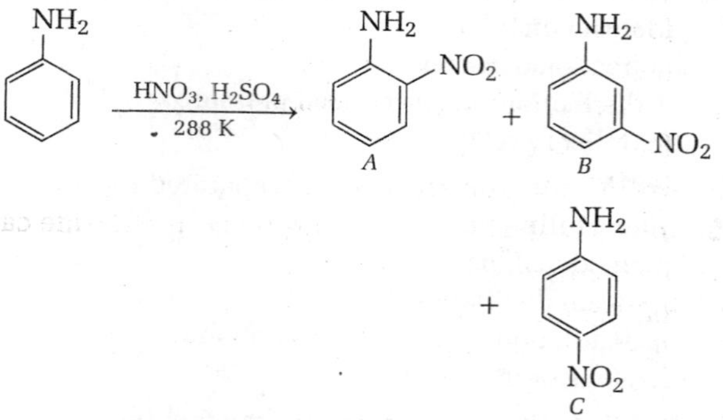

Consider the given reaction, percentage yield of [JEE Main 2021, March]
(a) $C > A > B$ (b) $A > C > B$
(c) $B > C > A$ (d) $C > B > A$

62. Partition coefficient of succinic acid between ether and water 2. 100 mL of water has 4 g succinic acid. It is to be extracted into ether. Select the correct statement(s).
(a) 66.66% acid is extracted if 100 mL of ether is used at one time
(b) 75.00% acid is extracted if 100 mL of ether is used in two parts of 50 mL each
(c) 80.50% acid is extracted if 100 mL of ether is used in four parts of 25 mL each
(d) All of the above are correct statements

63. A gaseous hydrocarbon gives upon combustion 0.72 g of water and 3.08 g of CO_2. The empirical formula of the hydrocarbon is [JEE Main 2013]
(a) C_2H_4 (b) C_3H_4
(c) C_6H_5 (d) C_7H_8

Objective Questions Type II [One or more than one correct option(s)]

In each of the questions below, four choices are given, of which one or more than one are correct.

1. Detection of the chlorine is possible without preparing sodium extract in
(a) 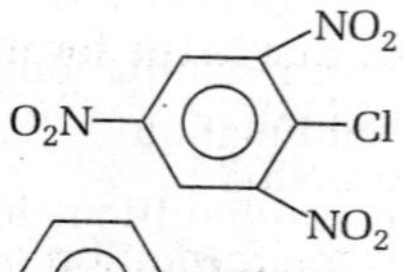

(b) $CHCl_3$
(c) 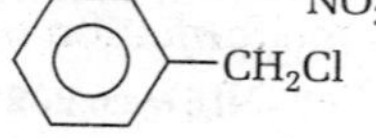

(d) $CH_3{=}CHCH_2Cl$

2. Which of the organic compound will give red colour in Lassaigne's test ?
(a) NaCNS
(b) $NH_2—\overset{S}{\overset{\|}{C}}—NH_2$
(c) $NH_2—\overset{O}{\overset{\|}{C}}—NH_2$
(d) 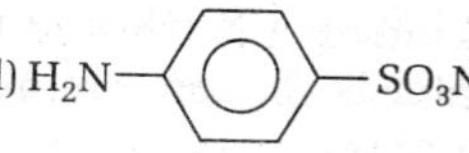

3. p-chloroaniline and aniline hydrochloride can't be distinguished by
(a) Sandmeyer reaction
(b) $NaHCO_3$
(c) $AgNO_3$
(d) Carbylamine test

4. Which of the following test can be used for identification of 1° amine?
(a) Carbylamine test
(b) Hofmann mustard oil reaction
(c) $NaNO_2/HCl$
(d) Fehling's solution

5. p-chloroaniline and anilinium hydrochloride can be distinguished by
(a) $AgNO_3$
(b) Beilstein's test
(c) $NaHCO_3$
(d) Carbylamine reaction

6. An organic compound is boiled with HNO_3, cooled and then treated with $AgNO_3$, a white precipitate is obtained. The compound can be

(a) 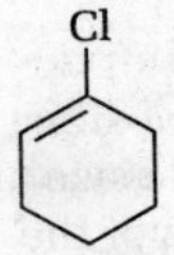
(b) 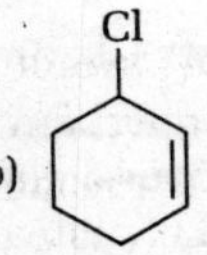
(c) 
(d) $CH_3-\overset{\overset{O}{\|}}{C}-Cl$

7. Which of the following will not give white precipitate with ammoniacal silver nitrate solution ?
(a) $CH_3-C\equiv C-CH_3$
(b) 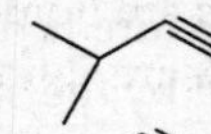
(c) 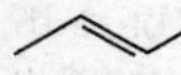
(d) 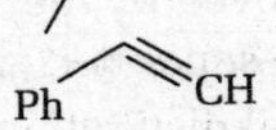

8. The product of acid hydrolysis of P and Q can't be distinguished by

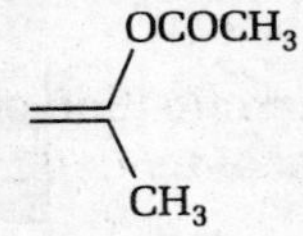
(P)

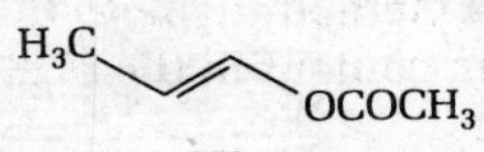
(Q)

(a) Lucas reagent
(b) 2, 4-DNP
(c) Fehling's solution
(d) $NaHSO_3$

Numerical Value Questions

All these questions have a Numerical value as their answer, solve the questions and write your answer.

1. A sample of 0.50 g of organic compound was treated according to Kjeldahl's method. The ammonia evolved was absorbed in 50 mL of 0.5 M H_2SO_4. The residual acid required 60 mL of 0.5 M solution of NaOH for neutralisation. Find the percentage composition of nitrogen in the compound.

2. In Carius method 0.099 g organic compound gave 0.287 g AgCl. The percentage of chlorine in the compound will be ....

3. The vapour density of the methyl ester of an organic monocarboxylic acid is 37. What is the molecular weight of the acid ?

4. An organic compound with molecular formula C_6H_8 on reductive ozonolysis gives 2 moles of 2-oxopropanal. How many compounds are possible ?

5. 0.24 g of an organic compound gave 0.22 g CO_2 on complete combustion. If it contains 1.66% hydrogen, then the percentage of C is ....

Comprehension Based Questions

In these questions, a passage has been given followed by questions based on it. You have to answer the questions based on the passage given.

Passage **1** Read the following passage and answer the questions given thereafter.

In the identification of organic compounds, preliminary investigation includes detection of specific elements like nitrogen, sulphur and halogens. Research scholar ***A*** as well as Research scholar ***B*** prepared sodium extract for the detection of nitrogen (as they were told). In analysis there was red colour formation for the compound of scholar ***A*** and blue colour for the compound of scholar ***B***. Further analysis indicated 36.84% nitrogen in ***A*** (molar mass 76 g mol^{-1}) and 46.67% nitrogen in ***B*** (molar mass 60 g mol^{-1})

1. Elements in the compound analysed by ***A*** could be
(a) C, N, S (b) C, N (c) C, N, Cl (d) C, N, O

2. Red colour obtained by ***A*** can be due to the formation of
(a) $Fe(OH)_3$
(b) $Fe(CNS)_3$
(c) $[Fe(CNS)_2]^+$
(d) $[Fe(CNS)]^{2+}$

3. Blue colour in ***B*** can be due to the formation of
(a) $Fe[Fe(CN)_6]^-$
(b) $Fe[Fe(CN)_6]^+$
(c) $Fe[Fe(CN)_6]^{2-}$
(d) $Fe[Fe(CN)_6]^{2+}$

***Passage* 2** Thin-Layer Chromatography (TLC)

As the name implies, adsorbent is the thin layer of silica gel or alumina spread over a glass plate of suitable size and plate thus formed as TLC plate on which solution of the mixture is placed in the form of a spot about 2 cm above one end of the TLC plate. This treated TLC plate is placed in a closed jar having a solvent.

As the solvent moves up the plate, individual components move up along the plate to different distances depending on the degree of adsorption and separation takes place. R_f, **retention factor,** which gives relative adsorption of each component in the mixture is defined by equation,

$$R_f = \frac{\text{distance moved by the spot centre from the base line}}{\text{distance moved by the solvent from the base line}}$$

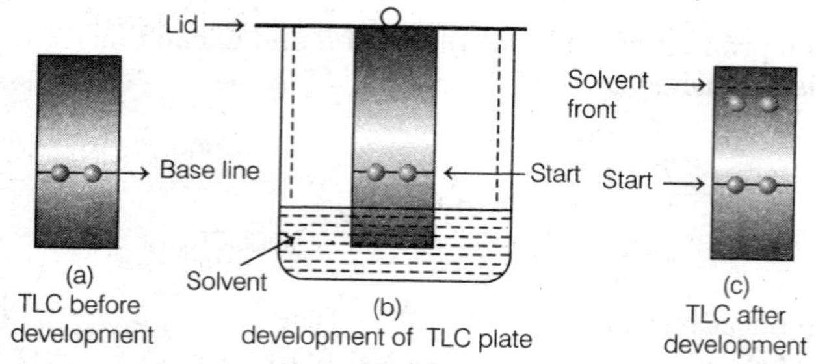

Read the above passage and answer the questions at the end of it.

1. R_f value does not depend on
   (a) type of plate (b) eluent
   (c) temperature (d) pressure
2. Some of the spots in TLC analysis are colourless. In case of amino acids colourless spots can be made visible by
   (a) ninhydrin (b) sulphuric acid
   (c) anthraquinone (d) quinol
3. R_f values of A and B are 0.65 and 0.42 respectively. Which of these will elute first?
   (a) A (b) B
   (c) Equally (d) Cannot be decided

***Passage* 3** *Read the following passage and answer the questions given at the end of it.*

Bonding organic compounds are generally covalent. Therefore, like inorganic compounds, no direct method is available for the detection of elements. In sodium-fusion method covalent bonds of hetro atoms are broken by heating of organic compounds with sodium metal. This results in the formation of inorganic ions involving these elements; these ions can in turn be readily identified by the inorganic qualitative methods.

1. Detection of elements in organic compound is done using sodium-fusion method which is also called
   (a) Middleton's fusion method
   (b) Lassaigne fusion method
   (c) Hofmann's method
   (d) Hinsberg's method
2. Instead of sodium, one can also use following in the detection of elements in organic compounds
   (a) $NaHCO_3$ (b) Na_2CO_3/Zn
   (c) $NaHCO_3/Zn$ (d) $CaCO_3$
3. Detection of chlorine is possible without preparing sodium extract in
   (a) 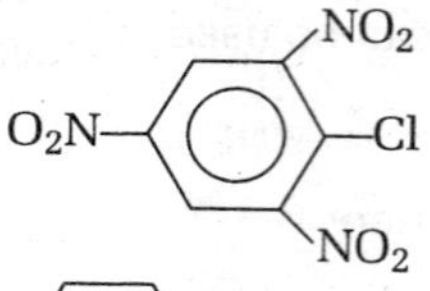

   (b) $CHCl_3$
   (c) 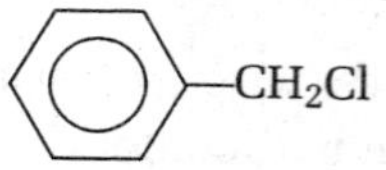

   (d) $CH_2{=}CHCH_2Cl$

***Passage* 4** A mixture contains the three compounds shown in the table below :

	Solubility (g/100 mL) **in H_2O**	**in ether**
1. 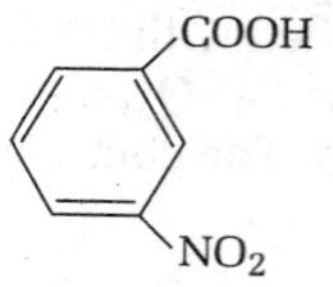	0.31	25.0
2. 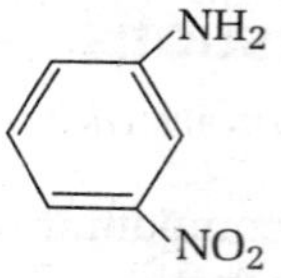	0.11	5.5
3. 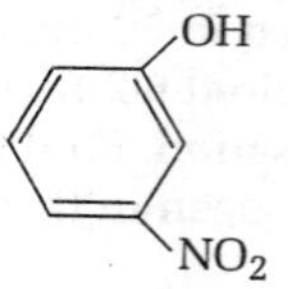	3.02	106

1. The mixture is dissolved in small amount of ether. To this is added an equal volume of 0.01 M HCl(*aq*). After shaking, two layers are formed—an aqueous layer and an ether layer. The layers are then separated. Which of the compounds will be found in the aqueous layer?
   (a) 1 only (b) 2 only
   (c) 3 only (d) 2 and 3
2. To the ether layer is added an equal volume of 0.01 M NaOH(*aq*). Again, two layers are formed. After separating them, which of the compounds will be found in the aqueous layer?
   (a) 1 only (b) 3 only
   (c) 1 and 3 (d) 2 and 3
3. This aqueous layer is evaporated to dryness leaving a solid residue of mass 0.31 g. Ten millilitres of aqueous acid of pH 3 are added. After stirring, the residue is smaller. What is the identity of the residue?
   (a) 1 only (b) 2 only
   (c) 3 only (d) 1 and 3

Matrix-Match Type

Given below are Matching Type Questions, with two columns (each having some items) each . Each item of Column I has to be matched with the items of Column II.

1. Match the element (in Column I) with the method (in Column II) used to determine its percentage.

Column I (Element)	Column II (Method)
A. Nitrogen	1. Carius method
B. Sulphur	2. Duma's method
C. Carbon	3. Iodine method
D. Oxygen	4. Leibig's combustion method
E. Phosphorus	5. Ignition method

2. Match the compound (in Column I) with the reagent used to test them (in Column II).

Column I (Compound)	Column II (Reagent)
A. Na_2S	1. $HNO_3/AgNO_3$
B. $Na_3[Fe(CN)_6]$	2. $FeCl_3$
C. NaCNS	3. $(CH_3COO)_2Pb$
D. NaI	4. $FeCl_2$

3. Match the organic substance (in Column I) with the method of determination of its molar mass (in Column II).

Column I (Substance)	Column II (Method)
A. An organic acid	1. Platinum-salt method
B. A base	2. Victor-Meyer method
C. Non-electrolyte	3. Silver-salt method
D. A volatile substance	4. Cryoscopic method

4. Match the compound in Column I with the compond obtained with sodium fusion test in Column II.

Column I (Compound)	Column II (Compound obtained with sodium fusion test)
A. 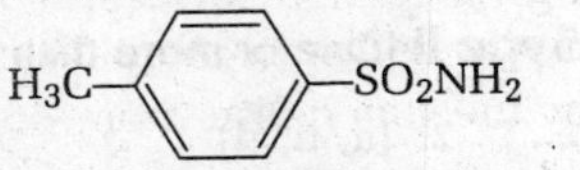	1. $[Fe(CNS)]^{2+}$
B. 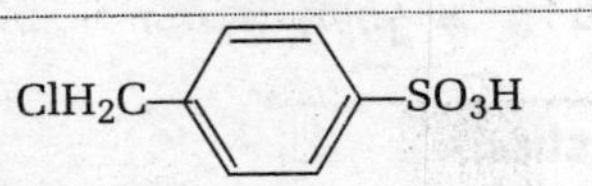	2. $[Fe(CN)_5NO]^{2-}$
C. $NH_2\overset{\overset{O}{\Vert}}{C}NH_2$	3. $Fe^{III}[Fe^{II}(CN)_6]^-$
D. 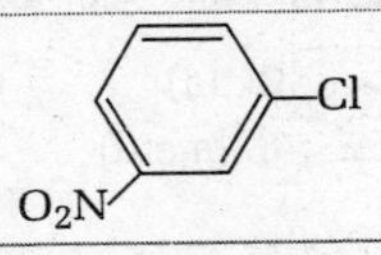	4. $[Ag(NH_3)_2]^+$

5. Match the compound in Column I with the characteristics tests in Column II. **[JEE Main 2021, March]**

Column I (Test/Reagents/ Observations(s))	Column II (Species detected)
A. Lassaigne's Test	1. Carbon
B. Cu(II) oxide	2. Sulphur
C. Silver nitrate	3. N, S, P and halogen
D. The sodium fusion extract gives black precipitate with acetic acid and lead acetate	4. Halogen specifically

Single Integer Answer Questions

Answer of these questions is a single digit lying between 0 to 9.

1. Total number of atoms in empirical formula of acetic acid is ....

2. When one mole of acetone is completely combusted ratio of CO_2 and H_2O formed is ....

3. An organic compound weighing 0.203 g gave on combustion 0.378 g of CO_2 and 0.128 g of H_2O. Thus, percentage of hydrogen is ....

4. Magnitude of charge on Prussian blue $Fe[Fe(CN)_6]$ is ....

5. An organic compound weighing x g containing 46.67% nitrogen on heating with NaOH gave NH_3 NH_3 which is neutralised by 200 mL of 1 N HCl. Thus, x is

6. Deep violet colour formed when sodium extract of the organic compound containing sulphur is treated with sodium nitroprusside has structure $Na_2[Fe(CN)_xNOS]$ where x is

7. Acetic acid is converted into silver salt and 4.64 g of the silver salt on decomposition gave silver ...... g.

8. Haemoglobin (molecular weight 64000) is a chromoprotein having x atoms of Fe in each molecule. Analysis showed 0.35% Fe. Thus, x is ... .

Answers

Objective Questions Type I [Only one correct option]

1. (c)	**2.** (d)	**3.** (b)	**4.** (a)	**5.** (b)	**6.** (a)	**7.** (c)	**8.** (b)	**9.** (a)	**10.** (b)
11. (d)	**12.** (a)	**13.** (c)	**14.** (a)	**15.** (d)	**16.** (b)	**17.** (d)	**18.** (d)	**19.** (d)	**20.** (a)
21. (a)	**22.** (b)	**23.** (a)	**24.** (b)	**25.** (c)	**26.** (a)	**27.** (c)	**28.** (b)	**29.** (c)	**30.** (a)
31. (d)	**32.** (b)	**33.** (c)	**34.** (b)	**35.** (a)	**36.** (a)	**37.** (b)	**38.** (d)	**39.** (b)	**40.** (c)
41. (d)	**42.** (c)	**43.** (d)	**44.** (b)	**45.** (a)	**46.** (d)	**47.** (d)	**48.** (d)	**49.** (c)	**50.** (a)
51. (a)	**52.** (d)	**53.** (d)	**54.** (a)	**55.** (d)	**56.** (b)	**57.** (b)	**58.** (d)	**59.** (a)	**60.** (c)
61. (d)	**62.** (d)	**63.** (d)							

Objective Questions Type II [One or more than one correct option(s)]

1. (a, c, d) **2.** (a, b, d) **3.** (a, b, d) **4.** (a, b, c) **5.** (a, c)
6. (b, c, d) **7.** (a, b, d) **8.** (a, b, d)

Numerical Value Questions

1. (56) **2.** (71) **3.** (74) **4.** (3) **5.** (25)

Comprehension Based Questions

Passage 1 – **1.** (a) **2.** (d) **3.** (a)
Passage 2 – **1.** (b) **2.** (b) **3.** (b)
Passage 3 – **1.** (b) **2.** (b) **6.** (a,c,d)
Passage 4 – **1.** (b) **2.** (b) **3.** (b)

Matrix-Match Type

1. A→(2); B→(1); C→(4); D→(3); (E)→5
2. A→(3); B→(4); C→(2); D→(1);
3. A→(3); B→(1); C→(4); D→(2)
4. A→(1,3); B→(1,2); C→(3,4); D→(1,2,3)
5. A→(3); B→(1); C→(4); D→(2)

Single Integer Answer Questions

1. (4) **2.** (1) **3.** (7) **4.** (1) **5.** (6) **6.** (5) **7.** (3) **8.** (4)

Solutions

Objective Questions Type I [Only one correct option]

1. (*c*) $Fe[Fe(CN)_6]^-$

Prussian blue is formed when Fe^{3+} salts react with $[Fe^{II}(CN)_6]^{4-}$

$$Fe^{3+} + [Fe(CN)_6]^{4-} \longrightarrow Fe^{III}[Fe^{II}(CN)_6]^-$$

Thus, $x = 3$
$y = 2$

2. (*d*) Sodium extract has $= NaCNS$

$$FeCl_3 + NaCNS \longrightarrow [Fe(CNS)]Cl_2 + NaCl$$

3. (*b*) $Na_2S + (CH_3COO)_2Pb \longrightarrow \underset{\text{Black}}{PbS\downarrow} + 2CH_3CO\overset{-}{O}\overset{+}{N}a$

$$Na_2S + Na_2[Fe(CN)_5NO] \longrightarrow \underset{\text{Violet-purple}}{Na_4[Fe(CN)_5NOS]}$$

4. (*a*) $Ca(OH)_2 + CO_2 \longrightarrow \underset{\text{Milky (I)}}{CaCO_3} + H_2O$

$$CaCO_3 + H_2O + CO_2 \longrightarrow \underset{\text{Soluble (II)}}{Ca(HCO_3)_2}$$

5. (*b*) $Na_3PO_4 + 12(NH_4)_2MoO_4 + 21HNO_3 \longrightarrow \underset{\text{Yellow ppt.}}{(NH_4)_3PO_4 \cdot 12MoO_3}\downarrow + 21NH_4NO_3 + 3NaNO_3 + 12H_2O$

6. (*a*) $S \xrightarrow[\Delta]{HNO_3} H_2SO_4 \xrightarrow{BaCl_2} BaSO_4$

9. (*a*) $PO_4^{3-} \xrightarrow{Mg} Mg_3(PO_4)_2 \xrightarrow{\Delta} Mg_2P_2O_7$

10. (*b*)

CH_3NH_2	CH_3OH
Molar mass = 31	Molar mass = 32
= 38.71%	C% = 37.5%

11. (*d*) Total amount $= 3 + 1 = 4\,g$

	Moles	Ratio
% of C = 75%	6.25	1
% of H = 25%	25.0	4

Thus, formula is CH_4.

12. (*a*)

(a) $C_6H_6Cl_6 \equiv (CHCl)_6 \qquad Cl_\% = \dfrac{35.5\times 100}{48.5}$

(b) $CH_3Cl \qquad Cl_\% = \dfrac{31.5\times 100}{50.5}$

(c) $C_6H_5Cl \qquad Cl_\% = \dfrac{35.5\times 100}{112.5}$

(d) $C_2H_4Cl_2 \equiv (CH_2Cl)_2 \qquad Cl_\% = \dfrac{35.5\times 100}{49.5}$

$$Cl_\% \propto \frac{1}{\text{Denominator (which is minimum in (a))}}$$

13. (*a*)

(a) $CH_2O \equiv C_2H_4O_2$

(b) CH_4N_2O, molar mass (60)

$C_2H_4O_2$, molar mass (60)

(c) $C_4H_4O_2$ is not related to molar mass and also not to formula

(d) $C_4H_8O_4 \equiv (C_2H_4O_2)_2$

14. (*a*)

(a) $CH_3CH_2OH = \dfrac{24\times 100}{46} = 52.17$

(b) $CH_3CHO = \dfrac{24\times 100}{44} = 54.54$ (increases)

(c) $CH_3COOH = \dfrac{24\times 100}{60} = 40\%$

(d) $CO_2 = \dfrac{12\times 100}{44} = \dfrac{24\times 100}{88} = 27.27\%$

15. (*d*) In chromatography technique, the purification of a compound is independent of the physical state of the pure compound.

16. (*b*) Equivalent of dibasic acid = equivalent of NaOH

$$\frac{0.63}{E} = \frac{100\times 0.1}{1000}$$

$$E = 63$$

$\therefore$ Molar mass $= 63\times 2 = 126$ g mol^{-1}

18. (*d*) $\dfrac{\text{Equivalent weight of silver salt}}{\text{Equivalent weight of silver}} = \dfrac{\text{Weight of silver salt}}{\text{Weight of silver}}$

$$\frac{E}{108} = \frac{100}{27}$$

$$E = 400$$

Equivalent weight of acid $= 400 - 107 = 293$

Molar mass $= 293\times 2 = 586$

19. (*d*) $(CH_3)_3CCl$ gives a precipitate with $AgNO_3$ solution because it forms stable carbocation. (i.e. tertiary) that readily combines with $AgNO_3$ to give precipitates of AgCl.

$$CH_3-\underset{CH_3}{\overset{CH_3}{\underset{|}{\overset{|}{C}}}}-Cl + AgNO_3 \longrightarrow (CH_3)_3\overset{+}{C} + \underset{\text{(White ppt.)}}{AgCl}$$

$CH_2{=}CH{-}Cl$ forms unstable carbocation.

Hence, it does not readily react with $AgNO_3$.

20. (*a*) $\Delta T_f = \text{molality} \times K_f$

$$0.54 = 1\times K_f$$

$\therefore \quad K_f = 0.54°$ molal^{-1}

Also $\quad \Delta T_f = \dfrac{100 K_f w(\text{solute})}{m(\text{solute}) W(\text{solvent})}$

$$0.054 = \frac{1000\times 0.54\times 0.18}{m\times 10}$$

$$m = 180 \text{ g mol}^{-1}$$

21. (*a*) If NaCNS is formed in sodium extract then red colour is formed.

$$NaCNS + FeCl_3 \longrightarrow \underset{\text{Red}}{[Fe(CNS)]Cl_2} + NaCl$$

22. (*b*)

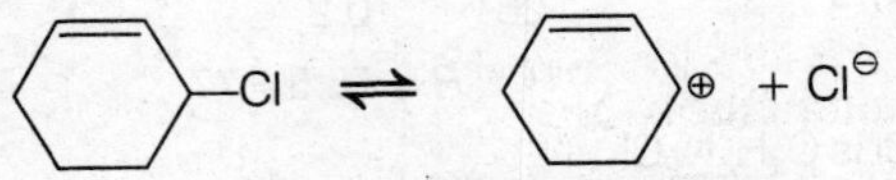

Allylic carbocation (resonance stabilised)

$$Cl^- + Ag^+ \longrightarrow \underset{\text{(White ppt.)}}{AgCl\downarrow}$$

Also gives white ppt. but it is inorganic salt.

23. (*a*) Prussian blue colour is formed.

$$Na_4[Fe(CN)_6] + FeCl_3 \longrightarrow 3NaCl + NaFe^{III}[Fe^{II}(CN)_6]$$

25. (*c*) Percentage of N $= \dfrac{1.4NV}{w\text{ (compound)}}$

$$= \frac{1.4\times 1\times 200}{6}$$

$$= 46.66\%$$

26. (*a*) When 0.35 g Fe = molar mass is 100

$$4\times 56 \text{ g Fe} = \frac{100\times 4\times 56}{0.35}$$

$$= 64000 \text{ D}$$

27. (*c*)

	%	Moles	Ratio	Empirical formula
C	20	1.66	1	
H	6.66	6.66	4	CH_4N_2O
N	46.66	3.33	2	
O	26.67	1.66	1	

$A \xrightarrow{NaOH/\Delta} NH_3$, thus ($-CONH_2$) group hence A is NH_2CONH_2.

28. (*b*) Let molar mass of compound = 100

Sulphur atom = 26.7%

When 26.7 g sulphur, molar mass = 100 g mol^{-1}

When 64 g sulphur, molar mass $= \dfrac{100\times 64}{26.7}$

$$= 239.7 \simeq 240$$

29. (*c*) When molar mass is 100 then protein content is 0.22%

$\therefore \quad$ Molar mass of protein $= \dfrac{100}{0.22}\times 181$

$$= 82273$$

30. (*a*) The reagents that can selectively precipitate S^{2-} and SO_4^{2-} in aqueous solution is $CuCl_2$.

Reaction $S^{2-} + CuCl_2 \longrightarrow CuS + Cl^-$

31. (*d*) H_2O decomposes RMgBr forming RH

1.4 L of RH at STP = 1 g

$\therefore$ 22.4 L of RH at STP $= \frac{22.4}{1.4} = 16$ g

Thus, RH is CH_4.

Hence, RMgBr is CH_3MgBr.

32. (*b*)
$$\underset{(R+28+35.5)}{RN_2Cl} \xrightarrow[Cu]{\Delta} RCN + \underset{28\text{ g}}{N_2}$$
$$\frac{R+63.5}{28} = \frac{1}{0.2}$$
$\therefore$ $R = 76.5 \approx 77$

RN_2Cl is $C_6H_5N_2Cl$.

41. (*d*) Let A extracted into ether = x g

A left in water = $(5-x)$ g

Conc. of A in water $= \left(\frac{5-x}{50}\right)$

Conc. of A in ether $= \frac{x}{50}$

Given, $\frac{C_A\text{ (ether)}}{C_A\text{ (water)}} = 20 = \frac{\frac{x}{50}}{\frac{5-x}{50}} = \frac{x}{5-x}$

$\therefore$ $x = 4.8$ g

42. (*c*) Organic compound solution has been cooled to 20°C.

100 mL H_2O can dissolve = 10 g

50 mL H_2O can dissolve = 5 g

Solute taken = 30 g

Hence, solute crystallised = 25 g

52. (*d*) For detection of NO^{2-}, the following test is used.
$$NO^{2-} + CH_3COOH \longrightarrow HNO_2 + CH_3COO^-$$

55. (*d*) In soap industries, glycerol is separated from spent lye using distillation under reduced pressure.

So, option (d) is correct.

(a) **Fractional distillation** is used to separate two liquids when difference in their boiling points is not much.
e.g. Separation of different fractions of crude oil in petroleum refinery.

(b) **Differential extraction** is based on different solubilities of an organic compound in different solvents. In this process same solvent is repeatedly used (continuous extraction) for extraction of the compound.

(c) **Steam distillation** method is used to separation substances which are steam volatile and are immiscible with water.
e.g. Separation of aniline water mixture.

60. (*c*) $\underbrace{RNH_2}_{28\text{ g}} + HNO_2 \longrightarrow \underset{22400\text{ mL at NTP}}{N_2 + H_2O}$

Actual pressure = 715 − 15 = 700 mm
$$\frac{p_1V_1}{T_1} = \frac{p_2V_2}{T_2}$$
STP given
$$V_1 = \frac{T_1p_2V_2}{T_2p_1} = \frac{273 \times 700 \times 55}{300 \times 760} = 46.09\text{ mL}$$
Thus, $N_{\%} = \frac{28 \times 46.09 \times 100}{22400 \times 0.35} = 16.46$

61. (*d*) $C > B > A$

63. (*d*) Let consider C_xH_y

where, x = number of carbon atoms

y = number of hydrogen atoms

For gaseous hydrocarbon,
$$C_xH_y + \left(x + \frac{y}{4}\right)O_2 \longrightarrow xCO_2 + \frac{y}{2}H_2O$$
No. of moles of $H_2O = \frac{0.72}{18} = 0.04$

No. of mole of $CO_2 = \frac{3.08}{44} = 0.07$

Coefficient of water $= \frac{y}{2} = 0.04 \times 100$

$y = 8$

and $x = 0.07 \times 100 = 7$

$x = 7$

Hence, the empirical formula is C_7H_8.

02

IUPAC Nomenclature

Objective Questions Type I [Only one correct option]

In each of the questions below, four choices are given of which only one is correct.

1. Mesityl oxide is a common name of **[JEE Main 2021, March]**
(a) 2,4-dimethyl pentan-3-one
(b) 3-methyl cyclohexane carbaldehyde
(c) 2-methyl cyclohexanone
(d) 4-methyl pent-3-en-2-one

2. In the following compounds number of 1° (primary) carbons is

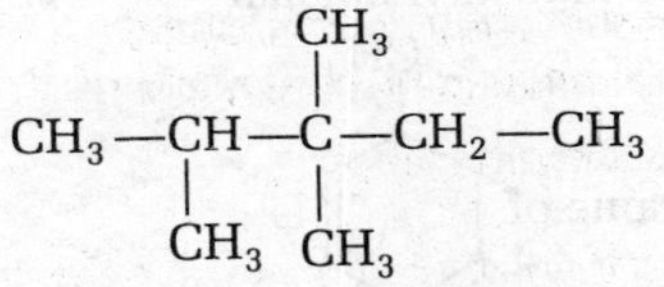

(a) 3 (b) 4 (c) 5 (d) 6

3. *Neo*-pentyl group is named as based on IUPAC system on
(a) *iso*-pentyl
(b) *neo*-pentyl
(c) 2,2-dimethylpropyl
(d) 1,1-dimethyl

4. Parent hydrocarbon of the following alkane is

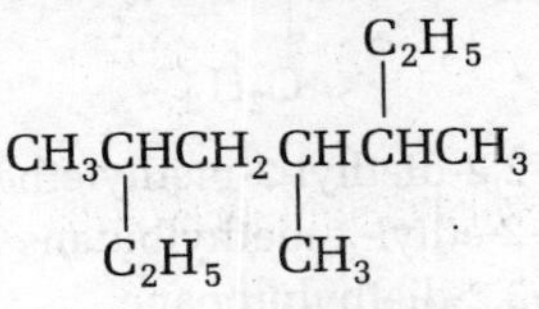

(a) hexane (b) octane
(c) unidecane (d) nonane

5. Based on "1993 Recommendations" $H_2C{=}CHCH_2CH_2CH_3$ is named as
(a) 1-pentene
(b) pent-1-ene
(c) 4-pentene
(d) pent-4-ene

6. IUPAC name of the following compound is

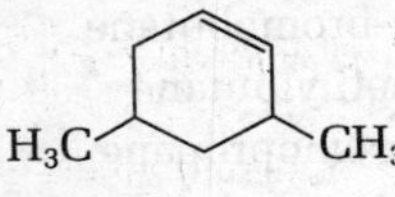

(a) 3,5-dimethylcyclohexene
(b) 3,5-dimethyl-1-cyclohexene
(c) 1,5-dimethyl-5-cyclohexene
(d) 1,3-dimethyl-5-cyclohexene

7. Structure of 2-methyl-2-cyclohexen-1-ol is

(a) 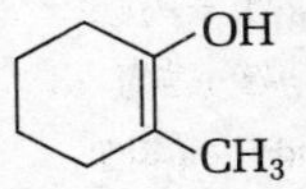
(b) 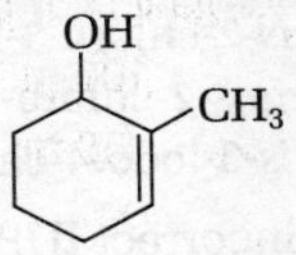
(c) 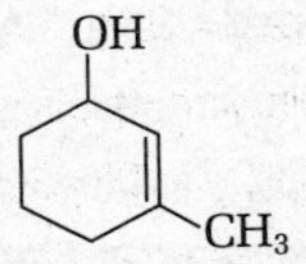
(d) 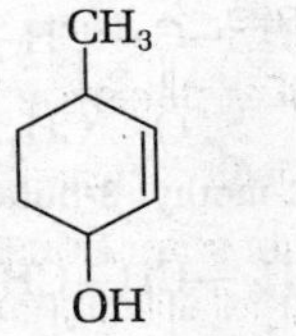

8. Bicyclo [1.1.0] butane is

(a) 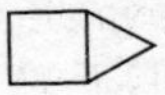
(b) 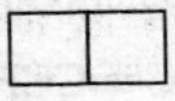
(c) 
(d) 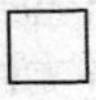

9. Systematic nomenclature of

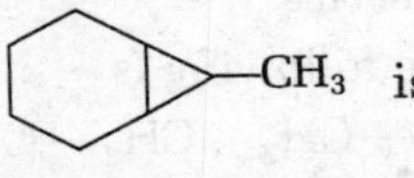

is

(a) 1-methylbicyclo (4.1.0) heptane
(b) 2-methylbicyclo (4.1.0) heptane
(c) 4-methylbicyclo (4.1.0) heptane
(d) 7-methylbicyclo (4.1.0) heptane

10. Structure of bicyclo (2.1.1) hexane is

(a) 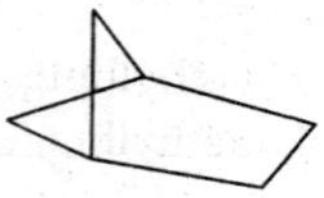

(b) 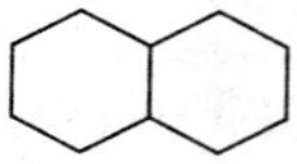

(c) 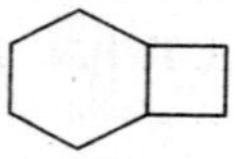

(d) 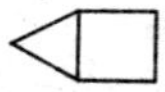

11. The IUPAC name for

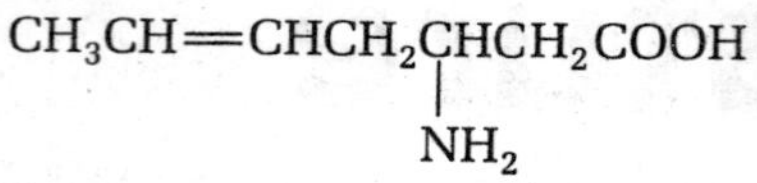

(a) 5-amino-2-heptenoic acid
(b) 5-amino-hex-2-ene-carboxylic acid
(c) 3-amino-5-heptenoic acid
(d) β-amino-δ-heptenoic acid

12. IUPAC name of $(CH_3)_2CH—CH_2—CH_2Br$ is
(a) 1-bromo-pentane
(b) 2-methyl-1-4-bromobutane
(c) 1-bromo-3-methylbutane
(d) 2-methyl-3-bromopropane

13. IUPAC name of the compound

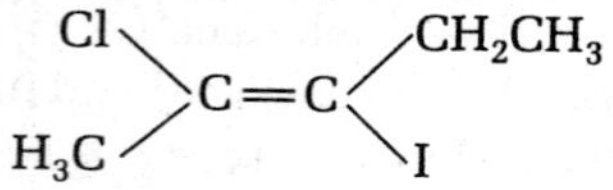

is

(a) *trans*-3-iodo-4-chloro-3-pentene
(b) *cis*-2-chloro-3-iodo-2-pentene
(c) *trans*-2-chloro-3-iodo-2-pentene
(d) *cis*-3-iodo-4-chloro-3-pentene

14. The incorrect IUPAC name is

(a) 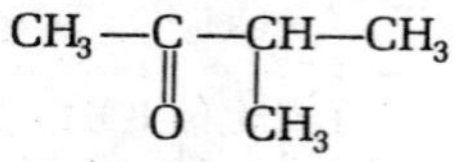

2-methyl-3-butanone

(b) 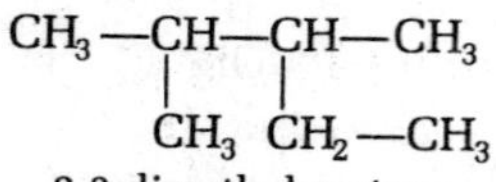

2,3-dimethylpentane

(c) $CH_3—C{\equiv}CCH(CH_3)_2$
4-methyl-2-pentyne

(d) 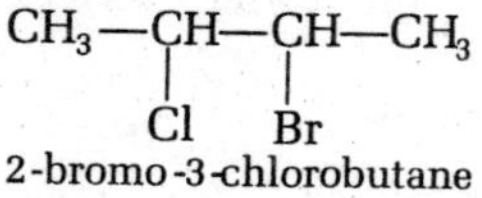

2-bromo-3-chlorobutane

15. IUPAC name of the following is
$CH_2{=}CH—CH_2—CH_2—C{\equiv}CH$
(a) 1,5-hexenyne
(b) 1-hexene-5-yne
(c) 1-hexyne-5-ene
(d) 1,5-hexyenene

16. Names of some compounds are given. Which one is not correct in IUPAC system?

(a) 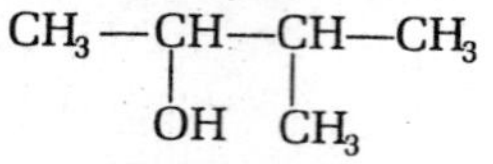

3-methyl-2-butanol

(b) $CH_3—C{\equiv}C—CH(CH_3)_2$
4-methyl-2-pentyne

(c) 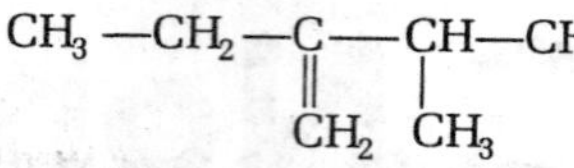

2-ethyl-3-methyl-but-1-ene

(d) 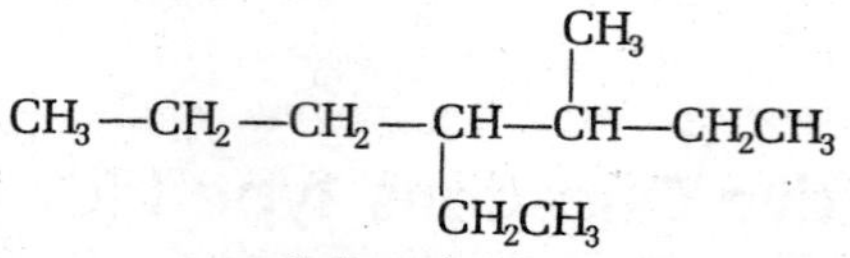

3-methyl-4-ethyl heptane

17. The IUPAC name of following compound is

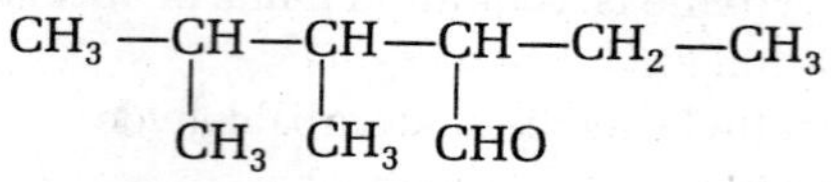

(a) 2-ethyl-3,4-dimethylpentanal
(b) 2,3-dimethyl-4-aldo hexane
(c) 3-aldol-4,5-dimethyl hexane
(d) 1,3,4,5-tetraethyl butanal

18. IUPAC name of 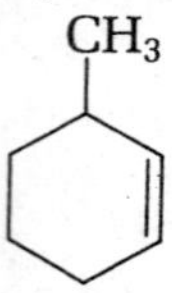 is

(a) 3-methylcyclohexene
(b) 1-methylcyclohex-2-ene
(c) 6-methylcyclohexene
(d) 1-methylcyclohex-5-ene

19. IUPAC name of

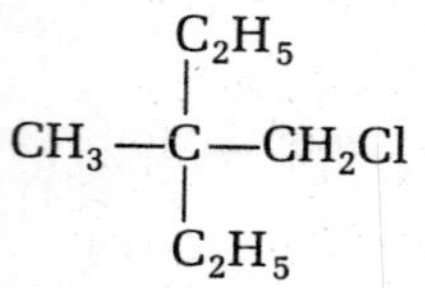

is

(a) 1-chloro-2,2-diethyl-2-methylethane
(b) 1-chloro-2-ethyl-2-methylbutane
(c) 1-chloro-2,2-diethylpropane
(d) 3-chloro-2,2-diethylpropane

20. The IUPAC name of 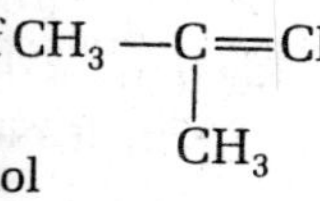 is

(a) 2-methyl-3-butenol
(b) 3-methyl-2-butenol
(c) 3-methyl-3-butenol
(d) 2-methyl-2-butenol

21. Which one of the following contains *iso*-propyl group?
(a) 2,2,3,3-tetramethylpentane
(b) 2-methylpentane
(c) 2,2,3-trimethylpentane
(d) 3,3-dimethylpentane

22. The IUPAC name of the following compound is

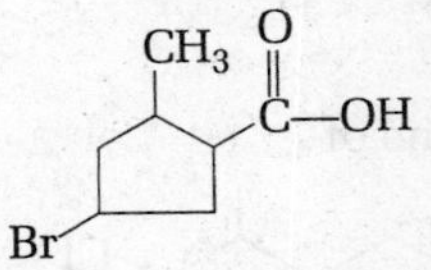

[JEE Main 2020, Sep.]

(a) 3-bromo-5-methylcyclopentane carboxylic acid
(b) 3-bromo-5-methylcyclopentanoic acid
(c) 5-bromo-3-methylcyclopentanoic acid
(d) 4-bromo-2-methylcyclopentane carboxylic acid

23. Which one of the following structures has the IUPAC name 3-ethynyl-2-hydroxy-4-methylhex-3-en-5-ynoic acid? **[JEE Advanced 2020]**

(a) 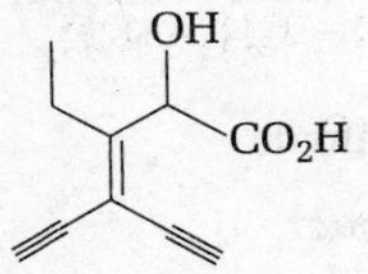

(b) 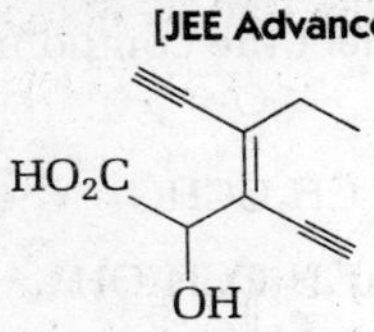

(c) 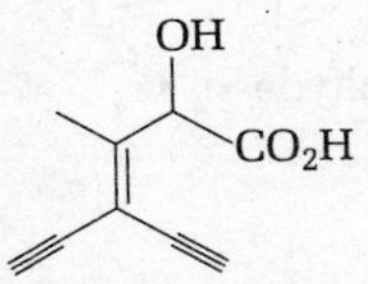

(d) 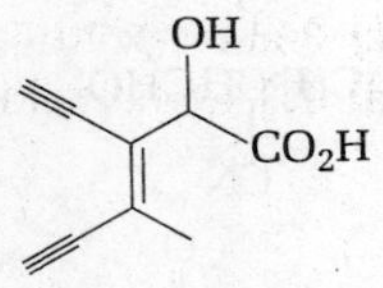

24. IUPAC name for the compound

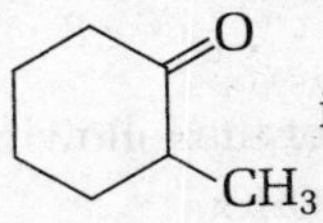

is

(a) α-methylcyclohexanone
(b) 2-methylcyclohexanone
(c) heptanone-2
(d) methylcyclohexanone

25. Which is not the correct nomenclature?
(a) Ethanedioic acid
(b) 4-pentanone
(c) Pentanedial
(d) Pent-2-ene

26. IUPAC name of the following compound is

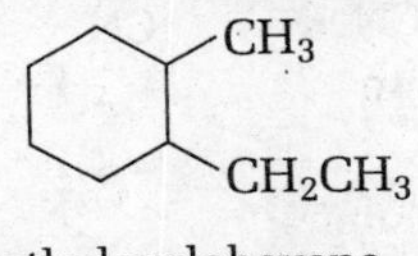

(a) 1-ethyl-2-methylcyclohexane
(b) 1-methyl-2-ethylcyclohexane
(c) 1-methyl-6-ethylcyclohexane
(d) 1-ethyl-6-methylcyclohexane

27. C_5H_{12} has a symmetrical structure with one quaternary carbon. Its name is
(a) *n*-pentane (b) 2-methylbutane
(c) 2,2-dimethylpropane (d) 1-methylbutane

28. 2,2,3,3-tetramethylbutane reacts with Cl_2 such that one H-atom is replaced by Cl-atom. IUPAC name of the product obtained is
(a) 2-chloromethyl-2,2,3-tetramethylbutane
(b) 1-chloro-2,2,3,3-tetramethylbutane
(c) Both are acceptable
(d) None is acceptable

29. By acidic hydrolysis —CN group changes to $-\overset{\text{O}}{\overset{\|}{\text{C}}}\text{OH}$

I. $CH_3\underset{\underset{\text{CN}}{|}}{\text{CH}}CHO \xrightarrow{H_3O^+} CH_3\underset{\underset{\text{COOH}}{|}}{\text{CH}}CHO$

II. $CH_3\underset{\underset{\text{OH}}{|}}{\text{CH}}CN \xrightarrow{H_3O^+} CH_3\underset{\underset{\text{OH}}{|}}{\text{CH}}COOH$

III. $CH_3\overset{\overset{\text{O}}{\|}}{\text{C}}CN \xrightarrow{H_3O^+} CH_3\overset{\overset{\text{O}}{\|}}{\text{C}}COOH$

In which case(s), preference group of nomenclature changes?
(a) I and II (b) II and III
(c) I and III (d) Only I

30. Following reactions are possible

I. $CH_2{=}CHCOOH \xrightarrow{\Delta} CH_2{=}CH_2$

II. 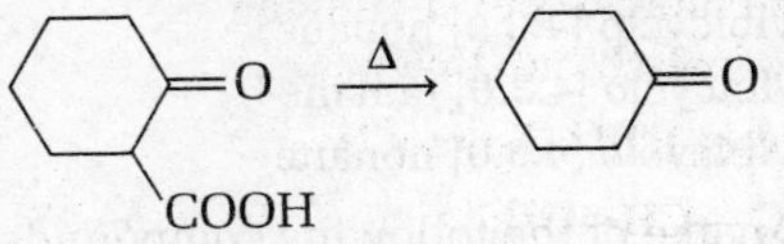

III. $CH_3CH(COOH)_2 \xrightarrow{\Delta} CH_3CH_2COOH$

In which case(s), parent compound loses its preference?
(a) I and II (b) I, II and III
(c) II and III (d) I and III

31. *R*Cl changes to *R*CN on reaction with KCN. Propanenitrile is obtained on reaction of KCN with
(a) 1-chloroethane (b) 1-chloropropane
(c) 2-chloropropane (d) None is correct

32. *A* 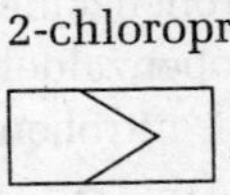, *A* is named as
(a) bicyclo [2. 2. 1] heptane
(b) bicyclo [2. 2. 2] hexane
(c) bicyclo [2. 2. 1] hexane
(d) bicyclo [2. 1. 0] hexane

33. IUPAC name of vinyl acetylene is
(a) 1-butene-3-yne (b) 1-butyne-3-ene
(c) Both are correct (d) None is correct

34. C_6H_{14} has two tertiary carbons. The IUPAC name is

(a) *n*-hexane (b) 2-methylpentane
(c) 3-methylpentane (d) 2,3-dimethylbutane

35. What is the IUPAC name of the following compound?

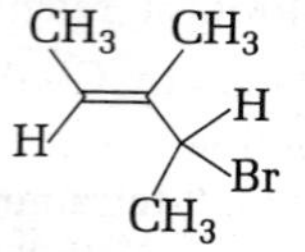

[JEE Main 2019, Jan.]

(a) 3-bromo-3-methyl-1,2-dimethylprop-1-ene
(b) 3-bromo-1,2-dimethylbut-1-ene
(c) 2-bromo-3-methylpent-3-ene
(d) 4-bromo-3-methylpent-2-ene

36. IUPAC name of the following is

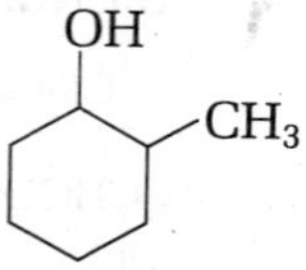

(a) 2-methylcyclohexanol
(b) 2-methyl-1-cyclohexanol
(c) 1-hydroxyl-2-methylcyclohexane
(d) 2-hydroxy-1-methylcyclohexane

37. IUPAC name of the following cycloalkane is

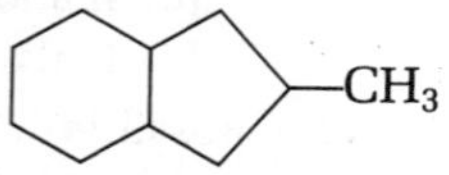

(a) 8-methylbicyclo [4.3.0] nonane
(b) 1-methylbicyclo [4.3.0] nonane
(c) 3-methylbicyclo [4.3.0] nonane
(d) 4-methylbicyclo [4.3.0] nonane

38. The IUPAC name of the following compounds is

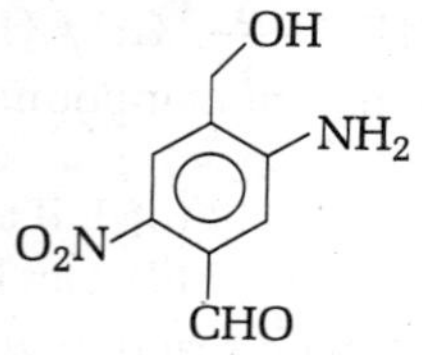

[JEE Main 2020, Sep.]

(a) 2-nitro-4-hydroxymethyl-5-amino benzaldehyde
(b) 3-amino-4-hydroxymethyl-1-5- nitrobenzaldehyde
(c) 5-amino-4-hydroxymethyl 1-2-nitrobenzaldehyde
(d) 4-amino-2-formyl-5-hydroxymethyl -nitrobenzene

39. PCl_5 causes cleavage of ether linkage $R—O—R'$ forming RCl, $R'Cl$ and $POCl_3$.

$C_5H_{12}O$ on reaction with PCl_5 forms 2-chloropropane and 1-chloroethane as main compounds.

Thus, $C_5H_{12}O$ is named as

(a) 1-ethoxypropane
(b) 2-ethoxypropane
(c) 1-ethylpropane
(d) 2-ethylpropane

40. Structure of bicyclo (2.2.2) octane is

(a) 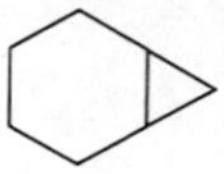 (b) 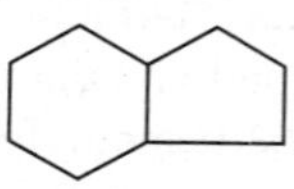

(c) 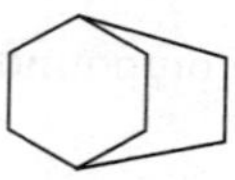 (d) 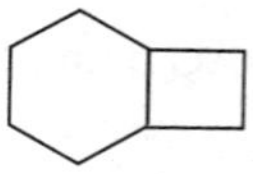

41. The IUPAC name of

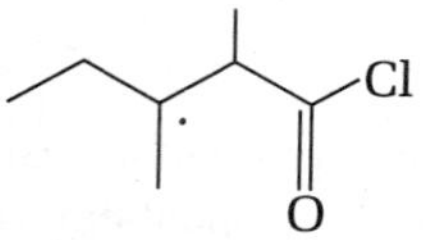

is

(a) 3,4-dimethylpentanoyl chloride
(b) 1-chloro-1-oxo-2,3-dimethylpentane
(c) 2-ethyl-3-methylbutanoyl chloride
(d) 2,3-dimethylpentanoyl chloride

42. Select the compound with incorrect principal group

(a) $CH_3\overset{O}{\overset{\|}{C}}CHO$ Aldehyde
(b) $CH_3\underset{O}{\underset{\|}{C}}CH_2OH$ Alcohol
(c) $CH_3\underset{CN}{\underset{|}{CH}}CHO$ Aldehyde
(d) $CH_3\underset{CN}{\underset{|}{CH}}\overset{O}{\overset{\|}{C}}OH$ Carboxylic acid

43. The IUPAC name for the following compound is

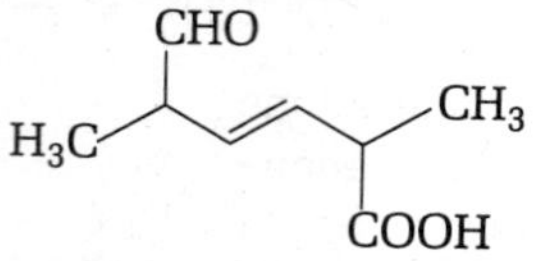

[JEE Main 2020, Sep.]

(a) 6-formyl-2-methyl-hex-3-enoic acid
(b) 2, 5-dimethyl-6-oxo-hex-3-enoic acid
(c) 2, 5-dimethyl-6-carboxy-hex-3-enal
(d) 2, 5-dimethyl-5-carboxy-hex-3-enal

44. 3-cyano-1,5-pentanedinitrile has following structure

(a) $\underset{CN}{\underset{|}{CH_2}}—CH_2—\underset{CN}{\underset{|}{CH}}—CH_2—\underset{CN}{\underset{|}{CH_2}}$
(b) $\underset{CN}{\underset{|}{CH_2}}—\underset{CN}{\underset{|}{CH}}—\underset{CN}{\underset{|}{CH_2}}$
(c) $\underset{CN}{\underset{|}{CH_2}}—\underset{CN}{\underset{|}{CH}}—CH_2—\underset{CN}{\underset{|}{CH_2}}$
(d) $\underset{NO_2}{\underset{|}{CH_2}}—CH_2—\underset{CN}{\underset{|}{CH}}—CH_2—\underset{NO_2}{\underset{|}{CH_2}}$

45. Propane-1,2,3-tricarboxylic acid is

(a) $HOOC-CH(COOH)-COOH$ (COOH above, CHCOOH, COOH below)

(b) CH_2COOH above, CHCOOH, COOH below

(c) CH_2COOH above, CHCOOH, CH_2COOH below

(d) None of these

46. The IUPAC name for the following compound is **[JEE Main 2019, April]**

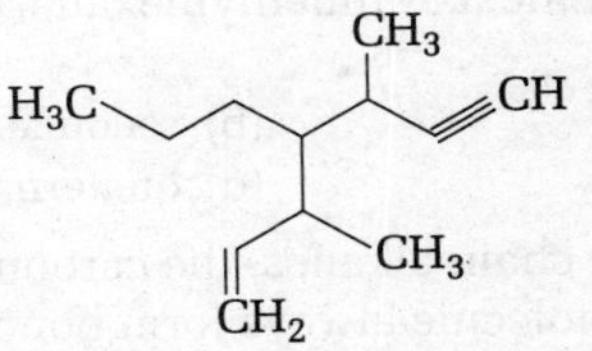

(a) 3-methyl-4-(3-methylprop-1-enyl)-1-heptyne
(b) 3, 5-dimethyl-4-propylhept-6-en-1-yne
(c) 3-methyl-4-(1-methylprop-2-ynyl)-1-heptene
(d) 3, 5-dimethyl-4-propylhept-1-en-6-yne

47. Pent-4-yne-2-ol has the structure as

(a) $CH_3CH(OH)CH_2C\equiv CH$

(b) $CH\equiv CCH_2CH(OH)CH_3$

(c) Both (a) and (b)
(d) None of the above

48. In the following compound, groups designated as *A*, *B*, *C* will be numbered as

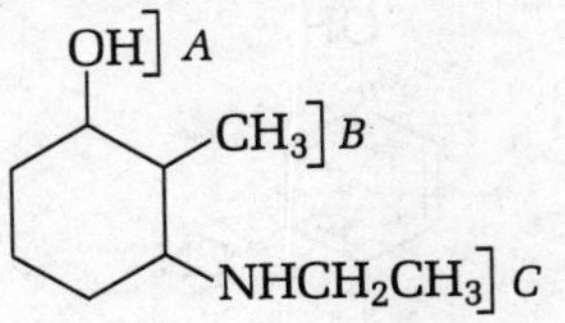

(a) 3, 2, 1 (b) 6, 1, 2
(c) 3, 1, 2 (d) 1, 2, 3

49. In the following compound, groups designated as *A*, *B*, *C* will be numbered as

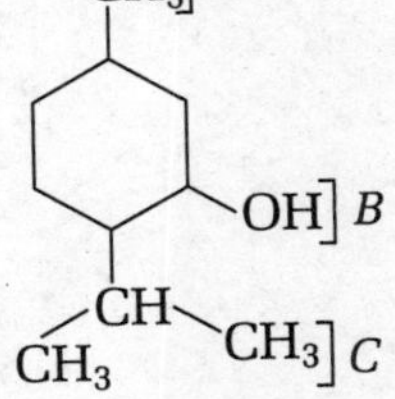

(a) 1, 2, 4 (b) 4, 2, 1
(c) 5, 1, 2 (d) 3, 1, 6

50. Following compound is named as

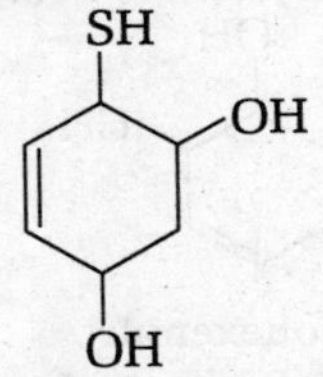

(a) 6-mercaptocyclohex-4-ene-1,3-diol
(b) 1-mercaptocyclohex-2-ene-4,6-diol
(c) 1-mercaptocyclohex-5-ene-2,4-diol
(d) 4-mercaptocyclohex-2-ene-1,5-diol

51. IUPAC name of the following compound is

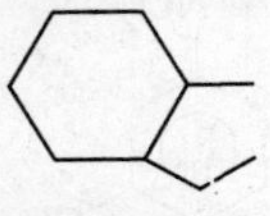

(a) 1-ethyl-2-methylcyclohexane
(b) 2-ethyl-1-methylcyclohexane
(c) 6-ethyl-1-methylcyclohexane
(d) 1-ethyl-6-methylcyclohexane

52. When Cl_2 reacts with C_5H_{10}, one H is replaced by Cl giving only one type of $C_5H_9Cl \cdot C_5$ is

(a)  (b) 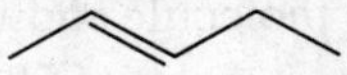

(c) 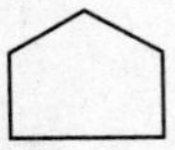 (d) 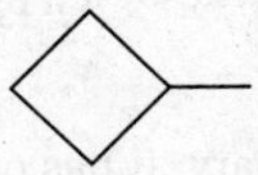

53. Which class represents oxiranes?

(a) 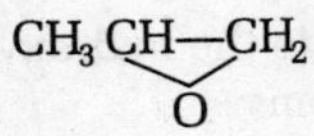 (b) $CH_3\overset{O}{\overset{\|}{C}}-O-\overset{O}{\overset{\|}{C}}CH_3$

(c) 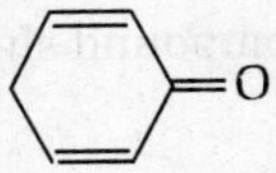 (d) ---SiO_2—O—SiO_2----

54. The IUPAC name of the following compound is

$H_3C-\underset{}{CH}(CH_3)-CH(OH)-CH_2-COOH$ **[JEE Main 2019, April]**

(a) 4,4 - dimethyl -3-hydroxybutanoic acid
(b) 2-methyl-3-hydroxypentan-5-oic acid
(c) 3- hydroxy -4- methylpentanoic acid
(d) 4-methyl-3-hydroxypentanoic acid

55. Number of primary, secondary and tertiary hydrogen in the following are respectively

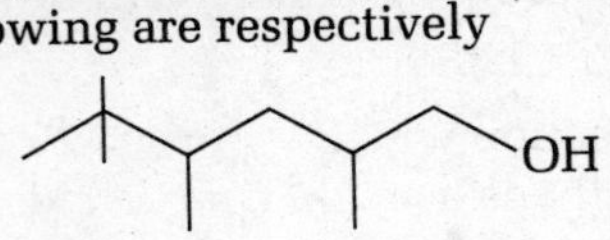

	1°	2°	3°
(a)	18	2	2
(b)	16	4	2
(c)	17	2	2
(d)	17	2	1

56. IUPAC name of the following compound is

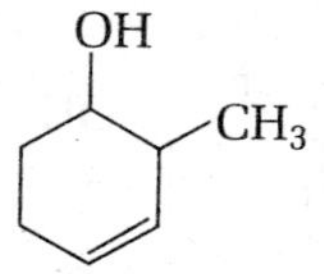

(a) 2-methyl-3-cyclohexenol
(b) 3-methyl-1-cyclohexen-4-ol
(c) 4-hydroxy-3-methyl-1-cyclohexene
(d) 2-hydroxy-1-methylcyclohexene

57. The correct IUPAC name of the following compound is **[JEE Main 2019, April]**

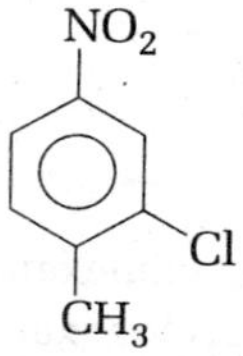

(a) 2-methyl-5-nitro-1-chlorobenzene
(b) 3-chloro-1-methyl-1-nitrobenzene
(c) 2-chloro-1-methyl 1-4-nitrobenzene
(d) 5-chloro-4-methyl 1-1-nitrobenzene

58. The molecule shown is a .... alcohol because

$$\underset{\large |\atop \large OH}{CH_3CH_2CHCH_2CH_3}$$

(a) primary, it has one —OH group
(b) primary, its —OH group is on the central carbon
(c) secondary; the carbon bonded to the —OH group is bonded to two other carbons
(d) secondary, each group bonded to the hydroxyl carbon contains two carbon atoms

59. What is the IUPAC name of the compound shown?

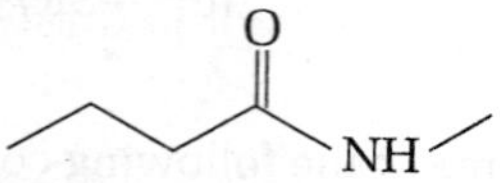

(a) 1-methylpropanamide (b) N-methyl propanamide
(c) N-butylethanamide (d) N-methylbutanamide

60. IUPAC name of the following compound is

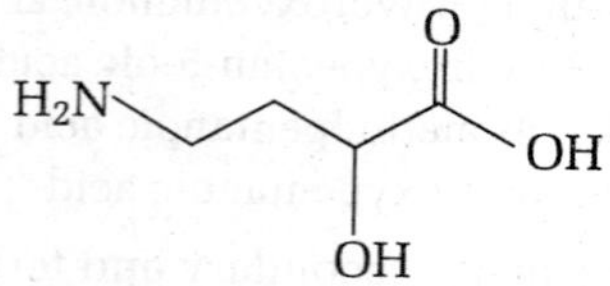

(a) γ-amino-α-hydroxybutyric acid
(b) 4-amino-2-hydroxybutanoic acid
(c) α-amino-γ-hydroxybutyric acid
(d) 1-amino-3-hydroxybutanoic acid

61. 3-butenoic acid (or but-3-enoic acid) is represented as

(a) 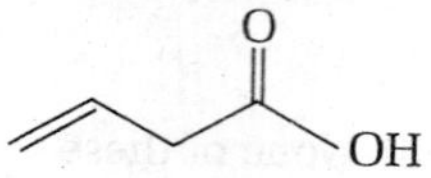 (b) 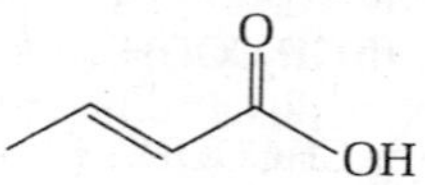

(c) 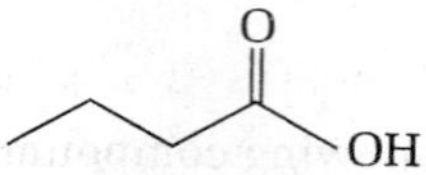 (d) None of these

62. In the molecule 3,3-dimethylhexane, carbon number two is
(a) primary (b) secondary
(c) tertiary (d) quaternary

63. In a straight chain alkanes, the carbon atoms on each end of the molecule always form bonds with .... atoms of hydrogen, the carbons within the molecule always form bonds with .... hydrogen atoms.
(a) 4, 4 (b) 4, 2
(c) 3, 3 (d) 3, 2

64. A hydrocarbon of molecular weight 72 g mol^{-1} has a 2-methyl group. Its IUPAC name is
(a) 2-methyl butane
(b) 2,3-dimethyl propane
(c) 2,2-dimethyl propane
(d) *n*-pentane

65. Molar ratio of C, H and O are same in the compound of molar mass 58 g mol^{-1}. It can be
(a) propanal (b) propanone
(c) 1,2-ethanedial (d) propenol

66. The IUPAC name of the following compound is

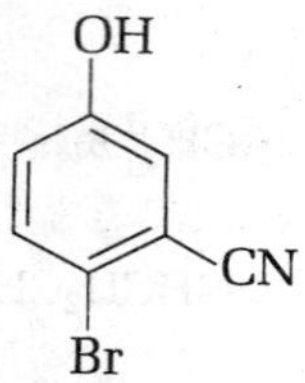

[IIT JEE 2009]

(a) 4-bromo-3-cyanophenol
(b) 2-bromo-5-hydroxybenzonitrile
(c) 2-cyano-4-hydroxybromobenzene
(d) 6-bromo-3-hydroxybenzonitrile

Objective Questions Type II [One or more than one correct option(s)]

In each of the questions below, four choices are given, of which one or more than one are correct.

1. Which of the following statements is/are wrong?
(a) C_nH_{2n} is the general formula of alkanes.
(b) In homologous series, all members have the same physical properties.
(c) IUPAC means International Union of Physics and Chemistry.
(d) Butane contains two 1°C atoms and two 2°C atoms.

2. Which of the following statements is/are correct?
(a) Homologous series can be represented by a general formula.
(b) The chemical properties of an organic compound depend on the functional group.
(c) Groups obtained by the removal of one H-atom from the alkane are called alkyl groups.
(d) Alkynes consists of one double-bond in their molecules.

3. Which of the following statements is/are wrong?
(a) Acetic acid is the systematic name of vinegar.
(b) $Me-\overset{O}{\overset{\|}{C}}-OH$ is an an unsaturated compound.
(c) Prefixes like *n*-, *iso*, sec-, *tert*, *neo*-, etc., are used in IUPAC system.
(d) The systematic names of acids are formed by dropping -e of the name of parent alkane and adding -oic acid.

4. Which of the following statements is/are correct?
(a) $R-\overset{O}{\overset{\|}{C}}-O-\overset{O}{\overset{\|}{C}}-R$ is an unsaturated compound.
(b) Neohydrocarbons contain a 3°C atom.
(c) The IUPAC name of *iso*-propyl alcohol is propan-2-ol.
(d) The IUPAC name of (CH_3CN) is ethanenitrile.

5. Which of the following statement is/are correct?
(a) Methane was name as fire damp as it forms explosive mixture with air.
(b) Primary suffixes are added to the root word to show saturation or unsaturation in a C-atom.
(c) The IUPAC name of valeric acid is pentanoic acid.
(d) The common name of hexanoic acid is caproic acid.

6. The IUPAC name(s) of the following compound is (are) **[JEE Advanced 2017]**

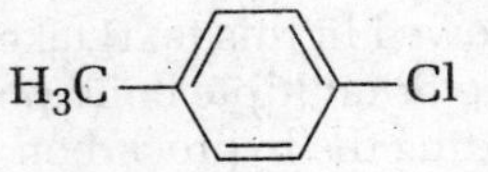

(a) 4-methylchlorobenzene
(b) 4-chlorotoluene
(c) 1-chloro-4-methylbenzene
(d) 1-methyl-4-chlorobenzene

7. Which of the following statements is/are correct?
(a) The common name of ($HOOC-CH_2-COOH$) is malonic acid.
(b) The common name of 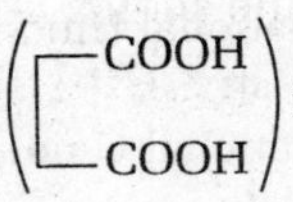 is succinic acid.

(c) The IUPAC name of ($CH_2{=}CH-OCOCH_3$) is vinyl acetate.
(d) The IUPAC name of acrylonitrile is pro-2-ene-nitrile.

8. Which of the following statements is/are correct?
(a) The common name of benzene-1, 2-diol is catechol.
(b) The common name of benzene-1, 3-diol is resorcinol.
(c) The common name of benzene-1, 4-diol is quinol.
(d) The common name of benzene-1, 4-diol is hydroquinone.

Numerical Value Questions

All these questions have a Numerical value as their answer, solve the questions and write your answer.

1. How many 1° carbon atom will be present in a simplest hydrocarbon having two 3° and one 2° carbon atom?

2. Calculate the total carbon atoms are present in parent carbon chain in the given following compound?

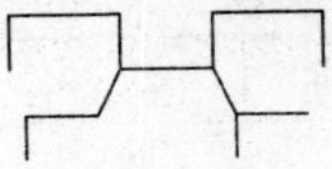

3. 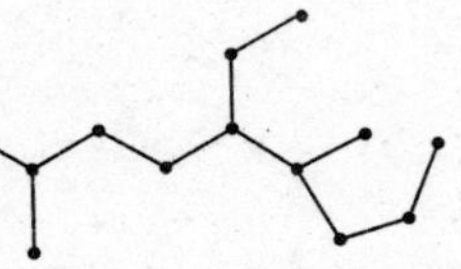

Observe the above structure and count the number of $-CH_3$ (methyl group) present in given alkane.

4. How many total number of substituent are present in the following compound?

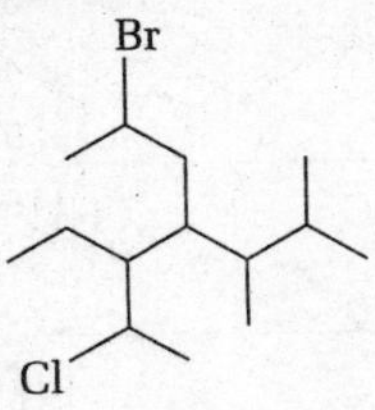

5. 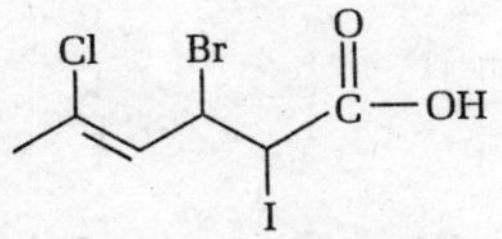

Total number of substituent present in the above compound.

Comprehension Based Questions

In these questions, a passage has been given followed by questions based on it. You have to answer the questions based on the passage given.

***Passage* 1** In 1993, the IUPAC published A Guide to Nomenclature of Organic Compounds Recommendations 1993, R. Panico, W.H. Powell and Jean-Claude Richer, Blackwell Science. This publication advocated one major change that affects the nomenclature of relatively simple compounds.

The 1993 recommendations prefer the principal group or multiple bond position with a number preceding the suffix itself whereas the 1979 recommendations (generally followed in this text) take into account the principal group or multiple bond position with a number preceding the hydrocarbon name.

The 1993 recommendations have not been generally adopted thus, names that adhere to either set of recommendations are acceptable.

Read the above passage and answer the following questions.

1. IUPAC stands for
(a) Indian Union of Pure and Applied Chemists
(b) International Union of Pure and Applied Chemistry
(c) International Union of Pure and Applied Chemists
(d) Italian Union of Pure and Applied Chemists

2. $CH_3CH{=}CHCH_3$ is named as based on 1993 recommendations
(a) 2-butene (b) but-2-ene
(c) Both (a) and (b) (d) None of these

***Passage* 2** IUPAC nomenclature of organic compounds is interesting in many cases. Cyanide in the longest chain is nitrile while as a side chain it is cyano.

Read the above passage and answer the following questions.

1. Write the IUPAC name of the following.

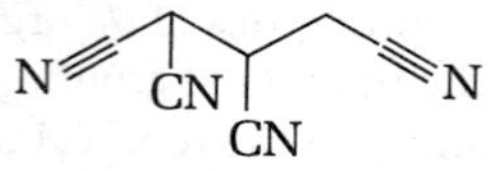

(a) 1,2,3,4-tetracyanobutane
(b) 3,4-dicyano 1,5-pentanedinitrile
(c) 3,3-dicyano 1,5-pentanedinitrile
(d) None of the above

2. In which of the following compounds

$CH_3CH(CN)CHO$	$CH_3CH(CN)COOH$	$CH_3CH(CN)CH_2OH$
I	II	III

—CN is in longest chain?
(a) I and II (b) Only I (c) Only III (d) I, II and III

Matrix-Match Type

Given below are Matching Type Questions, with two columns (each having some items) each . Each item of Column I has to be matched with the items of Column II.

1. Match the functional group (in Column I) with the order of IUPAC nomenclature *p, q, r, ...* (preference in Column II).

	Column I	Column II
A.	—COOH	1. *p*
B.	—OH	2. *q*
C.	—CHO	3. *r*
D.	C=C	4. *s*
E.	C≡C	5. *t*
F.	C—C(=O)—C	6. *u*

2. Match the alkyl groups (in Column I) with their IUPAC nomenclature (in Column II).

Column I	Column II
A. $CH_2{=}\overset{\vert}{C}{-}CH_3$	1. 2-methylpropyl
B. $-CH_2C(CH_3)_3$	2. 1,1-dimethylethyl
C. $-C(CH_3)_3$	3. 3-methylbutyl
D. $-CH_2CH_2CH(CH_3)_2$	4. Isopropenyl
E. $-CH_2CH(CH_3)_2$	5. 2,2-dimethylpropyl

3. Match the parent hydrocarbons in Column I with groups in Column II.

Column I (Parent hydrocarbons)		Column II (Compound or group)	
A.	butane	1.	$CH_3CH_2C{\equiv}CH$
B.	pentane	2.	$CH_2{=}CH{-}CH_2CH_3$
C.	yne	3.	$CH_3CH_2CH_2CH{=}CH_2$
D.	ene	4.	$CH_2{-}CH_2{=}CH_2{-}CH_2{-}CH_3$

4. Match the compound in Column I with the functional group in Column II.

Column I (Compound)	Column II (Functional group)
A. 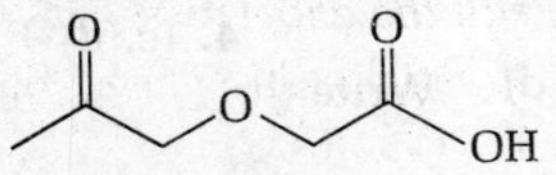	1. Carbonyl
B. 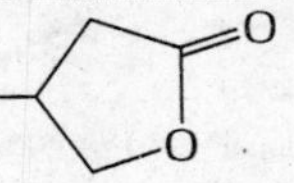	2. Alkoxy
C. 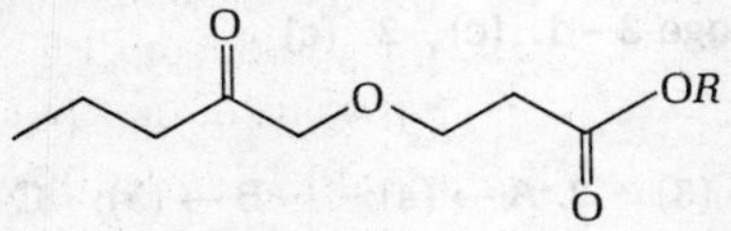	3. Carboxylic
D. 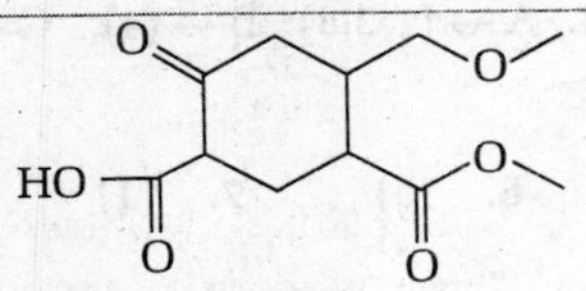	4. Ester

Single Integer Answer Questions

Answer of these questions is a single digit lying between 0 to 9.

1. In the following, yne is at position ....

2. In the following, methyl is at position ....

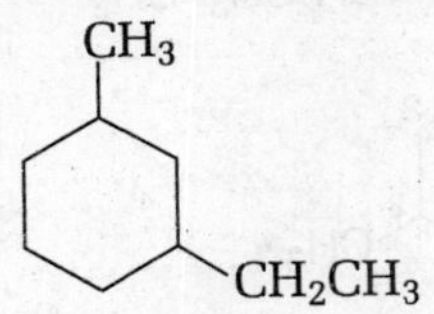

3. Following is named as bicyclo [x.y.z] hept-2-ene

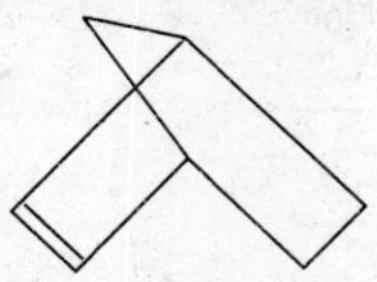

Thus, $(x + y + z)$ is ....

4. In the following principal group is at C_1. Sum of positions of other groups is ....

5. Minimum number of carbon atoms in neosystem is ....

6. The total number of C—C sigma bond(s) in mesityl oxide ($C_6H_{10}O$) is .... **[JEE Main 2021, March]**

7. In the following, number of methyl group(s) as side chain is (are) ....

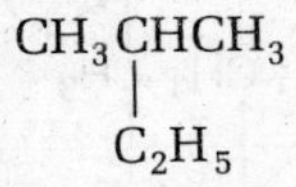

8. In the following, keto group is at position ....

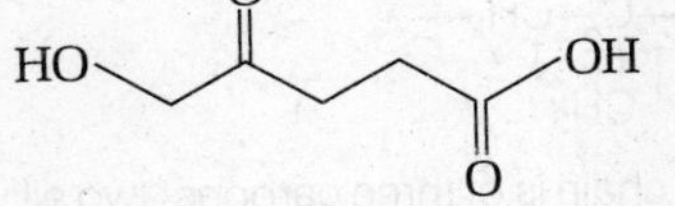

Answers

Objective Questions Type I [Only one correct option]

1. (d)	2. (c)	3. (c)	4. (b)	5. (a)	6. (a)	7. (b)	8. (c)	9. (d)	10. (a)
11. (c)	12. (c)	13. (c)	14. (a)	15. (b)	16. (d)	17. (a)	18. (a)	19. (b)	20. (b)
21. (b)	22. (b)	23. (d)	24. (b)	25. (c)	26. (a)	27. (c)	28. (b)	29. (d)	30. (a)
31. (a)	32. (a)	33. (a)	34. (d)	35. (d)	36. (a)	37. (d)	38. (c)	39. (b)	40. (c)
41. (d)	42. (b)	43. (b)	44. (b)	45. (a)	46. (d)	47. (c)	48. (d)	49. (c)	50. (a)
51. (b)	52. (c)	53. (a)	54. (c)	55. (c)	56. (a)	57. (c)	58. (c)	59. (d)	60. (b)
61. (a)	62. (b)	63. (d)	64. (a)	65. (c)	66. (c)				

Objective Questions Type II [One or more than one correct option(s)]

1. (a, b, c) 2. (a, b, c) 3. (a, b, c) 4. (c, d) 5. (a, b, c, d)
6. (a, b, c) 7. (a, b, d) 8. (a, b, c, d)

Numerical Value Questions

1. (4) 2. (8) 3. (2) 4. (4) 5. (4)

Comprehension Based Questions

Passage 1 – 1. (b) 2. (c) **Passage 2** – 1. (c) 2. (c)

Matrix-Match Type

1. A → (1); B → (4); C → (2); D → (5); E → (6); F → (3)
2. A → (4); B → (5); C → (2); D → (3); E → (1)
3. A → (1,2); B → (3,4); C → (1); D → (2,3,4)
4. A → (1,2,3); B → (4); C → (1,2,3); D → (1,2,3,4)

Single Integer Answer Questions

1. (4) 2. (3) 3. (5) 4. (7) 5. (5) 6. (5) 7. (1) 8. (4)

Solutions

Objective Questions Type I [Only one correct option]

1. (*d*)

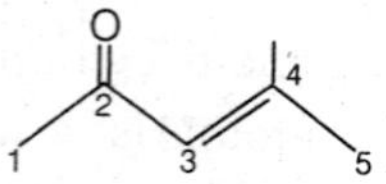

Mesityl oxide

IUPAC [4-methylpent-3-en-2-one]

2. (*c*) 1° carbons are attached directly to one carbon

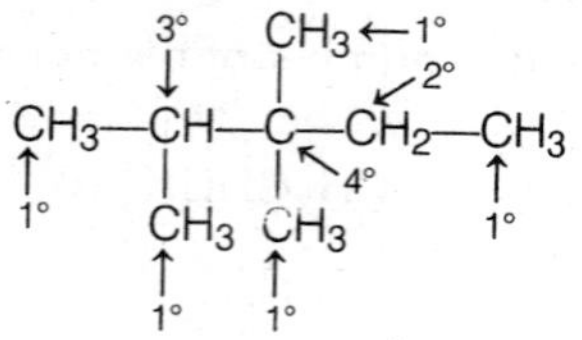

3. (*c*)

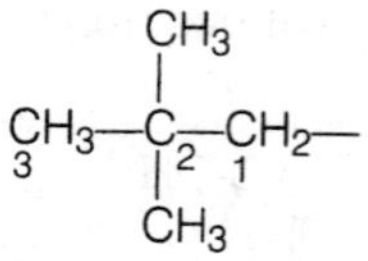

Longest chain is of three carbons; two alkyl groups at C_2—

4. (*b*) —C_2H_5 is expanded to —CH_2CH_3

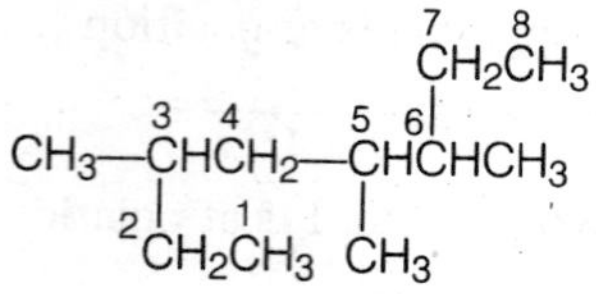

6. (*a*)

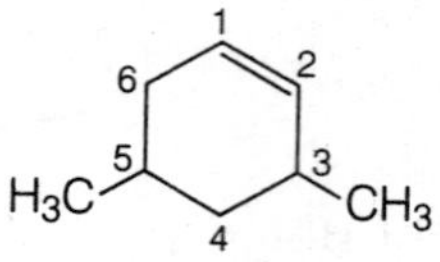

7. (*b*)

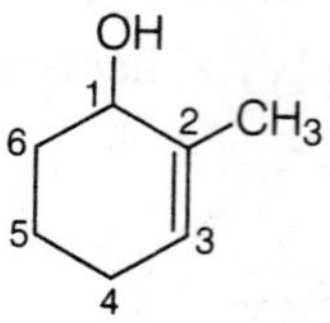

9. (*d*)

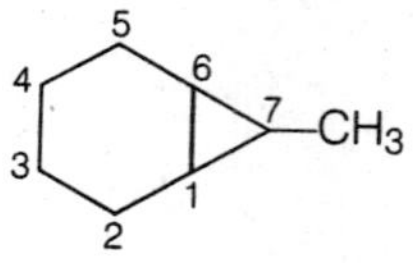

10. (*a*)

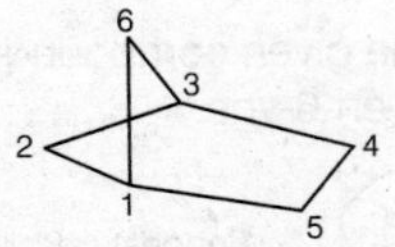

11. (*c*)

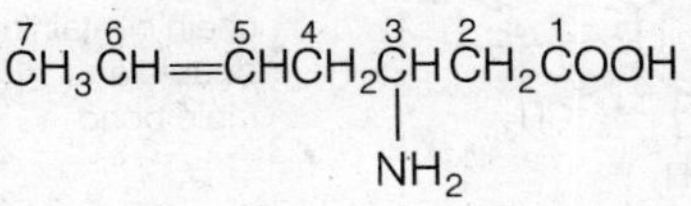

12. (*c*)

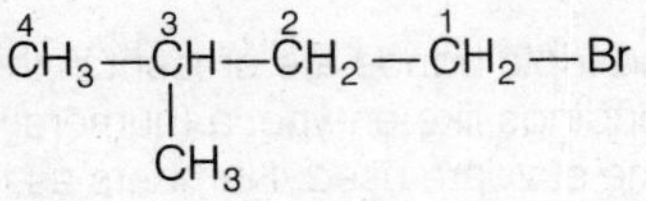

13. (*c*)

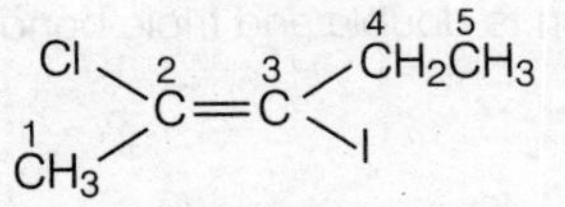

14. (*a*)

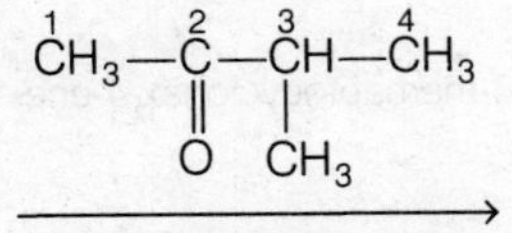

Counting from left side

Correct name is 3-methyl-2-butanone.

15. (*b*)

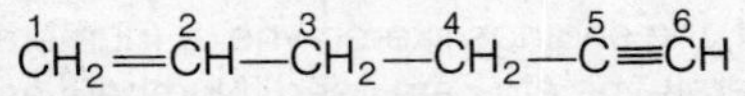

16. (*d*) Substituents are written in alphabetical order 4-ethyl-3-methylheptane

17. (*a*)

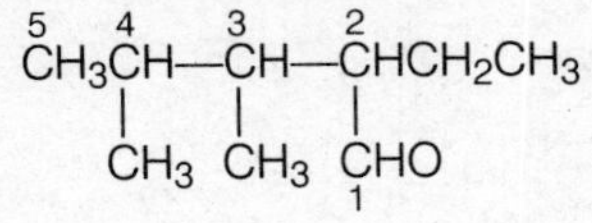

19. (*b*)

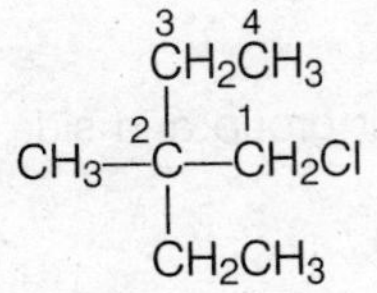

20. (*b*)

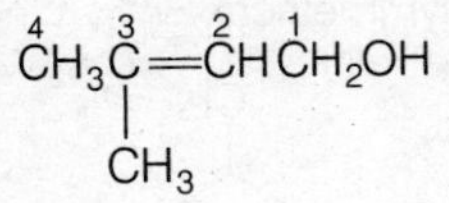

21. (*b*) (a)

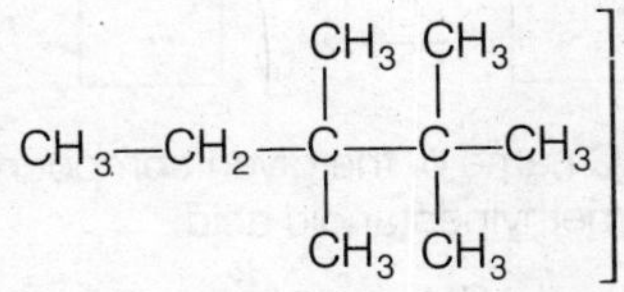

t-butyl

(b)

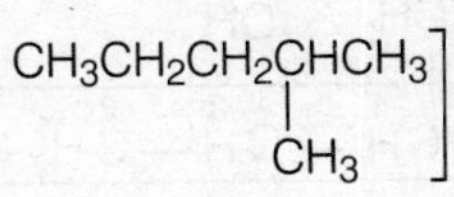

Isopropyl

(c)

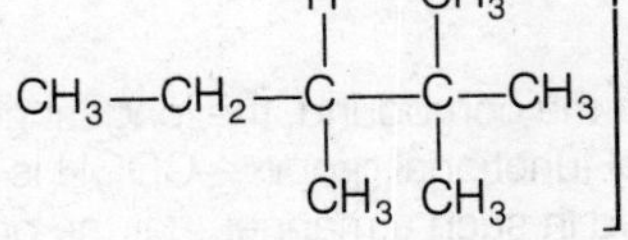

t-butyl

(d)

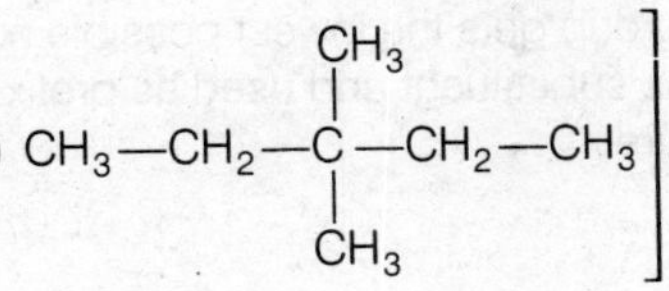

t-butyl

22. (*d*) The IUPAC name of the given compound.

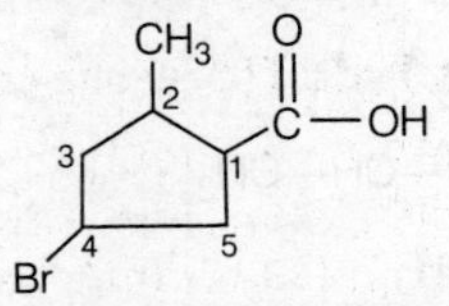

4-bromo-2-methylcyclopentane carboxylic acid

23. (*d*)

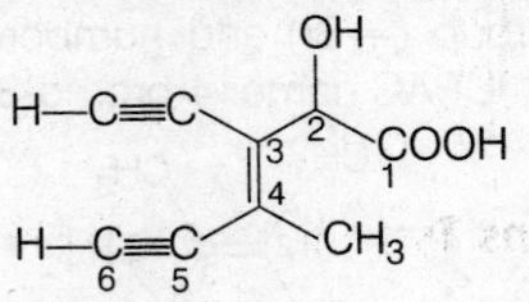

3-ethynyl-2-hydroxy-4-methylhex-3-en-5-ynoic acid

27. (*c*)

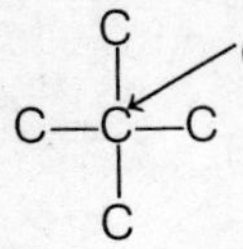

Quaternary carbon

28. (*b*)

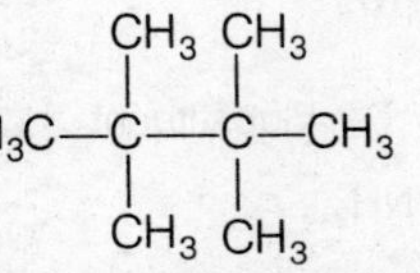

All H-atoms are equivalents

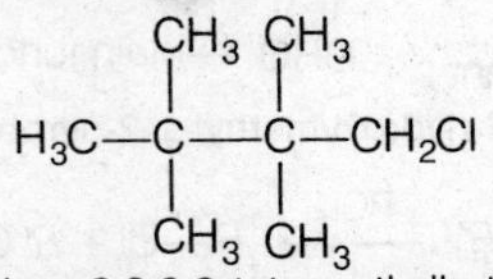

1-chloro-2,2,3,3-tetramethylbutane

29. (*d*) Seniority order is

—COOH, (most)

—CHO

—CN

—OH

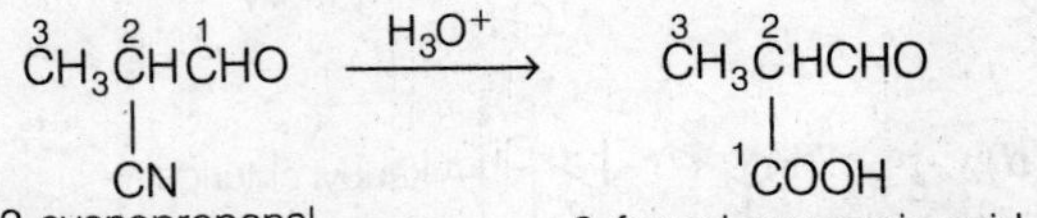

2-cyanopropanal   2-formyl propanoic acid

30. (*a*) I. $CH_2{=}CHCOOH \xrightarrow{\Delta} CH_2{=}CH_2 + CO_2$

II.

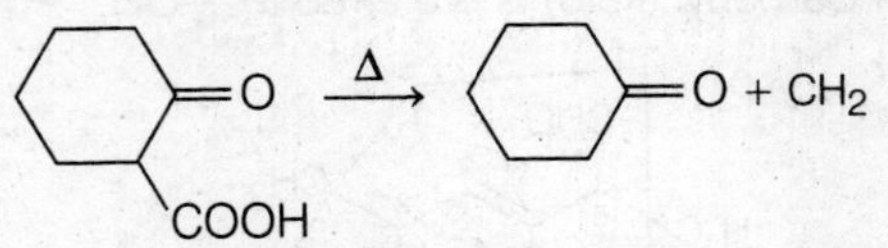

III. No CO_2 evolved (No reaction)

31. (*a*) $RCl \xrightarrow{KCN} RCN$

$CH_3CH_2Cl \longrightarrow CH_3CH_2CN$

Propane nitrile

32. (*a*)

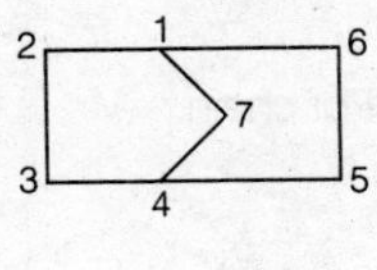

33. (*a*) $\overset{1}{C}H_2=\overset{2}{C}H-\overset{3}{C}\equiv\overset{4}{C}H$

34. (*d*)

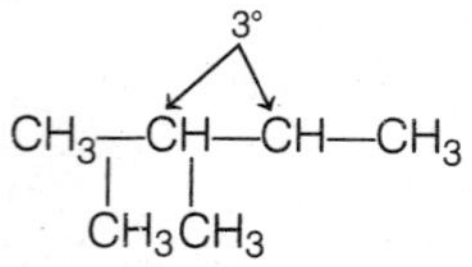

35. (*d*) While naming the compound, alkene gets priority over functional group (—Br) and numbering starts from alkene side. Hence, IUPAC name: 4-bromo-3-methylpent-2-ene.

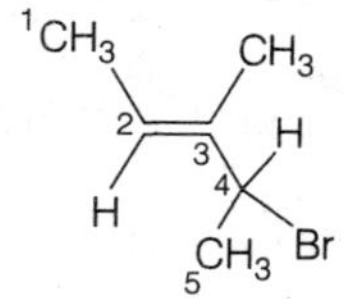

37. (*d*)

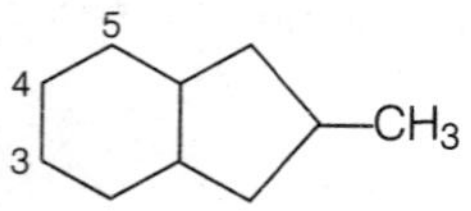

38. (*c*)

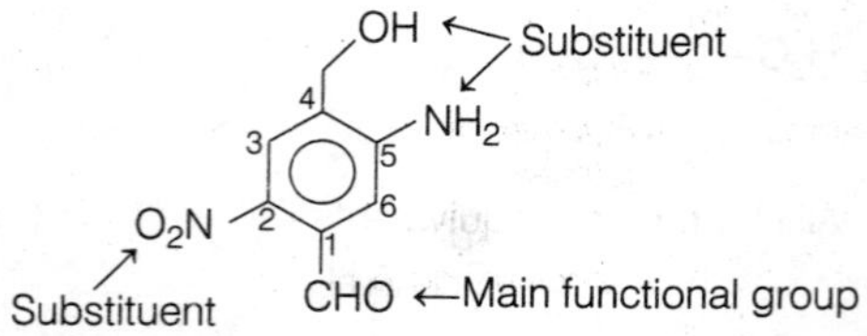

5-amino-4-hydroxymethyl-1-2-nitrobenzaldehyde

39. (*b*) $R—O—R' \xrightarrow{PCl_5} R—Cl + R'Cl + POCl_3$

2-chloropropane

O is replaced by two Cl-atoms one each on alkyl group.

Thus, $C_5H_{12}O$ is

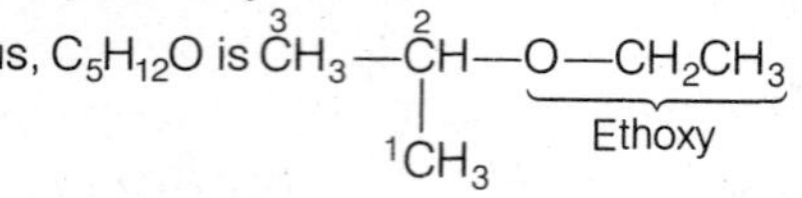

41. (*d*)

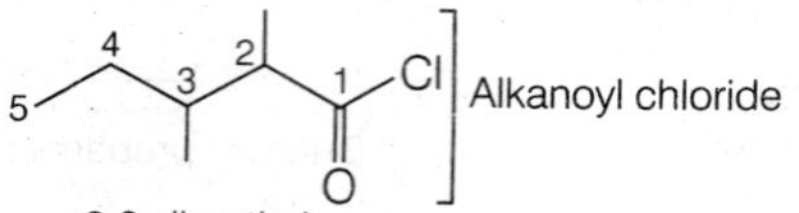

2,3-dimethyl

42. (*b*) Carbonyl (keto) is preferred to —OH.

43. (*b*)

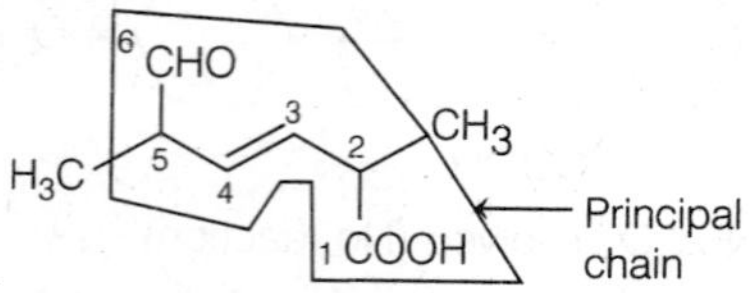

IUPAC name is 2, 5-dimethyl-6-oxo-3-enoic acid.

44. (*b*)

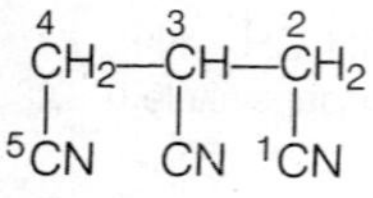

—CN (in longest chain) is part of chain.

46. (*d*) The IUPAC name for the given compound is 3, 5-dimethyl-4-propylhept-1-en-6-yne.

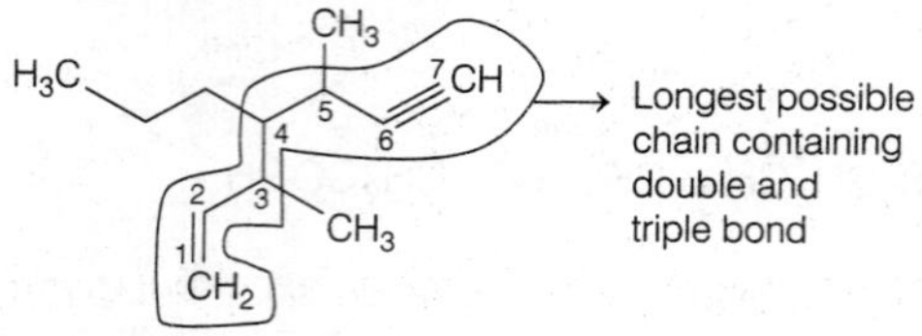

If both double and triple bonds are present in the compound, the endings like-en-yne, a (numeral) dien-(numeral)-yne etc., are used. Numbers as low as possible are given to double and triple bonds as a set.

50. (*a*)

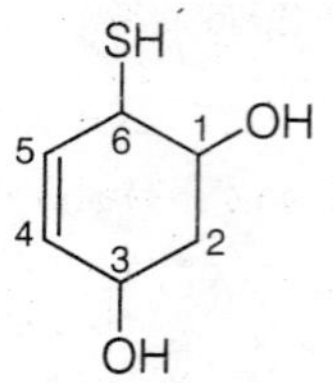

6-mercaptocyclohex-4-ene-1, 3-diol

If both double and triple bonds are present in the compound, the endings like-en-yne, a (numeral) dien-(numeral)-yne etc., are used. Numbers as low as possible are given to double and triple bonds as a set.

51. (*b*)

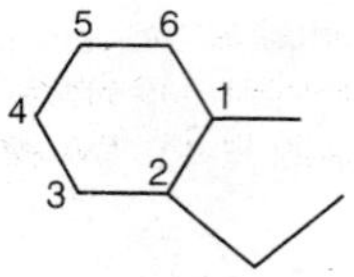

Counting is from the smaller group and side chains are written in alphabetical order.
2-ethyl-1-methylcyclohexane

52. (*c*) Given compound is symmetrical.

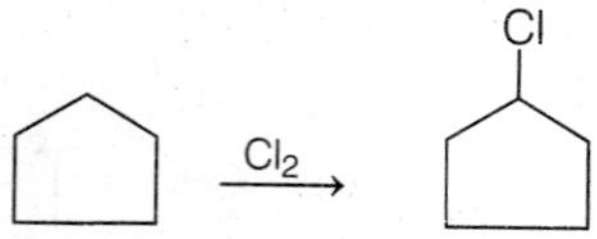

54. (*c*) The IUPAC name of the given compound is 3-hydroxy-4-methylpentanoic acid.

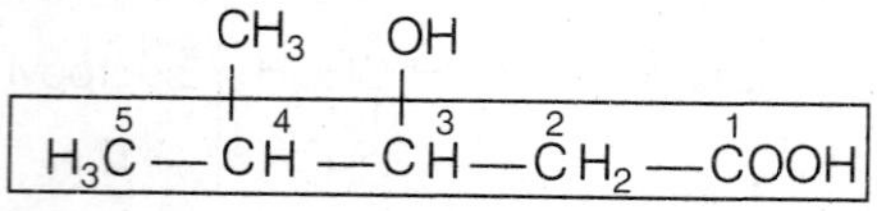

Principal chain

While naming the compound, the longest chain that have principal functional group —COOH is choosen and numbered in such a manner that the principal functional group gets the lowest possible number. —OH act as substituent and used as prefix in nomenclature.

55. (*c*)

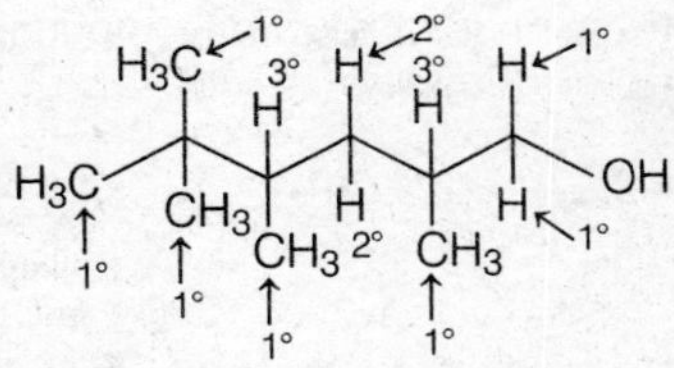

1° — 17 (attached to C directly, attached to one C)

2° — 2 (attached to C directly, attached to two C)

3° — 2 (attached to C directly and attached to three C)

56. (*a*)

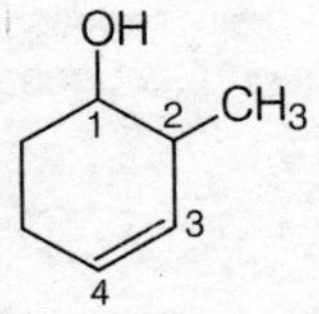

2-methyl-3-cyclohexenol

57. (*c*) The IUPAC name of the given compound is

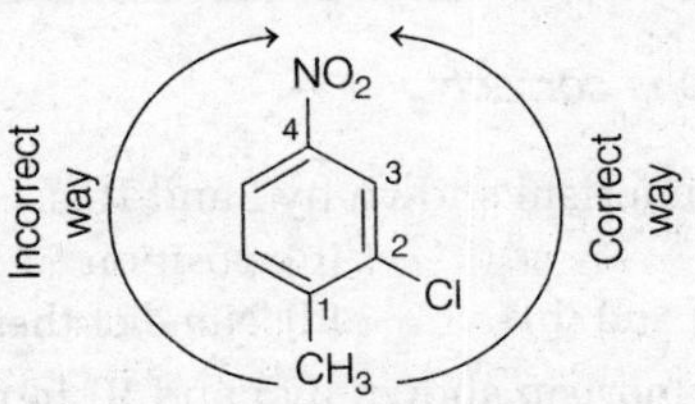

2- chloro-1-methyl-4-nitrobenzene

Here, the given compound contains two or more functional groups. So, the numbering is done in such a way that the sum of the locants is the lowest.

59. (*d*)

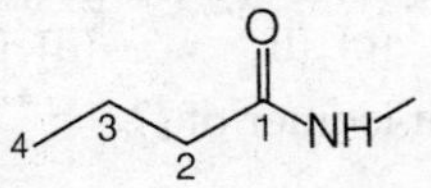

Derivative of butanoic acid.

60. (*b*)

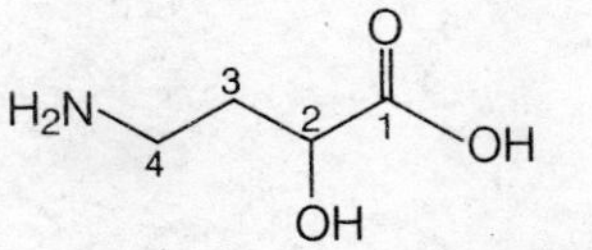

Derivative of butanoic acid.

—OH at C_2

—NH_2 at C_4

61. (*a*)

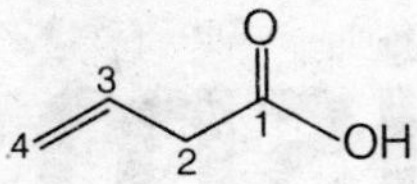

62. (*b*)

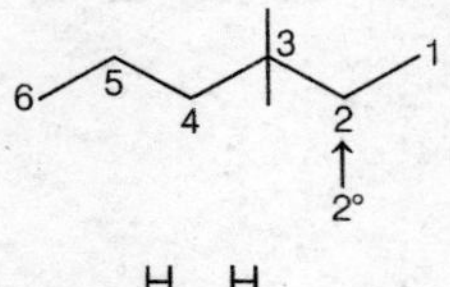

63. (*d*)

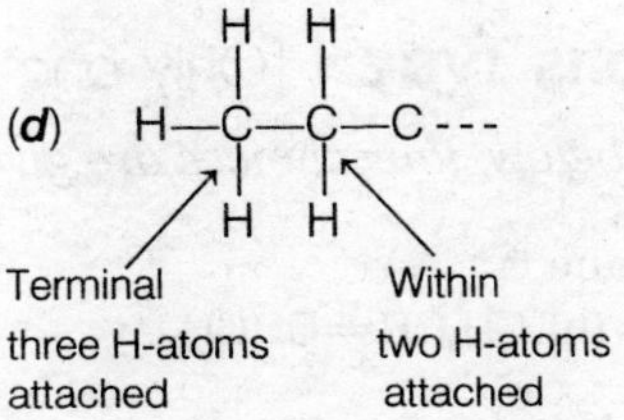

64. (*a*)

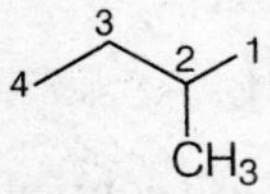

2-methyl butane

C_5H_{12} molar mass = 72 g mol^{-1}

65. (*c*) Empirical formula weight of CHO = 29 g

Molar mass = 58 g mol

Molecular formula = $C_2H_2O_2$,

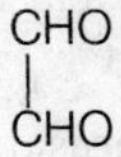

03

Isomerism

Objective Questions Type I [Only one correct option]

In each of the questions below, four choices are given of which only one is correct.

1. Chain isomer of cyclobutane is
(a) $CH_3CH_2CH{=}CH_2$
(b) $CH_3CH{=}CHCH_3$
(c) 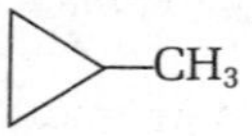
(d) $CH_3\underset{\displaystyle CH_3}{\underset{|}{C}}{=}CH_2$

2. Alkane, C_5H_{12}, in which all H-atoms are equivalent is
(a) *n*-pentane
(b) 2-methylbutane
(c) 2,2-dimethylpropane
(d) cyclopentane

3. Nuclear isomers (alicyclic) of C_6H_{12} are
(a) 1
(b) 2
(c) 3
(d) 4

4. In presence of $AlCl_3$/HCl, *n*-butane changes to another nuclear isomer that can be
(a) isobutane
(b) isobutene
(c) 1-butene
(d) 2-butene

5. Chain isomer of butyl group can be
(a) $CH_3\underset{\displaystyle CH_3}{\underset{|}{C}H}CH_2-$
(b) $CH_3CH_2\underset{\displaystyle CH_3}{\underset{|}{C}H}-$
(c) $CH_3-\overset{\displaystyle CH_3}{\overset{|}{\underset{\displaystyle CH_3}{\underset{|}{C}}}}-$
(d) All are correct

6. Consider the following structures,

I: $CH_3CH_2CH_2CH_2Cl$

II: $CH_3\underset{\displaystyle Cl}{\underset{|}{C}H}CH_2CH_3$

III: $CH_3\underset{\displaystyle CH_3}{\underset{|}{C}H}CH_2Cl$

IV: $CH_3-\overset{\displaystyle CH_3}{\overset{|}{\underset{\displaystyle Cl}{\underset{|}{C}}}}-CH_3$

Type of isomerism shown by I and II is
(a) chain
(b) position
(c) Both (a) and (b)
(d) None of these

7. Type of isomerism shown by I and III in question 6 (above) is
(a) chain
(b) position
(c) Both (a) and (b)
(d) None of these

8. Position isomer of III in question 6 (above) is
(a) I
(b) II
(c) III
(d) IV

9. Which is not the position isomer of I?

I. 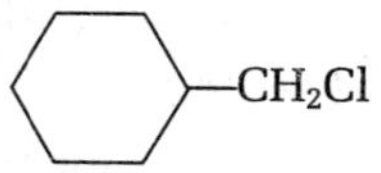

(a) 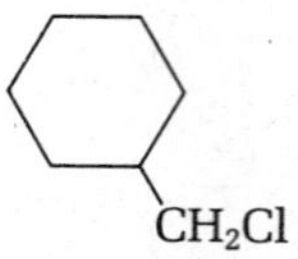
(b) 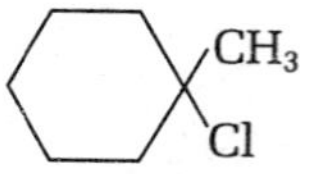
(c) 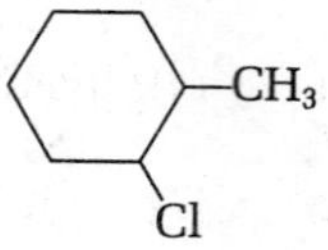
(d) 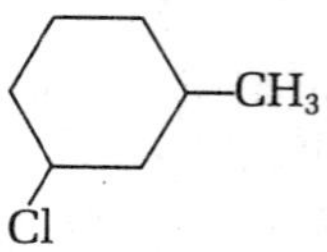

10. Compound with molecular formula C_3H_6O can show [JEE Main 2021, March]
(a) positional isomerism
(b) both positional isomerism and metamerism
(c) metamerism
(d) functional group isomerism

11. Functional isomers of the molecular formula $C_5H_8O_2$ can be
(a) 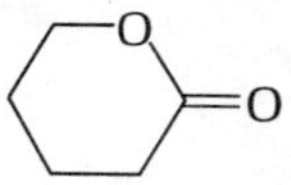
(b) 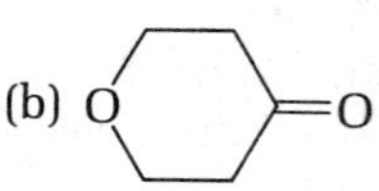
(c) Both (a) and (b)
(d) None of these

12. C_4H_8O is decomposed by PCl_5 forming 2,3-dichlorobutane. C_4H_8O can be
(a) 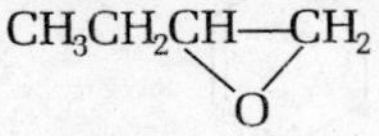 (b) 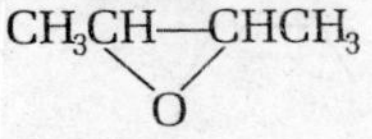
(c) $CH_3CH_2CH_2CHO$ (d) $CH_3CH_2\overset{O}{\overset{\|}{C}}CH_3$

13. A dibasic acid *A* with a dipole moment decolourises Br_2 water. Functional isomer of *A* is an ester *B*. *A* and *B* are

	A	*B*
(a)	CHCOOH ‖ CHCOOH	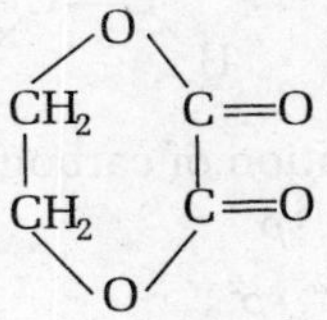
(b)	CHCOOH ‖ HOOCCH	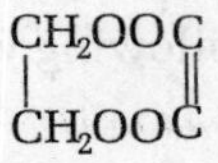
(c)	CHCOOH ‖ CHCOOH	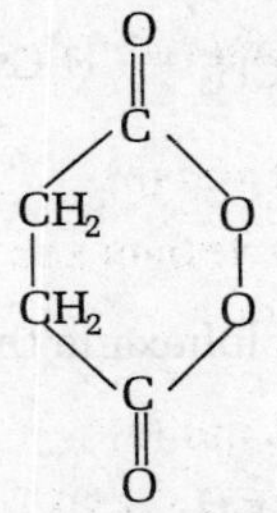

(d) None of the above

14. Which is not the functional isomer of the molecular formula C_4H_8O?
(a) 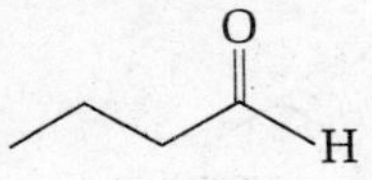 (b) 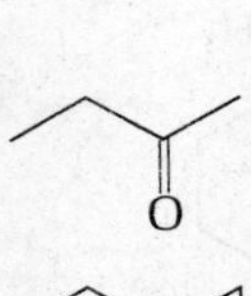
(c) 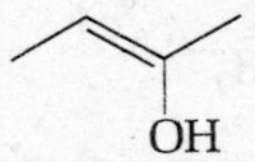 (d) 

15. Number of esters of the molecular formula $C_3H_6O_2$ can be
(a) 4 (b) 3 (c) 2 (d) 1

16. A tertiary-ether of molecular formula $C_5H_{12}O$ is
(a) $CH_3CH_2\underset{OCH_3}{\underset{|}{C}}HCH_3$ (b) $(CH_3)_3COCH_3$
(c) $CH_3CH_2OCH(CH_3)_2$ (d) $CH_3CH_2OCH_2CH_2CH_3$

17. 2-pentanone and 3-pentanone are
(a) position isomers
(b) metamers
(c) Both (a) and (b)
(d) None of the above

18. Metamer of the compound *A* is
A : 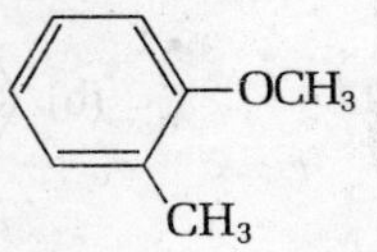
(a) 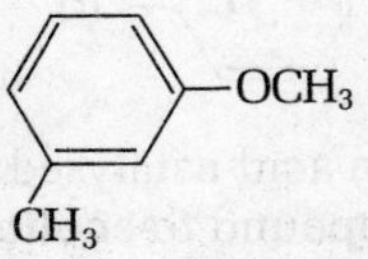 (b) 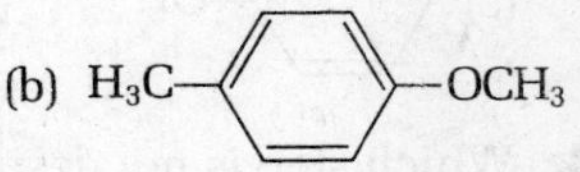
(c) 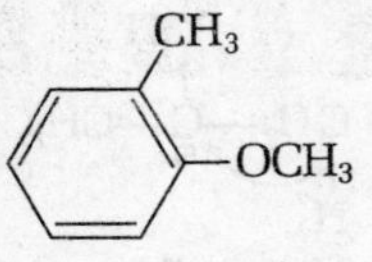 (d) 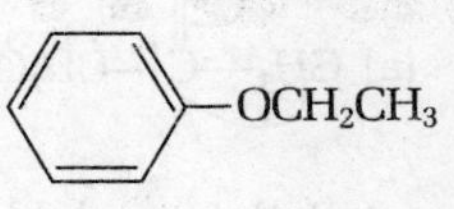

19. Functional isomer of the compound *A* (in question 18) is
(a) 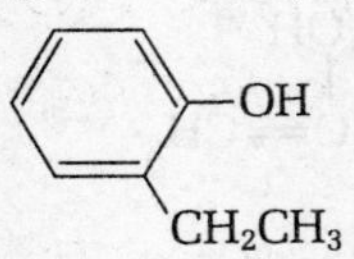 (b) 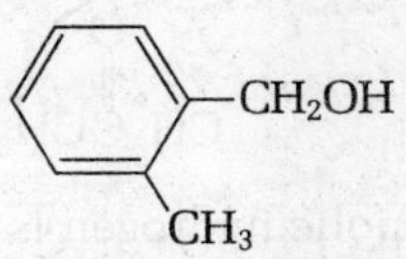
(c) Both (a) and (b) (d) None of these

20. Position isomer of the compound *A* [in question (18)] is
(a) 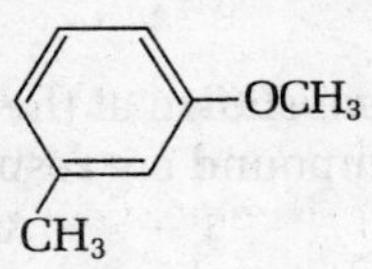 (b) 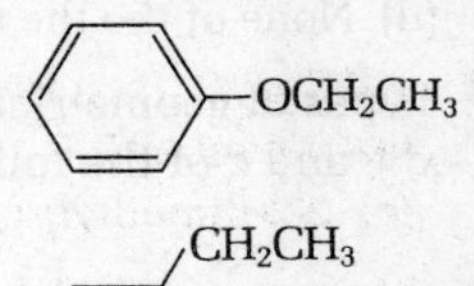
(c) 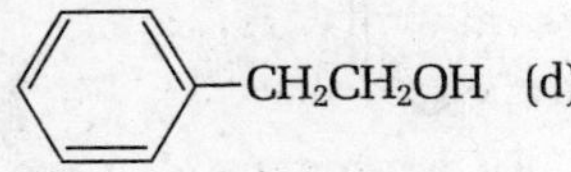 (d) 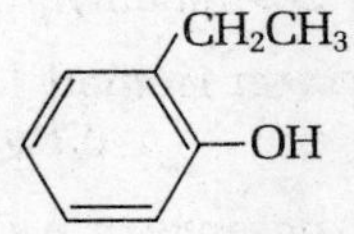

21. Carbanion of the following compound is
$$CH_3\overset{O}{\overset{\|}{C}}CH_2CH_2CH_3$$
(a) $CH_3\overset{O}{\overset{\|}{C}}\underset{\ominus}{C}HCH_2CH_3$ (b) $CH_3\overset{O}{\overset{\|}{C}}CH_2\underset{\ominus}{C}HCH_3$
(c) $\underset{\ominus}{C}H_2\overset{O}{\overset{\|}{C}}CH_2CH_2CH_3$ (d) $CH_3\overset{O}{\overset{\|}{C}}CH_2CH_2\underset{\ominus}{C}H_2$

22. Which carbon has most acidic hydrogen?
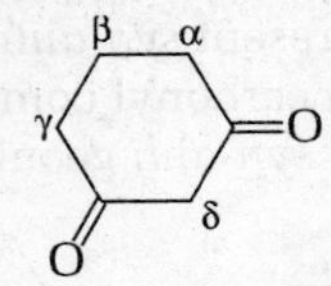
(a) C_α (b) C_β
(c) C_γ (d) C_δ

23. Which is the most predominant out of the following?

(a) 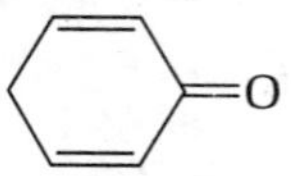

(b) 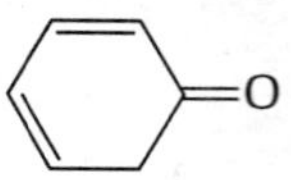

(c) 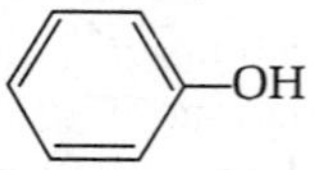

(d) 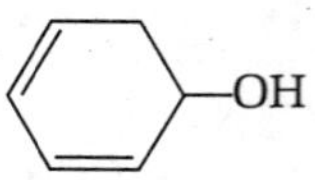

24. Which step is not desirable in acid-catalysed conversion of a carbonyl compound to enolic form?

(a) 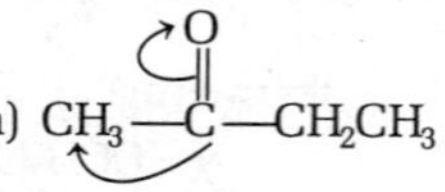

(b) 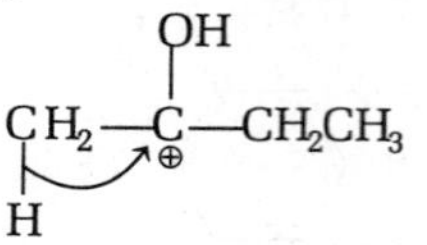

(c) Both (a) and (b)

(d) None of these

25. In the following acid catalysed reaction

$$CH_3\overset{O}{\overset{\|}{C}}CH_3 \overset{H^+}{\rightleftharpoons} CH_3\overset{OH}{\overset{|}{C}}=CH_2$$

enolic hydrogen is from

(a) acetone itself

(b) proton-catalyst

(c) Both (a) and (b)

(d) None of the the above

26. Types of geometrical isomerism shown at the points *x*, *y* and *z* of the following compound are respectively

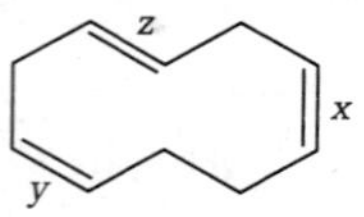

	x	*y*	*z*
(a)	*cis*	*trans*	*trans*
(b)	*cis*	*cis*	*trans*
(c)	*cis*	*trans*	*cis*
(d)	*trans*	*cis*	*trans*

27. Which of the following compounds shows geometrical isomerism? **[JEE Main 2020, Sep.]**

(a) 2-methylpent-2-ene

(b) 4-methylpent-2-ene

(c) 4-methylpent-1-ene

(d) 2-methylpent-1-ene

28. Carbonyl compounds react with NH_2OH forming oximes which represent *syn-anti* geometrical isomerism. Which carbonyl compound forms oxime but does not show *syn-anti* geometrical isomerism?

(a) 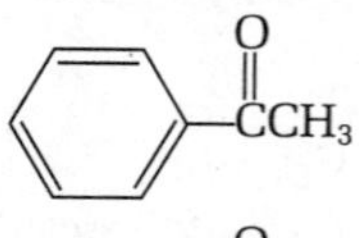

(b) 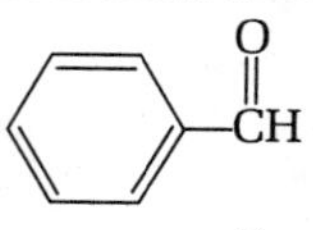

(c) 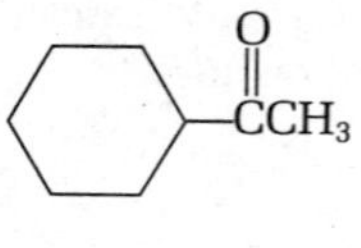

(d) 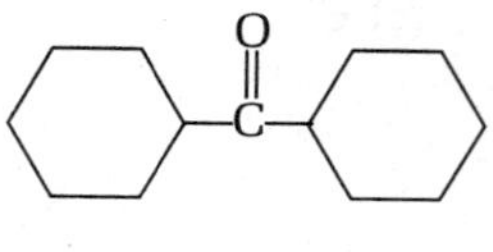

29. *Cis-trans* isomerism is shown by

(a) 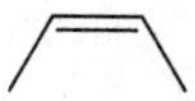

(b) 

(c) 

(d) 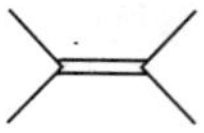

30. In the following molecules, **[JEE Main 2021, March]**

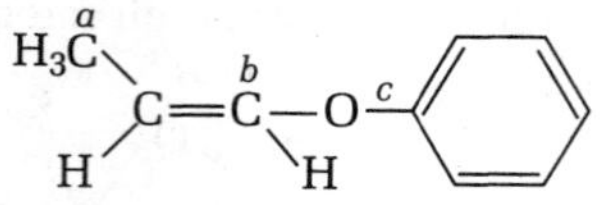

Hybridisation of carbon *a*, *b* and *c* respectively are

(a) sp^3, *sp*, *sp*

(b) sp^3, sp^2, *sp*

(c) sp^3, sp^2, sp^2

(d) sp^3, *sp*, sp^2

31. Out of the following which are chiral?

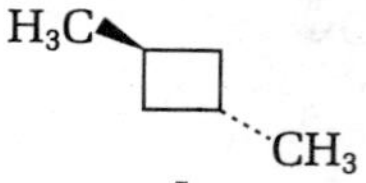
I

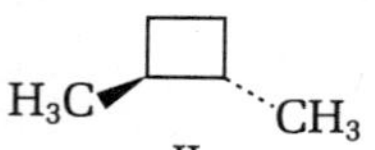
II

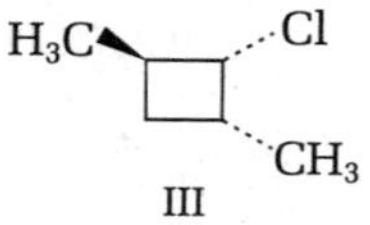
III

(a) I and II

(b) II and III

(c) I and III

(d) Only III

32. Dimethylcyclohexane that has a plane of symmetry is

(a) 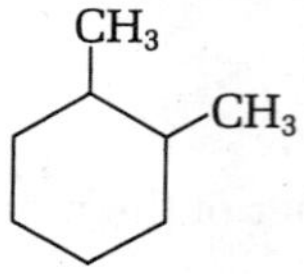

(b) 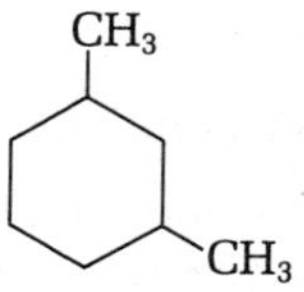

(c) 

(d) 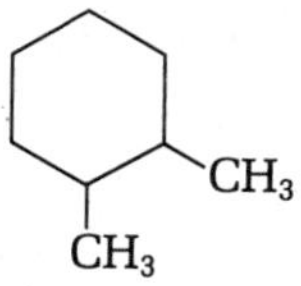

33. C_8H_{16} that can form *cis-trans* geometrical isomerism and has also a chiral centre is

(a) 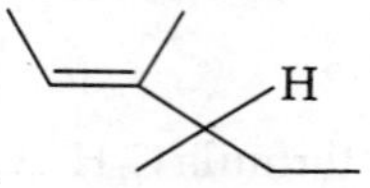

(b) 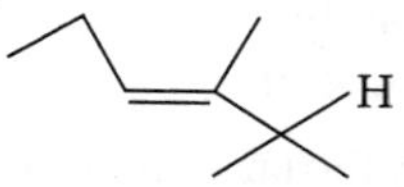

(c) Both (a) and (b)

(d) None of these

34. Consider the following statements,

I. A compound and its enantiomer can be distinguished by their effects on polarised light

II. Enantiomers are not superimposable

III. Dissymmetry is the necessary and sufficient condition for the existence of enantiomers.

Select the correct statement(s).

(a) I and II

(b) I and III

(c) II and III

(d) I, II and III

35. Select the correct statement(s).
(a) Optical isomers are also called enantiomers
(b) Molecules that are not superimposable on their mirror images are dissymmetric
(c) Both are correct
(d) None of the above is correct

36. Select the correct statement(s).
(a) Relative configuration *D* or *L* is based on glyceraldehyde
(b) Diastereomers are optically inactive compounds
(c) Both are correct
(d) None of the above statements is correct

37. Following compound *A*,

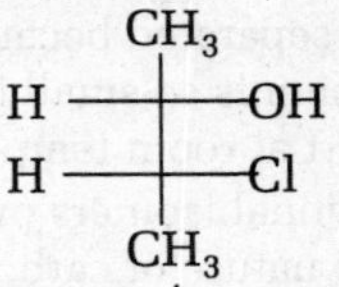

A

(a) is called *threo*-enantiomer
(b) is called *erythro*-enantiomer
(c) is called diastereomer
(d) is a racemic compound

38. Fischer projection of a compound can be represented as

(a) 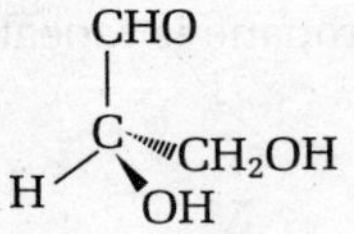
(b) 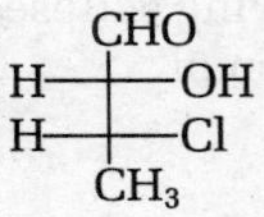

(c) Both (a) and (b)
(d) None of these

39. Following compound *A*

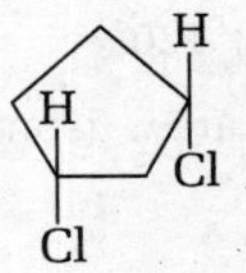

A

(a) is a *meso* compound
(b) is a diastereomer
(c) is a *threo*-enantiomer
(d) is a *trans*-isomer

40. Following stereo-structure of tartaric acid represents

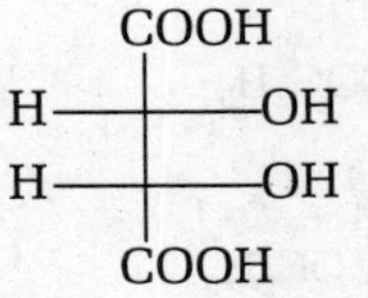

(a) *d*-or *l*-form
(b) racemic form
(c) *meso* form
(d) *trans*-form

41. In the following structure

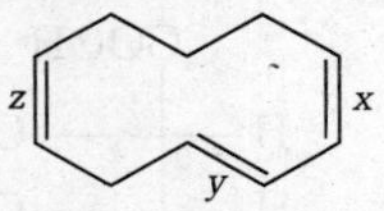

(a) *x*, *y* and *z* represent *Z*-configurations
(b) *x*, *y* and *z* represent *E*-configurations
(c) *x* and *z* represent *E*-configurations while *y* represents *Z*-configurations
(d) *x* and *z* represent *Z*-configurations while *y* represents *E*-configurations

42. Assign correct configurations to following stereo compounds

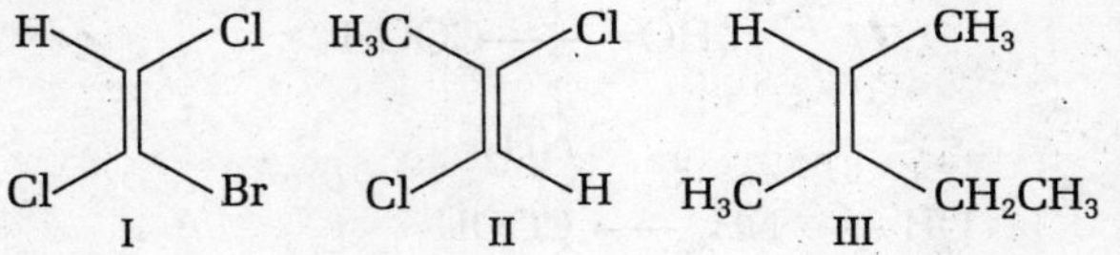

I II III

	I	II	III
(a)	*E*	*E*	*E*
(b)	*Z*	*Z*	*Z*
(c)	*Z*	*E*	*Z*
(d)	*E*	*Z*	*E*

43. 2-butyne can be reduced to (*A*) by Li/NH_3 and to (*B*) by Pd-C/H_2

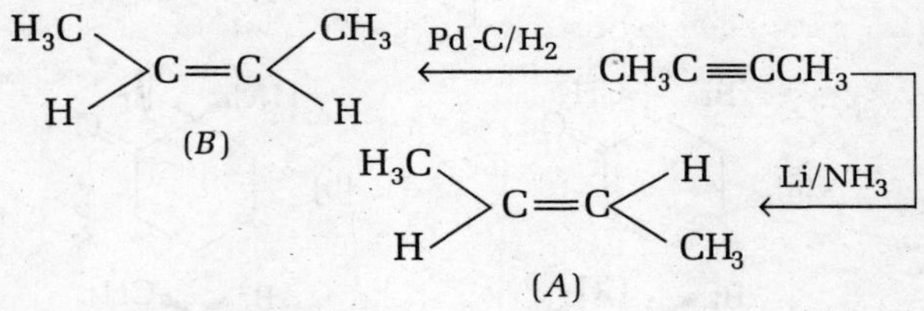

Configurations of *A* and *B* are respectively
(a) *E*, *Z* (b) *Z*, *E* (c) *Z*, *Z* (d) *E*, *E*

44. *cis*-3-hexene is
(a) *Z*-3-hexene
(b) *E*-3-hexene
(c) Both (a) and (b) are correct
(d) None of the two is correct

45. *trans*-3-methyl-2-pentene is
(a) *E* (b) *Z*
(c) Both (a) and (b) (d) None of these

46. Select the correct statement.
(a) *R*, *S* system of nomenclature indicates the configuration of the chirality centre
(b) *R*, *S* system of nomenclature indicates the configuration of the achirality centre
(c) *E*, *Z* system of nomenclature indicates the configuration of the chirality centre
(d) *E*, *Z* system of the nomenclature indicates the configuration of the achirality centre

47. Following configuration of the tartaric acid represents

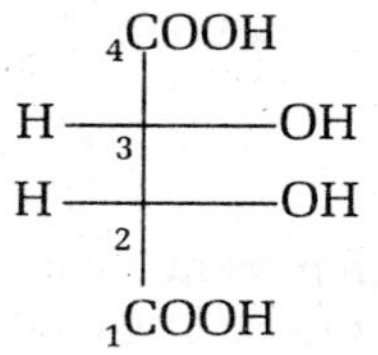

(a) 2*R*, 3*R* (b) 2*R*, 3*S*
(c) 2*S*, 3*S*, (d) 2*S*, 3*R*

48. For the following compound, sequence followed is (best priority to the first one)

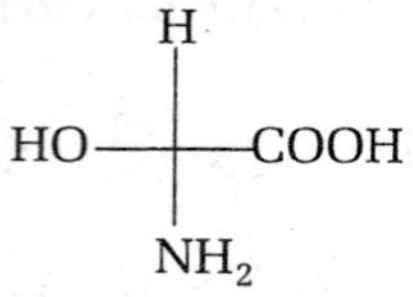

(a) OH ⟶ NH_2 ⟶ COOH
(b) OH ⟶ COOH ⟶ NH_2
(c) COOH ⟶ NH_2 ⟶ OH
(d) COOH ⟶ OH ⟶ NH_2

49. Three-dimensional representation of the *R*-enantiomer of

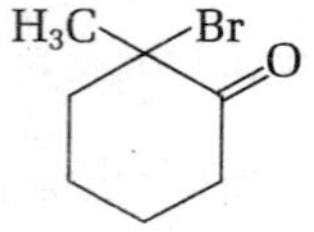

is

(a) 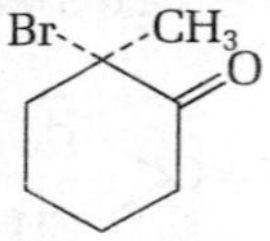 (b) 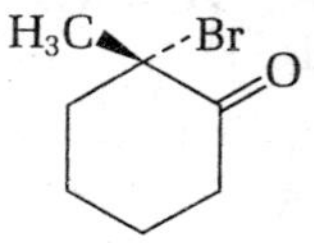

(c) 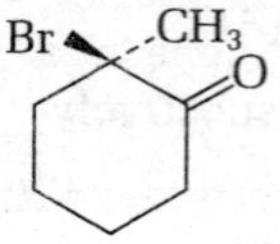 (d) 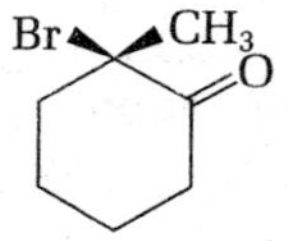

50. (2*R*, 3*R*)-2,3-butanediol is

(a) 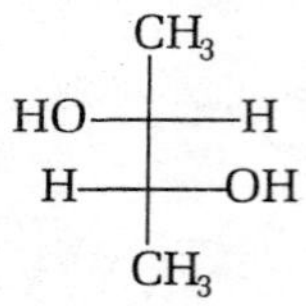 (b) 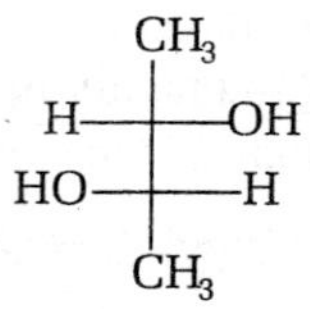

(c) 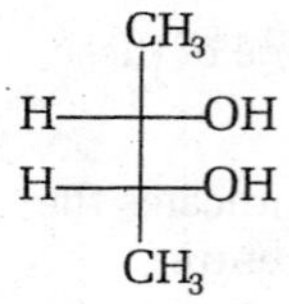 (d) 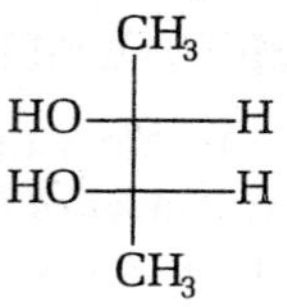

51. The order of stability for the conformations of *n*-butane is

(a) *anti* > *gauche* > eclipsed (partial) > eclipsed (fully)
I II III IV

(b) IV > III > II > I
(c) III > II > I > IV
(d) II > III > I > IV

52. Sawhorse staggered representation of ethane is

(a) 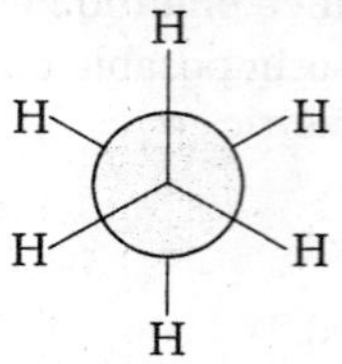 (b) 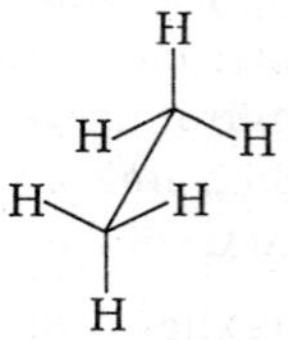

(c) 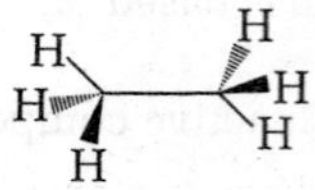 (d) All of these

53. Select the correct statement(s).
(a) Staggered and eclipsed conformers cannot be physically separated because the energy difference between them is so small that most readily interconvert at room temperature
(b) Conformational isomers owe their existence to the tetrahedral nature of carbon bonding and the fact that the σ-bond is cylindrically symmetrical
(c) Both the statements are correct
(d) None of the above statement is correct

54. Which form has maximum energy?
(a) Eclipsed (b) Staggered
(c) *Gauche* (d) Equal

55. Following eclipsed form of propane is repeated after rotation of

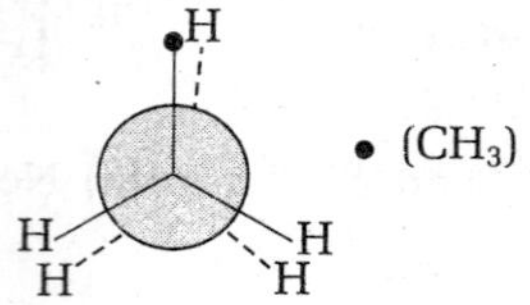

(a) 60° (b) 120° (c) 180° (d) 360°

56. HCN and HNC are ... isomers.
(a) functional (b) tautomers
(c) chain (d) position

57. $CH_3\overset{O}{\overset{\|}{C}}CH_2\overset{O}{\overset{\|}{C}}OCH_2CH_3 \overset{D^+}{\rightleftharpoons} A$, ($D^+$ is catalyst). *A* is

(a) $CH_3\overset{OH}{\overset{|}{C}}{=}CH\overset{O}{\overset{\|}{C}}OC_2H_5$
(b) $CH_3\overset{O}{\overset{\|}{C}}CH{=}\overset{OH}{\overset{|}{C}}OC_2H_5$
(c) $CH_3\overset{OD}{\overset{|}{C}}{=}CH\overset{O}{\overset{\|}{C}}OC_2H_5$
(d) formation of *A* is not possible

58. Functional isomers of $CH_3\overset{O}{\overset{\|}{C}}OH$ are
(a) 2 (b) 3 (c) 4 (d) 5

59. $C_6H_4Cl_2 + Cl_2 \xrightarrow{Fe} C_6H_3Cl_3$
X (Dichlorobenzene) — Y (Trichlorobenzene)

Only one structural isomer of *Y* is formed. Hence, *X* is
(a) *o*-isomer
(b) *p*-isomer
(c) *m*-isomer
(d) None of the above

60. $C_5H_{12} + Cl_2 \xrightarrow{Light} C_5H_{11}Cl \xrightarrow{Na/ether} C$
A — B

Only one structure of *B* is possible. *A*, *B* and *C* are

(a)
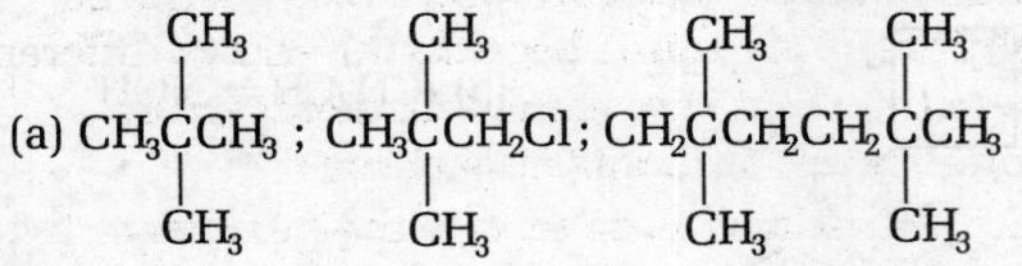

(b)
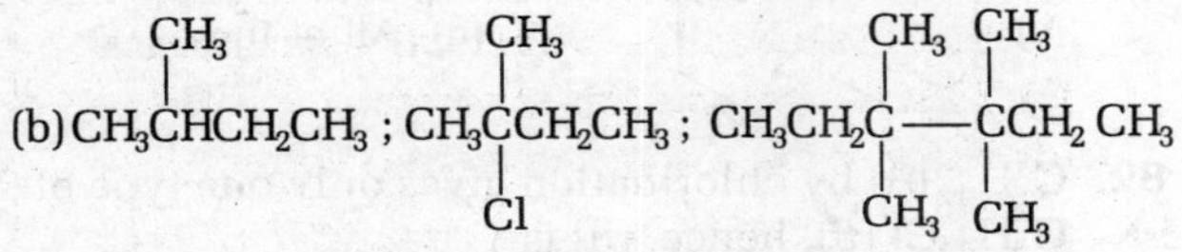

(c) Both (a) and (b) are correct
(d) None of the above

61. $C_4H_{10}O$ (ether) + $PCl_5 \longrightarrow RCl + R'Cl + POCl_3$
*R*Cl gives haloform test, *R'*Cl does not. Hence, ether is
(a) ethoxy ethane
(b) 1-methoxy propane
(c) 2-methoxy propane
(d) None of the above

62. 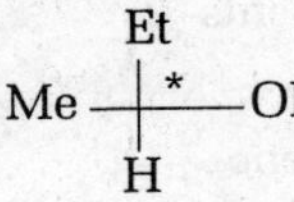 has chiral centre (*). It is
(a) *R* (b) *S*
(c) Both (a) and (b) (d) None of these

63. Number of optically active isomers of tartaric acid
CH(OH)COOH
|
CH(OH)COOH
is
(a) 2 (b) 3 (c) 4 (d) 5

64. C_4H_8 can have total of ...... isomers (geometrical not included)
(a) 3 (b) 4
(c) 5 (d) 6

65. 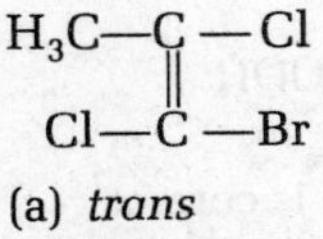 is
(a) *trans* (b) *Z*
(c) both are correct (d) None is correct

66. 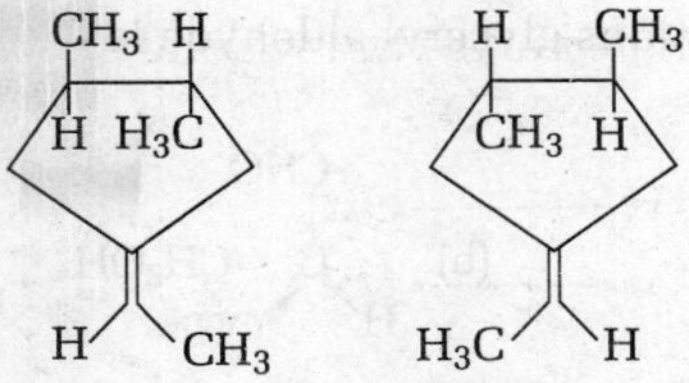 are
(a) enantiomers (b) diastereomers
(c) geometrical isomers (d) same structure

67. The compound, whose stereo-chemical formula is written below, exhibits *x* geometrical isomers and *y* optical isomers.

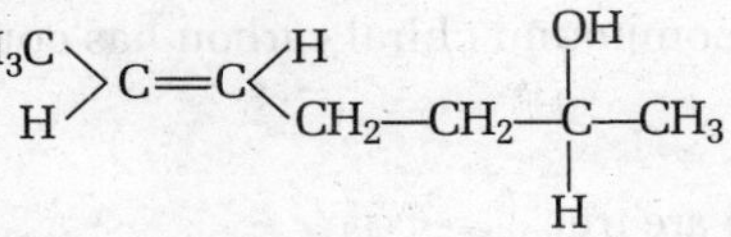

The values of *x* and *y* are
(a) 4 and 4 (b) 2 and 2
(c) 2 and 4 (d) 4 and 2

68. The number of optically active isomers possible for
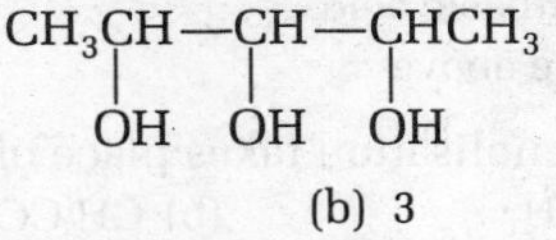 is
(a) 2 (b) 3
(c) 6 (d) 8

69. How many asymmetric carbon atoms are present in
(i) 1,2-dimethylcyclohexane,
(ii) 3-methylcyclopentene and
(iii) 3-methylcyclohexene?
(a) two, one, one (b) one, one, one
(c) two, none, two (d) two, none, one

70. As organic compound of formula $C_nH_{2n}O$ has an acyclic skeleton with no carbon-carbon multiple bonds. If the molecular weight of the compound is 58, which of the following may be the structure of the compound?
(a) $CH_2{=}CH{-}O{-}CH_3$ (b) 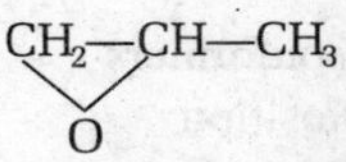
(c) $H_3C{-}CO{-}CH_3$ (d) $CH_2{=}CH{-}CH_2OH$

71. The following compound can exhibit

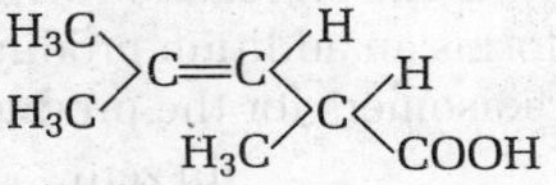

(a) geometrical isomerism
(b) geometrical and optical isomerism
(c) optical isomerism
(d) tautomerism

72. By Fischer projections glyceryl aldehyde is represented as

(a) 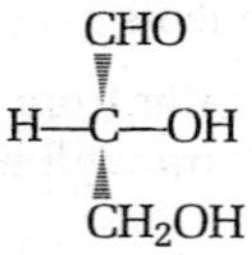

(b) 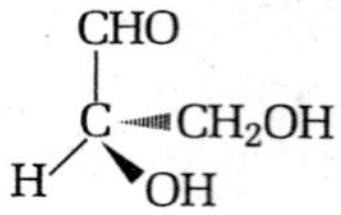

(c) Both are true
(d) None is true

73. 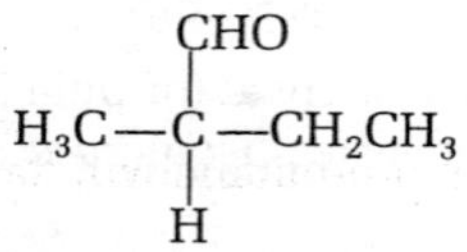

In this compound chiral carbon has configuration
(a) *R*
(b) *S*
(c) both are true
(d) none is true

74. $C_4H_4O_4$ can be
(a) a cyclic ester of dibasic acid
(b) a *cis*-dibasic acid
(c) a *trans*-dibasic acid
(d) All of the above

75. Maximum enolisation takes place of
(a) CH_3COCH_3
(b) CH_3COCH_2CHO
(c) $CH_3COCH_2COCH_3$
(d) 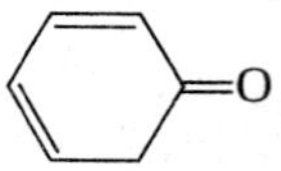

76. What are the type of isomers in following pairs?

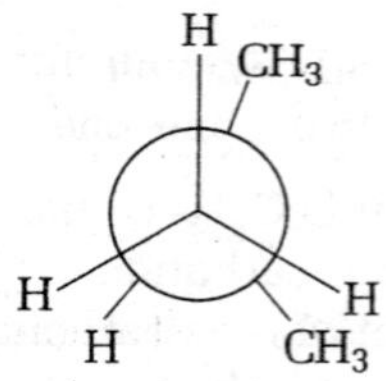

I

and

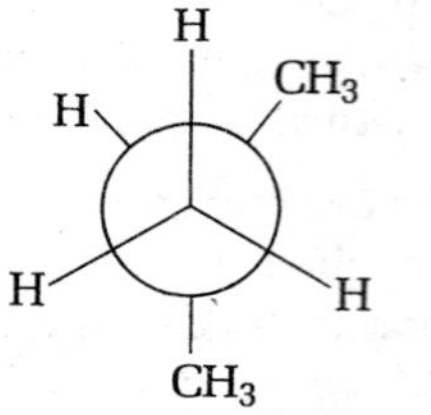

II

(a) Conformers
(b) Position
(c) Optical
(d) Geometrical

77. 3-methyl-pent-2-ene on reaction with HBr in presence of peroxide forms an addition product. The number of possible stereoisomers for the product is **[JEE Main 2017]**
(a) six
(b) zero
(c) two
(d) four

78. Type of isomerism shown by the product of the reaction between benzaldehyde and hydroxyl amine is
(a) *syn* and *anti* geometrical
(b) *cis* and *trans* geometrical
(c) *E* and *Z* geometrical
(d) None is correct

79. $C_4H_4O_4$ can be
(a) a cyclic ester
(b) *cis*- and *trans*- dibasic acid
(c) *gem*-α,β-unsaturated dibasic acid
(d) All of the above are correct

80. Number of chiral carbon atoms in 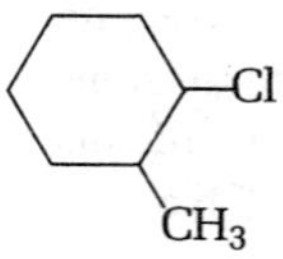 is
(a) 2
(b) 3
(c) 4
(d) 1

81. Which will form geometrical isomers?
(a) 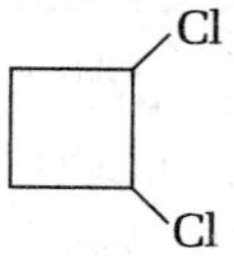
(b) $CH_3CH{=}NOH$
(c) 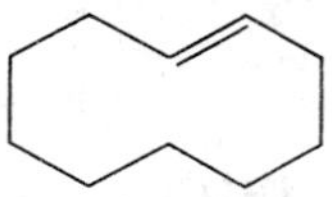
(d) All of these

82. $C_5H_{12}(A)$ by chlorination gives only one type of $C_5H_{11}Cl$ (*B*), hence, (*A*) is
(a) *n*-pentane
(b) isopentane
(c) neopentane
(d) All are true

83. $C_6H_4Cl_2(A)$, dichlorobenzene is chlorinated (without using directive influence rule) to give $C_6H_3Cl_3(B)$. Which are correct statements?
(a) *ortho*-isomer of *A* will form two types of *B*
(b) *meta*-isomer of *A* will form three types of *B*
(c) *para*-isomer of *A* will form one type of *B*
(d) All of the above are correct statements

84. Geometrical isomerism is possible in
(a) acetone-oxime
(b) isobutene
(c) acetophenone-oxime
(d) benzophenone-oxime

85. $C_6H_{10}O_3(A) \xrightarrow{H_3O^+} C_4H_6O_3(B) + C_2H_6O(C)$ *A*, *B* and *C* all give iodoform test. *A* and *B* also form oximes, *A* is neutral but *B* gives CO_2 with $NaHCO_3$. Hence, *A* can be
(a) $CH_3COCH_2COOC_2H_5$
(b) $CH_3CH_2COCH_2COOCH_3$
(c) $CH_3CH_2CH_2COCOOCH_3$
(d) 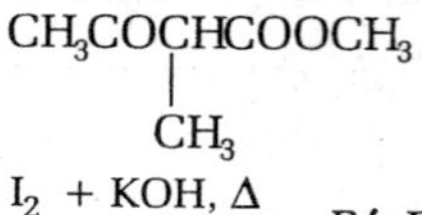

86. Product *B* (of Q. No. 85) $\xrightarrow[\text{(II) } H^+ \text{ (III) } \Delta]{\text{(I) } I_2 + KOH, \Delta}$ *B′*, *B′* is
(a) $CH_2(COOH)_2$
(b) CH_3COOH
(c) 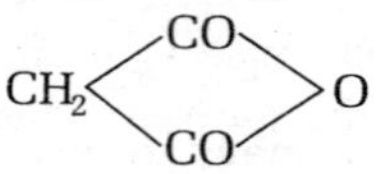
(d) None is correct

87. Which is most volatile isomer of nitrophenol?
(a) *o*-
(b) *m*-
(c) *p*-
(d) Equal

88. Tautomerism is not exhibited by

(a) 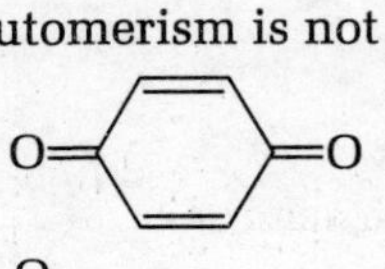   (b) 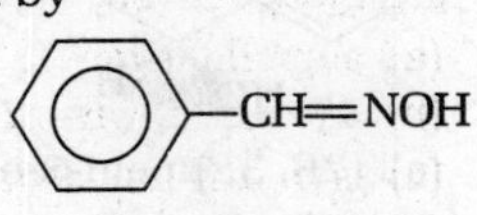

(c) 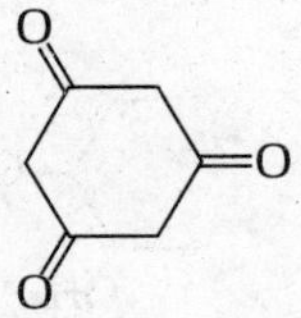   (d) 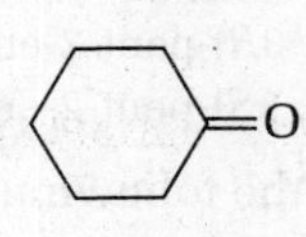

89. Carbon chain splits into two or more parts by ozonolysis in the following except in

(a) 1,3-cyclobuta-di-*ene*
(b) 1,2-dimethylcyclohexene
(c) benzene
(d) isobutene

90. Total number of isomers of $C_4H_{10}O$ will be

(a) 4 (b) 5 (c) 6 (d) 7

91. Which will give colour with $FeCl_3$?

(a) 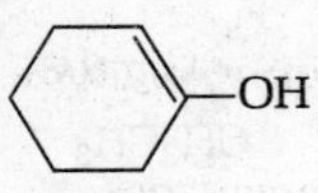   (b) $CH_3\overset{OH}{C}{=}CH\overset{O}{\overset{\|}{C}}OC_2H_5$

(c) 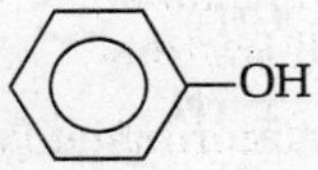   (d) All of these

92. The absolute configuration of 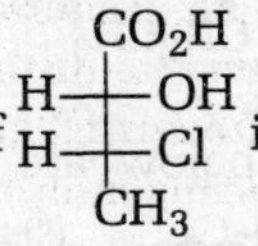 is **[JEE Main 2016]**

(a) (2*S*, 3*R*) (b) (2*S*, 3*S*)
(c) (2*R*, 3*R*) (d) (2*R*, 3*S*)

93. Chirality is lost when

(a) $CH_3\underset{OH}{CH}COOH$ is heated

(b) 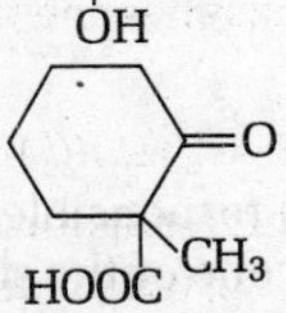 is heated

(c) $CH_3\underset{OH}{CH}CH_2COOH$ is heated

(d) $CH_3\underset{CH_2COOH}{CH}COOH$ is heated

94. Select the correct statements.

(a) 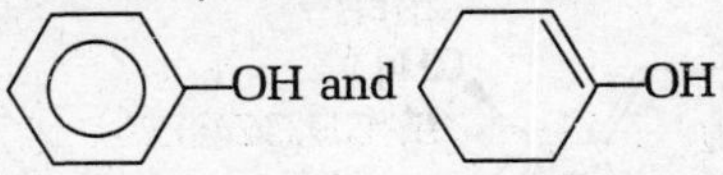 both give colour with neutral $FeCl_3$ solution

(b) 2-pentanone and 3-pentanone are position as well as metamers

(c) Product formed when benzaldehyde reacts with hydroxylamine shows geometrical isomerism

(d) All of the above are correct statements

95. The α-D-glucose and β-D-glucose differ from each other due to difference in carbon atom with respect to its

(a) conformation
(b) configuration
(c) number of OH groups
(d) size of hemiacetal ring

96. The most stable configuration of *n*-butane will be

(a) skew boat
(b) eclipsed
(c) gauche
(d) staggered-anti

97. Tautomerism will be exhibited by

(a) $(CH_3)_3CNO$
(b) $(CH_3)_2NH$
(c) R_3CNO_2
(d) RCH_2NO_2

98. The (*R*) and (*S*) enantiomers of an optically active compound differ in

(a) their solubility in achiral solvents
(b) their reactivity with achiral reagents
(c) their optical rotation of plane polarised light
(d) their melting points

99. α and β-glucose are examples of

(a) isomers (b) anomers
(c) isotropic (d) All of these

100. The number of enantiomers of the compound $CH_3CHBrCHBrCOOH$ is

(a) 2 (b) 3
(c) 4 (d) 6

101. One among the following will show optical activity

(a) 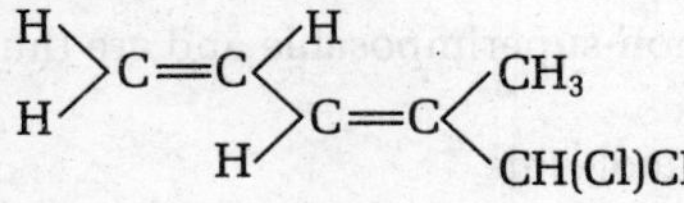

(b) 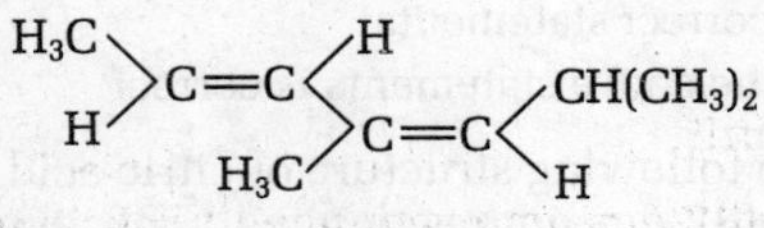

(c) 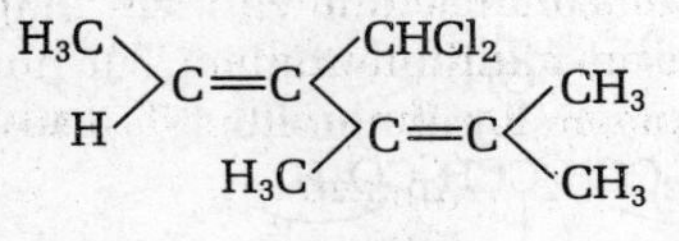

(d) 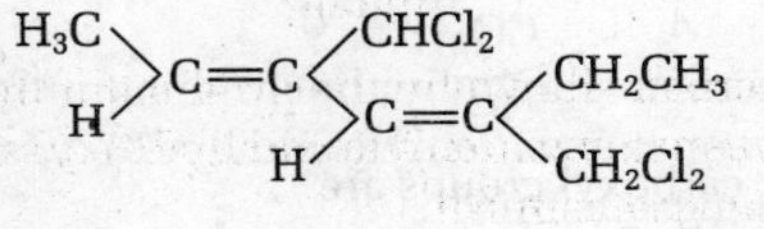

102. Acid-catalysed hydration of an unknown compound X, C_6H_{12}, yielded as the major product a racemic mixture $Y, C_6H_{14}O$. Which (if any) of the following is (are) likely candidates(s) for X ?

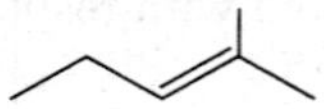
1

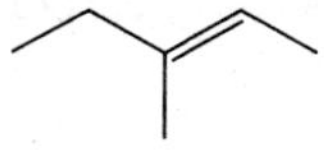
2

3

(a) Only 3 (b) Only 4
(c) 1 and 3 (d) None of these

103. Among the following compounds, geometrical isomerism is exhibited by **[JEE Main 2020, Sep.]**

(a) 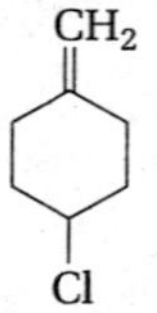

(b) 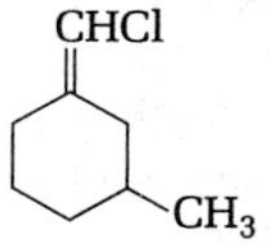

(c) 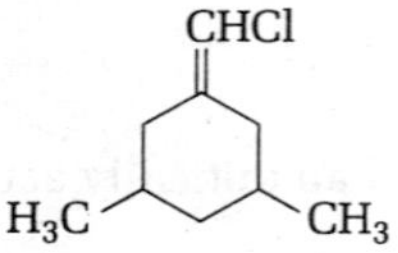

(d) 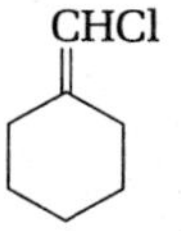

104. Chirality centres in I and II respectively are

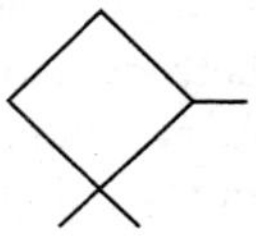
I

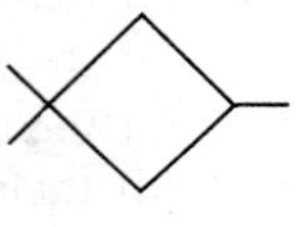
II

	I	II
(a)	1	1
(b)	1	2
(c)	2	1
(d)	1	0

105. Write the correct statements about I, II and III.

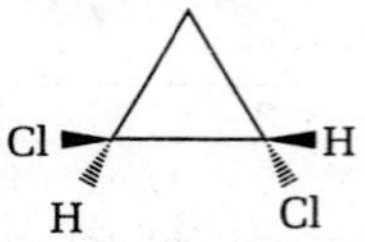
I

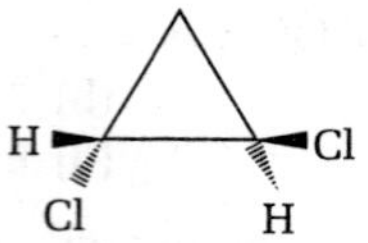
II

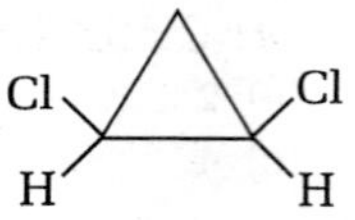
III

(a) I and II are non-superimposable and are thus chiral molecules
(b) III is achiral molecule
(c) Both are correct statements
(d) None of the above statements is correct

106. Consider the following structure of citric acid (a tribasic acid)

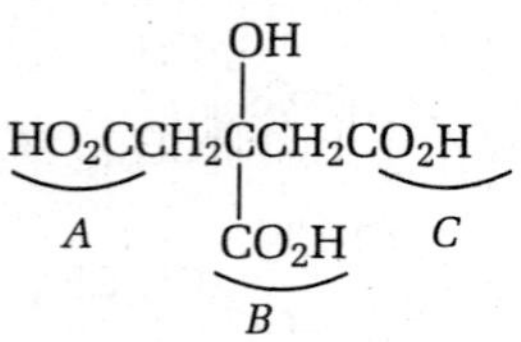

Enantiotropic carboxyl groups are
(a) *A, B* (b) *B, C* (c) *A, C* (d) *A, B, C*

107. 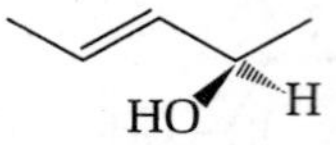 is named as

(a) (2*R*, 3*E*)-pent-3-en-2-ol
(b) (2*S*, 3*E*)-3 pent-3-en-2-ol
(c) (2*E*, 3*R*)-pent-2-en-3-ol
(d) (2*E*, 3*S*)-pent-2-en-3-ol

108. Out of the following

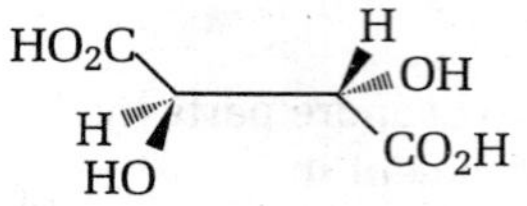
I

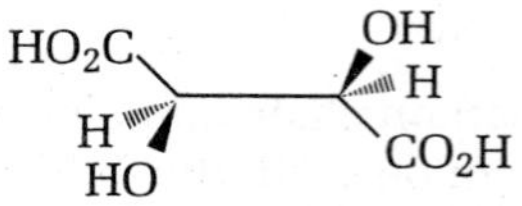
II

(a) Both I and II are *meso*-tartaric acid
(b) I is (*R*, *R*) and II is (*S*, *S*) tartaric acid
(c) I is (*R*, *S*) and II is (*S*, *R*) tartaric acid
(d) I is *meso*- and II is (*R*, *R*) tartaric acid

109. The structure of (*S*)-2-fluorobutane is best represented by

(a) $CH_3\overset{F}{\overset{|}{C}}HCH_2CH_3$

(b) 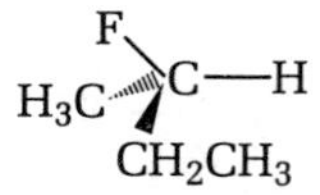

(c) 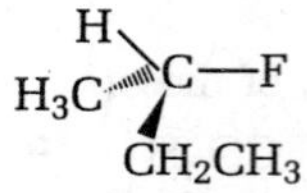

(d) 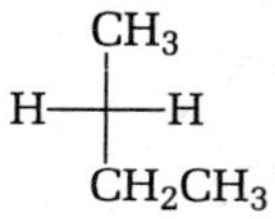

110. I and II (below) are

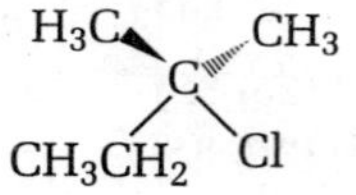
I

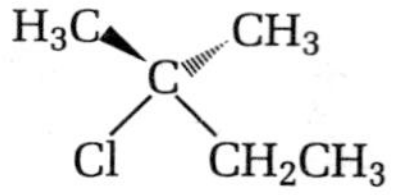
II

(a) enantiomer
(b) achiral, identical
(c) chiral, identical
(d) *meso*

111. The *S* enantiomer of ibuprofen is responsible for its pain-relieving properties. Which one of the structures shown is (*S*)-ibuprofen?

(a) 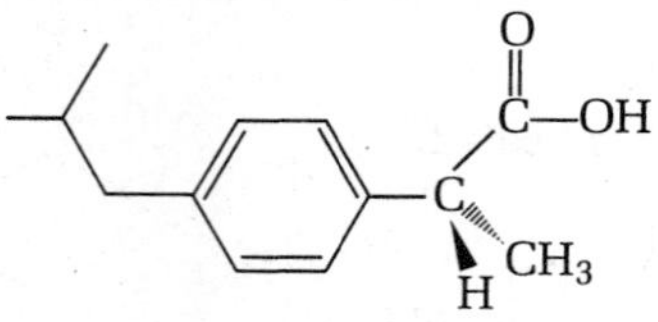

(b) 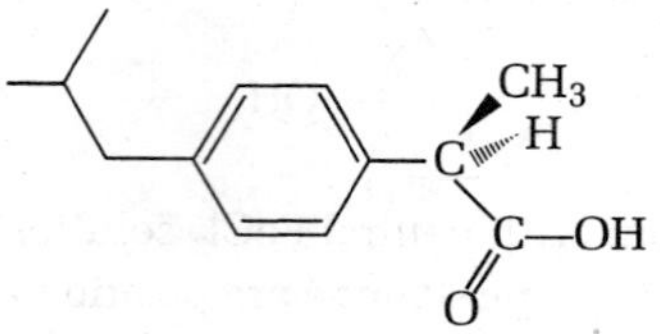

(c) 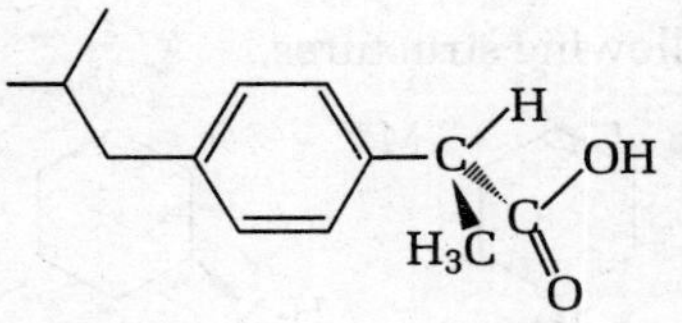

(d) 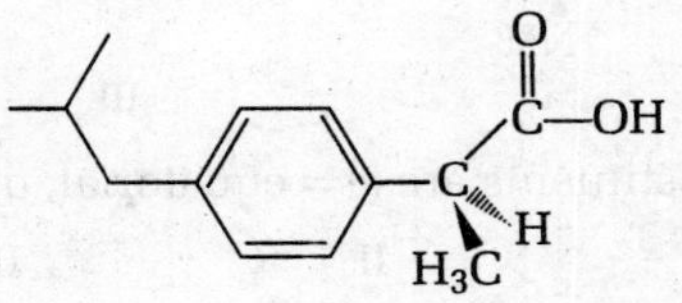

112. Which one of the following is a diastereomer of (*R*)-4-bromo-*cis*-2-hexene?
(a) (*S*)-4-bromo-*cis*-2-hexene
(b) (*R*)-4-bromo-*trans*-2-hexene
(c) (*S*)-5-bromo-*trans*-2-hexene
(d) (*R*)-5-bromo-*trans*-2-hexene

113. The reaction sequence

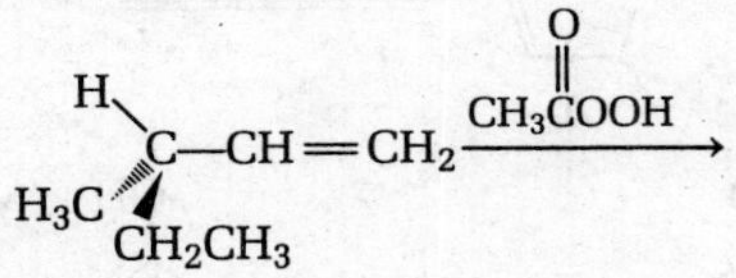

will yield
(a) a pair of product that are enantiomers
(b) a single product that is optically active
(c) a pair of products that are diastereomers
(d) a pair of products one of which is *meso*

114. Which of the following depict the same stereoisomer?

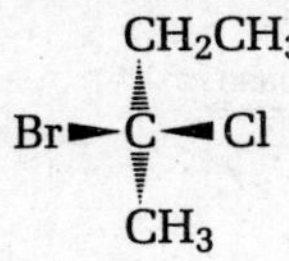
1

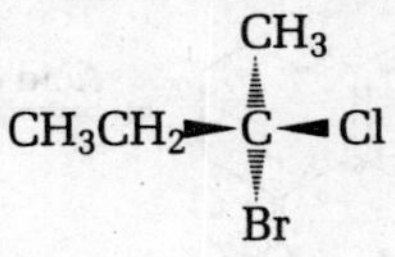
2

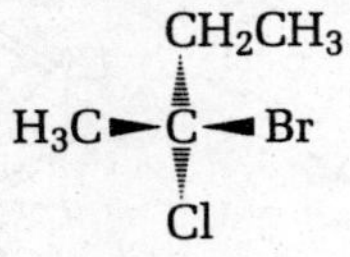
3

(a) 1 and 2
(b) 1 and 3
(c) 2 and 3
(d) 1, 2 and 3

115. Which of the following compounds are *meso* forms?

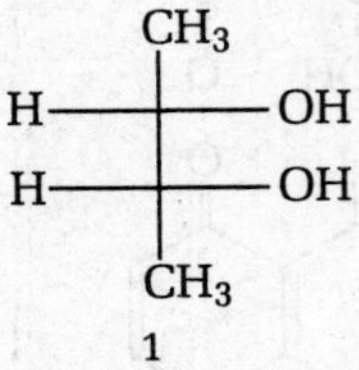
1

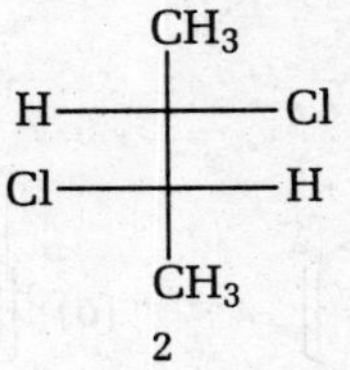
2

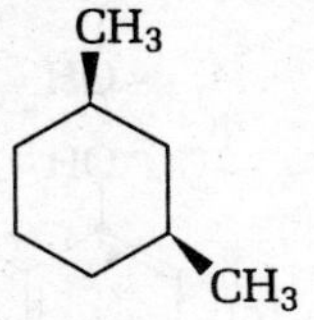
3

(a) Only 1
(b) 1 and 3
(c) 1 and 2
(d) 2 and 3

116. The 2,3-dichloropentane whose structure is shown is

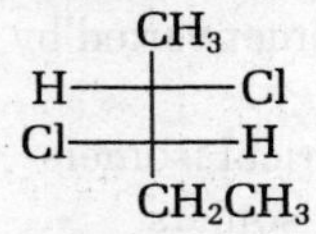

(a) 2 *R*, 3*R* (b) 2 *R*, 3*S* (c) 2*S*, 3*R* (d) 2*S*, 3*S*

117. Newman projections *P*, *Q*, *R* and *S* are shown below :

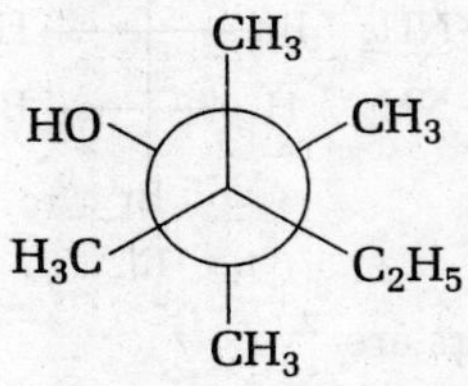
(*P*)

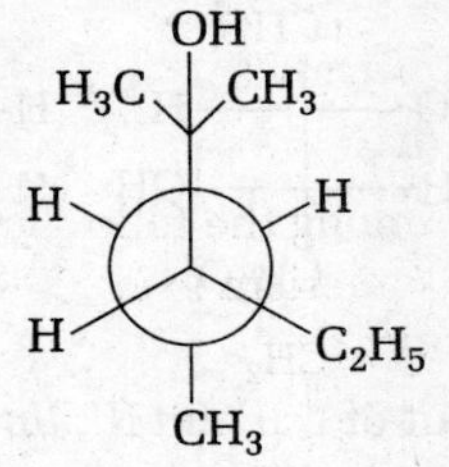
(*Q*)

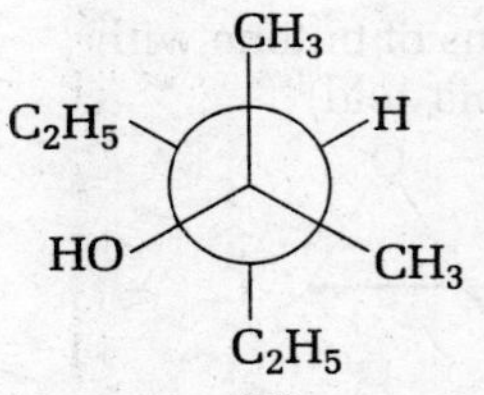
(*R*)

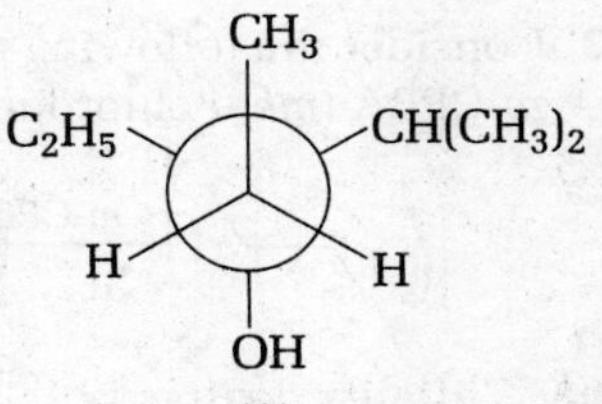
(*S*)

Which one of the following options represents identical molecules? **[JEE Advanced 2020]**
(a) *P* and *Q* (b) *P* and *S* (c) *Q* and *R* (d) *R* and *S*

118. Rank the following groups in order of *R*, *S* precedence (4 is highest)
$-CH(CH_3)_2$ $-CH_2CH_2Br$ $-CH_2Br$ $-C(CH_3)_3$

	A	*B*	*C*	*D*
	4	**3**	**2**	**1**
(a)	*C*	*B*	*C*	*A*
(b)	*A*	*D*	*B*	*C*
(c)	*C*	*D*	*A*	*B*
(d)	*C*	*D*	*B*	*A*

119. A *meso* compound
(a) is an achiral molecule that contains chirality centres
(b) contains a plane of symmetry or a centre of symmetry
(c) is optically inactive
(d) is characterised by all of the above

120. *A* is named as

(*A*) 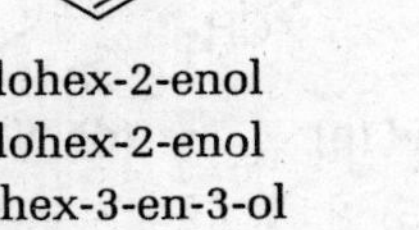

(a) (*R*)-1-ethylcyclohex-2-enol
(b) (*S*)-1-ethylcyclohex-2-enol
(c) *S*-3-ethylcyclohex-3-en-3-ol
(d) None of the above

121. Term atropisomers is used for stereoisomers
(a) that can be interconverted by rotation about single bonds
(b) that are geometrical isomers
(c) that are optical isomers
(d) that are enantiomers

122. Consider the following structures

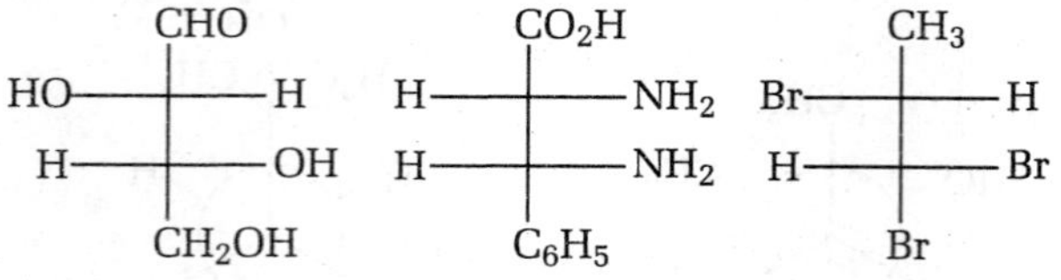

I II III

Out of I, II and III, *threo* isomers are
(a) I and II (b) II and III
(c) I and III (d) Only II

123. Consider the following reactions of butene with *m*-CPBA (*meta* chloroperbenzoic acid)

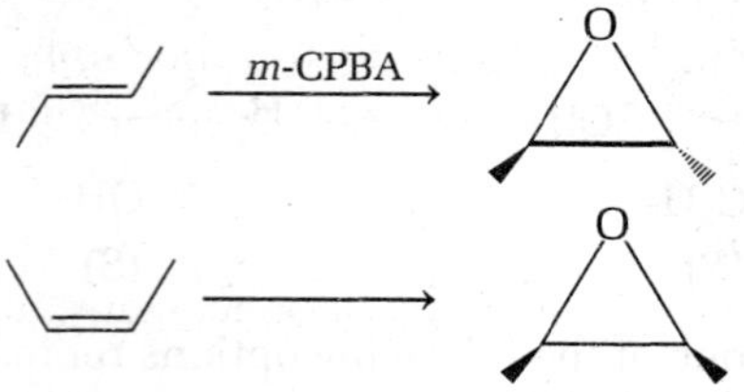

This is an example of
(a) stereoselective reaction (b) stereospecific reaction
(c) Both (a) and (b) (d) None of these

124. Consider the reduction of 2-methyl cyclohexanone with $LiAlH_4$

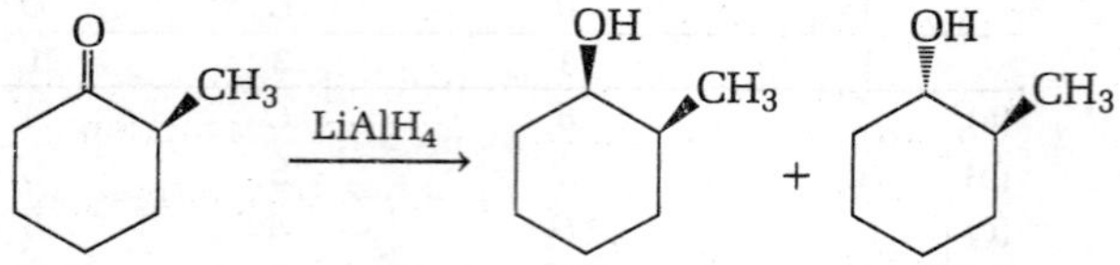

cis *trans*

This is an example of
(a) stereospecific reaction (b) stereoselective reaction
(c) Both (a) and (b) (d) None of these

125. Which of these are chiral molecules without a chiral centre?

(a) 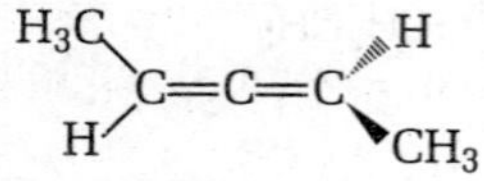 (b) 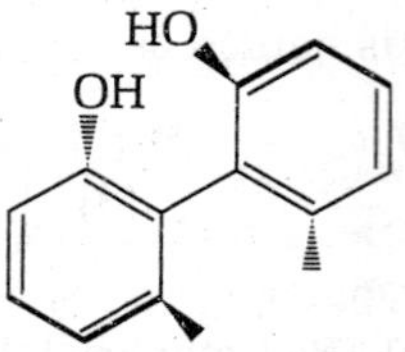

(c) Both (a) and (b) (d) None of these

126. Consider the following structures,

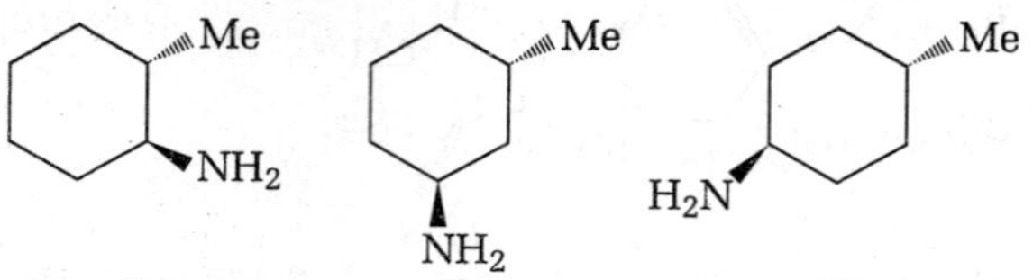

I II III

Positions of substituents are (e = equatorial, a = axial)

	I	II	III
(a)	e, e	e, e	a, e
(b)	e, e	a, e	a, e
(c)	e, e	e, e	e, e
(d)	a, e	a, e	a, e

127. In presence of an acid or base, *A* changes to

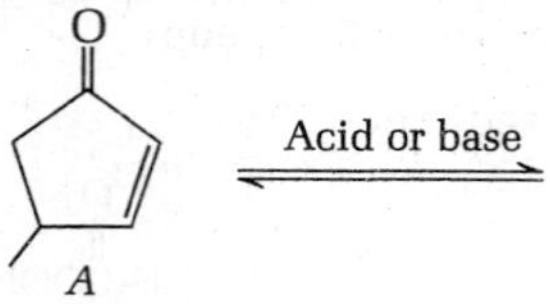

A

(a) 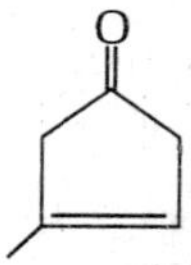 (b) 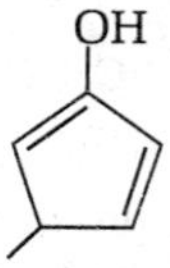

(c) Both (a) and (b) (d) None of these

128. In the following reaction,

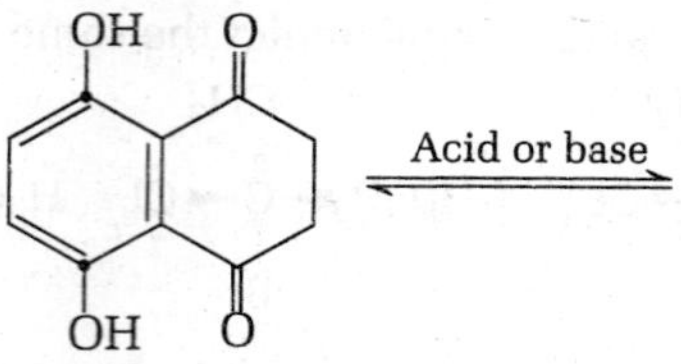

(• $= {}^{13}C$) product formed is

(a) 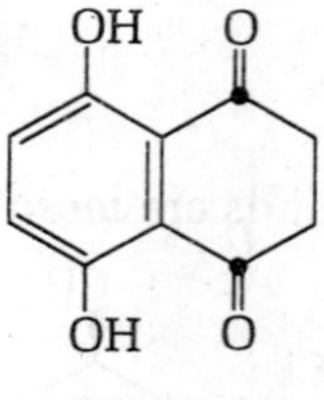 (b) 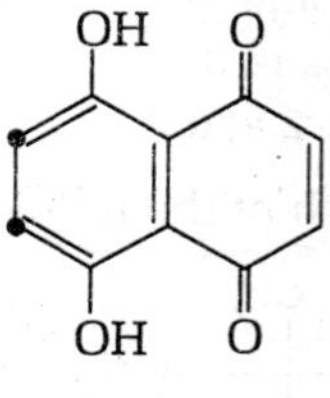

(c) 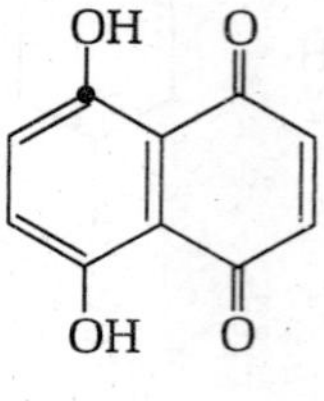 (d) 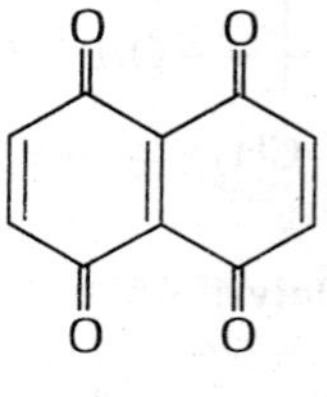

Objective Questions Type II [One or more than one correct option(s)]

In each of the questions below, four choices are given, of which one or more than one are correct.

1. Which will give colour with $FeCl_3$?

(a) 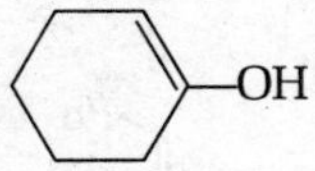 (b) $CH_3C(OH){=}CHCOC_2H_5$ (C=O)

(c) 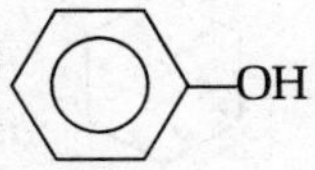 (d) 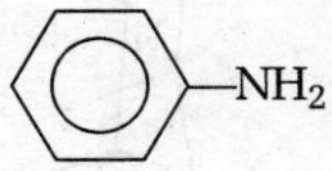

2. $\begin{matrix} CHCOOH \\ \| \\ CHCOOH \end{matrix}$ (maleic acid) can form

(a) optical isomer (b) geometrical isomer
(c) position isomer (d) functional isomer

3. 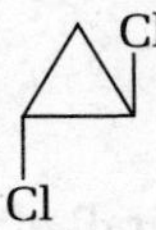 and 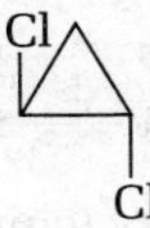 are ..... isomer

(a) position (b) optical
(c) geometrical (d) diastereomer

4. Which can show tautomerism?

(a) $CH_2CH_2NO_2$ (b) 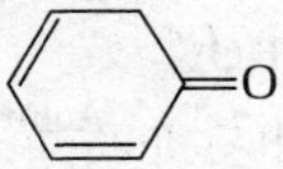

(c) 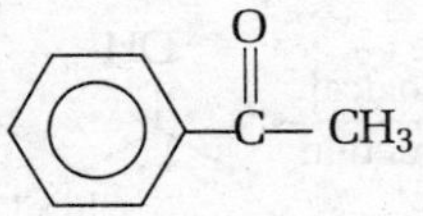 (d) HCN

5. Which will show geometrical isomerism?

(a) $CH_3CH{=}NOH$ (b) 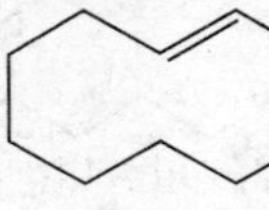

(c) $(H_3C)_2C{=}NOH$ (d) $HO{-}N{=}N{-}OH$

(a) *d* and *d* (b) *l* and *l*
(c) *R* and *R* (d) *R* and *S*

6. In which case, chiral carbon is generated?

(a) $CH_3COCH_3 + HCN \xrightarrow{H_3O^+}$

(b) $CH_3CHO + HCN \xrightarrow{H_3O^+}$

(c) $CH_3COCOOH + HCN \xrightarrow{H_3O^+}$

(d) 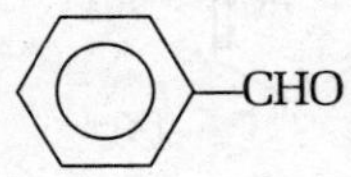 $+ HCN \xrightarrow{H_3O^+}$

7. Chirality is lost when

(a) $CH_3CH(OH)COOH$ is heated

(b) 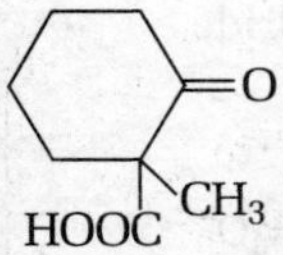 is heated

(c) $CH_3CH(OH)CH_2COOH$ is heated

(d) $CH_3CH(CH_2COOH)COOH$ is heated

8. Which are correct statements?

(a) methyl malonic acid is converted into propanoic acid on heating
(b) succinic acid forms succinic anhydride on heating
(c) 3-hydroxy propanoic acid forms acrylic acid on heating
(d) CH_3COCH_2COOH forms acetone on heating

9. Select the correct statements.

(a) 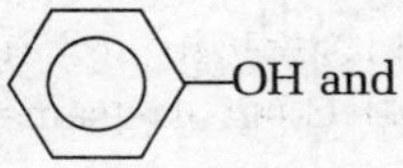 and 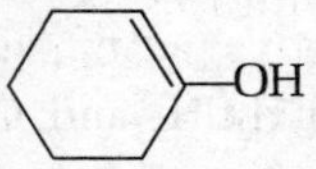 both give colour with neutral $FeCl_3$ solution
(b) 2-pentanone and 3-pentanone are position as well as metamers
(c) product formed when benzaldehyde reacts with hydroxylamine shows geometrical isomerism
(d) 1,2-dibromocyclohexane shows geometrical and optical isomerism.

10. $\underset{\text{(Ether)}}{C_5H_{12}O(A)} \xrightarrow[KOH]{PCl_5} B + C$, *B* and *C* (both alcohols) gives haloform test. Hence, *A* is

(a) 2-methoxy butane
(b) 1-ethoxy propane
(c) 2-ethoxy propane
(d) 1-methoxy butane

11. $A(C_4H_6) \xrightarrow{H_2/Pt} B(C_4H_8) \xrightarrow{O_3/H_2O/Zn} C \xrightarrow{HCN} D$

D has chiral carbon and can be hydrolysed to lactic acid. Hence *A*, is

(a) $CH_3C{\equiv}CCH_3$ (b) $CH_2{=}CHCH{=}CH_2$
(c)  (d) 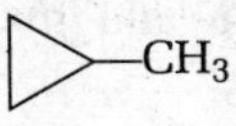

12. $C_4H_6O_4(A) \xrightarrow{\Delta} C_3H_6O_2(B) \xrightarrow[\Delta]{\text{Sodalime}} (C)$, C is hydrocarbon occupying 0.75 L per gram approximately. Hence, A and B respectively are

(a) methyl malonic acid, propanoic acid
(b) succinic acid, succinic anhydride
(c) maleic acid, maleic anhydride
(d) tartaric acid, propanoic anhydride

13. 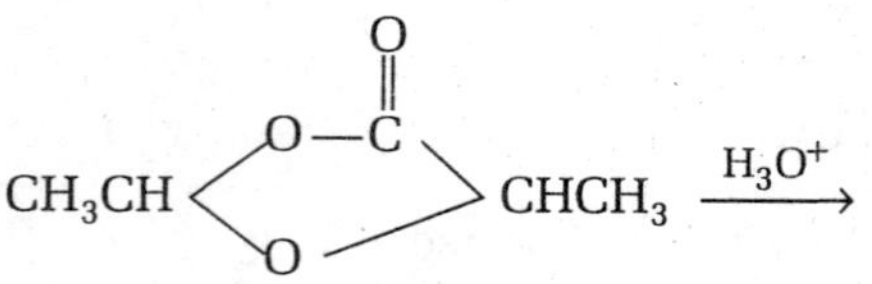 product can be

(a) $CH_3CH(OH)_2, CH_3CH(OH)COOH$
(b) CH_3CHO, $CH_3CH(OH)COOH$
(c) CH_3CH_2COOH, CH_3CH_2OH
(d) $CH_3CH(OH)COOH, CH_3CH_2OH$

14. Dipole moment of *o*-, *m*- and *p*-dichlorobenzene will be in the order

(a) *o*- < *m*- < *p*- (b) *o*- < *p*- < *m*-
(c) *p*- < *m*- < *o*- (d) equal

15. Which is the incorrect statement?

(a) 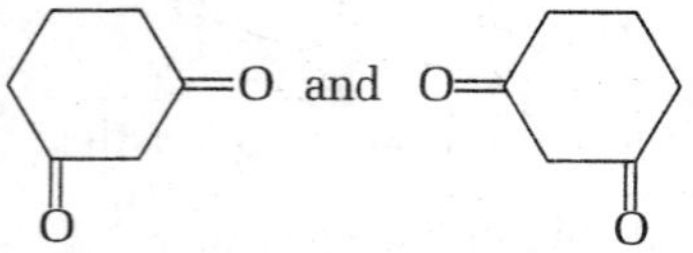 are enantiomers

(b) 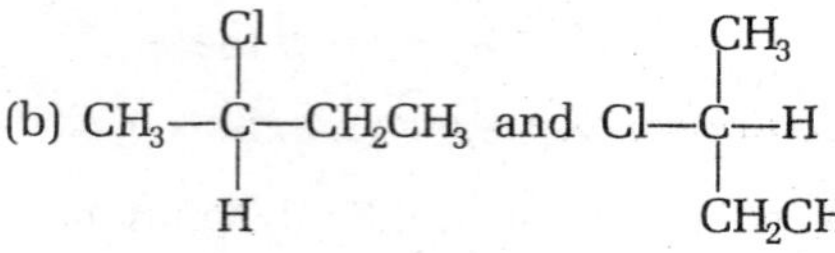 are same structures

(c) argol (sodium potassium tartrate) will show optical isomerism

(d) CH_3CHO on reaction with HCN gives racemic mixture

16. Assign a configuration, *R* or *S* to each of these compounds

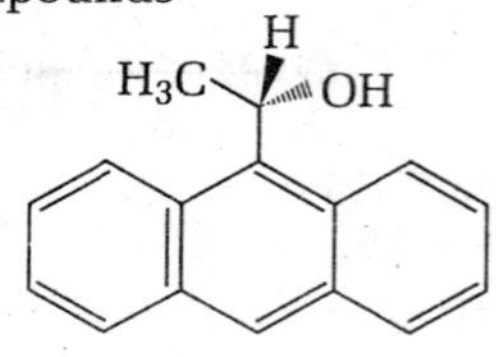

A

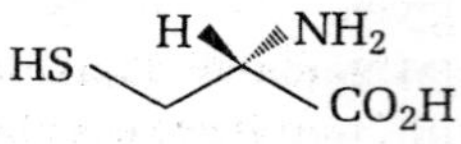

B

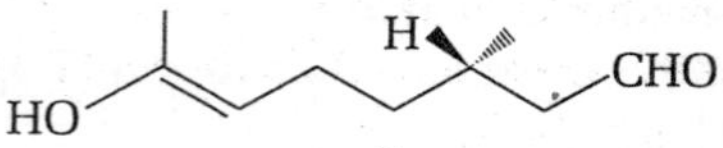

C

	A	*B*	*C*
(a)	*R*	*R*	*S*
(b)	*R*	*S*	*R*
(c)	*S*	*R*	*R*
(d)	*R*	*R*	*R*

17. Select chiral molecules out of *A*, *B*, *C* and *D*

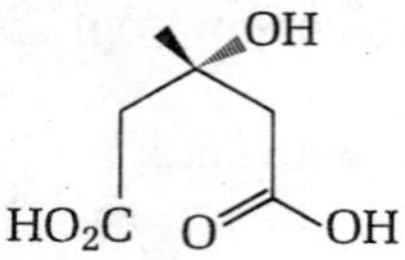

A

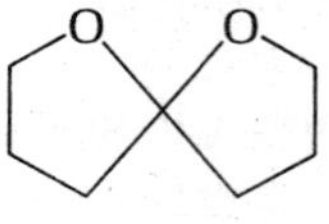

B

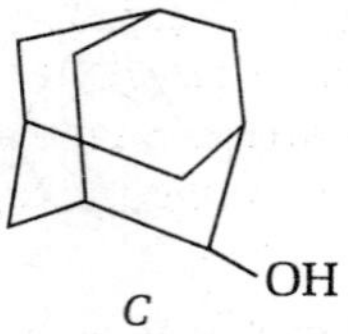

C

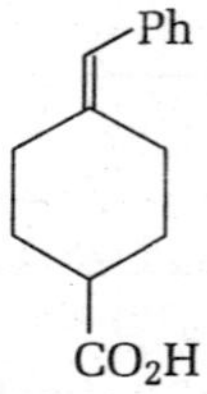

	A	*B*	*C*	*D*
(a)	not	yes	not	yes
(b)	not	not	yes	not
(c)	yes	not	yes	yes
(d)	yes	yes	not	not

18. Select correct stereochemistry (chiral/achiral) of the reactants and products

(a) 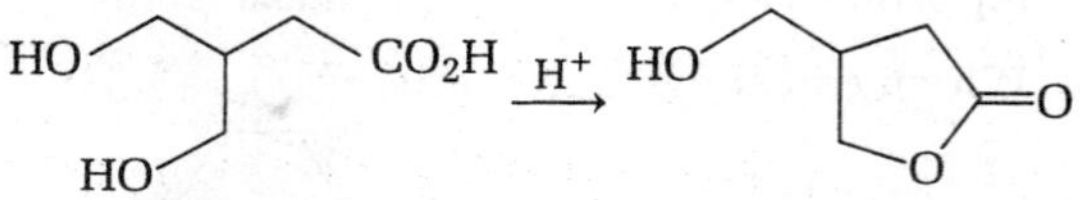

Achiral Chiral

(b) 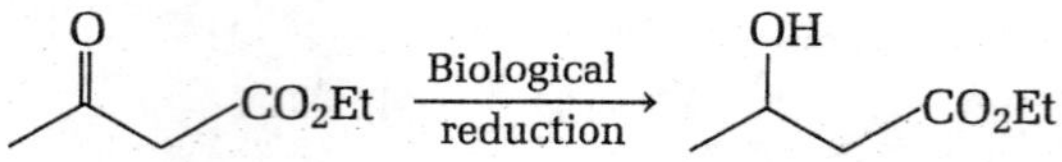

Achiral Chiral

(c) 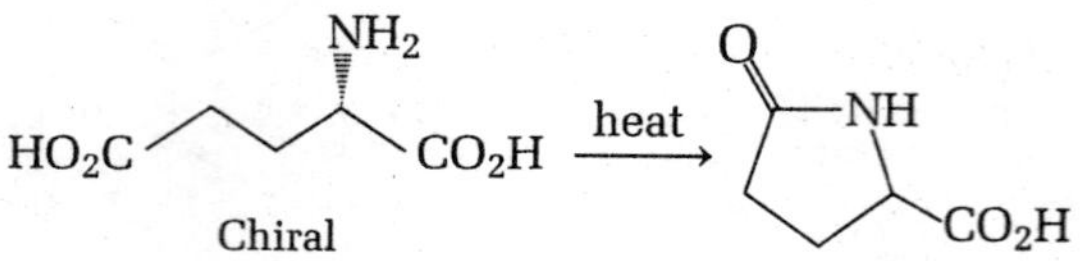

Chiral Chiral

(d) 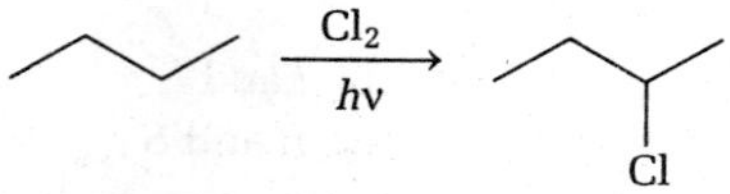

Achiral Achiral

19. Following compound (*P*) is subjected to reaction with $C_6H_5COCl(X)$.

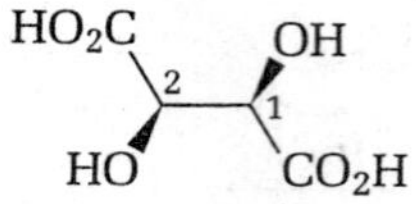

(*P*)

+

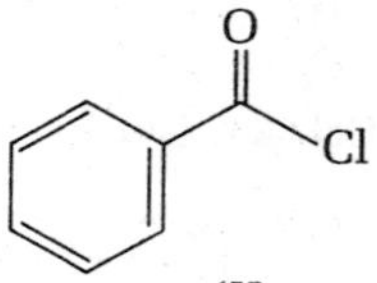

(*X*)

Select the correct statement(s).

(a) There is no cleavage or formation of bonds a the chiral centres and thus, both acylation go with retention

(b) There is cleavage and formation of bond at (1) at the chiral centre and thus, configuration at (1) inverted, but at (2) there is no change

(c) There is cleavage and formation of bond at (2) at the chiral centre and thus, configuration at (2) is inverted but at (1) there is no change

(d) There is cleavage and formation of bonds at both chiral centres and thus, configuration at both chiral centres are inverted

20. Select the correct statement(s).

(a) Hydrogenation of *A* is faster than that of *B* because *B* contains a more sterically hindered double bond

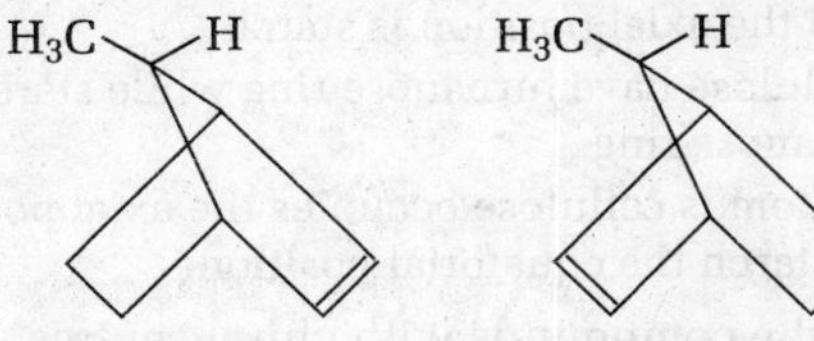

(*A*) (*B*)

(b) Hydrogenation of *B* is faster than that of *A* due to smaller free energy of *B*

(c) Hydrogen can add to *C* to either top face or the bottom face of the double bond.

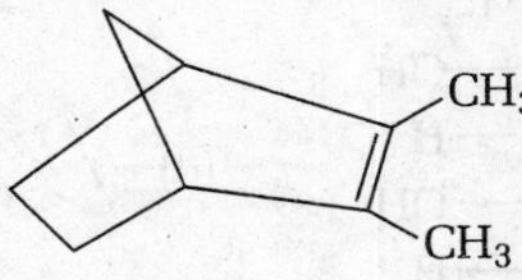

(d) Hydrogen can add to (*C*) only at top face

21. Consider the following structure

I II III

Select the true statement(s).

(a) I and II are enantiomers as they are nonsuperimposable mirror images

(b) I and II have the *E* configuration at the double bond

(c) II and III are identical

(d) I and III are identical

22. Select the correct statement(s).

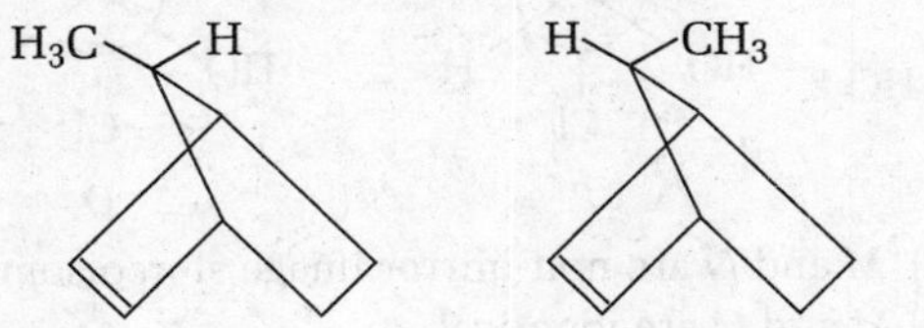

I II

(a) I and II are enantiomers

(b) I and II are stereoisomers

(c) I and II are achiral

(d) I and II are chiral

23. Consider the following epoxides I, II and III and select correct statements about them

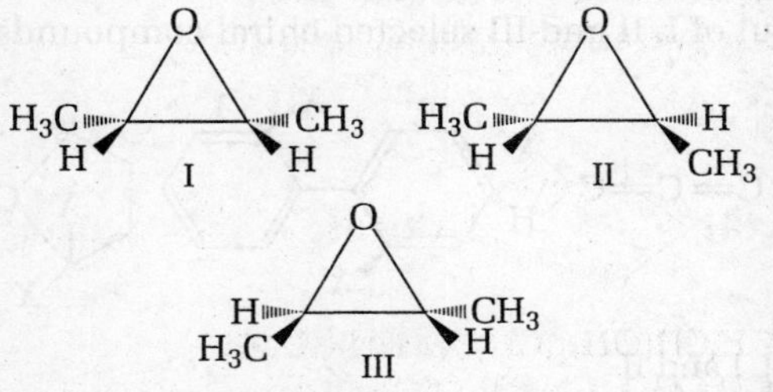

(a) I is *cis*-isomer and is achiral

(b) II and III are *trans*-isomers and are achiral

(c) II and III are *trans*-isomers and are chiral

(d) II and III are nonsuperimposable enantiomeric forms

24. Out of I and II, which is stabilised by intramolecular hydrogen-bonding?

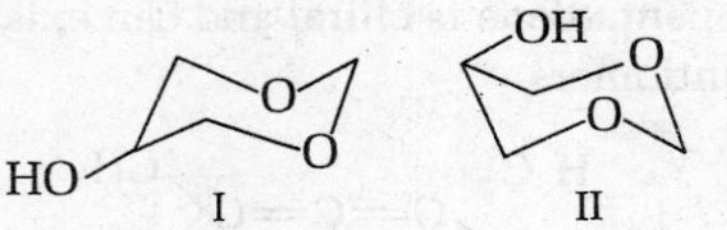

I II

(a) Only I (b) Only II

(c) I and II (d) None of these

25. Isomers of trichlorocyclopropane can be

(a) 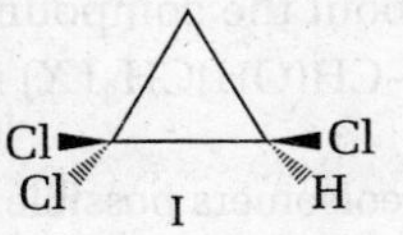 (b) 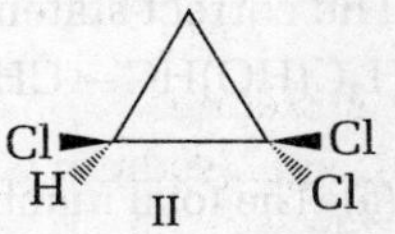

(c) 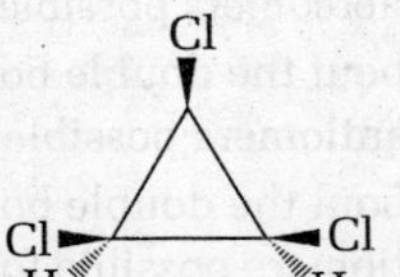 (d) 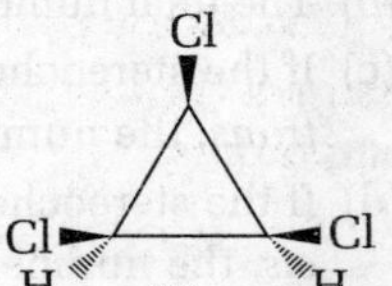

26. In the above question (No. 25)

(a) I and II are enantiomers

(b) III and IV are enantiomers

(c) III is *cis* and IV is *trans*-isomer

(d) I and II are chiral while III and IV are achiral

27. Consider the following molecules,

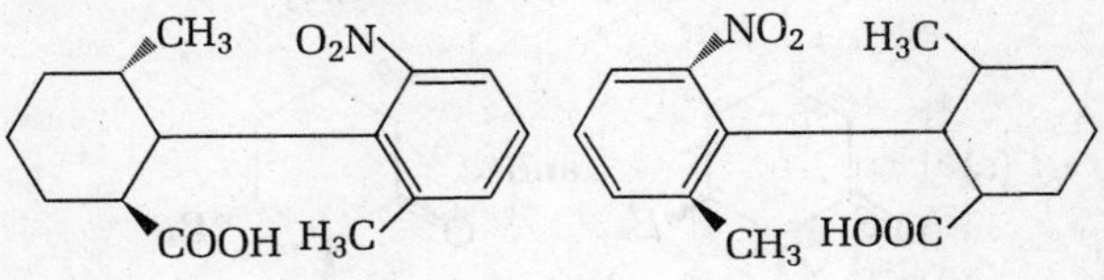

Select the correct statement(s).

(a) There is restricted rotation about (C—C) single bond
(b) I and II can be isolated as enantiomers
(c) I and II are enantiomers of the class called astropisomers
(d) Heating of I or II will give racemic mixture

28. Out of I, II and III selected chiral compounds

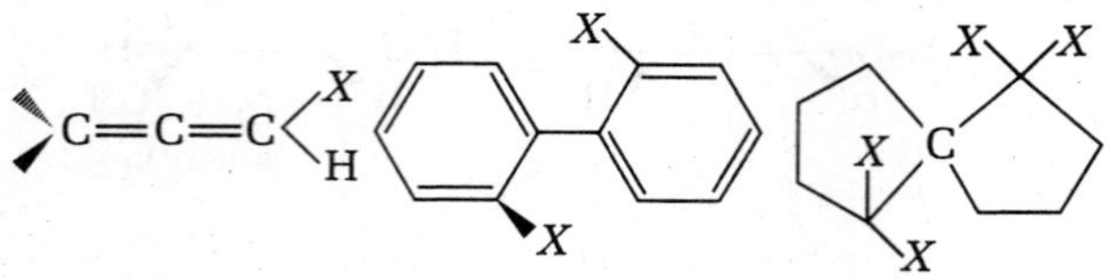

(a) I and II
(b) II and III
(c) I and III
(d) I, II and III

29. Select the correct statement(s).

(a) Enantiomers in which there is restricted rotation about (C—C) single bond are called astropisomers
(b) 2,3-pentadiene is chiral and can existas pair of enantiomers

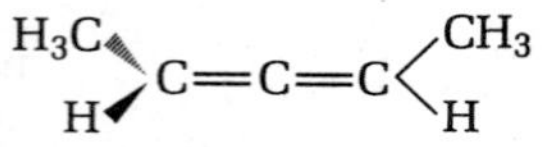

(c) 2,3-pentadiene can exist as *CTS* and *trans*-isomers
(d) 2,3-pendadiene is achiral and *meso* compound

30. The correct statement(s) about the compound $H_3C(HO)HC—CH{=}CH—CH(OH)CH_3\,(X)$ is (are) **[IIT JEE 2009]**

(a) The total number of stereoisomers possible for *X* is 6.
(b) The total number of diastereomers possible for *X* is 3.
(c) If the stereochemistry about the double bond in *X* is *trans*, the number of enantiomers possible for *X* is 4.
(d) If the stereochemistry about the double bond in *X* is *cis*, the number of enantiomers possible for *X* is 2.

31. Which of the following pairs of compounds could be separated by recrystallisation or distillation?

(a) *meso*-tartaric acid and (±) tartaric acid

(b) 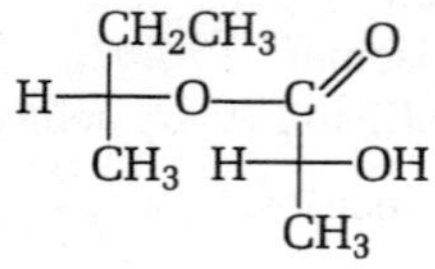 and 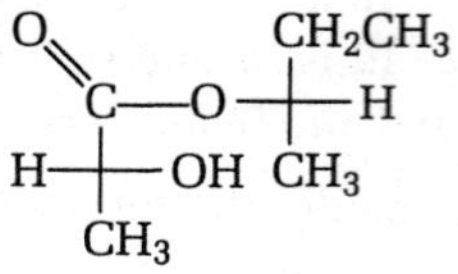

(c) 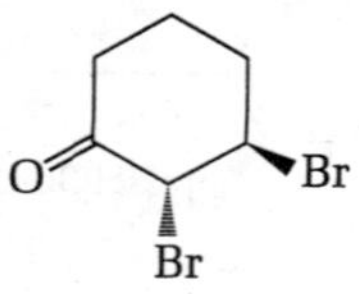 and 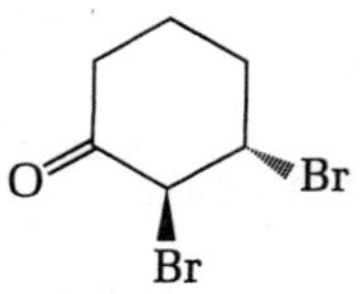

(d) 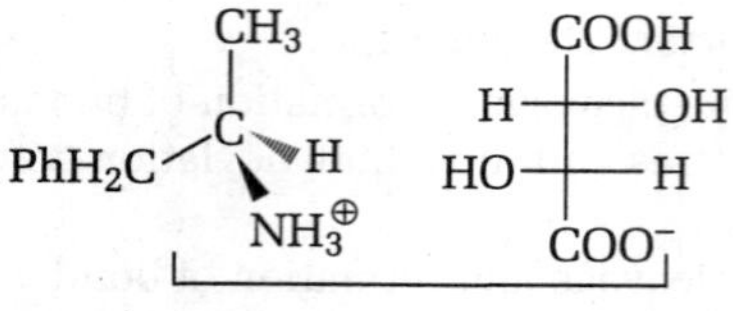 and

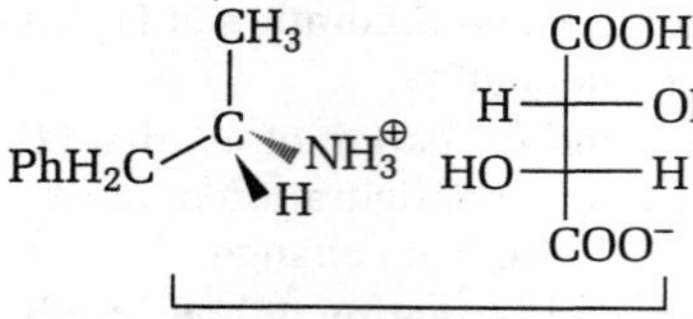

in acid base salt

32. Select the correct alternates.

(a) Cellulose and starch both have same repeating unit a six-members ring containing an oxygen atom and three —OH groups joined by an oxygen atom
(b) O-atom occupies the equatorial position in cellulose and the axial position is starch
(c) Cellulose have furnanose ring while starch have pyranose ring.
(d) O-atom is cellulose occupies the axial position and in starch the equatorial position.

33. Select the compounds with chiral centres.

(a) 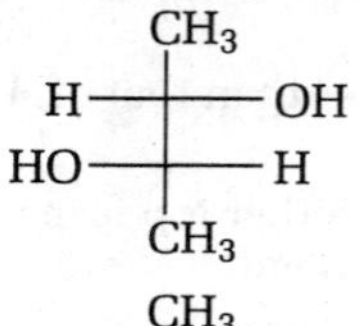

(b) 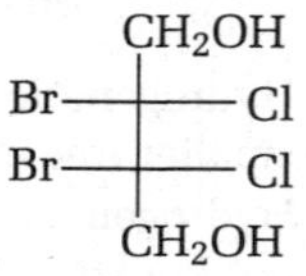

(c) 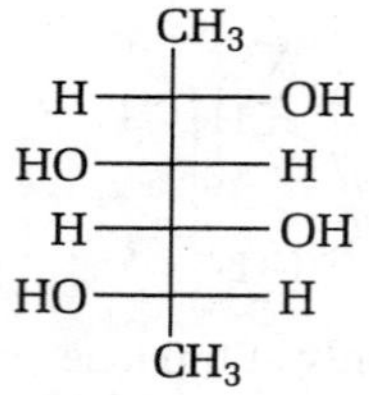

(d) 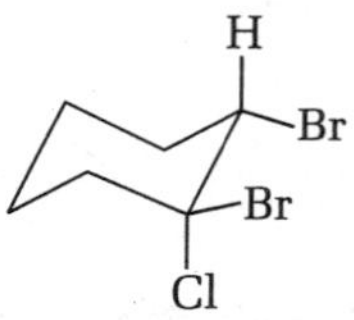

34. Which of the given statement(s) about *N*, *O*, *P* and *Q* with respect to *M* is (are) correct? **[IIT JEE 2012]**

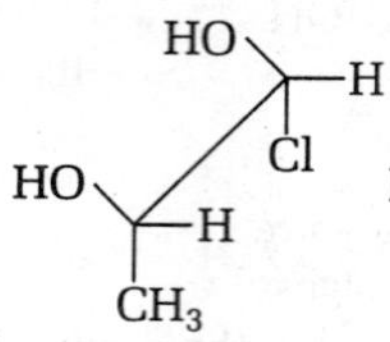

M

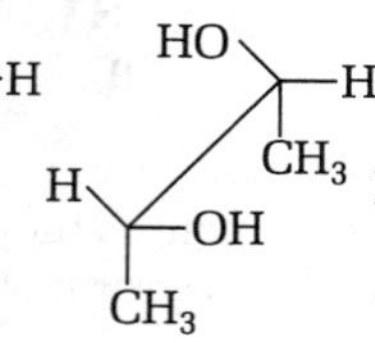

N

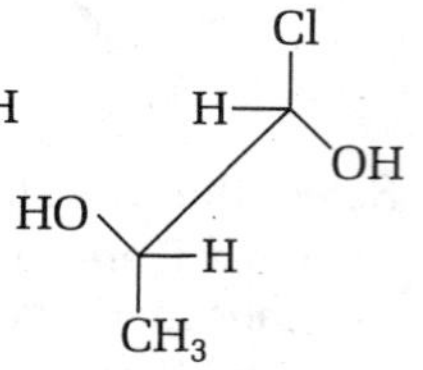

O

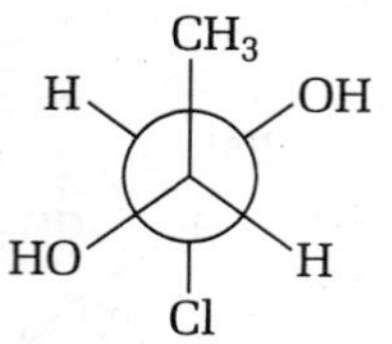

P

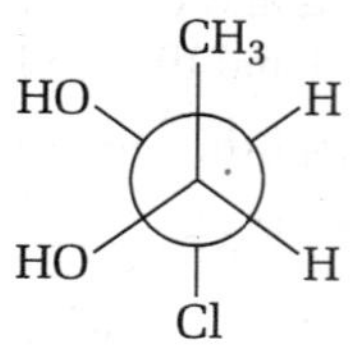

Q

(a) *M* and *N* are non-mirror image stereoisomers
(b) *M* and *O* are identical
(c) *M* and *P* are enantiomers
(d) *M* and *Q* are identical

Numerical Value Questions

All these questions have a Numerical value as their answer, solve the questions and write your answer.

1. Calculate inantiomeric excess from the given data ;
(i) *sp* rotation = 20° (in percentage)
(ii) optical rotation = 18°

2. Calculate the optical rotation from the given data.
$sp = 20\%$, $D = 90\%$, $L = 10\%$

3. If two chiral center present in symmetrical molecule. Find the total number of optical isomer?

4. If molecule has no planar of symmetry and molecule has '*n*' assymetric carbons atoms. How many number of *meso* form are present ?

5. How many total chiral center present in 1, 2, 3, 4 tetrahydroxy pentanol?

6. Find the number of stereo-isomers of 1, 2-dihydroxy cyclopentane.
(Hint : Number of stereoisomers = $2^n - 1$)

Comprehension Based Questions

In these questions, a passage has been given followed by questions based on it. You have to answer the questions based on the passage given.

***Passage* 1** *Following passage is about the type of isomerism. Answer the questions at the end of it.*

Tautomerism is due to spontaneous interconversion of two isomeric forms with different functional groups into one each other. The term tautomer means constitutional isomers that undergo such rapid interconversion that they cannot be independently isolated.

1. *A* (given below) can be identified by some of the following reagents

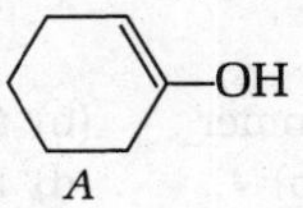

A

I. NH_2OH
II. Neutral $FeCl_3$
III. Br_2 water
IV. $[Ag(NH_3)_2]OH$
Select suitable reagents
(a) I and II
(b) I and III
(c) II and III
(d) II and IV

2. In the following D^+ catalysed tautomerisation, final product is

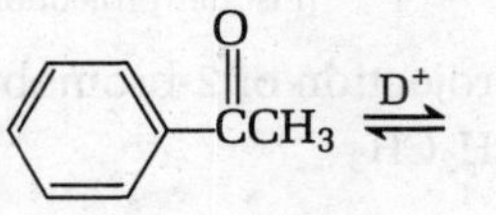

(a) 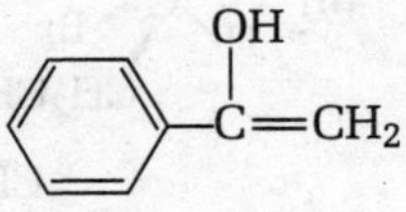

(b) 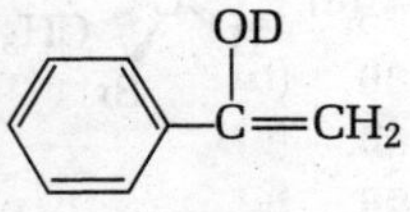

(c) 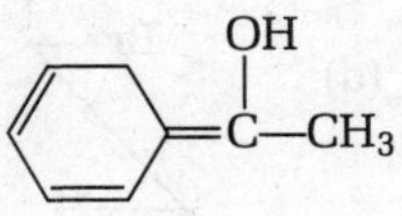

(d) 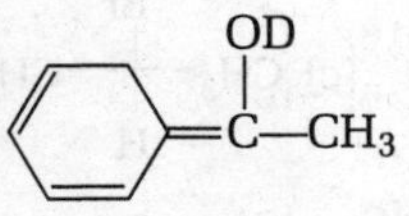

3. What is relation between (I), (II) and (III)?

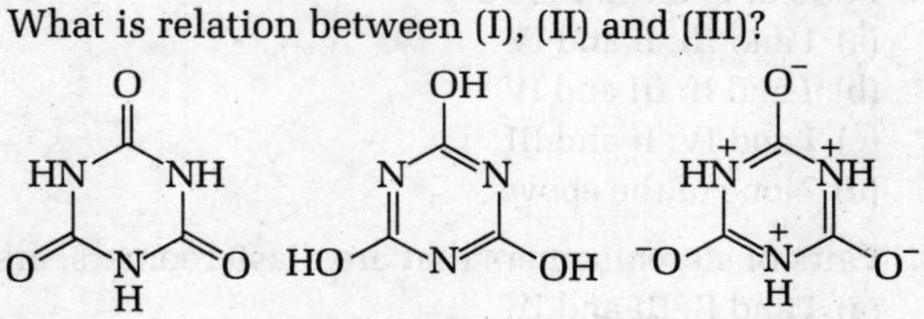

(I) (II) (III)

(a) I and II are tautomers
(b) III is conjugate base of II
(c) III is resonance structure of I
(d) No relation exists

***Passage* 2** By the term *syn* addition, we actually mean the addition of electrophile and nucleophile on the available sites, and by the term *anti* addition, we mean the addition of these *trans* to available sites.
Based on this write-up, answer the questions given.

1. *Syn* and *anti* addition can take place in

(a) 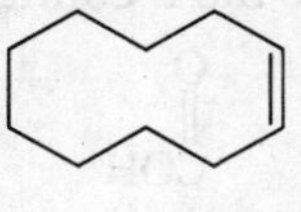
(b) 
(c) 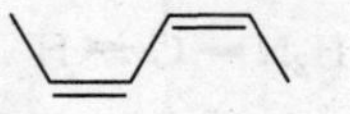
(d) 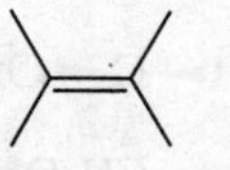

2. Addition of alkaline $KMnO_4$ to an alkene is *syn*. Thus,
(a) maleic acid is converted to *meso*-tartaric acid
(b) fumaric acid is converted to *meso*-tartaric acid
(c) maleic acid is converted to racemic mixture
(d) fumaric acid is converted to racemic mixture

3. Addition of Br_2 water to an alkene is *anti*. $(CHO)_4$ on reaction with Br_2 forms *meso* $(CHO)_4Br_2$. Thus, $(CHO)_4$ is
(a) maleic acid
(b) fumaric acid
(c) Both (a) and (b)
(d) None of these

***Passage* 3** 2,4-dichlorohexane has two chiral centres indicated by (*)

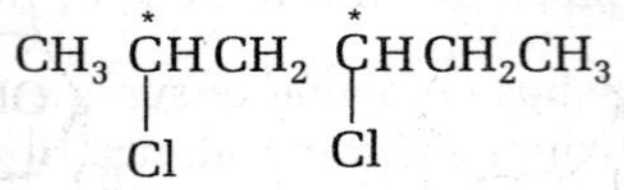

Their Fischer projections can be written as

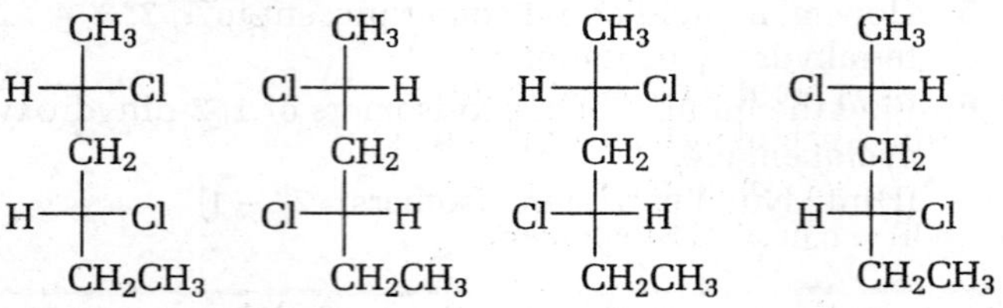

I II III IV

Based on these structures, answer the questions at the end.

1. Pairs of enantiomers are
   (a) I and III; II and IV
   (b) I and II; III and IV
   (c) I and IV; II and III
   (d) None of the above

2. Pairs of stereoisomers that are diastereomers, are
   (a) I and II; III and IV
   (b) I and III; II and IV
   (c) I and III; I and IV; II and III; II and IV
   (d) I and IV; II and III

3. Pair of *erythro*-enantiomers is
   (a) I and II
   (b) III and IV
   (c) I and III
   (d) II and IV

***Passage* 4** The naturally occurring enantiomer of glyceraldehyde has the D-configuration, and the most naturally occurring amino acids have the L-configuration.

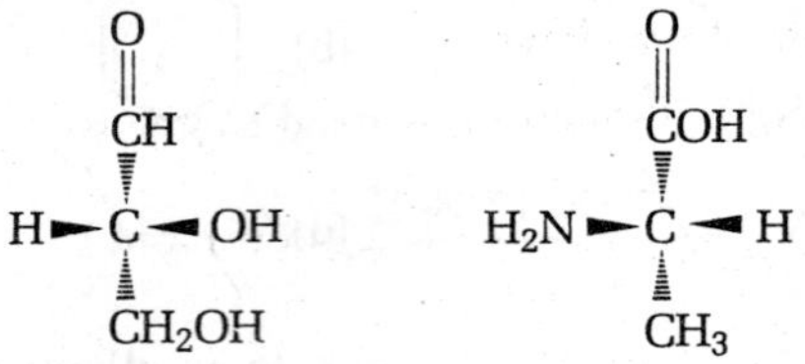

D-glyceraldehyde L-serine

Any asymmetric compound which can be converted to or prepared from D-glyceraldehyde will have D-configuration.

1. Following compound has the configuration at (1) and (2) indicated carbons

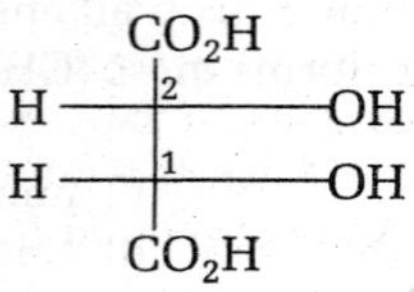

(a) D, D (b) D, L
(c) L, L (d) L, D

2. Following isomer of optically active tartaric acid has D, L-configurations at C_1 and C_2 indicated carbons. Thus, its configuration is

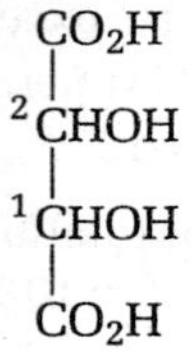

(a) 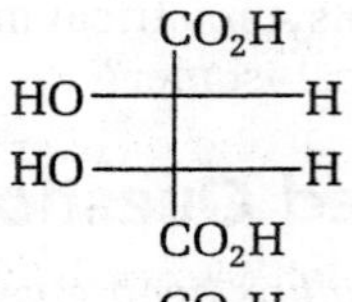 (b) 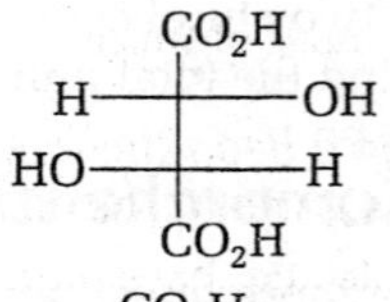

(c) 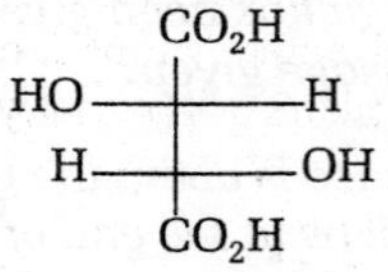 (d) 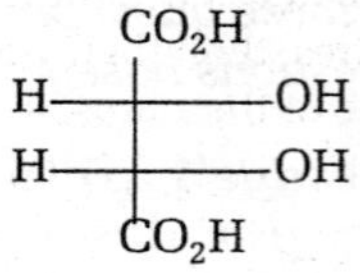

3. In the following compound, relative configuration has been indicated

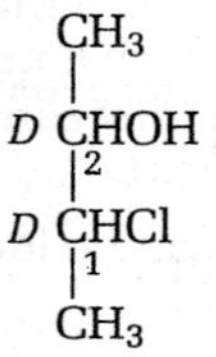

Thus, it is
(a) *erythro* enantiomer (b) *threo* enantiomer
(c) Both (a) and (b) (d) None of these

***Passage* 5**

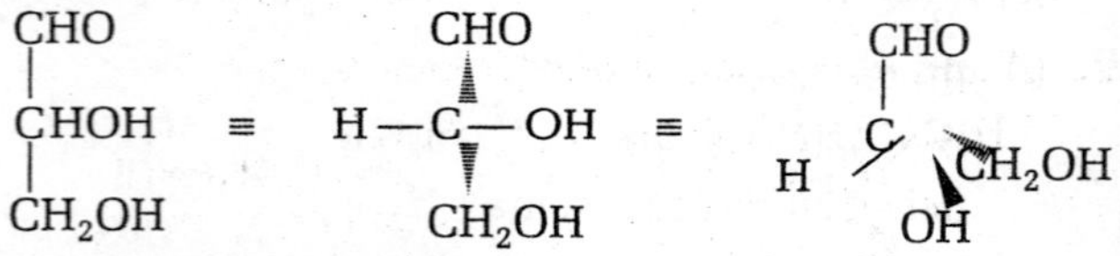

Three dimensional representation

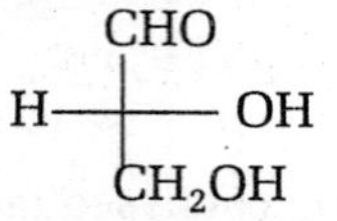

Projected form
(Fischer projection)

1. Fischer projection of 2-bromobutane is

(a) 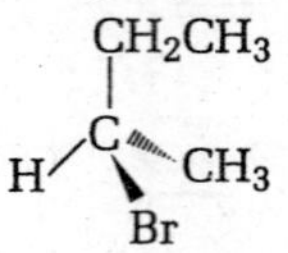 (b) 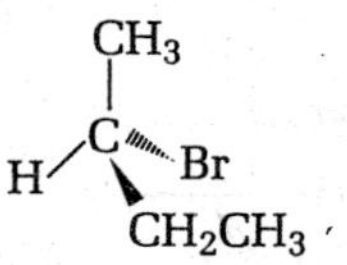

(c) 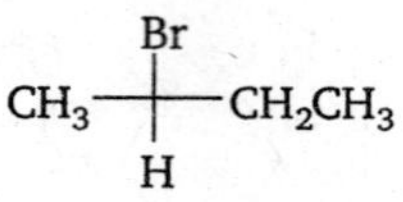 (d) 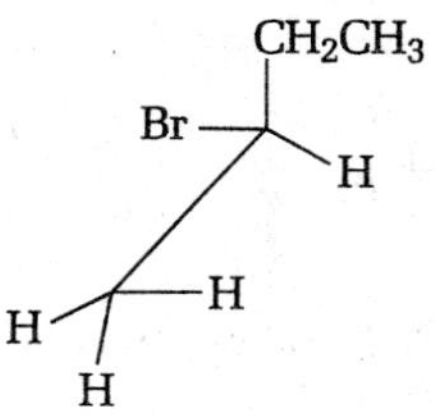

2. Fischer projection of *A* is

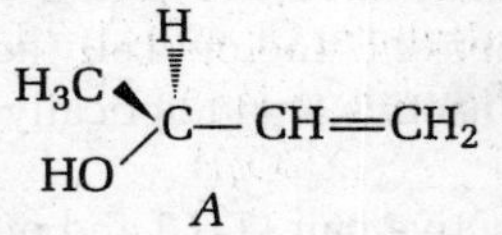

A

(a) 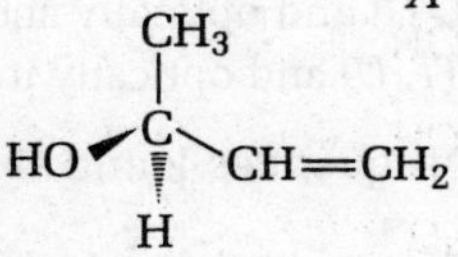 (b) 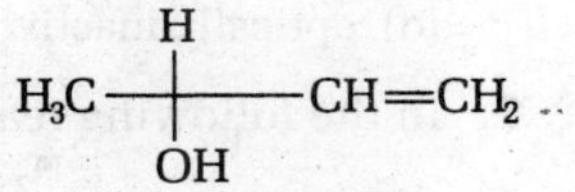

(c) Both of these (d) None of these

***Passage* 6** *Read the following passage and answer the questions given at the end.*

Many molecules have more than one chiral centres. If there are *n* chiral centres, then there are 2^n stereoisomers, number can be less if some of the stereoisomers have plane of symmetry. The molecule

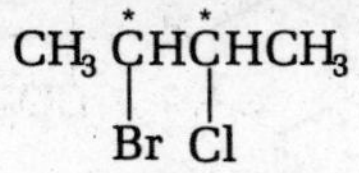

has two chiral centres hence, there are four stereoisomers or two pairs of enantiomers

1. Select the pair of diastereomers out of the following.

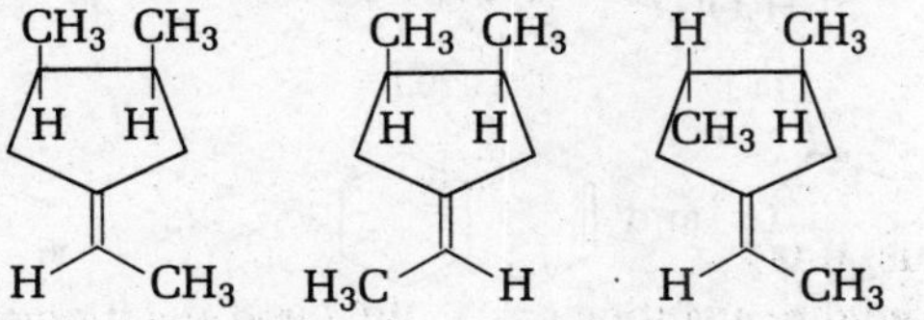

A *B* *C*

(a) *A* and *C* (b) *B* and *C*

(c) *A* and *B* (d) None of these

2. (*A* and *B*) is a pair of diastereomers,

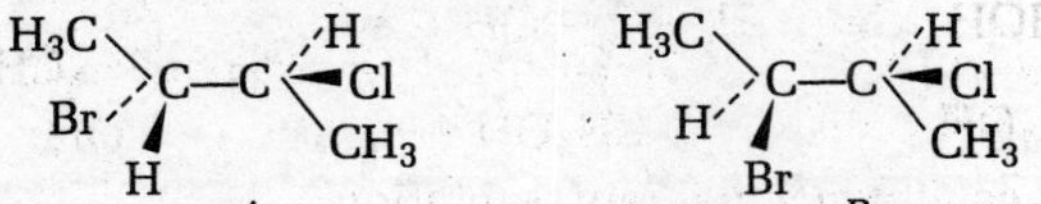

A *B*

They are represented by Fischer projections as

A *B*

(a) 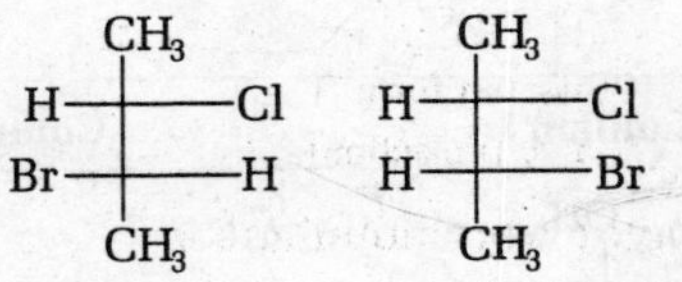

(b) 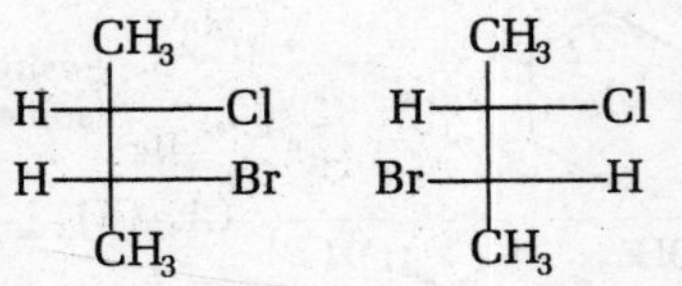

(c) 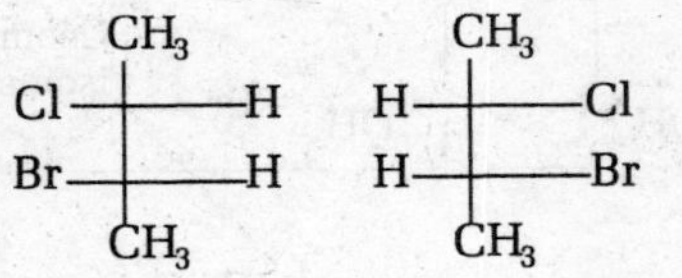

(d) None of the above

3. Following pair of *A* and *B* represents

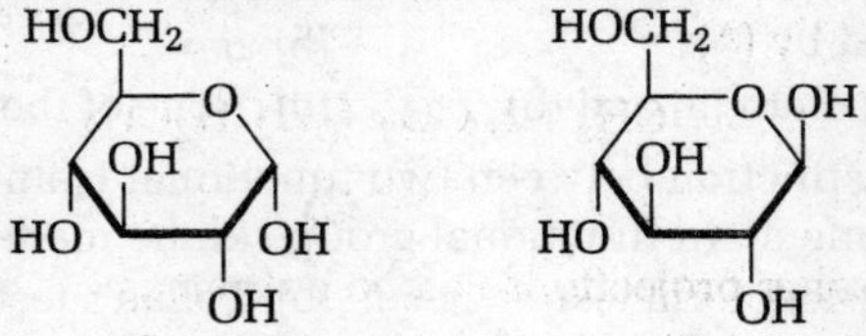

A *B*

(a) a pair of same compounds

(b) a pair of racemic compounds

(c) a pair of epimers

(d) a pair of diastereomers

***Passage* 7** A graduate student was studying enzymatic reductions of cyclohexanones when she encontered some interesting chemistry. When she used an enzyme and NADPH to reduce the following ketone, the product was optically active. On purification of the product so that no enzyme, NADPH or other contaminates were present, product did not lose its optical activity.

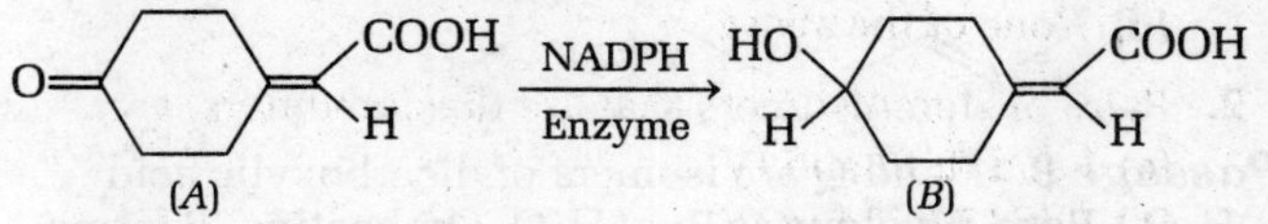

(*A*) (*B*)

Optically active

Answer the following questions.

1. Optical activity in the product was due to presence of

(a) one chiral centre (b) two chiral centres

(c) three chiral centres (d) no chiral centre

2. The product formed is

(a) an example of a chiral compound with no chiral centres

(b) like the allenes, it is classified as an "extended tetrahedron"

(c) Both (a) and (b)

(d) None of the above

3. If the alternate method is used as given

$$A \xrightarrow{Ni/H_2} \text{product } (C)$$

then (*C*) is

(a) racemic mixture and is optically inactive

(b) meso compound

(c) *d*(+)

(d) *l*(–)

***Passage* 8** *Read the following short write-up and answer the questions at the end of it.*

Two substances having the same molecular formula, C_4H_8O, were examined in the gaseous state by electron diffraction. The carbon-oxygen distance was found to be 1.43 Å in the compound *A* and 1.24 Å in compound *B*.

C—O bond length = 143 pm

C—O bond length = 123 pm

1. Keto-enol tautomerism occurs in
   (a) A (b) B
   (c) Both (a) and (b) (d) None of these
2. Distinction between two functional isomers of the same main functional group can be made by
   (a) iodoform test (b) Tollen's test
   (c) Br_2 water (d) phthalein test
3. Probable structures of A and B can be

(a) 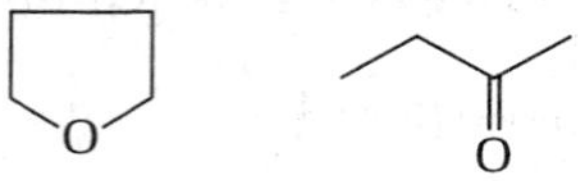

(b) 

(c) 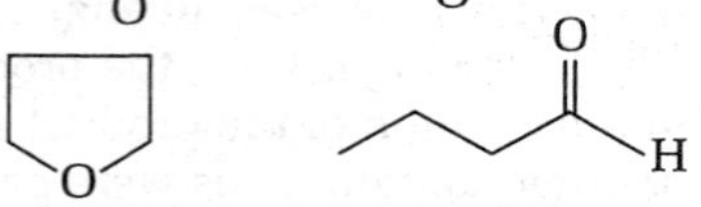

(d) 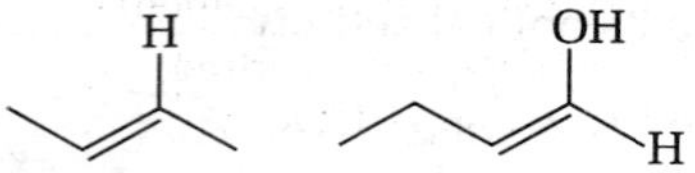

Passage 9 P and Q are isomers of dicarboxylic acid $C_4H_4O_4$. Both decolourise Br_2 / H_2O. On heating, P forms the cyclic anhydride.

Upon treatment with dilute alkaline $KMnO_4$. P as well as Q could produce one or more than one form S, T and U.

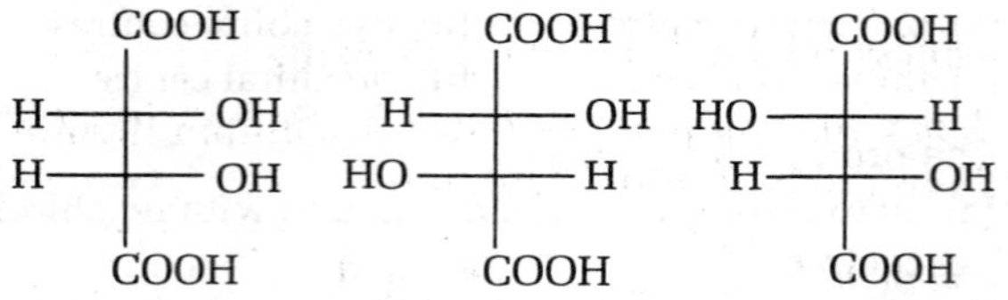

S T U

[JEE Advanced 2013]

1. Compounds formed from P and Q are, respectively
   (a) optically active S and optically active pair (T, U)
   (b) optically inactive S and optically inactive pair (T, U)
   (c) optically active pair (T, U) and optically active S
   (d) optically inactive pair (T, U) and optically inactive S
2. In the following reaction sequences V and W are respectively $Q \xrightarrow[\Delta]{H_2/Ni} V$

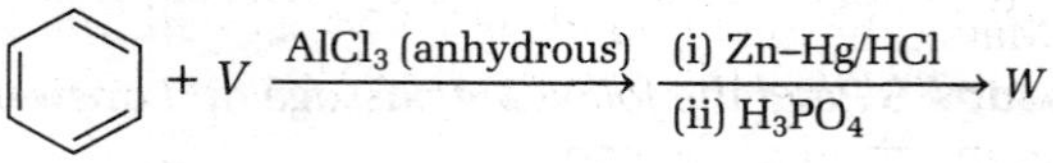

V W

(a) 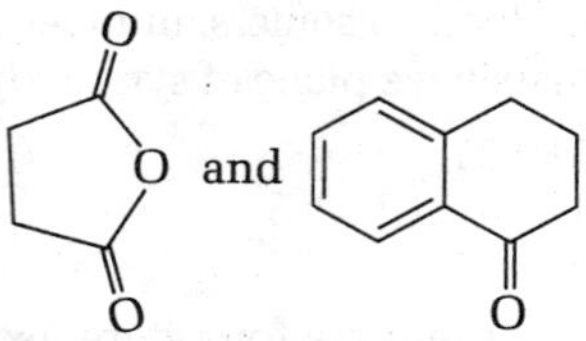

(b) 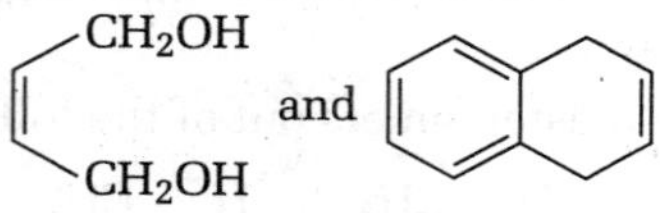

(c) 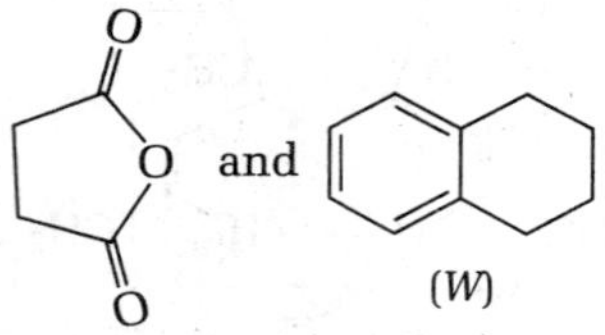

(W)

(d) 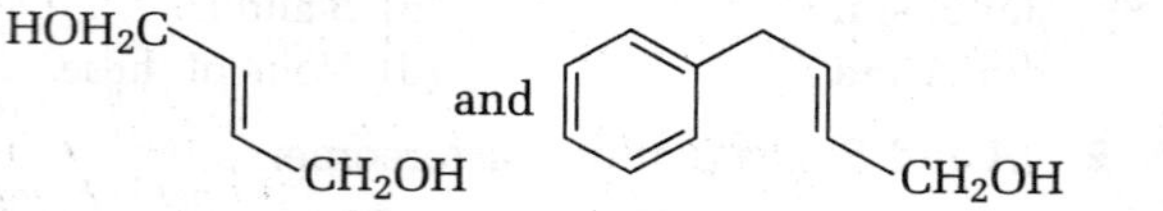

Matrix-Match Type

Given below are Matching Type Questions, with two columns (each having some items) each . Each item of Column I has to be matched with the items of Column II.

1. Match the pair of compounds in Column I with the isomerism shown by them in Column II.

Column I	Column II
A. 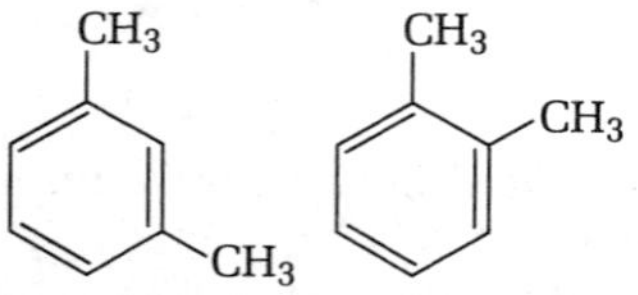	1. Metamerism
B. $CH_3\overset{O}{\overset{\parallel}{C}}CH_2CH_2CH_3, CH_3CH_2\overset{O}{\overset{\parallel}{C}}CH_2CH_3$	2. Tautomerism
C. 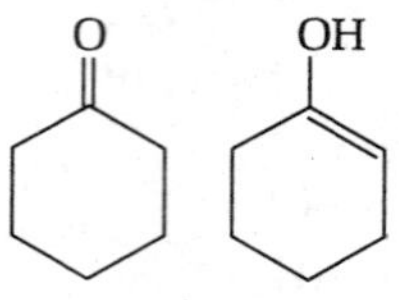	3. Position isomerism
D. 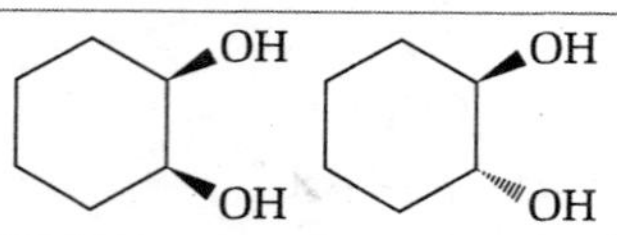	4. Geometrical isomerism

2. Match the compound in Column I with the possible isomers given by it in Column II.

Column I		Column II
A. CH_3CH_2CHO	1.	Optical
B. $CH_3CH{=}CHCH_3$	2.	Functional
C. $CH_3CH_2CH(OH)CH_3$	3.	Geometrical
D. $CH_3—CH_3$	4.	Conformer

3. Match the compounds is Column I with the number of isomers (specified) formed by them in Column II.

Column I		Column II
A. Position isomers of benzyl chloride	1.	(2)
B. Chain isomers of pentane	2.	(3)
C. Optical isomers of 2-butanol	3.	(4)
D. Alcohols and ethers of $C_4H_{10}O$	4.	(7)

4. Match the compounds in Column I with number of stereo centres in Column II.

	Column I		Column II
A.	2-butene	1.	Zero
B.	2-butanol	2.	One
C.	1-chloro-2,3-dimethyl cyclohexane	3.	Two
D.	Isobutene	4.	Three

5. Match the compound in Column I with the possible isomerism given by it in Column II.

	Column I (Compound)		Column II (Type of isomerism)
A.	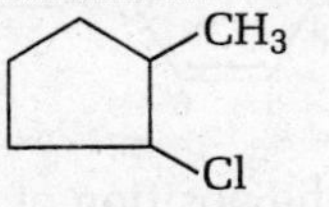	1.	Functional
B.		2.	Optical
C.	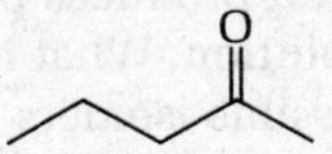	3.	Chain
D.	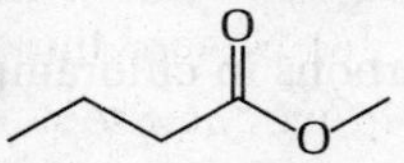	4.	Metamerism

6. Consider the following reactions,

$$\underset{(P)}{CH_3\overset{O}{\overset{\|}{C}}CH_2\overset{O}{\overset{\|}{C}}OC_2H_5} \xrightarrow{H_3O^+} (Q) + (R)$$

Tautomerises ⇅

$[CO_2 \text{ with } NaHCO_3]$

Match the compounds *P* to *S* in Column I with their properties in Column II.

Column I	Column II
A. *P*	1. Colour with $FeCl_3$ solution
B. *Q*	2. Br_2 water is decolourised
C. *R*	3. Yellow ppt. with NaOH/ I_2
D. *S*	4. Brick effervescence with $NaHCO_3$

7. Consider the following reactions,

$C_4H_4O_4$ has three isomeric dibasic acid, *P*, *Q*, *R* and a cyclic ester (*S*)

$$\text{isomer } (R) \xrightarrow{\Delta} \text{monobasic acid}$$

Isomer (*Q*) has zero dipole moment.

Match the compounds *P* to *S* (in Column I) with their properties (in Column II).

Column I		Column II
A. *P*	1.	Optically inactive compounds with Baeyer's reagent.
B. *Q*	2.	Resovable racemic mixture with Baeyer's reagent.
C. *R*	3.	Br_2 water is decolourised.
D. *S*	4.	One of the hydrolysis products give white precipitate with $CaCl_2$ solution in acetic acid medium.

Single Integer Answer Questions

Answer of these questions is a single digit lying between 0 to 9.

1. The number of chiral carbons in chloramphenicol is ……… . **[JEE Main 2020]**

2. The number of chiral centres in penicillin is …… . **[JEE Main 2020]**

3. How many stereogenic centres are there in the following naturally occurring antioxidant? (Glutathione)

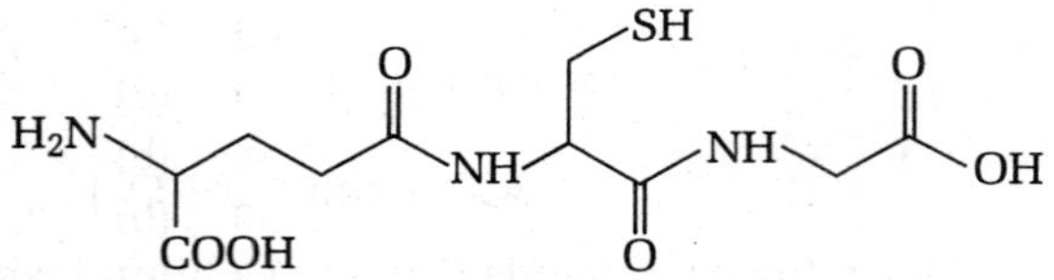

4. The number of chiral centres present in [*B*] is …… . **[JEE Main 2020, Sep.]**

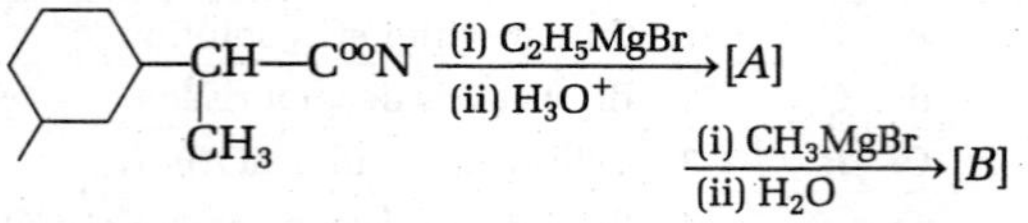

5. The number of chiral centres present in threonine is ……… . **[JEE Main 2020, Sep.]**

6. Identify the position (by number) of the stereogenic centre in the following.

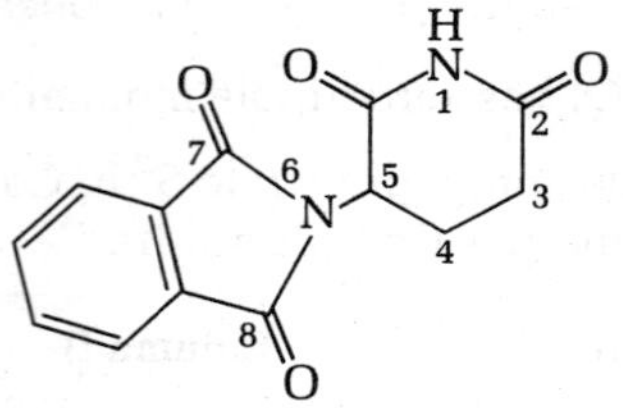

7. Which carbonyl group is most enolised in the following compound?

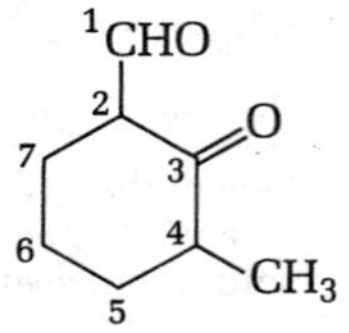

8. Following molecule is *trans*- at $(x + y)$ position of $(C{=}C)$ bond. What is the value of $(x + y)$?

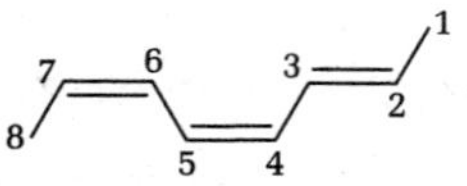

9. For the given compound *X*, the total number of optically active stereoisomers is ……… . **[JEE Advanced 2018]**

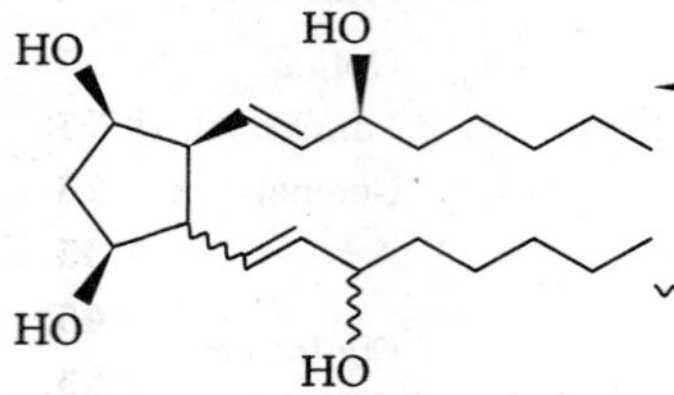

This type of bond indicates that the configuration at the specific carbon and the geometry of the double bond is fixed.

This type of bond indicates that the configuration at the specific carbon and the geometry of the double bond is not fixed.

10. Which compound shows stereoisomerism, position and functional isomerism?

$CH_3CH(OH)CH{=}CHCH_3$ (1), $CH_3CH_2CH_2C(=O)CH_3$ (2),

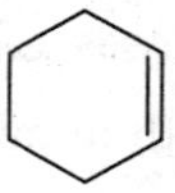

(3), $CH_3CH_2CH(Cl)CH_2CH_2CH_3$ (4)

$CH_3CH_2OCH_2CH(OH)CH_3$ (5), CH_3CH_2COOH (6)

11. A mixture contains 6 g of (+) 2-butanol and 5 g of (–) 2-butanol. What is the percentage of enantiomeric excess (e.e.)?

12. In the following reaction, optically activity of the chiral compound is retained in the product,

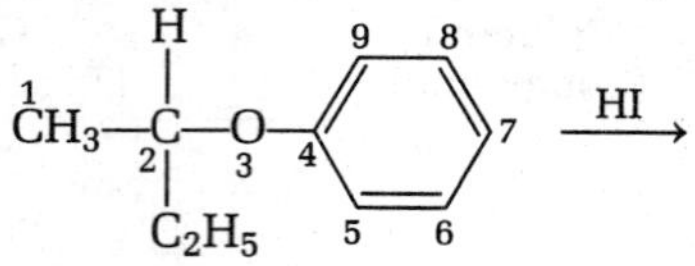

What is the sum of the position of bonds cleaved?

13. An organic compound $(C_8H_{10}O_2)$ rotates plane-polarised light. It produces pink colour with neutral $FeCl_3$ solution. What is the total number of all the possible isomers for this compound? **[JEE Advanced 2020]**

14. Which group/atom has maximum preference in deciding *R*, *S* configuration?

$-H$ (1), $-CH_3$ (2), $-SH$ (3), $-CHO$ (4), $-COOH$ (5),

$-NH_2$ (6), $-OH$ (7), $-C{\equiv}CH$ (8)

Answers

Objective Questions Type I [Only one correct option]

1. (c)	2. (c)	3. (d)	4. (a)	5. (d)	6. (b)	7. (a)	8. (d)	9. (a)	10. (d)
11. (c)	12. (b)	13. (a)	14. (c)	15. (c)	16. (b)	17. (c)	18. (d)	19. (c)	20. (a)
21. (a)	22. (d)	23. (c)	24. (b)	25. (b)	26. (b)	27. (b)	28. (d)	29. (a)	30. (c)
31. (b)	32. (c)	33. (a)	34. (d)	35. (c)	36. (a)	37. (b)	38. (b)	39. (a)	40. (c)
41. (d)	42. (c)	43. (a)	44. (a)	45. (b)	46. (a)	47. (d)	48. (a)	49. (c)	50. (a)
51. (a)	52. (b)	53. (c)	54. (a)	55. (b)	56. (b)	57. (c)	58. (b)	59. (b)	60. (a)
61. (c)	62. (b)	63. (a)	64. (c)	65. (c)	66. (a)	67. (b)	68. (d)	69. (a)	70. (c)
71. (c)	72. (a)	73. (a)	74. (d)	75. (d)	76. (a)	77. (d)	78. (a)	79. (d)	80. (a)
81. (d)	82. (c)	83. (d)	84. (c)	85. (a)	86. (b)	87. (a)	88. (a)	89. (b)	90. (d)
91. (d)	92. (a)	93. (c)	94. (d)	95. (b)	96. (d)	97. (d)	98. (c)	99. (b)	100. (c)
101. (a)	102. (d)	103. (b)	104. (d)	105. (c)	106. (c)	107. (a)	108. (d)	109. (c)	110. (b)
111. (d)	112. (b)	113. (c)	114. (d)	115. (b)	116. (d)	117. (c)	118. (c)	119. (d)	120. (a)
121. (a)	122. (c)	123. (b)	124. (a)	125. (c)	126. (a)	127. (c)	128. (a)		

Objective Questions Type II [One or more than one correct option(s)]

1. (a, b, c)	2. (b, c, d)	3. (b, c)	4. (a, b, c, d)	5. (a, b, d)
6. (b, c, d)	7. (c)	8. (a, b, c, d)	9. (a, b, c, d)	10. (c)
11. (a, b)	12. (a)	13. (b)	14. (c)	15. (b, c, d)
16. (d)	17. (a)	18. (a, b, c)	19. (a)	20. (a, c)
21. (a, b, d)	22. (b, d)	23. (a, c, d)	24. (b)	25. (a, b, c,d)
26. (a, c, d)	27. (a, b, c, d)	28. (d)	29. (a, b)	30. (a, d)
31. (a, b, d)	32. (a, b)	33. (a, b, c)	34. (a, b, c)	

Numerical Value Questions

1. (90) 2. (16) 3. (2) 4. (0) 5. (3) 6. (3)

Comprehension Based Questions

Passage 1 – 1. *(c)* **2.** *(b)* **3.** *(a,c)*

Passage 2 – 1. *(a,b,d)* **2.** *(a,d)* **3.** *(b)*

Passage 3 – 1. *(b)* **2.** *(c)* **3.** *(a)*

Passage 4 – 1. *(a)* **2.** *(c)* **3.** *(a)*

Passage 5 – 1. *(c)* **2.** *(b)*

Passage 6 – 1. *(a,b)* **2.** *(a)* **3.** *(c,d)*

Passage 7 – 1. *(d)* **2.** *(c)* **3.** *(a)*

Passage 8 – 1. *(b)* **2.** *(a,b)* **3.** *(a,c)*

Passage 9 – 1. *(b)* **2.** *(a)*

Matrix-Match Type

1. A→(3); B→(1); C→(2); D→(4)
2. A→(2); B→(3); C→(1); D→(4)
3. A→(3); B→(2); C→(1); D→(4)
4. A→(3); B→(2); C→(1); D→(4)
5. A→(2,3); B→(1,3,4); C→(1,3,4); D→(1,3,4)
6. A→(1,2); B→(1,3); C→(1,4); D→(4)
7. A→(3); B→(3,4); C→(3); D→(1,2,3)

Single Integer Answer Questions

1. (2)	2. (3)	3. (2)	4. (2)	5. (2)	6. (5)	7. (3)	8. (5)	9. (7)	10. (1)
11. (9)	12. (5)	13. (1)	14. (3)						

Solutions

Objective Questions Type I [Only one correct option]

1. (*c*)

Cyclobutane
(a chain of four carbon atoms)

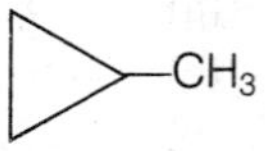

A chain of three carbon atoms

2. (*c*) All H are equivalents. It means it is symmetrical.

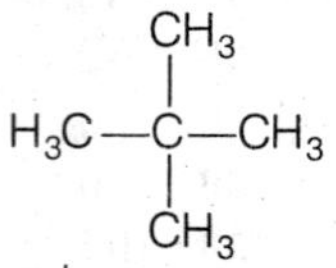

3. (*d*) C_6H_{12} (alicyclic) can be

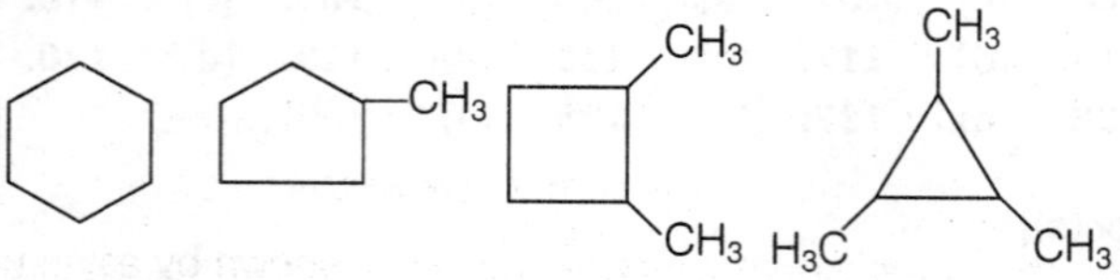

4. (*a*)

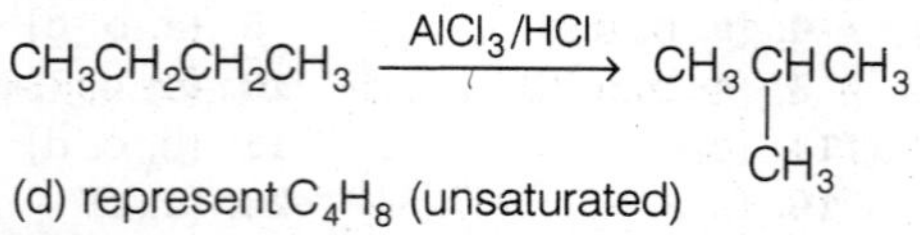

(b), (c), (d) represent C_4H_8 (unsaturated)
Thus, incorrect.

5. (*d*) All are chain-isomers.

(a) 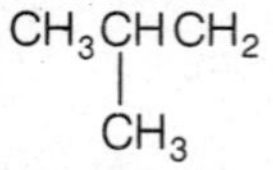 — 2-methylpropyl

(b) 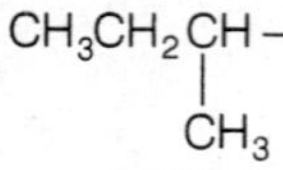 — 1-methylpropyl

(c) 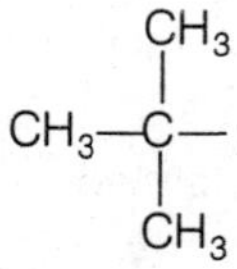 1,1-dimethylethyl

6. (*b*) Position of — Cl differs.

7. (*a*) $CH_3CH_2CH_2CH_2Cl$
1-chlorobutane

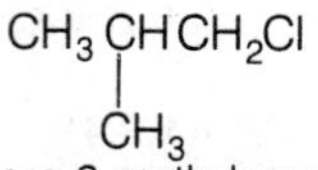

1-chloro-2-methylpropane

Position of Cl— atom is fixed.
They differ in chain.

8. (*d*)

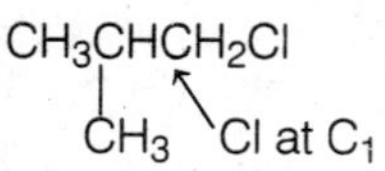

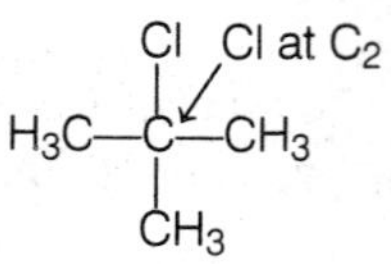

Thus, IV is position isomer of III.

9. (*a*) Remain (b), (c) and (d) are position isomers of I.

10. (*d*) $C_3H_6O \Rightarrow CH_3—CH_2—CH=O$
and 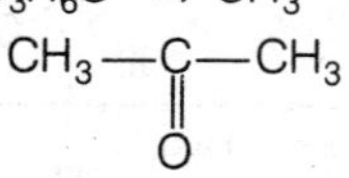

They are functional group isomerism.

11. (*c*)

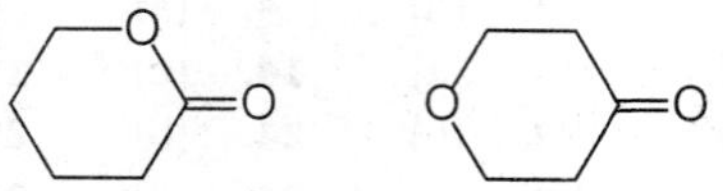

Cyclic ester   Cyclo keto ether

12. (*b*) (a)

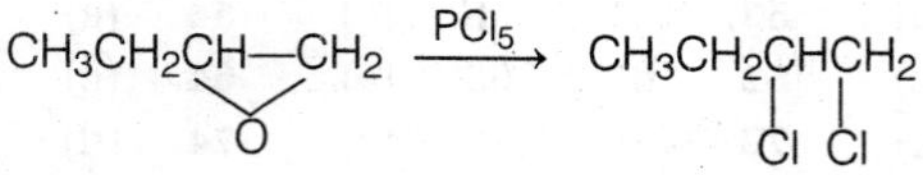

1,2-dichlorobutane

(b)

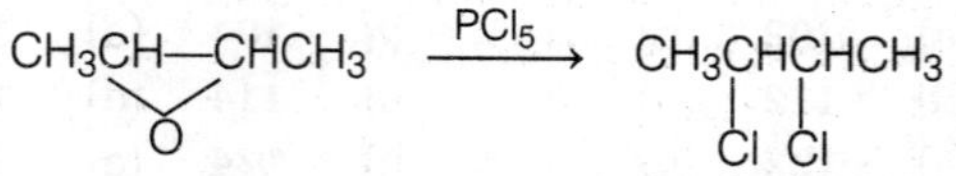

2,3-dichlorobutane

(c) $CH_3CH_2CH_2CHO \xrightarrow{PCl_5} CH_3CH_2CH_2CHCl_2$
1,1-dichlorobutane

(d)

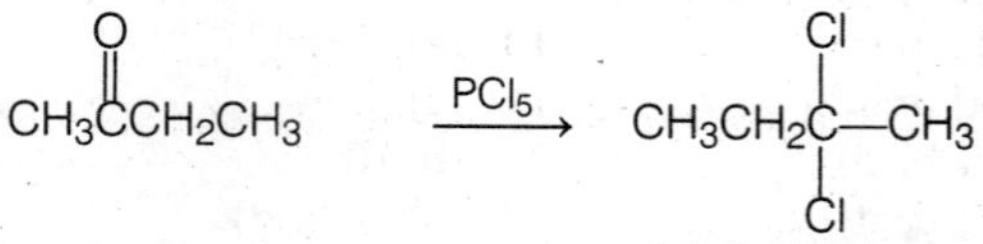

2,2-dichlorobutane

13. (*a*)
(*A*) is a dibasic acid, it means two —COOH groups (*A*) has a dipole moment, means it exists as *cis*-isomer.
(*A*) decolourises Br_2 water. means it has (C=C) bond.
(b) has zero dipole moment
(c) has a dipole moment, but other compound is not an ester.

14. (*c*) (c) is tautomer of (b).

15. (*c*) CH_3COOCH_3, $HCOOCH_2CH_3$
Thus, two esters only.

16. (*b*) Tertiary ether has alkoxy group (*R*O—) attached to tertiary carbon.

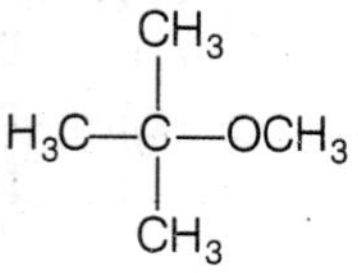

17. (*c*)

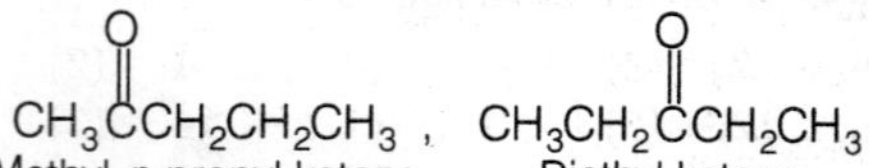

Methyl-*n*-propyl ketone   Diethyl ketone

Position of keto group differs thus position isomers.
Alkyl groups on both sides of keto group differ, thus metamers.

18. (*d*)
(a), (b) and (c) are position isomers.
(d) is a metamer.

19. (*c*) *A* :

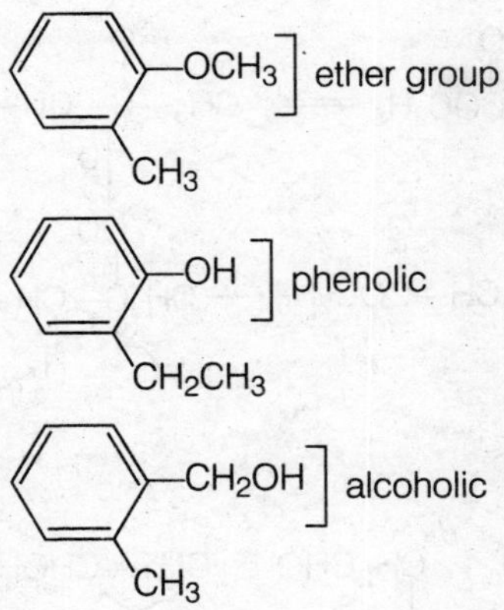

21. (*a*) Carbonyl group is electron-withdrawing. It can withdraw most acidic H, from adjacent carbon.

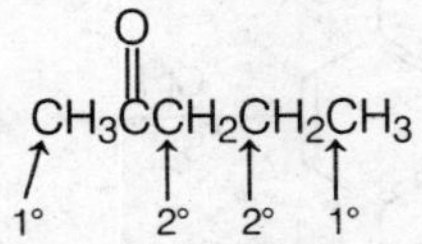

Acidic nature of H attached at : 1° < 2° < 3° carbon

Thus, carbanion formed is $CH_3\overset{O}{\overset{\|}{C}}\underset{\ominus}{C}HCH_2CH_3$.

22. (*d*)

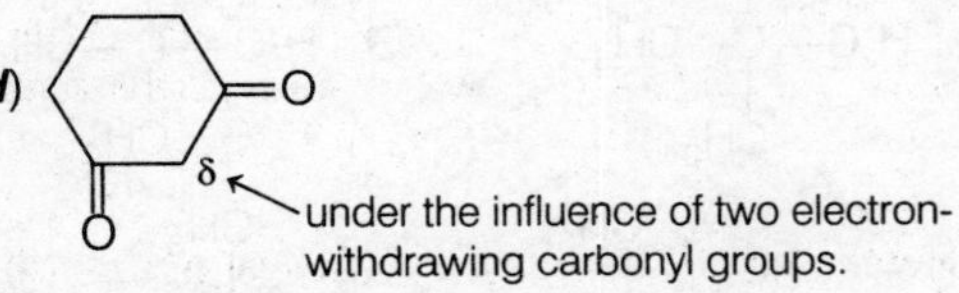

23. (*c*) Most stable due to conjugation.

24. (*b*)

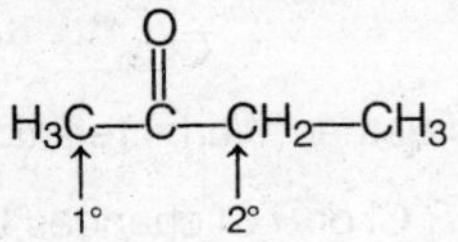

H at 2° carbon is more acidic.

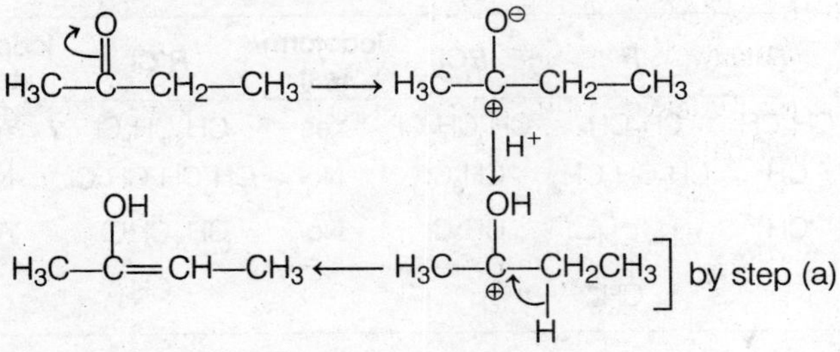

Thus, H from 2° carbon is lost.

Thus, (b) is not desirable.

25. (*b*) If we take D^+

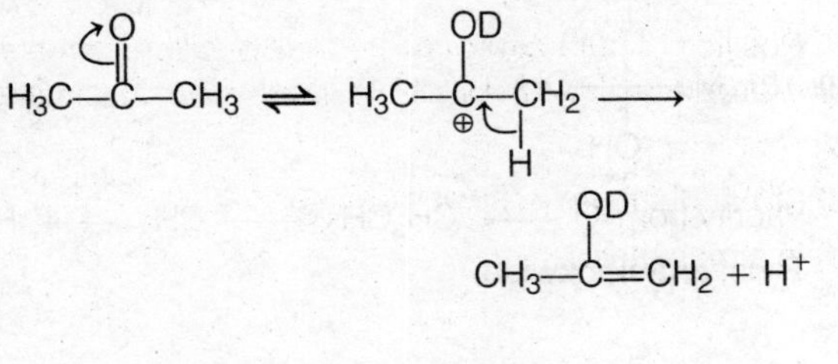

Then, H^+ is released.

Thus, enolic hydrogen is from proton-catalyst.

26. (*b*)

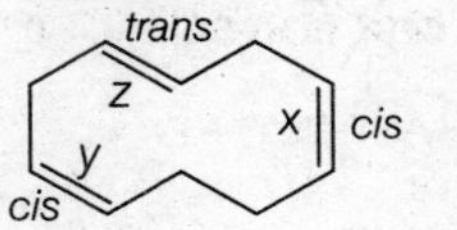

Thus, *cis*, *cis*, *trans*

27. (*b*) Only 4-methylpent-2-ene shows geometrical isomerism.

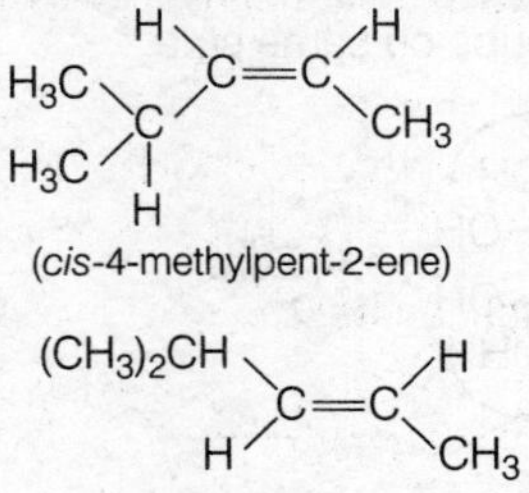

(*cis*-4-methylpent-2-ene)

(*trans*-4-methylpent-2-ene)

28. (*d*) *syn-anti* geometrical isomerism is shown by asymmetrical oximes. All form oximes.

Oximes of (a), (b) and (c) give *syn-anti* geometrical isomerism.

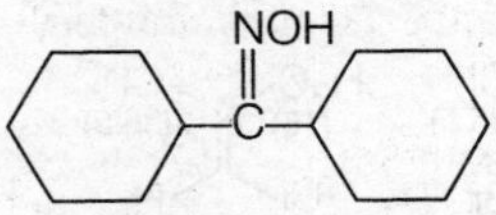

does not give *syn-anti* geometrical isomerism.

29. (*a*)

(a)

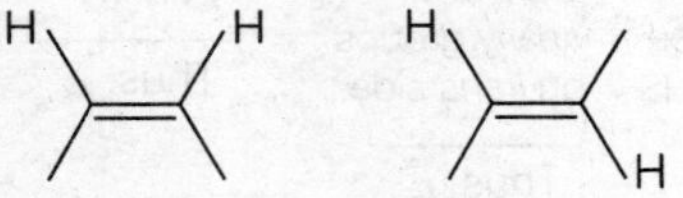

cis- *trans-*

(b)

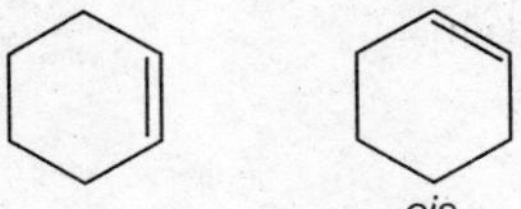

cis

Only *cis*- is formed

(c)

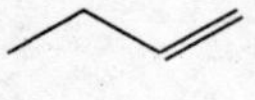

not possible

(d)

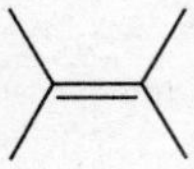

not possible

(*b*)

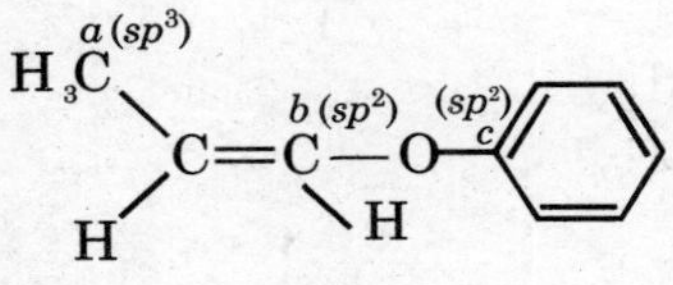

31. (*b*)

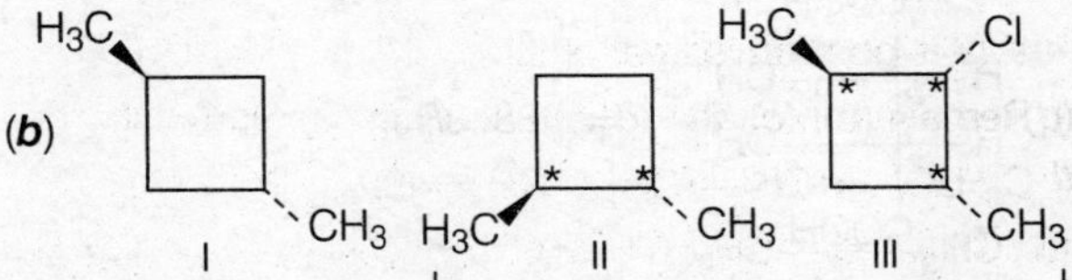

I No chiral carbon

II III C* are chirals

Thus, II and III.

33. (*a*)

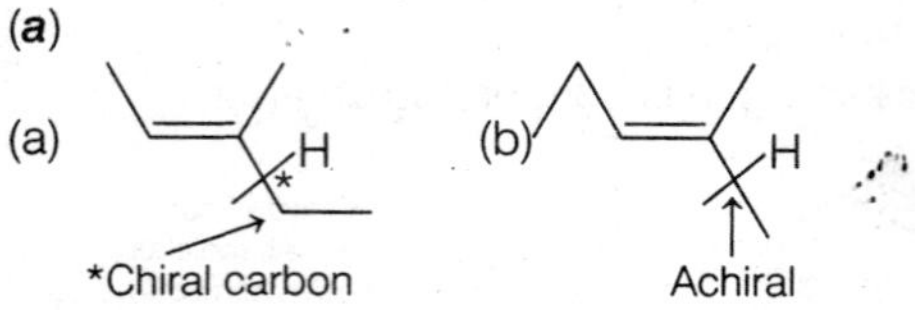

37. (*b*)

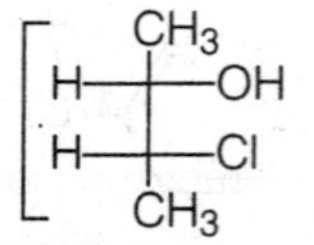

Similar groups on same side.

40. (*c*)

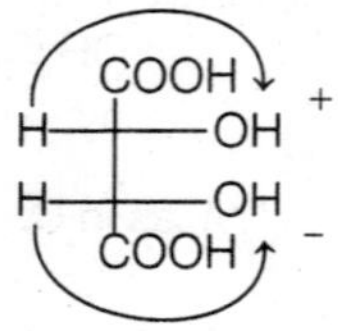

= Zero

41. (*d*)

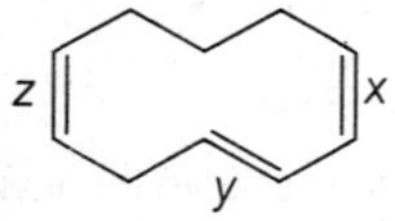

x : *cis* or *Z*

y : *trans* or *E*

z : *cis* or *Z*

42. (*c*)

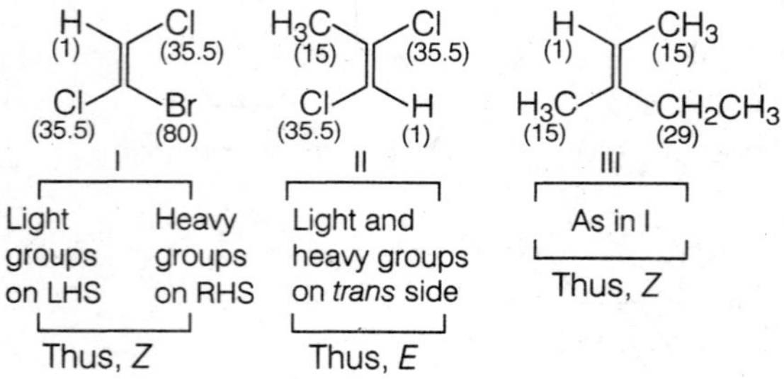

43. (*a*) $Li/NH_3 \Rightarrow$ *E*-alkene (*A*)

$H_2/Pd\text{-}C \Rightarrow$ *Z*-alkene (*B*)

44. (*a*)

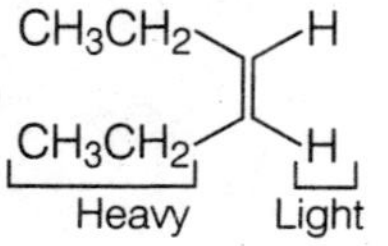

Thus, *Z*-isomer

45. (*b*)

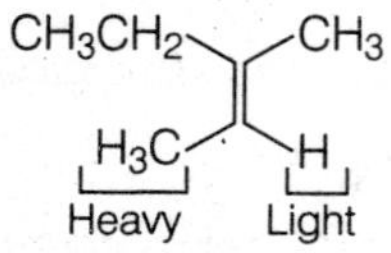

Thus, *Z*-isomer

47. (*d*)

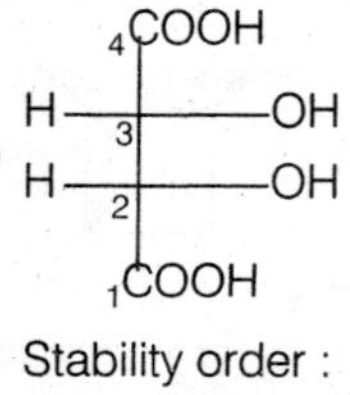

$\Rightarrow$ 2*S*, 3*R*

51. (*a*) Stability order :

anti > *gauche* > eclipsed > eclipsed
(Partially) (Fully)

57. (*c*)

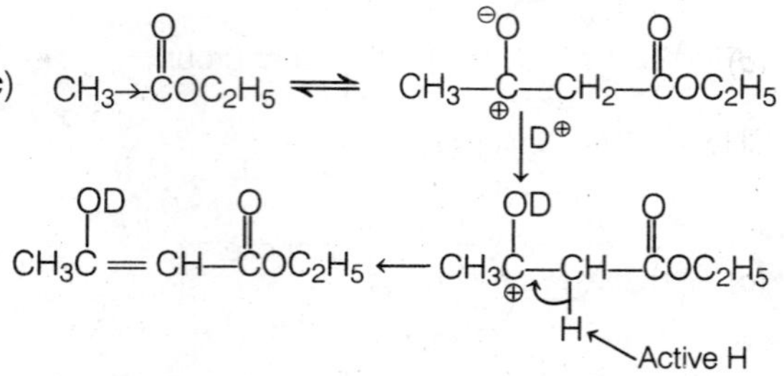

58. (*b*) 3; isomers

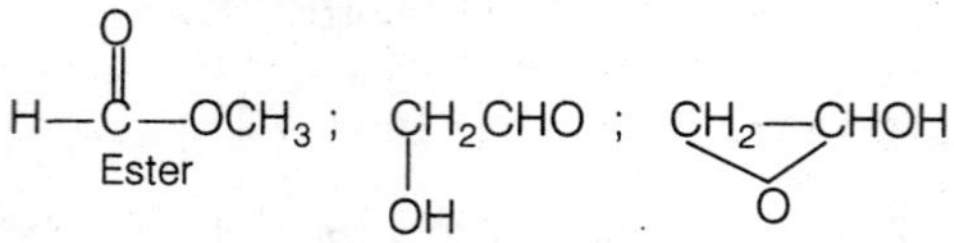

59. (*b*)

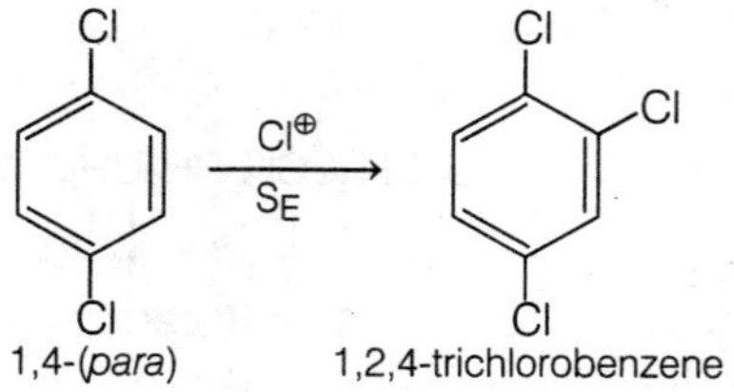

60. (*a*) Only one structure of *B* means *B* is neopentyl chloride.

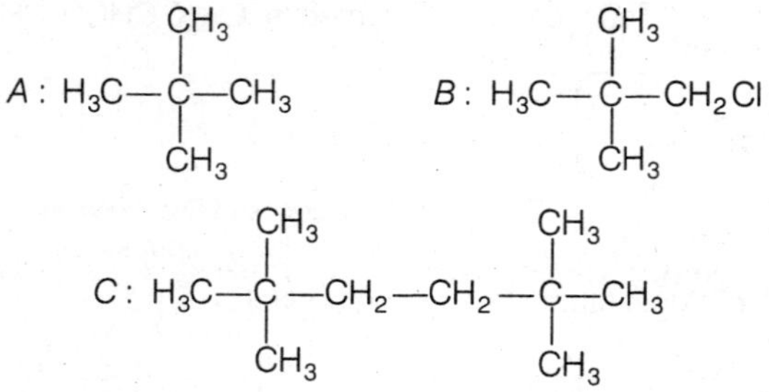

New (C—C) bond by Na/ether (Wurtz) reaction.

61. (*c*) Ether can be *R*—O—*R*′. *R* Cl or *R*′Cl changes to *R*OH or *R*′ OH which can give/cannot give iodoform test.

R	*R*′	*R*Cl	Iodoform test	*R*′Cl	Iodoform test
CH_3CH_2	CH_3CH_2	CH_3CH_2Cl	Yes	CH_3CH_2Cl	Yes
CH_3	$CH_3CH_2CH_2$	CH_3Cl	No	$CH_3CH_2CH_2Cl$	No
CH_3	$CH_3\underset{CH_3}{\underset{\vert}{C}}H—$	CH_3Cl	No	$CH_3\underset{CH_3}{\underset{\vert}{C}}HCl$	Yes

Thus, ether is $CH_3\underset{CH_3}{\underset{\vert}{C}}HOCH_3$.

62. (*b*)

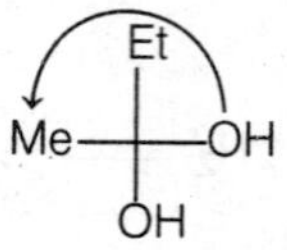

Priority from O $\longrightarrow$ CH_3CH_2 $\longrightarrow$ CH_3 $\longrightarrow$ H(*S*)

Thus, **anticlockwise**.

64. (*c*) 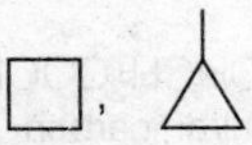

$CH_3CH_2CH{=}CH_2, CH_3CH{=}CHCH_3, CH_3C(CH_3){=}CH_2$

65. (*c*) Structure is *trans*, but by

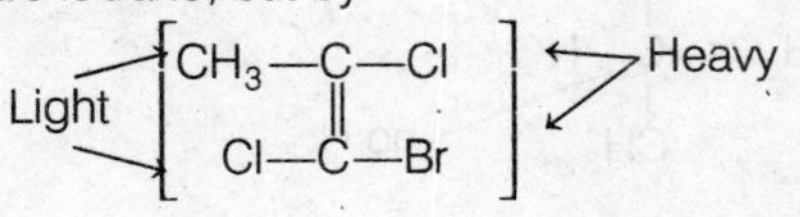

it is *Z*.

67. (*b*) $x = cis$ and *trans* (2)
$y = d$ and *l* (2)

68. (*d*) 3 chiral centre

$(2)^3 = 8$

69. (*a*) (i) (ii) (iii)

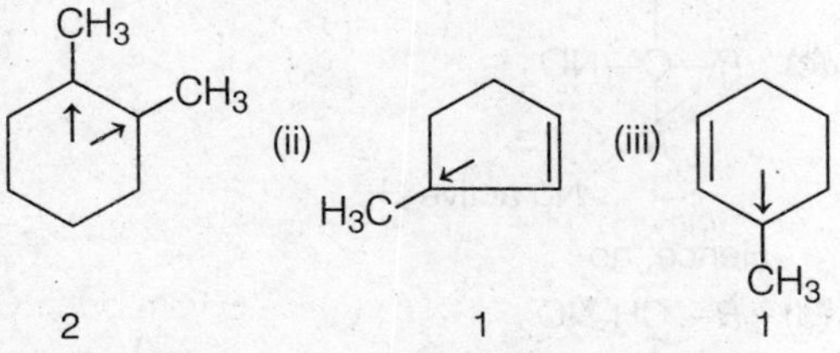

(↑) are asymmetric carbon atoms.

71. (*c*)

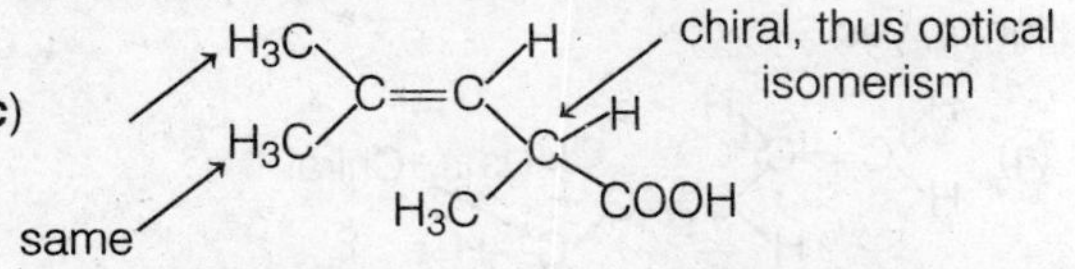

same groups, hence, geometrical isomers are not possible

73. (*a*)

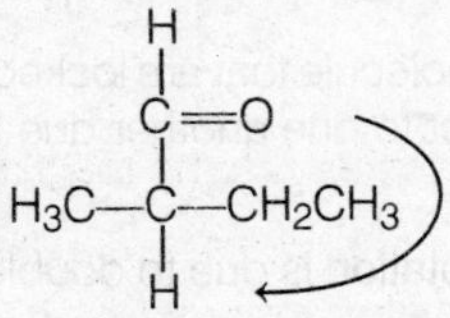

Clockwise thus, *R*.

74. (*d*)

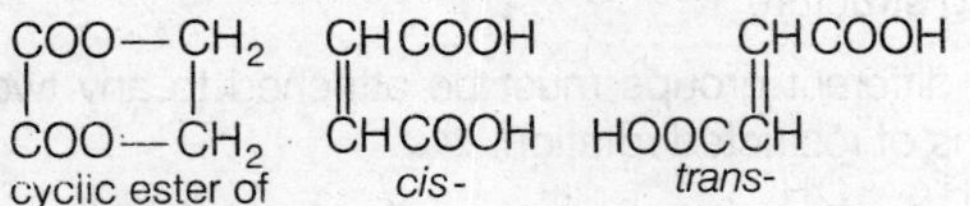

cyclic ester of oxalic acid — *cis*- — *trans*-

75. (*d*)

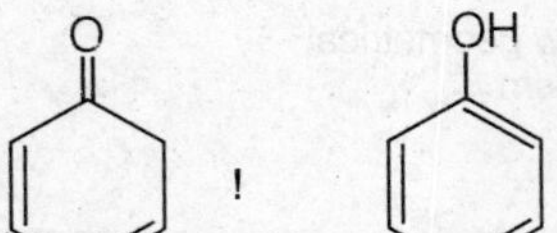

maximum stable due to delocalisation of π-electrons in conjugate system.

77. (*d*) The number of stereoisomers in molecules which are not divisible into two equal halves and have *n* number of asymmetric C-atoms $= 2^n$.

3-methyl-pent-2-ene on reaction with HBr in presence of peroxide forms an addition product, i.e.
2-bromo-3-methyl pentane. It has two chiral centres.
Therefore, 4 stereoisomers are possible

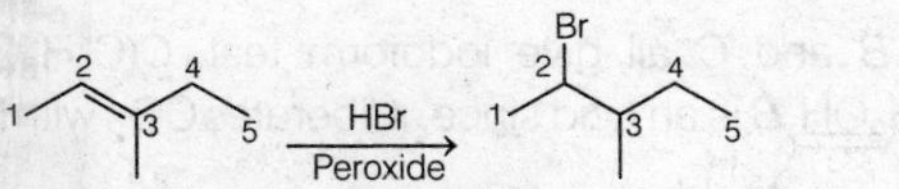

3-methylpent-2-ene — Anti-Markownikoff's addition Four stereoisomers are possible (As molecule has two chiral centres and asymmetric).

78. (*a*)

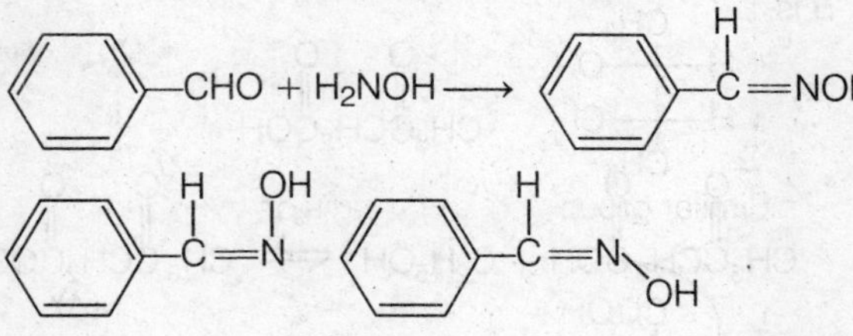

syn — *anti*

79. (*d*) (a) 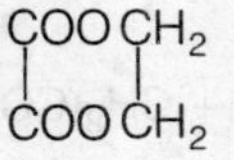 as in Q. (74) (b) as in Q. (74)

(c) 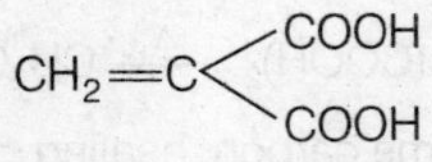

gem-α, β-unsaturated acid

80. (*a*) 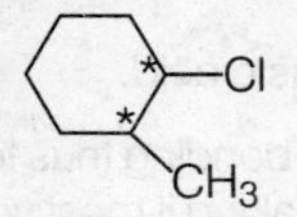 two chiral centres

81. (*d*) (a)

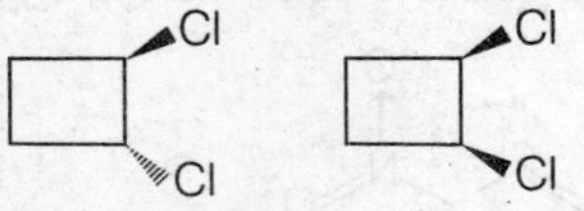

trans- — *cis*-

(b) *syn* — *anti*

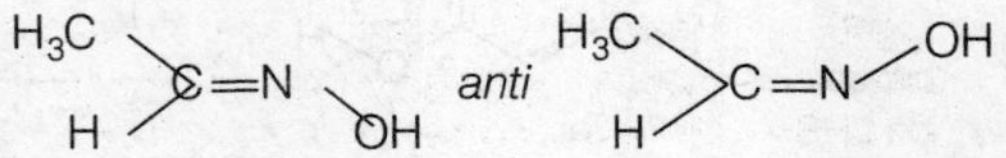

(c)

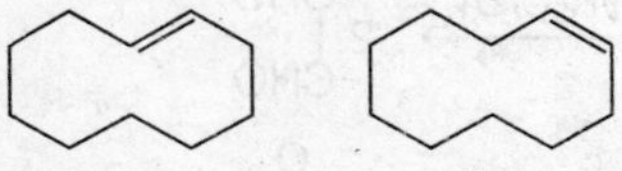

trans- — *cis*-

82. (*c*)

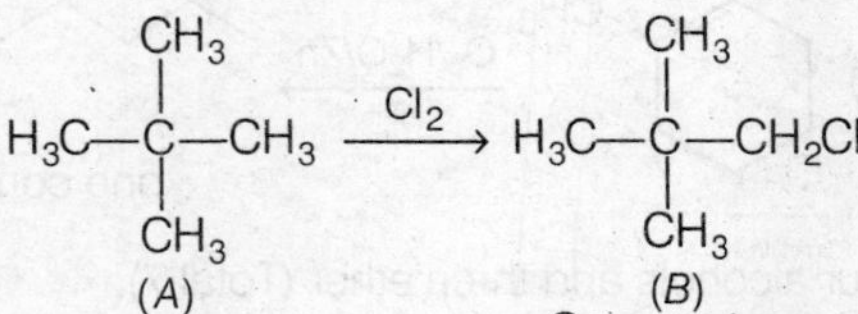

(*A*) — (*B*) Only one type

84. (*c*) (a) 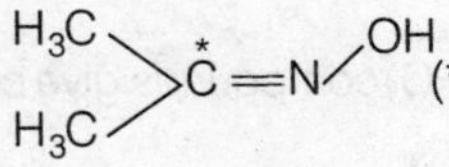 (*) carbon has same groups, No

(b) 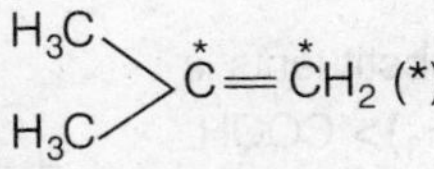 (*) carbons have same groups, No

(c) 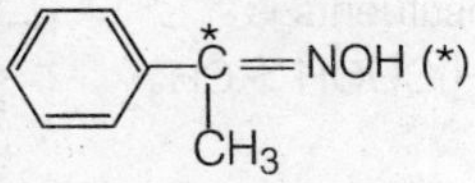 (*) carbon has different groups, Yes

(d) 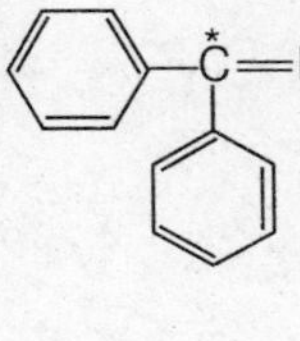 (*) as in (a), (b)

85. (*a*) *A*, *B* and *C* all give iodoform test. $C(C_2H_6O)$ is thus, CH_3CH_2OH. *B* is an acid since, it liberates CO_2 with $NaHCO_3$.

B has also ($CH_3\overset{O}{\overset{\|}{C}}$) group, iodoform test being positive. Thus, *B* is

$$CH_3\overset{O}{\overset{\|}{C}}CH_2\overset{O}{\overset{\|}{C}}OH$$

$$CH_3\overset{O}{\overset{\|}{C}}CH_2\overset{O}{\overset{\|}{C}}OH + C_2H_5OH \underset{}{\overset{H_3O^+}{\rightleftharpoons}} \underset{(A)}{CH_3\overset{O}{\overset{\|}{C}}CH_2\overset{O}{\overset{\|}{C}}OC_2H_5}$$

86. (*b*) *B* (above) is

$$CH_3\overset{O}{\overset{\|}{C}}CH_2\overset{O}{\overset{\|}{C}}OH \xrightarrow{I_2/KOH,\ \Delta} \text{iodoform} + CH_2(COOK)_2$$

$$\xrightarrow{H_3O^+} CH_2(COOH)_2 \xrightarrow{\Delta} CH_3COOH$$

If two —COOH groups are on same carbon, heating eliminates one CO_2.

$$\textit{gem}\ \text{dibasic} \xrightarrow{\Delta} \text{monobasic acid.}$$

87. (*a*) In *o*-isomer, there is intramolecular H-bonding thus force of attraction between molecules is weak, making it most volatile.

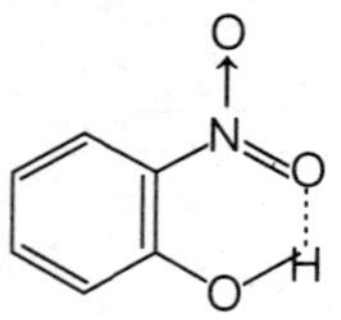

89. (*b*) (a)

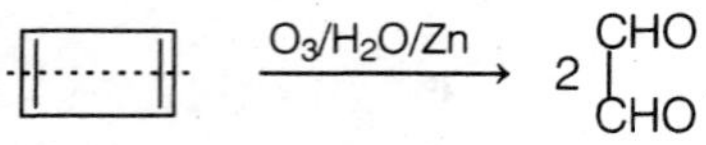

(b)

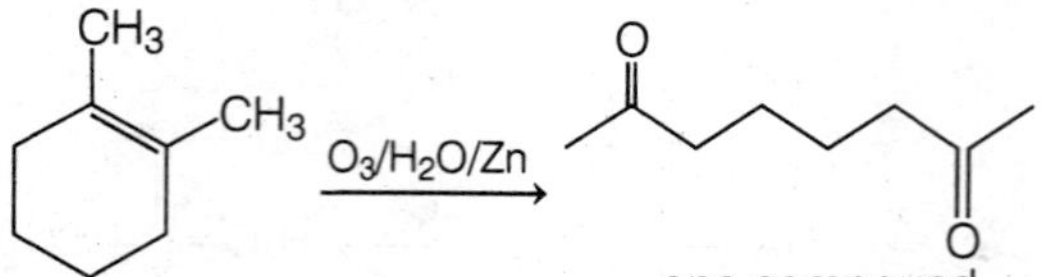

one compound

90. (*d*) Four alcohols and three ether (Total 7).

91. (*d*) Phenol and enolic ($-\overset{OH}{\overset{|}{C}}=C$) compounds give colour with $FeCl_3$.

92. (*a*) For C-2, order of priority of substituents is

OH > CH(Cl)(CH_3) > COOH

For C-3, order of priority of substituents is

Cl > CH(OH)COOH > CH_3

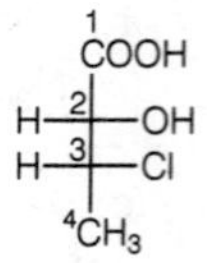

Hence, according to CIP rules,

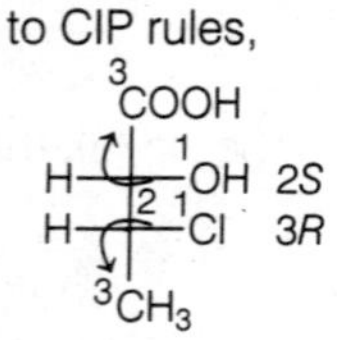

93. (*c*) $CH_3\underset{OH}{\underset{|}{C}}HCH_2COOH \xrightarrow{\Delta} CH_2{=}CHCH_2COOH$ (↓ Chiral)

No chiral carbon

94. (*d*)

(a) True (b) True (c) True

97. (*d*)

(a)

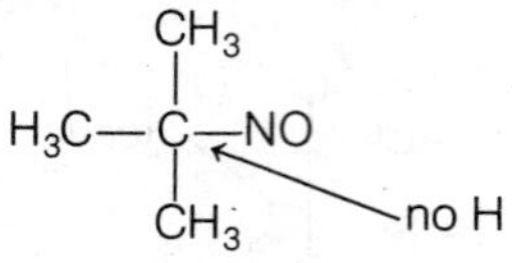

Hence, no

(b)

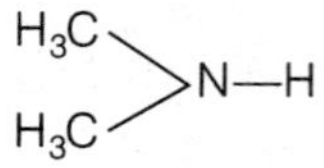

Hence, no

(c)

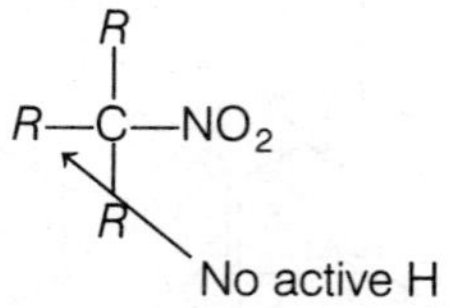

Hence, no

(d) $R-\underset{H}{\underset{\uparrow}{C}}H_2NO_2$

Hence, yes

101. (*a*)

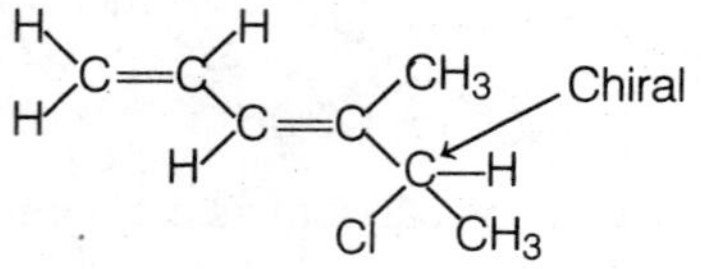

103. (*b*) Geometric isomers are molecule that are locked into their saptial positions with respect to one another due to double bond or a ring structure.

The presence of restricted rotation is due to double bond or a ring structure.

Two different groups must be attached to any two carton atoms of restricted rotation.

(a)

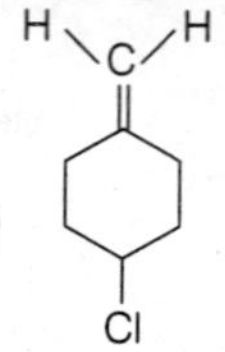

not show geometrical isormerism

(b)

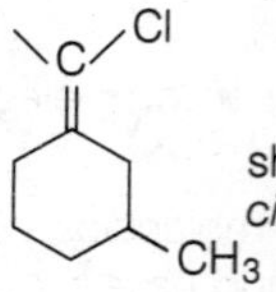

show geometrical (possible *cis* and *trans* isomer) isomerism

and

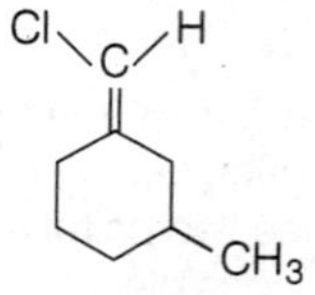

(c) 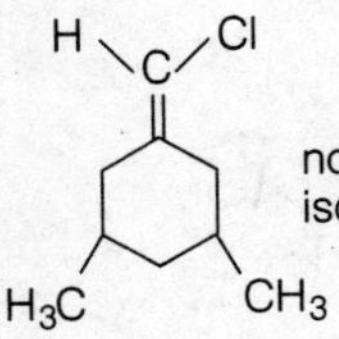

not show geometrical isomerism

(d) 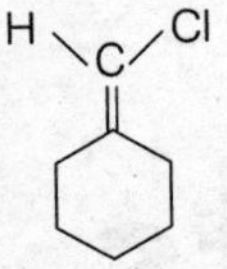

not shows geometrical isomerism

It is also *S*.

104. (*d*)

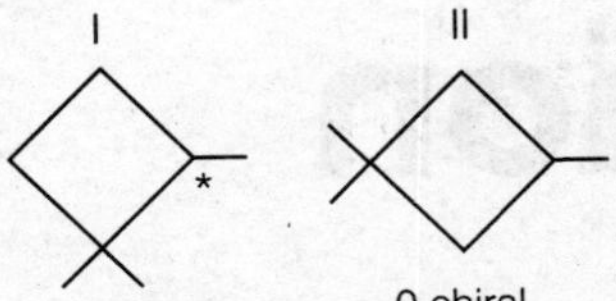

1 chiral centre   0 chiral centre

107. (*a*)

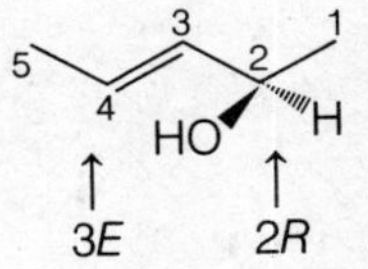

116. (*d*)

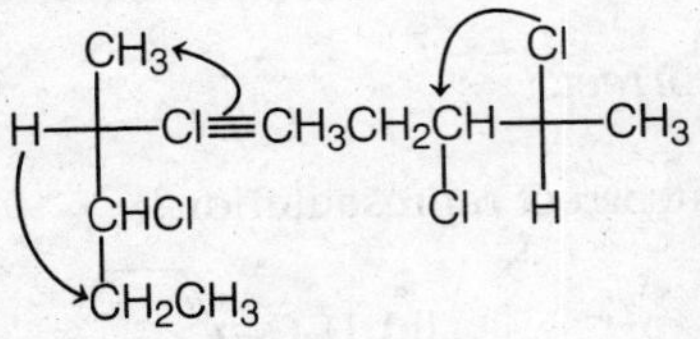

anticlockwise thus, *S*.

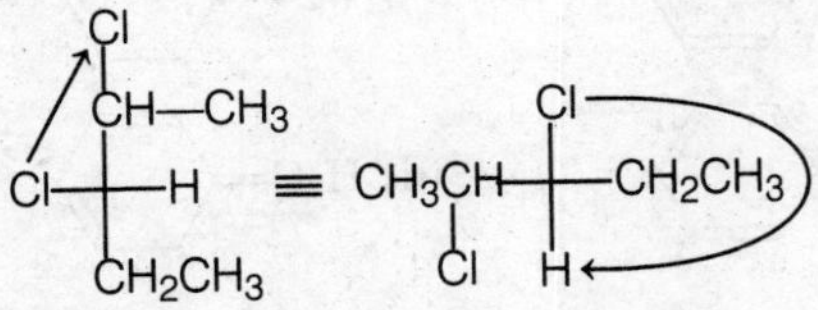

117. (*c*) IUPAC name of *P*, *Q*, *R* and *S* are :

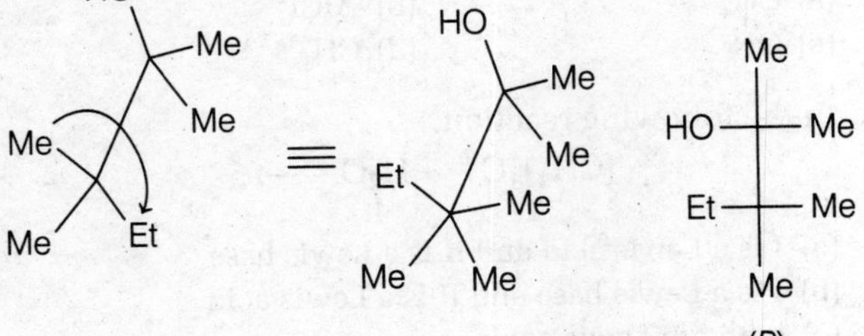

(*P*)

2,3,3-trimethyl pentan-2-ol

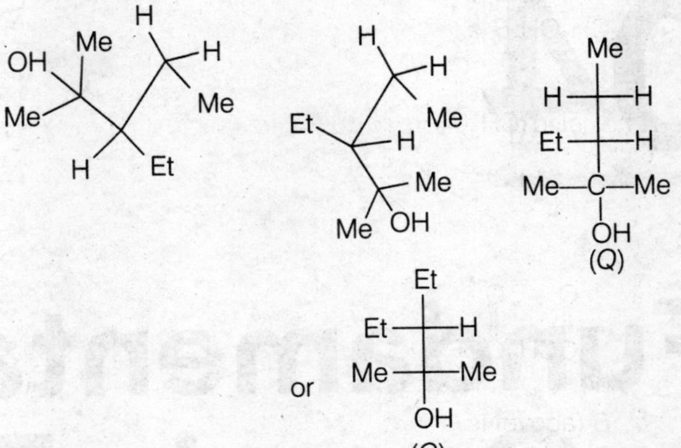

3-ethyl-methyl pentan-2-ol

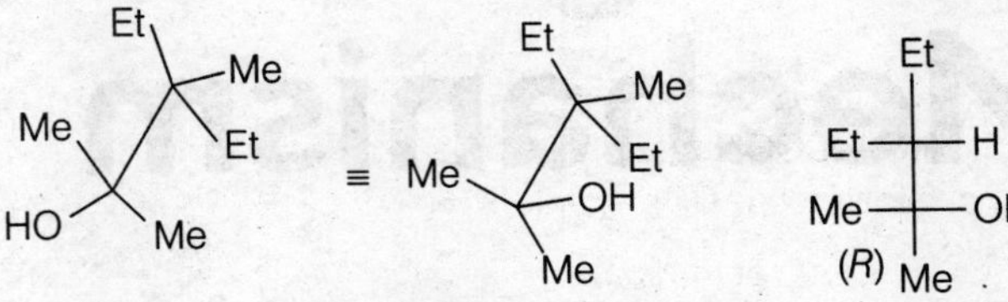

3-ethyl, 2-methyl pentan-2-ol

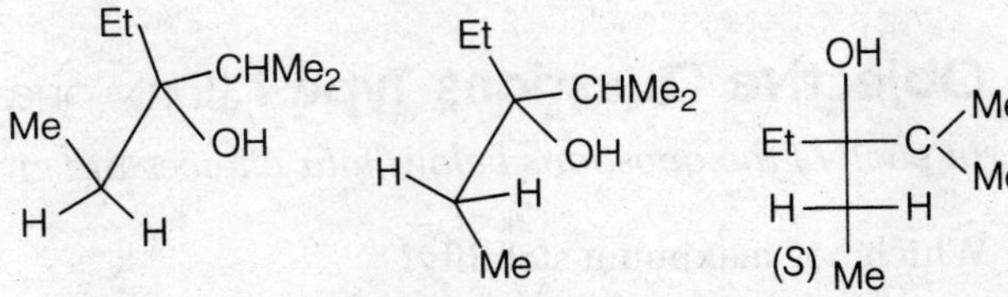

3-ethyl, 2-methyl pentan-3-ol

120. (*a*)

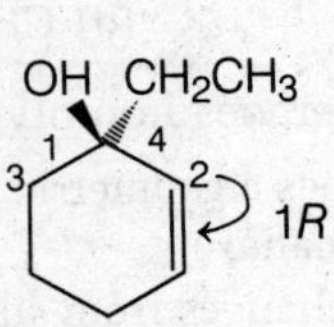

123. (*b*) *E*-alkene gives *trans* epoxide and 2-alkene gives *cis*-epoxide. Hence, streospecific reaction.

128. (*a*) There is enolisation of the keto ring

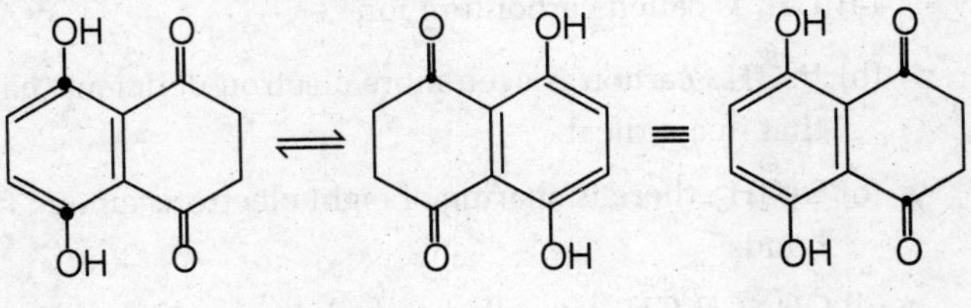

04

Fundamental Concepts in Organic Reaction Mechanism

Objective Questions Type I [Only one correct option]

In each of the questions below, four choices are given of which only one is correct.

1. Which has maximum stability?

(a) $CH_2=CH\dot{C}H_2$ (b) $(CH_3)_3\dot{C}$

(c) $(CH_3)_2\dot{C}H$ (d) $CH_3\dot{C}H_2$

2. When CH_3Cl undergoes homolytic bond-fission

(a) carbon undergoes a geometric change from tetrahedral to planar

(b) hybridisation changes from sp^3 to sp^2

(c) Both (a) and (b) take place

(d) None of the above takes place

3. Select the incorrect statement.

(a) $\overset{\oplus}{C}H_3$ is called carbonium ion

(b) In $\overset{\oplus}{C}H_3$, carbon is even more electron deficient than that in a radical

(c) In $\overset{\oplus}{C}H_5$, there is sharing of eight electrons among five bonds

(d) $\overset{\oplus}{C}H_3$, $CH_3\overset{\oplus}{C}H_2$ are called carbenium ions based on IUPAC nomenclature

4. Select the correct statement(s) about carbene.

(a) It is obtained by photolysis of diazomethane or ketene

(b) It can be inserted into alkene forming cycloalkane

(c) It can exist as singlet or triplet

(d) All of the above statements are true

5. Which is the incorrect representation?

(a) 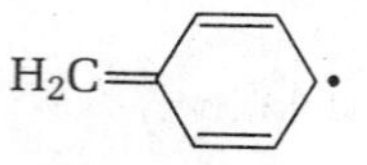

(b) 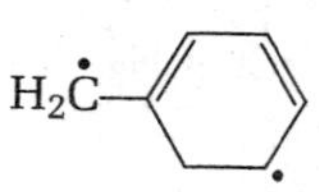

(c) 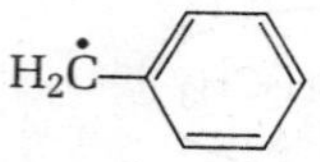

(d) 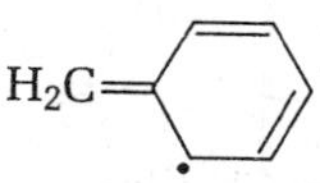

6. Which of the following compounds can react with the Lewis base Cl^- in a Lewis acid-base reaction?

(a) CH_4 (b) $AlCl_3$

(c) OH^- (d) CH_3^-

7. In the following reaction,

$$\underset{\text{I}}{(CH_3)_3C^{\oplus}} + \underset{\text{II}}{H_2O} \longrightarrow$$

(a) I is a Lewis acid and II is a Lewis base

(b) I is a Lewis base and II is a Lewis acid

(c) both are Lewis acids

(d) both are Lewis bases

8. Select the incorrect comparison as nucleophile.

(a) $(CH_3)_3CO^{\ominus} < OH^{\ominus}$

(b) $H_2O < NH_3$

(c) $RO^{\ominus} < RS^{\ominus}$

(d) $R_3P > R_3N$

9. Which of the following compounds is not aromatic? [JEE Main 2019]

(a) 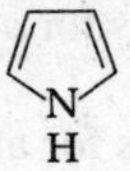 (b) 

(c)  (d) 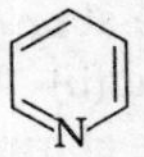

10. Select the incorrect statement.
(a) Homolytic fission results in the formation of free radicals
(b) Heterolytic fission results in the formation of Lewis acid and Lewis base
(c) Completion of the octet provides a major driving force for the Lewis acid-base reaction
(d) Steric bulky group increases nucleophilicity

11. Which is the most stable carbocation?

(a) $(CH_3)_3\overset{\oplus}{C}$ (b) 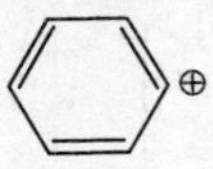

(c) 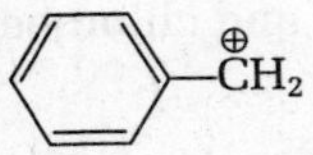 (d) $(CH_3)_2\overset{\oplus}{C}H$

12. Which comparison is not correct as indicated?

(a) 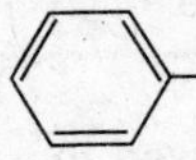—OH > CH_3OH (acidic nature)

(b) 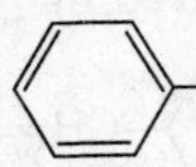—NH_2 > CH_3NH_2 (basic nature)

(c) 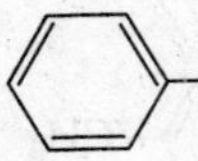—$\overset{\oplus}{C}H_2$ > $CH_3\overset{\oplus}{C}H_2$ (stability)

(d) 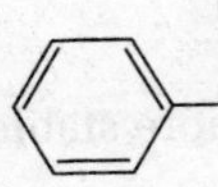—$\overset{O}{\overset{\|}{C}}OH$ > $CH_3\overset{O}{\overset{\|}{C}}OH$ (acidic nature)

13. Which is maximum acidic?

(a)  (b) 

(c) 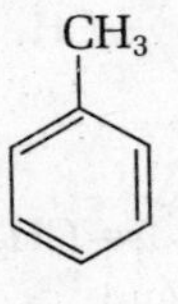 (d) 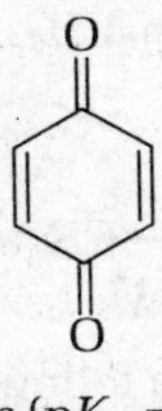

14. Increasing order of pK_a values ($pK_a = -\log K_a$) of H_2O, CH_3OH and C_6H_5OH is
(a) $H_2O < CH_3OH < C_6H_5OH$
(b) $CH_3OH < H_2O < C_6H_5OH$
(c) $C_6H_5OH < H_2O < CH_3OH$
(d) $C_6H_5OH < CH_3OH < H_2O$

15. Select the incorrect statement.
(a) Electron-withdrawing inductive effect of the carbonyl group in —COOH group weakens the O—H bond and favours ionisation of a carboxylic acid compared with an alcohol
(b) Inductive effect of the chlorine destabilises the acid and stabilises the conjugate base
(c) Aniline is a weaker base than ammonia
(d) Phenol is a weaker acid than water

16. Which has maximum stabilisation energy as a result of resonance?

(a) 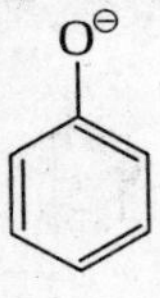 (b) 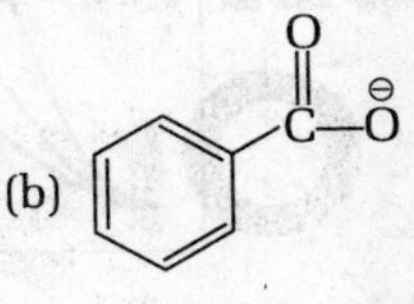

(c) $CH_2=CH\overset{\ominus}{C}H_2$ (d) $CH_3\overset{\ominus}{C}H_2$

17. Which group decreases acidic nature of phenol?
(a) $—CH_3$ (b) $—NO_2$
(c) $—\overset{O}{\overset{\|}{C}}CH_3$ (d) $—\overset{O}{\overset{\|}{C}}H$

18. In the following compound which hydrogen is most acidic?

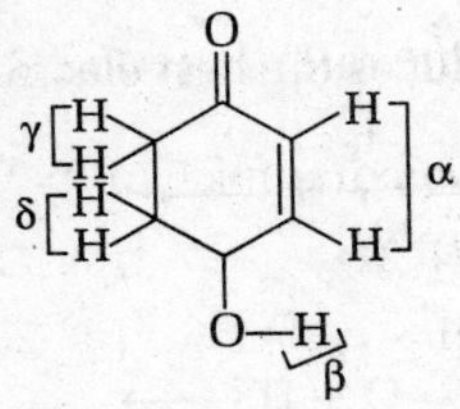

(a) α (b) β
(c) γ (d) δ

19. Select the incorrect statement.
(a) Branching at the electron-deficient carbon strongly stabilises carbocations
(b) Greater the stability of carbocation, easier the formation
(c) Greater the stability of carbocation, smaller the heat of formation
(d) Greater the stability of carbocation, greater the heat of formation

20. Which is not the primary carbocation?

(a) $CH_3—\underset{CH_3}{\overset{CH_3}{\overset{|}{\underset{|}{C}}}}—\overset{\oplus}{C}H_2$ (b) 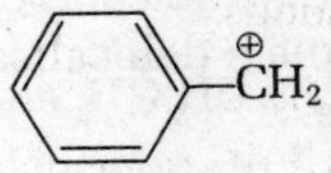

(c) $CH_3—\underset{\oplus}{\overset{CH_3}{\overset{|}{C}}}—CH_3$ (d) $CH_3—\underset{CH_3}{\underset{|}{CH}}—\overset{\oplus}{C}H_2$

21. Which is not the correct representation of the π-electron transfer?

(a) $CH_3CH{=}CH_2$ (b) $CH_2{=}CHCH_2CH_3$

(c) $CH_3CH{=}CHCN$ (d) $CH_3\overset{O}{\overset{\|}{C}}CH_2CH{=}CH_2$

22. Potential energy of the tertiary carbocation is represented by the point

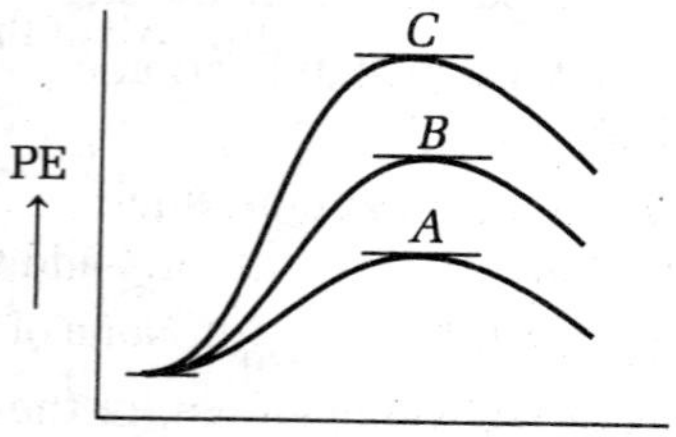

(a) *A* (b) *B*
(c) *C* (d) any of *A, B, C*

23. Ethynic hydrogen is released most easily in

(a) 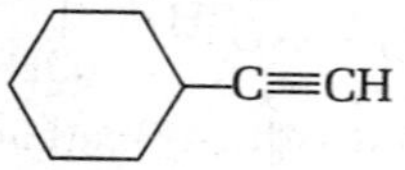 (b) 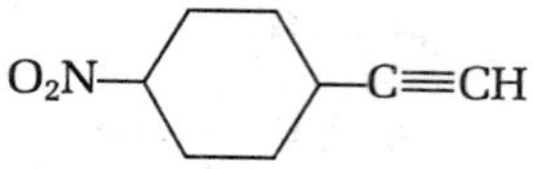

(c) 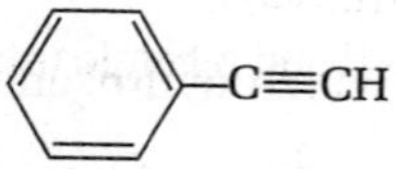 (d) 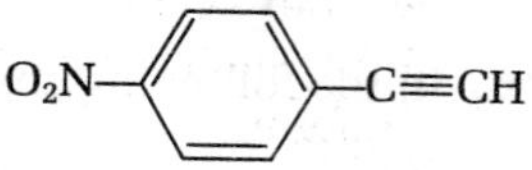

24. Which produces the best electrophile?

(a) $(H)(H)C{=}O + H^+ \longrightarrow$

(b) $(H_3C)(H)C{=}O + H^+ \longrightarrow$

(c) $(H_3C)(H_3C)C{=}O + H^+ \longrightarrow$

(d) no specific criterion

25. Which does not contain conjugate system?

(a) $CH_2{=}CHCl$ (b) $CH_2{=}CHCHO$

(c) $CH_3CH{=}CH_2$ (d) 

26. Identify the compound out of the following in which complete delocalisation of π-electrons does not take place.

(a)  (b) 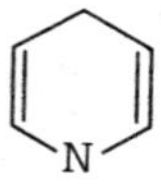

(c) 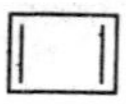 (d) 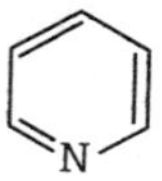

27. Select the correct statement(s).

(a) $-NO_2$ group activates benzene nucleus for attack of electrophile at *ortho*- and *para*-sites
(b) $-NH_2$ group activates benzene nucleus for attack of electrophile at *ortho*- and *para*-sites
(c) Both (a) and (b)
(d) None of the above

28. Which is not the resonance structure of aniline?

(a) 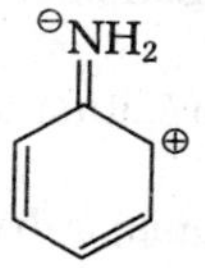 (b) 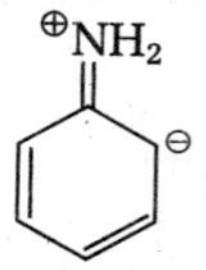

(c) 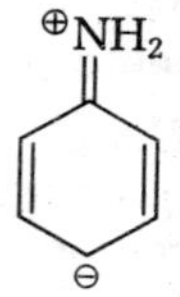 (d) 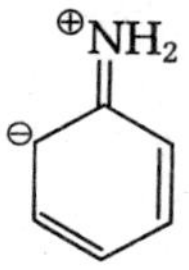

29. Low reactivity of vinyl chloride and chlorobenzene is due to

(a) positive mesomeric effect
(b) negative mesomeric effect
(c) greater electronegativity of chlorine
(d) lower electronegativity of chlorine

30. Maximum hyperconjugation is observed in

(a) 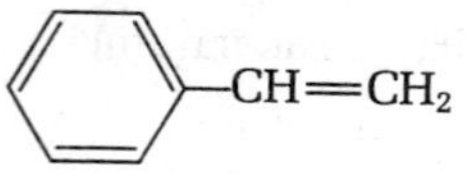 (b) 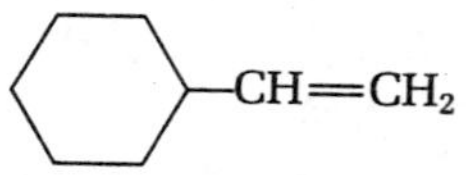

(c) $(CH_3)_3C{-}CH{=}CH_2$ (d) 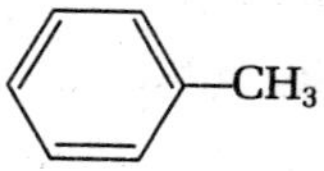

31. Following carbocation changes to more stable carbocation which is

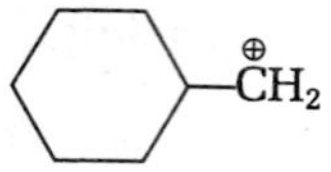

(a) 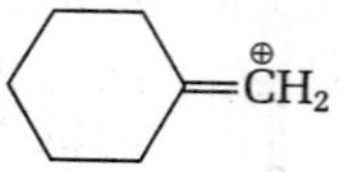 (b) 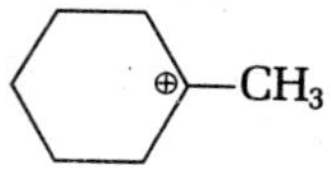

(c) 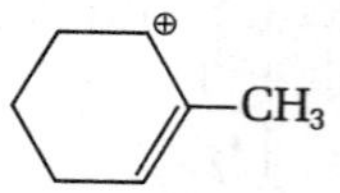 (d) 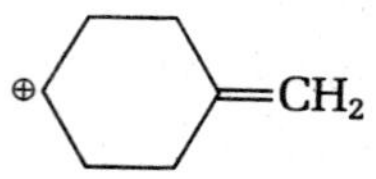

32. Consider the following reactions :

(A) $(CH_3)_3CCH(OH)CH_3 \xrightarrow{\text{Conc. } H_2SO_4}$

(B) $(CH_3)_2CHCH(Br)CH_3 \xrightarrow{\text{Alc. KOH}}$

(C) $(CH_3)_2CHCH(Br)CH_3 \xrightarrow{(CH_3)_3O^-K^{\oplus}}$

(D) $(CH_3)_2\underset{OH}{\underset{|}{C}}{-}CH_2{-}CHO \xrightarrow{\Delta}$

Which of these reaction(s) will not produce Saytzeff product? **[JEE Main 2020]**
(a) (A), (C) and (D) (b) (B) and (D)
(c) (C) Only (d) (D) Only

33. In the following reaction, most stable intermediate is

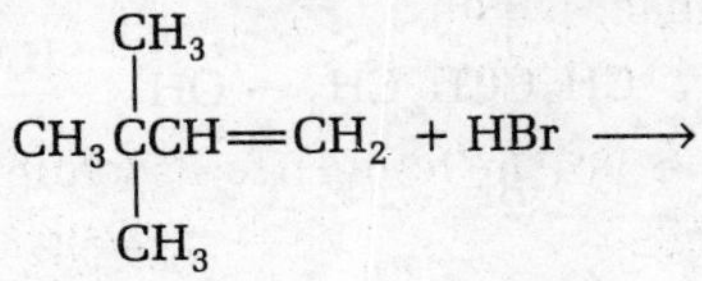

(a) 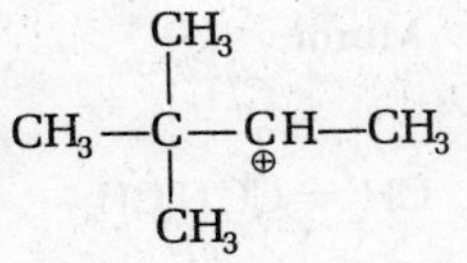 (b) 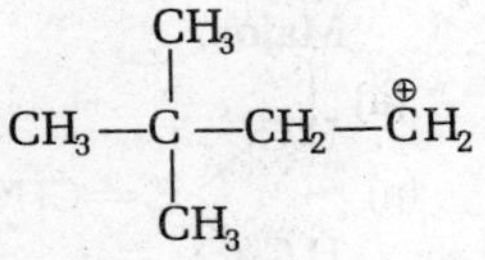
(c) 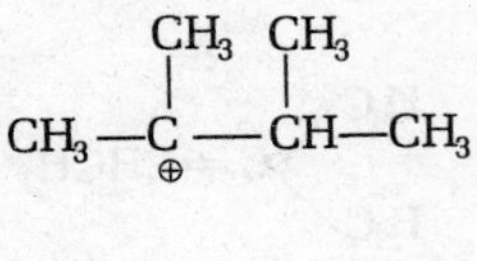 (d) 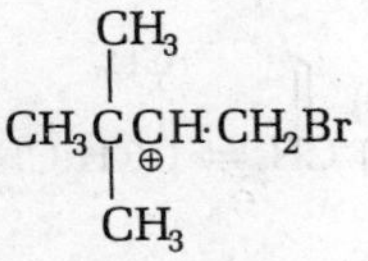

34. Select the alkene(s) in which addition of HX is strictly regiospecific.

I. 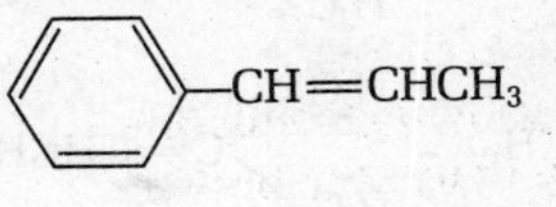 II. 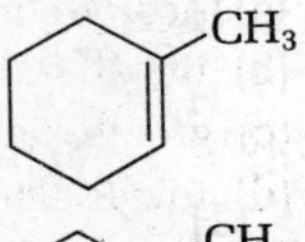

III. $CH_3CH{=}CH_2$ IV. 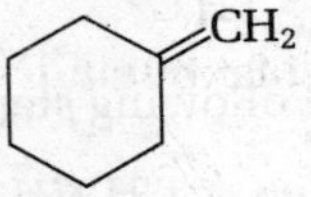

(a) I (b) I, II
(c) I, II, III (d) II, III, IV

35. In the following reaction,

$\overset{1}{C}H_3\overset{2}{C}H{=}\overset{3}{C}H\overset{4}{C}H{=}\overset{5}{C}H\overset{6}{C}H_3 + HBr \longrightarrow$

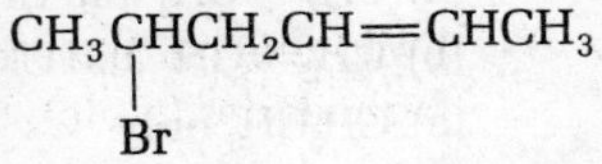

addition is called
(a) 2,3-addition (b) 1,2-addition
(c) 1,4-addition (d) 4,5-addition

36. The correct pair(s) of the ambident nucleophiles is (are) **[JEE Main 2021, March]**
(A) AgCN/KCN (B) RCOOAg/RCOOK
(C) $AgNO_2/KNO_2$ (D) AgI/KI
(a) (B) and (C) (b) Only (A)
(c) (A) and (C) (d) Only (B)

37. In the following conjugated system $CH_3CH{=}CHCH{=}CHCH_3$ addition is considered at the
(a) sp^2-hybridised carbon
(b) sp^3-hybridised carbon
(c) sp-hybridised carbon
(d) sp^2 or sp^3-hybridised carbon

38. 1,2 or 1,4-addition can take place at
(a)  (b) 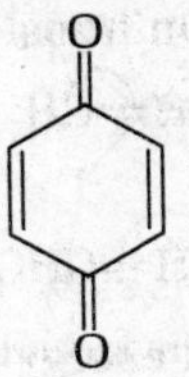
(c)  (d) All of these

39. Which gives more stable product?
(a) 1,2-addition (b) 1,4-addition
(c) Both (a) and (b) (d) None of these

40. Select the correct statement(s) for the following reaction.

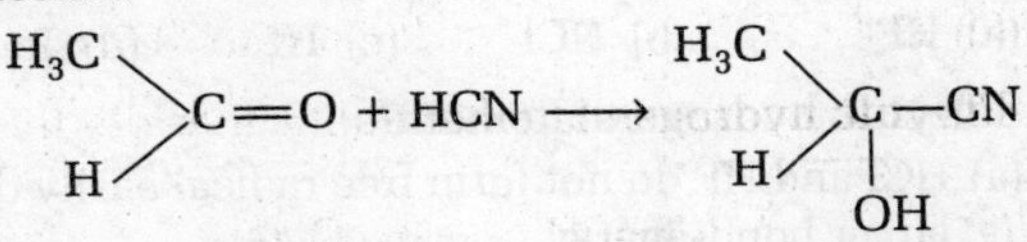

(a) Addition takes place at the carbonyl carbon and thus, addition is regioselective
(b) A chiral carbon is produced and racemic mixture is formed
(c) Geometry of the reactant is different from that of the product
(d) All of the above statements are true

41. Which is not observed in nucleophilic addition reaction?
(a) Bond angle decreases and repulsion increases
(b) Bond angle and repulsion both decrease
(c) Repulsion and free energy both increase
(d) Repulsion increases and free energy decreases

42. The increasing order of reactivity of the following compounds towards aromatic electrophilic substitution reaction is **[JEE Main 2019]**

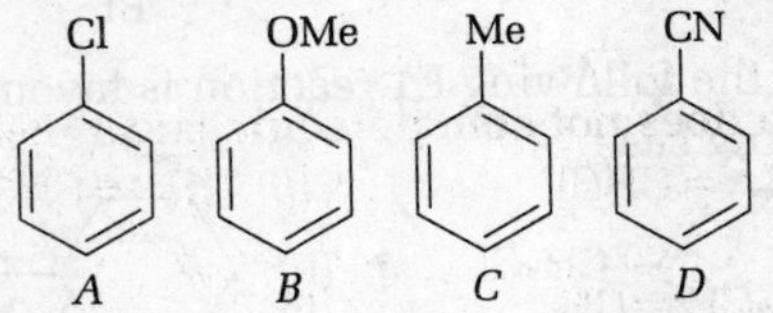

A *B* *C* *D*

(a) $A < B < C < D$ (b) $B < C < A < D$
(c) $D < A < C < B$ (d) $D < B < A < C$

43. Which is the possible structure?
(a) 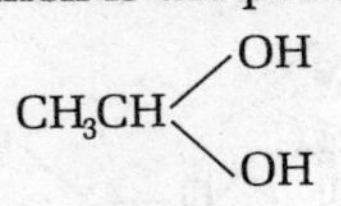 (b) 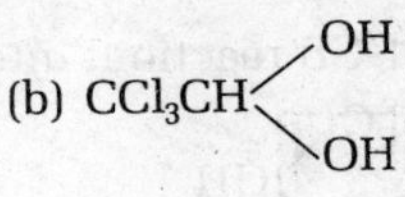
(c) 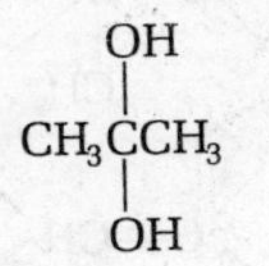 (d) None of these

44. In the following reaction,

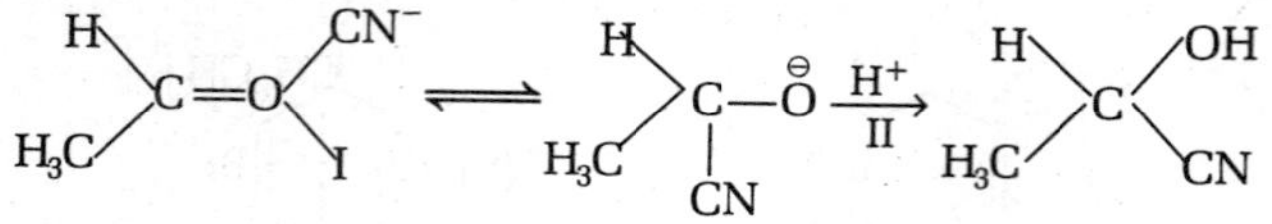

(a) step I is slow, II is fast
(b) step I is fast, II is slow
(c) Both steps I and II are fast
(d) Both steps I and II are slow

45. The addition of HBr in the presence of peroxides is called
(a) radical addition reaction
(b) carbocation addition reaction
(c) nucleophilic addition reaction
(d) electrophilic addition reaction

46. In which peroxide effect is not observed?
(a) HF (b) HCl (c) HI (d) In all cases

47. Select the correct statement(s).
(a) HCl and HF do not form free radical easily due to larger bond-energy
(b) HI with a minimum bond energy is very reactive and instead forms I_2
(c) Both (a) and (b)
(d) None of the above

48. In which case product formed is identical in the absence or presence of peroxide?
(a) $CH_3CH{=}CH_2$ (b) $CH_3CH{=}CHCH_3$
(c) 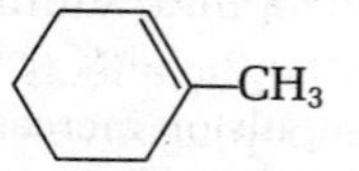 (d) 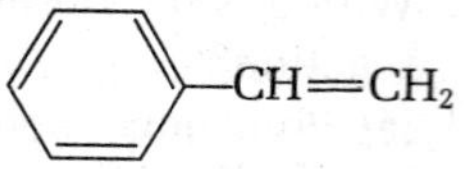

49. In the addition of HBr to propene in presence of peroxide, most stable free radical formed is
(a) $CH_3\dot{C}HCH_3$ (b) $BrCH_2\dot{C}HCH_3$
(c) $\dot{C}H_2CH_2CH_3$ (d) $\dot{C}H_2CH(Br)CH_3$

50. Out of the following E1 reaction is favoured in the following case
(a) 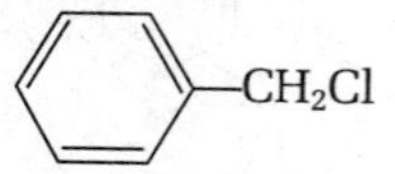 (b) 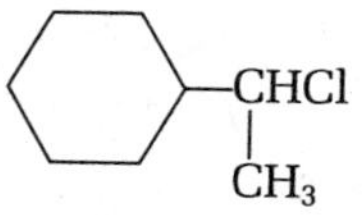
(c) 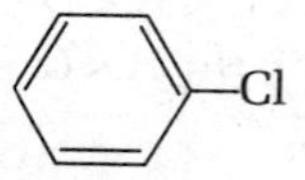 (d) CH_3CH_2Cl

51. In E1-CB reaction, intermediate is
(a) 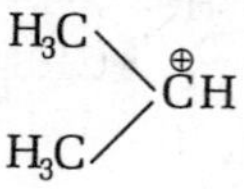 (b) 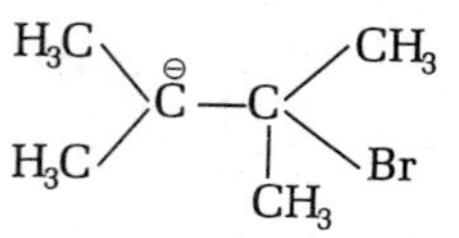
(c) $CH_3CH_2\overset{\oplus}{C}HCH_3$ (d) 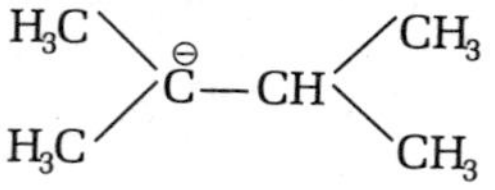

52. E2 reaction is called
(a) β-elimination (b) 1,2-elimination
(c) Both (a) and (b) (d) None of these

53. Major and minor product of E2 reaction of

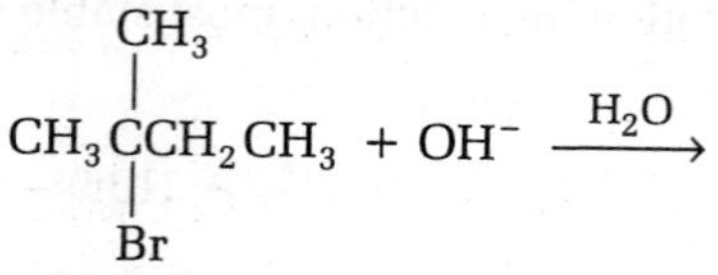

are

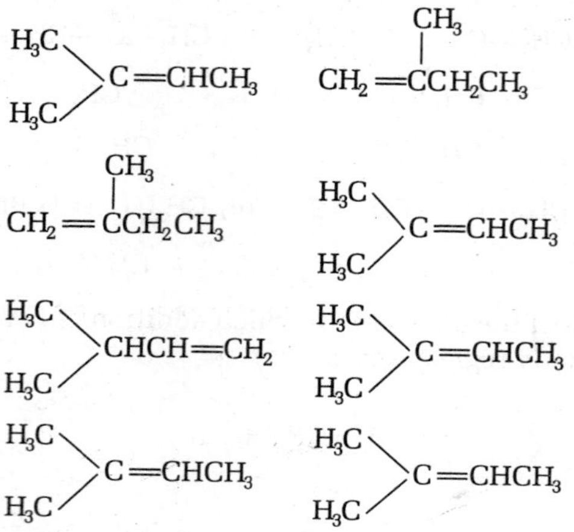

54. Following step is

$$CH_3CH_3 + Cl^{\bullet} \longrightarrow CH_3\dot{C}H_2 + HCl$$

(a) chain initiation (b) chain propagation
(c) chain termination (d) chain disproportionation

55. $CH_3\dot{C}H_2$ disproportionates to
(a) $CH_2{=}CH_2$ and CH_3CH_3
(b) $CH_2{=}CH_2$ and $CH_3CH_2CH_2CH_3$
(c) CH_3CH_3 only
(d) $CH_2{=}CH_2$ only

56. Which H is abstracted most easily from

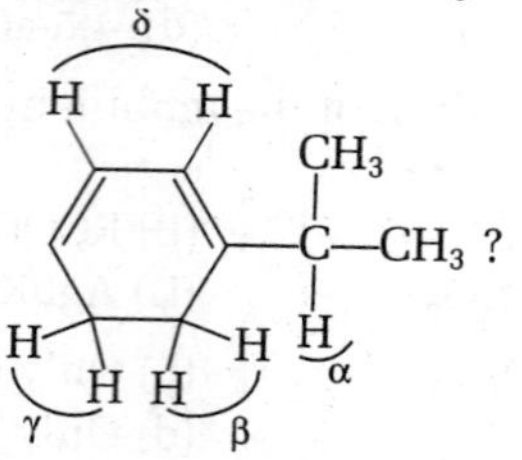

(a) α (b) β (c) γ (d) δ

57. $CH_2{=}CHCH_3$ undergoes free radical substitution using NBS. Product formed is
(a) $CH_3CH{=}CHBr$ (b) $CH_3CH(Br)CH_2Br$
(c) $CH_2{=}CHCH_2Br$ (d) $CH_2{=}C(Br)CH_3$

58. Following ion is called

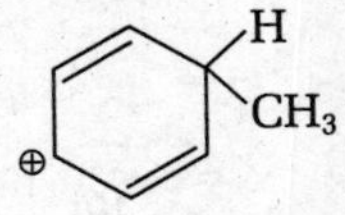

(a) σ-complex (b) carbonium ion
(c) arenium ion (d) nucleophile

59. Conc. HNO_3 forms NO_2^+ in the presence of

(a) conc. H_2SO_4 (b) Fe
(c) $FeBr_3$ (d) $AlCl_3$

60. Which is not the resonance structure of a carbocation?

(a) 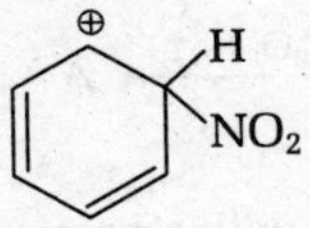
(b) 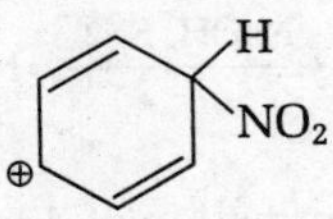
(c) 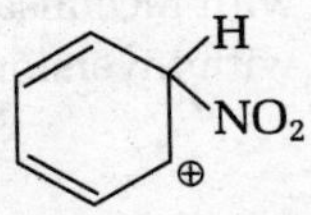
(d) 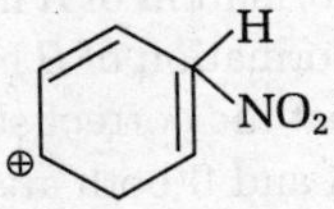

61. Which has least free energy?

(a) 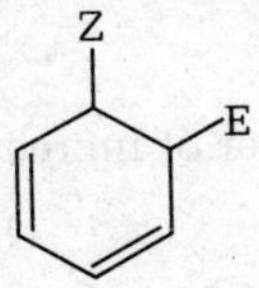
(b) 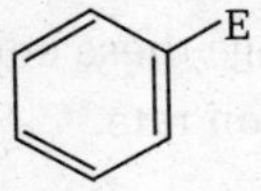
(c) 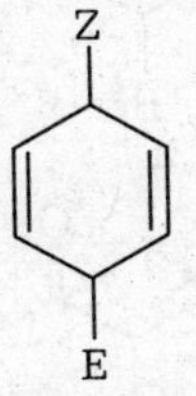
(d) 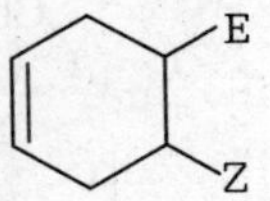

62. Intermediate electrophile in the following reaction is

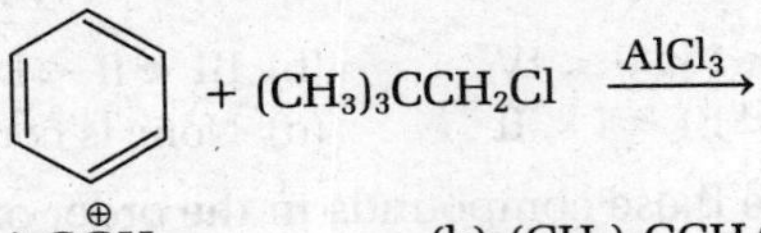

(a) $(CH_3)_3C\overset{\oplus}{C}H_2$ (b) $(CH_3)_2\underset{\oplus}{C}CH_2CH_3$
(c) 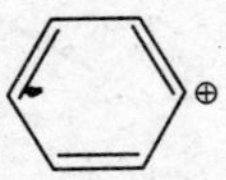 (d) None of these

63. Product(s) of the following S_N1 reaction is/are

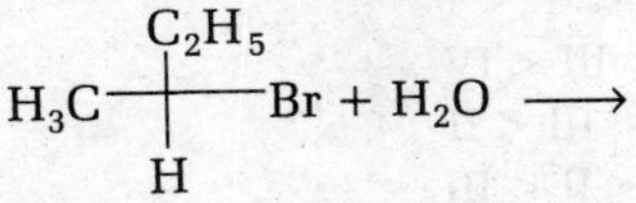

(a) 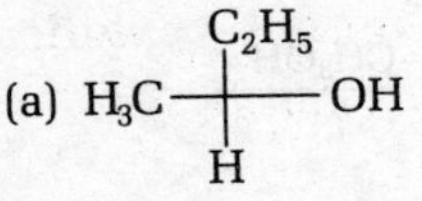 (b) 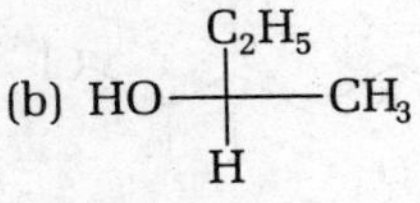
(c) Both (a) and (b) (d) None of these

64. Indicate the alkyl halides out of the following which can undergo S_N1 reaction,

I. 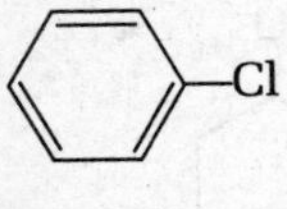 II. 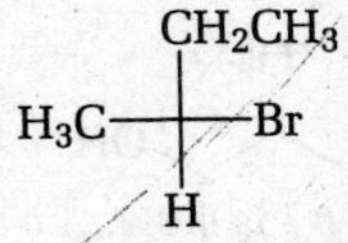

III. $CH_2=CHCl$ IV. $CH_2=CHCH_2I$

(a) I, II (b) II, III
(c) I, III (d) II, IV

65. Classify the following reactions,

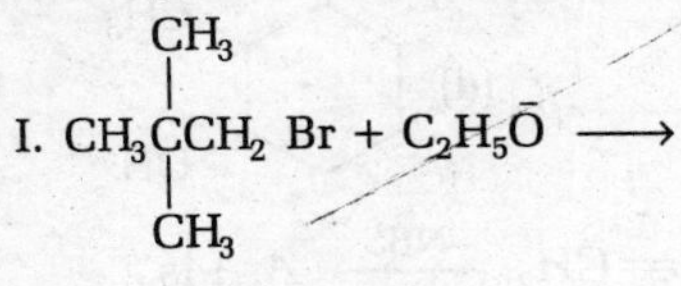

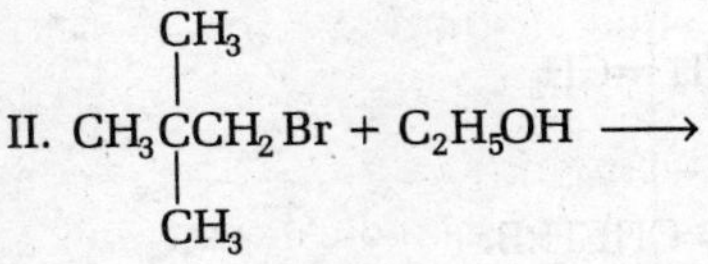

(a) I. S_N1, II. S_N2 (b) I. S_N2, II. S_N1
(c) Both S_N1 (d) Both S_N2

66. Select the incorrect statement(s).

(a) S_N1 reactions also take place with some elimination
(b) S_N2 reactions with chiral compounds give racemic mixture
(c) S_N1 reaction is faster in more polar solvents
(d) All of the above are incorrect statements

67. Which one of the following has all the effects, namely inductive, mesomeric and hyperconjugative?

(a) CH_3Cl
(b) $CH_3CH=CH_2$
(c) 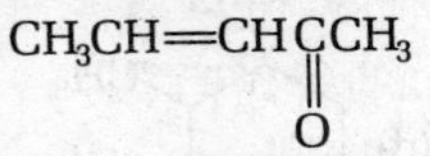
(d) $CH_2=CH-CH=CH_2$

68. Relative stabilities of the following carbocation will be in the order

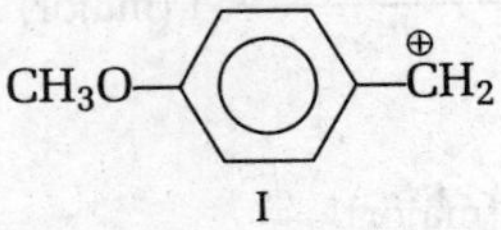 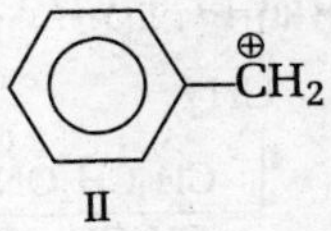

I II

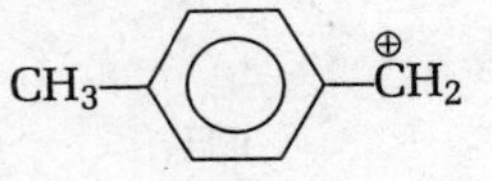 $CH_3\overset{\oplus}{C}H_2$

III IV

(a) I < II < III < IV
(b) IV < III < II < I
(c) IV < II< III < I
(d) II < IV < III < I

69. Which is dehydrated to a maximum extent using conc. H_2SO_4?

(a) 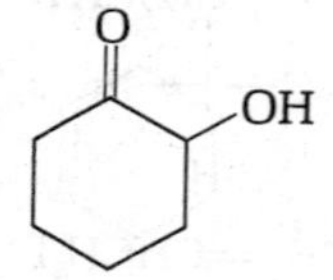
(b) 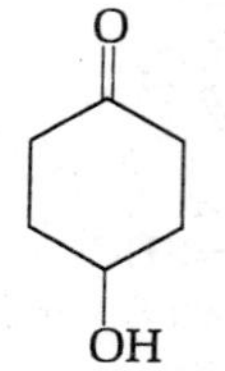
(c) 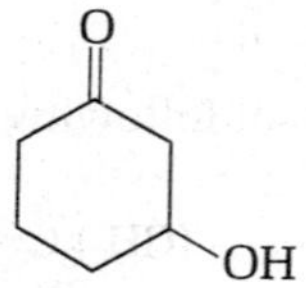
(d) 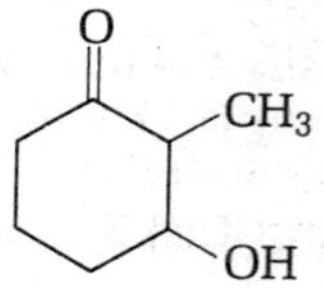

70. $CH_2{=}CHCH_2CH{=}CH_2 \xrightarrow{NBS} A$, A is

(a) $CH_2{=}CHCH(Br)CH{=}CH_2$
(b) $CH_2{=}CHCH{=}CHCH_2Br$
(c) $CH_2{=}CHCH_2CH{=}CHBr$
(d) None of the above is correct

71. 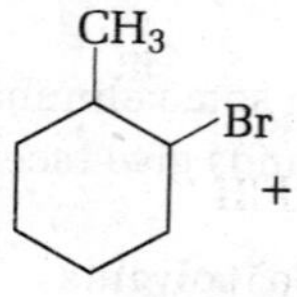 $+ CH_3OH \xrightarrow{CH_3OH} A$; A(predominant A) is

(a) 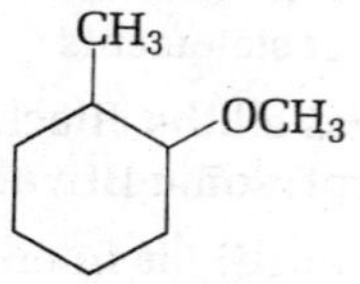
(b) 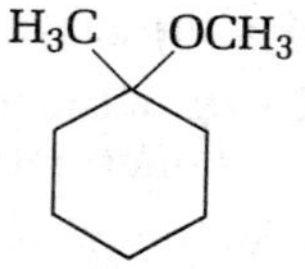
(c) 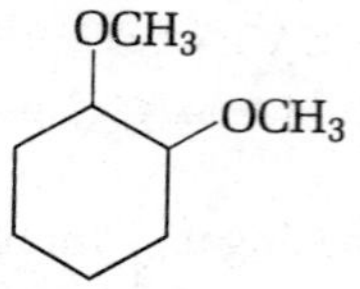
(d) 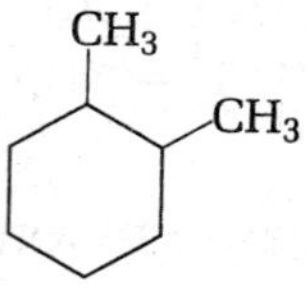

72. $CH_3C(CH_3)_2Br + CH_3CH_2OH \xrightarrow{CH_3CH_2OH} A$ (major)

$\xrightarrow[(CH_3CH_2OH)]{CH_3CH_2ONa} B$ (major)

Possible products can be

I. $CH_3C(CH_3)_2OCH_2CH_3$ II. $CH_3C(CH_3){=}CH_2$

A and B can be respectively
(a) I, II
(b) II, I
(c) II in both cases
(d) I in both cases

73. Most stable free radical is

(a) 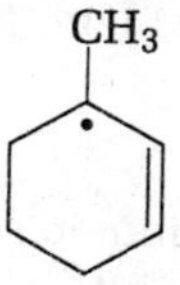
(b) 
(c) 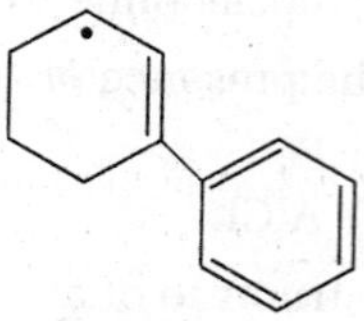
(d) 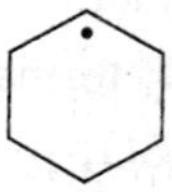

74. 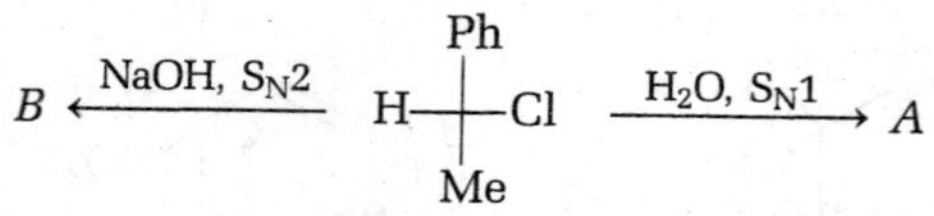

I. Formation of A has proceeded with racemisation.
II. Formation of B has proceeded with inversion.
Select the correct statement.
(a) I and II both are correct
(b) Only I is correct
(c) Only II is correct
(d) None of the above is correct

75. Arrange these compounds in order of increasing S_N2 reaction rate.

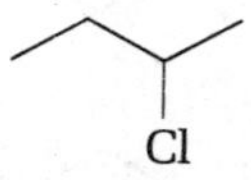
I

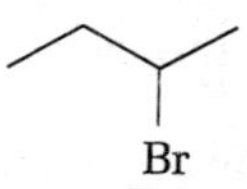
II

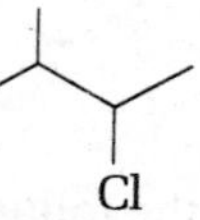
III

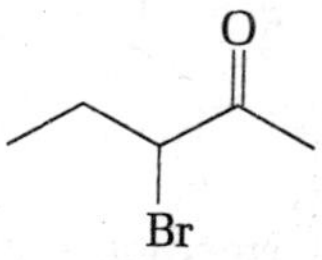
IV

(a) III < I < II < IV
(b) III < II < I < IV
(c) IV < III < I < II
(d) None is correct

76. Arrange these compounds in the order of increasing S_N1 reaction rate.

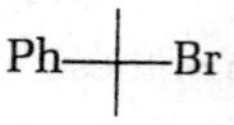
I

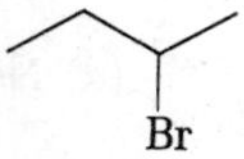
II

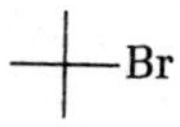
III

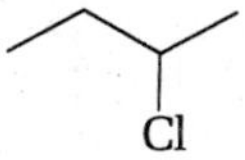
IV

(a) IV < II < III < I
(b) I < II < III < IV
(c) IV < I < III < II
(d) IV < I < II < III

77. 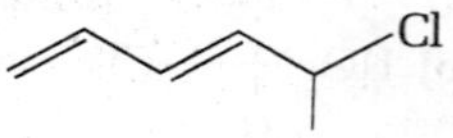 $+ H_2O \xrightarrow{CH_3OH}$

In this reaction we get ... types of substituted alcohols (stereoisomers not considered)
(a) one
(b) two
(c) three
(d) four

78. $PhCH_2\underset{OTs}{C}H\overset{CH_3}{C}HCH_3 \xrightarrow[t\text{-}BuOH]{(CH_3)_3CO^{\ominus}} A$. Predominant A is

(a) $PhCH{=}CH\underset{CH_3}{C}HCH_3$ (b) $PhCH_2CH{=}\underset{CH_3}{C}CH_3$

(c) $PhCH_2CH_2\underset{CH_3}{C}{=}CH_2$ (d) None is correct

79. 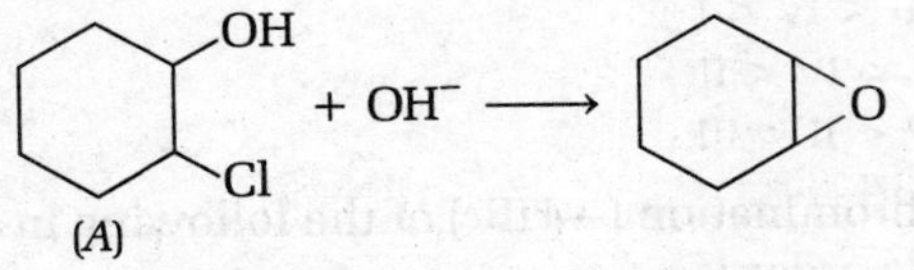

This reaction is possible when A is

(a) *cis* (b) *trans*

(c) Both (a) and (b) (d) None of these

80. 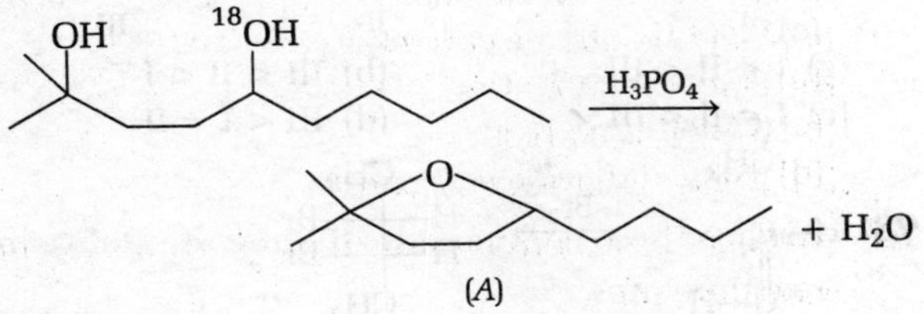

^{18}O will be in

(a) A (b) H_2O

(c) Both (a) and (b) (d) None of these

81. 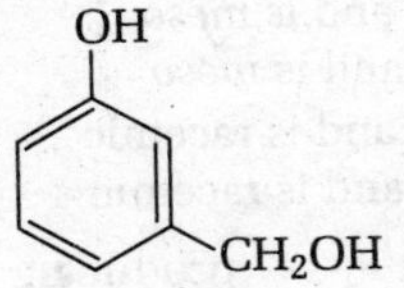 $\xrightarrow[\text{(ii) } CH_3I]{\text{(i) } K_2CO_3} A$; A is

(a) 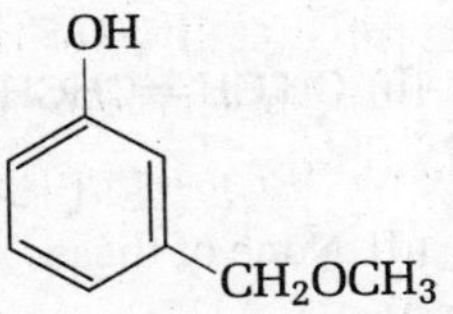 (b) 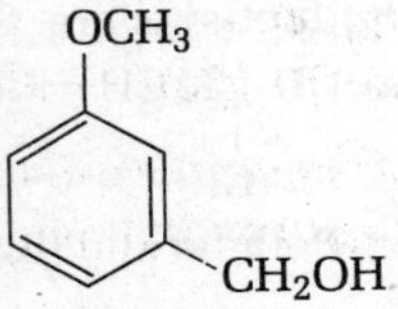

(c) 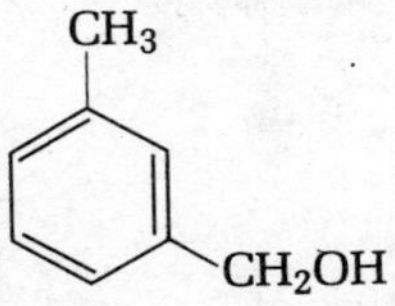 (d) 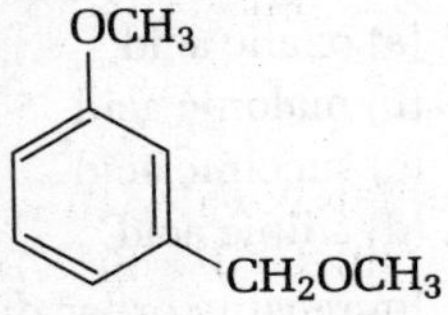

82. Which of the following molecules is least resonance stabilised? **[JEE Main 2017]**

(a) 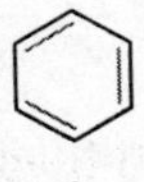 (b) 

(c) 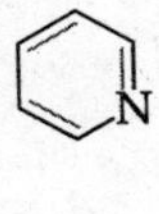 (d) 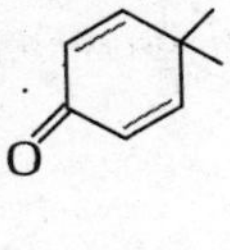

83. 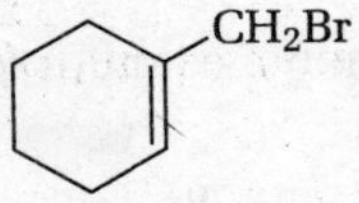 $\xrightarrow[\Delta]{EtOH}$ products. Expected products are

A: 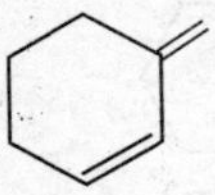, B: 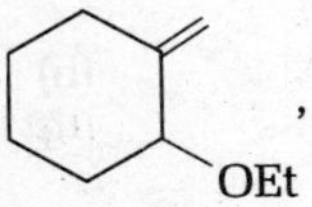, C: 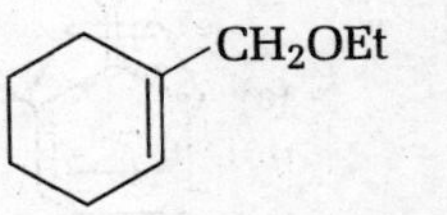

Select the correct alternates.

(a) *A, B, C* (b) *A, C*

(c) *B, C* (d) *A, B*

84. The order of ease of heterolysis of following *t*-butyl compound is

$(CH_3)_3C—OH$ (I) $(CH_3)_3C—OAc$ (II) $(CH_3)_3C—Cl$ (III)

(a) I < II < III (b) III < II < I

(c) I < III < II (d) II < I < III

85. There is formation of precipitate almost instantly when alcoholic $AgNO_3$ reacts with

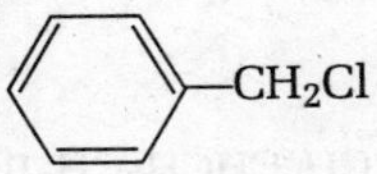 $CH_3\overset{CH_3}{\underset{CH_3}{C}}—Cl$ 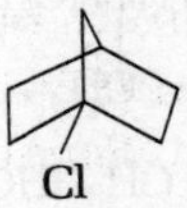

I II III

(a) I, II and III (b) I and II

(c) II and III (d) I and III

86. Acidic nature of CH_3OH(I), CH_3SH(II) and CH_3NH_2(III) is in order

(a) III < II < I (b) III < I < II

(c) I < II < III (d) II < I < III

87. Basic nature of H_3O^+, H_2O and OH^- is in order

(a) $H_3O^+ < H_2O < OH^-$ (b) $H_2O < OH^- < H_3O^+$

(c) $OH^- < H_2O < H_3O^+$ (d) $OH^- = H_3O^+ = H_2O$

88. $\overset{\ominus}{C}H_3$, $\overset{\ominus}{N}H_2$, $\overset{\ominus}{O}H$ and $\overset{\ominus}{F}$ in increasing pK_b values are

(a) $\overset{\ominus}{C}H_3 < \overset{\ominus}{N}H_2 < \overset{\ominus}{O}H < \overset{\ominus}{F}$

(b) $\overset{\ominus}{F} < \overset{\ominus}{O}H < \overset{\ominus}{N}H_2 < \overset{\ominus}{C}H_3$

(c) $\overset{\ominus}{O}H < \overset{\ominus}{N}H_2 < \overset{\ominus}{C}H_3 < \overset{\ominus}{F}$

(d) None of the above is correct

89. Most stable carbocation is

(a) $CH_2{=}\overset{\oplus}{C}H$ (b) 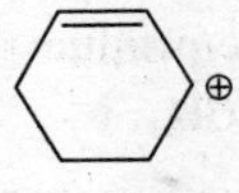

(c) 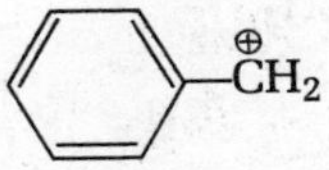 (d) $(CH_3)\overset{\oplus}{C}$

90. Least reactive is

(a) CH_2N_2 (b) $CH_2{=}C{=}O$

(c) $:CH_2$ (d) $\cdot\dot{C}H_2$

91. 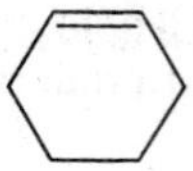 + NBS $\longrightarrow$ *A*; *A* is

(a) 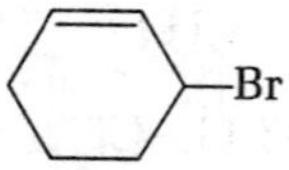
(b) 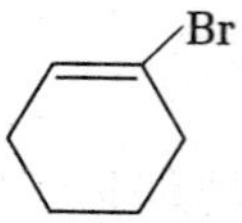
(c) 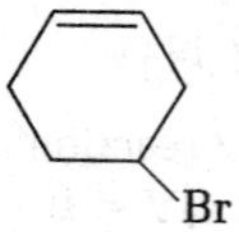
(d) 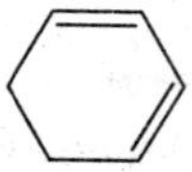

92. Basic strength of $CH{\equiv}\overset{\ominus}{C}$(I); $CH_2{=}\overset{\ominus}{C}H$(II) and $CH_3\overset{\ominus}{C}H_2$(III) will be in order
(a) I < II < III
(b) II < III < I
(c) III < II < I
(d) III < I < II

93. $CH_3CH(CH_3)CH{=}CH_2$ + HBr $\longrightarrow$ *A*, *A* (predominant) is
(a) $CH_3CH(CH_3)CH(Br)CH_3$
(b) $CH_3CH(CH_3)CH_2CH_2Br$
(c) $CH_3C(Br)(CH_3)CH_2CH_3$
(d) None is correct

94. Which reacts fastest with conc. HCl?
(a) 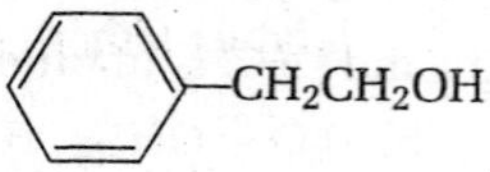
(b) 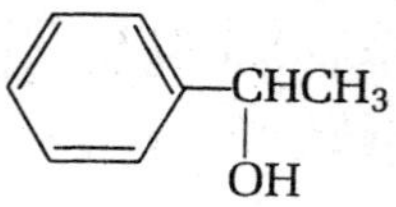
(c) $CH_3C(CH_3)_2$—OH
(d) $CH_2{=}CHCH_2OH$

95. Stability of following alkenes in the increasing order is

$CH_3CH{=}CHCH_3$ (I)

$CH_3C(CH_3){=}C(CH_3)CH_3$ (II)

$CH_3C(CH_3){=}CH_2$ (III)

$CH_3C(CH_3){=}CHCH_3$ (IV)

(a) I < III < IV < II
(b) I < II < III < IV
(c) IV < III < II < I
(d) II < III < IV < I

96. Dehydration of the following in increasing order is

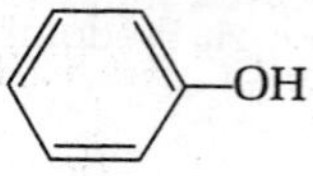
I
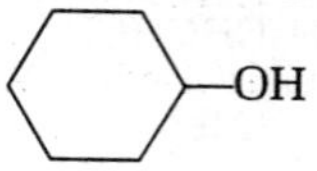
II
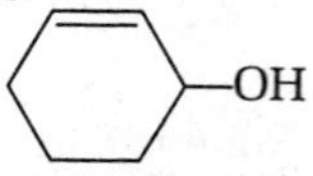
III
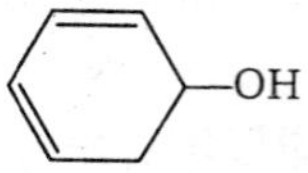
IV

(a) I < II < III < IV
(b) II < III < IV < I
(c) I < III < IV < II
(d) I < IV < II < III

97. Dehydrobromination (—HBr) of the following in increasing order is

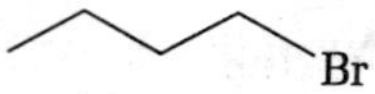
I
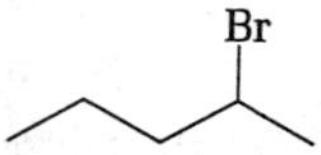
II
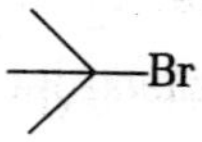
III

(a) I < II < III
(b) III < II < I
(c) I = II < III
(d) III < I = II

98. 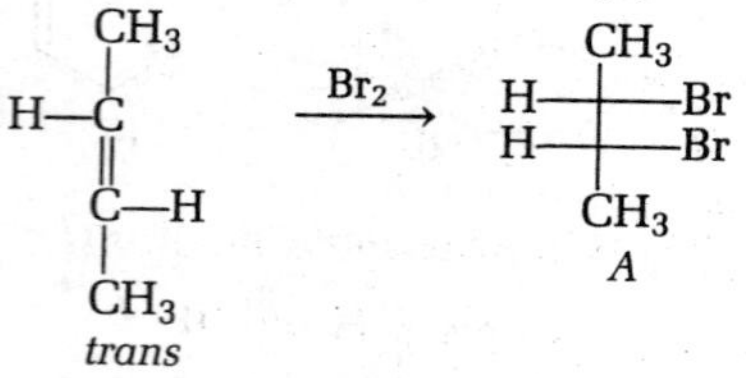

Which is the true statement?
(a) *A* is formed by *anti* addition and is *meso*
(b) *A* is formed by *syn* addition and is *meso*
(c) *A* is formed by *anti* addition and is racemic
(d) *A* is formed by *syn* addition and is racemic

99. $CH_3CH_2CH{=}CH_2$ + *t*-BuOCl $\longrightarrow$ products;
Product(s) is/are
(a) $CH_3CH(Cl)CH{=}CH_2$
(b) $CH_3CH{=}CHCH_2Cl$
(c) Both (a) and (b)
(d) None of these

100. Strongest acid out of the following is
(a) oxalic acid
(b) malonic acid
(c) succinic acid
(d) adipic acid

101. Increasing order of basic nature of

NH_3(I), CH_3NH_2(II) and 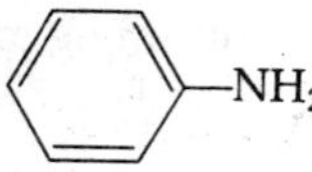 (III) is

(a) III < II < I
(b) I < II < III
(c) III = II < I
(d) III < I < II

102. $CH_2{=}CHCH{=}CH_2 \xrightarrow{CCl_3Br}$ product of 1,4-addition is

(a) $BrCH_2CH{=}CHCH_2CCl_3$ (b) $CH_2{=}CHCH(Br)CH_2CCl_3$

(c) $CH_2{=}CHCH(CCl_3)CH_2Br$ (d) None of these

103. Increasing order of the following for S_E reaction is

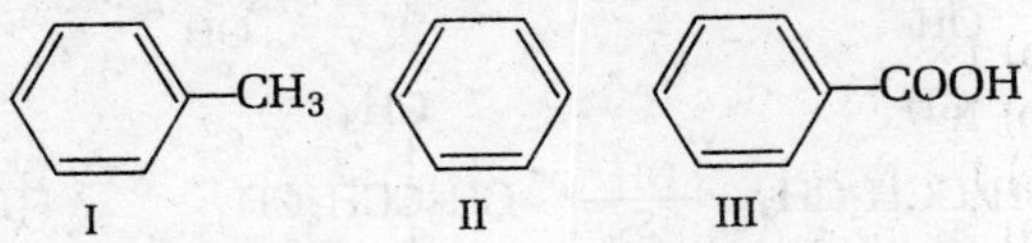

I II III

(a) I < II < III
(b) III < II < I
(c) II < III < I
(d) I < III < II

104. Electrophile $\overset{\oplus}{N}O_2$ attacks the following

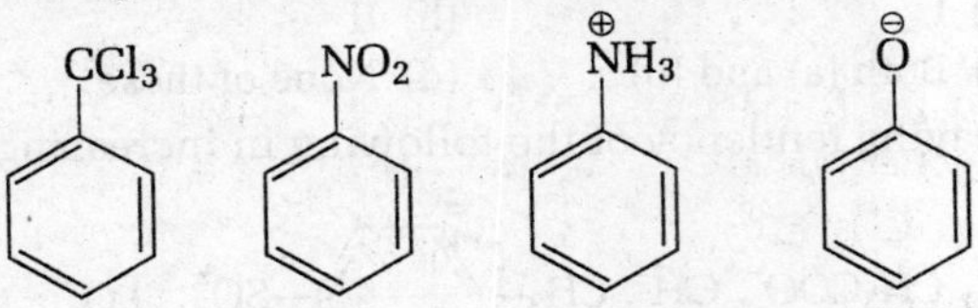

I II III IV

In which cases $\overset{\oplus}{N}O_2$ will be at *meta*-position?

(a) II and IV (b) I, II and III
(c) II and III (d) I only

105. 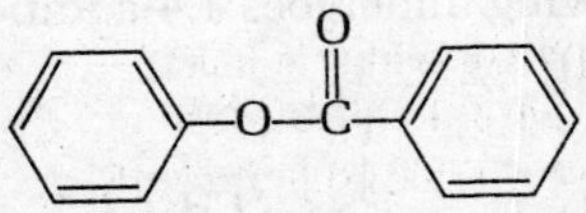 $+ NO_2^+ \longrightarrow$ Product of this reaction by single S_E reaction

(a) 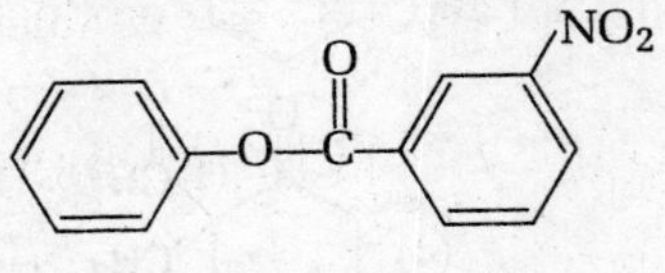

(b) 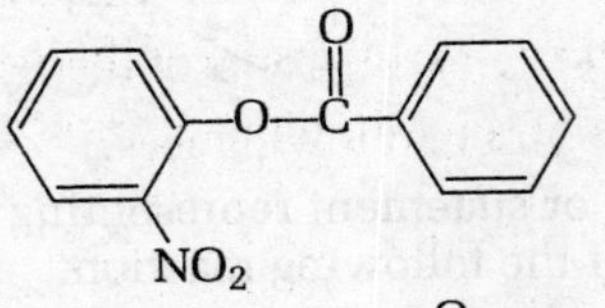

(c) 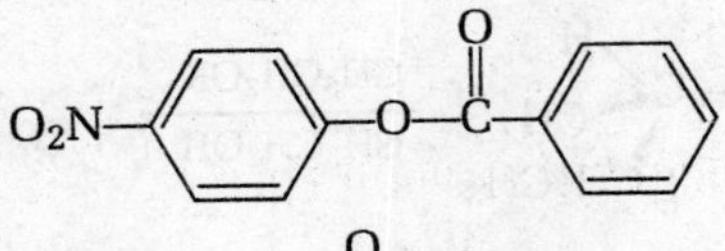

(d) 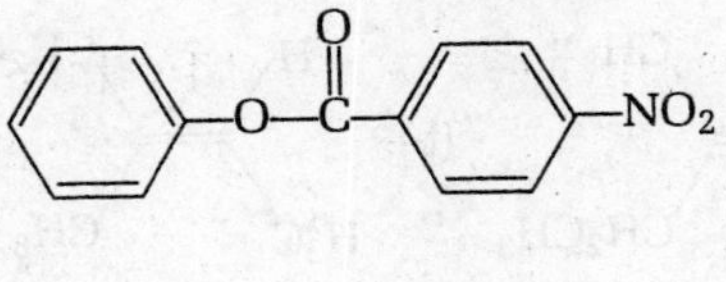

106. I. $CH_3CH_2CH_2CH_2Cl$, II. $CH_3CH_2CH(Cl)CH_3$,

III. $CH_3CH(CH_3)CH_2Cl$ IV. $CH_3C(CH_3)_2{-}Cl$

Increasing tendency for S_N1 and S_N2 reaction is

(*A*) S_N1 : I < III < II < IV (*B*) S_N2 : IV < II < III < I

(a) *A* and *B* both are correct (b) only *A* is correct
(c) only *B* is correct (d) Both are incorrect

107. The major product of the following reaction is **[JEE Advanced 2017]**

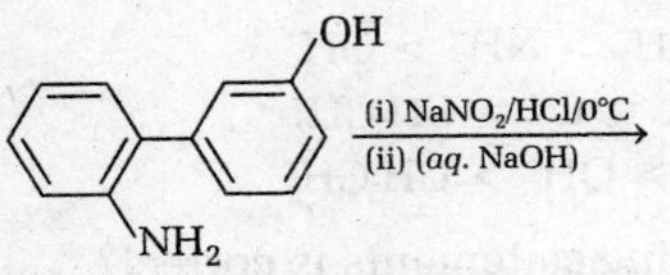

(a) 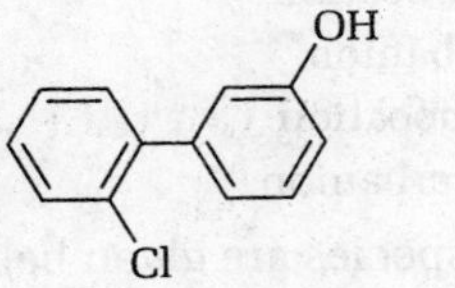 (b) 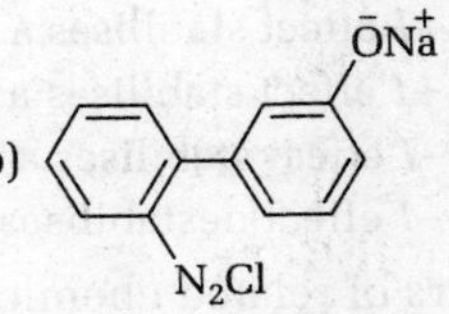

(c) 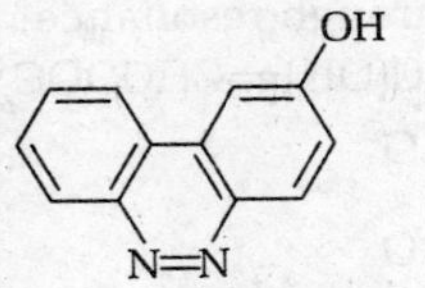 (d) 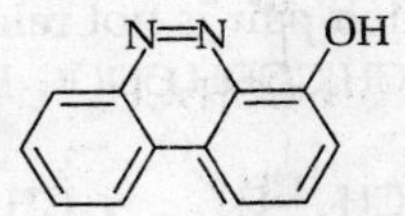

108. $CH_3CH(CH_3)CH(Br)CH_3 \xrightarrow[\text{Williamson}]{S_N2,\ C_2H_5ONa}$ product (ether); ether is

(a) $CH_3CH(CH_3){-}CH(OC_2H_5)CH_3$ (b) $CH_3C(OC_2H_5)(CH_3)CH_2CH_3$

(c) Both (a) and (b) (d) None is correct

109. 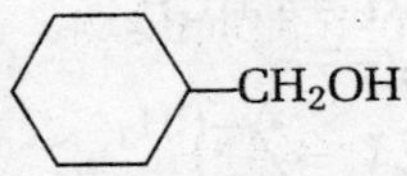 on dehydration with conc. H_2SO_4 forms predominantly

(a) 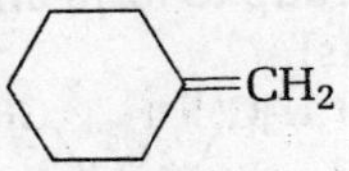 (b) 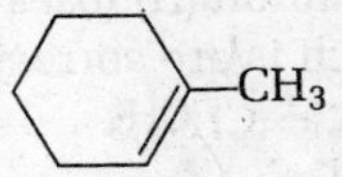

(c) 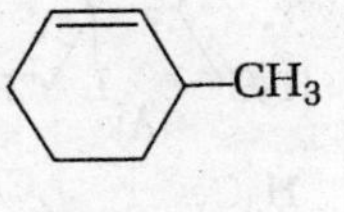 (d) 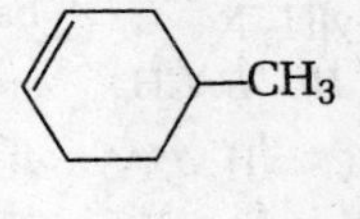

110. Stability order of ...... is in order

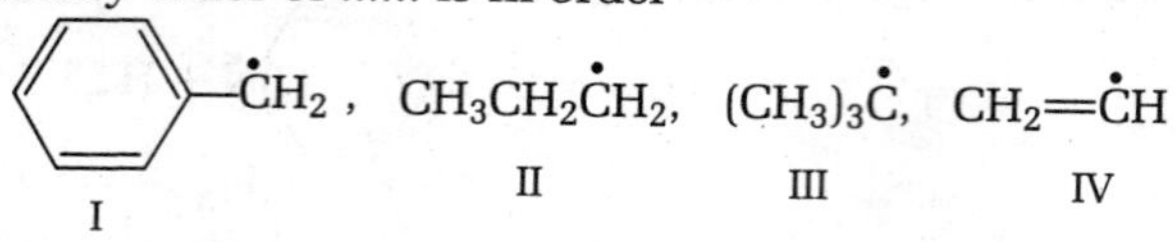

(a) IV < II < III < I (b) IV < II < I < III
(c) I < II < III < IV (d) IV < I < III < II

111. Increasing values of dissociation constant K_a of CH_3COOH(I), HCOOH (II) and C_6H_5COOH (III) are
(a) I < II < III (b) III < II < I
(c) I < III < II (d) II < III < I

112. What is the decreasing order of strength of the bases OH^-, NH_2^-, $HC{\equiv}C^-$ and $CH_3{-}CH_2^-$?
(a) $CH_3CH_2^- > NH_2^- > HC{\equiv}C^- > OH^-$
(b) $HC{\equiv}C^- > CH_3CH_2^- > NH_2^- > OH^-$
(c) $OH^- > NH_2^- > HC{\equiv}C^- > CH_3CH_2^-$
(d) $NH_2^- > HC{\equiv}C^- > OH^- > CH_3CH_2^-$

113. Which of the following statements is correct?
(a) +*I* effect stabilises a carbocation
(b) +*I* effect stabilises a carbanion
(c) –*I* effect stabilises a carbocation
(d) –*I* effect destabilises a carbanion

114. Pairs of related chemical species are given below. Which pair is not related through resonance?
(a) $CH_3COCH_2COOC_2H_5$, $CH_3C(OH){=}CHCOOC_2H_5$
(b) 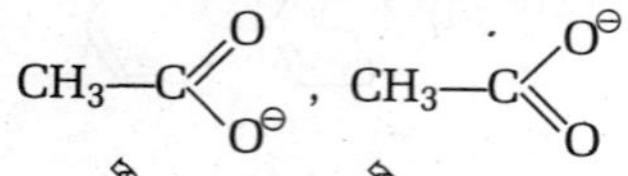
(c) 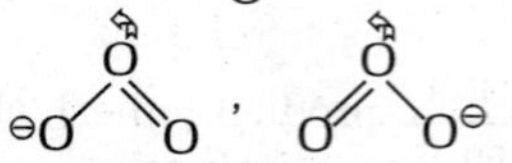
(d) 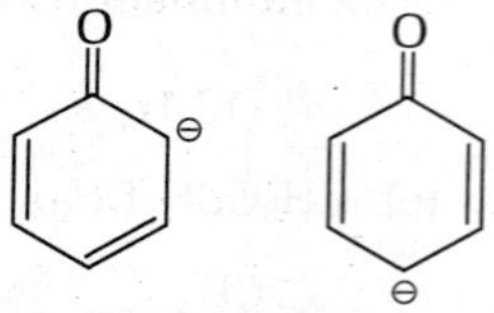

115. Most stable radical is
(a) $CH_2{=}\dot{C}H$ (b) $CH_2{=}CH\dot{C}H_2$
(c) 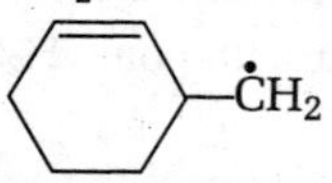 (d) 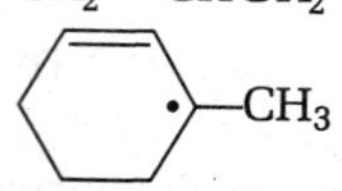

116. Carbanion (*A*) loses a leaving group to form alkene. Which is/are correct statement(s)?

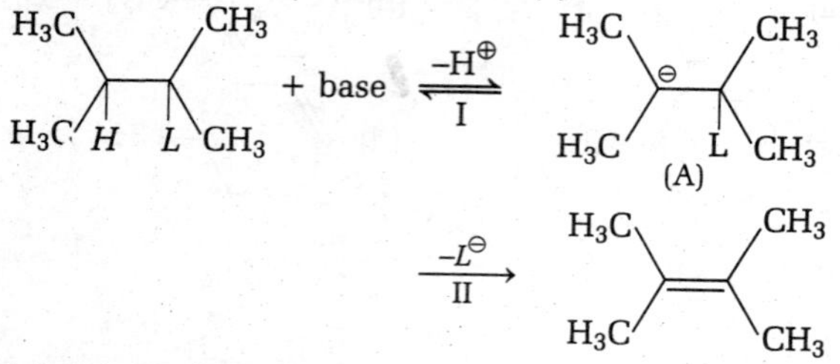

(a) It is E1-CB type (b) It is E2 type
(c) It is E1 type (d) None of these

117. Maximum dehydration takes place of
(a) 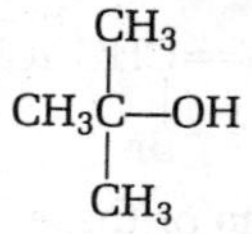 (b) 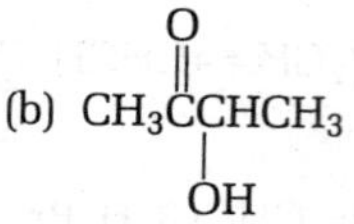
(c) 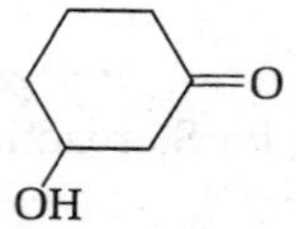 (d) 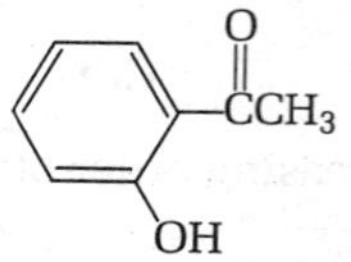

118. 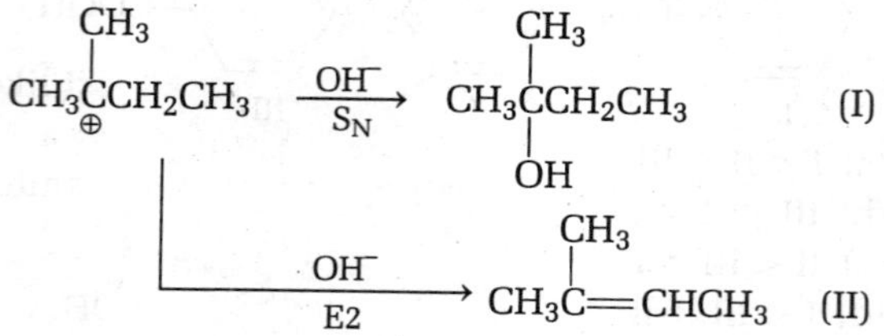

Which is predominant?
(a) I (b) II
(c) Both (a) and (b) (d) None of these

119. Leaving tendency of the following in increasing order is

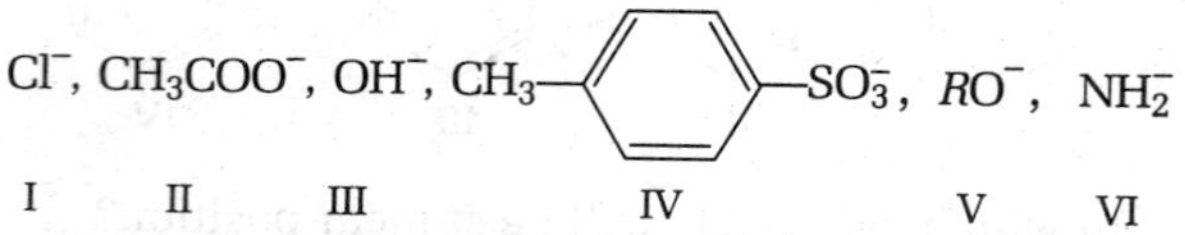

(a) VI < V < III < II < IV < I (b) I < II < III < VI < V < IV
(c) I < III < V < II < IV < VI (d) cannot be decided

120. Which one of the following undergoes 1,4-addition with CH_3SK (in ethanol)?
(a) 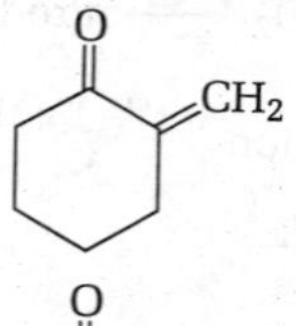 (b) 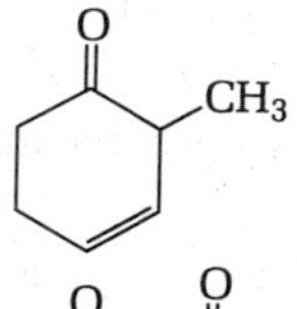
(c)  (d) 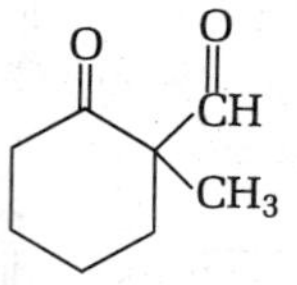

121. Select the formula or statement representing the major product(s) of the following reaction.

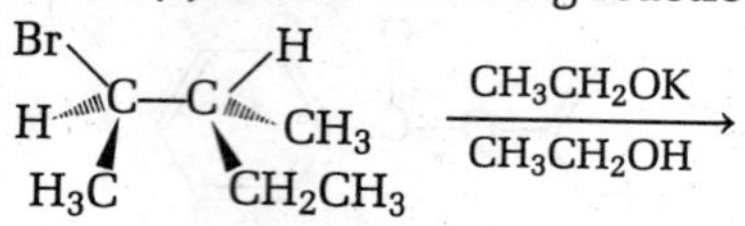

(a) 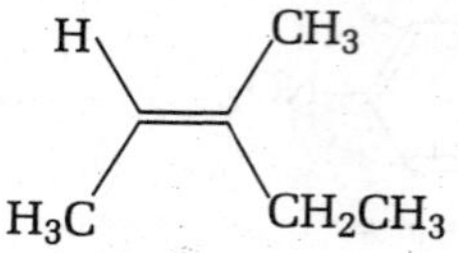 (b) 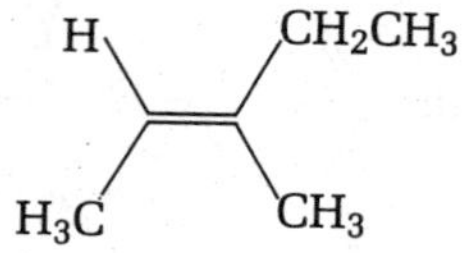

(c) $H_2C{=}CHCH(CH_3)CH_2CH_3$
(d) Both (a) and (b) in approximately equal amounts

122. Which of the following statements concerning E2 reactions of alkyl halide is true?

(a) The rate of an E2 reaction depends only on the concentration of alkyl halide

(b) The rate of an E2 reaction depends on the concentration of the base

(c) The C—H bond and the C—X bond (X = halogen) bond are broken in the same step

(d) Alkyl chlorides generally react faster than alkyl halide

123. Which of the following alcohols would be most likely to undergo dehydration with rearrangement by a process involving a methyl migration (methyl shift)?

(a) 

(b) 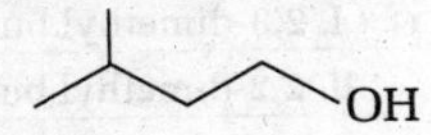

(c) 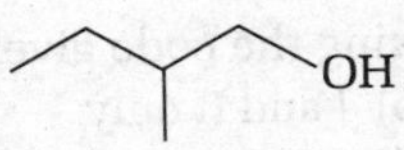

(d) 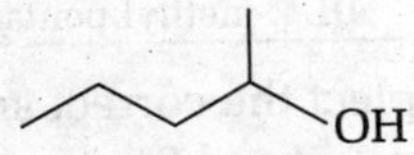

124. Consider the following reaction,

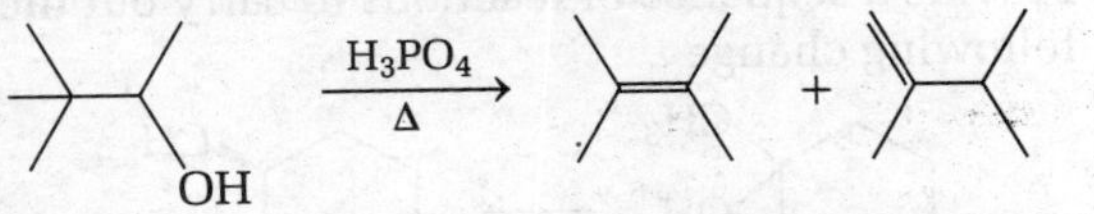

Which response contains all the correct statements about this process?

I. Dehydration

II. Carbon skeleton migration

III. E2 mechanism

IV. Most stable carbocation forms

(a) I, III (b) I, II, III (c) I, II, IV (d) I, III, IV

125. Which one of the following will give 2-methyl-1-butene as the only alkene on treatment with $KOC(CH_3)_3$ in dimethyl sulphoxide?

(a) 1-bromo-2-methylbutane

(b) 2-methyl-1-butanol

(c) 2-bromo-2-methylbutanol

(d) 2-methyl-2-butanol

126. Consider the following statements,

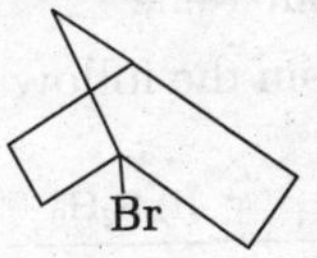

does not undergo S_N reaction when treated with $C_2H_5O^-$ because

I. Br^- is a poor leaving group.

II. The geometry of the molecule does not permit formation of carbocation at bridge head.

III. The geometry of the molecule does not permit backside attack by $C_2H_5O^-$ at the bridge head.

Which of the statement given above is/are correct?

(a) I and II (b) II and III (c) Only II (d) Only III

127. In the following case

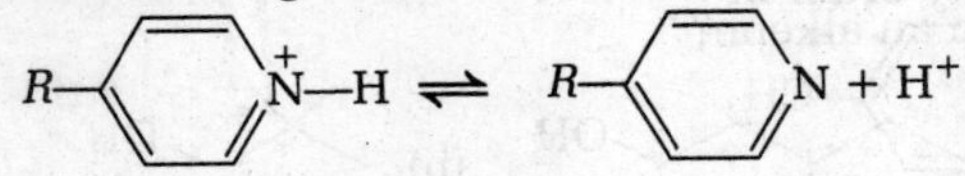

pK_a is maximum when R is

(a) H (b) NH_2 (c) CN (d) CH_3

128. Major product of the following reaction is

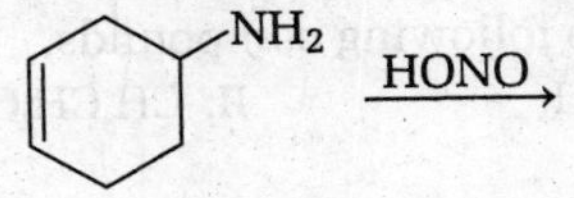

(a) 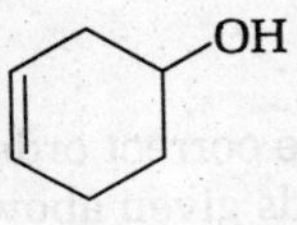

(b) 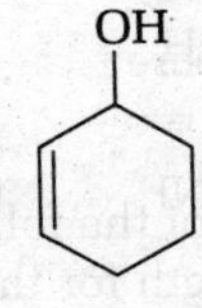

(c) 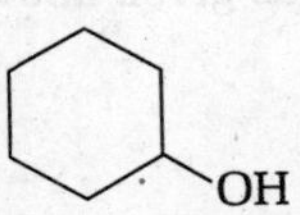

(d) None of these

129. Optically pure 2(S)-butanol is subjected to the following reaction,

$$2(S)\text{—BuOH} \xrightarrow{\text{Na}} ? \xrightarrow{\text{MeI}}$$

which of the following statements is correct for stereochemical outcome of the reaction?

(a) The reaction proceeds with inversion

(b) The reaction proceeds with racemisation

(c) The reaction proceeds with complete retention of configuration

(d) The reaction leads to destruction of chirality in the molecule

130. Which alkyl halide undergoes E2 elimination at the fastest rate?

(a) 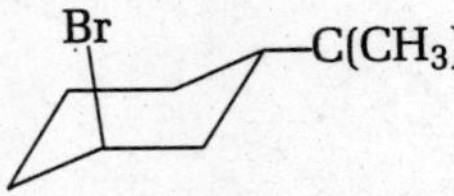

(b) 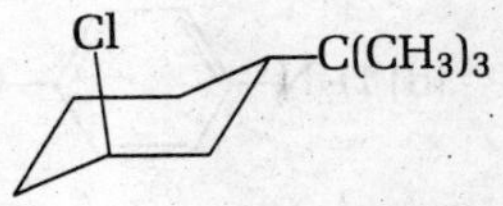

(c) 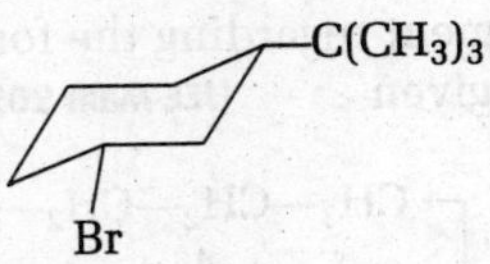

(d) 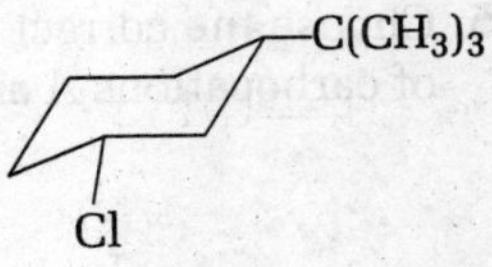

131. Arrange the following alcohols in order of decreasing reactivity (faster ⟶ slowest) toward dehydration with 85% H_2SO_4.

I: $(CH_3)_2CHCH_2CH_2OH$

II: $(CH_3)_2C(OH)CH_2CH_3$

III: $(CH_3)_2CHCH(OH)CH_3$

(a) II > III > I (b) I > III > II

(c) II > I > III (d) I > II > III

132. Which of the following alcohols cannot be prepared from an alkene?

(a) 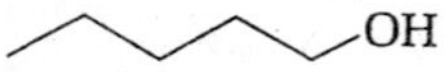 (b) 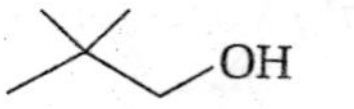

(c) 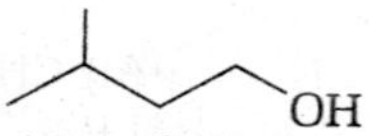 (d) 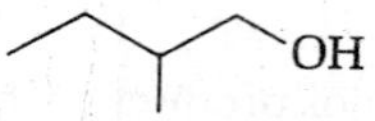

133. Consider the following compounds,

I. $CH_2(F)CH_2OH$, II. CH_3CH_2OH

III. $CH_3CH(F)OH$, IV. $CH_2(Cl)CH_2OH$

Which one of the following is the correct order of acidic strength for the compounds given above?

(a) IV > III > I > II
(b) II > I > IV > III
(c) II > IV > I > III
(d) III > I > IV > II

134. Which one of the following compounds undergoes predominantly S_N2 reaction with aqueous NaOH in polar aprotic solvents?

(a) 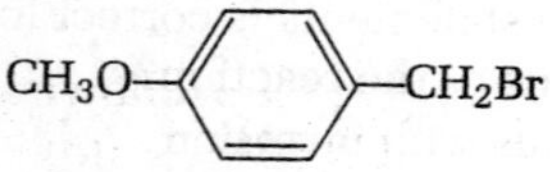

(b) 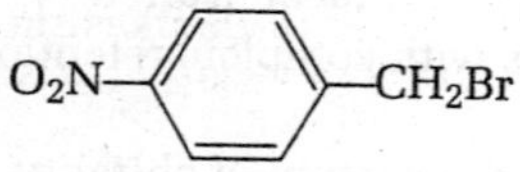

(c) 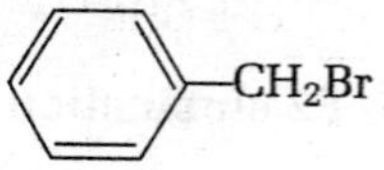

(d) 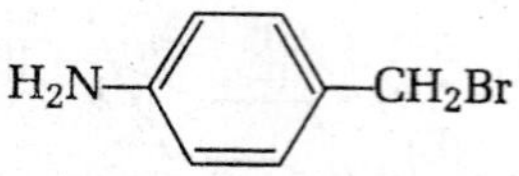

135. Choose the correct statement regarding the formation of carbocations *A* and *B* given **[JEE Main 2021, March]**

$$CH_3-CH_2-CH=CH_2+HBr \rightarrow \begin{cases} CH_3-CH_2-CH_2-\overset{+}{C}H_2+Br^- \quad (A) \\ CH_3-CH_2-\overset{+}{C}H-CH_3+Br^- \quad (B) \end{cases}$$

(a) Carbocation *B* is more stable and formed relatively at faster rate
(b) Carbocation *A* is more stable and formed relatively at slow rate
(c) Carbocation *B* is more stable and formed relatively at slow rate
(d) Carbocation *A* is more stable and formed relatively at faster rate

136. The dehydration of *n*-butanol with acid gives

(a) a mixture of 1-and-2-butenes in equal amount
(b) 1-butene as the major product involving primary carbocation as the intermediate
(c) 2-butene as the major product involving a proton shift to form a more stable secondary carbocation
(d) 2-butene as the major product involving a hydride shift to form a more stable secondary carbocation

137. Which of the following pairs are correctly matched for the number of monochlorinated products (ignoring stereoisomers) obtained from the listed isomeric hexanes?

Isomer	Number of monochlorinated products
I. 2,3-dimethyl butane	Two
II. 2,2-dimethyl butane	Three
III. 2-methyl pentane	Five

Select the correct answer using the code given below.

(a) I, II and III (b) I and II only
(c) II and III only (d) I and III only

138. Provide a sequence of reactions to carry out the following change

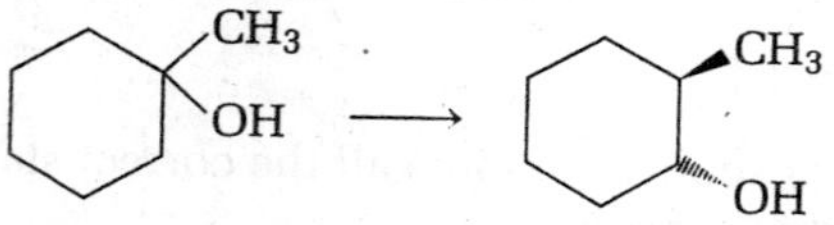

(a) $\xrightarrow[\Delta]{\text{Conc. } H_2SO_4} \xrightarrow[OH^-]{B_2H_6,\ H_2O_2}$

(b) $\xrightarrow[\Delta]{\text{Conc. } H_2SO_4} \xrightarrow{H_3O^+}$

(c) $\xrightarrow[\Delta]{\text{Conc. } H_2SO_4} \xrightarrow{Hg(OOCCH_3)_2}$

(d) $\xrightarrow[\Delta]{\text{Conc. } H_2SO_4} \xrightarrow{MnO_4^-,\ OH^-}$

139. Alkene + Cl_2 $\longrightarrow$ 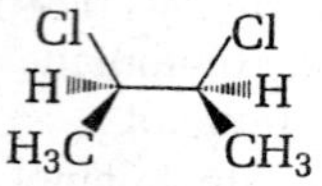

In the above reaction alkene is

(a) *Z*-but-2-ene (b) *E*-but-2-ene
(c) *Z*-but-1-ene (d) *E*-but-1-ene

140. Major organic product formed from the following sequence of reactions is

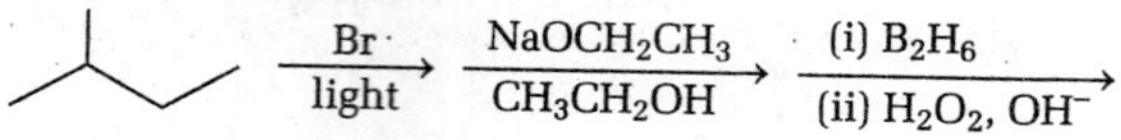

(a) 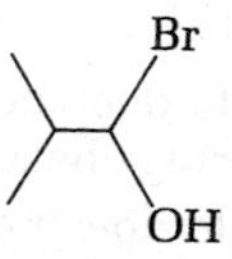 (b) 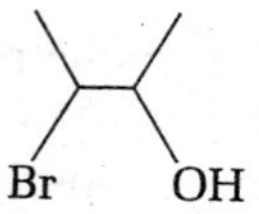

(c) 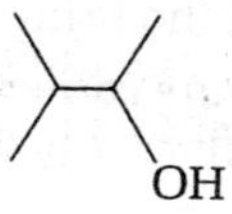 (d) 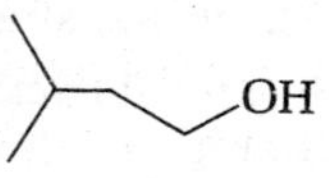

141. The reaction,

$$(CH_3)_2C{=}CH_2 + \dot{B}r \longrightarrow (CH_3)_2\dot{C}\,CH_2Br$$

is an example of $a(n)$—step in a radical chain reaction.

(a) Initiation (b) Termination
(c) Propagation (d) Heterolytic cleavage

142. Addition of HCl to 3,3-dimethyl-1-butene yields two products, one of which has a rearranged carbon skeleton. Which of the following cations are intermediates in that reaction?

$(CH_3)_3\overset{\oplus}{C}CHCH_2Cl$ (I), $(CH_3)_3C\overset{\oplus}{C}HCH_3$ (II)

$(CH_3)_2\overset{\oplus}{C}C(CH_3)_2$ with Cl on the second carbon (III), $(CH_3)_2\overset{\oplus}{C}CH(CH_3)_2$ (IV)

(a) I, II (b) I, III
(c) II, III (d) II, IV

143. Which compound undergoes nucleophilic substitution with NaCN at the fastest rate?

(a) 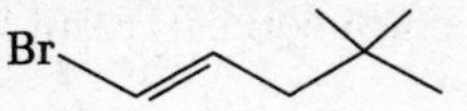

(b) 

(c) 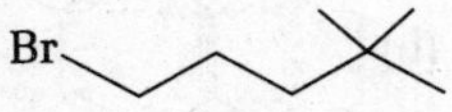

(d) 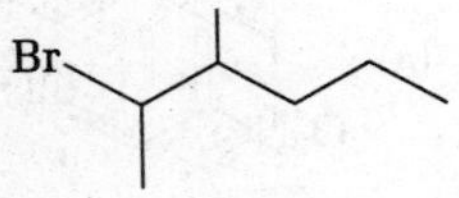

144. For the reaction,

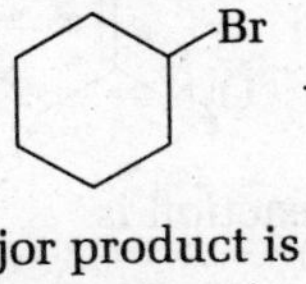

$+ CH_3CH_2ONa \longrightarrow$

the major product is formed by

(a) a S_N1 reaction (b) an S_N2 reaction
(c) an E1 reaction (d) an E2 reaction

145. Which of the following statements pertaining to an S_N2 reaction are true?

I. The rate of reaction is independent of the concentration of the nucleophile.
II. The nucleophile attacks carbon on the side of the molecule opposite the group being displaced.
III. The reaction proceeds with simultaneous bond formation and bond rupture.
IV. Partial racemisation of an optically active substrate results.

Select the alternate from the following.

(a) I, IV
(b) I, III, IV
(c) II, III
(d) All of the above

146. Which of the following alkyl halides would be most likely to give a rearranged product under S_N1 conditions?

(a) 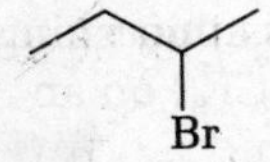

(b) 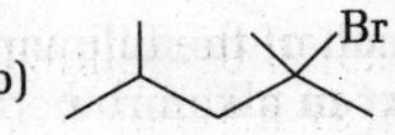

(c) 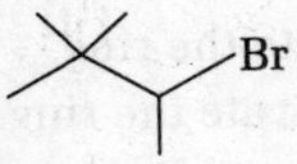

(d) 

147. From each of the following pairs select the compound that will react faster with sodium iodide in acetone

2-chloropropane (I) or 2-bromopropane (II)

1-bromobutane (III) or 2-bromobutane (IV)

(a) I, III (b) I, IV (c) II, III (d) II, IV

148. Which of the following phrases are not correctly associated with an S_N1 reaction?

I. Rearrangement is possible.
II. Rate is affected by solvent polarity.
III. The strength of the nucleophile is important in determining rate.
IV. The reactivity series is : tertiary > secondary > primary.
V. Proceeds with complete inversion of configuration.

Select the correct alternate from the following.

(a) III, V (b) II, III, V (c) V only (d) III only

149. Rank the following in the order of decreasing rate of solvolysis with aqueous ethanol (fastest ⟶ slowest)

I: $CH_2{=}C(CH_3){-}Br$

II: 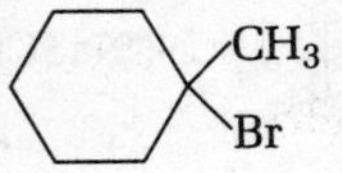

III: $CH_2CH(Br)CH_2CH(CH_3)_2$

(a) II > I > III (b) I > II > III
(c) II > III > I (d) I > III > II

150. Which one of the following alkyl halides would be expected to give the highest substitution-to-elimination ratio (most substitution, least elimination) on treatment with sodium ethoxide in ethanol?

(a) 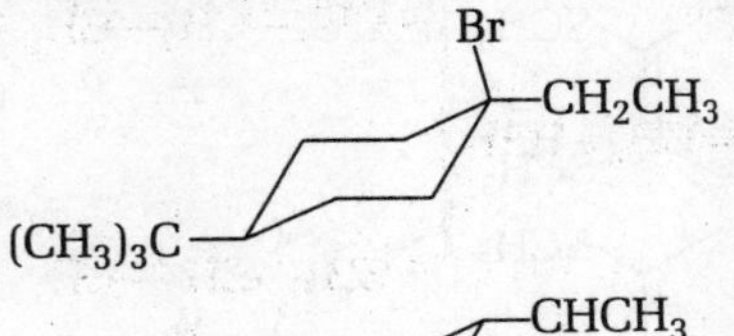

(b) 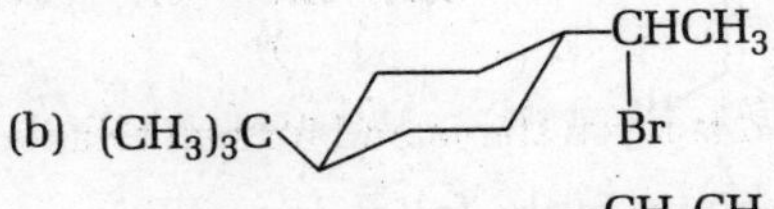

(c) 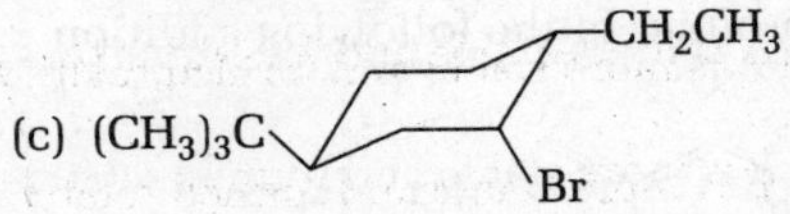

(d) 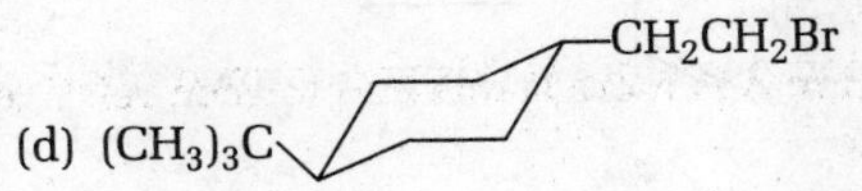

151. Consider the following statements concerning the effect of trifluoromethyl group, —CF_3, on an electrophilic aromatic substitution.

I. The CF_3 group will activate the ring.
II. The CF_3 group will deactivate the ring.
III. The CF_3 group will be a *meta* director.
IV. The CF_3 group will be an *ortho, para* director.

Which of these statements are correct?

(a) I, III (b) I, IV
(c) II, III (d) II, IV

152. Which of the following resonance structures is not a contributor to the cyclohexadienyl cation (carbocation σ complex) intermediate in the nitration of benzene?

(a) 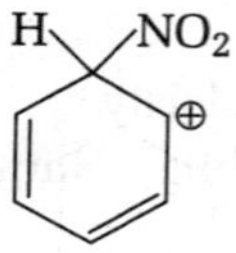

(b) 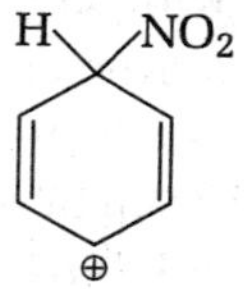

(c) 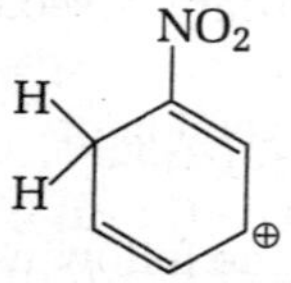

(d) None of the above (all are contributors)

153. Identify the principal organic product of the following reaction

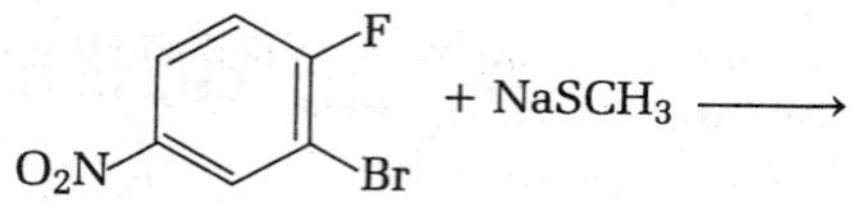

(a) 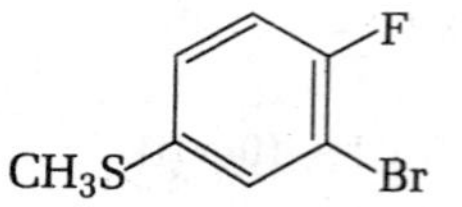

(b) 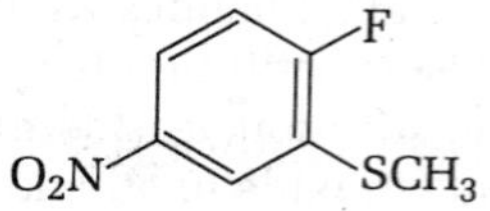

(c) 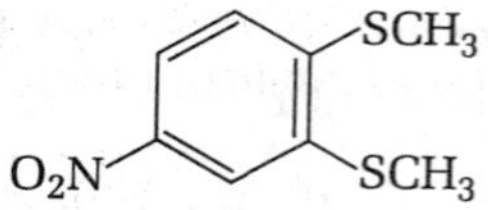

(d) 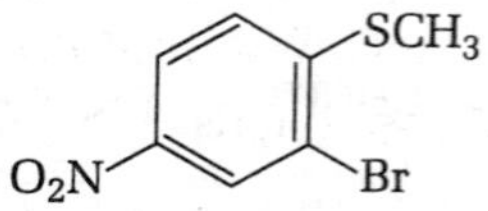

154. Predominant product in the following addition reaction is

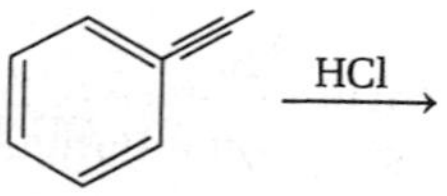

(a) 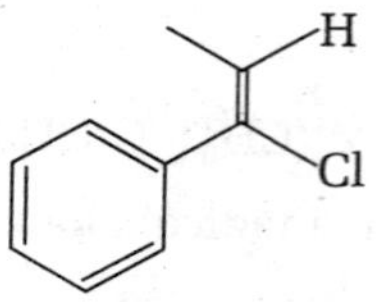

(b) 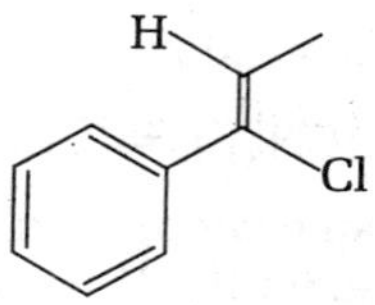

(c) 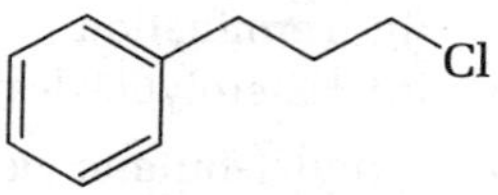

(d) 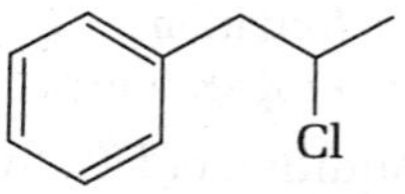

155. Which of the following statements is correct?

(a) $CH_3CH_2S^{\ominus}$ is a stronger base and more nucleophilic than $CH_3CH_2O^{\ominus}$
(b) $CH_3CH_2S^{\ominus}$ is a stronger base and less nucleophilic than $CH_3CH_2O^{\ominus}$
(c) $CH_3CH_2S^{\ominus}$ is a weaker base and less nucleophilic than $CH_3CH_2O^{\ominus}$
(d) $CH_3CH_2S^{\ominus}$ is a weaker base and more nucleophilic than $CH_3CH_2O^{\ominus}$

156. Intermediate of the following reaction is

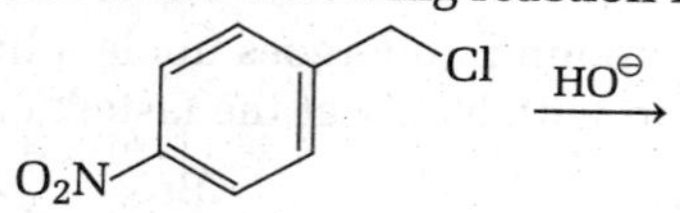

(a) 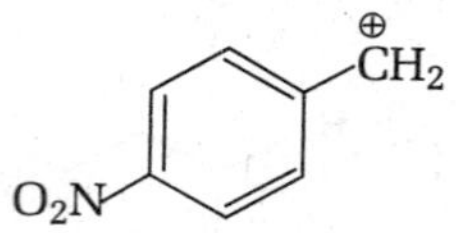

(b) 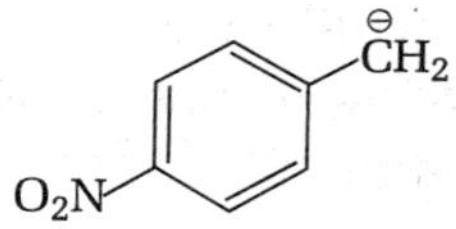

(c) 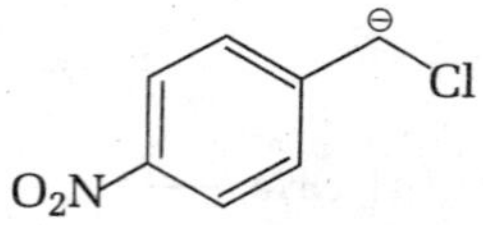

(d) 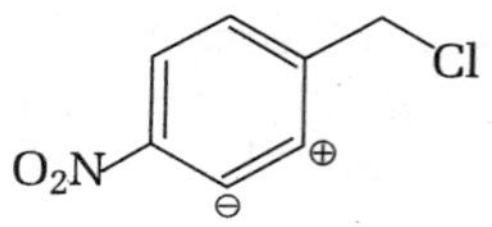

157. Final product of the above reaction is

(a) 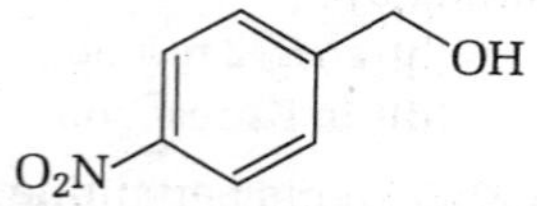

(b) 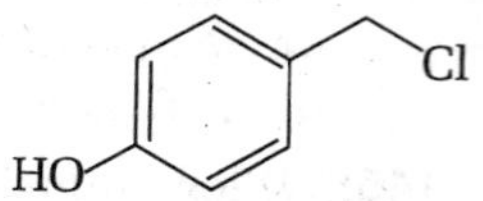

(c) 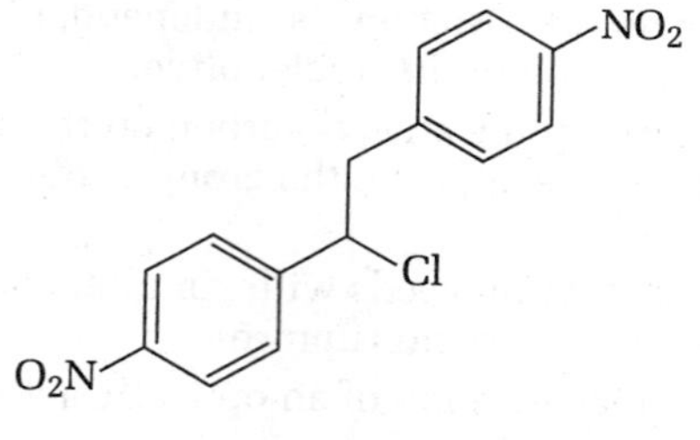

(d) 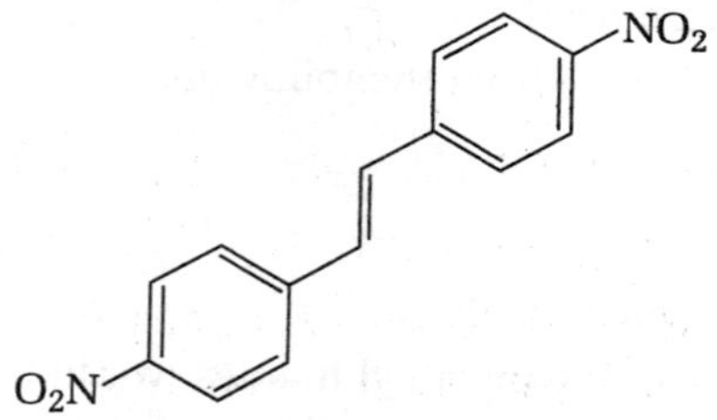

158. Addition of Br_2 to 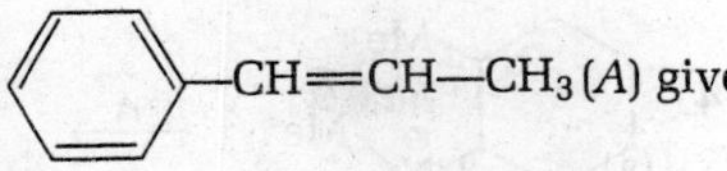 (A) gives

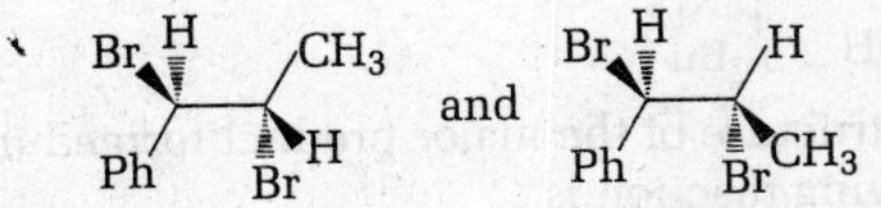

(B) and (C)

Select the correct statements.

(a) B is predominant when A is *trans* and C is predominant when A is *cis*

(b) B is predominant when A is *cis* and C is predominant when A is *trans*

(c) Both are correct statements

(d) None of the above are correct statements

159. Consider the following molecules,

I. *trans*-1,2-dichlorocyclopropane

II. *cis*-1,2-dichlorocyclopropane

III. 1,1,2-trichlorocyclopropane

In which of the above molecules is/are the set(s) of methylene hydrogen (s) diastereotopic?

(a) I only (b) I and III

(c) II and III (d) II only

160. The reaction is described as,

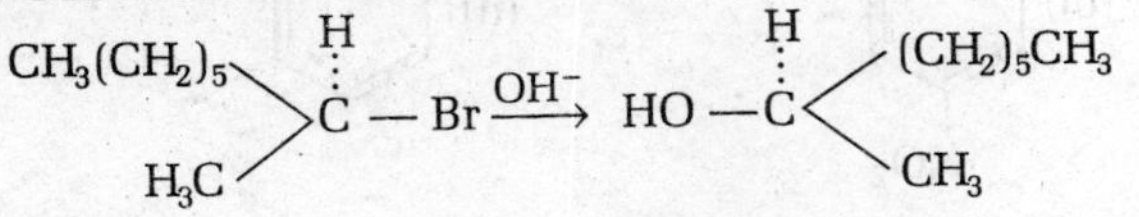

(a) S_E2 (b) S_N1

(c) S_N2 (d) S_N0

161. In a ring substitution of C_6H_5Z, the main product obtained is *meta* the group Z is

(a) —COOH (b) —Cl

(c) $—NH_2$ (d) $—CH_3$

162. Which of the following compounds will react by unimolecular nucleophilic substitution mechanism?

(A) 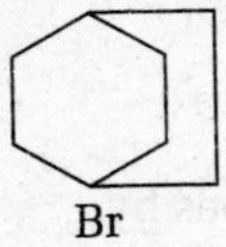 (B) 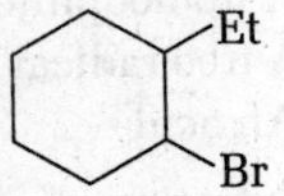

(C) 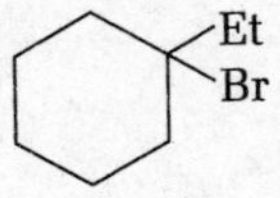 (D) Et_3CBr

(a) A, B, C (b) A, C, D

(c) B, C, D (d) A, B, D

163. Which of the following is applied in this reaction?

$$CH_3CHBrCH_2CH_3 \xrightarrow{\text{Alc. KOH}}$$

(i) $CH_3CH{=}CHCH_3$ major product

(ii) $CH_2{=}CHCH_2CH_3$ minor product

(a) Hofmann's rule (b) Kharasch effect

(c) Saytzeff's rule (d) Markownikoff's rule

164. Which one of the following C—H bonds is the weakest for homolytic fission?

(a) $CH_3—H$ (b) $(C_6H_5)CH_2—H$

(c) $C_6H_5—H$ (d) $(C_6H_5)_3C—H$

165. Of the given resonating structures of formic acid:

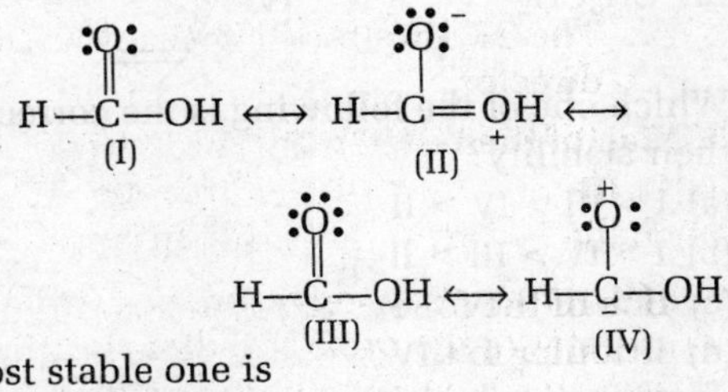

The most stable one is

(a) IV (b) III (c) II (d) I

166. Consider the following molecules

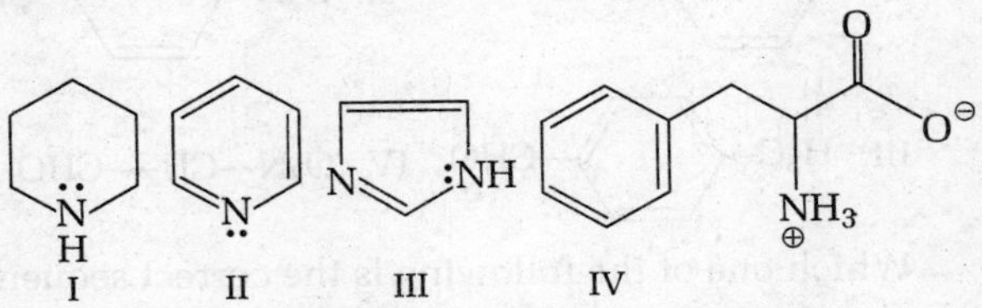

What is the correct order of their basicity?

(a) I > III > II > IV (b) IV > II > III > I

(c) I > III > IV > II (d) IV > II > I > III

167. An S_N2 reaction at an asymmetric carbon of a compound always gives which one of the following?

(a) An enantiomer of the substrate

(b) A product with opposite optical rotation

(c) A mixture of diastereomers

(d) A single stereoisomer

168. Consider the following species:

I. 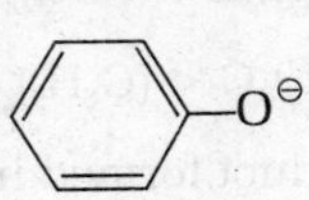 II. CH_3OH

III. $OH^{\ominus}$ IV. $CH_3COO^{\ominus}$ V. $CH_3S^{\ominus}$

What is the correct sequence of the species given above in decreasing order of nucleophilicity in an aqueous solution?

(a) V > III > I > IV > II (b) IV > II > III > I > V

(c) V > II > I > IV > III (d) IV > III > II > I > V

169. Consider the following compounds,

I. 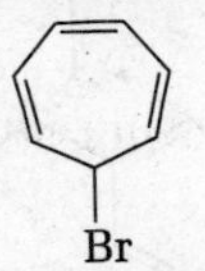 II.  III. 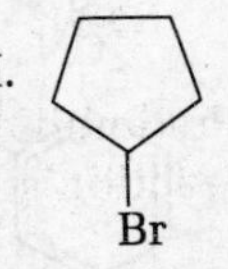

What is the correct sequence of the compounds given above in decreasing order of their S_N1 reactivity?

(a) I > II > III (b) I > III > II

(c) II > III > I (d) III > I > II

170. Consider the following carbanions,

I. $(CH_3)_3C\overset{\ominus}{C}H_2$ II. 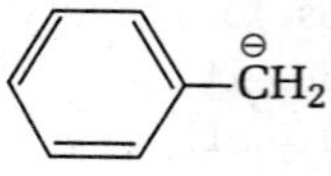

III. $CH_3\overset{\ominus}{C}H_2$ IV. 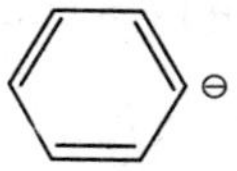

Which one of the following is the correct order of their stability?
(a) I > III > IV > II
(b) I > IV > III > II
(c) II > III > IV > I
(d) II > III > I > IV

171. Consider the following four carbonyl compounds,

I. 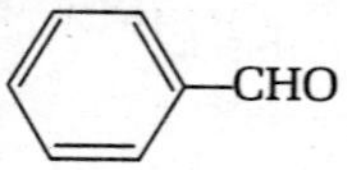 II. 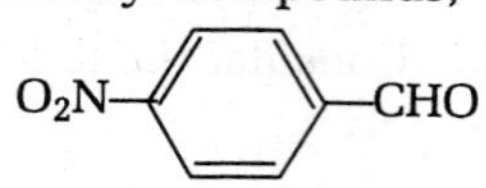

III. 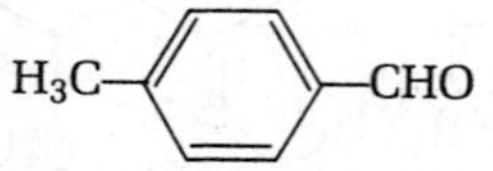 IV. $O_2N—CH_2—CHO$

Which one of the following is the correct sequence of decreasing order of reactivity towards nucleophilic addition reaction of the above compounds?
(a) III > I > II > IV (b) IV > II > I > III
(c) II > IV > I > III (d) IV > III > II > I

172. The increasing order of stability of the following free radicals is
(a) $(CH_3)_2\dot{C}H < (CH_3)_3\dot{C} < (C_6H_5)_2\dot{C}H < (C_6H_5)_3\dot{C}$
(b) $(C_6H_5)_3\dot{C} < (C_6H_5)_2\dot{C}H < (CH_3)_3\dot{C} < (CH_3)_2\dot{C}H$
(c) $(C_6H_5)_2\dot{C}H < (C_6H_5)_3\dot{C} < (CH_3)_3\dot{C} < (CH_3)_2\dot{C}H$
(d) $(CH_3)_2\dot{C}H < (CH_3)_3\dot{C} < (C_6H_5)_3\dot{C} < (C_6H_5)_2\dot{C}H$

173. The structure of the major product formed in the following reaction is

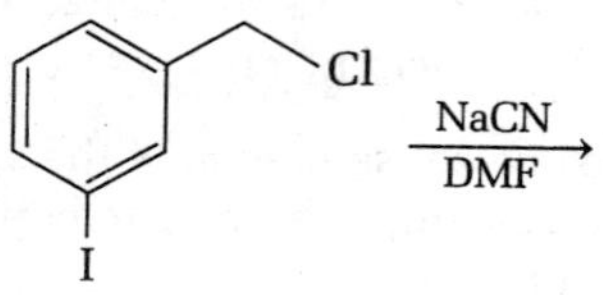

(a) 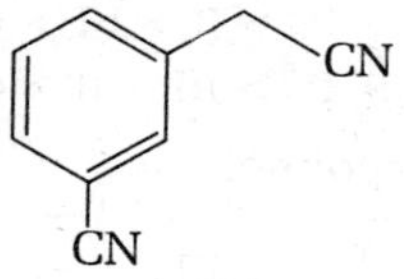 (b) 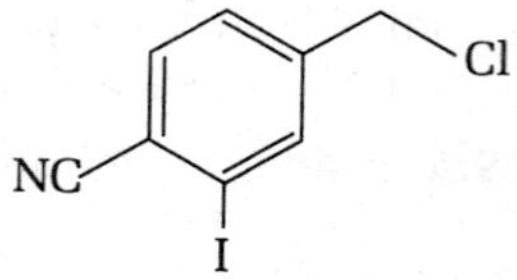

(c) 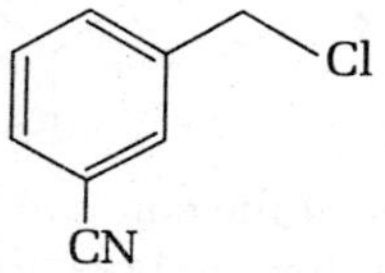 (d) 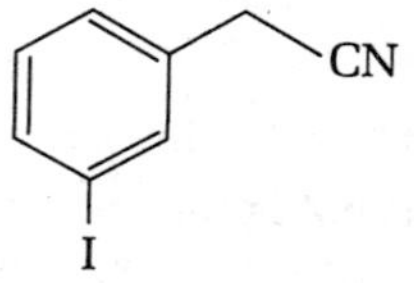

174. 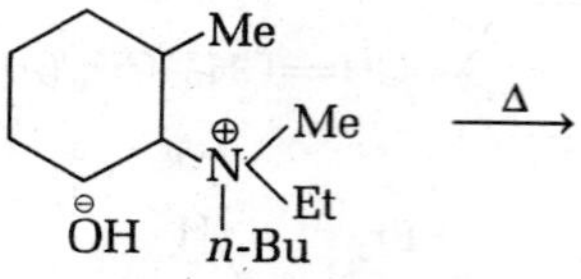

The structure of the major product formed in the following reaction is

(a)  (b) $CH_2{=}CH_2$

(c) 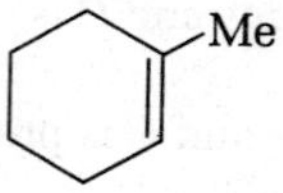 (d) 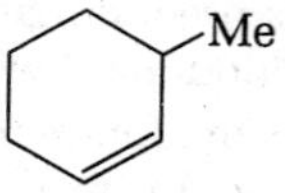

175. Which of the following would react most readily with nucleophiles?

(a)  (b) 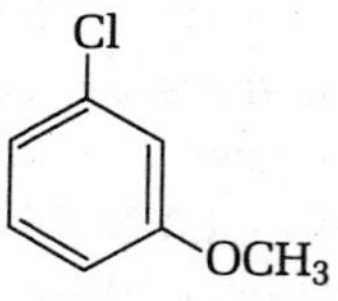

(c) 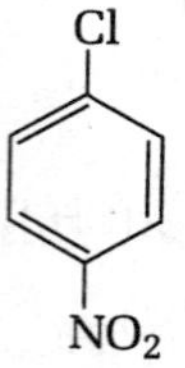 (d) 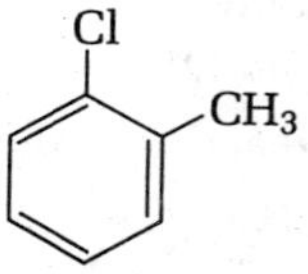

176. Geometry of methyl free radical is
(a) pyramidal
(b) planar
(c) tetrahedral
(d) linear

177. In which of the following ways does the hydride ion tend to function?
(a) An electrophile
(b) A nucleophile
(c) A free radical
(d) An acid

178. Dehydration of alcohol usually goes by
(a) E1 mechanism
(b) E2 mechanism
(c) E1 cb mechanism
(d) S_N2 mechanism

179.

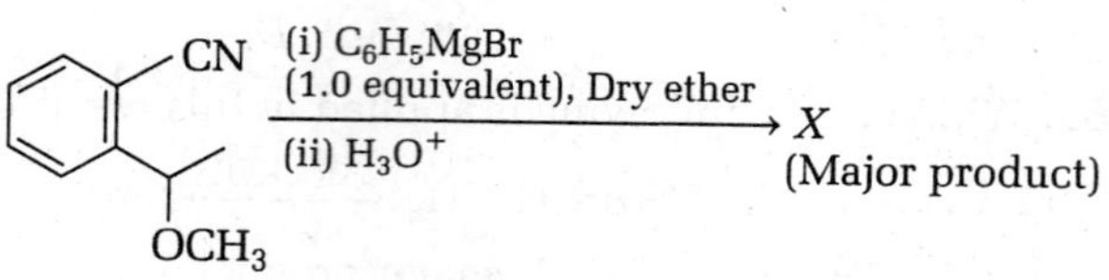

The structure of X is **[JEE Main 2021, March]**

(a) 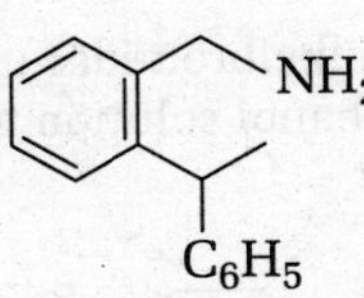 (b) 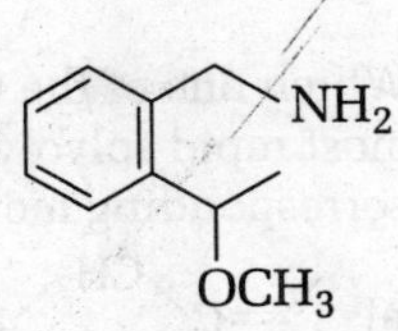

(c) 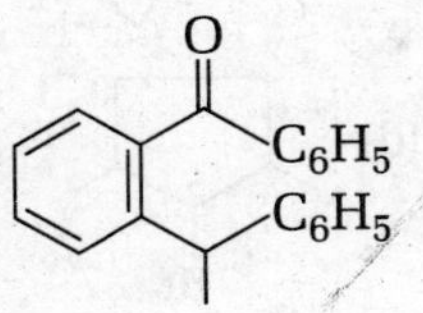 (d) 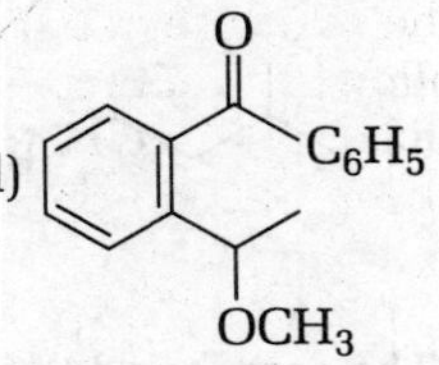

180. Which of the following will be easily nitrated?

(a) 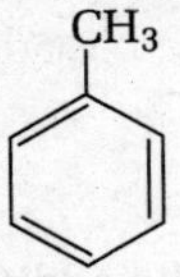 (b) 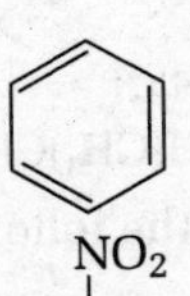

(c) CH_3NO_2 (d) 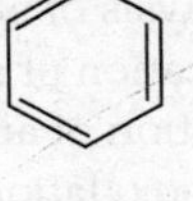

181. Following reaction,

$$(CH_3)_3CBr + H_2O \longrightarrow (CH_3)_3COH + HBr$$

is an example of

(a) elimination reaction
(b) free radical substitution
(c) nucleophilic substitution
(d) electrophilic substitution

182. In electrophilic aromatic substitution reaction, the nitro group is *meta* directing because it

(a) decreases electron density at *ortho* and *para* positions
(b) decreases electron density at *meta* position
(c) increases electron density at *meta* position
(d) increases electron density at *ortho* and *para* positions

183. The electrophile involved in the sulphonation of benzene is

(a) SO_3^+ (b) SO_3^{2-}
(c) H_3^+O (d) SO_3

184. Which of the following species does not exert a resonance effect?

(a) $C_6H_5NH_2$ (b) $C_6H_5\overset{+}{N}H_3$
(c) C_6H_5OH (d) C_6H_5Cl

185. Among the following, which is least acidic?

(a) Phenol
(b) *o*-cresol
(c) *p*-nitrophenol
(d) *p*-chlorophenol

186. Inductive effect involves

(a) displacement of σ-electrons
(b) delocalisation of π-electrons
(c) delocalisation of σ-electrons
(d) displacement of π-electrons

187. The basicity of aniline is less than that of cyclohexylamine. This is due to

(a) +*R*-effect of —NH_2 group
(b) –*I* effect of —NH_2 group
(c) –*R* effect of —NH_2 group
(d) hyperconjugation effect

188. The compound which gives the most stable carbocation ion on dehydration is

(a) $CH_3CH(CH_3)CH_2OH$ (b) $(CH_3)_3COH$
(c) $CH_2{=}CHCH_2CH_2OH$ (d) $CH_3CHOHCH_2CH_3$

189. Which of the following carbocations is most stable?

(a) $C_6H_5\overset{+}{C}H_2$ (b) $(CH_3)_3\overset{+}{C}$
(c) $(CH_3)_2\overset{+}{C}H$ (d) $CH_3\overset{+}{C}H_2$

190. Relative stabilities of the following carbocations will be in the order

$\overset{\oplus}{C}H_3$ (*A*) $CH_3\overset{\oplus}{C}H_2$ (*B*) $\overset{\oplus}{C}H_2OCH_3$ (*C*)

(a) $C > B > A$ (b) $C < B < A$
(c) $B > C > A$ (d) $C > A > B$

191. Which of the following shows S_N1 reaction most readily?

(a) 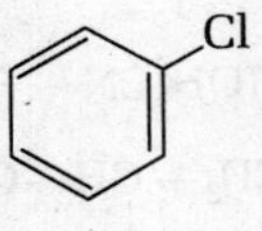 (b) 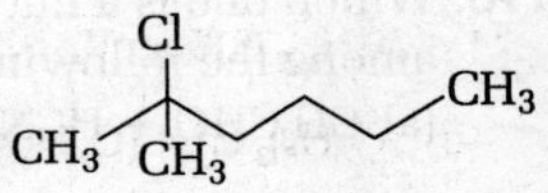

(c) 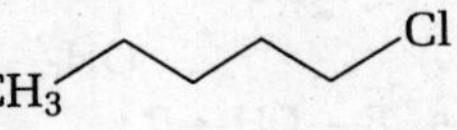 (d) 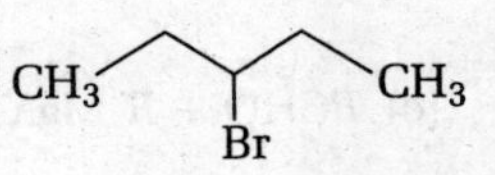

192. Formic acid is a stronger acid than acetic acid. This can be explained using

(a) +*M* effect (b) –*I* effect (c) +*I* effect (d) –*M* effect

193. Most stable carbocation is

(a) 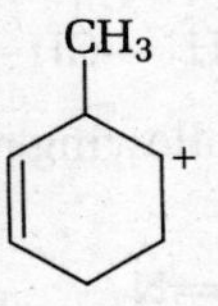 (b) 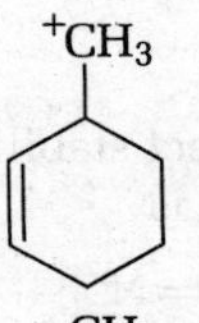

(c) 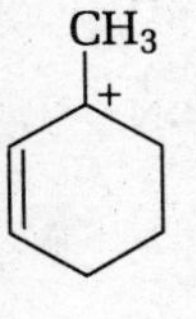 (d) 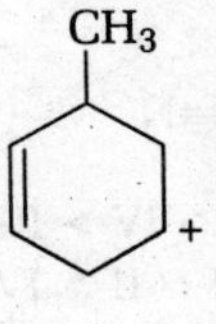

194. The product '*A*' and '*B*' formed in above reactions are **[JEE Main 2021, March]**

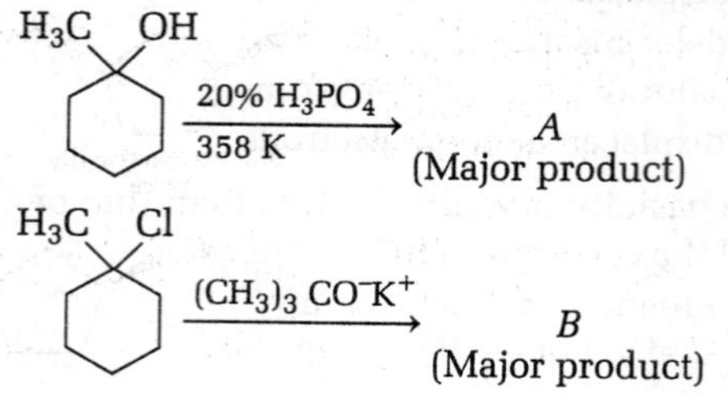

(a) A- 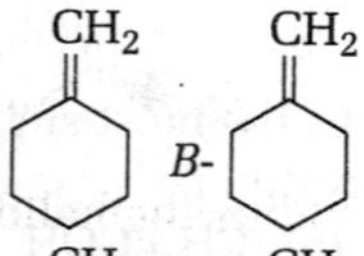
(b) A- 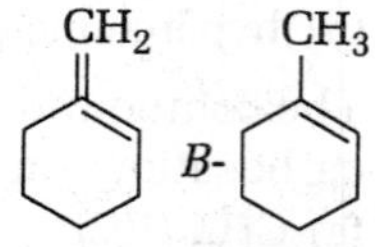
(c) A- 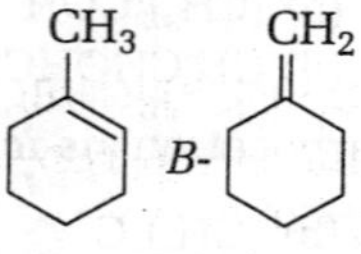
(d) A- 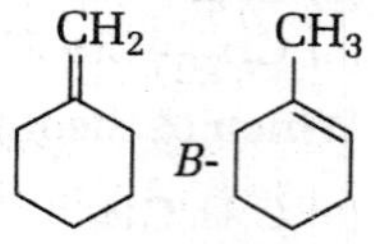

195. Which of the following is the most reactive towards electrophilic reagent?

(a) 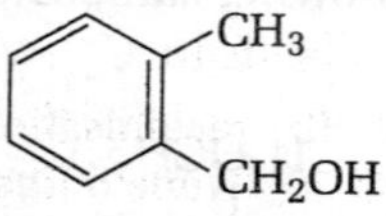
(b) 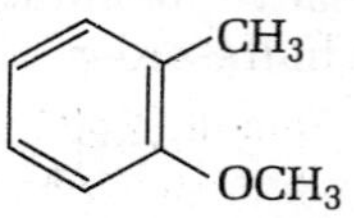
(c) 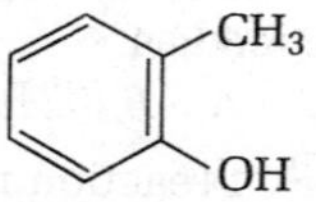
(d) 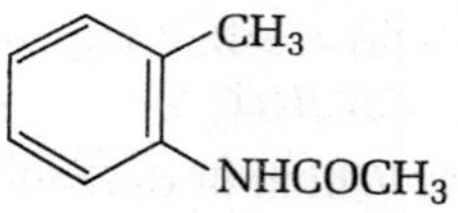

196. Which one is a nucleophilic substitution reaction among the following?

(a) $CH_3CHO + HCN \longrightarrow CH_3CH(OH)CN$

(b) $CH_3—CH{=}CH_2 + H_2O \xrightarrow{H^+} CH_3—CH(OH)—CH_3$

(c) $RCHO + R'MgX \longrightarrow R—CH(OH)—R'$

(d) $CH_3—CH_2—CH(CH_3)—CH_2Br + NH_3 \longrightarrow CH_3—CH_2—CH(CH_3)—CH_2NH_2$

197. The correct stability order of the following resonance structure is **[IIT JEE 2009]**

$H_2C{=}\overset{+}{N}{=}\overset{-}{N}$ (I) $\quad H_2\overset{+}{C}—N{=}\overset{-}{N}$ (II)

$H_2\overset{-}{C}—\overset{+}{N}{\equiv}N$ (III) $\quad H_2\overset{-}{C}—N{=}\overset{+}{N}$ (IV)

(a) I > II > IV > III
(b) I > III > II > IV
(c) II > I > III > IV
(d) III > I > IV > II

198. Which one of the following alkylbromides undergoes most rapid solvolysis in methanol solution to give corresponding methyl ether?

(a) 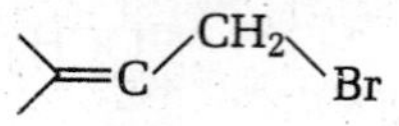
(b) 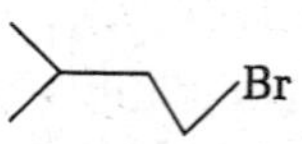
(c) 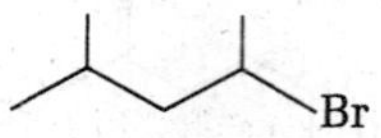
(d) 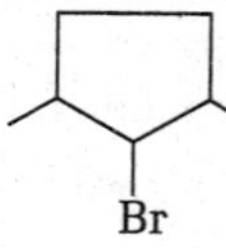

199. The compound that does not undergo hydrolysis by S_N1 mechanism is
(a) $CH_2{=}CHCH_2Cl$
(b) C_6H_5Cl
(c) $C_6H_5CH_2Cl$
(d) $C_6H_5CH(CH_3)Cl$

200. Which of the following is nucleophilic addition reaction?
(a) Hydrolysis of ethyl chloride by NaOH
(b) Purification of acetaldehyde by $NaHSO_3$
(c) Alkylation of anisol
(d) Decarboxylation of acetic acid

201. Given are cyclohexanol (I), acetic acid (II), 2,4,6-trinitrophenol (III) and phenol (IV). In these the order of decreasing acidic character will be
(a) III > IV > II > I
(b) III > II > IV > I
(c) II > III > I > IV
(d) II > III > IV > I

202. The correct order of acidity of the following compound is
(a) $RCOOH > C_2H_2 > H_2O > ROH$
(b) $RCOOH > ROH > H_2O > C_2H_2$
(c) $RCOOH > ROH > C_2H_2 > H_2O$
(d) $RCOOH > H_2O > ROH > C_2H_2$

203. $\overset{\ominus}{:}CH_2—C(=\ddot{O}:)—CH_3$ and $CH_2{=}C(—:\ddot{O}:^-)—CH_3$ are
(a) resonating structures
(b) tautomers
(c) geometrical isomers
(d) optical isomers

204. Which of the following carbon atoms is likely to possess tetrahedral geometry?

$H_2\overset{4}{C}{=}\overset{3}{C}H—\overset{2}{C}H_2—\overset{1}{C}OOH$

(a) 1
(b) 2
(c) 3
(d) 4

205. The arrangement of $(CH_3)_3C—$, $(CH_3)_2CH—$, $CH_3CH_2—$ when attached to benzene or unsaturated group in increasing order of inductive effect is
(a) $(CH_3)_3C— < (CH_3)_2CH— < CH_3CH_2—$
(b) $CH_3CH_2— < (CH_3)_2CH— < (CH_3)_3C—$
(c) $(CH_3)_2CH— < (CH_3)_3C— < CH_3CH_2—$
(d) $(CH_3)_3C— < CH_3CH_2— < (CH_3)_2CH—$

206. Among the given compounds, the most susceptible to nucleophilic attack at the carbonyl group is
(a) CH_3COCl (b) CH_3COOCH_3
(c) CH_3CONH_2 (d) $CH_3COOCOCH_3$

207. Which of the following is produced during nucleophilic addition reaction?
(a) Atoms (b) Anions
(c) Free radical (d) Cation

208. Which of the following species is paramagnetic in nature?
(a) Carbocation (b) Free radical
(c) Carbene (d) Nitrene

209. In the following carbocation; H/CH_3 that is most likely to migrate to the poistively charged carbon is

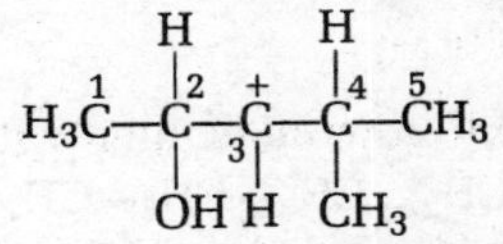

[IIT JEE 2009]

(a) CH at C-4 (b) H at C-4
(c) CH_3 at C-2 (d) H at C-2

210. Among the following compounds, the most acidic is **[IIT JEE 2011]**
(a) *p*-nitrophenol (b) *p*-hydroxybenzoic acid
(c) *o*-hydroxybenzoic, acid (d) *p*-toluic acid

211. The ascending order of stability of the carbanion $\bar{C}H_3(P), C_6H_5\bar{C}H_2(Q), (CH_3)_2\bar{C}H(R)$ and $H_2\bar{C}—CH{=}CH_2(S)$ is
(a) $P < R < S < Q$ (b) $R < P < S < Q$
(c) $R < P < Q < S$ (d) $P < R < Q < S$

212. The descending order of stability of the carbocations $C_6H_5\overset{+}{C}H_2$ (I), p-$(CH_3O)C_6H_4\overset{+}{C}H_2$ (II), p-$(NO_2)C_6H_4\overset{+}{C}H_2$ (III) and p-$(CH_3)C_6H_4\overset{+}{C}H_2$ (IV) is
(a) IV > II > I > III (b) II > IV > III > I
(c) II > IV > I > III (d) IV > II > III > I

213. The correct order of increasing reactivity of C—X bond towards nucleophile in the following compound is

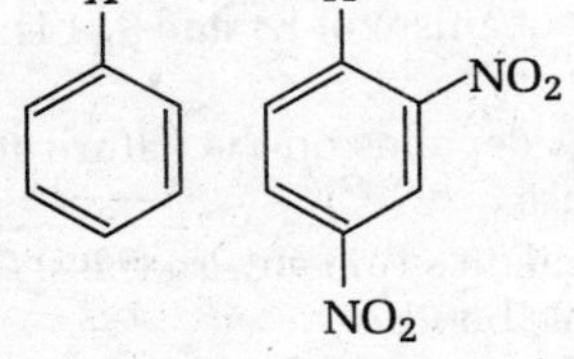

$(CH_3)_3C—X$ (III) $(CH_3)_2CH—X$ (IV)

I II III (IV)

(a) III < II < I < IV (b) I < II < IV < III
(c) II < III < I < IV (d) IV < III < I < II

214. In the following reaction sequence, the correct structure (s) of *X* is **[JEE Advanced 2018]**

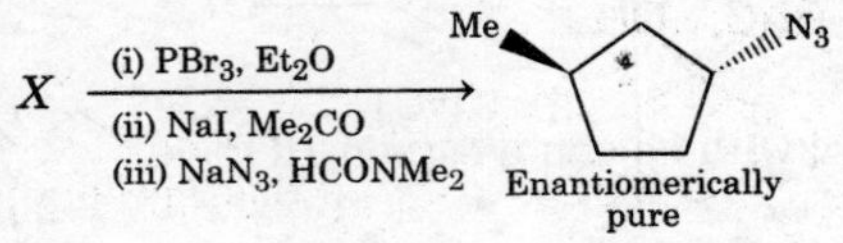

(a) 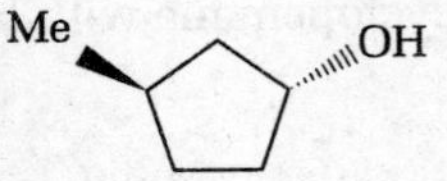 (b) 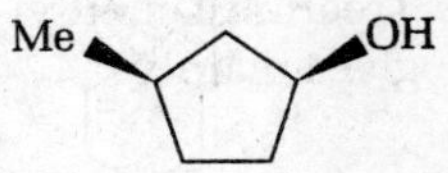

(c) 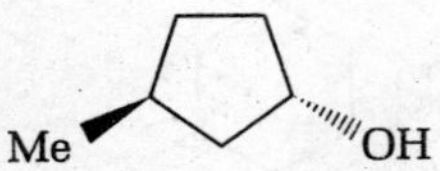 (d) 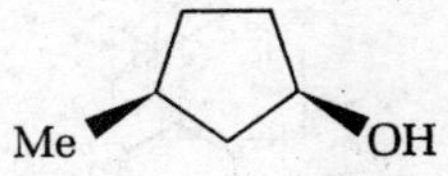

215. The S_N1 reactivity of the following halides will be in the order
(i) $(CH_3)_3CBr$ (ii) $(C_6H_5)_2CHBr$
(iii) $(C_6H_5)_2C(CH_3)Br$ (iv) $(CH_3)_2CHBr$ (v) C_2H_5Br
(a) (ii) > (i) > (iii) > (v) > (iv)
(b) (i) > (iii) > (v) > (ii) > (iv)
(c) (v) > (i) > (ii) > (iv) > (iii)
(d) (iii) > (ii) > (i) > (iv) > (v)

216. S_N1 reaction of alkyl halides leads to
(a) retention of configuration (b) racemisation
(c) inversion of configuration (d) None of these

217. The following reaction is described as

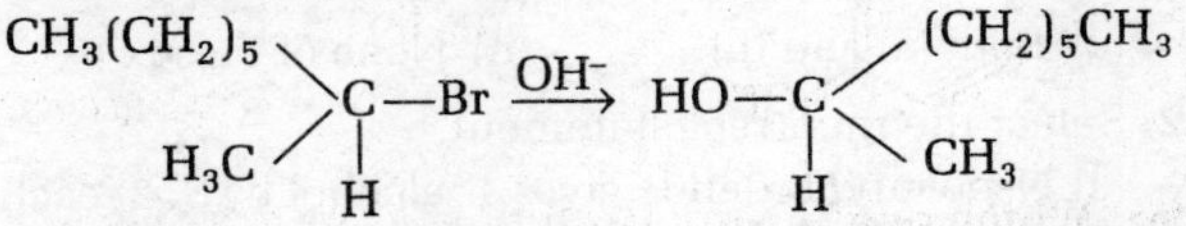

(a) S_E2 (b) S_N2 (c) S_N1 (d) S_N0

218. Consider the following reaction,

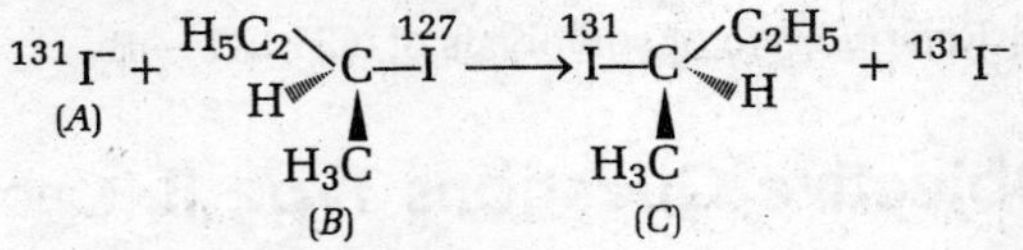

(*S*)-2-iodobutane

Select the incorrect statement for this reaction.
(a) Reaction is first-order in (*A*) and first-order in (*B*)
(b) It follows S_N2 mechanism
(c) (*C*) is (*R*)-2-iodobutane with complete inversion
(d) Intermediate is carbocation and racemisation takes place

219. In the following reaction

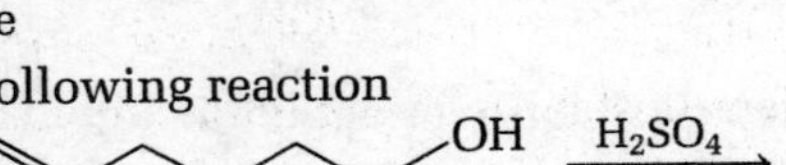

Product is

(a) a racemic mixture of 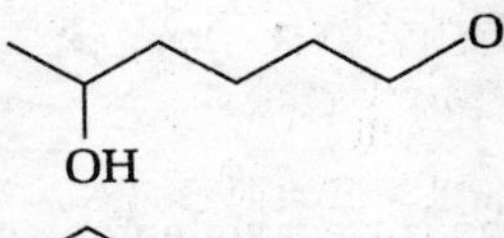

(b) a racemic mixture of 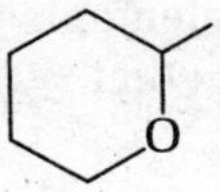

(c) a racemic mixture of 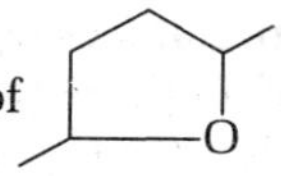

(d) diol with no chiral carbon 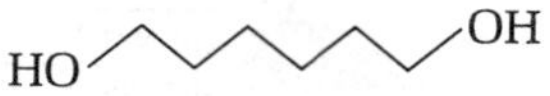

220. Treating 1-methyl-1-vinylcyclopentane with HCl gives mainly

(a) 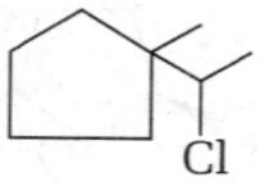 (b) 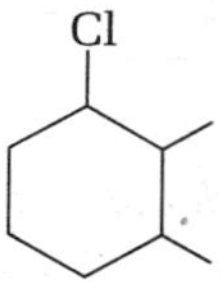

(c) 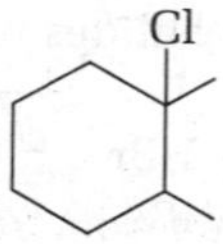 (d) 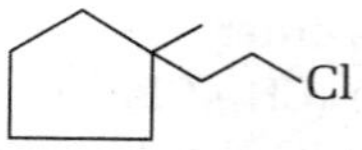

221. In the following reaction.

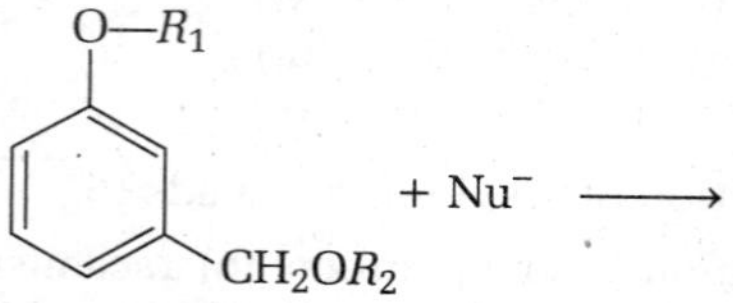

Nu^- (nucleophile) replaces

(a) R_1 (b) R_2
(c) Both (a) and (b) (d) None of these

222. Select the incorrect statement.

(a) Neopentyl bromide gives 1° alcohol by S_N2 reaction and 3° alcohol by S_N1 reaction
(b) Intramolecular S_N2 reaction is favoured in 2-bromoethanol
(c) Relative rate of solvolysis of $(CH_3)_3C—Br$, I

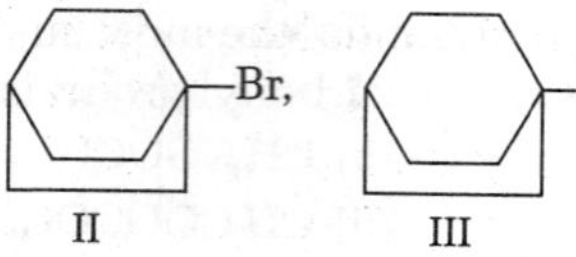 is in order III < II < I

(d) Et_2CBr and 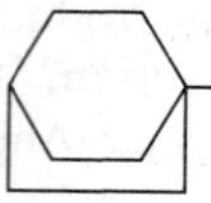 react by S_N1 mechanism.

223. A solution of (–)-1-chloro-1-phenylethane in toluene racemises slowly in the presence of a small amount of $SbCl_5$, due to the formation of **[JEE Main 2013]**

(a) carbanion (b) carbene
(c) carbocation (d) free radical

224. The order of stability of the following carbocations

$CH_2{=}CH—\overset{+}{C}H_2$ (I); $CH_3—CH_2—\overset{+}{C}H_2$ (II); 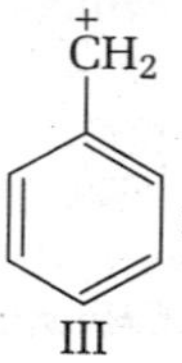 (III) is

(a) III > II > I (b) II > III > I **[JEE Main 2013]**
(c) I > II > III (d) III > I > II

225. KI in acetone undergoes S_N2 reaction with each *P, Q, R* and *S*. The rates of the reaction vary as

$H_3C—Cl$ (*P*) 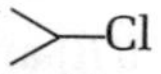 (*Q*)  (*R*) 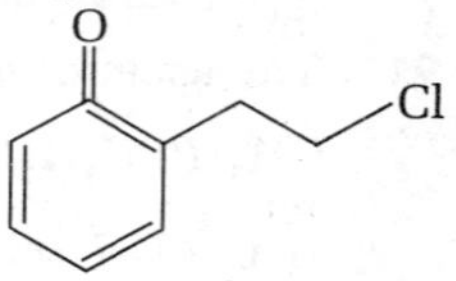 (*S*)

[JEE Advanced 2013]

(a) *P* > *Q* > *R* > *S* (b) *S* > *P* > *R* > *Q*
(c) *P* > *R* > *Q* > *S* (d) *R* > *P* > *S* > *Q*

Objective Questions Type II [One or more than one correct option(s)]

In each of the questions below, four choices are given, of which one or more than one are correct.

1. Consider the following reactions,

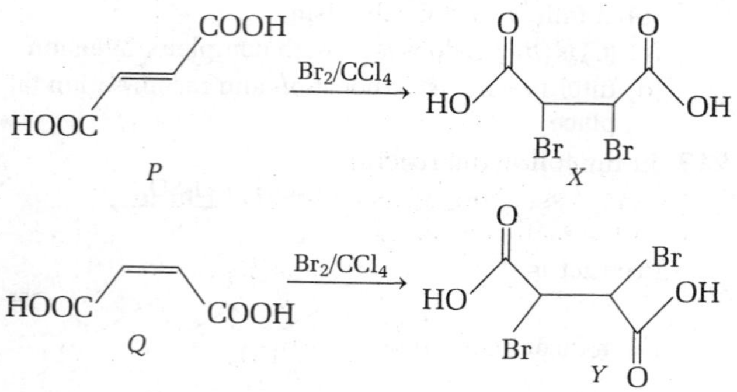

The correct statements with respect to the above pair of reactions are that

(a) The reactions are stereospecific
(b) (*X*) is erythro and (*Y*) is threo isomer
(c) (*X*) is threo and (*Y*) is erythro isomer
(d) Each of (*P*) and (*Q*) gives a mixture of (*X*) and (*Y*)

2. Select the correct statement(s) about elimination reaction.

(a) The first step in the mechanism of E1 and S_N1 is identical
(b) The rate of E1 reactions depends on the nature and concentration of the base
(c) In E1 elimination, Hofmann's rule govern the orientation of the double bond
(d) E2 elimination of adjacent groups on a six membered ring proceeds best when the leaving groups are anti, *viz.*, *trans*-diaxial

3. The IUPAC name(s) of the following compound is (are) [JEE Advanced 2017]

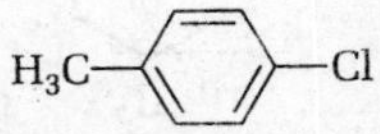

(a) 4-methylchlorobenzene
(b) 4-chlorotoluene
(c) 1-chloro-4-methylbenzene
(d) 1-methyl-4-chlorobenzene

4. Select the correct statement(s).
(a) Bridgehead halides are inert to both S_N1 and S_N2 displacements
(b) The first step in both S_N1 and E1 reactions is the same
(c) S_N2 displacements proceed with retention of configuration
(d) E2 eliminations are favoured by use of a solvent of low polarity and high concentration of a strong base.

5. Choose the correct option(s) that give(s) an aromatic compound as the major product. [JEE Advanced 2019]

(a) 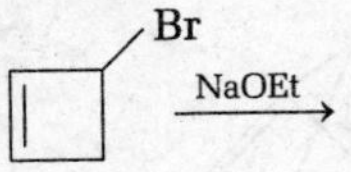

(b) 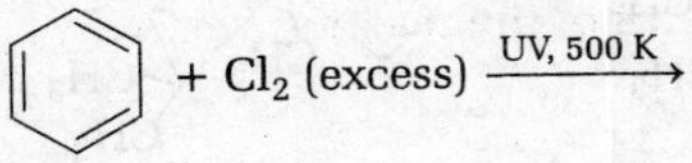

(c) 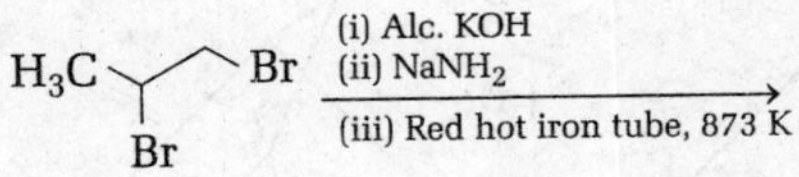

(d) 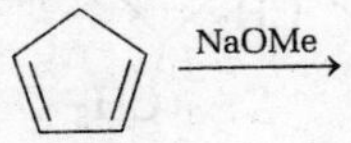

6. When cyclohexyl bromide is treated with a base, it does undergo E2 reaction to give cyclohexene. Select the correct statement(s) in this reaction.
(a) Cyclohexyl bromide has the chair conformation with the bromine atom equatorial
(b) E2 reaction is not possible in this conformation as E2 reaction requires the reacting C—H and C—Br bonds to be antiperiplanar
(c) There is changing of conformation to an unfavourable axial conformation

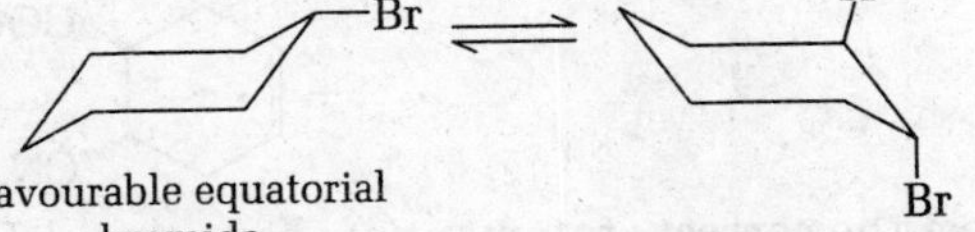

Favourable equatorial bromide

Favourable axial bromide

(d) There is cleavage of ring to minimise strain

7. Select the correct statement(s).
(a) Hydrogenation of (*A*) or (*B*) gives a mixture *cis*-1, 4- and *trans*-1, 4-cyclohexane

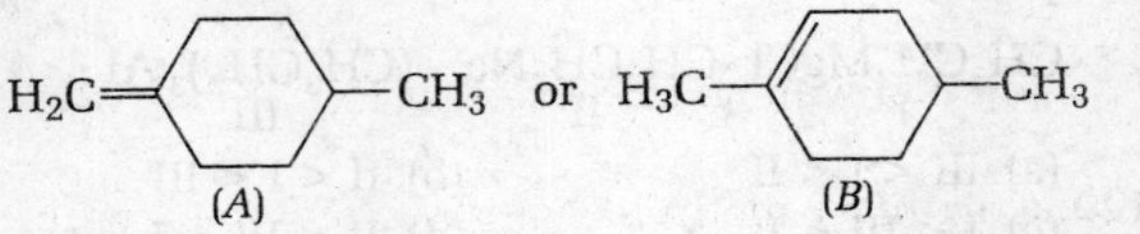

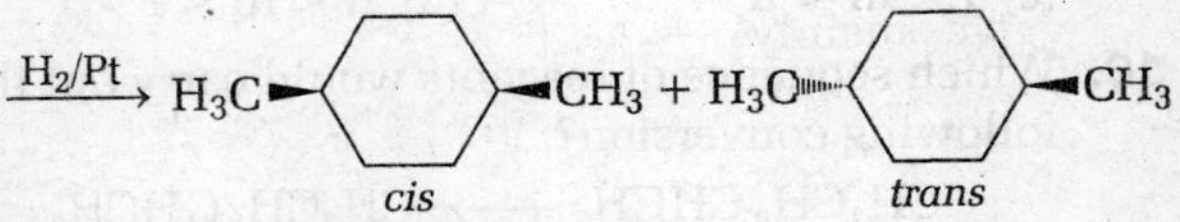

(b) Hydrogenation of (*C*) forms *cis*-isomer

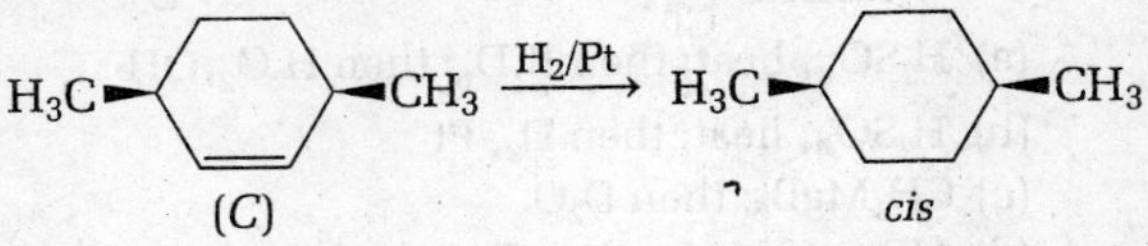

(c) Hydroboration-oxidation of (*D*) occurs from the axial direction to give major product

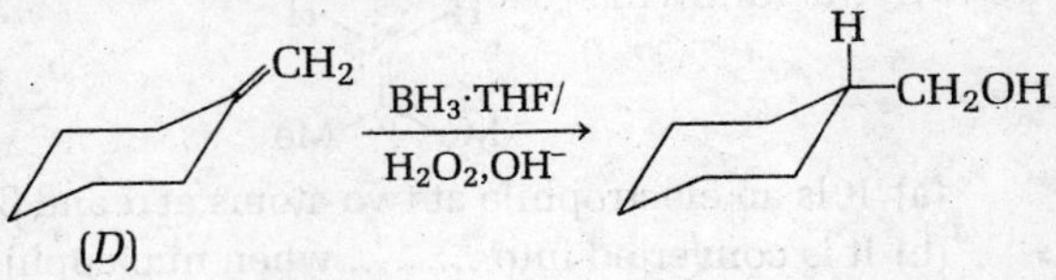

(d) Hydroboration-oxidation of (*D*) occurs from the equatorial direction to give major product.

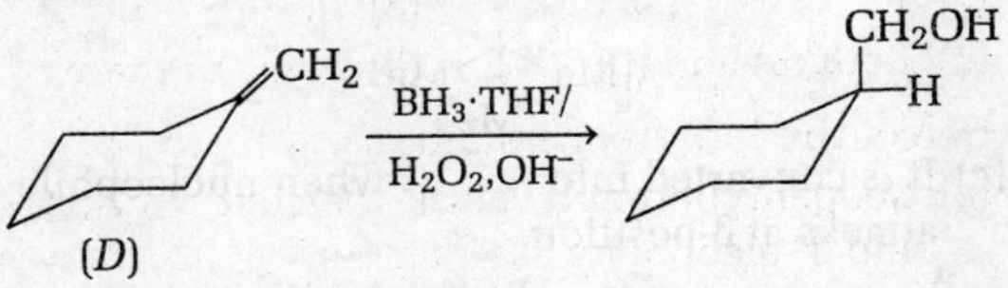

8. Two products formed by addition of HBr to 1,2-dimethylcyclohexene

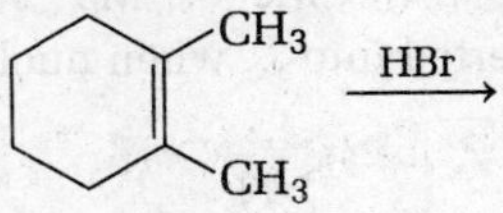

(a) are *cis*-and *trans*-1, 2-dimethylcyclohexyl bromide

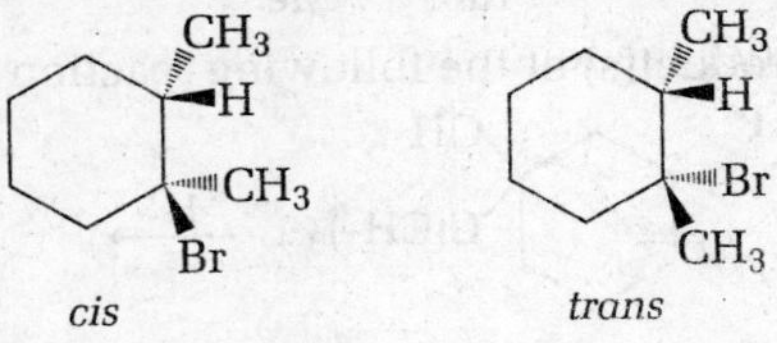

(b) cannot be regioisomers
(c) can also be formed by addition of HBr to 1,6-dimethylcyclohexene

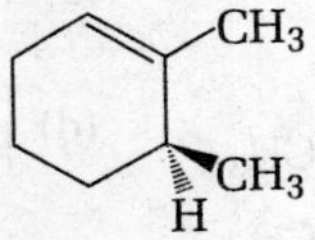

(d) have two chiral centres each

9. Rank the following species in order of increasing polarity of the carbon-metal bond (least ⟶ most polar)

CH_3CH_2MgCl (I) CH_3CH_2Na (II) $(CH_3CH_2)_3Al$ (III)

(a) III < I < II (b) II < I < III
(c) I < III < II (d) II < III < I

10. Which sequence of reagents would carry out the following conversion?

$CH_3CH_2CH(OH)CH_3 \longrightarrow CH_3CH_2CH(D)CH_3$

(a) H_2SO_4, heat; then B_2D_6; then H_2O_2, OH^-
(b) H_2SO_4; heat; then D_2, Pt
(c) CH_3MgBr; then D_2O
(d) HBr; then Mg; then D_2O

11. Select the correct statement(s) about following.

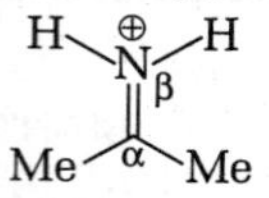

(a) It is an electrophile at two atoms at α and β
(b) It is converted into .... when nucleophile attacks at α-position

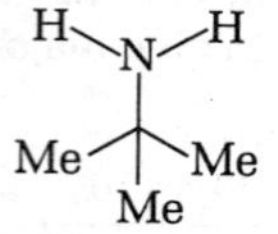

(c) It is converted into .... when nucleophile attacks at β-position.

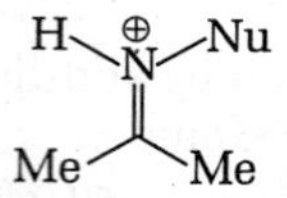

(d) It is converted into ... when nucleophile attacks at β-position.

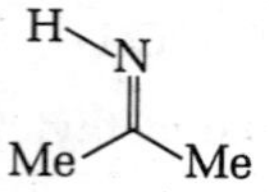

12. End product(s) of the following reaction is/are

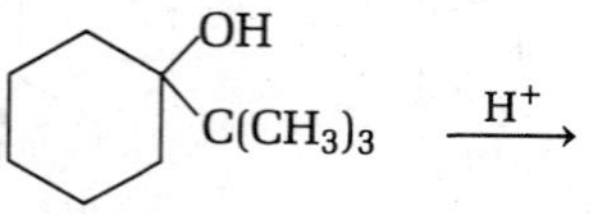

(a) 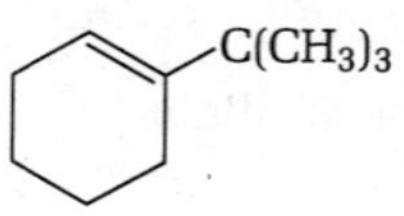 (b) 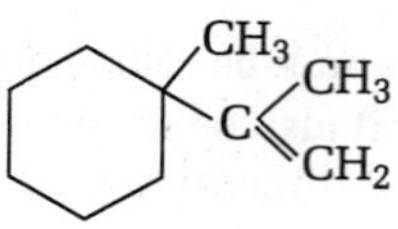

(c) 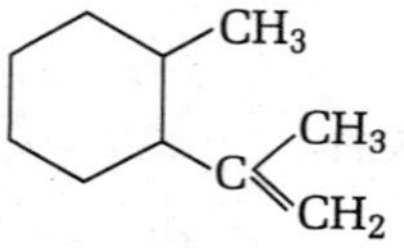 (d) 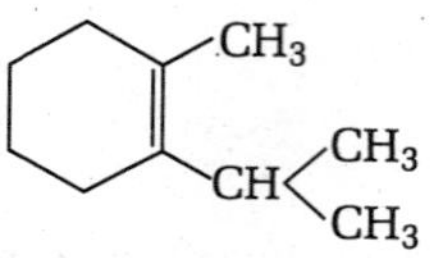

13. For the following compounds, the correct statement(s) with respect to nucleophilic substitution reactions is/are **[JEE Main 2017]**

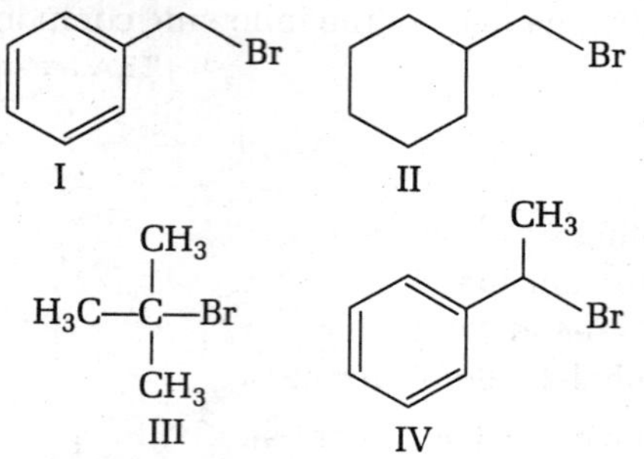

(a) I and II follow S_N1 mechanism
(b) I and II follow S_N2 mechanism
(c) compound IV undergoes inversion of configuration
(d) The order of reactivity for I, III and IV is IV > I > III

14. End product of the following reaction is

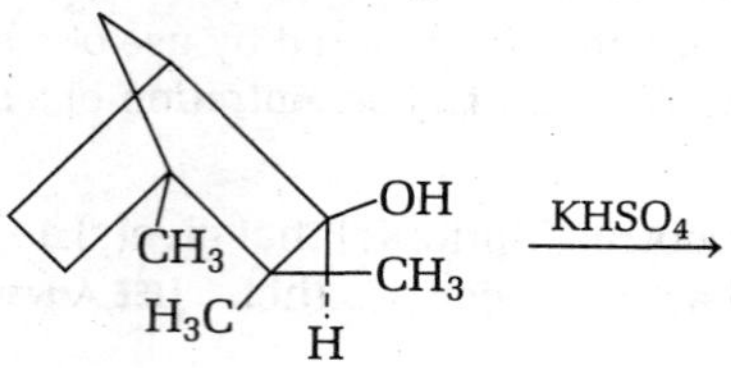

(a) 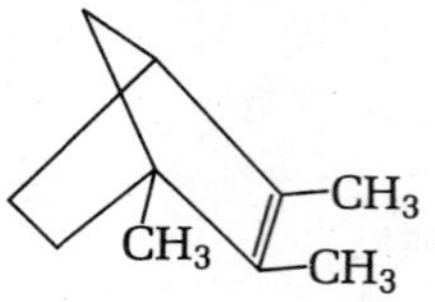 (b) 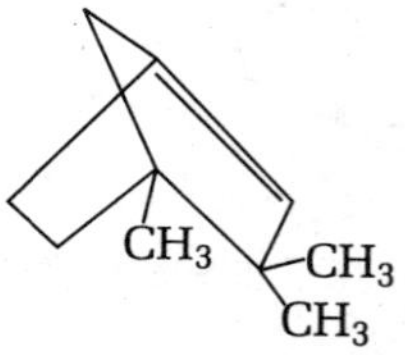

(c) 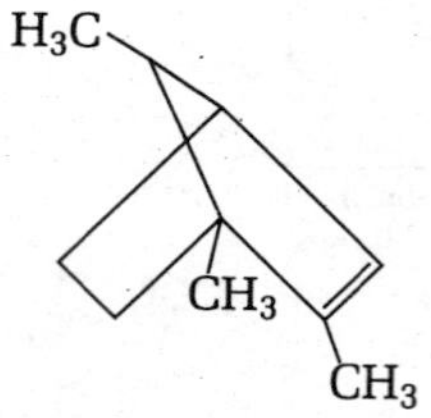 (d) 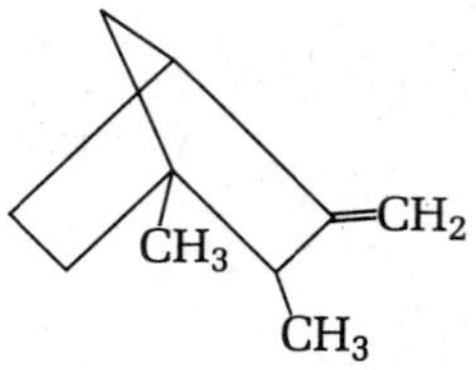

15. Consider the reactions *A* and *B*,

A. 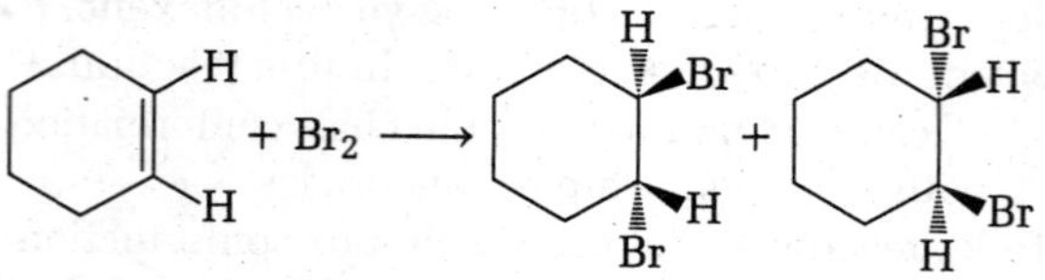

B. 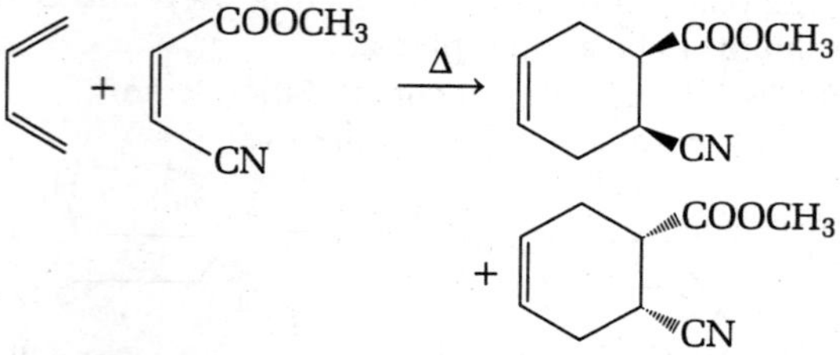

Select the correct statement(s) about *A* and *B*.

	A	*B*
(a)	Stereospecific *trans*	Stereoselective *cis*
(b)	Stereoselective *trans*	Stereoselective *cis*
(c)	Stereospecific *cis*	Stereoselective *trans*
(d)	Enantiospecific *trans*	Enantiospecific *cis*

16. 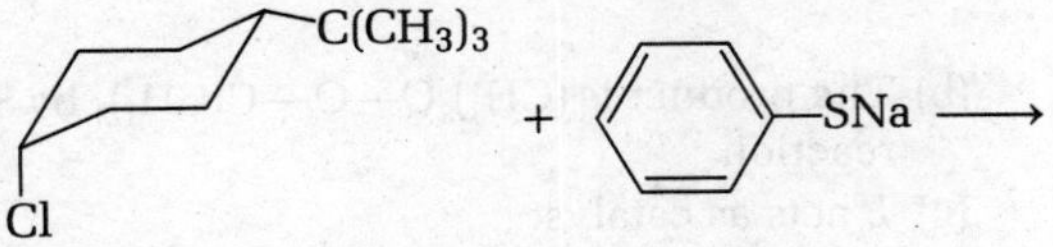

trans-4-*tert*-butylcyclohexyl chloride

Select the correct statement(s).

(a) Product is 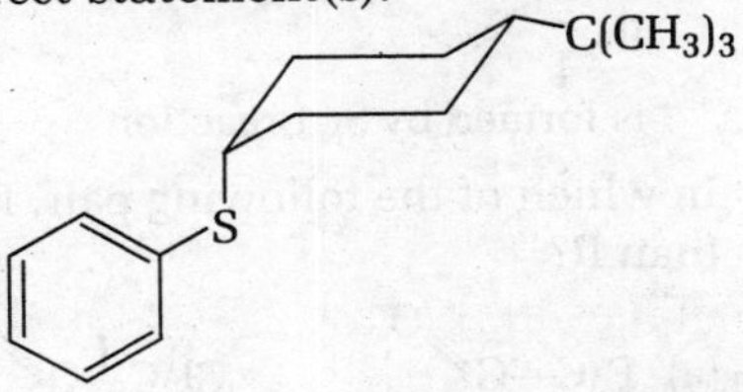

(b) Product is 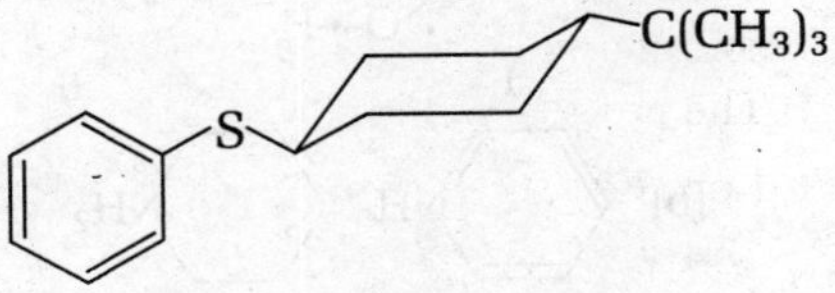

(c) S_N2 mechanism is followed

(d) There is inversion of configuration

17. In the following reaction,

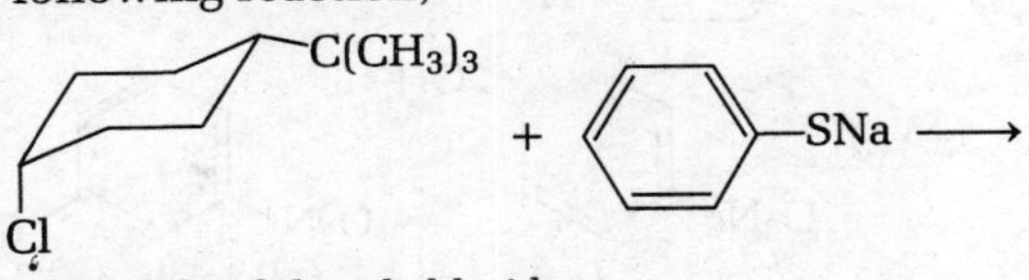

cis-4-*tert*-butylcyclohexyl chloride

(a) Product formed has inverted configuration

(b) S_N2 mechanism is followed

(c) Product is 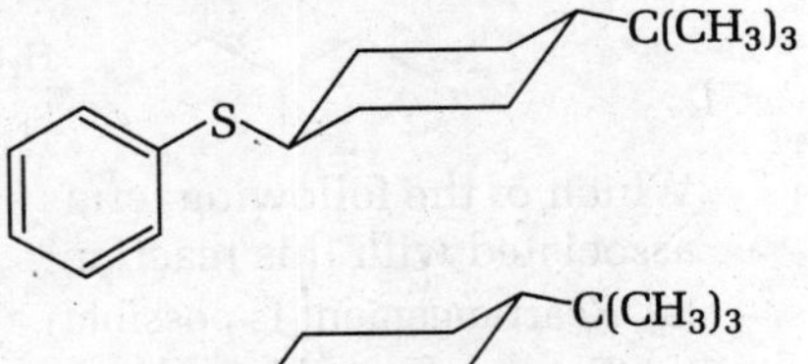

(d) Product is 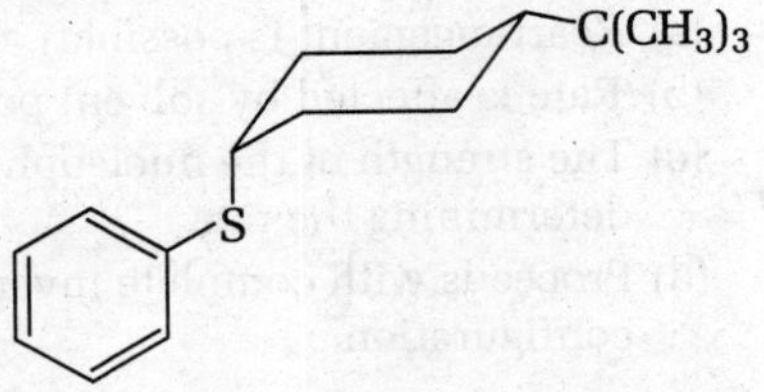

18. Select the correct statement(s) about the following reaction.

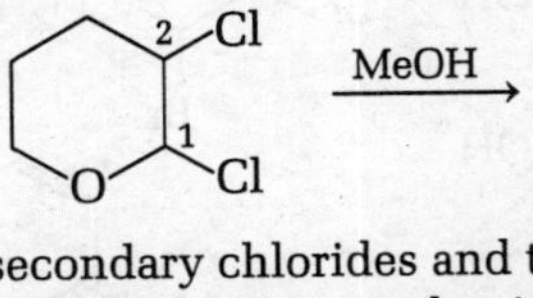

(a) Both are secondary chlorides and the one that leaves is next to oxygen by S_N1 mechanism replacing Cl by OMe

(b) Both are secondary chlorides and the one that leaves is at C—2 by S_N1 mechanism

(c) Both are secondary chlorides and the one that leaves is next to oxygen by S_N2 mechanism

(d) Both are secondary chloride and are replaced by S_N1 at C—1 and by S_N2 at C—2

19. In the following reaction,

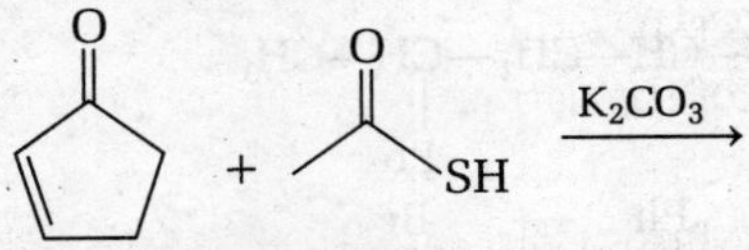

(a) there is straight forward conjugate addition of sulphur nucleophile and product is

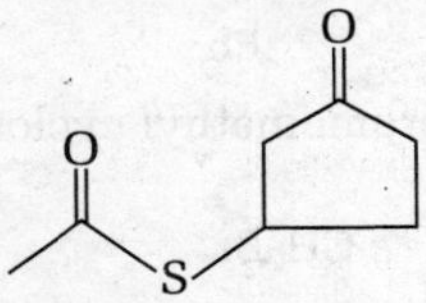

(b) one stereogenic centre is formed

(c) product is *racemic* mixture

(d) product is *meso* compound

20. Arrange the following intermediates in order of decreasing basicity.

Strongest ⟶ Weakest

$H_2C{=}CHNa$ (I) CH_3CH_2Na (II) CH_3CH_2ONa (III) $HC{\equiv}CNa$ (IV)

(a) II > I > IV > III (b) IV > I > II > III

(c) III > IV > I > II (d) III > II > IV > I

21. For the following reaction,

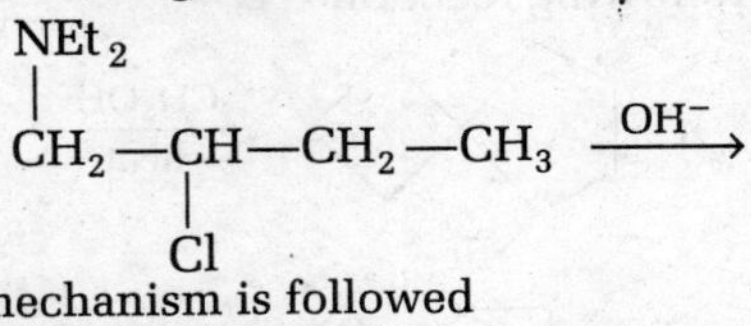

(a) S_N2 mechanism is followed

(b) rearrangement takes place

(c) product is 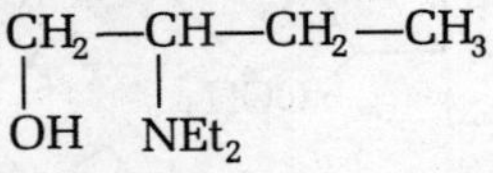

(d) product is 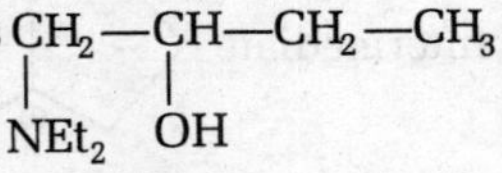

22. 2,4-diphenyl-2-pentene (*X*) is the only product upon treatment of the following alkyl halide (*Y*) with potassium *t*-butoxide

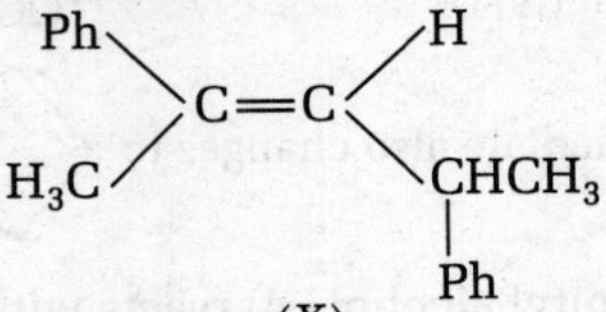

(*X*)

Y is

(a) 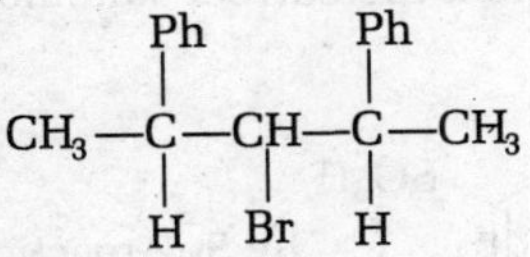

(b) 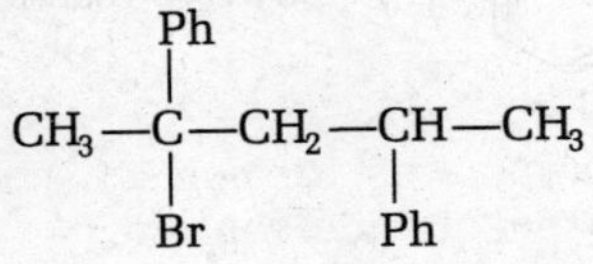

(c) 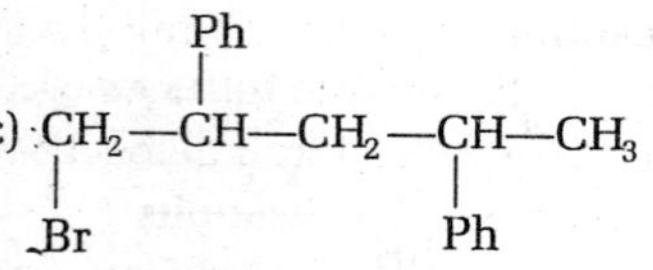

(d) 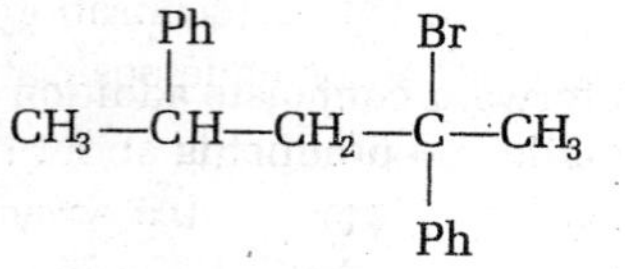

23. Solvolysis of bromomethyl cyclopentane in methanol gives

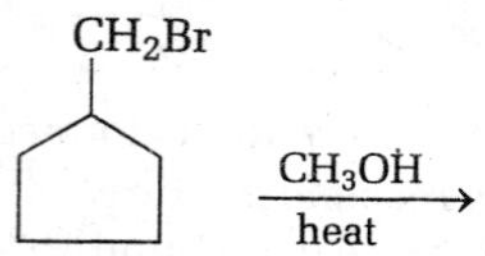

(a) 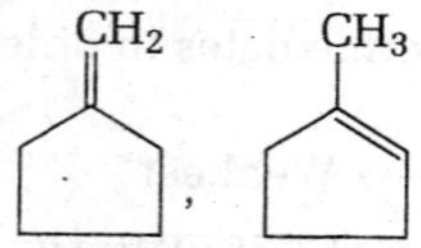
(b) 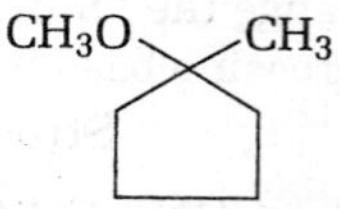

(c) 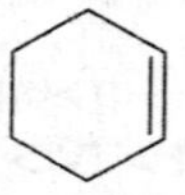
(d) 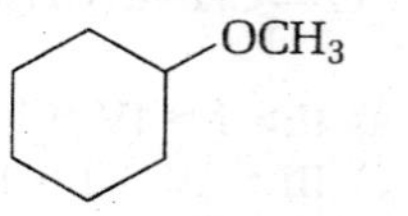

24. In the following reaction

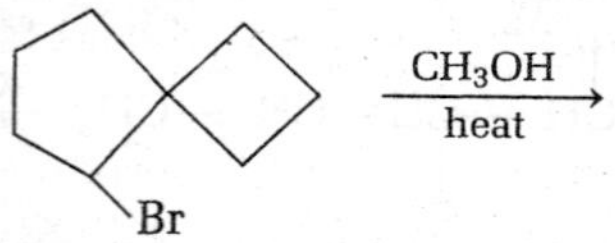

(a) product is 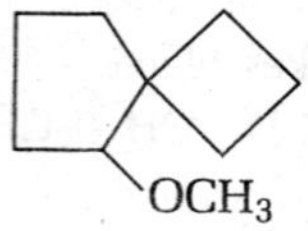 by S_N reaction

(b) it involve intermediate 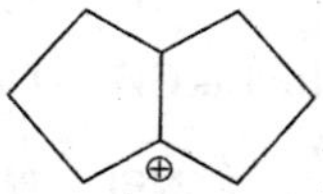

(c) intermediate changes to 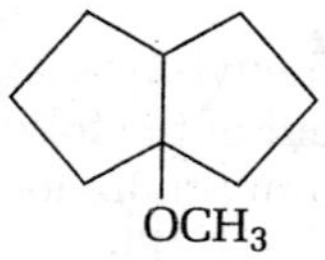

(d) intermediate also changes to 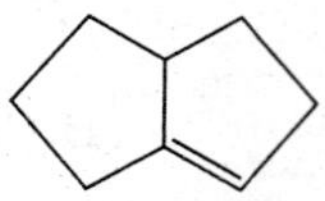

25. Tertiary butyl alcohol (*A*) reacts with *p*-bromo benzene sulphonic acid (*B*). Select the correct statement(s) for this reaction.

(a) The product is

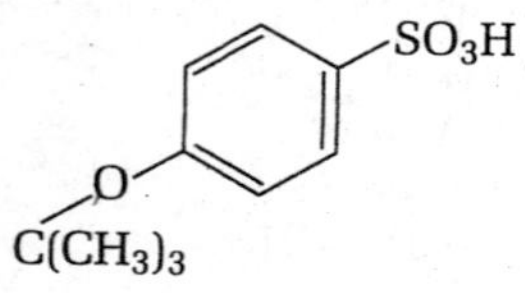 by S_N2 reaction

(b) The product is $(CH_3)_3C—O—C(CH_3)_3$ by S_N2 reaction

(c) *B* acts as catalyst

(d) 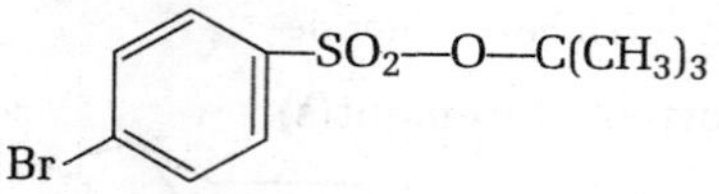

is formed by S_N1 reaction

26. In which of the following pair, I is more acidic than II?

(a) 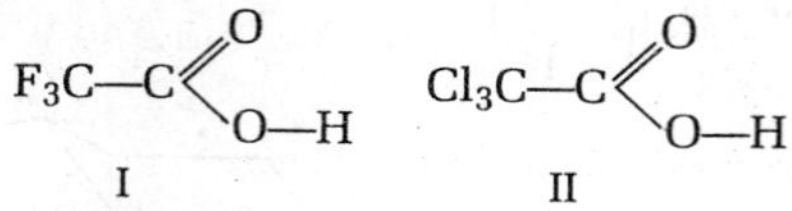

(b) 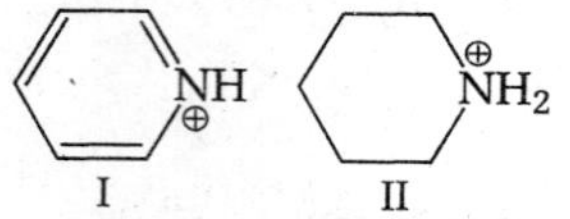

(c) 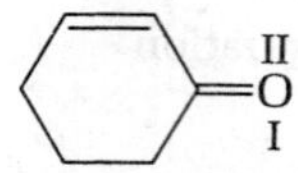

(d) 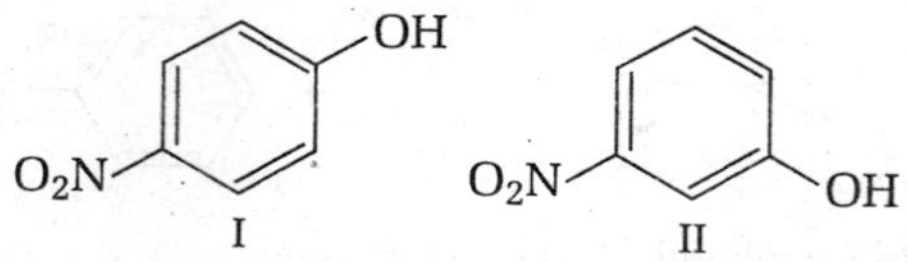

27. Taking the following example

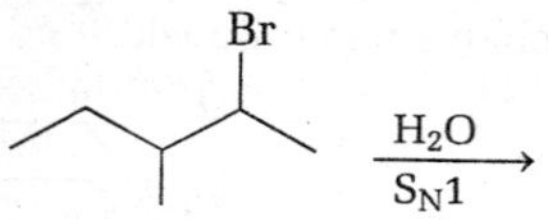

Which of the following terms are correctly associated with this reaction?

(a) Rearrangement is possible
(b) Rate is affected by solvent polarity
(c) The strength of the nucleophile is important in determining the rate
(d) Proceeds with complete inversion of configuration

28. Select the correct statements about the following reaction.

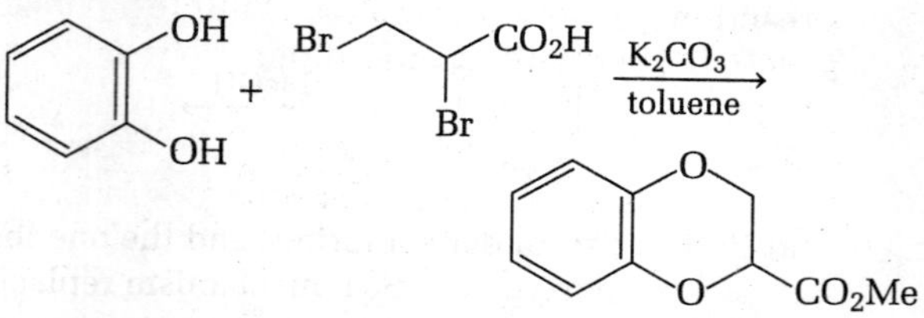

(a) Carbonate is a strong base to depronate phenols
(b) 1° bromide is displaced by S_N2 reaction and 2° bromide is displaced by S_N1 reaction
(c) Both bromides are displaced by S_N1 reaction
(d) Both bromides are displaced by S_N2 reaction

29. The correct statement(s) for the following addition reactions is (are) [JEE Advanced 2017]

(i) 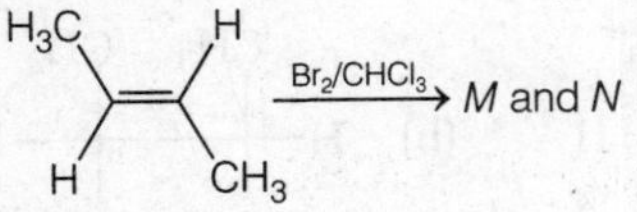

(ii) 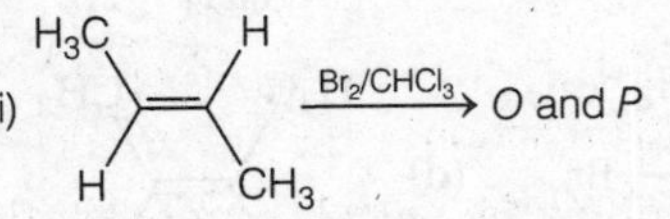

(a) (M and O) and (N and P) are two pairs of enantiomers

(b) Bromination proceeds through *trans*-addition in both the reactions

(c) O and P are identical molecules

(d) (M and O) and (N and P) two pairs of diastereomers

30. The hyperconjugative stabilities of *tert*-butyl cation and 2-butene, respectively, are due to [JEE Advanced 2013]

(a) $\sigma \to p$ (empty) and $\sigma \to \pi^*$ electron delocalisations

(b) $\sigma \to \sigma^*$ and σ-π electron delocalisations

(c) $\sigma \to p$ (filled) and σ-π electron delocalisations

(d) p (filled) $\to \sigma^*$ and σ-π^* electron delocalisations

31. Reagent(s) which can be used to bring about the following transformation is (are) [JEE Advanced 2016]

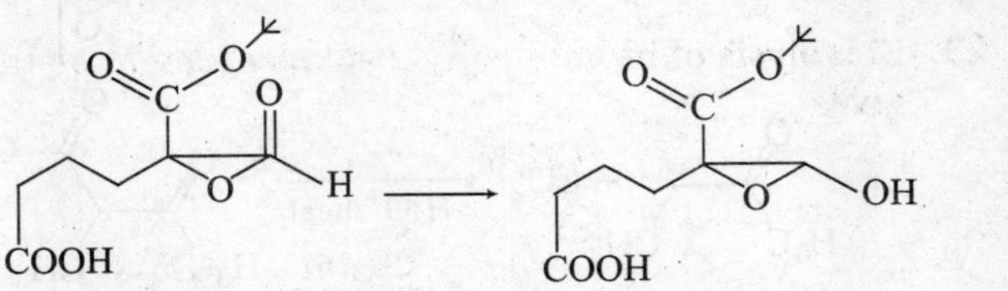

(a) $LiAlH_4$ in $(C_2H_5)_2O$ (b) BH_3 in THF

(c) $NaBH_4$ in C_2H_5OH (d) Raney Ni/H_2 in THF

Numerical Value Questions

All these questions have a Numerical value as their answer, solve the questions and write your answer.

1. Total number of isomers formed, when 2-methyl butane is subjected to monochlorination.

2. When 3-bromo-2, 2-dimethylbutane is treated with alcoholic KOH, the number of possible alkene isomers formed is ....

3. The number of πe^- present in benzyne is ....

4. When *m*-dichlorobenzene is treated with one mole of $Cl_2/FeCl_3$, the number of mono-chlorinated possible product are ....

5. Cyclic hydrocarbon molecule '*A*' has all the carbon and hydrogen in a single plane. All the carbon-carbon bonds are of same length less than 1.54 Å (C—C), but more than 1.34 Å (C—C). The C=C bond angle will be (in degree).

6. During the preparation of chloroform from ethanol by treating with Cl_2/base the number of base molecule consumed is ....

7. The number of substitution products formed, when metabromo anisole is treated with KNH_2/NH_3 ....

8. When 3,3-dimethyl-2-butanol is treated with HBr, the number of 3° carbons present in the major product formed is ....

Comprehension Based Questions

In these questions, a passage has been given followed by questions based on it. You have to answer the questions based on the passage given.

Passage 1 *Read the following short write up and answer the questions at the end of it.*

The S_N2 reaction goes with inversion of configuration at the carbon atom under attack but the S_N1 reaction generally goes with racemisation.

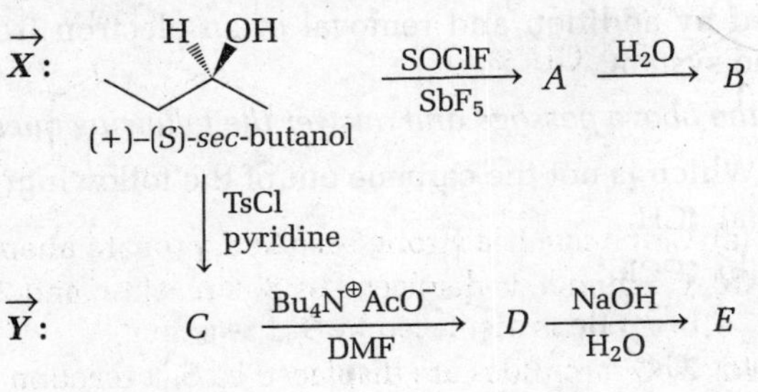

1. S_N1 reaction is

(a) X (b) Y

(c) Both (a) and (b) (d) None of these

2. B is

(a) pure (+) *S*-*sec*-butanol

(b) pure (–) *R*-*sec*-butanol

(c) *racemic* (±) *sec*-butanol

(d) None of the above is correct

3. E is

(a) pure (+) *S*-*sec*-butanol

(b) pure (–) *R*-*sec*-butanol

(c) racemic (±) *sec*-butanol

(d) None of the above is correct

Passage 2 *The following questions relate to the reaction sequence outlined below.*

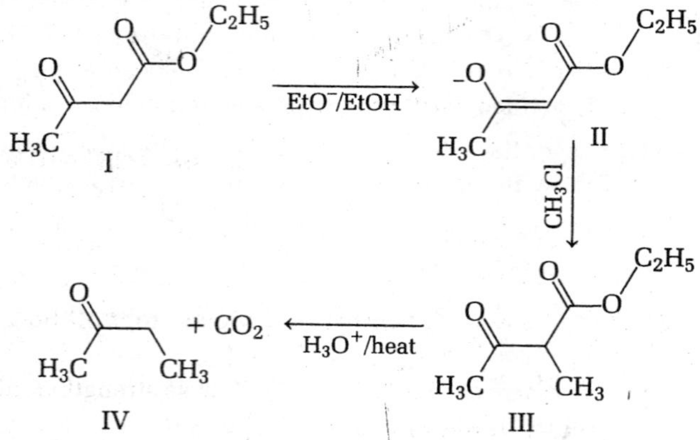

1. The first step in the sequence could be enhanced by
   (a) replacing the hydrogens at the alpha position by two alkyl groups.
   (b) replacing one of the hydrogens at the alpha position by a chlorine atom.
   (c) replacing one of the carbonyl groups with iodine atoms.
   (d) using ethanoate/ethanoic acid instead of ethoxide/ethanol.
2. Although sodium methoxide is readily available, it was not used in the first step because
   (a) it is not as strong a base as ethoxide
   (b) it would cause an undesired transesterification
   (c) it would be more difficult to hydrolyse a methyl ester than an ethyl ester
   (d) a hindered base is needed to protect the carbonyl group
3. The third step involves
   I. protonation of O in the C=O of the ester group
   II. S_N2 substitution of OC_2H_5 by OH
   III. heat-induced decarboxylation
   (a) I and II (b) I and III (c) II and III (d) I, II and III

Passage 3 Alkenes are characterised by C=C bonds. As such, they are subjected to electrophilic addition reactions. Most electrophilic additions obey Markownikoff's rule. However, there are some exceptions. Examples of alkenes are given below.

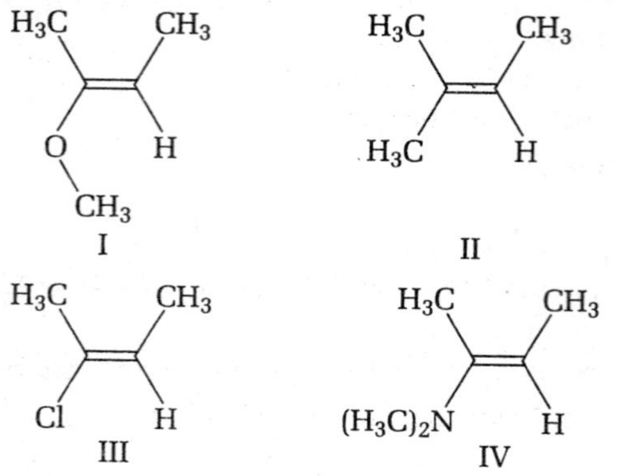

1. When HBr adds to compound 2 above, the main product is

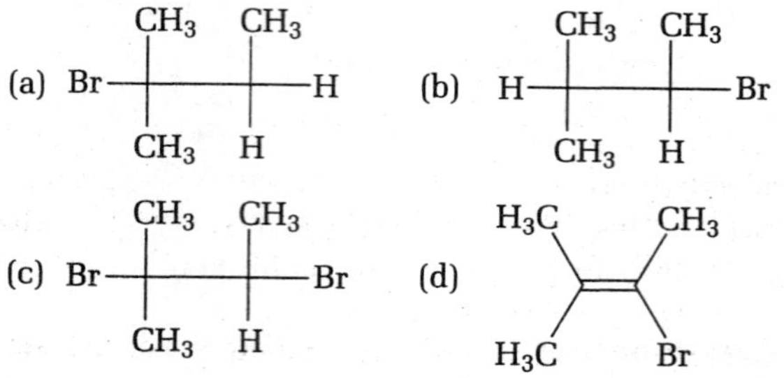

2. What is the major product of the following reaction?

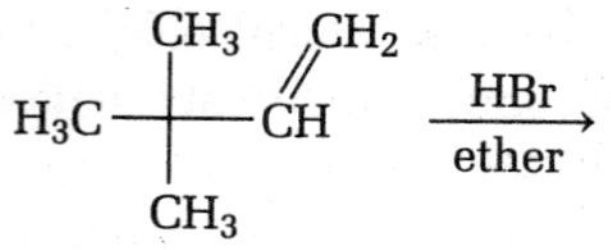

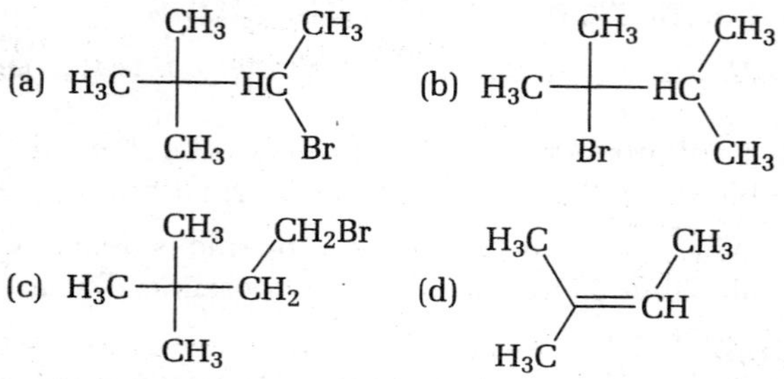

3. What is the major product of the following reaction?

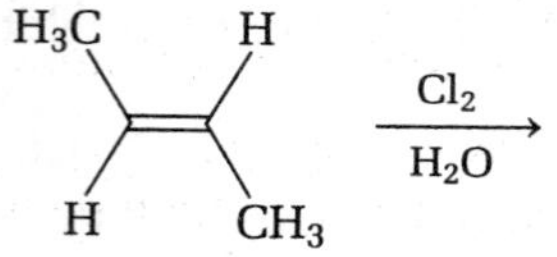

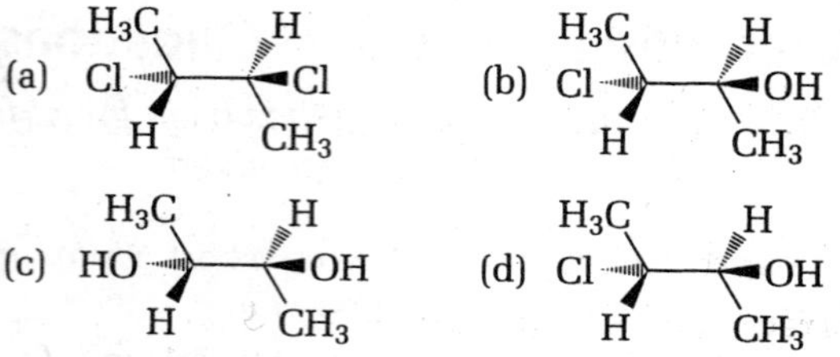

Passage 4 There is another class of intermediate called carbene. There are also radical anion and radical cation formed by addition and removal of an electron from the π-bond system.

Read the above passage and answer the following questions.

1. Which is not the carbene out of the following?
   (a) $:CH_2$
   (b) $:CCl_2$
   (c) 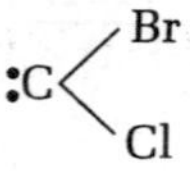
   (d) CCl_3

2. Consider the following structures of *A* and *B*.

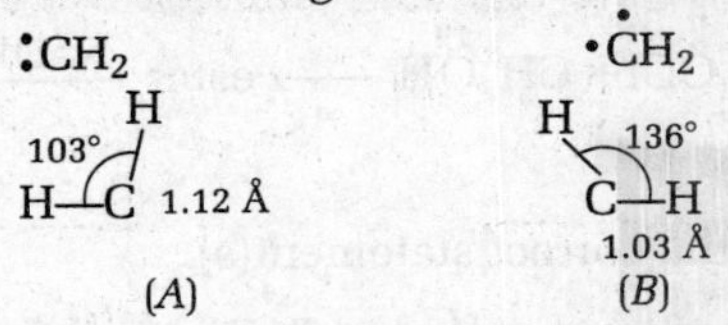

Select the correct statement about (*A*) and (*B*).

(a) (*A*) represents singlet and (*B*) represents triplet carbenes
(b) (*A*) resembles carbocation and is less stable than (*B*) which is a free diradical
(c) Non-bonding electron repulsions in *A* and *B* are identical
(d) All of the above are correct statements

3. Following chart is for the matching of intermediates with their structural properties. Which intermediate has been mismatched?

	Number of			
	σ-bond s	Unshared electron pairs	Hybrid orbitals	Hybrid state
(a) Carbocation	3	0	3	sp^2
(b) Carbanion	3	1	4	sp^3
(c) Radical	3	0	3	sp^2
(d) Singlet carbene	3	1	3	sp

Passage **5** The reaction of an electrophile with a nucleophile is the same as the reaction of a Lewis acid with a Lewis base and is termed as Lewis acid-base association reaction, as a result of which each atom in the product completes its octet (except H which completes its duplet).

Read the above passage and answer the following questions.

1. Consider the following reaction between an electrophile and nucleophile,

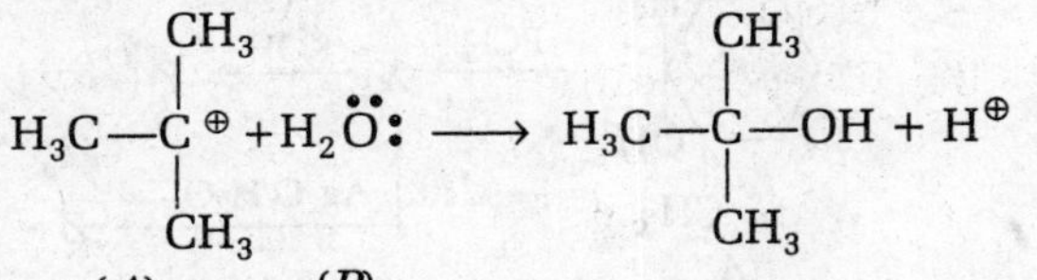

Incorrect statement(s) is/are

(a) It is a Lewis acid-base association reaction
(b) It is a Lowry-Bronsted acid-base reaction
(c) Driving force that makes ΔG negative is the completion of the octet of C and O atoms in the product
(d) *A* is an electrophile and *B* is a nucleophile

2. In which case additional reagent is required to generate an electrophile?

(a) 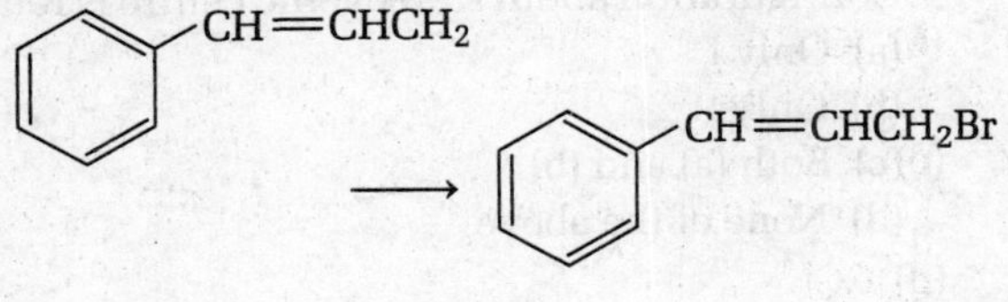

(b) 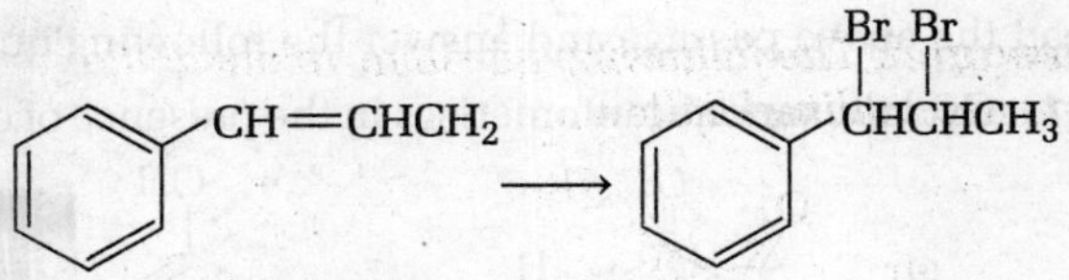

(c) 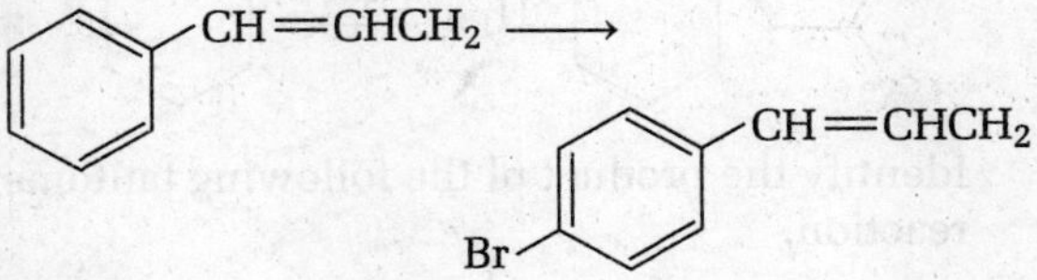

(d) In all cases

3. Which is not the correct increasing order of the property indicated?

(a) $CH_3OH < CH_3CO_2^{\ominus} < CH_3O^{\ominus}$ (base strength and nucleophile strength)
(b) $F^{\ominus} < Cl^{\ominus} < Br^{\ominus} < I^{\ominus}$ (base strength and nucleophile strength)
(c) 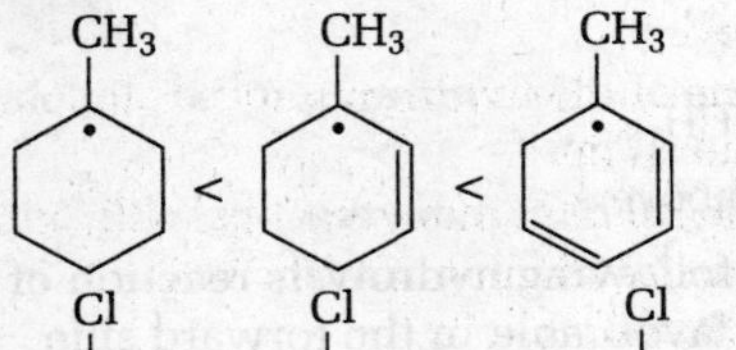 (stability of free radicals)
(d) 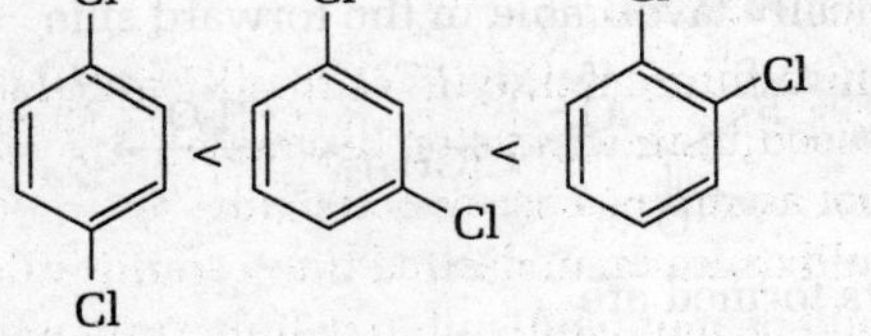 (dipole moment)

Passage **6** Reaction mechanism plays an important role in deciding the nature of product and *vice-versa*. To decide rate-determining step or nature of the product or to study reaction mechanism, reactants are radiated with isotopes and by locating the position of isotopes in the final product, reaction mechanism is worked out. In the following esterification, alcoholic O has been isotopically labelled with O-18 and in the final product O-18 goes with ester indicating that alcohol behaves as an acid and *R*COOH behaves as a base.

Actual

$$R\text{—}\overset{\overset{O}{\|}}{C}\text{—O}\,\vdots\,\text{H} + R'\text{—}\overset{18}{O}\text{—H}\,\vdots \longrightarrow R\text{—}\overset{\overset{O}{\|}}{C}\text{—}\overset{18}{O}\text{—}R' + H_2O$$

↑ This is cleaved ↑ This is cleaved

We expected

$$R\text{—}\overset{\overset{O}{\|}}{C}\,\vdots\,\text{—O—H} + R'\text{—}\overset{18}{O}\,\vdots\,\text{—H} \longrightarrow R\text{—}\overset{\overset{O}{\|}}{C}\text{—O—}R' + H_2O^{18}$$

Since H_2O does not contain $\overset{18}{O}$, it means esterification does not follow mechanism as we expected.

Read the above passage and answer the following questions.

1. Cyclohexanone tautomerises in the presence of catalyst (H^+)

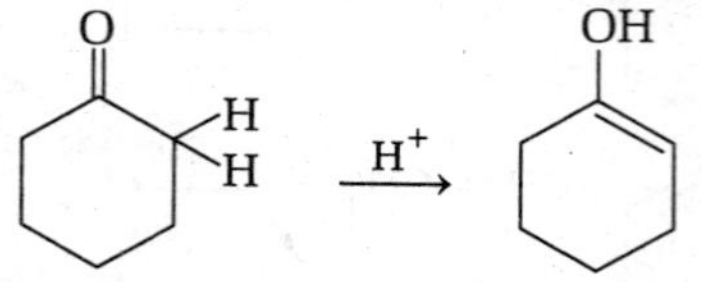

Identify the product of the following tautomerisation reaction.

$$TCH_2-\overset{O}{\overset{\|}{C}}-CH_2H \underset{}{\overset{D^+}{\rightleftharpoons}} \text{(T is tritium)}$$

(a) $TCH_2-\overset{OH}{\overset{|}{C}}=CH_2$

(b) $TCH_2-\overset{OD}{\overset{|}{C}}=CH_2$

(c) $CH_2=\overset{OT}{\overset{|}{C}}-CH_3$

(d) All of the above

2. Consider the following hydrolysis reaction of ester which is practically favourable in the forward side

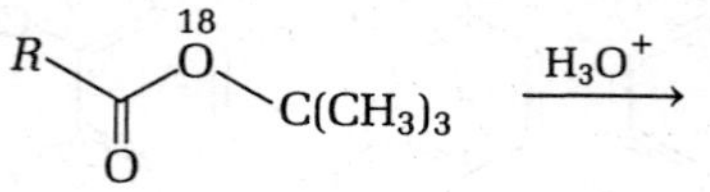

Products formed are

(a) 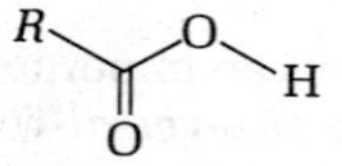 $(CH_3)_3C\overset{18}{O}H$

(b) 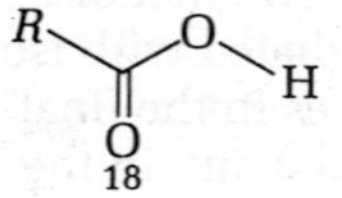 $(CH_3)_3COH$

(c) 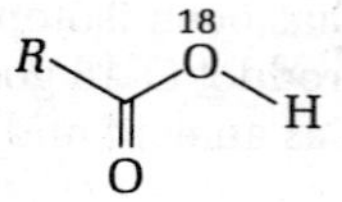 $(CH_3)_3COH$

(d) 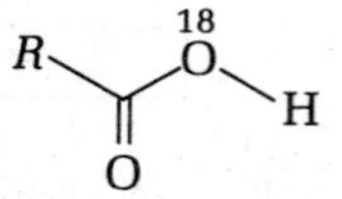 $(CH_3)_3C\overset{18}{O}H$

3. Consider the following reactions involving esterification followed by saponification.

I. 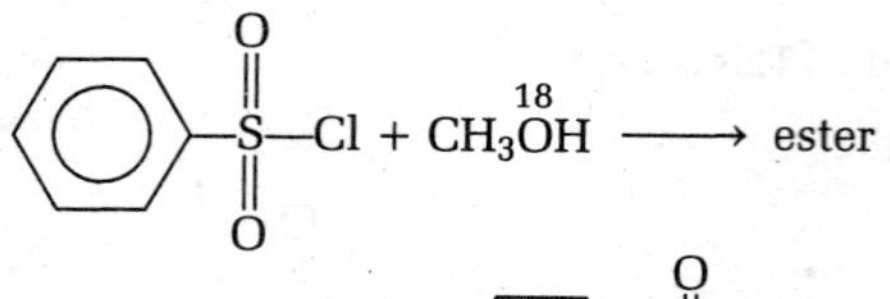

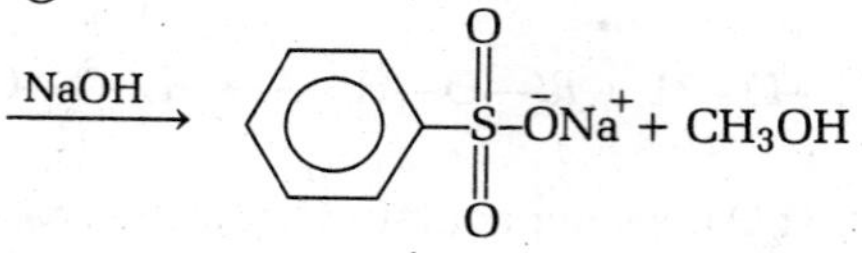

A_1 A_2

II. $CH_3\overset{O}{\overset{\|}{C}}Cl + CH_3\overset{18}{O}H \longrightarrow \text{ester} \xrightarrow{NaOH} \underset{B_1}{CH_3\overset{O}{\overset{\|}{C}}ONa} + \underset{B_2}{CH_3OH}$

Select the correct statement(s).

(a) $\overset{18}{O}$ is present in A_1 and B_1

(b) $\overset{18}{O}$ is present in A_2 and B_2

(c) $\overset{18}{O}$ is present in A_1 and B_2

(d) $\overset{18}{O}$ is present in B_1 and A_2

Passage 7 Following passage describes the reaction taking place in the compounds with stereogenic centre. Based on these facts.

Answer the questions.

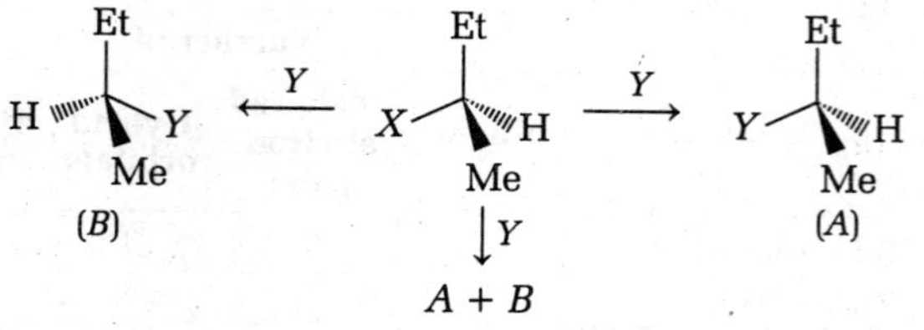

There are three outcomes for reaction at chiral centre. If A is only the compound, it is said to be stereospecific retention of configuration. If B is only the compound, it is said to be stereospecific inversion of configuration. If a mixture of above two situations occurs equally then process is known as non-stereospecific reaction or racemisation. These reactions occur through S_N1 and S_N2 mechanism.

1. In the following reactions, compounds X, Y and Z are formed with inversion/retention/racemisation w.r.t. original compound (A)

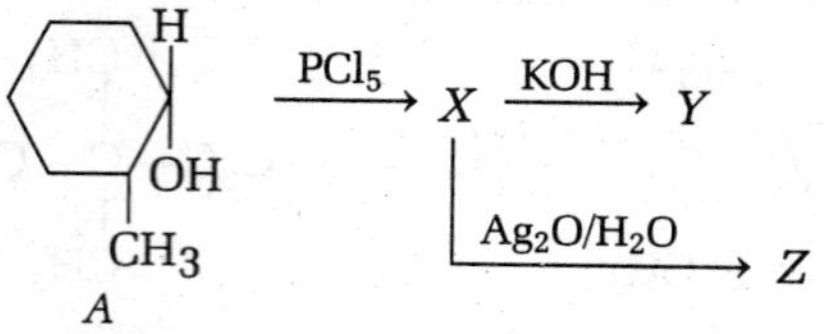

	X	Y	Z
(a)	in	re	in
(b)	in	re	re
(c)	in	in	re
(d)	re	in	in

2. R—OH has stereogenic centre and is optically active. It is subjected to following reaction

I. $ROH \xrightarrow{PCl_5} \xrightarrow{KOH}$ II. $ROH \xrightarrow{PCl_5} \xrightarrow{Ag_2O/H_2O}$

Configuration about stereogenic centre is retained in

(a) Only I

(b) Only II

(c) Both (a) and (b)

(d) None of the above

3. Consider the following reactions and select the correct alternate.

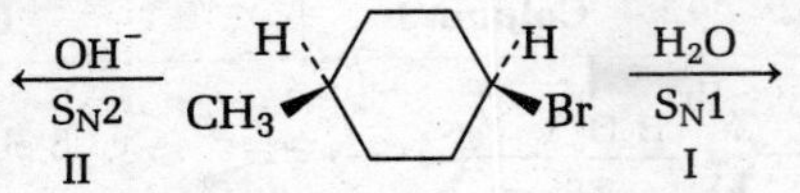

(a) there is inversion in both
(b) there is retention in both
(c) there is inversion in I and retention in II
(d) there is racemisation in I and inversion in II

***Passage* 8** Hydrolysis of the nitrogen mustard *bis* (2-chloroethyl) methyl amine (*A*) gives (*B*)

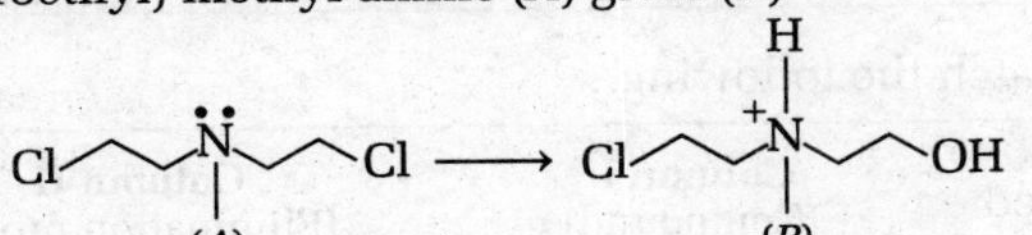

(*A*) (*B*)

Answer the following questions.

1. Intermediate of the reaction is

(a) 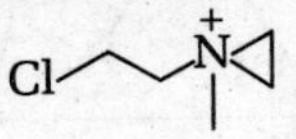 formed by internal S_N2 reaction

(b) 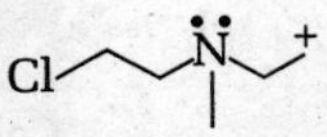 formed by cleavage of C—Cl bond in S_N1 reaction

(c) 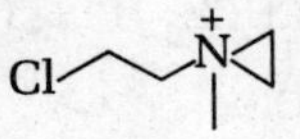 formed by internal S_N1 reaction

(b)  formed by cleavage of (C—Cl) bond in S_N1 reaction

2. (*B*) is formed from the intermediate by
(a) S_N2 reaction in which H_2O is a nucleophile and Cl is a leaving group
(b) S_N2 reaction in which H_2O is a nucleophile and nitrogen is the leaving group
(c) S_N1 reaction in which H_2O is a nucleophile and Cl is a leaving group
(d) S_N1 reaction in which H_2O is a nucleophile and nitrogen is a leaving group.

Matrix-Match Type

Given below are Matching Type Questions, with two columns (each having some items) each . Each item of Column I has to be matched with the items of Column II.

1. Match the following.

Column I (Reaction)	Column II (Type)
A. $(CH_3)_3CCH_2CHCH_3$ (Br on CH) $\xrightarrow{t\text{-butoxide}, \Delta}$ $(CH_3)_3CCH_2CH{=}CH_2$	1. Nucleophilic addition
B. $(CH_3)_3CCH_2OH \xrightarrow[\Delta]{\text{Anhyd. } ZnCl_2/\text{conc. HCl}}$ $(CH_3)_2CCH_2CH_3$ (Cl on C)	2. E2
C. 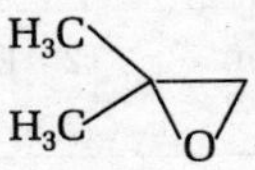 $\xrightarrow{CH_3OH/CH_3O^{\ominus}}$ $(CH_3)_3CCH_2OCH_3$	3. S_N1
D. $C_6H_5CHO + HCN \xrightarrow{Ba(CN)_2}$ C_6H_5CHCN (OH on CH)	4. S_N2

2. Match the following.

Column I (Reaction)	Column II (Intermediate)
A. 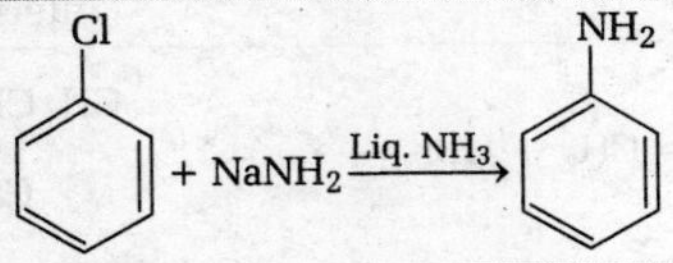	1. Free radical
B. 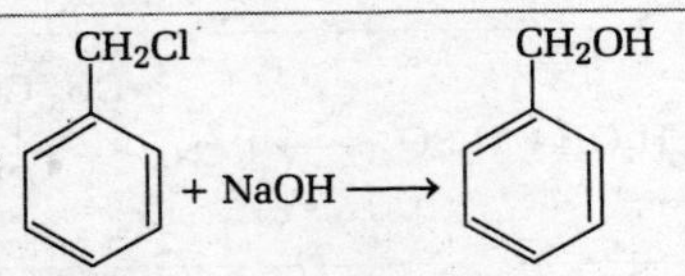	2. Carbanion
C. $CH_3\overset{O}{\overset{\Vert}{C}}CH_2\overset{O}{\overset{\Vert}{C}}OCH_2CH_3 \xrightarrow[\text{(ii) } RX]{\text{(i) } CH_3CH_2O^{\ominus}}$ $CH_3\overset{O}{\overset{\Vert}{C}}\underset{R}{\underset{\vert}{C}}H\overset{O}{\overset{\Vert}{C}}OCH_2CH_3$	3. Carbocation
D. 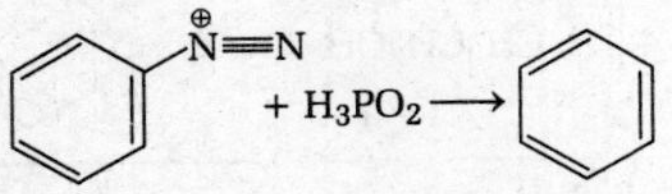	4. Benzyne

3. Match the following.

Column I (Reaction)	Column II (Type)
A. $CH_3CH{=}CH_2 + HCl \longrightarrow CH_3\underset{\mid}{C}HCH_3$ (with Cl)	1. S_N1
B. $CH_3CH{=}CH_2 + HBr \xrightarrow{(R)_2O_2} CH_3CH_2CH_2Br$	2. Dipolar addition
C. $(CH_3)_2CCH_2OH \xrightarrow[\text{conc. HCl}]{\text{Anhyd. } ZnCl_2} (CH_3)_2\underset{\mid}{C}CH_2CH_3$ (with Cl)	3. Electrophilic addition
D. $CH_2{=}CH_2 + CH_2N_2 \longrightarrow$ 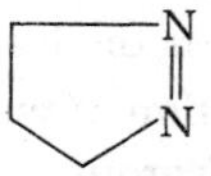	4. Free radical addition

4. Match the following.

Column I (Reaction)	Column II (Directing influence)
A. $-\overset{\oplus}{N}H_3$	1. *o, p*-director due to resonance
B. $-CCl_3$	2. *m*-director due to inductive effect
C. $-CH_3$	3. *o, p*-director due to hyperconjugation
D. $-NH_2$	4. *m*-director due to reverse hyperconjugation.

5. Match the following.

Column I (Reaction)	Column II (Most stable intermediate)
A. $CH_3\underset{\mid}{C}HCH{=}CH_2 + HBr \longrightarrow$ (with CH_3)	1. $CH_3CH\overset{\oplus}{C}HCH_3$ (with CH_3)
B. $CH_3\underset{\mid}{C}HCH_2CH_2OH + H_2SO_4 \longrightarrow$ (with CH_3)	2. $CH_3\overset{\oplus}{C}CH_2CH_3$ (with CH_3)
C. 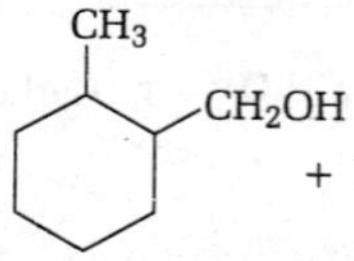 $+ H_2SO_4 \longrightarrow$	3. 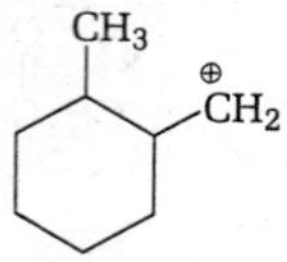
D. 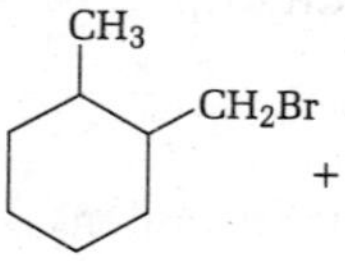 $+ CH_3CH_2OH$	4. 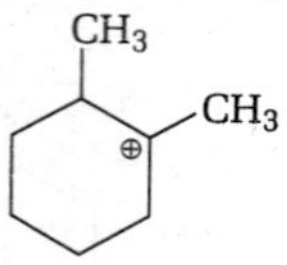

6. Match the following.

Column I	Column II
A. 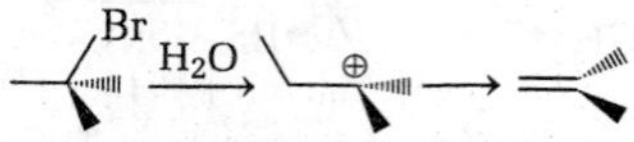	1. β-elimination
B. Two step leads to the elimination	2. 1,2-elimination
C. All bond breaking and formation occur in one single step	3. E1 mechanism
D. 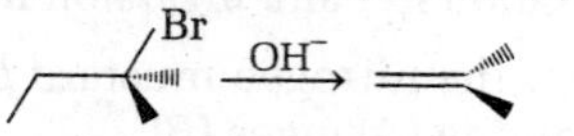	4. E2 mechanism

7. Match the following.

Column I (Compound)	Column II (Elimination product)
A. 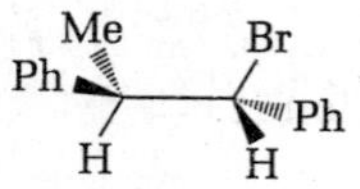 (1*S*, 2*R*)	1. 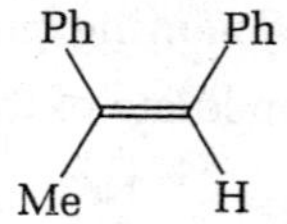
B. 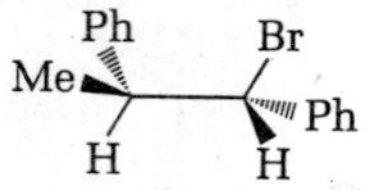 (1*S*, 2*S*)	2. 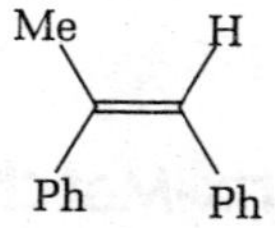
C. 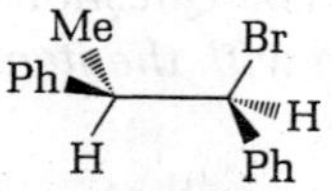 (1*R*, 2*R*)	3. 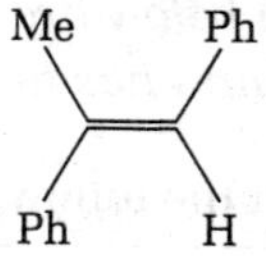
D. 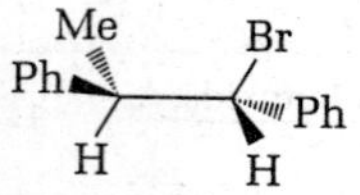 (1*R*, 2*S*)	4. 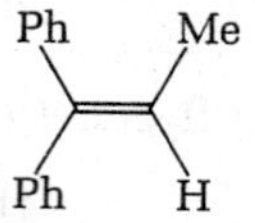

8. Match the following.

Column I	Column II
A. $CH_3{-}CHBr{-}CD_3$ on treatment with alc. KOH gives $CH_2{=}CH{-}CD_3$ as a major product.	1. E1 reaction
B. $Ph{-}CHBr{-}CH_3$ reacts faster than $Ph{-}CHBr{-}CD_3$	2. E2 reaction
C. $Ph{-}CH_2{-}CH_2Br$ on treatment with $C_2H_5OD/C_2H_5O^-$ gives $Ph{-}CD{=}CH_2$ as the major product	3. E1CB reaction
D. $PhCH_2CH_2Br$ and $PhCD_2CH_2Br$ react with same rate	4. First order reaction

9. Match the following.

Column I		Column II	
A.	$(C_6H_5)(p\text{-}BrC_6H_4)\overset{*}{C}=C(H)(Br) \xrightarrow{(CH_3)_3CO^-K^+}$ ($\overset{*}{C}$ is C^{13})	1.	$Br\text{-}C_6H_4\text{-}\overset{*}{C}\equiv C\text{-}C_6H_5$
B.	$(C_6H_5)(p\text{-}BrC_6H_4)\overset{*}{C}=C(Br)(H) \xrightarrow{(CH_3)_3CO^-K^+}$	2.	$C_6H_5\text{-}\overset{*}{C}\equiv C\text{-}C_6H_4\text{-}Br$
C.	C_6H_4XY (X and Y ortho) $\xrightarrow[NH_3]{NH_2^{\ominus}}$	3.	$C_6H_4(NH_2)(Y)$ (NH_2 and Y meta)
D.	C_6H_4XY (X and Y para) $\xrightarrow[NH_3]{NH_2^{\ominus}}$	4.	$C_6H_4(NH_2)(Y)$ (NH_2 and Y para)

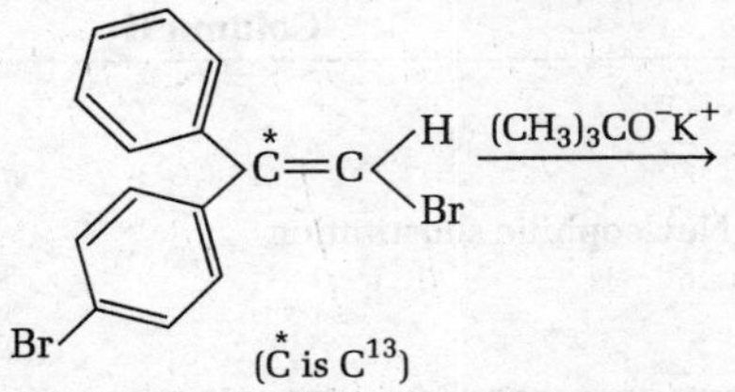

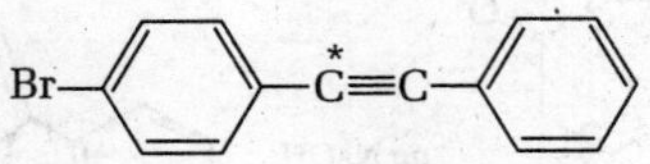

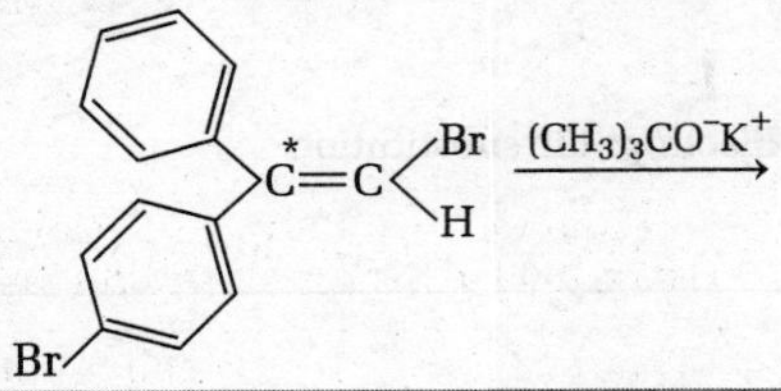

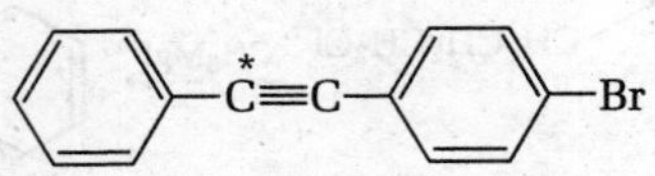

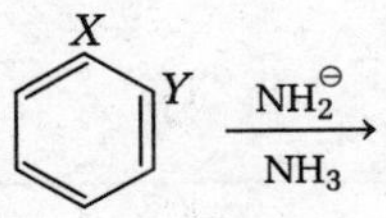

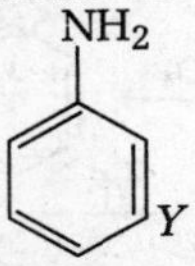

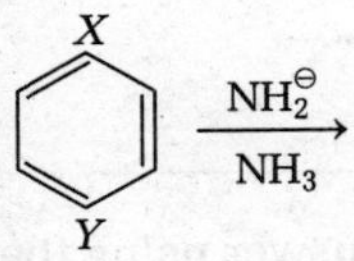

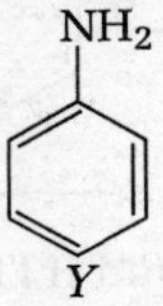

10. Match the compounds/ions in Column I with their properties/reactions in Column II.

Column I	Column II
A. C_6H_5CHO	1. gives precipitate with 2,4-dinitrophenylhydrazine.
B. $CH_3C\equiv CH$	2. gives precipitate with $AgNO_3$.
C. CN^-	3. is a nucleophile.
D. I^-	4. is involved in cyanohydrin formation.

11. Match the reaction in Column I with appropriate options in Column II. **[IIT JEE 2010]**

Column I	Column II
A. $C_6H_5\text{-}N_2Cl + C_6H_5\text{-}OH \xrightarrow[NaOH/H_2O]{0°C} C_6H_5\text{-}N=N\text{-}C_6H_4\text{-}OH$	1. Racemic mixture
B. $H_3C\text{-}C(OH)(CH_3)\text{-}C(OH)(CH_3)\text{-}CH_3 \xrightarrow{H_2SO_4} H_3C\text{-}C(=O)\text{-}C(CH_3)_3$	2. Addition reaction
C. $C_6H_5\text{-}C(=O)\text{-}CH_3 \xrightarrow[(ii)\ H_3O^+]{(i)\ LiAlH_4} C_6H_5\text{-}CH(OH)\text{-}CH_3$	3. Substitution reaction
D. $HS\text{-}C_6H_{10}\text{-}Cl \xrightarrow{Base}$ (bicyclic sulfide, S bridge)	4. Coupling reaction
	5. Carbocation intermediate

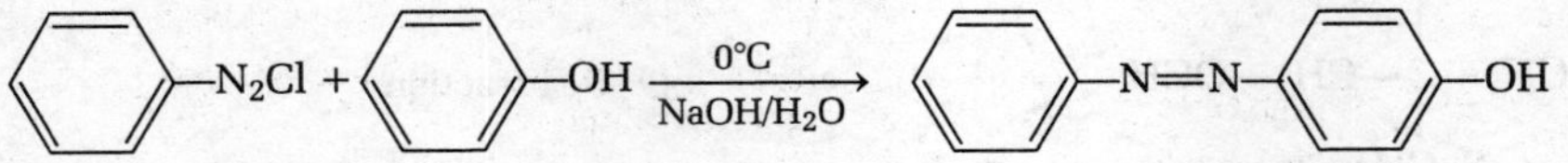

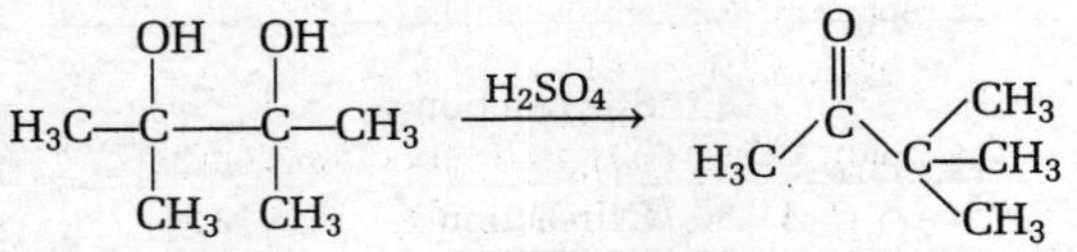

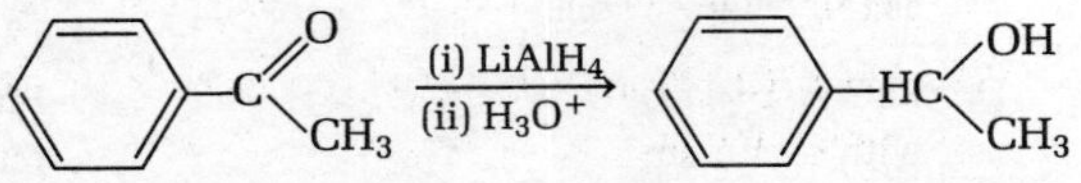

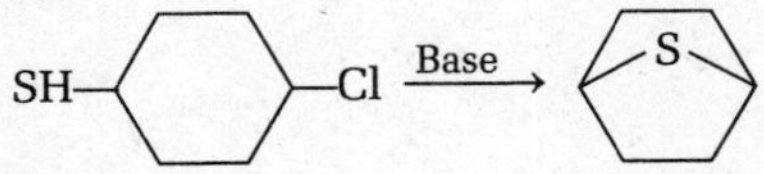

12. Match the reaction in Column I with appropriate types of steps/reactive intermediate involved in these reactions as given in Column II. **[IIT JEE 2011]**

	Column I		Column II
A.	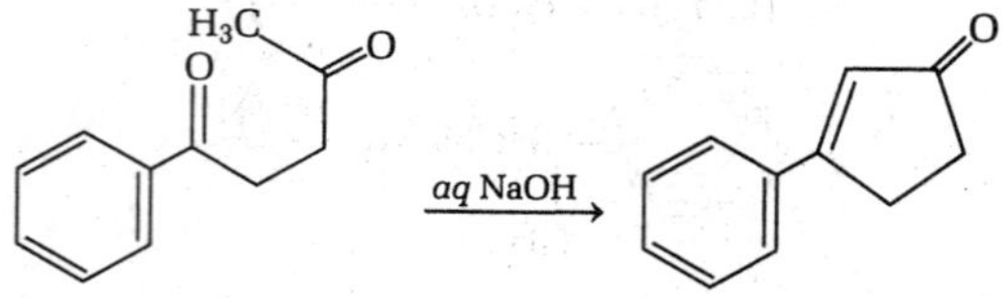	1.	Nucleophilic substitution
B.	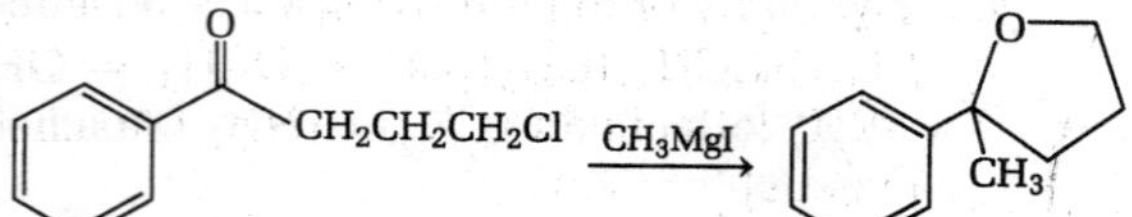	2.	Electrophilic substitution
C.	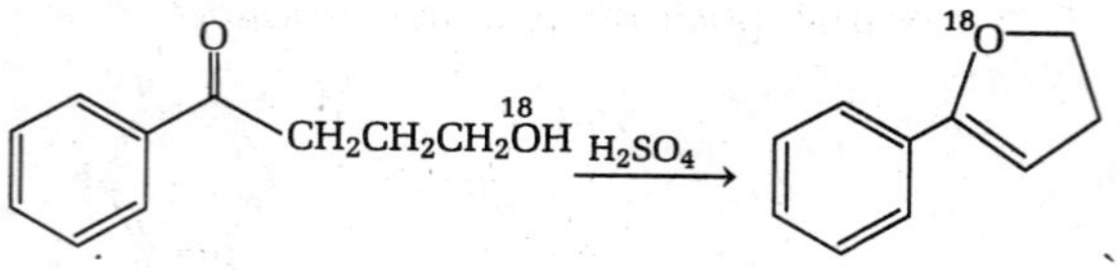	3.	Dehydration
D.	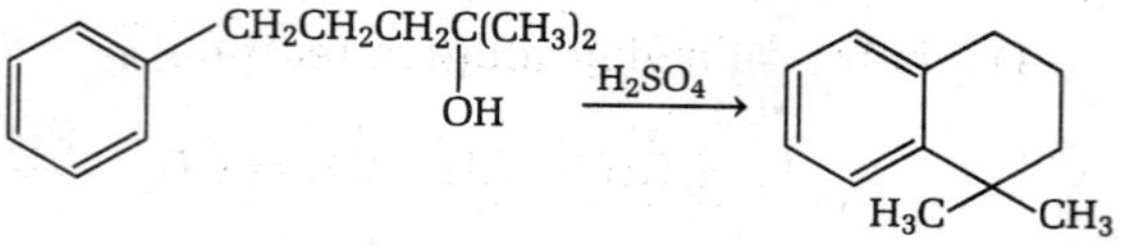	4.	Nucleophilic addition

13. Match Column I (Reactions) with Column II (Types of Reaction) and select the correct answer using the codes given below the lists.

	Column I		Column II
A.	$CH_3-C(CH_3)_2-CH_2-CH(Br)CH_3 \xrightarrow{t\text{-butoxides}/\Delta} CH_3-C(CH_3)_2-CH_2-CH=CH_2$	1.	Nucleophilic substitution
B.	$CH_3-C(CH_3)_2-CH_2OH \xrightarrow[\text{Conc. HCl}/\Delta]{\text{Anhyd. } ZnCl_2} CH_3-C(Cl)(CH_3)-CH_2-CH_3$	2.	E2 reaction
C.	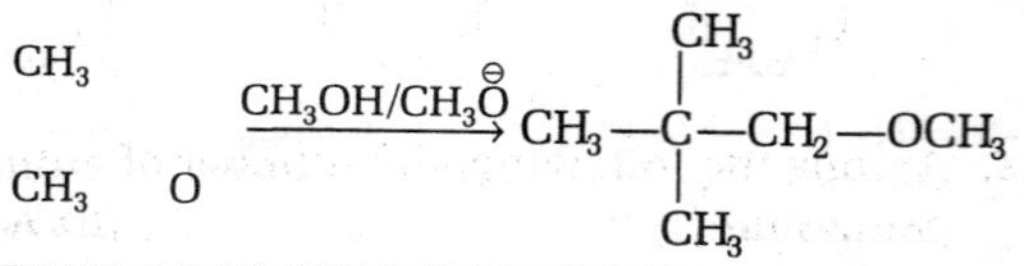	3.	S_N1 reaction
D.	$C_6H_5-\overset{O}{\overset{\parallel}{C}}-H + HCN \xrightarrow{Ba(CN)_2} C_6H_5-CH(OH)-CN$	4.	S_N2 reaction
		5.	E1 reaction

Single Integer Answer Questions

Answer of these questions is a single digit lying between 0 to 9.

1. Number of bonds to $C^{\oplus}$ in carbonium ions is ....

2. $CH_3CH\overset{\oplus}{C}HCH_3$ (with CH_3 on the second carbon). In this carbocation $H^{\ominus}$ can shift to carbon at .... to form most stable carbocation.

3. Number of α-hydrogen in given compound is

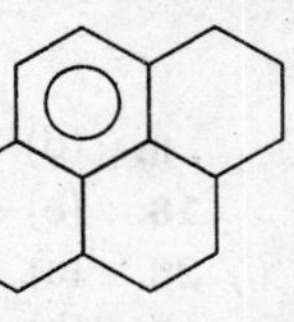

4. How many resonance structure are there for anthrocene?

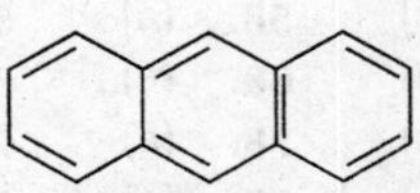

5. How many of the following would give E1 reactions?

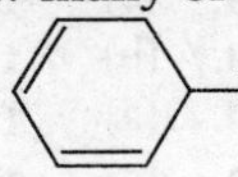
–Br,
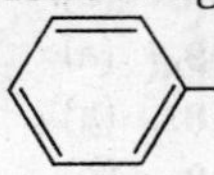
–Br, CH_3Br, CH_3CH_2Br

$(CH_3)_3CBr$,
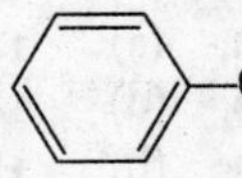
–CH_2Br,
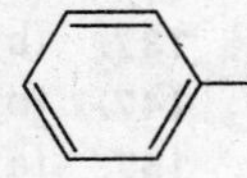
–CH_2CH_2Br

6. In the following reaction,

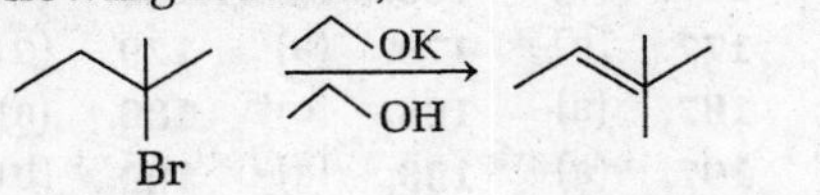

(A) (B)

What is the concentration of A if

$1\times10^{-5}\ Ms^{-1} = 2\times10^{-6}\ s^{-1}\ [A]$?

7. In the following how many are better leaving group, than CN^-?

$I^-, Br^-, Cl^-, OH^-, CH_3COO^-, CH_3O^-, C_6H_5SO_3^-, NH_2^-$

8. How many of the following S_N reactions will give product by rearrangement ?

I. $(CH_3)_3C—Cl + H_2O \longrightarrow$

II.
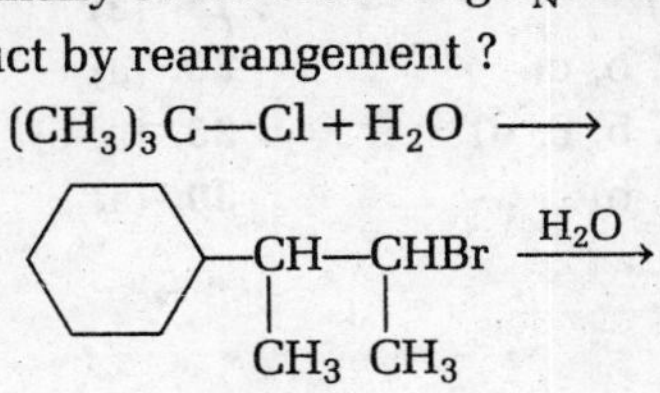

III.
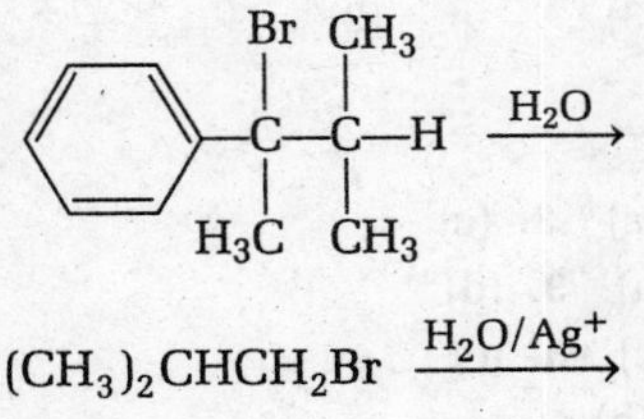

IV. $(CH_3)_2CHCH_2Br \xrightarrow{H_2O/Ag^+}$

V. $(CH_3)_3CCH_2Br \xrightarrow{H_2O/Ag^+}$

VI.
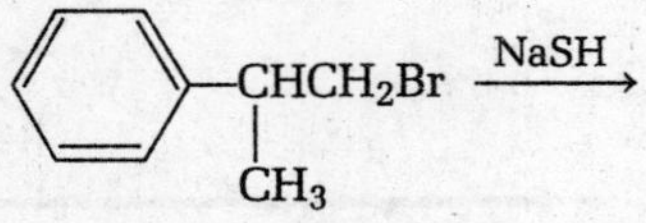

9. How many of the following show +*I*-effect?
CH_3, CH_3CH_2, $(CH_3)_2CH$, $—OCH_3$, $—OH$, $—NO_2$, $—NH_2$ (attached to CH_3), $—NH_2$ (attached to benzene nucleus)

10. In the bromination of following compound, Br goes to which position as major product?

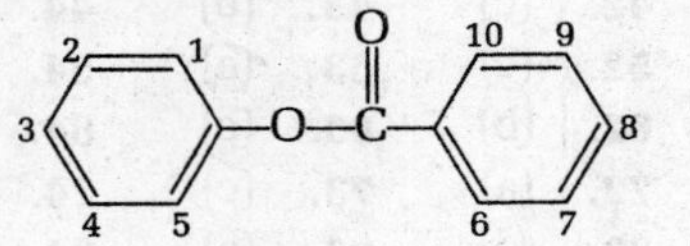

11. In the following addition reaction,

$\overset{5}{C}H_3\overset{4}{C}H_2—\overset{3}{C}H(CH_3)—\overset{2}{C}H=\overset{1}{C}H_2 \xrightarrow{H_3O^+}$

—OH group occupies which position?

12. How many of the following are stronger acids than phenol?

CH_3OH,
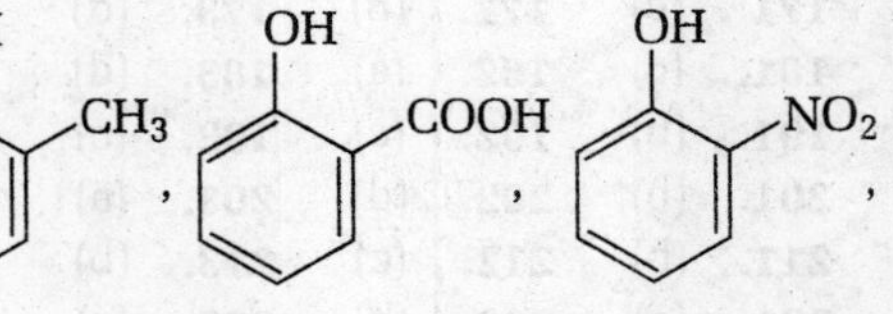

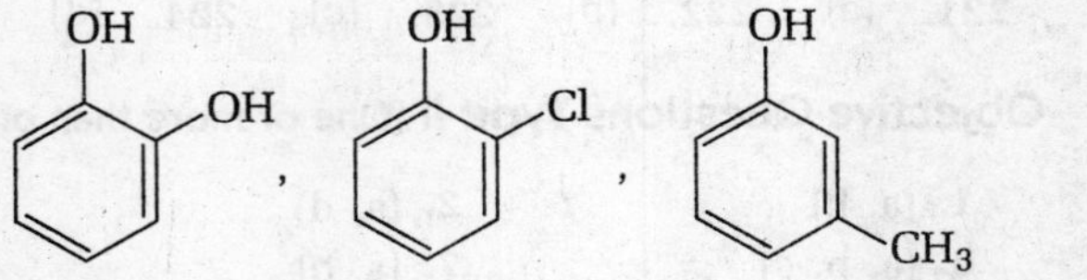

13. Among the following, the number of aromatic compound(s) **[JEE Advanced 2017]**

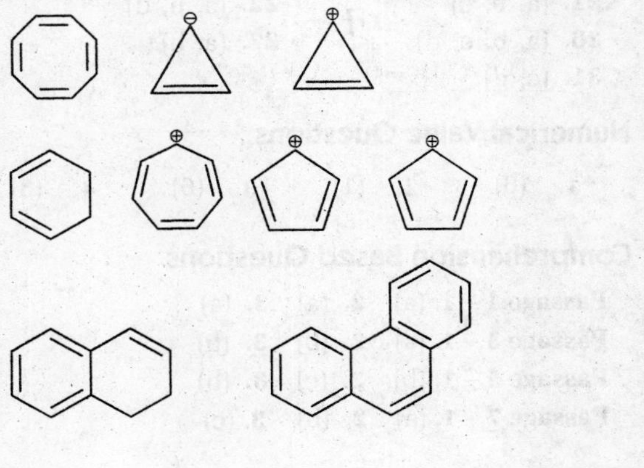

14. Identify total number of compounds which shows the correct direction of inductive effect

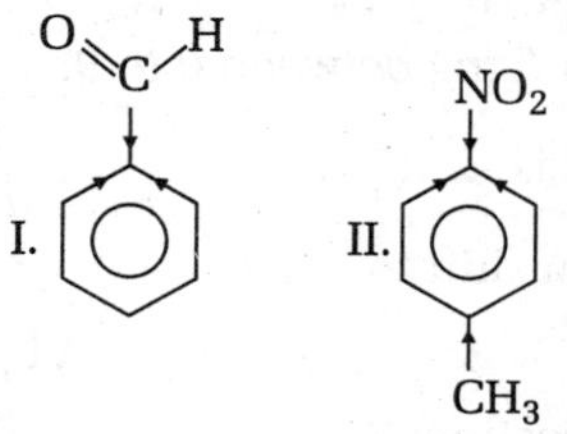

Answers

Objective Questions Type I [Only one correct option]

1. (a)	**2.** (c)	**3.** (a)	**4.** (d)	**5.** (b)	**6.** (b)	**7.** (a)	**8.** (d)	**9.** (b)	**10.** (d)
11. (c)	**12.** (b)	**13.** (a)	**14.** (c)	**15.** (d)	**16.** (b)	**17.** (a)	**18.** (b)	**19.** (a)	**20.** (c)
21. (c)	**22.** (a)	**23.** (d)	**24.** (a)	**25.** (c)	**26.** (b)	**27.** (b)	**28.** (a)	**29.** (a)	**30.** (d)
31. (b)	**32.** (c)	**33.** (c)	**34.** (a)	**35.** (b)	**36.** (c)	**37.** (a)	**38.** (b)	**39.** (b)	**40.** (d)
41. (a)	**42.** (c)	**43.** (b)	**44.** (a)	**45.** (a)	**46.** (d)	**47.** (c)	**48.** (b)	**49.** (b)	**50.** (b)
51. (b)	**52.** (c)	**53.** (a)	**54.** (b)	**55.** (a)	**56.** (a)	**57.** (c)	**58.** (a)	**59.** (a)	**60.** (c)
61. (b)	**62.** (b)	**63.** (c)	**64.** (d)	**65.** (b)	**66.** (b)	**67.** (a)	**68.** (c)	**69.** (d)	**70.** (b)
71. (b)	**72.** (a)	**73.** (c)	**74.** (a)	**75.** (c)	**76.** (a)	**77.** (c)	**78.** (a)	**79.** (d)	**80.** (a)
81. (b)	**82.** (d)	**83.** (a)	**84.** (a)	**85.** (b)	**86.** (b)	**87.** (a)	**88.** (a)	**89.** (a)	**90.** (c)
91. (a)	**92.** (a)	**93.** (c)	**94.** (b)	**95.** (a)	**96.** (a)	**97.** (a)	**98.** (a)	**99.** (c)	**100.** (a)
101. (d)	**102.** (a)	**103.** (b)	**104.** (b)	**105.** (c)	**106.** (a)	**107.** (c)	**108.** (a)	**109.** (b)	**110.** (a)
111. (c)	**112.** (a)	**113.** (a)	**114.** (a)	**115.** (d)	**116.** (b)	**117.** (c)	**118.** (a)	**119.** (a)	**120.** (c)
121. (b)	**122.** (a)	**123.** (a)	**124.** (b)	**125.** (a)	**126.** (b)	**127.** (b)	**128.** (b)	**129.** (c)	**130.** (a)
131. (a)	**132.** (b)	**133.** (b)	**134.** (b)	**135.** (a)	**136.** (b)	**137.** (b)	**138.** (a)	**139.** (a)	**140.** (c)
141. (d)	**142.** (d)	**143.** (c)	**144.** (b)	**145.** (d)	**146.** (c)	**147.** (b)	**148.** (d)	**149.** (b)	**150.** (d)
151. (c)	**152.** (c)	**153.** (c)	**154.** (a)	**155.** (c)	**156.** (c)	**157.** (a)	**158.** (b)	**159.** (d)	**160.** (c)
161. (d)	**162.** (b)	**163.** (c)	**164.** (d)	**165.** (b)	**166.** (a)	**167.** (d)	**168.** (a)	**169.** (b)	**170.** (a)
171. (c)	**172.** (b)	**173.** (d)	**174.** (b)	**175.** (c)	**176.** (b)	**177.** (b)	**178.** (a)	**179.** (d)	**180.** (a)
181. (c)	**182.** (a)	**183.** (d)	**184.** (b)	**185.** (b)	**186.** (a)	**187.** (a)	**188.** (c)	**189.** (a)	**190.** (a)
191. (b)	**192.** (c)	**193.** (c)	**194.** (c)	**195.** (c)	**196.** (d)	**197.** (a)	**198.** (a)	**199.** (b)	**200.** (b)
201. (b)	**202.** (d)	**203.** (a)	**204.** (b)	**205.** (a)	**206.** (a)	**207.** (b)	**208.** (b)	**209.** (d)	**210.** (c)
211. (b)	**212.** (c)	**213.** (b)	**214.** (b)	**215.** (d)	**216.** (b)	**217.** (b)	**218.** (d)	**219.** (b)	**220.** (c)
221. (a)	**222.** (b)	**223.** (c)	**224.** (d)	**225.** (b)					

Objective Questions Type II [One or more than one correct option(s)]

1. (a, b)	**2.** (a, d)	**3.** (b, c)	**4.** (a, b, d)	**5.** (b, d)
6. (a, b, c)	**7.** (a, b)	**8.** (a, b, c)	**9.** (a)	**10.** (d)
11. (a, b, c)	**12.** (a, b)	**13.** (a, b, c, d)	**14.** (a)	**15.** (a)
16. (a, c, d)	**17.** (a, b, c)	**18.** (a)	**19.** (a, b, c)	**20.** (a)
21. (a, b, c)	**22.** (a, b, d)	**23.** (a, b, c, d)	**24.** (a, b, c, d)	**25.** (b, c)
26. (a, b, c, d)	**27.** (a, b)	**28.** (a, d)	**29.** (a, b)	**30.** (a)
31. (c, d)				

Numerical Value Questions

1. (6)	**2.** (1)	**3.** (6)	**4.** (3)	**5.** (120)	**6.** (4)	**7.** (3)	**8.** (2)

Comprehension Based Questions

Passage 1 – 1. (a) **2.** (a) **3.** (a)

Passage 2 – 1. (b) **2.** (a) **3.** (c)

Passage 3 – 1. (a) **2.** (b) **3.** (b)

Passage 4 – 1. (d) **2.** (a) **3.** (d)

Passage 5 – 1. (b) **2.** (c) **3.** (b)

Passage 6 – 1. (b) **2.** (c) **3.** (c)

Passage 7 – 1. (a) **2.** (b) **3.** (c)

Passage 8 – 1. (a) **2.** (b)

Matrix-Match Type

1. A→(2); B→(3); C→(4); D→(1)
2. A→(5); B→(3); C→(2); D→(1)
3. A→(3); B→(4); C→(1); D→(2)
4. A→(4); B→(2); C→(3); D→(1)
5. A→(2); B→(1); C→(4); D→(4)
6. A→(1,2,3); B→(1,2,3); C→(1,2,4); D→(1,2,4)
7. A→(3); B→(1); C→(2); D→(3)
8. A→(2); B→(2); C→(3,4); D→(1,4)
9. A→(1); B→(2); C→(3); D→(3,4)
10. A→(1,4); B→(2); C→(3,4); D→(2,3)
11. A→(3,4); B→(5); C→(1,2); D→(3)
12. A→(3,4,5); B→(1,4); C→(3,4); D→(2,3)
13. A→(2); B→(3); C→(4); D→(1)

Single Integer Answer Questions

1. (1) 2. (4) 3. (6) 4. (4) 5. (6) 6. (3) 7. (0) 8. (2) 9. (1) 10. (3)
11. (2) 12. (3) 13. (4) 14. (1)

Solutions

Objective Questions Type [Only one correct option]

1. (*a*) Stability of free radicals is in order :

$$1° < 2° < 3°$$

(a) $CH_2{=}CH\dot{C}H_2$ (1°) but allylic and its extra stability is due to resonance

$$CH_2{=}CH\dot{C}H_2 \longleftrightarrow \dot{C}H_2{-}CH{=}CH_2$$

(b) $(CH_3)_3\dot{C}$ 3° alkyl

(c) $(CH_3)_2\dot{C}H$ 2° alkyl

(d) $CH_3\dot{C}H_2$ 1° alkyl

Thus, (d) < (c) < (b) < (a) maximum.

2. (*c*) $CH_3 : Cl \longrightarrow \dot{C}H_3 + \dot{C}l$

$\dot{C}H_3$: Methyl free radical *sp*2-hybridised (with singly occupied *p*-orbital)

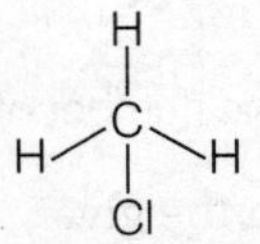

*sp*3-hybridised carbon tetrahedral bond angle 109°28′

Bond angle 120° with three coplanar (C—H) bonds

3. (*a*) (a) $\overset{\oplus}{C}H_3$ is called carbocation, thus (a) is incorrect.

(b) $\overset{\oplus}{C}H_3$ has six bonding electrons thus is more electron-deficient than $\dot{C}H_3$ which has six bonding electrons and one unpaired electron.

Thus, (b) is true.

(c) $CH_4 + H^+ \longrightarrow \overset{\oplus}{C}H_5$

CH_4: 8 bonding electrons with four C—H bonds; $\overset{\oplus}{C}H_5$: 8 bonding electrons with five C—H bonds

Thus, (c) is also true.

(d) $\overset{\oplus}{C}H_3, CH_3\overset{\oplus}{C}H_2$ — Carbenium ion.

Thus, (d) is also true.

(a) is only incorrect.

5. (*b*)

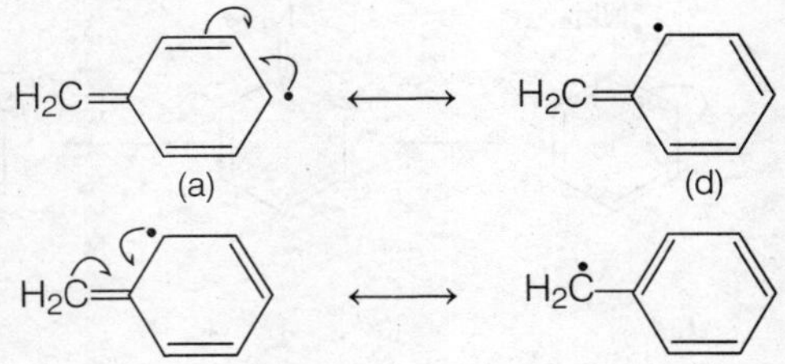

6. (*b*) (a) $CH_4 + Cl^- \longrightarrow$ no reaction

(b) $AlCl_3 + Cl^- \longrightarrow AlCl_4^-$

$AlCl_3$: Electron-deficient Al (Lewis acid); Cl^-: Lewis base

(c) $OH^- + Cl^- \longrightarrow$ no reaction

(d) $CH_3^- + Cl^- \longrightarrow$ no reaction

7. (*a*) $(CH_3)_3C^{\oplus} + H_2\ddot{O}:$

$(CH_3)_3C^{\oplus}$: Electron-deficient carbon thus, Lewis acid; $H_2\ddot{O}:$ Electron-rich thus, Lewis-base

8. (*d*) Nucleophilic strength increases down the group then

$$R_3P > R_3N$$

but given comparison $R_3P < R_3N$ is incorrect.

9. (*b*) Not aromatic 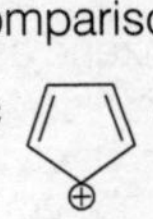 $4e^-$ It follow an Huckle rule

10. (*d*) Steric bulky groups decreases nucleophilicity. Thus, (d) is incorrect.

11. (*c*) Benzyl carbocation is most stable due to resonance

(a) 3° alkyl (b) 3° vinylic least stable

(c) 1° benzyl most stable (d) 2° alkyl

Order is : (b) < (d) < (a) < (c)

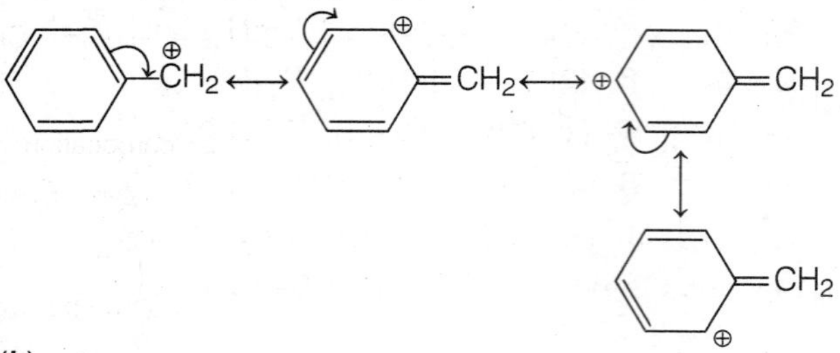

12. (*b*)

(a) 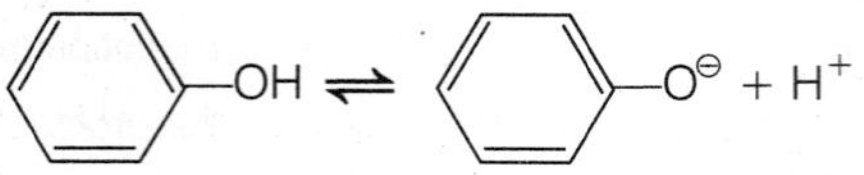

Phenolate ion is resonance stabilised thus, equilibrium is in towards formation of H^+.

Thus, 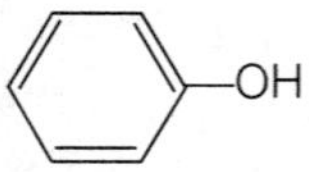 —OH > CH_3OH (acidic)

(b) C_6H_5 is electron-withdrawing and lone-pair on N-atom is used in delocalisation of π-electrons while CH_3 is electron-donating making N-atom more electron-rich. Thus, CH_3NH_2 is more basic than $C_6H_5NH_2$.

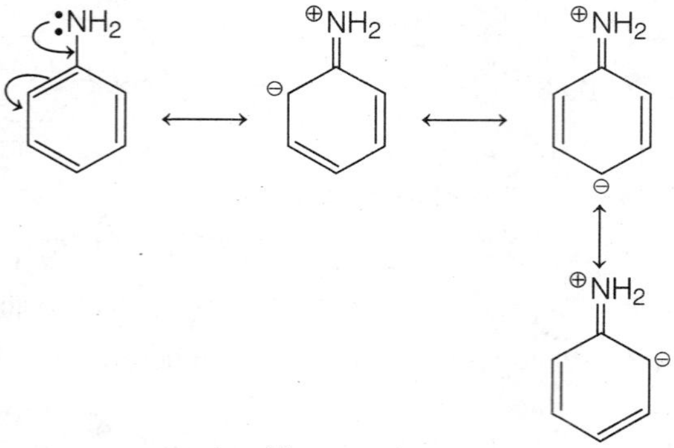

$CH_3 \rightarrow \ddot{N}H_2$

Given comparison is incorrect.

(c) 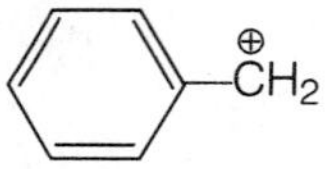 resonance stabilised

Thus, (c) is correct.

(d) 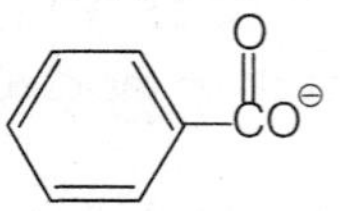

Resonance stabilisation in benzene as well as in carboxylate ion. Thus, (d) is correct.

13. (*a*) 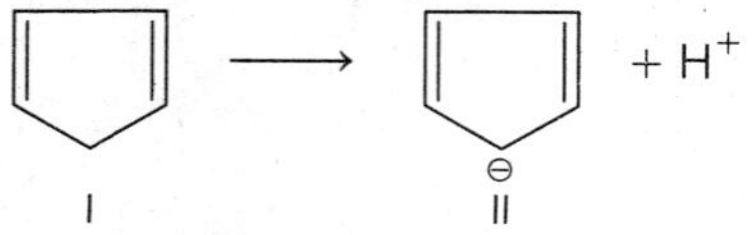

Cyclopentadienyl anion (II) is stable due to resonance and I (non-aromatic) changes to II (aromatic).

Thus, stability is increased. Thus, I maximum acidic.

14. (*c*) H—$\ddot{O}$—H Acidic

$CH_3 \rightarrow \ddot{O}$—H —$CH_3$ is electron-repelling group, increases basic nature. Thus, $CH_3OH > H_2O$ (basic)

$CH_3OH < H_2O$ (acidic K_a)

Thus, $CH_3OH > H_2O$ (pK_a)

$C_6H_5 \leftarrow \ddot{O}$—H—$C_6H_5$ is electron-withdrawing group, increases acidic nature.

Thus, $C_6H_5OH > H_2O$ (acidic K_a)

$C_6H_5OH < H_2O$ (pK_a)

Thus, pK_a of $C_6H_5OH < H_2O < CH_3OH$

15. (*d*) 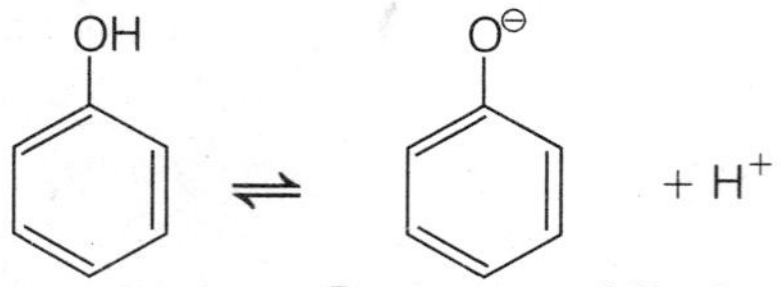

Resonance stabilised phenolate ion

Thus, C_6H_5OH is stronger acid than water.

Thus, (d) is incorrect statement.

16. (*b*) 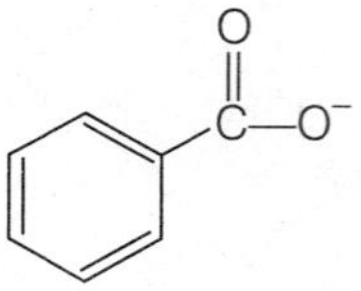

Resonance in benzene nucleus as well as in carboxylate ion. Thus, maximum stable.

Thus, maximum resonance energy.

17. (*a*) Electron-donating groups (as —CH_3) decrease acidic nature (and increase basic nature) while electron-withdrawing groups (as —CHO, —NO_2, —$COCH_3$) increase acidic nature (and decrease basic nature)

20. (*c*) is 3° carbocation

Carbocation is of $(3-n)°$ where, n is the number of H-atoms at $C^{\oplus}$.

21. (*c*) —CN is electron-withdrawing group, thus, π-electron shift in (c) takes place as $CH_3 \rightarrow CH{=}CH \rightarrow CN$

Thus, given π-electron transfer is incorrect.

22. (*a*) 3° carbocation is most stable thus, least PE.

23. (*d*) Ethynic H is attached to (—C≡C—) system.

—NO_2 is electron-withdrawing and (C—H) is weakened to a greater extent. Since, benzene nucleus is also resonance stabilised, hence, (d).

24. (*a*) 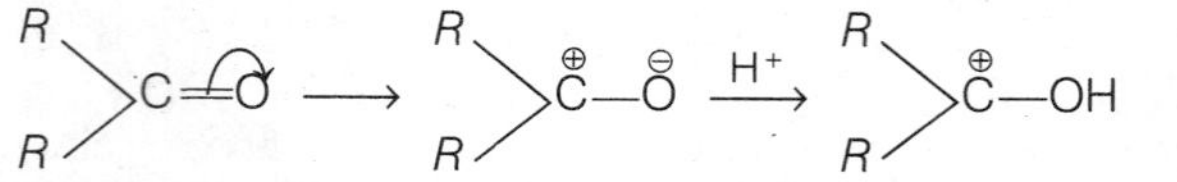

Alkyl groups decrease positive charge on carbon atom. Thus, electrophile formed in (a) is the best electrophile.

26. (*b*) (a)
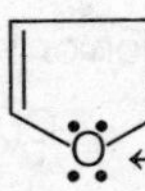

← Lone-pair is used in delocalisation

(b)
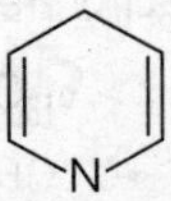

No delocalisation

27. (*b*) $—NO_2$ group is *meta*-directing, deactivating.
$—NH_2$ group is *ortho*-, *para*-directing, activating.

29. (*a*) $+M$ effect increases, reactivity decreases due to —Cl group attached.

31. (*b*)
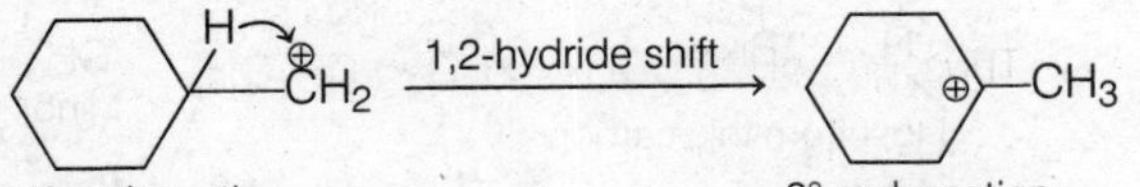

32. (*c*) In a β-elimination reaction, a leaving group (like Cl^-) leaves along with a hydrogen (as H^+) from a β-position. Among available β-positions, H^+ removal is preferred to take place from the β-position having least H atoms according to Saytzeff's rule.

But in reaction (c),

the major product is not Saytzeff 's product

because the given base, $CH_3—\overset{CH_3}{\underset{CH_3}{C}}—O^-$ is bulky and ∴due to

steric hinderance removes H^+ from— CH_3 group.

In this case reaction occurs as :

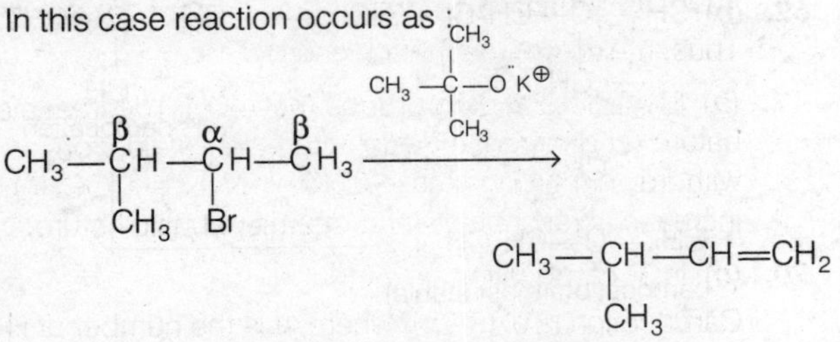

The major product is called Hofmann product.

The rest of the given reactions produce Saytzeff products as follows :

(a)
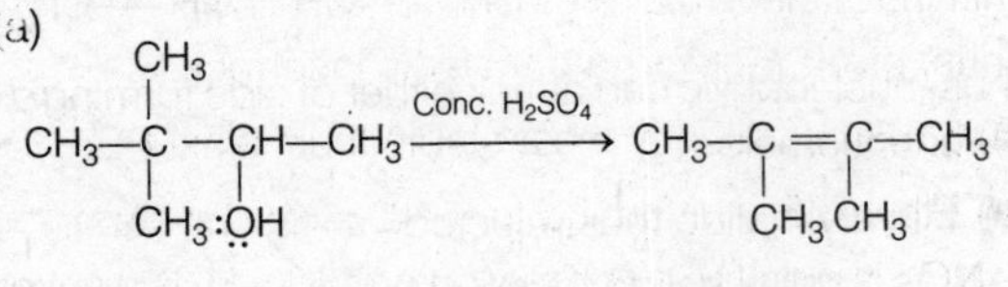

(b)
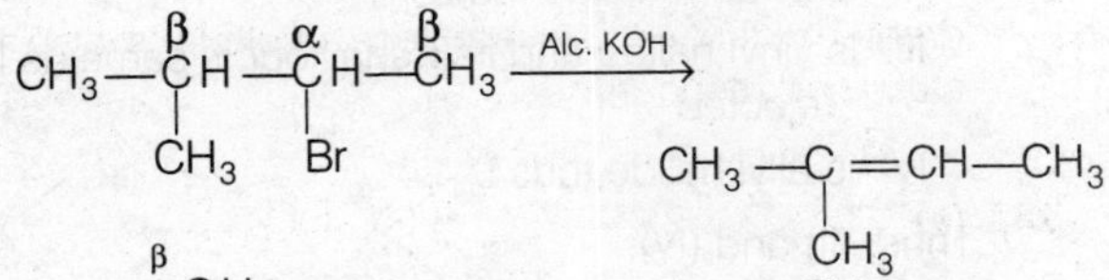

(d)
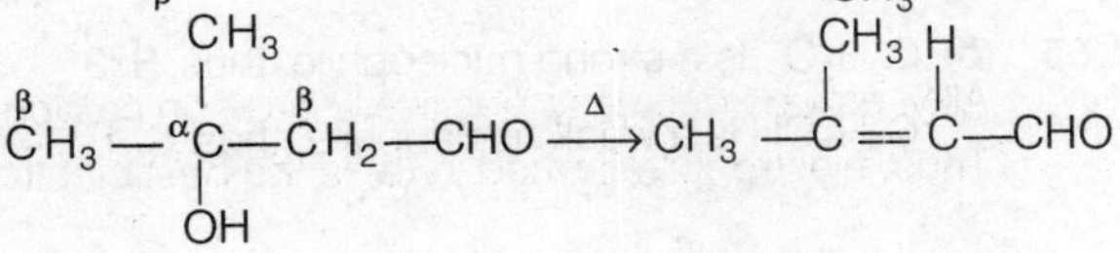

33. (*c*)
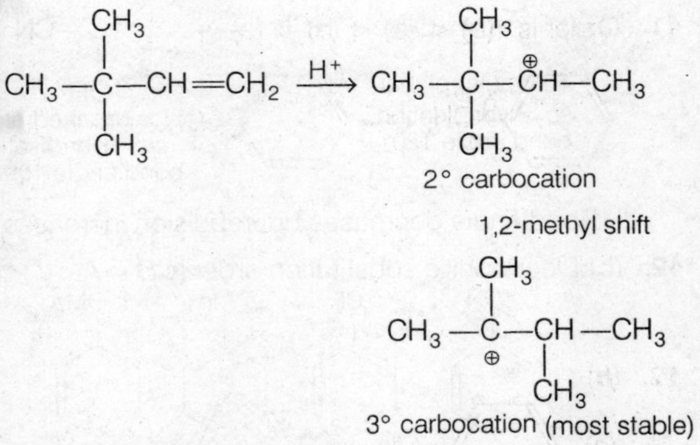

34. (*a*) Addition is regiospecific if one of the products is predominant.

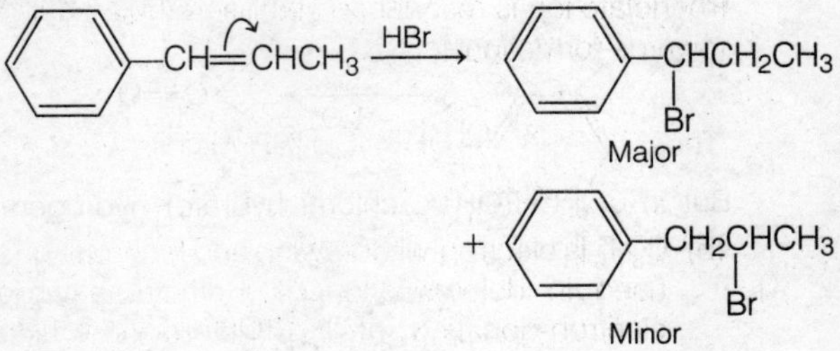

35. (*b*) $CH_3CH=CHCH=CHCH_3 \xrightarrow{HBr} CH_3\underset{Br}{CH}\,CH_2CH=CHCH_3$

It is called 1,2-addition.

36. (*c*) Ambident nucleophile

(A) KCN and AgCN (C) $AgNO_2$ and KNO_2

38. (*b*)1,2- and 1,4-addition takes place in conjugated system.

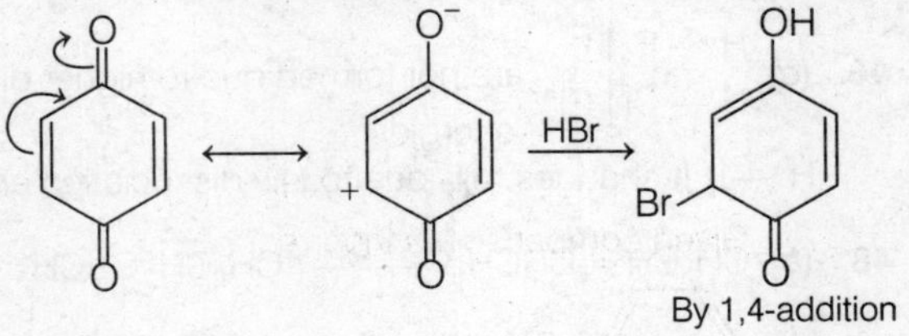

By 1,4-addition

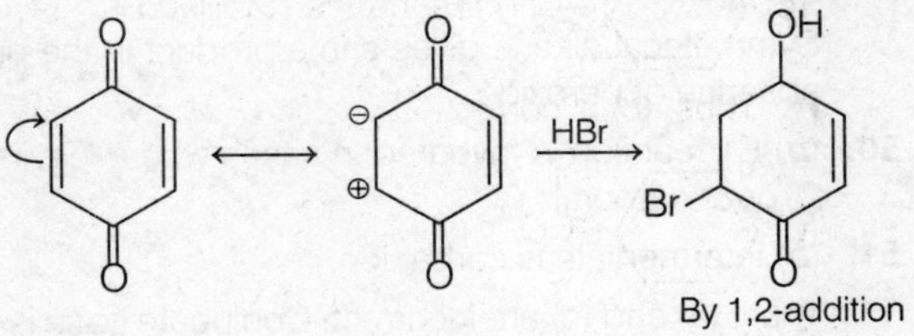

By 1,2-addition

40. (*d*)

(a) is true.
(b) is also true.
(c) is also true.

41. (*a*)

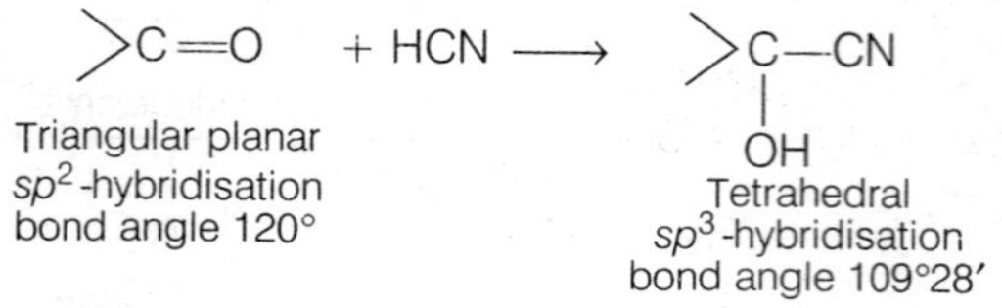

Bond angle decreases but repulsion increases.

42. (*c*) Electrophilic substitution order is $D < A < C < B$.

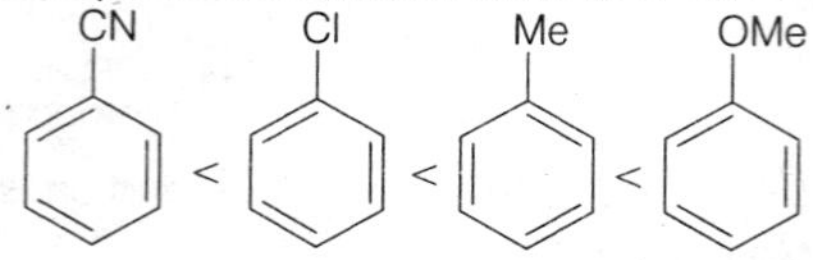

43. (*b*) Two —OH groups at the geminal (same) carbon are not possible.

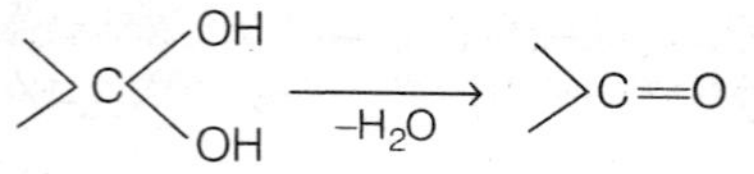

But in $CCl_3CH(OH)_2$, (chloral hydrate) hydrogen bonding stabilises it.

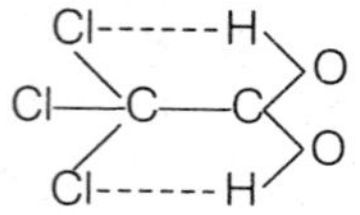

44. (*a*) It is nucleophilic addition.

45. (*a*) Radicals are intermediates.

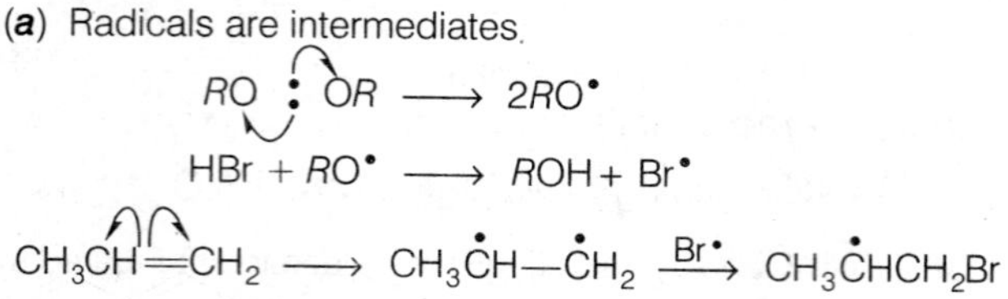

46. (*d*) H — F, H — Cl ($F^\bullet$, $Cl^\bullet$) are not formed due to higher dissociation energies.

H — I] It changes to I_2 due to low dissociation energy.

48. (*b*) $CH_3CH{=}CHCH_3 \xrightarrow{HBr} CH_3CH_2CH(Br)CH_3$

Symmetrical alkene gives same product in the presence or absence of peroxide.

50. (*b*) E1 reaction is favoured in cases where leaving group is 2° or 3° carbon.

51. (*b*) Intermediate is carbanion.

Thus, (a) and (c) are incorrect. Conjugate base is formed by loss of H^+.

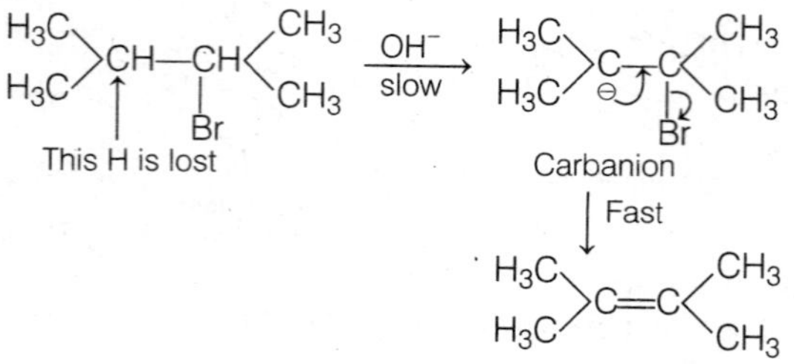

52. (*c*) E2 reaction is also called β-elimination or 1, 2-elimination.

53. (*a*)

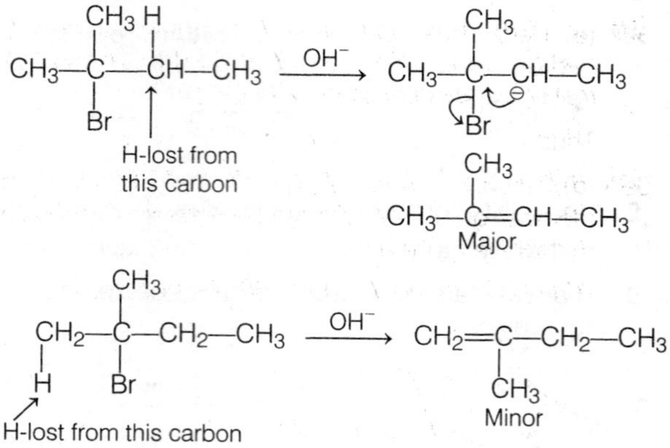

55. (*a*) $CH_3-\dot{C}H_2 \xrightarrow{\text{Oxidation}} CH_2{=}CH_2 + H^\bullet$

$\xrightarrow{H^\bullet,\ \text{reduction}} CH_3-CH_3$

56. (*a*) BE of allylic 3° (C—H) bond is least thus, it is abstracted most easily.

57. (*c*) $CH_2{=}CH-CH_3 \longrightarrow CH_2{=}CH-CH_2Br$
Vinylic Allylic

BE of allylic (C—H) < BE of vinylic (C—H)

59. (*a*) $H\overset{\ominus}{O}-\overset{\oplus}{N}O_2 + H_2SO_4 \longrightarrow H_2O + HSO_4^{\ominus} + NO_2^{\oplus}$

61. (*b*) Most stable due to conjugation.

Thus, least energy.

62. (*b*)

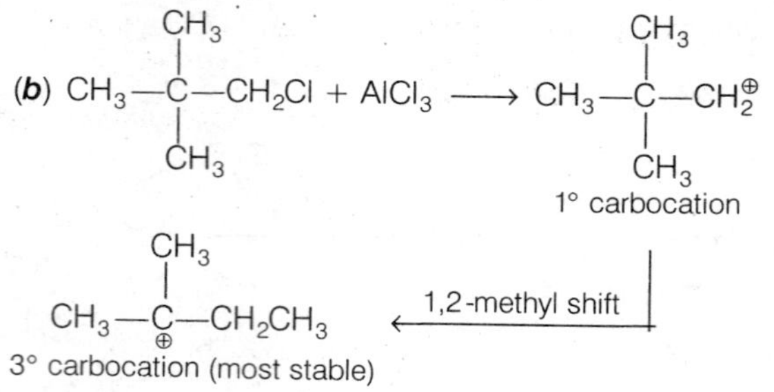

63. (*c*)

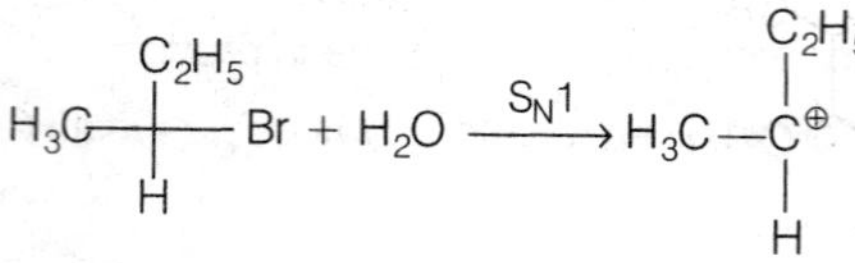

Thus, nucleophilic can attack either of side forming *d*(+) and *l*(−) enantiomers.

64. (*d*) I. is aryl halide thus rejected

II. is 2° alkyl halide thus S_N1

III. is vinyl halide and its behaviour is same as I thus rejected

IV. is allyl halide thus S_N1

Thus, (II) and (IV).

65. (*b*) $C_2H_5O^-$ is a strong nucleophile, thus, S_N2

C_2H_5OH is a weak nucleophile, thus, S_N1

66. (*b*) If there is S_N2 reaction on chiral centre, inversion takes place thus, statement (b) is incorrect.

68. (*c*) Benzyl carbocation is more stable than alkyl ($CH_3\overset{\oplus}{C}H_2$) CH_3O— and —CH_3 both stabilise benzyl carbocation (CH_3O — is more stabilising than CH_3—).

Thus, IV < II < III < I

69. (*d*) Carbonyl group makes methylene group acidic. Nearer the position of carbonyl group, greater the acidic nature of methylene group.

H and OH are eliminated from *vic*-position.

(a) 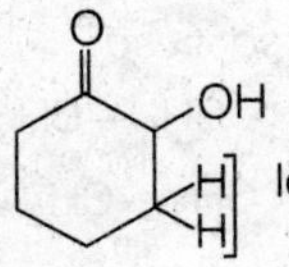 less acidic

(b) 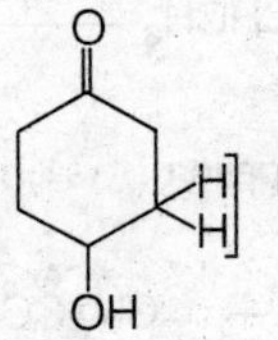 less acidic

(c) 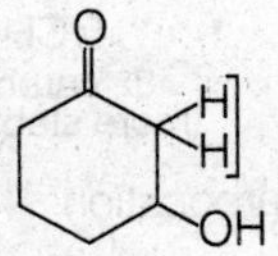 more acidic, dehydration is favoured.

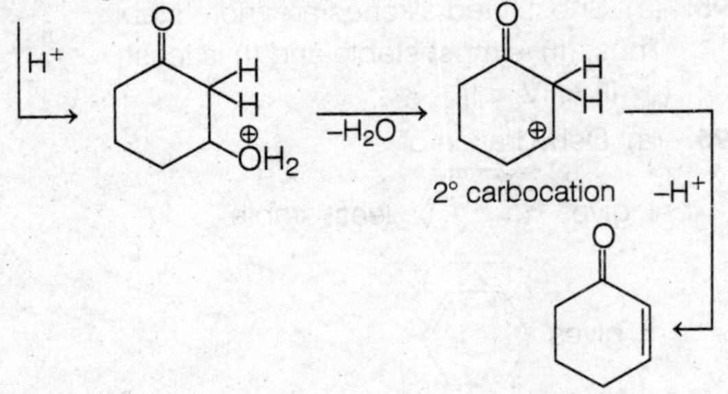

(d) 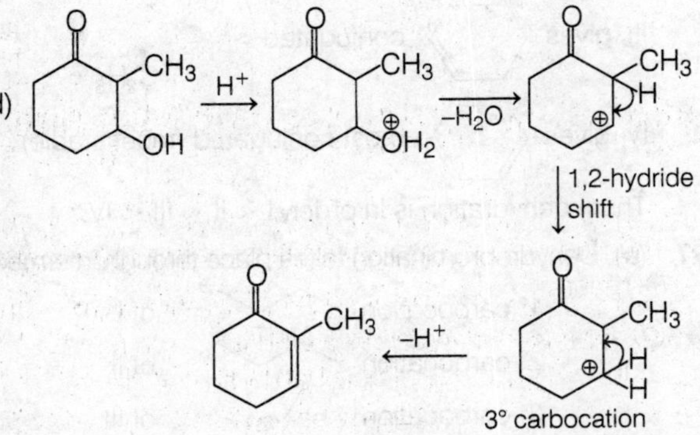

3° carbocation is more stable (in (d)) than 2° carbocation in (c) thus, dehydration is maximum in (d).

70. (*b*) due to increase in conjugation.

71. (*b*) 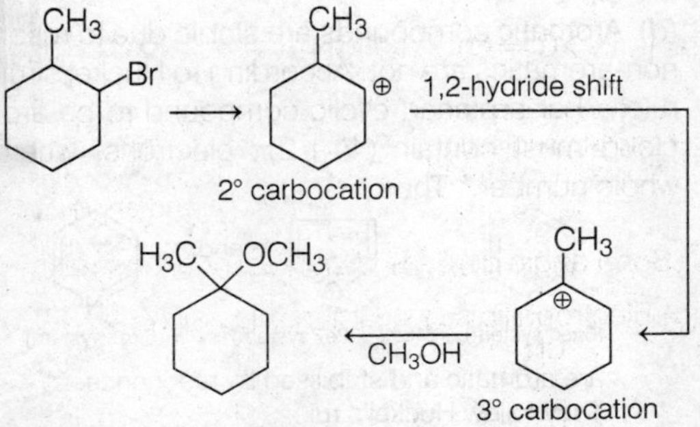

72. (*a*) $CH_3CH_2O^-$ is a strong nucleophile and causes dehydrohalogenation.

73. (*c*) due to conjugation.

74. (*a*) S_N2 mechanism causes inversion, thus, II is true S_N1 mechanism proceeds through carbocation hence products formed are enantiomers and racemisation takes place thus, I is true.

75. (*c*) 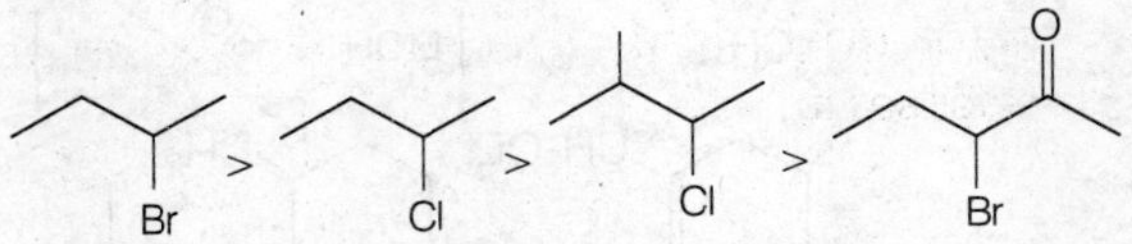

77. (*c*) 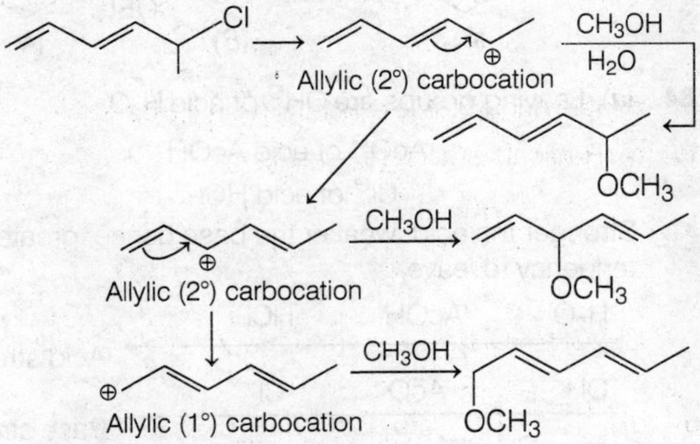

Thus, three types of substituted products.

78. (*a*) due to conjugation with phenyl group.

80. (*a*) 3° alcohol (without $\overset{18}{O}$) is more basic than 2° alcohol (with $\overset{18}{O}$). Thus, OH group of 3° alcohol and H of 2° alcohol take part in dehydration. Thus, $\overset{18}{O}$ is retained in epoxide (*A*).

81. (*b*) Phenolic H is more acidic than alcohol H thus, $\overset{\oplus}{C}H_3$ is attached to phenoxide.

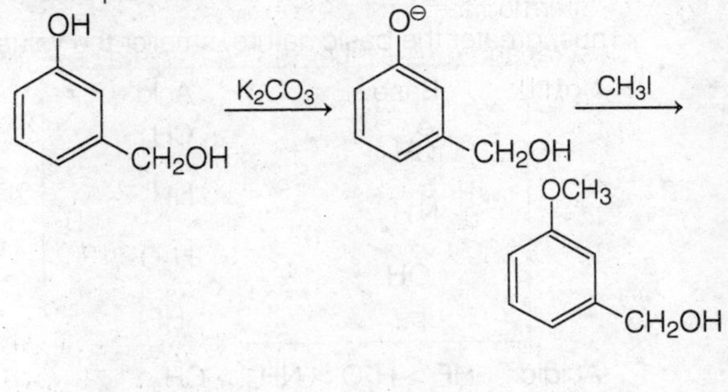

82. (*d*) Aromatic compounds are stable due to resonance while non-aromatics are not. According to Huckel's rule (or $4n+2$ rule), "For a planar, cyclic compound to be aromatic, its π cloud must contain $(4n+2)\pi$ electrons, where, n is any whole number." Thus,

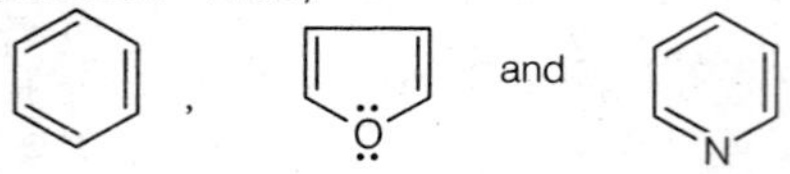

($6\pi e^-$ system) ($4\pi e^- + 2e^-$ system) ($6\pi e^-$ system)

are aromatic and stabilised by resonance.
They follow Huckel's rule.

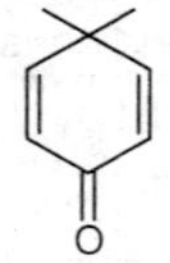

is non-aromatic, hence, least stabilised by resonance.

83. (*a*)

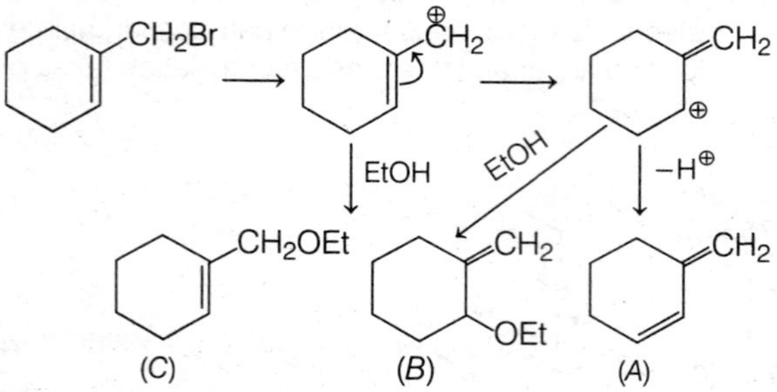

84. (*a*) Leaving groups are $OH^{\ominus}$ of acid H_2O

$AcO^{\ominus}$ of acid AcOH

$Cl^{\ominus}$ of acid HCl

Stronger the acid, weaker the base hence, greater the tendency to leave.

H_2O AcOH HCl ⟶ Acid strength

OH^- AcO^- Cl^- ⟵ Base strength

⟶ Leaving tendency

85. (*b*)

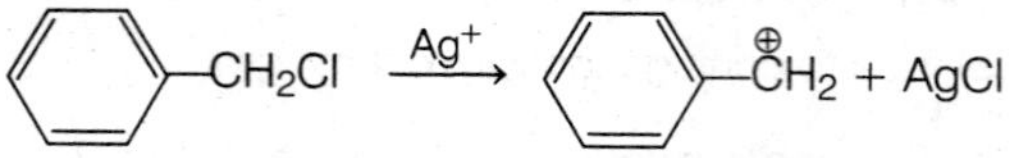

$$(CH_3)_3CCl \xrightarrow{Ag^+} (CH_3)_3C^{\oplus} + AgCl$$

Stable 3° carbocation

Thus, I and II

88. (*a*) $pK_b = -\log K_b$

Thus, greater the basic nature, smaller the value of pK_b

Base	Acid
$\overset{\ominus}{C}H_3$	CH_4
$\overset{\ominus}{N}H_2$	NH_3
$\overset{\ominus}{O}H$	H_2O
$F^{\ominus}$	HF

Acidic : $HF > H_2O > NH_3 > CH_4$

Basic : $F^- < OH^- < \bar{N}H_2 < \bar{C}H_3$

pK_b : $F^- > OH^- > \bar{N}H_2 > \bar{C}H_3$

89. (*a*) Stability $CH_2{=}\overset{\oplus}{C}H >$

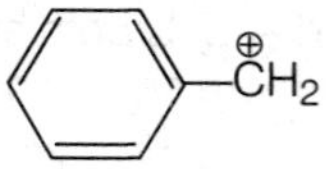

90. (*c*) due to paired electron

91. (*a*) due to substitution at allylic position

92. (*a*) $CH{\equiv}CH$ (sp) $CH_2{=}CH_2$ (sp^2) $CH_3{-}CH_3$ (sp^3)

Electronegativity of carbon $sp > sp^2 > sp^3$

Acidic $CH{\equiv}CH > CH_2{=}CH_2 > CH_3{-}CH_3$

Basic $CH{\equiv}C^{\ominus} < CH_2{=}CH^{\ominus} < CH_3{-}CH_2^{\ominus}$
(I) (II) (III)

93. (*c*)

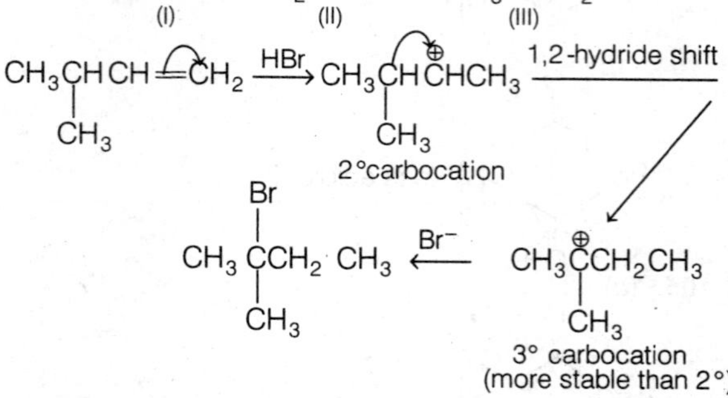

94. (*b*) Due to formation of 2° benzylic carbocation.

95. (*a*) Substituted alkenes are more stable.
Thus, (II) is most stable and (I) is least,
I < III < IV < II.

96. (*a*) Dehydration of

I gives  least stable

II gives 

III gives 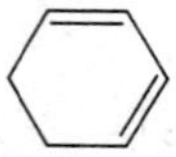 conjugated

IV gives 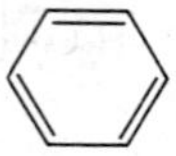 most conjugated (most stable)

Thus, dehydration is in order, I < II < III < IV.

97. (*a*) Dehydrobromination takes place through intermediates :

1° carbocation 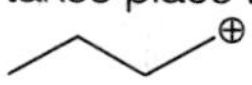 of I

2° carbocation  of II

3° carbocation 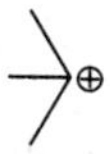 of III

Stability of carbocations 1° < 2° < 3° greater the stability, easier the formation.

99. (*c*) $CH_3CH_2CH{=}CH_2 + t\text{-}BuOCl \longrightarrow CH_3\overset{\ominus}{C}HCH{=}CH_2 + Cl^{\oplus} + BuOH$

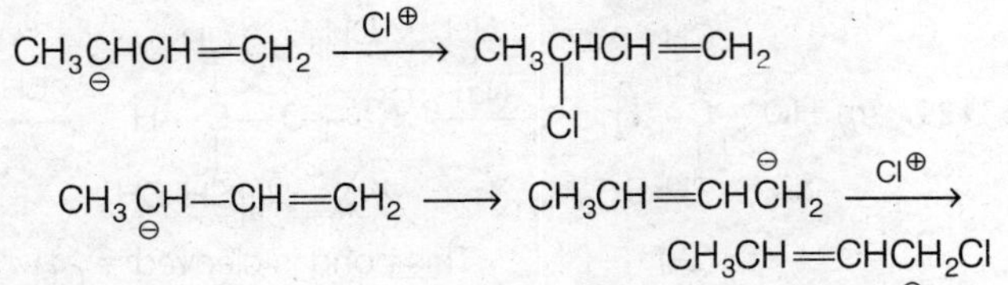

102. (*a*)

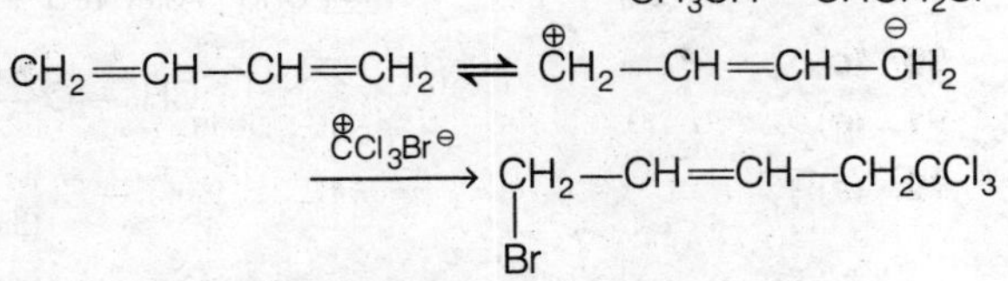

103. (*b*) —CH_3 is activating group

—COOH is deactivating group

Thus, III < II < I

104. (*b*)

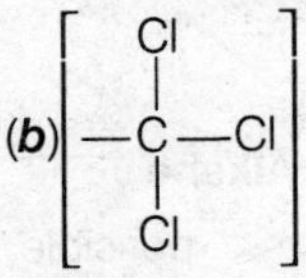

m directing $[—\overset{\oplus}{N}H_3]$ and $[—NO_2]$

m-directing.

105. (*c*)

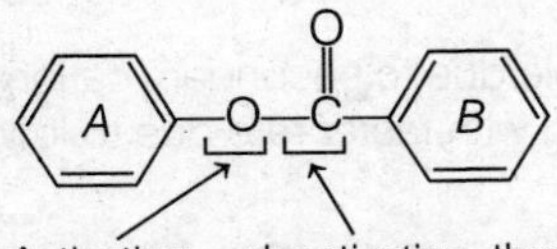

Activating deactivating, thus, $NO_2^{\oplus}$ attacks ring (*A*)

But at *p*-site due to avoid steric effect.

106. (*a*) S_N1: 1° < 2° < 3°

S_N2: 3° < 2° < 1°

Thus, S_N1 : I < III < II < IV

S_N2 : IV < II < III < I

107. (*c*)

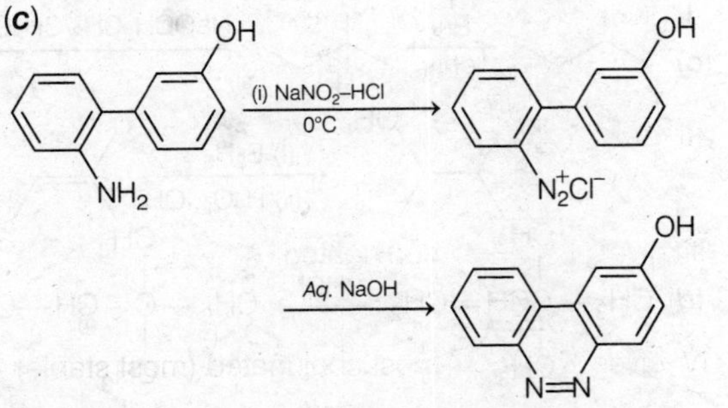

108. (*a*) In S_N2 reaction, no carbocation is formed.

109. (*b*)

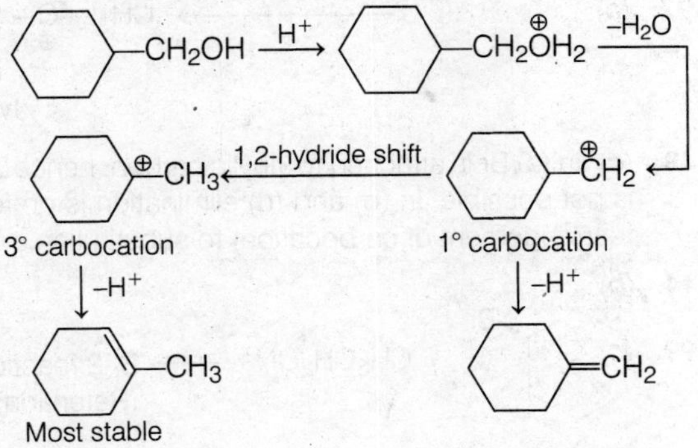

110. (*a*) Vinyl (IV) is least stable

Benzyl (I) is most stable due to resonance 3° alkyl(III) is more stable than 1° alkyl (II). Thus, order is IV < II < III < I

111. (*c*) CH_3COOH (inductive effect of —CH_3 decreases acid strength) is less basic than HCOOH

C_6H_5COOH (resonance effect of —C_6H_5 ring) is more acidic than CH_3COOH

$$\underset{I}{CH_3COOH} < \underset{III}{C_6H_5COOH} < \underset{II}{HCOOH}$$

112. (*a*)

Base	Acid
OH^-	H_2O
NH_2^-	NH_3
$HC\equiv C^-$	$HC\equiv CH$
$CH_3CH_2^-$	CH_3CH_3

Acid strength $H_2O > CH\equiv CH > NH_3 > CH_3CH_3$

Base strength $OH^- < CH\equiv C^- < NH_2^- < CH_3CH_2^-$

(If acid (HX) is strong, its conjugate base (X^-) is weak)

113. (*a*) + *I* effect stabilises a carbocation.

114. (*a*) represents pair of tautomers.

115. (*d*) 3° allylic radical.

117. (*c*) Elimination of H and OH takes place from *vic*-position in dehydration process.

(a)

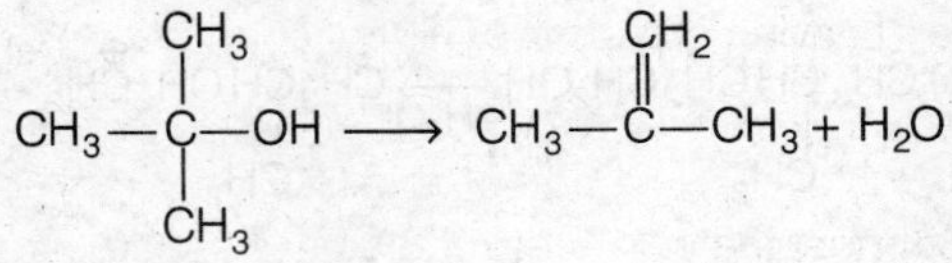

(b)

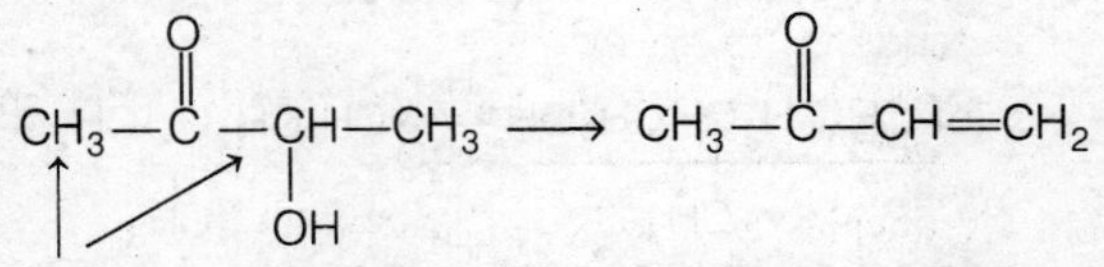

Carbonyl group makes methylene group more acidic, but H (from indicated position) is not involved in dehydration.

(c)

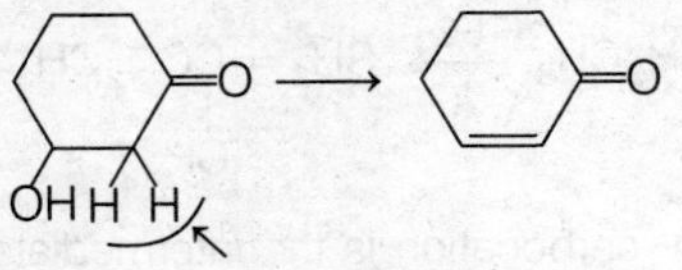

Indicated H is acidic and involved in dehydration. Thus, maximum dehydration.

(d) no dehydration.

118. (*a*) Reactant (3° carbocation) is most stable and S_N reaction is preferred over elimination (E2).

119. (*a*) If acid (HX) is strong, conjugate base (X^-) is weak and is a good leaving group.

Base (X^-) $\underset{I}{Cl^-}$ $\underset{II}{CH_3COO^-}$ $\underset{III}{OH^-}$

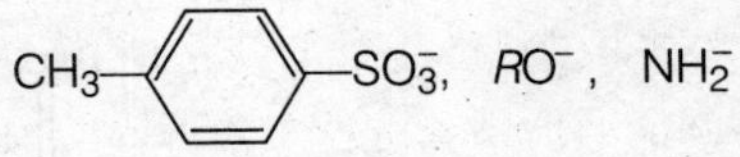

IV V VI

Acid (*HX*) HCl (I′), CH_3COOH (II′), H_2O (III′),

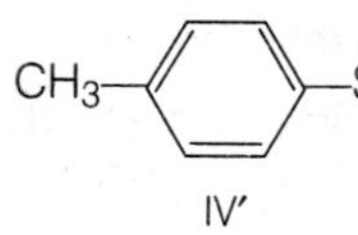

CH_3–C₆H₄–SO_3H (IV′), *R*OH (V′), NH_3 (VI′)

I′ > IV′ > II′ > III′ > V′ > VI′

Leaving tendency VI < V < III < II < IV < I

120. (*c*)

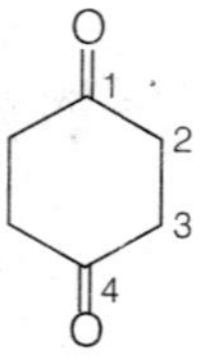

(1, 4 addition)

121. (*b*) More substituted with less steric effect.

123.

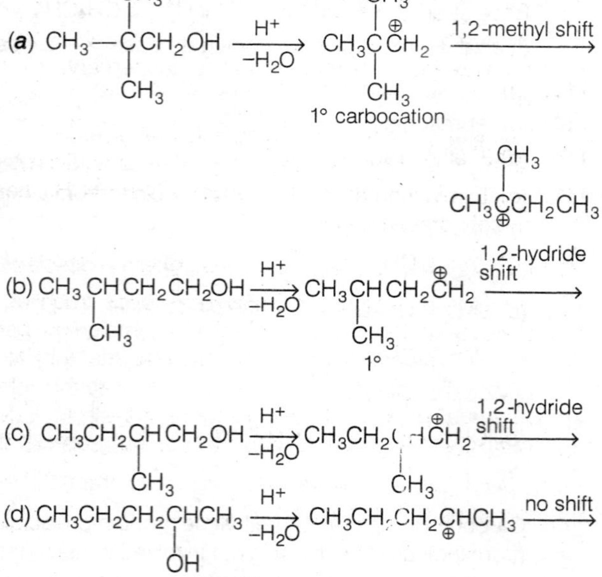

125. (*a*)

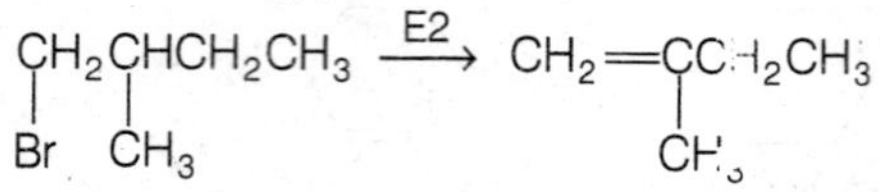

In (b), (c), (d), carbocation is the intermediate which can undergo 1,2-methyl or 1,2-hydride shift to give more stable carbocation.

127. (*b*) $pK_a = -\log K_a$; pK_a is maximum means least acidic or maximum basic. Thus, —NH_2 group.

128. (*b*)

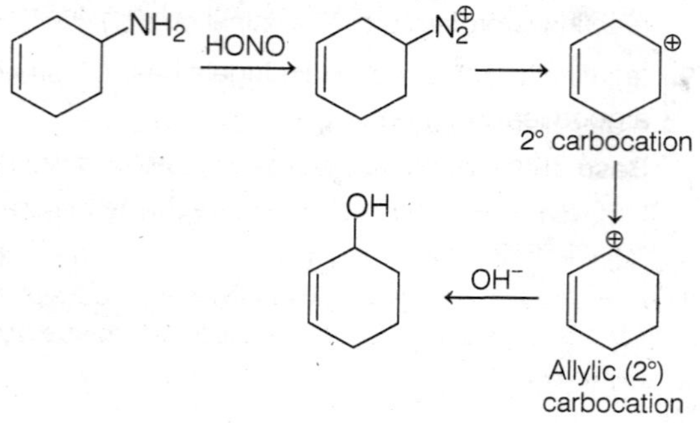

129. (*c*)

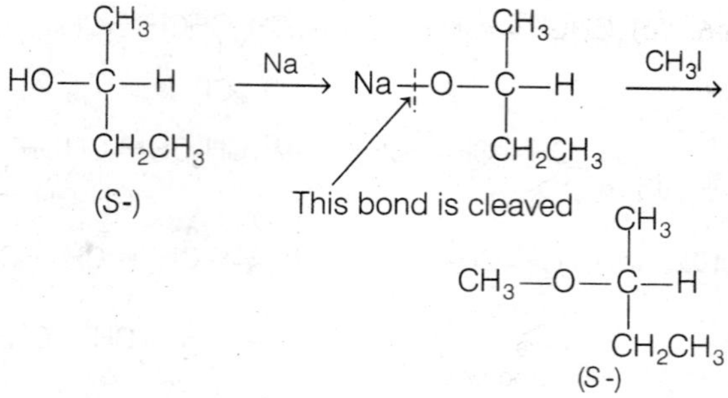

Thus, no change.

130. (*a*) Axial equitorial gives faster E2 elimination

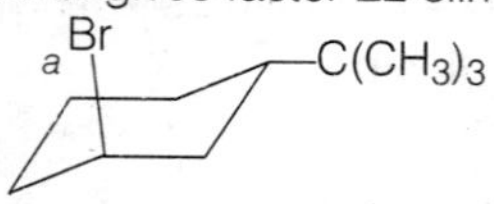

132. (*b*)

	Alcohol	Alkene	
(a)			possible
(b)			not possible

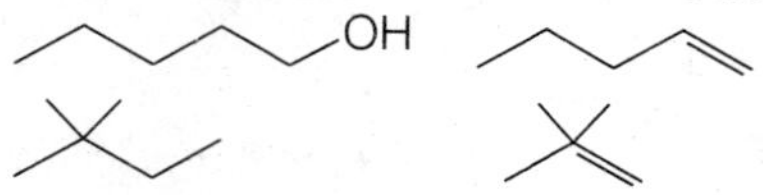

135. (*a*) This is more stable due to secondary cation formation and formed with faster rate due to low activation energy.

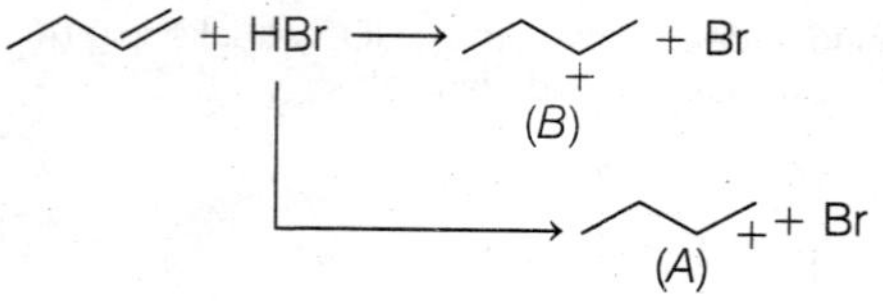

138. (*a*) Hydration takes place such that –OH goes to least substituted carbon.

140. (*c*)

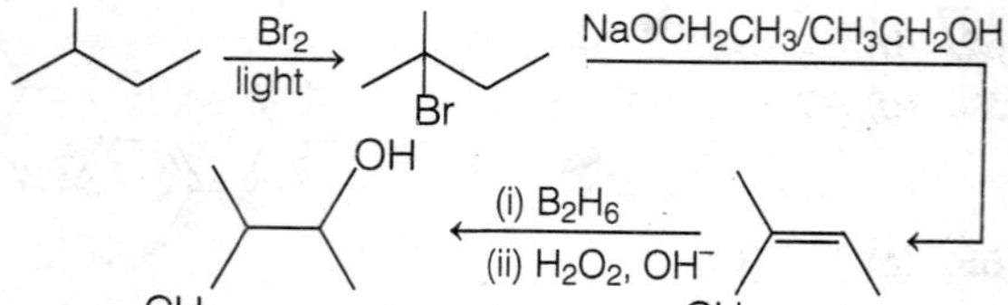

142. (*d*)

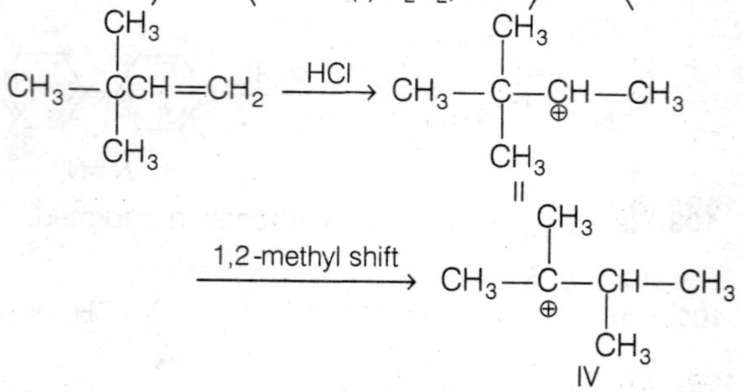

143. (*c*) In (a) Br is attached to vinylic carbon, hence S_N reaction is not possible. In (b) and (d) elimination is preferred (with rearrangement of carbocation) to substitution.

144. (*b*)

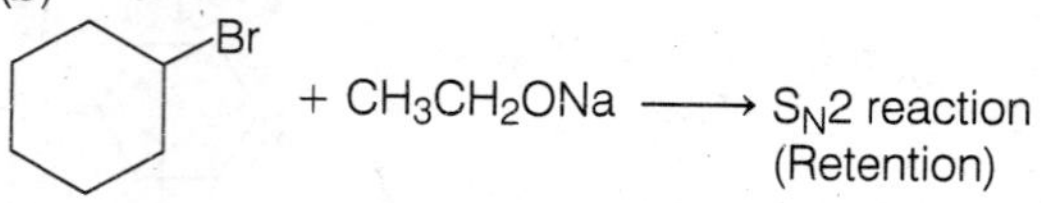

146. (*c*) (a)
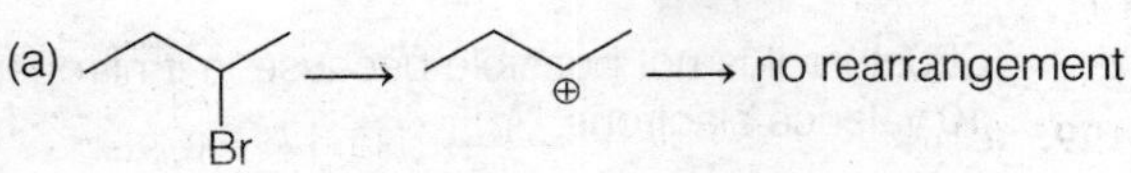

(b)
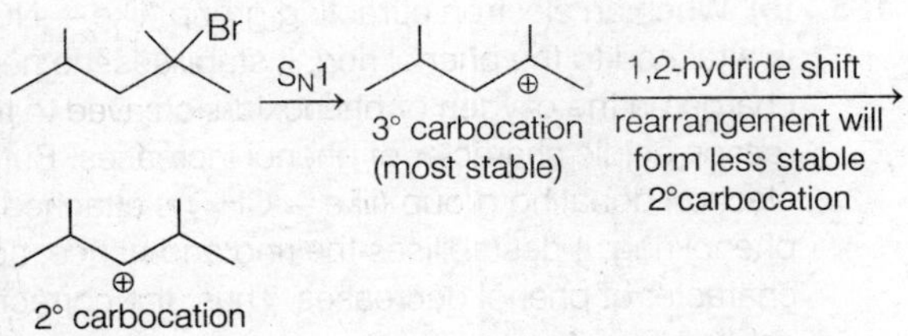

(c)
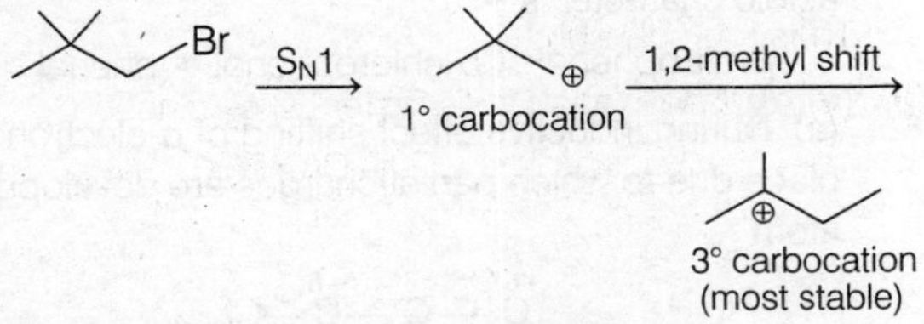

150. (*d*) In 1° alkyl halide, elimination is least.

151. (*c*)
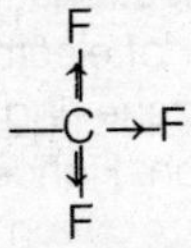
is an electron-withdrawing group thus deactivating and *meta*-directing.

154. (*a*) Addition by Markownikoff's rule to give product with less steric hindrance.

156. (*c*)
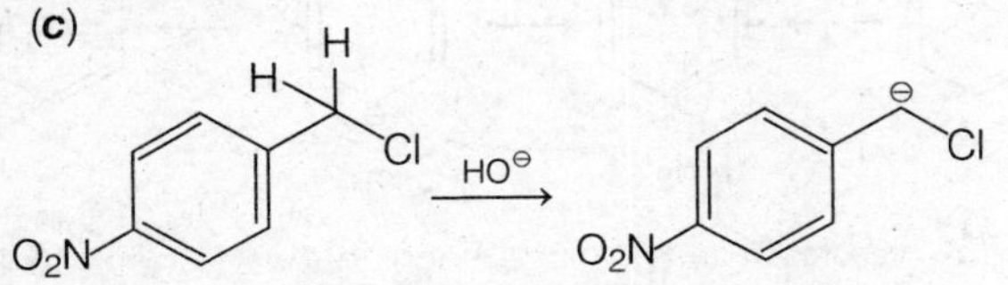

160. (*c*) Due to inversion, reaction is S_N2

162. (*b*) S_N1 reaction is favourable at 3° carbon, thus, *A*, *C*, *D*.

164. (*d*) $(C_6H_5)_3C—H \longrightarrow (C_6H_5)_3C^{\oplus}$
Resonance stabilised carbocation (most stable)

166. (*a*)
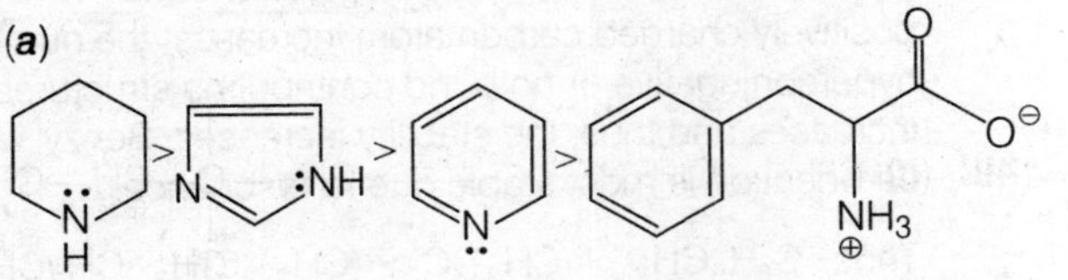

169. (*b*)
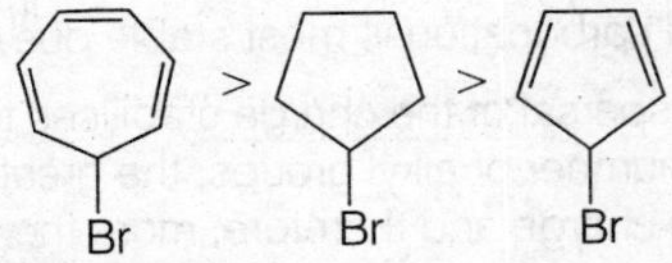

172. (*b*) Free radicals stability
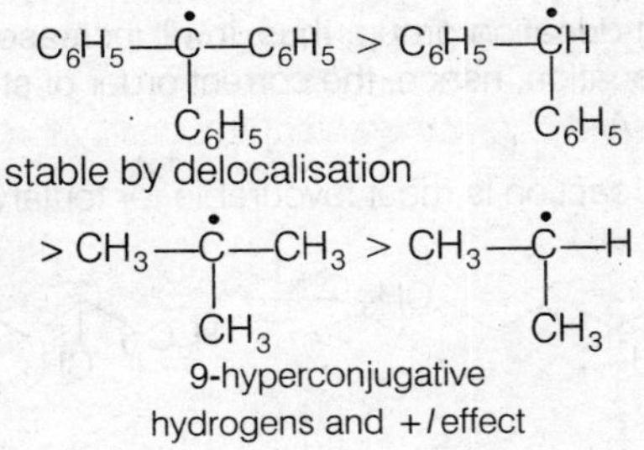

173. (*d*)
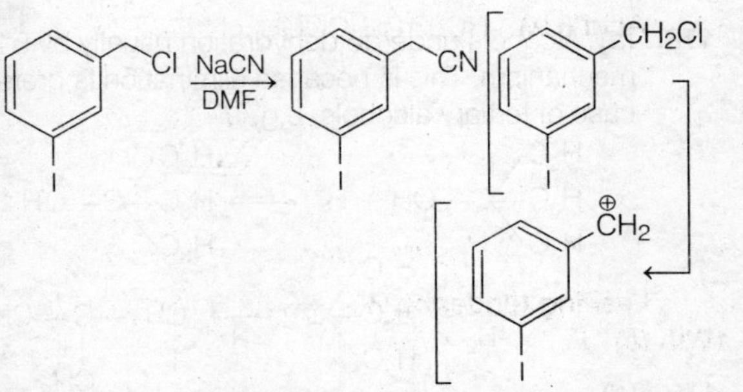

Benzyl carbocation is stable due to resonance. Thus, S_N reaction takes place.

174. (*b*)
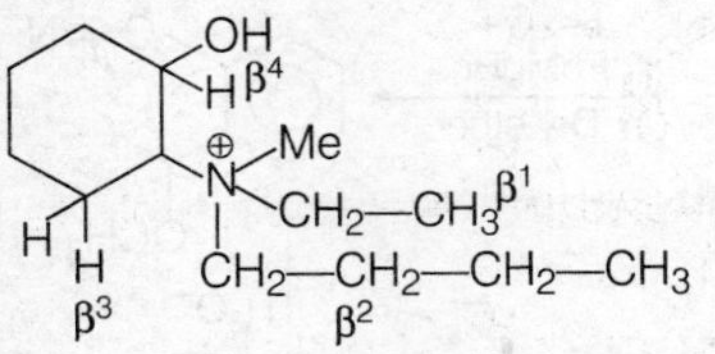

There are four β-hydrogens, in this quarternary ammonium salt.

On heating quarternary ammonium salt gives Hofmann elimination (abstraction of most acidic hydrogen which is β[1]). Hence, major product is $CH_2{=}CH_2$, (least substituted alkene).

175. (*c*) Nucleophile always attacks on electron deficient site.

Presence of electron withdrawing groups such as NO_2, CHO, etc., decreases the electron density on benzene nucleus, hence, such groups activate the ring towards nucleophilic attack. While presence of electron releasing groups such as *R* or *OR* increases the electron density, thus, deactivates the nucleus towards nucleophilic attack.

—NO_2 group activates the ring more than Cl towards nucleophilic attack, hence

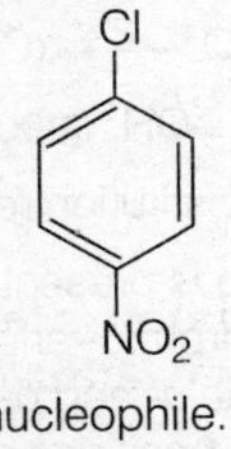

reacts readily with nucleophile.

176. (*b*) Number of hybrid orbitals = number of σ-bonds + number of *lps* in $\dot{C}H_3$
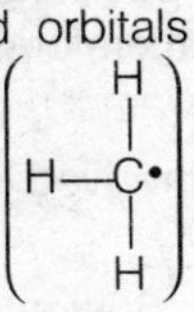

; σ-bonds = 3, *lps* = 0

∴ Number of hybrid orbitals = 3 + 0 = 3

Hence, hybridisation is sp^2 and geometry is planar.

(Methyl free radical is highly reactive due to the presence of one unpaired electron.)

177. (*b*) Hydride ion is formed when hydrogen accept a proton, so it has a tendency to donate electron, hence it functions as nucleophile.

178. (*a*) Alcohols undergo dehydration usually by E1 mechanism. This is because elimination is preferred in case of tertiary alcohols, e.g.

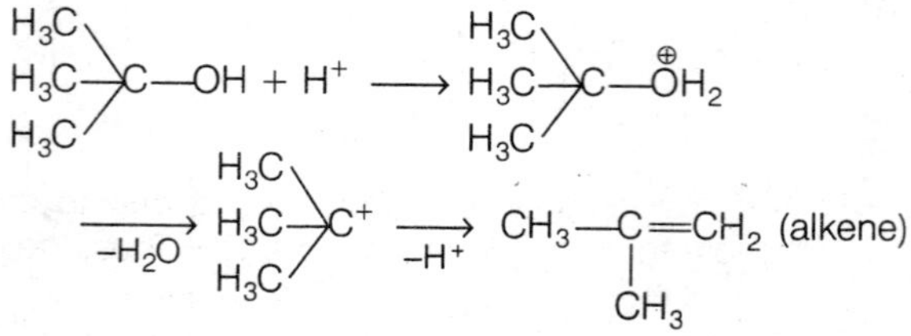

179. (*d*)

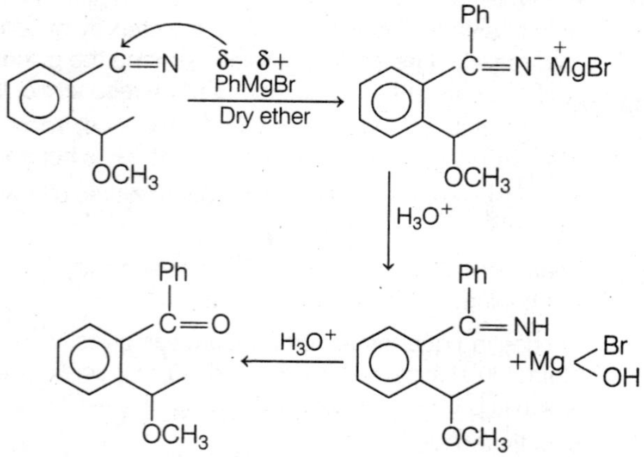

180. (*a*) Nitration of aromatic compounds takes place by an electrophile. The electrophile will be more attracted towards electron rich positions in benzene ring. Hence, electron donating groups will be easily nitrated.

Toluene will be most easily nitrated among these compounds due to presence of electron donating group (i.e. $-CH_3$).Nitrobenzene will be most slowly nitrated due to the presence of electron withdrawing group (i.e. NO_2).

CH_3NO_2 will be formed by free radical substitution of CH_4.

181. (*c*) $(CH_3)_3CBr + H_2O \longrightarrow (CH_3)_3COH + HBr$

Br is substituted by $-OH^-$ (nucleophile)

S_N1 (unimolecular substitution reaction)

182. (*a*) When nitro group is present in the benzene nucleus, it withdraws electrons from *o*- and *p*-positions. Thus, the electron density at the *o*- and *p*-positions decreases, *m*-positions become positions of comparatively higher electron density and therefore, electrophilic attack occurs at *m*-positions.

183. (*d*) The electrophile involved in the sulphonation of benzene is SO_3.

$$2H_2SO_4 \longrightarrow SO_3 + H_3O^+ + HSO_4^-$$

184. (*b*) Among the given species $C_6H_5\overset{+}{N}H_3$ does not exert a resonance effect.

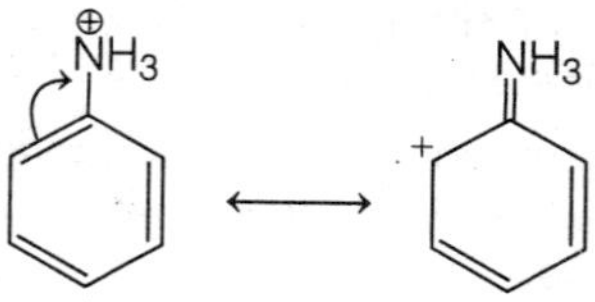

I II

Structure II is not possible because in it nitrogen contains 10 valence electrons.

185. (*b*) When an electron attracting group (like $-NO_2$, $-Cl$) is attached to the phenol ring, it stabilises the negative charge on the oxygen of phenoxide ion. Due to this reason acidic character of phenol increases. But when an electron donating group (like $-CH_3$) is attached to the phenol ring, it destabilises the ring and hence, acidic character of phenol decreases. Thus, the correct order of acidic character is

p-nitrophenol > *p*-chlorophenol > phenol > *o*-cresol

186. (*a*) During inductive effect shifting of σ-electrons takes place due to which partial charges are developed on the atom

$$\overset{+\delta''}{C}-\overset{+\delta'}{C}-\overset{+\delta}{C}-\overset{-\delta}{Cl}$$

187. (*a*) $-NH_2$ has $+R$ effect, it donates electrons to the benzene ring. As a result, the lone pair of electron on the N-atom gets delocalised over the benzene ring and thus, it is less readily available for protonation. Hence, aniline is a weaker base than cyclohexylamine.

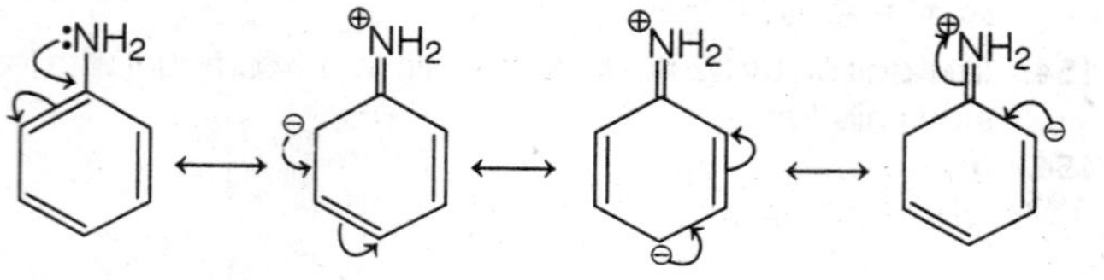

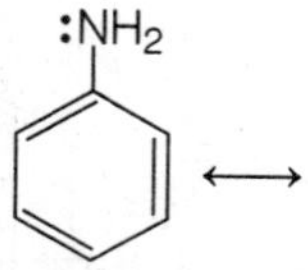

⟷ Resonance structure of aniline

188. (*c*) $CH_2{=}CH\overset{\oplus}{C}HCH_3$ is resonance stabilised.

189. (*a*) As the number of alkyl group attached to the positively charged carbon atom increases, the number of hyperconjugative or no bond contributing structures increases and thus, the stability increases. Benzyl carbocation is most stable due to resonance.

Thus, $C_6H_5\overset{\oplus}{C}H_2 > (CH_3)_3\overset{\oplus}{C} > (CH_3)_2\overset{\oplus}{C}H > CH_3\overset{\oplus}{C}H_2$

but benzyl carbocation is most stable due to resonance.

190. (*a*) The dispersal of the charge stabilises the carbocation. More the number of alkyl groups; the greater the dispersal of positive charge and therefore, more the stability of carbocation, thus, $CH_3\overset{+}{C}H_2 > \overset{+}{C}H_3$ $O-CH_3$ is also an electron-donating group, thus, it will increase the stability of carbocation, hence, the correct order of stability is $C > B > A$.

191. (*b*) S_N1 reaction is most favourable for tertiary substrate.

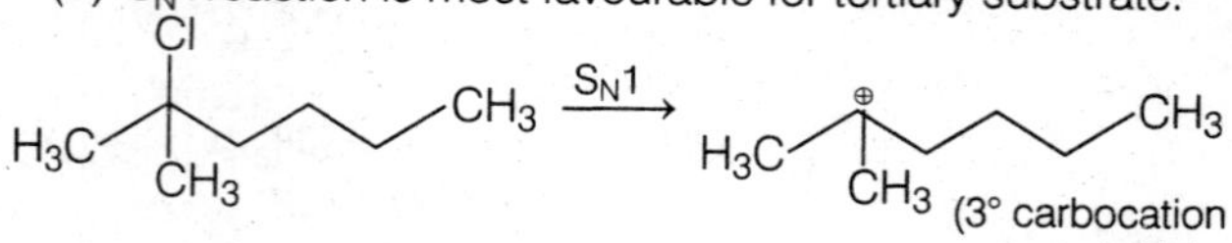

(3° carbocation most stable)

192. (*c*) Due to $+I$ effect CH_3COOH is a weaker acid than formic acid.

193. (*c*)

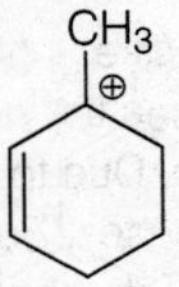

tert allyl carbocation > 2° allyl > 1° allyl > 3° > 2° > 1

194. (*c*)

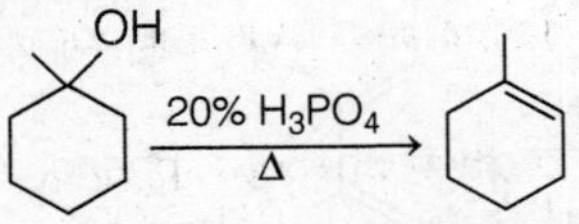

(saytzeff product)

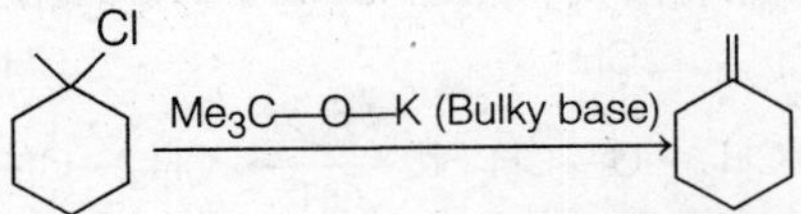

(Hofmann product)

195. (*c*) $+R$ effect of OH > OCH_3

Hence, 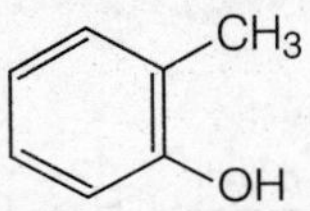 2-methyl phenol is more reactive towards electrophilic reagent.

196. (*d*) $CH_3-CH_2-CH(CH_3)-CH_2Br + NH_3 \longrightarrow CH_3-CH_2-CH(CH_3)-CH_2NH_2$

Br^- is replaced by NH_2^-.

It is an example of nucleophilic substitution reaction.

197. (*a*) $H_2C{=}\overset{+}{N}{=}\overset{-}{N} > H_2\overset{+}{C}-N{=}\overset{-}{N} > H_2\overset{-}{C}-N{=}\overset{+}{N} > H_2\overset{-}{C}-\overset{+}{N}{\equiv}N$

198. (*a*) 1-bromo-3-methyl; prop-2-ene reacts most readily both by S_N1 because the bromine is allylic.Since, CH_3OH is a weak nucleophilic and weak nucleophilic favours S_N1.

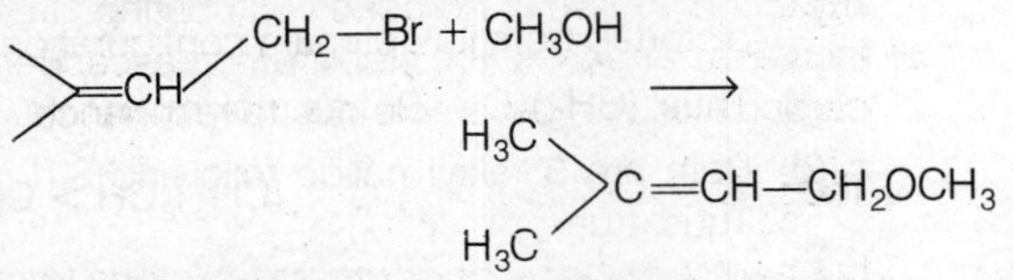

199. (*b*) Aryl halides doesn't undergo hydrolysis by S_N1 mechanism.

200. (*b*) Addition of sodium hydrogen sulphite to acetaldehyde is an example of nucleophilic addition reaction.

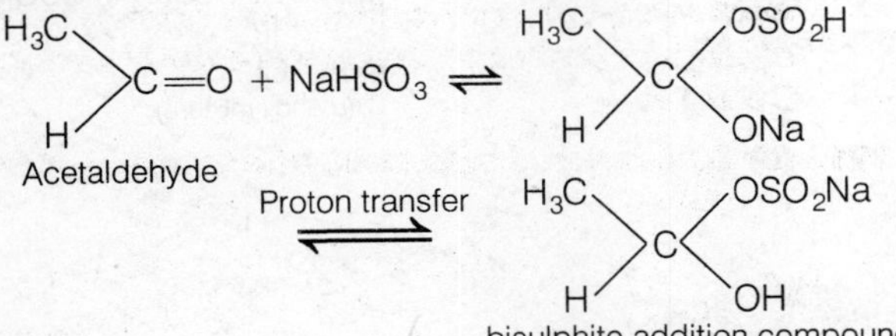

201. (*b*)

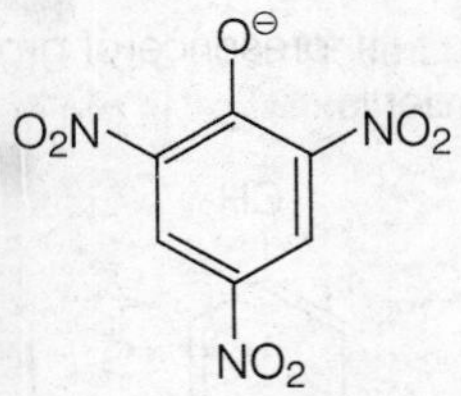

Maximum resonance stabilised and due to three $—NO_2$ groups, more acidic than CH_3COOH. Thus, the decreasing order of acidic strength, III > II > IV > I.

202. (*d*) Higher the tendency to lose a proton, higher will be the acidic character. Besides it, higher the stability of conjugate base, more will be acidic character. Among the given, carboxylate ion ($RCOO^-$) is stabilised by resonance, thus it is more stable and hence, *R*COOH is the most acidic. C_2H_2, on the other hand, gives $HC{\equiv}C^-$ ion which is not so stable, thus it is a weak acid. Thus, the order of acidic character is $RCOOH > H_2O > ROH > C_2H_2$.

203. (*a*)

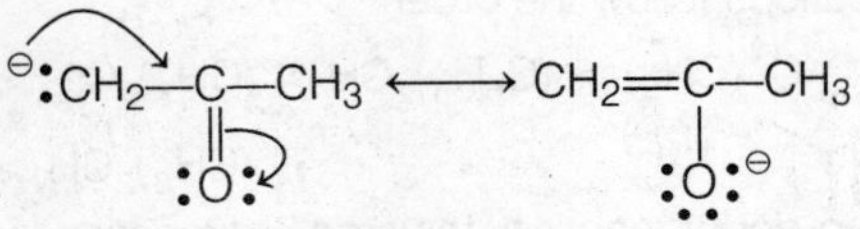

Hence, these are resonating structures.

204. (*b*) $\overset{4}{H_2C}{=}\overset{3}{CH}-\overset{2}{CH_2}-\overset{O}{\overset{\|}{C}}-O-H$ (sp^2, sp^2, sp^3, sp^2)

sp^3-hybridised carbon atom is likely to posses tetrahedral geometry.

205. (*a*) The inductive effect of the alkyl group on a saturated carbon chain follows the order

$(CH_3)_3C— > (CH_3)_2CH— > CH_3CH_2— > CH_3$

However, when an alkyl group is attached to an unsaturated system such as double bond or a benzene ring, the order of inductive effect is actually reversed. This effect is called hyperconjugation effect or Baker-Nathan effect. Now, the reactivity order is

$(CH_3)_3C— < (CH_3)_2CH— < CH_3—CH_2— < CH_3—$

206. (*a*) Cl^- is a weakest base, therefore good leaving group.

207. (*b*) Anions are formed during nucleophilic reaction as

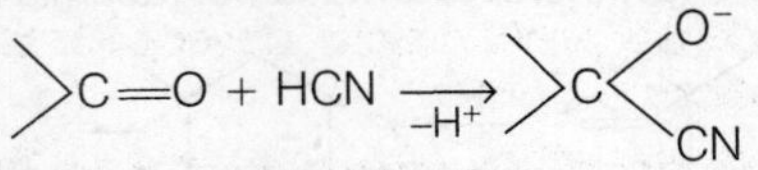

209. (*d*) Migratory order H > Ph > CH_3

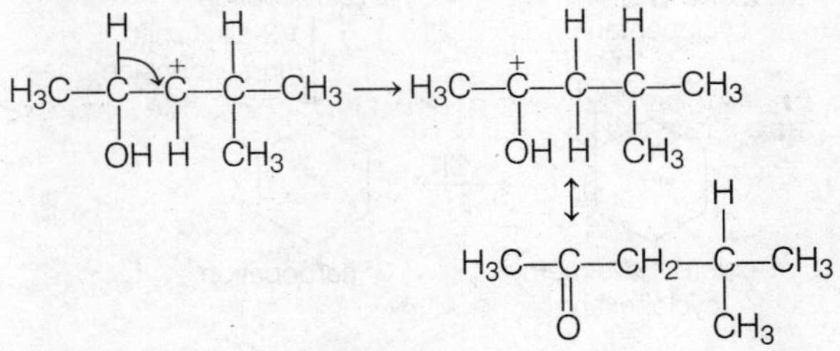

212. (*c*) Stability of carbocations is enhanced by

(i) presence of conjugation, (ii) presence of groups having $+I$ effect. So, the correct order is

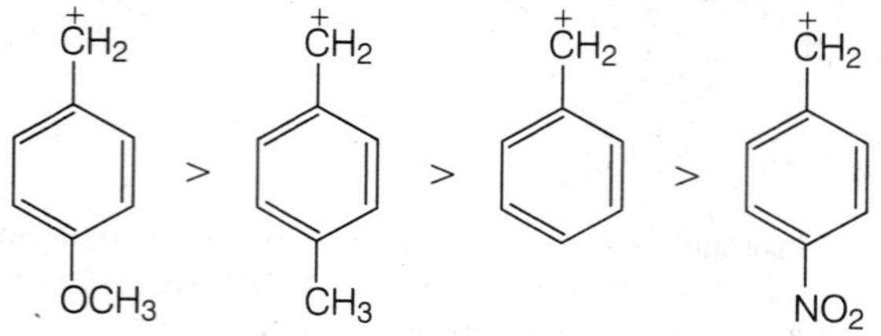

213. (*b*) Based on carbocation stability..Alkyl halides (3° > 2°) are more reactive than aryl halides towards nucleophilic substitution. Among I and II compounds, II has more reactivity due to $-I$ effect of two —NO_2 groups.

215. (*d*) In S_N1 (unimolecular nucleophilic substitution)reactions,

$$\text{Rate} \propto [\text{substrate}]$$

Rate determining step is the formation of carbocation and depends on the stability of carbocation formed. The stability of carbocations follow the order

$$(C_6H_5)_2C^+(CH_3) > (C_6H_5)_2\overset{+}{C}H > (CH_3)_3C^+$$
$$(CH_3)_2\overset{+}{C}H > CH_3CH_2^+$$

Thus, the order of reactivity towards S_N1 reaction is:

(iii) > (ii) > (i) > (iv) > (v)

217. (*b*)

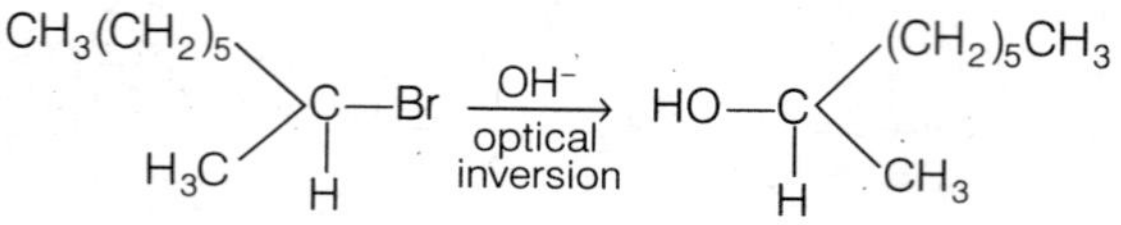

In this reaction inversion takes place. Hence, it is an example of S_N2 reaction. In this mechanism, the attack of OH^- ion takes place from the back side while, the Br^- ion leaves from the front side.

219. (*b*)

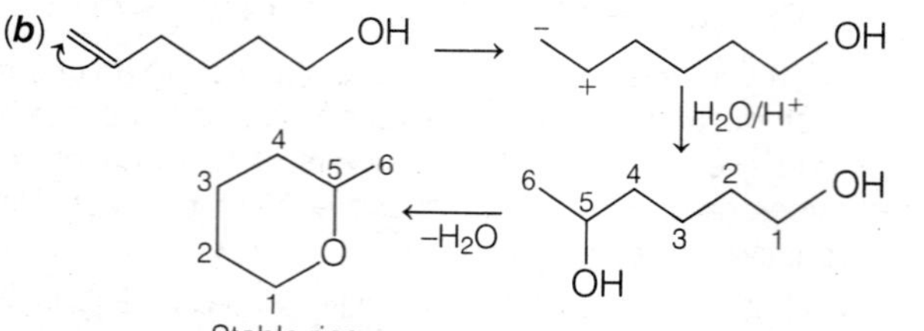

C_5 is chiral carbon, hence enantiomers are formed in equal amounts. Thus, there is formation of racemic mixture.

220. (*c*)

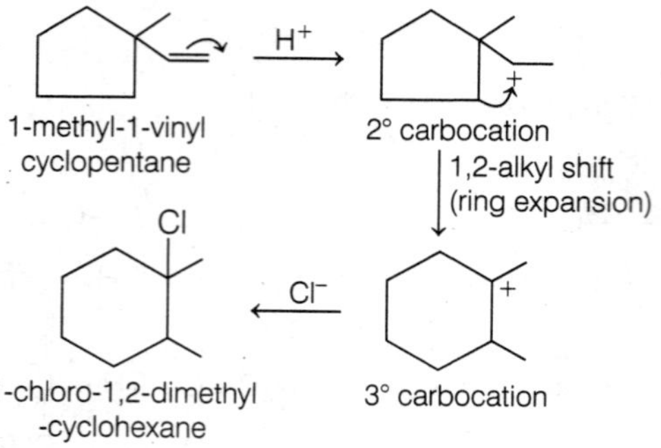

Since, product formed has chiral carbon hence there is formation of racemic mixture.

221. (*a*)

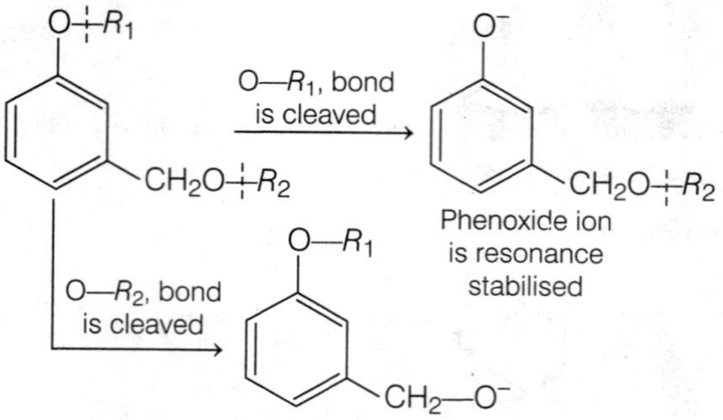

Methoxide ion is not resonance stabilised.

222. (*b*) (a)

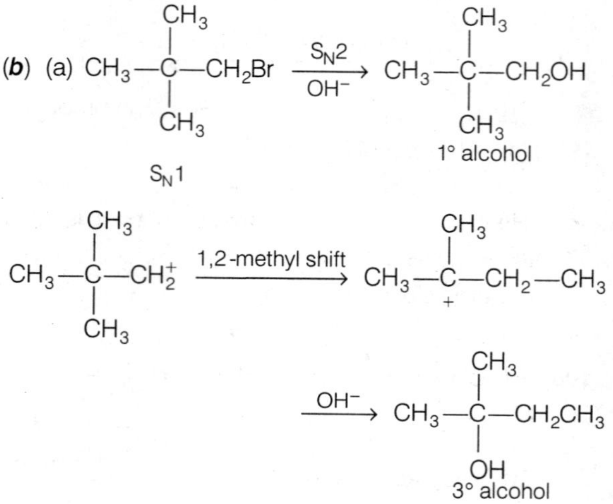

(b) Unstable three membered ring is formed 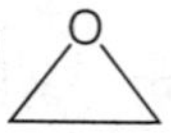

Thus, incorrect.

(c) Bridge head halides are essentially inert under S_N1 conditions. Intermediate carbocation cannot attain the coplanarity needed for optimum formation of its sp^2 bonds and the transition state is correspondingly distorted from its optimum configuration.

Thus, $(CH_3)_3C$—Br has maximum rate. Thus, true.

(d) Both are 3° alkyl halide following S_N1 mechanism. Thus, true.

223. (*c*) This carbocation is attacked by Cl^- from both side. It produce a racemic mixture.

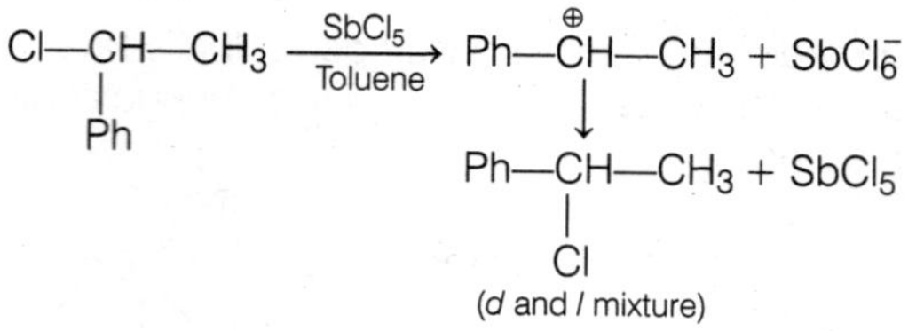

05

Alkanes

Objective Questions Type I [Only one correct option]

In each of the questions below, four choices are given of which only one is correct.

1. Carbon of CH_4 is called

(a) alkyl primary carbon (b) super primary carbon
(c) methyl carbon (d) quaternary carbon

2. Which of the following will have at least one quaternary carbon?

(a) C_5H_{12} (b) C_4H_{10} (c) C_3H_8 (d) C_2H_6

3. Which isomerism is not shown by alkanes ?

(a) Nuclear (b) Chain
(c) Position (d) Functional

4. Following conformation of *n*-butane is called

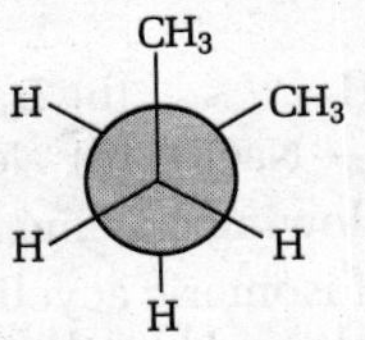

(a) eclipsed (b) *gauche* (staggered)
(c) *anti* (staggered) (d) skew

5. C_8H_{18} with two quaternary carbon atoms will have

(a) one $-CH_2$ and six $-CH_3$ groups
(b) one $-CH_2$ and five $-CH_3$ groups
(c) two $-CH_2$ and four $-CH_3$ groups
(d) six $-CH_3$ groups

6. Following reaction is of the type

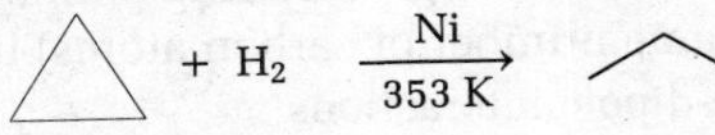

(a) nucleophilic addition
(b) nucleophilic substitution
(c) electrophilic addition
(d) electrophilic substitution

7. *R*—*X* can be reduced to *R*—H by (Zn—Cu) couple/ C_2H_5OH as a result of

(a) nascent hydrogen
(b) molecular hydrogen
(c) electron-transfer from the metal to the substrate followed by the addition of protons from the solvent
(d) all the above are correct statements

8. Which reaction is not correct?

(a) $CH_3\underset{\overset{|}{Cl}}{CH}CH_3 \xrightarrow{LiAlH_4} CH_3CH_2CH_3$

(b) $(CH_3)_3CCl \xrightarrow{LiAlH_4} (CH_3)_3CH$

(c) $(CH_3)_3CCl \xrightarrow{NaBH_4} (CH_3)_3CH$

(d) $CH_3I + HI \xrightarrow{420\text{ K}} CH_4 + I_2$

9. $R\overset{\overset{O}{\|}}{C}CH_3$ (ketone) can be reduced to RCH_2CH_3 (alkane) by

I. $LiAlH_4$, II. P/HI, III. Zn(Hg) / conc. HCl,
IV. N_2H_4 / C_2H_5ONa,

Select the correct reagents.

(a) I, II and III (b) I, III and IV
(c) I, II and IV (d) II, III and IV

10. Following reaction is called

$$CH_3\overset{\overset{O}{\|}}{C}CH_3 \xrightarrow[450\text{ K}]{NH_2-NH_2/C_2H_5ONa} CH_3CH_2CH_3$$

(a) Wolff-Kishner reduction
(b) Clemmensen reduction
(c) Mozingo reduction
(d) Cannizzaro reduction

11. $\underset{A}{C_5H_{11}Br} \xrightarrow[\text{(ii) } D_2O]{\text{(i) Mg/ether}} \underset{B}{C_5H_{11}D}$

Only one type of B is formed. Thus, A is

(a) $CH_3CH_2CH(Br)CH_2CH_3$ (b) $CH_3CH(Br)CH(CH_3)CH_3$

(c) $CH_3-C(CH_3)_2-CH_2Br$ (d) $CH_3CH_2CH(CH_3)CH_2Br$

12. Only one type of hydrocarbon is formed by Wurtz reaction using

(a) CH_3CH_2Cl (b) 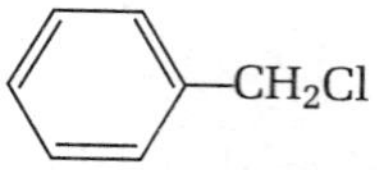

(c) $CH_3CH(Cl)CH_3$ (d) in all cases

13. Using C_2H_5Cl/Na by Wurtz reaction in addition to C_4H_{10}, C_2H_4 and C_2H_6 are also formed. It is due to

(a) oxidation

(b) reduction

(c) disproportionation

(d) auto-oxidation

14. Intermediate of the Wurtz reaction is

$$CH_3CH_2Br \xrightarrow{\text{Na/ether}}$$

(a) $CH_3\dot{C}H_2$ (b) $Br^{\bullet}$

(c) $CH_3CH_2\underset{\bullet}{C}HCH_3$ (d) $CH_3CH_2CH_2\dot{C}H_2$

15. $(CH_3)_3COH + CH_3MgBr \longrightarrow$ Hydrocarbon (A), (A) is

(a) $(CH_3)_3CCH_3$ (b) $(CH_3)_3CH$

(c) CH_4 (d) None of these

16. Consider the following reactions for the formation of alkanes

I. $CH_3COOK(aq) \xrightarrow{\text{Current}} CH_3CH_3$ (at anode)

II. $CH_3Cl \xrightarrow{\text{Na/ether}} CH_3CH_3$

III. $CH_3Cl \xrightarrow[\text{(ii) } CH_3Cl]{\text{(i) Li/ether/CuI}} CH_3CH_3$

These reactions are

	I	II	III
(a)	Kolbe	Wurtz	Fittig
(b)	Kolbe	Fittig	Wurtz
(c)	Kolbe	Fittig	Corey-House
(d)	Kolbe	Wurtz	Corey-House

17. In the following reaction,

$$R_2CuLi \xrightarrow{R'X} R-R' + RCu + LiX$$

Nature of R and R' should be

(a) any alkyl, 2° alkyl

(b) any alkyl, methyl/1° alkyl/2° cycloalkyl

(c) 1° alkyl, methyl/1° alkyl/2° cycloalkyl

(d) 2° alkyl, any alkyl

18. In the following reaction X can be

$$RCH{=}CH_2 \xrightarrow{B_2H_6} (RCH_2CH_2)_3B \xrightarrow{X} RCH_2CH_3$$

(a) $AgNO_3/NaOH$ (b) CH_3CH_2COOH

(c) Both (a) and (b) (d) None of these

19. Select the correct option. **[JEE Main 2021, Feb.]**

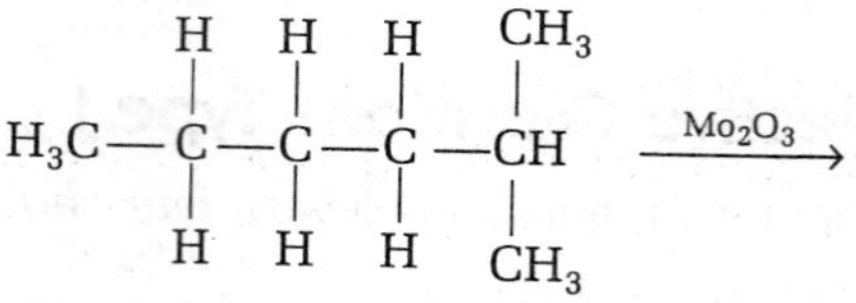

(a) 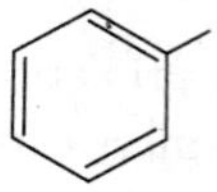 (b) 

(c) 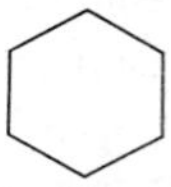 (b) 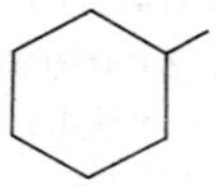

20. Partial reduction of A is selectively done using

(a) $Sia_2BH/AcOH$ (b) B_2H_6/CH_3CH_2COOH

(c) $B_2H_6/AgNO_3-NaOH$ (d) $NaBH_4$

21. Consider the following statements,

I. In a group of isomeric acyclic compounds, normal compound always has the highest boiling point. and melting point.

II. Greater the branching in alkanes, lower is the boiling point.

III. Melting point of alkanes depends upon the packing of molecules in the crystalline lattice.

Select the correct statement(s).

(a) I and II (b) II and III

(c) I and III (d) I, II and III

22. Alkyl halides have higher boiling points than alkanes (having same number of carbon atoms) because of

(a) dipole-dipole interactions

(b) decreased surface area

(c) packing of molecules

(d) All of the factors above

23. As branching in alkane increases, boiling point decreases due to

(a) decreased surface for intermolecular attraction

(b) dipole-dipole interactions

(c) Both (a) and (b)

(d) None of the above

24. Which is incorrect comparison of the boiling point of alkanes?

(a) 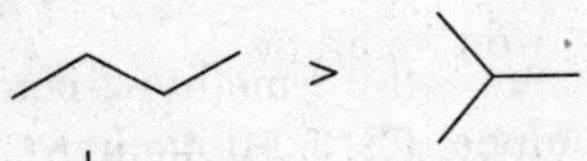

(b) 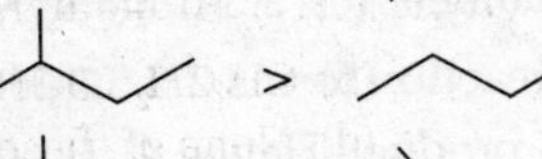

(c) 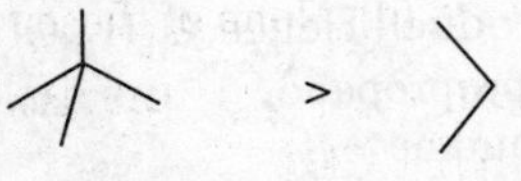

(d) None of the above

25. During the free redical chlorination of methane, which of the following reactions has the lowest collision frequency ?

(a) $Cl\bullet + \bullet CH_3 \longrightarrow CH_3Cl$

(b) $Cl\bullet + Cl_2 \longrightarrow Cl_2 + Cl\bullet$

(c) $\bullet CH_3 + CH_4 \longrightarrow CH_4 + \bullet CH_3$

(d) $\bullet CH_3 + Cl_4 \longrightarrow CH_3Cl + Cl\bullet$

26. Which is the most stable free radical (which is most easily formed)?

(a) $CH_2{=}CH\dot{C}H_2$ (b) $CH_3\dot{C}H_2$

(c) $(CH_3)_2\dot{C}H$ (d) $(CH_3)_3\dot{C}$

27. Which C—H bond has the minimum bond energy in the following?

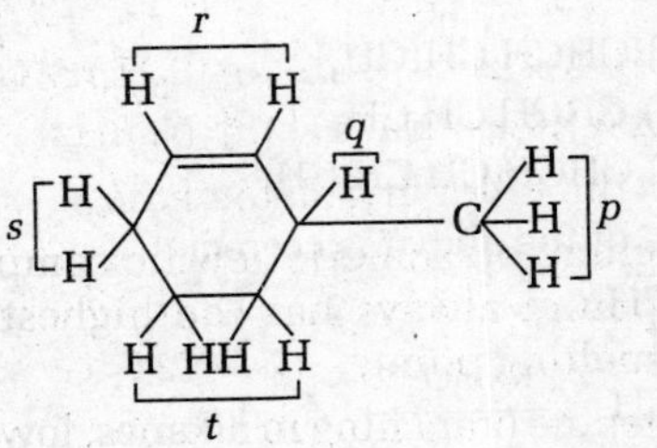

(a) *p* (b) *q* (c) *r* (d) *s*

28. Monochlorination of the following produces a chiral carbon

(a) 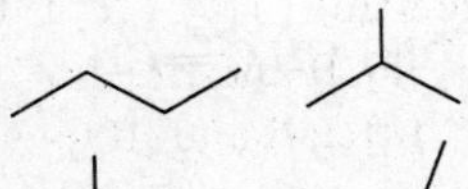

(b) 

(c) 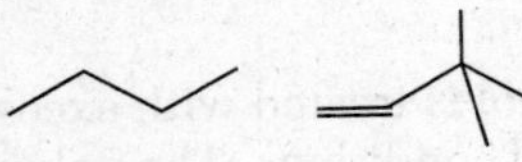

(d) 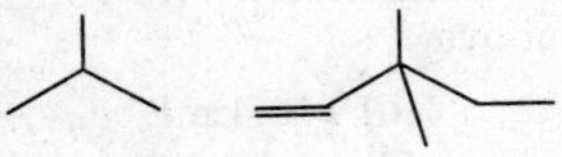

29. During the combustion of ethane, the hybrid state of carbon changes from :

(a) sp^3 to sp (b) sp^2 to sp^3

(c) sp to sp^3 (d) sp^2 to sp^2

30. In the iodination of alkane, some HIO_3 is also added so that

(a) reaction is made faster

(b) reaction is made reversible

(c) HI formed is oxidised to I_2

(d) reaction is selective

31. Indicate suitable reagents *x*, *y* and *z* for the following transformations

$$(CH_3)_3CH \xrightarrow{x} (CH_3)_3C{-}OH$$

$$CH_4 \xrightarrow{y} CH_2O$$

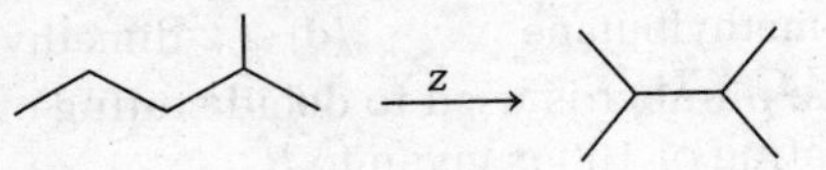

	x	*y*	*z*
(a)	$KMnO_4$	$AlCl_3$ / HCl	CH_3Cl / $AlCl_3$
(b)	$AlCl_3$/HCl	$KMnO_4$	CH_3Cl/ $AlCl_3$
(c)	$KMnO_4$	O_3	$AlCl_3$ / HCl
(d)	$KMnO_4$	$AlCl_3$/HCl	O_3

32. Intermediate of the following isomerisation is

$$CH_3CH_2CH_2CH_3 \xrightarrow{AlCl_3/HCl} CH_3\underset{\underset{CH_3}{|}}{C}HCH_3$$

(a) $CH_3CH_2\overset{\oplus}{C}HCH_3$ (b) $(CH_3)_3C^{\oplus}$

(c) Both (a) and (b) (d) None of these

33. *n*-octane in the presence of Cr_2O_3/Al_2O_3 at 873 K changes to

(a) 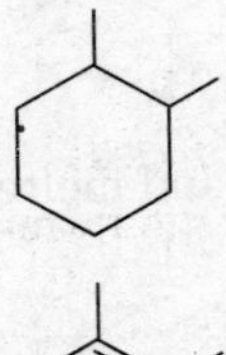

(b) 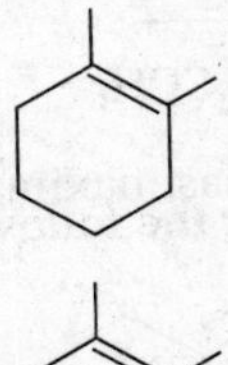

(c) 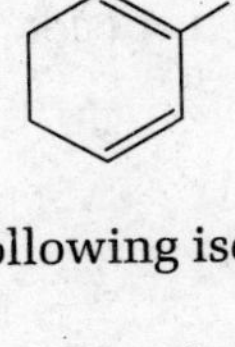

(d) 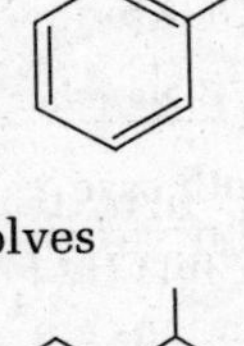

34. Following isomerisation involves

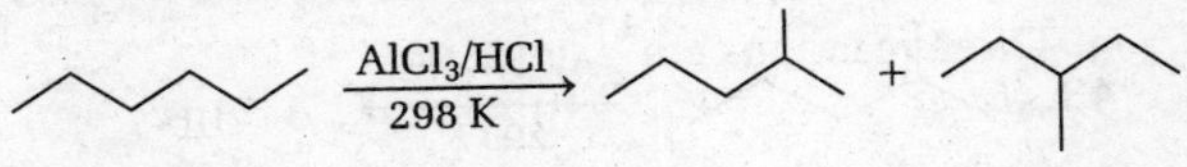

(a) 1,2-hydride or methyl shift

(b) 1,2-methyl shift only

(c) 1,2-hydride only

(d) reduction

35. Cracking of ethane gives mixture of
(a) C_2H_4 and H_2 (b) C_2H_4, H_2 and CH_4
(c) H_2 and CH_4 (d) only CH_4

36. $(CH_3)_3CMgCl$ on reaction with D_2O produces
(a) $(CH_3)_3CD$ (b) $(CH_3)_3COD$
(c) $(CD_3)_3CD$ (d) $(CD_3)_3COD$

37. Which of the following has the lowest boiling point?
(a)  (b) 
(c)  (d) 

38. Which of the following compound has highest boiling point?
(a) *n*-hexane (b) *n*-pentane
(c) 2-methylbutane (d) 2,2-dimethylpropane

39. Cetane number is used to decide rating of *A* ...., ... and rating of 100 is given to *B*.
A and *B* are
(a) diesel, isooctane
(b) diesel, hexadecane
(c) gasoline, isooctane
(d) gasoline, hexadecane

40. Aqueous solution of potassium acetate is electrolysed. Possible organic products are
(a) CH_3CH_3 (b) CH_3COOCH_3
(c) $CH_3CH_2CH_2CH_3$ (d) (a) and (b)

41. Which of the alkane is synthesised from single alkyl halide?
(a)  (b) 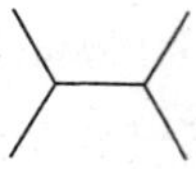
(c) 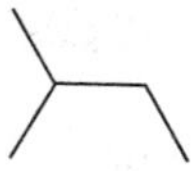 (d) 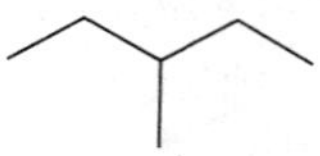

42. Which has maximum boiling point and melting point out of
 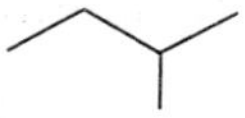 
I II III
(a) I in both case (b) I and II
(c) I and III (d) II and I

43. 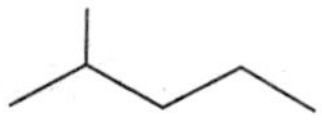 $\xrightarrow[298\ K]{AlCl_3—HCl}$ *A*, *A* is
(a) 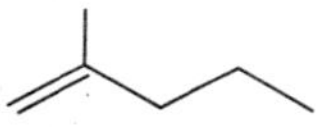 (b) 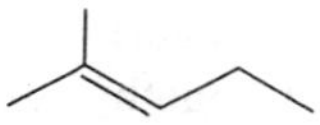
(c) 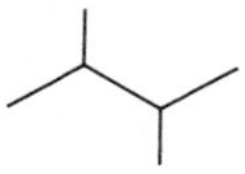 (d) 

44. Octane rating is decided by octane number and is given 100 when centper cent anti-knocking property of the petroleum product. Which is given octane number 100?
(a) *Iso*-octane (b) Heptane
(c) Tetraethyl lead (d) Octane

45. C_6H_{12} (A) has chirality but on hydrogenation A is converted into $C_6H_{14}(B)$ in which chirality disappears. Hence, *A* is
(a) 3-methyl-1-pentene (b) 2-methyl-2-pentene
(c) 2,3-dimethyl-2-butene (d) 3,3-dimethyl-1-butene

46. $C_5H_{11}Cl$ by Wurtz reaction forms 2,2,5,5-tetramethylhexane as the main product. Hence, $C_5H_{11}Cl$ is
(a) 2,2-dimethyl-1-chloropropane
(b) 2-methyl-1-chlorobutane
(c) Both (a) and (b)
(d) None of the above true

47. C_8H_{18} (*A*) on chlorination forms only one type of $C_8H_{17}Cl$ (*B*). Hence, *A* can be
(a) 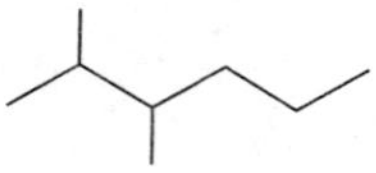 (b) 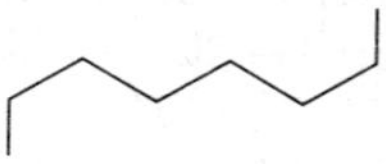
(c) 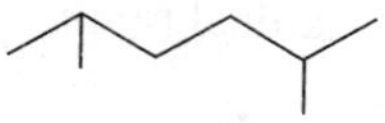 (d) 

48. $(CH_3)_2CHBr \xrightarrow[\text{(ii) CuI, (iii) } (CH_3)_2CHCH_2Br]{\text{(i) Li}} A$
This is Corey-House method of synthesis of *A* which is
(a) $(CH_3)_2CHCH_2CH(CH_3)_2$
(b) $(CH_3)_2CHCH_2CH_2CH_3$
(c) $(CH_3)_2CHCH_2CH_2CH_2CH_3$
(d) None of the above is correct

49. $CH_3—CH(CH_3)—CH_3$ (i.e. $(CH_3)_3CH$) $\xrightarrow{KMnO_4}$ *A*, *A* is
(a) $CH_3CH(CH_3)COOH$ (b) $CH_3C(CH_3){=}CH_2$
(c) $CH_3—C(CH_3)(OH)—CH_3$ (d) CH_3COCH_3

50. 0.21 g of but-3-ynll-2-ol is treated with excess of C_2H_5MgBr at standard conditions. The volume of gas evolved is
(a) 134.4 mL (b) 146.4 mL
(c) 67.2 mL (d) 73.2 mL

51. R—Mg—Br + $(CH_3)_2CHOH \longrightarrow$ hydrocarbon (A). A occupies 1.4 L per g at NTP. Hence, R—Mg—Br is

(a) CH_3—Mg—Br (b) 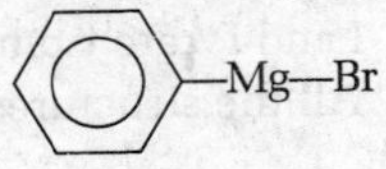

(c) 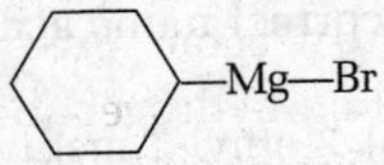 (d) None of these

52. Scheme I. Mg/ether/D_2O
Scheme II. CaO/NaOD (sodalime)
Which is used to replace Br by D in bromocyclohexane?

(a) Only I (b) Only II
(c) Both (a) and (b) (d) None of these

53. 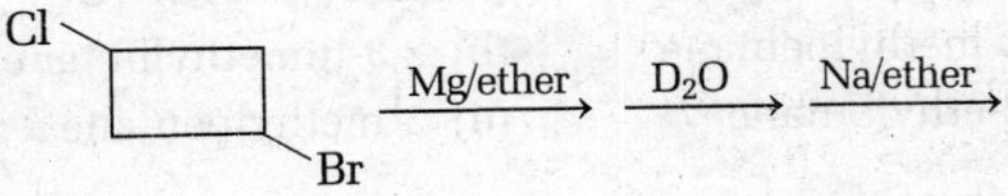 (A), A is

(a) 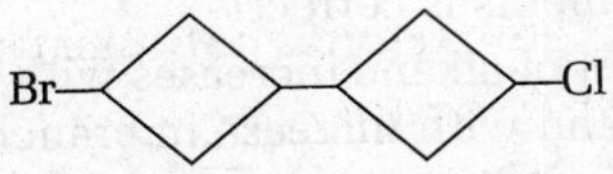

(b) 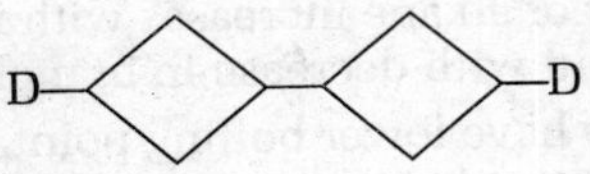

(c) 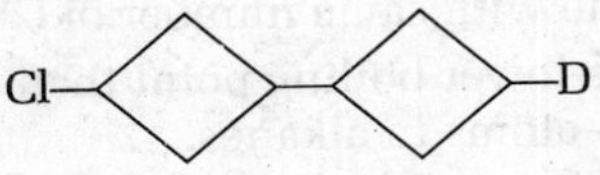

(d) 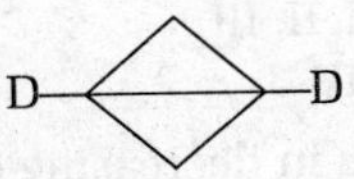

54. $CH_3CH_2Cl + LiAlH_4 \longrightarrow CH_3CH_3$
This reduction process follows

(a) S_N1 mechanism (b) S_N2 mechanism
(c) E1 mechanism (d) E2 mechanism

55. $(R)_2LiCu \xrightarrow{R'\,Br} R—R' + R—Cu + LiBr$
This is called Corey-House method of synthesising alkanes. This, follows

(a) S_N 1 mechanism (b) S_N 2 mechanism
(c) E2 mechanism (d) E1-CB mechanism

56. In (Q. 55) above, R' should be

(a) a methyl (b) 1° alkyl
(c) 2° cycloalkyl (d) All are true

57. Cetane number and octane number are zero respectively for

(a) 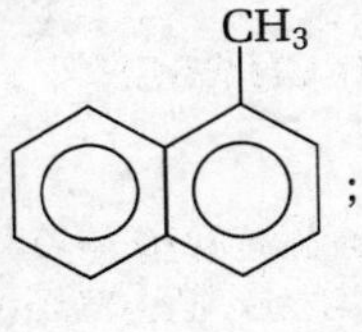 ; 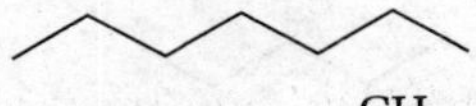

(b) 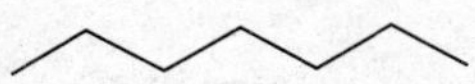 ; 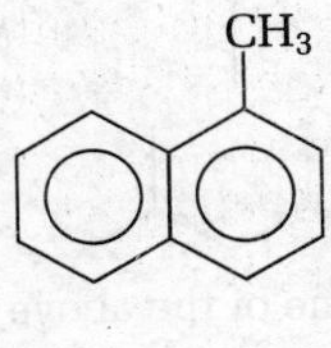

(c) 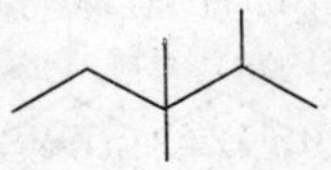 ; 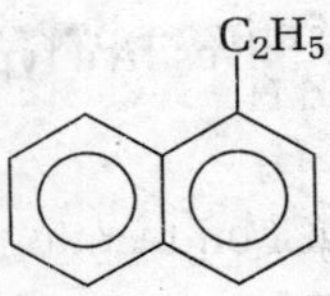

(d)  ; 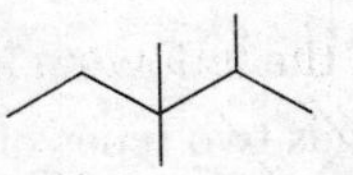

58. Octane number can be improved without causing toxic effect by

(a) TEL (b) RDX
(c) MTBE (d) None of these

59. Out of the following which structures represent the same compound

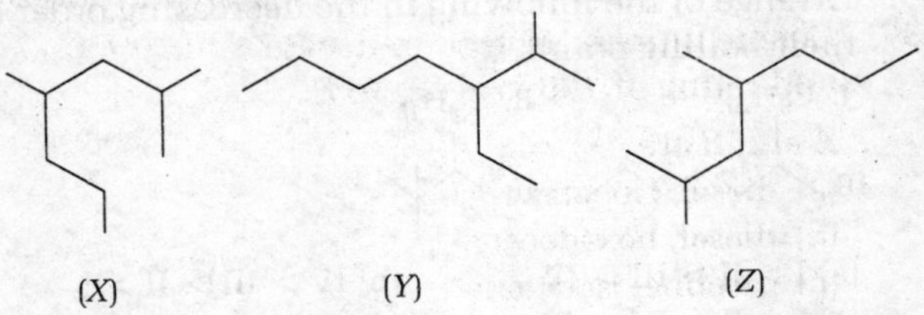

(X) (Y) (Z)

(a) X, Z (b) X, Y (c) Y, Z (d) X, Y, Z

60. Consider the following statement(s).

I. Melting points tend to increase with increasing molecular mass within a series.

II. Many symmetrical molecules have unusually high melting points.

III. Boiling points tend to be lower for highly branched molecules that approach spherical proportions because they have less molecular surface available for van der Waals' attractions.

Select the correct statement(s).

(a) I and II (b) I and III
(c) II and III (d) I, II and III

61. Which has maximum melting point and boiling point out of n-pentane (I), *iso*-pentane (II) and *neo*-pentane (III)?

(a) I and II (b) II and I
(c) III and I (d) II and III

62. Which of the following has maximum boiling point?

(a) 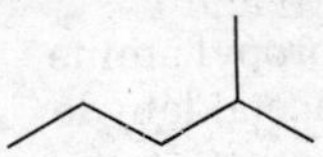 (b) 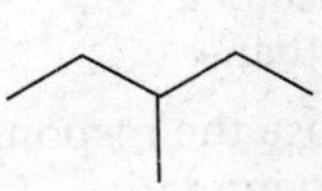

(c) 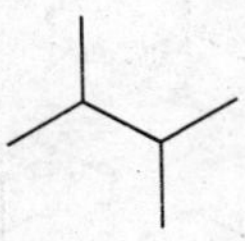 (d) 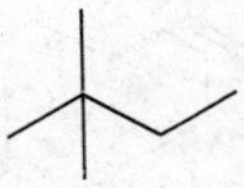

63. Which C_6H_{14} gives five types of $C_6H_{13}Cl$?

(a)  (b) 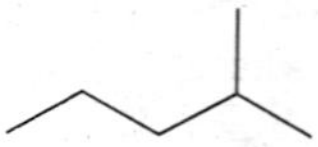

(c) 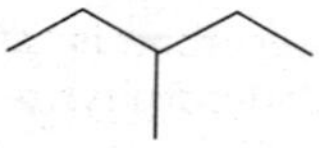 (d) 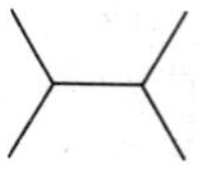

64. $C_6H_{12}(A)$ has two types of alkenes that can be reduced to one type of C_6H_{14} (B). B is

(a)  (b) 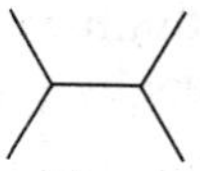

(c) 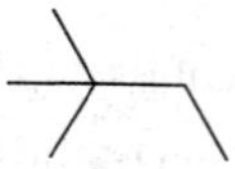 (d) 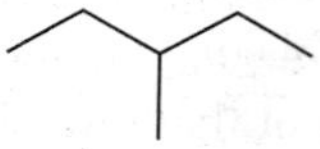

65. Arrange of the following in the decreasing order of their boiling points :

I. C_9H_{20} II. C_9H_{18}

III. 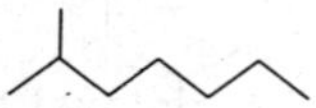 II. 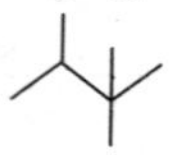

(a) I > II > III > IV (b) IV > III > II > I
(c) I > II > IV > III (d) III > IV > II > I

66. The alkane is not obtained from

(a) hydroxylation of ethyne (b) $C_2H_5OH \xrightarrow[150°C]{HI/Red\ P}$

(c) butanone $\xrightarrow[Reflux]{Zn/Hg\text{-}HCl}$

(d) electrolysis of sodium propanoate solution

67. Which of the following gives methane (CH_4) on hydrolysis?

(a) Fe_3O_4 (b) Al_2O_3 (c) CaC_2 (d) Al_4C_3

68. Domestic cooking gas consists of mostly

(a) butane and isobutane
(b) methane and ethane
(c) ethylene and carbon monoxide
(d) acetylene and hydrogen

69. Both CH_4 and C_2H_6 can be prepared in one step by the reaction of

(a) CH_3Br (b) CH_3CH_2OH (c) CH_3OH (d) CH_3COCH_3

70. The product formed by heating sodium propionate with sodalime is

(a) acetone (b) propyl amine
(c) ethane (d) acetaldehyde

71. Choose the response that best describes the following compounds

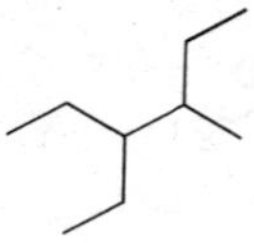 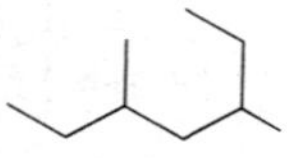 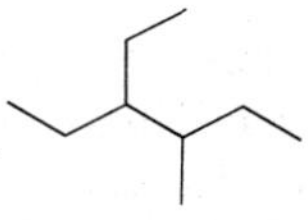 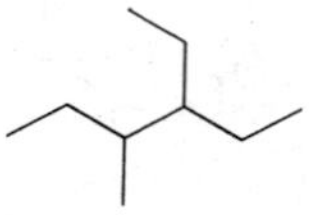

I II III IV

(a) I, III and IV represent the same compound
(b) I and III are isomers of II and IV
(c) I and IV are isomers of II and III
(d) All the structures represent the same compound

72. Which of the following is a correct name according to the IUPAC rules?

(a) 2-methylcyclohexane (b) 2-ethyl-2-methylpentane
(c) 3,4-dimethylpentane (d) 3-ethyl-2-methylpentane

73. Following are the structures of four isomers of hexane. Which of the names given correctly identifies a fifth isomer?

$CH_3CH_2CH_2CH_2CH_2CH_3$ $(CH_3)_3CCH_2CH_3$
$(CH_3)_2CHCH_2CH_2CH_3$ $(CH_3)_2CHCH(CH_3)_2$

(a) 2-methylpentane (b) 2,3-dimethylbutane
(c) 2-ethylbutane (d) 3-methylpentane

74. Which of the statements is correct?

I. Melting point of alkane increases with increase of C–atoms and with increase in branching.
II. Boiling point of alkane increases with increase of C–atoms but with decrease in branching.
III. Cycloalkanes have lower boiling point than normal alkane with same number of C–atoms.
IV. Alkenes have lower boiling point than same number of C–atoms in alkanes.

(a) I, II (b) I, II, III
(c) III, IV (d) IV

75. Rank the following substances in decreasing order of heats of combustion (most exothermic → least exothermic).

 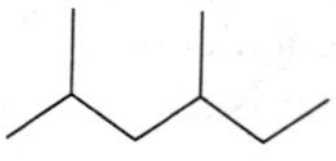 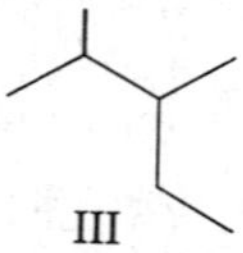

I II III

(a) II > I > III (b) II > III > I (c) III > I > II (d) III > II > I

76. What is the total number of σ-bonds present in the molecule shown?

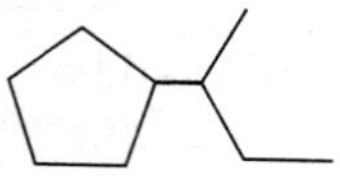

(a) 18 (b) 26 (c) 27 (d) 30

77. Which of the following substances is not an isomer of 3-ethyl-2-methylpentane?

(a) 

(b) 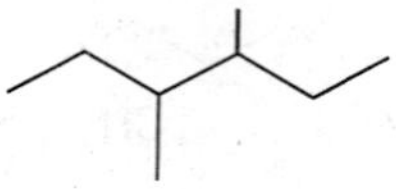

(c) 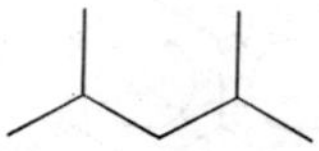

(d) None of the above (all are isomers)

78. Which of the following plots is (are) correct for the given reaction ? **[JEE Advanced 2020]**

($[P]_0$ is the initial concentration of P)

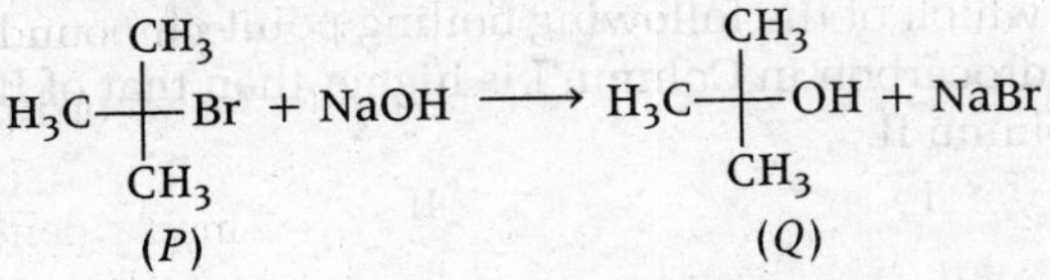

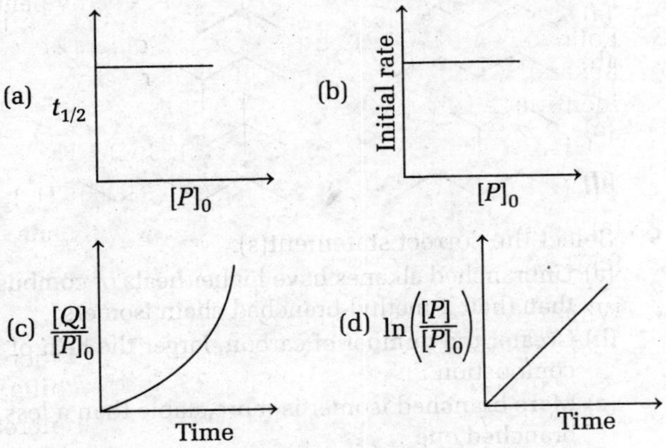

79. What is the correct IUPAC name of the alkyl group shown?

$$\begin{array}{l} \quad CH_2CH_3 \\ -CHCH_2CH(CH_3)_2 \end{array}$$

(a) 1-ethyl-3-methylbutyl (b) 1-ethyl-3,3-dimethyl propyl
(c) 4-ethyl-2-methylbutyl (d) 5-methylhexyl

80. $C_4H_8Cl_2(A) \xrightarrow{\text{Hydrolysis}} C_4H_8O(B)$

B forms oxime with NH_2OH but does not give Tollen's test. Compound (A) and (B) are respectively **[JEE Main 2021, Feb.]**

(a) 2, 2-dichlorobutane and 2-butanone
(b) 2, 2-dichlorobutane and 2-butanal
(c) 1, 1-dichlorobutanc and 2-butanal
(d) 1, 2-dichlorobutane and 2-butanone

81. In the following reaction,

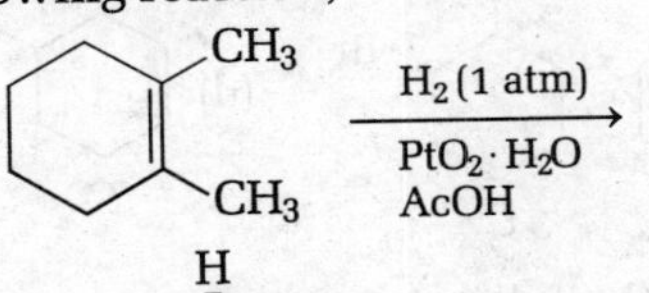

I. Product is

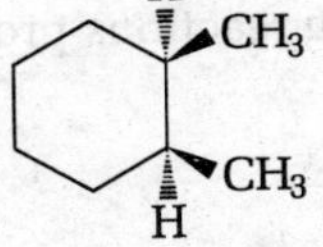

II. Product is

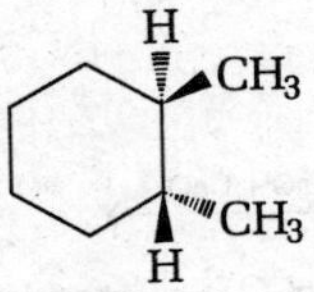

III. Addition is *syn*

IV. Addition is *anti*

V. Addition is stereoselective

Select the correct statement(s).

(a) I, III and V (b) II, IV and V
(c) I, IV and V (d) II, III and V

82. Select the correct statement(s).

(a) The hydroxylation of the hydrocarbon is carried out in the liver, catalysed by an iron-porphyrin-containing enzyme.
(b) Iron changes its oxidation state from V to IV and to III
(c) Intermediate is a radical
(d) All of the above are correct statements

83. The deuterium kinetic isotope effect for chlorination of an alkane is defined as

(a) $= \dfrac{\text{rate of homolytic cleavage of C — H bond by Cl}^\bullet}{\text{rate of homolytic cleavage of C — D bond by Cl}^\bullet}$

(b) $= \dfrac{\text{rate of homolytic cleavage of C — D bond by Cl}^\bullet}{\text{rate of homolytic cleavage of C — H bond by Cl}^\bullet}$

(c) Both (a) and (b)
(d) None of the above

84. The reactions, P to Q, Q to R and R to product are **[JEE Advanced 2017]**

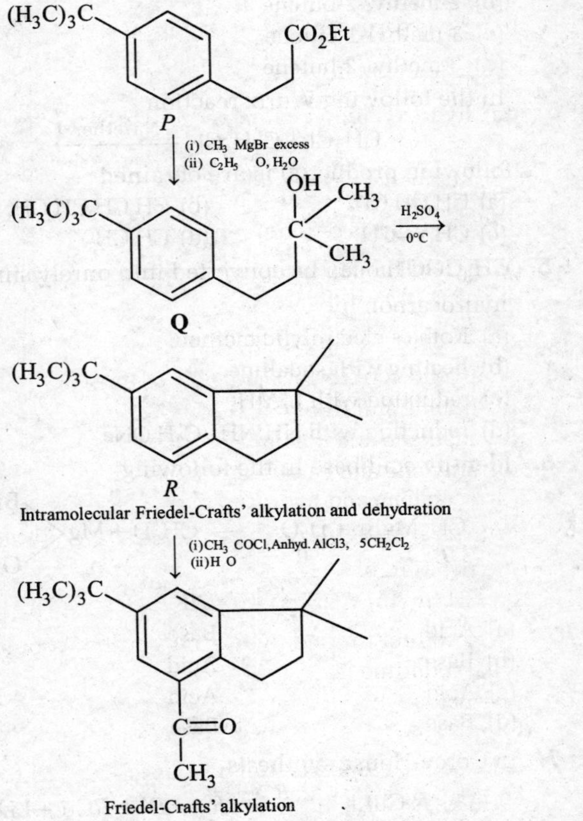

(a) Dehydration and Friedel-Crafts acylation
(b) Aromatic sulphonation and Friedel-Crafts acylation
(c) Friedel-Crafts alkylation, dehydration and Friedel-Crafts acylation
(d) Friedel-Crafts alkylation and Friedel-Crafts acylation

Objective Questions Type II [One or more than one correct option(s)]

In each of the questions below, four choices are given, of which one or more than one are correct.

1. Following conversion can be carried out by (X)

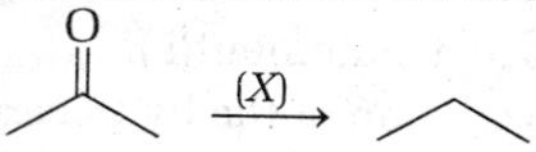

(X) can be

(a) red P/HI (b) NH_2NH_2/C_2H_5ONa
(c) Zn(Hg)/conc. HCl (d) $LiAlH_4$

2. Select in correct products formed.

(a) 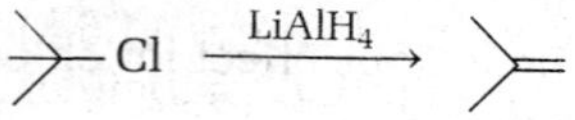

(b) 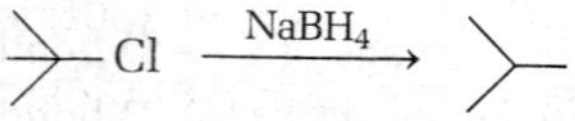

(c) 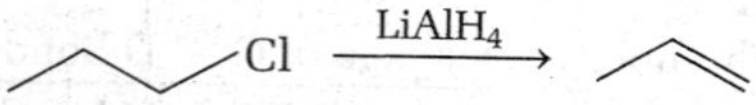

(d) 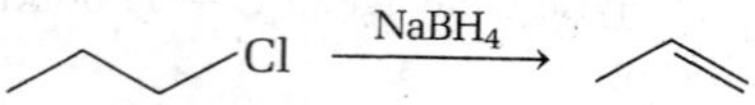

3. 2-methylbutane can be formed by hydrogenation of

(a) 2-methyl-1-butene
(b) 2-methyl-2-butene
(c) 3-methyl-1-butene
(d) 3-methyl-2-butene

4. In the following Wurtz reaction

$$CH_3Cl + C_2H_5Cl \xrightarrow{Na/ether}$$

following product(s) is/are obtained

(a) $CH_3CH_2CH_3$ (b) $CH_3CH_2CH_2CH_3$
(c) $CH_2{=}CH_2$ (d) CH_3CH_3

5. CH_3COONa can be converted into purely single hydrocarbon by

(a) Kolbe's electrolytic method
(b) heating with sodalime
(c) reduction with $LiAlH_4$
(d) reduction with NH_2NH_2/C_2H_5ONa

6. Identify acid/base in the following

$$\underset{I}{CH_3MgBr} + \underset{II}{D_2O} \longrightarrow CH_3D + Mg\langle^{Br}_{OD}$$

	I	II
(a)	Acid	Base
(b)	Base	Acid
(c)	Acid	Acid
(d)	Base	Base

7. In Corey-House synthesis

$$\underset{\text{(Gilman reagent)}}{R_2CuLi} \xrightarrow{R'X} R - R' + RCu + LiX$$

$R{-}R'$ is formed good yield if R' is

(a) methyl (b) 1° alkyl
(c) 2° cycloalkyl (d) 3° alkyl

8. In which of the following boiling point of hydrocarbon in Column I is higher than that of II in Column II.

I II

(a) 

(b) 

(c) 

(d) 

9. Select the correct statement(s).

(a) Unbranched alkanes have higher heats of combustion than their 2-methyl-branched chain isomers
(b) Greater the number of carbon, larger the heat of combustion
(c) More branched isomer is more stable than a less branched one
(d) Reactivity of (C—H) bond in halogenation reaction is $1° > 2° > 3°$

10. Choose the correct option(s) for the following set of reactions **[JEE Advanced 2019]**

$$C_6H_{10}O \xrightarrow[\text{(ii) } H_2O]{\text{(i) MeMgBr}} Q \xrightarrow{\text{Conc. HCl}} \underset{\text{(Major)}}{S}$$

$$Q \xrightarrow{20\%\ H_3PO_4,\ 360\ K} \underset{\text{(Major)}}{T} \xrightarrow[\text{(ii) } Br_2,\ h\nu]{\text{(i) } H_2,\ Ni} \underset{\text{(Major)}}{R} \xrightarrow[\Delta]{\text{HBr, Benzoyl peroxide}} \underset{\text{(Major)}}{U}$$

(a) 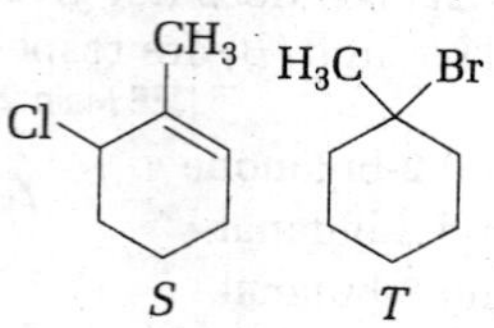
S T

(b) 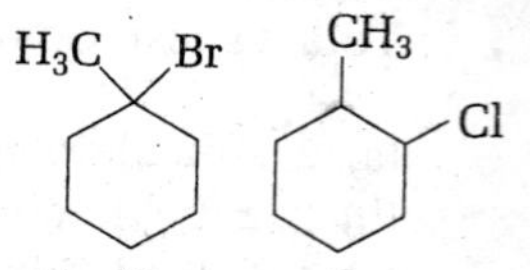
U S

(c) 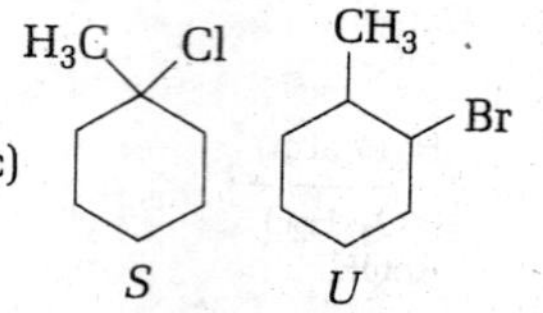
S U

(d) 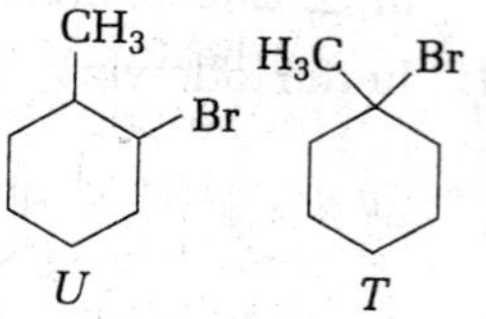
U T

11. Which of the following reactions produce(s) propane as a major product? **[JEE Advanced 2019]**

(a) 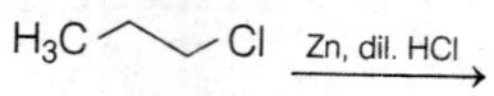

(b) 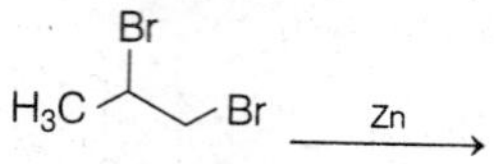

(c) 

(d) 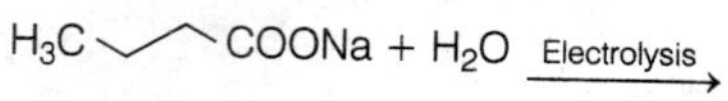

Numerical Value Questions

All these questions have a Numerical value as their answer, solve the questions and write your answer.

1. Find the sum of $N + M$ in the given reaction ?

$$\text{Propane} \xrightarrow{Cl_2/h\nu} \underset{C_3H_6Cl_2}{N} \xrightarrow[\text{distillation}]{\text{Fractional}} \underset{\text{(Isomeric product)}}{M}$$

2. The total number of stable conformers with non-zero dipole moment for the following compound is

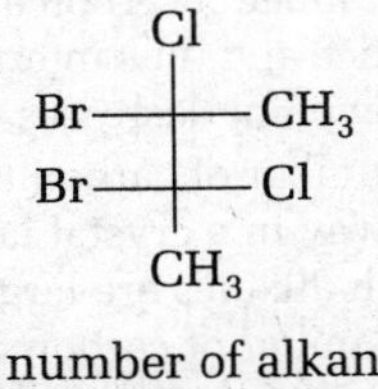

3. The total number of alkane possible by dehydrobromination of 3-bromo-3-cyclopentyl-hexane using alcoh. KOH.

4. 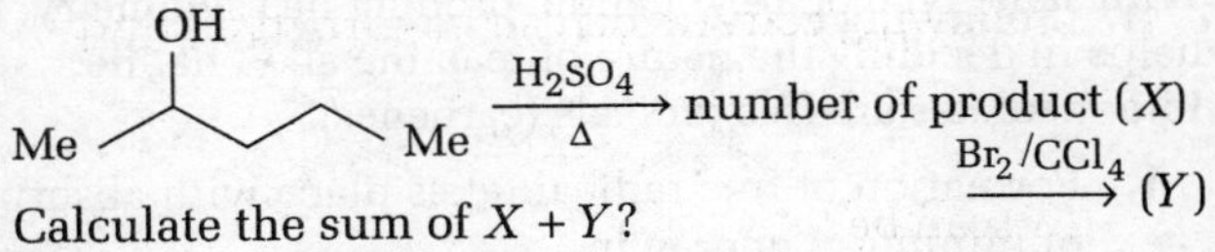

Calculate the sum of $X + Y$?

5. What volume of ethane is formed from 38 g of sodium propionate by fusion with lime ?

6. The energy difference between staggered and eclipsed conformations of ethane is 11.5 kJ mol^{-1}. Assuming entropy contribution negligible, the ratio of staggered: eclipsed conformers at 300K is ....

7. A sample of 1.79 mg of compound of molar mass 90 g mol^{-1}, when treated with CH_3MgI release 1.34 mL of gas at STP. The number of active hydrogen in the molecule is ....

Comprehension Based Questions

In these questions, a passage has been given followed by questions based on it. You have to answer the questions based on the passage given.

Passage 1 Carboxylic acids are also the major source of hydrocarbons. Heating of sodium salt ($RCOONa$) with sodalime NaOH hydrocarbon. Decarboxylation takes place on heating itself when there are two carboxylic groups are on the gem position keto group or double bond on β-carbon.

Based on this answer, the questions are given at the end.

1. 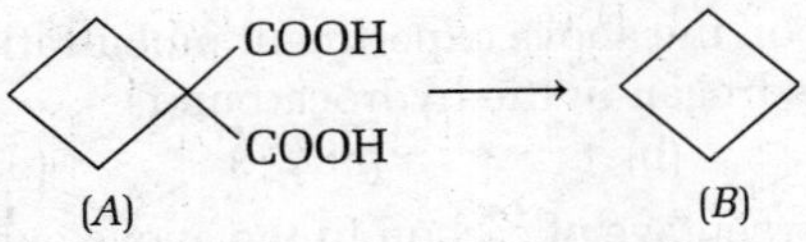

A is to be converted into B. It can be performed by

(a) heating with sodalime in two stages
(b) heating in the absence of sodalime
(c) heating and then using sodalime
(d) A cannot be converted into B

2. Consider the following reactions,

$$\underset{A}{CH_3\overset{O}{\overset{\|}{C}}CH_3} \xrightarrow[\Delta]{NaOH/I_2} \xrightarrow[\Delta]{\text{Sodalime}} B$$

B is identified as a gas that can

(a) be ethane
(b) be methane
(c) occupy 1.4 L per gram at NTP
(d) also called Marsh gas

3. Products A, B and C of the following reaction is

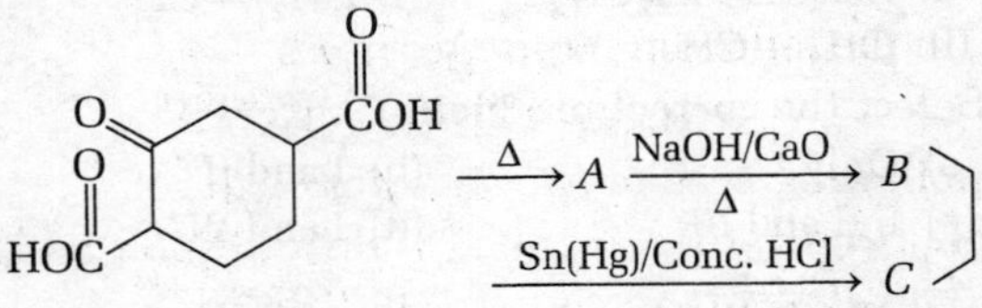

(a) 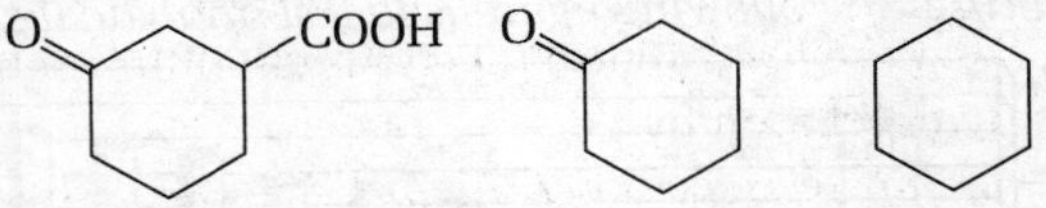

(b) 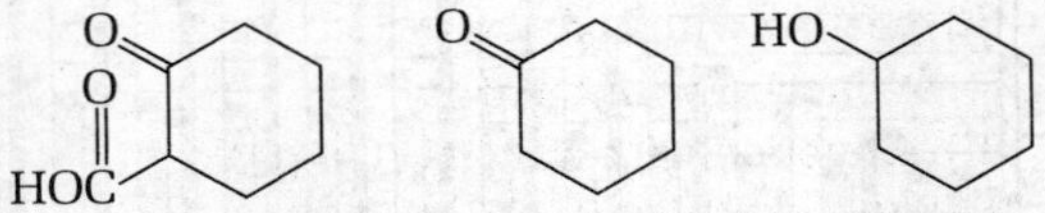

(c) 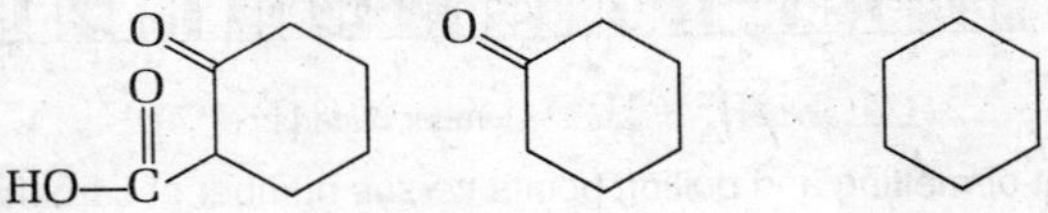

(d) 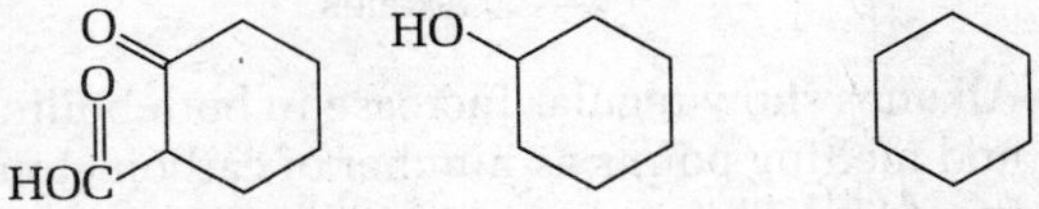

Passage 2 *Following passage describes the applications of Wurtz reaction in the synthesis of alkane. Read this passage and answer the given questions.*

An ethereal solution of an alkyl halide (preferably the bromide or iodide) is treated with sodium

$$2R{-}X + 2Na \xrightarrow{\text{Ether}} R{-}R + 2NaX$$

$$2CH_3{-}Br + 2Na \xrightarrow{\text{Ether}} CH_3{-}CH_3 + 2NaBr$$

$$CH_3CH_2Br + 2Na + CH_3Br \xrightarrow{\text{Ether}} CH_3CH_2—CH_3 + 2NaBr$$

In this reaction, product has new (C—C) bond.

With same type of alkyl halide, product has symmetry, this helps in deciding the nature of reacting alkyl halide. Intermediates are free radicals (carbenes).

1. Formation of free radical takes place with absorption of minimum energy in

(a) $CH_3CH_2CH_2CH_2Br$ (b) $CH_3CH(CH_3)CH_2Br$

(c) $CH_3CH(Br)CH_2CH_3$ (d) $(CH_3)_3C—Br$

2. Which of the following can be obtained in good yield by Wurtz reaction?

(a)  (b) 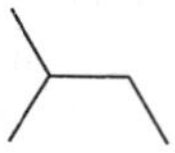

(c) 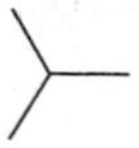 (d) 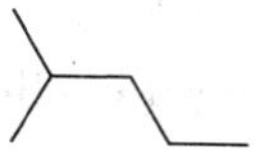

3. CH_3CH_2Br undergoes Wurtz reaction. We may expect some of the following products

I. $CH_3CH_2CH_2CH_3$ II. $CH_2{=}CH_2$
III. $CH_3—CH_3$

Select the correct product(s).

(a) Only I (b) I and II
(c) I, II and III (d) I and III

Passage 3 *Following figure is to test analytical skill.*

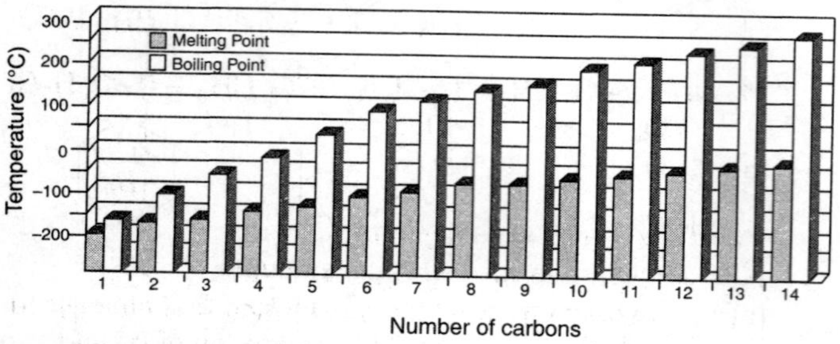

A plot of melting and boiling points *versus* number of carbons for the $C_1—C_{14}$ alkanes

1. Alkanes show regular increase in both boiling points and melting points as number of carbon atoms increases. This is due to

(a) presence of H-bonding
(b) presence of weak van der Waals' forces
(c) permanent dipole-dipole interaction
(d) presence of electronegative C-atoms

2. Force of attraction between alkane molecules which give a increase in melting point and boiling point results from

(a) induced polarisation of electron clouds in molecules
(b) greater electronegative difference between C and H
(c) larger C—C internuclear distance
(d) internal energy itself

3. Select the correct alternate(s).

(a) As branching increases, the molecule tends to become spherical, thereby resulting in a decreased surface for intermolecular attraction and thus boiling point decreases
(b) Melting point depends upon the packing of molecules in the crystalline lattice
(c) Alkanes with even number of carbon atoms fit together better in a crystal lattice and thus intermolecular forces decreases and melting point decreases
(d) Alkanes with odd number of carbon atoms fit together in a better way in a crystal lattice and thus melting point of such alkanes are larger than those of alkanes with even number of carbon atoms

Passage 4 *Read the following passage and answer the questions given at the end.*

Combustion is used in the quantitative determination of elemental compositions, called **elemental analysis.** Combustion has been used for this purpose since the beginning of the modern era of chemistry. The results of combustion analysis led early chemists to the realisation that most compounds contain their constituent elements in definite whole-number ratios.

1. Consider the following experiment based on combustion

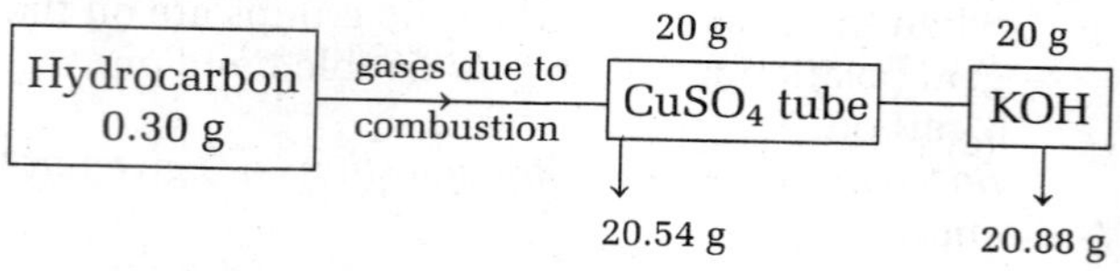

Based on the above experiment molar ratio of carbon and hydrogen in the hydrocarbon is

(a) 1 : 1 (b) 1 : 2 (c) 1 : 3 (d) 1 : 4

2. Mass percentage of carbon in the above experiment is

(a) 80% (b) 20% (c) 40% (d) 16.67%

3. A hydrocarbon was combusted with excess of O_2 and the gaseous mixture was placed at 25°C and then run into KOH and pyrogallol solution. Following observations were made.

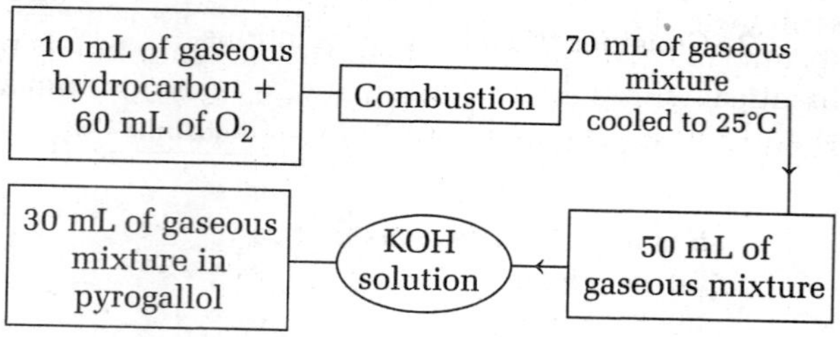

Thus, hydrocarbon is

(a) CH_4 (b) C_2H_6 (c) C_2H_4 (d) C_2H_2

***Passage* 5** *Read the following passage and answer the questions given at the end.*

Alkanes of low molecular mass are in great demand for a variety of purposes—especially as motor fuels—and alkanes available directly from wells do not satisfy the demand. The petroleum industry has developed methods (called *catalytic cracking*) for converting alkanes of high molecular mass into alkanes and alkenes of lower molecular mass. The petroleum industry has also developed processes (called *reforming*) for converting unbranched alkanes into branched-chain ones, which have superior ignition properties as motor fuels.

1. Which is a reforming process?

(a) 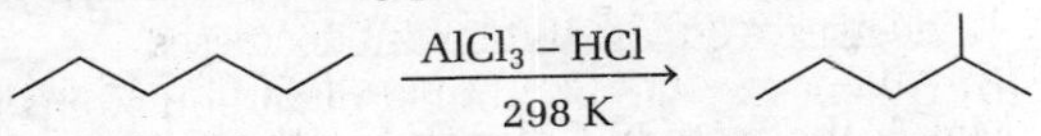

(b) 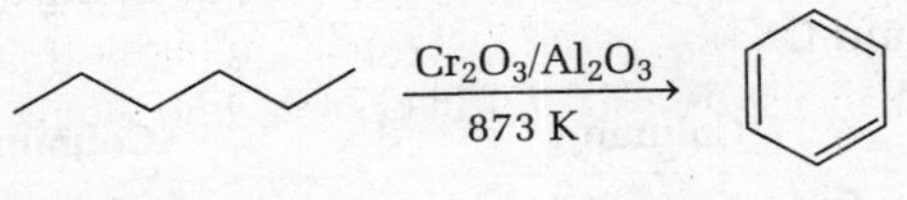

(c) Both (a) & (b)
(d) None of the above

2. Select the correct statement(s).
(a) Octane number is the knocking quality of a gasoline
(b) Cetane-number is the knocking quality of diesel
(c) MTBE is the major additives used for improving octane-number
(d) Safety of oils in different countries is decided by flash point

3. Methyl tertiary butyl ether (MTBE), $(CH_3)_3COCH_3$ is a gasoline additive and is prepared by
(a) $(CH_3)_2C{=}CH_2 \xrightarrow[H^+]{CH_3OH}$
(b) $(CH_3)_3COH + CH_3Cl \longrightarrow$
(c) $(CH_3)_3CONa + CH_3Br \longrightarrow$
(d) $(CH_3)_3CBr + CH_3ONa \longrightarrow$

***Passage* 6** Our understanding of multistep reaction is incomplete; we cannot realistically predict rates unless we know which step is rate-determining. One experimental method for finding the rate-determining step is using **isotope effects,** which are changes in reaction rates resulting from using different isotopes. The isotope most commonly used is deuterium (D), the isotope of hydrogen with mass number 2, which has a proton and a neutron in its nucleus. Although the chemistry of deuterium is nearly identical with that of hydrogen, bonds to deuterium are slightly stronger than bonds to hydrogen, and the activation energy for abstraction of a deuterium atom is slightly higher than for a hydrogen atom.

1. Select the correct statement(s).
If all hydrogen atoms in methane are replaced by deuterium atoms
(a) rate of chlorination is decreased
(b) rate of chlorination is increased
(c) activation energy of formation of free radical is decreased
(d) activation energy of formation of free radical is increased

2. Consider the following reaction

$$CH_3{-}CD_2{-}CH_3 \xrightarrow{Cl_2}$$

Most stable intermediate of this reaction is
(a) $CH_3CD_2\dot{C}H_2$
(b) $CH_3\underset{\displaystyle Cl}{CD}\dot{C}H_2$
(c) $CH_3\dot{C}DCH_3$
(d) $CH_3\dot{C}DCH_2Cl$

3. Consider the following reaction

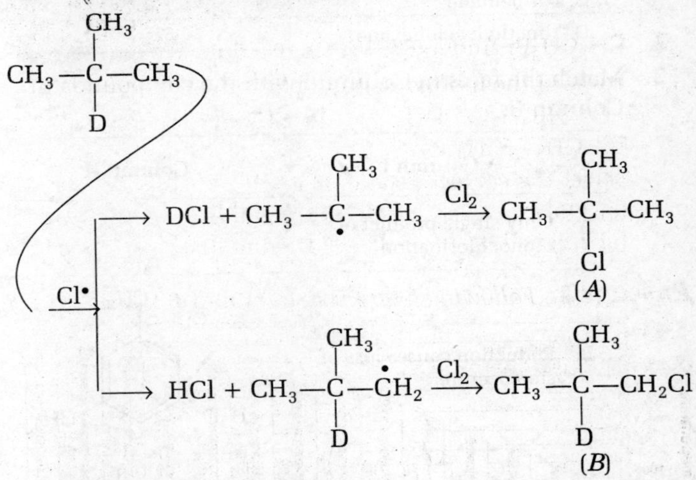

Select the correct statement(s).
(a) *A* and *B* are formed in equal amounts
(b) Intermediate from which *B* is formed first changes to more stable 2° free radical by migration of D^- and then Cl_2 reacts
(c) Only *A* is formed
(d) Only *B* is formed

Matrix-Match Type

Given below are Matching Type Questions, with two columns (each having some items) each . Each item of Column I has to be matched with the items of Column II.

1. Match the hydrocarbons in Column I with the name of 3° carbon in Column II.

Column I	Column II
A. Neopentane	1. 3
B. Isopentane	2. 2
C. 2, 3-dimethylbutane	3. 1
D. 1, 2, 3-trimethyl cyclohexane	4. 0

2. Match the hydrocarbons in Column I with the name of halogen derivatives it can give by monohalogenation in Column II.

Column I	Column II
A. Neopentane	1. 5
B. Isopentane	2. 4
C. *n*-pentane	3. 3
D. methylcyclohexane	4. 1

3. Match the facts in Column I with the compounds in Column II.

Column I	Column II
A. Only single product of monochlorination	1. 
B. Reduction causes loss of stereocentre	2. 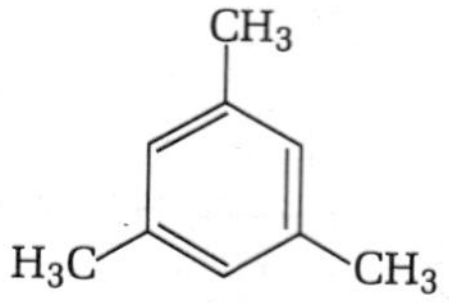
C. Chlorination induces one chiral centre	3. 2,2,3,3-tetramethyl butane
D. Compound has zero octane rating	4. $CH_3-\underset{H}{\overset{CH=CH_2}{C}}-CH_2CH_3$

4. Match the facts in Column I with the compounds in Column II.

Column I	Column II
A. Order of reactivity toward *X*.	1. $R_3CH > R_2CH_2 > RCH_3$
B. Stability of free radicals formed by abstraction of H.	2. $-CH_3 > RCH_3 > CH_2{=}CH_2$
C. Heating leads to decarboxylation.	3. 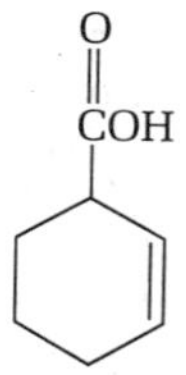
D. Heating and then reduction with Pt/H_2 forms cyclohexane.	4. 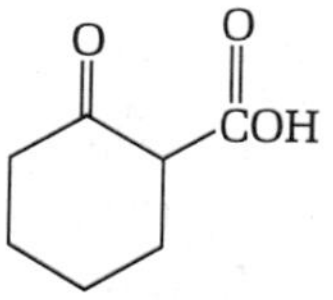

Single Integer Answer Questions

Answer of these questions is a single digit lying between 0 to 9.

1. In the following synthesis, how many π-bonds are formed?

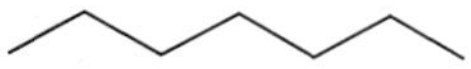 $\xrightarrow[873\text{ K}]{Cr_2O_3\text{-}Al_2O_3}$

2. Singlet ($:CH_2$) can be inserted between C—H bonds in alkanes. How many products are formed by random insertion of methylene singlet in *n*-pentane?

3. MTBE is the major additive used for the improvement of octane number. How many carbon atoms are there in MTBE?

4. How many types of *R*—Cl are obtained by dichlorination of 2-methylpropane?

5. In the following reaction, how many types of carbon containing compounds are formed?

$$CH_3CH_2COOK(aq) \xrightarrow{\text{Current}}$$

6. How many product will formed in the following reaction?

$$CH_3-Cl + CH_3-CH_2-Cl \xrightarrow[\text{dry other}]{Na}$$

7. .... types of hydrocarbons are formed when CH_3CH_2Br reacts with sodium in presence of ether.

8. Number of moles of oxygen required for complete combustion of one mole of pentane is ....

9. 15 g of CH_3MgBr is decomosed by H_2O to give ...... g of CH_4.

10. The maximum number of isomers (including stereoisomers) that are possible on mono-chlorination of the following compound, is

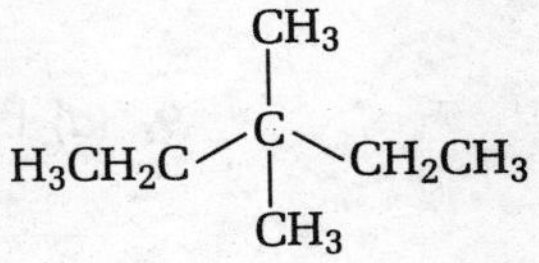

[JEE Main 2011]

Answers

Objective Questions Type I [Only one correct answer]

1. (b)	**2.** (a)	**3.** (d)	**4.** (b)	**5.** (d)	**6.** (c)	**7.** (c)	**8.** (b)	**9.** (d)	**10.** (a)
11. (c)	**12.** (b)	**13.** (c)	**14.** (a)	**15.** (c)	**16.** (d)	**17.** (c)	**18.** (c)	**19.** (a)	**20.** (a)
21. (d)	**22.** (a)	**23.** (a)	**24.** (b)	**25.** (a)	**26.** (a)	**27.** (b)	**28.** (c)	**29.** (a)	**30.** (c)
31. (c)	**32.** (c)	**33.** (d)	**34.** (a)	**35.** (b)	**36.** (a)	**37.** (c)	**38.** (a)	**39.** (b)	**40.** (d)
41. (b)	**42.** (c)	**43.** (c)	**44.** (a)	**45.** (a)	**46.** (a)	**47.** (d)	**48.** (a)	**49.** (c)	**50.** (a)
51. (a)	**52.** (a)	**53.** (b)	**54.** (b)	**55.** (b)	**56.** (d)	**57.** (a)	**58.** (c)	**59.** (a)	**60.** (d)
61. (c)	**62.** (b)	**63.** (b)	**64.** (b)	**65.** (a)	**66.** (a)	**67.** (d)	**68.** (a)	**69.** (a)	**70.** (c)
71. (a)	**72.** (d)	**73.** (d)	**74.** (a)	**75.** (a)	**76.** (c)	**77.** (c)	**78.** (a)	**79.** (a)	**80.** (a)
81. (a)	**82.** (a)	**83.** (a)	**84.** (c)						

Objective Questions Type II [One or more than one correct answer(s)]

1. (a, b, c)	**2.** (c, d)	**3.** (a, b, c)	**4.** (a, b, d)	**5.** (b)
6. (b)	**7.** (a, b, c)	**8.** (a, b, c)	**9.** (a, b, c)	**10.** (c, d)

Numerical Value Questions

1. (8) **2.** (3) **3.** (0) **4.** (9) **5.** (10) **6.** (100) **7.** (3)

Comprehension Based Questions

Example 1 – 1. (c) **2.** (b,c,d) **3.** (a)

Example 2 – 1. (d) **2.** (a) **3.** (c)

Example 3 – 1. (b) **2.** (a) **3.** (a,b)

Example 4 – 1. (c) **2.** (a) **3.** (c)

Example 5 – 1. (a) **2.** (b,c,d) **3.** (a,c)

Example 6 – 1. (b,d) **2.** (c) **3.** (a)

Matrix-Match Type

1. (A)→(4); (B)→(3); (C)→(2); (D)→(1)

2. (A)→(4); (B)→(2); (C)→(3); (D)→(1)

3. (A)→(1,2); (B)→(1,2); (C)→(3,4); (D)→(3)

4. (A)→(1,2,3,4); (B)→(1,3); (C)→(1,3,4); (D)→(1,2,3,4)

Single Integer Answer Questions

1. (3) **2.** (3) **3.** (5) **4.** (4) **5.** (5) **6.** (4) **7.** (3) **8.** (8) **9.** (2) **10.** (5)

Solutions

Objective Questions Type I [Only one correct option]

2. (*a*)

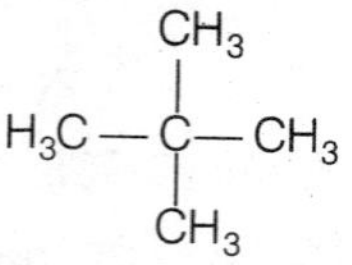

Quaternary (4°) carbon has no H attached to it. Thus, central (4°) carbon is attached to four carbon atoms.

4. (*b*) *Gauche* (staggered)

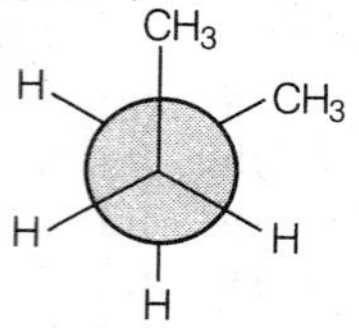

$\theta = 60°$

5. (*d*) Two quaternary carbons can be at terminal

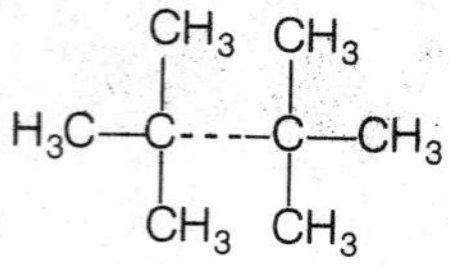

By structure two $(CH_3)_3C—$ are joined by C—C bond.

Thus, C_8H_{18} is

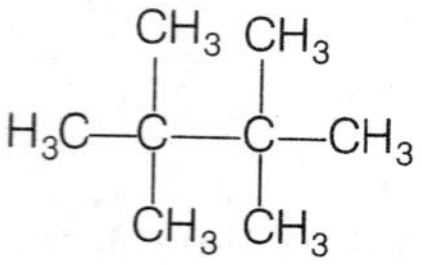

It has six-methyl groups

6. (*c*) To minimise strain, there is opening of ring (bond angle changes from 60° to 109° 28′) and electrophilic addition of H^+ takes place

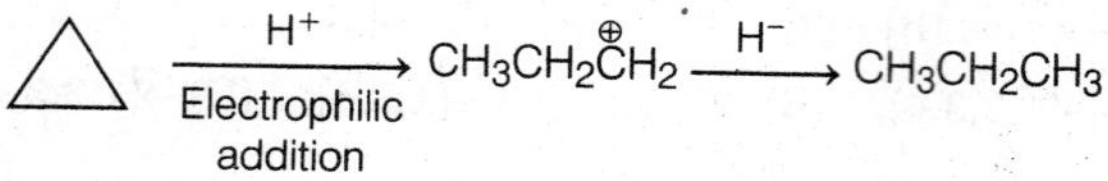

7. (*c*)

$$Zn \longrightarrow Zn^{2+} + 2e^-$$

$$R—X + e^- \longrightarrow X^- + R^{\bullet}$$

$$R^{\bullet} + e^- \longrightarrow R\!:^-$$

$$R\!:^- + C_2H_5OH \longrightarrow RH + C_2H_5O^-$$

8. (*b*) $LiAlH_4$ converts 3° alkyl halide into alkene

$$(CH_3)_3CCl \xrightarrow{LiAlH_4} (CH_3)_2C{=}CH_2$$

Thus, (b) is incorrect.

9. (*d*)

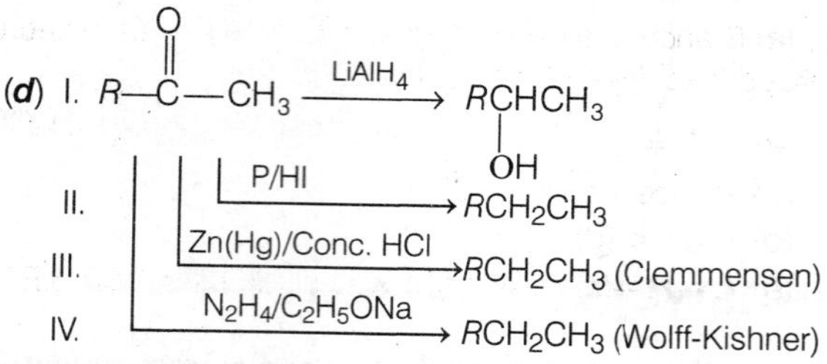

Thus, II, III, IV.

10. (*a*) Wolff-Kishner reduction

$$CH_3—\overset{O}{\overset{\|}{C}}—CH_3 \xrightarrow[450\,K]{NH_2—NH_2/C_2H_5ONa} CH_3CH_2—CH_3$$

11. (*c*) If one type of *B* is formed, it means *A* is also of one type

Thus *A* is $\underset{(A)}{(CH_3)_3CCH_2Br} \xrightarrow{Mg} (CH_3)_3CCH_2MgBr \xrightarrow{D_2O} \underset{(B)}{(CH_3)_3CCH_2}$

12. (*b*) (a)

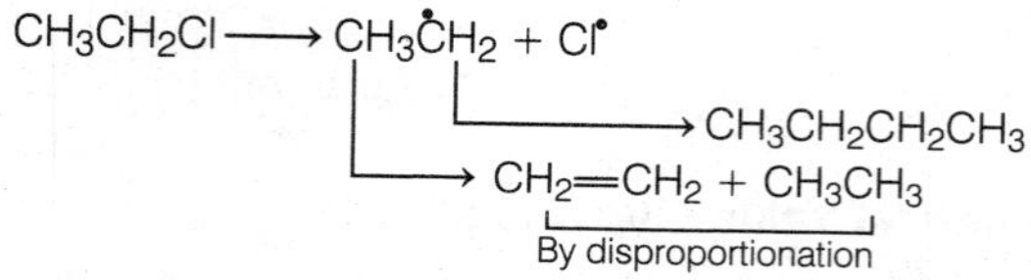

(b)

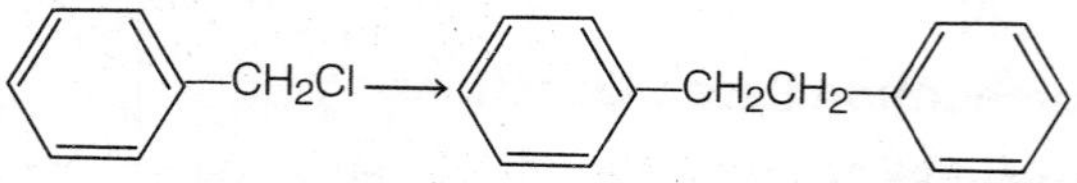

(c)

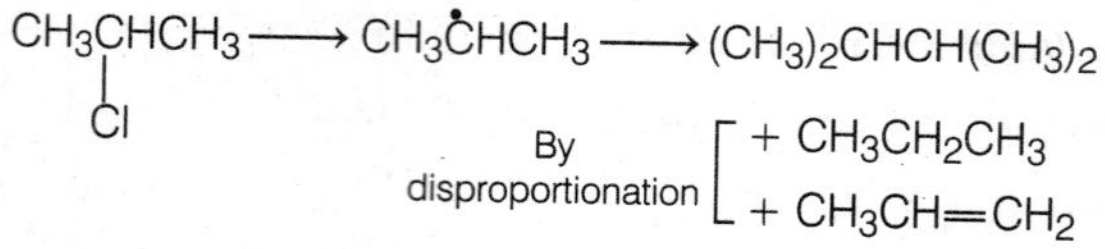

13. (*c*)

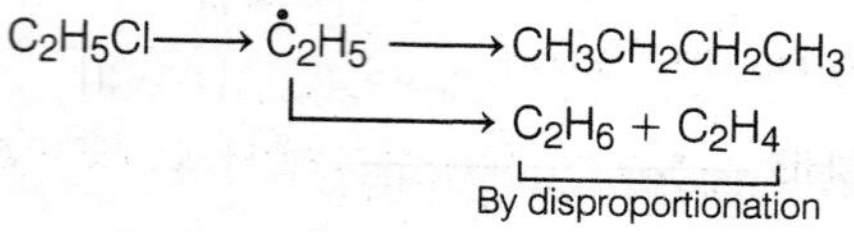

15. (*c*)

$$RMgX \xrightarrow{\text{Active H}} RH$$

$$CH_3MgBr \xrightarrow{(CH_3)_3COH} CH_4$$

Note $(CH_3)_3COH$ is a source of active H and decomposes *RMgX*.

19. (*a*)

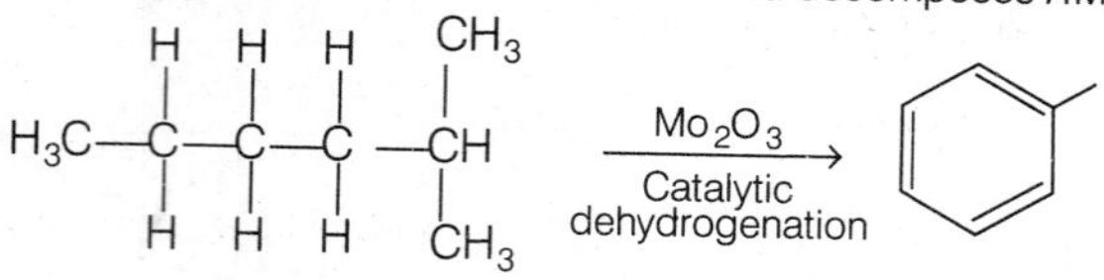

20. (*a*) 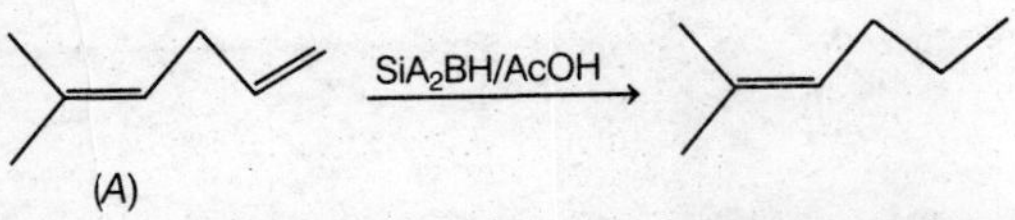

(*A*)

23. (*a*) Branch of alkane increases, boiling point are decreases due to lower intermolecular attraction.

26. (*a*) $CH_2{=}CH\dot{C}H_2$ (allyl free radial) is stable due to resonance stability order is

(b) < (c) < (d) < (a)

27. (*b*) C—H—(at position q) is 2° allylic thus least B.E.

28. (*c*) 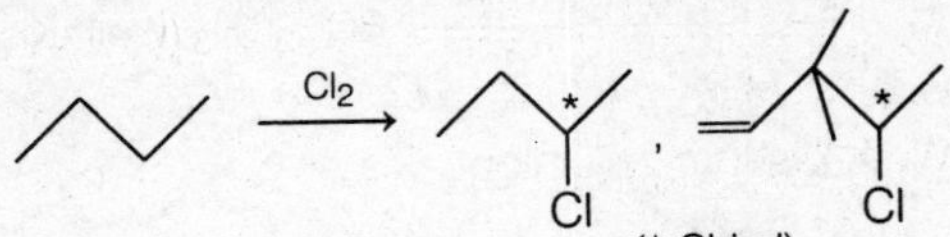

(* Chiral)

30. (*c*) $HIO_3 + 5HI \longrightarrow 3I_2 + 3H_2O$

32. (*c*) $CH_3CH_2CH_2CH_3 \xrightarrow{AlCl_3/HCl} CH_3CH_2\overset{\oplus}{C}HCH_3 \longrightarrow CH_3\overset{\oplus}{C}H—CH_3$ (with CH_3 on CH)

or

$CH_3—\overset{\oplus}{C}(CH_3)—CH_3$

34. (*a*) 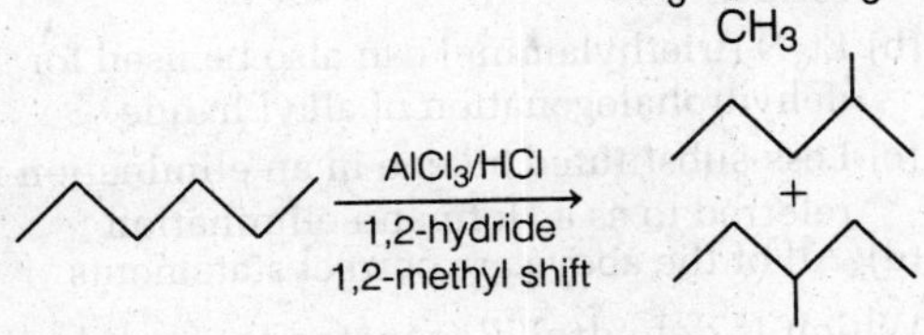

40. (*d*) Refer Kolbe's electrolysis

42. (*c*) Maximum boiling point and melting point

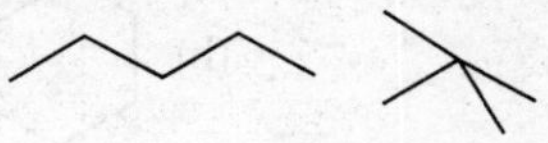

I III

48. (*a*) Corey-House method

$(CH_3)_2CHBr \xrightarrow[\text{(ii) CuI (iii) }(CH_3)_2CHCH_2Br]{\text{(i) Li}} (CH_3)_2CHCH_2CH(CH_3)_2$

50. (*a*) $H\overset{4}{C} \equiv \overset{3}{C}—\overset{2}{C}H(OH)—\overset{1}{C}H_3$ (It contains two active H atoms.)

One mole of compound, i.e. 70 g gives 2 mol of C_2H_6 gas. Seventy grams of compound $\Rightarrow 2 \times 22.4$ litres of C_2H_6 gas at standard condition.

$\therefore$ 0.21 g of the compound $= \dfrac{2 \times 22.4 \times 0.21}{70}$

$= 0.1344$ litres $= 134.4$ mL

51. (*a*) 1.4 L at NTP is occupied by = 1g

hence, 22.4 L at NTP is occupied by = 16 g

Thus, hydrocarbon is CH_4 and *R* is CH_3

52. (*a*) 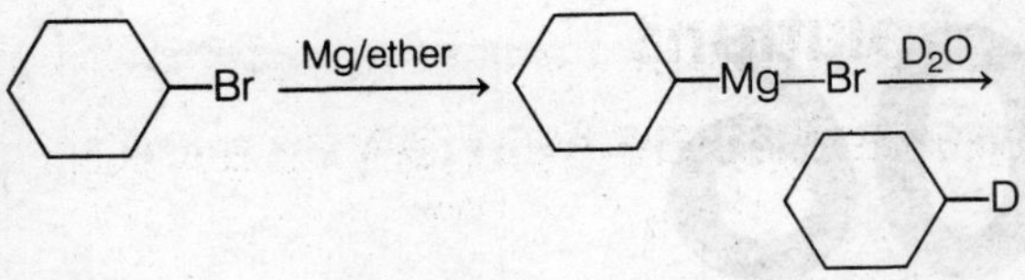

53. (*b*) B.E. of (C—Br) is lower than that of (C—Cl)

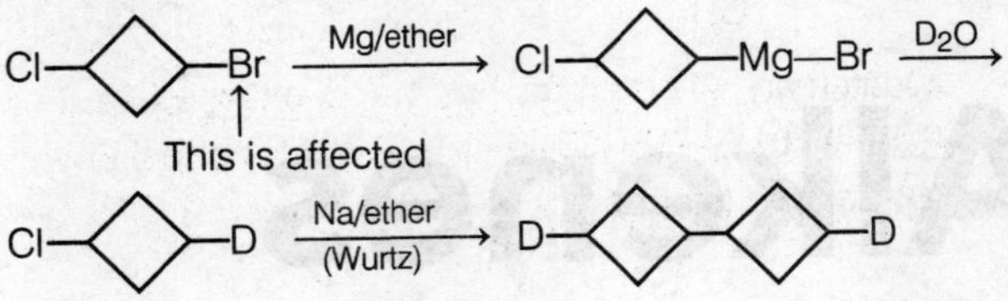

57. (*a*) Zero octane number

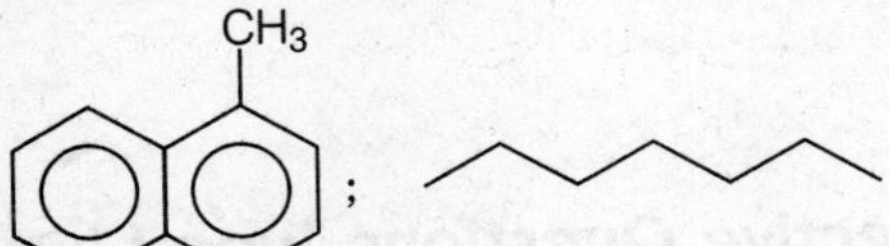

63. (*b*)  gives five type

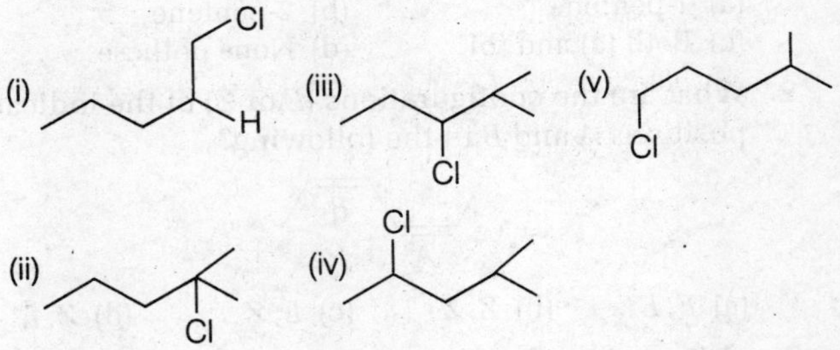

64. (*b*) 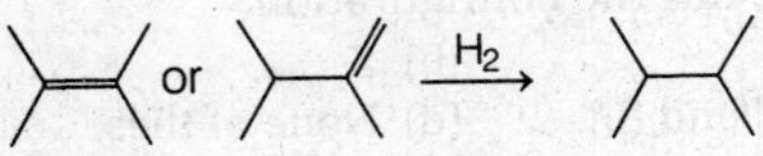

67. (*d*) $Al_4C_3 \xrightarrow{\text{Hydrolysis}} CH_4$

75. (*a*) Order :

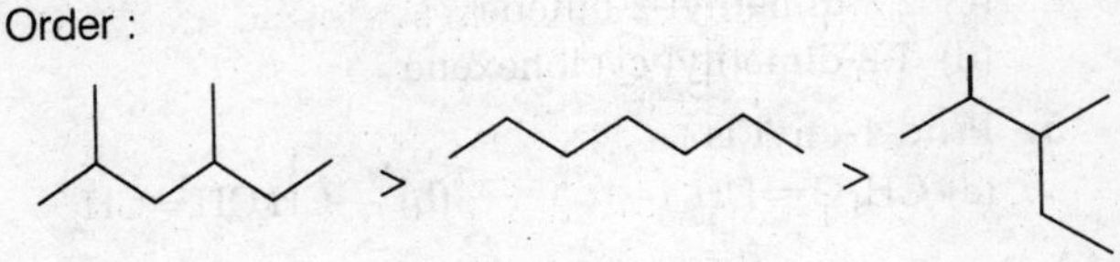

78. (*a*) 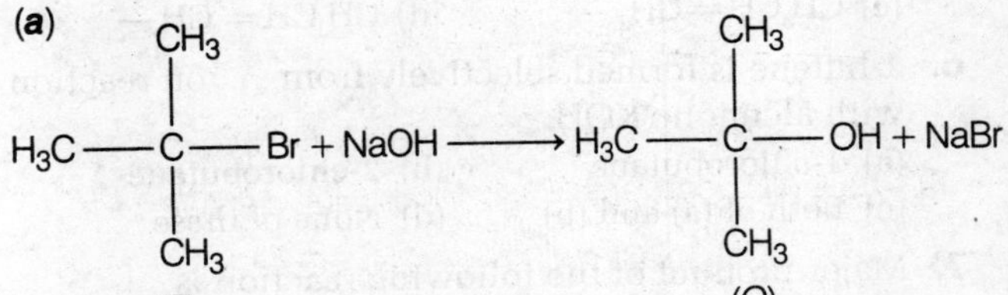

(*P*) (*Q*)

80. (*a*) 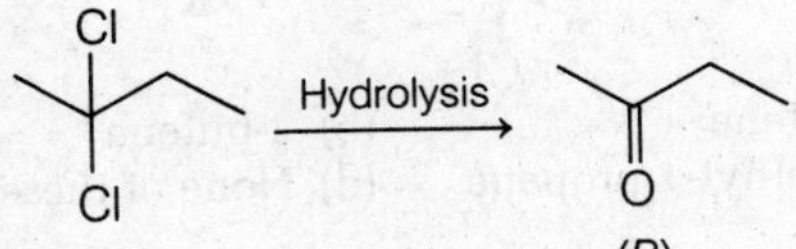

(*A*) (*B*)

06

Alkenes

Objective Questions Type I [Only one correct option]

In each of the questions below, four choices are given of which only one is correct.

1. Which of the following has stereocentre?
   (a) 1-pentene (b) 2-pentene
   (c) Both (a) and (b) (d) None of these

2. What are the configurations (E or Z) of the indicated positions A and B in the following?

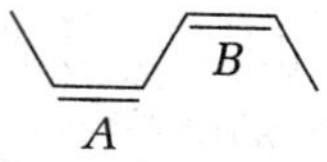

   (a) E, E (b) Z, Z (c) E, Z (d) Z, E

3. *cis*-2-pentene has the configuration
   (a) E (b) Z
   (c) Both of (a) and (b) (d) None of these

4. Stereoisomers are not formed in
   (a) 2-butene (b) 2-pentene
   (c) 2,3-dimethyl-2-butene
   (d) 1,2-dimethyl-cyclohexene

5. Prop-1-enyl is
   (a) $CH_3\underset{|}{C}{=}CH_2$ (b) $—CH_2CH{=}CH_2$
   (c) $CH_3CH{=}CH_2$ (d) $CH_3CH{=}CH—$

6. 1-butene is formed selectively from . . . on reaction with alcoholic KOH.
   (a) 1-chlorobutane (b) 2-chlorobutane
   (c) Both of (a) and (b) (d) None of these

7. Major product of the following reaction is

$$CH_3CH_2\underset{\underset{Cl}{|}}{C}HCH_3 \xrightarrow[\Delta]{\text{Alc. KOH}}$$

   (a) 1-butene (b) 2-butene
   (c) 2-methyl-1-propene (d) None of these

8. Select the correct statement(s).
   (a) The more stable the alkene, the more easily it is formed
   (b) Et_3N (triethylamine) can also be used for the dehydrohalogenation of alkyl halide
   (c) Less-substituted alkene in an elimination reaction is referred to as a Hofmann elimination
   (d) All of the above are correct statements

9. Which is dehydrohalogenated to a maximum extent?

   (a) 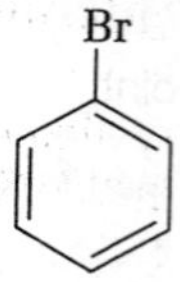
   (b) 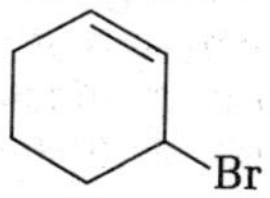
   (c) 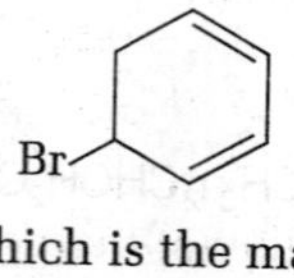
   (d) 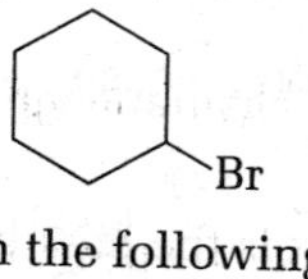

10. Which is the major product in the following?

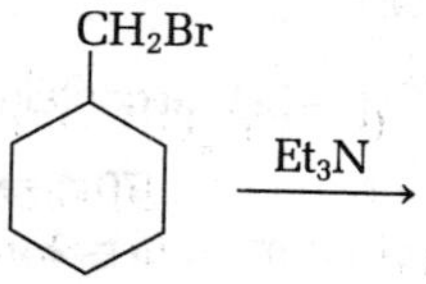

   (a) 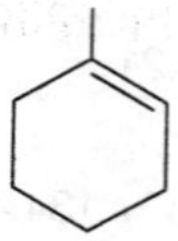
   (b) 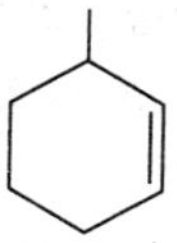
   (c) 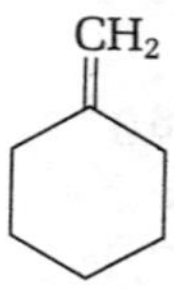
   (d) 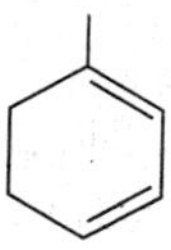

11. Dehydration takes place to a maximum extent in

(a) 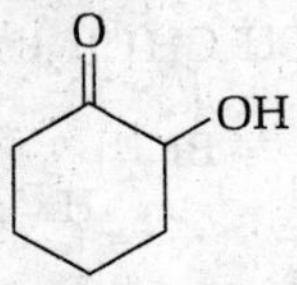
(b) 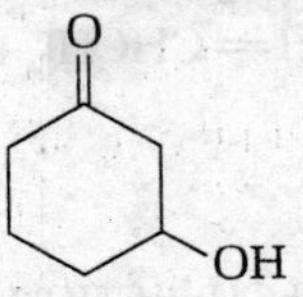

(c) 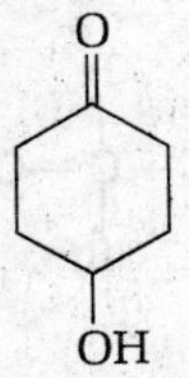
(d) 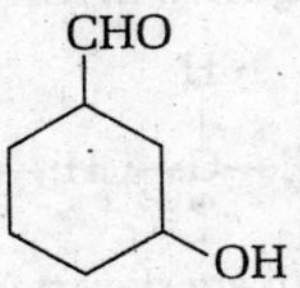

12. Identify the dehydration product in the following compound

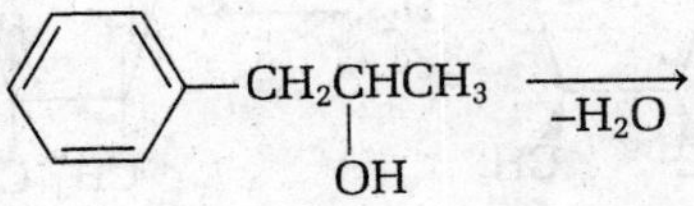

(a) 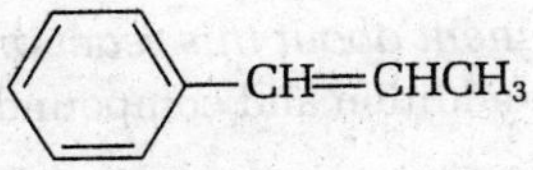

(b) 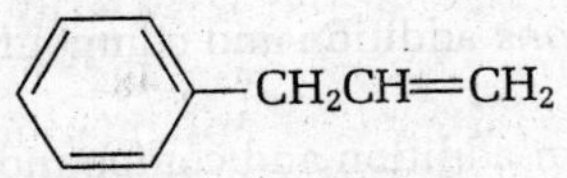

(c) Both of (a) and (b)
(d) None of the above

13. Select the correct statement(s).
(a) Dehydration of secondary and tertiary alcohols follows E1 mechanism while that of primary alcohol follows E2 mechanism
(b) Dehydration of secondary and tertiary alcohols follows E2 mechanism while that of primary alcohol follows E1 mechanism
(c) Primary carbocation is formed easily
(d) Dehydration of 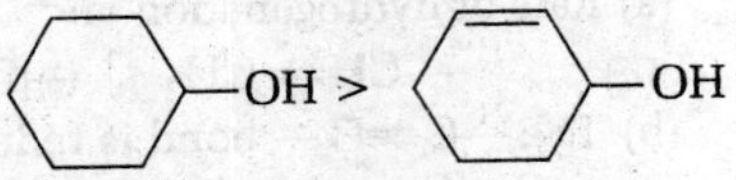

14. What is the possible product in the following reaction?

$$CH_3CH_2OH \xrightarrow{H^+}$$

(a) $CH_2{=}CH_2$ (b) $CH_3CH_2OCH_2CH_3$
(c) Both (a) and (b) (d) None of these

15. Major product of the dehydration of the following is

$$(CH_3)_3C\underset{\displaystyle OH}{\underset{|}{C}}HCH_3$$

(a) $(CH_3)_3CCH{=}CH_2$
(b) $(CH_3)_2CH\underset{\displaystyle CH_3}{\underset{|}{C}}{=}CH_2$
(c) $(CH_3)_2C{=}C(CH_3)_2$
(d) $CH_3CH_2CH{=}CHCH_2CH_3$

16. Following conversion can be carried out using

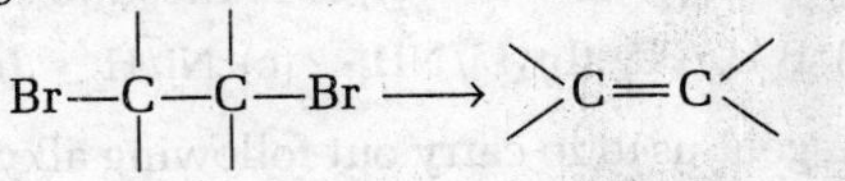

(a) Zn/CH_3OH (b) NaI/acetone
(c) Both of (a) and (b) (d) None of these

17. Possible intermediate of the following reaction is

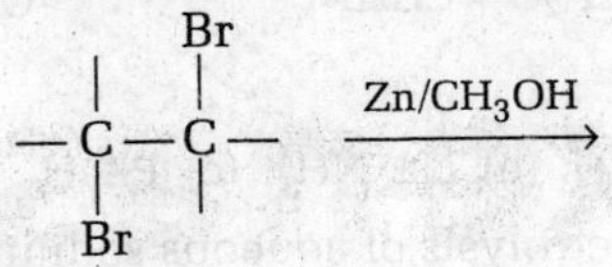

(a) 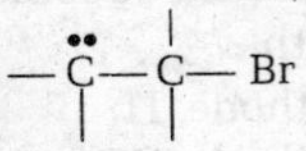 (b) 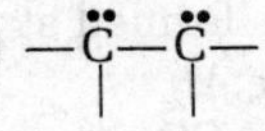
(c) 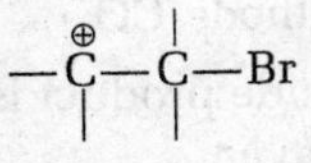 (d) 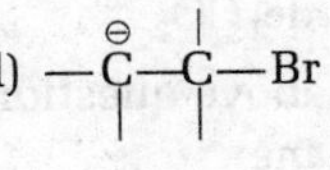

18. In the following reaction *A* is

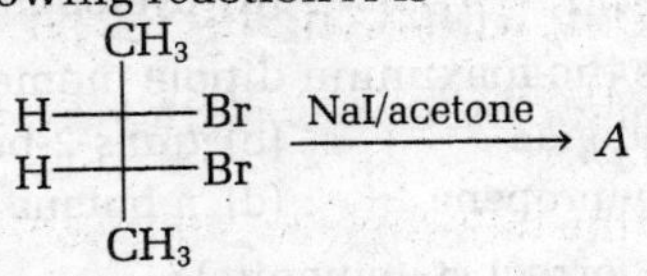

(a) 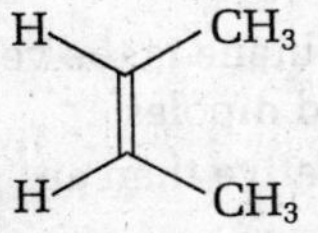 (b) 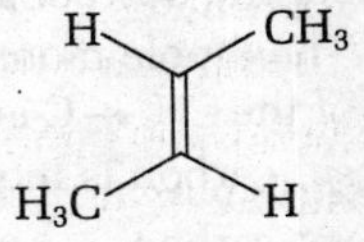

(c) Both of (a) and (b) (d) None of these

19. In the following reaction *A* is

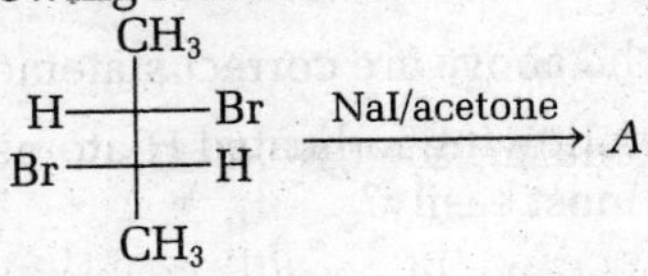

(a) 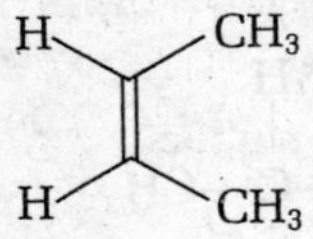 (b) 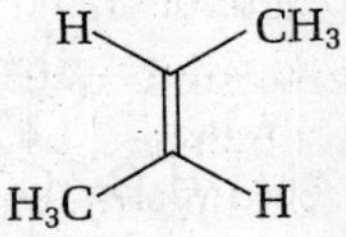

(c) 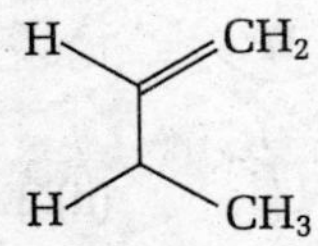 (d) 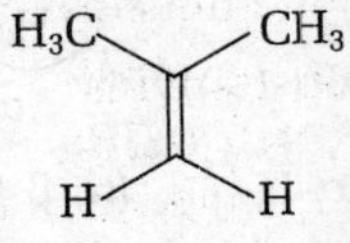

20. Identify species in which elimination of two Br atoms is stereoselective

(a) $CH_3CH_2CHBr_2$ (b) $CH_3\underset{Br}{C}H\underset{Br}{C}H_2$
(c) $CH_3CH_2\underset{Br}{C}H\underset{Br}{C}H_2$ (d) $CH_3\underset{Br}{C}H\underset{Br}{C}HCH_3$

21. P-2 catalyst consists of
(a) nickel boride
(b) palladium/carbon
(c) Both of (a) and (b)
(d) None of the above

22. Alkyne ($R-C\equiv C-R$) is reduced to *cis*-alkene using
(a) B_2H_6/H^+ (b) Li/NH_3 (c) Ni/H_2 (d) CH_3OH/Na

23. Reagent used to carry out following alkyne to alkene is

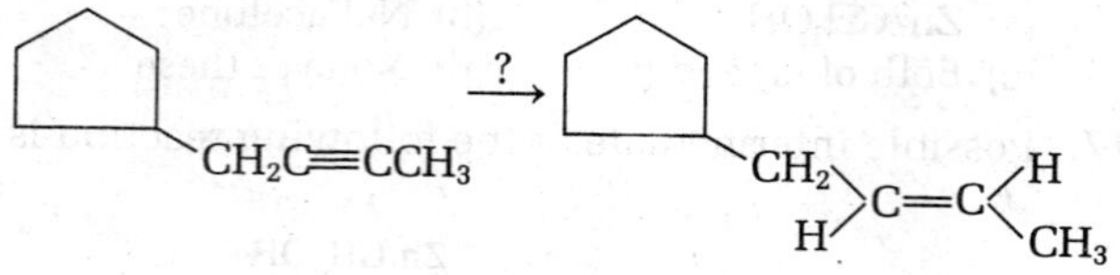

(a) Pd -C/H_2 (b) Na/NH_3 (c) P-2/H_2 (d) Ni/H_2

24. By the electrolysis of aqueous sodium succinate, ethene is formed at . . . along with . . .
(a) anode, H_2
(b) cathode, H_2
(c) anode, CO_2
(d) cathode, CO_2

25. In the above question (No. 24), side product is
(a) ethane
(b) ethyne
(c) butane
(d) cyclobutane

26. Which has the maximum dipole moment?
(a) *cis*-2-butene
(b) *trans*-2-butene
(c) 2-methylpropene
(d) *n*-butane

27. Select the correct statement(s).
(a) The dipole moment of *cis*-2-butene is the vector sum of the CH_3-C and C—H bond dipoles
(b) sp^2-carbon is more electronegative than an sp^3-carbon
(c) NBS is used for brominating alkenes at the allylic position
(d) All of the above are correct statements

28. Out of the following indicated H-atoms, which H is abstracted most easily?

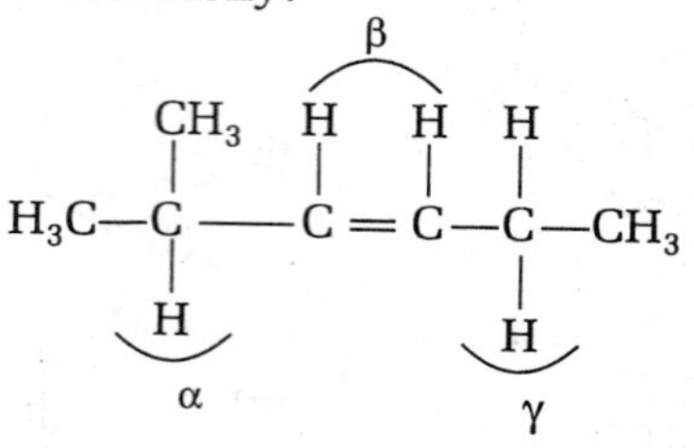

(a) α-H (b) β-H (c) γ-H (d) Equally

29. Following reaction is of the type

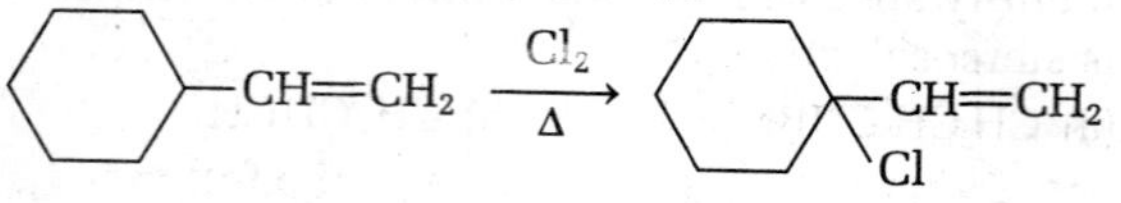

(a) S_N1
(b) S_N2
(c) E1
(d) free-radical substitution

30. $CH_2=CHCH_3 \xrightarrow{SeO_2} A$; *A* is/are
(a) HCHO, CH_3CHO
(b) $CH_2=CHCHO$
(c) CHO–CHO, HCHO
(d) CHO–CHO, HCOOH

31. Slow step in the following addition reaction is
$CH_3CH=CHCH_3 + HBr \longrightarrow CH_3\underset{Br}{CH}CH_2CH_3$
(a) $CH_3CH=CHCH_3 + H-Br \longrightarrow H_3C-\overset{H}{\underset{\oplus}{C}}-CH_2CH_3$
(b) $H_3C-\overset{H}{\underset{\oplus}{C}}-CH_2-CH_3 + Br^{\ominus} \longrightarrow H_3C-\overset{H}{\underset{Br}{C}}-CH_2CH_3$
(c) Both are slow steps
(d) Both are fast steps

32. Consider the following addition reaction

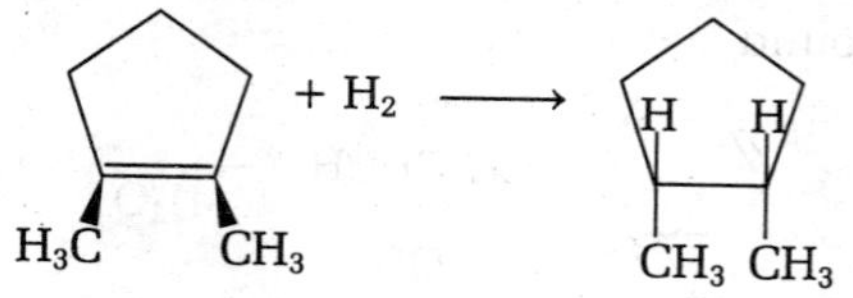

Select the correct statement about this reaction.
(a) This is a case of *syn*-addition and compound formed is racemic
(b) This is a case of *trans*-addition and compound formed is *meso*
(c) This is a case of *syn*-addition and compound formed is *meso*
(d) All of the above are correct statements

33. Wilkinson's catalyst consists of
(a) nickel boride
(b) palladium/carbon
(c) sodium/ethanol
(d) $RhCl(Ph_3P)_3$

34. Reducing agent in Birch reduction is
(a) $NaBH_4 \cdot PtCl_2$
(b) Na/liquid NH_3-EtOH
(c) $RhCl(Ph_3P)_3$
(d) N_2H_4

35. Select the correct statement(s).
(a) Rate of hydrogenation of
$-CH=CH_2 \quad -CH=CH-$
(b) The $-C\equiv C-$ bond is reduced more readily than $-\overset{|}{C}=\overset{|}{C}-$ bond
(c) Birch reaction is effective for reduction of terminal double (C=C) bonds
(d) All of the above are correct alternates

36. Product formed in the following reaction

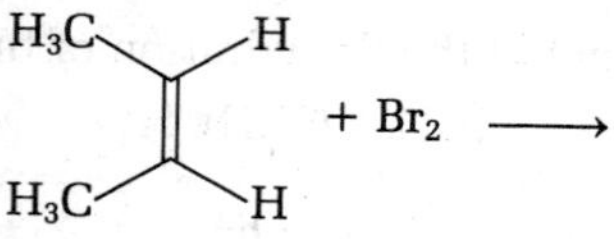

(a) is a racemic mixture
(b) is a *meso*-compound
(c) is an achiral compound
(d) None is correct

37. Select the correct statement(s).
(a) Addition of Br_2 to alkene is stereoselective
(b) Addition takes place through the formation of a bridged bromonium ion
(c) Both (a) and (b) are correct statements
(d) None of the above is a correct statement

38. *Meso*-compound is formed when Br_2 adds to
(a) *cis*-2-butene (b) *trans*-2-butene
(c) 1-butene (d) any alkene

39. Distinction between ethene and ethane can be made using
(a) $AgNO_3/NH_4OH$ (b) Cu_2Cl_2/NH_4OH
(c) $K_2Cr_2O_7/H_2SO_4$ (d) Br_2 water

40. When Br_2 adds to 2-butene, intermediate formed is
(a) $CH_3\overset{\oplus}{C}H—\underset{Br}{\underset{|}{C}}HCH_3$ (b) 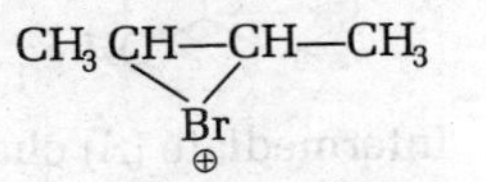
(c) $CH_3\overset{\oplus}{C}H\cdot CH_2CH_2Br$ (d) $CH_3\overset{\oplus}{C}H—\overset{\oplus}{C}HCH_3$

41. Following reaction is
$$CH_3CH{=}CH_2 + HBr \longrightarrow$$
(a) stereoselective (b) stereospecific
(c) regioselective (d) nucleophilic addition

42. In which case regioselectivity is observed when HBr reacts with
(a) 2-pentene (b) 2-hexene
(c) 1-pentene (d) in all cases

43. Which is the intermediate of the following reaction?
$$(H_3C)_2C{=}CH_2 + HBr \longrightarrow$$
(a) $(H_3C)_2CH—\overset{\oplus}{C}H_2$ (b) $(H_3C)_2\overset{\oplus}{C}—CH_3$
(c) Both (a) and (b) (d) None of these

44. Major addition product of the following reaction is
$$(CH_3)_3CCH{=}CH_2 \xrightarrow{HBr/\,CH_3NO_2}$$
(a) $(CH_3)_3CCH_2CH_2Br$ (b) $(CH_3)_3C\underset{Br}{\underset{|}{C}}HCH_3$
(c) $(CH_3)_2\underset{Br}{\underset{|}{C}}CH(CH_3)_2$ (d) $(CH_3)_2\underset{Br}{\underset{|}{C}}CH_2CH_2CH_3$

45. $CH_2{=}CH—CH{=}CH_2$ reacts with HBr forming 1-bromo-2-butene by
(a) 1,4-addition (b) 1,2-addition
(c) 1,3-addition (d) 2,3-addition

46. Consider the following reagents
I. Br_2 water; II. Alkaline $KMnO_4$
III. HCO_3H; IV. OsO_4 in ether solution/H_2O_2
Reagents used to make distinction between alkane and alkene are
(a) I and II (b) II and III (c) I and III (d) I and IV

47. Select the incorrect statement.
(a) Hydroxylation (glycol formation) can be affected by cold alkaline $KMnO_4/HCO_3H/OsO_4$ in ether
(b) Addition of 2 —OH by $KMnO_4$ is *anti*
(c) Addition of 2 —OH by HCO_3H is *anti*
(d) Addition of 2 —OH by $KMnO_4$ is *syn*

48. Hydroxylation of alkene can be affected by
I. OsO_4 in ether/H_2O_2 II. HCO_3H
III. $KMnO_4/OH^-$
In which case racemic mixture is formed when *cis*-2-butene reacts with
(a) I (b) II
(c) III (d) any of I, II and III

49. In the following compound,
$$(H_3C)_2\underset{A}{C{=}}CHCH_2\underset{B}{CH{=}}CH_2$$
which (C=C) bond is more nucleophilic?
(a) *A*
(b) *B*
(c) Equally nucleophilic
(d) C=C is never nucleophilic

50. Which is the incorrect reaction?
(a) 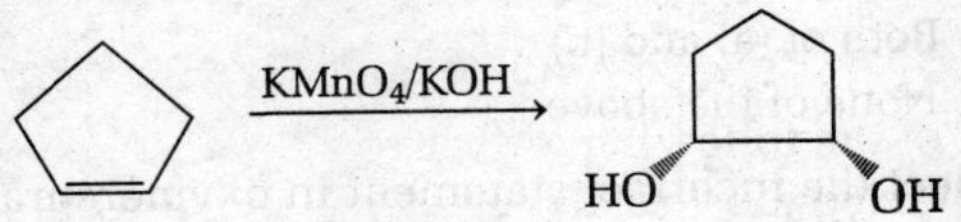
(b) 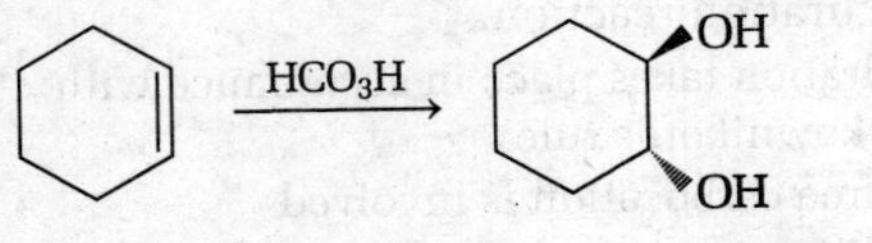
(c) 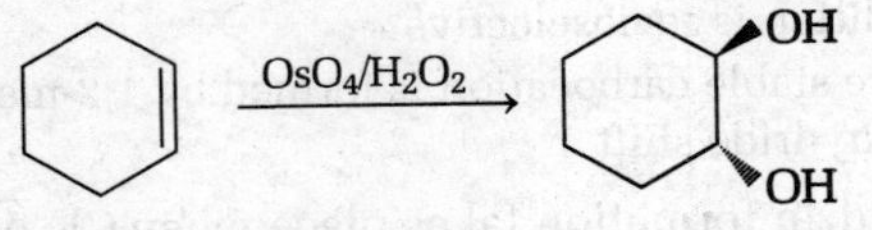
(d) 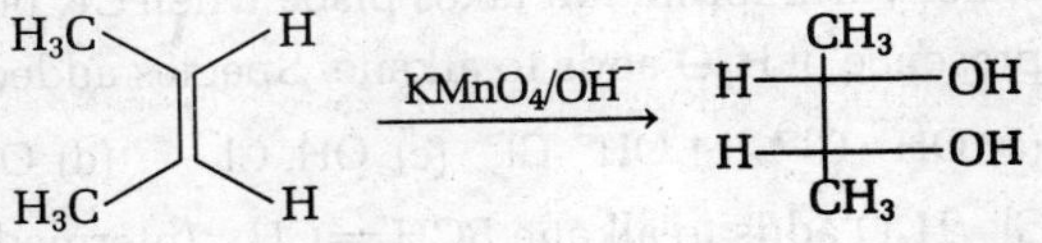

51. Hydration of alkene takes place in the following steps
$$RCH{=}CH_2 \xrightarrow[I]{H_3O^{\oplus}} R\overset{\oplus}{C}HCH_3 \xrightarrow[II]{H_2O} R\underset{\oplus OH_2}{\underset{|}{C}}HCH_3 \xrightarrow[III]{H_2O} R\underset{OH}{\underset{|}{C}}HCH_3$$
Rate determining step (slow step) is
(a) I (b) II (c) III (d) I and III

52. Which is regioselective?

I. $RCH{=}CHR \xrightarrow{H_2O/H^+}$

II. $RCH{=}CHR \xrightarrow{HBr}$

(a) Only I (b) Only II
(c) Both of (a) and (b) (d) None of these

53. Hydration of *A* gives predominantly

(*A*) $CH_3CH(CH_3)CH{=}CH_2$

(a) $CH_3CH(CH_3)CH(OH)CH_3$ (b) $CH_3CH(CH_3)CH_2CH_2OH$
(c) $CH_3C(OH)(CH_3)CH_2CH_3$ (d) $CH_3CH(CH_2OH)CH_2CH_3$

54. To prepare only *B* from *A*, reagent used is

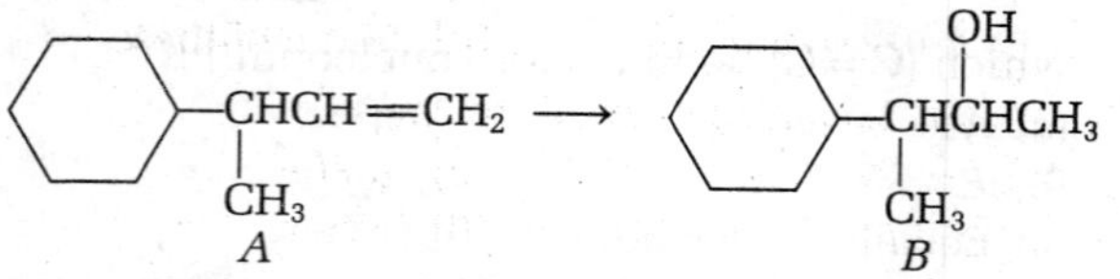

(a) H_2O/H^+
(b) $Hg(OAc)_2/NaBH_4–NaOH$
(c) Both of (a) and (b)
(d) None of the above

55. Select the incorrect statement in oxymercuration-demercuration reaction.
(a) Hydration takes place in accordance with Markownikoff's rule
(b) No free carbocation is involved
(c) Addition is regioselective
(d) More stable carbocation is formed by 1,2-methyl or 1,2-hydride shift

56. Halohydrin formation takes place when Cl_2 or Br_2 in presence of H_2O adds to alkene. Species added are
(a) $OH^{\ominus}, Cl^{\ominus}$ (b) $OH^{\ominus}, Cl^{\oplus}$ (c) OH, Cl (d) $\overset{\oplus}{O}H, Cl^{\oplus}$

57. Cl_2/H_2O adds to alkene $RCH{=}CH_2$. Intermediate formed is
(a) $R\underset{\oplus}{C}HCH_2Cl$ (b) $RCH(OH)\overset{\oplus}{C}H_2$
(c) 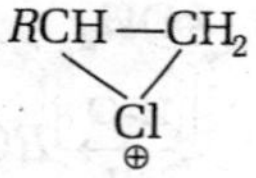 (d) 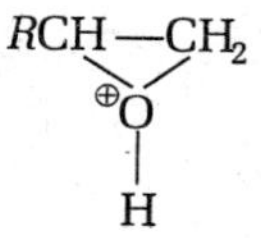

58. In which case addition of Br_2/H_2O is highly regioselective?
(a) $CH_3CH{=}CHCH_2CH_3$
(b) $(CH_3)_2C{=}CH_2$
(c) $CH_3CH{=}CHCH_3$
(d) $CH_2{=}CH_2$

59. Chlorohydrin formed when Cl_2/H_2O adds to cyclohexene has configuration

(a) 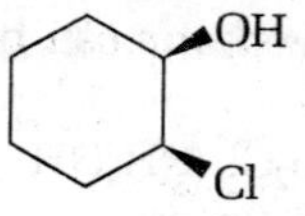 (b) 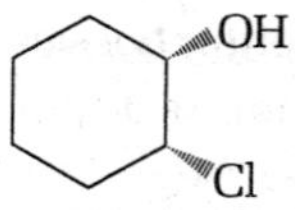
(c) 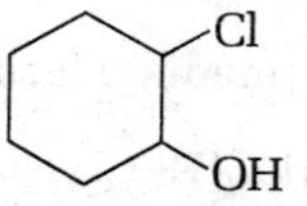 (d) 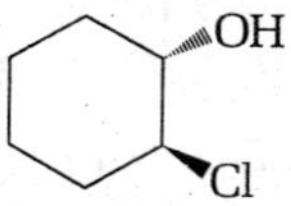

60. Intermediate (*A*) changes to chlorohydrin due to attack of H_2O (nucleophile). Select the correct statement about this reaction.

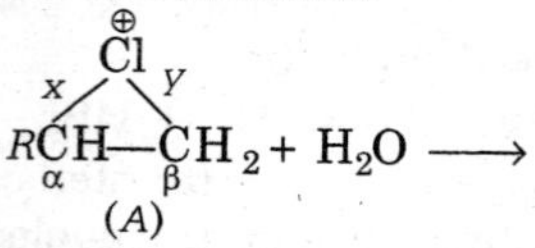

(a) H_2O attacks α-carbon and bond (*y*) is cleaved
(b) H_2O attacks β-carbon and bond (*x*) is cleaved
(c) H_2O attacks α-carbon and bond (*x*) is cleaved
(d) H_2O attacks β-carbon and bond (*y*) is cleaved

61. $(CH_3)_2CHCH{=}CH_2$ changes to *A*, *B* and *C* by using

$(CH_3)_2CHCH_2CH_2OH$ (*A*), $(CH_3)_2CHCH(OH)CH_3$ (*B*),

$(CH_3)_2C(OH)CH_2CH_3$ (*C*)

(a) H_2O/H^+, $BH_3\cdot THF/H_2O_2\cdot NaOH$, $Hg(OAc)_2/NaBH_4\cdot NaOH$
(b) H_2O/H^+, $Hg(OAc)_2/NaBH_4\cdot NaOH$, $BH_3\cdot THF/H_2O_2\cdot NaOH$
(c) $BH_3\cdot THF/H_2O_2\cdot NaOH$, $Hg(OAc)_2/NaBH_4\cdot NaOH$, H_2O/H^+
(d) $BH_3\cdot THF/H_2O_2\cdot NaOH$, H_2O/H^+, $Hg(OAc)_2/NaBH_4\cdot NaOH$

62. In which case carbocation is the intermediate?
(a) Alkene + $H_2O/H^+ \longrightarrow$
(b) Alkene + $BH_3\cdot THF/H_2O_2\cdot NaOH \longrightarrow$
(c) Alkene + $Hg(OAc)_2/NaBH_4\cdot NaOH$
(d) In all the above cases

63. Same type of alcohol is formed by
I. H_2O/H^+;
II. $BH_3 \cdot THF/H_2O_2 \cdot NaOH$
III. $Hg(OAc)_2/NaBH_4 \cdot NaOH$
when alkene is
(a) $CH_3CH=CHCH_3$
(b) $CH_3CH=CH_2$
(c) $(CH_3)_2CHCH=CH_2$
(d) $CH_3CH_2CH=CH_2$

64. Select the correct configuration in the following addition reaction.

(a) 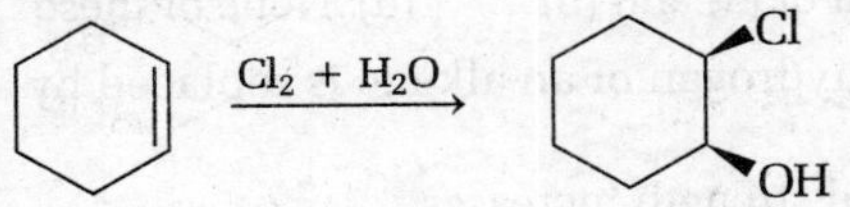

(b) 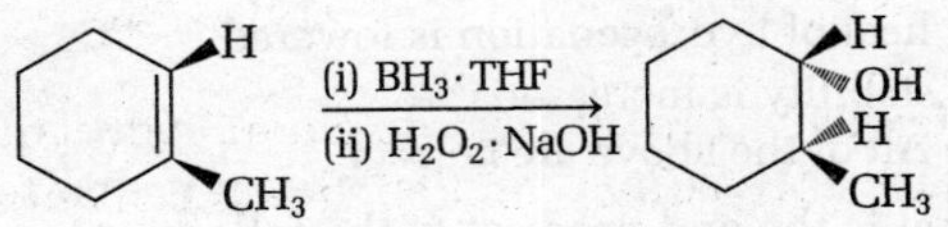

(c) 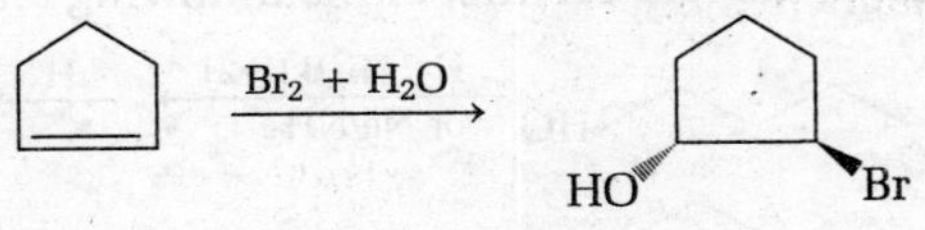

(d) Configurations (b) and (c) are correct

65. To convert *A* into *B*

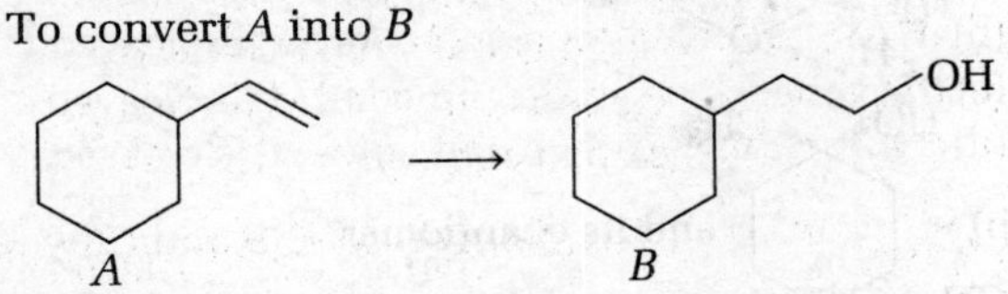

Reagent used is
(a) $Hg(OAc)_2/NaBH_4 \cdot NaOH$
(b) $BH_3 \cdot THF/H_2O_2 \cdot NaOH$
(c) Both of (a) and (b)
(d) None of the above

66. Consider the following addition reaction,

$$CH_3CH=CH_2 + HBr \longrightarrow CH_3CH_2CH_2Br$$

This
(a) takes place by free-radical mechanism
(b) takes place in presence of peroxide
(c) follows anti-Markownikoff's rule
(d) follows all these statements

67. General name for $:CH_2$ is
(a) carbene
(b) carbocation
(c) carbanion
(d) carbonium ion

68. Write the correct statement about $:CCl_2$
(a) it is an electrophile — Lewis base
(b) it is a nucleophile — Lewis base
(c) it is an electrophile — Lewis acid
(d) it is a nucleophile — Lewis acid

69. In the following cycloaddition reaction, intermediate of *A* is

$CH_2=CHCH=CH_2 + CH_2=CH_2 \longrightarrow$ 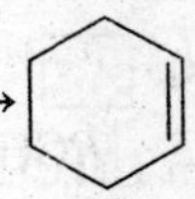
A B C

(a) $CH_2=CH-\overset{\oplus}{C}H-\overset{\ominus}{C}H_2$
(b) $\overset{\oplus}{C}H_2-CH=CH-\overset{\ominus}{C}H_2$
(c) $CH_2=CH-\overset{\ominus}{C}H-\overset{\oplus}{C}H_2$
(d) None of the above

70. Above reaction (in question 69) is an example of
(a) 1,4-addition reaction (b) Diels-Alder reaction
(c) Both (a) and (b) (d) None of these

71. Polymerisation of alkenes takes place through
(a) free-radical mechanism (b) ionic mechanism
(c) S_N1 mechanism (d) S_N2 mechanism

72. Which of the following polymers does not use alkene?
(a) SBR (b) Bakelite
(c) Both (a) and (b) (d) None of these

73. Fibres have polymers of the type
(a) Kel-F (b) lucite
(c) orlon (d) teflon

74. Which is not the Friedel-Crafts' reaction?

(a) 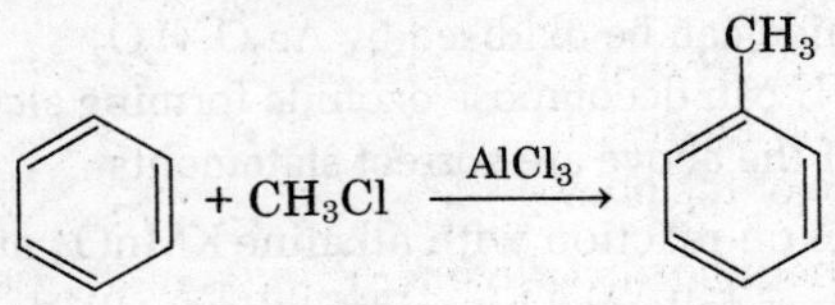

(b) $(CH_3)_3CCl + CH_2=CH_2 \xrightarrow{AlCl_3} (CH_3)_3CCH_2CH_2Cl$
(c) Both (a) and (b)
(d) None of the above

75. Monomer of natural rubber is
(a) styrene (b) butadiene
(c) isoprene (d) chloroprene

76. $C_{10}H_{16}(A)$ changes $C_{10}H_{16}O_2(B)$ by ozonolysis. If *B* is symmetrical then (*A*) is

(a) 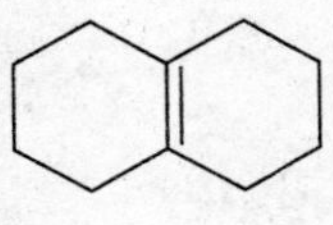 (b) 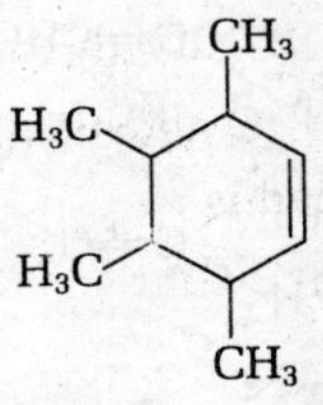

(c) 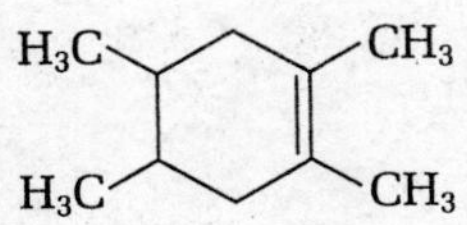 (d) 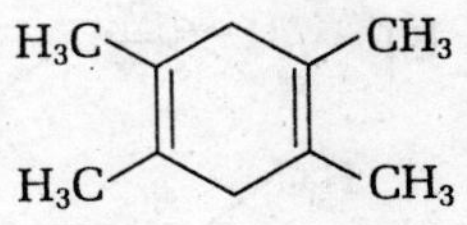

77. By oxidation ozonolysis $A(C_4H_8)$ changes to CH_3COOH. Thus, A is

(a)  (b) 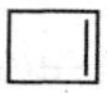

(c) $CH_3CH{=}CHCH_3$ (d) $CH_3CH_2CH{=}CH_2$

78. $A \xrightarrow{O_3/Zn,\ H_2O} (CH_3)_2CO + HCHO + \begin{matrix} CHO \\ | \\ CHO \end{matrix}$

Thus, A is

(a) $(CH_3)_2CHCH{=}CHCH{=}CH_2$

(b) $(CH_3)_2C{=}CHCH{=}CH_2$

(c) $CH_3CH{=}CHCH{=}CHCH{=}CH_2$

(d) None of the above

79. $A(C_4H_6) \xrightarrow[1\ mol]{H_2/Ni} B(C_4H_8) \xrightarrow{O_3/H_2O/Zn} CH_3CHO$

Thus, A and B are respectively

	(A)	(B)
(a)		
(b)	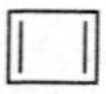	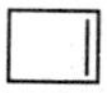
(c)	$CH_3CH_2C{\equiv}CH$	$CH_3CH{=}CHCH_3$
(d)	$CH_2{=}CHCH{=}CH_2$	$CH_3CH{=}CHCH_3$

80. Select the correct statement(s).

(a) Ozonide is reduced by Zn/CH_3COOH so that H_2O_2 is not formed

(b) Ozonide can be oxidised by Ag_2O, H_2O_2

(c) $LiAlH_4$ can decompose ozonide forming alcohol

(d) All of the above are correct statements

81. But-2-ene on reaction with alkaline $KMnO_4$ at elevated temperature followed by acidification will give **[JEE Main 2019, April]**

(a) $CH_3{-}\underset{OH}{\underset{|}{CH}}{-}\underset{OH}{\underset{|}{CH}}{-}CH_3$

(b) one molecule of CH_3CHO and one molecule of CH_3COOH

(c) 2 molecules of CH_3COOH

(d) 2 molecules of CH_3CHO

82. Which is the most stable alkene?

(a) $(H_3C)_2C{=}CHCH_3$

(b) $\underset{H}{\overset{H_3C}{>}}C{=}C\underset{H}{\overset{CH_2CH_3}{<}}$

(c) $\underset{H}{\overset{H_3C}{>}}C{=}C\underset{CH_2CH_3}{\overset{H}{<}}$

(d) $(H_3C)_2CHCH{=}CH_2$

83. Which has least heat of hydrogenation?

(a) 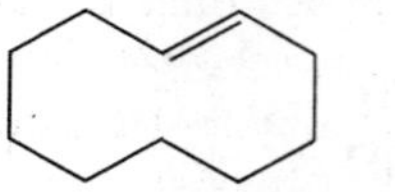 (b) 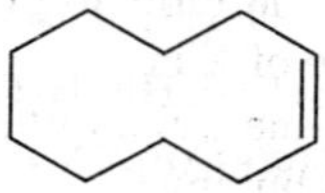

(c) 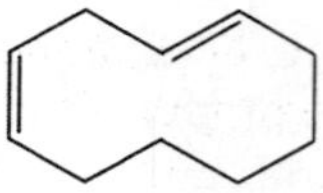 (d) Equal

84. Stabilities of isomeric alkenes are compared based on following factors

(a) degree of substitution (b) van der Waals' strain

(c) Both of (a) and (b) (d) None of these

85. When hydrogen of an alkene is replaced by alkyl/aryl group

(a) bond strength increases

(b) heat of hydrogenation is lowered

(c) stability is increased

(d) All of the above are correct

86. What is the end product of the following reaction?

 $\xrightarrow[\text{or } Na/NH_3]{H_2,\ Ni_2B\ (P\text{-}2)} \xrightarrow{H^+} \xrightarrow[H^+]{\Delta}$

(a) 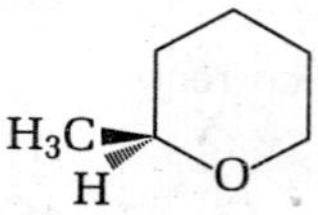 and its enantiomer

(b) 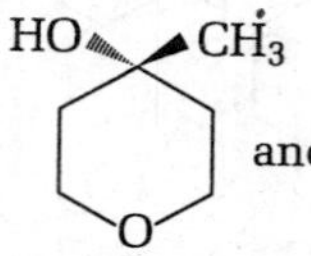 and its enantiomer

(c) Both (a) and (b)

(d) None of the above

87. Ethylene can be separated from acetylene by passing the mixture through

(a) fuming H_2SO_4 (b) pyrogallol

(c) ammoniacal Cu_2Cl_2 (d) charcoal powder

88. End product of the following reaction is

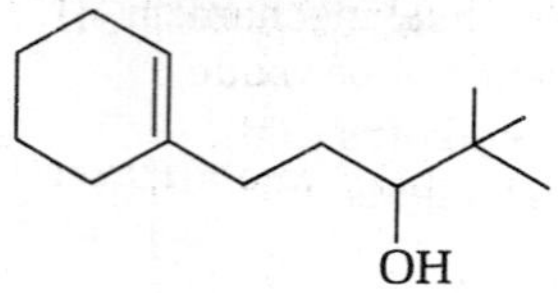 $\xrightarrow[\text{Heat}]{\text{Conc. } H_2SO_4}$

(a) 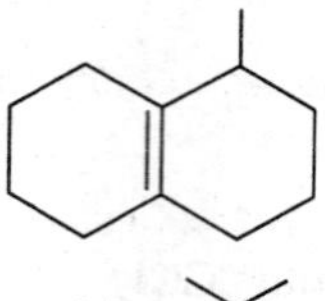 (b) 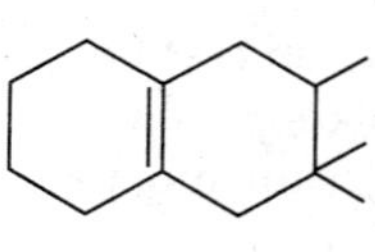

(c) 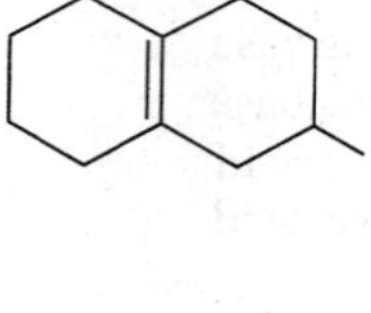 (d) 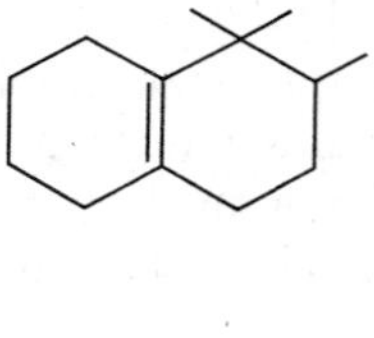

89. One mole of alkene X on ozonolysis gave one mole of acetaldehyde and one mole of acetone. The IUPAC name of X is
(a) 2-methyl-2-butene (b) 2-methyl-1-butene
(c) 2-butene (d) 1-butene

90. Among the following, the alkene on ozonolysis giving rise to only one aldehyde as the product is
(a) 1-butene (b) propane
(c) 2-butene (d) 2-methylprop-1-ene

91. $CH_2{=}CH{-}CH{=}CH_2 + \begin{matrix} CHCOOH \\ \| \\ CHCOOH \end{matrix} \longrightarrow$ Product X

by reaction R; X and R are

(a) 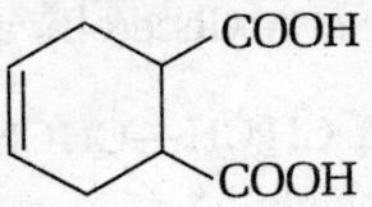 Diels-Alder

(b) 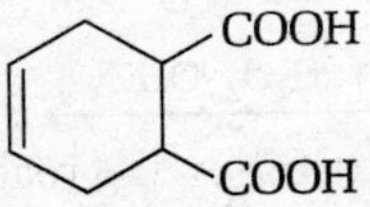 Friedel-Crafts'

(c) 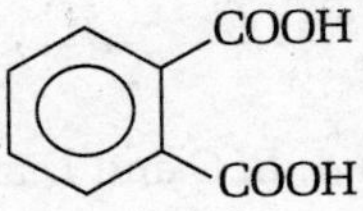 Diels-Alder

(d) 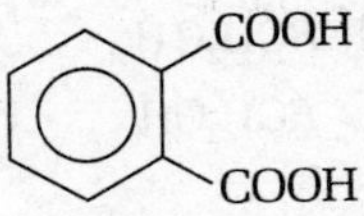 Friedel-Crafts'

92. $CCl_3CH{=}CH_2 \xrightarrow{Cl_2\,+\,H_2O} A$; A is
(a) $CCl_3\underset{OH}{\underset{|}{C}H}CH_2Cl$ (b) $CCl_3CH\underset{Cl}{\underset{|}{C}H_2}OH$
(c) $CCl_3\underset{Cl}{\underset{|}{C}H}\underset{Cl}{\underset{|}{C}H_2}$ (d) $CCl_3\underset{OH}{\underset{|}{C}H}\underset{OH}{\underset{|}{C}H_2}$

93. $CH_3CH{=}CH_2 \xrightarrow[H_2O_2\,/OH]{NaBD_4}$ Product X; X is
(a) $CH_3\underset{OH}{\underset{|}{C}H}CH_2D$ (b) $CH_3\underset{D}{\underset{|}{C}H}CH_2OH$
(c) $CH_3\underset{OD}{\underset{|}{C}H}CH_3$ (d) None is correct

94. 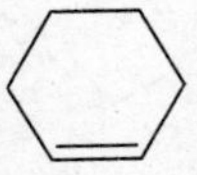 + $Br_2 \longrightarrow A$, A will have configuration

(a) 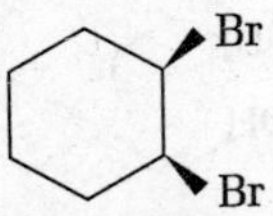 (b) 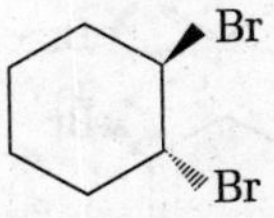

(c) Both (a) and (b) (d) None is true

95. $B \xleftarrow{\text{Lindlar}/H_2} R{-}C{\equiv}C{-}R \xrightarrow{Na/NH_3} A$, A and B are geometrical isomers ($R{-}CH{=}CH{-}R$)
(a) A is *cis*, B is *trans* (b) A is *trans*, B is *cis*
(c) A and B both are *cis* (d) A and B both are *trans*

96.  $\xrightarrow[H_2O_2]{OsO_4} A$, A is
(a) *meso*-diol (b) racemic diol
(c) Both are correct (d) None is correct

97. Lindlar's catalyst is
(a) specially active form of nickel
(b) palladium-calcium carbonate partially deactivated
(c) platinum oxide reduced by H_2 to platinum
(d) copper powder

98. $\underset{cis}{CH_3CH{=}CHCH_3} \xrightarrow{X} Y$ (non-resolvable) then X can be
(a) Br_2 water
(b) HCO_3H
(c) OsO_4/H_2O_2
(d) None of the above

99. $CH_3\overset{CH_3}{\overset{|}{C}}{=}CH\overset{CH_3}{\overset{|}{\underset{CH_3}{\underset{|}{C}}}}CH_3 \xrightarrow{NaIO_4/KMnO_4}$ Products;

products are
(a) $CH_3\overset{O}{\overset{\|}{C}}CH_3$, $(CH_3)_3CCOOH$
(b) $CH_3\overset{O}{\overset{\|}{C}}CH_3$, $(CH_3)_3CCHO$
(c) $CH_3\overset{O}{\overset{\|}{C}}OH$, $(CH_3)_3CCOOH$
(d) None of the above is correct

100. An alkene on ozonolysis yields only ethanal. There is an isomer of this, which on ozonolysis yields
(a) propanone and methanal
(b) propanone and ethanal
(c) ethanal and methanal
(d) only propanone

101. Which one of the following has the smallest heat of hydrogenation per mole?
(a) 1-butene (b) *trans*-2-butene
(c) *cis*-2-butene (d) 1,3-butadiene

102. Consider the following,

$$A \xrightarrow{O_3/H_2O} CH_3\overset{O}{\overset{\|}{C}}CH_3 + CH_3COOH + CH_3\underset{O}{\underset{\|}{C}}COOH,$$

A can be

(a) $CH_3\overset{\overset{\large CHCH_3}{\|}}{C}CH{=}C{<}^{CH_3}_{CH_3}$ (b) $CH_3\overset{\overset{\large C(CH_3)_2}{\|}}{C}CH{=}CHCH_3$

(c) Both (a) and (b) (d) None is correct

103. The major product of the following addition reaction is $H_3C{-}CH{=}CH_2 \xrightarrow{Cl_2/H_2O}$ **[JEE Main 2019]**

(a) $CH_3{-}\underset{\large Cl}{\underset{|}{CH}}{-}\underset{\large OH}{\underset{|}{CH_2}}$

(b) $CH_3{-}\underset{\large OH}{\underset{|}{CH}}{-}\underset{\large Cl}{\underset{|}{CH_2}}$

(c) 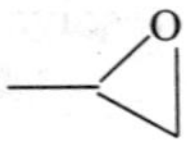

(d) 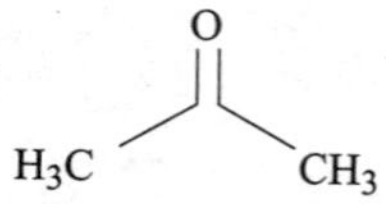

104. Which of the following reactions are correct?

I. $\underset{\text{1-octene}}{C_6H_{13}CH{=}CH_2} + BrCCl_3 \xrightarrow{\text{Peroxide}} C_6H_{13}\underset{\large Br}{\underset{|}{CH}}CH_2CCl_3$

II. $RCH{=}CH_2 + CCl_4 \xrightarrow{\text{Peroxide}} R\underset{\large Cl}{\underset{|}{CH}}CH_2CCl_3$

(a) Only I (b) Only II
(c) Both (a) and (b) (d) None is correct

105. Most stable intermediate of the hydration of isopentene $CH_3\underset{\large CH_3}{\underset{|}{CH}}CH{=}CH_2$ is

(a) $CH_3\overset{\large CH_3}{\overset{|}{C}H}\overset{\oplus}{C}HCH_3$ (b) $CH_3\overset{\large CH_3}{\overset{|}{\overset{\oplus}{C}}}CH_2CH_3$

(c) Both (a) and (b) (d) None is correct

106. Identify end products A, B and C of the following.

$CH_3CH{=}CH_2 \xrightarrow[\text{(ii) } H_2O]{\text{(i) } D^+} A$

$CH_3CH{=}CH_2 \xrightarrow[\text{(ii) } D_2O]{\text{(i) } D^+} B$

$CH_3CH{=}CH_2 \xrightarrow[\text{(ii) } D_2O]{\text{(i) } D^+} C$

(a) $CH_3\underset{\large OH}{\underset{|}{CH}}CH_3$ in all cases

(b) $CH_3CH(OH)CH_2D$, $CH_3CH(OD)CH_3$, $CH_3CH(OD)CH_2D$

(c) $CH_3\underset{\large OD}{\underset{|}{CH}}CH_3$ in all cases

(d) $CH_3\underset{\large OD}{\underset{|}{CH}}CH_2D$ in all cases

107. $CH_3CH{=}CHCH_3 + CHCl_3 + t\text{-BuOK} \longrightarrow A$; A is

(a) $CH_3CH{-}CHCH_3$ (ring with CH_2)
(b) $CH_3CH{-}CHCH_3$ (ring with CCl_2)
(c) $CH_3\underset{\large OBu}{\underset{|}{CH}}{-}\underset{\large Cl}{\underset{|}{CH}}CH_3$
(d) $CH_3CH{-}CHCH_3$ (ring with O)

108. $RCH{=}CH_2 \xrightarrow{BH_3\cdot THF} A \xrightarrow[D]{H_2O_2/OH^-} B$; $A \xrightarrow{CH_3COOH} C$

In this sequence of reactions A, B, C and D are

	A	B	C
(a)	$(RCH_2CH_2)_3B$,	RCH_2CH_2OH,	RCH_2CH_3,
(b)	$(RCH_2CH_2)_3B$,	$R\underset{\large OH}{\underset{|}{CH}}CH_3$,	RCH_2CH_3,
(c)	$(R\underset{|}{CH}CH_3)_3B$,	$R\underset{\large OH}{\underset{|}{CH}}CH_3$,	RCH_2CH_3,

(d) None of the above is correct

109. 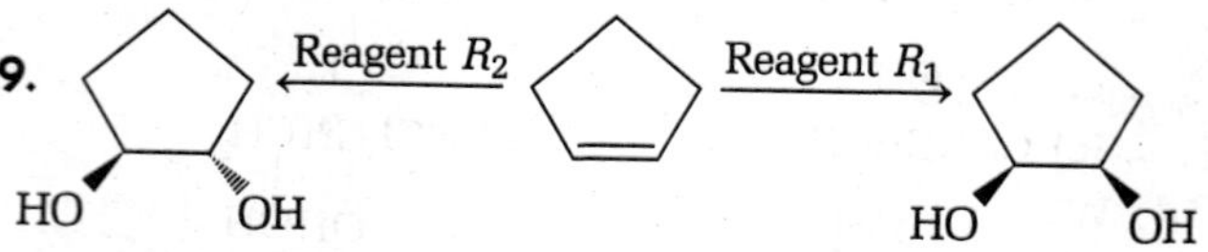

R_1 and R_2 are

(a) cold alkaline $KMnO_4$, OsO_4/H_2O_2
(b) cold alkaline $KMnO_4$, HCO_2H
(c) cold alkaline $KMnO_4$, $C_6H_5CO_3H$
(d) $C_6H_5CO_3H$, HCO_3H

110. $B \xleftarrow[H_2O_2]{OsO_4}$  $\xrightarrow{Br_2} A$, A and B are

(a) 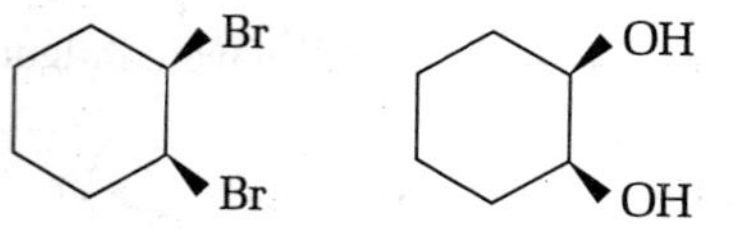

(b) 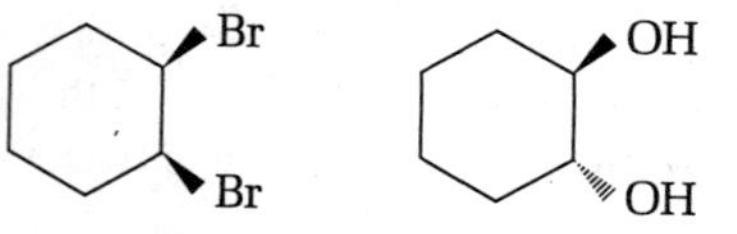

(c) 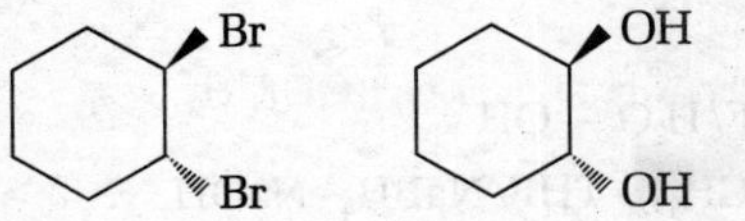

(d) 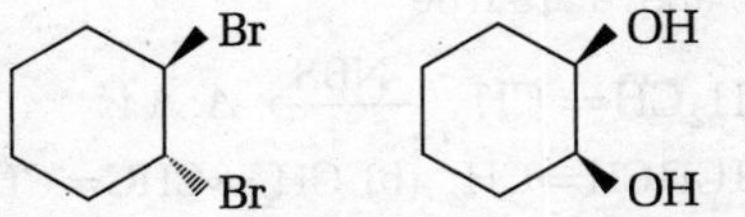

111. Monomer *A* of a polymer on ozonolysis yields two moles of HCHO and one mole of CH_3COCHO. Deduce the structure of *A*

(a) $CH_2=CH-CH\equiv CCHO$ (b) $CH_2=C(CH_3)-CH=CH_2$

(c) $CH_2=CH-C(CH_3)_2-CH_3$ (d) $CH_2=CH-CH=CH_2$

112. 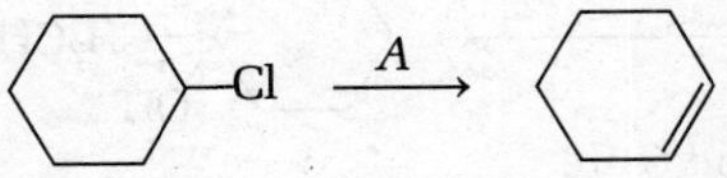 , *A* is

(a) Et_3N (b) NH_3

(c) alcoholic KOH (d) All of these

113. 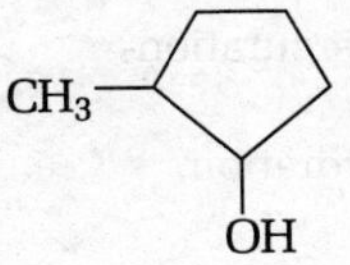 $\xrightarrow[\text{heat}]{H_2SO_4}$ *A* (major), *A* is

(a) 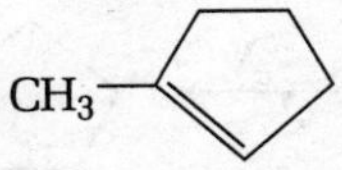 (b) 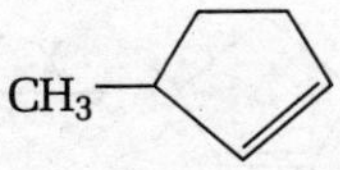

(c) 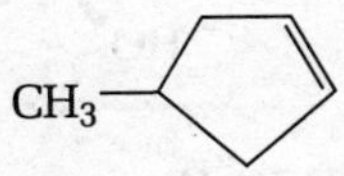 (d) 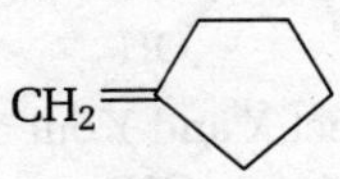

114. Which one of the following alkenes when treated with HCl yields majorly an anti Markownikov product? **[JEE Main 2019, April]**

(a) $Cl-CH=CH_2$

(b) $H_2N-CH=CH_2$

(c) $CH_3O-CH=CH_2$

(d) $F_3C-CH=CH_2$

115. 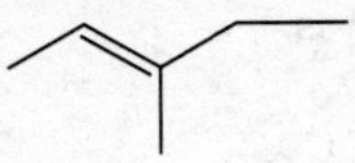 $\xrightarrow[H_2O]{Cl_2}$ *A*, *A* is

(a) 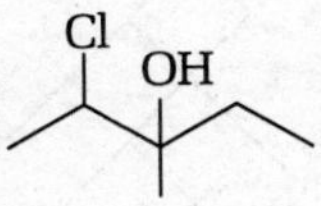 (b) 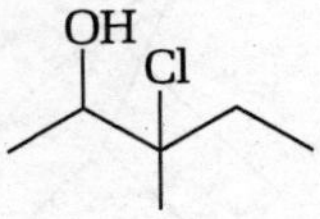

(c) 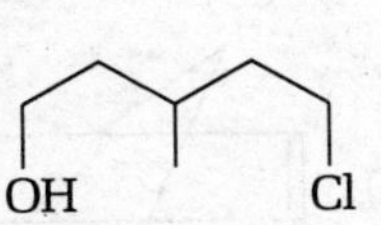 (d) 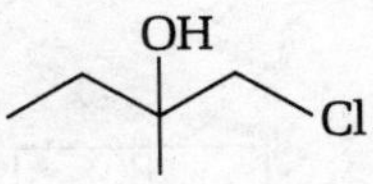

116. 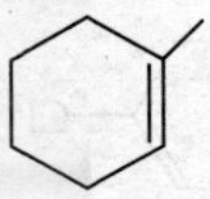 $\xrightarrow[H_2O_2/OH^-]{BD_3/THF}$ Product *A*, *A* is

(a) 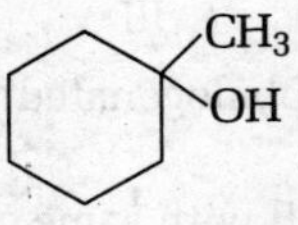 (b) 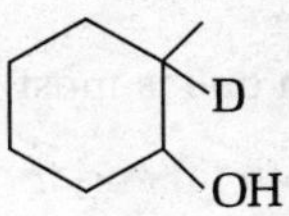

(c) 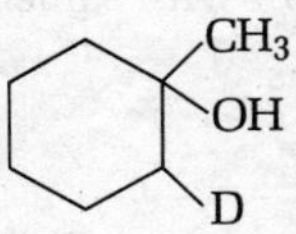 (d) 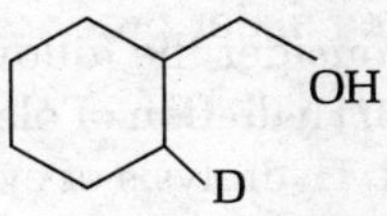

117. $R-CH=CH_2 + CCl_4 \xrightarrow{\text{Peroxide}} A$; *A* is

(a) $RCH(Cl)CH_2CCl_3$ (b) $RCH(CCl_3)CH_2Cl$

(c) Both (a) and (b) (d) None is correct

118. Which one of the following has least heat of hydrogenation?

(a) 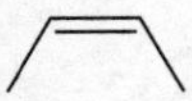 (b) 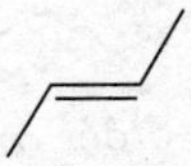

(c) 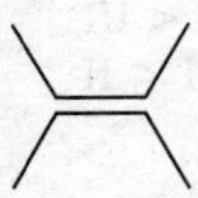 (d) 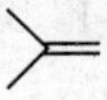

119. 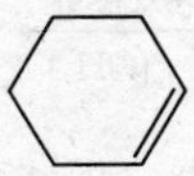 $\xrightarrow[\Delta]{A}$ 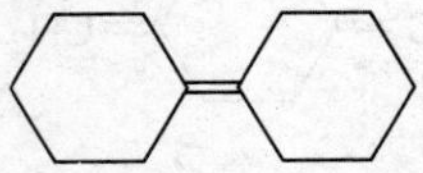 , *A* can be

(a) conc. H_2SO_4 (b) alc. KOH

(c) Et_3N (d) *t*-BuOK

120. Degree of unsaturation in 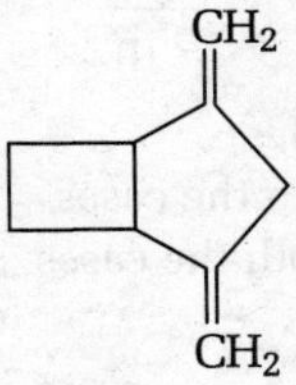 is

(a) 2 (b) 3 (c) 4 (d) 5

121. $B \xleftarrow[\Delta]{Na/NH_3}$ 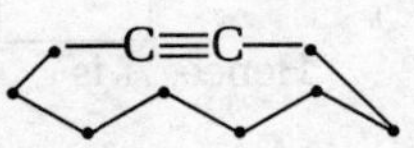 $\xrightarrow[\text{Lindlar's catalyst}]{H_2} A$

A and *B* are

(a) 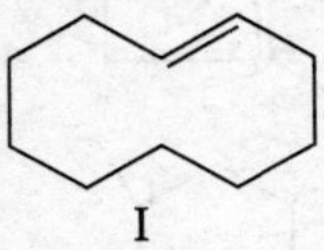 in both cases

I

(b) 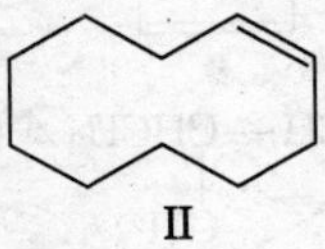 in both cases

II

(c) *A* is I, *B* is II

(d) *A* is II, *B* is I

122. 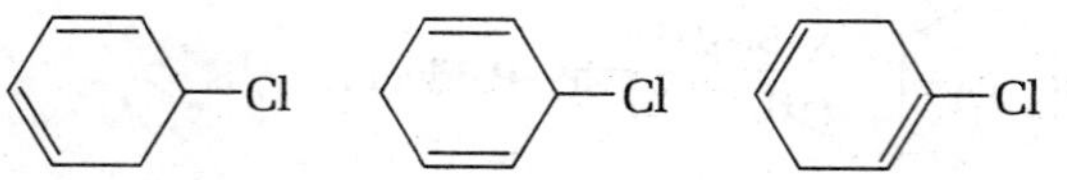

I II III

Which one is most easily dehydrohalogenated?

(a) I (b) II
(c) III (d) All with same ease

123. Consider the following methods
I. Hydration of olefins
II. Hydrolysis of cyanides
III. Reduction of carbonyl compounds
Which of these methods can be used to prepare alcohols?

(a) I, II and III (b) I and II
(c) II and III (d) I and III

124. Dehydrohalogenation of

I.  II. 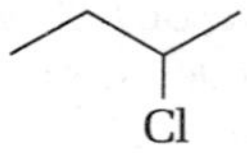

III. 

will be in order

(a) III < I < II (b) I < II < III
(c) III < II < I (d) I < III < II

125. In the reaction,

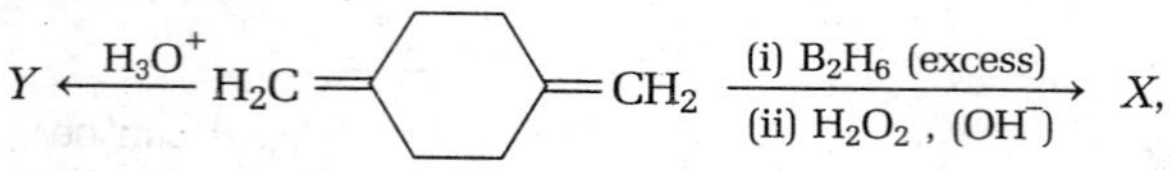

X and *Y* are

(a) 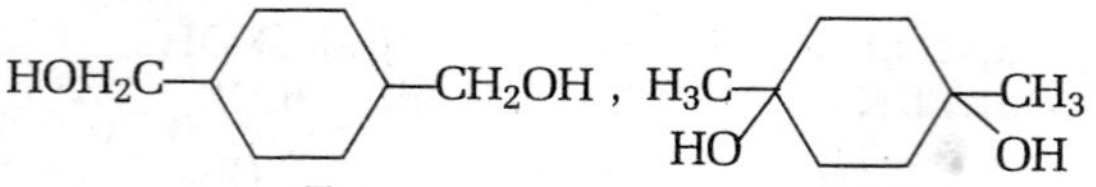

(I) (II)

(b) II and I
(c) I in both the cases
(d) II in both the cases

126. C_9H_{14} (*A*) (Santene) 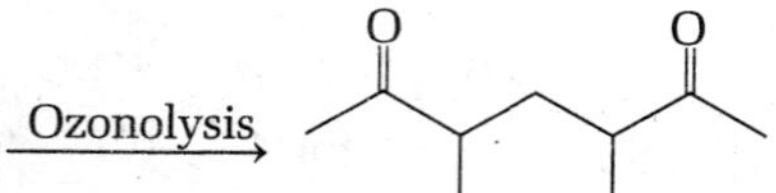 Hence, *A* is

Hence, *A* is

(a) 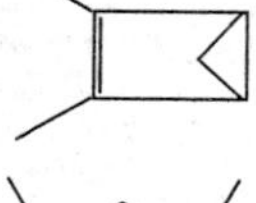 (b) 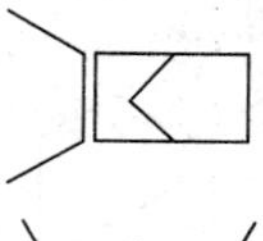

(c) 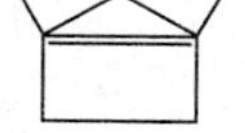 (d) 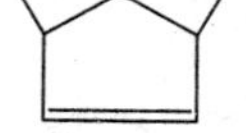

127. 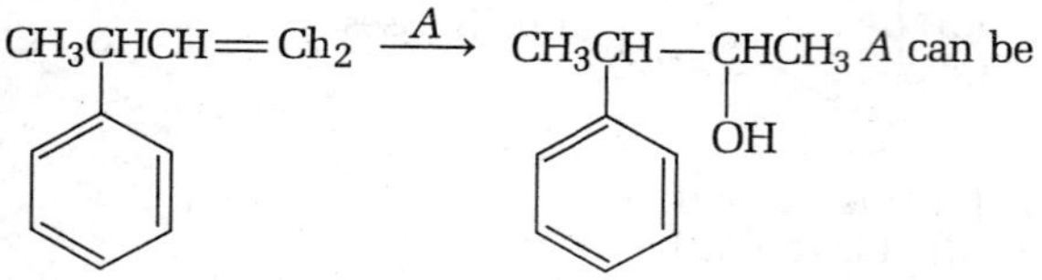

(a) H_2O/H^+
(b) $BH_3 \cdot THF/H_2O_2—OH^-$
(c) $Hg(OCOCH_3)_2 \cdot THF/NaBH_4 \cdot NaOH$
(d) All of the above are true

128. $CH_2= CHCH_2CH= CH_2 \xrightarrow{NBS} A$, *A* is

(a) $CH_2=CHCH(Br)CH=CH_2$ (b) $CH_2=CHC=CHCH_2Br$
(c) $CH_2=CHCH_2CH=CHBr$ (d) $CH_2=CHCH_2C(Br)=CH_2$

129. 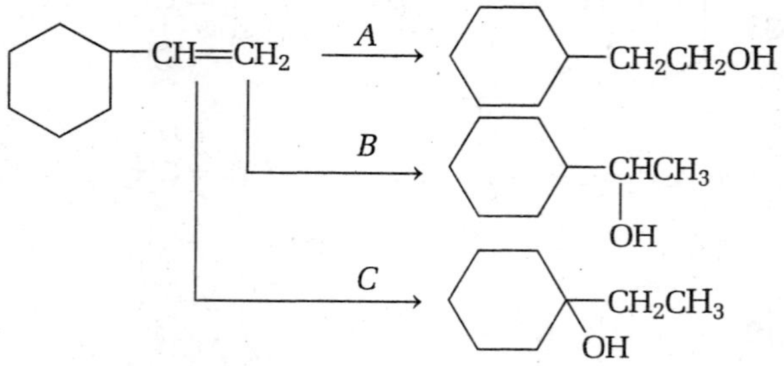

Schemes; *A*, *B* and *C* are

(a) simple hydration
(b) hydroboronation, mercuration-demercuration, hydration
(c) hydration, hydroboronation, mercuration-demercuration
(d) mercuration-demercuration, hydration, hydroboronation

130. 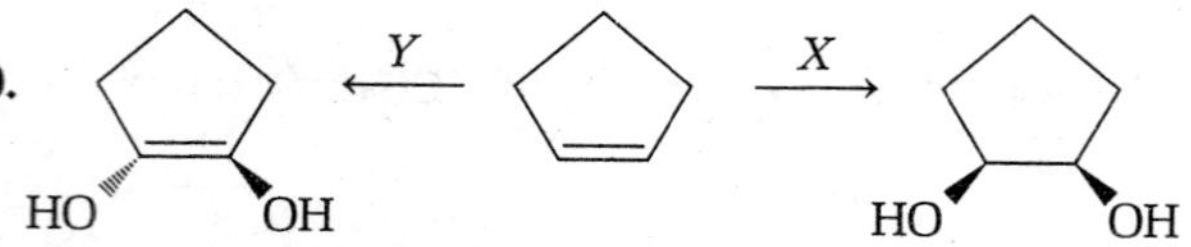

Select *X* and *Y* out of

I. MnO_4^-/OH^- II. HCO_3H

	X	*Y*
(a)	I	II
(b)	II	I
(c)	I	I
(d)	II	II

131. 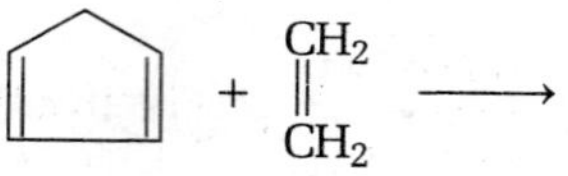 *A*; *A* is

(a) 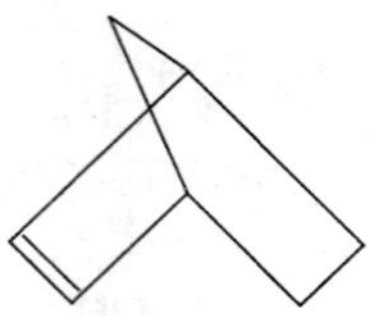 (b) 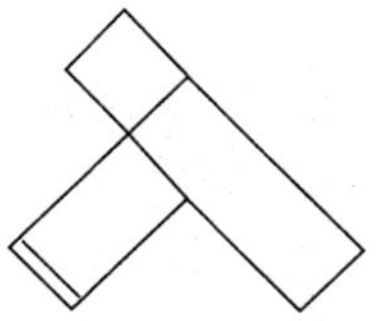

(c) 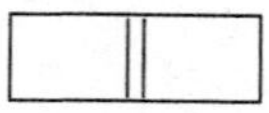 (d) 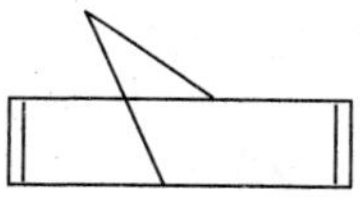

132. 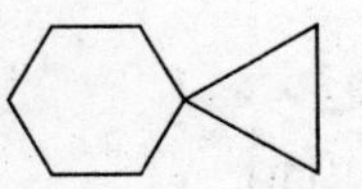 $+ H_2 \longrightarrow A$, A can be

(a) 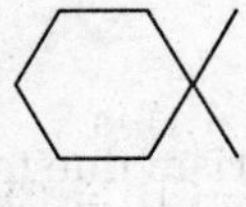
(b) 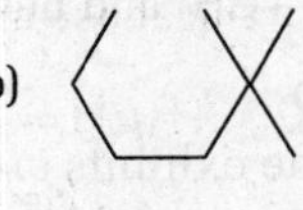
(c) 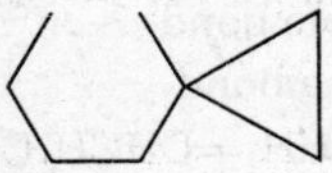
(d) no reaction

133. 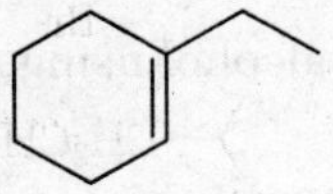 $\xrightarrow{SeO_2} A$; A is

(a) 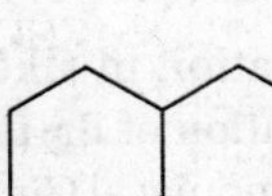
(b) 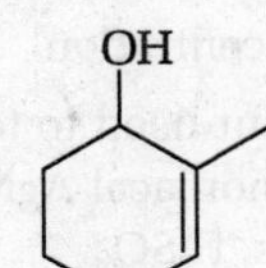
(c) 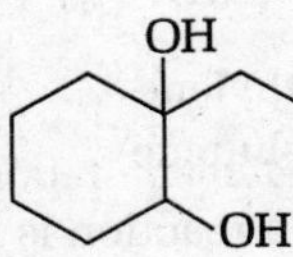
(d) 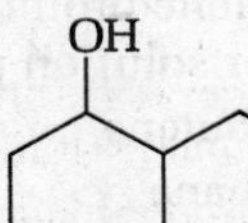

134. 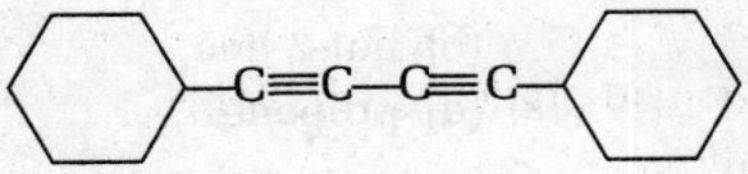 $\xrightarrow{Li/NH_3} A$; A is

(a) 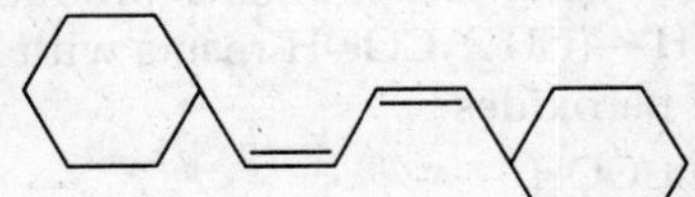
(b) 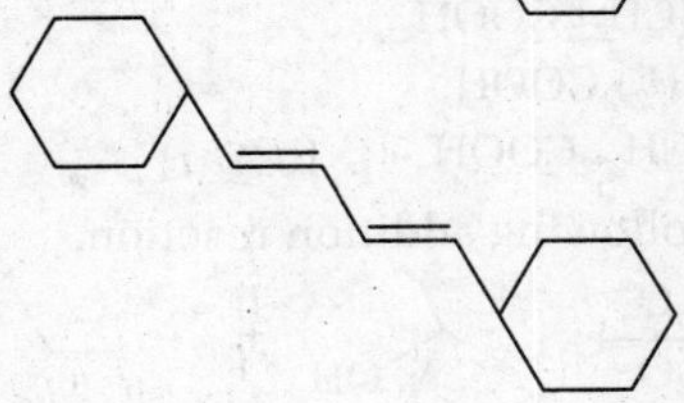
(c) Both (a) and (b)
(d) None of the above is correct

135. 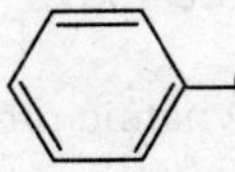 $—CH=CHCH_3 \xrightarrow{H_2O/H^+} A$ (predominant), A is

(a) 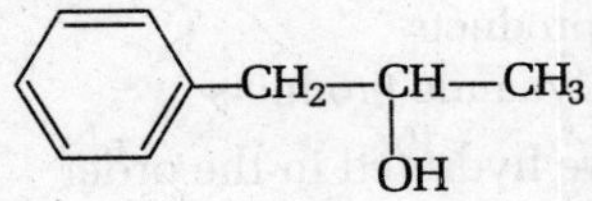
(b) 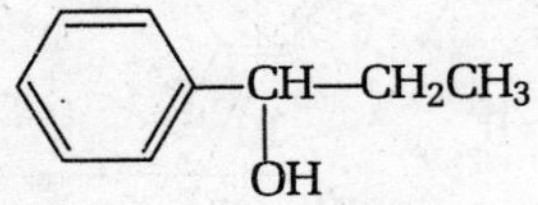
(c) 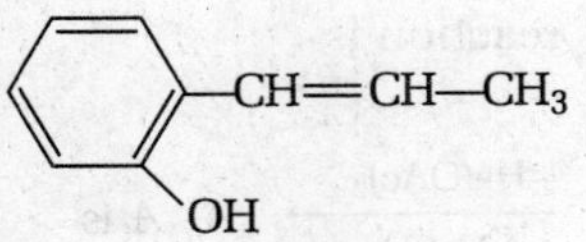
(d) 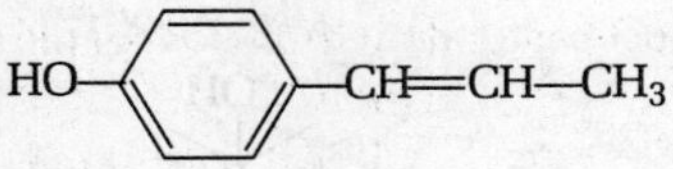

136. 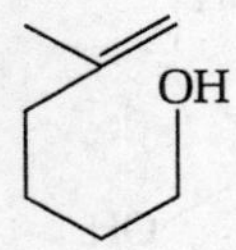 $+ Br_2 \xrightarrow{CH_2Cl_2} A$; A is

(a) 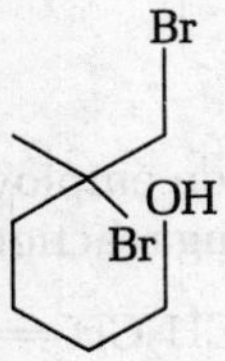
(b) 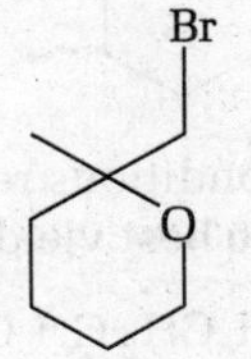
(c) 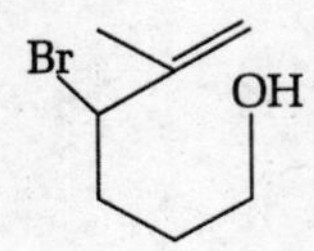
(d) 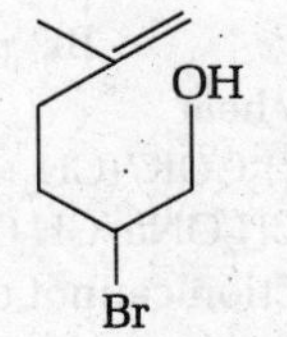

137. $2HCHO +$  $\xrightarrow{H^+} A$, A is

(a) 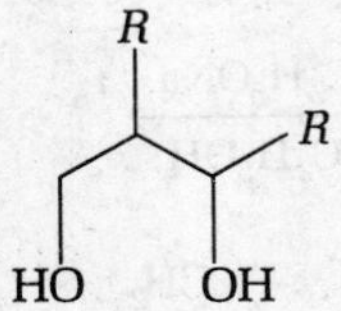
(b) 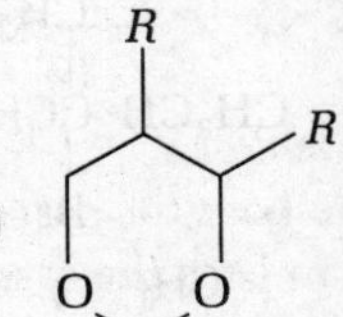
(c) 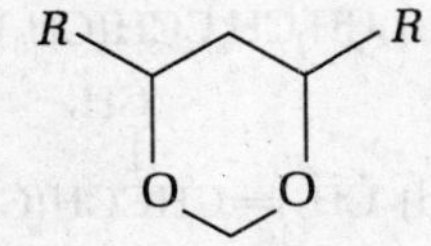
(d) 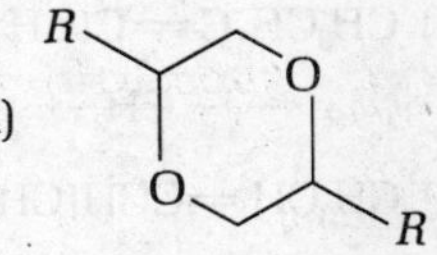

138. Which is hydrated to maximum extent?

(a) *cis*-$CH_3CH=CHCH_3$
(b) *trans*-$CH_3CH=CHCH_3$
(c) *trans* 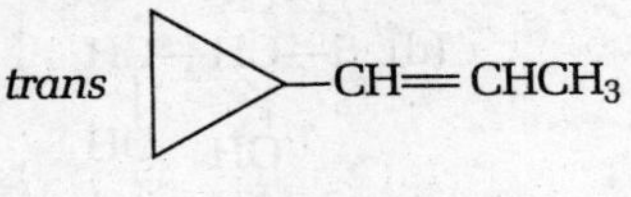
(d) 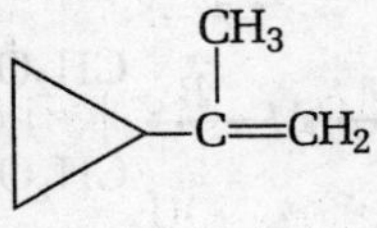

139. End product of this reaction is

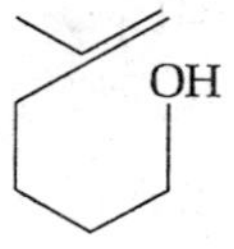

$\xrightarrow[NaBH_4]{Hg(OAc)_2}$ A, A is

(a) 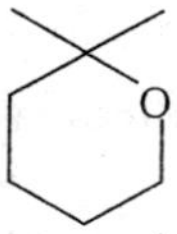

(b) 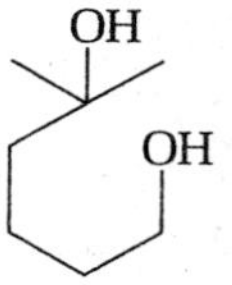

(c) 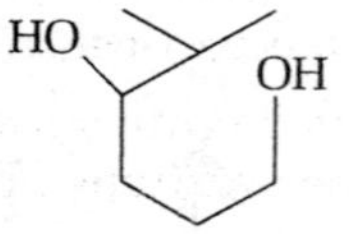

(d) 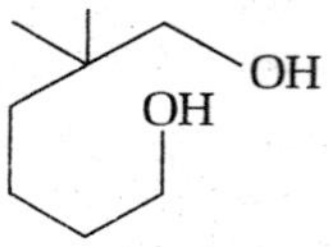

140. Which conditions/reagents would you employ to obtain the best yields in the following reaction?

$$CH_3CH_2\underset{\underset{Br}{|}}{CH}\,CH_3 \xrightarrow{?} CH_3CH_2CH{=}CH_2$$

(a) H_2O/heat
(b) $(CH_3)_3COK/(CH_3)_3COH$, heat
(c) CH_3CH_2ONa/CH_3CH_2OH, heat
(d) Reaction cannot occur as shown

141. Which of the following names is incorrect?
(a) 1-butene
(b) *trans*-2-butene
(c) (Z)-2-chloro-2-pentene
(d) 1,1-dimethylcyclopentene

142. Select the major product of the reaction.

$$CH_3CH_2\overset{\overset{CH_3}{|}}{\underset{\underset{Br}{|}}{C}}CH(CH_3)_2 \xrightarrow[C_2H_5OH]{C_2H_5ONa} ?$$

(a) $CH_3CH_2\overset{\overset{CH_3}{|}}{C}{=}C(CH_3)_2$
(b) $CH_3CH_2\overset{\overset{CH_2}{||}}{C}CH(CH_3)_2$
(c) $CH_3CH{=}\overset{\overset{CH_3}{|}}{C}CH(CH_3)_2$
(d) $CH_2{=}CH\overset{\overset{CH_3}{|}}{C}CH(CH_3)_2$

143. The alkene R—$CH{=}CH_2$ reacts readily with B_2H_6 and the product on oxidation with alkaline hydrogen peroxide produces
(a) R—CH_2—CHO
(b) R—CH_2—CH_2—OH
(c) $R-\underset{\underset{CH_3}{|}}{C}{=}O$
(d) $R-\underset{\underset{OH}{|}}{CH}-\underset{\underset{OH}{|}}{CH_2}$

144. In a reaction

$$CH_2{=}CH_2 \xrightarrow[\text{acid}]{\text{Hypochlorous}} M \xrightarrow{R} \begin{matrix} CH_2OH \\ | \\ CH_2OH \end{matrix}$$

M and R are
(a) CH_3CH_2Cl and NaOH
(b) $CH_2Cl\cdot CH_2OH$ and (aq)$NaHCO_3$
(c) CH_3CH_2OH and HCl
(d) CH_2—CH_2 (bridged by O) and heat

145. But-2-ene exhibits *cis-trans* isomerism due to
(a) rotation around C_2—C_3 double bond
(b) rotation around C_3—C_4 sigma bond
(c) rotation around C_1—C_2 bond
(d) restricted rotation around C=C bond

146. In the preparation of alkene from alcohol using Al_2O_3 which is effective factor?
(a) Porosity of Al_2O_3
(b) Temperature
(c) Concentration
(d) Surface area of Al_2O_3

147. A reagent used to test for unsaturation in alkenes is
(a) ammoniacal $AgNO_3$
(b) solution of Br_2 in CCl_4
(c) conc. H_2SO_4
(d) ammoniacal Cu_2Cl_2

148. Ethylidene bromide on heating with metallic sodium in ether solution produces
(a) 1-butene
(b) ethylene
(c) ethane
(d) 2-butene

149. Anti-Markownikoff's rule addition reaction is not observed in
(a) pent-2-ene
(b) but-2-ene
(c) but-1-ene
(d) propene

150. Which of the following compounds is produced when $CH_2{=}CH{-}(CH_2)_2COOH$ reacts with HBr in the presence of peroxides?
(a) $CH_3CH(CH_2)_2COOH$
(b) $CH_3CHCH_2(CH_2)_2COOH$
(c) $CH_3CHBr(CH_2)_2COOH$
(d) $BrCH_2CH_2(CH_2)_2COOH$

151. Consider the following addition reaction,

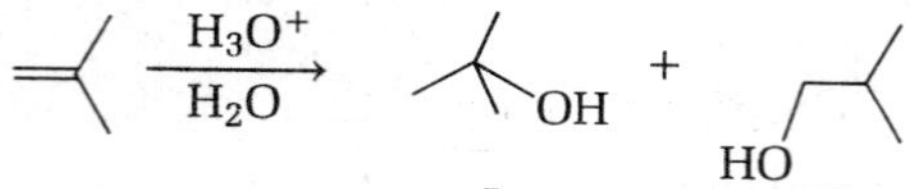

I II

Select the correct statement based on the above reaction.
(a) I is kinetic product and II is thermodynamic product
(b) I is thermodynamic product and II is kinetic product
(c) Both are kinetic products
(d) Both are thermodynamic products

152. Following olefins are hydrated in the order

I II III

(a) I < II < III
(b) III < II < I
(c) I ≈ II < III
(d) I = II = III

153. Major product of the following reaction is

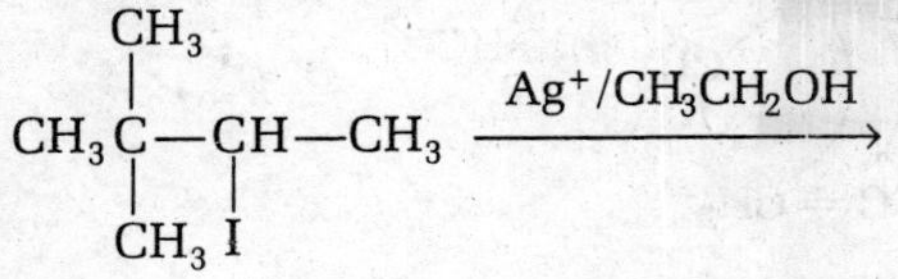

(a) $(CH_3)_3CCH{=}CH_2$ (b) 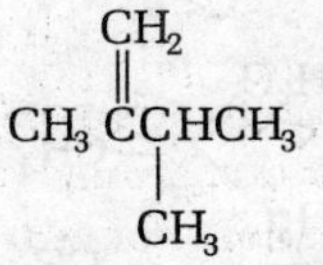

(c) 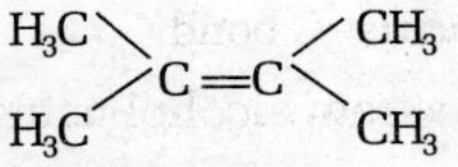 (d) 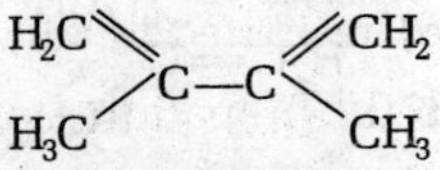

154. Consider conversion of *cis*- and *trans*-2-butene into butane

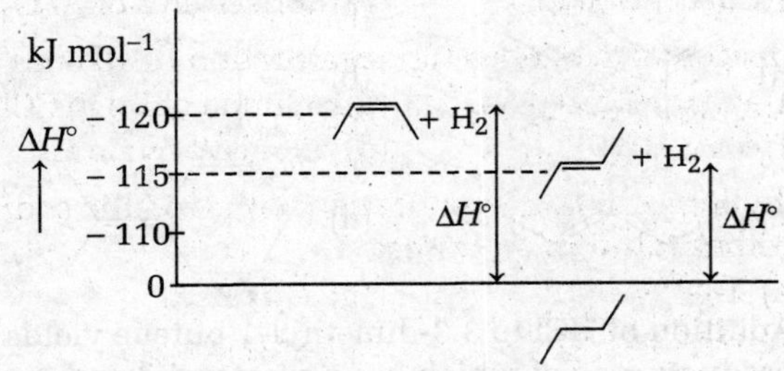

Thus, for *cis*-2-butene ⟶ *trans*-2-butene, $\Delta H°$ is

(a) $-$ 235 kJ mol^{-1}

(b) + 235 kJ mol^{-1}

(c) + 5 kJ mol^{-1}

(d) $-$ 5 kJ mol^{-1}

155. Consider the following elimination reactions.

X : 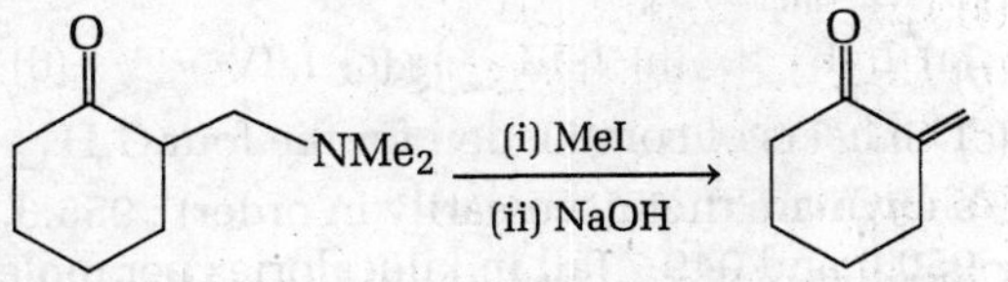

Y : 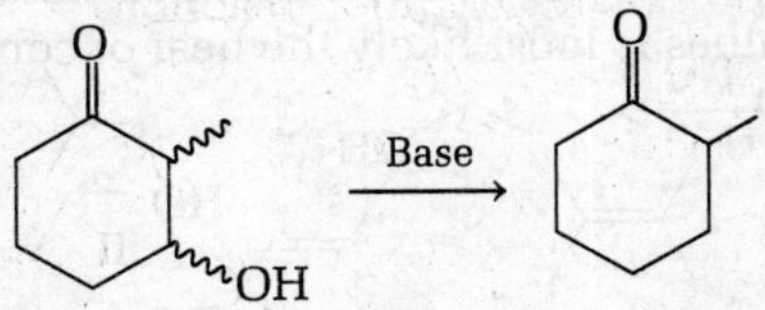

Z : 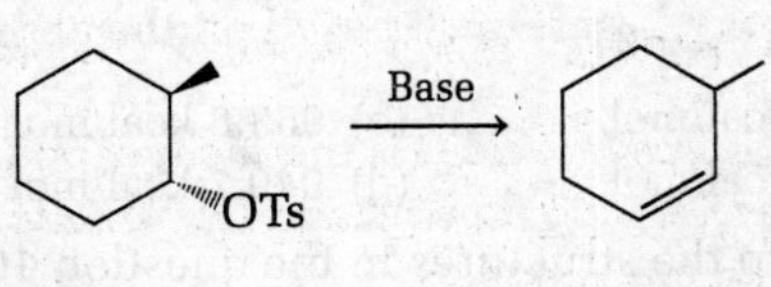

These are

	X	*Y*	*Z*
(a)	E1CB	E2	E1CB
(b)	E2	E1CB	E1CB
(c)	E1CB	E1CB	E2
(d)	E1CB	E1CB	E1CB

156. Rank the following alkenes in the order of decreasing heats of hydrogenation (largest first)

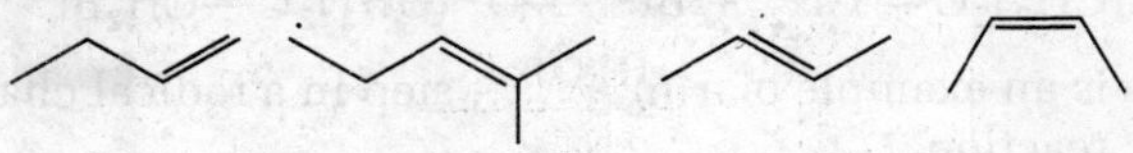

1 2 3 4

(a) 2 > 3 > 4 > 1 (b) 1 > 3 > 4 > 2

(c) 1 > 4 > 3 > 2 (d) 2 > 4 > 3 > 1

157. The product from the reaction of 1-pentene with Cl_2 in H_2O is named

(a) 1-chloro-2-pentanol (b) 1-chloro-1-pentanol

(c) 2-chloro-2-pentanol (d) 2-chloro-1-pentanol

158. In the reaction of hydrogen bromide with an alkene (in the absence of peroxides), the first step of the reaction is the .... to the alkene.

(a) fast addition of an electrophile

(b) slow addition of an electrophile

(c) fast addition of a nucleophile

(d) slow addition of a nucleophile

159. The reaction of propene with HOCl (Cl_2 + H_2O) proceeds through the intermediate **[JEE Main 2016]**

(a) $CH_3-\overset{+}{C}H-CH_2-Cl$ (b) $CH_3-CH(OH)-\overset{+}{C}H_2$

(c) $CH_3-CHCl-\overset{+}{C}H_2$ (d) $CH_3-\overset{+}{C}H-CH_2-OH$

160. Which, if any, of the following alcohols cannot be prepared from an alkene?

(a) 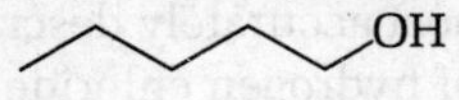 (b) 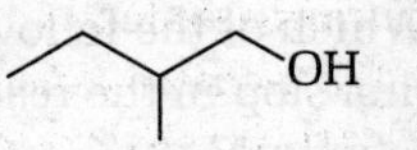

(c) 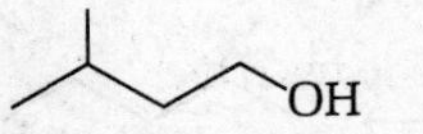 (d) 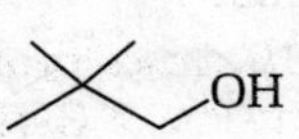

161. Which of the species shown is the most stable form of the intermediate in the electrophilic addition of Cl_2 in water to cyclohexene to form a halohydrin? Electron pairs have been omitted for convenience and their absence should not be considered as part of the problem.

(a) 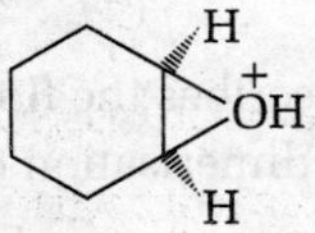 (b) 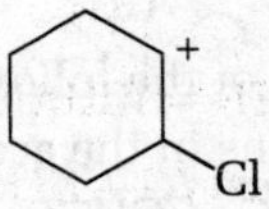

(c) 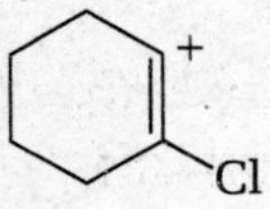 (d) 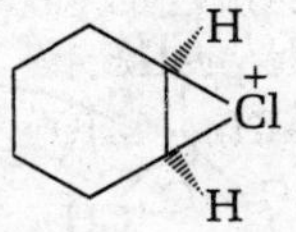

162. Treatment of 2-methyl-2-butene with HBr in the presence of a peroxide yields

(a) a primary alkyl bromide

(b) a secondary alkyl bromide

(c) a tertiary alkyl bromide

(d) a *vicinal* dibromide

163. The reaction,

$(CH_3)_2C{=}CH_2 + Br^{\bullet} \longrightarrow (CH_3)_2\dot{C}{-}CH_2Br$

is an example of a (n) .... step in a radical chain reaction.

(a) initiation
(b) termination
(c) propagation
(d) heterolytic cleavage

164. A hydrocarbon '*A*' on ozonolysis gives two isomeric forms '*B*' and '*C*'. *B* on oxidation gives '*D*'. silver salt of *D* contains 59.6% Ag. Structure of hydrocarbon is

(a) $CH_3{-}CH{=}C(CH_3){-}CH_3$

(b) $CH_3{-}CH_2{-}CH{=}C(CH_3){-}CH_3$

(c) $CH_3{-}CH_2{-}CH_2{-}CH{=}C(CH_3){-}CH_2{-}CH_3$

(d) $CH_3{-}CH(CH_3){-}CH{=}C(CH_3){-}CH_2{-}CH_3$

165. Which of the following most accurately describes the first step in the reaction of hydrogen chloride with 1-butene?

(a) 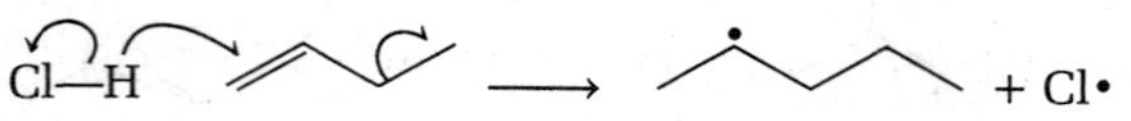

(b) 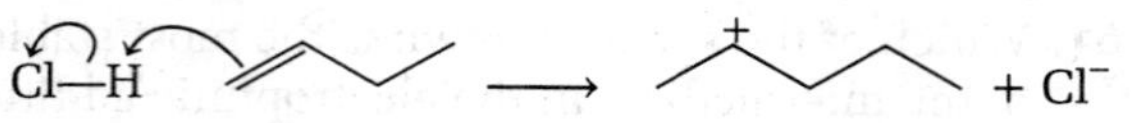

(c) 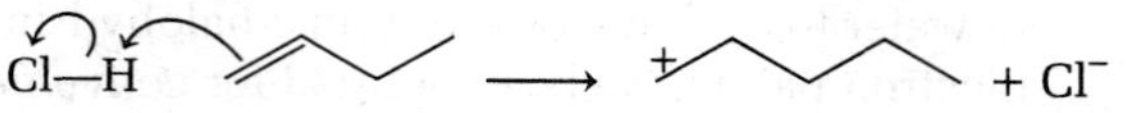

(d) 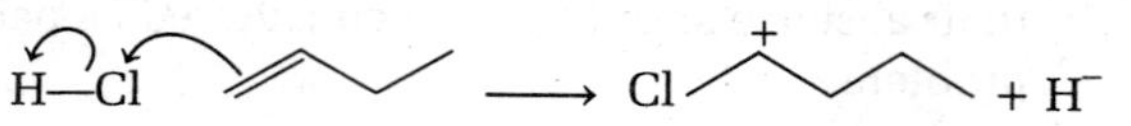

166. Which of the following best describes the flow of electrons in the acid-catalysed dimerisation of $(CH_3)_2C{=}CH_2$?

(a) 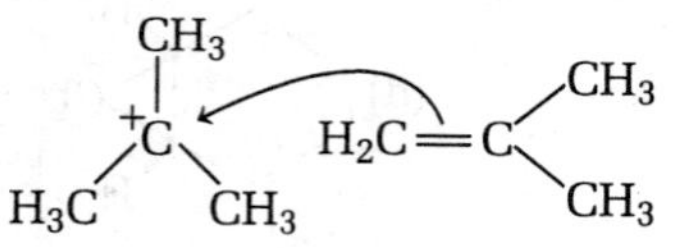

(b) 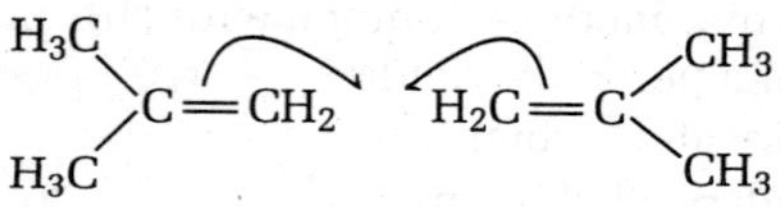

(c) 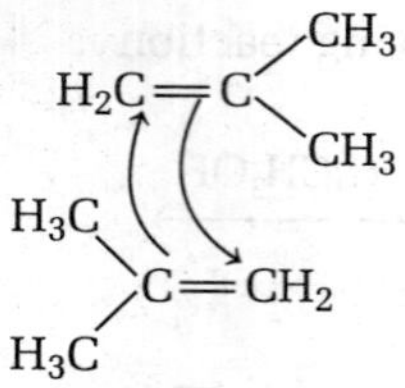

(d) 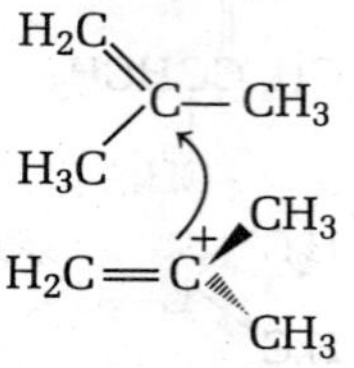

167. Which one of the following compounds gives acetone $(CH_3)_2C{=}O$ as one of the products of its ozonolysis?

(a) 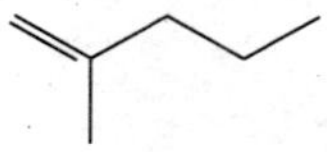
(b) 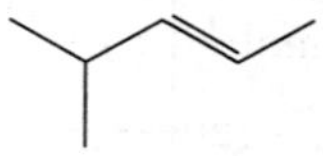
(c) 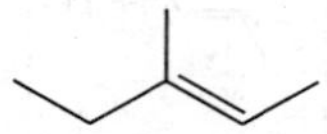
(d) 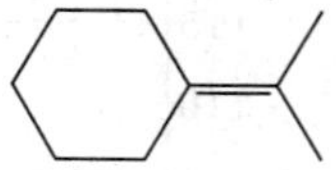

168. Addition of HCl to 3,3-dimethyl-1-butene yields two products, one of which has a rearranged carbon skeleton. Which of the following cations are intermediates in that reaction?

I: $(CH_3)_3C\overset{+}{C}HCH_2Cl$ II: $(CH_3)_3C\overset{+}{C}HCH_3$

III: $(CH_3)_2C(Cl)\overset{+}{C}(CH_3)_2$ IV: $(CH_3)_2\overset{+}{C}CH(CH_3)_2$

(a) I, II (b) I, III (c) I, IV (d) II, IV

169. The heats of combustion for the four C_6H_{12} isomers shown are (not necessarily in order) : 955.3, 953.6, 950.6 and 949.7 (all in kilocalories per mole). Which of these values is most likely the heat of combustion of isomer 1?

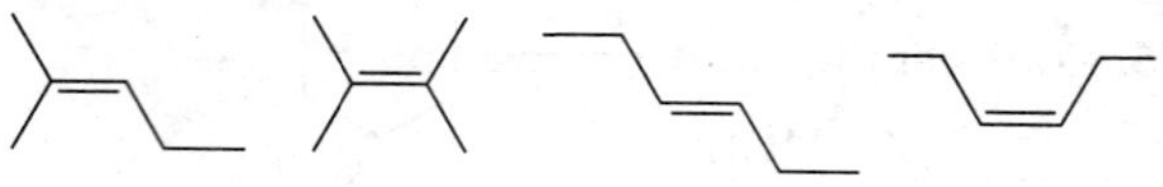

1 2 3 4

(a) 955.3 kcal/mol (b) 953.6 kcal/mol
(c) 950.6 kcal/mol (d) 949.7 kcal/mol

170. Referring to the structures in the question 169 what can be said about isomers 3 and 4?

(a) 3 is more stable by 1.7 kcal/mol
(b) 3 is more stable by 3.0 kcal/mol
(c) 4 is more stable by 1.7 kcal/mol
(d) 3 is more stable by 0.9 kcal/mol

171. Which of the following compounds will exhibit geometrical isomerism? **[JEE Main 2015]**

(a) 1-phenyl-2-butene (b) 3-phenyl-1-butene

(c) 2-phenyl-1-butene (d) 1, 1-diphenyl-1-propane

172. In the dehydrohalogenation of 2-bromobutane, which conformation leads to the formation of *cis*-2-butene?

(a) 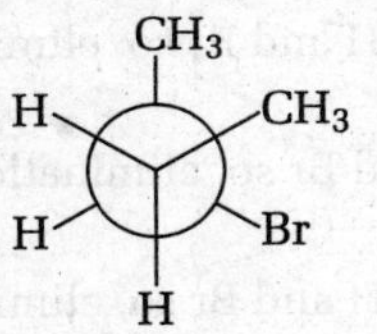

(b) 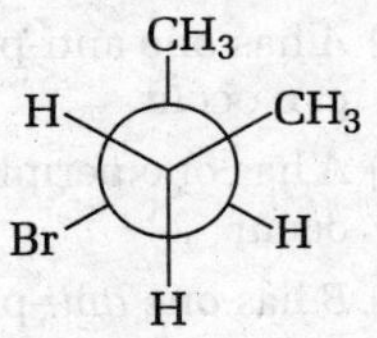

(c) 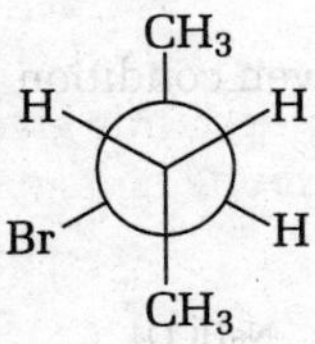

(d) 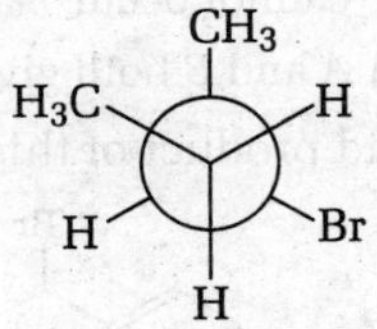

173. Which of the following alcohols would be most likely to undergo dehydration with rearrangement by a process involving a methyl migration (methyl shift)?

(a) 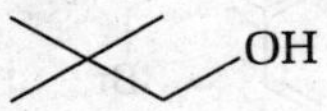

(b) 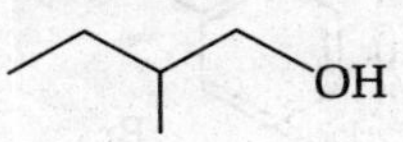

(c) 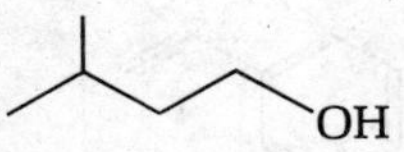

(d) 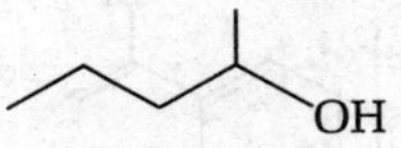

174. Rank the following alcohols in order of decreasing reactivity (fastest → slowest) toward dehydration with 85% H_3PO_4

$\underset{1}{(CH_3)_2CH_2CH_2CH_2OH}$; $\underset{2}{(CH_3)_2\overset{OH}{C}CH_2CH_3}$;

$\underset{3}{(CH_3)_2CH\overset{OH}{C}HCH_3}$

(a) 2 > 3 > 1 (b) 1 > 3 > 2

(c) 2 > 1 > 3 (d) 1 > 2 > 3

175. Consider the following reaction

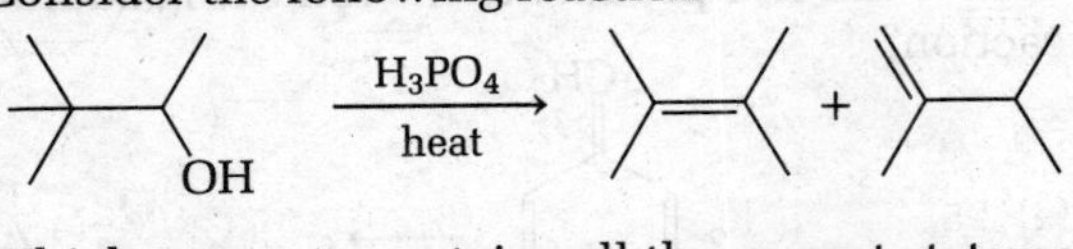

Which response contains all the correct statements about this process and no incorrect ones?

I. Dehydration

II. E2 mechanism

III. Carbon skeleton migration

IV. Most stable carbocation forms

V. Single-step reaction

(a) I and III (b) I, II and III

(c) I, II and V (d) I, III and IV

176. Select the formula or statement representing the major product(s) of the following reaction

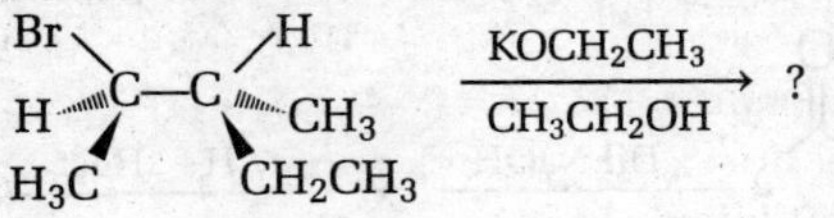

(a) 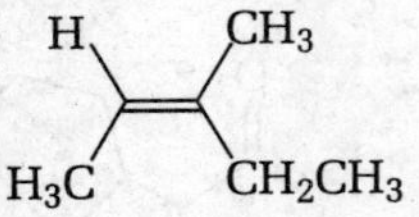

(b) 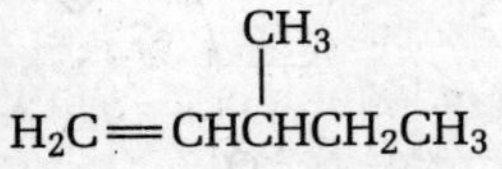

(c) 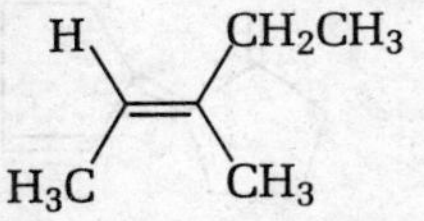

(d) Both (a) and (b) form in approximately equal amounts

177. Which one of the following statements concerning E2 reactions of alkyl halides is true?

(a) The rate of an E2 reaction depends only on the concentration of the alkyl halide

(b) The rate of an E2 reaction depends only on the concentration of the base

(c) The C—H bond and the C—*X* (*X*=halogen) bond are broken in the same step

(d) Alkyl chlorides generally react faster than alkyl bromides

178. Which alkyl halide undergoes E2 elimination at the fastest rate?

(a) 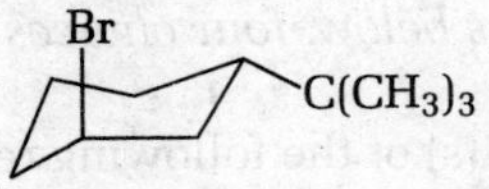

(b) 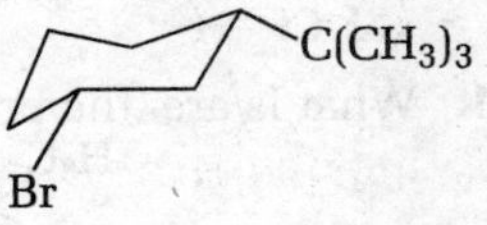

(c) 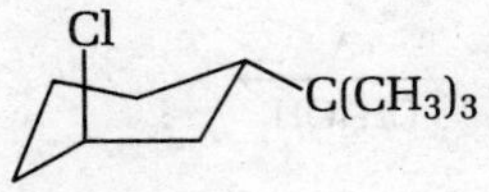

(d) 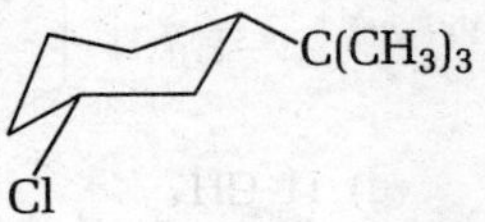

179. What is the relationship between the pair of compounds shown?

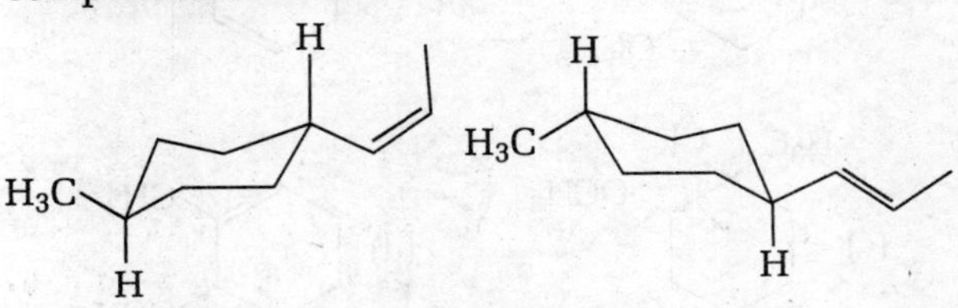

(a) Identical : superimposable without bond rotations

(b) Conformations

(c) Stereoisomers

(d) Constitutional isomers

180. Consider the above reaction, the product 'X' and 'Y' respectively are **[JEE Main 2021, March]**

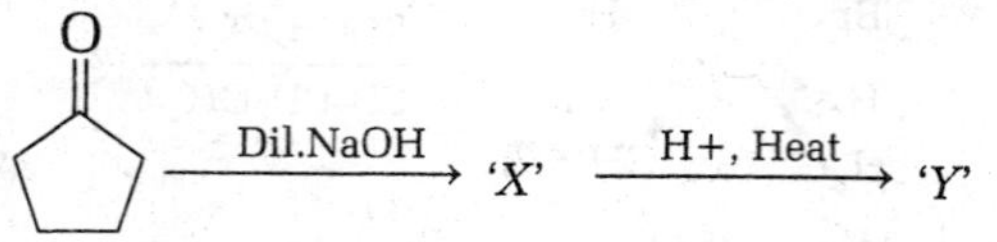

(a) 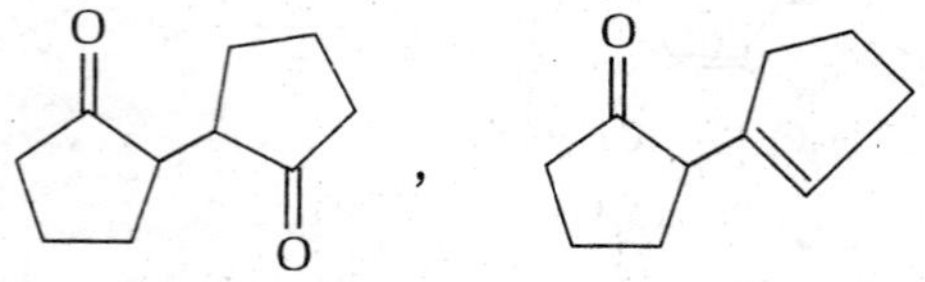

(b) 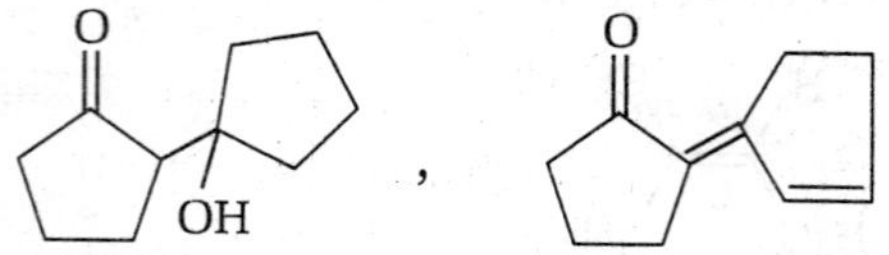

(c) 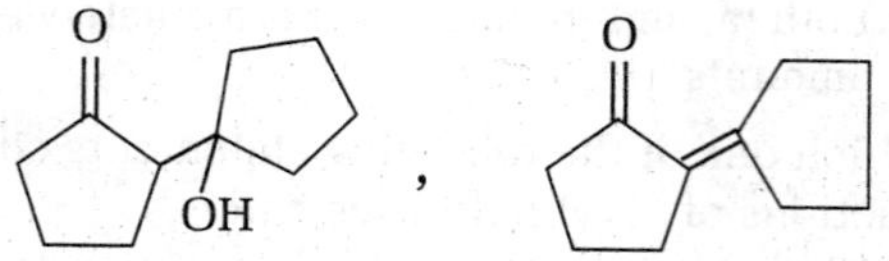

(d) 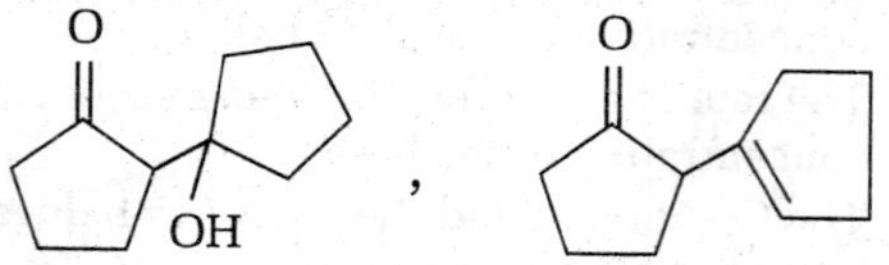

181. Alkene (*C*) is formed from (*A*) and not from (*B*)

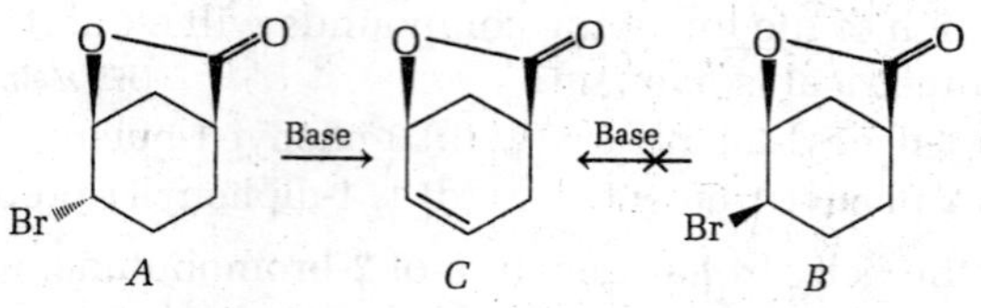

It is due to

(a) *A* has one anti-periplanar H and Br so, elimination can occur

(b) *A* has one periplanar H and Br so, elimination can occur

(c) *B* has one *anti*-periplanar H and Br so, elimination cannot occur

(d) *A* and *B* both give *C* under given condition

182. End product of this reaction is

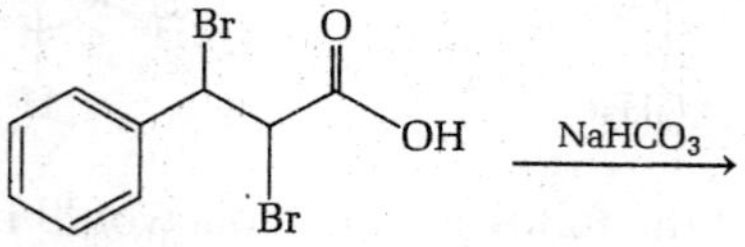

(a) 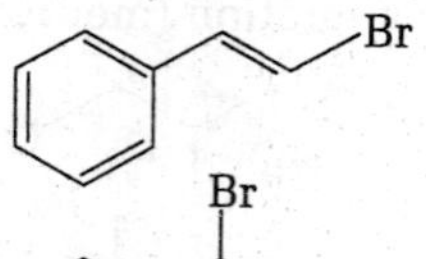

(b) 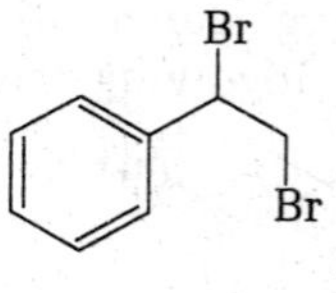

(c) 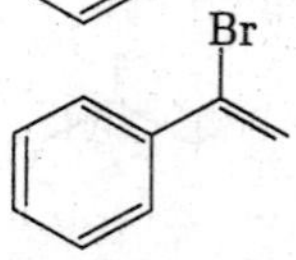

(d) 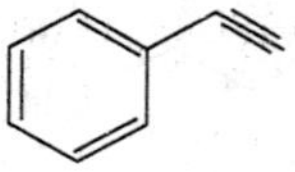

Objective Questions Type II [One or more than one correct option(s)]

In each of the questions below, four choices are given, of which one or more than one are correct.

1. What is/are the product(s) of the following reaction?

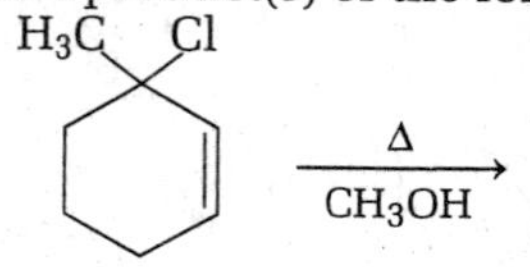

(a) 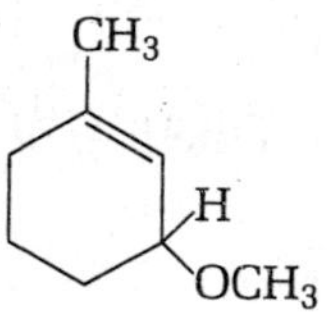

(b) 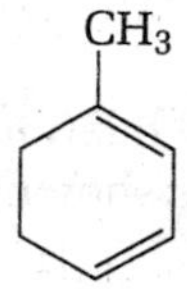

(c) 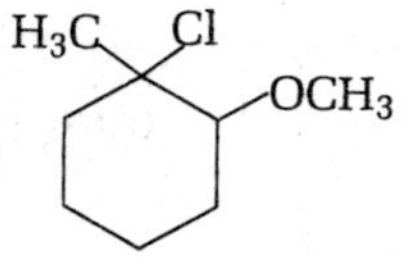

(d) 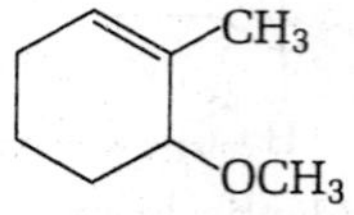

2. Compound (*A*) in presence of aqueous H_2SO_4 changes into

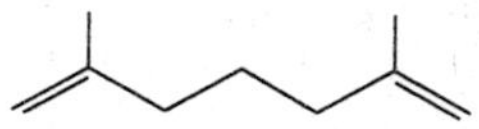

A

(a) 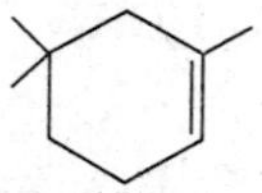

(b) 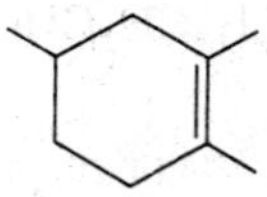

(c) 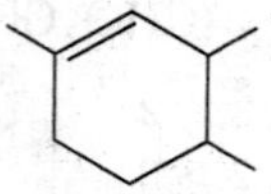

(d) 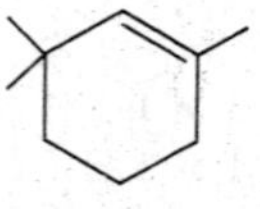

3. What is the end-product of the following addition reaction?

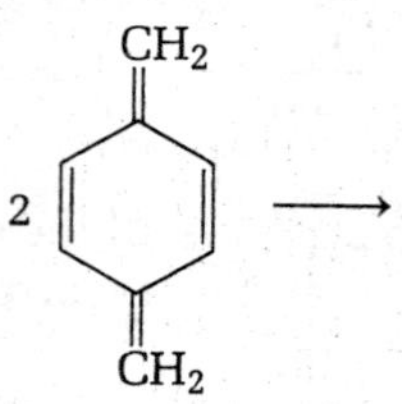

(a) 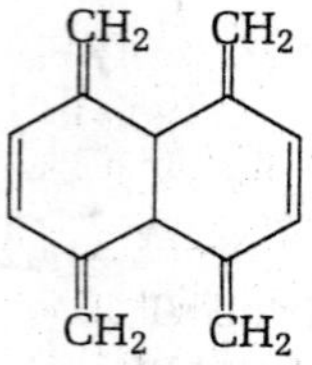

(b) 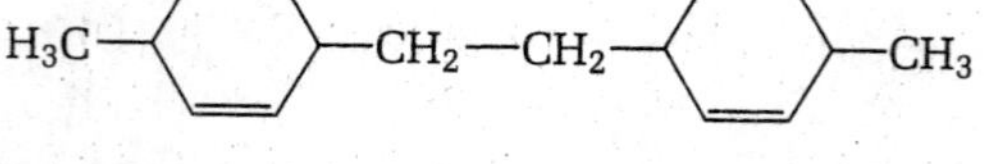

(c) 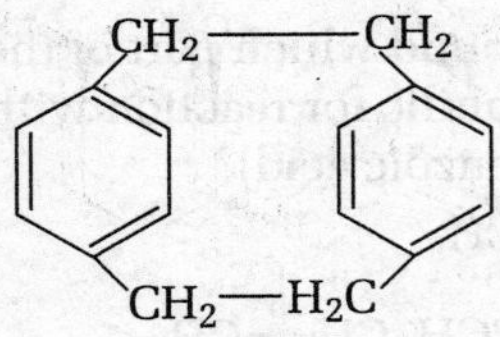

(d) 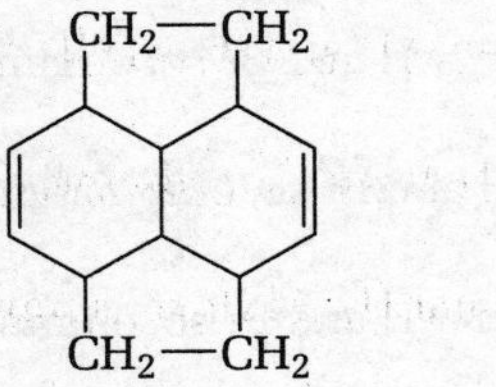

4. End-product of the following reaction is

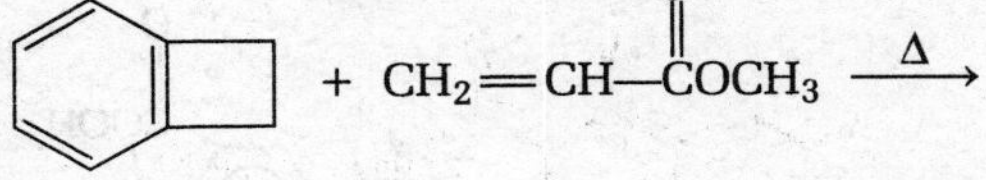

(a) 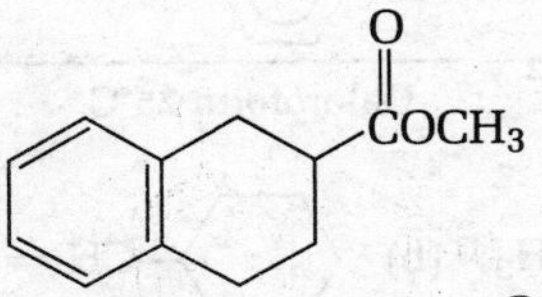

(b) 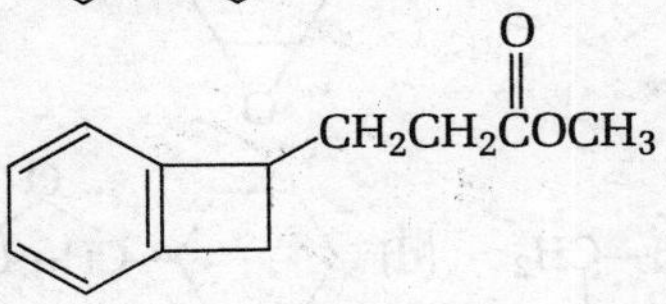

(c) 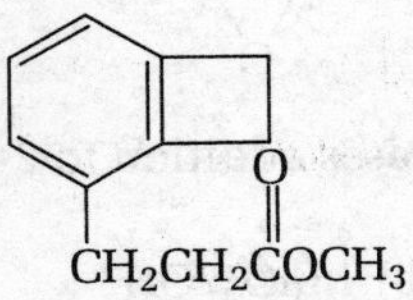

(d) 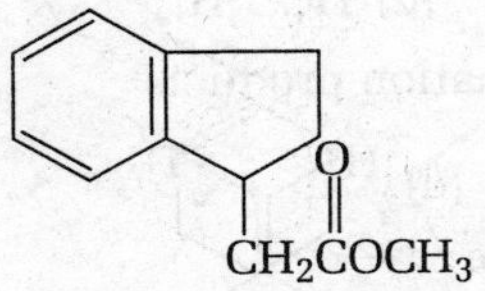

5. Radioactive (^{82}Br—^{82}Br) adds to 1-bromocyclohexene. Product

(a) is 1,1,2-tribromocyclohexene
(b) has radioactive bromine in *vicinal* position
(c) has radioactive bromine *trans* to each other
(d) has radioactive bromine *cis* to each other

6. Major product(s) in the following reaction is/are

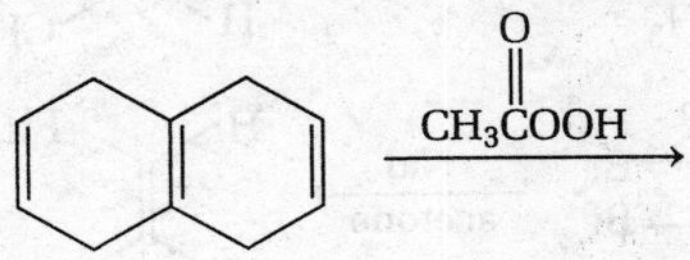

(a) 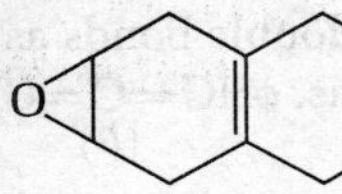 (b) 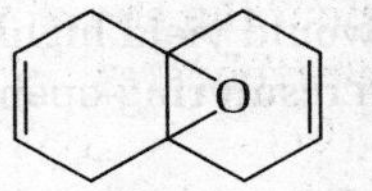

(c) 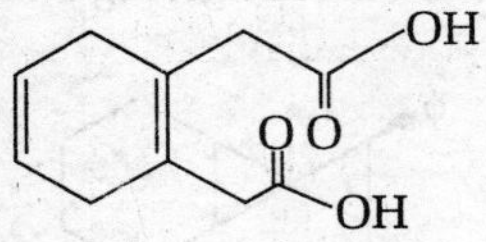 (d) 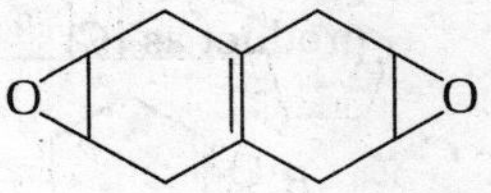

7. 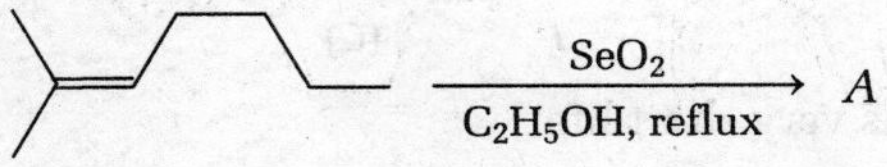

A can be

(a) 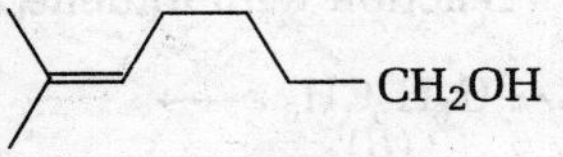 (b) 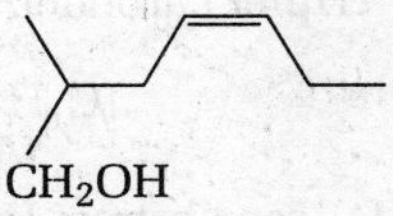

(c) 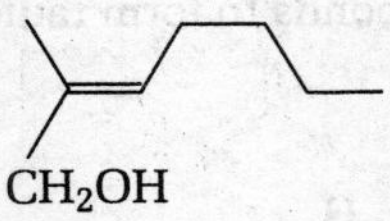 (d) 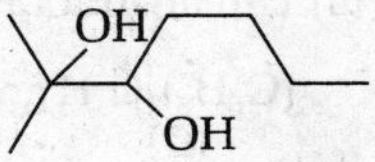

8. Product(s) of the following reaction is/are

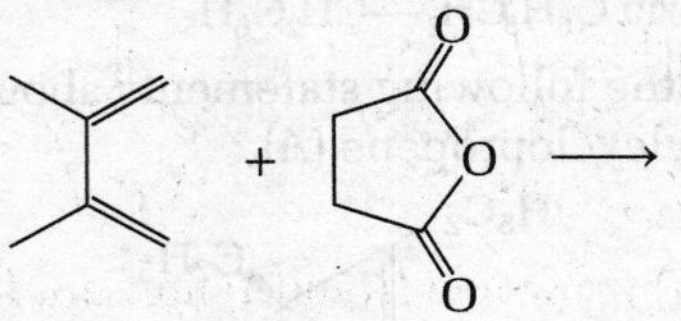

(a) 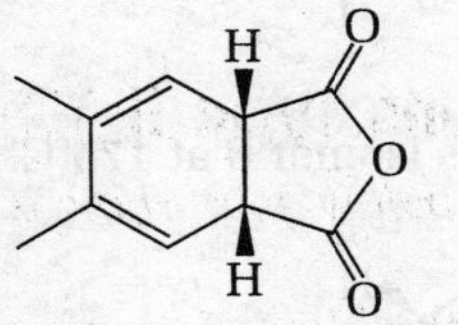 (b) 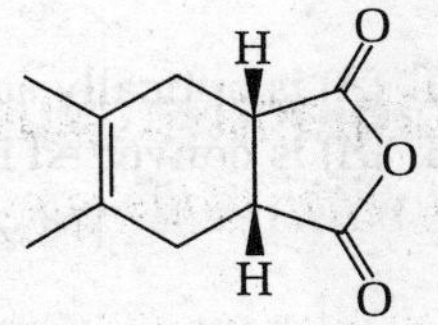

(c) 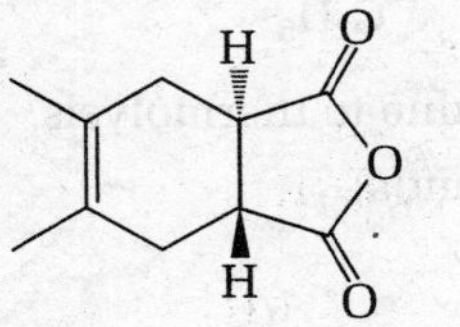 (d) 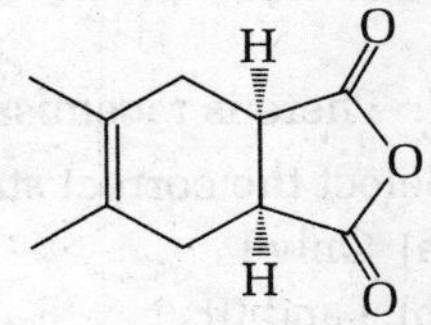

9. In the compound (*A*) (C=C) bonds involved in Diels-Alder reaction are

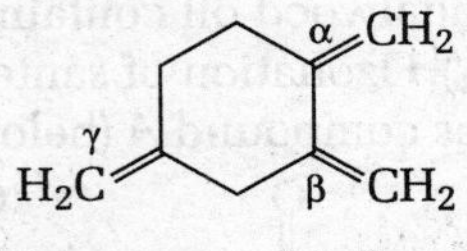

(a) α, β (b) α, γ (c) β, γ (d) α, β, γ

10. Three membered ring carbenes (*A*)

(*A*)

(a) would yield highly strained double bonds as in (*B*) as a result ring-opening reactions, $\phi HC{=}C{=}CH\phi$ (*B*)

(b) (*B*) can also combine with alkene giving addition product as (*C*)

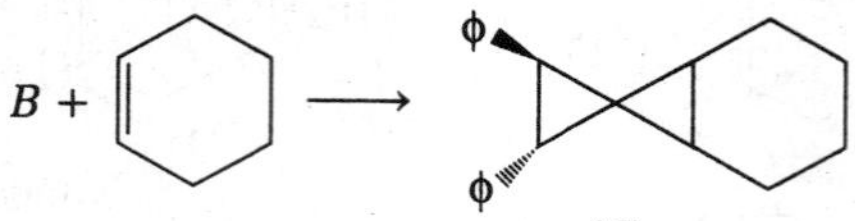

(*C*)

(c) (*A*) has very short life

(d) (*C*) has two stereocentres

11. Triplet carbene(*A*) in a reaction with toluene(*B*)

$$\underset{(A)}{(C_6H_5)_2\dot{C}\cdot} + \underset{(B)}{C_6H_5CH_3} \longrightarrow$$

(a) can abstract H from C—H bonds to form radical pairs $\underset{(C)}{(C_6H_5)_2\dot{C}H}$ and $\underset{(D)}{(C_6H_5\dot{C}H_2)}$

(b) can form $(C_6H_5)_2CH—CH_2C_6H_5$

(c) can form $(C_6H_5)_2CH—CH(C_6H_5)_2$

(d) can form $C_6H_5CH_2—CH_2C_6H_5$

12. Consider the following statements about 1,2-diethylcyclopropene (*A*)

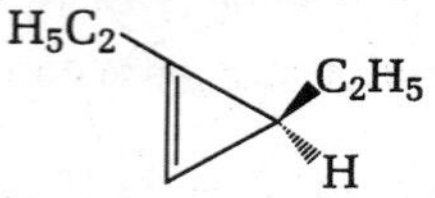

I. (*A*) is optically active.

II. (*A*) is converted into its isomer *B* at 175°C.

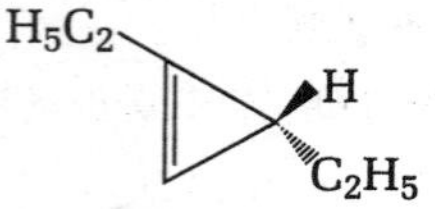

III. There is racemisation due to thermolysis

Select the correct statement(s).

(a) Only I

(b) I and III

(c) II and III

(d) I, II and III

13. East Indian sandalwood oil contains a hydrocarbon santene (C_9H_{14}). Ozonation of santene followed by hydrolysis gives compound *A* (below).

(A) 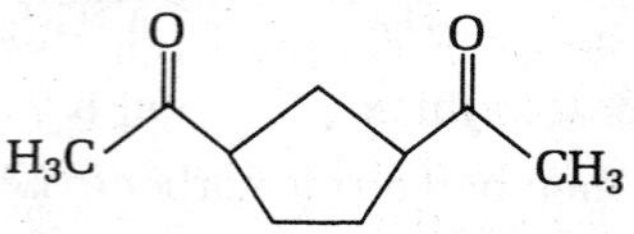

Select the correct statement(s).

(a) *A* gives iodoform test

(b) Degree of unsaturation in santene is 3°

(c) Both of the above

(d) None of the above

14. In the following compound which part of the alkene is more nucleophilic for reaction with *m*CPBA (*meta* chloro peroxy benzoic acid)?

$$CH_3\overset{\displaystyle CH_3}{\underset{\displaystyle CH_3}{C}}\overset{\alpha}{=}\overset{\displaystyle CH_3}{C}CH_2CH\overset{\beta}{=}CH_2$$

(a) $C\overset{\alpha}{=}C$

(b) $C\overset{\beta}{=}C$

(c) Equally nucleophilic

(d) Only electrophilic character

15. Identify the product of the following reaction

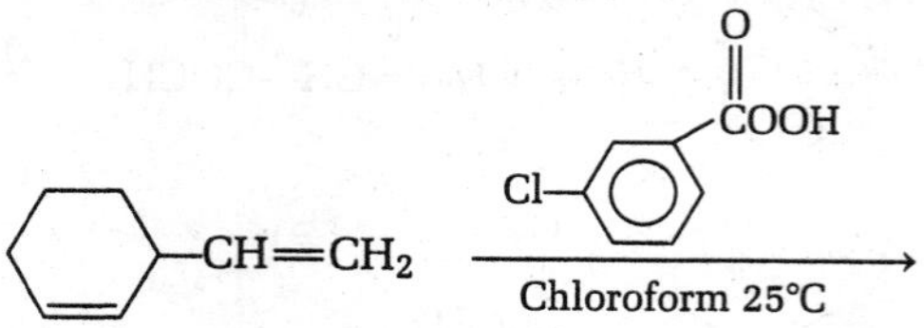

(a) 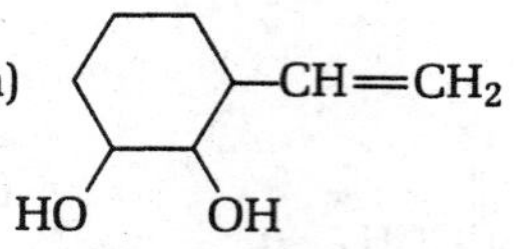

(b) 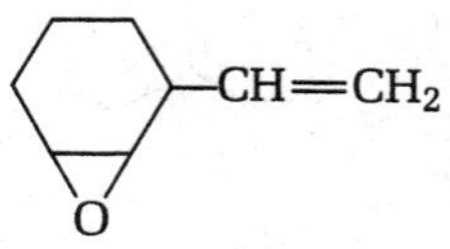

(c) 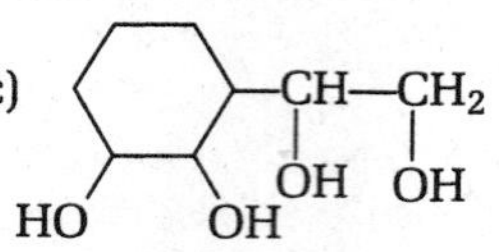

(d) 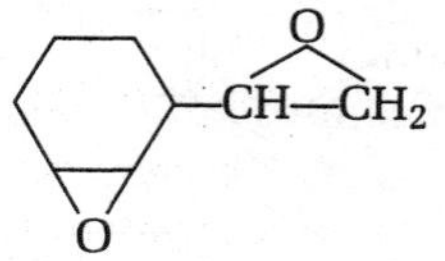

16. In which of the following cases addition to 2-butene is stereoselective?

(a) D_2

(b) MnO_4^-/OH^-

(c) Br_2

(d) HCO_3H

17. Select the correct elimination products

(a) 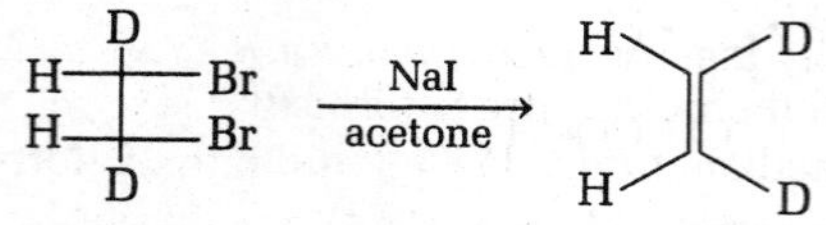

(b) 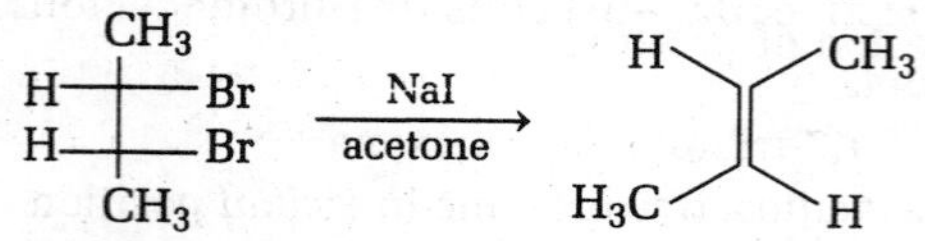

(c) 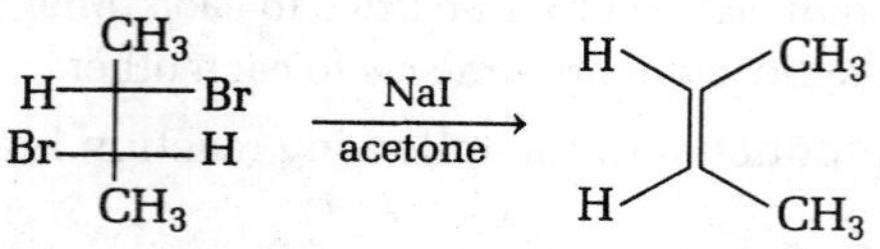

(d) 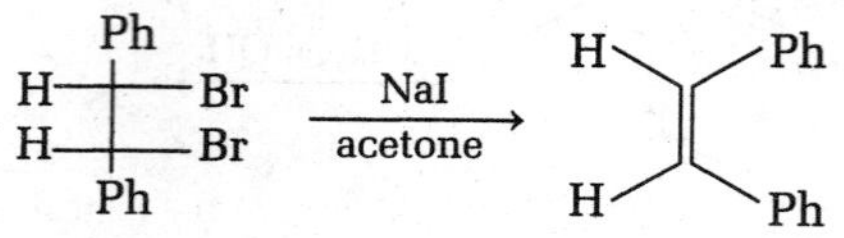

18. Consider the following alkene and select the correct alternate(s). $CH_3CHCH{=}CH_2$ (with CH_3 on the second carbon)

(a) A 3° alcohol is formed by acidic hydration
(b) A 1° alcohol is formed by hydroboration-oxidation
(c) A racemic mixture of 2° alcohols is formed by oxymercuration-demercuration
(d) A racemic mixture of 1° alcohols is formed by oxymercuration-demercuration

19. Which pair have approximately equal stability?
(a) $CH_3CH{=}CH_2$ and $CH_3CH{=}CHCH_3$
(b) $CH_3CH{=}CH_2$ and $CH_3CH_2CH{=}CH_2$
(c) $CH_3CH_2CH{=}CH_2$ and $(CH_3)_2CHCH{=}CH_2$
(d) *cis* $CH_3CH{=}CHCH_3$, *trans* $CH_3CH{=}CHCH_3$

20. Consider the following graph,

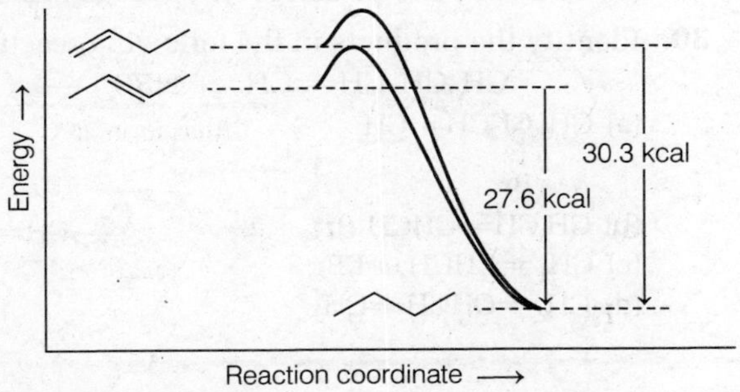

From this it is clear that
(a) *cis*-2-butene is more stable than 1-butene by 2.7 kcal
(b) *trans*-2-butene is more stable than 1-butene by 2.7 kcal
(c) *trans*-2-butene is more stable than *cis*-2-butene by 11 kJ
(d) *trans*-2-butene is more stable than 1-butene by 11 kJ

21. Addition of Br_2 to an alkene is stereoselective which means that in all cases
(a) *trans*-isomer is formed
(b) optically active isomer is formed if chiral centre is formed
(c) optically inactive racemic mixture or *meso* isomer is formed if chiral centre is formed
(d) intermediate bridged bromonium ion is formed

22. Select the correct alternate(s) in respect of relative formation of products.

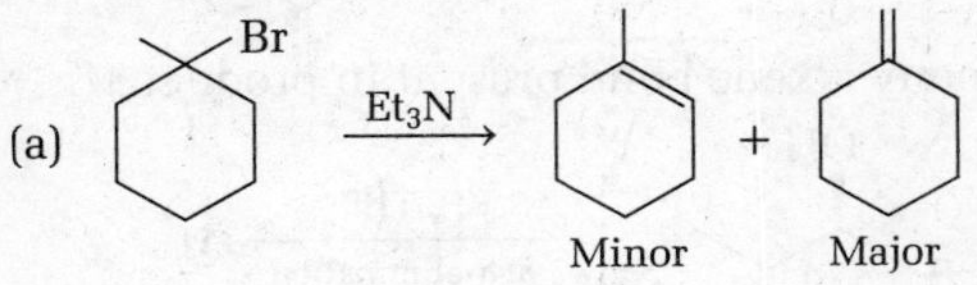

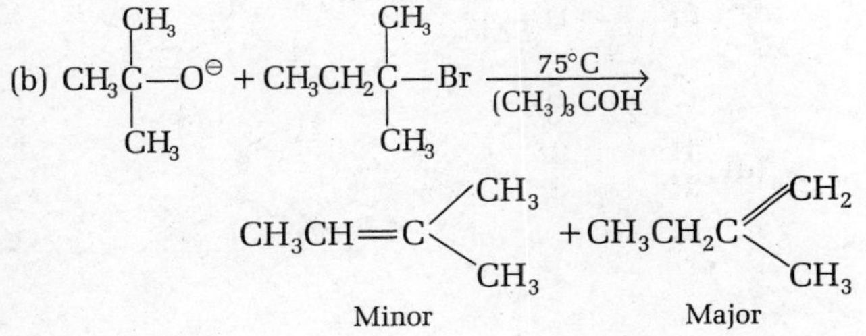

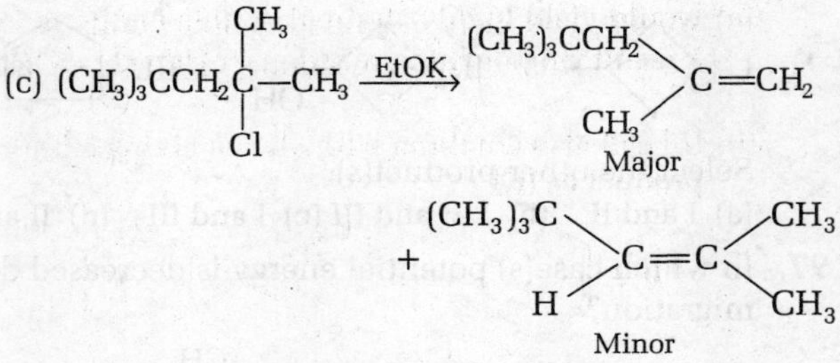

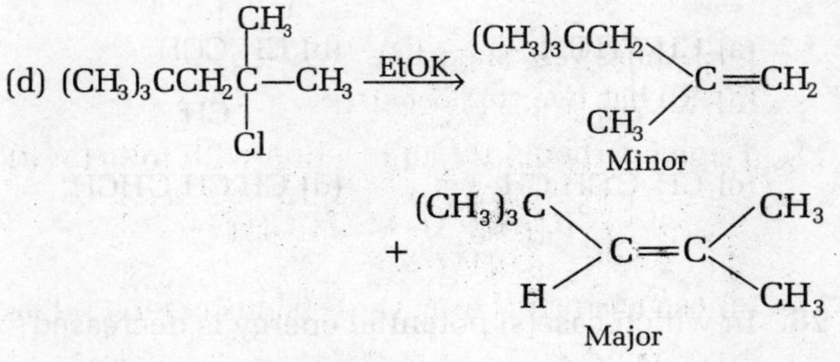

23. Reaction of reddish brown bromine with alkenes is used as a qualitative test to distinguished between alkenes and alkanes. The result is
(a) bromine water is decolourised by alkenes
(b) a trace of alkyne in alkene is not affected
(c) benzene also decolourises Br_2 water
(d) cyclopropane decolourises Br_2 water

24. Which of the following pairs can be distinguished by Br_2 water?
(a) Benzene and cyclohexene
(b) Cyclohexane and cyclohexene
(c) Cyclopropane and propene
(d) Benzene and propene

25. *B* and *C* are two possible products of dehydration of *A*

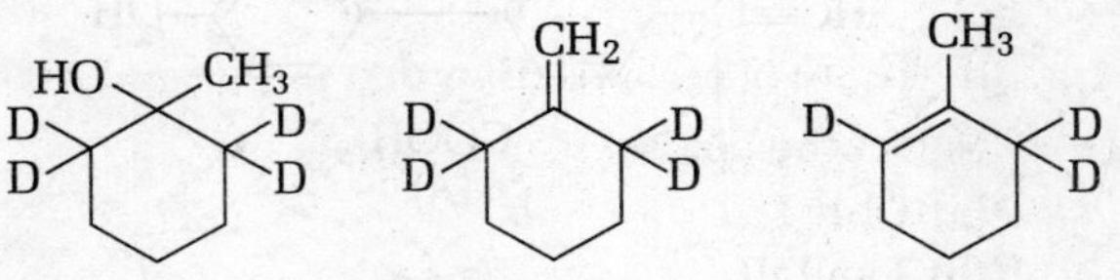

A *B* *C*

Select the correct statement(s).
(a) *B* is formed at faster rate since C—H bond is cleaved at a faster rate than C—D bond
(b) *B* is formed at a slower rate since C—H bond is cleaved at a slower rate than C—D bond
(c) *C* is formed at a faster rate since intermediate is 3° carbocation
(d) *B* is formed at a slower rate since intermediate is 1° carbocation

26. A graduate student wanted to make methylene cyclobutane, and he tried the following reaction

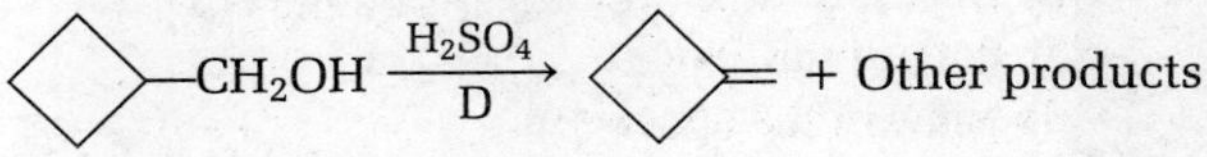

Other products can be

I. 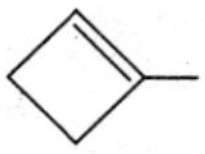 II. 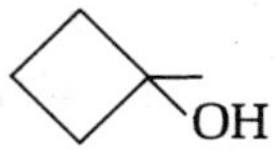 III. 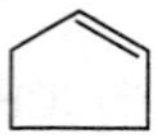

Select the other product(s).
(a) I and II (b) I, II and III (c) I and III (d) II and III

27. In which case(s) potential energy is decreased due to migration?

(a) $CH_3CH(CH_3)\dot{C}H_2$ (b) $CH_3C(CH_3)_2\dot{C}H_2$

(c) $CH_3\dot{C}(CH_3)CH_2CH_3$ (d) $CH_3CH_2\dot{C}HCH_3$

28. In which case(s) potential energy is decreased?

(a) $CH_3\overset{\oplus}{C}HCH{=}CH_2$ (b) 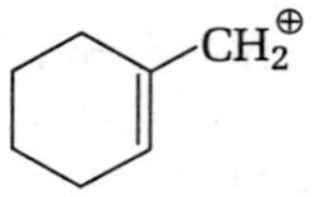

(c) 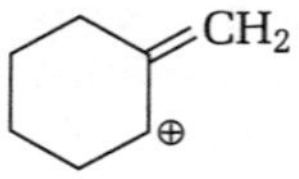 (d) 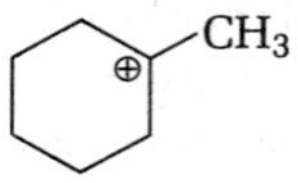

29. The correct statement(s) for the following addition reactions is (are) [JEE Advanced 2017]

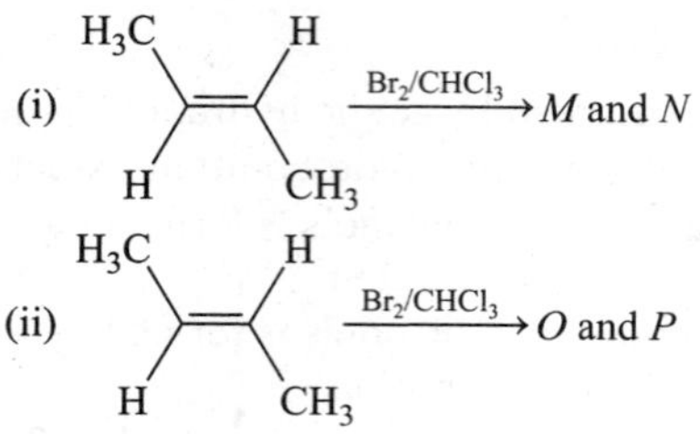

(a) (*M* and *O*) and (*N* and *P*) are two pairs of enantiomers
(b) Bromination proceeds through *trans*-addition in both the reactions
(c) *O* and *P* are identical molecules
(d) (*M* and *O*) and (*N* and *P*) two pairs of diastereomers

30. Identify the products in the following reaction

$$CH_3CH_2CH{=}CH_2 + NBS \longrightarrow$$

(a) $CH_3CH(Br)CH{=}CH_2$
(b) $CH_3CH{=}CHCH_2Br$
(c) $CH_2{=}CHCH_2CH_2Br$
(d) $CH_2{=}CHCH{=}CH_2$

Numerical Value Questions

All these questions have a Numerical value as their answer, solve the questions and write your answer.

1. How many moles of ethane can be liberates when one mole of compound *A* is treated with excess of CH_3MgI ....

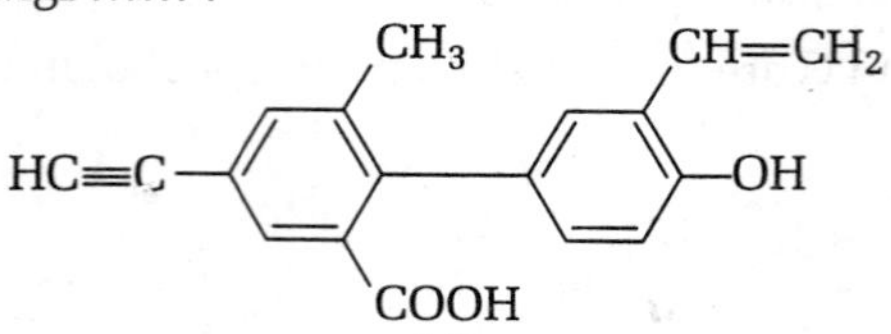

(*A*)

2. Among H_2O, C_2H_5OH, , , , how many compound will liberate methane on treatment with CH_3MgBr ?

3. How many products or alkene break after ozonolysis of 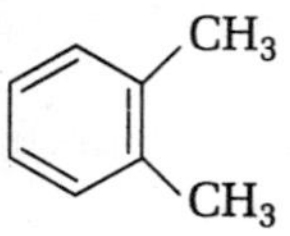 ?

4. How many possible product will be formed in wittig reaction of 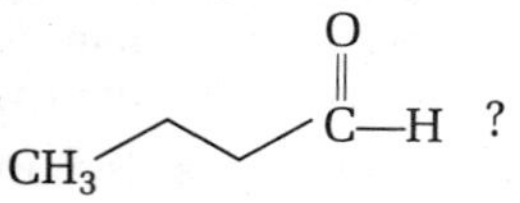 ?

5. How many double bond present in benzyne?

6. How many double bond present in the product when *n*-bromopropane react with alc. NaOH and HBr/acetic acid?

7. Count the number of electrons in the given ring?

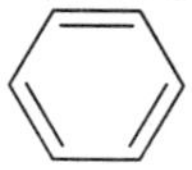

8. How many alkene bond present in product *M*?

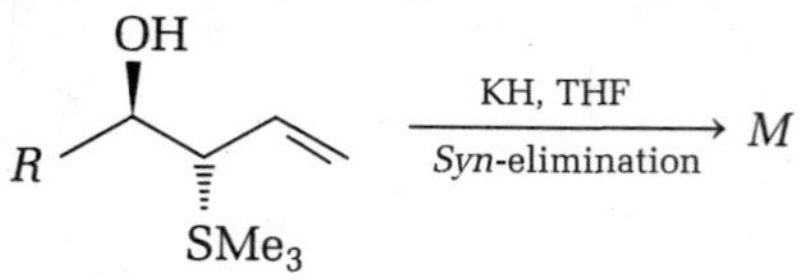

Comprehension Based Questions

In these questions, a passage has been given followed by questions based on it. You have to answer the questions based on the passage given.

***Passage* 1** Reduction of an alkyne to the double bond stage can yield a *cis*-alkene or a *trans*-alkene (except in cases where triple bond is at the end of the chain)

Read the above passage and answer the following questions.

1. Shown below is the final step in a synthesis of the important perfume constituent, *cis*-Jasmone. Which reagents would you choose to carryout this last step?

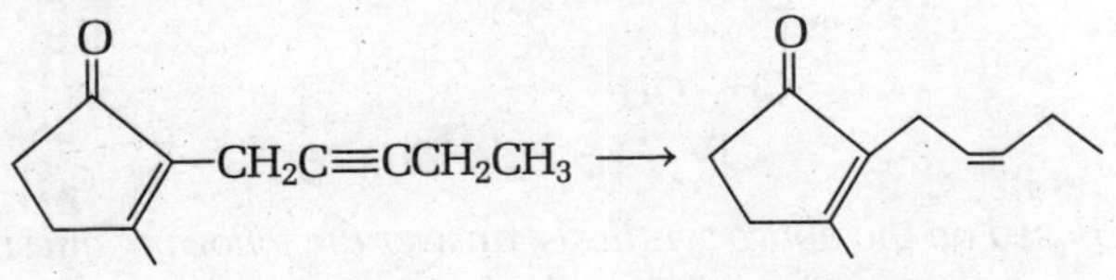

(*A*) *cis*-jasmone

(a) Li / NH_3 (b) Lindlar's catalyst
(c) Na/C_2H_5OH (d) Pt / H_2

2. 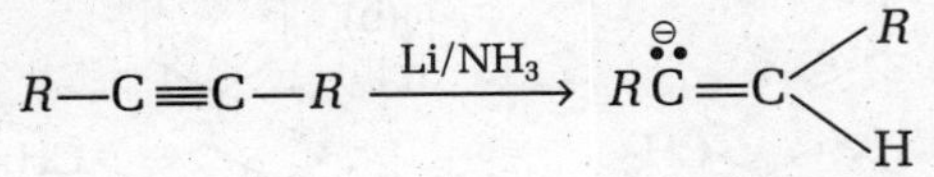

Vinylic anion (intermediate)

Select the correct statement(s).
(a) *trans* form of vinylic anion is more stable
(b) *cis*-form of vinylic anion is more stable
(c) Rate-determining step occurs prior to the step in which vinylic anion reacts
(d) Rate-determining step occurs after vinylic anion has reacted

3. Consider the following reactions,

$$CH_3C\equiv CCH_3 \xrightarrow{H_2/\text{Lindlar}} \xrightarrow{D_2/Pd} Y$$
$$CH_3C\equiv CCH_3 \xrightarrow[\text{dry ice}]{Li/NH_3} \xrightarrow{D_2/Pd} X$$

Select the correct alternate.
(a) *X* and *Y* both are *meso* forms
(b) *X* and *Y* both are racemic mixture
(c) *X* is *meso* form and *Y* is a racemic mixture
(d) *X* is racemic mixture and *Y* is a *meso* form

***Passage* 2** Following figure is given to test analytical ability. Based on it, answer the questions at the end of it.

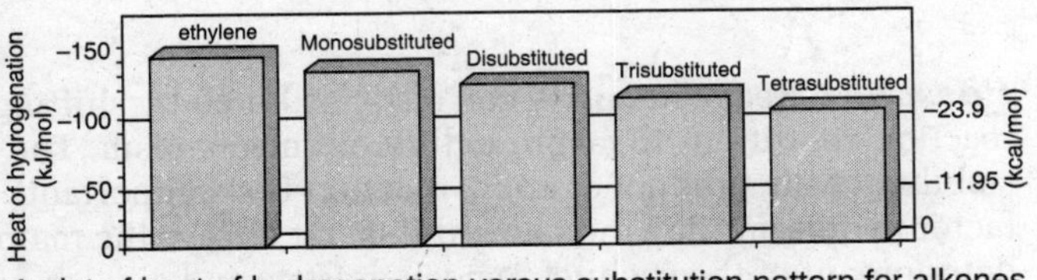

A plot of heat of hydrogenation *versus* substitution pattern for alkenes

1. Which undergoes catalytics hydrogenation much faster?

(a) 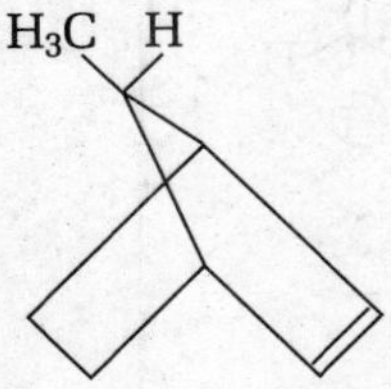

(b) 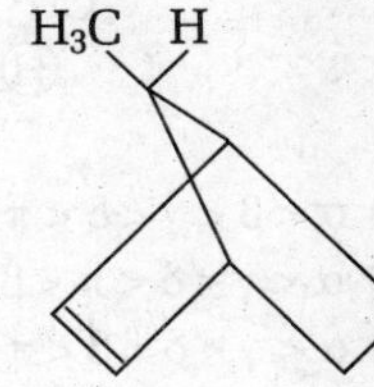

(c) Equally (d) Cannot be predicted

2. 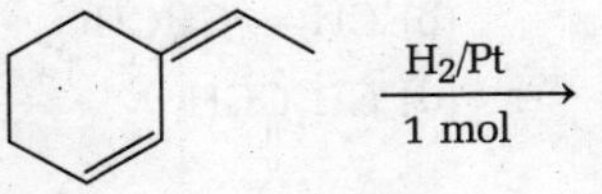

(a) 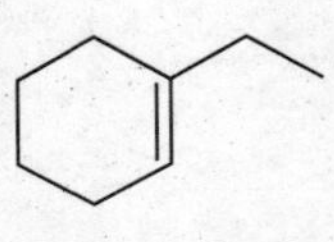 (b) 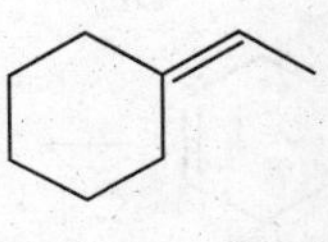

(c) 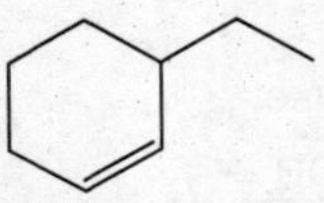 (d) 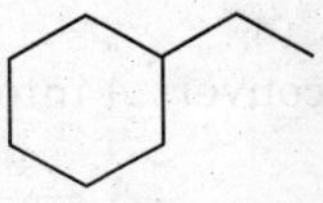

3. Following reaction is spontaneous (in forward direction) because

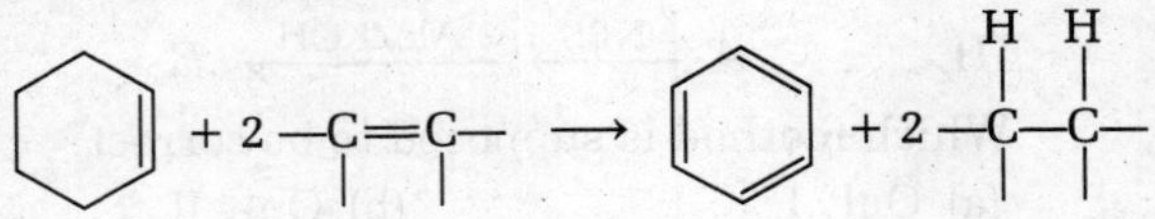

since
(a) it is a redox reaction
(b) it is a disproportionation reaction
(c) there is formation of benzene which is stabilised by resonance
(d) saturated open chain compound is formed

***Passage* 3** Following data have been given to determine relative reactivity of alkenes.

Bond dissociation energies of different type of C—H bonds

Hydrocarbon	Type of hydrogen	Bond energy ΔH, kcal mol^{-1}
$H_3C—H$	methyl	105
$H_2C=CH—H$	vinylic	108
$H_2C=CH\,CH_2—H$	allylic	86
$CH_3CH_2CH_2—H$	1°	98
$(CH_3)_2CH—H$	2°	96
$(CH_3)_3C—H$	3°	93

1. Increasing order of reactivity of different types of hydrogen in the following compound is

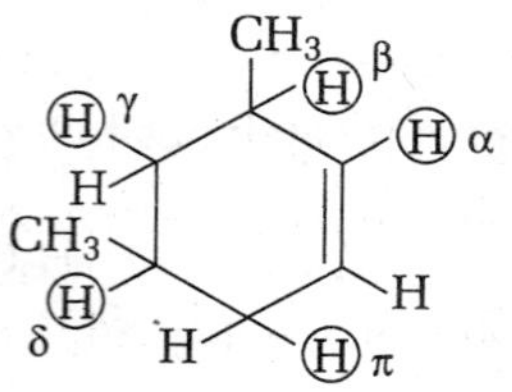

(a) $\alpha < \beta < \gamma < \delta < \pi$
(b) $\alpha < \gamma < \delta < \pi < \beta$
(c) $\alpha < \gamma < \delta < \beta < \pi$
(d) $\gamma < \alpha < \delta < \pi < \beta$

2. SeO_2 converts propene into

(a) $CH_2{=}CHCH_2OH$ (b) $CH_2{=}CHCHO$
(c) $CH_2{=}C(OH)CH_3$ (d) $CH_3C(=O)CH_3$

3. 

A B

To convert A into B, we can use

I. $A \xrightarrow{Br_2} \xrightarrow{\text{Alc. KOH}} B$

II. $A \xrightarrow{KOH} \xrightarrow{\text{Conc. } H_2SO_4} B$

III. $A \xrightarrow{NBS} \xrightarrow{\text{Alc. KOH}} B$

Which method is supposed to be correct?
(a) Only I (b) Only II
(c) Only III (d) None of these

***Passage* 4** 2-bromo-4-methylpentane can be converted into different products by E1, E2, S_N1 and S_N2 reactions

Reagent I. $NaOH/H_2O$ II. $NaOH/EtOH$ III. $KOH/(CH_3)_3COH$

1. 4-methyl-2-pentanol can be formed by use of
(a) I — S_N1 (b) II — S_N2
(c) III — S_N2 (d) I — S_N2

2. 4-methyl-1-pentene can be formed by use of
(a) I — E2 (b) II — E2
(c) III — E1 (d) III — E2

3. 4-methyl-2-pentene can be formed by use of
(a) I — E2 (b) II — E2
(c) III — E2 (d) II — E1

***Passage* 5** Alkenes are nucleophilic in nature due to π-electrons and can undergo electrophilic addition reaction. Alkenes can be converted to desired alcohol depending on the type of reagents.

Addition of water to (I) below gives different types of alcohols, and addition can be regioselective.

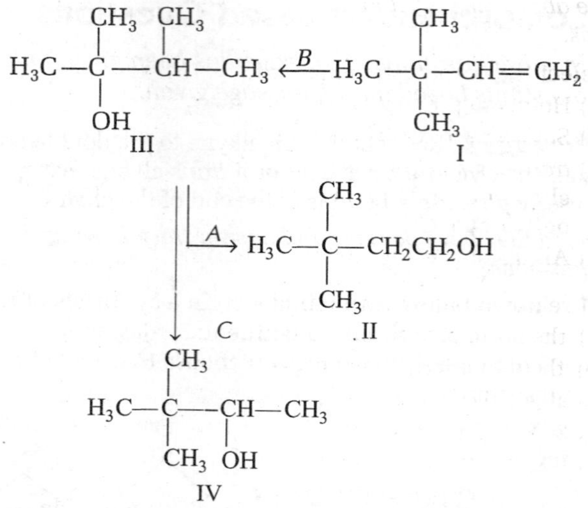

Based on the above synthesis, answer the following questions.

1. Product is identical by reagents X, Y and Z in Q. 1 if alkene is

(a) 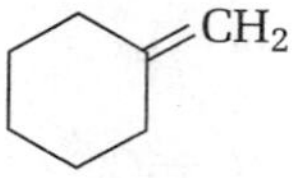 (b) 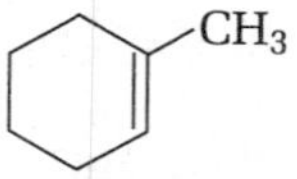

(c) 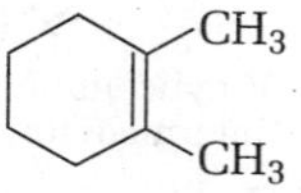 (d) 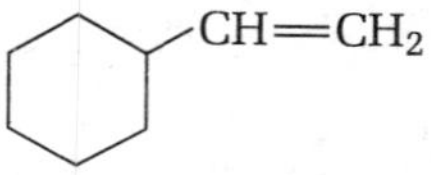

2. Consider the following alkene and select the correct alternate(s).

$CH_3CH(CH_3)CH{=}CH_2$

(a) a 3° alcohol is formed by acidic hydration
(b) a 1° alcohol is formed by hydroboration-oxidation
(c) a racemic mixture of 2° alcohol is formed by oxymercuration-demercuration
(d) a racemic mixture of 1° alcohols is formed by oxymercuration-demercuration

3. Which is hydrated to a maximum extent?
(a) *cis* $CH_3CH{=}CHCH_3$
(b) *trans* $CH_3CH{=}CHCH_3$
(c) *trans* 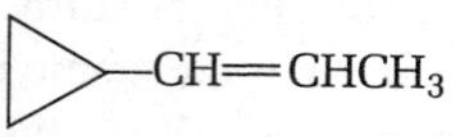
(d) 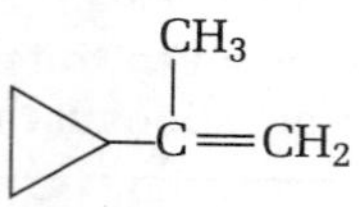

***Passage* 6** Regiochemistry can also be altered by shifting reaction conditions to favour a different mechanism. The stability of the product of an E2 reaction is an important factor in determining the rate but it is not always the main determinant of the product regiochemistry; and a less-stable product is sometimes formed more rapidly.

Read the above passage and answer the following questions.

1. Select the correct statement(s).
   (a) Hofmann product is favoured if base is large
   (b) Saytzeff product is favoured if base is small
   (c) *trans*-2-methylbromocyclohexane by E2 elimination gives 3-methyl cyclohexene as the only product
   (d) All the above are correct statements

2. E1 reaction takes place with
   (a) the formation of carbocation
   (b) the formation of pentavalent transition state
   (c) attack of nucleophile and migration of leaving group simultaneously
   (d) formation of carbanion

Passage 7 The elimination of *HX* from a vinyl halide produces an alkyne. Three pathways can be adopted for elimination at sp^2-hybridised atoms.

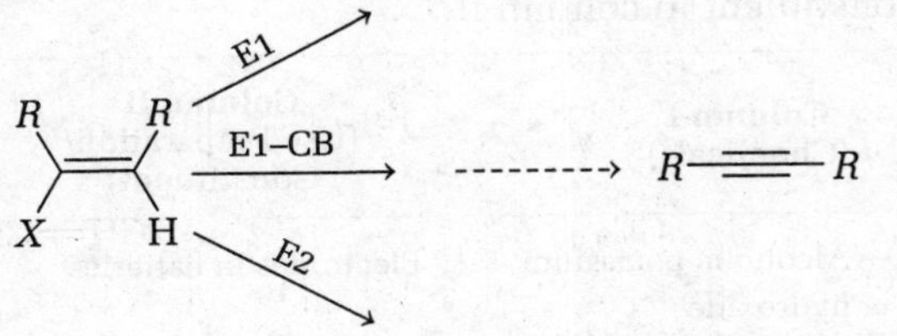

Based on the above three pathways, answer the following questions.

1. Intermediate divalent vinyl cation

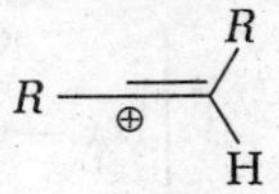

   (a) is *sp*-hybridised
   (b) is unstable because it has an access to only six valence electrons
   (c) undergoes E1 elimination more difficulty than in an alkyl halide
   (d) follows all the above statements

2. Formation of benzyne from bromobenzene takes place through
   (a) E1 mechanism with phenyl cation as the intermediate

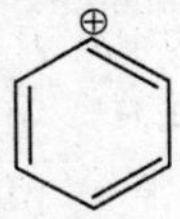

   (b) E1–CB mechanism with phenyl anion as the intermediate

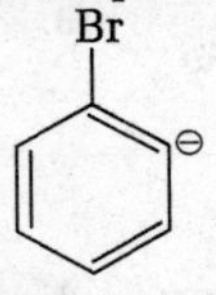

   (c) E2 mechanism with a concerted pathway
   (d) E2–CB mechanism with phenyl anion as the intermediate

Matrix-Match Type

Given below are Matching Type Questions, with two columns (each having some items) each . Each item of Column I has to be matched with the items of Column II.

1. Match the compounds in Column I with suitable properties/reagent, in Column II for distinction.

Column I	Column II
A. *cis*-but-2-ene, *trans*-but-2-ene	1. Alkaline $KMnO_4$
B. *n*-butane, propane	2. Dipole moment
C. Ethene, ethane	3. Melting point
D. But-1-ene, but-2-ene	4. Ozonolysis

2. Match the compounds in Column I with their heat of hydrogenation in Column II.

Column I	Column II
A. $CH_2=CH_2$	1. -27.6 kcal mol^{-1}
B. $CH_3CH=CH_2$	2. -28.6 kcal mol^{-1}
C. $CH_3CH=CHCH_3$ *cis*	3. -30.1 kcal mol^{-1}
D. $CH_3CH=CHCH_3$ *trans*	4. -32.8 kcal mol^{-1}

3. Match the contents in Column I with degree of unsaturation in Column II.

Column I	Column II
A. Cyclobutane	1. 4
B. Cyclohexene	2. 3
C. Benzene	3. 2
D. 1,4-cyclobutadiene	4. 1

4. Match the compounds in Column I with their ozonolysis product by $O_3/H_2O/Zn$ in Column II.

Column I	Column II
A. But-1-ene	1. $OHCCH_2—CH_2CHO$
B. But-2-ene	2. CH_3CHO
C. 2-methylprop-1-ene	3. CH_3CH_2CHO, HCHO
D. Cyclobutene	4. CH_3COCH_3, HCHO

5. Match the following.

Column I (Method/Reagent)	Column II 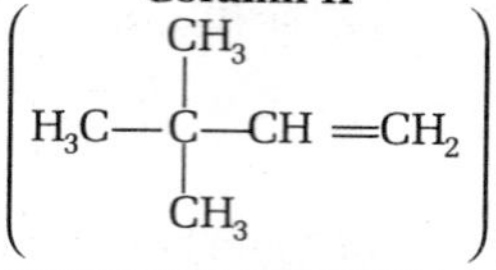
A. Hydrocarboration/ $BH_3 \cdot THF / H_2O_2 \cdot OH^-$	1. 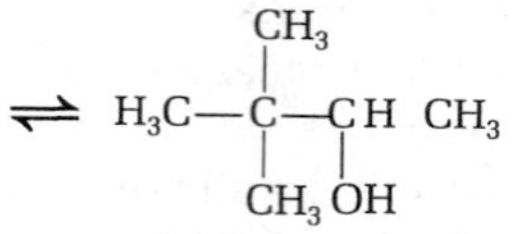 (Major or minor)
B. Oxymercuration-demercuration $(CH_3COO)_2 Hg / H_2O, H^+$	2. 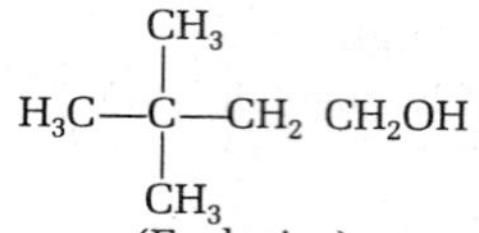 (Exclusive)
C. Hydration/H_3O^+	3. 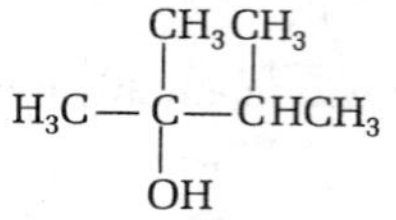 (Major)
D. Dehydration/conc. H_2SO_4	4. 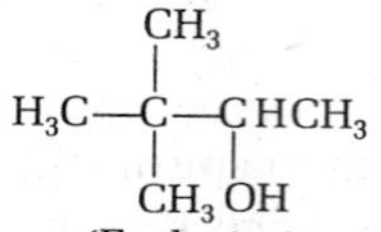 (Exclusive)

6. Match the following.

Column I (Reagent)	Column II (Product)
A. MnO_4^-/OH^-	1. 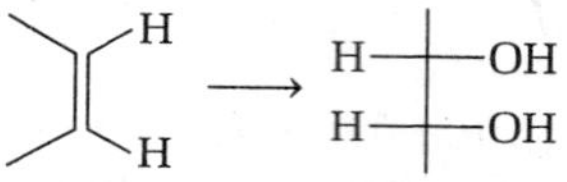
B. HCOOH, H_2O_2	2. 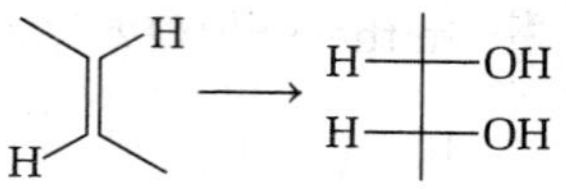
C. $OsO_4/H_2O/Na_2SO_3$	3. 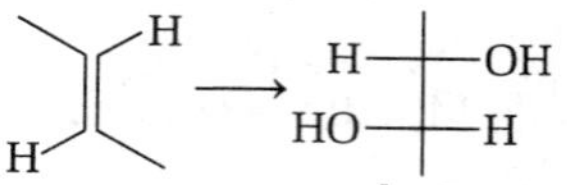 and enantiomer
D. *m*-CPBA	4. 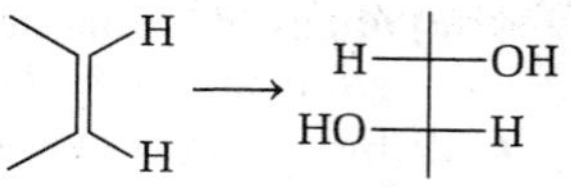 and enantiomer

7. Match the chemicals in column I with the same of its constituent in column II.

Column I (Chemicals)	Column II (Use/Preparation/ Constituent)
A. Alcoholic potassium hydroxide	1. Electrodes in batteries
B. $Pd/BaSO_4$	2. Obtained by addition reaction
C. BHC (Benzene hexachloride)	3. Used for β-elimination reaction
D. Polyacetylene	4. Lindlar's catalyst

Single Integer Answer Questions

Answer of these questions is a single digit lying between 0 to 9.

1. Ozonolysis of the following will form number of product(s).

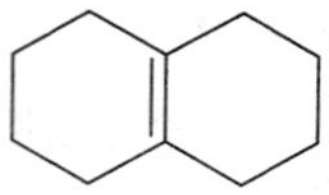

2. Oxidation number of Hg obtained after mercuration-demercuration of an alkene is …… .

3. Total number of double bonds formed in the following addition reaction is ……

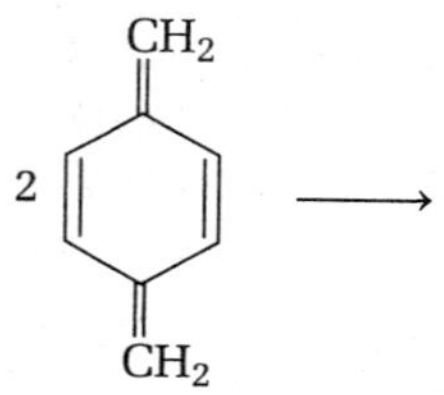

4. Cyclohexene can reduce olefinic bond to alkane and itself oxidised to a new compounds. How many π-electrons are there in new compound?

5. In the following structure how many isomers are there in *E*-forms?

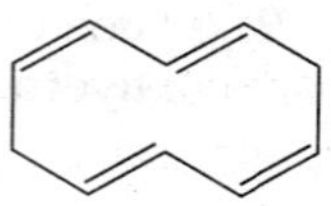

6. In the following sequence of reactions

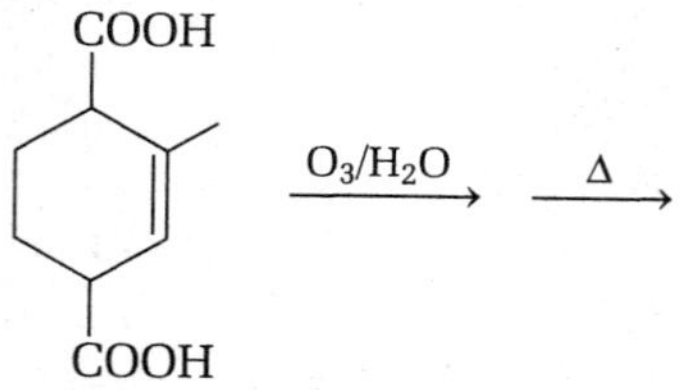

How many —COOH groups are present in the product formed?

7. In the hydroboronation-oxidation, 1-butene converted to 1-butanol. How many moles of BH_3 are used per mole of butene?

8. In the following reaction (C $=$C) bond in the product is at (x, y) position. What is the value of $(x + y)$?

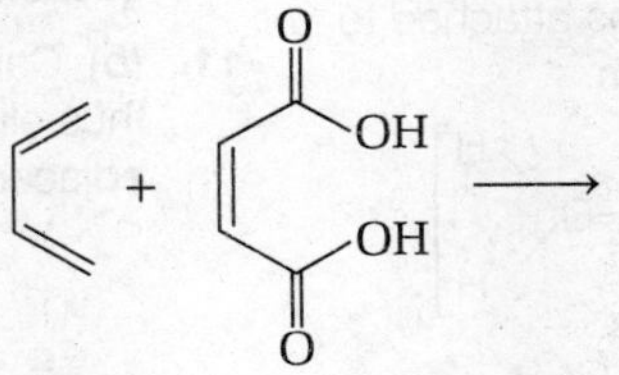

Answers

Objective Questions Type I [Only one correct option]

1. (b)	2. (b)	3. (b)	4. (c)	5. (d)	6. (a)	7. (b)	8. (d)	9. (c)	10. (c)
11. (b)	12. (a)	13. (a)	14. (c)	15. (c)	16. (c)	17. (a)	18. (b)	19. (a)	20. (d)
21. (a)	22. (a)	23. (b)	24. (c)	25. (c)	26. (c)	27. (d)	28. (a)	29. (d)	30. (b)
31. (a)	32. (c)	33. (d)	34. (b)	35. (d)	36. (a)	37. (c)	38. (b)	39. (d)	40. (b)
41. (c)	42. (c)	43. (b)	44. (c)	45. (a)	46. (a)	47. (b)	48. (b)	49. (a)	50. (c)
51. (a)	52. (d)	53. (c)	54. (b)	55. (d)	56. (b)	57. (c)	58. (a)	59. (d)	60. (c)
61. (c)	62. (a)	63. (a)	64. (d)	65. (b)	66. (d)	67. (a)	68. (c)	69. (b)	70. (c)
71. (a)	72. (b)	73. (c)	74. (d)	75. (c)	76. (a)	77. (c)	78. (b)	79. (d)	80. (d)
81. (c)	82. (a)	83. (a)	84. (c)	85. (d)	86. (a)	87. (c)	88. (d)	89. (a)	90. (c)
91. (a)	92. (b)	93. (b)	94. (b)	95. (b)	96. (a)	97. (b)	98. (c)	99. (a)	100. (a)
101. (d)	102. (c)	103. (b)	104. (c)	105. (b)	106. (b)	107. (b)	108. (a)	109. (b)	110. (d)
111. (b)	112. (d)	113. (a)	114. (d)	115. (a)	116. (b)	117. (a)	118. (c)	119. (a)	120. (c)
121. (d)	122. (a)	123. (d)	124. (b)	125. (a)	126. (b)	127. (c)	128. (b)	129. (b)	130. (a)
131. (a)	132. (a)	133. (b)	134. (b)	135. (b)	136. (b)	137. (b)	138. (d)	139. (a)	140. (b)
141. (d)	142. (a)	143. (b)	144. (b)	145. (d)	146. (b)	147. (b)	148. (d)	149. (b)	150. (d)
151. (c)	152. (c)	153. (c)	154. (d)	155. (c)	156. (c)	157. (a)	158. (b)	159. (a)	160. (d)
161. (d)	162. (b)	163. (c)	164. (b)	165. (b)	166. (a)	167. (d)	168. (a)	169. (b)	170. (a)
171. (c)	172. (a)	173. (a)	174. (a)	175. (d)	176. (c)	177. (c)	178. (a)	179. (c)	180. (c)
181. (a)	182. (a)								

Objective Questions Type II [One or more than one correct option(s)]

1. (b)	2. (a)	3. (a)	4. (a)	5. (a, b, c)
6. (b)	7. (c)	8. (b, d)	9. (a)	10. (a, b, c, d)
11. (a, b, c, d)	12. (d)	13. (c)	14. (a)	15. (b)
16. (a, b, c, d)	17. (b, c)	18. (a, b, c)	19. (b, c)	20. (b, d)
21. (c, d)	22. (a, b, c)	23. (a, d)	24. (a, b, d)	25. (a)
26. (b)	27. (a, b)	28. (a, b, c)	29. (a, b)	30. (a, b)

Numerical Value Questions

1. (3) 2. (4) 3. (3) 4. (2) 5. (2) 6. (1) 7. (5) 8. (2)

Comprehension Based Questions

Passage 1 – 1. (b) 2. (a,c) 3. (d) Passage 2 – 1. (a) 2. (a) 3. (c) Passage 3 – 1. (b) 2. (b) 3. (c)

Passage 4 – 1. (d) 2. (b, d) 3. (b) Passage 5 – 1. (c) 2. (a, b, c) 3. (d) Passage 6 – 1. (d) 2. (a)

Passage 7 – 1. (d) 2. (b)

Matrix-Match Type

1. (A)→(2); (B)→(3); (C)→(1); (D)→(4)
2. (A)→(4); (B)→(3); (C)→(2); (D)→(1)
3. (A)→(4); (B)→(3); (C)→(1); (D)→(2)
4. (A)→(3); (B)→(2); (C)→(4); (D)→(1)
5. (A)→(2); (B)→(4); (C)→(1,3); (D)→(1,2,3,4)
6. (A)→(1,3); (B)→(2,4); (C)→(1,3); (D)→(2,4)
7. (A)→(3); (B)→(4); (C)→(2); (D)→(1)

Signle Integer Answer Questions

1. (1) 2. (0) 3. (6) 4. (3) 5. (2) 6. (1) 7. (3) 8. (9)

Solutions

Objective Questions Type I [Only one correct option]

1. (*b*) Stereocentre (carbon) has different groups attached to it and which can show geometrical isomerism.

(a) $CH_3CH_2CH_2CH{=}CH_2$ (1-pentene)

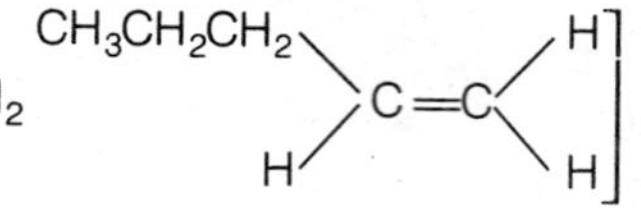

Identical

(b) $CH_3CH{=}CHCH_2CH_3$ (2-pentene)

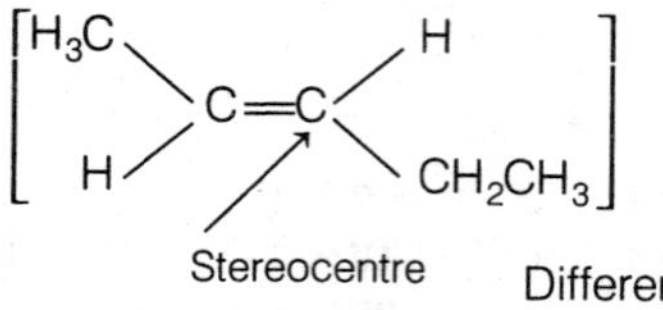

Different

2. (*b*)

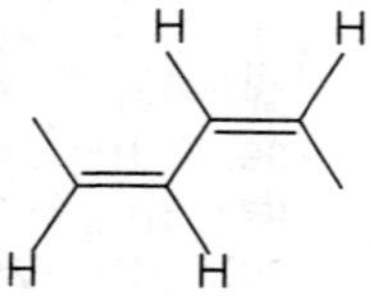

both are *Z*.

3. (*b*)

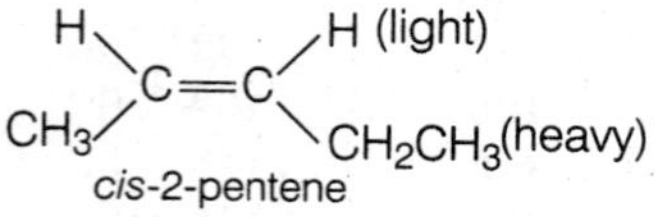

Light groups are on same side.
Heavy groups are also on same side.

4. (*c*) (a)

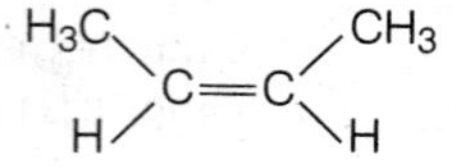

cis-and-*trans* (Yes)

(b)

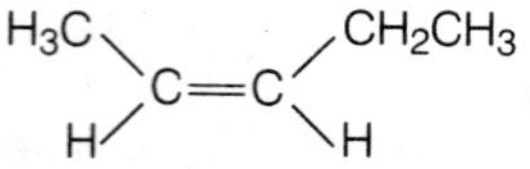

cis-and-*trans* (Yes)

(c)

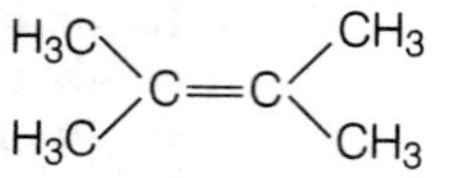

cis-and-*trans* (No)

5. (*d*) (a) 2-methyl-eth-1-enyl (1-methyl ethyl)
(b) Prop-2-enyl (c) Prop-1-ene (d) Prop-1-enyl

6. (*a*) (a) $CH_3CH_2CH_2CH_2Cl \xrightarrow{\text{Alc. KOH}} CH_3CH_2CH{=}CH_2$ (But-1-ene)

(b) $CH_3CH_2\underset{Cl}{CH}CH_3 \longrightarrow CH_3CH{=}CHCH_2$ (But-2-ene) + But 1-ene

7. (*b*) $CH_3CH_2\underset{Cl}{CH}CH_3 \xrightarrow[\Delta]{\text{Alc. KOH}} CH_3-CH{=}CH-CH_3$ (But-2-ene)

9. (*c*) Greater the conjugation, greater the stability.

10. (*c*) Et_3N is a bulky base and poor nucleophile and gives least substituted product (Hofmann elimination).

11. (*b*) Carbonyl group increases acidic nature of adjacent H, thus elimination is preferred. (H and OH are eliminated from adjacent carbon).

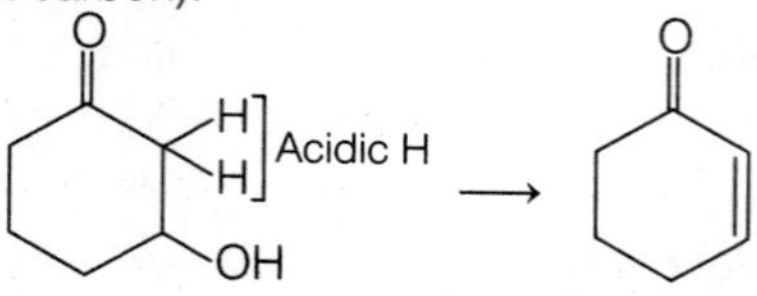

12. (*a*)

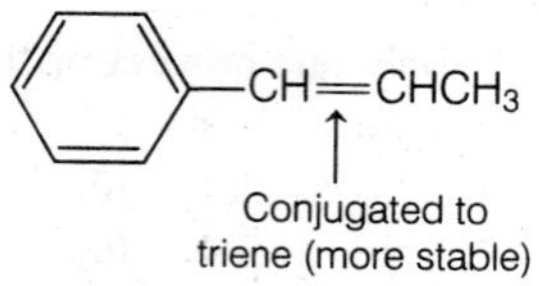

14. (*c*)

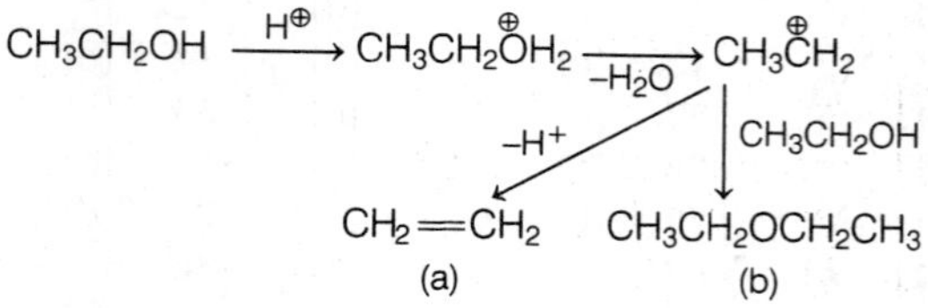

15. (*c*)

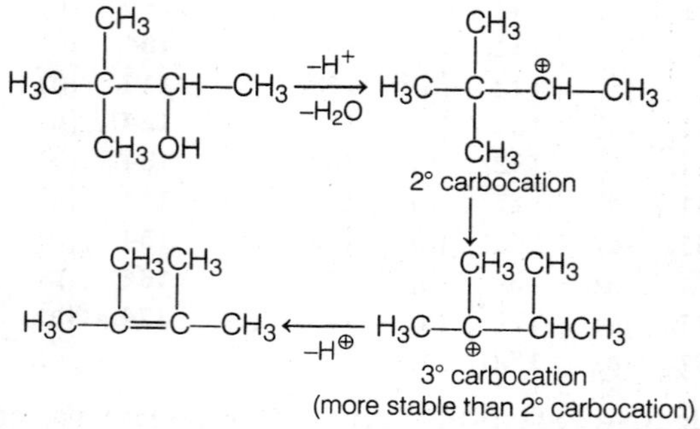

16. (*c*)

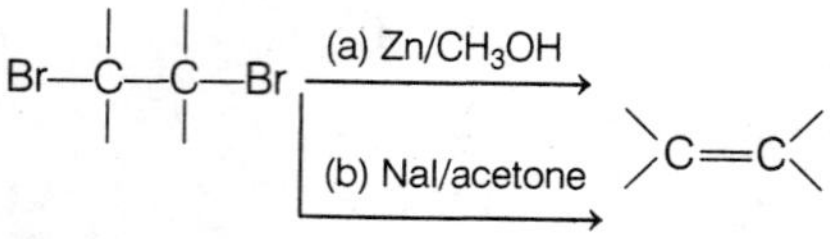

Both (a) and (b)

17. (*a*) $Zn \longrightarrow Zn^{2+} + 2e^-$

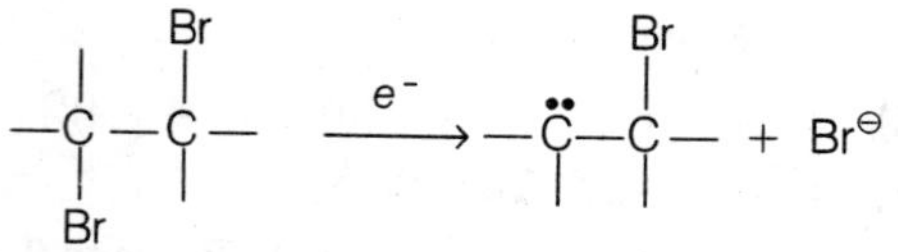

18. (*b*) Addition to the alkene and elimination of two bromine atoms from the dibromide are predominantly *trans*.

$$cis + Br_2 \rightleftharpoons d \text{ and } l$$
$$trans + Br_2 \rightleftharpoons meso$$

19. (*a*) As in question 18.

22. (*a*)

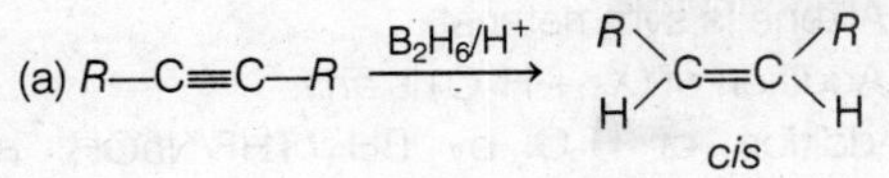

24. (*c*)

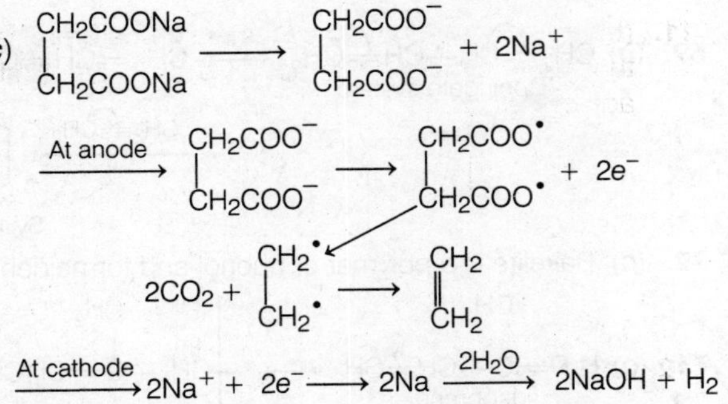

25. (*d*)

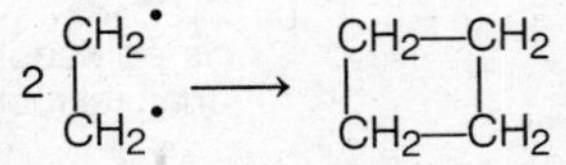

28. (*a*) H at is 3° allylic position and has (C—H) bond energy and is abstracted most easily and most stable carbocation is formed.

29. (*d*)

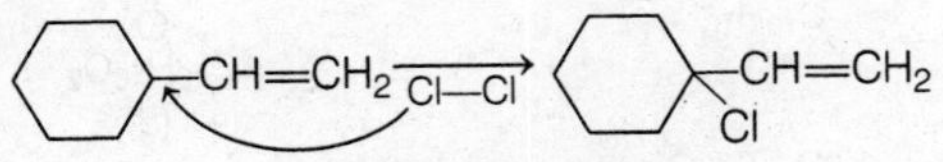

Free-radical mechanism

30. (*b*) SeO_2 oxidises —CH_3 to —CHO at allylic position.

31. (*a*) Addition of electrophile to alkene is the slow step.

36. (*a*) Addition of Br_2 is selectively *anti*.
Thus, product formed is a mixture of *d*-and-*l* and thus racemic.

37. (*c*) Refer mechanism.

38. (*b*) *cis*-2-butene + Br_2 $\longrightarrow$ *d*-and *l*- by *anti*-addition
trans-2-butene + Br_2 $\longrightarrow$ *meso* by *anti*-addition

39. (*d*) Ethane + Br_2 $\longrightarrow$ no reaction
Ethene + Br_2 $\longrightarrow$ Br_2 water is decolourised.

40. (*b*)

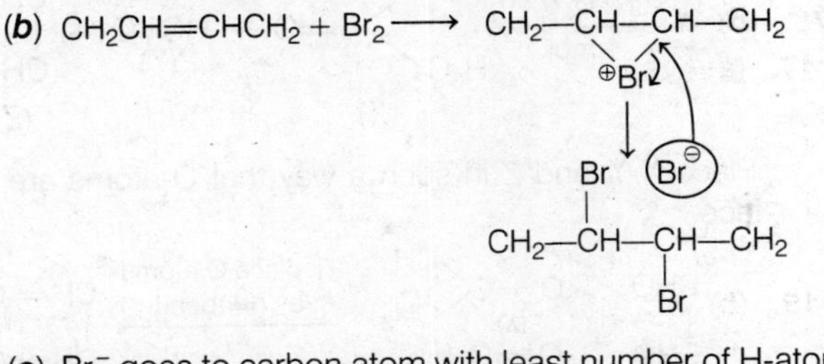

41. (*c*) Br^- goes to carbon atom with least number of H-atoms. (Markownikoff's rule).
2-bromopropane is formed predominantly.

43. (*b*)

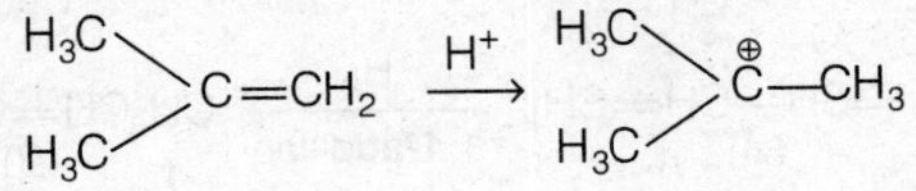

44. (*c*)

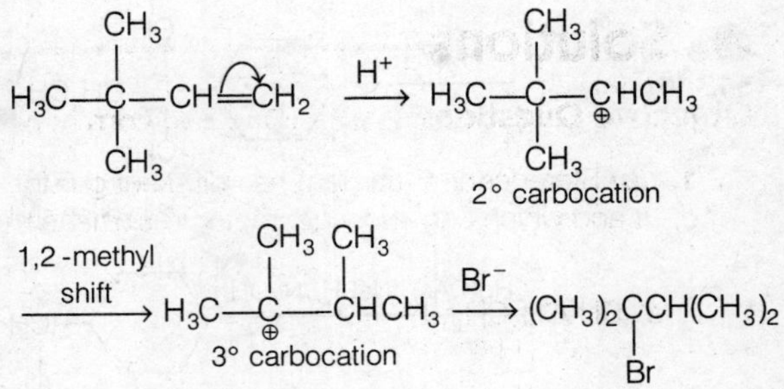

45. (*a*) $CH_2{=}CH{-}CH{=}CH_2 \longrightarrow \overset{-}{C}H_2{-}CH{=}CH{-}\overset{+}{C}H_2 \xrightarrow{H^+Br^-} CH_3{-}CH{=}CH{-}CH_2Br$
By 1,4-addition
(1-bromo-2-butene)

46. (*a*) I and II are decolourised by ethene.

47. (*b*) Addition of two—OH by $KMnO_4$ is *syn* then (b) is incorrect.

48. (*b*)

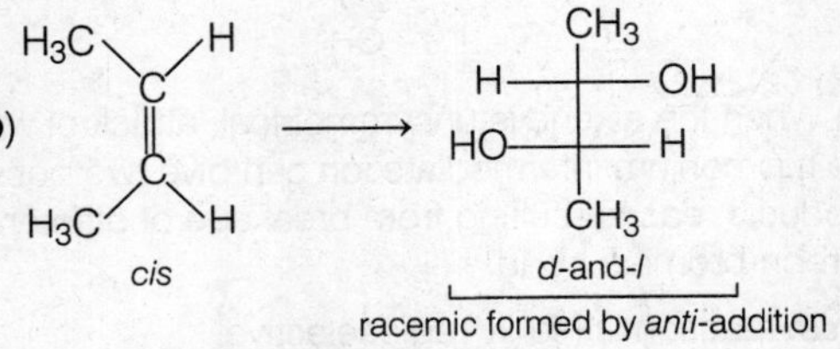

Addition of two (—OH) by

I. OsO_4/H_2O_2 in ether is *syn*.

II. HCO_3H is *anti*.

III. $KMnO_4/OH^-$ is *syn*.

49. (*a*) More substituted (C=C) is more nucleophilic.

50. (*c*) Addition of OsO_4/H_2O_2 is *syn* thus *meso*-isomer is formed. Thus (c) is incorrect.

51. (*a*) First step is also known as slow step or rate determine step.

52. (*d*) Alkene is symmetrical and product formed is same whether electrophile goes to which carbon.

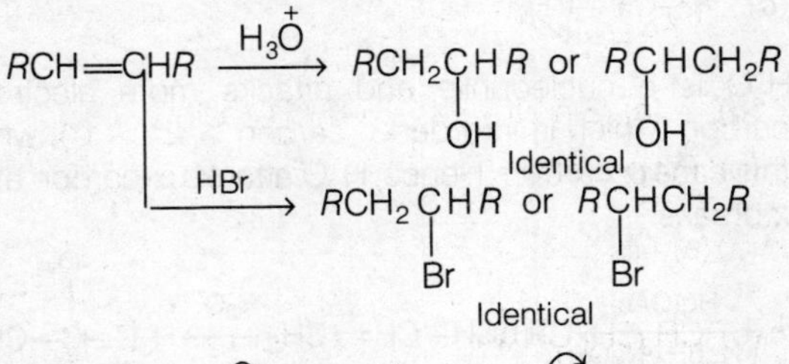

53. (*c*)

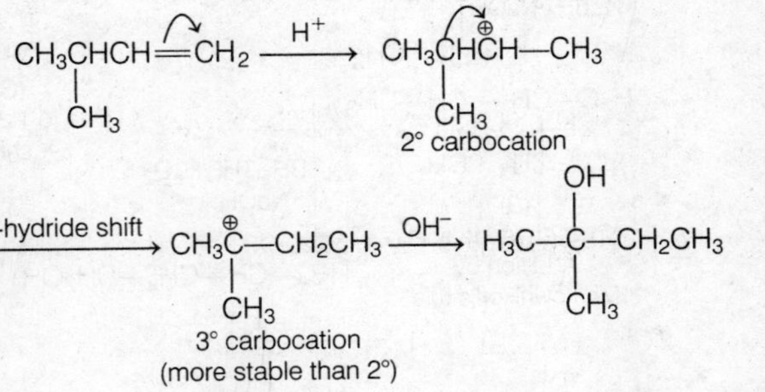

54. (*b*)

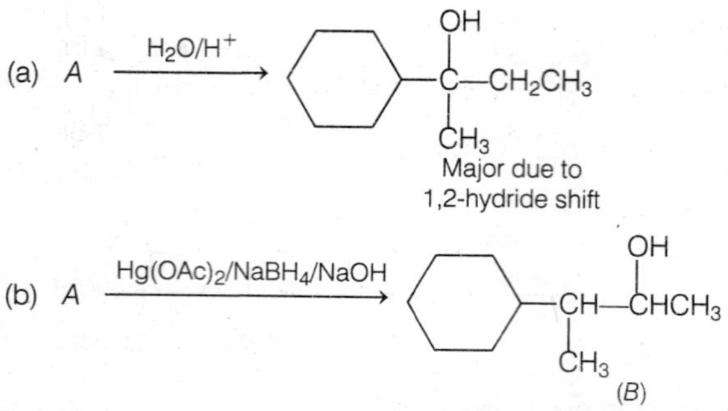

55. (*d*) There is no 1,2-hydride or 1,2-methyl shift.

56. (*b*) $H_2O + X_2 \longrightarrow HOX + HX$

$HOX \longrightarrow OH^{\ominus} + X^{\oplus}$

57. (*c*)

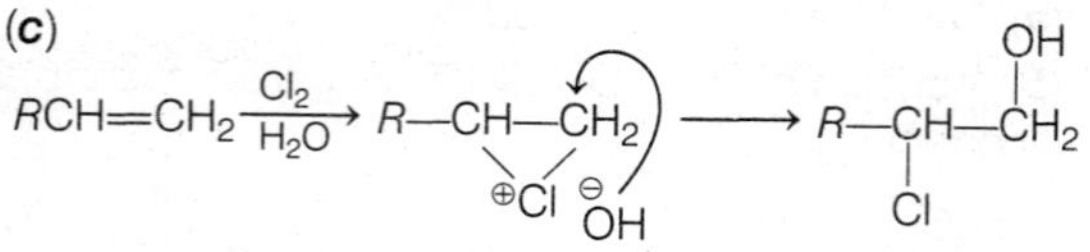

58. (*a*) When the alkene is unsymmetrical, attack of water on the bromonium intermediate ion can give two possible products, each resulting from breakage of different carbon-bromine bond.

Thus, reaction is highly regioselective.

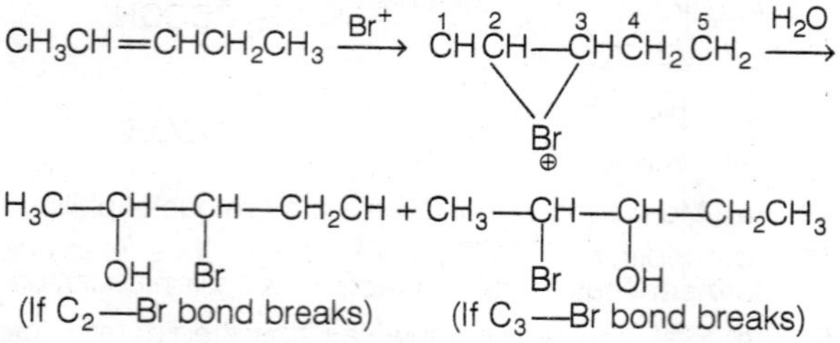

59. (*d*) Addition of $(H_2O + Cl_2)$ is *anti*.

60. (*c*)

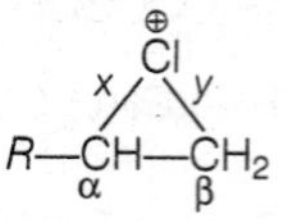

H_2O is a nucleophile and attacks more electropositive carbon (which is in order 3° carbon > 2° > 1°), which is in this case α-carbon. Hence, H_2O attacks α-carbon and bond *x* breaks.

61. (*c*)

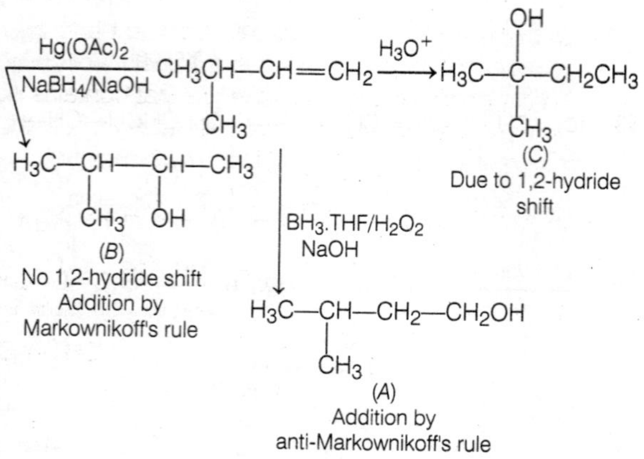

63. (*a*) Alkene is symmetrical.

64. (*d*) Addition of $(X_2 + H_2O)$ is *anti*.

65. (*b*) Addition of H_2O by BH_3/THF/NaOH, H_2O_2 is by anti-Markownikoff's rule.

69. (*b*)

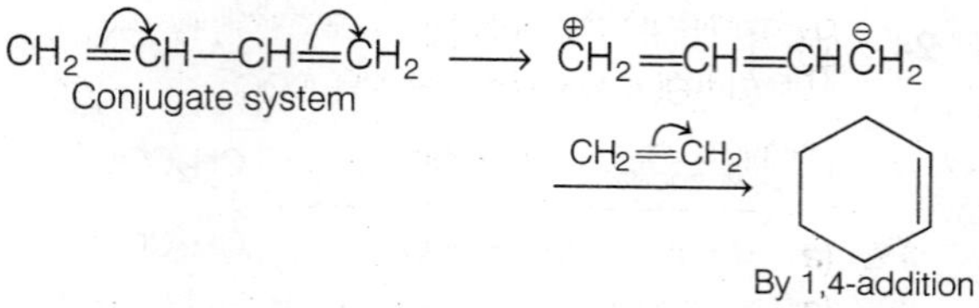

72. (*b*) Bakelite is a polymer of phenol and formaldehyde.

75. (*c*)

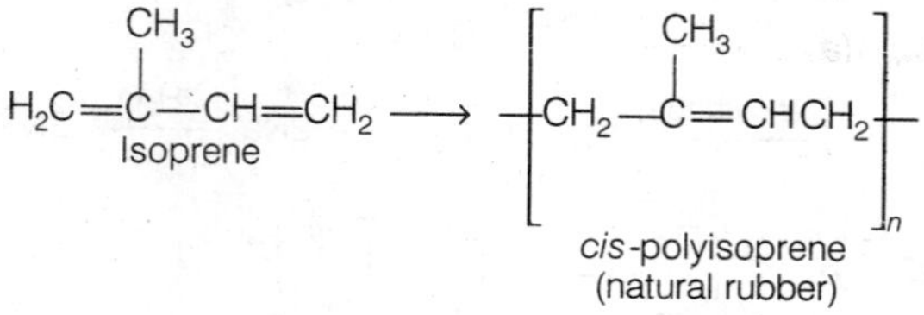

76. (*a*)

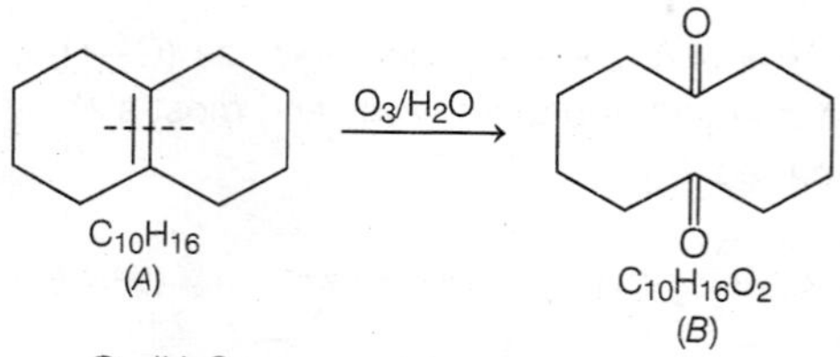

77. (*c*) (a) $\xrightarrow{O_3/H_2O}$ no ozonolysis

(b)

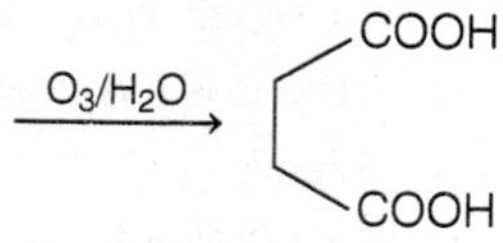

(c) $\xrightarrow{O_3/H_2O} 2CH_3COOH$

(d) $\xrightarrow{O_3/H_2O} CO_2 + CH_3CH_2COOH$

Note If ozonolysis is without Zn, H_2O_2 formed causes oxidation of —CHO to —COOH. HCOOH is further oxidised to CO_2.

78. (*b*)

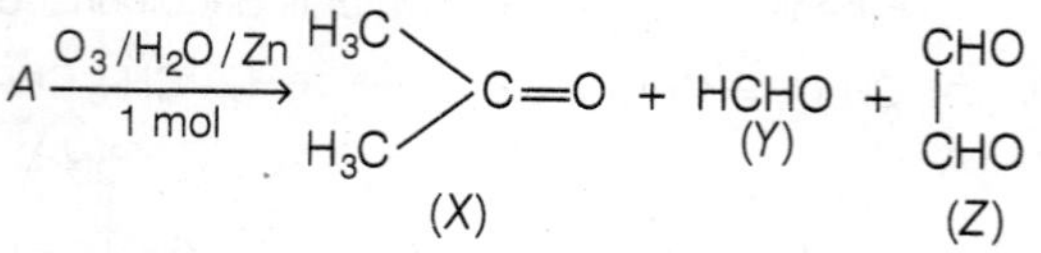

Place *X*, *Y*, and *Z* in such a way that O-atoms are face to face.

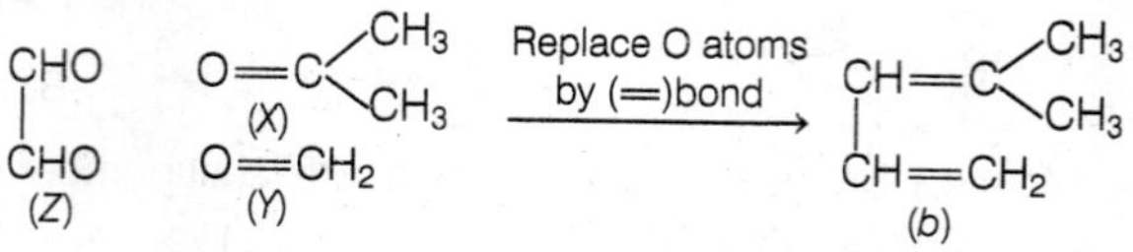

79. (*d*) $A(C_4H_6) \xrightarrow[1\ mol]{H_2/Ni} B(C_4H_8) \xrightarrow{O_2/H_2O/Zn} CH_3CHO$

$\underset{(A)}{CH_2{=}CH{-}CH{=}CH_2} \xrightarrow[1,4\text{-addition}]{H_2} \underset{(B)}{CH_3CH{=}CHCH_3}$

$\xrightarrow{O_3/H_2O/Zn} CH_3CHO$

81. (*c*) But-2-ene on reaction with alkaline $KMnO_4$ at elevated temperature followed by acidification will give acetic acid (CH_3COOH).

Hot alkaline solution of potassium permanganate followed by acidification oxidatively cleaved alkenes.

The reaction proceed as follows :

$$\underset{\text{But-2-ene}}{CH_3—CH{=}CH—CH_3} \xrightarrow[H_3O^+]{\text{Alk. } KMnO_4,\text{ heat}} \underset{\text{Acetic acid}}{2CH_3COOH}$$

82. (*a*) Substituted alkenes are more stable.

83. (*a*) *trans*-isomer has least heat of hydrogenation.

86. (*a*)

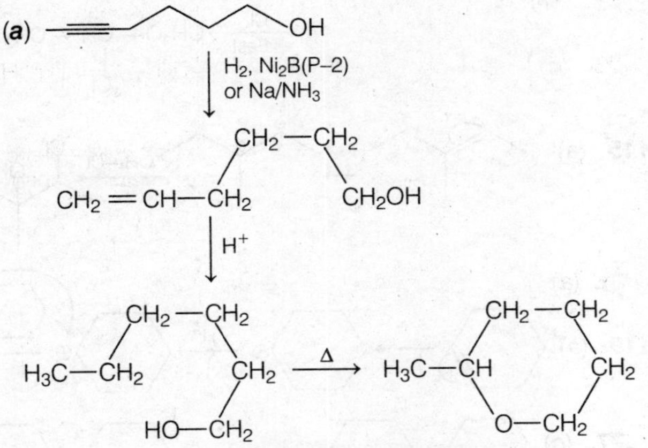

88. (*d*)

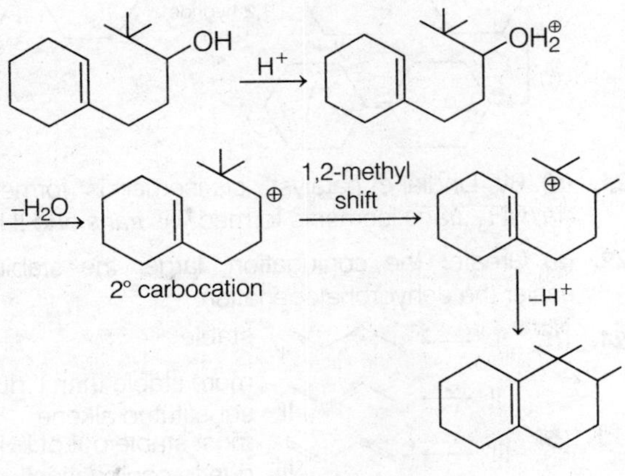

92. (*b*)

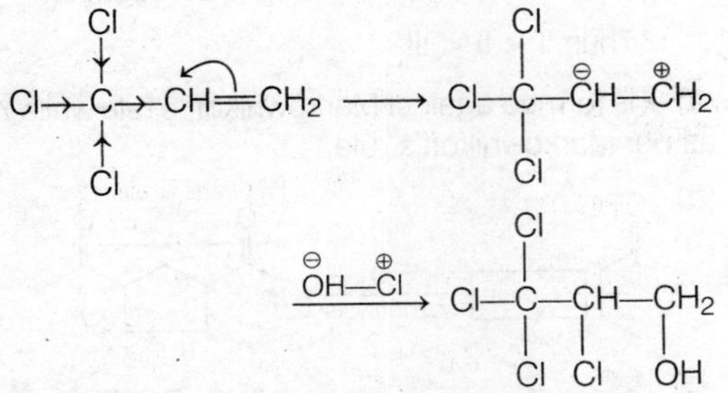

CCl_3^- is an electron-withdrawing group causing π-electron shift from C_1 to C_2 and addition is opposite to Markownikoff's rule.

93. (*b*) $NaBD_4$ is a source of D^- (isotopic hydride).

94. (*b*)

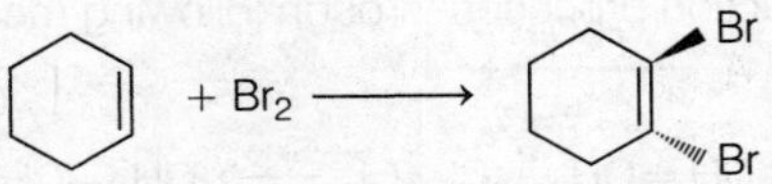

(*Anti* addition)

96. (*a*)

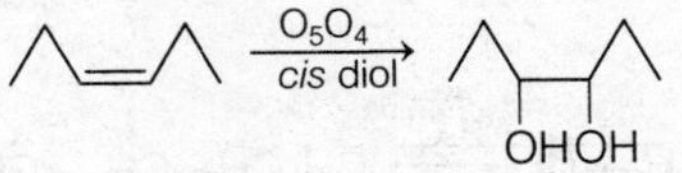

(*Meso* compound)

99. (*a*) C=C bond cleaves.

100. (*a*) Alkene is $CH_3CH{=}CHCH_3$. Isomeric alkene can be

Which on ozonolysis would give CH_3COCH_3 (propanone) and HCHO (methanal).

102. (*c*) (a)

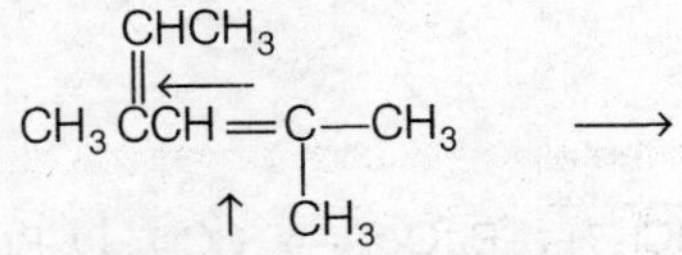

⟶ Indicates where bonds are cleaved

$$CH_3\overset{O}{\overset{\|}{C}}CHO \xrightarrow{\text{Oxidation}} CH_3\overset{O}{\overset{\|}{C}}COOH$$

$$+$$

$$CH_3CHO \xrightarrow{\text{Oxidation}} CH_3COOH$$

$$+$$

$$(CH_3)_2CO$$

(H_2O_2) is one of the products under given conditions, which causes oxidation of —CHO to —COOH.

(b)

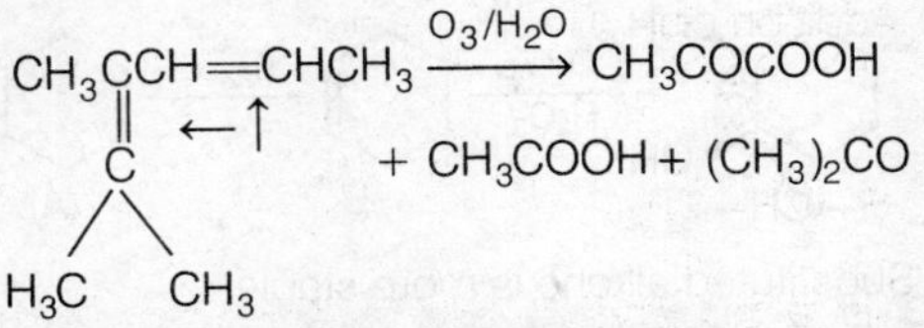

103. (*b*) The major product of the given addition reaction is

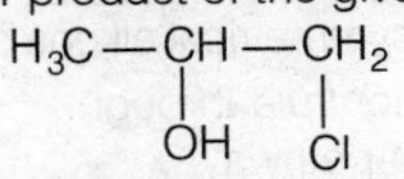

In this reaction, H_2O is used as a solvent and the major product of the reaction will be a *vicinal* halohydrin. A halohydrin is an organic molecule that contains both OH group and a halogen. In a *vicinal* halohydrin, the OH and halogen are bonded to adjacent carbons.

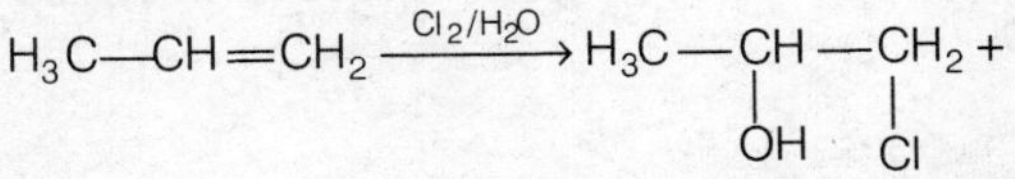

A chlorohydrin (major product)

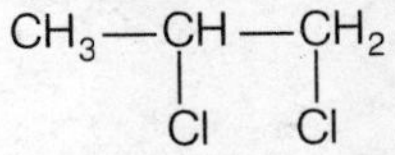

(Minor product)

The reaction proceeds through following mechanism :

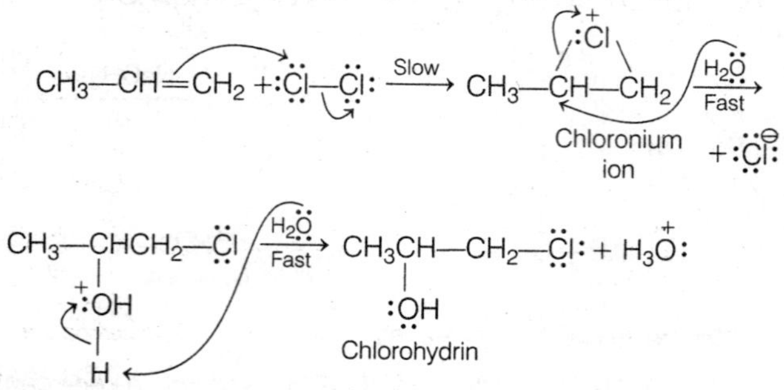

105. (*b*)

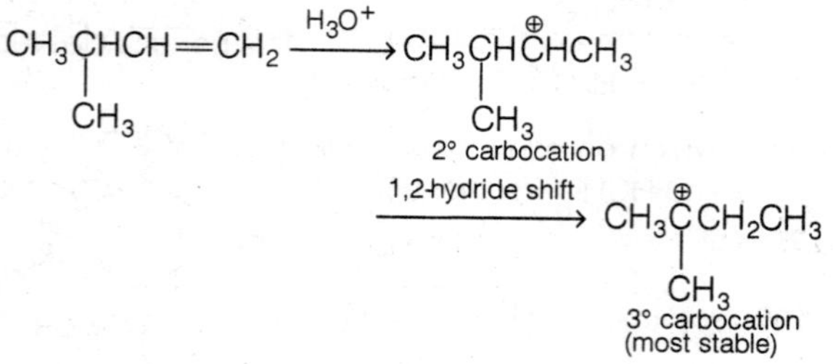

107. (*b*)

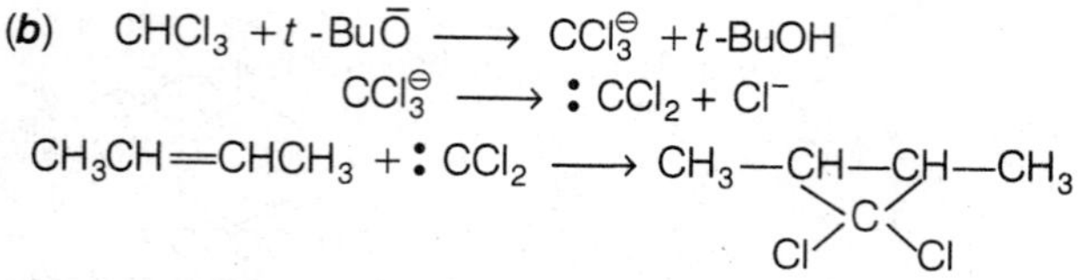

108. (*a*)

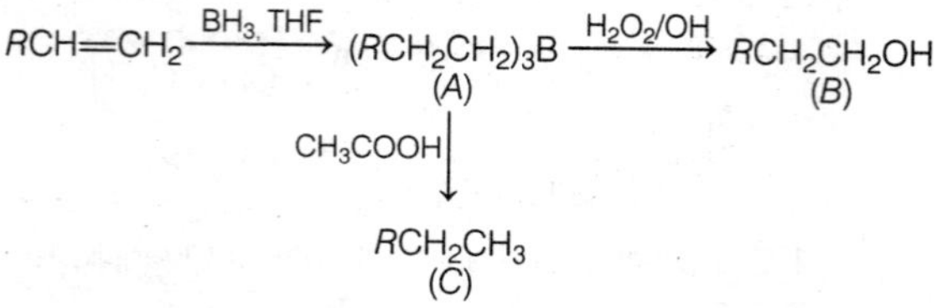

110. (*d*)

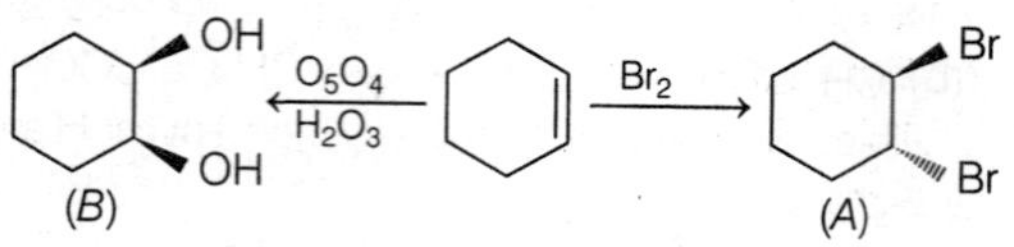

113. (*a*) Substituted alkene is more stable.

114. (*d*) Attachment of electron donating group (+ *R* or + *I*) with sp^2-carbon of an unsymmetrical alkene supports Markownikov's addition rule through electrophilic-addition-pathway.

But, attachment of electron-withdrawing group (– *R* or – *I*) for the same will follow anti-Markownikov's pathway (even in absence of organic peroxide which favours free radical addition) through electrophilic addition pathway.

The product formed by given alkenes when treated with HCl.

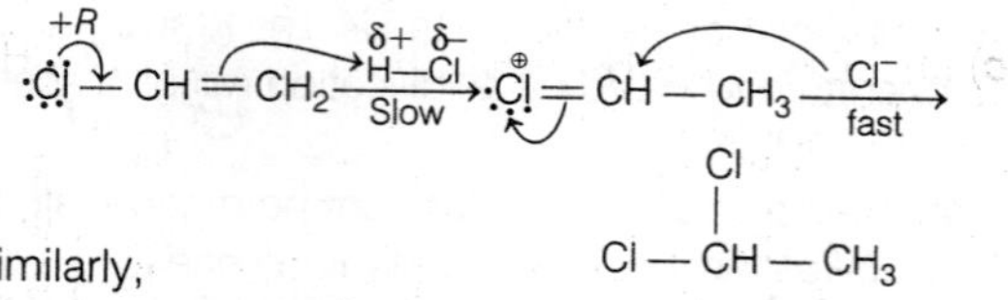

Similarly,

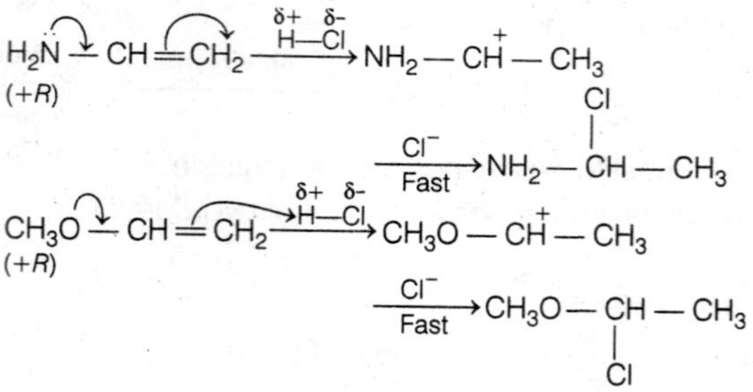

115. (*a*)

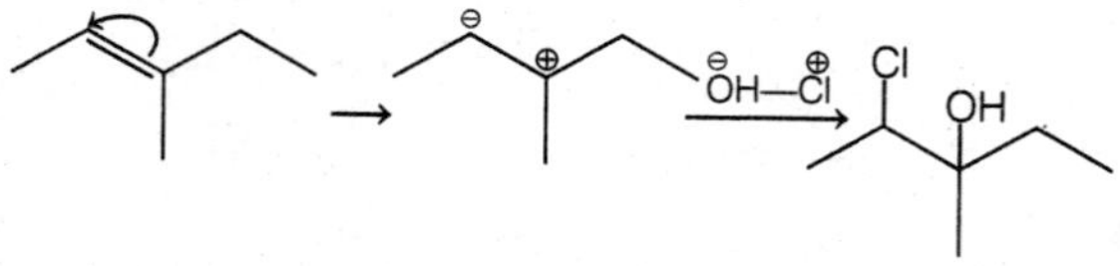

119. (*a*)

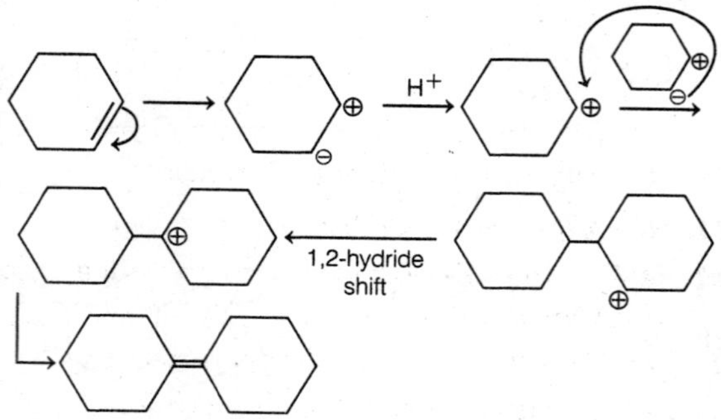

121. (*d*) By Lindlar's catalyst, *cis*-isomer is formed and by Na/NH_3, *trans* isomer is formed. I is *trans* and II is *cis*.

122. (*a*) Greater the conjugation, larger the stability hence, easier the dehydrohalogenation.

124. (*b*)

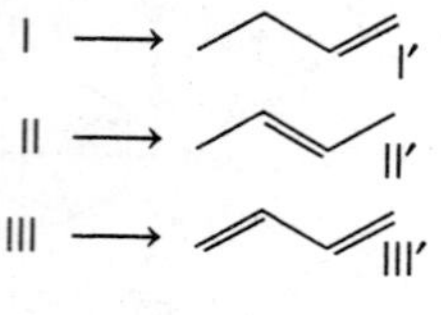

I → I′ stable

II → II′ more stable than I′ due to substituted alkene

III → III′ most stable out of I′, II′ and III′ due to conjugation

Thus, I < II < III

125. (*a*) *X* is formed against Markownikoff's rule while *Y* is formed as per Markownikoff's rule.)

126. (*b*)

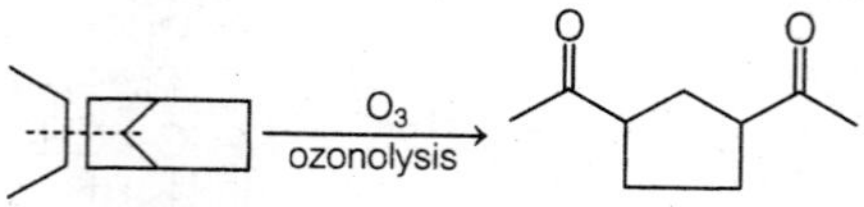

127. (*c*) (a)

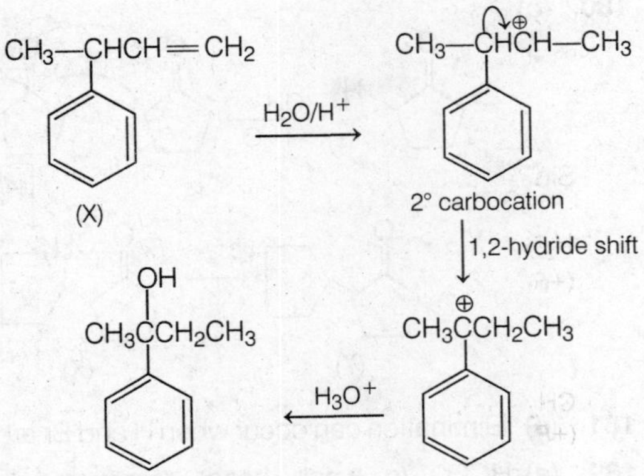

(b) *X*

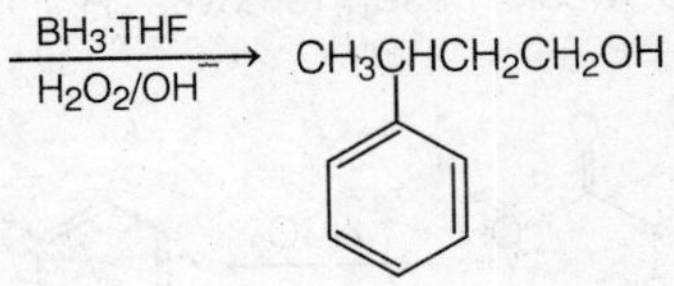

(c) *X*

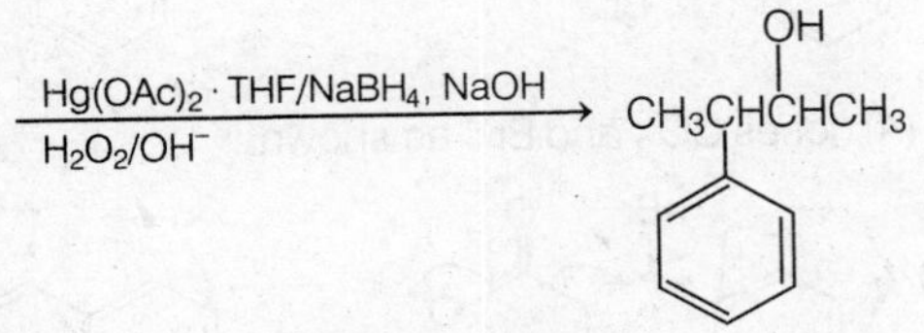

128. (*b*) Conjugated and Br at allylic position.

131. (*a*) by Diels-Alder reaction.

132. (*a*) Three-membered ring cleaves due to strain, no effect on six-membered ring.

133. (*b*) There is oxidation at allylic position by SeO_2.

134. (*b*) By Li/NH_3, *trans*-isomer is formed.

135. (*b*)

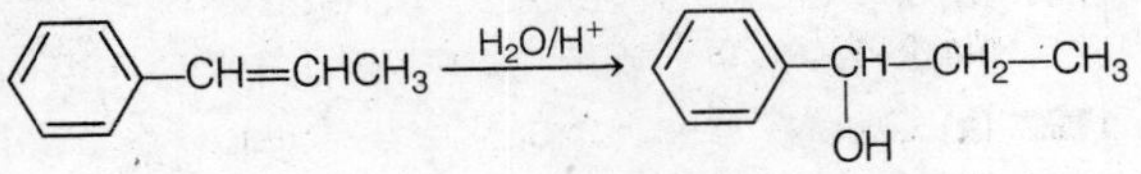

136. (*b*)

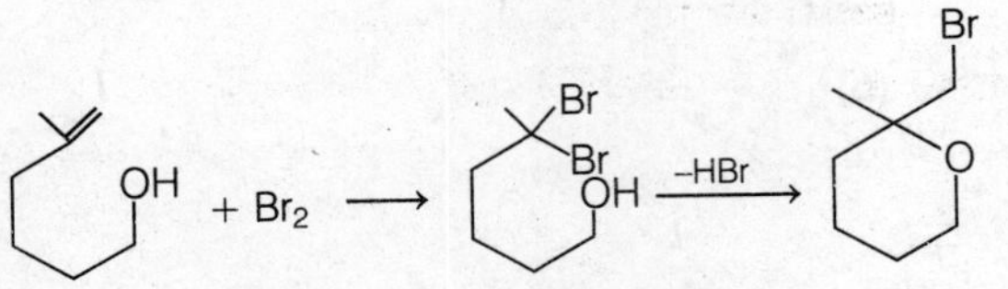

138. (*d*) Most stable 3° carbocation is formed in (*d*)

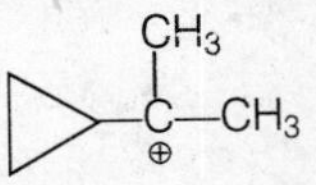

This is thus hydrated to maximum extent.

139. (*a*)

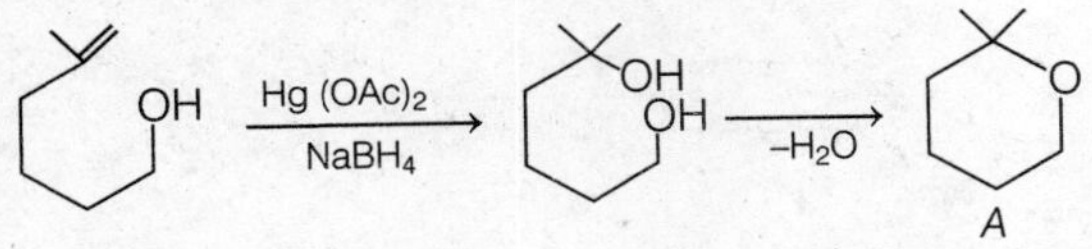

141. (*d*) Position of ene is not given.

144. (*b*)

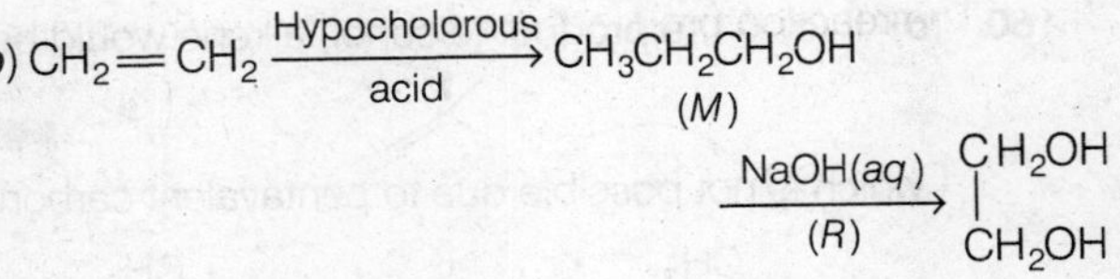

153. (*c*)

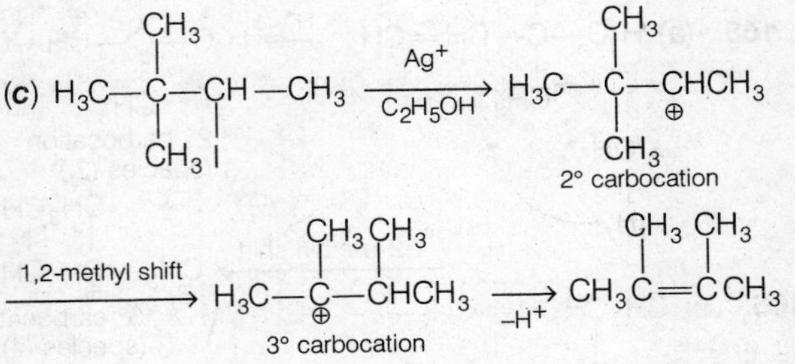

155. (*c*) *X* :

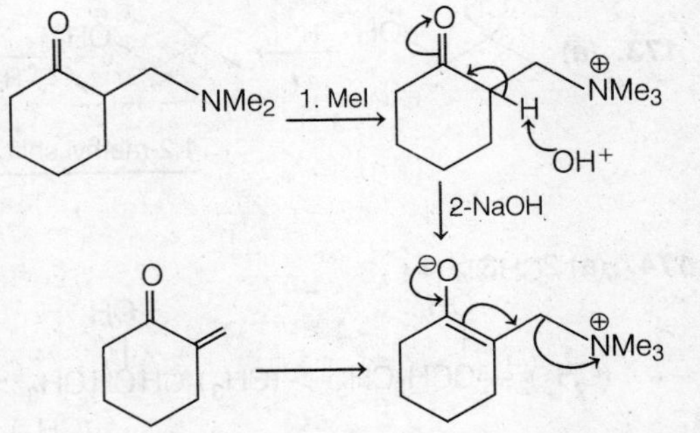

This is E1CB after methylation at nitrogen and the double bond has to go when the leaving group was

Y :

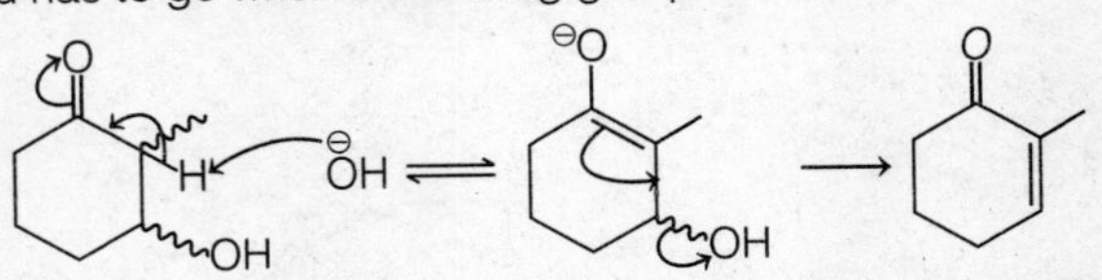

This is also E1CB and reaction ends up conjugated with the carbonyl group.

Z : This is E2 and there is a requirement for H and OTs to be *anti*-planar.

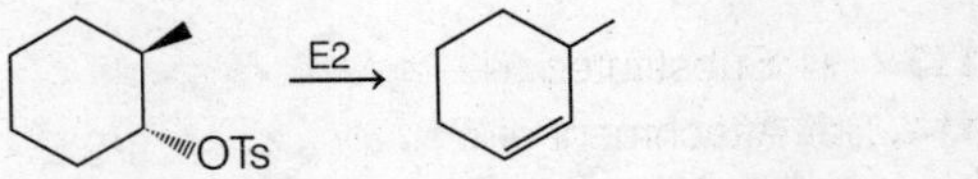

156. (*c*)

Order :

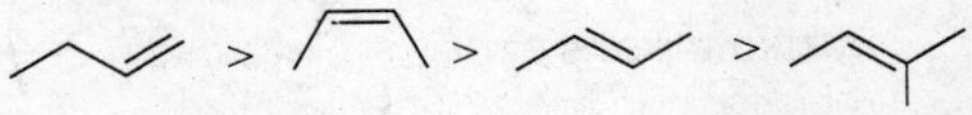

159. (*a*)

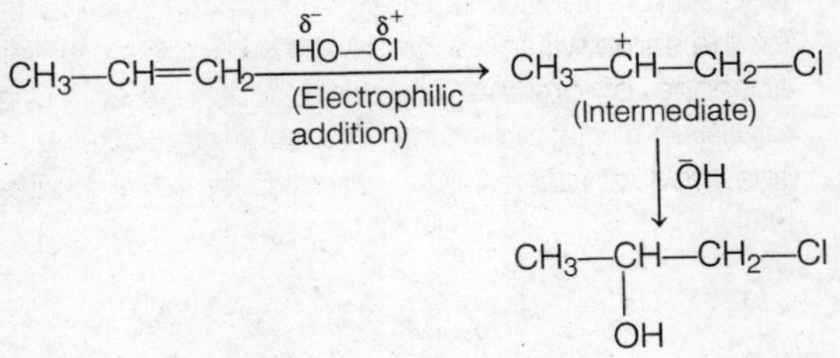

160. (*d*) If (*d*) is the product (alcohol) alkene would be

which is not possible due to pentavalent carbon.

168. (*a*)

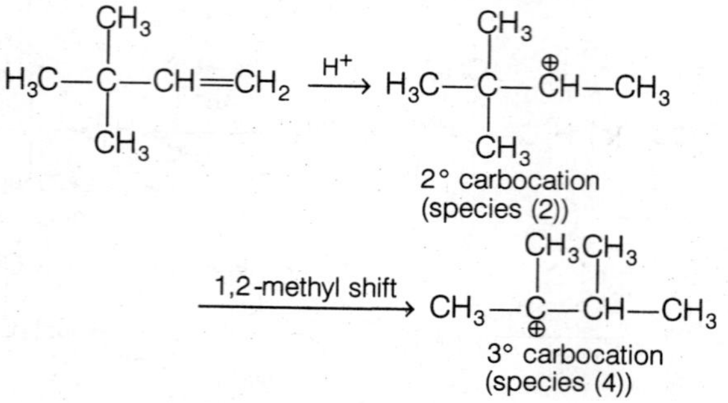

173. (*a*)

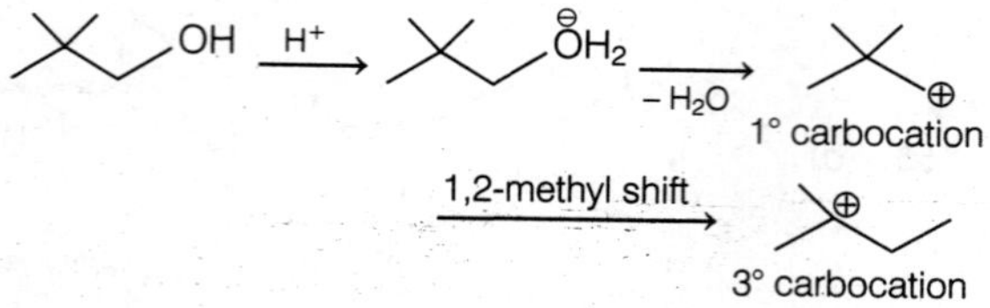

174. (*a*) 2 > 3 > 1

$(CH_3)_2$—C(OH)CH_2CH_3 > $(CH_3)_2$CHCH(OH)CH_3 > $(CH_3)_2CH_2CH_2CH_2OH$

180. (*c*)

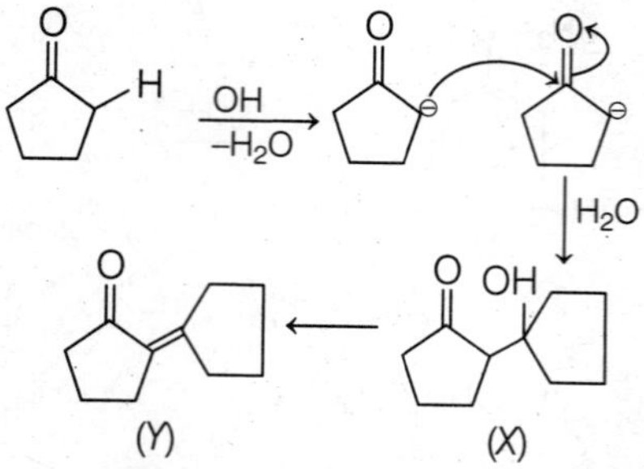

181. (*a*) Elimination can occur when H and Br are anti-periplanar.

182. (*a*) HCO_3^- (a weak base) removes H^+ from —CO_2H formin9g (*A*).

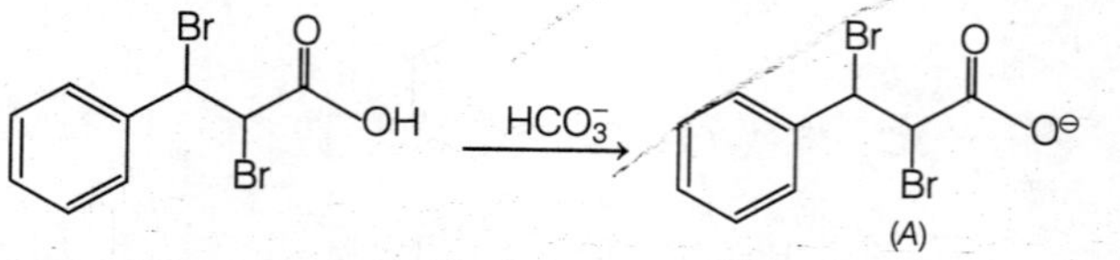

(*A*) loses CO_2 and $Br^\ominus$ as shown.

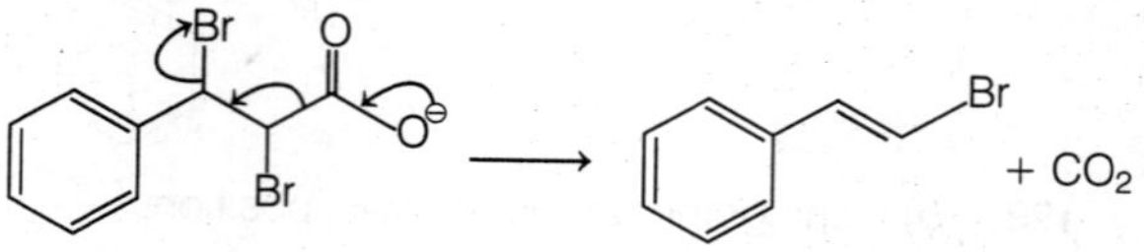

07

Alkynes

Objective Questions Type I [Only one correct option]

In each of the questions below, four choices are given of which only one is correct.

1. Anions of CaC_2 and Mg_2C_3 respectively are

(a) C^-, C^{2-}
(b) C^{2-}, C^{3-}
(c) C_2^{2-}, C_3^{2-}
(d) C_2^{2-}, C_3^{4-}

2. Structure of C_3^{4-} is

(a) $^{2-}C{=}C{=}C^{2-}$
(b) $^{-}C{\equiv}C{-}C^{3-}$
(c) $^{-}C{\equiv}C{-}C^{2-}$
(d) $^{2-}C{-}\underset{|}{\overset{|}{C}}{-}C^{2-}$

3. $R\underset{Br}{\underset{|}{C}}H\underset{Br}{\underset{|}{C}}HR$ can be dehydrobrominated to $RC{\equiv}CR$ by $NaNH_2$.

It follows

(a) E1 mechanism
(b) E2 mechanism
(c) S_N1 mechanism
(d) E1CB mechanism

4. 2-hexyne changes to 1-hexyne by using

(a) $NaNH_2/H_2O$
(b) KOH/CH_3CH_2OH
(c) Both (a) and (b)
(d) None of the above

5. Which salt can be converted into alkyne by Kolbe's method?

(a) Sodium acetate
(b) Sodium succinate
(c) Sodium maleate
(d) Sodium formate

6. *cis-trans* isomerism is not possible in alkynes because of

(a) 180° bond-angle at the carbon–carbon triple bond
(b) greater electronegativity of *sp*-hybridised carbon
(c) shorter bond length of carbon–carbon triple bond
(d) lesser stability of *sp*-hybridised state

7. Carbon–carbon bond-length in alkyne is shortest due to following facts

(a) increase in *s*-character of the *sp*-hybridised carbon
(b) electrons are closer to the nucleus of the *sp*-hybridised carbon
(c) Both (a) and (b) statements are correct
(d) None of the above statement is correct

8. In the following compound

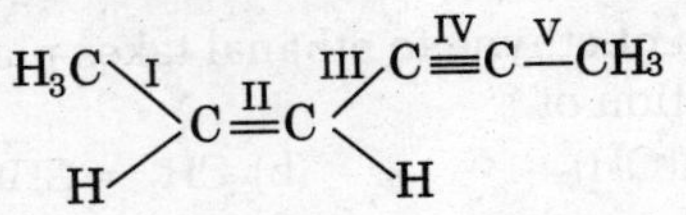

(C—C) bond-lengths in increasing order are

(a) I < II < III < IV < V
(b) I < III < II < IV < V
(c) IV < II < I < III < V
(d) IV < II < III < V < I

9. Which C—H bond is cleaved homolytically most easily?

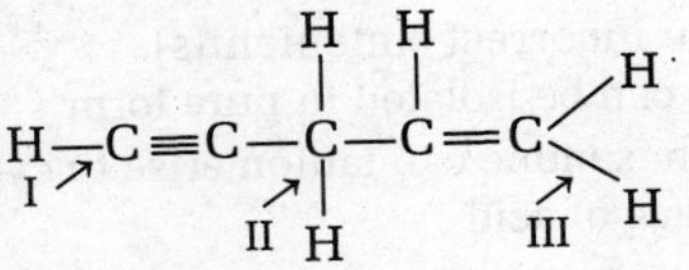

(a) I
(b) II
(c) III
(d) Equally

10. Which compound has maximum carbon-carbon bond energy?

(a) Ethane
(b) Ethene
(c) Ethyne
(d) Equal

11. Consider the following reaction,

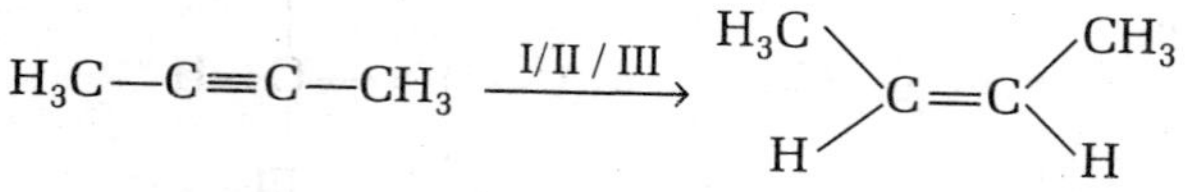

I. H_2/Ni_2B
II. H_2/Pd-$CaCO_3$ in quinoline
III. Na/NH_3 or $LiAlH_4$

This reaction takes place by

(a) I or II (b) I or III
(c) II or III (d) I, II or III

12. P-2 catalyst is

(a) Pd/$CaCO_3$ in quinoline (b) Ni_2B
(c) PtO_2 (d) $LiAlH_4$

13. *Anti*-addition of hydrogen atoms to the triple bond takes place by

(a) H_2/Pd-$CaCO_3$ in quinoline
(b) Li/NH_3
(c) Ni_2B/H_2
(d) RhO_2

14. Alkynes are reduced to *trans*-alkene by Na/NH_3. Reduction is due to

(a) nascent hydrogen (b) molecular hydrogen
(c) atomic hydrogen (d) solvated electrons

15. Which is the following molecules is not linear

(a) $H_2C=C=O$ (b) $O=C=C=C=O$
(c) $HC\equiv C-C\equiv CH$ (d) $HC\equiv CH$

16. Hydration of ethyne to ethanal takes place through the formation of

(a) $CH_3CH(OH)_2$ (b) $CH_2=CHOH$
(c) $CH_2=CHO^-$ (d) $CH\equiv C^{\ominus}$

17. The correct order of C—H bond length in CH_3-CH_3, $CH_2=CH_2$ and $CH\equiv CH$ is

(a) $CH\equiv CH < CH_2=CH_2 < CH_3-CH_3$
(b) $CH_2=CH_2 < CH_3-CH_3 < CH\equiv CH$
(c) $CH_3-CH_3 < CH_2=CH_2 < CH\equiv CH$
(d) All are equal

18. Select the incorrect statement(s).

(a) Enols can be isolated in pure form
(b) Cyclohexanone can tautomerise to cyclohexenol in presence of acid
(c) Hydration of alkynes takes place through the formation of enolic compounds
(d) $HgSO_4 / H_2SO_4$ is used for hydration

19. In the following reaction reactant *A* is

$$A \xrightarrow{HgSO_4/H_2SO_4} CH_3CH_2CH_2\overset{O}{\overset{\|}{C}}H$$

(a) 1-butyne (b) 2-butyne
(c) Both (a) and (b) (d) None of these

20. Only one type of carbonyl compound is obtained by hydration of the following alkynes

(a) $CH\equiv CH$ or $CH_3C\equiv CH$
(b) $CH_3C\equiv CH$ or $CH_3CH_2C\equiv CH$
(c) $CH\equiv CH$ or $CH_3C\equiv CCH_3$
(d) in all the above cases

21. Select the incorrect statement(s).

(a) Alkynes are less reactive than alkenes towards addition of Br_2
(b) 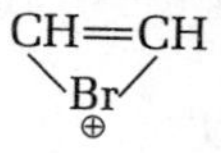 is more stable than 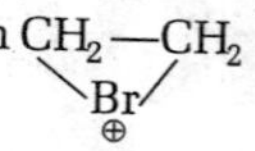
(c) Addition of Br_2 to acetylene is stereoselective
(d) Degree of unsaturation of alkynes is 2

22. When Br_2 (in CCl_4) reacts with C_2H_2,

(a) addition is stereoselective
(b) predominant product is *trans*-isomer
(c) Br_2 is decolourised
(d) All of the facts given above are followed

23. Formation of acetylene from calcium acetylide can be represented as

$$Ca^{2+}C\equiv C^{2-} + 2HOH \longrightarrow H-C\equiv C-H + 2OH + Ca^{2+}$$

(a) The weaker acid (acetylene) is displaced from its salt by neutral substance (water).
(b) The stronger acid (acetylene) is displaced from its salt by a weaker acid (water).
(c) The weaker acid (acetylene) is displaced from its salt by a stronger acid (water).
(d) The weak acid (acetylene) is displaced from its salt by another weak acid (water).

24. Consider the following statements.

I. Vinyl acetate is used in plastic industry.
II. Vinyl cyanide and butadiene form buna-N synthetic rubber.
III. In the addition of HBr or Br_2 to an alkyne, second addition is usually faster than the first.
IV. Bromoalkene is more reactive than an alkyne.

Select the correct statements.

(a) I and II (b) II and III
(c) I and III (d) III and IV

25. When HBr adds to 1-butyne in the presence of peroxide

(a) anti-Markownikoff rule is followed
(b) free radical is the intermediate
(c) Both (a) and (b) are correct
(d) None of the above is correct

26. Methine H-atom is present in

(a) $CH_3C\equiv CCH_3$
(b) CH_4
(c) $CH_3CH=CHCH_3$
(d) $CH\equiv CH$

27. Which is the ethinylation reaction?

(a) $CH_3C{\equiv}CCH_3 + HCHO \xrightarrow[CH_3OH]{CH_3ONa}$

(b) $CH_3C{\equiv}CH + (CH_3)_2CO \xrightarrow[CH_3OH]{CH_3ONa}$

(c) $CH{\equiv}CH + CH_3CH_2Cl \xrightarrow[CH_3OH]{CH_3ONa}$

(d) All of the above

28. Following compound (*A*) is subjected to oxidation by CrO_3/CH_3COOH.

$$\underset{A}{CH{\equiv}CCH_2CH_2CH{=}CHCH_3}$$

Products formed are

(a) CO_2, $HO_2CCH_2CH_2CO_2H$, CH_3CO_2H

(b) CO_2, $HO_2CCH_2CH_2CH{=}CHCH_3$

(c) $CH{\equiv}CCH_2CH_2CO_2H$, CH_3CO_2H

(d) HCO_2H, $HO_2CCH_2CH_2CO_2H$, CH_3CO_2H

29. C_8H_{10} (*A*) by oxidative cleavage forms C_3H_5COOH (*B*). Thus, *A* and *B* are

(a) $\underset{A}{CH_2{=}CHCH_2C{\equiv}CCH_2CH{=}CH_2}$, $\underset{B}{CH_2{=}CHCH_2COOH}$

(b) 

(c) Both (a) and (b) are correct

(d) None of the above is correct

30. Suitable reagent that can convert *A* into *B* is

$$\underset{A}{CH_3C{\equiv}CCH{=}CH_2} \longrightarrow \underset{B}{CH_3C{\equiv}C\underset{OH}{CH}\underset{OH}{CH_2}}$$

(a) alkaline $KMnO_4$

(b) neutral $KMnO_4$

(c) HCO_3H

(d) CrO_3/CH_3COOH

31. Strongest base is

(a) $CH_3CH_2^{\ominus}$ (b) $CH_2{=}CH^{\ominus}$

(c) $CH{\equiv}C^{\ominus}$ (d) can't be predicted

32. Which has most electronegative carbon atom?

(a) CH_3CH_3

(b) $CH{\equiv}CH$

(c) $CH_3CH{=}CH_2$

(d) CH_4

33. $CH_3C{\equiv}CCH_3$ and $CH_3CH_2C{\equiv}CH$ can be distinguished by

(a) ammoniacal $AgNO_3$

(b) ammoniacal Cu_2Cl_2

(c) Both (a) and (b)

(d) None of the above

34. Proton release by different hydrocarbons is in order

$$\underset{\substack{I\\ \text{easiest}}}{\equiv C{-}H} > \underset{II}{=\overset{|}{C}{-}H} > \underset{III}{-\overset{|}{\underset{|}{C}}{-}H}$$

Which factor causes easy removal of proton?

(a) Bond-strength of C—H bond : I < II < III

(b) Bond-strength of C—H bond : I > II > III

(c) Electronegativity of C in I < II < III

(d) Electronegativity of C in I > II > III

35. $\underset{I}{CH_3C{\equiv}C{-}Na} + RX \xrightarrow{S_N2} \underset{II}{CH_3C{\equiv}CR} + NaX$

Reaction follows S_N2 mechanism. Select the correct statement.

(a) II is formed in good yield by S_N2 reaction if *RX* is 1°

(b) If *R—X* is 2° alkyl halide then *R—X* changes to alkene by E2 mechanism

(c) Both (a) and (b) are correct

(d) None of the above is correct

36. Good yield of carbonyl compound is formed in oxidative hydroboration by using

(a) $BH_3 \cdot THF$ (b) $LiAlH_4$

(c) Sia_2BH (d) $H_2SO_4/HgSO_4$

37. In oxidative-hydroboration, intermediate is

(a) enol (b) carbene (c) carbocation (d) carbanion

38. Select the correct statement(s).

(a) When BH_3 adds to alkyne ($RC{\equiv}CR$) product formed is *cis*-isomer by *syn*-addition.

(b) Enol formed tautomerises to carbonyl compound.

(c) Only aldehydes are formed from terminal alkynes by oxidative hydroboration.

(d) All the above are correct statements

39. $CH_3CH_2C{\equiv}CH \underset{B}{\overset{A}{\rightleftharpoons}} CH_3C{\equiv}CCH_3$, *A* and *B* are

(a) alcoholic KOH and $NaNH_2$

(b) $NaNH_2$ and alcoholic KOH

(c) $NaNH_2$ and Lindlar catalyst

(d) Lindlar catalyst and $NaNH_2$

40. $CH{\equiv}CH \xrightarrow[Cu_2Cl_2]{NH_4Cl}$ product. Product is

(a) $CuC{\equiv}CCu$ (b) $CH_2{=}CHC{\equiv}CH$

(c) $CH{\equiv}CCu$ (d) $CuC{\equiv}CNH_4$

41. An organic compound of molecular formula C_4H_6, *A* forms precipitates with ammoniacal silver nitrate and ammoniacal cuprous chloride. '*A*' has an isomer '*B*', one mole of which reacts with one mole of Br_2 to form 1,4-dibromo-2-butene. '*A*' and '*B*' are

(a) $CH_3CH_2C{\equiv}CH$ and $CH_2{=}CHCH{=}CH_2$

(b) $CH_3C{\equiv}CCH_3$ and $CH_3CH{=}C{=}CH_2$

(c) 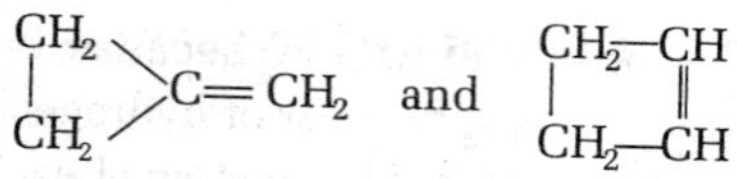

(d) $CH_3C\equiv CCH_3$ and 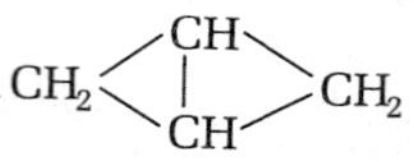

42. 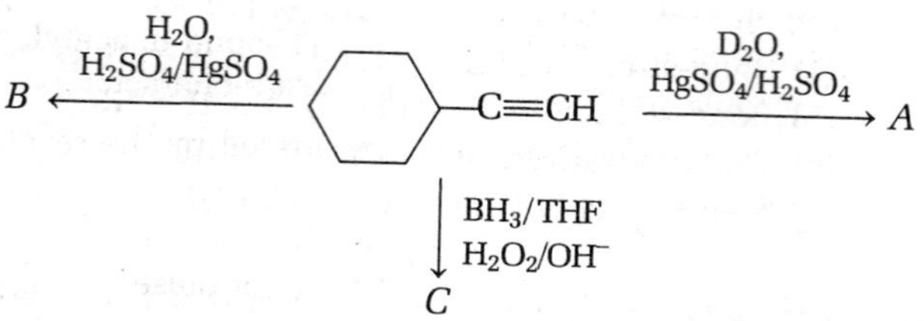

A, *B* and *C* are

(a) 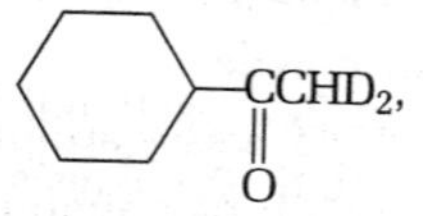
(*X*)

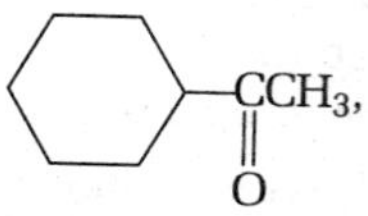
(*Y*)

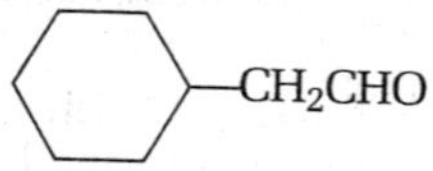
(*Z*)

(b) *Y*, *X* and *Z*
(c) *Y* in all cases
(d) *Z* in all cases

43. $\underset{(X)}{CH\equiv CH} + \underset{(Y)}{2CH_3COOH} \longrightarrow A \xrightarrow{\Delta} B + C$, *B* can be obtained from (*X*) by hydration and *C* can be obtained from (*Y*) by heating with P_2O_5. Hence, *A* is

(a) $CH_2=CH-O-\overset{O}{\overset{\|}{C}}CH_3$

(b) $CH_3CH(O-\overset{O}{\overset{\|}{C}}CH_3)_2$

(c) $CH_3CH_2COOCH_3$

(d) None of the above

44. What is the product of the following reaction?

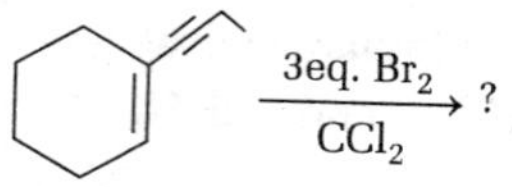

(a) 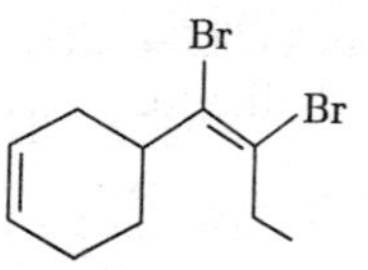
(b) 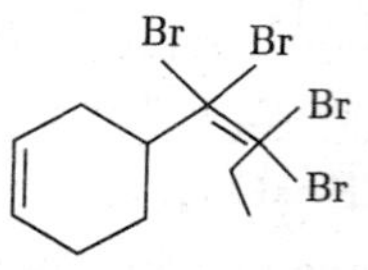

(c) 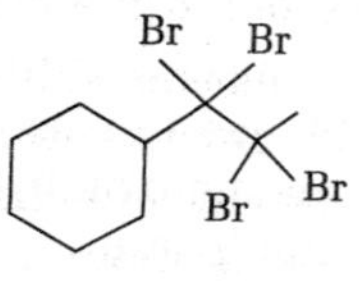
(d) 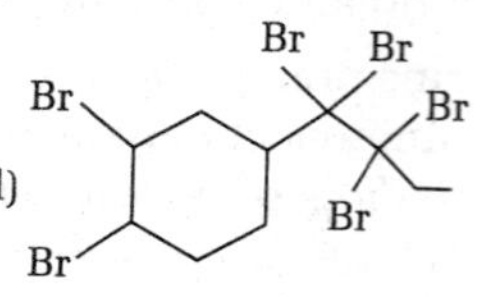

45. $CH\equiv CH + 2HCHO \xrightarrow{CH_3O^-} X$, *X* is

(a) $HOH_2CC\equiv C\ CH_2OH$
(b) $HOH_2CC\equiv C\ CH_2OCH_3$
(c) Both (a) and (b)
(d) None of the above

46. $A + CH_3MgBr \xrightarrow{H_3O^+} CH_3CH_2CH_2OH$,

hence, $CH\equiv CH \xrightarrow[\text{(ii) } A]{\text{(i) } NaNH_2} B$, *B* is

(a) $CH\equiv CCH_2CH_2OH$
(b) $CH\equiv C\cdot CH_2OH$
(c) $CH\equiv C\cdot CHO$
(d) $CH\equiv C\cdot COOH$

47. The major product (*Y*) in the following reaction is **[JEE Main 2020, Jan.]**

$$CH_3-\overset{CH_3}{\overset{|}{CH}}-C\equiv CH \xrightarrow[H_2O]{HgSO_4,\ H_2SO_4} X \xrightarrow[\text{(ii) Conc. } H_2SO_4/\Delta]{\text{(i) } C_2H_5MgBr,\ H_2O} Y$$

(a) $CH_3-\overset{CH_3}{\overset{|}{C}}=\underset{CH_2CH_3}{\underset{|}{C}}-CH_3$

(b) $CH_3-\overset{CH_3}{\overset{|}{CH}}-\underset{CH_3}{\underset{|}{C}}=CH-CH_3$

(c) $H_3C-\overset{CH_2}{\overset{\|}{C}}-\underset{C_2H_5}{\underset{|}{CH}}-CH_3$

(d) $CH_3-\overset{CH_3}{\overset{|}{CH}}-\underset{CH_2CH_3}{\underset{|}{C}}=CH_2$

48. In the following hydration reaction,

$$R-C\equiv C-H \underset{H_2SO_4}{\overset{Hg^{2+},\ SO_4^{2-}}{\rightleftharpoons}} R-\overset{O}{\overset{\|}{C}}-CH_3$$

mercuric sulphate is used (instead of mercuric acetate as in alkene). It is due to

(a) sulphate is a very poor nucleophile
(b) it does not compete with H_2O which traps the carbocation to yield a vinyl alcohol
(c) Both (a) and (b)
(d) None of the above

49. 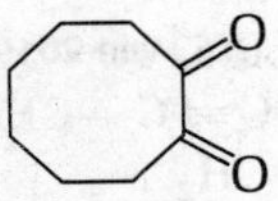 $\xrightarrow[HgO]{N_2H_4}$ A, A is

(a) 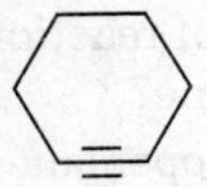 (b) 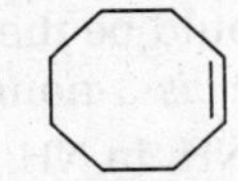

(c) 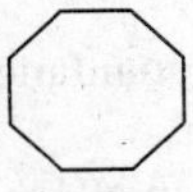 (d) 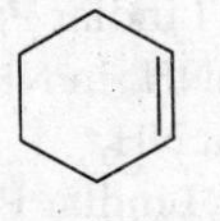

50. $CH \equiv CH \xrightarrow[CH_3O^-]{2HCHO} \xrightarrow{Li/NH_3} A$, A is

(a) 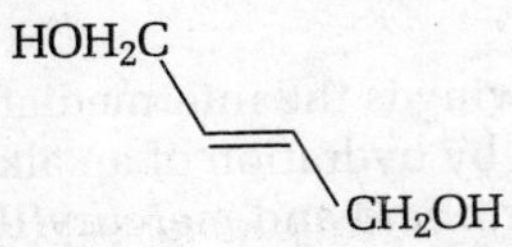

(b) 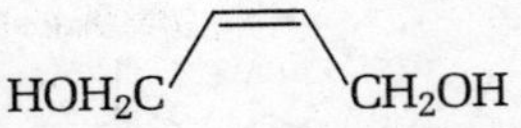

(c) 

(d) 

51. The *trans*-alkenes are formed by the reduction of alkynes with **[JEE Main 2018]**

(a) H_2-Pd/C, $BaSO_4$ (b) $NaBH_4$
(c) Na/liq. NH_3 (d) Sn-HCl

52. The cylindrical shape of an alkyne is due to

(a) three sigma C—C bonds
(b) three pi C—C bonds
(c) two sigma C—C and one pi C—C bonds
(d) one sigma C—C and two pi C—C bonds

53. 1-butyne and hot alkaline $KMnO_4$ reacts to produce

(a) CH_3CH_2COOH
(b) $CH_3CH_2COOH + CO_2$
(c) $CH_3CH_2COOH + HCOOH$
(d) $CH_3CH_2CH_2COOH$

54. What is the product when 1-butyne reacts with excess of HBr?

(a) 2,2-dibromobutane (b) 2-bromobutane
(c) 1,1,2,2-tetrabromobutane (d) 1,2-dibromobutene

55. Identify (Y) in the series

$$CH \equiv CH \xrightarrow{O_3/NaOH} (X) \xrightarrow{Zn/CH_3COOH} (Y)$$

(a) CH_3OH (b) $CH_2COOH—CH_2COOH$
(c) CH_3CH_2COOH (d) $CH_2OH—CH_2OH$

56. Acetylene and HI react to produce

(a) CH_3CH_2I (b) $CH_2=CHI$
(c) CH_3CHI_2 (d) CH_3CH_3

57. Acetylene hydrocarbons are acidic because

(a) acetylene contains least number of hydrogen atoms
(b) acetylene has only one hydrogen atom at each carbon atom
(c) acetylene belongs to the class of alkynes with formula C_nH_{2n-2}
(d) sigma electron density of C—H bond in acetylene is nearer a carbon which has 50% *s*-character

58. Ethylidine chloride can be prepared by the reaction of HCl and

(a) C_2H_4 (b) C_2H_2
(c) C_2H_5 (d) All of these

59. Iodoform (CHI_3) reacts with Ag powder to produce

(a) methane (b) ethane
(c) butane (d) ethyne

60. When CH_4, C_2H_2, C_2H_4 and C_2H_6 gases are passed through the Wolf-bottle of containing ammoniacal $AgNO_3$, then which one of the following gas does not come out from the bottle?

(a) CH_4 (b) C_2H_2 (c) C_2H_4 (d) C_2H_6

61. C_2H_4 and C_2H_2 can be distinguished by

(a) conc. H_2SO_4 (b) Cl_2 in CCl_4
(c) ammoniacal $CuCl_2$ (d) dilute alkaline $KMnO_4$

62. The product formed when acetylene is passed through red hot tube is

(a) cyclohexane (b) ethane
(c) neoprene (d) benzene

63. Alkaline $KMnO_4$ oxidises acetylene to

(a) acetic acid (b) ethyl alcohol
(c) ethylene glycol (d) oxalic acid

64. The IUPAC name for the compound shown is

$$CH_3\underset{\displaystyle|}{\overset{CH_2CH_3}{CH}}CH_2C \equiv CCH(CH_3)_2$$

(a) 2, 6-dimethyl-3-octyne
(b) 6-ethyl-2-methyl-3-heptyne
(c) 2-ethylpropyl isopropyl acetylene
(d) 2-ethyl-6-methyl-4-heptyne

65. Which of the following statements best explains the greater acidity of terminal alkynes ($RC \equiv CH$) compared with monosubstituted alkenes ($RCH = CH_2$)?

(a) The *sp*-hybridised carbons of the alkyne are less electronegative than the sp^2 carbons of the alkene
(b) The two π-bonds of the alkyne are better able to stabilise the negative charge of the anion by resonance
(c) The *sp*-hybridised carbons of the alkyne are more electronegative than the sp^2 carbons of the alkene
(d) The question is incorrect–alkenes are more acidic than alkynes

66. Referring to the following equilibrium (R = alkyl group)

$$RCH_2CH_3 + RC{\equiv}C:^- \rightleftharpoons RCH_2\ddot{C}H_2^- + RC{\equiv}C{-}H$$

(a) $K < 1$; the equilibrium would lie to the left
(b) $K > 1$; the equilibrium would lie to the right
(c) $K = 1$; equal amounts of all species would be present
(d) Not enough information is given; the structure of R must be known

67. Which of the following is an effective way to prepare 1-pentyne?

(a) 1-pentene $\xrightarrow[\text{(ii) NaNH}_2\text{, heat}]{\text{(i) Cl}_2}$

(b) Acetylene $\xrightarrow[\text{(ii) CH}_3\text{CH}_2\text{CH}_2\text{Br}]{\text{(i) NaNH}_2}$

(c) 1, 1-dichloropentane $\xrightarrow[\text{(ii) H}_2\text{O}]{\text{(i) NaNH}_2/\text{NH}_3}$

(d) All of the above are effective

68. Which alkyne yields butanoic acid ($CH_3CH_2CH_2CO_2H$) as the only organic product on treatment with ozone followed by hydrolysis?
(a) 1-butyne (b) 4-octyne (c) 1-pentyne (d) 2-hexyne

69. Which of the following produces a significant amount of acetylide ion on reaction with acetylene?
(a) Conjugate base of CH_3OH ($pK_a = 16$)
(b) Conjugate base of H_2($pK_a = 35$)
(c) Conjugate base of H_2O ($pK_a = 16$)
(d) Both (a) and (c)

70. Which of the following is the product of the reaction of 1-hexyne with 1 mole of Br_2?

(a) 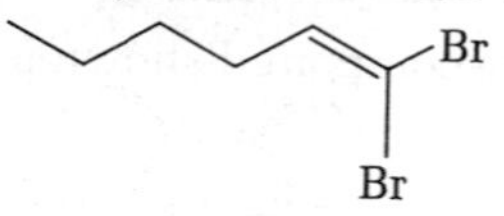
(b) 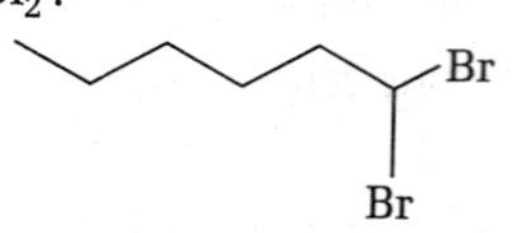
(c) 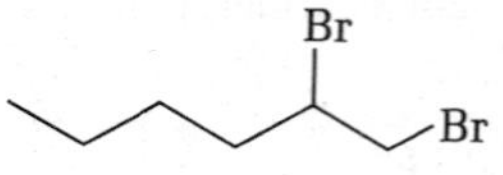
(d) 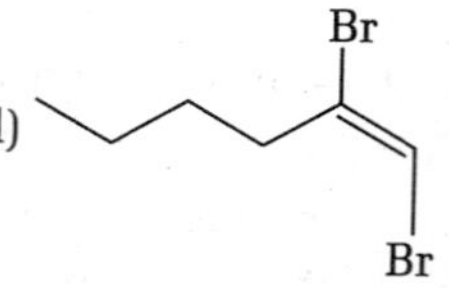

71. Choose the sequence of steps that describes the best synthesis of 1-butene from ethanol
(a) (1) $NaC{\equiv}CH$; (2) H_2, Lindlar Pd
(b) (1) $NaC{\equiv}CH$; (2) Na, NH_3
(c) (1) HBr, heat; (2) $NaC{\equiv}CH$; (3) H_2, Lindlar Pd
(d) (1) HBr, heat; (2) $KOC(CH_3)_3$, DMSO;
(3) $NaC{\equiv}CH$; (4) H_2, Lindlar Pd

72. Consider the following reactions,

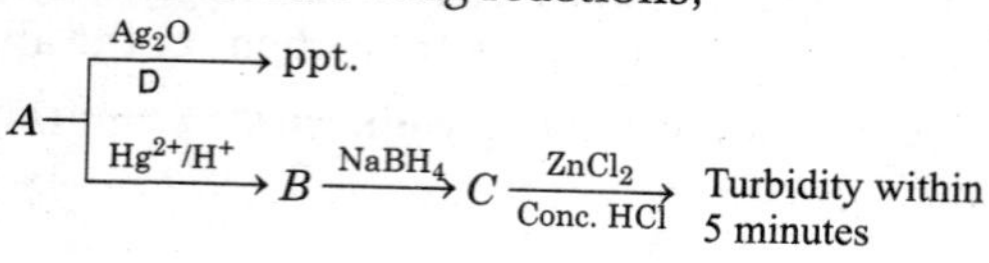

A is [JEE Main 2019, April]
(a) $CH{\equiv}CH$
(b) $CH_3{-}C{\equiv}C{-}CH_3$
(c) $CH_3{-}C{\equiv}CH$
(d) $CH_2{=}CH_2$

73. Which would be the best sequence of reactions to use to prepare *cis*-3-nonene from 1-butyne?
(a) (1) $NaNH_2$ in NH_3; (2) 1-bromopentane; (3) H_2, Lindlar Pd
(b) (1) $NaNH_2$ in NH_3; (2) 1-bromopentane; (3) Na, NH_3
(c) (1) H_2, Lindlar Pd; (2) $NaNH_2$ in NH_3; (3) 1-bromopentane
(d) (1) Na, NH_3; (2) $NaNH_2$ in NH_3; (3) 1-bromopentane

74. Which one of the following is the intermediate in the preparation of a ketone by hydration of an alkyne in the presence of sulphuric acid and mercury(II) sulphate?

(a) 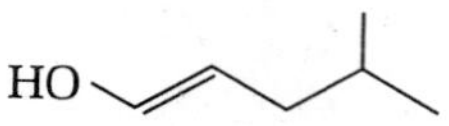

(b) 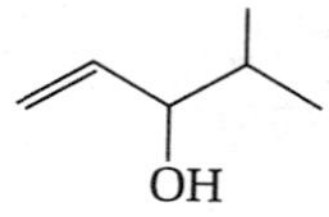

(c) 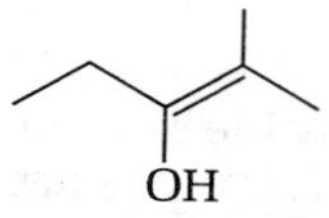

(d) 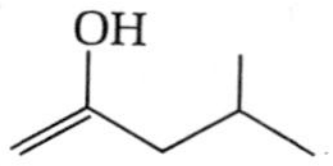

75. The major product of the following reaction is

$$CH_3C{\equiv}CH \xrightarrow[\text{(ii) DI}]{\text{(i) DCl (1 equiv.)}}$$

[JEE Main 2019, April]
(a) $CH_3CD(Cl)CHD(I)$
(b) $CH_3CD_2CH(Cl)(I)$
(c) $CH_3CD(I)CHD(Cl)$
(d) $CH_3C(I)(Cl)CHD_2$

76. The major product $[R]$ in the following sequence of reactions is

$$HC{\equiv}CH \xrightarrow[\text{(ii) } (H_3C)((CH_3)_2CH)CH{-}Br]{\text{(i) LiNH}_2/\text{ether}} [P] \xrightarrow[\text{(ii) NaBH}_4]{\text{(i) HgSO}_4/\text{H}_2\text{SO}_4} [Q] \xrightarrow[\Delta]{\text{Conc. H}_2\text{SO}_4} [R]$$

[JEE Main 2020, Sep.]
(a) $(H_3C)((CH_3)_2CH)C{=}CH{-}CH_3$
(b) $(H_3C)((CH_3)_2CH)CH{-}CH{=}CH_2$
(c) $(H_3C)(H_3CCH_2)C{=}C(CH_3)_2$
(d) $H_2C{=}C((CH_3)_2CH){-}CH_2{-}CH_3$

77. Which acid-base reaction is not possible?
(a) $CH{\equiv}CH + NH_2^{\ominus} \rightleftharpoons CH{\equiv}C^{\ominus} + NH_3$
(b) $CH{\equiv}CH + RO^{\ominus} \rightleftharpoons CH{\equiv}C^{\ominus} + ROH$

(c) $CH_3COOH + RO^{\ominus} \rightleftharpoons CH_3COO^{\ominus} + ROH$
(d) $ROH + NH_2^{\ominus} \rightleftharpoons RO^{\ominus} + NH_3$

78. Which is the most stable anion?
(a) Acetylide (b) Vinylic
(c) Alkyl (d) Equal stability

79. Which of the following is Lindlar catalyst ? **[JEE Main 2021, March]**
(a) Zinc chloride and HCl
(b) Cold dilute solution of $KMnO_4$
(c) Sodium and liquid NH_3
(d) Partially deactivated palladised charcoal

80. The correct order for acid strength of compounds $CH\equiv CH$, $CH_3—C\equiv CH$ and $CH_2=CH_2$ is as follows **[JEE Main 2019, Jan.]**
(a) $CH_3—C\equiv CH > CH_2=CH_2 > HC\equiv CH$
(b) $CH_3—C\equiv CH > CH\equiv CH > CH_2=CH_2$
(c) $HC\equiv CH > CH_3—C\equiv CH > CH_2=CH_2$
(d) $CH\equiv CH > CH_2=CH_2 > CH_3—C\equiv CH$

81. The synthesis of 3-octyne is achieved by adding a bromoalkane into a mixture of sodium amide and an alkyne. The bromoalkane and alkyne respectively are **[JEE Main 2010]**
(a) $BrCH_2CH_2CH_2CH_2CH_3$ and $CH_3CH_2C\equiv CH$
(b) $BrCH_2CH_2CH_3$ and $CH_3CH_2CH_2C\equiv CH$
(c) $BrCH_2CH_2CH_2CH_2CH_3$ and $CH_3C\equiv CH$
(d) $BrCH_2CH_2CH_2CH_3$ and $CH_3CH_2C\equiv CH$

82. Number of sp^2-hybridised carbon in *B*.

$$HC\equiv CH \xrightarrow[\Delta]{Fe} (A) \xrightarrow[AlCl_3]{CO,\ HCl} (B)$$

(a) 7 (b) 5 (c) 6 (d) 1

Objective Questions Type II [One or more than one correct option(s)]

In each of the questions below, four choices are given, of which one or more than one are correct.

1. What are *A*, *B* and *C* in the following reaction?

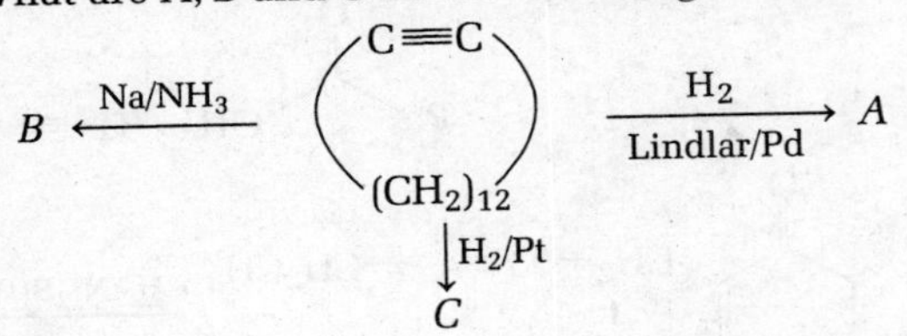

(a)
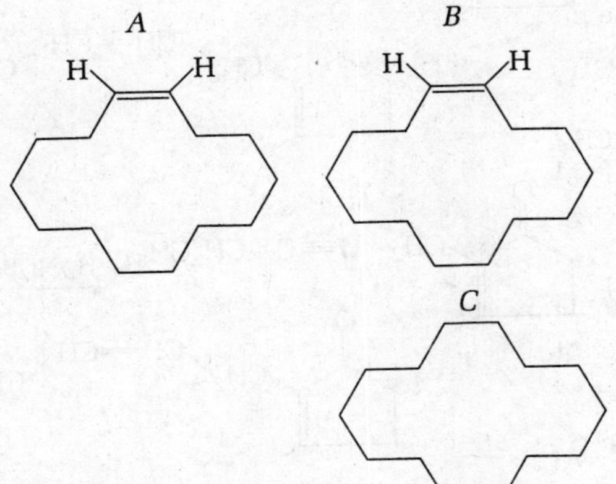

(b)
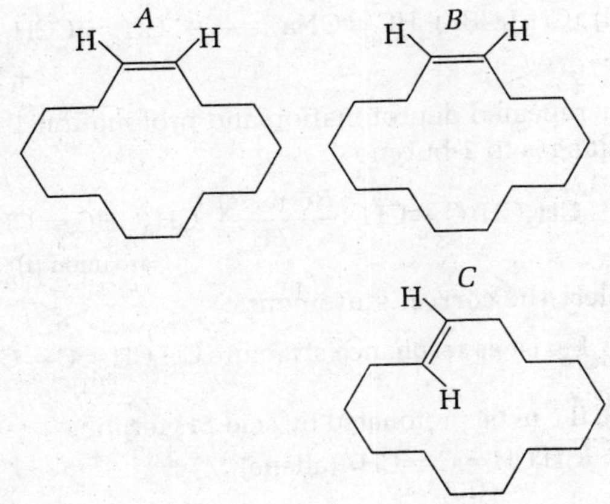

(c)
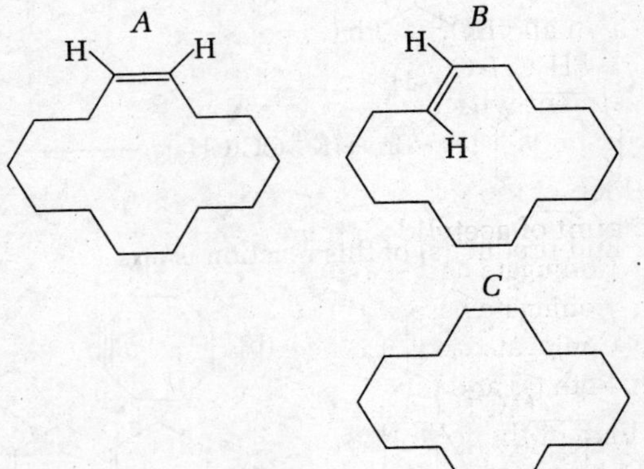

(d)
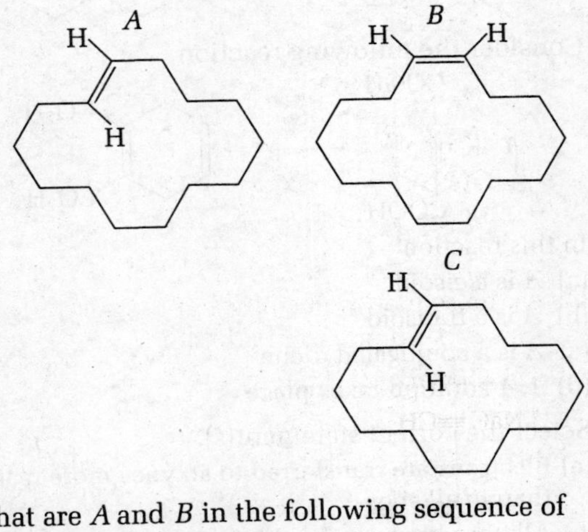

2. What are *A* and *B* in the following sequence of reactions?

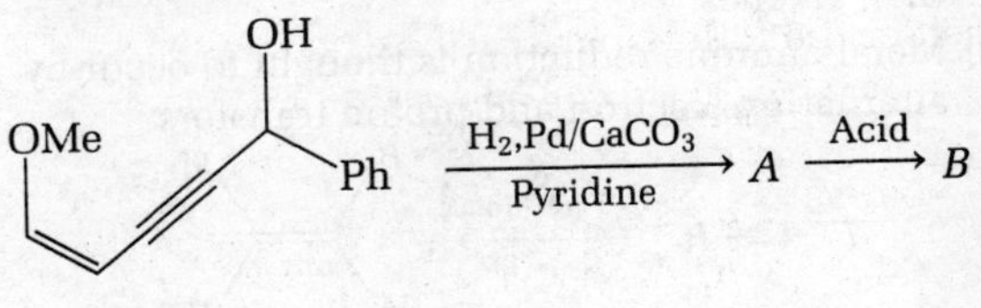

A B

(a) 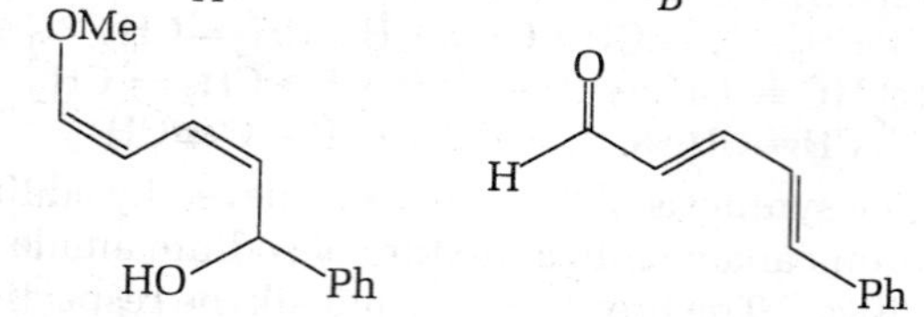

(b) 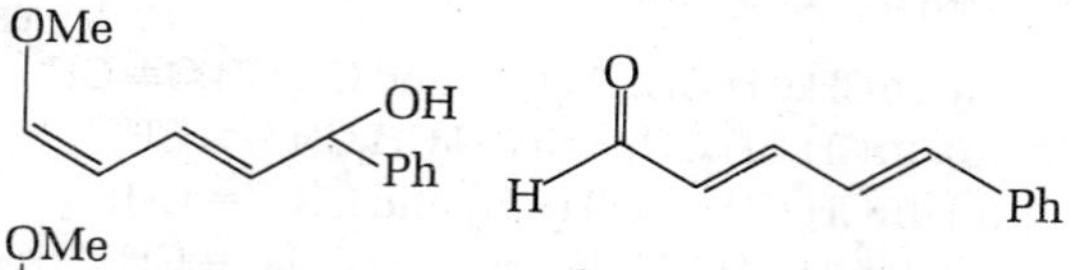

(c) 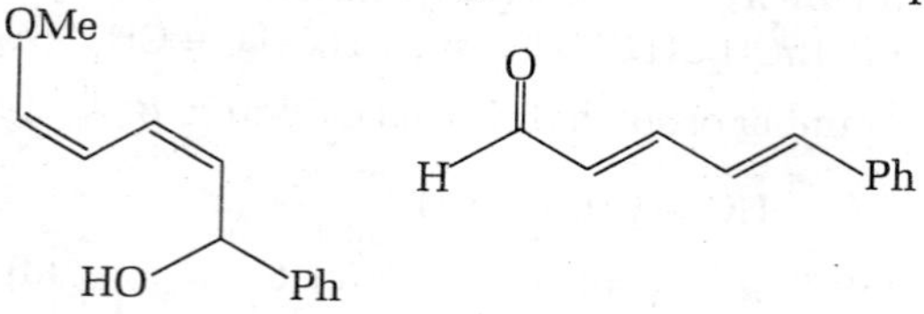

(d) 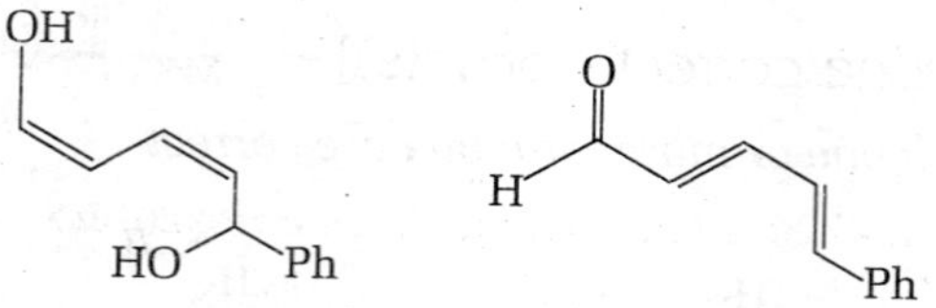

3. 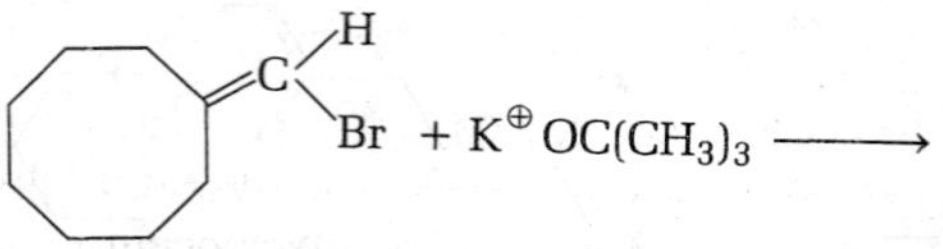

End-product(s) of this reaction is/are

(a) 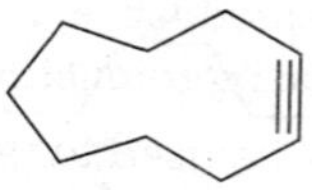 (b) 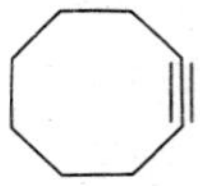

(c) 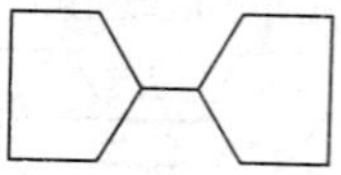 (d) 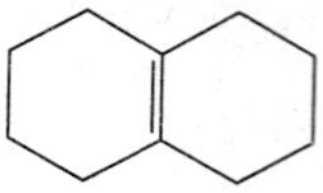

4. Consider the following reaction,

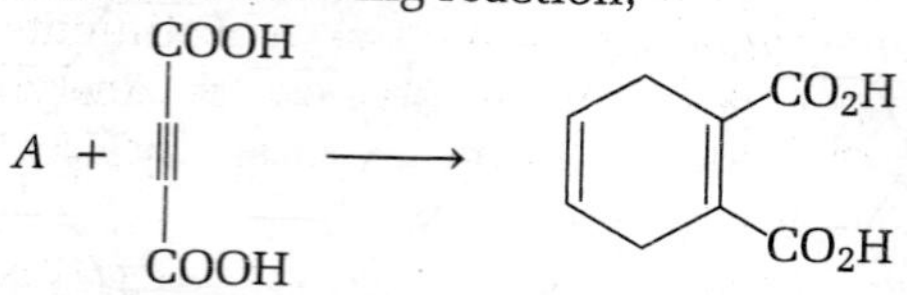

In this reaction

(a) *A* is a cisoid

(b) *A* is a transoid

(c) *A* is a conjugated diene

(d) 1, 4-addition takes place

5. Select the correct statement(s).

(a) Electrons are transferred to alkynes more readily than to alkenes

(b) Alkynes have greater reactivity towards nucleophiles than alkenes

(c) Metal-ammine reduction is thought to occur by alternating electron and proton transfers

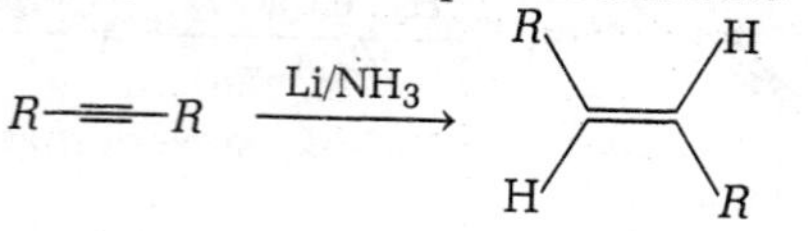

(d) The *trans* anion is formed faster than *cis* anion due to steric effect.

6. Select the correct statement(s).

(a) Diisobutyl aluminium hydride reduces alkynes to alkenes.

(b) Lithium aluminium hydride is effective only when the alkyne has a hydroxyl group in the α-position

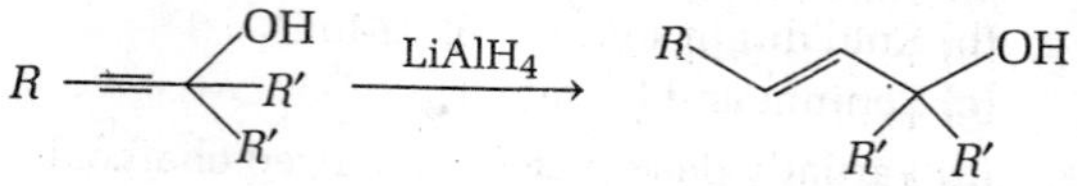

(c) In reaction (b), *cis*-isomer is selectively formed.

(d) Lithium aluminium hydride selectively reduces alkynes to alkanes.

7. Select the reactions giving correct set of products.

(a) 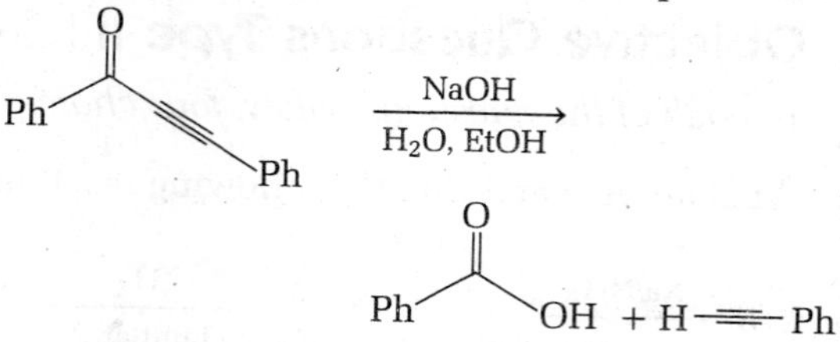

(b) 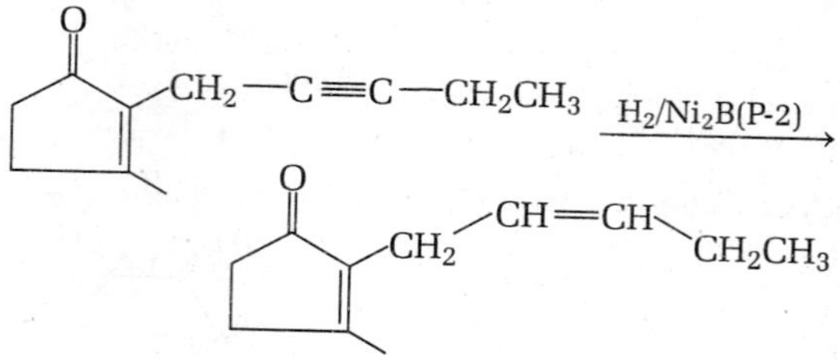

(c) 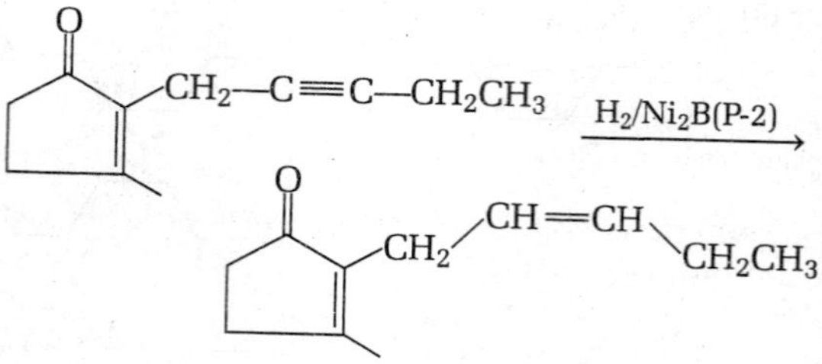

(d) $(CH_3)_3CBr + HC\equiv\overset{\ominus}{C}Na^{\oplus} \longrightarrow CH_2{=}\underset{}{C}(CH_3)CH_3 + HC\equiv CH$

8. By repeated deprotonation and protonation 1-butyne changes to 2-butyne

$$CH_3CH_2C\equiv CH \xrightarrow[-BH]{B^{\ominus}\text{ (base)}} CH_3\overset{}{\underset{\ominus}{C}}HC\equiv CH$$

Carbanion (I)

Select the correct statements.

(a) I exist as resonance structure $CH_3CH{=}C{=}\overset{\ominus}{C}H$ (II)

(b) II can be protonated by acid *BH* forming $CH_3CH{=}C{=}CH_2$ (allene) (III)

(c) III can be deprotonated by $B^{\ominus}$ forming $CH_3\overset{\ominus}{C}=C=CH_2$ which exists as resonance structure (IV) $CH_3C\equiv C\overset{\ominus}{C}H_2$ and changing to $CH_3C\equiv CCH_3$

(d) Above conversion does not take place

9. In the following reaction 2-pentyne $\xrightarrow{A}$ 1-pentyne, A is

(a) $NaNH_2/H_2O$

(b) NH_3 (liquid)

(c) H_3O^+

(d) $HgSO_4/H_2SO_4$

10. Consider the following reaction

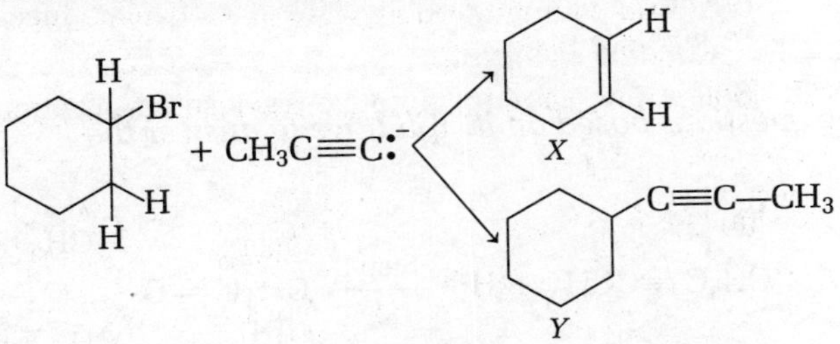

Select the correct statement(s).

(a) Y is the major product by S_N2 reaction

(b) Y is the minor product by S_N2 reaction

(c) X is the major product by E2 reaction

(d) X is the minor product by E2 reaction

11. In the following reaction, hydrocarbons are

$$CH_3CH_2C\equiv C{:}^{\ominus} + CH_3\underset{\mid \atop Br}{C}HCH_3 \xrightarrow{E2}$$

(a) $CH_3CH_2C\equiv CCH(CH_3)_2$

(b) $CH_3CH_2C\equiv CH$

(c) $CH_3CH=CH_2$

(d) $CH_3C\equiv CCH_3$

12. Dehydrohalogenation of *geminal* or *vicinal* dihalide is a two-step reaction

$$\underset{\text{Dihalide}}{R_2C_2H_2X_2} \xrightarrow[\text{I}]{\text{Base} \atop -HX} \xrightarrow[\text{II}]{\text{Base} \atop -HX} R{-}C\equiv C{-}R$$

Select the correct statement(s).

(a) Step I is slow and step II is fast

(b) Step I is fast and step II is slow

(c) Intermediate is vinyl halide

(d) Step II (involving second dehydrohalogenation) occurs only under extremely basic condition

13. Choose the correct option(s) for the following reaction sequence **[JEE Advanced 2019]**

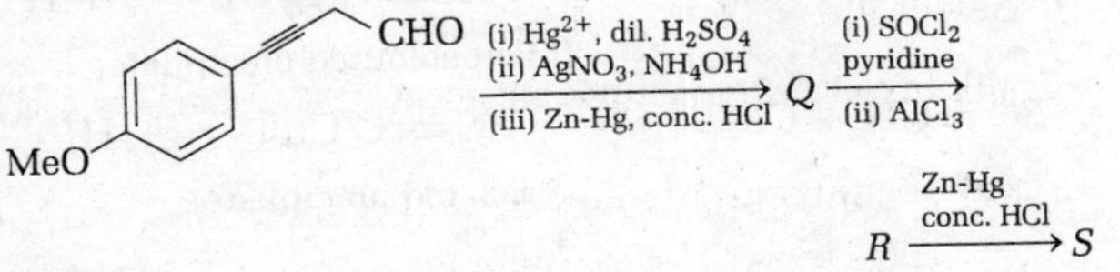

Consider Q, R and S as major products.

(a)

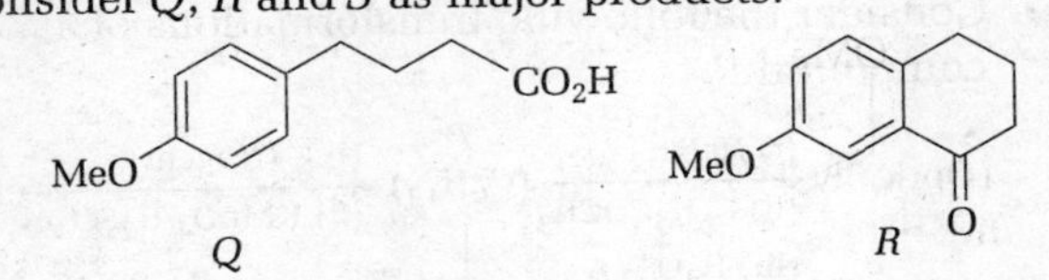

(b)

(c)

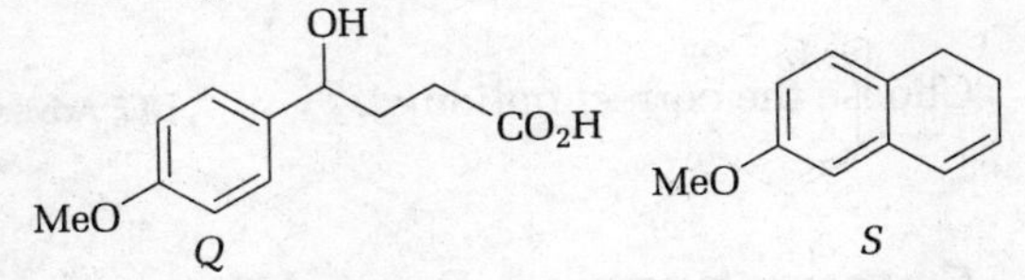

(d)

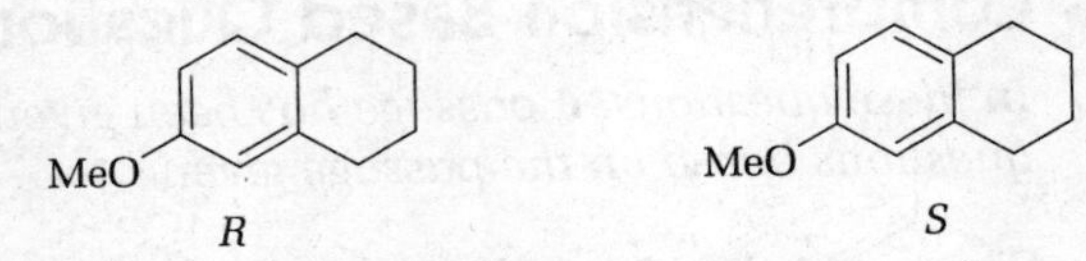

14. Consider the following addition reaction

Select the correct statement(s).

(a) It gives predominantly the *anti*-addition product

(b) Protonation and nucleophilic attack occur simultaneously

(c) It gives predominantly the *cis* product

(d) Nucleophilic attack is faster than protonation

15. Following synthetic method can be used to prepare higher alkynes from lower terminal alkyne.

$$RC\equiv CH \xrightarrow{NaNH_2} RC\equiv C^{\ominus}Na^{\oplus} \xrightarrow[S_N2]{R'I} RC\equiv CR'$$

$R'X$ for S_N2 reaction to give $RC\equiv CR'$ in good yield must be primary, with no bulky substituents or branches close to the reaction centre. Acetylide (alkynide) ions can be decomposed by H_2O to regenerate alkyne

$$RC\equiv C^{\ominus}Na^{\oplus} + H_2O \rightleftharpoons RC\equiv CH + NaOH$$

Following methods have been suggested to synthesise A

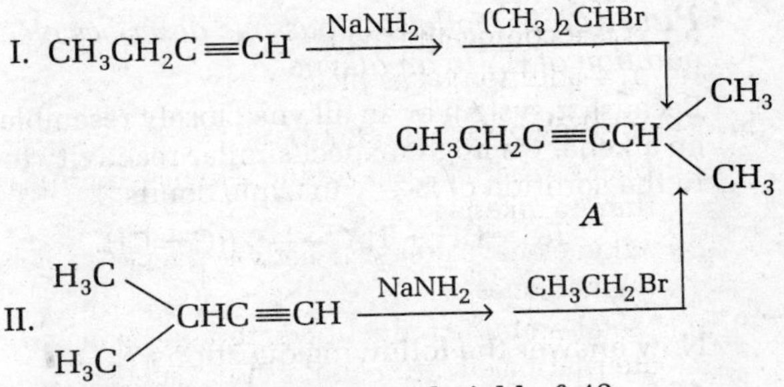

Which can be used to give good yield of A?

(a) Only I

(b) Only II

(c) Both (a) and (b)

(d) None of these

16. Consider the following transformations of a compound *P*.

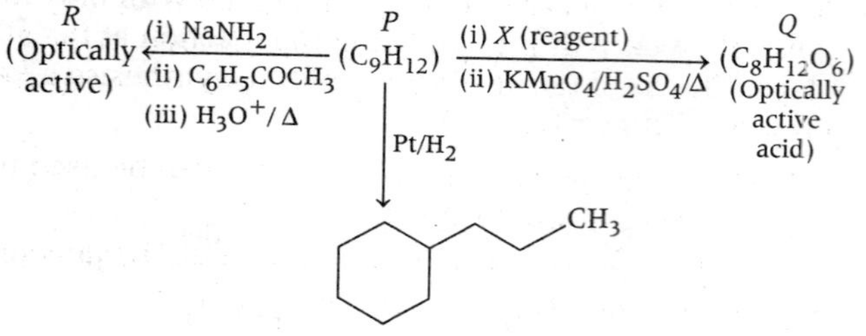

Choose the correct option(s). **[JEE Advanced 2020]**

(a) *P* is 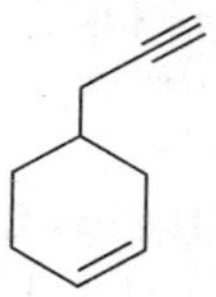

(b) *X* is Pd-C/quinoline/H_2

(c) *P* is 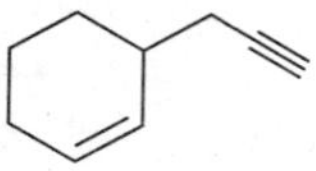

(d) *R* is 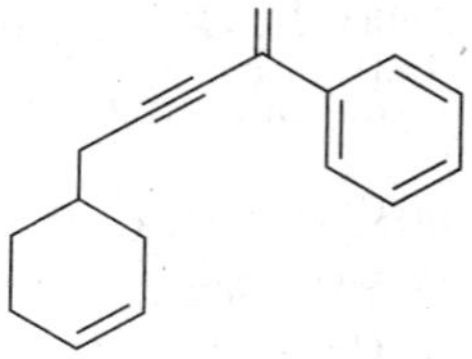

Comprehension Based Questions

In these questions, a passage has been given followed by questions based on it. You have to answer the questions based on the passage given.

***Passage* 1** *Read the following passage and answer the questions at the end of it.*

Alkynes can be stereoselectively reduced to give *Z*- or *E*-alkenes using different types of reagents.

$$R{-}C{\equiv}CR \longrightarrow \underset{cis\text{ - or }trans}{RCH{=}CHR}$$

1. Select the correct statement(s).

I. Reduction with Lindlar's catalyst gives selectively *trans*-isomer due to formation of radical anion.

II. Reduction with Lindlar's catalyst gives selectively *cis*-isomer since metal catalyst ensures that the two H-atoms add to the same face of the alkene in a *syn*-addition.

III. Solvated electrons from Li/NH_3 add to the alkyne to produce a radical anion with bulky *R* groups far apart from each other due to repulsion thus, producing selectively *trans*-isomer.

(a) I and II
(b) II and III
(c) I and III
(d) I, II and III

***Passage* 2** *Following passage describes electrophilic addition of* HX *to an alkyne.*

Because π-system of an alkyne closely resembles that of an alkene, we might expect similar reactivity to result in the addition of H—*X* to triple bonds.

$$RC{\equiv}CH + HX \longrightarrow R\underset{\displaystyle X}{\underset{|}{C}}{=}CH_2$$

Now answer the following questions.

1. Consider the addition of HBr to 2-butyne

$$CH_3C{\equiv}CCH_3 + H^+ \xrightarrow{\text{Step I}} \underset{(A)}{CH_3\overset{\oplus}{C}{=}C}\begin{matrix}CH_3\\H\end{matrix} \xrightarrow[\text{step II}]{Br^-}$$

Select the correct statement(s).

(a) Intermediate *A* is called vinyl cation–an unstable intermediate
(b) *A* is less stable than sp^2-hybridised carbocation
(c) *A* is formed in a slow step
(d) *A* is more stable than sp^2-hybridised carbocation

2. Nucleophilic attack of Br^- on *A* results in the formation of

(a) 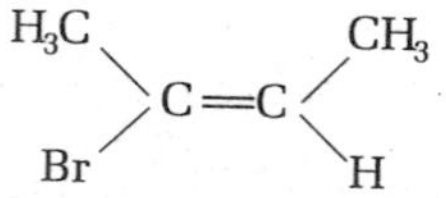

(major)

(b) 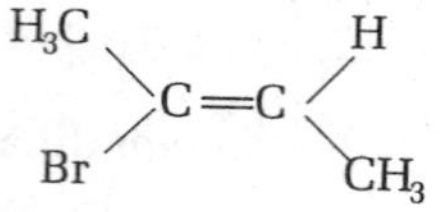

(minor)

(c) Both (a) and (b)
(d) None of the above

***Passage* 3** *Following chemical tests can be used to make distinction of terminal alkynes from internal alkynes and alkenes.*

Silver (I) and copper (I) salts react with terminal alkynes to form silver and copper acetylides. Silver and copper acetylides are bonded more covalently than other acetylides, however and they are much less basic and less nucleophilic.

$$RC{\equiv}CH + Ag^+ \longrightarrow \underset{\text{(Light coloured precipitate)}}{RC{\equiv}CAg\downarrow} + H^+$$

$$RC{\equiv}CH + Cu^+ \longrightarrow \underset{\text{(Brick red precipitate)}}{RC{\equiv}C\,Cu\downarrow} + H^+$$

Heavy metals acetylides can be used to purify alkynes-say a mixture of 1-hexyne and 2-hexyne.

Answer the following questions.

1. Following pairs can be distinguished by the given reagent. Which reagent(s) is/are not for specific distinction?

Pair	Reagent
(a) $CH_3C{\equiv}CH$, $CH_3CH{=}CH_2$	Br_2 water
(b) $CH_3C{\equiv}CCH_3$, $CH_3CH_2C{\equiv}CH$	$[Ag(NH_3)_2^+]$
(c) $CH{\equiv}CH$, $CH_3C{\equiv}CH$	$[Cu(NH_3)_2^+]$
(d) $CH_3CH_2CH_3$, $CH_3CH{=}CH_2$	$[Ag(NH_3)_2^+]$

2. Consider a mixture of 1-hexene and 1-hexyne.

Hydrocarbon	B.P.	pK_a
1-hexene	337 K	x
1-hexyne	344 K	$y < x$

We can suggest different methods to separate the mixture

I. Distillation

II. Mixture $\xrightarrow{NaNH_2}$ $\xrightarrow{\text{Filter}}$ $RC{\equiv}CNa \xrightarrow{HCl} RC{\equiv}CH$

↓ Residue

1-hexene (filtrate)

III. Mixture + $[Cu(NH_3)_2^+]$ $\xrightarrow{\text{Filter}}$ $R{\equiv}CCu$ ↓ $\xrightarrow{HCl} RC{\equiv}CH$

↓

1-hexene (filtrate)

Correct method(s) is/are

(a) I and II (b) II and III

(c) III only (d) III only

***Passage* 4** Your goal is to synthesise *4,4-dimethyl -2-pentyne. You have following reagents* $CH_3C{\equiv}CH$, $(CH_3)_3CBr$, $(CH_3)_3CC{\equiv}CH$, CH_3I, NH_3(liquid), $NaNH_2$.

Answer the following questions.

1. Two suitable paths are possible

I. $CH_3C{\equiv}CH \xrightarrow{NaNH_2} \xrightarrow{(CH_3)_3CBr}$

II. $(CH_3)_3CC{\equiv}CH \xrightarrow{NaNH_2} \xrightarrow{CH_3I}$

Better path is

(a) Only I (b) Only II

(c) either of two (d) None of these

2. Select the correct statement.

(a) Reaction in I is S_N2 (b) Reaction in II is S_N2

(c) Reaction in II is E2 (d) Reaction in II is E1

3. There is formation of alkene in

(a) I by E1 (b) II by E1

(c) I by E2 (d) II by E2

***Passage* 5 Reduction of Alkynes** Alkynes normally react with two equivalents of hydrogen to produce alkanes. However, it is possible to react an alkyne with only one equivalent of hydrogen and stop the reaction at the alkene stage. Choice of the catalyst enables to synthesise alkene of desired configuration.

1. Some of the catalysts given below can be used to convert alkyne to alkene.

I. P-2 catalyst (Ni_2B) II. $Pd/CaCO_3$/quinoline

III. Li / NH_3 (liquid) IV. $LiAlH_4$

Choice can be

(a) I and II (b) I, II and III

(c) I, III and IV (d) I, II, III and IV

2. The *anti*-stereochemistry of sodium-ammonia reduction appears as a result of

(a) greater stability of vinyl radical in the *trans*-configuration

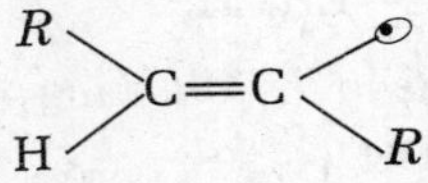

(b) greater stability of vinyl radical in the *cis*-configuration

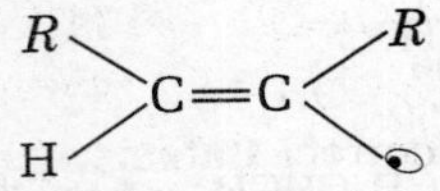

(c) greater stability of *cis*-alkene

(d) greater stability of *trans*-alkene

3. Oleic acid (*A*), stearic acid (*B*) and elaidic acid (*C*) are naturally occurring compounds, which can be isolated from various fats and oils. Each can be prepared by hydrogenation of a compound known as stearolic acid (*D*), $CH_3(CH_2)_7C{\equiv}C(CH_2)_7COOH$. Suggest structures of (*A*), (*B*) and (*C*) if they are obtained by reduction as given

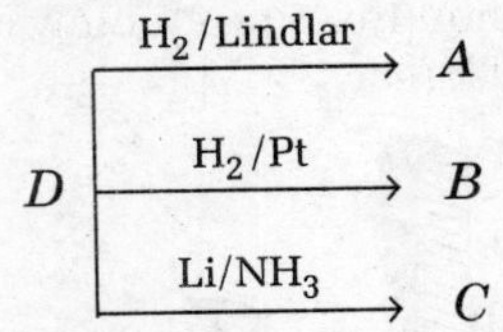

(a) $CH_3(CH_2)_{16}COOH$ in all cases

(b) $CH_3(CH_2)_7CH{=}CH(CH_2)_7COOH$ in all cases

(c) $CH_3(CH_2)_7CH{=}CH(CH_2)_7COOH$ (*trans*) in all cases

(d) *A* : *cis*; *B* : $CH_3(CH_2)_{16}COOH$; *C* : *trans*

***Passage* 6** An acyclic hydrocarbon *P*, having molecular formula C_6H_{10} gave acetone as the only organic product through the following sequence of reactions, in which *Q* is an intermediate organic compound.

$$\underset{(C_6H_{10})}{P} \xrightarrow[\text{(ii) } NaBH_4\text{/ethanol} \quad \text{(iii) Dil. acid}]{\text{(i) Dil. } H_2SO_4/HgSO_4}$$

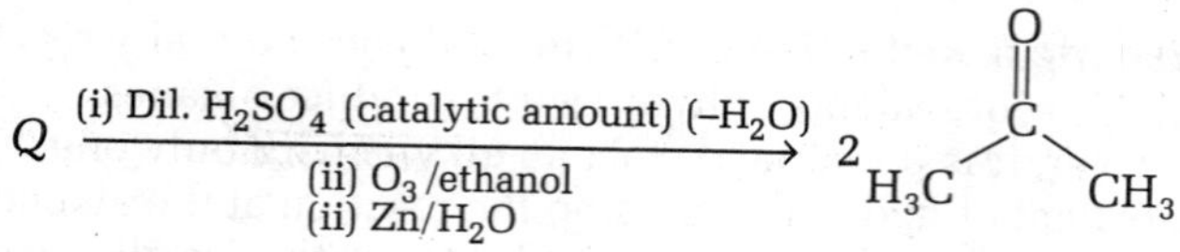

1. The structure of the compound P is
(a) $CH_3CH_2CH_2CH_2—C≡C—H$
(b) $H_3CH_2C—C≡C—CH_2CH_3$
(c) 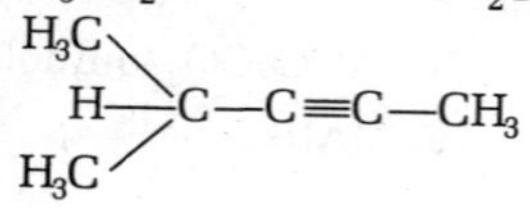
(d) 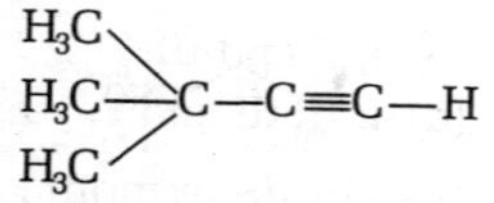

2. The structure of the compound Q is
(a) 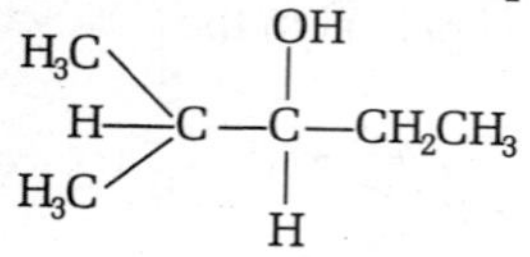
(b) 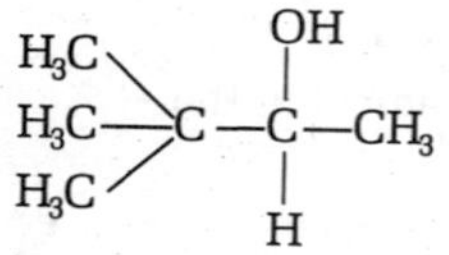
(c) 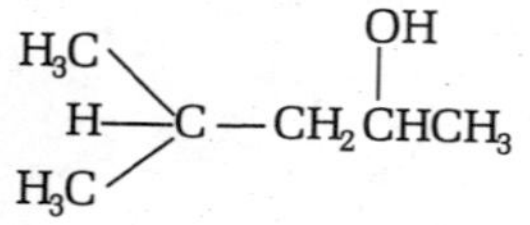
(d) $CH_3CH_2CH_2\underset{}{CH}(OH)CH_2CH_3$

***Passage* 7** Following figure gives ΔH_f° (standard heat of formation) of different types of isomers of unsaturated compound C_nH_{2n-2}. Based on it answer the questions.

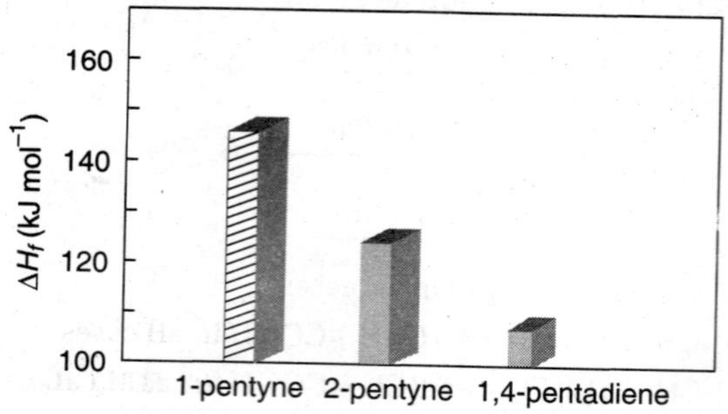

1. Which reaction is exothermic?
(a) 2-pentyne ⟶ 1-pentyne
(b) 1-pentyne ⟶ 2-pentyne
(c) 1,4-pentadiene ⟶ 2-pentyne
(d) All of the above

2. Which is most stable isomer?
(a) 1-pentyne
(b) 2-pentyne
(c) 1,4-pentadiene
(d) Additional data is required to decide relative stability

3. Given graphical data shows that
(a) alkynes are less stable than isomeric dienes
(b) *sp*-hybridisation state is less stable than the *sp*^{2}-hybridisation state
(c) triple bond like a double bond is more stable in the interior of a carbon chain than at the end
(d) 2-pentyne is acidic

***Passage* 8** *Following passage is about the newly discovered fourth allotrope of carbon.*

Now there seems to be yet a fourth crystalline allotrope of carbon, the polyyne form. Reported in 1995 by Richard Lagow at The University of Texas, the polyyne allotrope consists of linear chains of up to 500 *sp*-hybridised carbons joined by alternating single and triple bonds.
It is prepared by laser-induced vaporisation of graphite in the presence of trifluoromethyl radicals (• CF_3) to "cap" the ends of the long acetylenic chains and thereby stabilise the molecules.

—C≡C—C≡C—C≡C—C≡C—C≡C—C≡C—C≡C—

Polyyne allotrope of carbon

Read the above passage and answer the questions.

1. Other three allotropes of carbon can be out of
I. graphite II. coal
III. diamond IV. fullerene
Correct alternate is
(a) I, II and III
(b) I and III
(c) I, III and IV
(d) I, II and IV

2. Types of hybridisation in the bonding of various allotropes are

	Graphite	Diamond	Fullerene	Polyyne
(a)	*sp*^{3}	*sp*^{3}	*sp*^{2}	*sp*
(b)	*sp*^{2}	*sp*^{3}	*sp*^{2}	*sp*
(c)	*sp*	*sp*^{2}	*sp*^{2}	*sp*
(d)	*sp*^{3}	*sp*^{2}	*sp*	*sp*

3. Select the correct statement(s).
(a) Diamond is a covalent network solid composed of *sp*^{3}-hybridised atoms linked together in a vast, three-dimensional lattice of cyclohexane-like rings.
(b) Graphite is composed of *sp*^{2}-hybridised atoms joined in two-dimensional sheets of benzene like rings.
(c) Fullerene contains 60 *sp*^{2}-hybridised carbon atoms in 32 five and six-membered rings that are joined into the spherical shape of a soccer ball.
(d) Polyyne is a conjugate system joined by *sp*-*sp* bonding

***Passage* 9.** Treatment of benzene with CO/HCl in the presence of anhydrous $AlCl_3/CuCl$ followed by reaction with AcO/NaOAc gives compound X as the major product. Compound X upon reaction with Br_2/Na_2CO_3, followed by heating at 473 K with moist KOH furnishes Y as the major product. Reaction of X with H_2/Pd-C, followed by H_3PO_4 treatment gives Z as the major product.

1. The compound Y is **[JEE Advanced 2018]**

(a) 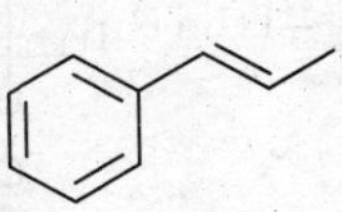

(b) 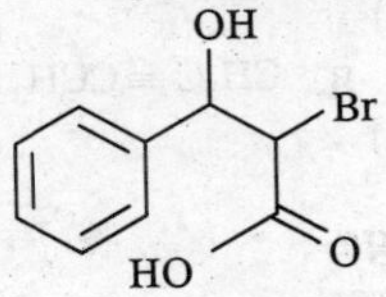

(c) 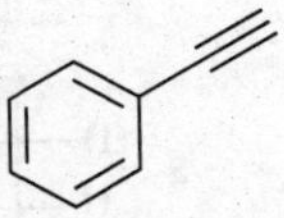

(d) 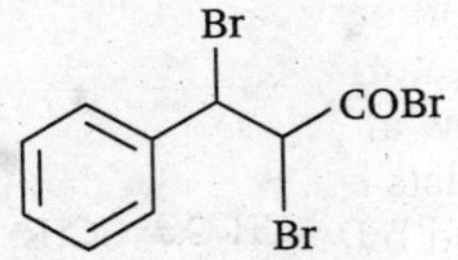

2. The compound Z is

(a) 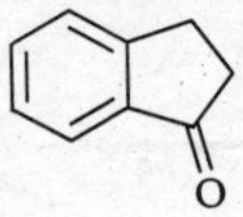

(b) 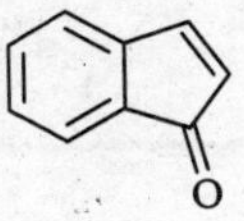

(c) 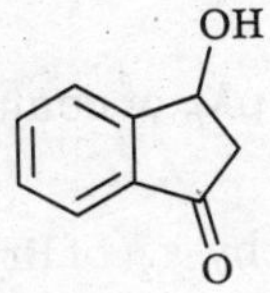

(d) 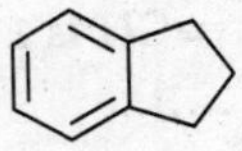

***Passage* 10.**

$$C_8H_6 \xrightarrow[H_2]{Pd\text{-}BaSO_4} C_8H_8 \xrightarrow[(ii)\ H_2O_2, NaOH, H_2O]{(i)\ B_2H_6} X$$

$$C_8H_6 \xrightarrow{H_2O,\ HgSO_4, H_2SO_4} C_8H_8O \xrightarrow[(ii)\ H^+,\ Heat]{(i)\ EtMgBr,\ H_2O} Y$$

[JEE Advanced 2015]

1. Compound X is

(a) 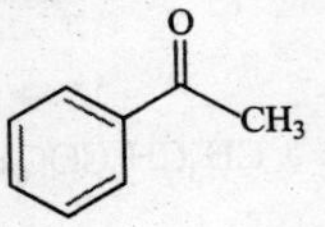

(b) 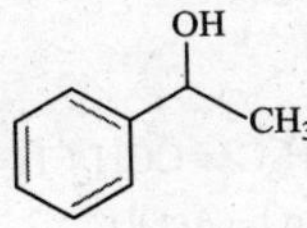

(c) 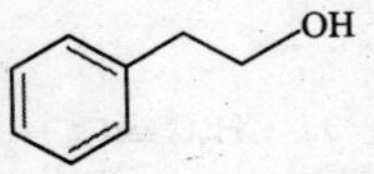

(d) 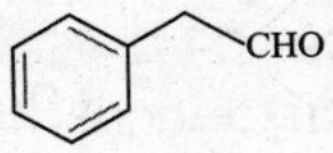

2. The major compound Y is

(a) 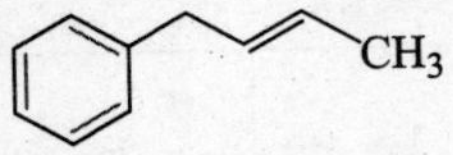

(b) 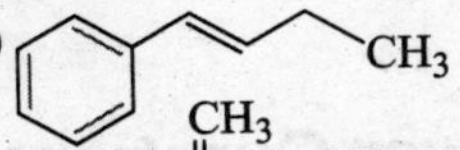

(c) 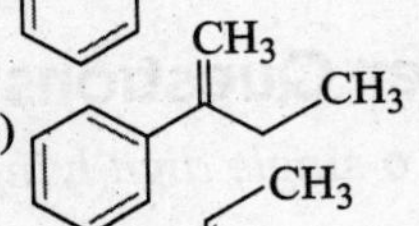

(d) 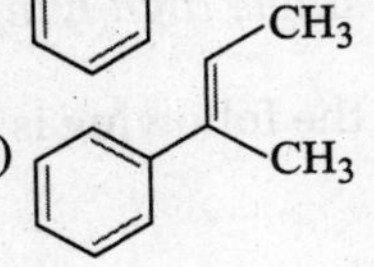

Matrix-Match Type

Given below are Matching Type Questions, with two columns (each having some items) each . Each item of Column I has to be matched with the items of Column II.

1. Match the hydrocarbons in Column I with the properties shown by them in Column II.

Column I	Column II
A. Ethyne	1. Reacts with 1 mole H_2 to form alkane
B. Propyne	2. Reacts with 2 moles H_2 to form alkane
C. Cyclopropane	3. Reacts with Cu_2Cl_2/NH_4OH
D. Cyclobutene	4. Has sp^3 and sp-hydridised carbon

2. Match the pair of hydrocarbons in Column I with the reagent/property in Column II to make distinction between them.

Column I	Column II
A. Ethane and ethene	1. Dipole moment
B. 1-butyne, 2-butyne	2. Br_2-water
C. Ethane and ethyne	3. $NH_4OH / AgNO_3$
D. *cis*-and *trans*- 2-butene	4. $BH_3 \cdot THF / NaOH - H_2O_2$

3. Match the following.

Column I (Alkyne + Reagent)	Column (II (Final product)
A. $R—C\equiv C—R$ + Pd/C/H_2 $\longrightarrow$	1. (R)(H)C=C(H)(R)
B. $R—C\equiv C—R$ + Li/NH_3 $\longrightarrow$	2. RCH_2CH_2R
C. $RC\equiv CR$ + Pd/$CaCO_3$/PbO/H_2 $\longrightarrow$	3. (R)(H)C=C(R)(H)
D. $R—C\equiv C—R$ + $\xrightarrow[CH_3COOH]{BH_3.THF}$	4. $RCH_2\overset{O}{\overset{\Vert}{C}}CH_3$

4. Match the following.

Column I (Alkynes)	Column II (Product of oxidative cleavage)
A. $CH_3C{\equiv}CCH_2CH_3 \xrightarrow[\Delta,\ H_2O]{MnO_4^-/OH^-}$	1. CH_3COOH
B. $CH_3C{\equiv}CCH_2CH{=}CHCH_3 \xrightarrow{CrO_3/AcOH}$	2. CH_3CH_2COOH
C. $CH_3C{\equiv}CCH_3 \xrightarrow{O_3/H_2O}$	3. $CH_3C{\equiv}CCH_2COOH$
D. $CH_3CH_2C{\equiv}CH \xrightarrow{O_3/H_2O}$	4. CO_2

5. Match the following.

Column I	Column II
A. $CH_3C{\equiv}CCH_3 \xrightarrow[Ni_2B\ (P\text{-}2)]{H_2} \xrightarrow{D_2/Pt}$	1. 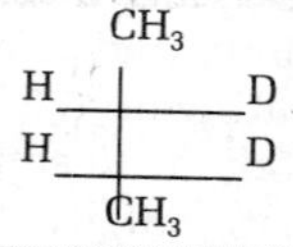
B. $CH_3C{\equiv}CCH_3 \xrightarrow{Na/EtOH} \xrightarrow{D_2/Pt}$	2. 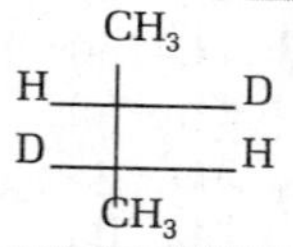
C. $CH_3C{\equiv}CCH_3 \xrightarrow{Li/NH_3} \xrightarrow{D_2/Pt}$	3. 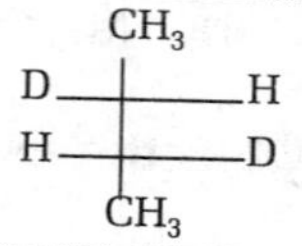
D. $CH_3C{\equiv}CCH_3 \xrightarrow{LiAlH_4} \xrightarrow{D_2/Pt}$	4. 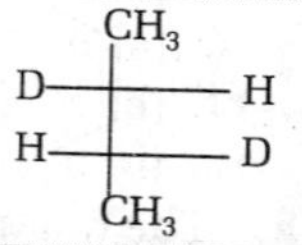

Single Integer Answer Questions

Answer of these questions is a single digit lying between 0 to 9.

1. Number of acidic hydrogens in the following is

$$CH_3\overset{O}{\overset{\|}{C}}CH_2\overset{O}{\overset{\|}{C}}CH_2C{\equiv}CH$$ ....

2. Mg_2C_3 is decomposed by H_2O forming propyne, numerical value of charge on C_3 is ....

3. Degree of unsaturation of C_3H_4 is ....

4. How many compounds are formed upon the ozonolysis of the following triyne?

5. How many carboxylic acids are formed in the following reaction?

$$RC{\equiv}CCH_2CH{=}CHR \xrightarrow{CrO_3\ \text{in AcOH}}$$

6. K_a of $RC{\equiv}CH$ is 1×10^{-5}. Hence, pK_b of conjugate base is ....

7. 1.35 g of 2-butyne is decolourised by x g of Br_2 water. x is ....

8. Degree of unsaturation in C_yH_8 is two. The value of y is ....

9. One mole of 1,2-dibromopropane on treatment with X moles of $NaNH_2$ followed by treatment with ethyl bromide gave a pentyne. The value of X is

10. Total number of hydroxyl groups present in a molecule of the major product P is .... **[JEE Advanced 2019]**

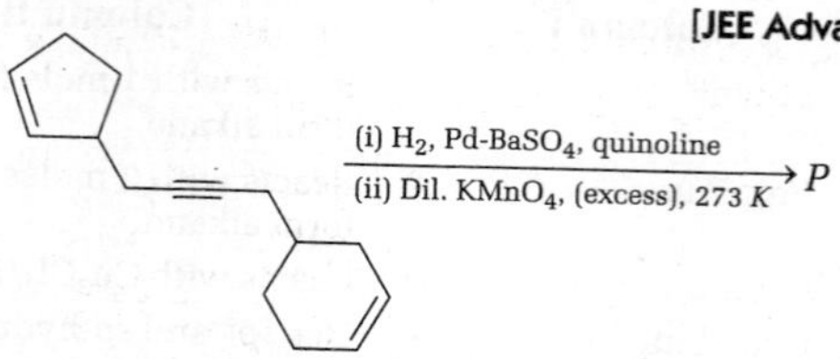

Answers

Objective Questions Type I [Only one correct option]

1. (d)	**2.** (b)	**3.** (b)	**4.** (a)	**5.** (c)	**6.** (a)	**7.** (c)	**8.** (d)	**9.** (b)	**10.** (c)
11. (a)	**12.** (b)	**13.** (b)	**14.** (d)	**15.** (a)	**16.** (a)	**17.** (a)	**18.** (a)	**19.** (d)	**20.** (d)
21. (b)	**22.** (b)	**23.** (c)	**24.** (a)	**25.** (c)	**26.** (d)	**27.** (b)	**28.** (c)	**29.** (b)	**30.** (c)
31. (a)	**32.** (b)	**33.** (c)	**34.** (d)	**35.** (c)	**36.** (c)	**37.** (a)	**38.** (d)	**39.** (a)	**40.** (b)
41. (a)	**42.** (a)	**43.** (b)	**44.** (c)	**45.** (a)	**46.** (a)	**47.** (a)	**48.** (c)	**49.** (a)	**50.** (a)
51. (c)	**52.** (d)	**53.** (b)	**54.** (a)	**55.** (d)	**56.** (c)	**57.** (d)	**58.** (b)	**59.** (d)	**60.** (b)
61. (c)	**62.** (d)	**63.** (d)	**64.** (a)	**65.** (c)	**66.** (a)	**67.** (d)	**68.** (b)	**69.** (b)	**70.** (d)
71. (c)	**72.** (c)	**73.** (a)	**74.** (d)	**75.** (d)	**76.** (c)	**77.** (b)	**78.** (a)	**79.** (d)	**80.** (c)
81. (d)	**82.** (a)								

Objective Questions Type II [One or more than one correct option(s)]

1. (c)	**2.** (a)	**3.** (a)	**4.** (a, c)	**5.** (a, b, c, d)
6. (a, b)	**7.** (a, c, d)	**8.** (a, b, c)	**9.** (a)	**10.** (b, c)
11. (b, c)	**12.** (a, c, d)	**13.** (a, b)	**14.** (a, b)	**15.** (b)
16. (b, c)				

Comprehension Based Questions

Passage 1 – 1. (b)
Passage 2 – 1. (a,b,c) 2. (c)
Passage 3 – 1. (a,c,d) 2. (d)
Passage 4 – 1. (b) 2. (b) 3. (c)
Passage 5 – 1. (d) 2. (a) 3. (b)
Passage 6 – 1. (d) 2. (b)
Passage 7 – 1. (b) 2. (c) 3. (a,b,c)
Passage 8 – 1. (c) 2. (b) 3. (a,b,c,d)
Passage 9 – 1. (c) 2. (a)
Passage 10 – 1. (c) 2. (d)

Matrix-Match Type

1. A→(3); B→(4); C→(1); D→(2)
2. A→(2); B→(4); C→(3); D→(1)
3. A→(2); B→(1); C→(3); D→(4)
4. A→(1,4); B→(2,3); C→(1,4); D→(2,3)
5. A→(1,2); B→(1,3); C→(1); D→(2,4)

Single Integer Answer Questions

1. (3)	**2.** (4)	**3.** (2)	**4.** (4)	**5.** (2)	**6.** (9)	**7.** (8)	**8.** (5)	**9.** (2)	**10.** (6)

Solutions

Objective Questions Type I [Only one correct option]

1. (*d*) $CaC_2 \equiv Ca^{2+} + C_2^{2-}\ (^-C{\equiv}C^-)$

$Mg_2C_3 \equiv 2Mg^{2+} + C_3^{4-}\ (^{3-}C{-}C{\equiv}C^-)$

2. (*b*) $(^{3-}C{-}C{\equiv}C^-)$

4. (*a*) $\underset{\text{2-hexyne}}{CH_3CH{=}CHCH_2CH_2CH_3} \xrightarrow[H_2O]{NaNH_2} \underset{\text{1-hexyne}}{CH_3{=}CHCH_2CH_2CH_2CH_3}$

5. (*c*) $\begin{matrix} CHCOONa \\ \| \\ CHCOONa \end{matrix} \xrightarrow{\text{Current}} \begin{matrix} CHCOO^- \\ \| \\ CHCOO^- \end{matrix} + 2Na^+$

At anode $\begin{matrix} CHCOO^- \\ \| \\ CHCOO^- \end{matrix} \longrightarrow \begin{matrix} CH \\ \||| \\ CH \end{matrix} + 2CO_2 + 2e^-$

At cathode $2Na^+ + 2e^- \longrightarrow 2Na$

$2Na + 2H_2O \longrightarrow 2NaOH + H_2$

8. (*d*)

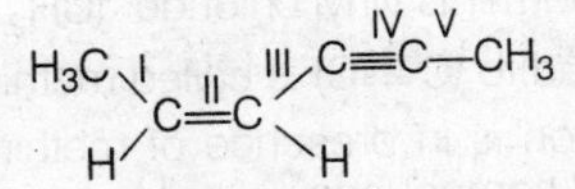

C—C bond length $\propto \dfrac{1}{\text{hybridisation}}$

IV < II < III < V < I

10. (*c*) $\underset{\text{Ethane}}{(C{-}C)} < \underset{\text{Ethene}}{(C{=}C)} < \underset{\text{Ethyne}}{(C{\equiv}C)}$

11. (*a*) $H_3C{-}C{\equiv}C{-}CH_3 \xrightarrow{\text{I or II}}$ *cis*-but-2-ene

$\xrightarrow{\text{III}}$ *trans*-but-2-ene.

13. (*b*)

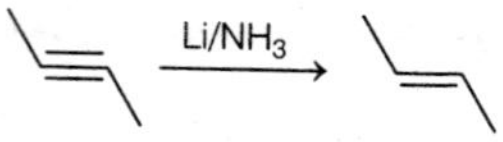

14. (*d*) $NH_3 + Na \longrightarrow \underbrace{NH_3.e^- \text{ (deep blue colour)}}_{\text{Solvated electrons}} + Na^+$

Solvated electrons reduce alkynes to *trans*-alkene. The *anti* stereochemistry of the sodium-ammonia reduction appears is to result from the greater stabilty of the vinyl radical in the *trans*-configuration where the alkyl groups are farther apart.

An electron is added to the *trans*-radical to give a *trans*-vinyl anion, which is quickly protonated to the *trans*-vinyl anion, *trans*-alkene.

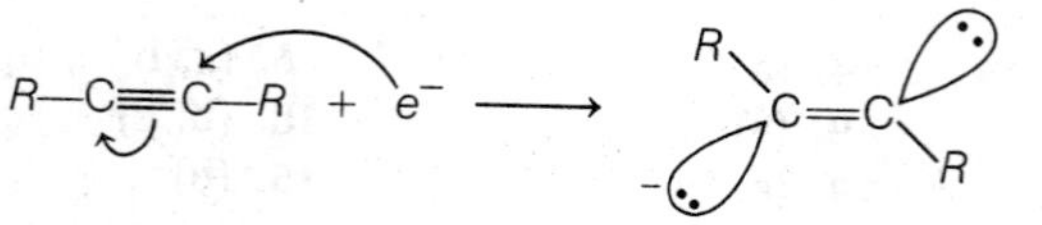

16. (*b*) $CH{\equiv}CH + \overset{\oplus}{H}{-}\overset{\ominus}{O}H \longrightarrow \underset{\text{Vinyl alcohol}}{CH_2{=}CHOH}$

17. (*a*) $\underset{sp}{HC{\equiv}CH} < \underset{sp^2}{CH_2{=}CH_2} < \underset{sp^3}{CH_3{-}CH_3}$

18. (*a*) Enols are unstable and exist in equilibrium with keto form.

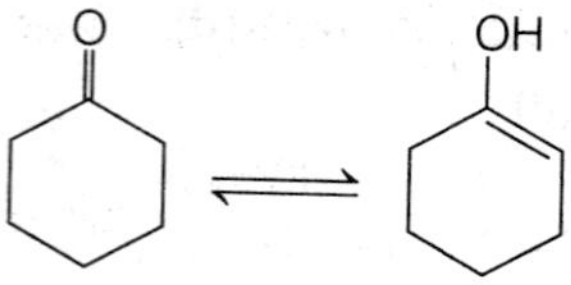

19. (*d*) $CH_3CH_2C{\equiv}CH \xrightarrow[HgSO_4/H_2SO_4]{H_2O} CH_3CH_2\overset{O}{\overset{\|}{C}}CH_3$

or $CH_3C{\equiv}CCH_3$

21. (*b*) CH=CH (bridged by $\overset{\oplus}{Br}$) is less stable.

22. (*b*) $HC{\equiv}CH \xrightarrow[CCl_4]{Br_2}$ $\underset{trans}{\overset{Br}{\underset{H}{>}}C{=}C\overset{H}{\underset{Br}{<}}}$

24. (*c*) PVC is polyvinyl chloride.

Thus, monomer is vinyl chloride ($CH_2{=}CHCl$).

26. (*d*) H attached to ($C{\equiv}C$) is called methine hydrogen.

27. (*b*) Ethinylation is in presence of methine H and a reacts with carbonyl compounds.

28. (*c*) $CH{\equiv}CCH_2CH_2CH{=}CHCH_3$

↑ This is not cleaved; ↑ This is cleaved by CrO_3/CH_3COOH

↓

$CH{\equiv}CCH_2CH_2COOH + CH_3COOH$

29. (*b*)

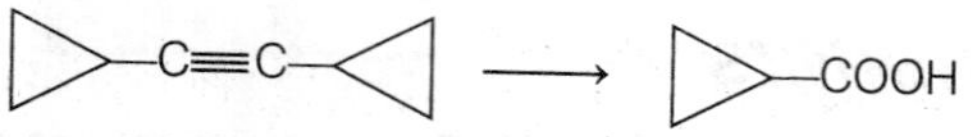

$\underset{A}{C_8H_{10}}$ $\underset{B}{C_3H_5COOH}$

Formation of *B* indicates that *A* is symmetrical.

30. (*c*)
(a) and (b) react with ($C{=}C$) and ($C{\equiv}C$) bond.
(d) Cleaves ($C{=}C$) bond forming acid without affecting ($C{\equiv}C$) bond.
(c) HCO_3H (perexy formic acid reacts with ($C{=}C$) bond forming diol.)

31. (*a*) If acid is weak, conjugate base is strong. Greater the s-character of C-atom in hydrocarbon, greater the electronegativity, hence stronger the acid.

	$HC\equiv CH$ ↑ sp	$CH_2{=}CH_2$ ↑ sp^2	$CH_3{-}CH_3$ ↑ sp^3
s-character	50%	33%	25%
Electronegativity of carbon	Maximum		
Acidic nature	Maximum		
Conjugate base	$CH{\equiv}C^{\ominus}$	$CH_2{=}\overset{\ominus}{C}H$	$CH_3\overset{\ominus}{C}H_2$

33. (*c*) $CH_3C{\equiv}CCH_3 \xrightarrow{AgNO_3 \text{ in } NH_3 \,|\, Cu_2Cl_2 \text{ in } NH_3}$ No reaction

$CH_3CH_2C{\equiv}CH \xrightarrow{AgNO_3 \text{ in } NH_3} \underset{\text{White ppt.}}{CH_3CH_2C{\equiv}CAg}$

$CH_3CH_2C{\equiv}CH \xrightarrow{Cu_2Cl_2 \text{ in } NH_3} \underset{\text{Red ppt.}}{CH_3CH_2C{\equiv}CCu}$

34. (*d*) Electronegativity : $\underset{sp}{HC{\equiv}CH} > \underset{sp^2}{H_2C{=}CH_2} > \underset{sp^3}{H_3C{-}CH_3}$

37. (*a*) $3CH_3C{\equiv}CH \xrightarrow{BH_3 \cdot THF} \left(CH_3CH{=}\underset{H}{\underset{|}{C}}{-}\right)_3 B$

$\xrightarrow{H_2O_2/OH^-} \underset{\text{Unstable}}{CH_3CH{=}\underset{H}{\underset{|}{C}}OH} \xrightarrow{\text{Tautomerises}} CH_3CH_2CHO$

38. (*d*) $CH_3C{\equiv}C{-}CH_3 \xrightarrow{BH_3 \cdot THF} \left(H{-}\overset{H_3C}{\overset{|}{C}}{=}\overset{CH_3}{\overset{|}{C}}{-}\right)_3 B$

cis-isomer formed by *syn*-addition

$\xrightarrow{H_2O_2/OH^-} \underset{\text{Enol}}{H{-}\overset{CH_3}{\overset{|}{C}}{=}\overset{CH_3}{\overset{|}{C}}{-}OH} \xrightarrow{\text{Tautomerises}} CH_3CH_2\overset{O}{\overset{\|}{C}}CH_3$

$$CH_3C{\equiv}CH \xrightarrow[H_2O_2/OH^-]{BH_3 \cdot THF} CH_3CH_2CHO \text{ (Q. 37)}$$

Thus, (a), (b) and (c) are correct.

39. (*a*) $CH_3CH_2C{\equiv}CH \xrightarrow[NaNH_2]{Alc.\ KOH} CH_3C{\equiv}CCH_3$

40. (*b*) $CH{\equiv}CH \longrightarrow \overset{\oplus}{C}H{=}\overset{\ominus}{C}H \xrightarrow[CH_2Cl_2]{NH_4Cl}$

$$CH{\equiv}C{-}CH{=}CH_2$$

41. (*a*) $CH_3CH_2C{\equiv}CH \longleftarrow$ terminal alkyne

(gives white precipitate with $AgNO_3/NH_4OH$ and red precipitate with Cu_2Cl_2/NH_4OH)

$$CH_2{=}CHCH{=}CH_2 \longrightarrow \overset{\oplus}{C}H_2{-}CH{=}CH{-}\overset{\ominus}{C}H_2 \xrightarrow{Br_2} \underset{Br}{CH_2}{-}CH{=}CH{-}\underset{Br}{CH_2}$$

1,4-dibromo-2-butene

42. (*a*)

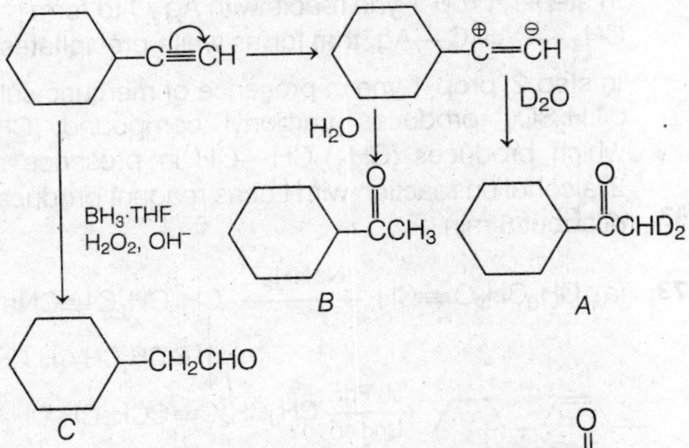

43. (*b*) $CH{\equiv}CH + CH_3COO^{\ominus}H^{\oplus} \longrightarrow CH_3CH(O\overset{O}{\overset{\|}{C}}CH_3)_2$ (*A*)

$\xrightarrow{H_2O/H_2SO_4,\ HgSO_4} CH_3CHO\ (B) + (CH_3CO)_2O\ (C)$; $A \xrightarrow{\Delta} B + C$

$$2CH_3COOH \xrightarrow{P_2O_5} (CH_3CO)_2O$$

44. (*c*)

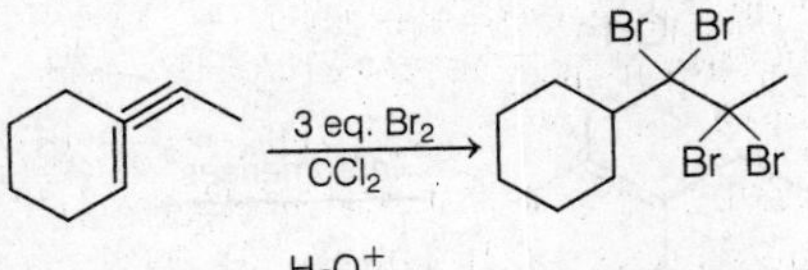

46. (*a*) $A + CH_3MgBr \xrightarrow{H_3O^+} CH_3CH_2CH_2OH$

Thus, *A* is 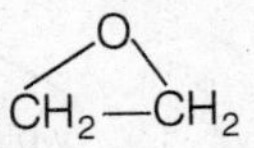

$$CH{\equiv}CH \xrightarrow{NaNH_2} CH{\equiv}C^{\ominus} \xrightarrow{A} CH{\equiv}CCH_2CH_2OH$$

47. (*a*)

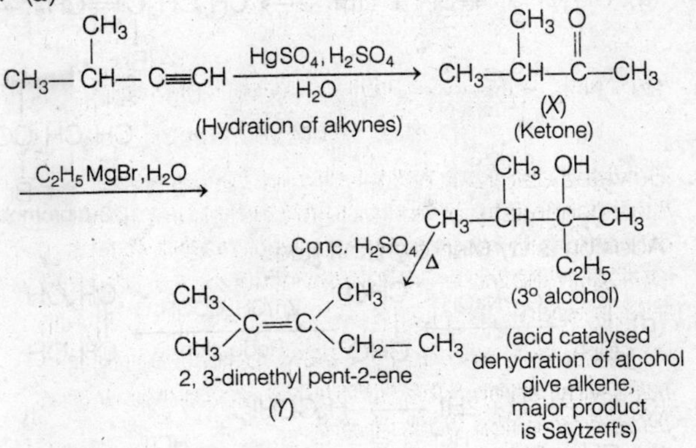

48. (*c*)

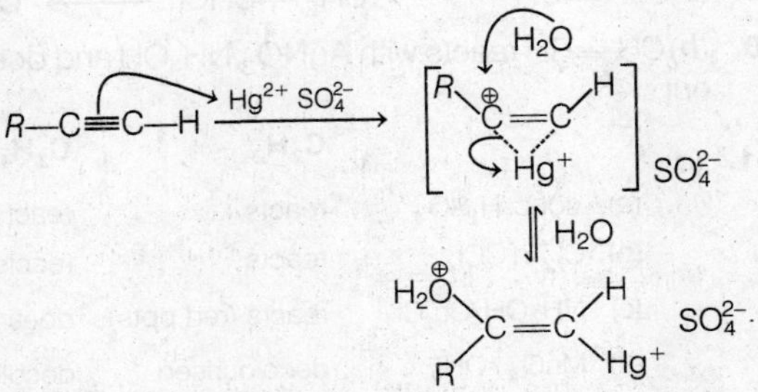

50. (*a*) $CH{\equiv}CH \xrightarrow{2HCHO} HOH_2C{-}C{\equiv}C{-}CH_2OH \xrightarrow{Li/NH_3} HOH_2C{-}CH{=}CH{-}CH_2OH$

(*trans*)

51. (*c*) Sodium metal in liquid ammonia reduces alkynes with anti stereochemistry to give *trans* alkenes. The reduction is selectively *anti* since the vinyl radical formed during reduction is more stable in *trans* configuration.

Mechanism

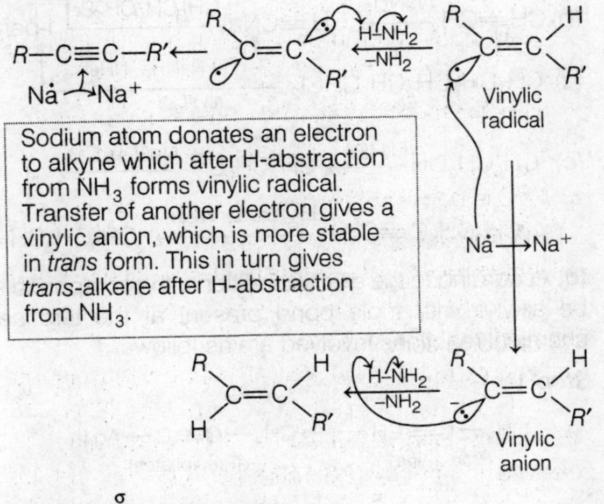

52. (*d*) $-C\overset{\sigma}{\underset{2\pi}{\equiv}}C-$ 2π and 1σ

53. (*b*) $CH_3CH_2C{\equiv}CH \longrightarrow CH_3CH_2COOH + HCOOH \rightarrow CO_2$

54. (*a*) $CH_3CH_2C{\equiv}CH + HBr \longrightarrow CH_3CH_2\underset{\underset{Br}{|}}{C}{=}CH_2 \xrightarrow{HBr} CH_3CH_2\overset{\overset{Br}{|}}{\underset{\underset{Br}{|}}{C}}CH_3$

2,2-dibromobutane

Addition is by Markownikoff rule.

55. (*d*) $\begin{matrix}CH\\ |||\\ CH\end{matrix} \xrightarrow{O_3/NaOH} \begin{matrix}CHO\\ |\\ CHO\end{matrix} \xrightarrow[\text{Reduction}]{Zn/CH_3COOH} \begin{matrix}CH_2OH\\ |\\ CH_2OH\end{matrix}$

56. (*c*) $HC{\equiv}CH + 2HI \longrightarrow H_3CCHI_2$

58. (*b*) $CH{\equiv}CH \xrightarrow{HCl} CH_2{=}CHCl \xrightarrow{HCl} CH_3CHCl_2$

60. (*b*) $CH{\equiv}CH$ reacts with $AgNO_3/NH_4OH$ and does not come out.

61. (*c*)

		C_2H_2	C_2H_4
(a)	conc. H_2SO_4	reacts	reacts
(b)	Cl_2 in CCl_4	reacts	reacts
(c)	NH_4OH/Cu_2Cl_2	reacts (red ppts)	does not react
(d)	MnO_4^-/OH^-	decolourised	decolourised

63. (*d*) $CH{\equiv}CH \xrightarrow{MnO_4^-/OH^-} \begin{matrix}COOH\\ |\\ COOH\end{matrix}$

66. (*a*) RCH_2CH_3 is a weak acid and cannot protonate $RC{\equiv}C^{\ominus}$. Thus, $K < 1$.

67. (*d*) (a) $\underset{\text{1-pentene}}{CH_3CH_2CH_2CH{=}CH_2} \xrightarrow{Cl_2} CH_3CH_2CH_2\underset{\underset{Cl}{|}}{CH}\underset{\underset{Cl}{|}}{CH_2} \xrightarrow{NaNH_2} CH_3CH_2CH_2C{\equiv}CH$

(b) $CH{\equiv}CH \xrightarrow{NaNH_2} CH{\equiv}CNa \xrightarrow{CH_3CH_2CH_2Br}$ 1-pentyne

(c) $CH_3CH_2CH_2CH_2CHCl_2 \xrightarrow[\text{(ii) } H_2O]{\text{(i) } NaNH_2,\ NH_3}$ 1-pentyne

71. (*c*) $CH_3CH_2OH \xrightarrow{HBr} CH_3CH_2Br \xrightarrow{NaC{\equiv}CH} CH_3CH_2C{\equiv}CH \xrightarrow{H_2/Pd\ \text{Lindlar}} CH_3CH_2CH{=}CH_2$

72. (*c*) According to the given conditions, the compound should be alkyne with triple bond present at the terminal. The chemical reactions involved are as follows

***Step* 1**

$\underset{\underset{(A)}{\text{Prop-1-yne}}}{CH_3{-}C{\equiv}CH} \xrightarrow{Ag_2O} \underset{\text{(Precipitates)}}{CH_3{-}C{\equiv}C{-}Ag\downarrow}$

***Step* 2**

$CH_3{-}C{\equiv}CH \xrightarrow[\text{Dil. } H_2SO_4]{Hg^{2+}} \left[CH_3{-}\overset{\overset{OH}{|}}{C}{=}CH_2 \xrightleftharpoons{\text{Tautomerisation}} CH_3{-}\overset{\overset{O}{||}}{C}\,CH_3\right]$

(Propan-2-one) (*B*)

$\xrightarrow{NaBH_4} CH_3{-}\underset{\underset{OH}{|}}{CH}{-}CH_3$ (*C*) (2° alcohol)

$\xrightarrow{\text{Conc. HCl + } ZnCl_2} CH_3{-}\underset{\underset{Cl}{|}}{CH}{-}CH_3$

Turbidity within 5 minutes (Insoluble in Lucas reagent)

In step-1, prop-1-yne reacts with Ag_2O to form $CH_3{-}C{\equiv}C{-}Ag$, that forms white precipitates.

In step 2, prop-1-yne in presence of mercuric sulphate and dil. H_2SO_4 produces carbonyl compound $(CH_3)_2C{=}O$, which produces $(CH_3)_2CH{-}OH$ in presence of $NaBH_4$. 2°alcohol on reaction with Lucas reagent produces turbidity in about 5 min.

73. (*a*) $CH_3CH_2C{\equiv}CH \xrightarrow{NaNH_2} CH_3CH_2C{\equiv}CNa \xrightarrow{BrCH_2CH_2CH_2CH_2CH_3} CH_3CH_2C{\equiv}CCH_2CH_2CH_2CH_2CH_3 \xrightarrow[\text{Lindlar}]{H_2/Pd}$

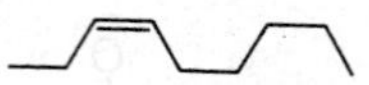

3-nonene

74. (*d*) (a)

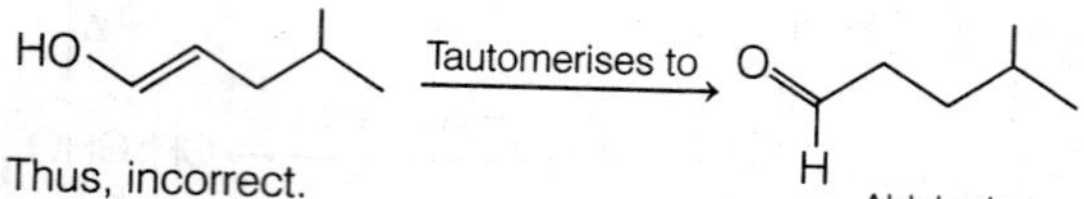

Aldehyde

Thus, incorrect.

(b)

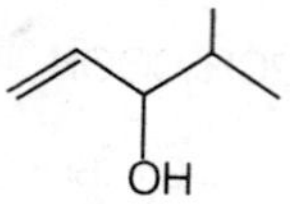

it is not enol. Thus, incorrect.

(c)

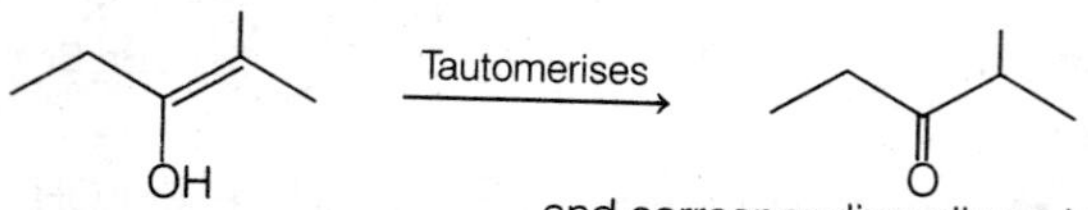

and corresponding alkyne is

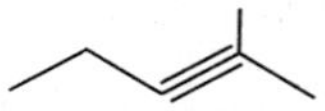

which is incorrect.

(d) 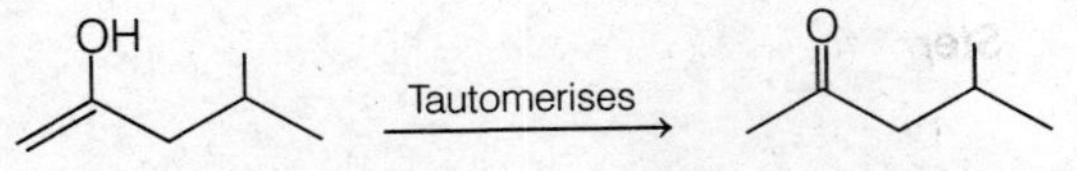

and corresponding alkyne is

75. (*d*) The major product obtained in the given reaction is $CH_3C\ (I)\ (Cl)\ CHD_2$.

$$CH_3C\equiv CH \xrightarrow[\text{2. DI}]{\text{1. DCl (1 equiv.)}} CH_3C\ (I)(Cl)CHD_2$$

Addition in unsymmetrical alkynes takes place according to Markownikoff's rule. Reaction proceed as follows :

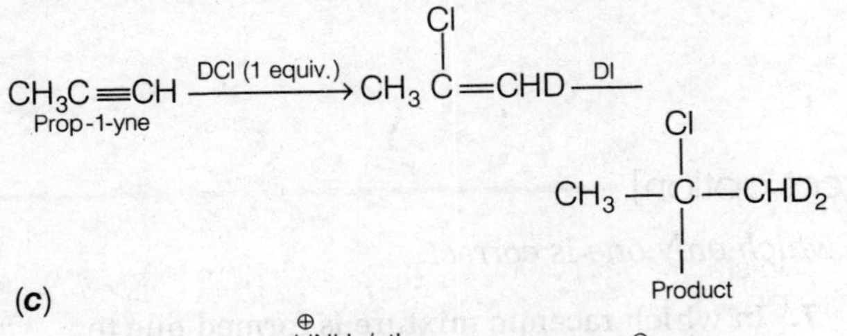

76. (*c*)

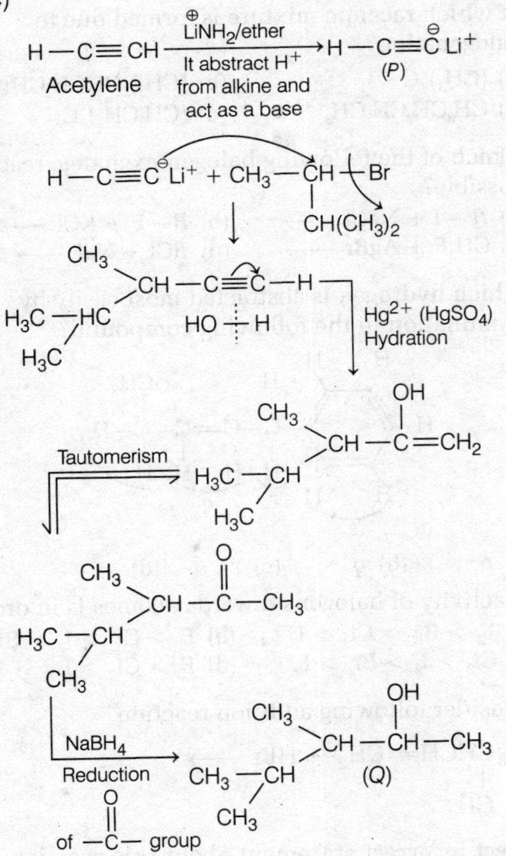

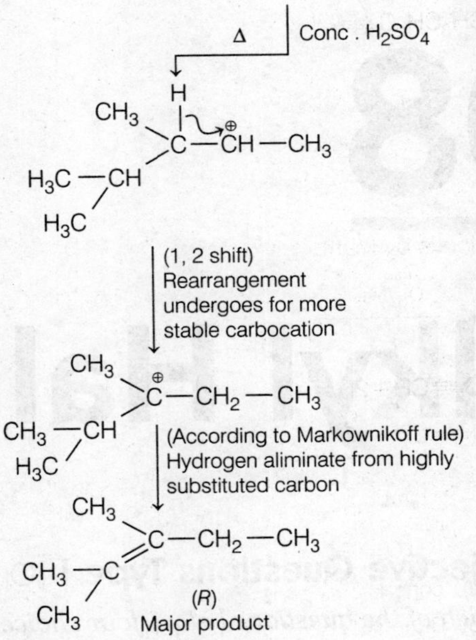

So,correct option is (c).

77. (*b*) $HC\equiv CH + RO^{\ominus} \rightleftharpoons HC\equiv C^{\ominus} + ROH$

(Not possible)

79. (*d*) Partially deactivated palladised charcoal ($H_2/Pd/CaCO_3$) is Lindlar catalyst.

80. (*c*) Ethene ($H_2C=CH_2$) is sp^2-hybridised and ethyne ($HC\equiv CH$) is *sp*-hybridised. In ethyne, the *sp*-hybridised carbon atom possesses maximum *s*-character and hence, maximum electronegativity.

Due to which, it attracts the shared electron pair of C—H bond to a greater extent and makes the removal of proton easier. Hence, alkyne is much more acidic than alkene. Presence of electron donating group in alkyne ($H_3C—C\equiv CH$) decreases the acidic strength of compound. Hence, the correct order of acidic strength is

$$HC\equiv CH > H_3C—C\equiv CH > CH_2=CH_2$$

82. (*a*)

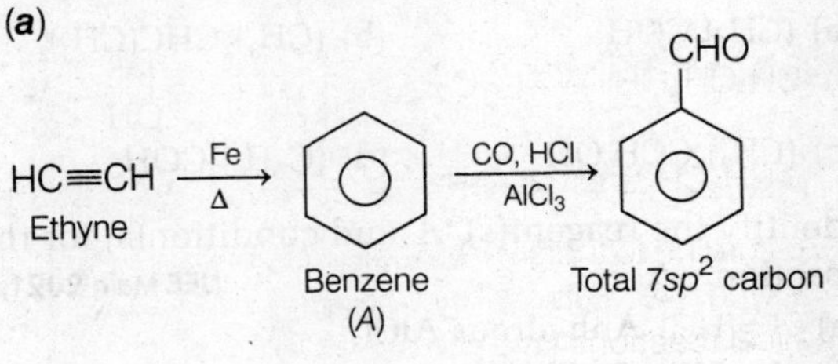

08

Alkyl Halides

Objective Questions Type I [Only one correct option]

In each of the questions below, four choices are given of which only one is correct.

1. Which is maximum reactive towards HCl ?

(a) $CH_2{=}CHCH_2OH$ (b) $CH_3CH_2CH_2OH$

(c) $CH_3\underset{OH}{\underset{|}{C}}HCH_3$ (d) $CH_2{=}CHOH$

2. When 3-methyl-2-butanol reacts with $HCl/ZnCl_2$ most stable intermediate formed is

(a) $(CH_3)_2CH\overset{\oplus}{C}HCH_3$ (b) $(CH_3)_2\overset{\oplus}{C}CH_2CH_3$

(c) $(CH_3)_2CHCH_2\overset{\oplus}{C}H_2$ (d) $CH_3\underset{\oplus CH_2}{\underset{|}{C}}HCH_2CH_3$

3. Which mechanism (S_N1 or S_N2) is followed in the protonation of CH_3CH_2OH and $(CH_3)_2CHOH$?

(a) S_N1 in both (b) S_N2 in both

(c) S_N1 and S_N2 (d) S_N2 and S_N1

4. Which is not the tertiary alcohol?

(a) $(CH_3)_3COH$ (b) $(CH_3)_2CH\underset{OH}{\underset{|}{C}}(CH_3)_2$

(c) $(CH_3)_3CCH_2OH$ (d) $(C_6H_5)_3COH$

5. Identify the reagent(s) '*A*' and condition(s) for the reaction **[JEE Main 2021, March]**

(a) $A = HCl$, Anhydrous $AlCl_3$

(b) $A = HCl$, $ZnCl_2$

(c) $A = Cl_2$, UV light

(d) $A = Cl_2$ dark, Anhydrous $AlCl_3$

6. Which is not the intermediate in the halogenation of toluene at benzylic position?

(a) 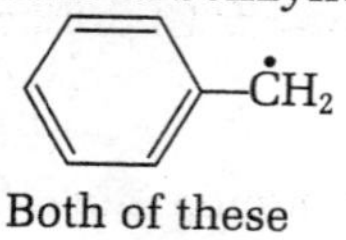 (b) 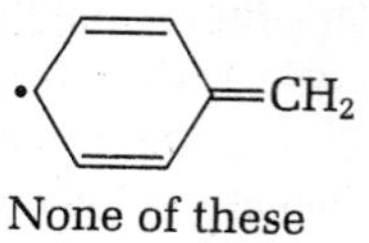

(c) Both of these (d) None of these

7. In which racemic mixture is formed due to halogenation?

(a) $(CH_3)_4C$ (b) $(CH_3)_2CHCH_2CH(CH_3)_2$

(c) $CH_3CH_2CH_2CH_3$ (d) $(CH_3CH_2)_4C$

8. Which of the following halogen-exchange reactions is possible?

(a) $R{-}I + NaCl \longrightarrow$ (b) $R{-}F + KCl \longrightarrow$

(c) $CH_3F + AgBr \longrightarrow$ (d) $RCl + NaI \longrightarrow$

9. Which hydrogen is abstracted most easily by bromination in the following compound?

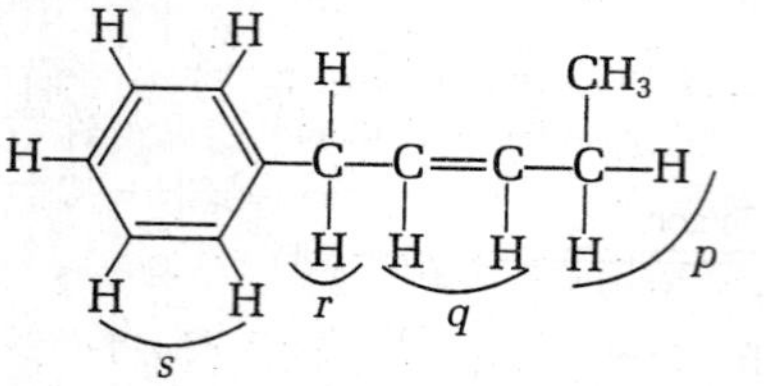

(a) *p* (b) *q* (c) *r* (d) *s*

10. Reactivity of halogens towards alkanes is in order

(a) $F_2 > Br_2 > Cl_2 > I_2$ (b) $F_2 > Cl_2 > I_2 > Br_2$

(c) $Cl_2 > I_2 > Br_2 > F_2$ (d) $F_2 > Cl_2 > Br_2 > I_2$

11. Consider following addition reaction,

$$CH_3\underset{CH_3}{\underset{|}{C}}HCH{=}CH_2 + HBr \longrightarrow$$

Select incorrect statement about this reaction.

(a) It follows electrophilic addition mechanism

(b) Most stable intermediate is the carbocation

$$CH_3\underset{CH_3}{\underset{|}{C}}H\overset{\oplus}{C}HCH_3$$

(c) Final product is $(CH_3)_2\underset{\displaystyle Br}{\underset{|}{C}}CH_2CH_3$

(d) In presence of benzoyl peroxide final product is $(CH_3)_2CHCH_2CH_2Br$

12. Intermediate (*A*) given below can change to

$H_3C{-}\overset{\displaystyle CH_3}{\overset{|}{\underset{\displaystyle CH_3}{\underset{|}{C}}}}{-}\underset{\oplus}{C}HCH_3$ (*A*)

(a) $H_3C{-}\overset{\displaystyle CH_3}{\overset{|}{\underset{\displaystyle CH_3}{\underset{|}{C}}}}{-}CH_2\overset{\oplus}{C}H_2$ by 1,2-hydride shift

(b) $H_3C{-}\overset{\displaystyle CH_3}{\overset{|}{\underset{\displaystyle \underset{\oplus}{C}H_2}{\underset{|}{C}}}}{-}CH_2CH_3$ by 1,3-hydride shift

(c) $H_3C{-}\overset{\displaystyle CH_3}{\overset{|}{\underset{\oplus}{C}}}{-}\underset{\displaystyle CH_3}{\underset{|}{C}}HCH_3$ by 1,2-methyl shift

(d) $H_3C{-}\overset{\displaystyle CH_3}{\overset{|}{\underset{\oplus}{C}}}{-}CH_2CH_2CH_3$ by 1,3-methyl shift

13. Best yield of alkyl halide (R—X) is formed in $RCO_2Ag + X_2 \longrightarrow RX + CO_2 + AgX$ when X_2 is

(a) Cl_2 (b) Br_2
(c) I_2 (d) F_2

14. Addition of HBr gives same product in the presence or absence of peroxide when alkene is

(a) 1-butene (b) isobutene
(c) 2,3-dimethyl-2-butene (d) propene

15. Maximum yield of following alkyl bromide is formed by Borodine-Hunsdiecker reaction

(a) CH_3CH_2Br (b) $(CH_3)_2CHBr$
(c) $(CH_3)_3CBr$ (d) C_6H_5Br

16. $CHCl_3$ is one of the products in the following reaction when *A* is

$A + Cl_2 + NaOH \xrightarrow{\Delta}$

(a) $CH_3\overset{\displaystyle O}{\overset{\|}{C}}OH$ (b) $CH_3\overset{\displaystyle OH}{\overset{|}{C}}HCH_3$
(c) $CH_3CH_2\underset{\displaystyle OH}{\underset{|}{C}}HCH_2CH_3$ (d) in all cases

17. Westron and westrosol respectively are

(a) $CHCl_2CHCl_2, CCl_2{=}CCl_2$
(b) $CCl_2{=}CCl_2, CHCl_2CHCl_2$
(c) $CHCl_2CHCl_2, CCl_2{=}CHCl$
(d) $CCl_2{=}CHCl, CHCl_2CHCl_2$

18. Moth repellent is

(a) perchloroethane (b) *p*-dichlorobenzene
(c) Both (a) and (b) (d) None of these

19. Fire extinguisher under the trade name pyrene is

(a) CCl_4 (b) CO_2 (c) H_2O (d) $COCl_2$

20. Ozone-layer is not depleted by

(a) CF_2Cl_2 (b) C_7H_{16}
(c) Freon-12 (d) All of these

21. Select correct statement (s).

(a) Strongest force of attraction in alkyl halide is the London force
(b) London force is a surface attraction
(c) Molecules with larger surface area have higher b.p.
(d) All of the above are correct statements

22. Which has maximum boiling point?

(a) CH_3OH (b) CH_3CH_2I (c) CH_3CH_2Cl (d) CH_3CH_2Br

23. Boiling point of alkyl halides is influenced by

(a) London force of attraction
(b) dipole-dipole attraction
(c) Both of the above
(d) None of the above

24. Select correct statement (s) about following reaction

$C_2H_5\bar{O} + CH_3CH_2\overset{\displaystyle Br}{\overset{|}{C}}HCH_3 \xrightarrow{C_2H_5OH}$

(a) It is termed as β-elimination reaction
(b) $C_2H_5\bar{O}$ is a Bronsted-base
(c) Products are 1-butene and 2-butene
(d) All of the above are correct statements

25. β-elimination is not possible in

(a) $CHCl_3$ (b) $(CH_3)_3CBr$
(c) $(CH_3)_2CHBr$ (d) $(CH_3)_2CHCH_2Br$

26. Following alkyl halides change to carbocation by E1 mechanism.

(a) $CH_3\underset{\displaystyle CH_3}{\underset{|}{C}}HCH_2Cl$ (b) $CH_3\underset{\displaystyle CH_3}{\underset{|}{C}}HCl$
(c) Both (a) and (b) (d) None of these

27. Slow and fast steps are respectively

$CH_3\underset{\displaystyle Br}{\underset{|}{C}}HCH_3 \xrightarrow{I} CH_3\underset{\oplus}{C}HCH_3 \xrightarrow{II} CH_3CH{=}CH_2$

(a) I and II (b) II and I
(c) Both are slow steps
(d) Both are fast steps

28. Select incorrect statement.

(a) Reactivity of alkyl halides towards E1 or E2 reaction is 3° > 2° > 1° alkyl halide
(b) E1 reaction is stereospecific
(c) Dehydrohalogenation is *trans*-elimination
(d) E1 and S_N1 reactions are competitive

29. 1-methyl ethylene oxide when treated with an excess of HBr produces : **[JEE Main 2020, Jan.]**

(a) 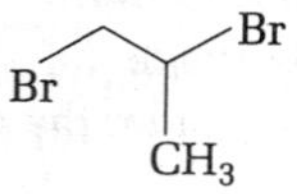
(b) 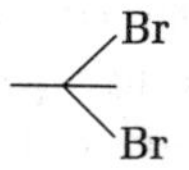
(c) 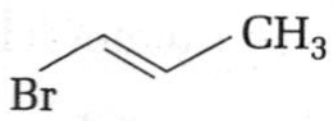
(d) 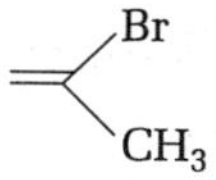

30. Following reactions take place in presence of

I. 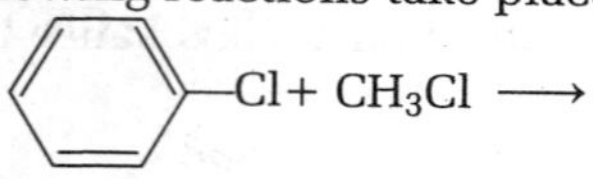

II. $CH_3\underset{|}{C}HCH_3$ (Cl) + $CH_3CH_2\bar{O} \longrightarrow$

(a) $AlCl_3, AlCl_3$ (b) $AlCl_3, CH_3CH_2OH$
(c) $OH^-, AlCl_3$ (d) $CH_3CH_2OH, AlCl_3$

31. Among the following compounds, which one has the shortest C—Cl bond? **[JEE Main 2020, Sep.]**

(a) H_3C—Cl
(b) 
(c) 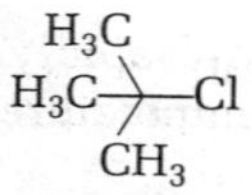
(d) 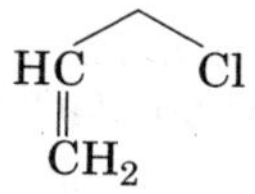

32. *A* is formed when benzene reacts with .... in presence of $AlCl_3$

A : 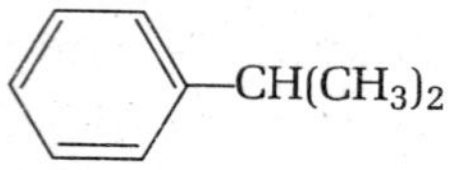

(a) $(CH_3)_2CHBr$ (b) $CH_3CH_2CH_2Br$
(c) Both (a) and (b) (d) None of these

33. In the following reaction σ-complex is

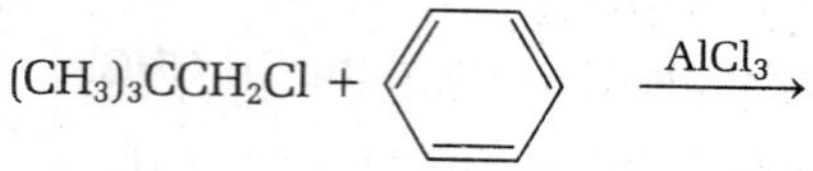

(a) 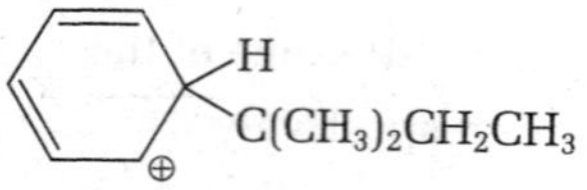
(b) 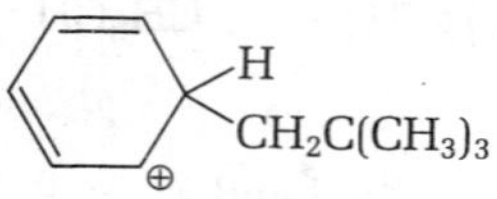
(c) 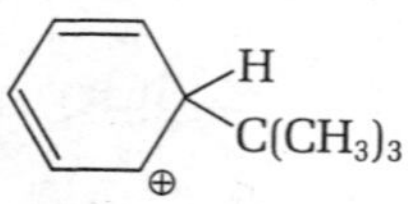
(d) None of the above

34. Find the major product *A*. **[JEE Main 2021, March]**

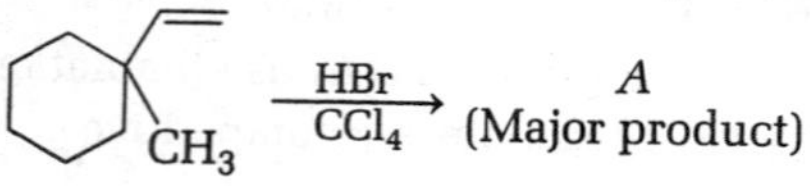

(a) 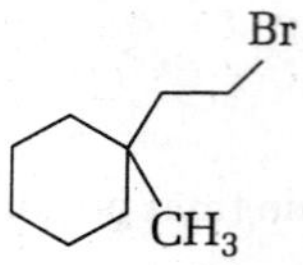
(b) 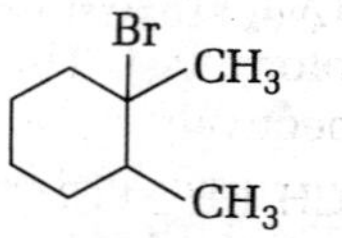
(c) 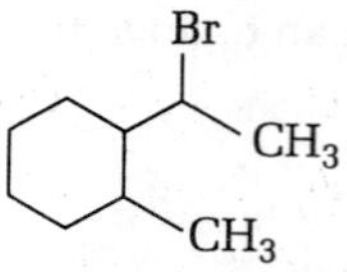
(d) 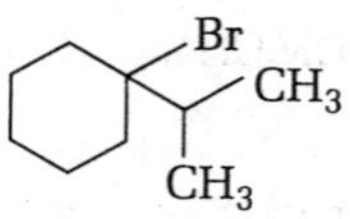

35. What is the final product of the following reaction?

$CH_3CH{=}CH_2 + NBS \longrightarrow \xrightarrow{AgCN}$ (major)

(a) $CH_3CH{=}CHCN$ (b) $CH_3CH{=}CHNC$
(c) $CH_2{=}CHCH_2CN$ (d) $CH_2{=}CHCH_2NC$

36. In the following intramolecular S_N reaction nucleophile is

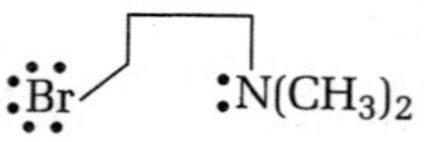

(a) Br (b) N
(c) Both (a) and (b) (d) None of these

37. Which of the following cannot form Grignard reagent?

(a) CH_3CH_2Br (b) $CH_2{=}CHBr$
(c) $HC{\equiv}CCH_2Br$ (d) $CH_2{=}CHCH_2Br$

38. To replace circled hydrogen by deuterium (D), reagents used are

$CH_2{=}CHCH_2{-}\text{(H)} \xrightarrow{I} \xrightarrow{II} \xrightarrow{III} CH_2{=}CH\cdot CH_2D$

	I	II	III
(a)	Br_2/CCl_4	Na	D_2O
(b)	NBS	Mg/ether	D_2O
(c)	Br_2	Mg/ether	D_2O
(d)	HBr	Mg/ether	D_2O

39. Which reaction is not expected to occur?

(a) $[(CH_3)_3C]_2{-}CuLi \xrightarrow{C_2H_5{-}Br}$

(b) $(C_2H_5)_2{-}CuLi \xrightarrow{(CH_3)_3C{-}Br}$

(c) Both (a) and (b)

(d) None of the above

40. Following reaction is of the type

$R_2CuLi + R'X \longrightarrow R{-}R' + LiX + RCu$

(a) S_N1 (b) E1 (c) E2 (d) S_N2

41. Which is not the Wurtz-Fittig reaction?

(a) 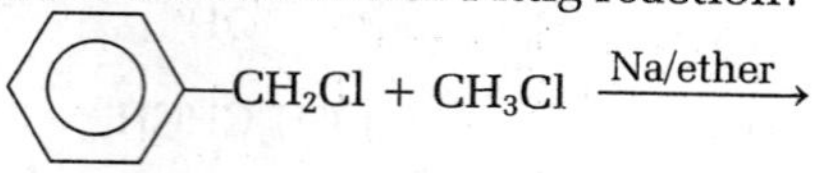

(b) 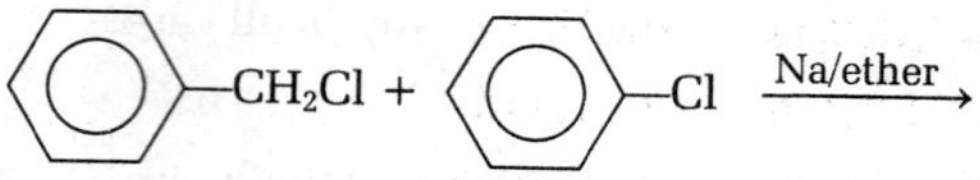

(c) 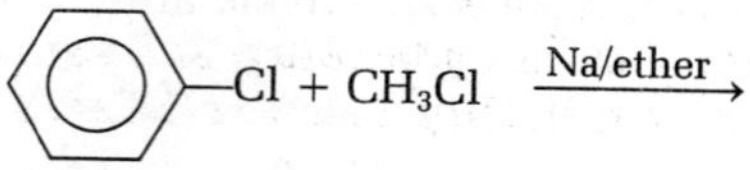

(d) None of the above

42. $C_2H_4Cl_2$ by hydrolysis forms C_2H_4O which gives iodoform test. Thus, $C_2H_4Cl_2$ and C_2H_4O are respectively

(a) 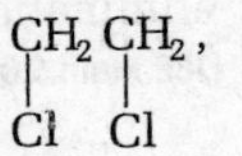 , CH_3CHO (b) CH_3CHCl_2, 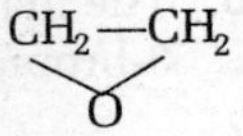

(c) CH_3CHCl_2, CH_3CHO (d) 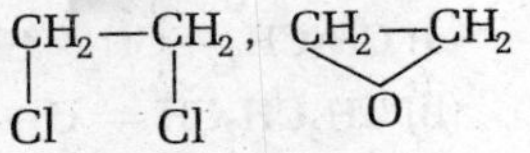

43. $C_3H_6Cl_2(A)$ by hydrolysis form $C_3H_6O(B)$. B gives iodoform test if A is

(a) 1,1-dichloropropane (b) 1,2-dichloropropane
(c) 1,3-dichloropropane (d) 2,2,-dichloropropane

44. Which can be debrominated?

(a) 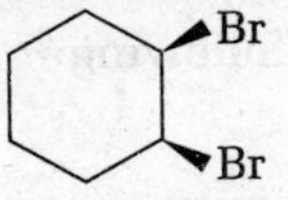 (b) 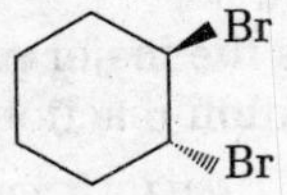

(c) Both (a) and (b) (d) None of these

45. Which gives stereoselective elimination product?

(a) CH_2Br-CH_2Br (b) 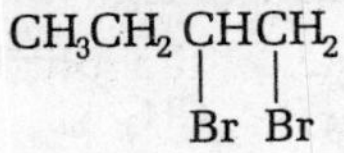

(c) 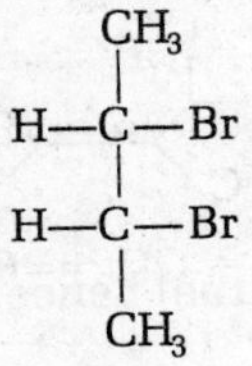 (d) CH_3CHBr_2

46. Following reaction is of the type

$:\overset{s}{C}Cl_3 \longrightarrow :CCl_2 + Cl^-$

(a) β-elimination (b) α-elimination
(c) 1,2-elimination (d) E2-elimination

47. Which addition is *syn* type?

(a) $:CCl_2$ + *cis*-2-butene $\longrightarrow$
(b) $:CCl_2$ + *trans*-2-butene $\longrightarrow$
(c) Both (a) and (b)
(d) None of the above

48. In the following reaction,

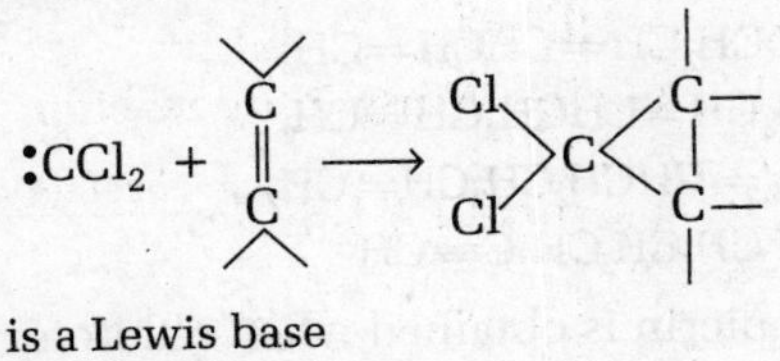

(a) $:CCl_2$ is a Lewis base
(b) $:CCl_2$ is a Lewis acid
(c) alkene is a Lewis base
(d) empty orbital of the carbene acts as a Lewis acid while unshared electron pair acts as Lewis base

49. Which is not the correct statement?

(a) Chloretone is an insecticide
(b) $COCl_2$ is called phosgene
(c) Chloropicrin is used as an insecticide
(d) CCl_4 is used as fire extinguisher under the name pyrene

50. Select the correct intermediate in Riemer-Tiemann reaction

(a) 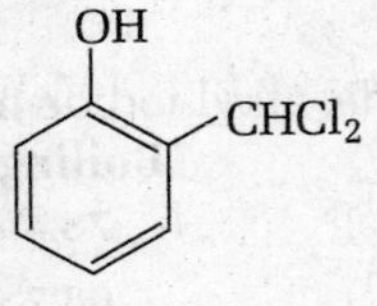 (b) 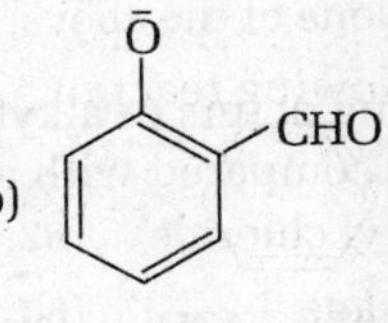

(c) 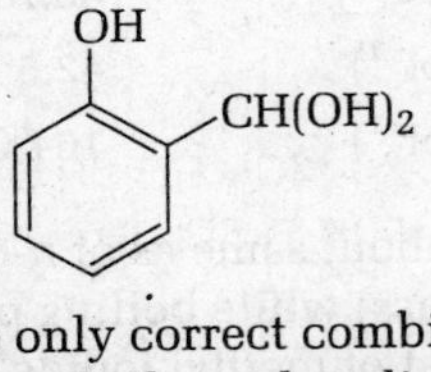 (d) 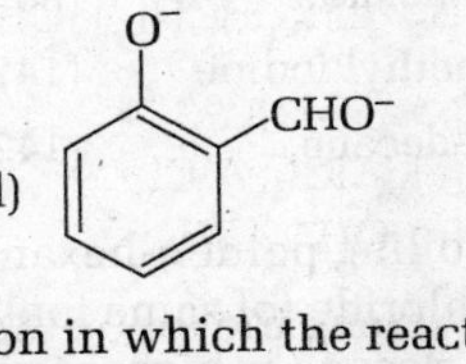

51. The only correct combination in which the reaction proceeds through radical mechanism is **[JEE Advance 2017]**

(a) toluene, $Br_2/h\nu$, substitution
(b) acetophenone, naoh / CO_2, haloform
(c) benzaldehyde, $Br_2/h\nu$, carboxylation
(d) phenol, NaOH/Br_2, condensation

52. Which S_N2 reaction will occur most rapidly? (Assume the concentration and temperatures are all the same).

(a) $CH_3O^- + CH_3CH_2F \rightarrow$
(b) $CH_3O^- + CH_3CH_2I \rightarrow$
(c) $CH_3O^- + CH_3CH_2Cl \rightarrow$
(d) $CH_3O^- + CH_3CH_2Br \rightarrow$

53. $CH_3CH=CHCH(CH_3)_2 \xrightarrow{HBr}$ **[JEE Main 2020 Sep.]**

(a) $CH_3CH(Br)CH_2CH(CH_3)_2$
(b) $CH_3CH_2CH(Br)CH(CH_3)_2$
(c) $Br(CH_2)_3CH(CH_3)_2$
(d) $CH_3CH_2CH_2C(Br)(CH_3)_2$

54. Consider the following reaction,

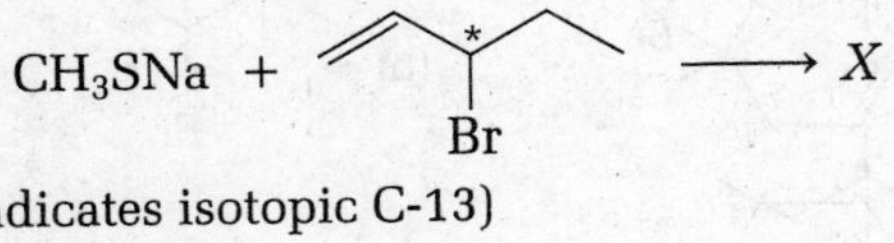

(* indicates isotopic C-13)

(X) is

(a) 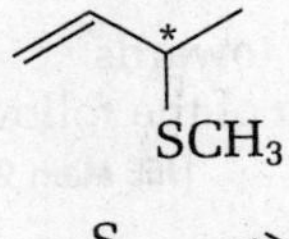 (b) 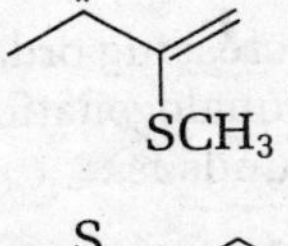

(c)  (d) 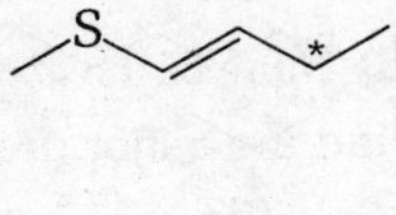

55. Select the correct statement(s) about following reaction

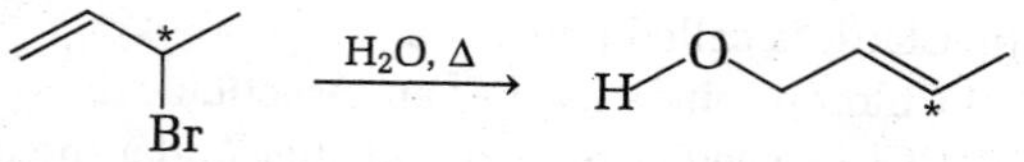

(a) It is unimolecular nucleophilic substitution reaction
(b) It takes place with allylic rearrangement
(c) Both (a) and (b)
(d) None of the above

56. Boiling points of alkyl chloride, alkyl iodide have been compared with alkane.

		Boiling point
n-butyl chloride	(92.5 g mol^{-1})	78.4°C
n-hexane	(86.2 g mol^{-1})	68.7°C
methyl iodide	(142 g mol^{-1})	42.5°C
n-decane	(142 g mol^{-1})	164°C

Boiling point n-hexane is about same as of n-butyl chloride (of same molar mass) while boiling point of n-decane is higher than that of methyl iodide (of same molar mass). It is due to
(a) greater molecular volumes of alkanes than alkyl iodide
(b) compensation of polar effects and molecular volumes in alkyl chloride and alkanes
(c) Both (a) and (b)
(d) None of the above

57. A will give ... by E1 reaction 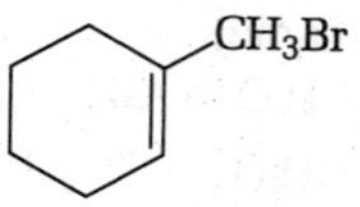 (A)

(a) 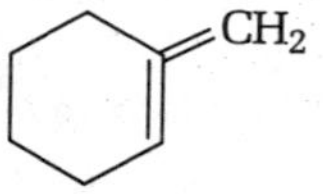 (b) 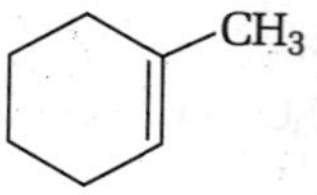

(c) 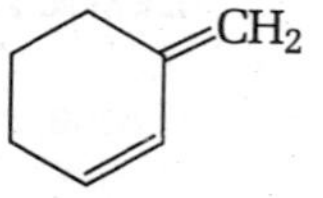 (d) 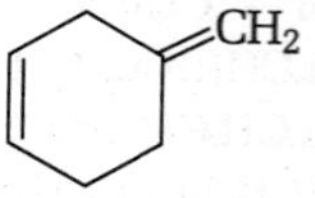

58. Which cannot undergo E2 reaction?

(a) 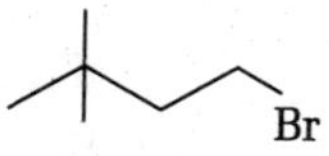 (b) 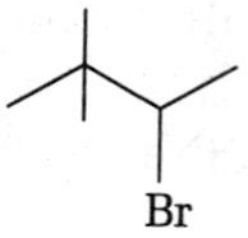

(c) 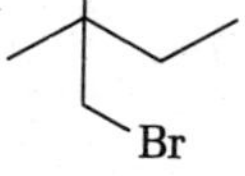 (d) None of these

59. The decreasing order of reactivity towards dehydrohalogenation (E_1) reaction of the following compounds is : **[JEE Main 2020, Jan]**

(A) 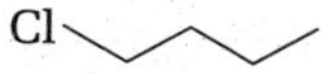 (B) 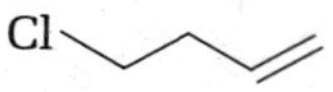

(C) 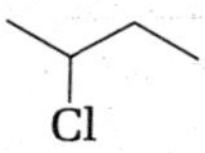 (D) 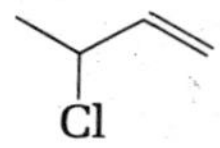

(a) $B > A > D > C$ (b) $B > D > A > C$
(c) $D > B > C > A$ (d) $B > D > C > A$

60. The major product obtained from E_2-elimination of 3-bromo-2-fluoropentane is **[JEE Main 2020, Sep.]**

(a) $CH_3CH_2-CH(Br)-CH_2=CH_2$
(b) $CH_3CH_2CH=C(CH_3)-F$
(c) $CH_3-CH=CH-CH(F)-CH_3$
(d) $CH_3-CH_2-C(Br)=CH-CH_3$

61. What is the major product of the following elimination reaction?

$$(CH_3)_3CCH_2CH(Br)(CH_3)_2 \xrightarrow{E1}$$

(a) 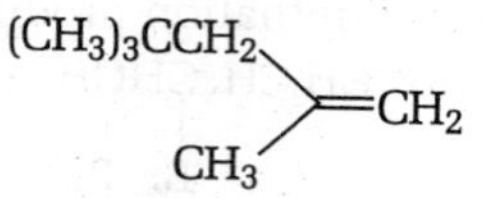 (c) 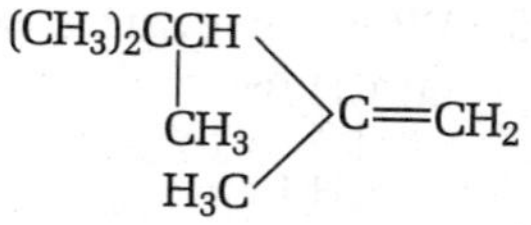

(b) 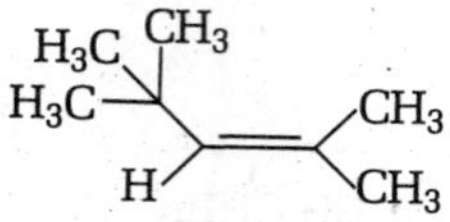 (d) 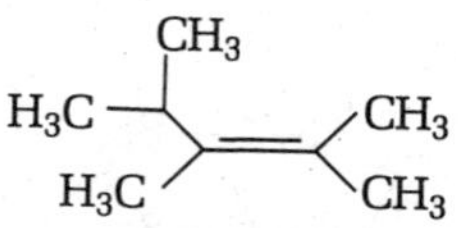

62. $CH_3CH_2Br \xrightarrow{NH_3} CH_3CH_2NH_2$ (true) hence,

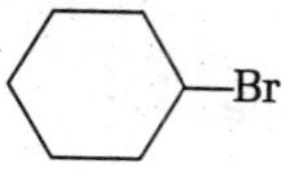 $+ NH_3 \longrightarrow$ A, A is

(a) 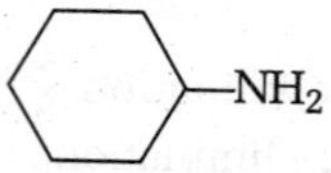 (b) 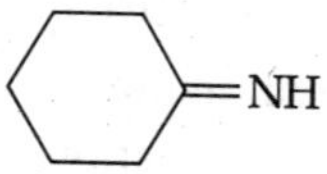

(c)  (d) None of these

63. $CH_3CH_2CH(Br)CH_2CH=CH_2 \xrightarrow{\text{alcoholic KOH}}$ A (predominant), A is
(a) $CH_3CH_2CH=CHCH=CH_2$
(b) $CH_3CH=CHCH_2CH=CH_2$
(c) $CH_2=CHCH_2CH_2CH=CH_2$
(d) $CH_3CH_2CH_2CH_2C\equiv CH$

64. Chloropicrin is obtained when chloroform reacts with...........and reaction is...........
(a) nitrous acid, S_N
(b) nitric acid, S_E
(c) picric acid, S_N
(d) nitric acid, S_N

65. Order of hydrolysis of the following in increasing order is

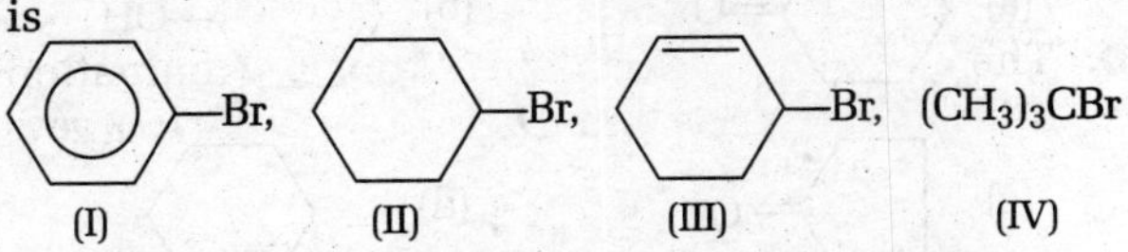

(a) I < II < III < IV
(b) I < IV < II < III
(c) IV < III < II < I
(d) I < II < IV < III

66. The monomer used in the manufacture of teflon is
(a) $CHCl_2—CHF_2$
(b) $F_2C═CF_2$
(c) $Cl_2C═CF_2$
(d) $—F_2CH—CHF_2$

67. Monomer of neoprene is
(a) isoprene
(b) chloroprene
(c) vinyl chloride
(d) vinyl acetylene

68. Which one of the following cannot undergo nucleophilic substitution reaction under ordinary condition?
(a) Allyl chloride
(b) Benzyl chloride
(c) *n*-propyl chloride
(d) Vinyl chloride

69. The most suitable reagent for producing dichlorocarbene from chloroform is
(a) sodium acetate
(b) potassium-*t*-butoxide
(c) triethyl amine
(d) pyridine

70. $CHCl_3 + OH^- \longrightarrow HCOO^-$. Intermediate of this reaction can be
(a) $:\!CCl_3^-$
(b) $:\!CCl_2$
(c) Both (a) and (b)
(d) None of these

71. $(CH_3)_3CCH_2Cl \xrightarrow[\Delta]{AlCl_3} X$ (predominant), X is
(a) $(CH_3)_2\underset{\underset{Cl}{|}}{C}CH_2CH_3$
(b) $CH_3CH_2\underset{\underset{Cl}{|}}{C}HCH_2CH_3$
(c) Both are correct
(d) None is correct

72. RCl + AgCN $\longrightarrow A \xrightarrow{\text{Redn.}} B$; A and B are
(a) RCN, RCH$_2$NH$_2$
(b) RNC, RNHCH$_3$
(c) RCN, RNHCH$_3$
(d) RNC, RCH$_2$NH$_2$

73. The major product in the following reaction is

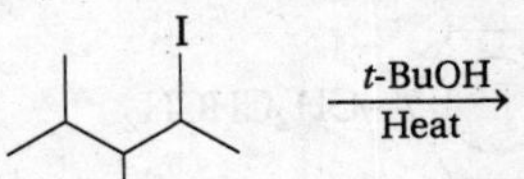

[JEE Main 2020, Sep.]

(a) 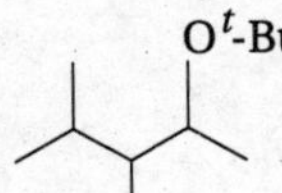

(b) 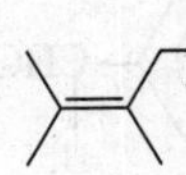
(c) 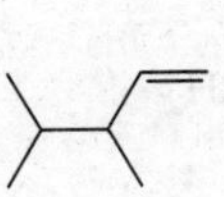
(d) 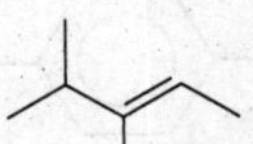

74. 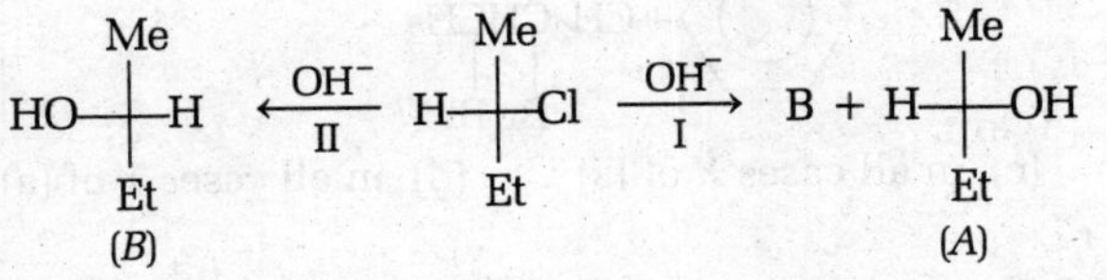

Steps I and II are
(a) Both S_N1
(b) Both S_N2
(c) I: S_N1, II: S_N2
(d) I: S_N2, II: S_N1

75. $CH_3CH_2\underset{\underset{Br}{|}}{C}HCH_3 \xrightarrow{NaNH_2}$ 1-butene and 2-butene

Which are the correct statements?
(a) 1-butene is Hofmann product
(b) 2-butene is Saytzeff product
(c) Both (a) and (b)
(d) None of the above

76. $(CH_3)_3C\cdot CH═CH_2 \xleftarrow{II} (CH_3)_3C\underset{\underset{Cl}{|}}{C}HCH_3 \xrightarrow{I} (CH_3)_2C═C(CH_3)_2$

In this reaction
(a) I is E1, II E2
(b) I is E2, II is E1
(c) Both are E1
(d) Both are E2

77. 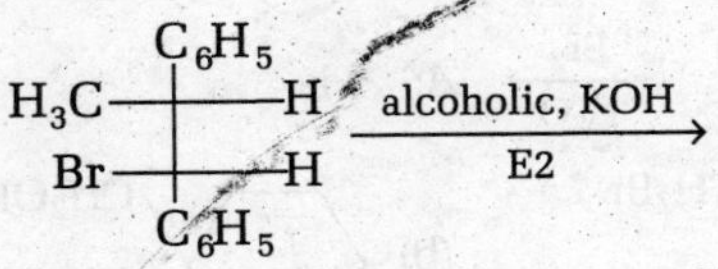

A, A is

(a) 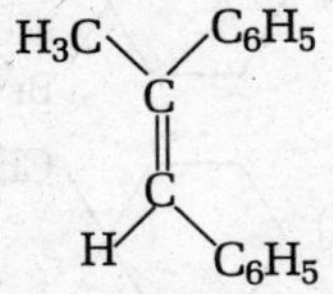

(b) 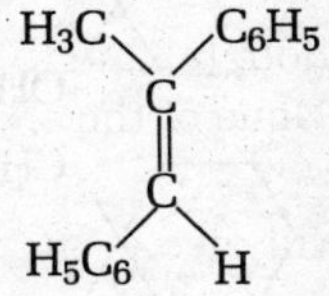

(c) 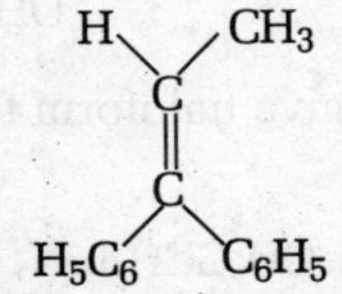

(d) None is correct

78. $\underset{A}{C_3H_6Cl_2} \xrightarrow[\text{(ii) } H_3O^+ \text{ (iii) } \Delta]{\text{(i) KCN}} CH_3\underset{\underset{CH_3}{|}}{C}HCOOH$. Hence, A is
(a) 1,1-dichloropropane
(b) 1,2-dichloropropane
(c) 2,2-dichloropropane
(d) 1,3-dichloropropane

79. Major product of the following S_N1 reaction is

$CH_3\underset{\underset{Br}{|}}{C}H\underset{\underset{CH_3}{|}}{C}HCH_3 + \bar{O}C_2H_5 \longrightarrow$

(a) $CH_3\underset{\underset{OC_2H_5}{|}}{C}H\overset{\overset{CH_3}{|}}{C}HCH_3$
(b) $CH_3\underset{\underset{CH_3}{|}}{C}HCH_2CH_2OC_2H_5$
(c) $CH_3CH_2\underset{\underset{OC_2H_5}{|}}{\overset{\overset{CH_3}{|}}{C}}CH_3$
(d) None is correct

80. $CH_3\overset{CH_3}{\underset{CH_3}{C}}Cl + C_2H_5ONa \longrightarrow$

Major product of this reaction is

(a) $CH_3\overset{CH_3}{\underset{CH_3}{C}}OC_2H_5$ (b) $CH_3-\underset{CH_3}{C}=CH_2$

(c) $CH_3CH_2\underset{CH_3}{CH}CH_2OC_2H_5$ (d) None is correct

81. Increasing rate of dehydrohalogenation is

(a) $RF < RCl < RBr < RI$

(b) $RI < RBr < RCl < RF$

(c) $RCl < RF < RBr < RI$

(d) $RF < RI < RCl < RBr$

82. 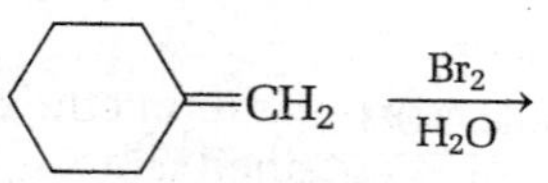 A; A is

(a) 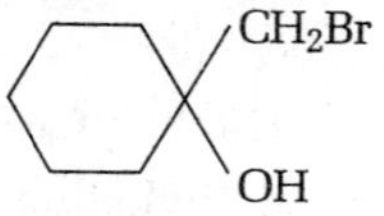 (b) 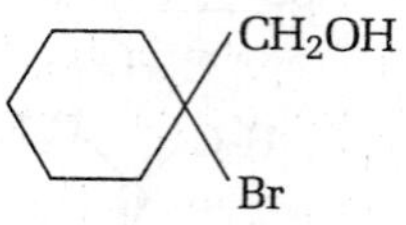

(c) 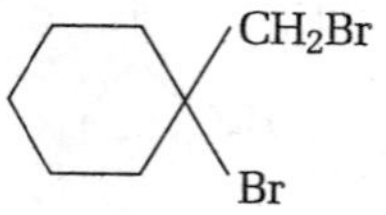 (d) 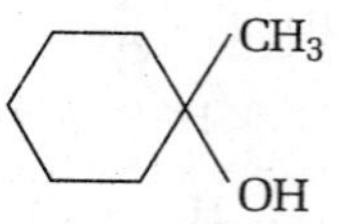

83. Which of the following will give haloform test?

(a) $CH_3\overset{O}{\overset{\|}{C}}CCl_3$ (b) $CH_3\underset{OH}{C}CH_2I$

(c) $CH_3\underset{O}{\underset{\|}{C}}CH_2Cl$ (d) All of these

84. $CH_3\overset{\oplus}{\underset{CH_3}{C}}CH_2CH_3$ can undergo elimination to give major product as

(a) $CH_3\underset{CH_3}{C}=CHCH_3$ (b) $CH_3\underset{CH_2}{\underset{\|}{C}}CH_2CH_3$

(c) $CH_3\underset{CH_3}{CH}CH=CH_2$ (d) None of these

85. End product of the following sequence of reactions is

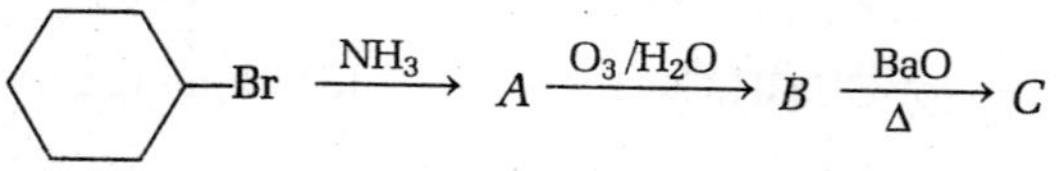

(a) 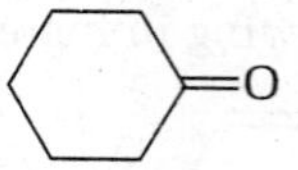 (b) 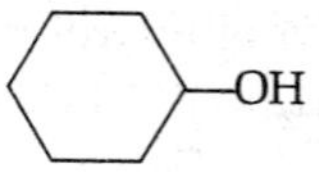

(c) 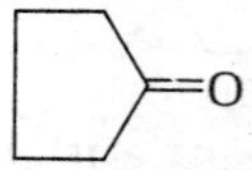 (d) 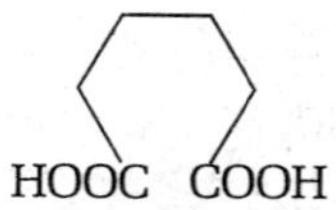

86. Consider the reaction sequence given below :

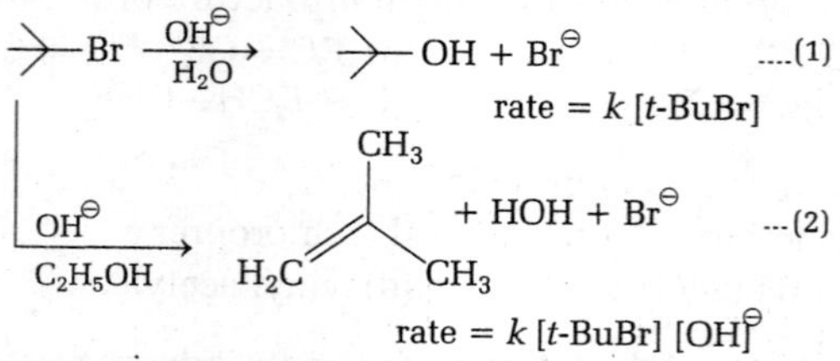

Which of the following statements is true ?

[JEE Main 2020, Sep.]

(a) Changing the base from $\overset{-}{O}H$ to $\overset{-}{O}R$ will have no effect on reaction (2)

(b) Changing the concentration of base will have no effect on reaction (1)

(c) Doubling the concentration of base will double the rate of both the reactions

(d) Changing the concentration of base will have no effect on reaction (2)

87. 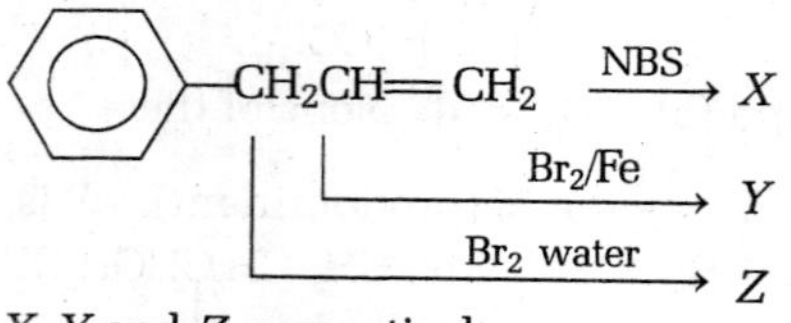

X, Y and Z, respectively are

(a) X : 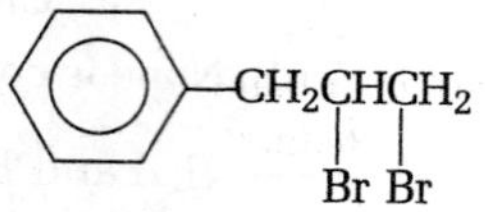

Y : 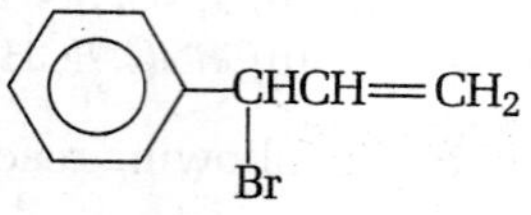

Z : 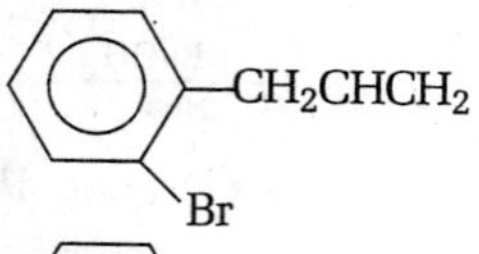

(b) X : 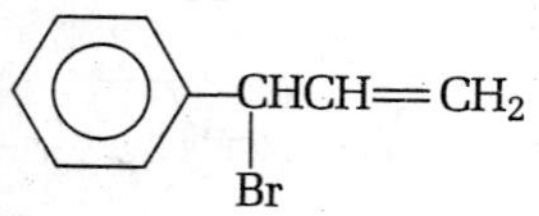

Y : 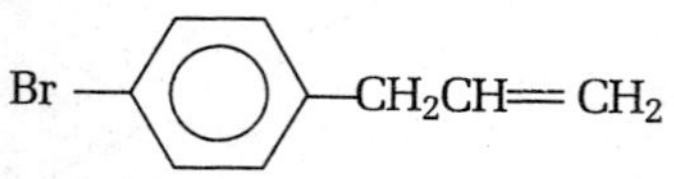

Z : 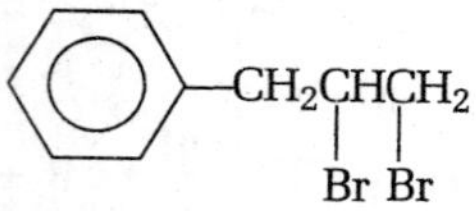

(c) in all cases X of (a) (d) in all cases Y of (a)

88. $CH_2{=}CHCH_2CH{=}CH_2 \xrightarrow{NBS} A$. A is

(a) $CH_2{=}CHCH(Br)CH{=}CH_2$

(b) $CH_2{=}CHCH{=}CHCH_2Br$

(c) $CH_2{=}CHCH_2CH{=}CHBr$

(d) $CH_2{=}CHCH_2C(Br){=}CH_2$

89. 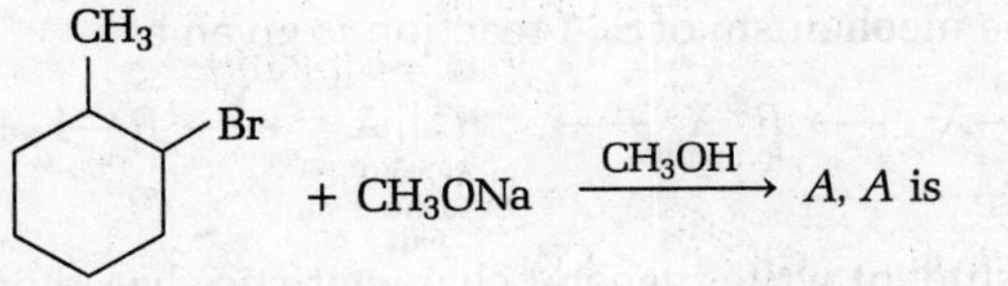

(a) 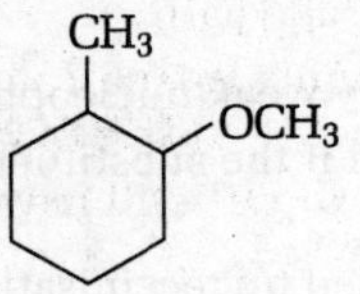

(b) 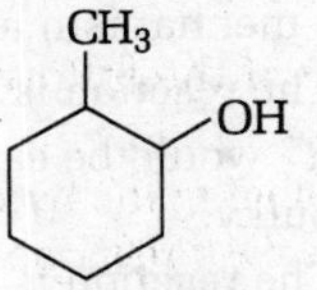

(c) 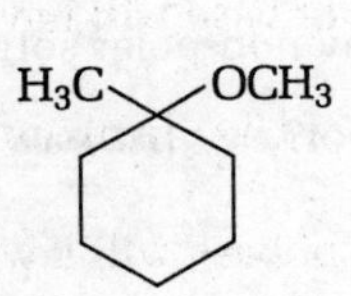

(d) 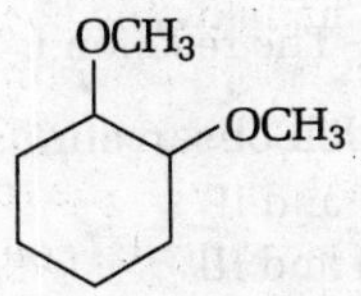

90. $\underset{(major)}{B} \xleftarrow[(CH_3CH_2OH)]{CH_3CH_2ONa} CH_3C(CH_3)_2{-}Br \xrightarrow{CH_3CH_2OH} \underset{(major)}{A}$,

A and B are

(a) $CH_3C(CH_3)_2{-}OCH_2CH_3$ in both cases

(b) $CH_3C(CH_3){=}CH_2$ in both cases

(c) $CH_3C(CH_3)_2{-}OCH_2CH_3$ and $CH_3{-}C(CH_3){=}CH_2$

(d) $H_3C{-}C(CH_3){=}CH_2$ and $CH_3C(CH_3)_2{-}OCH_2CH_3$

91. 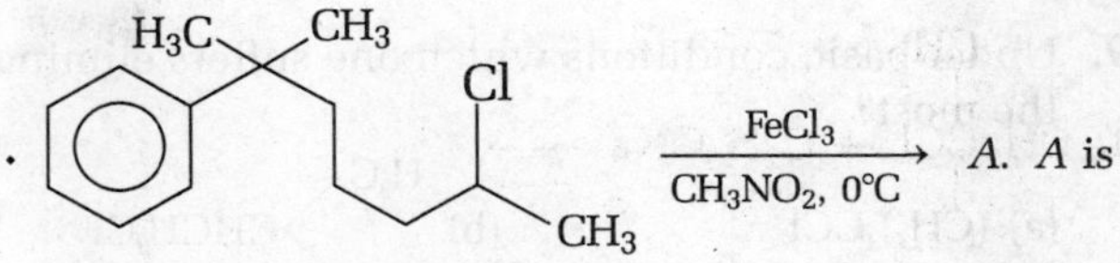

(a) 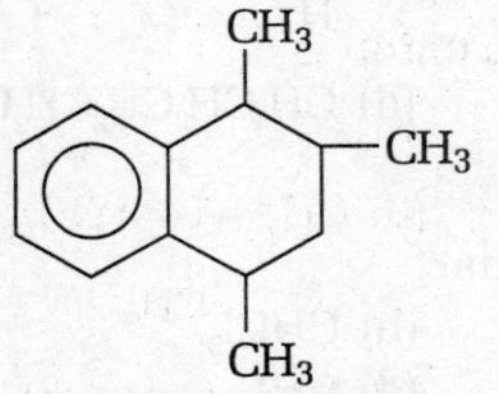 (b) 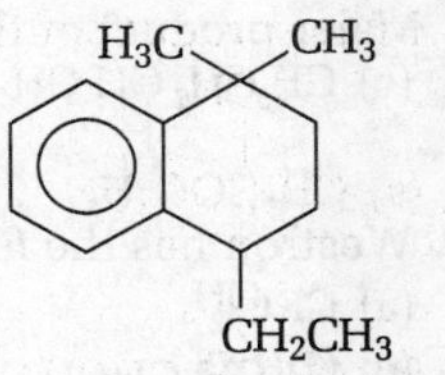

(c) Both (a) and (b) (d) None is correct

92. The reaction,

$CH_2{=}CHCH_3 + HBr \longrightarrow CH_3{-}CHBr{-}CH_3$ is

(a) nucleophilic addition

(b) electrophilic addition

(c) electrophilic substitution

(d) free radical addition

93. 2-bromopentane is heated with potassium ethoxide in ethanol. The major product obtained is

(a) 2-ethoxypentane (b) 1-pentene

(c) *trans*-2-pentene (d) *cis*-2-pentene

94. Ethyl chloride is converted into diethyl ether by

(a) Wurtz synthesis

(b) Grignard reaction

(c) Perkin's reaction

(d) Williamson's synthesis

95. Which of the following reacts with chloroform and base to form phenyl isocyanide?

(a) Phenol (b) Benzene

(c) Nitrobenzene (d) Aniline

96. Iodoform is formed on warming iodine and Na_2CO_3 with

(a) C_2H_5OH (b) CH_3OH

(c) CH_3COOH (d) $HCOOCH_3$

97. Slow oxidation of $CHCl_3$ in air produces

(a) formic acid (b) $COCl_2$

(c) formyl chloride (d) trichloro acetic acid

98. Which of the following has maximum chlorine atoms?

(a) Chloral (b) Chloroform

(c) DDT (d) Carbon tetrachloride

99. Under basic conditions which one suffers elimination the most?

(a) $(CH_3)_3CCl$ (b) $(H_3C)_2CHCH_2Cl$

(c) $CH_3CH_2CH(Cl)CH_3$ (d) $CH_3CH_2CH_2CH_2Cl$

100. Westron has the formula

(a) CF_2Cl_2 (b) $CHCl_3$

(c) $C_2H_2Cl_4$ (d) CHF_3

101. When CH_3CH_2Br reacts with sodium acetylide, the main product is

(a) 2-butene (b) 2-butyne

(c) 1-butene (d) 1-butyne

102. Alkyl halides can be converted into Grignard reagents by

(a) boiling them with Mg ribbon in alcoholic solution

(b) refluxing them with magnesium powder in dry ether

(c) refluxing them with $MgCl_2$ solution

(d) warming them with $MgCl_2$

103. When chlorine reacts with ethyl alcohol, it forms

(a) chloroform (b) chloral

(c) ethyl chloride (d) carbon tetrachloride

104. The increasing order of the boiling points of the major products *A*, *B* and *C* of the following reactions will be **[JEE Main 2020, Sep.]**

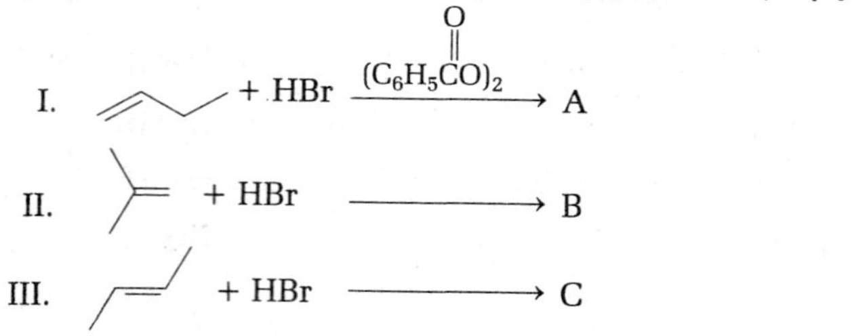

(a) II < III < I (b) III < I < II

(c) I < II < III (d) I < III < II

105. What is the decreasing stability order (most stable → least stable) of the following carbocations?

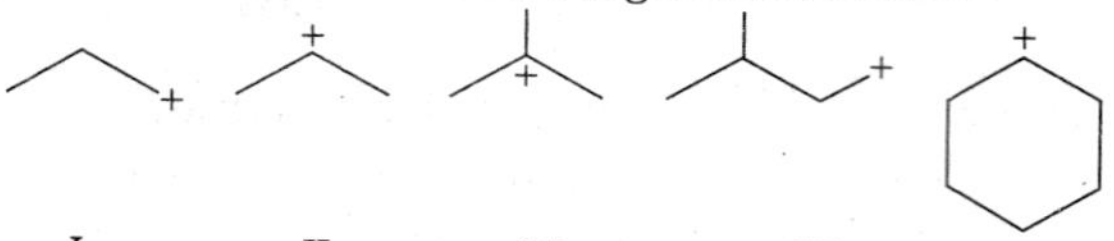

I II III IV V

(a) I > II > I > IV > V (b) I ≈ IV > II ≈ V > III

(c) III > II ≈ V > I ≈ IV (d) III > I ≈ IV > II ≈ V

106. What are the chain-propagating steps in the free radical chlorination of methane?

I. $Cl_2 \longrightarrow 2Cl\bullet$

II. $Cl\bullet + CH_4 \longrightarrow CH_3Cl + H\bullet$

III. $Cl\bullet + CH_4 \longrightarrow \bullet CH_3 + HCl$

IV. $H\bullet + Cl_2 \longrightarrow HCl + Cl\bullet$

V. $\bullet CH_3 + Cl_2 \longrightarrow CH_3Cl + Cl\bullet$

IV. $\bullet CH_3 + CH_4 \longrightarrow CH_4 + \bullet CH_3$

(a) II and IV (b) I and II

(c) III and V (d) I, III and V

107. Which of the following is least able to serve as a nucleophile in a chemical reaction?

(a) Br^- (b) OH^- (c) NH_3 (d) CH_3^+

108. The mechanism of S_N1 reaction is given as :

$$R{-}X \longrightarrow \underset{\text{Ion pair}}{R^{\oplus}\ddot{X}} \longrightarrow \underset{\text{Solvent Separated ion pair}}{R^{\oplus}||\ddot{X}} \xrightarrow{Y} R{-}Y + \ddot{X}$$

A student writes general characteristics based on the given mechanism as :

I. The reaction is favoured by weak nucleophiles.

II. $R^{\oplus}$ would be easily formed if the substituents are bulky.

III. The reaction is accompanied by recemisation.

IV. The reaction is favoured by non-polar solvents.

Which observations are correct? **[JEE Main 2020, Sep.]**

(a) I and II

(b) I and III

(c) I, II and III

(d) II and IV

109. Which compound undergoes nucleophilic substitution with NaCN at the fastest rate?

(a) 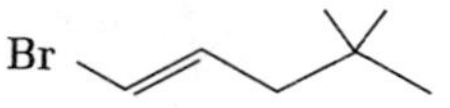

(b) 

(c) 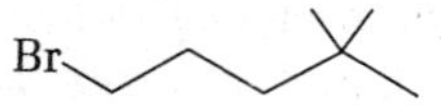

(d) 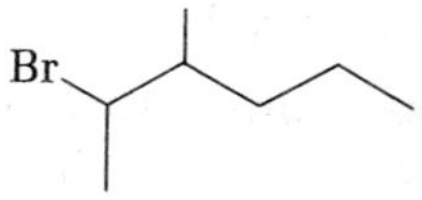

110. For the reaction,

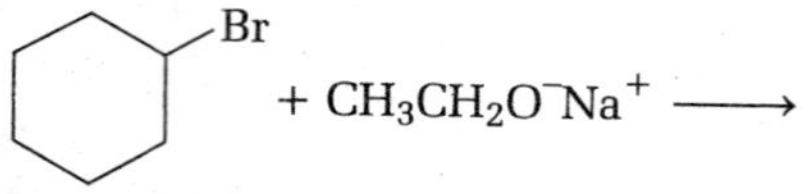

The major product is formed by

(a) S_N1 reaction (b) E1 reaction

(c) S_N2 reaction (d) E2 reaction

111. Which of the following statements pertaining to an S_N2 reaction are true?

I. The rate of reaction is independent of the concentration of the nucleophile.

II. The nucleophile attacks carbon on the side of the molecule opposite the group being displaced.

III. The reaction proceeds with simultaneous bond formation and bond rupture.

IV. Partial racemisation of an optically active substrate results.

(a) I and IV (b) I, III and IV

(c) II and III (d) All of these

112. Which one of the following alkyl halides would be expected to give the highest substitution-to-elimination ratio (most substitution, least elimination) on treatment with sodium ethoxide in ethanol?

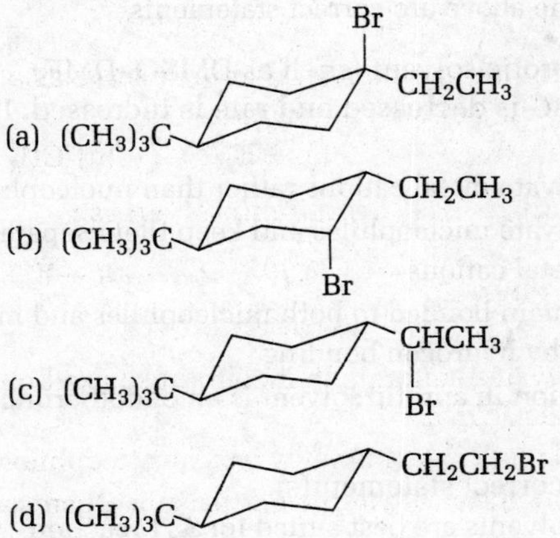

113. Which of the following phrases are not correctly associated with S_N1 reaction?

I. Rearrangement is possible.
II. Rate is affected by solvent polarity.
III. The strength of the nucleophile is important in determining rate.
IV. The reactivity series is tertiary > secondary > primary.
V. Proceeds with complete inversion of configuration.

(a) III and V
(b) Only V
(c) II, III and V
(d) Only III

114. Rank the following in order of decreasing rate of solvolysis with aqueous ethanol (fastest → slowest)

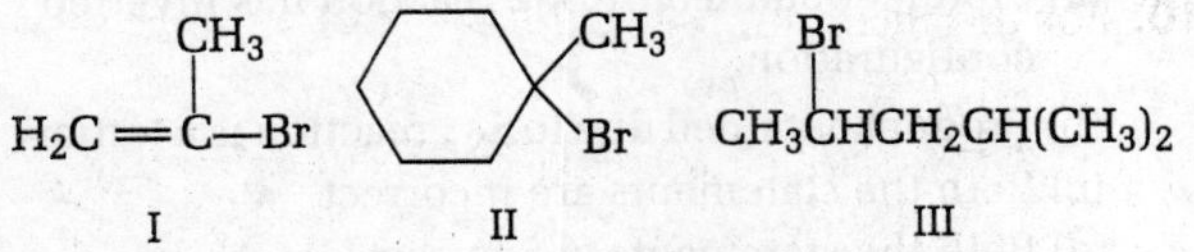

I II III

(a) II > I > III (b) I > II > III
(c) II > III > I (d) I > III > II

115. Rank the following species in order of decreasing nucleophilicity in a polar protic solvent (most → least nucleophilic)

$CH_3CH_2CH_2O^-$ (I) $CH_3CH_2CH_2S^-$ (II) $CH_3CH_2\overset{O}{\overset{\|}{C}}O^-$ (III)

(a) III > I > II (b) II > III > I
(c) I > III > II (d) II > I > III

116. From each of the following pairs select the compound that will react faster with sodium iodide in acetone

2-chloropropane (I) or 2-bromopropane (II)

1-bromobutane (III) or 2-bromobutane (IV)

(a) I and III (b) I and IV
(c) II and III (d) II and IV

117. Select the reagent that will yield the greater amount of substitution on reaction with 1-bromobutane.

(a) CH_3CH_2OK in dimethyl sulphoxide (DMSO)
(b) $(CH_3)_3COK$ in dimethyl sulphoxide (DMSO)
(c) Both (a) and (b) will give comparable amounts of substitution
(d) Neither (a) nor (b) will give any appreciable amount of substitution

118. The reaction of (*R*)-1-chloro-3-methylpentane with sodium iodide in acetone will yield 1-iodo-3-methylpentane that is

(a) *R* (b) *S*
(c) a mixture of *R* and *S* (d) *meso*

119. What is the principal product of the following reaction

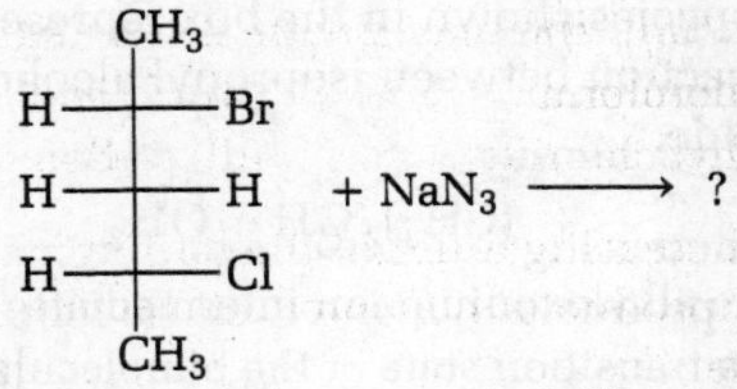

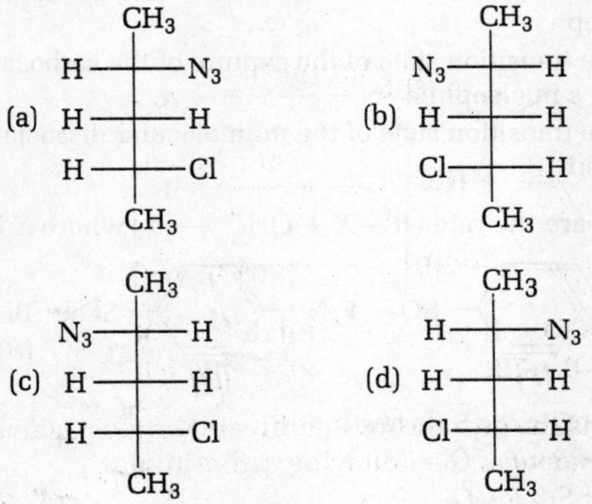

120. Which of the following statements is true?

(a) $CH_3CH_2S^-$ is both a stronger base and more nucleophilic than $CH_3CH_2O^-$.
(b) $CH_3CH_2S^-$ is a stronger base but is less nucleophilic than $CH_3CH_2O^-$.
(c) $CH_3CH_2S^-$ is a weaker base but is more nucleophilic than $CH_3CH_2O^-$.
(d) $CH_3CH_2S^-$ is both a weaker base and less nucleophilic than $CH_3CH_2O^-$.

121. The decreasing order of reactivity of the following organic molecules towards $AgNO_3$ solution is **[JEE Main 2020, Sep.]**

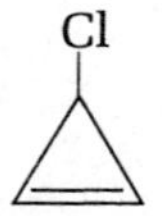
A

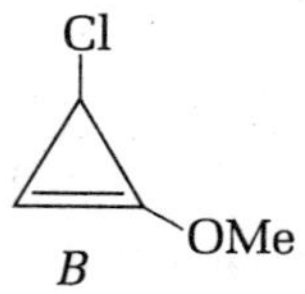
B

$CH_3CH(Cl)CH_3$
C

$CH_3CH(Cl)CH_2NO_2$
D

(a) (*A*) > (*B*) > (*C*) > (*D*) (b) (*C*) > (*D*) > (*A*) > (*B*)
(c) (*B*) > (*A*) > (*C*) > (*D*) (d) (*A*) > (*B*) > (*D*) > (*C*)

122. An alkane with a molecular formula C_6H_{14} reacts with chlorine in the presence of light and heat to give four constitutionally isomeric monochlorides of molecular formula $C_6H_{13}Cl$. What is the most reasonable structure for the starting alkane ?

(a) $CH_3CH_2CH_2CH_2CH_2CH_3$ (b) $(CH_3)_2CHCH_2CH_2CH_3$
(c) $CH_3CH(CH_2CH_3)_2$ (d) $(CH_3)_3CCH_2CH_3$

123. The species shown in the box represents .... of the reaction between isopropyl alcohol and hydrogen bromide.

$$(CH_3)_2\overset{\delta+}{C}H\cdots\overset{\delta+}{O}H_2$$

(a) the alkyloxonium ion intermediate
(b) the transition state of the bimolecular proton transfer step
(c) the transition state of the capture of the carbocation by a nucleophile
(d) the transition state of the unimolecular dissociation step

124. Compare the rate ($R—X + OH^- \longrightarrow$) where *X* is

(*P*)

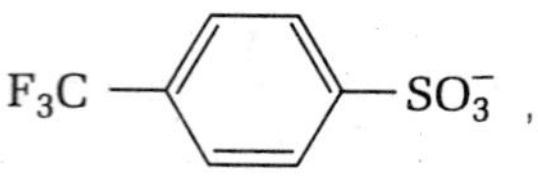
(*Q*)

Br^- (*R*), I^- (*S*)

(a) $P < Q < R < S$ (fastest)
(b) $S < R < P < Q$
(c) $R < S < P < Q$
(d) $R < P < Q < S$

125. Select the correct statement(s).

(a) OH^- and RO^- are both stronger bases and more powerful nucleophiles than their conjugate acids H_2O and *ROH*
(b) NH_3 is both a stronger base and more powerful nucleophile than H_2O
(c) RS^- is less basic but more strongly nucleophilic than RO^-
(d) All of the above are correct statements

126. In polar aprotic solvent (such as DMSO, DMF, acetone), ΔG is decreased and rate is increased. It is because

(a) they solvate metal cations rather than nucleophiles
(b) they solvate nucleophiles and keep them separated from metal cations
(c) they remain bonded to both nucleophiles and metal cations by hydrogen bonding
(d) dissolution in aprotic solvent is an endothermic process

127. Select the correct statement(s).

(a) Protic solvents are best suited for S_N1 reaction
(b) Protic solvent solvate nucleophiles thereby lowering the energy of nucleophiles, increasing ΔG and decreasing the reaction rate
(c) Crown ether increases reactivity of nucleophile by solvating its cation
(d) All of the above statements are correct

128. Consider the following reaction,

$$\xleftarrow[S_N1]{C_2H_5OH} CH_3\overset{CH_3}{\underset{CH_3}{C}}CH_2Br \xrightarrow[S_N2]{C_2H_5O^-}$$

$(CH_3)_3CCH_2Br$ shows S_N2 reaction with $C_2H_5O^-$ and S_N1 reaction with C_2H_5OH as given above. Select incorrect statement.

(a) Product obtained by S_N2 reaction has inverted configuration
(b) Product obtained due to S_N1 reaction is a tertiary ether
(c) Both the statements are incorrect
(d) Both the statements are correct

129. Ammonolysis of alkyl halides followed by the treatment with NaOH solution can be used to prepare primary, secondary and tertiary amines. The purpose of NaOH in the reaction is **[JEE Main 2021, March]**

(a) to remove basic impurities
(b) to activate NH_3 used in the reaction
(c) to remove acidic impurities
(d) to increase the reactivity of alkyl halide

Objective Questions Type II [One or more than one correct option(s)]

In each of the questions below, four choices are given, of which one or more than one are correct.

1. Consider the following reaction

$$(CH_3)_3CBr \xrightarrow[C_2H_5OH]{C_2H_5ONa} (H_3C)_2C{=}CH_2$$

Select correct statement(s) about this reaction.

(a) It is called α-elimination since Br atom is lost from α-carbon

(b) It is called β-elimination since Br atom is lost from α-carbon

(c) It is called β-elimination since Br atom is lost from β-carbon

(d) β-elimination is the reverse of an addition to an **alkene**

2. Select the correct reactions taking place by E_2 mechanism.

(a) 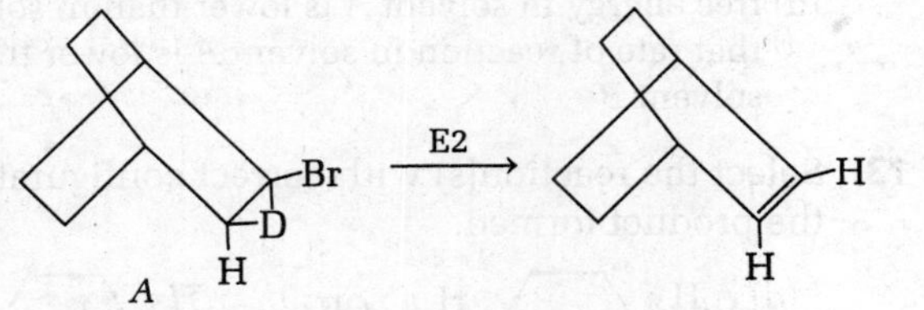

(b) 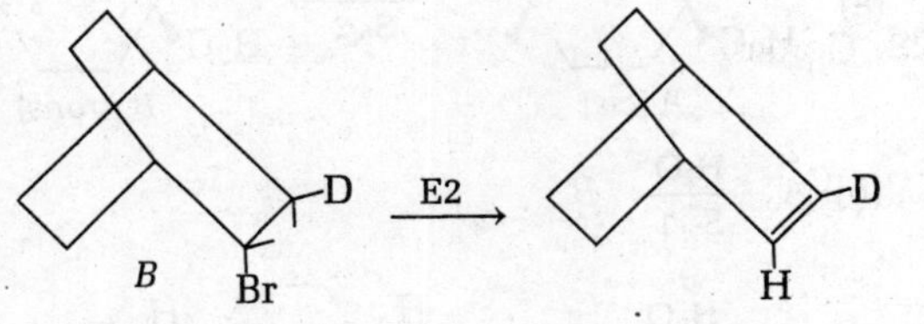

(c) 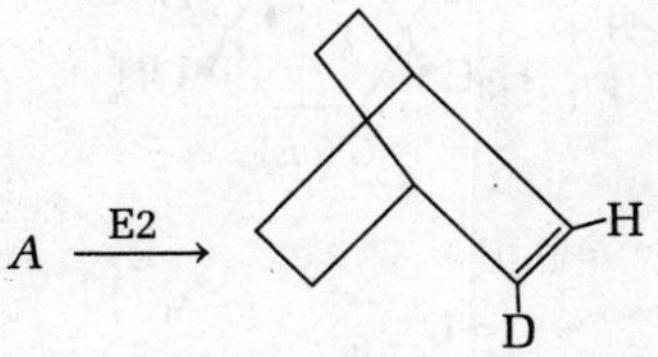

(d) 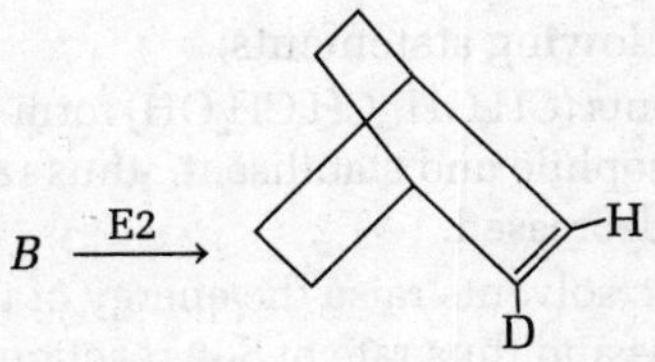

3. Select the final product(s) of the following reaction,

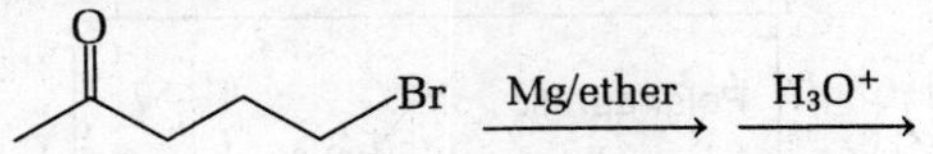

(a) 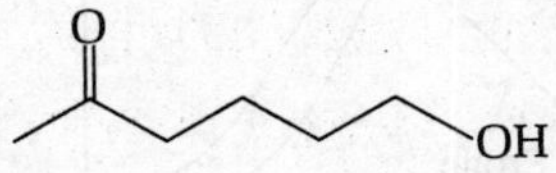

(b) 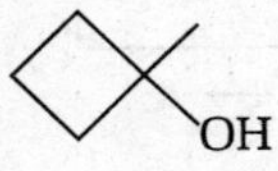

(c) 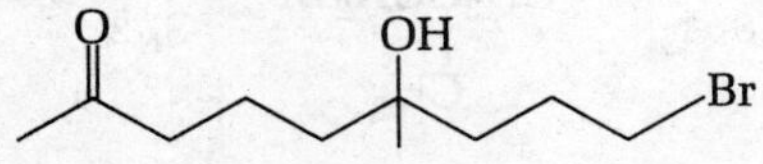

(d) 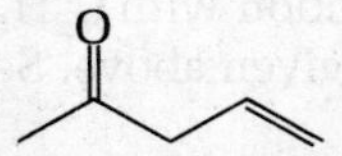

4. Questions are based on the Mitsunobu reaction a general method for performing S_N reactions of alcohols

$$R{-}OH + HX \xrightarrow[(DEAD)]{PH_3P} R{-}X + O{=}PPH_3 + EtO{-}\overset{O}{\overset{\|}{C}}{-}\underset{H}{N}{-}\underset{H}{N}{-}\overset{O}{\overset{\|}{C}}{-}OEt$$

DEAD is Di-Ethyl Azo Dicarboxylate

$$EtO{-}\overset{O}{\overset{\|}{C}}{-}N{=}N{-}\overset{O}{\overset{\|}{C}}{-}OEt$$

OH of R—OH can be replaced by X by using HX ($HX = R'\overset{O}{\overset{\|}{C}}OH$, ArOH, HN_3, RSH)) by a new reaction called

(a) Schmidt reaction (b) HVZ reaction

(c) Mitsunobu reaction (d) Saytzeff reaction

5. Select the correct statement(s).

(a) DEAD undergoes a reduction–oxidation reaction in the presence of the acidic component

(b) Intermediate $[ROPPh_3]^+$ is formed

(c) Reaction proceeds with inversion

(d) Reaction proceeds through formation of carbocation

6. Two types of stereoisomers are formed in the following substitution reactions (assume no migration)

(a) $H{-}\overset{Et}{\underset{Me}{C}}{-}Br + OH^- \xrightarrow{S_N1}$

(b) $H{-}\overset{Me}{\underset{Me}{C}}{-}Br + H_2O \xrightarrow{S_N1}$

(c) 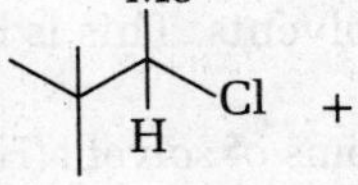 $+ OH^- \xrightarrow{S_N1}$

(d) 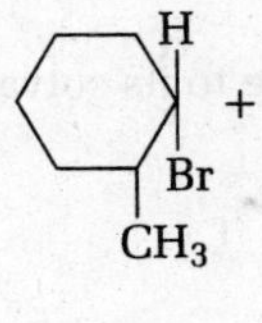 $+ OH^- \xrightarrow{S_N1}$

7. Consider the following reaction,

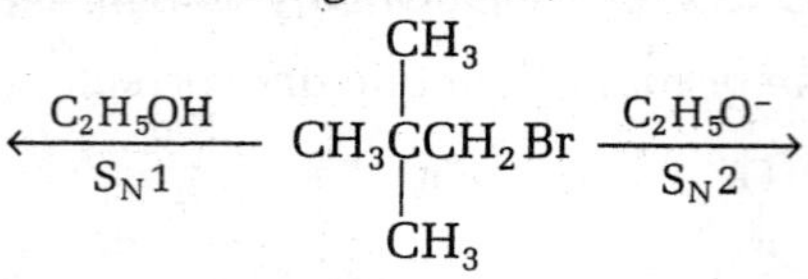

$(CH_3)_3CCH_2Br$ shows S_N2 reaction with $C_2H_5O^-$ and S_N1 reaction with C_2H_5OH as given above. Select correct statement(s).
(a) Product obtained by S_N2 reaction has inverted configuration
(b) Product obtained due to S_N1 reaction is a tertiary ether
(c) Product obtained by S_N1 reaction has inverted configuration
(d) Product obtained due to S_N2 reaction is a tertiary ether

8. Rate of S_N1 reaction is increased based on by following factors because
(a) good leaving groups (more stable anions) lower the energy of the transition state leading to carbocation formation thus increasing the reaction rate
(b) a nonbasic nucleophile (like H_2O) will prevent a competitive E2 reaction
(c) polar solvents stabilise the carbocation intermediate by solvation, thereby increasing the reaction rate
(d) All of the above

9. Select the correct statement(s).
(a) Isomerisation of a less stable carbocation to a more stable carbocation by 1,2-alkyl shift is called Wagner-Meerwein rearrangement
(b) Isomerisation to a more stable carbocation is accompanied with decrease in potential energy
(c) Greater stability of benzyl, allyl and tertiary carbocations is due to hyperconjugation
(d) Carbocation is more electron deficient than alkyl radical

10. Select the correct statement(s).
(a) Stability order of carbocations in gaseous phase and solution are different
(b) The enthalpies of dissociation are much lower in solution
(c) Polar solvents stabilise the nucleophile
(d) Increase in conjugation increases stabilisation of the carbocation

11. S_N1 reactions take place much more rapidly in polar solvents than in non-polar solvents. This is because of hydration of nucleophile
(a) by electron-rich oxygen atoms of solvent (H_2O) molecules
(b) stabilisation of carbocation due to its solvation by electron-rich oxygen atoms
(c) Both of the above
(d) None of the above

12. Following diagram illustrates the effect of solvent on the reaction rate for S_N1 reaction. It is indicated that

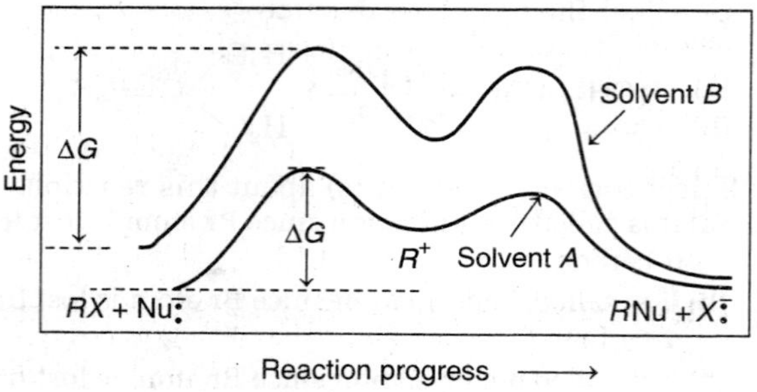

(a) solvent A is more polar than solvent B
(b) solvent B is more polar than solvent A
(c) free energy in solvent A is lower than in solvent B so that rate of reaction in solvent A is higher than that in solvent B
(d) free energy in solvent A is lower than in solvent B so that rate of reaction in solvent A is lower than that in solvent B

13. Select the reaction(s) with correct configuration of the product formed.

(a) 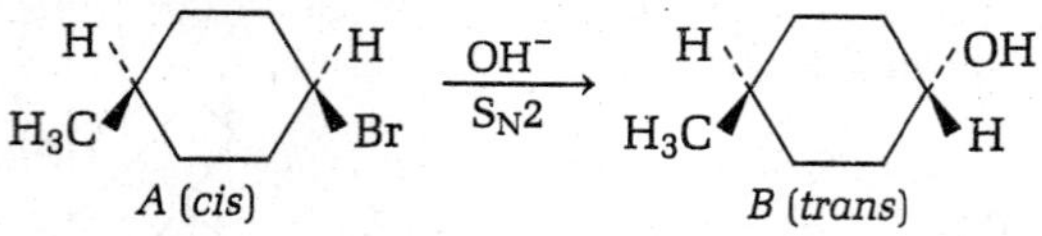

(b) $A \xrightarrow[S_N1]{H_2O} B$

(c) $A \xrightarrow[S_N1]{H_2O} B +$ 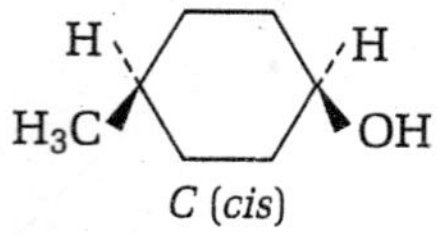

(d) $A \xrightarrow[S_N1]{H_2O} C$

14. Consider the following statements,
I. Protic solvents (CH_3OH, CH_3CH_2OH) form H-bonds to the nucleophile and stabilise it, thus rate of S_N2 reaction is decreased.
II. Polar aprotic solvents raise the energy of the nucleophiles and thus rate of S_N2 reaction is increased as in the following figure

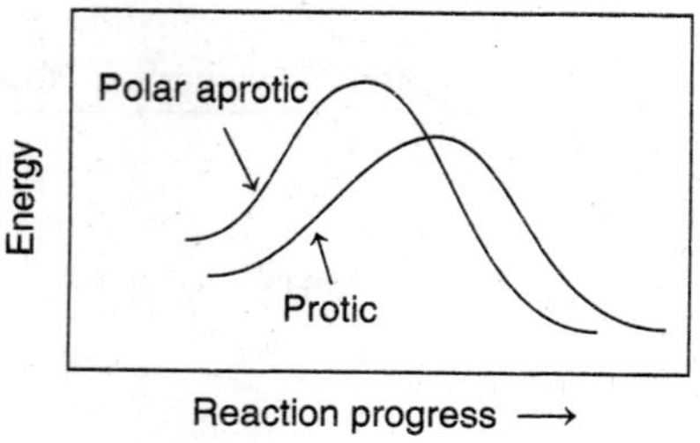

III. Reactivity of nucleophile in presence of crown ether (solvent) is increased for S_N1 and S_N2 reactions.

Select the correct statement(s)

(a) I and II
(b) II and III
(c) I and III
(d) I, II and III

15. Select the correct statement(s) about the following reaction.

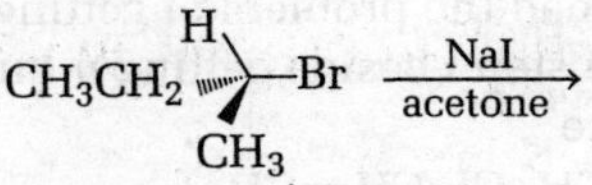

(a) It can proceed *via* S_N2 mechanism
(b) Configuration about chiral carbon is retained
(c) A racemic mixture is formed
(d) Reaction is stereospecific

Numerical Value Questions

All these questions have a Numerical value as their answer, solve the questions and write your answer.

1. $CH_3-C(Br)_2-C(Br)_2-CH_3 \xrightarrow{(a)NaNH_2} \xrightarrow{(b)CH_2} CH_3-C\equiv C-C\equiv C-CH_3$

a and b mole consumed.

Value of $a+b=$

2. How many isomer of C_4H_9Br when reacts with $NaNH_2$ diastereomers will form? (excluding stereoisomer)

3. 1, 2-dibromopropane on treatment with X moles of $NaNH_2$ followed by treatement with C_2H_5Br gives a pentyne. The value of X is ....

4. In the following sequence of reactions

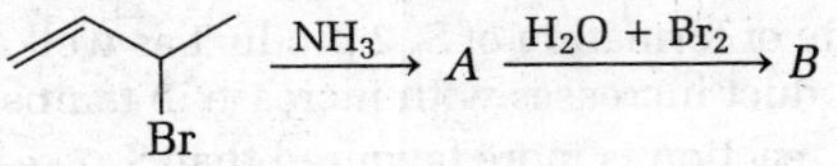

How many types of products(B) are formed?

5. What is the position of $\bar{O}C_2H_5$ in the major product in the following reaction?

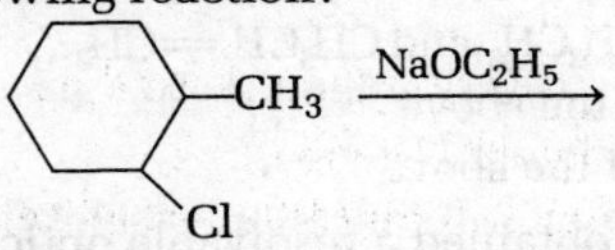

6. Which of the following will be halogenated first on treatment with HBr ?

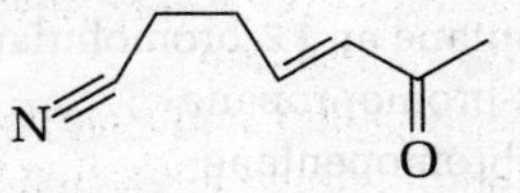

7.

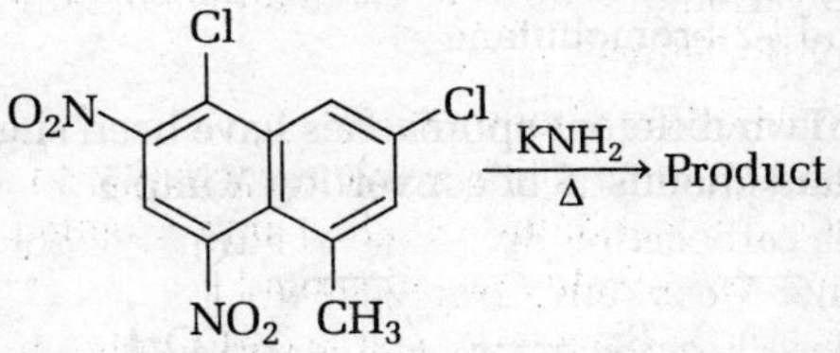

8.

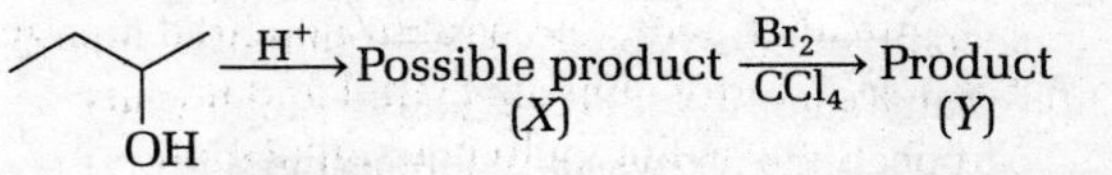

The total number of possible product $(X+Y)$ are

Comprehension Based Questions

In these questions, a passage has been given followed by questions based on it. You have to answer the questions based on the passage given.

***Passage* 1** To convert 1-bromopropane into 1-bromobutane, chemists A and B designed two paths.

Chemist A

$CH_3CH_2CH_2Br \xrightarrow[\text{Wurtz}]{CH_3Br + Na} CH_3CH_2CH_2CH_3$ (Step I)

$\xrightarrow[Br_2]{h\nu} CH_3CH_2CH_2CH_2Br$ (Step II)

Chemist B

$CH_3CH_2CH_2Br \xrightarrow{Mg/ether} CH_3CH_2CH_2MgBr$ (Step I)

$\xrightarrow{(i)\ HCHO,\ (ii)\ H_3O^+} CH_3CH_2CH_2CH_2OH$ (Step II)

$\xrightarrow{HBr} CH_3CH_2CH_2CH_2Br$ (Step III)

Based on these methods, answer the following questions.

1. Chemist *A* had the problem of getting so many side products in step I beside getting *n*-butane. These side products are
   (a) $CH_3CH_2CH_3, CH_3CH{=}CH_2$
   (b) $CH_3CH_2CH_3, CH_3CH{=}CH_2, CH_3CH_3, CH_4$
   (c) $CH_3CH_2CH_3, CH_3CH{=}CH_2, CH_3CH_3, CH_3(CH_2)_4CH_3$
   (d) $CH_3CH_3, CH_3CH{=}CH_2$
2. One of the side products of step I of chemist *A* also decolourised Br_2 water. This side product is .... and is formed by
   (a) $CH_2{=}CH_2$, by coupling of $\dot{C}H_3$ to CH_3CH_3 and $CH_2{=}CH_2$
   (b) $CH_3CH{=}CH_2$, by disproportionation of $CH_3CH_2\dot{C}H_2$ to $CH_3CH_2CH_3$ and $CH_3CH{=}CH_2$
   (c) Both of the above
   (d) None of the above
3. Chemist *A* obtained a resolvable optically inactive mixture in step II, as major product. This mixture contains
   (a) 1-bromobutane and 2-bromobutane
   (b) *d*- and *l*-2-bromopropane
   (c) *d*-and *l*-3-bromopentane
   (d) *d*- and *l*-2-bromobutane

***Passage* 2** Two different approaches have been suggested by chemist *A* and chemist *B* of converting *X* into *Y*

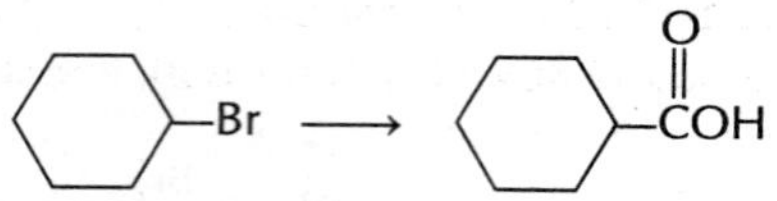

(X) (Y)

Chemist *A* $X \xrightarrow[\text{step I}]{\text{Mg/ether}} \xrightarrow[\text{(ii) } H_3O^+\text{, step II}]{\text{(i) } CO_2} Y$

Chemist *B* $X \xrightarrow[\text{step I}]{\text{NaCN}} \xrightarrow[\text{step II}]{H_3O^+} Y$

Answer the following questions based on above methods.

1. Correct method is of
   (a) chemist *A*
   (b) chemist *B*
   (c) both (a) and (b)
   (d) None of these
2. Select the correct statement(s).
   (a) Chemist *B* also gets cyclohexene as the side-product in step I due to dehydrohalogenation since $NC^{\ominus}$**:** is a strong nucleophile
   (b) Chemist *B* also gets cyclohexanol as the side-product in step II due to hydration of cyclohexene
   (c) Both of the above
   (d) None of the above

***Passage* 3** *Read the following passage and answer the questions at the end of it.*

A secondary alkyl halide can form both substitution and elimination products under S_N2 and E2 conditions. The relative amounts of the two products depend on the base strength (and the bulk) of the nucleophile.

1. Consider the following reaction,

$$\underset{\substack{|\\ Cl}}{CH_3CHCH_3} + CH_3CH_2O^- \xrightarrow{CH_3CH_2OH} \underbrace{\underset{S_N2\text{ product}}{CH_3\overset{\substack{OCH_2CH_3\\|}}{C}HCH_3}}_{A} + \underbrace{\underset{\text{E2 product}}{CH_3CH{=}CH_2}}_{B} + CH_3CH_2OH + Cl^-$$

The reaction is studied at 300 K and 350 K. Rates of the formation of *A* and *B* have been given below in the figure.

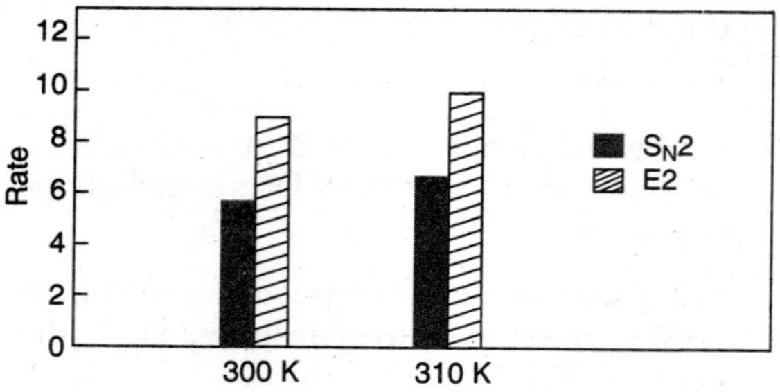

Select the correct statement(s) based on the above figure.
   (a) Rate of formation of S_N2 product as well as of E2 product increases with increase in temperature
   (b) E2 reaction is more favoured than S_N2 reaction on increasing temperature
   (c) Temperature coefficient of the elimination reaction in the given temperature range is about 1.05
   (d) Rate constant is independent of temperature

2. Consider the following reactions on primary alkyl halides.

A. $CH_3CH_2CH_2CH_2Br + CH_3O^- \xrightarrow{CH_3OH}$

B. $CH_3\underset{\substack{|\\ CH_3}}{C}HCH_2Br + CH_3O^- \xrightarrow{CH_3OH}$

C. $CH_3CH_2CH_2CH_2Br + (CH_3)_3CO^- \xrightarrow{(CH_3)_3COH}$

Major products of these reactions are

	A	*B*	*C*
(a)	$CH_3CH_2CH{=}CH_2$	$CH_3\underset{\substack{|\\ CH_3}}{C}{=}CH_2$	$CH_3CH_2CH{=}CH_2$
(b)	$CH_3CH{=}CHCH_3$	$CH_3\underset{\substack{|\\ CH_3}}{C}{=}CH_2$	$CH_3CH{=}CHCH_3$

(c) $CH_3CH_2CH_2CH_2OCH_3$ $CH_3CH(CH_3)OCH_3$ $CH_3CH_2CH_2CH_2OC(CH_3)_3$

(d) $CH_3CH_2CH_2CH_2OCH_3$ $CH_3C(CH_3){=}CH_2$ $CH_3CH_2CH{=}CH_2$

3. Consider the following S_N2 / E2 reactions on 2-chloropropane

$$B \xleftarrow[CH_3CH_2OH]{CH_3CH_2O^-} (CH_3)_2CHCl \xrightarrow[CH_3COOH]{CH_3COO^-} A$$

Select the correct alternate(s).

(a) Major products *A* and *B* are the substitution products
(b) Major products *A* and *B* are the elimination products
(c) Major *A* is the substitution product and major *B* is the elimination products
(d) Major *A* is the elimination product and major *B* is the substitution product

***Passage* 4** Following reaction energy diagram have been given for testing analytical skill.

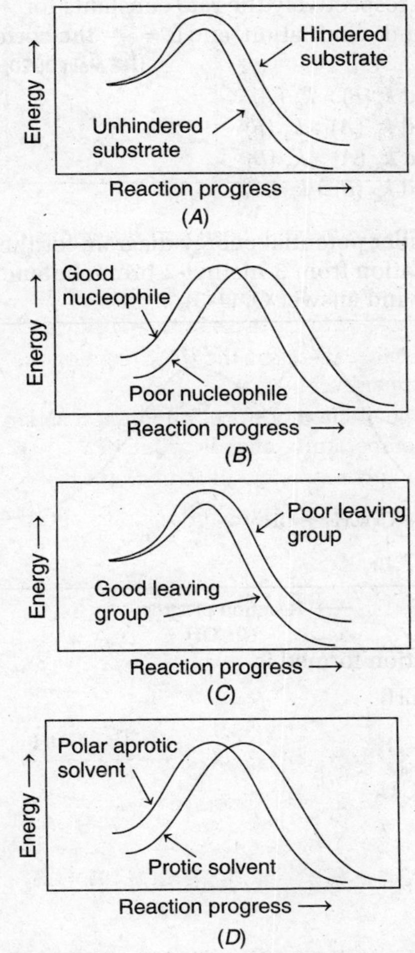

Reaction energy diagrams showing the effects of (*A*) substrate structure, (*B*) nucleophile, (*C*) leaving group, and (*D*) solvent on

Questions 1 to 3 are based on the above diagrams.

1. From the graph *A*, it is concluded that
(a) steric hindrance raises the energy of the transition state, thus increasing ΔG and decreasing reaction rate.
(b) $(CH_3)_3CCl$ and $(CH_3)_2CHCl$ are good substrates for S_N2 reaction
(c) free energy of the CH_3Cl and $(CH_3)_2CHCl$ is quite different at the start as well as after the reaction
(d) carbocation is the intermediate in the S_N2 reaction

2. Consider the diagram *B* and select correct statement(s).
(a) Energy of the good nucleophiles (say OH^-, NH_2^-) is higher than those of poor nucleophiles (say Cl^-, I^-)
(b) ΔG of good nucleophiles is higher than those of poor nucleophiles
(c) Rate of the reaction ($CH_3Cl + OH^- \longrightarrow$) is larger than that of the reaction ($CH_3Cl + CH_3COO^-$)
(d) All of the above are correct statements

3. Refer diagram *D*. In polar aprotic solvent (such as DMSO, DMF, acetone), ΔG is decreased and rate is increased. It is because.
(a) they solvate metal cations rather than nucleophiles
(b) they solvate nucleophiles and keep them separated from metal cations
(c) they remain bonded to both nucleophiles and metal cations by hydrogen bonding
(d) dissolution in aprotic solvent is an endothermic process

***Passage* 5** Following two synthetic paths have been designed to prepare 2-ethoxypentane from 2-pentanol. Observe each step and answer the questions at the end of it.

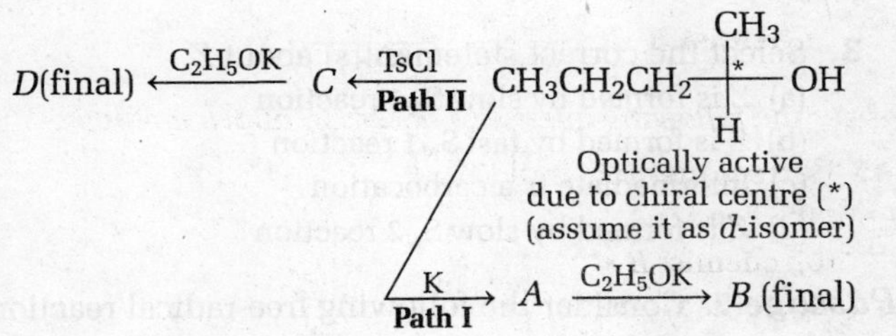

Ts is Tosyl

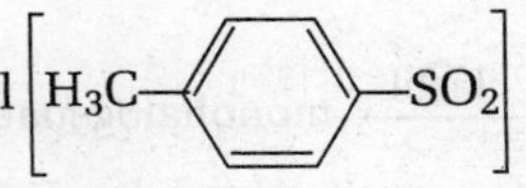

1. Which has inverted configuration?
(a) *B*
(b) *D*
(c) Both (a) and (b)
(d) None of the above

2. Select the correct statement(s).

(a) In path I, configuration in the product B is retained as TsO^- is a good leaving group

(b) In path II, configuration in the product D inverted since (C—O) bond is cleaved and TsO^- is a good leaving group

(c) A is $R—\bar{O}K^+$ (R is alkyl chiral part) and on reaction with C_2H_5OTs, $RO^-C_2H_5^+$ is formed

(d) C is $R—O—Ts$ and its S_N2 reaction gives inverted product due to cleavage of $R—O$ bond

***Passage* 6** Answer the following questions based on the figure given in which reactions of R—LG (where LG is a good leaving group) with B : (a base and/or nucleophile) are studied.

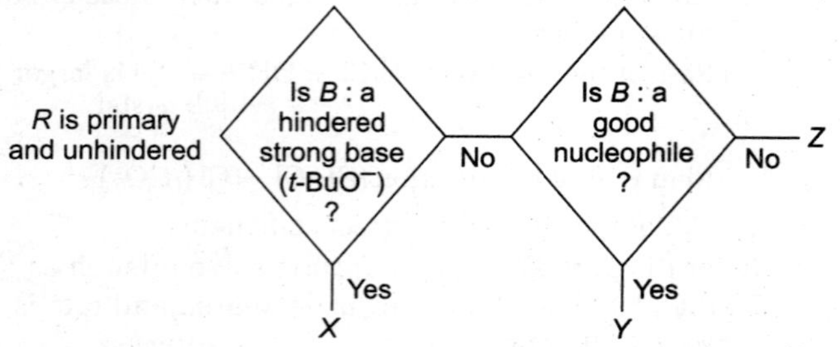

R—LG + B:⟶

1. Select the correct statement about X.

(a) X is an alkene by E2 reaction

(b) X is an alkene by E1 reaction

(c) X is (RB) by S_N1 reaction

(d) X is (RB) by S_N2 reaction

2. Select the correct statement(s) about Y.

(a) Y is formed by flow S_N2 reaction

(b) Y is formed by fast S_N2 reaction

(c) Y is an alkene

(d) Y is (RB)

3. Select the correct statement(s) about Z.

(a) Z is formed by slow S_N1 reaction

(b) Z is formed by fast S_N1 reaction

(c) Intermediate is a carbocation

(d) Z is formed by slow S_N2 reaction

***Passage* 7.** Consider the following free-radical reaction

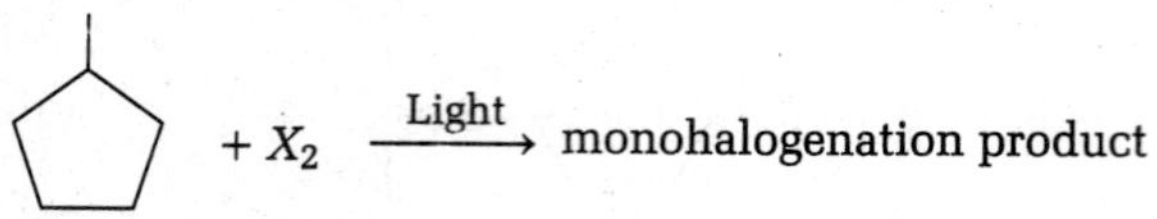

1. Light is involved in which of the following reaction steps?

(a) Initiation only

(b) Propagation only

(c) Termination only

(d) Initiation and propagation

2. Which of the following statements about the reaction is not true?

(a) Halogen atoms are consumed in the first propagation step

(b) Halogen atoms are regenerated in the second propagation step

(c) Hydrogen atoms are produced in the first propagation step

(d) Chain termination occurs when two radicals react with each other

3. For the following reactions :

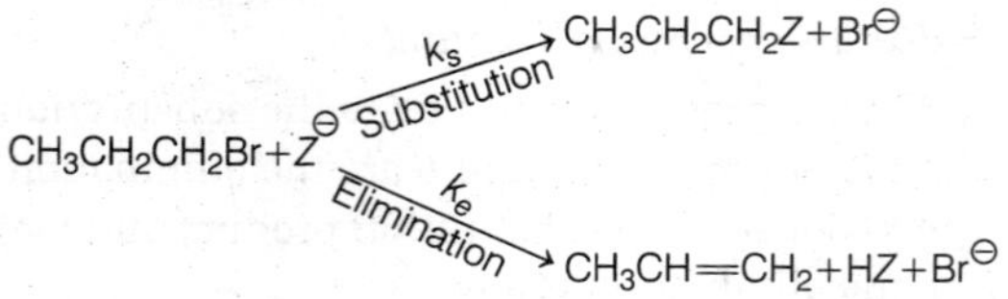

where,

$Z^{\ominus} = CH_3CH_2O^{\ominus}$ (A) or $H_3C—C(CH_3)_2—O^{\ominus}$ (B)

k_s and k_e, are respectively the rate constants for substitution and elimination, and $\mu = \frac{k_s}{k_e}$, the correct option is .... **[JEE Main 2020, Jan.]**

(a) $\mu_B > \mu_A$ and $k_e(B) > k_e(A)$

(b) $\mu_B > \mu_A$ and $k_e(A) > k_e(B)$

(c) $\mu_A > \mu_B$ and $k_e(A) > k_e(B)$

(d) $\mu_A > \mu_B$ and $k_e(B) > k_e(A)$

***Exmaple* 8.** Consider potential energy diagram for the formation of carbocation from 3-methyl-2-bromobutane during S_N1 reaction and answer Q. (1-3).

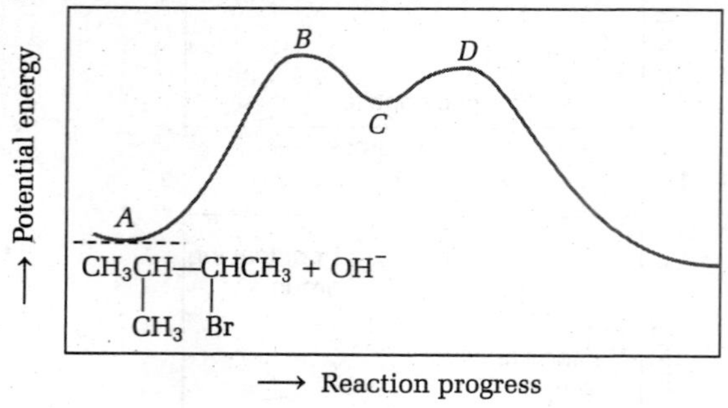

1. Initial carbocation formed is

(a) $CH_3CH\overset{\oplus}{C}HCH_3$
$\quad\;\; |$
$\quad CH_3$

(b) $CH_3CHCH_2\overset{\oplus}{C}H_2$
$\quad\;\; |$
$\quad CH_3$

(c) $CH_3\overset{\oplus}{C}CH_2CH_3$
$\quad\;\; |$
$\quad CH_3$

(d) this S_N reaction takes place without formation of carbocation

2. There is some dip in potential energy from *B* to *C* in the given figure. This is due to

(a) 1,2-hydride shift to form more stable 1° carbocation

$$CH_3CH(CH_3)\overset{\oplus}{C}HCH_2(H) \longrightarrow CH_3CH(CH_3)CH_2\overset{\oplus}{C}H_2$$

(b) 1,2-hydride shift to form more stable 3° carbocation

$$CH_3\overset{\oplus}{C}H(H)CH(CH_3)CH_3 \longrightarrow CH_3\overset{\oplus}{C}(CH_3)CH_2CH_3$$

(c) presence of strong nucleophile OH^-

(d) solvation of Br^- by H-bonding

3. Alkyl halide (R—Br) has chiral centre, as is evident from the structure, and by S_N reaction we expect the product (alcohol) as to be chiral or mixture of optically active *d*, *l* (±) isomers due to inversion. But we get optically inactive achiral alcohol as the major product. This indicates that

(a) reaction is S_N1 which result in the formation of carbocation $CH_3CH(CH_3)\overset{\oplus}{C}HCH_3$

(b) there is 1,2-hydride shift leading to isomerisation to the more stable 3° carbocation $CH_3\overset{\oplus}{C}(CH_3)CH_2CH_3$

(c) nucleophile is attached to 3° carbon (having two identical methyl groups and the alcohol is thus a chiral)

(d) All the above facts are true

Matrix-Match Type

Given below are Matching Type Questions, with two columns (each having some items) each . Each item of Column I has to be matched with the items of Column II.

1. Match the species in Column I with their commercial names in Column II.

	Column I		Column II
A.	CCl_3NO_2	1.	Freon-12
B.	CCl_4	2.	Chloretone
C.	$(CH_3)_2C(OH)CCl_3$	3.	Pyrene
D.	CCl_2F_2	4.	Chloropicrin

2. Match the list I with the list II. **[JEE Advanced 2018]**

	List-I		List-II
P.	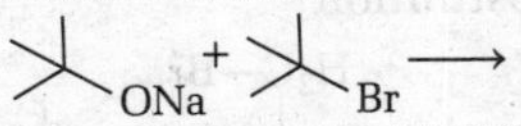	1.	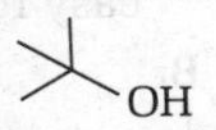
Q.	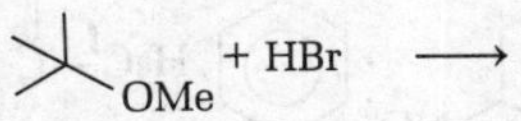	2.	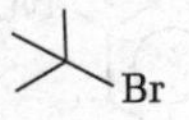
R.	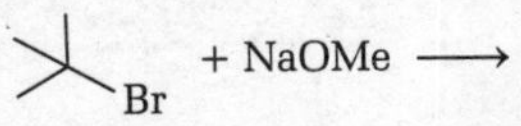	3.	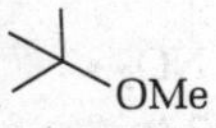
S.	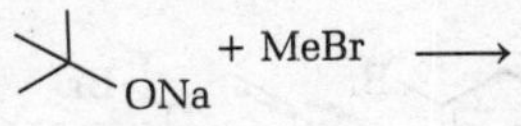	4.	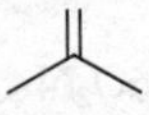
		5.	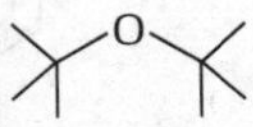

3. Match the chemical conversion in Column I with the appropriate reagents in Column II. **[JEE Advanced 2013]**

	Column I	Column II
A.	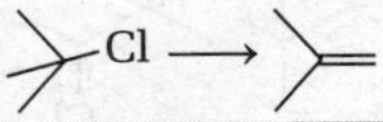	1. (i) $Hg(OAc)_2$; (ii) $NaBH_4$
B.	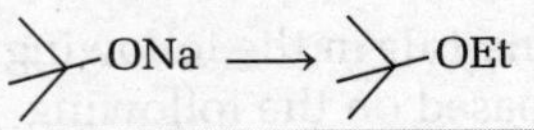	2. NaOEt
C.	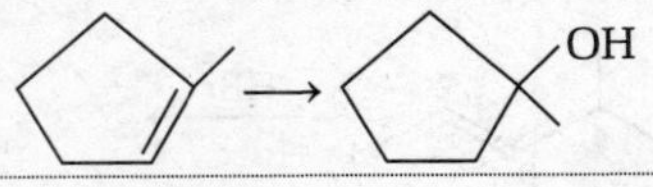	3. Et–Br
D.	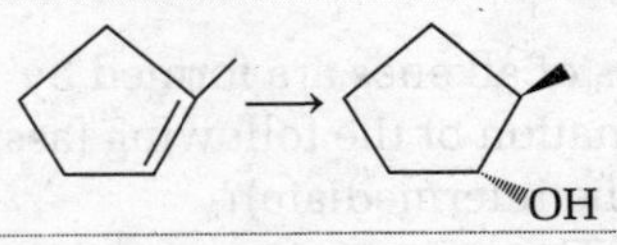	4. (i) BH_3; (ii) H_2O_2/NaOH

4. Match the following.

Column I (Type)	Column II (Reaction)
A. $Y^{\ominus}$: acts as a nucleophile.	1. $\overset{\ominus}{Y}: + R_2\overset{\oplus}{C}CHR_2' \longrightarrow R_2C(Y)CHR_2'$
B. $Y^{\ominus}$: acts as a base.	2. $\overset{\ominus}{Y}: + R_2\overset{\oplus}{C}CHR_2' \longrightarrow R_2C{=}CR_2'$
C. Enolate formation	3. $\overset{\ominus}{Y}: + R_2CHC(=O)R' \longrightarrow R_2CHC(O^-)(R)R'$
D. Nucleophilic addition	4. $\overset{\ominus}{Y}: + R_2CHC(=O)R' \longrightarrow R_2C{=}C(O^-)R'$

5. Match the following.

Column I (Reaction)	Column II (Type)
A. $CF_3CH{=}CH_2 + HCl \longrightarrow$	1. Markownikoff's addition
B. $CH_3CH{=}CH_2 + HBr \xrightarrow{\text{Benzoyl peroxide}}$	2. Anti-Markownikoff's addition
C. $CH_3CH_2CH_2Cl \xrightarrow{H_2O/S_N1}$	3. Primary carbocation
D. $CH_3CH{=}CH_2 + HCl \xrightarrow{\text{Benzoyl peroxide}}$	4. Secondary carbocation

6. Match the following.

Column I (Reaction)	Column II (Types)
A. H—C(Me)(Et)—Br $\xrightarrow{OH^-}$ HO—C(Me)(Et)—H	1. Carbocation
B. H—C(Me)(Et)—Br $\xrightarrow{\bar{O}C_2H_5}$ H_5C_2O—C(Me)(Et)—H + H—C(Me)(Et)—OC_2H_5	2. $\left(\frac{dx}{dt}\right) = k$[reactant]
C. $CH_3CH(CH_3)CH_2CH_2Br \xrightarrow{\bar{O}C_2H_5}$ $CH_3C(CH_3)H{=}CHCH_3$	3. Optical rotation
D. $CH_3CH(CH_3)CH{=}CH_2 + HBr \longrightarrow CH_3C(Br)(CH_3)CH_2CH_3$	4. Rearrangement

Single Integer Answer Questions

Answer of these questions is a single digit lying between 0 to 9.

1. How many of the compounds will form chiral alkyl chloride on chlorination?

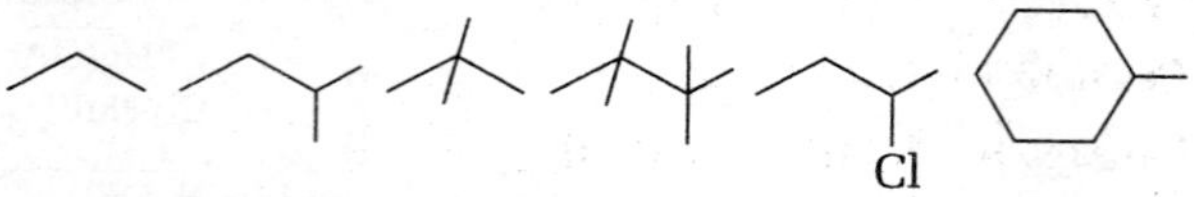

2. What is the position of Br in the following addition reaction (based on the following numbering)

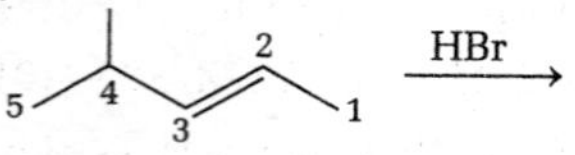

3. How many types of alkenes are formed by dehydroboromination of the following (assume carbocation as the intermediate)?

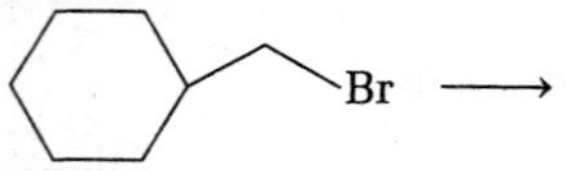

4. The total number of alkenes possible by dehydrobromination of 3-bromo-3-cyclopentylhexane using alcoholic KOH is **[IIT JEE 2011]**

5. In the following sequence of reaction,

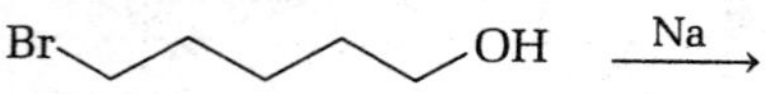

n-member ring is formed. What is the value of n?

6. How many of the following are better leaving groups than OH^-?

$Cl^-, Br^-\ I^-, CH_3COO^-, CH_3O^-, NH_2^-, HCO_3^-$

7. In the following monobromination reaction, the number of possible chiral products is **[JEE Advance 2016]**

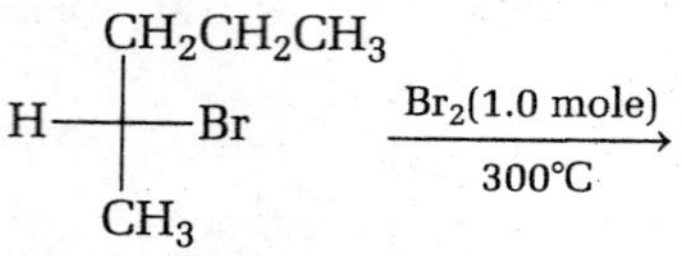

(1.0 mole)
(enantiomerically pure)

8. How many of the following halides will not go for easy nucleophilic substitution?

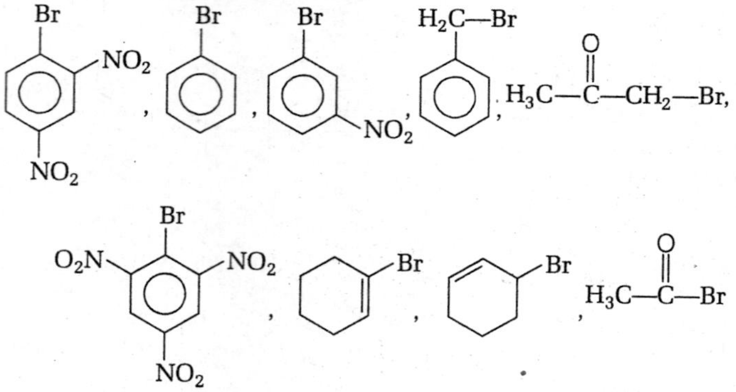

Answers

Objective Questions Type I [Only one correct option]

1. (a)	2. (b)	3. (a)	4. (c)	5. (c)	6. (b)	7. (c)	8. (d)	9. (c)	10. (d)
11. (c)	12. (c)	13. (b)	14. (c)	15. (a)	16. (b)	17. (c)	18. (c)	19. (a)	20. (b)
21. (d)	22. (b)	23. (c)	24. (d)	25. (a)	26. (c)	27. (a)	28. (b)	29. (a)	30. (b)
31. (b)	32. (c)	33. (a)	34. (d)	35. (d)	36. (b)	37. (c)	38. (b)	39. (b)	40. (d)
41. (a)	42. (c)	43. (d)	44. (a)	45. (c)	46. (b)	47. (c)	48. (d)	49. (a)	50. (a)
51. (a)	52. (c)	53. (d)	54. (c)	55. (c)	56. (c)	57. (c)	58. (c)	59. (c)	60. (b)
61. (a)	62. (c)	63. (a)	64. (b)	65. (d)	66. (b)	67. (b)	68. (d)	69. (b)	70. (c)
71. (a)	72. (b)	73. (b)	74. (c)	75. (c)	76. (a)	77. (a)	78. (c)	79. (c)	80. (b)
81. (a)	82. (a)	83. (d)	84. (a)	85. (c)	86. (b)	87. (b)	88. (b)	89. (c)	90. (c)
91. (b)	92. (b)	93. (c)	94. (d)	95. (d)	96. (a)	97. (b)	98. (c)	99. (a)	100. (c)
101. (d)	102. (b)	103. (b)	104. (a)	105. (c)	106. (c)	107. (d)	108. (c)	109. (c)	110. (d)
111. (c)	112. (d)	113. (a)	114. (c)	115. (d)	116. (c)	117. (a)	118. (a)	119. (c)	120. (c)
121. (c)	122. (c)	123. (d)	124. (b)	125. (d)	126. (c)	127. (d)	128. (a)	129. (c)	

Objective Questions Type II [One or more than one correct option(s)]

1. (b, d)	2. (a, b)	3. (a, c)	4. (c)	5. (a, b, c)
6. (a, c, d)	7. (b)	8. (a, c)	9. (a, b, c, d)	10. (b, c, d)
11. (b)	12. (a, c)	13. (a, c)	14. (d)	15. (a, d)

Numerical Value Questions

1. (5) 2. (2) 3. (3) 4. (2) 5. (1) 6. (5) 7. (4) 8. (8)

Comprehension Based Questions

Passage 1 – 1. (c) 2. (b) 3. (d)

Passage 2 – 1. (a) 2. (c)

Passage 3 – 1. (a,b,c) 2. (d) 3. (c)

Passage 4 – 1. (a) 2. (d) 3. (a)

Passage 5 – 1. (b) 2. (a,b,c,d)

Passage 6 – 1. (a) 2. (b,d) 3. (d)

Passage 7 – 1. (a) 2. (c) 3. (d)

Passage 8 – 1. (a) 2. (b) 3. (d)

Matrix-Match Type

1. A→(4); B→(3); C→(2); D→(1)
2. A→(1,4); B→(2); C→(4); D→(3)
3. A→(2); B→(3); C→(1); D→(4)
4. A→(1,3); B→(2,4); C→(3,4); D→(3)
5. A→(2,3); B→(2); C→(3,4); D→(1,2,3)
6. A→(3); B→(1,2,3); C→(1,2,4); D→(1,4)

Single Integer Answer Questions

1. (3) 2. (4) 3. (5) 4. (6) 5. (5) 6. (6) 7. (5) 8. (3)

Solutions

Objective Questions Type I [Only one correct option]

1. (*a*) $CH_2{=}CH\overset{\oplus}{C}H_2$ (intermediate) is resonance stabilised.

2. (*b*)

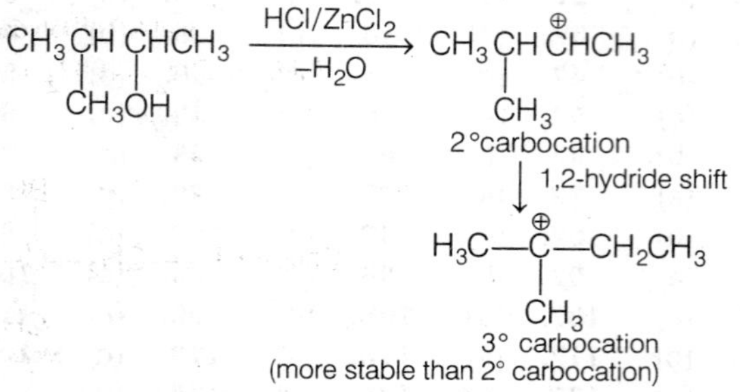

4. (*c*) 3° alcohol has no H-atom at (C—OH).

5. (*c*) For substitution at allylic position in the given compound, the reagent used is $Cl_2/h\nu$ light. The reaction is free radical halogenation.

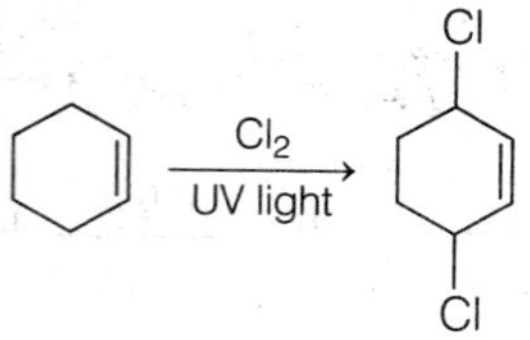

6. (*b*)

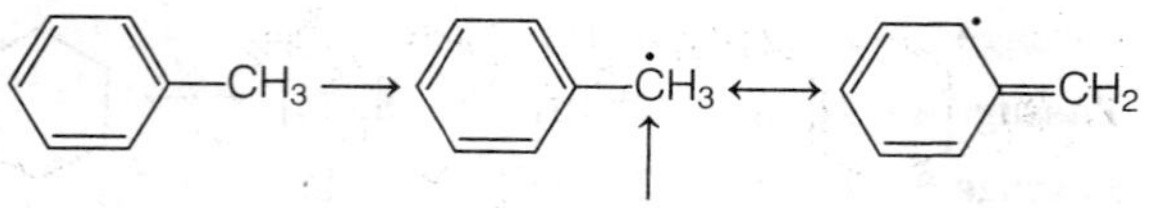

7. (*c*) $CH_3CH_2CH_2CH_3 \xrightarrow{Cl_2} CH_3\overset{*}{C}(Cl)HCH_2CH_3$

(* is chiral carbon)
Thus, racemic mixture.

8. (*d*) NaI is the best for halogen-exchange reaction.

9. (*c*) Since, this H is allylic as well as benzylic.

11. (*c*)

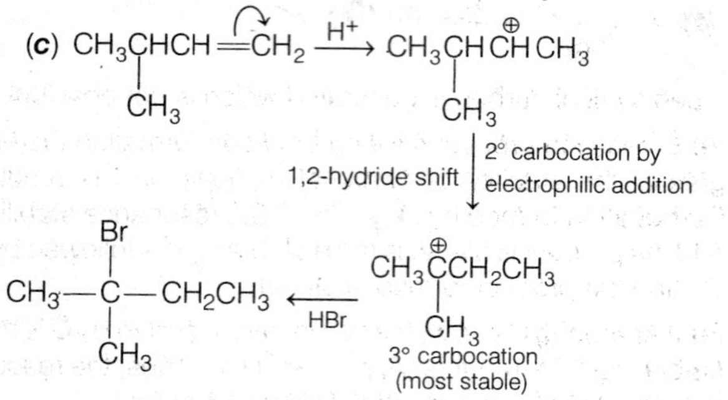

12. (*c*) 3° carbocation is formed by 1,2-methyl shift.

13. (*b*) $RCO_2Ag + Br \longrightarrow RBr + CO_2 + AgBr$
(Best yield)

14. (*c*) $H_3C{-}C(CH_3){=}C(CH_3){-}CH_3$ is symmetrical thus same product is formed in the presence or absence of peroxide.

15. (*a*) Borodine-Hunsdiecker reaction
1° alkyl bromide gives maximum yield.

16. (*b*) Haloform reaction is given by
CH_3CH_2OH, $CH_3CH(OH)$, CH_3CHO, $CH_3{-}C(CH_3){=}O$

22. (*b*) Maximum boiling point: I > Br > Cl > OH.

25. (*a*) It lacks β-carbon.

27. (*a*) $CH_3CH(Br)CH_3 \xrightarrow{\text{Slow}} CH_3\overset{\oplus}{C}HCH_3 \xrightarrow{\text{Fast}} CH_3CH{=}CH_2$

29. (*a*) The given reaction is completed as follows :

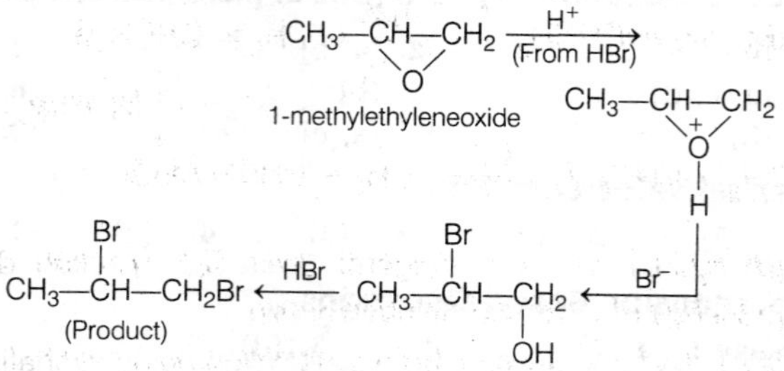

31. (*b*) In option (b) vinyl chloride, C—Cl bond is shortest due to resonance of lone pair of — Cl (chlorine atom).
Due to resonance C — Cl bond aquire partial double bond character.
Hence, vinyl chloride have least C — Cl bond length.

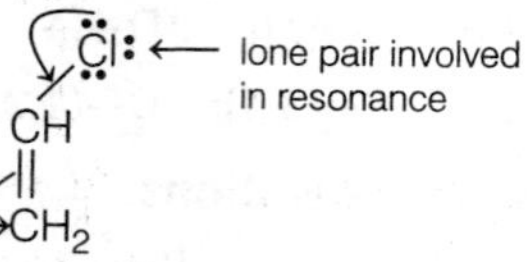

32. (*c*)

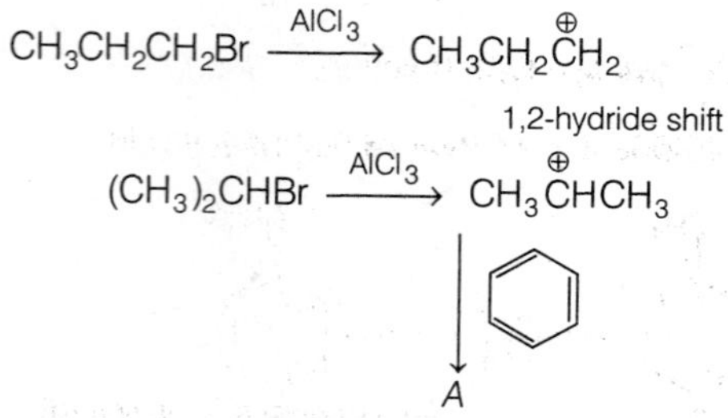

33. (*a*)

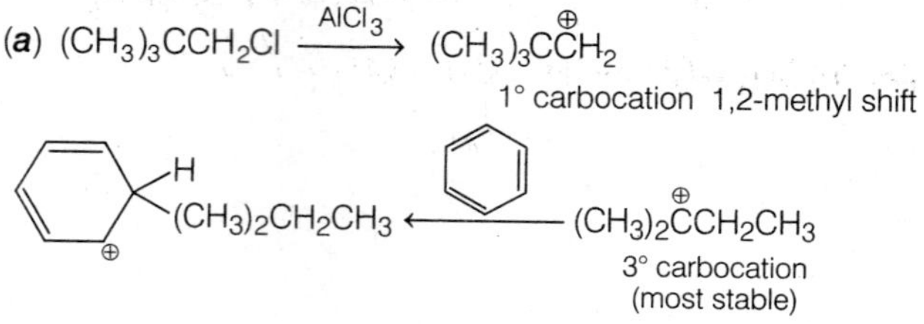

34. (*d*)

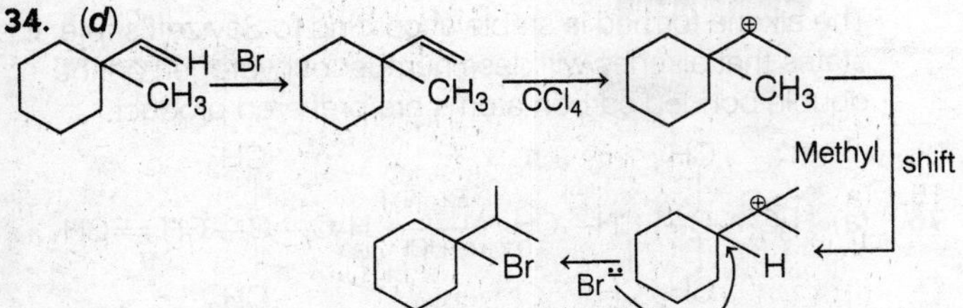

35. (*d*) $CH_2{=}CHCH_3 \xrightarrow{NBS} CH_2{=}CHCH_2Br \xrightarrow{AgCN} CH_2{=}CHCH_2NC$

Allylic position is affected

37. (*c*) $H{-}C{\equiv}CCH_2Br \xrightarrow{Mg}$

↑

Thus, H is acidic, thus (C—Br) does not react with Mg.

38. (*b*) $CH_2{=}CHCH_2{-}H \xrightarrow[I]{NBS} CH_2{=}CHCH_2Br \xrightarrow[II]{Mg/ether} CH_2{=}CHCH_2MgBr \xrightarrow[III]{D_2O} CH_2{=}CHCH_2D$

40. (*d*) R_2CuLi (Gilmann reagent) gives S_N2 reaction due to presence of $-R^{\ominus}$ act as nucleophile.

41. (*a*) It is Wurtz reaction, both alkyl halide being aliphatic.

42. (*c*) $CH_3CHCl_2 \xrightarrow{KOH} CH_3CHO$

43. (*d*) $CH_3{-}C(Cl)_2{-}CH_3 \xrightarrow{KOH} CH_3{-}C(OH)_2{-}CH_3 \xrightarrow{-H_2O} CH_3COCH_3$ gives iodoform test

(*A*) (*B*)

47. (*c*) $:CCl_2$ give *syn* type reaction.

49. (*a*) Chloretone is preservative not insecticicle.

51. (*a*)

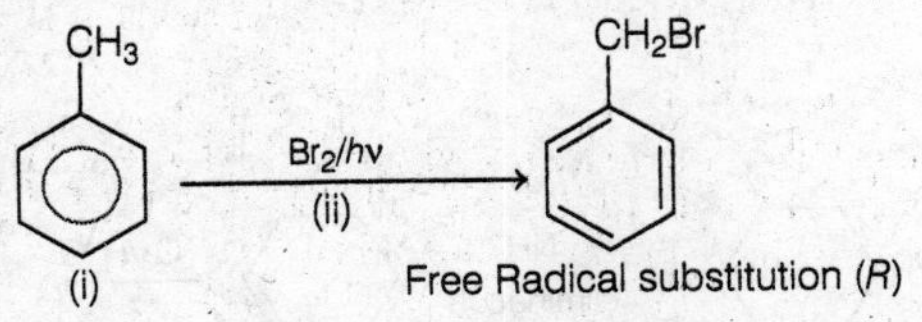

53. (*d*) $CH_3{-}CH{=}CH{-}CH(CH_3){-}CH_3 \xrightarrow{HBr}$

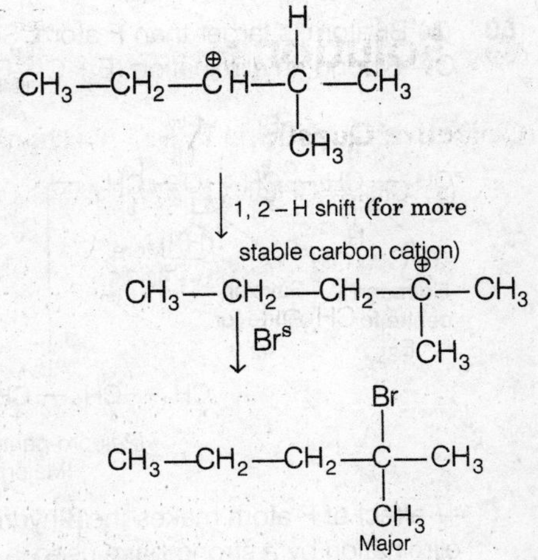

54. (*c*)

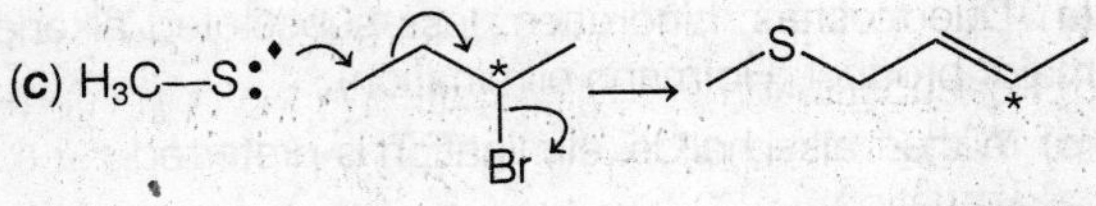

55. (*c*)

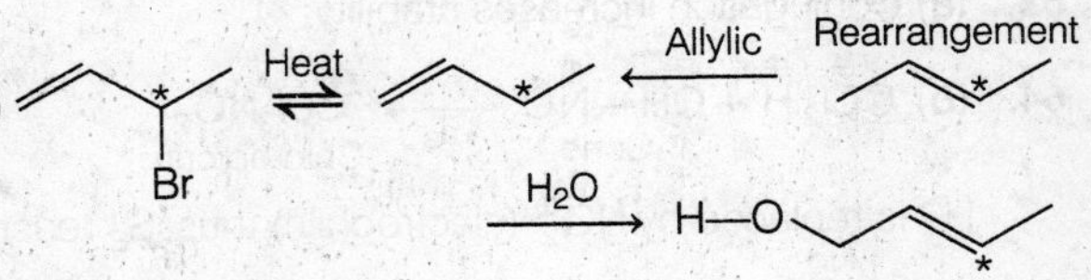

57. (*c*)

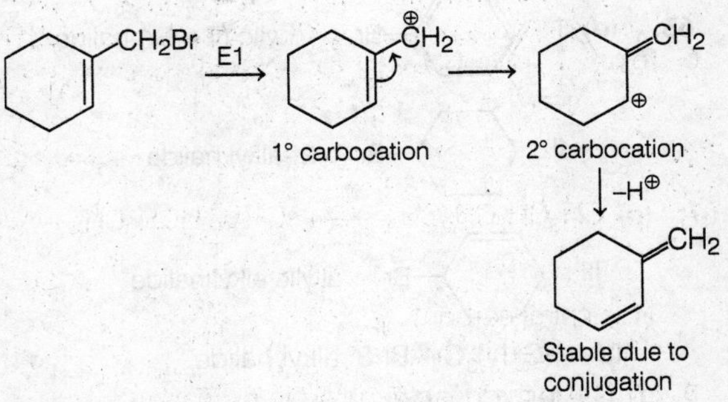

58. (*c*)

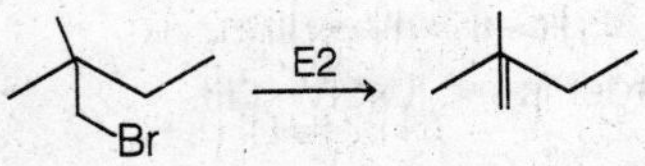

pentavalent carbon is generated which is not possible.

59. (*c*) E_1 reaction proceeds *via* carbocation formation, therefore greater the stability of carbocation faster is the reaction. Carbocation formed by *D*, 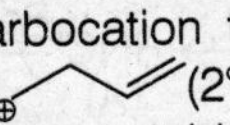 (2°, resonance stabilised and the product is diene) is most stable  followed by *B*, (1° and the product formed is diene).

Further among C and *A*, the carbocation formed by *C* is more stable 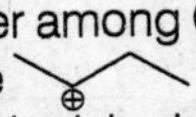 (2°) than *A*, 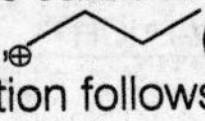 (1°). Thus, the reactivity towards dehydrohalogenation follows the order :

D > *B* > *C* > *A*

60. (*b*) Br atom is larger than F atom. So, C—Br is weaker than C—F bond. In elimination (E_2), C—Br bond will be cleared.

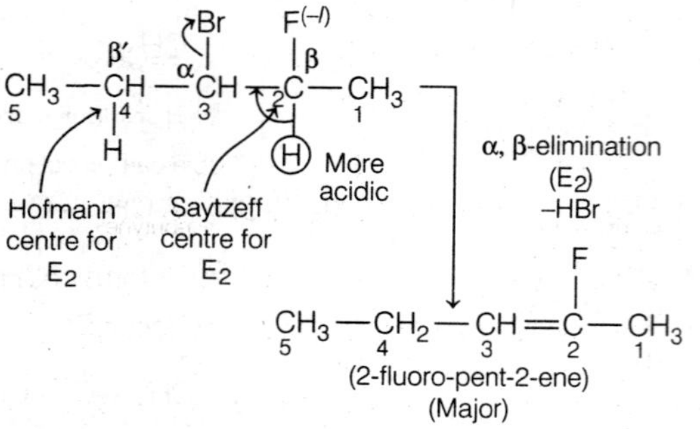

–*I*-effect of F atom makes the β-hydrogen more acidic for its elimination by a strong base used in E_2.

61. (*a*) Due to steric hindrance, less substituted alkene is the major product (Hofmann elimination).

62. (*c*) With 2° alkyl halide, elimination is preferred.

63. (*a*) Conjugation increases stability.

64. (*b*) $\overset{\ominus}{C}Cl_3\overset{\oplus}{H} + \overset{\ominus}{O}H—\overset{\oplus}{N}O_2 \longrightarrow CCl_3NO_2$
Conc. Chloropicrin

H^+ is replaced by $NO_2^{\oplus}$ (electrophile) thus, S_E reaction.

65. (*d*) I : 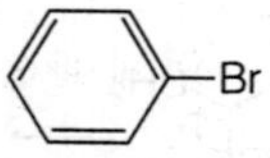 vinylic (C—Br) halide

II : 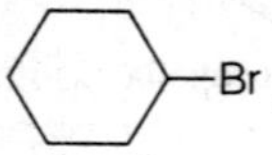 2° alkyl halide

III : 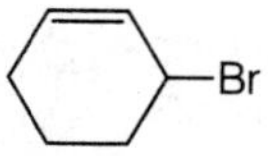 allylic alkyl halide

IV : $(CH_3)_3C$—Br 3° alkyl halide

BE (C — Br)

I > II > IV > III

Thus, hydrolysis order is I < II < IV < III.

69. (*b*) $CHCl_3 \xrightarrow{KtO^-Bu} :CCl_2$
Carbene

72. (*b*) $RCl + AgCN \longrightarrow \underset{(A)}{RNC} \xrightarrow{\text{Reduction}} \underset{(B)}{RNHCH_3}$

73. (*b*) Complete reaction is as follows :

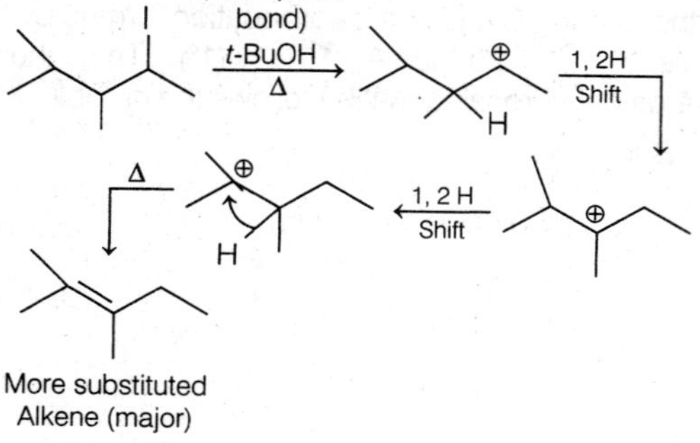

The alkene formed is stable according to Saytzeff's rule. It states that alkenes with less number of hydrogen on the double bonded carbon atoms are preffered product.

76. (*a*)

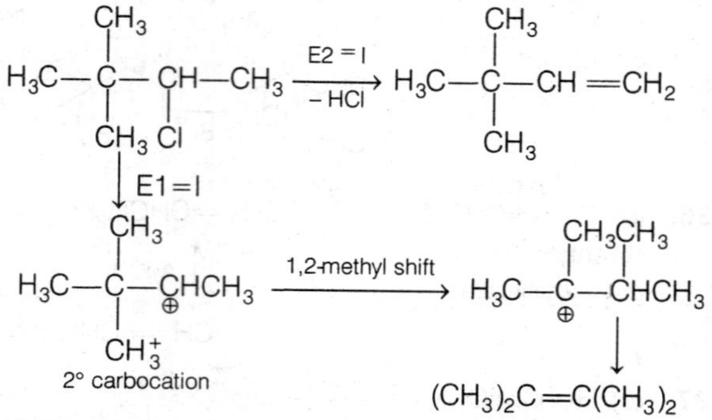

78. (*c*) End product indicates that *A* has $(CH_3)_2CH$ group.

Thus, *A* can be $(CH_3)_2CHCl_2 \xrightarrow{KCN} (CH_3)_2CH(CN)_2$

$\xrightarrow{H_3O^+} (CH_3)_2CH(COOH)_2 \xrightarrow{\Delta} (CH_3)_2CHCOOH$

when two —COOH groups are on same carbon, heating eliminates CO_2.

79. (*c*)

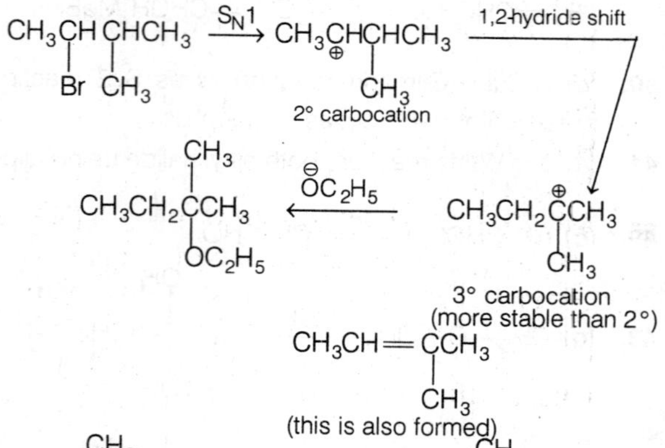

80. (*b*)

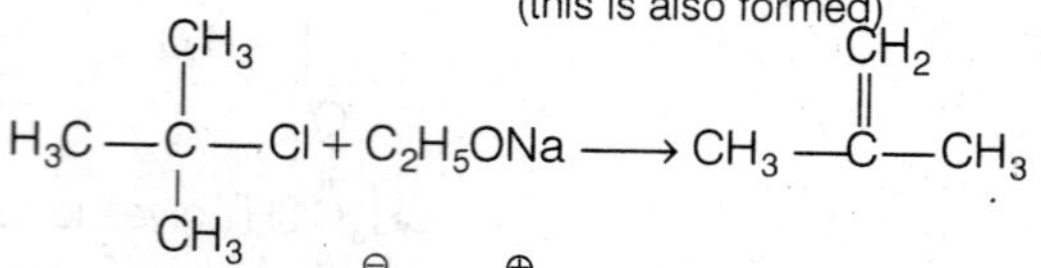

82. (*a*) $Br_2 + H_2O \longrightarrow \overset{\ominus}{O}H—\overset{\oplus}{Br}$

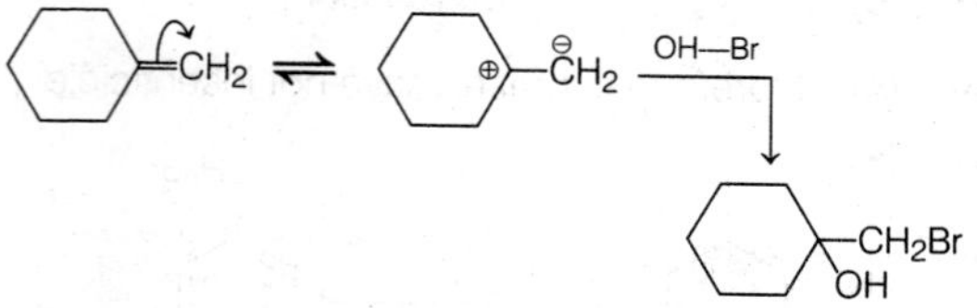

85. (*c*)

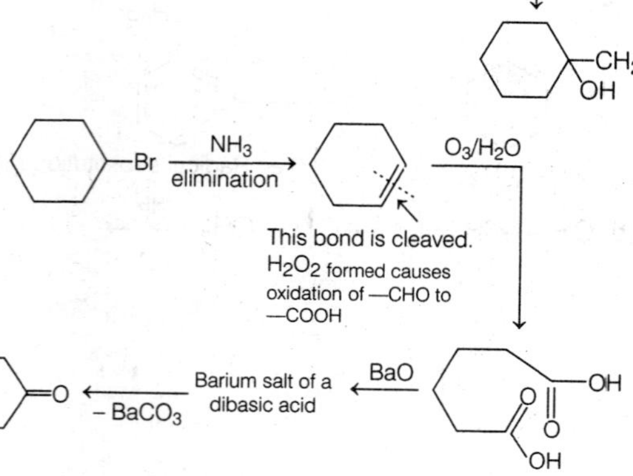

86. (*b*) **Reaction (1)**

Rate $= k[t\text{-BuBr}]$, it is a first order nucleophilic substitution reaction (S_N1), so, rate of this reaction will depend only on the concentration of the substrate, i.e. *t*-BuBr.

So, option (b) is correct, but option (c) is not correct.

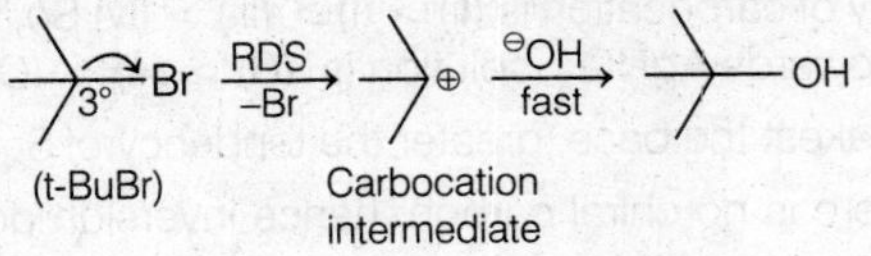

Reaction (2)

Rate $= k\ [t\text{-ByBr}]\ [\underset{\text{(base)}}{OH^-}]$, it is a second order α, β-elimination reaction (E_2), because *t*-BuBr undergoes dehydrohalogenation (—HBr) with a strong base (alcoholic or ethanolic OH^-) to give an alkene. So, rate of the reaction depends on concentrations of substrate (*t*-ByBr) and base (OH/alc.). So, option (a) is not correct.

$\ddot{O}R$ is a stronger base than $\ddot{O}H$. So, use of $\ddot{O}R$ will make the E_2 reaction faster. Hence, option (a) is also not correct.

87. (*b*) 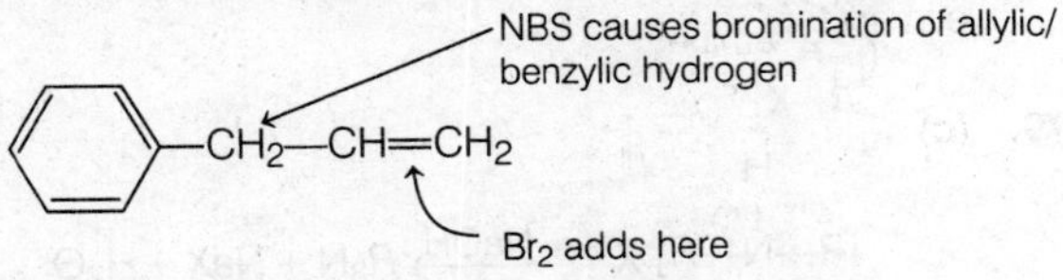

Br_2/Fe causes S_E at *ortho*/*para* position.

88. (*b*) 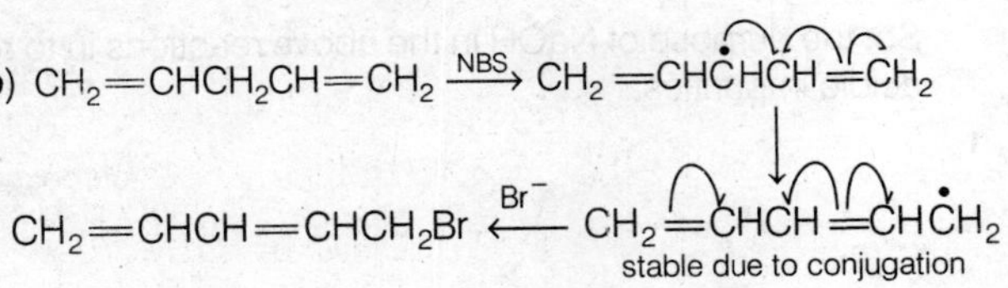

89. (*c*) 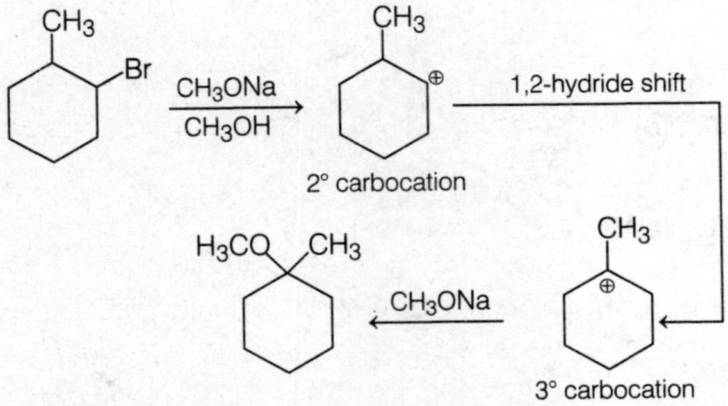

91. (*b*) Intramolecular Friedel–Crafts reaction.

95. (*d*) Carbylamine reaction.

98. (*c*) (a) CCl_3CHO chloral (b) $CHCl_3$ chloroform

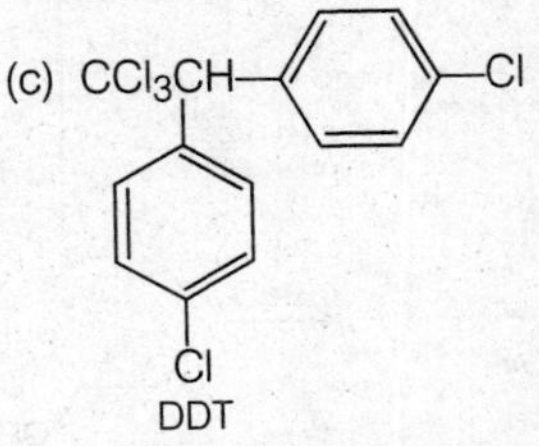

(d) CCl_4 carbon tetrachloride

99. (*a*) Tertiary alkyl halide produces most stable 3° carbocation as an intermediate.

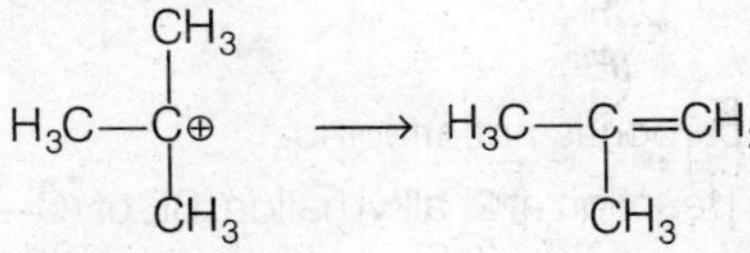

101. (*d*) $CH{\equiv}\overset{-}{C}\overset{+}{N}a + CH_3CH_2Br \longrightarrow \underset{\text{1-butyne}}{CH{\equiv}CCH_2CH_3}$

103. (*b*) When chlorine react with ethyl alcohol, it form chloral.

104. (*a*) Complete reaction of I, II and III are as follow:

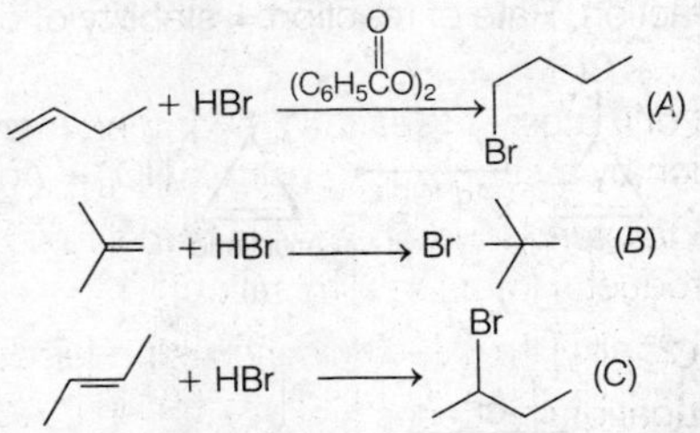

RX are polar, therefore intermolecular forces of attraction (e.g., dipole-dipole and van der Waals') are stronger in *RX*.

Hence, the boiling point of *RX* is greater than those of hydrocarbons of comparable molecular masses.

Branching decreases the surface area as in alkane because the branched *C* chains are more spherical -like, which results in lower boiling point. $\text{B.P} \propto \dfrac{1}{\text{Branching}}$

Hence, the boiling point of isomeric *RX* decreases with increase in branching, hence the order will be II < III < I.

107. (*d*) Due to electron deficient carbon.

108. (*c*) $R{-}X \longrightarrow \overset{\oplus}{R}\ddot{X} \longrightarrow \overset{\oplus}{R}||\ddot{X} \xrightarrow{\ddot{Y}} R{-}Y + \ddot{X}$

It indicates $R^{\oplus}$ (carbocation) formation takes place and $R^{\oplus}$ got stabilised by electronic factors and polar solvent molecules because solvent separation of $R^{\oplus}$ is possible.

So, statement (D) is not correct.

Here, $\ddot{X}$ (leaving group) of *R*—*X* is substituted by $\ddot{Y}$, (nucleophile) *via* the formation of carbocation ($R^{\oplus}$) intermediate. So, it is an S_N1 reaction.

S_N1 mechanism supports weaker nucleophiles. So, statement (A) is correct.

S_N1 reaction is accompanied by inversion and retention in configuration, i.e. racemisation provided '*R*' of *R*—*X* is chiral. So, statement (C) is correct.

Attachment of bulkier substituents or 3°-nature of the carbon atom of C—*X* bond of *R*—*X* will favour formation of $R^{\oplus}$ (carbocation). So, statement (B) is also correct.

114. (*c*) Solvolysis order :

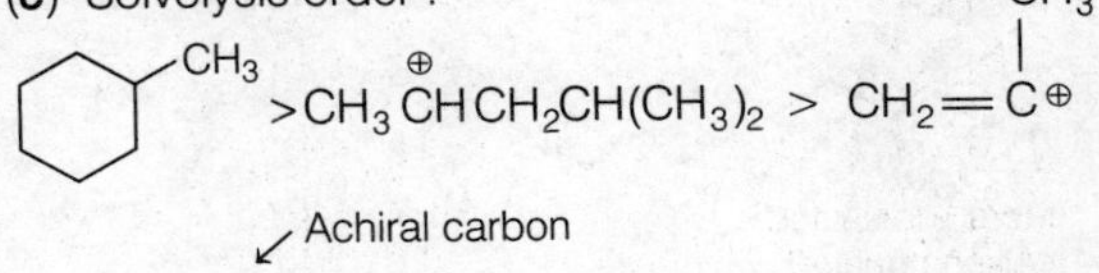

118. (**a**)

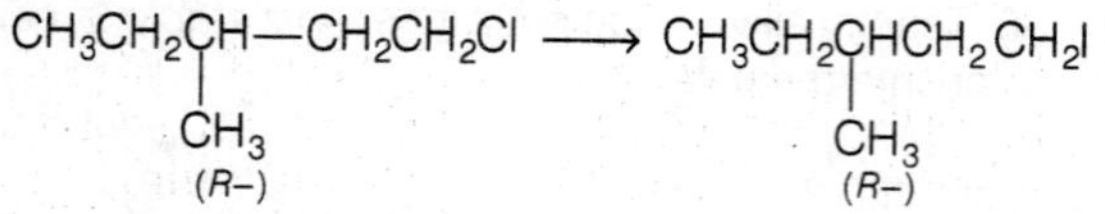

Achiral carbon is not affected.

119. (**c**) S_N1-reaction at 2° alkyl halide. BE of (C—Br) < (C—Cl). Thus (C—Br) is affected.

121. (**c**) General reaction :

$$AgNO_3 + X(\text{Halogen}) \longrightarrow AgX + NO_3^{2-}$$

It follows S_N1 reaction.

In S_N1 reaction, Rate of reaction ∝ stability of carbocation

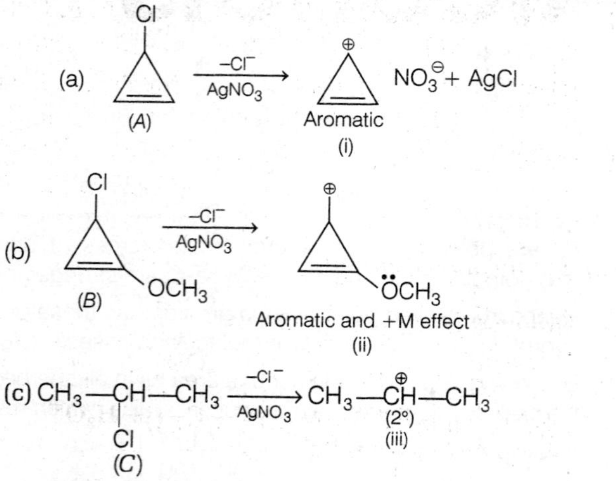

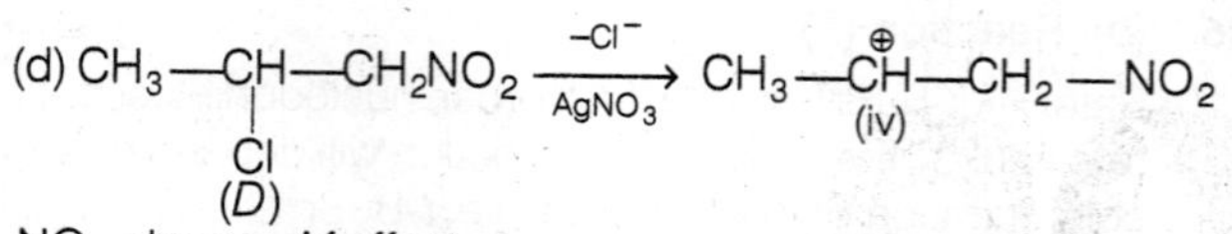

NO_2 shows $-M$ effect

Stability of carbocation is (ii) > (i) > (iii) > (iv) So, the reactivity order towards $AgNO_3$ solution is (*B*) > (*A*) > (*C*) > (*D*).

124. (**b**) Weakest the base, greater the tendency of S_N reaction.

128. (**a**) There is no chiral carbon, hence inversion does not take place.

129. (**c**)

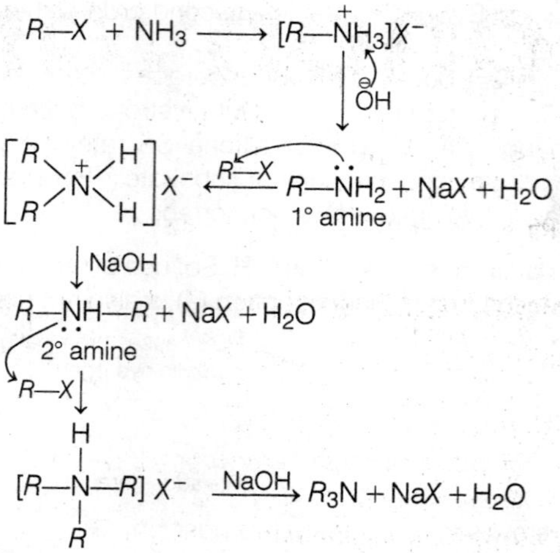

So, the purpose of NaOH in the above reactions in to remove acidic impurities.

09

Monohydric Alcohols

Objective Questions Type I [Only one correct option]

In each of the questions below, four choices are given of which only one is correct.

1. Hydration
(a) takes place through carbocation
(b) is a reversible process
(c) follows S_N1 mechanism
(d) follows all of the above

2. Which is hydrated to a maximum extent?
(a) $CH_3-\underset{CH_3}{\overset{CH_3}{\overset{|}{\underset{|}{C}}}}-CH=CH_2$
(b) $CH_3-CH=CH_2$
(c) $CH_2=CH_2$
(d) $CH\equiv CH$

3. In the following reaction most stable intermediate is

$$\overset{CH_3}{\overset{|}{CH_3CH}}CH=CH_2 + H_2O \xrightarrow{H^+}$$

(a) $\overset{CH_3}{\overset{|}{CH_3CH}}CH_2\overset{\oplus}{C}H_2$ (b) $\overset{CH_3}{\overset{|}{CH_3CH}}\underset{\oplus}{C}HCH_3$
(c) $CH_3\underset{\oplus}{\overset{CH_3}{\overset{|}{C}}}CH_2CH_3$ (d) $\overset{CH_3}{\overset{|}{CH_3CH}}CH_2\overset{\ominus}{C}H_2$

4. In the hydration of an alkene carbocation is formed from
(a) carbanion
(b) oxonium ion
(c) hydroxide ion
(d) hydride ion

5. Following reaction represents

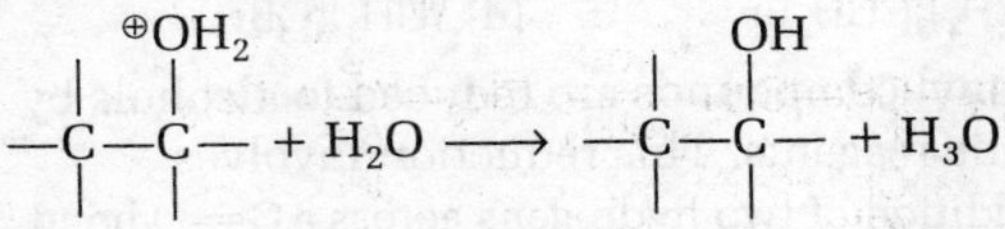

(a) Lowry-Bronsted protonic acid-base reaction
(b) Lewis acid-base reaction
(c) Both (a) and (b)
(d) None of the above

6. The synonym for water gas when used in the production of methanol is **[JEE Main 2019, April]**
(a) natural gas (b) laughing gas
(c) *syn* gas (d) fuel gas

7. In the following reaction,

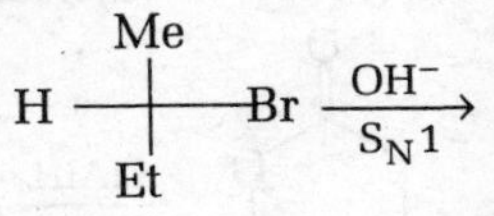

product formed
(a) retains configuration (b) inverts configuration
(c) is a racemic mixture (d) is a *meso* compound

8. In the following reaction,

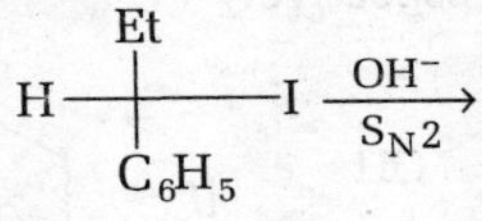

product formed
(a) retains configuration (b) inverts configuration
(c) is a racemic mixture (d) is a *meso* compound

9. Main products formed during a reaction of 1-methoxy naphthalene with hydroiodic acid are **[JEE Main 2021, March]**

(a) 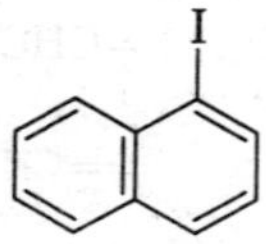 and CH_3OH

(b) 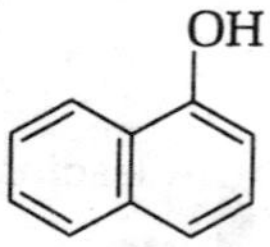 and CH_3I

(c) 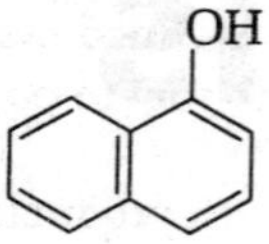 and CH_3OH

(d) 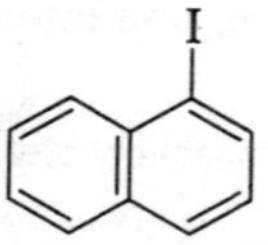 and CH_3I

10. Alkene is also formed as the major product in the hydrolysis of the following with NaOH

(a) CH_3CH_2Br (b) $(CH_3)_2CHBr$

(c) $(CH_3)_3CCH_2Br$ (d) $(CH_3)_3CBr$

11. Carbonyl compounds are reduced to alcohols by hydride reagents. This reduction involves

(a) addition of two hydrogens across a C=O bond

(b) reduction of carbonyl group to an alkoxide which is protonated to alcohol

(c) Both (a) and (b)

(d) None of the above

12. $CH_3\overset{O}{\overset{\|}{C}}CH_2\overset{O}{\overset{\|}{C}}OCH_3$ is reduced to $CH_3\underset{OH}{\underset{|}{C}H}CH_2\overset{O}{\overset{\|}{C}}OCH_3$ by

(a) $LiAlH_4$ (b) $NaBH_4$

(c) Both (a) and (b) (d) None of these

13. 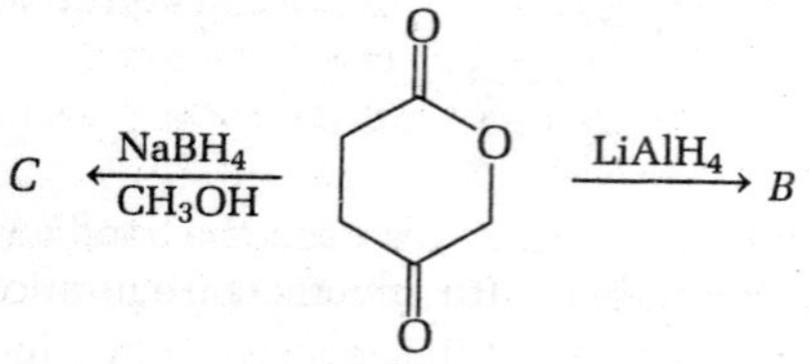

(A)

B and *C* are respectively

(a) I : 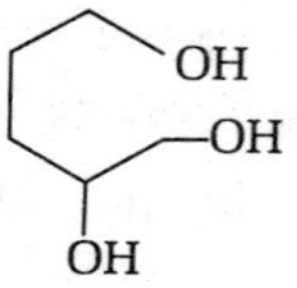 II : 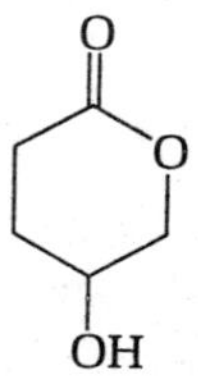

(b) II, I (c) I in both cases

(d) II in both cases

14. $C_4H_8O(A)$ changes to 3° alcohol by reduction with $LiAlH_4$. Thus, *A* is

(a) $CH_3\overset{O}{\overset{\|}{C}}CH_2CH_3$ (b) $CH_3CH_2CH_2CHO$

(c) $(CH_3)_2C\text{—}CH_2$ (epoxide, O bridging) (d) $CH_3CH\text{—}CHCH_3$ (epoxide, O bridging)

15. 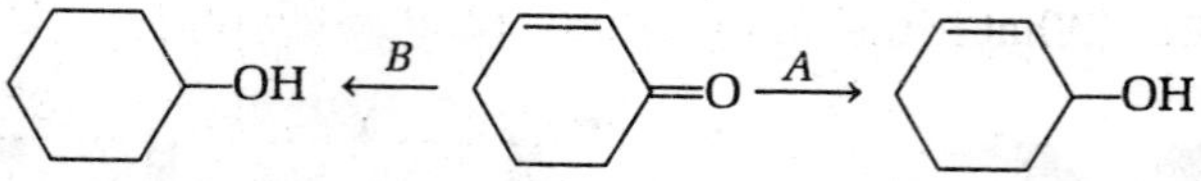

A and *B* are respectively

(a) $H_2/Pt; LiAlH_4/H_2O$ (b) $H_2/Pt; H_2/Pt$

(c) $LiAlH_4/H_2O; LiAlH_4/H_2O$ (d) $LiAlH_4/H_2O; H_2/Pt$

16. Select the incorrect statement about hydroboration-oxidation.

(a) Addition is against Markownikoff rule

(b) Intermediate is a carbocation

(c) It does not involve rearrangement

(d) Addition of boron and hydrogen to double bond is a *syn*-addition

17. 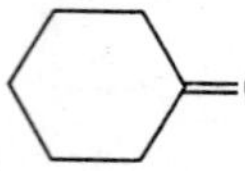 changes to 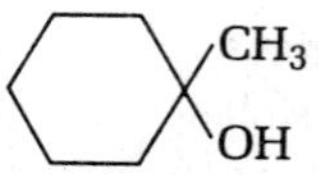 by

(a) $H_3O^{\oplus}$ (b) $BH_3 \cdot THF/H_2O_2$, NaOH

(c) $LiAlH_4$ (d) $NaBH_4$

18. *A* changes to .... with hydroboration-oxidation

$A : CH_3CH{=}\overset{CH_3}{\overset{|}{C}}CH_3$

(a) $CH_3\underset{OH}{\underset{|}{C}H}\underset{CH_3}{\underset{|}{C}H}CH_3$ (b) $CH_3CH_2\overset{OH}{\overset{|}{\underset{CH_3}{\underset{|}{C}}}}CH_3$

(c) $CH_3CH_2\underset{CH_3}{\underset{|}{C}H}CH_2OH$ (d) None of these

19. Addition of the following reagents to alkenes is stereospecific.

I. Br_2 II. $KMnO_4$ III. $BH_3 \cdot THF/H_2O_2 \cdot NaOH$

Select the correct reagents.

(a) I, II (b) II, III

(c) I, III (d) I, II, III

20. Alcohol containing least number of carbon which can be prepared using Grignard reagent is

(a) $(CH_3)_2CHOH$ (b) $(CH_3)_3COH$

(c) CH_3OH (d) CH_3CH_2OH

21. C_2H_4O (*A*) reacts with CH_3MgBr followed by decomposition with $H_3O^{\oplus}$ to give 2° alcohol. Thus, *A* is

(a) $CH_2{=}CHOH$ (b) CH_3CHO

(c) $CH_2\text{—}CH_2$ (epoxide, O bridging) (d) None of these

22. C_2H_4O (*A*) reacts with CH_3MgBr followed by decomposition with $H_3O^{\oplus}$ to give 1° alcohol. Thus, *A* is

(a) $CH_2=CHOH$ (b) CH_3CHO

(c) 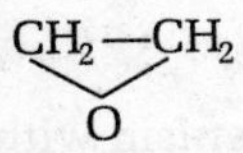 (d) None of these

23. What is the end-product of the following?

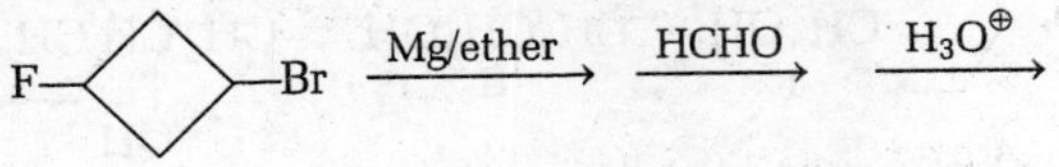

(a) 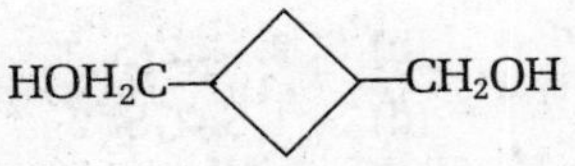

(b) 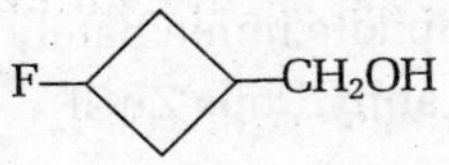

(c) 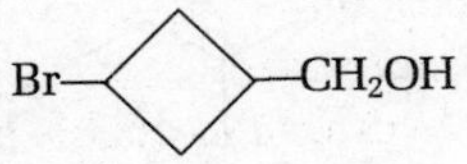

(d) 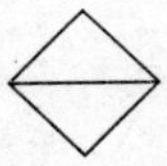

24. Consider the following reactions,

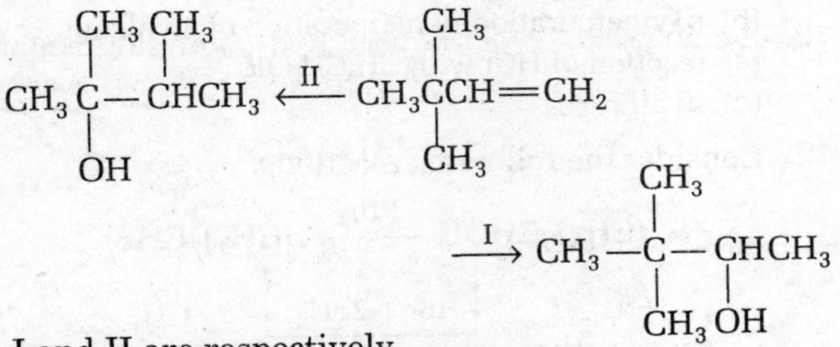

I and II are respectively

(a) hydroboration-oxidation, hydration
(b) hydroboration-oxidation, oxymercuration-demercuration
(c) oxymercuration-demercuration, hydration
(d) hydration, oxymercuration-demercuration

25. Use of methanol may cause

(a) blindness and death due to its oxidation to methanoic acid
(b) blindness and death due to its oxidation to carbon dioxide
(c) deficiency of calcium due to formation of salt
(d) disorder of blood hormones

26. Formation of alcohol by oxymercuration-demercuration of alkenes

(a) involves carbocations and rearrangement
(b) involves carbanions and rearrangement
(c) is stereospecific
(d) does not involve rearrangement and carbocation

27. Following alkene will give same product by any method out of hydration, hydroboration-oxidation and oxymercuration- demercuration

(a) $CH_3CH=CH_2$ (b) $CH_3CH=CHCH_3$

(c) $CH_3CHCH=CH_2$ with CH_3 on the second carbon (d) 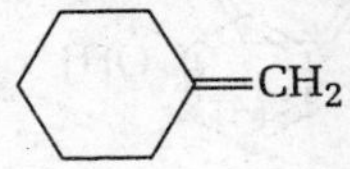

28. Select the incorrect alternate.

(a) Methanol is very toxic to humans, leading to blindness and even death
(b) 98% methanol – H_2O mixture is called rectified spirit
(c) Methanol is used as a premium fuel to power racing car engines
(d) Ethanol is mixed with petroleum products to produce non-lead gasoline for use in internal combustion engine

29. Boiling points of alcohols are generally high. This is due to

(a) hydrogen bonding intermolecular attractions
(b) dipole-dipole attractions
(c) Both (a) and (b)
(d) None of the above

30. Boiling point of CH_3CH_2OH (351 K) is much higher than that of isomeric ether. $(CH_3)_2O$ (248 K). This indicates

(a) hydrogen bonds are much stronger intermolecular attractions than dipole-dipole attractions
(b) dipole-dipole attractions are much stronger than hydrogen bonds
(c) $(CH_3)_2O$ has two hydrophobic groups while CH_3CH_2OH has one
(d) $(CH_3)_2O$ has two hydrophilic groups while CH_3CH_2OH has one

31. Select the incorrect statement.

(a) The O—H bond lengths are about the same in water and methanol
(b) The bond angle C—O—H in methanol and bond angle H—O—H in water are about the same
(c) Both water and methanol have sp^3 hybridised oxygen atom
(d) The bulky methyl group counteracts the bond angle compression caused by non-bonding lone pairs of electrons

32. Increasing order of dipole-moments of (I) ethanol, (II) methoxymethane and (III) propane is

(a) I < II < III (b) III < I < II
(c) III < II < I (d) III < II = I

33. Solubility of alcohol in water is due to

(a) hydrophobic —*R* group
(b) hydrophilic — OH group
(c) hydrophilic —*R* group
(d) hydrophobic —OH group

34. In the following dehydration of alcohol (A) leading to the formation of styrene (B)

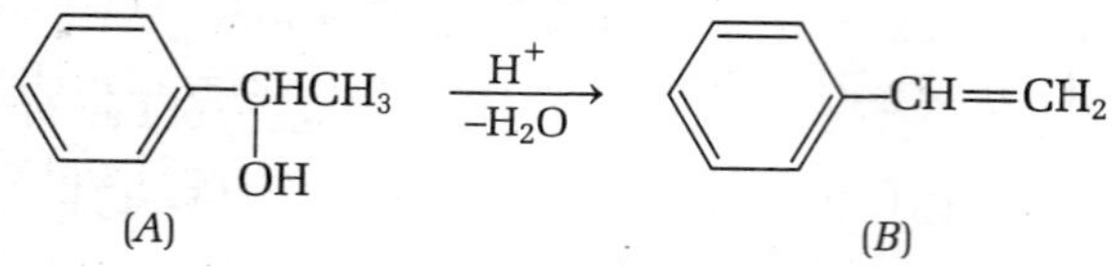

(a) intermediate is carbocation
(b) carbocation is resonance stabilised
(c) it takes place rapidly
(d) All the above are correct statements

35. The major product of the following reaction is

$CH_3CH{=}CHCO_2CH_3 \xrightarrow{LiAlH_4}$ **[JEE Main 2019, April]**

(a) $CH_3CH{=}CHCH_2OH$
(b) $CH_3CH_2CH_2CH_2OH$
(c) $CH_3CH_2CH_2CO_2CH_3$
(d) $CH_3CH_2CH_2CHO$

36. Which is incorrect order of dehydration of alcohol?

(a) 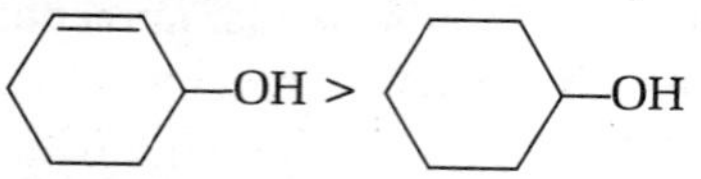

(b) 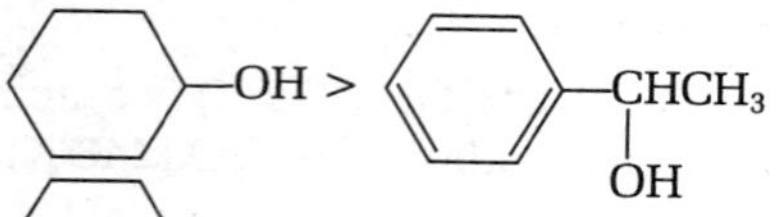

(c) 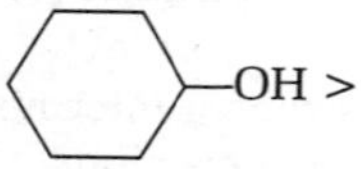 $> CH_3CH_2OH$

(d) $CH_3CH_2CH(OH)CH_3 > CH_3CH_2CH_2CH_2OH$

37. Dehydration product of 1-butanol is
(a) 1-butene (b) 2-butene
(c) isobutene (d) None of these

38. Consider the following reactions,

I. $CH_3CH_2CH(OH)CH_3 \xrightarrow{H^+} A$ (major)

II. $CH_3C(CH_3)_2CH(OH)CH_3 \xrightarrow{H^+} B$ (major)

A and B (both alkenes) are respectively

(a) $CH_3CH{=}CHCH_3$, $CH_3C(CH_3)_2CH{=}CH_2$

(b) $CH_3CH_2CH{=}CH_2$, $CH_3C(CH_3)_2CH{=}CH_2$

(c) $CH_3CH{=}CHCH_3$, $CH_3C(CH_3){=}C(CH_3)CH_3$

(d) $CH_3CH_2CH{=}CH_2$, $CH_3C(CH_3){=}C(CH_3)CH_3$

39. Alcohols given below follow mechanism with HCl/anhydrous $ZnCl_2$

CH_3OH (I), CH_3CH_2OH (II), $CH_3CH(OH)CH_3$ (III)

(a) S_N1, S_N2, S_N2 (b) S_N2, S_N2, S_N1
(c) S_N2, S_N1, S_N1 (d) S_N1, S_N1, S_N2

40. $C_4H_{10}O$ gives white precipitate immediately with conc. HCl in presence of anhydrous $ZnCl_2$. Alcohol can be

(a) 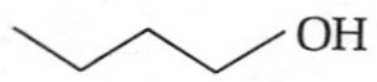 (b) 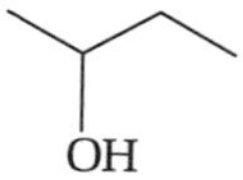

(c) 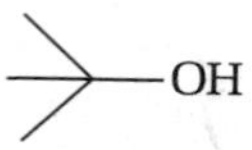 (d) 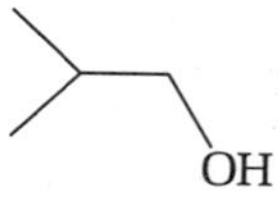

41. Carbocation is not the intermediate in
(a) hydroboration-oxidation of an alkene
(b) oxymercuration-demercuration of an alkene
(c) reaction of HCl with CH_3CH_2OH
(d) in all cases

42. Consider the following reactions,

$(CH_3)_2CHOH \xrightarrow[I]{PBr_3} (CH_3)_2CHBr$; $(CH_3)_2CHOH \xrightarrow[II]{HBr + ZnCl_2} (CH_3)_2CHBr$

These reactions are of the type

	I	II		I	II
(a)	S_N1	S_N2	(b)	S_N2	S_N1
(c)	S_N2	S_N2	(d)	S_N1	S_N1

43. Best reagent to convert an alcohol to an alkyl chloride is
(a) $SOCl_2$ (b) PCl_3 (c) PCl_5 (d) HCl

44. Strongest conjugate base is
(a) $(CH_3)_3CO^-$ (b) $(CH_3)_2CHO^-$
(c) $CH_3CH_2O^-$ (d) CH_3O^-

45.

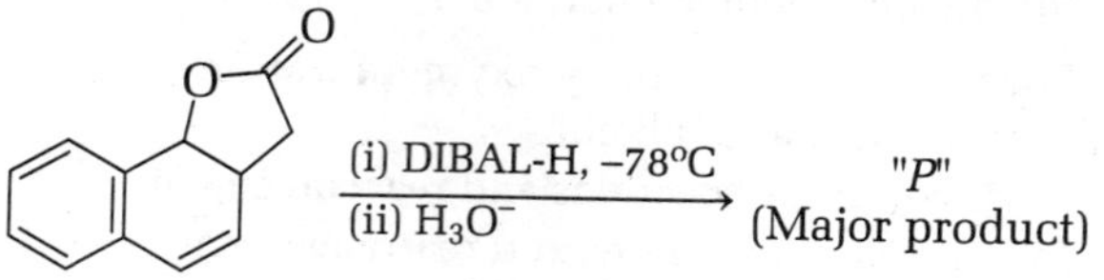

The product (P) in the above reaction is

[JEE Main 2021, March]

(a) 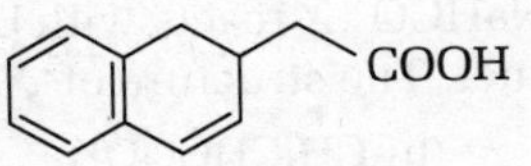 (b) 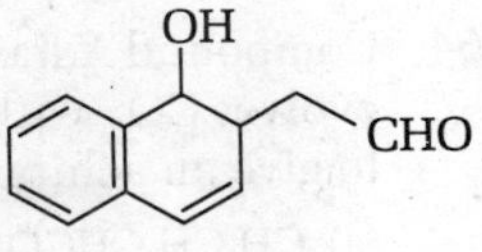

(c) 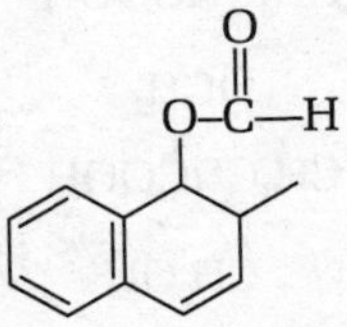 (d) 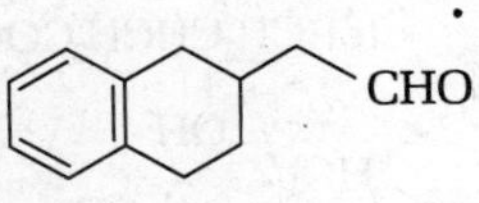

46. Which has maximum pK_a value?

(a) 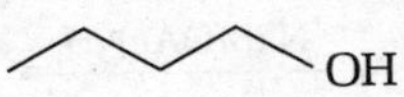 (b) 

(c) 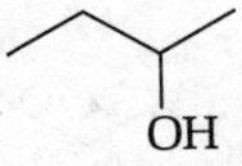 (d) 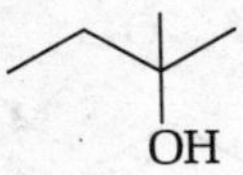

47. Reagents that can convert R—OH, into R—Cl without changing the configuration about chiral carbon are

(a) $SOCl_2$, TsCl
(b) $SOCl_2$, PCl_5
(c) PCl_5, TsCl
(d) TsCl, PCl_5, $SOCl_2$

48. In which case chiral carbon (*) retains its configuration?

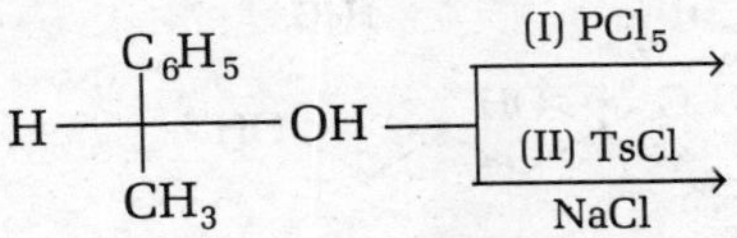

(a) In path I (b) In path II
(c) In both of these (d) In none of these

49. Which reaction is not reversible?

(a) $RCOOH + R'OH \xrightarrow{H^+} RCOOR' + H_2O$
(b) $CH_3CH_2CH_2OH \xrightarrow{H^+} CH_3CH{=}CH_2 + H_2O$
(c) $PCl_5 \longrightarrow PCl_3 + Cl_2$
(d) $CH_3OH + O_2 \longrightarrow CO_2 + H_2O$

50. Ester formation of CH_3COOH takes place to maximum extent when alcohol is

(a) CH_3OH (b) CH_3CH_2OH
(c) $(CH_3)_2CHOH$ (d) $(CH_3)_3COH$

51. Consider the following reactions,

I. $CH_3\overset{O}{\overset{\|}{C}}OH \xrightarrow{PCl_5} \xrightarrow{CH_3OH} CH_3\overset{O}{\overset{\|}{C}}OCH_3$

II. $\xrightarrow{H_3O^+/CH_3OH}$

Which path is not reversible?

(a) I
(b) II
(c) Both I and II
(d) None of the above

52. In the following reaction which bonds are cleaved?

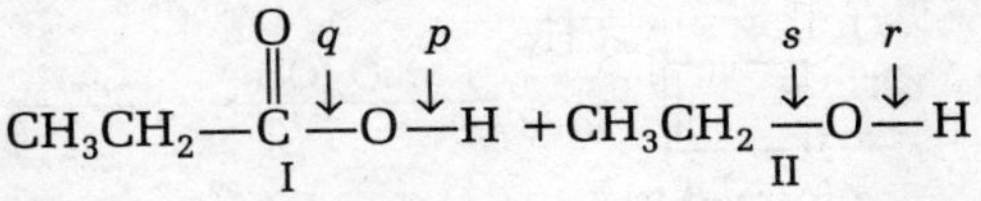

(a) Bond p of I and s of II (b) Bond q of I and r of II
(c) Bond p of I and r of II (d) Bond q of I and s of II

53. Isotopic O of I goes with

$$\underset{II}{CH_3\overset{O}{\overset{\|}{C}}OH} + \underset{I}{CH_3CH_2\overset{18}{O}H} \longrightarrow \underset{III}{CH_3\overset{O}{\overset{\|}{C}}OCH_2CH_3} + \underset{IV}{H_2O}$$

(a) IV (b) III
(c) Both (a) and (b) (d) None of these

54. Consider oxidation of the following alcohols

I. $CH_2{=}CHCH_2OH \xrightarrow{A} CH_2{=}CHCHO$
II. $(CH_3)_3COH \xrightarrow{B} CH_3\underset{CH_3}{\underset{|}{C}}{=}CH_2$
III. $CH_3CH_2OH \xrightarrow{C} CH_3CO_2H$
IV. $CH_3CH{=}CHCH_3 \xrightarrow{D} CH_3CO_2H$

A, B, C and D are oxidising agents which are respectively

	A	B	C	D
(a)	MnO_2	Cu/Δ	H_2CrO_4	$KMnO_4$/Δ
(b)	Cu/Δ	MnO_2	H_2CrO_4	$KMnO_4$/Δ
(c)	MnO_2	Cu/Δ	$KMnO_4$/Δ	H_2CrO_4
(d)	MnO_2	H_2CrO_4	Cu/Δ	$KMnO_4$

55. Jones reagent is

(a) MnO_2
(b) CrO_3 in aqueous acetone
(c) N_2O_4 in $CHCl_3$
(d) PCC

56. The major product of the following reaction is **[JEE Main 2019, April]**

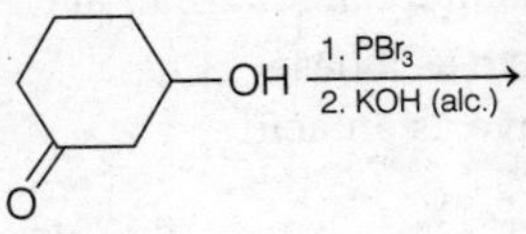

(a) 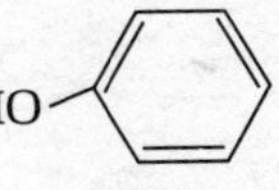 (b) 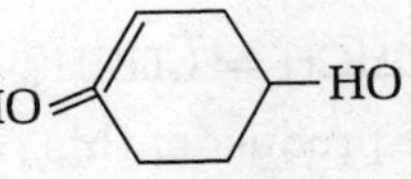

(a) 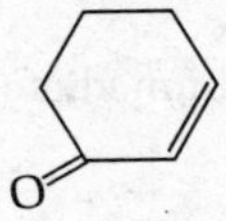 (b) 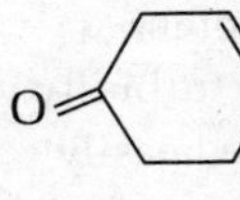

57. Consider the following tests,

I : Iodoform test II : Victor Meyer test
III : Lucas test

CH_3OH and CH_3CH_2OH can be distinguished by

(a) I and II (b) I and III
(c) I only (d) III only

58. Consider the following reaction,

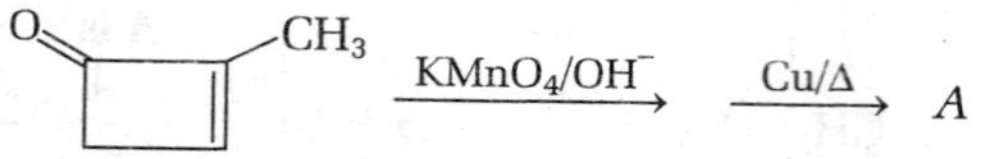

A formed is

(a) 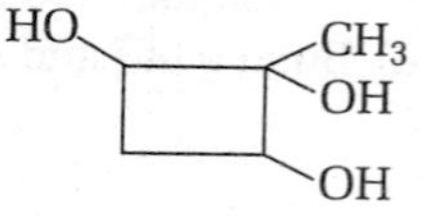 (b) 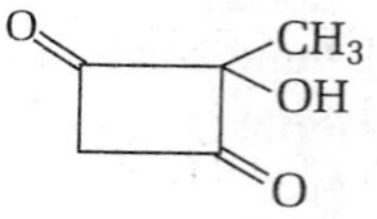

(c) 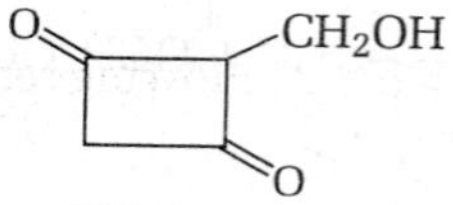 (d) 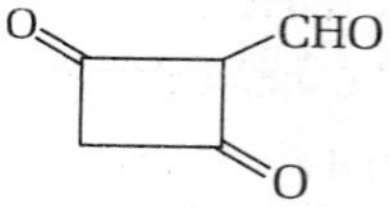

59. $CH_3-\underset{CH_3}{\overset{CH_3}{C}}-CH=CH_2 \longrightarrow CH_3-\underset{CH_3}{\overset{CH_3}{C}}-\underset{OH}{CH}-CH_3$

This change can be done by

(a) acid catalysed hydration
(b) oxymercuration-demercuration
(c) hydroboration-oxidation
(d) any method mentioned above

60. 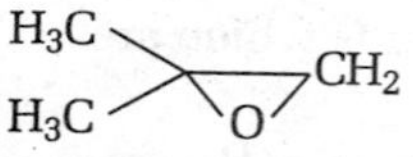 $\xrightarrow{LiAlH_4}$ *A*, *A* is

(a) $CH_3\underset{CH_3}{CH}CH_2OH$ (b) $CH_3CH_2CH_2CH_2OH$

(c) $CH_3\underset{CH_3}{\overset{CH_3}{C}}-OH$ (d) no reaction

61. 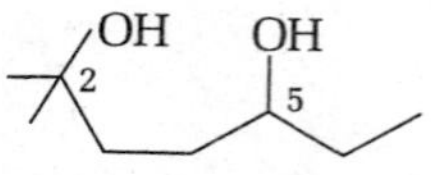 In this diol

(a) OH at C_2 is more basic than that of at C_5
(b) OH at C_2 is more acidic than at C_5
(c) Both behave as a base
(d) Both behave as an acid

62. $CH_3\overset{CH_2CH_3}{CH}CH=CHCH_3 \xrightarrow{H_3O^+}$

Major product of this reaction

(a) is optical isomer
(b) gives white turbidity with HBr immediately
(c) is dehydrated easily
(d) obeys all the above facts

63. Consider the following methods,

I. Hydration of olefins
II. Hydrolysis of cyanides
III. Reduction of carbonyl compounds

Which of these can be used to prepare alcohols?

(a) I, II and III (b) I and II (c) II and III (d) I and III

64. Compound *X* has molecular formula $C_4H_8O_3$. It evolves CO_2 with *aq*. $NaHCO_3$ *X* reacts with $LiAlH_4$ to give an achiral product. The structure of '*X*' is

(a) $CH_3CH_2\underset{OH}{CH}COOH$ (b) $CH_3\underset{OCH_3}{CH}COOH$

(c) $CH_3\underset{OH}{CH}CH_2COOH$ (d) $CH_3\underset{CH_2OH}{CH}COOH$

65. In the following reaction, (*X*) is

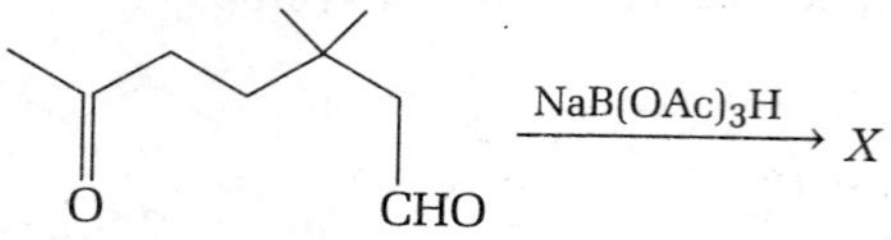

(a) 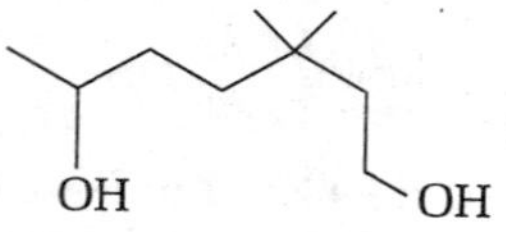 (b) 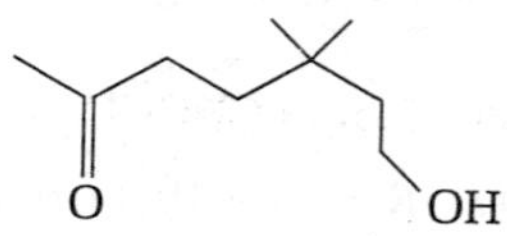

(c) 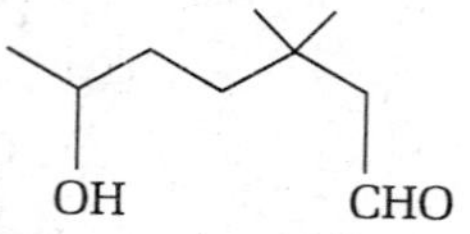 (d) 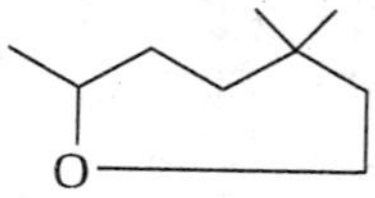

66. 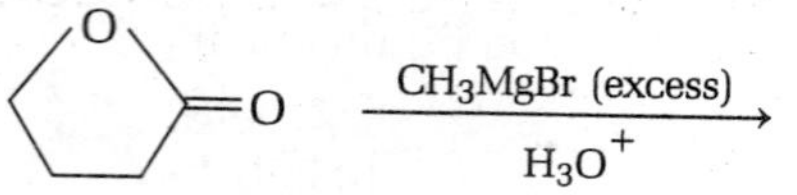

(a) 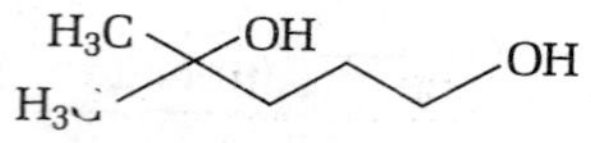

(b) 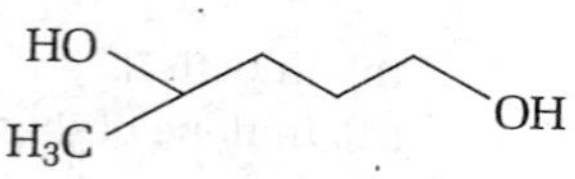

(c) 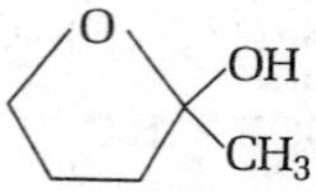

(d) 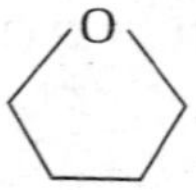

67. 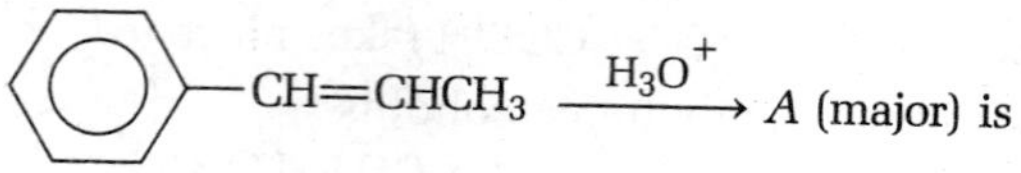

(a) 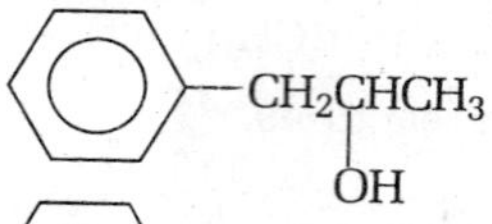

(b) 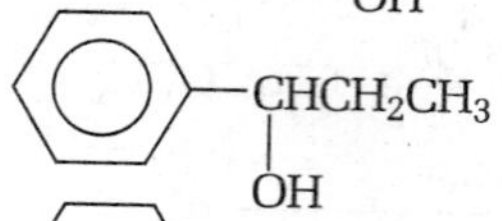

(c) 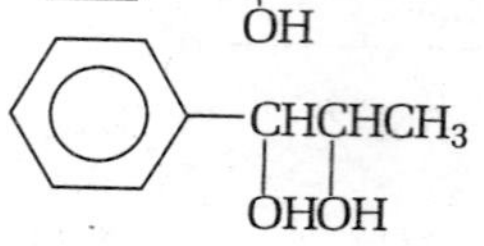

(d) 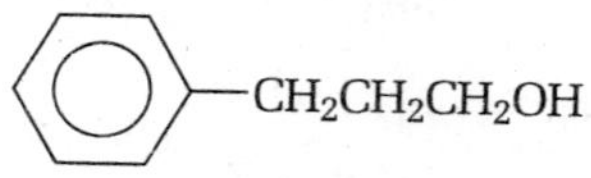

68. 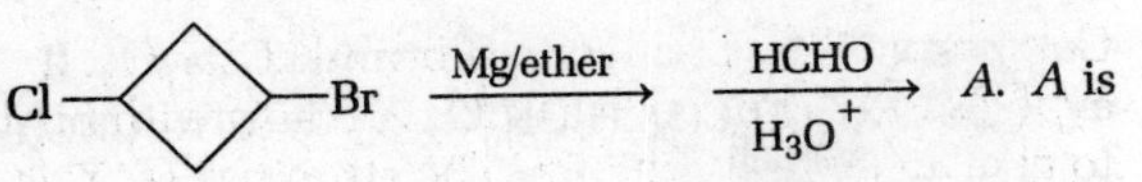 A. A is

(a) 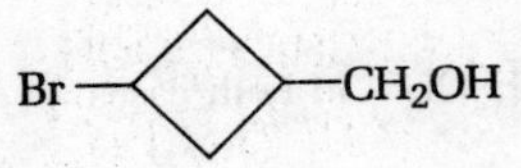

(b) 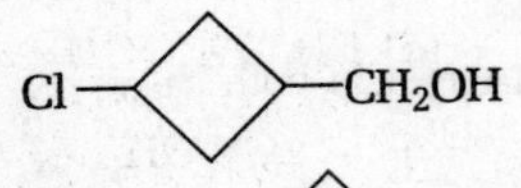

(c) 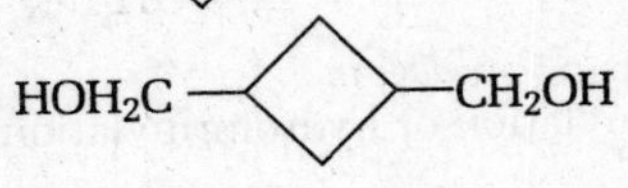

(d) 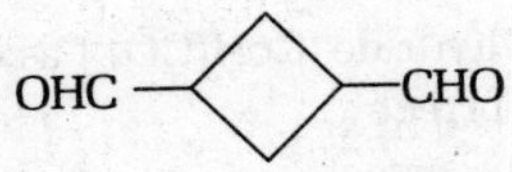

69. $CH_2{=}CH\underset{OH}{\underset{|}{C}H}CH_2CH_2OH \xrightarrow{MnO_2} A$. A is

(a) $CH_2{=}CH\overset{\|}{\underset{O}{C}}CH_2CH_2OH$ (b) $CH_2{=}CH\underset{OH}{\underset{|}{C}H}CH_2CHO$

(c) $CH_2{=}CH\underset{O}{\underset{\|}{C}}CH_2CHO$ (d) $CH_2{=}CH\underset{O}{\underset{\|}{C}}CH_2\overset{O}{\overset{\|}{C}}OH$

70. 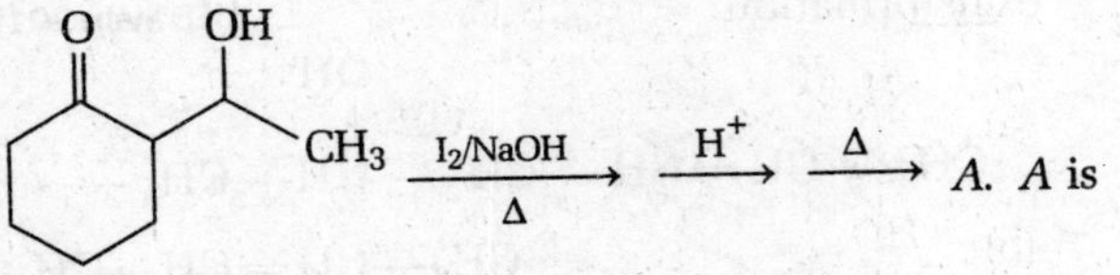 A. A is

(a) 

(b) 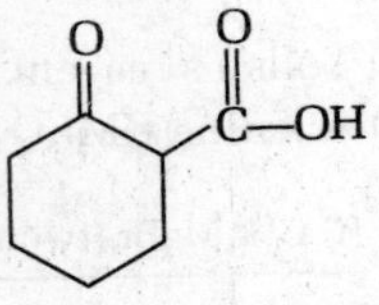

(c) 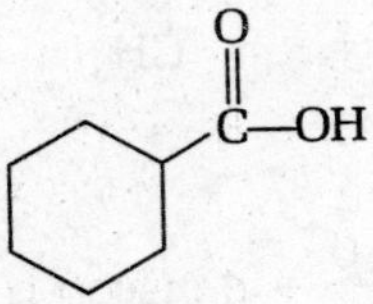

(d) 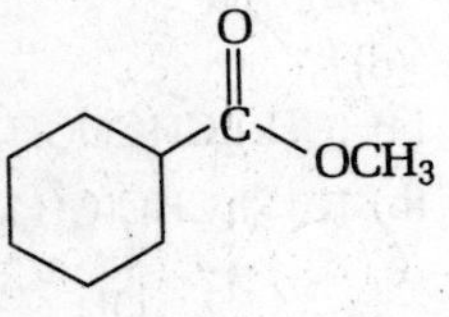

71. 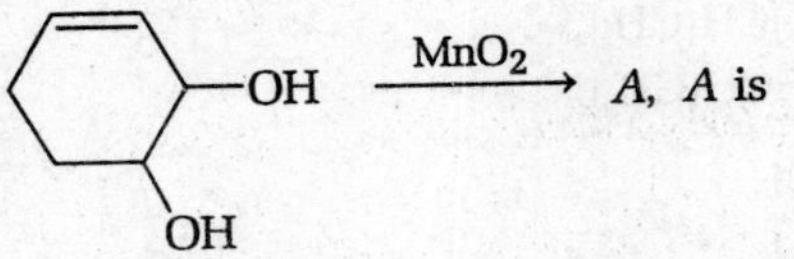 A, A is

(a) 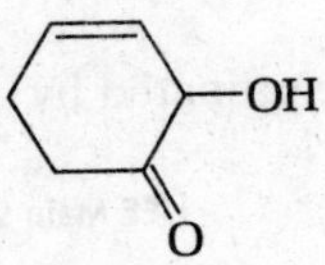

(b) 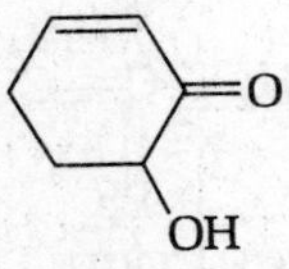

(c) 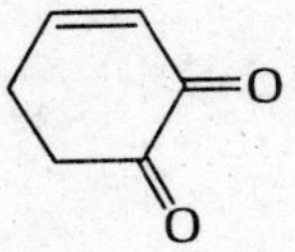

(d) 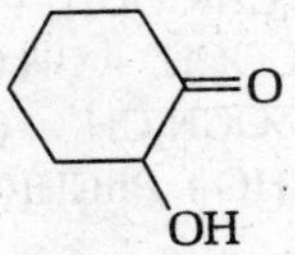

72. 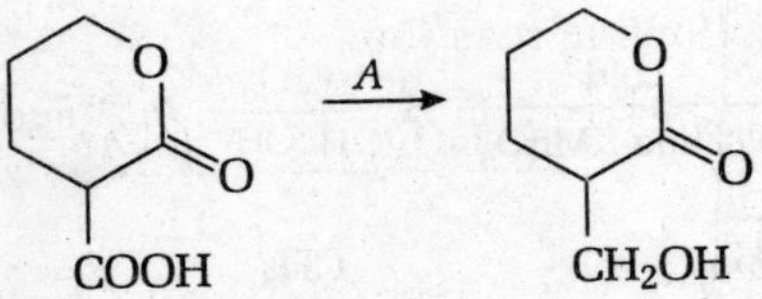 A is

(a) B_2H_6/H_2O

(b) $LiAlH_4$

(c) CH_3OH/Na

(d) P/HI

73. The major product formed in the following reaction is

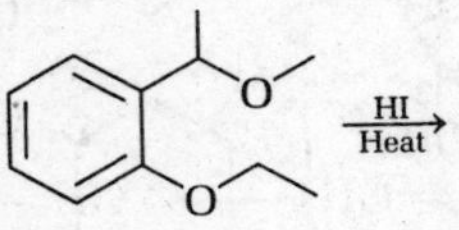

[JEE Main 2018]

(a) 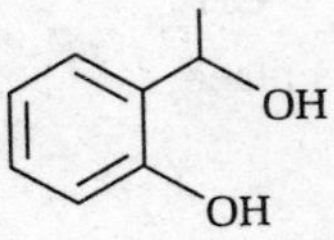

(b) 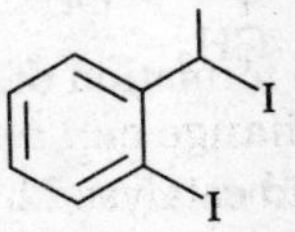

(c) 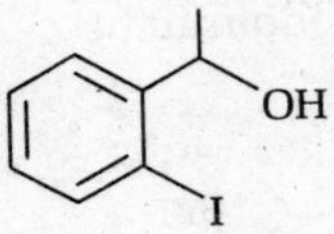

(d) 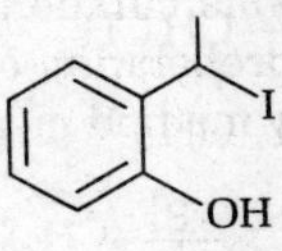

74. $(C_2H_5O)_2CO \xrightarrow[H_3O^+]{CH_3MgBr\ (excess)} A$. A (alcohol) can also be obtained by

(a) $CH_3CH_2CHO \xrightarrow[H_3O^+]{CH_3MgBr\ (2\ mol)}$

(b) $CH_3\overset{O}{\overset{\|}{C}}OC_2H_5, \xrightarrow[H_3O^+]{CH_3MgBr\ (2\ mol)}$

(c) $CH_3\overset{O}{\overset{\|}{C}}CH_3 \xrightarrow[H_3O^+]{CH_3MgBr\ (1\ mol)}$

(d) as in (b) and (c)

75. Ester $A(C_4H_8O_2) + \underset{(2\ parts)}{CH_3MgBr} \xrightarrow{H_3O^+} \underset{(alcohol\ B)}{C_4H_{10}O}$

Alcohol B reacts fastest with Lucas reagent. Hence, A and B are

(a) $CH_3\overset{O}{\overset{\|}{C}}OC_2H_5$, $(CH_3)_3COH$

(b) $H\overset{O}{\overset{\|}{C}}OC_3H_7$, $(CH_3)_2CHOH$

(c) $CH_3\overset{O}{\overset{\|}{C}}OC_2H_5$, $(CH_3)_2CHOH$

(d) $H\overset{O}{\overset{\|}{C}}OC_3H_7$, $(CH_3)_3COH$

76. 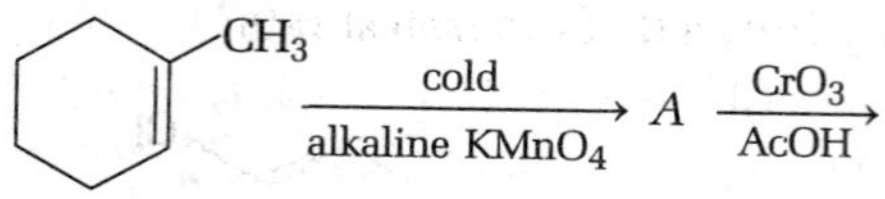 B, A and B are

(a) 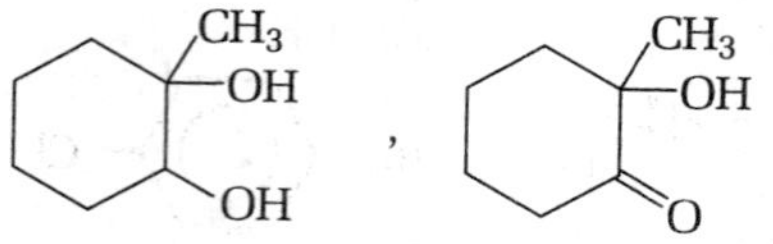

(b) 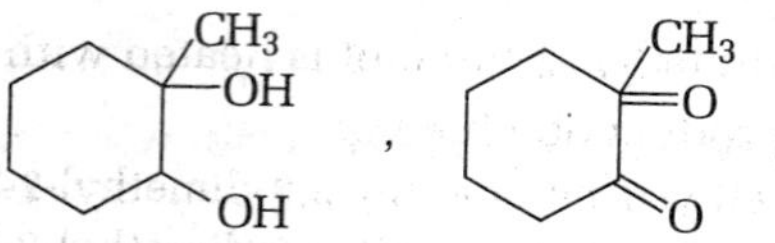

(c) 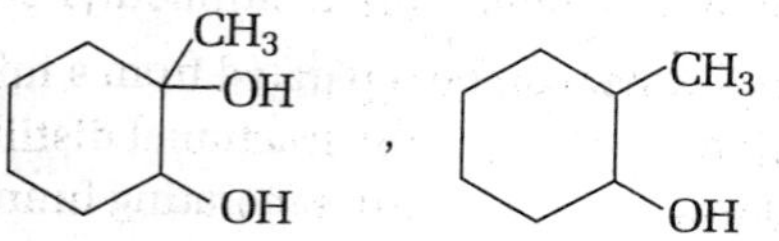

(d) no formation of A and B takes place

77. $CH_3C(CH_3)_2—CH(OH)CH_3 \xrightarrow{HBr} A$ (predominant). A is

(a) $(CH_3)_3CCH(Br)CH_3$ (b) $(CH_3)_2CBrCH(CH_3)_2$
(c) Both (a) and (b) (d) None is correct

78. Which of the following compounds give most stable carbocation (intermediate) on dehydration?

(a) $CH_3C(CH_3)_2—OH$ (b) $CH_3CH(CH_3)CH_2CH_2OH$
(c) $CH_3CH(OH)CH_2CH_3$ (d) $CH_3CH_2CH_2CH_2OH$

79. $CH_3C(CH_3)_2—CH(OH)CH_3 \xrightarrow{H_2SO_4,\ \Delta} CH_3C(CH_3)=C(CH_3)CH_3$

This involves
(a) retropinacol rearrangement
(b) Wagner-rearrangement
(c) Both (a) and (b)
(d) None of the above

80. 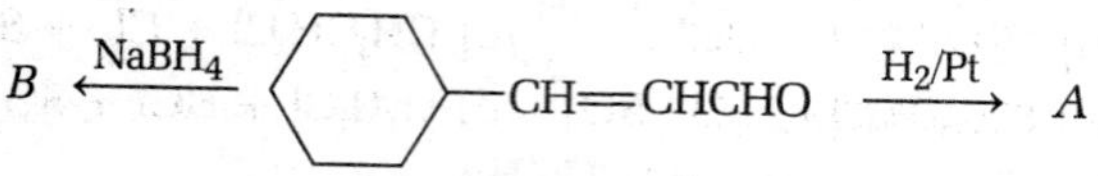

A and B are respectively

(a) 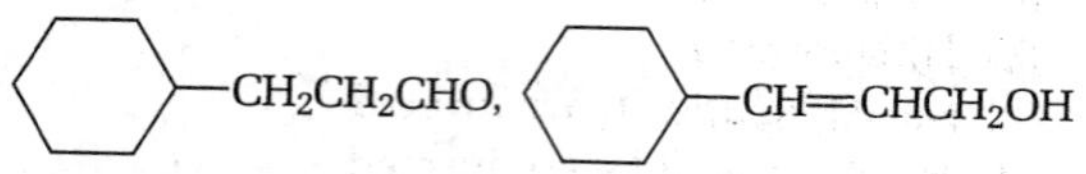

(b) 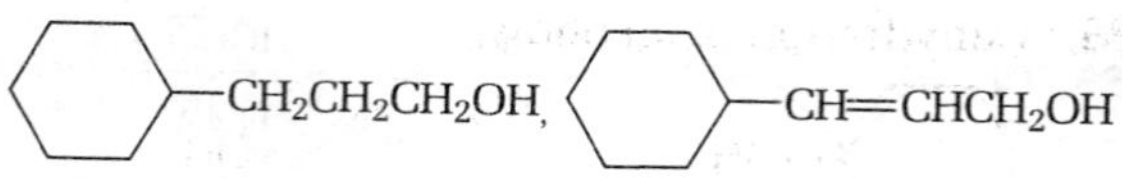

(c) 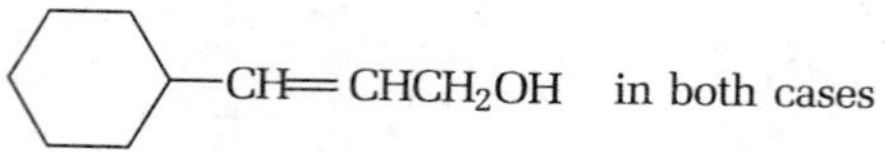

(d) 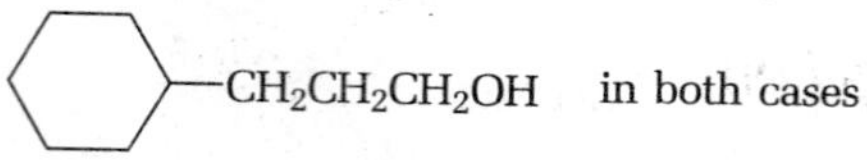

81. Oxo process
(a) is simply carbonylation or hydroformylation reaction.
(b) uses cobalt carbonyl hydride $[CoH(CO)_4]$ as catalyst.
(c) Both (a) and (b) are correct
(d) Both (a) and (b) are incorrect

82. $CH_3CH=CH_2 \xrightarrow[125°,\ pressure]{CO,\ H_2,\ [CoH(CO)_4]} \xrightarrow[Cu\text{-}Zn]{H_2}$ Product

This represents oxo method of alcohol synthesis. Product can be

(a) $CH_3CH_2CH_2CH_2OH$ (b) $CH_3CH(CH_3)CH_2OH$
(c) Both are true (d) None is true

83. Which is the most suitable reagent for the following transformation? **[JEE Main 2019, Jan.]**

$$CH_3—CH=CH—CH_2—CH(OH)—CH_3 \longrightarrow CH_3—CH=CH—CH_2CO_2H$$

(a) Tollen's reagent (b) $I_2/NaOH$
(c) Alkaline $KMnO_4$ (d) CrO_2Cl_2/CS_2

84. $B \xleftarrow[(ii)\ H_3O^+]{(i)\ CH_3MgBr\ (two\ mol)} A \xrightarrow{H_3O^+} CH_3CH(CH_3)COOH$, B is

(a) $(CH_3)_2CHCOCH_3$
(b) $(CH_3)_2CHC(OH)(CH_3)_2$
(c) $(CH_3)_2CHCOCH(CH_3)_2$
(d) $(CH_3)_2CHCH(OH)CH(CH_3)_2$

85. $CH_3CH_2—C(OH)(Ph)—CH_3$ cannot be prepared by **[JEE Main 2019, Jan.]**

(a) $CH_3CH_2COCH_3 + PhMgX$
(b) $PhCOCH_3 + CH_3CH_2MgX$
(c) $PhCOCH_2CH_3 + CH_3MgX$
(d) $HCHO + PhCH(CH_3)\ CH_2MgX$

86. Dehydration of alcohols,

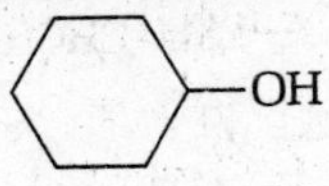

I

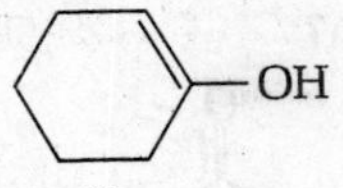

II

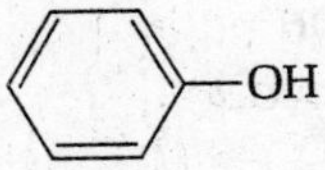

III

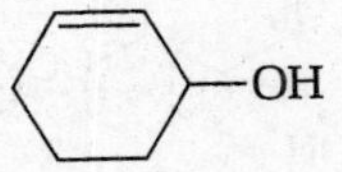

IV

will be in order

(a) I < II < III < IV (b) I > II > III > IV
(c) III < II < I < IV (d) II < III < IV < I

87. CH_3MgBr + 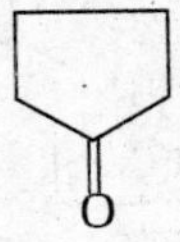 $\xrightarrow{H_3O^+} A \xrightarrow{HBr} B \xrightarrow{Mg/ether} C \xrightarrow[H_3O^+]{HCHO} D$, D is

(a) 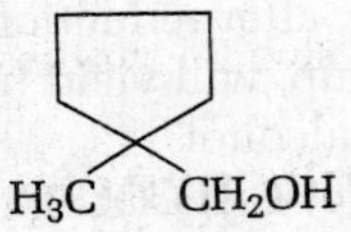
(b) 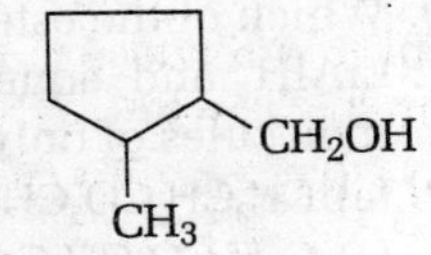
(c) 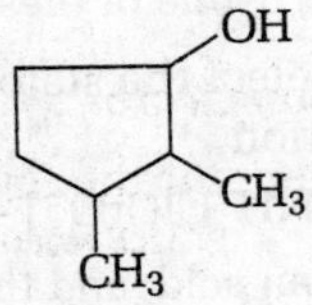
(d) 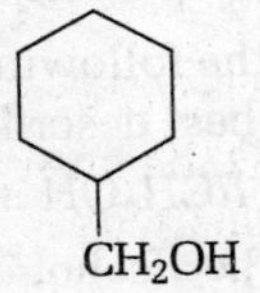

88. $RMgBr + A \xrightarrow{H_3O^+} CH_3CH_2CH_2OH$, R and A are

(a) CH_3CH_2— and HCHO (b) CH_3— and 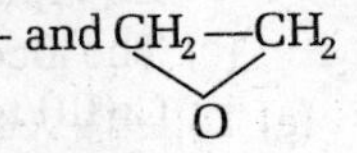
(c) Both (a) and (b) (d) None of these

89. In the following case configuration about chiral C(*) is retained.

(a) 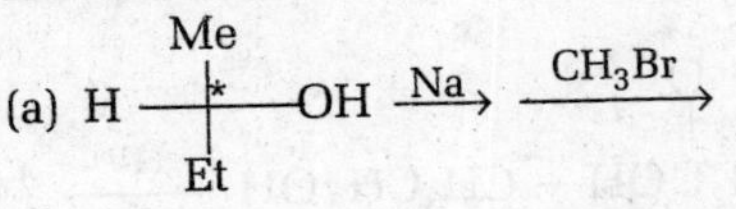

(b) 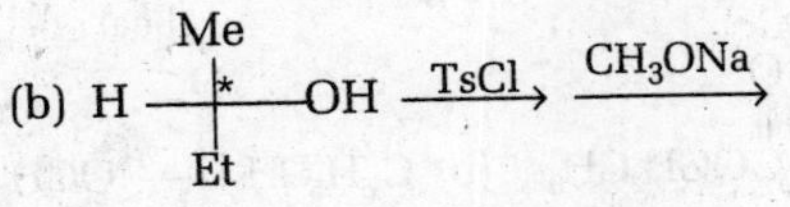

(c) 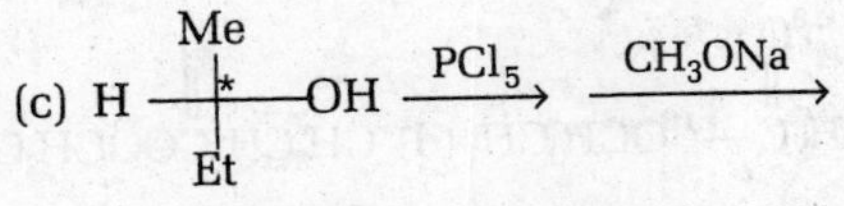

(d) in none of the above case

90. 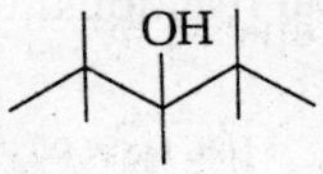 $\xrightarrow{\text{Conc. } H_2SO_4}$ products can be

(a) 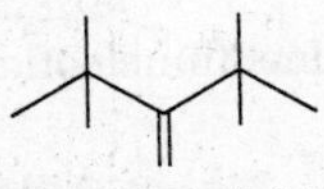
(b) 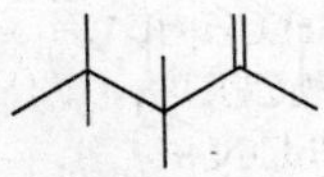
(c) Both (a) and (b) (d) None is correct

91. Which is hydrolysed at the fastest rate?

(a) 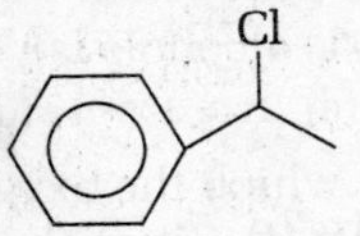
(b) 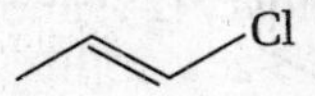
(c) 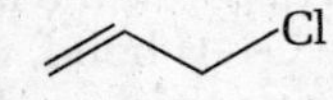
(d) 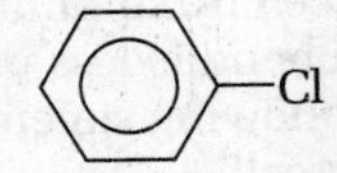

92. When 3,3-dimethyl 2-butanol is heated with H_2SO_4, the major product obtained is

(a) 3,3-dimethyl-1-butene (b) 3,3-dimethyl-2-butene
(c) 2,3-dimethyl-1-butene (d) 2,3-dimethyl-2-butene

93. Methanol and water can be separated from a mixture by

(a) distillation (b) fractional distillation
(c) evaporation (d) separating funnel

94. Chlorine and ethyl alcohol react to produce

(a) ethyl chloride (b) ethyl tetrachloride
(c) chloroform (d) chloral

95. An alcohol gave Lucas test in about 5 minutes. When the alcohol was treated with hot concentrated H_2SO_4 it gave an alkene of molecular formula C_4H_8 which on ozonolysis gave C_2H_4O. The structure of alcohol is

(a) $CH_3CHOHCH_2CH_3$ (b) $CH_3CH_2CH_2CH_2OH$
(c) $CH_3CHOHCH_2CH_2CH_3$ (d) $(CH_3)_3C—OH$

96. In the reaction given below, the product C is

$$CaC_2 \xrightarrow{H_2O} A \xrightarrow[HgSO_4]{\text{dil. } H_2SO_4} B \xrightarrow{H_2/Ni} C$$

(a) C_2H_5OH (b) CH_3CHO (c) CH_3OH (d) CH_3COOH

97. Butanol has higher boiling point than diethyl ether due to

(a) strong covalent bonding
(b) intermolecular hydrogen bonding
(c) electrovalent bonding
(d) intramolecular hydrogen bonding

98. The alcohol manufactured from water gas is

(a) butanol (b) ethanol
(c) methanol (d) isobutanol

99. Which one of the following gives iodoform test?

(a) Formaldehyde (b) Benzaldehyde
(c) Ethanol (d) Benzyl alcohol

100. When ethyl alcohol (C_2H_5OH) reacts with thionyl chloride in the presence of pyridine, the products obtained are

(a) $CH_3CH_2Cl + HCl$ (b) $CH_3CH_2Cl + Cl_2 + SO_2$
(c) $CH_3CH_2Cl + H_2O + SO_2$ (d) $C_2H_5Cl + HCl + SO_2$

101. When sodium is added to ethanol

(a) no action occurs
(b) H_2 is formed
(c) $NaOC_2H_5$ and O_2 are formed
(d) $NaOC_2H_5$ and H_2 are formed

102. The correct order of boiling point of primary (1°), secondary (2°) and tertiary (3°) alcohols is
(a) 1° > 2° > 3° (b) 2° > 1° > 3° (c) 2° > 3° > 1° (d) 3° > 2° > 1°

103. Thiols are alcohol analogs in which the oxygen has been replaced by sulphur (*e.g.*, CH_3SH). Given the fact that the S—H bond is less polar than the O—H bond, which of the following statements comparing thiols and alcohols is correct?
(a) Hydrogen bonding forces are weaker in thiols
(b) Hydrogen bonding forces are stronger in thiols
(c) Hydrogen bonding forces would be the same
(d) No comparison can be made without additional information

104. Rank the transition states that occur during the following reaction steps in order of increasing stability (least → most stable) :
I. $H_3C—\overset{+}{O}H_2 \longrightarrow CH_3^+ + H_2O$
II. $(CH_3)_3C—\overset{+}{O}H_2 \longrightarrow (CH_3)_3C^+ + H_2O$
III. $(CH_3)_2CH—\overset{+}{O}H_2 \longrightarrow (CH_3)_2\overset{+}{C}H + H_2O$
(a) I < II < III (b) II < III < I (c) I < III < II (d) II < I < III

105. Rank the following substances in order of increasing boiling point (lowest → highest) :
$\underset{1}{CH_3CH_2CH_2CH_2OH}$ $\underset{2}{(CH_3)_2CHOCH_3}$ $\underset{3}{(CH_3)_3COH}$
$\underset{4}{(CH_3)_4C}$
(a) 1 < 3 < 2 < 4 (b) 2 < 4 < 3 < 1
(c) 4 < 2 < 3 < 1 (d) 2 < 3 < 1 < 4

106. Which one of the following reacts with HBr at the fastest rate?
(a) 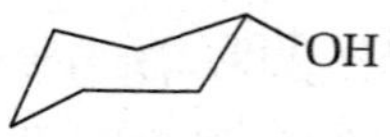
(b) 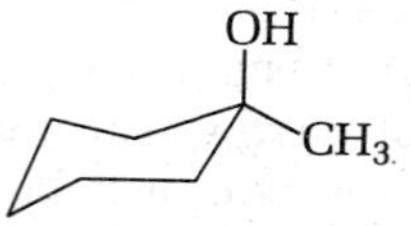
(c) 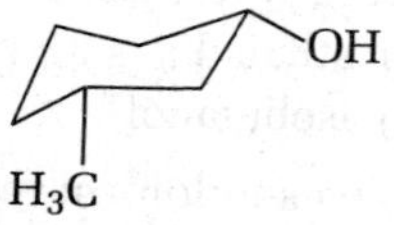
(d) 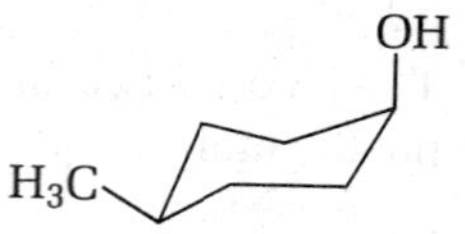

107. Ethanethiol (CH_3CH_2SH) is a gas at room temperature, but ethanol is a liquid. The reason for this is
(a) the C—S—H bonds in ethanethiol are linear
(b) the C—O—H bonds in ethanol are linear
(c) ethanethiol has a higher boiling point
(d) ethanethiol is less polar

108. Which of the following would yield a secondary alcohol after the indicated reaction, followed by hydrolysis if necessary?
(a) $LiAlH_4$ + a ketone
(b) CH_3CH_2MgBr + an aldehyde
(c) 2-butene + aqueous H_2SO_4
(d) All of the above

109. What is the major product of the following reaction?
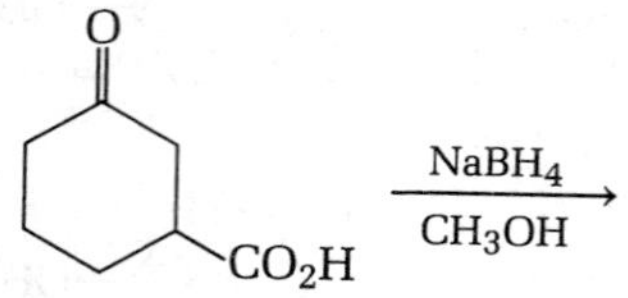
(a) 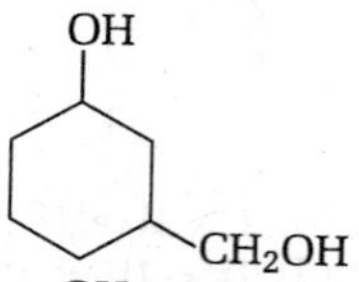
(b) 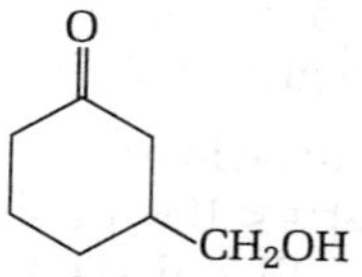
(c) 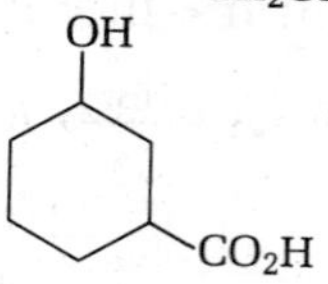
(d) 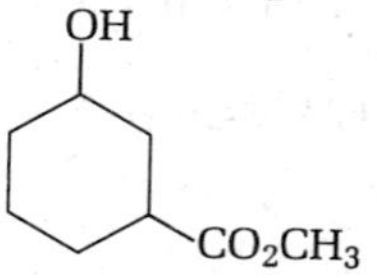

110. Which of the esters shown, after reduction with $LiAlH_4$ and aqueous workup, will yield two molecules of only a single alcohol?
(a) $CH_3CH_2CO_2CH_2CH_3$ (b) $C_6H_5COCH_2C_6H_5$
(c) $C_6H_5CO_2CH_2C_6H_5$ (d) None of these

111. For the following reaction, select the statement that best describes the situation
$$RCH_2OH + PCC\ [C_5H_5NH^+ClCrO_3^-] \longrightarrow$$
(a) The alcohol is oxidised to an acid, and the Cr(VI) is reduced
(b) The alcohol is oxidised to an aldehyde, and the Cr(VI) is reduced
(c) The alcohol is reduced to an aldehyde, and the Cr(III) is oxidised
(d) The alcohol is oxidised to a ketone, and the Cr(VI) is reduced

112. What is the product from the following esterification?
$$C_6H_5CH_2\overset{O}{\overset{\|}{C}}OH + CH_3CH_2\overset{18}{O}H \xrightarrow[\text{heat}]{H^+} ?$$
(a) $C_6H_5CH_2\overset{O}{\overset{\|}{C}}OCH_2CH_3$ (b) $C_6H_5CH_2\overset{O}{\overset{\|}{C}}—^{18}OCH_2CH_3$
(c) $C_6H_5CH_2\overset{^{18}O}{\overset{\|}{C}}—^{18}OCH_2CH_3$ (d) $CH_3CH_2\overset{^{18}O}{\overset{\|}{C}}OOCH_2C_6H_5$

113. The following substance acts as a coenzyme in which of the following biological reactions?
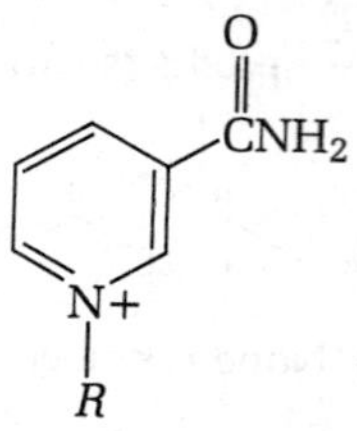
(R = adenine dinucleotide)

(a) Alcohol oxidation (b) Ketone reduction
(c) Aldehyde reduction (d) None of these

114. Which of the following alcohols gives the best yield of dialkyl ether on being heated with a trace of sulphuric acid?
(a) 1-pentanol (b) Cyclopentanol
(c) 2-pentanol (d) 2-methyl-2-butanol

115. What is the major organic product of the following sequence of reactions?

$$(CH_3)_2CHCH_2OH \xrightarrow{PBr_3} \xrightarrow{Mg} \xrightarrow{H_2C\overset{O}{—}CH_2} \xrightarrow{H_3O^+}$$

(a) $(CH_3)_2CH\overset{OH}{C}HCH_2CH_3$ (b) $(CH_3)_2CHCH_2\overset{OH}{C}HCH_3$
(c) $(CH_3)_2CHCH_2CH_2OH$ (d) $(CH_3)_2CHCH_2CH_2CH_2OH$

116. What is the product of the following reaction?

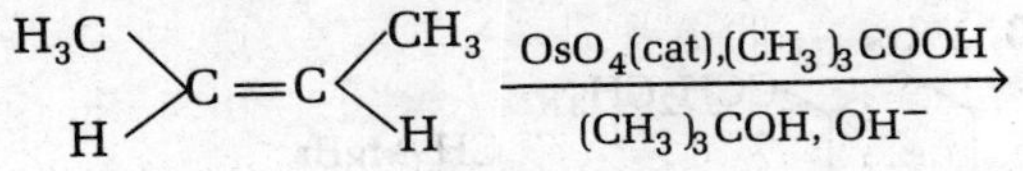

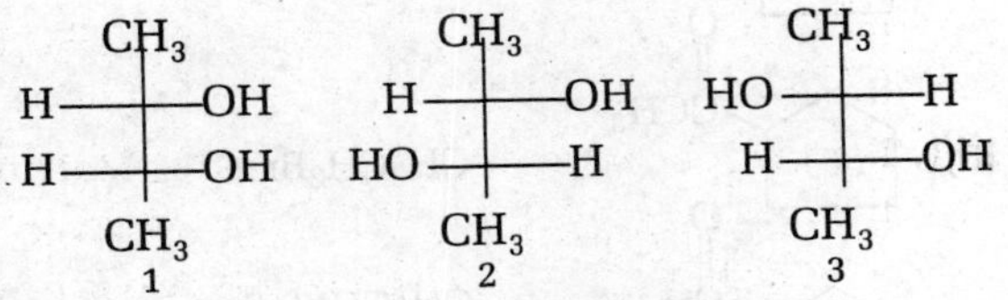

(a) Only 1 (b) Only 2
(c) Only 3 (d) A 1 : 1 mixture of 2 and 3

117. Which reaction is the best method for preparing (*R*)-2-butanol?

(a) $CH_3CH_2\overset{O}{\overset{\|}{C}}CH_3 \xrightarrow[\text{(ii) } H_2O]{\text{(i) } LiAlH_4\text{, diethyl ether}}$

(b) 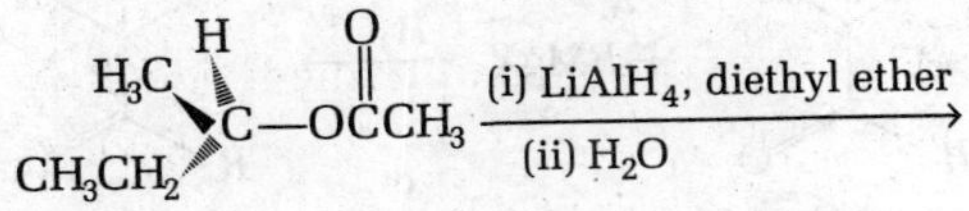

(c) $CH_3CH_2\overset{O}{\overset{\|}{C}}H \xrightarrow[\text{(ii) } H_3O^+]{\text{(i) } CH_3MgBr\text{, diethyl ether}}$

(d) $CH_3\overset{O}{\overset{\|}{C}}H \xrightarrow[\text{(ii) } H_2O^+]{\text{(i) } CH_3CH_2Li\text{, diethyl ether}}$

118. An organic compound *B* is formed by the reaction of ethyl magnesium iodide (CH_3CH_2MgI) with a substance *A*, followed by treatment with dilute aqueous acid. Compound *B* does not react with PCC or PDC in dichloromethane. Which of the following is a possible candidate for *A*?

(a) $CH_3\overset{O}{\overset{\|}{C}}H$ (b) $H_2C{=}O$
(c) $H_2\overset{O}{C—}CH_2$ (d) $CH_3CH_2\overset{O}{\overset{\|}{C}}CH_3$

119. Which of the following reagents would carry out the following transformation? (D=^{2}H, the mass-2 isotope of hydrogen)

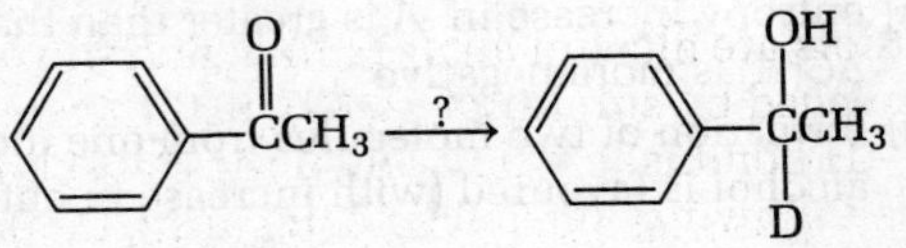

(a) $NaBD_4$ in CH_3OH (b) $NaBD_4$ in CH_3OD
(c) $LiAlH_4$, then D_2O (d) $LiAlD_4$, then D_2O

120. Which sequence of steps describes the best synthesis of 2-methyl-3-pentanone?

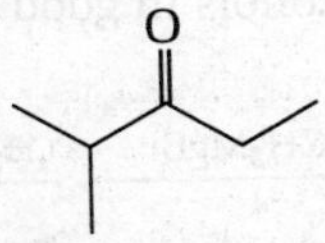

2-methyl-3-pentanone

(a) 1. 1-propanol + $(CH_3)_2CHMgBr$, diethyl ether
2. H_3O^+
3. PDC, CH_2Cl_2
(b) 1. 1-propanol + $Na_2Cr_2O_7$, H_2SO_4, H_2O, heat
2. $SOCl_2$
3. $(CH_3)_2CHCl$, $AlCl_3$
(c) 1. 1-propanol + PCC, CH_2Cl_2
2. $(CH_3)_2CHLi$, diethyl ether
3. H_3O^+
4. $Na_2Cr_2O_7$, H_2SO_4, H_2O, heat
(d) 1. 2-propanol + $Na_2Cr_2O_7$, H_2SO_4, H_2O, heat
2. $CH_3CH_2CH_2Li$, diethyl ether
3. H_3O^+
4. PCC, CH_2Cl_2

121. LD_{50} of ethanol is 10.6 g/kg. This LD_{50} is used to evaluate chemical toxicity and is the amount of
(a) a substance per kilogram body weight that is lethal to 50% of the test animal
(b) a substance per kilogram substance weight that is lethal to 0.50% of the body weight
(c) a substance per gram body weight that is lethal to 50% of the test animal
(d) none of the term defined is not correct

122. Consider the following reaction,
A : Substitution to give the ether–a bimolecular dehydration

$$\underset{\text{ethanol}}{2CH_3CH_2OH} \xrightarrow{H_2SO_4,\ 410\ K} CH_3CH_2OCH_2CH_3 + H_2O$$

B : Elimination to give the alkene –a unimolecular dehydration

$$CH_3CH_2OH \xrightarrow{H_2SO_4,\ 450\ K} CH_2{=}CH_2 + H_2O$$

We observe that temperature control is necessary to get the required product. Difference in the nature of the product due to change in temperature is because of

(a) entropy increase in A is greater than that in B. Thus, $\Delta G(A)$ is more negative
(b) formation of two molecules from one molecule of alcohol is favoured (with increase in entropy) in B which makes ΔG more negative at higher temperature as $\Delta G = \Delta H - T\Delta S$
(c) entropy change in both reactions remains constant, temperature is control is to cleave a particular type of bond
(d) None of the above statements is correct

Objective Questions Type II [One or more than one correct option(s)]

In each of the questions below, four choices are given, of which one or more than one are correct.

1. Which of the following methods are feasable for the preparation of alcohols in good yield?

(a) 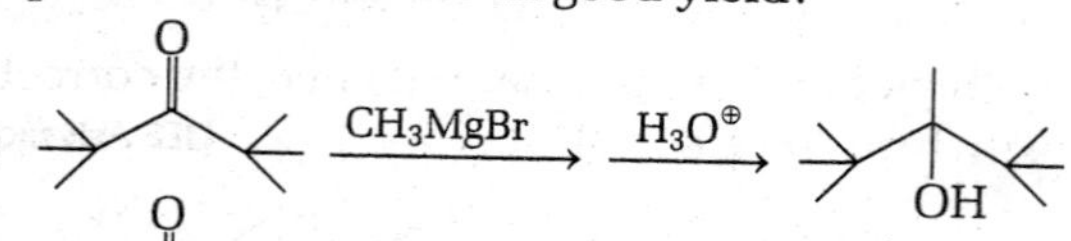

(b) 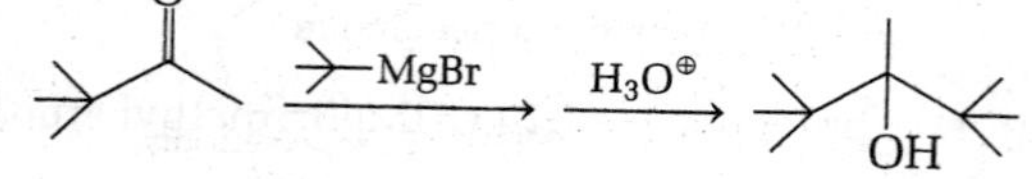

(c) 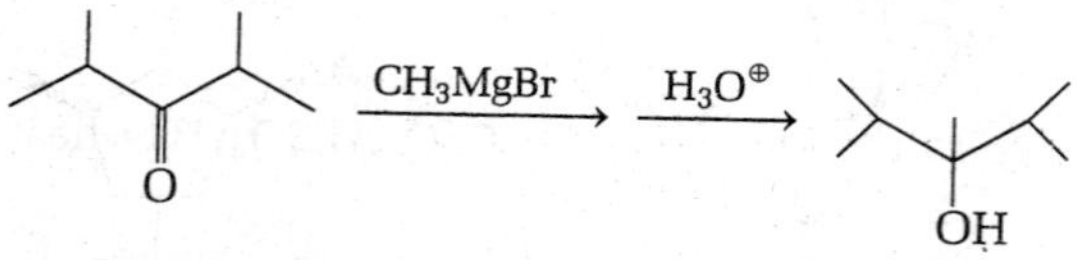

(d) 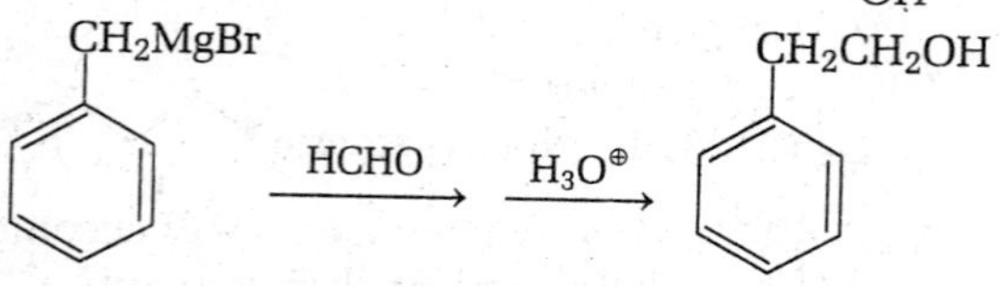

2. Select the correct synthetic methods.

(a) 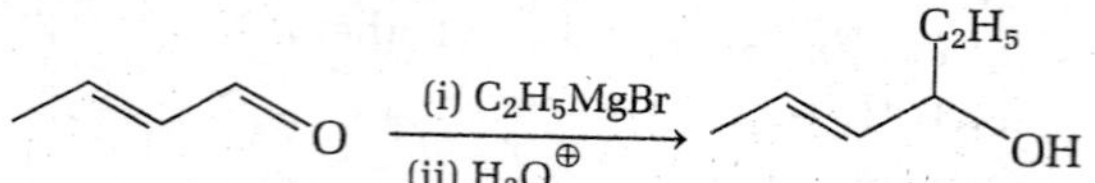

(b) 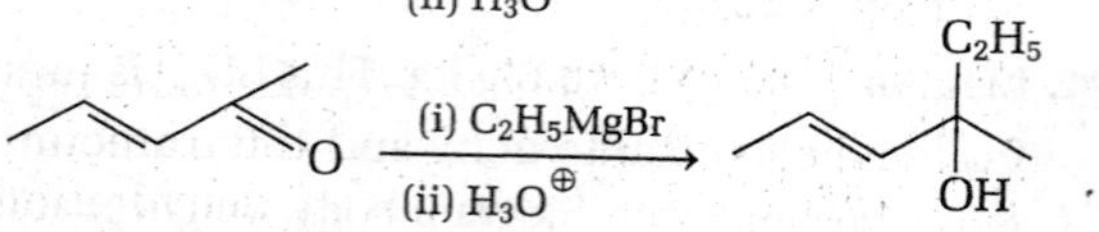

(c) 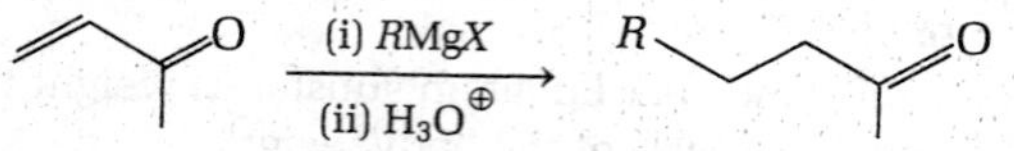

(d) 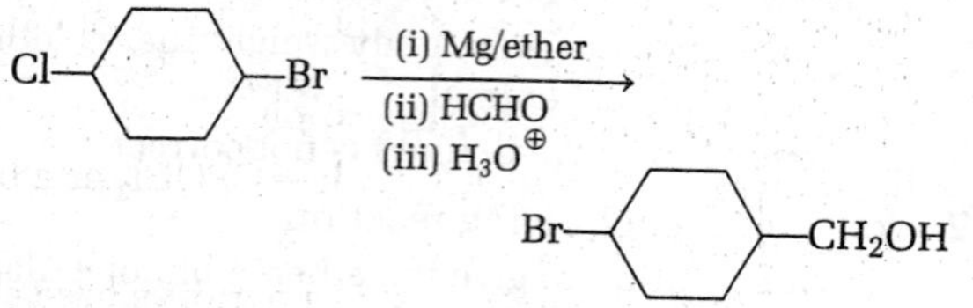

3. For the following transformation

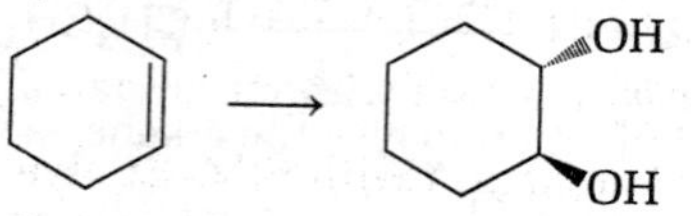

reagents can be

(a) H_2O_2
(b) $KMnO_4/OH^-$
(c) CH_3CO_3H/H_3O^+
(d) m-CPBA$/H_3O^+$

4. To synthesise alcohol A, possible reactants can be

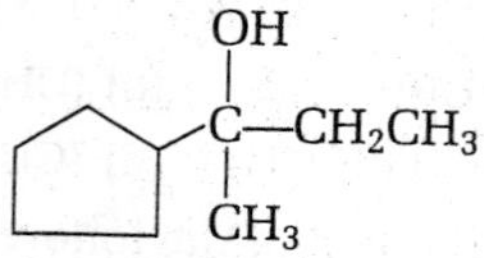

(a) 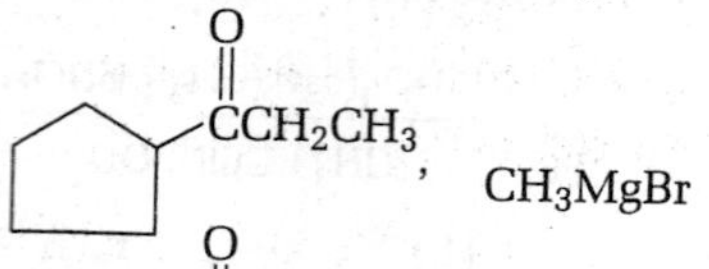

(b) 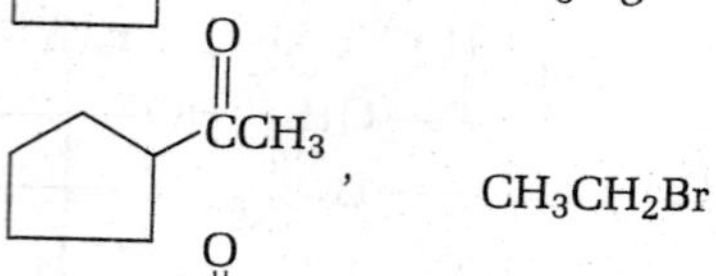

(c) 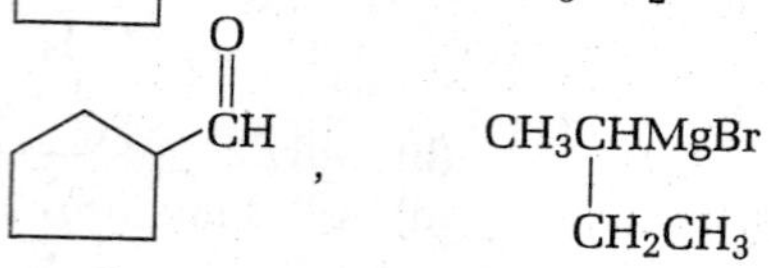

(d) 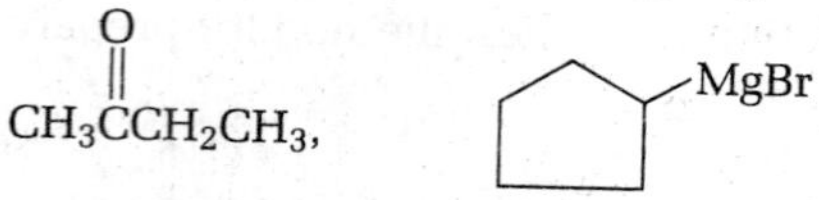

5. In the following reaction, select the correct statement(s).

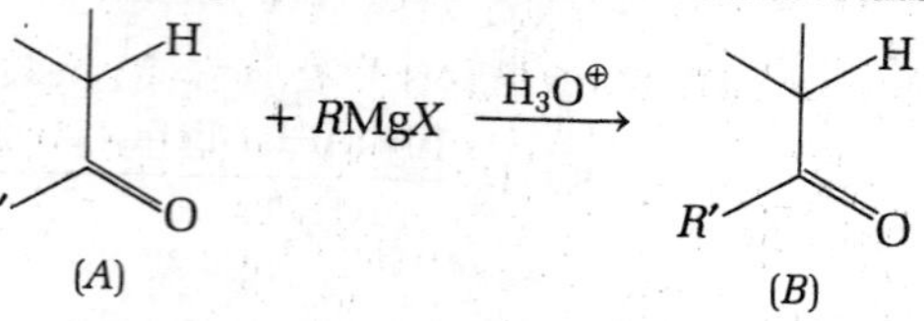

(A) (B)

(a) Due to the presence of at least one H atom an α-carbon atom, enolisation can take place giving the intermediate (C) which tautomerise to (B)

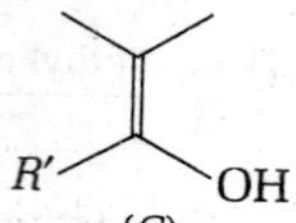

(C)

(b) The Grignard reagent acts as a base rather than as a nucleophile and abstracts an active hydrogen, giving the enolate
(c) Formation of (B) from (A) is simply a side reaction and other product formed is

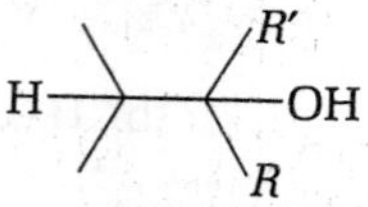

(d) Formation of (B) is not possible

6. In the following reaction

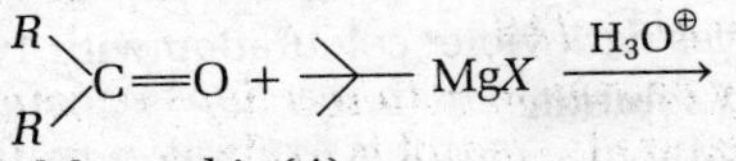

(a) alcohol formed is (*A*)

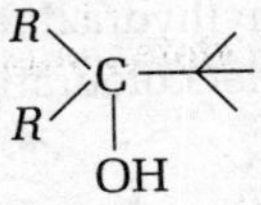

(*A*)

(b) reduction can occur by hydride-ion transfer due to hydrogen atom an β-carbon of the Grignard reagent forming (*B*)

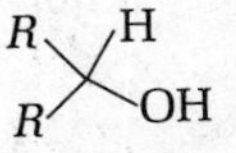

(*B*)

(c) (*A*) is side-product and (*B*) is major product
(d) (*B*) is side-product and (*A*) is major product

7. End product of the following reaction is

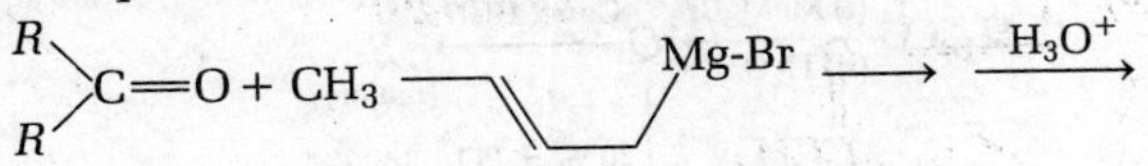

(a) 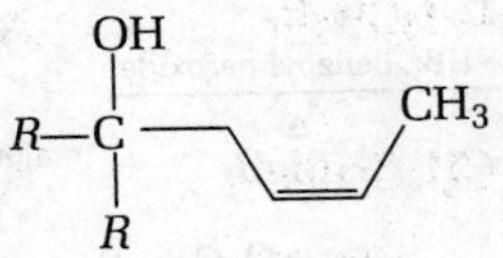
(b) 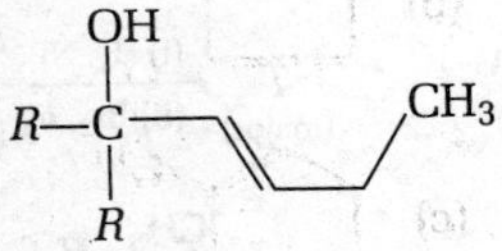
(c) 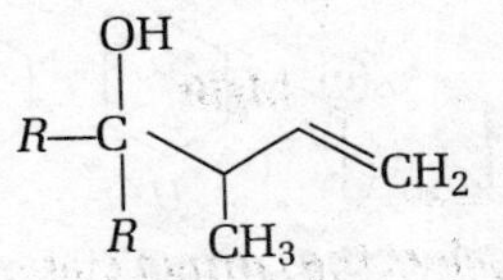
(d) 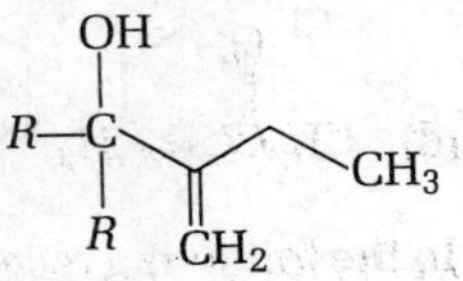

8. Compound (*A*) given below is to be synthesised.

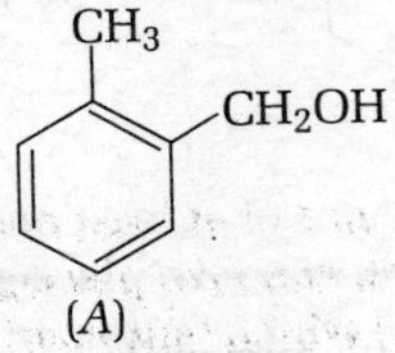

(*A*)

Suitable routes are

(a) 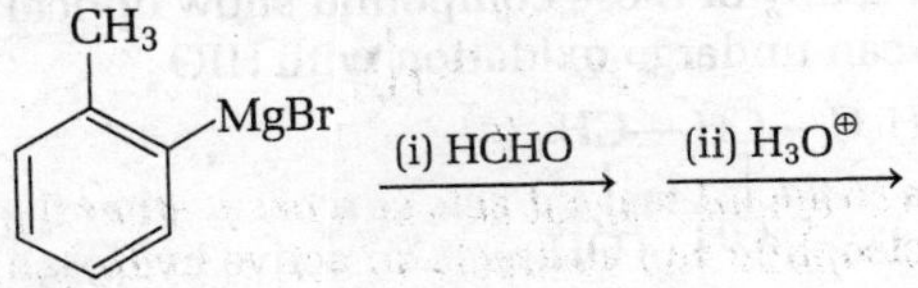

(b) 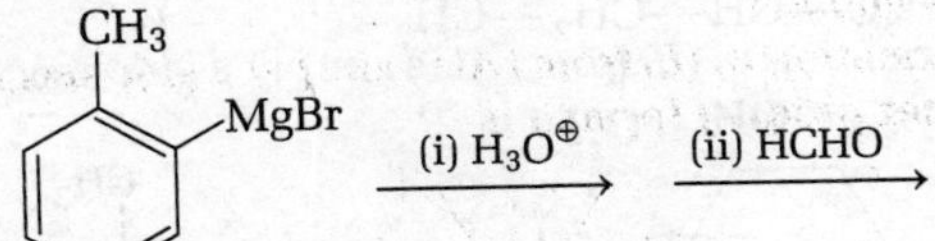

(c) 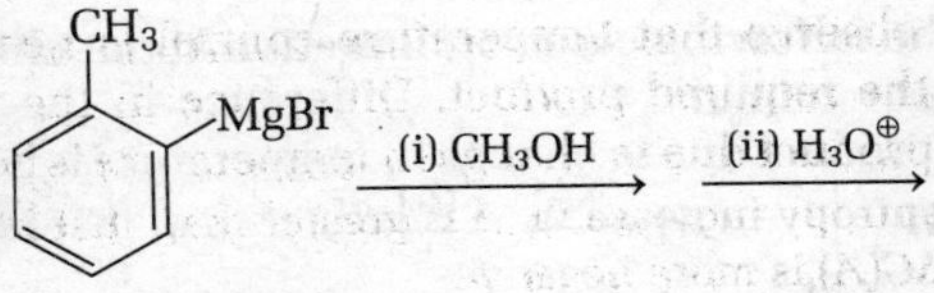

(d) 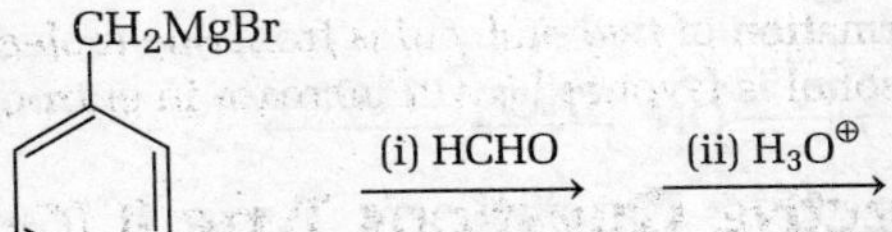

9. The (O—H) group in alcohols can be replaced by :
(a) $SOCl_2$ (b) Cl_2
(c) PCl_5 (d) $P+Cl_2$

10. In the following reaction sequence, the correct structure (s) of *X* is (are) **[JEE Advanced 2018]**

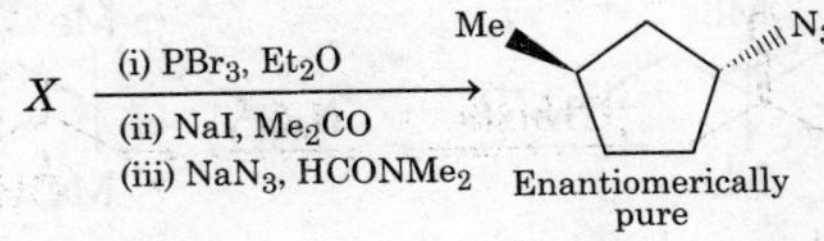

(a) 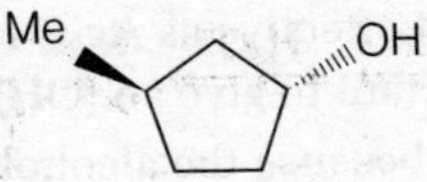
(b) 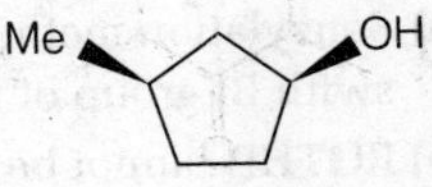
(c) 
(d) 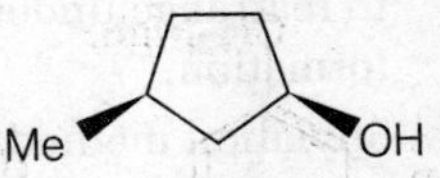

11. Which of the following reagents will accomplish *trans*-hydroxylation of an olefinic bond?
(a) *m*-chloroperbenzoic acid/$H_3O^{\oplus}$
(b) O_3/Zn
(c) $B_2H_6/H_2O_2, OH^{\ominus}$
(d) OsO_4/Na_2CO_3

12. Dehydration of alcohols take place more rapidly with $POCl_3$ than with H_2SO_4. Select the correct statement(s) about the following dehydration reaction.

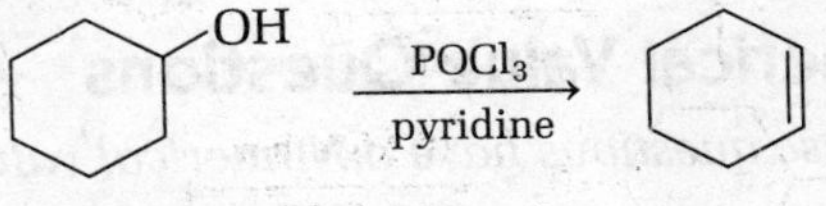

(a) It does not involve carbocation
(b) It involves *R*—$OPOCl_2$ with —$OPOCl_2$ as a better leaving group
(c) It involves E2 mechanism as pyridine base abstracts proton from the adjacent carbon at the same time at which —$OPOCl_2$ is leaving
(d) It is E1 reaction without formation of carbocation

13. Esters on reaction with EtMgBr give
(a) 1° alcohols (b) 2° alcohls
(c) 3° alcohols (d) Hydroxy ketone

14. In the following case configuration about chiral C(*) is not retained

(a) 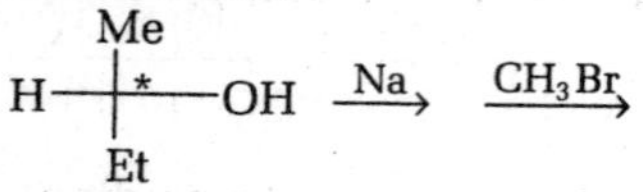

(b) 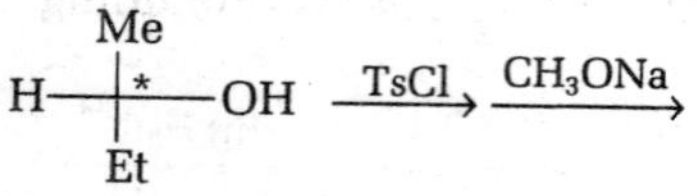

(c) 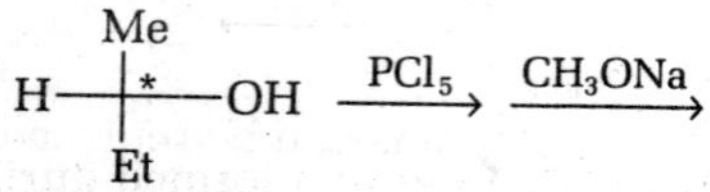

(d) in none case

15. In the conversion of (*A*) to (*B*), the best method for the protection of (OH) group is silylation method because :

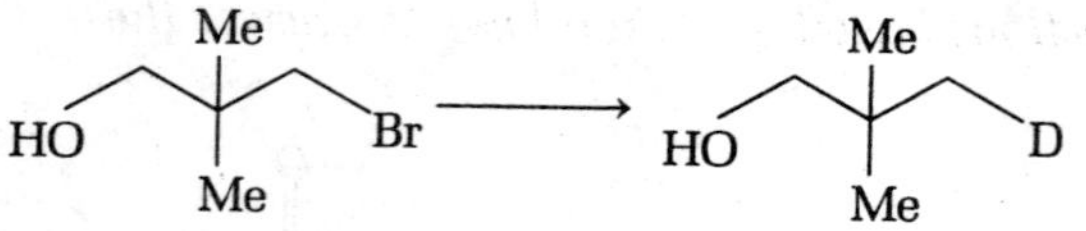

(a) Benzylation method is not effective as Ag_2O react swith Br group of the reactant to give an (OH) group.

(b) ROTHP cannot be uiased because the alcohol is likely to rearrange under the acidic conditions of ether formation.

(c) Silylation method is effective since (OH) group is not sterically hindered.

(d) The reaction can be carried out without protecting (OH) group, as shown below

$(A) \xrightarrow[2.\ D_2O]{1,\ Mg/ether} (B)$

16. The correct statement(s) about the following reaction sequence is (are)

Cumene $(C_9H_{12}) \xrightarrow[(ii)\ H_3O^+]{(i)\ O_2} P \xrightarrow{CHCl_3/NaOH}$

Q(major) + R(minor), $Q \xrightarrow[PhCH_2Br]{NaOH} S$ **[JEE Advanced 2016]**

(a) *R* is steam volatile

(b) *Q* gives dark violet colouration with 1% aqueous $FeCl_3$ solution

(c) *S* gives yellow precipitate with 2, 4-dinitrophenylhydrazine

(d) *S* gives dark violet colouration with 1% aqueous $FeCl_3$ solution

17. HBO, oxymercuration-demercuration and acid catalysed hydration will give different products in

(a) 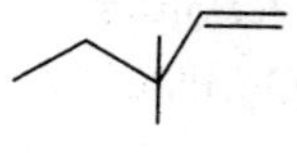

(b) 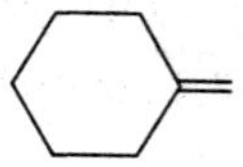

(c) 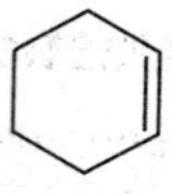

(d) 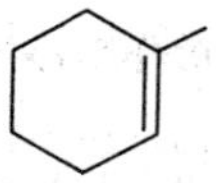

18. Choose the correct option(s) for the following set of reactions.

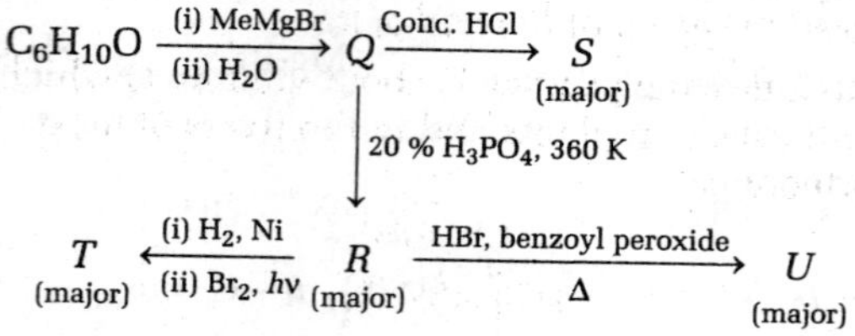

(a) 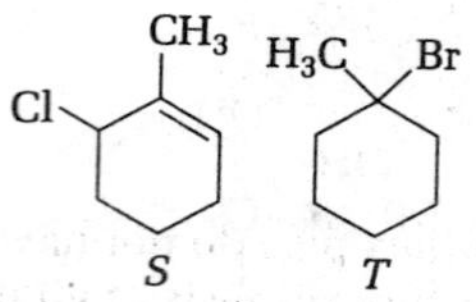

(b) 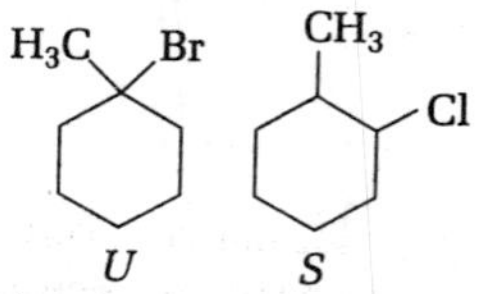

(c) 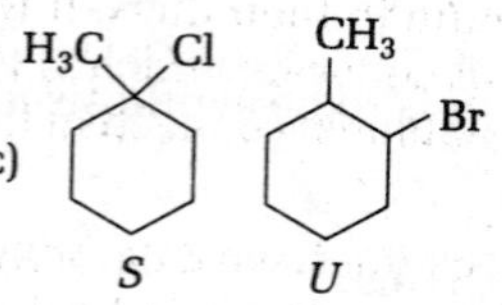

(d) 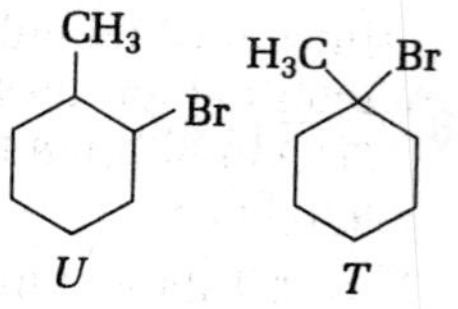

Numerical Value Questions

All these questions have a Numerical value as their answer, solve the questions and write your answer.

1. The alcohol $PH-CH(CH_3)-CH(OH)-CH_3$ is heated with concentrate H_2SO_4 to effect dehydration. How many isomeric products are possible ?

2. Which alcoholic group is most reactive for dehydration by concentrated H_2SO_4 in the given compound ?

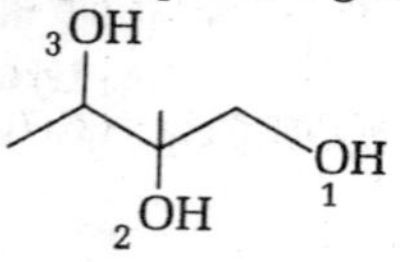

3. How many of these compound show optical activity that can undergo oxidation with HIO_4?

(i) $H_3C-CH(OH)-CH_3(OH)$

(ii) $H_3C-CH(OH)-CH_2(OH)-CH_2$

(iii) 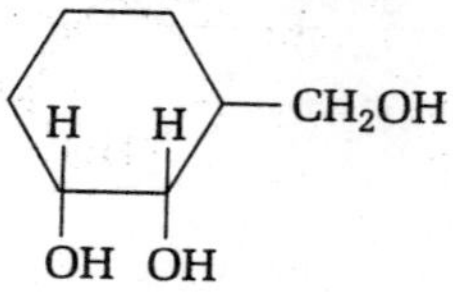

(iv) $H_3C-C(CH_3)(OH)-CH_2(OH)$

4. The number of alcohols giving iodoform test among the following is :
$CH_3CH_2OH, CH_3OH, CH_3CH_2CH_2OH, (CH_3)_2CHOH,$
$CH_3CH_2CH_2CH_2OH, CH_3CH_2CH(OH)CH_3,$
$CH_3CH(OH)CH(CH_3)_2, (C_2H_5)_2 CHOH, (CH_3)_3COH.$

5. $C_5H_{12}O$ is a monohydric alcohol. How many isomers of this alcohol are possible ? How many of these contain chiral centers as well as can exhibit enantiomerism ?

6. How many reagents give allylic/benzylic oxidation and form —OH group in given reagents.
$LiAlH_4, PCC, NaBH_4, SeO_2, MnO_2, POC$

7. 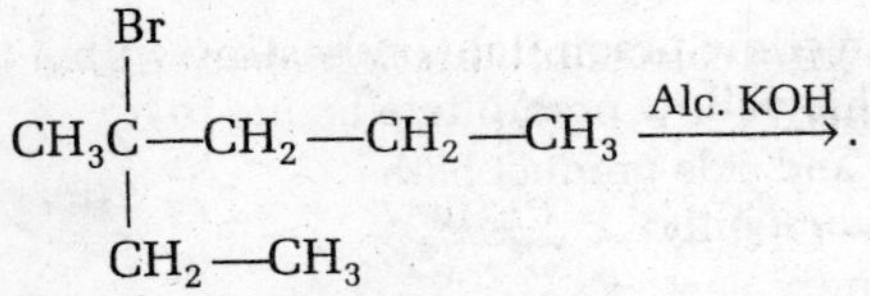

The total number of E_2-products (including stereoisomers)

8. 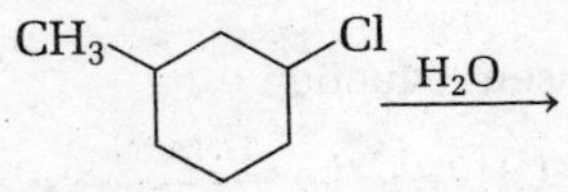

The total number of S_N1 product formed during given reaction will be including stereoisomer of reactant ?

Comprehension Based Questions

In these questions, a passage has been given followed by questions based on it. You have to answer the questions based on the passage given.

***Passage* 1** *Read the passage and answer the questions given at the end of it.*

The following passage is about vitamin C which is synthesised in plants and in the livers of most vertebrates.

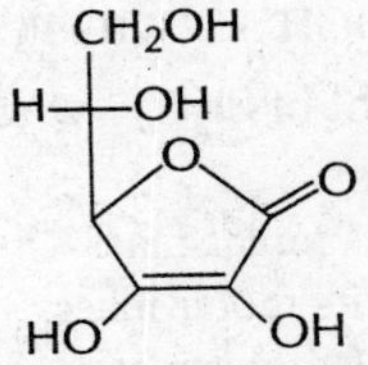

Humans, monkeys and guinea pigs do not have the enzymes necessary for the biosynthesis of vitamin C, so they must include the vitamin in their diets. It is also required for the synthesis of collagen, which is the structural protein of skin, tendons, connective tissue and bone.

1. Although vitamin C does not have a carboxylic acid group, it is an acidic compound. Acidic character is shown by
(a) $—CH_2OH$ group (b) CHOH
(c) 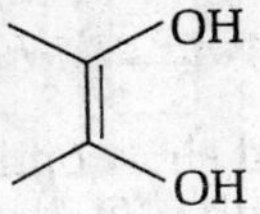 (d) All of these

2. Oxidation of vitamin C under mild condition gives
(a) 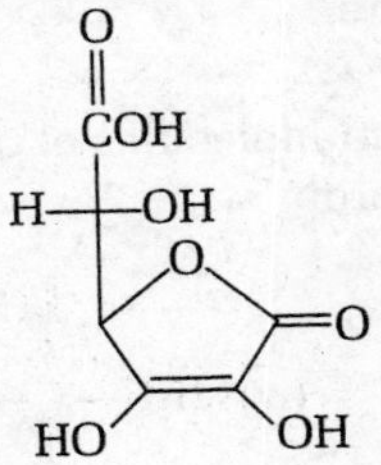 (b) 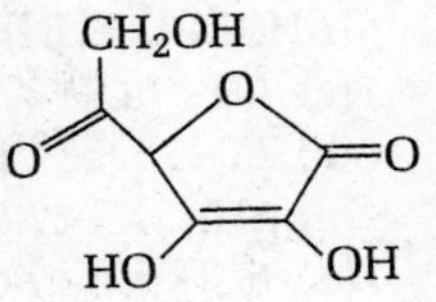
(c) 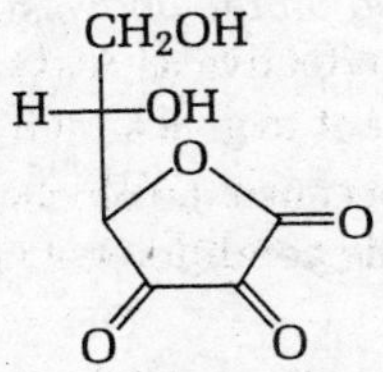 (d) 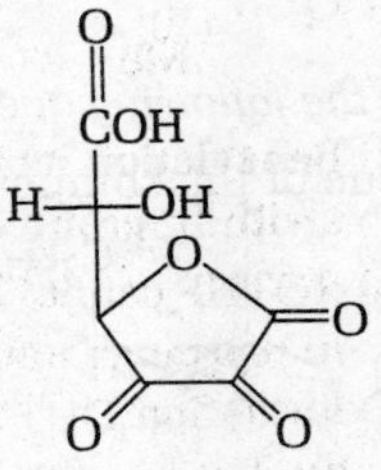

3. If vitamin C is hydrolysed
(a) lactone ring is opened and vitamin C activity is retained
(b) lactone ring is opened and vitamin C activity is lost
(c) lactone ring is opened and by at the same time is changed to another lactone
(d) no ring opening is possible

***Passage* 2** A research scholar synthesised alcohol by the hydration of 1-butene. He was unaware of the fact that the vessel he used had some coating of a metal, and in addition to alcohol (b.p. 100°C) he also got a compound (*X*). *X* (b.p. 80°C) forms bisulphite compound as well as 2,4-dinitrophenylhydrazone. He however was successful in the separation, based on physical and chemical properties.

Read the above technical report and answer the following questions.

1. Which alcohol does research scholar want to synthesise and what is the other product?
(a) $CH_3CH_2CH_2CH_2OH, CH_3CH_2CH_2CHO$
(b) $CH_3CH_2CH(OH)CH_3, CH_3CH_2C(=O)CH_3$
(c) $CH_3CH_2CH_2CH_2OH, CH_3CH_2CH(OH)CH_3$
(d) $CH_3CH_2CH_2CH_2OH, CH_3CH_2CH{=}CH_2$

2. He also got yellow precipitate on heating with $NaOH/I_2$. This yellow precipitate is due to
   (a) alcohol, and side product both
   (b) side product only
   (c) alcohol only
   (d) None of the above
3. Carbonyl compound can be converted into required alcohol by
   (a) Clemmensen reduction
   (b) $LiAlH_4$
   (c) Wolff-Kishner reduction
   (d) All of the above

***Passage* 3** (X) reacts with (i) C_2H_5Mg / Br (ii) H_3O^+ to form two different compounds (Y) and (Z).

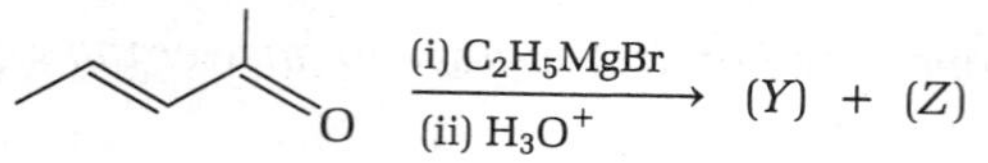

(X)

Answer the following questions based on the above synthesis.

1. One of the compounds (say Y) is

(a) 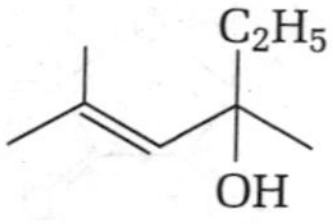 (b) 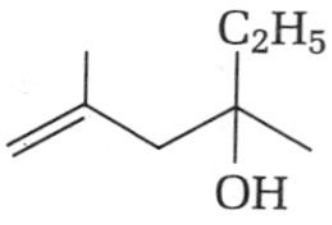

(c) 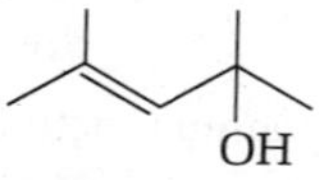 (d) None of these

2. Compound Z is

(a) 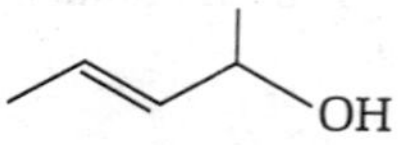 (b) 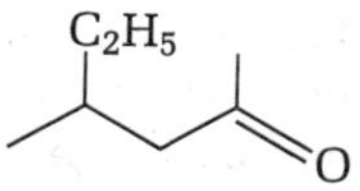

(c) 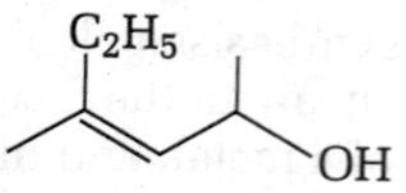 (d) None of these

3. If (X) reacts with excess of C_2H_5MgBr/H_3O^+ final product would have been

(a) 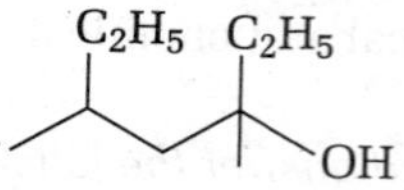 (b) 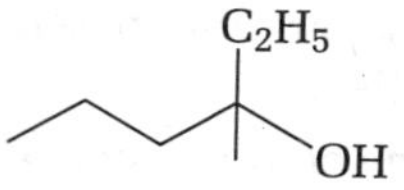

(c) 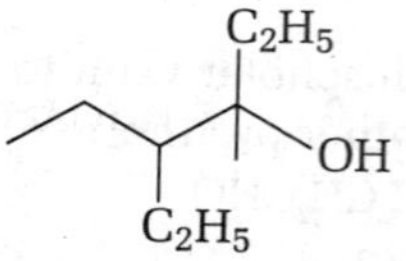 (d) 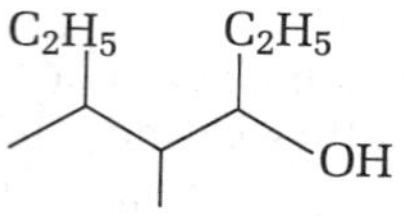

***Passage* 4** Chromium in the +6 oxidation state, Cr(VI), is a very important and effective oxidant in the organic laboratory. The major drawback to the use of reagents based on this species is that the product, Cr(III), is toxic. Chromium is just one Passage of a toxic heavy metal that requires quite expensive disposal procedures.

The development of environmentally safe reagents that can be used to replace more toxic materials in organic reactions in an area that deserves and is receiving considerable research attention, especially in industrial laboratories. All chemists need to be conscious of the effect on the environment of each reaction that they run.

1. Cr(VI) is reduced to Cr(III) and can oxidise
   (a) a secondary alcohol to a ketone
   (b) a primary alcohol to an aldehyde
   (c) a tertiary alcohol to an alkene
   (d) SO_3 to SO_4^{2-}
2. Cyclohexanol is oxidised to cyclohexanone by $Cr_2O_7^{2-}/H^+$ and Cr^{3+} being toxic heavy metal, its use is causing environmental problem. Recently a new oxidant has been suggested that is environment-friendly and can affect the following oxidation

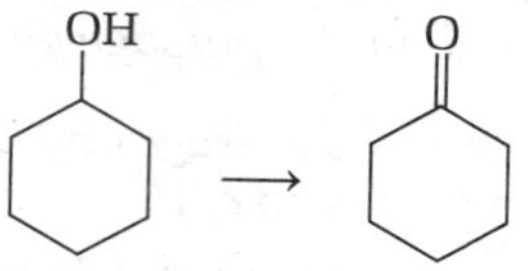

   This is
   (a) $KMnO_4/H^+$ (b) Ag_2O
   (c) $NaOCl/CH_3COOH$ (d) PCC
3. Equivalent weight of $Cr_2O_7^{2-}$ when reduced to Cr^{3+} in acidic medium is
   (a) one-third of its molar mass
   (b) one-fourth of its molar mass
   (c) one-sixth of its molar mass
   (d) one-half of its molar mass

***Passage* 5** Following diagram is given to test analytical skill. Take the graphical data into consideration to answer the questions at the end of it.

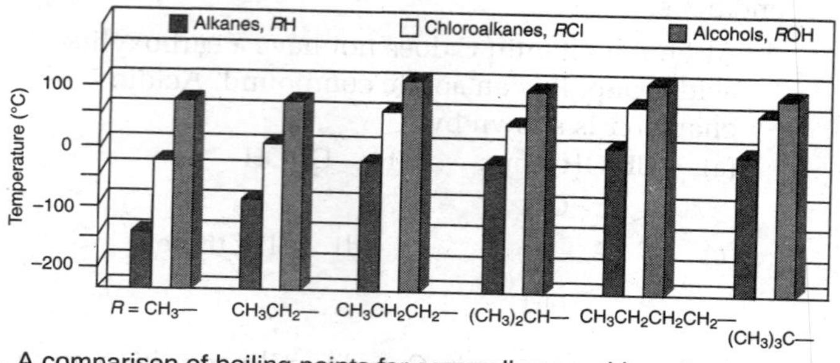

A comparison of boiling points for some alkanes, chloroalkanes, and alcohols

1. Force of attraction between molecules of one class (RH, RCl, ROH) is in the order
   (a) $RH < ROH < RCl$
   (b) $ROH < RH < RCl$
   (c) $RH < RCl < ROH$
   (d) $RCl < RH < ROH$

2. BP of the isomeric C_4H_9OH (butanol) is in order
(a) 1-butanol < 2-butanol < 2-methyl-2-propanol
(b) 1-butanol < 2-methyl-2-propanol < 2-butanol
(c) 2-butanol < 1-butanol < 2-methyl-2-propanol
(d) 2-methyl-2-propanol < 2-butanol < 1-butanol

3. Which of the following mixture can be separated by distillation or fractional distillation method at 1 atmospheric pressure?
(a) CH_3CH_2OH and H_2O (b) $(CH_3)_2CHOH, (CH_3)_2CHCl$
(c) Both (a) and (b) (d) None of the above

***Passage* 6** A research scholar synthesised the compound *A* in the laboratory.

A : 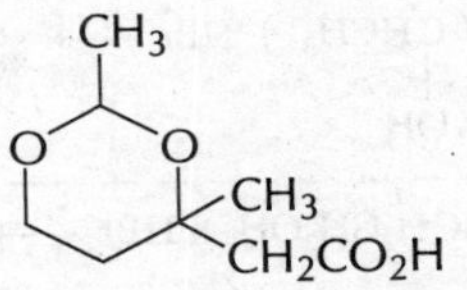

He wanted to study this compound in acidic medium and kept for some time in it. After an hour, when isolated the compound, to his surprise, he got the mixture of two compounds *B*, *C*. He studied their properties and compared them with *A*.

	A	*B*	*C*
• reaction with $NaHCO_3$	brisk effervescence	no	no
• blue litmus	red	no	no
• NaOI	no	no	yellow precipitate
• $[Ag(NH_3)_2]^+$	no	no	silver-mirror
• clue	original	$A \xrightarrow{H_3O^+} B + C,$	carbon = 54.55% hydrogen = 9.1%

1. Compound *C* is
(a) $CH_3\overset{O}{\overset{\|}{C}}CH_3$ (b) CH_3CH_2CHO
(c) HCHO (d) CH_3CHO

2. *B* is formed due to
(a) cleavage of C—O bond followed by esterification between —COOH and —OH present
(b) decarboxylation of —COOH group
(c) oxidation of $—CH_2COOH$ into —COOH
(d) None of the above is correct

***Passage* 7** Consider the following reaction,

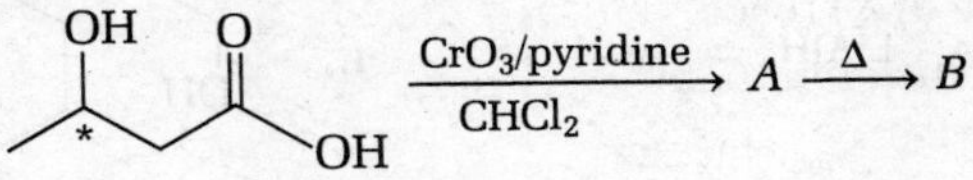

1. *A* is
(a) 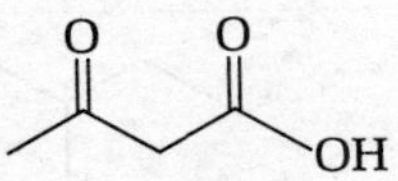 (b) 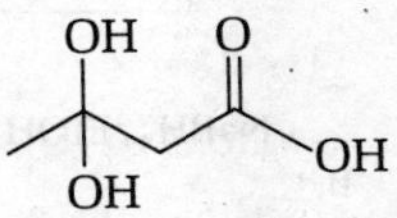
(c) 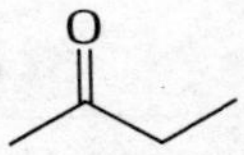 (d) 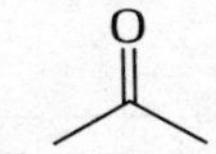

2. *B* is
(a) 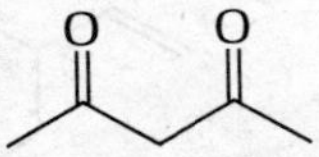 (b) 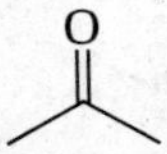
(c) 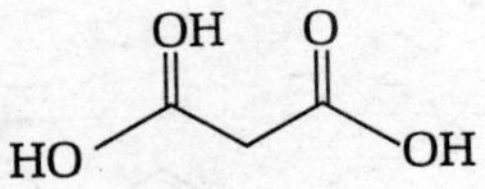 (d) 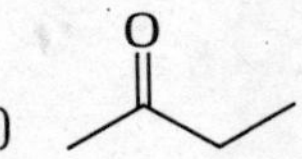

Matrix-Match Type

Given below are Matching Type Questions, with two columns (each having some items) each . Each item of Column I has to be matched with the items of Column II.

1. Match the species in Column I with the corresponding properties in Column II.

Column I	Column II
A. CH_3OH	1. Gives ketone on reaction with Cu.
B. CH_3CH_2OH	2. Gives white ppt. with Lucas reagent immediately.
C. $(CH_3)_2CHOH$	3. Cannot be synthesised using Grignard's reagent
D. $(CH_3)_3COH$	4. Gives iodoform test

2. Match the species in Column I with the corresponding method of synthesis in Column II.

Column I	Column II
A. $(CH_3)_3C\underset{OH}{\underset{\mid}{C}}HCH_3$	1. $(CH_3)_3CCH{=}CH_2 + H_3O^+$
B. $(CH_3)_2\underset{OH}{\underset{\mid}{C}}CH(CH_3)_2$	2. $(CH_3)_3CCH{=}CH_2$ + $Hg(OAc)_2 \cdot THF$ $\cdot H_2O / NaBH_4, OH^-$
C. $(CH_3)_3CCH_2CH_2OH$	3. $(CH_3)_3CCH{=}CH_2 + BH_3 \cdot THF$ $/H_2O_2, OH^-$
D. $(CH_3)_3C\underset{OCH_3}{\underset{\mid}{C}}HCH_3$	4. $(CH_3)_3CCH{=}CH_2 + Hg(OAc)_2 \cdot$ $THF \cdot CH_3OH / NaBH_4, OH^-$

3. Match the reagent in Column I that gives the desired product in Column II from

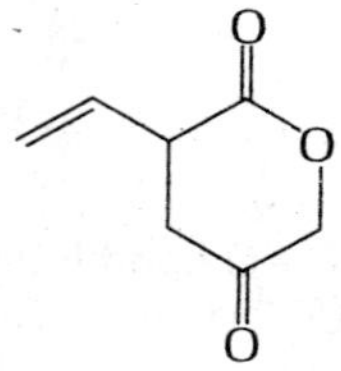

Column I	Column II
A. $LiAlH_4$	1. 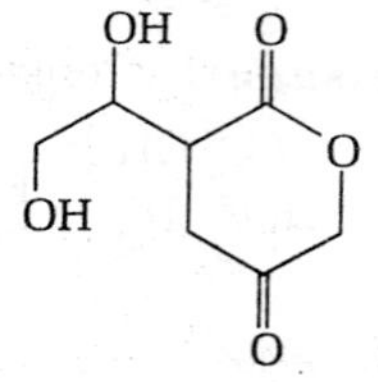
B. $NaBH_4/EtOH$	2. 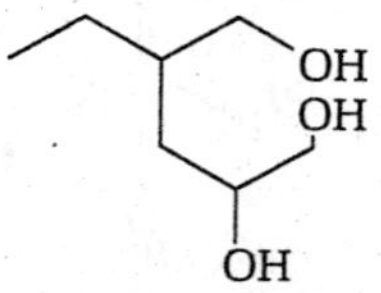
C. H_2/Pt	3. 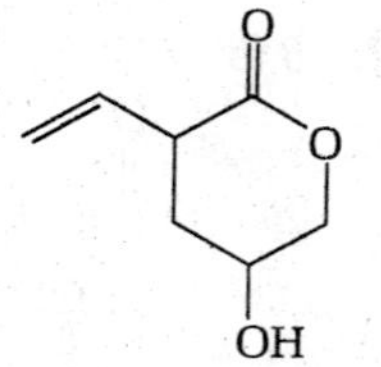
D. $KMnO_4/OH^-$	4. 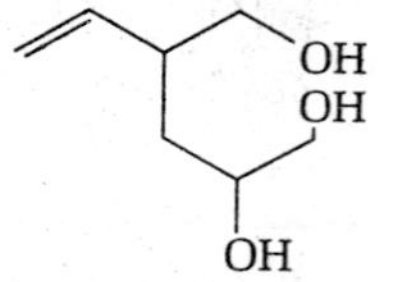

4. Match the following.

Column I (Reaction)	Column II (Product)
A. 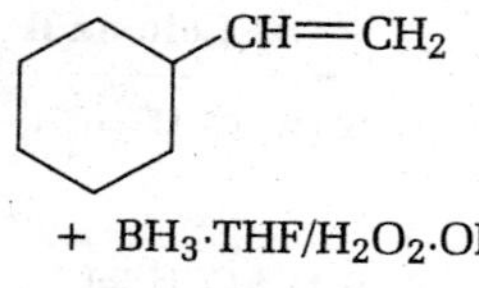 + $BH_3 \cdot THF/H_2O_2 \cdot OH^-$	1. 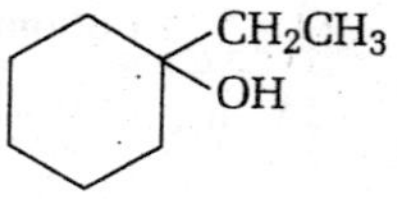
B. 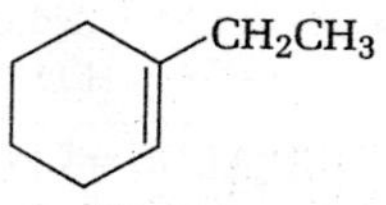 + $Hg(OAc)_2 \cdot THF/H_2O$	2. 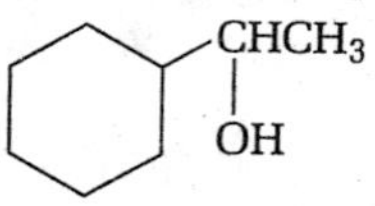
C. 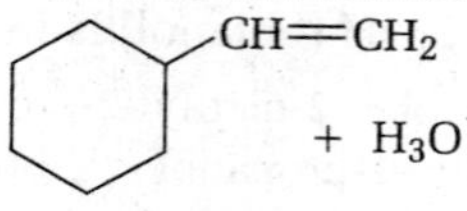 + H_3O^+	3. 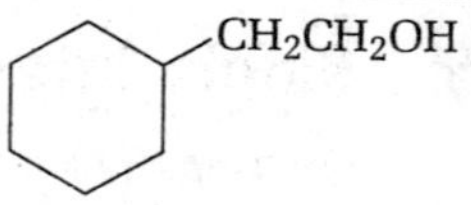
D. 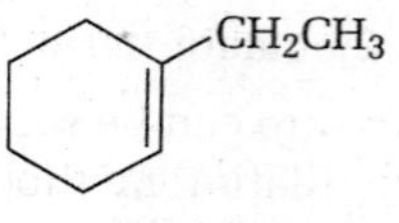 + $BH_3 \cdot THF/H_2O_2 \cdot OH^-$	4. 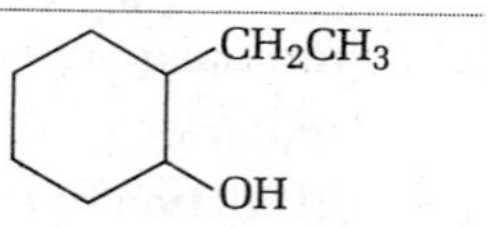

5. Match the following.

Column I (Reaction)	Column II (Product)
A. $CH_3CH(CH_3)CH(OH)CH_3 + HBr \longrightarrow$	1. $CH_3CH(CH_3)CH(Br)CH_3$
B. $CH_3CH(CH_3)CH_2CH_2OH + HBr \longrightarrow$	2. $CH_3CH(CH_3)CH_2CH_2Br$
C. $CH_3CH(CH_3)CH(OH)CH_3 + PBr_3 \longrightarrow$	3. $CH_3C(Br)(CH_3)CH_2CH_3$
D. $CH_3CH(CH_2OH)CH_2CH_3 + HBr \longrightarrow$	4. $CH_3CH(CH_2Br)CH_2CH_3$

6. Match the following.

Column I (Alcohol/intermediate)	Column II (Grignard synthesis)
A. $CH_3CH_2CH_2OH$	1. $CH_2{-}CH_2$ (O) $+ CH_3MgBr \xrightarrow{H_3O^+}$
B. $CH_3CH(OH)CH_3$	2. $CH_3CH_2MgBr + HCHO \xrightarrow{H_3O^+}$
C. $CH_3C(CH_3)(OH)CH_3$	3. $CH_3C(=O)OCH(CH_3)CH_3 + 2CH_3MgBr \xrightarrow{H_3O^+}$
D. CH_3CHO (intermediate)	4. $HC(=O)CH_2CH_3 + 2CH_3MgBr \xrightarrow{H_3O^+}$

Single Integer Answer Questions

Answer of these questions is a single digit lying between 0 to 9.

1. The number of isomer(s) with stereogenic centre in $C_4H_{10}O$ is ....
2. $(CH_3)_2CHOH$ is oxidised to a carbonyl compound by $Cr_2O_7^{2-}/H^+$ which is itself reduced to green coloured salt with oxidation number ....
3. Alcoholic group at position .... reacts fastest with Lucas' reagent.

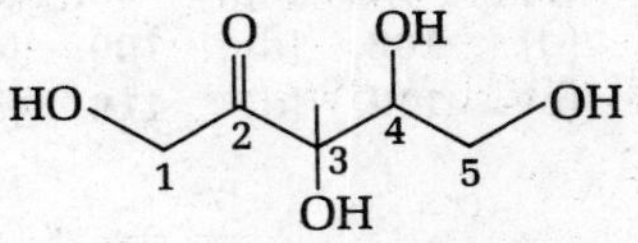

4. Alcoholic group at position is oxidised to carbonyl group by copper metal.

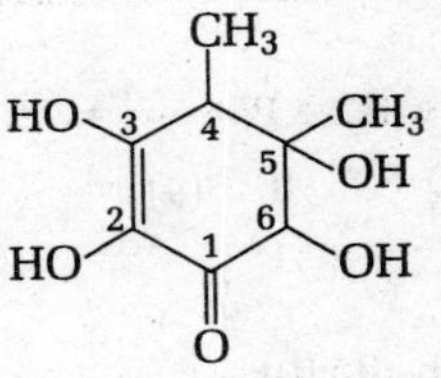

5. The final state of mercury in the following reaction is ....

$$CH_3\underset{\displaystyle CH_3}{\underset{|}{C}H}CH=CH_2 \xrightarrow{Hg(OAc)_2 \cdot THF/H_2O}$$

6. 30 g of CH_3MgBr reacts with excess of $CH_3CH_2CH_2OH$ forming x g of a gas. x is ....
7. $KMnO_4/H^+$ oxidises 1° alcohol to acid. What is change in oxidation number of Mn?
8. Vitamin C is also called ascorbic acid and has hydroxy group? How many types of groups are present in the product formed by mild oxidation of vitamin C?
9. In the following reaction, 6.2 g of $CH_3CO\overset{18}{O}H$ reacts with 4.6 g CH_3CH_2OH.

$$CH_3CO\overset{18}{O}H + CH_3CH_2OH \longrightarrow CH_3COOC_2H_5 + H_2O$$

How much water is formed?

10. In the following hydration of alkene, what is the position of —OH group based on given numbering?

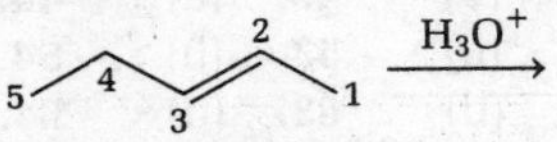

11. The number of hydroxyl group(s) in Q is **[JEE Advanced 2015]**

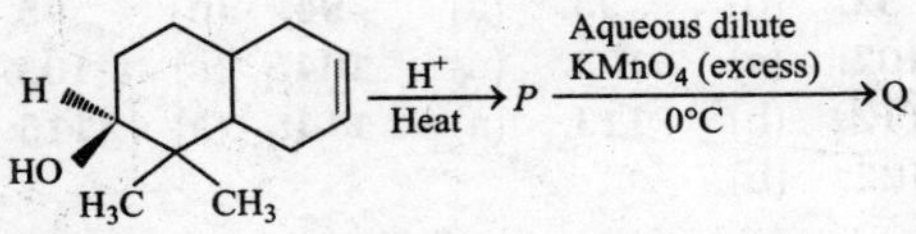

12. How many cyclic (including stereo isomers) alcohols are possible for the compound with molecular formula C_4H_7OH.
13. If (dl) or (±) 3-methyl butanoic acid were esterified by reaction with (dl) or (±) 2-butanol, how many optically active compounds would be present in the final equilibrium reaction mixture?
14. An organic compound ($C_8H_{10}O_2$) rotates plane-polarised light. It produces pink colour with neutral $FeCl_3$ solution. What is the total number of all the possible isomers for this compound ? **[JEE Advanced 2020]**
15. Schemes 1 and 2 describe the conversation of P to Q and R to S, respectively. Scheme 3 describes the synthesis of T from Q and S. The total number of Br atoms in the a molecule of T is ....**[JEE Advanced 2019]**

Scheme 1

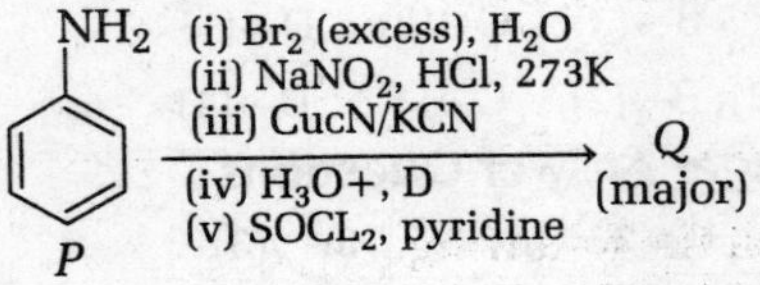

Scheme 2

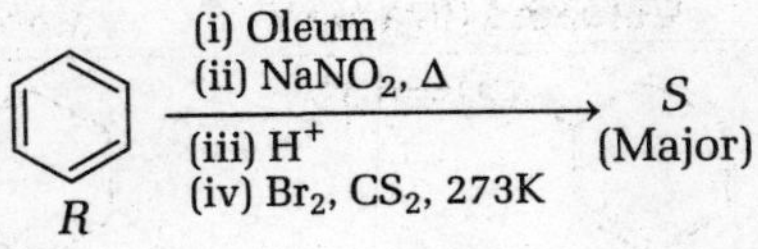

Scheme 3

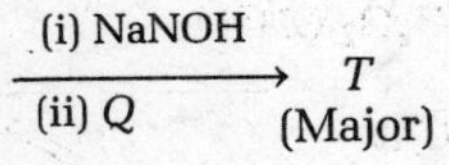

Answers

Objective Questions Type I [Only one correct option]

1. (d)	**2.** (a)	**3.** (c)	**4.** (b)	**5.** (a)	**6.** (c)	**7.** (c)	**8.** (b)	**9.** (b)	**10.** (d)
11. (c)	**12.** (b)	**13.** (a)	**14.** (c)	**15.** (d)	**16.** (b)	**17.** (a)	**18.** (a)	**19.** (d)	**20.** (d)
21. (b)	**22.** (c)	**23.** (b)	**24.** (c)	**25.** (a)	**26.** (d)	**27.** (b)	**28.** (b)	**29.** (c)	**30.** (a)
31. (b)	**32.** (c)	**33.** (b)	**34.** (d)	**35.** (a)	**36.** (b)	**37.** (b)	**38.** (c)	**39.** (b)	**40.** (c)
41. (d)	**42.** (b)	**43.** (a)	**44.** (a)	**45.** (b)	**46.** (d)	**47.** (b)	**48.** (a)	**49.** (d)	**50.** (a)
51. (a)	**52.** (b)	**53.** (b)	**54.** (a)	**55.** (b)	**56.** (c)	**57.** (c)	**58.** (b)	**59.** (b)	**60.** (c)
61. (a)	**62.** (d)	**63.** (d)	**64.** (d)	**65.** (b)	**66.** (a)	**67.** (b)	**68.** (b)	**69.** (a)	**70.** (a)
71. (b)	**72.** (a)	**73.** (d)	**74.** (d)	**75.** (a)	**76.** (a)	**77.** (b)	**78.** (a)	**79.** (c)	**80.** (b)
81. (c)	**82.** (c)	**83.** (b)	**84.** (b)	**85.** (d)	**86.** (c)	**87.** (d)	**88.** (c)	**89.** (a)	**90.** (c)
91. (a)	**92.** (d)	**93.** (a)	**94.** (d)	**95.** (a)	**96.** (a)	**97.** (b)	**98.** (c)	**99.** (c)	**100.** (d)
101. (d)	**102.** (a)	**103.** (a)	**104.** (c)	**105.** (c)	**106.** (b)	**107.** (d)	**108.** (d)	**109.** (c)	**110.** (c)
111. (b)	**112.** (b)	**113.** (a)	**114.** (a)	**115.** (d)	**116.** (a)	**117.** (b)	**118.** (d)	**119.** (a)	**120.** (c)
121. (a)	**122.** (b)								

Objective Questions Type II [One or more than one correct option(s)]

1. (b, c)	**2.** (a, b, c)	**3.** (c, d)	**4.** (a, b, d)	**5.** (a, b, c)
6. (a, b, d)	**7.** (c)	**8.** (a, d)	**9.** (a, c, d)	**10.** (b)
11. (a)	**12.** (a, b, c)	**13.** (b, c)	**14.** (b, c)	**15.** (a, b, c)
16. (b, c)	**17.** (a)	**18.** (c, d)		

Numerical Value Questions

1. (4) **2.** (2) **3.** (2) **4.** (4) **5.** (8) **6.** (2) **7.** (5) **8.** (4)

Comprehension Based Questions

Passage 1 – 1. (c) **2.** (c) **3.** (b)

Passage 2 – 1. (b) **2.** (a) **3.** (b)

Passage 3 – 1. (a) **2.** (b) **3.** (a)

Passage 4 – 1. (a) **2.** (c) **3.** (c)

Passage 5 – 1. (c) **2.** (d) **3.** (b)

Passage 6 – 1. (d) **2.** (a)

Passage 7 – 1. (a) **2.** (b)

Matrix-Match Type

1. A→(3); B→(4); C→(1); D→(2)

2. A→(2); B→(1); C→(3); D→(4)

3. A→(4); B→(3); C→(2); D→(1)

4. A→(3); B→(2); C→(2,3); D→(4)

5. A→(1,3); B→(2); C→(1); D→(4)

6. A→(4); B→(3); C→(2); D→(1)

Single Integer Answer Questions

1. (1)	**2.** (3)	**3.** (3)	**4.** (6)	**5.** (0)	**6.** (4)	**7.** (5)	**8.** (3)	**9.** (2)	**10.** (4)
11. (4)	**12.** (7)	**13.** (4)	**14.** (6)	**15.** (4)					

Solutions

Objective Questions Type I [Only one correct option]

2. (*a*) Intermediate is most stable carbocation, thus hydrated to maximum extent.

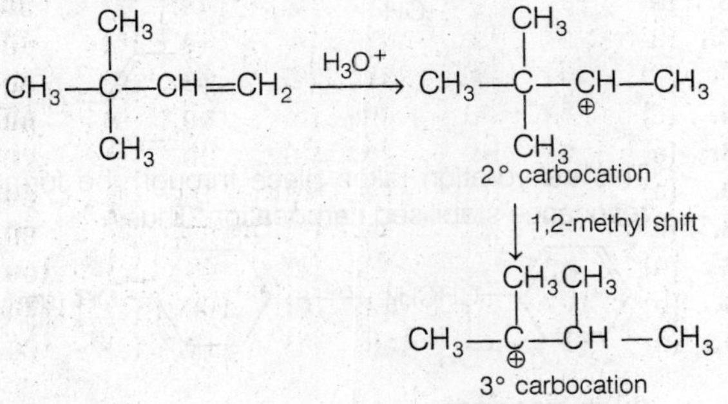

3. (*c*)

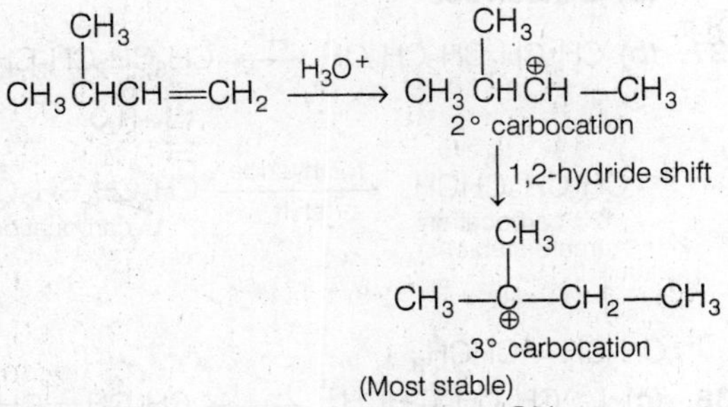

5. (*a*)

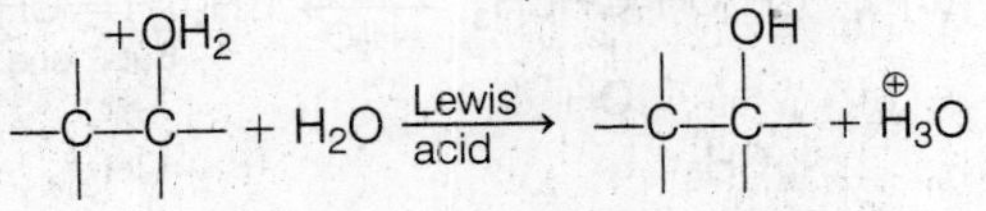

6. (*c*) The production of methanol from water gas is as follows:

$$\underset{\substack{\text{Water gas} \\ \text{or} \\ \textit{syn gas}}}{[CO + H_2] + H_2} \xrightarrow[300\text{ atm}, 300^\circ C]{ZnO + Cr_2O_3} \underset{\text{Methanol}}{CH_3OH}$$

It is an industrial process used for the production of methanol where volume ratio of the reactant gases is maintained as:

syn gas : $H_2 = 2:1$ and $ZnO\text{-}Cr_2O_3$ act as catalysts

Thus, water gas is also called *syn* gas because it is used for synthesis of methanol.

7. (*c*) S_N1 reaction is through the formation of carbocation. Thus, nucleophile can attack on either side forming racemic mixture.

8. (*b*) S_N2 reaction takes place by nucleophilic attack on the backside resulting in the formation inverted product.

9. (*b*)

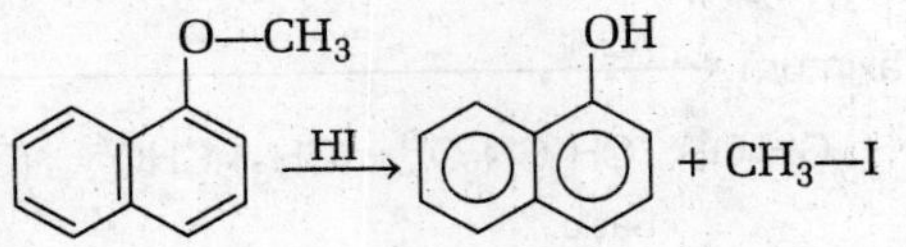

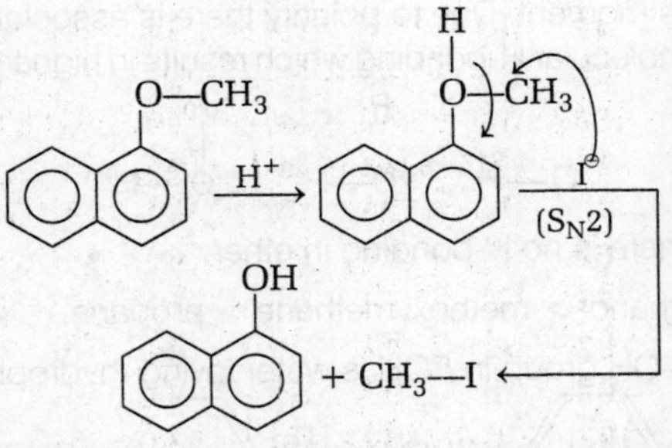

10. (*d*) Due to formation of stable carbocation intermediate.

12. (*b*) $LiAlH_4$ reduces ketonic as well as ester group, only $NaBH_4$ give product.

13. (*a*)

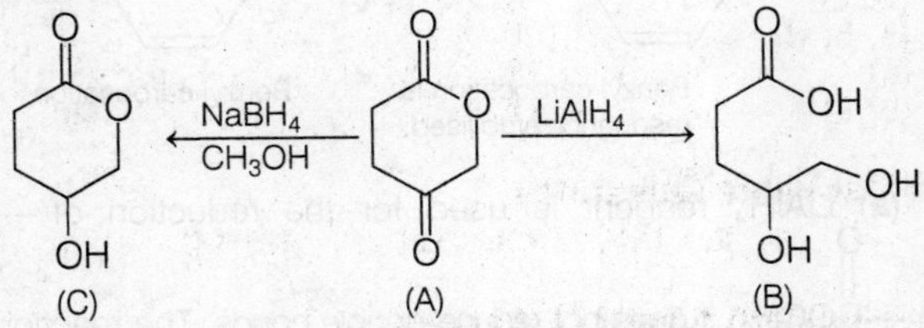

14. (*c*)

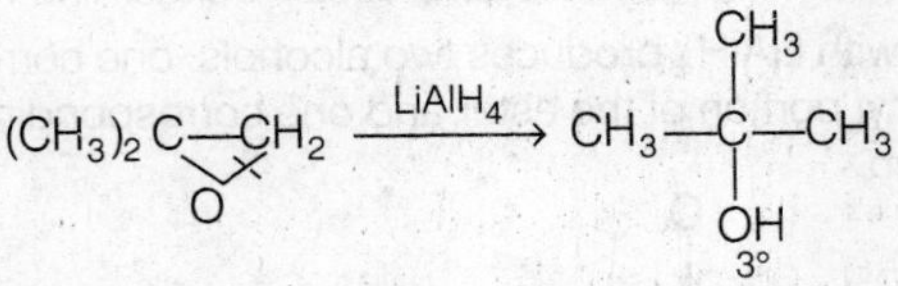

15. (*d*) $LiAlH_4$ does not attack (C=C) bond.

17. (*a*)

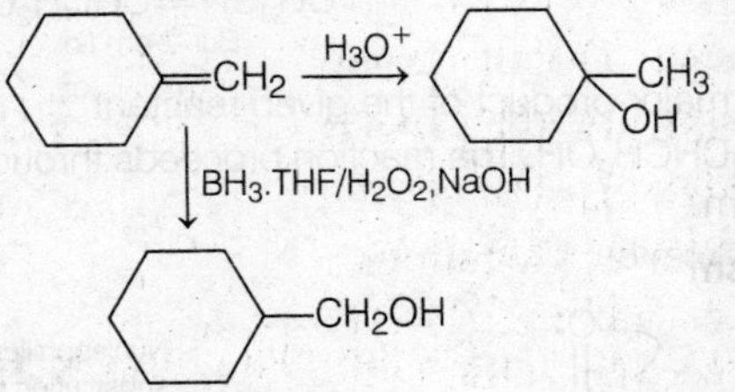

21. (*b*) $CH_3CHO \xrightarrow[\text{(ii) } H_3O^+]{\text{(i) } CH_3MgBr} \underset{\substack{| \\ OH \\ 2^\circ}}{CH_3CHCH_3}$

23. (*b*)

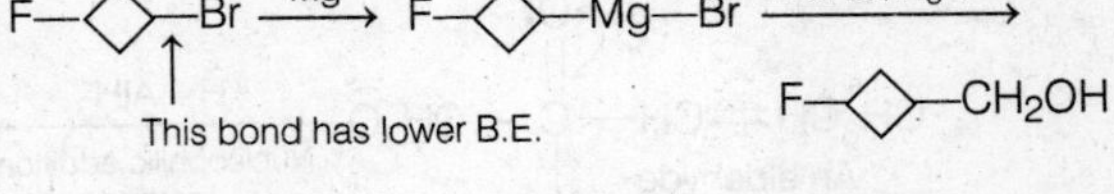

27. (*b*) $CH_3CH{=}CHCH_3$ is symmetrical and gives same product by any of the given method adopted.

28. (*b*) Rectified spirit contains 98% ethanol-water (not methanol) mixture.

29. (*c*) R—O—H has polarity as $R—\overset{\delta^-}{O}—H^{\delta^+}$ and thus molecule has dipole moment. Due to polarity there is association by intermolecular H-bonding which results in higher boiling point.

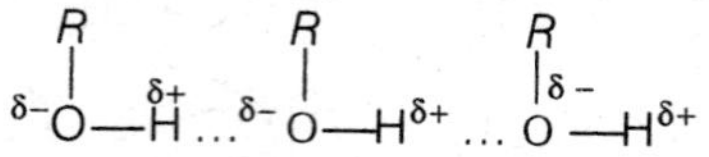

30. (*a*) There is no H-bonding in ether.

32. (*c*) ethanol > methoxymethane > propane.

33. (*b*) —OH group in *R*OH is water loving (hydrophilic).

34. (*d*)

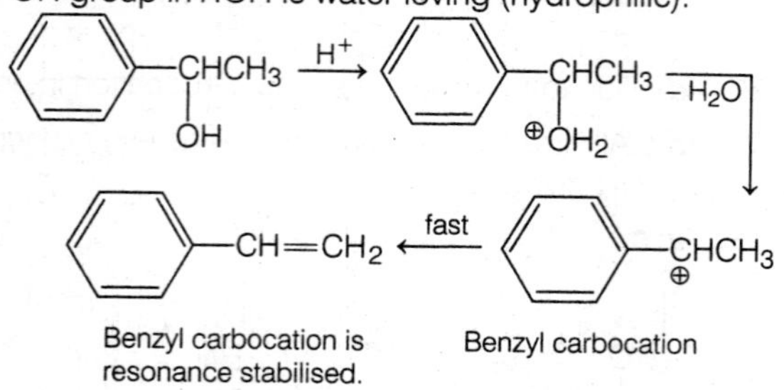

35. (*a*) $LiAlH_4$ reagent is used for the reduction of —CHO, $—\overset{O}{\overset{\|}{C}}OCH_3$. It does not reduce double bonds. The reaction of an ester with $LiAlH_4$ produces two alcohols, one corresponding to the acyl portion of the ester and one corresponding to the alkyl portion.

$$CH_3CH{=}CH\overset{O}{\overset{\|}{C}}—OCH_3 \xrightarrow{LiAlH_4} \underset{\text{But-2-en-1-ol}}{CH_3CH{=}CHCH_2OH} + \underset{\text{Methanol}}{CH_3OH}$$

Thus, the major product of the given reactant $CH_3CH{=}CHCH_2OH$. The reaction proceeds through following mechanism.

Mechanism

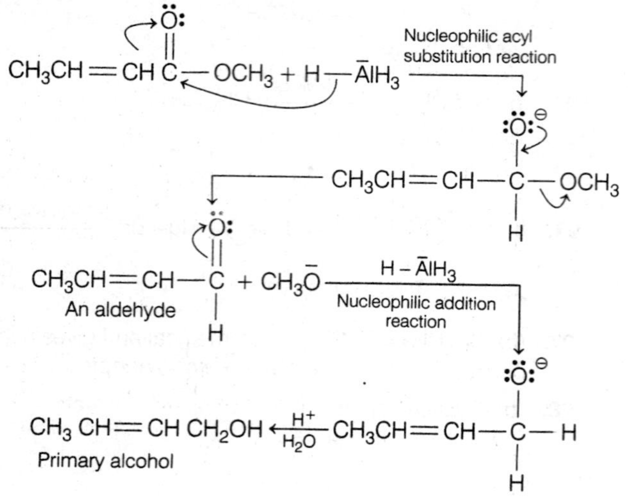

36. (*b*)

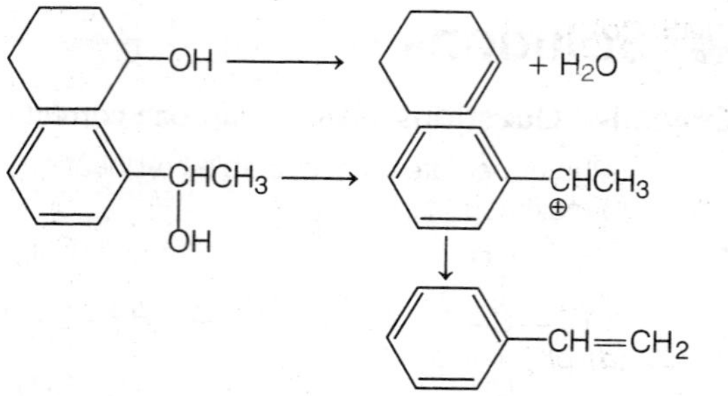

This dehydration takes place through the formation of resonance stabilised carbocation. Thus,

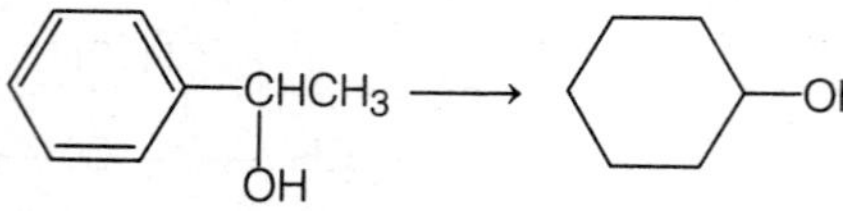

(b) is incorrect.

37. (*b*)

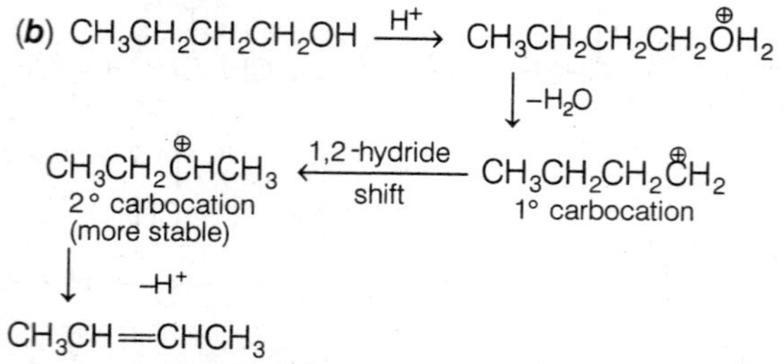

38. (*c*) I. $CH_3CH_2\underset{OH}{CH}CH_3 \xrightarrow{-H_2O} \underset{\text{But-2-ene}}{CH_3CH{=}CHCH_3}$

II.

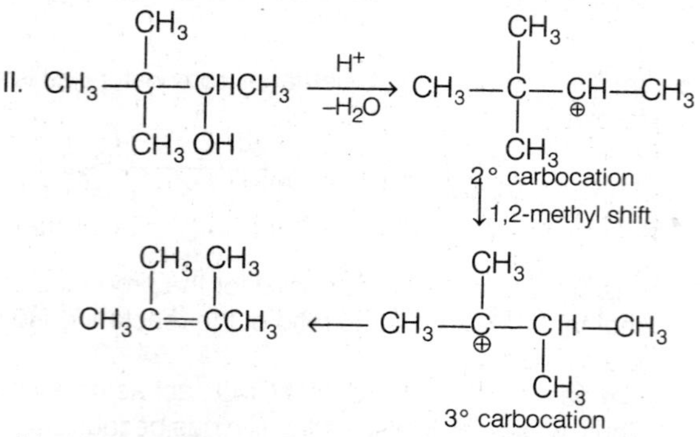

39. (*b*) 1° alcohol : S_N2 2°, 3° alcohol : S_N1

40. (*c*) 3° alcohol is most basic reacts with conc. HCl forming white precipitate.

43. (*a*) $ROH + SOCl_2 \longrightarrow RCl + SO_2\uparrow + HCl\uparrow$

SO_2 and HCl escape easily. Thus, reacts faster.

44. (*a*) CH_3OH CH_3CH_2OH $(CH_3)_2CHOH$ $(CH_3)_3COH$

Maximum ← Acidic

(a) $CH_3O^\ominus$ $CH_3CH_2O^\ominus$ $(CH_3)_2CHO^\ominus$ $(CH_3)_3CO^\ominus$

Basic → Maximum

If acid is weak, its conjugate base is strong.

45. (*b*)

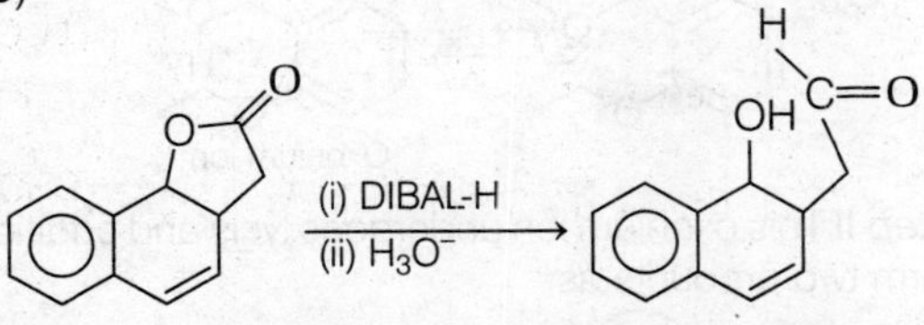

DIBAL can not reduce double bond. It can reduce cyclic ester.

46. (*d*) $pK_a = -\log K_a$

If K_a is high, pK_a is low.

1° alcohol 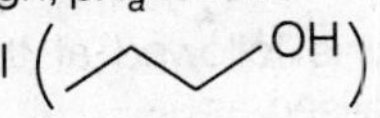 is the strongest acid thus has maximum K_a value.

3° alcohol 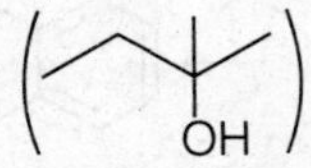 is the weakest acid and thus has minimum K_a value and maximum pK_a value.

49. (*d*) CO_2 escapes thus reaction is not reversible.

50. (*a*) Due to smaller size of alcohol.

52. (*b*) $CH_3CH_2-\overset{O}{\overset{\|}{C}}\overset{q}{\vdots}O-H + CH_3CH_2\overset{r}{\vdots}\overset{18}{O}-H$

$$CH_3CH_2\overset{O}{\overset{\|}{C}}-\overset{18}{O}-CH_2CH_3 + H_2O$$

If oxygen of CH_3CH_2OH is labelled with ^{18}O, then it goes with ester formed, indicating cleavage of bond *q* in I and *r* in II.

54. (*a*)

I. $CH_3{=}CH_2CH_2OH \xrightarrow{MnO_2} CH_3CH_2CHO$ (Allylic oxidation)

II. $(CH_3)_3COH \xrightarrow[\Delta]{Cu} CH_3-\underset{CH_3}{\underset{|}{C}}{=}CH_2 + H_2O$

III. $CH_3CH_2OH \xrightarrow{H_2CrO_4} CH_3\overset{O}{\overset{\|}{C}}-OH$ (Overoxidation)

IV. $CH_3CH{=}CHCH_3 \xrightarrow[\Delta]{KMnO_4} CH_3-\overset{O}{\overset{\|}{C}}-OH$

56. (*c*) PBr_3 reagent is used for the substitution of —Br group while alc. KOH reagent is used to carry out elimination reaction.

The given reaction proceed in following manner:

Step I In presence of PBr_3, alcohols undergo substitution reactions to give halides. Reagent PBr_3 is usually generated *insitu* by the reaction of red phosphorus with bromine.

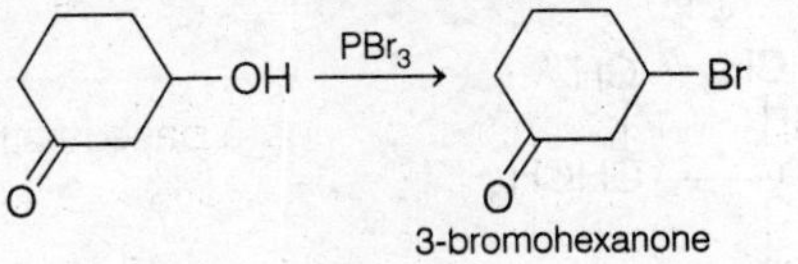

Step II 3-bromohexanone in presence of alc. KOH undergoes elimination reaction and gives cyclohex-2-en-1-one.

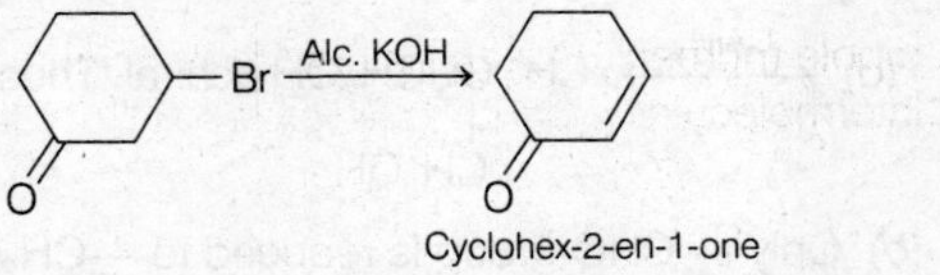

57. (*c*) Both are 1° alcohols and respond to tests II and III but iodoform test is given by CH_3CH_2OH.

58. (*b*)

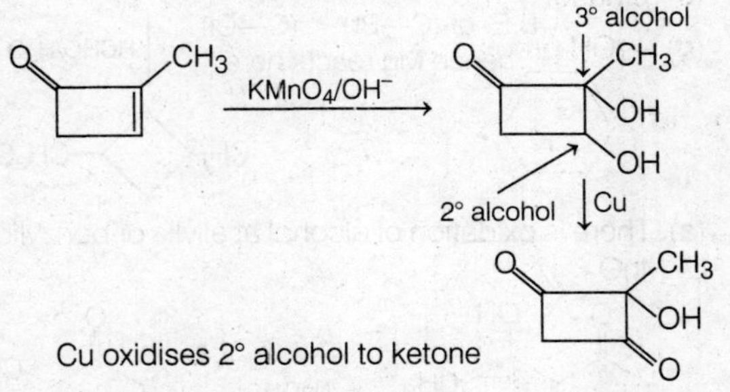

Cu oxidises 2° alcohol to ketone

59. (*b*) Oxymercuration-demercuration hydrates alkenes without rearrangement.

60. (*c*)

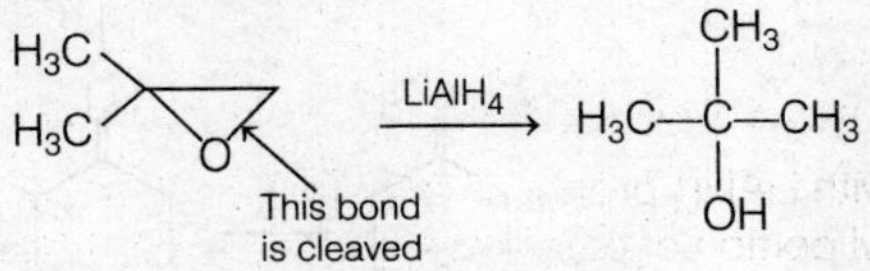

61. (*a*) Basic number of alcohols is in order : 3° > 2° > 1° Alcohol at C_2(3°) is more basic than at C_5(2°).

62. (*d*)

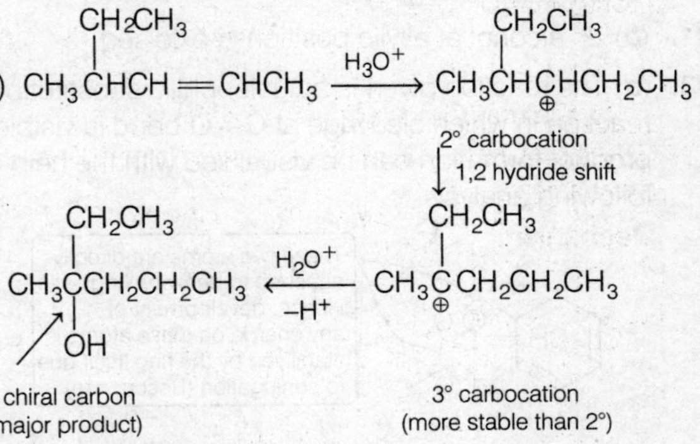

Major product has chiral carbon thus shows optical isomerism ⇒ (a) is true,

It is 3° alcohol reacting fastly with HBr (Lucas test) ⇒ (b) is true.

It is dehydrated easily ⇒ (c) is true.

64. (*d*) *X* evolves CO_2 with aq $NaHCO_3$ indicating —COOH

$$X \xrightarrow{LiAlH_4} \text{achiral}$$

(a) $\xrightarrow{LiAlH_4} CH_3CH_2\underset{OH}{\underset{|}{C}}HCH_2OH$ chiral Thus, false.

(b) $\xrightarrow{LiAlH_4} CH_3\underset{OCH_3}{\underset{|}{C}}HCH_2OH$ chiral Thus, false.

(c) $\xrightarrow{LiAlH_4}$ $CH_3CH(OH)CH_2CH_2OH$ chiral Thus, false.

(d) $\xrightarrow{LiAlH_4}$ $CH_3CH(CH_2OH)CH_2OH$ achiral. Thus true.

65. (*b*) Only — CHO group is reduced to $—CH_2OH$

68. (*b*)

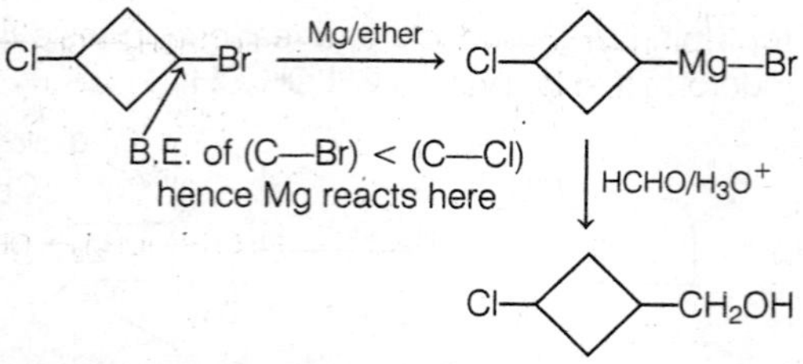

69. (*a*) There is oxidation of alcohol at allylic or benzylic position by MnO_2.

70. (*a*)

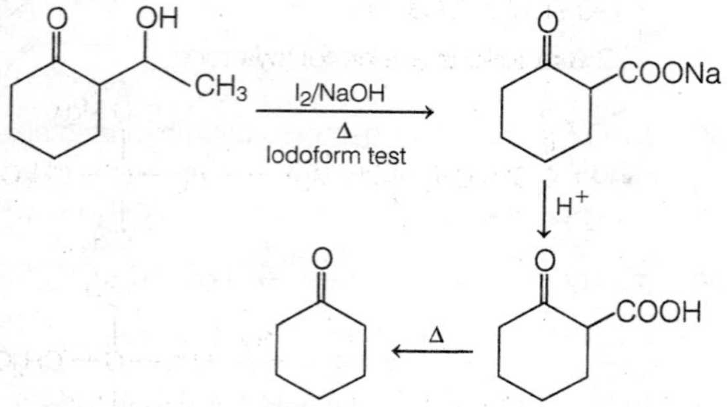

When there is a keto group at β-position *wrt* —COOH, CO_2 is lost due to heating.

71. (*b*) 2° alcohol at allylic position is oxidised.

73. (*d*) The reaction given is a nucleophilic substitution reaction in which cleavage at C—O bond is visible. The product formation can be visualised with the help of following analysis.

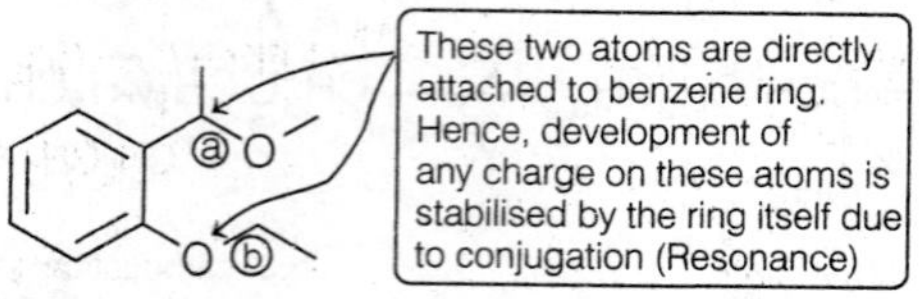

If any one properly visualise the fact written with figure above, than a conclusion can be made that C—O bonds marked (a) and (b) in the figure will undergo heterolysis during the reaction.

The reaction can be represented as

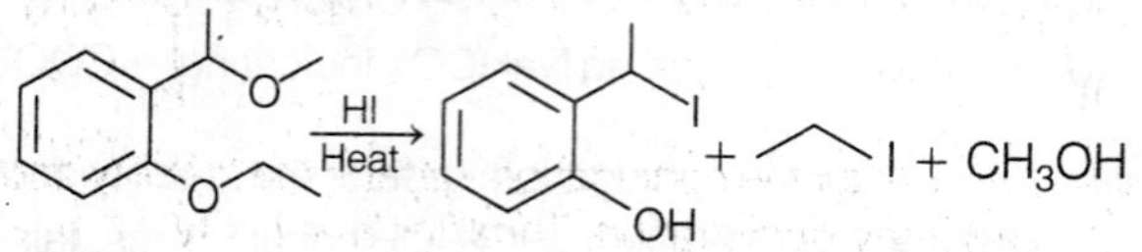

Mechanism

***Step* I** The reaction begins with the attack of H^+ of HI on oxygen to form oxonium ion as

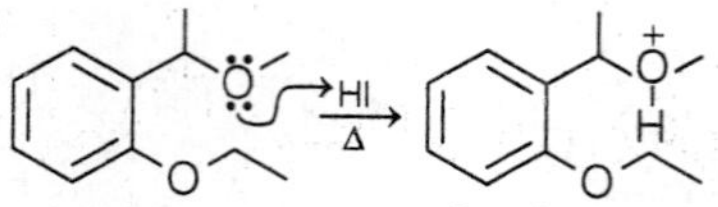

Oxonium ion

***Step* II** This oxonium ion undergoes lysis and addition of I^- to form two products as

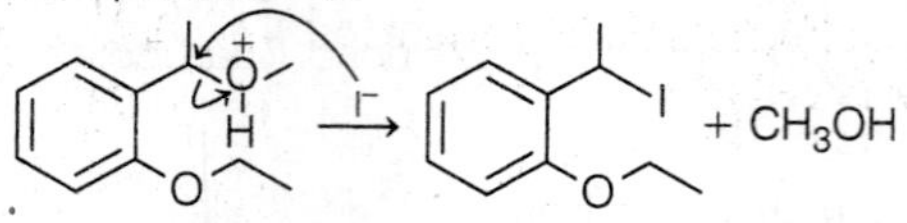

***Step* III** Similar pathway is followed at the other oxygen atom, which can be visualised as

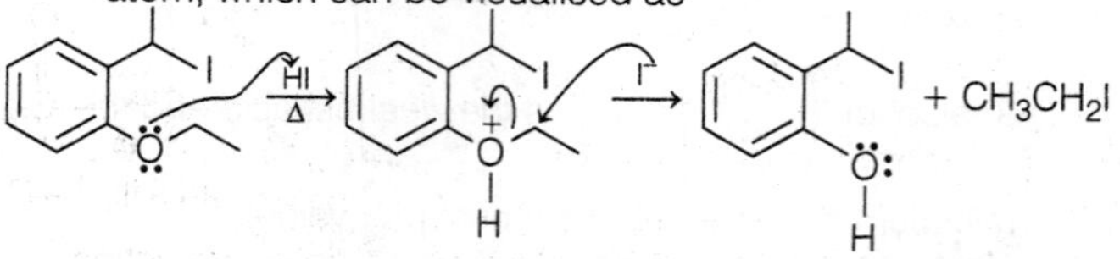

Note Mechanism of a reaction is always a logical sequencing of events which may occur simultaneously as well.

74. (*d*) $(C_2H_5O)_2C{=}O \xrightarrow{CH_3MgBr} CH_3COC_2H_5$ (This is (b)) $\xrightarrow{CH_3MgBr} CH_3COCH_3 \xrightarrow[H_3O^+]{CH_3MgBr} (CH_3)_3COH$ (3° alcohol)

75. (*a*) Alcohol *B* is 3° (reacts fastest with Lucas reagent).

$$CH_3COC_2H_5 \xrightarrow{CH_3MgBr} CH_3COCH_3 \xrightarrow[H_3O^+]{CH_3MgBr} (CH_3)_3COH$$

76. (*a*)

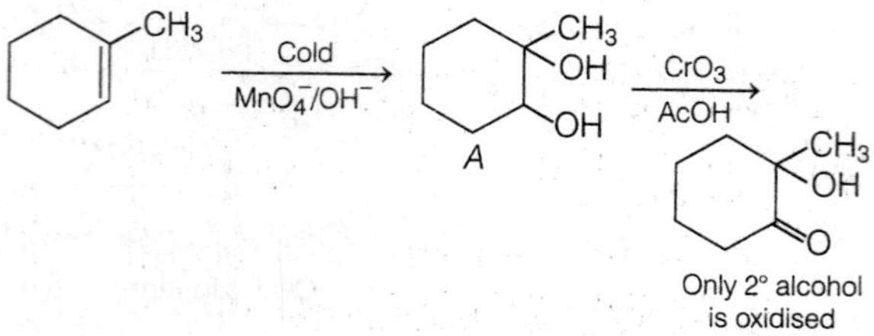

77. (*b*)

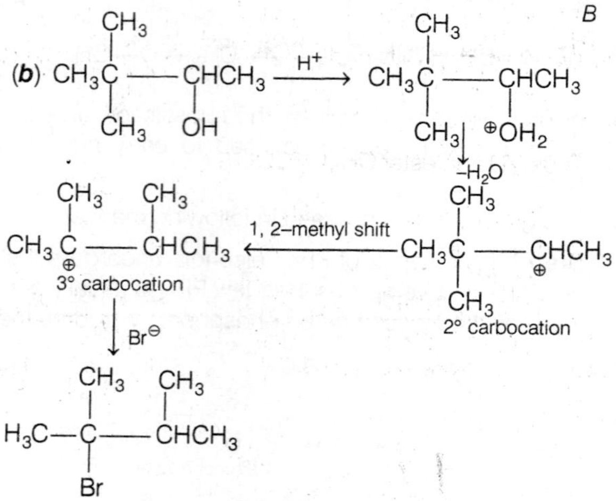

80. (*b*)

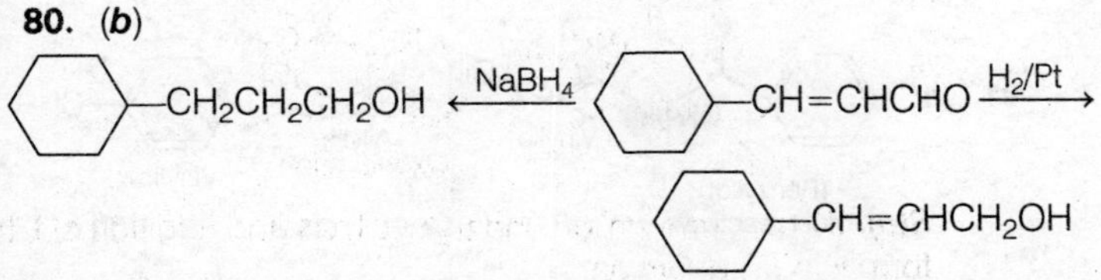

83. (*b*) The most suitable reagent to carry out given transformation is I_2/NaOH

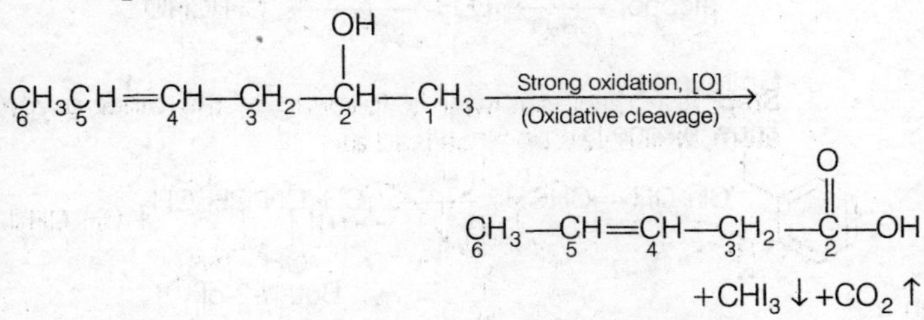

Here, the haloform reaction will give following reaction:

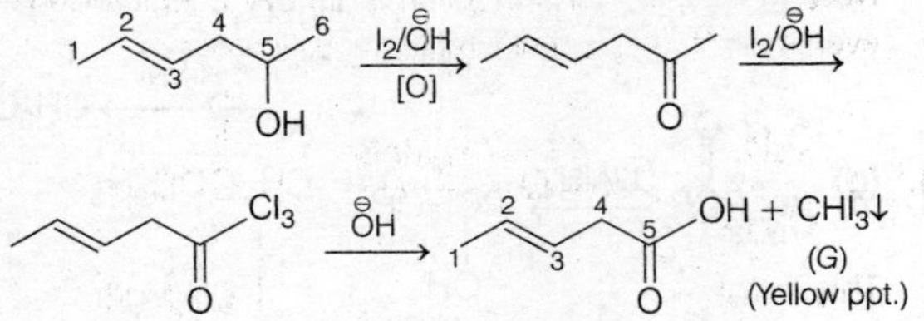

(i) Tollen's reagent ($AgNO_3$ + NH_4OH) is a mild oxidising agent. It does not react with $-\underset{OH}{\underset{|}{CH}}-CH_3$ group (2°-alcohol).

(ii) Alkaline $KMnO_4$ cannot perform the oxidative cleavage, rather it will hydroxylate the C=C.

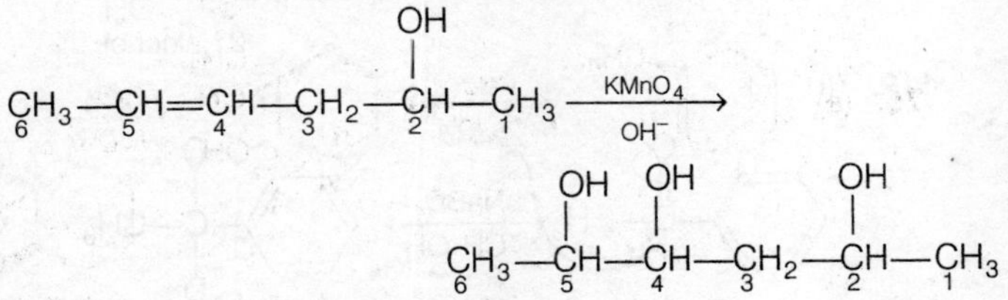

(iv) CrO_2Cl_2 / CS_2 will not react here.

84. (*b*) $A \xrightarrow{H_3O^+} CH_3\underset{CH_3}{\underset{|}{C}}HCOOH$

Thus, *A* is an ester $CH_3\underset{CH_3}{\underset{|}{C}}HCOOR$

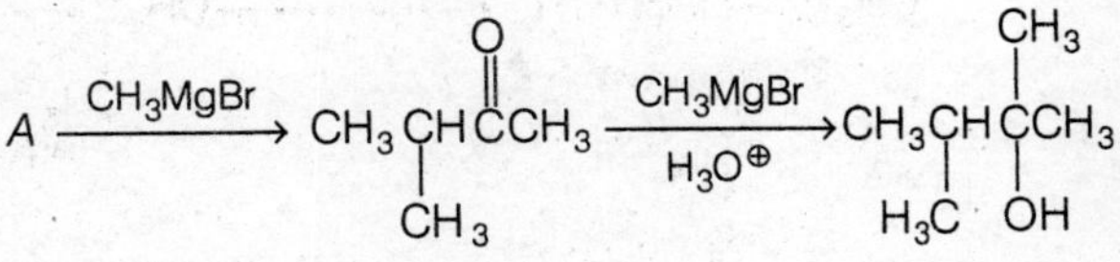

85. (*b*)

(d) $CH_3CH_2-\overset{OH}{\underset{Ph}{C}}-CH_3$ cannot be prepared by HCHO and $PhCH(CH_3)CH_2MgX$ This can be easily illustrated by following reaction.

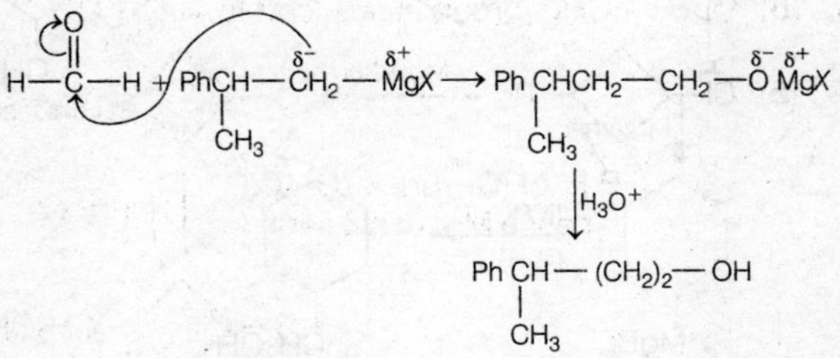

The obtained product is not the required substance. While option (a), (b) and (c) can readily prepare the required substance.

The reactions are as follows :

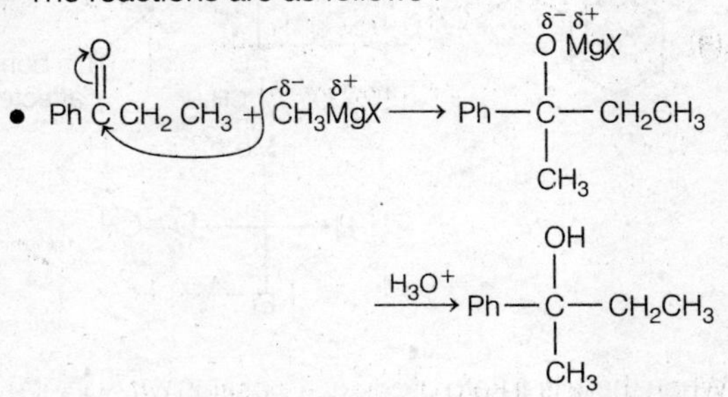

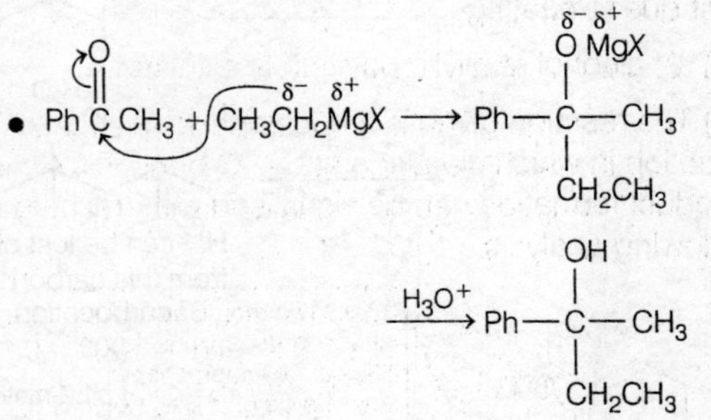

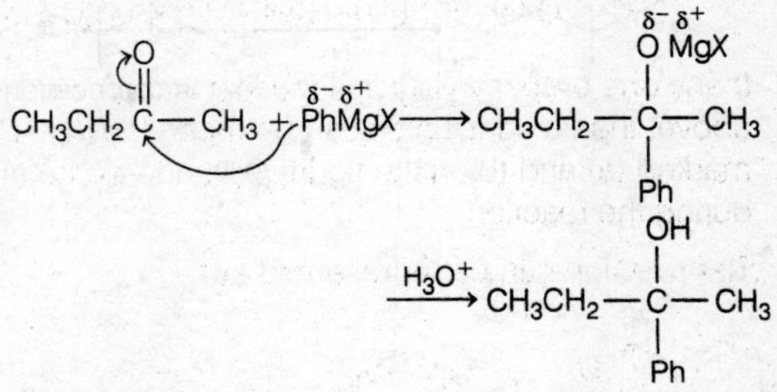

86. (*c*) Greater the conjugation, greater the stability and thus larger the dehydration. Thus III < II < I < IV

87. (*d*)

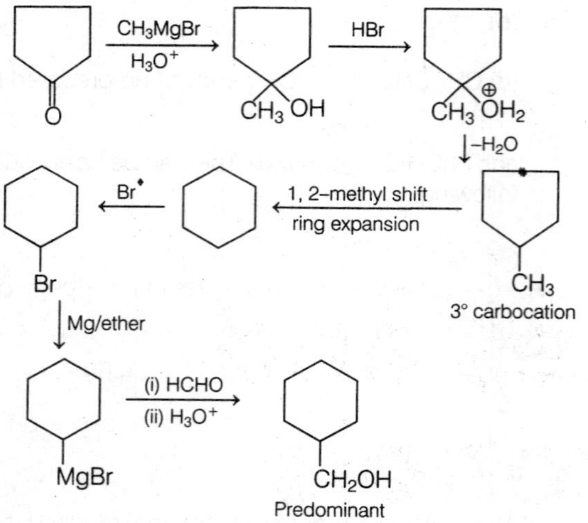

89. (*a*)

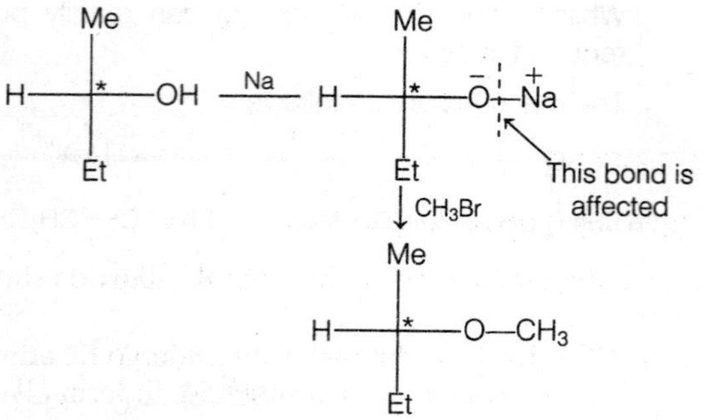

90. (*c*)

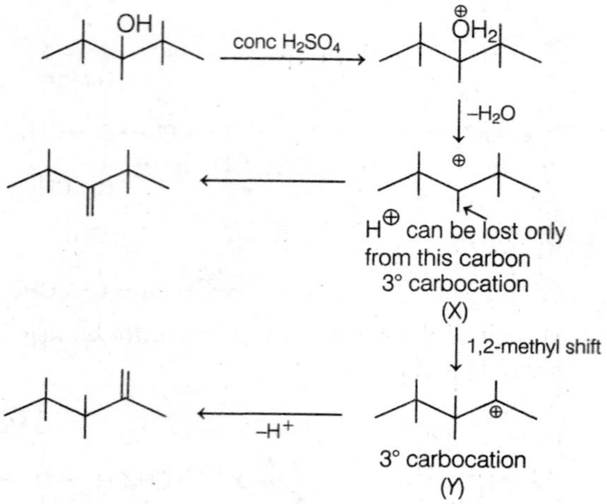

91. (*a*)

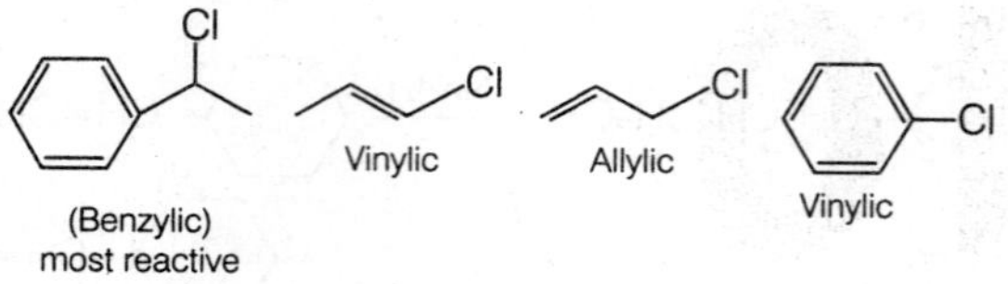

95. (*a*) Alcohol is 2° (Lucas test)

$$\text{alcohol} \xrightarrow[-H_2O]{} C_4H_8 \xrightarrow{O_3/Zn} CH_3CHO$$

Go reversely :

Thus, alkene is

$$CH_3CH{=}CHCH_3 \xrightarrow{H_2O} CH_3\underset{\underset{OH}{|}}{CH}\,CH_2CH_3$$

Butan-2-ol

96. (*a*) $CaC_2 \xrightarrow{H_2O} CH{\equiv}CH \xrightarrow[HgSO_4]{\text{Dil } H_2SO_4} CH_3CHO$

$$\xrightarrow{H_2/Ni} CH_3CH_2OH$$

108. (*d*) (a) $R\overset{\overset{O}{\|}}{C}R \xrightarrow{LiAlH_4} R\underset{\underset{OH}{|}}{C}HCH_3$

2° alcohol

(b) $\underset{\text{But-1-ene}}{CH_3CH_2CH{=}CH_2} \xrightarrow{H_3O^+} CH_3CH_2\underset{\underset{OH}{|}}{C}HCH_3$

2° alcohol

(c) $CH_3CH_2MgBr + RCHO \xrightarrow{H_3O^+} CH_3CH_2\underset{\underset{OH}{|}}{C}H\,R$

2° alcohol

119. (*a*)

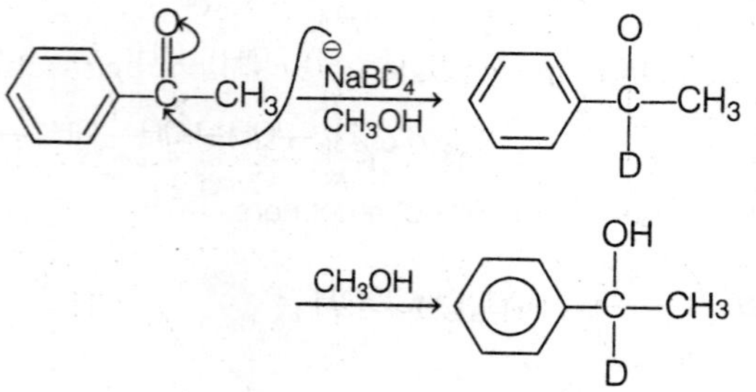

10

Ethers, Oxiranes and Polyhydric Alcohols

Objective Questions Type I [Only one correct option]

In each of the questions below, four choices are given of which only one is correct.

1. Major addition product of the following reaction is

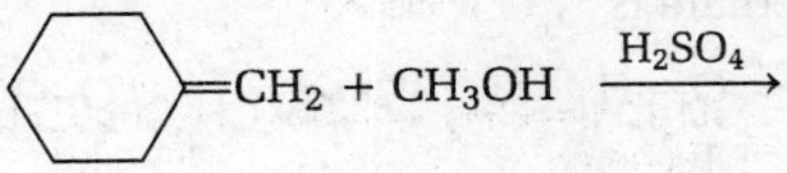

(a) 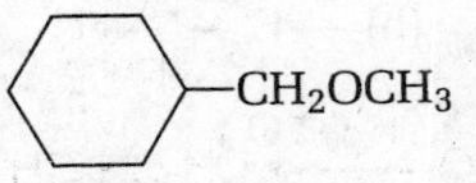

(b) 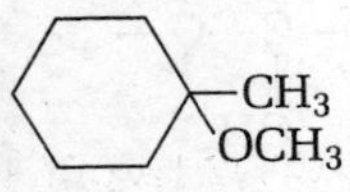

(c) 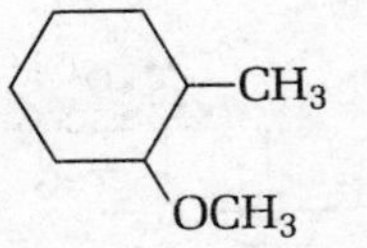

(d) 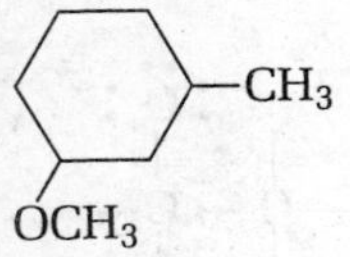

2. Most stable intermediate in the following reaction is

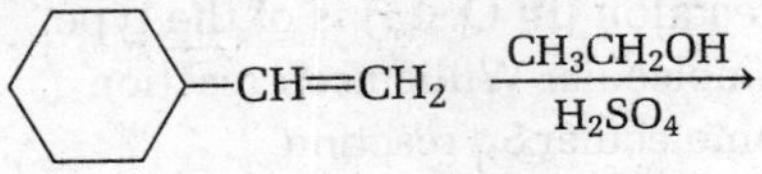

(a) 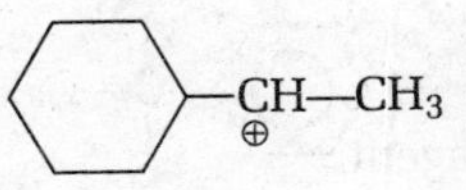

(b) 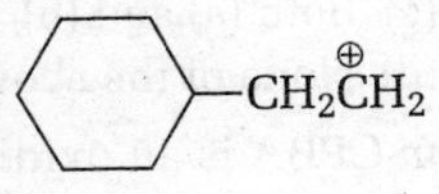

(c) 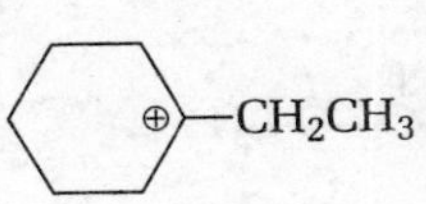

(d) 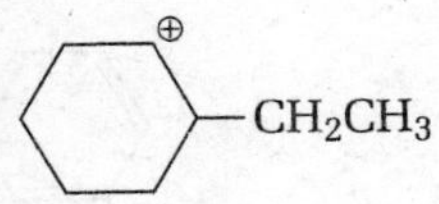

3. Select the incorrect statement(s) about the following reaction of ether synthesis.

$$RX + R'ONa \longrightarrow ROR' + NaX$$

(a) It follows S_N2 mechanism

(b) Alkyl halide (RX) should be 2° or 3° while alkoxide (RO^-Na^+) should be 1°

(c) Alkyl halide should be 1° while alkoxide should be 2° or 3°.

(d) 2° and 3° alkyl halides may undergo E2 elimination in the presence of a strong base to form alkenes.

4. Consider the following reactions,

I. 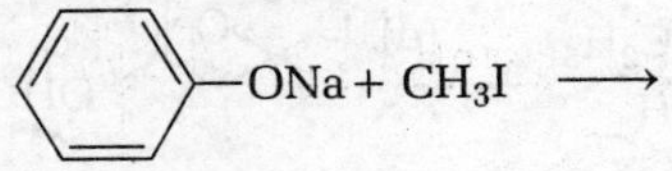

II. 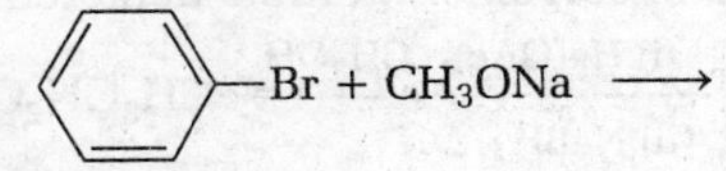

III. $(CH_3)_3C—Cl + CH_3ONa \longrightarrow$

IV. $(CH_3)_3C—ONa + CH_3Cl \longrightarrow$

Which of the above methods cannot be used in the synthesis of ether?

(a) I, IV

(b) I, III

(c) II, IV

(d) II, III

5. Ether (A) can be prepared by bimolecular dehydration of alcohols as shown

$$(CH_3)_2CHOH + CH_3OH \xrightarrow{H_2SO_4} \underset{(A)}{(CH_3)_2CHOCH_3}$$

Intermediate of this reaction is

(a) $(CH_3)_2\overset{\oplus}{C}H$ (b) $\overset{\oplus}{C}H_3$

(c) $CH_3CH_2\overset{\oplus}{C}H_2$ (d) $CH_3\overset{\oplus}{C}H_2$

6. Which is the leaving group in the following reaction?

$$CH_3OH + CH_2N_2 \xrightarrow{HBF_4}$$

(a) H_2O (b) N_2 (c) $\overset{\oplus}{C}H_3$ (d) $H^{\oplus}$

7. Above reaction (in Q. 6) is of the type
(a) S_N1 (b) S_N2 (c) E1 (d) E2

8. Select the correct statement(s) about the following reaction.

$$2\,ROH \xrightarrow{H^+} ROR + H_2O$$

(a) It is an example of S_N reaction in which protonated alcohol is the substrate and second molecule of alcohol is the nucleophile
(b) This reaction can be S_N1 if protonated alcohol loses water before attack of second molecule
(c) This reaction can be S_N2 if alcohol is 1°
(d) All of the above statements are correct

9. 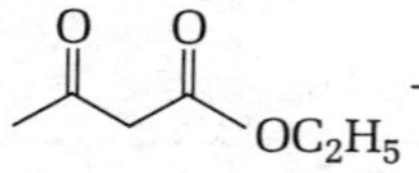 $\xrightarrow[H^+]{\text{Ethylene glycol}}$ A (Major product) **[JEE Main 2021, March]**

The product "A" in the above reaction is

(a) 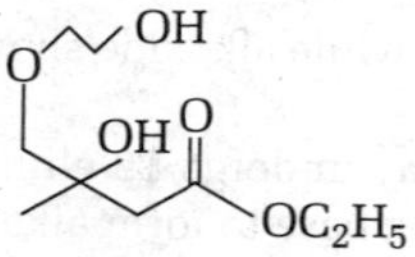 (b) 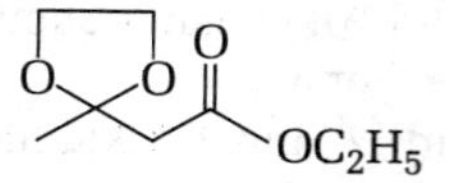

(c) 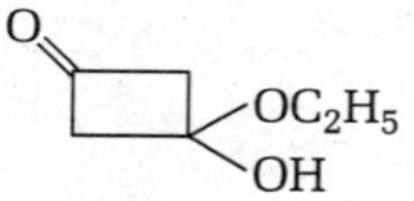 (d) 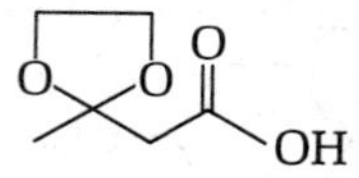

10. Following step of solvomercuration–demercuration is

$$CH_2{=}CH_2 \xrightarrow[\text{(ii) } NaBH_4,\ OH^-]{\text{(i) } Hg(OAc)_2,\ CH_3OH} CH_3CH_2OCH_3$$

(a) oxidation reaction
(b) reduction reaction
(c) disproportionation reaction
(d) solvation reaction

11. When ethylene glycol is heated with oxalic acid in the presence of conc. H_2SO_4, the product formed is **[JEE Main 2021, Feb.]**

(a) 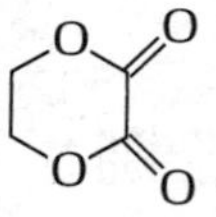 (b) 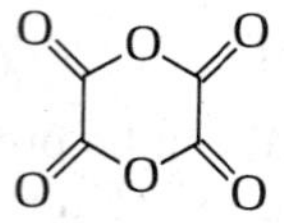

(c) 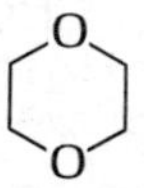 (d) 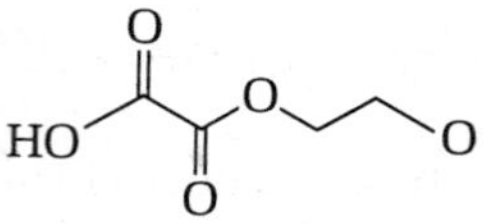

12. Indicate the reagent in the following conversion

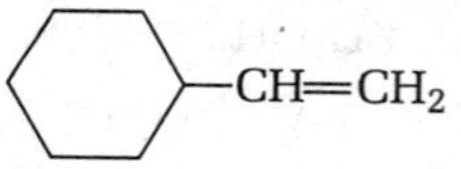 ⟶ 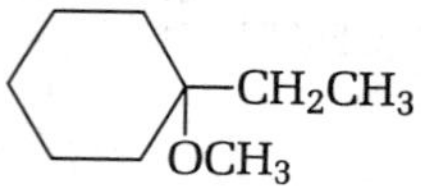

(a) H_3O^+/CH_3OH (b) CH_3ONa
(c) $Hg(OAc)_2$, CH_3OH (d) None of these

13. Select the incorrect statement about solvomercuration- demercuration of alkenes.
(a) It involves carbocation as the intermediate
(b) It involves no rearrangement
(c) It involves addition of water according to Markownikoff's rule
(d) Regiochemistry is very identical as in alcohol

14. Alkene can be converted to oxirane by oxidation using
(a) *m*-CPBA
(b) trifluoroperoxyacetic acid
(c) oxygen/Ag (catalyst)
(d) All of the above

15. In the following reaction,

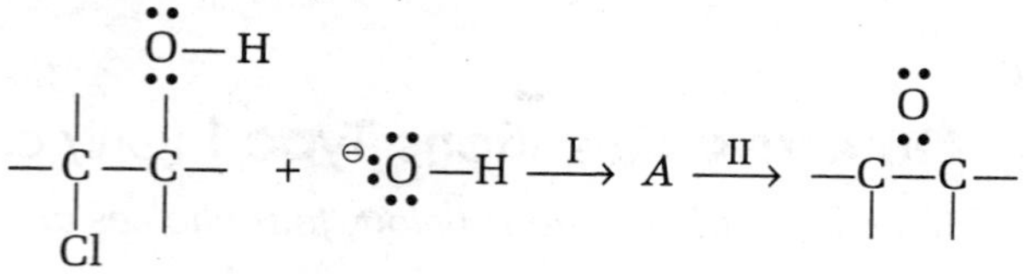

intermediate is

(a) 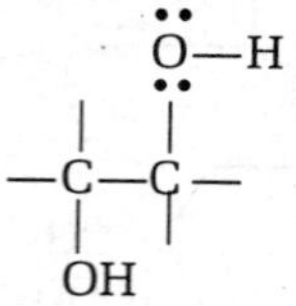 (b) 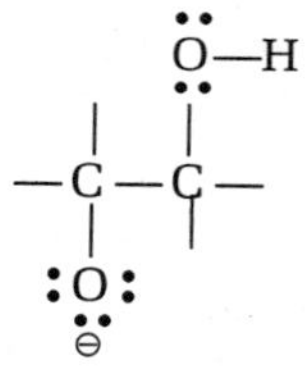

(c) 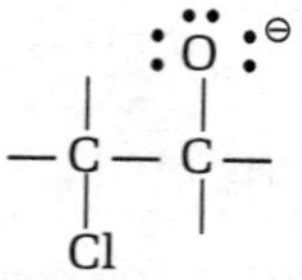 (d) 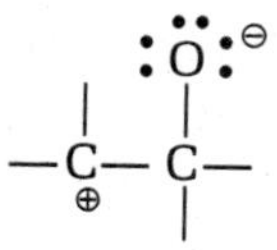

16. Above reaction (in Q. 15) is of the type
(a) intramolecular Williamson reaction
(b) intramolecular S_N reaction
(c) Both (a) and (b)
(d) None of the above

17. *m*-CPBA is an oxidising agent

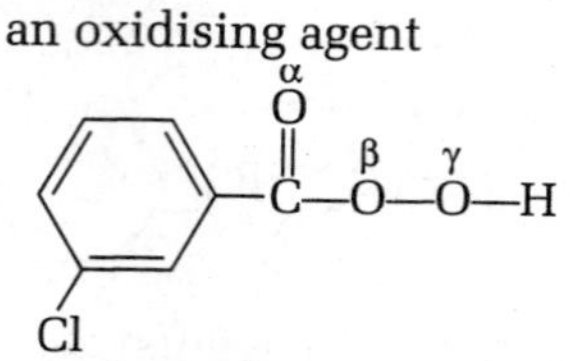

which oxygen adds to alkene?
(a) α-type (b) β-type
(c) γ-type (d) Any of the oxygen

18. Which oxygen of *m*-CPBA (in Q. 17) changes to carbonyl oxygen?
(a) α-type (b) β-type
(c) γ-type (d) α and β both

19. In H_2O, there is bond-angle HOH of 104.5° due to repulsion, but in ether bond-angle *ROR* is 109.5°. It is due to
(a) H is polar while *R* is non-polar
(b) H is non-polar while *R* is polar
(c) repulsion between the bulkier alkyl groups almost counterbalances the effect of lone pair-lone pair interactions
(d) None of the explanations given above is correct

20. Select the correct statement(s).
(a) Ethers are strongly polar compounds
(b) Ethers have lower boiling points than the isomeric alcohols
(c) Dipole moment of ether is the sum of the two polar C—O bonds with a substantial contribution from the two lone pairs of electrons.
(d) All of the above statements are correct

21. Ether is a good solvent for Grignard reagent. Which property makes it good solvent?
(a) It acts as a base towards acidic magnesium
(b) It makes H-bonding with Grignard reagent
(c) It acts as an acid towards basic magnesium
(d) It is electron-rich

22. Increasing order of dipole moment of (I) ethanol (II) propane and (III) methoxy-methane is
(a) I < II < III (b) II < III < I
(c) II < I < III (d) I < III < II

23. In the halogenation of the following ether in dark which H is affected?

$$\overset{\gamma}{C}H_2{=}\overset{\beta}{C}H\overset{\alpha}{C}H_2OCH_2CH{=}CH_2$$

(a) α (b) β (c) γ (d) β, γ together

24. Following reaction is of the type

$$Br^{\ominus} + R{-}\overset{\oplus}{\ddot{O}}(H){-}R' \longrightarrow RBr + R'OH$$

(a) S_N1 with tertiary alkyl group
(b) S_N2 with primary alkyl group
(c) Both (a) and (b)
(d) None of the above types

25. In the following reaction,

$$I^- + CH_3CH_2CH_2 \overset{\alpha}{—} \overset{\oplus}{\ddot{O}}(H) \overset{\beta}{—} CH(CH_3)CH_3 \longrightarrow$$

(a) α-bond is cleaved due to nucleophilic attack by $I^{\ominus}$ ion since, $(CH_3)_2CHOH$ is weak base (a good leaving group)
(b) β-bond is cleaved due to nucleophilic attack by $I^{\ominus}$ ion since, $CH_3CH_2CH_2OH$ is a weak base (a good leaving group)
(c) α-bond is cleaved due to electrophilic attack of $I^{\ominus}$ ion
(d) β-bond is cleaved due to electrophilic attack of $I^{\ominus}$ ion

26. Reaction of $CH_3O\ CH_2CH_3$ is maximum with
(a) HF (b) HCl (c) HBr (d) HI

27. HI cleaves ether (*A*) forming

A :
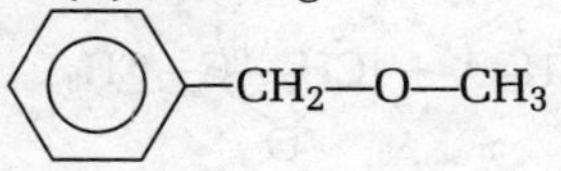

(a)
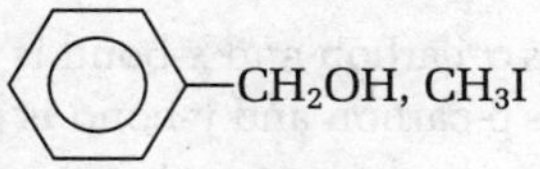

(b)
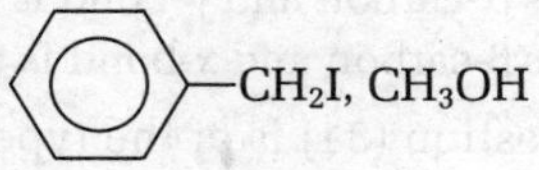

(c)
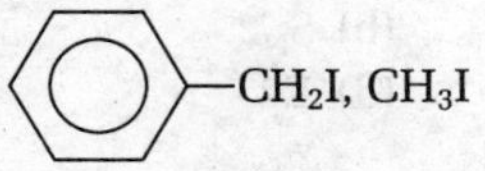

(d)
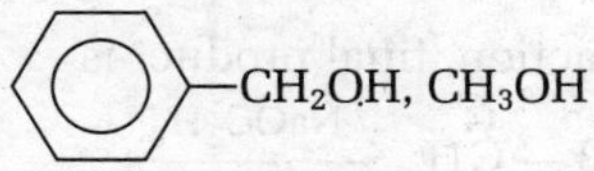

28. Which is the most stable carbocation in the protonation of

$$(CH_3)_3C{-}O{-}CH_2CH_3\,?$$

(a) $(CH_3)_3C{-}\overset{\oplus}{O}(H){-}CH_2CH_3$ (b) $(CH_3)_3C^{\oplus}$
(c) $CH_3\overset{\oplus}{C}H_2$ (d) $(CH_3)_3CO^{\oplus}$

29. Oxiranes are cleaved under acidic and basic conditions because of
(a) strain produced due to decrease in bond-angle to 61.5° from normal value of 109.5°.
(b) strong H^+ and OH^-
(c) formation of oxonium ion
(d) formation of carbocation

30. Which is the correct statement about following reaction?

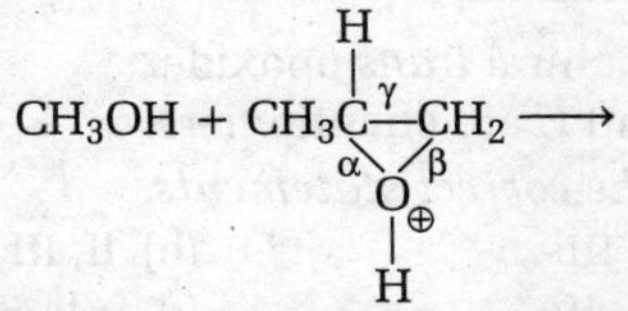

(a) α-bond is cleaved when product formed is $CH_3CH(OH){-}CH_2OCH_3$
(b) β-bond is cleaved when product formed is $CH_3CH(OCH_3){-}CH_2OH$
(c) α-bond is cleaved when product formed is $CH_3\ CH(OCH_3){-}CH_2OH$
(d) β-bond is cleaved when product formed is $CH_3CH(OH){-}CH_2OCH_3$

31. Select the correct statement for the following reaction.

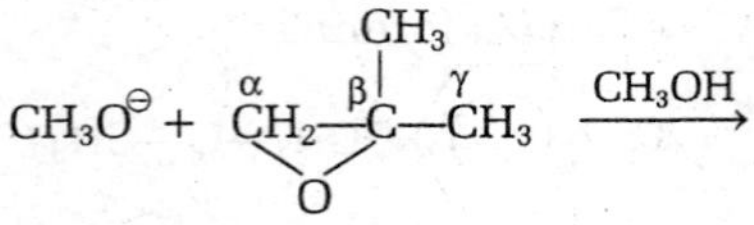

(a) nucleophile attacks α-carbon and *x*-bond is cleaved
(b) nucleophile attacks β-carbon and *y*-bond is cleaved
(c) nucleophile attacks α-carbon and *y*-bond is cleaved
(d) nucleophile attacks β-carbon and *x*-bond is cleaved

32. Above reaction in question (31) is of the type
(a) S_N1 (b) S_N2
(c) E1 (d) E2

33. In the following reaction, final product is

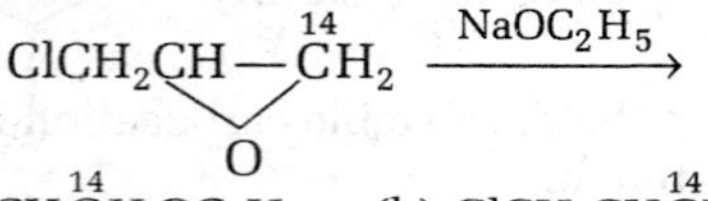

(a) $ClCH_2CH(OH)\overset{14}{C}H_2OC_2H_5$ (b) $ClCH_2CH(OC_2H_5)\overset{14}{C}H_2ONa$
(c) $\overset{14}{C}H_2—CHCH_2OC_2H_5$ (epoxide, O bridging) (d) $CH_2—CH\overset{14}{C}H_2OC_2H_5$ (epoxide, O bridging)

34. Consider the following structures of epoxides

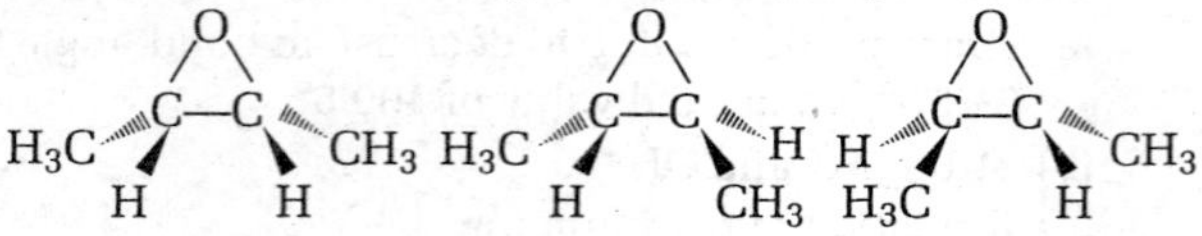

A B C

I. *A* is achiral *cis* epoxide.
II. *B* is chiral *trans* epoxide.
III. *C* is chiral *trans* epoxide.
IV. *B* and *C* are enantiomers.
Select the correct statements.
(a) I, II, III (b) II, III, IV
(c) I, III, IV (d) All of these

35.

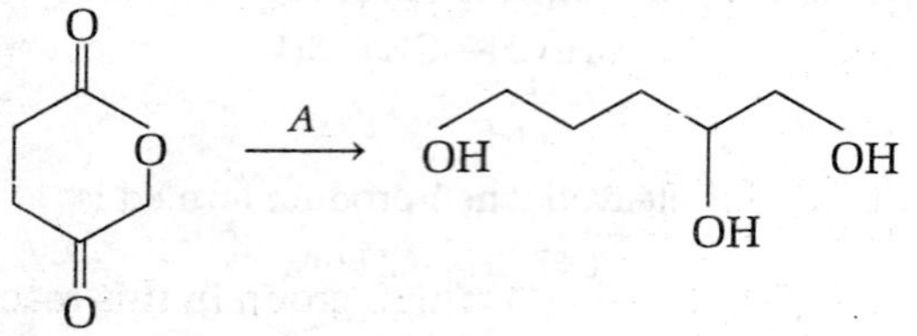

Reagent *A* used in this change is
(a) B_2H_6 (b) $LiAlH_4$
(c) Sn/HCl (d) CH_3OH/Na

36. 2-butene

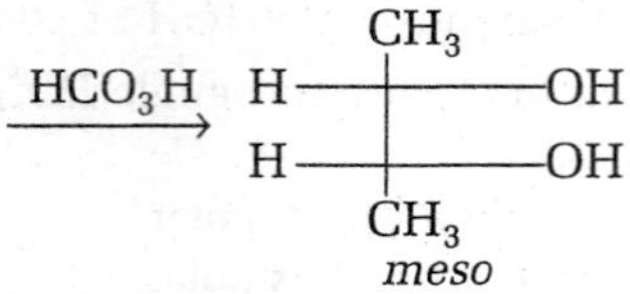

Hence,

2-butene is
(a) *cis*-
(b) *trans*-
(c) Both (a) and (b)
(d) None of the above is correct

37.

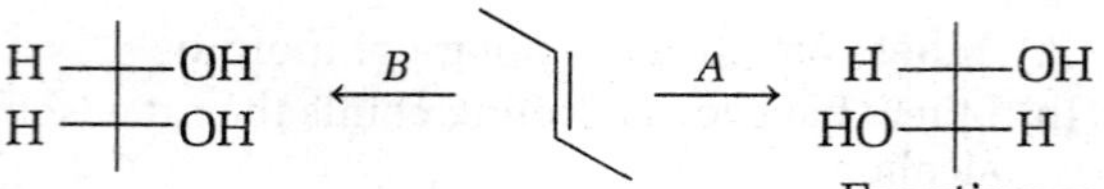

Enantiomer

A and *B* are
(a) HCO_3H, MnO_4^-/OH^-
(b) OsO_4/Na_2SO_3, MnO_4^-/OH^-
(c) MnO_4^-/OH^-, HCO_3H
(d) MnO_4^-/OH^-, *m*CPBA

38. Which of the following is found in waxes?
(a) $CH_3(CH_2)_{27}COO(CH_2)_{21}CH_3$
(b) $CH_3(CH_2)_{26}COO(CH_2)_{21}CH_3$
(c) $CH_3(CH_2)_{26}COO(CH_2)_{22}CH_3$
(d) All of the above are found in waxes

39. Among the compounds *A* and *B* with molecular formula $C_9H_{18}O_3$, *A* is having higher boiling point the *B*. The possible structures of *A* and *B* are
[JEE Main 2020, Jan.]

(a) *A* =

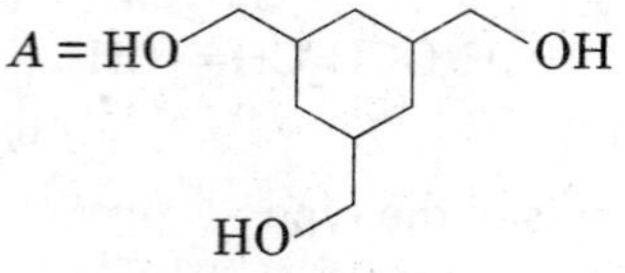

B =

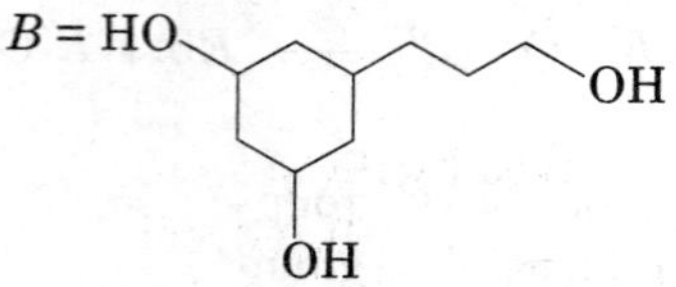

(b) *A* =

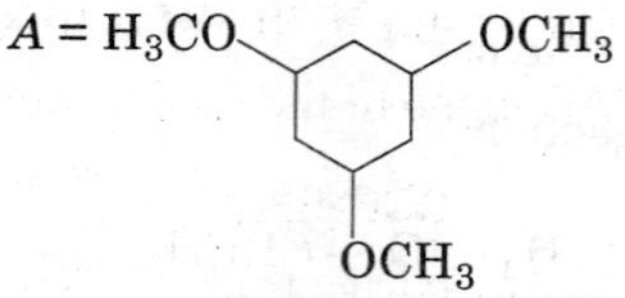

B =

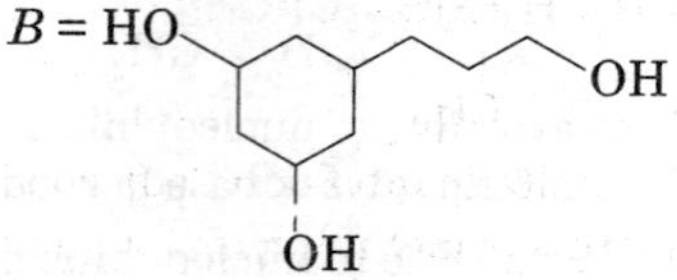

(c) $A =$ 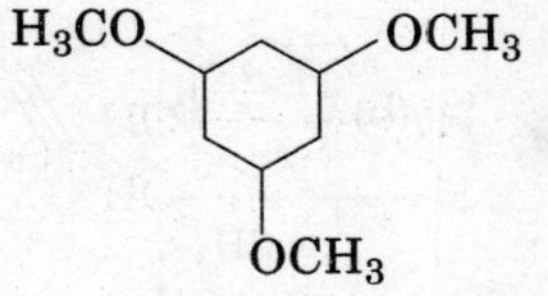

$B =$ 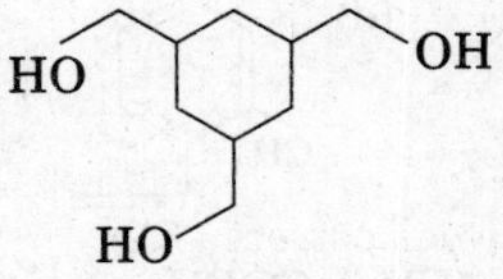

(d) $A =$ 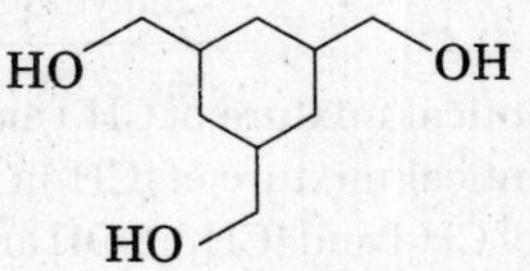

$B =$ 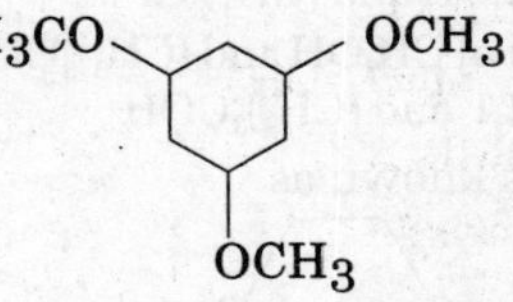

40. Glycerol + A $\xrightarrow{530\text{ K}, \Delta}$ allyl alcohol, A can be

I. oxalic acid II. formic acid III. allyl chloride

(a) I, II and III (b) I and III (c) II and III (d) I and II

41. Glycerol + HNO_3 $\xrightarrow[\text{cold}]{H_2SO_4}$ product, product is

(a) trinitroglycerine (b) glyceryl trinitrate

(c) TNT (d) glycerol mononitrate

42. $CH_2{=}CHCH_2Cl \xrightarrow{HClO} X$ is

(a) $\underset{Cl}{CH_2}\underset{OH}{CH}\underset{Cl}{CH_2}$ (b) $\underset{OH}{CH_2}\underset{Cl}{CH}\underset{Cl}{CH_2}$

(c) $CH_2{-}CHCH_2Cl$ (with O bridging the two carbons) (d) $CH_3\underset{Cl}{CH}CH_3$

43. Which is not cleaved by HIO_4?

I. Glycerol II. Glycol

III. 1,3-propanediol IV. Methoxy-2-propanol

(a) I, II, III, IV (b) I, II (c) II, III (d) III, IV

44. An acceptable IUPAC name of the compound shown is

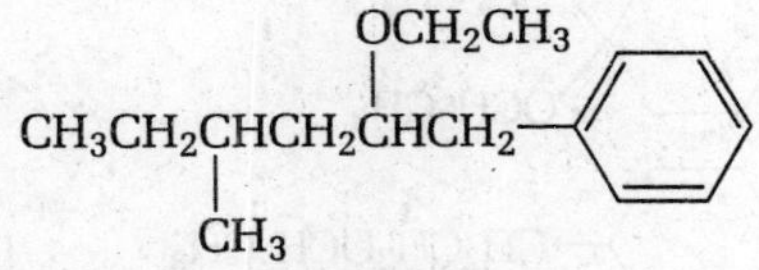

(a) 1-benzyl-3methylpentyl ethyl ether

(b) ethyl 3-methyl-1-methylphenyl-2 hexyl ether

(c) ethyl 4-methyl-1-phenyl-2-hexyl ether

(d) 5-ethoxy-3-methyl-6-phenylhexane

45. The best choice of reactant(s) for the following conversion is

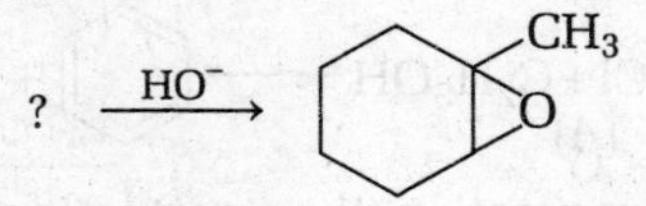

(a) 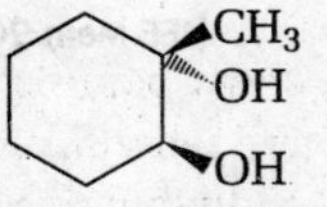 (b) 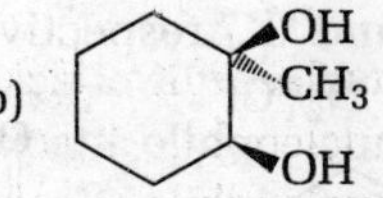

(c) 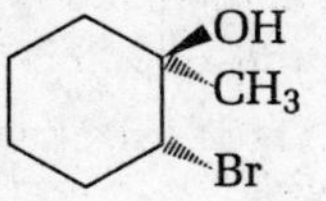 (d) 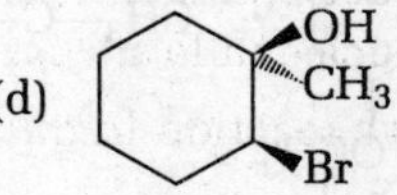

46.  $\xrightarrow[CH_3OH]{Hg(OAc)_2} \xrightarrow{NaBH_4} A$, A is

(a) 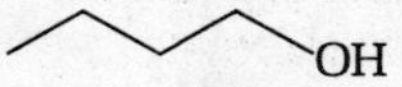 (b) 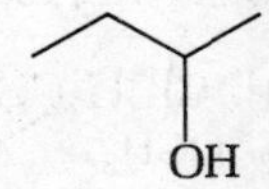

(c) 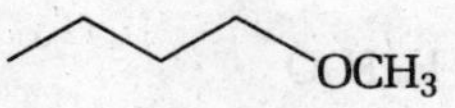 (d) 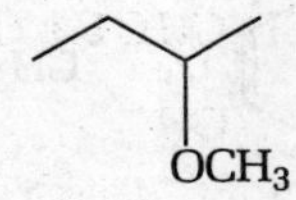

47. To prepare phenyl *t*-butyl ether, best synthesis is

(a) 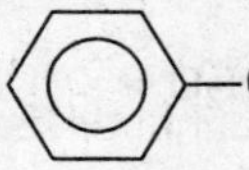 —ONa + $(CH_3)_3C{-}Cl$

(b) 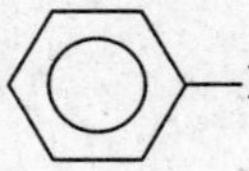 —Br + $(CH_3)_3CONa$

(c) $CH_2{=}C(CH_3)_2 \xrightarrow{Hg(OAc)_2} \xrightarrow{NaBH_4}$ 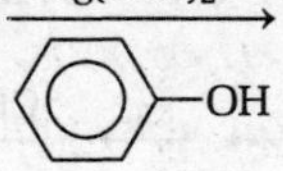

(d) None of the above is suitable

48. Decreasing order of reactivity of the following alkyl halides in the Williamson's ether synthesis is

$(CH_3)_3CCH_2Br\ (A)$, $ClCH_2CH{=}CH_2\ (B)$,

$ClCH_2CH_2CH_3\ (C)$, $BrCH_2CH_2CH_3\ (D)$

(a) $B > D > C > A$

(b) $A > B > C > D$

(c) $D > C > B > A$

(d) $C > D > B > A$

49. $ROH + CH_2N_2 \longrightarrow$ Which group in this reaction are removed

(a) CH_3

(b) R

(c) N_2

(d) CH_2

50. $C_7H_7N_2OCl + C_2H_5OH \longrightarrow$ 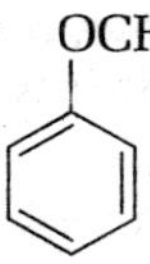 $+ N_2 +$ "X" + "Y"
(A)

In the above reaction, the structural formula of (A), "X" and "Y" respectively are **[JEE Main 2021, March]**

(a) 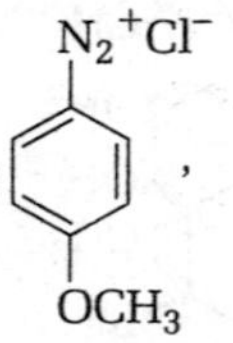 , $CH_3-\overset{O}{\overset{\|}{C}}-H$, HCl

(b) 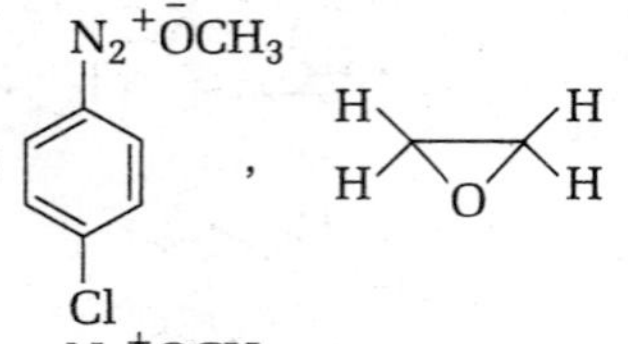 , HCl

(c) 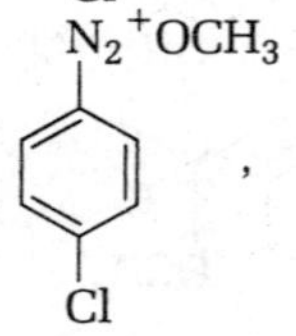 , $CH_3-\overset{O}{\overset{\|}{C}}-H$, H_2O

(d) 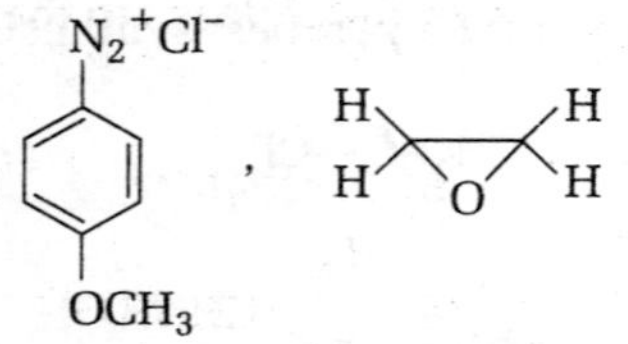 , H_2O

51. Consider the following synthesis,

I. $\xrightarrow[CH_3OH]{Hg(OAc)_2} \xrightarrow{NaBH_4}$ II. $\xrightarrow{H_3O^+} \xrightarrow{Na} \xrightarrow{CH_3Br}$

III. $\xrightarrow[H_2O_2/OH^-]{BH_3 \cdot THF} \xrightarrow{Na} \xrightarrow{CH_3Br}$

This change $CH_3\underset{}{\overset{CH_3}{\overset{|}{C}}}HCH=CH_2 \longrightarrow CH_3\overset{CH_3}{\overset{|}{C}}H\underset{OCH_3}{\underset{|}{C}}HCH_3$ can be made by using

(a) I, II and III (b) I and II (c) I and III (d) I only

52. To convert $CH_3CH=CH_2$ into $CH_3CH_2CH_2OCH_3$, process given in Q. 51 can be

(a) I (b) II (c) III (d) I and II

53. 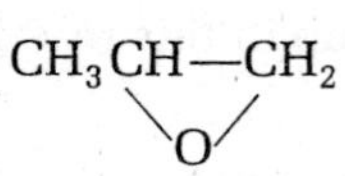 $\xrightarrow[H^+]{LiAlH_4}$ A, A can be

(a) $CH_3\underset{OH}{\underset{|}{C}}HCH_3$ (b) $CH_3CH_2CH_2OH$

(c) Both (a) and (b) (d) None is correct

54. What will be the major product when *m*-cresol is reacted with propargyl bromide ($HC\equiv C-CH_2Br$) in presence of K_2CO_3 in acetone? **[JEE Main 2019, April]**

(a) 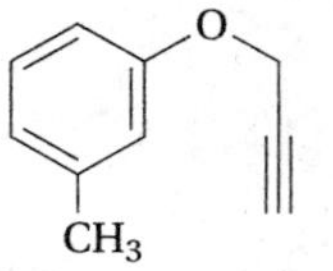 (b) 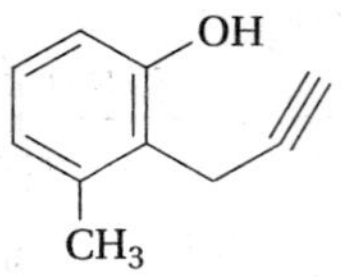

(c) 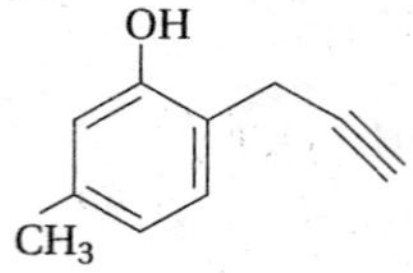 (d) 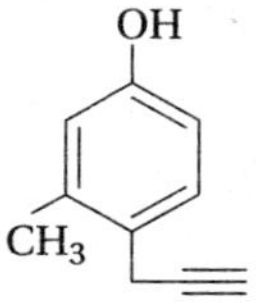

55. $B\ (\text{mix}) \xleftarrow{\text{Conc. HI}} (CH_3)_3COCH_3 \xrightarrow{\text{Anhydrous HI}} A\ (\text{mix})$

(a) A and B are identical mixture of CH_3I and $(CH_3)_3COH$
(b) A and B are identical mixture of $(CH_3)_3CI$ and CH_3OH
(c) A is a mixture of CH_3I and $(CH_3)_3COH$ and B is a mixture of CH_3OH and $(CH_3)_3CI$
(d) A is a mixture of CH_3OH and $(CH_3)_3CI$ and B is a mixture of CH_3I and $(CH_3)_3COH$

56. This polyether is known as

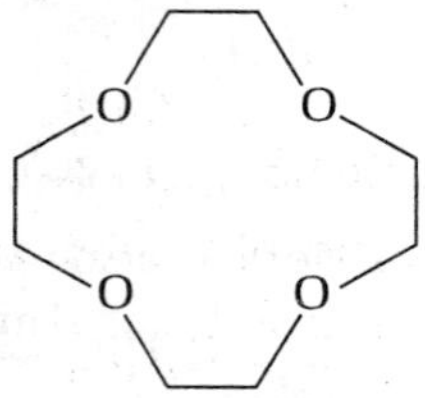

(a) 12-crown-4 (b) 18-crown-6
(c) 8-crown-4 (d) 4-crown-8

57.  $\xrightarrow{CH_3ONa}$ A, A can be

(a)  (b) 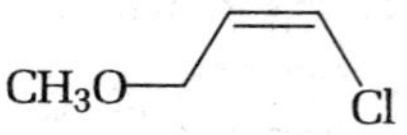

(c) 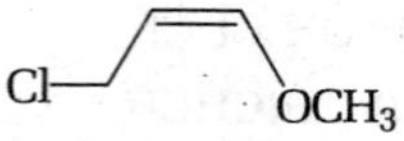 (d) no reaction

58. 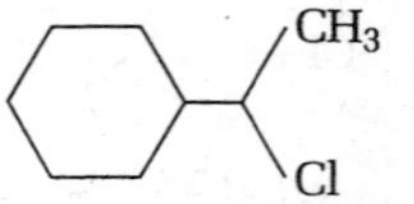 $\xrightarrow[CH_3CH_2ONa]{Ag^+}$ A, A (predominant) is

(a) 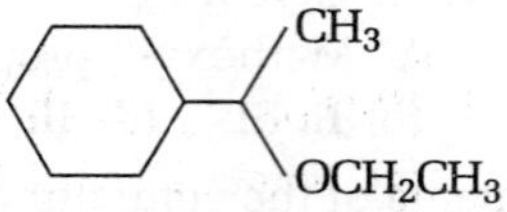

(b) 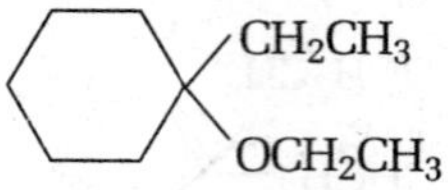

(c) 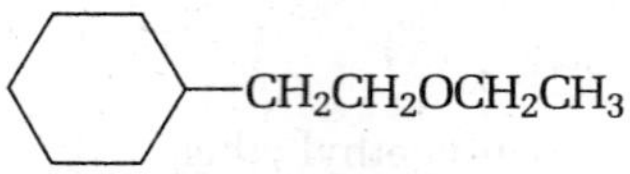

(d) 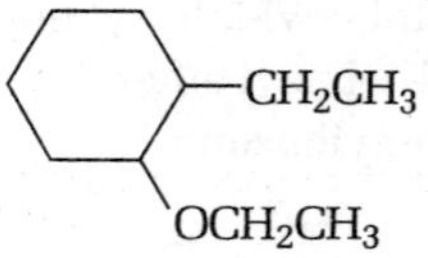

59. 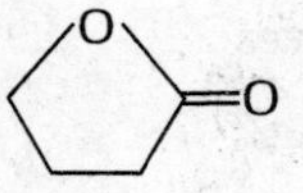 $\xrightarrow[H_3O^+]{CH_3MgBr\text{ (excess)}}$ A, A can be

(a) 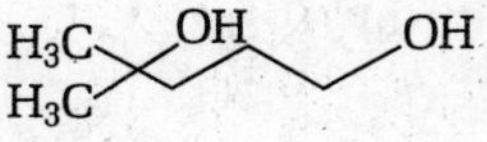 (b) 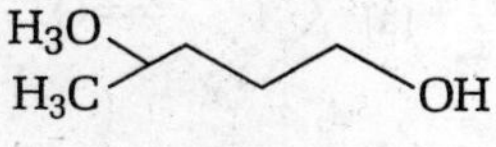

(c) 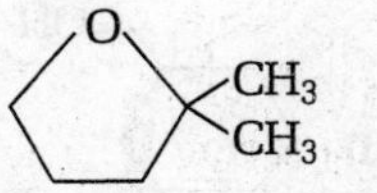 (d) 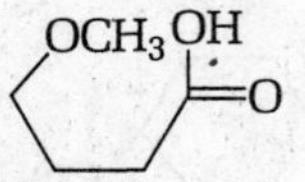

60. Which route provides a better synthesis of ether?

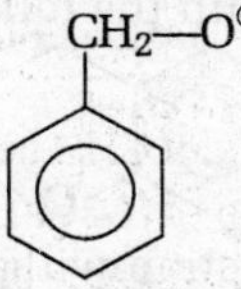 + $CH_3CH(Br)CH_2CH_3 \xrightarrow{I}$,

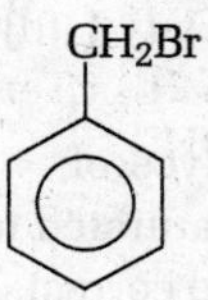 + $CH_3CH(O^\ominus)CH_2CH_3 \xrightarrow{II}$

(a) I (b) II
(c) Of equal importance (d) None of these

61. Dehydration product of 1,4-diol given below will be

$CH_3CH(OH)CH_2CH_2CH_2(^{18}OH) \xrightarrow{H_3PO_4}$

(a) 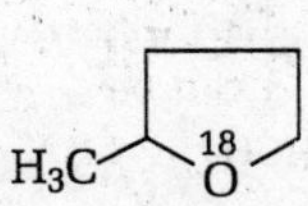 (b) 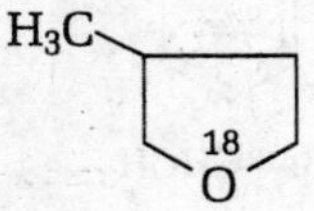

(c) 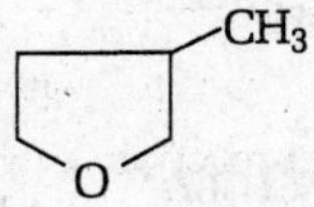 (d) 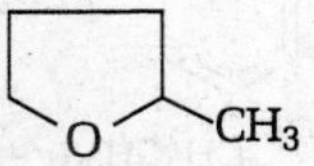

62. 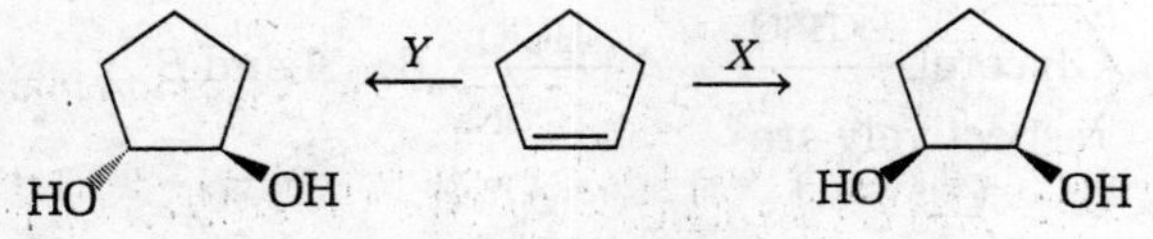

Select X and Y out of I. MnO_4^-/OH^- II. HCO_3H
(a) I and II (b) II and I (c) II and II (d) I and I

63. 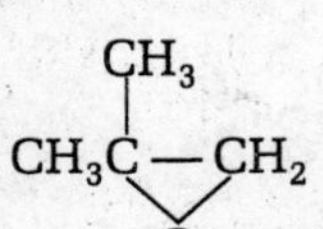 $\xrightarrow[CH_3OH]{CH_3ONa}$ X, X is

(a) $CH_3C(CH_3)(OH)CH_2OCH_3$ (b) $CH_3C(CH_3)(OCH_3)CH_2OH$

(c) $CH_3CH(OCH_3)—CH(CH_3)HOH$ (d) None is correct

64. In the following reaction sequence, structures of A and B, respectively will be **[JEE Main 2020, Jan.]**

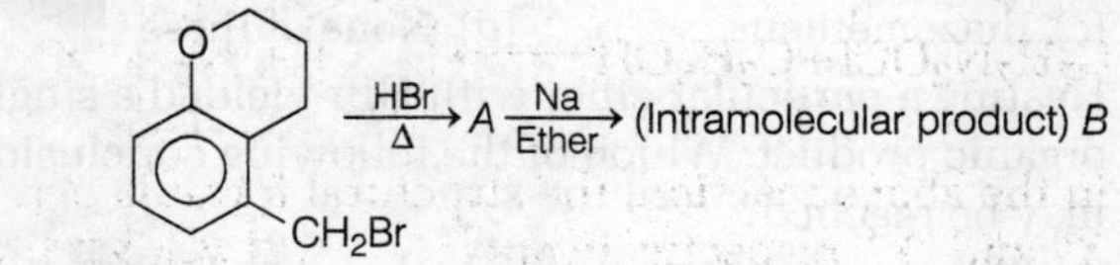

(a) 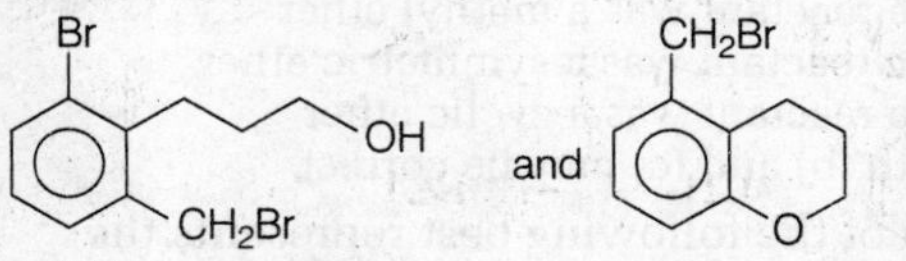

(b) 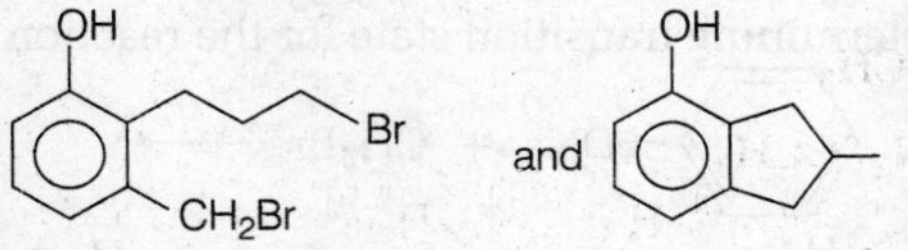

(c) 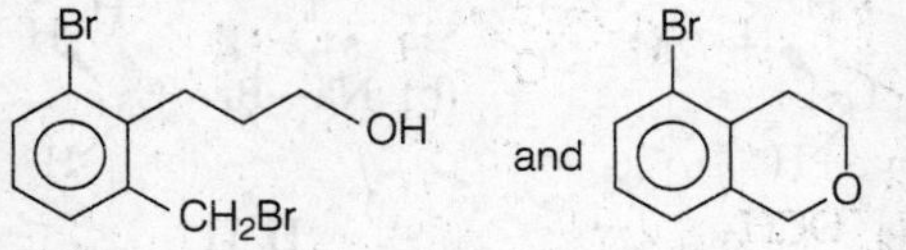

(d) 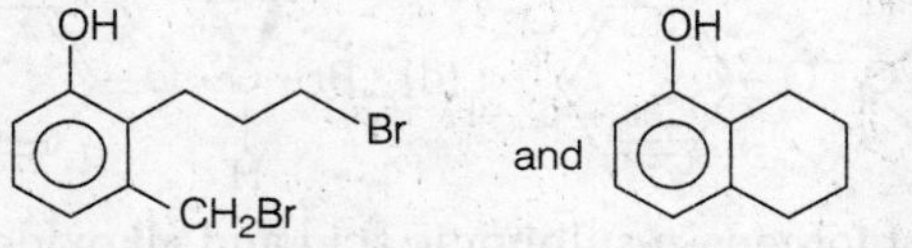

65. Reaction of 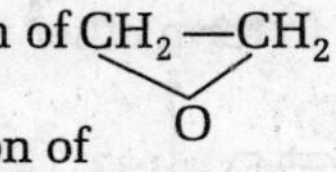 with RMgX leads to the formation of
(a) RCHOHR (b) $RCHOHCH_3$
(c) RCH_2CH_2OH (d) R_2CHCH_2OH

66. For the preparation of t-butyl methyl ether, which one of the following methods should be recommended?

(a) $CH_3OH + HO—C(CH_3)_2—CH_3 \xrightarrow{Conc.\ H_2SO_4}$

(b) $CH_3—C(CH_3)_2—Br + CH_3OH \xrightarrow{NaOH}$

(c) $CH_3Br + Na^+O^-—C(CH_3)_2—CH_3$

(d) $CH_3O^-Na^+ + CH_3—C(CH_3)_2—Br$

67. Diethyl ether can be isomeric with
(a) 1-butanol (b) 2-butanol
(c) 2-methyl-2-propanol (d) All of these

68. Higher homologues of ethers can be prepared by
(a) alkyl halides (b) Grignard reagent
(c) diazomethene (d) None of these

69. Heating a particular ether with HBr yielded a single organic product. Which of the following conclusions may be reached?
(a) The reactant was a methyl ether
(b) The reactant was a symmetric ether
(c) The reactant was a cyclic ether
(d) Both (b) and (c) may be correct

70. Which of the following best represents the rate-determining transition state for the reaction shown?

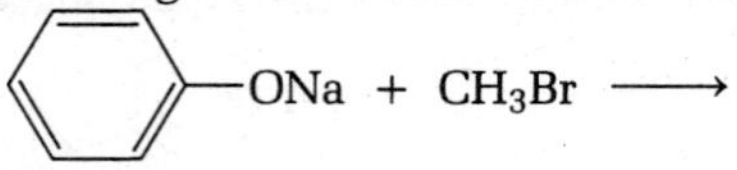

(a) 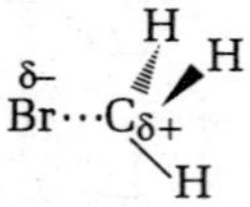 (b) 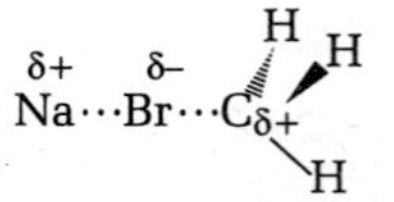

(c) 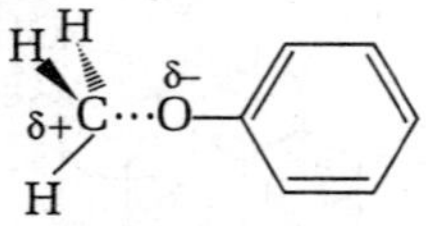 (d) 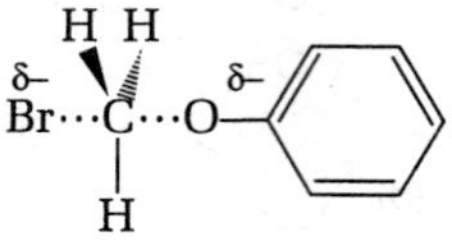

71. Ester of toluene-*p*-sulphonic acid and alkoxide react in the presence of sodium to form ether

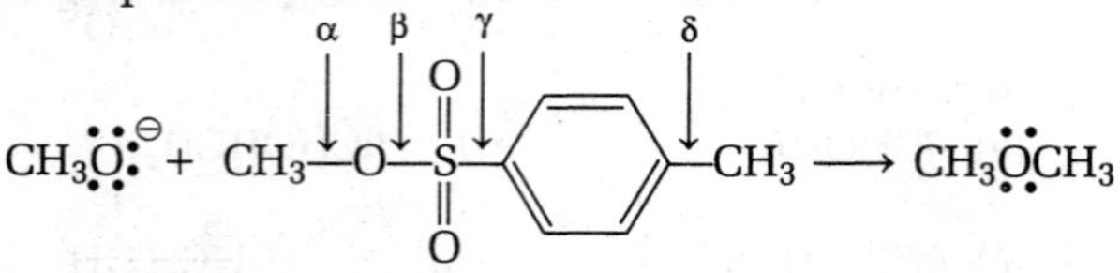

Which bond is cleaved and why?
(a) α-bond since, toluene-*p*-sulphonate is a good leaving group
(b) β-bond since, $CH_3O^\ominus$ is a better leaving group
(c) γ-bond since, it has least bond-energy
(d) δ-bond since, hyperconjugation makes —CH_3 a better leaving group

72. The major product of the following reaction is

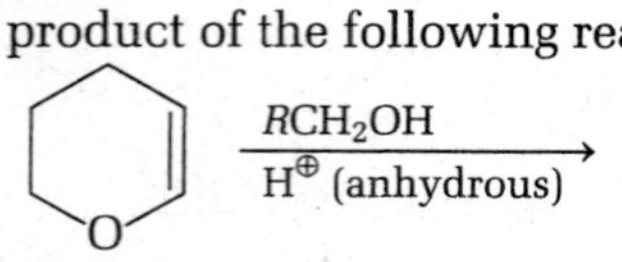

(a) a hemiacetal (b) an acetal (c) an ether (d) an ester

73. Which method is not useful for the synthesis of required ether?

(a) 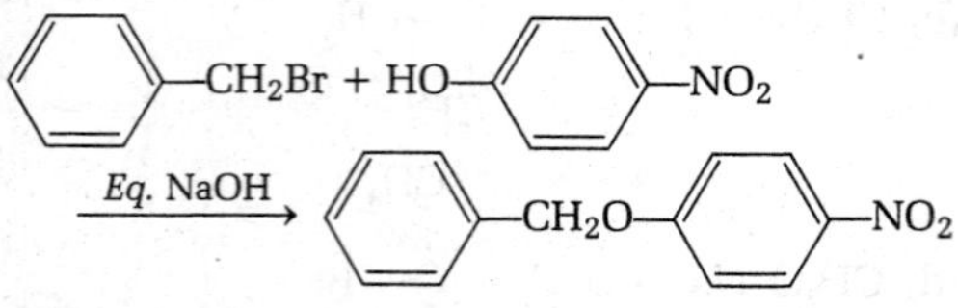

(b) $C_2H_5ONa + (CH_3)_2SO_4 \longrightarrow C_2H_5OCH_3$

(c) 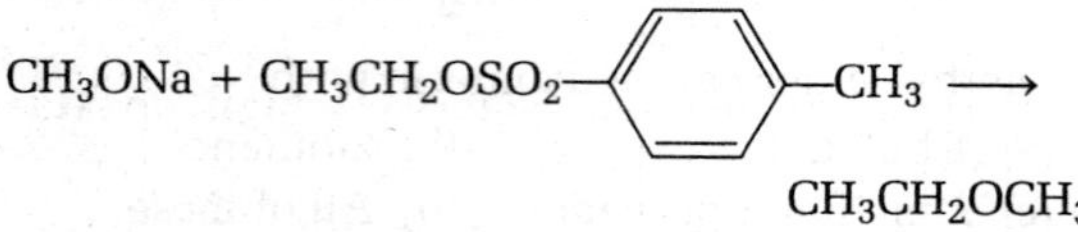

(d) $(CH_3)_3CBr + CH_3CH_2ONa \longrightarrow (CH_3)_3COCH_2CH_3$

74. Air oxidation of tetrahydrofuran gives

(a) 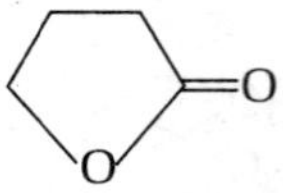 (b) 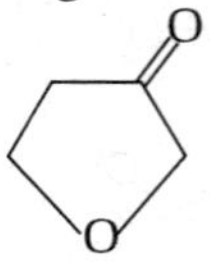

(c) 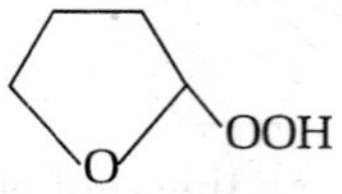 (d) 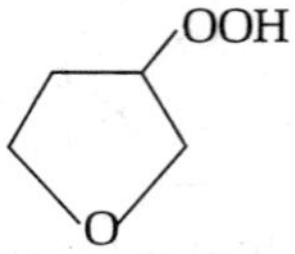

75. Consider the reaction of HI with the following

I.  II. 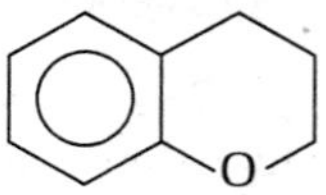

Which forms di-iodide on reaction with HI (excess)?
(a) I and II (b) Only II (c) Only I (d) None of these

76. Select the correct statement.
(a) Phospholipids are esters of glycerol
(b) Glyceryl tristearate is an unsaturated fat
(c) Both the above statements are correct
(d) Both the above statements are incorrect

77. The major product of the following reaction is

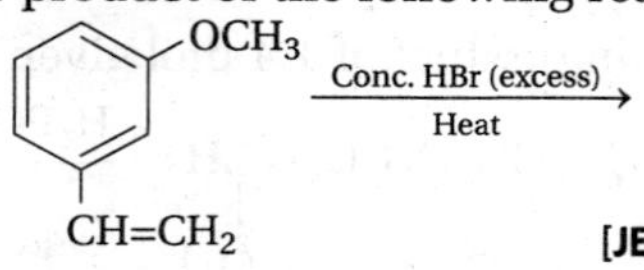

[JEE Main 2019, April]

(a) 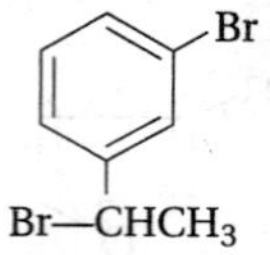 (b) 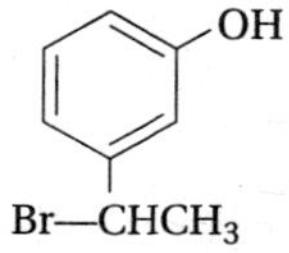

(c) 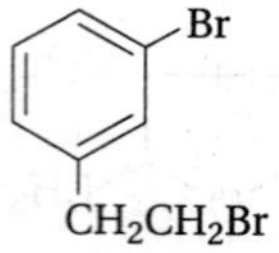 (d) 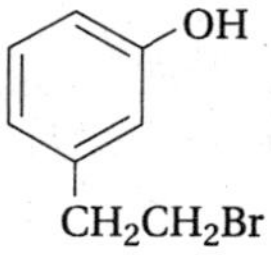

78. Glycerol $\xrightarrow{KHSO_4} A \xrightarrow{HClO} B$, *A* and *B* respectively are

(a) $CH_2{=}CHCHO$; $CH_2(Cl)CH(OH)CHO$

(b) $CH_2{=}CHCHO$; $CH_2(OH)CH(Cl)CHO$

(c) CH_3CH_2CHO ; $CH_3CH_2CH(OH)Cl$

(d) $CH_2{=}CHCHO$; $CH_2(ClO)CH_2CHO$

Objective Questions Type II [One or more than one correct option(s)]

In each of the questions below, four choices are given, of which one or more than one are correct.

1. In the following reaction, what is/are the true statement(s).

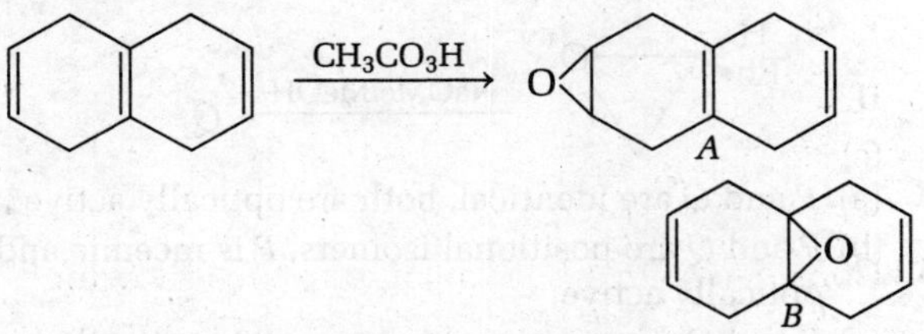

(a) Major product is *A* and formed faster
(b) Major product is *B* and formed faster
(c) Epoxidation is an electrophilic addition, oxygen is transferred to the more electron-rich, more highly substituted double bond
(d) A tetrasubstituted double bond reacts faster than a disubstituted one

2. In the following compound, by epoxidation

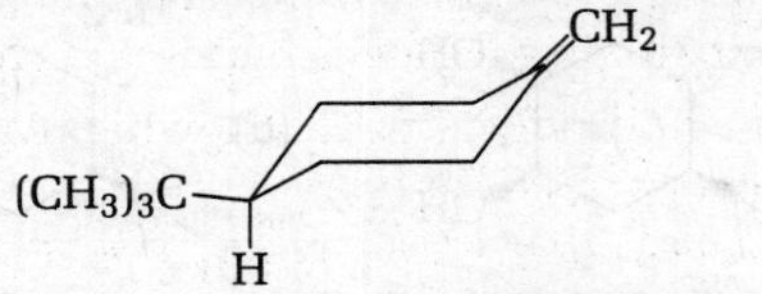

(a) major product is the stereoisomer that corresponds to transfer of oxygen from the equatorial direction

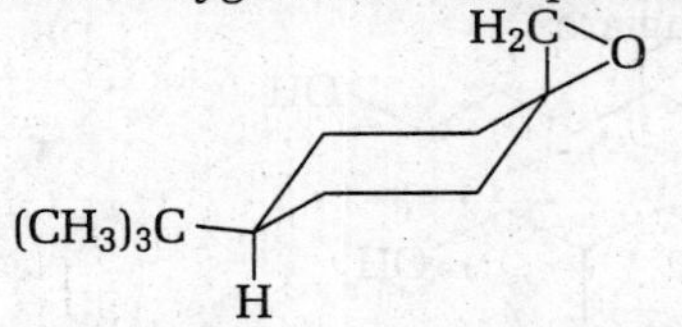

(b) minor product is the stereoisomer that corresponds to transfer of oxygen from the axial direction

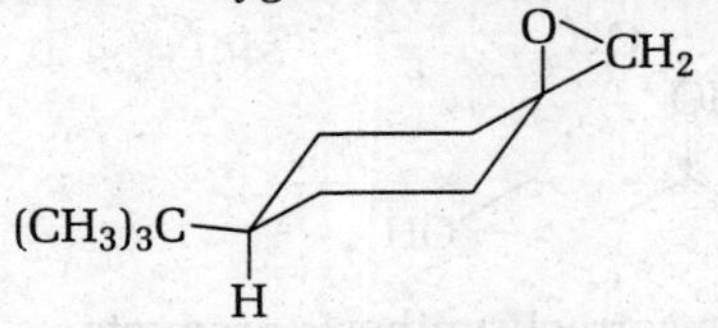

(c) major product is the stereoisomer that corresponds to transfer of oxygen from the axial direction
(d) minor product is the stereoisomer that corresponds to the transfer of oxygen from the equatorial direction

3. Reagent(s) which can be used to bring about the following transformation is/are **[JEE Advanced 2016]**

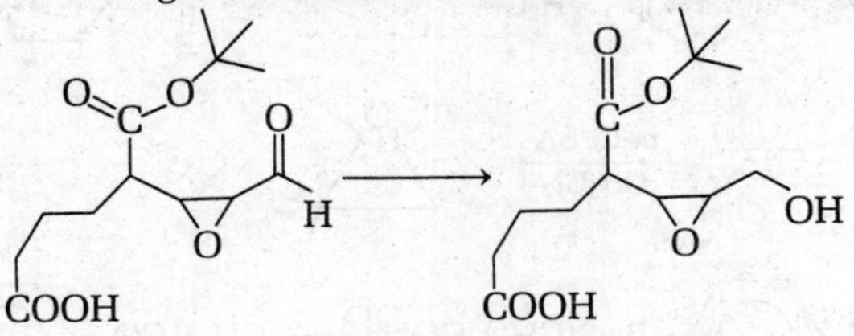

(a) $LiAlH_4$ in $(C_2H_5)_2O$
(b) BH_3 in THF
(c) $NaBH_4$ in C_2H_5OH
(d) Raney Ni/H_2 in THF

4. In the following reaction,

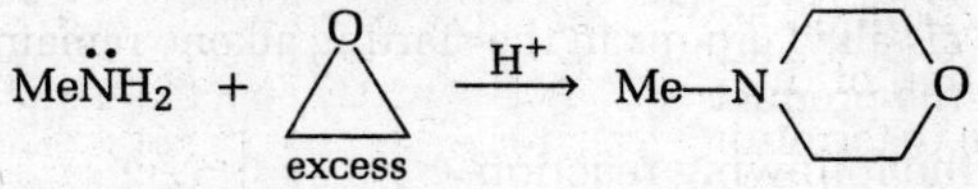

intermediates can be

(a) 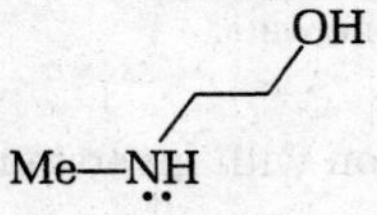

(b) 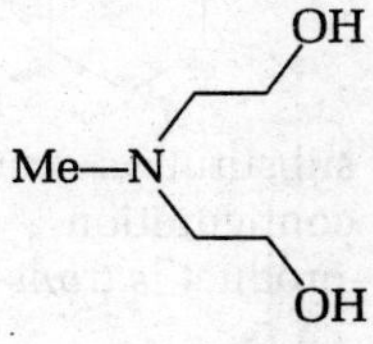

(c) 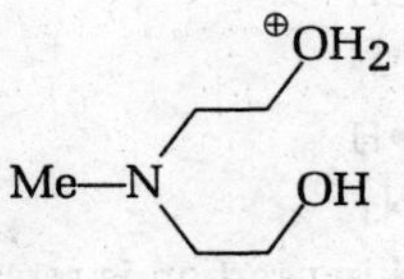

(d) 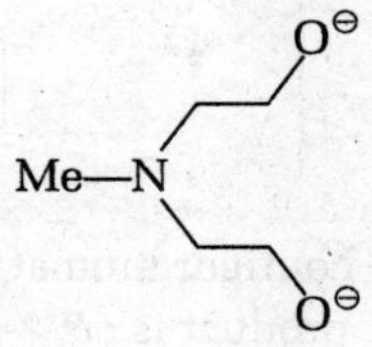

5. Product of the following reaction is

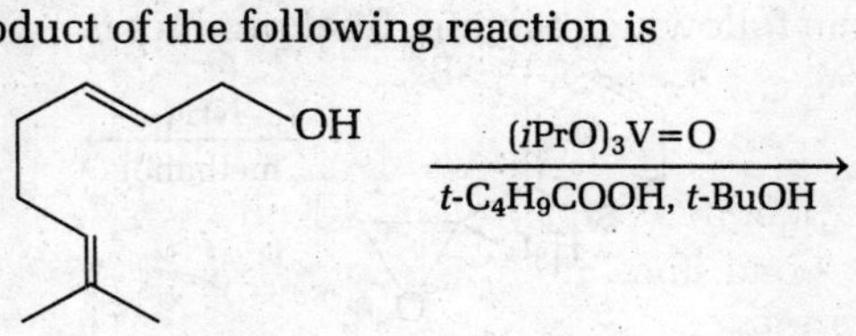

(a) 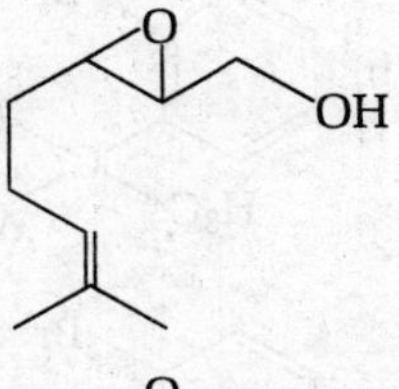

(b) 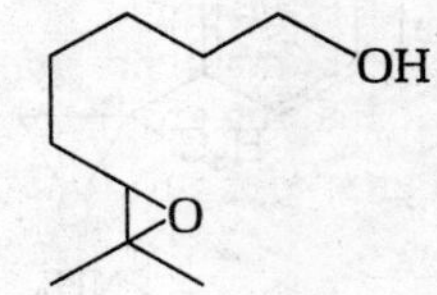

(c) 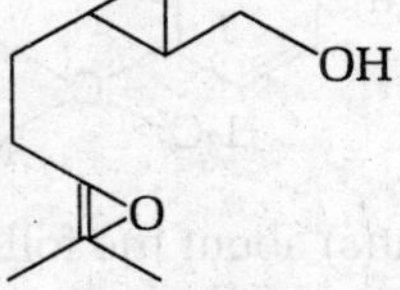

(d) no reaction

6. Select the correct statement(s). Epoxidation of
(a) (Z)-2-butene gives the *meso* (achiral) epoxide
(b) (Z)-2-butene gives a mixture of two enantiomeric epoxides
(c) (E)-2-butene gives a mixture of two enantiomeric epoxides
(d) (E)-2-butene gives the *meso* (achiral) epoxide

7. In the following reaction,

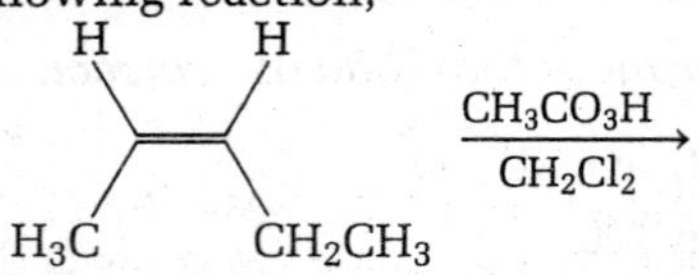

(a) two enantiomeric epoxides are formed in equal amounts
(b) there is stereospecific *syn* addition
(c) product is *meso* isomer
(d) *cis* alkyl groups in the starting alkene remain *cis* in the product

8. In the following reaction

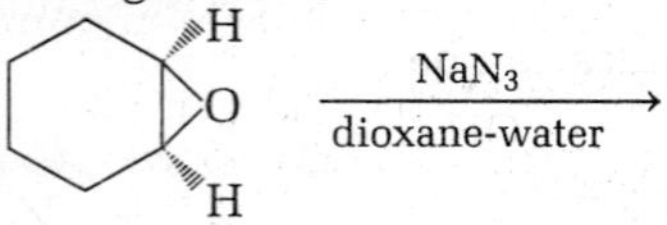

(a) substitution occurs at carbon with inversion of configuration
(b) product is *trans*-2-azidocyclohexanol

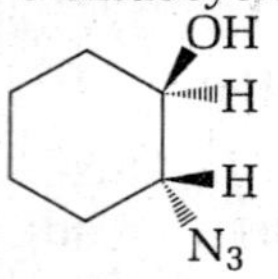

(c) configuration at the attacking carbon is retained
(d) product is *cis*-2-azidocyclohexanol

9. In the following reaction, final product is

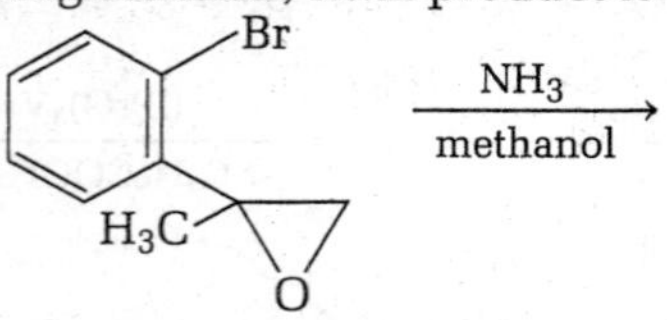

(a) 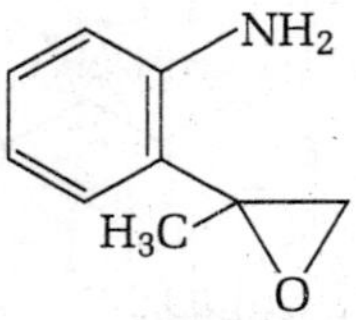
(b) 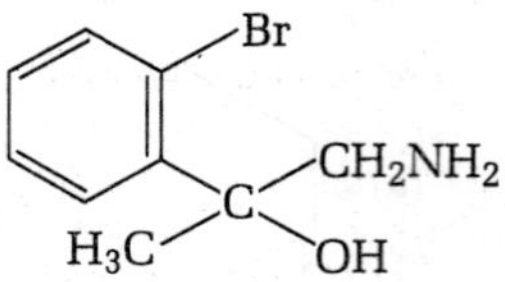

(c) 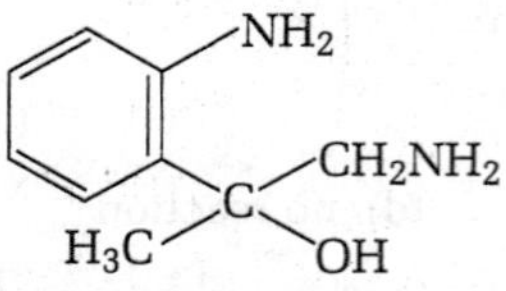
(d) 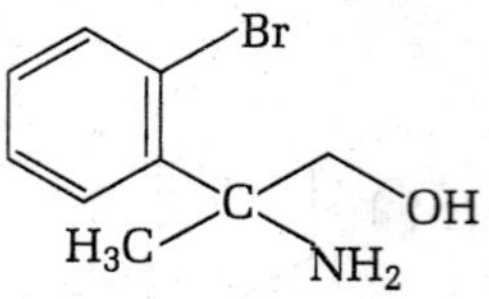

10. Select the correct statement(s) about the following reaction.

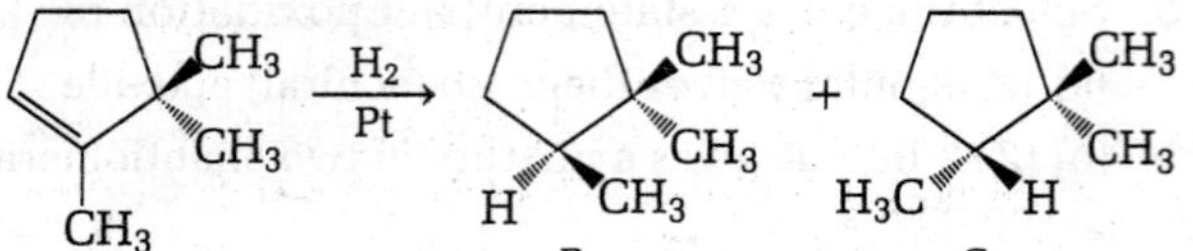

A *B* *C*

(a) *A*, *B* and *C* are achiral
(b) *A* is achiral but *B* and *C* are chiral
(c) *B* and *C* are enantiomers and product is optically inactive due to racemisation
(d) *B* and *C* are identical compounds

11. For the reactions shown below, identify the correct statement with regard to the products formed.

I. 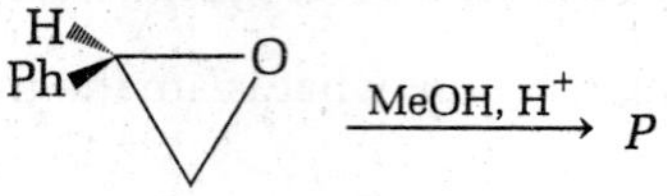

II. 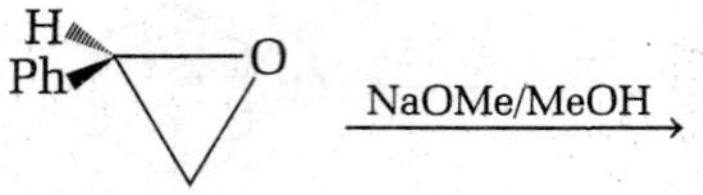

(a) *P* and *Q* are identical, both are optically active
(b) *P* and *Q* are positional isomers, *P* is racemic and *Q* is optically active
(c) *P* and *Q* are positional isomers, *P* is optically active and *Q* is racemic
(d) *P* and *Q* are positional isomers, both are optically active

12. Identify the diols which are cleaved by HIO_4.

(a) 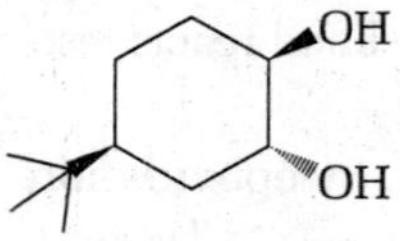
(b) 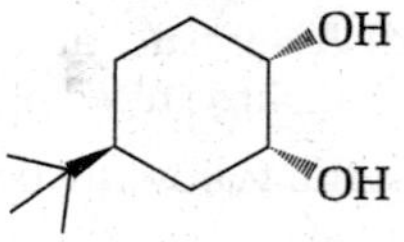

(c) 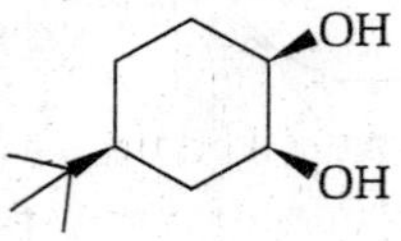
(d) 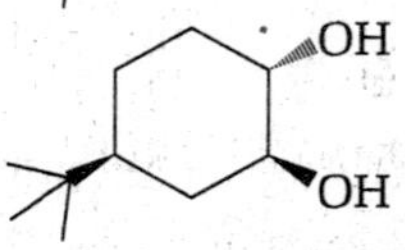

13. Diols which react with CrO_3 in aqueous H_2SO_4 and yield products that readily undergo decarboxylation on heating are

(a) 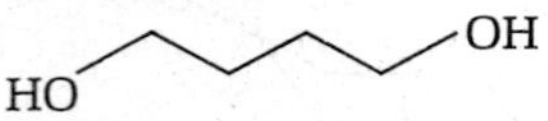

(b) 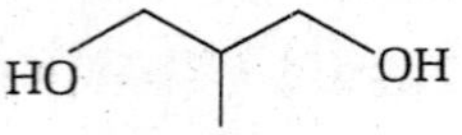

(c) 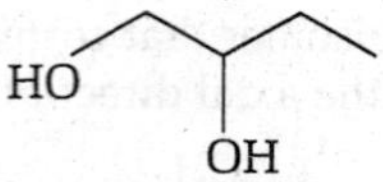

(d) 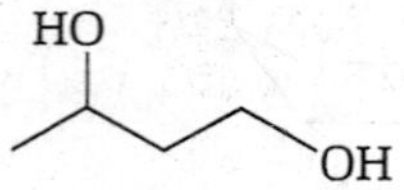

14. Select the correct synthesis products.

(a) 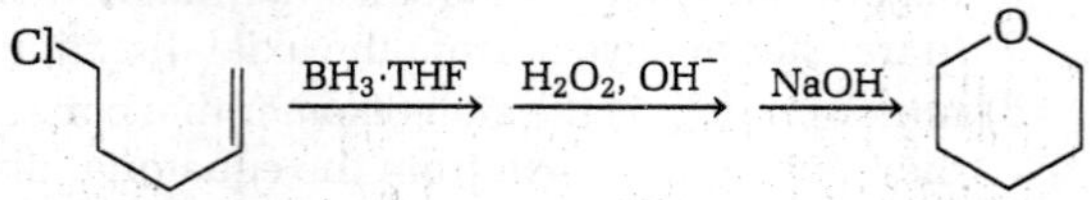

(b) 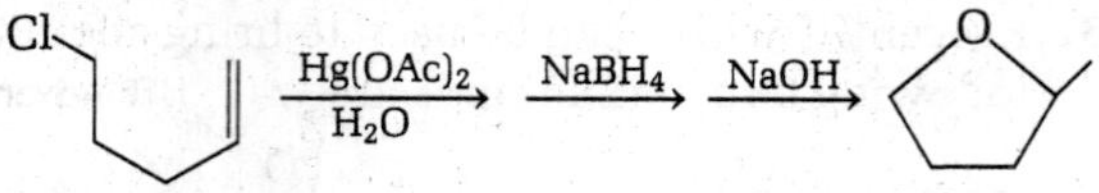

(c) 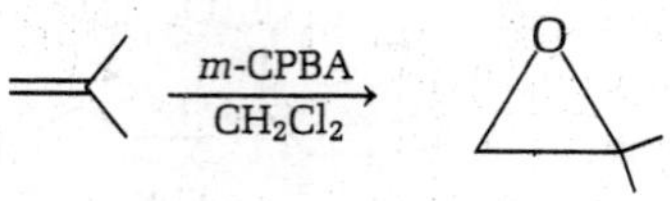

(d) 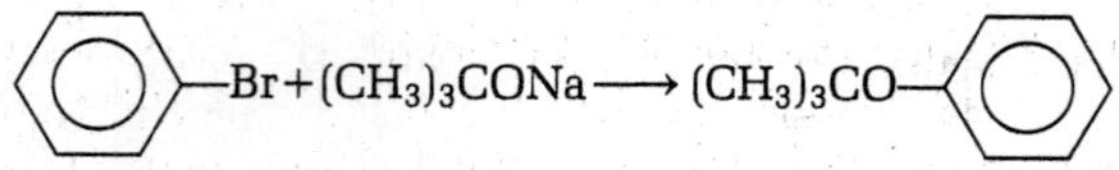

Numerical Value Questions

All these questions have a Numerical value as their answer, solve the questions and write your answer.

1. In the following reaction specify the positon of $\overset{\ominus}{O}C_2H_5$

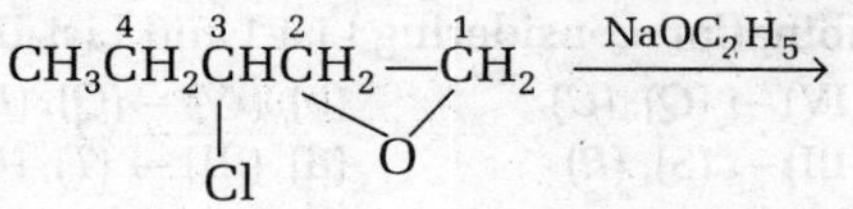

2. By CH_3CO_3H, (C=C) is oxidised to epoxide (C–C bridged by O). What is the sum of position of (C=C) oxidised in the major product in following reactant?

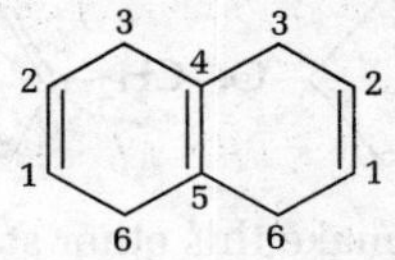

3. A *n*-membered ring is formed in the following synthesis. The value of *n*is ....

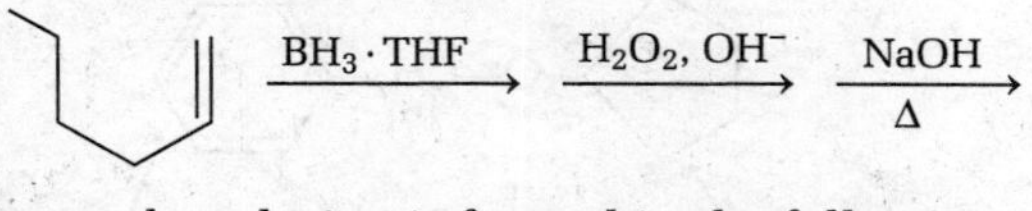

4. A *n*-membered, ring is formed in the following synthesis. The value of *n* is ......

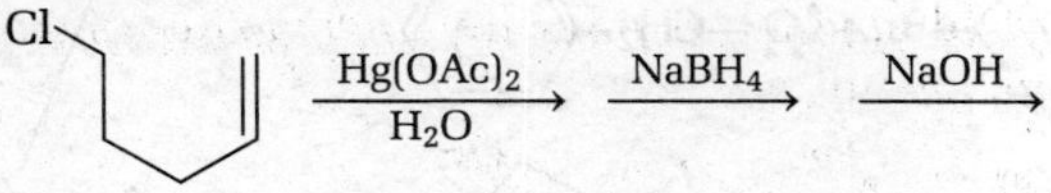

5. In the following reaction, how many carbon atoms are there in the carbocation as the intermediate?

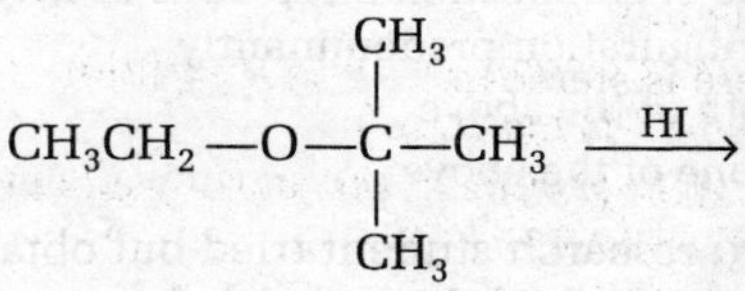

6. C_7H_8O represents aromatic compounds. How many isomers are possible?
7. How many different ether isomer are possible for C_3H_6O ?
8. 0.218 g of the acetyl derivative of a polyhydric alcohol (molecular mass =92) requires 0.168 g of KOH for hydrolysis. Calculate the number of (—OH) group in the alcohol.
9. How many mole of methyl magnesium iodide in ether will react with a molecule of ethyl chloro formate to form a 3° alcohol?
10. A 5.2 g of polyhydric alcohol was treated with an CH_3MgBr to produce 3.36 litre of CH_4 at STP. Calculate number of OH groups present in polyhydric alcohol (molar mass of alcohol $=104\ mol^{-1}$).

Comprehension Based Questions

In these questions, a passage has been given followed by questions based on it. You have to answer the questions based on the passage given.

***Passage* 1** Ether *X* (below) is found to have some medicinal application in l (–) isomer and is entitled as chiral-drug.

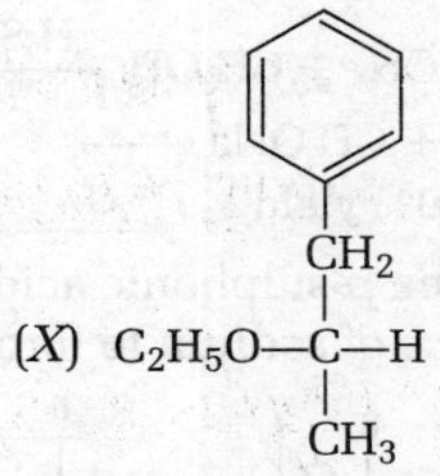

Two research students tried this project by two different methods but taking the identical stereoisomer *d*(+) alcohol.

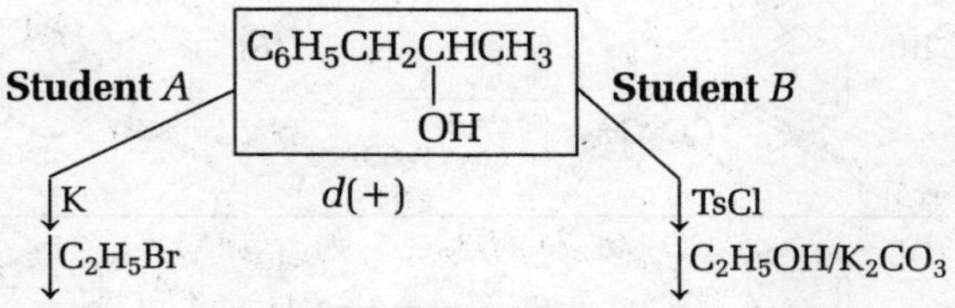

1. Research student (*A*) would have obtained the required isomer because of
   (a) cleavage of C—O bond which results in the formation of carbocation on which attack can take place either of side
   (b) steric hindrance on the original isomer so that attack of C_2H_5Br takes place from back side
   (c) Both of the above
   (d) None of the above since configuration is retained

2. Research student *B* would have obtained the required isomer because of
   (a) cleavage of C—O bond after TsCl has reacted and TsO^- is a better leaving group which results in the formation of carbocation
   (b) there is probability of nucleophilic attack on either side of carbocation but results in inverted configuration predominantly
   (c) Both of the above
   (d) None of the above
3. A third research student tried but obtained the compound which lacked chiral centre.
   This would have been due to
   (a) formation of *d*(+) and *l*(–) in equal amounts
   (b) wrong selection of the reactants as

$$C_6H_5CH_2\underset{\displaystyle Br}{\underset{|}{C}}HCH_3 + C_2H_5ONa$$

   (c) Both of the above
   (d) None of the above

Passage 2 List-I includes starting materials and reagents of selected chemical reactions. List-I gives structures of compounds that may be formed as intermediate product and/or final products from the reactions of List-I. **[JEE Advanced, 2019]**

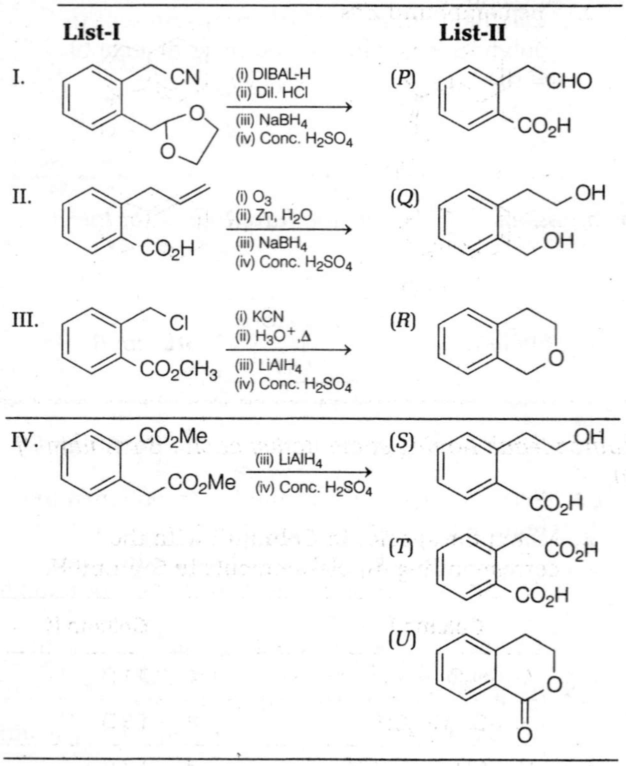

1. Which of the following options has the correct combination considering List-I and List-II?
   (a) (II) → (*P*), (*S*), (*T*)
   (b) (II) → (*P*), (*S*), (*U*)
   (c) (I) → (*S*), (*Q*), (*R*)
   (d) (I) → (*Q*), (*T*), (*U*)
2. Which of the following options has the correct combination considering List-I and List-II ?
   (a) (IV) → (*Q*), (*U*)
   (b) (IV) → (*Q*), (*R*)
   (c) (III) → (*S*), (*R*)
   (d) (III) → (*T*), (*U*)

Passage 3 *Following passage describes the route to prepare alkoxy alkane by Williamson synthesis. Go into the detail and answer the questions at the end of it.*

Suppose the target is

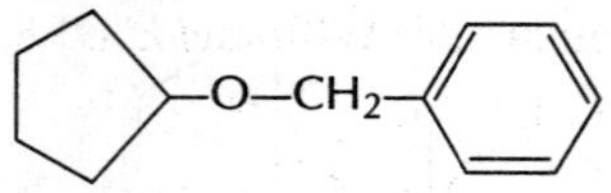

and we are asked to make this ether starting from alkyl halides. The two ways to prepare the target ether are as follow

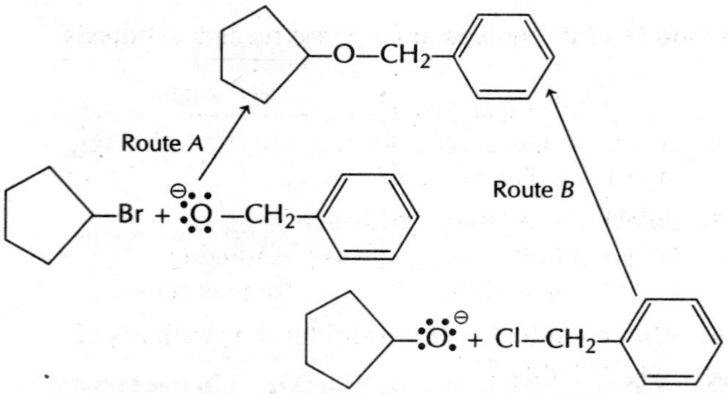

Route *B* is the obvious choice.

1. Methyl tertiary butyl ether (MTBE) is an important gasoline additive for improving octane number. Select the best method of its synthesis out of the following.
   (a) $(CH_3)_3CONa + CH_3I \longrightarrow$
   (b) $(CH_3)_2C{=}CH_2 + CH_3OH \xrightarrow{H_2SO_4}$
   (c) $(CH_3)_3CBr + CH_3ONa \longrightarrow$
   (d) all give 100% yield
2. Ester of toluene-*p*-sulphonic acid and alkoxide react in the presence of sodium to form ether

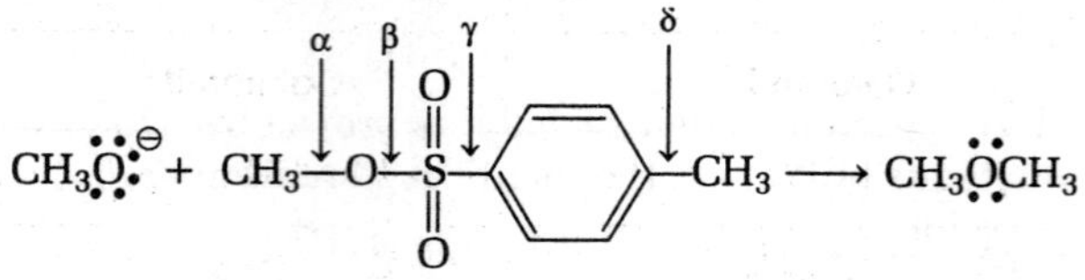

Which bond is cleaved and why?
(a) α-bond since toluene-*p*-sulphonate is a good leaving group
(b) β-bond since $CH_3O^{\ominus}$ is a better leaving group
(c) γ-bond since it has least bond-energy
(d) δ-bond since hyperconjugation makes $—CH_3$ a better leaving group

***Passage* 4** Consider the following cyclic ether

A : 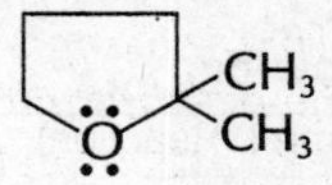

We can design two processes to synthesise it.

Method *P* Intramolecular Williamson ether synthesis

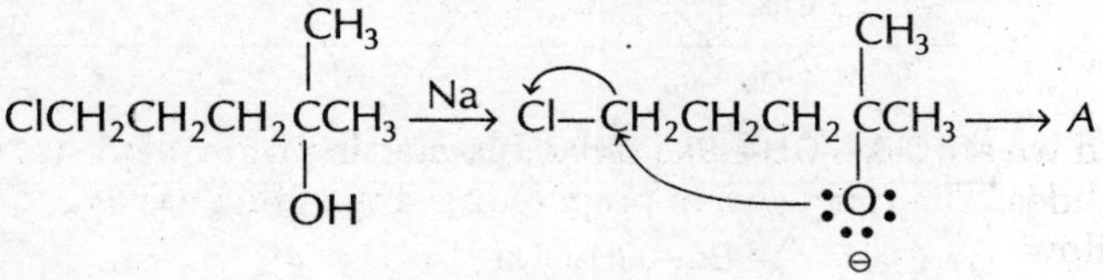

Method *Q* Intramolecular Grignard reagent synthesis.

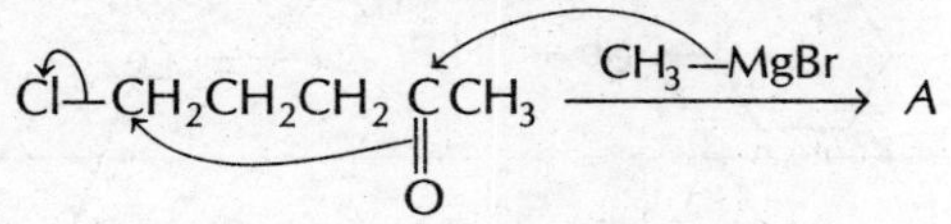

1. Select the required synthesis.
(a) Method *P*
(b) Method *Q*
(c) Both (a) and (b)
(d) None of these

2. Which method is not useful for the synthesis of required ether?

(a) 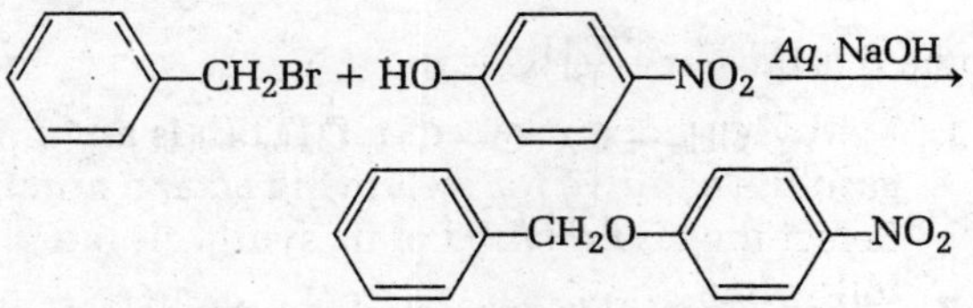

(b) $C_2H_5ONa + (CH_3)_2SO_4 \longrightarrow C_2H_5OCH_3$

(c) $CH_3ONa + CH_3CH_2OSO_2—C_6H_4—CH_3 \longrightarrow CH_3CH_2OCH_3$

(d) $(CH_3)_3CBr + CH_3CH_2ONa \longrightarrow (CH_3)_3COCH_2CH_3$

***Passage* 5.** Treatment of benzene with CO / HCl in the presence of anhydrous $AlCl_3$ / CuCl followed by reaction with Ac_2O / NaOAc gives compound *X* as the major product. Compound *X* upon reaction with Br_2 / Na_2CO_3 followed by heating at 473 K with moist KOH furnishes *Y* as the major product. Reaction of *X* with H_2 / Pd - C, followed by H_3PO_4 treatment gives *Z* as the major product. **[JEE Advanced 2018]**

1. The compound *Y* is

(a) 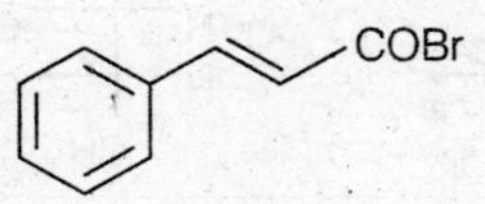
(b) 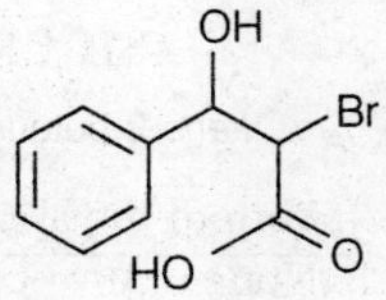
(c) 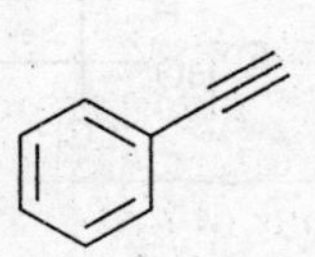
(d) 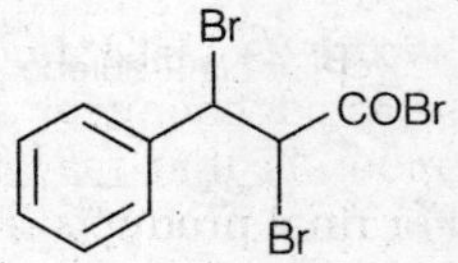

2. The compound *Z* is

(a) 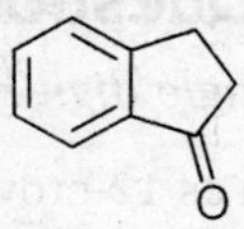
(b) 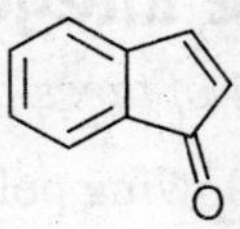
(c) 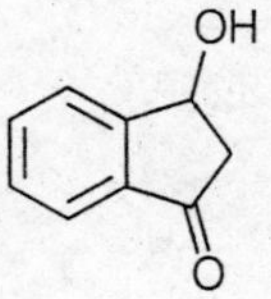
(d) 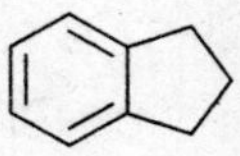

Matrix-Match Type

Given below are Matching Type Questions, with two columns (each having some items) each . Each item of Column I has to be matched with the items of Column II.

1. Match the species in Column I with the corresponding bond-angles in Column II.

Column I	Column II
A. CH_3OH	1. 104.5°
B. CH_3OCH_3	2. 109.5°
C. H_2O	3. 108.9°
D. CH_4	4. 110°

2. Match the species in Column I with the corresponding dipole-moments in Column II.

Column I	Column II
A. H_2O	1. 0.1 D
B. CH_3CH_2OH	2. 1.3 D
C. $CH_3—O—CH_3$	3. 1.7 D
D. $CH_3CH_2CH_3$	4. 1.9 D

3. Match the species in Column I with the corresponding boiling point in Column II.

Column I	Column II
A. CH_3CH_2OH	1. 373 K
B. $CH_3—O—CH_3$	2. 298 K
C. H_2O	3. 351 K
D. $CH_3CH_2—O—CH_2CH_3$	4. 348 K

4. Match the following.

Column I (Reaction)	Column II (Product)
A. *trans*-2-butene $\xrightarrow{mCPBA}$	1. 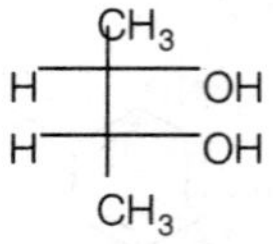
B. *cis*-2-butene $\xrightarrow{mCPBA}$	2. 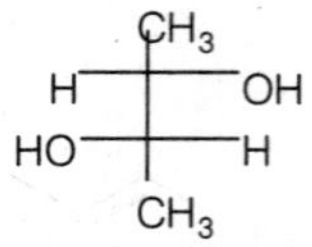
C. *trans*-2-butene $\xrightarrow{MnO_4^-/OH^-}$	3. 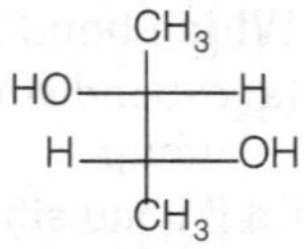
D. *cis*-2-butene $\xrightarrow{MnO_4^-/OH^-}$	4. 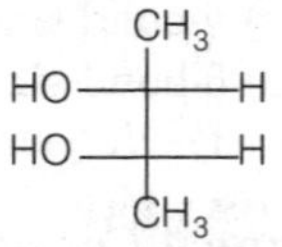

5. Match the following.

Column I (Reaction)	Column II (Type)
A. $CH_3-\overset{CH_3}{\underset{CH_3}{C}}-ONa + CH_3CH_2Br$	1. S_N2
B. $CH_3-\overset{CH_3}{CH}-Br + CH_3CH_2ONa$	2. S_N1
C. 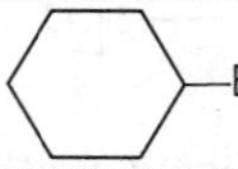—Br + CH_3ONa	3. E 1
D. 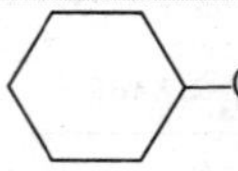—ONa + CH_3Br	4. E2

Single Integer Answer Questions

Answer of these questions is a single digit lying between 0 to 9.

1. The following polyether is known as 12-crown-*x* where, *x* is ....

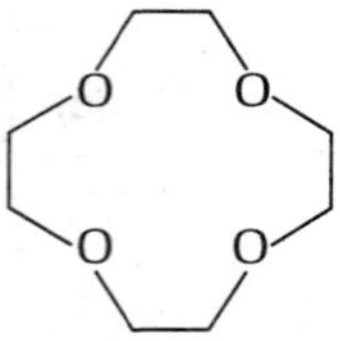

2. Total number of isomeric ethers of the molecular formula $C_4H_{10}O$ is ....

3. Number of isomeric ethers with chiral carbon in molecular formula $C_5H_{12}O$ is ....

4. 11.19 g of CH_3CH_2OH gives *x* g of $(CH_3CH_2)_2O$ on dehydration. *x* is ....

5. Ethene is oxidised to glycol by cold alkaline $KMnO_4$ which is reduced to new salt with oxidation number of Mn ....

6. In the following reaction, iodide goes to carbon ....

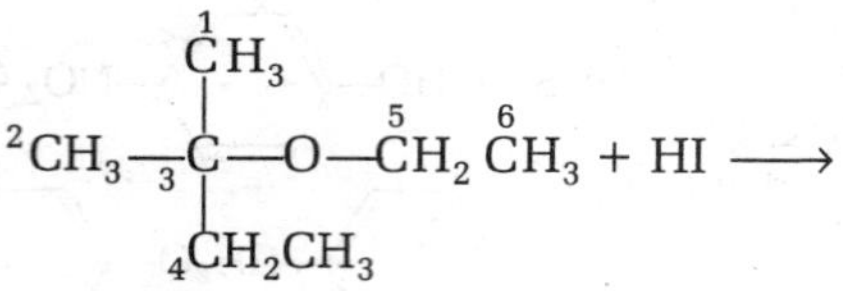

7. When glycerol is subjected to periodate oxidation, *y* types of products are formed. *y* is ....

8. Periodate is reduced to new salt (in Q. 7) with oxidation number of iodide equal to ....

9. How many ethers cannot be prepared by Williamson's synthesis?

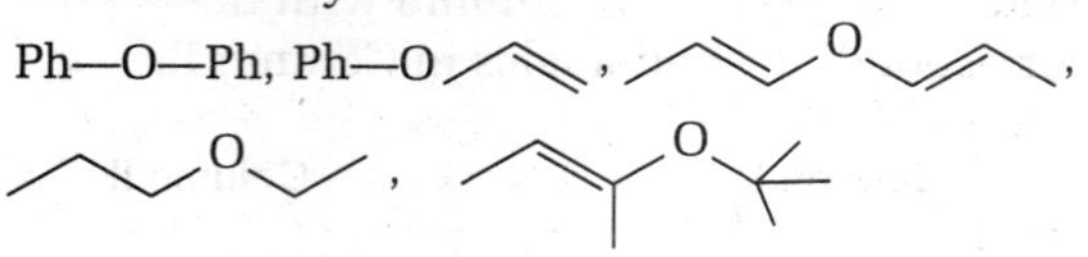

Answers

Objective Questions Type I [Only one correct option]

1. (b)	**2.** (c)	**3.** (b)	**4.** (d)	**5.** (a)	**6.** (b)	**7.** (b)	**8.** (d)	**9.** (b)	**10.** (b)
11. (a)	**12.** (a)	**13.** (a)	**14.** (d)	**15.** (c)	**16.** (c)	**17.** (c)	**18.** (b)	**19.** (c)	**20.** (d)
21. (a)	**22.** (b)	**23.** (a)	**24.** (c)	**25.** (b)	**26.** (a)	**27.** (b)	**28.** (b)	**29.** (a)	**30.** (c)
31. (b)	**32.** (b)	**33.** (d)	**34.** (b)	**35.** (b)	**36.** (b)	**37.** (c)	**38.** (b)	**39.** (d)	**40.** (d)
41. (b)	**42.** (b)	**43.** (d)	**44.** (b)	**45.** (a)	**46.** (d)	**47.** (c)	**48.** (d)	**49.** (c)	**50.** (a)
51. (d)	**52.** (c)	**53.** (b)	**54.** (a)	**55.** (c)	**56.** (a)	**57.** (b)	**58.** (b)	**59.** (a)	**60.** (b)
61. (a)	**62.** (a)	**63.** (a)	**64.** (d)	**65.** (c)	**66.** (b)	**67.** (c)	**68.** (b)	**69.** (a)	**70.** (c)
71. (a)	**72.** (c)	**73.** (d)	**74.** (c)	**75.** (c)	**76.** (c)	**77.** (b)	**78.** (b)		

Objective Questions Type II [One or more than one correct option(s)]

1. (b, c)	**2.** (a, b)	**3.** (c, d)	**4.** (a, b, c)	**5.** (a)
6. (a)	**7.** (a, b, d)	**8.** (a, b)	**9.** (b)	**10.** (a, b, c)
11. (d)	**12.** (a, d)	**13.** (b, d)	**14.** (a, b, c)	

Numerical Value Questions

1. (1)	**2.** (9)	**3.** (6)	**4.** (5)	**5.** (4)	**6.** (5)	**7.** (4)	**8.** (3)	**9.** (3)	**10.** (3)

Comprehension Based Questions

Passage 1 – 1. (d) **2.** (c) **3.** (b)

Passage 2 – 1. (b) **2.** (b)

Passage 3 – 1. (a) **2.** (a)

Passage 4 – 1. (c) **2.** (d)

Passage 5 – 1. (c) **2.** (a)

Matrix-Match Type

1. A→(3); B→(4); C→(1); D→(2)

2. A→(4); B→(3); C→(2); D→(1)

3. A→(3); B→(2); C→(1); D→(4)

4. A→(1,4); B→(2,3); C→(2,3); D→(1,4)

5. A→(1); B→(2,3); C→(2,3); D→(1)

6. A→(1,2,3); B→(3); C→(2); D→(1,4)

Single Integer Answer Questions

1. (4)	**2.** (3)	**3.** (1)	**4.** (9)	**5.** (4)	**6.** (3)	**7.** (2)	**8.** (5)	**9.** (4)

Solutions

Objective Questions Type I [Only one correct option]

1. (*b*) Cyclohexylidene $=CH_2$ → $\overset{\oplus}{}$ cyclohexyl $-\overset{\ominus}{C}H_2$ $\xrightarrow{H^+}$ 3° carbocation ($\overset{\oplus}{}$ $-CH_3$) $\xrightarrow{CH_3O^{\ominus}}$ 1-methyl-1-methoxycyclohexane ($-CH_3$, OCH_3)

3° carbocation

2. (*c*) Cyclohexyl $-CH=CH_2$ $\xrightarrow{H^+}$ cyclohexyl $-\overset{\oplus}{C}H-CH_3$

2° carbocation

↓ 1,2-hydride shift

$\overset{\oplus}{}$ cyclohexyl $-CH_2-CH_3$

3° carbocation (most stable)

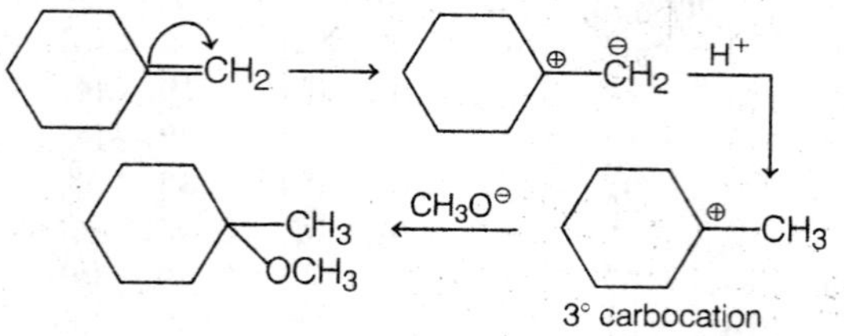

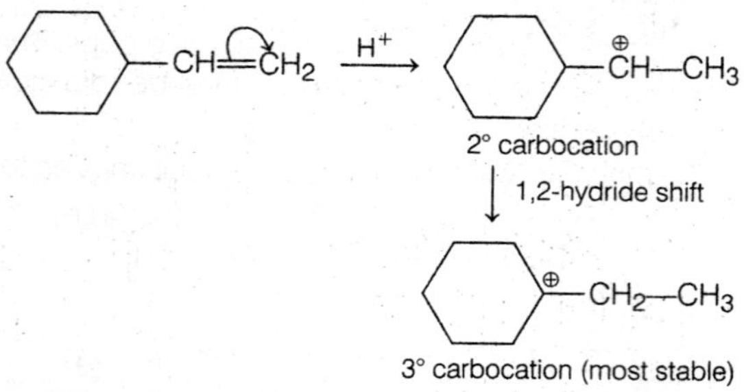

3. (*b*) If *RX* is 2° or 3°, *R*ONa will cause elimination. Thus, (b) is incorrect statement.

4. (*d*) I is correct.
II is incorrect since C—Br bond is most stable.
III is incorrect since elimination takes place.

6. (*b*) N_2 escapes easily.

11. (*a*) Ethylene glycol (OH, OH) + oxalic acid (HO—C=O, HO—C=O) $\xrightarrow[-H_2O]{\text{Conc. } H_2SO_4}$ cyclic oxalate ester

12. (*a*) Cyclohexyl $-CH=CH_2$ $\xrightarrow{H_3O^+/CH_3OH}$ 1-ethyl-1-methoxycyclohexane ($-CH_2CH_3$, OCH_3)

21. (*a*) $R_2O:$ (Base) MgRX (Acid)

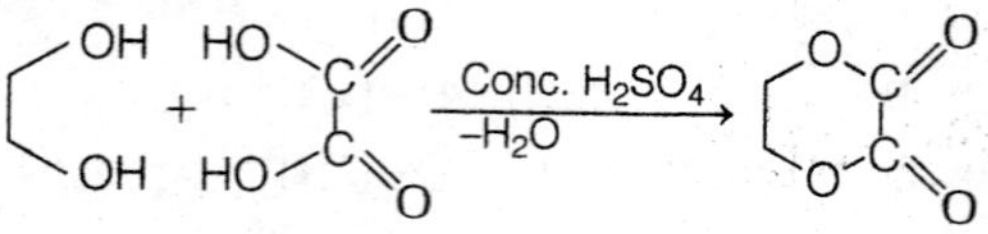

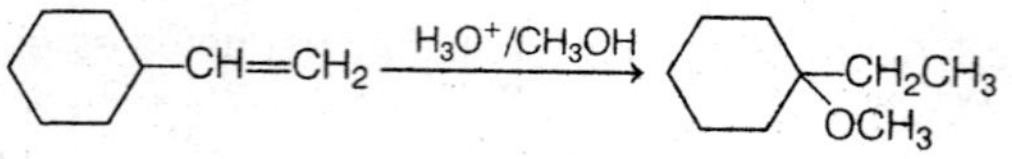

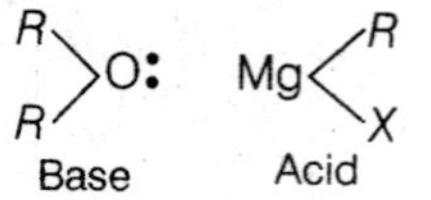

23. (*a*) β, γ hydrogens are vinylic with maximum (C—H) B.E.

25. (*b*) $CH_3CH_2CH_2CH_2-\overset{\oplus}{O}(H)-CH(CH_3)_2$ ⟶ $CH_3CH_2CH_2OH + (CH_3)_2\overset{\oplus}{C}H$

Weak base

(more stable carbocation)

27. (*b*) $C_6H_5-CH_2 \mid OCH_3$ $\xrightarrow{H^+}$ $C_6H_5-\overset{\oplus}{C}H_2 + CH_3O^{\ominus}$

Resonance stabilised carbocation

Thus, products are $C_6H_5-CH_2I + CH_3OH$

31. (*a*) $CH_3O^{\ominus}$ + $CH_2-CH(CH_3)-CH_3$ (epoxide, O) ⟶ CH_3O—C(H)—C(CH_3)(OH_3)—CH_3

33. (*d*) $ClCH_2\,CH-\overset{14}{C}H_2$ (epoxide, O) + $CH_3CH_2O^{\ominus}$ attack at least substituted site

$CH_2-\overset{14}{C}HCH_2OCH_2CH_3$ (epoxide, O) $\xleftarrow[\text{Williamson's reaction}]{\text{Intramolecular}}$ $Cl-CH_2-CH(O^{\ominus})-\overset{14}{C}H_2OCH_2CH_3$

37. (*c*) H—C—OH / H—C—OH $\xleftarrow{HCO_3H}$ alkene $\xrightarrow{MnO_4^-/OH^-}$ H—C—OH / HO—C—H

Enantiomer

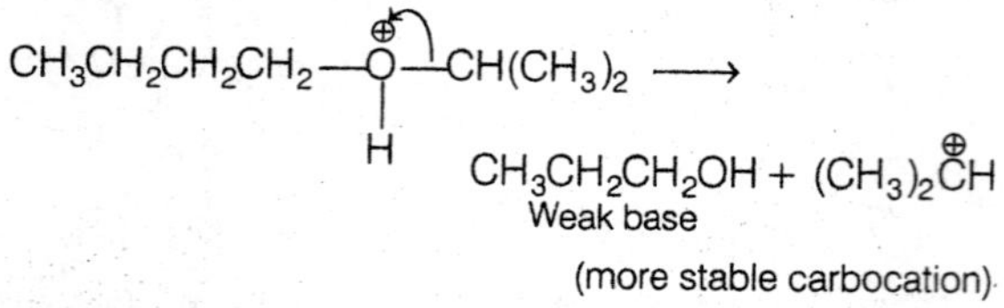

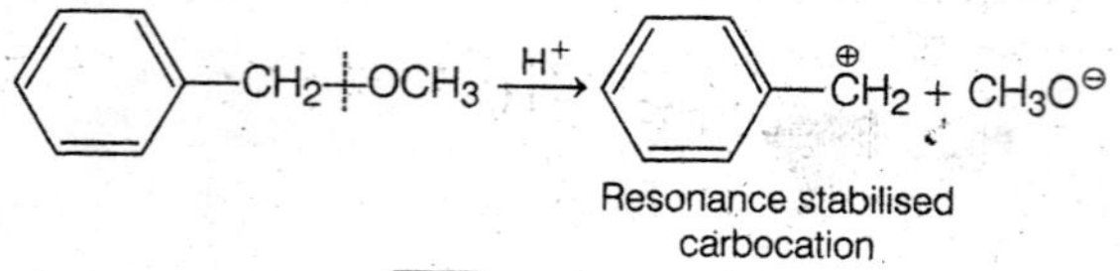

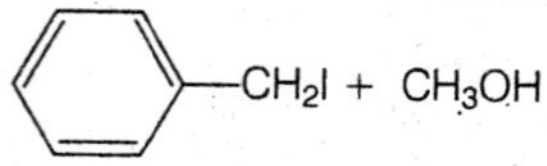

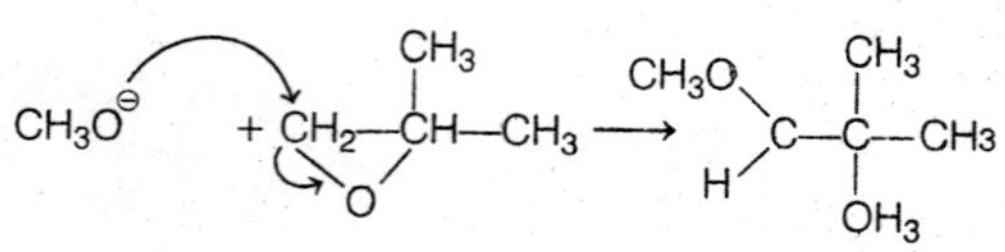

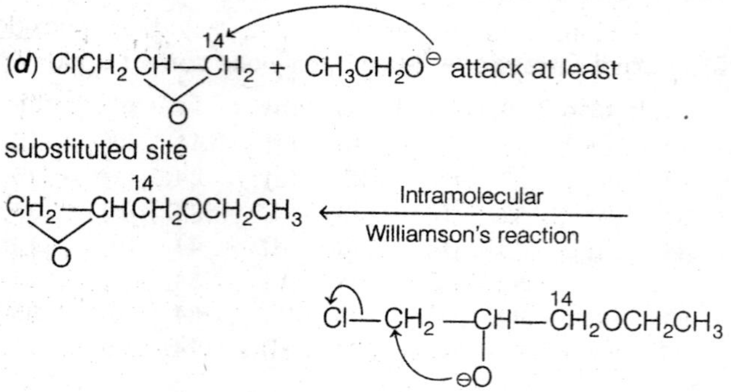

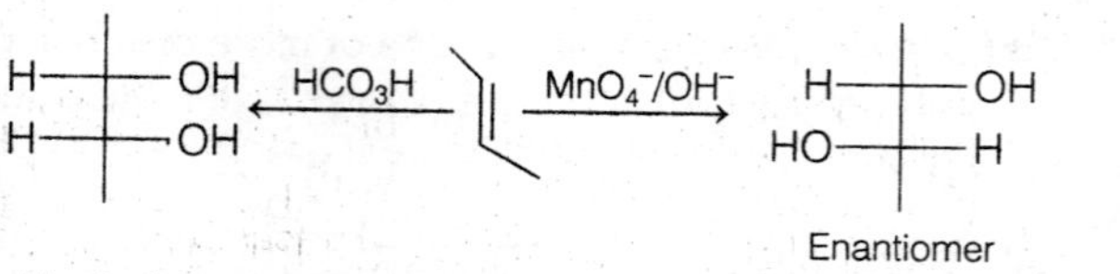

39. (*d*) Alcohols have higher boiling point than ethers of same molecular mass due to possibility of intermolecular hydrogen bonds in alcohols and not in ethers.

So, *A* is alcohol derivative and *B* is ether derivative.

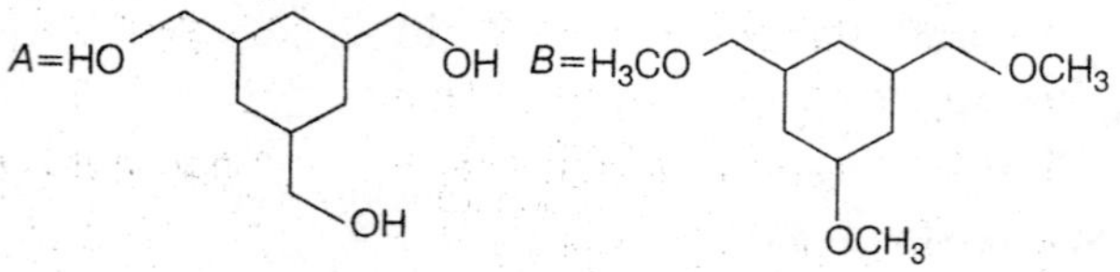

A=HO—CH_2CH_2—cyclohexane(—CH_2OH)—CH_2CH_2—OH   *B*=H_3CO—CH_2CH_2—cyclohexane(—CH_2OCH_3)—CH_2CH_2—OCH_3

41. (*b*) $CH_2OH-CH-OH-CH_2-OH + 3HNO_3 \xrightarrow[\text{Cold}]{\text{Conc.}H_2SO_4} CH_2-ONO_2 / CH-ONO_2 / CH-ONO_2$

45. (*a*) trans-diol (OH, CH_3, OH) $\xrightarrow[S_N2]{HO^-}$ epoxide (CH_3, O)

50. (*a*) $N_2^+Cl^-$-C$_6$H$_4$-OCH_3 (*A*) $+ CH_3-CH_2-OH \longrightarrow C_6H_5OCH_3 + CH_3CHO + HCl + N_2$

(*X*) (*Y*)

Anisole

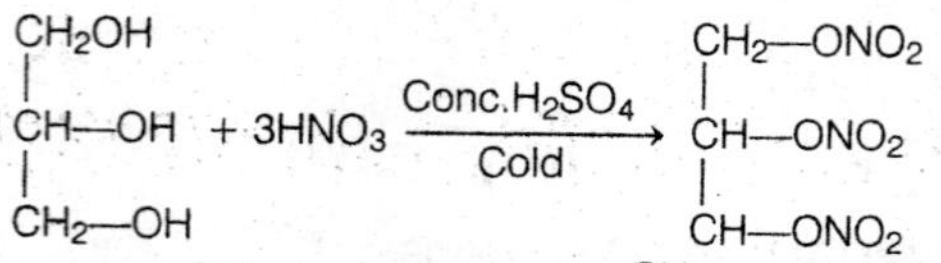

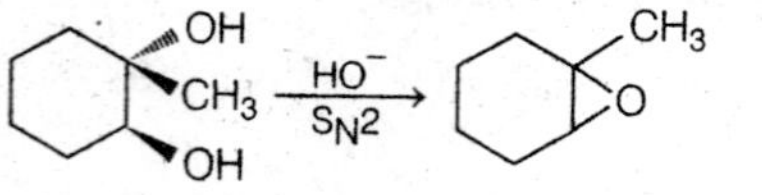

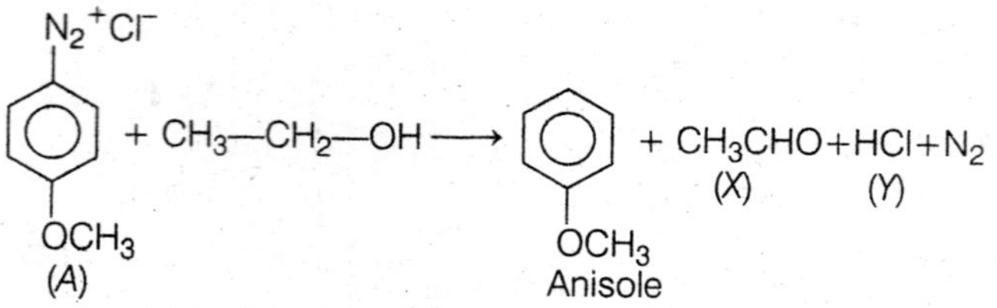

54. (*a*) The major product when *m*-cresol reacts with propargyl bromide ($HC\equiv C-CH_2Br$) in presence of K_2CO_3 in acetone is given in the following reaction:

m-cresol (OH) $\xrightarrow{\text{Step 1: 1. } K_2CO_3}$ phenoxide (O^-) $\xrightarrow[-Br^{\ominus}]{\text{Step 2: } Br-CH_2-C\equiv CH}$ $O-CH_2-C\equiv CH$ (*m*-tolyl)

Major product

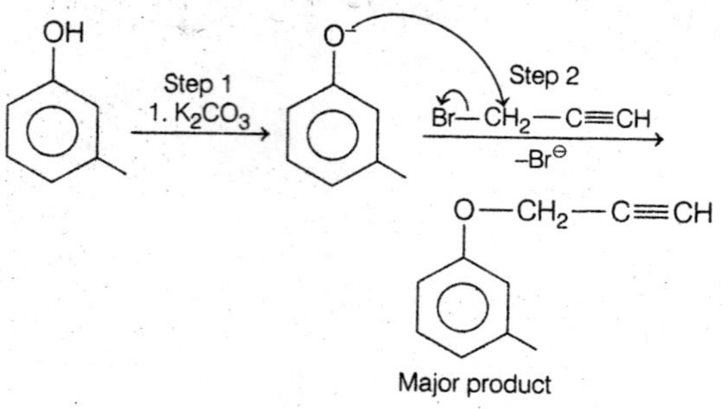

In **step 1** K_2CO_3 act as a base and abstract H-atom from —OH group.

This leads to the formation of substituted phenoxide ion (highly stable).

In **step 2** substituted phenoxide ion on reaction with $Br—CH_2—C≡CH$ gives the required product.

55. (*c*)

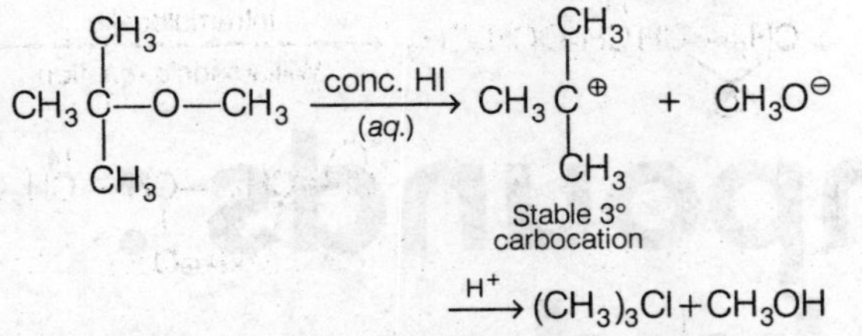

with anhydrous HI, bond-cleavage takes place such that halide remains with smaller alkyl group forming CH_3I and $(CH_3)_3COH$.

56. (*a*) Polyether is represented as,

X crown Y

↑ ↑

Total number of carbon and oxygen atoms — Number of oxygen atoms

57. (*b*)

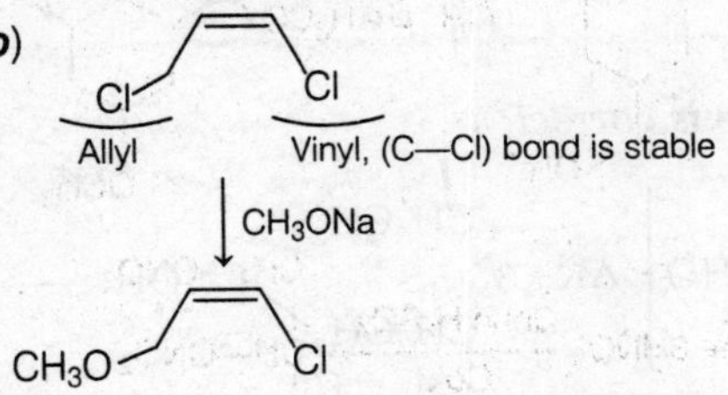

61. (*a*) 2° alcohol is more basic than 1°.

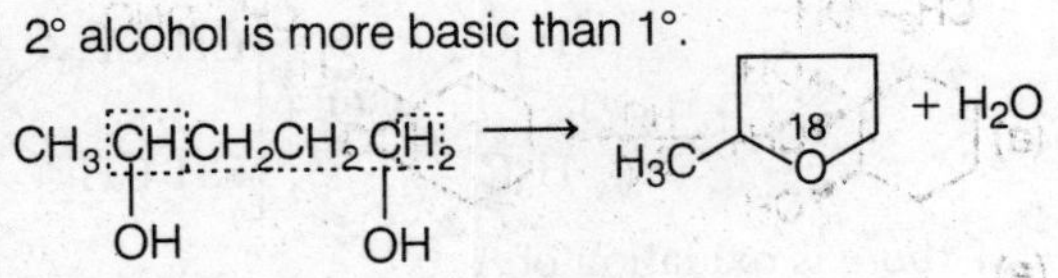

62. (*a*) By *X*, *cis* diol is formed thus, I

By *Y*, *trans* diol is formed thus, II

63. (*a*)

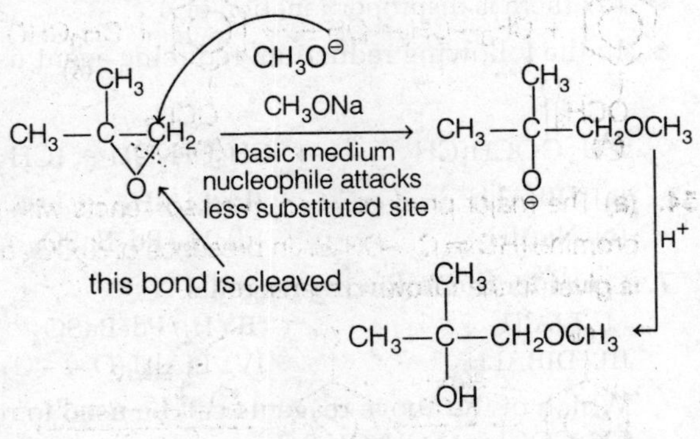

64. (*d*) The given reaction can be completed as follows :

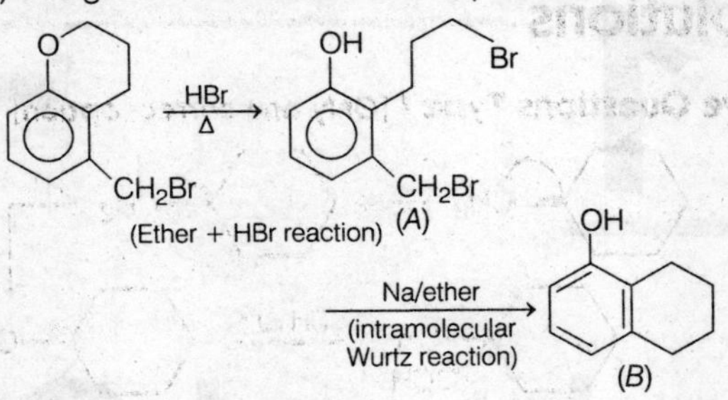

73. (*d*) Elimination is favoured.

77. (*b*) Ethers are least reactive functional groups. The cleavage of C—O bond in ethers take place under drastic conditions with excess of HX.

The major product obtained in the reaction is as follows:

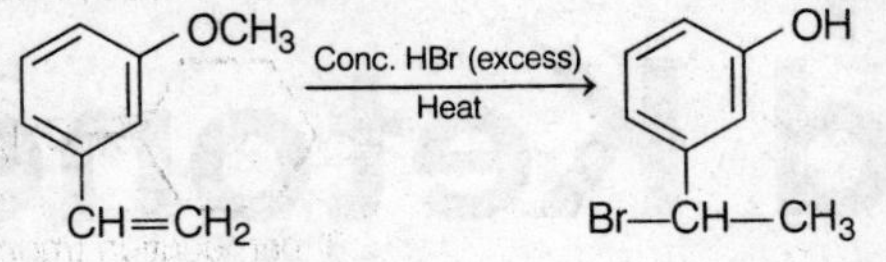

As conc. HBr is in excess. So, reaction will take place at both the substituents.

Mechanism

***Step* 1** Protonation of ether to form oxonium ion.

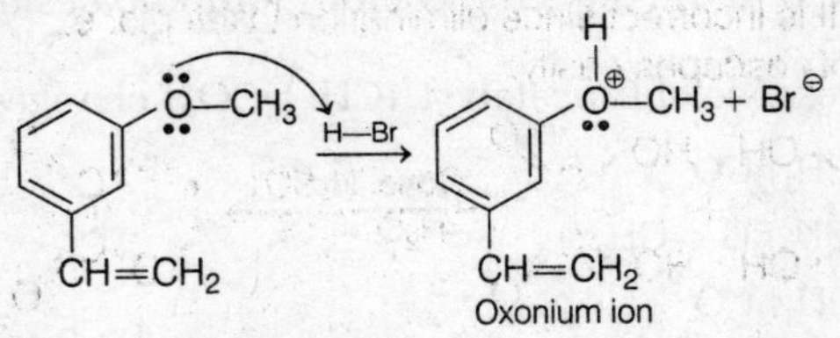

***Step* 2** Attack of nucleophile at the protonated ether.

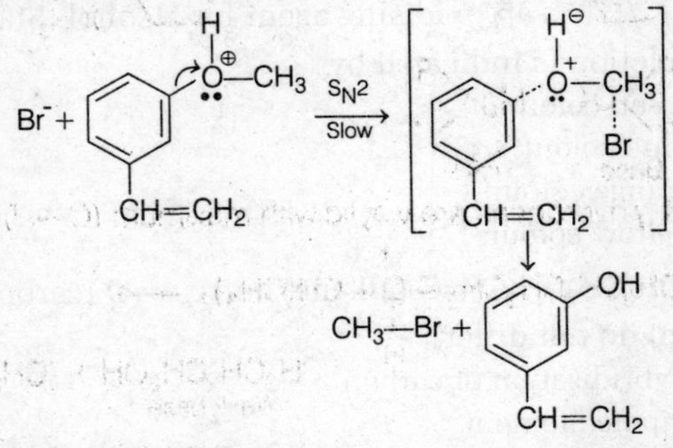

***Step* 3** As HBr is in excess, so, reaction will also take place at alkene.

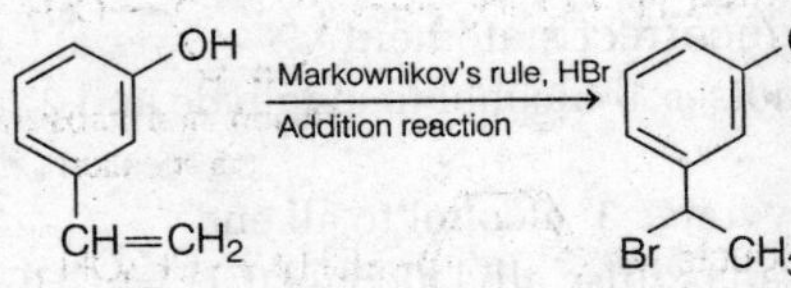

11

Carbonyl Compounds : Aliphatic Aldehydes and Ketones

Objective Questions Type I [Only one correct option]

In each of the questions below, four choices are given of which only one is correct.

1. In presence of Cu catalyst, $(CH_3)_3COH$ changes to

(a) $(CH_3)_2CO$
(b) $(CH_3)_2C{=}CH_2$
(c) $(CH_3)_2CO$
(d) $CH_3CH_2CH{=}CH_2$

2. $Cr_2O_7^{2-}/H^+$ is an oxidising agent for alcohol. Stage of completion is indicated by

(a) green colour
(b) blue colour
(c) orange colour
(d) yellow colour

3. In which case, C=C (alkene) and C=O (carbonyl group) do not differ?

(a) Hybridisation of carbon
(b) Dipole moment
(c) Energy of double bond
(d) Bond length of double bond

4. Select the incorrect statement.

(a) PCC oxidises 1° alcohol to aldehyde and 2° alcohol to ketone
(b) Cu dehydrates 3° alcohol to alkene
(c) MnO_2 can oxidise allyl alcohol ($CH_2{=}CHCH_2OH$) to acrolein ($CH_2{=}CHCHO$)
(d) Oppenauer oxidation method is used to oxidise 1° alcohol to aldehyde

5. In the following reaction,

$$\underset{(A)}{\left[\begin{matrix}H_3C\\H_3C\end{matrix}\!\!>\!CHO\right]_3\!Al} + 3\underset{(B)}{\begin{matrix}CH_3CH_2\\CH_3CH_2\end{matrix}\!\!>\!CHOH} \longrightarrow 3\begin{matrix}H_3C\\H_3C\end{matrix}\!\!>\!CO + \left[\begin{matrix}CH_3CH_2\\CH_3CH_2\end{matrix}\!\!>\!CO\right]_3\!Al$$

(a) there is oxidation of *A*
(b) there is oxidation of *B*
(c) there is reduction of *B*
(d) there is disproportionation of *A*

6. In the following reduction, reducing agent used is

$$CH_3\overset{O}{\overset{\|}{C}}OCH(CH_3)_2 \longrightarrow CH_3CH_2OH + (CH_3)_2CHOH$$

(a) DIBALH
(b) $LiAlH_4$
(c) $NaAlH_4$
(d) $H_2/Pd\text{-}BaSO_4$

7. Consider the following reagents,

I. $LiAlH_4$
II. $H_2/Pd\text{-}BaSO_4$
III. DIBALH
IV. $LiAlH(O{-}t{-}C_4H_9)_3$

Which of the above reagents can be used to reduce CH_3COCl into CH_3CHO ?

(a) I and II
(b) II and III
(c) I and IV
(d) II, III and IV

8. $$\underset{(A)}{C_5H_{10}Cl_2} + NaOH \longrightarrow \underset{(B)}{C_5H_{10}O}$$

B is an aldehyde with no α-hydrogen. Thus, *A* is

(a) $(CH_3)_3CCHCl_2$ (b) $CH_3CH_2\underset{CH_3}{\underset{|}{C}H}CHCl_2$

(c) $CH_3\underset{CH_3}{\underset{|}{C}H}CH_2CHCl_2$ (d) $CH_3\underset{Cl}{\underset{|}{\overset{Cl}{\overset{|}{C}}}}CH_2CH_2CH_3$

9. $C_3H_6Cl_2$ on reaction with NaOH forms C_3H_6O. Which gives yellow precipitate on heating with NaOH and I_2. Thus, $C_3H_6Cl_2$ is

(a) 1,1-dichloropropane (b) 1,2-dichloropropane
(c) 2,2-dichloropropane (d) 1,3-dichloropropane

10. $NaAlH_4$ reduces an ester into HCHO and $(CH_3)_2CHOH$. Thus, ester is

(a) $HCOOCH(CH_3)_2$ (b) $(CH_3)_2CHCOOCH_3$
(c) $HCOOCH_2CH_2CH_3$ (d) $CH_3CH_2COOCH_3$

11. Which of the following nitriles will form aldehyde on reaction with Grignard reagent?

(a) HCN (b) CH_3CN
(c) $(CH_3)_2CHCN$ (d) $CH_2{=}CHCN$

12. An acid chloride on reaction with $H_2/Pd\text{-}BaSO_4$ changes to $(CH_3)_2CHCHO$. This acid chloride on reaction with CH_3MgBr/H_3O^+ gives

(a) $(CH_3)_3COH$
(b) $(CH_3)_2CHOH$
(c) $(CH_3)_2CHCOCH_3$
(d) $(CH_3)_2CHCHO$

13. $NaAlH_4$ reduces an ester into HCHO and $(CH_3)_2CHOH$. This ester changes to .... on reaction with CH_3MgBr/H_3O^+.

(a) $(CH_3)_2CHCOCH_3$ (b) CH_3CHO
(c) CH_3COCH_3 (d) CH_3CH_2CHO

14. Consider the following reactions,

I. $CH_3\overset{O}{\overset{\|}{C}}Cl \xrightarrow{CH_3MgBr} \xrightarrow{H_3O^+} CH_3\overset{O}{\overset{\|}{C}}CH_3$

II. $CH_3\overset{O}{\overset{\|}{C}}Cl \xrightarrow{(CH_3)_2CuLi} CH_3\overset{O}{\overset{\|}{C}}CH_3$

Pure yield of CH_3COCH_3 is obtained in

(a) Only I (b) Only II
(c) Both (a) and (b) (d) None of these

15. Grignard reagent can convert the following into carbonyl compound except in

(a) $CH_3\overset{O}{\overset{\|}{C}}Cl$ (b) $H\overset{O}{\overset{\|}{C}}OCH_3$
(c) $CH_3C{\equiv}N$ (d) CH_3CH_2OH

16. In the following reaction,

$$\underset{(A)}{(RCOO)_2Ca} + \underset{(B)}{(R'COO)_2Ca} \longrightarrow CH_3\underset{CH_3}{\underset{|}{C}H}\overset{O}{\overset{\|}{C}}CH_3$$

A and *B* are

(a) $CH_3\underset{CH_3}{\underset{|}{C}H}COOH$, $CH_3\overset{O}{\overset{\|}{C}}CH_2COOH$

(b) $\left(CH_3\underset{CH_3}{\underset{|}{C}H}COO\right)_2Ca$, $\left(CH_3\overset{O}{\overset{\|}{C}}CH_2COO\right)_2Ca$

(c) $\left(CH_3\underset{CH_3}{\underset{|}{C}H}COO\right)_2Ca$, $(CH_3COO)_2Ca$

(d) $(CH_3COO)_2Ca$, $\left(CH_3\underset{CH_3}{\underset{|}{C}H}\overset{O}{\overset{\|}{C}}CH_2COO\right)_2Ca$

17. Compound $A(C_5H_{10}O)$ gives yellow precipitate on heating with $Ca(OH)_2$ and I_2, calcium salt thus, formed forms *B* on heating

B. $(CH_3)_2CH\overset{O}{\overset{\|}{C}}CH(CH_3)_2$

Thus, *A* is

(a) $(CH_3)_2CH\overset{O}{\overset{\|}{C}}CH_3$ (b) $(CH_3)_2CHCH_2CHO$

(c) $CH_3CH_2\overset{O}{\overset{\|}{C}}CH_2CH_3$ (d) $CH_3\overset{O}{\overset{\|}{C}}CH_2CH_2CH_3$

18. What is *A* in the following reaction?

$A \xrightarrow[\text{(ii) } H_2O/Zn]{\text{(i) } O_3}$ 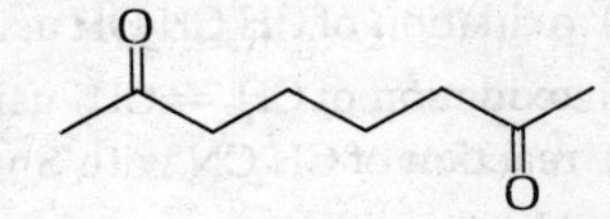

(a) 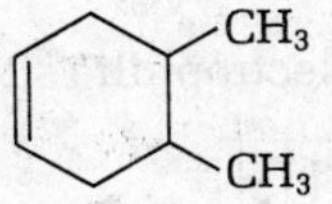 (b) 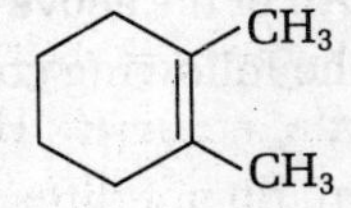

(c) 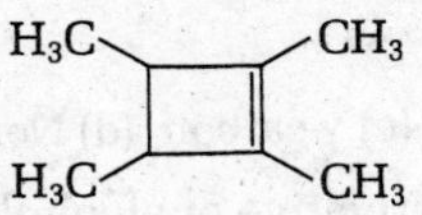 (d) 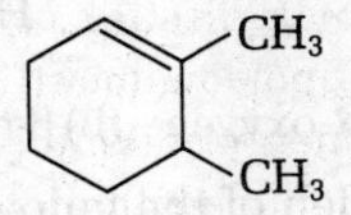

19. By oxo-process

$$(CH_3)_2C{=}CH_2 + CO + H_2 \longrightarrow A$$

A formed is

(a) $(CH_3)_2CHCH_2CHO$ (b) $(CH_3)_2CH\overset{O}{\overset{\|}{C}}CH_3$

(c) $(CH_3)_2CHCH_2CH_3$ (d) $(CH_3)_2CH\underset{CH_3}{\underset{|}{C}H}CH_3$

20. Catalyst used in oxo-process is
(a) $Fe(CO)_5$ (b) $Co(CO)_5$
(c) $CrH(CO)_4$ (d) $[CoH(CO)_4]$

21. Which does not produce aldehyde in the following reactions?
(a) $RCN \xrightarrow{\text{Reduction}/H_3O^+}$ (b) $RCN \xrightarrow{SnCl_2/H_3O^+}$
(c) $RCN \xrightarrow{Sn/HCl}$ (d) $HCN \xrightarrow[H_3O^+]{CH_3MgBr}$

22. Which is the incorrect reaction?
(a) $CH_3CH{=}CH_2 \xrightarrow{\text{Oxo method}} CH_3CH_2CH_2CHO$
(b) $RCN \xrightarrow{\text{DIBALH}} RCHO$
(c) $(HCOO)_2Ca \xrightarrow{\Delta} HCHO$
(d) $CH_3\overset{O}{\overset{\|}{C}}Cl \xrightarrow{(CH_3)_2CuLi} CH_3CH_2\overset{O}{\overset{\|}{C}}CH_3$

23. Following synthesis is effective when
$CH_3COCl + R_2Cd \longrightarrow RCOCH_3 + RCdCl$
R is of the type
(a) $(CH_3)_2CH—$
(b) $(CH_3)_3CCH_2—$
(c) $(C_6H_5)_2CH—$
(d) All of these

24. Identify A in the following sequence of reactions,
$C_3H_5N(A) \xrightarrow{H_3O^+} \xrightarrow{PCl_5} \xrightarrow{(CH_3)_2CuLi} CH_3CH_2\overset{O}{\overset{\|}{C}}CH_3$
(a) CH_3CH_2CN (b) CH_3CH_2NC
(c) $CH_2{=}CHCH{=}NH$ (d) None of these

25. CH_3CHO can be prepared by
(a) oxidation of CH_3CH_2OH using $Cr_2O_7^{2-}/H^+$
(b) oxidation of $CH_2{=}CH_2$ using $PdCl_2 \cdot CuCl_2 / H_2O$
(c) reaction of CH_3CN with $Sn/HCl/H_3O^+$
(d) All of the above

26. In the following compound, electrophilic site is
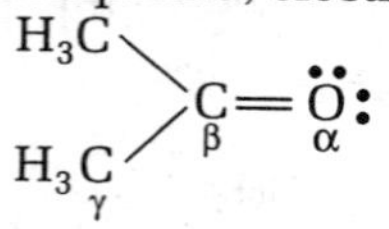

(a) α-oxygen (b) β-carbon (c) γ-carbon (d) None of these

27. Which of the following derivative of alcohols is unstable in an aqueous base? **[JEE Main 2020, Sep.]**
(a) 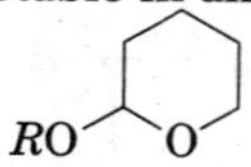

(b) 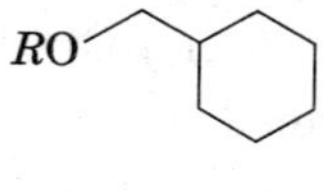

(c) 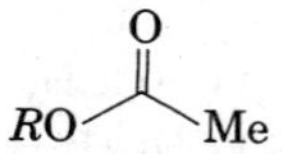

(d) $RO—CMe_3$

28. Select the incorrect statement(s).
(a) Protonation increases electrophilic nature of the carbonyl group
(b) Aldehydes are more reactive than ketones
(c) Carbonyl compounds cannot form hydrogen-bonding with H_2O
(d) Chloral hydrate formation is possible due to hydrogen bonding

29. Boiling points of carbonyl compounds are higher than those of alkanes due to
(a) hydrogen bonding
(b) dipole-dipole interactions
(c) van der Waals' forces
(d) All of the above

30. Reactivity of HCHO (I), CH_3CHO (II) and C_6H_5CHO(III) is in order
(a) I > III > II (b) III > II > I
(c) I = II > III (d) I > II > III

31. Silver-mirror test is not positive with
(a) benzaldehyde (b) acetaldehyde
(c) acetone (d) fructose

32. HCHO reduces Fehling's solution giving red precipitate of
(a) Ag^{2+} (b) Cu^{2+} (c) $HCOO^-$ (d) Cu^+

33. For the following transformation
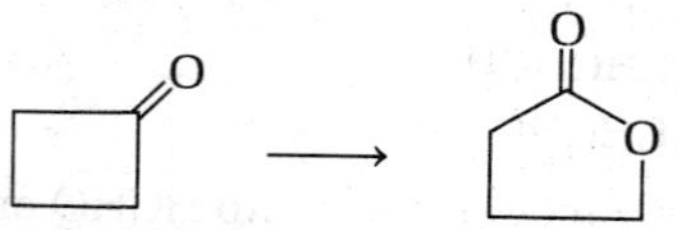

reagent used is
(a) SeO_2 (b) $C_6H_5CO_3H$
(c) ClO^- (d) Se

34. Identify A and B in the following
$CH_3CH_2\overset{O}{\overset{\|}{C}}CH_3 \xrightarrow{C_6H_5CO_3H} \xrightarrow{H_3O^+} A + B$

	A	B
(a)	$CH_3CH_2CO_2H$,	CH_3OH
(b)	CH_3CO_2H,	CH_3CH_2OH
(c)	CH_3CO_2H	CH_3OH
(d)	CH_3CO_2H,	CH_3CO_2H

35. Identify correct product of the following oxidation reaction
$CH_3CH_2COCH_3 \xrightarrow{SeO_2}$
(a) CH_3CH_2COCHO (b) $CH_3CO \cdot COCH_3$
(c) CH_3COCH_2CHO (d) CH_3CH_2COOH

36. In the following reaction,

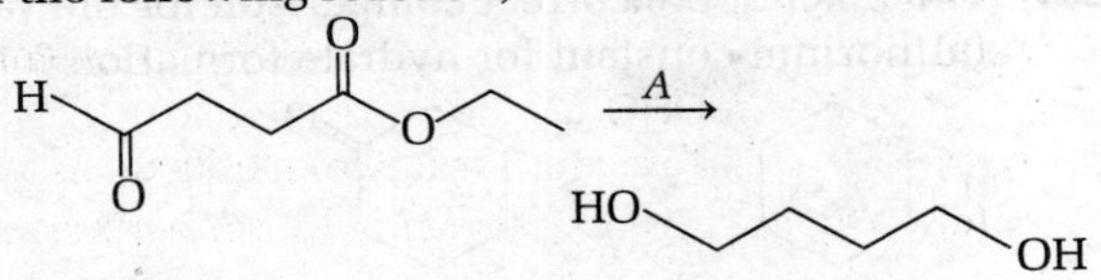

reagent A is

(a) $NaBH_4$ (b) $LiAlH_4$

(c) H_2/Ni (d) Mg/benzene/H_2O

37. Nucleophile and Lewis acid in $LiAlH_4$ are respectively

(a) H^-, AlH_4^- (b) Li^+, AlH_4^- (c) H^-, Li^+ (d) H^+, Al^{3+}

38. Which of the following alcohols cannot be obtained by a hydride reduction of an aldehyde or a ketone?

(a) 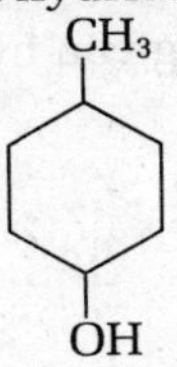 (b) 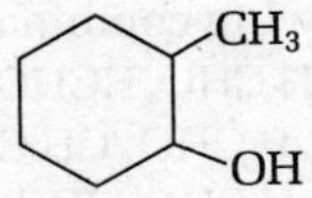

(c) 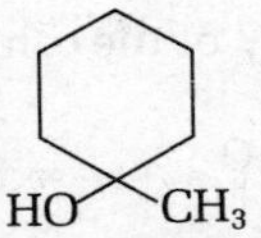 (d) All of these

39. In the following, A, B and C are respectively

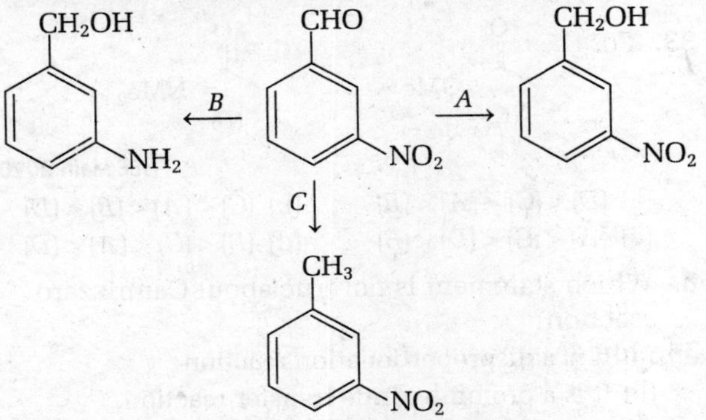

(a) $NaBH_4$ / C_2H_5OH; $LiAlH_4$/ether; N_2H_4/glycol, OH^-

(b) $LiAlH_4$/ether, $NaBH_4$/C_2H_5OH, N_2H_4/glycol, OH^-

(c) N_2H_4/glycol, OH^- in all cases

(d) $LiAlH_4$/C_2H_5OH in all cases

40. Reagents used in Clemmensen reduction and Wolff-Kishner reduction are respectively

(a) Zn(Hg)–conc. HCl; N_2H_4–glycol, OH^-

(b) $LiAlH_4$, $NaBH_4$

(c) $NaBH_4$; $LiAlH_4$

(d) Pd-C/H_2; Li/NH_3

41. Nucleophilic attack on carbonyl carbon changes its hybridisation from

(a) sp to sp^2 (b) sp^2 to sp^3

(c) sp^3 to sp^2 (d) sp to sp^3

42. In the following reaction,

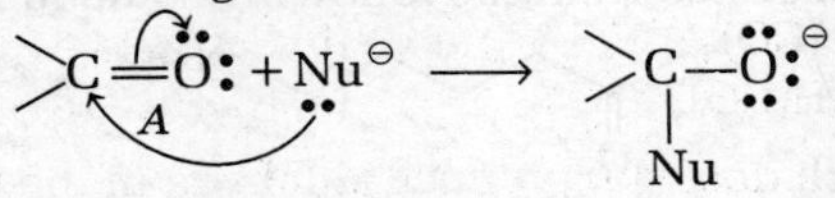

rate is maximum, when A is

(a) HCHO (b) CH_3CHO (c) $(CH_3)_2CO$ (d) C_6H_5CHO

43. Which is maximum reactive towards nucleophilic attack of H_2O forming hydrate?

(a) 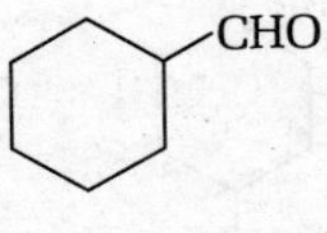 (b) 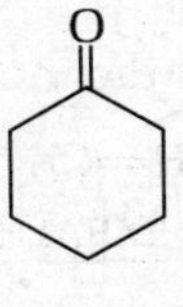

(c) 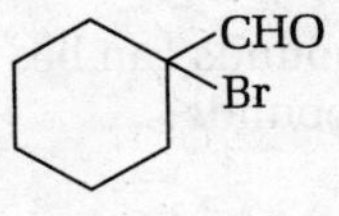 (d) 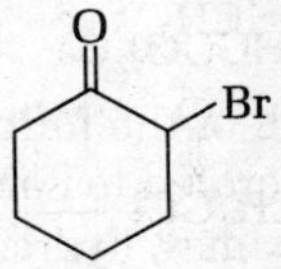

44.

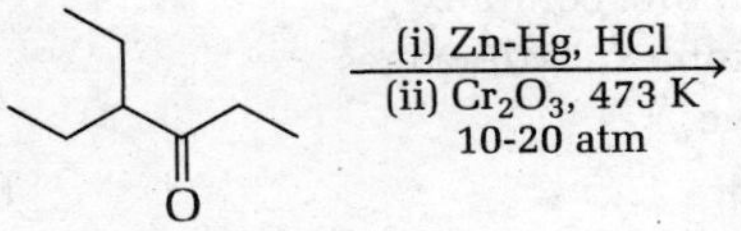

(JEE Main 2021, Feb.)

(a)  (b) 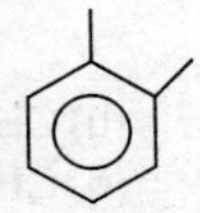 (c) 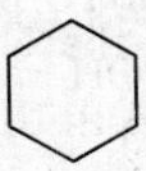 (d) 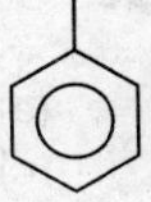

45. Select the incorrect statement.

(a) Carbonyl compounds are attacked by nucleophiles

(b) An aldehyde has a greater partial positive charge on its carbonyl carbon

(c) Protonation of a carbonyl compound decreases electrophilic nature and thus, nucleophilic attack is retarded

(d) Hydration of CCl_3CHO is more than that of CH_3CHO

46. Propanal reacts with amino methane forming

(a) *anti*-imine

(b) *syn*-imine

(c) Both (a) and (b)

(d) None of the above

47. Imine (A) can be prepared by

A : 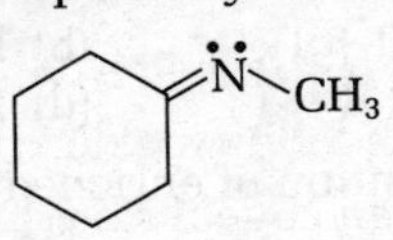

(a) 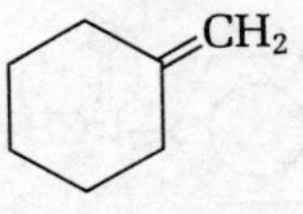, CH_3CHO (b) 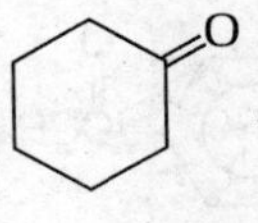, CH_3NH_2

(c) 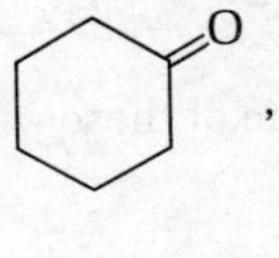, CH_3NHCH_3 (d) None of these

48. Imine formed from the following compound is

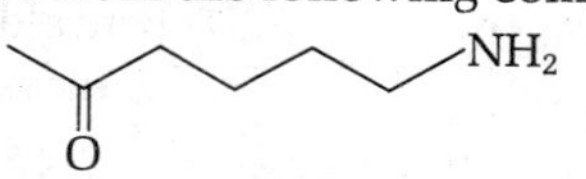

(a) 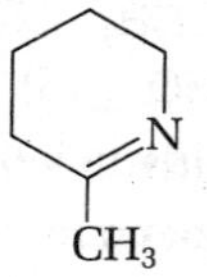
(b) 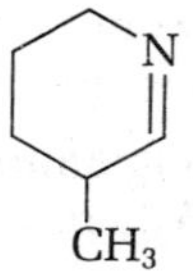
(c) 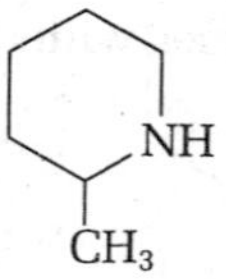
(d) 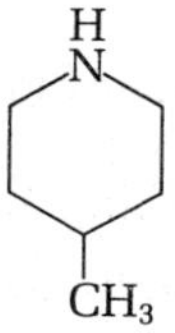

49. Which of the following compounds can be regenerated to carbonyl compounds?
(a) Oximes, hydrazones
(b) Oximes, bisulphite complex
(c) Bisulphite complex, hydrazones
(d) All of the above

50. $CH_3CN \xrightarrow[\text{(iii) Pd/BaSO}_4]{\text{(i) } H_3O^+ \text{ (ii) } SOCl_2}$ **[JEE Main 2021, Feb.]**

(a) CH_3COOH (b) CH_3COCl
(c) CH_3CHO (d) CH_3CH_2OH

51. CH_3CN reacts with two moles of CH_3MgBr followed by hydrolysis in each stage. Final product is

(a) $CH_3\overset{\overset{O}{||}}{C}CH_3$ (b) $CH_3\overset{\overset{O}{||}}{C}OH$
(c) $(CH_3)_3COH$ (d) $(CH_3)_2CHOH$

52. Aldehyde group can be protected against alkaline oxidising agents by
(a) acetal formation (b) mercaptal formation
(c) cyclic acetal formation (d) All of these

53. Hydration formation of the following is in order

$\underset{\text{I}}{CCl_3CHO}$, $\underset{\text{II}}{CF_3CHO}$, $\underset{\text{III}}{CH_3\overset{\overset{O}{||}}{C}CH_3}$, $\underset{\text{IV}}{CCl_3\overset{\overset{O}{||}}{C}CH_3}$

(a) I < II < III < IV (b) III < IV < I < II
(c) III < IV < II < I (d) IV < III < I < II

54. Trace the position of enriched oxygen (^{18}O) in

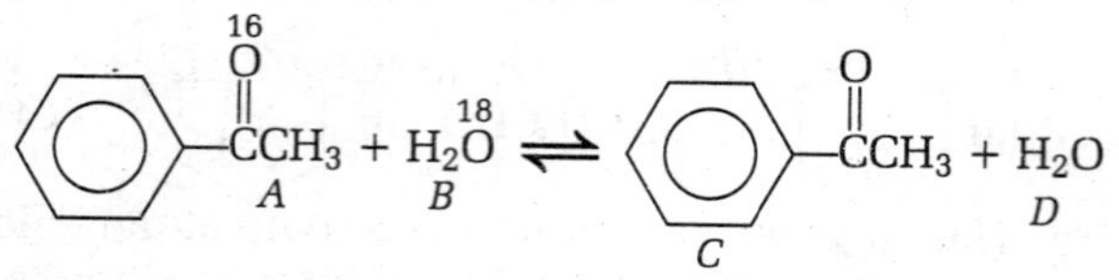

(a) *C* (b) *D*
(c) Both (a) and (b) (d) None of these

55. Which is not the correct comparison for the value of equilibrium constant for hydrate formation ?

(a) 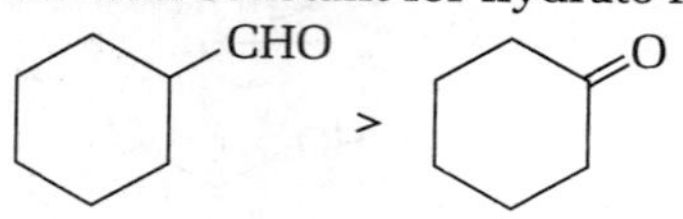

(b) 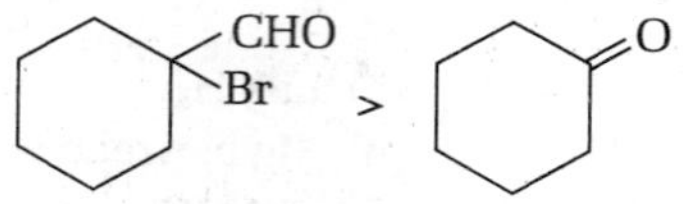

(c) 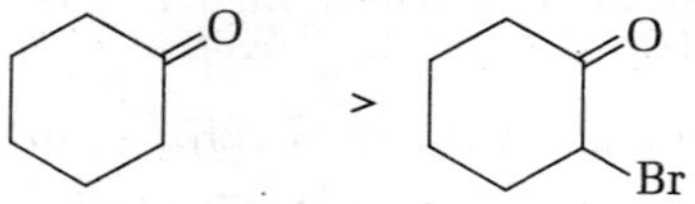

(d) $CH_3CHO > CH_3COCH_3$

56. Crossed Cannizzaro reaction can be given by the following combination
(a) CH_3CHO, $HCHO$
(b) C_6H_5CHO, CH_3CHO
(c) C_6H_5CHO, $HCHO$
(d) All of these

57. The increasing order of the acidity of the α-hydrogen of the following compounds is

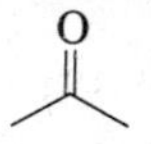

(*A*)

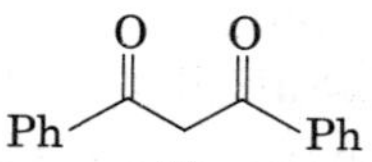

(*B*)

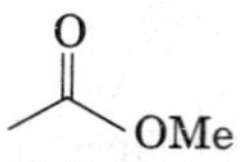

(*C*)

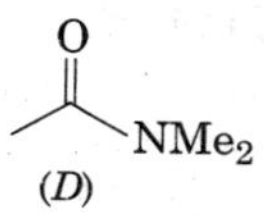

(*D*)

[JEE Main 2020, Sep.]

(a) $(D) < (C) < (A) < (B)$ (b) $(C) < (A) < (B) < (D)$
(c) $(A) < (C) < (D) < (B)$ (d) $(B) < (C) < (A) < (D)$

58. Which statement is not true about Cannizzaro reaction?
(a) It is a disproportionation reaction
(b) It is a proton-hydride transfer reaction
(c) It is given by all the carbonyl compounds
(d) It takes place with 50% aqueous or ethanolic solution

59. By Cannizzaro reaction *A* changes to *B* and *C* as given

$$A \xrightarrow{50\%\ NaOH} \underset{B}{\begin{matrix} COONa \\ | \\ COONa \end{matrix}} + \underset{C}{\begin{matrix} CH_2OH \\ | \\ COONa \end{matrix}}$$

Thus, *A* is

(a) $\begin{matrix} CHO \\ | \\ COOH \end{matrix}$ (b) $\begin{matrix} CHO \\ | \\ CHO \end{matrix}$ (c) $\begin{matrix} CH_2OH \\ | \\ CHO \end{matrix}$ (d) $\begin{matrix} CH_2OH \\ | \\ CH_2OH \end{matrix}$

60. Which is the best hydride donor?

(a) $C_6H_5—\underset{\underset{OH}{|}}{\overset{\overset{H}{|}}{C}}—O^{\ominus}$ (b) $C_6H_5—\underset{\underset{O^{\ominus}}{|}}{\overset{\overset{H}{|}}{C}}—O^{\ominus}$

(c) $C_6H_5-CH_2-Cl$ (d) $C_6H_5-CH{=}O$

61. $C_3H_6O \xrightarrow{OH^-} \xrightarrow[\Delta]{NaHSO_4} CH_3CH_2CH{=}C(CH_3)CHO$

Thus, C_3H_6O is

(a) CH_3COCH_3 (b) CH_3CH_2CHO

(c) $CH_2{=}CHCH_2OH$ (d) $CH_3C(OH){=}CH_2$

62. Aldol condensation reaction is not given by

(a) $C_6H_5CH_2CHO$ (b) C_6H_5CHO

(c) CH_3CHO (d) CH_3COCH_3

63. Resonance form of enolate ion (A) of acetone

$\overset{\ominus}{C}H_2-C(=O)-CH_3$ (A) is

(a) $CH_2{=}C(O^{\ominus})-CH_3$ (b) $\overset{\ominus}{C}H_2-C(OH){=}CH_2$

(c) Both (a) and (b) (d) None of these

64. What is the final product of the following crossed aldol condensation?

$CH_3CHO + CH_3CH_2COCH_3 \xrightarrow{OH^-} \xrightarrow{\Delta}$

(a) $CH_3CH{=}CHCH_2COCH_3$ (b) $CH_3CH_2C(CH_3){=}CHCH_3$

(c) $CH_3CH{=}C(CH_3)COCH_3$ (d) $CH_3CH{=}CHCH{=}CHCH_3$

65. $CH_3CHO + 3HCHO \xrightarrow[I]{OH^-} (CH_2OH)_3CCHO$

$\xrightarrow[II]{OH^-} (CH_2OH)_4C + (CH_2OH)_3CCOONa$

Reactions at stages I and II are respectively

(a) Cannizzaro, aldol (b) aldol, aldol

(c) Cannizzaro, Cannizzaro (d) aldol, Cannizzaro

66. Benzophenone and benzaldehyde can be distinguished by

(a) Tollen's solution (b) Fehling's solution

(c) iodoform test (d) 2,4-DNP solution

67. Acetaldehyde and benzaldehyde can be distinguished by

(a) Tollen's reagent (b) Fehling's solution

(c) iodoform test (d) Both (b) and (c)

68. Benzoin is formed by

(a) bezophenone (b) benzaldehyde

(c) acetophenone (d) quinone

69. Which of the following does not give iodoform test ?

(a) CH_3CHO (b) $C_6H_5COCH_3$

(c) CH_3COCH_3 (d) C_6H_5CHO

70. Grignard reagent forms 3° alcohol with

(a) benzophenone (b) acetophenone

(c) acetone (d) All of these

71. The reaction of aldehydes and ketones with $LiAlH_4$ and $NaBH_4$ is

(a) nucleophilic addition

(b) nucleophilic substitution

(c) elimination

(d) electrophilic substitution

72. $CH_3CHO + LiAlH_4 \longrightarrow CH_3CH_2OH$

Nucleophile added in this reaction is

(a) AlH_4^- (b) Li^+ (c) H^+ (d) H^-

73. $CH_3COCH_2CH_2CH_2Cl \xrightarrow[(ii)\ H_3O^+]{(i)\ CH_3MgBr} A$, A is

(a) $CH_3C(CH_3)(OH)CH_2CH_2CH_2Cl$ (b) $CH_3COCH_2CH_2CH_2CH_3$

(c) 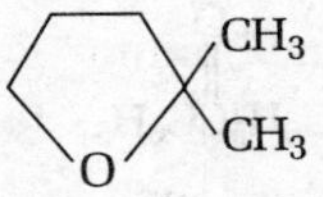

(d) 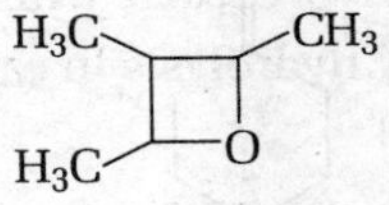

74. 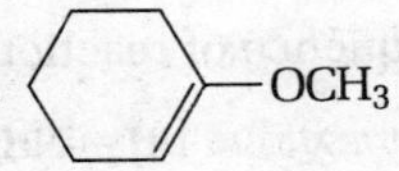 $\xrightarrow{H_3O^{\oplus}} A$, A is

(a) 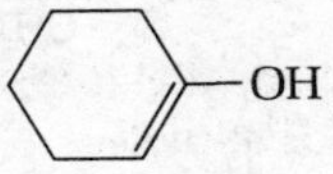 (b) 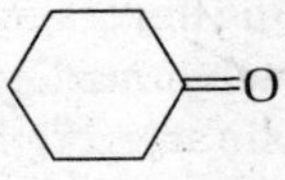

(c) 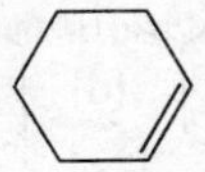 (d) 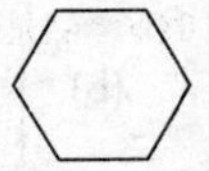

75. Maximum hydration takes place that of

(a) CF_3COCF_3 (b) CH_3COCH_3

(c) $CH_3CH(Cl)COCH_3$ (d) $C_6H_5COC_6H_5$

76. The increasing order of the reactivity of the following compounds in nucleophilic addition reaction is :

Propanal, Benzaldehyde, Propanone, Butanone

[JEE Main 2020, Sep.]

(a) Benzaldehyde < Butanone < Propanone < Propanal

(b) Butanone < Propanone < Benzaldehyde < Propanal
(c) Propanal < Propanone < Butanone < Benzaldehyde
(d) Benzaldehyde < Propanal < Propanone < Butanone

77. Hydrolysis product of *A* (given below) is

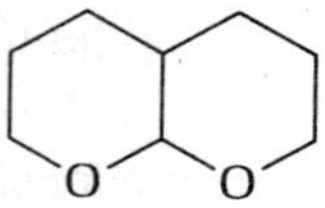

(a) 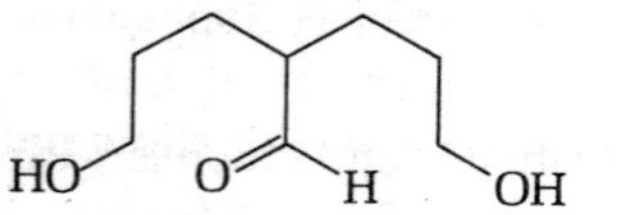

(b) 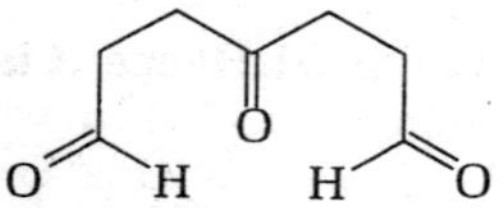

(c) 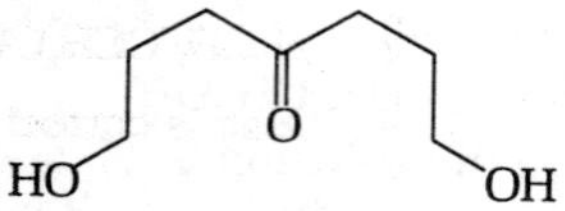

(d) ring is stable hence, no hydrolysis

78. Enolisation is maximum in case of

(a) 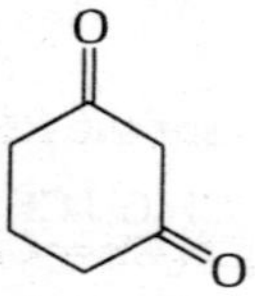

(b) 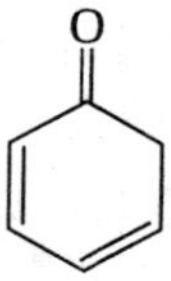

(c) 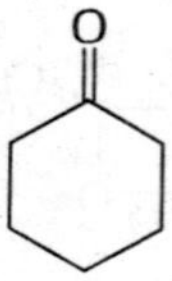

(d) $C_6H_5\overset{O}{\overset{\|}{C}}C_6H_5$

79. End product in the following sequence of reaction is

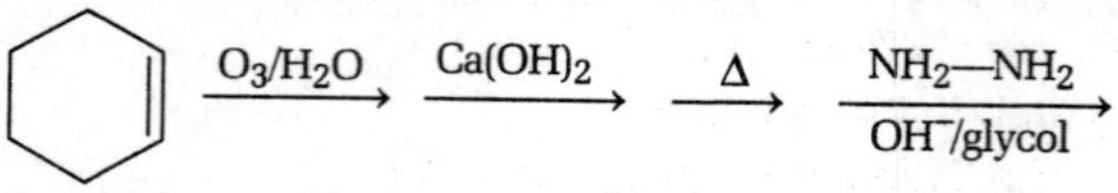

(a) 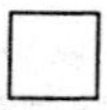 (b) 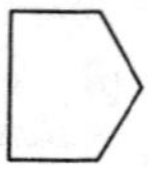 (c) 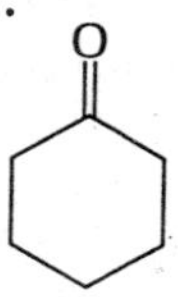 (d) 

80. $2\begin{array}{l}COOH\\|\\CHO\end{array} \xrightarrow{NaOH} \begin{array}{l}COOH\\|\\CH_2OH\end{array} + \begin{array}{l}COOH\\|\\COONa\end{array}$; it is

(a) crossed Cannizzaro reaction
(b) intermolecular Cannizzaro reaction
(c) intramolecular Cannizzaro reaction
(d) None of the above

81. Fehling's solution can make distinction between

(a) CH_3CHO and C_6H_5CHO
(b) CH_3CHO and $CH_3\underset{\|}{\underset{O}{C}}CH_2OH$
(c) $CH_3\underset{OH}{\underset{|}{C}H}\underset{O}{\underset{\|}{C}}CH_3$ and HCHO
(d) CH_3CHO and HCHO

82. 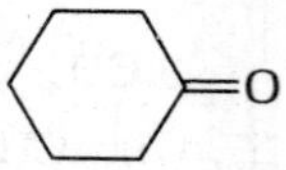 $\xrightarrow[\text{(aldol)}]{NaOH,\ \Delta}$ *A*, *A* can be

(a) 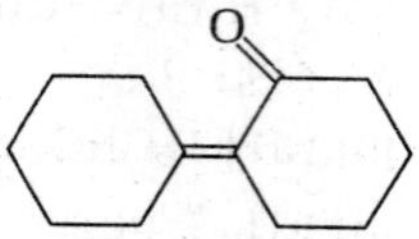 (b) 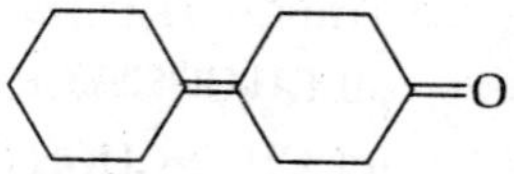

(c) 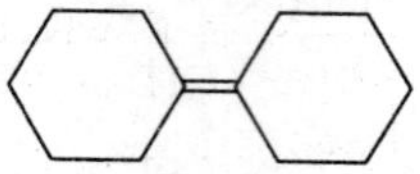 (d) 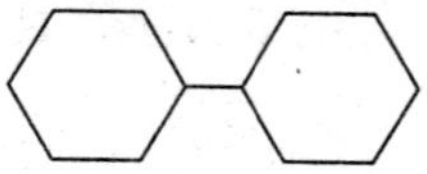

83. $CH_3CH_2CHO \xrightarrow[\text{(aldol)}]{NaOH,\ \Delta} A$, *A* is

(a) $CH_3CH_2CH{=}CHCH_2CHO$ (b) $CH_3CH_2CH{=}\overset{CH_3}{\overset{|}{C}}CHO$

(c) $CH_3CH_2\underset{OH}{\underset{|}{C}H}CH_2CH_2CHO$ (d) $CH_3CH_2\underset{OH}{\underset{|}{C}H}\overset{CH_3}{\overset{|}{C}H}CHO$

84. Greatest amount of hydration is in

(a) 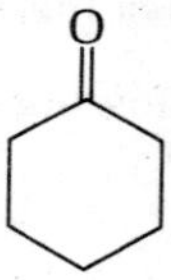 (b) 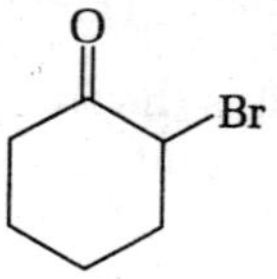

(c) 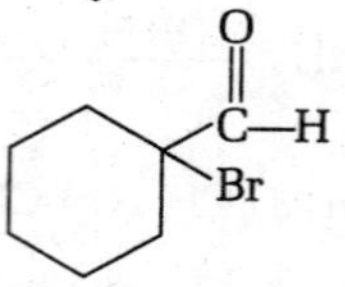 (d) equal

85. $2D-\overset{D}{\overset{|}{C}}=O + OH^- \xrightarrow{\text{Cannizzaro}}$ *X* and *Y* (*Y* is alcohol, D is deuterium)
X and *Y* will have structure

(a) $D-\overset{O}{\overset{\|}{C}}-O^-$, $D-\overset{D}{\overset{|}{\underset{D}{\underset{|}{C}}}}-OH$

(b) $D-\overset{O}{\overset{\|}{C}}-O^-$, $D-\overset{D}{\overset{|}{\underset{H}{\underset{|}{C}}}}-OH$

(c) $H-\overset{O}{\overset{\|}{C}}-O^-$, $D-\overset{D}{\overset{|}{\underset{D}{\underset{|}{C}}}}-OH$

(d) None of the above are correct

86. $CH_3MgBr + CH_2{=}CH{-}\overset{O}{\overset{\|}{C}}{-}H \xrightarrow{H_3O^+}$ product (1 : 4 addition). It is

(a) $CH_2{=}CH{-}C(OH)(CH_3){-}H$ (b) $CH_2CH{=}CH{-}CH_3$ with OH on the first carbon

(c) $CH_3CH_2CH_2CHO$ (d) None is correct

87. Aldehyde $A(C_4H_8O) \xrightarrow[\text{Tischenko}]{\text{Al-}t\text{-butoxide}} B(\text{ester}) \xrightarrow{H_3O^+}$

$(H_3C)_2CHCOOH + (H_3C)_2CHCH_2OH$

A and *B* are

(a) $(H_3C)_2CHCHO$, $(H_3C)_2CHCOOCH_2CH(CH_3)_2$

(b) $(H_3C)_2CHCHO$, $CH_3CHCOOCH(CH_3)_2$

(c) Both (a) and (b)

(d) None of the above is correct

88. $CH_2{-}CHCH_3$ (epoxide, bridged by O) $+ PCl_5 \longrightarrow A$,

$CH_3CH_2CHO + PCl_5 \longrightarrow B$, *A* and *B* are

(a) *vic* halides (b) *gem* halides

(c) *A gem* halide, *B vic* halide

(d) *A vic* halide, *B gem* halide

89. $CH_3CN \xrightarrow[\text{(ii) } H_3O^+]{\text{(i) } CH_3MgBr \text{ (2 mol)}} A \xrightarrow{\text{conc. } H_2SO_4} B$; *A* and *B* are

(a) CH_3COCH_3, 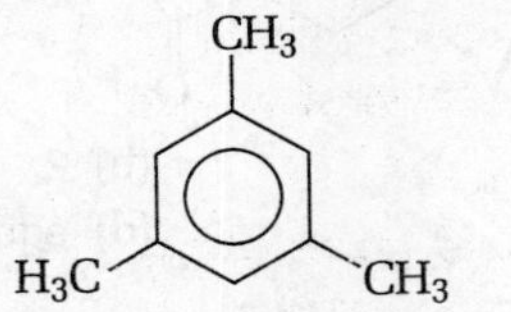

(b) $(CH_3)_3COH$, $(CH_3)_2C{=}CH_2$

(c) $(CH_3)_2CHOH$, $CH_3CH{=}CH_2$

(d) None of the above is correct

90. Which one of the following is correct regarding an acetal?

(a) It is the condensation product from 2 molecules of aldehyde

(b) It is the condensation product from 2 molecules of ketone

(c) It is the condensation product from 2 molecules of alcohol

(d) It is a diether

91. The reaction $C_6H_4CH{=}CHCHO$ with $NaBH_4$ yields

(a) $C_6H_5CH_2CH_2CH_2OH$ (b) $C_6H_5CH{=}CHCH_2OH$

(c) $C_6H_5CH_2CH_2CHO$ (d) $C_6H_5CH_2CHOHCH_3$

92. A, β-hydroxy carbonyl compound is obtained by the action of NaOH on

(a) $R_3C{\cdot}CHO$ (b) C_6H_5CHO

(c) CH_3CHO (d) HCHO

93. $\underset{A}{C_6H_{10}O_3}$ (keto ester) $\xrightarrow[\Delta]{NaOH + I_2}$ yellow ppt. + *B*

$B \xrightarrow{H^+} C \xrightarrow[-CO_2]{\Delta} CH_3COOH$. Hence, *A* is

(a) $CH_3\overset{O}{\overset{\|}{C}}CH_2\overset{O}{\overset{\|}{C}}OC_2H_5$ (b) $CH_3CH_2\overset{O}{\overset{\|}{C}}CH_2\overset{O}{\overset{\|}{C}}OCH_3$

(c) Both are correct (d) None is correct

94. Oppenauer oxidation

(a) is used to prepare ketone

(b) uses aluminium *t*-butoxide as catalyst

(c) Both are correct

(d) None of the above is correct

95. Suggest suitable oxidising reagents for the following conversions

I. $CH_3CH_2CH{=}CHCH_2OH \longrightarrow CH_3CH_2CH{=}CHCHO$

II. 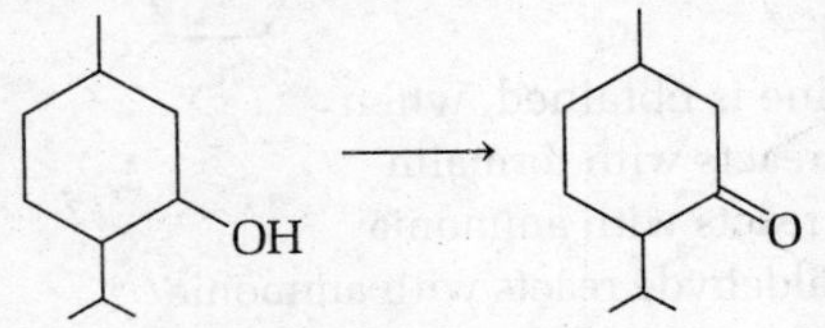

(a) MnO_2 in I and CrO_3 (in glacial acetic acid) in II

(b) CrO_3 in I and MnO_2 in II

(c) Both are correct

(d) None of the above is correct

96. Aldehyde group can be protected

(a) by acetal formation against attack by alkaline oxidising agents

(b) by mercaptal formation against attack by acidic oxidising agents

(c) Both statements are correct

(d) None of the above is correct

97. $CH_3CH{=}CH\,CHO \xrightarrow[\text{aldol}]{OH^-} \xrightarrow{\Delta} A$, *A* is

(a) $CH_3(CH{=}CH)_3CHO$

(b) $CH_3CH_2CH_2(CH{=}CH)_2CHO$

(c) $CH_3(CH_2CH_2)_3CH{=}CH{-}CHO$

(d) None of the above is correct

98. Mixture of CH_3CH_2OH and CH_3CHO can be separated by using

(a) $NaHSO_3$ (b) NH_2OH

(c) HCN (d) $NH_2{-}NH_2$

99. End product of the following sequence of reactions is

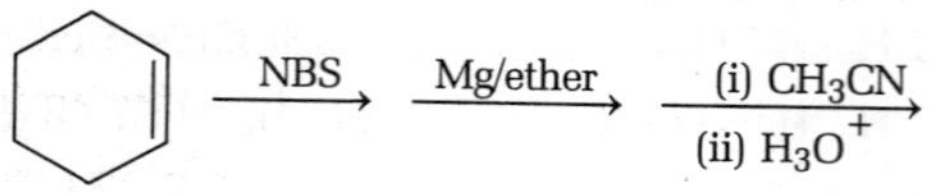

(a) 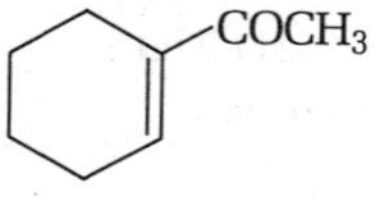

(b) 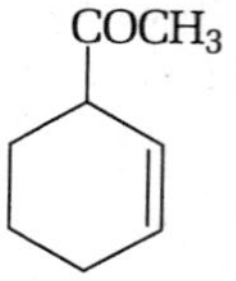

(c) 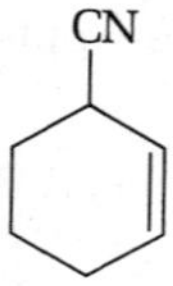

(d) 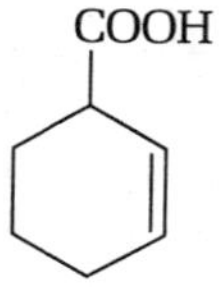

100. 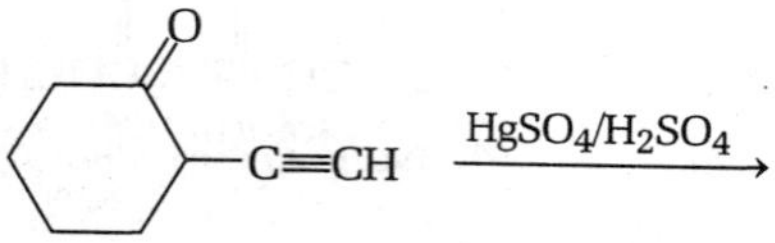

A, *A* is

(a) 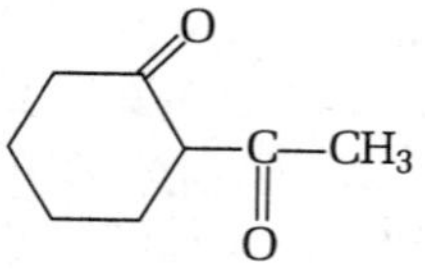

(b) 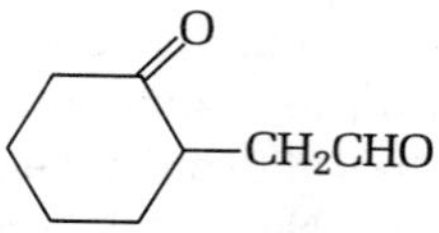

(c) 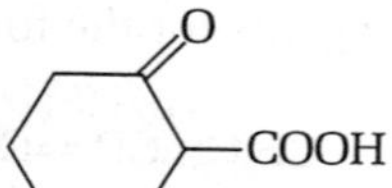

(d) 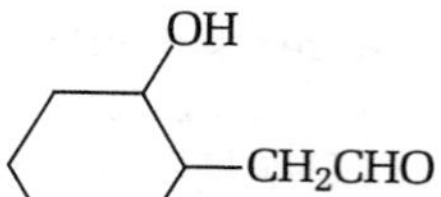

101. Urotropine is obtained, when
(a) urea reacts with formalin
(b) urea reacts with ammonia
(c) formaldehyde reacts with ammonia
(d) acetone reacts with ammonia

102. At room temperature, formaldehyde changes to
(a) trioxane which does not reduce Tollen's reagent
(b) paraldehyde
(c) hexose
(d) None of the above is correct

103. What are *A*, *B* and *C* in the following?

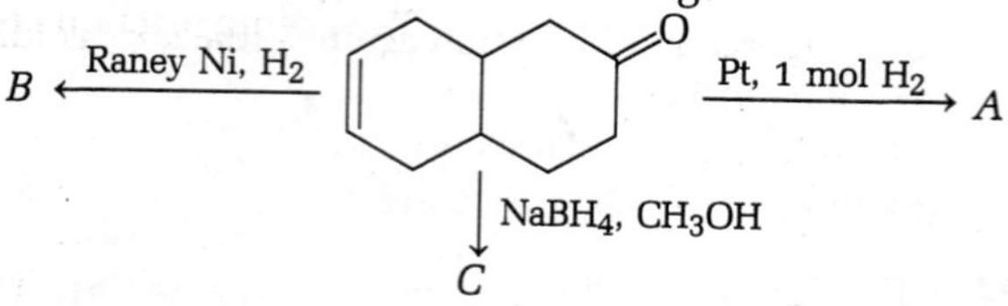

(a) 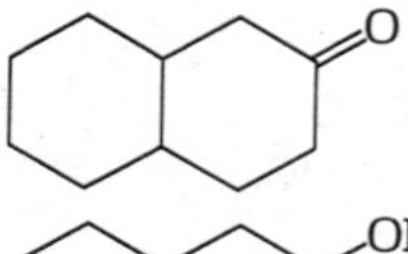

in all cases

(b) 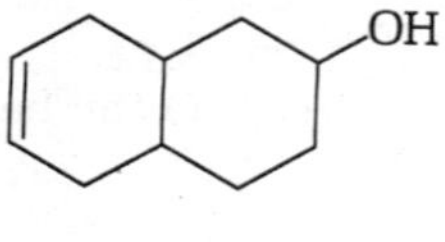

in all cases

(c) 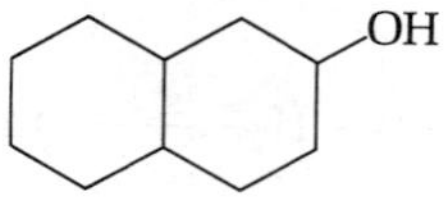

in all cases

(d) *A* : 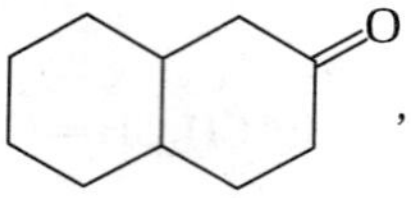

, *B* : 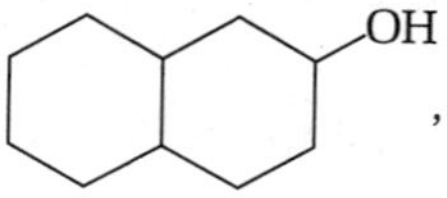

,

C : 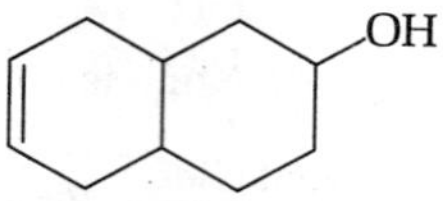

104. Which of the following gives aldol condensation reaction?
(a) $(CH_3)_3CCHO$
(b) CCl_3CHO
(c) 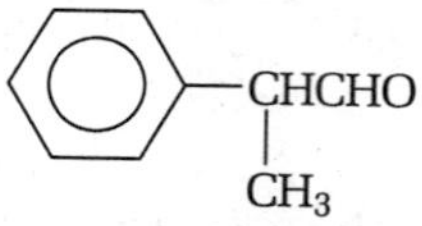

(d) 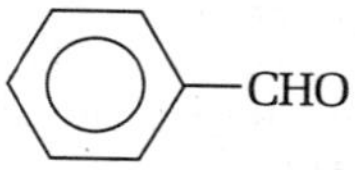

105. $CH_3—\underset{\underset{O}{\|}}{C}—CH_2—CH_2—CH_2—\underset{\underset{O}{\|}}{C}—CH_3 \xrightarrow{OH^-,\ \Delta} A$
(formed by aldol condensation) is

(a) 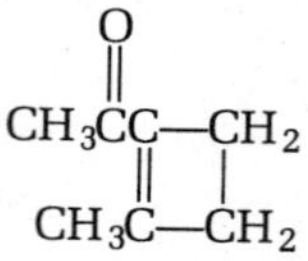

(b) 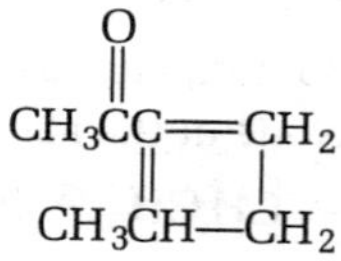

(c) 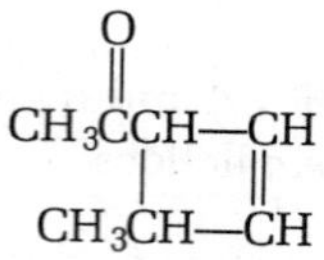

(d) None of these

106. Following is hydrated maximum at the position

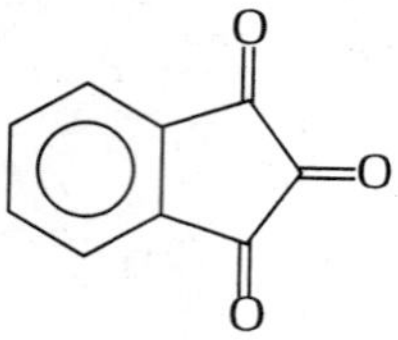

(a) 1
(b) 2
(c) 3
(d) equal

107. $C_2H_5O—\overset{\overset{O}{\|}}{C}—OC_2H_5 \xrightarrow{2CH_3MgBr} A$. Product *A* formed can
(a) give iodoform test
(b) further react with CH_3MgBr / H_3O^+ to give *t*-butyl alcohol
(c) be obtained by the ozonolysis of 2,3-dimethyl-2-butene
(d) give all the above reactions

108. 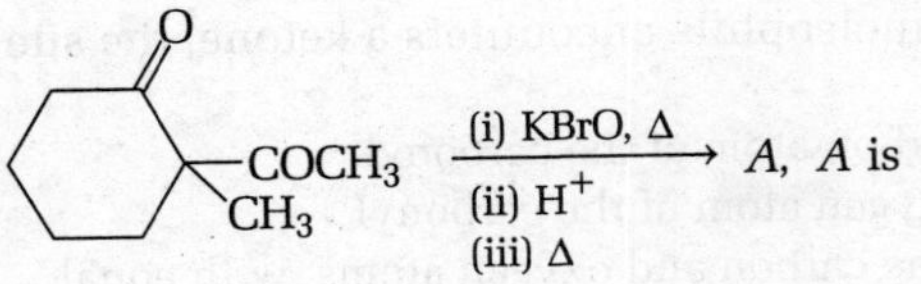

(a) 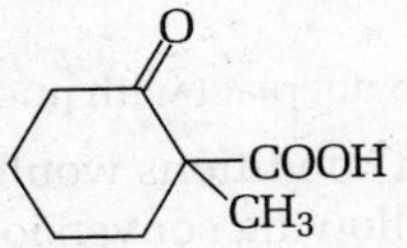 (b) 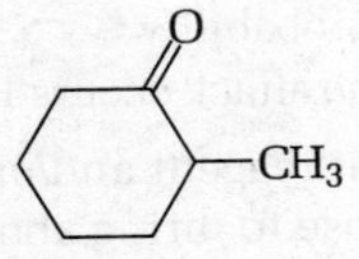

(c) 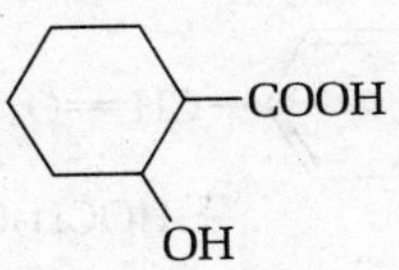 (d) 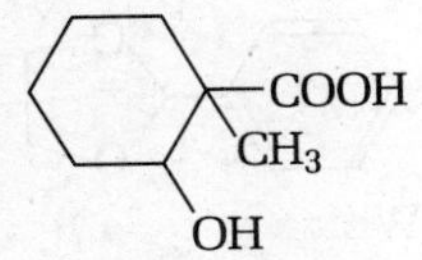

109. Product of the following reaction is

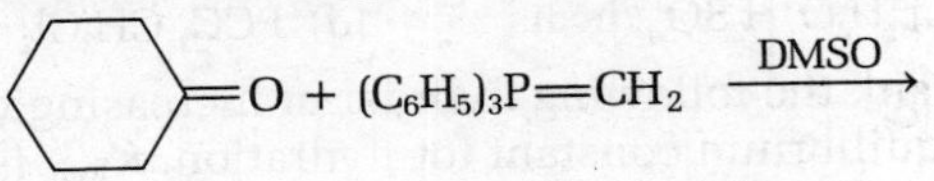

(a) 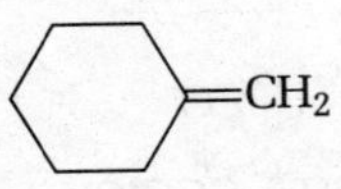 (b) 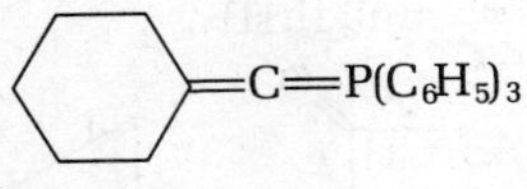

(c) Both (a) and (b) (d) None of these

110. $2CH_3\overset{O}{\overset{\|}{C}}OC_2H_5 \xrightarrow{C_2H_5ONa} A$, A is formed by Claisen condensation; which is/are true about A?

(a) A forms oximes (b) A shows tautomerism
(c) A shows iodoform test (d) All true

111. In the reaction $CH_3CHO + HCN \longrightarrow CH_3CH(OH)CN$, a chiral centre is produced. This product is

(a) *meso* compound (b) *laevo* rotatory
(c) *dextro* rotatory (d) racemic mixture

112. Which one of the following product is formed when calcium salt of adipic acid is heated?

(a) 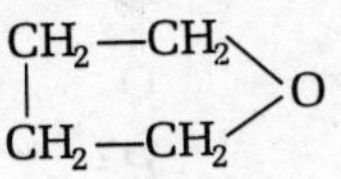 (b) 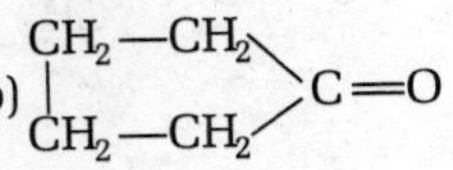

(c) 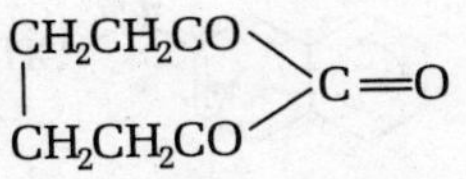 (d) 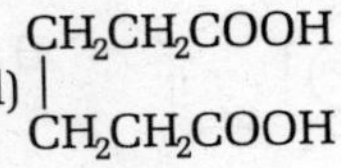

113. Aldol condensation will not take place in

(a) HCHO (b) CH_3CH_2CHO
(c) CH_3CHO (d) CH_3COCH_3

114. Ketones $[R-\underset{\underset{O}{\|}}{C}-R_1]$, where, $R = R_1$ = alkyl group, can be obtained in one step by

(a) hydrolysis of esters
(b) oxidation of primary alcohol
(c) oxidation of secondary alcohol
(d) reaction of acid halide with alcohols

115. In the reaction

$$CH_3CN + 2H \xrightarrow[SnCl_2]{HCl} X \xrightarrow{\text{Boiling } H_2O} Y$$, The term Y is

(a) acetone (b) ethanamine
(c) acetaldehyde (d) dimethyl amine

116. Cyanohydrin of which of the following forms lactic acid?

(a) HCHO (b) CH_3CHO
(c) CH_3CH_2CHO (d) CH_3COCH_3

117. Which pair can be distinguished by using Tollen's reagent?

(a) Ethanol and propanol
(b) Ethanoic acid and propanone
(c) Ethanoic acid and propanal
(d) Methanol and methanoic acid

118. Acetaldehyde does not respond to

(a) Tollen's test (b) Benedict's test
(c) Lucas test (d) iodoform test

119. The reaction sequence.

$$CH_3CH_2COOH \xrightarrow{SOCl_2} A \xrightarrow{LiAlH(O-tBu)_3} B \xrightarrow{HOCH_2CH_2OH} C$$. 'C' is most likely to be

(a) 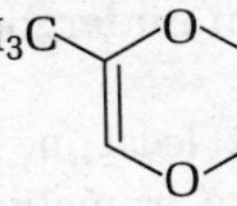 (b) 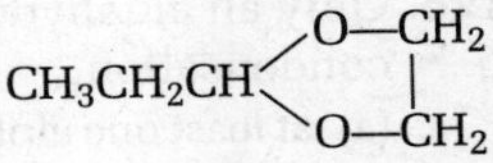

(c) CH_3CH_2CHO (d) 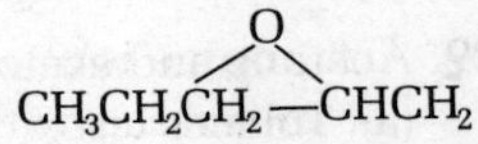

120. An olefin on ozonolysis yields a mixture of acetone and methyl ethyl ketone. The possible structure of the olefin is

(a) 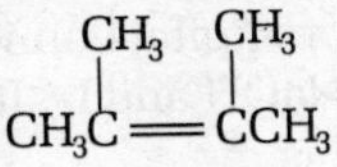 (b) 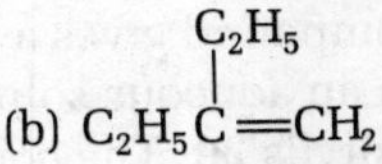

(c) 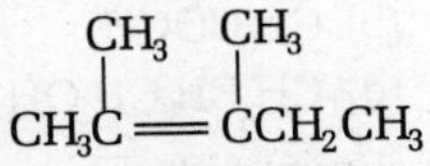 (d) $CH_3CH{=}CHCH_3$

121. The major products of the following reaction are

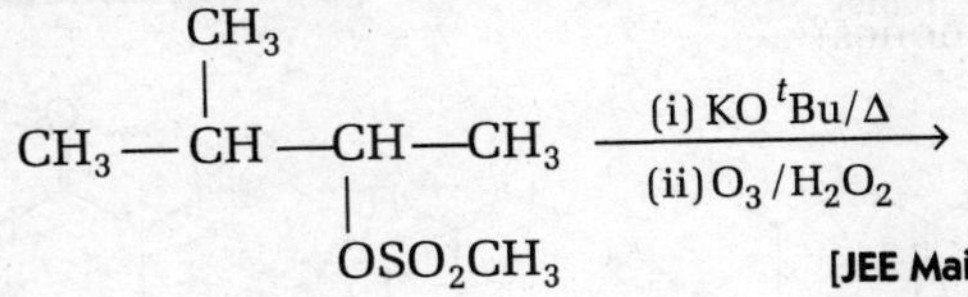

[JEE Main 2020, Sep.]

(a) 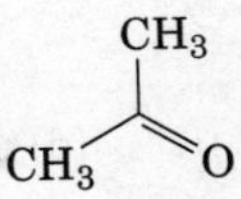 $+ CH_3CHO$ (b) 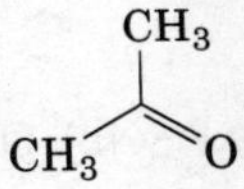 $+ CH_3COOH$

(c) 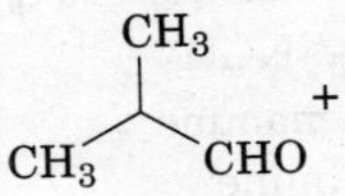 $+ HCHO$ (d) 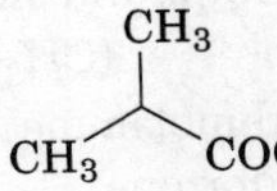 $+ HCOOH$

122. Pure propanone can be prepared by ozonolysis of
(a) 1,2-dimethyl-2-butene (b) 1-pentene
(c) 2-methyl-2-butene (d) 2,3-dimethyl-2-butene

123. Which of the following reacts with iodine in presence of Na_2CO_3 to produce iodoform?
(a) CH_3COONH_4 (b) CH_3COCH_3
(c) CH_3OCH_3 (d) CH_3OH

124. Acetone and methyl magnesium bromide react to produce a product which on hydrolysis gives
(a) *n*-butyl alcohol (b) secondary butyl alcohol
(c) tertiary butyl alcohol (d) None of these

125. When acetaldehyde is heated with Fehling's solution, it gives a precipitate of
(a) Cu_2O (b) $Cu + Cu_2O + CuO$
(c) Cu (d) CuO

126. Schiff's reagent is
(a) rosaniline solution in water decolourised by SO_2
(b) resorcinol solution in dilute HCl
(c) ammoniacal silver nitrate
(d) alkaline $CuSO_4$ stabilised by Rochelle salt

127. Monomer of trioxan is
(a) formaldehyde (b) isoprene
(c) acetone (d) acetaldehyde

128. Only an aldehyde having ... can undergoes the aldol condensation.
(a) at least one alpha H-atom (b) at least one beta H-atom
(c) no alpha H-atom (d) an aromatic ring

129. Acetone and acetophenone can be distinguished by
(a) Tollen's test
(b) DNP test
(c) Schiff's reagent
(d) Saturated solution of $NaHSO_3$

130. A compound gives a yellow precipitate on warming with an aqueous solution of NaOH and I_2. Its vapour density is 29. The compound is
(a) CH_3CH_2CHO (b) CH_3COCH_3
(c) $CH_3CHOHCH_3$ (d) $CH_3CH_2CH_2OH$

131. Which of the compounds shown is (are) correctly named as pentane derivatives, either as pentanals or pentanones?

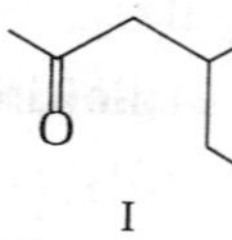
I

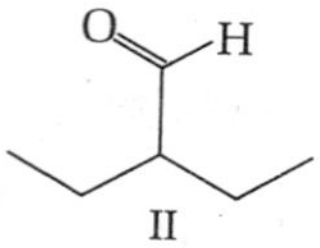
II

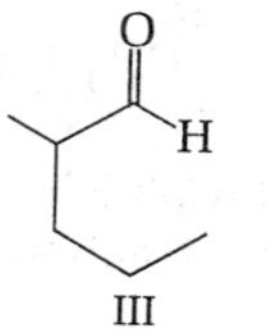
III

(a) Only I (b) Only II (c) Only III (d) I and III

132. The compound shown is best classified as a(an)
$$(CH_3)_3CCH_2CH{=}NCH_3$$
(a) carbinolamine (b) enamine
(c) hydrazone (d) imine

133. When a nucleophile encounters a ketone, the site of attack is
(a) the carbon atom of the carbonyl
(b) the oxygen atom of the carbonyl
(c) both the carbon and oxygen atoms, with equal probability
(d) no attack occurs-ketones do not react with nucleophiles

134. What reagent and/or reaction conditions would you choose to bring about the following conversion?

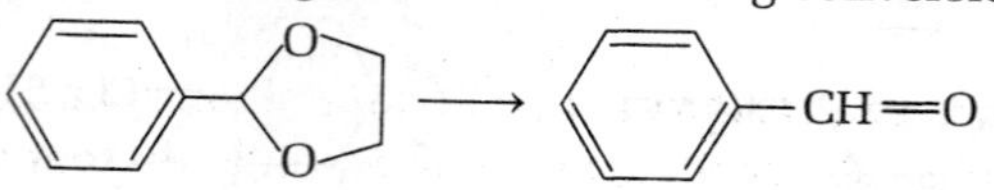

$+ HOCH_2CH_2OH$

(a) $LiAlH_4, H_2O$ (b) H_2O, NaOH, heat
(c) H_2O, H_2SO_4, heat (d) PCC, CH_2Cl_2

135. Rank the following in order of increasing value of the equilibrium constant for hydration, K_{hyd} (smallest value first)

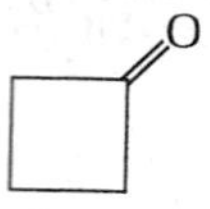
I

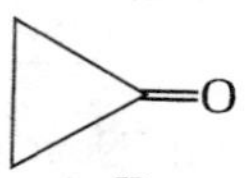
II

$(CH_3)_3C\overset{O}{\overset{\|}{C}}C(CH_3)_3$
III

(a) I < II < III (b) III < I < II
(c) II < I < III (d) II < III < I

136. Final proudct of the reaction is

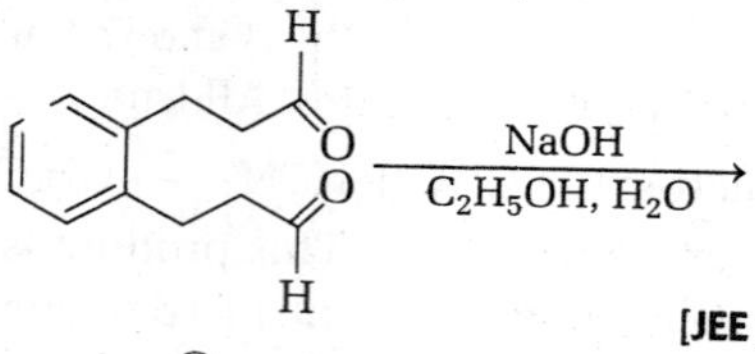

[JEE Main 2021, Feb.]

(a) 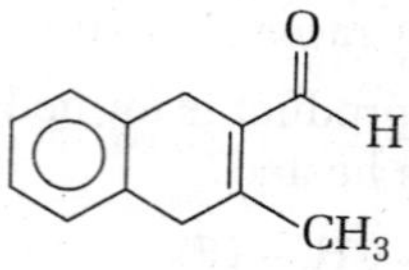 (b) 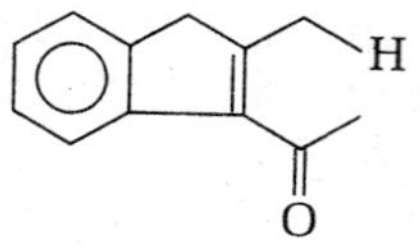

(c) 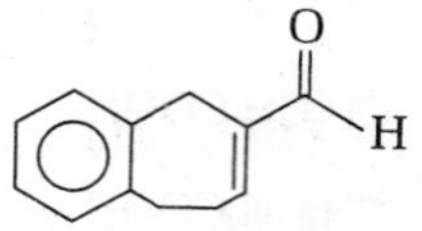 (d) 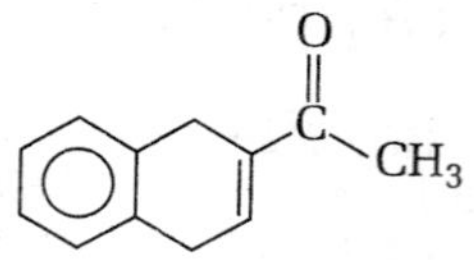

137. Which of the following pairs of reactants is most effective in forming an enamine?
(a) $CH_3CH_2\overset{O}{\overset{\|}{C}}H + [(CH_3)_2CH]_2NH$
(b) $(CH_3)_3C\overset{O}{\overset{\|}{C}}H + (CH_3)_2NH$
(c) 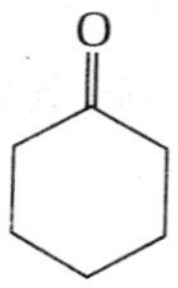 $+ (CH_3)_3CNH_2$
(d) None of the above forms an enamine

Objective Questions Type II [One or more than one correct option(s)]

In each of the questions below, four choices are given, of which one or more than one are correct.

1. Consider the following reaction,

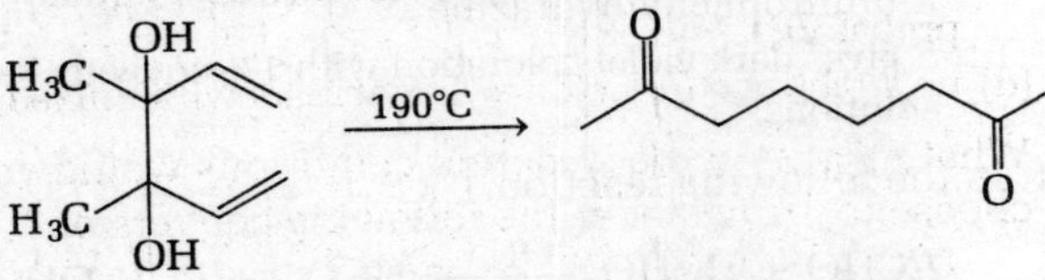

Select correct statement(s) about the reaction.

(a) It is called enol-keto tautomerisation reaction

(b) It is oxy-cope rearrangement

(c) It is a case of 1, 2-methyl shift

(d) It is a case of 1, 2-hydride shift

2. In the following reaction *A* and *B* are

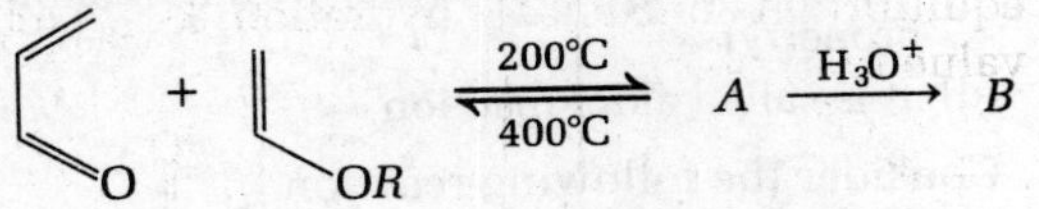

	A	*B*
(a)	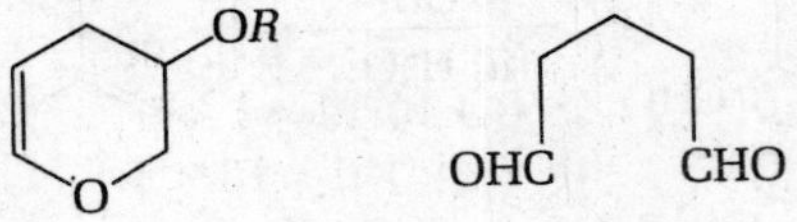	
(b)	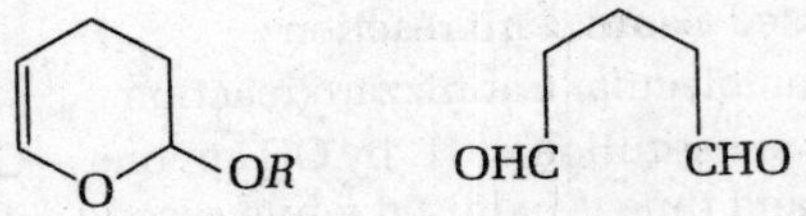	
(c)		
(d)	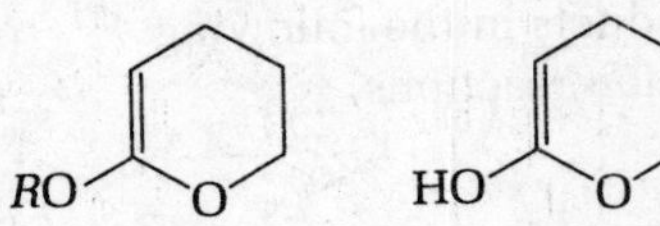	

3. (*A*) can be converted into (*B*) by

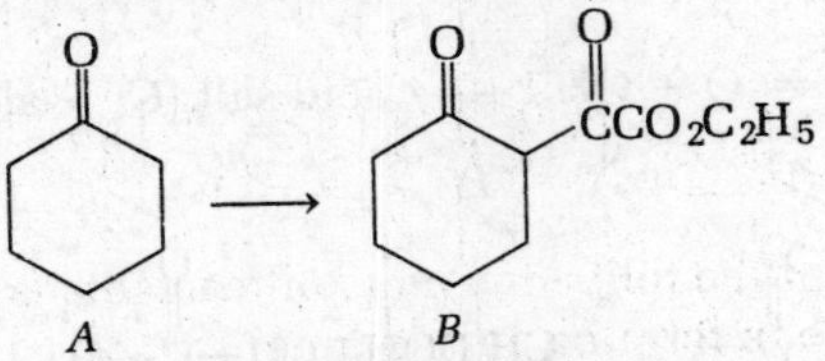

(a) reaction with ethyl carbonate in presence of $C_2H_5OH/NaOC_2H_5$

(b) condensation with diethyloxalate in presence of $C_2H_5OH/NaOC_2H_5$

(c) reaction with oxalic acid followed by reaction with C_2H_5OH

(d) reaction with sodium oxalate followed by reaction with C_2H_5OH

4. (*A*) given below is to be converted into methyl derivative by reaction with (i) C_2H_5ONa/C_2H_5OH (ii) CH_3I. Methylation takes place at position

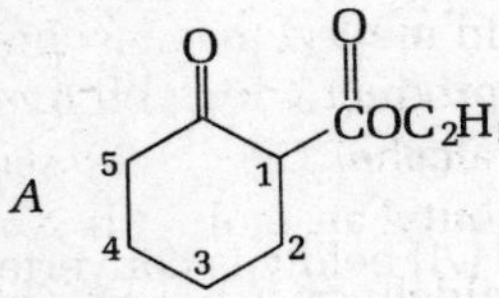

(a) 1 (b) 2

(c) 5 (d) 3

5. Select major product of the following reaction

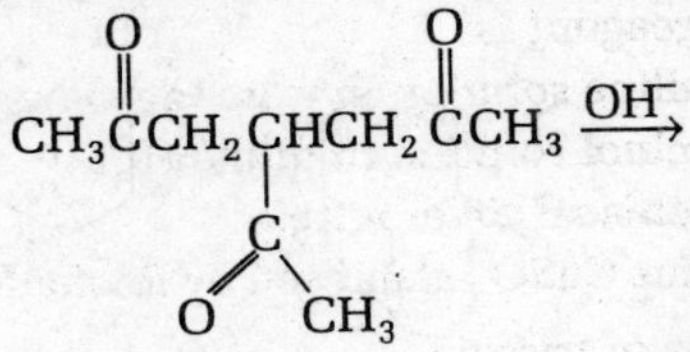

(a) 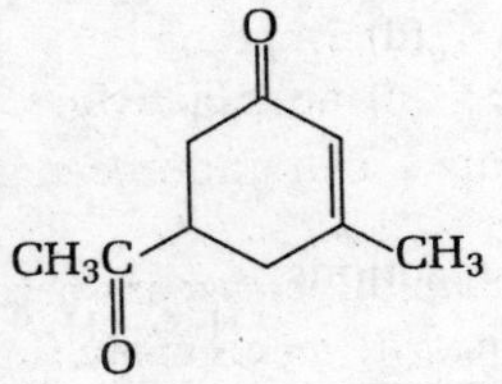

(b) 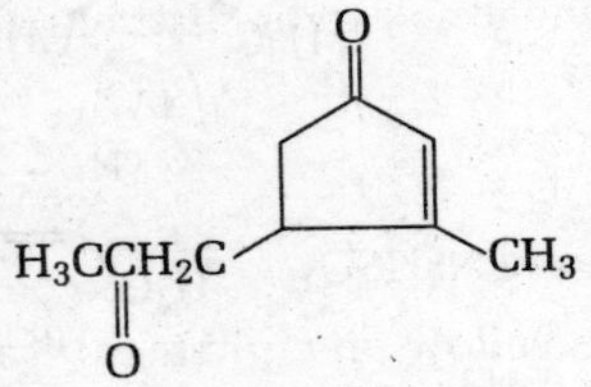

(c) 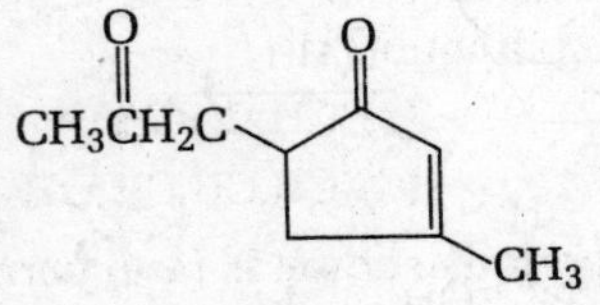

(d) 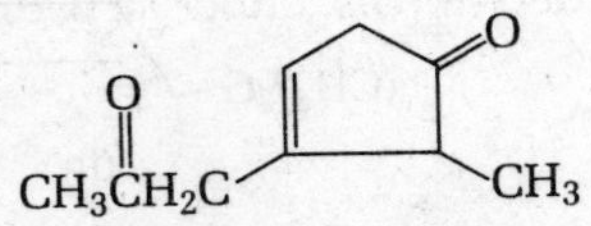

6. Which is the major product in the following reaction?

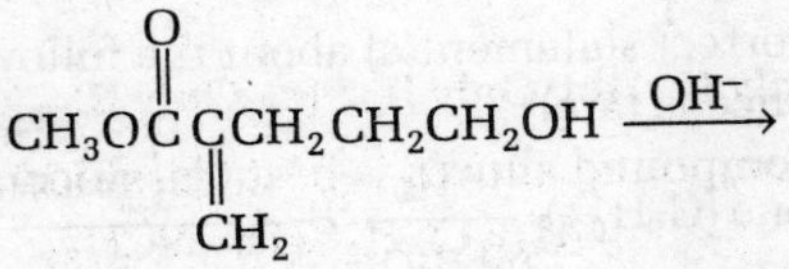

(a) 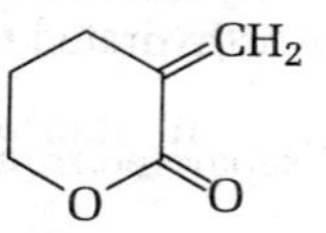

(b) 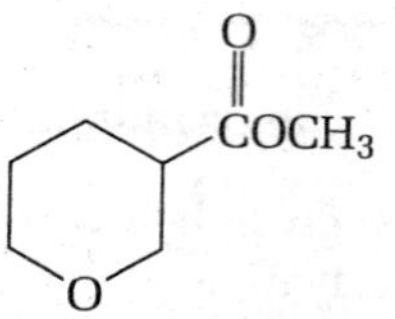

(c) 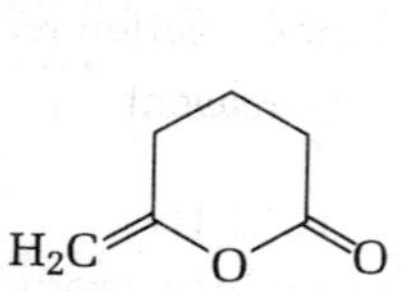

(d) 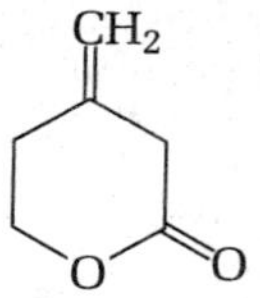

7. Compound (*A*) below is converted into

(*A*) 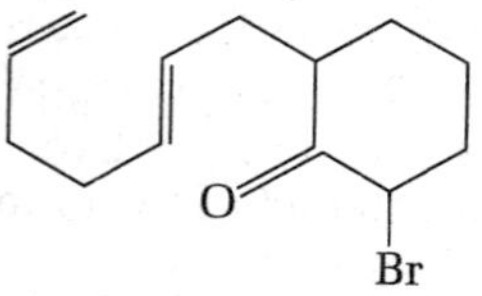

(a) 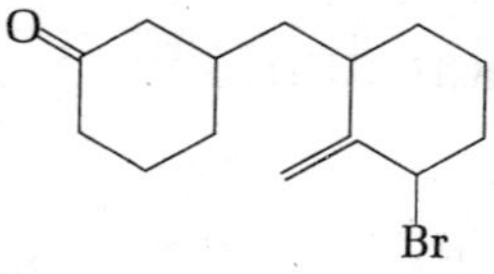

(b) 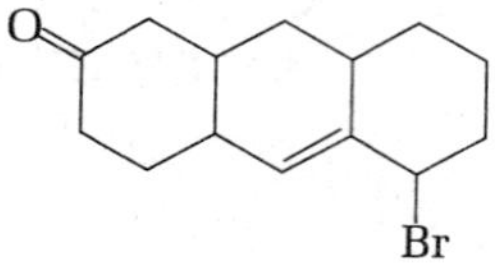

(c) 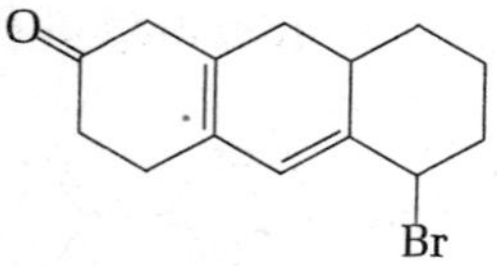

(d) 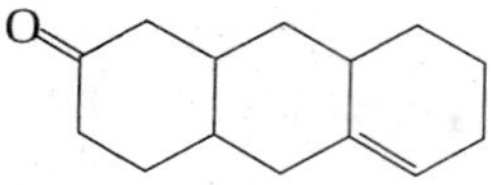

8. Consider the following reactions,

I. 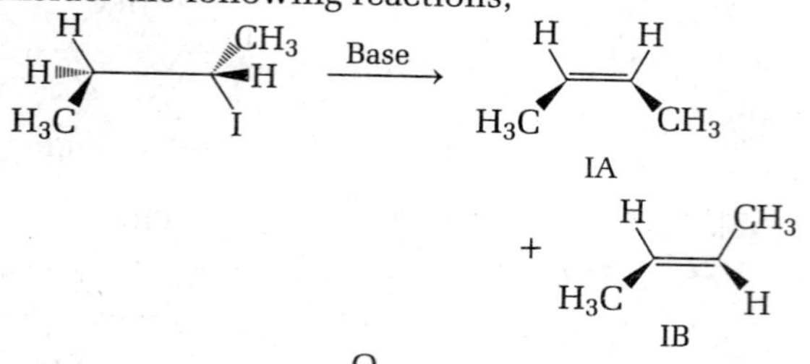

II. 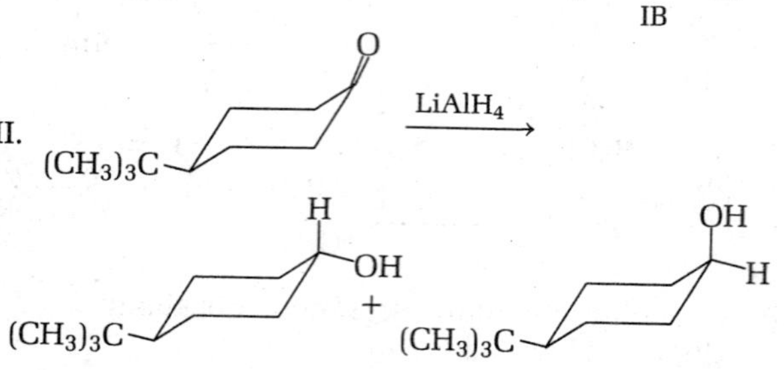

Major products are

(a) IA and IIA
(b) IB and IIB
(c) IA and IIB
(d) IB and IIA

9. The correct statement(s) about the following reaction sequence is (are) **[JEE Advanced 2016]**

$$\text{Cumene } (C_9H_{12}) \xrightarrow[\text{(ii) } H_3O^+]{\text{(i) } O_2} P \xrightarrow{CHCl_3/NaOH} Q\text{ (major)} + R\text{ (minor)}$$

$$Q \xrightarrow[PhCH_2Br]{NaOH} S$$

(a) *R* is steam volatile
(b) *Q* gives dark violet coloration with 1% aqueous $FeCl_3$ solution
(c) *S* gives yellow precipitate with 2, 4-dinitrophenylhydrazine
(d) *S* gives dark violet coloration with 1% aqueous $FeCl_3$ solutions

10. In the following reaction,

$$RCHO + HCHO \xrightarrow{OH^-} HCO_2^- + RCH_2OH$$

HCHO is a hydride donor while another *R*CHO is a hydride acceptor.

(a) It is called crossed redox reaction (Cannizzaro)
(b) It is a disproportionation reaction
(c) Nucleophilic addition reactivity is highest for HCHO hence, it is always oxidised at the expense of other aldehyde (with non-enolisable property)
(d) It is called aldol reaction

11. Consider the following reaction,

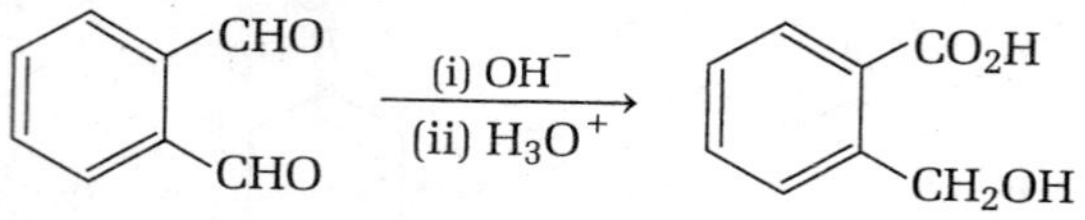

This

(a) is crossed Cannizzaro reaction
(b) is intramolecular Cannizzaro reaction
(c) causes substitution of H^- by OH^- in one —CHO group and thus is oxidised while second —CHO undergoes an addition of H^- and is thus reduced to alcohol
(d) resembles aldol type condensation reaction

12. Identify the products in the following disproportionation reactions.

$$2H{-}\overset{\displaystyle D}{\overset{|}{C}}{=}O + OH^- \longrightarrow \text{acid salt } (A) + \text{alcohol } (B)$$

$$2D{-}\overset{\displaystyle D}{\overset{|}{C}}{=}O + OH^- \longrightarrow \text{acid salt } (C) + \text{alcohol } (D)$$

	A	*B*	*C*	*D*
(a)	$D{-}\overset{\overset{\displaystyle O}{\|}}{C}{-}O^-$	CH_2DOH	$D{-}\overset{\overset{\displaystyle O}{\|}}{C}{-}O^-$	CH_2DOH
(b)	$H{-}\overset{\overset{\displaystyle O}{\|}}{C}{-}O^-$	CH_3OH	$H{-}\overset{\overset{\displaystyle O}{\|}}{C}{-}O^-$	CH_2DOH
(c)	$H{-}\overset{\overset{\displaystyle O}{\|}}{C}{-}O^-$	CH_2DOH	$D{-}\overset{\overset{\displaystyle O}{\|}}{C}{-}O^-$	CH_2DOH
(d)	$D{-}\overset{\overset{\displaystyle O}{\|}}{C}{-}O^-$	CH_2DOH	$D{-}\overset{\overset{\displaystyle O}{\|}}{C}{-}O^-$	CD_3OH

13. Compound (A) given below can undergo intramolecular aldol condensation reaction.

A : 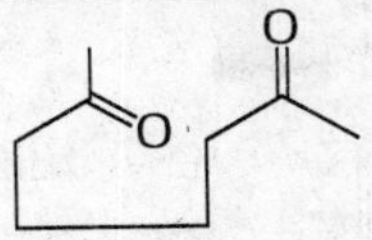

Product formed is

(a) 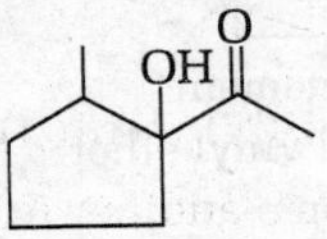 (b) 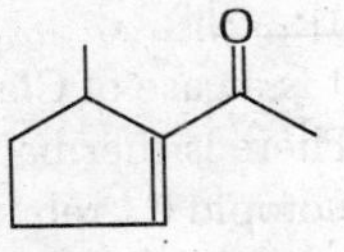

(c) 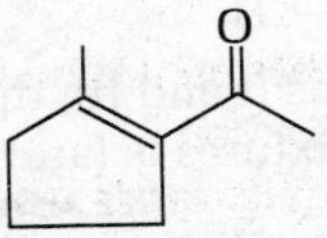 (d) 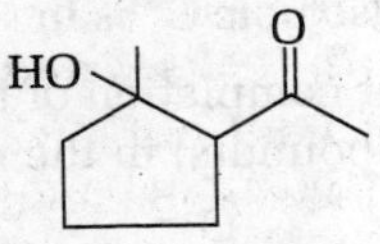

14. Following reaction takes place in two steps.

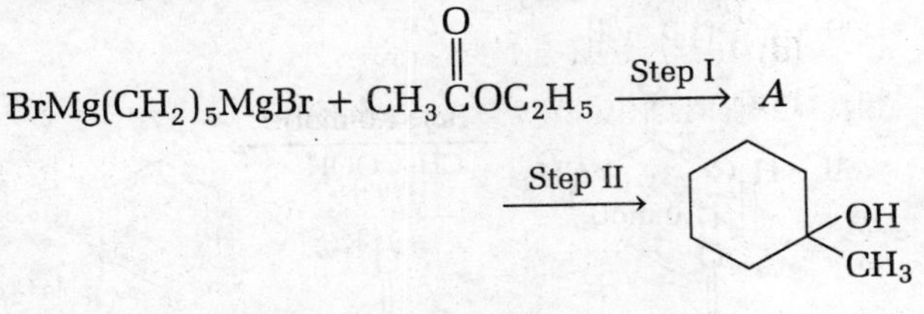

Select correct statement(s) about A.

(a) A contains nucleophile as well as carbonyl group

(b) A contains ester group

(c) A contains only carbonyl group

(d) A can be represented as $BrMg(CH_2)_5\overset{O}{\overset{\|}{C}}CH_3$

15. Consider the following intramolecular aldol condensation reaction.

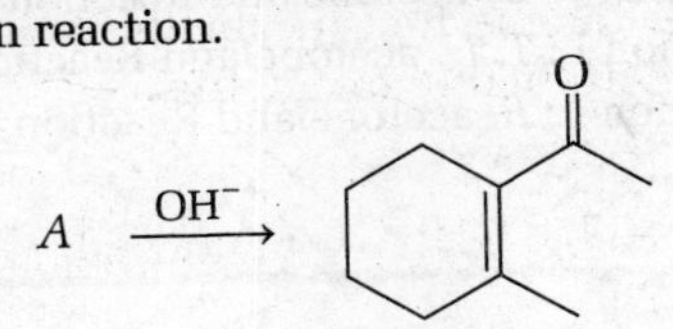

A can be

(a) 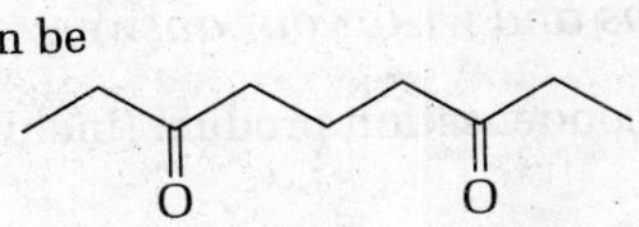

(b) 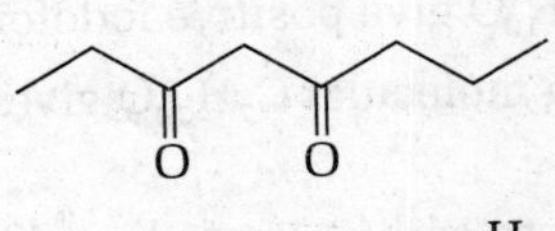

(c) 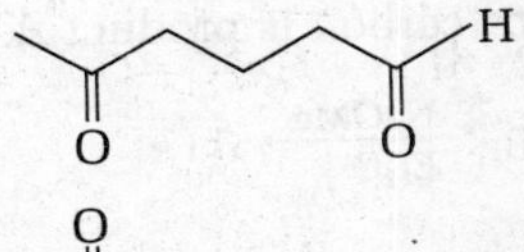

(d) 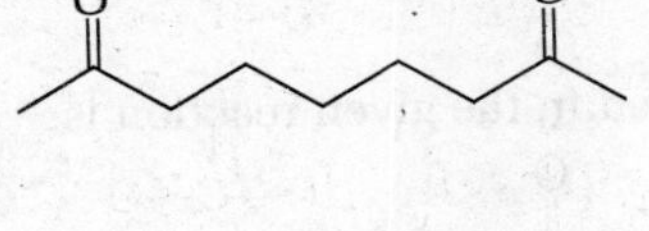

16. Select the correct statements.

(a) Cyclopropanone is completely hydrated in aqueous solution while cyclohexanone is hydrated to a few percent

(b) Carbonyl compounds can be separated from acids by enamine formation

(c) CCl_3CHO undergoes aldol condensation reaction

(d) $CH_3\underset{CH_3}{\underset{|}{C}}HCHO$ reduces Tollen's reagent

17. Compounds P and R upon ozonolysis produce Q and S, respectively. The molecular formula of Q and S is C_8H_8O. Q undergoes Cannizzaro reaction but not haloform reaction, whereas S undergoes haloform reaction but not Cannizzaro reaction. **[JEE Advanced 2017]**

(i) $P \xrightarrow[\text{(ii) } Zn/H_2O]{\text{(i) } O_3/CH_2Cl_2} \underset{(C_8H_8O)}{Q}$

(ii) $R \xrightarrow[\text{(ii) } Zn/H_2O]{\text{(i) } O_3/CH_2Cl_2} \underset{(C_8H_8O)}{S}$

The option(s) with suitable combination of P and R, respectively, it(are)

(a) 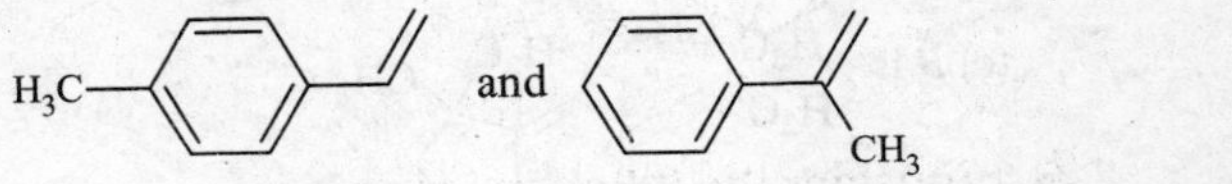

(b) 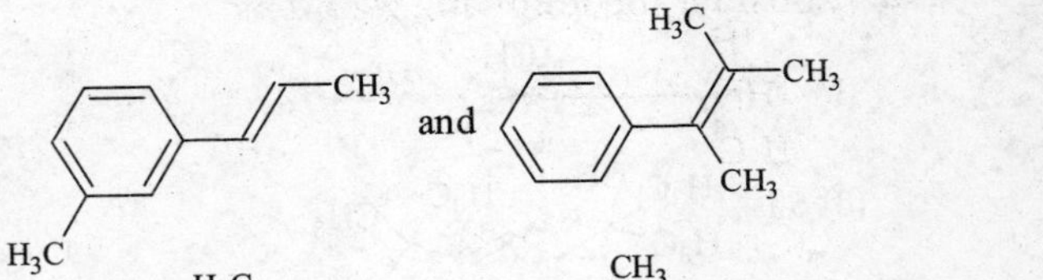

(c) 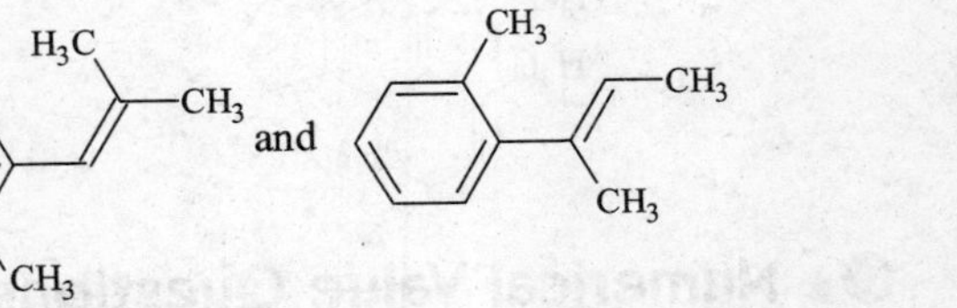

(d) 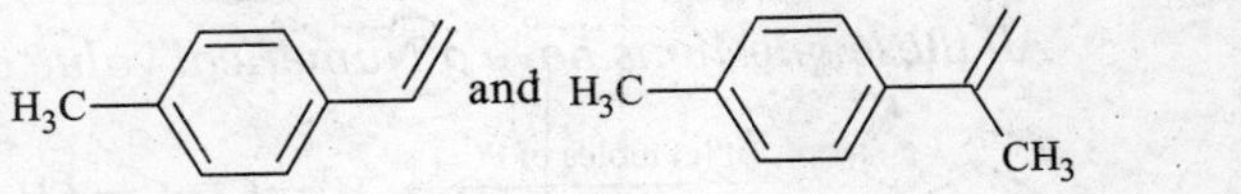

18. Consider the following statements about Wolff-Kishner reduction,

I. It involves hydrazone intermediate.

II. It involves double bond migration under basic conditions and loss of N_2.

III. Reaction is thermodynamically spontaneous as N_2 is formed.

Correct statements are

(a) I and II (b) II and III

(c) I and III (d) I, II and III

19. In the reaction scheme shown below. Q, R and S are the major products **[JEE Advanced 2020]**

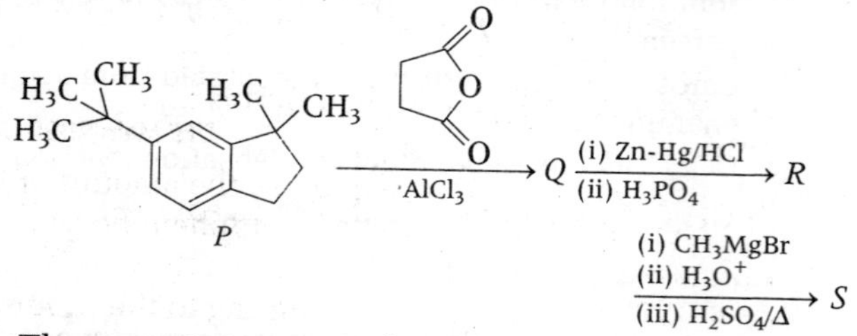

The correct structure of

(a) S is

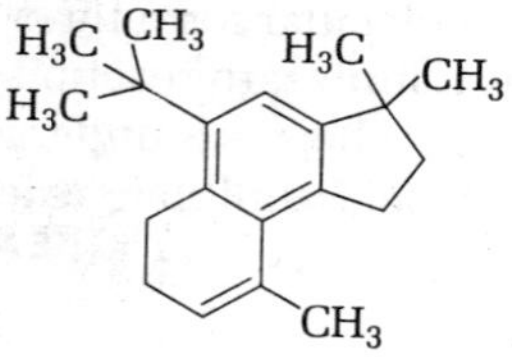

(b) Q is

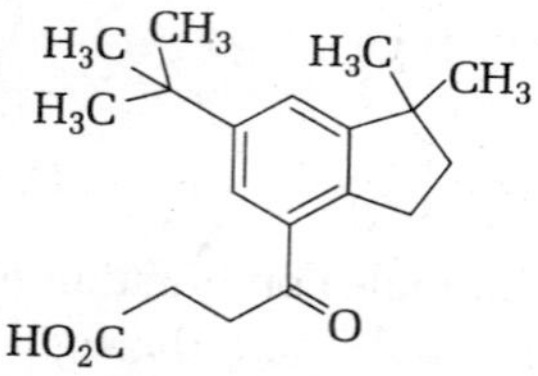

(c) R is

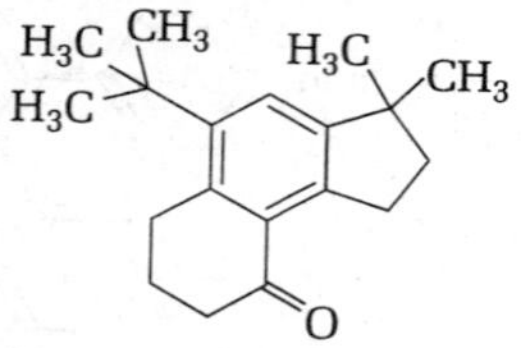

(d) S is

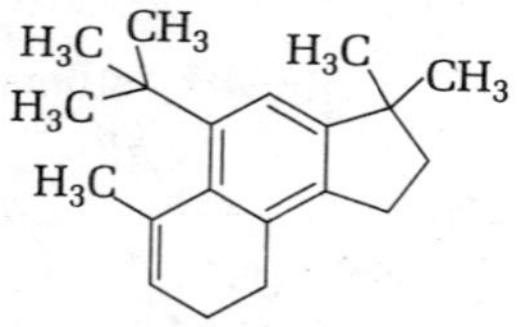

20. Write the correct statements about the following reaction.

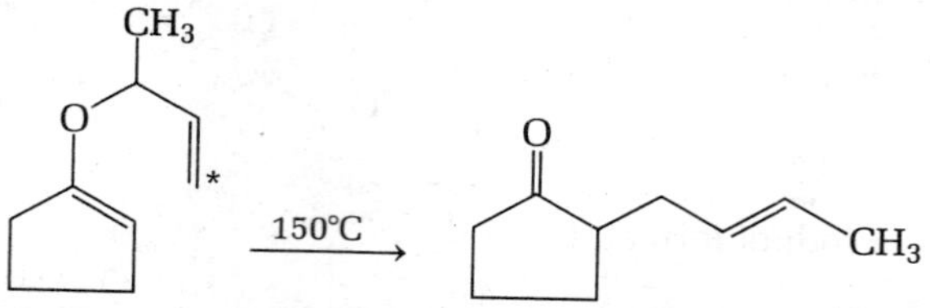

(a) It is a case of Claisen rearrangement
(b) There is thermal shift in allyl vinyl ether
(c) Isotopic C* retains its position
(d) Isotopic C* is in side chain —CH_3

21. After completion of the reactions (I and II), the organic compound(s) in the reaction mixtures is (are) **[JEE Advanced 2013]**

I. 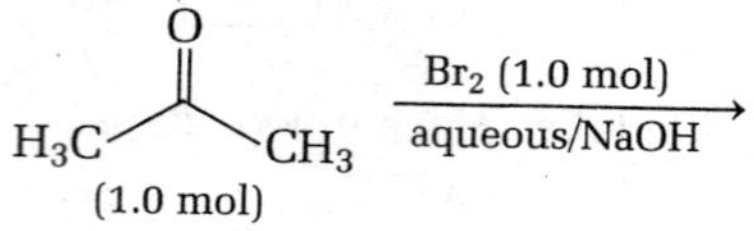

II. 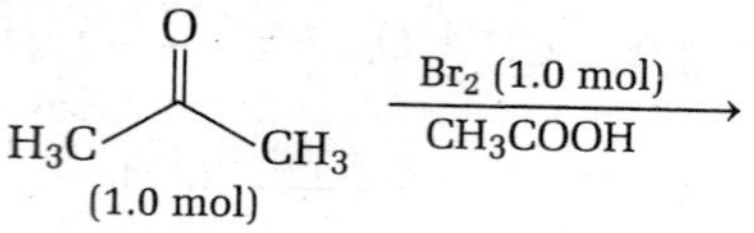

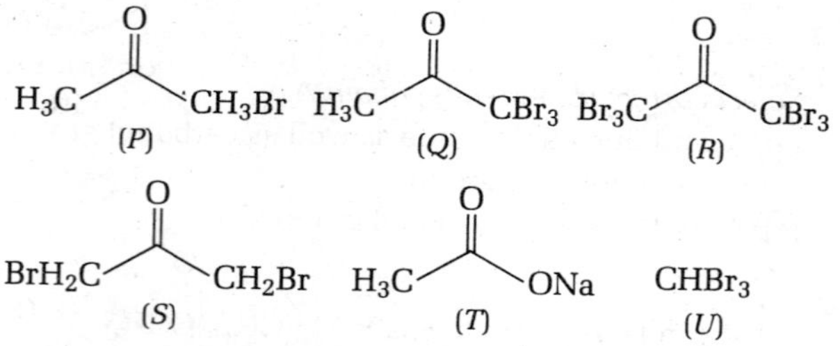

(a) Reaction I : P and Reaction II : P
(b) Reaction I : U, acetone and Reaction II : Q, acetone
(c) Reaction I : T, U, acetone and Reaction II : P
(d) Reaction I : R, acetone and Reaction II : S, acetone

Numerical Value Questions

All these questions have a Numerical value as their answer, solve the questions and write your answer.

1. 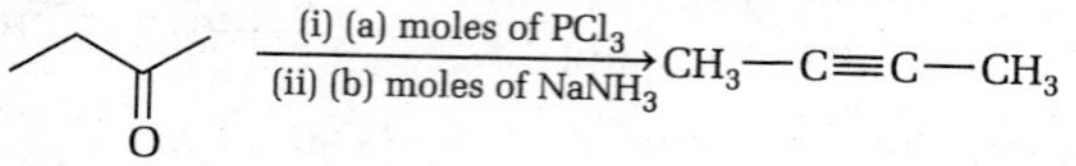

Sum of $(a + b = ?)$

2. 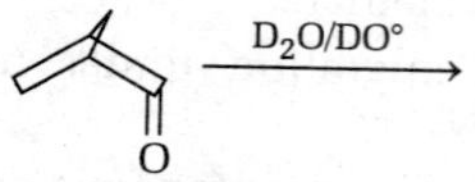

How many hydrogen replaced by (D)?

3. The number of isomers of carbonyl compound of $C_5H_{10}O$ that give positive iodoform test (includnig siereoisomer) are ....

4. $CH_3\overset{O}{\overset{\|}{C}}CH_3 + CH_3CH_2\overset{O}{\overset{\|}{C}}CH_3 \xrightarrow[\Delta]{KOH(aq.)} (A)$

(A) = number of aldol condensation product (including stereoisomers).

5. How many isomers of $C_4H_{10}O$ give positive iodoform test?

6. How many isomers having molecular $C_7H_{14}O$ gives Cannizzaro reaction?

7. Calculate total number of sp^3 carbon is product A.

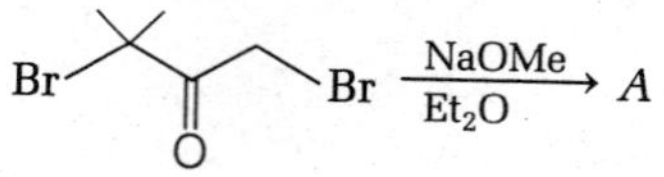

8. Possible product formed in the given reaction is

$Ph—CH_2—\overset{O}{\overset{\|}{C}}—CH_3 \xrightarrow[\text{(ii) NaOEt}]{\text{(i) } Br_2 \cdot AcOH}$

9. Number of reagent which are suitable for given conversion is

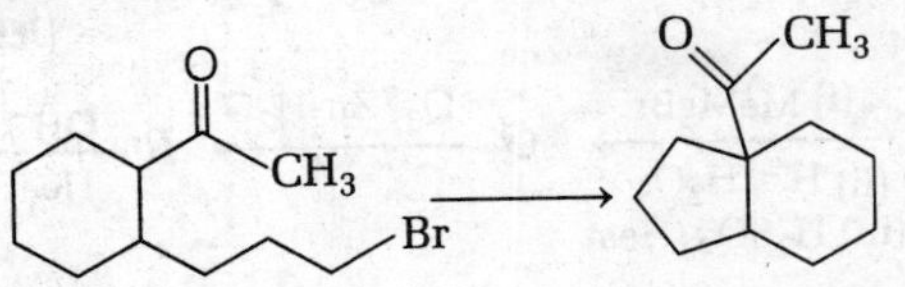

LOA, 78°C, NaH, CH_3Li, CH_3—MgBr, 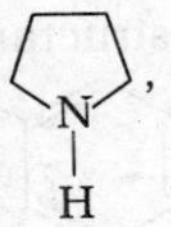, H^+

10.

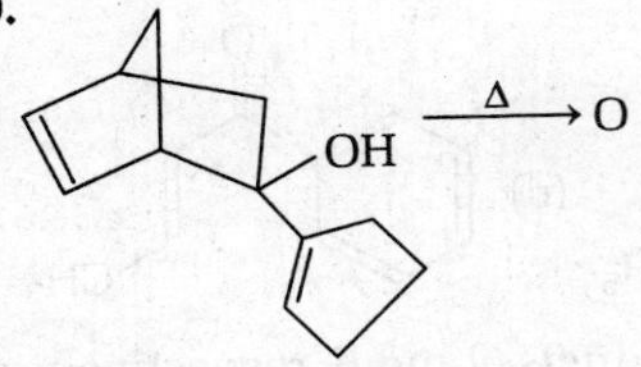

Number of 5 membered rings in the compound O.

11. Consider the following reactions :

$$A \xrightarrow[\text{(ii) } H_3O^+]{\text{(i) } CH_3MgBr} B \xrightarrow[573\text{ K}]{Cu} \text{2-methyl- 2- butene}$$

The mass percentage of carbon in A is ......

[JEE Main 2020, Jan.]

12. In the following reaction sequence, the amount of D (in g) formed from 10 moles of acetophenone is ...... (Atomic weights in g/mol H = 1, C = 12, N = 14, O = 16, Br = 80). The yield (%) corresponding to the product in each step is given in the parenthesis).

[JEE Advanced 2018]

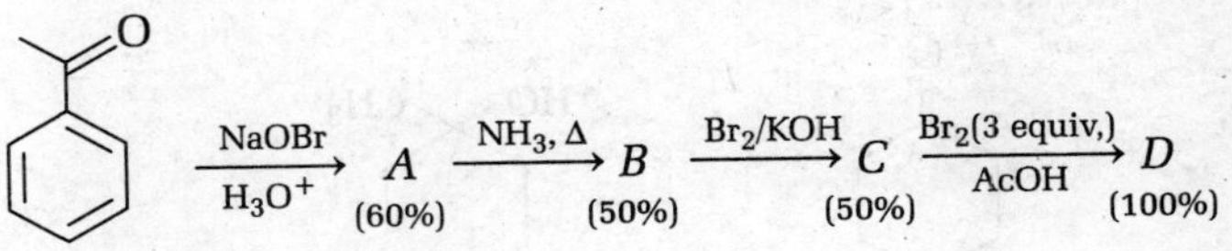

Comprehension Based Questions

In these questions, a passage has been given followed by questions based on it. You have to answer the questions based on the passage given.

***Passage* 1** A research scholar studying isotopic effect using tracer technique isolated the compound A. After sometime A changed to B along with the compound C under the given conditions.

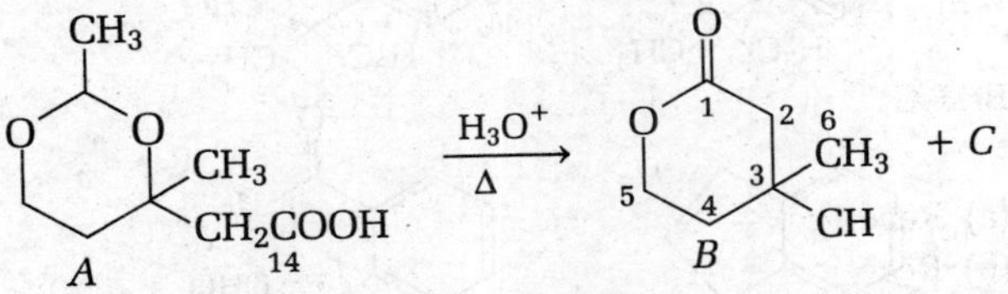

Answer the following questions based on the above experimental study.

1. Product C

(a) reduces Tollen's reagent

(b) reduces Fehling's solution

(c) can be obtained by hydration of ethyne with $H_2SO_4/HgSO_4$

(d) can be converted into 2-propanol with CH_3MgBr / H_3O^+

2. A changes to B

(a) due to hydrolysis of acetal (A) giving a diol and C

(b) due to oxidation of (A)

(c) due to reduction of (A)

(d) due to hydrolysis of acetal (A) giving a diol and free acid (in same molecule) which undergoes cyclic ester formation

3. ^{14}C of A appears in (B) at

(a) C_1

(b) C_3

(c) C_5

(d) None of the above (goes with C)

***Passage* 2** A is to be converted into B through

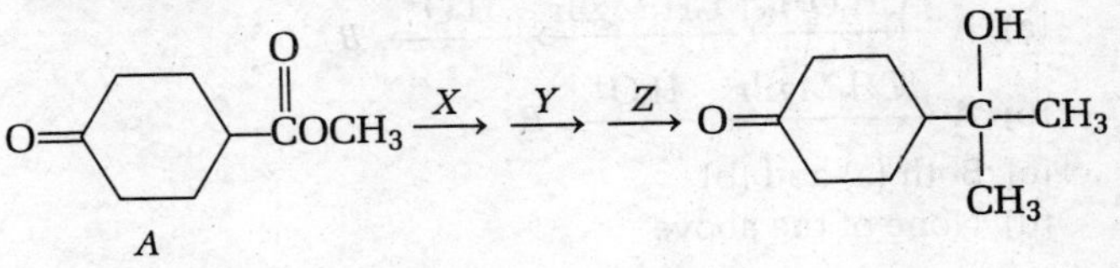

Some reagents have been suggested.

I. CH_2OH—CH_2OH II. $LiAlH_4$/ether, H_3O^+

III. CH_3MgBr IV. H_3O^+

Answer the following questions.

1. Steps X, Y and Z use reagents as

(a) III (two moles), I and IV

(b) I, III (two moles) and IV

(c) IV, III (two moles) and IV

(d) I, II and III (two moles)

2. If only II is used, product formed would be

(a) 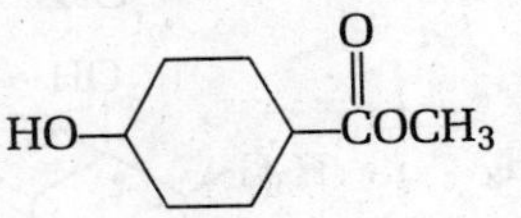

(b) 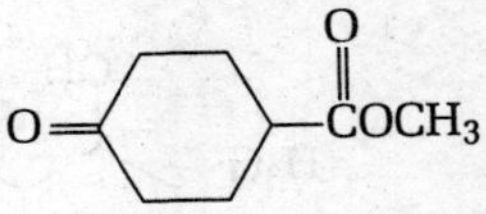

(c) 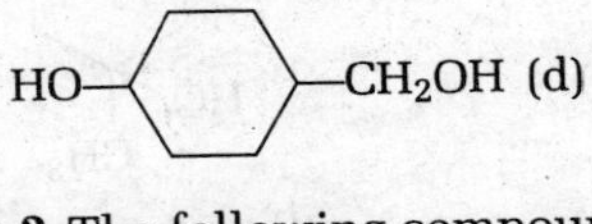

(d) 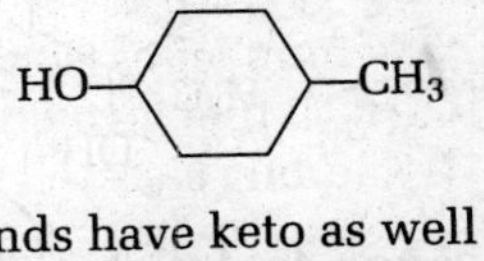

***Passage* 3** The following compounds have keto as well as aldehyde group if one group is to be changed into desired alcohol, then other will have to be protected (shield) carrying the necessary reactions and finally removing the protecting group. *A* can be converted into *B* by protection of —CHO.

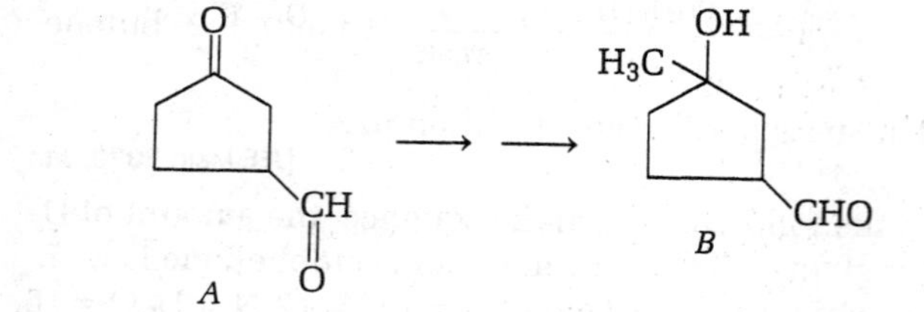

Read the above passage and answer the following questions.

1. Group can be protected by .... due to formation of ....

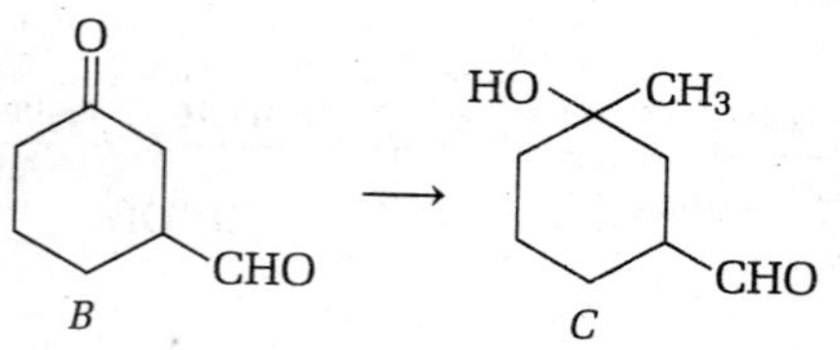

(a) diol, acetal
(b) thiol, mercaptal
(c) Both (a) and (b)
(d) None of these

2. *A* can be converted to *B* by

(a) $A \xrightarrow{\begin{array}{c}CH_2OH \\ | \\ CH_2OH\end{array}} \xrightarrow{CH_3MgBr} \xrightarrow{H_3O^+} B$

(b) $A \xrightarrow{CH_3MgBr} \xrightarrow{H_3O^+} B$

(c) Both (a) and (b)

(d) None of the above

3. 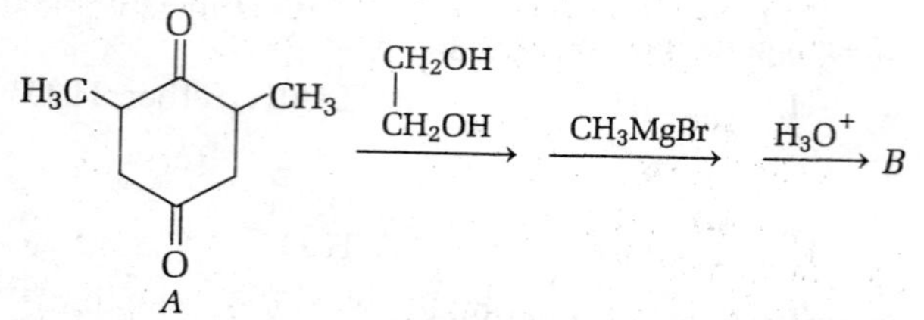

B is identified as

(a) 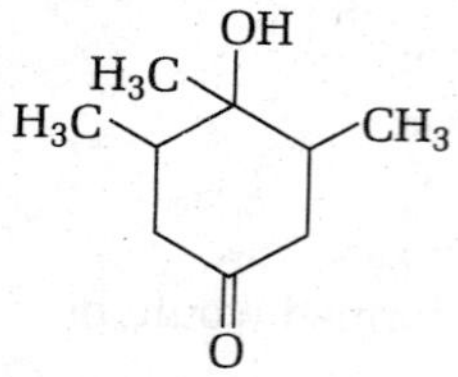
(b) 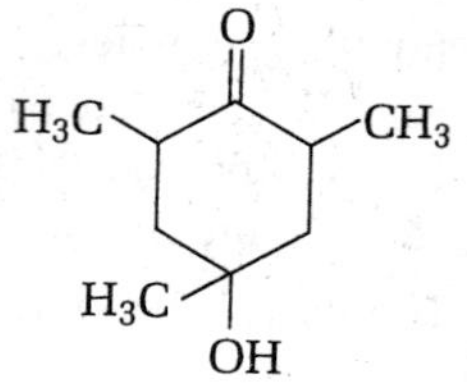
(c) 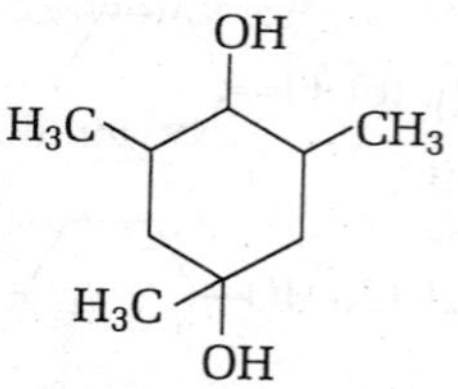
(d) 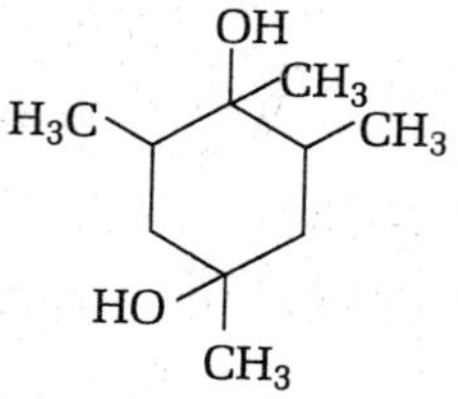

***Passage* 4** A carbonyl compound *P*, which gives positive iodoform test, undergoes reaction with MeMgBr followed by dehydration to give an olefin *Q*. Ozonolysis of *Q* leads to a dicarbonyl compound *R*, which undergoes intramolecular aldol reaction to give predominantly *S*. **[JEE Main 2009]**

$$P \xrightarrow[\text{(ii) } H^+, H_2O \text{ (iii) } H_2SO_4/\text{Heat}]{\text{(i) MeMgBr}} Q \xrightarrow{O_3/Zn\text{-}H_2O} R \xrightarrow[\text{Heat}]{OH^-} S$$

1. The structure of the carbonyl compound *P*, is

(a) 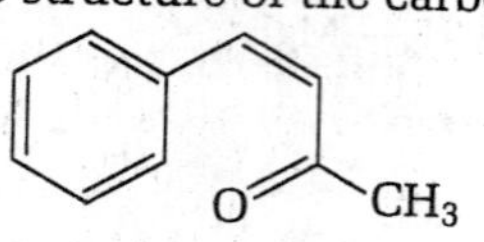
(b) 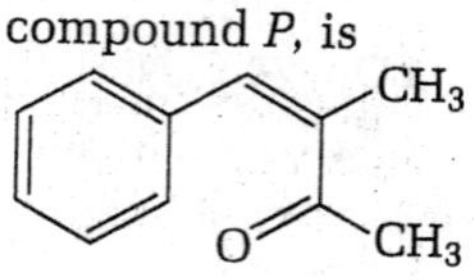
(c) 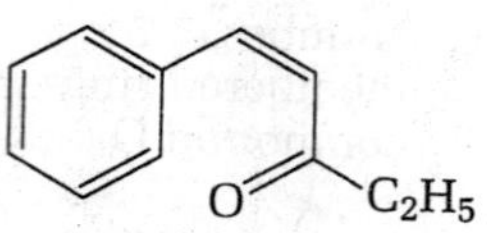
(d) 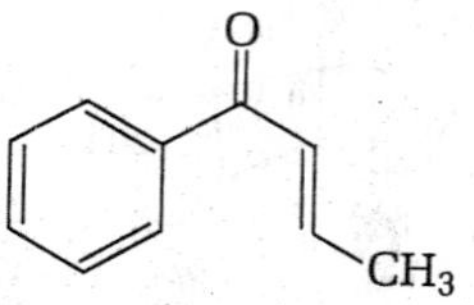

2. The structure of the products *Q* and *R*, respectively, are

(a) 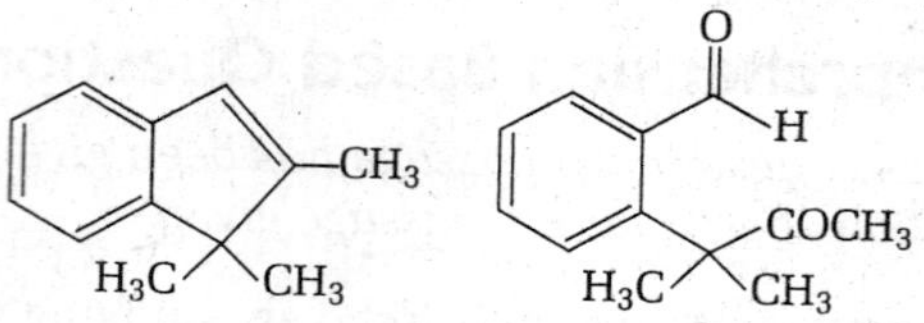
(b) 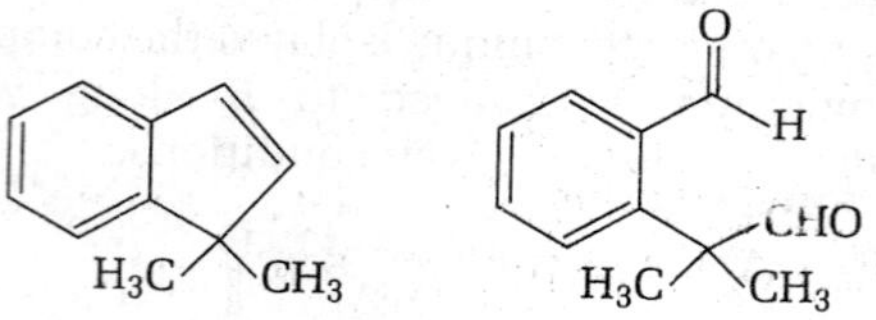
(c) 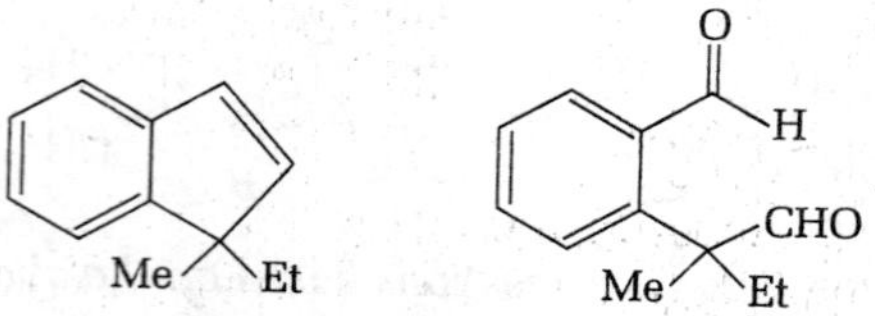
(d) 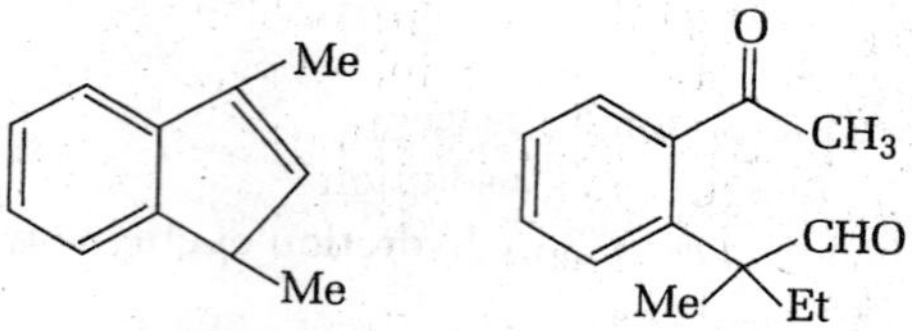

3. The structure of the product *S*, is

(a) 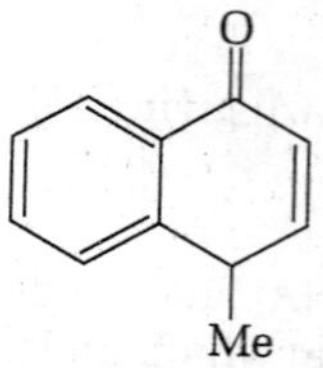
(b) 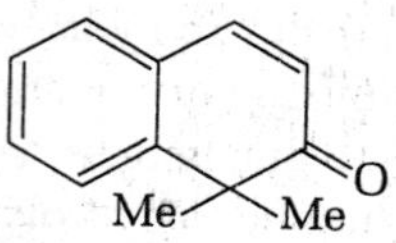
(c) 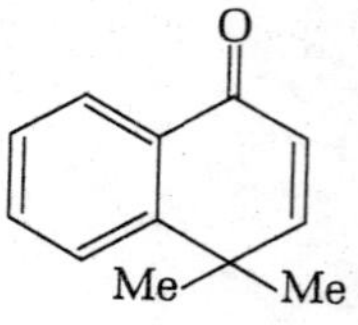
(d) 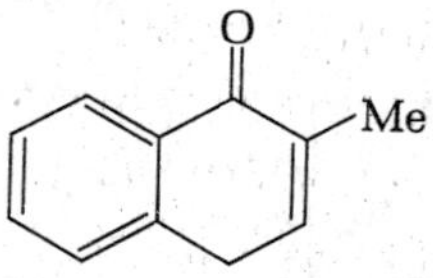

Passage 5 Crossed Cannizzaro reaction can be of preparative utility of one if the aldehyde (which is used in excess) acts as the hydride donor and reduces the other aldehyde to the alcohol.

$$\underset{\text{Hydride donor}}{RCHO} + \underset{\text{Hydride acceptor}}{R'CHO} \longrightarrow R\overset{O}{\overset{\|}{C}}O^- + R'CH_2OH$$

Following questions are based on the above experimental facts and the graph of the relative reactivity of different carbonyl compounds.

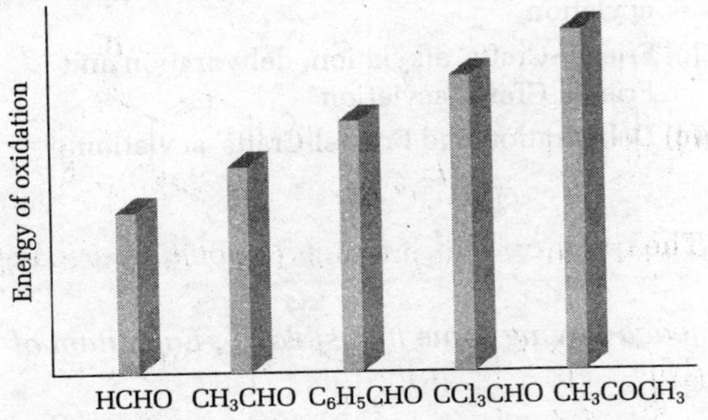

1. Consider the reaction between CH_3CHO and HCHO in basic medium.

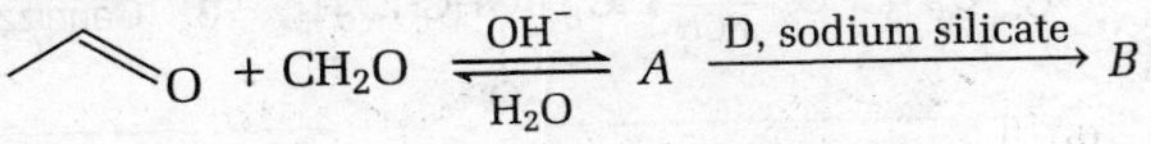

A and *B* are respectively

(a) 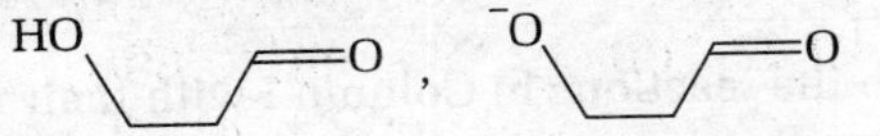

(b) 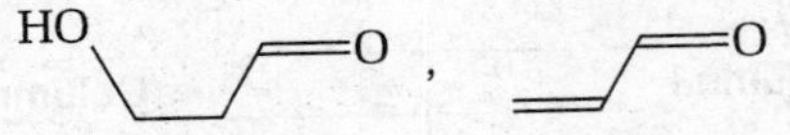

(c) 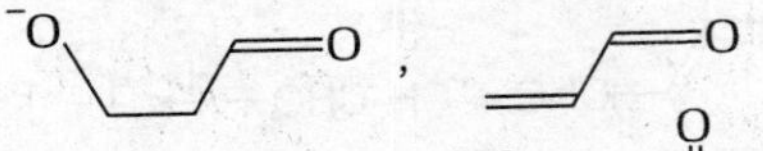

(d) 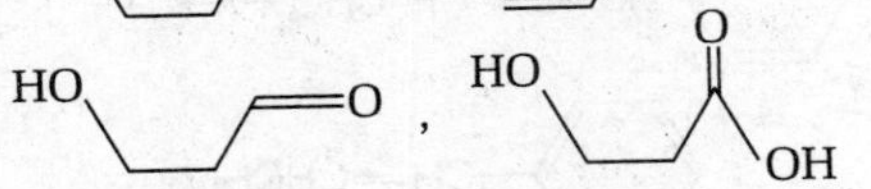

2. What are the products of the following crossed Cannizzaro reaction?

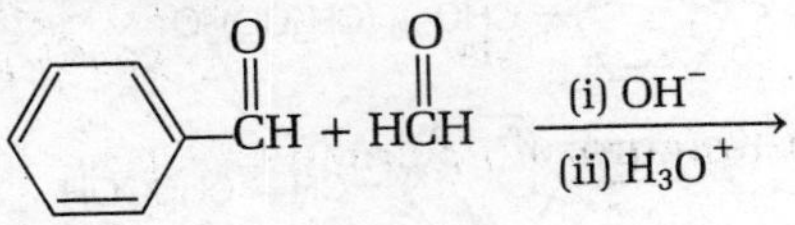

(a) 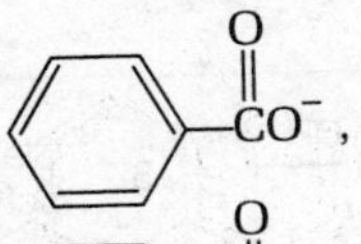 CH_3OH

(b) 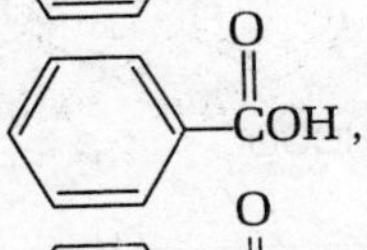 CH_3O^-

(c) 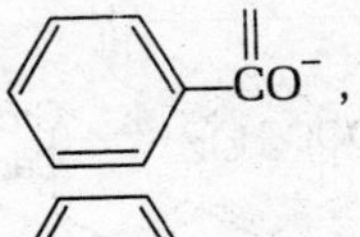 CH_3O^-

(d) 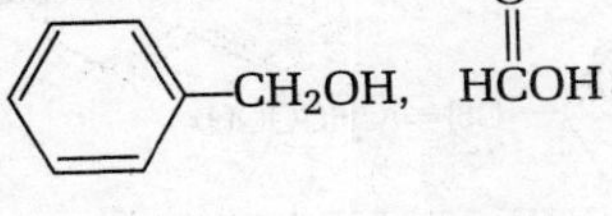

3. Products when *A* reacts with HCHO in presence of OH^- are

$$A + HCHO + OH^- \longrightarrow D + E$$

	D	*E*
(a)	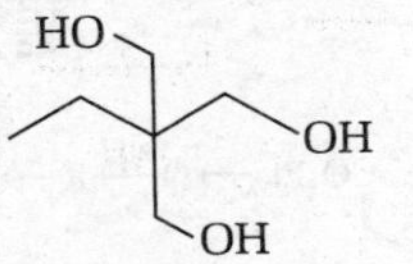	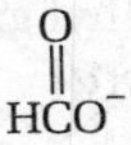
(b)	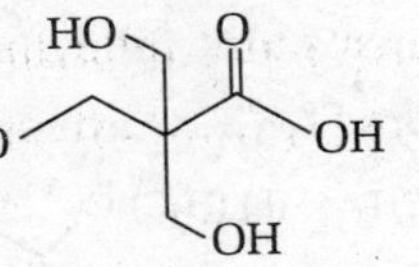	CH_3OH
(c)	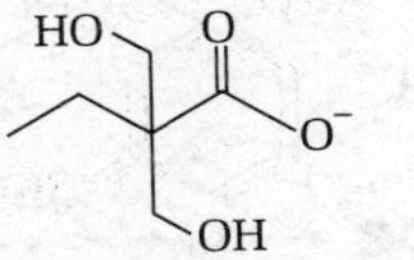	CH_3OH
(d)	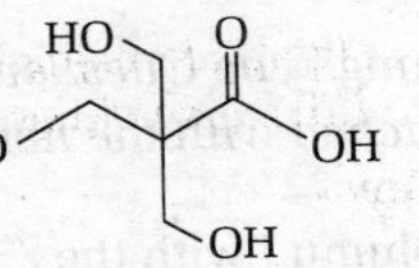	CO_2

Passage 6 Reaction of Grignard reagent and carbonyl compound is a good synthetic method of preparing 1°, 2° and 3° alcohols.

Answer the questions based on synthesis of alcohol from Grignard reagent and carbonyl compounds.

1. Consider the following reaction using isotopically labelled Cl(35), Cl(37) and C(14)

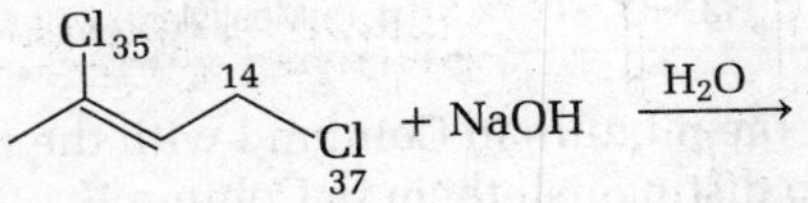

What is/are the product(s) of this S_N reaction?

(a) 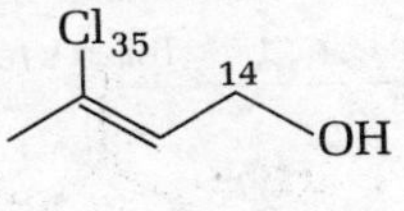

(b) 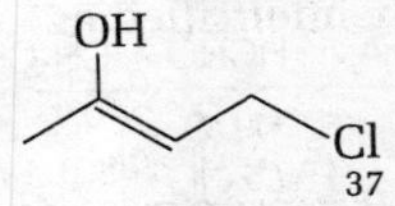

(c) 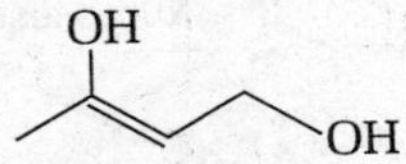

(d) 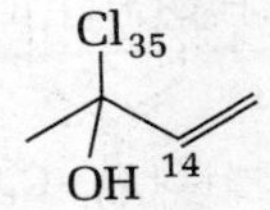

2. What is/are final product(s) of the following?

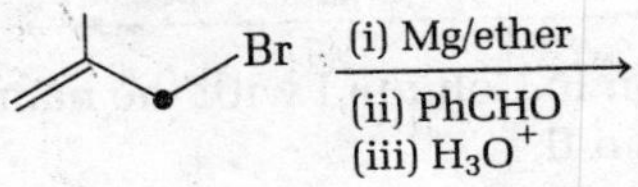

(• isotopic C-14)

(a) 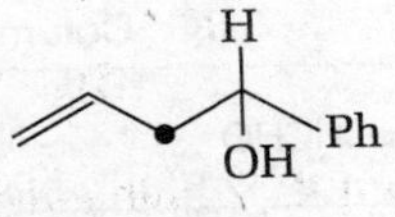

(b) 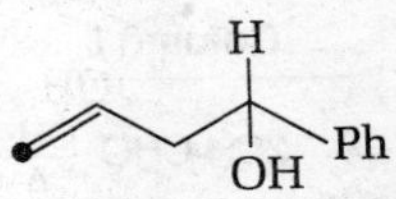

(c) Both (a) and (b)

(d) None of these

***Passage* 7.** The reaction of compound P with CH_3MgBr (excess) in $(C_2H_5)_2O$ followed by addition of H_2O gives Q. The compound Q on treatment with H_2SO_4 at 0° C gives R. The reaction of R with CH_3COCl in the presence of anhydrous $AlCl_3$ in CH_2Cl_2 followed by treatment wi compound S. [Et in compound P is ethyl group]. **[JEE Advanced 2017]**

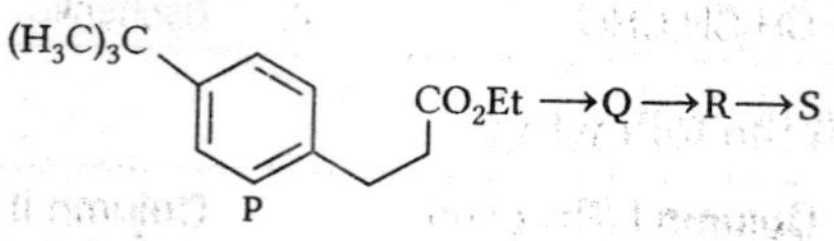

P

1. The product S is

(a) 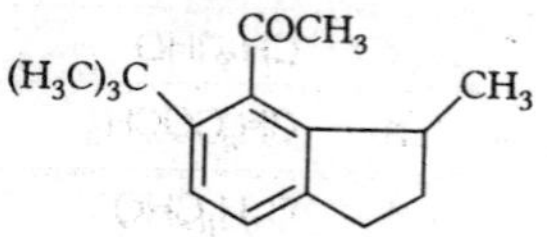

(b) 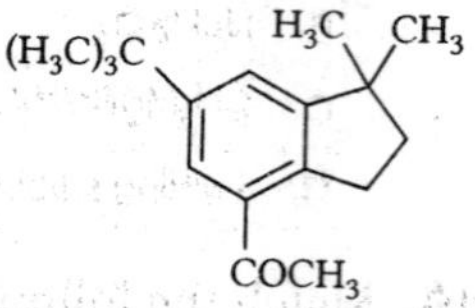

(c) 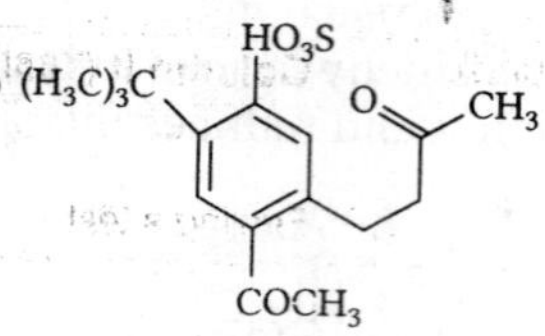

(d) 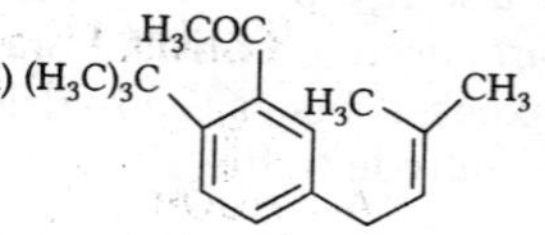

2. The reactions, Q to R and R to S, are

(a) Aromatic sulphonation and Friedel-Crafts acylation

(b) Friedel-Crafts' alkylation and Friedel-Crafts acylation

(c) Friedel-Crafts' alkylation, dehydration and Friedel-Crafts' acylation

(d) Dehydration and Friedel-Crafts' acylation

Matrix-Match Type

Given below are Matching Type Questions, with two columns (each having some items) each . Each item of Column I has to be matched with the items of Column II.

1. Match the species in Column I with the corresponding reaction shown in Column II.

	Column I		Column II
A.	HCHO	1.	Benzoin condensation
B.	CH_3CHO	2.	Iodoform test
C.	$CH_3\overset{O}{\overset{\|\|}{C}}CH_3$	3.	Cannizzaro reaction
D.	C_6H_5CHO	4.	Mesitylene with conc. H_2SO_4

2. Match the mixture in Column I with the reagents used to distinguish them in Column II.

	Column I		Column II
A.	$HCHO + CH_3CHO$	1.	Tollen's reagent
B.	$CH_3\overset{O}{\overset{\|\|}{C}}CH_3 + (CH_3)_3COH$	2.	Lucas test
C.	$C_6H_5CHO + C_6H_5\overset{O}{\overset{\|\|}{C}}CH_3$	3.	Iodoform test
D.	$CH_3CH_2OH + CH_3CHO$	4.	Cannizzaro reaction

3. Match the reaction in Column I with the name of reaction in Column II.

Column I		Column II
A. $2CH_3CHO \xrightarrow[\Delta]{OH^-} CH_3CH{=}CHCHO$	1.	Gattermann-Koch
B. $2HCHO \xrightarrow{OH^-} HCOO^- + CH_3OH$	2.	Benzoin
C. $C_6H_5CHO \xrightarrow[KCN]{Alc.} C_6H_5\underset{OH}{\underset{\|}{C}}HCHC_6H_5$	3.	Cannizzaro
D. $C_6H_5 + CO + HCl \xrightarrow{AlCl_3} C_6H_5CHO$	4.	Aldol

4. Match the reactions in Column I with their names in Column II.

Column I		Column II
A. 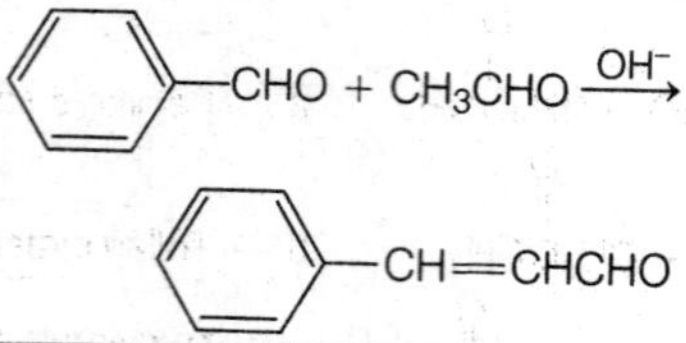	1.	Perkin
B. 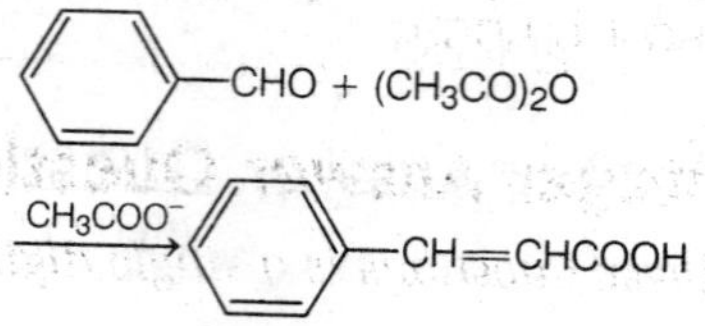	2.	Knoevenagel
C. 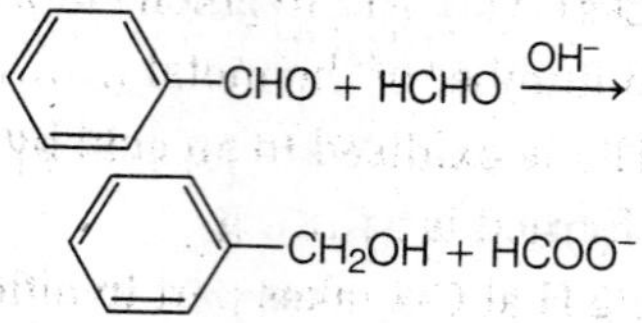	3.	Claisen Schmidt
D. 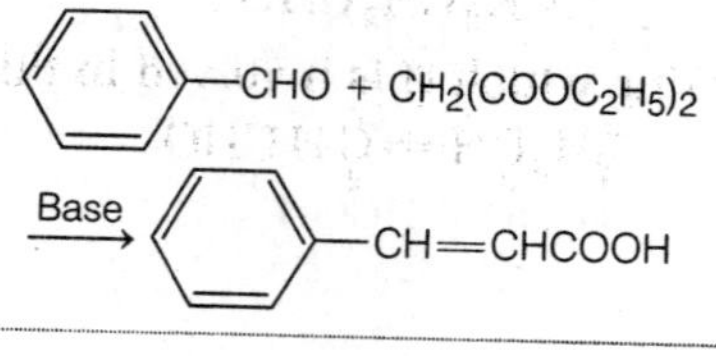	4.	Crossed Cannizzaro

5. Match the following.

	Column I (Compound)		Column II (Test)
A.	$H\overset{O}{\overset{\|}{C}}OH$	1.	Fehling's test
B.	$CH_3\overset{O}{\overset{\|}{C}}H$	2.	Silver mirror test
C.	$CH_3\overset{O}{\overset{\|}{C}}CH_3$	3.	Iodoform test
D.	$C_6H_5\overset{O}{\overset{\|}{C}}H$	4.	Benedict's test

6. Match the following.

	Column I (Compound)		Column II (Synthesis)
A.	$CH_3CH_2CH_2OH$	1.	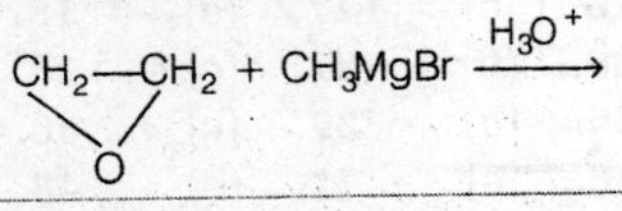
B.	$CH_3\underset{OH}{\underset{\|}{C}H}CH_3$	2.	$CH_3MgBr + CH_3CHO \xrightarrow{H_3O^+}$
C.	$CH_3-\overset{CH_3}{\overset{\|}{\underset{CH_3}{\underset{\|}{C}}}}-OH$	3.	$CH_3\overset{O}{\overset{\|}{C}}CH_3 + CH_3MgBr \xrightarrow{H_3O^+}$
D.	CH_3CH_2OH	4.	$HCHO + CH_3MgBr \xrightarrow{H_3O^+}$

7. Match the following.

	Column I (Pair for distinction)		Column II (Reagent used)
A.	$CH_3CHO + HCHO$	1.	I_2 / NaOH / Δ
B.	$CH_3CHO + CH_3\overset{O}{\overset{\|}{C}}CH_3$	2.	Fehling's solution
C.	$HCHO + CH_3\overset{O}{\overset{\|}{C}}CH_3$	3.	Tollen's reagent
D.	$C_6H_5CHO + CH_3\overset{O}{\overset{\|}{C}}CH_3$	4.	$Cr_2O_7^{2-}/H^+/\Delta$

8. Match the following.

	Column I (Compound)		Column II (Reaction)
A.	HCHO	1.	Aldol
B.	CH_3CHO	2.	Cannizzaro
C.	CH_3COCH_3	3.	Haloform
D.	CH_3CH_2CHO	4.	Tischenko

9. Match the following.

	Column I (Reagent)		Column II (Compound)
A.	NH_2NH_2	1.	HCHO
B.	$NaHSO_3$	2.	CH_3CHO
C.	CH_3MgBr/H_3O^+	3.	CH_3COCH_3
D.	Fehling's solution	4.	C_6H_5CHO

10. Match the following.

	Column I (Reaction)		Column II (Name)
A.	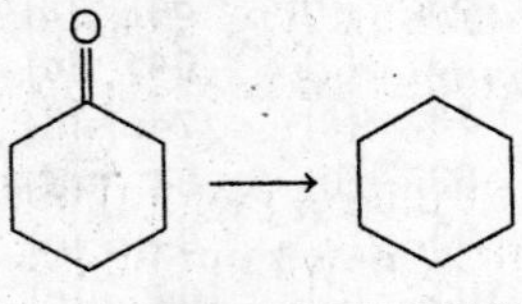	1.	Wolff-Kishner
B.	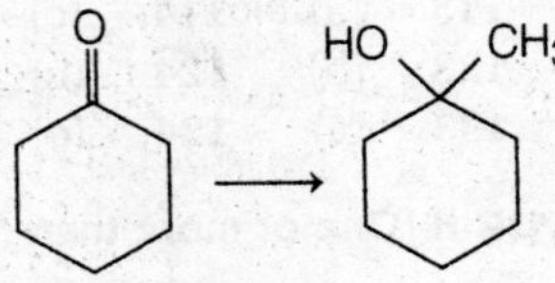	2.	Clemmensen
C.	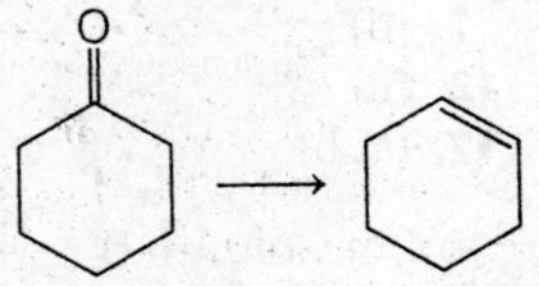	3.	H_3O^+/Δ
D.	$CH_3\overset{O}{\overset{\|}{C}}CH_3 \longrightarrow (CH_3)_3COH$	4.	CH_3MgBr/H_3O^+

Single Integer Answer Questions

Answer of these questions is a single digit lying between 0 to 9.

1. CH_3CHO reduces $Cr_2O_7^{2-}/H^+$ to green coloured salt with oxidation number of the metal ....

2. 4.4 g of CH_3CHO is oxidised to an acid by Tollen's reagent. Acid formed is .... g.

3. In the following H at C-2 takes part in aldol reaction.

$$\overset{3}{C}H_3\overset{2}{C}H_2\overset{1}{C}HO$$

In the following which H is involved in this reaction?

$$\underset{4}{C}H_3\underset{3}{C}H{=}\underset{2}{C}H\underset{1}{C}HO$$

4. The total number of nitrogen atom (s) in urotropine is ....

5. In the following H at C—X is involved in crossed aldol reaction.

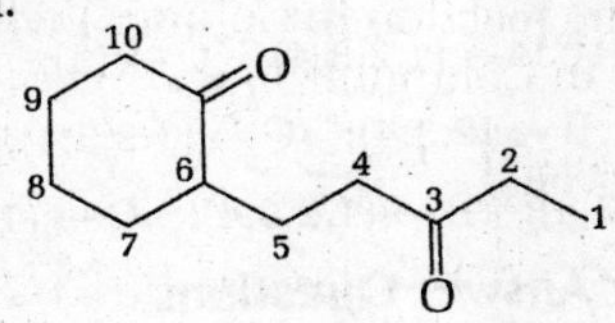

X is ....

6. Which carbonyl is changed to enolic form?

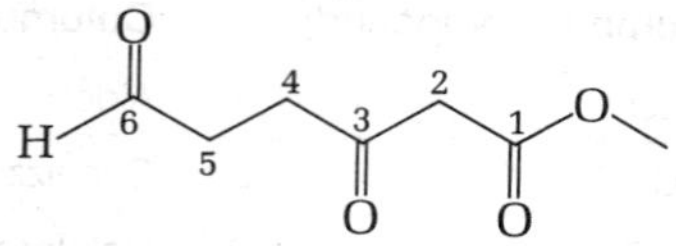

7. Oxidation number of the metal of Tollen's reagent after reduction becomes ....

8. Oxidation number of the metal of Fehling's solution after reduction becomes ....

9. In the scheme given below, the total number of intramolecular aldol condensation products formed from 'Y' is [JEE Main 2011]

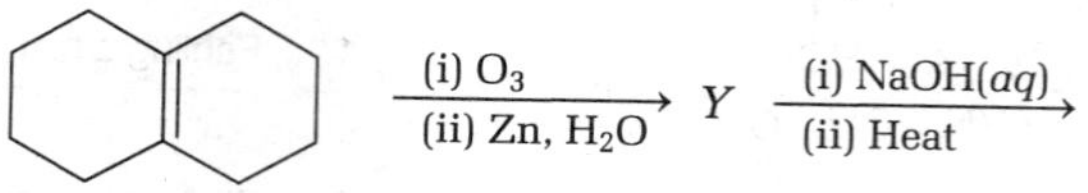

10. The number of $>C=O$ groups present in a tripeptide Asp-Glu-Lys is .... [JEE Main 2020, Sep.]

Answers

Objective Questions Type I [Only one correct option]

1. (b)	2. (a)	3. (a)	4. (d)	5. (b)	6. (b)	7. (d)	8. (a)	9. (c)	10. (a)
11. (a)	12. (c)	13. (b)	14. (b)	15. (d)	16. (c)	17. (a)	18. (b)	19. (a)	20. (d)
21. (c)	22. (d)	23. (b)	24. (a)	25. (d)	26. (b)	27. (c)	28. (c)	29. (b)	30. (d)
31. (c)	32. (d)	33. (b)	34. (b)	35. (a)	36. (b)	37. (c)	38. (c)	39. (a)	40. (a)
41. (b)	42. (a)	43. (c)	44. (d)	45. (c)	46. (c)	47. (b)	48. (a)	49. (d)	50. (c)
51. (c)	52. (d)	53. (b)	54. (a)	55. (c)	56. (c)	57. (a)	58. (c)	59. (a)	60. (b)
61. (b)	62. (b)	63. (a)	64. (c)	65. (c)	66. (a)	67. (d)	68. (b)	69. (d)	70. (d)
71. (a)	72. (d)	73. (c)	74. (b)	75. (a)	76. (b)	77. (a)	78. (b)	79. (b)	80. (b)
81. (a)	82. (a)	83. (b)	84. (d)	85. (a)	86. (c)	87. (a)	88. (d)	89. (b)	90. (d)
91. (b)	92. (c)	93. (a)	94. (c)	95. (a)	96. (c)	97. (a)	98. (a)	99. (b)	100. (b)
101. (c)	102. (a)	103. (d)	104. (c)	105. (a)	106. (b)	107. (d)	108. (b)	109. (a)	110. (d)
111. (d)	112. (b)	113. (a)	114. (c)	115. (c)	116. (b)	117. (c)	118. (c)	119. (b)	120. (c)
121. (d)	122. (d)	123. (b)	124. (c)	125. (a)	126. (a)	127. (a)	128. (b)	129. (d)	130. (b)
131. (c)	132. (d)	133. (a)	134. (c)	135. (b)	136. (c)	137. (a)			

Objective Questions Type II [One or more than one correct option(s)]

1. (b)	2. (a, b)	3. (a)	4. (a)	5. (a)
6. (a)	7. (d)	8. (d)	9. (b, c)	10. (a, c)
11. (b, c)	12. (d)	13. (d)	14. (a, d)	15. (d)
16. (a, b, d)	17. (a, b)	18. (d)	19. (b, d)	20. (a, b, d)
21. (c)				

Numerical Value Questions

1. (3)	2. (2)	3. (2)	4. (4)	5. (7)	6. (5)	7. (3)	8. (3)	9. (1)	10. (2)
11. (67)	12. (495)								

Comprehension Based Questions

Passage 1 – 1. (a,b,c,d) 2. (d) 3. (a) **Passage 2** – 1. (b) 2. (c) **Passage 3** – 1. (c) 2. (a) 3. (a)
Passage 4 – 1. (b) 2. (a) 3. (b) **Passage 5** – 1. (b) 2. (d) 3. (a) **Passage 6** – 1. (a) 2. (c)
Passage 7 – 1. (b) 2. (b)

Matrix-Match Type

1. A → (3); B → (2); C → (4); D → (1)
2. A → (4); B → (2); C → (3); D → (1)
3. A → (4); B → (3); C → (2); D → (1)
4. A → (3); B → (1); C → (4); D → (2)
5. A → (1,2,4); B → (1,2,3,4); C → (3); D → (2,4)
6. A → (1); B → (2); C → (3); D → (4)
7. A → (1); B → (2,3,4); C → (1,2,3,4); D → (1,3,4)
8. A → (2); B → (1,3,4); C → (2,4); D → (1,4)
9. A → (1,2,3,4); B → (1,2,3,4); C → (1,2,3,4); D → (1,2)
10. A → (1,2); B → (4); C → (3); D → (4)

Single Integer Answer Questions

1. (3)	2. (6)	3. (4)	4. (4)	5. (2)	6. (3)	7. (0)	8. (1)	9. (1)	10. (5)

Solutions

Objective Questions Type I [Only one correct option]

1. (*b*) $CH_3-\underset{CH_3}{\overset{CH_3}{\overset{|}{\underset{|}{C}}}}-OH \xrightarrow[-H_2O]{Cu} CH_3-\overset{CH_3}{\overset{|}{C}}=CH_2$

2. (*a*) $CH_3CH_2OH \xrightarrow{Cr_2O_7^{2-}/H^+} CH_3CHO + \underset{\text{Green}}{Cr^{3+}}$

3. (*a*) $\underset{sp^2}{>C=O}$ $\qquad$ $\underset{sp^2}{>C=C<}$

They do not differ in hybridisation of carbon.

6. (*b*) $RCOOR' \xrightarrow{LiAlH_4} R'OH + RCH_2OH$

7. (*c*) $CH_3COCl \longrightarrow CH_3CHO$

Used H_2 /Pd-$BaSO_4$, DiBALH, LiAlH (O -*t* -C_4H_9)$_3$

8. (*a*) $(CH_3)_3CCHCl_2 + NaOH \longrightarrow (CH_3)_3CCH(OH)_2 \xrightarrow{-H_2O} (CH_3)_3C-CHO$

α-C with no H

9. (*c*) C_3H_6O (carbonyl compound) gives iodoform test (yellow ppt with I_2/NaOH) thus it has $-\overset{O}{\overset{\|}{C}}CH_3$.

$-\overset{O}{\overset{\|}{C}}-$ group is due to hydrolysis of $-\underset{Cl}{\overset{Cl}{\overset{|}{\underset{|}{C}}}}-$.

Then $C_3H_6Cl_2$ is

$CH_3-\underset{Cl}{\overset{Cl}{\overset{|}{\underset{|}{C}}}}-CH_3 \xrightarrow{2NaOH} CH_3-\overset{O}{\overset{\|}{C}}-CH_3$

2,2-dichloropropane

10. (*a*) $H-\overset{O}{\overset{\|}{C}}-OCH(CH_3)_2 \xrightarrow{NaAlH_4} H-\overset{O}{\overset{\|}{C}}-H + (CH_3)_2CHOH$

12. (*c*) $R\overset{O}{\overset{\|}{C}}Cl \xrightarrow{H_2/Pd/BaSO_4} RCHO$ Thus, RCOCl is

$(CH_3)_2CH\overset{O}{\overset{\|}{C}}-Cl \xrightarrow{H_2/Pd/BaSO_4} (CH_3)_2CHCHO$

$(CH_3)_2CH\overset{O}{\overset{\|}{C}}-Cl \xrightarrow{CH_3MgBr} (CH_3)_2CH\overset{O}{\overset{\|}{C}}-CH_3$

13. (*b*) Ester is $H-\overset{O}{\overset{\|}{C}}-OCH(CH_3)_2 \xrightarrow{CH_3MgBr} CH_3CHO$

14. (*b*) In (I) CH_3COCH_3 changes to $(CH_3)_3COH$ on reaction with CH_3MgBr.

15. (*d*) $CH_3CH_2OH + RMgBr \longrightarrow RH$

16. (*c*) $(RCOO)_2Ca + (R'COO)_2Ca \longrightarrow R'COR$

$\underset{R'}{\underline{(CH_3)_2CH}}\overset{O}{\overset{\|}{C}}-\underset{R}{\underline{CH_3}}$

R is CH_3.

R' is $(CH_3)_2CH$.

17. (*a*) $A\ (C_5H_{10}O)$ gives iodoform test thus *A* is

$R\overset{O}{\overset{\|}{C}}CH_3 \xrightarrow[\Delta]{Ca(OH)_2/I_2} (R\overset{O}{\overset{\|}{C}}O)_2Ca + CHI_3$

$\xrightarrow{\Delta} R\overset{O}{\overset{\|}{C}}R\ (B)\ \ \underset{(B)}{(CH_3)_2CH\overset{O}{\overset{\|}{C}}CH(CH_3)_2}$

Thus, *R* is $(CH_3)_2CH$ on comparison.

Thus, *A* is $(CH_3)_2CH\overset{O}{\overset{\|}{C}}CH_3$.

18. (*b*) Ozonolysis product is symmetrical and single product with same number of C-atoms.

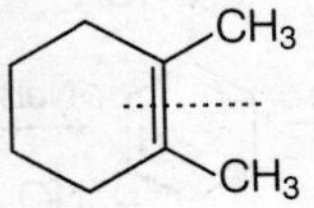

21. (*c*) $RCN \xrightarrow{Sn/HCl} RCH=NH$

22. (*d*) Product is $CH_3\overset{O}{\overset{\|}{C}}CH_3$.

24. (*a*) $CH_3CH_2CN \xrightarrow{H_3O^+} CH_3CH_2\overset{O}{\overset{\|}{C}}OH \xrightarrow{PCl_5} CH_3CH_2\overset{O}{\overset{\|}{C}}Cl \xrightarrow{(CH_3)_2Cu} CH_3CH_2\overset{O}{\overset{\|}{C}}-CH_3$

26. (*b*) $>C=O \rightleftharpoons >\overset{\oplus}{C}-O^-$

Electrophilic $\quad$ Nucleophile

27. (*c*)

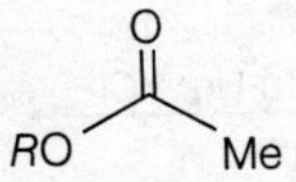

derivative of alcohols is unstable in an aqueous basic solution and undergoes hydrolysis to give alcohol and carboxylate.

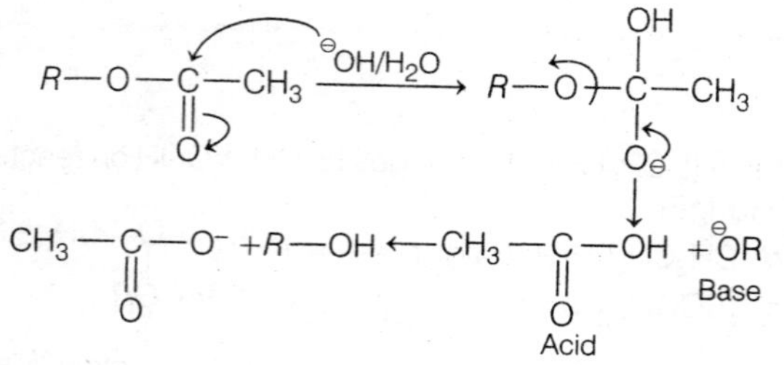

(It is a hydrolysis of ester in basic medium).

30. (*d*) HCHO > CH_3CHO > PHCHO (reactivity order)

32. (*d*) $HCHO \xrightarrow[\Delta]{Cu^{2+}/OH^-} CO_2 + Cu^+$

$Cu^{2+} + e^- \longrightarrow \underset{\text{Red ppt.}}{Cu^+}$

33. (*b*) $C_6H_5CO_3H$ (peroxybenzoic acid) oxidises ketone into ester (Baeyer-Villiger oxidation).

34. (*b*) $CH_3CH_2\overset{O}{\overset{\|}{C}}CH_3 \xrightarrow{C_6H_5CO_3H} CH_3CH_2O\overset{O}{\overset{\|}{C}}CH_3 \xrightarrow{H_3O^+} CH_3CH_2OH + CH_3COOH$

(Oxygen is inserted between carbonyl carbon and larger alkyl group)

35. (*a*) $CH_3CH_2COCH_3 \xrightarrow{SeO_2} CH_3CH_2COCHO$

39. (*a*)

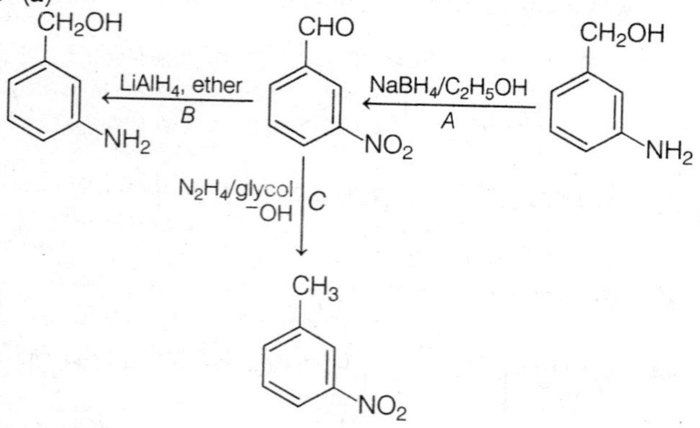

41. (*b*)

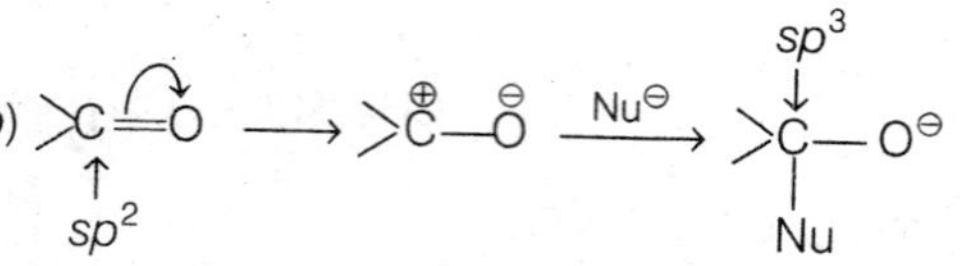

43. (*c*) —Br (EWG) increases positive charge on carbonyl carbon for nucleophilic attack.

44. (*d*)

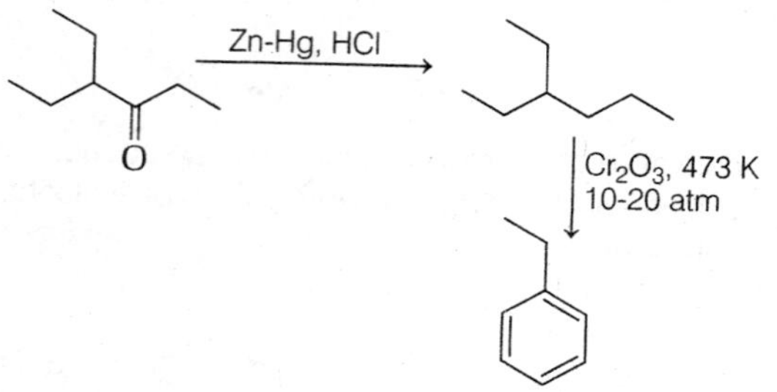

45. (*c*) $>C=O \rightleftharpoons >\overset{\oplus}{C}-\overset{\ominus}{O} \xrightarrow{H^+} >\overset{\oplus}{C}-OH$

Due to protonation, electrophilic nature of carbonyl carbon is increased, hence nucleophilic attack is increased. Thus, statement (c) is incorrect.

46. (*c*) $CH_3-CH_2-\underset{H}{\underset{|}{C}}=O + H_2NCH_3 \longrightarrow CH_3-CH_2-\underset{H}{\underset{|}{C}}H=\underset{CH_3}{\underset{|}{N}}$

syn and anti

50. (*c*)

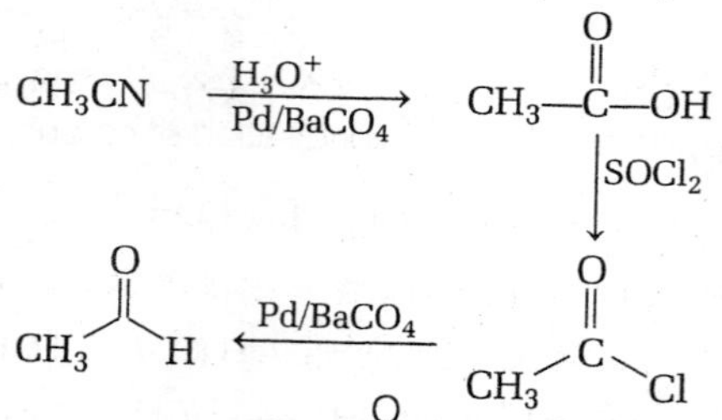

51. (*c*) $CH_3CN \xrightarrow[H_3O^+]{CH_3MgBr} CH_3\overset{O}{\overset{\|}{C}}CH_3 \xrightarrow[H_3O^+]{CH_3MgBr} (CH_3)_3COH$

53. (*b*) Hydration of (*R*CHO) is larger than that of $R-\overset{O}{\overset{\|}{C}}CH_3$.
(EWG) increases hydration. Thus, II > I
Then IV > III.
III < IV < I < II

56. (*c*) There should not be H at α -C (or α -C absent) for Cannizzaro reaction.

57. (*a*)

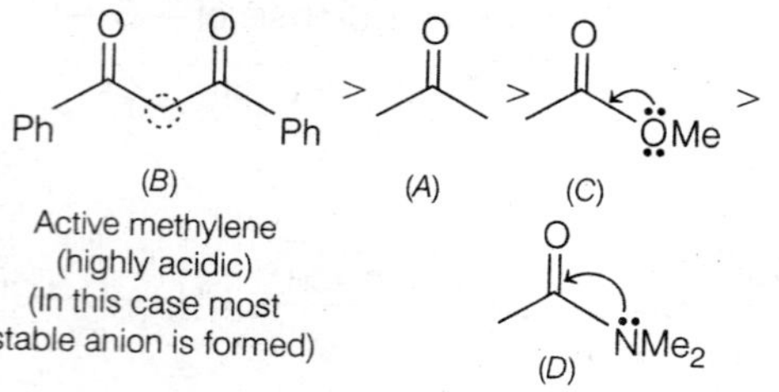

(*B*) Active methylene (highly acidic) (In this case most stable anion is formed) > (*A*) > (*C*) >

(*D*) Lower-M (mesomeric) effect as compaired to $-\overset{}{C}(=O)-$group

Compound (*B*) is a active methylene compound is highly resonance stabilised. This compound possessing a methylene bridge located between two strong electron withdrawing groups (such as carbonyl group). So, it is highly acidic in nature.

Compounds (*C*) and (*D*) having electron donating group. Which decreases the acidity and compound (*A*) is more acidic than (*C*) and (*D*) because it does not contain any electron releasing group.

Hence, option (a) is correct.

(*D*) < (*C*) < (*A*) < (*B*)

58. (*c*) Only aldehydes without H at α-C or without α-C gives Cannizzaro reaction.

60. (*b*)
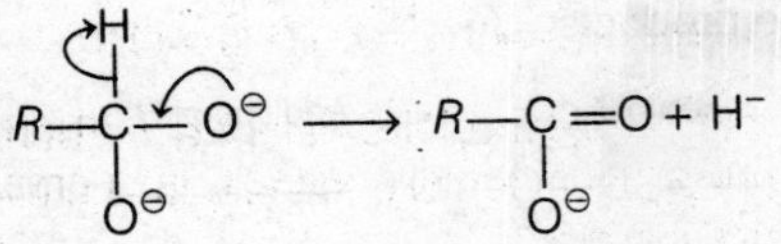

62. (*b*) C_6H_5CHO has no H at α-carbon thus no aldol condensation.

63. (*a*) In resonance form, position of atoms remains unchanged. Only electrons shift
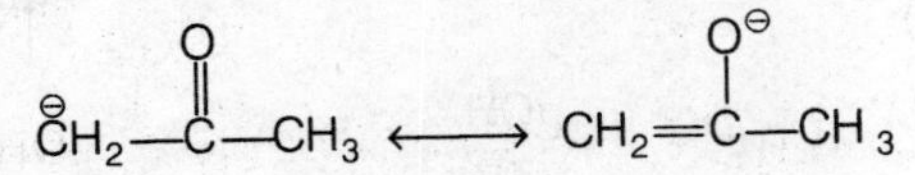

64. (*c*)
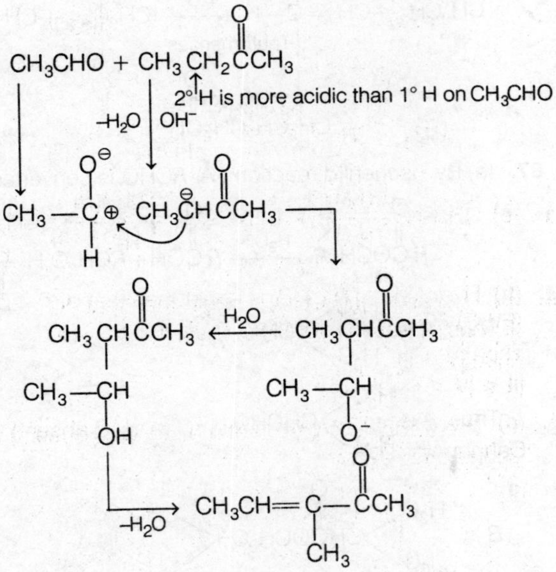

65. (*c*)
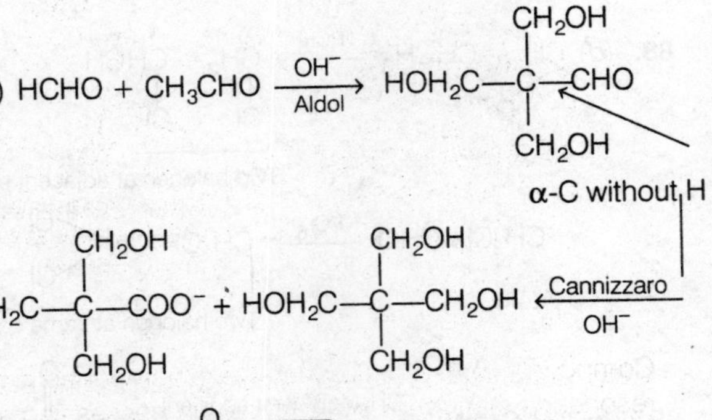

70. (*d*)
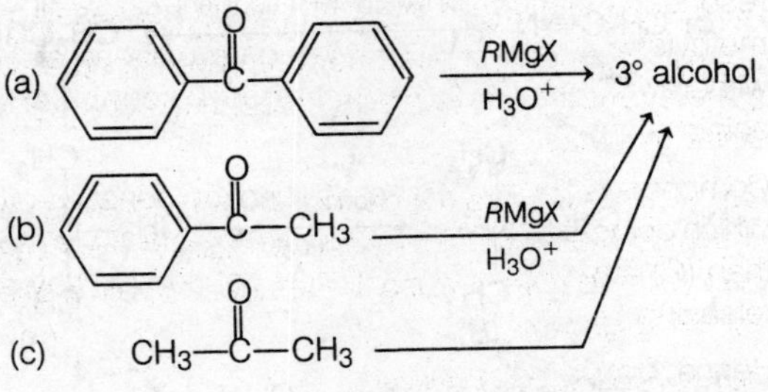

72. (*d*) $LiAlH_4 \rightleftharpoons Li^{\oplus} + (AlH_4^{\ominus}) \rightleftharpoons AlH_3 + H^{\ominus}$

73. (*c*)
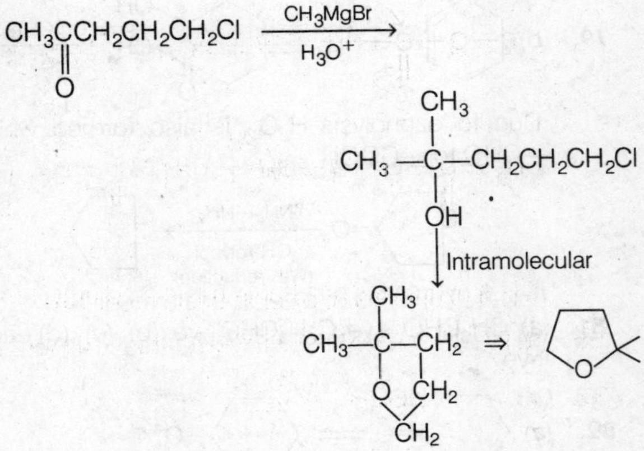

74. (*b*)
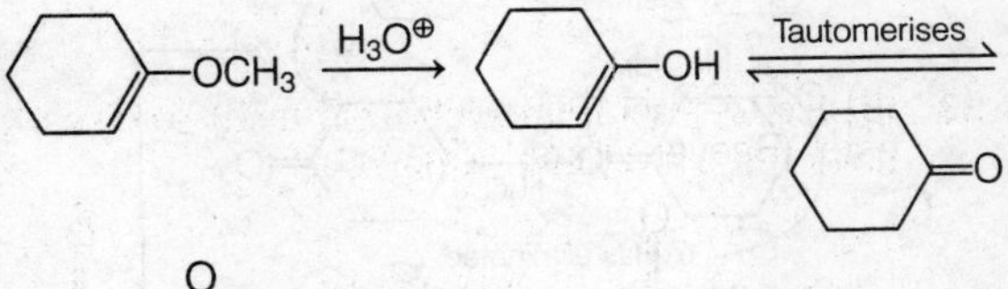

75. (*a*)
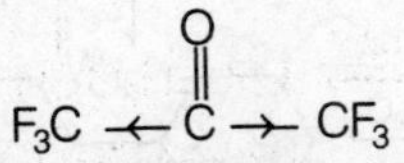

CF_3 is electron withdrawing group making carbonyl carbon more electrophilic for nucleophilic addition.

76. (*b*) Reactivity order toward nucleophilic addition reaction is aldehydes > ketones.

Due to the following reasons aldehydes are more reactive than ketones.

(i) **Inductive effect** An alkyl group has electron donating ($+I$) inductive effect. Hence, greater the number of alkyle group attached to carbonyl group, greater the electron density on carbonyl carbon. Thus, it lowers the attack of nucleophile and hence, reactivity decreases.

(ii) **Steric effect** Increase in the number of alkyl group attached to carbon results in the attack of nucleophile on carbonyl group becomes more and more difficult due to steric hinderance. Therefore, due to two bulky R groups, ketones are less reactive than aldehydes.

So, the correct reactivity order is
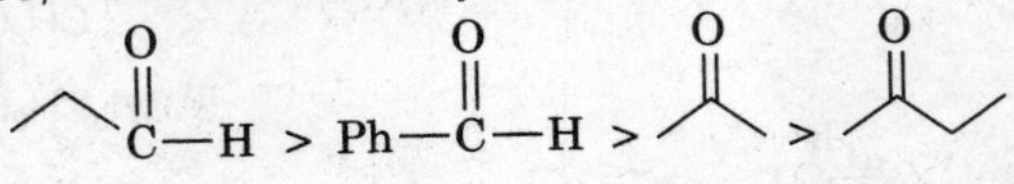

77. (*a*)
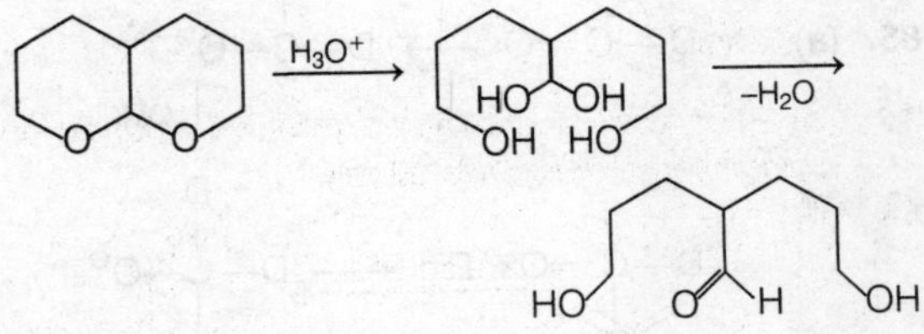

78. (*b*)
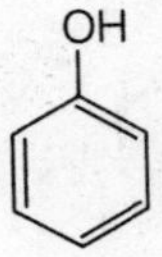

Maximum stable due to conjugation thus maximum enolisation.

79. (*b*)

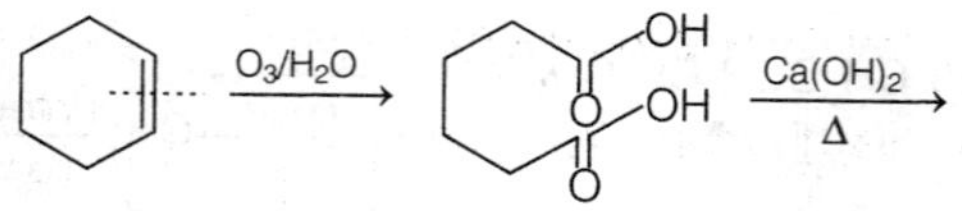

Due to ozonolysis H_2O_2 is also formed which oxidise —CHO to —COOH

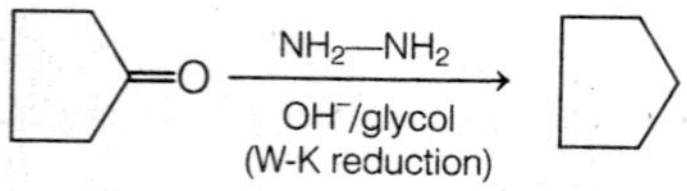

81. (*a*) CH_3CHO +ve, C_6H_5CHO –ve. (b), (c), (d) each species +ve

82. (*a*)

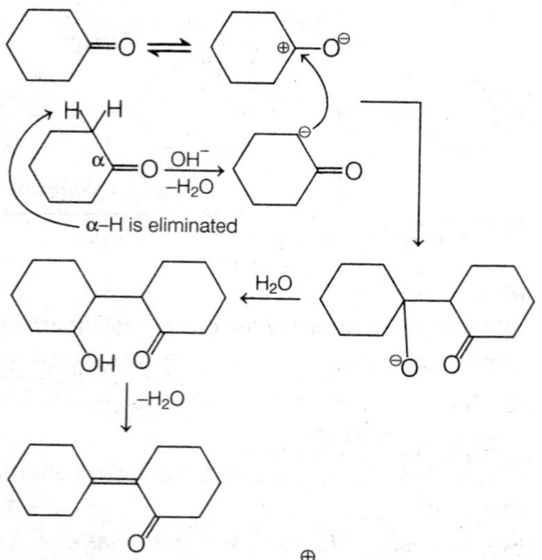

83. (*b*)

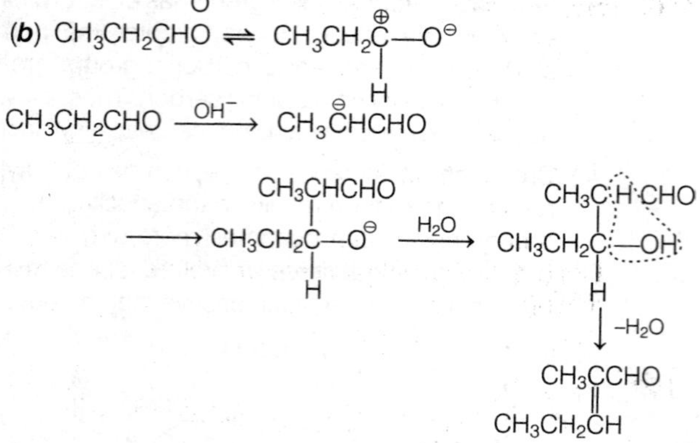

85. (*a*)

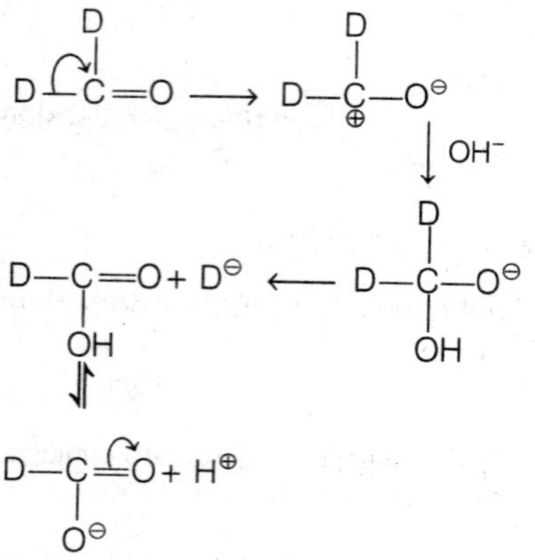

One of the products

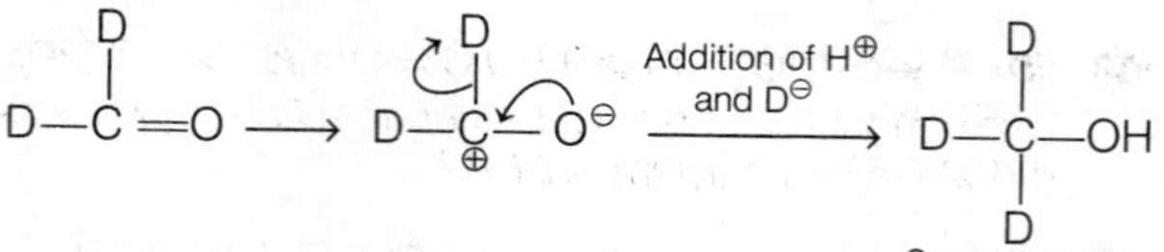

Second product

86. (*c*)

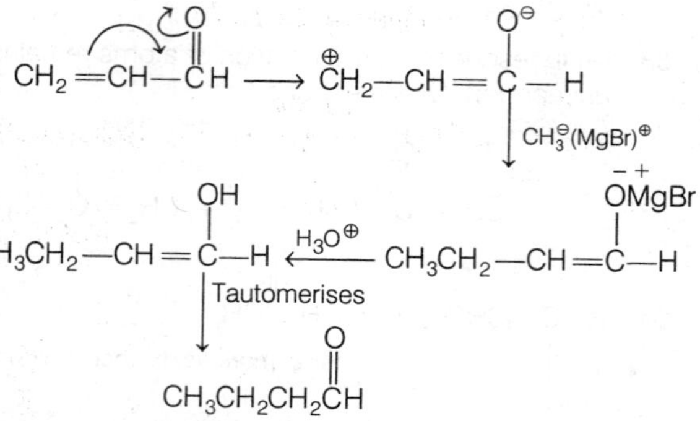

87. (*a*) By Tischenko reaction (*A*) *R*CHO is converted into (*B*)

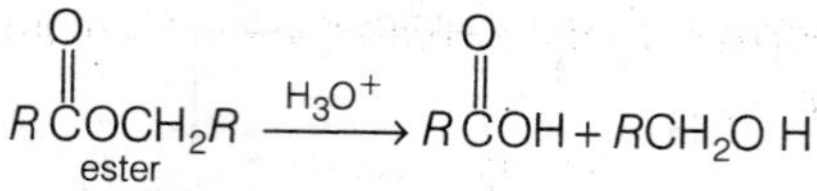

Thus, *R* is

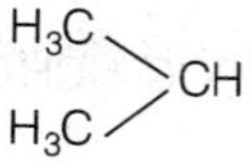

Thus, *A* is

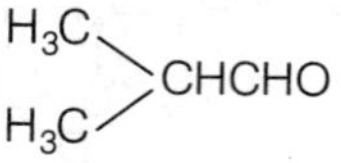

B is

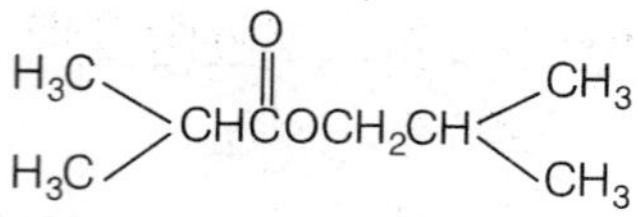

88. (*d*)

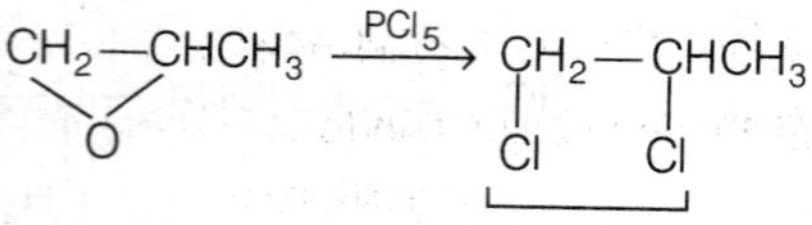

Two halogen at adjacent position (*vic*)

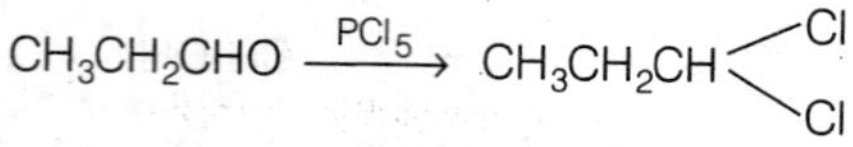

Two halogen at same carbon (*gem*)

89. (*b*)

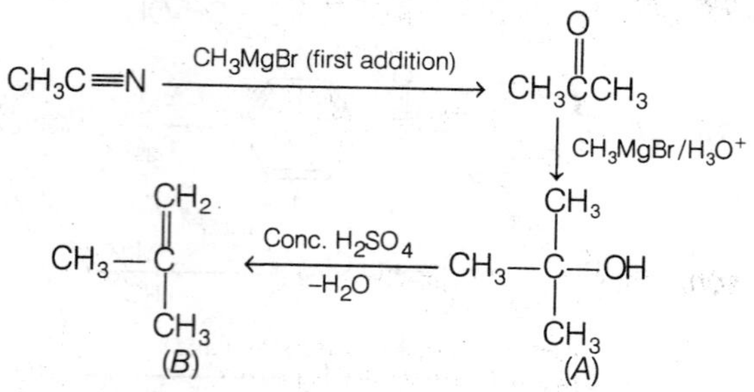

91. (*b*) (C=C) is not reduced. —CHO is reduced to —CH_2OH.

92. (*c*) β-hydroxy carbonyl compound is formed by condensation of carbonyl compound with at least one H at α-carbon.

93. (*a*) *A* gives iodoform test thus *A* has group $-\overset{O}{\overset{\|}{C}}CH_3$. *C* eliminates CO_2 on heating hence, *C* has two —COOH groups at same (*gem*) position.

Only (a) has $\left(-\overset{O}{\overset{\|}{C}}CH_3\right)$

$$\underset{(A)}{CH_3\overset{O}{\overset{\|}{C}}CH_2\overset{O}{\overset{\|}{C}}OC_2H_5} \xrightarrow[\Delta]{NaOH/I_2} CHI_3 \text{ (yellow ppt)} + \underset{(B)}{Na\overset{+}{}\overset{-}{O}\overset{O}{\overset{\|}{C}}CH_2\overset{O}{\overset{\|}{C}}\overset{-}{O}\overset{+}{Na}}$$

$$\xrightarrow{H^+} \underset{(C)}{HO\overset{O}{\overset{\|}{C}}CH_2\overset{O}{\overset{\|}{C}}OH} \xrightarrow{\Delta} CH_3\overset{O}{\overset{\|}{C}}OH$$

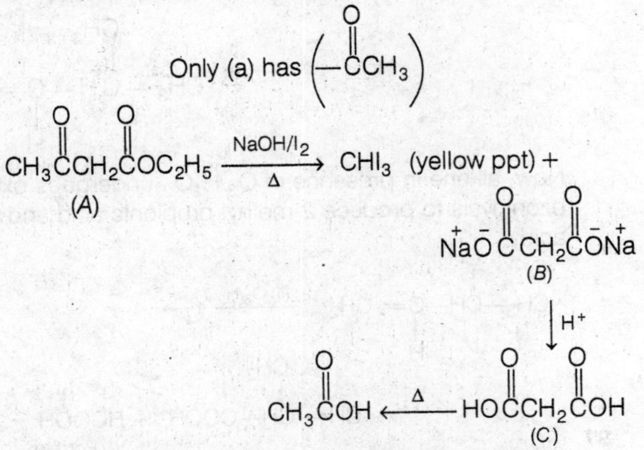

97. (*a*) Vinyl α-H is not involved due to maximum (C—H) bond energy.

$$CH_3CH{=}CH{-}\overset{H}{\underset{\|}{C}}{=}O + H{-}CH_2CH{=}CHCHO \longrightarrow CH_3CH{=}CH{-}\overset{H}{\underset{OH}{C}}{-}\underset{H}{CH}{-}CH{=}CHCHO$$

$$\xrightarrow{-H_2O} CH_3{-}CH{=}CH{-}CH{=}CH{-}CH{=}CH{-}CHO$$

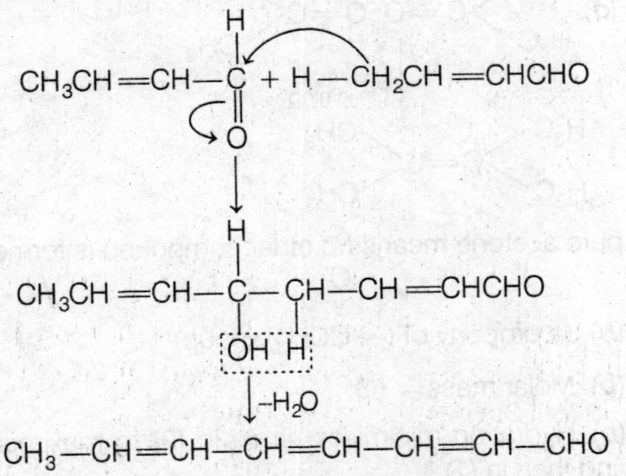

98. (*a*) CH_3CHO forms bisulphite (crystalline) complex.

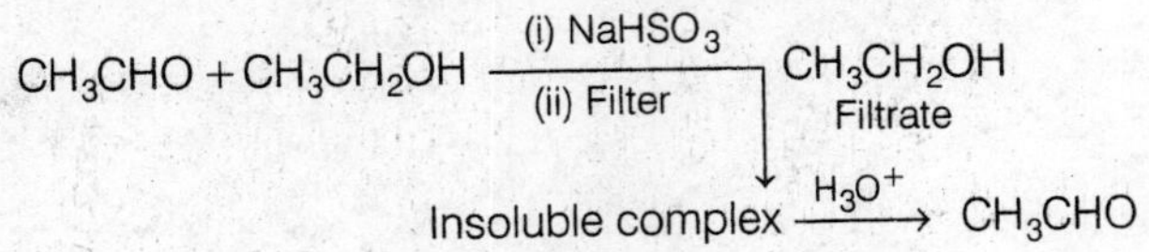

$$CH_3CHO + CH_3CH_2OH \xrightarrow[\text{(ii) Filter}]{\text{(i) } NaHSO_3} \underset{\text{Filtrate}}{CH_3CH_2OH}$$

$$\text{Insoluble complex} \xrightarrow{H_3O^+} CH_3CHO$$

99. (*b*) Cyclohexene $\xrightarrow[\text{Allylic substitution}]{NBS}$ 3-bromocyclohexene (—Br) $\xrightarrow{Mg/ether}$ cyclohexenyl—MgBr $\xrightarrow[\text{(ii) } H_3O^+]{\text{(i) } CH_3CN}$ cyclohexenyl—$\overset{O}{\overset{\|}{C}}CH_3$

100. (*b*) 2-(C≡CH)cyclohexanone ⟶ 2-($\overset{\ominus}{C}{=}\overset{\oplus}{C}H$)cyclohexanone $\xrightarrow{H_2O}$ 2-(CH=CHOH)cyclohexanone

(C=O) is electron withdrawing group hence π-electrons are migrated as given

2-(CH=CHOH)cyclohexanone $\xrightarrow{\text{Tautomerises}}$ 2-(CH_2CHO)cyclohexanone

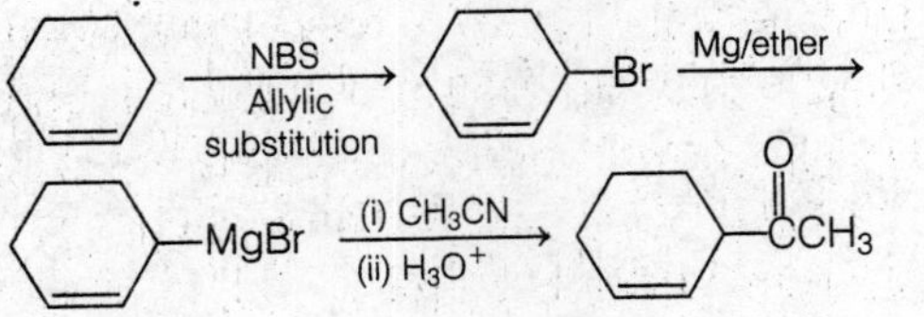

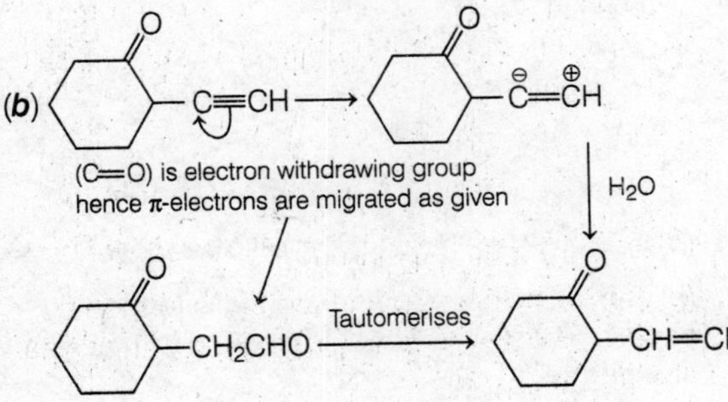

104. (*c*) (due to H at α-carbon)

105. (*a*) $CH_3\underset{O}{\underset{\|}{C}}{-}CH_2{-}CH_2{-}CH_2{-}\underset{O}{\underset{\|}{C}}{-}CH_3 \xrightarrow[\text{condensation}]{\text{Intramolecular}}$

H-atom at α-carbon is condensed with this carbonyl group

$$CH_3\underset{O}{\underset{\|}{C}}\overset{\ominus}{C}H{-}CH_2CH_2\overset{\oplus}{\underset{HO}{C}}{-}CH_3 \longrightarrow \text{ring: } CH_3\overset{O}{\overset{\|}{C}}CH{-}CH_2,\ HO{-}\underset{CH_3}{C}{-}CH_2 \xrightarrow{-H_2O} CH_3\overset{O}{\overset{\|}{C}}C{-}CH_2,\ \underset{CH_3}{C}{-}CH_2$$

107. (*d*)

$$\underset{\text{Diethyl carbonate}}{C_2H_5{-}O{-}\overset{O}{\overset{\|}{C}}{-}O{-}C_2H_5} \xrightarrow[\text{(ii) } H_3O^+]{\text{(i) } CH_3MgBr \text{ (2 moles)}} CH_3\overset{CH_3}{C}{=}\overset{CH_3}{C}CH_3 \xrightarrow{O_3/Zn} CH_3{-}\overset{O}{\overset{\|}{C}}{-}CH_3$$

$$\xrightarrow{CH_3MgBr/H_3O^+} \underset{3^\circ \text{ alcohol}}{(CH_3)_3COH}$$

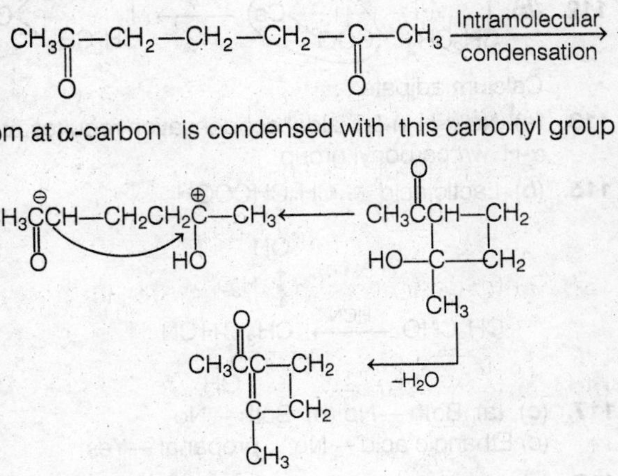

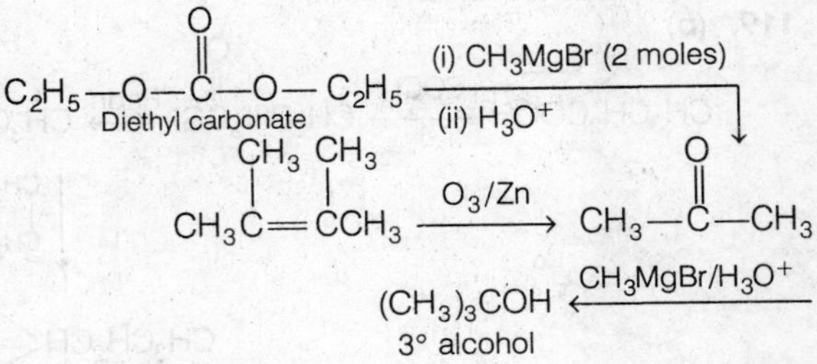

(a) True, (b) True, (c) True

108. (*b*) 2-methyl-2-acetylcyclohexanone ($COCH_3$, CH_3) $\xrightarrow[\text{(ii) } H^+]{\text{(i) KBrO, haloform test}}$ 2-methyl-2-carboxycyclohexanone ($COOH$, CH_3) $\xrightarrow{\Delta}$ 2-methylcyclohexanone (CH_3)

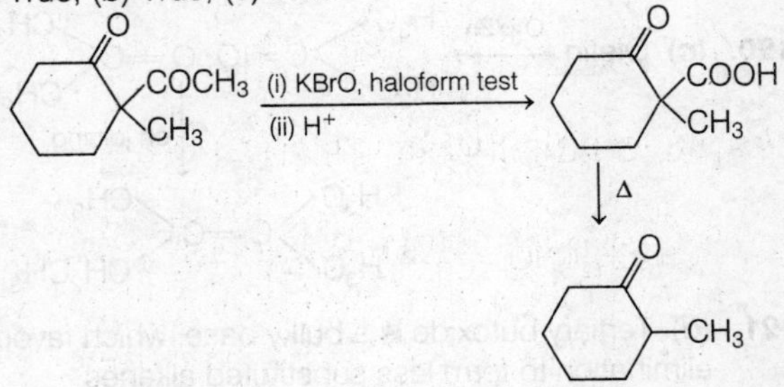

If keto group is at β-position *wrt* COOH, CO_2 is lost due to heating.

109. (*a*)

$$\text{Cyclohexanone}{=}O + (C_6H_5)P{=}CH_2 \xrightarrow{DMSO} \text{Cyclohexane}{=}CH_2$$

(Wittig reaction)

110. (*d*) *A* is $CH_3\overset{O}{\overset{\|}{C}}CH_2\overset{O}{\overset{\|}{C}}OC_2H_5$

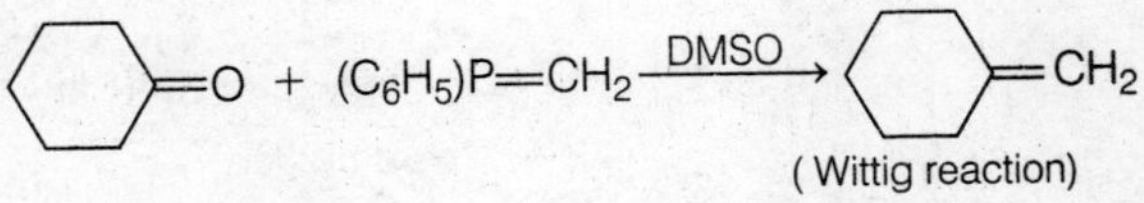

Enol due to H at α-carbon

Oximes due to carbonyl group, iodoform test due to CH_3CO, group.

111. (*d*) $CH_3CHO + HCN \longrightarrow H{-}\overset{CH_3}{\underset{CN}{C}}{-}OH$

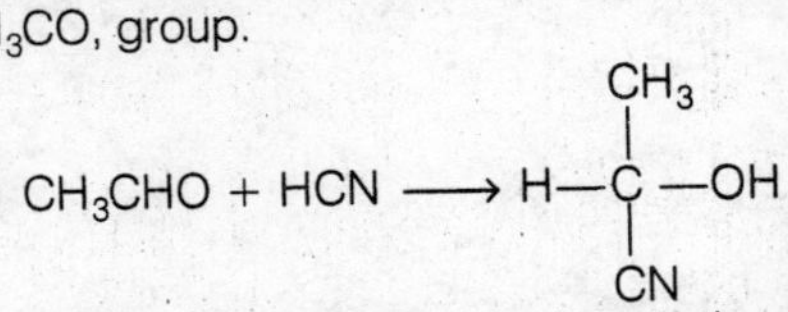

(*d*) and (*l*) are formed in equal parts thus racemic mixture.

112. (*b*) 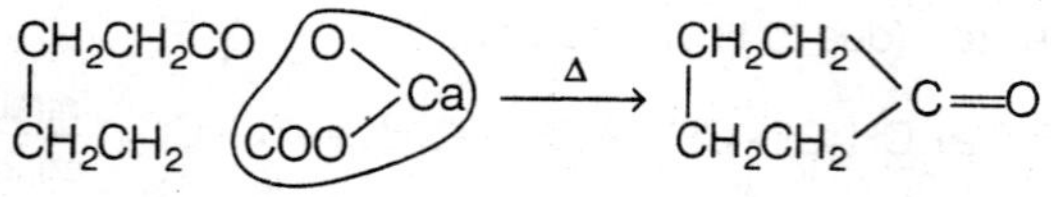

Calcium adipate

113. (*a*) No α-H in (a), aldol condensation requires at least one α-H *wrt* carbonyl group.

116. (*b*) Lactic acid 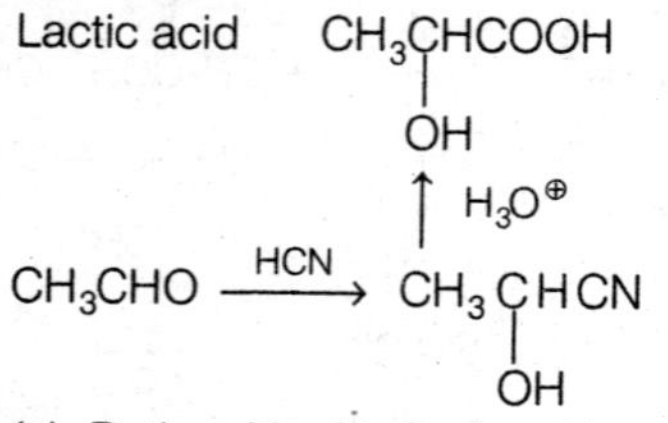

117. (*c*) (a) Both —No (b) Both —No
(c) Ethanoic acid —No, propanal —Yes

118. (*c*) Lucas test is for alcohol.

119. (*b*)

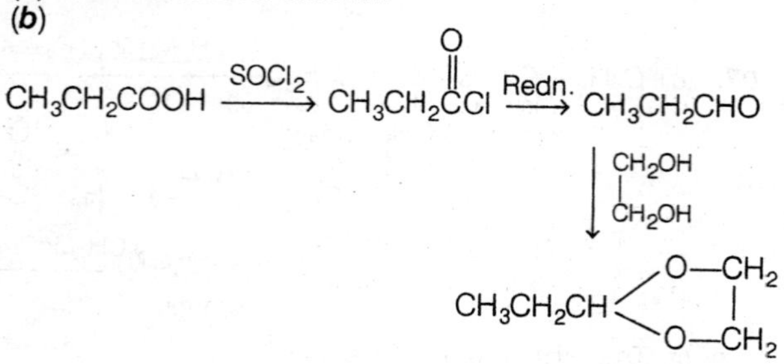

120. (*c*) Olefin 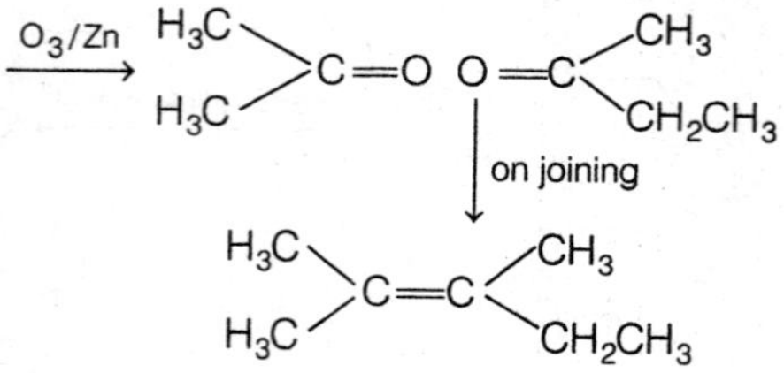

121. (*d*) Tertiary butoxide is a bulky base, which favour elimination to form less substituted alkenes (Hofmann-product).

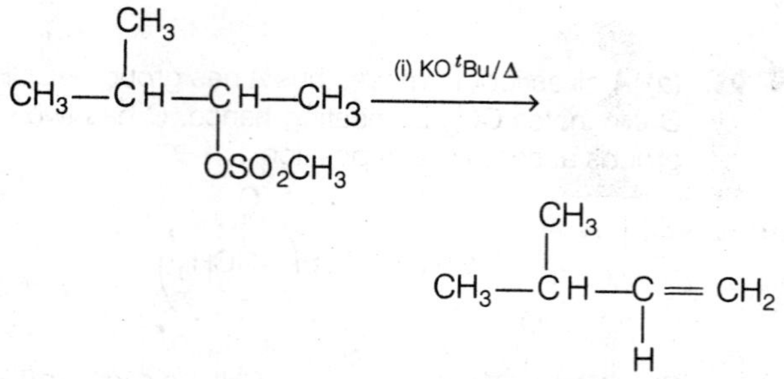

Now, alkene in presence of O_3/H_2O_2 undergoes oxidative ozonloysis to produce 2-methyl propionic acid and formic acid.

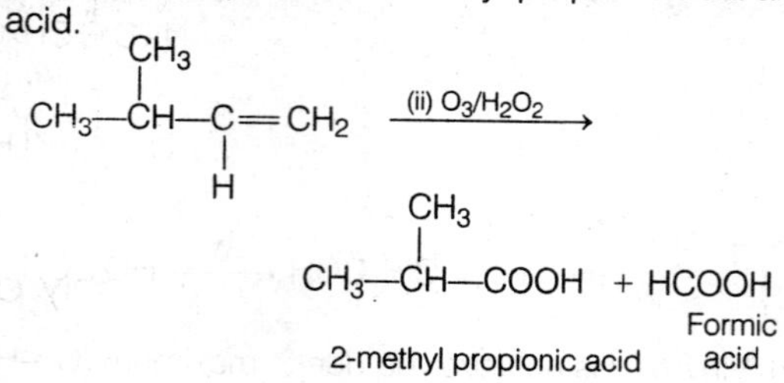

122. (*d*) 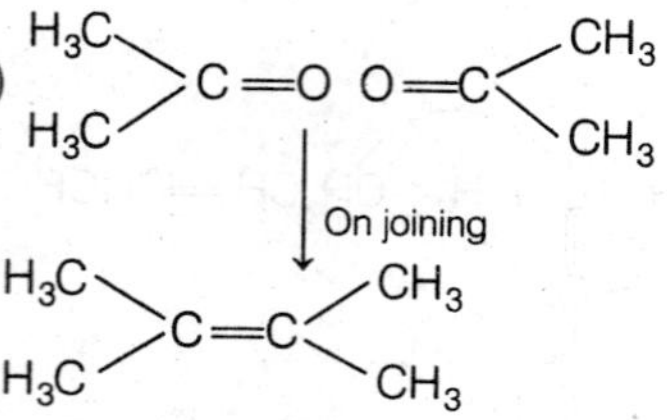

pure acetone means no other compound is formed.

123. (*b*) (a property of $(-\overset{O}{\overset{\|}{C}}CH_3)$ group)

130. (*b*) Molar mass = 58.

135. (*b*) Hydration minimises strain in (2) to maximum extent and then in (1).

12 Carboxylic Acids

Objective Questions Type I [Only one correct option]

In each of the questions below, four choices are given of which only one is correct.

1. RCH_2OH is oxidised to $R\overset{O}{\overset{\|}{C}}OH$ by $Cr_2O_7^{2-}/H_3O^+$. Intermediate formed and final state of $Cr_2O_7^{2-}$ are respectively

(a) $R\overset{O}{\overset{\|}{C}}H, Cr^{3+}$ (b) $R\overset{O}{\overset{\|}{C}}H, CrO_3$

(c) $R\overset{O}{\overset{\|}{C}}OH, Cr^{3+}$ (d) $R\overset{O}{\overset{\|}{C}}OH, CrO_3$

2. Suitable oxidising agent for the following change is ...... and predominant product is ......

$$CH_3\overset{O}{\overset{\|}{C}}CH_2CH_3 \longrightarrow CH_3\overset{O}{\overset{\|}{C}}OH \text{ and } CH_3CH_2\overset{O}{\overset{\|}{C}}OH$$

(a) $MnO_4^-/OH^-, CH_3CH_2\overset{O}{\overset{\|}{C}}OH$ (b) $Cr_2O_7^{2-}/H^+, CH_3\overset{O}{\overset{\|}{C}}OH$

(c) $MnO_4^-/OH^-, CH_3\overset{O}{\overset{\|}{C}}OH$ (d) $Cr_2O_7^{2-}/H^+, CH_3CH_2\overset{O}{\overset{\|}{C}}OH$

3. $CH_3\overset{O}{\overset{\|}{C}}CH_3$ can be converted to $CH_3\overset{O}{\overset{\|}{C}}OH$ by following methods

I. $CH_3\overset{O}{\overset{\|}{C}}CH_3 \xrightarrow[\Delta, H^+]{I_2/NaOH}$ II. $CH_3\overset{O}{\overset{\|}{C}}CH_3 \xrightarrow{Cr_2O_7^{2-}/H^+}$

III. $CH_3\overset{O}{\overset{\|}{C}}CH_3 \xrightarrow{Ag(NH_3)_2^+}$

Which methods can be effective?

(a) I, III (b) II, III (c) I, II (d) I, II, III

4. Alkaline $KMnO_4$ oxidises following alcohol into carboxylic acid.

(a) $CH_2{=}CHCH_2OH$ (b) $HC{\equiv}CCH_2OH$

(c) CH_3CH_2OH (d) 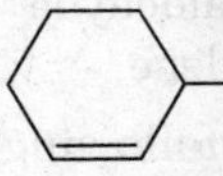$-CH_2OH$

5. Which reaction does not have the correct oxidising agent?

(a) $CH_2{=}CHCHO \xrightarrow{[Ag(NH_3)_2]^+} CH_2{=}CHCO_2H$

(b) $CH_2{=}CHCHO \xrightarrow{MnO_4^-/OH^-} CH_2{=}CHCO_2H$

(c) $CH_3CH_2OH \xrightarrow{Cr_2O_7^{2-}/H^+} CH_3CO_2H$

(d) All of the above

6. Grignard reagent is a source of

(a) carbocation

(b) carbanion

(c) Both (a) and (b)

(d) None of the above

7. Carbonation of an organometallic reagent

(a) is a one-carbon homologation

(b) involves its carbanionic centre attacking the electron-deficient carbonyl carbon

(c) Both of the above are correct

(d) None of the above is correct

8. The mechanism of carbonation is analogous to that of addition to

(a) aldehydes and ketones (b) nitriles

(c) alcohols (d) amines

9. Which of the following cannot be used for the synthesis of a carboxylic acid?

(a) 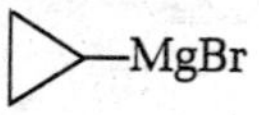   (b) $CH_2{=}CHCH_2MgBr$

(c) $CH_3\overset{O}{\overset{\|}{C}}CH_2MgBr$ (d) 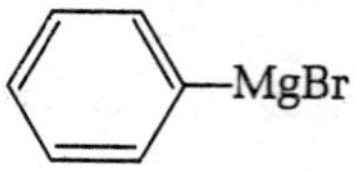

10. Indicate correct synthesis of carboxylic acid from organometallic compound.

(a) $CH_3MgBr \xrightarrow{CO_2} \xrightarrow{H_3O^+}$

(b) $CH_3M\ gBr \xrightarrow[\text{(ii) } CO_2]{\text{(i) } H_3O^+}$

(c) $CH_3\overset{O}{\overset{\|}{C}}CH_2CH_2M\ gBr \xrightarrow[\text{(ii) } H_3O^+]{\text{(i) } CO_2}$

(d) All of the above

11. In the reaction,

$$CH_3COOH \xrightarrow{LiAlH_4} A \xrightarrow{PCl_5} B \xrightarrow{\text{Alc. KOH}} C$$

The product C is **[JEE Main 2014]**

(a) acetaldehyde (b) acetylene
(c) ethylene (d) acetyl chloride

12. For the following reaction,

$$R{-}C{\equiv}N \xrightarrow{H_3O^+} R\overset{O}{\overset{\|}{C}}OH$$

(a) there is protonation of the electronegative nitrogen followed by attack of water at the electron-deficient carbon
(b) an amide is formed as an intermediate
(c) nitrogen atom is expelled as ammonium ion
(d) All of the above are true

13. $CH_2{=}CHCO_2H$ can be obtained in the folllowing synthesis

(a) $CH_2{=}CHCN \xrightarrow{H_3O^+}$ (b) $CH_2{=}CHCN \xrightarrow{OH^-}$
(c) Both (a) and (b)   (d) None of these

14. In which case yield of the carboxylic acid is maximum?

(a) $CH_3CH_2CH_2CH_2Br \xrightarrow{\text{KCN, DMSO}} \xrightarrow{H_3O^+}$

(b) $CH_3\underset{Br}{\underset{|}{C}}HCH_2CH_3 \xrightarrow{\text{KCN, DMSO}} \xrightarrow{H_3O^+}$

(c) $CH_3{-}\underset{CH_3}{\underset{|}{\overset{CH_3}{\overset{|}{C}}}}{-}Br \xrightarrow{\text{KCN, DMSO}} \xrightarrow{H_3O^+}$

(d) Equivalent yield

15. In which cases RCO_2H is not the product?

I. $RCN \xrightarrow{H_3O^+}$ II. $RCN \xrightarrow{OH^-}$
III. $RCN \xrightarrow{DIBALH}$ IV. $RCN \xrightarrow{SnCl_2/HCl}$
V. $RCN \xrightarrow{LiAlH_4}$

(a) All except III
(b) All except III, V
(c) All except I
(d) All except I, II

16. Which of the following methods does give a carboxylic acid without homologation?

(a) $RCH_2OH \xrightarrow{Cr_2O_7^{2-}/H_3O^+}$

(b) $RCH_2Br \xrightarrow{CN^-,\ H_3O^+}$

(c) $CH_3OH \xrightarrow[Co(CO)_8]{\text{CO, pressure}}$

(d) $CH_3CH_2ONa \xrightarrow[\text{pressure}]{CO,\ \Delta} \xrightarrow{H_3O^+}$

17. Isobutyric acid can be synthesised by two methods

I. $CH_3\underset{CH_3}{\underset{|}{C}}HBr \xrightarrow{CN^-} \xrightarrow{H_3O^+}$

II. $CH_3CH{=}CH_2 + CO + H_2O \xrightarrow[600\ K]{H_3PO_4}$

Which of the above methods can be adopted?

(a) I
(b) II
(c) Both (a) and (b)
(d) None of the above

18. $A(C_8H_{10})$ by ozonolysis forms $B(C_4H_6O_2)$, A and B can be

(a) $HC{\equiv}C(CH_2)_4C{\equiv}CH, CH_2{=}CHCH_2CO_2H$
(b) $HC{\equiv}C(CH_2)_4C{\equiv}CH, CH_3CH{=}CHCO_2H$
(c) 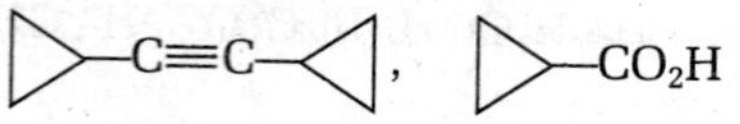
(d) $CH_2{=}CHCH_2C{\equiv}CCH_2CH{=}CH_2$, $CH_2{=}CHCH_2CO_2H$

19. Consider the following two reactions,

$$\underset{cis}{CH_3CH{=}CHCH_3} \xrightarrow[H_3O^+]{\text{I}: MnO_4^-,\ OH^-,\ \Delta}$$

$$\text{II} \downarrow MnO_4^-, OH^-$$

Select the correct statement(s) about these reactions.

(a) racemic mixture is formed in I and *meso* form in II
(b) *meso* form is formed in I and racemic mixture in II
(c) *meso* form is formed in I and C=C bond cleaved in II
(d) C=C bond is cleaved in I and *meso* form is formed in II

20. In which case number of carbon atoms is retained?

(a) $CH_3CH{=}CHCH_3 \xrightarrow{O_3/H_2O/Zn}$

(b) $CH_3C{\equiv}CCH_3 \xrightarrow[\Delta]{KMnO_4,\ OH^-}$

(c) 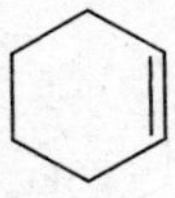 $\xrightarrow{MnO_4^-,\ OH^-,\ \Delta}$

(d) $CH_3CH_2CH{=}CH_2 \xrightarrow{O_3/H_2O}$

21. Acid hydrolysis of an ester is reversible because

(a) alcohol and acid react together to form ester

(b) protonation of ester makes carbonyl carbon more reactive for nucleophilic attack

(c) proton being strong nucleophile, favours hydrolysis

(d) H_3O^+ is a nucleophile as well as electrophile

22. Alkaline hydrolysis of ester is irreversible because of

(a) carboxylate ion (a nucleophile) cannot attack alcohol (a nucleophile)

(b) base, being strong electrophile favours hydrolysis

(c) Both (a) and (b)

(d) None of the above

23. In the above reaction, the reagent "A" is

[JEE Main 2021, March]

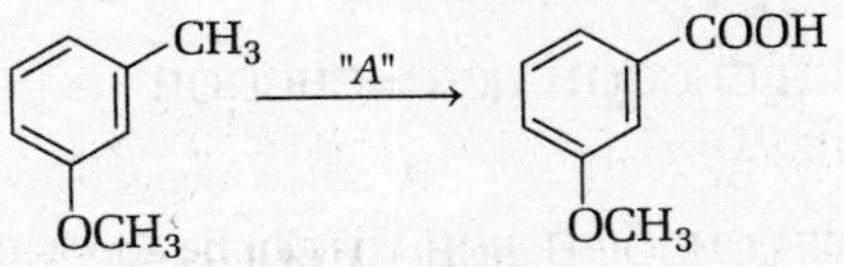

(a) $NaBH_4, H_3O^+$ (b) $LiAlH_4$

(c) Alkaline $KMnO_4, H^+$ (d) HCl, Zn-Hg

24. Which is the leaving group in the hydrolysis of $CH_3\overset{\overset{O}{\|}}{C}OC_2H_5$?

(a) $C_2H_5^+$ (b) $C_2H_5O^-$ (c) $CH_3\overset{\overset{O}{\|}}{C}O$ (d) CH_3

25. Which cannot be used for the synthesis of a carboxylic acid?

(a) $CH_3CN \xrightarrow{H_3O^+}$ (b) $CH_3\overset{\overset{O}{\|}}{C}Cl \xrightarrow{H_3O^+}$

(c) $CH_3\overset{\overset{O}{\|}}{C}OC_2H_5 \xrightarrow{OH^-}$ (d) $CH_3\overset{\overset{O}{\|}}{C}O\overset{\overset{O}{\|}}{C}CH_3 \xrightarrow{H_3O^+}$

26. What is the end-product *A* in the following sequence of reactions?

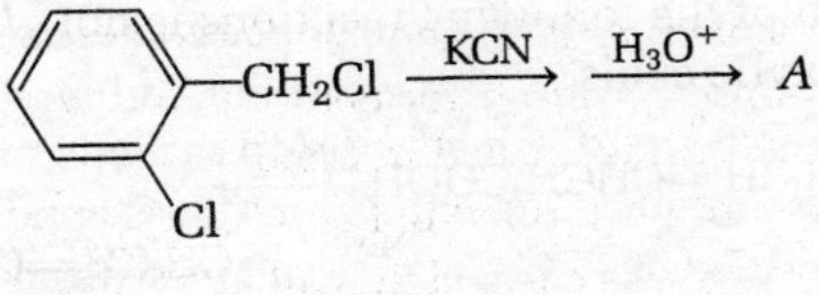

(a) 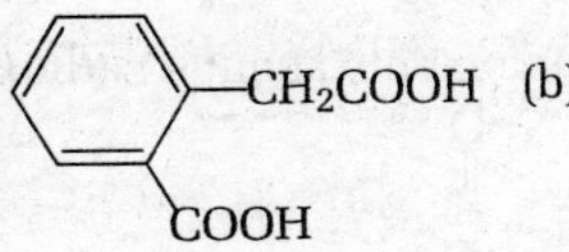 (b) 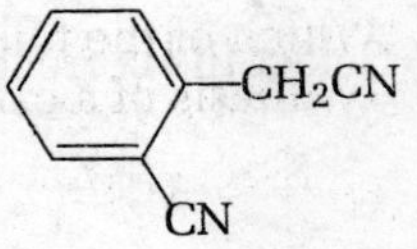

(c) 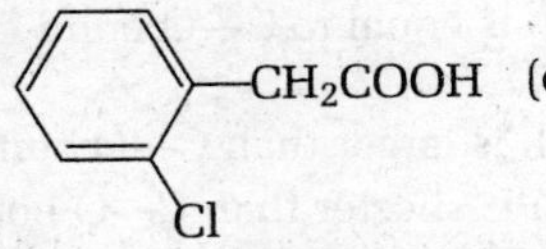 (d) 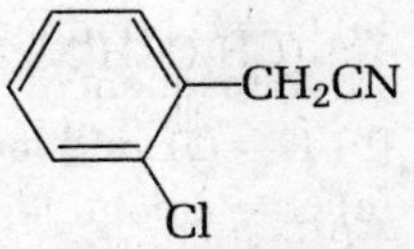

27. In the following sequence of reactions identify *A*

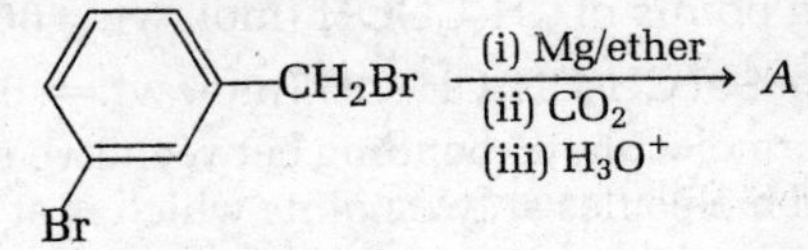

(a) 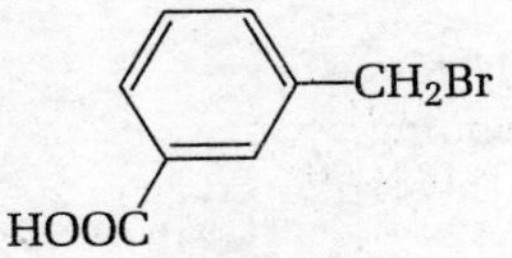

(b) 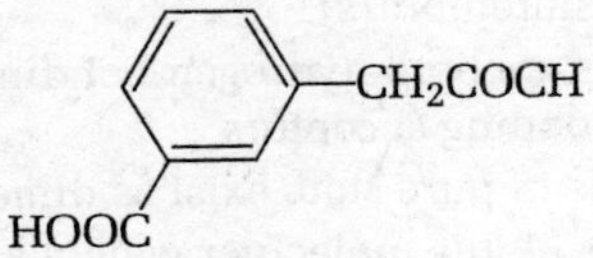

(c) 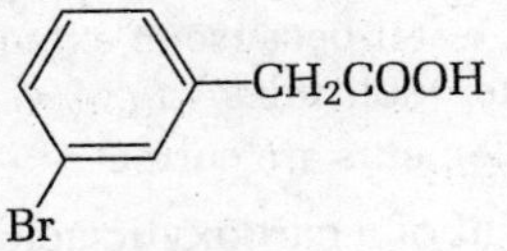

(d) 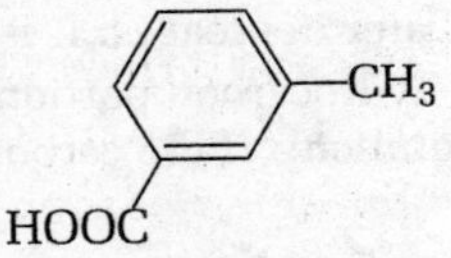

28. Consider the following reactions,

I. $H_3CCl_3 \xrightarrow{OH^\ominus}$

II. $H_3CCHO \xrightarrow{[Ag(NH_3)_2]^+OH^\ominus}$

III. $H_3CCO_2C_2H_5 \xrightarrow{OH^\ominus}$

Carboxylic acid salt is the final product only in the reaction(s).

(a) I, II and III (b) II and III

(c) Only II (d) Only III

29. Identify '*Z*' in the following sequence of reactions.

$$CH_3COOH \xrightarrow{NH_3} X \xrightarrow{\Delta} Y \xrightarrow{P_2O_5} Z$$

(a) CH_4 (b) CH_3CHO

(c) CH_3CN (d) $CH_3COO^-NH_4^+$

30. Which acid has —COOH group?

(a) Carbolic acid (b) Picric acid

(c) Anthranilic acid (d) Sulphanilic acid

31. Select the correct statements about a carboxylic acid

$$R-\overset{\overset{\large O}{\|}}{C}-O-H$$

(a) C=O bond length is equal to C—O bond length due to resonance
(b) C=O bond length is larger than C—O bond length
(c) C=O bond length is shorter than C—O bond length
(d) C—O, C=O and O—H bond lengths are equal

32. Boiling points of CH_3COOH (mol. wt. = 60) is higher than that of $CH_3CH_2CH_2OH$ (mol. wt. = 60) due to
(a) intermolecular H-bonding between two carboxylic acid molecules at two points which is at one point only in alcohol
(b) strong van der Waals' forces
(c) intramolecular H-bonding
(d) None of the above

33. Select the correct statement(s).
(a) Carboxylic acids are both hydrogen-bonding donors and hydrogen-bonding acceptors
(b) Carboxylic acids in pure state exist as dimers
(c) Carboxylic acids of low molecular weight are infinitely soluble in water because of extensive H-bonding with water molecules
(d) All of the above statements are correct

34. As the molecular weight of a carboxylic acid increases, solubility in water decreases. It is due to
(a) hydrophobicity of the hydrocarbon portion overweighs the hydrophilicity of the carboxyl group
(b) hydrophobicity of the carboxyl group overweighs the hydrophilicity of the hydrocarbon portion
(c) ionisation of the carboxylic acid is increased
(d) carboxylic acid exists as dimer

35. Increasing order of the boiling points of CH_3COOH (I), $CH_3CH_2CH_2OH$ (II) and CH_3CH_2CHO (III) is
(a) I < II < III (b) III < II < I
(c) II < I < III (d) III < I = II

36. Consider the following carboxylic acids

I. $CH_2=CHCH_2\overset{O}{\overset{\|}{C}}OH$ II. $CH_3\overset{O}{\overset{\|}{C}}CH_2\overset{O}{\overset{\|}{C}}OH$

III. 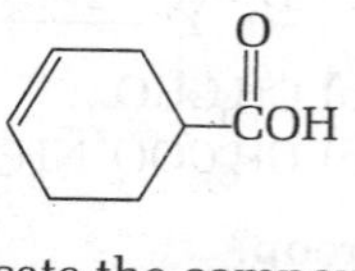   IV. 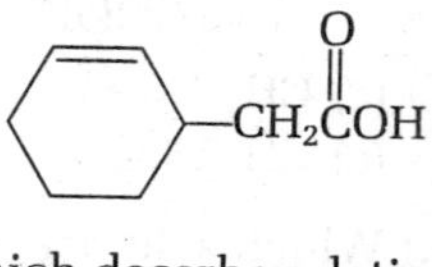

Indicate the compounds in which decarboxylation takes place on heating.
(a) III, IV (b) I, III
(c) II, IV (d) I, II

37. 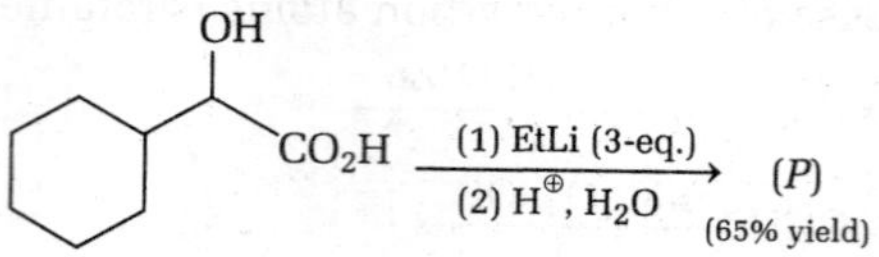

Product (P) of the reaction is

(a) 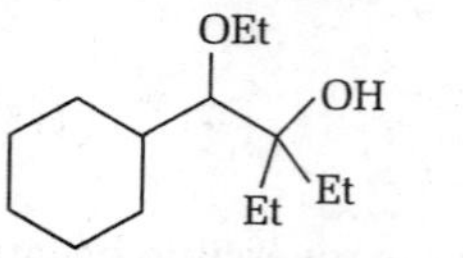   (b) 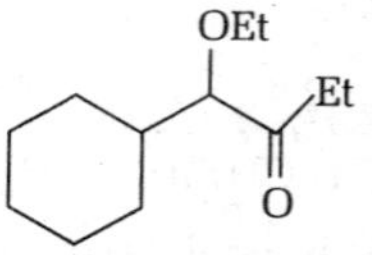

(b) 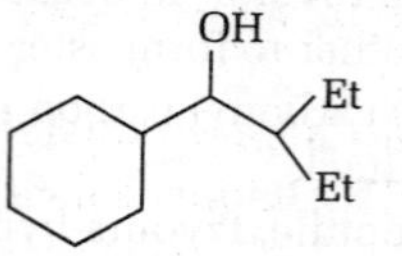   (d) 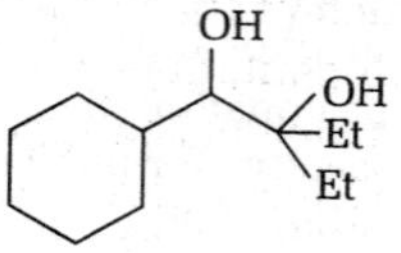

38. In the following sequence of reactions, A and B are respectively

$$RCH_2CH_2COOH \xrightarrow[\text{(ii) } H_2O]{\text{(i) P, } Br_2} A \xrightarrow[\text{(ii) } H^+]{\text{(i) } NaOC_2H_5} B$$

(a) $R\underset{Br}{\underset{|}{C}}HCH_2COOH$, $RCH=CHCOOH$
(b) $R\underset{Br}{\underset{|}{C}}HCH_2COOH$, $R\underset{OC_2H_5}{\underset{|}{C}}HCH_2COOH$
(c) $RCH_2\underset{Br}{\underset{|}{C}}HCOOH$, $RCH=CHCOOH$
(d) $RCH_2\underset{Br}{\underset{|}{C}}HCOOH$, $RCH_2\underset{OC_2H_5}{\underset{|}{C}}HCOOH$

39. Hell-Volhard-Zelinsky reaction is used to prepare A (from RCH_2CH_2COOH) and actually takes place through formation of B which is hydrolysed to get A. A and B are respectively
(a) $RCH_2\underset{Br}{\underset{|}{C}}HCOOH$, $RCH_2\underset{Br}{\underset{|}{C}}HCOBr$
(b) $R\underset{Br}{\underset{|}{C}}HCH_2COOH$, $R\underset{Br}{\underset{|}{C}}HCOBr$
(c) $R\underset{Br}{\underset{|}{C}}HCH_2COOH$, $RCH=CHCOOH$
(d) $RCH\underset{Br}{\underset{|}{C}}HCOOH$, $RCH=CHCOOH$

40. Which of the following reactions is not given by carboxylic acids?

(a) $CH_3CH=CHCH_2COOH \xrightarrow{LiAlH_4} CH_3CH=CHCH_2CH_2OH$

(b) $CH_3CH_2CO_2H \xrightarrow{\Delta} CH_3CH_3 + CO_2$

(c) 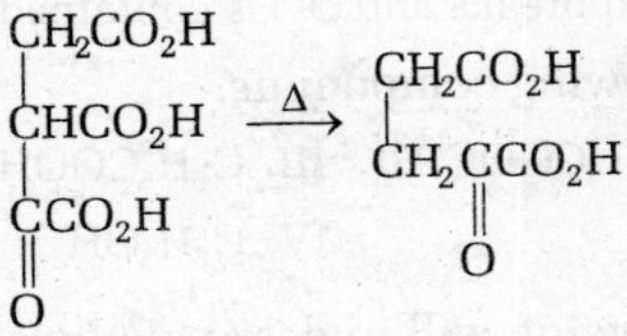

(d) $CH_3\underset{\underset{Br}{|}}{C}HCO_2H \xrightarrow{NaOC_2H_5} CH_2{=}CHCO_2H$

41. Which of the following calcium salt will give cyclopentanone on heating?

(a) Calcium succinate (b) Calcium adipate
(c) Calcium glucarate (d) Calcium oxalate

42. Select the incorrect statement.

(a) NaOH is strong enough to remove the proton from phenols and carboxylic acids.
(b) $NaHCO_3$ is only strong enough to remove the proton of carboxylic acids.
(c) Mixture of phenol and succinic acid can be separated using $NaHCO_3$.
(d) Mixture of phenol and succinic acid can be separated using NaOH.

43. Fehling's solution can make distinction between following pairs :

I. $CH_3COOH, HCOOH$ II. $CH_3COOH, HCHO$
III. $C_6H_5CHO, HCHO$ IV. $CH_3CHO, HCHO$

Select the correct pairs.

(a) I, II, III (b) II, III, IV
(c) II, III (d) II only

44. Which is the incorrect statement?

(a) Electron-withdrawing group stabilises the anion ($RCOO^-$) and thus, acidic nature of RCOOH is increased.
(b) Electron-pumping group stabilises the anion ($RCOO^-$) and thus, acidic nature of RCOOH is increased.
(c) Bond-lengths C=O and C—O$^{\ominus}$ in the following are equal.

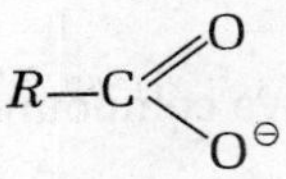

(d) Electron-pumping group destabilises the anion ($RCOO^-$). and thus, acidic nature of RCOOH is decreased

45. Which has maximum value of equilibrium constant?

(a) $CH_3COOH + H_2O \rightleftharpoons CH_3COO^- + H_3O^+$
(b) $HCOOH + H_2O \rightleftharpoons HCOO^- + H_3O^+$
(c) $C_6H_5COOH + H_2O \rightleftharpoons C_6H_5COO^- + H_3O^+$
(d) $CF_3COOH + H_2O \rightleftharpoons CF_3COO^- + H_3O^+$

46. In which case Hell-Volhard-Zelinsky reaction can take place

(a) 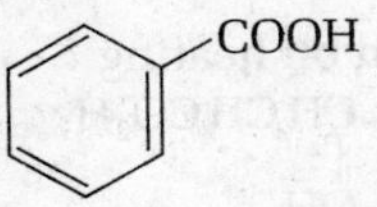
(b) 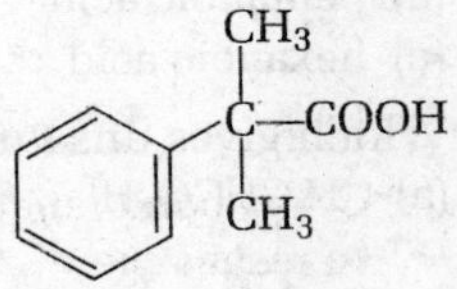
(c) 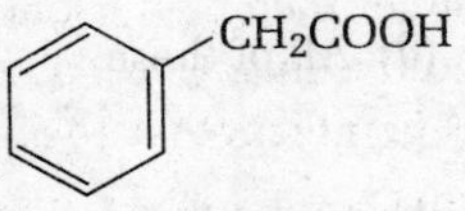
(d) $(CH_3)_3C—COOH$

47. The correct set of reagents for the following conversion is

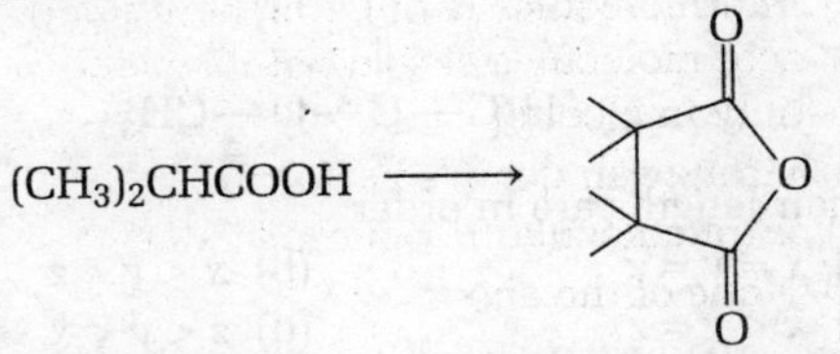

(a) P_4/I_2, Na, conc. H_2SO_4 (b) P_2O_5, $LiAlH_4$
(c) P_2O_5/Δ, H_2O, P_4/I_2, Na (d) P_4/O_2, Na, P_2O_5/Δ

48. When salicylic acid is nitrated,

(a) —COOH group is knocked out and product is picric acid
(b) —OH group is knocked out and product is *m*-nitrobenzoic acid
(c) —OH and —COOH groups both are knocked out and product is 1,3,5-trinitrobenzoic acid
(d) product is 2-hydroxy 5-nitrobenzoic acid

49. In which case van't Hoff factor is less than 1?

(a) Acetic acid or benzoic acid is taken is benzene solvent
(b) Benzoic acid is dissolved in aqueous solution at 50°C
(c) Glucose is dissolved in aqueous solution
(d) Potassium chloride is dissolved in aqueous solution

50. Considering the above chemical reaciton, identify the product '*X*'. **[JEE Main 2021, March]**

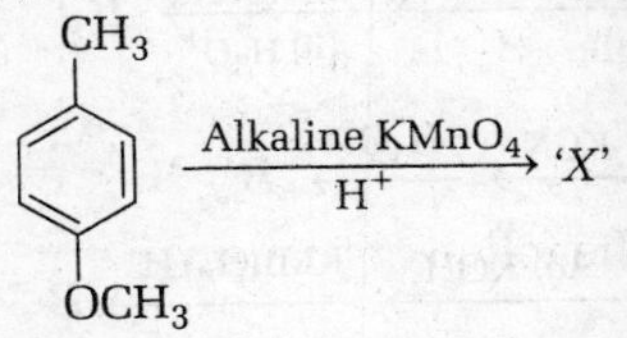

(a) *X* - 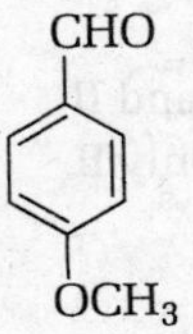
(b) *X* - 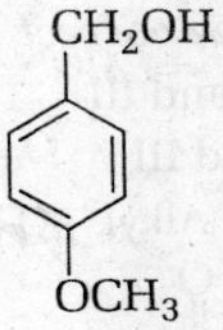
(c) *X* - 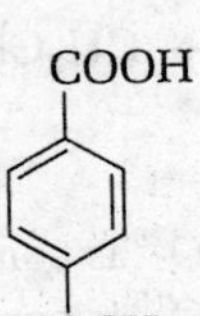
(d) *X* - 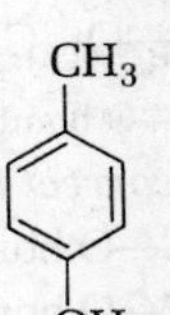

51. IUPAC name of valeric acid is
(a) pentanoic acid (b) butanoic acid
(c) hexanoic acid (d) benzoic acid

52. Which gives unsaturated acid on heating ?
(a) $CH_3CH(OH)CO_2H$ (b) $CH_2(OH)CH_2CO_2H$
(c) $CH_2(OH)CH_2CH_2CO_2H$ (d) All of these

53. In the following there are three carbon–oxygen bonds denoted by *x*, *y* and *z*

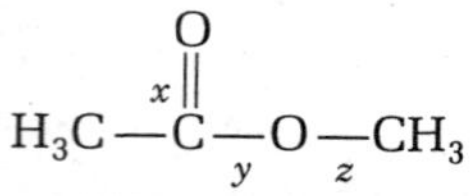

Their lengths are in order
(a) $x = y = z$ (b) $x < y < z$
(c) $x < y = z$ (d) $z < y < x$

54. The correct order of acidity for the following compounds is **[JEE Advanced 2016]**

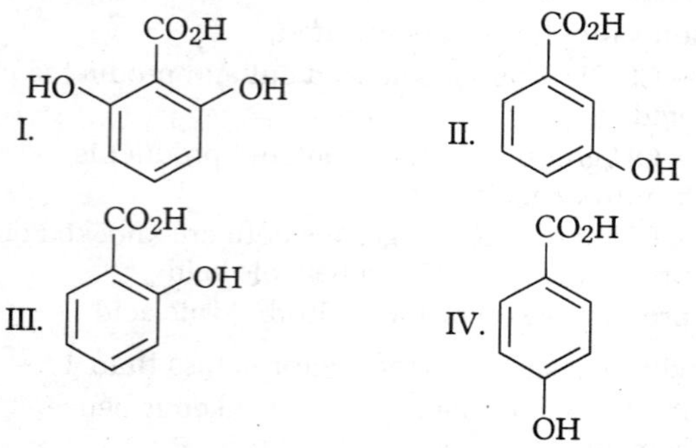

(a) I > II > III > IV (b) III > I > II > IV
(c) III > IV > II > I (d) I > III > IV > II

55. 4-bromo-1-butanol (*A*) can be converted into 5-hydroxy pentanoic acid (*B*) by following method(s)

I. $A \xrightarrow{Mg/ether} \xrightarrow[(ii)\ H_3O^+]{(i)\ CO_2} B$

II. $A \xrightarrow{KCN} \xrightarrow{H_3O^+} B$

III. $A \xrightarrow{Aq.\ KOH} \xrightarrow{KMnO_4/H^+} B$

Select the correct alternate.
(a) I, II and III (b) I and II
(c) II and III (d) Only II

56. 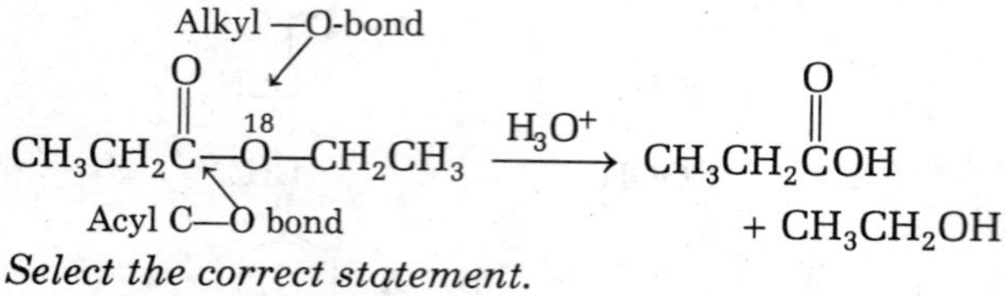

Select the correct statement.
(a) Alkyl C—O bond breaks and O^{18} is contained in acid
(b) Alkyl C—O bond breaks and O^{18} is contained in alcohol
(c) Acyl C—O bond breaks and O^{18} is contained in alcohol
(d) Acyl C—O bond breaks and O^{18} is contained in acid

57. Consider the following compounds,
I. $CH_3C(OH)=CHCOOC_2H_5$ III. C_6H_5COOH
II. $C_6H_5CH_2NH_2$ IV. C_6H_5OH

Which of the following will undergo methylation using diazomethane?
(a) I, II and IV (b) II and III
(c) II and IV (d) I, III and IV

58. An optically active compound '*X*' has molecular formula $C_4H_8O_3$. It evolves CO_2 with *aq.* $NaHCO_3$. '*X*' reacts with $LiAlH_4$ to give an achiral compound. '*X*' is
(a) $CH_3CH_2CH(OH)COOH$ (b) $CH_3CH(OMe)COOH$
(c) $CH_3CH(CH_2OH)COOH$ (d) $CH_3CH(OH)CH_2COOH$

59. 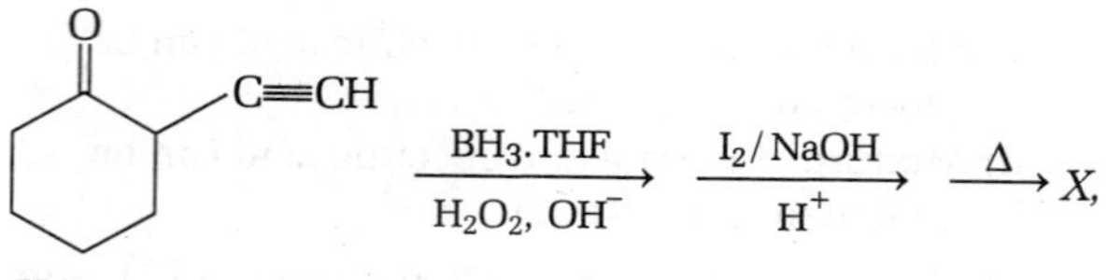

X is

(a) 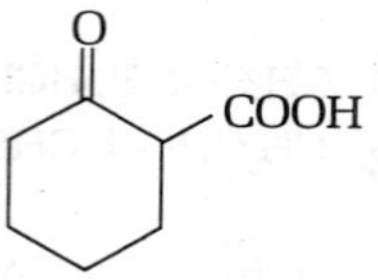

(b) 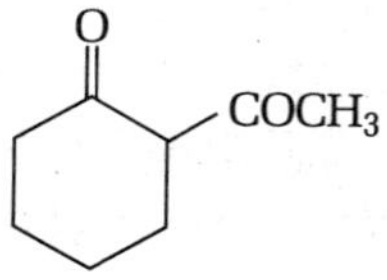

(c) 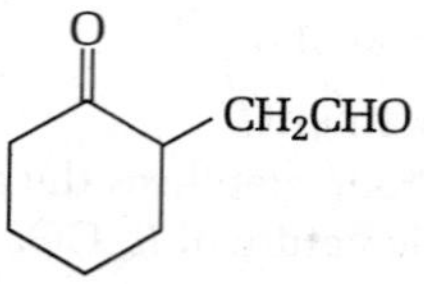

(d) 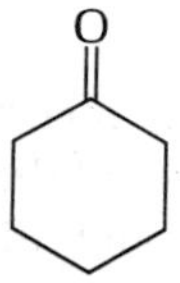

60. Consider the following compounds,

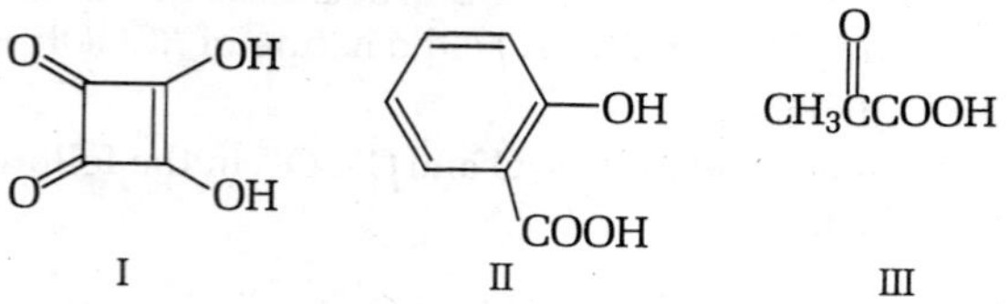

Which of the above compounds reacts with $NaHCO_3$ giving CO_2?
(a) I, II and III (b) I and III (c) II and III (d) I and II

61. Which is the strongest acid?
(a) CH_3COOH (b) CH_3COOOH
(c) $CH_3CH(CH_3)CH_2COOH$ (d) CH_3CH_2COOH

62. $CH_3\overset{\overset{O}{\|}}{C}O^-$ ion is stabilised by
(a) resonance effect of the carbonyl group
(b) inductive effect of the methyl group
(c) Both of the above are correct
(d) None of the above is correct

63. End product due to hydrolysis of (*A*) and subsequent heating is

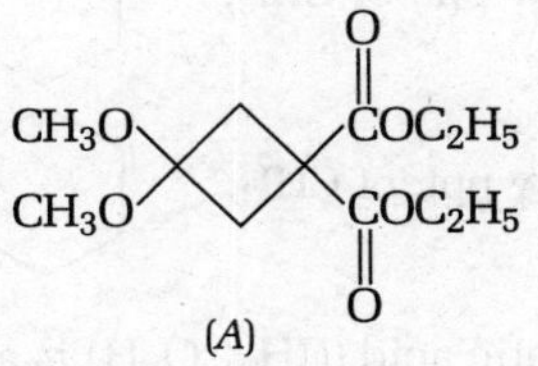

(*A*)

(a) 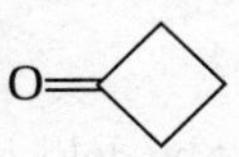 (b) 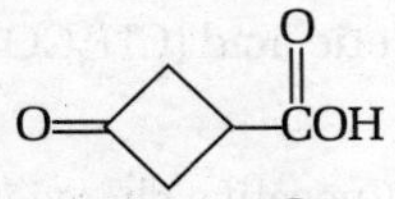

(c) 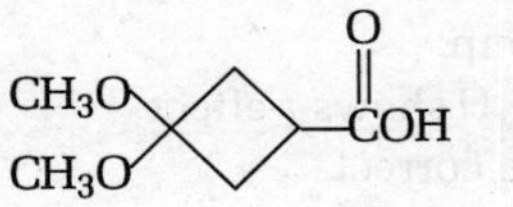 (d) 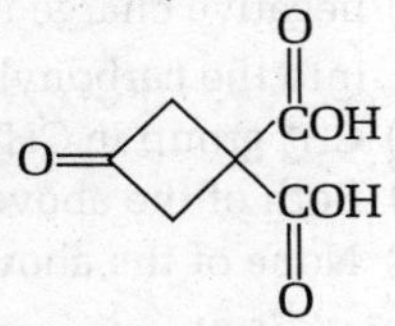

64. What is the product of following reaction?

Hex - 3 - ynal $\xrightarrow[\text{(ii) PBr}_3 \;\text{(iii) Mg/ether}\;\text{(iv) CO}_2/\text{H}_3\text{O}^+]{\text{(i) NaBH}_4}$? **[JEE Main 2020]**

(a) 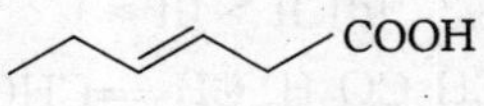

(b) 

(c) 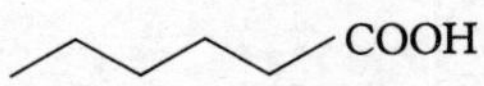

(d) 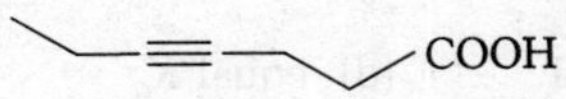

65. Consider the following reactions,

I. $CH_3MgBr \xrightarrow[H_3O^+]{CH_2-CH_2 \text{ (epoxide, O)}} \xrightarrow[\Delta]{MnO_4^-/H^+}$

II. $CH_3CH_2Br \xrightarrow{KCN} \xrightarrow{H_3O^+}$

III. $CH_3CH_2\overset{\overset{O}{\|}}{C}OC_2H_5 \xrightarrow[H_3O^+]{CH_3MgBr\text{ (2 mol)}}$

Propanoic acid is the final product in
(a) I, II and III
(b) I and II
(c) I and III
(d) II and III

66. Identify the final product in the following

$CH_3\underset{\underset{OH}{|}}{C}HCOOH \xrightarrow{\Delta}$

(a) 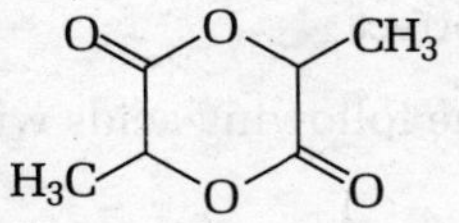 (b) $CH_2{=}CHCO_2H$

(c) $CH_3\overset{\overset{O}{\|}}{C}CO_2H$ (d) CH_3CH_2OH

67. When alanine is heated we get

(a) 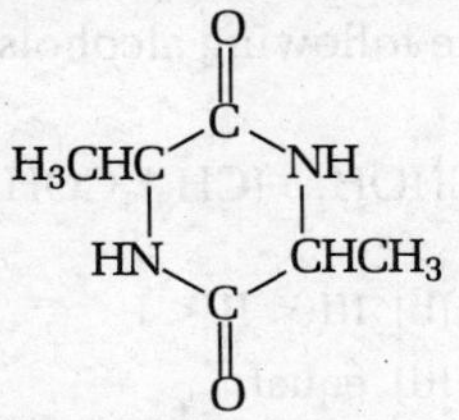 (b) $CH_2{=}CHCO_2H$

(c) $CH_3CH_2NH_2$ (d) no effect

68. Alkaline hydrolysis of CH_3CN forms
(a) CH_3COOH (b) CH_3COO^-
(c) $HCOO^-$ (d) HCOOH

69. Acid present in red ant is
(a) CH_3COOH (b) HCOOH
(c) HCN (d) H_3PO_4

70. $CH_3CH_2COOH \xrightarrow[\Delta]{NaN_3 \,+\, \text{conc. } H_2SO_4} A$ by reaction R_1

$CH_3CH_2COOH \xrightarrow[\Delta]{Br_2/P} B$ by reaction R_2

Which is the correct alternate?

	A	*B*	R_1	R_2
(a)	$CH_3CH_2NH_2$	$CH_3\underset{\underset{Br}{\vert}}{C}HCOOH$	Schmidt	HVZ
(b)	$CH_3CH_2CONH_2$	CH_3CH_2COBr	HVZ	Schmidt
(c)	$CH_3CH_2NH_2$	CH_3CH_2COBr	HVZ	Schmidt

(d) None of the above is correct

71. Maximum dehydration to form α,β-unsaturated acid takes place in
(a) lactic acid
(b) glycolic acid
(c) 3-hydroxy propanoic acid
(d) alanine

72. $CH_3-\overset{\overset{O}{\|}}{C}-\bullet H + CH_3CH_2OH \xrightarrow{H^+}$ ester(*A*) + water(*B*), *A* and *B* are

(• is isotopic oxygen)

(a) $CH_3-\overset{\overset{O}{\|}}{C}-OC_2H_5$, $H_2\bullet$

(b) $CH_3—\overset{O}{\overset{\|}{C}}—\bullet C_2H_5$, H_2O
(c) Both (a) and (b) are correct
(d) None of the above is correct

73. Ease of esterification of the following acids with CH_3OH

$$\underset{I}{HCOOH},\quad \underset{II}{CH_3COOH},\quad \underset{III}{CH_3CH_2COOH}$$

(a) III < II < I (b) I < II < III
(c) II < I < III (d) equal

74. Ease of esterification of the following alcohols with HCOOH

$$\underset{I}{CH_3CH_2OH},\quad \underset{II}{(CH_3)_2CHOH},\quad \underset{III}{(CH_3)_3COH}$$

(a) I < II < III (b) III < II < I
(c) II < I < III (d) equal

75. The carboxylic acid which has maximum solubility in water is
(a) phthalic acid (b) succinic acid
(c) malonic acid (d) salicylic acid

76. $CH_3COOH + HCOOH \xrightarrow[570\ K]{MnO}$

Main product of this reaction is
(a) CH_3CHO (b) CH_3COCH_3
(c) HCHO (d) $(CH_3CO)_2O$

77. $CH_3CH_2ONa \xrightarrow[\text{pressure (ii) } H^+]{\text{(i) CO, } \Delta} A$

$$CH_2{=}CH_2 + CO + H_2O \xrightarrow[670\ K]{H_3PO_4} B$$

A and *B* are
(a) CH_3CH_2COOH in both cases
(b) CH_3CH_2CHO in both cases
(c) CH_3CH_2COOH, CH_3CHO
(d) CH_3CHO, CH_3COOH

78. $H—C(\overset{\alpha}{=}O)(\overset{\beta}{—}O—H)$ $\quad H—C(\overset{\gamma}{=}O)(\overset{\delta}{—}O^{\ominus})$

(C—O) bond length designated by α, β, γ and δ are in order
(a) α = γ < β = δ (b) α < β < γ = δ
(c) α < γ = δ < β (d) All ot these are equal

79. End products of the following sequence of reactions are

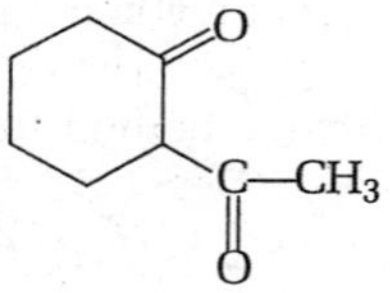

$\xrightarrow{\text{(i) } I_2 + \text{NaOH, } \Delta \text{ (ii) } H^+ \text{ (iii) } \Delta}$

(a) yellow ppt. of CHI_3, 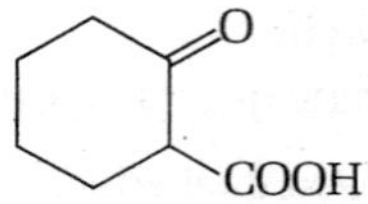

(b) yellow ppt. of CHI_3, 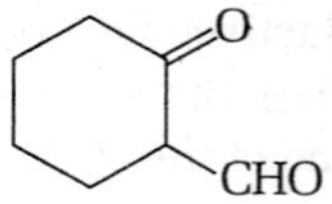

(c) yellow ppt. of CHI_3, 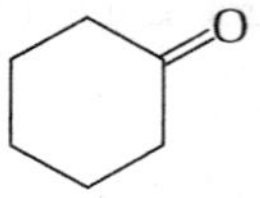

(d) yellow ppt. of CHI_3, 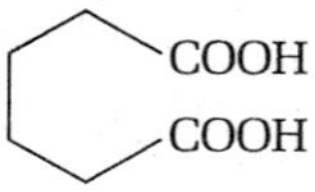

80. Peroxyacetic acid (CH_3CO_3H) is a weaker acid than acetic acid (CH_3CO_2H) since
(a) negative charge in $CH_3\overset{O}{\overset{\|}{C}}OO^-$ can't be delocalised into the carbonyl group
(b) CH_3 group in CH_3CO_3H shows *I*-effect
(c) Both of the above are correct
(d) None of the above is correct

81. For the following acids,

$$\underset{I}{(CH_3)_3CCH_2CO_2H};\quad \underset{II}{(CH_3)_3\overset{\oplus}{N}CH_2CO_2H};\quad \underset{III}{CH_3COOH}$$

pK_a value will be in order
(a) I > II > III (b) I < II < III
(c) I > III > II (d) II > III > I

82. Strongest acid out of CH_3CO_2H, $CH_2{=}CHCO_2H$,

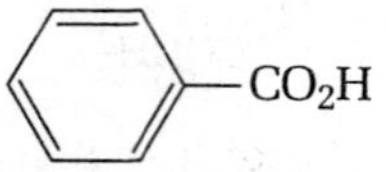 is

(a) CH_3CO_2H (b) $CH_2{=}CHCO_2H$
(c) 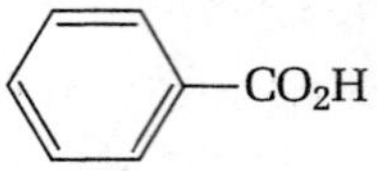 (d) equal K_a

83. End product of this conversion

$$CH_3\overset{O}{\overset{\|}{C}}CH_2CH_2CH_2CO_2H \xrightarrow[\text{(ii) } H_2O,\ H^+]{\text{(i) NaBH}_4} \text{is}$$

(a) 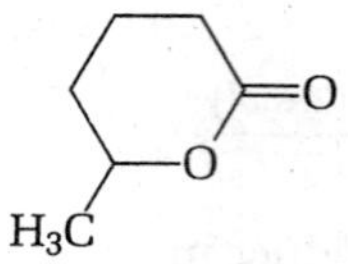 (b) 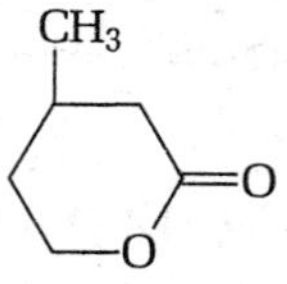

(c) 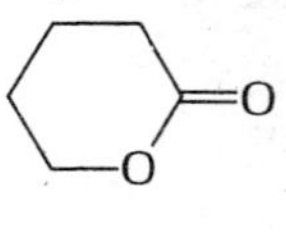 (b) $CH_3\underset{OH}{\underset{|}{C}H}CH_2CH_2CH_2CO_2H$

84. When acetic acid reacts with ketene, product formed

(a) ethyl acetate (b) aceto-acetic ester

(c) acetic anhydride (d) no reaction

85. Least pK_a value is of

(a) oxalic acid (b) pyruvic acid

(c) malonic acid (d) succinic acid

86. Which dicarboxylic acid in presence of a dehydrating agent is least reactive to give an anhydride? **[JEE Main 2019, Jan.]**

(a) 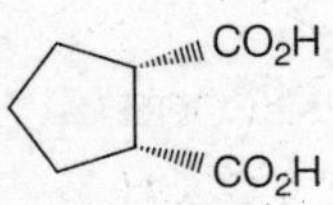

(b) 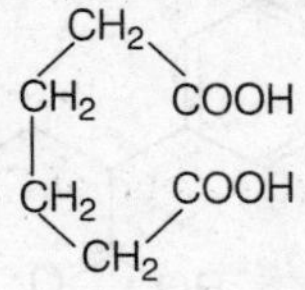

(c) 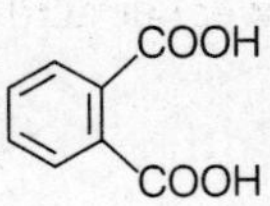

(d) 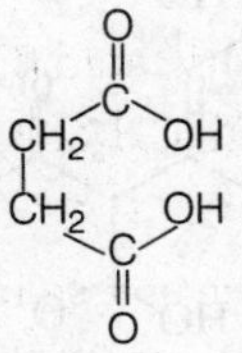

87. CH_3Br can be prepared by

(a) $CH_3COOAg + Br_2 \xrightarrow{\Delta}$

(b) $CH_3COOH \xrightarrow{P/Br_2} \xrightarrow{\text{Sodalime}, \Delta}$

(c) Both (a) and (b)

(d) None of the above

88. In case of Hofmann bromamide degradation reaction, intermediate RNCO is formed by

(a) intramolecular migration

(b) intermolecular migration

(c) hydrolysis of $RCONH_2$

(d) None of the above is correct

89. Decarboxylation will not take place on heating of

(a) methyl malonic acid (b) succinic acid

(c) acetoacetic acid (d) In all cases

90. When RCOOH reacts with $NaHCO_3$, CO_2 is formed. CO_2 contains carbon of

(a) RCOOH

(b) $NaHCO_3$

(c) Both (a) and (b)

(d) None of the above

91. Which of the following is a correct IUPAC name for the compound shown?

$$(CH_3CH_2)_2C(CO_2H)CH_2CH(CH_2CH_3)_2$$

(a) 1,1,3-triethylhexanoic acid

(b) 2,2,4-triethylhexanoic acid

(c) 3,5-diethyl-3-heptylcarboxylic acid

(d) 3,5,5-triethyl-6-hexanoic acid

92. Rank the following substances in order of decreasing acid strength (strongest → weakest)

$CH_3CH_2CH_2CO_2H$ (I) $\quad CH_3CH{=}CHCO_2H$ (II)

$CH_3CH_2CH_2CH_2OH$ (III) $\quad CH_3C{\equiv}CCO_2H$ (IV)

(a) IV > II > I > III

(b) I > II > IV > III

(c) III > I > II > IV

(d) II > IV > I > III

93. Which of the following compounds will undergo decarboxylation on heating?

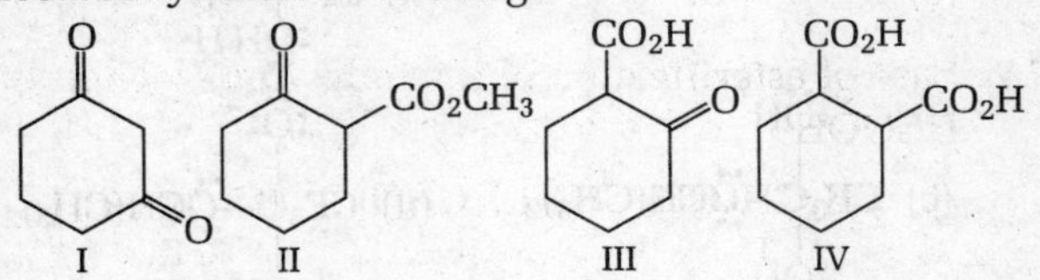

I II III IV

(a) II and III

(b) III and IV

(c) III only

(d) I and IV

94. Which of the following is least likely to form a lactone?

(a) $CH_3CH(OH)CH_2CH_2CO_2H$ (b) 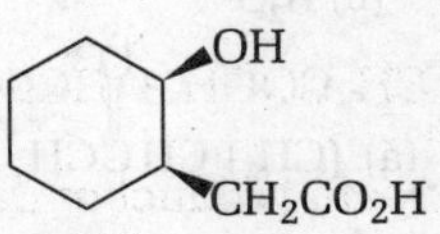

(c) 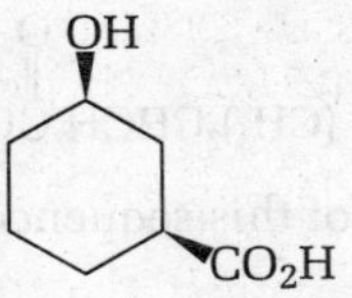 (d) 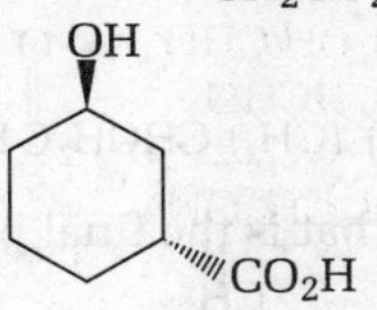

95. Compare the two methods shown for the preparation of carboxylic acids

Method 1 $RBr \xrightarrow[\text{diethyl ether}]{Mg} RMgBr \xrightarrow[\text{(ii) } H_3O^+]{\text{(i) } CO_2} RCO_2H$

Method 2 $RBr \xrightarrow{NaCN} RCN \xrightarrow[\text{heat}]{H_2O, HCl} RCO_2H$

Which one of the following statements correctly describes this conversion?

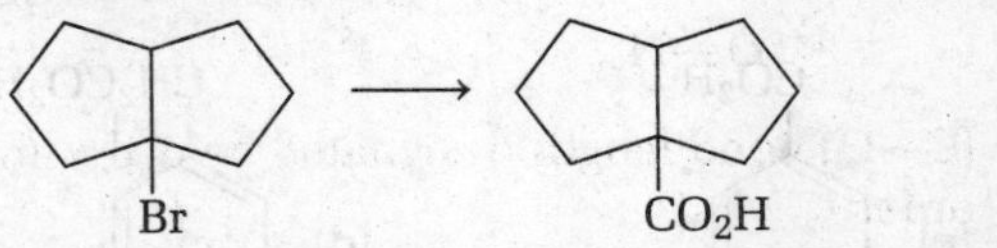

(a) Both method 1 and method 2 are appropriate for carrying out this conversion.

(b) Neither method 1 nor method 2 is appropriate for carrying out this conversion.

(c) Method 1 will work well, but method 2 is not appropriate.

(d) Method 2 will work well, but method 1 is not appropriate.

96. Which one of the following is not an intermediate in the generally accepted mechanism for the reaction shown?

$$CF_3\overset{\overset{\displaystyle O}{\|}}{C}OH + CH_3\underset{\underset{\displaystyle OH}{|}}{C}HCH_3 \xrightarrow{H_2SO_4} CF_3\overset{\overset{\displaystyle O}{\|}}{C}O\underset{\underset{\displaystyle CH_3}{|}}{C}HCH_3 + H_2O$$

(a) 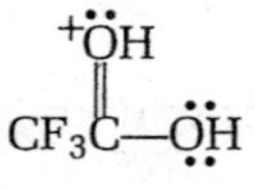

(b) 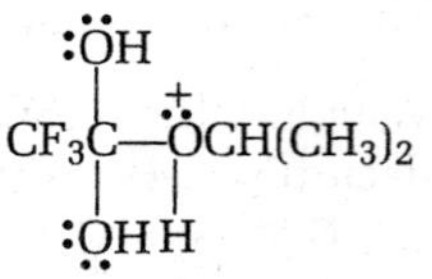

(c) 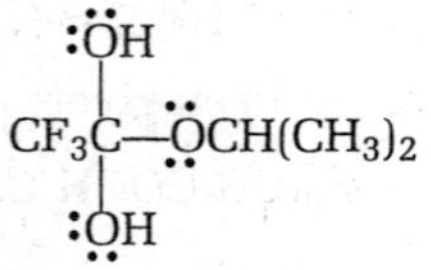

(d) 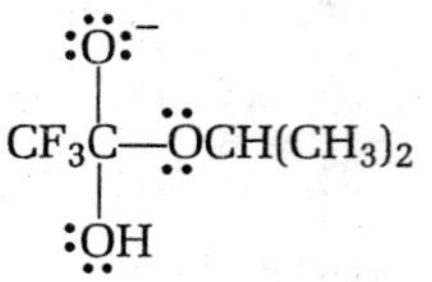

97. Identify compound *C* in the following sequence

$$(CH_3)_2CHCH_2C{\equiv}N \xrightarrow[\text{heat}]{H_2O,\ HCl} \text{compound } A \xrightarrow[\text{(ii) } H_2O]{\text{(i) } LiAlH_4} \text{compound } B \xrightarrow[CH_2Cl_2]{PCC} \text{compound } C$$

(a) $(CH_3)_2CH\overset{\overset{\displaystyle O}{\|}}{C}CH_3$

(b) $(CH_3)_2CHCH{=}C(OH)_2$

(c) $(CH_3)_2CHCH_2\overset{\overset{\displaystyle O}{\|}}{C}H$

(d) $(CH_3)_2CHCH_2\overset{\overset{\displaystyle O}{\|}}{C}OH$

98. What is the final product (*B*) of this sequence?

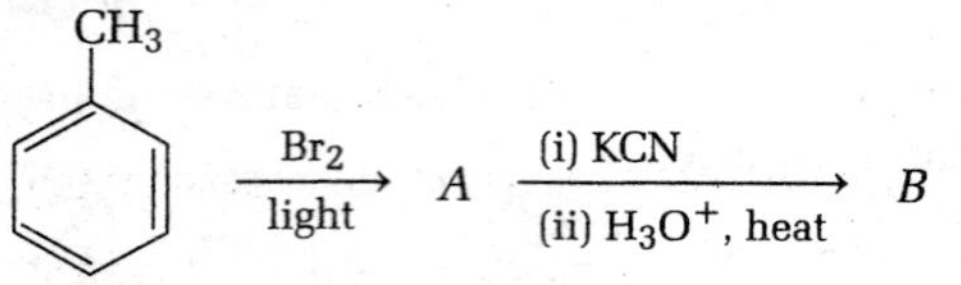

(a) 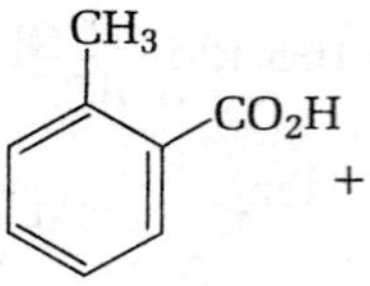 + *para*

(b) 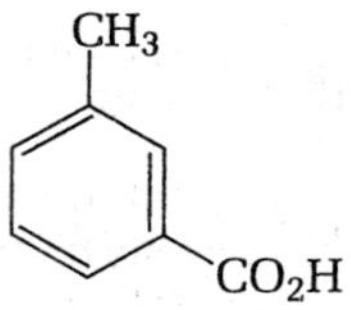

(c) 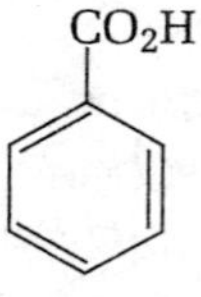

(d) 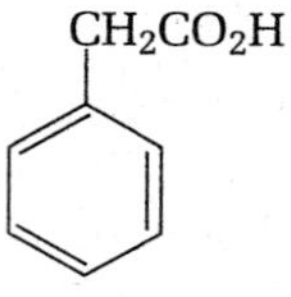

99. Which one of the following undergoes decarboxylation (loses carbon dioxide) most readily on being heated?

(a) 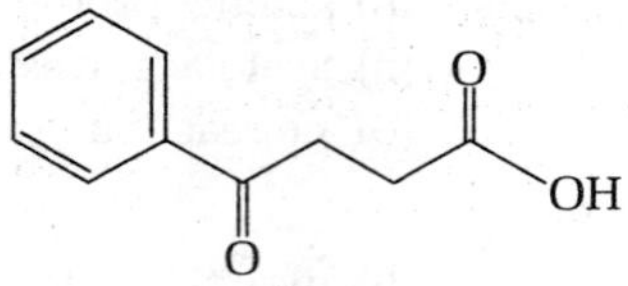

(b) 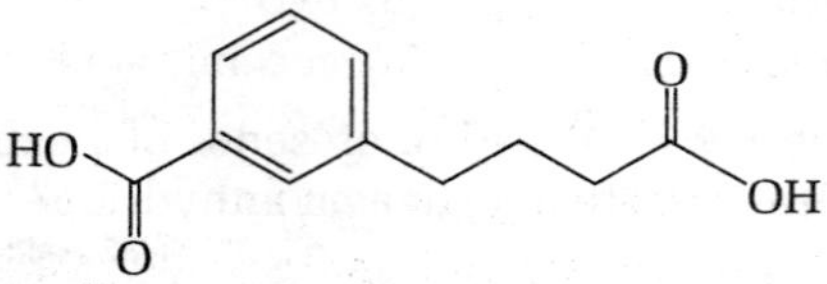

(c) 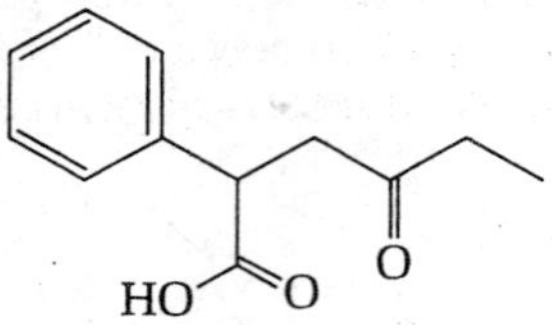

(d) 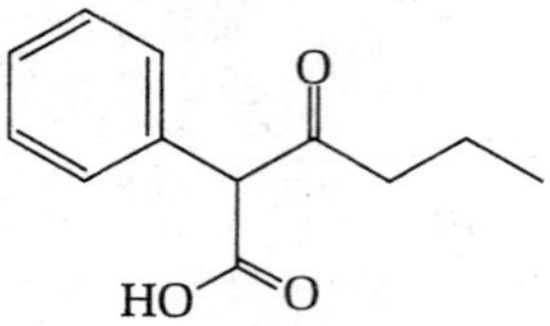

100. Which of the compounds yields a δ-lactone after being reduced with sodium borohydride?

(a) 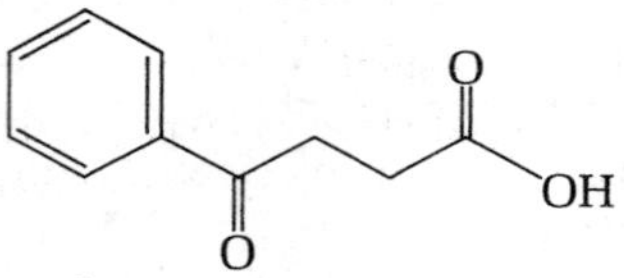

(b) 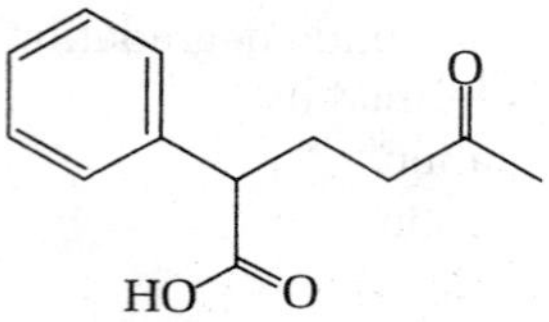

(c) Both (a) and (b)

(d) None of the above

101. What is compound *Z*?

$$CH_3CH_2CH_2Br \xrightarrow{NaCN} X \xrightarrow[\text{heat}]{H_3O^+} Y \xrightarrow[H^+]{CH_3CH_2OH} Z$$

(a) $CH_3CH{=}CH\overset{\overset{\displaystyle O}{\|}}{C}OH$

(b) $CH_3CH_2CH_2CH(OCH_2CH_3)_2$

(c) $CH_3CH_2\underset{\underset{\displaystyle OCH_2CH_3}{|}}{C}HC{\equiv}N$

(d) $CH_3CH_2CH_2\overset{\overset{\displaystyle O}{\|}}{C}OCH_2CH_3$

102. Compared to phenol ($pK_a = 10.02$) acetic acid ($pK_a = 4.76$) is more acidic. This is due to
(a) stabilisation of negative charge on carboxylate ion by induction
(b) resonance effect
(c) Both (a) and (b)
(d) None of the above

103. Consider the following statements,
I. In both the alcohol and carboxylic acid series, the smaller anion can be better solvated, leading to a larger acidity of the corresponding conjugate acid.
II. **Acid strength of**

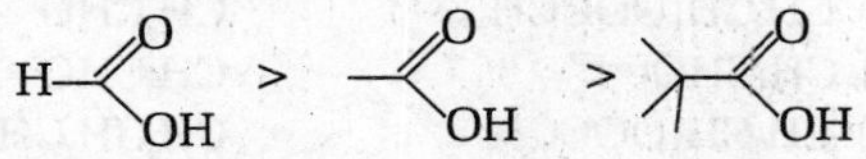

III. **Acid strength of**

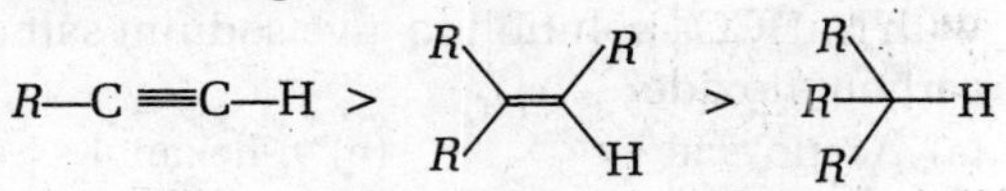

Select the correct statements.
(a) I, II and III (b) I and II
(c) II and III (d) I and III

104. The correct order of acid strength of the following carboxylic acids is **[JEE Advanced 2019]**

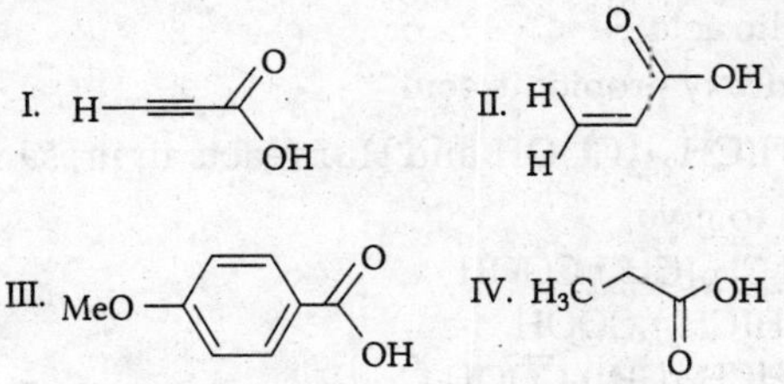

(a) III > II > I > IV (b) I > II > III > IV
(c) II > I > IV > III (d) I > III > II > IV

105. In the following multisteps synthesis, products *B*, *C* and *D* are

$$CH_3CH_2\overset{O}{\overset{\|}{C}}\underset{*}{C}H_2\overset{O}{\overset{\|}{C}}OH \xrightarrow{\Delta} A \xrightarrow[\Delta]{I_2/NaOH} B + C$$

($\underset{*}{C}$ is C-14) $\xrightarrow[\Delta]{CaO/NaOH} D$

(a) $CH_3CH_2\overset{O}{\overset{\|}{C}}\underset{*}{C}H_3$, $CH_3CH_2\overset{O}{\overset{\|}{C}}ONa$, $\underset{*}{C}HI_3$

(b) $CH_3CH_2\overset{O}{\overset{\|}{C}}ONa$, CHI_3, $CH_3\underset{*}{C}H_3$

(c) $CH_3CH_2\overset{O}{\overset{\|}{C}}O\,Na$, CHI_3, CH_3CH_3

(d) $CH_3CH_2\overset{O}{\overset{\|}{C}}ONa$, $\underset{*}{C}HI_3$, CH_3CH_3

106. Arrange the following in the increasing order of their acidic strength ? **[JEE Main 2021, Feb.]**

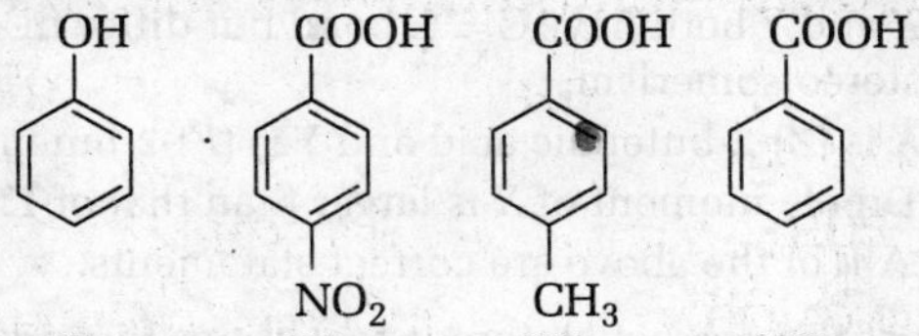

(I) (II) (III) (IV)

(a) I < III < IV < II (b) III < II < IV < I
(c) I < II < III < IV (d) IV < III < II < I

107. Acids with their pK_a values have been given

CH_2COOH	CH_2COOH	CH_2COOH	CH_2COOH	CH_2COOH
NO_2	CN	Cl	OH	H
pK_a: 1.68	2.46	2.86	3.83	4.74

Which group has maximum electron-withdrawing (acid strength increasing) tendency ?
(a) NO_2 (b) H (c) CN (d) OH

108. Consider the following acid-base equilibria,
I. $CH_3CO_2H + (CH_3)_3CO^- \rightleftharpoons CH_3CO_2^- + (CH_3)_3COH$
II. $CH_3CO_2H + Br^- \rightleftharpoons CH_3CO_2^- + HBr$
III. $CH_3CO_2H + CH{\equiv}C^{\ominus} \rightleftharpoons CH_3CO_2^- + CH{\equiv}CH$
IV. $CH_3CO_2H + NO_3^- \rightleftharpoons CH_3CO_2^- + HNO_3$
$\Delta G°$ has negative values for the above equilibria
(a) I, II (b) III, IV
(c) I, III (d) II, IV

109. Arrange the following acids in increasing pK_a values

I. $CH_3CH_2\overset{O}{\overset{\|}{C}}OH$ II. $CH_2{=}CH\overset{O}{\overset{\|}{C}}OH$

III. $CH{\equiv}C\overset{O}{\overset{\|}{C}}OH$

(a) I < II < III (b) III < II < I
(c) I < III < II (d) III < I < II

110. Select the correct order of acidic nature of

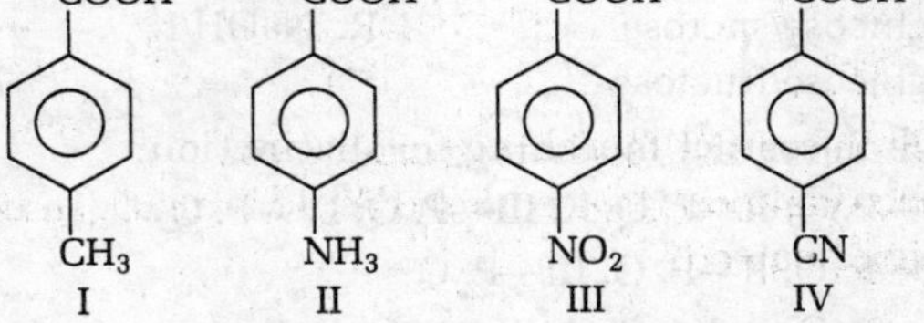

(a) III > IV > I > II (b) IV > III > II > I
(c) II > I > IV > III (d) I > II > III > IV

111. $CH_3C{\equiv}CCO_2H \xrightarrow{H_2,\ \text{Lindlar Pd}} X$

$\quad | \xrightarrow{Li/NH_3} Y$

Select the correct statement about X and Y.

(a) X and Y both have C=C bond but differ in stereoisomerism.

(b) X is (Z)-2-butenoic acid and Y is (E)-2-butenoic acid.

(c) Dipole moment of X is larger than that of Y.

(d) All of the above are correct statements.

112. Select the correct statement (s) about formic acid

(a) More stable conformation is *anti*

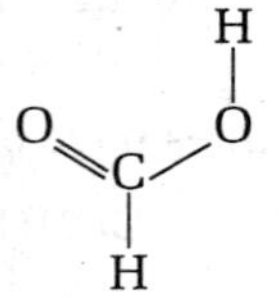

(b) A dipole moment of zero can mean that a molecule has a centre of symmetry

(c) It forms dimer by H-bonding

(d) All of the above are correct statements

113. Which one of the following order of acid strength is correct?

(a) $RCOOH > HOH > CH{\equiv}CH > ROH$

(b) $RCOOH > CH{\equiv}CH > HOH > ROH$

(c) $RCOOH > ROH > HOH > CH{\equiv}CH$

(d) $RCOOH > HOH > ROH > CH{\equiv}CH$

114. In the following sequence of reactions,

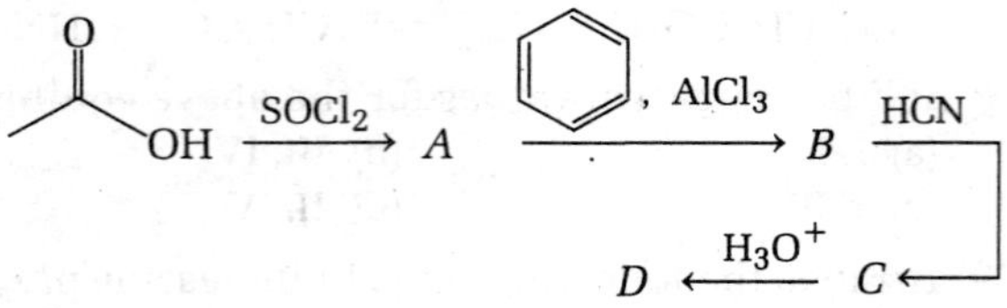

Select the correct statements about D.

(a) D has chiral centre

(b) D is α-hydroxy acid

(c) Both of the above

(d) None of the above

115. Consider the following pairs and reagents,

Pairs	Reagents
I. CH_3COOH / $HCOOH$	P. Tollen's
II. CH_3CHO / CH_3COCH_3	Q. Fehling's
III. glucose/sucrose	R. NaOH/I_2
IV. glucose/fructose	

Which is correct matching for distinction?

(a) I—P, Q; II—P, Q, R; III—P, Q; IV—P, Q

(b) I—P, Q; II—P, Q; III—P, Q

(c) I—P, Q, R; II—P, Q; III—P, Q, R, IV—P

(d) I—P, Q; II—P; Q; III—P; IV—Q

116. Consider the following reactions,

I. $CH_3NC \xrightarrow{H_3O^+}$ II. $CHCl_3 \xrightarrow{NaOH/H_3O^+}$

III. $CCl_4 \xrightarrow{H_3O^+}$

HCOOH is obtained in

(a) I, II and III (b) II and III

(c) I and II (d) I and III

117. $CH{\equiv}CH$ on reaction with CH_3COOH in presence of Hg^{2+} gives X which is hydrolysed to Y. X and Y are

	X	Y
(a)	$CH_3CH(OOCCH_3)_2$	CH_3COCH_3
(b)	$CH_3CH(OOCCH_3)_2$	CH_3CHO
(c)	CH_3CHO	CH_3CHO
(d)	$CH_3CH(OOCCH_3)_2$	CH_3CH_2CHO

118. Which one of the following compounds will react with $NaHCO_3$ solution to give sodium salt and carbon dioxide?

(a) Acetic acid (b) n-hexanol

(c) Phenol (d) Both (b) and (c)

119. $CH_3COOH \xrightarrow{Br_2/P} X \xrightarrow[\text{(ii) } H_3O^+]{\text{(i) KCN}} Y$, Y is identified as

(a) succinic acid

(b) malonic acid

(c) glycolic acid

(d) α-hydroxy propionic acid

120. $CH_2{=}CH(CH_2)_2COOH$ and HBr reacts in presence of peroxide to give

(a) $BrCH_2CH_2(CH_2)_2COOH$

(b) $CH_3CH(CH_2)_2COOH$

(c) $CH_3CHCH_2(CH_2)_2COOH$

(d) $CH_3CHBr(CH_2)_2COOH$

121. The acid which does not contain —COOH group is

(a) ethanoic acid (b) picric acid

(c) lactic acid (d) palmitic acid

122. Compound '*A*' reacts with PCl_5 to produce '*B*' which on treatment with KCN followed by hydrolysis produce propionic acid. Compound '*A*' is

(a) C_2H_5OH (b) C_2H_6

(c) C_3H_8 (d) C_2H_5Cl

123. Carboxylic acids react with diazomethane to yield

(a) alcohols (b) amides

(c) amines (d) esters

124. Identify the product Z in series

$CH_3CN \xrightarrow{Na/C_2H_5OH} X \xrightarrow{HNO_2} Y \xrightarrow[\text{reagent}]{\text{Baeyer's}} Z$

(a) CH_3CHO (b) CH_3CONH_2

(c) CH_3COOH (d) $CH_3CH_2\ NHOH$

125. Carboxylic acid undergoes ionisation due to
(a) hydrogen bonding
(b) absence of α-hydrogen
(c) high reactivity of α-hydrogen
(d) resonance stabilisation of carboxylate ion

126. (*A*) given below is to be converted into (*B*)

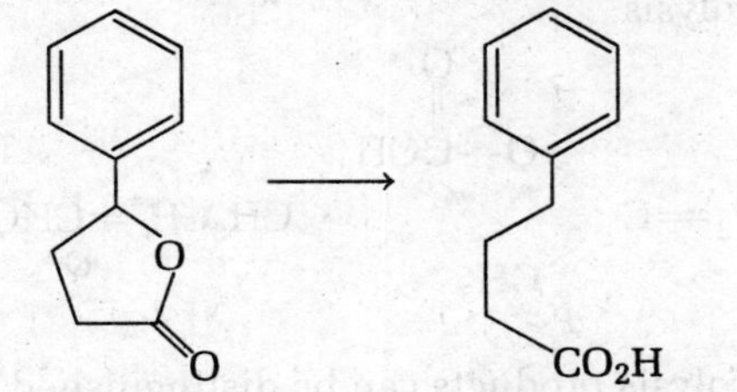

(*A*) (*B*)

Suitable reagent is
(a) $LiAlH_4$
(b) $NaBH_4/CH_3OH$
(c) Na/C_2H_5OH
(d) H_2, Pd/C

127. Major product *H* in the given reaction sequence is

$$CH_3—CH_2—CO—CH_3 \xrightarrow{^{\ominus}CN} G \xrightarrow{95\%\ H_2SO_4} H$$

[IIT JEE 2012]

(a) $CH_3—CH=C(CH_3)—COOH$
(b) $CH_3—CH=C(CH_3)—CN$
(c) $CH_3—CH_2—C(OH)(CH_3)—COOH$
(d) $CH_3—CH=C(CH_3)—CO—NH_2$

128. The compound that undergoes decarboxylation most readily under mild condition is **[IIT JEE 2012]**

(a) 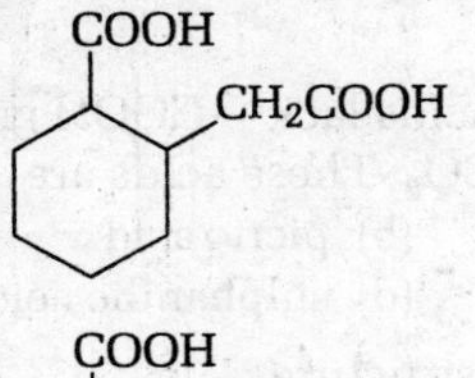
(b) 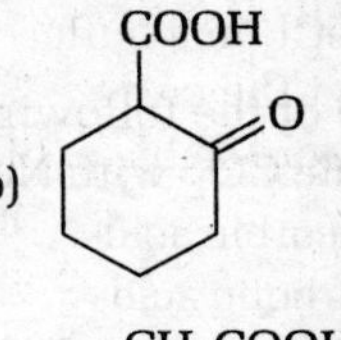
(c) 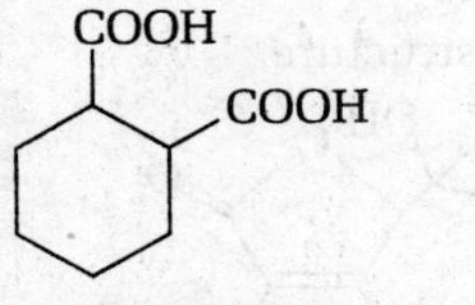
(d) 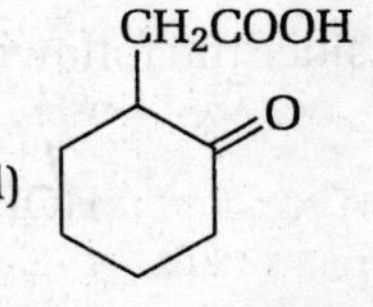

129. An organic compound *A* upon reacting with NH_3 gives *B*. On heating, *B* gives *C*. *C* in the presence of KOH reacts with Br_2 to give $CH_3CH_2NH_2$. Compound *A* is **[JEE Main 2013]**
(a) CH_3COOH
(b) $CH_3CH_2CH_2COOH$
(c) $CH_3—CH(CH_3)—COOH$
(d) CH_3CH_2COOH

Objective Questions Type II [One or more than one correct option(s)]

In each of the questions below, four choices are given, of which one or more than one are correct.

1. Select the correct conversion.

(a) 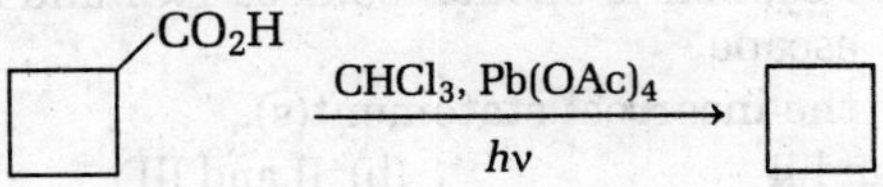

(b) 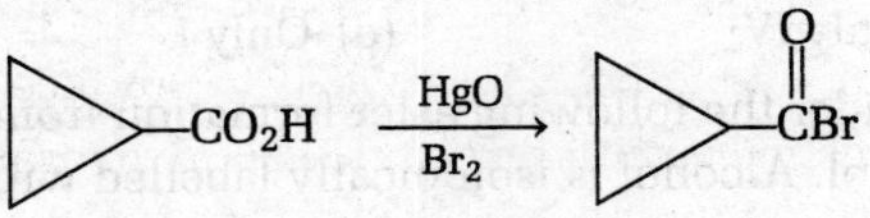

(c) 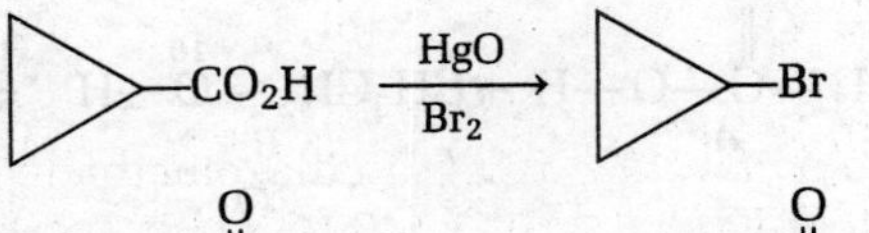

(d) 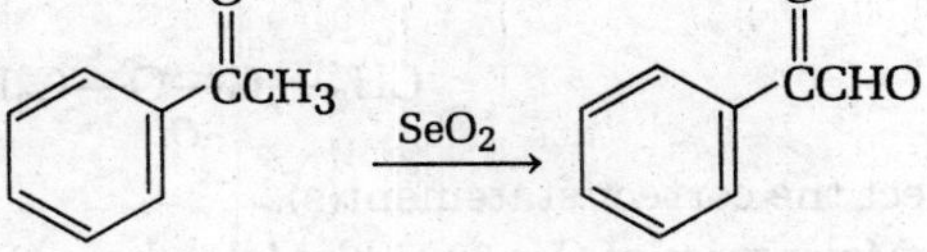

2. 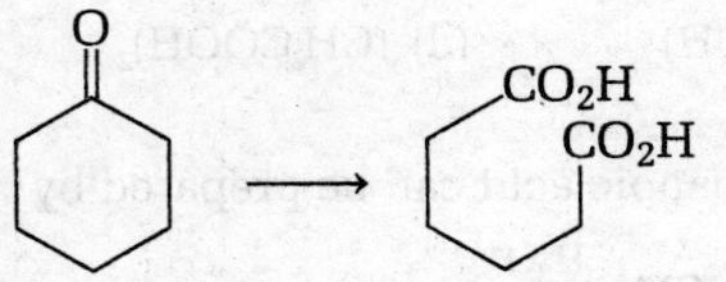

Above oxidation takes place through the formation of

(a) 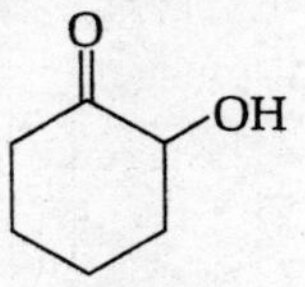
(b) 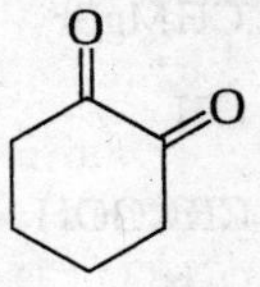
(c) 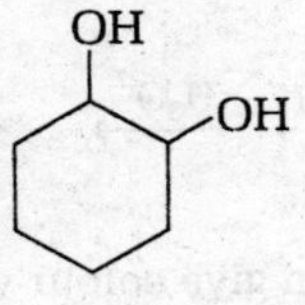
(d) 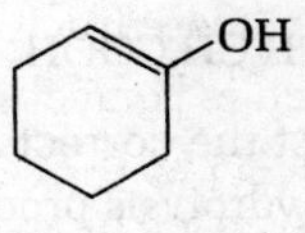

3. Following conversion can be carried out by using

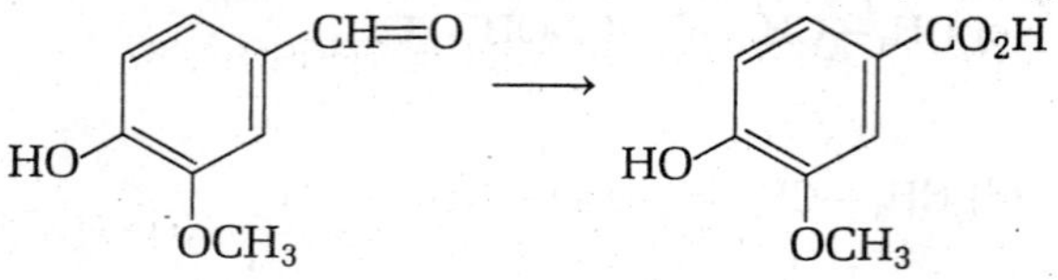

(a) $KMnO_4$ in *t*-butanol and an aqueous NaH_2PO_4 buffer
(b) NaClO in a buffer
(c) Ag_2O/NaOH, HCl
(d) $FeCl_3$ in a buffer

4. Some of the following acids lack —COOH group but liberate CO_2 with $NaHCO_3$. These acids are
(a) ascorbic acid (b) picric acid
(c) carbolic acid (d) sulphanilic acid

5. Consider the following structure,

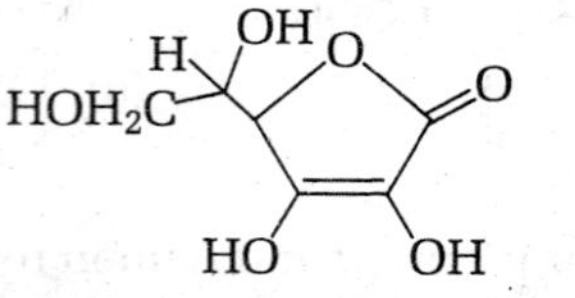

Select the acidic hydrogen in this compound.
(a) 1° alcoholic group (b) 2° alcoholic group
(c) enolic group (d) None of these

6. HCOOH and CH_3COOH have similarity in
(a) both liberate CO_2 with $NaHCO_3$
(b) alkanoate ion is stabilised by resonance
(c) (C—O) and (C═O) bond length are equal in (RCOO$^-$)
(d) both reduce Tollen's reagent

7. In which case decarboxylation takes place as heating?
(a) $CH_3CH{=}CHCOOH$ (b) $CH_3\overset{O}{\overset{\|}{C}}CH_2COOH$
(c) $CH_3CH(COOH)_2$ (d) $(CH_2COOH)_2$

8. 2-hydroxy propanoic acid can be prepared by
(a) $CH_3CHO + HCN \xrightarrow{H_3O^+}$
(b) $CH_3\underset{OH}{\underset{|}{C}}HMgBr \xrightarrow[H_3O^+]{CO_2}$
(c) $CH_3\underset{NH_2}{\underset{|}{C}}HCOOH \xrightarrow{HNO_2}$
(d) $CH_3CH_2COOH \xrightarrow{P/Br_2} \xrightarrow{KOH} \xrightarrow{H_3O^+}$

9. Select the correct statement(s).
(a) Hydrolysis products of aspirin give colour with $FeCl_3$
(b) Different types of acids are formed by hydrolysis of CH_3CN and its isomer.
(c) Ascorbic acid has chiral carbon
(d) Acetic anhydride is formed when ketene reacts with acetic acid.

10. Following reactants P and Q are subjected to hydrolysis

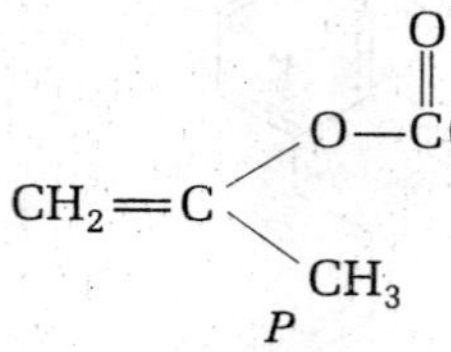

P

$CH_3CH{=}CHO\overset{O}{\overset{\|}{C}}CH_3$

Q

Hydrolysis products can be distinguished using
(a) Lucas reagent
(b) 2,4-DNP
(c) Fehling's solution
(d) Tollen's reagent

11. Consider the following reaction,

$$R\overset{O}{\overset{\|}{C}}OH + SOCl_2 \longrightarrow R—\overset{O}{\overset{\|}{C}}—Cl + HCl + SO_2$$

Consider the following statements about this reaction.
I. It is S_N2 at carbonyl carbon from where OH is a leaving group.
II. It is S_N2 at sulphur from where Cl is the leaving group.
III. Intermediate is resonance stabilised.

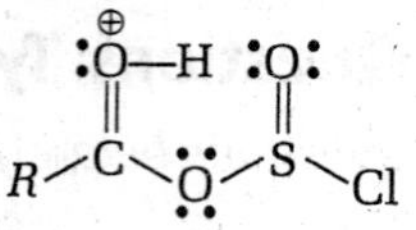

IV. Reaction is spontaneous as HCl and SO_2 gases escape.

Select the incorrect statement(s).
(a) I and II (b) II and III
(c) Only IV (d) Only I

12. Consider the following ester formation from acid and alcohol. Alcohol is isotopically labelled with ^{18}O.

$$\underset{A}{CH_3—\overset{O}{\overset{\|}{C}}—O—H} + \underset{B}{CH_3CH_2—\overset{18}{O}—H} \overset{H^+}{\rightleftharpoons} \underset{C}{CH_3—\overset{O}{\overset{\|}{C}}—O—C_2H_5} + \underset{D}{H_2O}$$

Select the correct statement(s).
(a) Molar mass of C is 88 (b) Molar mass of D is 20
(c) Molar mass of C is 90 (d) None of these

Numerical Value Questions

All these questions have a Numerical value as their answer, solve the questions and write your answer.

1. Find the total number of different products obtained when 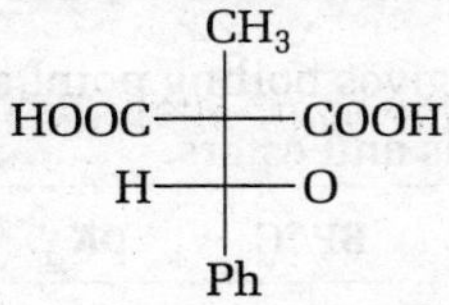 is heated strongly.

2. What is the number of conventical sigma-bonds present in maleic anhydride ?

3. What is the value of $x + y$?

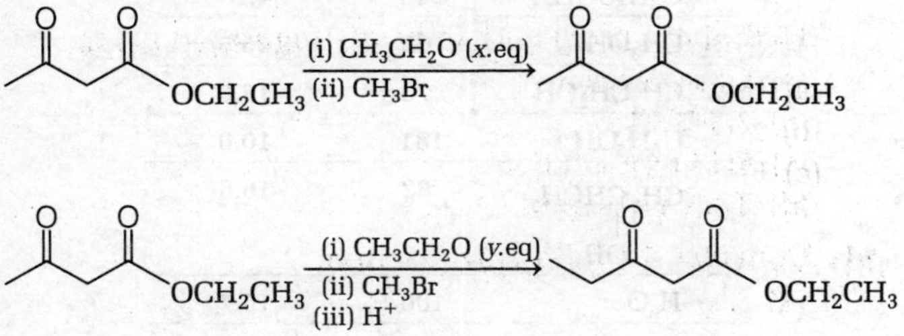

4. What is the value of x ?

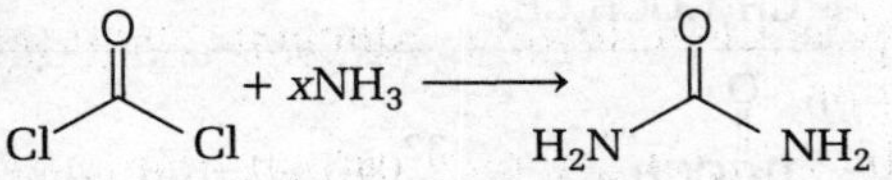

5. 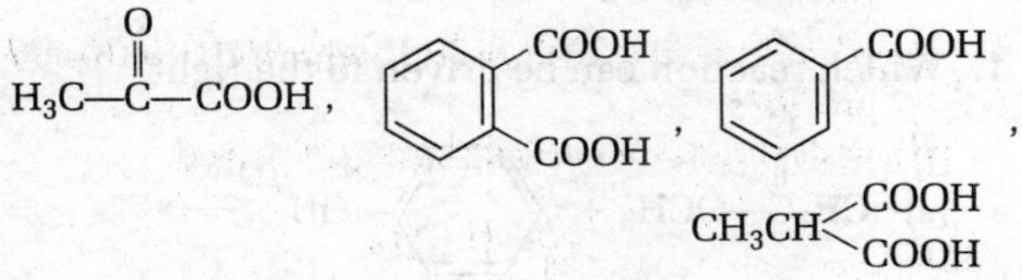

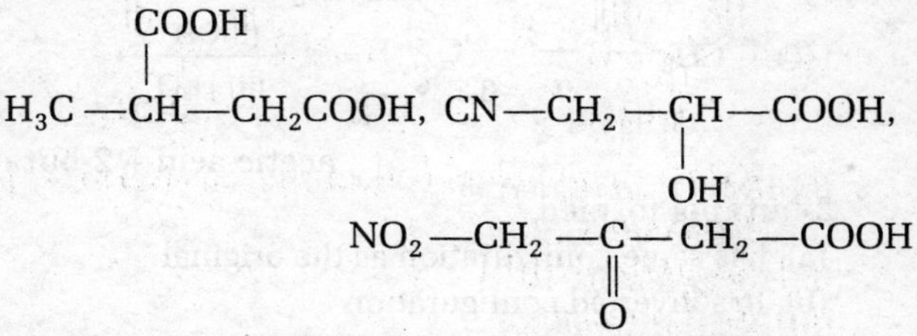

Number of compounds that can rather easily be decarboxylated is ....

6. How many mole of CO_2 will released when following compound treated with heat.

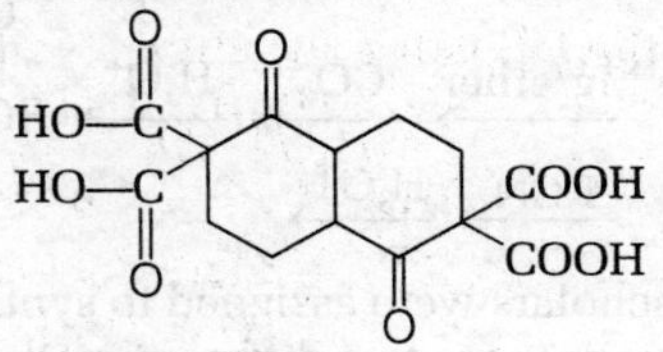

7. 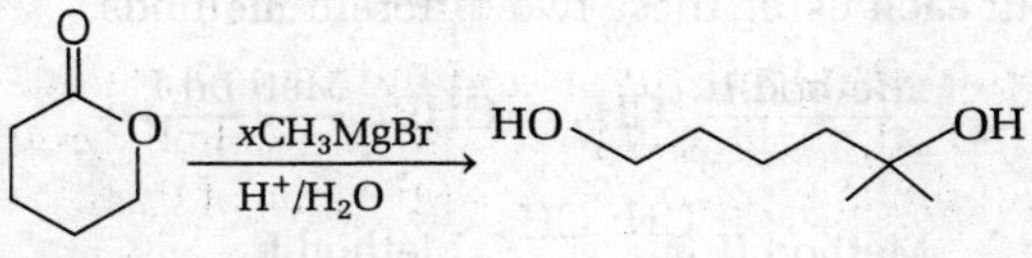

Find the value of x.

8. 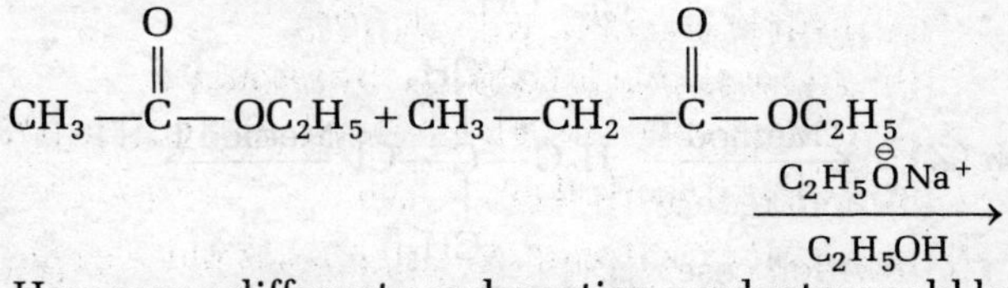

How many different condensation products would be form by above reaction ?

Comprehension Based Questions

In these questions, a passage has been given followed by questions based on it. You have to answer the questions based on the passage given.

***Passage* 1** The esterification reaction of an alcohol with an acid or its derivatives is strongly affected by steric hindrance. Bulky groups on either partner slow down the reaction considerably and in certain cases stereochemistry as well as nature of the products is changed.

Read the above experimental facts and answer the following questions.

1. 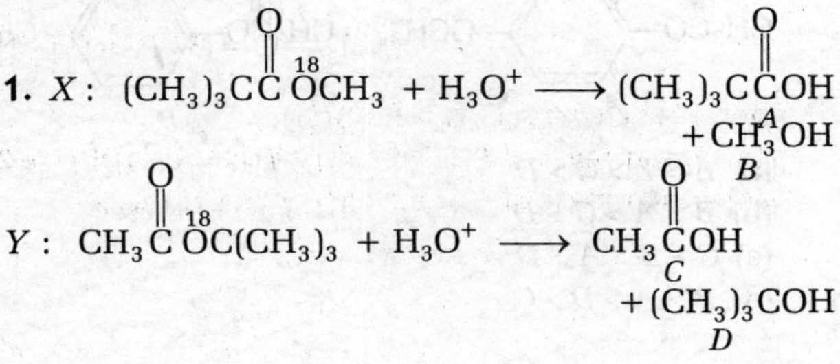

Select the correct statement(s).

(a) ^{18}O appears in A

(b) ^{18}O appears in B

(c) ^{18}O appears in C

(d) ^{18}O appears in D

2. Refer Q. (1).

Equilibrium Y is spontaneous ($\Delta G° = -$ ve) because

(a) $(CH_3)_3CO^{\ominus}$ (alkoxide) a strong nucleophile is formed

(b) $(CH_3)_3C^{\oplus}$ (3° carbocation) is formed

(c) $CH_3\overset{O}{\overset{\|}{C}}O^{\ominus}$ formed is stabilised by resonance

(d) $CH_3\overset{O}{\overset{\|}{C}}OH$ is a weak acid.

3. Optically pure (+)-2-butyl acetate is subjected to hydrolysis under basic condition.

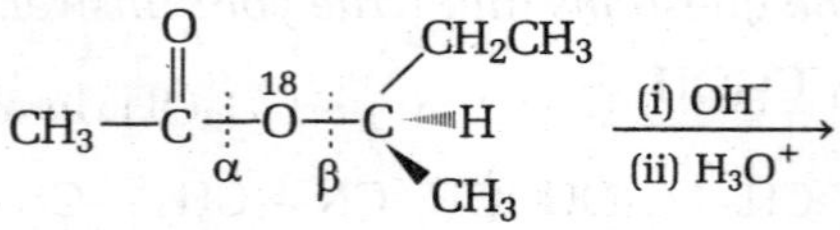

acetic acid + 2-butanol.

2-butanol formed.
(a) has same configuration as the original
(b) has inverted configuration
(c) is racemised
(d) None of the above is true

***Passage* 2** Carboxylic acid can be synthesised by using different methods.

Method I $RX \xrightarrow{Mg/ether} \xrightarrow{CO_2} \xrightarrow{H_3O^+} RCOOH$ (RC(=O)OH);

Method II $RX \xrightarrow{KCN} \xrightarrow{H_3O^+}$

Three research scholars were assigned to synthesise different acids but each using these two different methods.

Mr (X) : $\xleftarrow{\text{Method II}} CH_2{=}CHBr \xrightarrow{\text{Method I}}$;

Mr (Y) : $\xleftarrow{\text{Method II}}$ $CH_2(Cl)CH_2(OH)$ $\xrightarrow{\text{Method I}}$

Mr (Z) : $\xleftarrow{\text{Method II}}$ $H_3C{-}C(CH_3)_2{-}Cl$ $\xrightarrow{\text{Method I}}$

Answer the following questions based on the above study.

1. Best yield is in method I by
(a) X (b) Y
(c) Z (d) None of these

2. Select the products of X, Y, Z by method I.

	X	Y	Z
(a)	$CH_2{=}CHCOOH$	RH	$(CH_3)_3CCOOH$
(b)	$CH_2{=}CHCOOH$	RH	$(CH_3)_2C{=}CH_2$
(c)	$CH_2{=}CHCOOH$	$CH_2(OH)COOH$	$(CH_3)_3CCOOH$
(d)	$CH_2{=}CHCOOH$	RH	$(CH_3)_3CH$

3. The following are the drawbacks faced by X, Y, Z in their syntheses either by method I or method II.
A. method II used by X cannot be used as Br is attached to vinylic carbon
B. method II used by Y cannot be used as CN^- replace both Cl^- and OH^- group
C. method I used by Y cannot be used as $RMgX$ is decomposed by OH group
D. method II used by Z cannot be used as CN^- being a strong nucleophile can eliminate HCl

Select the correct drawbacks.
(a) A, B, C (b) A, C, D (c) A, B, D (d) A, B, C, D

***Passage* 3** Following table gives boiling point and pK_a values of some alcohols, acids and esters.

Component	BP/°C	pK_a
HCOOH	101	3.75
CH_3COOH	118	4.76
CH_3CH_2COOH	141	4.85
C_6H_5COOH	249	4.2
CH_3OH	65	15.5
CH_3CH_2OH	78	15.9
C_6H_5OH	181	10.0
$CH_3CH(OH)CH_3$	82	16.5
H_2O	100	15.7
$CH_3COCH_2CH_3$ (ester, C=O)	77	—
$HCOCH_3$ (ester, C=O)	32	—

1. Which reaction can be driven to the right?

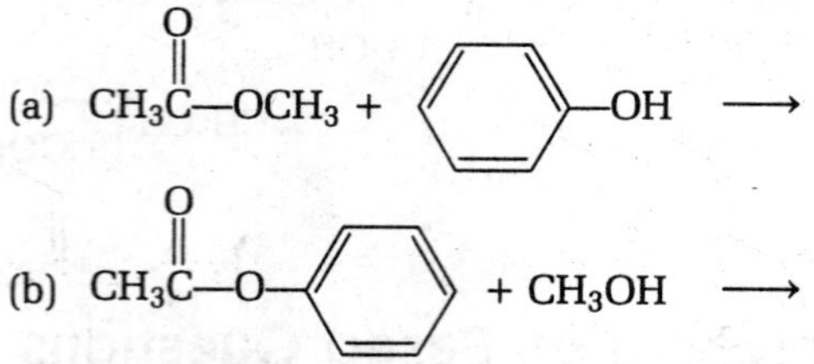

(c) Both of the above
(d) None of the above

2. List the following esters in order of decreasing reactivity towards hydrolysis

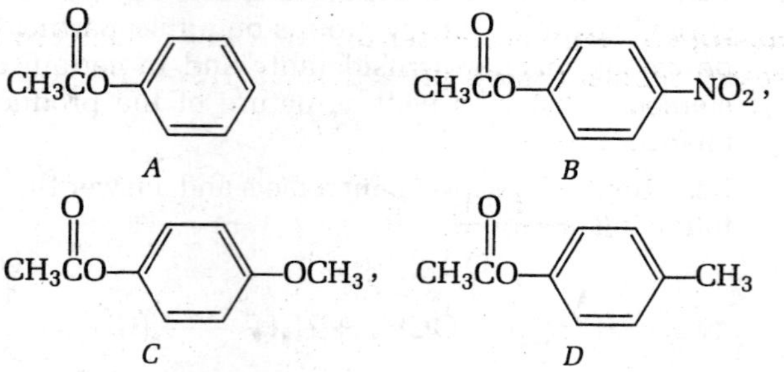

(a) $A > B > C > D$
(b) $B > A > C > D$
(c) $C > B > A > D$
(d) $B > A > D > C$

3. Although carboxylic acids are unreactive to alcohols alone, they can usually be esterified in the presence of a small quantity of concentrated sulphuric acid or about 3% HCl.

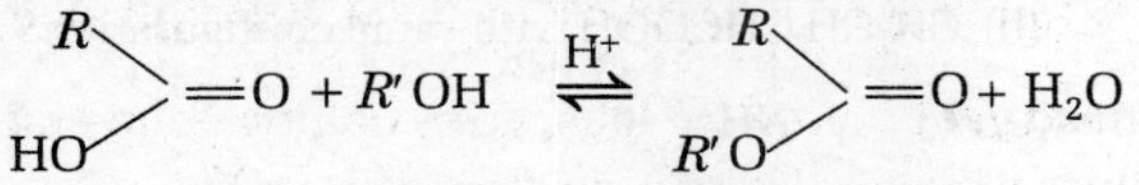

Consider the following statement(s) about this reaction.

I. It is called Fischer esterification reaction.

II. The reaction must be carried out with excess alcohol to drive it towards the product.

III. The reaction is spontaneous if water is removed by azeotropic distillation with toluene or benzene.

IV. Process is reversible if it is made through formation of *R*COCl and then acylation of alcohol.

Select the incorrect statement(s).

(a) I and II (b) II and III (c) Only III (d) Only IV

Passage 4 An organic acid *P* ($C_{11}H_{12}O_2$) can easily be oxidised to a dibasic acid which reacts with ethylene glycol to produce a polymer dacron. Upon ozonolysis, *P* gives a aliphatic ketone as one of the products. *P* undergoes the following reaction sequences to furnish *R via Q*. The compound *P* also undergoes another set of reactions to product *S*. **[JEE Advanced 2018]**

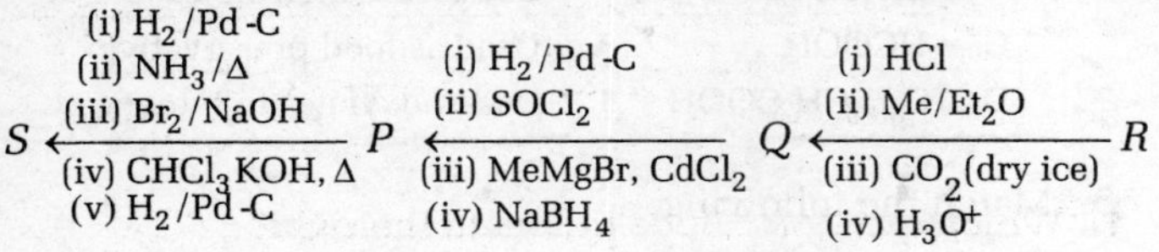

1. The compound *R* is

(a) 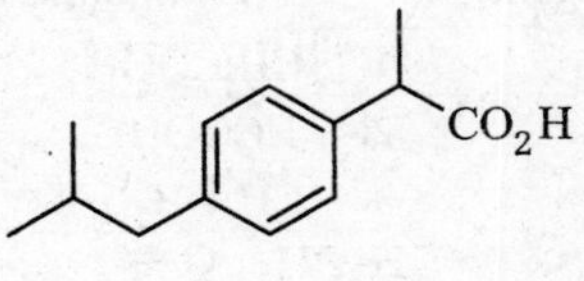 (b) 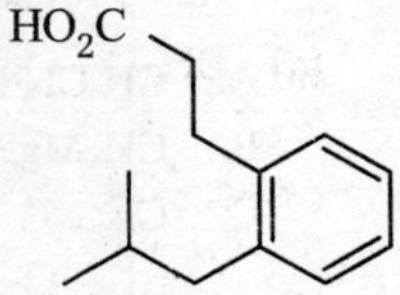

(c) 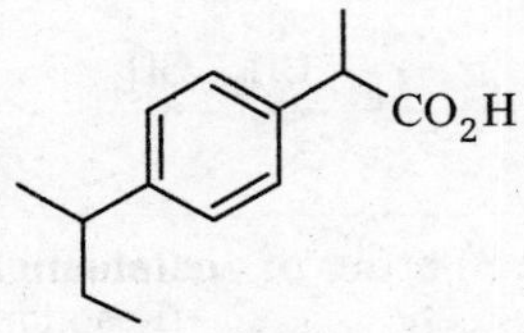 (d) 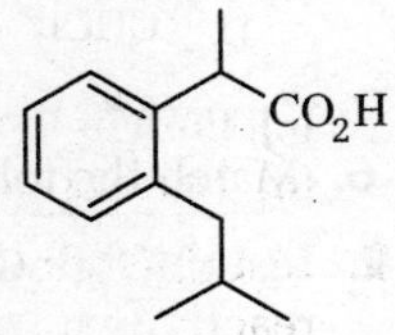

Passage 5 *Para* acetyl benzoic acid was reduced by three research scholars using different reducing agents.

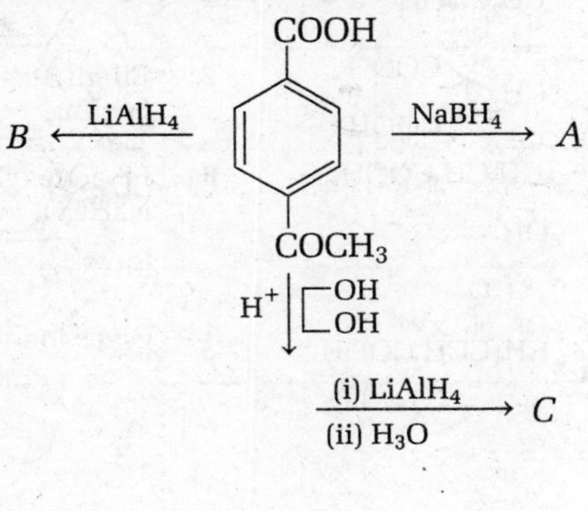

1. *A*, *B* and *C* respectively are

(a) 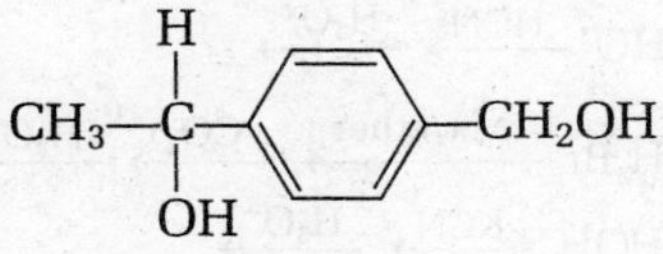 in all cases

(b) 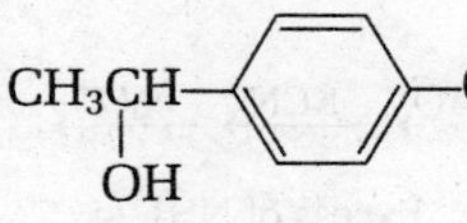 in all cases

(c) 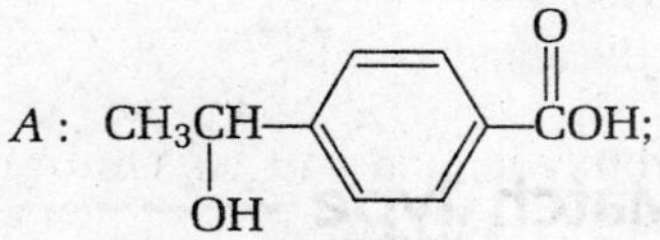

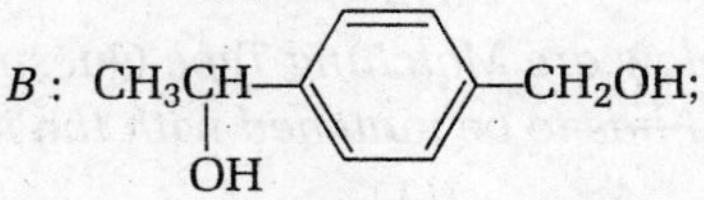

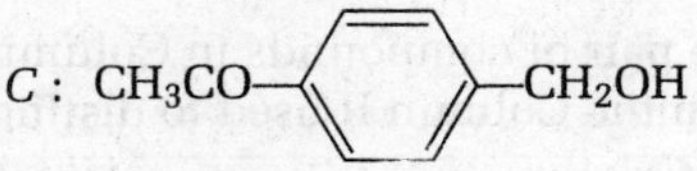

(d) 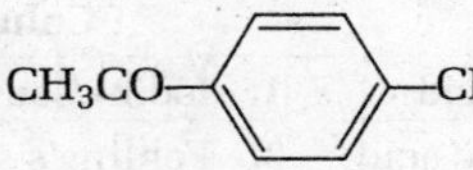 in all cases

Passage 6 Alkyl halides undergo S_N reactions as well as E1, E2 and ECB reactions, depending on the nature of substrate and nucleophile.

Carboxylic acids can be converted into α-bromo carboxylic acids and thus it can be used as an intermediate in the synthesis of so many other compounds.

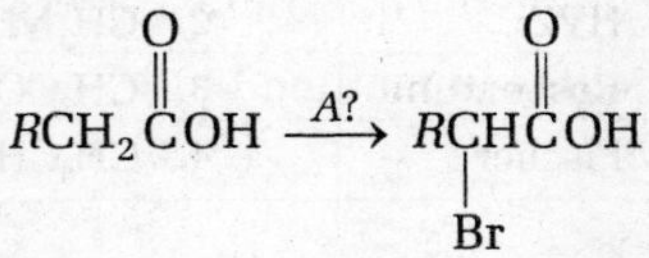

Based on the above intermediate, answer the following questions.

1. One sub-intermediate is also formed in the above reaction

(a) 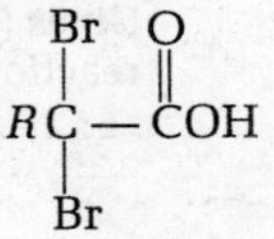

(b) 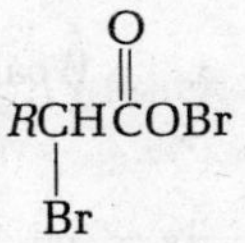

(c) 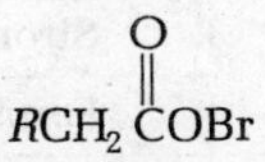

(d) no sub intermediate is formed

2. (Refer Q. 4) Product of Q. 4 can also be synthesised by

(a) $RCH_2CHO \xrightarrow{HCN} \xrightarrow{H_3O^+}$

(b) $RCH_2CH_2Br \xrightarrow{Mg/ether} \xrightarrow{CO_2} \xrightarrow{H_3O^+}$

(c) $RCH_2\underset{\underset{Br}{|}}{C}HOH \xrightarrow{KCN} \xrightarrow{H_3O^+}$

(d) $RCH{=}CH_2 \xrightarrow{HBrO} \xrightarrow{KCN} \xrightarrow{H_3O^+}$

3. $CH_3CH_2\underset{\underset{Br}{|}}{C}HCOOH \xrightarrow[S_N2]{\text{Excess of } NH_3}$ Product is

(a) $CH_3CH_2\underset{\underset{NH_2}{|}}{C}HCOONH_4$ with same configuration

(b) $CH_3CH_2\underset{\underset{NH_2}{|}}{C}HCOOH$ with same configuration

(c) $CH_3CH_2\underset{\underset{NH_2}{|}}{C}HCOONH_4$ with inverted configuration

(d) $CH_3CH_2\underset{\underset{NH_2}{|}}{C}HCOOH$ with inverted configuration

Matrix-Match Type

Given below are Matching Type Questions, with two columns (each having some items) each . Each item of Column I has to be matched with the items of Column II.

1. Match the pair of compounds in Column I with the reagents in the Column II used to distinguish them.

Column I	Column II
A. Phenol, benzoic acid	1. Iodine/sodium hydroxide
B. Acetic acid, formic acid	2. Fehling's solution
C. Acetic acid, acetaldehyde	3. Tollen's reagent
D. Benzaldehyde, formic acid	4. Neutral ferric chloride

2. Match the name-reactions in Column I that convert acetic acid into given compounds in Column II.

Column I	Column II
A. Schmidt	1. $CH_2(Br)COOH$
B. HVZ	2. CH_3NH_2
C. Rosenmund	3. CH_3COOCH_3
D. Fischer	4. CH_3CHO (through CH_3COCl)

3. Match the acids in Column I with the properties shown in Column II.

Column I	Column II
A. 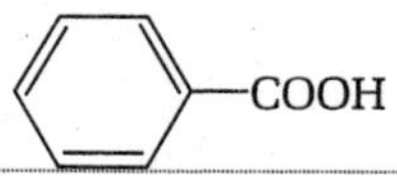	1. Gives (HVZ) reaction
B. 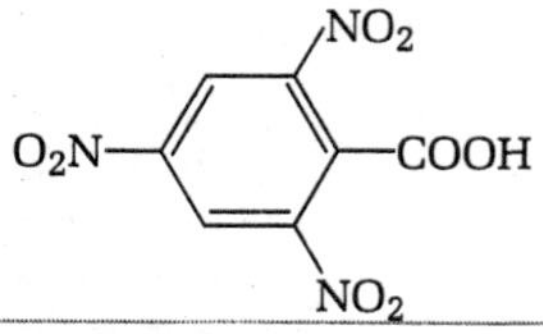	2. Weakest acid
C. CH_3COOH	3. Strongest acid
D. $(CH_3)_3C—COOH$	4. Forms dimer

4. Match the acids in Column I with the properties shown in Column II.

Column I	Column II
A. C_6H_5COOH	1. Red colour, with neutral $FeCl_3$
B. CH_3COOH	2. Reduces Tollen's reagent
C. HCOOH	3. Used as food preservative
D. $C_6H_5CH_2COOH$	4. Decarboxylates to toluene

5. Match the following.

Column I (Starting reagent)	Column II (Compound formed)
A. CH_3CN	1. CH_3COOH
B. CH_3MgBr	2. HCOOH
C. CH_3NC	3. CH_3NH_2
D. $CHCl_3$	4. $CH_3\overset{\overset{O}{\|}}{C}CH_3$

6. Match the following.

Column I (Acid)	Column II (Reaction)
A. $\begin{matrix}CH_2COOH\\ \vert\\ CH_2COOH\end{matrix}$	1. Eliminates H_2O due to heating
B. $CH_2\begin{matrix}\diagup COOH\\ \diagdown COOH\end{matrix}$	2. Eliminates CO_2 due to heating
C. $\begin{matrix}CH_2CH_2COOH\\ \vert\\ OH\end{matrix}$	3. Liberates CO_2 with $NaHCO_3$
D. $CH_3\overset{\overset{O}{\|}}{C}CH_2COOH$	4. Gives iodoform test

7. Match the following.

Column I (Pair to be distinguished by chemical tests)		Column II (Reagent used)	
A.	$HCOOH + CH_3COOH$	1.	Tollen's reagent
B.	$HCOOH + C_6H_5COOH$	2.	Neutral $FeCl_3$
C.	$CH_3COOH + C_6H_5COOH$	3.	MnO_4^- / H^+
D.	$HCOOH + \begin{matrix} COOH \\ \vert \\ COOH \end{matrix}$	4.	Fehling's solution

8. Match the following.

Column I (Acid)		Column II (Reaction)	
A.	$CH_3\overset{O}{\overset{\Vert}{C}}CH_2COOH$	1.	CO_2 lost due to heating
B.	$CH_3\underset{OH}{\underset{\vert}{C}H}COOH$	2.	Iodoform test positive
C.	$\underset{OH}{\underset{\vert}{C}H_2}CH_2COOH$	3.	α, β-unsaturated acid formed due to heating
D.	$HOOC—CH_2\overset{O}{\overset{\Vert}{C}}\underset{OH}{\underset{\vert}{C}H}CH_2COOH$	4.	Lactide formation due to heating

9. Match the following.

Column I (Acid)		Column II (Nature)	
A.	Maleic acid	1.	α, β-unsaturated acid
B.	Succinic acid	2.	gives stereoisomer
C.	Acrylic acid	3.	dibasic acid
D.	Crotonic acid	4.	decolourises Br_2 water and alkaline $KMnO_4$

Single Integer Answer Questions

Answer of these questions is a single digit lying between 0 to 9.

1. 0.5 mole of 1,4-butanedioic acid is heated. Mass of the final product is decreased by .... g.

2. Number of isomers (including geometrical isomers) of the formula $C_4H_8O_4$ is/are ....

3. Number of —OH group(s) in tartaric acid is ....

4. Number of —OH and —COOH groups in citric acid is ....

5. $HO\overset{O}{\overset{\Vert}{C}}(CH_2)_n\overset{O}{\overset{\Vert}{C}}OH \xrightarrow{\Delta}$ product

At what value of (n) given compound will not evolved CO_2 gas ?

6. How many optical isomers are possible of the formula $C_4H_8O_3$?

7. An acid is formed in the following process

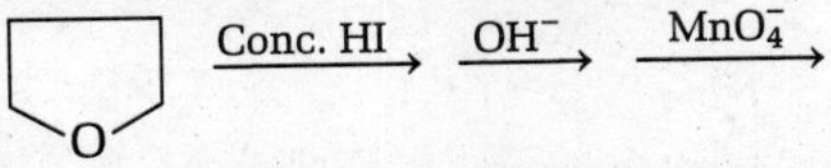

How many —COOH groups are present in the final product?

8. In the following reaction, (C═C) in the product is at (α, β) position. What is the value of ($\alpha + \beta$)?

$$CH_2{=}CHCH{=}CH_2 + \begin{matrix} CHCOOH \\ \Vert \\ CHCOOH \end{matrix} \longrightarrow$$

9. $C_4H_8O_3$ gives iodoform test and liberated CO_2 with $NaHCO_3$. What is the position of OH group?

10. In the following reaction,

$$CH_3CH_2COOH \xrightarrow{P/Br_2} \xrightarrow[H_3O^+]{KOH} \xrightarrow{\Delta} A$$

How many oxygen atoms are present in the product A?

11. How many acidic H are present in 3-pentanone?

12. How many functional groups are present in the final product in the following?

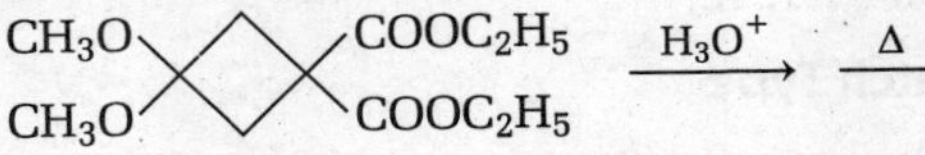

13. On standing in dilute aqueous acid A change to B

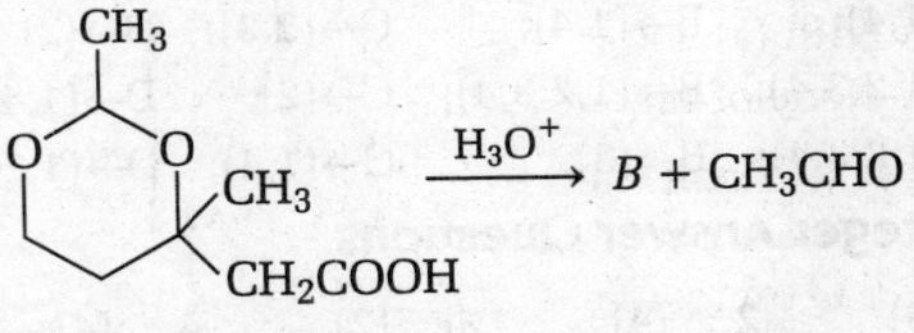

How many O-atoms are present in B?

14. The total number of carboxylic acid groups in the product P is **[JEE Advanced 2013]**

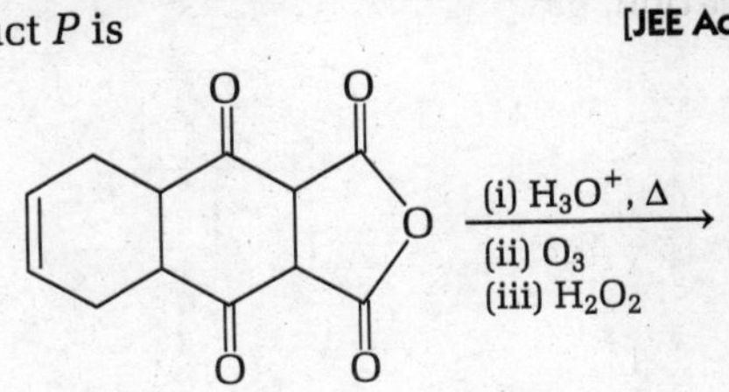

15.

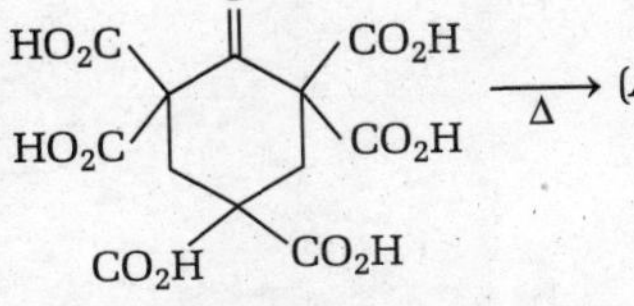

(A) moles of CO_2 evolved during given reaction ? So, the value of (A) is ....

Answers

Objective Questions Type I [Only one correct option]

1. (a)	2. (b)	3. (c)	4. (c)	5. (b)	6. (b)	7. (c)	8. (a)	9. (c)	10. (a)
11. (c)	12. (d)	13. (a)	14. (a)	15. (c)	16. (a)	17. (b)	18. (c)	19. (d)	20. (c)
21. (b)	22. (a)	23. (c)	24. (b)	25. (c)	26. (c)	27. (c)	28. (a)	29. (c)	30. (c)
31. (a)	32. (a)	33. (d)	34. (a)	35. (d)	36. (d)	37. (d)	38. (c)	39. (a)	40. (b)
41. (b)	42. (d)	43. (c)	44. (b)	45. (d)	46. (c)	47. (d)	48. (a)	49. (a)	50. (c)
51. (a)	52. (b)	53. (b)	54. (a)	55. (d)	56. (c)	57. (d)	58. (c)	59. (d)	60. (a)
61. (a)	62. (c)	63. (b)	64. (d)	65. (b)	66. (a)	67. (a)	68. (b)	69. (b)	70. (a)
71. (c)	72. (a)	73. (a)	74. (b)	75. (c)	76. (a)	77. (a)	78. (c)	79. (c)	80. (a)
81. (a)	82. (c)	83. (a)	84. (c)	85. (a)	86. (b)	87. (d)	88. (a)	89. (b)	90. (a)
91. (b)	92. (a)	93. (a)	94. (d)	95. (c)	96. (d)	97. (c)	98. (d)	99. (c)	100. (b)
101. (d)	102. (c)	103. (a)	104. (b)	105. (d)	106. (a)	107. (a)	108. (c)	109. (b)	110. (a)
111. (d)	112. (a)	113. (d)	114. (c)	115. (b)	116. (c)	117. (b)	118. (a)	119. (b)	120. (a)
121. (b)	122. (a)	123. (d)	124. (c)	125. (d)	126. (c)	127. (a)	128. (b)	129. (d)	

Objective Questions Type II [One or more than one correct option(s)]

1. (a, c, d)	2. (a, b)	3. (a, b, c)	4. (a, b, d)	5. (a)
6. (a, b, d)	7. (a, b, c)	8. (a, c, d)	9. (a, b, c, d)	10. (b, d)
11. (b)	12. (a)			

Numerical Value Questions

1. (3)	2. (5)	3. (3)	4. (6)	5. (3)	6. (4)	7. (2)	8. (4)

Comprehension Based Questions

Passage 1 – 1. (b,c) 2. (b) 3. (a)

Passage 2 – 1. (a) 2. (a) 3. (b)

Passage 3 – 1. (b) 2. (d) 3. (d)

Passage 4 – 1. (a)

Passage 5 – 1. (c)

Passage 6 – 1. (b) 2. (a) 3. (c)

Matrix-Match Type

1. A→(4); B→(3); C→(1); D→(2)

2. A→(2); B→(1); C→(4); D→(3)

3. A→(4); B→(3); C→(1); D→(2)

4. A→(3); B→(1); C→(2); D→(4)

5. A→(1,4); B→(1,4); C→(2,3); D→(2)

6. A→(1,3); B→(2,3); C→(1,3); D→(2,3,4)

7. A→(1,2,3,4); B→(1,2,3,4); C→(2); D→(1,4)

8. A→(1,2); B→(2,4); C→(3); D→(1,3)

9. A→(1,2,3,4); B→(3); C→(1,4); D→(1,2,4)

Single Integer Answer Questions

1. (9)	2. (4)	3. (2)	4. (4)	5. (2)	6. (4)	7. (2)	8. (9)	9. (3)	10. (4)
11. (4)	12. (2)	13. (3)	14. (2)	15. (5)					

Solutions

Objective Questions Type I [Only one correct option]

1. (*a*) RCH_2OH is oxidised to $R\overset{O}{\overset{\|}{C}}OH$ through intermediate $R\overset{O}{\overset{\|}{C}}H$ and $Cr_2O_7^{2-}$ is reduced to Cr^{3+} (green)

$$RCH_2OH \longrightarrow RCHO \longrightarrow RCOOH$$
$$Cr_2O_7^{2-} \longrightarrow Cr^{3+}$$

2. (*b*) $CH_3-\overset{O}{\overset{\|}{C}}-CH_2-CH_3 \xrightarrow[\Delta]{Cr_2O_7^{2-}/H^+} CH_3\overset{O}{\overset{\|}{C}}OH$

This is also oxidised (CH_2); This bond breaks (between C=O and CH_2)

3. (*c*) I. $CH_3-\overset{O}{\overset{\|}{C}}-CH_3 + I_2 + NaOH \xrightarrow{\Delta} CH_3COONa \xrightarrow{H^+} CH_3COOH$

II. $\xrightarrow{Cr_2O_7^{2-}/H^+} CH_3COOH$

III. $\xrightarrow{[Ag(NH_3)_2]^+}$ no reaction

Thus, I and II.

4. (*c*) Alkaline $KMnO_4$ also causes hydroxylation of $(C{=}C)$ and $(C{\equiv}C)$ bond.

5. (*b*) $CH_2{=}CHCHO \xrightarrow{MnO_4^-/OH^-} \underset{OH}{CH_2}-\underset{OH}{C}HCOOH$

This is also affected. (the $CH_2{=}CH$ double bond)

6. (*b*) $R-MgX \longrightarrow \underset{\text{Carbanion}}{R^\ominus} + (MgX)^\oplus$

7. (*c*) $\underset{\text{One C-atom}}{CH_3}-Mg-Br + CO_2 \xrightarrow{H_3O^+} \underset{\text{Two C-atom}}{CH_3COOH}$

Thus, one carbon homologation.

Thus, (a) is correct.

$$O{=}C{=}O \longrightarrow O{=}\overset{\oplus}{C}-O^\ominus$$
$$\overset{\ominus}{C}H_3(MgBr)^\oplus$$

Attack at electron deficient carboxy carbon.

$$O{=}\underset{CH_3}{\underset{|}{C}}-OH \xleftarrow{H_3O^+} O{=}\underset{CH_3}{\underset{|}{C}}-O-Mg-Br$$

Thus, (b) is also correct.

8. (*a*) $R-\overset{H}{\overset{|}{C}}{=}O \longrightarrow R-\overset{H}{\overset{|}{\underset{\oplus}{C}}}-O^\ominus$

$R-\overset{O}{\overset{\|}{C}}-R \longrightarrow R-\overset{O^\ominus}{\overset{|}{\underset{\oplus}{C}}}-R$

9. (*c*) Grignard reagent and carbonyl group are present in the same substance. Thus impossible.

$$CH_3\underset{O}{\underset{\|}{C}}CH_2MgBr$$

10. (*a*) (a) $CH_3MgBr \xrightarrow{CO_2/H_3O^+} CH_3COOH$

(b) $CH_3MgBr \xrightarrow{H_3O^+} CH_4 \xrightarrow{CO_2}$ no reaction

Grignard reagent is decomposed by H_3O^+ in first step. Thus, incorrect.

(c) Carboxyl group and grignard reagent both are present in same substance. Thus, incorrect.

11. (*c*) This problem is based on successive reduction, chlorination and elimination reaction. To solve such problem, use the function of the given reagents.

(i) $LiAlH_4$ causes reduction

(ii) PCl_5 causes chlorination

(iii) Alc. KOH causes elimination reaction

$$CH_3COOH \xrightarrow{LiAlH_4} \underset{(A)}{CH_3CH_2OH}$$
$$\xrightarrow{PCl_5} \underset{(B)}{CH_3CH_2Cl} \xrightarrow[-HCl]{\text{Alc. KOH}} \underset{\substack{(C)\\ \text{Ethylene}}}{CH_2{=}CH_2}$$

13. (*a*) $CH_2{=}CHCN \xrightarrow{H_3O^+} CH_2{=}CHCOOH$

$\xrightarrow{OH^-} CH_2{=}CHCOO^-$ salt is formed in (b)

14. (*a*) When alkyl halide is 2° or 3° dehalogenation takes place with strong nucleophile as CN^- giving alkene as major product. Thus (a) when alkyl halide is 1°.

15. (*c*) (I) $RCN \xrightarrow{H_3O^+} RCOOH$

(II) $RCN \xrightarrow{OH^-} RCOO^-$

(III) $RCN \xrightarrow{DIBAH} RCHO$

(IV) $RCN \xrightarrow{SnCl_2/HCl} RCHO$

(V) $RCN \xrightarrow{LiACH_4} RCH_2NH_2$

Thus, I gives RCO_2H.

16. (*a*) $RCH_2OH \xrightarrow{Cr_2O_7^{2-}/H_3O^+} RCOOH$ same number of carbon atom.

17. (*b*) In I alkene is also formed alkyl halide being 2°.

18. (*c*) *B* has half of the C-atoms as in *A* thus *A* is symmetrical.

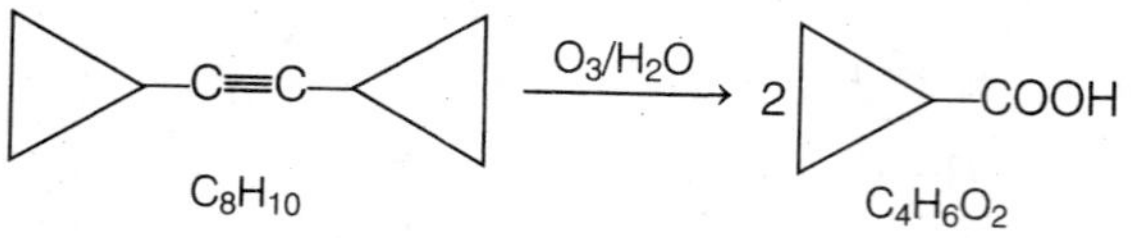

19. (*d*)

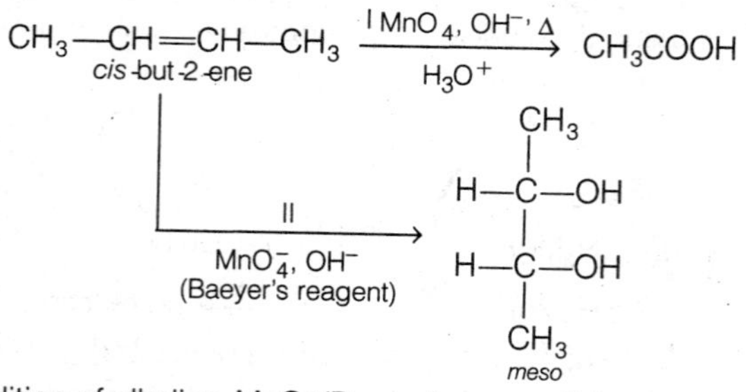

Addition of alkaline MnO_4^-(Baeyer's reagent) is *syn*, thus *cis*-but-2-ene gives *meso*-isomer.

20. (*c*)

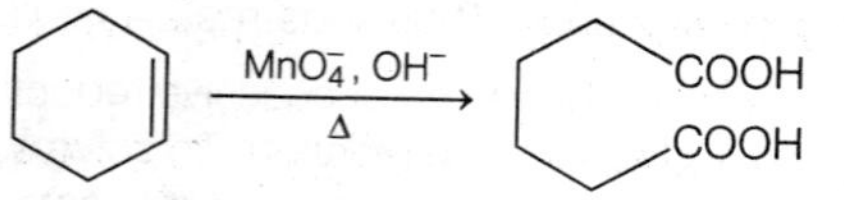

21. (*b*)

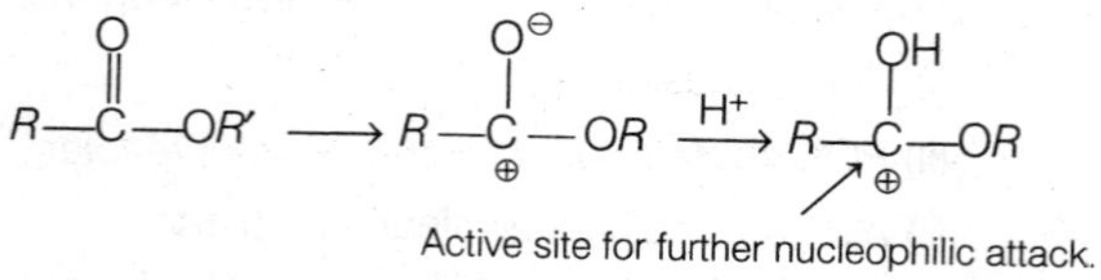

22. (*a*) Refer mechanism

23. (*c*)

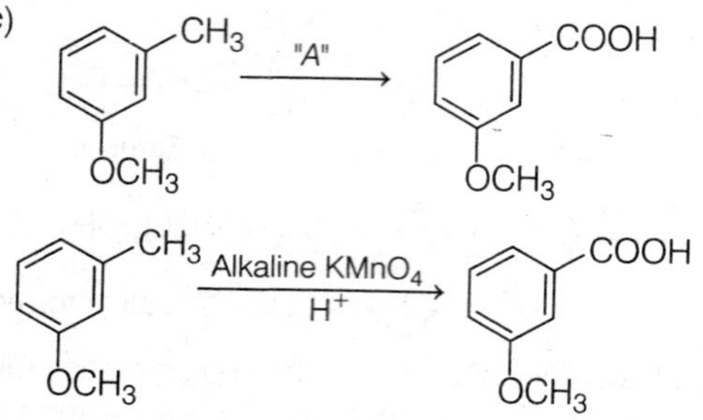

24. (*b*)

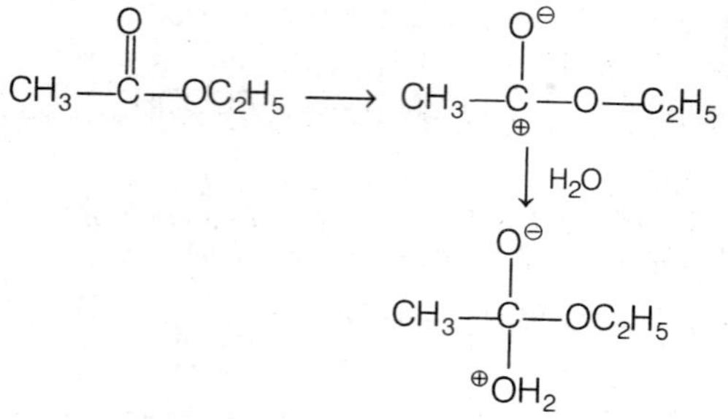

25. (*c*) It gives carboxylate ion ($RCOO^-$).

26. (*c*) Cl attached to benzene ring does not undergo S_N reaction, thus benzylic halide reacts with CN^-.

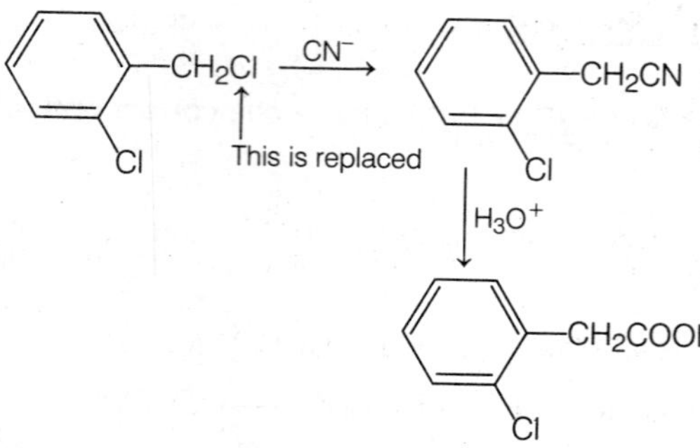

27. (*c*)

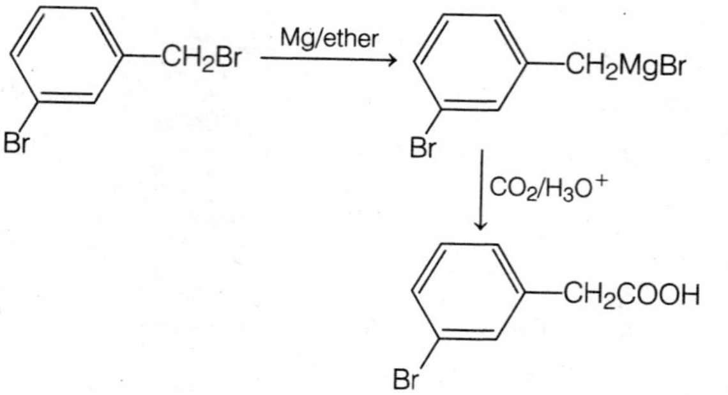

28. (*a*) $CH_3CHO + \underset{\text{(Tollen's reagent)}}{2[Ag(NH_3)_2]^+} + 3OH^- \longrightarrow CH_3COO^- + 2Ag + 4NH_3 + 2H_2O$

$H_3CCCl_3 \xrightarrow{OH^-} CH_3COO^-$

$H_3CCO_2C_2H_5 \xrightarrow{OH^-} H_3CCOO^- + C_2H_5OH$

(Base hydrolysis of ester)

29. (*c*) $CH_3COOH \xrightarrow{NH_3} \underset{'X'}{CH_3\,\overset{-}{COO}\overset{+}{NH_4}} \xrightarrow[-H_2O]{\Delta}$

$\underset{'Y'}{CH_3CONH_2} \xrightarrow[-H_2O]{P_2O_5} \underset{'Z'}{CH_3CN}$

(Methyl cyanide)

30. (*c*)

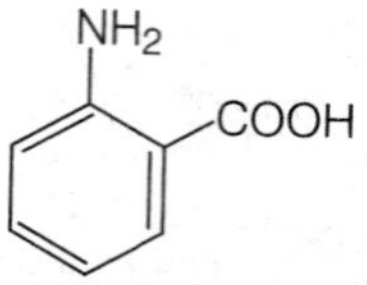

32. (*a*)

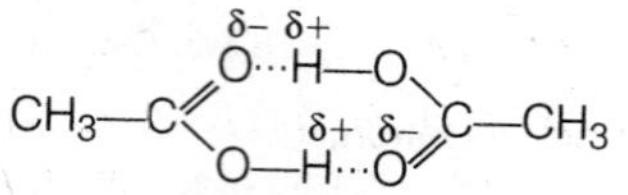

Dimer by intermolecular H-bonding.

34. (*a*)

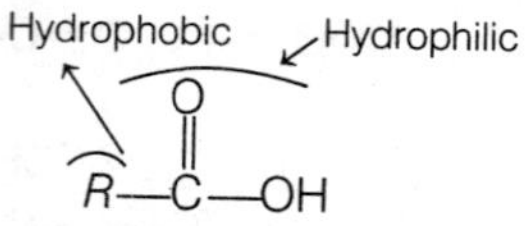

36. (*d*) Decarboxylation takes place in cases in which their is keto group at β-position or a (C═C) at (β, γ)-position or two —COOH group at *gem* (same) position

Decarboxylation takes place in I and II

(I) $\underset{\gamma}{CH_2}{=}\underset{\beta}{CH}{-}CH_2\overset{O}{\overset{\|}{C}}OH$ Yes, as (C═C) in β, γ-position

(II) $CH_3\overset{O}{\overset{||}{C}}CH_2\overset{O}{\overset{||}{C}}OH$ (β at CH_3C, α at CH_2)

Yes, keto group at β-position

(III) 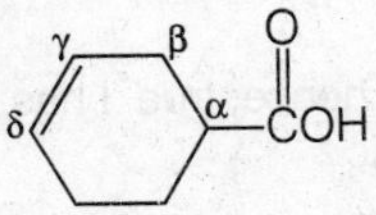 No as (C=C) in γ,δ-position

(IV) 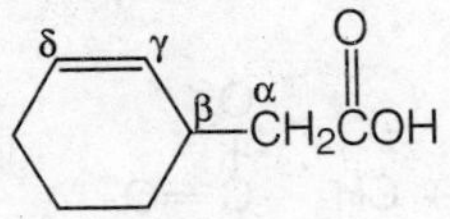

Thus, I and II.

38. (*c*) $RCH_2CH_2COOH \xrightarrow[\text{HVZ-reaction}]{P/Br_2} RCH_2\underset{Br}{CH}COOH \xrightarrow{NaOC_2H_5} RCH{=}CHCOOH$

($\bar{O}C_2H_5$ is a strong nucleophile)

41. (*b*) 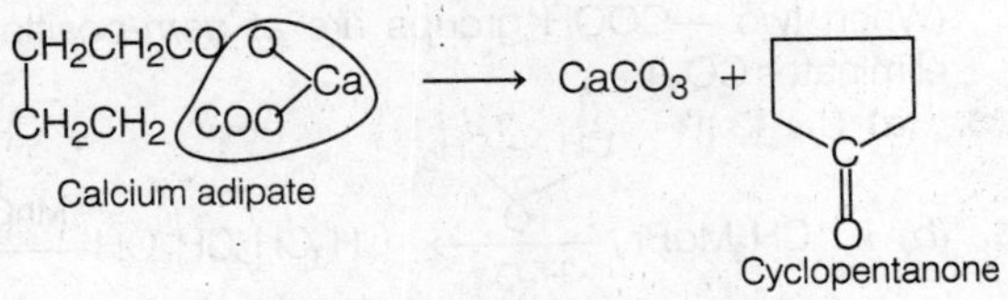

42. (*d*) Phenol and succinic acid both are soluble in NaOH and thus cannot be separated using NaOH.

43. (*c*) Fehling's solution is reduced by

CH_3COOH	No
$HCOOH$	Yes
$HCHO$	Yes
C_6H_5CHO	No
CH_3CHO	Yes

Thus, pair I can be distinguished
Pair II can be distinguished
Pair III can be distinguished
Pair IV cannot be distinguished

45. (*d*) Due to electron-withdrawing F-atom.

46. (*c*) HVZ-reaction in which H at α-C w.r.t.—COOH group is replaced by halogen atom, takes place in carboxylic acid with at least one H at α-C only out of given acids, only (c) has H at α-C.

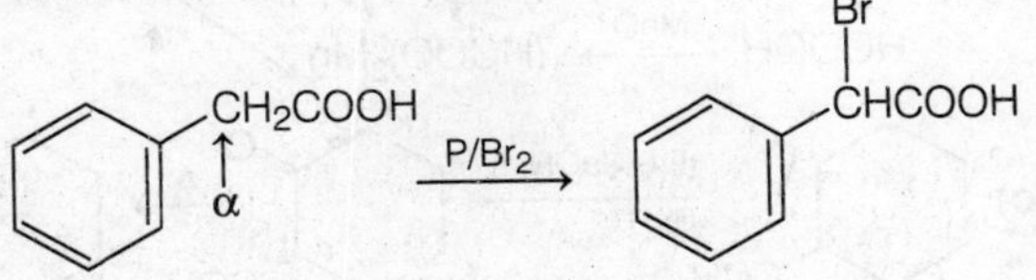

47. (*d*) 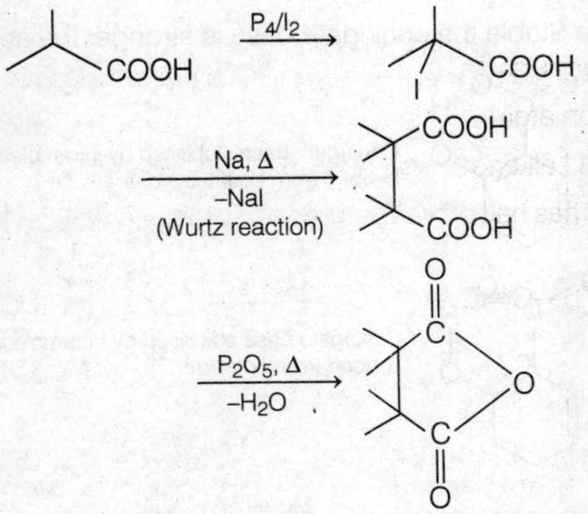

48. (*a*) 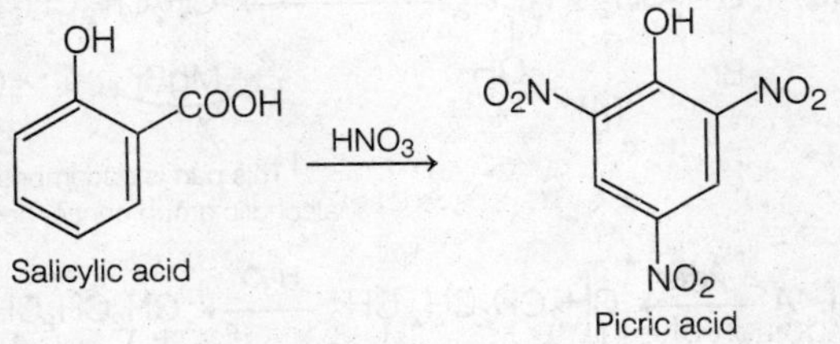

Explanation as in (d).

49. (*a*) CH_3COOH forms dimer due to intermolecular H-bonding.

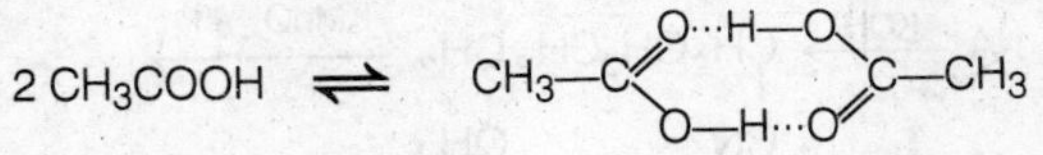

i (van't half factor) $= [1 + (y - 1)x]$

y = number of product for one mole of reactant $= 1/2$

x = degree of association

$$\therefore \quad i = 1 + \left(\frac{1}{2} - 1\right) x = \left(1 - \frac{x}{2}\right)$$

Thus, $i < 1$.

50. (*c*) 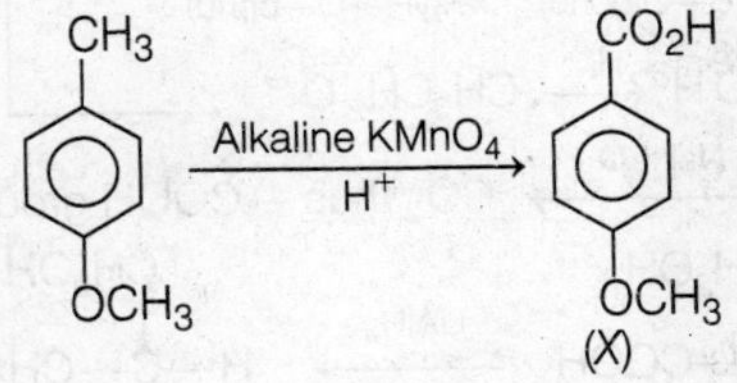

51. (*a*) Valeric acid is $CH_3CH_2CH_2CH_2\overset{O}{\overset{||}{C}}OH$.

52. (*b*) (a) α-hydroxy acid forms lactide by intermolecular loss of H_2O.

(b) β-hydroxy acid forms unsaturated acids by intramolecular loss of H_2O.

(c) γ-hydroxy acid form γ-lactam.

54. (*a*) More Stable the conjugate base is stronger the acid.

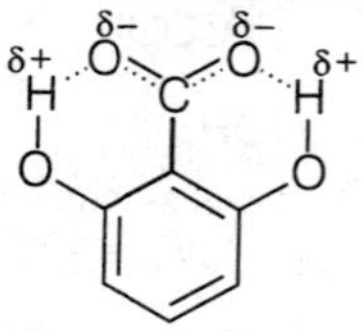

Conjugate base stabilised by intramolecular H-bond from both the sides.

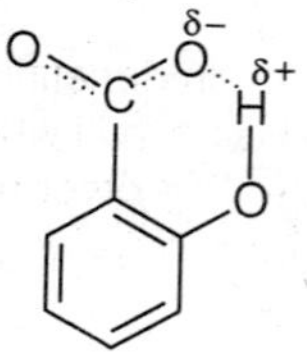

Conjugate base stabilised by intramolecular H-bond from one side.

55. (*d*) I.

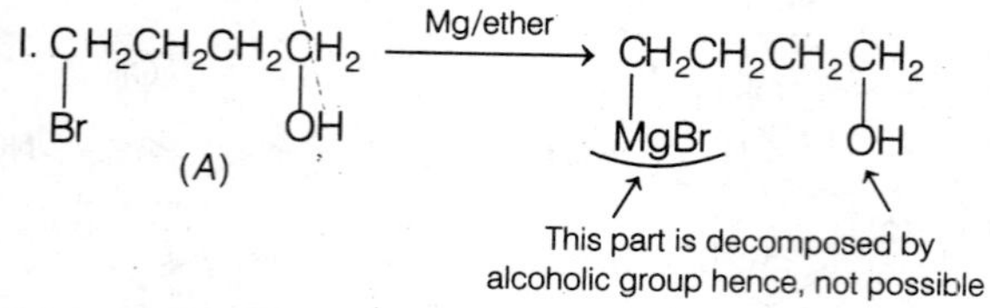

II.

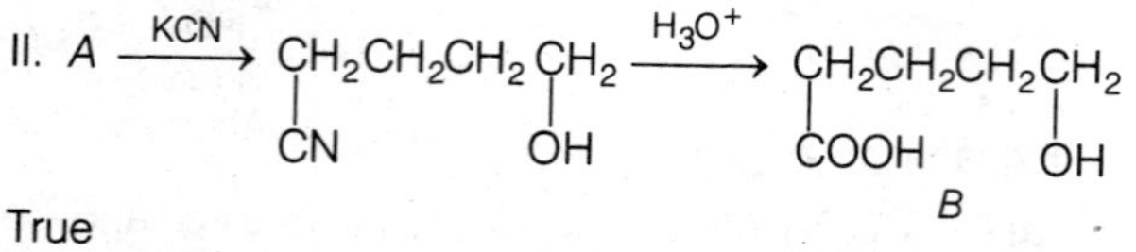

True

III :

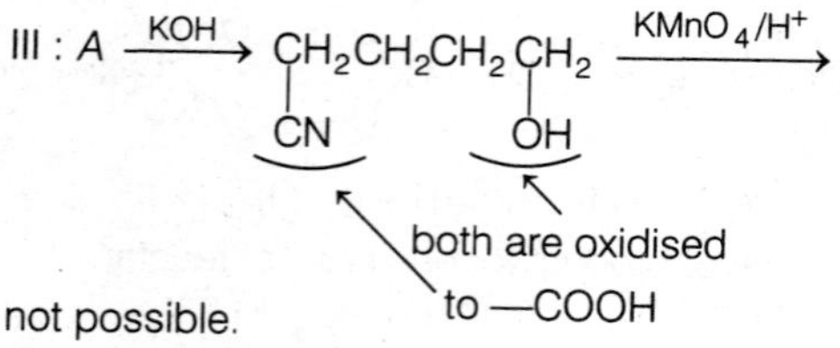

not possible.

56. (*c*)

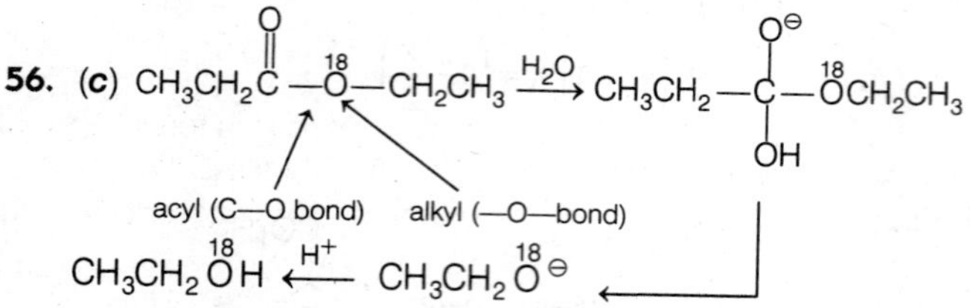

58. (*c*) $X \xrightarrow{NaHCO_3} CO_2$ thus —COOH group.

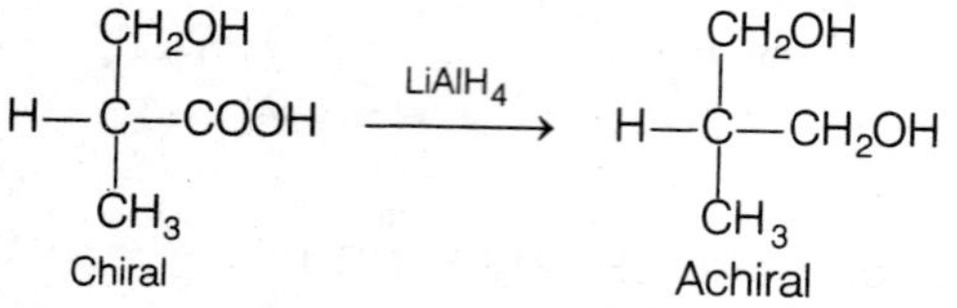

This is reduced to $—CH_2OH$

59. (*d*)

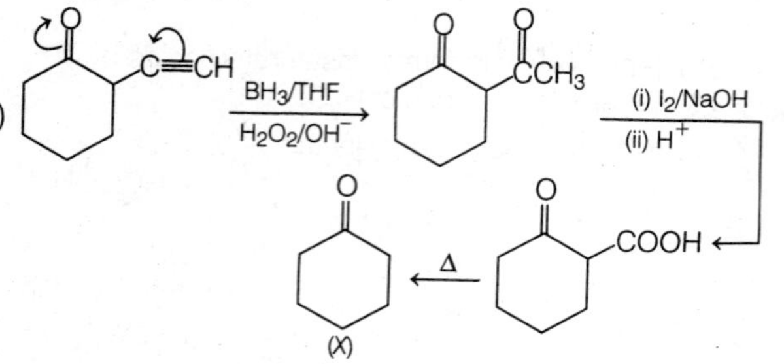

(C=O) group is electron-withdrawing hence, π-electron migration is from terminal carbon to internal carbon as shown.

Also when keto group is at β-position w.r.t. —COOH group, heating eliminates CO_2.

60. (*a*) II, III have —COOH group hence, true. I has keto groups which make —OH group acidic.

Thus, (a) I, II, III.

62. (*c*)

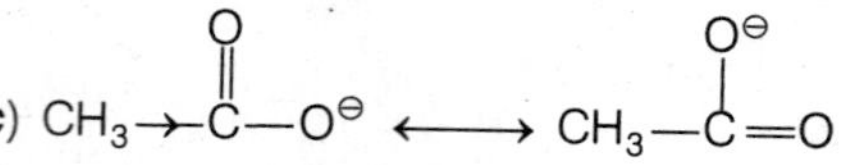

63. (*b*)

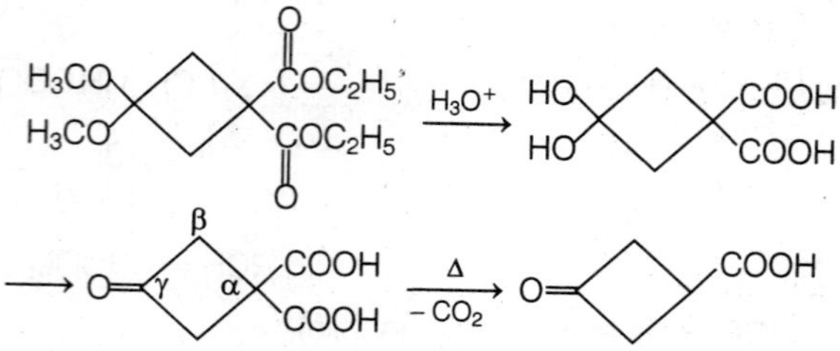

(When two —COOH groups are at *gem*-position, heating eliminates CO_2).

65. (*b*)

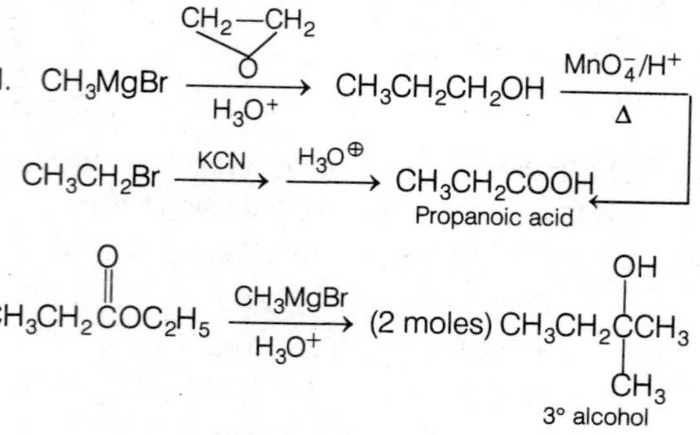

66. (*a*) Reactant is α-hydroxy acid which forms cyclic lactide.

67. (*a*)

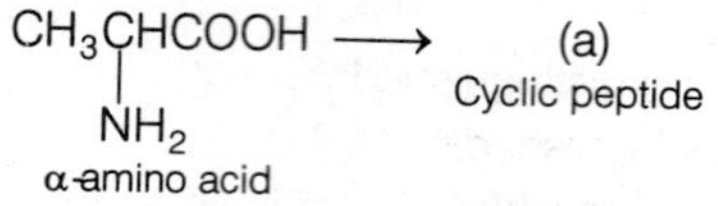

72. (*a*) $CH_3CH_2O^\ominus$ (alkoxy) group replaces OH group of

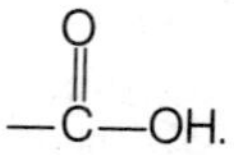

76. (*a*)

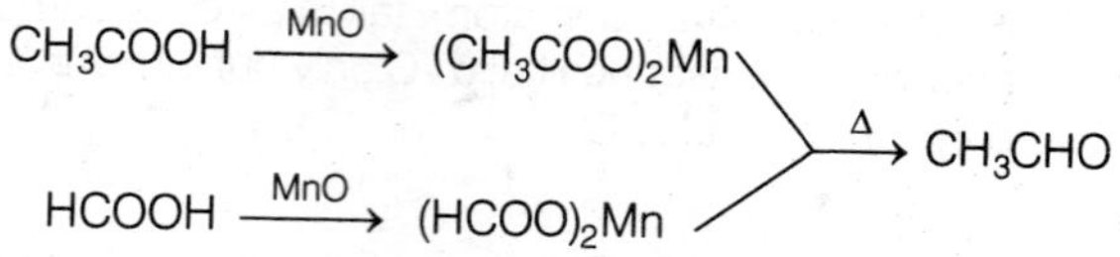

79. (*c*)

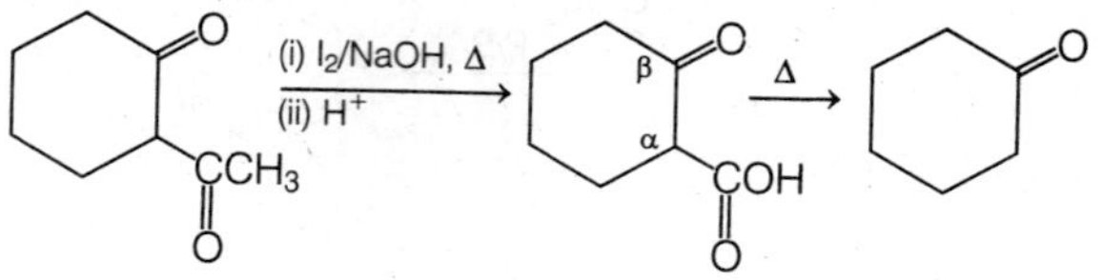

When keto group is at β-position w.r.t. —COOH, heating eliminates, CO_2.

81. (*a*) Greater the acid strength, smaller the value of pK_a.

82. (*c*) 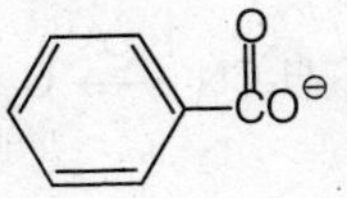 is stabilised due to resonance.

83. (*a*)

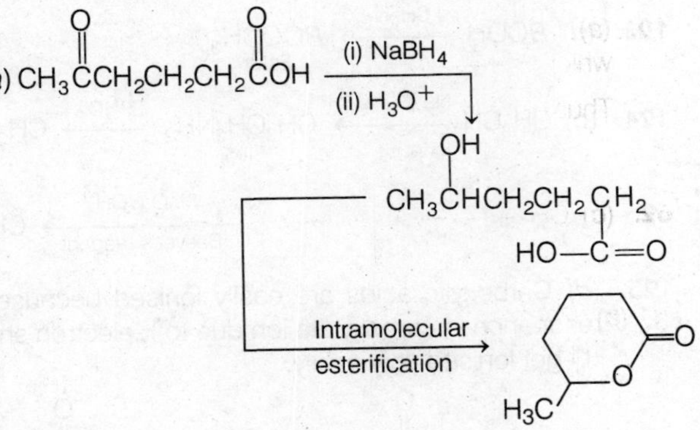

85. (*a*) Strongest acid is oxalic acid thus, have least pK_a value.

86. (*b*) Heating of $(CH_2)_4<^{COOH}_{COOH}$ (adipic acid) with a dehydrating agent, decarboxylates ($—CO_2$) to give a ketone (cyclopentanone), not an anhydride.

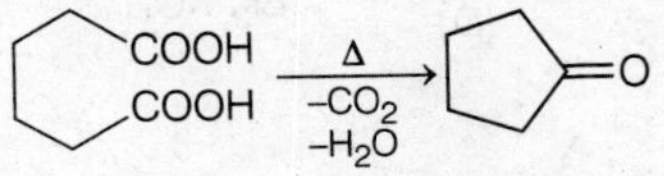

88. (*a*) $R\overset{O}{\overset{\|}{C}}NH_2 \xrightarrow{Br_2} R—\overset{O}{\overset{\|}{C}}NHBr \longrightarrow R—N{=}C{=}O$

94. (*d*) Being in *trans*-position.

95. (*c*) CN^- is a strong nucleophile and causes elimination.

97. (*c*) $RC{\equiv}N \xrightarrow[\Delta]{HCl/H_2O} R\overset{O}{\overset{\|}{C}}OH \xrightarrow{LiAlH_4} RCH_2OH \xrightarrow[CH_2Cl_2]{PCC} RCHO$

—CN changes to —CHO

98. (*d*) (Br_2/light) changes benzyl hydrogen to —Br.

104. (*b*) Acidic nature depends upon nature of electron withdrawing group and electronegativity. Electronegativity further depends on % *s* character.

Higher the *s*-character, greater will be the electronegativity and hence tendency to loose H increases thus acidic character also increases.

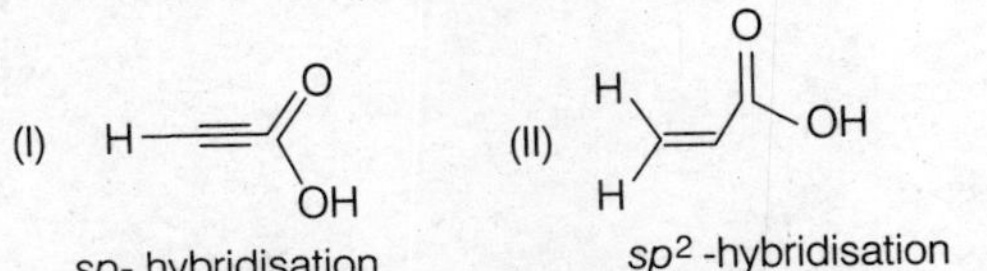

(I) *sp*- hybridisation (50% *s* character) (pK_a = 1.86)

(II) sp^2 -hybridisation (30-33% *s* character) (pK_a = 4.3)

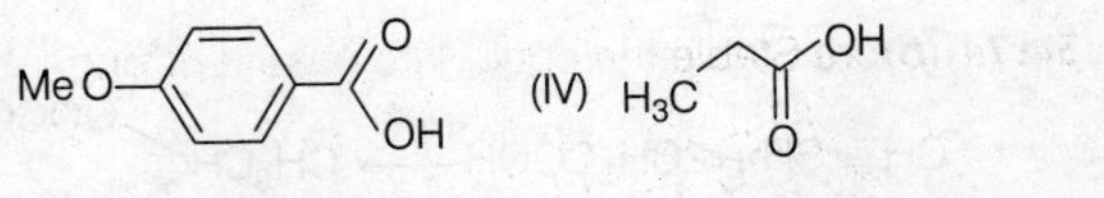

(III) sp^2 -hybridisation (Resonance effect) (pK_a = 4.5)

(IV) sp^3 -hybridisation (25% *s*-character) (pK_a = 4.8)

Hence, acidic order I > II > III > IV.

II is more acidic than III since electron donating group ($—OCH_3$) is attached to benzene ring in III which decreases the acidic character. On the other hand, pK_a value also determined acidic nature, lower pK_a value gives maximum acidic character.

Hence, option (b) is correct.

105. (*d*) $CH_3CH_2\overset{O}{\overset{\|}{C}}\overset{*}{C}H_2\overset{O}{\overset{\|}{C}}OH \xrightarrow{\Delta} \underset{A}{CH_3CH_2\overset{O}{\overset{\|}{C}}\overset{*}{C}H_3} \xrightarrow[\Delta]{I_2/NaOH}$

$\underset{(D)}{CH_3CH_3} \xleftarrow[\Delta]{CaO/NaOH} \underset{(B)}{CH_3CH_2\overset{O}{\overset{\|}{C}}O\overset{-}{N}\overset{+}{a}} + \underset{(C)}{\overset{*}{C}HI_3}\downarrow$

106. (*a*) Acidic strength of phenol is less then carboxylic acid. So, (I) is least acidic. Now,

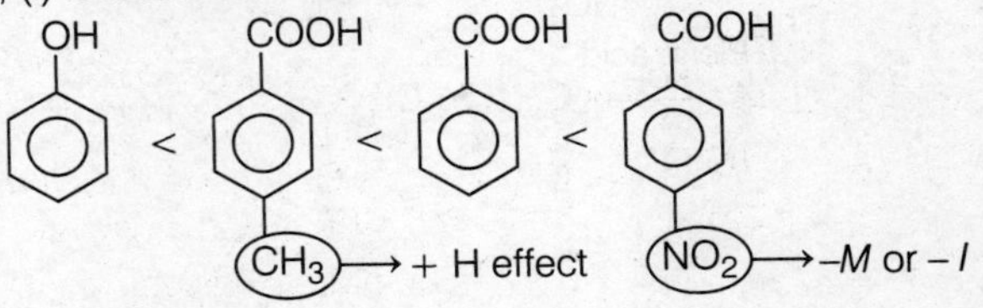

107. (*a*) $\underset{NO_2}{\underset{|}{C}}H_2COOH$ has maximum pK_a.

Thus, most acidic. Thus, $—NO_2$.

108. (*c*) Equilibria I and III are spontaneous in forward direction formation of stable compounds). Thus, $\Delta G° = -$ ve.

(C—F bond energy is maximum, does not react with Mg).

111. (*d*)

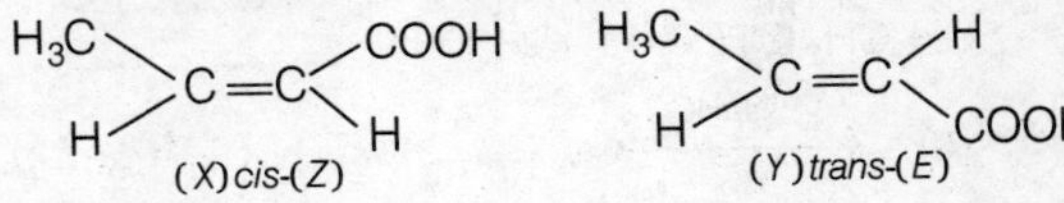

(a) true (b) true (c) true

114. (*c*)

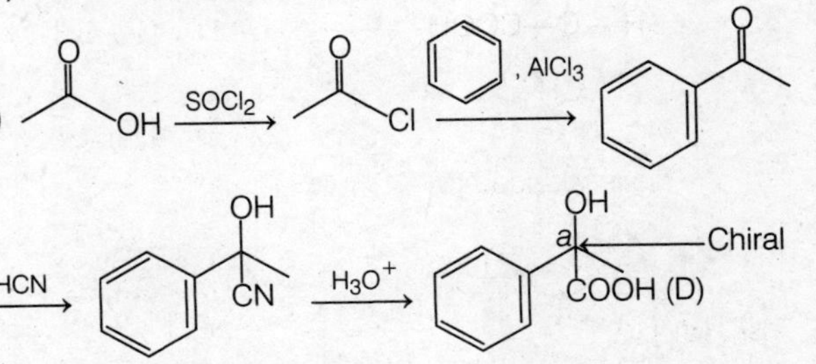

116. (*c*) (I) $CH_3NC \xrightarrow{H_3O^+} CH_3NH_2 + HCOOH$

(II) $CHCl_3 \xrightarrow{NaOH} H\overset{O}{\overset{\|}{C}}O\overset{-}{N}\overset{+}{a} \xrightarrow{H_3O^+} HCOOH$

(III) $CCl_4 \xrightarrow{H_3O^+}$ no hydrolysis

117. (*b*)

$$CH\equiv CH + 2CH_3COOH \xrightarrow{Hg^{2+}} \underset{(X)}{CH_3CH(OOCCH_3)_2} \xrightarrow{H_3O^+}$$

$$CH_3CH(OH)_2 \longrightarrow \underset{(Y)}{CH_3CHO}$$

118. (*a*) Carboxylic acids i.e. acetic acid are decomposed by $NaHCO_3$ to liberate CO_2.

119. (*b*) $X = \underset{\displaystyle Br}{CH_2COOH}$ $\quad Y = \underset{\displaystyle COOH}{CH_2COOH}$

120. (*a*) $CH_2{=}CHCH_2CH_2\overset{O}{\overset{\|}{C}}OH \xrightarrow{\text{HBr, peroxide}} \underset{\displaystyle Br}{CH_2}CH_2CH_2CH_2\overset{O}{\overset{\|}{C}}OH$

121. (*b*)

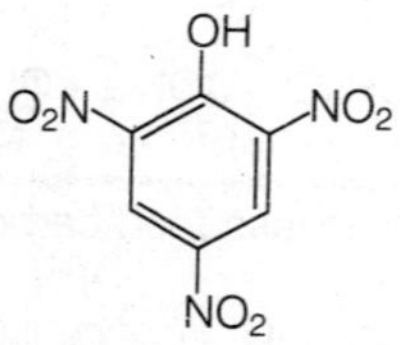

Picric acid

122. (*a*) Only possible compound that can react with PCl_5 is

$$C_2H_5OH \xrightarrow{PCl_5} C_2H_5Cl \xrightarrow{KCN} C_2H_5CN \xrightarrow{H_3O^+} \underset{\text{Propanoic acid}}{C_2H_5COOH}$$

123. (*d*) $R\overset{O}{\overset{\|}{C}}OH \xrightarrow{CH_2N_2} \underset{\text{Ester}}{R\overset{O}{\overset{\|}{C}}OCH_3}$

124. (*c*) $CH_3CN \xrightarrow{Na/C_2H_5OH} \underset{(X)}{CH_3CH_2NH_2} \xrightarrow{HNO_2} \underset{(Y)}{CH_3CH_2OH}$

$$\xrightarrow[\text{Baeyer's reagent}]{MnO_4^-/OH^-} \underset{(Z)}{CH_3COOH}$$

125. (*d*) Carboxylic acids are easily ionised because there is resonance in carboxylate ion due to π-electron shifting. So H^+ get ionised very easily.

129. (*d*) $\underset{(A)}{CH_3CH_2{-}\overset{O}{\overset{\|}{C}}{-}OH} \xrightarrow{NH_3} \underset{(B)}{CH_3CH_2{-}\overset{O}{\overset{\|}{C}}{-}\overset{\ominus}{O}\overset{\oplus}{N}H_4}$

$$\xrightarrow{\Delta,\ -H_2O} \underset{(C)}{CH_3CH_2{-}\overset{O}{\overset{\|}{C}}{-}NH_2} \xrightarrow{Br_2/KOH} \underset{(D)}{CH_3CH_2NH_2}$$

13

Functional Derivatives of Carboxylic Acids

Objective Questions Type I [Only one correct option]

In each of the questions below, four choices are given of which only one is correct.

1. $CH_3CH_2\overset{O}{\overset{\|}{C}}CH_3$ undergoes oxidation by CH_3CO_3H and then hydrolysed

$$CH_3CH_2\overset{O}{\overset{\|}{C}}CH_3 \xrightarrow{CH_3CO_3H} \xrightarrow{H_3O^+}$$

Products are

(a) $CH_3CH_2\overset{O}{\overset{\|}{C}}OH$ and CH_3OH (b) $CH_3\overset{O}{\overset{\|}{C}}OH$ and CH_3CH_2OH

(c) $CH_3CH_2OCH_3$ and CH_3OH (d) CH_3OCH_3 and CH_3OH

2. Which is hydrolysed to the maximum extent?

(a) 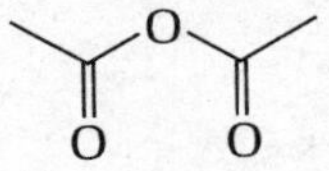 (b) 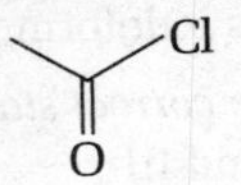

(c) 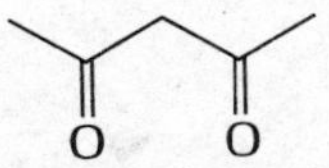 (d) 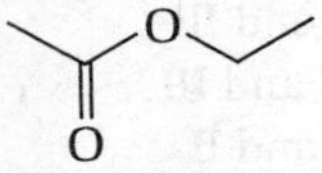

3. Which is more basic oxygen in an ester?

$$R-\overset{\overset{\alpha}{O}}{\overset{\|}{C}}-\overset{\beta}{O}-R'$$

(a) Carbonyl oxygen α

(b) Carboxyl oxygen β

(c) Equally basic

(d) Both are acidic oxygen

4. Which is γ-butyrolactone?

(a) 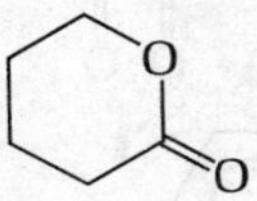 (b) 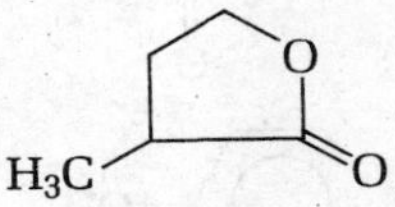

(c) 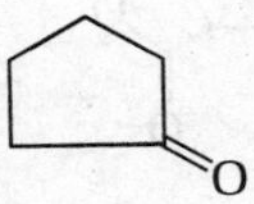 (d) 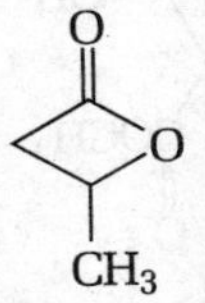

5. β-butyrolactone is

(a) 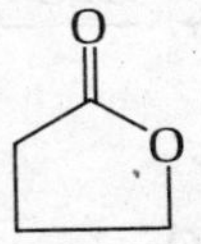 (b) 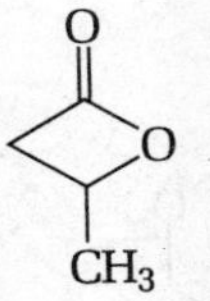

(c) 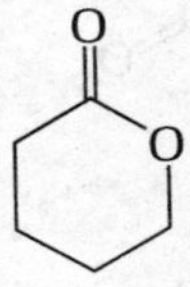 (d) 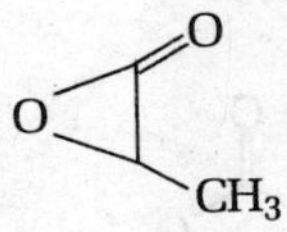

6. What is the end product of following reaction?

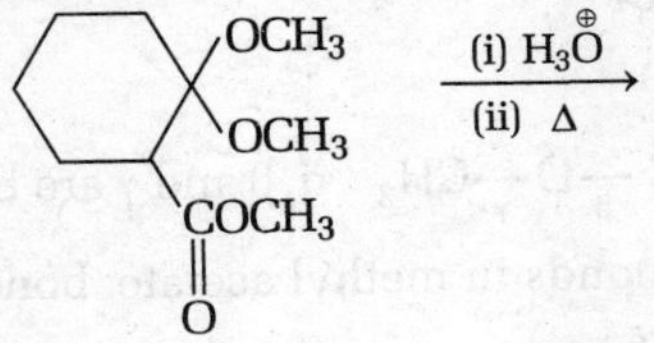

(a) 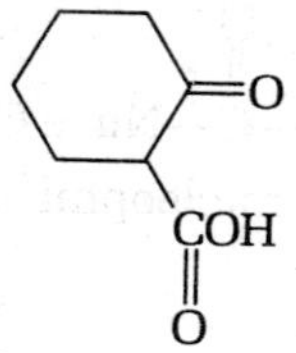
(b) 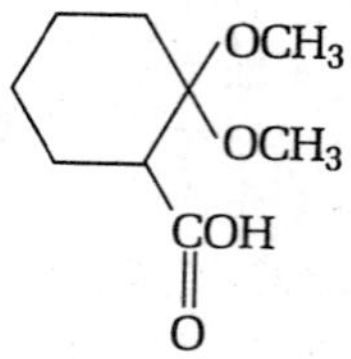

(c) 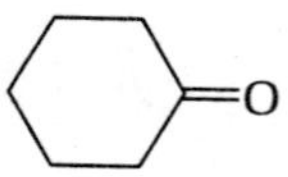
(d) 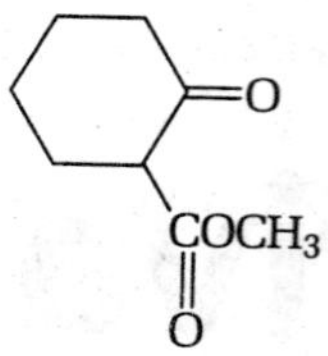

7. 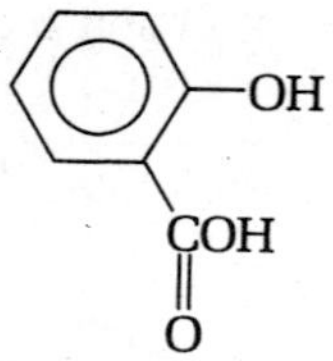 $\xrightarrow{CH_3COCl}$ Aspirin (*A*); *A* has structure

(a) 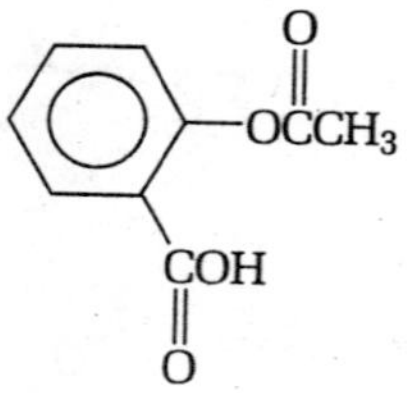
(b) 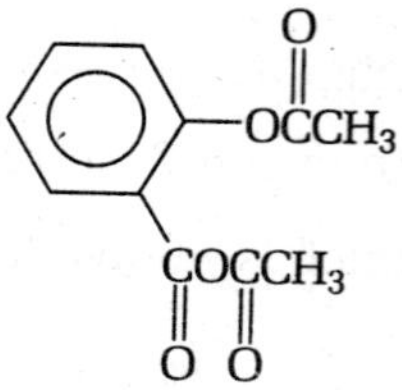

(c) 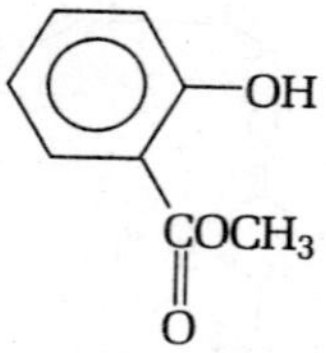
(d) 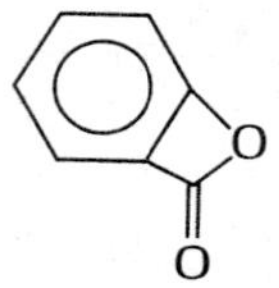

8. 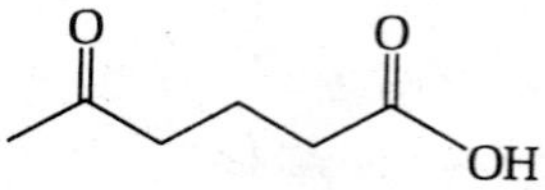 $\xrightarrow{NaBH_4}$ $\xrightarrow{H_3O^+}$ *A*; *A* is

(a) 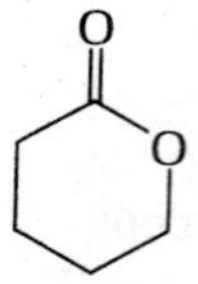
(b) 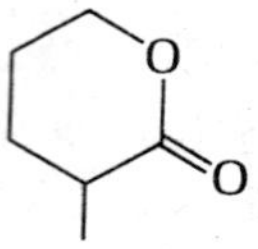

(c) 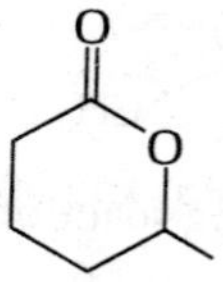
(d) 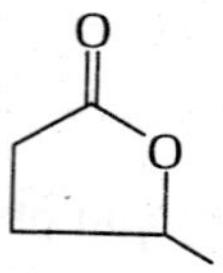

9. $CH_3\overset{\alpha}{—}\overset{\overset{O}{\|}}{C}\underset{\beta}{—}O\underset{\gamma}{—}CH_3$ α, β and γ are three types of (C—O) bonds in methyl acetate; bond lengths are in the order

(a) $\alpha > \beta > \gamma$
(b) $\alpha < \beta < \gamma$
(c) $\alpha = \beta = \gamma$
(d) $\alpha < \beta = \gamma$

10. Consider the following reactions,

$$I \xrightarrow{H_2,\ Pd/BaSO_4},\ II \xrightarrow{LiAlH_4},\ III \xrightarrow{LiAlH(Ot\text{-}Bu)_3}$$

$R\overset{\overset{O}{\|}}{C}H$ is obtained from $RCOCl$ using

(a) I, II and III
(b) I and II
(c) I and III
(d) II and III

11. In which of the following, —COOH group is not present? **[JEE Main 2021, Feb.]**

(a) Benzoic acid
(b) Sorbic acid
(c) Sulphonic acid
(d) Aspirin

12. Acidic hydrolysis is least that of

(a) 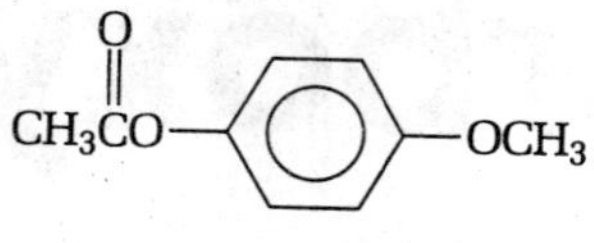

(b) 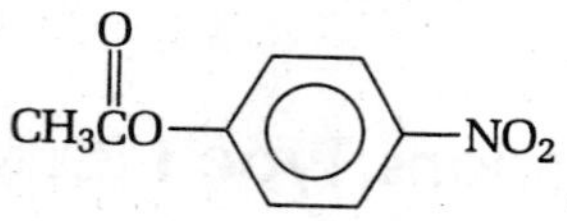

(c) 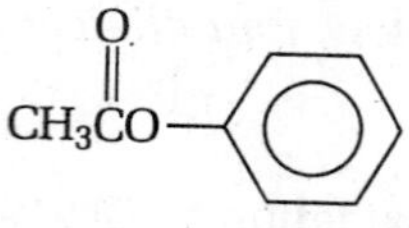

(d) 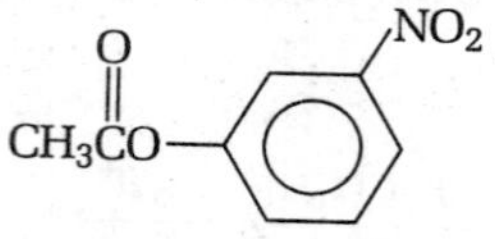

13. $CH_3\overset{\overset{O}{\|}}{C}OC_2H_5 \xrightarrow[\text{(ii) } H^+]{\text{(i) } C_2H_5ONa} A$

Consider the following statements about *A*.

I. Enolic form can be acetylated.
II. Enolic form decolourises Br_2 water.
III. Gives iodoform test

Select the correct statements.

(a) I, II and III
(b) I and III
(c) II and III
(d) I and II

14. The increasing order of the reactivity of the following with $LiAlH_4$ is

(A) 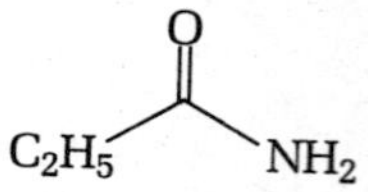
(c) 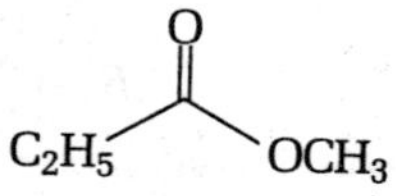

(C) 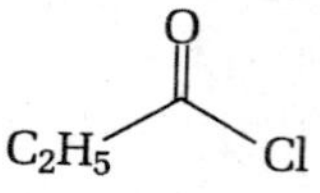
(d) 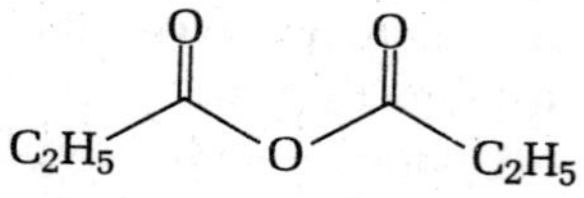

(a) (*A*) < (*B*) < (*D*) < (*C*)
(b) (*A*) < (*B*) < (*C*) < (*D*)
(c) (*B*) < (*A*) < (*D*) < (*C*)
(d) (*B*) < (*A*) < (*C*) < (*D*)

15. $CH_3\overset{O}{\overset{\|}{C}}O-\underset{CH_2CH_3}{\overset{H}{\underset{*}{C}}}-CH_3$ (ester) has chiral carbon (*).

Alkaline hydrolysis gives an acid salt and an alcohol. Select the correct statement about alcohol.

(a) Configuration about chiral carbon is retained
(b) Configuration about chiral carbon is inverted
(c) Product (alcohol) loses chirality
(d) None of the above statements is correct

16. $CH_3\overset{O}{\overset{\|}{C}}CH_2CH_2\overset{O}{\overset{\|}{C}}OCH_2CH_3 \xrightarrow[\text{(ii) } H_3O^+]{\text{(i) } CH_3CH_2MgI \text{ (one equivalent)}} A$; A is

(a) $CH_3\overset{O}{\overset{\|}{C}}CH_2CH_2\overset{O}{\overset{\|}{C}}CH_2CH_3$ (b) $CH_3\underset{CH_2CH_3}{\overset{OH}{C}}CH_2CH_2\overset{O}{\overset{\|}{C}}OCH_2CH_3$

(c) 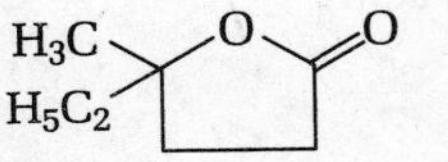 (d) 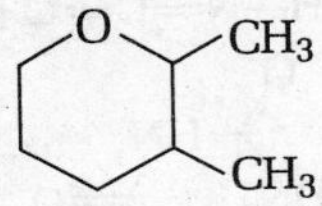

17. 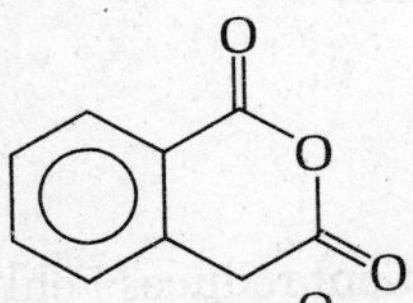 $\xrightarrow[HCl]{CH_3OH \text{ (excess)}} A$, A is

(a) 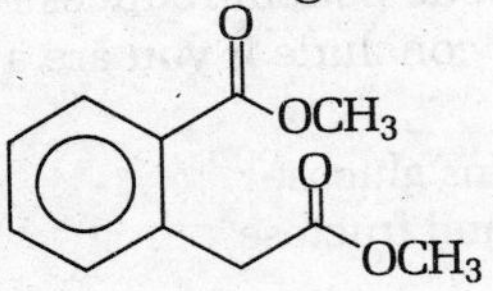 (b) 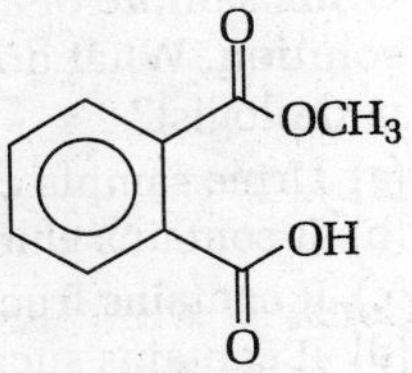

(c) 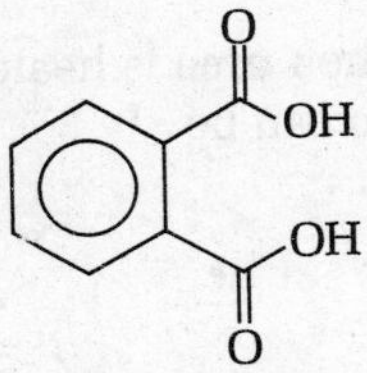 (d) 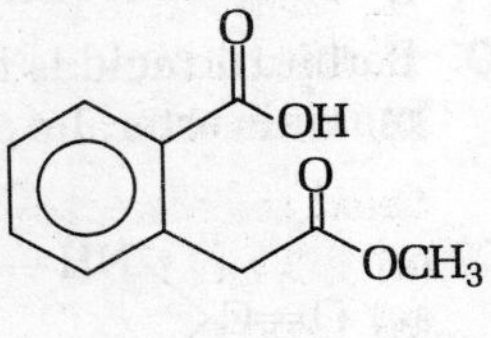

18. Which of the following compounds would be expected to decarboxylate when heated?

(a) 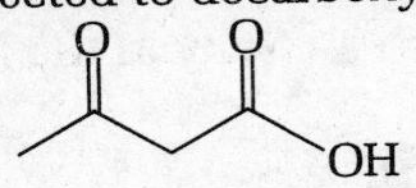

(b) 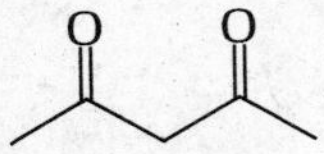

(c) 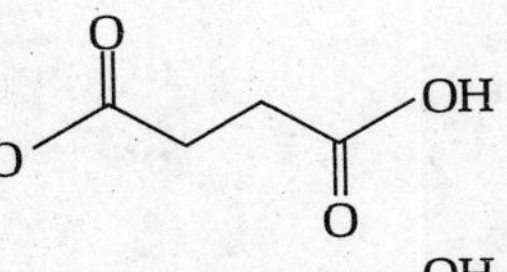

(d) 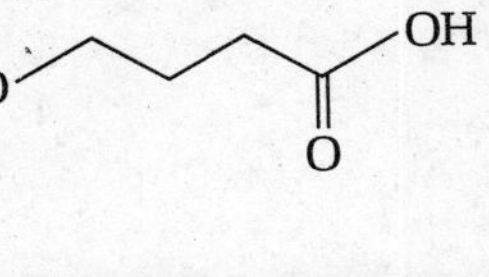

19. $CH_3-\overset{O}{\overset{\|}{C}}-Cl + Nu^- \longrightarrow CH_3-\overset{O}{\overset{\|}{C}}-Nu + Cl^-$

The reactivity order of different nucleophiles (NH_2^-, CH_3COO^-, OH^-) is in order

(a) $NH_2^- < CH_3COO^- < OH^-$
(b) $CH_3COO^- < OH^- < NH_2^-$
(c) $NH_2^- < OH^- < CH_3COO^-$
(d) $CH_3COO^- < NH_2^- < OH^-$

20. $B \xleftarrow[CH_3OH]{NaBH_4}$ 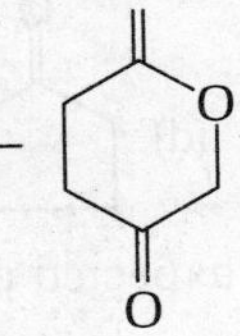 $\xrightarrow{LiAlH_4} A$, A and B are

(a) 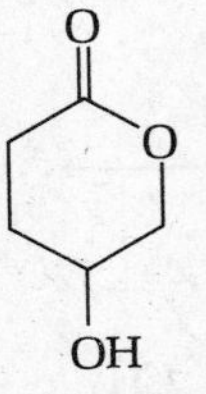 in both cases

(b) 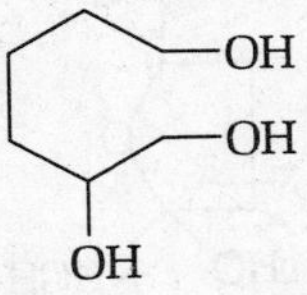 in both cases

(c) 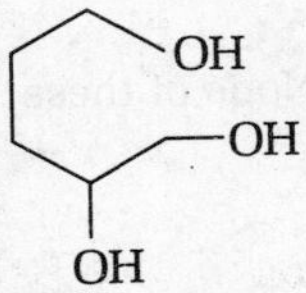 and 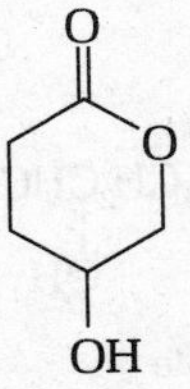

(d) formation of A and B is not possible

21. $R-\overset{O}{\overset{\|}{C}}-NH_2 + KOH + Br_2 \longrightarrow$

Intermediates of this reaction are except

(a) $R-N{=}C{=}O$ (b) $R-\overset{O}{\overset{\|}{C}}-\ddot{N}$

(c) $R-\overset{O}{\overset{\|}{C}}-\underset{H}{\underset{|}{N}}-Br$ (d) Both (a) and (c)

22. 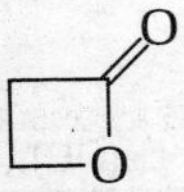 $\xrightarrow{CH_3OH} A$, A is

(a) $\underset{OH}{\underset{|}{CH_2}}-\underset{COOCH_3}{\underset{|}{CH_2}}$ (b) $\underset{OCH_3}{\underset{|}{CH_2}}-\underset{COOH}{\underset{|}{CH_2}}$

(c) Both (a) and (b) (d) None of these

23. 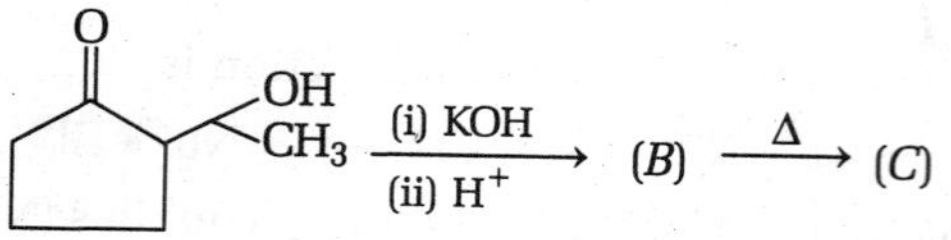

Hence, the product (*C*) in the above sequence of reaction, is

(a) 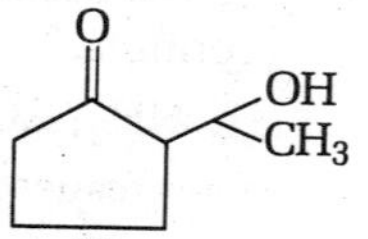

(b) 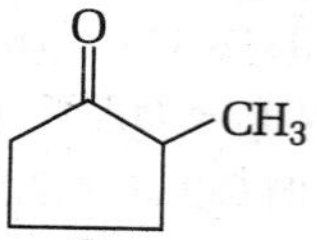

(c) 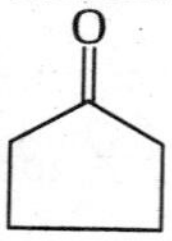

(d) 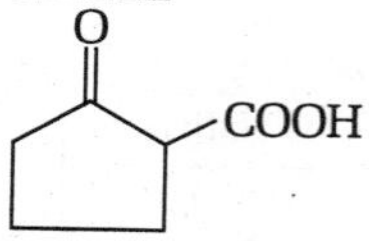

24. Give the structure of the expected product of the following reaction.

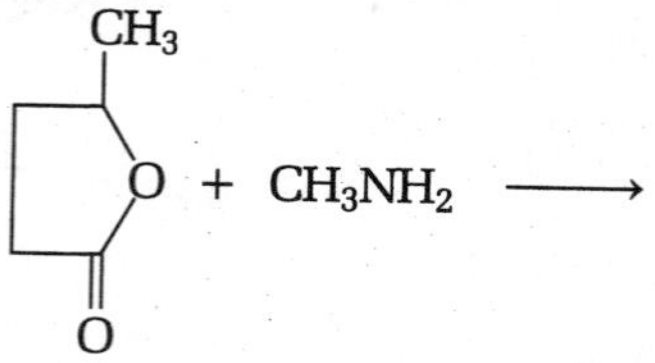

(a) 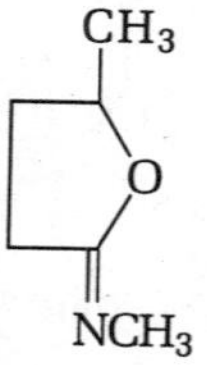

(b) 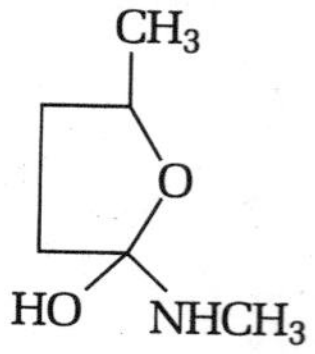

(c) $CH_3NHC(=O)CH_2CH_2CH(OH)CH_3$ (d) None of these

25. 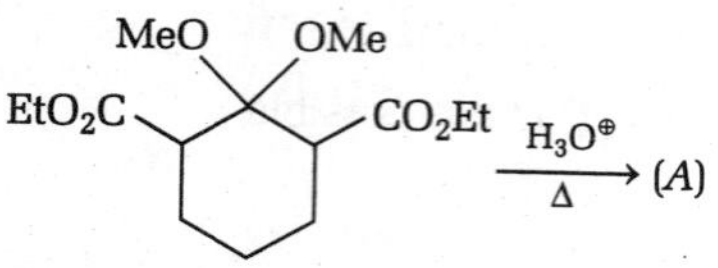

Product (*A*) obtained is

(a) 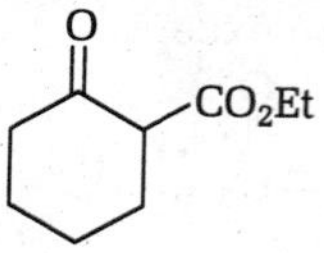

(b) 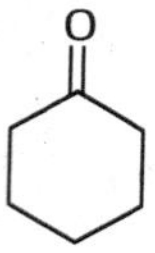

(c) 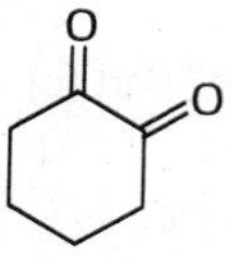

(d) 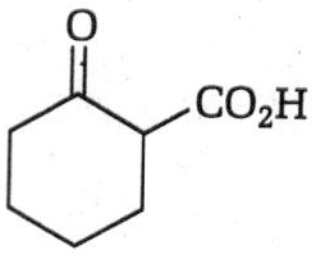

26. 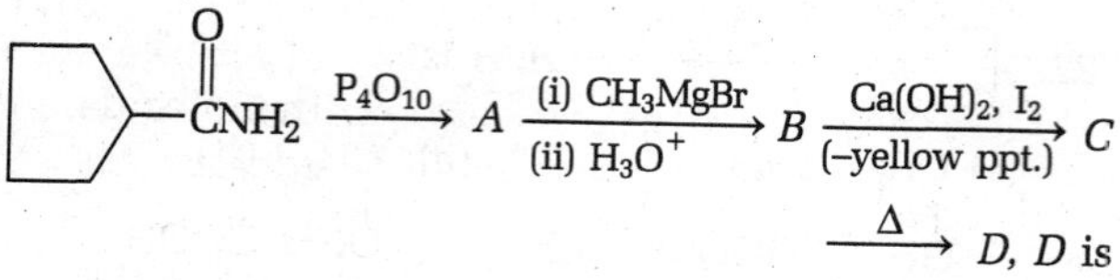

(a) 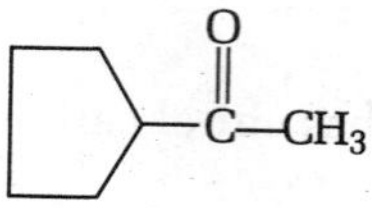

(b) 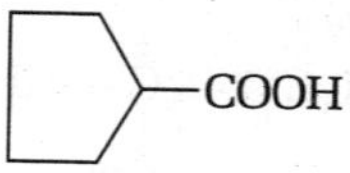

(c) 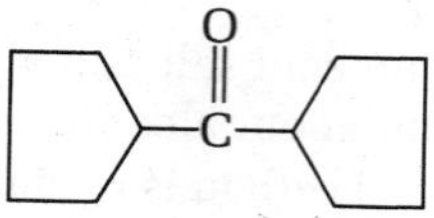

(d) 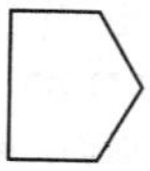

27. Biuret obtained on heating urea at about 400 K is

(a) $NH_2\overset{O}{\overset{\|}{C}}NH\overset{O}{\overset{\|}{C}}NH_2$ (b) $NH_2\overset{O}{\overset{\|}{C}}\overset{O}{\overset{\|}{C}}NH_2$

(c) $NH_2\overset{O}{\overset{\|}{C}}OH$ (d) $NH_2\overset{O}{\overset{\|}{C}}ONH_4$

28. When urea is heated rapidly, the product is

(a) $NH_2\overset{O}{\overset{\|}{C}}NH\overset{O}{\overset{\|}{C}}NH_2$ (biuret)

(b) H—N=C=O (cyanic acid)

(c) 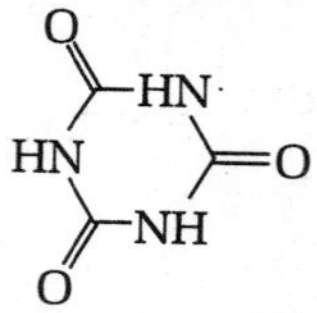 (cyanuric acid)

(d) None of the above

29. Urine sample of a diabetic patient reduces Fehling solution. What do you conclude if you are a pathologist?

(a) Urine sample contains glucose

(b) It contains glucose and fructose

(c) It contains fructose

(d) It contains sucrose

30. Barbituric acid is formed, when urea is heated with malonic ester. Its enolic form can be

(a) 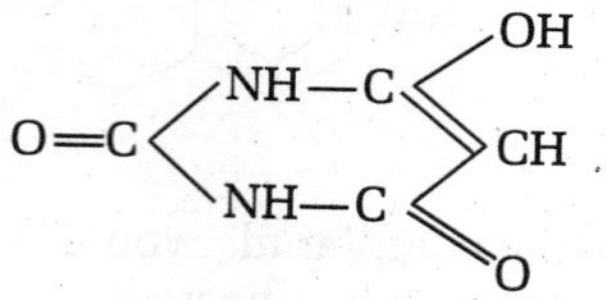

(b) 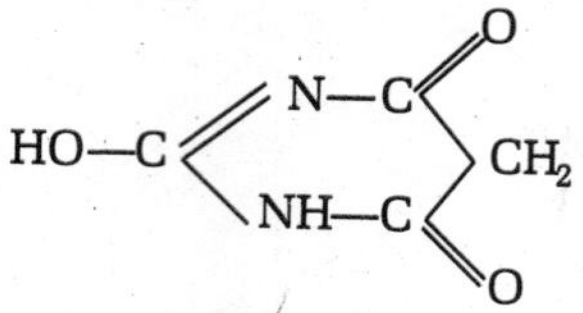

(c) Both (a) and (b)

(d) None of the above

31. Enolic form of acetoacetic ester reacts with urea forming methyl uracil which is

(a) 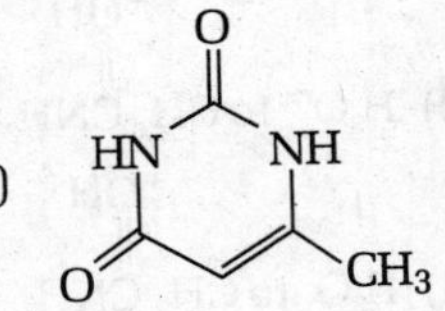

(b) 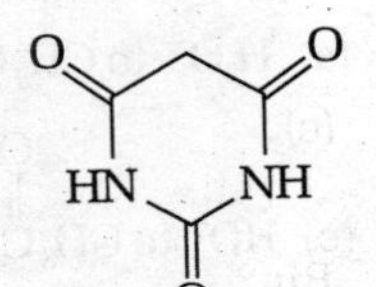

(c) 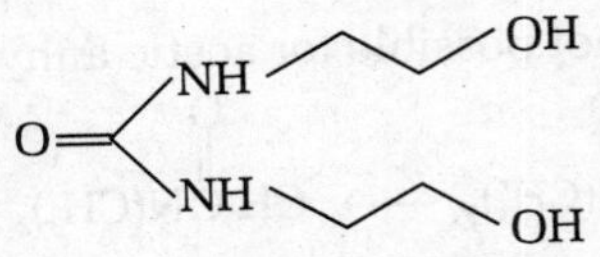

(d) None of these

32. The correct order of acid strength of the following carboxylic acids is **[JEE Advanced 2019]**

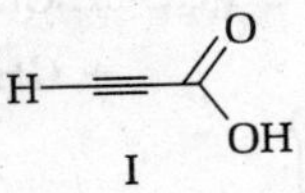
I

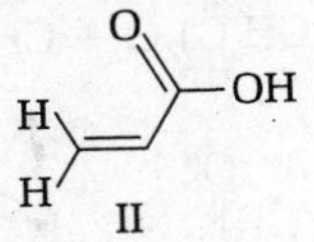
II

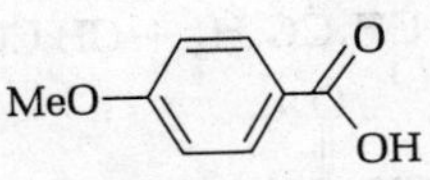
III

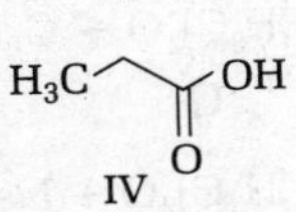
IV

(a) I > III > II > IV (b) III > II > I > IV
(c) I > II > III > IV (d) II> I > IV > III

33. Which is used in medicine as hypnotics?
(a) Methyl uracil (b) Barbituric acid
(c) 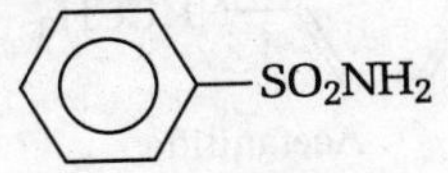 (d) Cyanuric acid

34. Urea is a carbamide of
(a) carbonic acid (b) carbamic acid
(c) Both (a) and (b) (d) None of these

35. Consider the following substances.

$HO-\underset{\underset{O}{\|}}{C}-OH$ I

$RO-\underset{\underset{O}{\|}}{C}-OH$ II

$H_2N-\underset{\underset{O}{\|}}{C}-OH$ III

$Cl-\underset{\underset{O}{\|}}{C}-OH$ IV

Which can give CO_2 on heating? Select the correct alternate from the following.
(a) I and II
(b) II and III
(c) Only I
(d) All of these

36. Urea is a stronger base than other amides. It is attributed to
(a) presence of two $-NH_2$ groups
(b) presence of a ketonic group
(c) resonance stabilisation of cation formed by protonation
(d) hydrolysis to NH_3

37. The major product of following reaction is

$$R-C\equiv N \xrightarrow[\text{(ii) } H_2O]{\text{(i) AlH (Bu)}_2} ?$$

(a) $RCHO$ (b) $RCONH_2$
(c) $RCOOH$ (d) RCH_2NH_2

38. Urea is hydrolysed in presence of acids, bases, or the enzyme urease, giving following products.
I. NH_4^+, CO_2 II. NH_3, CO_3^{2-} III. NH_3, CO_2
Products given in I, II and III are formed respectively in the presence of
(a) H^+, OH^- enzyme urease (b) OH^-, H^+ enzyme urease
(c) H^+, enzyme urease, OH^- (d) OH^-, H^+ enzyme urease

39. Ester formation is called
(a) Claisen condensation (b) aldol condensation
(c) Fischer esterification (d) *trans*-esterification

40. Pyrolysis of ester (A) gives

$$A: RCH_2CH_2O\underset{\underset{O}{\|}}{C}R' \xrightarrow{\Delta}$$

(a) $RCH{=}CH_2, R'COOH$ (b) $RCH{=}CH_2, R'H, CO_2$
(c) $RC{\equiv}CH, H_2, R'RCOOH$ (d) $RCH_3, R'\overset{O}{\overset{\|}{C}}CH_3$

41. Consider the following chemical tests

I. substance $\xrightarrow{\Delta} \xrightarrow{CuSO_4}$ violet colour

II. substance $\xrightarrow{NaOH, \Delta} \xrightarrow{HCl}$ white fumes

III. substance $\xrightarrow{NaNO_2 + HCl}$ N_2 gas

Which can identify urea exclusively?
(a) I and II (b) II and III
(c) Only I (d) Only II

42. Select incorrect statement(s).
(a) CH_3CN is named as methane nitrile
(b) Urea is an amide of carbamic acid
(c) Urea is excreted in the urine as the end product of protein metabolism
(d) Urea is a diamide

43. Which one of the following esters cannot undergo Claisen self-condensation?
(a) $CH_3CH_2CH_2CH_2COOC_2H_5$ (b) $C_6H_5COOC_2H_5$
(c) $C_6H_5CH_2COOC_2H_5$ (d) $C_6H_{11}CH_2COOC_2H_5$

44. An ester (A) with molecular formula $C_9H_{10}O_2$ was treated with excess of CH_3MgBr and the complex so formed was treated with H_2SO_4 to give an olefin (B). Ozonolysis of (B) gave a ketone with molecular formula $C_8H_8O(C)$ which shows positive iodoform test. The structure of (A) is
(a) $C_6H_5COOC_2H_5$ (b) $C_6H_5CH_2COOCH_3$
(c) $H_3COCH_2COC_6H_5$ (d) p-$H_3COC_6H_4COCH_3$

45. Acetaldoxime reacts with P_2O_5 to produce
(a) ethyl cyanide (b) propyl cyanide
(c) methyl cyanide (d) None of these

46. Which of the following is used for inducing sleep?
(a) Chloroquine
(b) Paracetamol
(c) Barbituric acid derivatives
(d) Bithional

47. The compound used as a preservative for food products (such as tomato ketchup and fruit juices) is
(a) sodium benzoate (b) formic acid
(c) sodium salicylate (d) sodium acetate

48. Schotten-Baumann reaction can be used to synthesise
(a) ester (b) ether
(c) acid (d) alcohol

49. For the reaction, $CH_3COCl \xrightarrow{H_2/Pd} X$, then X is
(a) CH_3CHO (b) CH_3COOH
(c) CH_3COCH_3 (d) CH_3CH_2OH

50. The compounds A and B in the following reaction are, respectively.

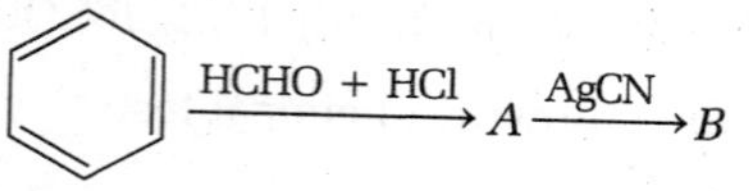

(a) A = Benzyl alcohol, B = Benzyl isocyanide
(b) A = Benzyl alcohol, B = Benzyl cyanide
(c) A = Benzyl chloride, B = Benzyl isocyanide
(d) A = Benzyl chloride, B = Benzyl cyanide

51. Choose the response that matches the correct functional group classification with the following group of structural formulae.

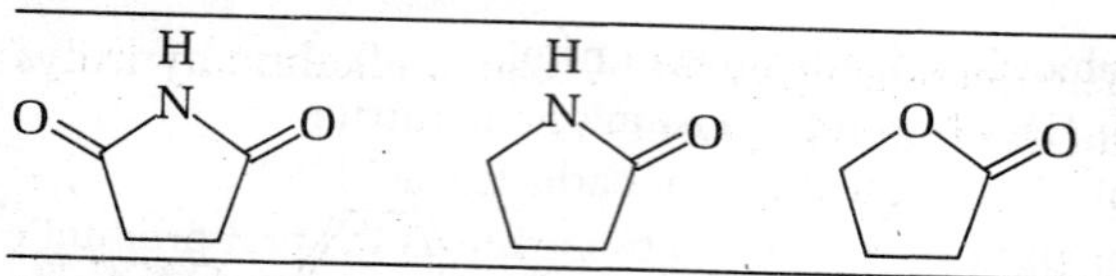

(a) Anhydride	Lactam	Lactone
(b) Lactam	Imide	Lactone
(c) Imide	Lactone	Anhydride
(d) Imide	Lactam	Lactone

52. Choose the best sequence of reactions for the transformation given.

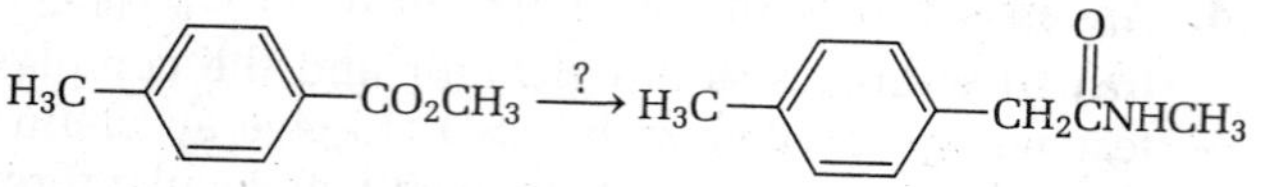

(a) H_3O^+; $SOCl_2$; CH_3NH_2
(b) HO^-/H_2O; PBr_3; Mg; CO_2; H_3O^+; $SOCl_2$; CH_3NH_2
(c) $LiAlH_4$; H_2O; HBr; Mg; CO_2; H_3O^+; $SOCl_2$; CH_3NH_2
(d) None of the above would yield the desired product.

53. A key step in the hydrolysis of acetamide in aqueous acid proceeds by nucleophilic addition of
(a) H_3O^+ to $CH_3\overset{\overset{O}{\|}}{C}NH_2$ (b) H_3O^+ to $CH_3\overset{\overset{+OH}{\|}}{C}NH_2$
(c) HO^- to $CH_3\overset{\overset{O}{\|}}{C}NH_2$ (d) H_2O to $CH_3\overset{\overset{+OH}{\|}}{C}NH_2$

54. Which reaction is not possible for acetic anhydride?
(a) $(CH_3\overset{\overset{O}{\|}}{C})_2O + 2HN(CH_3)_2 \longrightarrow CH_3\overset{\overset{O}{\|}}{C}N(CH_3)_2 + CH_3CO_2^-H_2\overset{+}{N}(CH_3)_2$
(b) $(CH_3\overset{\overset{O}{\|}}{C})_2O + CH_3CH_2OH \longrightarrow CH_3\overset{\overset{O}{\|}}{C}OCH_2CH_3 + CH_3CO_2H$
(c) $(CH_3\overset{\overset{O}{\|}}{C})_2O + C_6H_6 \xrightarrow{AlCl_3} CH_3\overset{\overset{O}{\|}}{C}C_6H_5 + CH_3CO_2H$
(d) $(CH_3\overset{\overset{O}{\|}}{C})_2O + NaCl \longrightarrow CH_3\overset{\overset{O}{\|}}{C}Cl + CH_3CO_2^-Na^+$

55. All but one of the following compounds react with aniline to give acetanilide. Which one does not?

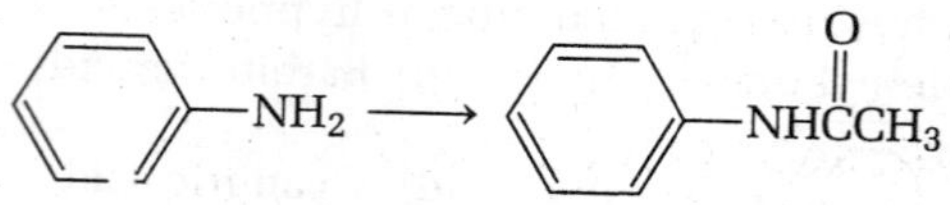

Aniline Acetanilide

(a) 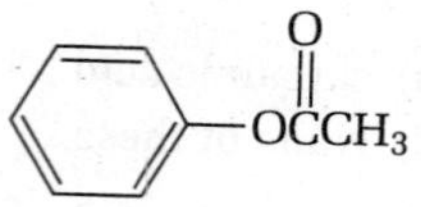

(b) $CH_3\overset{\overset{O}{\|}}{C}H$

(c) 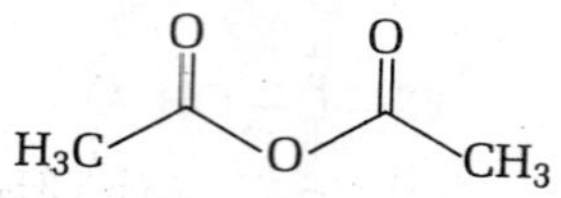

(d) 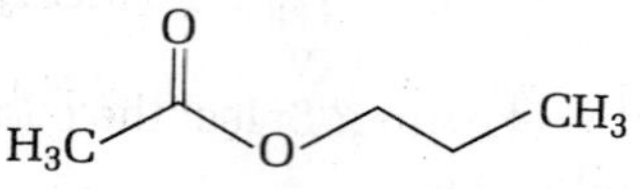

56. Identify product Z in the following reaction sequence
$$H_2C{=}CHCH_2Br \xrightarrow{NaCN} Y \xrightarrow[\text{(ii) } H_3O^+]{\text{(i) } C_6H_5MgBr,\ \text{Diethyl ether}} Z$$
(a) $H_2C{=}CHCH_2\overset{\overset{O}{\|}}{C}C_6H_5$ (b) $H_2C{=}CHCH_2\overset{\overset{OH}{|}}{C}HC_6H_5$
(c) $H_2C{=}CHCH_2\overset{\overset{O}{\|}}{C}NHC_6H_5$ (d) $H_2C{=}CHCH_2NH\overset{\overset{O}{\|}}{C}C_6H_5$

57. Which of the following best describes the nucleophilic addition step in the acid-catalysed hydrolysis of acetonitrile (CH_3CN)?

(a) 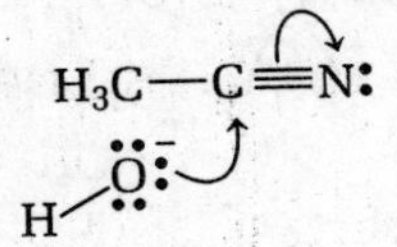
(b) 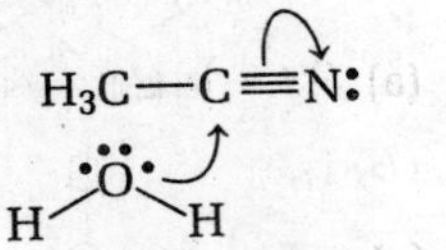
(c) 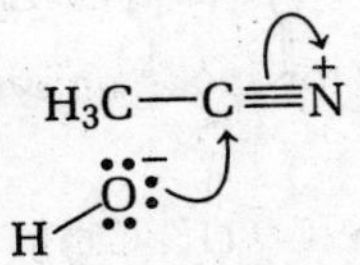
(d) 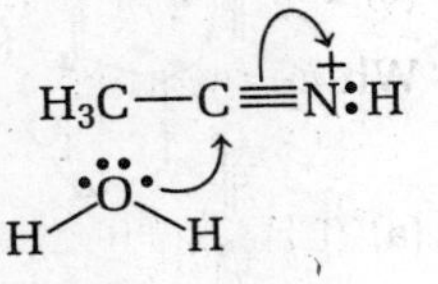

58. Saponification (basic hydrolysis) of will 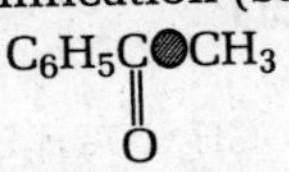
yield : [● = mass-18 isotope of oxygen]

(a) 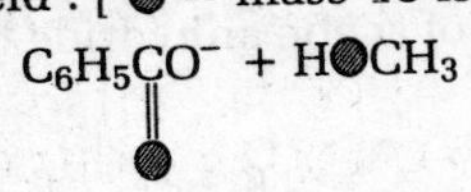
(b) 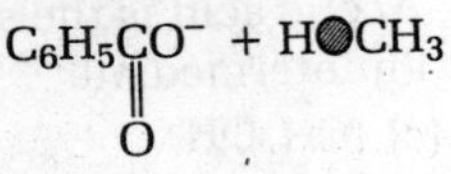
(c) 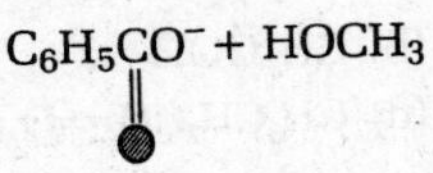
(d) 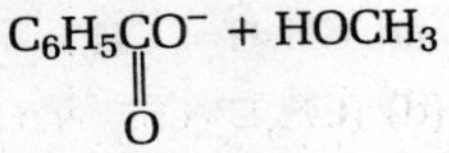

59. Which of the following compounds is the strongest acid?

(a) $HCO_2CH_2CH_3$
(b) $CH_3CH_2O_2CCH_2CO_2CH_2CH_3$
(c) $CH_3CH_2O_2CCH_2CH_2CO_2CH_2CH_3$
(d) $CH_3CO_2CH_2CH_3$

60. Which of the following will yield a ketone and carbon dioxide following saponification, acidification, and heating?

(a) 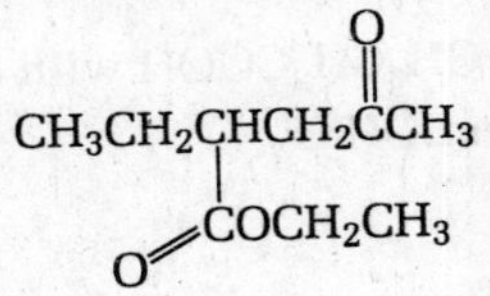
(b) 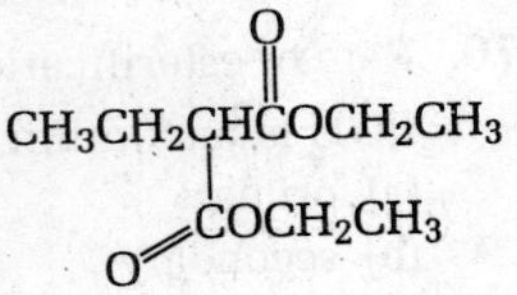
(c) 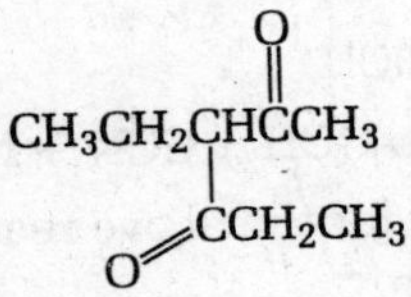
(d) 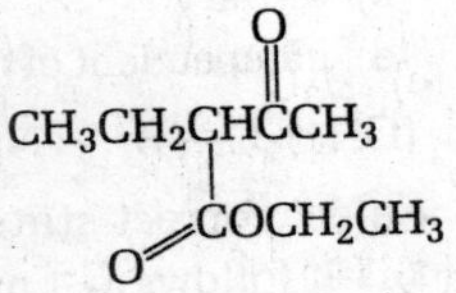

61. What is the final product of this sequence?

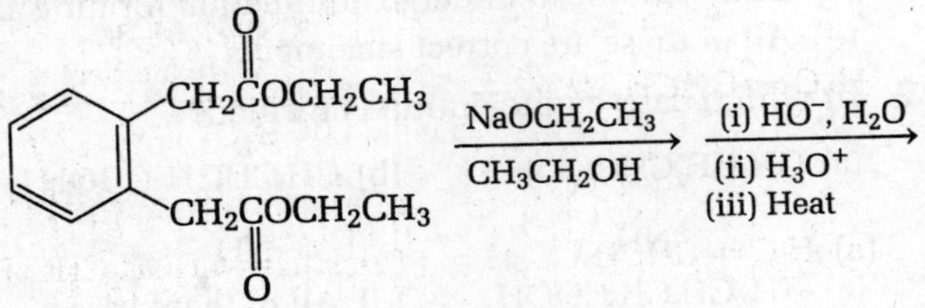

(a) 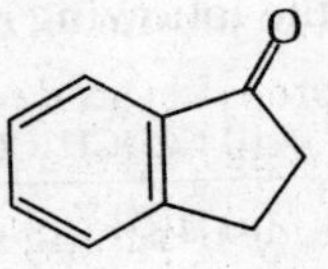
(b) 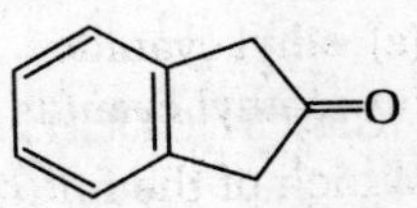
(c) 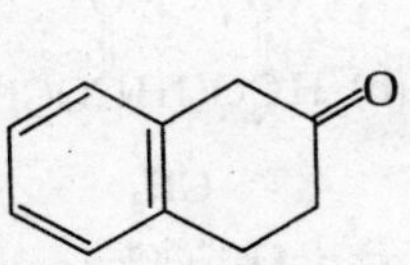
(d) 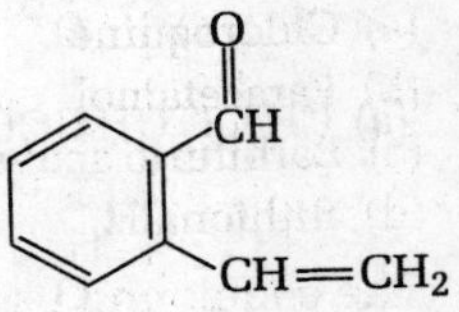

62. What is the final product of the following sequence of reactions?

$$CH_2(CO_2CH_2CH_3)_2 + (CH_3)_2C{=}CH\overset{O}{\overset{\|}{C}}CH_3 \xrightarrow[\text{Ethanol}]{NaOCH_2CH_3} \xrightarrow[\text{(ii) } H_3O^+ \text{ (iii) Heat}]{\text{(i) KOH}}$$

(a) 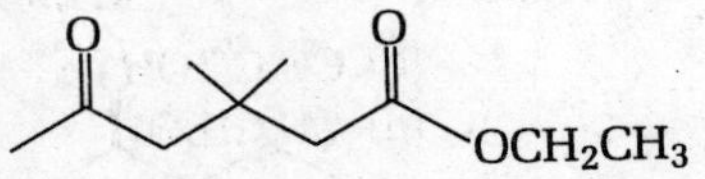
(b) 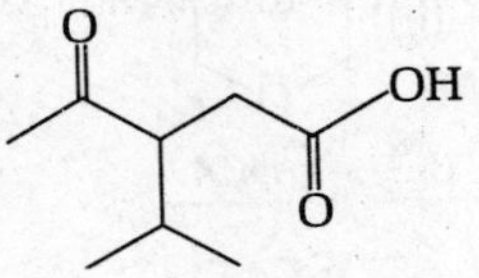
(c) 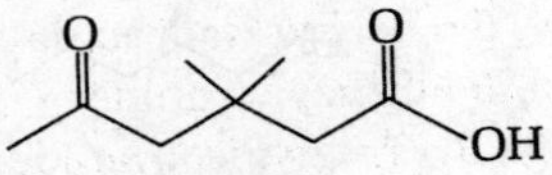
(d) 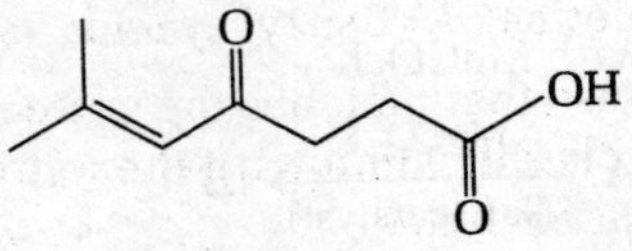

63. The decreasing order of case of alkaline hydrolysis for the following esters is

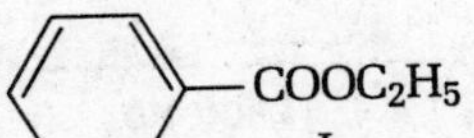
I
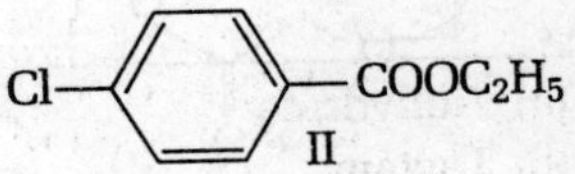
II
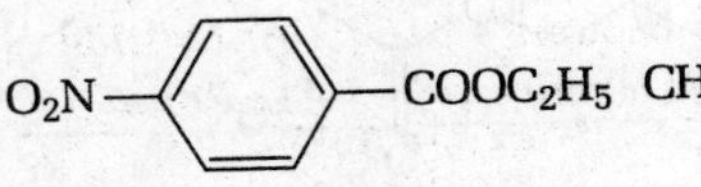
III
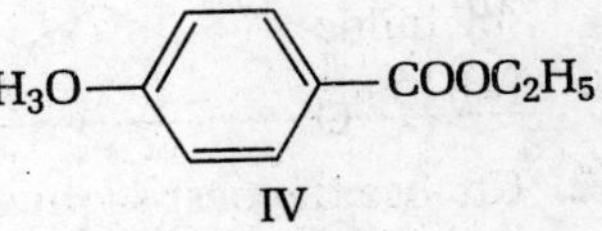
IV

(a) III > II > IV > I
(b) III > II > I > IV
(c) II > III > I > IV
(d) IV > II > III > I

64. What is the major product of the following reaction?

$$CH_3CH_2\overset{O}{\overset{\|}{C}}OCH_3 + H\overset{O}{\overset{\|}{C}}OCH_3 \xrightarrow[\text{(ii) } H_3O^+]{\text{(i) } NaOCH_2CH_3} ?$$

(a) $CH_3O\overset{O}{\overset{\|}{C}}\underset{CH_3}{\underset{|}{C}H}\overset{O}{\overset{\|}{C}}OCH_3$
(b) $H\overset{O}{\overset{\|}{C}}O\underset{CH_3}{\underset{|}{C}H}\overset{O}{\overset{\|}{C}}OCH_3$
(c) $HOCH_2\underset{CH_3}{\underset{|}{C}H}\overset{O}{\overset{\|}{C}}OCH_3$
(d) $H\overset{O}{\overset{\|}{C}}\underset{CH_3}{\underset{|}{C}H}\overset{O}{\overset{\|}{C}}OCH_3$

65. 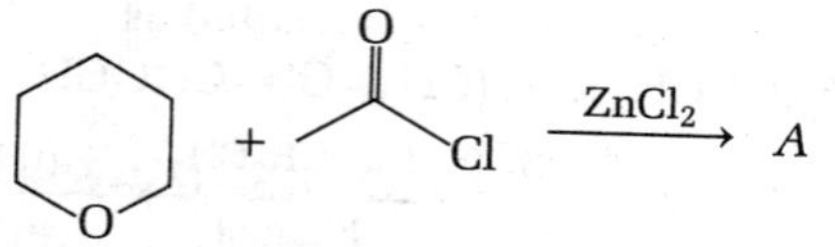

(A) is

(a) 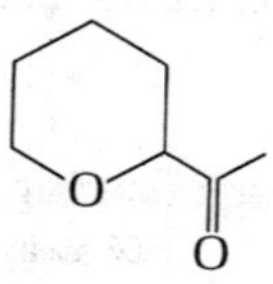
(b) 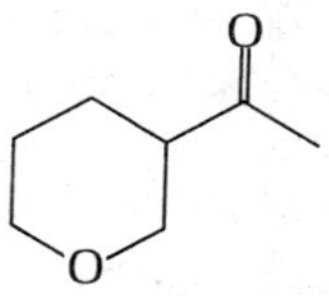
(c) 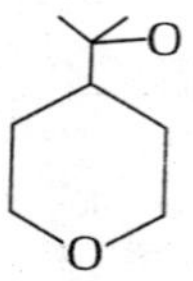
(d) 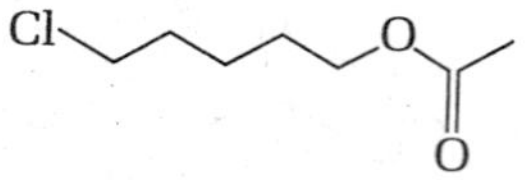

66. A (Q-65) reacts with $MeCO_2K$

$$A \xrightarrow[\text{NaI (catalyst)}]{MeCO_2K} B$$

B formed is

(a) 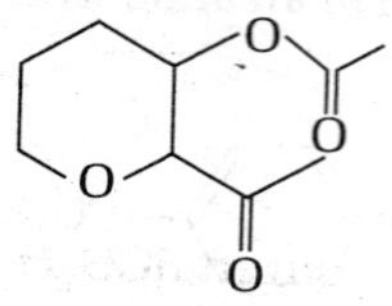
(b) 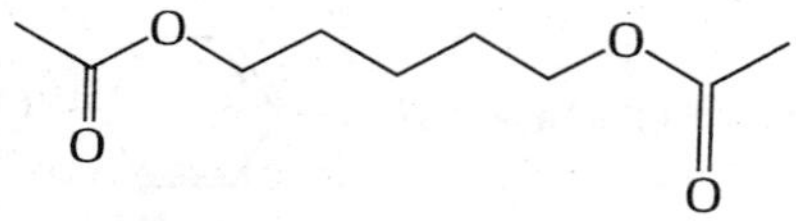
(c) 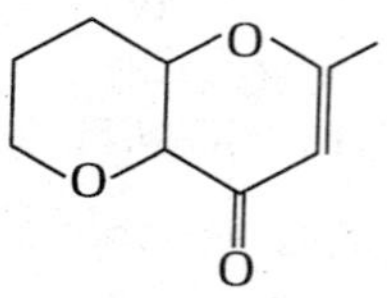
(d) 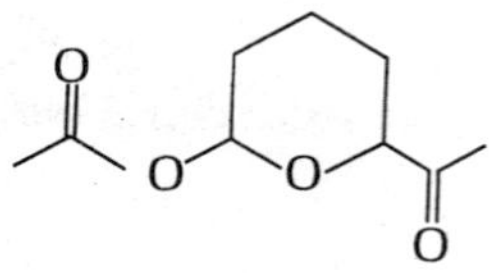

67. Acetoacetic ester (A) changes to (B) by the reaction

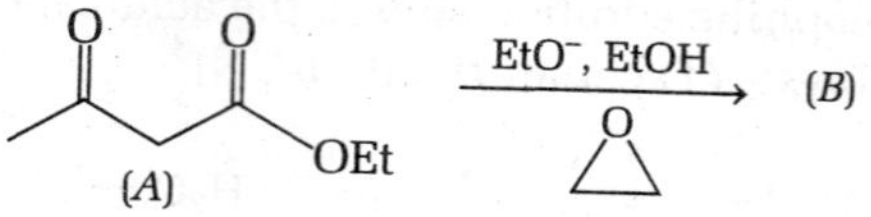

(B) is

(a) 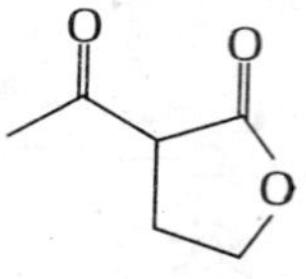
(b) 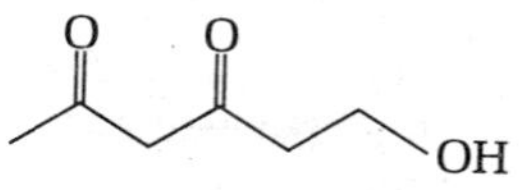
(c) 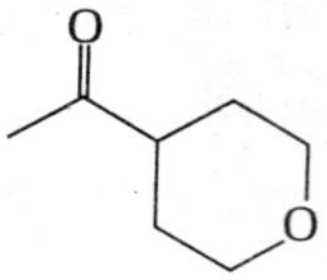
(d) 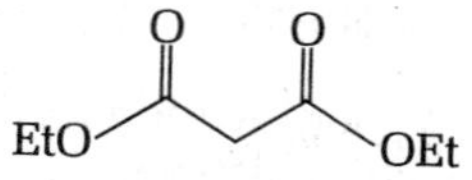

68. Acetic acid is the source of acetic anhydride through an intermediate

(a) $CH_3\overset{OH}{\overset{|}{C}}{=}CH_2$
(b) $CH_3\overset{O}{\overset{\|}{C}}OH$
(c) $CH_2{=}C{=}O$
(d) $CH_3CH_2CH{=}O$

69. Cyclopentanone on reaction with CH_3CO_3H forms

(a) 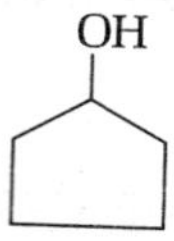
(b) 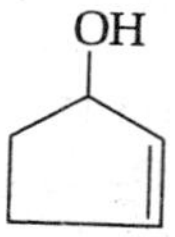
(c) 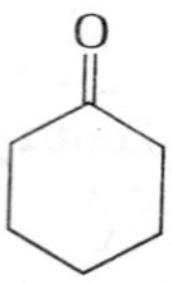
(d) 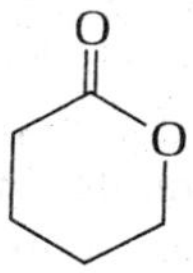

70. Rate of esterification of CH_3CH_2COOH with alcohol ROH is maximum when ROH is
(a) primary
(b) secondary
(c) tertiary
(d) independent of nature of ROH

71. $(CH_3)_3C{-}Br + NaCN \longrightarrow (CH_3)_3CCN + NaBr$
Select correct statement(s) for the above reaction.
(a) It follows S_N1 mechanism
(b) Intermediate is carbocation
(c) Carbocation can undergo elimination forming alkene
(d) All of these are correct statements

72. In which case cyclic amide is formed?

(a) $CH_3CH_2\underset{NH_2}{\underset{|}{C}H}COOH$
(b) $CH_3\underset{NH_2}{\underset{|}{C}H}CH_2COOH$
(c) $\underset{NH_2}{\underset{|}{C}H_2}CH_2CH_2COOH$
(d) All of these cases

73. Select the correct statement(s).

(a) Carboxylic acids have higher boiling points than isomeric esters because of dimer formation by intermolecular H-bonding

(b) $R\overset{O}{\overset{\|}{C}}NH_2$ or $R\overset{O}{\overset{\|}{C}}NHR$ molecules are associated by H-bonding

(c) The presence of carbonyl group in acid derivative makes them polar compounds

(d) All of the above statements are correct

74. Nitriles have higher boiling points than esters of equivalent molecular weight due to

(a) hydrogen bonding in nitriles

(b) strong dipolar association between adjacent cyano group

(c) van der Waals' attraction in nitriles

(d) hydrolysis of cyanide group to carboxylic group

75. Indicate incorrect comparison of boiling point

(a) $HCOOH < CH_3COOH$

(b) $CH_3CONH_2 < CH_3\underset{}{\overset{OH}{\overset{|}{C}}}{=}NH$

(c) $CH_3CN < CH_3NC$

(d) $\underset{Cl}{\underset{|}{CH_2}}CHO > CH_3COCl$

76. Carboxylic acids are unreactive towards nucleophilic attack because of

(a) resonance delocalisation from the hydroxyl to the carboxyl group and proton removal by the nucleophile

(b) larger pK_a values

(c) dimer formation by intermolecular H-bonding

(d) lower pK_a values

77. Select the correct statement(s) about following reaction,

$$R{-}\overset{O}{\overset{\|}{C}}{-}X + \underset{\text{Nucleophile}}{Y:} \longrightarrow \underset{\text{Alkoxide}}{R{-}\underset{Y}{\underset{|}{\overset{O^{\ominus}}{\overset{|}{C}}}}{-}X} \xrightarrow[-X^{\ominus}]{} R{-}\overset{O}{\overset{\|}{C}}{-}Y$$

(a) Stronger nucleophile normally replaces the weaker nucleophile

(b) Better leaving group leaves from the alkoxide intermediate

(c) Most electron-deficient carbonyl carbon is the most easily attacked by the nucleophile

(d) All of the above are correct statements

78. Select the incorrect statement.

(a) Acid derivatives are hydrolysed more readily in either alkaline or acidic solution than in neutral solution

(b) Alkaline hydrolysis of ester is called saponification

(c) In hydrolysis of $R{-}\overset{O}{\overset{\|}{C}}{-}O{-}R'$, R' is the leaving group

(d) In nucleophilic attack at the carbonyl carbon, resulting intermediate is tetrahedral in nature

79. Acyl S_N reaction is not possible

$$R{-}\overset{O}{\overset{\|}{C}}{-}X + Y^{\ominus} \longrightarrow R{-}\overset{O}{\overset{\|}{C}}{-}Y + X^{\ominus} \text{ when}$$

(a) X is NH_2 and Y is Cl or OH

(b) X is OH and Y is NH_2

(c) X is Cl and Y is OH

(d) X is OR and Y is NH_2

80. Acylation of alcohol can be represented as

$$R{-}\overset{O}{\overset{\|}{C}}{-}Cl + R'OH \xrightarrow{\text{Pyridine}} R{-}\overset{O}{\overset{\|}{C}}{-}O{-}R' + HCl$$

Select the incorrect statement for the above reaction.

(a) Configuration of the alcohol (if chiral) is retained

(b) Pyridine absorbs HCl formed

(c) Product formed is a racemic mixture if R' has chiral carbon

(d) None of the above

81. The major product obtained in the following reaction is **[JEE Main 2019, Jan.]**

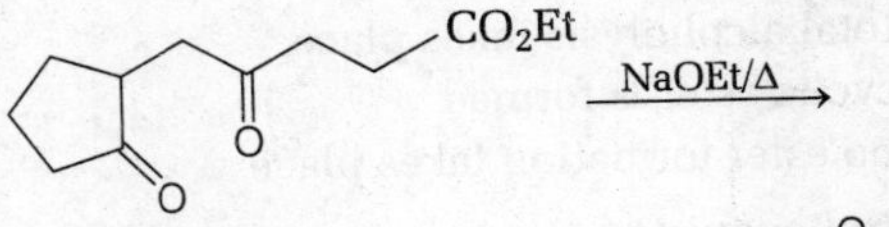

(a) 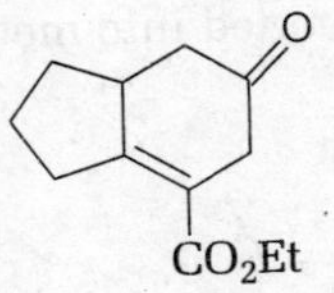

(b) 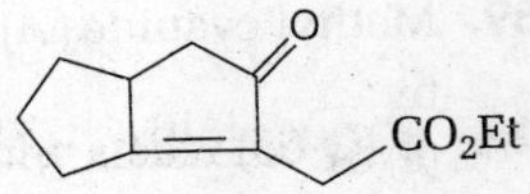

(c) 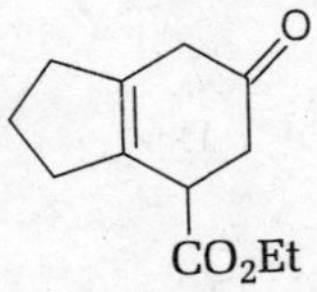

(d) 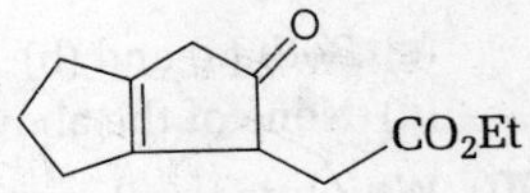

82. Which is the best reagent to convert RCO_2H into $RCOCl$?

(a) PCl_3 (b) PCl_5 (c) $SOCl_2$ (d) HCl

83. CH_3COCl reacts with Na_2O_2 (sodium peroxide) forming

(a) CH_3COONa (b) $(CH_3CO)_2O_2$

(c) $(CH_3CO)_2O$ (d) CH_3COOCH_3

84. $CH_3\underset{C_2H_5}{\underset{|}{\overset{*}{C}}}HOH$ reacts with CH_3COCl. Product formed

(a) has retained configuration about chiral carbon (*)

(b) is a racemic mixture

(c) loses chirality

(d) shows geometrical isomerism

85. CH_3COOH reacts with A forming $(CH_3CO)_2O$. A is

(a) CH_3COCl (b) $CH_3COOC_2H_5$
(c) $CH_2{=}C{=}O$ (d) All of these

86. $A \xrightarrow[H_3O^+]{LiAlH_4} HO(CH_2)_4OH$ (and no other organic compound), A is

(a) $CH_2COOC_2H_5$ | $CH_2COOC_2H_5$ (b) 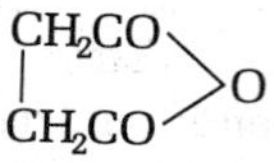

(c) Both of (a) and (b) (d) None of these

87. A can be acetylated using CH_3COCl or $(CH_3CO)_2O$. Which H of A can be acetylated

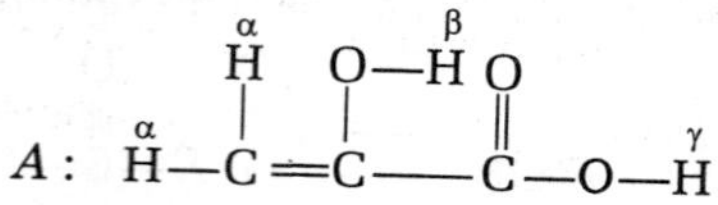

(a) α (b) β (c) γ (d) None of these

88. Succinic anhydride (A) reacts with one mole of CH_3OH per mole of A. In this reaction

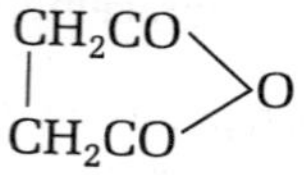

(a) half of the anhydride is converted into ester and other half becomes a COOH
(b) total alcoholysis takes place
(c) cyclic ester is formed
(d) no ester formation takes place

89. Methyl cyanide (A) can be converted into methylamine (B) by

(a) $A \xrightarrow{LiAlH_4} B$
(b) $A \xrightarrow[partial]{H_3O^+} \xrightarrow[\Delta]{Br_2/NaOH} B$
(c) Both (a) and (b)
(d) None of the above

90. Which is the 3° amide?

(a) 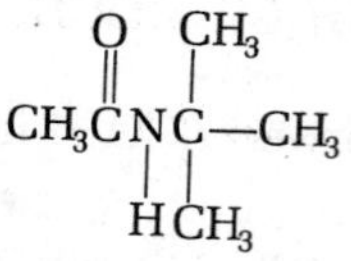 (b) 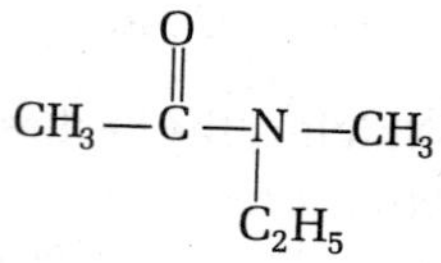

(c) 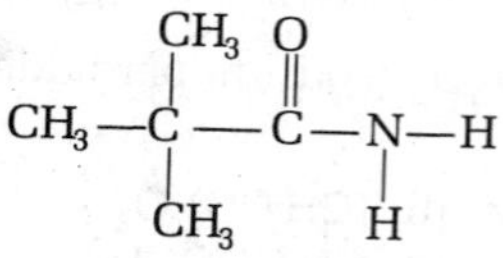 (d) 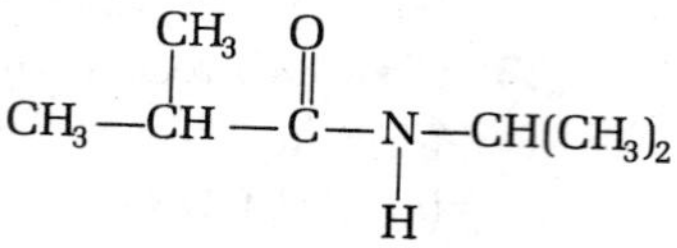

91. $R\overset{O}{\overset{\|}{C}}NH_2$ and $R\overset{O}{\overset{\|}{C}}OH$ can be best distinguished using

(a) KOH/Br_2
(b) $SOCl_2$
(c) NaOH
(d) neutral $FeCl_3$ solution

92. Consider the following statements.

I. Imides can be thought of as the nitrogen analogs of anhydrides.
II. Ethyl cyanide is reduced to ethyl amine by $LiAlH_4$.
III. Conversion of CH_3CONH_2 into CH_3NH_2 using KOH/Br_2 involves intramolecular migration of methyl group.

Select the correct statements.

(a) I and II (b) II and III (c) I and III (d) I, II and III

93. The major product of the following reaction is **[JEE Main 2019, April)**

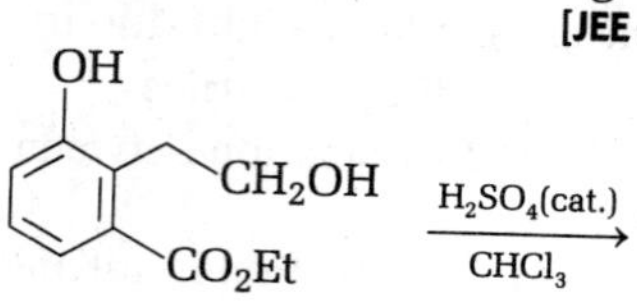

(a) 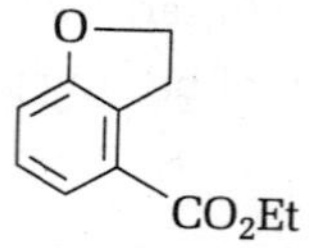 (b) 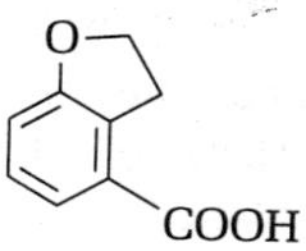

(c) 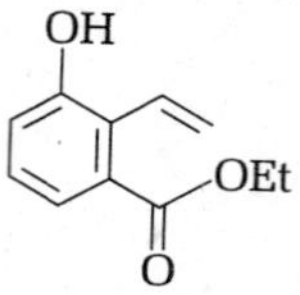 (d) 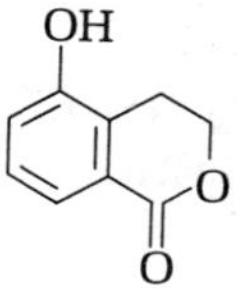

94. The major product of the following reaction is **[JEE Main 2019, April]**

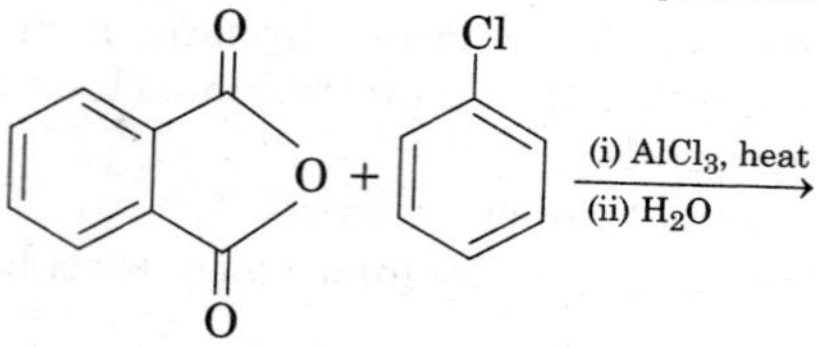

(a) 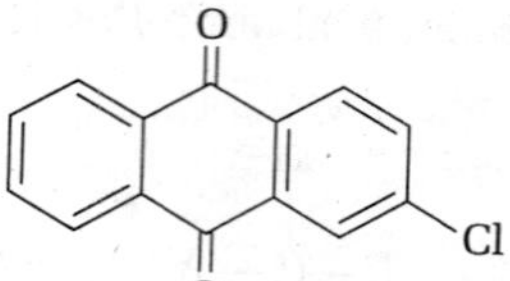 (b) 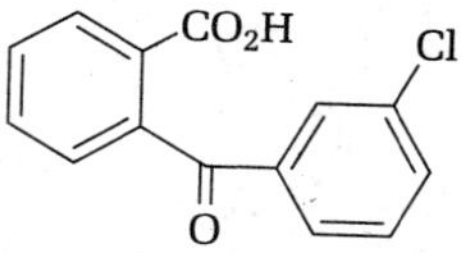

(c) 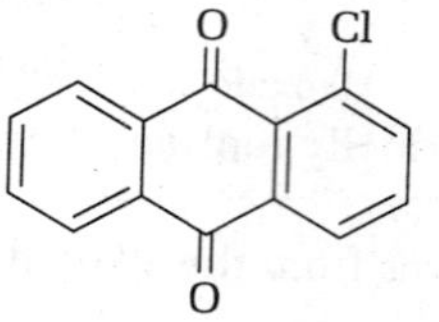 (d) 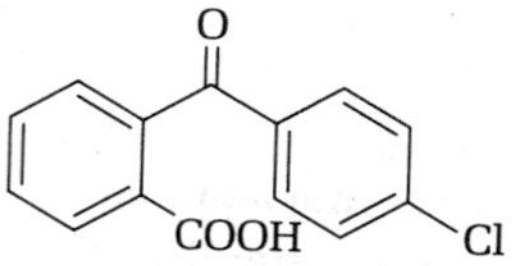

95. Consider the above chemical reaction and identify product "A". **[JEE Mains 2021, March]**

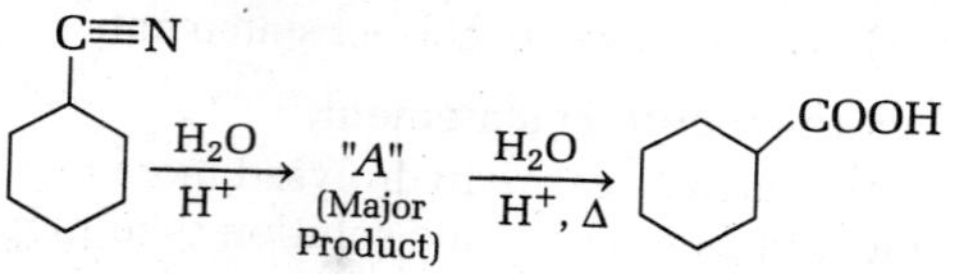

Consider the above chemical reaction and identify product "A".

(a) 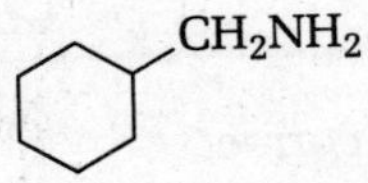
(b) 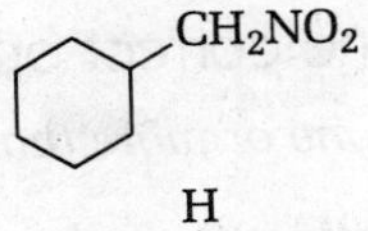
(c) 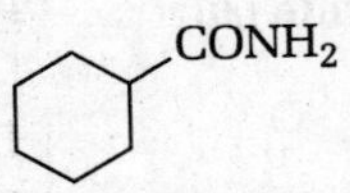
(d) 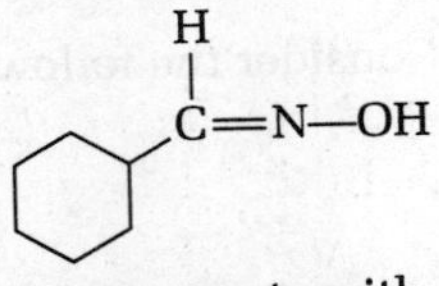

96. Barbituric acid is formed when urea reacts with
(a) diethyl malonate (b) acetoacetic ester
(c) formaldehyde (d) ethylene oxide

97. Following reaction is named as

$$CH_3\overset{O}{\overset{\|}{C}}OCH_2CH_3 \xrightarrow{CH_3OH} CH_3\overset{O}{\overset{\|}{C}}OCH_3 + CH_3CH_2OH$$

(a) alcoholysis
(b) *trans*-esterification
(c) saponification
(d) hydrolysis

98. $CH_3\overset{O}{\overset{\|}{C}}OCH_3(A)$ can be converted into $CH_3CHO(B)$ by following methods

I. $A \xrightarrow[H_3O^+]{DIBAH} B$

II. $A \xrightarrow{PCl_5} \xrightarrow{Pd/BaSO_4/H_2} B$

III. $A \xrightarrow{LiAlH_4} B$

IV. $A \xrightarrow[H_3O^+]{HMgBr} B$

Select the correct methods.
(a) I and III (b) II and III
(c) I and II (d) III and IV

99. Select correct statements for the following base-catalysed reaction

$$R-\overset{O}{\overset{\|}{C}}-\overset{18}{O}-CH_3 \xrightarrow{OH^{\ominus}} R-\overset{O}{\overset{\|}{C}}-O^{\ominus} + CH_3OH$$

(a) it is a straight forward nucleophilic acyl substitution (addition and then ejection)
(b) $\overset{18}{O}$ appears in methanol CH_3OH
(c) the reaction is not reversible
(d) All the above are correct statements

100. A cyclic ester is formed when following acid is heated
(a) $CH_3CH_2\underset{OH}{\underset{|}{C}H}CH_2COOH$ (b) $CH_3CH_2\underset{OH}{\underset{|}{C}H}COOH$
(c) $\underset{OH}{\underset{|}{C}H_2}CH_2CH_2COOH$ (d) All of these cases

101. Resonance-stabilised enolate anion of ester RCH_2COOCH_3 can be represented as
(a) $R\overset{\ominus}{\ddot{C}}H\overset{:O:}{\overset{\|}{C}}OCH_3$ (b) $RCH{=}\overset{:\ddot{O}:^{\ominus}}{\overset{|}{C}}OCH_3$
(c) Both (a) and (b) (d) None of these

102. In a Claisen condensation reaction (when an ester is treated with a strong base)
(a) a proton is removed from the α-carbon to form a resonance-stabilised carbanion of the ester
(b) carbanion acts as a nucleophile in a nucleophilic acyl substitution reaction with another ester molecule
(c) a new C—C bond is formed
(d) All of the above statements are correct

103. Select incorrect statement about Claisen condensation reaction
(a) product is always a β-keto ester
(b) mechanism is not different from the other nucleophilic acyl substitution
(c) esters that have at least one α-hydrogen give this reaction
(d) enolate carbanion is resonance stabilised

104. Ester $\xrightarrow{LiAlH_4}$ CH_3CH_2OH (only)

Ester $\xrightarrow[(ii)\ H_3O^+]{(i)\ NaOC_2H_5} A$

A is
(a) $CH_3\overset{O}{\overset{\|}{C}}CH_2\overset{O}{\overset{\|}{C}}OC_2H_5$ (b) $CH_3\overset{O}{\overset{\|}{C}}CH_2\overset{O}{\overset{\|}{C}}OH$
(c) $CH_3\overset{O}{\overset{\|}{C}}OH$ (d) None of the above

105. If the following reaction takes place

$$CH_3CH_2\overset{O}{\overset{\|}{C}}CH_2CH_3 \xrightarrow[C_6H_5CO_3H]{H_2SO_5\ \text{or}} CH_3CH_2\overset{O}{\overset{\|}{C}}OCH_2CH_3$$

then same treatment on *A* (below) gives

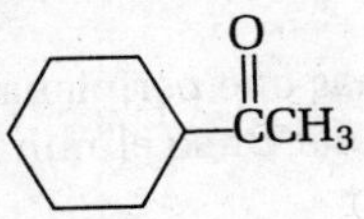

(a) 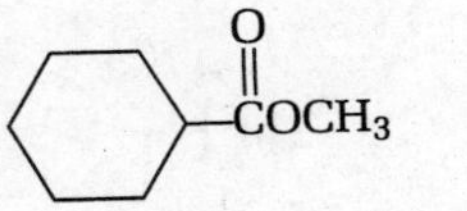 (b) 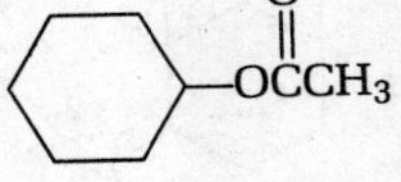
(c) 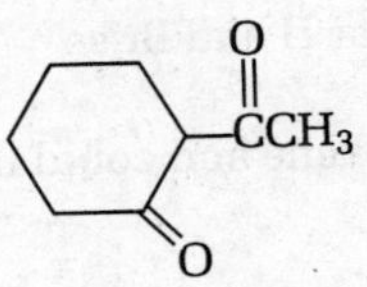 (d) 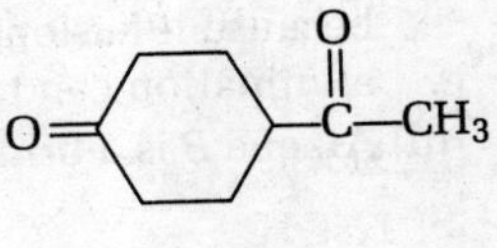

Objective Questions Type II [One or more than one correct option(s)]

In each of the questions below, four choices are given, of which one or more than one are correct.

1. Alkene *A* below can be obtained from .... on reaction with a base

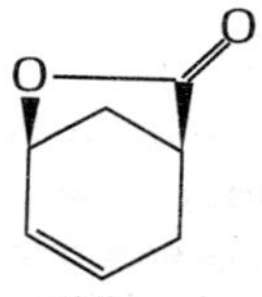

(*A*)

(a) 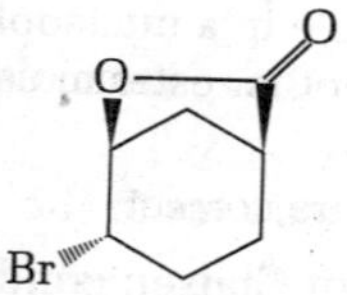

(b) 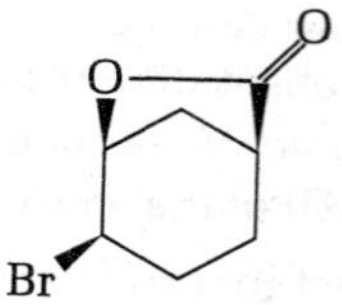

(c) 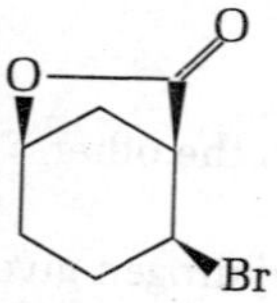

(d) 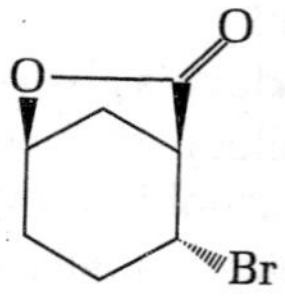

2. Alkene *B* below can be obtained from

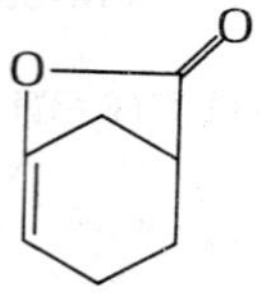

(*B*)

(a) 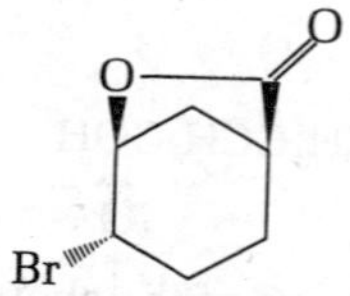

because it has one *anti*-periplanar H and Br so elimination can take place.

(b) 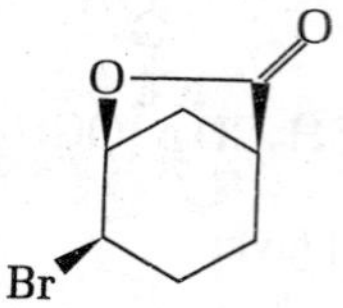

because it has one periplanar H and one *anti*-periplanar Br so elimination can take place

(c) 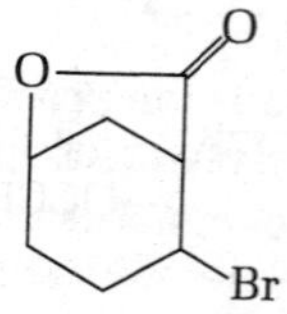

because it has one periplanar H and Br so elimination can take place

(d) Alkene *B* is a bridge head alkene and could not exist

3. Consider the following anhydride (*A*)

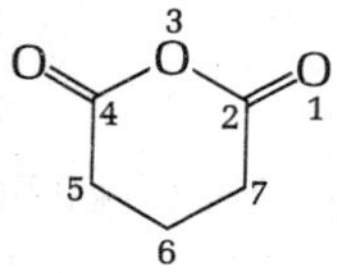

(*A*)

Select the correct statement(s) about (A).

(a) Nucleophilic attack takes place at (O – 1) or (O – 4)

(b) Nucleophilic attack takes place at (C – 2) or (C – 4)

(c) By nucleophilic attack (*A*) is converted into (*B*)

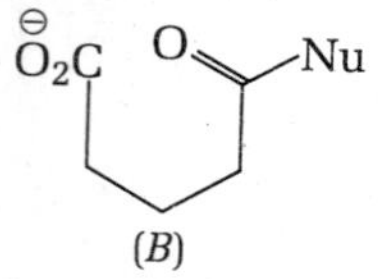

(*B*)

(d) By nucleophilic attack intermediate is

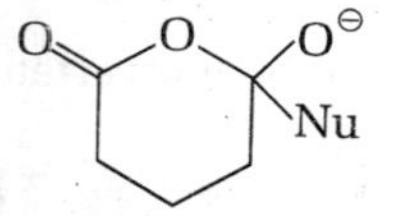

4. Select the correct statement(s) about (*A*)

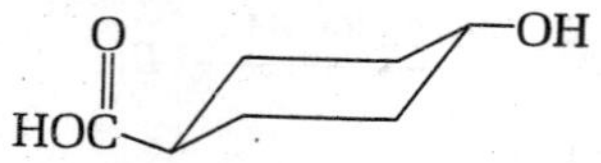

4-hydroxycyclohexane carboxylic acid

(a) Only *trans*-isomer of *A* is capable of forming a lactone

(b) In lactone formation, cyclohexane ring of *A* adopts a boat conformation

(c) Only *cis*-isomer of *A* is capable of forming a lactone

(d) Most stable conformation is chain conformation

5. The second-order rate constant k for saponification of 5-pentanolide (*A*) is over 20 times as great as that for 4-butanolide (*B*).

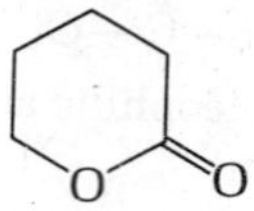

A

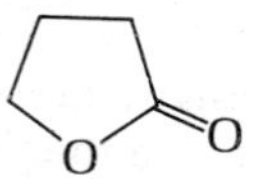

B

It is due to the fact.

(a) that addition of hydroxide to (*B*) introduces torsional strain in the intermediate with eclipsed bonds which is formed more slowly and is thus unstable

(b) that intermediate of alkaline hydrolysis of (*A*) has staggered bonds in a six-membered ring and is thus, free from strain

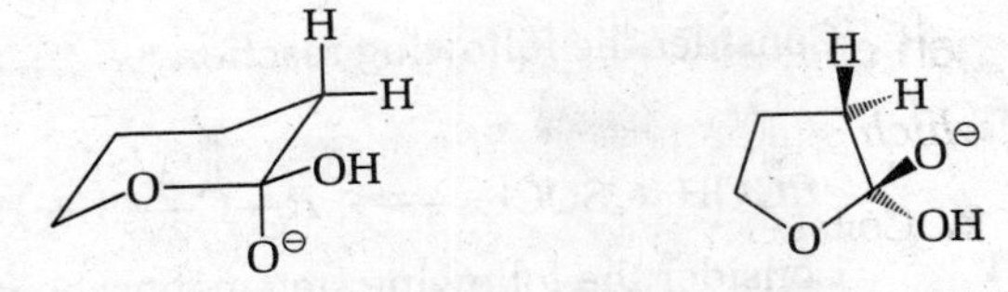

(c) that $OH^{\ominus}$ is strong base and it causes cleavage of (*A*) only

(d) that $OH^{\ominus}$ is a weak base and it causes cleavage of (*A*) only

6. End-product of the following reaction is

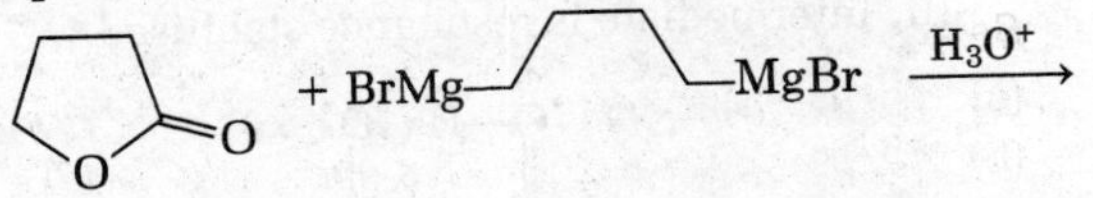

(a)
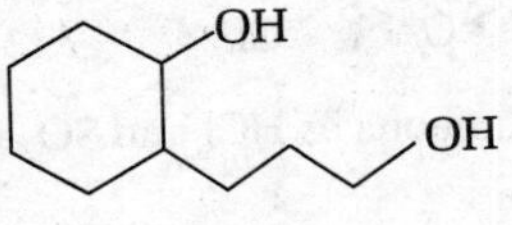

(b)
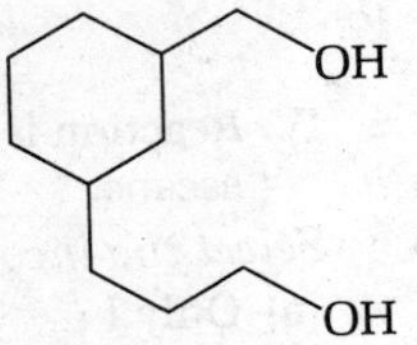

(c)
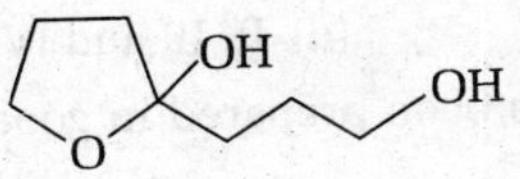

(d)
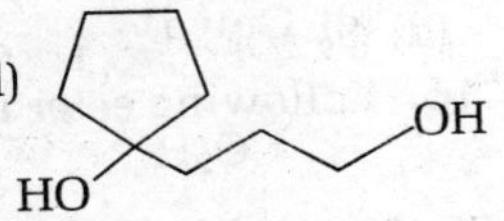

7. Identify the products of the following reactions

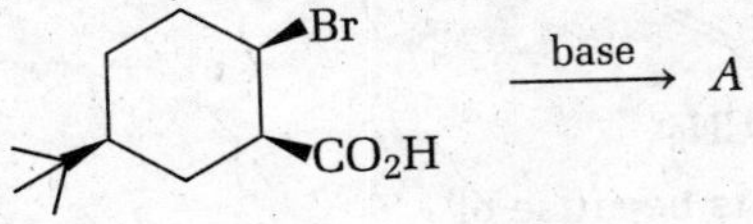

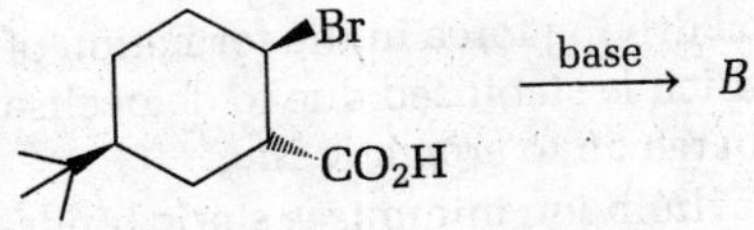

	A	B

(a)
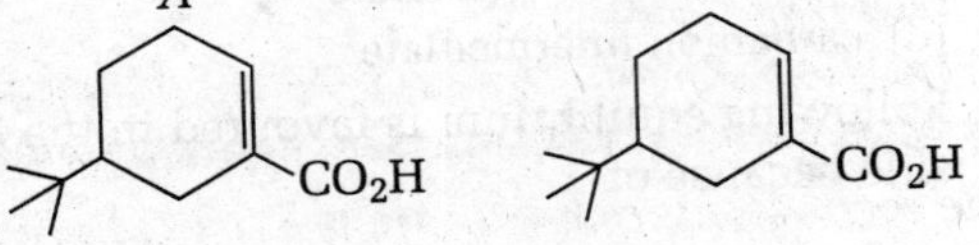

(b)

(c)
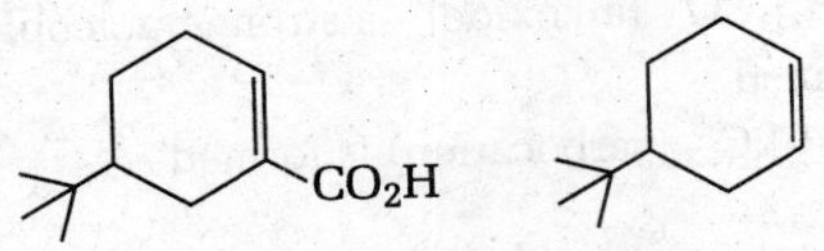

(d)
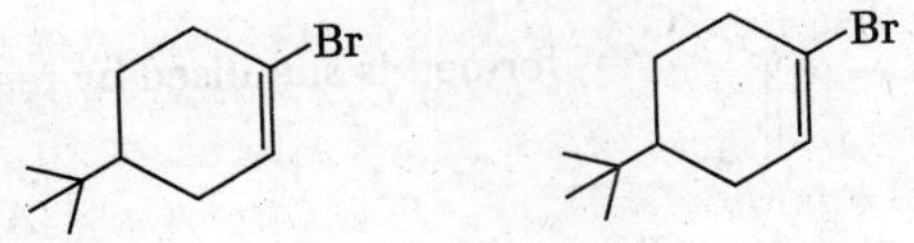

8. Select the correct statement(s).

(a) An enolate ion, being nucleophile reacts with CO_2 to form β-carboxy carboxyl compound

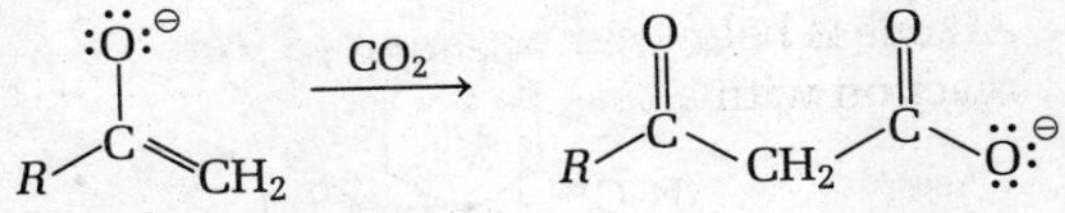

Enolate

(b) Above reaction is completely reversible

(c) β-keto ester can be prepared by using ethyl chloro formate or diethyl carbonate on reaction with carbanion

(d) Every dicarboxylic acid changes to mono carboxylic acid on heating

9. Following is one of the intermediates in the acid-catalysed hydrolysis of ester.

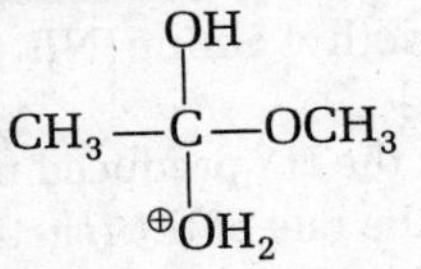

Select the correct statement(s)

(a) Intermediate is changed to ester back by elimination of water

(b) Intermediate is changed to acid by knocking $\bar{O}CH_3$

(c) Intermediate can go towards the side of ester formation or acid formation as pK_a of CH_3OH and H_2O are approximately equal

(d) Excess alcohol will derive the equilibrium towards the ester formation

10. Consider the following reaction,

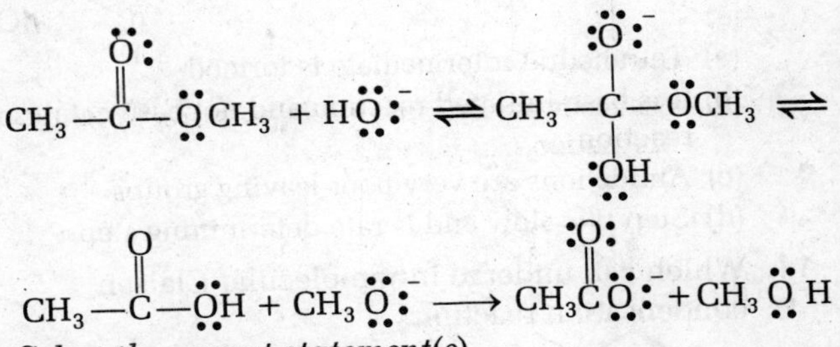

Select the correct statement(s).

(a) Nucleophilic attack of OH^- on carbonyl carbon takes place at a higher rate than that of H^+.

(b) Kinetics of the reaction can be studied using phenolphthalein as the indicator

(c) The reaction is called a hydroxide ion promoted reaction rather than a base-catalysed reaction

(d) Carboxylate ions formed are not attacked easily by nucleophiles, hence reaction is not reversible

11. With reference to the scheme given, which of the given, statements about *T, U, V* and *W* is/are correct. **[IIT JEE 2012]**

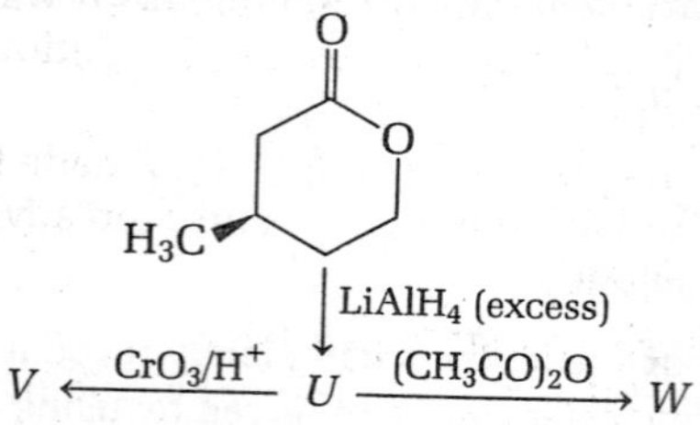

(a) *T* is soluble in hot aqueous NaOH
(b) *U* is optically active
(c) Molecular formula of *W* is $C_{10}H_{18}O_4$
(d) *V* gives effervescence on treatment with aqueous $NaHCO_3$

12. Recently solvolysis of acid chloride has been studied in presence of triethyl amine (NR_3). Addition of NR_3 ($R = C_2H_5$)
(a) neutralises the *HX* produced in the solvolysis reaction
(b) enhances the rate of the reaction
(c) results in the formation of an intermediate with a positive charge
(d) has no effect on the rate

13. Consider amide hydrolysis under basic conditions: Select correct statement(s).

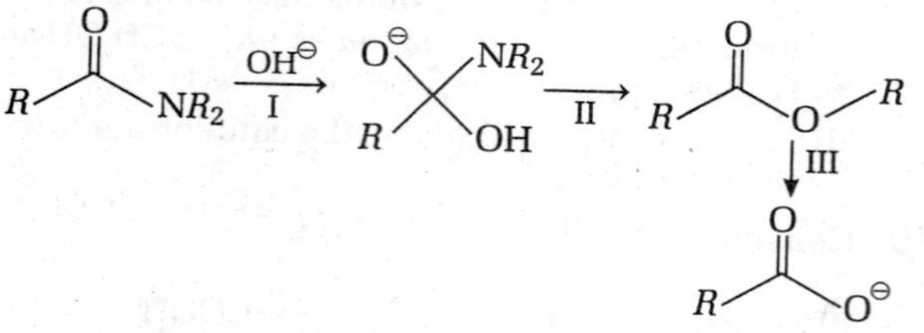

(a) Tetrahedral intermediate is formed
(b) It is base-initiated reaction and not base-catalysed reaction
(c) Amide ions are very poor leaving groups
(d) Step II is slow and is rate determining step

14. Which can undergo intramolecular Claisen condensation reaction?

(a) 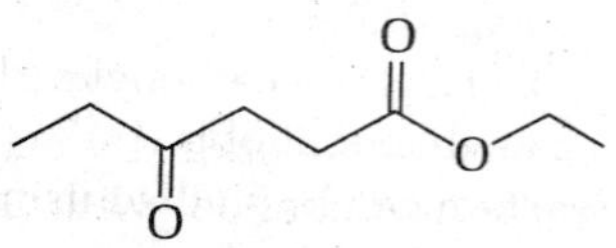

(b) 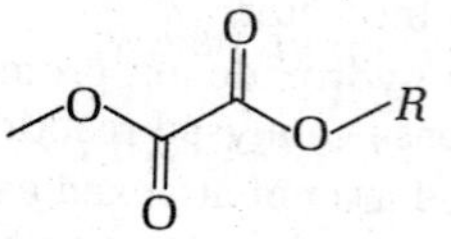

(c) 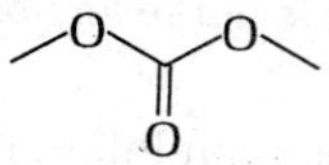

(d) 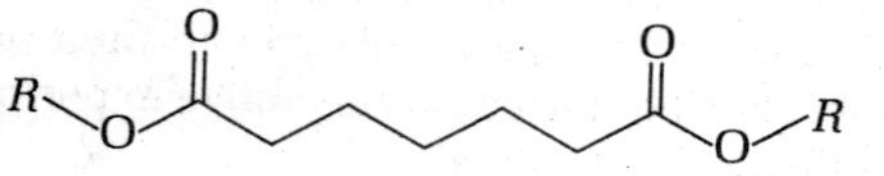

15. Consider the following reaction

$$R\overset{O}{\overset{\|}{C}}OH + SOCl_2 \longrightarrow R-\overset{O}{\overset{\|}{C}}-Cl + HCl + SO_2$$

Consider the following statements about this reaction
I. It is S_N2 at carbonyl carbon from where OH is a leaving group.
II. It is S_N2 at sulphur from where Cl is the leaving group.
III. Intermediate is resonance stabilised

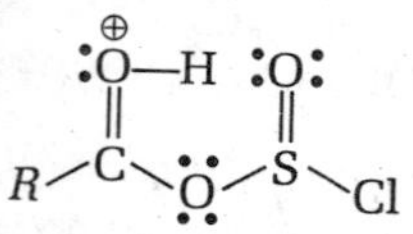

IV. Reaction is spontaneous as HCl and SO_2 gases escape.

Select the incorrect statement(s).
(a) Only I
(b) II and III
(c) Only IV
(d) II, III and IV

16. Following ester has been prepared in good yield as

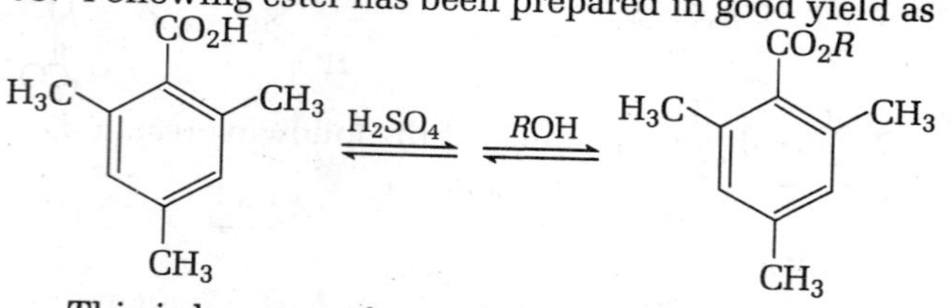

This is because of
(a) the driving force in the formation of acylium ion which is stabilised due to delocalisation of its charge on to aromatic ring
(b) acylium ion minimises steric hindrance
(c) carbocation intermediate
(d) carbanion intermediate

17. Following equilibrium is favoured in the forward side because of

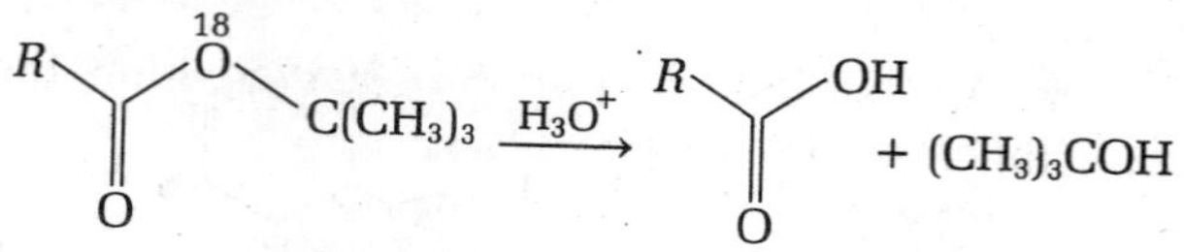

(a) $(CH_3)_3CO^{\ominus}$ (alkoxide)—a strong nucleophile is formed
(b) $(CH_3)_3C^{\oplus}$ (carbocation) is formed
(c) 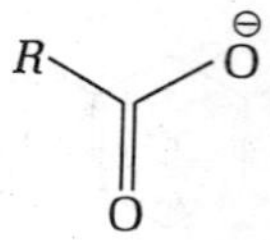 formed is stabilised by resonance
(d) 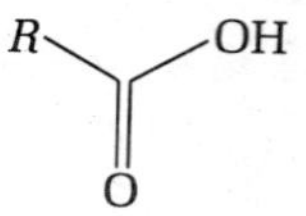 (a weak acid) is formed

18. Although carboxylic acids are unreactive to alcohols alone, they can usually be esterified in the presence of a small quantity of concentrated sulphuric acid or about 3% HCl.

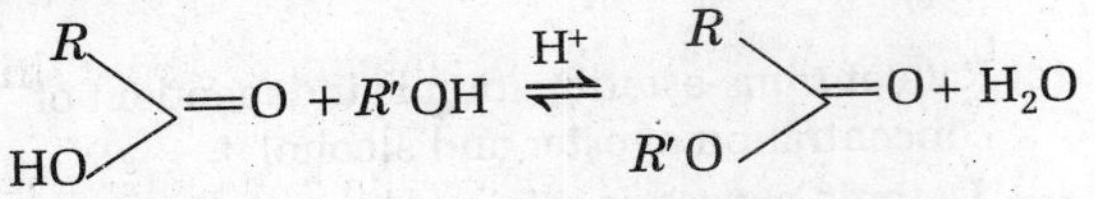

Consider the following statement(s) about this reaction.

I. It is called Fischer esterification reaction.

II. The reaction must be carried out with excess alcohol to drive it towards the product.

III. The reaction is spontaneous if water is removed by azeotropic distillation with toluene or benzene.

IV. Process is reversible if it is made through formation of RCOCl and then acylation of alcohol.

Select incorrect statement(s)

(a) I and II
(b) II and III
(c) Only III
(d) Only IV

Comprehension Based Questions

In these questions, a passage has been given followed by questions based on it. You have to answer the questions based on the passage given.

Passage 1 The following structure illustrates the alkaline hydrolysis of an ester which has a chiral centre in the alcoholic part. If the product is analysed for optical activity, one can decide the type of substitution on it.

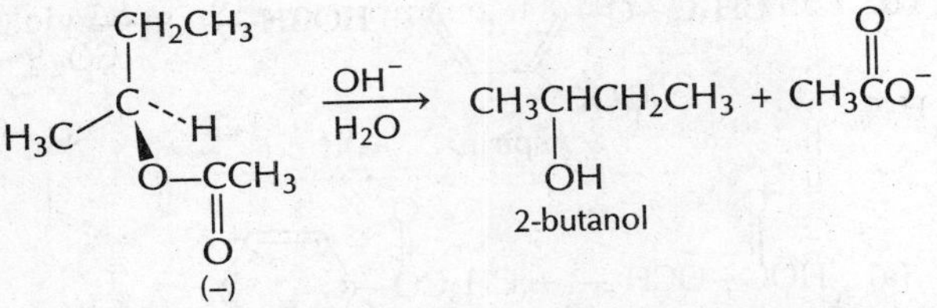

2-butanol formed may be with same configuration or inverted configuration or small specific rotation depending on S_N1 or S_N2 or nucleophilic acyl substitution or any other type.

1. Alcohol formed has same configuration as the ester, then mechanism followed is
(a) S_N1
(b) S_N2
(c) nucleophilic acyl substitution ($S_{N_{Ac}}$)
(d) E1CB

2. Alcohol formed is with (+) configuration, then mechanism followed is
(a) S_N1
(b) S_N2
(c) $S_{N_{Ac}}$
(d) E1CB

3. Alcohol formed has very small specific rotation then mechanism followed is
(a) S_N1
(b) S_N2
(c) $S_{N_{Ac}}$
(d) E1CB

Passage 2 The synthetic sweetener aspartame, known commercially as Nutra sweet, is a carboxylic acid.

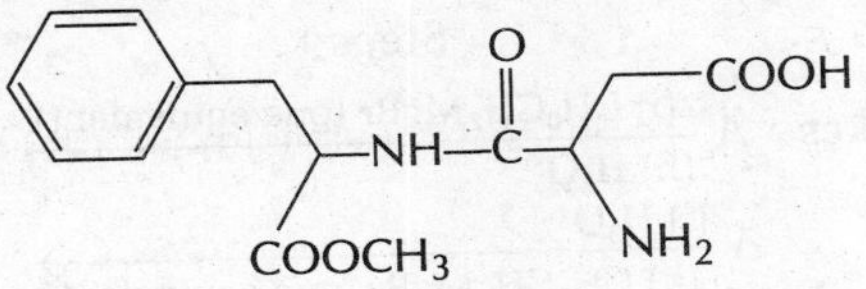

The following questions are based on aspartame.

1. Number of stereo centres present in it are
(a) 1
(b) 2
(c) 3
(d) 4

2. Other artificial (synthetic) sweeteners are
(a) sorbitol
(b) saccharin
(c) cyclamate
(d) xylitol

3. In aqueous solution, on standing it changes to

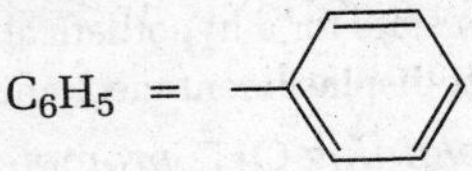

(a)

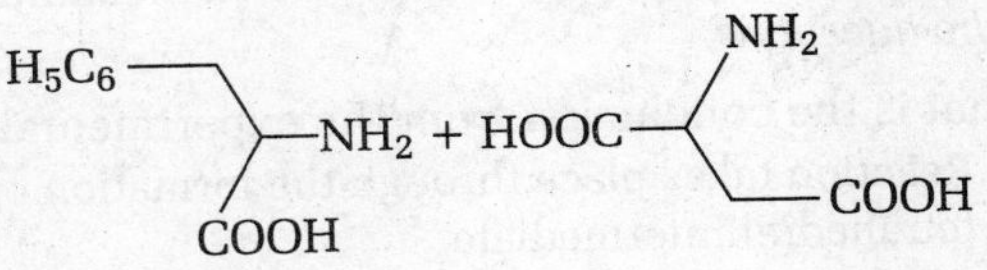

(b)

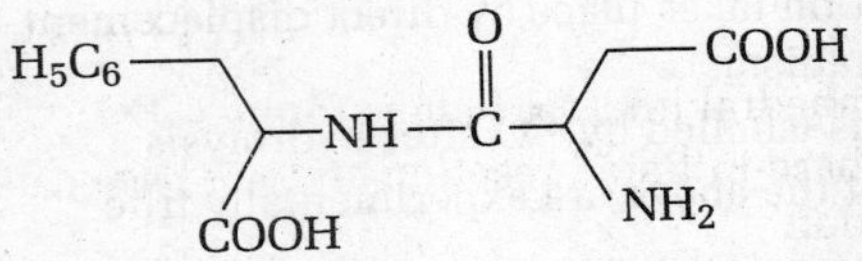

(c)

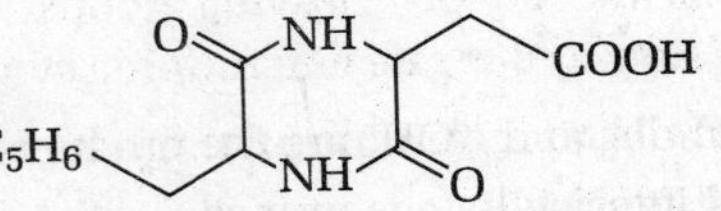

(d) no hydrolysis take place

Passage 3 Suppose we have some optically pure (+)-2-butyl acetate that has been "labelled" with the heavy ^{18}O isotope at one oxygen atom as shown below:

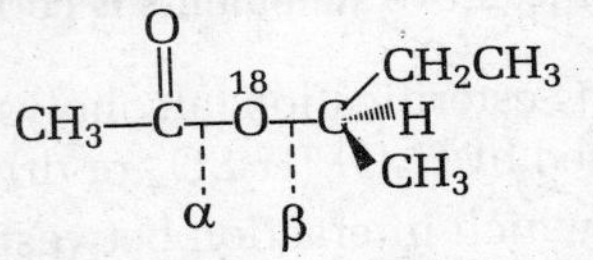

It is subjected to hydrolysis under basic condition. After hydrolysis is over, products are isolated and their nature are experimentally studied. Based on the above experiment, answer the following questions.

1. Which of the products will contain $\overset{18}{O}$?

(a) $CH_3-\overset{\overset{\displaystyle O}{\|}}{C}-\bar{O}$ (b) $CH_3CH_2\underset{\underset{\displaystyle OH}{|}}{C}HCH_3$

(c) Both (a) & (b) (d) None of these

2. Alcohol formed has same configuration as the ester, then mechanism followed is:

(a) S_N1 (b) S_N2

(c) nucleophilic acyl substitution ($S_{N_{Ac}}$)

(d) E1CB

3. Alcohol formed has very small specific rotation then mechanism followed is:

(a) S_N1 (b) S_N2 (c) $S_{N_{Ac}}$ (d) E1CB

Passage 4 It is said that nucleophilic acyl substitution reactions take place by a mechanism that involves the formation of a tetrahedral intermediate and its subsequent collapse.

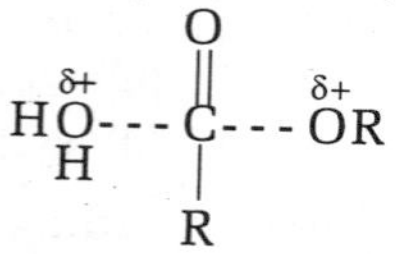

(Transition state for a hypothetical one-step direct displacement mechanism)

Read this passage explaining OH^- promoted mechanism and answer the questions.

1. What is the conclusion from the experimental study?
   (a) Reaction takes place through the formation of the tetrahedral intermediate
   (b) Reaction takes place by direct displacement mechanism
   (c) OH^- is labelled by ^{18}O after hydrolysis
   (d) All of the above are experimentally true

2. Select the correct statement(s).
   (a) $C_6H_5\overset{\overset{\displaystyle O}{\|}}{C}OCH_2CH_3$ and $^{18}OH^-$ are the products when tetrahedral intermediate is formed
   (b) $C_6H_5\overset{\overset{\displaystyle O}{\|}}{C}\overset{18}{O}H$ and $CH_3CH_2\bar{O}$ are the products when direct displacement mechanism is used
   (c) Both of the above statements are correct
   (d) None of the above statements is correct

Passage 5 *Trans*-esterification (alcoholysis-cleavage by an alcohol) is catalysed by H_3O^+ (H_2SO_4 or dry HCl) or by RO^- (CH_3CH_2ONa) in which interaction between an ester and an alcohol results in the exchange of alkoxide ion.

$$R-\overset{\overset{\displaystyle O}{\|}}{C}-\overset{18}{O}-R' + \underset{\text{Excess}}{R''\,OH} \xrightarrow{H_3O^+} R-\overset{\overset{\displaystyle O}{\|}}{C}-OR'' + R'OH$$

1. Select the correct statement(s).
   (a) It involves tetrahedral intermediate
   (b) Hybridisation of carbonyl carbon changes from sp^2 to sp^3
   (c) Rate of *trans*-esterification is independent of concentration of ester and alcohol
   (d) Isotopic oxygen is retained by new ester

2. Alcohol $R''OH$ is generally taken in large excess so as to
   (a) cleave $R'O$ — C bond
   (b) make $R''O$—a good leaving group
   (c) make $R'O$—a good leaving group
   (d) derive the equilibrium to the right

3. A *trans*-esterification reaction that blocks prostaglandin synthesis is responsible for the activity of aspirin (acetylsalicylic acid) as an anti-inflammatory agent. What are the products of following *trans*-esterification?

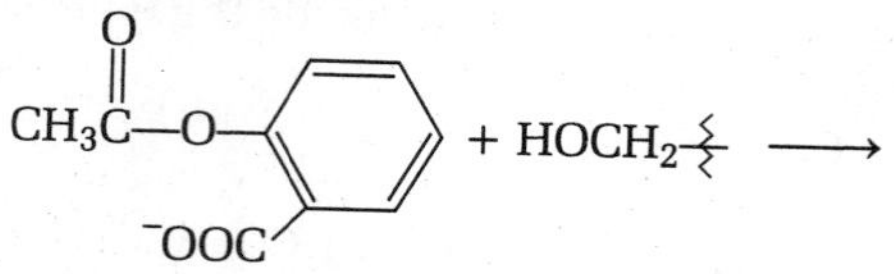

Aspirin

(a) 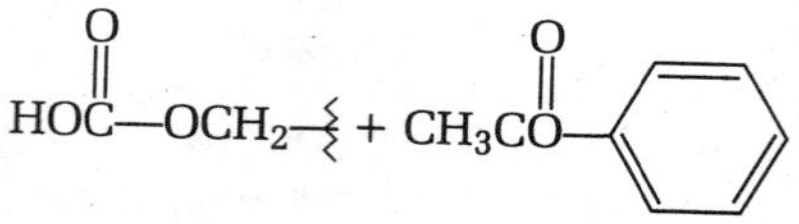

(b) 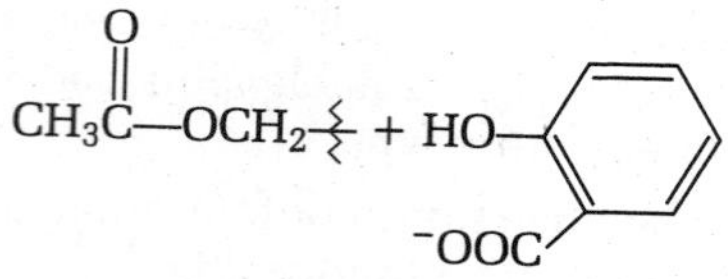

(c) 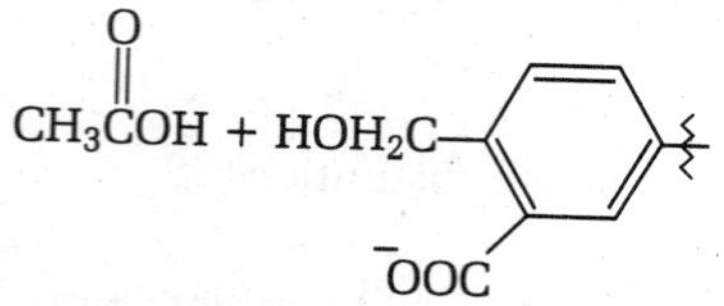

(d) None of the above

Passage 6 Two chemical engineers (CE) at MIT were working on the same keto ester (*A*)

A: 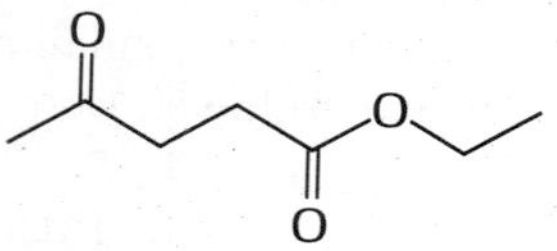

for the synthesis of carbonyl compounds using same Grignard reagent CH_3CH_2MgBr but changing some experimental steps.

CE	Steps	Product
Mr Petersykes	$A \xrightarrow[\text{(ii) } H_3O^+]{\text{(i) } CH_3CH_2MgBr \text{ (one equivalent)}}$	*X*
Mr Wade	$A \xrightarrow[\text{(ii) } CH_3CH_2MgBr \text{ (one equivalent)}]{\text{(i) } H_3O^+}$	*Y*

1. Identify the product *X* and *Y*.

	X	*Y*
(a)	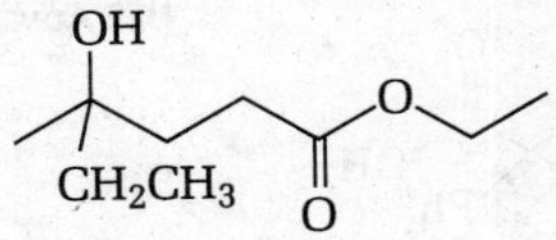	CH_3CH_3
(b)	CH_3CH_3	CH_3CH_3
(c)	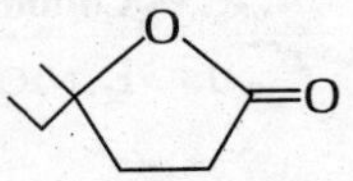	CH_3CH_3
(d)	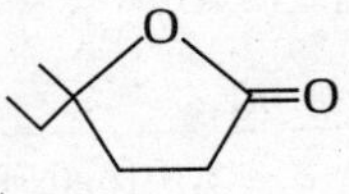	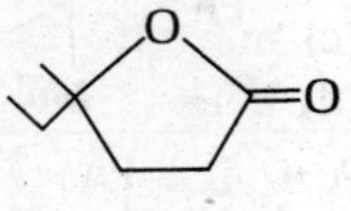

Passage 7 AIDS is a twentieth-century disease that has become a major medical problem in the world. The number of drugs that are effective in treating HIV infection and AIDS is small. The drug most used to treat **AIDS** patient is zidovudine, also known as **azidothymine,** or AZT. If fights an AIDS infection but does not cure it.

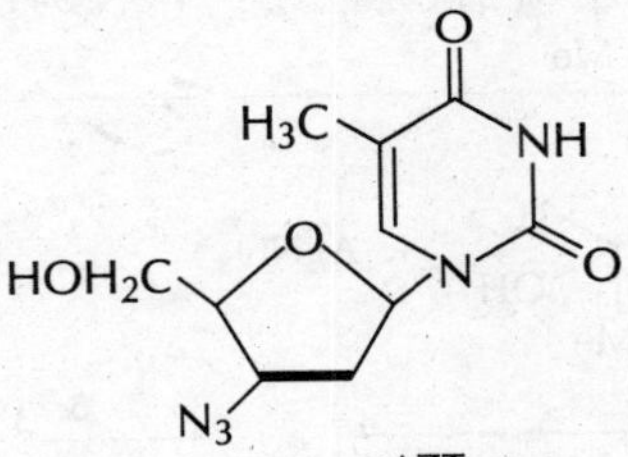

AZT

The following questions are based on AZT.

1. Which group is not present in AZT ?
   (a) Carbonyl (keto/aldehyde)
   (b) Oxirane
   (c) Peptide
   (d) Azide
2. Select the correct statement(s).
   (a) It can tautomerise
   (b) It can give white precipitate with Lucas reagent
   (c) It shows acidic property due to H attached to N
   (d) N_3^- can be replaced by Cl^-
3. Controlled hydrolysis of AZT gives
   (a) 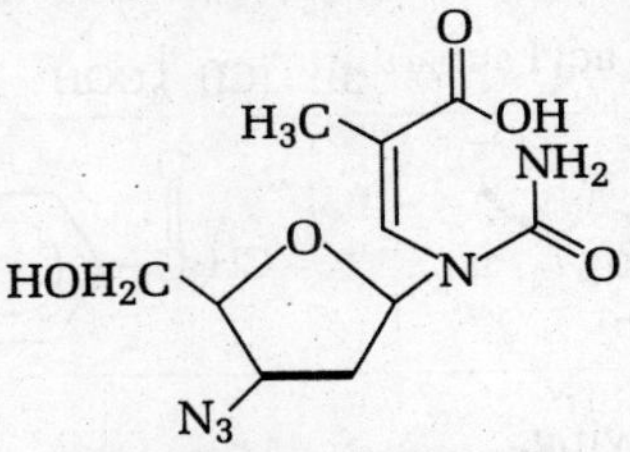
   which exists as Zwitter ion
   (b) 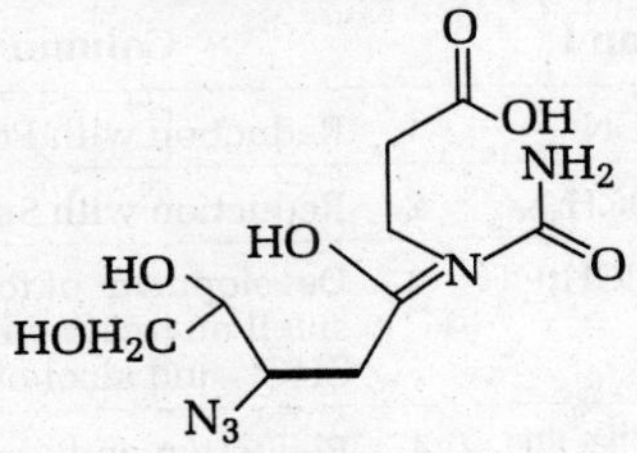
   (c) 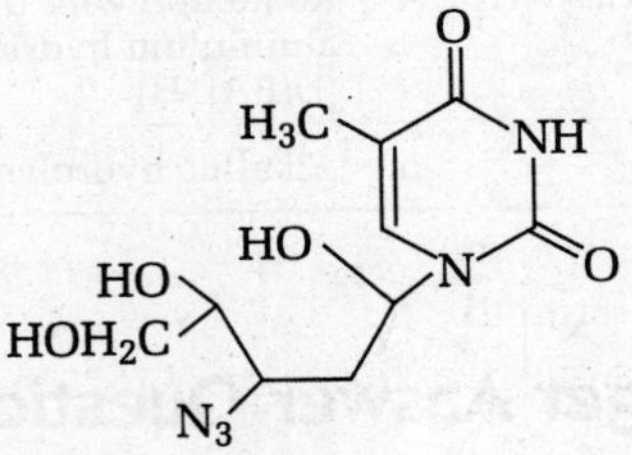
   (d) None of the above

Matrix-Match Type

Given below are Matching Type Questions, with two columns (each having some items) each . Each item of Column I has to be matched with the items of Column II.

1. Match the following.

Column I	Column II
A. $CH_3\overset{O}{\overset{\|\|}{C}}OCH_2CH_3$	1. Friedel-Crafts reaction
B. $CH_3\overset{O}{\overset{\|\|}{C}}_2O$	2. Acid formed due to acidic hydrolysis gives colour with neutral $FeCl_3$
C. $CH_3\overset{O}{\overset{\|\|}{C}}NH_2$	3. Gives a pungent gas on heating with NaOH
D. $CH_3\overset{O}{\overset{\|\|}{C}}Cl$	4. Can be converted into $(CH_3)_3COH$ on reaction with excess of CH_3MgBr/H_3O^+

2. Match of the following

Column I	Column II
A. $CH_3\overset{O}{\overset{\|\|}{C}}OCH_2CH_3$	1. Claisen condensation
B. $CH_3\overset{O}{\overset{\|\|}{C}}NH_2$	2. Biuret test
C. $NH_2\overset{O}{\overset{\|\|}{C}}NH_2$	3. Hydrolysed to carboxylic acid in acidic medium
D. CH_3CN	4. Decomposed by NaOH

3. Match the following.

Column I (Compound)		Column II (Product with Grignard reagent)
A. $(CH_3CO)_2O$	1.	$CH_3\overset{O}{\overset{\Vert}{C}}CH_3$
B. CH_3CN	2.	$(CH_3)_2CHOH$
C. $CH_3\overset{O}{\overset{\Vert}{C}}OC_2H_5$	3.	$(CH_3)_3COH$
D. $CH_3\overset{O}{\overset{\Vert}{C}}H$	4.	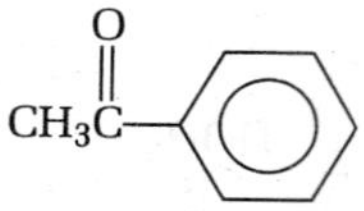

4. Match the following.

Column I		Column II
A. $CH_3CH_2CH_2CN$	1.	Reduction with Pd-C/H_2
B. $CH_3CH_2OCOCH_3$	2.	Reduction with $SnCl_2$/HCl
C. $CH_3CH{=}CHCH_2OH$	3.	Development of foul smell on treatment with $CHCl_3$ and alcoholic KOH
D. $CH_3CH_2CH_2CH_2NH_2$	4.	Reduction with disobutyl aluminium hydride (DIBAL-H)
	5.	Alkaline hydrolysis

5. The desired product X can be prepared by reacting the major product of the reactions in Column-I with one or more appropriate reagents in Column-II. **[JEE Advanced 2018]**

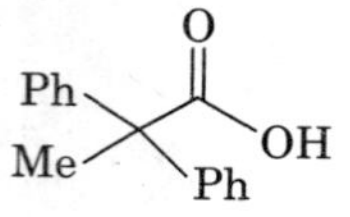

X

Column I		Column II
P. 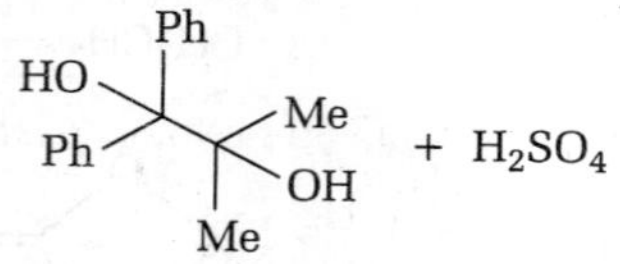	1.	I_2, NaOH
Q. 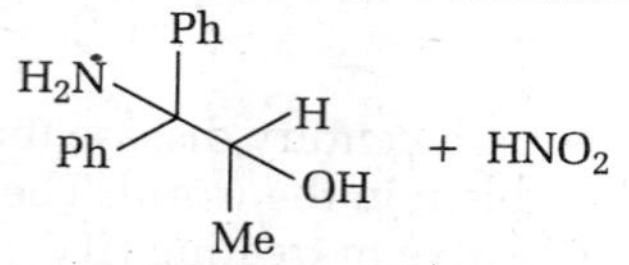	2.	$[Ag(NH_3)_2]OH$
R. 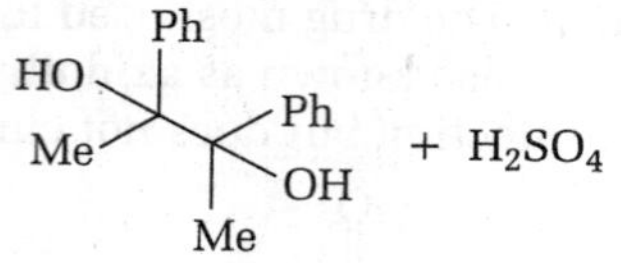	3.	Fehling solution
S. 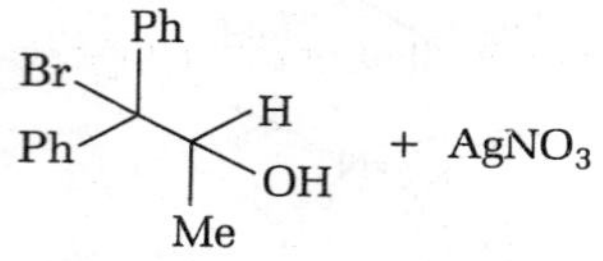	4.	HCHO, NaOH
	5.	NaOBr

Single Integer Answer Questions

Answer of these questions is a single digit lying between 0 to 9.

1. Total number of σ and π bonds and lone pair in ethane nitrile is ....

2. 4.53 g of NH_3 is obtained by decomposing x g urea with NaOH. x is ....

3. 1,2,3-tricyanopropane is actually is a chain of .... carbon atoms based on IUPAC nomenclature.

4. Dimethylhexanedionate forms β-keto ester of .... membered ring by Dieckmann reaction.

5. Which (at SN) phosgene derivative is maximum reactive toward nucleophilic attack?

$COCl_2$, $CO(OC_6H_4NO_2)_2$, $CO(OC_6H_5)_2$, $CO(OCH_3)_2$
(1) (2) (3) (4)

6. 0.1 mole of pure (*R*)-2-butyl acetate is hydrolysed under acidic condition.

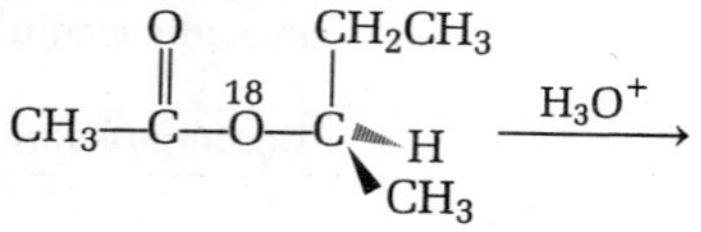

How much acid (in grams) is formed in this reaction?

7. How many geometrical isomers are possible if ascorbic acid assumes open chain structure?

8. By Baeyer-Villiger oxidation, carbonyl compound is converted into ester

$$\underset{4}{CH_3}\,\underset{3}{CH_2}\,\underset{2}{\overset{O}{\overset{\Vert}{C}}}\,\underset{1}{CH_3} \longrightarrow R\overset{O}{\overset{\Vert}{C}}OR'$$

What is the sum of C-atoms (position) in between which O atom is inserted?

9. 1 mole of urea is decomposed by HNO_2 forming N_2. How many moles of N_2 is/are formed?

10. Consider the following reaction

$$\underset{A}{CH_3COCH_2COOC_2H_5} \xrightarrow{H_3O^+} B + C$$

$$\underset{\text{Acid}}{B} \xrightarrow{\Delta} D$$

How many of A, B, C, D would give iodoform test?

11. The total number of carboxylic acid groups in the product P is **[JEE Advanced 2013]**

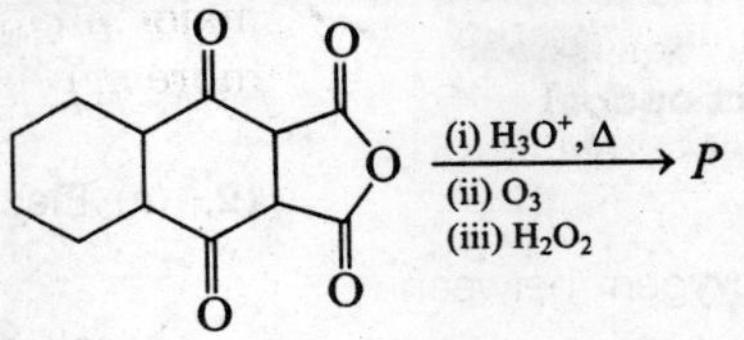

Answers

Objective Questions Type I [Only one correct option]

1. (b)	**2.** (b)	**3.** (a)	**4.** (b)	**5.** (b)	**6.** (c)	**7.** (a)	**8.** (c)	**9.** (b)	**10.** (c)
11. (c)	**12.** (a)	**13.** (a)	**14.** (a)	**15.** (a)	**16.** (c)	**17.** (a)	**18.** (a)	**19.** (b)	**20.** (c)
21. (b)	**22.** (a)	**23.** (c)	**24.** (c)	**25.** (b)	**26.** (c)	**27.** (a)	**28.** (c)	**29.** (a)	**30.** (c)
31. (a)	**32.** (c)	**33.** (b)	**34.** (c)	**35.** (d)	**36.** (c)	**37.** (a)	**38.** (a)	**39.** (c)	**40.** (a)
41. (c)	**42.** (a)	**43.** (b)	**44.** (a)	**45.** (c)	**46.** (a)	**47.** (a)	**48.** (a)	**49.** (d)	**50.** (c)
51. (d)	**52.** (c)	**53.** (d)	**54.** (d)	**55.** (b)	**56.** (a)	**57.** (d)	**58.** (b)	**59.** (b)	**60.** (d)
61. (b)	**62.** (c)	**63.** (b)	**64.** (d)	**65.** (d)	**66.** (b)	**67.** (a)	**68.** (c)	**69.** (d)	**70.** (a)
71. (d)	**72.** (b)	**73.** (d)	**74.** (b)	**75.** (c)	**76.** (a)	**77.** (d)	**78.** (c)	**79.** (a)	**80.** (c)
81. (b)	**82.** (c)	**83.** (b)	**84.** (a)	**85.** (c)	**86.** (b)	**87.** (b)	**88.** (a)	**89.** (b)	**90.** (b)
91. (c)	**92.** (c)	**93.** (d)	**94.** (d)	**95.** (c)	**96.** (a)	**97.** (b)	**98.** (c)	**99.** (d)	**100.** (a)
101. (c)	**102.** (d)	**103.** (b)	**104.** (a)	**105.** (b)					

Objective Questions Type II [One or more than one correct option(s)]

1. (a)	**2.** (d)	**3.** (b, c, d)	**4.** (b, c, d)	**5.** (a, b)
6. (d)	**7.** (c)	**8.** (a, b, c)	**9.** (c, d)	**10.** (a, b, c, d)
11. (a, c, d)	**12.** (a, c, d)	**13.** (a, b, c, d)	**14.** (a, d)	**15.** (b, c, d)
16. (a, b)	**17.** (b)	**18.** (d)		

Comprehension Based Questions

Passage 1 – 1. (c) **2.** (b) **3.** (a)

Passage 2 – 1. (b) **2.** (b,c) **3.** (b)

Passage 3 – 1. (b) **2.** (c) **3.** (a)

Passage 4 – 1. (a,c) **2.** (c)

Passage 5 – 1. (a,b) **2.** (d) **3.** (b)

Passage 6 – 1. (c)

Passage 7 – 1. (a) **2.** (a,c) **3.** (a)

Matrix-Match Type

1. A→(1,2,4); B→(1,3,4); C→(2,3); D→(1,2,4)

2. A→(1,2,4); B→(3,4); C→(2,4); D→(3,4)

3. A→(1,3,4); B→(1,3,4); C→(1,3,4); D→(2)

4. A→(1,2,4,5); B→(1,4,5); C→(1); D→(3)

5. A→(1,5); B→(2,3); C→(1,5); D→(2,3)

Single Integer Answer Questions

1. (5)	**2.** (8)	**3.** (5)	**4.** (8)	**5.** (1)	**6.** (6)	**7.** (2)	**8.** (3)	**9.** (2)	**10.** (4)
11. (2)									

Solutions

Objective Questions Type I [Only one correct option]

1. (*b*) $CH_3\overset{O}{\overset{\|}{C}}OOH$ (peroxy acid) inserts oxygen between carboxylic carbon and larger alkyl group.

$$CH_3CH_2-\overset{O}{\overset{\|}{C}}-CH_3 \xrightarrow{CH_3CO_3H} CH_3CH_2O\overset{O}{\overset{\|}{C}}CH_3 \xrightarrow{H_3O^{\oplus}} CH_3CH_2OH + CH_3\overset{O}{\overset{\|}{C}}OH$$

2. (*b*) $R-\overset{O}{\overset{\|}{C}}-X \xrightarrow{H_3O^+} R-\overset{O}{\overset{\|}{C}}OH + HX$

Best leaving group is $Cl^{\ominus}$ (conjugate base of strong acid).

4. (*b*) (a) 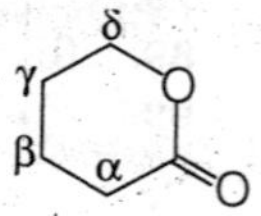 (b) 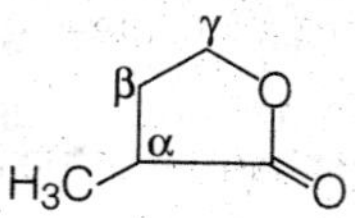

6. (*c*) 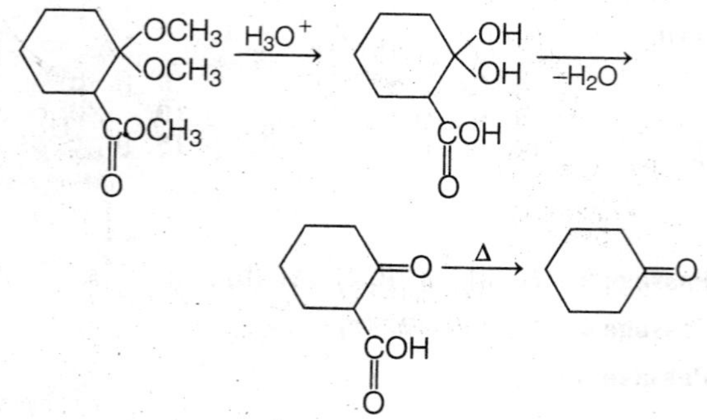

when keto group is at β–position *wrt* —COOH, heating causes loss of CO_2.

7. (*a*) H of phenolic group is acetylated.

8. (*c*) 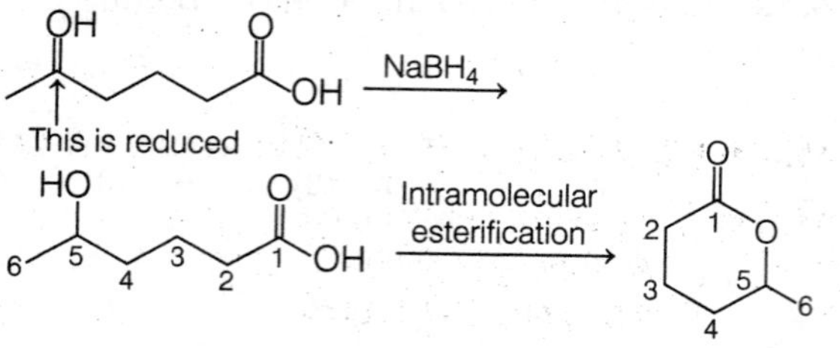

9. (*b*) α (double bond) < β (between single and double) < γ (purely single bond).

11. (*c*)

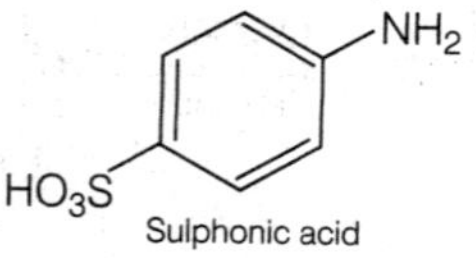

Sulphonic acid

12. (*a*) Electron-repelling group (—OCH_3) in *para* position deactivates ($CH_3\overset{O}{\overset{\|}{C}}O$—) group for hydrolysis.

13. (*a*) $CH_3\overset{O}{\overset{\|}{C}}OC_2H_5 + HCH_2\overset{O}{\overset{\|}{C}}OC_2H_5 \xrightarrow[\text{(ii) } H_3O^+]{\text{(i) } C_2H_5\overset{-\ +}{O}Na}$

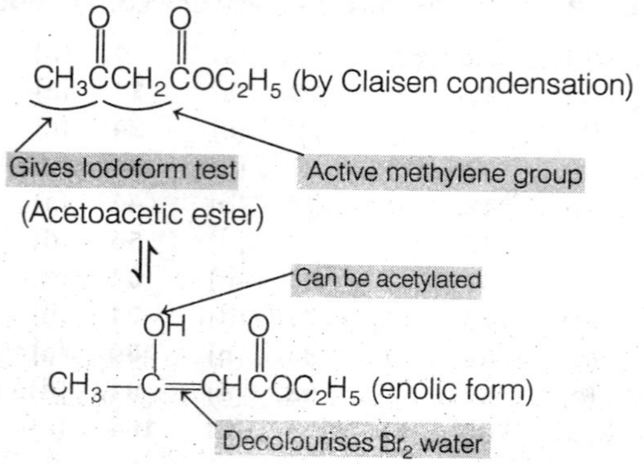

14. (*a*) All the given compounds are acid derivatives, thus contain carbonyl group in them. $LiAlH_4$ reduces these compounds through nucleophilic substitution *via* addition elimination (S_{NA} *E*) reaction. The rate of reaction depends upon the following factors :

(i) Size of alkyl group.
(ii) Steric hinderance around the $>C=O$ group.
(iii) (+) ve charge on the C-atom of $>C=O$ group.

The alkyl groups are more or less same in the given compounds. Thus, the reactivity order of given compounds depends upon 2nd and 3rd factor written above. The cumulative effect of these two factors results to leaving group ability (LGA) of the substituents in the following order :

$$\underset{\text{Good leaving group}}{Cl^-} > O^- - \overset{O}{\overset{\|}{C}} - CH_3 > \bar{O} - CH_3 > \underset{\text{Poor leaving group}}{NH_2}$$

This leaving group ability (weak conjugate base) corresponds directly to the reactivity order. Hence, the correct reactivity order is:

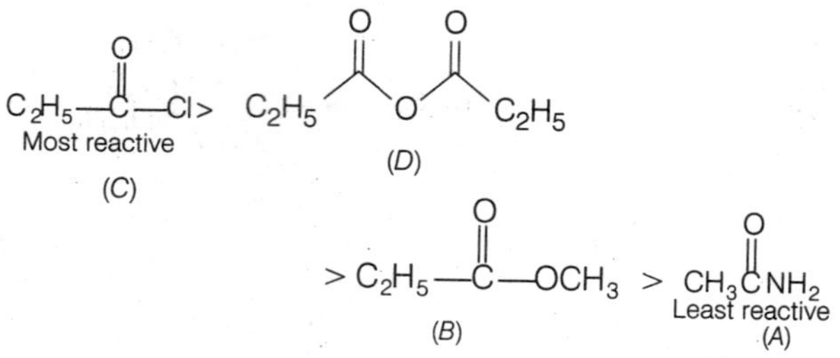

Note The $-I$ effect of —Cl and $+m$ effects of $-\ddot{N}H_2$—O—C(=O)—C_2H_5 and — OCH_3 groups while attached to —C(=O)— group to be reduced. Also add to the group leaving ability.

15. (*a*)

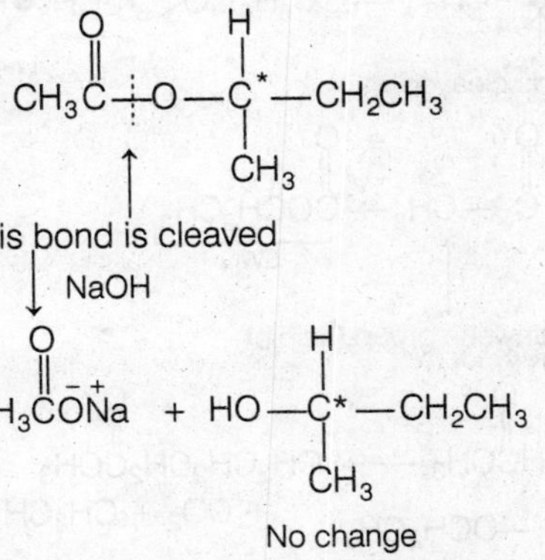

16. (*c*) Keto group is more reactive towards reagent. Hence, when its one equivalent is taken, keto group is converted to 3° alcohol.

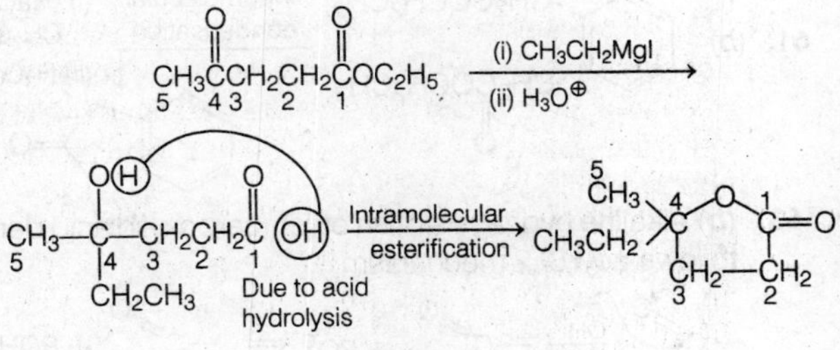

17. (*a*) Hydrolysis of cyclic ester gives **diacid** and then reaction with excess *T* forms normal ester.

18. (*a*)

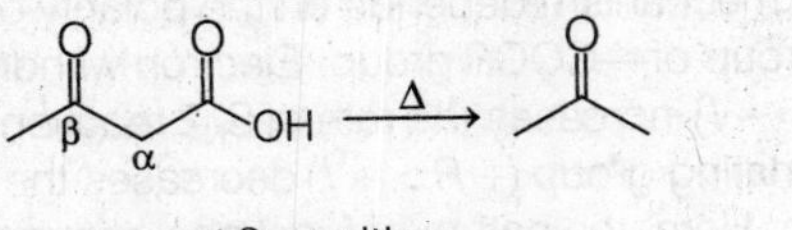

keto group at β-position

20. (*c*) $LiAlH_4$ reduces both ester and carbonyl group. $NaBH_4/CH_3OH$ reduces only carbonyl group.

22. (*a*)

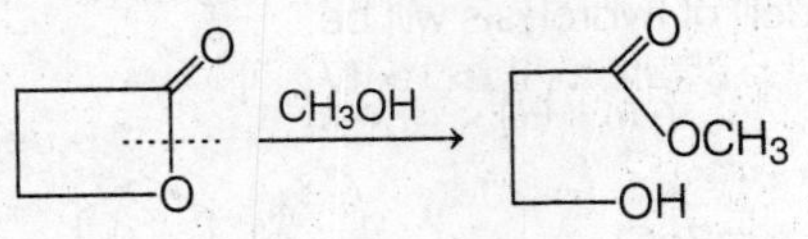

24. (*c*)

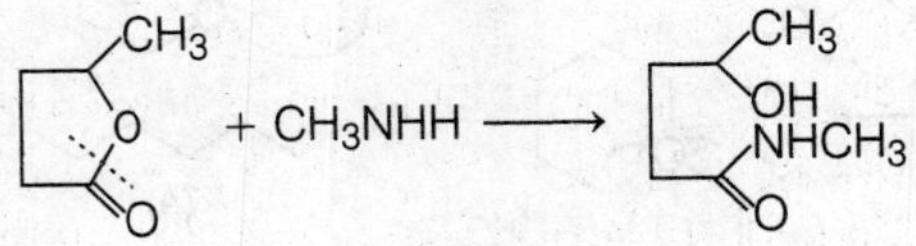

26. (*c*)

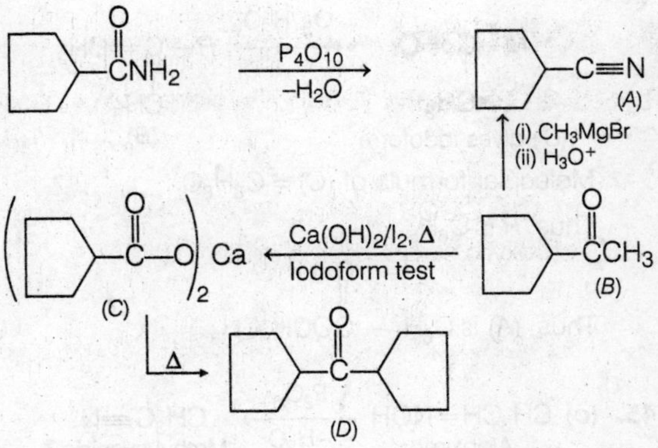

34. (*c*) $NH_2—C(=O)—OH$ (Carbamic acid) $HO—C(=O)—OH$ (Carbonic acid)

37. (*a*) DIBAL-H is diisobutyl aluminium hydride, $[(CH_3)_2CHCH_2]_2AlH$. It is a selective reducing agent. It reduces carboxylic acids, carboxylic acid derivatives and nitriles into aldehydes. It is an electrophilic reducing agent.

The mechanism of the reaction is as follows:

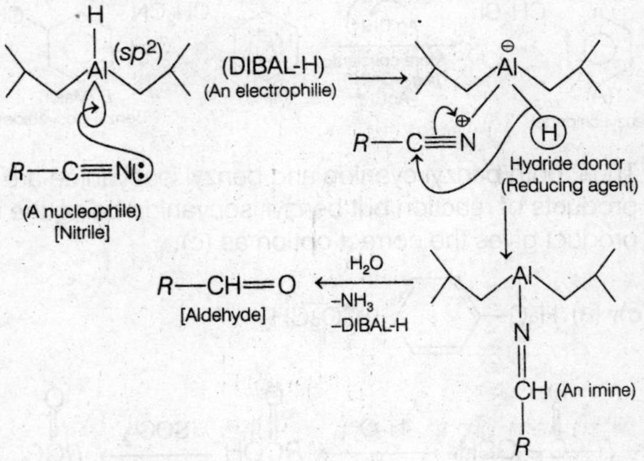

So, $R—CH(=O)$ is the correct answer.

40. (*a*) $RCH_2CH_2OC(=O)—R' \xrightarrow{\Delta} RCH=CH_2 + R'COOH$

41. (*c*) I. Biuret test only for urea
II. A property of amide
III. A property of NH_2 group

42. (*a*) CH_3CN is ethanenitrile

43. (*b*) $C_6H_5COOC_2H_5$ has no α-H *wrt* ester group.

44. (*a*) Ester, $RC(=O)OR' \xrightarrow[\text{(excess)}]{CH_3MgBr} RC(OH)(CH_3)—CH_3 \longrightarrow$

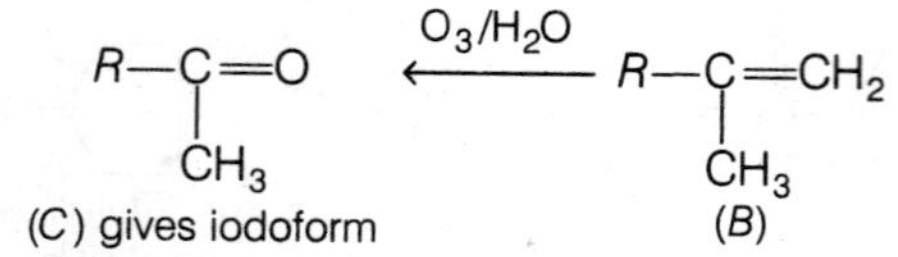

Molecular formula of (C) = C_8H_8O

Thus, R is C_6H_5.

Thus, (A) is $C_6H_5—\overset{O}{\overset{\|}{C}}OCH_2CH_3$.

45. (*c*) $CH_3CH=NOH \xrightarrow[-H_2O]{P_2O_5} CH_3C\equiv N$
Aldoxime — Methyl cyanide

49. (*d*) ($BaSO_4$ is absent hence, CH_3CHO formed is reduced to CH_3CH_2OH).

50. (*c*) The mechanism of the given reaction is as follows:

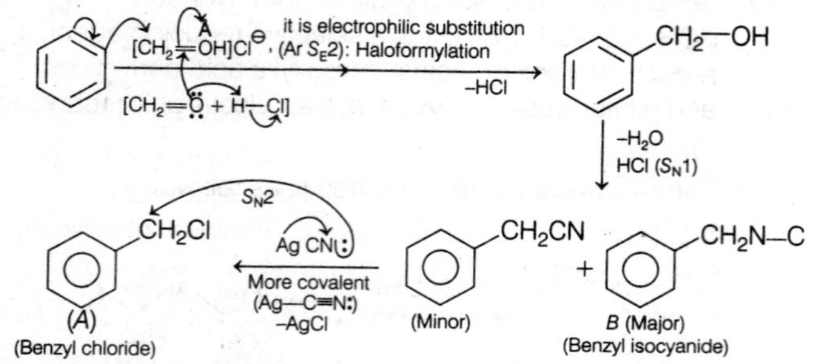

Thus, both benzyl cyanide and benzyl isocyanide are the products of reaction but benzyl isocyanide being the major product gives the correct option as (c).

52. (*c*) (a) 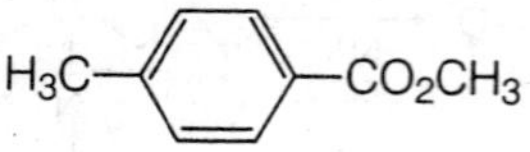

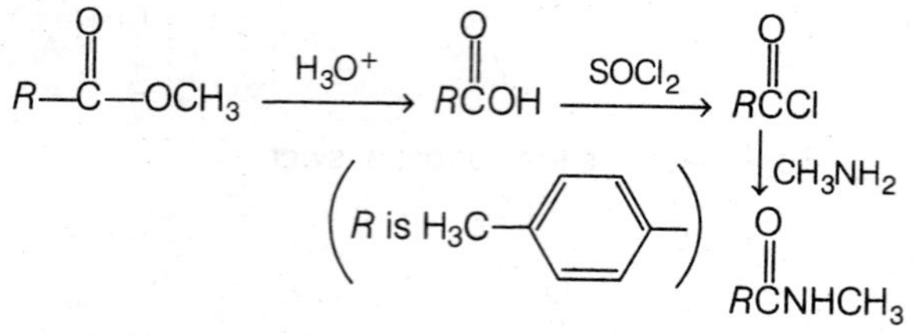

Thus, incorrect.

(c) $R—\overset{O}{\overset{\|}{C}}—OCH_3 \xrightarrow{LiAlH_4} RCH_2OH \xrightarrow{HBr}$

$RCH_2Br \xrightarrow{Mg/ether} RCH_2MgBr \xrightarrow[(ii)\ H_3O^+]{(i)\ CO_2}$

$RCH_2COOH \xrightarrow{SOCl_2} RCH_2COCl \xrightarrow{CH_3NH_2} RCH_2CONHCH_3$

56. (*a*) $H_2C=CHCH_2Br \xrightarrow{NaCN} H_2C=CHCH_2CN$

$\xrightarrow[(ii)\ H_3O^+]{(i)\ C_6H_5MgBr/ether} H_2C=CHCH_2\overset{O}{\overset{\|}{C}}C_6H_5$

58. (*b*) $C_6H_5\overset{O}{\overset{\|}{C}}—\overset{18}{O}—CH_3 \longrightarrow C_6H_5\overset{O}{\overset{\|}{C}}O^- + CH_3\overset{18}{O}H$

This bond is cleaved.

59. (*b*) $CH_3CH_2O\overset{O}{\overset{\|}{C}} \leftarrow CH_2 \rightarrow \overset{O}{\overset{\|}{C}}OCH_2CH_3$
EWG — EWG

Active methylene group (acidic)

60. (*d*) $CH_3CH_2CH(COOCH_2CH_3)\overset{O}{\overset{\|}{C}}CH_3 \xrightarrow{H—O—H} CH_3CH_2CH_2\overset{O}{\overset{\|}{C}}CH_3 + CO_2 + CH_3CH_2OH$

61. (*b*) 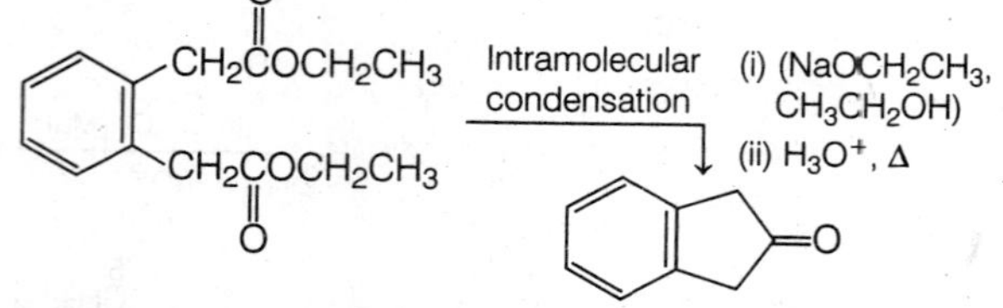

63. (*b*) Alkaline hydrolysis of an ester (carboxylic acid derivative) follows acyl S_N2 mechanism.

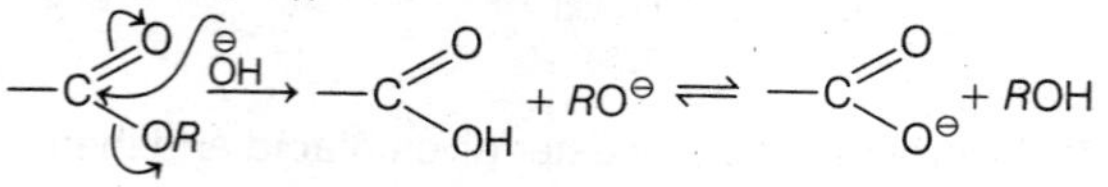

Rate of S_N2 mechanism depends on the polarity of $>C=O$ group of—COO*R* group. Electron withdrawing group ($-R > -I$) increases the rate of S_N2 reaction whereas electron donating group ($+R > +I$) decreases the rate of S_N2 reaction. Here, the nature of functional groups attached *para* to the benzene ring are:

$—NO_2 > —Cl > —OCH_3$
(–R) (–I) (+R)

So, the order of hydrolysis will be,

III > II > I > IV
(–R) (–I) (+R)

65. (*d*) 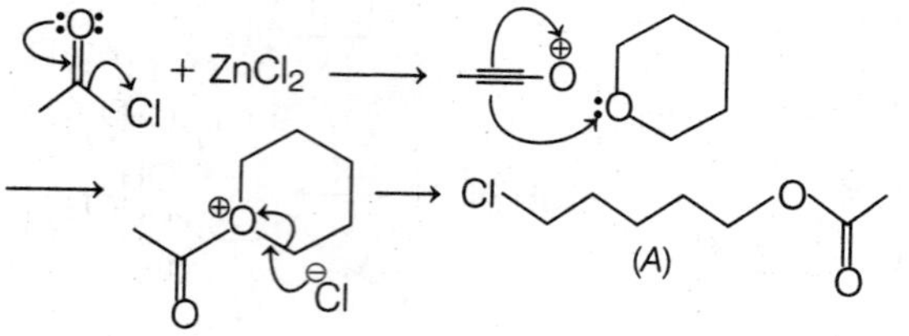

66. (*b*)

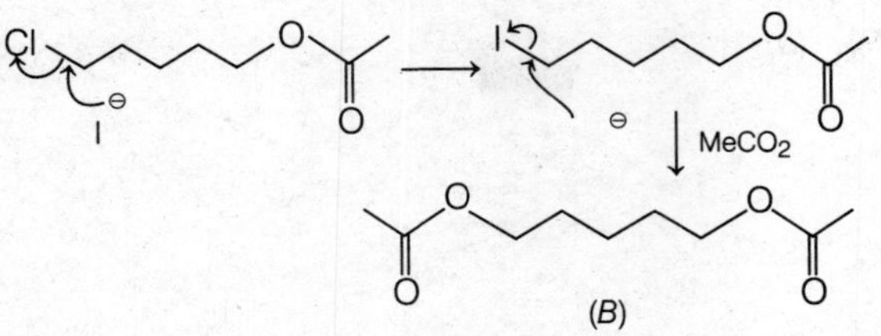

67. (*a*)

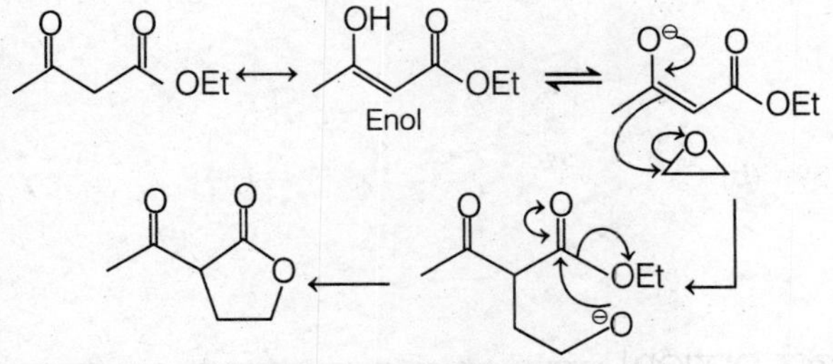

68. (*c*) $CH_3COOH + CH_2CO \longrightarrow (CH_3CO)_2O$

70. (*a*) Rate of esterification

$CH_3OH > 1° > 2° > 3°$

$$R\overset{O}{\overset{\|}{C}}OH + R'OH \longrightarrow R\overset{O}{\overset{\|}{C}}OR' + H_2O$$

Alcohol behaves as an acid.

80. (*c*) $R—\overset{O}{\overset{\|}{C}}—Cl + R'O—H$

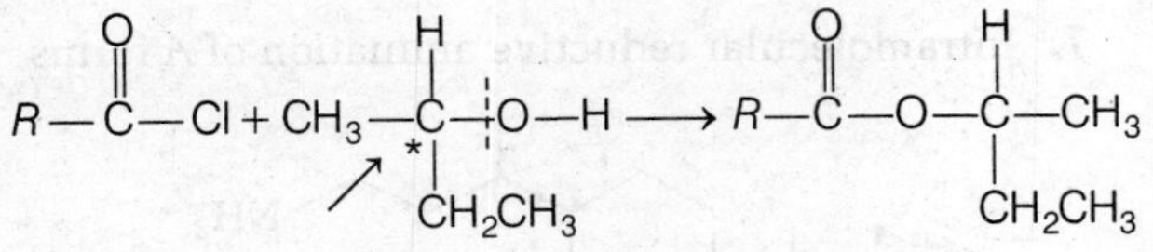

(a) is true, (b) is true

(c) due to chirality two types of ester can be formed.

Thus, (c)

81. (*b*) In presence of strong base, acidic H can easily be removed that result in formation of anion. The resulting anion undergoes intramolecular nucleophilic addition which on hydrolysis followed by heating gives the required product.

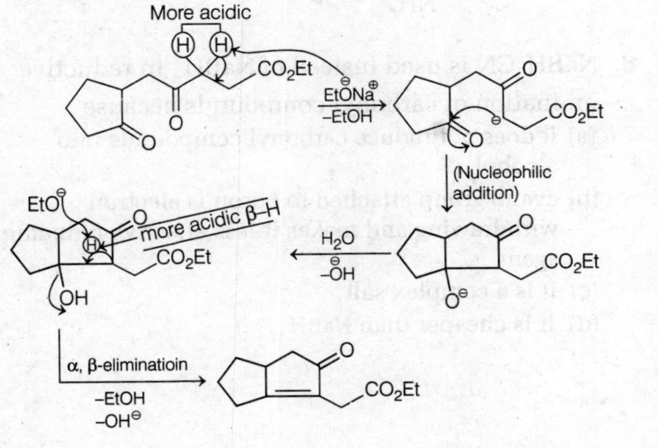

84. (*a*)

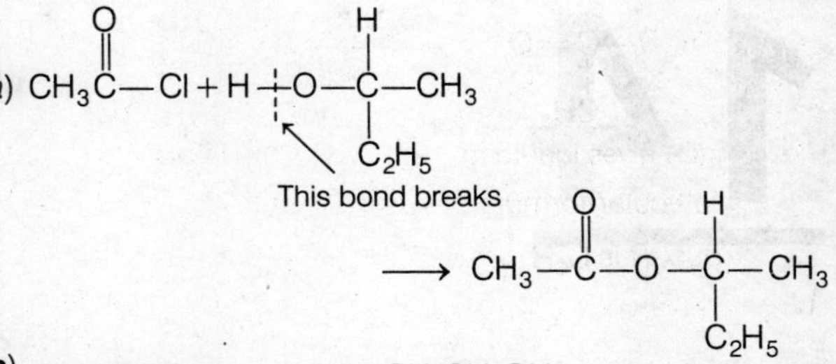

86. (*b*)

(a) $\begin{matrix} CH_2COOC_2H_5 \\ | \\ CH_2COOC_2H_5 \end{matrix} \xrightarrow{LiAlH_4} \begin{matrix} CH_2CH_2OH \\ | \\ CH_2CH_2OH \end{matrix} + 2C_2H_5OH$

(b)

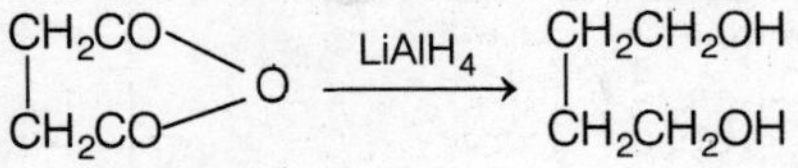

88. (*a*)

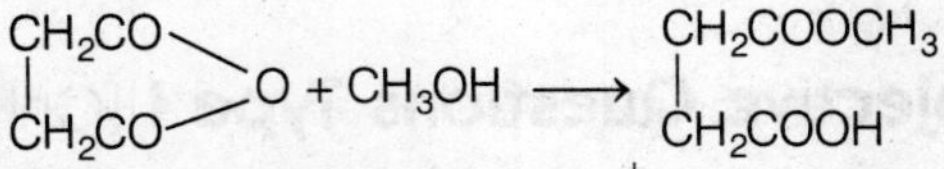

91. (*c*) $RCONH_2 \xrightarrow[\Delta]{NaOH} RCO\overset{-}{O}\overset{+}{Na} + NH_3\uparrow$

94. (*d*) The major product of the given reaction is (d).

This reaction proceed *via* Friedel-Craft acylation. Here, —Cl group present on chlorobenzene is *ortho* and *para*-directing. It can be easily understood by resonating structures of chlorobenzene.

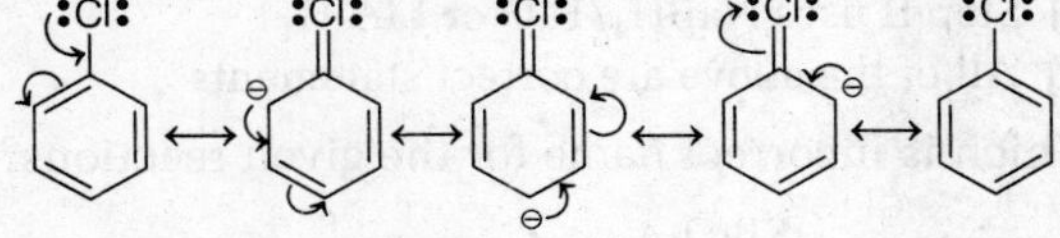

The given reaction proceed as follows :

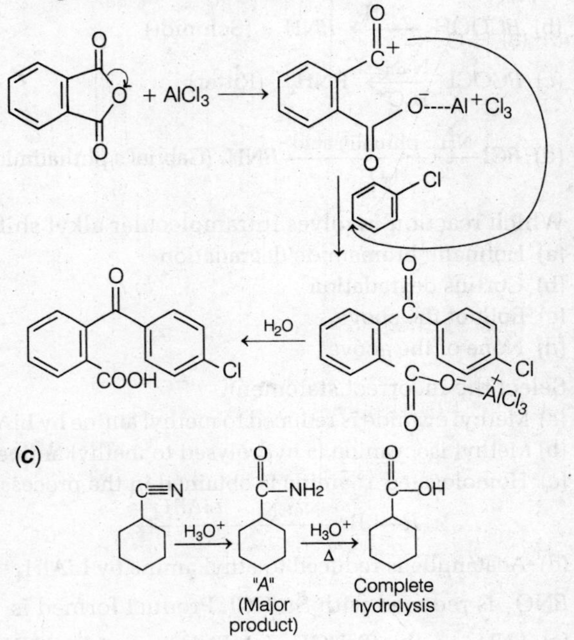

95. (*c*)

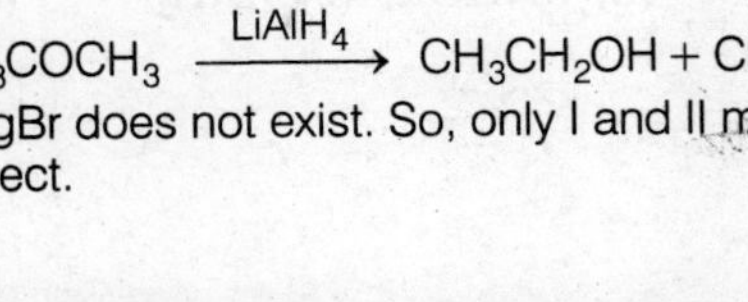

98. (*c*) $CH_3COCH_3 \xrightarrow{LiAlH_4} CH_3CH_2OH + CH_3OH$

HMgBr does not exist. So, only I and II methods are correct.

14

Amines

Objective Questions Type I [Only one correct option]

In each of the questions below, four choices are given of which only one is correct.

1. Select the correct statement(s) about the following reaction.

$$R\text{—Br} + NaN_3 \xrightarrow{\text{I}} RN_3 \xrightarrow{\text{II}} R\text{—}NH_2$$

(a) Step I is an S_N2 reaction
(b) R—Br should be 1° or 2° alkyl bromide
(c) Step II uses $NaBH_4/H_2O$ or $LiAlH_4$
(d) All of the above are correct statements

2. Which is incorrect name for the given reactions?

(a) $RCONH_2 \xrightarrow{KBrO, \Delta} RNH_2$ (Hofmann bromamide)

(b) $RCOOH \xrightarrow{N_3H} RNH_2$ (Schmidt)

(c) $RCOCl \xrightarrow[H_3O^+]{NaN_3} RNH_2$ (Ritter)

(d) $RCl \xrightarrow[H_3O^+]{NH_3,\text{ phthalic acid}} RNH_2$ (Gabriel's phthalimide)

3. Which reaction involves intramolecular alkyl shift?
(a) Hofmann bromamide degradation
(b) Curtius degradation
(c) Both of the above
(d) None of the above

4. Select the incorrect statement.
(a) Methyl cyanide is reduced to methyl amine by $LiAlH_4$
(b) Methyl isocyanide is hydrolysed to methyl amine
(c) Homologated 1° amine is obtained in the process

$$R\text{— Br} \xrightarrow{NaCN} \xrightarrow{LiAlH_4}$$

(d) Acetamide is reduced to ethyl amine by $LiAlH_4$

5. RNO_2 is reduced with Sn/HCl. Product formed is
(a) RNH_2 (b) $RNHOH$ (c) RNH_3^+ (d) R_2NH

6. RNH_2 can be converted into R_2NH (and no other amine) by
(a) its reaction with RX
(b) its reaction with $(CHCl_3/KOH, \Delta)$ followed by reduction
(c) its reaction with $(CHCl_3/KOH, \Delta)$ followed by hydrolysis
(d) All of the above

7. Intramolecular reductive amination of A forms

A :
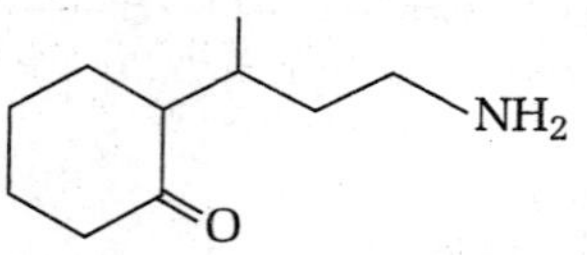

(a)
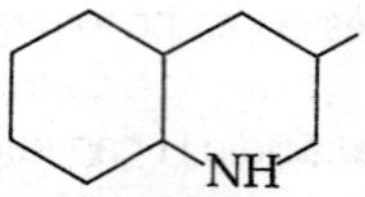

(b)
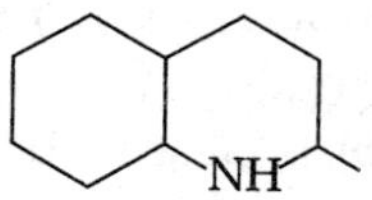

(c)
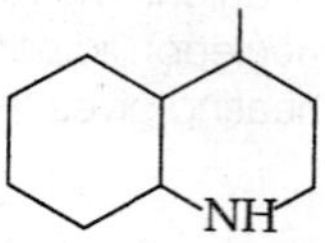

(d)
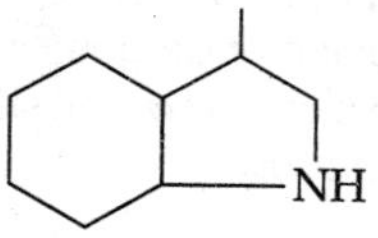

8. $NaBH_3CN$ is used instead of $NaBH_4$ in reductive amination of carbonyl compounds because
(a) it does not reduce carbonyl compounds into alcohol
(b) cyano group attached to boron is electron withdrawing and makes it less effective reducing agent
(c) it is a complex salt
(d) it is cheaper than $NaBH_4$

9. Identify product of the following reaction

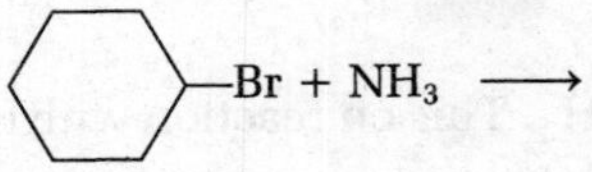

(a) 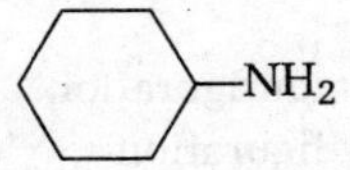 (b) 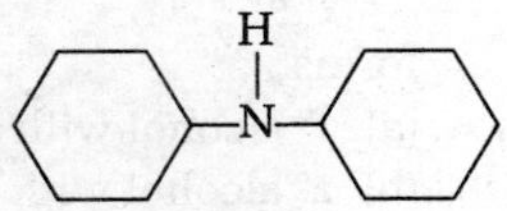

(c) NH_2Br (d) 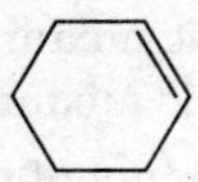

10. CH_3NHCH_3 by reduction amination using CH_2O changes to $(CH_3)_3N$ through an intermediate

(a) carbinolamine $CH_3—N—CH_3$ (N bearing CH_2OH)

(b) imine $CH_3N{=}CH_2$

(c) formyldimethylamine $CH_3—N—CH_3$ (N bearing CHO)

(d) None of the above

11. $C_2H_5NH_2$ and $C_6H_5NH_2$ can be best distinguished by

(a) NaOH

(b) azo dye test

(c) $CHCl_3$ / KOH

(d) Hinsberg's reagent

12. The reduction of which of the following compounds would yield secondary amine?

(a) Alkyl nitrile

(b) Carbylamine

(c) Primary amine

(d) Secondary nitro compound

13. In the following reaction, product formed is

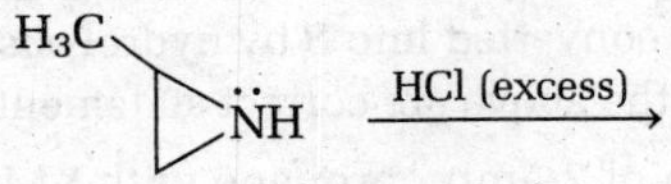

(a) 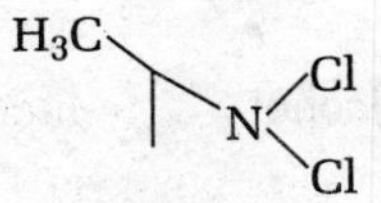 (b) 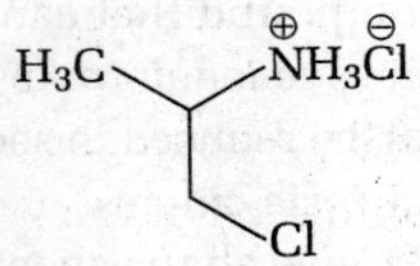

(c) 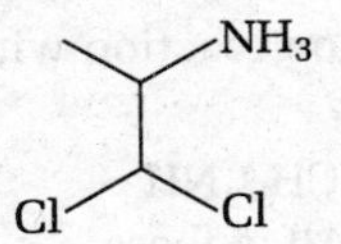 (d) 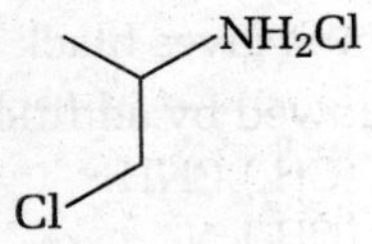

14. 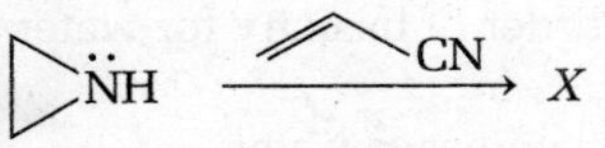

(*X*) is

(a) 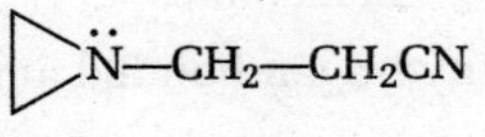 (b) 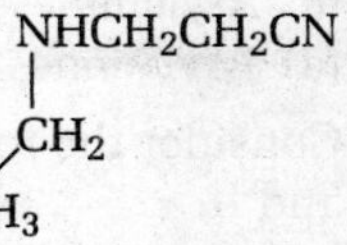

(c) $H_2N—CH_2—CH_2CN$ (d) None of these

15. CH_3NH_2 reacts with α, β-unsaturated ketone as shown

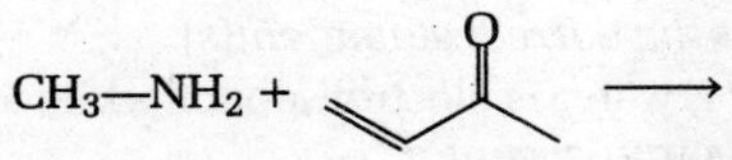

Select the correct statements out of I, II and III.

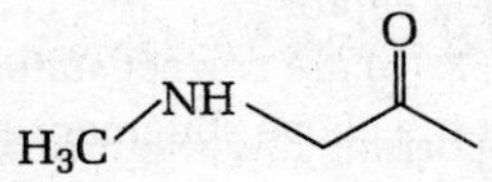

I. Product is by conjugate addition

II. It is called Michael reaction

III. Intermediate is Zwitter ion which tautomerises after the proton transfer

(a) I, II

(b) I, III

(c) II, III

(d) I, II, III

16. Amines are polar compounds because of the

(a) difference in electronegativity between N, C and H

(b) hydrogen bonding

(c) $—NH_2$ group

(d) alkyl group

17. Select the correct statement(s).

(a) Primary and secondary amines are hydrogen-bonding acceptors.

(b) All the three classes of amines are hydrogen-bonding donors.

(c) Tertiary amines cannot hydrogen-bond with other amine molecules because of the absence of a hydrogen bonded to nitrogen.

(d) All of the above are correct statements.

18. In the following compounds, the decreasing order of basic strength will be **[JEE Main 2019, April]**

(a) $C_2H_5NH_2 > NH_3 > (C_2H_5)_2NH$

(b) $(C_2H_5)_2NH > NH_3 > C_2H_5NH_2$

(c) $(C_2H_5)_2NH > C_2H_5NH_2 > NH_3$

(d) $NH_3 > C_2H_5NH_2 > (C_2H_5)_2NH$

19. Which is the general order of basicity for water and amines?
(a) Alkanamines < arylamines < water
(b) Alkanamines > arylamines > water
(c) Arylamines > alkanamines > water
(d) Arylamines > water > alkanamines

20. Consider the following hydrogen-bonded amines I and II,

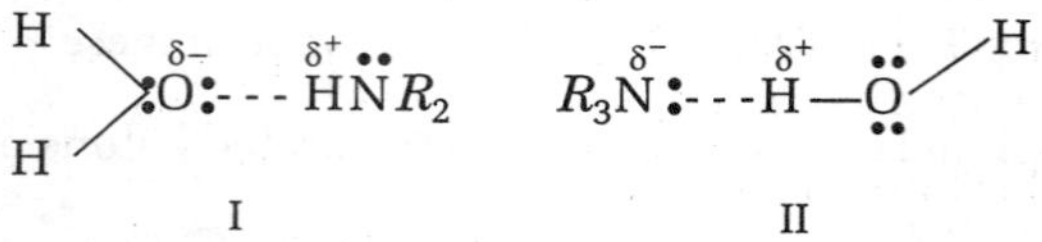

Select the correct statement(s).
(a) In I, water is electron-donor while amine is electron-acceptor
(b) In II, amine is electron-donor while water is electron-acceptor
(c) Both (a) & (b) are correct statements
(d) None of the above statement is correct

21. The increasing order of basicity of the following compounds is **[JEE Main 2018]**

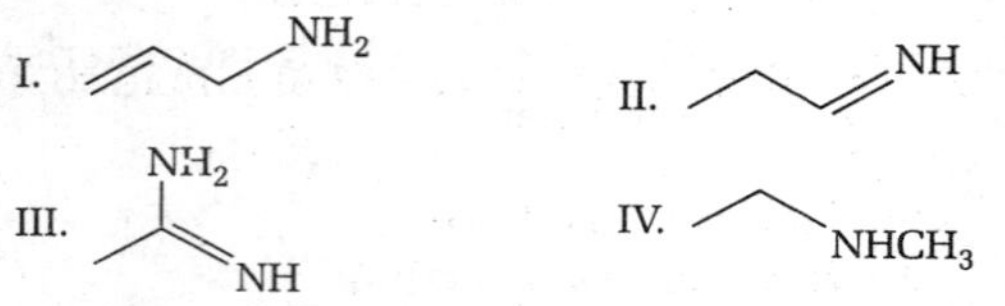

(a) (I) < (II) < (III) < (IV) (b) (II) < (I) < (III) < (IV)
(c) (II) < (I) < (IV) < (III) (d) (IV) < (II) < (I) < (III)

22. When $(CH_3)_3CNH_3^{\oplus}Cl^{\ominus}$ is heated, product is
(a) $(CH_3)_3CCl, NH_4Cl$ (b) $(CH_3)_2C{=}CH_2, NH_4Cl$
(c) $(CH_3)_3CNH_2, HCl$ (d) None of these

23. Select the correct statement (s) about the following reaction

$$[(CH_3)_3N^{\oplus}CH_2CH_3]OH^{\ominus} \xrightarrow{\Delta} (CH_3)_3N + CH_2{=}CH_2 + H_2O$$

(a) This reaction is called Hofmann elimination.
(b) OH^- ion functions as a base in an E2 elimination.
(c) Less substituted alkene is the predominant alkene.
(d) All of the above are correct statements.

24. Major alkene of the following reaction is

$$\underset{\overset{|}{^{\oplus}N(CH_3)_3OH^{\ominus}}}{CH_3CHCH_2CH_3} \xrightarrow{\Delta}$$

(a) $CH_3CH{=}CHCH_3$ (b) $CH_2{=}CHCH_2CH_3$
(c) $(CH_3)_2C{=}CH_2$ (d) $(CH_3)_2C{=}C(CH_3)_2$

25. Exhaustive methylation of $CH_3CH_2NH_2$ forms
(a) $(CH_3CH_2)_4N^{\oplus}OH^{\ominus}$ (b) $(CH_3CH_2)_2\overset{\oplus}{N}(CH_3)_2OH^{\ominus}$
(c) $(CH_3)_3N^{\oplus}(CH_2CH_3)OH^{\ominus}$ (d) None of these

26. Following 1° amine has chiral carbon as indicated

$$H-\overset{\overset{CH_3}{|}}{\underset{\underset{C_6H_5}{|}}{C^*}}-NH_2$$

This on reaction with $(NaNO_2 + HCl)$ forms
(a) 1° alcohol with retention of configuration
(b) 2° alcohol with inverted configuration
(c) racemic mixture of 2° alcohol
(d) racemic mixture of 1° alcohol

27. Major product of the following reaction is

$$\underset{\underset{CH_3}{|}}{CH_3\overset{\overset{NH_2}{|}}{CH}CHCH_3} + O{=}N{-}OH \longrightarrow$$

(a) $CH_3\overset{\overset{N=NOH}{|}}{CH}\underset{\underset{CH_3}{|}}{CH}CH_3$ (b) $CH_3\overset{\overset{OH}{|}}{\underset{\underset{CH_3}{|}}{C}}CH_2CH_3$

(c) $CH_3\overset{\overset{OH}{|}}{CH}\underset{\underset{CH_3}{|}}{CH}CH_3$ (d) $CH_3\underset{\underset{CH_3}{|}}{CH}CH_2CH_3$

28. Benzaldehyde reacts with CH_3NH_2 forming
(a) Schiff base (b) Hofmann base
(c) Saytzeff base (d) None of these

29. Consider the following reaction,

$$\underset{A}{CH_3CONH_2} \xrightarrow{I} \underset{B}{CH_3NH_2} \xrightarrow{II} \underset{C}{CH_3NC}$$

Select the correct statement(s).
(a) Reaction I is called Hofmann bromamide reaction
(b) Reaction II is called carbyl amine reaction
(c) A can be converted into isomeric C using P_2O_5 and C can be converted into B by hydrolysis
(d) All of the above are correct statements

30. Oxidation of 2-aminopropane with $KMnO_4$ forms a compound that can
(a) give iodoform test
(b) be reduced to secondary alcohol
(c) form oximes
(d) give all the above properties

31. Which gives black precipitate on reaction with CS_2 followed by addition of $HgCl_2$?
(a) $(CH_3)_3CNH_2$ (b) $(CH_3)_2NH$
(c) $(CH_3)_3N$ (d) All of these

32. $A + HNO_2 \longrightarrow B \xrightarrow{H_3O^+} A$; A is
(a) primary amine (b) secondary amine
(c) tertiary amine (d) quaternary ammonia salt

33. Primary, secondary and tertiary amines can be separated using **[JEE Main 2021, March]**
(a) *Para*-toluene sulphonyl chloride
(b) chloroform and KOH
(c) benzene sulphonic acid
(d) acetyl amide

34. Distinction between primary and secondary amines is made by
(a) carbyl amine reaction
(b) Hofmann mustard oil reaction
(c) Both (a) and (b)
(d) None of the above

35. Select the incorrect statement.
(a) Secondary amines are oxidised to tetra-alkyl hydrazine by $KMnO_4$.
(b) Caro's acid (H_2SO_5) oxidises secondary amine to nitrosamine.
(c) Nitrosamine is hydrolysed to secondary amine.
(d) Nitrosamine is oxidised to nitramine by CF_3CO_3H.

36. Which is soluble in $NaNO_2$ and dil. HCl mixture forming salt?
(a) $(CH_3)_3CNH_2$
(b) $(CH_3)_2CHNH_2$
(c) $(CH_3)_2NH$
(d) $(CH_3)_3N$

37. $C_4H_{11}N$ on reaction with HNO_2 forms tertiary alcohol. Thus, $C_4H_{11}N$ is
(a) primary amine
(b) secondary amine
(c) tertiary amine
(d) quaternary ammonium salt

38. Tertiary amine is oxidised to oxide by
(a) $KMnO_4$
(b) H_2O_2
(c) $K_2Cr_2O_7$
(d) All of these

39. Cope elimination
(a) is a *syn* elimination reaction
(b) is given by tertiary amine oxide containing β-hydrogen
(c) is intramolecular E2 reaction
(d) follows all the above facts

40. Cope elimination is an intramolecular E2 reaction because
(a) it is given by tertiary amine
(b) it is given by tertiary amine oxide containing β-hydrogen
(c) the nucleophile and leaving group are in the same molecule
(d) the less substituted alkene is the major product

41. Strongest base is
(a) $CH_2{=}CHCH_2NH_2$
(b) $CH{\equiv}C\,CH_2NH_2$
(c) $CH_3CH_2CH_2NH_2$
(d) 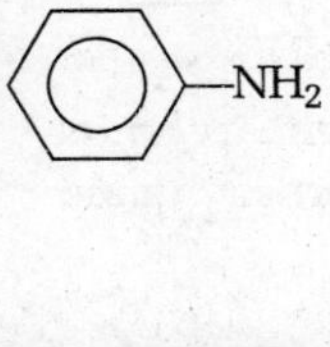

42. The order of basicity among the following compounds is **[JEE Advanced 2017]**

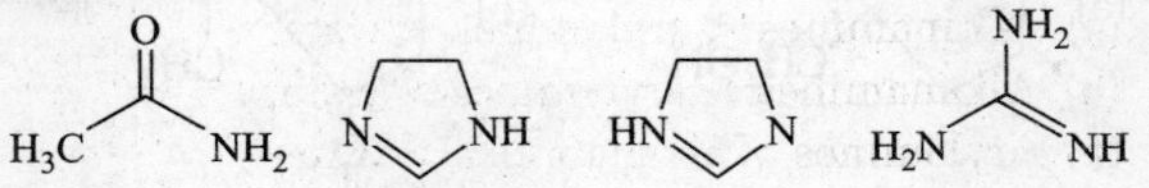

(I) (II) (III) (IV)

(a) II > I > IV > III
(b) I > IV > III > I
(c) IV > I > II > I
(d) IV > I > II > III

43. Strongest base is
(a) 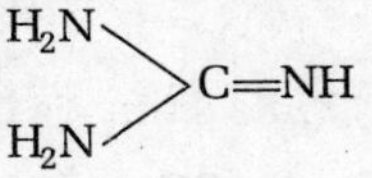
(b) 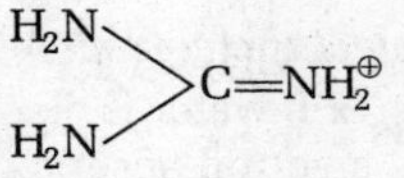
(c) 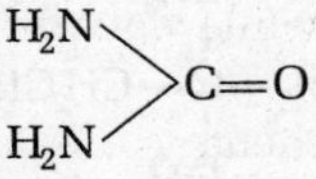
(d) 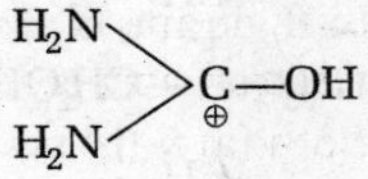

44. Which is the best leaving group?
(a) N_2
(b) $OH^{\ominus}$
(c) $NH_2^{\ominus}$
(d) $CH_3COO^{\ominus}$

45. $RCH_2CH_2NH_2$ does not undergo E2 elimination. It is attributed to
(a) formation of unstable alkene
(b) $NH_2^{\ominus}$ is a very poor leaving group
(c) $NH_2^{\ominus}$ is a very good leaving group
(d) maximum basic nature

46. Thermal decomposition of

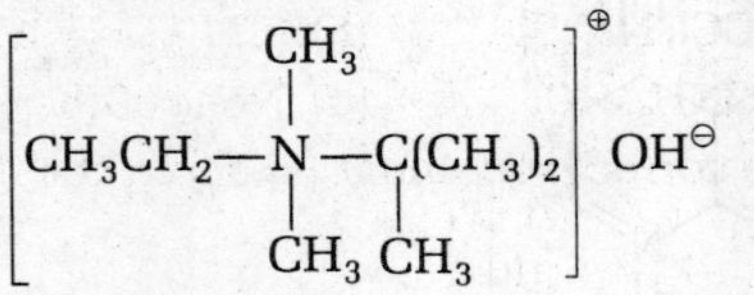

gives
(a) $CH_3CH{=}CH_2$
(b) $CH_2{=}CH_2$
(c) CH_3CH_3
(d) $CH_3CH_2CH_3$

47. A compound '*X*' on treatment with Br_2 / NaOH, provided C_3H_9N, which gives positive carbylamine test. Compound '*X*' is **[JEE Main 2019, Jan.]**
(a) $CH_3COCH_2NHCH_3$
(b) $CH_3CH_2CH_2CONH_2$
(c) $CH_3CON(CH_3)_2$
(d) $CH_3CH_2COCH_2NH_2$

48. 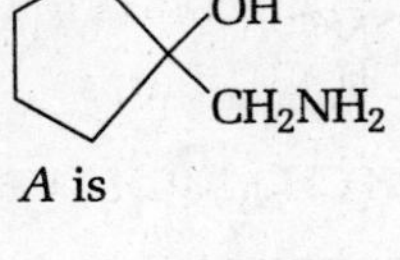 $\xrightarrow{HNO_2}$ *A* (major product);

A is

(a) 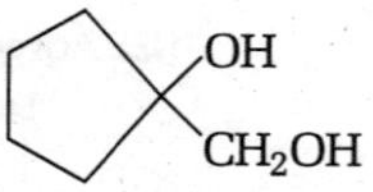
(b) 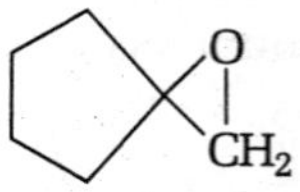

(c) 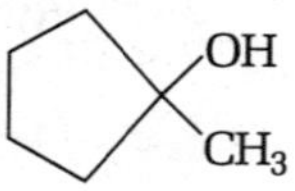
(d) 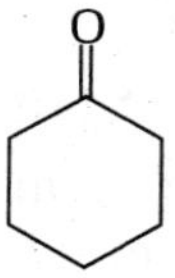

49. $CH_3-\overset{CH_3}{\underset{CH_3}{C}}-CH_2NH_2 \xrightarrow{HNO_2} A$ (major product)

A is

(a) $CH_3-\overset{CH_3}{\underset{CH_3}{C}}-CH_2OH$
(b) $CH_3-\overset{CH_3}{\underset{OH}{C}}-CH_2CH_3$
(c) $CH_3-\overset{CH_3}{\underset{CH_3}{C}}-CH_2N_2^{\oplus}$
(d) $CH_3-\overset{CH_3}{C}-CH=CH_2$

50. 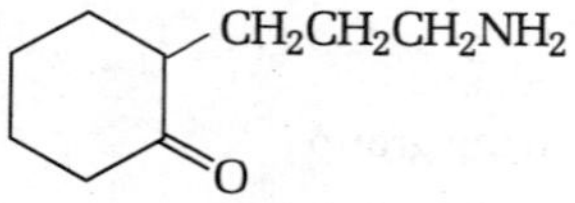 $\xrightarrow[\text{Raney Ni}]{H_2}$ *A*, *A* is

(a) 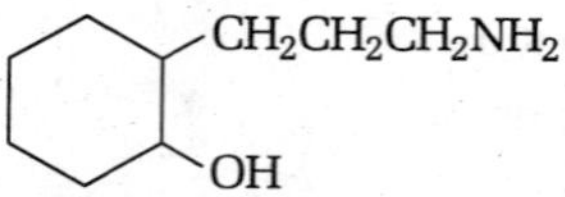

(b) 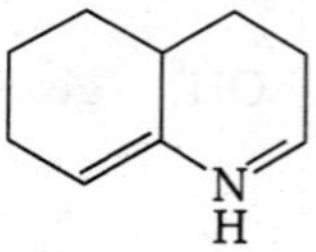

(c) 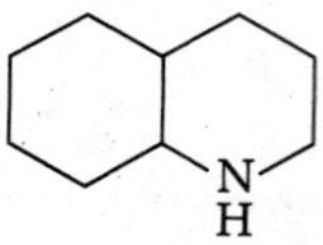

(d) 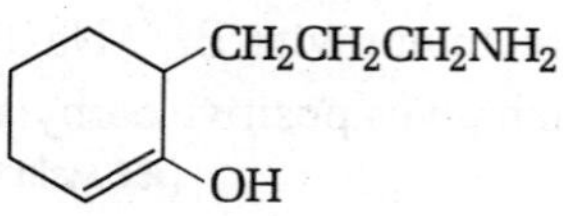

51. Consider the following comparison of basic nature of amines. Correct comparisons are

I. 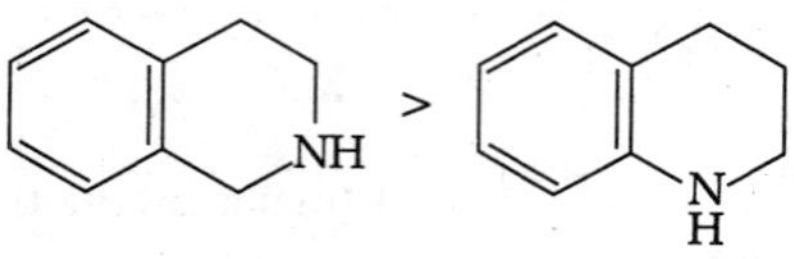

II. 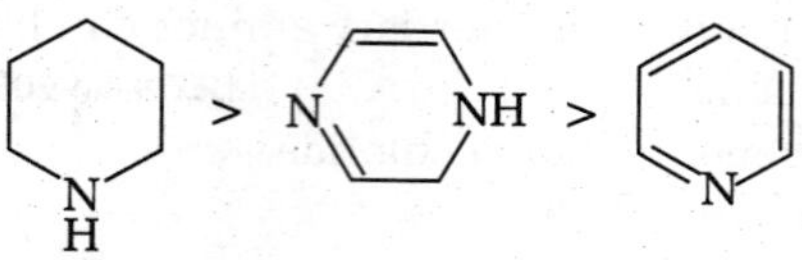

III. 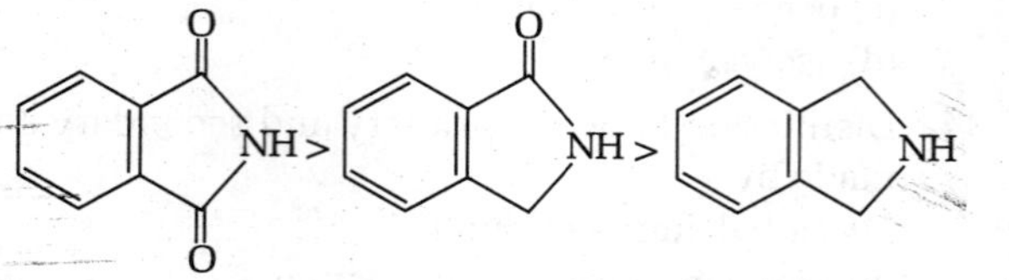

(a) I, II and III
(b) I and II
(c) II and III
(d) I and III

52. Hofmann's elimination product of (*A*) is

(*A*) 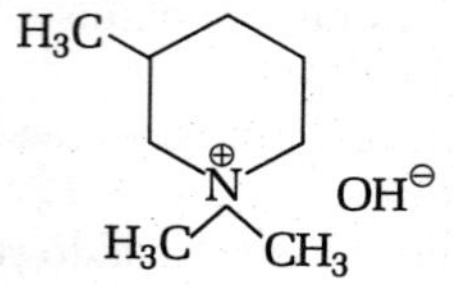

(a) 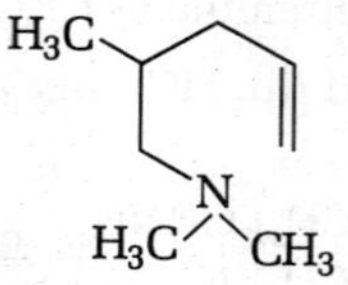
(b) 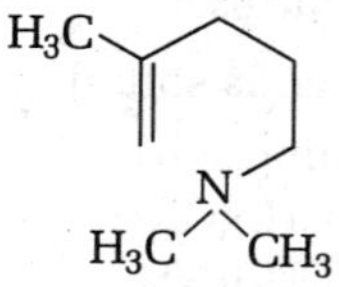

(c) 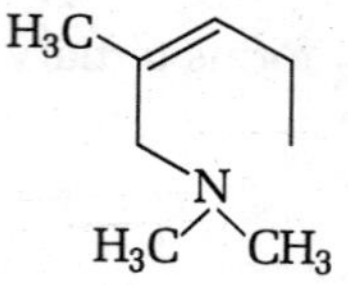
(d) 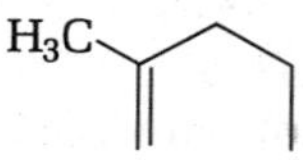

53. 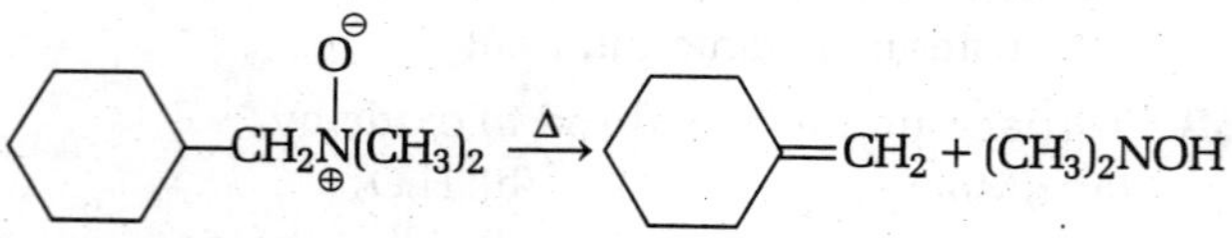

This is called

(a) Hofmann elimination
(b) Cope reaction
(c) Saytzeff reaction
(d) Carbyl amine reaction

54. Which of the following is least basic?

[JEE Main 2021, March]

(a) $(CH_3CO)N_2H_5$
(b) $(C_2H_5)_3N$
(c) $(CH_3CO_2)_2NH$
(d) $(C_2H_5)_2NH$

55. 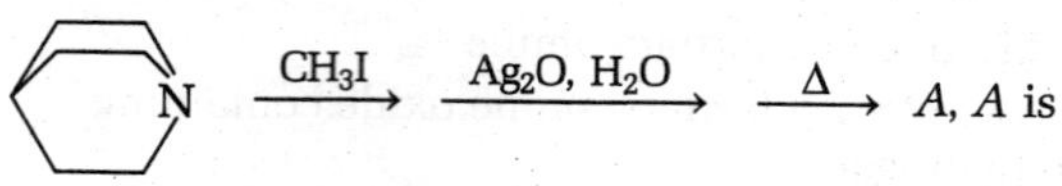

(a) 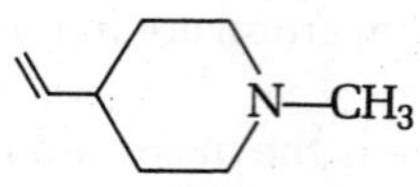
(b) 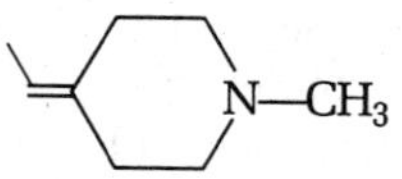

(c) 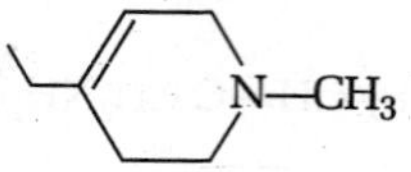
(d) 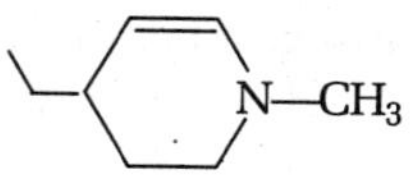

56. Which 'A' gives red colour in the reactions ?

$'A' \xrightarrow[\text{(ii) NaOH}]{\text{(i) HNO}_2} \text{red colour}$

(a) $CH_3CH_2NO_2$ (b) $(CH_3)_2CHNO_2$
(c) $(CH_3)_3CNO_2$ (d) 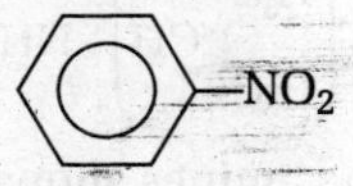

57. $CH_3CH_2CH_2NH_2 \xrightarrow{HNO_2} A \text{ (mixture)}$

Mixture can contain

(a) $CH_3CH_2CH_2OH$ (b) $CH_3CH(OH)CH_3$
(c) 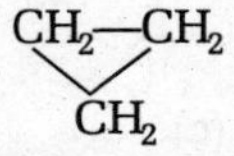 (d) All of these

58. Which of the following is Hofmann mustard oil reaction?

(a) Reaction of primary amine with $CHCl_3$
(b) Reaction of primary amine with $CHCl_3$ + KOH
(c) Reaction of primary amine with $CS_2 + HgCl_2$
(d) Reaction of aromatic amine with iodoform

59. $RCOOH \xrightarrow[\text{Reaction } R']{N_3H, \Delta} \text{product } P$

Product P and reaction R' are

(a) RNH_2, Schmidt
(b) $RCONH_2$, Schmidt
(c) $RCONH_2$, Hofmann
(d) NRH_2, Hofmann

60. $\underset{(X)}{C_4H_{11}N} + HNO_2 \longrightarrow C_4H_{10}O$ (3° alcohol) hence, X will give

(a) carbyl amine reaction
(b) Hofmann mustard oil reaction
(c) diazonium salt (as the intermediate) with HNO_2
(d) All of the above

61. Mixture of 1°, 2° and 3° amines can be separated by

(a) Hinsberg's method
(b) Hofmann's method
(c) distillation
(d) All of these

62. Which is not the correct reaction?

(a) 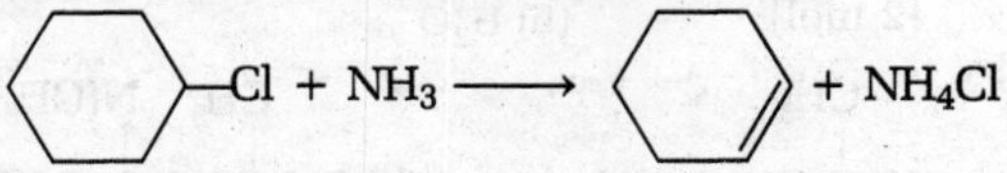
(b) 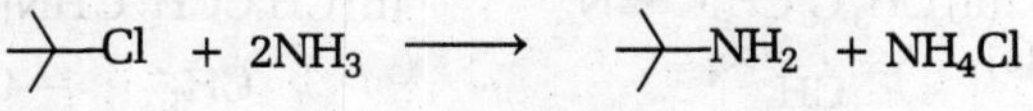
(c) 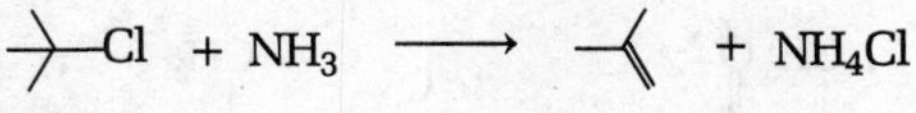
(d) 

63. Basic nature of the following is in order

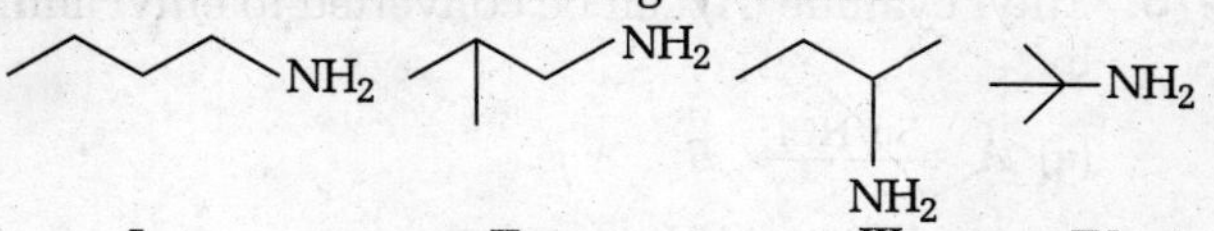

I II III IV

(a) I < II < III < IV (b) IV < II < III < I
(c) I < III < IV < II (d) II < IV < III < I

64. Dipole moment of $\underset{I}{CH_3CH_2CH_3}$, $\underset{II}{CH_3CH_2OH}$, $\underset{III}{CH_3CH_2NH_2}$ will be in order

(a) I < II < III (b) III < II < I
(c) I < III < II (d) II < III < I

65. Which is most volatile?

(a) $CH_3CH_2CH_2NH_2$ (b) $(CH_3)_3N$
(c) 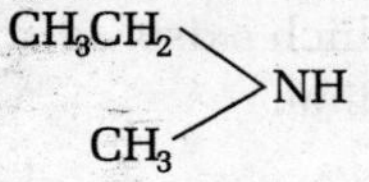 (d) CH_3OH

66. The major products A and B for the following reactions are, respectively **[JEE Main 2019, April]**

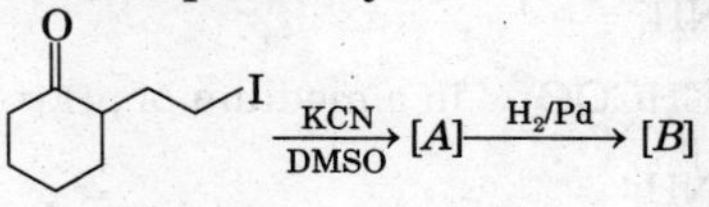

(a) 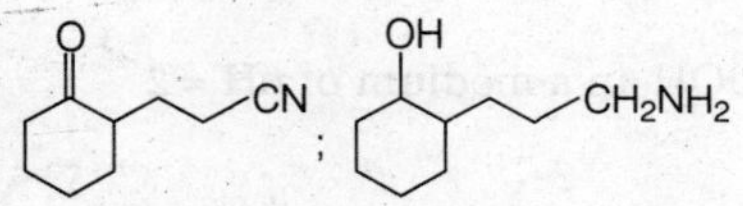

(b) 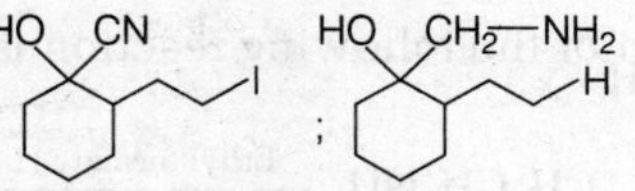

(c) 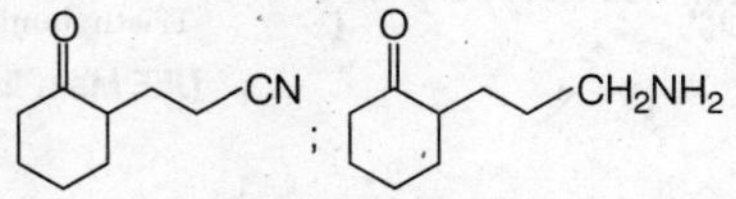

(d) 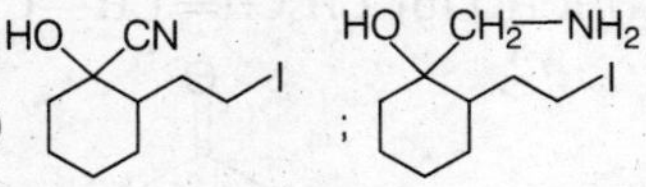

67. Maximum basic in gas phase is

(a) NH_3 (b) $CH_3CH_2NH_2$
(c) $(CH_3CH_2)_2NH$ (d) $(CH_3CH_2)_3N$

68. Which of the following amines can be prepared by Gabriel phthalimide reaction? **[JEE Main 2019, April]**

(a) n-butylamine (b) triethylamine
(c) t-butylamine (d) neo-pentylamine

69. Which is the best method of preparing 2° amine?

(a) $CH_3Cl + NH_3 \longrightarrow$
(b) $CH_3Cl \xrightarrow{KCN} \xrightarrow{Sn/HCl}$
(c) $CH_3Cl \xrightarrow{AgCN} \xrightarrow{LiAlH_4}$
(d) $CH_3NH_2 \xrightarrow[\Delta]{CHCl_3/KOH} \xrightarrow{Sn/HCl}$

70. Ethyl cyanide (A) can be converted to ethyl amine (B) by

(a) $A \xrightarrow{\text{Sn/HCl}} B$

(b) $A \xrightarrow{H_3O^+} \xrightarrow[\Delta]{NH_3} \xrightarrow[\Delta]{KBrO} B$

(c) $A \xrightarrow{LiAlH_4} B$

(d) (a) and (c) are correct

71. Best method of preparing 1° amines from alkyl halide is by

(a) Hofmann bromamide reaction
(b) reaction with NH_3
(c) Gabriel phthalimide reaction
(d) Sandmeyer reaction

72. Alanine forms Zwitter ion which exists as

(a) $CH_3CH(\overset{\oplus}{N}H_3)COO^-$ in acidic medium

(b) $CH_3CH(\overset{\oplus}{N}H_3)COOH$ in a medium of pH = 4

(c) $CH_3CH(NH_2)COO^{\ominus}$ in a medium of pH = 1

(d) $CH_3CH(NH_2)COOH$ in a medium of pH = 2

73. The major product of the following reaction is

$$CH_3CH(OH)CH_2CH_2NH_2 \xrightarrow[\text{Triethylamine}]{\text{Ethyl formate (1 equiv.)}}$$

[JEE Main 2019, April]

(a) $CH_3CH(OH)CH_2CH_2NHCHO$ (b) $CH_3CH{=}CH{-}CH_2NH_2$

(c) $CH_3{-}CH(OH){-}CH{=}CH_2$ (d) 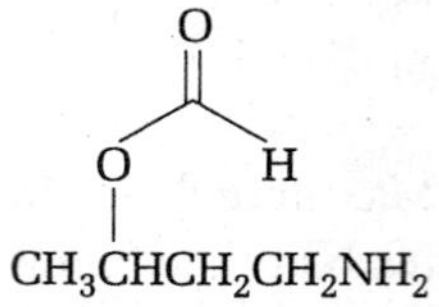

74. Which of the following is a secondary amine?

(a) 2- butanamine
(b) N-ethyl-2-pentanamine
(c) N-methylpiperidine
(d) N, N-dimethylcyclohexylamine

75. Ethylamine ($C_2H_5NH_2$) can be obtained from *N*-ethylphthalimide on treatment with **[JEE Main 2019, April]**

(a) $NaBH_4$
(b) NH_2NH_2
(c) H_2O
(d) CaH_2

76. In which of the following reaction does the amine behaves as an acid ?

(a) $(C_2H_5)_3\ddot{N} + BF_3$ (b) $CH_3NH_2 + H_2O$

(c) $((H_3C)_2CH)_2NH$ (d) $(C_2H_5)_2NH + H_2PtCl_6$

77. The amines shown are isomers. Choose the one with the lowest boiling point.

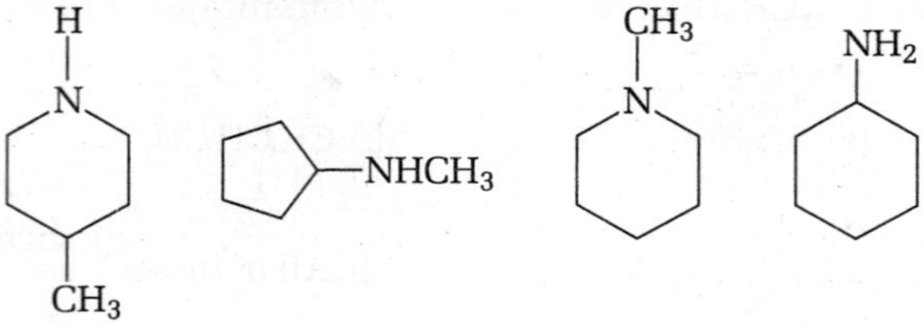

(a) (b) (c) (d)

78. Which of the following statements is not correct?

(a) Primary amine show intermolecular hydrogen bonding.
(b) Secondary amines show intermolecular hydrogen bonding.
(c) Tertiary amines show intermolecular hydrogen bonding.
(d) Amines have lower boiling points as compared to those of alochols and carboxylic acids of comparable molar mases.

79. The reaction,

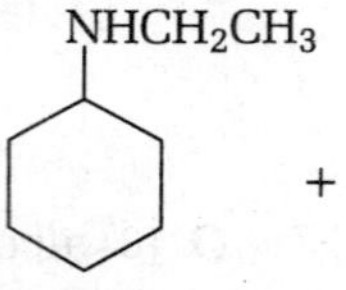

$+ CH_3I$ (excess) $\longrightarrow$?

gives as final product

(a) a primary amine
(b) a secondary amine
(c) a tertiary amine
(d) a quaternary ammonium salt

80. Identify product D in the following reaction sequence

$$CH_3C(CH_3)_2CH_2OH \xrightarrow[H_2O,\ \text{heat}]{K_2Cr_2O_7 \cdot H_2SO_4} A \xrightarrow{SOCl_2}$$

$$B \xrightarrow[(2\ \text{mol})]{(CH_3)_2NH} C \xrightarrow[\text{(ii) } H_2O]{\text{(i) } LiAlH_4,\ \text{diethyl ether}} D$$

(a) $CH_3C(CH_3)_2CH_2C{\equiv}N$ (b) $CH_3C(CH_3)_2CH_2CH(N(CH_3)_2)N(CH_3)_2$

(c) $CH_3C(CH_3)_2CH_2C(=O)N(CH_3)_2$ (d) $CH_3C(CH_3)_2CH_2CH_2N(CH_3)_2$

81. What will be the major product of each of the two reactions shown?

1. $CH_3CH_2CHCH_3$ with $^+N(CH_3)_3\,^-OH$ on C-2, heat

2. CH_3CH_2CHBr with CH_3 on C-2, heat, $+ CH_3CH_2ONa$

$\longrightarrow$ $\underset{X}{CH_3CH{=}CHCH_3}$ + $\underset{y}{CH_3CH_2CH{=}CH_2}$

(a) $1X, 2X$ (b) $1Y, 2X$
(c) $1X, 2Y$ (d) $1Y, 2Y$

82. The major products from the following sequence of reactions are

$$(CH_3)_2CHCH_2N(CH_2CH_3)_2 \xrightarrow{CH_3I} \xrightarrow[H_2O]{Ag_2O} \xrightarrow{heat} ?$$

(a) $(CH_3)_2CHCH_2NH_2 + H_2C{=}CH_2$
(b) $(CH_3)_2NCH_2CH_3 + H_2C{=}C(CH_3)_2$
(c) $(CH_3)_2CHCH_2\overset{CH_3}{N}CH_2CH_3 + H_2C{=}CH_2$
(d) $(CH_3)_3\overset{+}{N}CH_2CH_3I^- + H_2C{=}CH_2$

83. Hofmann bromamide degradation of benzamide gives product A, which upon heating with CHCl3 and NaOH gives product B. The structures of A and B are **[JEE Main 2021, March]**

(a) 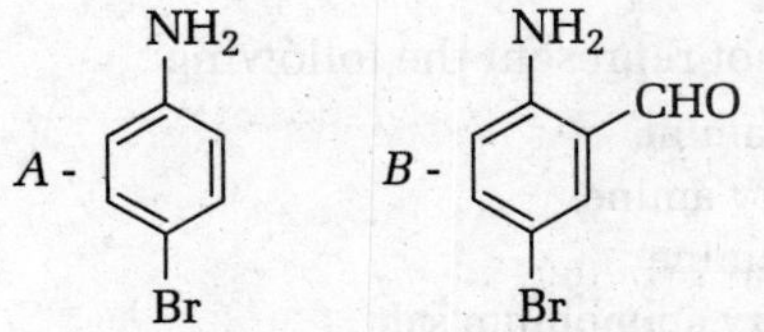

(b) 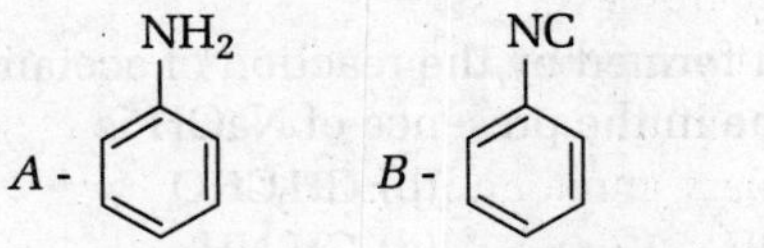

(c) 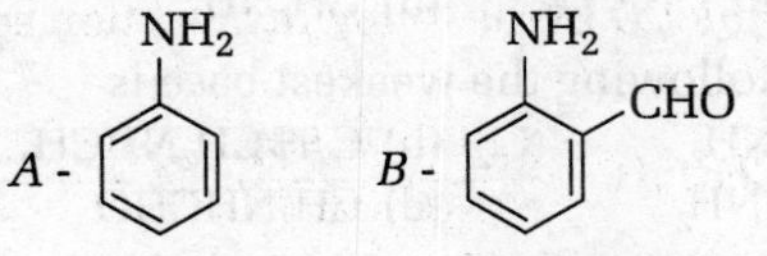

(d) 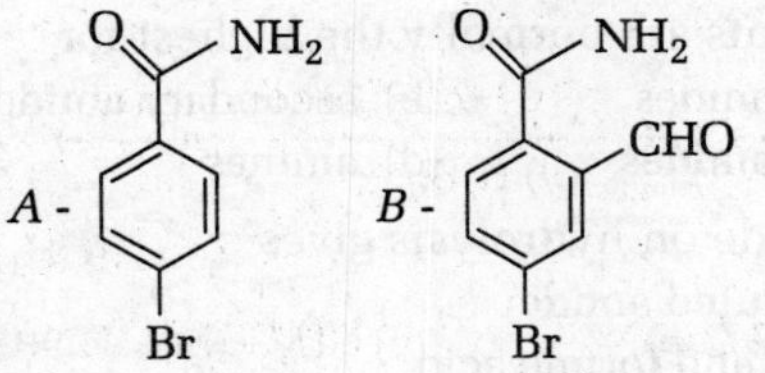

84. Which has maximum boiling point ?

(a) 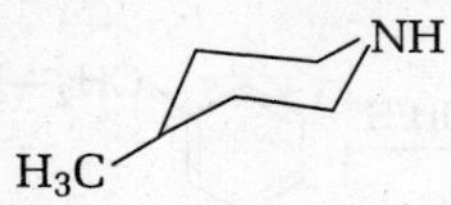 (b) 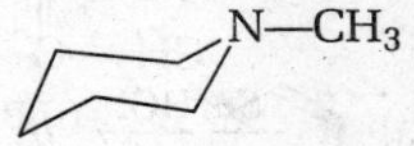

(c) $(CH_3)_3N$ (d) 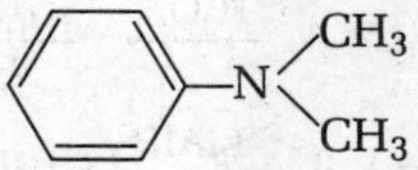

85. The major organic product formed from the following reaction is

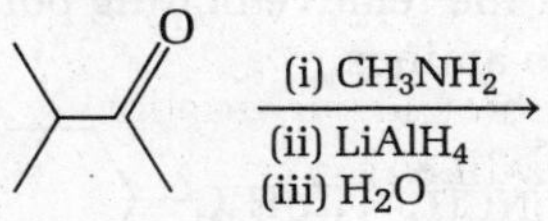

(a) 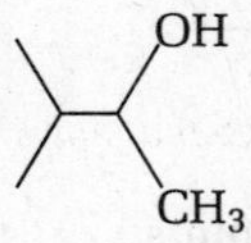 (b) 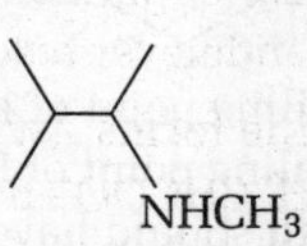

(c) 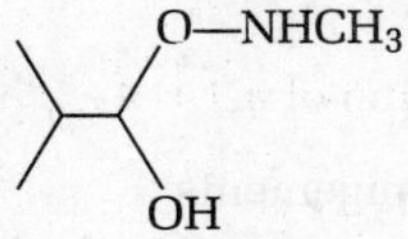 (d) 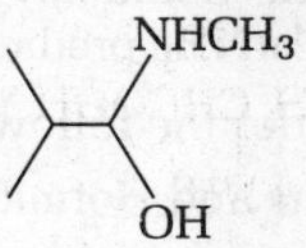

86. Primary amine reacts with carbon disulphide in presence of excess of mercuric chloride and produce isothiocyanate. This reaction is known as
(a) Hofmann bromamide reaction
(b) Hofmann mustard oil reaction
(c) carbyl amine reaction
(d) mercuration-demercuration reaction

87. Which of the following chemicals are used to manufacture methyl isocyanide that caused "Bhopal Tragedy"?

I. methyl amine II. chloroform/KOH
III. phosphine IV. dimethyl amine

(a) I and III
(b) III and IV
(c) I and II
(d) II and IV

88. Which of the following reaction does not involve Hofmann bromamide degradation ? **[JEE Main 2021, March]**

(a) 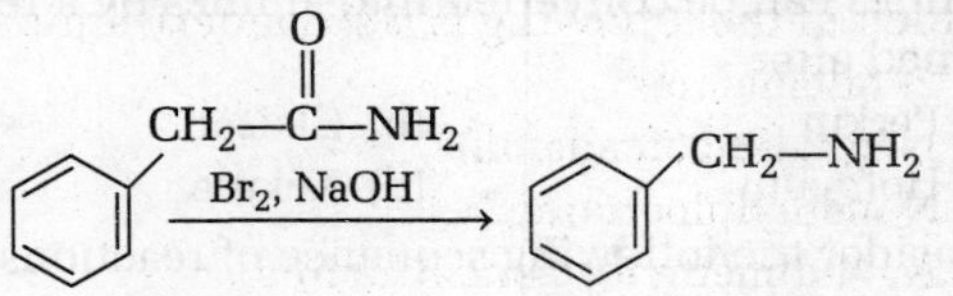

(b) 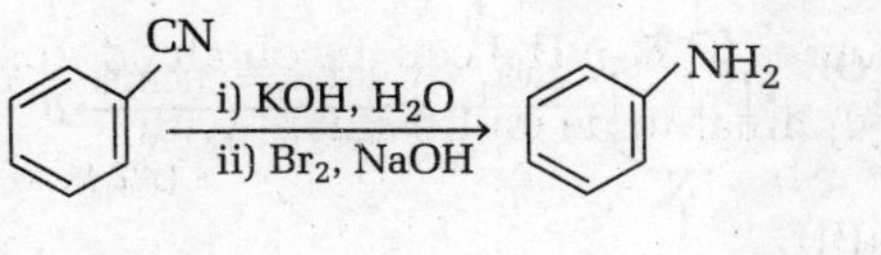

(c) 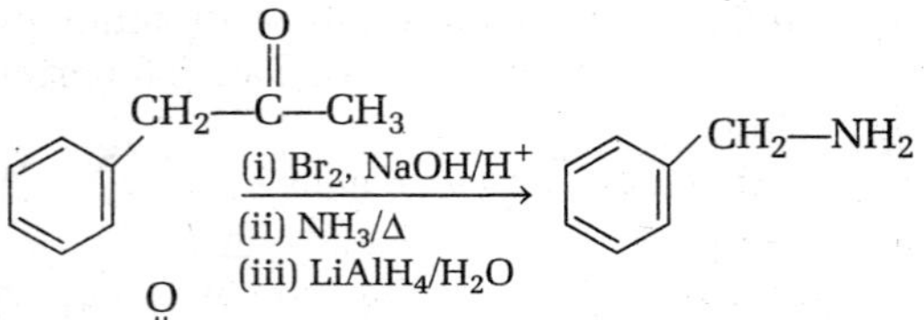

(d) 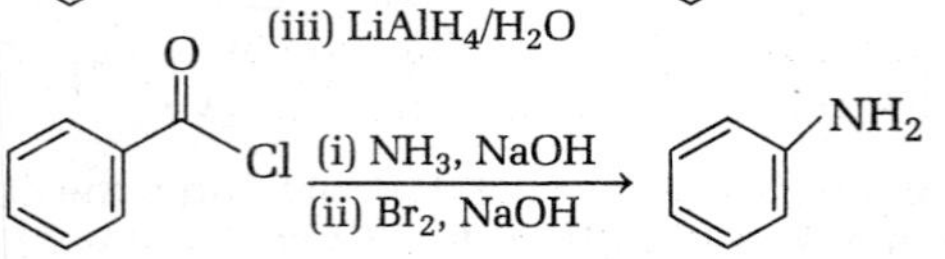

89. Predict about the relative boiling point of the following two amines.

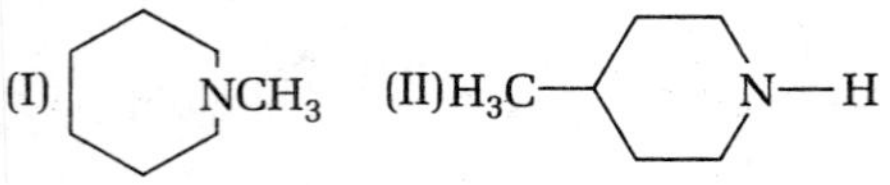

(a) Boiling point of I > II
(b) Boiling point of II > I
(c) Both should have equal boiling points
(d) It can't be predicted

90. Consider the following facts,

Curtius and Hofmann rearrangements

I. are synthetic methods of preparation of primary amines.
II. involve intramolecular alkyl/arylemigration.
III. involve isocyanate as an intermediate.
IV. take place with complete retention of stereochemical configuration in the migrating alkyl group.

Select the correct facts.

(a) I, II and III
(b) II, III and IV
(c) I, III and IV
(d) All of these

91. The compound obtained by heating a mixture of a primary amine and chloroform with ethanolic potassium hydroxide (KOH) is
(a) an isocyanide
(b) an halide
(c) an amide
(d) an amide and nitro compound

92. Amides can be converted into amines by a reaction named after
(a) Perkin (b) Claisen
(c) Hofmann (d) Kekule

93. Consider the following sequence of reactions

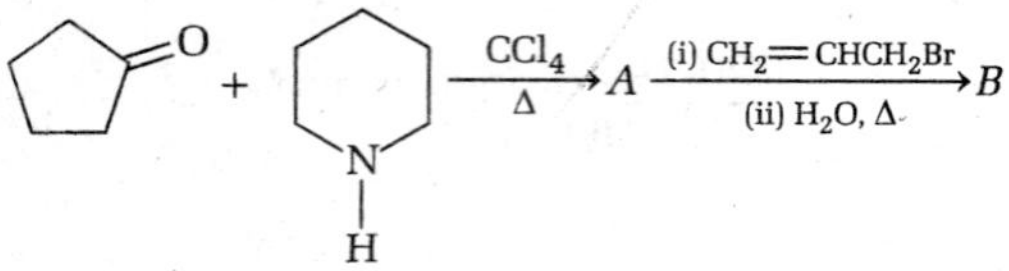

(a) 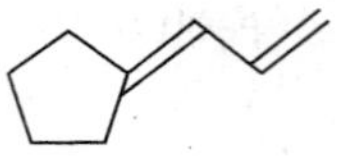 (b) 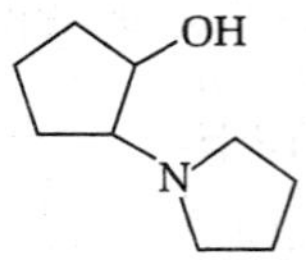

(c) 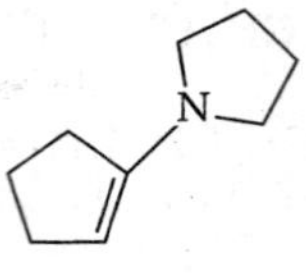 (d) 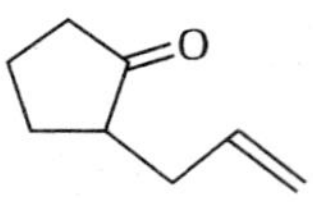

94. The most reactive amine towards dilute HCl is
(a) CH_3NH_2 (b) $(CH_3)_2NH$ (c) $(CH_3)_3N$ (d) $C_6H_5NH_2$

95. The major product of the following reaction is **[JEE Main 2019, Jan.]**

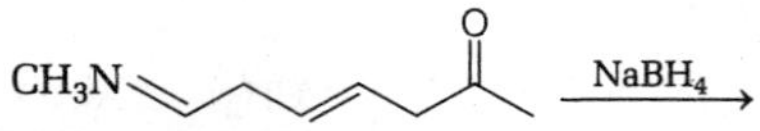

(a) 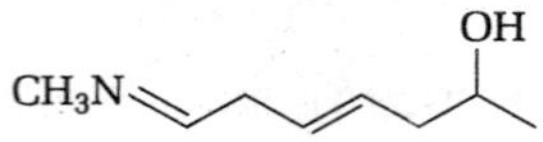

(b) 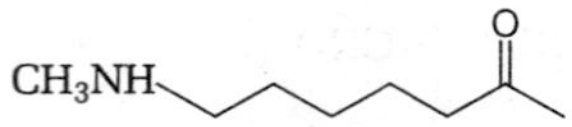

(c) 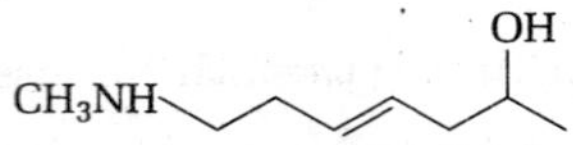

(d) 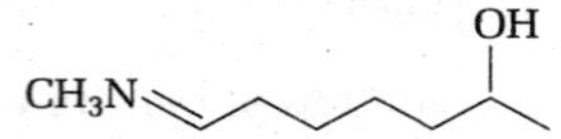

96. Secondary amine is formed by the reduction of
(a) methyl isocyanide (b) methyl cyanide
(c) nitrobenzene (d) nitrotoluene

97. C_3H_9N cannot represent the following
(a) primary amine
(b) secondary amine
(c) tertiary amine
(d) quaternary ammonium salt

98. The product formed by the reaction of acetamide with bromine in the presence of NaOH is
(a) CH_3CN (b) CH_3CHO
(c) CH_3CH_2OH (d) CH_3NH_2

99. Among the following the weakest base is
(a) $C_6H_5CH_2NH_2$ (b) $C_6H_5CH_2NHCH_3$
(c) $O_2N \cdot CH_2NH_2$ (d) CH_3NHCHO

100. Melting points are normally the highest for
(a) tertiary amides (b) secondary amides
(c) primary amides (d) amines

101. An isocyanide on hydrolysis gives
(a) N-substituted amide
(b) 1°-amine and formic acid
(c) carboxylic acid and ammonia
(d) an amide

102. Major product of the following reaction is

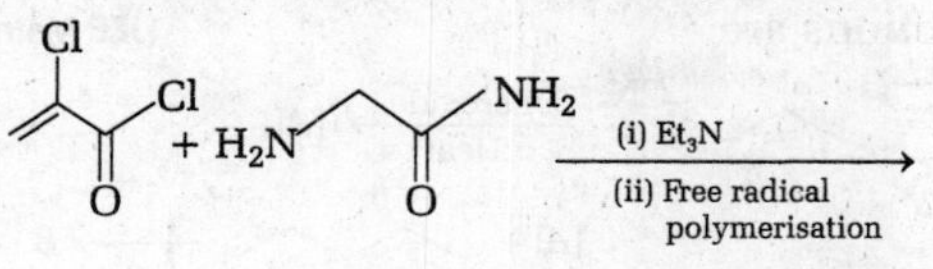

[JEE Main 2021]

(a) 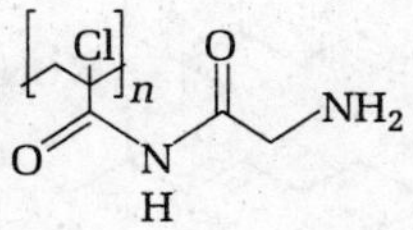
(b) 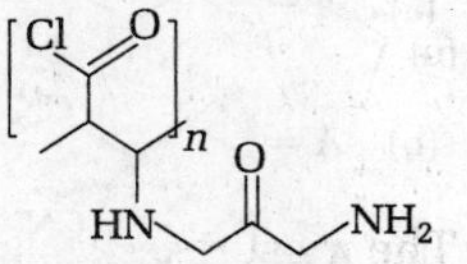
(c) 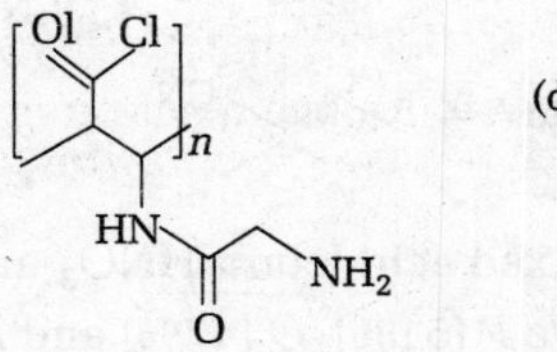
(d) 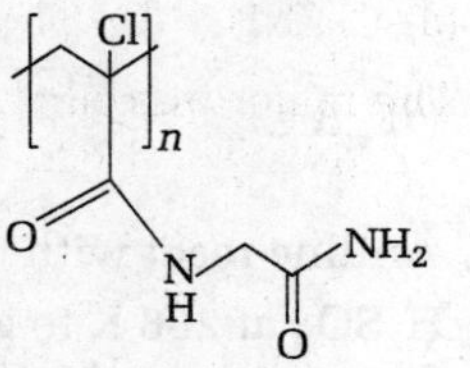

103. Pyridine is less basic than triethylamine because
(a) pyridine has aromatic character
(b) nitrogen in pyridine is sp^2-hybridised
(c) pyridine is a cyclic system
(d) in pyridine, lone pair of nitrogen is delocalised

104. The correct structure of product '*P*' in the following reaction is

$$\text{Asn}-\text{Ser}+\underset{\text{(Excess)}}{(CH_3CO)_2O}\xrightarrow{NEt_3}P$$

[JEE Main 2019, Jan.]

(a) 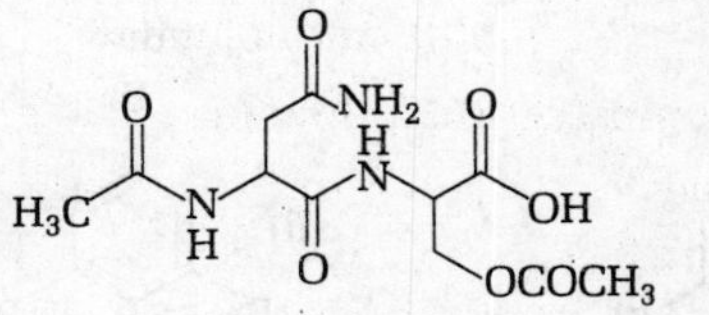
(b) 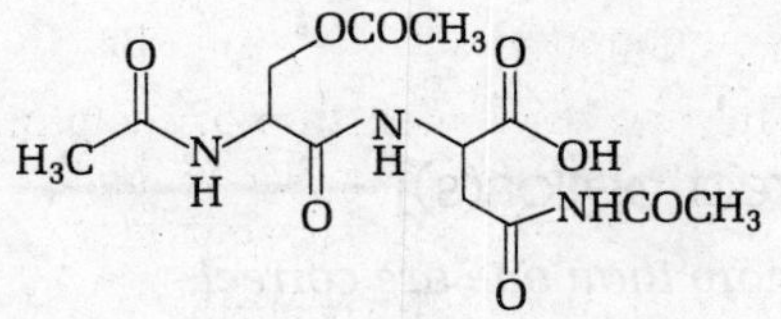
(c) 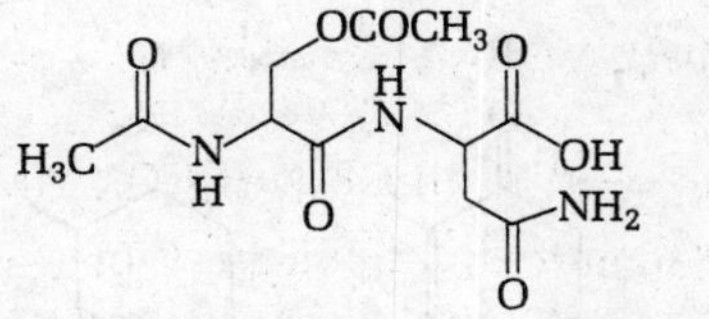
(d) 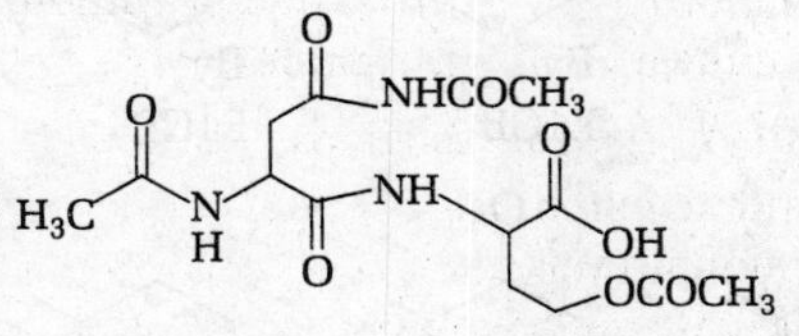

105. A primary amine on treatment with carbon disulphide and $HgCl_2$ produces black ppt and
(a) alkyl cyanide
(b) alkyl isothiocyanate
(c) alkyl cyanate
(d) carbylamine

106. A primary amine is formed from an amide by the treatment with bromine and alkali. The primary amine has
(a) 1 carbon atom less than amide
(b) 1 carbon atom more than amide
(c) 1 hydrogen atom less than amide
(d) 1 hydrogen atom more than amide

107. In the following sequence of reactions, the compound *C* formed would be

$$\underset{\underset{NH_2}{|}}{CH_3CHCH_3}\xrightarrow{HNO_2}A\xrightarrow{\text{Oxidation}}B\xrightarrow[H^+/H_2O]{CH_3MgI}C$$

(a) 1,1-dimethyl ethanol
(b) 1-butanol
(c) 2-butanol
(d) 2-methyl-2-propanol

108. Acetamide and ethyl amine are distinguished by reacting with
(a) Br_2 water
(b) acidic $KMnO_4$
(c) aq. NaOH and heat
(d) aq. HCl and heat

109. $C_2H_5NH_2\xrightarrow{HNO_2}A\xrightarrow{PCl_5}B\xrightarrow{NH_3}C.$
The compound '*C*' is identified as
(a) acetamide
(b) ethyl amine
(c) ethyl cyanide
(d) methyl amine

110. The reaction in which primary amine is not formed
(a) $CH_3NC\xrightarrow{LiAlH_4}$
(b) $CH_3CONH_2\xrightarrow{LiAlH_4}$
(c) $CH_3CN\xrightarrow{LiAlH_4}$
(d) $CH_3CONH_2\xrightarrow{KOH/Br_2}$

111. Which of the following is the weakest Bronsted base?
(a) 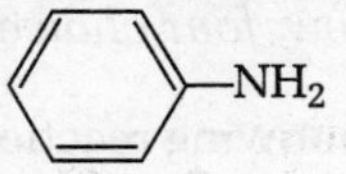
(b) 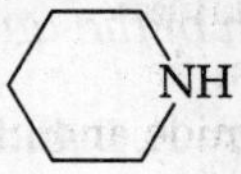
(c) 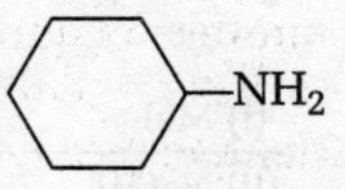
(d) CH_3NH_2

112. The product(s) of the following reaction sequence is (are) **[JEE Advanced 2016]**

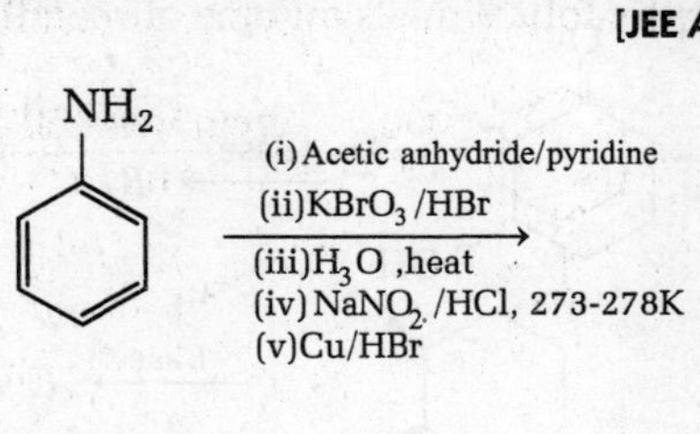

(a) 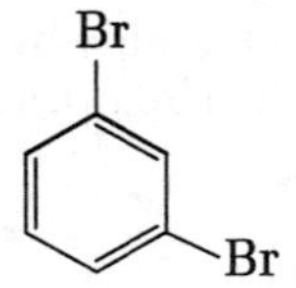 (b) 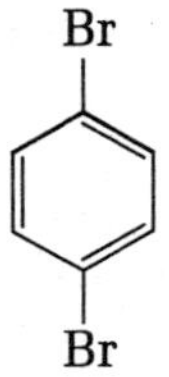

(c) 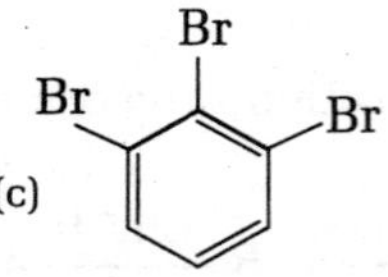 (d) 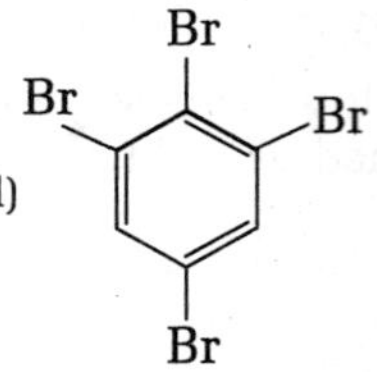

113. In order to prepare 1° amine with simultaneous addition of one CH_2 group in the C-chain, the reagent used is
(a) $NaNH_2$
(b) NaN_3
(c) KCN
(d) $C_6H_4(CO_2)N^-K^+$

114. The source of nitrogen in Gabriel synthesis of amine of
(a) NaN_3
(b) $NaNO_2$
(c) KCN
(d) $C_6H_4(CO_2)_2N^-K^+$

115. For preparing 2° amine, most appropriate method is
(a) $\underset{1^\circ}{NH_3 + 2RBr} \longrightarrow$
(b) $\underset{1^\circ}{2RBr} + NaCN \longrightarrow \xrightarrow{Pt/H_2}$
(c) $RNH_2 \xrightarrow{RCHO} \xrightarrow{Pt/H_2}$
(d) 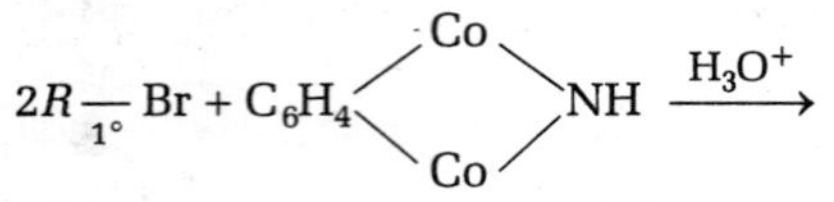

116. The major products *A* and *B* in the following reactions are **[JEE Main 2020, Jan.]**

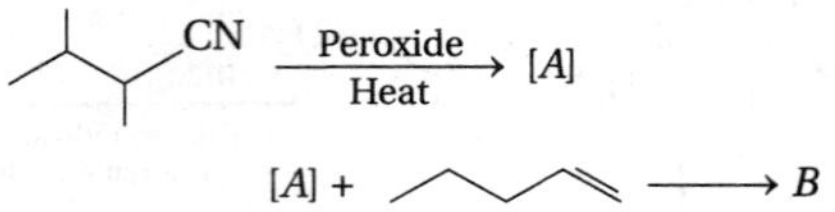

(a) $A =$ 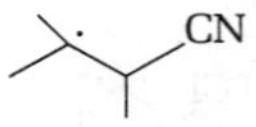 and $B =$ 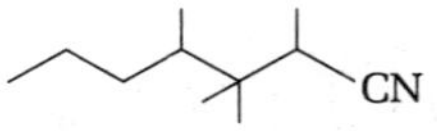
(b) $A =$ 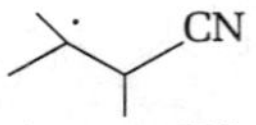 and $B =$ 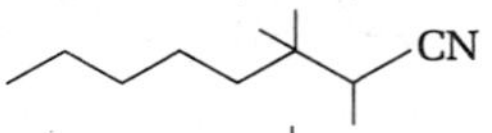
(c) $A =$ 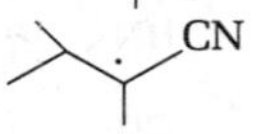 and $B =$ 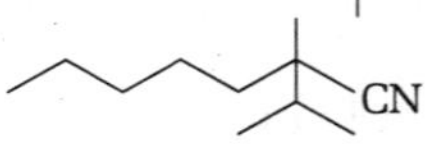
(d) $A =$ 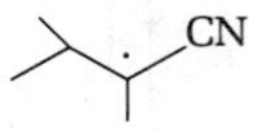 and $B =$ 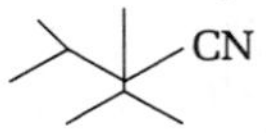

117. Aniline react with mixed acid (conc. HNO_3 and conc. H_2SO_4 at 288 K to give *P* (51%), *Q* (47%) and *R* (2%). The major product(s) of the following reaction sequence is (are) **[JEE advance 2018]**

$$R \xrightarrow[\text{(iii) } H_3O^+ \text{ (iv) } NaNO_2,\ HCl/273\text{-}278\ K \text{ (v) EtOH, } \Delta]{\text{(i) } Ac_2O,\text{ pyridine (ii) } Br_2,\ CH_3CO_2H} S \xrightarrow[\text{(iii) } NaNO_2,\ HCl/273\text{-}278\ K \text{ (iv) } H_3PO_2]{\text{(i) } Sn/HCl \text{ (ii) } Br_2/H_2O \text{ (excess)}} \text{Major product(s)}$$

(a) 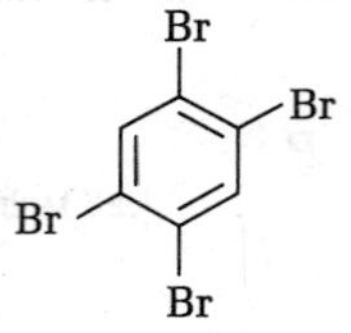 (b) 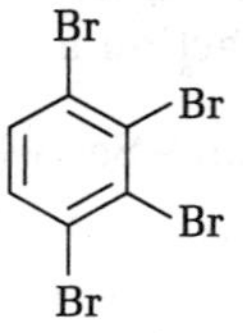

(c) 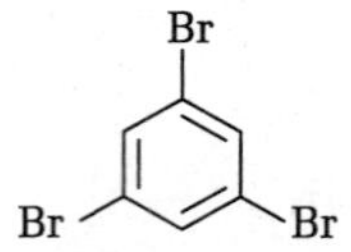 (d) 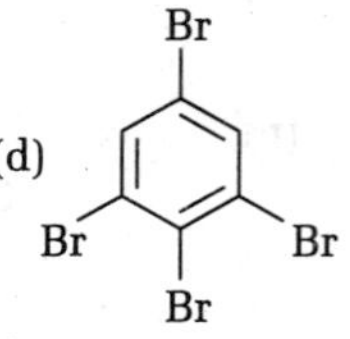

Objective Questions Type II [One or more than one correct option(s)]

In each of the questions below, four choices are given, of which one or more than one are correct.

1. What are *A*, *B* and *C* in the following reactions?

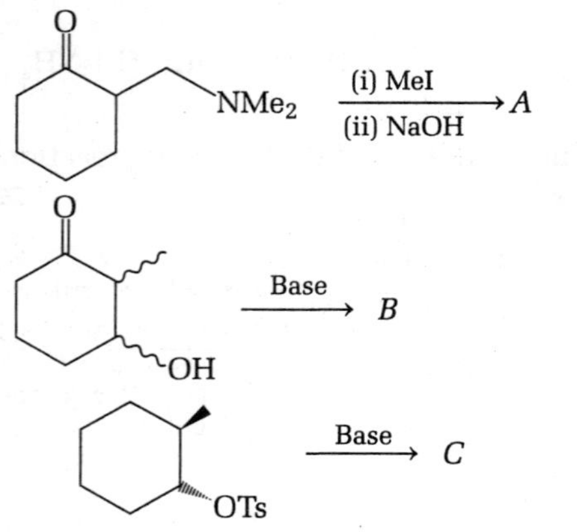

	A	*B*	*C*
(a)	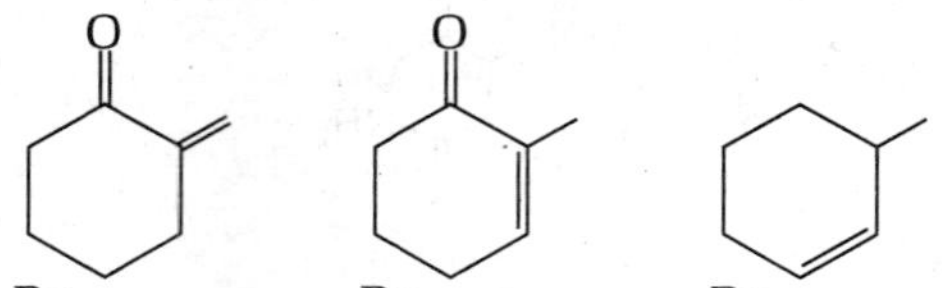		
	By E1CB	By E1CB	By E1CB
(b)	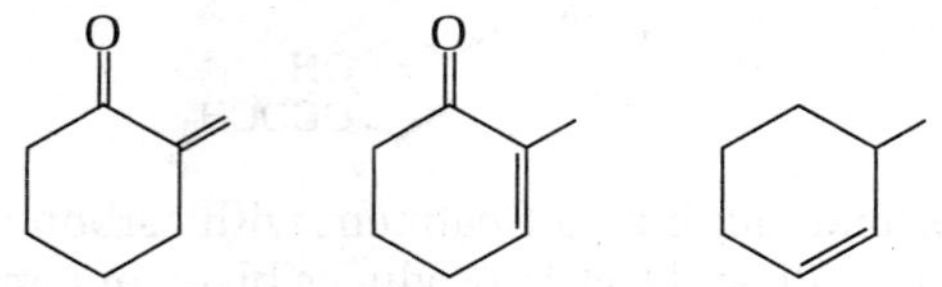		
	By E1CB	By E1CB	By E2

(c) 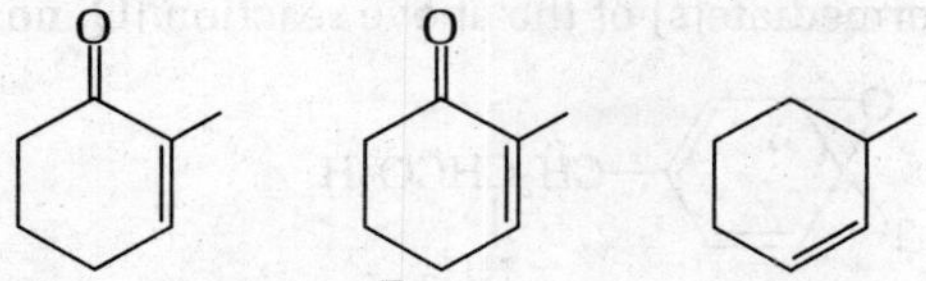

By E1CB   By E1CB   By E2

(d) 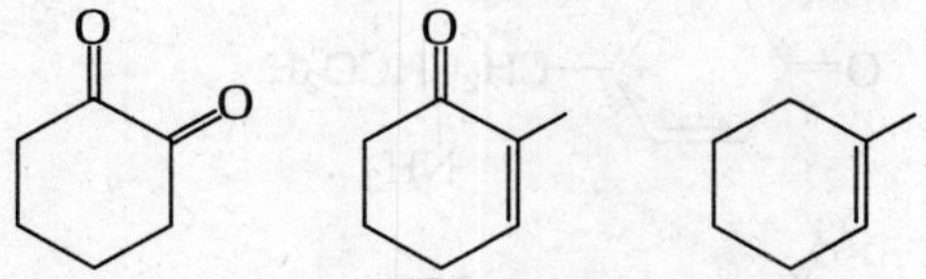

By E1CB   By E2   By E2

2. Final product of the following reaction is

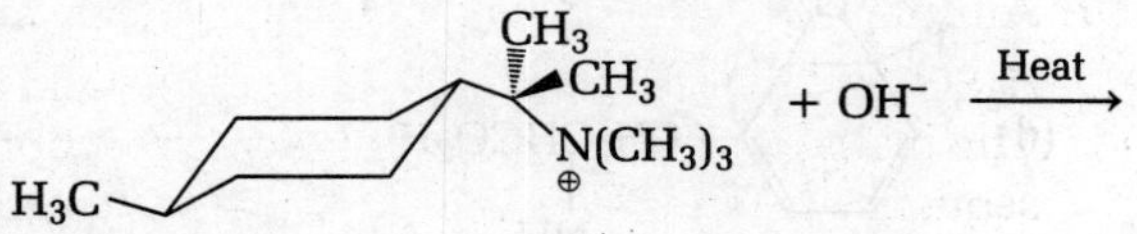

(a) 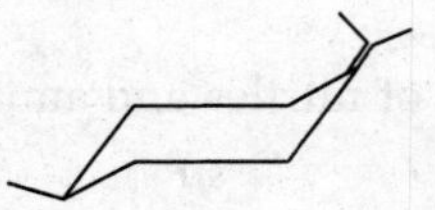
(b) 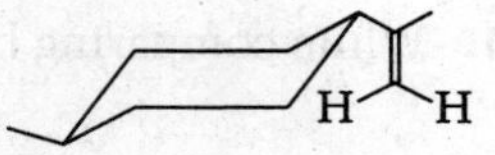

(c) 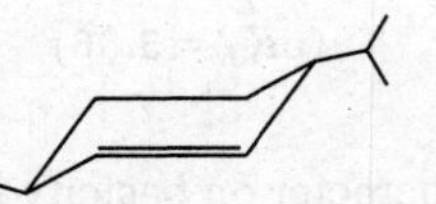
(d) 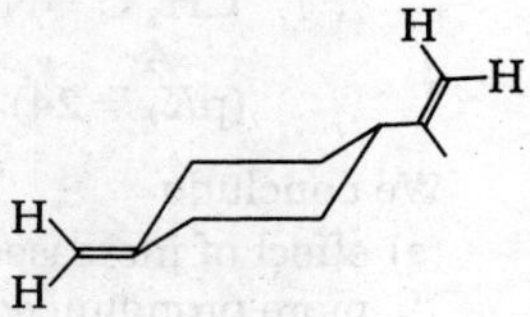

3. Select the correct statement(s).

(a) N-methyl piperidine (*A*) has higher boiling point than 4-methylpiperidine (*B*)

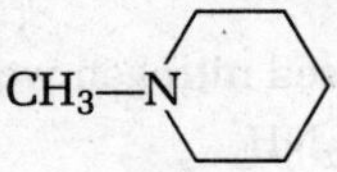

A

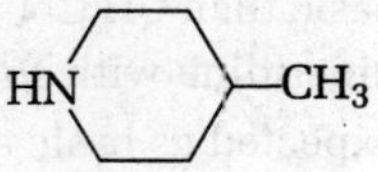

B

(b) (*B*) has higher boiling point than *A*

(c) (*A*) and (*B*) have same boiling point being isomeric amines

(d) There is formation of two diastereoisomeric quaternary ammonium chloride when 4-*tert*-butyl-N-methylpiperidine is treated with benzoyl chloride

4. Following compound *A* spontaneously changes into

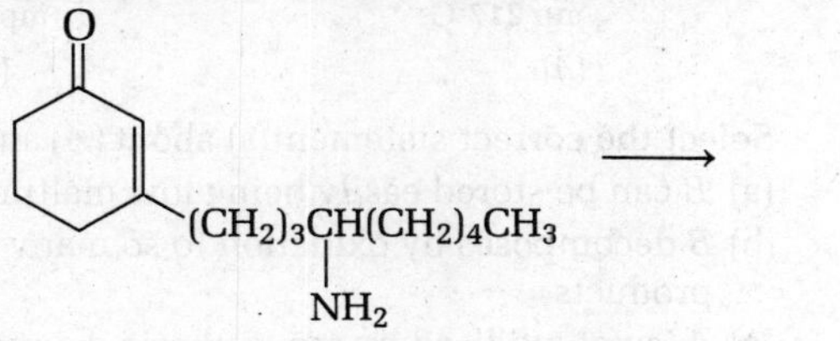

(a) 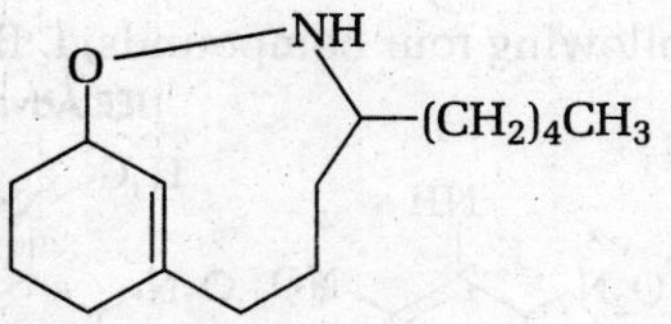

(b) 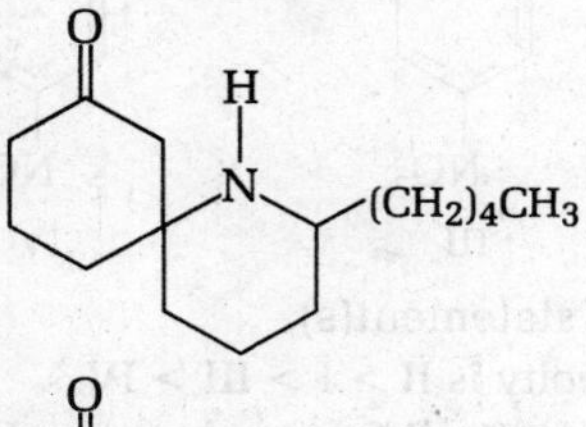

(c) 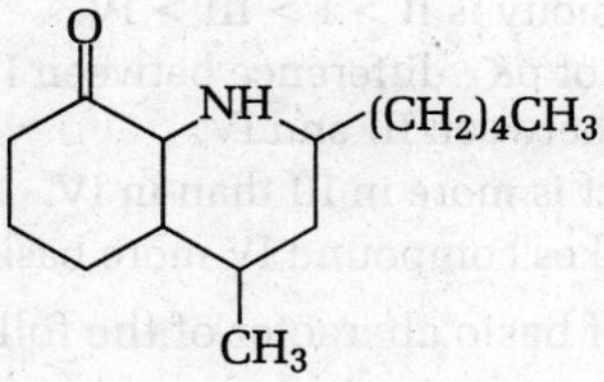

(d) 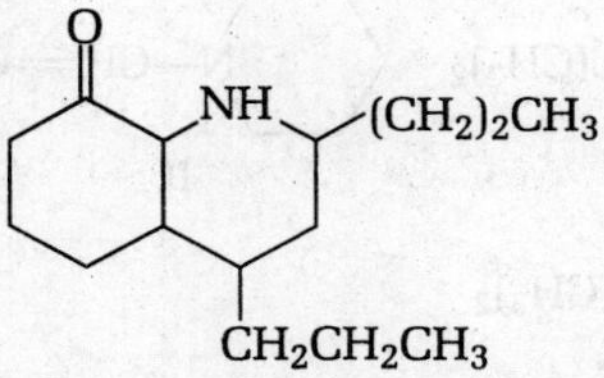

5. The major product of the reaction is **[JEE Advanced 2015]**

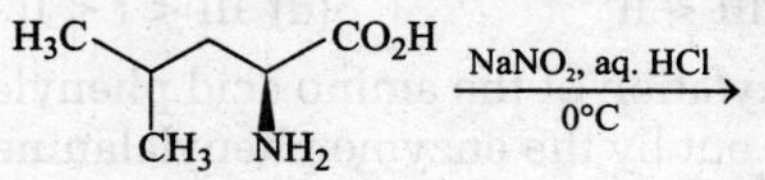

(a) 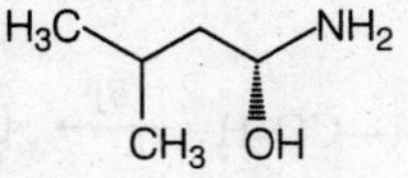
(b) 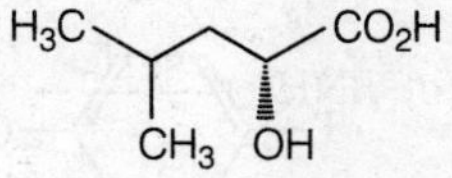

(c) 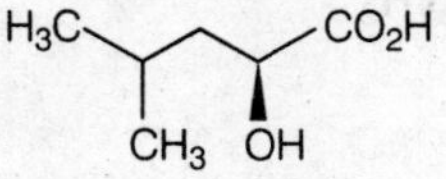
(d) 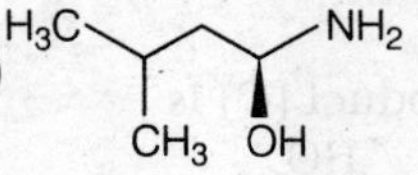

6. 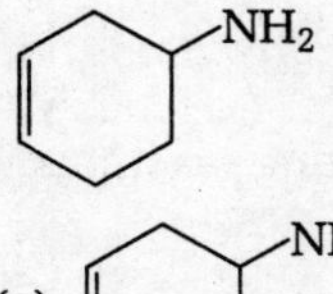 on reaction with HNO_2 forms

(a) 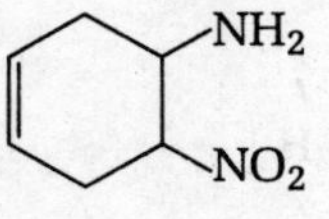
(b) 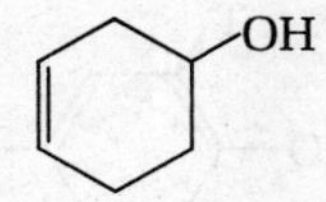

(c) 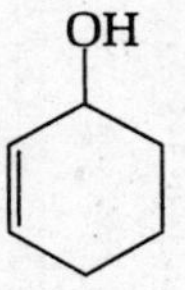
(d) 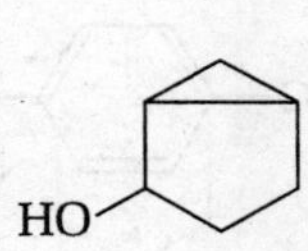

7. Consider the following four compounds, I, II, III, and IV. **[JEE Advanced 2020]**

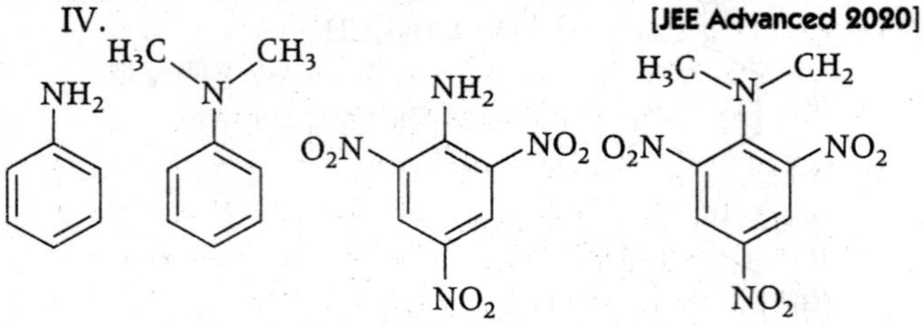

I II III IV

Choose the correct statement(s).

(a) The order of basicity is II > I > III > IV.
(b) The magnitude of pK_b difference between I and II is more than that between III and IV.
(c) Resonance effect is more in III than in IV.
(d) Steric effect makes compound IV more basic than III.

8. Increasing order of basic character of the following is

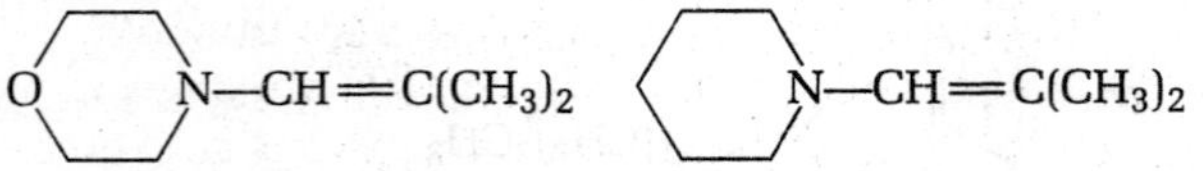

I II

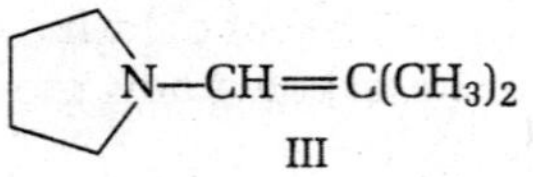

III

(a) I < II < III (b) III < II < I
(c) I < III < II (d) III < I < II

9. Hydroxylation of the amino acid phenylalanine (*A*) is carried out by the enzyme phenylalanine hydroxylase (*B*). The reaction was studied by use of tritium.

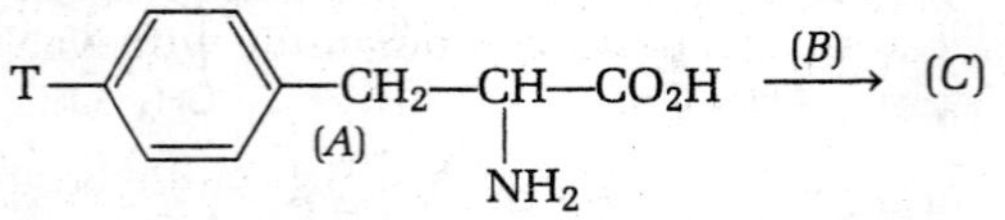

Product (*C*) is

(a) 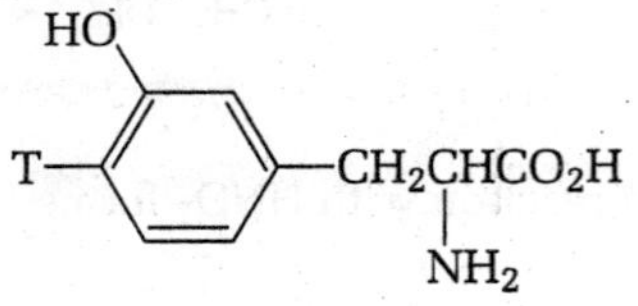

(b) 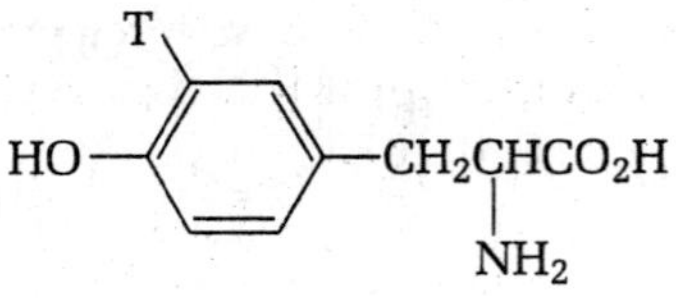

(c) 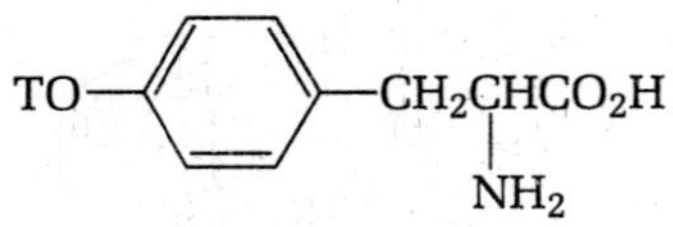

(d) 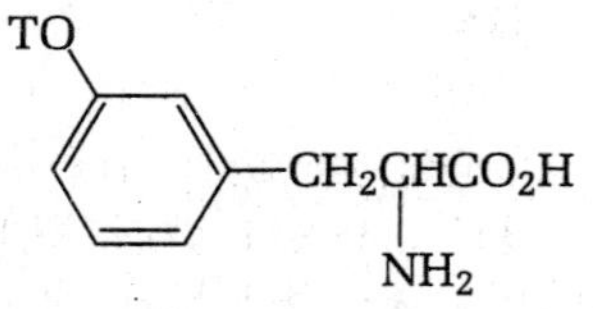

10. Intermediate(s) of the above reaction (Q. no. 9) is/are

(a) 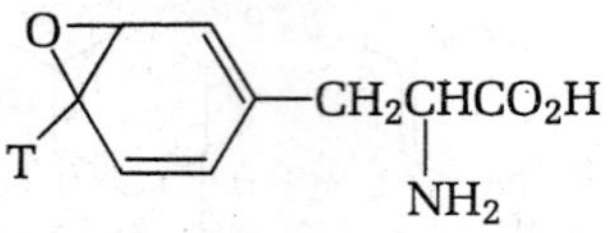

(b) 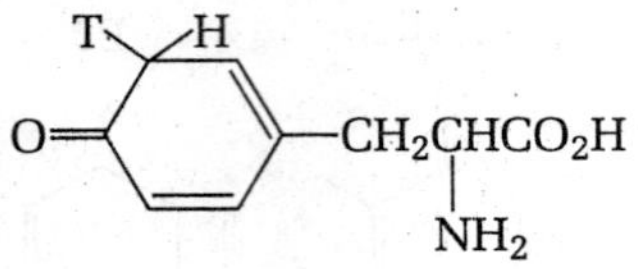

(c) 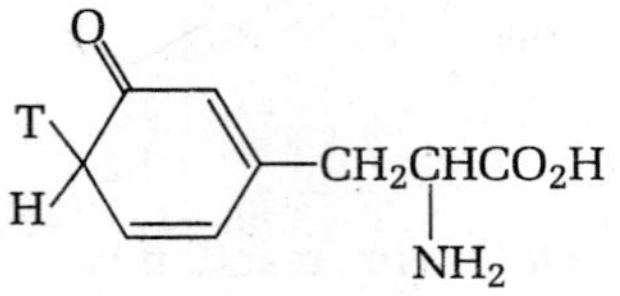

(d) 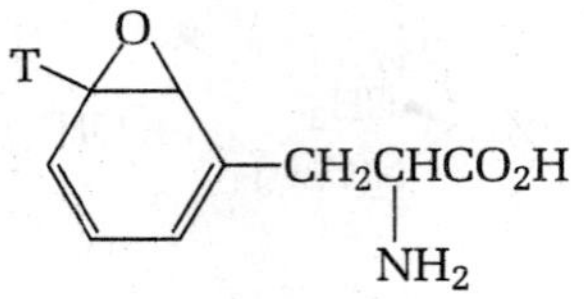

11. While comparing basicity of nitriles and amines

sp	sp^3
$CH_3C\equiv N$	$CH_3CH_2NH_2$
A	*B*
(pK_b = 24)	(pK_b = 3.36)

We conclude

(a) effect of increased *s*-character on basicity is even more pronounced in nitriles compared to amines
(b) concentrated mineral acid is required to protonate nitriles being a very weak base
(c) pyridine with sp^2-hybridised nitrogen would be more basic than CH_3CN
(d) piperidine with sp^3-hybridised nitrogen would be expected as basic as $CH_3CH_2NH_2$

12. Following drug ephedrine is widely used in cold and allergy medications.
(*A*) is the hydrochloride salt of (*B*).

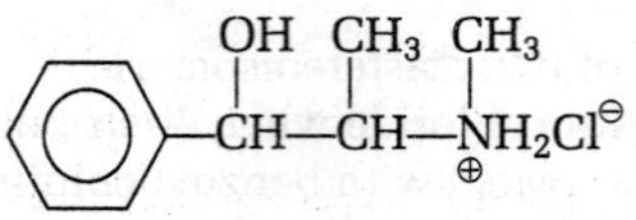

Ephedrine hydrochloride
mp 217°C
(*A*)

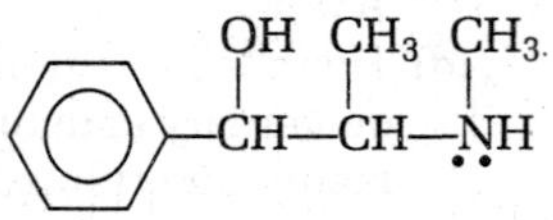

Ephedrine
mp 79°C
(*B*)

Select the correct statement(s) about (*A*) and (*B*).

(a) *B* can be stored easily being low melting solid
(b) *B* decomposes by oxidation to so many undesirable products
(c) *A* is not oxidised by atmospheric oxygen and is stable at high temperature
(d) *B* has fishy odour while there is no fishy odour in *A*

13. Select the correct statement(s).

(a) Most alkylamines are more basic than ammonia in aqueous solution

(b) pK_a of $Me_3\overset{\oplus}{N}H$ is higher than that of $\overset{\oplus}{N}H_4$

(c) Ammonium ion is stabilised by polarisation effect

(d) pK_b of CH_3NH_2 is higher than that of NH_3

14. Consider the following statements,

I. Ammonium ions in solution are stabilised not only by alkyl groups but also by hydrogen-bond donation to the solvent.

II. Primary ammonium ions are stabilised by hydrogen bonding more than tertiary ones.

III. Basicity order of amines in the gas phase is different from that in aqueous solution.

Select the correct statement(s).

(a) I and II

(b) I, II and III

(c) II and III

(d) Only II

Numerical Value Questions

All these questions have a Numerical value as their answer, solve the questions and write your answer.

1. $Ph-NH_2 \xrightarrow[0\text{-}5°C]{NaNO_2\ [H]} A \xrightarrow[\text{Dil. HCl}]{Ph\text{-}NH_2} X$

Find the sum of number of nitrogen atoms present in (X) and the total number of stereoisomers of (X) formed.

2.

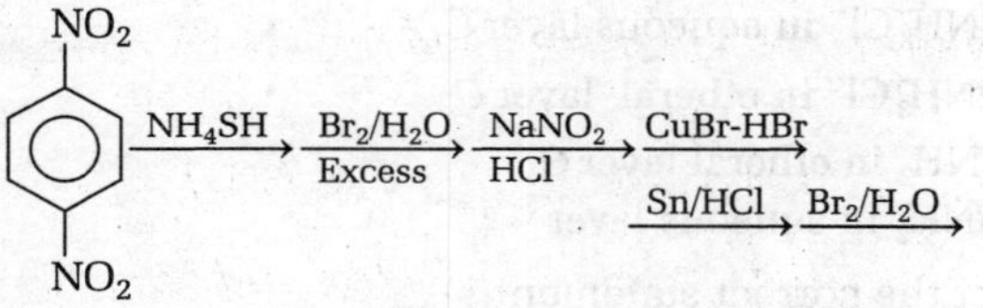

Find the total number of halogen atoms present in the major end product.

3.

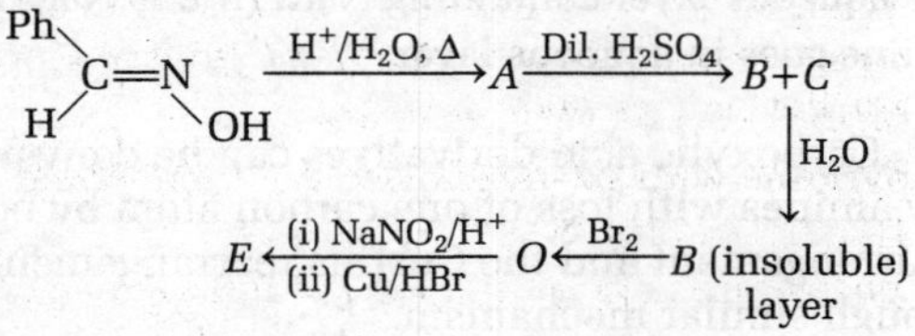

E has how many halogens?

4. One mole of 1-phenyl 1, 2 dibromoethane was treated with excess $NaNH_2$ in liquid NH_3 medium. How many moles of $NH_3(g)$ will evolve?

5. A unknown amine *A* with benzenesulphonyl chloride yields a derivative which dissolves in alkali. Compound *A* on reaction with nitrous acid gives on alcohol *B*, which responds to the haloform. Hydrochloride of *A* contains 37.2% of chlorine. Calculate the total number of carbon atoms present in compound *A* and *B*?

6. How many moles of NaOH will be consumed for conversion of 1 mole of ethanamide into methylamine following Hofmann bromamide process?

7. What is the number of different isomeric butenes obtained on diazotisation of normal butamine from diazotisation of normal butamine with $NaNO_2$ and HCl?

8. How many amino acid contains imino group in its structure?

Comprehension Based Questions

In these questions, a passage has been given followed by questions based on it. You have to answer the questions based on the passage given.

***Passage* 1** When alkyl halide and ammonia react, there is always formation of 1°, 2° and 3° amines even under controlled conditions. Given outline describes the technique to separate the mixture. Go through it and properties of the amines to answer the questions at the end.

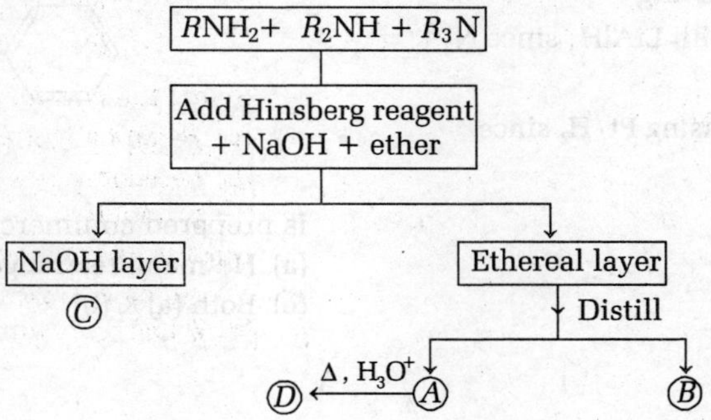

(a) sodium salt of 1° amine N-alkyl benzenesulphonamide
(b) sodium salt of 2° amine N,N-dialkyl benzenesulphonamide
(c) Both (a) and (b)
(d) None of the above

2. Ethereal layer contains
(a) 2° amine and 3° amine
(b) 3° amine and N,N-dialkyl benzene sulphonamide
(c) 1° amine, 2° amine
(d) only 3° amine

3. Distillation of ethereal layer gives
(a) *A* (N,N-dialkyl benzene sulphonamide) and *B* (3° amine)
(b) *A* (sodium salt of N-alkyl benzene sulphonamide) and *B* (3° amine)
(c) *A* (2° amine) and *B* (3° amine)
(d) None of the above

***Passage* 2** Two synthetic routes were planned to synthesise cyclohexylamine.

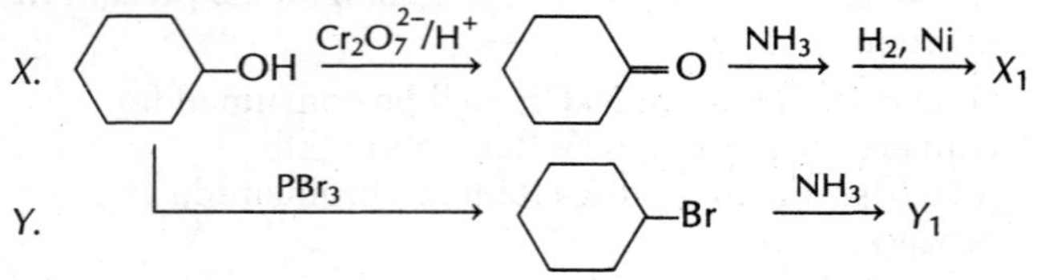

Taking all the aspects of 2° alcohol and 2° alkyl halide, answer the following questions.

1. Select the correct statement(s).
(a) Plan *Y* is preferred to plan *X* since it involves lesser number of steps
(b) Plan *X* is preferred to plan *Y* since plan *Y* also involves the elimination of HBr from 2° alkyl halide
(c) Plan *X* involves reductive amination which gives better yield
(d) Plan *Y* involves S_N reaction and being faster gives better yield

2. Cyclohexylbromide can also be converted into cyclohexylamine in good yield using
(a) NaN_3 followed by reduction with $LiAlH_4$ since N_3^- is a good nucleophile
(b) NaCN followed by reduction using Pt/H_2 since CN^- is a strong nucleophile
(c) Both of the above
(d) None of the above

***Passage* 3** It is often possible to take advantage of their basicity to purify amines by the following scheme.

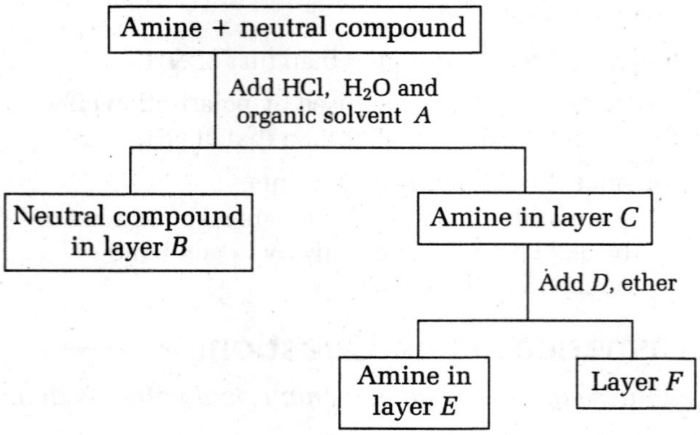

Answer the following questions.

1. Organic solvent (*A*) can be
(a) ketone (b) alcohol (c) ether (d) Any of these

2. Amine is in the form of
(a) $RNH_3^+Cl^-$ in aqueous layer *C*
(b) $RNH_3^+Cl^-$ in etheral layer *C*
(c) RNH_2 in etheral layer *C*
(d) RNH_2 in aqueous layer

3. Select the correct statement(s).
(a) Strong base *D* (say NaOH) is added
(b) Amine goes in etheral layer *E*
(c) *F* is aqueous layer containing NaCl (if *D* is NaOH)
(d) Amine goes in aqueous layer

***Passage* 4** Carboxylic acid derivatives can be converted into primary amines with loss of one carbon atom by both the Hofmann rearrangement and the Curtius rearrangement. Both proceed through similar mechanism.
Based on the above paragraph, answer the following questions.

1. Select the correct statement(s).
(a) Hofmann rearrangement involves a primary amide
(b) Hofmann rearrangement involves an acyl azide
(c) Curtius rearrangement involves an acyl azide
(d) Curtius rearrangement involves primary amide

2. The appetite-supporting drug **phentermine** (*A*)

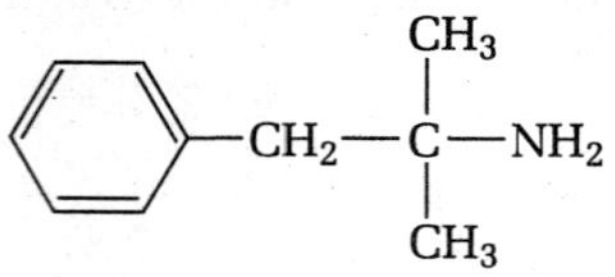

(*A*)

is prepared commercially by
(a) Hofmann rearrangement (b) Curtius rearrangement
(c) Both (a) & (b) (d) None of these

3. Following antidepressant drug tranylcypromine(*A*) is made by

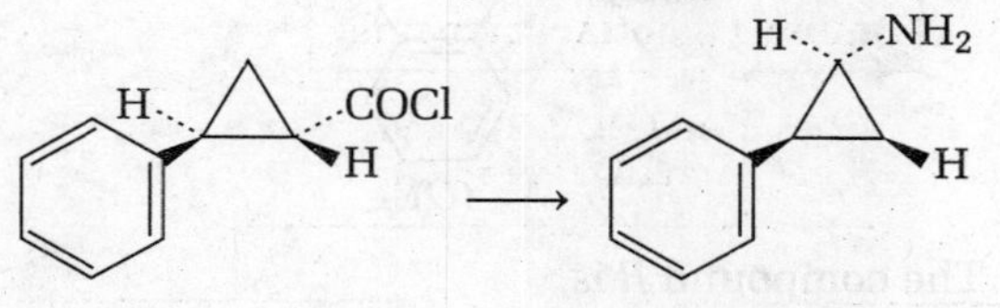

(*A*)

(a) (i) NH_3 (ii) $KBrO/\Delta$
(b) (i) H_2O (ii) N_3H, Δ
(c) (i) NaN_3 (ii) Δ
(iii) H_2O
(d) (i) H_2O (ii) Δ
(iii) NH_3

***Passage* 5** *Read the following passage about reactivity of amines with* $NaNO_2$ *and dil* HCl *and answer the questions at the end of it.*

RNH_2 reacts with HNO_2 (nitrous acid from $NaNO_2$ and dil. HCl) forming alcohols. Chemist *A* wanted to prepare 2-propanol and thus she worked out the synthesis from 2-aminopropane. Chemist *B* also wanted to prepare 2-propanol but she could not arrange 2-aminopropane but instead she tried the synthesis from 1-aminopropane.

1. What are the most stable intermediates of chemists *A* and *B*?

	A	*B*
(a)	$CH_3CH_2\overset{\oplus}{C}H_2$	$CH_3CH_2\overset{\oplus}{C}H_2$
(b)	$CH_3\overset{\oplus}{C}HCH_3$	$CH_3CH_2\overset{\oplus}{C}H_2$
(c)	$CH_3\overset{\oplus}{C}HCH_3$	$CH_3\overset{\oplus}{C}HCH_3$

(d) None of the above is correct

2. Some of the products have also been isolated by chemist *B*. She had put her views based on mechanism.

X : $CH_3CH_2CH_2Cl$ and $CH_3\underset{Cl}{\underset{|}{C}}HCH_3$: S_N reaction

Y : $CH_3CH{=}CH_2$ E_1

Z : $CH_2—CH_2$ E_1
CH_2

Correct alternates are

(a) *X*, *Y* (b) *Y*, *Z* (c) *X*, *Z* (d) *X*, *Y*, *Z*

3. 2-aminobutane is found to be optically active. On reaction with HNO_2 ($NaNO_2$ + HCl)

(a) it becomes optically inactive due to formation of pair of enantiomers
(b) it retains its configuration about chiral carbon
(c) its configuration is inverted
(d) nothing can be concluded on reaction with HNO_2

***Passage* 6** *Read the following technical report on "Bhopal Tragedy" in* 1984, *and answer the questions at the end of it.*

Sevin insecticide is made by the reaction of 1-naphthol with methyl isocyanate. A Union Carbide plant in Bhopal. (M.P.), once used this process to make sevin for use as an agricultural insecticide. On one day of December 1984, either by accident or by sabotage, a valve was opened that admitted water to a large tank of methyl isocyanate.

The pressure and temperature within the tank rose dramatically, and pressure-relief valves opened to keep the tank from bursting. A large quantity of methyl isocyanate rushed out through the pressure-relief valves, and the vapours flowed with the breeze into populated areas, killing about 3000 people and injuring over 10000. Generations born after have one type or other type of disease due to this disaster.

1. What is the structure of Sevin?

(a) 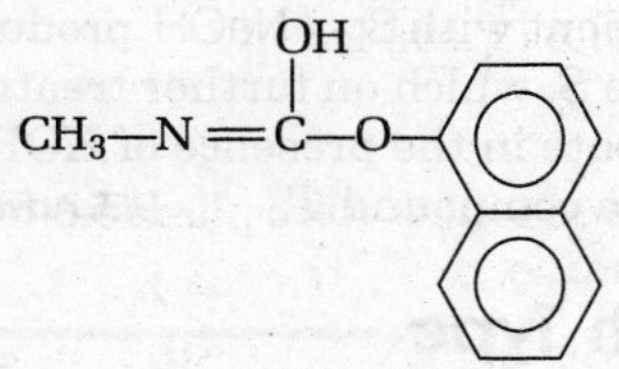

(b) 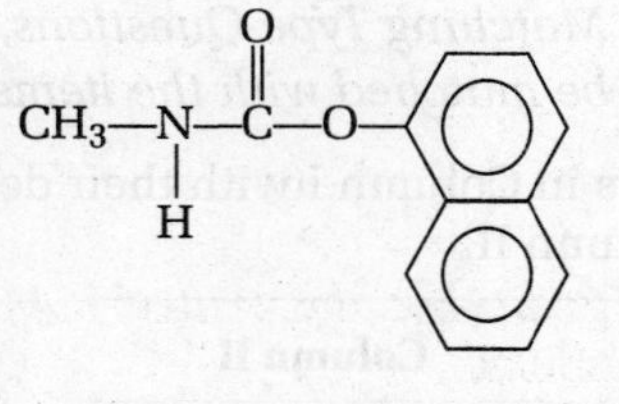

(c) 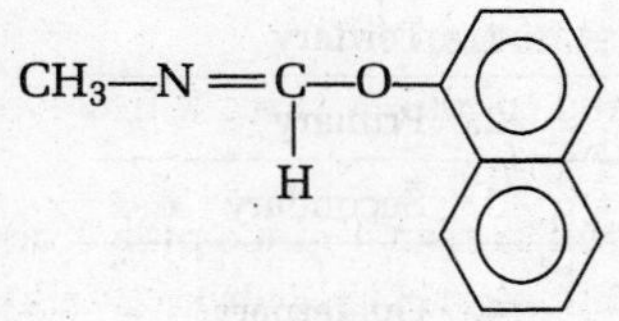

(d) 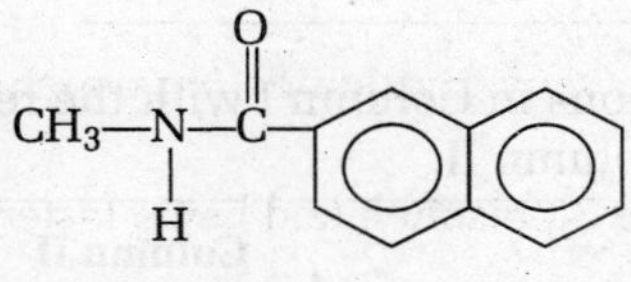

2. There are two types of double bonds in methyl isocyanate

$CH_3—N{=}C{=}O$

Which double bond takes part when 1-naphthol adds to it?

(a) N=C nitrogen being more basic and nucleophilic
(b) C=O oxygen being more electronegative
(c) Both due to resonance stabilisation
(d) None of the above explanation is correct

3. Sevin can also be synthesised without using CH_3CNO. This method is

A. 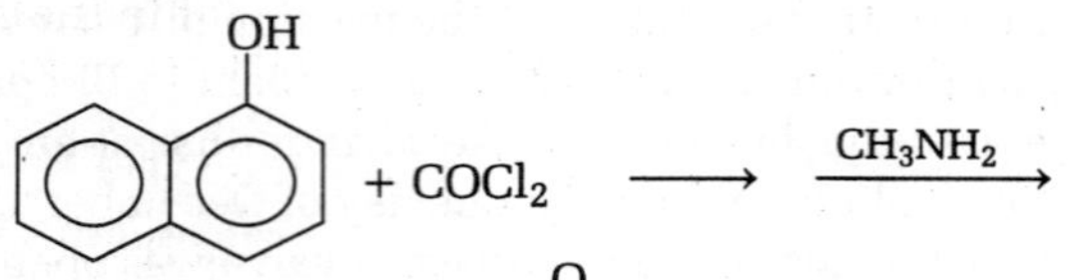

B. 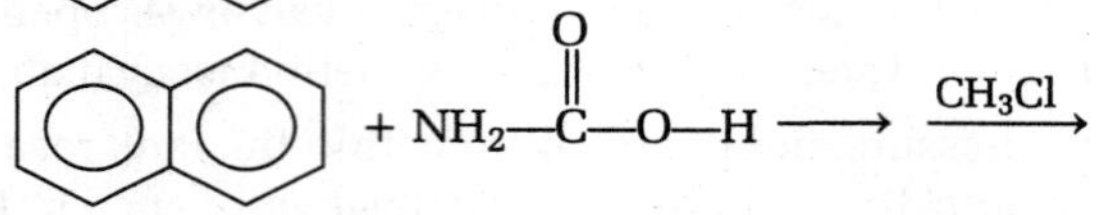

Select the correct synthesis.

(a) *A*
(b) *B*
(c) Both (a) and (b)
(d) None of these

***Passage* 7.** Treatment of compound *O* with $KMnO_4 / H^+$ gave *P*, which on heating with ammonia gave *Q*. The compound *Q* on treatment with Br_2 / NaOH produced *R*. On strong heating, *Q* gave *S*, which on further treatment with ethyl 2-bromopropanoate in the presence of KOH followed by acidification, gave a compound *T*. **[JEE Advanced 2016]**

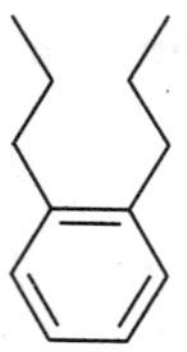

(*O*)

1. The compound *R* is

(a) 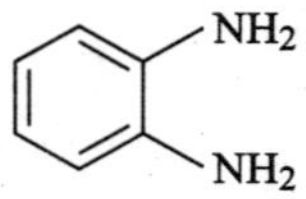
(b) 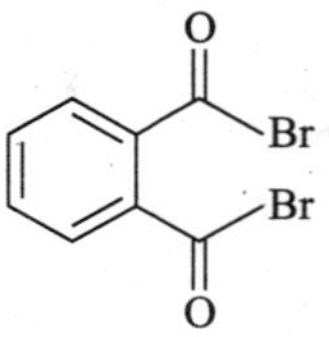
(c) 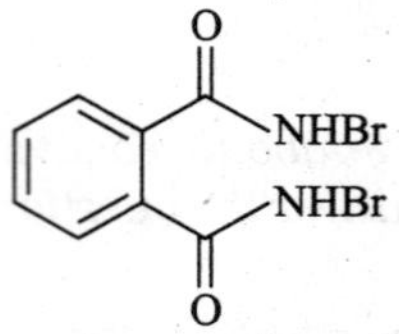
(d) 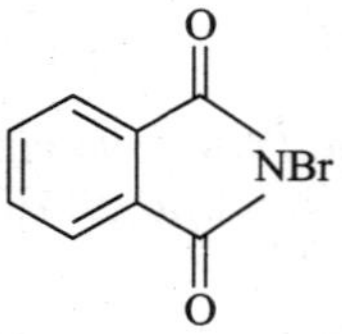

2. The compound *T* is
(a) glycine (b) alanine (c) valine (d) serine

Matrix-Match Type

Given below are Matching Type Questions, with two columns (each having some items) each . Each item of Column I has to be matched with the items of Column II.

1. Match the species in Column I with their degree (1°, 2°, 3°) in Column II.

Column I	Column II
A. $(CH_3)_3CNH_2$	1. Tertiary
B. $(CH_3)_2NH$	2. Primary
C. $(CH_3)_3N$	3. Secondary
D. $(CH_3)_4\overset{\oplus}{N}\overset{\ominus}{Cl}$	4. Quaternary

2. Match the reactions in Column I with the reacting substances in Column II.

Column I	Column II
A. Schmidt reaction	1. $RCONH_2 \xrightarrow[\Delta]{KBrO} RNH_2$
B. Carbyl amine reaction	2. $RNH_2 + CS_2 + HgCl_2 \rightarrow$ Black ppt.
C. Hofmann-bromamide degradation reaction	3. $RCOOH + N_3H \xrightarrow{\Delta} RNH_2$
D. Hofmann-mustard oil reaction	4. $RNH_2 + CHCl_3 + KOH \xrightarrow{\Delta} RNC$

3. Match the amines in Column I with the reactions shown in Column II.

Column I	Column II
A. 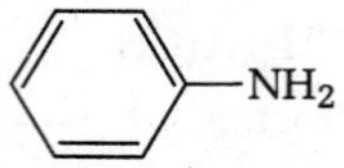	1. Cope elimination
B. CH_3NH_2	2. Azo dye formation
C. $(CH_3)_2NH$	3. Carbylamine reaction
D. $(CH_3CH_2)_3N$	4. Yellow oily liquid with HNO_2

4. Match the following.

Column I (Feature)	Column II (Reacting)
A. Intramolecular alkyl shift	1. Curtius degradation
B. Synthesis of 1° amine	2. Hofmann degradation
C. Retention of stereochemical configuration	3. Schmidt
D. Decarboxylation takes place	4. Gabriel

5. Match the following.

Column I (Reaction)	Column II (Product)
A. $CH_3CH_2CH_2NH_2 + HNO_2 \longrightarrow$	1. $CH_3CH_2CH_2OH$
B. $CH_3\underset{\substack{\vert \\ Cl}}{C}HCH_3 + H_2O \xrightarrow{S_N1}$	2. $CH_3\underset{\substack{\vert \\ OH}}{C}HCH_3$
C. $CH_3CH_2CH_2Cl + NaOH \xrightarrow{S_N2}$	3. $CH_3CH{=}CH_2$
D. $CH_3\underset{\substack{\vert \\ NH_2}}{C}HCH_3 + NHO_2$	4. $CH_2{-}CH_2$ / CH_2

6. Match the following.

Column I (Pair for distinction)	Column II (Reagent)
A. $CH_3CH_2NH_2$, $(CH_3)_2NH$	1. HNO_2 + β-naphthol
B. CH_3NH_2, 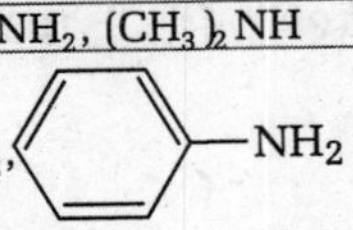	2. $NaNO_2$ + HCl
C. 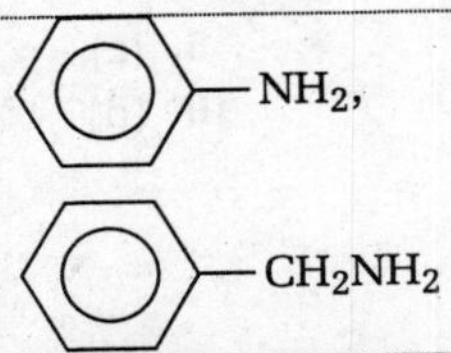	3. Hofmann mustard oil reaction
D. $(CH_3)_3N$, $CH_3CH_2CH_2CH_2NH_2$	4. Carbyl amine

7. Match the following.

Column I (Amine)	Column II (Reagent)
A. Primary amine	1. Hinsberg's reagent
B. Secondary amine	2. Diethyl oxalate
C. Tertiary amine	3. Carbyl amine reaction
D. Aniline	4. Nitrous acid

8. Match each of the compounds in Column I with its characteristic reaction(s) in Column II. **[JEE Advance 2016]**

Column I	Column II
A. $CH_3CH_2CH_2CN$	1. Reduction with Pd-C/H_2
B. $CH_3CH_2OCOCH_3$	2. Reduction with $SnCl_2$/HCl
C. $CH_3CH{=}CHCH_2OH$	3. Development of foul smell on treatment with chloroform and alcoholic KOH.
D. $CH_3CH_2CH_2CH_2NH_2$	4. Reduction with diisobutylaluminium hydride (DIBAL-H)
	5. Alkaline hydrolysis

Single Integer Answer Questions

Answer of these questions is a single digit lying between 0 to 9.

1. pK_b of a primary amine is 5, then pK_a of its conjugate acid is ....
2. CH_3COOH by Schmidt reaction forms primary amine. 1.55 g of such amine required .... g of CH_3COOH
3. When α-amine propanoic acid is heated, how many isomeric piperazines (including stereoisomers are obtained).
4. When β-aminobutanoic acid is heated how many diasteriosomers are obtained.
5. In the following exhaustive methylation as shown; how many π electrons are formed?

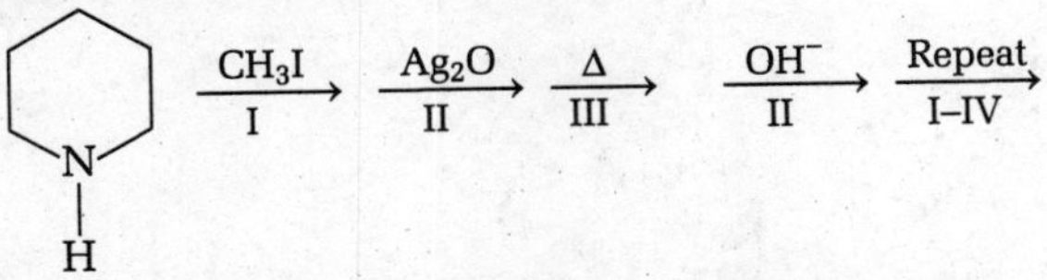

6. 2-amino 3-methyl butane reacts with HNO_2. The types of compounds formed are
7. The serial number of the amine with maximum basic character is

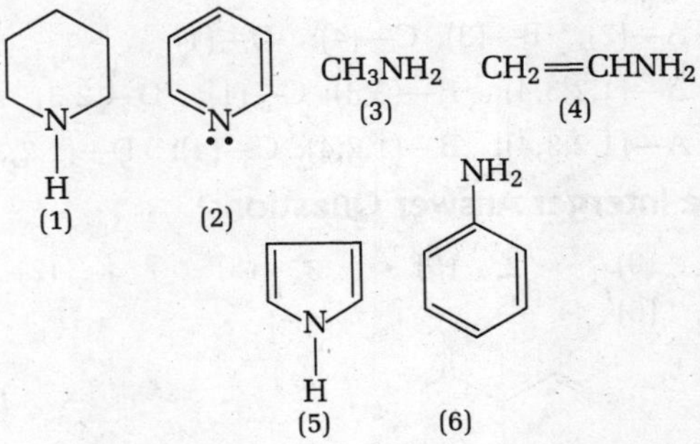

8. CH_3COOH reacts with N_3H. How many lone pairs are in the product formed?
9. Assuming every step as one step, how many steps are involved in conversion of ethyl amine into methyl amine (through acid amide formation)
10. $C_5H_{13}N(A)$ on reaction with HNO_2 forms 3° alcohol. What is the position of amino group in (A) ?
11. How many groups in the following make it less basic than NH_3?

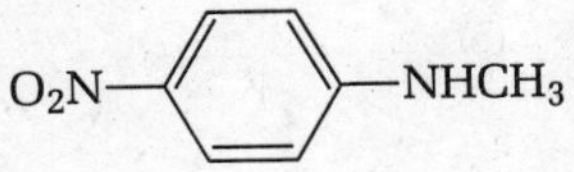

Answers

Objective Questions Type I [Only one correct option]

1. (d)	2. (c)	3. (c)	4. (a)	5. (c)	6. (c)	7. (c)	8. (b)	9. (d)	10. (a)
11. (b)	12. (b)	13. (b)	14. (a)	15. (d)	16. (a)	17. (d)	18. (c)	19. (b)	20. (c)
21. (c)	22. (b)	23. (d)	24. (b)	25. (c)	26. (c)	27. (b)	28. (a)	29. (d)	30. (d)
31. (a)	32. (b)	33. (a)	34. (c)	35. (b)	36. (d)	37. (a)	38. (b)	39. (d)	40. (c)
41. (c)	42. (d)	43. (a)	44. (a)	45. (b)	46. (b)	47. (b)	48. (d)	49. (b)	50. (c)
51. (b)	52. (a)	53. (b)	54. (c)	55. (a)	56. (a)	57. (d)	58. (c)	59. (a)	60. (d)
61. (d)	62. (b)	63. (a)	64. (c)	65. (b)	66. (c)	67. (d)	68. (a)	69. (d)	70. (b)
71. (c)	72. (b)	73. (a)	74. (b)	75. (b)	76. (c)	77. (c)	78. (c)	79. (d)	80. (d)
81. (b)	82. (c)	83. (b)	84. (a)	85. (b)	86. (b)	87. (c)	88. (c)	89. (b)	90. (d)
91. (a)	92. (c)	93. (d)	94. (c)	95. (c)	96. (a)	97. (d)	98. (d)	99. (c)	100. (c)
101. (b)	102. (d)	103. (b)	104. (d)	105. (b)	106. (a)	107. (d)	108. (c)	109. (b)	110. (a)
111. (a)	112. (b)	113. (c)	114. (d)	115. (c)	116. (c)	117. (d)			

Objective Questions Type II [One or more than one correct option(s)]

1. (d)	2. (b)	3. (b)	4. (b, c)	5. (c)
6. (a)	7. (c, d)	8. (b)	9. (b, c, d)	10. (d)
11. (a, b, c)	12. (b, c, d)	13. (a, b, c)	14. (b)	

Comprehension Based Questions

Passage 1 1. (a) 2. (b) 3. (a)

Passage 2 1. (b,c) 2. (a)

Passage 3 1. (c) 2. (a) 4. (a,b,c)

Passage 4 1. (a,c) 2. (a) 3. (c)

Passage 5 1. (c) 2. (d) 3. (a)

Passage 6 1. (b) 2. (a) 3. (a)

Passage 7 1. (a) 2. (b)

Matrix-Match Type

1. A—(2); B—(3); C—(1); D—(4)
2. A—(3); B—(4); C—(1); D—(2)
3. A—(2); B—(3); C—(4); D—(1)
4. A—(1,2); B—(1,2,3,4); C—(1,2); D—(3)
5. A—(1,2,3,4); B—(2,3); C—(1); D—(2,3)
6. A—(2,3,4); B—(1); C—(1); D—(2,3,4)
7. A—(1,2,3,4); B—(1,2,4); C—(4); D—(1,2,3,4)
8. A—(1,2,4,5); B—(1,4,5); C—(1); D—(3)

Single Interger Answer Questions

1. (9)	2. (3)	3. (3)	4. (2)	5. (4)	6. (6)	7. (1)	8. (1)	9. (9)	10. (8)
11. (6)									

Solutions

Objective Questions Type I [Only one correct option]

1. (*d*) $\underset{\text{1° or 2° Halide}}{R{-}X} + NaN_3 \xrightarrow[\text{Step I}]{S_N2} R\overset{}{N}{=}\overset{\oplus}{N}{=}\overset{\ominus}{N} \xrightarrow[\text{step II}]{NaBH_4} RNH_2$

2. (*c*) This method is used to prepare 3° alkyl 1° amine.

$$(CH_3)_3COH + HCN + H_2SO_4 \longrightarrow (CH_3)_3CNH_2$$

4. (*a*) $\underset{\text{Methyl cyanide}}{CH_3CN} \xrightarrow{LiAlH_4} \underset{\text{Ethyl amine}}{CH_3CH_2NH_2}$

5. (*c*) $RNO_2 \xrightarrow{Sn/HCl} RNH_2 \xrightarrow{H^+} RNH_3^+$

6. (*c*) $RNH_2 \xrightarrow[\Delta]{CHCl_3/KOH} RNC \xrightarrow{\text{Reduction}} RNHCH_3$

7. (*c*)

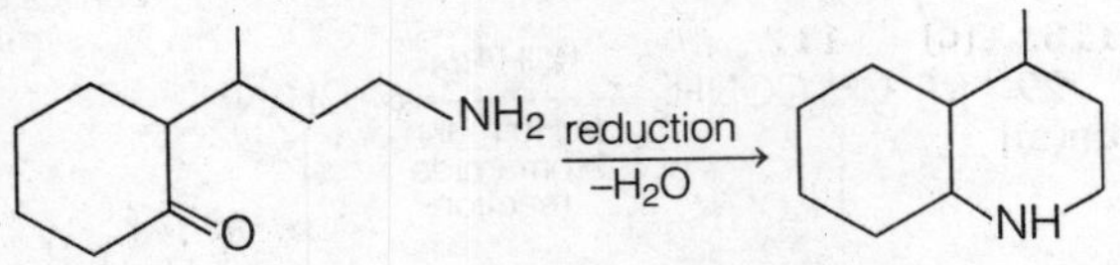

9. (*d*)

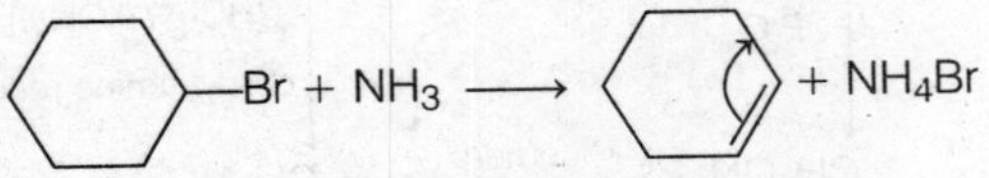

NH_3 (a strong nucleophile) causes loss of HX.

11. (*b*) $CH_3CH_2NH_2 \xrightarrow{HNO_2} CH_3CH_2OH$

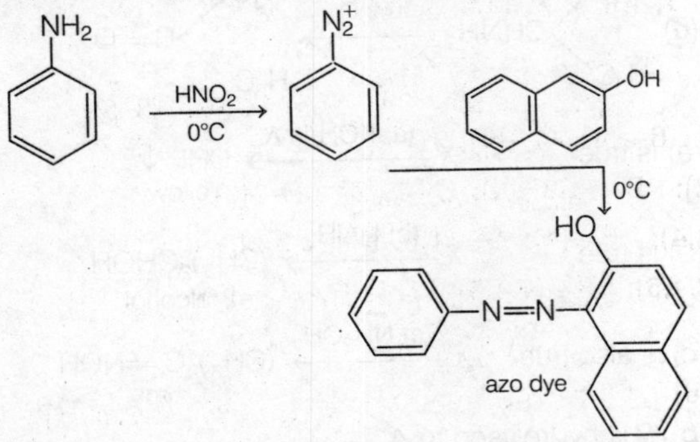

Only aromatic 1° amines give azo dye test.

12. (*b*)

(a) $CH_3CN \xrightarrow{[H]} \underset{1°}{CH_3CH_2NH_2}$

(b) $CH_3NC \xrightarrow{[H]} \underset{2°}{CH_3NHCH_3}$

13. (*b*)

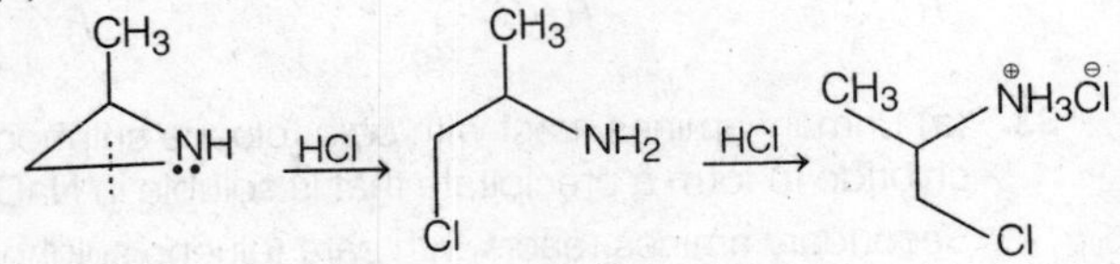

14. (*a*)

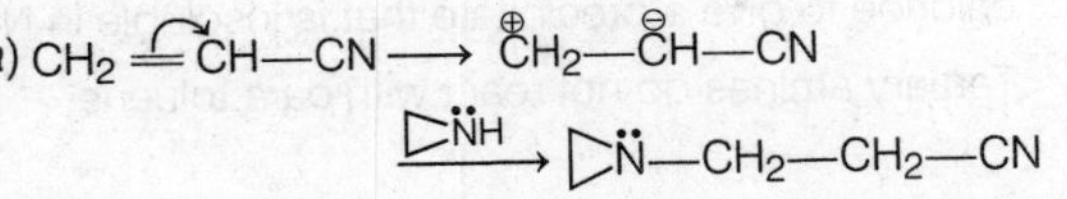

15. (*d*)

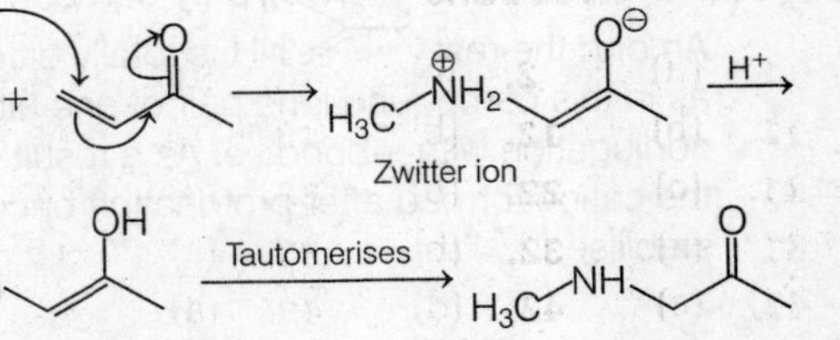

Thus I, II and III are true.

18. (*c*) Basic strength can be compared by the reaction of an alkanamine and ammonia with proton.

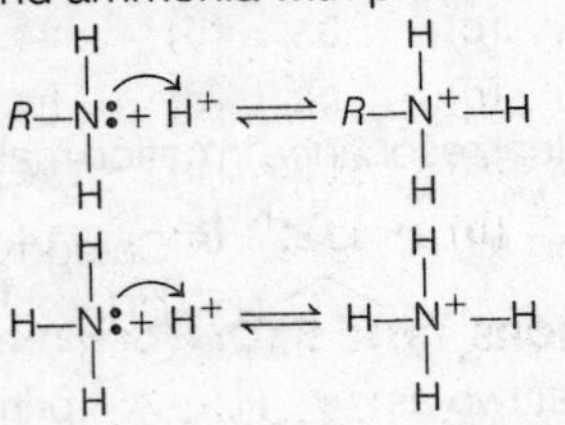

Basicity of an amine in aqueous solution depends upon the solubility of ammonium cation formed by accepting proton from water. The stability of ammonium cation depends upon the following factors.

(a) + *I* effect (b) Steric effect

(c) Solvation effect

In first case, on increasing the size of alkyl group + *I* effect increases and the positive charge of ammonium cation gets dispersed more easily, Therefore, order of basicity is 2° amine > 1° amine > ammonia. In second case, substituted ammonium cation is also stabilised by solvation with water molecules. Greater the size of ion, lesser will be the solvation and less stabilised is the ion.

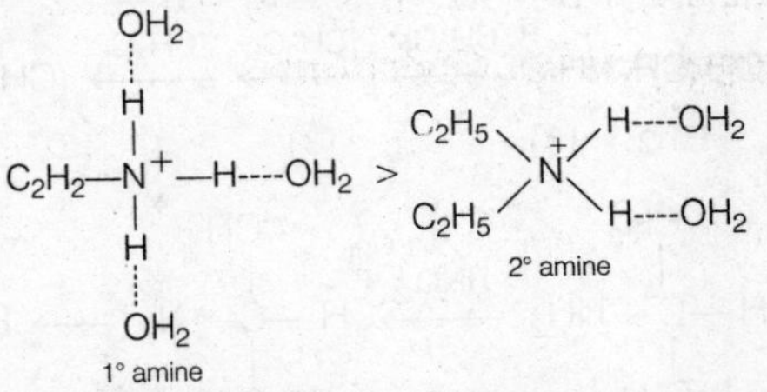

Considering both steric and solvation effect, it can be concluded that greater the number of H-atoms on the N-atom, greater will be the H-bonding and hence more stable is the ammonium cation. But in case of —C_2H_5 group, + *I* effect predominates over H-bonding. Therefore, order is 2° amine > 1° amine > ammonia i.e. $(C_2H_5)_2NH > C_2H_5NH_2 > NH_3$.

21. (*c*) Among the given compounds the basic nature depends upon their tendency to donate electron pair.

Among the given compounds in 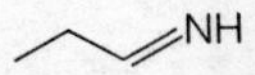 , Nitrogen is sp^2-hybridised. This marginally increases the electronegativity of nitrogen which in turn decreases the electron donation tendency of nitrogen. Thus making compound least basic.

Among the rest 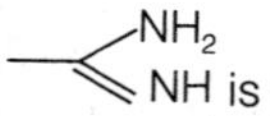 is totally different from others as in this compound lone pair of one nitrogen are in conjugation with π-bond i.e. As a result of this conjugation the cation formed after protonation becomes resonance stabilised

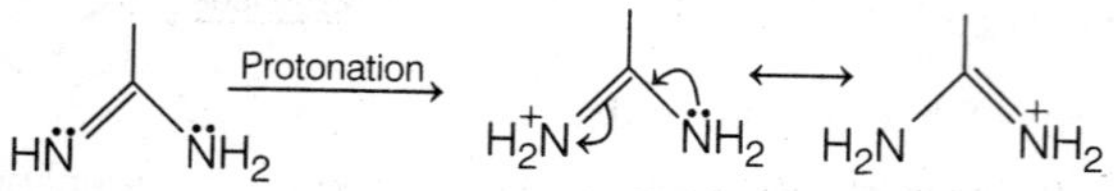

This equivalent resonance in cation makes 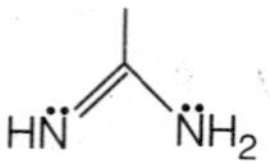 most basic among all.  Categorisation is very simple between rest two as 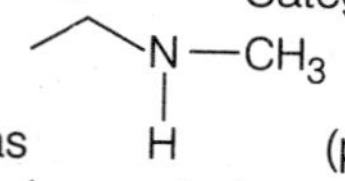 (primary amine) is less basic than (secondary amine).

Hence, the correct order is

(II) < (I) < (IV) < (III) i.e. option (c) is correct.

22. (*b*) $CH_3-C(CH_3)_2-\overset{\oplus}{N}H_3Cl^- \xrightarrow{\Delta} CH_3-C(=CH_2)-CH_3 + NH_4Cl$

23. (*d*)

(a) is true

(b) is true

(c) is also true since (CH_2) cannot be possible, thus $CH_2{=}CH_2$ is formed.

25. (*c*) $CH_3CH_2NH_2 \xrightarrow{CH_3Cl} \xrightarrow{CH_3Cl} \xrightarrow{CH_3Cl} (CH_3)_3N^+(CH_2CH_3)OH^-$

26. (*c*) 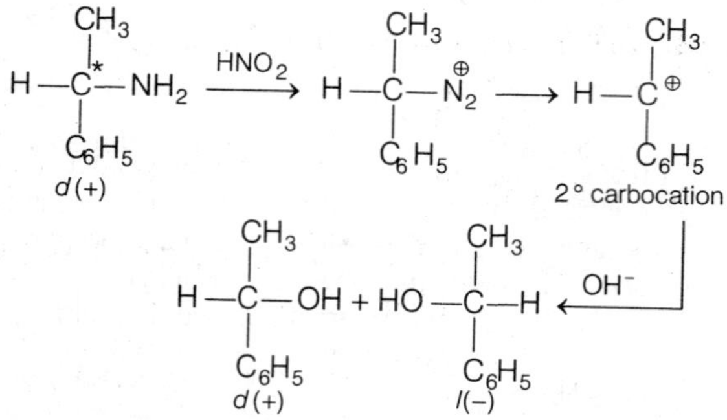

$d(+)$ and $l(-)$ 2° alcohols are formed in equal amounts thus, mixture is racemic.

27. (*b*) 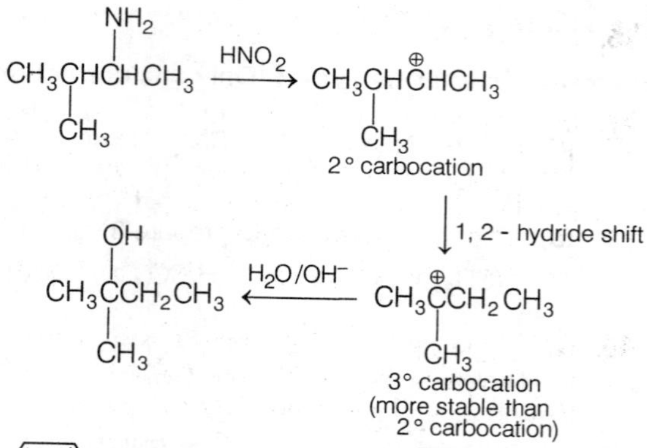

28. (*a*) 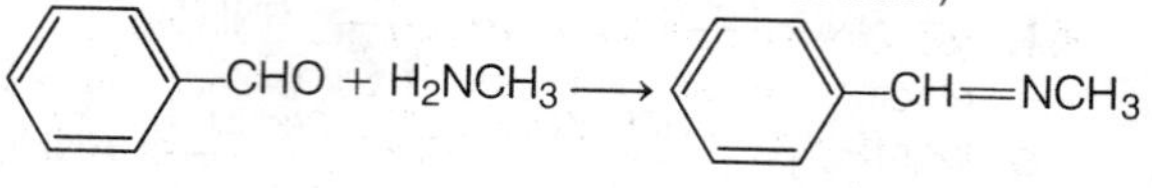

29. (*d*) 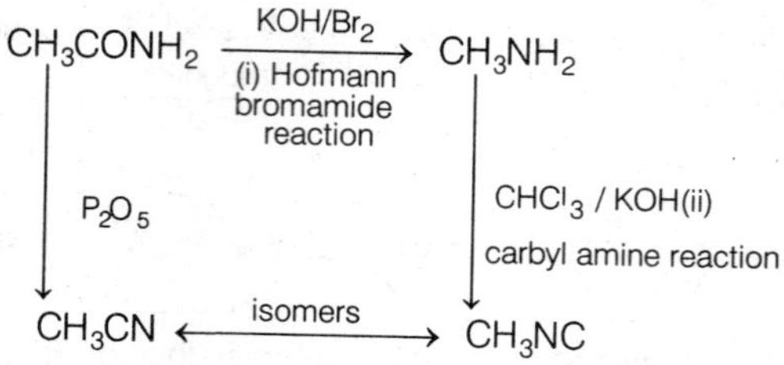

Thus, (a), (b) and (c) are true.

30. (*d*) $(H_3C)_2CHNH_2 \xrightarrow{KMnO_4} (H_3C)_2C{=}O$ (X)

(a) is true $\quad X \xrightarrow{\text{(a) } KOH/I_2\ \Delta} CHI_3\downarrow$ Yellow

(b) is true $\quad X \xrightarrow{\text{(b) } LiAlH_4} (CH_3)_2CHOH$ 2° alcohol

(c) is also true $\quad X \xrightarrow{\text{(c) } NH_2OH} (CH_3)_2C{=}NOH$ Oxime

32. (*b*) *B* is hydrolysed to *A*

$$A + HNO_2 \longrightarrow B \xrightarrow{H_3O^+} A$$

Thus, *B* is nitrosoamine formed when *A* (2° amine) reacts with HNO_2.

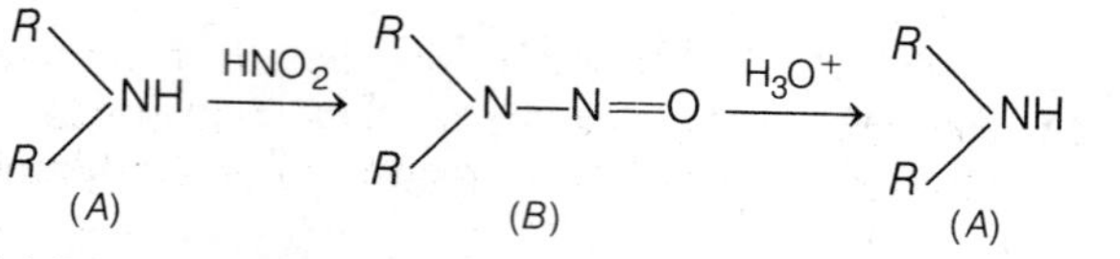

33. (*a*) Primary amines react with *para* toluene sulphonyl chloride to form a precipitate that is soluble in NaOH. Secondary amines reacts with *para* toluene sulphonyl chloride to give a precipitate that is insoluble in NaOH. Tertiary amines do not react with *para* toluene.

36. (*d*) $(CH_3)_3N \xrightarrow{HNO_2} \underset{\text{Soluble}}{(CH_3)_3NH^{\oplus}NO_2^{\ominus}}$

37. (*a*) $C_4H_{11}N \xrightarrow{HNO_2}$ 3° alcohol

Thus, $C_4H_{11}N$ has —NH_2 group. Thus, it is 1° amine. Since produce is 3° alcohol, hence $C_4H_{11}N$ is 3° butyl amine.

$$\underset{\text{1° amine}}{(CH_3)_3C—NH_2} \xrightarrow{HNO_2} \underset{\text{3° alcohol}}{(CH_3)_3C—OH}$$

40. (*c*) All the statements for the Cope elimination are true but intramolecular elimination take place when nucleophile and leaving groups are in the same molecule.

41. (*c*) Electron-repelling alkyl group increases electron-density of N-atom hence, basic nature is increased.

$CH_3CH_2CH_2NH_2$

42. (*d*) IV is most basic as conjugate acid is stabilised by resonance of two —NH_2.

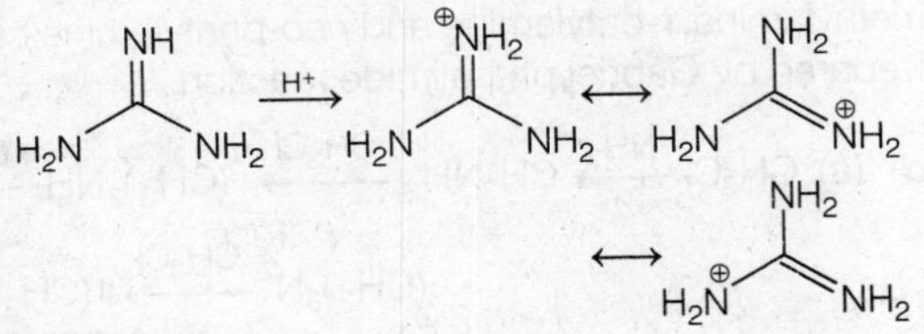

III is least basic as

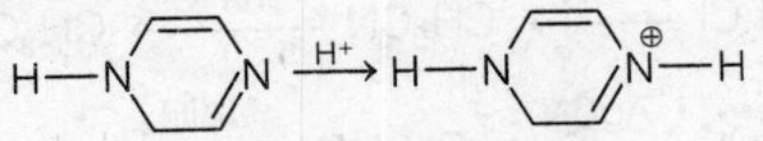

Destablised by –*I*-effect of sp^2-carbons.

46. (*b*) Least substituted alkene is formed. Hence, $CH_2=CH_2$ is formed.

47. (*b*) The molecular formula, C_3H_9N refers to four structural isomers of amines

(a) $CH_3CH_2CH_2NH_2$ (b) $CH_3–CH(NH_2)–CH_3$

Primary amine

(c) $CH_3–NH–CH_2CH_3$ Secondary amine (d) $CH_3–N(CH_3)–CH_3$ Tertiary amine

Here, only *a* and *b* (primary amines) can be prepared from their respective amides by Hofmann bromamide (Br_2/NaOH) method and can give positive carbylamine test.

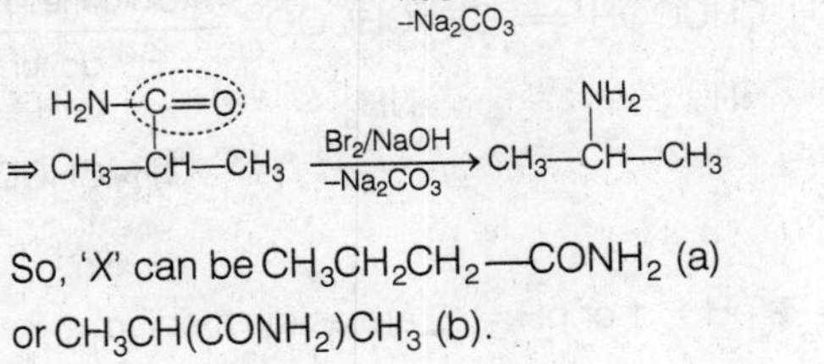

So, 'X' can be $CH_3CH_2CH_2—CONH_2$ (a) or $CH_3CH(CONH_2)CH_3$ (b).

48. (*d*)

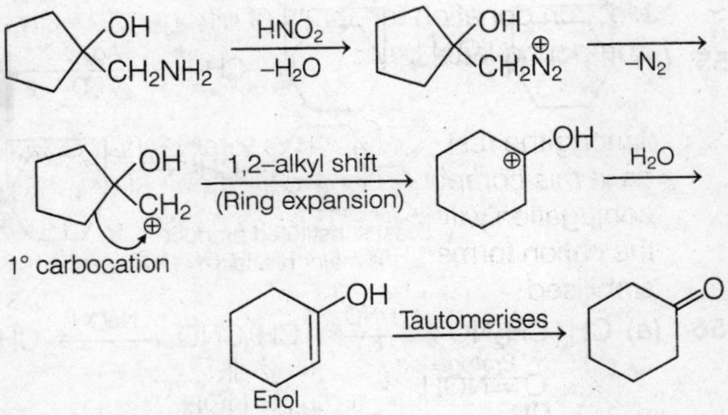

49. (*b*) (due to 1, 2-methyl shift)

50. (*c*)

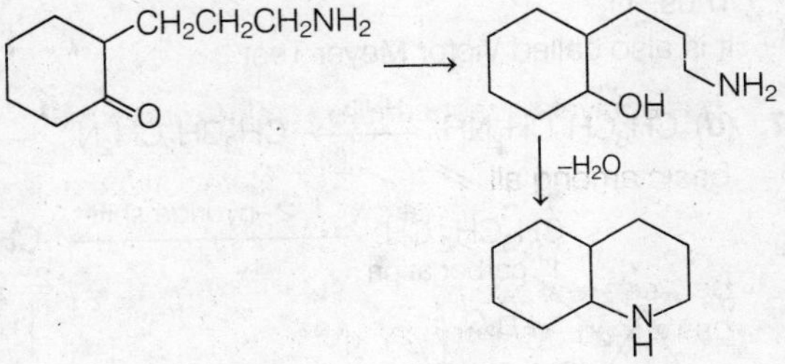

51. (*b*) (I)

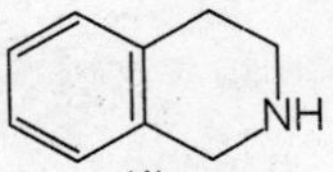

2° amine (aliphatic)

(*A*)

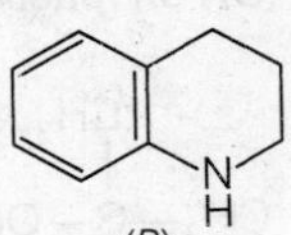

2° amine (aromatic) lone-pair on N is used in delocalisation of π-electrons

(*B*)

Thus, (*A*) is more basic than (*B*).

Thus, true

II : True

III : Carbonyl group is (EWG), thus electron density is decreased, first is least basic, last one is maximum basic, thus incorrect.

Thus I, II true.

54. (*c*) For the given compounds :

1. $CH_3—C(=O)—NH—C_2H_5$; L.P. on nitrogen is delocalised.

2. $CH_3CH_3\ddot{N}CH_2CH_3$ (with CH_3CH_3 on N); L.P. on nitrogen is localised.

3. $CH_3—C(=O)—\ddot{N}H—C(=O)—CH_3$; L.P. on Nitrogen is delocalised due to conjugation with both —C(=O)—

(Hence, least basic).

4. $CH_3—CH_3—\ddot{N}H—CH_2—CH_3$; L.P. on nitrogen is localised.

55. (*a*)

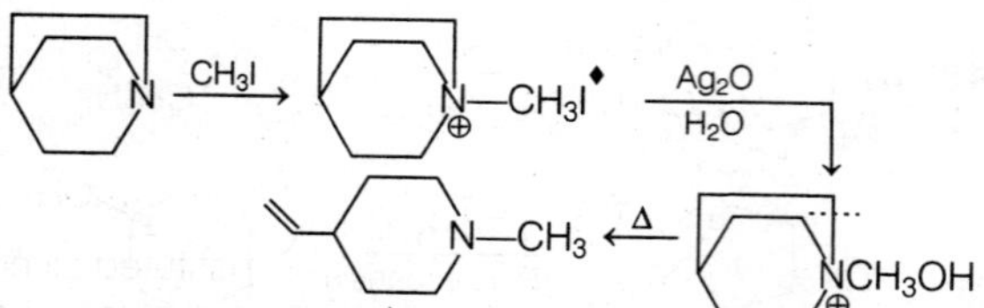

Least substituted product is major product

56. (*a*) $CH_3CH_2NO_2 \xrightarrow{HNO_2} CH_3CNO_2 \xrightarrow{NaOH} CH_3CNO_2$

O=NOH; NOH (Nitrolic acid, Blue); $N\bar{O}\overset{+}{Na}$ (Red)

Thus, 1°

It is also called Victor Meyer Test.

57. (*d*) $CH_3CH_2CH_2NH_2 \xrightarrow{HNO_2} CH_3CH_2CH_2N_2^{\oplus} \xrightarrow[-N_2]{}$

$CH_3CH_2\overset{\oplus}{C}H_2$ (1° carbocation) $\xrightarrow{1,\,2\text{–hydride shift}} CH_3\overset{\oplus}{C}HCH_3$ (2° carbocation)

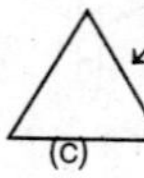

(c)

$\xrightarrow{H_2O} CH_3CH_2CH_2OH$ (a)

$\xrightarrow{H_2O} CH_3CH(OH)CH_3$ (b)

60. (*d*) —NH_2 group changes to —OH on reaction with HNO_2. Hence, (*X*) is 1° amine.

$CH_3-C(CH_3)_2-NH_2 \xrightarrow{HNO_2} CH_3-C(CH_3)_2-OH$

(*X*) 1° amine; 3° alcohol

Thus (a), (b), (c) are true.

62. (*b*) NH_3 (a strong nucleophile) causes elimination from 3° alkyl halide, thus (b) is incorrect.

63. (*a*) I (1° alkyl) < II (*iso* alkyl) < III (2° alkyl) < IV (3° alkyl)

64. (*c*) I < III < II

65. (*b*) $(CH_3)_3N$ least boiling point due to lack of H-bonding.

66. (*c*)

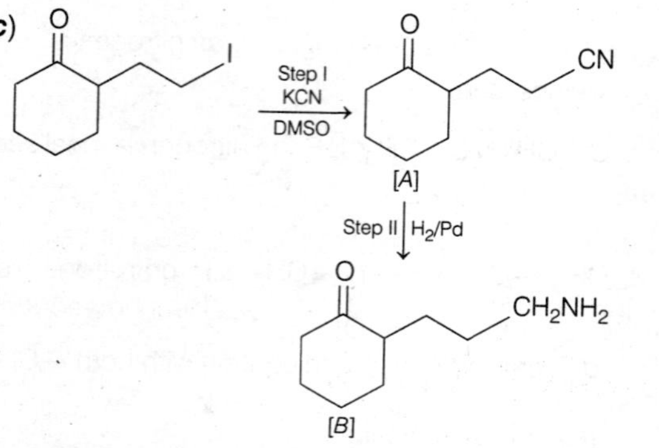

Step I involves the nucleophilic substitution reaction in which I (Iodine) is substituted by —CN group.

Step II H_2/Pd reagent is used for reduction process. Here, —CN group reduces itself to —CH_2NH_2

68. (*a*) *n*-butylamine ($CH_3CH_2CH_2CH_2NH_2$) can be prepared by Gabriel phthalimide reaction. This method produces only primary amines without the traces of secondary or tertiary amines. In this method, phthalimide is treated with ethanolic KOH, it forms potassium salt of phthalimide which on heating with alkyl halide followed by alkaline hydrolysis forms corresponding primary amines.

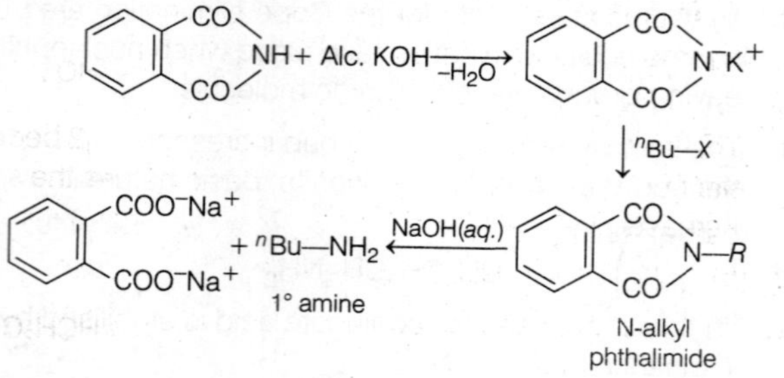

Triethylamine, *t*-butylamine and *neo*-pentylamine cannot be prepared by Gabriel phthalimide reaction.

69. (*d*) (a) $CH_3Cl \xrightarrow{NH_3} CH_3NH_2 \xrightarrow{CH_3Cl} (CH_3)_2NH \xrightarrow{CH_3Cl}$

$(CH_3)_3N \xrightarrow{CH_3Cl} (CH_3)_4N^{\oplus}Cl^{\ominus}$ mixture is formed

(b) $CH_3Cl \xrightarrow{KCN} CH_3CN \xrightarrow{Sn/HCl} CH_3CH_2NH_2$ 1° amine

(c) $CH_3Cl \xrightarrow{AgCN} CH_3NC \xrightarrow{LiAlH_4} CH_3NHCH_3$ 2° amine

$\overset{+}{C}H_3CN \xrightarrow{LiAlH_4} CH_3CH_2NH_2$ 1° amine

some 1° amine is also formed

(d) $CH_3NH_2 \xrightarrow[\Delta]{CHCl_3/KOH} CH_3NC \xrightarrow{Sn\ HCl} CH_3NHCH_3$ 2° amine (pure)

70. (*b*) $CH_3CH_2CN \longrightarrow CH_3CH_2NH_2$ one carbon less

(a) CH_3CH_2CN (*A*) $\longrightarrow CH_3CH_2CH_2NH_2$ incorrect propyl amine

(b) $\xrightarrow{H_3O^{\oplus}} CH_3CH_2\overset{O}{\overset{\|}{C}}OH \xrightarrow[\Delta]{NH_3} CH_3CH_2\overset{O}{\overset{\|}{C}}NH_2 \xrightarrow{\Delta,\ KBrO} CH_3CH_2NH_2$ (*B*)

Thus, true.

72. (*b*) $CH_3CH(NH_2)COOH \rightleftharpoons CH_3CH(\overset{\oplus}{N}H_3)COO^{\ominus}$ (Zwitter ion) $\xrightarrow[H^{\oplus}\ donor]{Acidic\ medium} CH_3CH(\overset{\oplus}{N}H_3)COOH$

(pH = 4, pH = 1 or pH = 2) are acidic medium.

73. (*a*) The mechanism of the given reaction is as follows

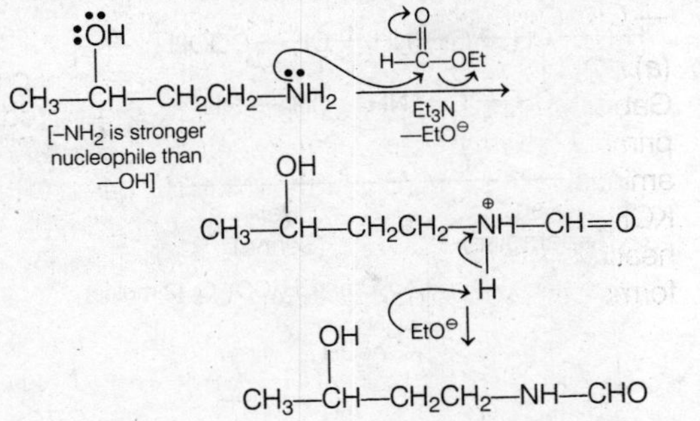

The basic mechanism of the reaction is acyl S_N2 because the nucleophile, $CH_3(OH)CH_2CH_2\ NH_2$ attacks the sp^2 carbon of the ester (H — CO_2Et) and gets substituted.

74. (*b*) (a) $CH_3CH_2CHCH_3$ with NH_2 — 1° (b) $CH_3CH_2CH_2CHCH_3$ with $NHCH_2CH_3$ — 2°

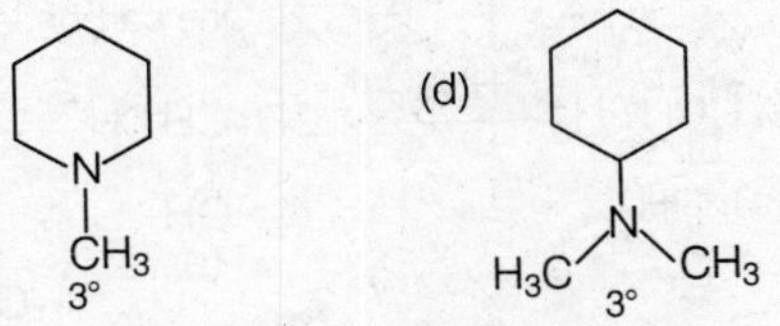

75. (*b*) The reaction for the production of ethylamine from *N*-ethylphthalimide can be takes place as follows

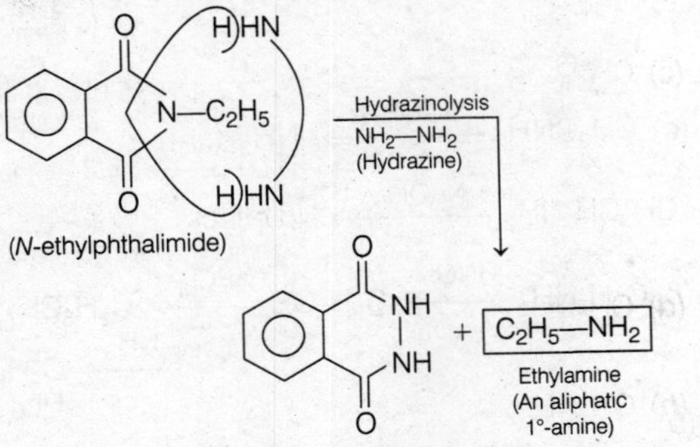

This reaction is the second step of Gabriel phthalimide synthesis for the preparation of aliphatic 1°-amines and amino acid. In this step concentrated alkali can also be used in place of hydrazine.

77. (c) 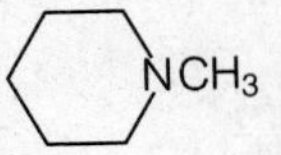 lacks H–atom at N–atom (3° amine) hence, no H–bonding. Thus, least boiling point.

80. (*d*)

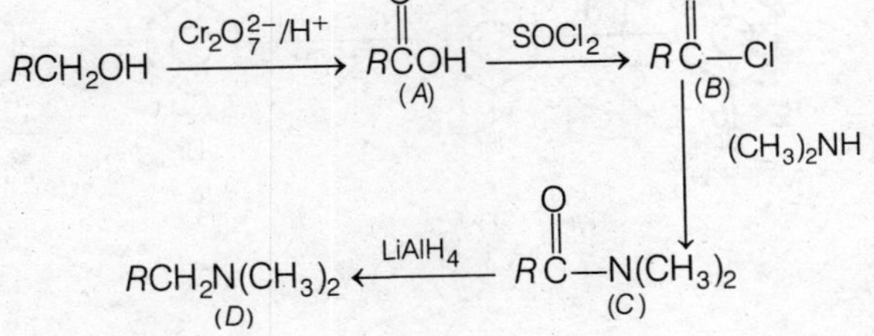

Thus, $CH_3-\overset{CH_3}{\underset{CH_3}{C}}-CH_2CH_2N(CH_3)_2$

81. (*b*) In (1) major product is least substituted alkene, i.e. *Y* and in (2) major product is substituted alkene, i.e. *X*. Thus 1*Y*, 2*X*.

82. (*c*)

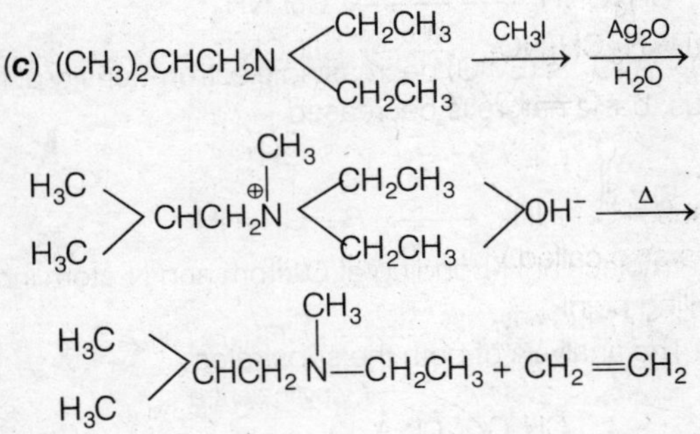

83. (*b*)

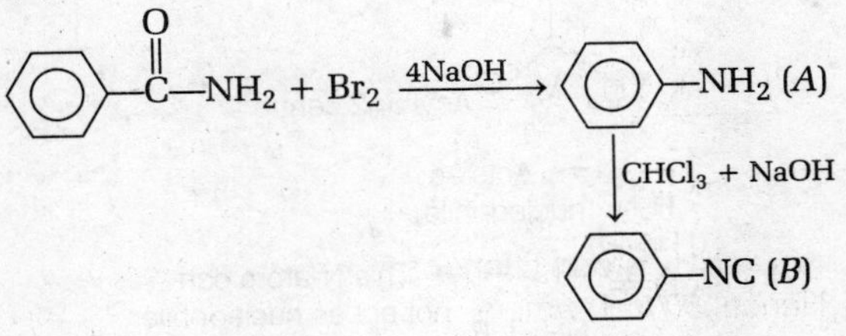

Carbylamine reaction

84. (*a*) (a) 2° amine due to intermolecular H-bonding; others lack active H for H-bonding.

87. (*c*) $CH_3NH_2 \xrightarrow[\Delta]{CHCl_3/KOH} CH_3NC$

88. (*c*) This reaction does not involve Hofmann bromamide degradation. Rest all options involve Hofmann bromamide degradation during the reaction of Br_2 + KOH with amide.

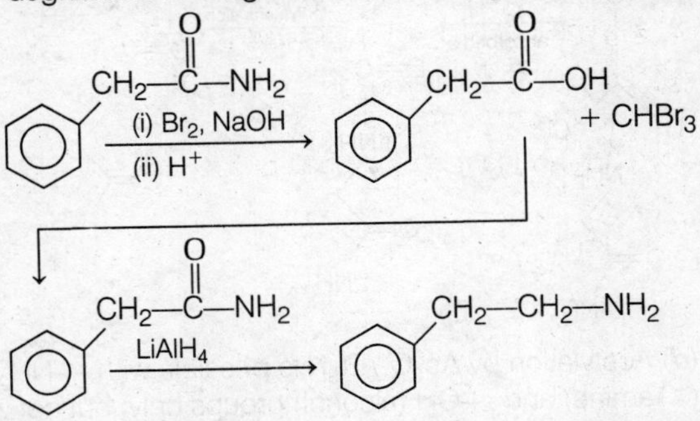

95. (*c*) $NaBH_4$ is a selective reducing agent. It can reduce group into alcohol, N-methyl imine group, Me—N=CH— into 2°-amine but cannot reduce an isolated C=C.

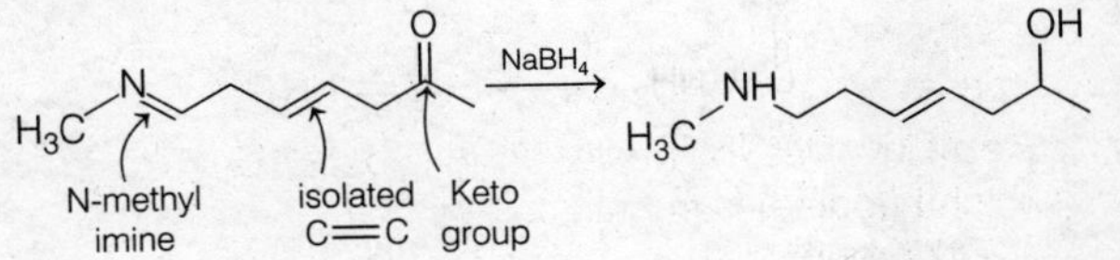

96. (*a*) $CH_3NC \xrightarrow{4H} CH_3NHCH_3$ (2° amine)

97. (*d*) $\underset{1°}{CH_3CH_2CH_2NH_2}$, $\underset{2°}{CH_3CH_2-NH-CH_3}$, $\underset{3°}{(CH_3)_3N}$

98. (*d*) $CH_3\overset{O}{\overset{\|}{C}}NH_2 \xrightarrow[\Delta]{NaOH/Br_2} CH_3NH_2$

99. (*c*) $-NO_2$ is (EWG) decreasing electron-density at N–atom thus, basic nature is decreased.

100. (*c*) $R-\overset{O}{\overset{\|}{C}}-NH_2 \longleftrightarrow R-\overset{OH}{\overset{|}{C}}=NH$

Intermolecular H-bonding at O-atom and N-atom increases boiling point.

102. (*d*) The analysis of both the substrates

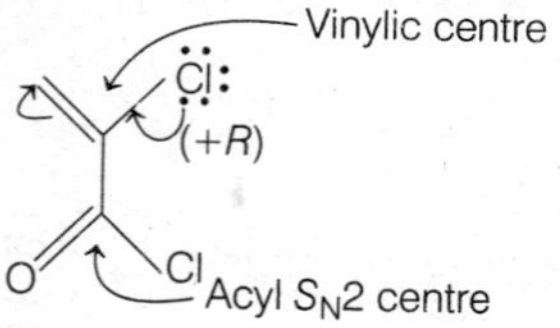

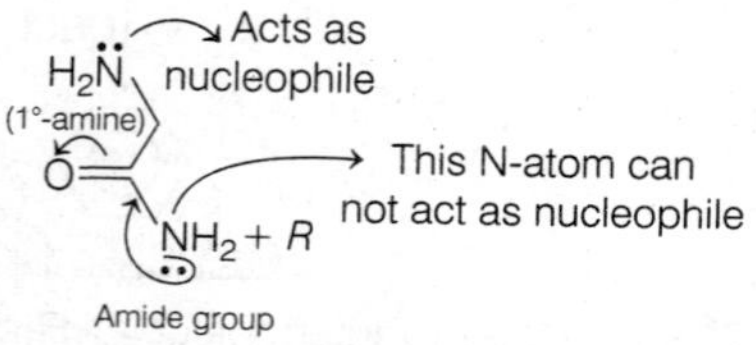

So, the reaction can take place as follows:

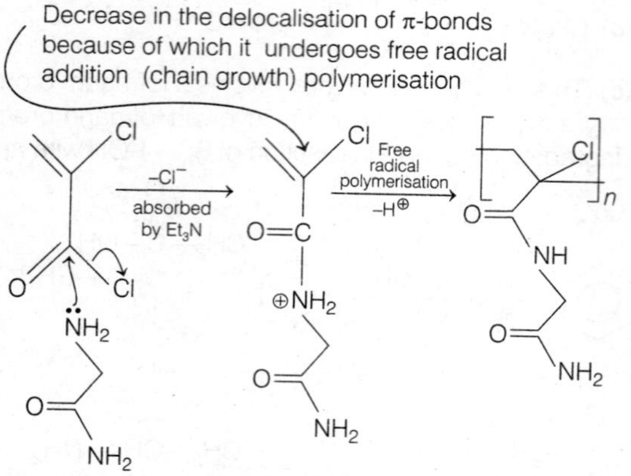

104. (*d*) Acetylation by Ac_2O /Et_3N is possible with $-NH_2$ (1°-amine) and $-OH$ (alcohol) groups only, but not with '$-NH_2$' part of $-\overset{O}{\overset{\|}{C}}-NH_2$ (amide) groups, because the *lp* of nitro $>C=O$

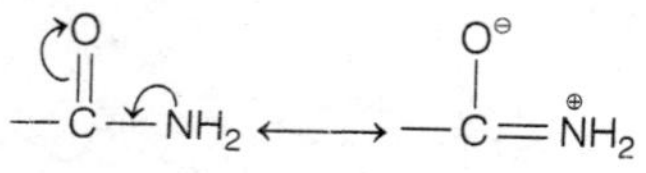

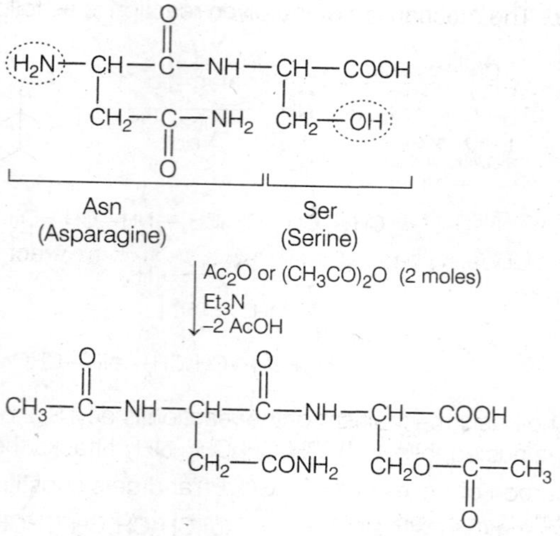

106. (*a*) $R-\overset{O}{\overset{\|}{C}}-NH_2 \xrightarrow[\Delta]{KOH/Br_2} \underset{\text{One carbon less}}{RNH_2}$

107. (*d*) $CH_3\underset{NH_2}{\underset{|}{C}}HCH_3 \xrightarrow{HNO_2} \underset{(A)}{CH_3\underset{OH}{\underset{|}{C}}HCH_3} \xrightarrow{\text{Oxidation}}$

$\underset{(B)}{CH_3-\underset{O}{\underset{\|}{C}}-CH_3} \xrightarrow[\text{(ii) } H_3O^+]{\text{(i) } CH_3MgBr} \underset{(C)}{CH_3-\overset{CH_3}{\overset{|}{\underset{CH_3}{\underset{|}{C}}}}-OH}$

108. (*c*) $CH_3\overset{O}{\overset{\|}{C}}NH_2 \xrightarrow{NaOH/\Delta} NH_3\uparrow$

$CH_3CH_2NH_2 \xrightarrow{NaOH/\Delta}$ No effect

109. (*b*) $C_2H_5NH_2 \xrightarrow{HNO_2} C_2H_5OH \xrightarrow{PCl_5} C_2H_5Cl \xrightarrow{NH_3} \underset{\text{Ethyl amine}}{C_2H_5NH_2}$

112. (*b*)

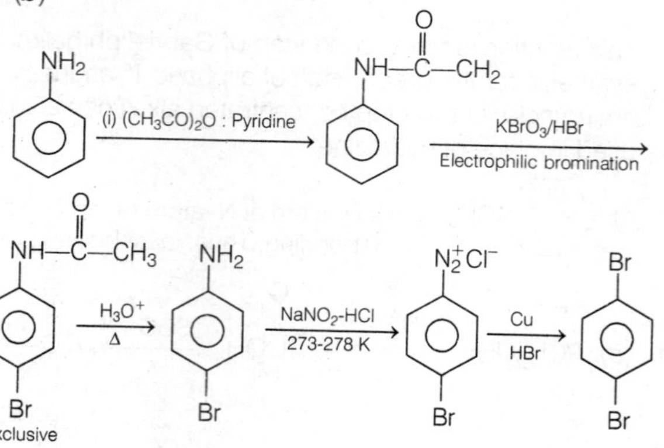

116. (*c*) The reaction is given as follows

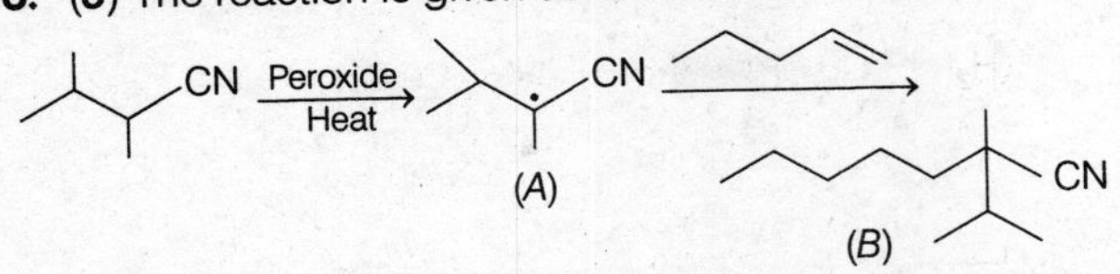

It can be proceed as

Peroxide on heating give radicals which abstract hydrogen from

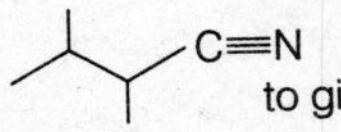

to give (A)

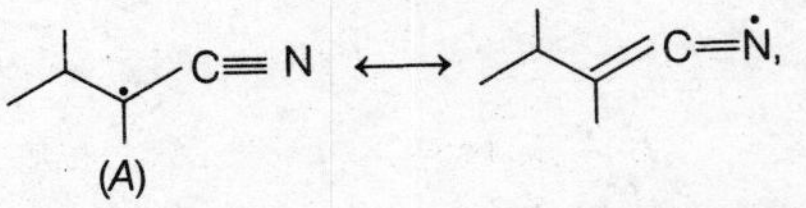

'*A*'which on addition to  (Anti-Markownikoff's)

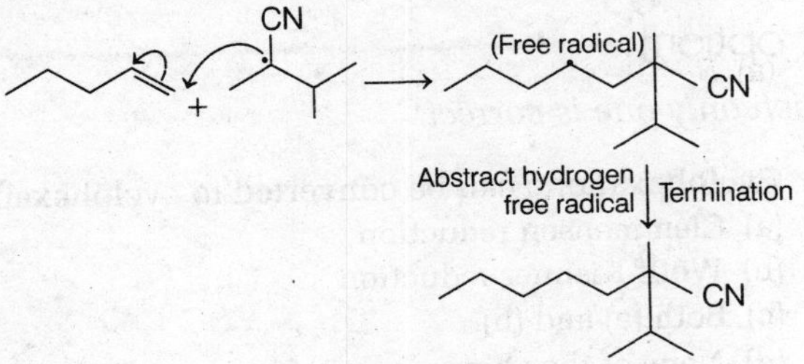

117. (*d*)

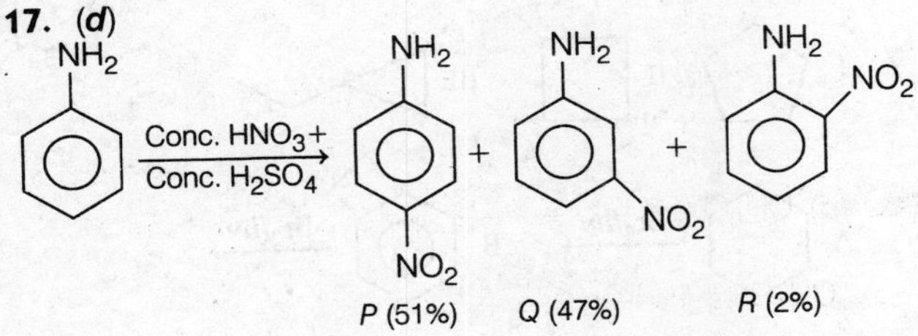

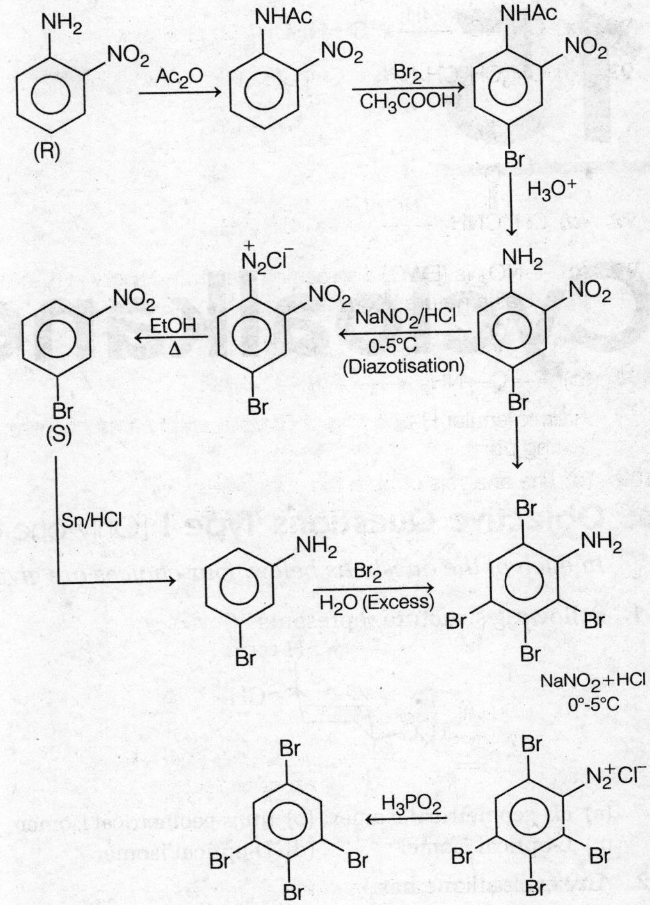

15

Cycloalkanes

Objective Questions Type I [Only one correct option]

In each of the questions below, four choices are given of which only one is correct.

1. Following structure represents

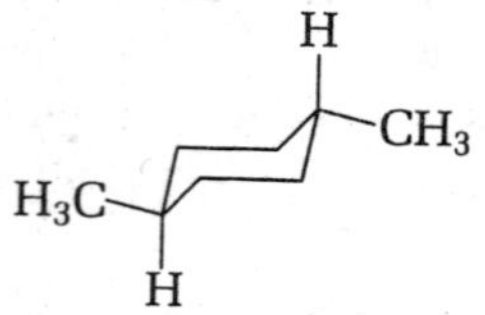

(a) *cis*-geometrical isomer (b) *trans*-geometrical isomer
(c) L-optical isomer (d) D-optical isomer

2. Any cycloalkane has
(a) equatorial hydrogen (b) axial hydrogen
(c) Both (a) and (b) (d) None of these

3. Structure of bicyclo (2.1.1) hexane is

(a) 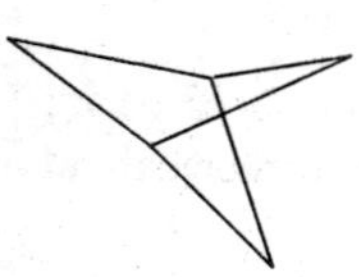

(b) 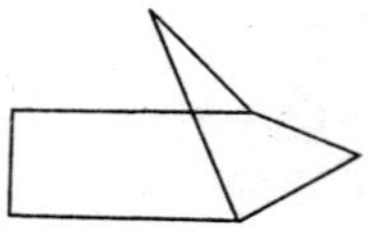

(c) 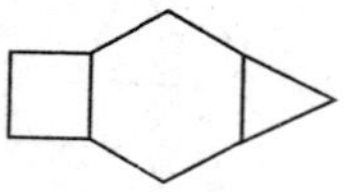

(d) 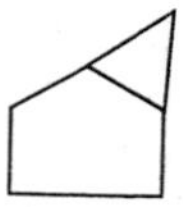

4. IUPAC name of the following structure is

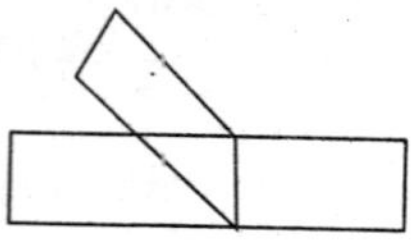

(a) bicyclo (2.2.2) octane (b) bicyclo (2.2.2) hexane
(c) bicyclo (2.1.1) hexane (d) bicyclo (2.2.1) heptane

5. Degree of unsaturation of cycloalkane is
(a) one (b) two
(c) three (d) four

6. Cyclohexanone can be converted to cyclohexane by
(a) Clemmensen reduction
(b) Wolff-Kishner reduction
(c) Both (a) and (b)
(d) None of the above

7. I. 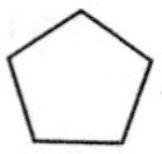 II. 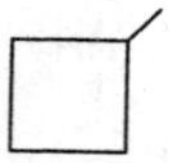 III. 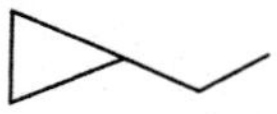

A. 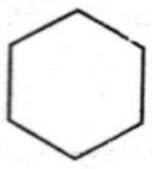 $\xrightarrow{Br_2/h\nu}$ B.  $\xrightarrow{Br_2/h\nu}$

C. 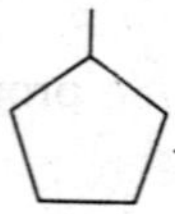 $\xrightarrow{Br_2/h\nu}$ D. 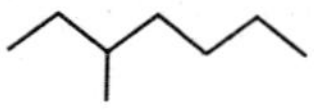 $\xrightarrow{Br_2/h\nu}$

E. 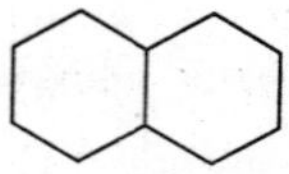 $\xrightarrow{Br_2/h\nu}$ F.  $\xrightarrow{Br_2/h\nu}$

Which of the following conversion gives product I, II and III ?
(a) A, B, C, D
(b) A, C, F
(c) A, C, D, E
(d) A, B, C, D, E

8. $CH_2{=}CH_2 + CH_2N_2 \xrightarrow{h\nu}$
In the above reaction
(a) intermediate is carbene
(b) product is cyclopropane
(c) leaving group is N_2
(d) All the facts are true

9. Select the incorrect statement.
(a) Diels-Alder reaction is a cycloaddition reaction
(b) Carbene can be added to ethene to form cyclopropane
(c) Both (a) and (b)
(d) None of the above

10. Diethyl malonate
(a) is a diester of a dibasic acid
(b) has active methylene group
(c) has acidic hydrogen
(d) satisfies all these facts

11. Methylcyclopropane undergoes free radical substitution reaction with Cl_2. Major product formed is

(a) 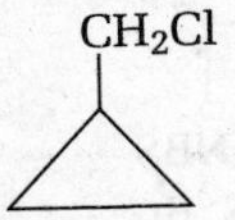

(b) 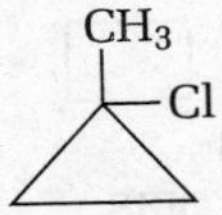

(c) $CH_3CHCH_2CH_2Cl$ (with Cl on C-2)
(d) $ClCH_2CH_2CH_2CH_2Cl$

12. The decreasing order of melting points of the following compounds is

I. 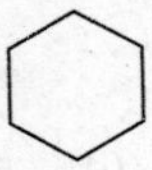
II. 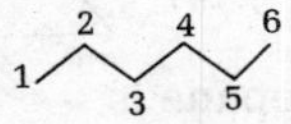

III. 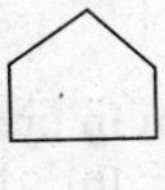
VI. 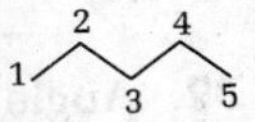

(a) I > II > III > IV
(b) IV > III. > II > I
(c) II > I > IV > III
(d) III > IV > I > II

13. Which has maximum melting point?
(a) Cyclooctane
(b) Cycloheptane
(c) Cyclohexane
(d) Cyclopentane

14. Select the incorrect variation of the given property.
(a) reactivity of halogens with cycloalkanes
$F_2 > Cl_2 > Br_2 > I_2$
(b) the ease of replacing a hydrogen
tertiary > secondary > primary > methyl
(c) the stability of cycloalkane
cyclopropane > cyclobutane > cyclopentane
(d) the strain in cycloalkane
cyclopropane > cyclobutane > cyclopentane

15. The major product formed in the followning reaction is

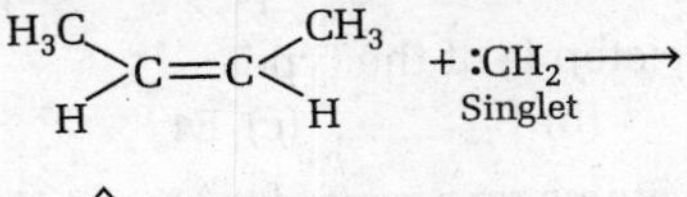

(a) 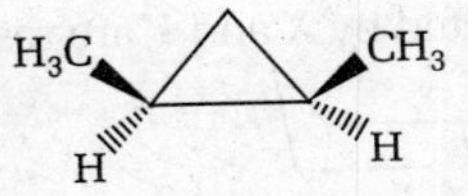

(b) 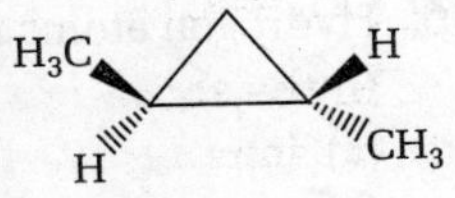

(c) 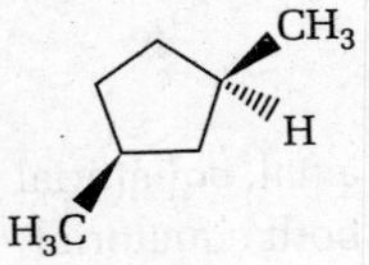

(d) 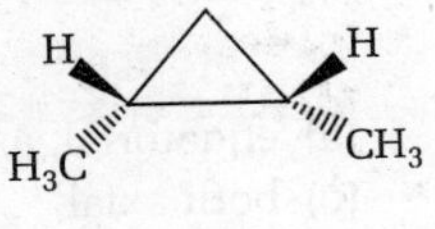

16. Select the correct statement(s).
(a) Ring strain is a form of potential energy that the cyclic molecule contains
(b) Greater the ring strain, greater the potential energy and thus smaller the stability
(c) Both the statements are correct
(d) None of the above statements is correct

17. Which has least heat of combustion per CH_2 group?
(a) Cyclopentane
(b) Cyclohexane
(c) Cycloheptane
(d) Cyclobutane

18. When strain in cyclobutane is minimised
(a) ring opening takes place
(b) hybridisation changes
(c) both of the above take place
(d) none of the above takes place

19. Heat of combustion (ΔH) of cis-1,2-dimethylcyclopropane is greater than that of *trans*-isomer because there is more eclipsing in the
(a) *cis*-isomer as the methyl groups are closer
(b) *cis*-isomer as the methyl groups are farther
(c) *trans*-isomer as the methyl groups are closer
(d) *trans*-isomer as the methyl groups are farther

20. Indicate the potential energy level of the chair form of cyclohexane

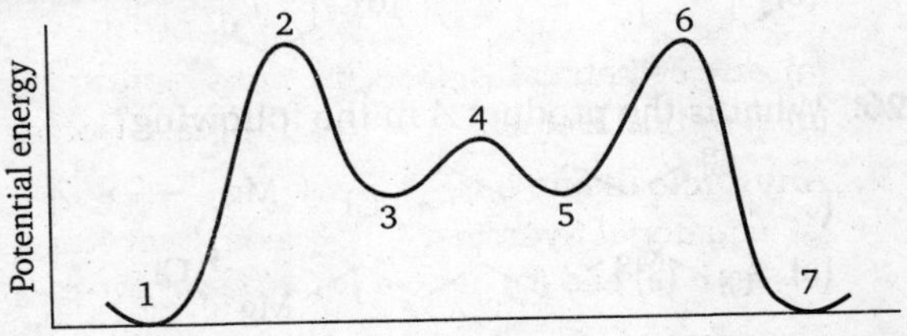

(a) 2, 6
(b) 3, 5
(c) 1, 7
(d) 4

21. Which of the following statements is wrong?
(a) The decreasing order of the numerical value of heat of combustion is

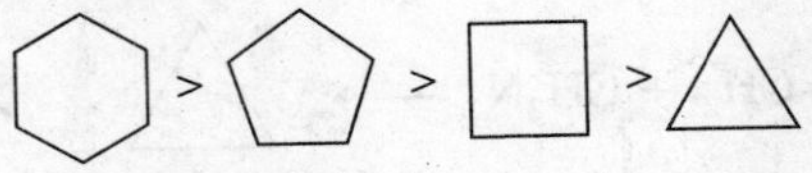

(b) Cycloalkanes are planar.
(c) Cyclopropane has higher heat of combustion per methylene (—CH_2—) group than that of cyclobutane.
(d) With the exception of cyclopropane, cycloalkanes are non-planar.

22. Identify the product of the following reaction

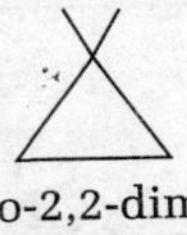 + Br_2 ⟶

(a) 1,3-dibromo-2,2-dimethylpropane
(b) 1,3-dibromo-3-methylbutane
(c) Both (a) and (b)
(d) None of the above

23. Diels-Alder reaction is of the type
(a) electrocyclic reaction
(b) cycloaddition reaction
(c) Both (a) and (b)
(d) None of the above

24. Factors that affect formation of cycloalkanes by intramolecular cyclisation are
(a) thermal stability
(b) entropy factor
(c) Both (a) and (b)
(d) None of the above

25. Consider the above chemical reaction and identify product "A". **[JEE Main 2021, March]**

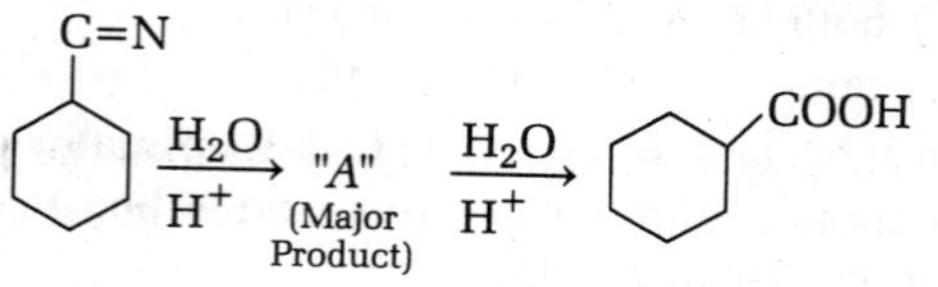

(a) 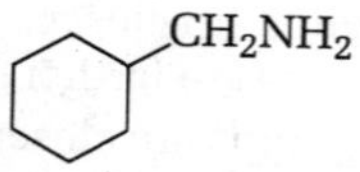
(b) 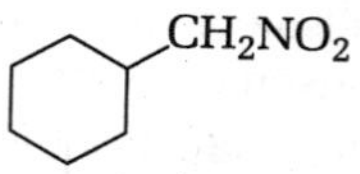
(c) 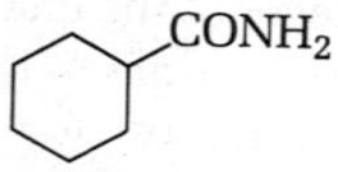
(d) 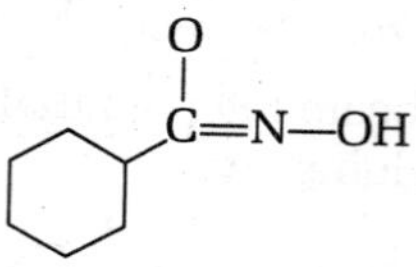

26. What is the product *A* in the following?

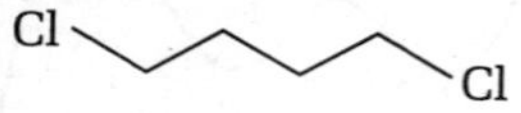 + Mg ⟶ *A*

(a) 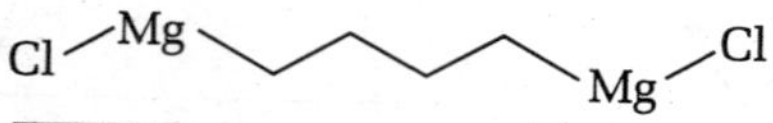
(b) 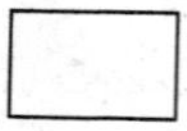
(c) 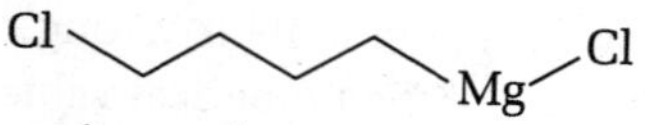
(d) 

27. $CH_2{=}CH_2 + CH_2N_2 \longrightarrow$ 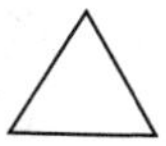

Intermediate in the above reaction is
(a) $\overset{\oplus}{C}H_2—\overset{\ominus}{C}H_2$
(b) $CH_2CH_2\overset{\oplus}{C}H_2\overset{\ominus}{N}_2$
(c) $\overset{\ominus}{C}H_2CH_2\overset{\oplus}{C}H_2$
(d) $:CH_2$

28. $CH_3CH{=}CHCH_3 + CHCl_3 \xrightarrow{(CH_3)_3CO^-K^+}$ 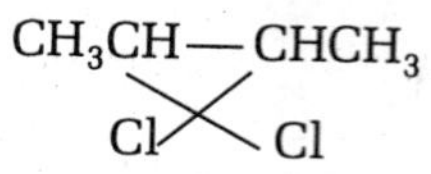

Intermediate in the above reaction is
(a) $:\overset{\ominus}{C}Cl_3$
(b) $:CCl_2$
(c) $CH_3\overset{\ominus}{C}H\overset{\oplus}{C}HCH_3$
(d) All of these

29. Which ring is cleaved on hydrogenation of the following compound?

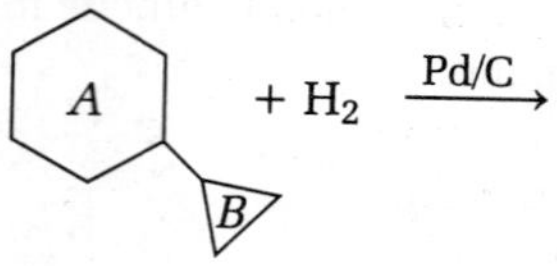

(a) *A*
(b) *B*
(c) Both *A* and *B*
(d) None of these

30. Suitable reagents *A* and *B* for the following reactions are

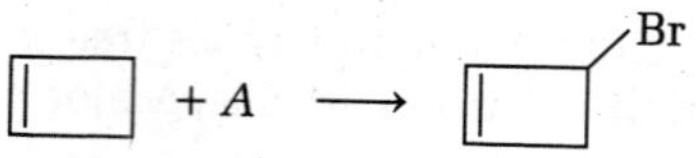

(a) Br, Br_2
(b) Br_2, NBS
(c) NBS, NBS
(d) NBS, Br_2

31. Which has maximum strain?
(a) 
(b) 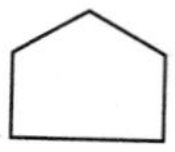
(c) 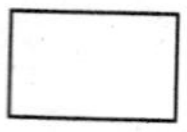
(d) 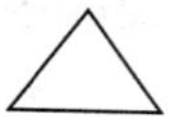

32. Angle strain in cyclopropane is
(a) 24°44′
(b) 9°44′
(c) 44′
(d) −5°16′

33. Angle strain in cyclohexane is larger than that of cyclopentane but is thermally stable. It is due to the fact that
(a) it exists in more stable boat form
(b) it exists in more stable chair form
(c) it exists in more stable skew form
(d) it exists in *cis* and *trans*-forms

34. If ring strain is larger, then
(a) larger the potential energy
(b) smaller the stability
(c) Both (a) and (b)
(d) None of the above

35. $\overset{\ominus}{\ddot{C}}H(COOC_2H_5)_2 + (CH_2)_2Br_2 \longrightarrow \underset{CH_2CH_2Br}{\overset{CH(COOC_2H_5)_2}{|}}$

The above step is of the type
(a) S_E
(b) S_N
(c) E1
(d) E2

36. Hydrogen atoms represented by *X* and *Y* are respectively

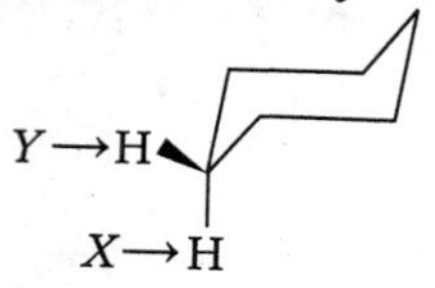

(a) equatorial, axial
(b) axial, equatorial
(c) both axial
(d) both equatorial

37. Which have equal potential energy?

I. 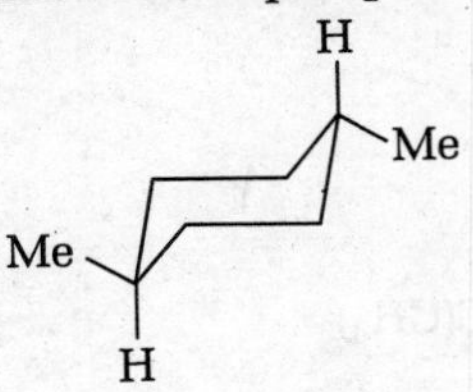

II. 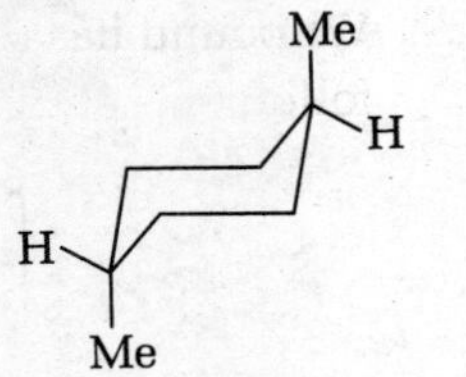

III. 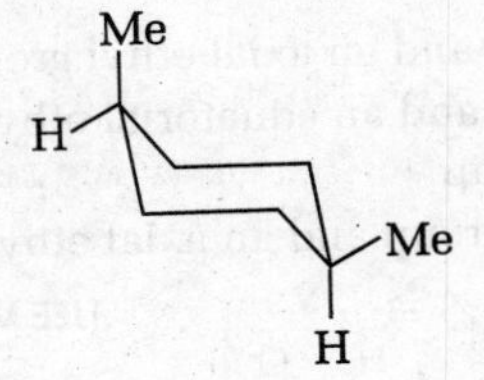

IV. 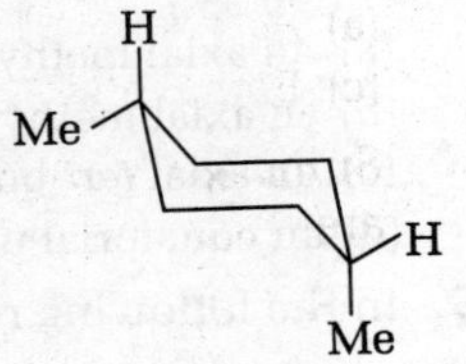

(a) I, II
(b) III, IV
(c) I, III
(d) II, IV

38. 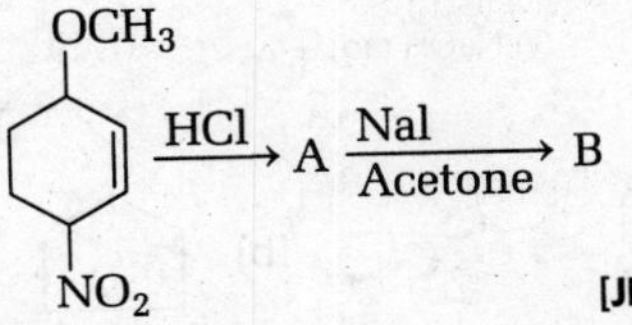

[JEE Main 2021, Feb.]

Find '*A*' and '*B*'

(a) *A* = 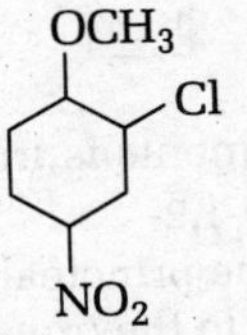 *B* = 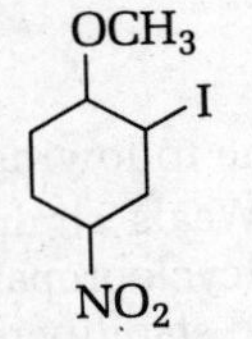

(b) *A* = 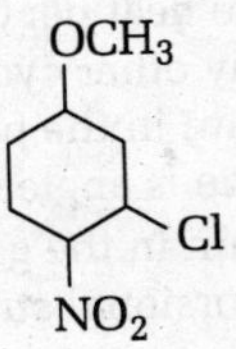 *B* = 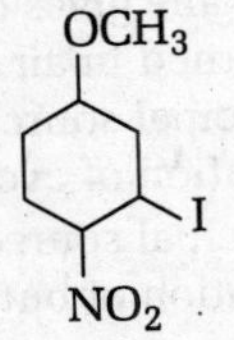

(c) *A* = 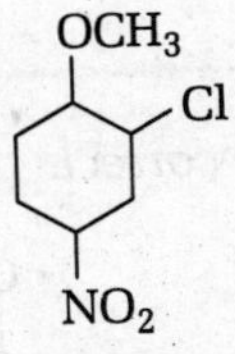 *B* = 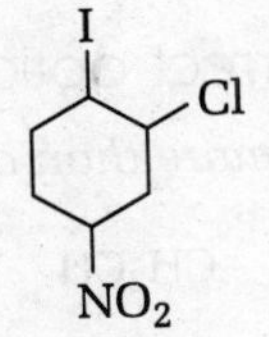

(d) *A* = 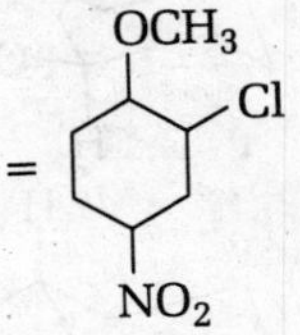 *B* = 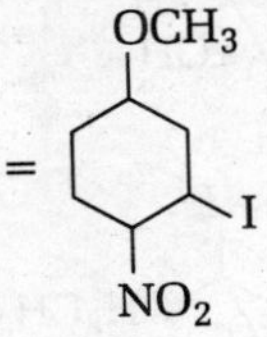

39. 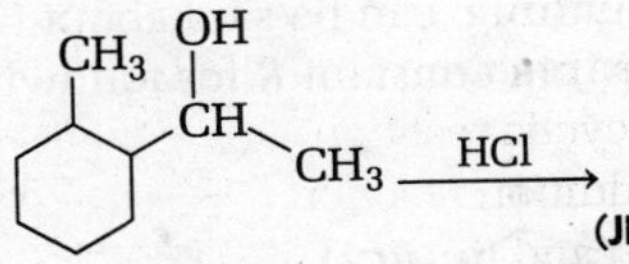

(JEE Main 2021, Feb.)

(a) 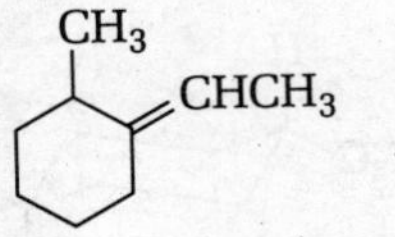
(b) 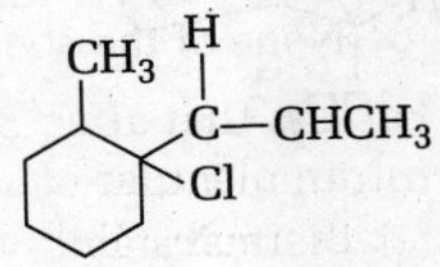
(c) 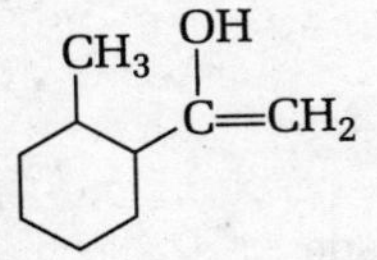
(d) 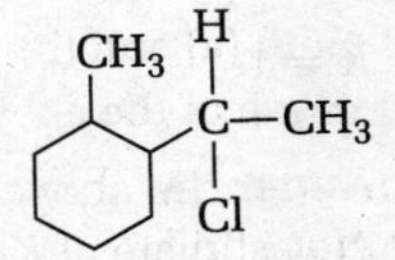

40. Number of rings in basketane is
(a) 5 (b) 6 (c) 7 (d) 8

41. Which of listed terms best describes the relationship between the methyl groups in the chair conformation of the substance shown?

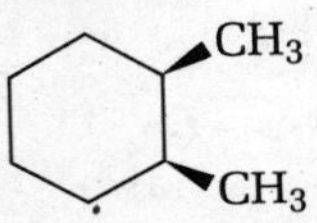

(a) Eclipsed (b) *Trans* (c) *Anti* (d) *Gauche*

42. Rank the following substances in order of decreasing heat of combustion (largest → smallest).

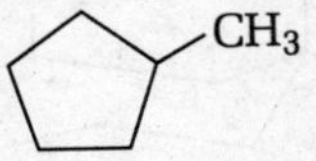
1

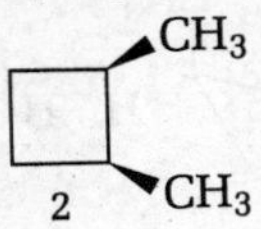
2

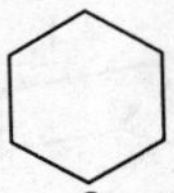
3

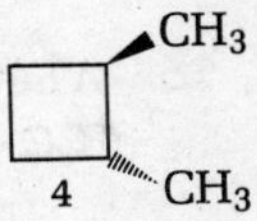
4

(a) 1 > 2 > 4 > 3
(b) 2 > 4 > 1 > 3
(c) 3 > 4 > 2 > 1
(d) 1 > 3 > 2 > 4

43. Which of the following statements best describes the most stable conformation of *trans*-1,3-dimethylcyclohexane?
(a) Both methyl groups are axial
(b) Both methyl groups are equatorial
(c) One methyl group is axial, the other equatorial
(d) The molecule is severely strained and cannot exist

44. Compare the stability of the following two compounds
A. *cis*-1-ethyl-3-methylcyclohexane
B. *trans*-1-ethyl-3-methylcyclohexane
(a) *A* is more stable
(b) *B* is more stable
(c) *A* and *B* are of equal stability
(d) No comparison can be made

45. What, if anything, can be said about the magnitude of the equilibrium constant K for following process?

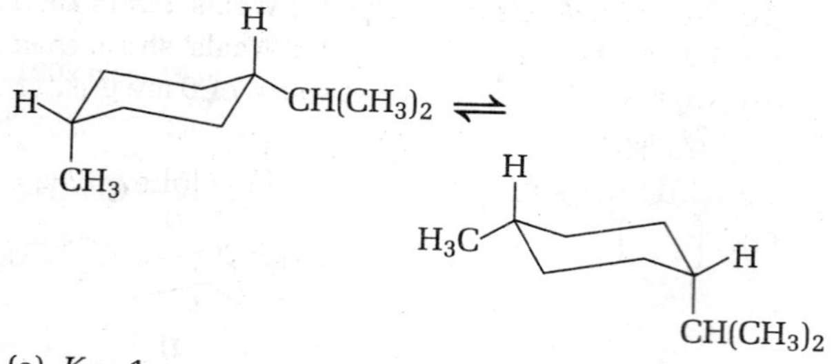

(a) $K = 1$
(b) $K > 1$
(c) $K < 1$
(d) No estimate of K can be made

46. Give the decreasing order of the stability of the following or increasing order of heat of combustion.

I. 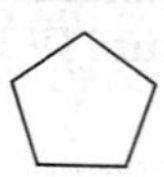 II. 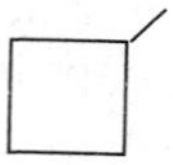 III. 

(a) I > II > III
(b) III > II > I
(c) II > III > I
(d) I > III > II

47. The two structures shown here are .... each other.

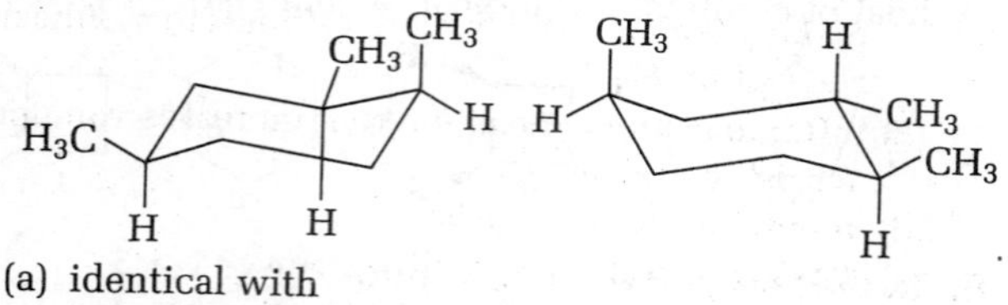

(a) identical with
(b) conformations of
(c) constitutional isomers of
(d) stereoisomers of

48. The most stable conformation of the following compound has

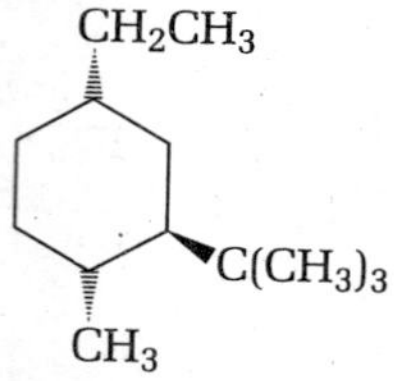

(a) an axial methyl group and an axial ethyl group
(b) an axial methyl group and an equatorial ethyl group
(c) an axial *tert*-butyl group
(d) an equatorial methyl group and an axial ethyl group

49. In the following reaction A is **[JEE Main 2020]**

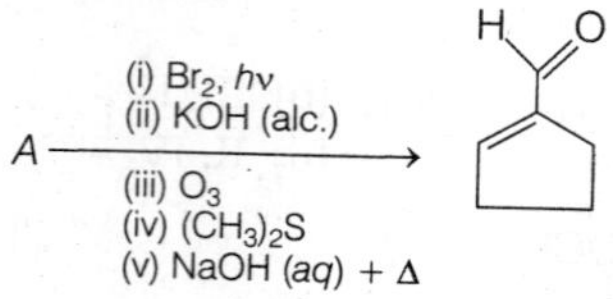

(a) 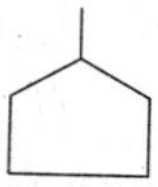 (b) 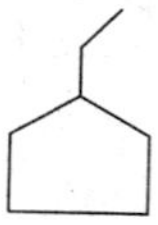

(c) 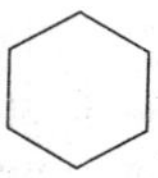 (d) 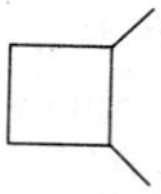

50. Which of the following statements is true?
(a) van der Waals' strain in *cis*-1,2-dimethylcyclopropane is the principal reason for its decreased stability relative to the *trans* isomer.
(b) Cyclohexane gives off more heat per CH_2 group on being burned in air than any other cycloalkane.
(c) The principal source of strain in the boat conformation of cyclohexane is angle strain.
(d) The principal source of strain in the gauche conformation of butane is torsional strain.

Objective Questions Type II [One or more than one correct option(s)]

In each of the questions below, four choices are given, of which one or more than one are correct.

1. Energy difference ($\Delta G°$) for equilibrium of monosubstituted cyclohexanes ($C_6H_{11}X$) is given below

X	$\Delta G°$ (equatorial-axial)
—H	0.0
—CN	– 0.2
—OH	– 1.0
—CH_3	– 1.7
—C_2H_5	– 2.9

Which of the following conformations is/are favourable?

(a) 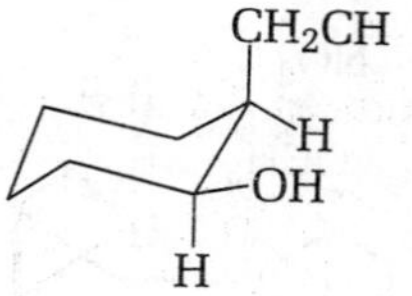 (b) 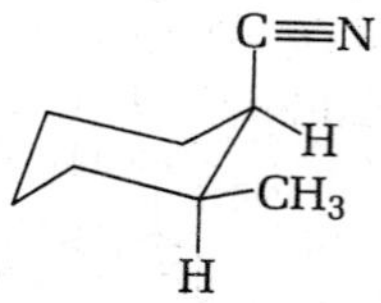

(c) 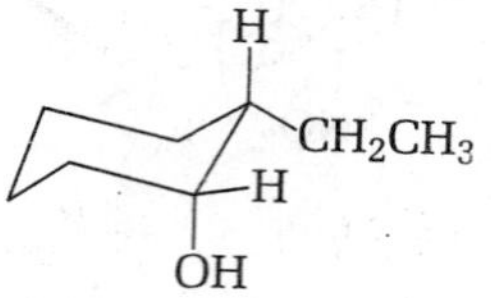 (d) 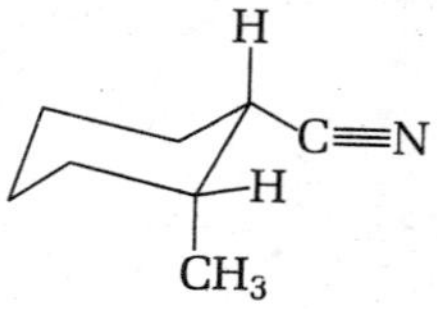

2. Select the correct conformers.

(a) 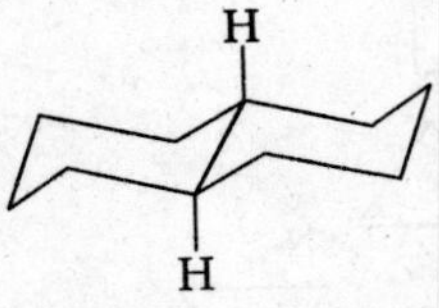
trans-decalin

(b) 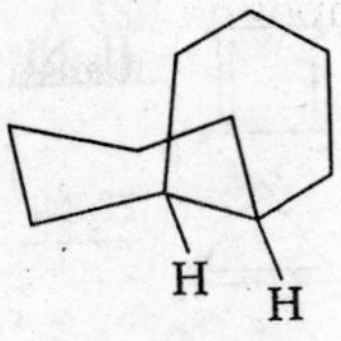
cis-decalin

(c) 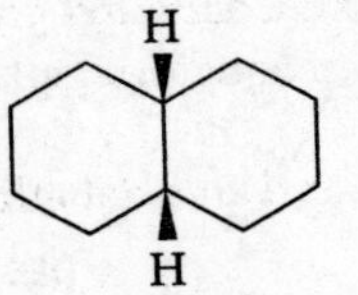
cis-decalin

(d) 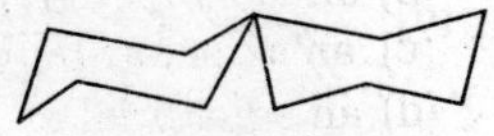
cis-decalin

3. Consider the following structures of 1, 3, 5-trimethyl cyclohexane

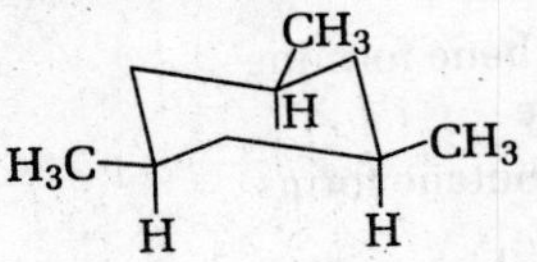
I

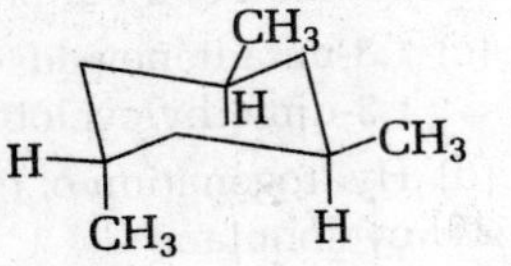
II

Select the correct statement(s).

(a) I is more stable stereoisomer with the greater number of its substituents in equatorial orientations
(b) II is more stable stereoisomer with the two substituents in equatorial and one in axial orientations
(c) I is *cis*-isomer and II is *trans*-isomer
(d) I is *trans*-isomer and II is *cis*-isomer

4. I and II in (Q. 3) can also be represented as

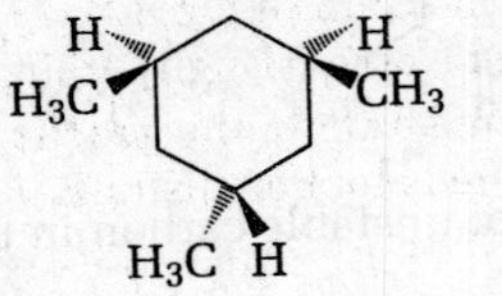
III

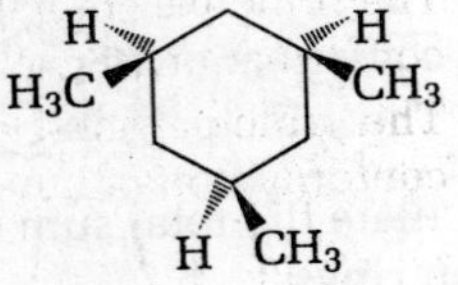
IV

(a)
(b) I is IV and II is III
(c) I and II both are III
(d) I and II both are IV

5. Consider the following structures *A* and *B*

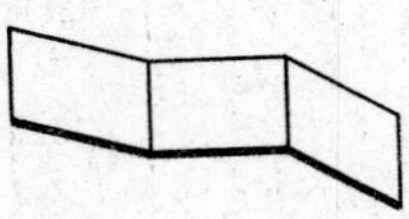
A

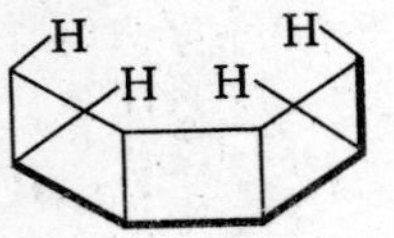
B

Select the correct statements about A and B.

(a) Both structures have approximately the same degree of angle strain and of torsional strain
(b) Structure *B* has more van der Waals' strain than *A*
(c) Structure *A* has more van der Waals' strain than *B*
(d) Angle strain and torsional strain of *B* are greater than that of *A*

6. Consider the structures **I** to **IV** of cyclohexanes,

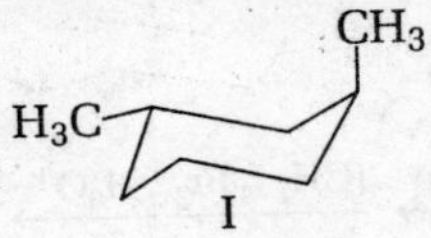
I

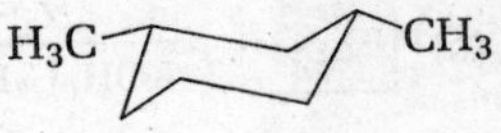
II

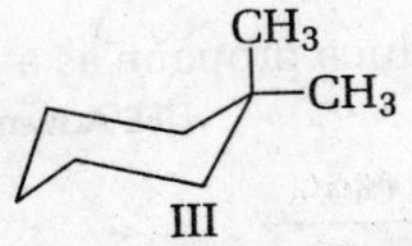
III

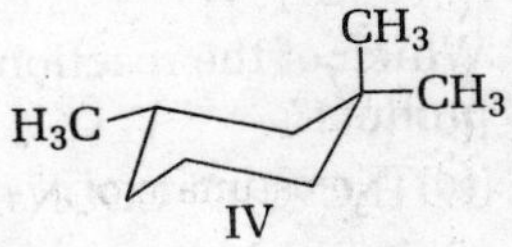
IV

Select the correct statement(s).

(a) I and II are stereoisomers of one another
(b) Heat of combustion of the structure IV is highest
(c) I is *trans*-stereoisomer
(d) I, II and III are constitutional isomers

7. Large rings with more than six C's are stable but difficult to prepare. On the other hand cyclopropanes have the greatest ring strain yet they are difficult to prepare. It is due to

(a) thermal stability which is determined by ring strain
(b) entropy factor that decreases with chain length, making it successively more difficult to synthesize rings of increasing size
(c) intramolecular cyclisation that increases van der Waals' repulsion
(d) torsional and angle strain

8. In the strongly acidic medium

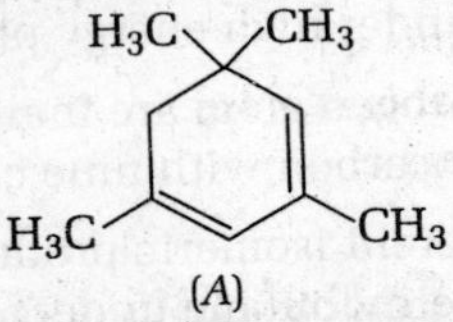
(*A*)

(a) *A* is converted completely into the allylic cation (*B*)

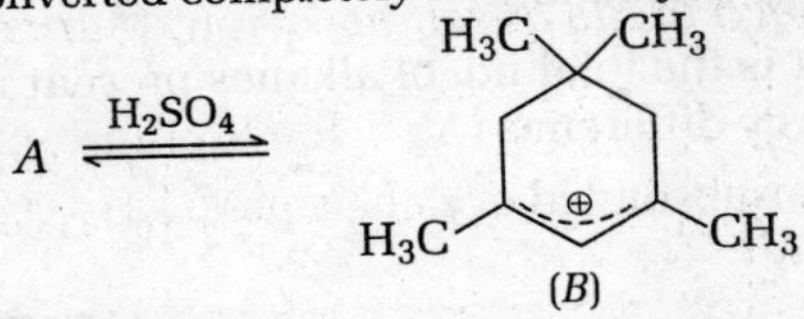
(*B*)

(b) *B* is stabilised by electron release from two methyl groups, one at each end of the allylic system
(c) *B* is converted into *A* on reaction with H_2O

$$B + H_2O \rightleftharpoons H_3O^{\oplus} + A$$

(d) *A* loses aromaticity

9. Cyclopentane can be obtained by following method(s)

(a) 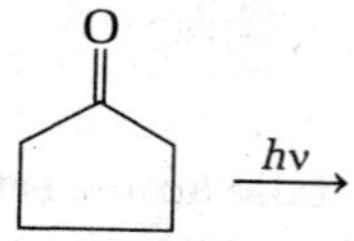

(b) 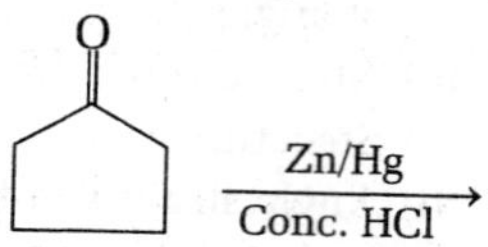

(c) 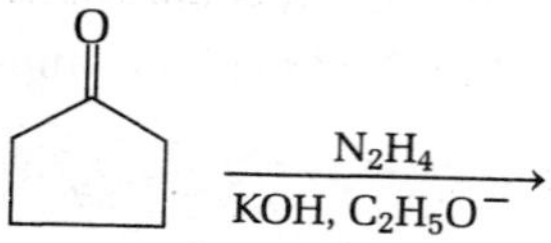

(d) $CH_2(CO_2C_2H_5)_2 \xrightarrow{2C_2H_5ONa} \xrightarrow{(CH_2)_4Br_2} \xrightarrow{H_3O^+} \xrightarrow{\Delta}$

10. Which of the reactions produce propane as a major product? **[JEE Advanced 2019]**

(a) 

(b) 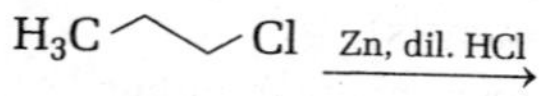

(c) 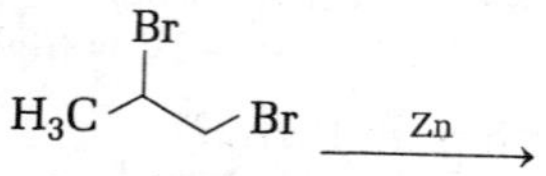

(d) 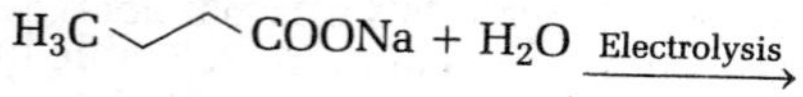

11. Select the correct formation of products.

(a) 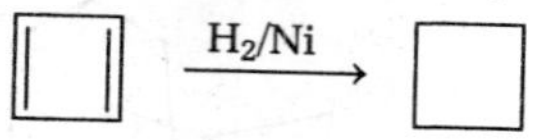

(b) 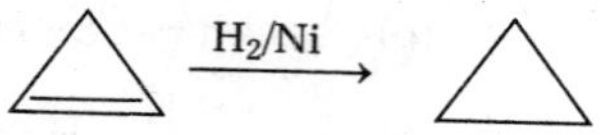

(c) 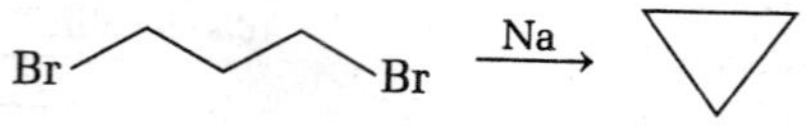

(d) 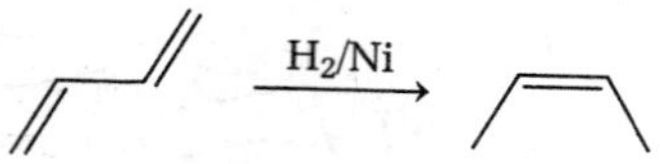

12. Select the correct statements.

(a) Electrocyclic addition of 1,3-pentadiene forms 3-methylcyclobutene

(b) 1,3-cyclohexadiene can be formed by electrocyclic addition of 1,3,5-hexatriene

(c) 1,3-butadiene adds to ethene forming 1,3-dimethylcyclobutene

(d) Hydrogenation of cyclobutene forms cyclobutane

Numerical Value Questions

All these questions have a Numerical value as their answer, solve the questions and write your answer.

1. The precentage of heptane in petrol (octane number 80) is ....

2. What are the bond angle in a chair conformer of cyclohexane?

3. How many monobrominated products (ignore stereoisomers) does 1, 3-dimethylcyclohexane can form with Br_2 under high energy photons?

4. How many hydrogen atom are there in nonane, the linear hydrocarbon with nine carbon atoms?

5. How many different isomeric products are obtained if 2-methylbutane undergoes monochlorination?

6. What is the total no. of alkanes present in product (Z)

$$CH_3Cl + C_2H_5Cl \xrightarrow{Na/dry\ ether} (Z)$$

7. How many total resonance structure can be drawn for the following anion (include those without separation of charge)?

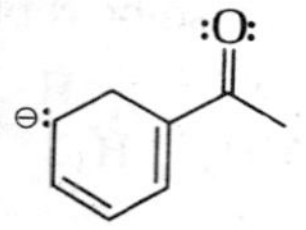

8. Calculate the total sum of unstable carbon in the given rings ?

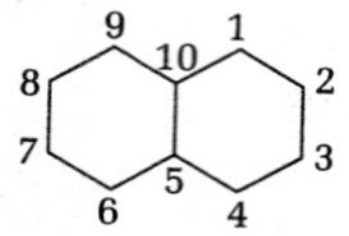

Comprehension Based Questions

In these questions, a passage has been given followed by questions based on it. You have to answer the questions based on the passage given.

***Passage* 1** Following figure is taken to test analytical ability.

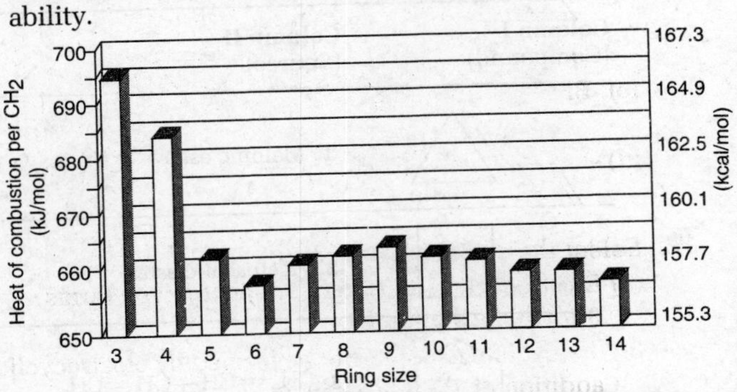

Heats of combustion per CH_2 for cycloalkanes as a function of ring size. By convention, the amount of energy released in an exothermic reaction has a negative sign. Thus, these heats of combustion are negative values.

1. Number of moles of oxygen required to combust one mole of cyclohexane is

(a) 3 (b) 5 (c) 7 (d) 9

2. From the above graph, maximum strain is in

(a) cyclopropane (b) cyclohexane

(c) cyclobutane

(d) heat of combustion is not related to strain

3. Select the correct statement(s).

(a) The more energy (strain) a compound contains, the more energy (heat) is released on combustion

(b) The more energy a compound contains, combustion reaction is less exothermic

(c) Combustion of methylcyclopentane is more exothermic than isomeric cyclohexane

(d) Combustion of methylcyclohexane is more exothermic than isomeric cyclopentane

***Passage* 2** Following figure is taken to test analytical ability.

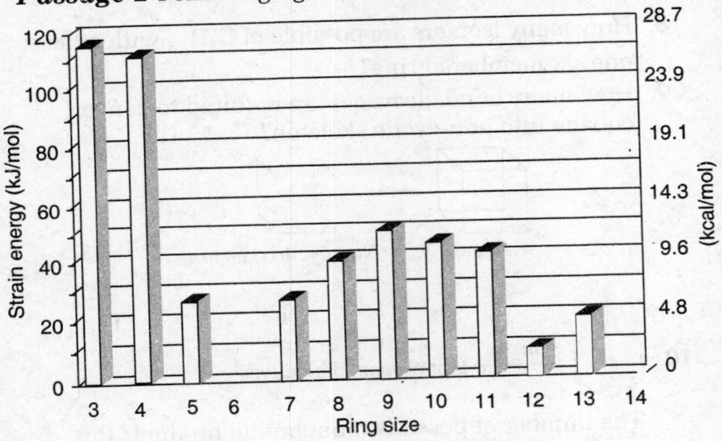

Cycloalkane strain energy as a function of ring size

1. If heat of combustion of long-chain alkane is 157.4 kcal per CH_2 group, then heat of combustion of cyclohexane is

(a) -944.4 kcal mol^{-1}

(b) $+944.4$ kcal mol^{-1}

(c) 26.2 kcal mol^{-1}

(d) $-$ 26.2 kcal mol^{-1}

2. If heat of combustion of long-chain alkane is 157.4 kcal per CH_2 group, then heat of combustion of cyclobutane is

(a) + 629.6 kcal

(b) $-$ 656.0 kcal

(c) $-$ 629.6 kcal

(d) + 656.0 kcal

3. Which ring is strain free and why?

(a) cyclopropane since it has internal bond angle of 60°

(b) cyclobutane since it has four C—C bonds of equal length and also bond angle of 90°

(c) cyclohexane since it can exist as more stable boat form

(d) cyclohexane since it can exist as more stable chair form

***Passage* 3** Disubstituted cycloalkanes can exist in different isomeric forms.

Answer the following questions.

1. 1,2-dimethyl cyclopentane can exist as

(a) geometrical isomer

(b) constitutional

(c) Both (a) and (b)

(d) None of the above

2. Disubstituted cyclopentane $\underset{(A)}{} \xrightarrow[\text{oxide}]{KMnO_4} \xrightarrow{\Delta}$ cyclopentane carboxylic acid. Thus, (A) is

(a)

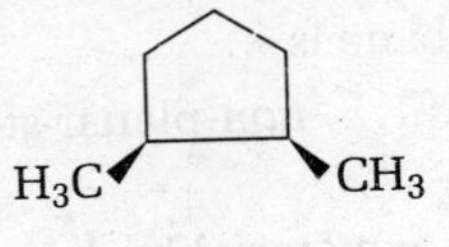

(b)

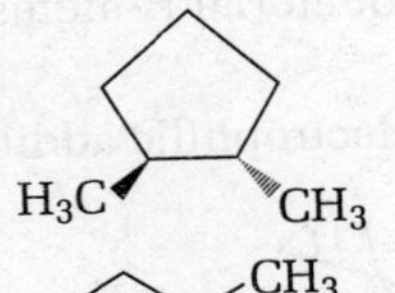

(c)

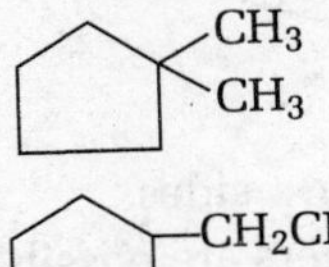

(d)

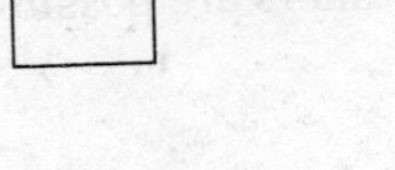

Matrix-Match Type

Given below are Matching Type Questions, with two columns (each having some items) each . Each item of Column I has to be matched with the items of Column II.

1. Match the following.

Column I (Hydrocarbon)	Column II (Feature)
A. 	1. Ring with maximum stability
B. 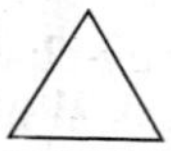	2. 1,3,5-cyclohexatriene is reduced to
C. 	3. Ring with maximum strain
D. $CH_3CH{=}CH_2$	4. Electrophilic addition reaction

2. Match the following.

Column I (Hydrocarbon)	Column II (Feature)
A. $CH_3CH{=}CH_2$	1. sp^3-hybridised carbon
B. CH_2 over $CH_2{-}CH_2$	2. sp^2-hybridised carbon
C. 	3. Decolourises Br_2 water
D. 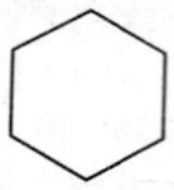	4. Exists in more than one form

3. Match the following.

Column I (Compound)	Column II (Source)
A. 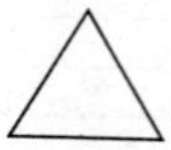	1. Malonic ester
B. 	2. Acetoacetic ester
C. 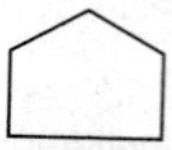	3. $CH_2{=}CH{-}CH{=}CH_2$
D. 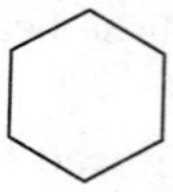	4. $CH_2{=}CHCH{=}CHCH{=}CH_2$

4. Match the following.

Column I (Cycloalkane)	Column II (Ring strain per CH_2 group)
A. Cyclopropane	1. 0.0 kcal
B. Cyclobutane	2. 1.3 kcal
C. Cyclopentane	3. 9.2 kcal
D. Cyclohexane	4. 6.6 kcal

Single Integer Answer Questions

Answer of these questions is a single digit lying between 0 to 9.

1. ...... membered cycloalkane has maximum stability.

2. Number of ring(s) in cubane is ....

3. Cyclohexane exists as .... non-planar strainless form.

4. There are total of .... equatorial H-atoms in cyclohexane.

5. Which ring is affected in electrophilic addition?

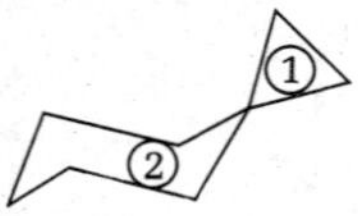

6. Norbornane has total of .... sides.

7. How many geometrical isomers are possible of decalin?

8. How many isomers are possible of C_8H_{16} with at least one six membered ring?

9. How many bond cleavages are required to convert cubane into non-cyclic skeleton?

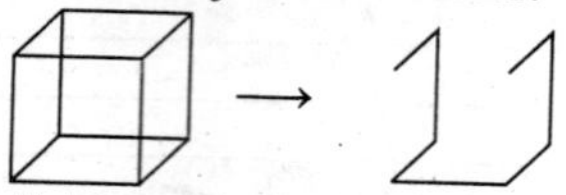

Cubane → Non-cyclic skeleton

10. 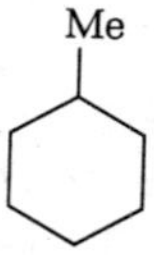

$\xrightarrow{Br_2/h\nu}$ Monobromo derivatives

The number of possible monobromo products is (excluding stereoisomers).

Answers

Objective Questions Type I [Only one correct option]

1. (b)	**2.** (c)	**3.** (b)	**4.** (a)	**5.** (a)	**6.** (c)	**7.** (b)	**8.** (d)	**9.** (d)	**10.** (d)
11. (b)	**12.** (a)	**13.** (c)	**14.** (c)	**15.** (a)	**16.** (c)	**17.** (b)	**18.** (a)	**19.** (a)	**20.** (c)
21. (b)	**22.** (c)	**23.** (b)	**24.** (c)	**25.** (c)	**26.** (a)	**27.** (d)	**28.** (b)	**29.** (b)	**30.** (d)
31. (d)	**32.** (a)	**33.** (b)	**34.** (c)	**35.** (b)	**36.** (b)	**37.** (b)	**38.** (a)	**39.** (b)	**40.** (a)
41. (d)	**42.** (b)	**43.** (c)	**44.** (a)	**45.** (c)	**46.** (a)	**47.** (d)	**48.** (d)	**49.** (c)	**50.** (d)

Objective Questions Type II [One or more than one correct option(s)]

1. (b, c) **2.** (a, b, c) **3.** (a, c) **4.** (b) **5.** (a, b)
6. (a, b, c, d) **7.** (a, b) **8.** (a, b, c) **9.** (b, c) **10.** (a, b)
11. (c, d) **12.** (a, b)

Numerical Value Questions

1. (20%) **2.** (109°) **3.** (5) **4.** (20) **5.** (6) **6.** (3) **7.** (3) **8.** (15)

Comprehension Based Questions

Passage 1. – **1.** (d) **2.** (a) **3.** (a,c) **Passage 2.** – **1.** (a) **2.** (b) **3.** (d) **Passage 3.** – **1.** (c) **2.** (d)

Matrix-Match Type

1. A → (1,2); B → (3,4); C → (4); D → (4)
2. A → (1,2,3); B → (1,3); C → (2,4); D → (1,4)
3. A → (1,2); B → (1,2,3); C → (1,2); D → (1,2,3,4)
4. A → (3); B → (4); C → (2); D → (1)

Single Integer Answer Questions

1. (6) **2.** (5) **3.** (2) **4.** (6) **5.** (1) **6.** (8) **7.** (2) **8.** (5) **9.** (5) **10.** (5)

Solutions

Objective Questions Type I [Only one correct option]

1. (*b*)

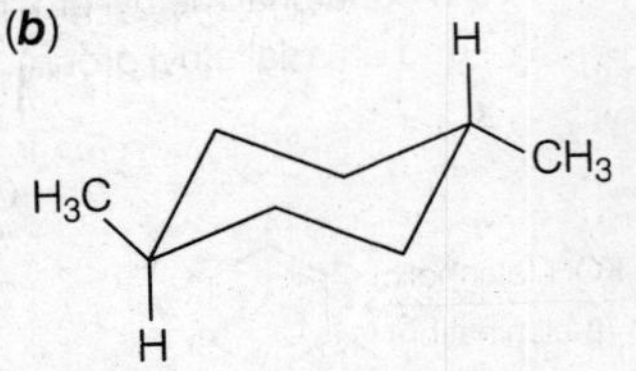

Both are equitorial position hence, it is trans-geometrical isomer.

3. (*b*) Bicyclo (2.1.1) hexane

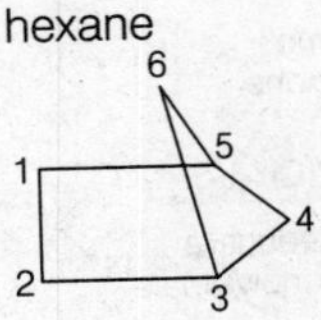

4. (*a*)

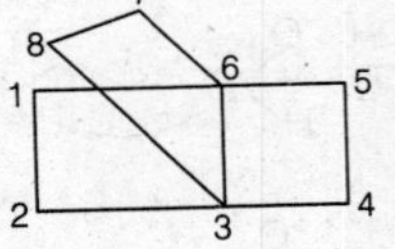

Bicyclo (2.2.2) octane

6. (*c*)

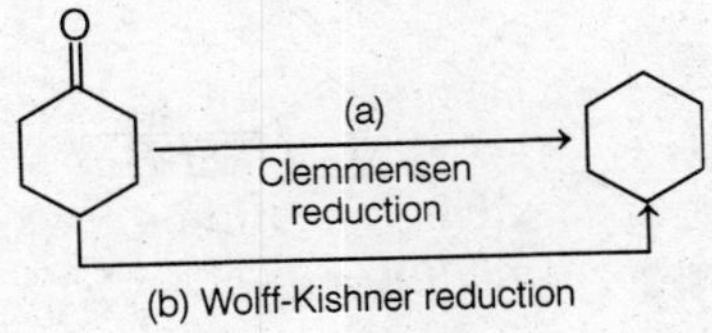

8. (*d*)

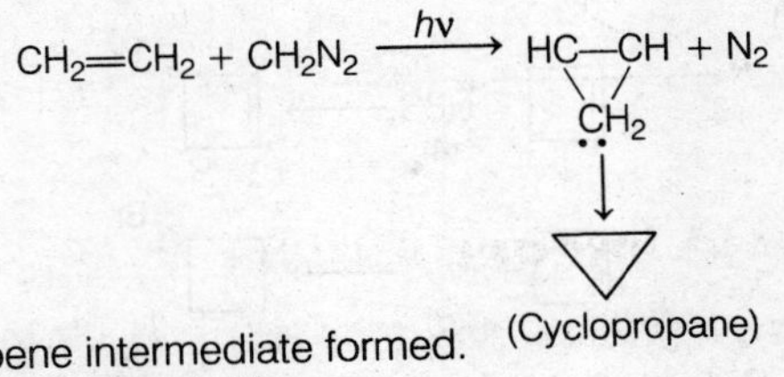

Carbene intermediate formed. Leaving group is N_2.

11. (*b*)

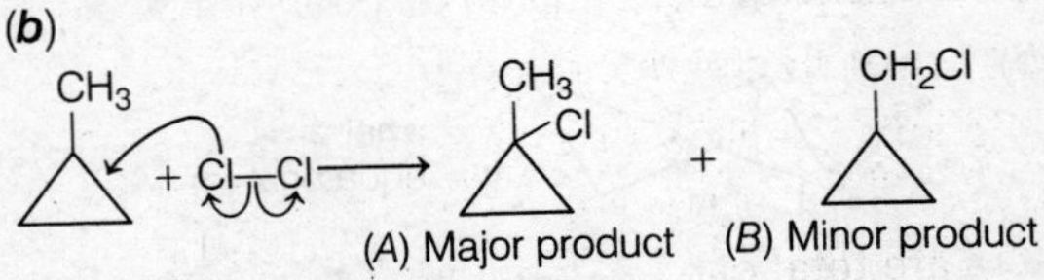

(*A*) 1-chloro-1-methylcyclopopane
(*B*) Chloromethylcyclopropane

15. (*a*)

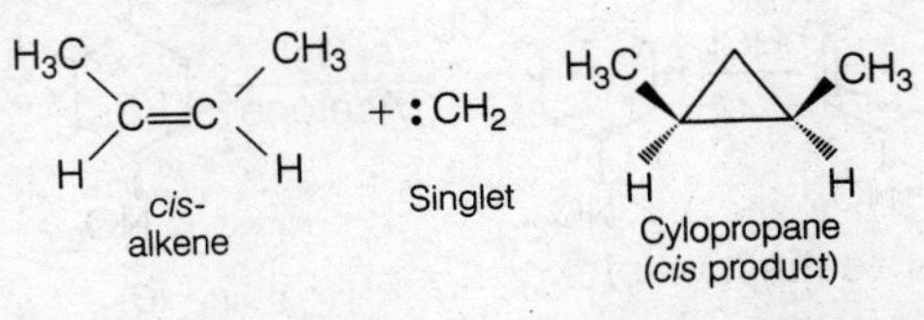

17. (*b*) Cyclohexane is most stable, hence have least heat of combustion per —CH_2 group.

17. (*b*) Cyclohexane is most stable, hence have least heat of combustion per — CH_2 group.

20. (*c*) Reactant (1) and product (7) same potential energy of cyclohexane, i.e. (1, 7).

21. (*b*) Only cyclopropane is the only cycloalkane that is planar. Cyclobutane (C_4H_8) and higher cycloalkanes adopt non-planar.

23. (*b*) Diel's-alder reaction is cycloaddition reaction. It is $4\pi + 2\pi$ (diene + dienophile) system addition reaction.

25. (*c*)

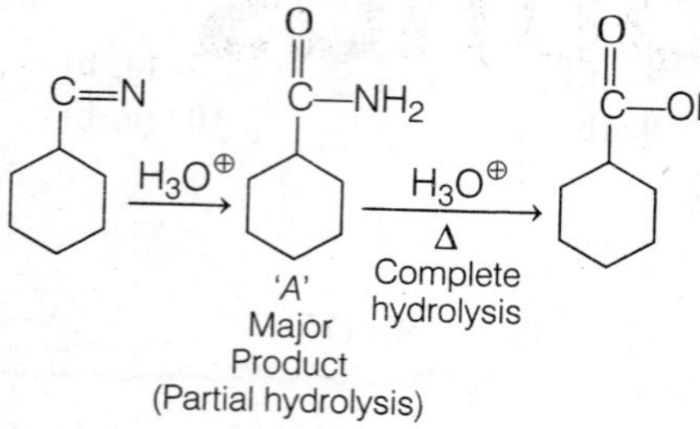

Cyclohexyl–C≡N $\xrightarrow{H_3O^{\oplus}}$ Cyclohexyl–C(=O)–NH_2 'A' Major Product (Partial hydrolysis) $\xrightarrow[\Delta]{H_3O^{\oplus}}$ Complete hydrolysis Cyclohexyl–C(=O)–OH

26. (*a*) Cl–$(CH_2)_5$–Cl + Mg ⟶ Cl–Mg–$(CH_2)_5$–Mg–Cl (*A*)

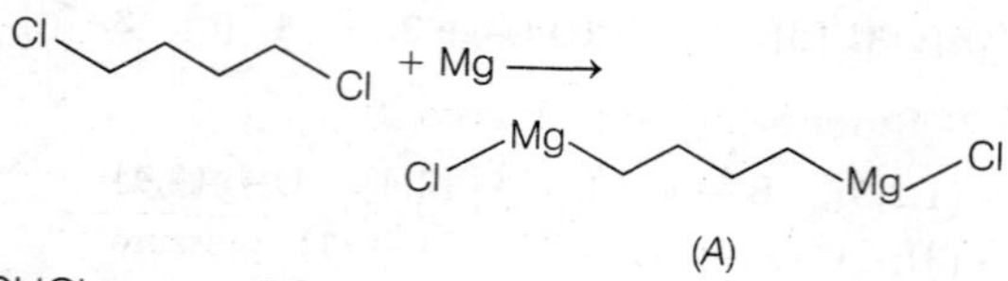

28. (*b*) $CHCl_3 \longrightarrow :CCl_2$ Carbene

$CH_3CH{=}CHCH_3 + :CCl_2 \xrightarrow{(CH_3)_3CO^-K^+}$ CH_3CH——$CHCH_3$ (bridged by CCl_2: Cl, Cl)

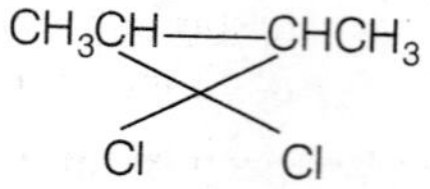

29. (*b*) Smaller ring have higher hydrogenation in nature.

30. (*d*)

Cyclobutene + NBS (*A*) ⟶ 3-Bromocyclobutene (Br)

Cyclobutane + Br_2 (*B*) ⟶ Bromocyclobutane (Br)

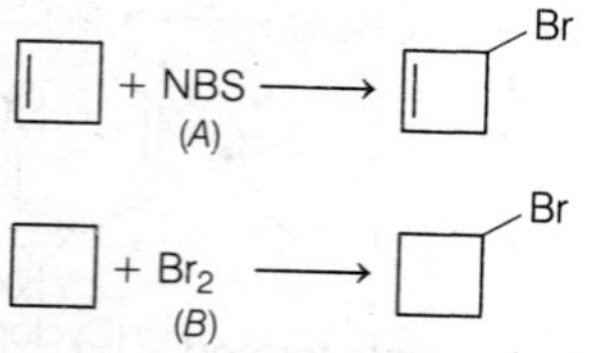

34. (*c*) Ring strain is larger, smaller the stability and larger the potential energy.

36. (*b*)

(Chair cyclohexane with H at *e* and H at *a*)

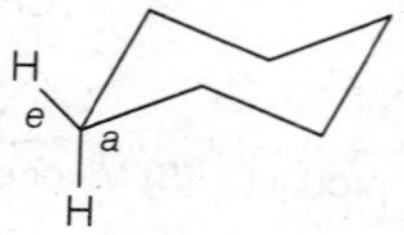

x = axial ;
y = equatorial (*e*)

38. (*a*)

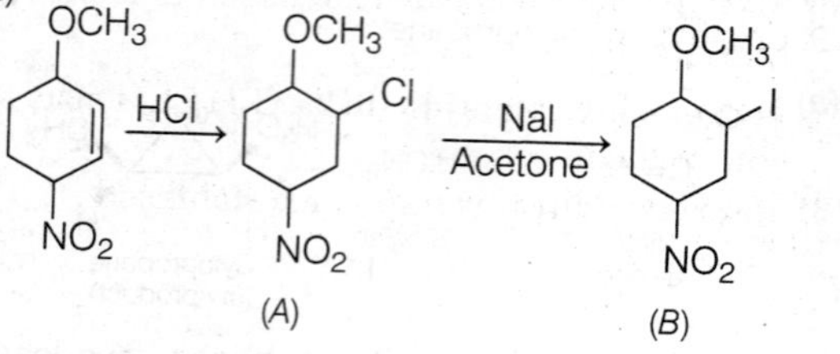

4-Nitro-1-methoxycyclohexene (OCH_3, NO_2) $\xrightarrow{HCl}$ (OCH_3, Cl, NO_2) (*A*) $\xrightarrow[\text{Acetone}]{NaI}$ (OCH_3, I, NO_2) (*B*)

39. (*b*)

CH_3 :ÖH / –CH–CH_3 (cyclohexane) $\xrightarrow{H^{\oplus}}$ CH_3 :$\overset{\oplus}{O}H_2$ –CH–CH_3 (Unstable) ⟶ CH_3 –$\overset{\oplus}{C}H$–CH_3, H (2° carbocation)

↓ 1,2 H^- shift

CH_3, –$\overset{\oplus}{C}$–CH–CH_3 (3° carbocation) $\xrightarrow{Cl^{\ominus}}$ CH_3, Cl, –CH_2–CH_3

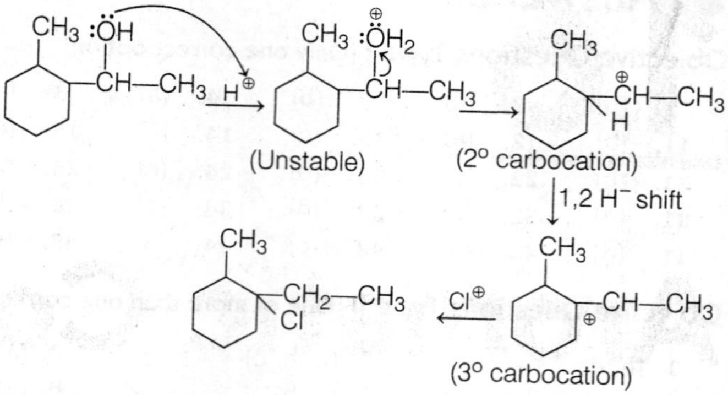

40. (*a*) Basketane ($C_{10}H_{12}$) contains five rings.

42. (*b*)

cis-1,2-Dimethylcyclobutane > *trans*-1,2-Dimethylcyclobutane > Methylcyclopentane > Cyclohexane

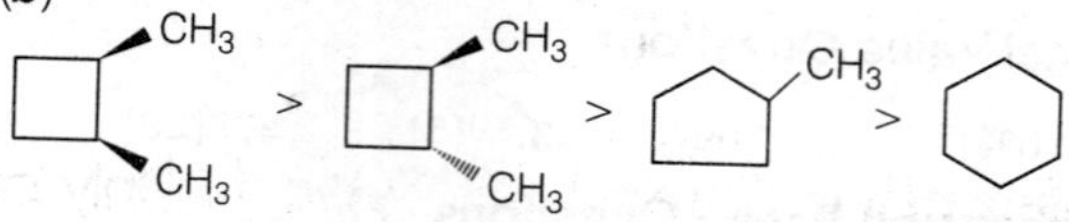

(Heat of combustion)

45. (*c*)

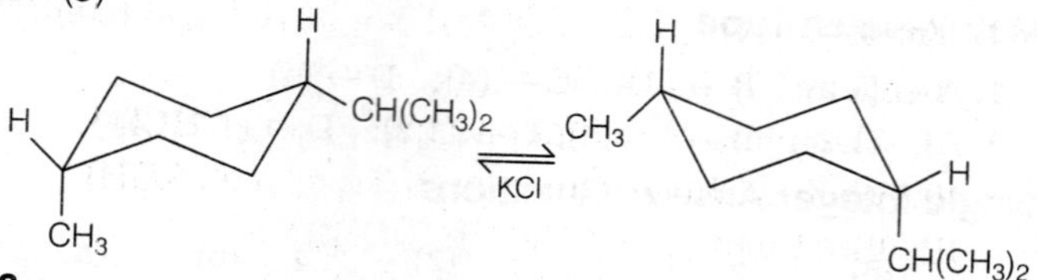

(Chair: H, $CH(CH_3)_2$; H, CH_3) $\underset{KCl}{\rightleftharpoons}$ (Chair: H, CH_3; H, $CH(CH_3)_2$)

48.

(CH_2CH_3, $C(CH_3)_3$, CH_3 cyclohexane) ⟷ (Chair: CH_3, $(CH_3)_3C$, CH_2CH_3)

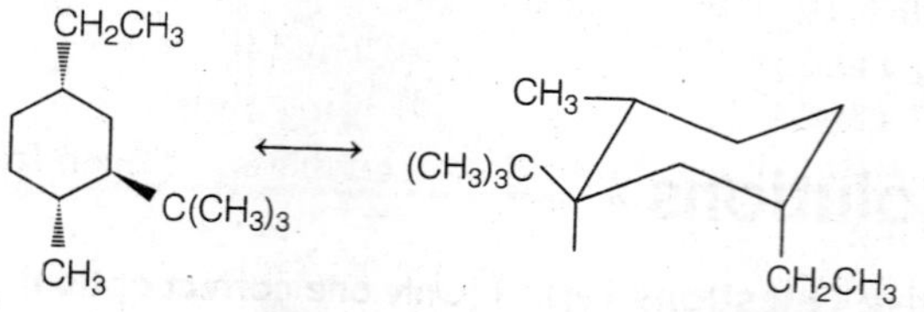

(An equatorial methyl group and an axial ethyl group).

49. (*c*)

Cyclohexane (*A*) $\xrightarrow[\text{(Free radical halogenation)}]{Br_2/h\nu}$ 1-bromo cyclohexane (Br) $\xrightarrow[(\beta\text{-elimination})]{\text{KOH (alcoholic)}}$ Cyclohex-1-ene (1, 2, 3, 4, 5, 6)

$\xrightarrow[\text{(Reductive ozonolysis)}]{O_3/(CH_3)_2S}$ OHC–$(CH_2)_4$–CHO (H, O … O, H)

(Intramolecular aldol condensation): OHC–$(CH_2)_3$–CH_2(α)–CHO $\xrightarrow[-H_2O]{:\ddot{O}H^- \text{(NaOH)}}$ OHC–$(CH_2)_3$–$\overset{\ominus}{C}H$–CHO ⟶ HO (1), CHO (5) cyclopentane (2, 3, 4) $\xrightarrow[-H_2O]{\Delta}$ Cyclopent-1-ene-1-carbaldehyde (H, O)

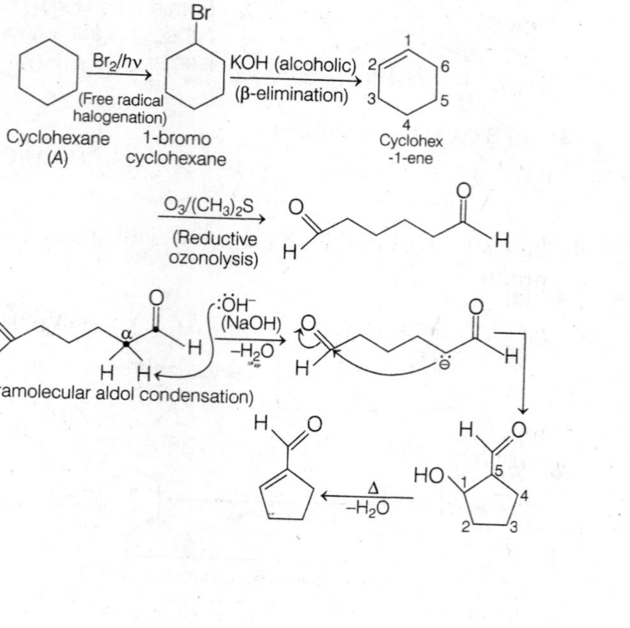

16

Aromatic Compounds

Objective Questions Type I [Only one correct option]

In each of the questions below, four choices are given of which only one is correct.

1. Acetophenone ($C_6H_5COCH_3$) can be reduced to ethyl benzene ($C_6H_5CH_2CH_3$) by

I. Clemmensen reduction [Zn(Hg)/conc. HCl]

II. Wolff-Kishner reduction (N_2H_4/glycol, KOH)

III. Birch reduction [(Na/NH_3)/CH_3OH]

Select the correct methods.

(a) I and III (b) II and III

(c) I and II (d) I, II and III

2. Benzene diazonium salt can be made nitrogen free using

(a) H_3PO_2 (b) HNO_2

(c) H_3PO_3 (d) H_3PO_4

3. *Neo*-pentyl chloride reacts with benzene in presence of a Lewis acid ($AlCl_3$) to form

(a) 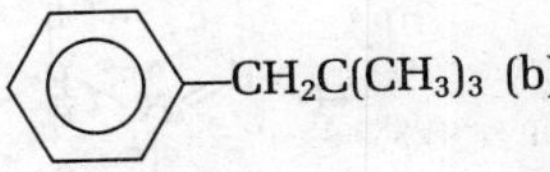

(b) 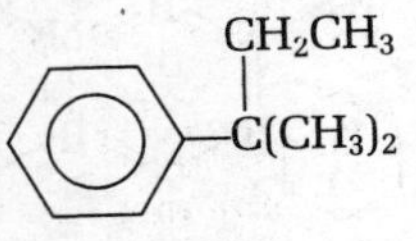

(c) 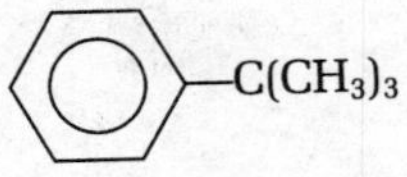

(d) 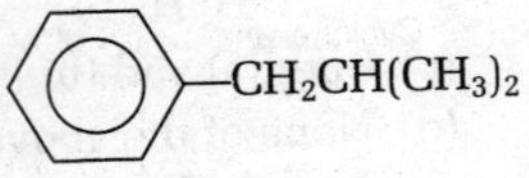

4. Benzene sulphonic acid is treated with steam. Final product is

(a) 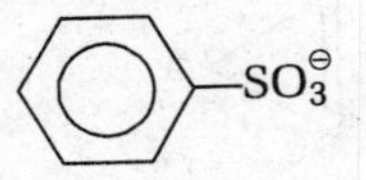

(b) 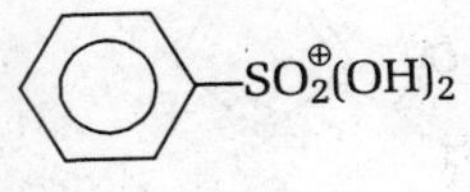

(c) 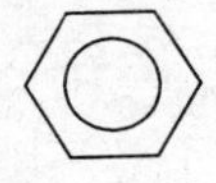

(d) 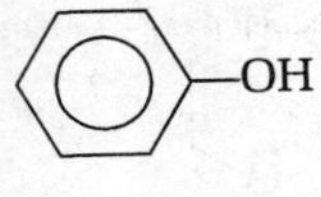

5. Cumene can be prepared by

(a)  $+ CH_3CH{=}CH_2 \xrightarrow[\text{pressure}]{H_3PO_4,\ \Delta}$

(b)  $+ CH_3CH_2CH_2Cl \xrightarrow{AlCl_3}$

(c) Both (a) and (b)

(d) None of the above

6. Birch reduction (dissolving metal reduction) of *o*-xylene gives

(a) 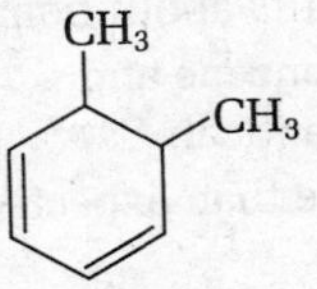

(b) 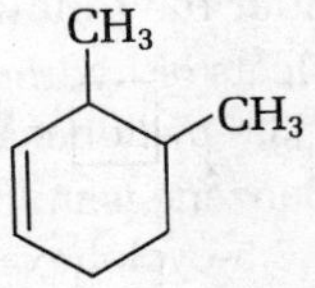

(c) 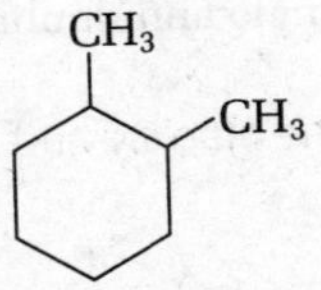

(d) 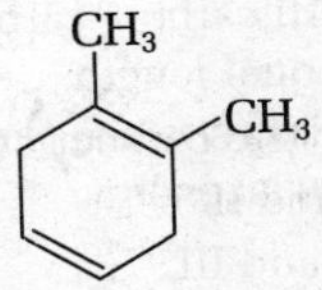

7. Select the incorrect statement.

(a) Toluene is oxidised to benzaldehyde by CrO_2Cl_2 followed by hydrolysis

(b) Tertiary butyl benzene is oxidised to benzoic acid by MnO_4^- / OH^-

(c) Benzene hexachloride (BHC, $C_6H_6Cl_6$) exists as chain and boat conformers

(d) Benzylic radical is resonance stabilised

8. Select the incorrect statement about the following carbocation.

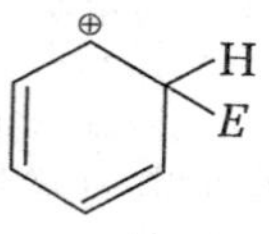

(a) It can lose proton forming an aromatic compound
(b) It can add a nucleophile forming an aromatic compound
(c) It is resonance stabilised
(d) All of the above

9. In the following fast reaction,

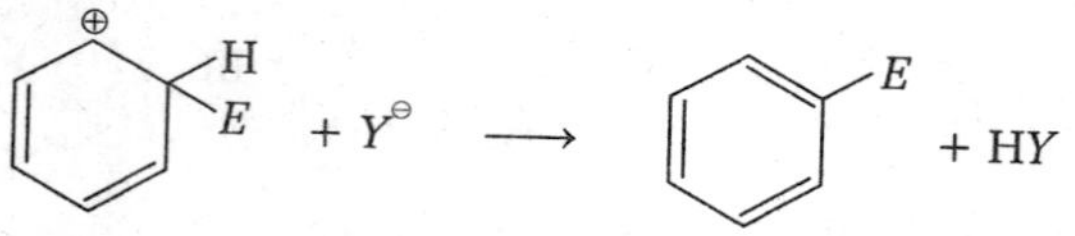

(a) energy is decreased and reaction is in forward direction
(b) energy is decreased and reaction is in backward direction
(c) energy is increased and reaction is in forward direction
(d) energy is increased and reaction is in backward direction

10. Which of the following is an aromatic compound ? **[JEE Main 2021, March]**

(a) 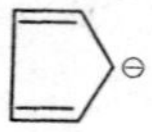
(b) 
(c) 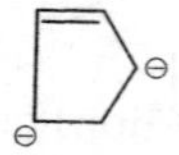
(d) 

11. Consider the following statements about benzene.
I. Heats of hydrogenation of benzene and 1,3,5-cyclohexatriene are identical.
II. Benzene is much more stable than expected for 1,3,5-cyclohexatriene.
III. All carbon–carbon bonds (single and double) have equal length.

Select the correct statements.
(a) I and II
(b) II and III
(c) I and III
(d) I, II and III

12. Select the incorrect statement.
(a) Benzene and 1,3,5-cyclohexatriene are same compounds
(b) Benzene has six delocalised π-electrons whereas cyclohexatriene has six localised π-electrons
(c) All C—H bonds have equal bond-length
(d) Benzene has a symmetrical, planar hexagonal structure

13. Aromaticity of the benzene ring is restored in the following case

(a) 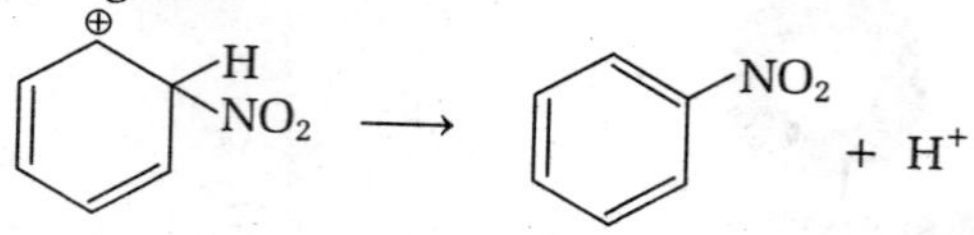
(b) 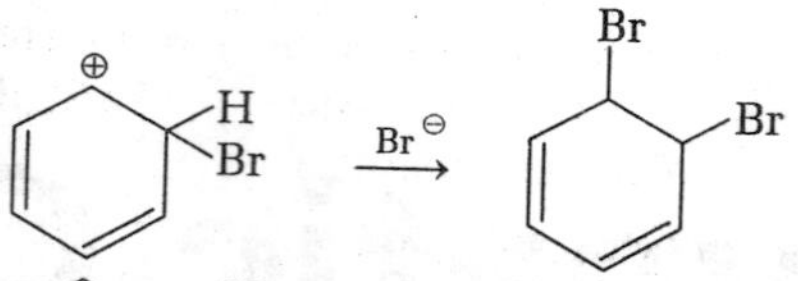
(c) 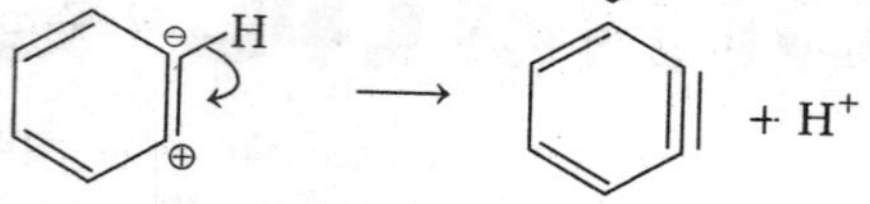
(d) All of the above cases

14. Select the correct statement(s).
(a) A compound with delocalised electrons is more stable than the compound would be if all its electrons were localised
(b) Six π-electrons delocalised in benzene are referred to as the aromatic sextet
(c) When a compound attains aromaticity, potential energy is decreased
(d) All of the above are correct statements

15. Which is a source of proton (H^+) in aqueous solution?

(a) 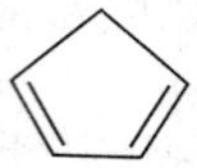
(b) 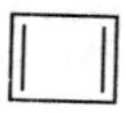
(c) 
(d) 

16. Resonance form of borazole (inorganic benzene) is

(a) 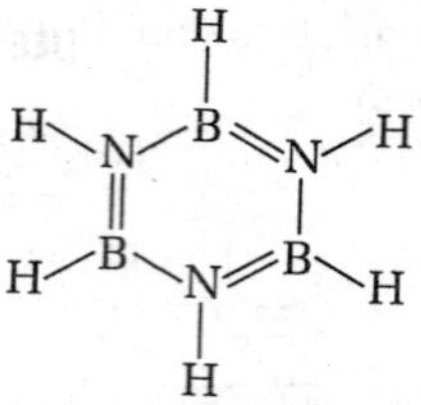
(b) 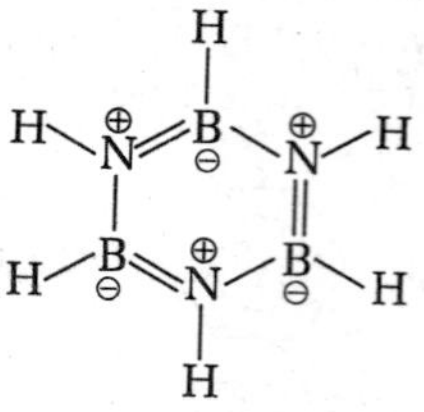
(c) Both (a) and (b)
(d) None of the above

17. Which of the following species should be aromatic by the Huckel rule?

(a) 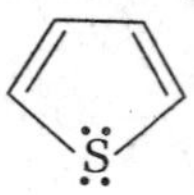
(b) 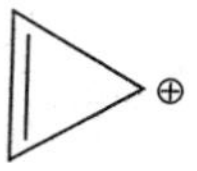
(c) 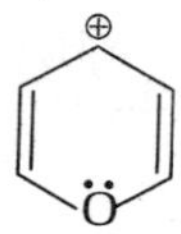
(d) All of these

18. Select the incorrect statement about *A* (imidazole).

A :
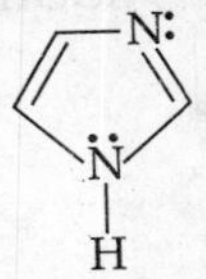

(a) It is a stronger base than pyrrole
(b) Nitrogen attached to hydrogen is protonated
(c) Nitrogen having no hydrogen is protonated
(d) It is an aromatic compound

19. Ferrocene contains
(a) cyclopentadienide anions complexed to iron
(b) phenyl anions complexed to iron
(c) benzyl carbocation complexed to magnesium
(d) benzyl carbanion complexed to iron

20. Increasing order of the dipole moment of the following is

I. 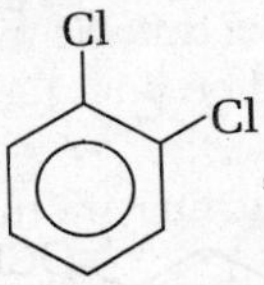 , II. 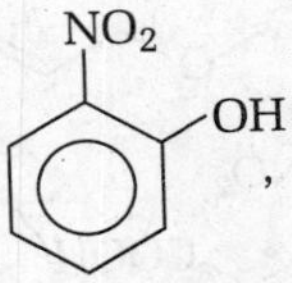 , III. 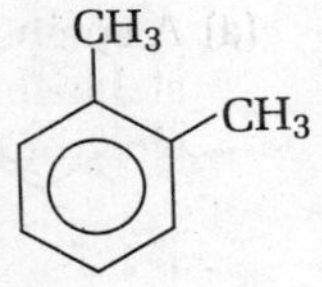

(a) I < II < III (b) II < III < I
(c) I < III < II (d) III < II < I

21. Consider the following statements,
I. All *meta*-directing groups are deactivating groups.
II. The activating substituents make the benzene ring more reactive towards S_E reaction.
III. Carbonyl groups are moderately deactivating substituents and withdraw electrons both inductively and by resonance.

Select the correct statements.
(a) I and II (b) I and III
(c) II and III (d) I, II and III

22. Consider the following reactions : **[JEE Main 2020]**

I. 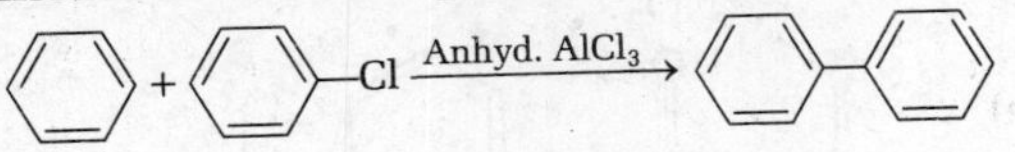

II. 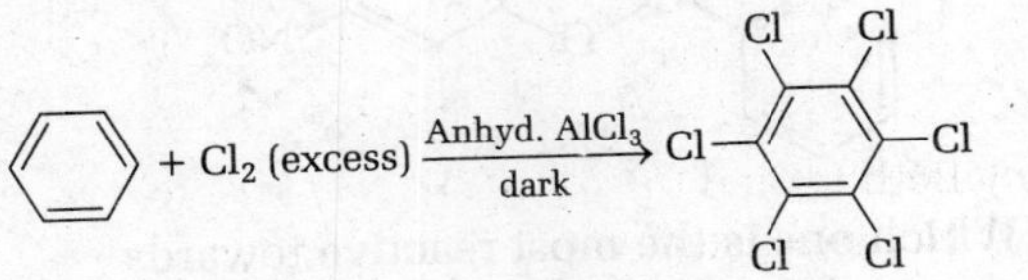

III. 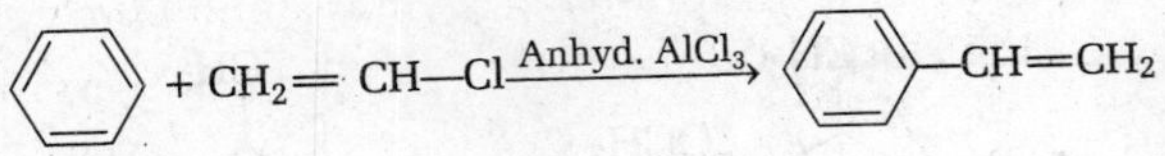

IV. 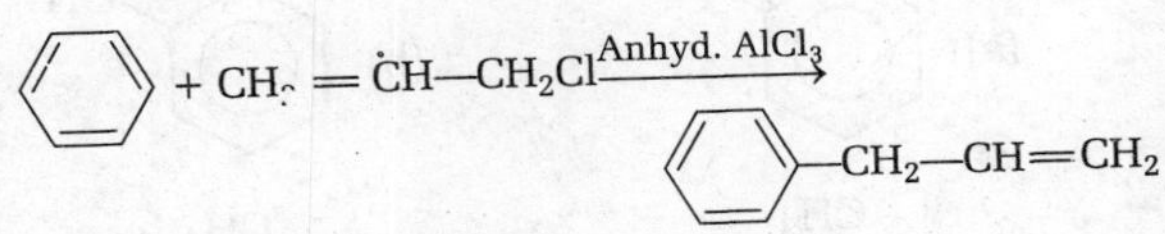

Which of these reactions are possible?
(a) (II) and (IV) (b) (I) and (IV)
(c) (II), (III) and (IV) (d) (I) and (II`)

23. Select the correct statement(s).
(a) The presence of a hydroxyl group on the benzene ring in phenol stabilises the arenium cation through delocalisation
(b) The presence of a cyano group on the benzene ring in benzonitrile destabilises the arenium cation relative to that from benzene itself
(c) Electron-donating groups are usually activating groups
(d) All of the above statements are correct

24. Nitration of the following takes place in the order

I.  II.  III. 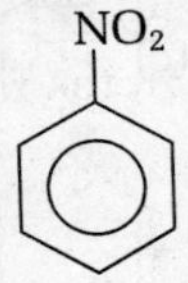

(a) I < II < III
(b) II < I < III
(c) I < III < II
(d) III < I < II

25. Which of the following structures cannot involve delocalisation to the amino substituent?

(a) 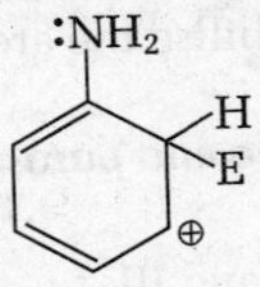
(b) 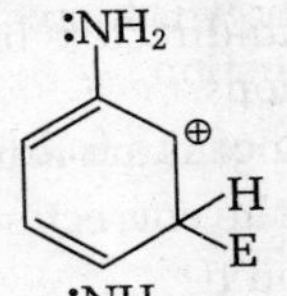
(c) 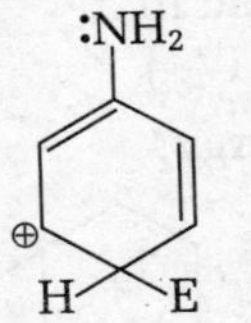
(d) 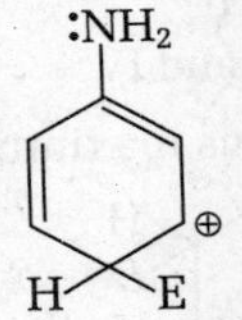

26. The major product of the following reaction is **[JEE Main 2019]**

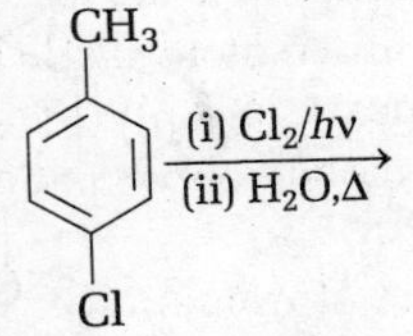

(a) 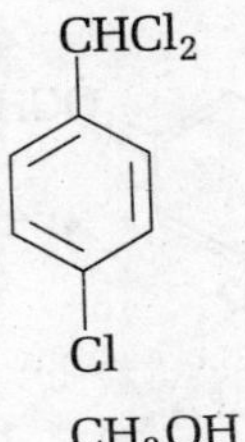
(b) 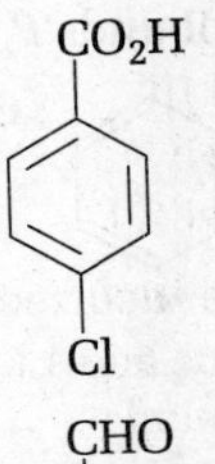
(c) 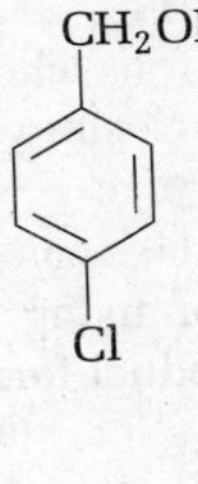
(d) 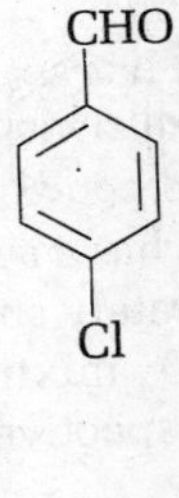

27. What is the major product expected from the chlorination of *p*-methylanisole?

(a) 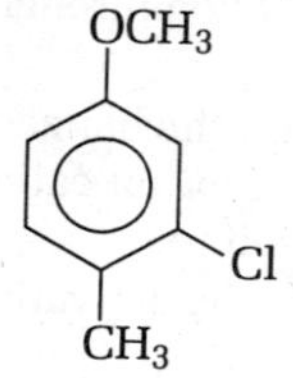
(b) 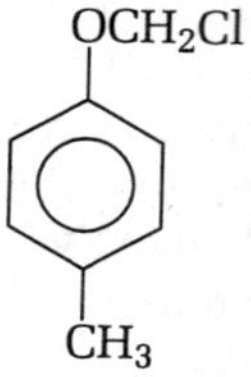
(c) 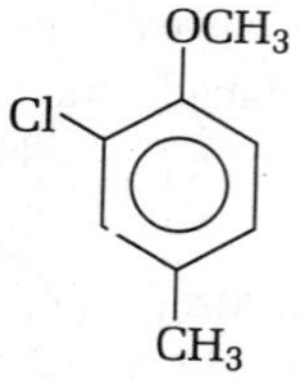
(d) 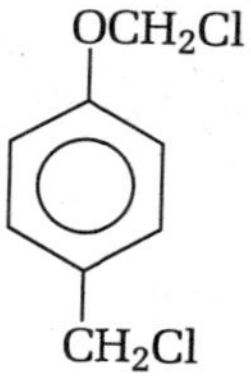

28. Consider the following statements.

I. Hyperconjugation helps in increasing electron-density at *ortho* and *para*-sites in case of alkyl groups.

II. Electron-donating groups are activators and *ortho* and *para*-directors because they stabilise the arenium cations.

III. Electron-withdrawing groups are activators and are *meta*-directors because they stabilise the arenium cations.

IV. Halogens are activators and *ortho* and *para*-directors.

Select the correct statements.

(a) I and II
(b) I, II and III
(c) II, III and IV
(d) I and IV

29. Which has maximum potential energy?

(a) 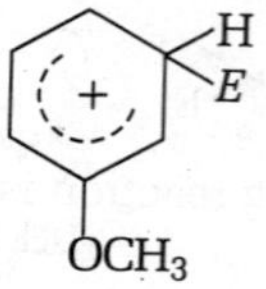
(b) 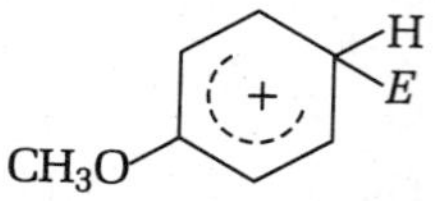
(c) 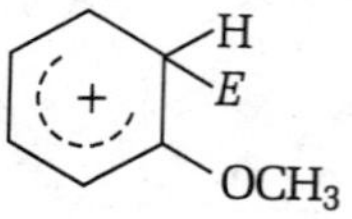
(d) 

30. The compounds *P*, *Q* and *S*

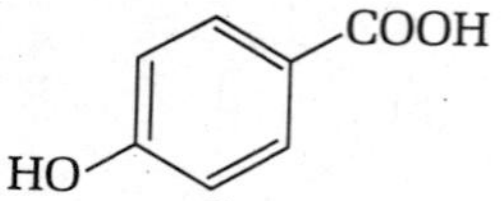
P

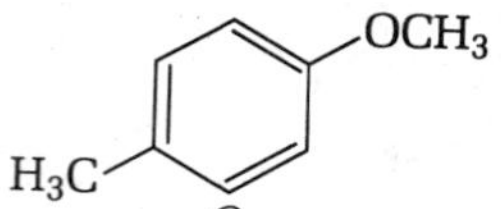
Q

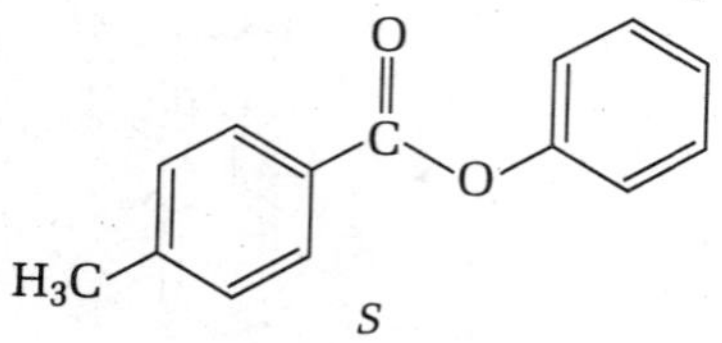
S

where separately subjected to nitration using HNO_3/H_2SO_4 mixture. The major product formed in each case respectively, is **[IIT JEE 2010]**

(a) 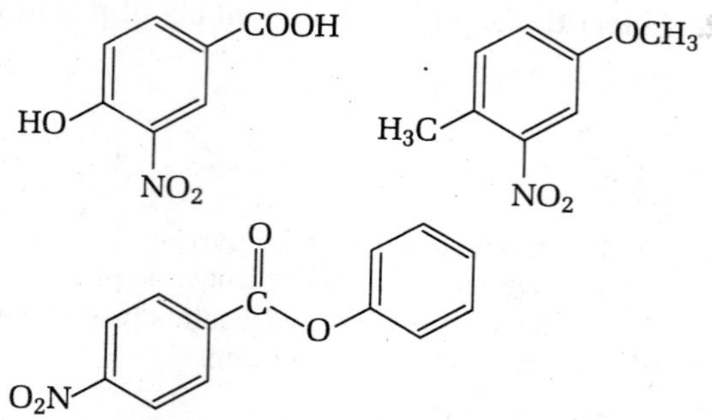
(b) 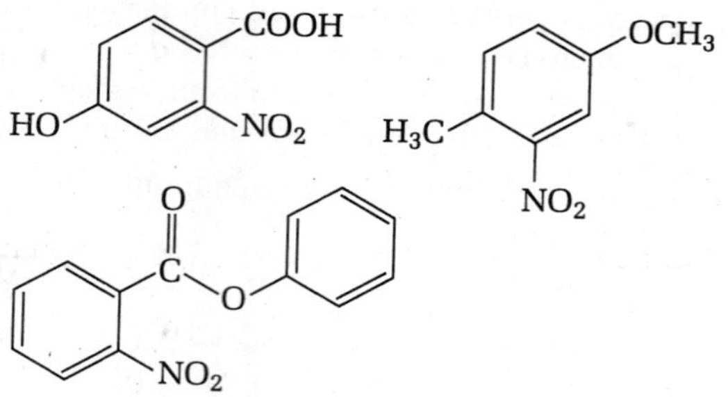
(c) 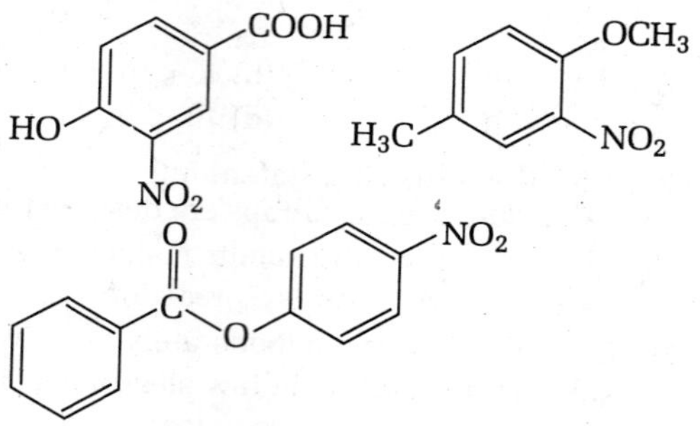
(d) 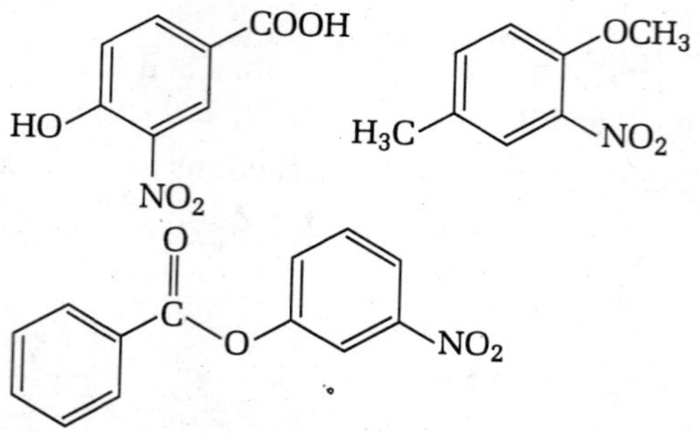

31. Which one is the most reactive towards electrophilic reagent?

(a) 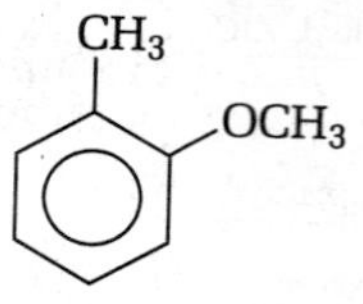
(b) 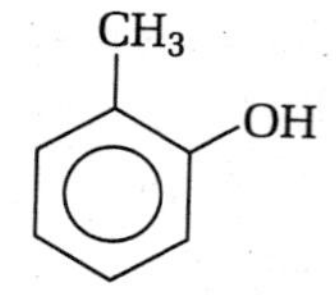
(c) 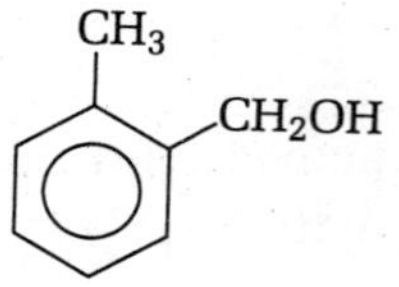
(d) 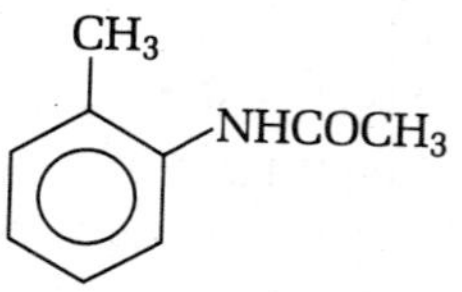

32. Increasing rate of S_N1 reaction in the following compounds is **[JEE Main 2019]**

(A) 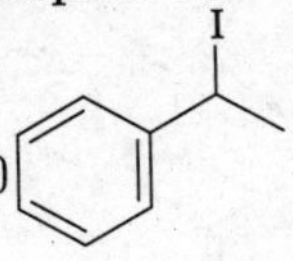
(C) 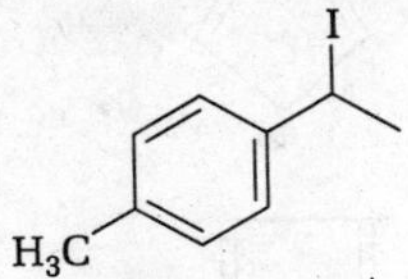

(B) 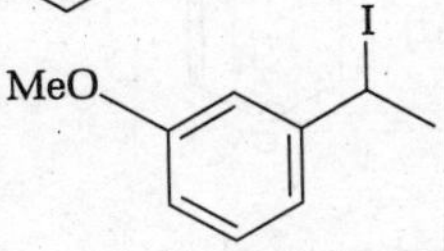

(D) 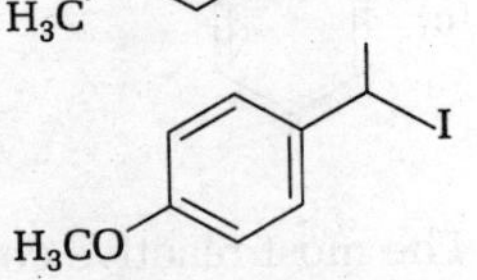

(a) (A) < (B) < (C) < (D) (b) (B) < (A) < (C) < (D)
(c) (A) < (B) < (D) < (C) (d) (B) < (A) < (D) < (C)

33. Compound (A), C_8H_9Br gives a white precipitate when warmed with alcoholic $AgNO_3$. Oxidation of (A) gives an acid (B), $C_8H_6O_4$. (B) easily forms anhydride on heating. Identify the compound (A). **[JEE Main 2013]**

(a) 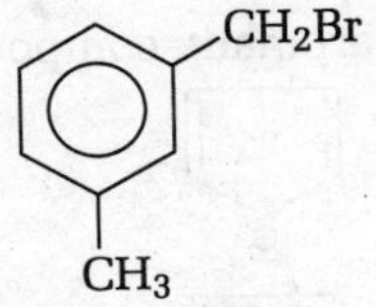

(b) 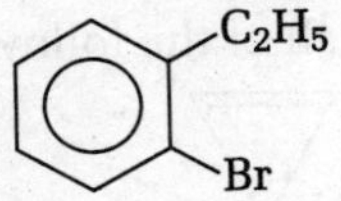

(c) 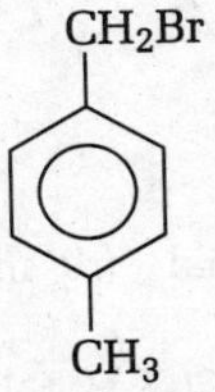

(d) 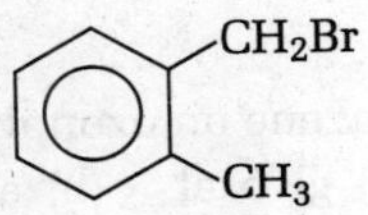

34. Which among the following groups when attached to benzene ring will direct the incoming electrophile predominantly to the *meta* position?

I. $—CH_3$ II. $—CH_2Cl$
III. $—NH_3^+$ IV. $—CCl_3$
V. $—NHCOCH_3$

(a) Only III (b) I, II and V (c) III and V (d) III and IV

35. Oxidation of toluene with CrO_3 in the presence of $(CH_3CO)_2O$ gives a product (A) which on treatment with aqueous NaOH produces

(a) C_6H_5CHO (b) $(C_6H_5CO)_2O$
(c) C_6H_5COONa (d) 2,4-diacetyl toluene

36. Among the following, the aromatic compounds are : **[JEE Main 2021, March]**

(A) 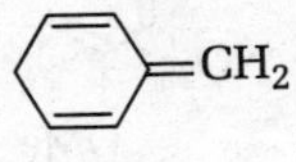

(B) 
(C) 
(D) 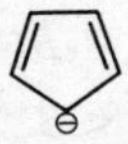

Choose the correct answer from the following options

(a) (A) and (B) only (b) (B) and (C) only
(c) (B), (C) and (D) only (d) (A), (B) and (C) only

37. Which of the following when treated with super heated steam under pressure gives benzene?

(a) Benzene sulphonic acid
(b) Benzyl chloride
(c) Bromobenzene
(d) Nitrobenzene

38. Most stable carbocation ion is

(a) $p\text{-}NO_2—C_6H_4—CH_2^+$
(b) $C_6H_5CH_2^+$
(c) $p\text{-}Cl—C_6H_4—CH_2^+$
(d) $p\text{-}CH_3O—C_6H_4—CH_2^+$

39. Which has unsaturation in side-chain ?

(a) Styrene (b) Mesitylene
(c) Xylene (d) Benzyl chloride

40. Most stable intermediate of the following reaction is

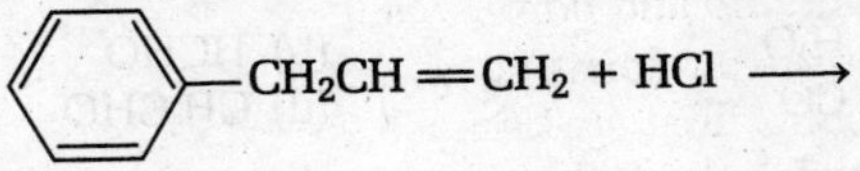

(a) 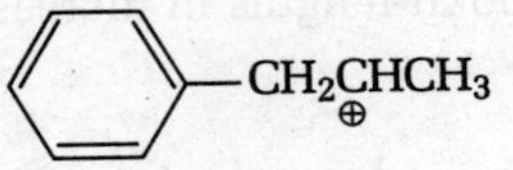

(b) 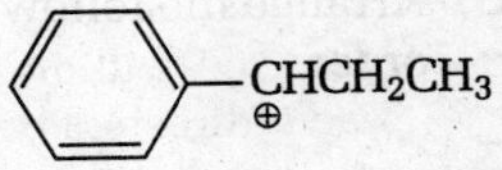

(c) 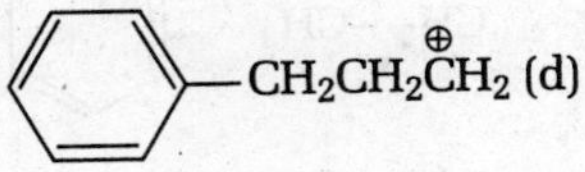

(d) 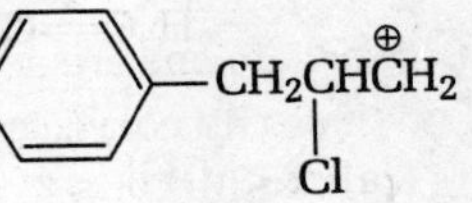

41. The major product of the following reaction is **[JEE Main 2019]**

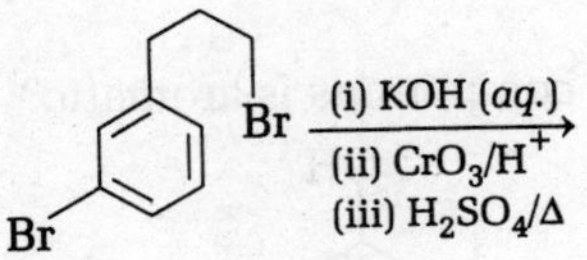

(a) 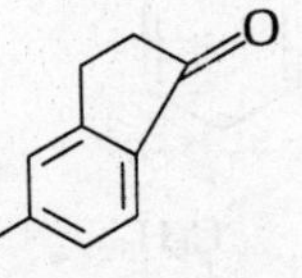

(b) 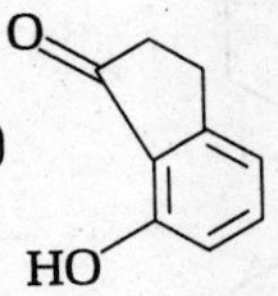

(c) 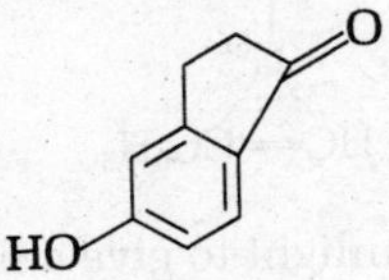

(d) 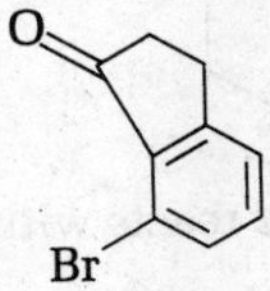

42. Out of

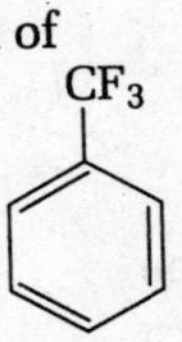

I
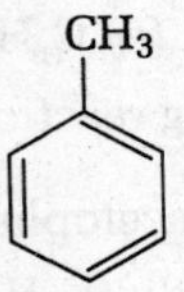

II
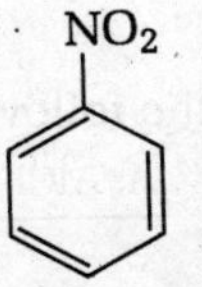

III
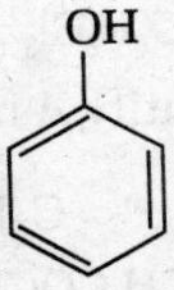

IV

m-directing group(s) is/are present in

(a) I and II (b) I and III
(c) I and IV (d) II and IV

43. Source of benzene is/are

(a) 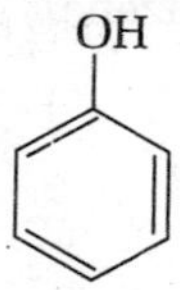 (b) 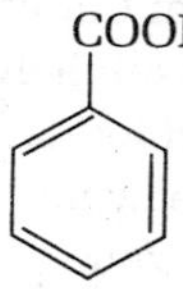

(c) 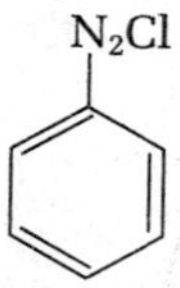 (d) All of these

44. Identify the reactant (A) in the following

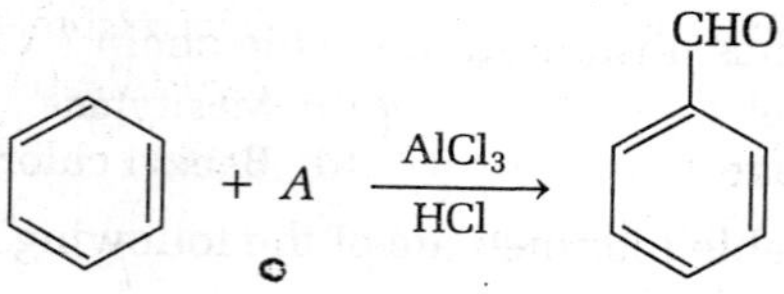

(a) H_2O (b) HCHO
(c) CO (d) CH_3CHO

45. Arrange the following bond-lengths in increasing order

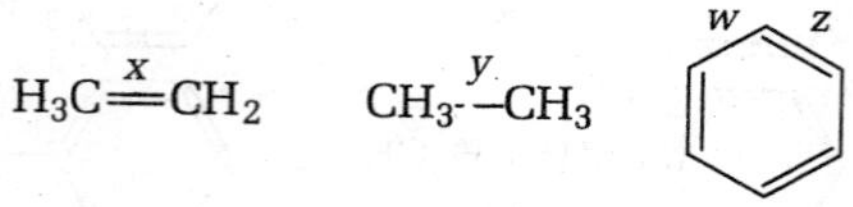

(a) $x < y < w < z$
(b) $x < y < z < w$
(c) $x < y < w = z$
(d) $x < w = z < y$

46. Which of the following compounds is aromatic?

(a) 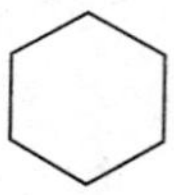 (b) 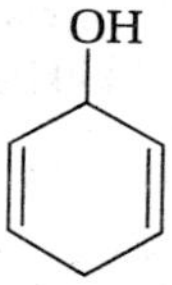

(c) 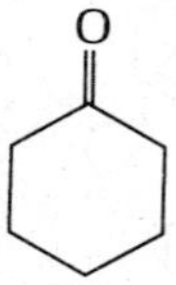 (d) 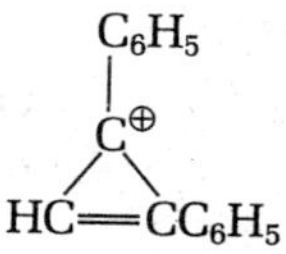

47. Benzene reacts with Cl_2 in sunlight to give a final product
(a) C_6H_5Cl (b) $C_6H_4Cl_2$
(c) $C_6H_3Cl_3$ (d) $C_6H_6Cl_6$

48. Identify A in the following reaction,

$$C_6H_6 \xrightarrow{A,\ AlCl_3} \text{acetophenone}$$

(a) CH_3COCl (b) C_6H_5COCl
(c) CH_3CHO (d) SO_2Cl_2

49. Which of the following shows aromaticity?

(a) 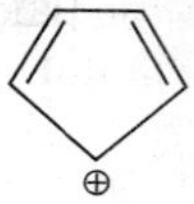 (b) 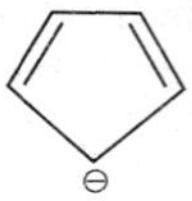

(c) 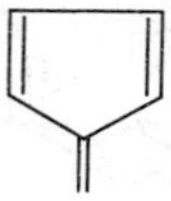 (d) 

50. The most reactive compound towards electrophilic nitration is
(a) toluene (b) benzene
(c) benzoic acid (d) nitrobenzene

51. Which of the following compounds shows aromatic properties?
(a) Valine (b) Leucine
(c) Seune (d) Tyrosine

52. Which of the following is an aromatic compound?

(a) 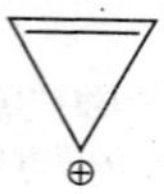 (b) 

(c) 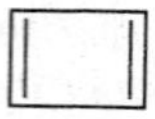 (d) 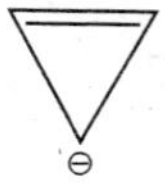

53. Benzene on ozonolysis gives
(a) glyoxal (b) acetone (c) ethanal (d) methanal

54. $A(C_8H_{10}) \xrightarrow{NO_2^+} B(C_8H_9NO_2) \xrightarrow{NO_2^+} C(C_8H_7(NO_2)_2$
One type Three type

A is thus
(a) ethyl benzene (b) m-xylene
(c) o-xylene (d) p-xylene

55. Aromatisation of n-heptane by passing over heated Al_2O_3 and Cr_2O_3 at 773 K gives
(a) benzene
(b) toluene
(c) xylene
(d) hepthylene

56. The increasing order of the pK_a values of the following compounds is **[JEE Main 2019]**

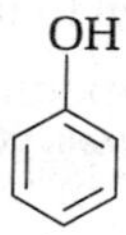 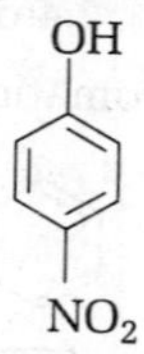 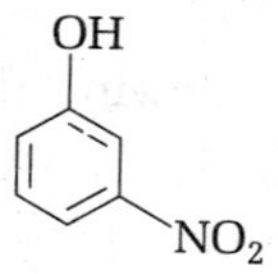 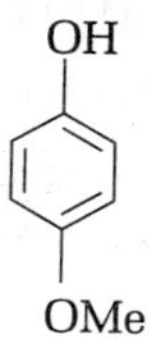

A B C D

(a) $D < A < C < B$ (b) $B < C < A < D$
(c) $C < B < A < D$ (d) $B < C < D < A$

57. The molecular formula of diphenyl methane is $C_{13}H_{12}$. How many structural isomers are possible when one of the hydrogen is replaced by a chlorine atom?

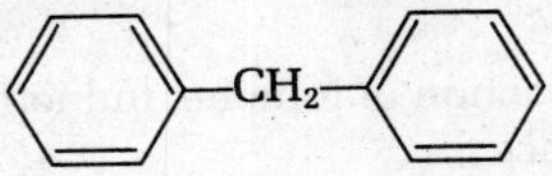

(a) 6 (b) 4 (c) 8 (d) 7

58. Benzene on oxidation with V_2O_5 produce
(a) toluene (b) benzaldehyde
(c) benzoic acid (d) maleic anhydride

59. The main components of middle oil fraction of coaltar distillation are
(a) benzene, phenol (b) phenol, naphthalene
(c) naphthalene, toluene (d) pyrrole

60. Benzene does not undergo addition reaction easily because
(a) it has six hydrogen atoms
(b) it has a cyclic structure
(c) double bonds present in benzene are strong
(d) resonance stabilised system is to be preserved

61. Which of the following compounds possesses the C—H bond with the lowest bond dissociation energy?
(a) Toluene (b) Benzene
(c) *n*-pentane (d) 2,2-dimethylpropane

62. The treatment of benzene with isobutene in the presence of sulphuric acid gives
(a) *iso*-butyl benzene (b) *tert*-butyl benzene
(c) *n*-butyl benzene (d) no reaction

63. In benzene molecule carbon atoms are inclined at an angle of
(a) 60° (b) 109° 28′
(c) 120° (d) 180°

64. Which of the following oils is obtained from benzene after fractional distillation of coal tar?
(a) Light oil (b) Heavy oil
(c) Middle oil (d) Anthracene oil

65. Which of the following is the most stable compound ?
(a) $Ph_3\overset{+}{C}$ (b) $Ph_2\overset{+}{C}H$
(c) $Ph_2\overset{+}{C}H_2$ (d) $Ph\overset{+}{C}H_2$

66. Which of the following will have the fastest rate of reaction with $Br_2/FeBr_3$?

(a) 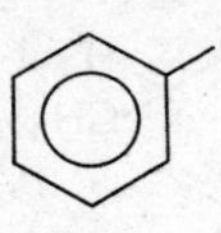

(b) 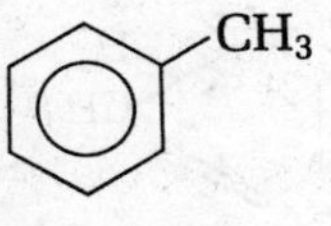

(c) 

(d) 

67. The major product obtained in the following reaction is [JEE Main 2017]

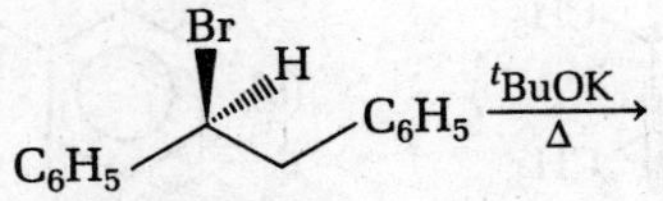

(a) (±) $C_6H_5CH(O^tBu)CH_2C_6H_5$
(b) $C_6H_5CH = CHC_6H_5$
(c) (+) $C_6H_5CH(O^tBu)CH_2C_6H_5$
(d) (−)$C_6H_5CH(O^tBu)CH_2C_6H_5$

68. In benzene, all the six C—C bonds have the same length because of
(a) isomerism (b) chain isomerism
(c) resonance (d) hybridisation

69. For nitration in benzene, we require
(a) conc. HNO_3 + conc. H_2SO_4
(b) conc. HNO_3
(c) conc. H_2SO_4 + fuming HNO_3
(d) KNO_2

70. Which one of the following acid does not form hydrocarbon with sodalime?
(a) Cinnamic acid
(b) Benzoic acid
(c) Picric acid
(d) Isophthalic acid

71. Which of the following species participates in sulphonation of benzene ring?
(a) SO_2^- (b) SO_3
(c) HSO_3^- (d) H_2SO_4

72.  + CH_2Cl_2 $\xrightarrow{AlCl_3}$ *A*; *A* is
(Excess)

(a) 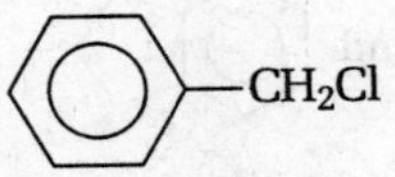

(b) 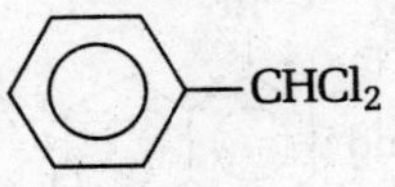

(c) 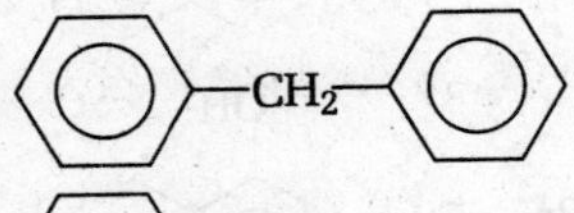

(d) 

73. The Birch reduction of toluene gives

(a) 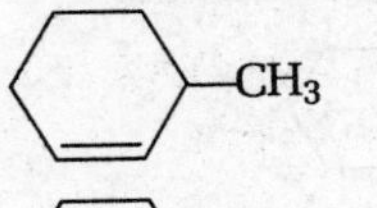

(b) 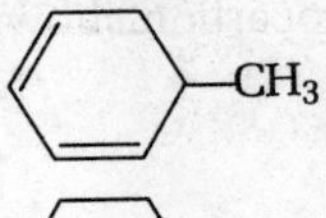

(c) 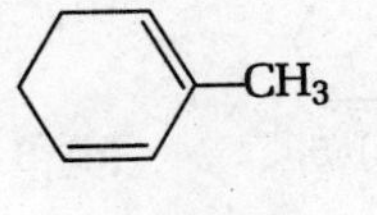

(d) 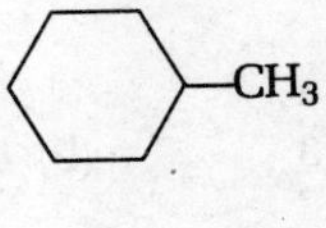

74. Ethyl benzene is heated with ZnO at about 873 K. Product is

(a) 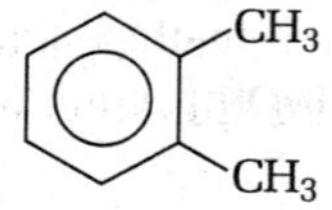

(b) 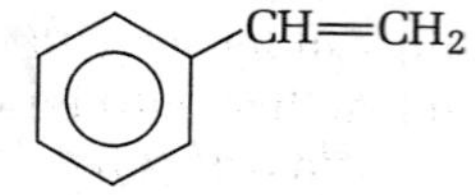

(c) 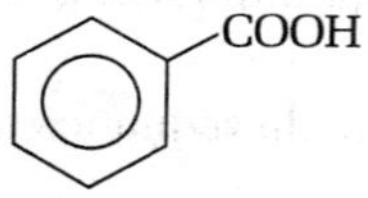

(d) 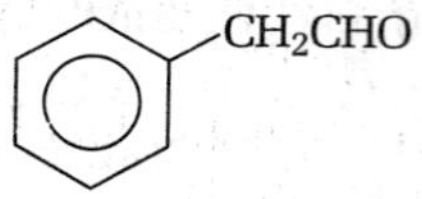

75. Which of the following compounds has a double bond that is conjugated with the π-system of the benzene ring?

(a) *p*-benzyltoluene (b) 2-phenyl-1-butene
(c) 3-phenylcyclohexene (d) 3-phenyl-1,4-pentadiene

76. When comparing the hydrogenation of benzene with that of a hypothetical 1,3,5-cyclohexatriene, benzene .... than the cyclohexatriene.

(a) absorbs 152 kJ/mol more heat
(b) gives off 152 kJ/mol more heat
(c) absorbs 152 kJ/mol less heat
(d) gives off 152 kJ/mol less heat

77. In the following reaction sequence, structures of *A* and *B*, respectively will be **[JEE Main 2020]**

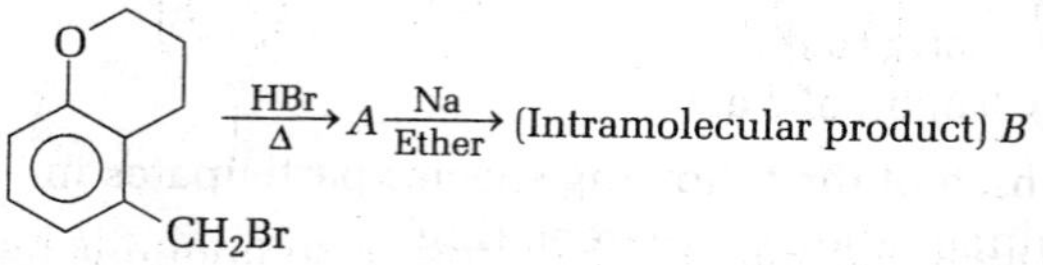

(a) 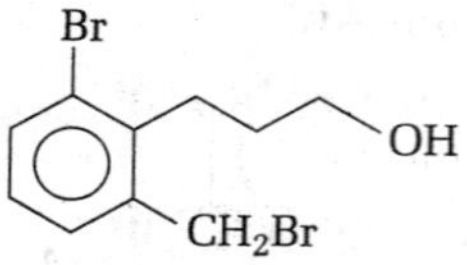

and 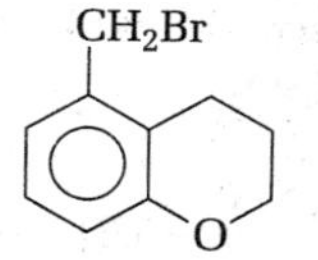

(b) 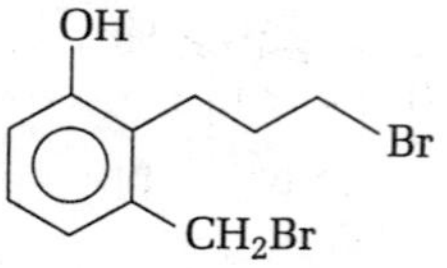

and 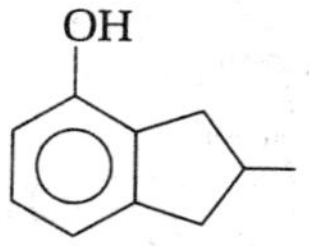

(c) 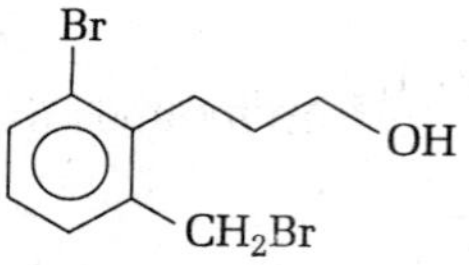

and 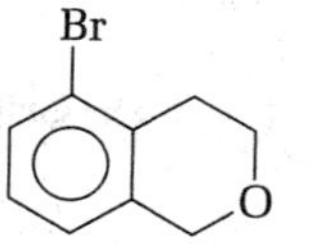

(d) 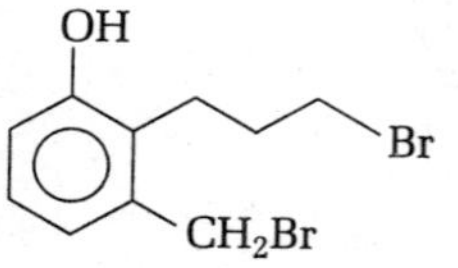

and 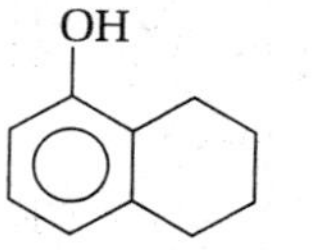

78. How many benzylic hydrogens are present in the hydrocarbon shown?

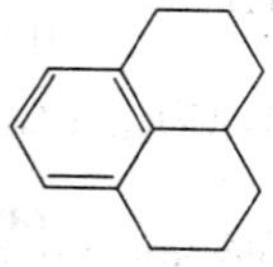

(a) 3 (b) 4 (c) 5 (d) 6

79. Select the correct statement(s).

(a) Alkyl group is *ortho* and *para* directing
(b) Rate of S_E reaction of toluene is faster than that of benzene
(c) In S_E reaction of toluene, inductive effect wins over resonance
(d) All of the above are correct statements

80. Select the correct statement(s).

(a) Addition of Br^- in the following leads to the loss of resonance energy that is associated with the aromatic ring

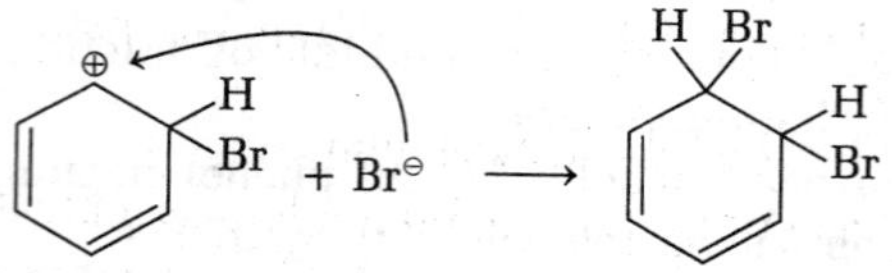

(b) The π-system of the benzene ring is the nucleophile
(c) The sulphur atom in SO_3 is electrophilic by virtue of the formal positive charge in each of the resonance structures
(d) All of the above are correct statements

81. Which is the Lewis-acid Lewis-base reaction?

(a) $R—Cl + AlCl_3 \longrightarrow \overset{\oplus}{R} + AlCl_4^{\ominus}$
(b) $2H_2SO_4 \rightleftharpoons H_3O^{\oplus} + HSO_3^{\ominus} + SO_3$
(c) $HNO_3 + H_2SO_4 \rightleftharpoons H_2NO_3^{\oplus} + HSO_4^{\ominus}$
(d) All of the above

82. Heat of hydrogenation of cyclohexene (one C=C bond) is -28.4 kcal mol^{-1}. Hence heat of hydrogenation of benzene (three C=C bonds) should be

(a) -85.2 kcal mol^{-1}
(b) -28.4 kcal mol^{-1}
(c) -49.3 kcal mol^{-1}
(d) -35.9 kcal mol^{-1}

83. Out of

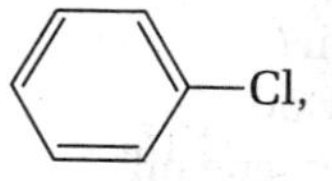

, $CH_2=CH—Cl$, 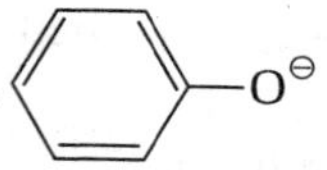

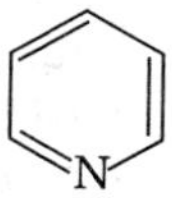

I II III IV

resonance stabilised compounds are

(a) I and II
(b) I, III and IV
(c) I, II, III and IV
(d) II, III and IV

84. In the alkylation of benzene, stable σ-complex can be

(a) 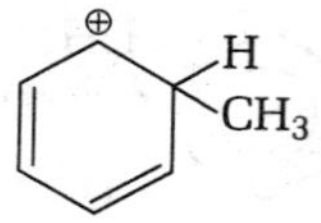

(b) 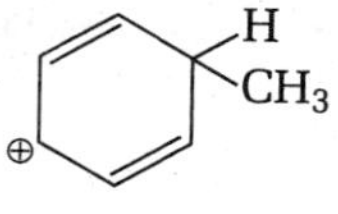

(c) 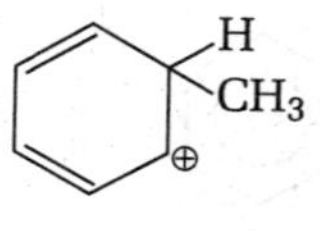

(d) All of these

85. Yellow precipitate of AgBr is formed on reaction with $AgNO_3$ with

(a) 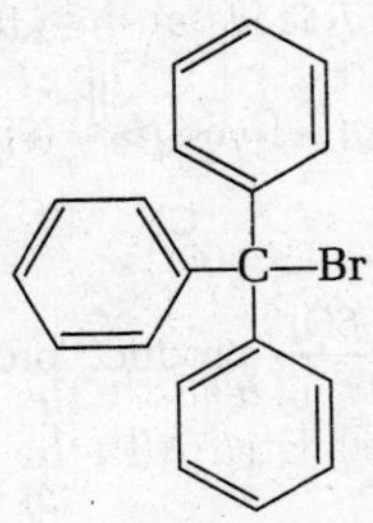
(b) 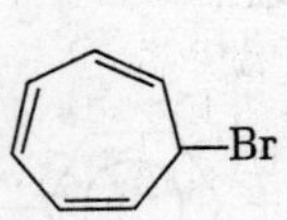

(c) Both (a) and (b)
(d) None of these

86. Consider the following statements.

I. —OH group in benzene nucleus is activating.
II. There is stabilisation of phenolate ion through resonance.
III. Rate of S_E in benzene is faster than that of phenol.

Select the correct statements.

(a) I and II
(b) I and III
(c) II and III
(d) I, II and III

87. Identify **ipso** carbon atom in

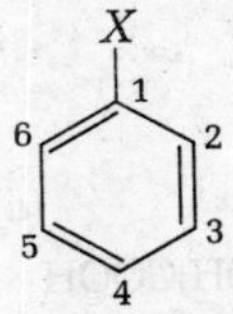

(a) C_1
(b) C_1 and C_4
(c) C_2 and C_6
(d) C_4

88. Which one of the following has the most nucleophilic nitrogen?

(a) 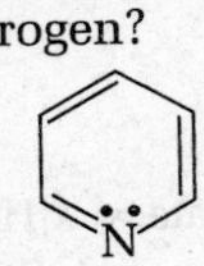
(b) 
(c) 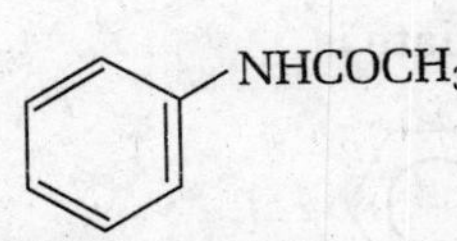
(d) 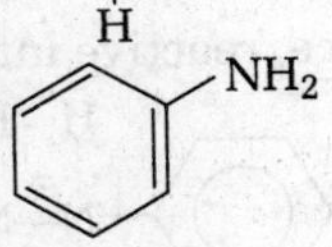

89. The product of the following reaction is

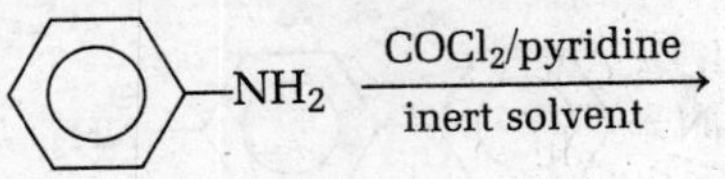

(a) 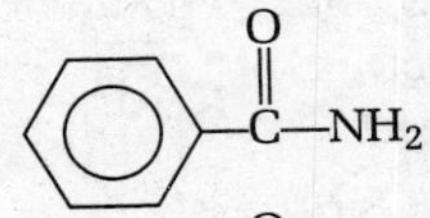
(b) 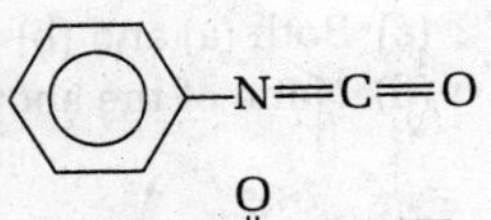
(c) 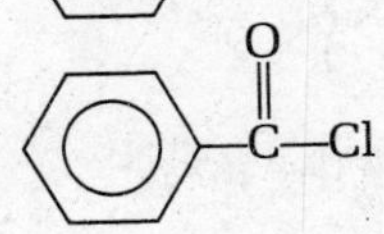
(d) 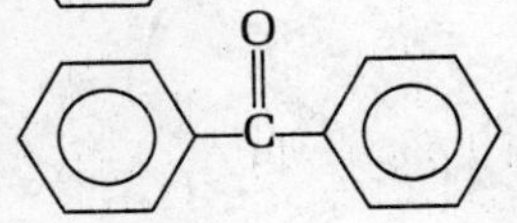

90. Which of the following statements is correct?

(a) Aniline is a stronger base than ethyl amine.
(b) Aniline is a stronger base than *p*-methoxyaniline.
(c) Aniline must be acetylated before nitration with an acid derivative.
(d) Aniline is soluble in an ammonium hydroxide solution.

91. The final product in the following sequence of reactions is

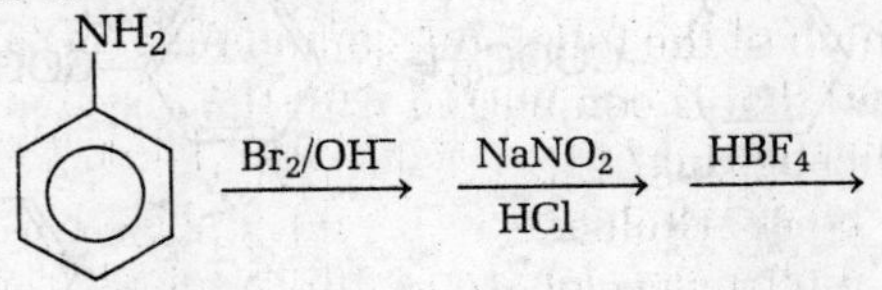

(a) 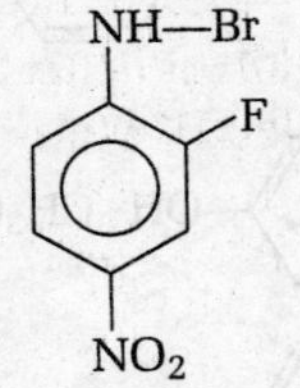
(b) 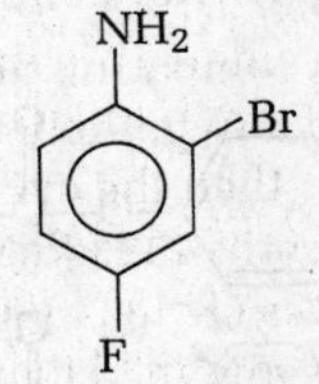
(c) 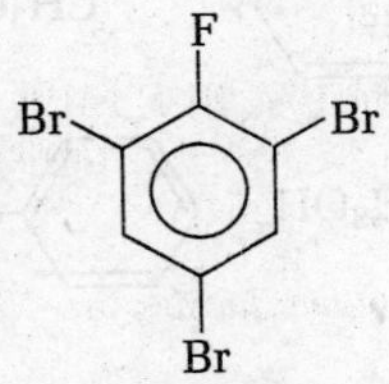
(d) 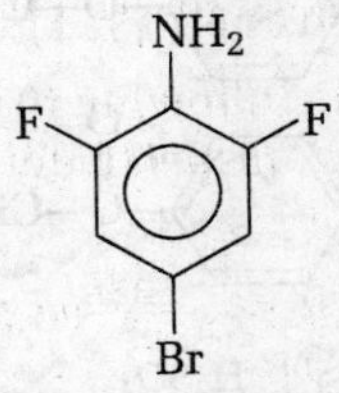

92. Which one among the following compounds has the highest value of dipole moment?

(a) 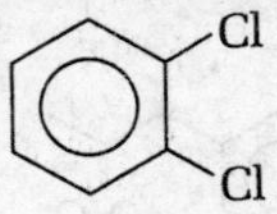
(b) 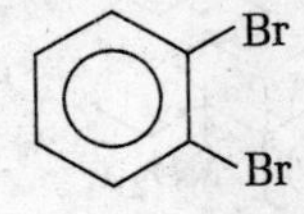
(c) 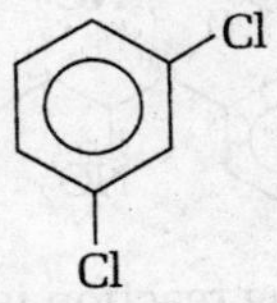
(d) 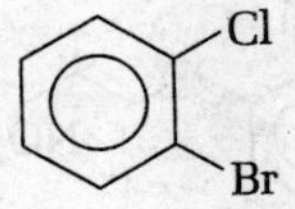

93. 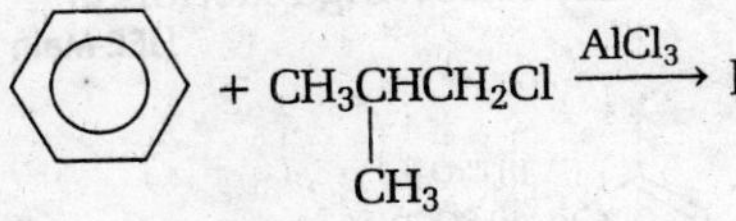 hydrocarbon (X), X is

(a) 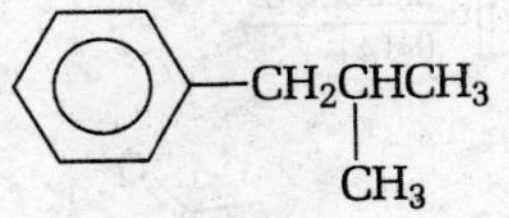
(b) 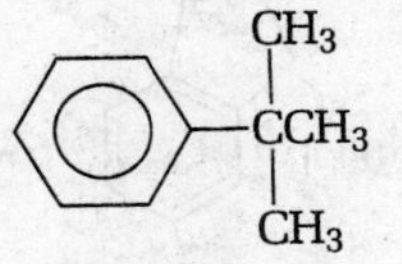
(c) 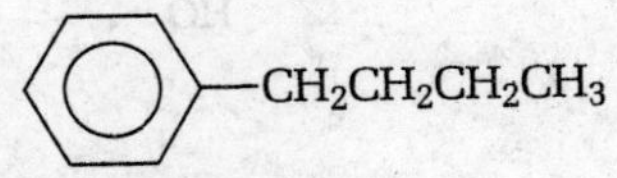
(d) All of the above are correct

94. Reactivity of (I) C_6H_5COCl, (II) $C_6H_5CONH_2$ and (III) $C_6H_5COOCH_3$ towards hydrolysis is in order

(a) I < II < III (b) III < II < I
(c) II < III < I (d) I < III < I

95. An ester (*A*) on acidic/hydrolysis gives (*B*) and (*C*). (*B*) gives violet colour and (*C*) gives blood red colour with neutral $FeCl_3$ solution (*A*), (*B*) and (*C*) are

(a) 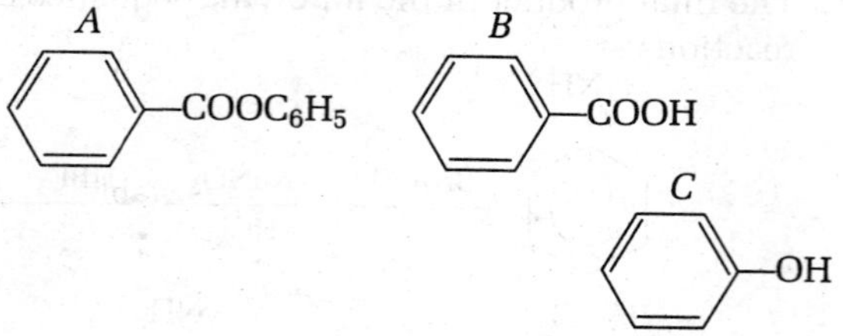

(b) 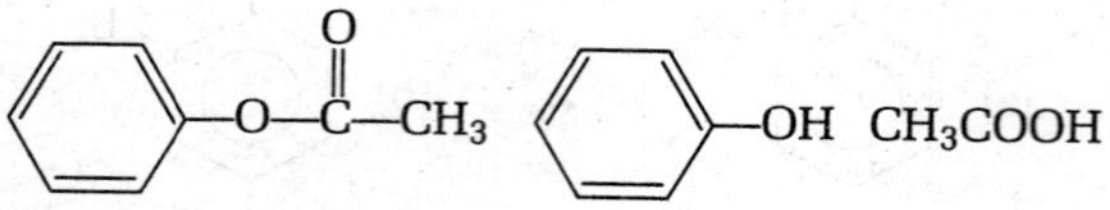

(c) 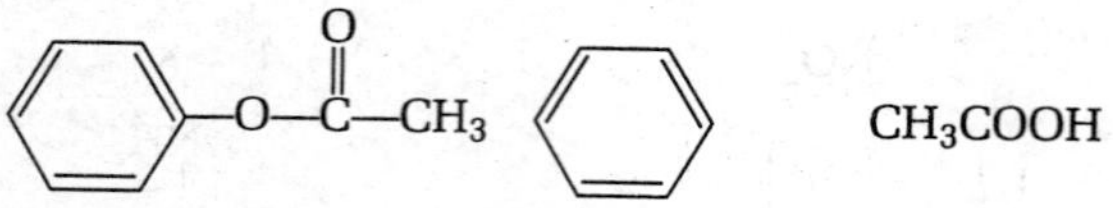

(d) 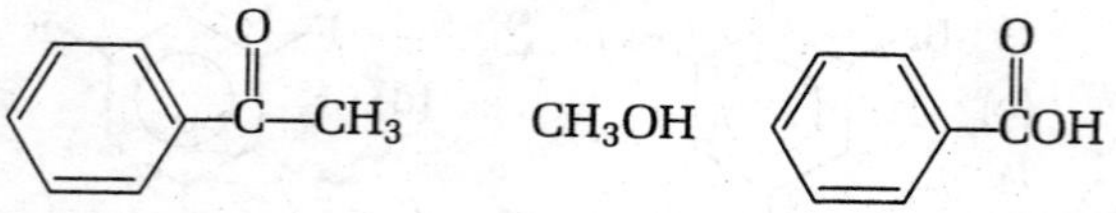

96. 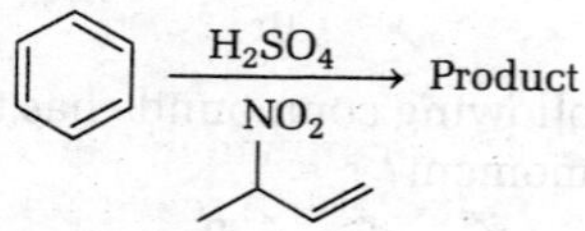

[JEE Main 2021, Feb.]

(a) 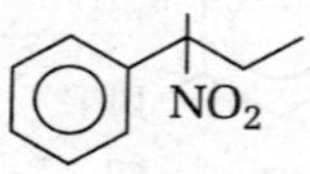

(b) 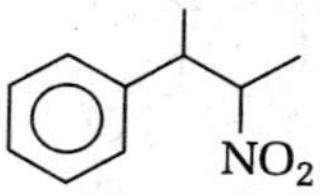

(c) 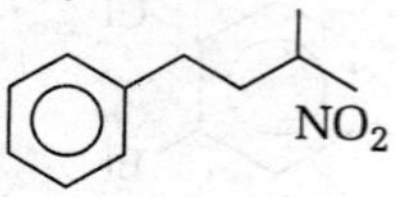

(d) 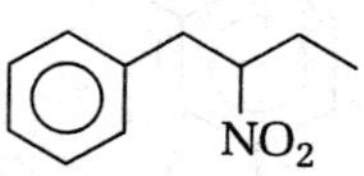

97. The major product of the following reaction is **[JEE Main 2019]**

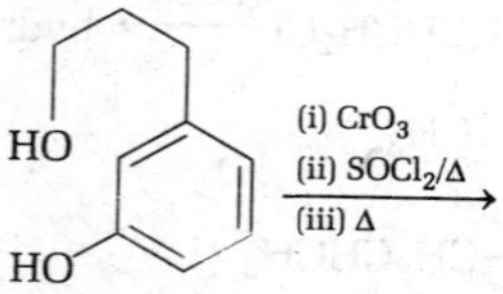

(a) 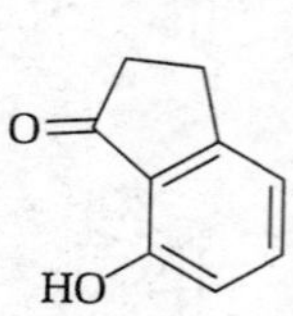

(b) 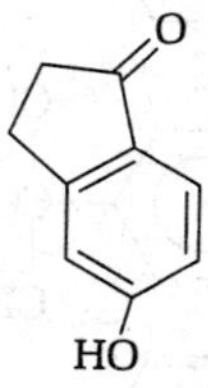

(c) 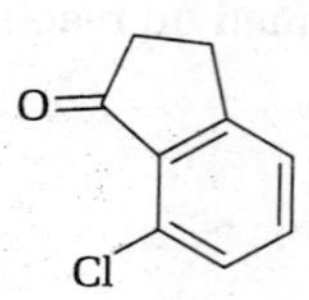

(d) 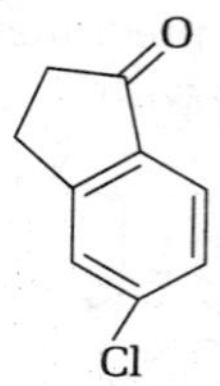

98. Chloral + 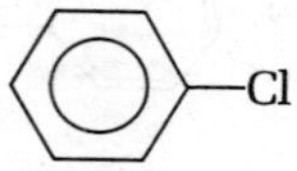 $\xrightarrow{\text{Conc. } H_2SO_4}$ product; product is

(a) lindane
(b) DDT
(c) teflon
(d) ethaneperchlorate

99. *p*-cresol reacts with chloroform in alkaline medium to give the compound *A* which adds hydrogen cyanide to form the compound *B*. The latter on acidic hydrolysis gives chiral carboxylic acid *C* which is

(a) 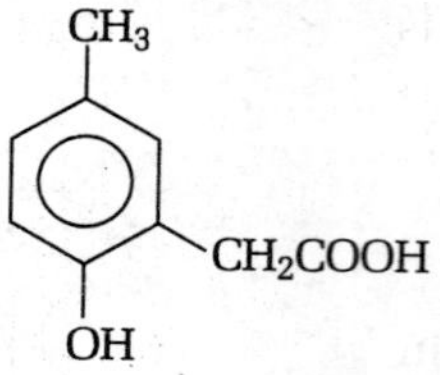

(b) 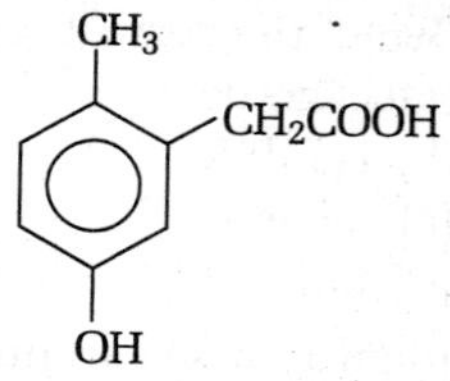

(c) 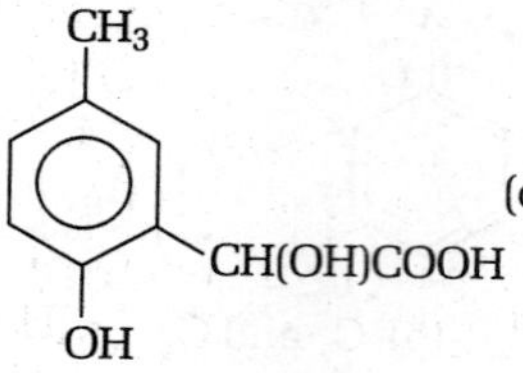

(d) 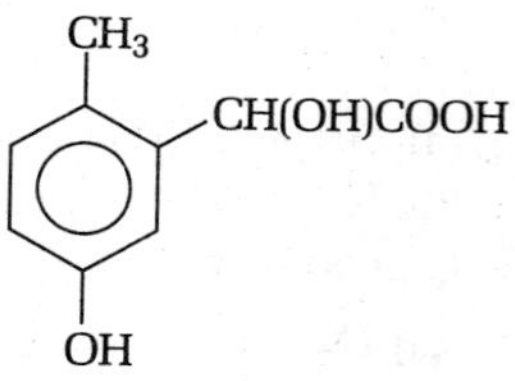

100. 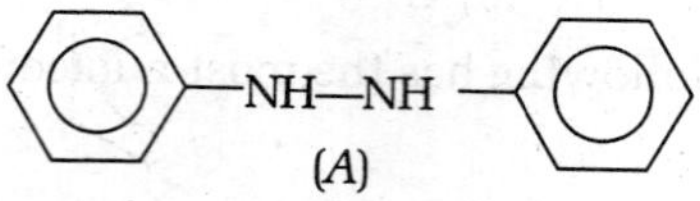 $\xrightarrow{H^+}$

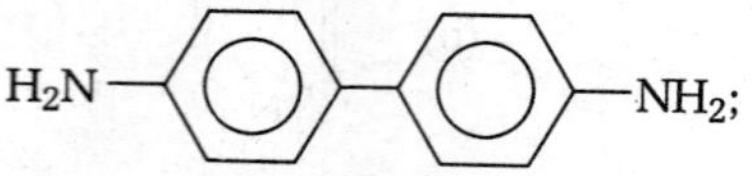 Rate $= k[H^+]^2 [A]$

Hence, reactive intermediate is

(a) 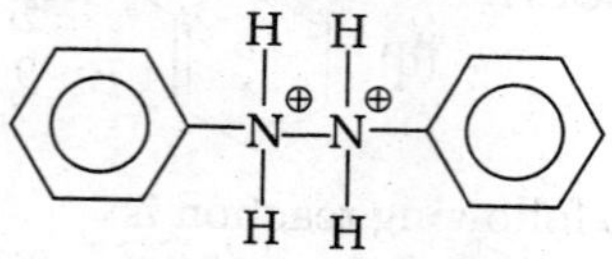

(b) 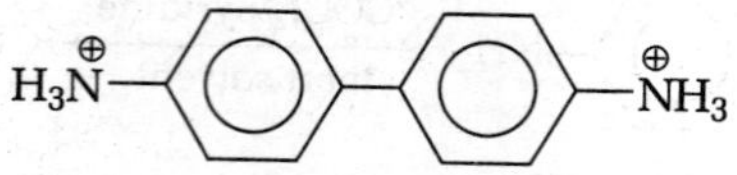

(c) Both (a) and (b) are correct
(d) None of the above is correct

101. 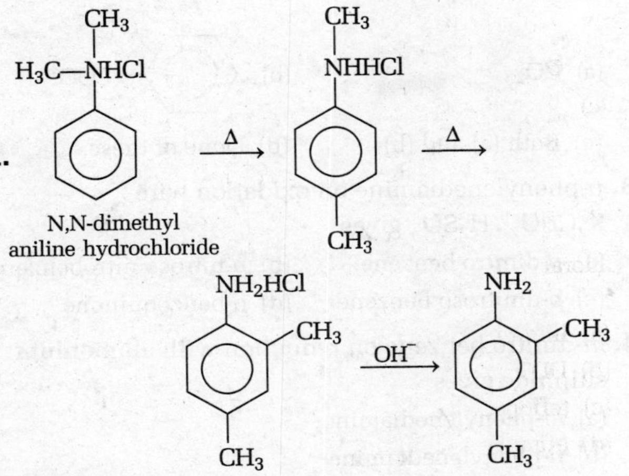

This is called
(a) Hofmann-Martius rearrangement
(b) Hofmann-degradation reaction
(c) Ulmann reaction
(d) Fries migration

102. Coupling of diazonium salts of the following takes place in order of

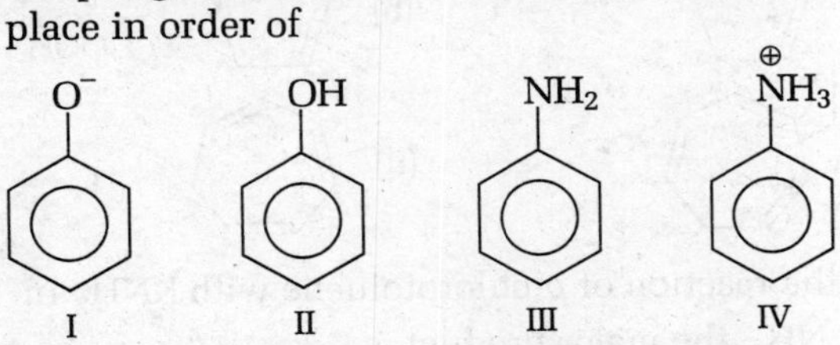

(a) IV < II < III < I
(b) IV > III < II < I
(c) II < IV < I < III
(d) I < II < III < IV

103. Consider *p*-amino phenol

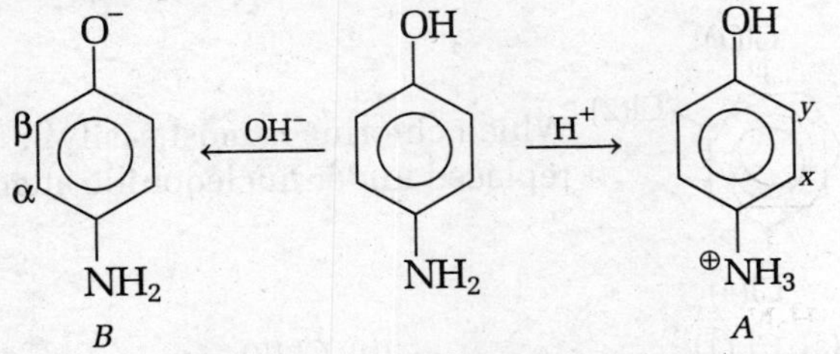

Which positions are activated in acidic and basic media for coupling?
(a) x in A and β in B
(b) x in A and α in B
(c) y in A and α in B
(d) y in A and β in B

104. Which one among the following carbocations has the longest half-life?

(a) 
(b) 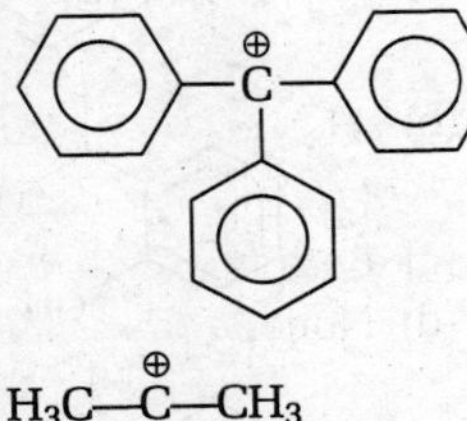
(c) 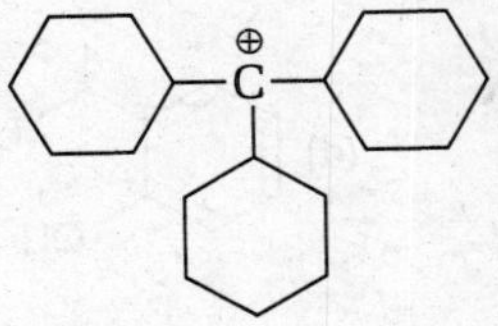
(d) $H_3C-\overset{\oplus}{C}(CH_3)-CH_3$

105. 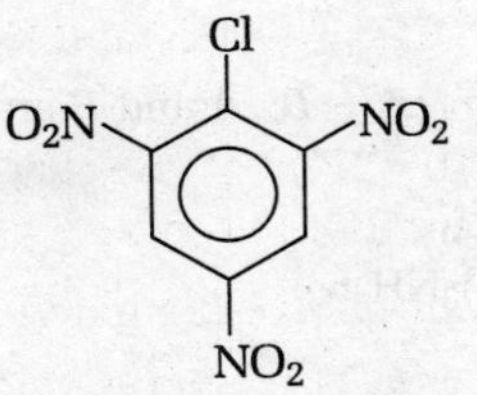

$+ H_2O \xrightarrow{\text{Warm}}$ product

Product can be
(a) picric acid
(b) phenol
(c) chlorobenzene
(d) no reaction since (C—Cl) bond is stable

106. 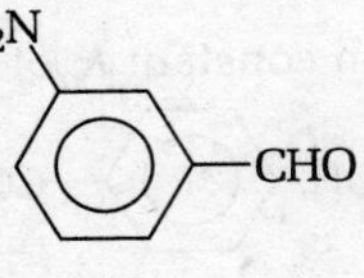

$\xrightarrow[\text{methanol}]{NaBH_4}$ A; A is

(a) 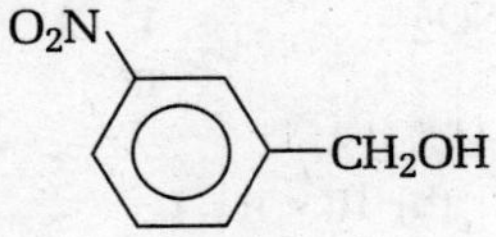

(b) 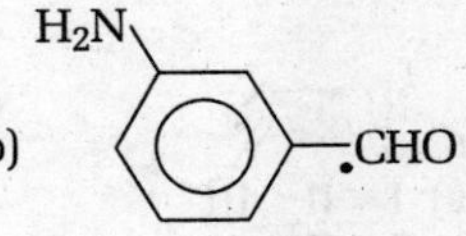

(c) 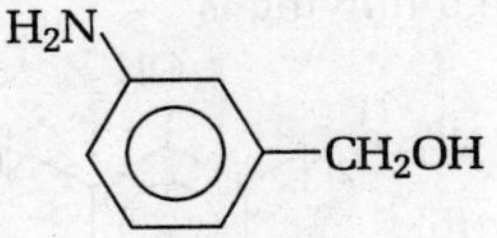

(d) 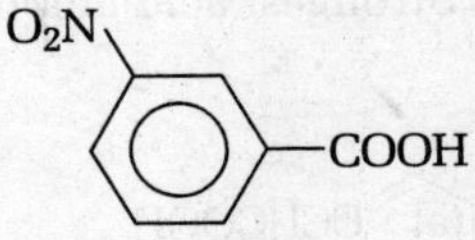

107. Phenol reacts with methyl chloroformate in the presence of NaOH to form product A. A reacts with Br_2 to form product B. A and B are respectively **[JEE Main 2018]**

(a) 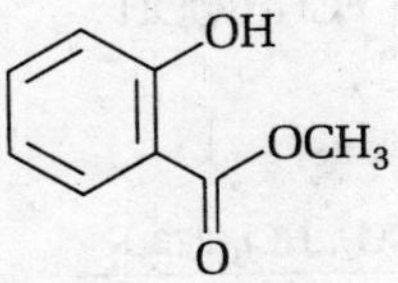

and 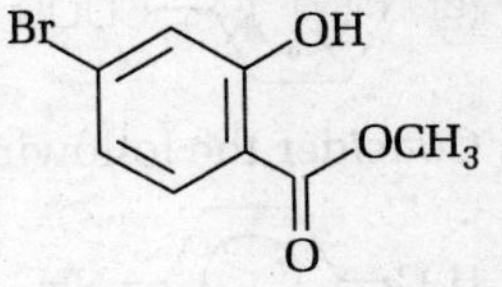

(b) 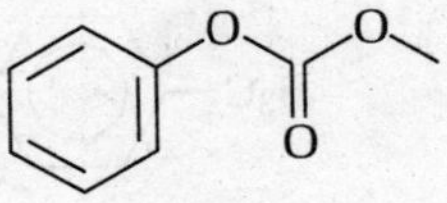
and 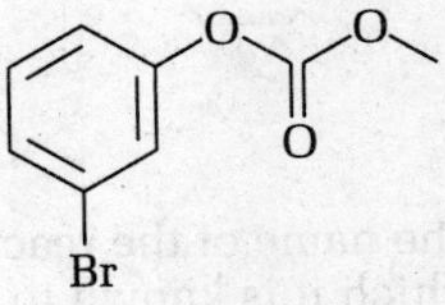

(c) 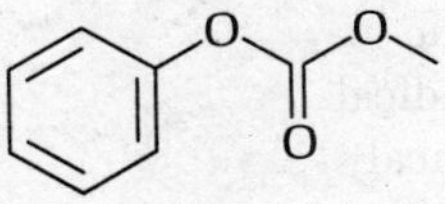
and 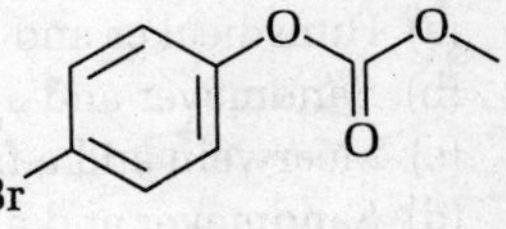

(d) 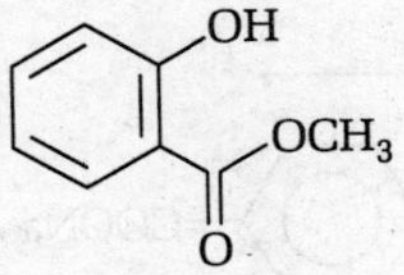

and 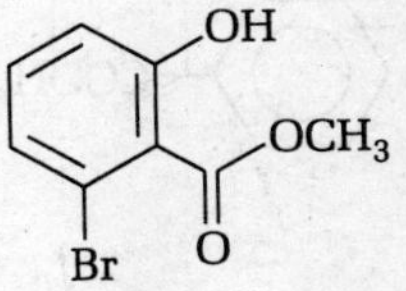

108. 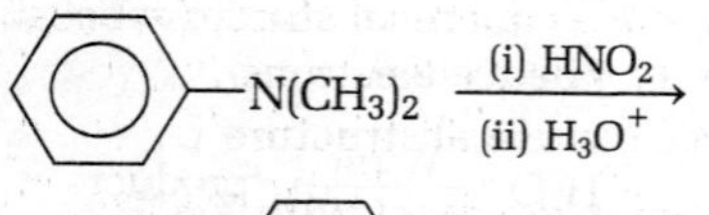

$A + B$; A and B are

(a) 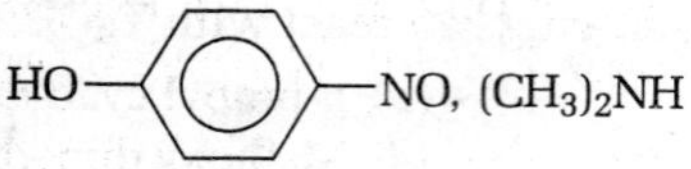

(b) 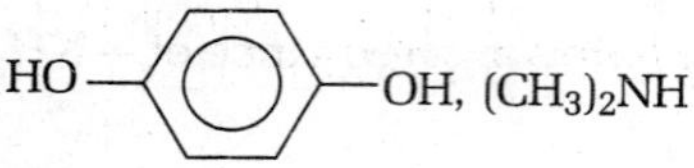

(c) 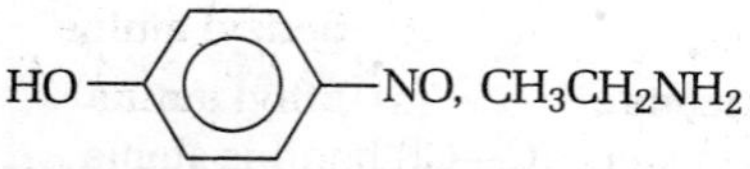

(d) None of the above is correct

109. Increasing values of dissociation constant K_a of

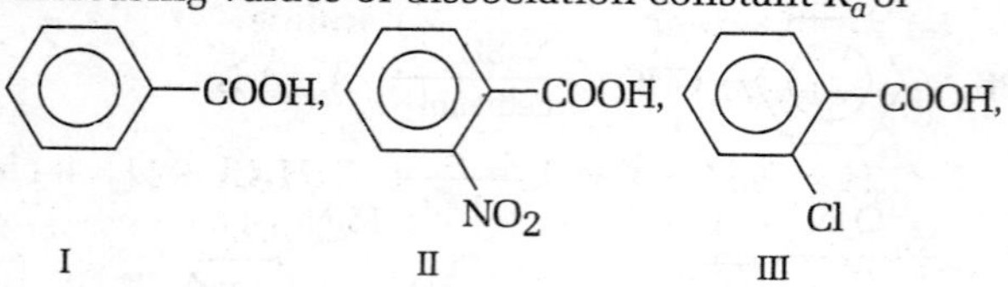

is

(a) I < II < III (b) III < II < I
(c) I < III < II (d) II < III < I

110. Strongest acid among the following is

(a) CCl_3COOH

(b) 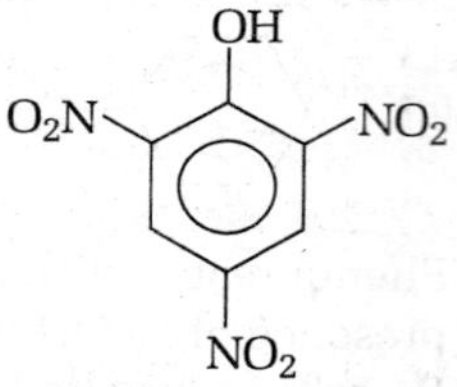

(c) 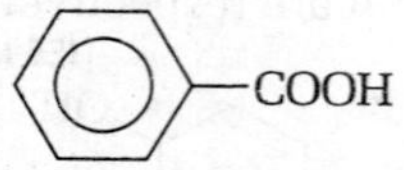

(d) FCH_2COOH

111. Consider the following reactions,

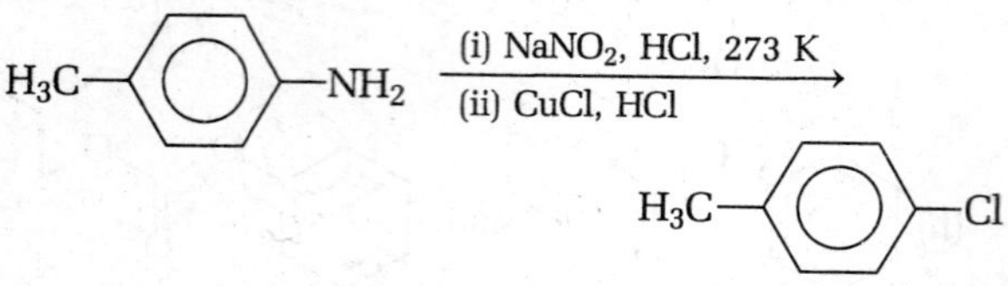

The name of the reaction and the intermediate *via.* which it is known to proceed, are respectively

(a) Hunsdiecker and benzyne
(b) Sandmeyer and a free radical
(c) Meerwein and a free radical
(d) Sandmeyer and a carbanion

112. 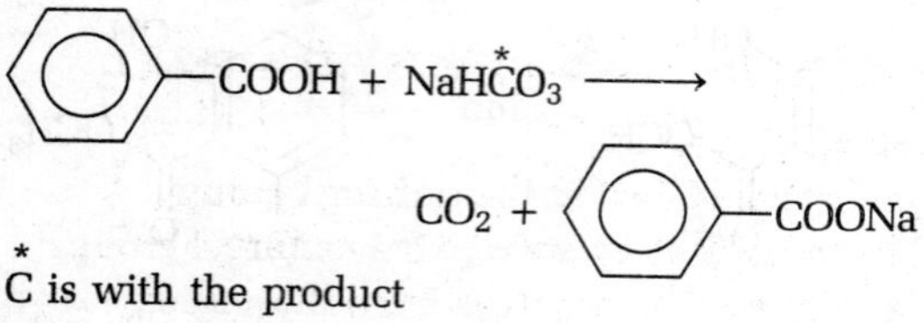

$\overset{*}{C}$ is with the product

(a) CO_2

(b) 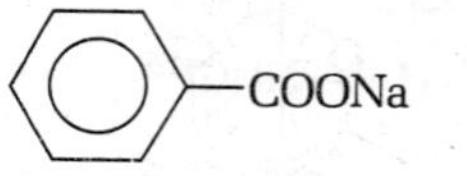

(c) Both (a) and (b) (d) None of these

113. *p*-phenylenediamine on oxidation with $K_2Cr_2O_7 \cdot H_2SO_4$ gives

(a) *p*-dinitro benzene (b) *p*-nitroso nitrobenzene
(c) *p*-dinitroso benzene (d) *p*-benzoquinone

114. *m*-dinitro benzene on reduction with ammonium sulphide gives

(a) *m*-phenylenediamine
(b) *p*-phenylenediamine
(c) *m*-nitroaniline
(d) *m*-phenylhydrazine

115. Which one of the following will be aromatic?

(a) 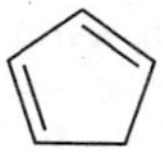

(b) 

(c) 

(d) 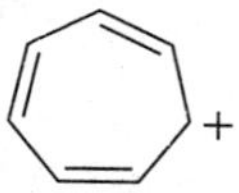

116. In the reaction of *p*-chlorotoluene with KNH_2 in liq. NH_3, the major product is

(a) *o*-toluidine (b) *m*-toluidine
(c) *p*-toluidine (d) *p*-chloroaniline

117. 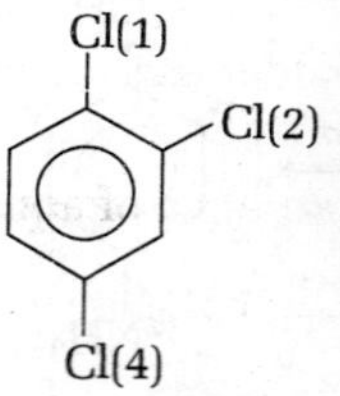

Which chlorine is most easily replaced under nucleophilic attack?

(a) Cl (1) (b) Cl (2)
(c) Cl (4) (d) Cl (1) and Cl (4)

118. The major product formed in the following reaction is **[JEE Main 2018]**

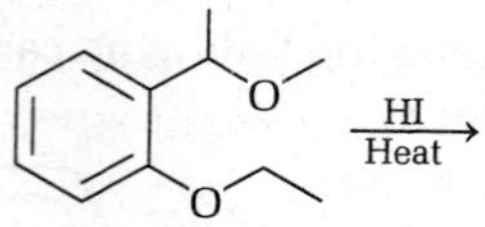

(a) 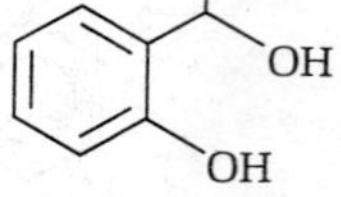

(b) 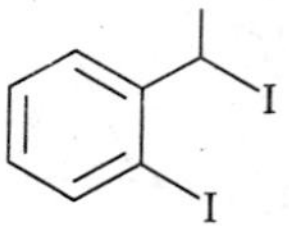

(c) 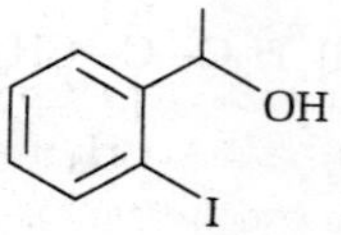

(d) 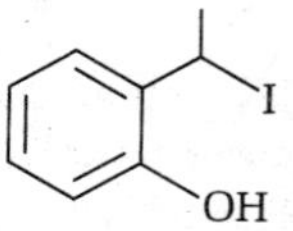

119. 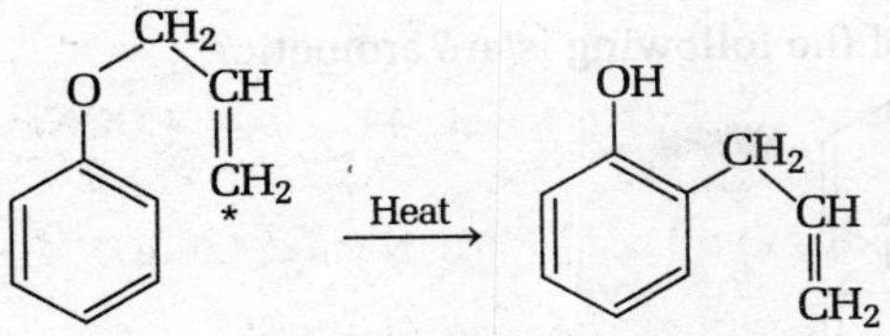

What is the name of this reaction?
(a) Fries rearrangement
(b) Claisen rearrangement
(c) Kolbe reaction
(d) Reimer-Tiemann reaction

120. Which is the correct structure of the product formed in (119) in terms of position of C*?

(a) 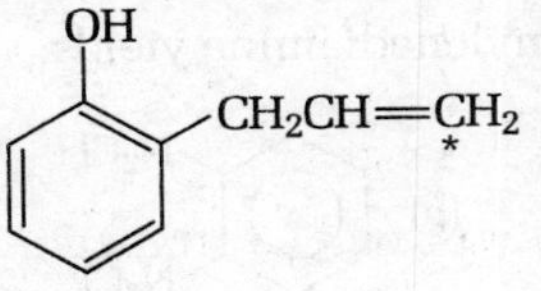

(b) 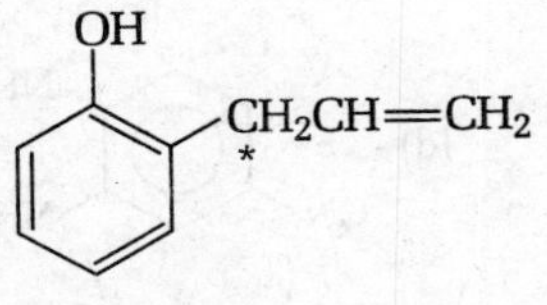

(c) Both (a) and (b)
(d) None of the above is correct

121. In the reaction sequence,

$$C_6H_6 \xrightarrow[\text{AlCl}_3\ (\text{anhy.})]{CH_3Cl} (X) \xrightarrow{KMnO_4} (Y),$$

the product (*Y*) is
(a) chlorobenzene (b) benzaldehyde
(c) benzoic acid (d) benzene

122. Thiophene reacts with HCHO in presence of aqueous HCl to give

(a) 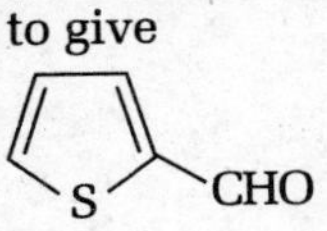 (b) 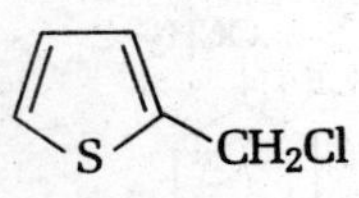

(c) 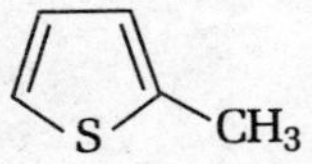 (d) 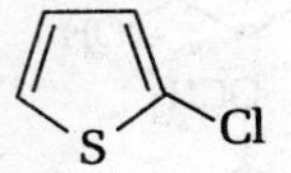

123. Examine the following two structures for the anilinium ion and choose the correct statement from the ones given below

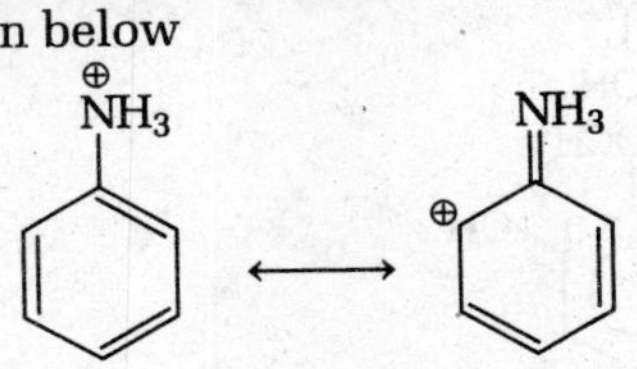

I II

(a) II is not an acceptable canonical structure because carbocation are less stable than ammonium ions
(b) II is not an acceptable canonical structure because it is non-aromatic
(c) II is not an acceptable canonical structure because the nitrogen has 10 valence electrons
(d) II is an acceptable canonical structure

124. Which of the following can react with TsCl?
(a) Glycerol (b) *n*-propyl cyanide
(c) Trimethylamine (d) Methoxy dimethyl amine

125. In which of the following resonance of —NH_2 is possible?
(a) *p*-toluidine (b) Benzyl amine
(c) 1-aminopropane (d) Ethyl amine

126. Liebermann's nitroso reaction is for the testing of
(a) phenol (b) benzoic acid
(c) nitrobenzene (d) aniline

127. The reaction,

$$C_6H_5N_2^+Cl^- + CuCl \xrightarrow[HCl]{\Delta} C_6H_5Cl + N_2 + CuCl$$

is known as
(a) Wurtz reaction (b) Sandmeyer reaction
(c) Gattermann reaction (d) Friedel-Crafts' reaction

128. Which of the following carboxylic acids undergoes decarboxylation easily?
(a) $C_6H_5COCH_2COOH$
(b) $C_6H_5COCOOH$
(c) $C_6H_5CH(OH)COOH$
(d) $C_6H_5CH(NH_2)COOH$

129. In the following compounds

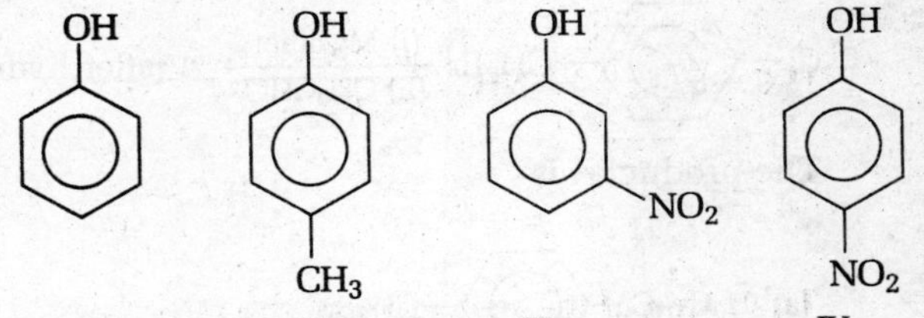

I II III IV

order of acidity is
(a) II < I < III < IV (b) III > IV > II > I
(c) IV < III < I < II (d) IV < III < II < I

130. In the Cannizzaro reaction given below

$$2PhCHO \xrightarrow{OH^-} PhCH_2OH + PhCO_2^-$$

The slowest step is
(a) the attack of OH^- at the carbonyl group
(b) the transfer of hydride to the carbonyl group
(c) the abstraction of proton from the carboxylic group
(d) the deprotonation of Ph—CH_2OH

131. The correct order of increasing basic nature for the following compounds is

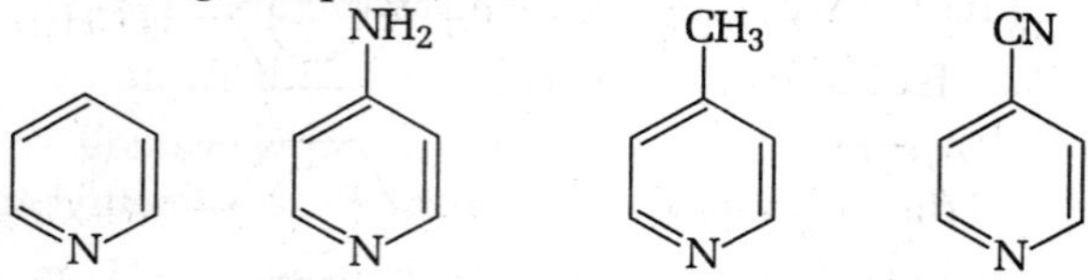

I II III IV

(a) IV < I < III < II (b) I < II < III < IV
(c) IV < III < II < I (d) II < IV < I < III

132. End product of the following reaction is

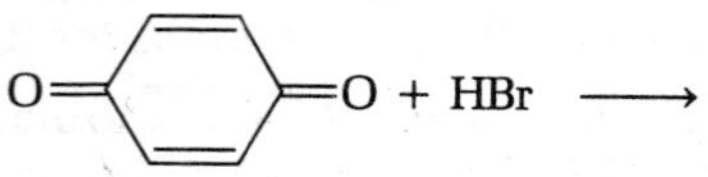

(a) 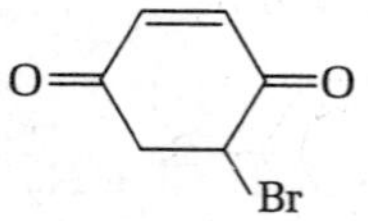 (b) 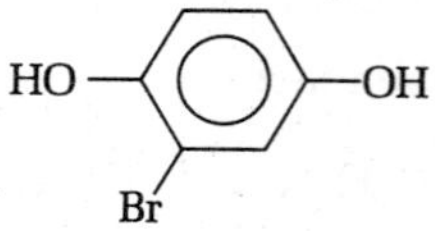

(c) 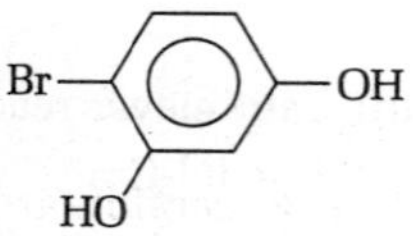 (d) 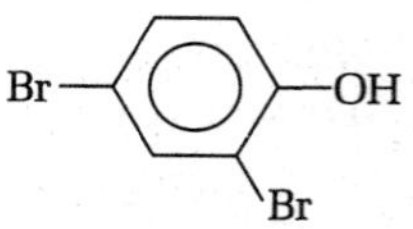

133. 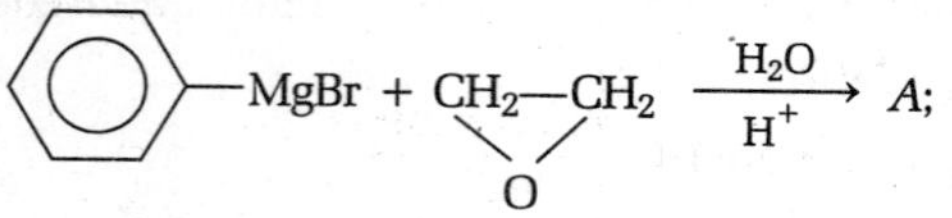 A; A is

(a) 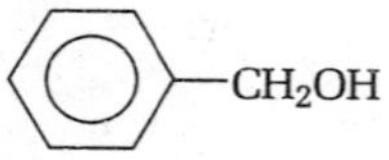 (b) 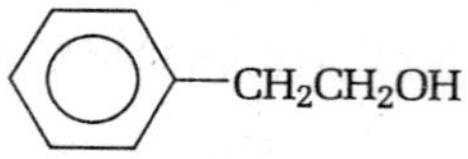

(c) 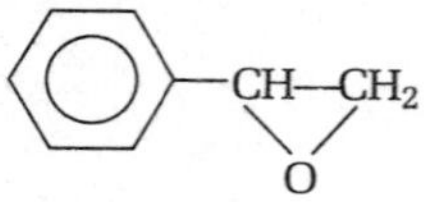 (d) no reaction

134. In the reaction,

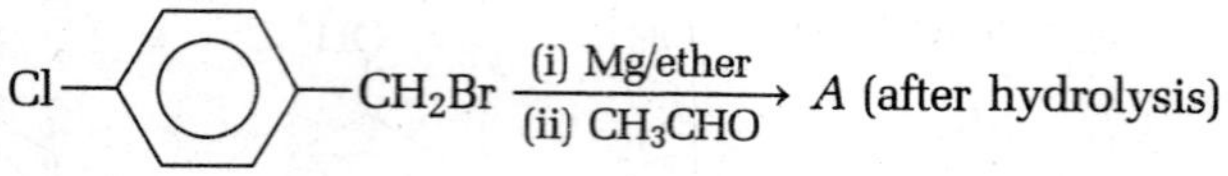

The product A is

(a) 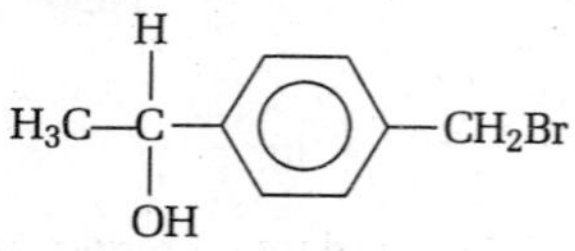

(b) 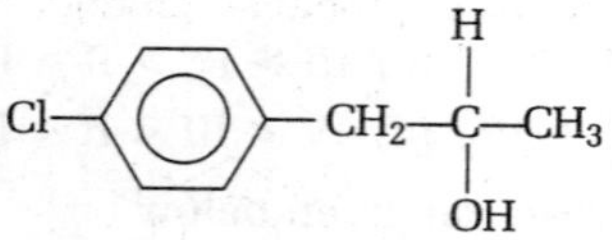

(c) 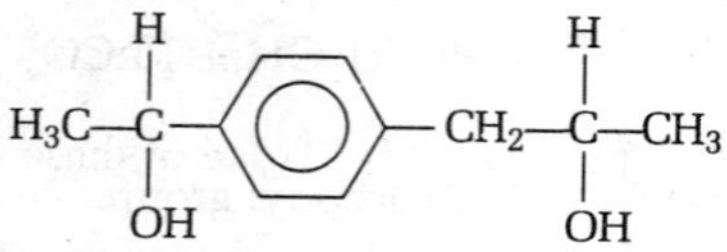

(d) 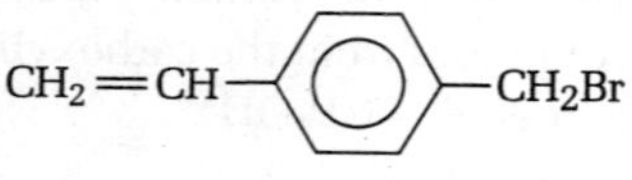

135. Which of the following is/are aromatic?

(a) 

(b) 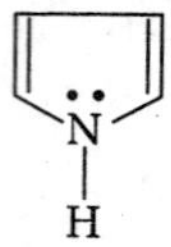

(c) 

(d) Both (a) and (b)

136. Diazotisation of o-phenylenediamine yields

(a) 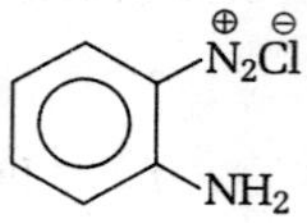 (b) 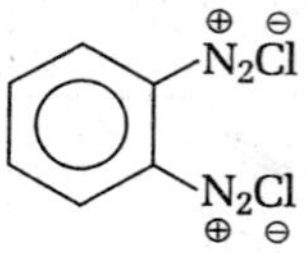

(c) 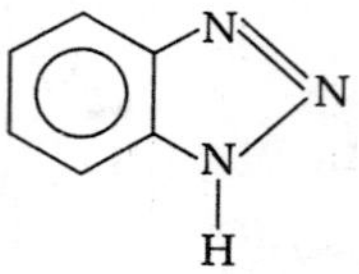 (d) 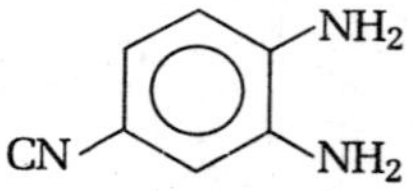

137. 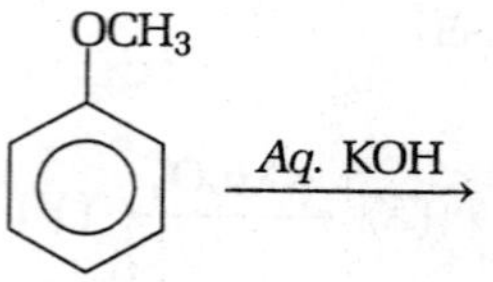 product; product is

(a) 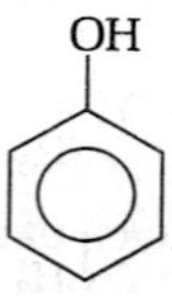 and CH_3OK (mixture)

(b) 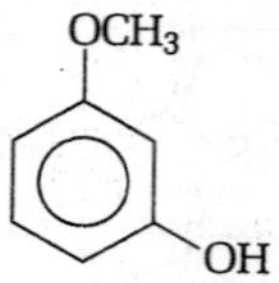

(c) 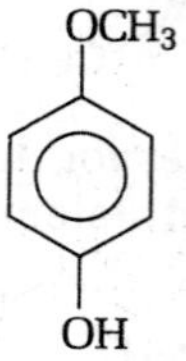

(d) 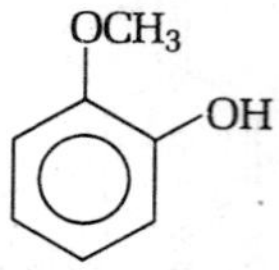

138. An organic compound of molecular formula $C_8H_{10}O$, on reaction with iodine and sodium hydroxide gives yellow precipitate. The most likely structure of the compound should be

(a) 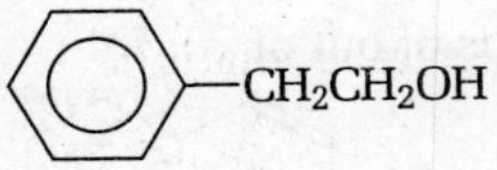

(b) 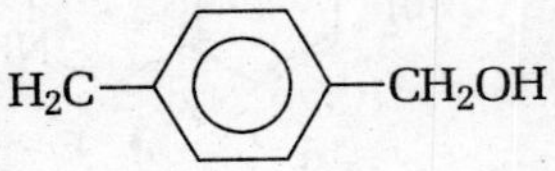

(c) 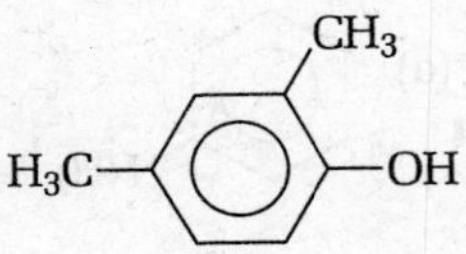

(d) 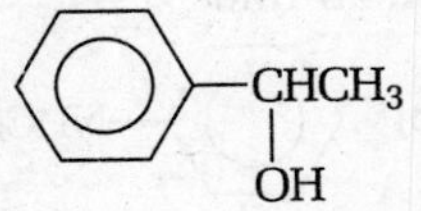

139. Identify (*A*) in the following reaction sequence :

$$\underset{\text{Gives positive iodoform test}}{(A)} \xrightarrow[\text{H}^+,\ \text{H}_2\text{O},\ \text{conc. H}_2\text{SO}_4/\Delta]{\text{CH}_3\text{MgBr}} (B) \xrightarrow{\text{O}_3/\text{Zn, H}_2\text{O}}$$

[JEE Main 2020]

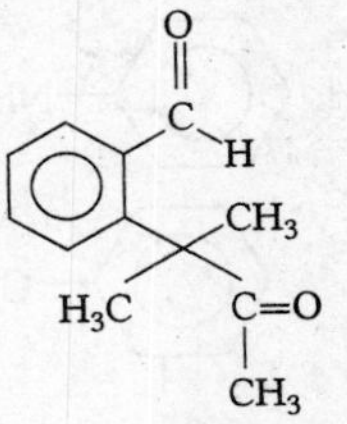

(a) 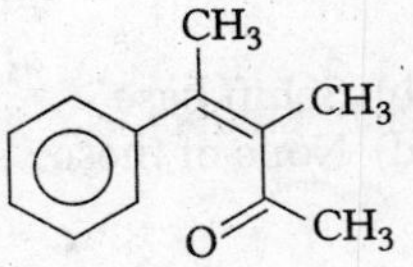 (b) 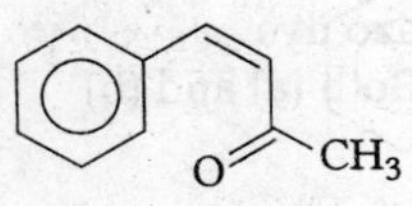

(c) 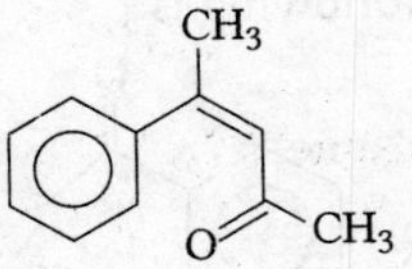 (d) 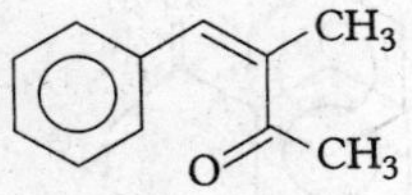

140. 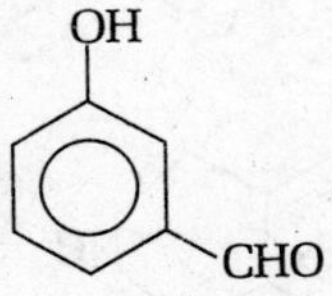 $\xrightarrow{\text{Br}_2,\ \text{Fe}}$ *A*; *A* can be

(a) 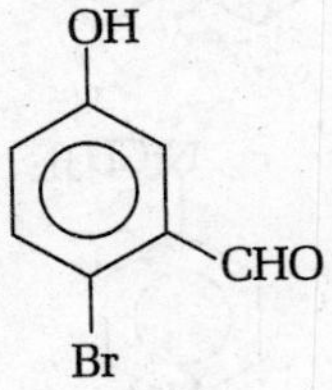 (b) 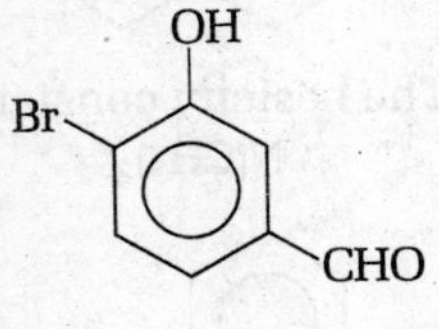

(c) 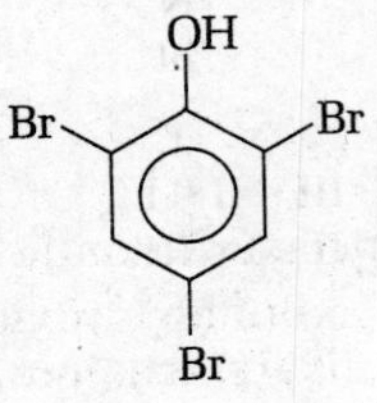 (d) no S_E reaction is possible

141. In which case, S_E will not be in *meta*-position?

(a) 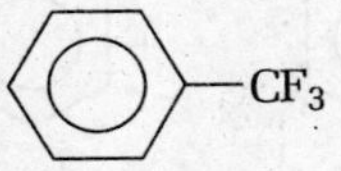 (b) 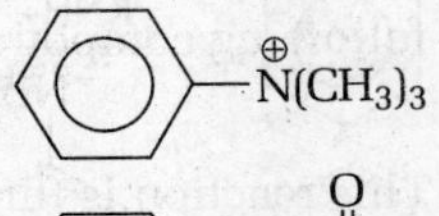

(c) 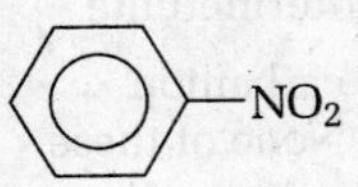 (d) 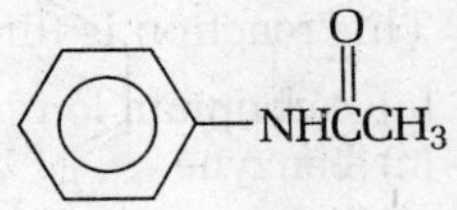

142. 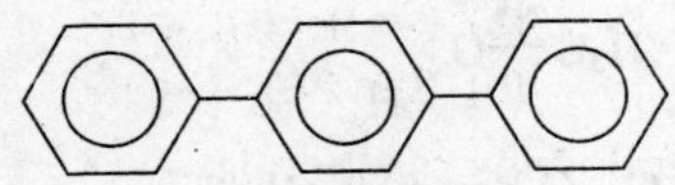 $\xrightarrow{\text{Br}_2,\text{Fe}}$ *A*; *A* is

(a) 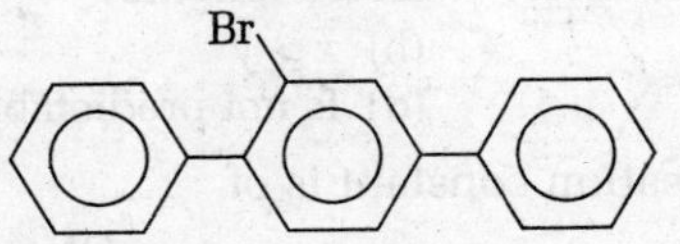

(b) 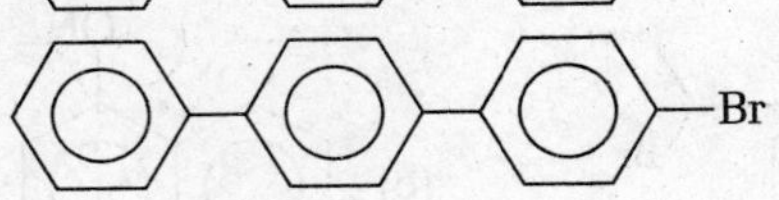

(c) Both (a) and (b)

(d) None of the above is correct

143. Major products of the following reaction are

[JEE Main 2019]

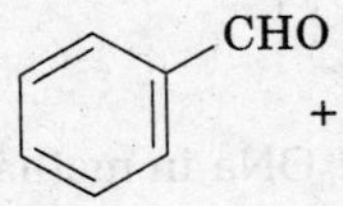 + HCHO $\xrightarrow[\text{(ii) H}_3\text{O}^+]{\text{(i) 50\% NaOH}}$

(a) CH_3OH and HCO_2H

(b) CH_3OH and 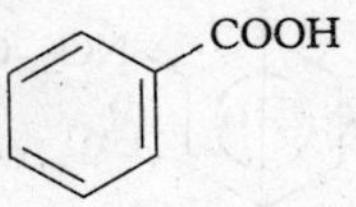

(c) HCOOH and 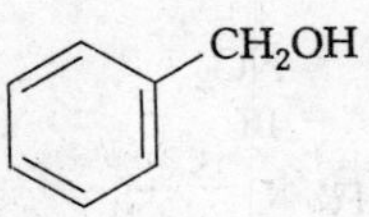

(d) 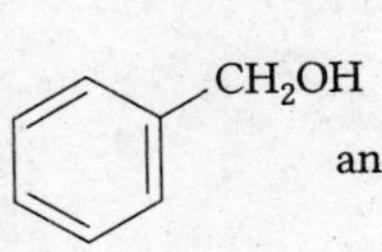 and 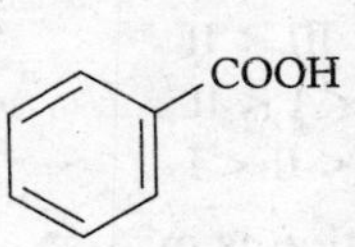

144. 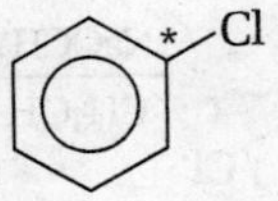 $\xrightarrow[\text{670 K}]{\text{NaOH, H}_2\text{O}}$ product; product is

(a) 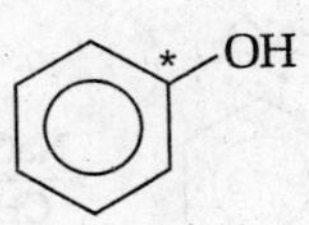 (b) 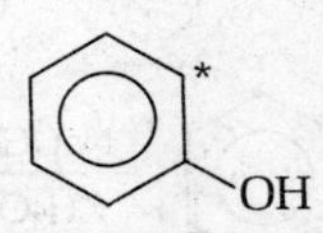

(c) Both (a) and (b) (d) None of these

145. 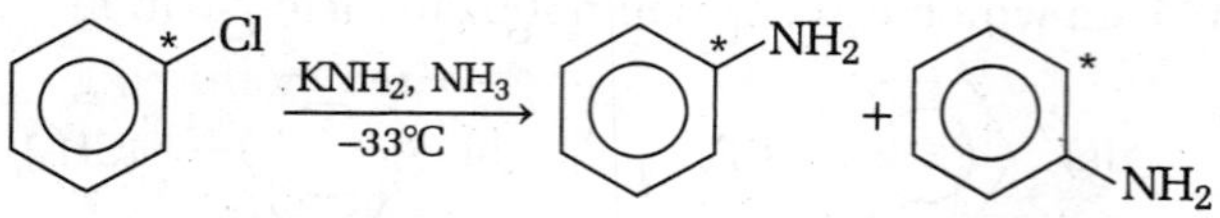

This reaction is through the intermediate

(a) carbonium ion (b) carbanion
(c) benzyne (d) None of these

146. 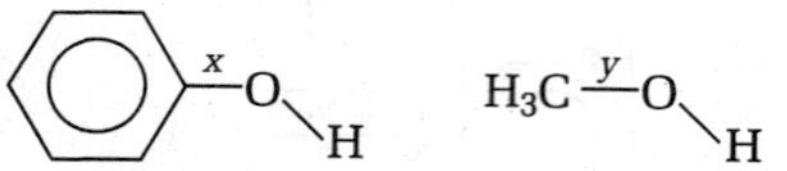

Which is true about C—O bond lengths?

(a) $x = y$ (b) $x > y$
(c) $x < y$ (d) Is not predictable

147. Maximum ionisation constant is of

(a) 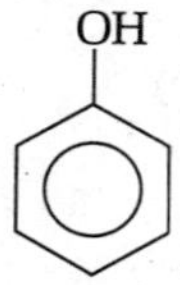 (b) 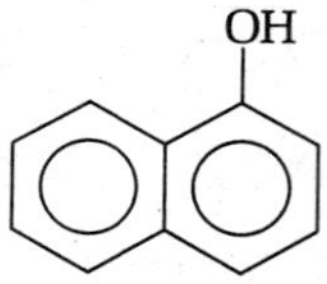

(c) 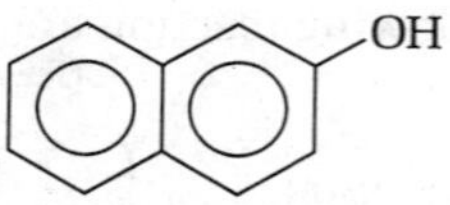 (d) 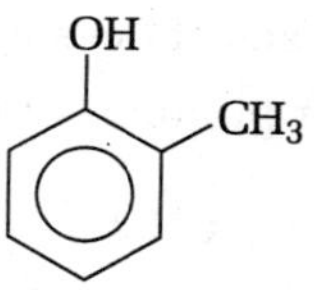

148. Increasing rate of reaction with CH_3ONa in methanol (by S_N) is in order of

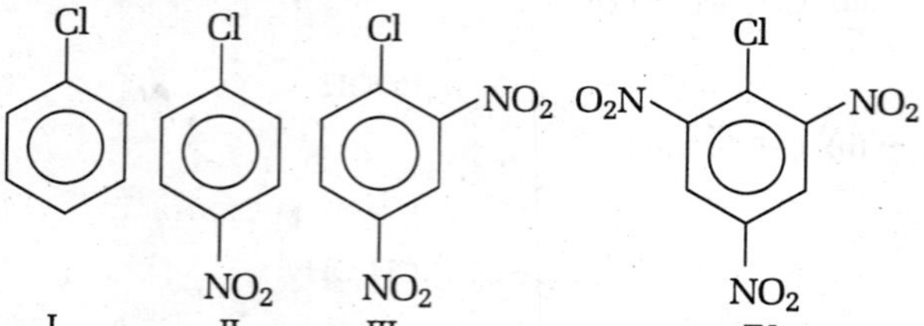

I II III IV

(a) I < II < III < IV
(b) IV < I < III < II
(c) IV < III < I < II
(d) IV < III < II < I

149. Fastest reaction is in

(a) 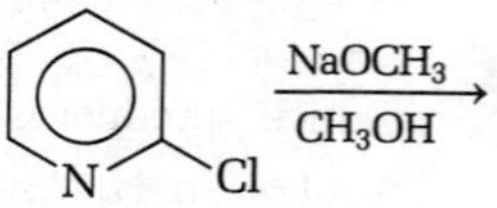 (b) 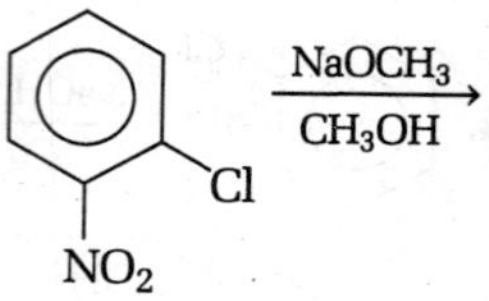

(c) 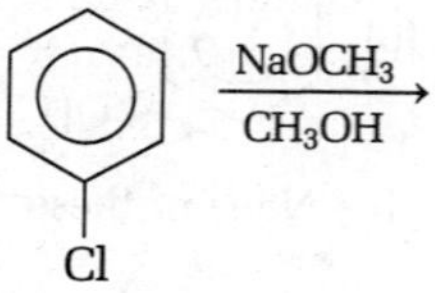 (d) 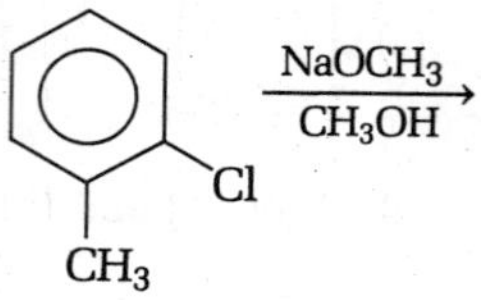

150. Maximum basic nature is of out of

(a) 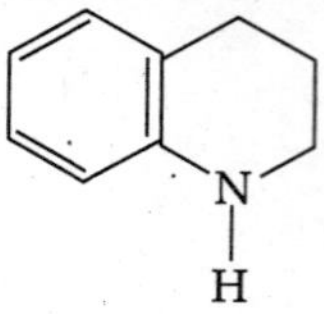 (b) 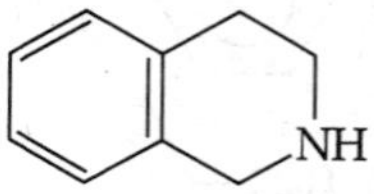

(c) CH_3NH_2 (d) 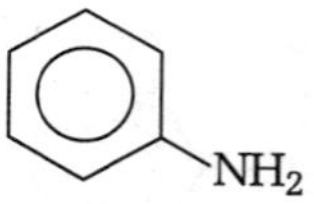

151. Which is a weaker base than aniline?

(a) 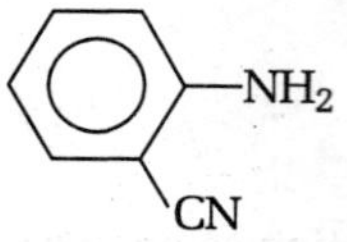 (b) 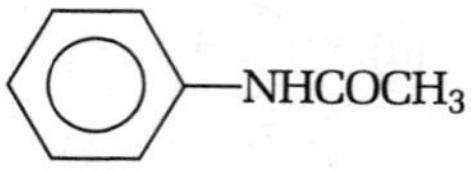

(c) 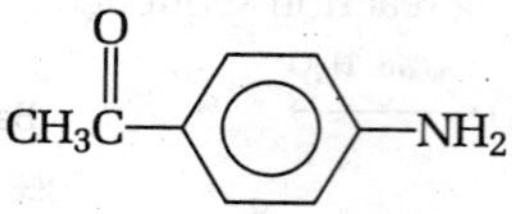 (d) All of these

152. 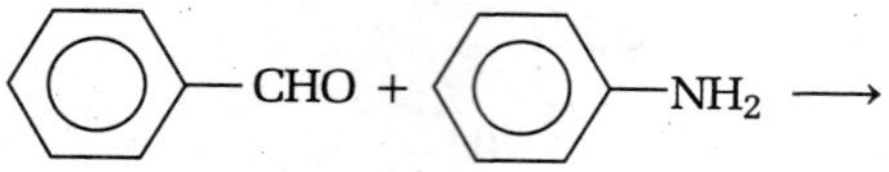

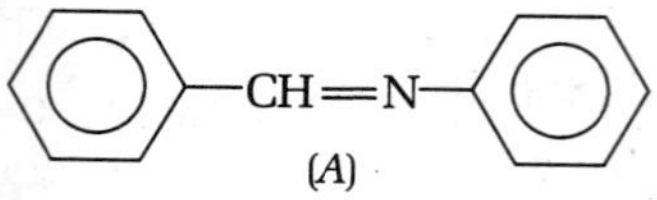

(A)

A is called

(a) azo dye (b) Schiff base
(c) Both (a) and (b) (d) None of these

153. Maximum basic out of the following is

(a) 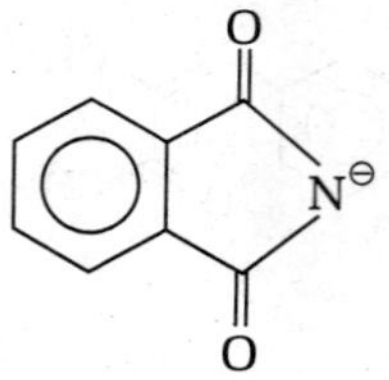 (b) 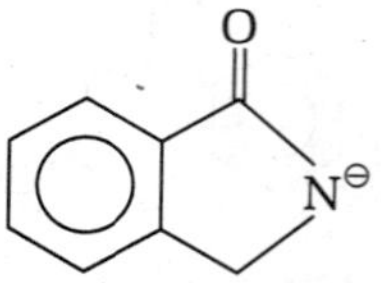

(c) 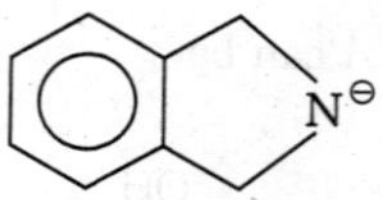 (d) 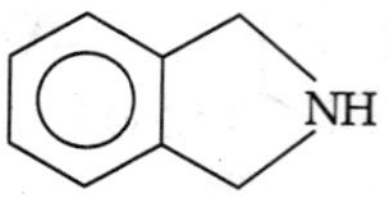

154. The basicity constant of

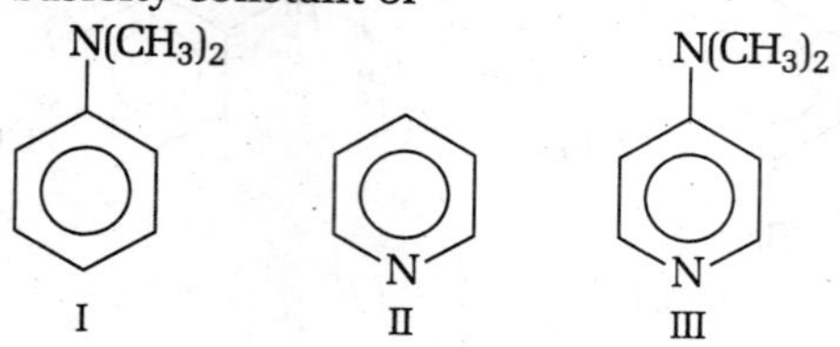

I II III

are in order

(a) I < II < III (b) III < II < I
(c) III < I < II (d) II < I < III

155. 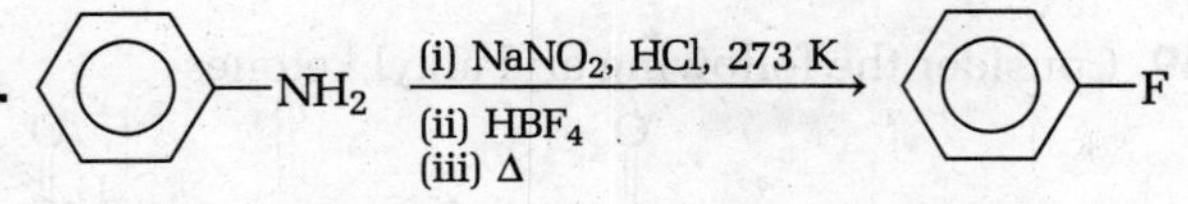

This reaction is called
(a) Sandmeyer (b) Gattermann
(c) Schiemann (d) Kolbe

156. Diazo coupling takes place in basic conditions. It is because of
(a) faster reaction in basic condition
(b) deprotonation of the phenolic and carboxyl group in the substrate activates the ring
(c) Both (a) and (b)
(d) None of the above

157. In which case, coupling takes place
(a) 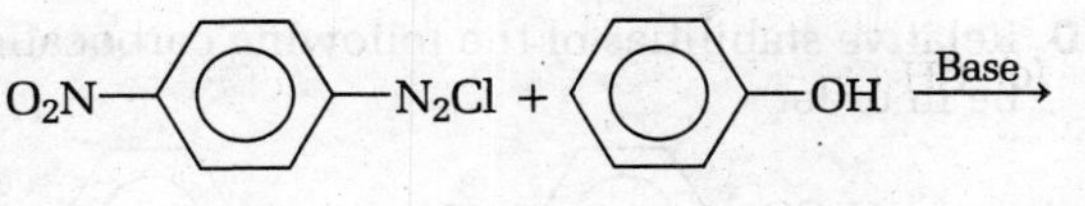
(b) 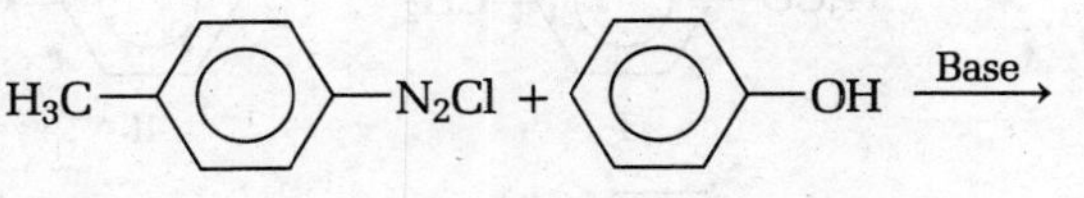
(c) in both cases (d) in none case

158. Phenol on treatment with CO_2 in the presence of NaOH followed by acidification produces compound X as the major product. X on treatment with $(CH_3CO)_2O$ in the presence of catalytic amount of H_2SO_4 produces: **[JEE Main 2018]**

(a) 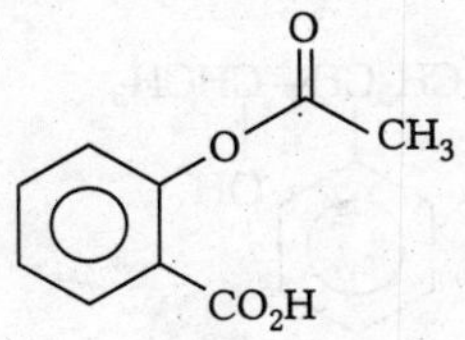
(b) 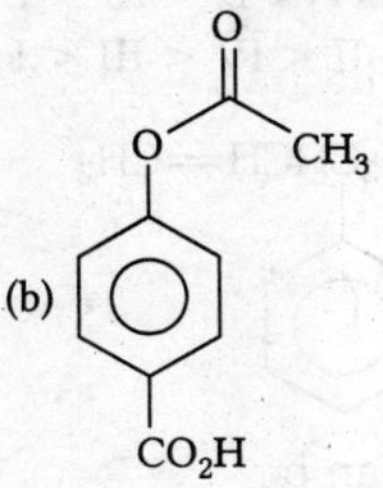
(c) 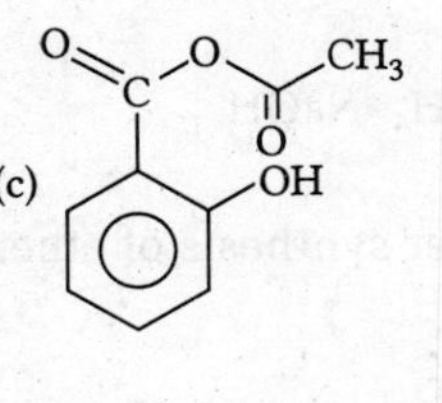
(d) 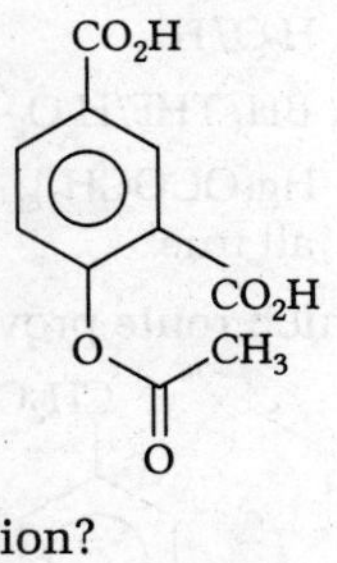

159. Which separates by sulphonation?
(a) *o*-xylene
(b) *m*-xylene
(c) *p*-xylene
(d) All of these

160. 2-phenyl ethanol can be prepared by reacting C_6H_5MgBr with
(a) methanol (b) ethanol
(c) ethyl acetate (d) ethylene oxide

161. O_2 gas is passed into hot cumene. The product is then treated with *aq.* H_2SO_4. The final product(s) formed is/are
(a) phenyl propionate
(b) phenyl isopropyl ether
(c) phenol and acetone
(d) *p*-isopropyl phenol

162. Which one of the following substances is not aromatic?
(a) 
(b) 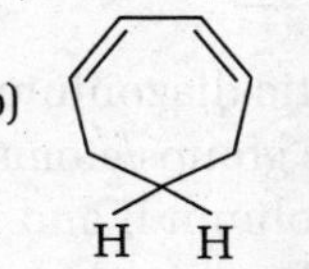
(c) 
(d) 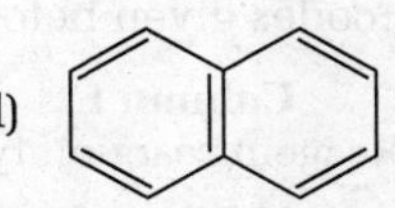

163. Consider the following groups,

I. $-O-\overset{O}{\overset{\|}{C}}-CH_3$ II. $-\overset{O}{\overset{\|}{C}}-O-CH_3$

III. $-NH-\overset{O}{\overset{\|}{C}}-CH_3$ IV. $-CF_3$

Which of these are *meta*-directing groups in S_E in benzene nucleus?
(a) II and IV (b) I, II and III
(c) I and III (d) I, II, III and IV

164. Consider the following statements regarding the reactions given below

$$C_6H_5CHO \xrightarrow[CH_3COONa,\ \Delta]{(CH_3CO)_2O} \xrightarrow{H_2O} C_6H_5CH{=}CHCOOH + CH_3COOH$$

I. The reaction is a representative example of Perkin reaction.
II. The anhydride having at least one α-H, provides an enolate ion for the reaction.
III. The acetate deprotonates the anhydride to form the nucleophile needed for the reaction.

Which of the above statements are correct?
(a) I, II and III (b) I and II
(c) II and III (d) I and III

165. Saponification of an ester (A) followed by neutralisation gives a compound (B), which gives violet coloration with $FeCl_3$. The ester (A) is

(a) ethyl salicylate
(b) ethyl acetate
(c) ethyl benzoate
(d) diethyl phthalate

166. Which one of the following compounds is most rapidly hydrolysed by S_N1 mechanism?

(a) $CH_3CH{=}CHCl$
(b) $ClCH_2CH{=}CH_2$
(c) 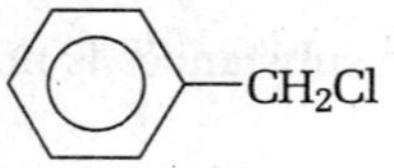
(d) $(C_6H_5)_3CCl$

167. Aromatic diazonium group can be replaced by various groups/atoms. In this context, match Column I with Column II and select the correct answer using the codes given below the columns.

Column I (Reagent/reaction types)		Column II	
A.	H_3PO_2	1.	Hydrogen
B.	Sandmeyer	2.	Hydroxyl group
C.	H_2O/Δ	3.	Aryl group
D.	Gomberg	4.	Chlorine

Codes

	A	B	C	D		A	B	C	D
(a)	4	3	2	1	(b)	1	4	2	3
(c)	1	2	3	4	(d)	2	3	4	1

168. Which of the following substituted benzene derivatives would furnish three isomers when one more substituent is introduced? (you are not to consider directive-influence rule).

I. 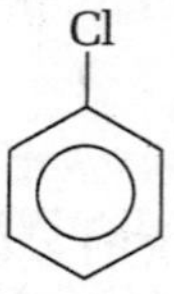
II. 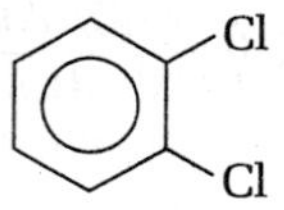
III. 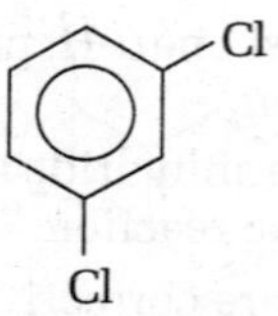
IV. 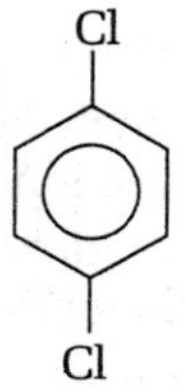

Select the correct answer using the codes given above.

Codes

(a) I, II and III
(b) Only I
(c) II and IV
(d) I and III

169. Consider the following aryl alkyl ketones

I. 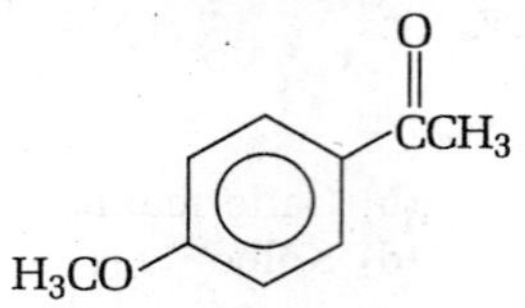
II. 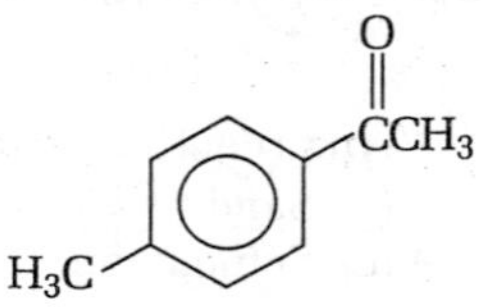
III. 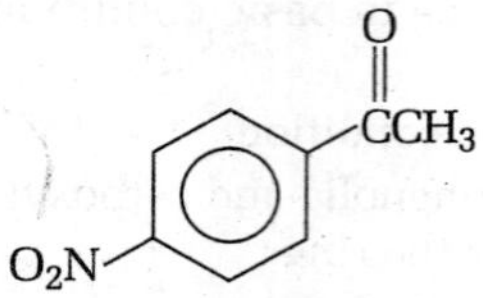

Friedel-Crafts' acylation can be used to obtain

(a) I, II and III
(b) I and II
(c) II and III
(d) I and III

170. Relative stabilities of the following carbocations will be in order

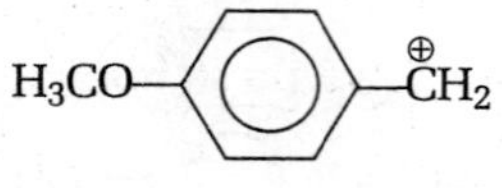
I

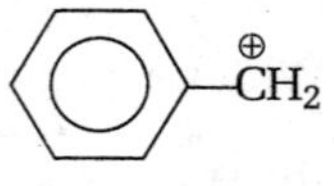
II

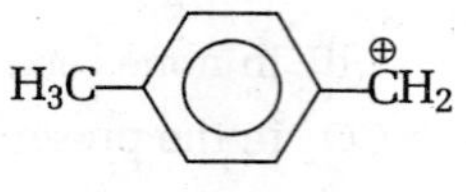
III

$CH_3\overset{\oplus}{C}H_2$
IV

(a) I < II < III < IV
(b) IV < III < II < I
(c) IV < II < III < I
(d) II < IV < III < I

171. 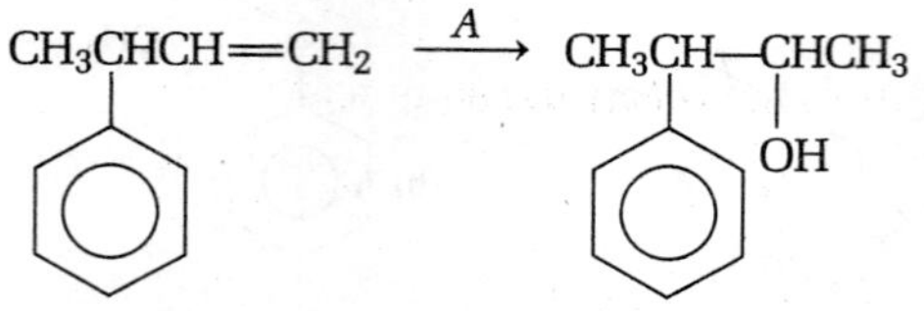

A can be

(a) H_2O/H^+
(b) $BH_3{\cdot}THF/H_2O_2{-}OH^-$
(c) $Hg(OCOCH_3)_2 \cdot THF / NaBH_4 \cdot NaOH$
(d) all true

172. Which route provides a better synthesis of ether?

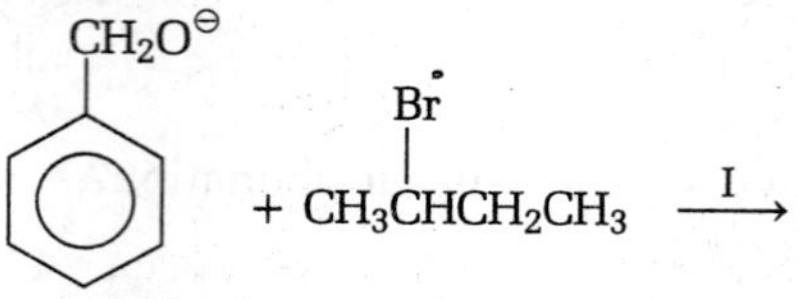

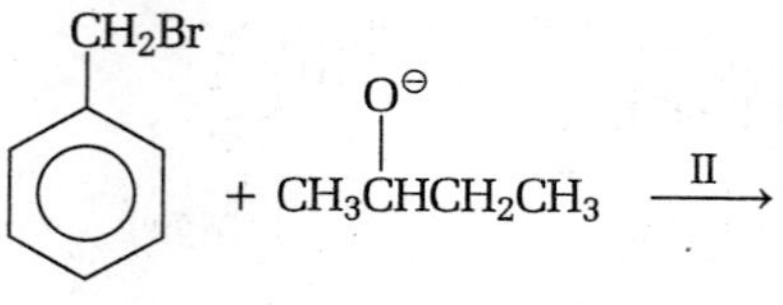

(a) Only I
(b) Only II
(c) Equal
(d) None of these

173. The correct order of acidity for the following compounds is [JEE Advanced 2016]

I. 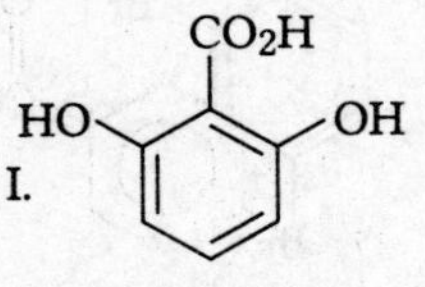

II. 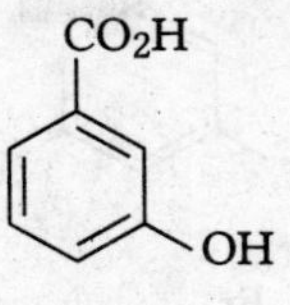

III. 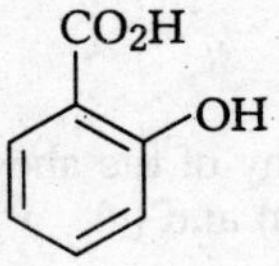

IV. 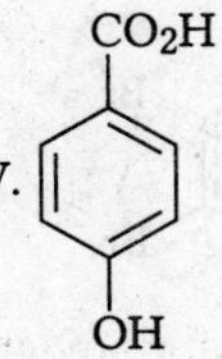

(a) I > II > III > IV
(b) III > I > II > IV
(c) III > IV > II > I
(d) I > III > IV > II

174. Which has maximum pK_a value in phenols?

(a) 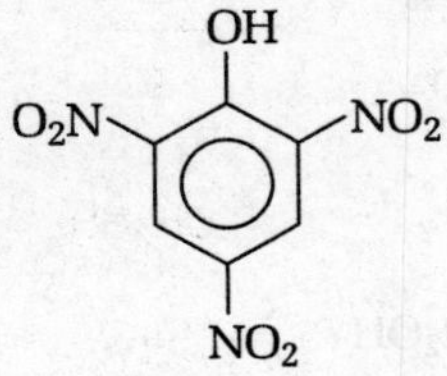

(b) 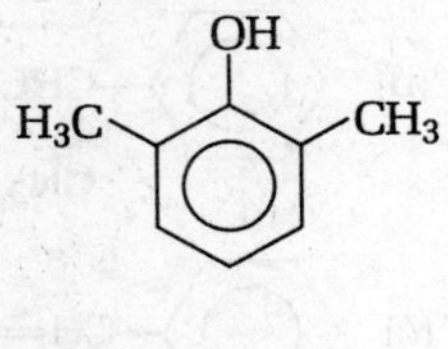

(c) 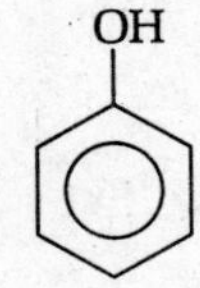

(d) 

175. In the following reaction sequence,

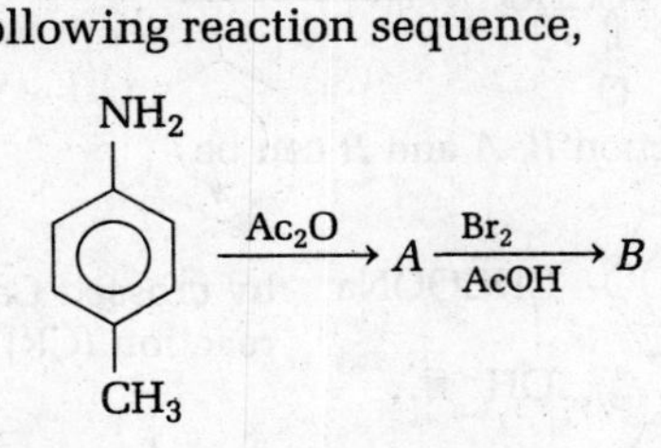

The major product *B* is [JEE Main 2020]

(a) 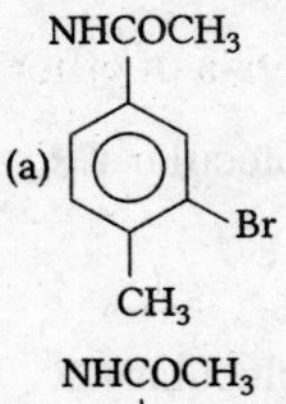

(b) 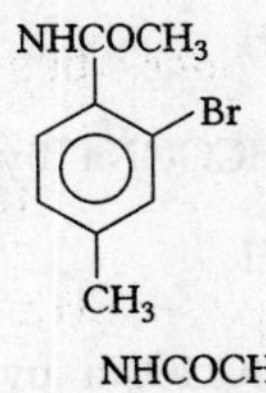

(c) 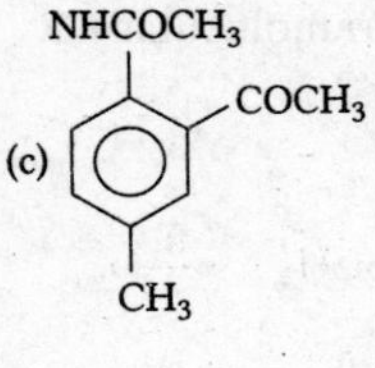

(d) 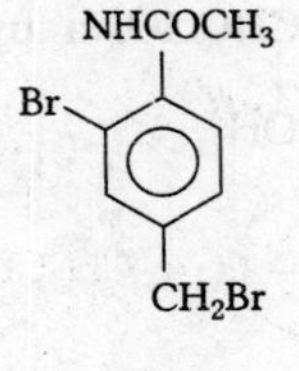

176. 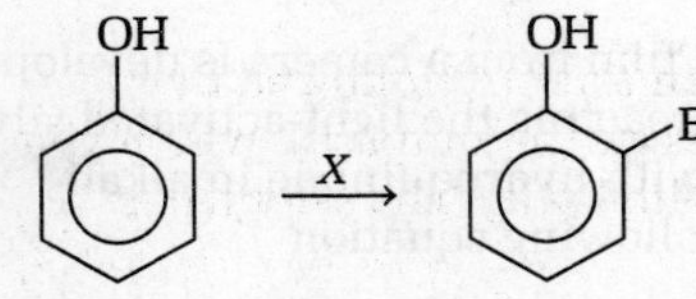

X can be
(a) Br_2 water
(b) Br_2/CS_2
(c) Both (a) and (b) are correct
(d) None of the above is correct

177. The reaction of

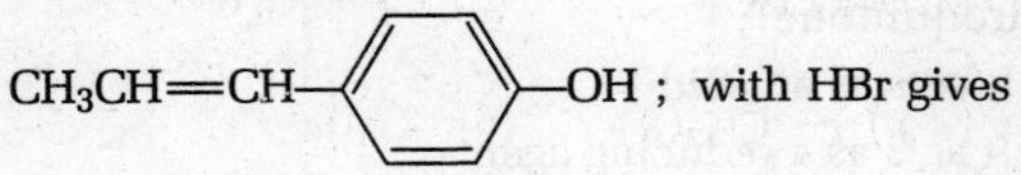

(a) 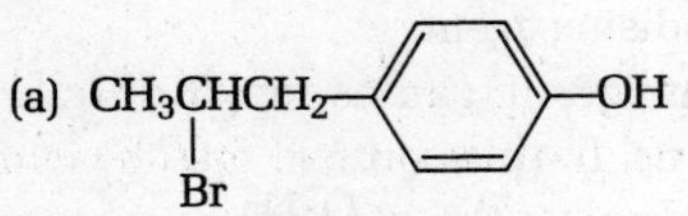

(b) 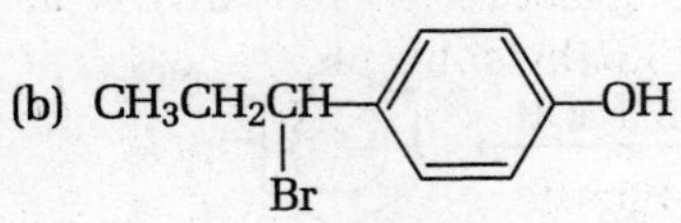

(c) 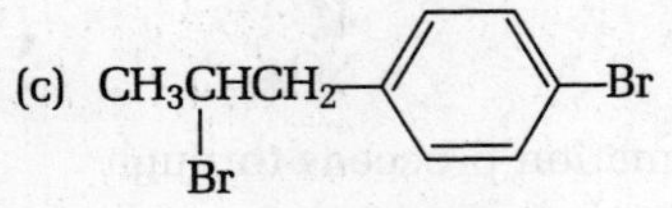

(d) 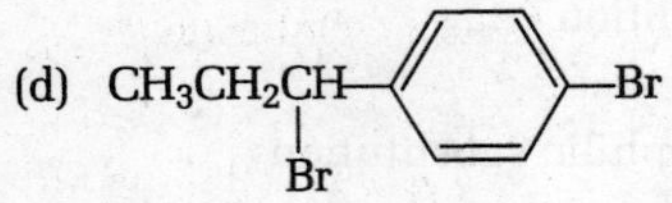

178. In the following compounds,

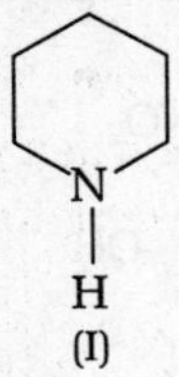
(I)

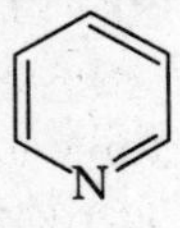
(II)

(III)

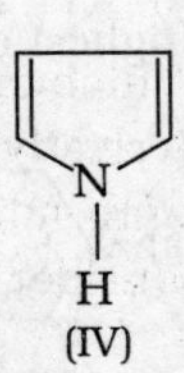
(IV)

The order of basic nature is
(a) IV > I > III > II
(b) III > I > IV > II
(c) II > I > III > IV
(d) I > III > II > IV

179. In a Cannizzaro reaction, the intermediate that will be the best hydride donor is

(a) 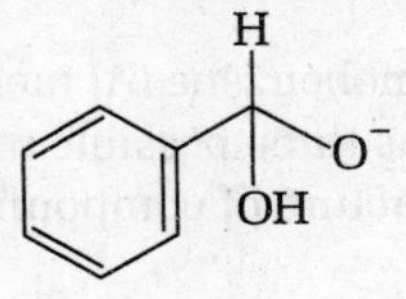

(b) 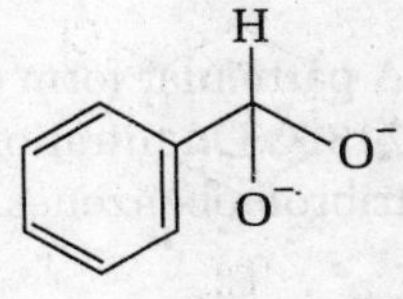

(c) 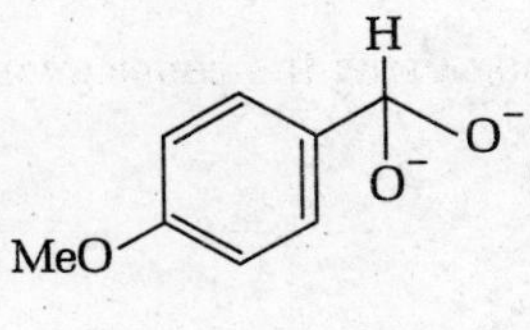

(d) 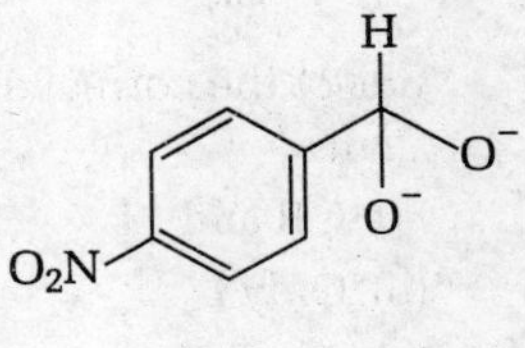

180. When an exposed film from a camera is developed, one step involves reacting the light-activated silver bromide crystals with hydroquinone in alkali according to the following equation

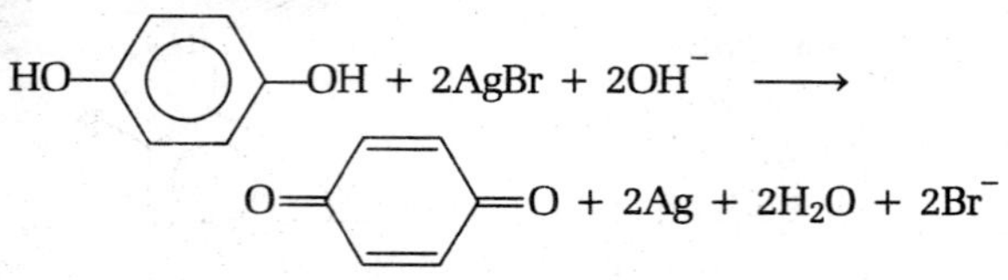

Which one of the following describes the role of the hydroquinone?

(a) It acts as an acid

(b) It acts as a reducing agent

(c) It acts as an oxidising agent

(d) It acts as a base

181.

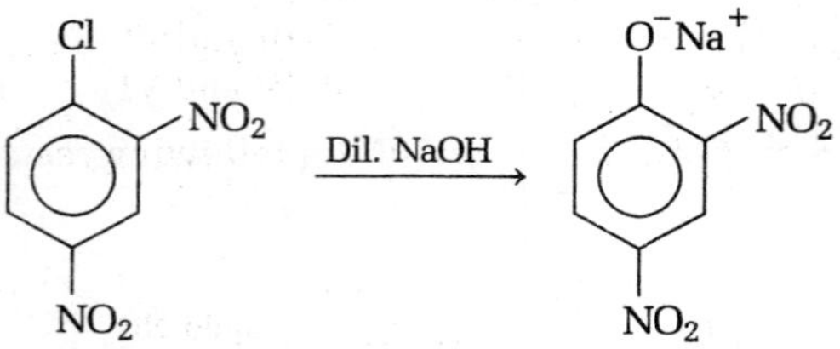

The above transformation proceeds through

(a) electrophilic addition

(b) benzyne intermediate

(c) activated nucleophilic substitution

(d) oxirane

182. Which one of the following compounds will have the highest dipole moment?

(a) 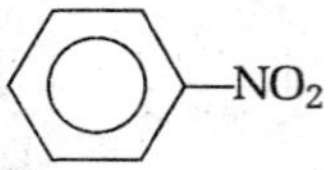

(b) 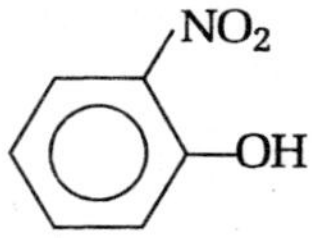

(c) 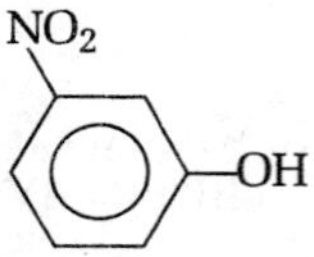

(d) 

183. A particular form of tribromobenzene (*A*) melts at 713 K. On nitration, it forms three possible mononitro tribromobenzenes. The structure of compound '*A*' is

(a) 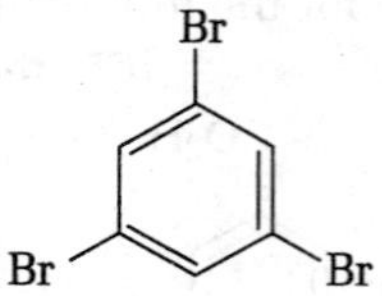

(b) 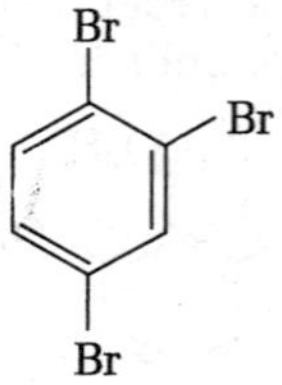

(c) 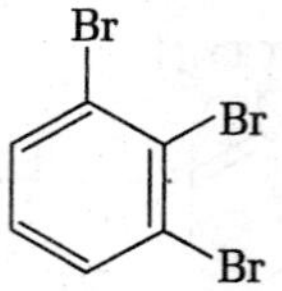

(d) any of the above at (a), (b) and (c)

184. 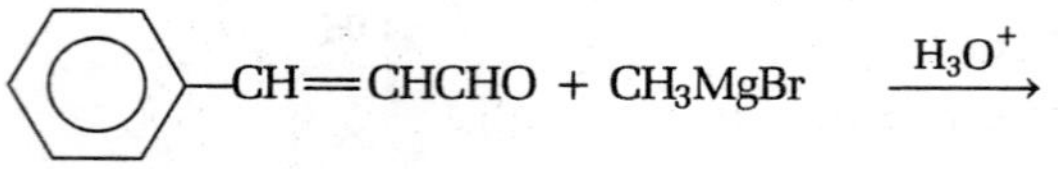 *A*,

A (formed by 1,4 -addition) is

(a) 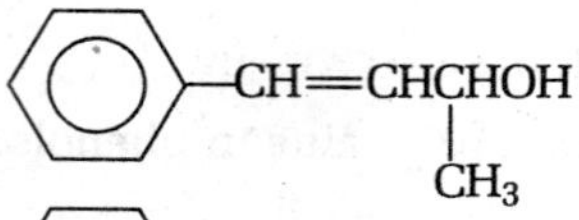

(b) 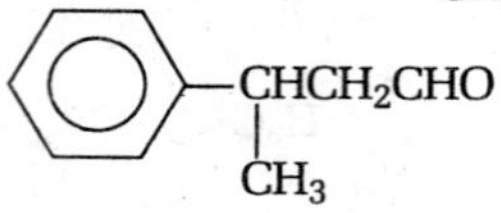

(c) 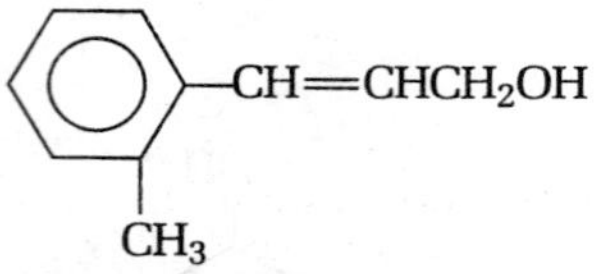

(b) None of the above is correct

185. 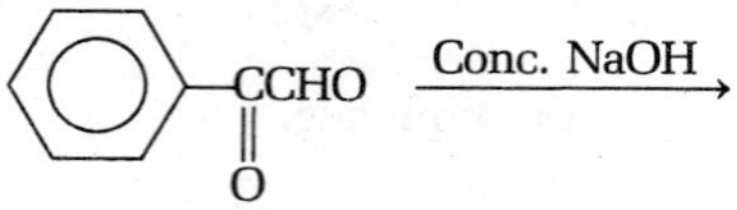

A by reaction *R*; *A* and *R* can be

(a) 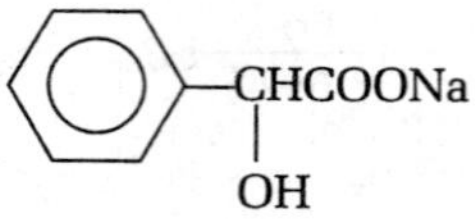 by crossed Cannizzaro reaction (CR)

(b) 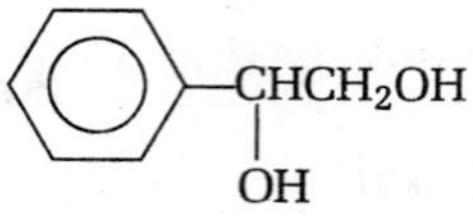 by intramolecular CR

(c) 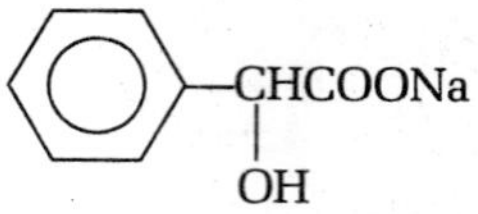 by intermolecular CR

(d) 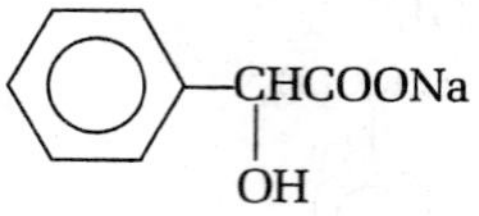 by intramolecular CR

186. 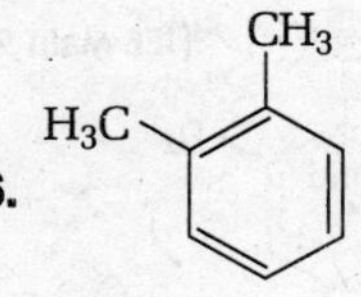 $\xrightarrow[C_2H_5OH]{Na,\ NH_3}$ A; A is

(a) 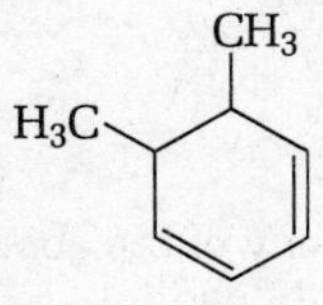
(b) 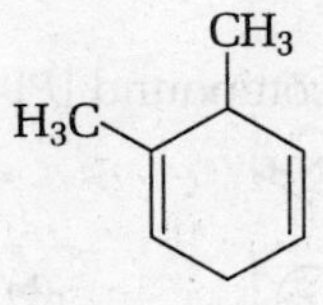
(c) 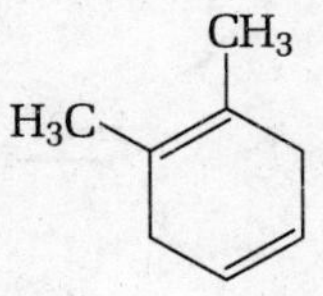
(d) 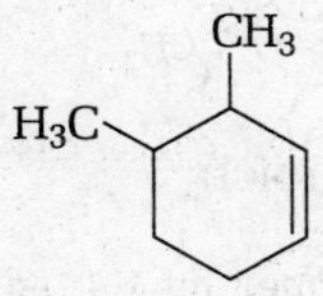

187. Which of the following are aromatic ?

I. 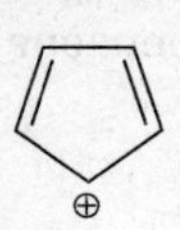 II. 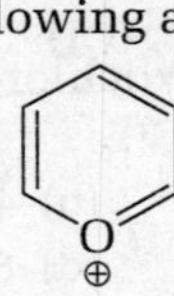 III. 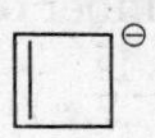

(a) I, II and III
(b) I and II
(c) II and III
(d) Only II

188. Which has maximum dipole moment?

(a) 
(b) 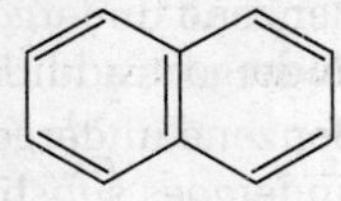
(c) 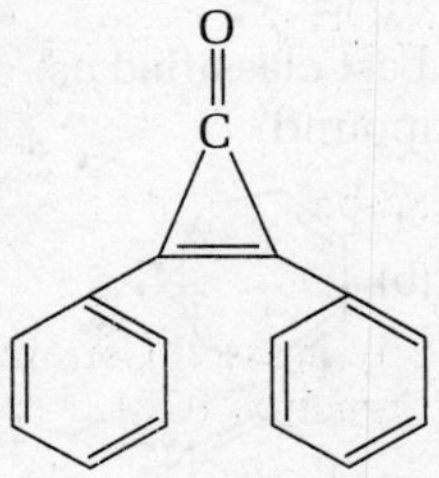
(d) 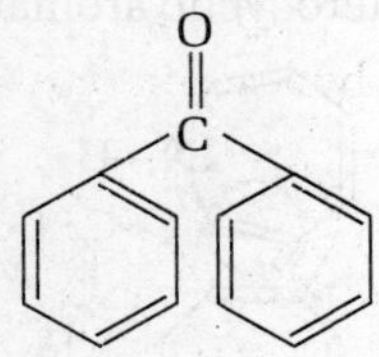

189. Which can lose a proton from methyl group most readily?

(a) 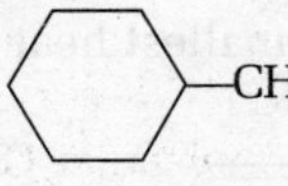
(b) 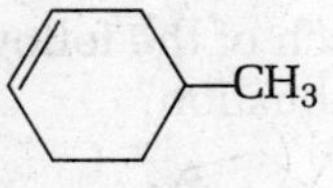
(c) 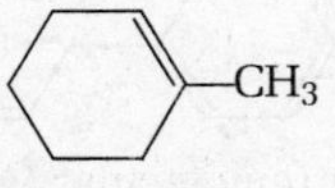
(d) 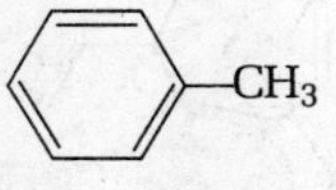

190.  $\xrightarrow{CF_3CO_3H}$ A; A is

(a) 
(b) 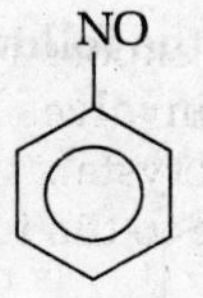
(c) 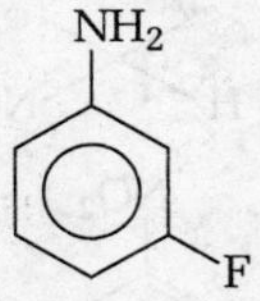
(d) 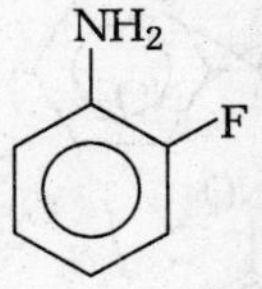

191. Consider the following groups,

I. Br II. $\overset{O}{\overset{\|}{C}}CH_3$ III. OCH_3 IV. OH

V. $NHCH_3$ V. $\overset{\oplus}{N}(CH_3)_3$

Which can donate electrons by resonance and can withdraw electrons inductively?

(a) I, IV and V
(b) II, III and VI
(c) I, III and V
(d) II, IV and VI

192. Cine substitution product in the following reaction is

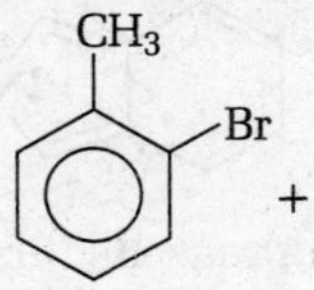 + $NaNH_2$ $\xrightarrow{\text{Liquid } NH_3}$

(a) 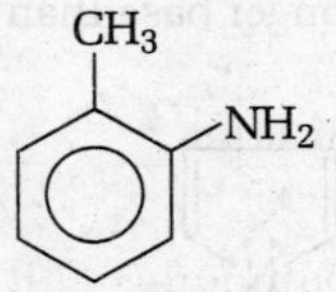
(b) 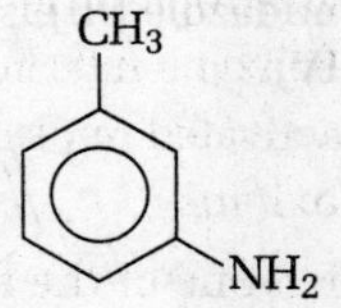
(c) 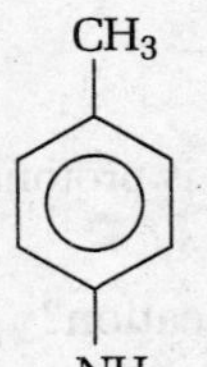
(d) 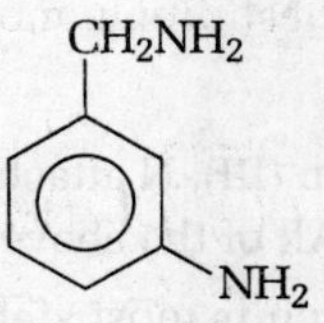

193. 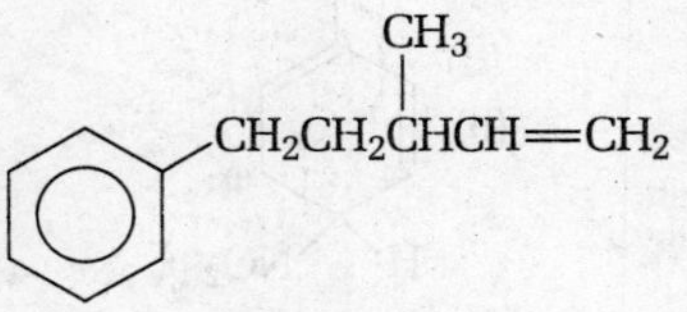 $\xrightarrow{H^+}$ A; A is

(a) 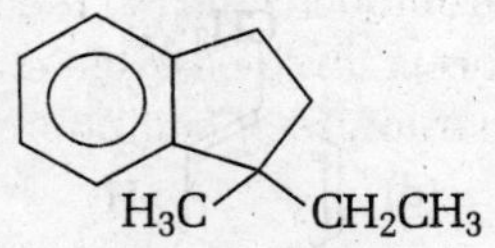
(b) 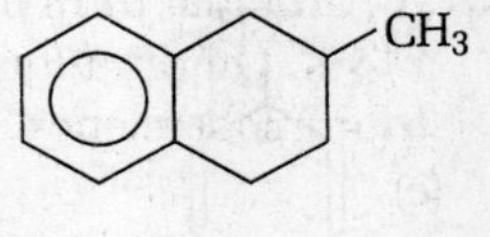
(c) 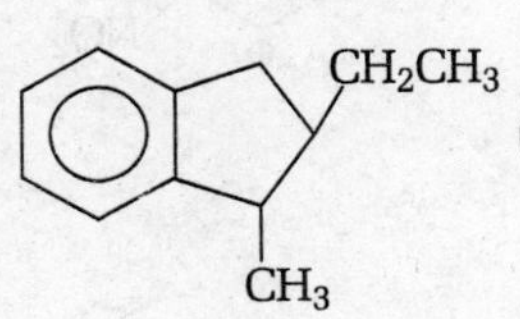
(d) 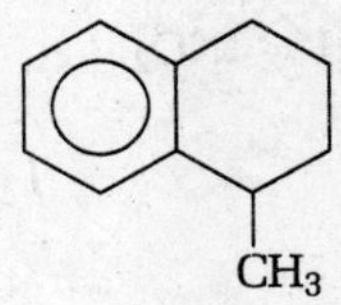

194. Consider the following statements,

I. 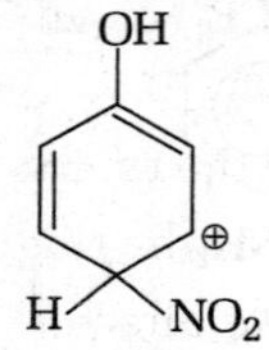 is more stable than 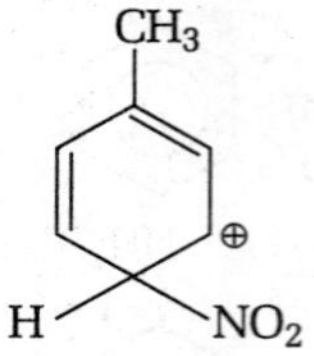

II. 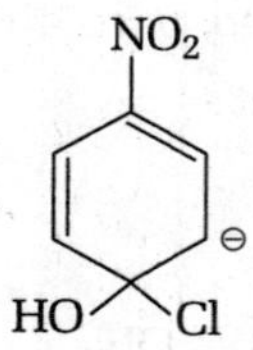 is more stable than 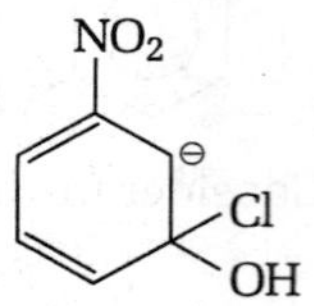

(a) I and II both are correct
(b) I and reverse of II are correct
(c) II and reverse of I are correct
(d) I and II both are incorrect

195. Select the correct statements,

(a) Indole (I) is more stable than isoindole (II)

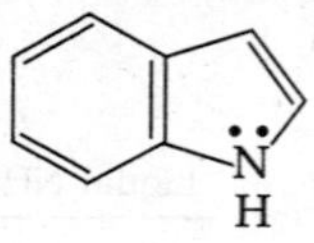
I

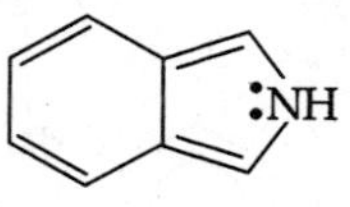
II

(b) Imidazole (III) is a much stronger base than pyrrole (IV)

III

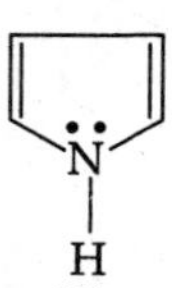
IV

(c) In (III), N attached to double bond is protonated.
(d) All of the above are correct

196. Which is most stable arenium carbocation?

(a) 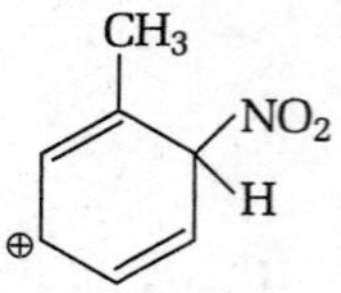
(b) 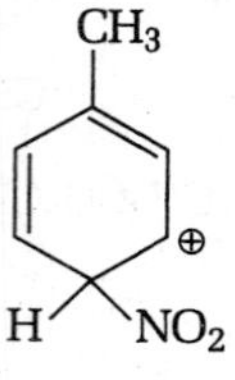
(c) 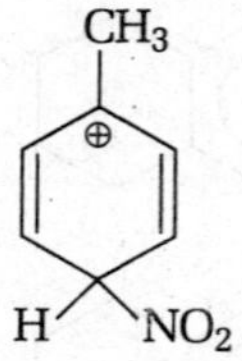
(d) 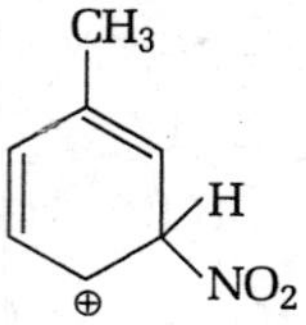

197. Consider the following reactions : **[JEE Main 2020]**

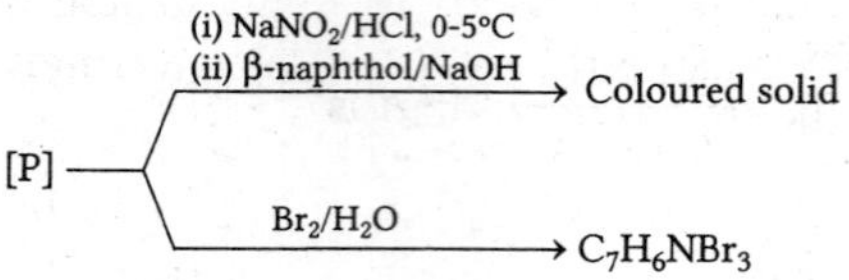

The compound [*P*] is

(a) 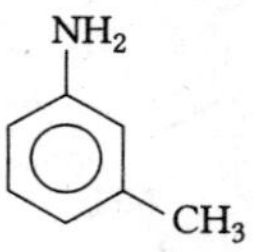
(b) 
(c) 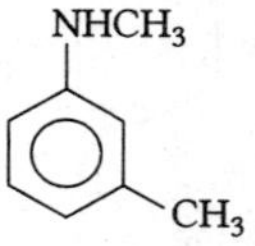
(d) 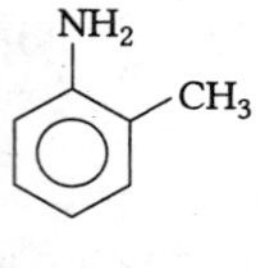

198. The number of possible dichloronitrobenzene isomers is

(a) 3
(b) 4
(c) 6
(d) 8

199. Which of the following statements is correct concerning the class of reactions to be expected for benzene and cyclooctatetraene?

(a) Both substances undergo addition reactions
(b) Both substances undergo substitution reactions.
(c) Benzene undergoes substitution; cyclooctatetraene undergoes addition
(d) Benzene undergoes addition; cyclooctatetraene undergoes substitution

200. Which of the following is best classified as heterocyclic aromatic compound?

(a) 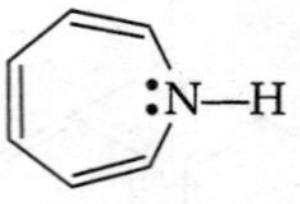
(b) 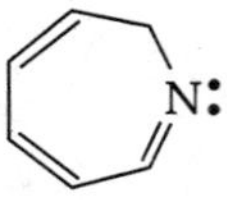
(c) 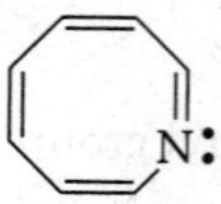
(d) 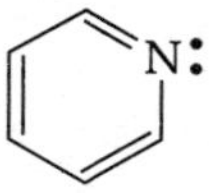

201. Which of the following has the smallest heat of combustion?

(a) 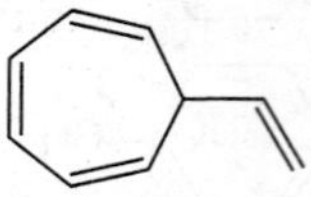
(b) 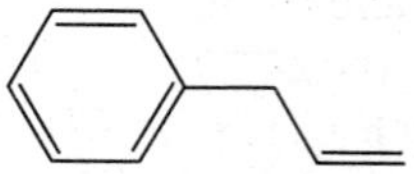
(c) 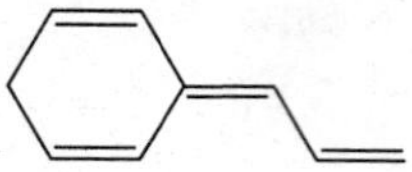
(d) 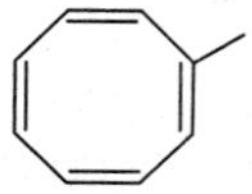

202. Which one of the following alcohols undergoes dehydration at the fastest rate on being heated with sulphuric acid? (The potential for rearrangement does not affect the rate).

(a) 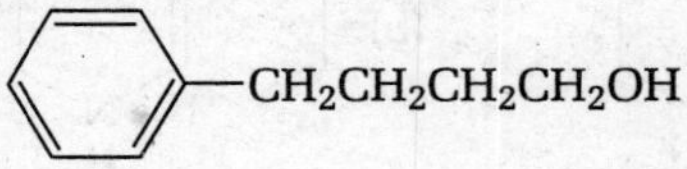

(b) 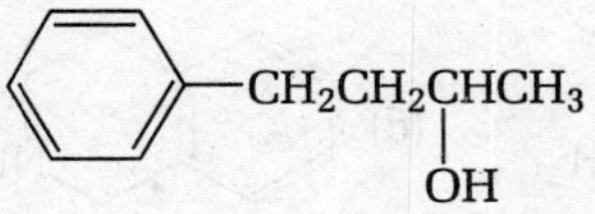

(c) 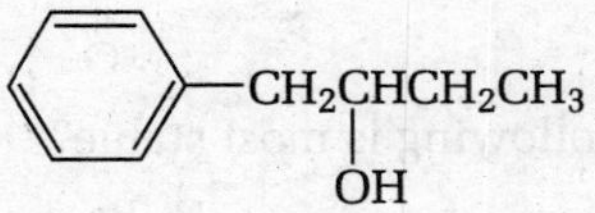

(d) 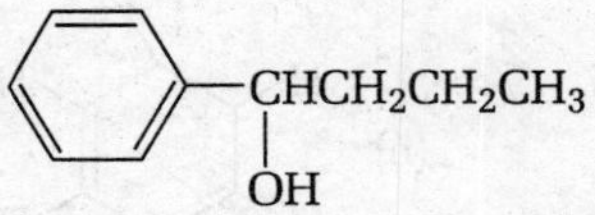

203. Ethylbenzene is treated with the reagents listed, in the order shown.

I. NBS, peroxides, heat II. $CH_3CH_2O^-$ III. B_2H_6

IV. H_2O_2, HO^-

The structure of the final product is

(a) $C_6H_5CH_2CH_2OH$

(b) $C_6H_5\underset{|}{\overset{Br}{C}}HCH_2OH$

(c) $C_6H_5\overset{OH}{\overset{|}{C}}HCH_3$

(d) $C_6H_5\overset{OH}{\overset{|}{C}}HCH_2OH$

204. Which of the following hydrogens is most easily abstracted (removed) on reaction with bromine atoms, Br•?

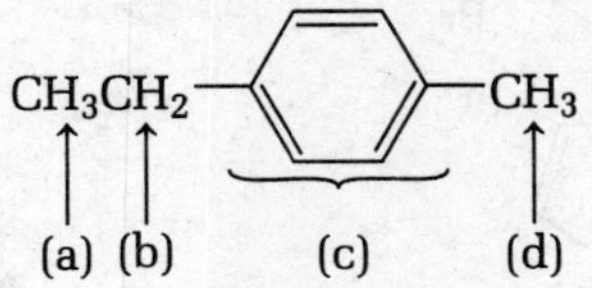

(a) $\underline{C}H_3—CH_2—$

(b) $\underline{C}H_2—$

(c) 

(d) 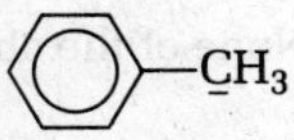

205. All the hydrocarbons shown below are very weak acids. One, however, is far more acidic than the others. Which one is the strongest acid?

(a) 

(b) 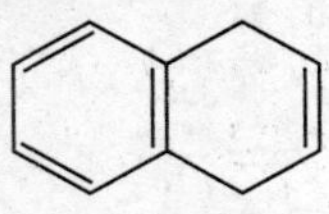

(c) 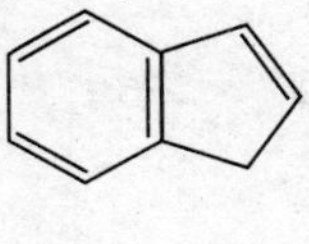

(d) 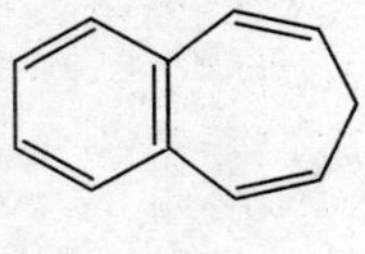

206. Consider the following statements concerning the effect of a trifluoromethyl group, CF_3, on an electrophilic aromatic substitution.

I. The CF_3 group will activate the ring.

II. The CF_3 group will deactivate the ring.

III. The CF_3 group will be a *meta* director.

IV. The CF_3 group will be an *ortho, para* director.

Which of the statements are correct?

(a) I and III

(b) I and IV

(c) II and III

(d) II and IV

207. Which of the following resonance structures is not a contributor to the cyclohexadienyl cation intermediate in the nitration of benzene ?

(a) 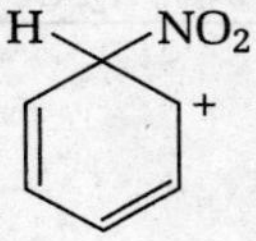

(b) 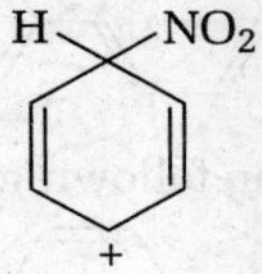

(c) 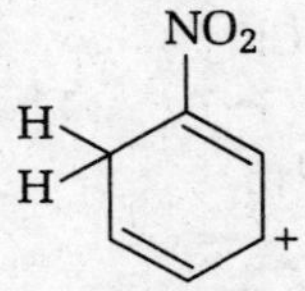

(d) None of these (all are contributors)

208. The major product in the following reaction is

[JEE Main 2019]

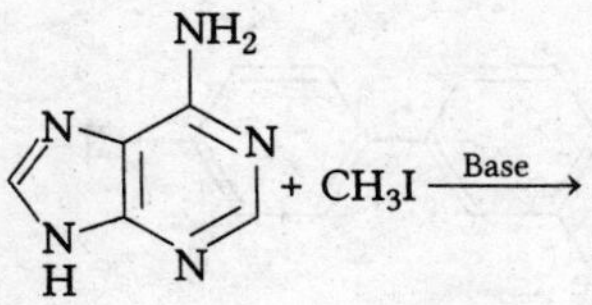

(a) 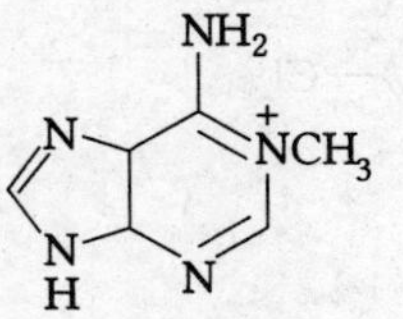

(b) 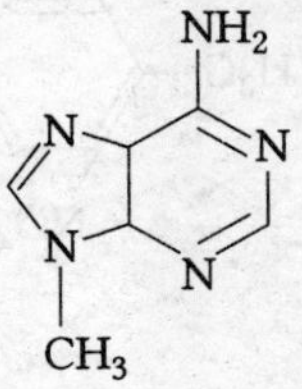

(c) 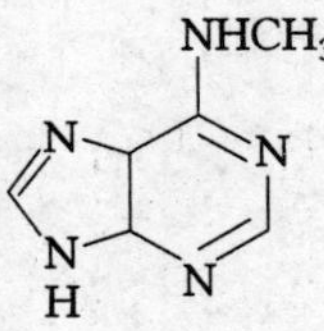

(d) 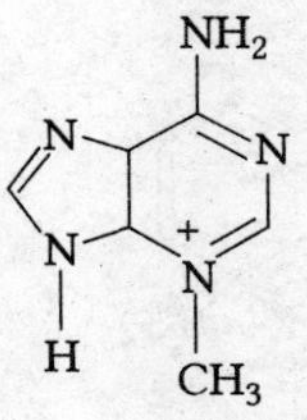

209. For the reaction

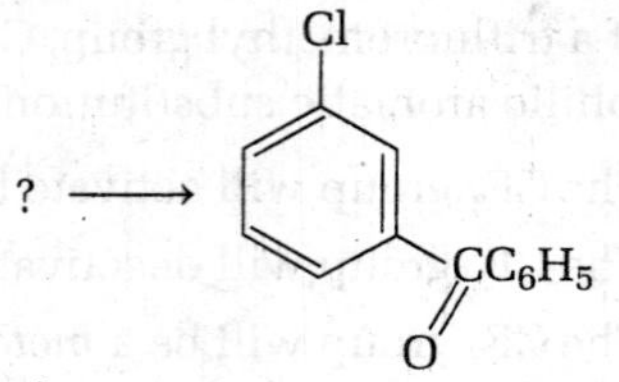

the best reactants are

(a) $C_6H_5Cl + C_6H_5\overset{O}{\overset{\|}{C}}Cl$, $AlCl_3$

(b) $C_6H_5\overset{O}{\overset{\|}{C}}C_6H_5 + Cl_2$, $FeCl_3$

(c) $C_6H_5CH_2C_6H_5$ + Cl_2, $FeCl_3$

(d) None of the above yields the desired product

210. The reaction

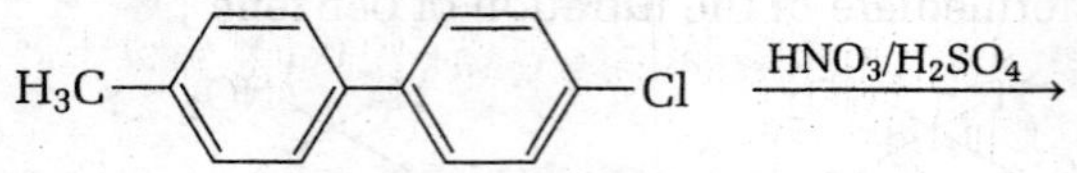

gives the following major product

(a) 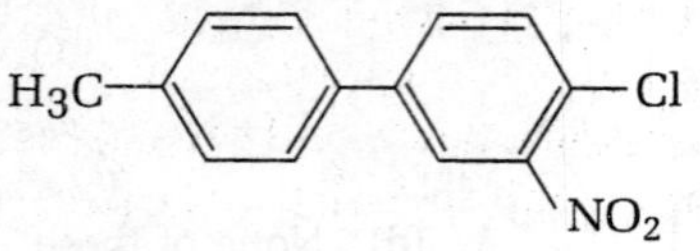

(b) 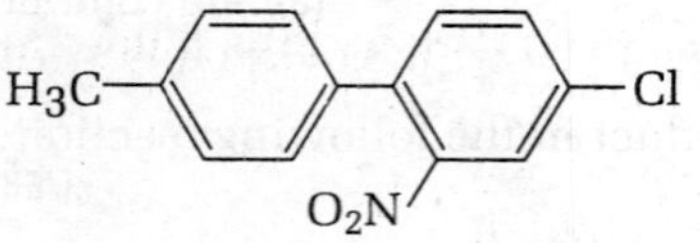

(c) 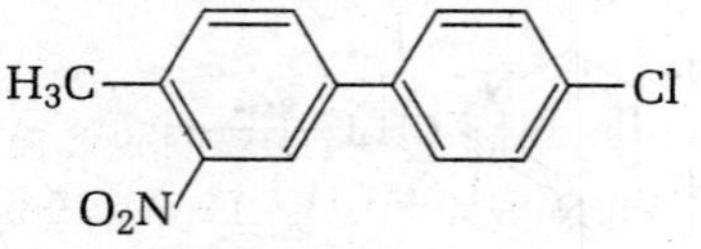

(d) 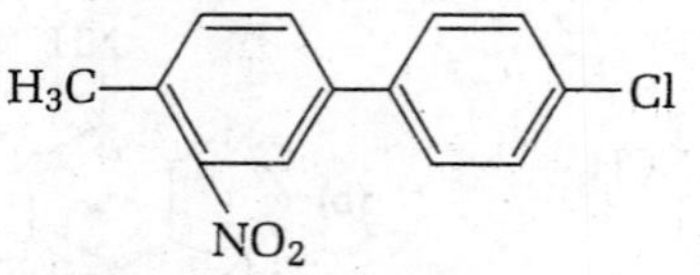

211. Which of the following compounds undergoes bromination of its aromatic ring (electrophilic aromatic substitution) at the fastest rate?

(a) 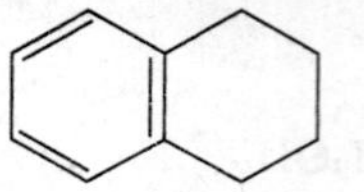

(b) 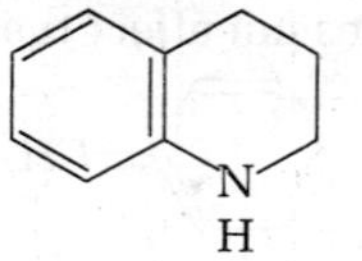

(c) 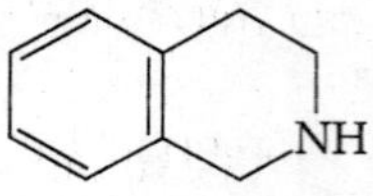

(d) 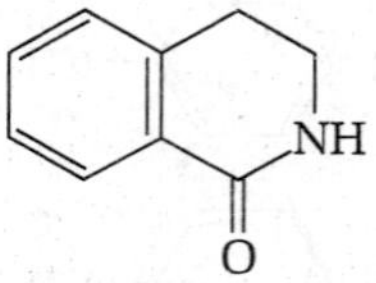

212. Which one of the following is most stable?

(a) 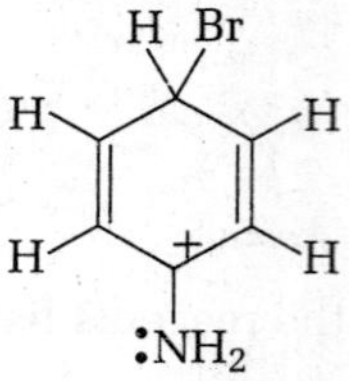

(b) 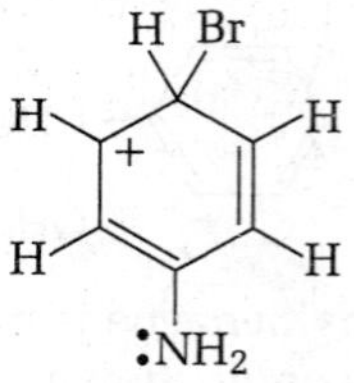

(c) 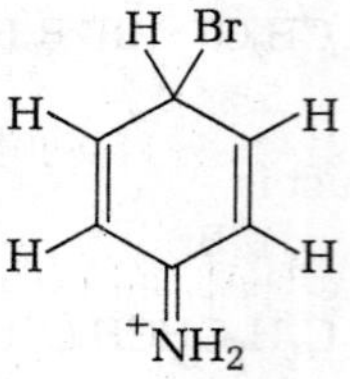

(d) 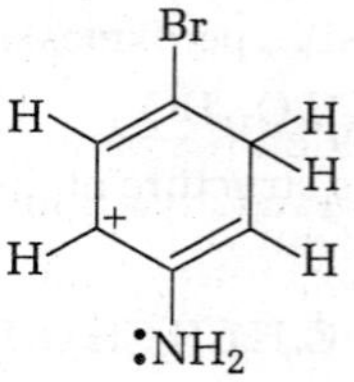

213. The major product of the reaction is

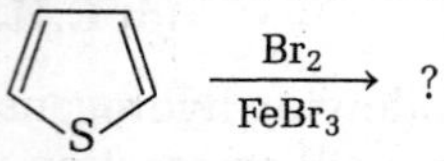

(a) 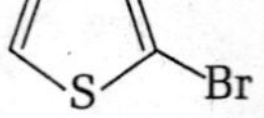

(b) 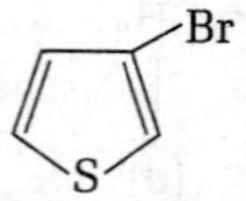

(c) an equal mixture of compound (a) and (b) would form

(d) None of the above; substitution would not occur

214. What is the product of the following reaction?

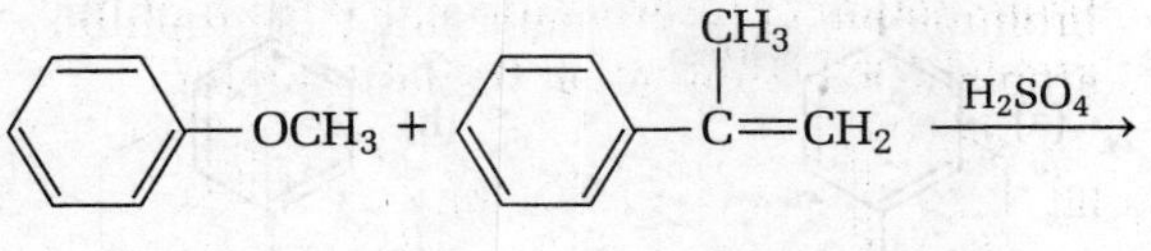

(a) 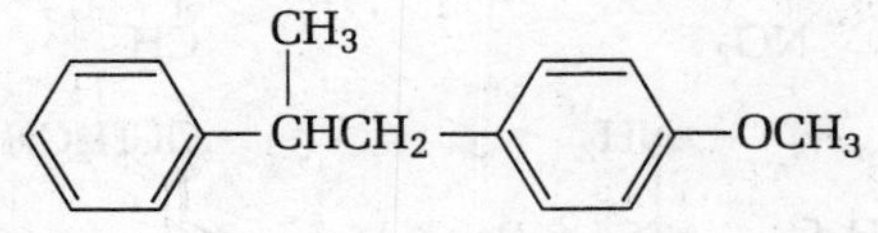

(b) 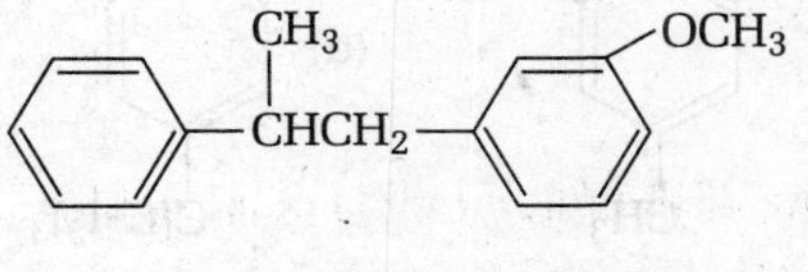

(c) 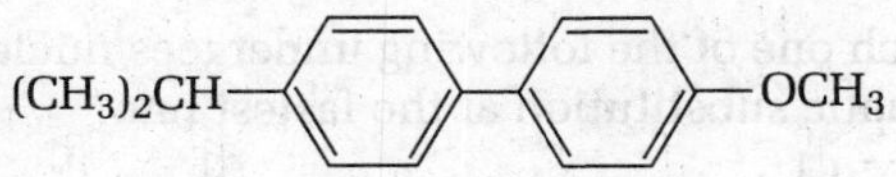

(d) 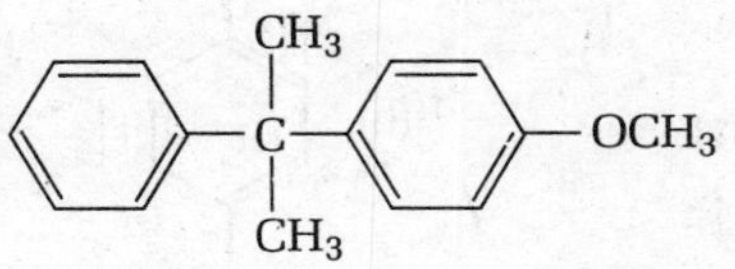

215. Which reactants combine to give the species shown as a reactive intermediate?

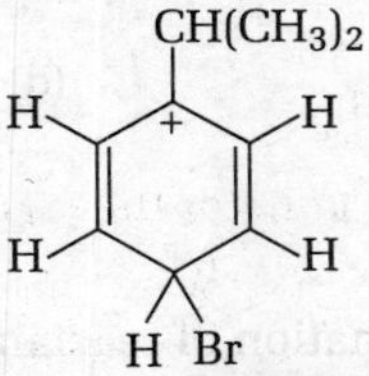

(a) Benzene, isopropyl bromide and HBr
(b) Bromobenzene, isopropyl chloride and $AlCl_3$
(c) Isopropylbenzene, Br_2 and $FeBr_3$
(d) Isopropylbenzene, Br_2, light and heat

216. Which sequence of steps describes the best synthesis of the compound shown?

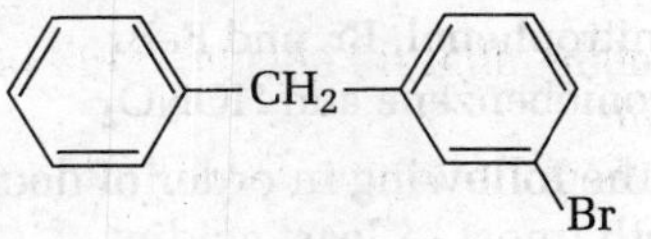

(a) 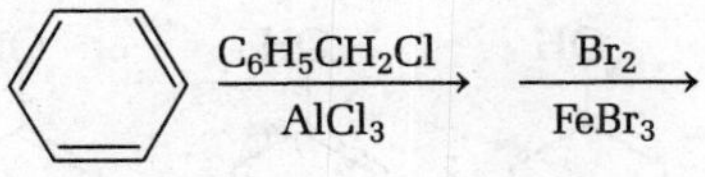

(b) 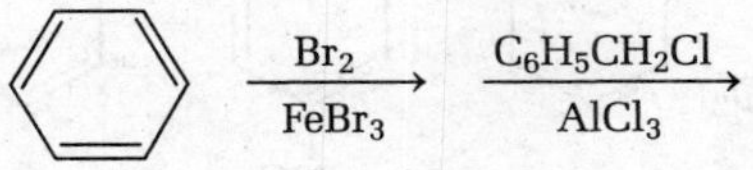

(c) 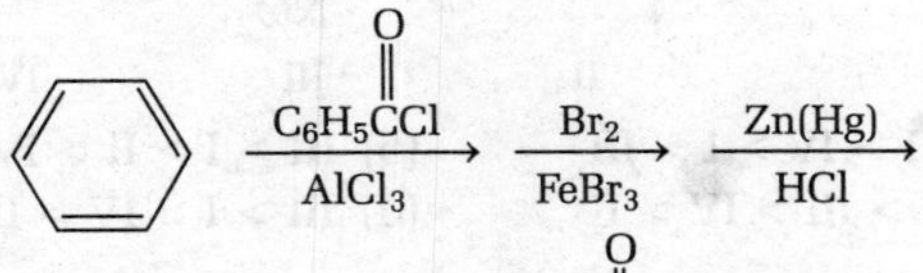

(d) 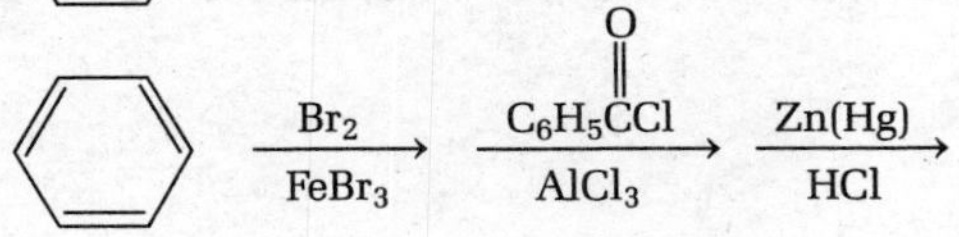

217. Which one of the following is the best synthesis of 2-chloro-4-nitrobenzoic acid?

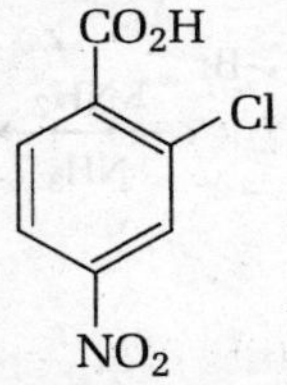

2-chloro-4-nitrobenzoic acid

(a) 1. Heat benzoic acid with HNO_3, H_2SO_4
2. Cl_2, $FeCl_3$, heat
(b) 1. Treat toluene with HNO_3, H_2SO_4
2. $K_2Cr_2O_7$, H_2O, H_2SO_4, heat
3. Cl_2, $FeCl_3$, heat
(c) 1. Treat toluene with HNO_3, H_2SO_4
2. Cl_2, $FeCl_3$, heat
3. $K_2Cr_2O_7$, H_2O, H_2SO_4, heat
(d) 1. Treat nitrobenzene with Cl_2, $FeCl_3$, heat
2. CH_3Cl, $AlCl_3$
3. $K_2Cr_2O_7$, H_2O, H_2SO_4, heat

218. The reaction

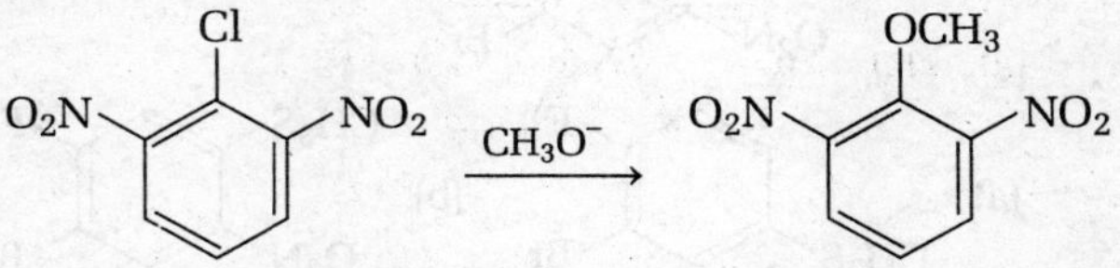

most likely occurs by which of the following mechanisms?
(a) Addition-elimination
(b) Elimination-addition
(c) Both (a) and (b)
(d) None of the above

219. Rank the following in order of decreasing rate of reaction with ethoxide ion ($CH_3CH_2O^-$) in a nucleophilic aromatic substitution reaction.

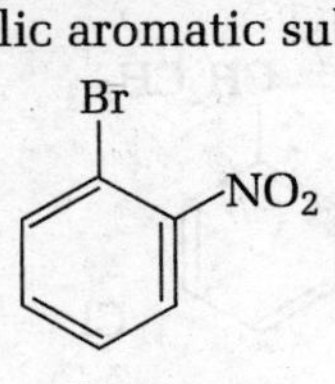
I

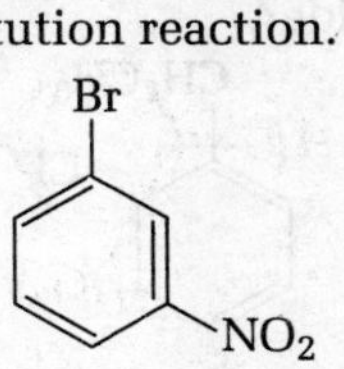
II

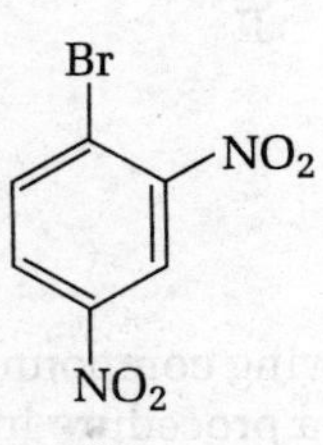
III

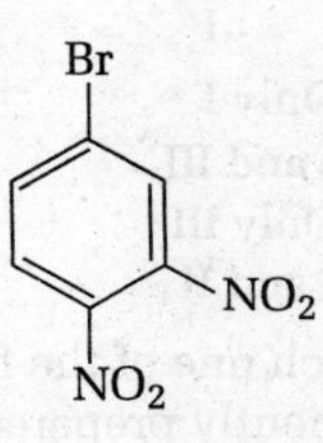
IV

(a) III > IV > I > II
(b) II > I > IV > III
(c) III > IV > II > I
(d) IV > III > II > I

220. The reaction

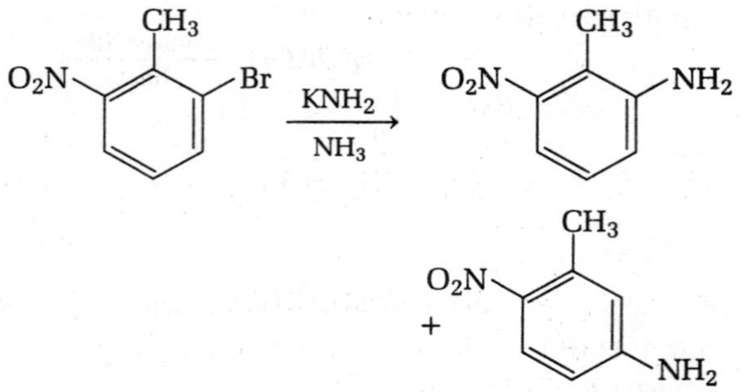

most likely involves which of the following aromatic substitution mechanisms?

(a) Addition-elimination
(b) Electrophilic substitution
(c) Elimination-addition
(d) Both (a) and (c)

221. Identify the principal organic product of the following reaction.

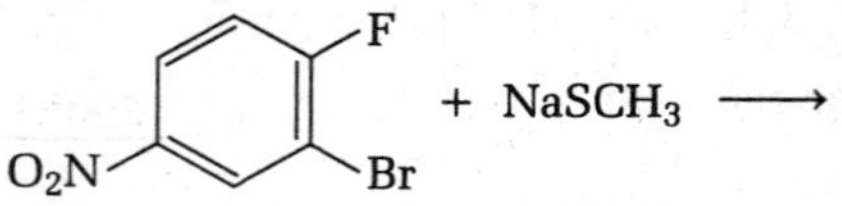

(a) 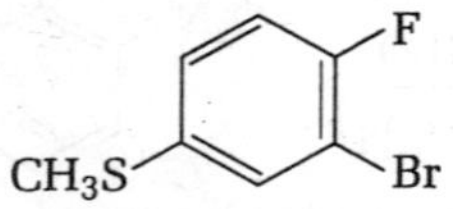 (b) 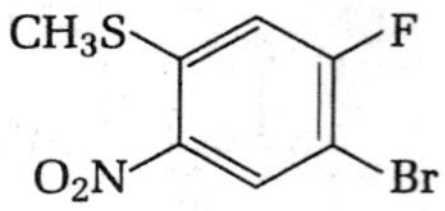

(c) 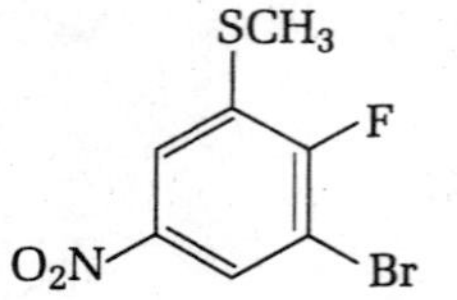 (d) 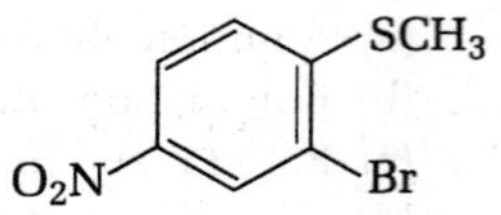

222. Which of the following compounds gives a single benzyne intermediate on reaction with sodium amide?

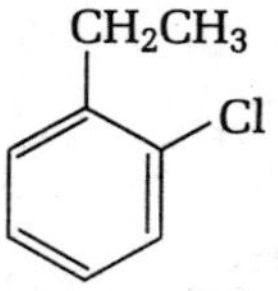
I

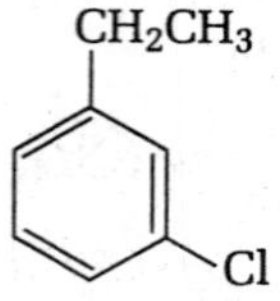
II

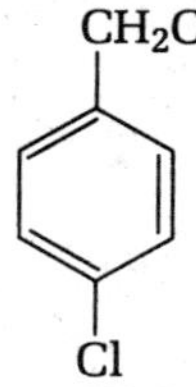
III

(a) Only I
(b) I and III
(c) Only III
(d) I and II

223. Which one of the following compounds can be efficiently prepared by a procedure in which nucleophilic aromatic substitution is the last step?

(a) 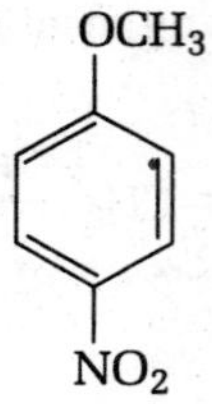 (b) 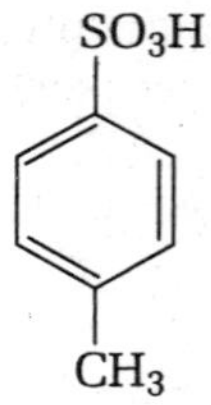

(c) 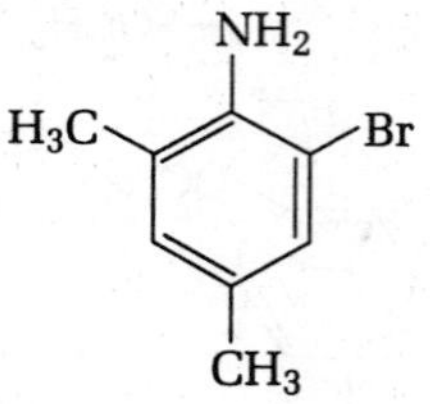 (d) 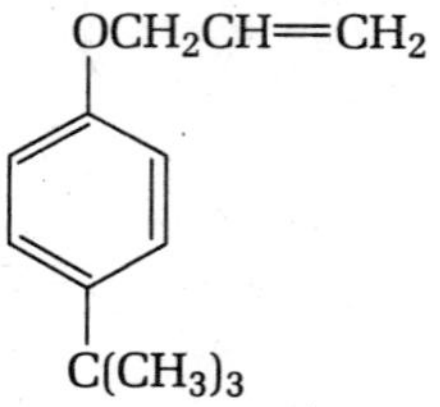

224. Which one of the following undergoes nucleophilic aromatic substitution at the fastest rate?

(a)  (b) 

(c)  (d) 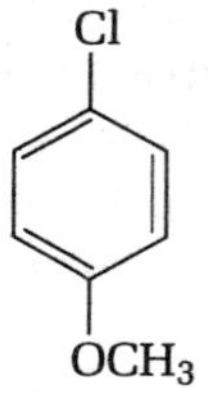

225. What combination of reactants will give the species shown as a reactive intermediate?

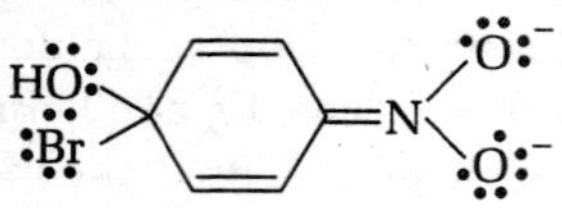

(a) 1-bromo-4-nitrobenzene and NaOH
(b) 4-nitrophenol and HBr
(c) 4-nitrophenol, Br_2 and $FeBr_3$
(d) Bromobenzene and $HONO_2$

226. Rank the following in order of decreasing acid strength (most → least acidic).

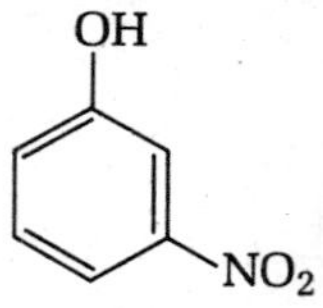
I

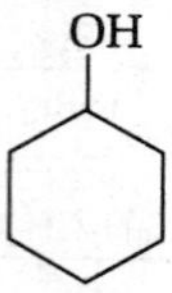
II

III

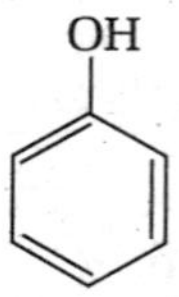
IV

(a) II > IV > I > III (b) III > I > II > IV
(c) I > III > IV > II (d) III > I > IV > II

227. Rank the following compounds in order of increasing acidity (weakest acid first)

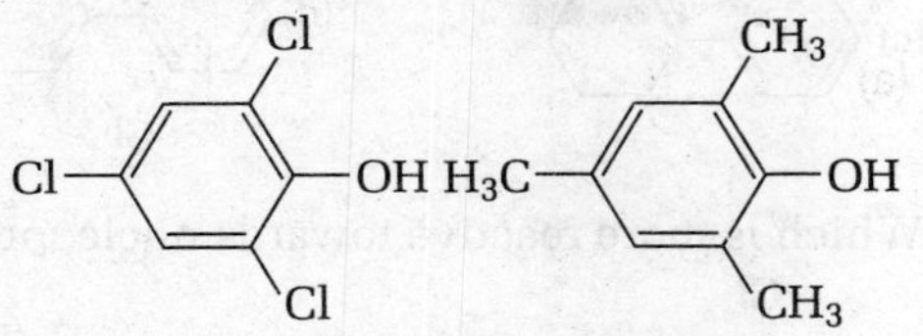

I II

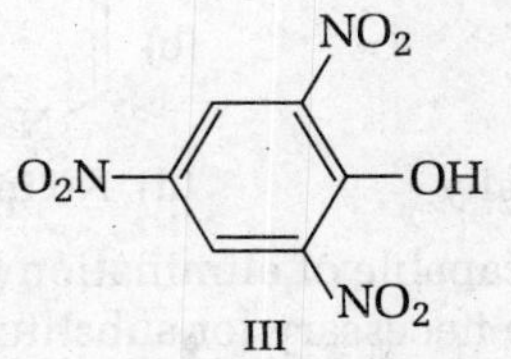

III

(a) II < III < I (b) III < II < I
(c) III < I < II (d) II < I < III

228. Which of the following reactions is a more effective method for preparing phenyl propyl ether?

I. $C_6H_5ONa + CH_3CH_2CH_2Br \longrightarrow$
II. $CH_3CH_2CH_2ONa + C_6H_5Br \longrightarrow$

(a) Reaction I is more effective
(b) Reaction II is more effective
(c) Both reaction I and II are effective
(d) Neither reaction I nor reaction II is effective

229. Which reactant gives the product shown on heating with aluminium chloride?

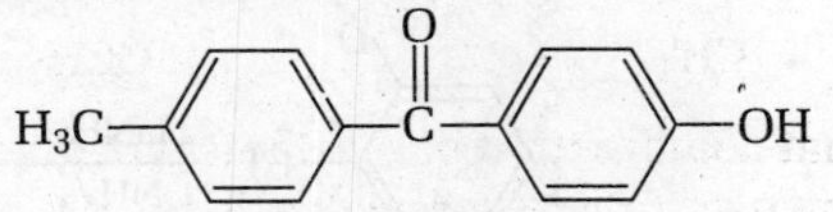

(a) 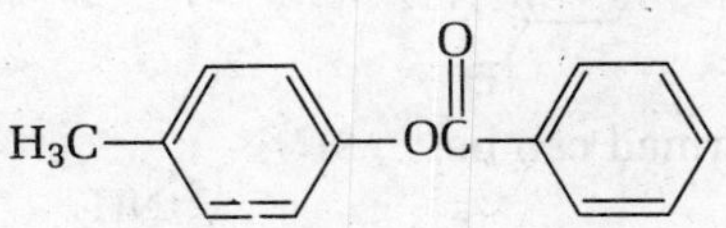

(b) 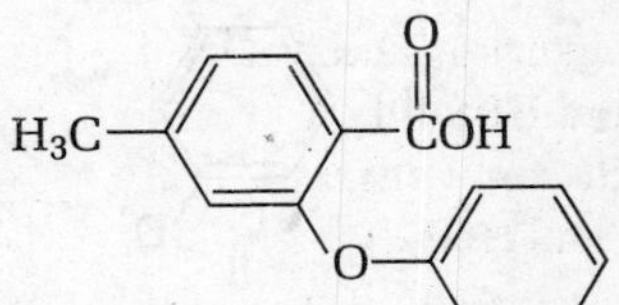

(c) 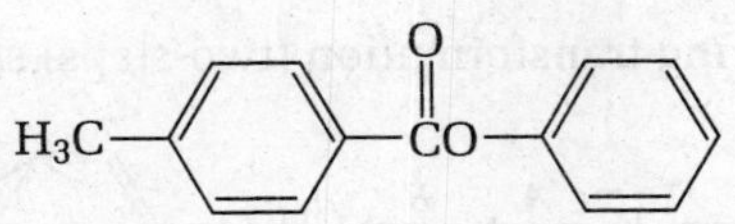

(d) 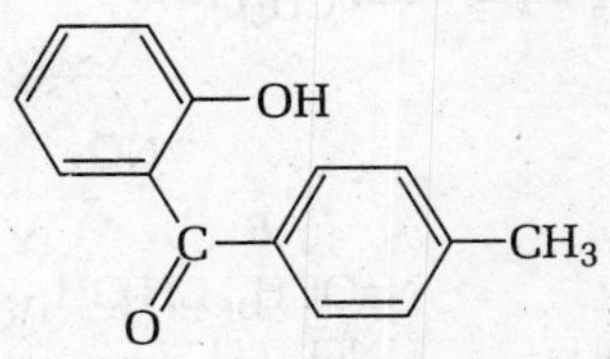

230. What are the products of the following reaction?

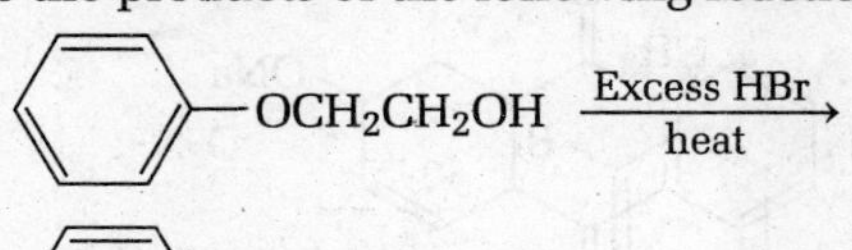

(a) 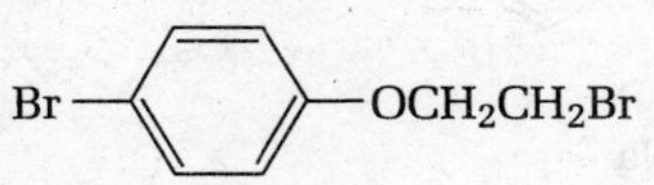

(b) 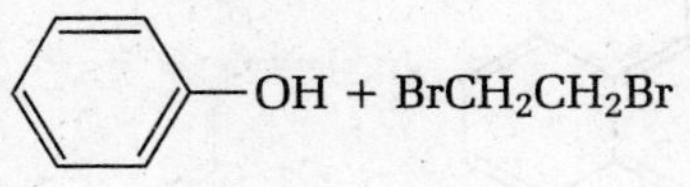

(c) 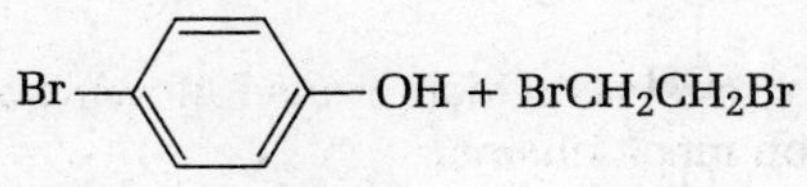

(d) 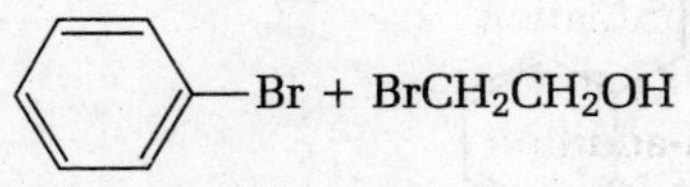

231. What is the product obtained by heating the following allylic ether of phenol?

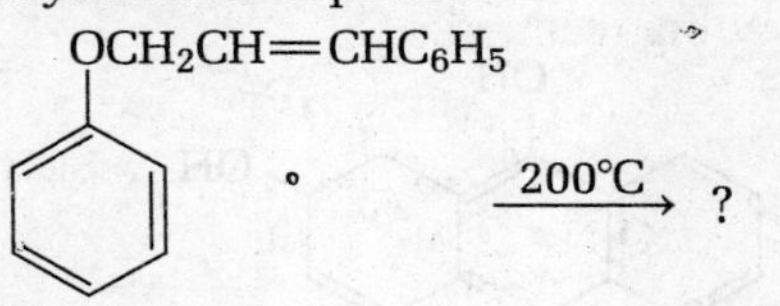

(a) 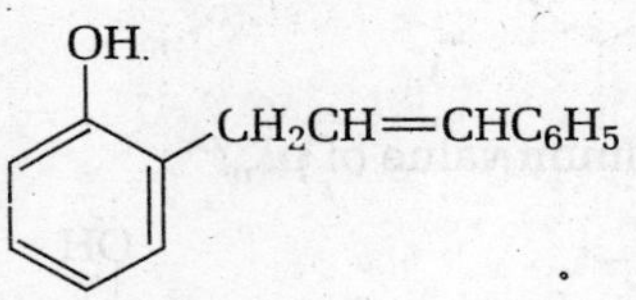

(b) 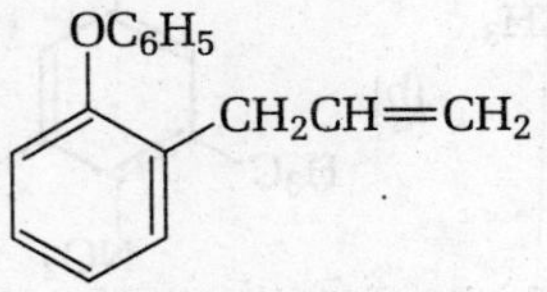

(c) 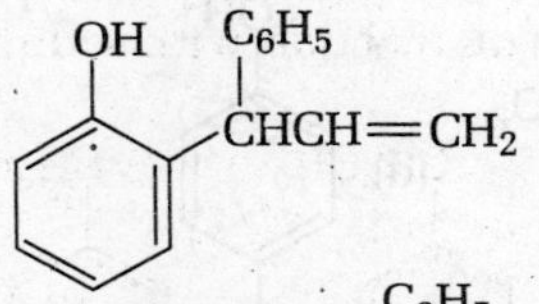

(d) 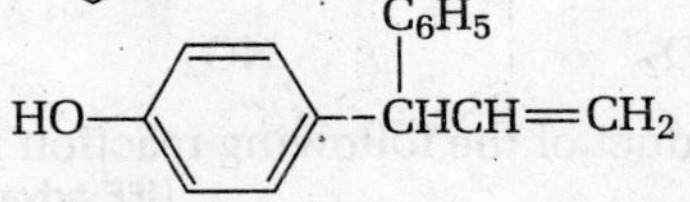

232. In presence of NaOH, *A* changes to

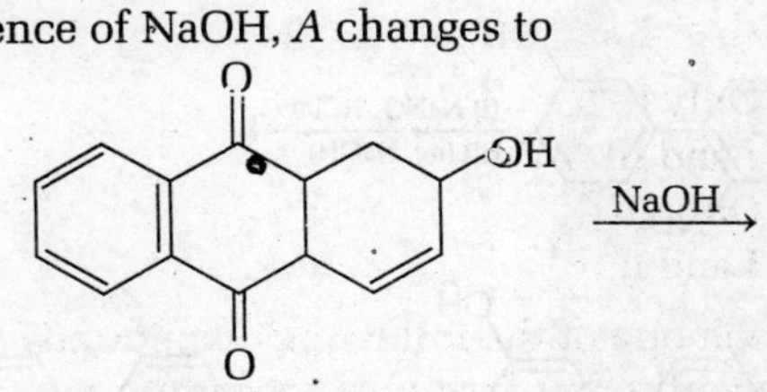

(A)

(a) 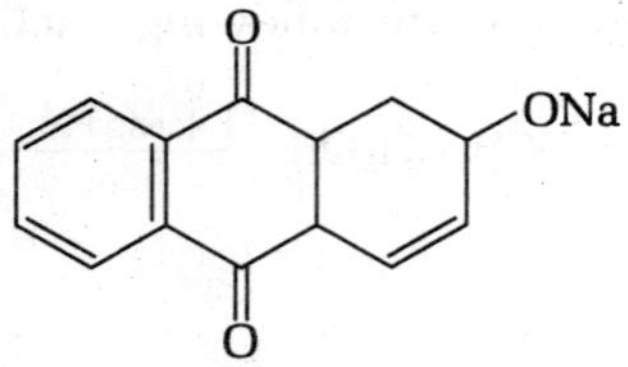

(b) 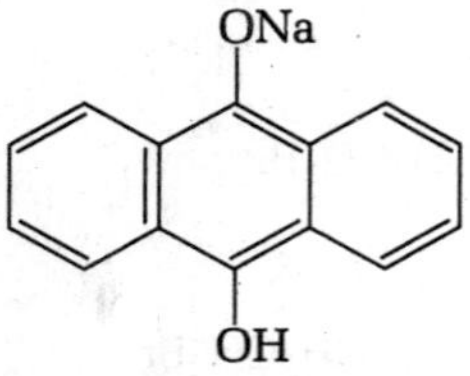

(c) 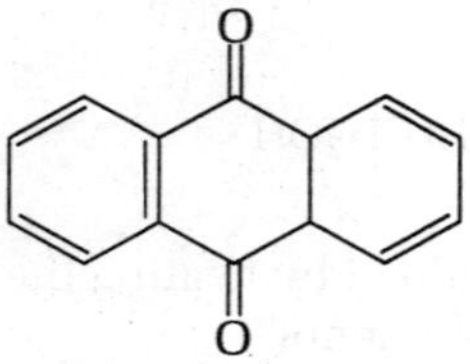

(d) 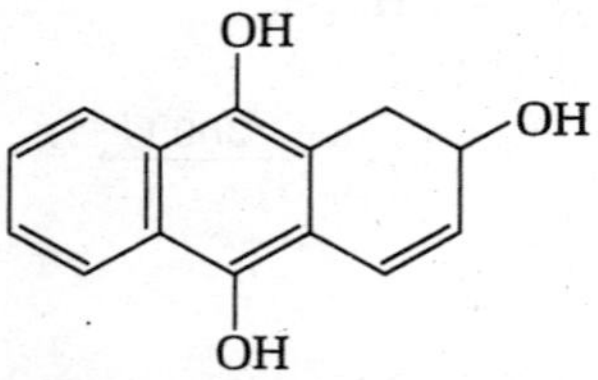

233. Which has maximum value of pK_a?

(a) 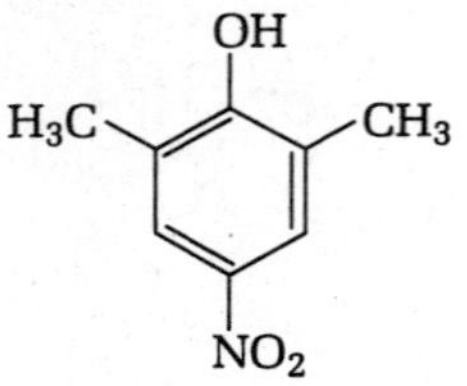
(b) 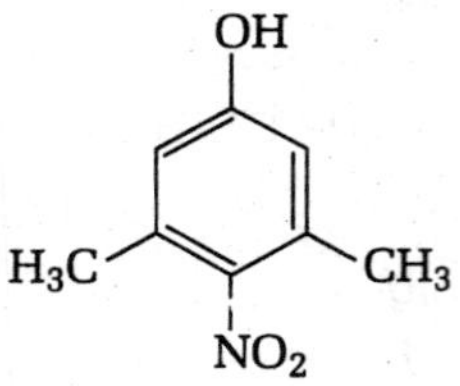

(c) 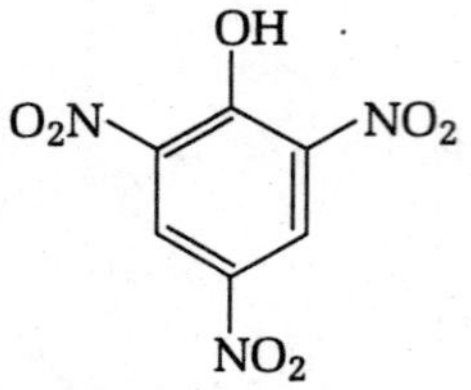
(d) 

234. The major product of the following reaction is **[JEE Advanced 2017]**

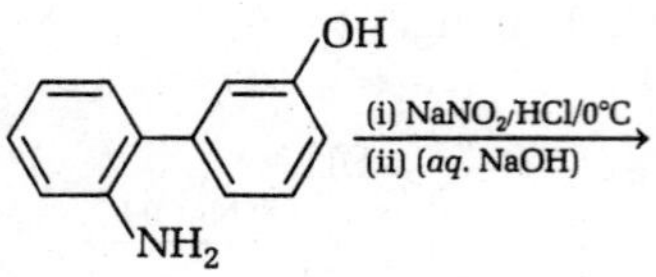

(a) 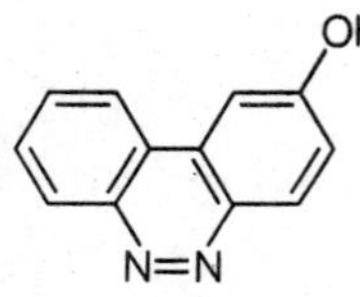
(b) 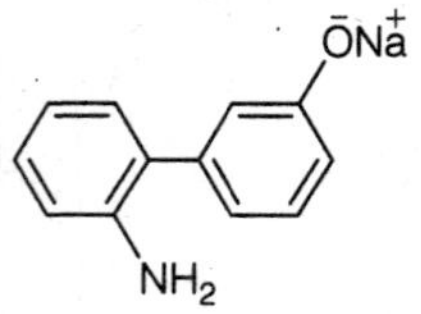

(c) 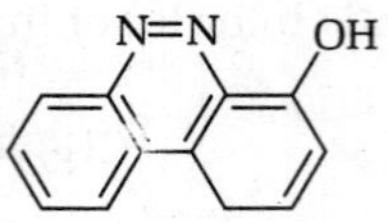
(d) 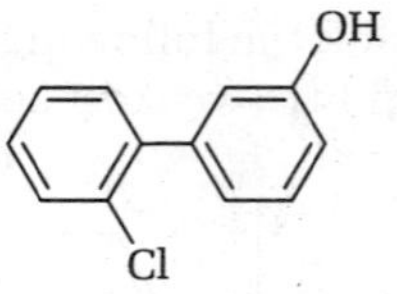

235. Which is more reactive towards nucleophiles?

(a) 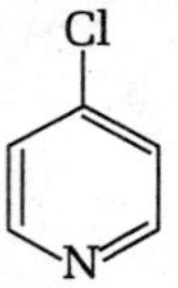
(b) 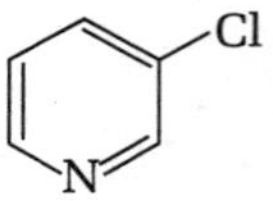

(c) Both equally
(d) No reactivity

236. Which is incapable of elimination giving benzyne intermediate necessary for substitution by the elimination-addition pathway?

(a) 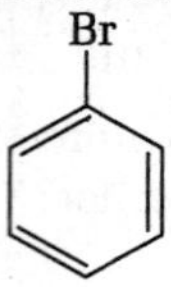
(b) 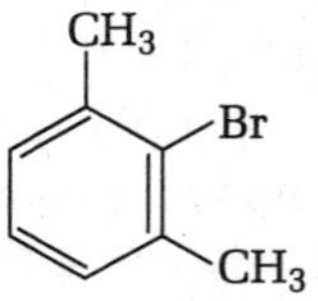

(c) 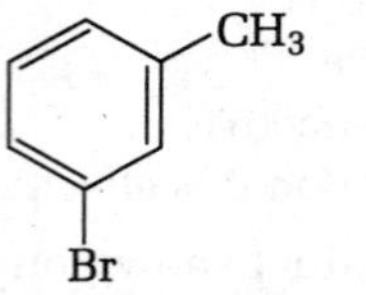
(d) 

237. In the following reaction

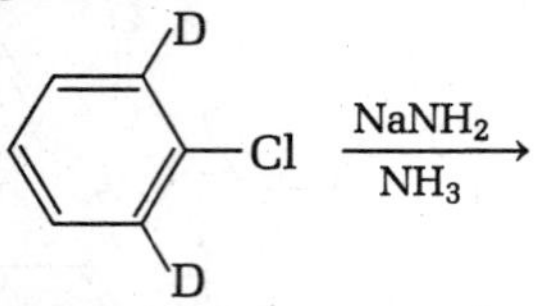

product(s) formed can be

(a) 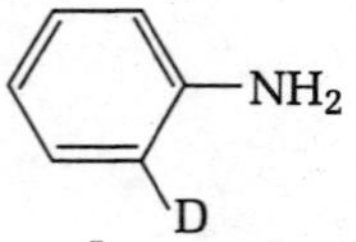
I

(b) 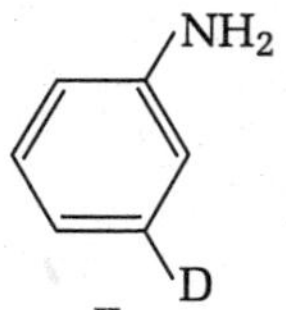
II

(c) I and II in 1 : 1 ratio
(d) I and II in 1 : 2 ratio

238. In the following transformation (two-steps) steps A and B are

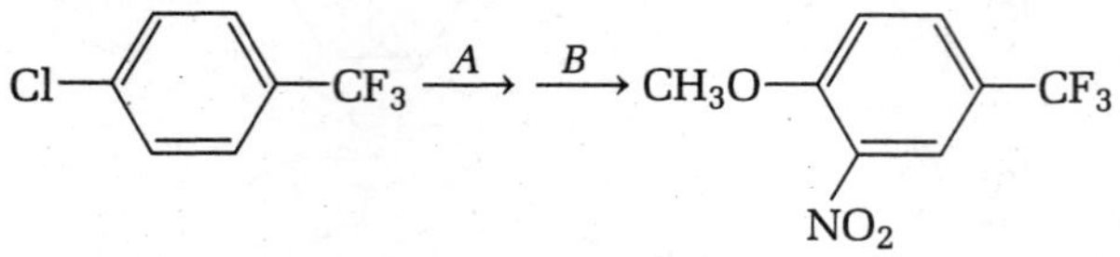

	A	B
(a)	HNO_3 / H_2SO_4	$NaOCH_3$, CH_3OH
(b)	$NaOCH_3$, CH_3OH	HNO_3 / H_2SO_4

(c) Both A and B in any order
(d) None of the above

239. Product(s) of the following reaction can be

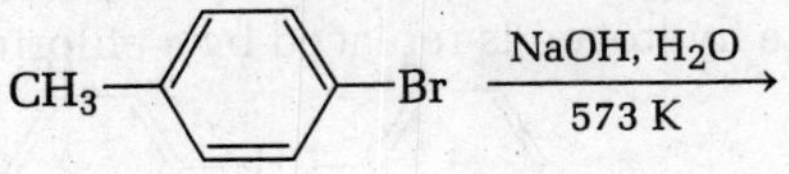

(a) 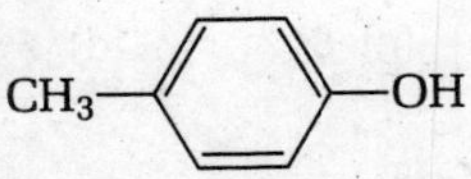 (b) 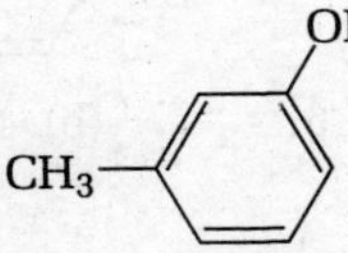

(c) Both (a) and (b) (d) None of these

240. Match the Column I with Column II and select the correct answer using the code given below.

Column I	Column II
A. Aldol condensation	1. Hydride ion transfer
B. Cannizzaro reaction	2. Organozinc compound
C. Reformatsky reaction	3. $CN^{\ominus}$ as catalyst
D. Benzoin condensation	4. Enolate ion

Codes

	A	B	C	D
(a)	4	1	2	3
(b)	2	3	4	1
(c)	4	3	2	1
(d)	2	1	4	3

241. Consider the following four carbonyl compounds.

I. 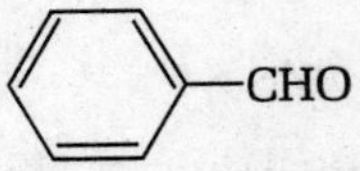 II. 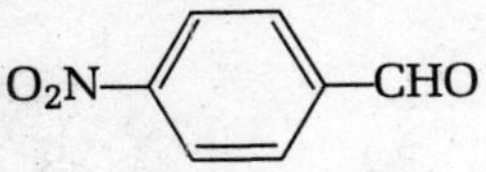

III. 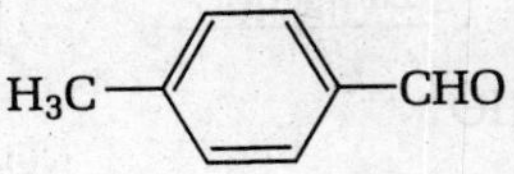 IV. NO_2-CH_2-CHO

Which one of the following is the correct sequence of decreasing order of reactivity towards the nucleophilic addition reactions of the above compounds?

(a) III > I > II > IV (b) IV > II > I > III

(c) II > IV > I > III (d) IV > III > II > I

242. Which one of the following compounds undergoes predominantly S_N2 reaction with *aq*. NaOH in polar aprotic solvents?

(a) 

(b) 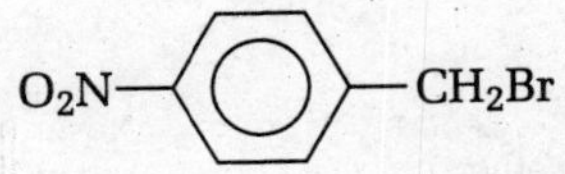

(c) 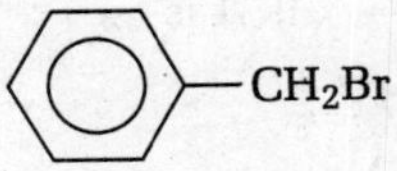

(d) 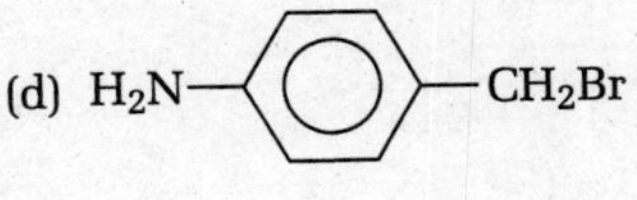

243. Which of the following compounds give benzoic acid on oxidation?

(a) Chlorophenol (b) Chlorotoluene

(c) Chlorobenzene (d) Benzyl chloride

244. *p*-nitrotoluene on further nitration gives

(a) 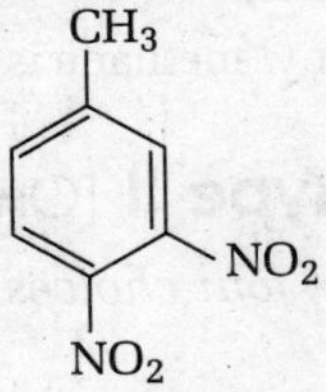 (b) 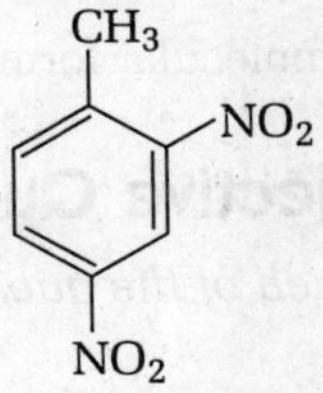

(c) 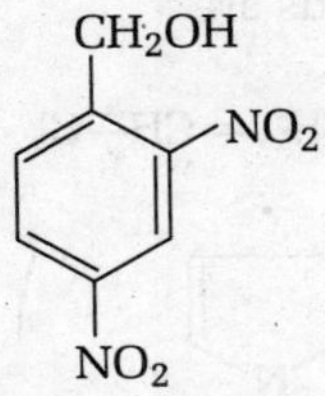 (d) 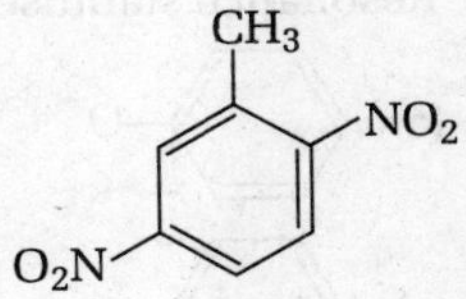

245. How will you get 2-bromo-4-nitro ethyl benzene from benzene? **[JEE Main 2021, March]**

(a) CH_3-CH_2-Cl / Anhyd. $AlCl_3$, Conc. HNO_3 / H_2SO_4, Br_2 / $FeBr_3$

(b) Conc. HNO_3 / H_2SO_4, CH_3-CH_2-Cl / Anhyd. $AlCl_3$, Br_2 / $FeBr_3$

(c) CH_3-CH_2-Cl / Anhyd. $AlCl_3$, Conc. H_2SO_4, Br_2 / $FeBr_3$

(d) None of the above

246. 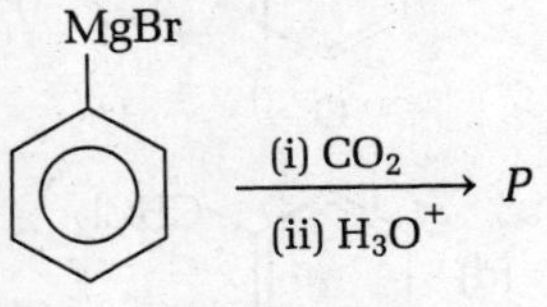

In the above reaction, product '*P*' is

(a)  (b) 

(c)  (d) $H_5C_6-\overset{\overset{O}{\|}}{C}-C_6H_5$

247. 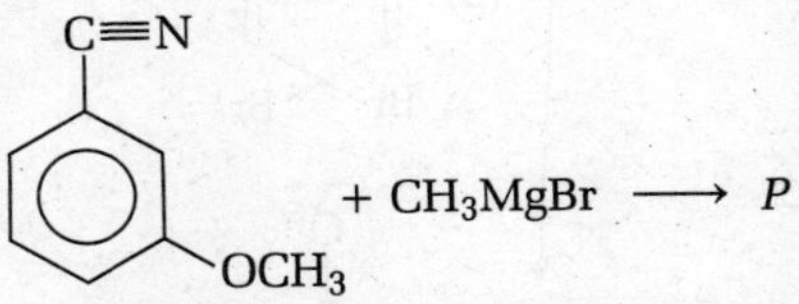

Product '*P*' in the above reaction is

(a) 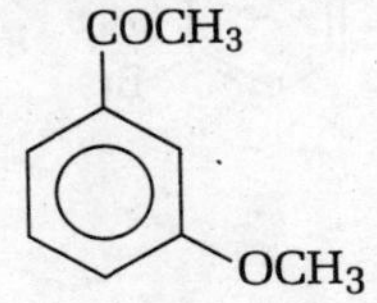 (b) 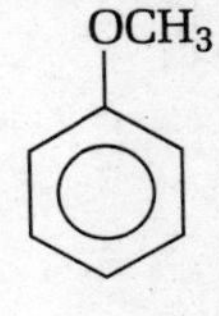

(c) 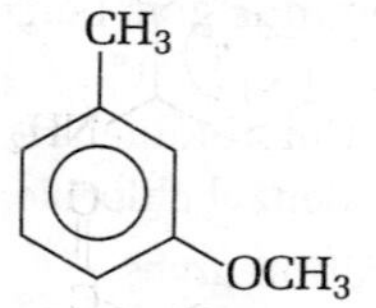

(d) 

248. The molecular formula of diphenyl methane is $C_{13}H_{12}$.

How many structural isomers are possible when one of the hydrogen is replaced by a chlorine atom?

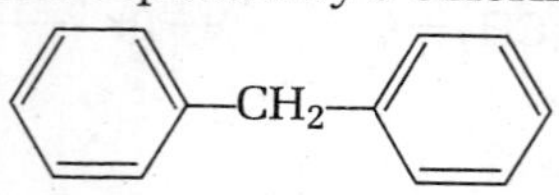

(a) 6 (b) 4 (c) 8 (d) 7

Objective Questions Type II [One or more than one correct option(s)]

In each of the questions below, four choices are given, of which one or more than one are correct.

1. Resonance stabilised compounds are

(a) 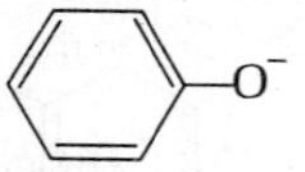

(b) $CH_2=CH-Cl$

(c) 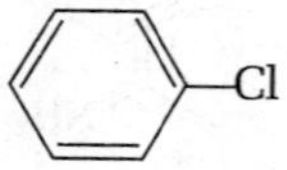

(d) 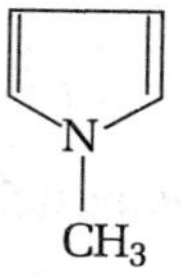

2. When phenol is reacted with $CHCl_3$ and NaOH followed by acidification, salicylaldehyde is obtained. Which of the following species are involved in the above mentioned reaction as intermediates?

(a) 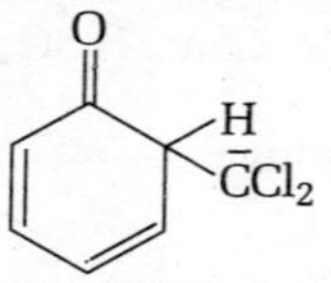

(b) 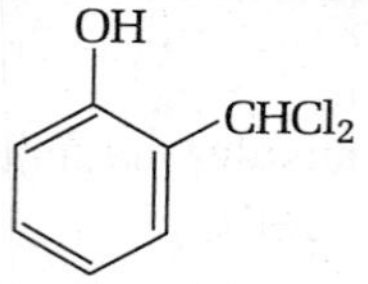

(c) 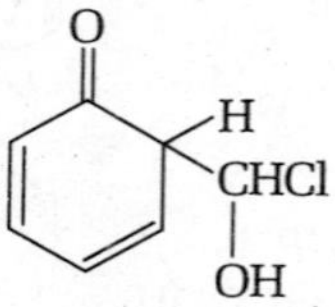

(d) 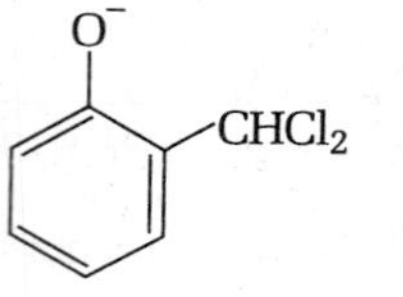

3. In the reaction, 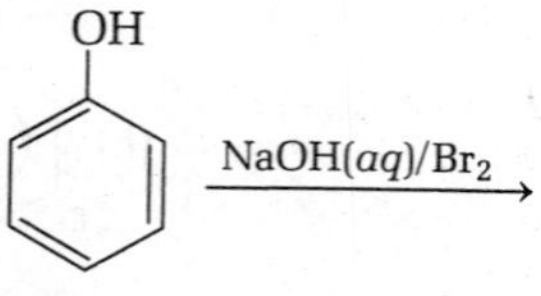

the intermediate(s) is (are) **[JEE Main 2010]**

(a) 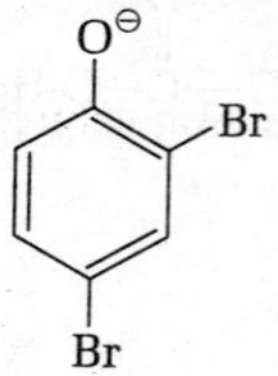

(b) 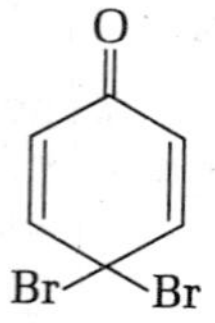

(c) 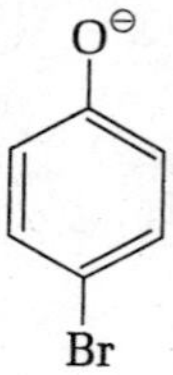

(d) 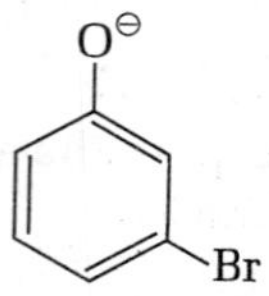

4. The reaction(s) leading to the formation of 1,3,5-trimethylbenzene is(are) **[JEE Advanced 2018]**

(a) 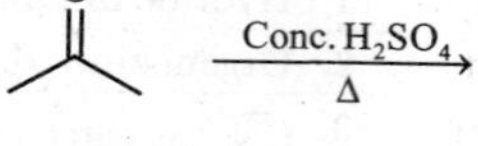

(b) 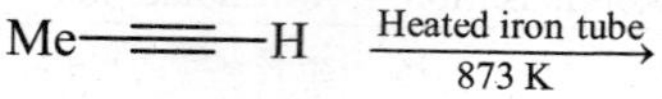

(c) 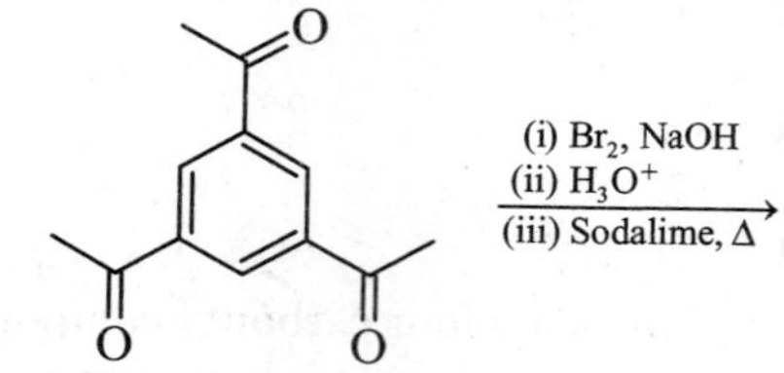

(d) 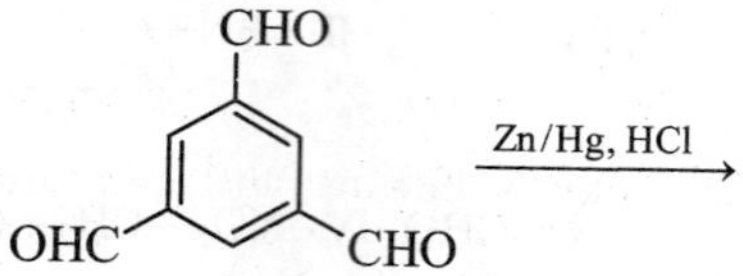

5. 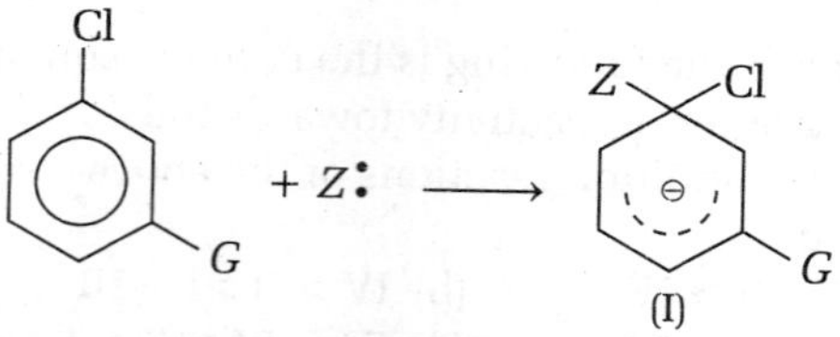

Which are the correct statements?

(a) If *G* is electron-withdrawing (like $-NO_2$) then, I is stabilised and S_N reaction is made favourable

(b) If *G* is electron-releasing (like $-NH_2$) then, I is destabilised and S_N reaction is retarded

(c) Both statements are true

(d) None is true

6. 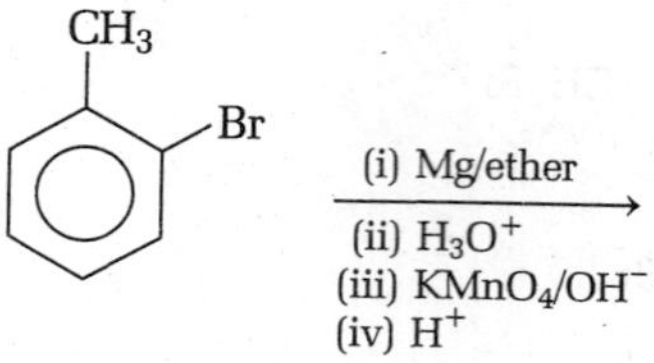

A; *A* is

(a) 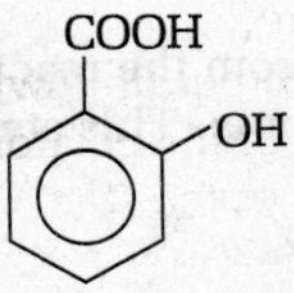
(b) 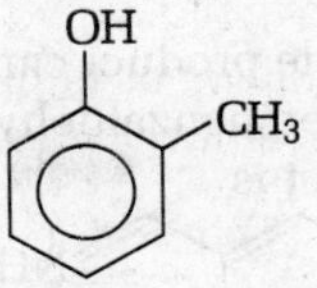
(c) 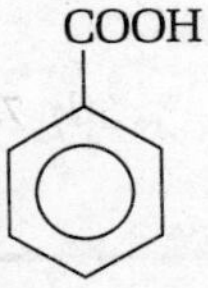
(d) 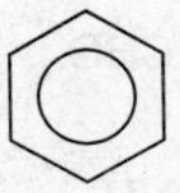

7. 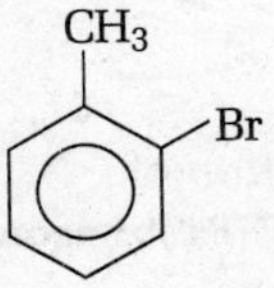 $\xrightarrow[\text{(ii) } CO_2/H_3O^+ \text{ (iii) } KMnO_4/OH^- \text{ (iv) } \Delta]{\text{(i) Mg/ether}}$ *A*; *A* is

(a) 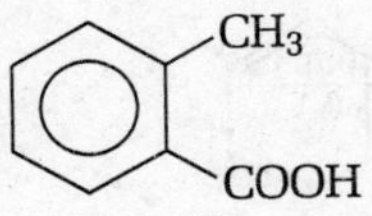
(b) 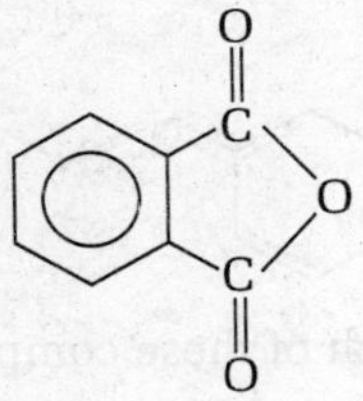
(c) 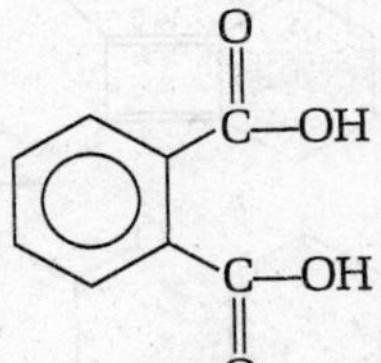
(d) 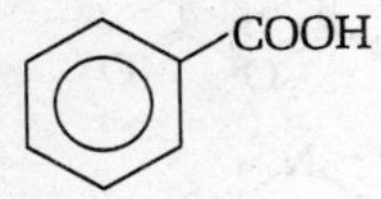

8. Among *P*, *Q*, *R* and *S*, the aromatic compound(s) is/are **[JEE Advanced 2013]**

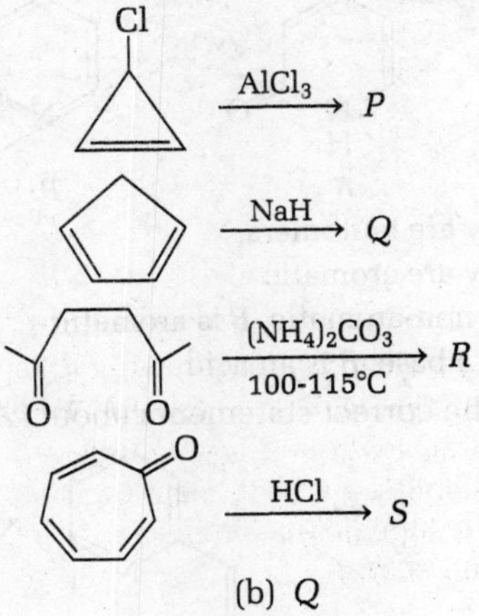

(a) *P*
(b) *Q*
(c) *R*
(d) *S*

9. 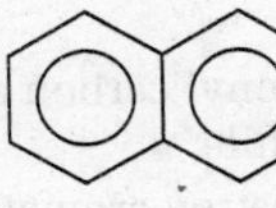 $\xrightarrow[\text{(ii) } NH_3, \Delta \text{ (iii) } KBrO, \Delta]{\text{(i) Air, } V_2O_5, \Delta}$ *A*; *A* is

(a) 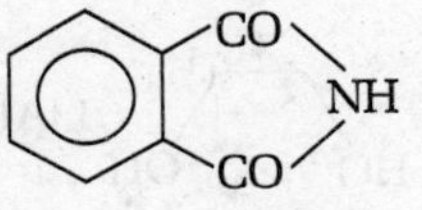
(b) 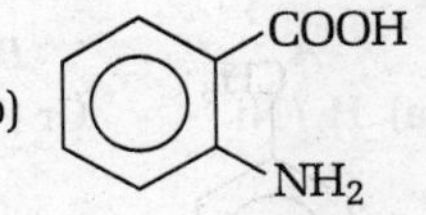
(c) 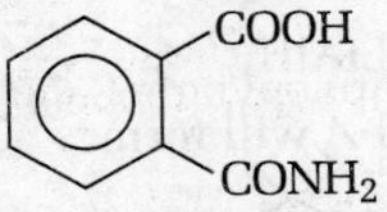
(d) 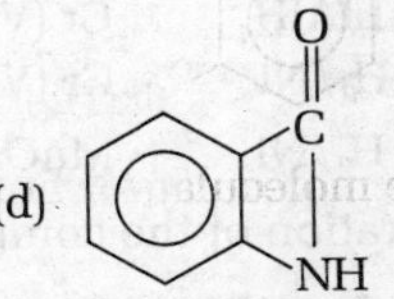

10. Anthranilic acid at pH = 2 exists as ...... and migrates towards ....

(a) 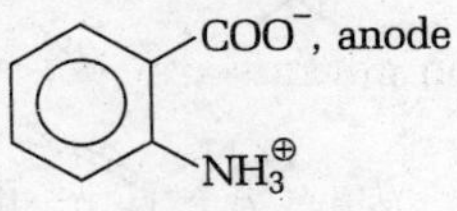

(b) 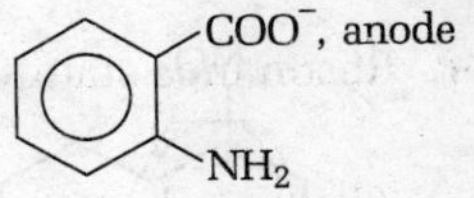

(c) 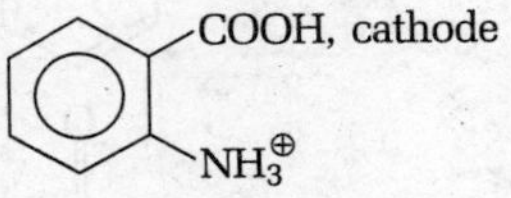

(d) 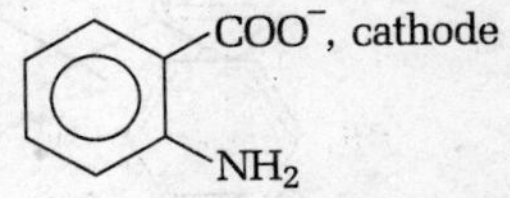

11. Oxidation of *A* gives *p*-benzoquinone; *A* can be

(a) 
(b) 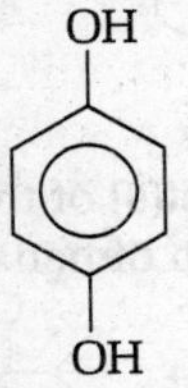
(c) 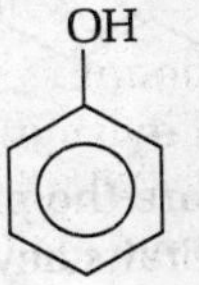
(d) 

12. Consider the following reaction,

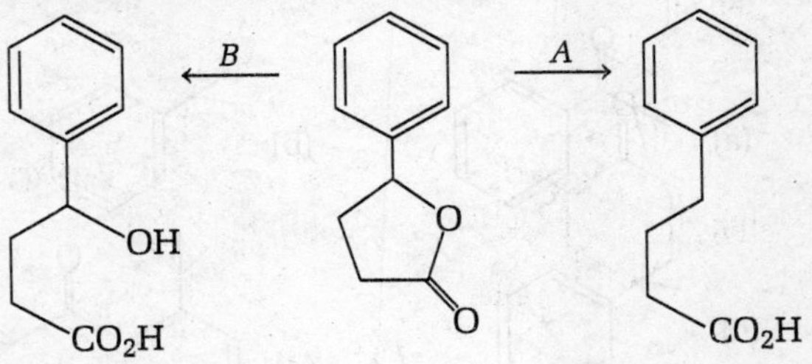

Reagents *A* and *B* are

	A	*B*
(a)	H_2, Pd / C	HCl
(b)	H_2, Pd / C	$NaOH/H_2O$
(c)	H_2, Pd / C	$LiAlH_4$
(d)	$LiAlH_4$,	$NaBH_4$

13. Reagents *A*, *B* and *C* in the following sequence of reactions are

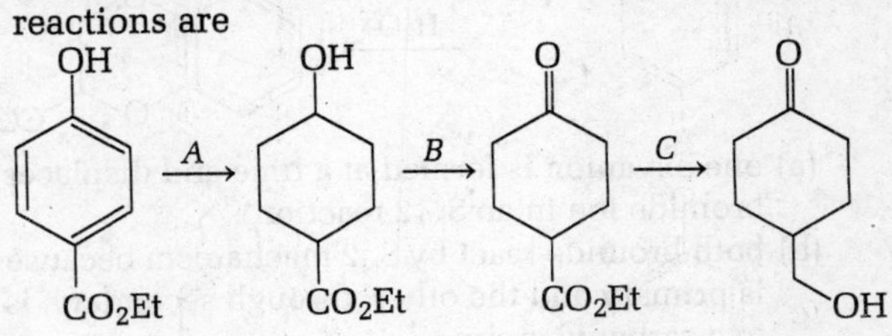

	A	*B*	*C*
(a)	H_2/Ni	Cr (VI)	 $/LiAlH_4/H_3O^{\oplus}$
(b)	$LiAlH_4$	Cr (VI)	BH_3
(c)	H_2/Ni	Cr (VI)	$LiAlH_4/H_3O^{\oplus}$
(d)	H_2/Ni	MnO_2	$LiAlH_4$

14. Nitration of the compound *A* will form

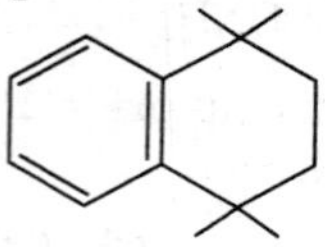

(a) 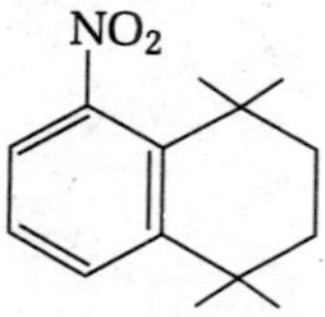
(b) 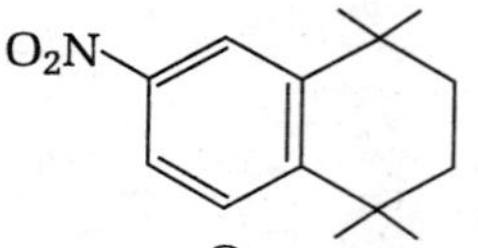
(c) 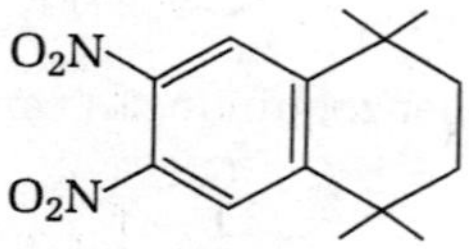
(d) 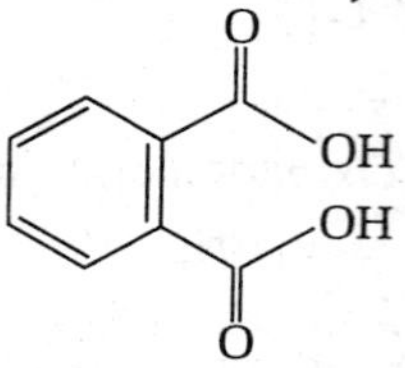

15. What is/are the product(s) of the following Friedel-Crafts acylation of benzene?

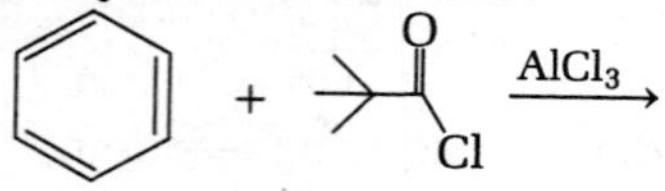

(a) 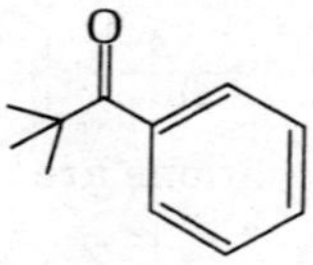
(b) 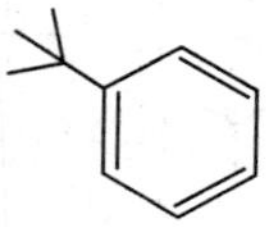
(c) 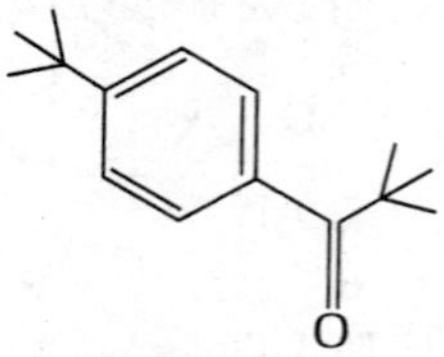
(d) 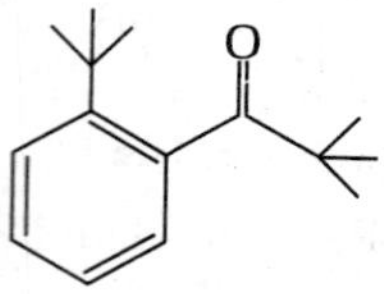

16. In the following reaction,

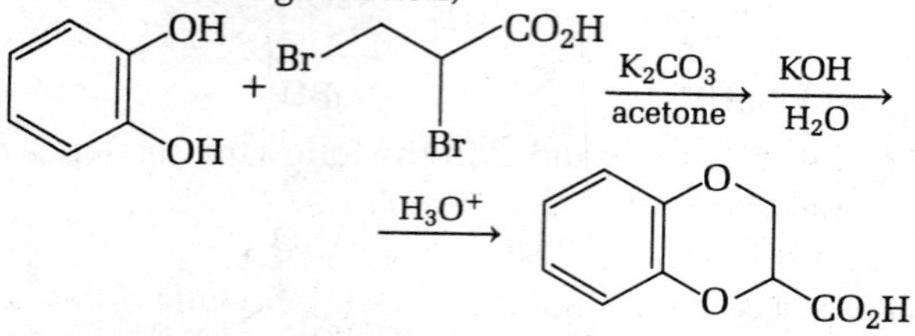

(a) one oxyanion is formed at a time and displaces a bromide ion in an S_N 2 reaction
(b) both bromide react by S_N2 mechanism because one is primary and the other, through secondary, is next to a carbonyl group
(c) primary bromide is displaced by S_N 2 and the secondary bromide (next to CO_2H) is displaced by S_N1 mechanism
(d) both bromide react by S_N1 mechanism

17. A stable product can be isolated from the reaction between benzaldehyde and ammonia. This stable product is

(a) 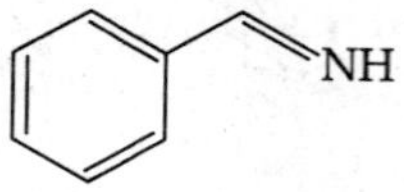
(b) 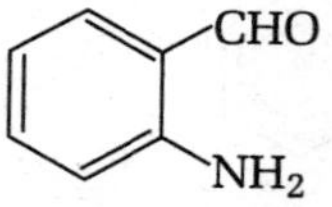
(c) 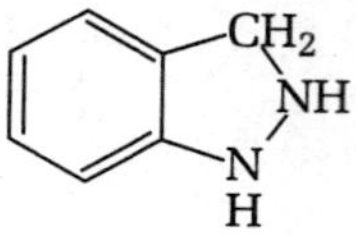
(d) 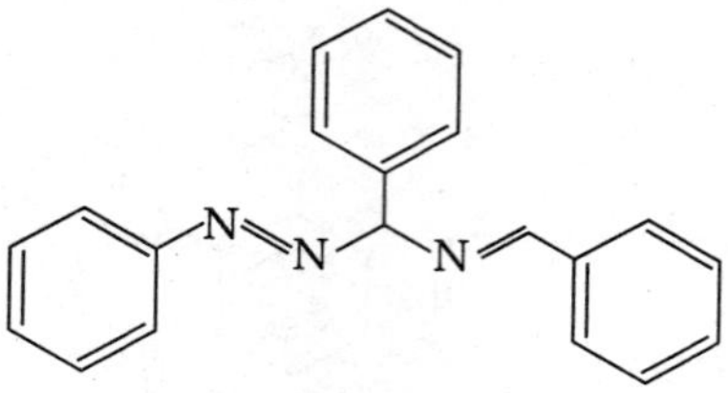

18. Which of these compounds are aromatic?

(a) 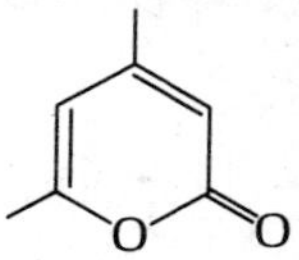
(b) 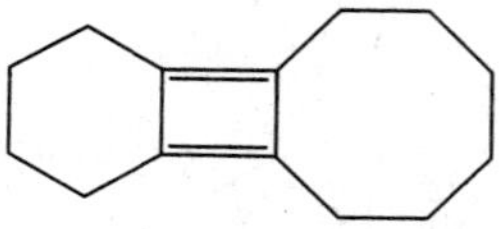
(c) 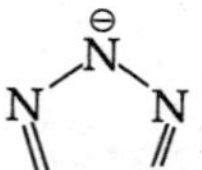
(d) 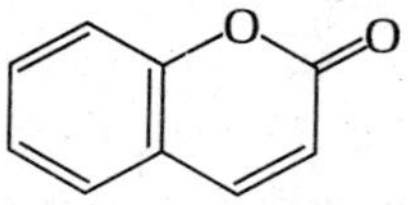

19. What is the relationship between *A* and *B*?

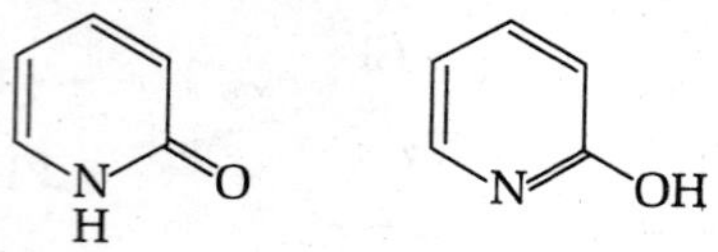

A *B*

(a) They are tautomers
(b) They are aromatic
(c) *A* is non-aromatic, *B* is aromatic
(d) *A* is a base, *B* is an acid

20. Select the correct statements about (*A*).

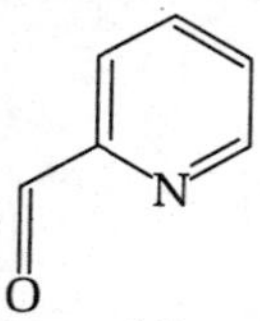

(*A*)

(a) nucleophilic attack occurs at the carbonyl carbon and not at the C=N group of the electrophile
(b) nucleophilic attack at C=N would destroy aromaticity of the pyridine ring
(c) nucleophilic attack occurs at the C=N group being less electrophilic than C=O
(d) there is no nucleophilic attack in either position of (*A*)

21. In the following reaction,

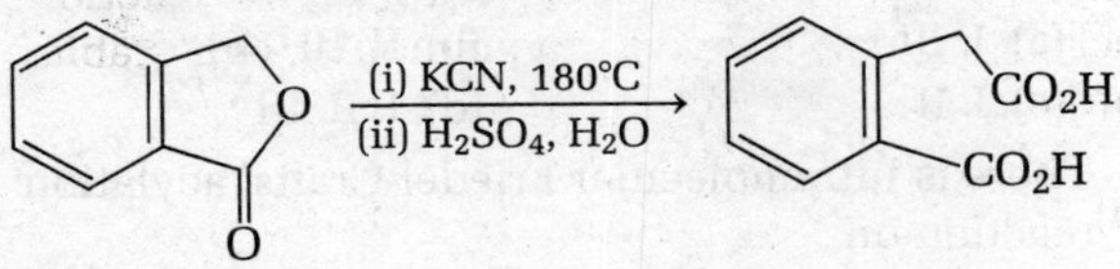

intermediates can be

(a) 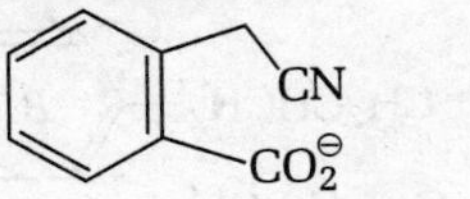 (b) 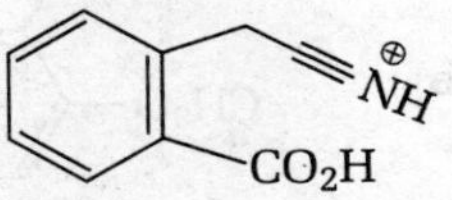

(c) 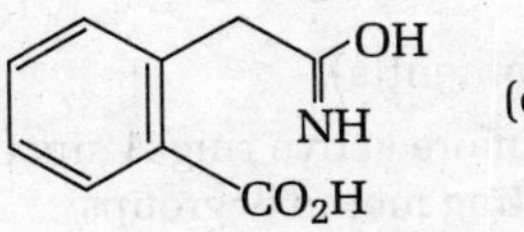 (d) 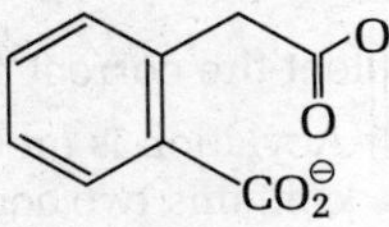

22. Identify the final product(s) of this reaction

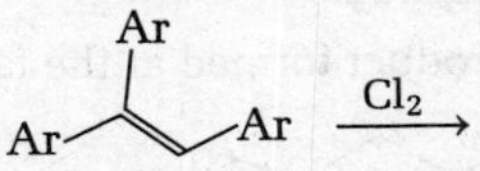

(a) 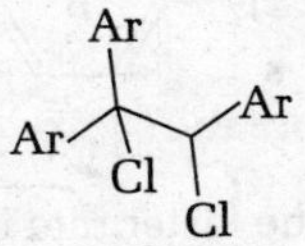 (b) 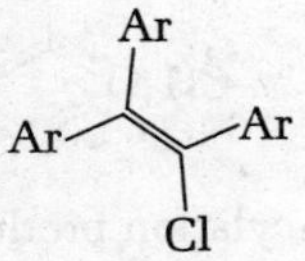

(c) 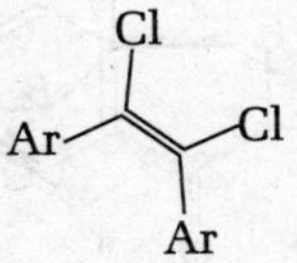 (d) 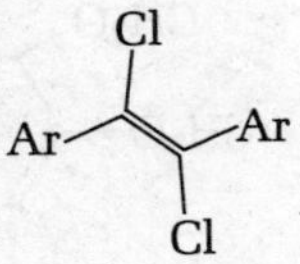

23. Consider the following reactions,

I. 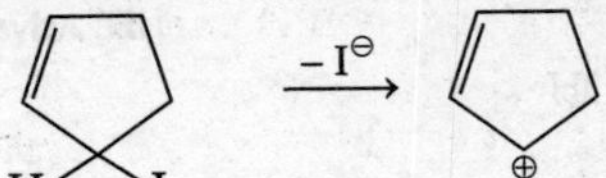
(A)

II. 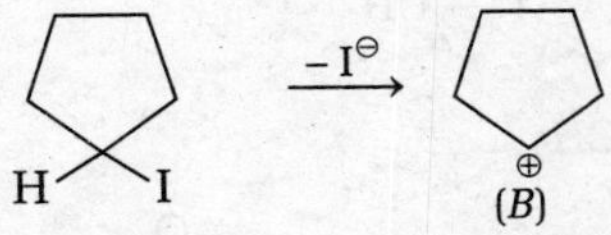
(B)

III. 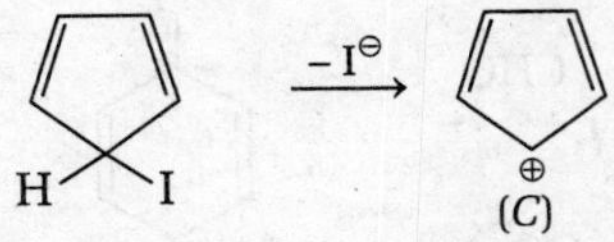
(C)

Select the correct statement(s).

(a) All the carbocations (A), (B) and (C) are secondary
(b) (A) is stabilised by conjugation with the double bond and is formed fastest
(c) (C) is least stable and is formed slowest
(d) (C) is conjugated cyclic system with four π-electrons and thus is antiaromatic

24. In the presence of aqueous sulphuric acid, styrene is converted into

(a) 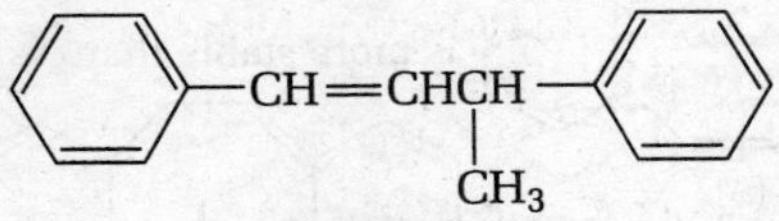
1,3-diphenyl-1-butene

(b) 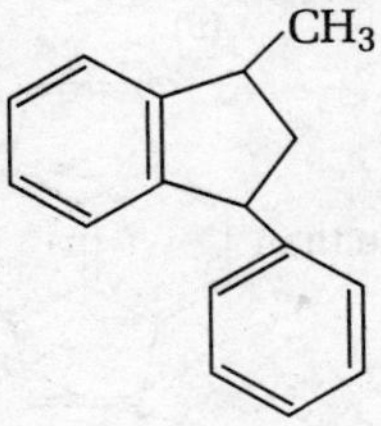 1-methyl-3-phenylindan

(c) 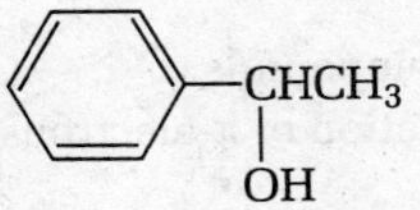

(d) 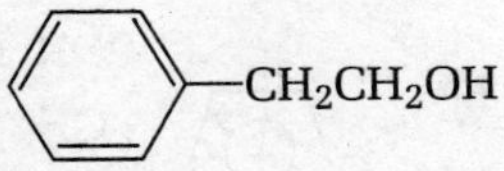

25. Chlorination of *m*-xylene takes place through the formation of carbocation intermediates

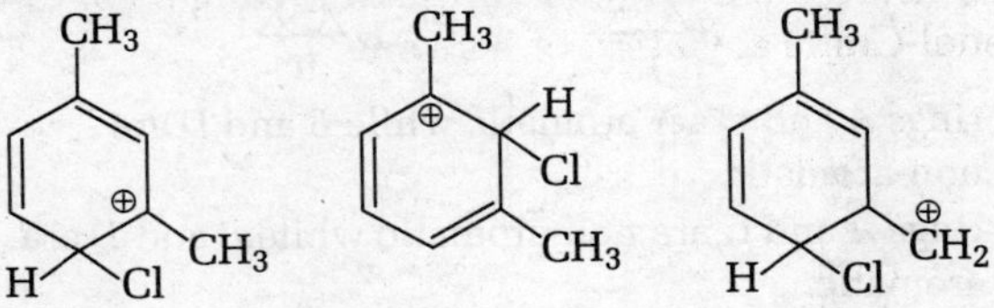
I II III

Most stable and least stable carbocations are
(a) II, III (b) I, III
(c) I, II (d) all have equal $\Delta G°$

26. Toluene (*A*) is to be converted into 3-bromo-5-nitrobenzoic acid (*B*)

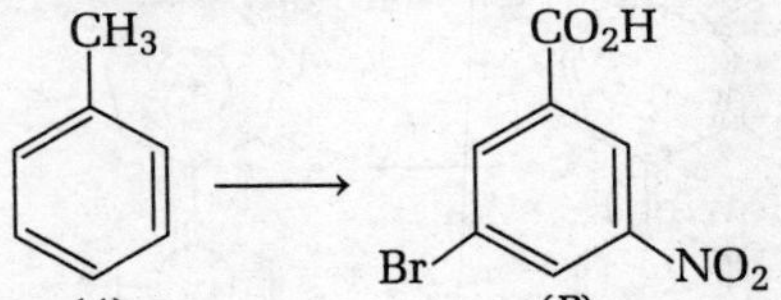
(A) (B)

It can be performed by using reagents
I. $Br_2/FeBr_3$, II. HNO_3/H_2SO_4, III. $K_2Cr_2O_7/H_2SO_4$, Δ
These reagents should be used in following order

(a) $A \xrightarrow{I} \xrightarrow{II} \xrightarrow{III} B$ (b) $A \xrightarrow{II} \xrightarrow{I} \xrightarrow{III} B$
(c) $A \xrightarrow{III} \xrightarrow{II} \xrightarrow{I} B$ (d) $A \xrightarrow{II} \xrightarrow{III} \xrightarrow{I} B$

27. Select the correct statement(s).

(a) 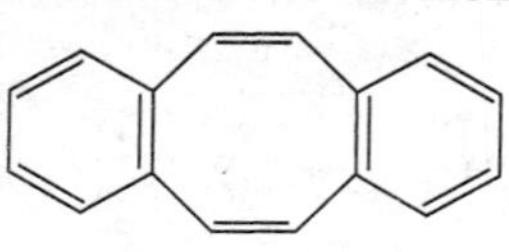 is more stable than 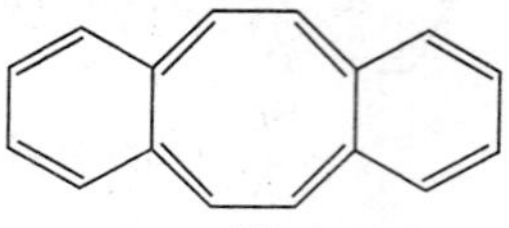

(A) (B)

(b) 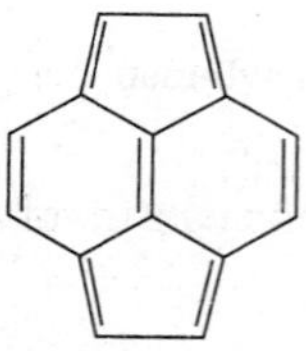 is more stable than 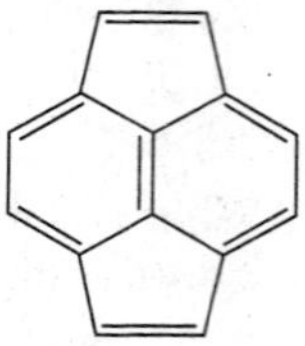

(C) (D)

(c) (*A*) to (*D*) all are aromatic compounds

(d) There is complete delocalisation of π-electrons in (*A*) to (*D*)

28. In structures I and II

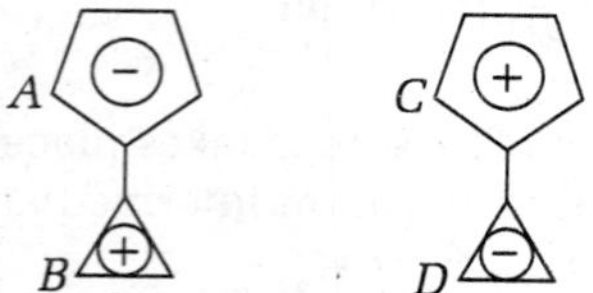

I II

(a) rings *A* and *C* are aromatic while *B* and *D* are non-aromatic

(b) rings *A* and *C* are non-aromatic while *B* and *D* are aromatic

(c) rings *A* and *B* are aromatic while *C* and *D* are non-aromatic

(d) all rings *A* to *D* are aromatic

29. Select the correct statement(s).

(a) Following structure can be stabilised by resonance involving a dipolar form

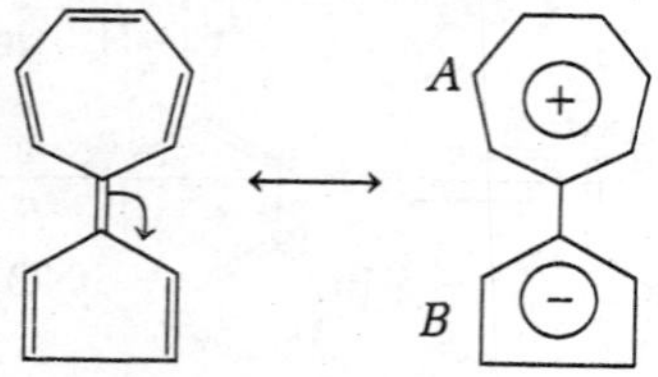

(b) Rings *A* and *B* both are aromatic

(c) Rings *A* and *B* both are non-aromatic

(d) Ring *A* is aromatic while ring *B* is non-aromatic

30. Consider the following compounds,

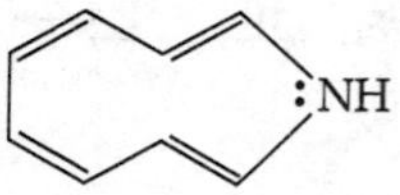 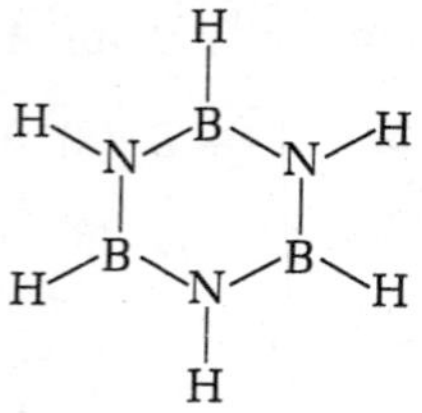 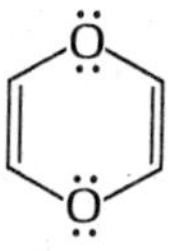

I II III

Out of these, aromatic compounds are

(a) I, III (b) II, III

(c) I, II (d) I, II, III

31. There is intramolecular Friedel-Crafts' acylation reaction on

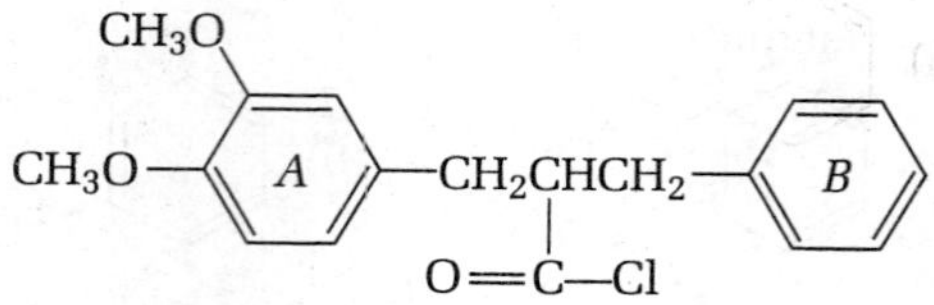

Select the correct statement(s).

(a) Acylation is on the more active ring *A* since it contains two activating methoxy groups

(b) Acylation is on the more active ring *B* since it lacks deactivating groups

(c) Acylation product formed at the faster rate is

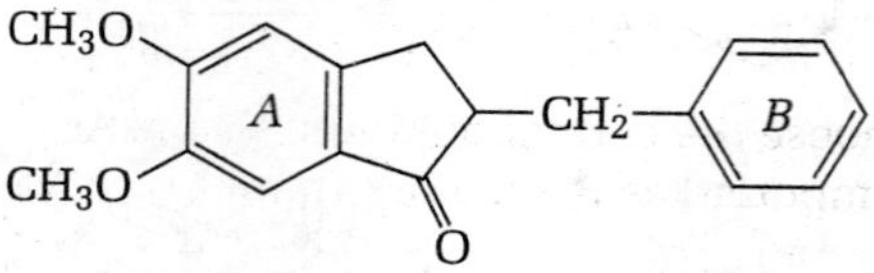

(d) Acylation product formed at the faster rate is/(are)

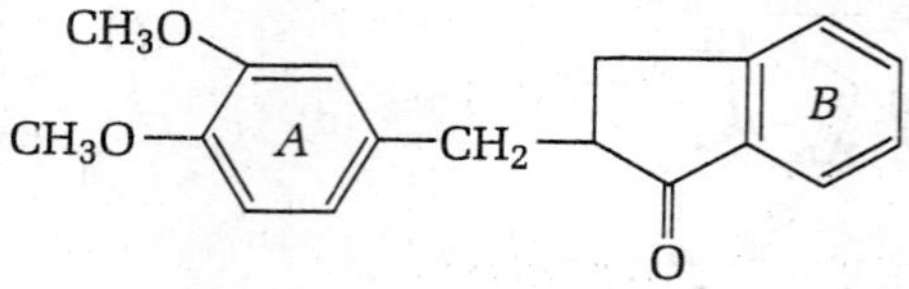

32. In the following reaction, the product(s) formed is **[JEE Advanced 2013]**

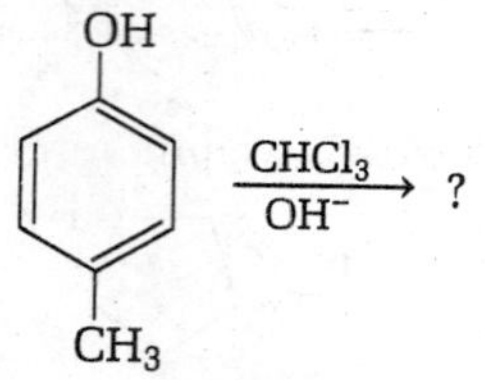

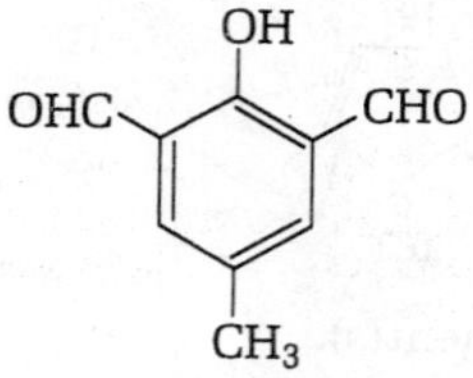 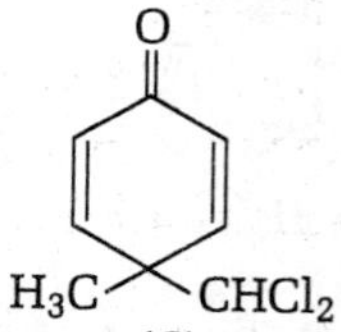

(*P*) (*Q*)

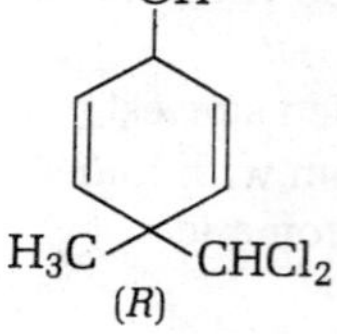 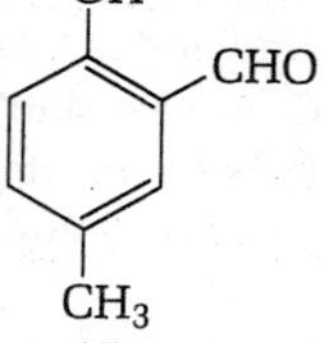

(*R*) (*S*)

(a) *P* (major) (b) *Q* (minor)

(c) *R* (minor) (d) *S* (major)

33. What is/are the end-product(s) of the following?

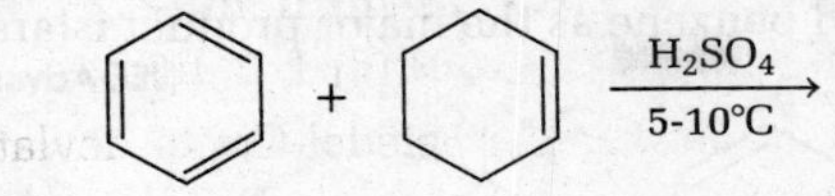

(a) 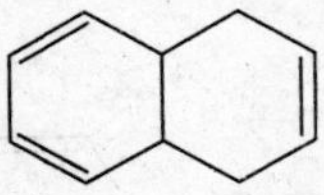

(b) 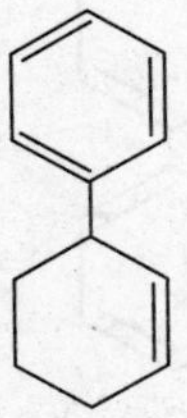

(c) 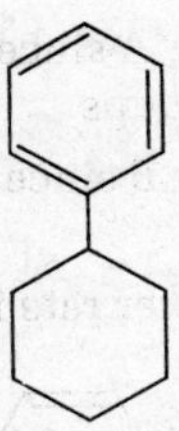

(d) 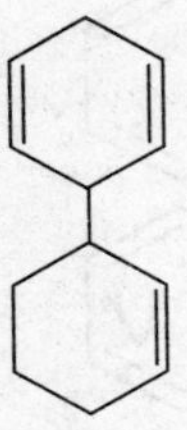

34. Choose the correct option(s) that give(s) an aromatic compound as the major product. **[JEE Advanced 2019]**

(a) 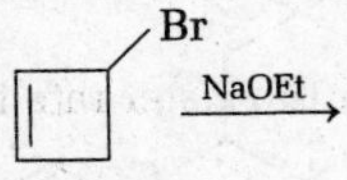

(b) 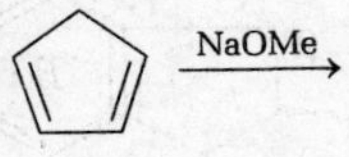

(c) 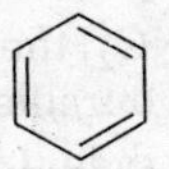 + Cl_2 (excess) $\xrightarrow{\text{UV, 500 K}}$

(d) 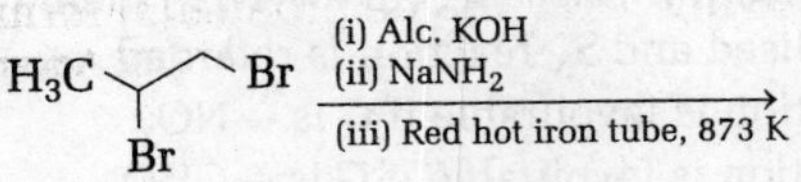

35. Which of the following compounds are antiaromatic?

(a) 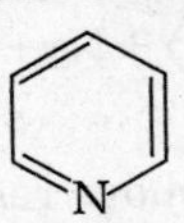

(b) 

(c) 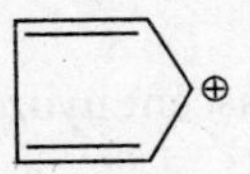

(d) 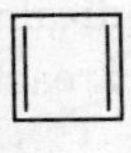

36. The major product(s) of the following reaction is (are) **[JEE Advanced 2013]**

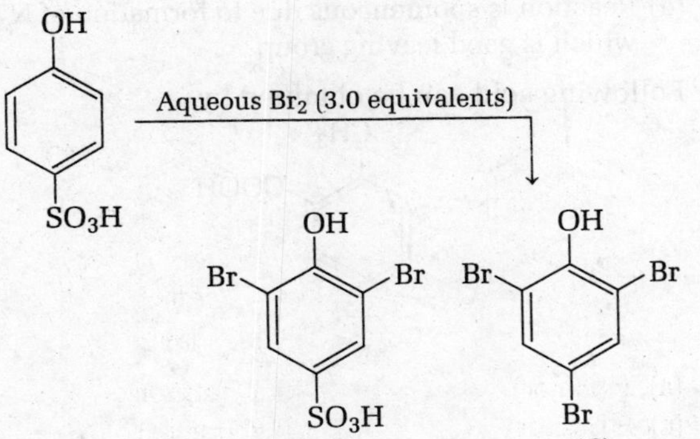

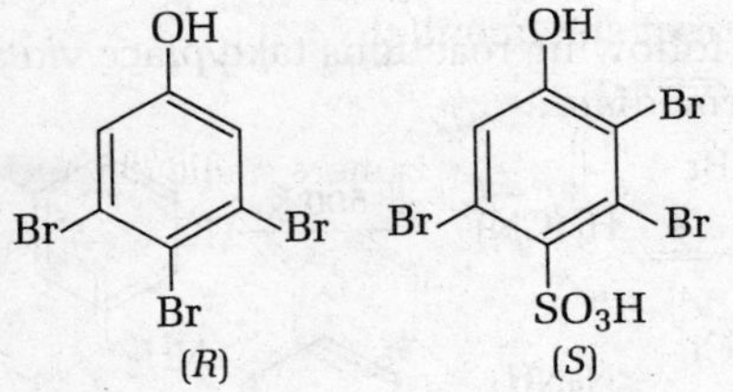

(a) *P*
(b) *Q*
(c) *R*
(d) *S*

37. Which of the following reactions can involve benzyne as the intermediate?

(a) 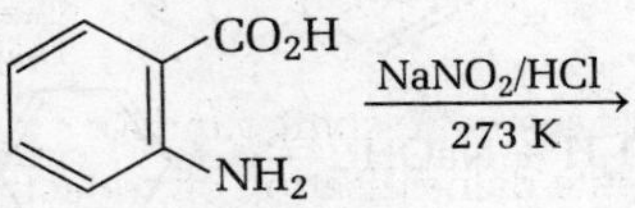

(b) 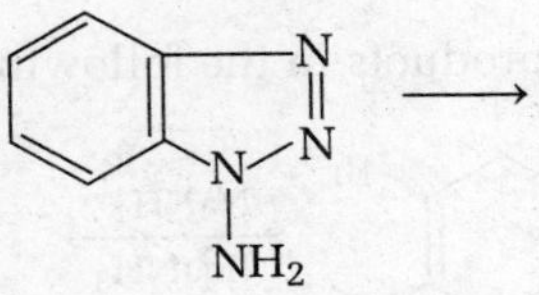

(c) 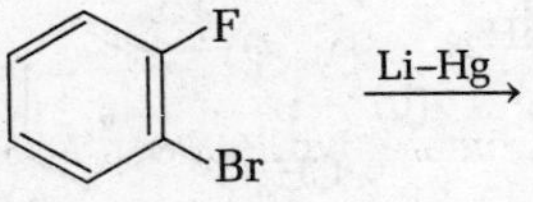

(d) 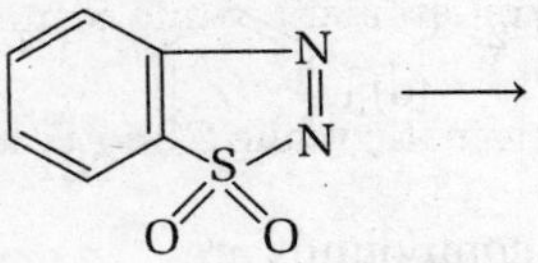

38. Aniline reacts with mixed acid (conc. HNO_3 and conc. H_2SO_4) at 288 K to give *P* (51%), *Q* (47%) and *R* (2%). The major product(s) of the following sequence is (are) **[JEE Advanced 2018]**

R $\xrightarrow[\text{(iii) } H_3O^+ \text{ (iv) } NaNO_2\text{, HCl/273-278 K (v) EtOH, }\Delta]{\text{(i) } Ac_2O\text{, pyridine (ii) } Br_2\text{, } CH_3CO_2H}$ *S* $\xrightarrow[\text{(iii) } NaNO_2\text{, HCl/273-278 K (iv) } H_3PO_2]{\text{(i) Sn/HCl (ii) } Br_2/H_2O \text{ (excess)}}$ Major product(s)

(a) 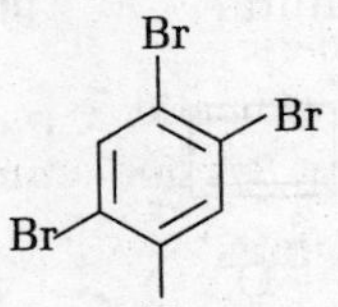

(b) 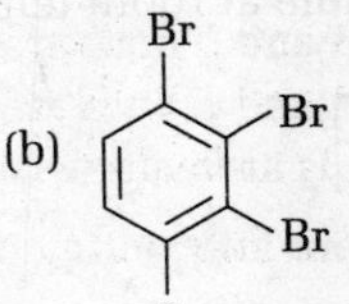

(c) 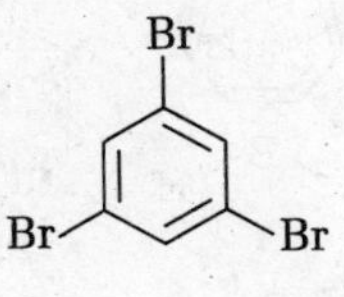

(d) 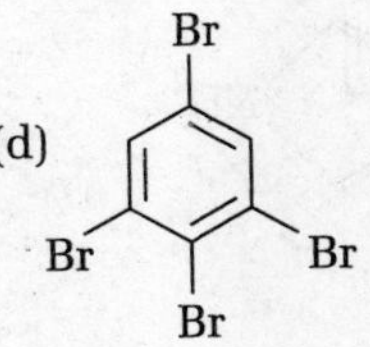

39. Which of the following reactions take place *via* a benzyne intermediate?

(a) 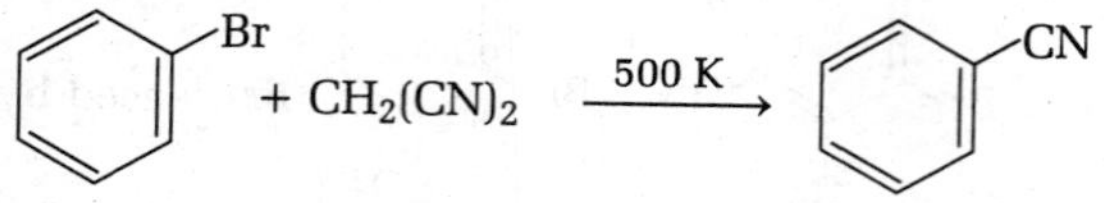

(b) 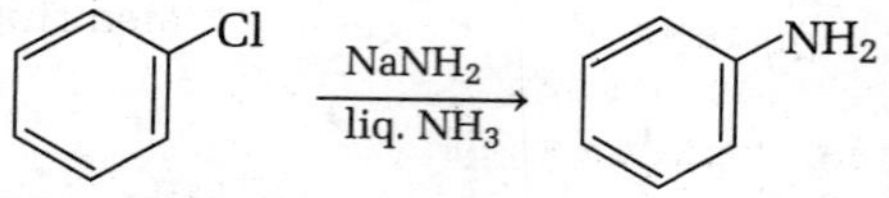

(c) 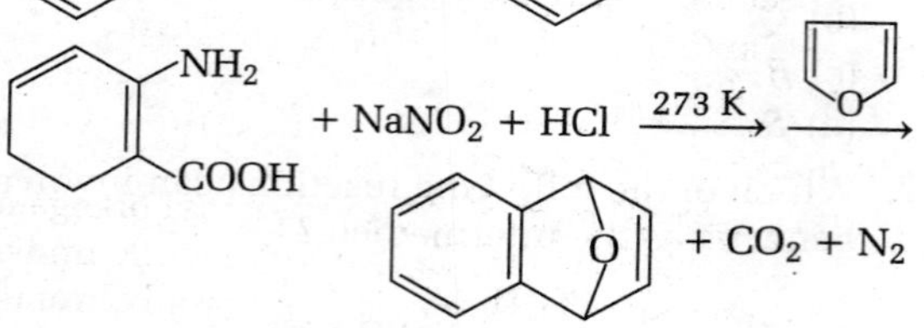

(d) 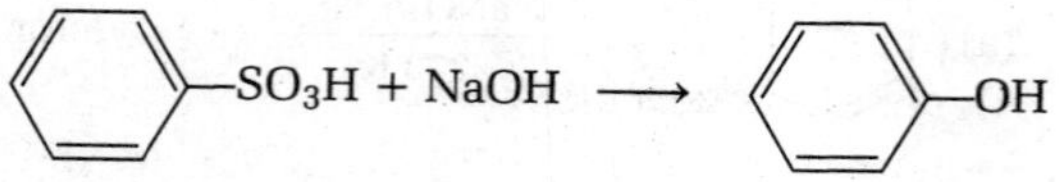

40. What is/are possible products in the following reaction?

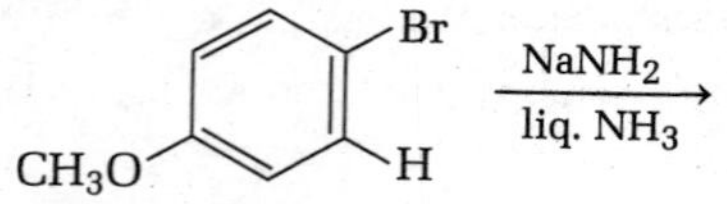

(a) 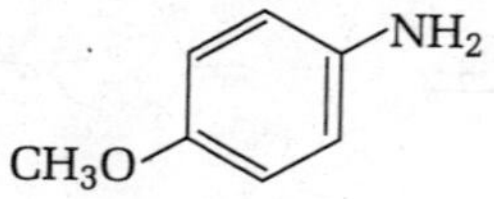

(b) 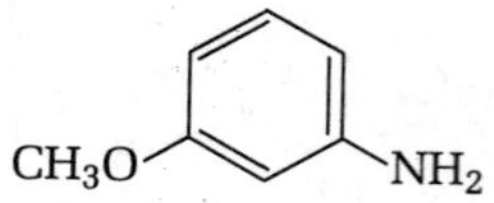

(c) 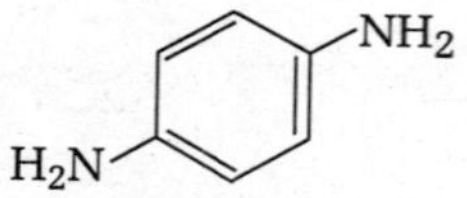

(d) 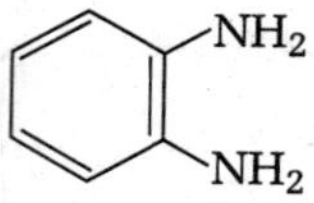

41. Resonance stabilised compounds are

(a) 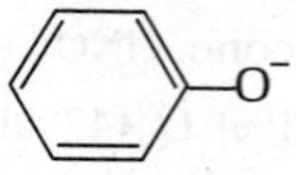

(b) $CH_2{=}CH{-}Cl$

(c) 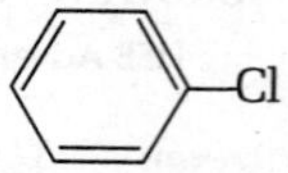

(d) 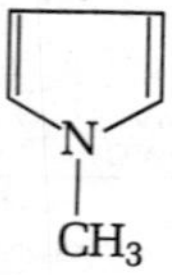

42. Which of the following molecules, in pure form, is (are) unstable at room temperature? **[IIT JEE 2012]**

(a) 

(b) 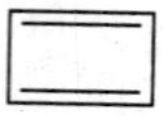

(c) 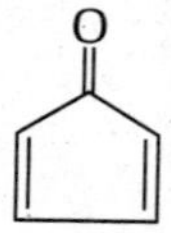

(d) 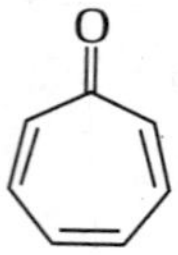

43. Among the following, reaction(s) which gives(give) *tert*-butyl benzene as the major product is(are) **[JEE Advanced 2016]**

(a) 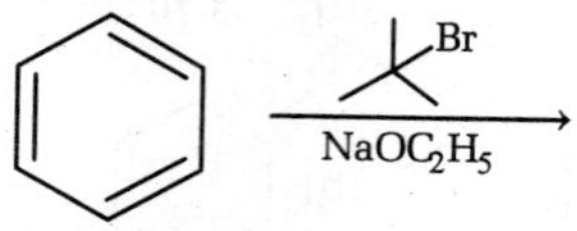

(b) 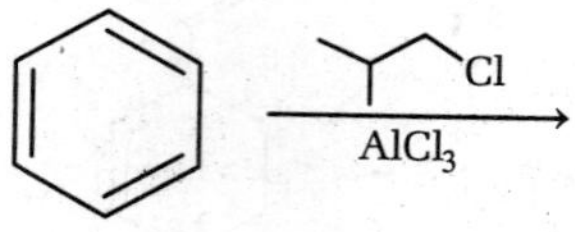

(c) 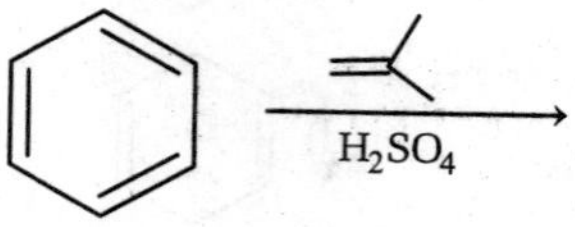

(d) 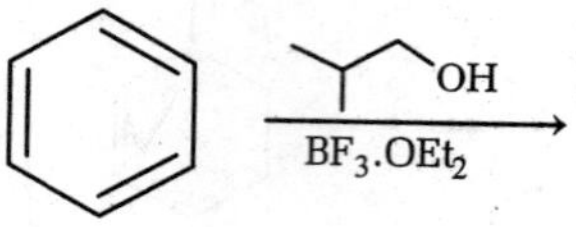

44. 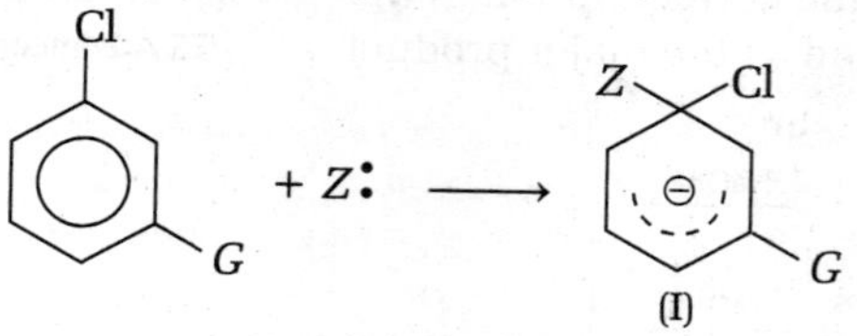

Which are correct statements?

(a) If G is electron-withdrawing (like —NO_2) then, I is stabilised and S_N reaction is made favourable

(b) If G is electron-releasing (like —NH_2) then, I is destabilised and S_N reaction is retarded

(c) S_E reaction is favourable if G is —NO_2

(d) S_E reaction is favourable if G is —CHO

45. 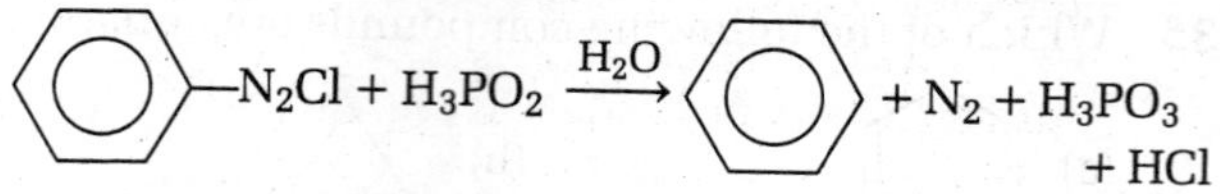

Select the correct statements about above reaction.

(a) It is free radical chain reaction

(b) It is a redox reaction in which nascent hydrogen is involved

(c) Basicity of oxyacid of phosphorus remains unchanged

(d) Reaction is spontaneous due to formation of N_2 which is good leaving group

46. Following acid can be obtained by

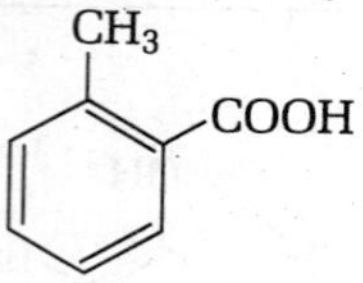

(a) 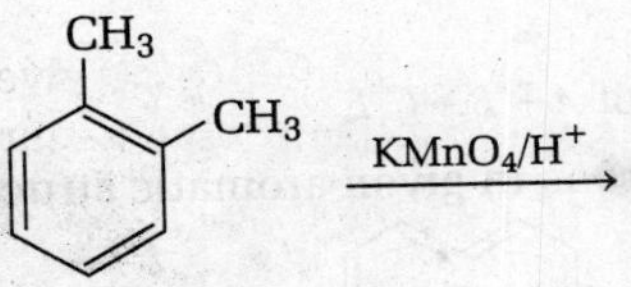

(b) 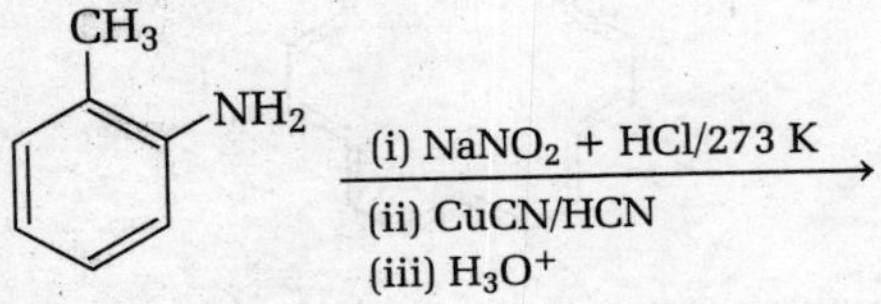

(c) 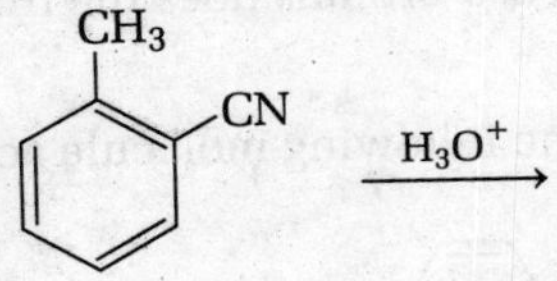

(d) 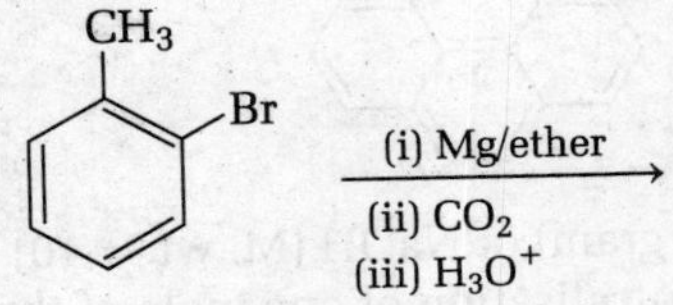

47. With respect to the compounds I-V, choose the correct statement(s). **[JEE Advanced 2021]**

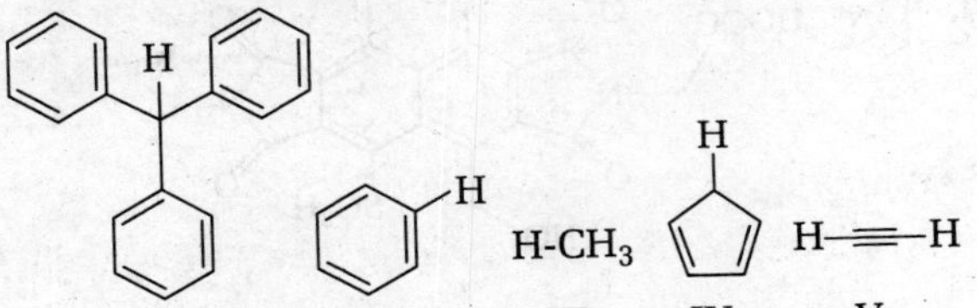

I. II. III. IV. V.

(a) The acidity of compoiund I is due to delocalisation in the conjugate base

(b) The conjugate base of compound IV is aromatic

(c) Compound II becomes more acidic, when it has a $—NO_2$ substituent

(d) The acidity of compounds follows the order I > IV > V > II > III

48. Following statements are related to reactions of arene diazonium salts.

I. They act as weak electrophiles in electrophiles aromatic substitutions.

II. Electrophilic character is increased by electron- donating groups.

III. Electrophilic character is increased by electron-withdrawing groups.

IV. They react with strongly activated rings as aniline phenol.

Select the correct statement(s).

(a) I and II (b) I and III
(c) I, II and IV (d) I, III and IV

49. Select the correct statement(s).

(a) Under alkaline conditions methyl orange-an azo dye, contains the azo chromophore while under acidic conditions it contains *p*-quinonoid chromophore

(b) Methyl orange is not a satisfactory dye for textiles being sensitive to acids.

(c) In acidic solution both N-atoms of azo group are protonated

(d) In basic solution, indicator is ionised to greater extent as compared to in acidic solution

50. The following compound on hydrolysis in aqueous acetone will give

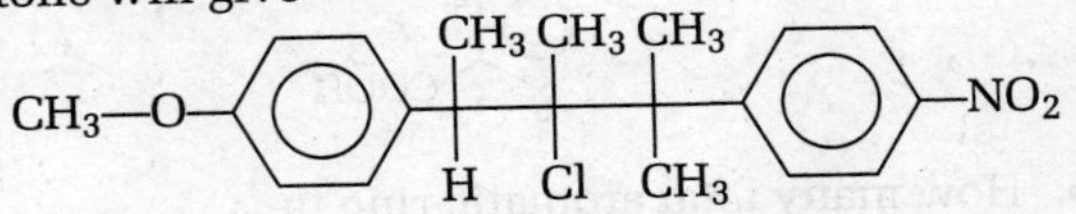

K. 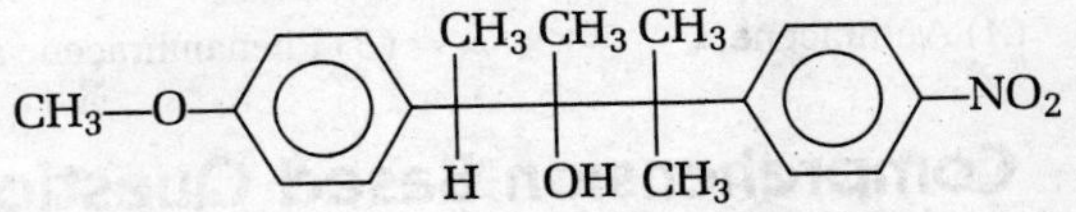

L. 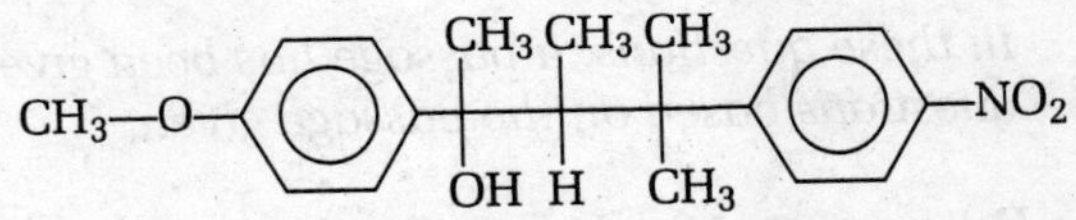

M. 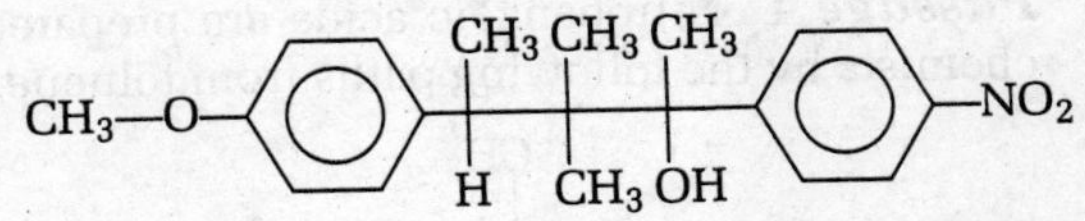

(a) mixture of (*K*) and (*L*) (b) mixture of (*K*) and (*M*)
(c) only (*M*) (d) only (*K*)

Numerical Value Questions

All these questions have a Numerical value as their answer, solve the questions and write your answer.

1. P, Q, R, S and T are the number of π electron in a, b, c, d and e respectively. What is the value of $P+Q+R+S+T$.

(i) Cyclopropenylium ion
(ii) Cyclopentadienide anion
(iii) Cycloheptatrienylium ion
(iv) Cyclooctatetraene dianion

2.

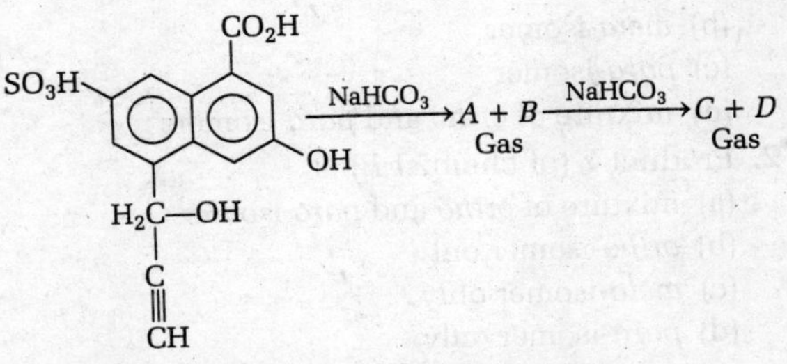

Sum of molecular mass of gas $(A + C)$ is ....

3. The number of resonance structures of N is

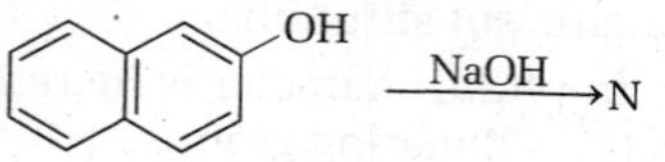

4. In how many reaction electrophilic aromatic substitution results in a major product with substitution in ring *A*.

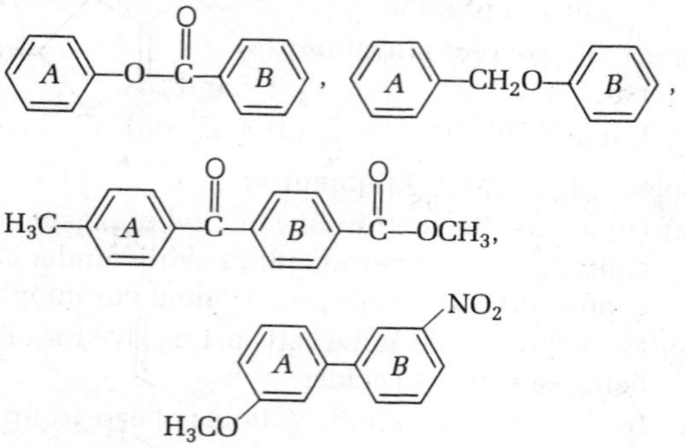

5. Nitration on of the given compound will take place at which of the carbon indicated by the numbers ?

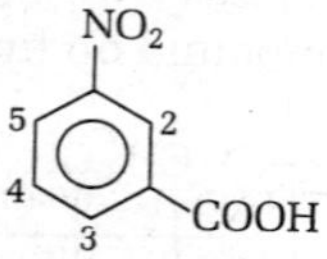

6. How many total aromatic ring in
(*A*) Anthracene (*B*) Phenanthracene and
(*C*) Naphthaline
Calculate the value of $A + B + C$?

7. How many electrons in given aromatic structure ?

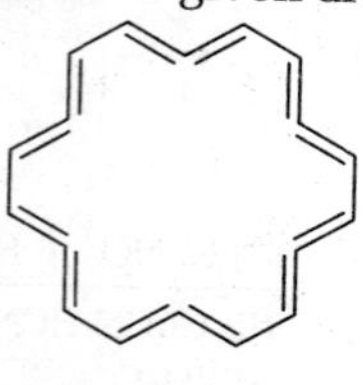

8. How many conjugated *p*-orbitals does the tropylium ion have?

9. The valve of '*n*' for the following molecule according to Huckel's rule is

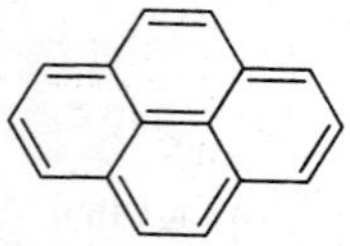

10. The amount (in gram) of NaOH (M. wt. = 40) required for complete neutralisation of one mole of the following compound is ....

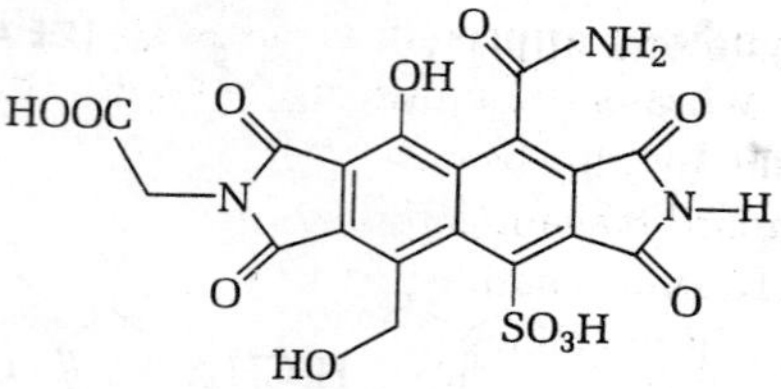

Comprehension Based Questions

In these questions, a passage has been given followed by questions based on it. You have to answer the questions based on the passage given.

Passage 1 Nitrobenzoic acids are prepared by two chemists by the following paths from toluene.

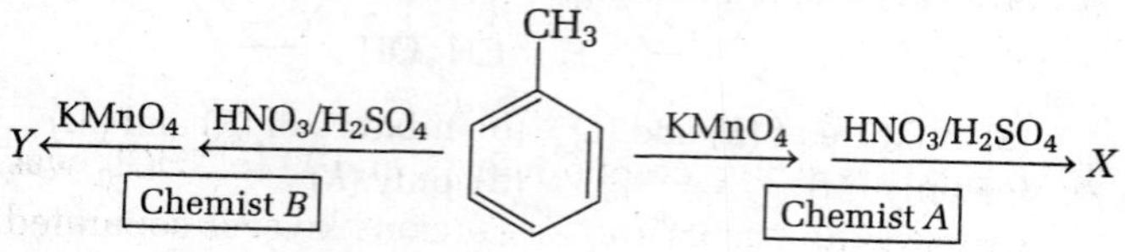

Answer the following questions.

1. Product *X* (of chemist *A*) is
   (a) *ortho*-isomer
   (b) *meta*-isomer
   (c) *para*-isomer
   (d) mixture of *ortho* and *para* isomers

2. Product *Y* (of chemist *B*) is
   (a) mixture of *ortho* and *para* isomer
   (b) *ortho*-isomer only
   (c) *meta*-isomer only
   (d) *para*-isomer only

3. Select the correct statement.
   (a) Yield of *Y* is larger than that of *X*
   (b) Yield of *Y* is smaller than that of *Y*
   (c) Yields of *X* and *Y* are equal
   (d) Nothing can be predicted

Passage 2 *Dr. John directed his graduate students to synthesise m-nitrobenzoic acid from nitrobenzene.*

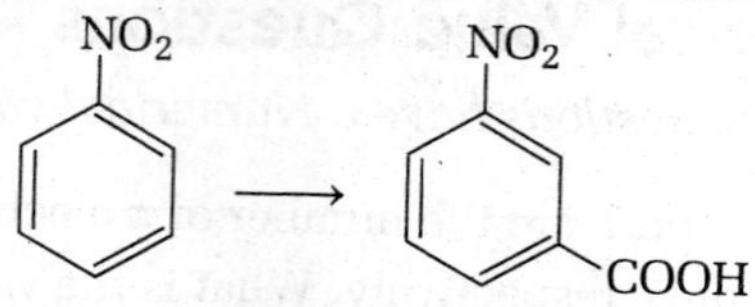

Each student had the idea of orientation but not all the reactions. They put first theoretical concept before their teacher.

Graduate student *A* He is proud of giving two-step synthesis

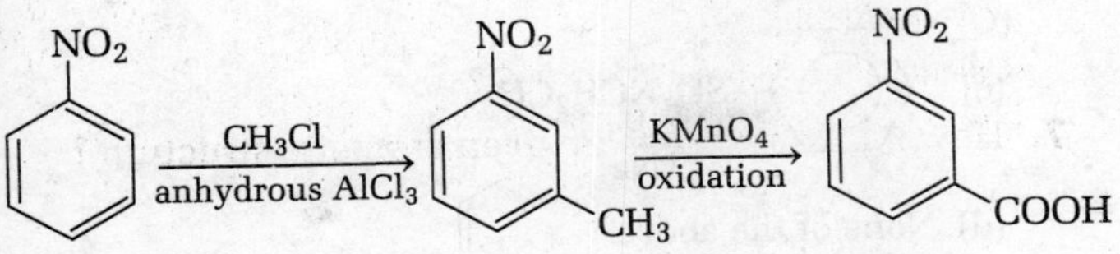

Graduate student B

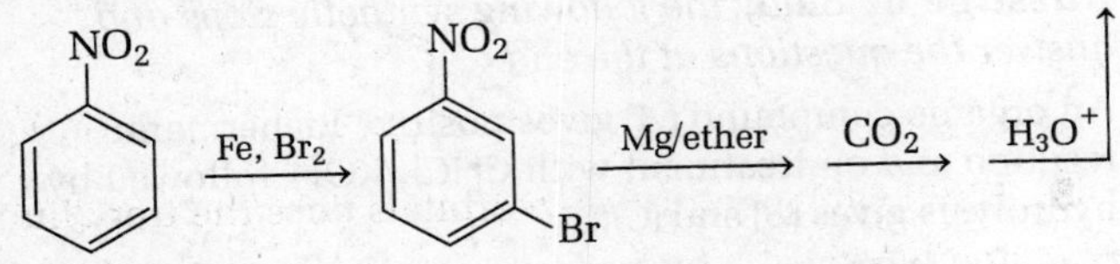

Graduate student C

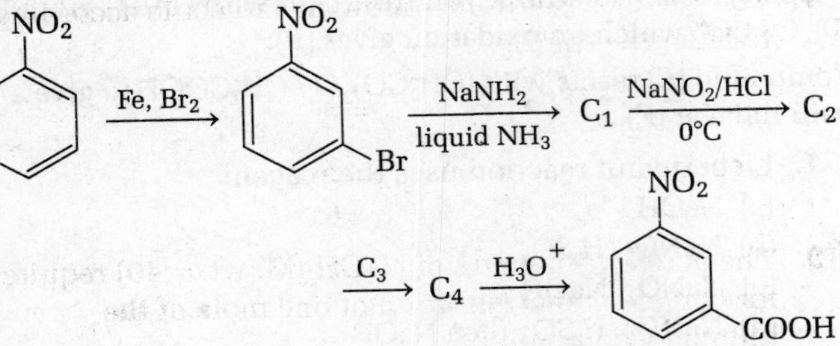

1. If the synthetic approach of the student B would be correct, what is the name of the reaction/reagent?
(a) Acidic hydrolysis
(b) Grignard reagent/carbonation
(c) Sandmeyer reaction
(d) None of the above

2. C_2 is converted to C_4 by a graduate student C, using C_3 which is .... by reaction.
(a) NaCN–Gattermann reaction
(b) CuCN/HCN – Gattermann reaction
(c) CuCN/HCN–Sandmeyer reaction
(d) $CH_3CN/AlCl_3$ – Friedel-Crafts' reaction

3. It happened that during the synthesis, C got the original compound from C_2. It was due to
(a) heating of C_2
(b) hydrolysis of C_2
(c) oxidation of C_2
(d) reaction of H_3PO_2 with C_2

Passage **3** In the following reactions sequence, the compound J is an intermediate.

$$I \xrightarrow[CH_3COONa]{(CH_3CO)_2O} J \xrightarrow[\text{(ii) } SOCl_2 \text{, (iii) anhyd. } AlCl_3]{\text{(i) } H_2,\ Pd/C} K$$

J $(C_9H_8O_2)$ gives effervescence on treatment with $NaHCO_3$ and positive Baeyer's test. **[IIT JEE 2012]**

1. The compound K, is

(a) 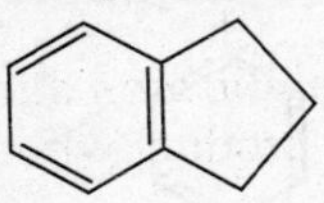
(b) 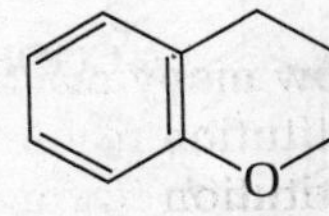
(c) 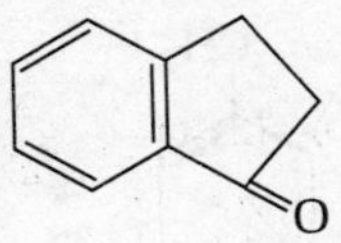
(d) 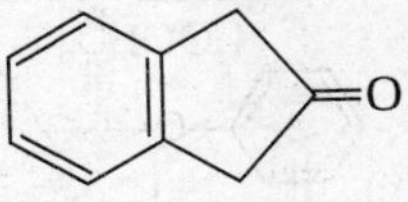

2. The compound I, is

(a) 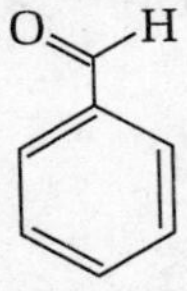
(b) 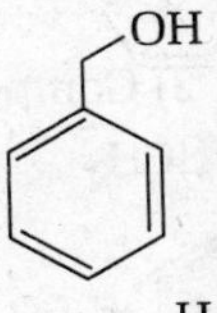
(c) 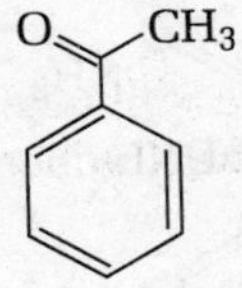
(d) 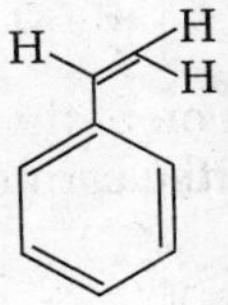

Passage **4** Mixture of organic compounds can be separated into individual components based on the solubility in different reagents, for example an acidic compound can be extracted into NaOH solution and a basic compound into HCl solution. Mixtures have been formed from the following compounds.

A. Naphthalene — *B*. *p*-dichlorobenzene
C. Aniline — *D*. Phenol
E. Benzoic acid — *F*. Methanol
G. 1-aminopropane — *H*. 2-propanol

Answer the questions based on the above compounds.

1. HCl can be used to separate mixture of
(a) A, B (b) C, D
(c) C, G (d) G, H

2. A mixture of two compounds (X and Y) in $CHCl_3$ was treated with NaOH and an aqueous layer is separated. $CHCl_3$ layer containing (Y) on heating with KOH gives unpleasant smell of $Z(C_8H_7N)$.
Compound in $CHCl_3$ layer is oxidised to the other components (Y) which on heating with sodalime forms hydrocarbon (W). Compound in NaOH layer on acidification followed by reaction with neutral

$FeCl_3$ gives buff-coloured precipitate. *X* is a good food-preserver. Thus, the compound (*X*) is

(a) 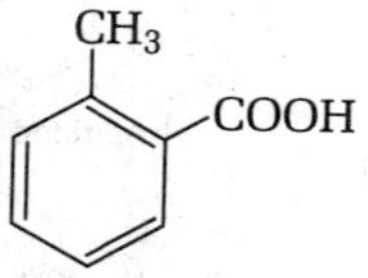

(b) 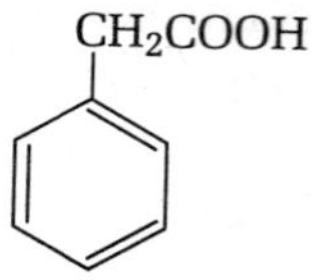

(c) 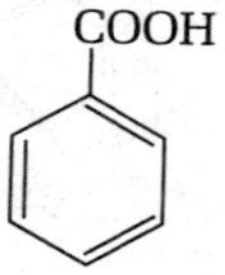

(d) 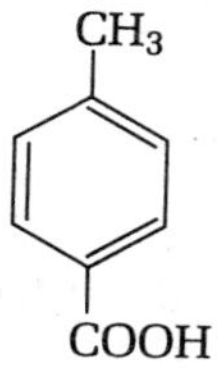

3. (Refer Q. 2) Compound *Y* is

(a) 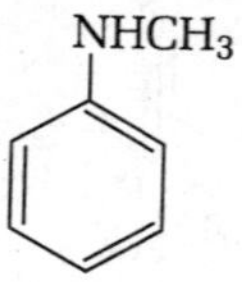

(b) 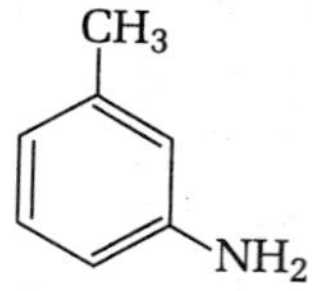

(c) 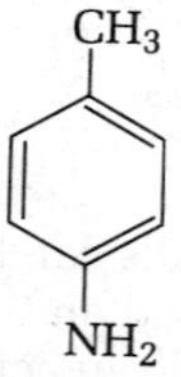

(d) 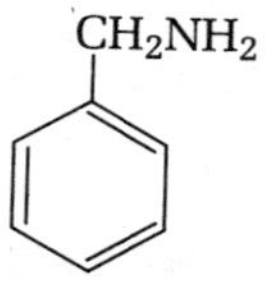

***Passage* 5** *Based on the following analysis scheme, answer the questions given.*

Mixture of two isomeric amines (C_2H_7N) *A* and *B* was treated with benzene sulphonyl chloride and NaOH and ether were added. Two layers were separated. Ethereal layer containing *A* on acidification followed by distillation generates *A*. Aqueous layer containing (*B*) followed by acidification and distillation generates (*B*).

1. Compound in ethereal layer is in the form

(a) 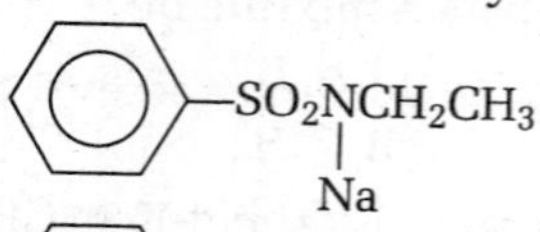

(b) 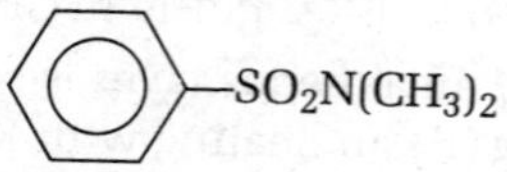

(c) Both (a) and (b)
(d) None of the above

2. Compound (*A*) is thus
(a) $(CH_3)_2NH$ (b) $CH_3CH_2NH_2$
(c) Both (a) and (b) (d) None of these

3. Compound in aqueous layer is in the form of

(a) 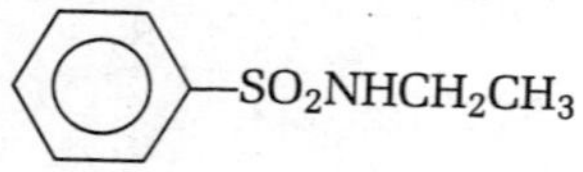

(b) 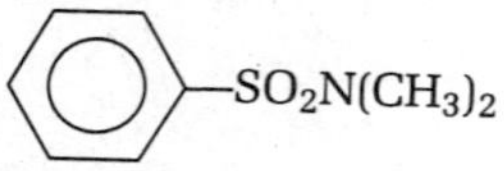

(c) 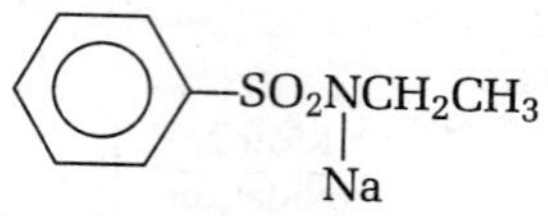

(d) None of the above

***Passage* 6** *Study the following synthetic steps and answer the questions at the end.*

An organic compound (*A*) gives positive Liebermann reaction and on treatment with $CHCl_3/KOH$ followed by hydrolysis gives (*B*) and (*C*).

Compound (*B*) gives colour with Schiff's reagent but not (*C*), which is steam volatile. (*C*) on treatment with $LiAlH_4$ gives (*D*), $C_7H_8O_2$ which on oxidation gives (*E*).

Compound (*E*) reacts with $(CH_3CO)_2O$ / CH_3COOH to give a pain reliever (*F*).

1. Liebermann reaction uses the reagent
(a) NaOH
(b) $NaNO_2/H_2SO_4$
(c) $NaNO_2/NaOH$
(d) $NaNO_2/H_2SO_4$ then NaOH

2. *B* and *C* are isomeric but *C* does not give colour with Schiff's reagent. It is due to the fact that
(a) *B* contains aldehyde group and *C* contains keto group in addition to phenolic group
(b) *B* contains keto group and *C* contains aldehyde group in addition to phenolic group
(c) carbonyl reactivity in *C* is masked by intramolecular H-bonding
(d) carbonyl group is lost in hydrolysis step

3. Compound *D*, *E* and *F* are respectively

D *E* *F*

(a) 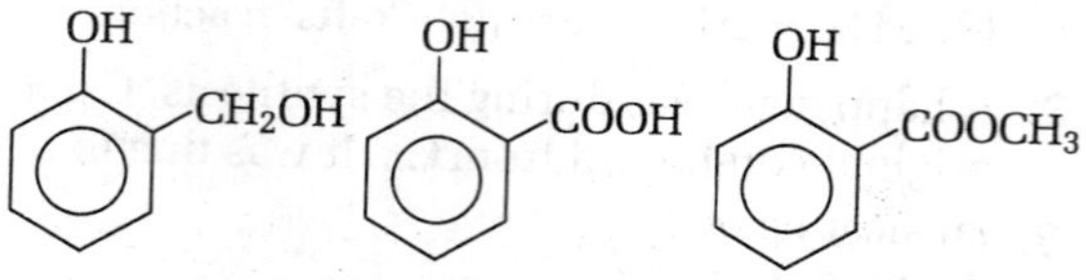

(b) 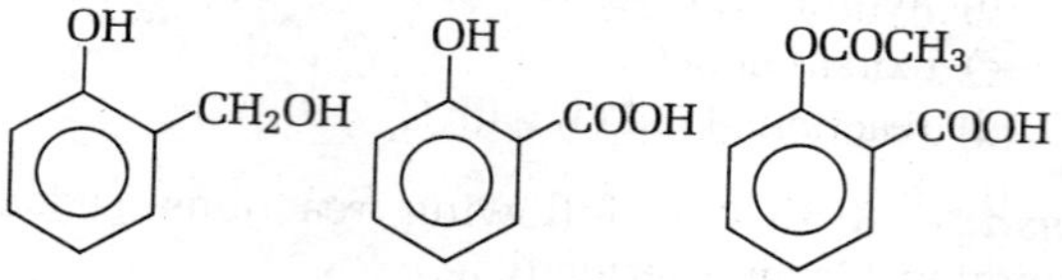

(c) 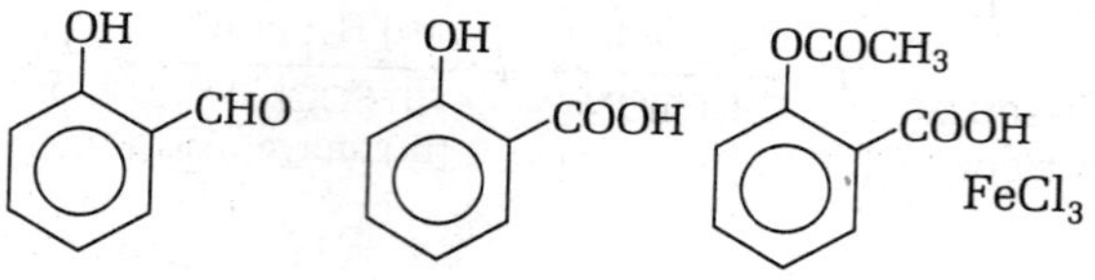

(d) 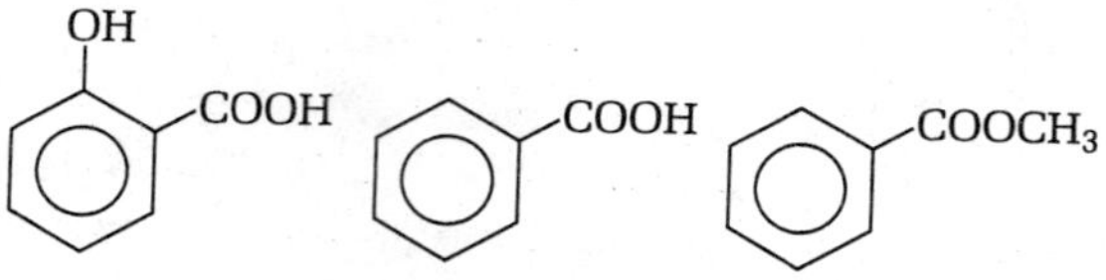

***Passage* 7** The following sequence of reactions is used to prepare two important compounds *A* and *B*.

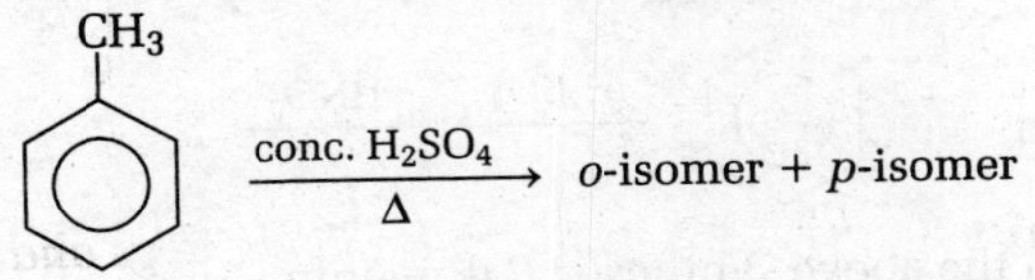

o-isomer $\xrightarrow{PCl_5}$ $\xrightarrow{NH_3}$ $\xrightarrow[35°C]{Aq.\ KMnO_4}$ $\xrightarrow{\Delta}$ A

p-isomer $\xrightarrow{PCl_5}$ $\xrightarrow{NH_3}$ $\xrightarrow[NaOCl]{Cl—OH}$ B

Based on above synthesis, answer the following questions.

1. Structure of *A* is

(a) 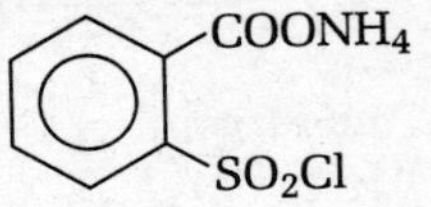

(b) 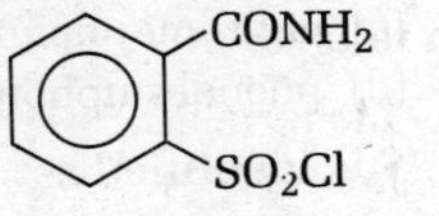

(c) 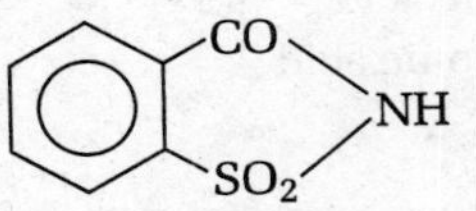

(d) 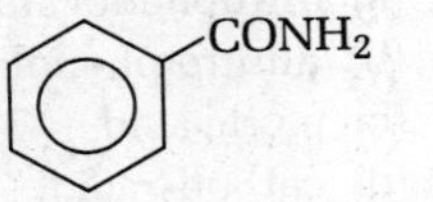

2. Structure of *B* is

(a) 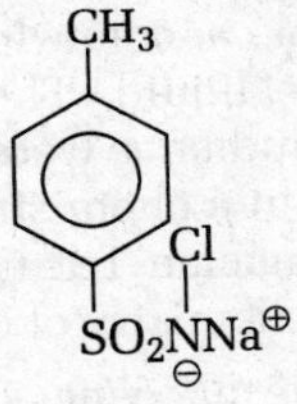

(b) 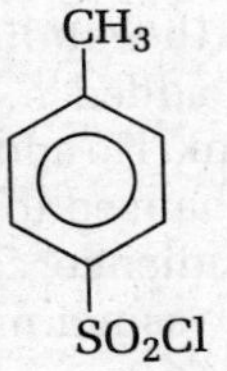

(c) 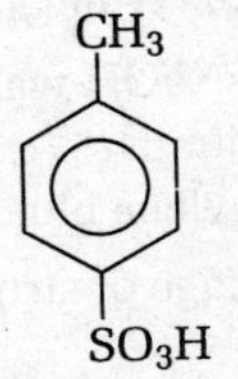

(d) 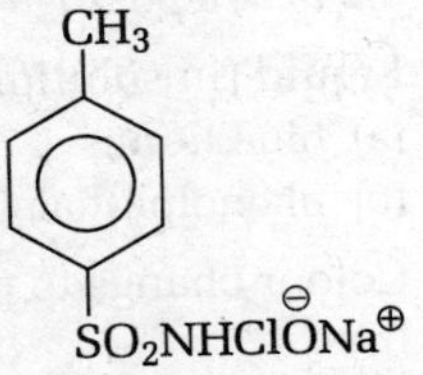

3. Compound *B* is found to have an antiseptic properties (a sulpha-drug). This property is due to the formation of

(a) benzene sulphonamide
(b) hypochlorous acid
(c) hydrochloric acid
(d) benzene sulphonic acid

***Passage* 8** In S_E (electrophilic substitution), arenium ion (a σ complex) is formed in a rate-determining step.

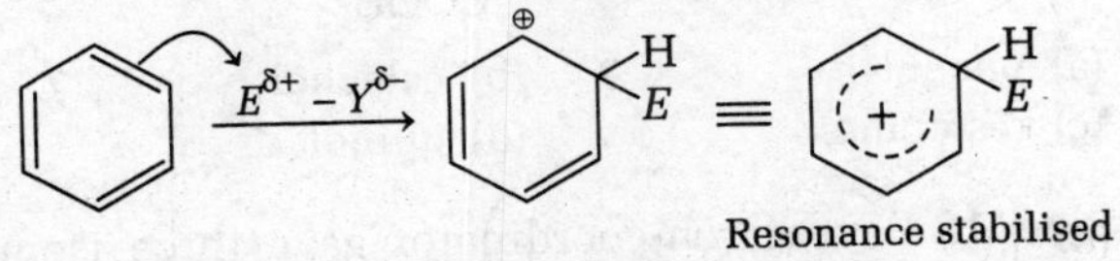

Free energy change associated with addition product and electrophilic substitution has been given in the diagram. *Answer the questions based on this.*

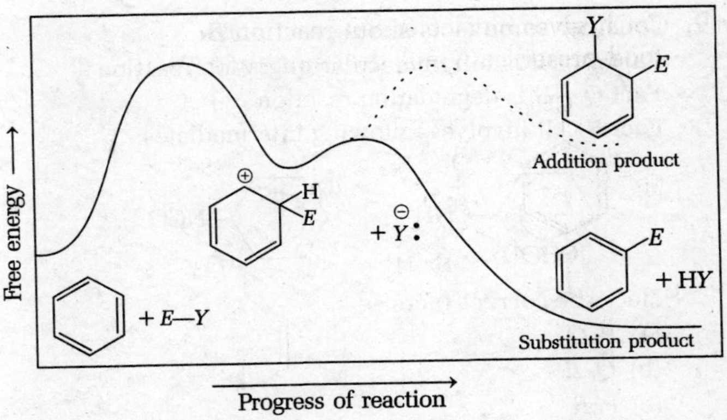

1. Which is not the resonance structure of σ-complex?

(a) 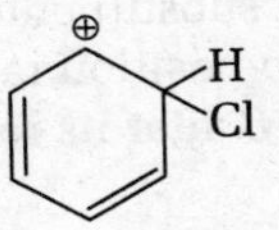

(b) 

(c) 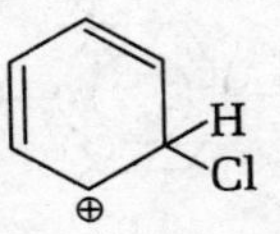

(d) 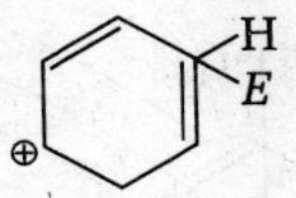

2. Which step is not favourable?

(a) 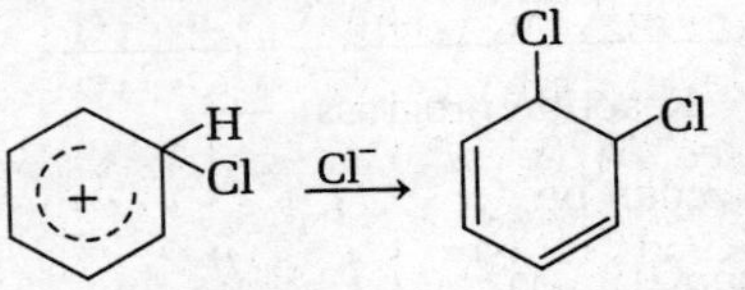

(b) 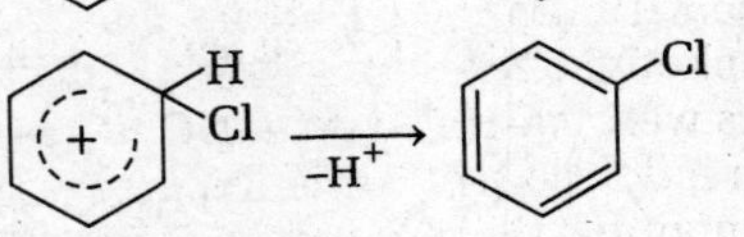

(c) Both (a) and (b)
(d) None of the above

***Passage* 9** Benzoic acid can be converted into aniline by different reagents.

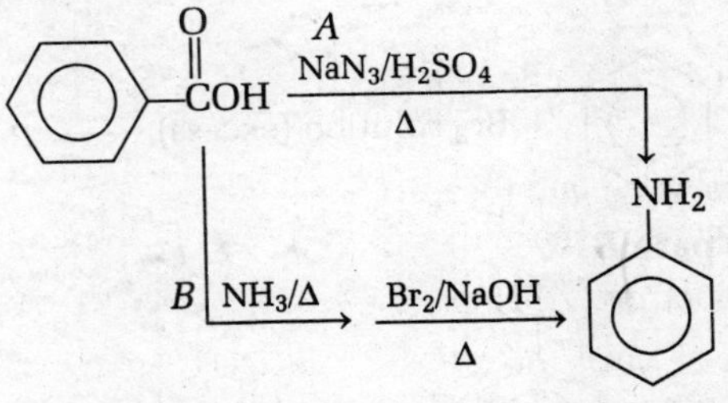

Following questions are based on the above reactions.

1. These reactions are called

	A	*B*
(a)	Hofmann	Schmidt
(b)	Schmidt	Hofmann
(c)	HVZ	Hofmann
(d)	Hofmann	HVZ

2. Consider some facts about reaction *B*

Fact *P*. It is intramolecular migration reaction

Fact *Q*. It is degradation reaction

Fact *R* It involves following intermediates

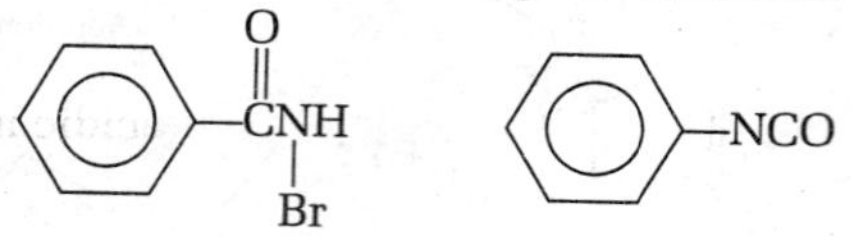

Select the correct facts.

(a) *P*, *Q*
(b) *Q*, *R*
(c) *P*, *R*
(d) *P*, *Q*, *R*

3. In presence of electron releasing substituents attached to benzene nucleus in *p*-position rate of reaction is increased in reaction *B* after its reaction with NH_3 as shown

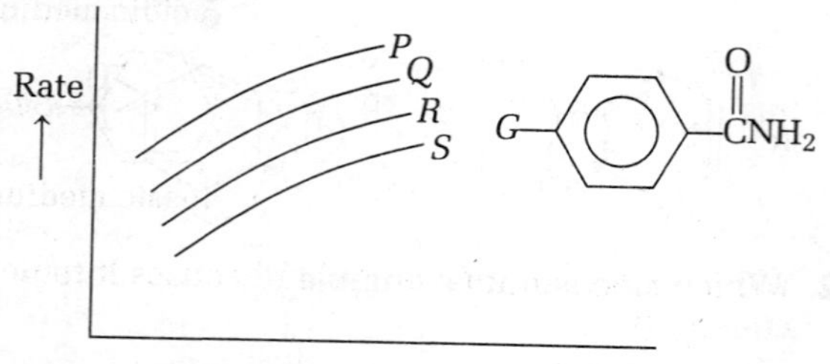

P, *Q*, *R* and *S* can be

	P	*Q*	*R*	*S*
(a)	$—NO_2$	—H	—Cl	$—NH_2$
(b)	$—OCH_3$	—H	$—NO_2$	—Cl
(c)	$—OCH_3$	—Cl	—H	$—NO_2$
(d)	$—OCH_3$	—H	—Cl	$—NO_2$

***Passage* 10** Mr Peter synthesised various compounds from phenol

Synthesis path *A*

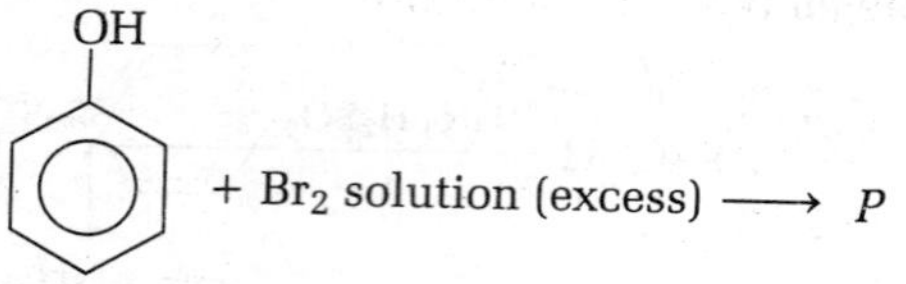

Synthesis path *B*

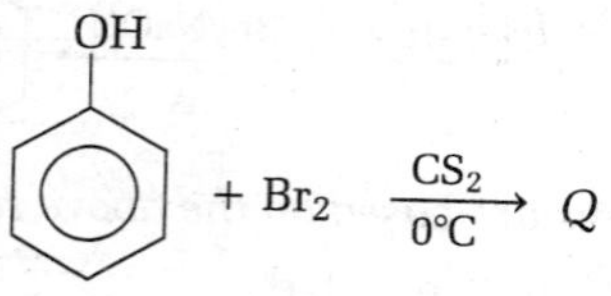

Synthesis path *C*

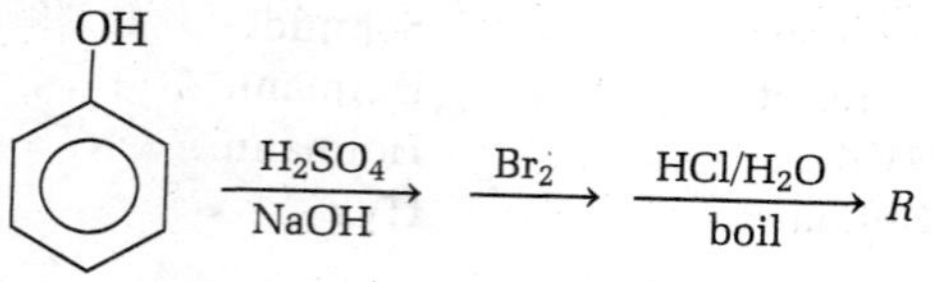

Synthesis path *D*

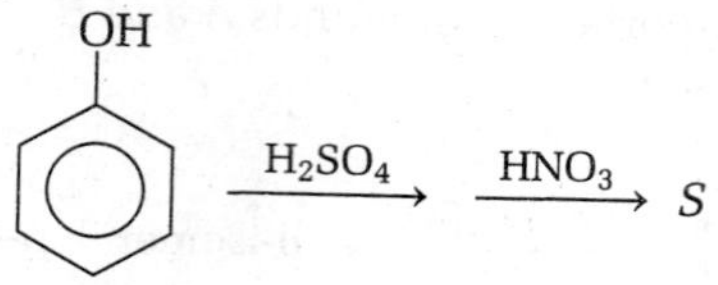

1. In the above synthesis, *P* is mainly
(a) mixture of *o*- and *p*-bromophenol
(b) 2,4,6-tribromophenol
(c) hypobromophenol
(d) *m*-bromophenol

2. *R* is identified as
(a) *o*-bromophenol
(b) *p*-bromophenol
(c) *m*-bromophenol
(d) phenol sulphonic acid

3. *S* is identified as
(a) nitrophenol sulphonic acid
(b) dinitro phenol sulphonic acid
(c) picric acid
(d) carbolic acid

***Passage* 11** A magician was giving a live colour-change show before the audience. He took a colourless NaOH solution and added a drop of some liquid. The solution changed to pink. He added water (as audience were told) and pink colour changed to colourless. But a chemistry student among the audience caught the magician red-handed by telling that it was not magic but the chemistry of colour.

Read the above passage and answer the following questions.

1. Liquid (in solution form) added to NaOH was that of
(a) blue litmus (b) red litmus
(c) phenolphthalein (d) methylene blue

2. Colour change to pink is due to change of structure from
(a) benzenoid to quinonoid
(b) quinonoid to benzenoid
(c) aromatic to aliphatic
(d) aliphatic to aromatic

3. Substance imparting pink colour in NaOH can be prepared by heating *A* (below) with conc. H_2SO_4 along with

(*A*)

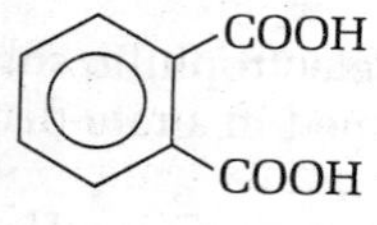

(a) phenol (b) catechol
(c) resorcinol (d) quinol

***Passage* 12** A research-coordinator gave three isomeric compounds to her three scholars *X*, *Y* and *Z* for their proper identification.

Molecular formula : $C_8H_{11}N$

Results of each are summarised as

Reaction	X	Y	Z
• $NaNO_2$ + HCl	$C_8H_{10}O$ (X_1)	$C_8H_{10}O$ (Y_1)	$C_8H_9N_2Cl$ (Z_1)
• $KMnO_4$	$C_7H_6O_2$	$C_8H_6O_2$	Ring is cleaved
• Iodoform test	X_1 gives iodoform test	No	No
• Coupling reaction	No	No	Yes
• Orientation	Singly substituted	Disubstituted S_E reaction slow	Disubstituted, S_E reaction fast

Questions given below are based on the above analysis.

1. Compound X is

(a) 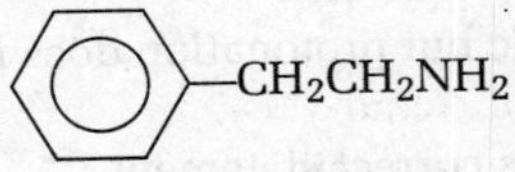 (b) 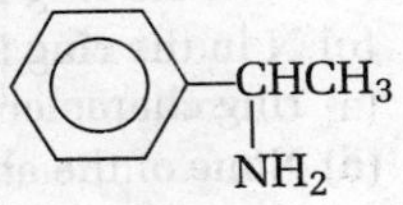

(c) Both (a) and (b)

(d) None of the above

2. Compound Y is

(a) 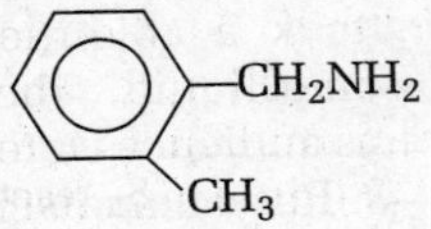 (b) 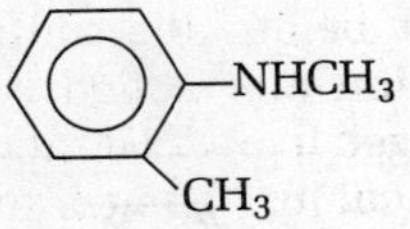

(c) 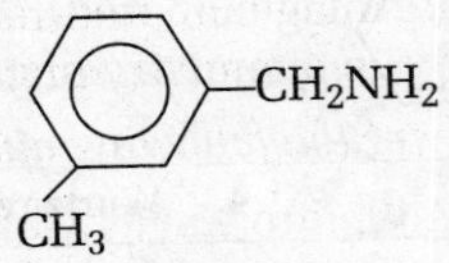 (d) 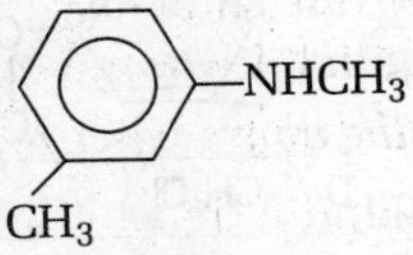

3. Compound Z is

(a) 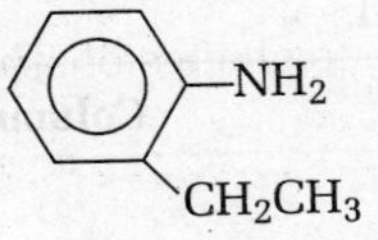 (b) 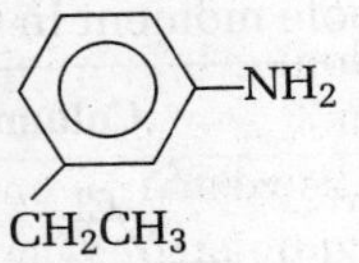

(c) 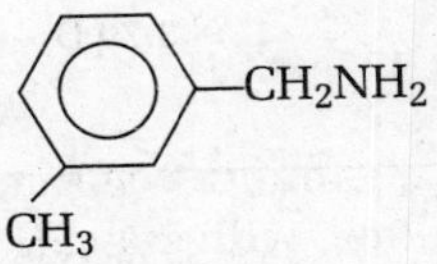 (d) 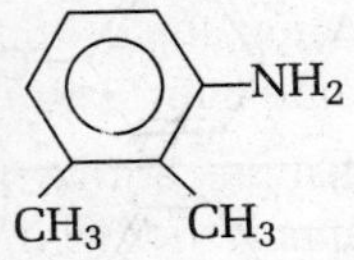

Passage 13 A textile designer was experimenting with different dyes. He found a substance that had a yellow colour he liked but the compound turned red in acid. Household ammonia restored the original yellow. The structure of the compound was confirmed as

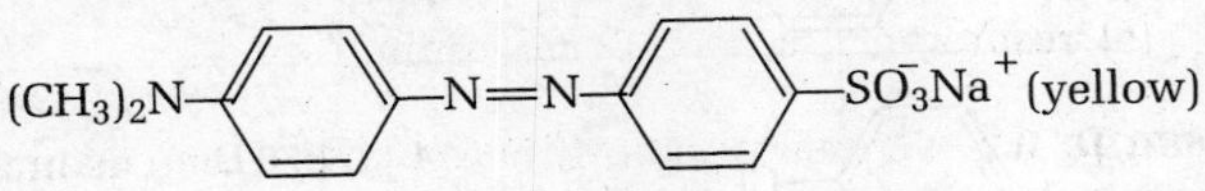

Answer the questions based on it.

1. Above dye can be synthesised from

(a) 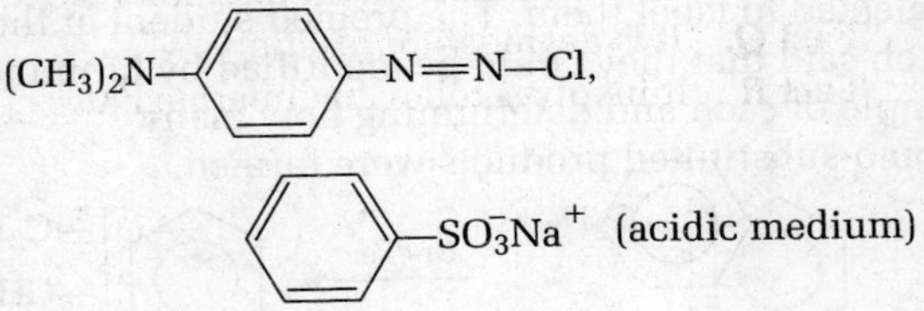

(b) 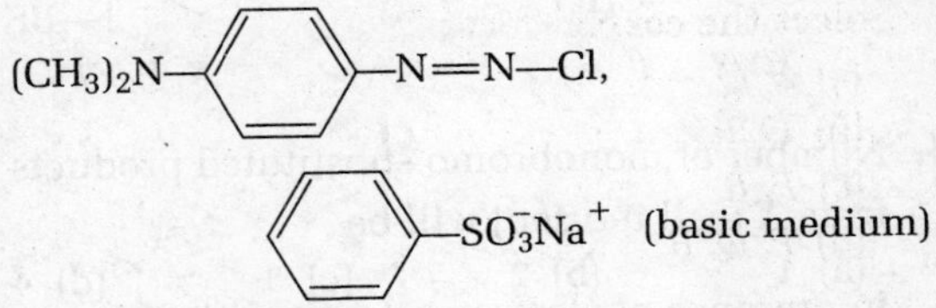

(c) 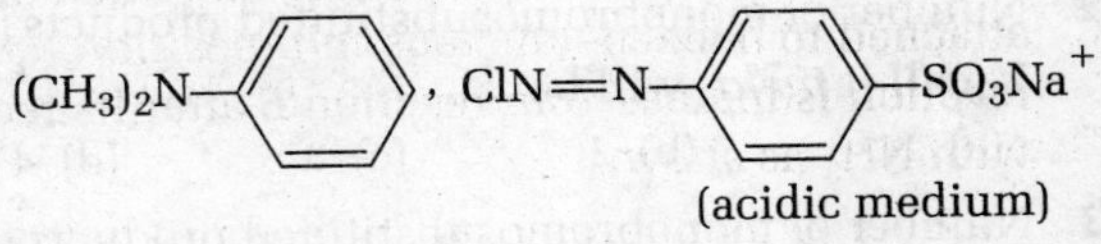

(d) 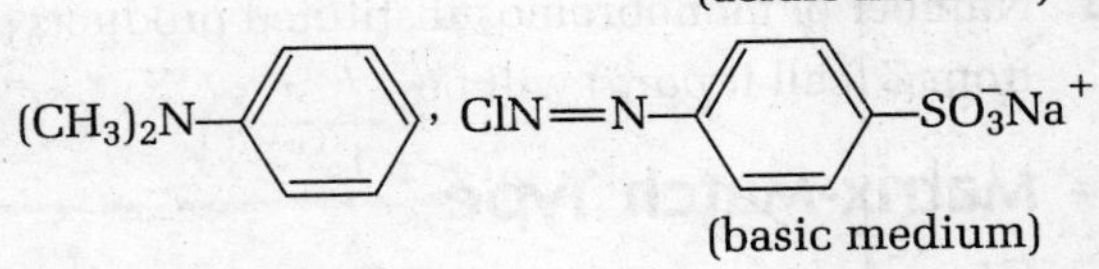

2. What feature of this compound causes it to be coloured?

(a) 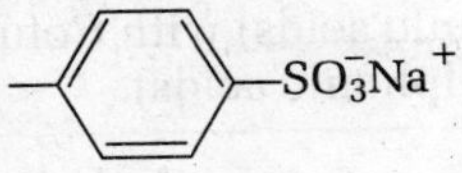

(b) 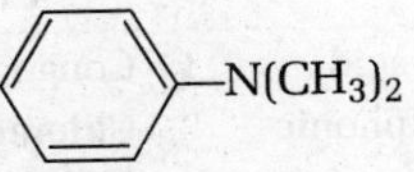

(c) diazo in conjugation with two aromatic rings

(d) 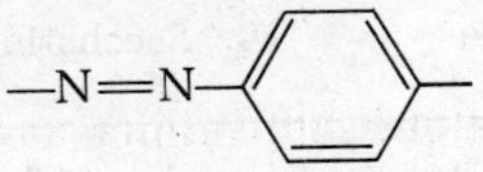

3. What is the structure of the compound when it is dissolved in acidic solution?

(a) 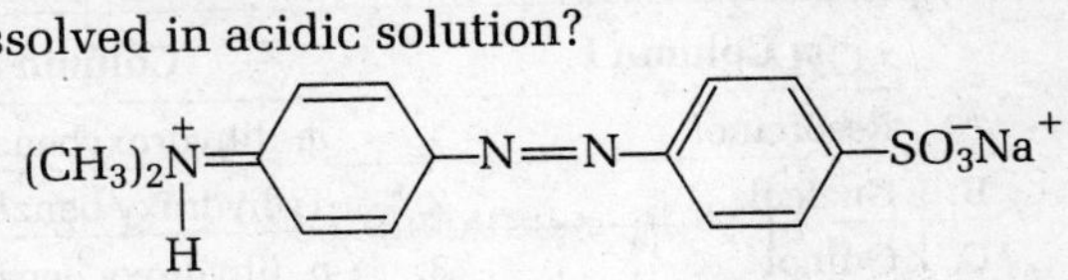

(b) 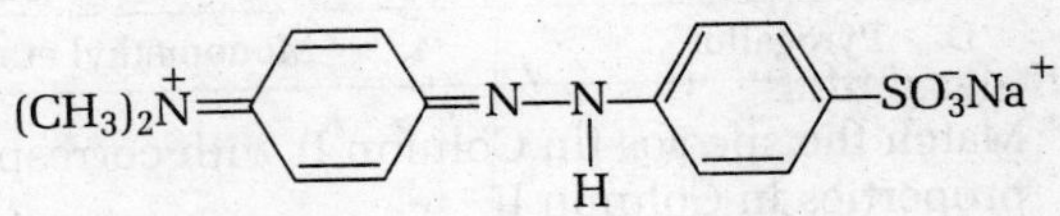

(c) 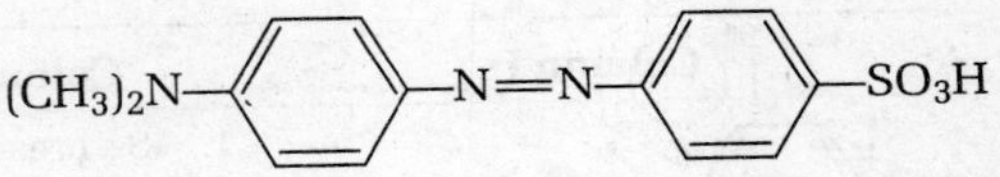

(d) 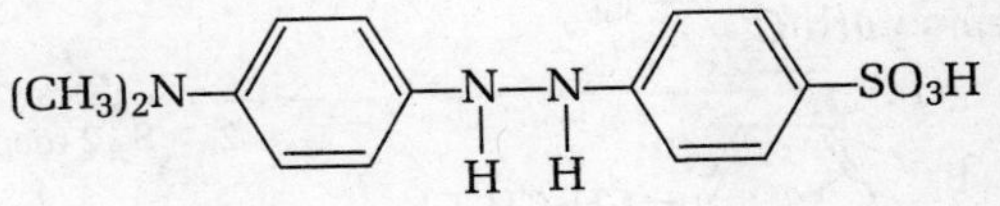

***Passage* 14** A student had prepared three ethyl-substituted benzaldehydes, *X*, *Y* and *Z*, but had neglected to label them. The premed student at the next batch said that they could be identified by brominating a sample of each and determining how many bromo-substituted products were formed.

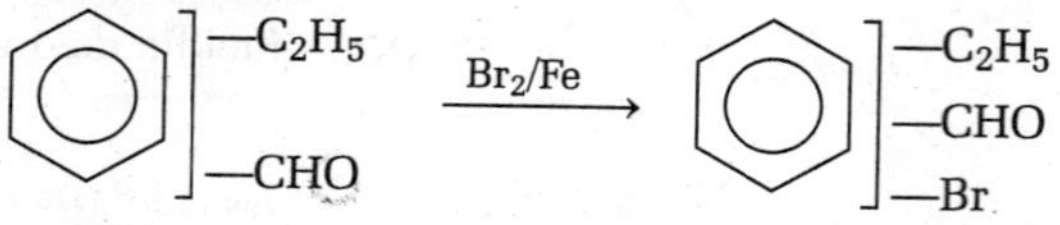

$X/Y/Z$ $\quad$ $X_1/Y_1/Z_1$

1. Number of monobromo substituted products (X_1) from X (call it *ortho*) will be
   (a) 1 (b) 2 (c) 3 (d) 4
2. Number of monobromosubstituted products (Y_1) from Y (call it *meta*) will be
   (a) 1 (b) 2 (c) 3 (d) 4
3. Number of monobromosubstituted products (Z_1) from Z (call it *para*) will be
   (a) 1 (b) 2 (c) 3 (d) 4

***Passage* 15** *Following compound has been synthesised recently*

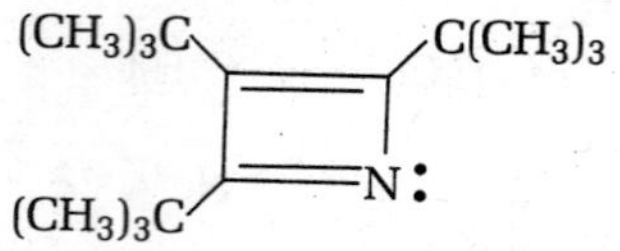

Answer the questions based on this structure.

1. This compound is
   (a) aromatic (b) antiaromatic
   (c) non-aromatic (d) simple alicyclic
2. Select the correct statement(s).
   (a) N in the ring is basic and ring is cleaved due to protonation
   (b) N in the ring is not protonated
   (c) N in the ring is basic but protonation does not affect ring character
   (d) None of the above is correct statement

Matrix-Match Type

Given below are Matching Type Questions, with two columns (each having some items) each . Each item of Column I has to be matched with the items of Column II.

1. Match Column I (sulphonic acids) with Column II (product formed from sulphonic acids).

	Column I		Column II
A.	*p*-toluene sulphonic acid	1.	Congo red dye
B.	*p*-amino benzene sulphonic acid	2.	Chloramine-T indicator
C.	*o*-toluene sulphonic acid	3.	Phenanacetin
D.	4-amino naphthalene sulphonic acid	4.	Saccharin

2. Match Column I (hydroxy compounds) with Column II (their names).

	Column I		Column II
A.	Resorcinol	1.	*m*-dihydroxybenzene
B.	Guaicol	2.	Trihydroxy benzene
C.	Quinol	3.	*p*-dihydroxy benzene
D.	Pyrogallol	4.	Monomethyl ether

3. Match the species (in Column I) with corresponding properties in Column II.

	Column I		Column II
A.	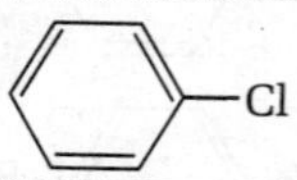	1.	S_N1 reaction
B.	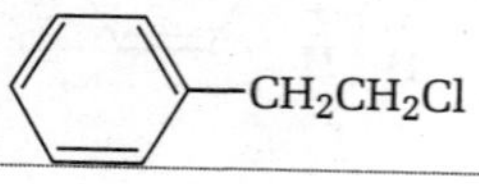	2.	S_N2 reaction
C.	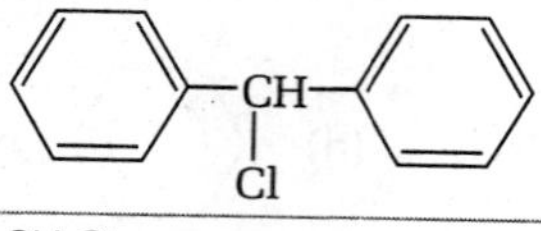	3.	S_E reaction
D.	CH_3Cl	4.	Wurtz reaction

4. Match the species in Column I with corresponding dipole moment in Column II.

	Column I		Column II
A.	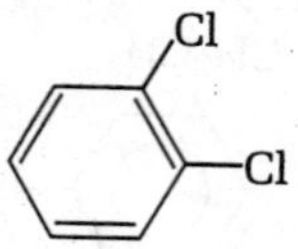	1.	3.79 D
B.	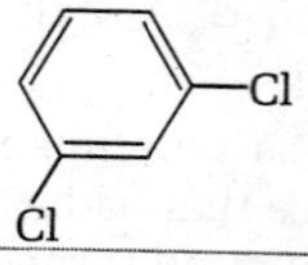	2.	6.00 D
C.		3.	0.00 D
D.	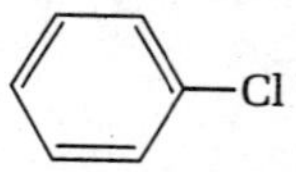	4.	1.76 D

5. Match the given reaction in Column I with the name of the reaction in Column II.

	Column I	Column II
A.	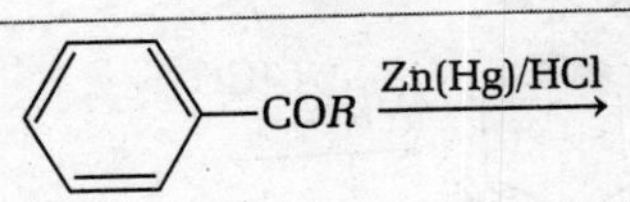	1. Gattermann aldehyde synthesis
B.	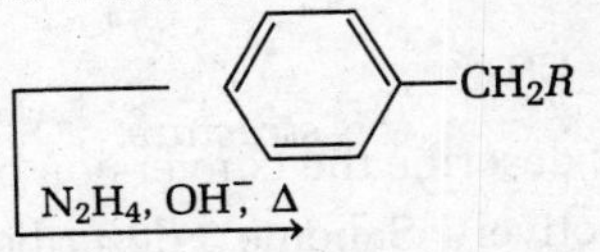	2. Gattermann-Koch reaction
C.	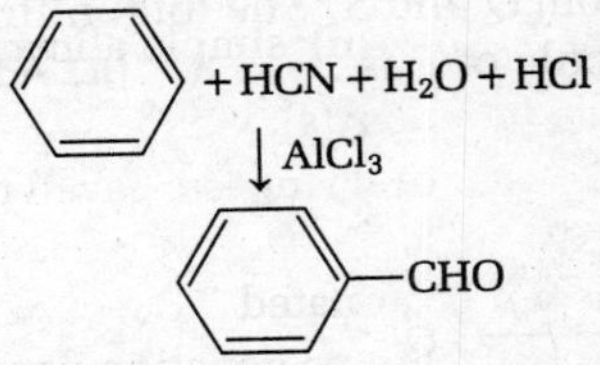	3. Clemmensen reduction
D.	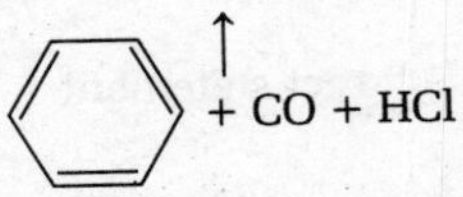	4. Wolff-Kishner reduction

6. Match the contents in Column I with the source of these contents in Column II.

	Column I	Column II
A.	BTX	1. Green oil
B.	Phenol	2. Heavy oil
C.	Cresols	3. Middle oil
D.	Anthracene	4. Light oil

7. 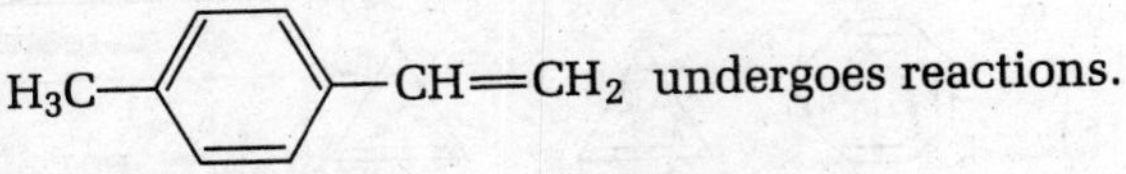 undergoes reactions.

Match the reactant in Column I with the product formed in Column II.

	Column I	Column II
A.	NBS	1. 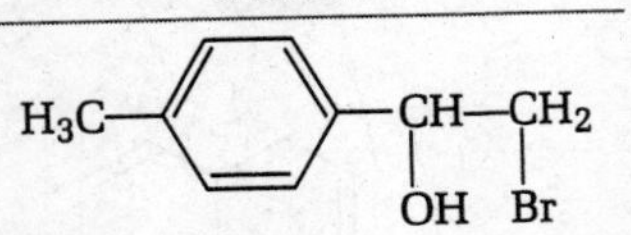
B.	Fe/Br_2	2. 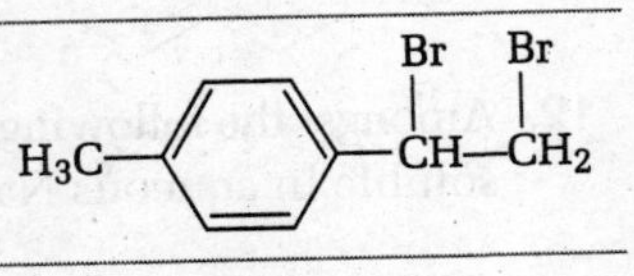
C.	Br_2 water	3. 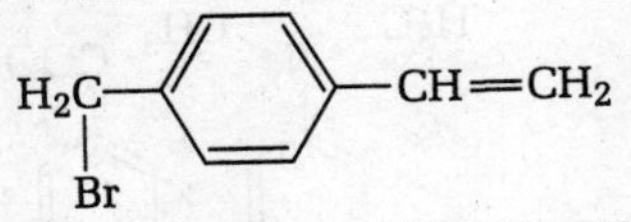
D.	$(Br_2 + H_2O)$	4. 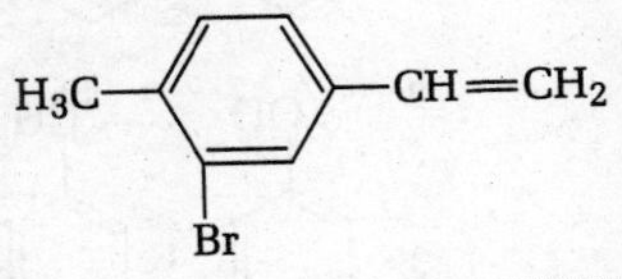

8. Match the species (in Column I) with corresponding properties (in Column II).

	Column I	Column II
A.	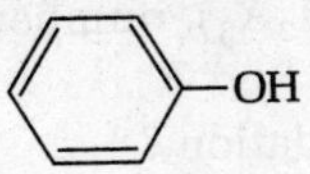	1. Neutral compound
B.	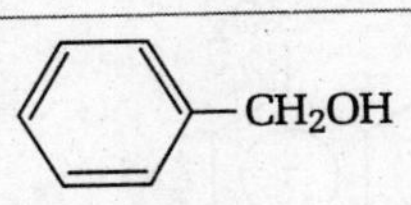	2. Gives iodoform test
C.	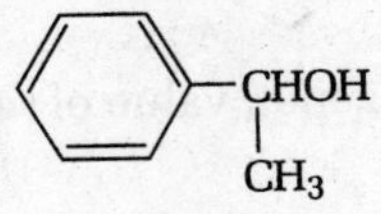	3. Gives violet colour with $FeCl_3$
D.	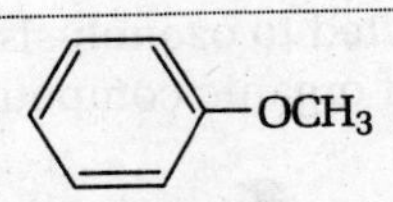	4. Oxidises to aldehyde by mild oxidant

9. Match the mixtures (in Column I) with the suitable reagents (in Column II) to make distinction.

	Column I	Column II
A.	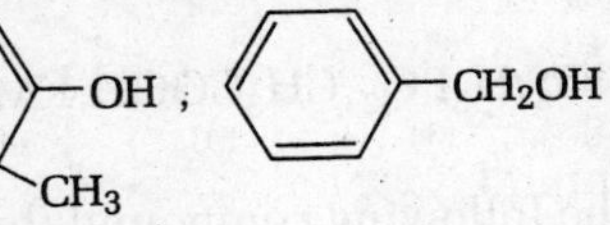	1. Volatile nature/ boiling points
B.	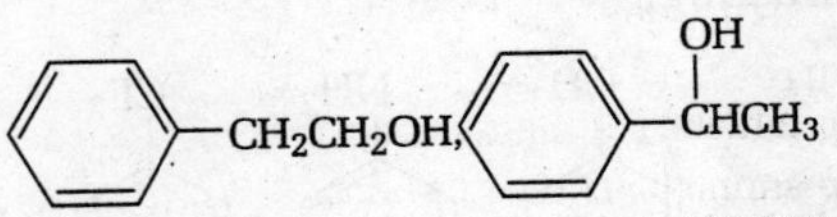	2. Neutral $FeCl_3$
C.	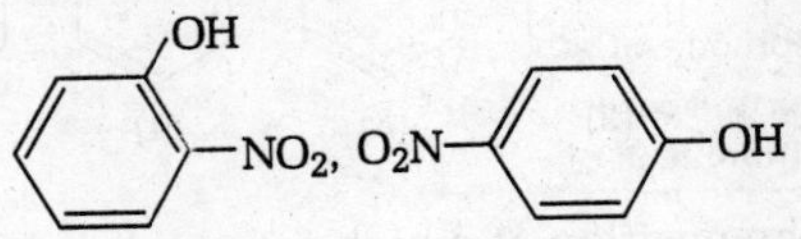	3. Iodoform test
D.	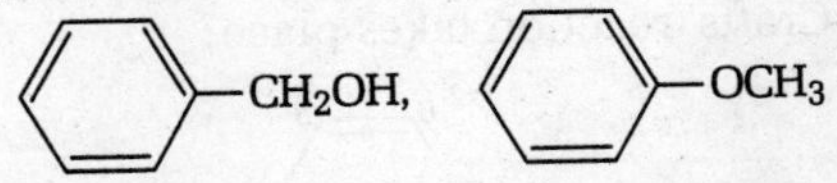	4. Oxidation by $KMnO_4$

10. Match the reacting species with phenol (in Column I) with the name of reaction (in Column II).

	Column I	Column II
A.	Phenol + $CHCl_3$ + KOH $\longrightarrow$	1. Friedel-Crafts reaction
B.	Phenol + NaOH + CO_2 $\longrightarrow$	2. Phthalein test
C.	Phenol + phthalic anhydride $\xrightarrow{\text{Conc. } H_2SO_4}$	3. Kolbe's reaction
D.	Phenol + NaOH $\xrightarrow{CH_3Cl/AlCl_3}$	4. Reimer-Tiemann reaction

Single Integer Answer Questions

Answer of these questions is a single digit lying between 0 to 9.

1. When *meta*-disubstituted benzene A $(C_6H_4X_2)$ is further converted into B $(C_6H_3X_3)$, number of isomers of B formed is ………

2. Which ring is affected in oxidation ?

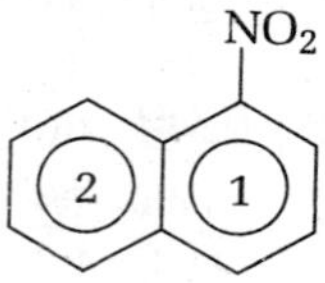

3. In borazole (inorganic benzene), value of $(4n+2)$ by Huckel rule is ………

4. 4.48 g of benzene is subjected to ozonolysis in presence of Zn. Amount of organic compound formed is ………

5. Which compound (at SN) is required to bring about following change?

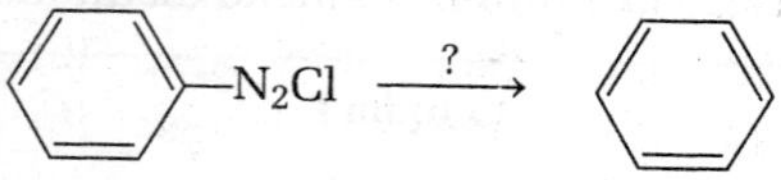

$\underset{(1)}{H_3PO_4}, \underset{(2)}{H_3PO_3}, \underset{(3)}{H_3PO_2}, \underset{(4)}{CH_3COOH}, \underset{(5)}{KMnO_4}, \underset{(6)}{Zn/HCl}$

6. Which of the following compound (by number) is *meta*-directing?

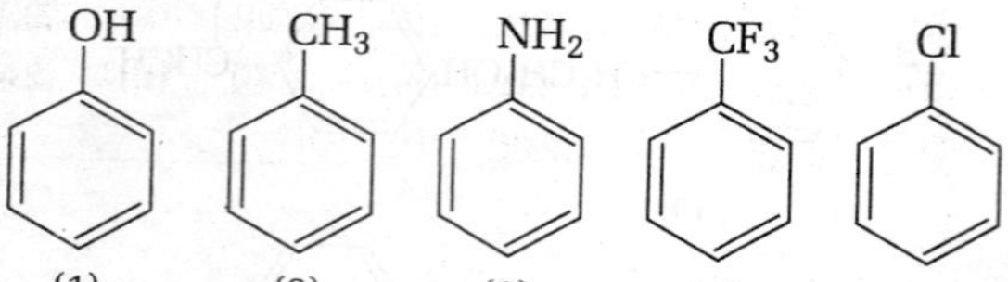

(1) (2) (3) (4) (5)

7. What is the position at which intramolecular Friedel-Crafts' reaction takes place?

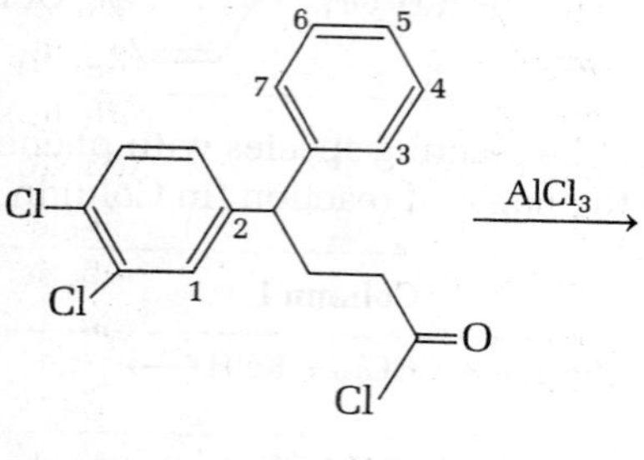

8. Which of the following are activating and electron donating groups?

$-NH_2, NHR, -NR_2, -OH, -OR, -F, -CHO,$
$-COOH, -CN, -NO_2, \overset{\oplus}{N}H_3, CF_3$

9. The position of the $-NO_2$ group in the following is ……

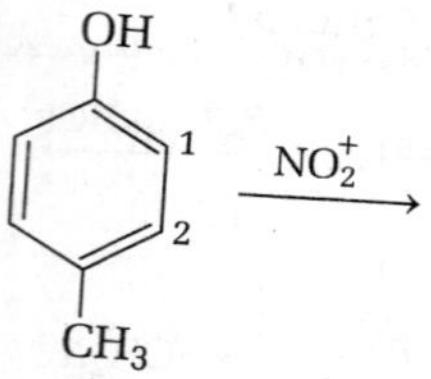

10. Schemes 1 and 2 describe the conversion of P to Q and R to S, respectively. Scheme 3 describes the synthesis of T from Q and S. The total number of Br atoms in a molecule of T is ……. **[JEE Advanced 2019]**

Scheme 1

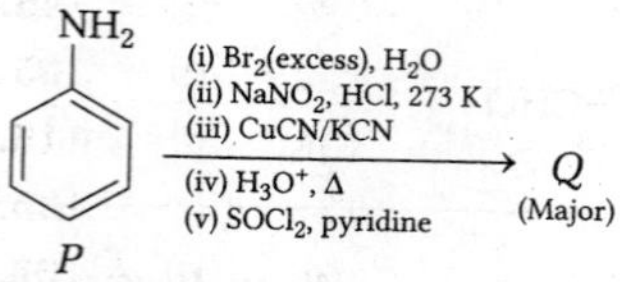

Scheme 2

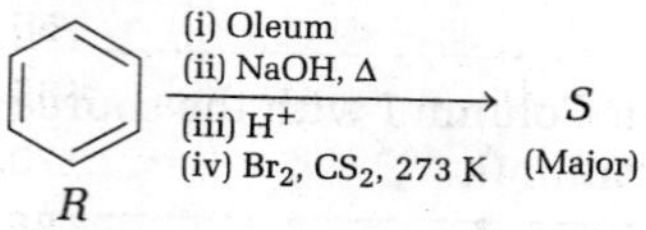

Scheme 3

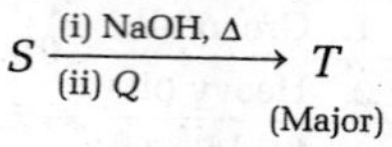

11. Among the following, the number of aromatic compound(s) is **[JEE Advanced 2017]**

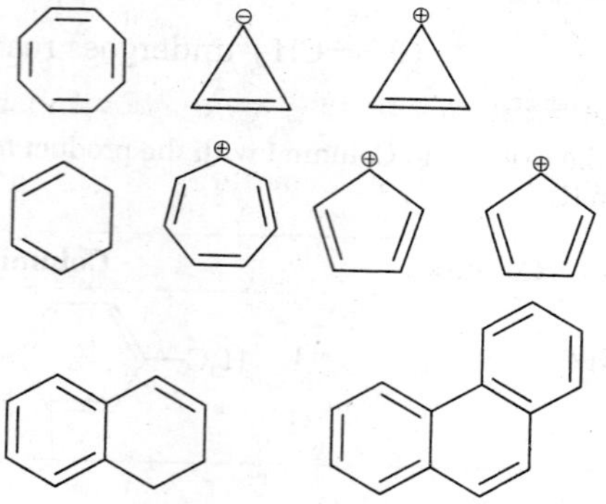

12. Amongst the following, the total number of compounds soluble in aqueous NaOH (at room temperature) is **[JEE Main 2020]**

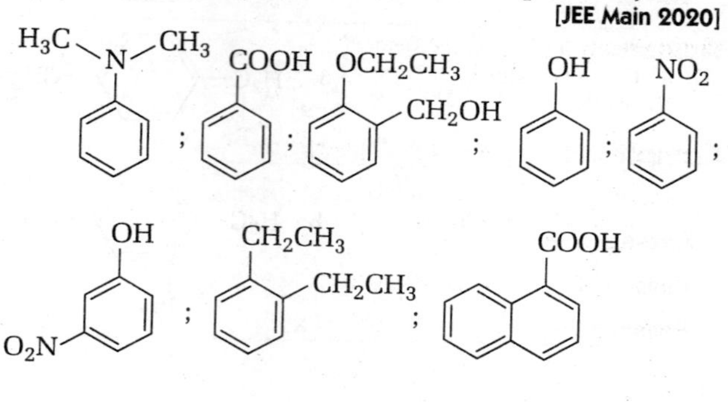

Answers

Objective Questions Type I [Only one correct option]

1. (c)	**2.** (a)	**3.** (b)	**4.** (c)	**5.** (c)	**6.** (d)	**7.** (b)	**8.** (b)	**9.** (c)	**10.** (a)
11. (b)	**12.** (a)	**13.** (a)	**14.** (c)	**15.** (a)	**16.** (b)	**17.** (d)	**18.** (b)	**19.** (a)	**20.** (c)
21. (d)	**22.** (a)	**23.** (d)	**24.** (d)	**25.** (a)	**26.** (d)	**27.** (c)	**28.** (a)	**29.** (a)	**30.** (c)
31. (b)	**32.** (b)	**33.** (d)	**34.** (d)	**35.** (a)	**36.** (b)	**37.** (a)	**38.** (d)	**39.** (a)	**40.** (b)
41. (a)	**42.** (b)	**43.** (d)	**44.** (c)	**45.** (d)	**46.** (d)	**47.** (d)	**48.** (a)	**49.** (b)	**50.** (a)
51. (d)	**52.** (a)	**53.** (a)	**54.** (d)	**55.** (b)	**56.** (b)	**57.** (b)	**58.** (a)	**59.** (b)	**60.** (d)
61. (a)	**62.** (b)	**63.** (c)	**64.** (a)	**65.** (a)	**66.** (a)	**67.** (b)	**68.** (c)	**69.** (a)	**70.** (c)
71. (b)	**72.** (c)	**73.** (c)	**74.** (b)	**75.** (b)	**76.** (d)	**77.** (d)	**78.** (c)	**79.** (d)	**80.** (d)
81. (a)	**82.** (c)	**83.** (c)	**84.** (d)	**85.** (c)	**86.** (a)	**87.** (a)	**88.** (a)	**89.** (b)	**90.** (c)
91. (c)	**92.** (a)	**93.** (b)	**94.** (b)	**95.** (b)	**96.** (c)	**97.** (b)	**98.** (b)	**99.** (c)	**100.** (a)
101. (a)	**102.** (a)	**103.** (a)	**104.** (b)	**105.** (a)	**106.** (a)	**107.** (c)	**108.** (a)	**109.** (c)	**110.** (b)
111. (b)	**112.** (a)	**113.** (d)	**114.** (c)	**115.** (d)	**116.** (b)	**117.** (a)	**118.** (d)	**119.** (b)	**120.** (b)
121. (c)	**122.** (b)	**123.** (b)	**124.** (a)	**125.** (a)	**126.** (a)	**127.** (b)	**128.** (a)	**129.** (a)	**130.** (b)
131. (a)	**132.** (b)	**133.** (b)	**134.** (b)	**135.** (d)	**136.** (c)	**137.** (b)	**138.** (d)	**139.** (d)	**140.** (b)
141. (d)	**142.** (a)	**143.** (c)	**144.** (c)	**145.** (c)	**146.** (c)	**147.** (b)	**148.** (a)	**149.** (a)	**150.** (b)
151. (d)	**152.** (b)	**153.** (c)	**154.** (a)	**155.** (c)	**156.** (b)	**157.** (a)	**158.** (a)	**159.** (b)	**160.** (d)
161. (c)	**162.** (b)	**163.** (a)	**164.** (d)	**165.** (a)	**166.** (d)	**167.** (b)	**168.** (d)	**169.** (b)	**170.** (c)
171. (c)	**172.** (b)	**173.** (a)	**174.** (b)	**175.** (b)	**176.** (b)	**177.** (b)	**178.** (d)	**179.** (c)	**180.** (b)
181. (c)	**182.** (b)	**183.** (b)	**184.** (b)	**185.** (d)	**186.** (c)	**187.** (d)	**188.** (c)	**189.** (d)	**190.** (a)
191. (a)	**192.** (b)	**193.** (a)	**194.** (a)	**195.** (d)	**196.** (c)	**197.** (a)	**198.** (c)	**199.** (c)	**200.** (d)
201. (b)	**202.** (d)	**203.** (a)	**204.** (b)	**205.** (c)	**206.** (c)	**207.** (c)	**208.** (b)	**209.** (b)	**210.** (c)
211. (b)	**212.** (c)	**213.** (a)	**214.** (d)	**215.** (c)	**216.** (c)	**217.** (c)	**218.** (a)	**219.** (a)	**220.** (c)
221. (d)	**222.** (b)	**223.** (a)	**224.** (a)	**225.** (a)	**226.** (d)	**227.** (d)	**228.** (a)	**229.** (c)	**230.** (b)
231. (c)	**232.** (b)	**233.** (b)	**234.** (a)	**235.** (a)	**236.** (b)	**237.** (c)	**238.** (a)	**239.** (c)	**240.** (a)
241. (b)	**242.** (c)	**243.** (d)	**244.** (b)	**245.** (a)	**246.** (b)	**247.** (a)	**248.** (b)		

Objective Questions Type II [One or more than one correct option(s)]

1. (a, b, c, d)	**2.** (a, b, d)	**3.** (a, b, c)	**4.** (a, b, d)	**5.** (c)
6. (c)	**7.** (b)	**8.** (b)	**9.** (b)	**10.** (c)
11. (a, b, c)	**12.** (b)	**13.** (a)	**14.** (b)	**15.** (a, b, c)
16. (a, b)	**17.** (d)	**18.** (a, c, d)	**19.** (a, b)	**20.** (a, b)
21. (a, b, c)	**22.** (b)	**23.** (a, c, d)	**24.** (a, b)	**25.** (b)
26. (c)	**27.** (a, d)	**28.** (c)	**29.** (a, b)	**30.** (c)
31. (a, c)	**32.** (c, d)	**33.** (d)	**34.** (b, d)	**35.** (c, d)
36. (b)	**37.** (a, b, c, d)	**38.** (d)	**39.** (b, c)	**40.** (a, b)
41. (a, b, c, d)	**42.** (b, c)	**43.** (b, c, d)	**44.** (a, b)	**45.** (a, b, d)
46. (b, c, d)	**47.** (a, b, c)	**48.** (d)	**49.** (a, b)	**50.** (c)

Numerical Value Questions

1. (38)	**2.** (90)	**3.** (9)	**4.** (3)	**5.** (4)	**6.** (8)	**7.** (36)	**8.** (6)	**9.** (3)	**10.** (160)

Comprehension Based Questions

Passage 1 – 1. (b) 2. (a) 3. (a)

Passage 2 – 1. (b) 2. (c) 3. (d)

Passage 3 – 1. (c) 2. (a)

Passage 4 – 1. (b) 2. (c) 3. (d)

Passage 5 – 1. (b) 2. (a) 3. (c)

Passage 6 – 1. (d) 2. (c) 3. (b)

Passage 7 – 1. (c) 2. (c) 3. (c)

Passage 8 – 1. (d) 2. (a)

Passage 9 – 1. (b) 2. (d) 3. (d)
Passage 10 – 1. (b) 2. (a) 3. (c)
Passage 11 – 1. (c) 2. (a) 3. (a)
Passage 12 – 1. (c) 2. (a) 3. (b)
Passage 13 – 1. (d) 2. (c) 3. (b)
Passage 14 – 1. (b) 2. (c) 3. (a)
Passage 15 – 1. (b) 2. (c)

Matrix-Match Type

1. A→(2); B→(3); C→(4); D→(1)
2. A→(1); B→(4); C→(3); D→(2)
3. A→(3); B→(2); C→(1); D→(4)
4. A→(2); B→(1); C→(3); D→(4)
5. A→(3); B→(4); C→(1); D→(2)
6. A→(4); B→(3); C→(2); D→(1)
7. A→(3); B→(4); C→(2); D→(1)
8. A→(3); B→(4); C→(2); D→(1)
9. A→(2); B→(3); C→(1); D→(4)
10. A→(4); B→(3); C→(2); D→(1)

Single Integer Answer Questions

1. (3) 2. (2) 3. (6) 4. (5) 5. (3) 6. (4) 7. (3) 8. (5) 9. (1) 10. (4)
11. (5) 12. (4)

Solutions

Objective Questions Type I [Only one correct option]

1. (c)

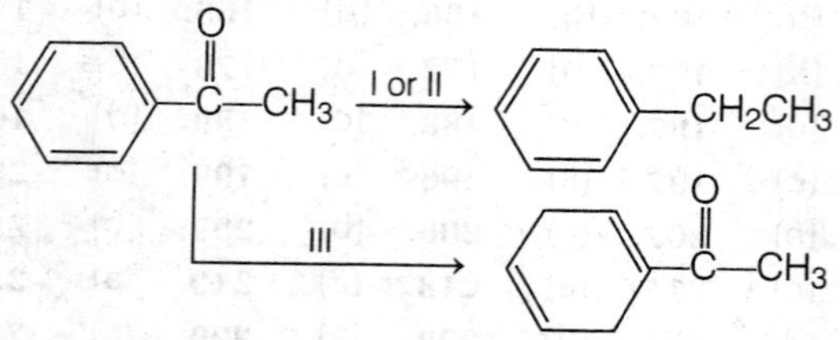

2. (a) $H_3PO_2 + H_2O \longrightarrow H_3PO_3 + 2H$

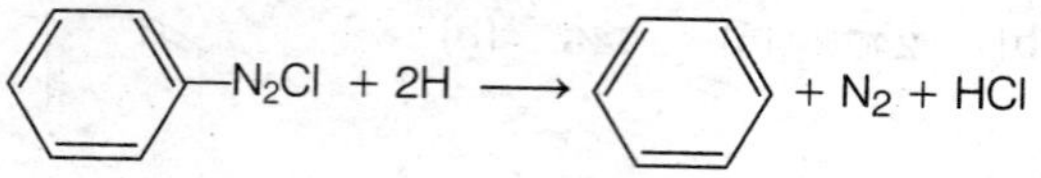

3. (b)

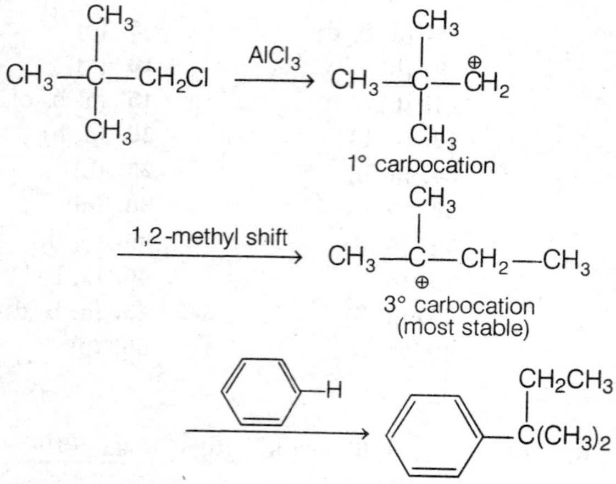

4. (c)

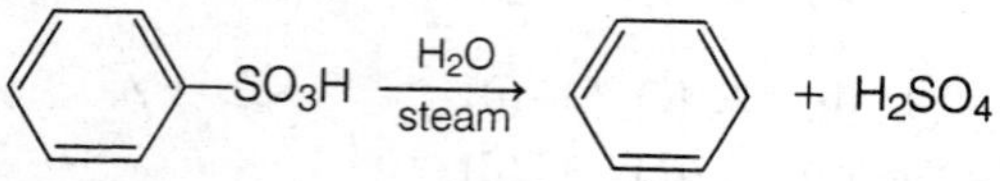

5. (c)

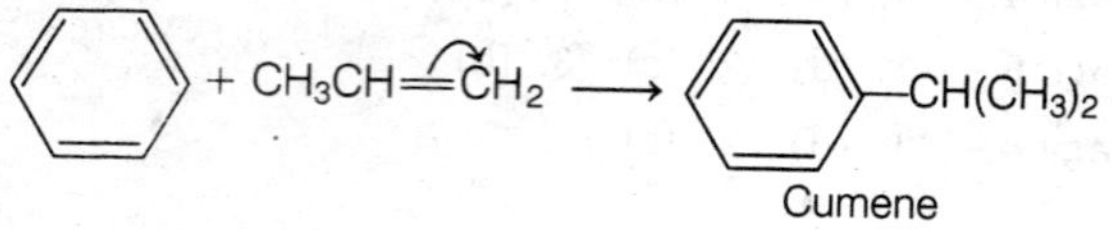

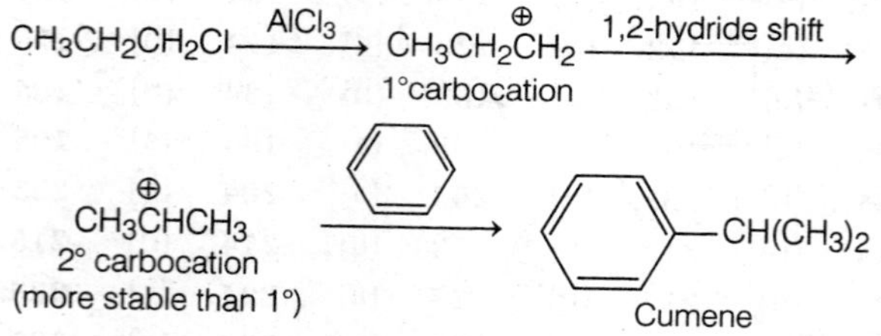

7. (b)

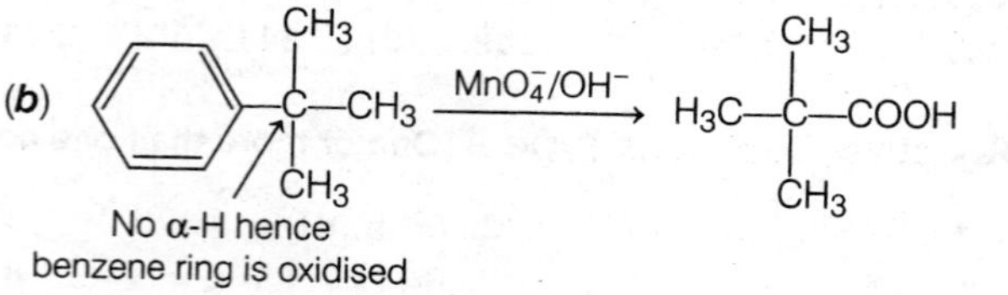

8. (b)

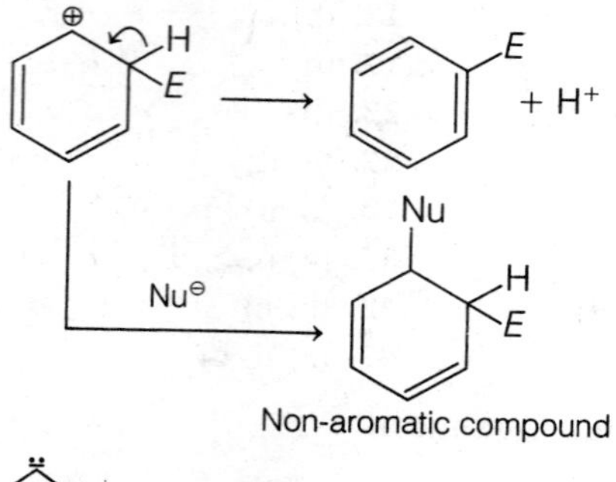

10. (a)

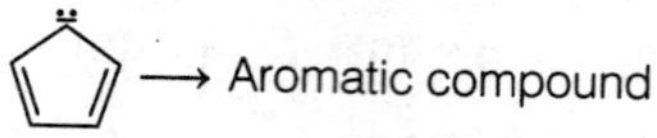

11. (b)

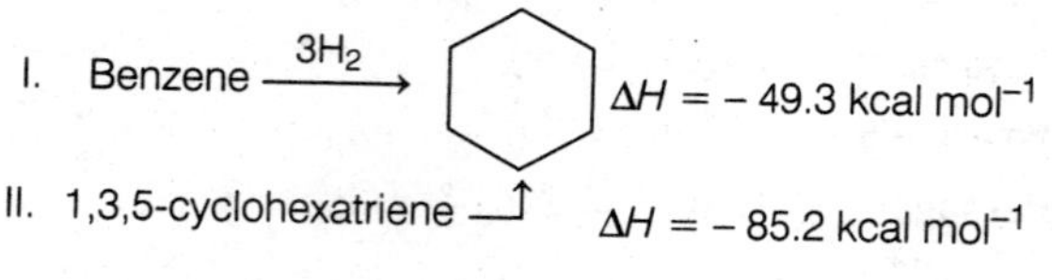

derived from

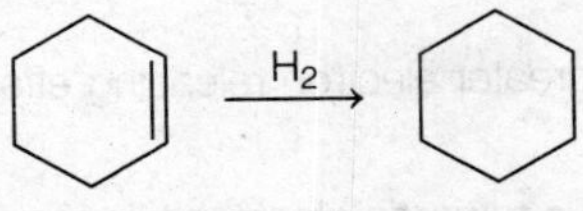

$\Delta H = -28.4$ kcal mol^{-1} for one (C=C) bond)

Thus, I is incorrect statement.

II. Based on heat of hydrogenation, benzene is more stable than 1,3,5-cyclohexatriene by $-85.2-(-49.3) = -35.9$ kcal.

Thus, II is correct.

III. Due to resonance all (C—C) and (C=C) bonds have equal length.

Thus III is also correct.

Thus, II and III are correct.

15. (*a*)

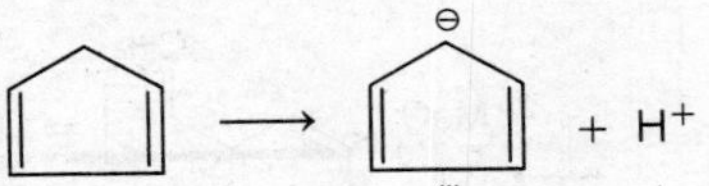

(I)

due to formation of (I), aromatic character is attained and it is stable.

19. (*a*)

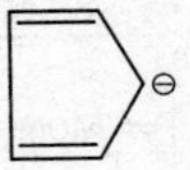

Cyclopentadiene anion

20. (*c*) I.

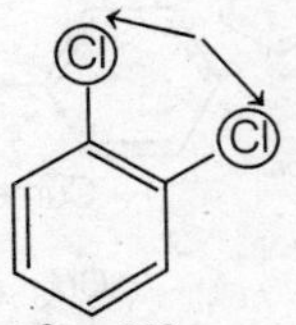

$\theta > 60°$

Due to large size of Cl atoms, dipole-dipole repulsion increases bond angle beyond 60°.

II.

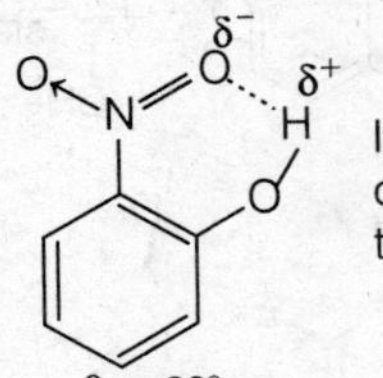

$\theta < 60°$

Intramolecular H-bonding decreases bond angle less than to 60°.

III.

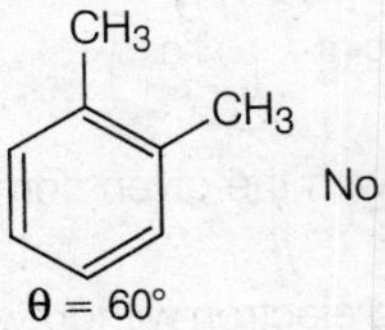

$\theta = 60°$

No repulsion hence

$$\mu = 2\mu_{C-X} \cos\left(\frac{\theta}{2}\right)$$

$$\mu \propto \cos\left(\frac{\theta}{2}\right)$$

or $$\mu \propto \left(\frac{1}{\theta}\right)$$

$\theta : \theta < 60° \quad \theta = 60° > \theta < 60°$

μ : I < III < II

22. (*a*) (I) and (III) are not possibe : Aryl halides and vinyl halides in the presence of anhyd. $AlCl_3$ do not act as electrophiles to give Friedel-Crafts' reaction with benzene. Therefore, these reactions are not possible.

II.

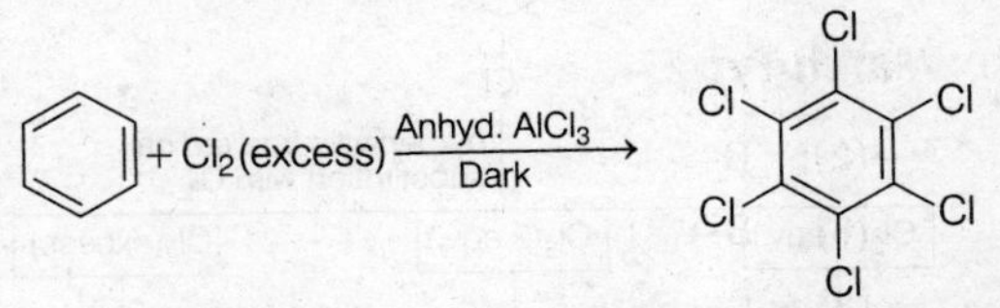

(This reaction is possible)

IV.

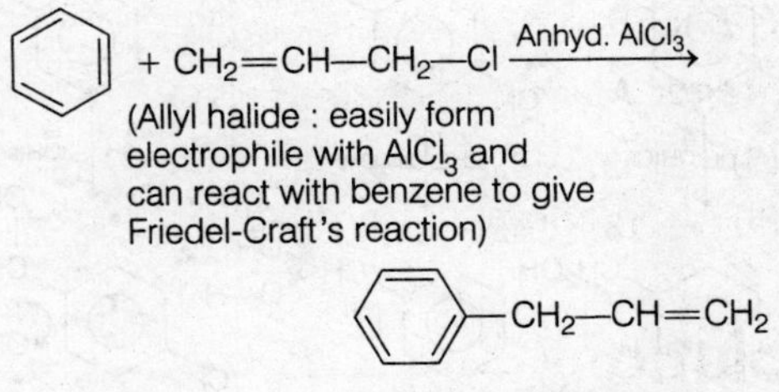

(Allyl halide : easily form electrophile with $AlCl_3$ and can react with benzene to give Friedel-Craft's reaction)

(This is also possible)

24. (*d*) Activating tendency $-NO_2 < -H < -CH_3$

Thus, nitration in III < I < II.

25. (*a*)

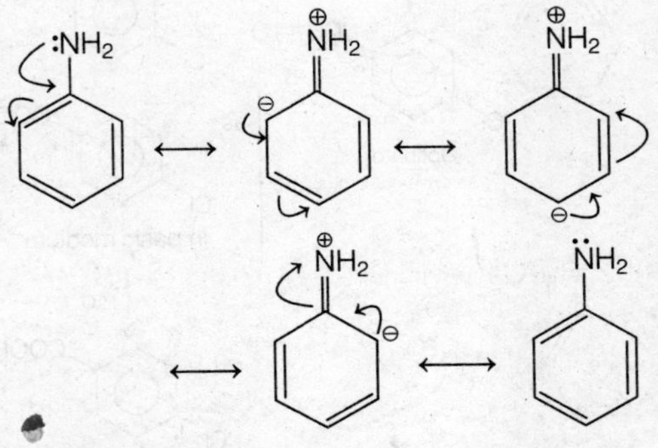

Resonance hybrid structure is

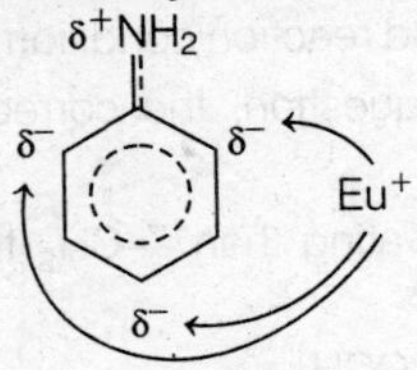

Eu^+ can attack at *o*-,and *p*-sites

Thus,

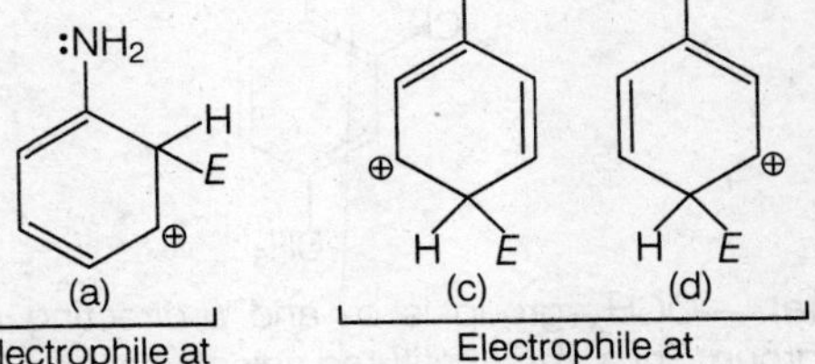

(a) Electrophile at *o*-position

(c) (d) Electrophile at *p*-position

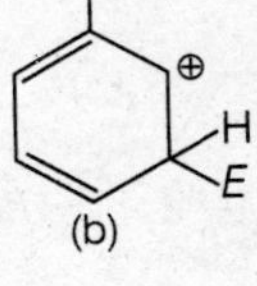

(b)

Electrophile at *m*-position is not formed.

26. (*d*)

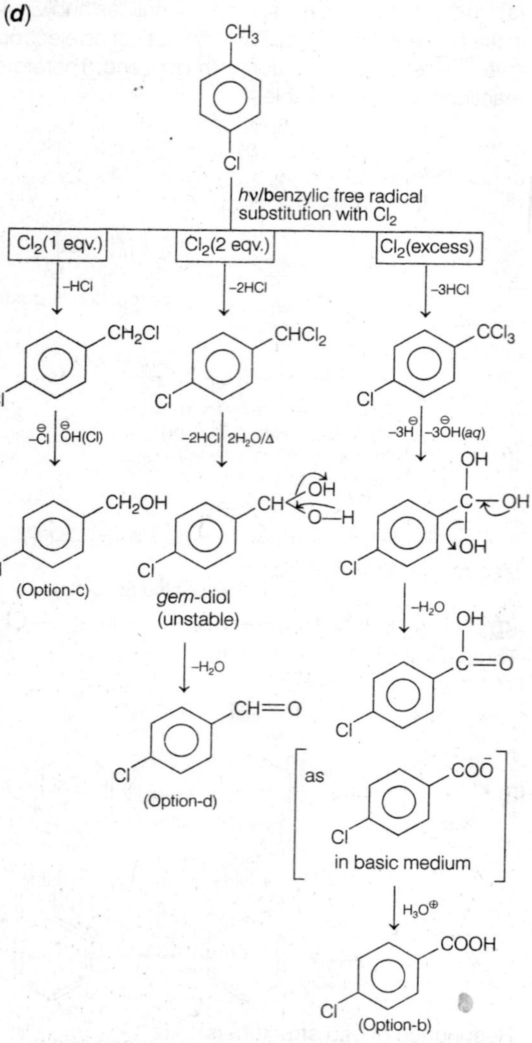

So, considering the second reaction condition, Cl^-, H_2O, Δ in the statement of the question, the correct answer is option (d).

27. (*c*) —OCH_3 is more activating than —CH_3 thus product formed is

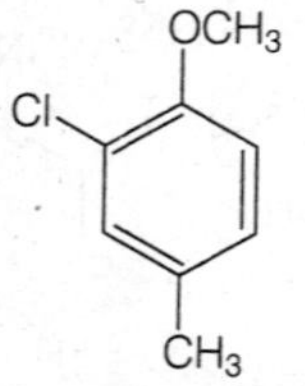

29. (*a*) —OCH_3 group is *o*- and *p*-directing and activating group. Thus, *m*-substituted anisole has maximum potential energy.

31. (*b*) Due to greater electron releasing effect. 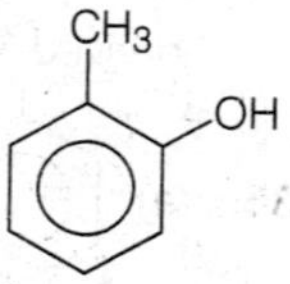 is most reactive towards electrophilic reagent.

32. (*b*) More stable the carbocation intermediate, higher will be the rate of S_N1 reaction.

The reaction involving carbocation intermediate formation for the given compounds are as follows:

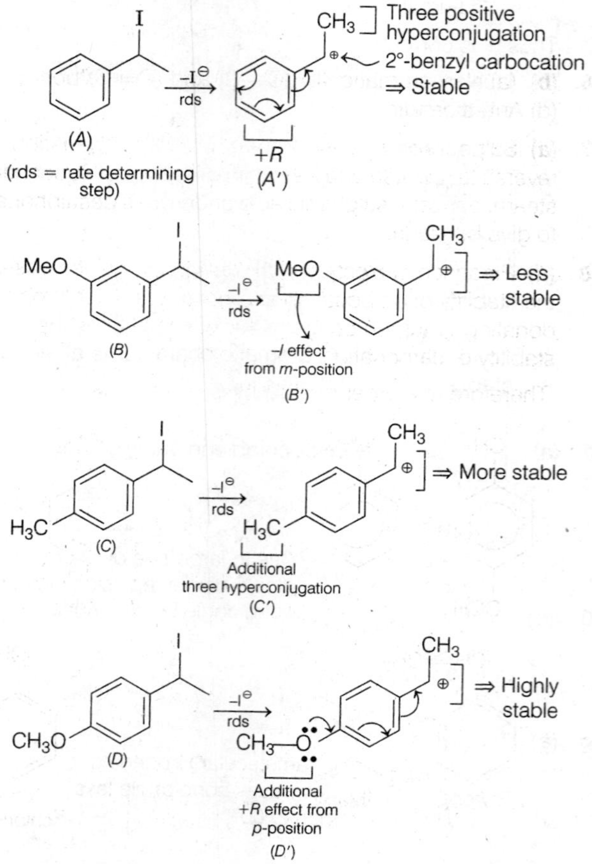

Stability of intermediates will follow the order

$$B' < A' < C' < D'$$

(−*I*) (−HPC=3) (+HPC=6) (+HPC=3, +*R*=1)

So, the rate of S_N1 reaction with the given compounds will be, *B* < *A* < *C* < *D*.

34. (*d*) —NH_3^+ and —CCl_3, being electron withdrawing groups, decrease the electron density at *ortho* and *para* positions. Hence, the incoming electrophile predominantly attack at *meta* position.

35. (*a*)

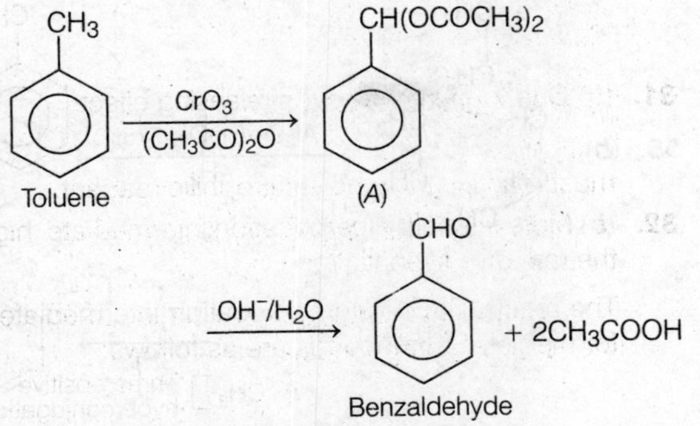

36. (*b*) (a) Non-aromatic, (b) Aromatic, (c) Aromatic, (d) Anti-aromatic

37. (*a*) Sulphonation unlike nitration and halogenation is a reversible reaction and hence, in presence of super heated steam, benzene sulphonic acid undergoes desulphonation to give benzene.

38. (*d*) Presence of electron withdrawing group decreases the stability of carbocation and presence of electron donating group on benzene nucleus increases the stability of carbocation.

Therefore, the order of stability is

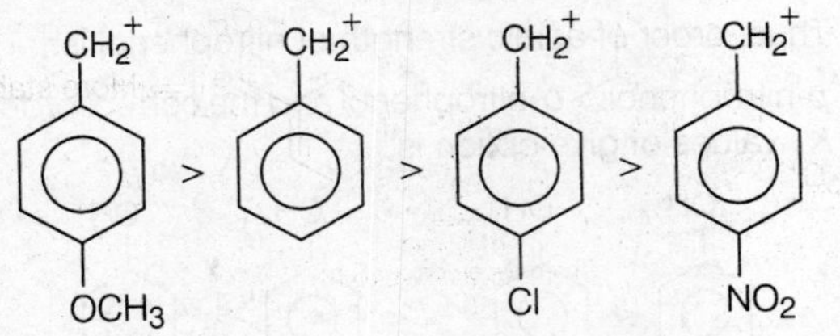

39. (*a*)

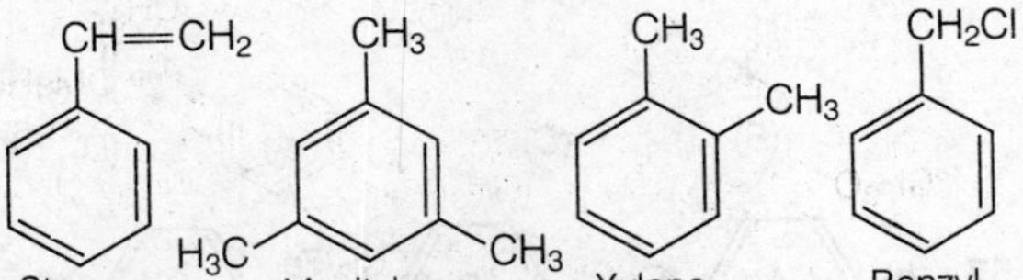

Styrene | Mesitylene | Xylene (*ortho*) | Benzyl chloride

40. (*b*)

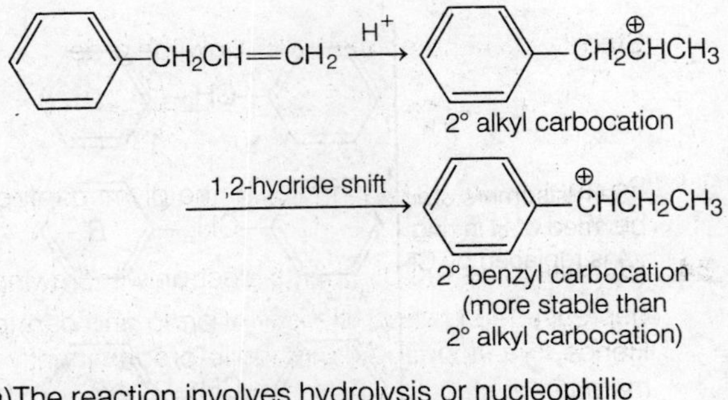

41. (*a*) The reaction involves hydrolysis or nucleophilic substitution in first step followed by oxidation and dehydration in last step. The most important fact is that, the Br group attached directly to aromatic ring will not undergo substitution in step 1.

The road map of the given reaction is as follows:

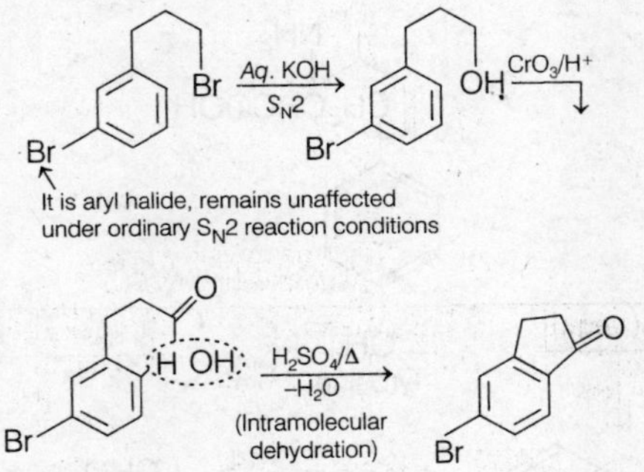

42. (*b*)

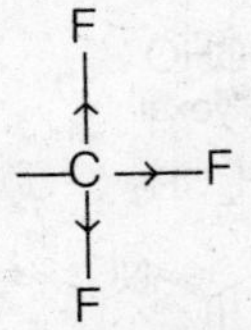

F is most electronegative element. Thus, —CF_3 group is electron withdrawing group.

Thus, *m*-directing.

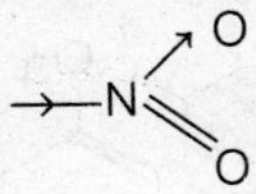

is *m*-directing.

43. (*d*)

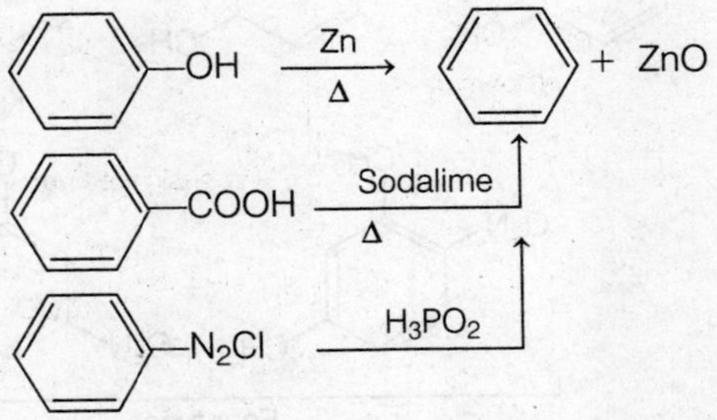

45. (*d*) Bond length in C=C < C—C open chain.

In benzene, there is delocalisation of π-electrons, then (C—C) = (C=C) in benzene but less than (C—C).

47. (*d*)

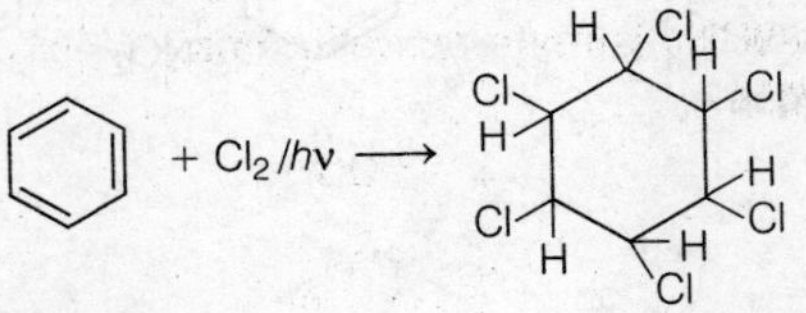

48. (*a*) $A = CH_3COCl$

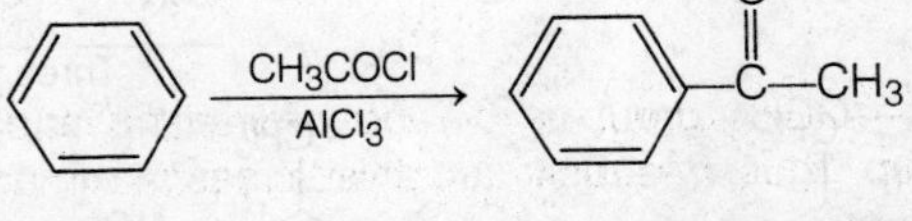

50. (*a*) —CH_3 is electron-repelling group (ERG) favours delocalisation effect, and thus S_E at *o*- and *p*-position.

—NO_2, —COOH are electron-withdrawing groups (EWG) and deactivate benzene nucleus for S_E reaction.

51. (*d*) Tyrosine is α-amino acid with aromatic benzene ring

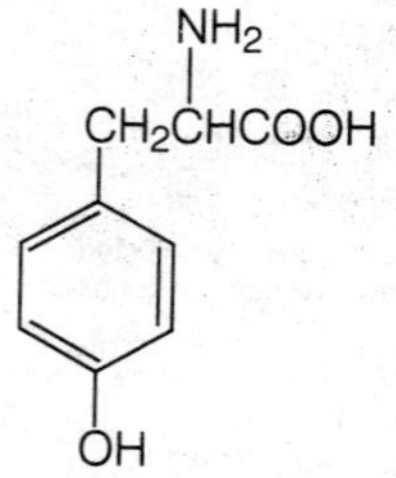

Tyrosine

53. (*a*)

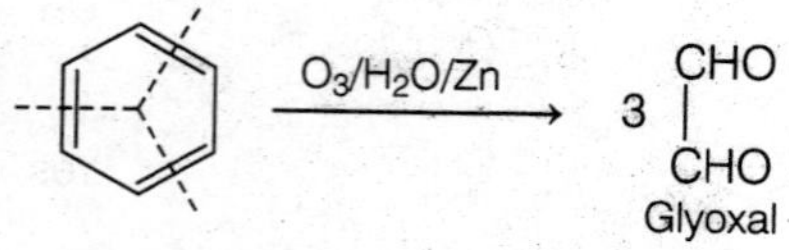

54. (*d*) (a)

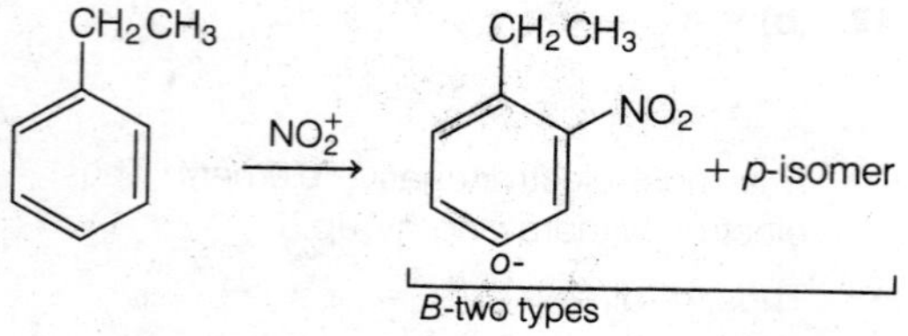

(b)

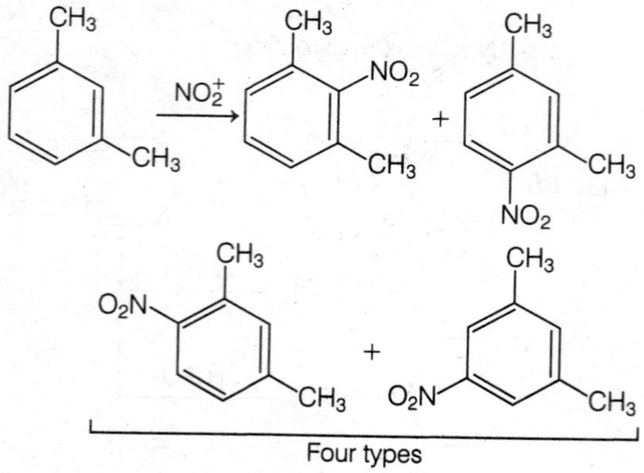

(c)

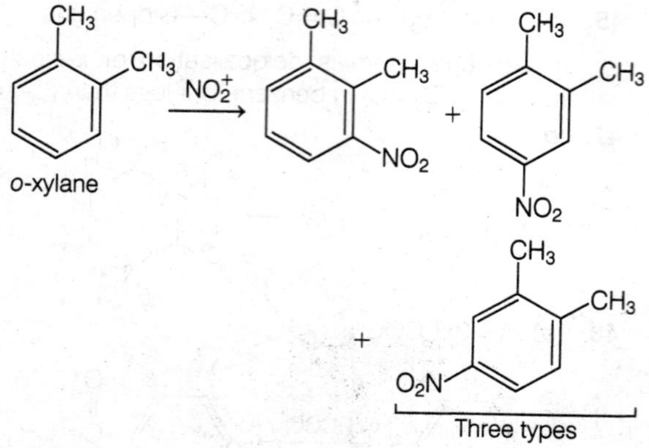

(d)

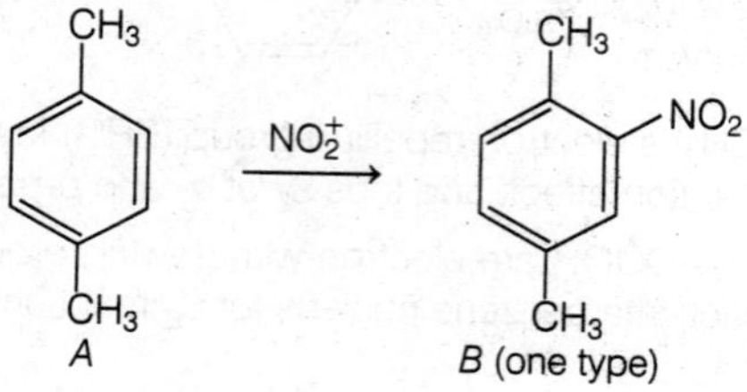

55. (*b*)

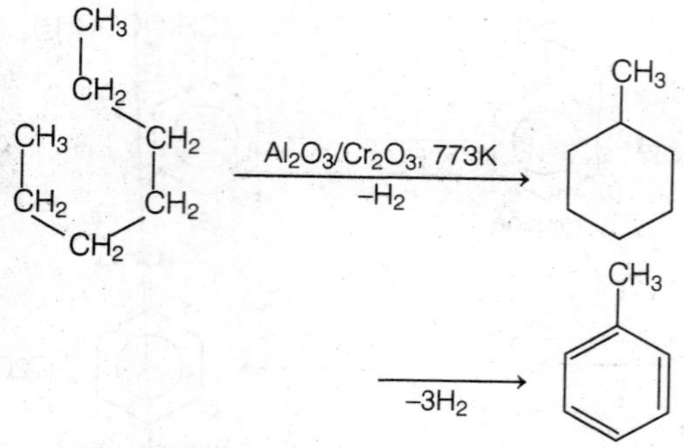

56. (*b*) Acidic strength is inversely proportional to pK_a value. The acidity of phenols is due to greater resonance stabilisation of phenoxide ion relative to phenol.

Therefore, any substituent which stabilises the phenoxide ion more by dispersal of negative charge will tend to increase the acidity of phenol.

Electron withdrawing groups (—NO_2) increases the acidic strength of phenol whereas electron donating group (—OCH_3) decreases the acidic strength of phenol. In case of —NO_2 group attached to phenol, the dispersal of negative charge is more pronounced at *o*- and *p*-position than at *m*-position.

Thus, order of acidic strength of nitrophenol is:

p-nitrophenol > *o*-nitrophenol and the correct order of the p K_a values of give option is

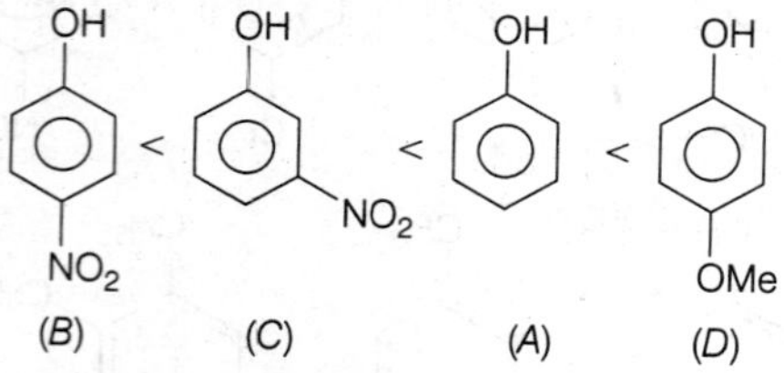

57. (*b*)

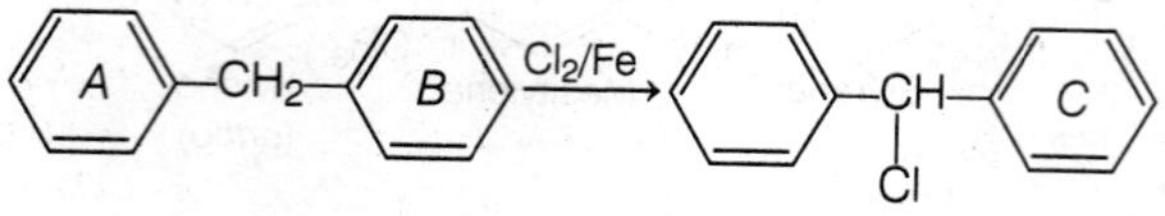

Same isomers are formed of H in ring *A* is replaced by Cl

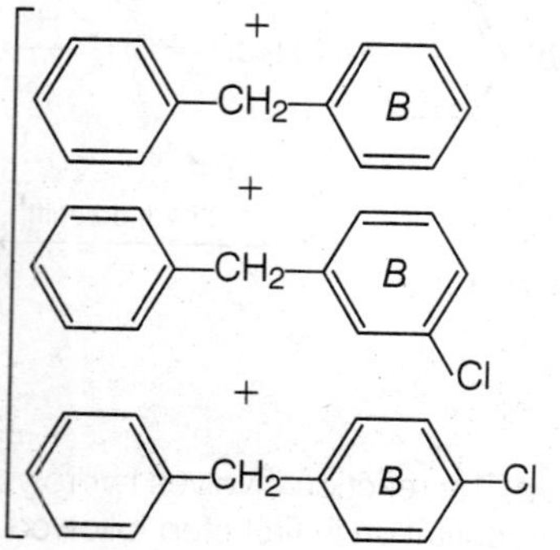

Thus, four isomers.

58. (*a*)

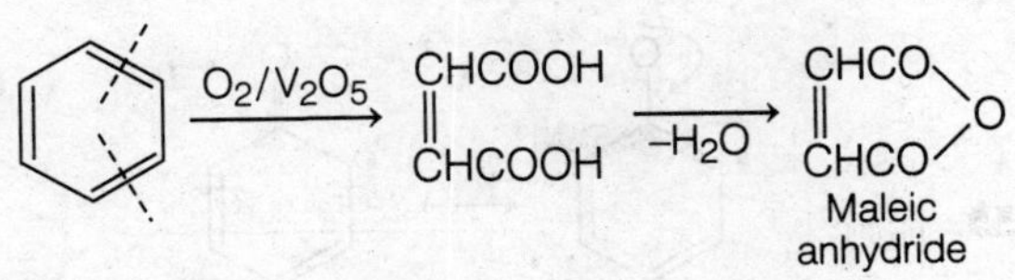

60. (*d*)

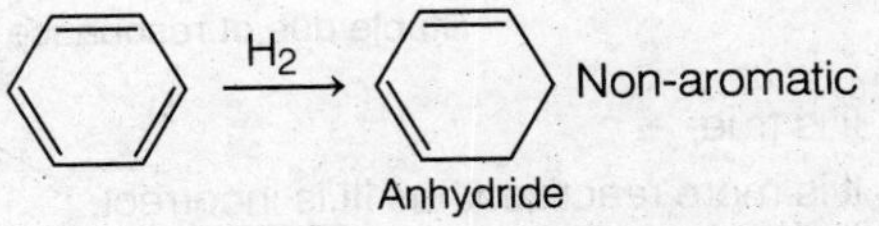

61. (*a*)

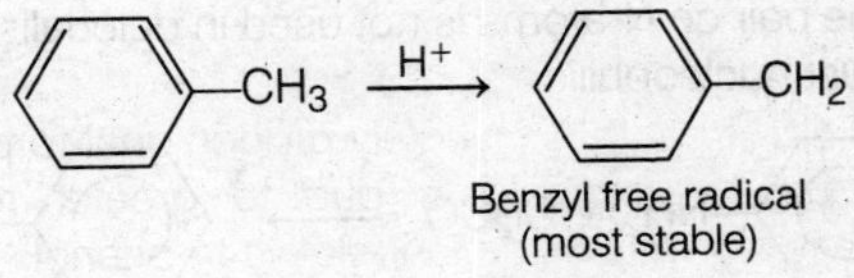

Thus, (C—H) bond energy is minimum.

62. (*b*)

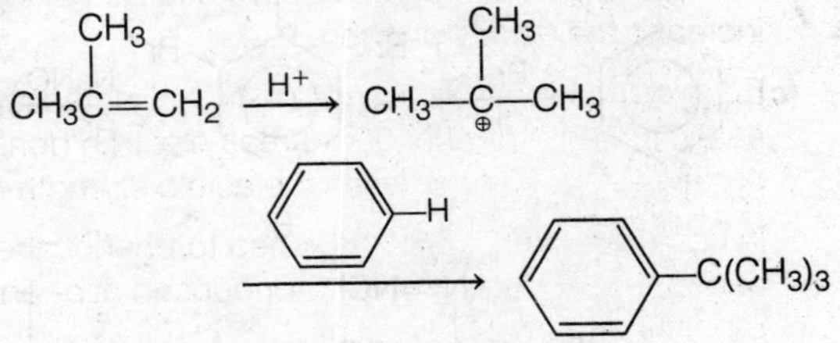

65. (*a*)

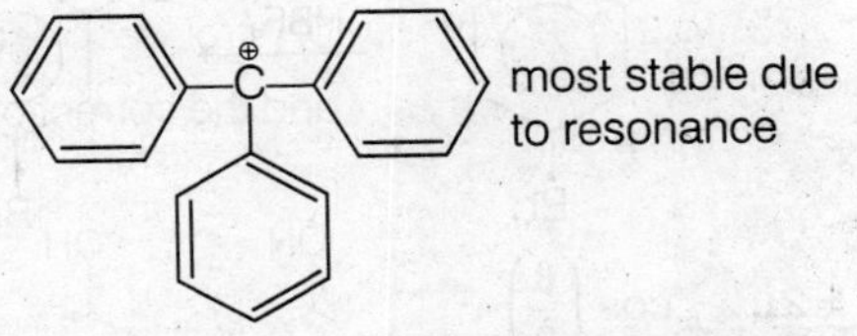

66. (*a*) (a) $—OCH_3$ activating, resonance effect wins over inductive effect w.r.t. (d)

(b) $—CH_3$ activiting, inductive effect wins over resonance effect w.r.t. (d)

(c) $—NO_2$ deactivating w.r.t. (d)

(d) —H

67. (*b*) An alkyl halide in presence of a bulkier base removes a proton from a carbon adjacent to the carbon bonded to the halogen. This reaction is called E2 (β-elimination reaction).

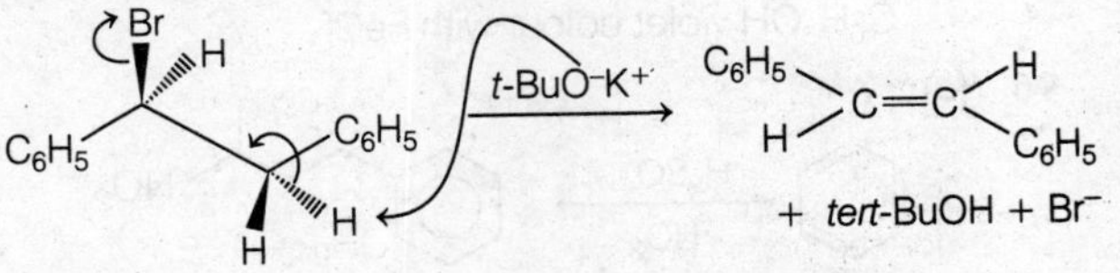

69. (*a*) $HNO_3 + H_2SO_4 \longrightarrow NO_2^+ + H_2O + HSO_3^-$

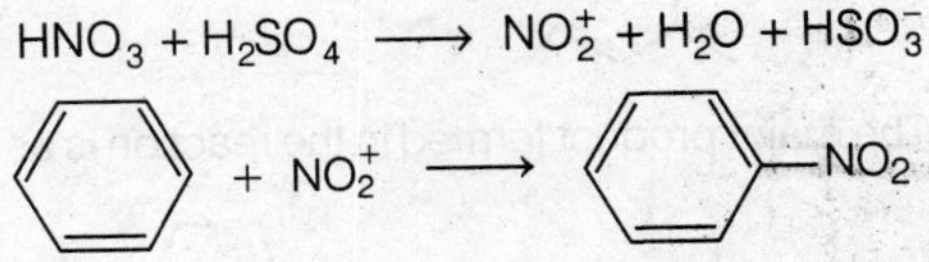

70. (*c*)

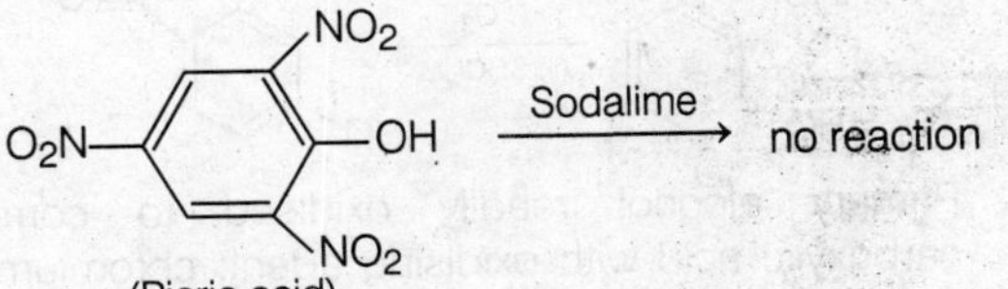

(Picric acid)

72. (*c*) Due to presence of two —Cl atoms reaction takes place by two benzene ring.

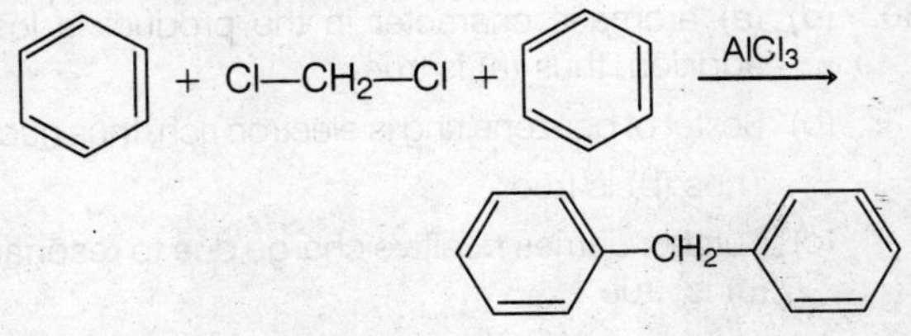

75. (*b*) (a)

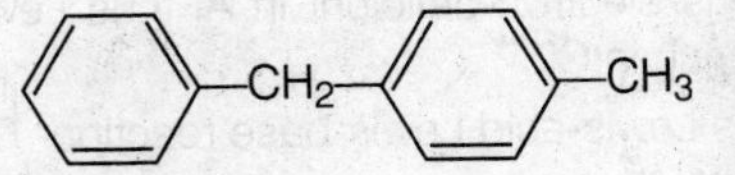

No

(b)

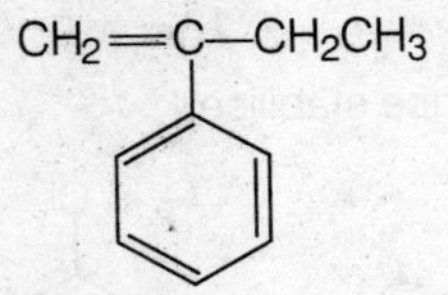

Yes

(c)

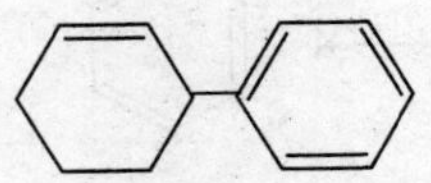

No

(d)

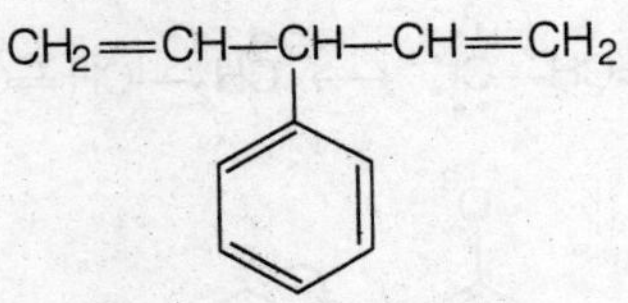

No

77. (*d*) The given reaction can be completed as follows :

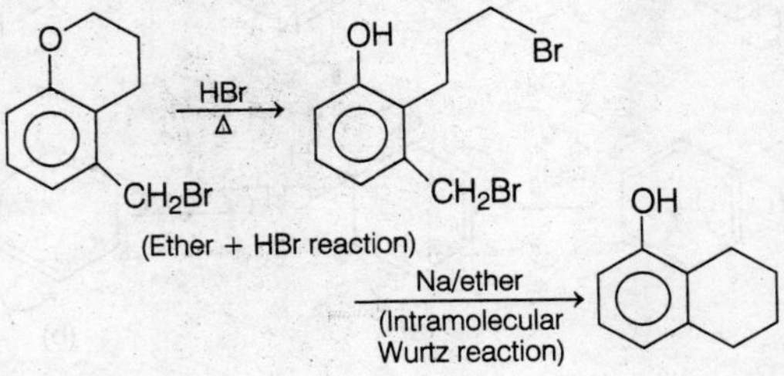

78. (*c*)

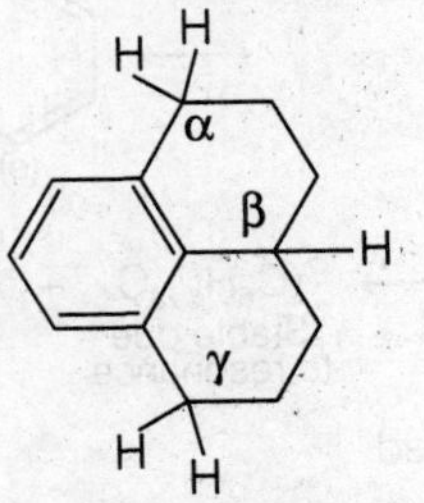

Benzylic carbon is adjacent to benzene ring. Positions are shown by α, β and γ, total H = 5.

79. (*d*)

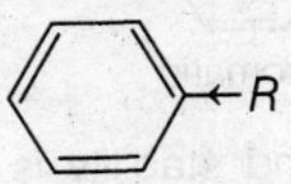

R is (ERG), increases rate for S_E at *o*-and *p*-positions compared to benzene.

(a) and (b) are thus true

(c) There is no resonance in —CH_3 group hence inductive effect is important thus true.

80. (*d*) (a) aromatic character in the product is lost due to addition, thus (a) is true.

(b) Sextet of benzene ring is electron rich, thus nucleophile. Thus (b) is true.

(c) Sulphur carries positive charge due to resonance, thus (c) is true.

81. (*a*) $AlCl_3$ is electron-deficient in Al thus Lewis-acid *R*Cl is electron rich in Cl.

Thus, it is Lewis-acid Lewis-base reaction RCl (Lewis base) + $AlCl_3$ (Lewis acid)

83. (*c*) All are resonance stabilised

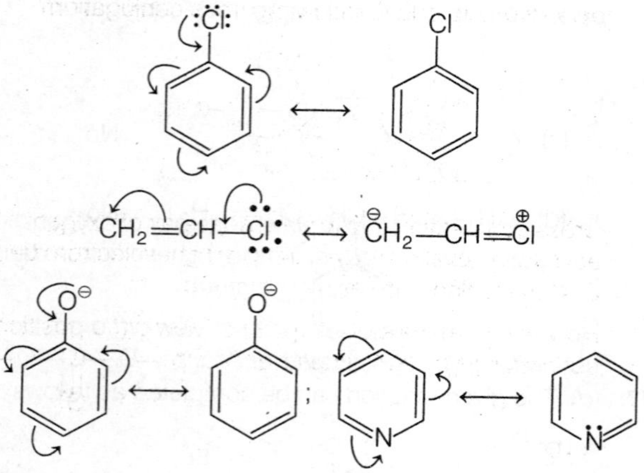

84. (*d*)

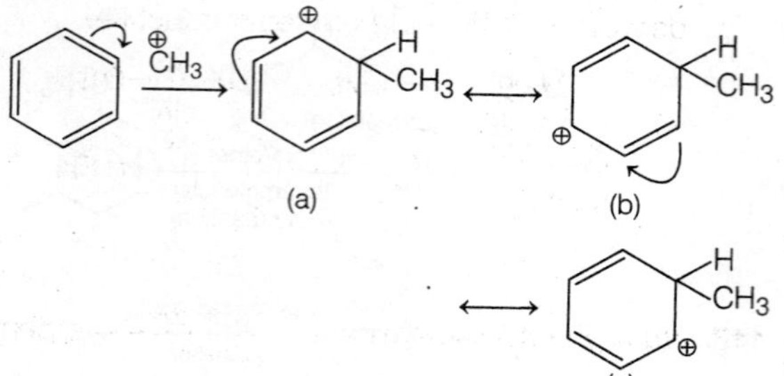

85. (*c*) $(C_6H_5)_3\overset{\oplus}{C}Br^{\ominus} + Ag^+ \longrightarrow (C_6H_5)_3\overset{\oplus}{C} + AgBr$

Stable due to resonance

Thus, this reaction is favoured.

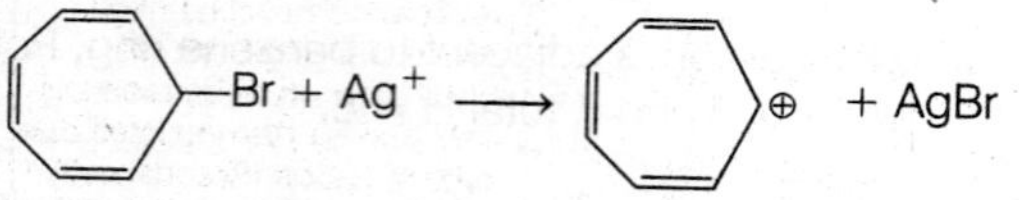

Aromatic

Aromatic character is attained and stability is obtained. Thus, reaction is favoured.

86. (*a*) —OH group is activating and resonance effect wins over inductive effect.

Thus, I is true.

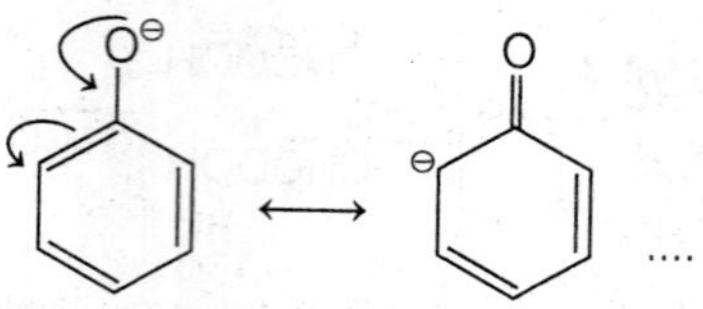

Stable due ot resonance

Thus, II is true.

Thus, II is more reactive, thus III is incorrect.

88. (*a*) Lone pair on N-atoms is not used in delocalisation and thus must nucleophilic.

89. (*b*)

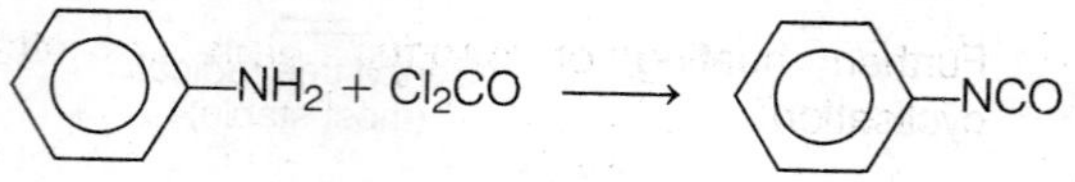

91. (*c*)

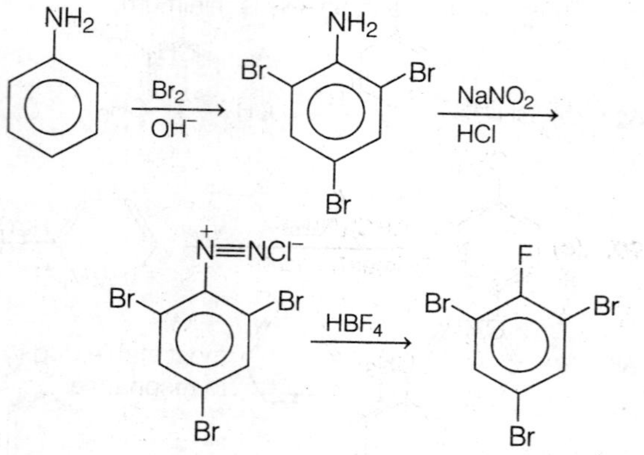

92. (*a*) $\mu = 2\mu_{c-x} \cos\left(\frac{\theta}{2}\right)$

where $\mu_{(c-x)}$ is the vector moment of the side $(c - x)$

$$\mu \propto \cos\left(\frac{\theta}{2}\right) \quad \text{or} \quad \mu \propto \left(\frac{1}{\theta}\right)$$

In case of *ortho*-isomer, θ is least hence μ is maximum. In case of Br atoms, repulsion is maximum due to its larger size than Cl atom. Angle increases, hence, μ decreases. Thus, μ(a) > μ(d) > μ(b) > μ(c).

94. (*b*) Cl is best leaving group.

95. (*b*) CH_3COOH blood red colour with $FeCl_3$.
C_6H_5OH violet colour with $FeCl_3$.

96. (*c*)

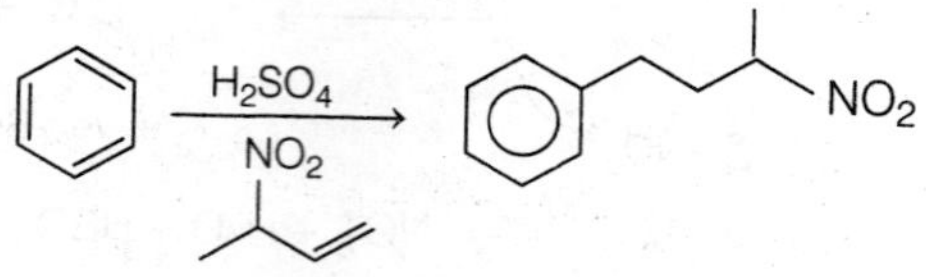

97. (*b*) The major product formed in the reaction is as follows :

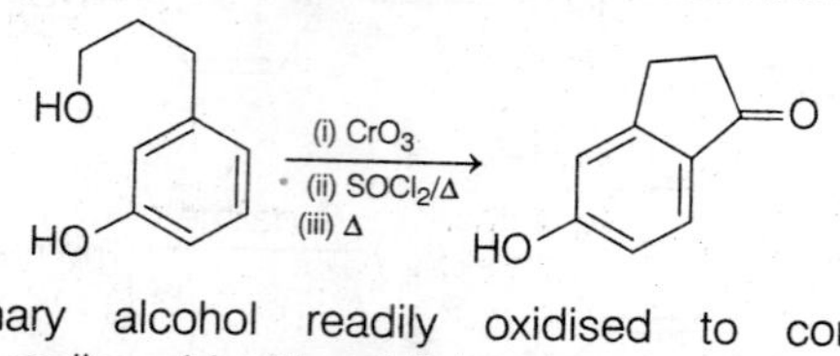

Primary alcohol readily oxidised to corresponding carboxylic acid with oxidising agent, chromium trioxide (CrO_3) in acidic medium.

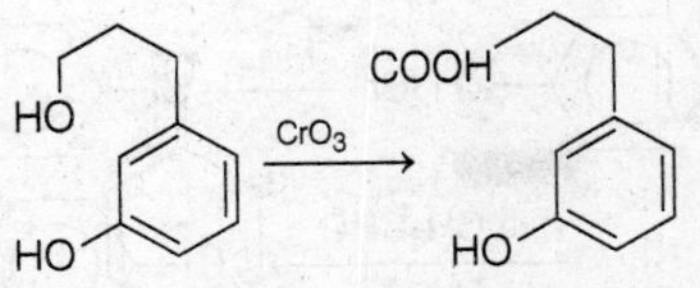

—OH group of carboxylic acid get substituted by —Cl in presence of $SOCl_2$ (Thionyl chloride).

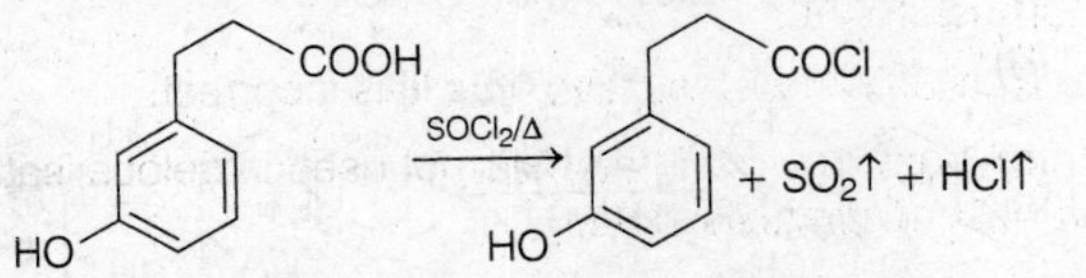

Further, heating of product leads to intramolecular cyclisation.

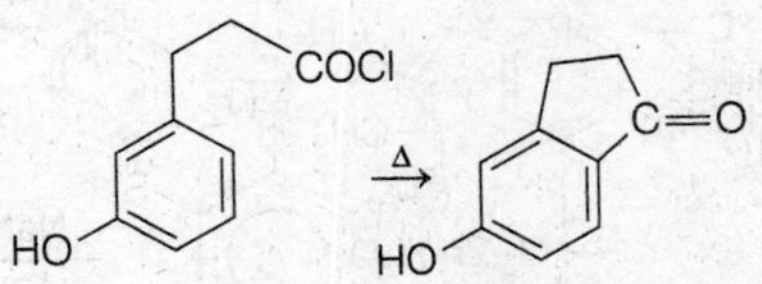

99. (*c*)

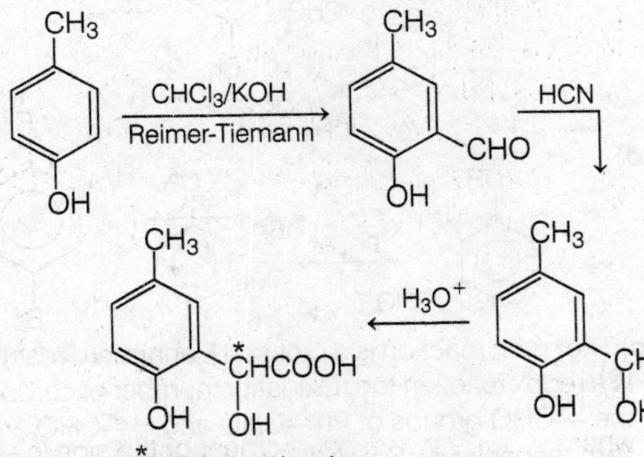

($\overset{*}{C}$-chiral carbon)

100. (*a*)

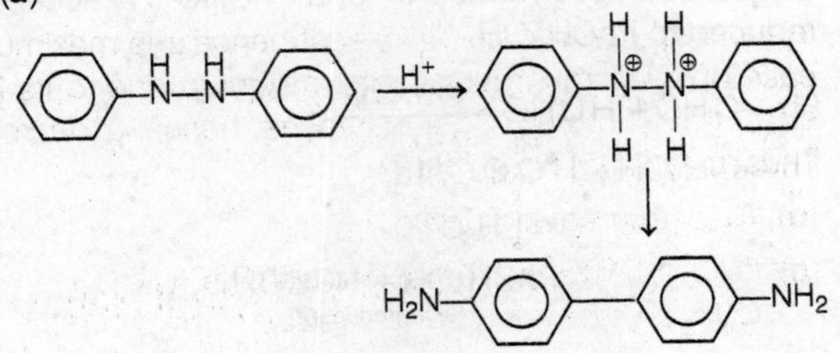

105. (*a*)

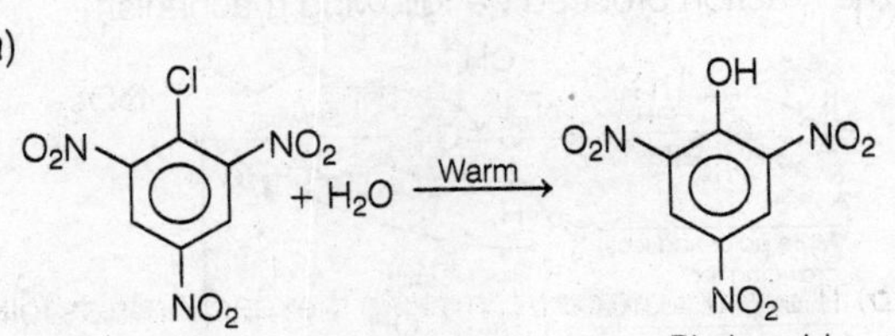

Picric acid

107. (*c*) Given

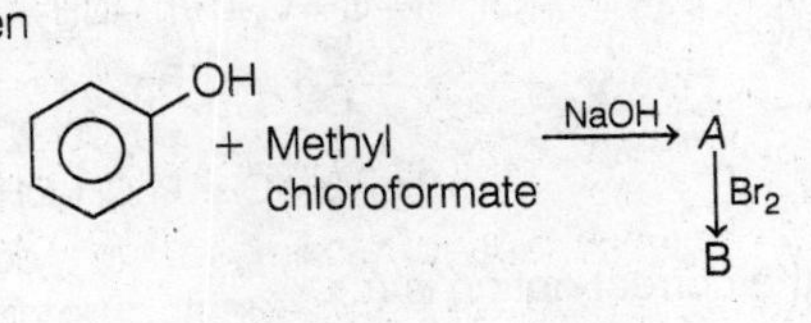

In the above road map, first reaction appears as acid base reaction followed by S_NAE (Nucleophilic substitution through Addition and Elimination). Both the steps are shown below

(i) **Acid base reaction**

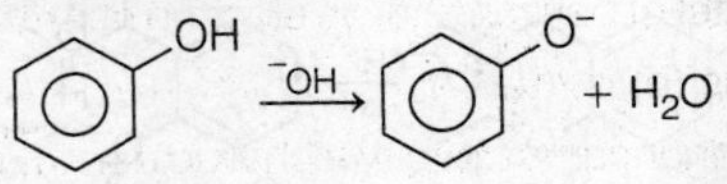

(ii) **S_NAE**

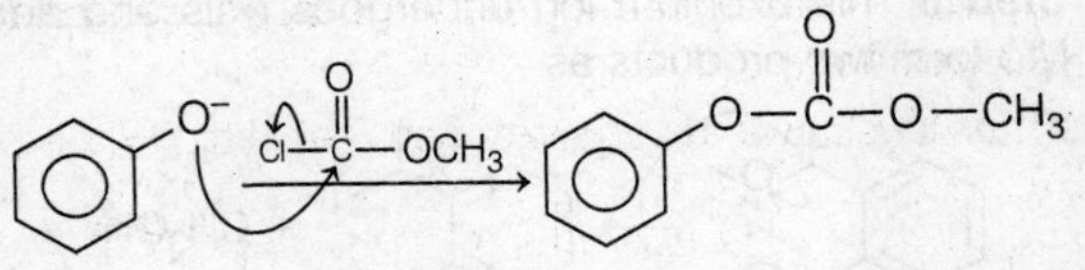

In the product of S_NAE the attached group is *ortho* and *para*-directing due to following cross conjugation

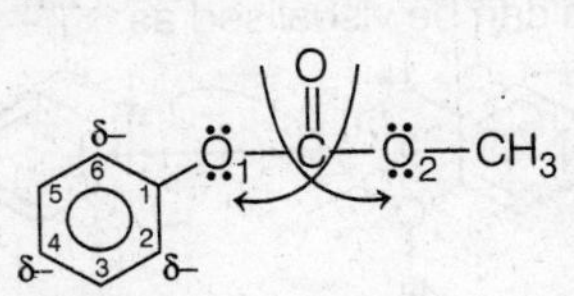

Cross conjugation due to which lone pair of oxygen 1 will be easily available to ring resulting to higher electron density at 2, 4, 6 position with respect to group.

However from the stability point of view *ortho* positions are not preferred by substituents as group —O—C(=O)—O—CH_3

is bulky.

Hence, on further bromination of S_NAE product *para* bromo derivative will be the preferred product i.e.

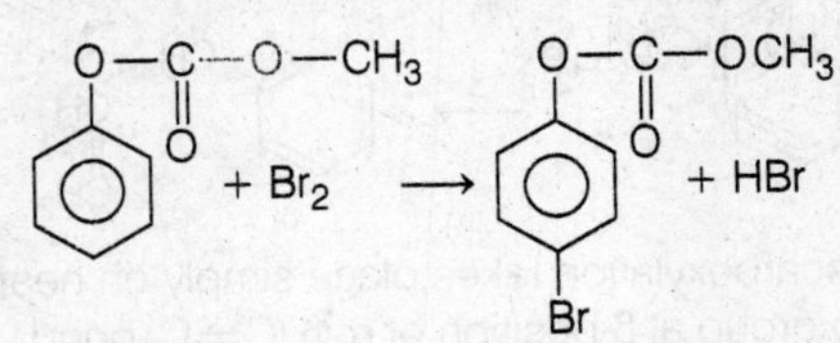

113. (*d*) *p*-phenylenediamine $\xrightarrow[\text{Oxidation}]{K_2Cr_2O_7\text{-}H_2SO_4}$ *p*-benzoquinone

118. (*d*) The reaction given is a nucleophilic substitution reaction in which cleavage at C—O bond is visible. The product formationc an be visualised with the help of following analysis.

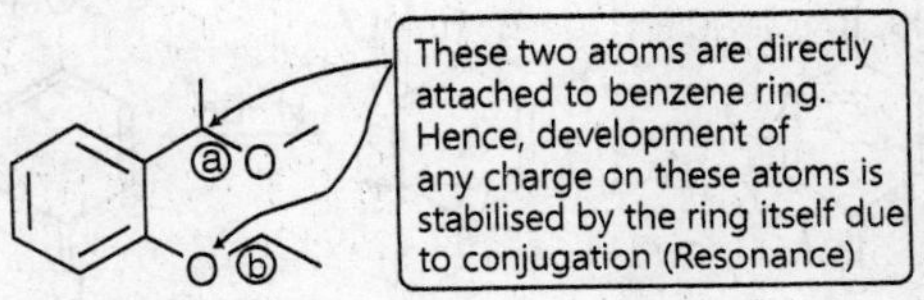

If any one properly visualise the fact written with figure above, than a conclusion can be made that C—O bonds marked (a) and (b) in the figure will undergo heterolysis during the reaction.

The reaction can be represented as

Mechanism

***Step* I** The reaction begins with the attack of H^+ of HI on oxygen to form oxonium ion as

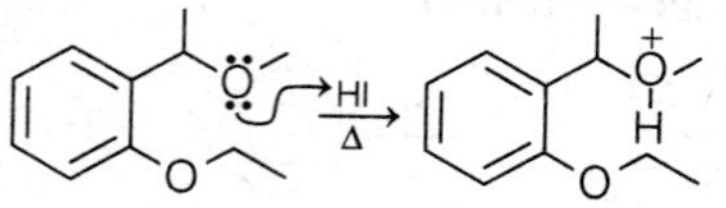

Oxonium ion

***Step* II** This oxonium ion undergoes lysis and addition of I^- to form two products as

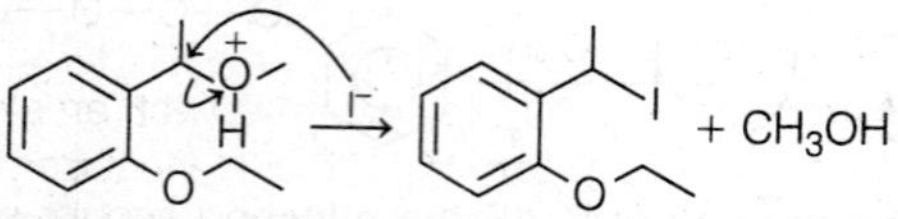

***Step* III** Similar pathway is followed at the other oxygen atom, which can be visualised as

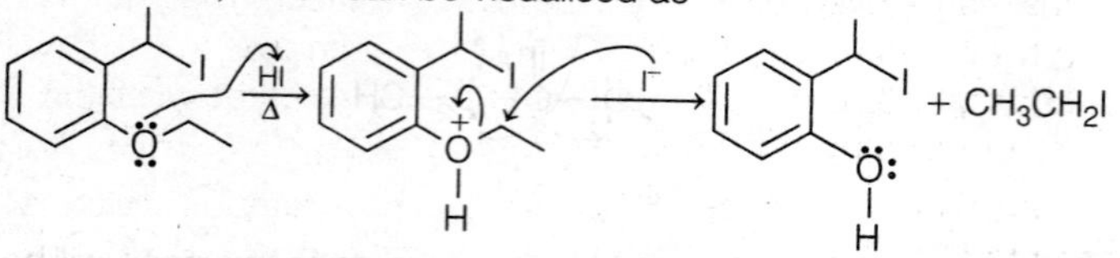

Mechanism of a reaction is always a logical sequencing of events which may occur simultaneously as well.

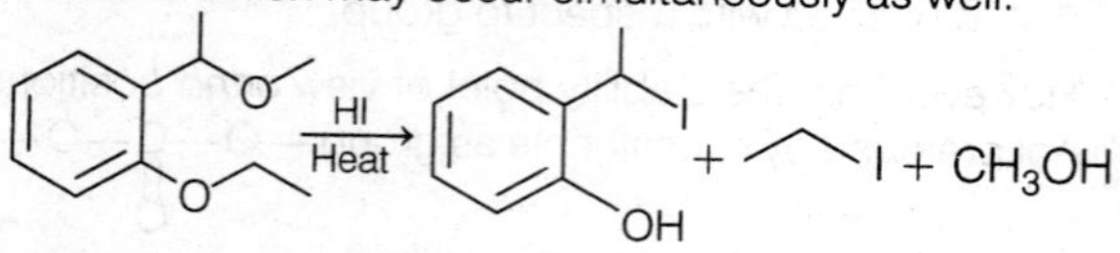

119. (*b*) Claisen rearrangement

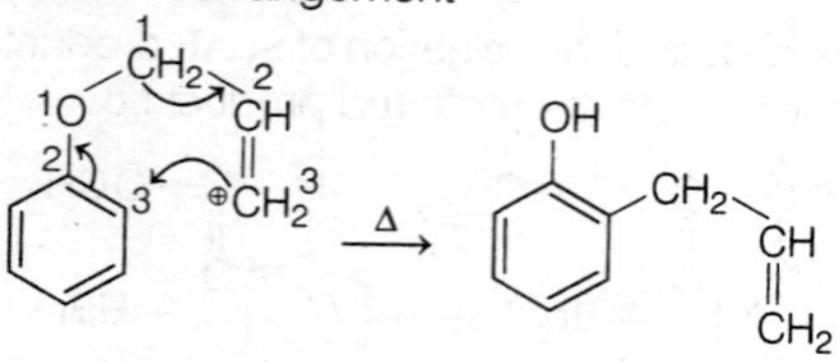

128. (*a*) Decarboxylation takes place simply on heating if there is keto group at β-position or α, β (C=C) bond

$$R\overset{O}{\underset{\beta}{\overset{\|}{C}}}CH_2\overset{O}{\overset{\|}{C}}OH \xrightarrow{\Delta} R\overset{O}{\overset{\|}{C}}CH_3$$

$$R\overset{\beta}{C}H=\overset{\alpha}{C}H\overset{O}{\overset{\|}{C}}OH \xrightarrow{\Delta} RCH=CH_2$$

132. (*b*)

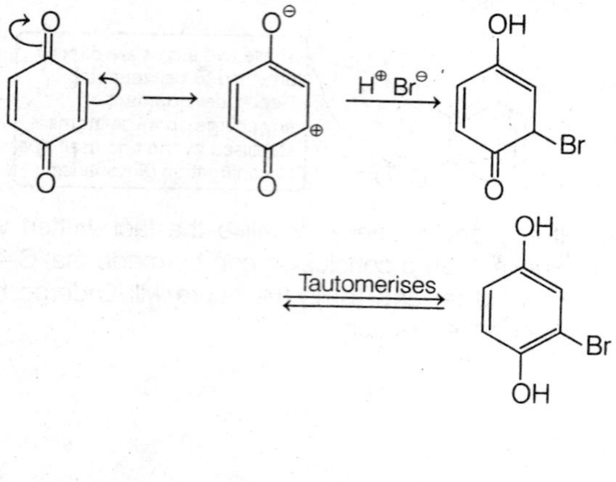

134. (*b*)

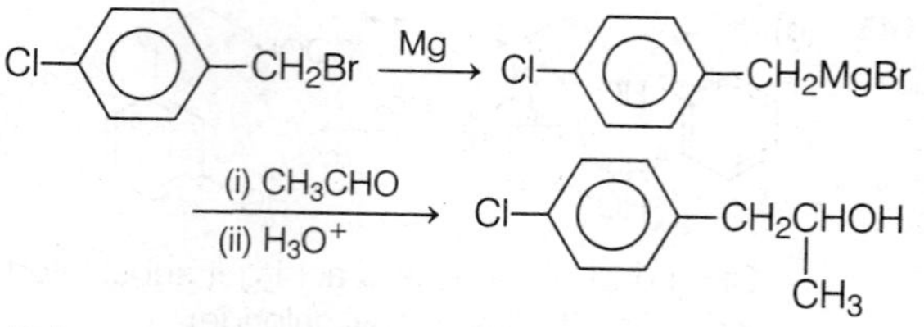

C—Br is more reactive than C—Cl.

139. (*d*)

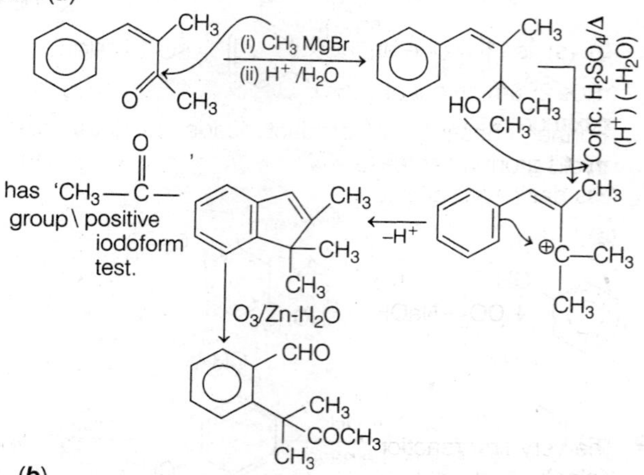

140. (*b*)

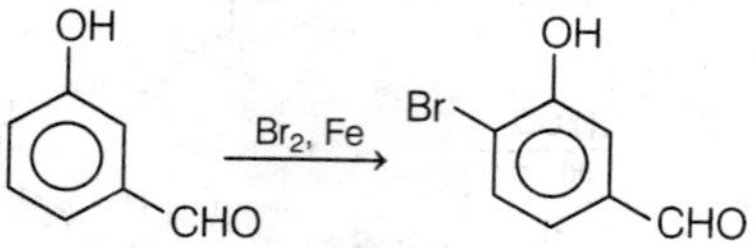

143. (*c*) The given reaction is a crossed Cannizzaro reaction which is a redox reaction too. Oxidation number of carbon atom of the —CHO groups of Ph—CHO and H—CHO are +1 and zero respectively. So, HCHO is the stronger reducing agent than PhCHO. As a result, HCHO is oxidised to HCOONa (by donation of hydride, H^-) and PhCHO (H^- acceptor) is reduced to $PhCH_2OH$.

$$Ph—\overset{+1}{C}HO + H\overset{0}{C}HO \xrightarrow{50\%\ NaOH} Ph—\overset{-1}{C}H_2OH + H\overset{+2}{C}O\overset{-}{O}\overset{+}{N}a$$

$$\downarrow H_3O^+$$

$$PhCH_2OH + HCOOH$$

(Major products)

The reaction proceed *via* following mechanism.

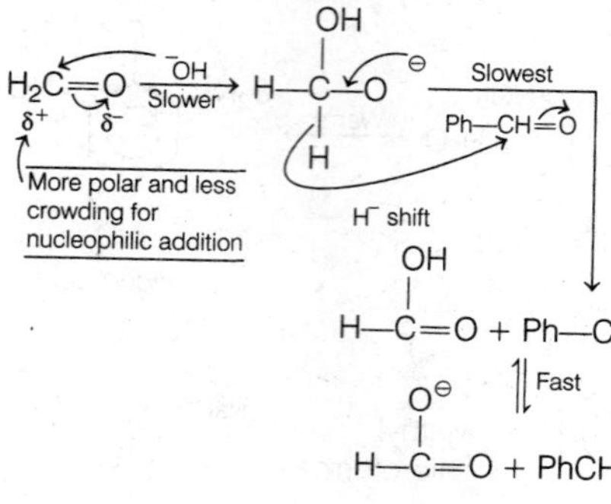

Thus, the correct option is (c).

145. (*c*)

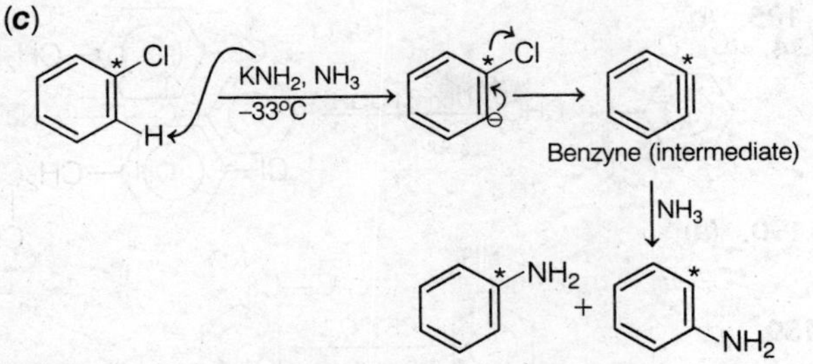

150. (*b*) (a) is 2° amine but attached to aromatic ring.

(b) is 2° amine but attached to aliphatic part. Thus, maximum basic.

151. (*d*) All groups decrease electron-density of nitrogen thus less basic than aniline.

158. (*a*)

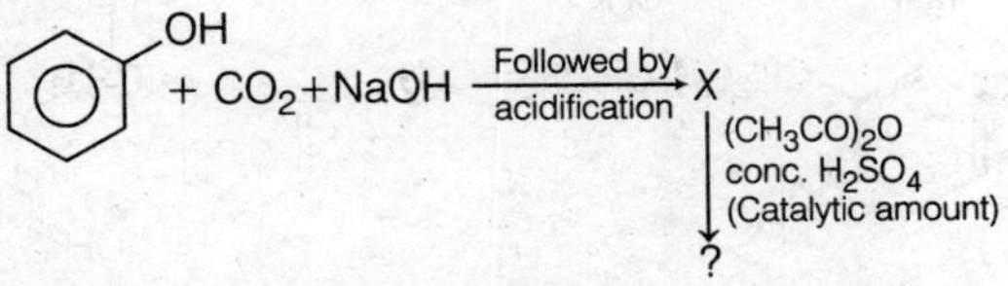

The very first reaction in the above road map looks like Kolbe's reaction which results to salicylic acid as

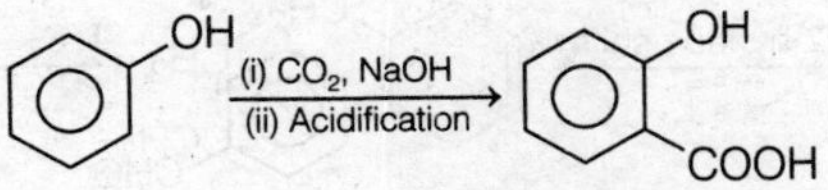

Salicylic acid
(X)

The salicylic acid with acetic anhydride $[(CH_3CO)_2O]$ in the presence of catalytic amount of conc. H_2SO_4 undergoes acylation to produce aspirin as

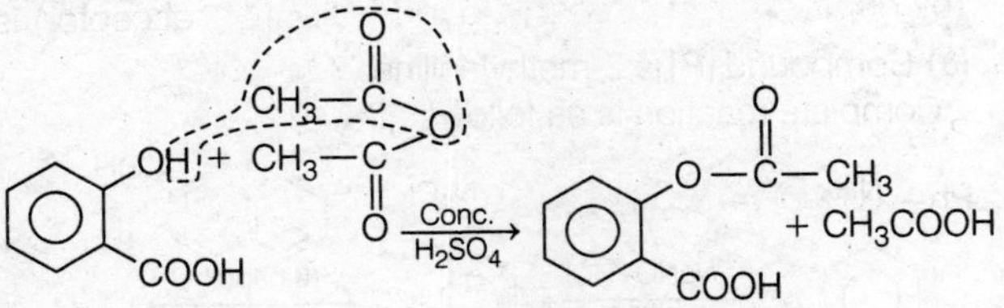

Acetyl salicylic acid (Aspirin)

Aspirin is a non-narcotic analgesic (Pain killer).

165. (*a*) Hydrolysis product of ester gives violet colour, thus, phenolic compound.

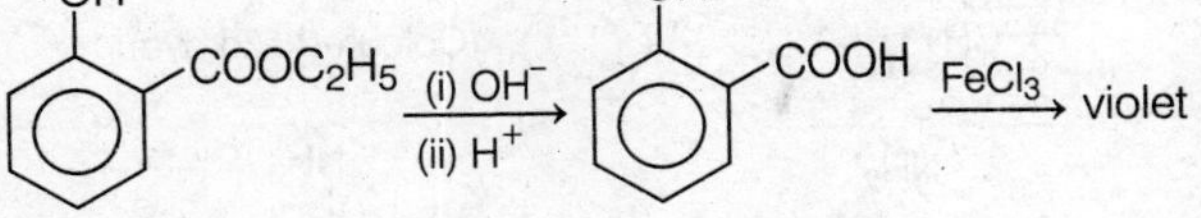

166. (*d*)

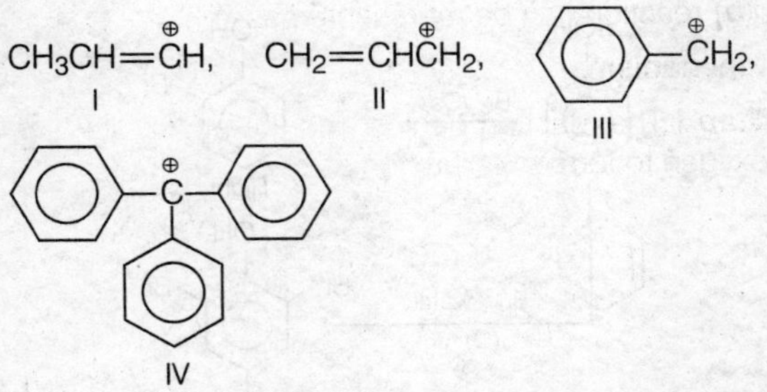

Carbocations given above are the intermediates of S_N1 reaction. Stability is in order I < II < III < IV. IV is stabilised to maximum extent due to resonance.

173. (*a*) —OH group displays both kinds of effect; an electron withdrawing acid-strengthening inductive effect from the *meta*-position and an electron-releasing acid weakening resonance effect from the *para*-position (at this position, resonance effect overweighs the inductive effect). Thus, III > IV. *o*-hydroxybenzoic acid (II) is far stronger than the corresponding *meta* and *para* isomers as the carboxylate ion is stabilised by intramolecular H-bonding.

2,6-dihydroxybenzoic acid (I) forms carboxylate ion which is further stabilised by intramolecular H-bonding,
Thus, correct order is I > II > III > IV

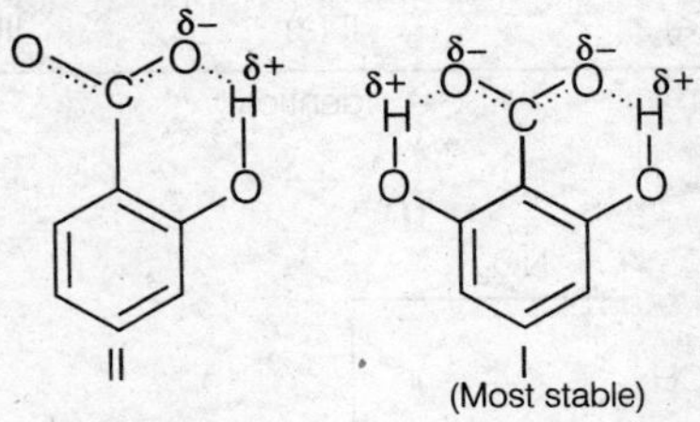

175. (*b*) The first step of the reaction is acylation.

In the second step of reaction, $-\ddot{N}H-\overset{O}{\overset{\|}{C}}-CH_3$ has +*R* (or +*M*) effect, so it acts as *ortho*/*para*-directing group. But, since *para* position has CH_3 group, substitution at *ortho* takes place. $-CH_3$ has weak *ortho*-/*para*- directing effect due to hyperconjugation, but it is suppressed due to

more predominant effect of $-\ddot{N}H-\overset{O}{\overset{\|}{C}}-CH_3$.

Thus, the complete reaction is given as follows :

176. (*b*)

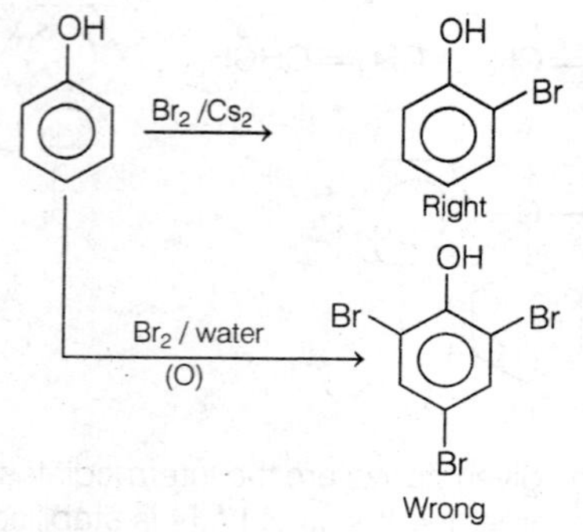

183. (*b*)

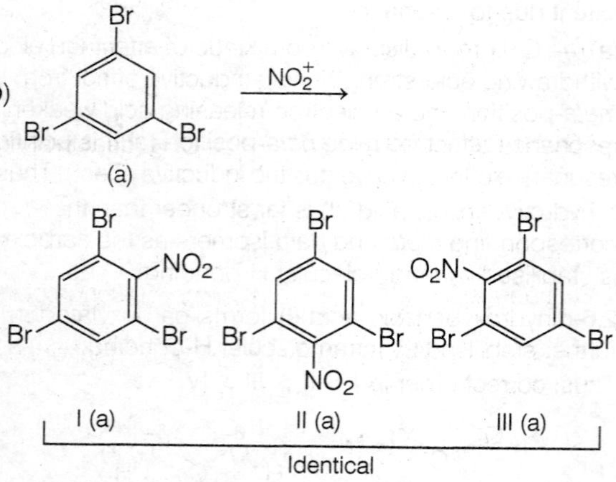

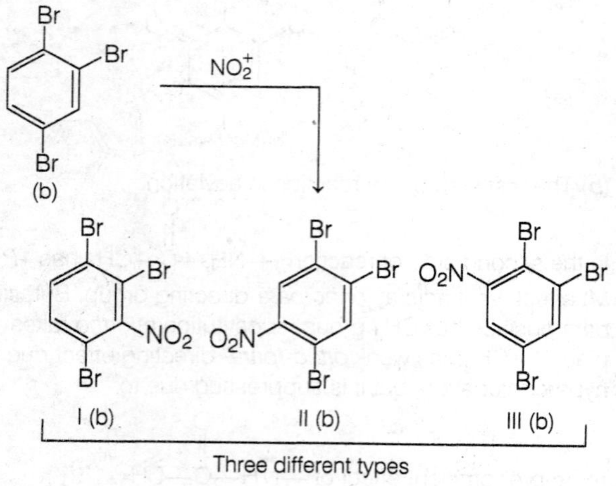

184. (*b*)

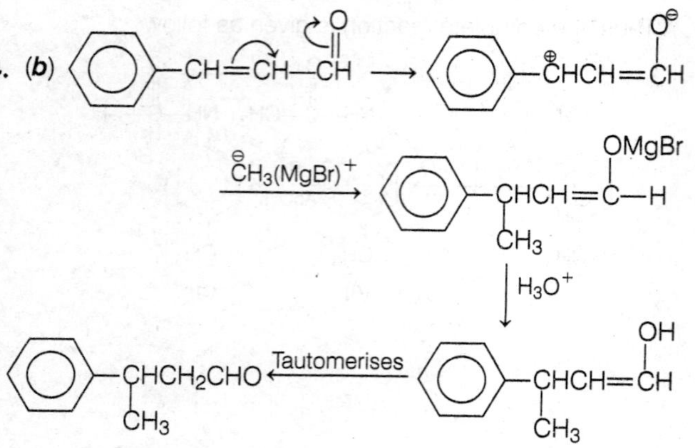

185. (*d*)

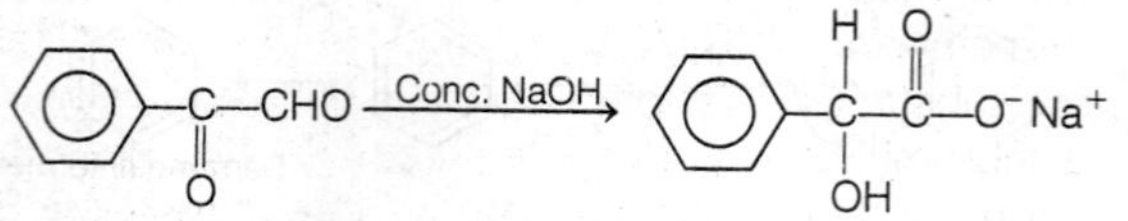

190. (*a*)

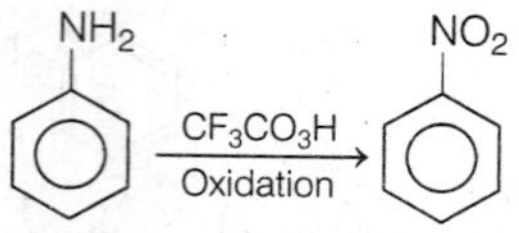

192. (*b*)

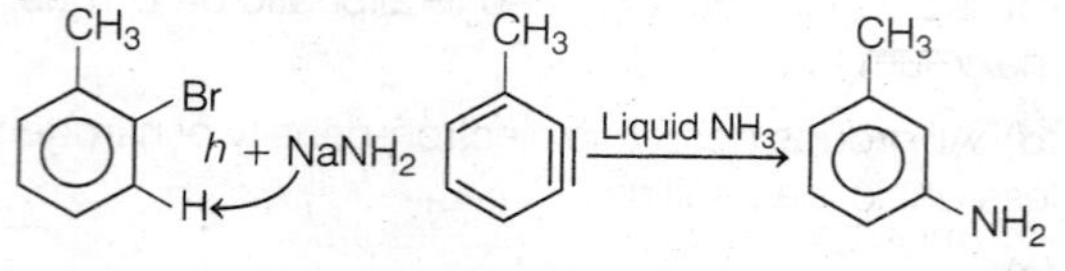

193. (*a*)

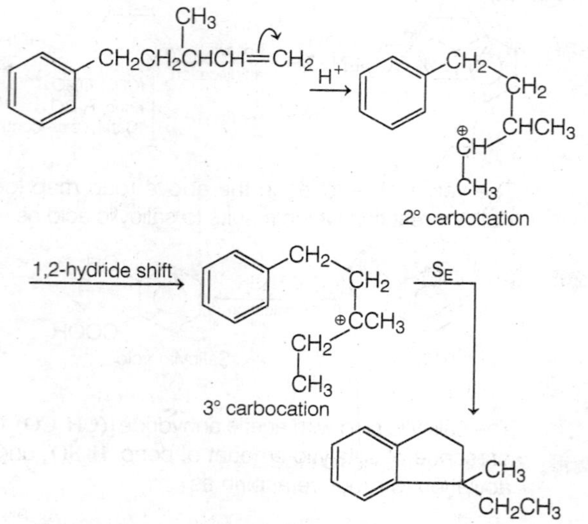

197. (*a*) Compound [*P*] is 3-methylaniline.
Complete reaction is as follows :

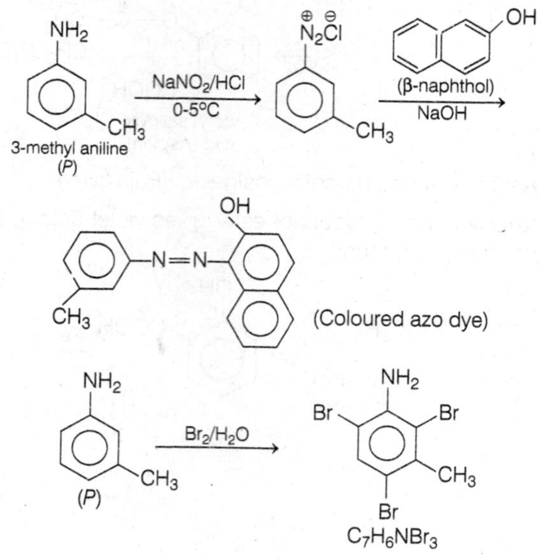

On comparing the formula $C_7H_6NBr_3$ with the formula of *m*-methylaniline (C_7H_9N), it is noticed that, three H atoms are substituted with three Br atoms (tribromination). To get a tribrominated product, all three activated positions of aniline (2 *ortho* and one *para*) must be free, where Br can come. Then, it can be concluded that the methyl group must be at *meta*-position only.

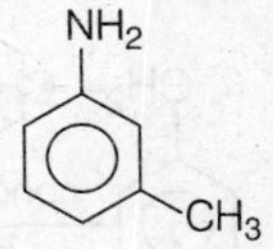

202. (*d*)

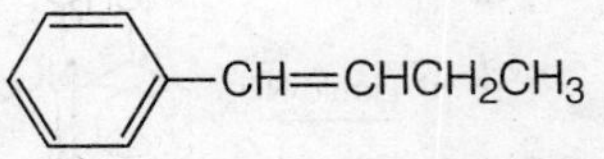

(most stable due to conjugation)

203. (*a*)

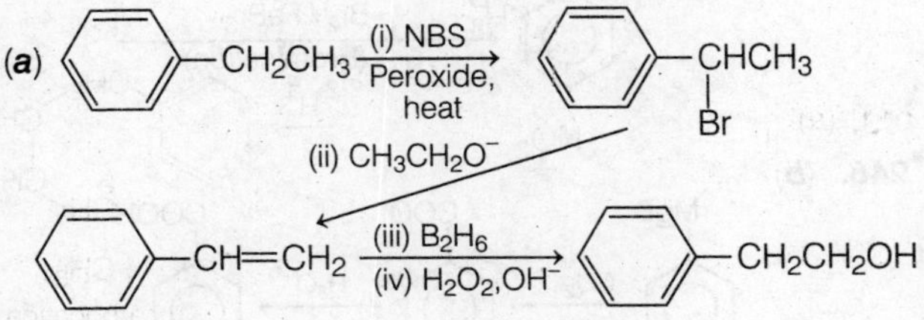

205. (*c*)

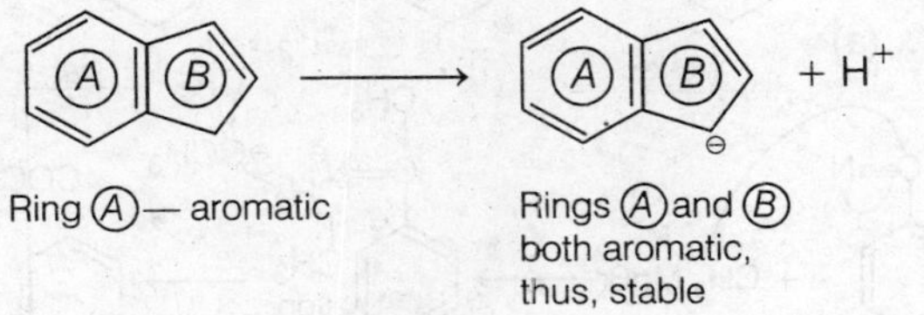

208. (*b*) N is more electronegative than 'C'. So, H of $\overset{\delta-}{N}$—$\overset{\delta+}{H}$ bond is more acidic than that of C—H bond in the ring. Again, sp^2-N is more electronegative ($s\% = 33.3$) than sp^3-N ($s\% = 25$) of the —NH_2 group.

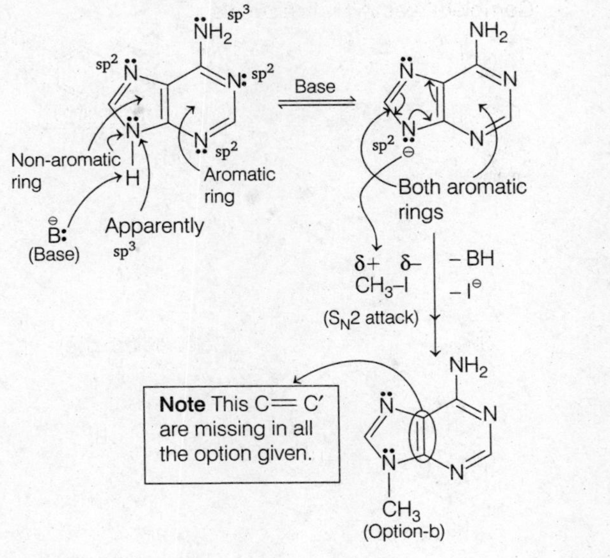

209. (*b*)

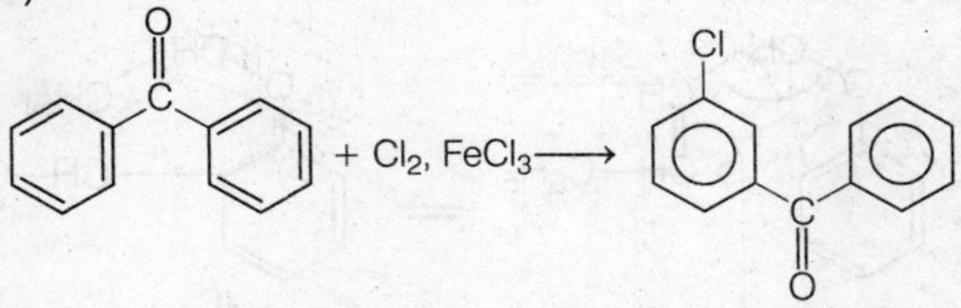

213. (*a*)

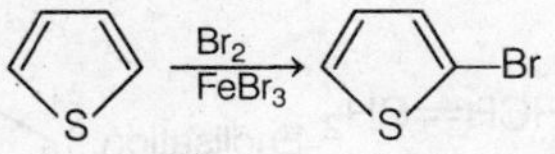

214. (*d*)

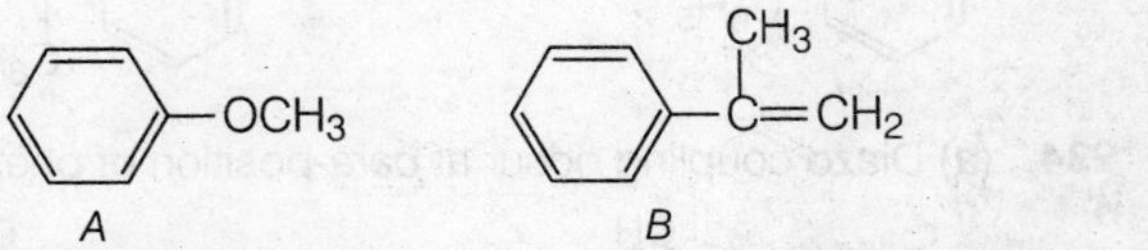

—OCH_3 (activating group) —C(—CH_3)=CH_2 (deactivating group)

B changes to

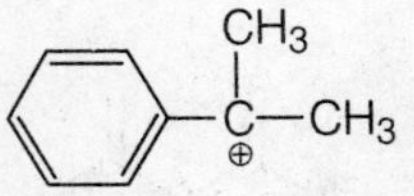

in presence of H_2SO_4.

Thus, there is S_E in ring *A* at *para* position (at *ortho* position, there is steric effect)

Thus,

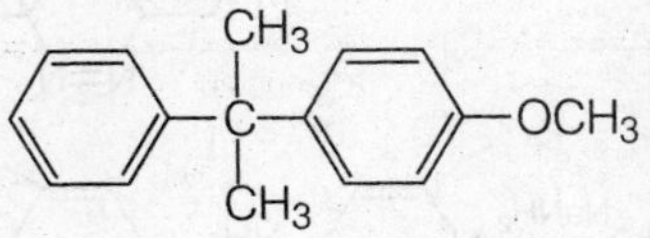

216. (*c*)

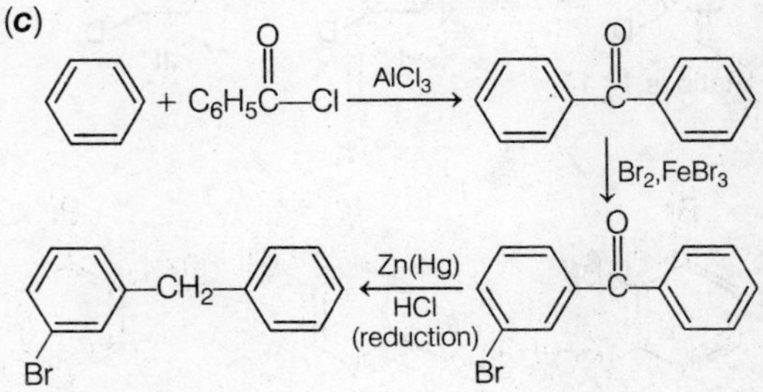

221. (*d*)

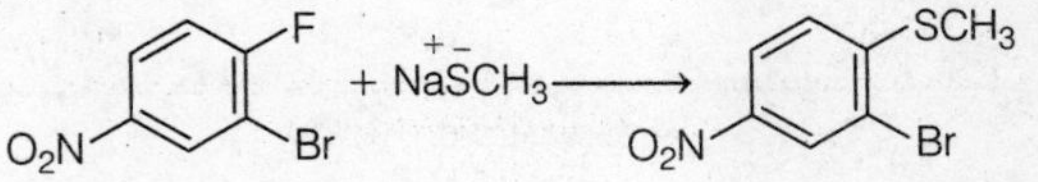

230. (*b*)

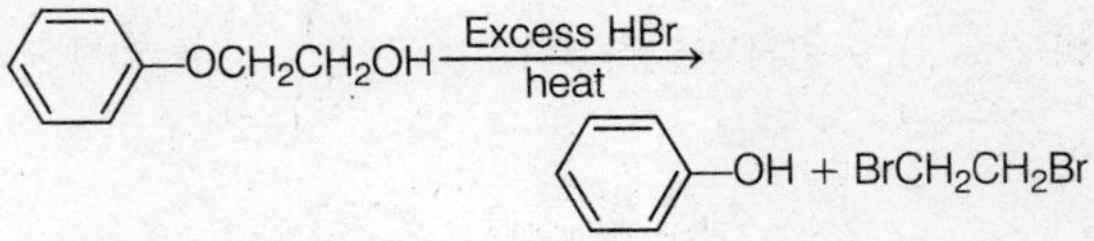

231. (*c*) By Claisen rearrangement

CH_2 CH CH—C_6H_5 ⇌ CH_2 CH CH—C_6H_5

OH CHCH=CH_2 C_6H_5 ← Enolisation — O H CHCH=CH_2 C_6H_5

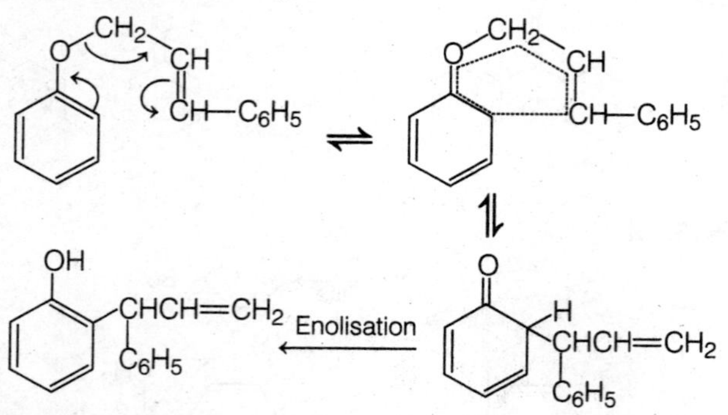

234. (*a*) Diazo coupling occur at *para*-position of phenol.

OH NH_2 —(i) $NaNO_2$/HCl/0°C (ii) NaOH→ OH $\overset{+}{N_2}Cl^-$ → OH N=N

237. (*c*)

D Cl D —$NaNH_2$ / NH_2→ NH_2 D (I) + NH_2 D (II)

Ratio is 1 : 1.

239. (*c*) CH_3 Br —NaOH→ CH_3 Benzyne —OH^-→ CH_3 OH and CH_3 HO

245. (*a*)

Benzene —CH_3—CH_2—Cl, $AlCl_3$ (Friedel Craft alkylation)→ CH_2—CH_3 —conc. HNO_3, H_2SO_4→ CH_2—CH_3 NO_2 —Br_2 / $FeBr_3$ (Bromination)→ CH_2—CH_3 Br NO_2

246. (*b*)

MgBr —CO_2→ COO^- —H_3O^+→ COOH

247. (*a*)

C≡N OCH_3 + $\overset{\ominus}{CH_3}$ $\overset{\oplus}{MgBr}$ → CH_3 C=$N^{\ominus}$ OCH_3 → $COCH_3$ OCH_3

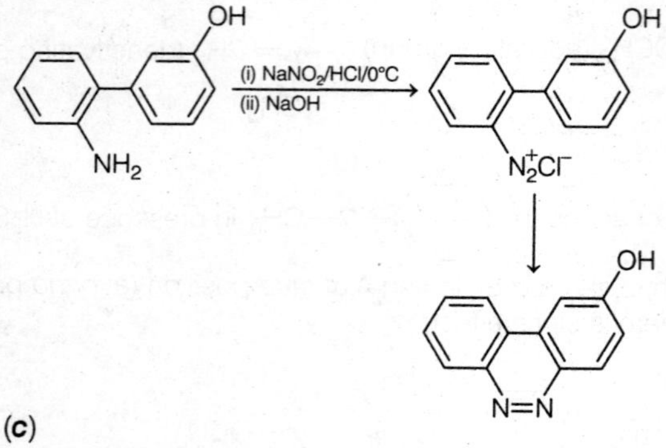

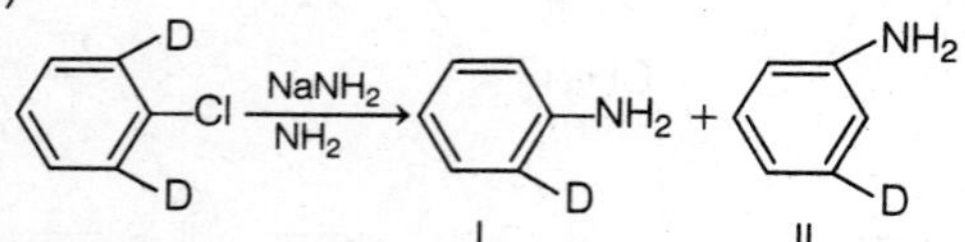

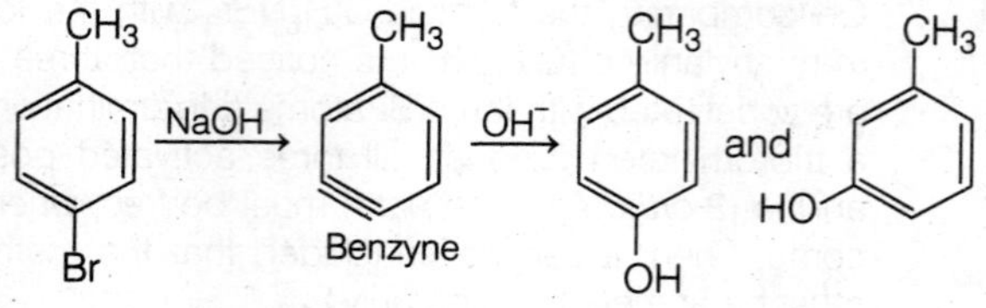

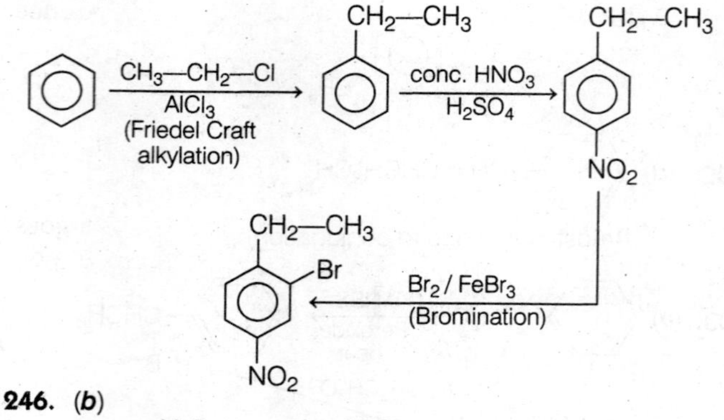

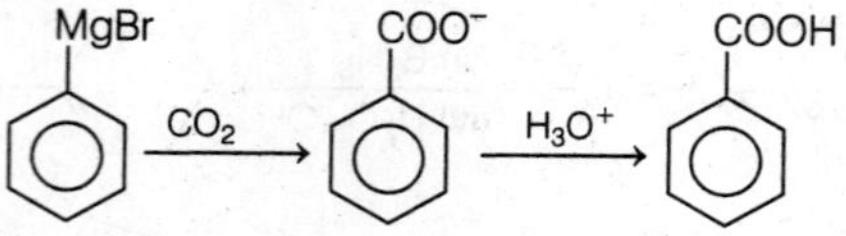

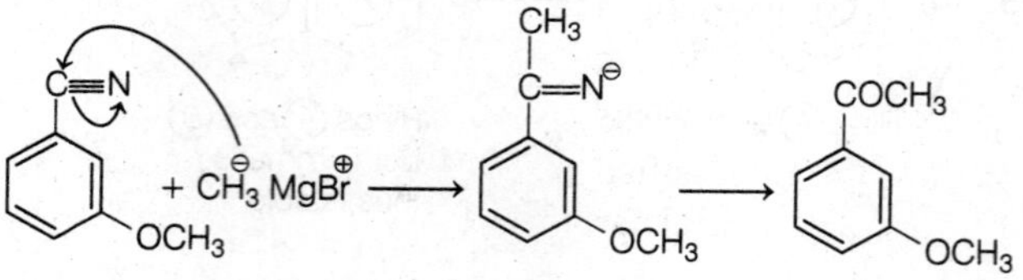

17

Biomolecules

Objective Questions Type I [Only one correct option]

In each of the questions below, four choices are given of which only one is correct.

1. Molecules such as erythrose and threose, which are stereoisomers but not mirror images, are referred to as a pair of ....; D- and L-threose are mirror images and are referred to as a pair of ....
(a) enantiomers; diastereomers
(b) diastereomers; enantiomers
(c) anomers; diastereomers
(d) diastereomers; anomers

2. A sugar is classified as a D-isomer if the hydroxyl group
(a) on the chiral carbon nearest to the carbonyl points to the left.
(b) on the chiral carbon nearest to the carbonyl points to the right.
(c) on the chiral carbon farthest from the carbonyl points to the left.
(d) on the chiral carbon farthest from the carbonyl points to the right.

3. All of the statements concerning monosaccharides are correct except.
(a) The number of stereoisomers possible is 2^n, where n is the number of chiral carbon atoms in the molecule.
(b) Monosaccharides with 5 or 6 carbon atoms exist in solution in cyclic form.
(c) The two different cyclic forms of a particular monosaccharide are called tautomers.
(d) A molecule is classified as a D or L isomer by the position of the hydroxyl group on the chiral centre farthest from the carbonyl group.

4. When a monosaccharide forms a ring by interaction of one of its hydroxyl group with its aldehyde group, the bond is referred to as a (an) .... linkage.
(a) ether (b) ester (c) acetal (d) hemiacetal

5. Glucose and galactose are having identical configuration in all the positions except position. **[JEE Main 2019]**
(a) C-3 (b) C-4 (c) C-2 (d) C-5

6. Plants obtain glucose by the process known as
(a) photosynthesis (b) respiration
(c) autolysis (d) dialysis

7. Consider the following statements,
I. Photosynthesis uses CO_2 that animals exhale as waste and generates O_2 that animals inhale.
II. Nearly all the O_2 in Earth's atmosphere has been released by photo-synthesis processes.
III. Cellulose is the major structural component of plants.

Select the correct alternates.
(a) I and II (b) II and III
(c) I, II and III (d) I and III

8. Which among the following pairs of vitamins is stored in our body relatively for longer duration? **[JEE Main 2021, March]**
(a) Thiamine and vitamin A
(b) Vitamin A and vitamin D
(c) Thiamine and ascorbic acid
(d) Ascorbic acid and vitamin D

9. Which is a furanose structure of D-glucose?

(a) 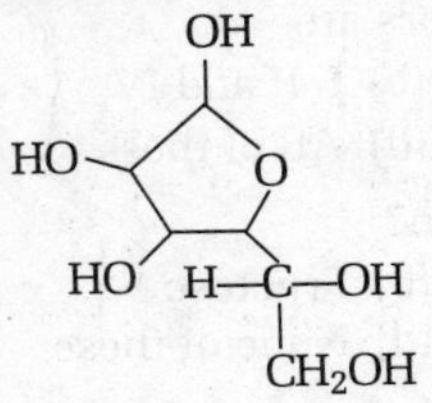

(b) 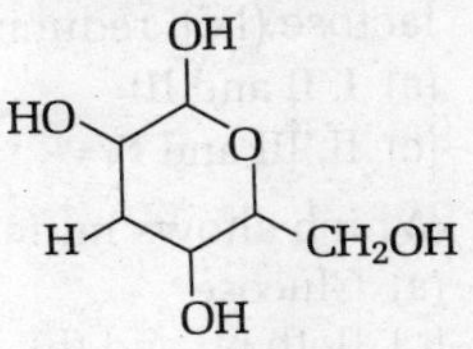

(c) Both (a) and (b) (d) None of these

10. Although D-galactose rotates plane-polarised light, its oxidation product, galactaric acid, due to HNO_3, does not. It is due to

(a) galactaric acid is a racemic mixture of D-and L-isomer
(b) galactaric acid is a meso compound
(c) Both (a) and (b) are correct
(d) None of the above is correct

11. Consider the following synthetic compounds,

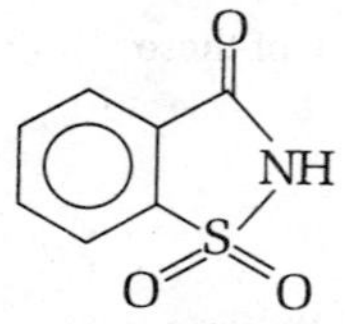

I (Saccharin)

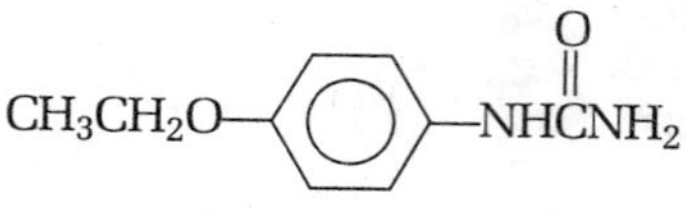

II (Dulcin)

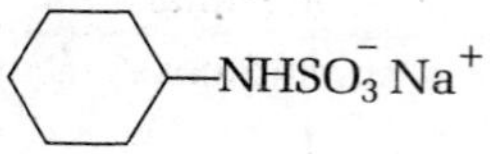

III (Sodium cyclamate)

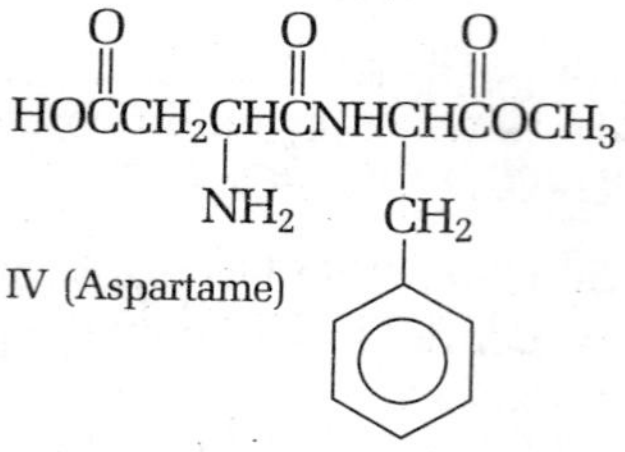

IV (Aspartame)

Which of the above examples are used as sweetening agents?

(a) I, III and IV (b) II, III and IV
(c) I, II and IV (d) All of these

12. Ketones do not reduce Tollen's reagents, but fructose with a keto group reduces it. It is attributed to

(a) enolisation of keto group of fructose and then, its transformation into aldehyde group in presence of OH^- which is present in Tollen's reagent
(b) >CHOH group which is also oxidised to keto group
(c) Both (a) & (b) statements are correct
(d) None of the above statement is correct

13. If α-D-glucopyranose is reacted with acetic anhydride at 373 K, the major product is the β-isomer of the pentaacetate. It is attributed to

(a) isomerisation of α-D into β-D-glucose at 373 K
(b) opening of glucopyranose ring
(c) Both the statements are correct
(d) None of the statement is correct

14. Out of maltose (I), cellobiose (II), sucrose (III) and lactose (IV), reducing sugars are

(a) I, II and III (b) I, II and IV
(c) II, III and IV (d) All of these

15. Which shows mutarotation?

(a) Glucose (b) Fructose
(c) Both (a) and (b) (d) None of these

16. The secondary structure of protein is stabilised by **[JEE Main 2021, March]**

(a) peptide bond (b) glycosidic bond
(c) hydrogen bonding (d) van der Waals' forces

17. Glucose is said to have — CHO group. Which of the following reactions is not expected with glucose?

(a) It does not form oxime
(b) It does not react with CH_3MgBr
(c) It does not reduce Tollen's reagent
(d) It does not form osazones

18. Fructose $\xrightarrow[\text{2. P/HI}]{\text{1. HCN/H}_3\text{O}^+}$ *A*. *A* is

(a) *n*-heptanoic acid
(b) 2-methyl hexanoic acid
(c) *n*-heptane
(d) 2-methyl hexane

19. Glucose $\xrightarrow[\text{2. P/HI}]{\text{1. HCN/H}_3\text{O}^+}$ *A*. *A* is

(a) *n*-heptanoic acid (b) 2-methyl hexanoic acid
(c) *n*-heptane (d) 2-methyl hexane

20. Blood sugar and grape sugar are respectively

(a) glucose, fructose (b) fructose, glucose
(c) glucose (of both) (d) fructose (of both)

21. Haworth's projection of α-D-glucose is

(a) 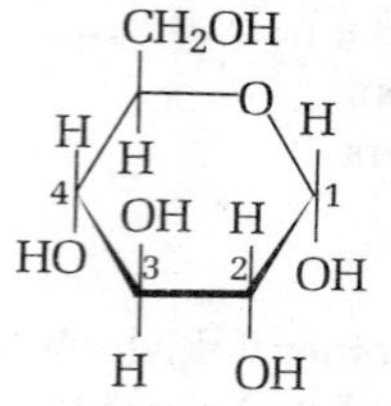

(b) 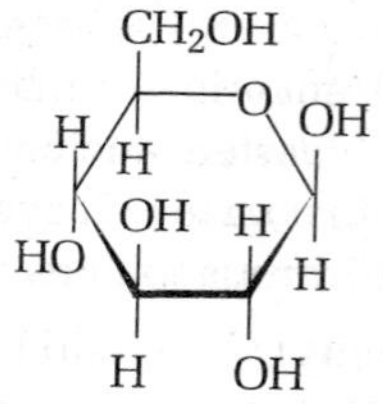

(c) Both (a) and (b) (d) None of these

22. Which of the following compounds will behave as a reducing sugar in an aqueous KOH solution? **[JEE Main 2017]**

(a) 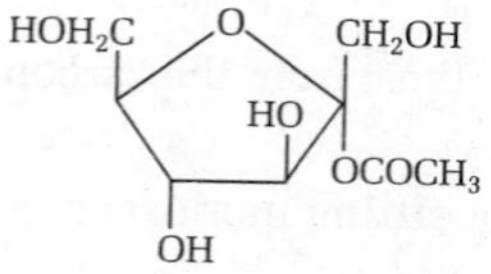

(b) 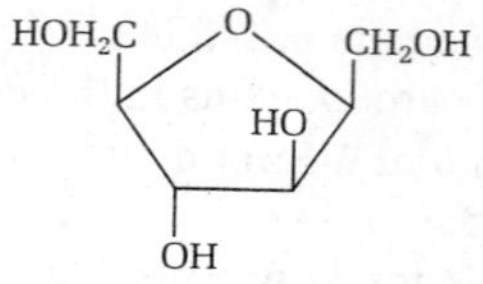

(c) 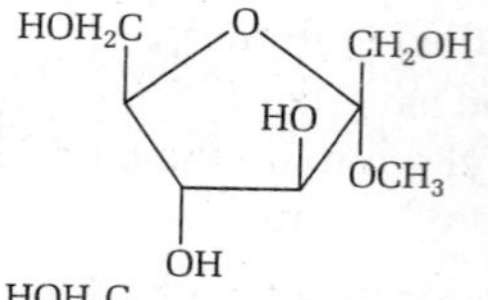

(d) 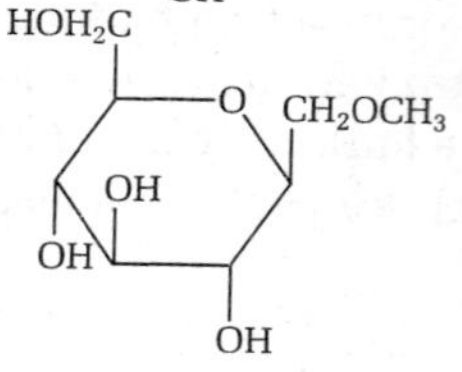

23. Periodic acid splits glucose and fructose into formic acid and formaldehyde. Ratio of formic acid and formaldehyde from glucose and fructose is

(a) 5/1 and 4/2
(b) 5/1 and 5/1
(c) 4/2 and 4/2
(d) No reaction

24. Chiral C-atoms in glucose and fructose are

(a) 4 in each
(b) 3 in each
(c) 4 in glucose and 3 in fructose
(d) 3 in glucose and 4 in fructose

25. Which gives only glucose by hydrolysis?

(a) sucrose
(b) raffinose
(c) maltose
(d) galactose

26. Which polysaccharide has α-glycoside linkage?

(a) amylose
(b) amylopetcin
(c) cellulose
(d) All of these

27. In the given reactions, the enzyme *A* and enzyme *B* respectively are **[JEE Main 2021, March]**

$$\underset{\text{Sucrose}}{C_{12}H_{22}O_{11}} + H_2O \xrightarrow{\text{Enzyme } A} \underset{\text{Glucose}}{C_6H_{12}O_6} + \underset{\text{Fructose}}{C_6H_{12}O_6}$$

$$\underset{\text{Glucose}}{C_6H_{12}O_6} \xrightarrow{\text{Enzyme } B} 2C_2H_5OH + 2CO_2$$

(a) Amylase and invertase
(b) Invertase and amylase
(c) Invertase and zymase
(d) Zymase and invertase

28. Methyl glucoside is stable towards HIO_4 such that it produces one molecule of formic acid by consuming two molecules of HIO_4. Other product formed is

(a) 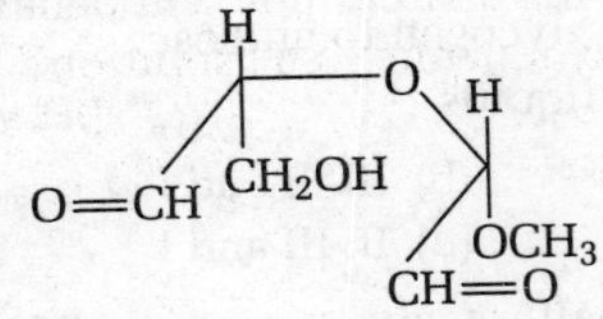

(b) 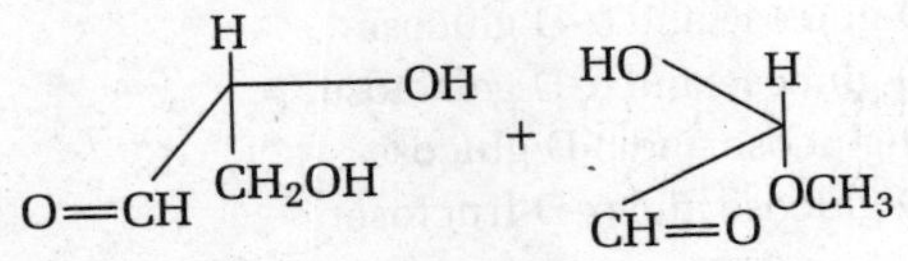

(c) Both (a) and (b)
(d) None of the above

29. Furanose form of glucoside (of a carbohydrate) given below is subjected to oxidative cleavage by periodic acid.

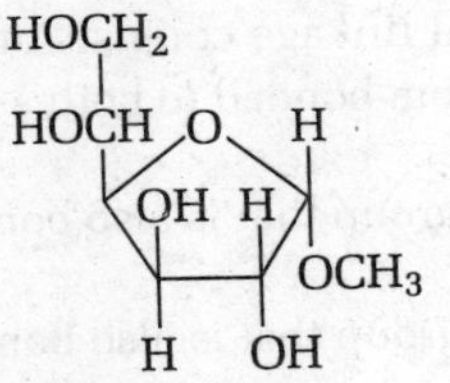

Product formed is HCHO and

(a) 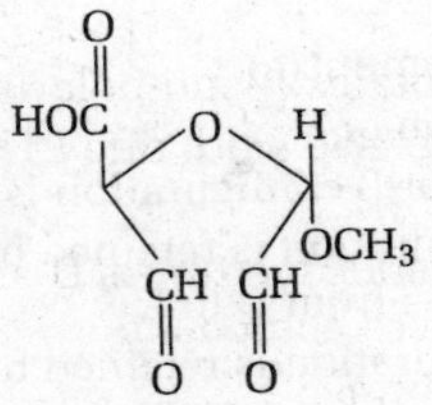

(b) 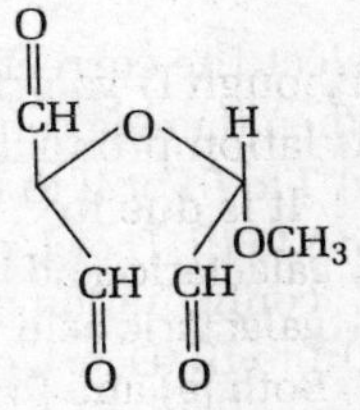

(c) 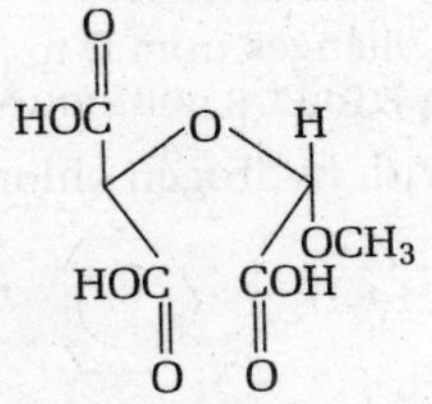

(d) None of these

30. Glucose on prolonged heating with HI gives **[JEE Main 2018]**

(a) *n*-hexane
(b) 1-hexene
(c) Hexanoic acid
(d) 6-iodohexanal

31. Consider the following pairs of substances *A*, *B* and *C*, *D*

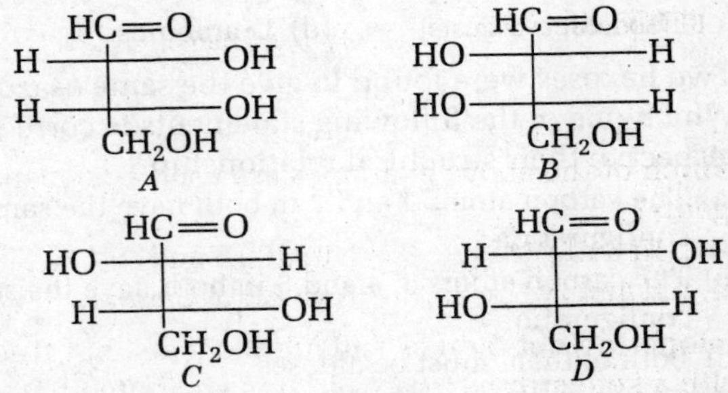

Consider the following facts about these stereoisomers

I. *A* and *B*, and *C* and *D* are also enantiomers and diastereomers
II. *A* and *C* and *B* and *D* are diastereomers
III. *A* and *C* represent D-configuration while *B* and *D* represent L-configuration
IV. *A* and *B* represent erythrose while *C* and *D* represent threose configuration

Select the correct facts.

(a) I and II
(b) II and III
(c) I, II and III
(d) II, III and IV

32. Consider the following transformation,

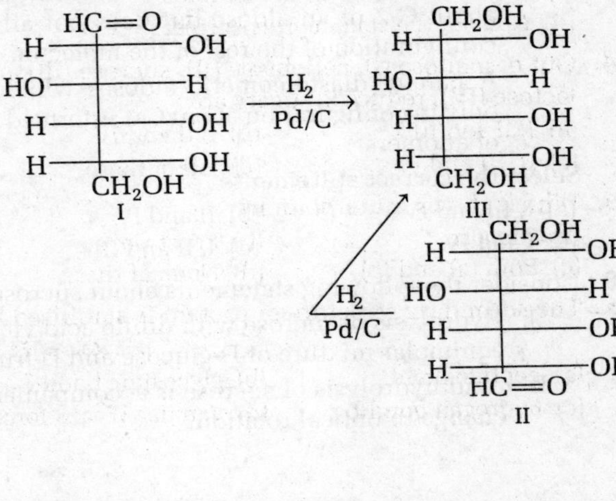

Select the correct statement(s).

When there is conversion of

(a) I to III or II to III, D or L configuration is retained

(b) I to III, D or L configuration is retained but II to III configuration changes from D to L

(c) I to III, D or L configuration is retained but II to III configuration changes from L to D

(d) I to III, configuration changes from D to L and that of II to III, changes from L to D

33. Glucose on treatment with hydrogen chloride in methanol affords

(a) pentamethyl glucose

(b) α-methyl glucoside

(c) β-methyl glucoside

(d) a mixture of α- and β-methyl glucosides

34. Which one of the following aldopentoses will yield a mixture of glucose and mannose on Kiliani homologation?

(a) D-ribose (b) D-xylose

(c) D-lyxose (d) D-arabinose

35. Two hexoses were found to give the same osazone. Which one of the following statements is correct with respect to their structural relationship?

(a) The carbon atoms 1 and 2 in both have the same configuration

(b) The carbon atoms 3, 4 and 5 in both have the same configuration

(c) Both of them must be aldoses

(d) They are epimeric at C-3

36. What is the number of asymmetric carbon atoms present in α-D-glucopyranose molecule?

(a) Two (b) Three

(c) Four (d) Five

37. Consider the following statements about carbohydrates.

I. Bromine water can be used to differentiate aldose from ketose.

II. All monosaccharides (aldose or ketose) are reducing sugars.

III. Osazone formation destroys the configuration about C-2 of an aldose but does not affect the configuration of the rest of the molecule.

IV. A pair of diastereomeric aldoses which differ only in configuration about C-2 is termed as pair of anomers.

Select the correct statements.

(a) I, III and IV (b) II and IV

(c) I and IV (d) I, II and III

38. Consider the following statements about sucrose.

I. Hydrolysis of sucrose with dilute acid yields an equimolar mixture of D-glucose and D-fructose.

II. Acid hydrolysis of sucrose is accompanied by a change in optical rotation.

III. In sucrose, the glycosidic linkage is between C_1 of glucose and C_2 of fructose.

IV. Aqueous solution of sucrose exhibits mutarotation.

Which of the statements given above are correct?

(a) I, II and III (b) I and IV

(c) II, III and IV (d) II and IV

39. Kiliani-Fischer synthesis converts an aldpentose to a

(a) mixture of aldohexose and ketohexose

(b) mixture of aldohexoses differing in configuration of C_6

(c) mixture of aldohexoses differing in configuration of C_2

(d) single aldohexose

40. Consider the following statements for monosaccharides.

I. They are optically active polyhydroxy carbonyl compounds.

II. Fructose is a ketose sugar and hence, it does not give red precipitate with Fehling solution.

III. α-D-[+]-glucose and β-D[+]-glucose are anomers.

IV. Glucose and mannose are epimers.

Which of the above statements are correct?

(a) I and II

(b) I, II and III

(c) I, II and IV

(d) I, III and IV

41. When a person is deprived of food, in which order does the body use the following sources to produce glucose?

I. Protein breakdown to amino acids used for gluconeogenesis

II. Conversion of glycogen to glucose

III. Catabolism of liquids

(a) I, II and III (b) III, II and I

(c) II, I and III (d) II, III and I

42. Two monomers in maltose are **[JEE Main 2020]**

(a) α-D-glucose and α-D-glucose

(b) α-D-glucose and α-D-galactose

(c) α-D-glucose and β-D-glucose

(d) α-D-glucose and α-D-fructose

43. Maltose on treatment with dilute HCl gives **[JEE Main 2019]**

(a) D-glucose and D-fructose

(b) D-fructose

(c) D-galactose

(d) D-glucose

44. A hemiacetal linkage consists of a

(a) carbon atom bonded to both an —OH and an —*OR* groups

(b) carbonyl group that is also bonded to a hydroxyl group

(c) carbonyl group that is also bonded to an ether linkage

(d) carbon atom bonded to two —OH groups

45. Two isomeric sugars that are cyclic and only differ in the position of the —OH group at the hemiacetal group are called
(a) enantiomers (b) mutarotations
(c) anomers (d) epimers

46. When a monosaccharide forms a cyclic hemiacetal, the carbon atom that contains the carbonyl group is identified as the ... carbon atom because
(a) D; the carbonyl group is drawn to the right
(b) L; the carbonyl group is drawn to the left
(c) anomeric; its substituents can assume an α or β position
(d) acetal; it forms bond to an —*OR* and an —*OR'*

47. The hormone which controls the processes like burning of fats, proteins and carbohydrates to liberate energy in the body is
(a) cortisone (b) thyroxine
(c) adrenalin (d) insulin

48. Glucose molecule reacts with '*X*' number of molecules of phenylhydrazine to yield osazone. The value of '*X*' is
(a) four (b) one
(c) two (d) three

49. If K_{a_1} and K_{a_2} are the ionisation constants of $H_3\overset{+}{N}CHRCOOH$ and $H_3\overset{+}{N}CHRCOO^-$, respectively, the pH of the solution at the isoelectric point is
(a) $pH = (pK_{a_1} + pK_{a_2})$ (b) $pH = (pK_{a_1} + pK_{a_2})^{1/2}$
(c) $pH = (pK_{a_1} + pK_{a_2})/2$ (d) $pH = (pK_{a_1} + pK_{a_2})^2$

50. Which of the following statement is not true for glucose? **[JEE Main 2020]**
(a) The pentaacetate of glucose does not react with hydroxylamine to give oxime
(b) Glucose exists in two crystalline forms α and β
(c) Glucose gives Schiff's test for aldehyde
(d) Glucose reacts with hydroxylamine to form oxime

51. The hormone that helps in the conversion of glucose to glycogen is
(a) cortisone (b) bile acids
(c) adrenalin (d) insulin

52. α-D-glucose and β-D-glucose have a specific rotation of +112° and +19° respectively. In aqueous solution the rotation becomes +52°. This is known as
(a) racemisation
(b) mutarotation
(c) inversion
(d) enolisation

53. The hydrolysis of sugar to glucose and fructose is catalysed by
(a) zymase (b) invertase
(c) diastase (d) maltase

54. Insulin is secreted by
(a) stomach (b) intestine
(c) pancreas (d) brain

55. Sucrose on treatment with HCl produces
(a) glucose (b) fructose
(c) Both (a) and (b) (d) laevulinic acid

56. Choose the response that provides the best match between the terms given and the structures shown.

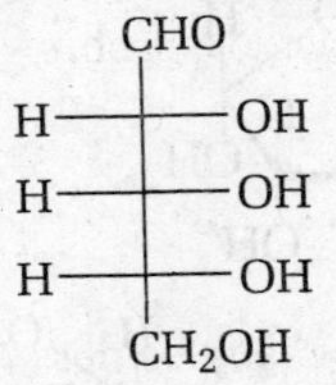
I

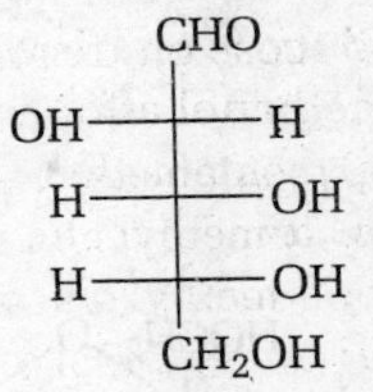
II

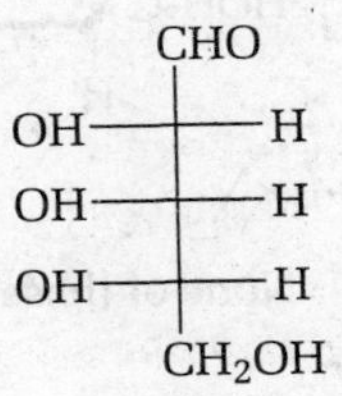
III

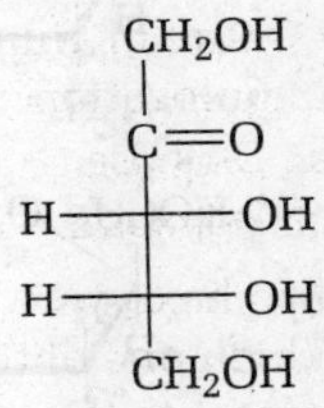
IV

	Diastereomers	Enantiomers
(a)	I, III and IV	I and III
(b)	I and II	I and III
(c)	I, II and III	I and III
(d)	I and IV	I and II

57. D-carbohydrate is
(a) always dextrorotatory
(b) always levorotatory
(c) always the anomer of the corresponding L carbohydrate
(d) None of the above

58. Two of the three compounds shown below yield the same product on reaction with warm HNO_3. The exception is

(a) 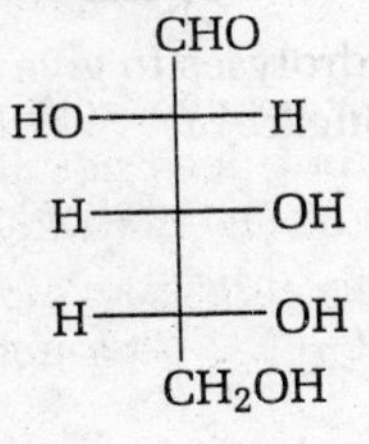

(b) 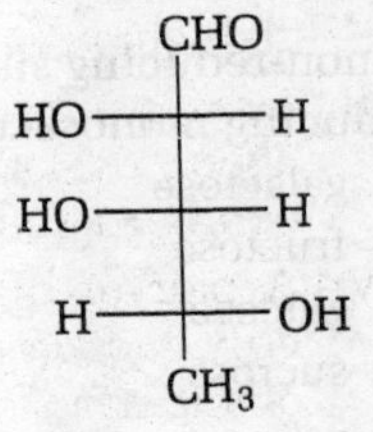

(c) 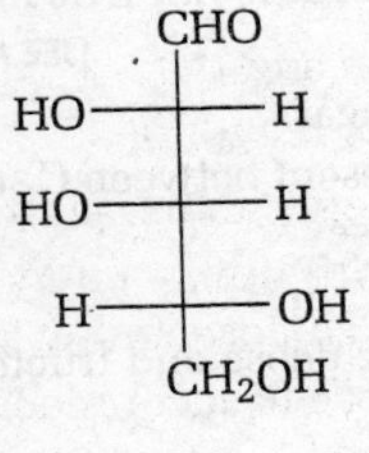

(d) None of these (all yield the same product)

59. The optical rotation of the α form of a pyranose is $+150.7°$; that of the β form is $+52.8°$. In solution, an equilibrium mixture of the anomers has an optical rotation of $+80.2°$. The percentage of the α-form at equilibrium is

(a) 28% (b) 32% (c) 68% (d) 72%

60. Which of the following represents the anomer of the compound shown?

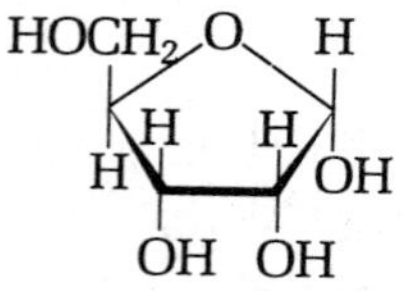

(a) 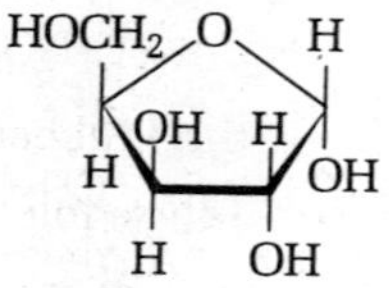

(b) 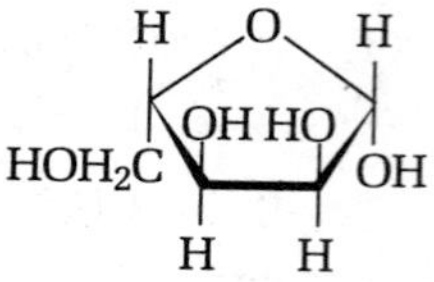

(c) 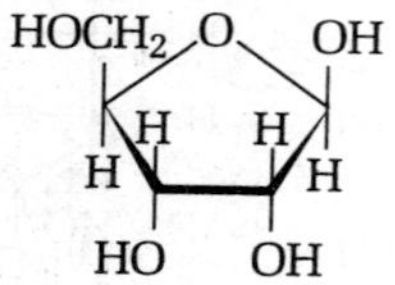

(d) None of these

61. All of the following can be classified as biomolecules except

(a) carbohydrates

(b) proteins

(c) lipids

(d) All of the above are biomolecules

62. Which functional group is least important in biochemistry?

(a) Amide (b) Amine

(c) Aromatic (d) Ester

63. Members of which class of biomolecules are the building blocks of proteins?

(a) Glycerols (b) Monosaccharides

(c) Fatty acids (d) Amino acids

64. A non-reducing sugar "*A*" hydrolyses to give two reducing monosaccharides. Sugar *A* is

(a) galactose

(b) fructose

(c) glucose

(d) sucrose

65. Which of the following statement is not true about sucrose? **[JEE Main 2019]**

(a) It is also named as invert sugar.

(b) The glycosidic linkage is present between C_1 of α-glucose and C_1 of β-fructose

(c) It is a non-reducing sugar

(d) On hydrolysis, it produces glucose and fructose

66. Cellulose upon acetylation with excess acetic anhydride/H_2SO_4 (catalytic) gives cellulose triacetate whose structure is

(a) 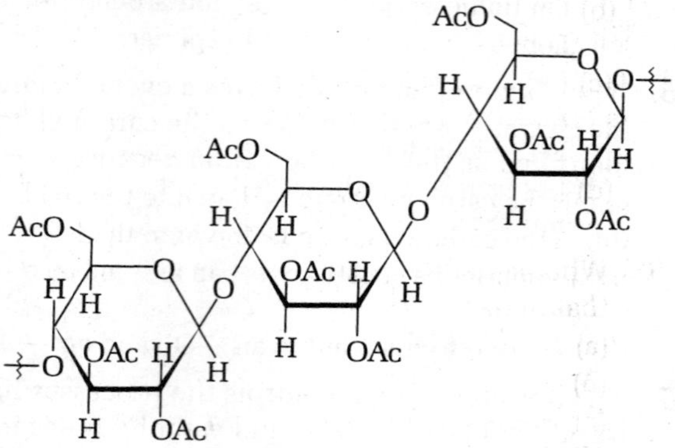

(b) 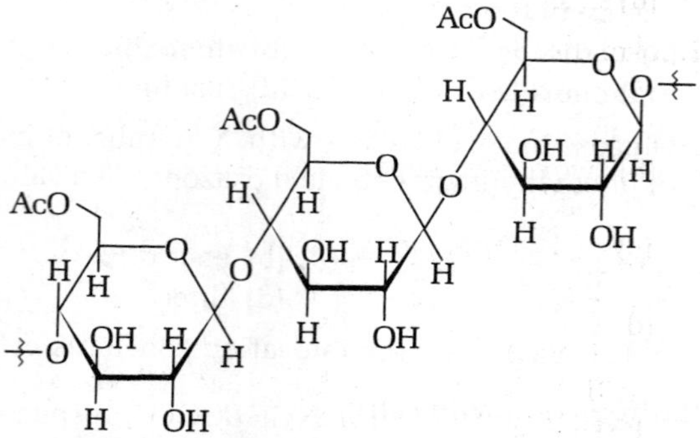

(c) 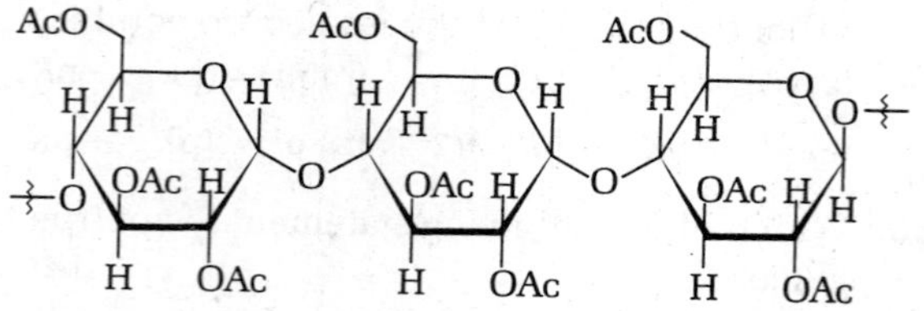

(d) 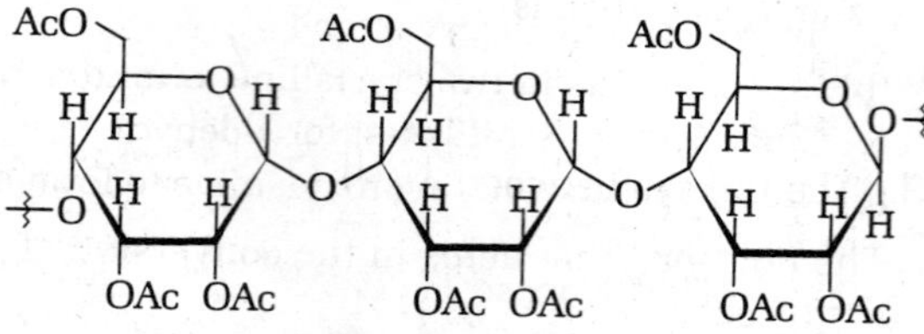

67. Sucrose is not a reducing sugar because its

(a) hemiacetal groups cannot be converted to aldehyde groups

(b) disaccharide bond is an α-1,4 linkage

(c) disaccharide bond is a β-1,4 linkage

(d) disaccharide bond is a 1,2 anomeric link

68. The most important goal of glucose metabolism is

(a) synthesis of oxidised coenzymes

(b) synthesis of glycogen for later use

(c) production of ATP as an energy source for all cells

(d) production of acetyl-SCoA for synthesis of lipids

69. Which one of the following statements is not true regarding (+) lactose?
(a) (+) lactose, $C_{12}H_{22}O_{11}$ contains 8-OH groups.
(b) On hydrolysis (+) lactose gives equal amount of D-(+)-glucose and D-(+)-galactose.
(c) (+) lactose is a β-glycoside formed by the union of molecule of D-(+)-glucose and a molecule of D-(+)-galactose.
(d) (+) lactose is reducing sugar and does not exhibit mutarotation.

70. What is nature of glucose-glucose linkage in starch that makes its so susceptible to acid hydrolysis?
(a) Starch is hemiacetal.
(b) Starch is acetal.
(c) Starch is polymer.
(d) Starch contains only few molecules of glucose.

71. α-maltose consists of
(a) one α-D-glucopyranose unit and one β-D-glucopyranose unit with 1-2 glycosidic linkage
(b) two α-D-glucopyranose units with 1-2 glycosidic linkage
(c) two β-D-glucopyranose units with 1-4 glycosidic linkage
(d) two α-D-glucopyranose units with 1-4 glycosidic linkage

72. In the following structure,

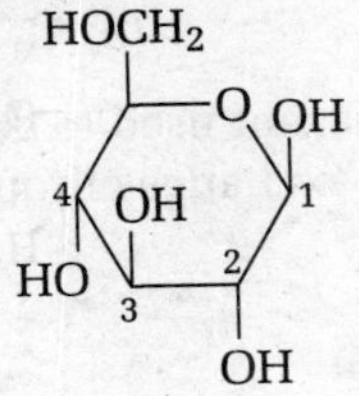

anomeric carbon is
(a) 1 (b) 2
(c) 3 (d) 4

73. The linkage between the two monosaccharide units in lactose is
(a) C_1 of β-D-glucose and C_4 of β-D-galactose
(b) C_1 of β-D-galactose and C_4 of β-D-glucose
(c) C_1 of α-D-galactose and C_4 of β-D-glucose
(d) C_1 of β-D-galactose and C_4 of α-D-glucose
(e) C_1 of α-D-glucose and C_4 of α-D-glucose

74. How glucose is related with fructose?
(a) Functional group isomerism
(b) Rotamers
(c) Positions isomerism
(d) Geometrical isomerism

75. How can you say that glucose is cyclic compound?
(a) Glucose undergoes Tollen's reaction
(b) Glucose reacts with phenyl hydrazine
(c) Glucose fails to react with sodium hydrogen sulphite
(d) Glucose reacts with nitric acid

76. A diabetic person carries a packet of glucose with him always, because
(a) glucose increases the blood sugar level slowly.
(b) glucose reduces the blood sugar level.
(c) glucose increases the blood sugar level almost instantaneously.
(d) glucose reduces the blood sugar level slowly.

77. Which of the following is a trisaccharide?
(a) Stachyrose (b) Sucrose
(c) Raffinose (d) Ribose

78. Among cellulose, poly (vinyl chloride), nylon and natural rubber, the polymer in which the intermolecular force of attraction is weakest is **[IIT JEE 2009]**
(a) nylon (b) poly (vinyl chloride)
(c) cellulose (d) natural rubber

79. The correct statement about the following disaccharide is **[IIT JEE 2010]**

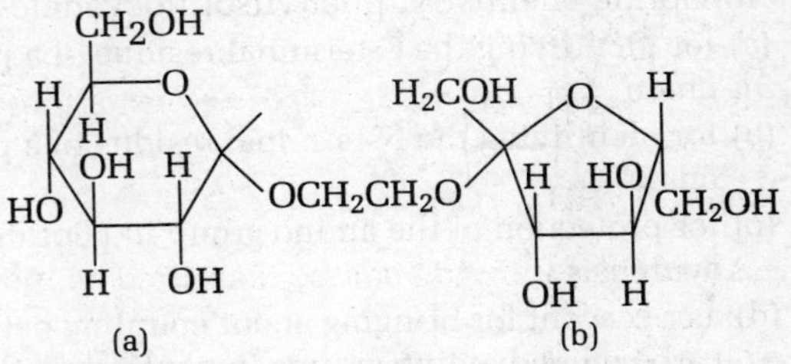

(a) ring (a) is pyranose with α-glycosidic link
(b) ring (a) is furanose with α-glycosidic link
(c) ring (b) is furanose with α-glycosidic link
(d) ring (b) is pyranose with β-glycosidic link

80. The following carbohydrate is **[IIT JEE 2011]**

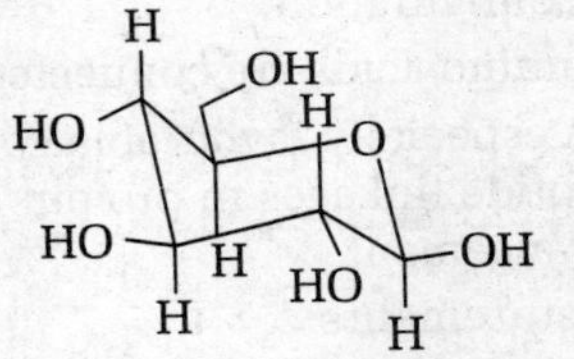

(a) a ketohexose (b) an aldohexose
(c) an α-furanose (d) an α-pyranose

81. Synthesis of each molecule of glucose in photosynthesis involves **[JEE Main 2013]**
(a) 18 molecules of ATP
(b) 10 molecules of ATP
(c) 8 molecules of ATP
(d) 6 molecular of ATP

82. The peptide bond joining amino acids into proteins is a specific example of the .... bond.
(a) amide
(b) carbonyl
(c) ester
(d) glycosidic

83. Two functional groups that are present in all amino acids are the .... group and the group.
(a) hydroxyl; amide
(b) carboxyl; amine
(c) carboxyl; phosphate ester
(d) acetal; amine

84. Serum albumin is an example of a (an)
(a) enzyme (b) structural protein
(c) storage protein (d) transport protein

85. Collagen is an example of a (an)
(a) enzyme (b) structural protein
(c) storage protein (d) transport protein

86. A tripeptide on complete hydrolysis gives glycine, alanine and phenylalanine. Using three-letter symbols, number of possible combinations are
(a) 3 (b) 4
(c) 5 (d) 6

87. In peptide chemistry, phenylisothiocyanate is used
(a) for identifying the C-terminal residue of a peptide chain
(b) for identifying the N-terminal residue of a peptide chain
(c) for protection of the amino group in peptide synthesis
(d) as a reagent for bringing about coupling between the carboxyl and amino groups in peptide synthesis

88. Consider the following statements concerning proteins
I. All natural amino acids which are constituents of proteins, are α-amino acids.
II. α-amino acids are all optically active and have L-configuration.
III. α-amino acids are connected by ester linkages.
IV. An especially favourable conformation for the peptide linkages in protein is the α-helix arrangement.

Of these statements
(a) I and II are correct (b) II and III are correct
(c) I and IV are correct (d) I, II, III and IV are correct

89. A component of folic acid (vitamin) is

(a) 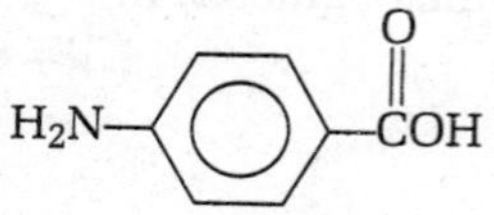
(b) 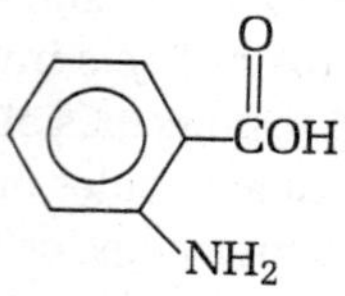
(c) 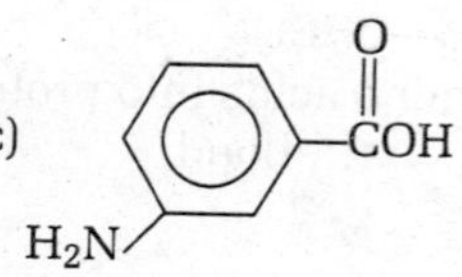
(d) $CH_3CH(NH_2)COOH$

90. Which phrase correctly completes the statement? Except for glycine, which is achiral, all the amino acids present in proteins...
(a) are chiral, but racemic
(b) are *meso* forms
(c) have the *L* configuration at their α carbon
(d) have the *R* configuration at their α carbon

91. Fischer projection of L-threonine is

(a) 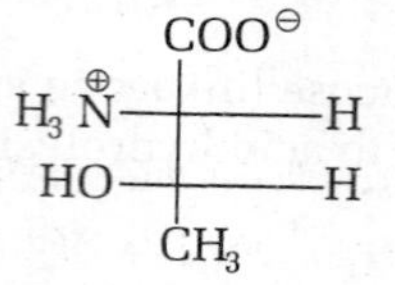
(b) 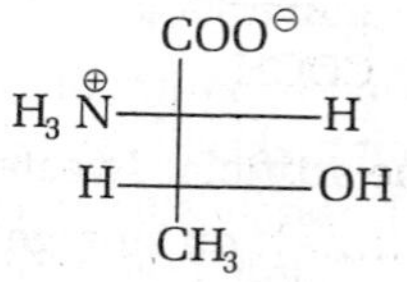
(c) 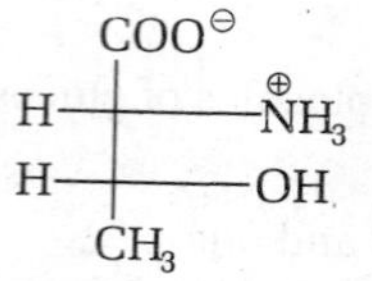
(d) 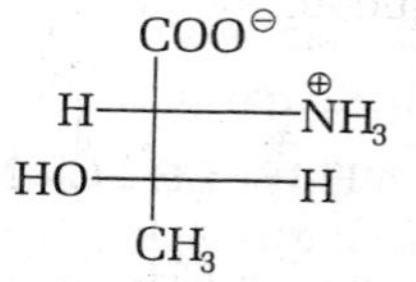

92. Assume that a particular amino acid has an isoelectric point of 6.0. In a solution of pH 1.0, which of the following species will predominate?
(a) $H_3\overset{+}{N}CH(R)CO_2H$ (b) $H_2NCH(R)CO_2H$
(c) $H_2\overset{+}{N}CH(R)CO_2^-$ (d) $H_3NCH(R)CO_2^-$

93. Ninhydrin is a reagent used to detect .... when separated by ion-exchange chromatography.
(a) amino acids
(b) amines
(c) Both (a) and (b)
(d) None of the above

94. One of the following amino acids was discovered in the amino acid sequence of the blood-clotting protein prothrombin, but in the isolation process another simple amino acid is detected. Amino acid present (in blood-clotting) is

(a) $CH_3CH(\overset{\oplus}{N}H_3)COO^{\ominus}$
(b) 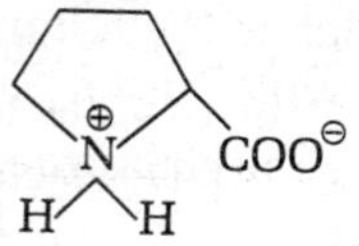
(c) $H_3\overset{\oplus}{N}—CH(COO^{\ominus})—CH_2—CH(COO^{\ominus})_2$
(d) 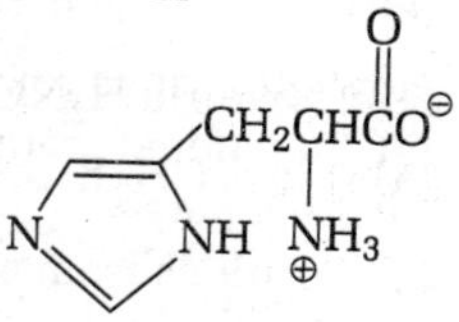

95. Which of the following amino acids is converted to benzyne on diazotisation?

(a) 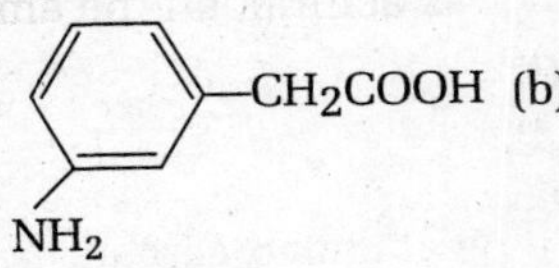 (b) 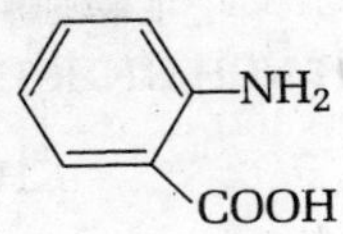

(c) 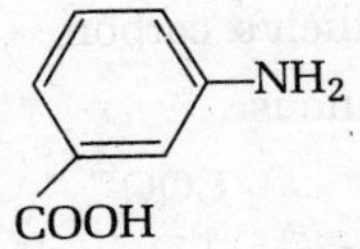 (d) 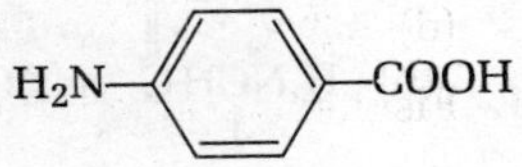

96. The artificial sweetener aspartame (A) is converted to .... on storage for extended periods of time in aqueous solution

$$H_3\overset{\oplus}{N}-\underset{CH_2CO_2^{\ominus}}{CH}-\overset{O}{\overset{\|}{C}}-NH-\underset{CH_2Ph}{CH}-\overset{O}{\overset{\|}{C}}-OCH_3 \longrightarrow \quad (A)$$

(a) $H_2N-\underset{CH_2CO_2H}{CH}-\overset{O}{\overset{\|}{C}}-NH-\underset{CH_2Ph}{CH}-\overset{O}{\overset{\|}{C}}-OCH_3$

(b) $H_2N-\underset{CH_2CO_2H}{CH}-\overset{O}{\overset{\|}{C}}OH + H_2N\underset{CH_2Ph}{CH}-\overset{O}{\overset{\|}{C}}OH + CH_3OH$

(c) 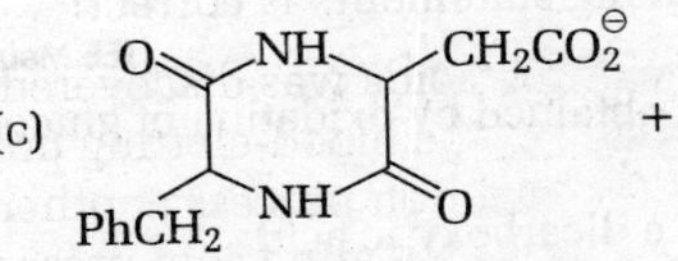 $+ CH_3OH$

(d) no change, remains as (A)

97. Which of the following reagents would be combined in the synthesis of Phe-Ala? [In phenylalanine (Phe), R in the generalised amino acid formula $H_2N\overset{R}{\overset{|}{C}}HCO_2H$ is $CH_2C_6H_5$ and in alanine (Ala) it is CH_3].

I. $HN\overset{CH_3}{\overset{|}{H}}CHCO_2H$ with $\underset{CH_2C_6H_5}{}$ — i.e. $\overset{CH_3}{\overset{|}{HNHCHCO_2H}}$, N-substituted with $CH_2C_6H_5$

II. $H_2N\overset{CH_3}{\overset{|}{C}}HCO_2\,CH_2C_6H_5$

III. $HNHC\underset{}{\overset{CH_2C_6H_5}{\overset{|}{H}}}CO_2H$

IV. $H_2N\underset{CH_2C_6H_5}{\overset{|}{C}}HCO_2CH_2C_6H_5$

(a) I and II (b) I and IV

(c) I and III (d) III and IV

98. Which amino acid can form covalent sulphur-sulphur bonds?

(a) Cysteine (b) Glycine

(c) Proline (d) Methionine

99. Simplest protein (Gly-Ala) has one peptide linkage. It is

(a) unipeptide (b) dipeptide

(c) tripeptide (d) oligopeptide

100. A protein is said to have following groups

I. $-NH_2$; II. $-\overset{O}{\overset{\|}{C}}OH$; III. $-\overset{O}{\overset{\|}{C}}NH-$

(a) I and II (b) I and III

(c) II and III (d) I, II and III

101. Consider the following compounds,

I. glycine; II. sulphanilic acid;

III. anthranilic acid,

Which can form dipolar (Zwitter ion)?

(a) I, II and III (b) I ad II

(c) II and III (d) I and III

102. Which is α-amino acid?

(a) 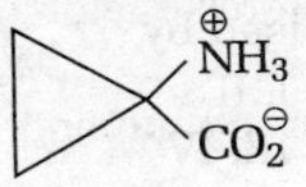 (b) 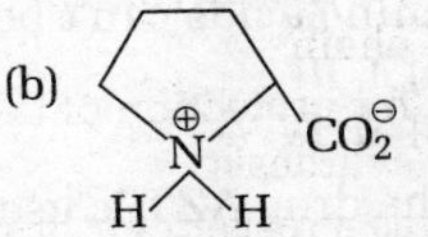

(c) Both (a) and (b) (d) None of these

103. Generally all the amino acids have primary amino function with the exception of

(a) alanine (b) proline

(c) leucine (d) isoleucine

(Q. No. 104-107) ***These questions are based on the following compounds***

I. Glycine $\underset{\oplus NH_3}{CH_2CO_2^{\ominus}}$

II. Proline 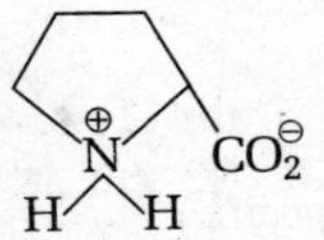

III. Serine $HOCH_2-\overset{\oplus NH_3}{\overset{|}{C}}HCO_2^{\ominus}$

IV. Aspartic acid $^{\ominus}O\overset{O}{\overset{\|}{C}}CH_2-\overset{\oplus NH_3}{\overset{|}{C}}HCO_2^{\ominus}$

V. Lysine $H_3\overset{\oplus}{N}(CH_2)_4\overset{\oplus NH_3}{\overset{|}{C}}HCO_2^{\ominus}$

104. Amino acid with basic side chain is

(a) I (b) III (c) V (d) IV

105. Amino acid with acidic side chain is
(a) II (b) IV
(c) V (d) I

106. Amino acids with non-polar side chains are
(a) I, II, III (b) II, III
(c) II, IV (d) II, IV, V

107. Amino acid with polar but non-ionised side chains is
(a) I (b) III
(c) V (d) None of these

108. $H_3\overset{\oplus}{N}CH_2\overset{O}{\overset{\|}{C}}O^{\ominus}$ (Zwitter ion or inner salt)
Select the correct statement(s).
(a) Glycine, as well as other amino acids, is amphoteric
(b) The acidic functional group is $—\overset{\oplus}{N}H_3$
(c) The basic functional group is $—CO_2^{\ominus}$
(d) All the above are correct statements

109. Consider the following synthetic methods
I. Strecker II. Rosenmund
III. Gabriel IV. Williamson
Amino acids can't be synthesised by
(a) I, III (b) I, II
(c) II, IV (d) III, IV

110. The drug **AZT** is used to treat AIDS patient. It has one or more of the linkages
(a) peptide (b) ether
(c) Both (a) and (b) (d) None of these

111. What are the products obtained by the following treatment of Ser-Tyr-Val-Ala with chymotrypsin?
(a) Serine + Tyr-Val-Ala
(b) Ser-Tyr + Valine + Alanine
(c) Ser-Tyr + Val-Ala
(d) Ser-Tyr-Val + Alanine

112. N-terminus or amino terminus of the peptide structure is on the
(a) left hand side
(b) right hand side
(c) both sides
(d) random way (non-specific)

113. C-terminus or carboxyl terminus of the peptide structure is on the
(a) left hand side
(b) right hand side
(c) both sides
(d) random way (non-specific)

114. In what order would the following amino acids be eluted with a buffer of pH 4 from a column containing an anion-exchange resin?
I. Histidine, II. Serine
III. Aspartic acid IV. Valine
(a) I > II > III > IV (b) I > IV > II > III
(c) I > III > II > IV (d) III > II > IV > I

115. (Gly-Ala) has structures
(a) $H_3\overset{\oplus}{N}CH_2\overset{O}{\overset{\|}{C}}NH\underset{CH_3}{\underset{|}{C}H}CO_2^{\ominus}$
(b) $H_3\overset{\oplus}{N}\underset{CH_3}{\underset{|}{C}H}\overset{O}{\overset{\|}{C}}—NHCH_2CO_2^{\ominus}$
(c) $\overset{\ominus}{O}_2C\underset{CH_3}{\underset{|}{C}H}NH—\overset{O}{\overset{\|}{C}}CH_2\overset{\oplus}{N}H_3$
(d) $\overset{\ominus}{O}_2CCH_2NH—\overset{O}{\overset{\|}{C}}\underset{CH_3}{\underset{|}{C}H}\overset{\oplus}{N}H_3$

116. Following acid(s) cannot form α-amino acid
I. benzoic acid II. glycolic acid
III. phenyl acetic acid IV. formic acid
(a) I, II (b) II, IV
(c) I, IV (d) II, III

117. The first cycle of the Edman degradation of the tetrapeptide Gly-Ala-Ile-Leu would give a PTH derivative of
(a) glycine (b) alanine
(c) isoleucine (d) leucine

118. Which is neutral amino acid?
(a) Serine (b) Glutamic acid
(c) Lysine (d) Histidine

119. Which of the following statements is correct? **[JEE Main 2020]**
(a) Gluconic acid is obtained by oxidation of glucose with HNO_3
(b) Gluconic acid is a dicarboxylic acid
(c) Gluconic acid can form cyclic (acetal/hemiacetal) structure
(d) Gluconic acid is a partial oxidation product of glucose

120. When the imidazole ring of histidine is protonated, nitrogen that is protonated is

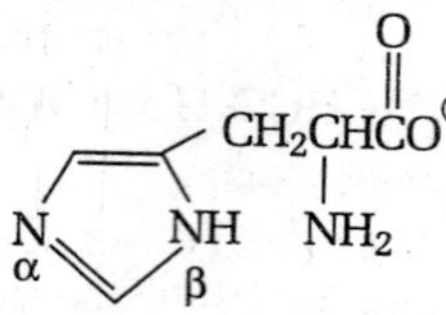

(a) at α (b) at β
(c) Both (a) and (b) (d) None of these

121. Peptides are amino acid polymers in which the individual amino acid units are called
(a) residue (b) monomer
(c) amide (d) C-terminal

122. A tripeptide has ...... peptide bonds.
(a) three (b) two
(c) four (d) one

123. To identify the N-terminal amino acid of peptide 1-fluoro-2,4-dinitrobenzene (DNFB) is used. This is called
(a) Van Slyke reagent
(b) Sorenson reagent
(c) Sanger reagent
(d) None of the above is correct

124. Following chart compares classification of proteins with their functions and examples. Which set has been matched incorrect?

	Protein	Example	Function
(a)	Transport proteins	Haemoglobin	Transport O_2 to the cells
(b)	Hormones	Insulin	Regulate glucose metabolism
(c)	Enzymes	Antibodies	Replicate and repair DNA
(d)	Contractile proteins	Actin, myosin	Cause contraction of muscles

125. 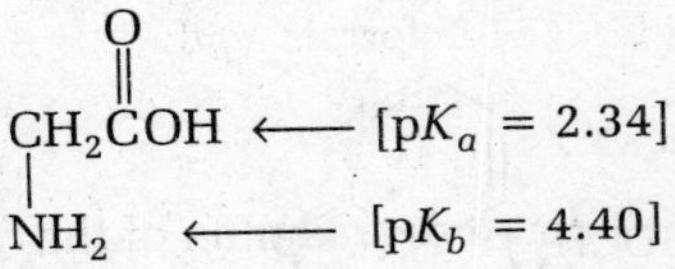

Hence, isoelectric point is
(a) 3.37 (b) 10.63
(c) 5.97 (d) 8.03

126. Some of the following are parts of essential amino acids:
A. Valine *B*. Leucine
C. Serine *D*. Proline
E. Lysine *F*. Aspartic acid
Select essential amino acids.
(a) *A*, *B*, *C* (b) *B*, *C*, *F*
(c) *A*, *C*, *D* (d) *A*, *B*, *E*

127. Most of the amino acids have chiral centres but not in
(a) glycine (b) alanine
(c) aspartic acid (d) glutamic acid

128. **Ala-Ser** is a
(a) dipeptide (b) unipeptide
(c) tripeptide (d) single amino acids

129. Select the correct statements.
(a) Oligopeptide is generally used for the peptides containing about four to ten amino acid residues
(b) Steric hindrance causes the *trans* configuration to be more stable than the *cis*-configuration so that α-carbons of adjacent amino acids are *trans* to each other.
(c) Both of the above are correct
(d) None of the above is correct

130. The type of bond that is most important in maintaining secondary structure of a protein is
(a) disulphide bridges
(b) hydrogen bonding within the backbone
(c) hydrogen bonding between *R* groups
(d) salt bridges

131. All of the following are examples of fibrous proteins except
(a) wool (b) fingernails (c) skin (d) insulin

132. The amino acid sequence of a protein is known as its
(a) primary structure (b) secondary structure
(c) tertiary structure (d) quaternary structure

133. In the tetrapeptide Ala–Cys–Val–Leu, the N-terminal amino acid is .... .
(a) ala (b) cys (c) val (d) leu

134. In the tetrapeptide Ala–Cys–Val–Leu, the C-terminal amino acid is ... .
(a) ala (b) cys (c) val (d) leu

135. All of the following can denature proteins without hydrolysis except
(a) heat (b) mechanical stress
(c) enzyme treatment (d) lowering of pH

136. All of the following are examples of denaturing proteins except
(a) souring of milk
(b) a mild sunburn
(c) using a curling iron on your hair
(d) digestion of a meal

137. Which hormone is an example of a polypeptide?
(a) Epinephrine (b) Thyroxine
(c) Growth hormone (d) Estrogen

138. One example of an amino acid derivative that acts as both a hormone and a neurotransmitter is
(a) epinephrine
(b) thyroxine
(c) growth hormone (GH)
(d) estrogen

139. Which of the following compounds is not an amino acid derivative hormone?
(a) Dopamine
(b) Epinephrine
(c) Thyroxine
(d) Norepinephrine

140. Which statement regarding polypeptide hormones is incorrect?
(a) This class of hormones includes all the regulatory hormones produced by the pituitary gland
(b) Vasopressin is an example
(c) Insulin is an example
(d) Sex hormones are included in this category

141. The increasing order of pK_a of the following amino acids in aqueous solution is Gly, Asp, Lys, Arg **[JEE Main 2019]**

(a) Asp < Gly < Arg < Lys
(b) Arg < Lys < Gly < Asp
(c) Gly < Asp < Arg < Lys
(d) Asp < Gly < Lys < Arg

142. The predominant form of histamine present in human blood is (pK_a, Histidine = 6.0) **[JEE Main 2018]**

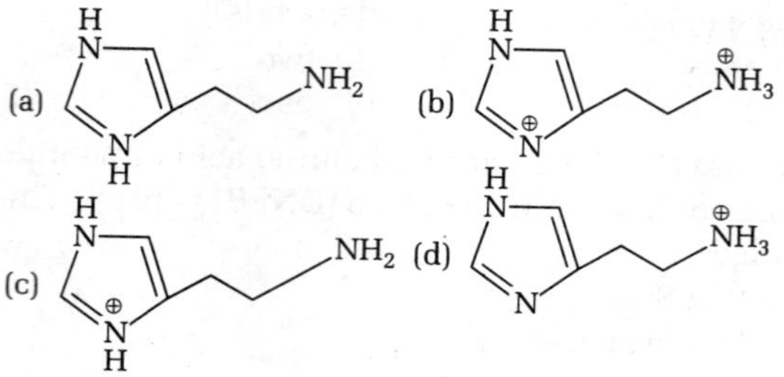

Objective Questions Type II [One or more than one correct option(s)]

In each of the questions below, four choices are given, of which one or more than one are correct.

1. In the following structure of lactose (carbohydrate)

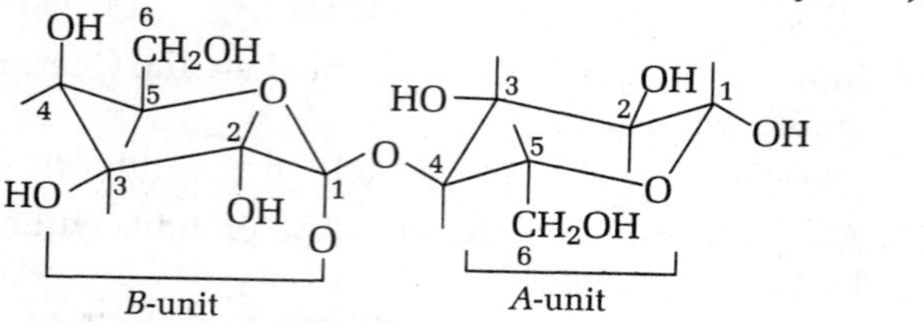

(a) there is free anomeric OH
(b) β-galactoside linkage is used
(c) *A* and *B* units are respectively D-glucose and D-galactose
(d) *A* and *B* are pyranoses joined through the C^4OH of the *A*-unit

2. Consider the following structure of sucrose,

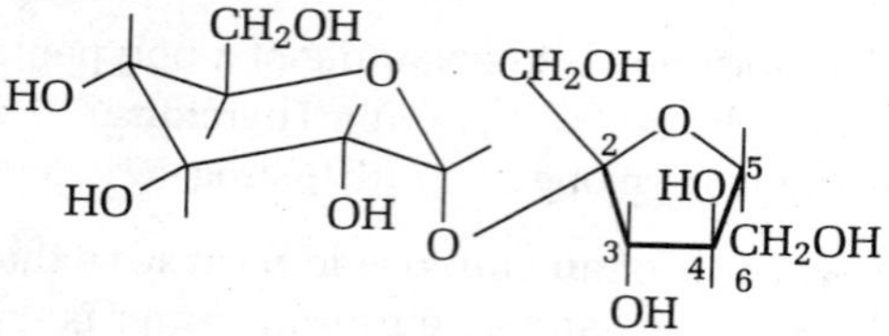

Select the correct statement(s) about this structure.

(a) There are two free anomeric OH
(b) D-glucose and D-fructose are linked by their anomeric OH
(c) The glucose unit and fructose unit both are pyranosides
(d) Structure can be named as α-D-glucopyranosyl-β-D-fructofuranoside or β-D-fructofuranosyl-α-D-glucopyranoside

3. Consider the following structure of gentiobiose,

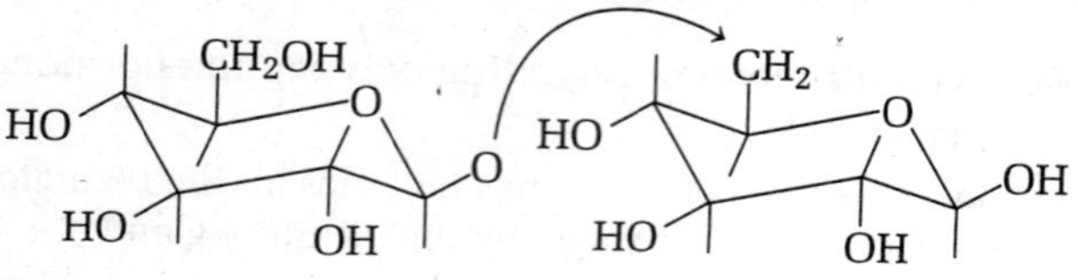

Select the correct statement(s).

(a) It is a β-disaccharide composed of two glucose units
(b) It undergoes mutarotation
(c) It is hydrolysed by emulsion to D-glucose
(d) It is a α-disaccharide composed of two glucose units

4. Consider the following structure of a nucleosides,

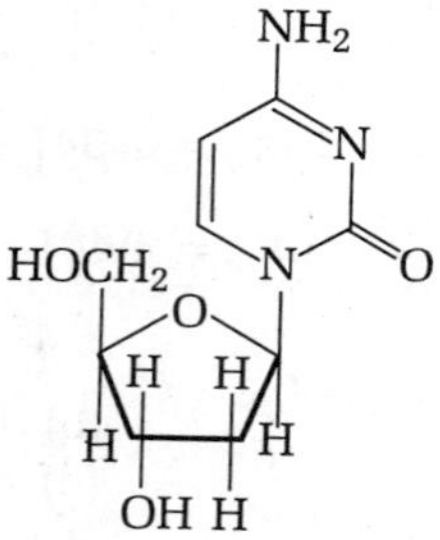

Select the correct statement(s).

(a) It represents an amino acid joined to sucrose
(b) It represents β-glycosides of D-ribofuranose
(c) It represents β-glycosides of D-deoxyribofuranose
(d) It represents α-glycosides of D-ribofuranose

5. Following structure

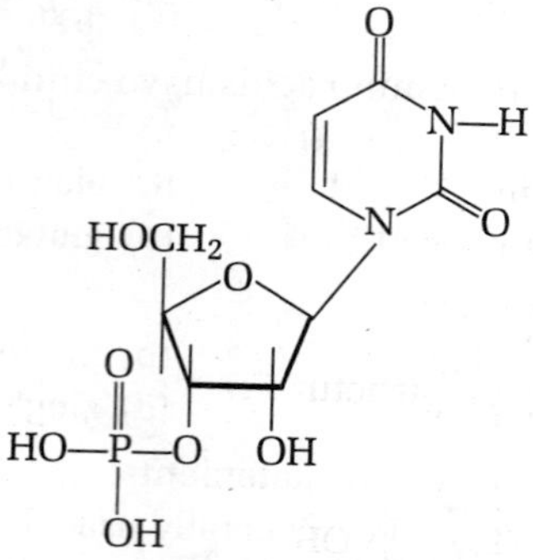

(a) represents a nucleotide
(b) represents a nucleoside
(c) has a base, a sugar and a phosphate group
(d) has an acid, a sugar and a phosphate group

6. The correct statement(s) about the following sugars X and Y is (are)

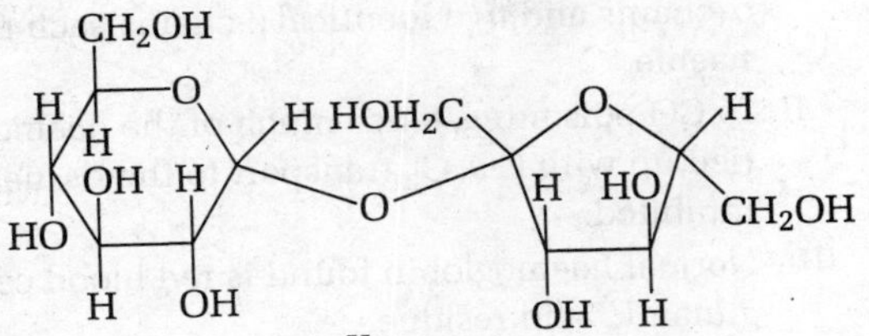

X

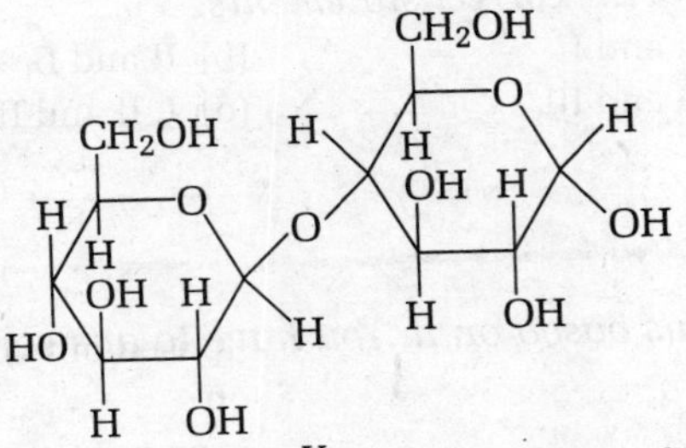

Y **[IIT JEE 2011]**

(a) X is a reducing sugar and Y is a non-reducing sugar
(b) X is a non-reducing sugar and Y is a reducing sugar
(c) The glucosidic linkages in X and Y are α and β, respectively
(d) The glucosidic linkages in X and Y are β and α, respectively

7. Which of the following statement(s) is(are) true? **[JEE Advanced 2019]**
(a) The two six-membered cyclic hemiacetal forms of D-(+)-glucose are called anomers
(b) Oxidation of glucose with bromine water gives glutamic acid
(c) Monosaccharides cannot be hydrolysed to given polyhydroxy aldehydes and ketones
(d) Hydrolysis of sucrose gives dextrorotatory glucose and laevorotatory fructose

8. The Fischer presentation of D-glucose is given below. **[JEE Advanced 2018]**

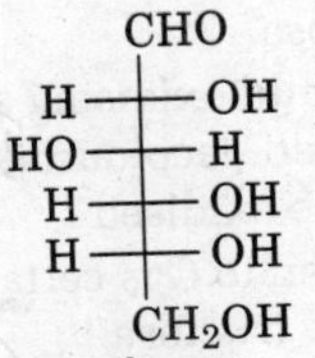

D-glucose

The correct structure(s) of β-L-glucopyranose is (are)

(a) 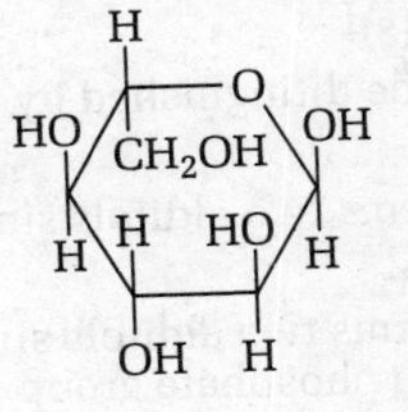

(b) 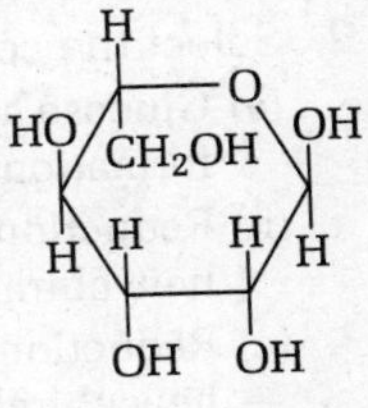

(c) 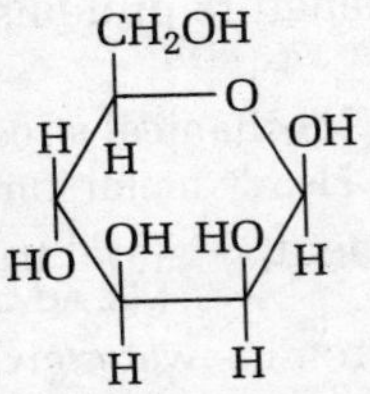

(d) 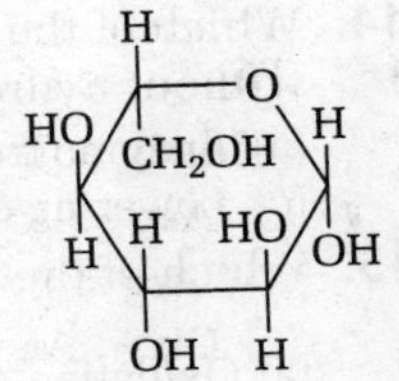

9. For 'invert sugar', the correct statement(s) is (are) (Given: specific rotations of (+) - sucrose, (+) - maltose, L-(−) -glucose and L-(+) -fructose in aqueous solution are $+66°$, $+140°$, $-52°$ and $92°$, respectively) **[JEE Advanced 2016]**
(a) Invert sugar is prepared by acid catalysed hydrolysis of maltose
(b) Invert sugar is an equimolar mixture of D-(+) -glucose and D-(−)- fructose
(c) Specific rotation of invert sugar is $-20°$
(d) On reaction with Br_2 water, invert sugar forms saccharic acid as one of the products

10. Which pair(s) of amino acids cannot have hydrophobic interactions?
(a) Leucine and alanine
(b) Arginine and glutamic acid
(c) Glycine and asparagine
(d) Glutamic acid and serine

11. Which types of interactions are directly involved in maintaining tertiary structure?
(a) Disulphide bridge
(b) Hydrogen bonding
(c) Peptide bonds
(d) Hydrophobic interactions

12. Which is/are correct pair(s) of matching?

	Protein	Property
(a)	Native protein	A protein that is usually water soluble, having hydrophilic exterior and hydrophobic interior and an overall rounded shape
(b)	Fibrous protein	A protein that is usually insoluble in water is very tough and has a long shape
(c)	Globular protein	A protein with the tertiary structure in which it normally occurs in living system
(d)	Conjugated protein	A protein that produces amino acids and other biomolecules or inorganic substances upon hydrolysis

13. When a glycoprotein is hydrolysed, the products would include
(a) amino acid
(b) carbohydrates
(c) lipids
(d) RNA

14. Which of the following can denature proteins without hydrolysis?

(a) Enzyme treatment (b) Mechanical stress
(c) Lowering of pH (d) Heavy metal ions

15. Which of the following statement(s) is(are) true? **[JEE Advance 2019]**

(a) Oxidation of glucose with bromine water gives glutamic acid
(b) The two six-membered cyclic hemiacetal forms of D-(+)-glucose are called anomers
(c) Monosaccharides cannot be hydrolysed to given polyhydroxy aldehydes and ketones
(d) Hydrolysis of sucrose gives dextrorotatory glucose and laevorotatory fructose

16. Consider the following statements about haemoglobin,

I. It has four separate peptide subunits : two identical α-chains and two identical β-chains each bonded to haeme.
II. In CO poisoning, since much of the haemoglobin is tied up with CO, O_2 transport to the tissues is inhibited.
III. Normal haemoglobin found is red blood cells has a glutamic acid residue.

Select the correct statements.

(a) I and II (b) II and II
(c) I and III (d) I, II and III

Comprehension Based Questions

In these questions, a passage has been given followed by questions based on it. You have to answer the questions based on the passage given.

***Passage* 1** Following two synthetic stages were assigned to two chemists *X* and *Y* to decide whether the isomeric compounds of molecular formula was a glucose or fructose.

	Chemist *X*	Chemist *Y*
	Isomer *A*	**Isomer *B***
• Molecular formula	$C_6H_{12}O_6$	$C_6H_{12}O_6$
• Tollen's reagent is	reduced	reduced
• Br_2 water	is decolourised	not decolourised
• *A* and *B* HCN $H_3\overset{\oplus}{O}$ P/HI	*n*-heptanoic acid	2-methyl hexanoic acid

Based on the above observations, answer the following question.

1. Compounds analysed by *X* and *Y* are

	A	*B*
(a)	glucose	fructose
(b)	glucose	glucose
(c)	fructose	glucose
(d)	fructose	fructose

***Passage* 2** Teacher in the +2 Lab instructed the students that

- distinction between an aldehyde and ketone can be made by Tollen's reagent and that between an unsaturated and saturated compound can be made by Br_2 water, and the students thus made identification of acetone, acetaldehyde (by Tollen's test) and also allyl alcohol and ethyl alcohol (by Br_2 water).
- After teacher had left the lab, one lab assistant gave glucose, (having aldehyde group) and fructose (having keto group) for identification.

Students used both of the reagents without waiting any another instruction. Following results were reported by

Student	Reagent	Result	Group/ Compound
A	Tollen's reagent	reduced to metallic silver	aldehyde/glucose
B	Tollen's reagent	reduced to metallic silver	aldehyde/glucose
C	Br_2 water	decolourised	some unsaturated compound
D	Br_2 water	no effect	some saturated compound

Student were told that no compound other that monosaccharide had been given.

Read the above experiment and answer the following questions.

1. Select the correct statement(s).

(a) Compound given to *A* and *B* is certainly glucose but it can be fructose
(b) Br_2 water is a mild oxidising agent and can oxidise glucose and itself decolourised. Fructose with a keto group cannot be oxidised
(c) Compound given to *C* is certainly glucose and given to *D* is certainly fructose
(d) Reducing property of fructose is due to its enolic form which exists in basic medium of the reaction

2. Select the correct statement(s).

(a) Glucose and fructose can be ditinguished by osazone formation
(b) Reduction of D-glucose forms two alditols since a new chiral centre is formed
(c) Reduction of D-fructose forms two alditols since a new chiral centre is formed
(d) Reduction of D-glucose forms D-mannitol and D-glucitol, the C-2 epimer of D-mannitol

***Passage* 3** Scientist at a biochemical lab at IIT Delhi extracted a compound of molecular formula $C_{14}H_{17}O_6N$, and was given the name Indican. It was subjected to hydrolysis in emulsion to D-glucose and indoxyl. Take the known structure of D-glucose as given and answer the following questions.

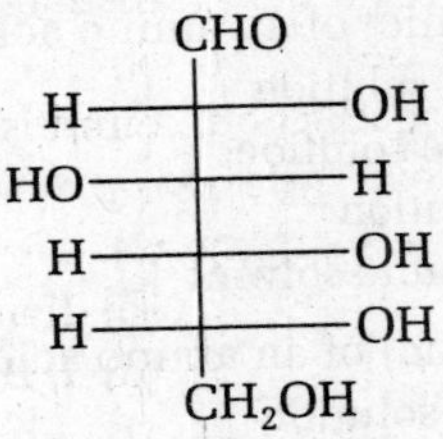

1. What is the formula of indoxyl?
   (a) C_8H_5N (b) C_8H_7NO
   (c) C_8H_5N (d) C_8H_7N

2. What is the structure of indican? (assume that it does not reduce Tollen's reagent)

(a)

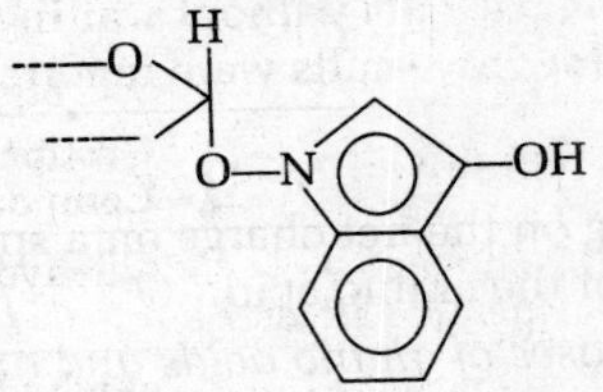

(b)

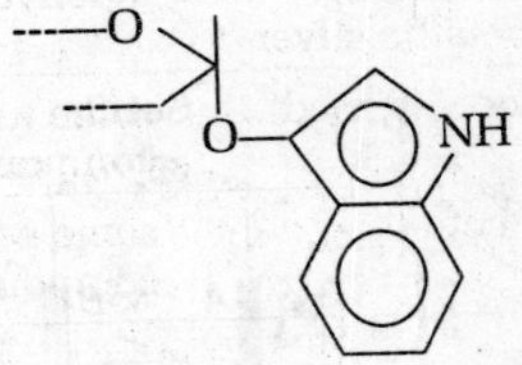

(c)

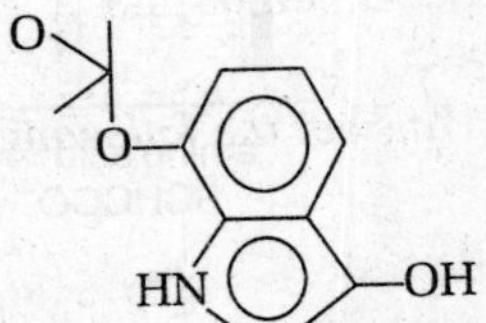

(d) None of the above

***Passage* 4** Say the word sugar and most people immediately think of sweet tasting candies, desserts and suck. With sucrose as a reference point, fructose is heavily twice as sweet, but lactose is only about one-sixth as sweet. The desire of many people to cut caloric intake has led to the development of synthetic sweeteners.

Based on the above passage, answer the following questions.

1. Which is incorrect grading of sugars?

	Sugar	Sweetness
(a)	Sucrose	1.00
(b)	Fructose	1.75
(c)	Lactose	6.00
(d)	Saccharin	3500

2. Which is not the synthetic sweetener?
   (a) Aspartame (b) Saccharin
   (c) Cyclamate (d) Fructose

***Passage* 5** Two diastereomers that differ in the configuration around one stereogenic centre only are called epimers. Anomers are stereoisomers of a cyclic monosaccharide that differ in the position of that OH group at the hemiacetal carbon.

Answer the following questions.

1. In the following,

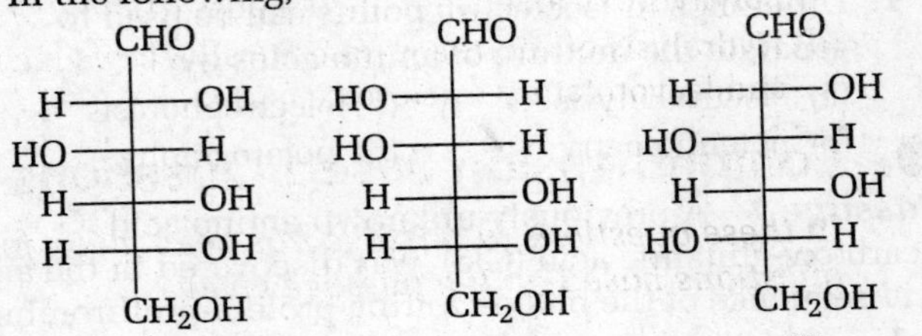

I II III

epimers can be
(a) I and II
(b) II and III
(c) I and III
(d) All of these

2. In the following,

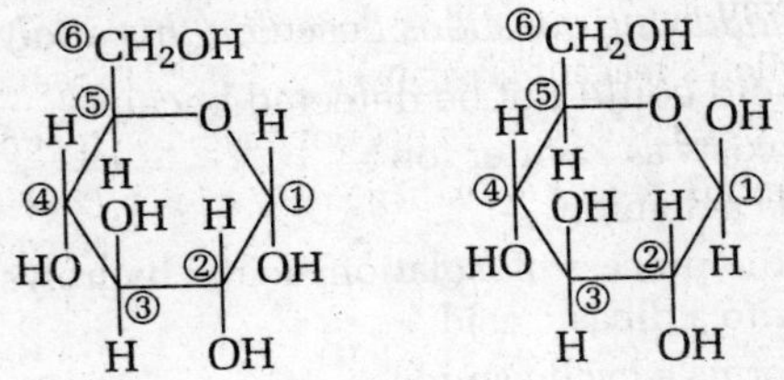

anomeric carbon is
(a) C_1 (b) C_2 (c) C_3 (d) C_4

***Passage* 6** You have been given a mixture of alanine, lysine and aspartic acid in a buffer at pH 6. The isoelectric point of

Alanine : 6
Lysine : 9.7
Aspartic acid : 2.8

A voltage is applied to this mixture.

Answer the following questions based on the above experimental facts.

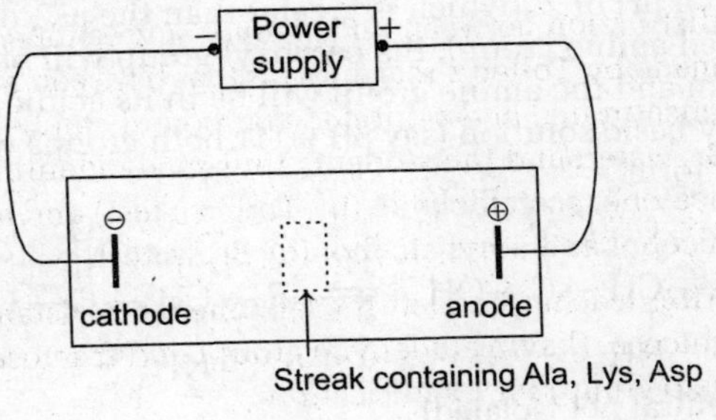

1. Consider the following statements,
   Under the influence of an electric field
   I. Ala does not move
   II. Aspartic acid is in anionic form and moves towards anode
   III. Lysine is in cationic form and moves towards cathode
   IV. Above method is based on electrodialysis

   Select the correct statements.
   (a) all but IV (b) all but III
   (c) all but I (d) all but I and IV
2. Difference in isoelectric points can be used to separate the mixture of amino acids by
   (a) electrodialysis (b) electrophoresis
   (c) potentiometry (d) polarography

***Passage* 7** A previously unknown amino acid γ-carboxy-glutamic acid (Gla) was discovered in the amino acid sequence of the blood-clotting protein prothrombin.

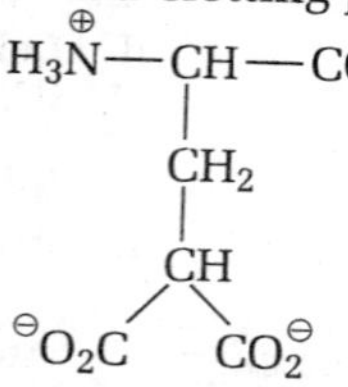

This amino acid escaped detection for many years.

Answer the following questions based on this analysis.

1. This acid could not be detected because
   (a) it exists as Zwitter ion
   (b) it is a dianion
   (c) in the process of isolation, acidic hydrolysis converts it into a dibasic acid
   (d) it forms a cyclic amide
2. Chiral centre(s) present is/are
   (a) 1 (b) 2 (c) 3 (d) 4

***Passage* 8** *Read the following passage and answer the questions at the end of it.*

Every amino acid has a carboxyl group and an amino group, and each group can exist in an acidic form or a basic form depending on the pH of the solution in which the amino acid is dissolved. The carboxyl groups of the amino acids have pK_a values of approximately 2; the protonated amino group have pK_a values near 9. Therefore, in a very acidic solution (pH near zero), both groups will be in their acidic forms. At a pH of 7, (which is greater than the pK_a of the protonated amino group), the carboxyl group will be in its basic form and the amino group will be in its acidic form. In a strongly basic solution (say pH = 11), both groups will be in the basic form.

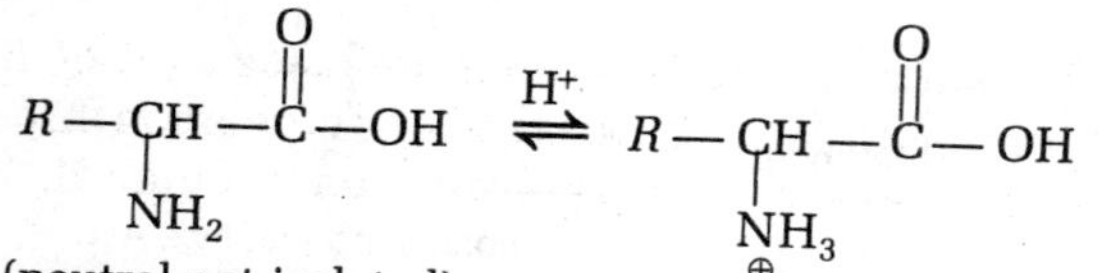

(neutral not isolated) (*A*)

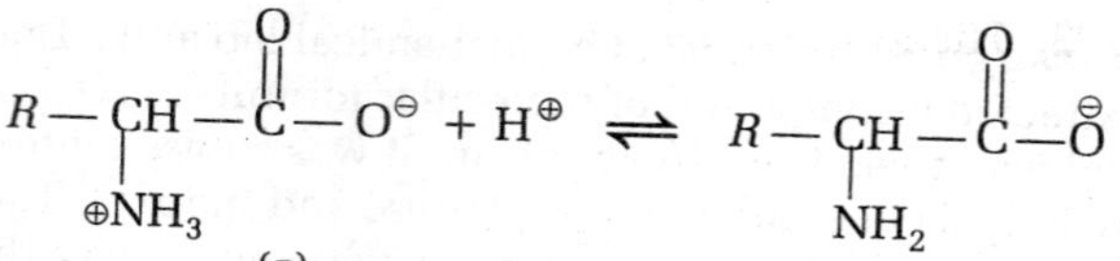

(*B*) (*C*)

1. Form *A* (cationic) of an amino acid exists in
   (a) fairly basic solution
   (b) fairly acidic solution
   (c) neutral solution
   (d) aprotic organic solvent
2. Form *C* (anionic) of an amino acid exists in
   (a) fairly basic solution
   (b) fairly acidic solution
   (c) neutral solution
   (d) aprotic organic solvent
3. Form *B* is called
   (a) Lewis acid
   (b) Lewis base
   (c) amphoteric
   (d) Zwitter ion

***Passage* 9** Depending on the net charge on a species, there can be migration of the amino acid.

Consider the following cases of amino acids and answer the questions at the end of it.

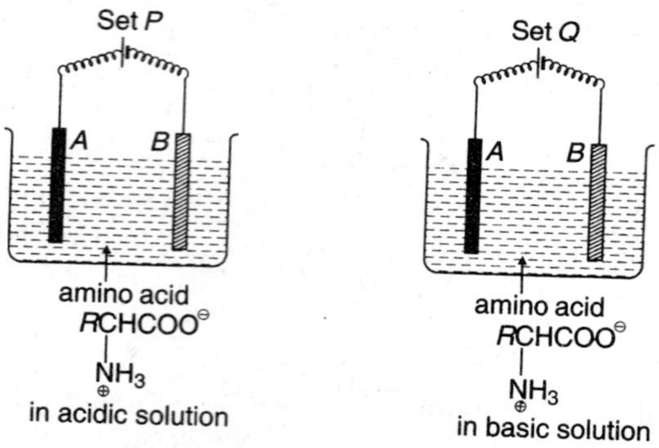

1. Consider the following equilibrium,

$$CH_3\underset{NH_2}{\underset{|}{C}H}COOH \rightleftharpoons CH_3\underset{\oplus NH_3}{\underset{|}{C}H}COO^{\ominus}$$

   and select the correct statement(s).
   (a) It is intramolecular Lewis acid-base reaction
   (b) It is intramolecular Lowry-Bronsted acid-base reaction
   (c) It is formation of Zwitter ion
   (d) All of the above are correct
2. At a certain pH, there is no migration of the amino acid. This pH is called
   (a) pK_a (= − log K_a), K_a = ionisation constant
   (b) pI = (− log I), I = isoelectric point
   (c) pK_w
   (d) pOH

3. Histidine (*A*) has pK_a values as indicated

(*A*) 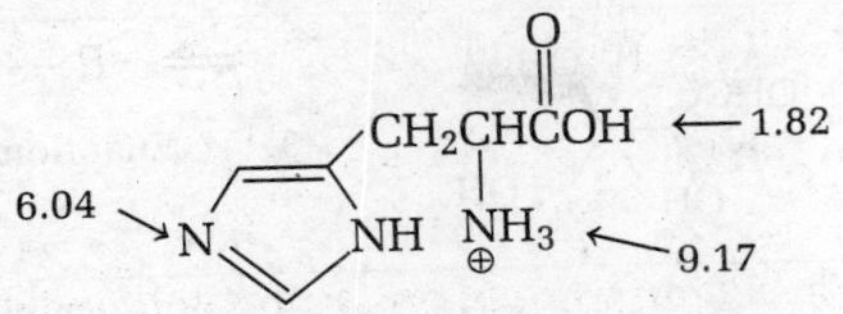

Following form is at pH

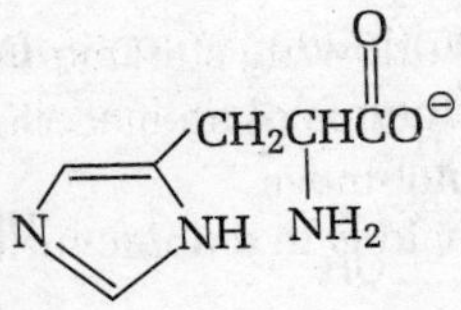

(a) 4 (b) 6 (c) 8 (d) 12

Matrix-Match Type

Given below are Matching Type Questions, with two columns (each having some items) each . Each item of Column I has to be matched with the items of Column II.

1. Match Column I (compound) with Column II (configuration) and select the correct answer using the codes gives below.

	Column I		Column II
A.	α-D-glucose and β-D-glucose	1.	Enantiomers
B.	D-glucose ad D-galactose	2.	Anomers
C.	Erythrose and threose	3.	Epimers
D.	D-(+)-glyceraldehyde and L-(−) glyceraldehyde	4.	Diastereomers

2. Match Column I with Column II and select the correct answer using the codes given below the Columns.

	Column I		Column II
A.	α- and β-glucose	1.	Mutarotation
B.	(+) and (−)-glucose	2.	Enantiomers
C.	D- and L-glucose	3.	Anomers
D.	α-form ⇌ open chain form; ⇅ β-form	4.	Configurational relationship

3. Match the column I of elements with column II of its biological effects in the following options **[JEE Main 2021, March]**

	Column I (Chemical compound)	Column II (Used as)
A.	Be	1. Treatment of cancer
B.	Mg	2. Extraction of metals
C.	Ca	3. Incendiary bombs and signals
D.	Ra	4. Windows of X-ray tubes.

4. Match the following.

	Column I (Carbohydrate)		Column II (Feature)
A.	Amylose	1.	Polysaccharide
B.	Cellulose	2.	α-glycosidic linkage
C.	Maltose	3.	β-glycosidic linkage
D.	Galactose	4.	Hydrolysed to glucose

5. Match column I of chemical compound with column II of its uses in the following options. **[JEE Main 2021, March]**

	Column I (Chemical Compound)		Column II (Used as)
A.	Sucralose	1.	Synthetic detergent
B.	Glyceryl ester of stearic acid	2.	Artificial sweetener
C.	Sodium benzoate	3.	Antiseptic
D.	Bithionol	4.	Food preservative

6. Match Column I (amino acids) with Column II (products obtained due to heating).

	Column I		Column II
A.	α-amino acid	1.	α, β-unsaturated acid
B.	β-amino acid	2.	Diketopiperazine
C.	γ-amino acid	3.	Lactam

7. Match of the following.

	Column I (Group)		Column II (Compound)
A.	$-NH_2$ group	1.	Glycine
B.	—OH group	2.	Picric acid
C.	—COOH group	3.	Tyrosine
D.	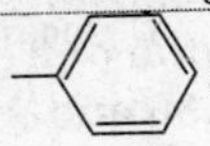 group	4.	Serine

8. The Fischer projection of D-erythrose is shown below :

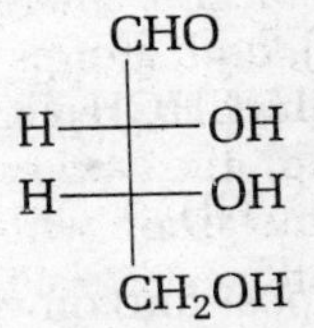

D-erythrose

D-erythrose and its isomers are listed as *P*, *Q*, *R*, and *S* in Column-I. Choose the correct relationship of *P*, *Q*, *R*, and *S* with D-erythrose from Column II.

	Column I		Column II
A.	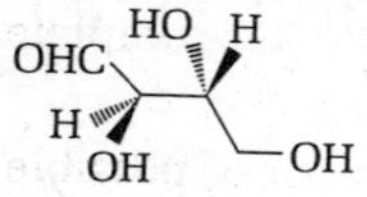	1.	Diastereomer
B.	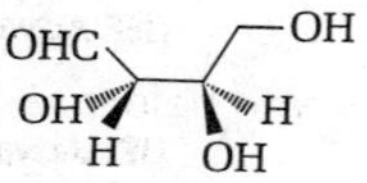	2.	Identical

	Column I		Column II
C.	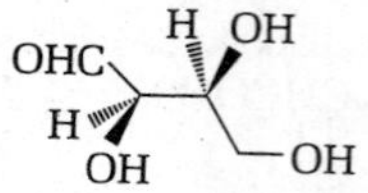	3.	Enantiomer
D.	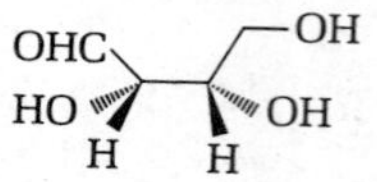		

Single Integer Answer Questions

Answer of these questions is a single digit lying between 0 to 9.

1. When the following aldohexose exists in its D-configuration, the total number of stereoisomers in its pyranose form, is

CHO
|
CHOH
|
CHOH
|
CHOH
|
CHOH
|
CH_2OH

[IIT JEE 2012]

2. Bromine water oxidises glucose to gluconic acid; how much gluconic acid is formed from 4.55 g of glucose?

3. At what carbon are the following sugar option of each other?

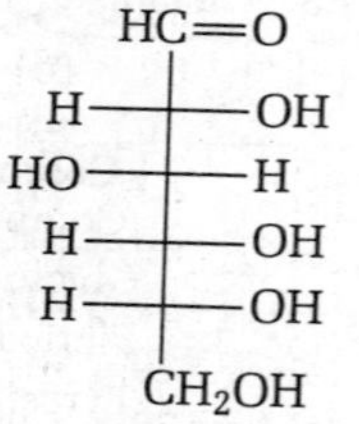

D-sucrose

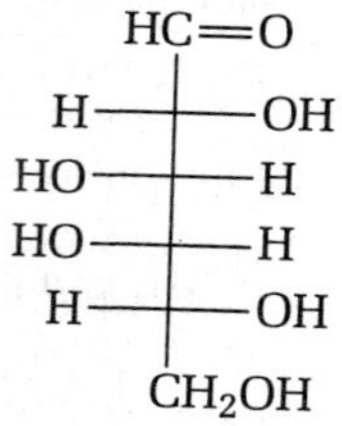

D-glucose

4. pK_{a_1} and pK_{a_2} of isoleucine are 2.36 and 9.64. Thus, isoelectric point of isoleucine is ....

5. The following acid on heating is converted into unsaturated acid.

$$\overset{4}{C}H_3\underset{\underset{NH_2}{|}}{\overset{3}{C}H}\overset{2}{C}H_2\overset{1}{C}OOH$$

Sum of C-atoms (position) on which unsaturation occurs is ....

6. The total number of basic group in the following form of lysine is ...... **[IIT JEE 2010]**

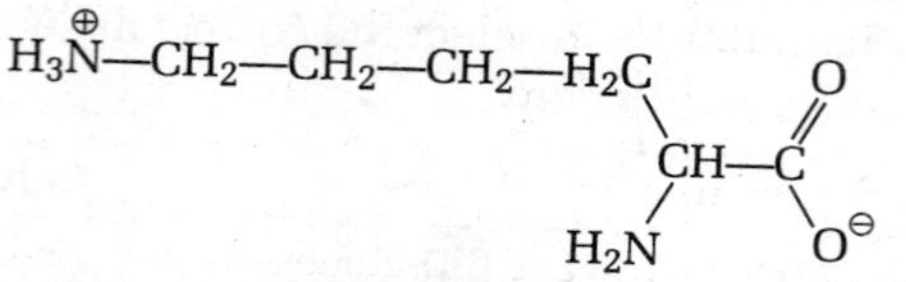

7. A decapeptide (Mol. wt. 796) on complete hydrolysis gives glycine (Mol. wt. 75), alanine and phenylalanine. Glycine contributes 47.0% to the total weight of the hydrolysed products. The number of glycine units present in the decapeptide is **[IIT JEE 2011]**

8. In the following drug used to treat AIDS how many functional groups are present?

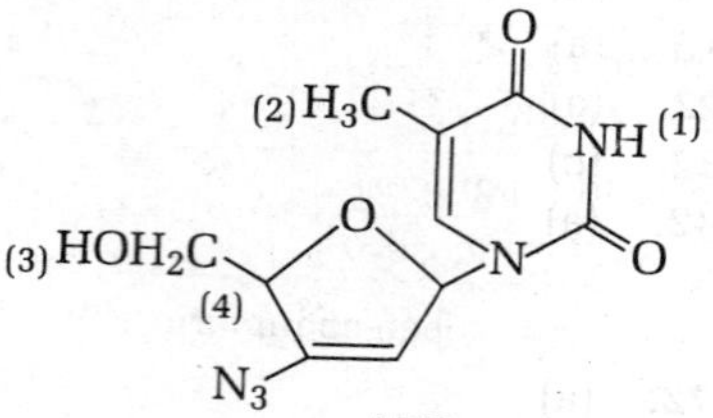

AZT

9. In controlled hydrolysis of AZT carboxylic acid is formed. Which bond (S. N.) is cleaned?

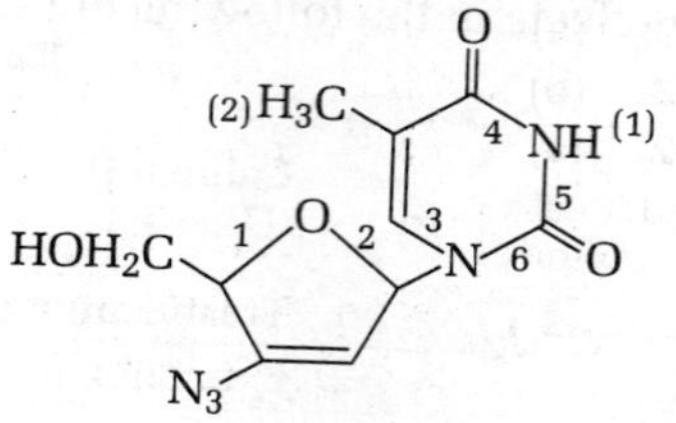

10. How many of the following form Zwitter ions? glycine, salicylic acid, sulphanilic acid, picric acid, carbolic acid, serine, alanine.

11. A tripeptide is formed from glycine, serine and alanine. How many possible combinations are possible?

12. How many of the following amino acids have heterocyclic ring also? Valine, leucine, tryptophan, tyrosine, histidine, serine, cysteine.

13. The substituents R_1 and R_2 for nine peptides are listed in the table given below. How many of these peptides are positively charged at pH = 7.0? **[IIT JEE 2012]**

$$H_3\overset{\oplus}{N}\text{—CONH—NH—}\underset{R_1}{\text{CH}}\text{—CONH—}\underset{R_2}{\text{CH}}\text{—CONH—}\underset{H}{\text{CH}}\text{—CO}\overset{\ominus}{O}$$
(with H below the N)

Peptide	R_1	R_2
I	H	H
II	H	CH_3
III	CH_2COOH	H
IV	CH_2CONH_2	$(CH_2)_4NH_2$
V	CH_2CONH_2	CH_2CONH_2
VI	$(CH_2)_4NH_2$	$(CH_2)_4NH_2$
VII	CH_2COOH	CH_2CONH_2
VIII	CH_2OH	$(CH_2)_4NH_2$
IX	$(CH_2)_4NH_2$	CH_2

14. A tetrapeptide has —COOH group on alanine. This produces glycine (Gly), valine (val), phenyl alanine (Phe) and alanine (Ala), on complete hydrolysis.

For this tetrapeptide, the number of possible sequencies (primary structures) with $—NH_2$ group attached to a chiral centre is ...... **[JEE Advanced 2013]**

15. The structure of a peptide is given below **[JEE Advanced 2020]**

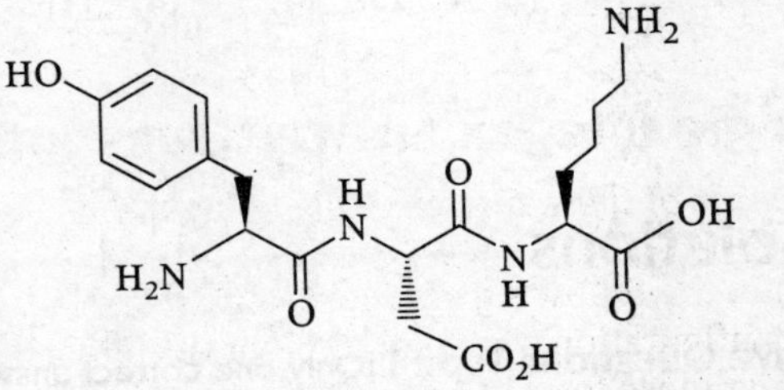

If the absolute values of the net charge of the peptide at pH = 2, pH = 6, and pH = 11 are $|z_1|, |z_2|$ and $|z_3|$, respectively, then what is $|z_1| + |z_2| + |z_3|$?

Answers

Objective Questions Type I [Only one correct option]

1. (b)	**2.** (d)	**3.** (c)	**4.** (d)	**5.** (b)	**6.** (a)	**7.** (c)	**8.** (b)	**9.** (a)	**10.** (b)
11. (d)	**12.** (a)	**13.** (a)	**14.** (b)	**15.** (c)	**16.** (c)	**17.** (b)	**18.** (b)	**19.** (a)	**20.** (c)
21. (a)	**22.** (a)	**23.** (a)	**24.** (c)	**25.** (c)	**26.** (a)	**27.** (c)	**28.** (a)	**29.** (b)	**30.** (a)
31. (d)	**32.** (c)	**33.** (d)	**34.** (d)	**35.** (b)	**36.** (d)	**37.** (d)	**38.** (a)	**39.** (c)	**40.** (d)
41. (c)	**42.** (a)	**43.** (d)	**44.** (a)	**45.** (c)	**46.** (c)	**47.** (d)	**48.** (d)	**49.** (c)	**50.** (c)
51. (d)	**52.** (b)	**53.** (b)	**54.** (c)	**55.** (c)	**56.** (b)	**57.** (d)	**58.** (b)	**59.** (a)	**60.** (c)
61. (d)	**62.** (c)	**63.** (d)	**64.** (c)	**65.** (b)	**66.** (a)	**67.** (d)	**68.** (c)	**69.** (d)	**70.** (b)
71. (d)	**72.** (a)	**73.** (b)	**74.** (a)	**75.** (c)	**76.** (c)	**77.** (c)	**78.** (d)	**79.** (d)	**80.** (d)
81. (a)	**82.** (a)	**83.** (b)	**84.** (d)	**85.** (b)	**86.** (d)	**87.** (d)	**88.** (c)	**89.** (a)	**90.** (c)
91. (b)	**92.** (a)	**93.** (c)	**94.** (c)	**95.** (b)	**96.** (c)	**97.** (c)	**98.** (a)	**99.** (b)	**100.** (d)
101. (a)	**102.** (c)	**103.** (b)	**104.** (c)	**105.** (b)	**106.** (a)	**107.** (b)	**108.** (d)	**109.** (d)	**110.** (c)
111. (c)	**112.** (a)	**113.** (b)	**114.** (b)	**115.** (a)	**116.** (c)	**117.** (a)	**118.** (a)	**119.** (d)	**120.** (a)
121. (a)	**122.** (b)	**123.** (b)	**124.** (c)	**125.** (c)	**126.** (d)	**127.** (a)	**128.** (a)	**129.** (c)	**130.** (b)
131. (d)	**132.** (a)	**133.** (a)	**134.** (d)	**135.** (c)	**136.** (d)	**137.** (c)	**138.** (a)	**139.** (a)	**140.** (d)
141. (d)	**142.** (d)								

Objective Questions Type II [One or more than one correct option(s)]

1. (a, b, c, d)	**2.** (b, d)	**3.** (a, b, c)	**4.** (b)	**5.** (a, c)
6. (b, c)	**7.** (a, c, d)	**8.** (d)	**9.** (b, c)	**10.** (b, c, d)
11. (b, d)	**12.** (a, b, d)	**13.** (a, b)	**14.** (b, c, d)	**15.** (b, c, d)
16. (d)				

Comprehension Based Questions

Passage 1 – 1. (a)

Passage 2 – 1. (a, b, c, d) 2. (c, d)

Passage 3 – 1. (b) 2. (b)

Passage 4 – 1. (c) 2. (d)

Passage 5 – 1. (a, c) 2. (a)

Passage 6 – 1. (a) 2. (b)

Passage 7 – 1. (c) 2. (a)

Passage 8 – 1. (b) 2. (a) 3. (d)

Passage 9 – 1. (b, c) 2. (b) 3. (d)

Matrix-Match Type

1. A → (2); B → (3); C → (4); D → (1)
2. A → (3); B → (2); C → (4); D → (1)
3. A → (4); B → (3); C → (2); D → (1)
4. A → (1,2,3); B → (1,3,4); C → (4); D → (4)
5. A → (2); B → (1); C → (4); D → (3)
6. A → (2); B → (1); C → (3)
7. A → (1,3, 4); B → (2,3,4); C → (1,3,4); D → (2,3)
8. A → (2); B → (1); C → (1); D → (3)

Single Integer Answer Questions

1. (8)	**2.** (6)	**3.** (4)	**4.** (6)	**5.** (5)	**6.** (2)	**7.** (6)	**8.** (4)	**9.** (4)	**10.** (4)
11. (6)	**12.** (2)	**13.** (4)	**14.** (4)	**15.** (5)					

Solutions

Objective Questions Type I [Only one correct answer]

1. (*b*) Erythrose and threose are stereoisomers but not mirror images, are referred to as a pair of diastereomers, while D- and L-threose are mirror images and are referred to as a pair of enantiomers.

5. (*b*) Glucose and galactose are having identical configuration at all the positions except at C_4 position. Both of them are diastereomers that differ in configuration at only one chirality center. Hence, these are called **epimers**. Structures of glucose and galactose are as follows:

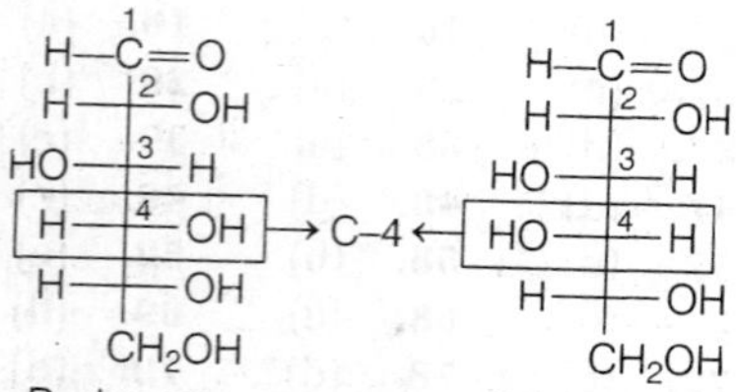

D-glucose D-galactose

8. (*b*) Vitamin A and D are the most suitable vitamins, which stored in our body for longer duration.

9. (*a*) Furanose structure of D-glucose is as follows

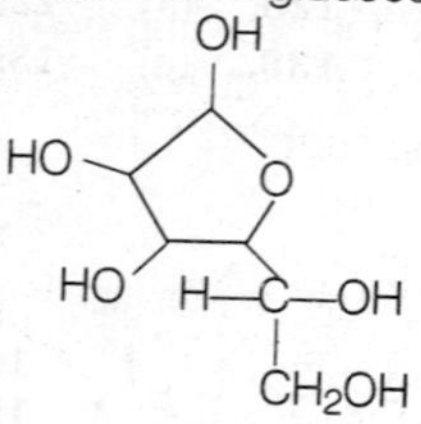

11. (*d*) Saccharin, dulcin, aspartame, sodium cyclamate. All are artificial sweetening agents.

14. (*b*) Sucrose is a non-reducing sugar. Hence maltose, lactose, cellobiose are reducing sugars.

16. (*c*) The secondary structure of protein includes two types: α-helix and β pleated sheet. In α-helix structure, the polypeptide chain is coil around due to presence of Intramolecular H-bonding.

18. (*b*)

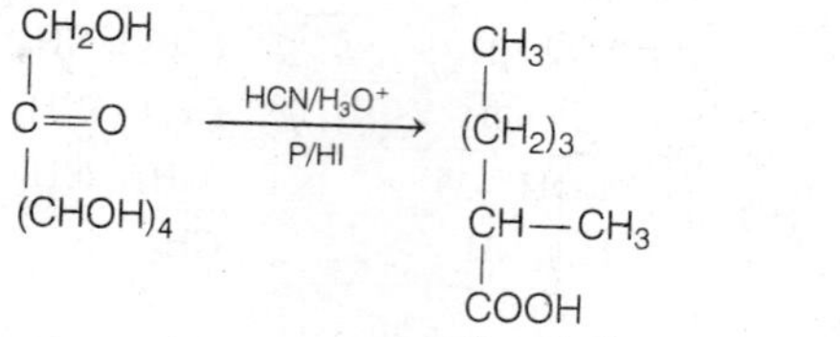

2-methyl hexanoic acid

19. (*a*)

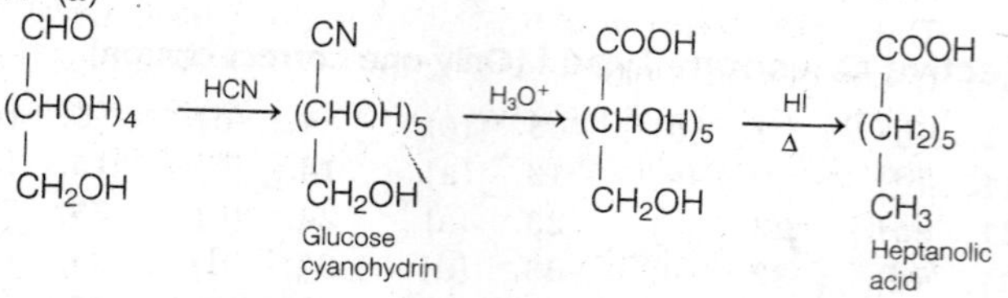

22. (*a*) Sugars that have an aldehyde, a ketone, a hemiacetal or a hemiketal group is able to reduce an oxidising agent. These sugars are classified as reducing sugars.

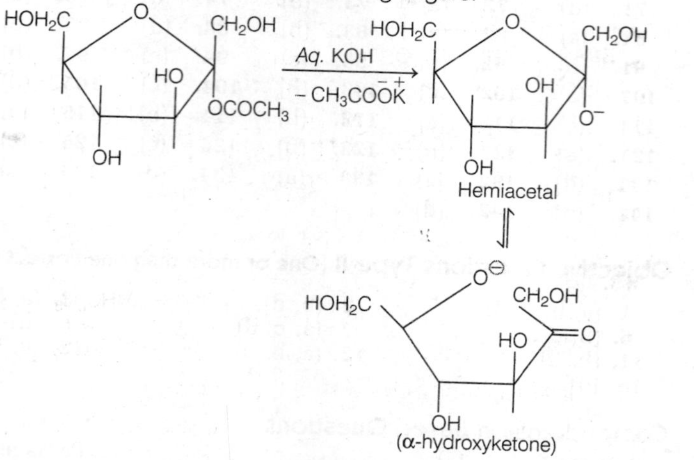

Hemiacetal can be easily reduced by oxidising agent such as Tollen's reagent.

24. (*c*) Glucose contain 4 and fructose contain 3 chiral C-atoms.

26. (*a*) Amlyose contain α-glycoside linkage.

27. (*c*) $C_{12}H_{22}O_{11} + H_2O \xrightarrow{\text{Invertase}} \underset{\text{Glucose}}{C_6H_{12}O_6} + \underset{\text{Fructose}}{C_6H_{12}O_6}$

$C_6H_{12}O_6 \xrightarrow{\text{Zymase}} 2C_2H_5OH + 2CO_2$

30. (*a*) HI is a strong reducing agent. It reduces both primary and secondary alcoholic groups of glucose along with the carbonyl group to produce *n*-hexane as

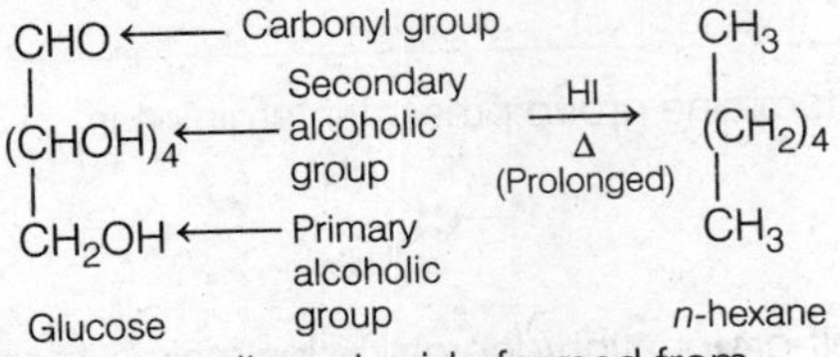

42. (*a*) Maltose is a disaccharide formed from monosaccharides α-D- glucose and α-D glucose *via* $C_1 — C_4$ glycosidic linkage.
It is shown in following structure:

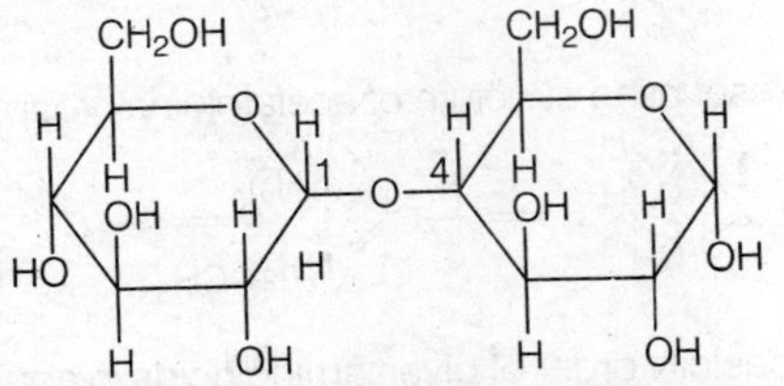

43. (*d*) Maltose on treatment with dil. HCl gives D-glucose. Hydrolysis of maltose yields two moles of α- D-glucose. Thus, it is composed of two α-D-glucose units in which C_1 of one glucose unit (I) is linked to C_4 of another glucose unit (II). The free aldehyde group can be produced at C_1 of second glucose in solution and it shows reducing properties.
So, it is a reducing sugar.

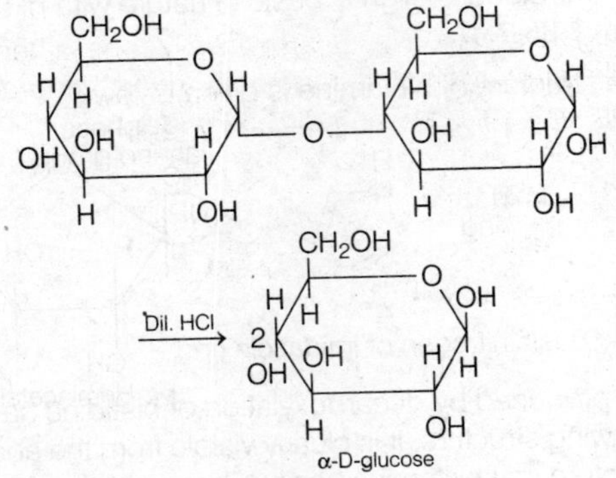

48. (*d*)

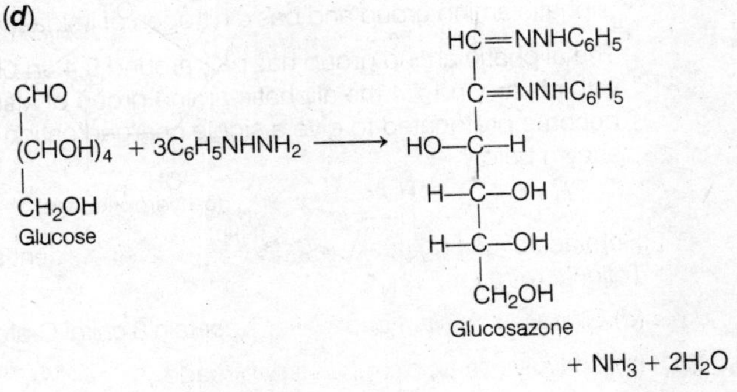

50. (*c*) The incorrect statement is (c). It can be corrected as follows : Glucose does not give Schiff's test due to absence of free —CHO in cyclic form.

The correct statements can be explained as follows :

(a) Pentaacetate of glucose does not react with hydroxylamine to give oxime. Because, the cyclic form (pyranose) of glucose after pentaacetate formation does not have free —CHO or >C=O group.

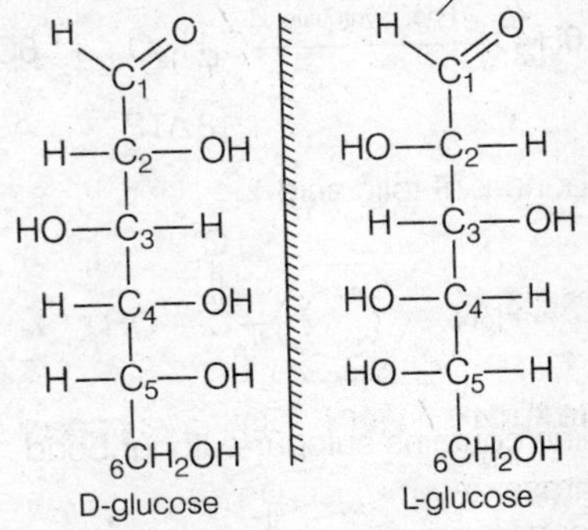

(b) Cyclic form of glucose has two diastereomeric forms which are named as α and β form. Each form its own crystal.

(d) Glucose reacts with hydroxylamine to form oxime.

51. (*d*) Insulin helps in the conversion of glucose to glycogen.

55. (*c*) $\underset{\text{Sucrose}}{C_{12}H_{22}O_{11}} + H_2O \xrightarrow{\text{HCl}} \underset{\text{D-glucose}}{C_6H_{12}O_6} + \underset{\text{D-fructose}}{C_6H_{12}O_6}$

60. (*c*)

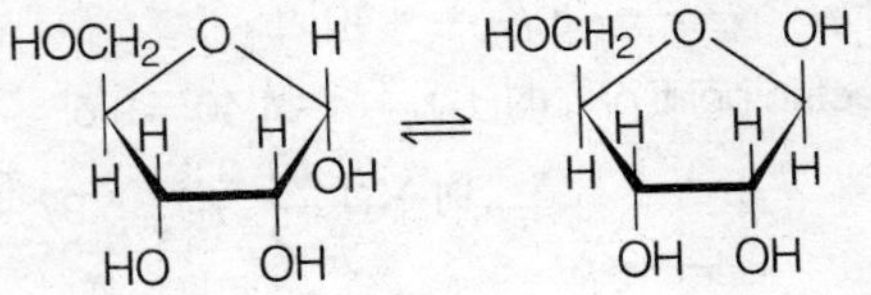

64. (*c*) $\underset{\text{(Non-reducing sugar)}}{\text{Sucrose}} \xrightarrow{H_2O} \underset{\text{(Reducing sugar)}}{\text{Glucose}} + \underset{\text{(Reducing sugar)}}{\text{Fructose}}$

65. (*b*) Statement-(b) is not true for sucrose. It is linked through a glycosidic linkage between C-1 of α-glucose and C-2 of β-fructose. Since, the reducing groups of glucose and fructose are involved in glycosidic bond formation, sucrose is a non-reducing sugar.

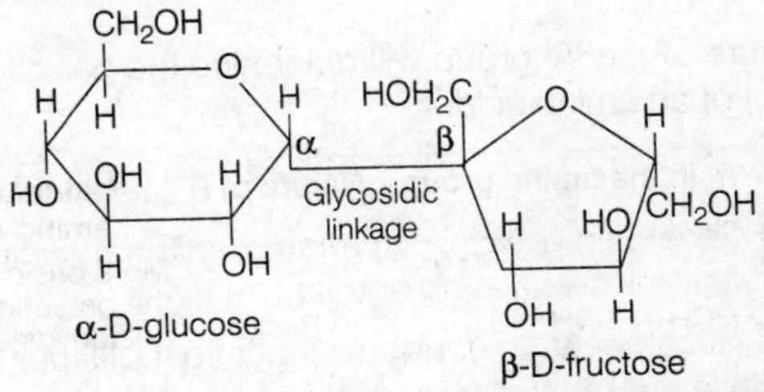

On hydrolysis with acids or enzyme, sucrose gives equimolar mixture of D-(+)-glucose and D-(–)-fructose.

$C_{12}H_{22}O_{11} + H_2O \xrightarrow{\text{HCl}} \underset{\text{D-(+)-glucose}}{C_6H_{12}O_6} + \underset{\text{D-(–)-fructose}}{C_6H_{12}O_6}$

67. (*d*) Sugar is not a reducing sugar because its disaccharide bond is a 1, 2 anomeric link.

71. (*d*) α-maltose contain two α-D-glucopyranose units with 1, 4-glycosidic linkage.

78. (*d*) Natural rubber has the weakest intermolecular force of attraction, i.e. van der Waals' force.

81. (*a*) 18 ATP

$$6CO_2 + 6H_2O \xrightarrow{\text{Photosynthesis}} \underset{\underset{18\,ATP}{\downarrow}}{C_6H_{12}O_6} + 6O_2$$

89. (*a*) Component of folic acid

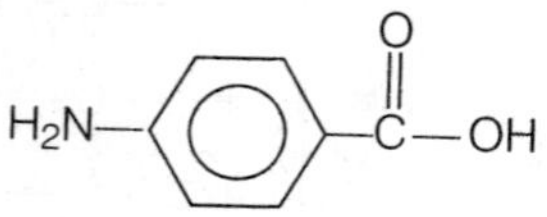

98. (*a*) Cysteine contains sulphur-sulphur bond

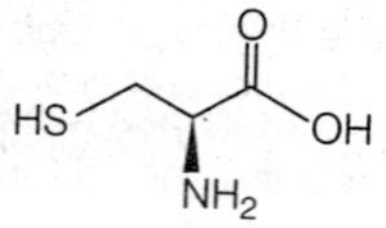

114. (*b*) Order : Histidine > Valine > Serine > Aspartic acid based on their anion-exhcnage resin.

125. (*c*)

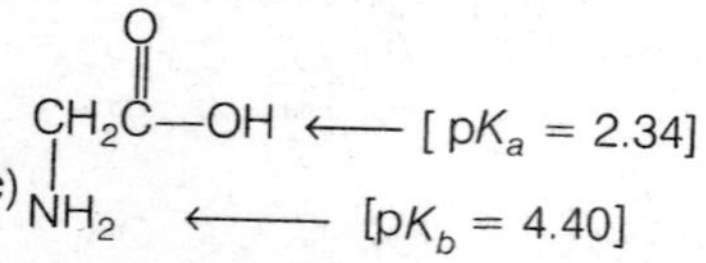

Isoelectric point $pK_a\,(NH_2) = 14 - 4.40 = 9.6$

$$PI = \frac{2.34 + 9.8}{2} = 5.97$$

Thus, $PI = 5.97$

127. (*a*) Glycine not contain any chiral center.

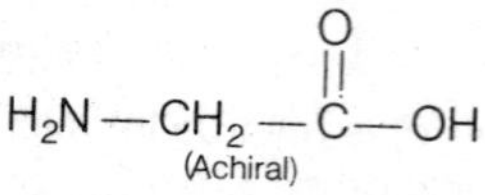

141. (*d*) Amino acid molecules can be represented as,

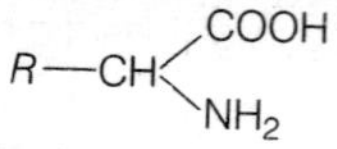

Nature of the '*R*' group will determine the basicity (hence, pK_a) of an amino acid.

	'*R*' in the amino group	Nature of *R*	Nature of the amino acids
1.	$-(CH_2)_3-NH-C(=\overset{+}{N}H_2)-NH_2$ (Arginine : Arg)	Basic	More basic (due to the presence of acetamidine group)
2.	$-CH_2-C(=O)-O^-$ (Aspartic acid: Asp)	Acidic	Acidic
3.	—H (Glycine) : Gly	Neutral	Neutral
4.	$-(CH_2)_4-\overset{+}{N}H_3$ (Lysine : Lys)	Basic	Basic

Acetamidine group present in arginine is

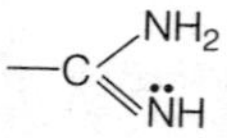

its self-protonation/deprotonation makes its conjugate acid very stable.

So, 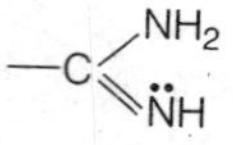 is a strongly basic in nature.

The resonating structure of acetamidine group is

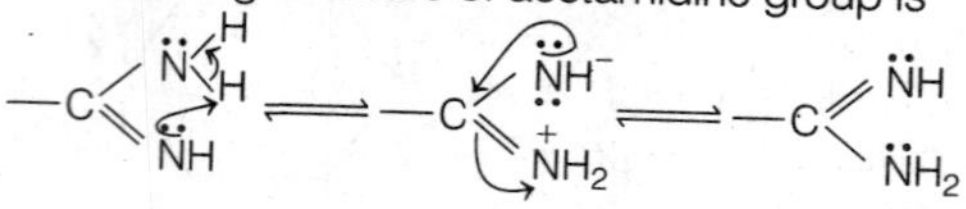

The basicity order of given amino acids in aqueous solution is as follows:

Asp < Gly < Lys < Arg

Thus, order of pK_a values is also,

	Asp	<	Gly	<	Lys	<	Arg
pK_a value :	(3)		(6)		(9.8)		(10.8)

142. (*d*) Our blood is slightly basic in nature with pH range from 7.35-7.4.

The structure of histamine is given below :

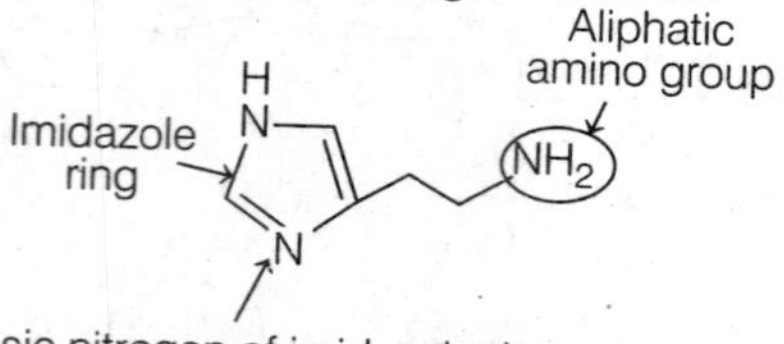

It is produced by decarboxylation of histidine having following structure. It is clearly visible from the above structure that histamine has two basic centres namely aliphatic amino group and basic nitrogen of imidazole ring.

The aliphatic amino group has pK_a around 9.4. In blood with pH around 7.4 the aliphatic amino group of histamine become protonated to give a single charged cation as shown below

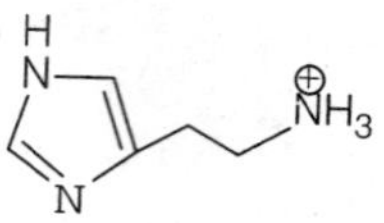

18

Polymers

Objective Questions Type I [Only one correct option]

In each of the questions below, four choices are given of which only one is correct.

1. Monomer of orlon is formed by following
(a) $CH\equiv CH + HCl \longrightarrow$
(b) $CH\equiv CH + HCN \longrightarrow$
(c) $CH_2=CHCl + KCN \longrightarrow$
(d) $CH_2=CH_2 + Cl_2 \longrightarrow$

2. Nitrile rubber is
(a) Buna-N
(b) Neoprene
(c) Buna-S
(d) PMMA

3. If polymer becomes more crystalline, then
(a) it becomes harder
(b) it becomes denser
(c) it becomes more resistant to heat
(d) All of the above properties are held true

4. Which are harder than steel and can conduct electricity?
(a) Oriented polymers
(b) Conventional polymers
(c) Both (a) and (b)
(d) None of the above

5. Which of the following properties is/are true for thermoplastics?
(a) The intermolecular forces of attraction are intermediate between elastomers and fibres
(b) They have cross-linking between them
(c) They cannot be molded by heating
(d) All of the above

6. Which of the following polymers have more than one monomer?
I. Nylon-6 II. Nylon-6, 6 III. Teflon IV. Buna-S
(a) I and II
(b) II and IV
(c) II and III
(d) I, II and IV

7. Condensation polymers are formed from monomers
(a) which have bifunctional groups
(b) which have multiple ($C=C$) or ($C\equiv N$) or ($C\equiv C$) bonds
(c) in which elimination can take place
(d) in which addition can take place

8. Molecular weight of the polymer can be controlled by
(a) chain-transfer
(b) chain-growth
(c) Both (a) and (b)
(d) None of the avove

9. Which is the best monomer for chain-growth polymer?
(a) Vinyl cyanide
(b) Vinyl chloride
(c) Styrene
(d) Vinyl acetate

10. Head-to-tail addition is not preferred in
(a) $CH_2=CHCl$
(b) $CH_2=CHCN$
(c) 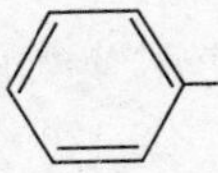 $-CH=CH_2$
(d) $HO\overset{O}{\overset{\|}{C}}(CH_2)_4\overset{O}{\overset{\|}{C}}OH$

11. Which polymer describes tail-to-tail addition?
(a) $-CH_2-\underset{X}{\underset{|}{CH}}-CH_2-\underset{X}{\underset{|}{CH}}-$
(b) $-\underset{X}{\underset{|}{CH}}-CH_2-CH_2-\underset{X}{\underset{|}{CH}}-$
(c) $-CH_2-\underset{X}{\underset{|}{CH}}-\underset{X}{\underset{|}{CH}}-CH_2-$
(d) All of the above

12. Cationic addition polymerisation reaction initiated by an acid is maximum in

(a) $H_3C-\underset{CH_3}{\overset{CH_3}{\underset{|}{\overset{|}{C}}}}-CH_3$ (b) $H_3C-\overset{CH_3}{\overset{|}{C}}=CH_2$

(c) $CH_3CH=CH_2$ (d) $H_2C=CH_2$

13. Arrange the following in increasing order of anionic addition polymerisation.

I: $H_2C=CH-Cl$ II: $H_2C=CH-C\equiv N$ III: $H_2C=CH-COCH_3$ (with C=O)

(a) I < II < III (b) II < I < III

(c) III < II < I (d) I < III < II

14. Lactam from which nylon-4 is synthesised, is

(a) 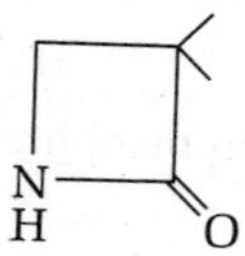 (b) 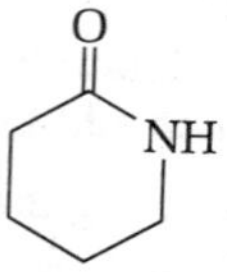

(c) 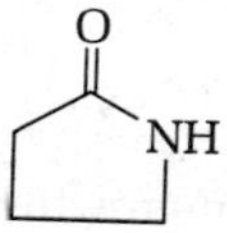 (d) 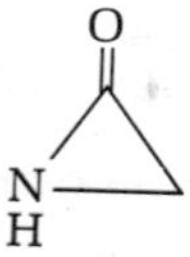

15. Consider the following monomers,

I: $H_2C=CH-CH_3$ II: $H_2C=C(CH_3)-CH_3$ III: $H_2C=CH-OCCH_3$ (with C=O)

IV: $H_2C=CH-C\equiv N$ V: 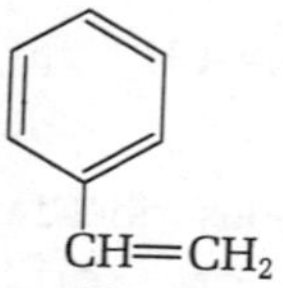

Which can undergo cationic and anionic addition polymerisation?

(a) I and II (b) II and IV

(c) II and V (d) III and V

16. Which of the following statements about low density polythene is false? **[JEE Main 2016]**

(a) It is a poor conductor of electricity

(b) Its synthesis required dioxygen or a peroxide initiator as a catalyst

(c) It is used in the manufacture of buckets, dustbins etc.

(d) Its synthesis requires high pressure

17. The formation of which of the following polymers involves hydrolysis reaction? **[JEE Main 2017]**

(a) Nylon-6 (b) Bakelite

(c) Nylon-6, 6 (d) Terylene

18. Number of chiral carbons in neoprene? **[JEE Main 2021, Feb.]**

(a) 0 (b) 1

(c) 2 (d) 3

19. In the following head-to-tail addition is preferred because

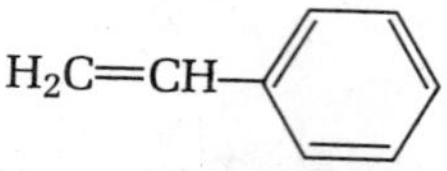 or $H_2C=CH-Cl$

(a) the propagating site preferentially attacks the less sterically hindered carbon of the alkene part

(b) radical intermediate is stabilised by resonance

(c) Both (a) and (b)

(d) None of the above

20. Preparation of bakelite proceeds *via* reactions **[JEE Main 2020]**

(a) Electrophilic addition and dehydration

(b) Condensation and elimination

(c) Nucleophilic addition and dehydration

(d) Electrophilic substitution and dehydration

21. Consider the following statements,

I. Cationic-polymerisation occurs in monomers with electron-donating substituents.

II. Anionic-polymerisation occurs in monomers with electron-withdrawing substituents.

III. Head-to-head chain-growth polymerisation occurs in polystyrene.

Select the correct statements.

(a) I and II

(b) I and III

(c) II and III

(d) I, II and III

22. In anionic polymerisation

(a) the initiator is a nucleophile like $NaNH_2$

(b) the alkene must contain an electron-withdrawing substituent

(c) Both (a) and (b) are true

(d) None of the above is true

23. Which polymer has 'chiral' monomer(s)? **[JEE Main 2020]**

(a) PHBV (b) Buna-N

(c) Nylon-6, 6 (d) Neoprene

24. Which of the following is a condensation polymer? **[JEE Main 2019]**

(a) Nylon-6, 6 (b) Neoprene

(c) Teflon (d) Buna - S

25. Which polymer is not correctly matched in terms of physical properties?
(a) Polyethylene — crystalline
(b) Rubber — amorphous
(c) Nylon — semicrystalline
(d) Bakelite — amorphous

26. Thermosetting polymers are except
(a) bakelite (b) PET
(c) epoxy resins (d) melmac

27. Which polymer (trade name) is used to make magnetic tapes?
(a) Dacron (b) Mylar (c) Lexan (d) Kevlar

28. Teflon is named as on the IUPAC pattern as
(a) poly (1,1,2,2-tetrafluoro ethene)
(b) poly (1,1,2,2-tetrafluoro ethane)
(c) poly (difluoro methylene)
(d) poly (tetrafluoro ethene)

29. Kevlar is used in the following except
(a) bullet proof vests
(b) crash helmets
(c) radial tyres
(d) shatter-resistant eyeglasses

30. Select the incorrect statement.
(a) Nylon is a step-growth condensation polymer
(b) Radical polymerisation usually yields atactic polymer
(c) Natural rubber is *trans*-polyisoprene
(d) *Gutta percha* is *trans*-polyisoprene

31. Monomer of buna-S and nylon-6, respectively are **[JEE Main 2021, Feb.]**
(a) Styrene and caprolactam
(b) Cyclohexane and caprolactam
(c) Ethylene glycol and styrene
(d) Styrene and amino acid

32. Which of the following is a thermosetting polymer? **[JEE Main 2019]**
(a) Bakelite (b) Buna-N (c) Nylon-6 (d) PVC

33. The correct name of the following polymer is

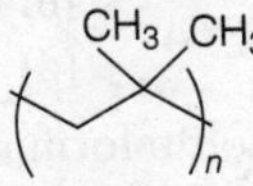

[JEE Main 2019]

(a) polyisobutane (b) polytert-butylene
(c) polyisoprene (d) polyisobutylene

34. The homopolymer formed from 4-hydroxybutanoic acid is **[JEE Main 2019]**
(a) $\left[-\overset{O}{\overset{\|}{C}}O(CH_2)_3-O- \right]_n$ (b) $\left[-\overset{O}{\overset{\|}{C}}(CH_2)_2\overset{O}{\overset{\|}{C}}- \right]_n$
(c) $\left[-\overset{O}{\overset{\|}{C}}(CH_2)_3-O- \right]_n$ (d) $\left[-\overset{O}{\overset{\|}{C}}(CH_2)_2\overset{O}{\overset{\|}{C}}-O- \right]_n$

35. Consider the following polymers,
I. Polyvinyl chloride
II. Polystyrene
III. Polyacetate
IV. Polysiloxanes
V. Polyisoprene

Out of the above, artificial chain-growth polymers are
(a) all except IV and V (b) all except III and IV
(c) all except I, II and V (d) all except IV

36. Which is not the step-growth polymer?
(a) Polysulphones (b) Polycarbonates
(c) Polyvinyl acetate (d) Polyethylene oxide

37. Acrylic acid is a monomer of so many polymers. Which is not the correct synthesis of this monomer?
(a) $HC{\equiv}CH + CO + H_2O \xrightarrow[473\text{ K, }100\text{ atm}]{NiBr_2}$
(b) $H_2C{=}CH_2 \xrightarrow{O_2/Ag} \xrightarrow{HCN} \xrightarrow[-H_2O]{448\text{ K}} \xrightarrow{H_3O^+}$
(c) $H_2C{=}CH{-}CH_3 \xrightarrow[593\text{ K}]{O_2} \xrightarrow[553\text{ K}]{O_2}$
(d) $H_2C{=}CH_2 \xrightarrow{HCN} \xrightarrow{H_3O^+}$

38. Acrylonitrile can be synthesised *via*
(a) $H_2C{=}CH{-}CH_3 + NO \xrightarrow{1000\text{ K, Ag}}$
(b) $H_2C{=}CHCH_3 + NH_3 + O_2 \xrightarrow[FeO,\ 3\text{ atm}]{700\text{ K}}$
(c) $H_2C{=}CH_2 \xrightarrow[Ag]{O_2} \xrightarrow{HCN} \xrightarrow[MgCO_3]{500\text{ K}}$
(d) All of the above

39. Terylene is a condensation polymer of ethylene glycol and
(a) benzoic acid (b) phthalic acid
(c) salicylic acid (d) terephthalic acid

40. Orlon is a hard, horny and a high melting material. Which of the following represents its structure?
(a) $\left(H_2C{-}\underset{COOC_2H_5}{\underset{|}{C}H} \right)_n$ (b) $\left(H_2C{-}\underset{Cl}{\underset{|}{C}H} \right)_n$
(c) $\left(H_2C{-}\underset{CN}{\underset{|}{C}H} \right)_n$ (d) $\left(H_2C{-}\overset{CH_3}{\overset{|}{\underset{COOCH_3}{\underset{|}{C}}}} \right)_n$

41. Which of the following is a biodegradable polymer?
(a) Cellulose (b) Polythene
(c) Polyvinyl chloride (d) Nylon-6

42. Substance having ester linkage is
(a) bakelite (b) polythene
(c) PVC (d) terylene

43. Caprolactam is the monomer of
(a) melamine (b) dacron
(c) nylon-6 (d) All of these

44. Glyptal polymer is obtained by the reaction of glycerol with
(a) malonic acid (b) acetic acid
(c) phthalic acid (d) maleic acid

45. Which of the following is not a synthetic fibre?
(a) Rubber (b) Nylon-6
(c) Nylon-6,6 (d) Nylon-6,10

46. The monomer of the polymer

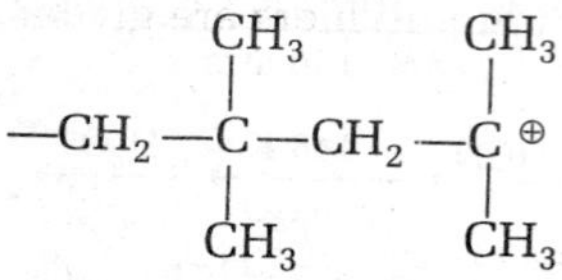

is

(a) $H_2C{=}C(CH_3)_2$ (b) $(CH_3)_3C{=}C(CH_3)_2$
(c) $CH_3CH{=}CHCH_3$ (d) $CH_3CH{=}CH_2$

47. Natural rubber is not used in making footwear for polar regions because
(a) natural rubber becomes soft at temperature lower than 10°C.
(b) natural rubber becomes brittle at temperature lower than 10°C.
(c) natural rubber melts at temperature lower than 10°C.
(d) natural rubber becomes stronger at temperature lower than 10°C.

48. Cationic polymerisation of styrene forming polystyrene always takes place
(a) head-to-tail
(b) head-to-head
(c) tail-to-tail
(d) anionic polymerisation and not cationic polymerisation (head-to-tail) takes place

49. Which of the following structures represents neoprene polymer? **[JEE Main 2021, Feb.]**

(a) 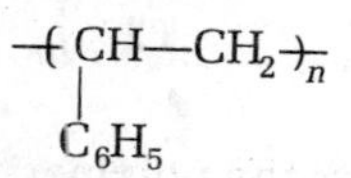

(b) 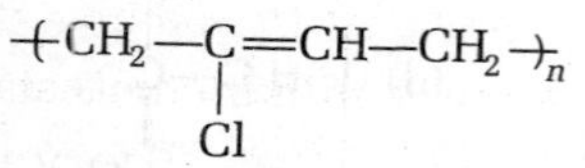

(c) 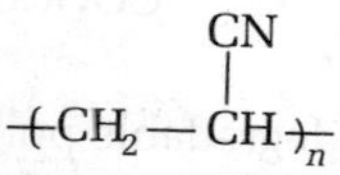

(d) 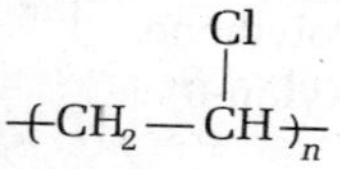

50. Arrange the following in increasing order of their intermolecular forces : Nylon-6,6 (I), Buna-S (II), Polythene (III)
(a) II < I < III (b) III < II < I
(c) I < II < III (d) II < III < I

51. Polymer used in bullet proof glass is
(a) PMMA (b) lexan
(c) nomex (d) kevlar

52. Glyptal polymer is obtained from glycol by reacting with
(a) malonic acid (b) phthalic acid
(c) maleic acid (d) terephthalic acid

53. Nylon-6,6 is obtained from
(a) adipic acid and hexamethylene diamine
(b) tetrafluoroethylene
(c) vinyl cyanide
(d) vinyl benzene

54. Which of the following type of forces are present in nylon-66?
(a) van der Waals' forces of attraction
(b) Hydrogen bonding
(c) Three dimensional network of bonds
(d) Metallic bonding

55. On complete hydrogenation natural rubber produces **[JEE Advanced 2016]**
(a) ethylene-propylene copolymer
(b) vulcanised rubber
(c) polypropylene
(d) polybutylene

56. The monomer (s) used to prepare polyvinyl polythene is
(a) vinyl chloride and ethane
(b) ethene
(c) 1,3-butadiene and acrylonitrile
(d) 1,3-butadiene

57. The polymer used in orthopaedic devices and in controlled drug release is
(a) orlon (b) PTFE
(c) SBR (d) PHBV

58. The first step in bakelite formation is
(a) aromatic nucleophilic substitution
(b) aromatic electrophilic substitution
(c) condensation
(d) electrophilic addition

59. Which of the following polymer is used in the manufacture of wood laminates? **[JEE Main 2021, March]**
(a) *cis*-polyisoprene
(b) Melamine formaldehyde resin
(c) Urea formaldehyde resin
(d) Phenol and formaldehyde resin

Objective Questions Type II [One or more than one correct option(s)]

In each of the questions below, four choices are given, of which one or more than one are correct.

1. Which of the following statements are correct about phenol-formaldehyde resin?
(a) Novalac or resol is a linear polymer and is used in the manufacture of adhesive.
(b) Bakelite is a cross-linked polymer and is used in making switches and plugs.
(c) Novolac is prepared when (P/F) (phenol/formaldehye) ratio is greater than 1, whereas bakelite is prepared when (P/F) ratio is less than 1.

2. Which of the following are used as chain transfer agents?
(a) CCl_4 (b) CBr_4
(c) Benzoquinone (d) Benzoyl peroxide

3. Nylon-5, 10 can be prepared by
(a) $H_2N(CH_2)_5NH_2$ + Decanoic acid (Sebacic acid)
(b) $HOOC(CH_2)_3COOH + H_2N(CH_2)_{10}NH_2$
(c) $H_2N(CH_2)_6NH_2 + HOOC(CH_2)_8COOH$
(d) $H_2N(CH_2)_{10}NH_2 + HOOC(CH_2)_4COOH$

4. By which of the following reaction sequence can nylon-5 be prepared?

(a) 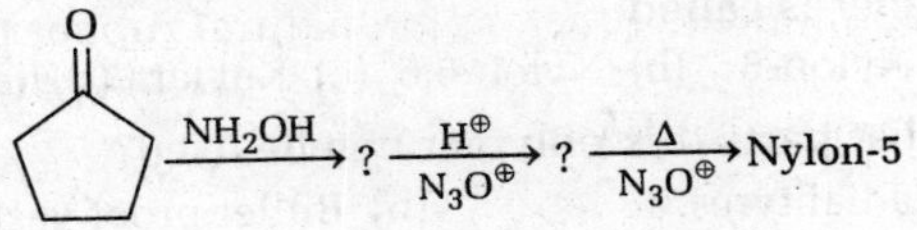

(b) 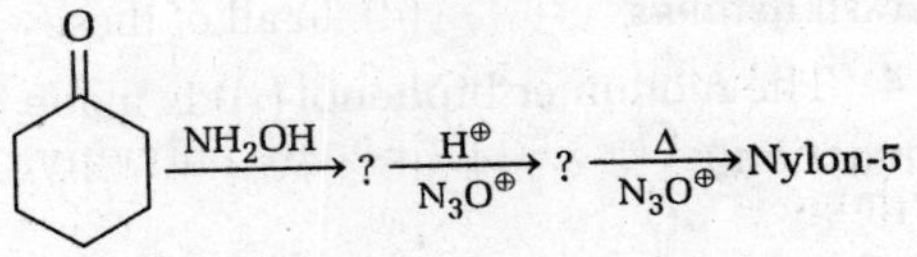

(c) 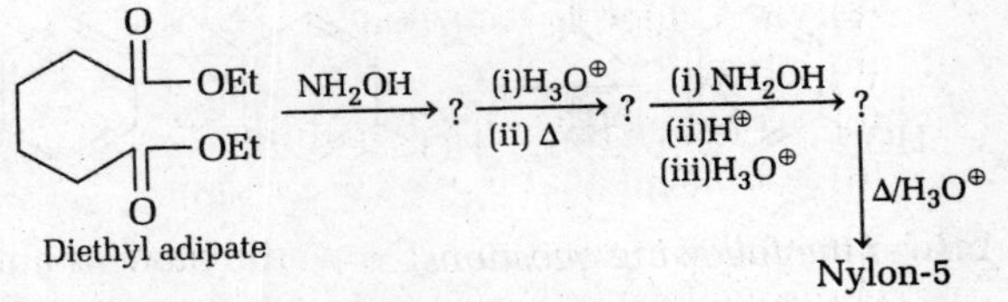

Diethyl adipate

(d) All of the above

5. Which of the following fibres are made of polyamides?
(a) Wool
(b) Natural silk
(c) Rayon
(d) Nylon

6. Which of the following can be used as plasticisers?
(a) Sodium hexametaphosphate
(b) Di-*n*-butylphthalate
(c) Tricresyl phosphate
(d) Diethyl phthalate

7. Structures of some common polymers are given. Which are correctly presented?
(a) Teflon $\text{+}CF_2—CF_2\text{+}_n$
(b) Neoprene $\left(CH_2—\underset{Cl}{\underset{|}{C}}{=}CH—CH_2—CH_2\right)_n$
(c) Terylene $\text{+}OC—C_6H_4—COOCH_2—CH_2—O\text{+}_n$
(d) Nylon-6, 6 $\text{+}NH(CH_2)_6NHCO(CH_2)_4—CO\text{+}_n$

8. Choose the correct option(s) from the following. **[JEE Advanced 2019]**
(a) Teflon is prepared by heating tetrafluorethene is presence of a persulphate catalyst at high pressure
(b) Natural rubber is polyisoprene containing *trans* alkene units
(c) Cellulose has only α-D-glucose units that are joined by glycosidic linkages
(d) Nylon-6 has amide linkages

Numerical Value Questions

All these questions have a Numerical value as their answer, solve the questions and write your answer.

1. The follownig chain-growth polymer is made up of how many difluoroethylene monomer units?

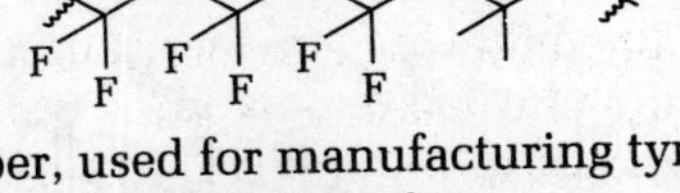

2. The rubber, used for manufacturing tyres, is vulcanised with sulphur of % …… .

3. For the formation of terylene, the number of moles of ethylene glycol required per mole of terephthalic acid is

4. An acidic resin can be made by the polymerization of 4-vinylpyridine initiated by AIBN and heat followed by treatment of the polymer with bromoacetate. How many (C=C) bonds are in conjugation with each other in 4-vinylpyridine ?

5. The total number of lone pairs of electrons in melamine is …… . **[JEE Main 2012]**

6. Buna-S-rubber is a polymer of styrene and 1, 3-butadiene. Calculate the total π-bonds present in the product?

7. The contour of a polymer chain modelled as a random coil, with $N = 1000$ and $l = 150$ pm, are closest to ... .

8. The degree of polymerisation ($< N >$) and the fraction of monomer consumed (P) is 0.5. For a polymerisation reaction. Calculate the value of $< N >$ using value of P.

Comprehension Based Questions

In these questions, a passage has been given followed by questions based on it. You have to answer the questions based on the passage given.

***Passage* 1** Kodel is a polyester fibre of a dibasic acid and polyhydroxy compound.

Answer the following questions.

1. Dibasic used is
   (a) oxalic acid
   (b) phthalic acid
   (c) terephthalic acid
   (d) succinic acid

2. Polyhydroxy compound is
   (a) glycol
   (b) glycerol
   (c) 1,4-cyclohexane dimethanol
   (d) tetra (hydroxy methyl) methane

3. If oxygen of alcohol is (^{18}O), then, this $\overset{18}{O}$ goes with ...... in polyester formation.
   (a) H_2O
   (b) polyester monomer
   (c) Both (a) and (b)
   (d) None of the above

***Passage* 2** Isobutylene can be polymerised by treated with liquid HF.

Answer the following questions.

1. Polymer formed is
   (a) 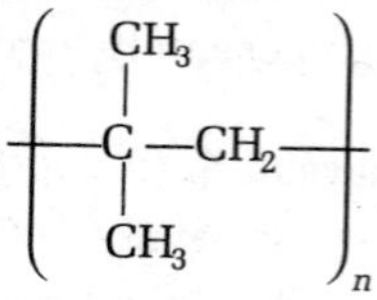
   (b) 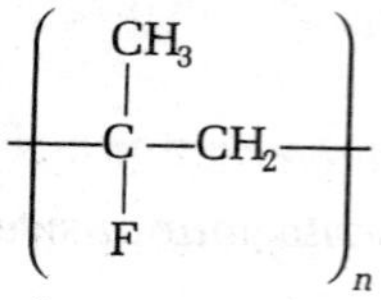
   (c) 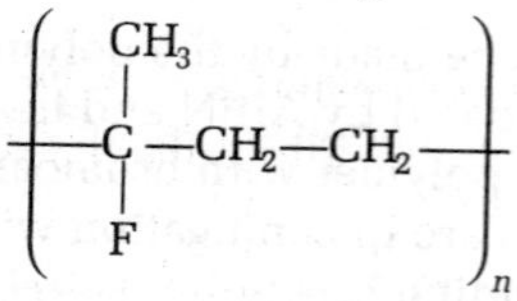
   (d) None of the above

2. Mechanism involved is
   (a) anionic polymerisation
   (b) cationic polymerisation
   (c) free radical polymerisation
   (d) None of the above

***Passage* 3** As a material scientist working for an auto manufacturer. You are considering three polymer samples for possible use in new models. Unfortunately the shipment of samples was in ware-house in a coastal city when a hurricane hit and the labels came off all the samples when the ware-house flooded. On examining one of the samples, it consists of long filament. When heated in the presence of acid, the filament decomposed, absorbing water to produce the following two compounds.

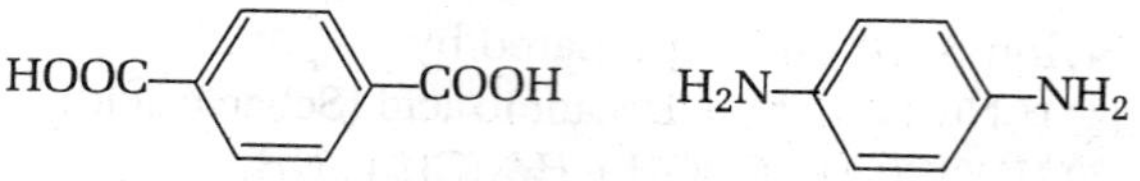

Answer the following questions.

1. Polymers under this category can be
   (a) an aramids (b) an alimids
   (c) carbomids (d) None of these

2. Polymer is called
   (a) Nylon-6 (b) Nylon-6,6 (c) Kevlar (d) Orlon

3. In what parts this polymer can be used?
   (a) Radial tyres (b) Bullet proof vests
   (c) Crash helmets (d) In all of these

***Passage* 4** The monomer biphenol (A) is made by the following reaction :

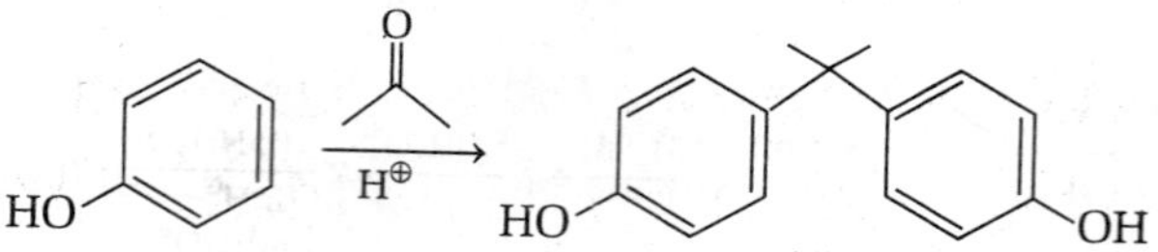

(A)

Answer the following questions.

1. Some of the facts about this reaction are
   I. Phenol is a nucleophilic aromatic compound
   II. It involves electrophilic aromatic substitution
   III. Phenol is *ortho, para*-directing and the *para* product is favoured for steric reasons.

   Select the correct facts.
   (a) I and II (b) I and III (c) II and III (d) I, II and III

2. It involves intermediate
   (a) 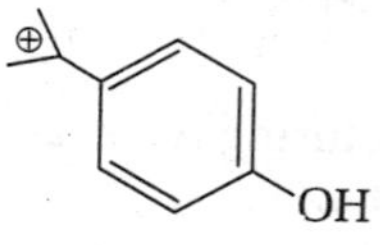
   (b) 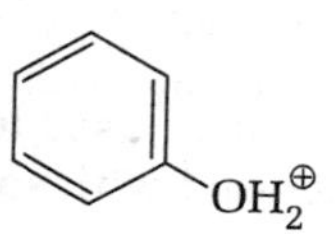
   (c) 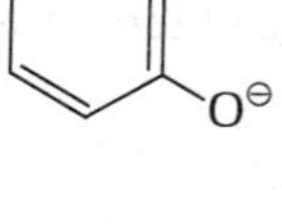
   (d) None of these

Matrix-Match Type

Given below are Matching Type Questions, with two columns (each having some items) each . Each item of Column I has to be matched with the items of Column II.

1. Match the polymer in Column I with their monomer in Column II.

Column I	Column II
A. Polyvinyl chloride	1. $CF_2=CF_2$
B. Polystyrene	2. $CH_2=CHCOOC_2H_5$
C. Teflon	3. $CH_2=CH—Cl$
D. Neoprene	4. 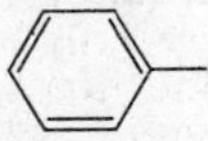 $—CH=CH_2$
E. Polyethyl acrylate	5. $CH_2=CH—C(Cl)=CH_2$

2. Match the following.

Column I (Polymer)	Column II (Monomer)
A. ABS	1. $CH_2=CHCN$
B. SBR	2. $CH_2=CH—CH=CH_2$
C. Polystyrene	3. 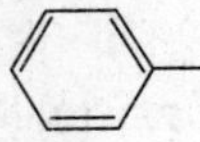 $—CH=CH_2$
D. Orlon	4. $CF_2=CF_2$
E. Teflon	

3. Match the copolymers in Column I with their monomers in Column II.

Column I	Column II
A. Saran	1. 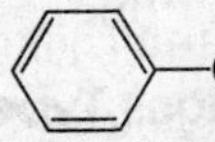 $—CH=CH_2$
B. SAN	2. $CH_{22}=CH—CH=CH_2$
	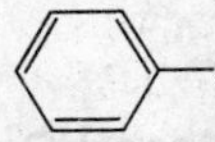 $—CH=CH_2$
	$CH_2=CH—CH=CH_2$,
	$CH_2=CHCN$
C. ABS	3. $CH_2=CHCl$, $CH_2=CCl_2$
	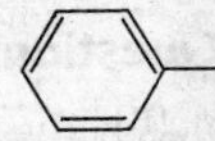 $—CH=CH_2$
D. SBR	4. $CH_2=CHCN$

4. The correct match between Column I and Column II is **[JEE Main 2019]**

Column I	Column II
A. High density polythene	I. Peroxide catalyst
B. Polyacrylonitrile	II. Condensation at high temperature and pressure
C. Novolac	III. Ziegler-Natta catalyst
D. Nylon-6	IV. Acid or base catalyst

Single Integer Answer Questions

Answer of these questions is a single digit lying between 0 to 9.

1. Melamine is polymerised with formaldehyde to make formica. Melamine is formed by heating cyanamide. How many molecules of cyanamide are involved in this formation?

2. An acidic resin can be made by the polymerisation of 4-vinylpyridine initiated by AIBN and heat followed by treatment of the polymer with. bromoacetate. How many (C=C) bonds are in conjugation with each other in 4-vinylpyridine?

3. When sodium metal is dissolved in a solution of naphthalene in THF, a green solution of radical anion is produced. This green solution initiates the polymerisation of butadiene to form a polymer. How many non-bonding electrons are there in radical anion?

4. How many main scientists are involved in the first synthesis of nylon?

5. How many monomers are present in polymer ABS?

6. How many N-atoms are present in momomer of Nylon-6,6?

7. The average end-to-end distance of a random coil polymer of 10^6 monomers (in units of segment length) is 10^x. Find x.

8. How many carbon-carbon bond in caprolactam?

Answers

Objective Questions Type I [Only one correct option]

1. (b) 2. (a) 3. (d) 4. (a) 5. (a) 6. (b) 7. (a) 8. (a) 9. (c) 10. (d)
11. (b) 12. (b) 13. (d) 14. (c) 15. (d) 16. (c) 17. (a) 18. (a) 19. (c) 20. (d)
21. (a) 22. (c) 23. (a) 24. (a) 25. (d) 26. (b) 27. (b) 28. (a) 29. (d) 30. (c)
31. (a) 32. (a) 33. (d) 34. (c) 35. (b) 36. (c) 37. (d) 38. (d) 39. (d) 40. (c)
41. (d) 42. (d) 43. (a) 44. (c) 45. (a) 46. (a) 47. (b) 48. (a) 49. (b) 50. (d)
51. (b) 52. (b) 53. (a) 54. (b) 55. (a) 56. (d) 57. (d) 58. (b) 59. (c)

Objective Questions Type II [One or more than one correct option(s)]

1. (a, b, c) 2. (a, b) 3. (a) 4. (a, c) 5. (a, b, d)
6. (b, c) 7. (a, c, d) 8. (a, d)

Comprehension Based Questions

Passage 1 – 1. (c) 2. (c) 3. (b)
Passage 2 – 1. (a) 2. (b)
Passage 3 – 1. (a) 2. (b) 3. (d)
Passage 4 – 1. (d) 2. (a)

Numerical Value Questions

1. (4) 2. (6) 3. (1) 4. (6) 5. (6) 6. (6) 7. (150) 8. (2)

Matrix-Match Type

1. (A) → (3); (B) → (4); (C) → (1); (D) → (5); (E) → (2)
2. (A) → (1,2,3); (B) → (2,3); (C) → (3); (D) → (1); E → (4)
3. (A) → (3); (B) → (4); (C) → (2); (D) → (1)
4. (A) → (3); (B) → (1); (C) → (4); (D) → (2)

Single Integer Answer Questions

1. (3) 2. (2) 3. (3) 4. (2) 5. (3) 6. (2) 7. (3) 8. (5)

Solutions

Objective Questions Type I

1. (*b*) $HC \equiv CH + HCN \longrightarrow \underset{\text{Orlon}}{H_2C = CH - CN}$

5. (*a*) Thermoplastics have intermolecular force of interaction in intermediate between elastomers and fibres.

13. (*d*) $\underset{\underset{C\equiv N}{|}}{H_2C = CH} > \underset{\underset{\underset{O}{||}}{COCH_3}}{H_2C = CH} > \underset{\underset{Cl}{|}}{H_2C = CH}$

14. (*c*) For the synthesis of nylon-4, lactam with four carbon atoms is required.

16. (*c*) High density polythene is used in the manufacture of buckets, dustbins etc.

17. (*a*) Nylon-6 or perlon is prepared by polymerisation of amino caproic acid at high temperature. Caprolactam is first hydrolysed with water to form amino acid which on heating undergoes polymerisation to give nylon-6.

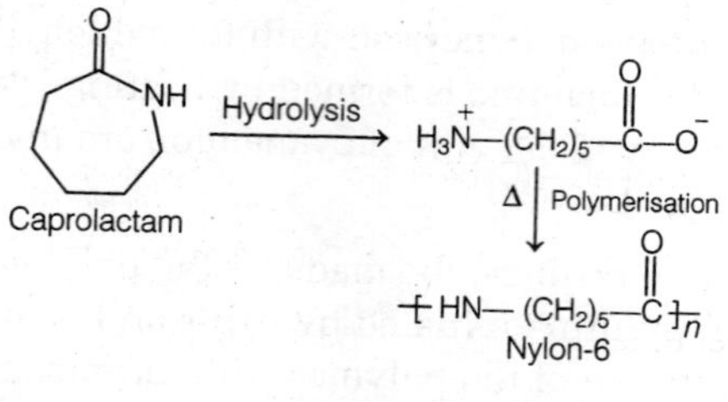

18. (*a*)

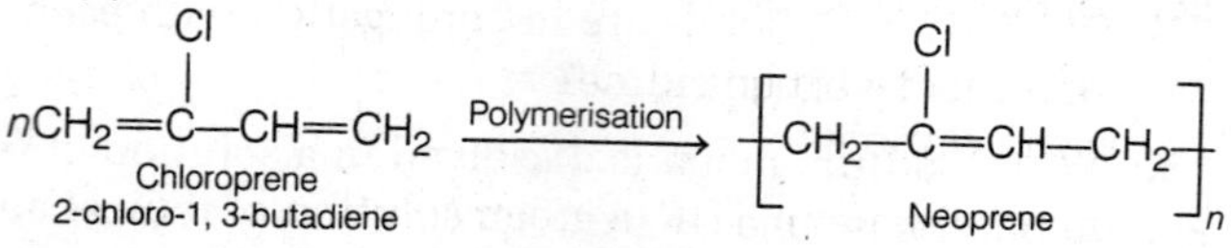

In neoprene no chiral carbon is present.

20. (*d*) Preparation of bakelite proceeds *via* electrophilic substitution and dehydration reactions.

It is shown below :

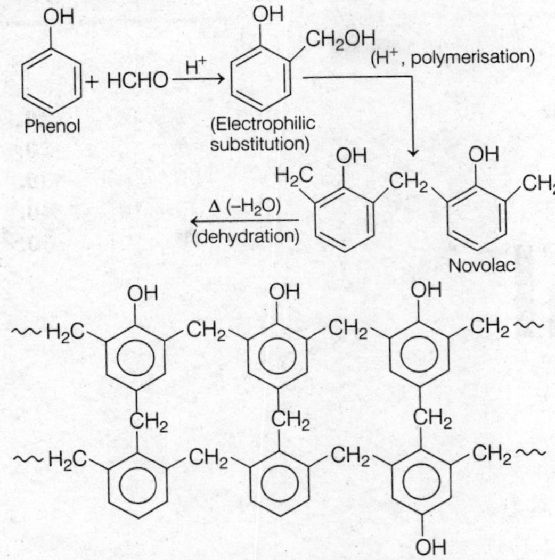

3D-cross-linked polymer (bakelite)

23. (*a*) PHBV, (Poly 3- hydroxybutyrate -co-3- hydroxyvalerate) is a copolymer of

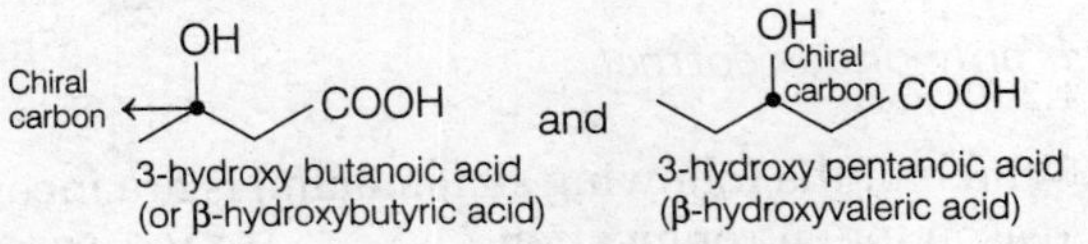

In both monomers, there is one chiral centre (shown by dark spot).

∴ Polymer contains chiral monomers.

24. (*a*) Nylon-6, 6 (an amide) is a condensation copolymer because it is obtained by condensation between adipic acid and hexamethylenediamine.

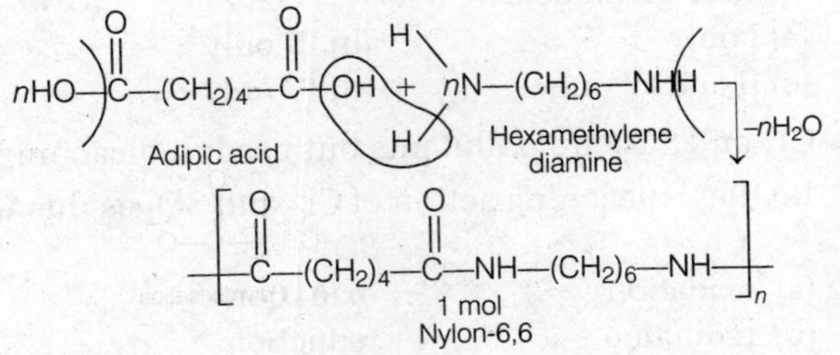

Neoprene, teflon and buna-S are addition polymers.

26. (*b*) PET polymer is thermoplastic polymers.

31. (*a*) Monomer of buna-S is styrene and monomer of nylon-6 is caprolactam.

32. (*a*) Bakelite is a thermosetting polymer. These polymers are cross-linked or heavily branched molecules which on heating undergo extensive cross linking in moulds and become infusible. Once they get set, they cannot be reshaped and reused.

33. (*d*) The correct name of the given polymer is polyisobutylene. It's monomer unit is isobutylene.

Reaction involved is as follows :

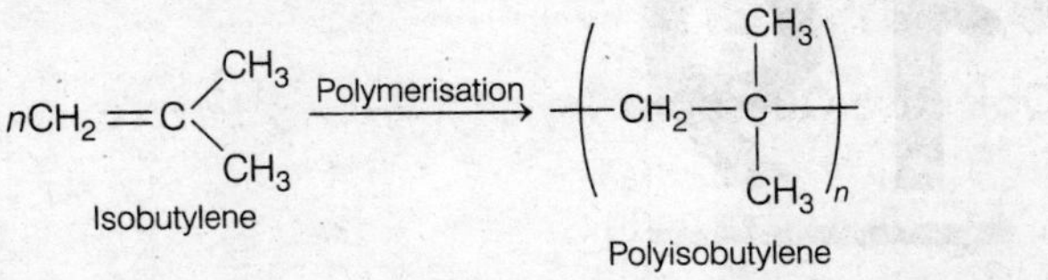

The above reaction proceed *via* addition polymerisation. Polymer is formed by the repeated addition of monomer molecules possessing double bond.

34. (*c*) On polymerisation, 4-hydroxy butanoic acid will produce a condensation homopolymer by loss of H_2O molecules.

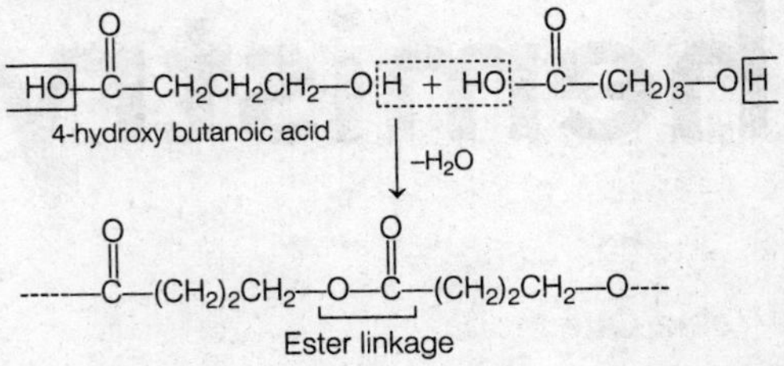

The homopolymer obtained can also be represented as

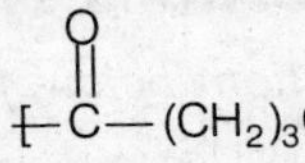

42. (*d*) Terylene contain ester linkage.

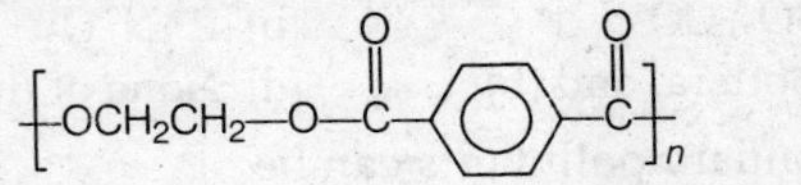

51. (*b*) Lexan is used for making bullet proof glass.

53. (a)

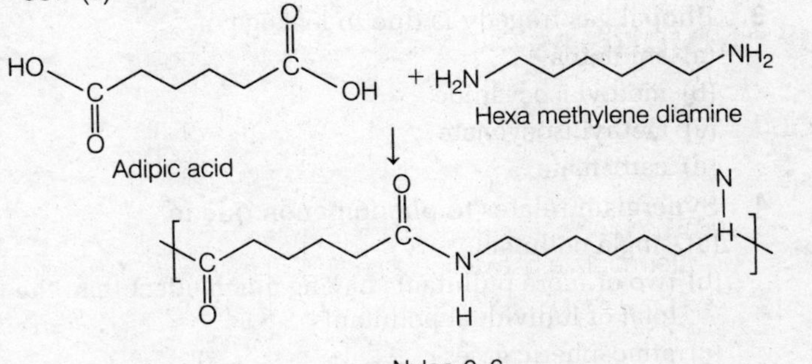

55. (*a*)

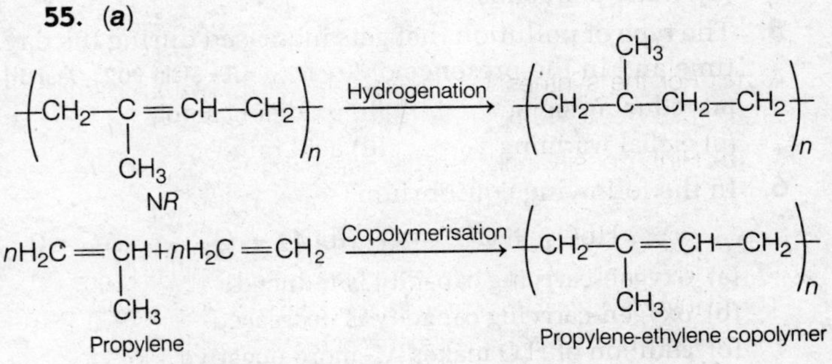

59. (*c*) Urea-HCHO resin is used in manufacture of wood laminates.

19

Environmental Chemistry

Objective Questions Type I [Only one correct option]

In each of the questions below, four choices are given of which only one is correct.

1. Primary pollutants can be
(a) SO_2, CO (b) PAN, O_3
(c) Both (a) and (b) (d) None of these

2. Secondary pollutants can be
(a) PAN (b) O_3
(c) Cl (d) All of these

3. Bhopal gas tragedy is due to leakage of
(a) ammonia
(b) methyl isocyanide
(c) methyl isocyanate
(d) carbamate

4. Synergism relates to phenomenon due to
(a) single pollutant
(b) two or more pullutants having much effect than the total of individual pollutants
(c) atmospheric gases
(d) water pollutants

5. The type of pollution that gets increased during the day time and in the presence of O_3 is **[JEE Main 2021, March]**
(a) reducing smog (b) oxidising smog
(c) global warming (d) acid rain

6. In the following equilibrium
$$HbO_2 + CO \rightleftharpoons HbCO + O_2 ; \quad \Delta G < 0$$
(a) oxygen-carrying capacity is reduced
(b) oxygen-carrying capacity is decreased
(c) addition of H_2O makes ΔG more negative
(d) temperature has no effect

7. Which of the following statement(s) is are incorrect reason for eutrophication ? **[JEE Main 2021, March]**
I. excess usage of fertilizers
II. excess usage of detergents
III. dense plant population in water bodies
IV. lack of nutrients in water bodies that prevent plant growth
Choose the most appropriate answer from the options given below
(a) I only (b) III only
(c) II and IV only (d) IV only

8. Cl_2 and SO_2 are pollutants but used in bleaching of textiles. Bleaching action of Cl_2 and SO_2 is due to

	Cl_2	SO_2
(a)	oxidation	oxidation
(b)	reduction	reduction
(c)	reduction	oxidation
(d)	oxidation	reduction

9. The statement leads are TRUE
I. Methane leads to both global warming and photochemical smog
II. Methane is generated from paddy fields
III. Methane is a stronger global warming gas than CO
VI. Methane is a part of reducing smog
Choose the most appropriate answer from the options given below
(a) I, II, III (b) I and II (c) II, III, IV (d) I, II, IV

10. BOD_5 is
(a) waste decomposed in 5 days
(b) oxygen used in 5 days
(c) microorganisms killed in 5 days
(d) dissolved oxygen left after 5 days

11. The pH of rain water, is approximately
(a) 7.5 (b) 6.5 [JEE Main 2019, Jan.]
(c) 5.6 (d) 7.0

12. Which reaction is not part of acid rain?
(a) $CO_2 + H_2O \longrightarrow H_2CO_3$
(b) $SO_3 + H_2O \longrightarrow H_2SO_4$
(c) $NO_2 + O_2 + H_2O \longrightarrow HNO_3$
(d) $ClONO_2 + H_2O \longrightarrow HOCl + HNO_3$

13. The statement that is not true about ozone is [JEE Main 2020, Sep.]
(a) in the stratosphere, CFCs release chlorine free radicals (Cl), which reacts with O_3 to give chlorine dioxide radicals
(b) in the atmosphere, it is depleted by CFCs
(c) in the stratosphere, it forms a protective shield against UV radiation.
(d) it is a toxic gas and its reaction with NO gives NO_2

14. Select the correct statement(s).
(a) CFCs are transporting agents for continuously generating $Cl^{\bullet}$ into stratosphere and damaging ozone layer.
(b) The upper stratosphere consists of considerable amount of O_3.
(c) Ozone in the stratosphere is a product of UV radiations acting on O_2 molecules.
(d) All of the above are correct statements.

15. The correct set of species responsible for the photochemical smog is [JEE Main 2019, April]
(a) N_2, NO_2 and hydrocarbons
(b) CO_2, NO_2, SO_2 and hydrocarbons
(c) NO, NO_2, O_3 and hydrocarbons
(d) N_2, O_2, O_3 and hydrocarbons

16. Eye irritation is caused by
(a) HCHO (b) $CH_2{=}CHCHO$
(c) PAN (d) All of these

17. Which is not the constituents of photochemical smog?
(a) *R*CHO (b) *R*COR (c) PAN (d) CF_2Cl_2

18. Thermal power plants can lead to [JEE Main 2020, Sep.]
(a) acid rain (b) blue baby syndrome
(c) ozone layer depletion (d) eutrophication

19. Biochemical oxygen demand (BOD) is the amount of oxygen required (in ppm) [JEE Main 2020, Jan.]
(a) for the photochemical breakdown of waste present in 1 m^3 volume of a water body.
(b) for sustaining life in a water body.
(c) by anaerobic bacteria to breakdown inorganic waste present in a water body.
(d) by bacteria to breakdown organic waste in a certain volume of a water sample.

20. The maximum prescribed concentration of copper in drinking water is [JEE Main 2019, April]
(a) 5 ppm (b) 0.5 ppm
(c) 0.05 ppm (d) 3 ppm

21. The amberlyst A-26 resin is a "green" oxidising agent. It oxidises
(a) 1° alcohol to aldehyde
(b) 2° alcohol to ketone
(c) Both (a) and (b)
(d) None of the above

22. Biodegradable polymers are
(a) TPA (b) PHB
(c) PHBV (d) All of these

23. Biodegradable polymers (PHA) are of the type
(a) PHB (b) PHBV
(c) Both (a) and (b) (d) None of these

24. The reaction that is not involved in the ozone layer depletion mechanism in the stratosphere is
(a) $CH_4 + 2O_3 \longrightarrow 3CH_2{=}O + 3H_2O$ [JEE Main 2019, Jan.]
(b) $Cl\dot{O}(g) + O(g) \longrightarrow \dot{C}l(g) + O_2(g)$
(c) $HOCl(g) \xrightarrow{h\nu} \dot{O}H(g) + \dot{C}l(g)$
(d) $CF_2Cl_2(g) \xrightarrow{h\nu} \dot{C}l(g) + \dot{C}F_2Cl(g)$

25. Rosenmund synthesis of CH_3CHO uses $BaSO_4$ which causes pollution. In "green" chemistry alternate method is
(a) $CH_3COCl + H_2 \xrightarrow{Pd}$
(b) $CH_2{=}CH_2 + O_2 \xrightarrow{Pd(II)/Cu(II)}$
(c) $(CH_3CO)_2O \xrightarrow{LiAlH_4}$
(d) $CH_3COCl \xrightarrow{LiAlH_4}$

26. When rain is accompanied by a thunderstrom, the collecte rain water will have a pH value ?
(a) Which depends upon the amount of dust in air
(b) Slightly lower than that when rain water is without thunderstorm
(c) Slightly higher than that when the thunderstorm is not there
(d) Uninfluenced by occurrence of thunderstorm

27. Find the incorrect statement.
(a) BOD value of clean water is less than 5 ppm.
(b) Drinking water pH should be between 5.5-9.5.
(c) Carbon, sulphur and nitrogen oxides are the most widespread air pollutants.
(d) Dissolved oxygen concentration below 5 ppm is ideal for the growth of fish.

28. Find the secondary pollutant among these
(a) PAN
(b) N_2O
(c) SO_2
(d) CO_2

29. The reaction responsible for radiant energy of the sun is
(a) nuclear fission
(b) nuclear fusion
(c) chemical reaction
(d) combustion

30. Alum's capacity of purify water is due to
(a) softens hard water
(b) pathogenic bacteria destroy
(c) impurities coagulation
(d) it improves taste

31. In the air, N_2 and O_2 occur naturally but they do not react to form oxides of nitrogen because
(a) oxides of nitrogen are unstable
(b) catalyst is required for the reaction
(c) the reaction is endothermic
(d) N_2 and O_2 do not react with each other

Comprehension Based Questions

In these questions, a passage has been given followed by questions based on it. You have to answer the questions based on the passage given.

***Passage* 1** General new methods of oxidation are based on green chemisry sodium hypochlorite (NaOCl the oxidant in household bleach) in aqueous CH_3COOH is also touted on "green" oxidising agent.

Answer the following questions.

1. Green chemistry means
(a) the use of green vegetables in synthesis
(b) the use of chemicals with green colour
(c) use of very fast reactions
(d) use of environmentally bengin methods to synthesise compounds

2. NaOCl in CH_3COOH is under "green" oxidising agent as
(a) waste products are NaCl and H_2O thus no harm to environment
(b) it is cheap and is easily available
(c) it forms NaOH and HCl are thus can be used
(d) it is a better oxidising agent

***Passage* 2** $K_2Cr_2O_7 / H_2SO_4, KMnO_4 / H_2SO_4, OsO_4$ and O_3 have been used as oxidising agents. But they generate carcinogenic by—products. Alternate reagents have been developed under "green" chemistry.

Answer the following questions.

1. $K_2Cr_2O_7/H_2SO_4$ etc generate carcinogenic by-products. These are
(a) Cr^{3+}
(b) Mn^{2+}
(c) H_2O
(d) CrO_3

2. Alternate reagent used for oxidation is
(a) Amberlyst A-26 resin-$HCrO_4^-$
(b) PCC
(c) Both (a) and (b)
(d) None of the above

***Passage* 3** Nylon-6,6 is prepared industrially from adipic acid and 1,6-diaminohexane. Adipic acid is synthesised starting from benzene. This synthesis has so many problems.

Answer the following questions.

1. In the following synthesis

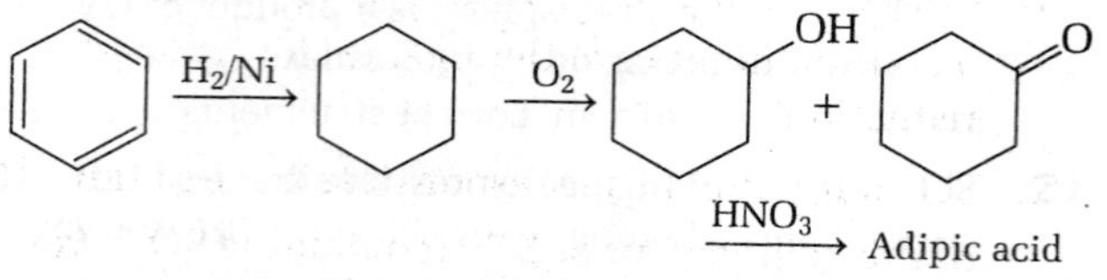

(a) benzene is a carcinogen and liver toxin
(b) N_2O (from HNO_3) depletes ozone layer
(c) N_2O also absorbs thermal energy from the earth's surface and thus causes global warming
(d) All of the above facts are true

2. Adipic acid can be synthesised using following steps of green chemistry from D-glucose (A).
(a) $A \xrightarrow{\text{biocatalyst}}$ 2,4-hexane dioicant $\xrightarrow{\Delta}$ adipic acid
(b) $A \xrightarrow{\text{biocatalyst}}$ 2,4-hexadienoic acid $\xrightarrow{H_2}$ adipic acid
(c) Both (a) and (b)
(d) None of the above

Matrix-Match Type

Given below are Matching Type Questions, with two columns (each having some items) each . Each item of Column I has to be matched with the items of Column II.

1. Match the species in Column I with their types in Column II.

Column I	Column II
A. DDT	1. Photochemical smog
B. $NaClO_3$	2. Disinfectant
C. Cl_2	3. Herbicides
D. PAN	4. Pesticides

2. Match the reactions in Column I with their order taking place in ozone depletion in Column II.

Column I	Column II
A. $ClO^{\bullet} + O \longrightarrow Cl^{\bullet} + O_2$	1. (1)
B. $Cl^{\bullet} + O_3 \longrightarrow ClO^{\bullet} + O_2$	2. (2)
C. $CF_2Cl_2 \longrightarrow Cl^{\bullet} + \dot{C}F_2Cl_2$	3. (3)
D. $O_2 \longrightarrow O^{\bullet} + O^{\bullet}$	4. (4)

3. Match the pollutants given in Column I with their effects give in Column II.

Column I	Column II
A. Phosphate fertilizers in water.	1. BOD level of H_2O increase
B. Methane in air.	2. Acid rain
C. Synthetic detergents in water.	3. Global warming
D. Nitrogen oxide in air.	4. Eutrophication

4. Match the term given in Column I with the compounds given in Column II.

Column I	Column II
A. Acid rain	1. $CHCl_2—CHF_2$
B. Photochemical smog	2. CO
C. Combination with haemoglobin	3. CO_2
D. Depletion of ozone layer	4. SO_2
	5. Unsaturated hydrocarbon

Single Integer Answer Questions

Answer of these questions is a single digit lying between 0 to 9.

1. $K_2Cr_2O_7$ used as oxidant causes pollution. What is oxidation number of the species formed by reduction?
2. SO_2 (air pollutant) is responsible for acid rain. 1000 L of this polluted air at STP (containing SO_2) was passed into H_2O and the resulting solution required 7.143×10^{-5} mol of $KMnO_4$ in acidic medium for complete reaction. What is concentration of SO_2 in ppm in air?
3. An approach to control industrial pollution is to recover waste products in usable form. Waste H_2S and SO_2 are recovered as elemental sulphur liquid. How much sulphur can be recovered if industrial waste contains 1.867 L SO_2 at STP in a given sample?
4. Iodine pentoxide is a very important reagent because it can oxidise carbon monoxide which is a major pollutant of the atmosphere to carbon dioxide in the absence of water. How many moles of carbon monoxide air oxidised per mole of I_2O_5?
5. Cl_2 and SO_2 are being used as bleaching agent in paper and textile industries. But they being pollutants are replaced by H_2O_2. How many moles of H_2O_2 are required in place of 64 g of Cl_2 ?
6. Ozone layer is being depleted by CFC. How many atoms are there in smallest of unit of CFC?
7. In the process of biological oxygen demand, oxygen used in ...... days.
8. How many, lone pairs (P) are present in ozone molecule and total resonance structure (Q). Calculate the sum of $P + Q$?
9. Temperature increases with height until the estimated to of the thermosphere at 5×10^x km. Find the value of x?
10. How many of gases are responsible for global warming?

$$CO_2, N_2O, CH_4, O_3, N_2, CFC, O_2, H_2$$

Answers

Objective Questions Type I [Only one correct option]

1. (a)	2. (d)	3. (c)	4. (d)	5. (b)	6. (a)	7. (d)	8. (d)	9. (a)	10. (b)
11. (c)	12. (d)	13. (a)	14. (d)	15. (c)	16. (d)	17. (d)	18. (a)	19. (d)	20. (d)
21. (c)	22. (d)	23. (c)	24. (a)	25. (b)	26. (b)	27. (d)	28. (a)	29. (b)	30. (c)
31. (c)									

Comprehension Based Questions

Passage 1 – **1.** (d) **2.** (a)

Passage 2 → **1.** (a) **2.** (a)

Passage 3 – **1.** (d) **2.** (b)

Matrix-Match Type

1. A → (4); B → (3); C → (2); D → (1)

2. A → (1); B → (4); C → (3); D → (2)

3. A → (1, 4); B → (3); C → (1); D → (2)

4. A → (3, 4); B → (4, 5); C → (2); D → (1)

Single Integer Answer Questions

1. (3)	2. (4)	3. (8)	4. (5)	5. (1)	6. (5)	7. (5)	8. (5)	9. (2)	10. (6)

Solutions

Objective Questions Type I [Only one correct option]

5. (*b*) In presence of ozone(O_3), oxidising smog gets increased during the day time because automobiles and factories produce main components of the photochemical smog (oxidising smog) results from the action of sunlight on unsaturated hydrocarbon and nitrogen oxide.

7. (*d*) The process in which nutrient enriched water bodies support a dense plant population which kills animal life by depriving it of oxygen and results in subsequent loss of biodiversity is known as eutrophication.

9. (*a*) Methane leads to both global warming and photochemical smog. Methane is generated in large amounts from paddy fields. CO_2 can be absorbed by photosynthesis, or by formation of acid rain etc., while no such activities are there for methane.

Hence, methane is stronger global warming gas than CH_4. Methane is not a part of reducing smog.

11. (*c*) In clean air, rain water picks up some acidic oxides like CO_2 and SO_2 (obtained from volcanic eruptions). These substance make the rain slightly acidic ($pH = 5.6 - 6$).

But, when rain falls through polluted air, it consumes oxides of sulphur (SO_x) and oxides of nitrogen (NO_x), mists of HCl etc. They make the rain more acidic (called acid rain) of pH range 3.5 to 5.6.

13. (*a*) Statement (a) is not true whereas all the given statements are true.

In the stratosphere, CFCs release chlorine free radicals ($Cl^\bullet$) which reacts with O_3 to give chlorine monoxide ($ClO^\bullet$) radicals but not chlorine dioxide radicals.

15. (*c*) The correct set of species responsible for the photochemical smog is NO, NO_2, O_3 and hydrocarbons. Photochemical smog appears in warm, dry and sunny climate which are obtained by the action of sunlight on unsaturated hydrocarbons and nitrogen oxides. Following reactions are involved during the formation of photochemical smog.

(i) $N_2(g) + O_2(g) \longrightarrow 2NO(g)$

(Originates from burning of fossil fuels)

(ii) $2NO(g) + O_2(g) \xrightarrow{\text{Sunlight}} 2NO_2(g)$

$NO_2(g) \xrightarrow{h\nu} NO(g) + \underset{\text{Nascent oxygen}}{[O]}$

(iii) $O(g) + O_2(g) \rightleftharpoons O_3(g)$

Reacts rapidly with NO

$O_3(g) + NO(g) \longrightarrow \underset{\text{Brown gas concentration}}{NO_2(g)} + \underset{\text{(in high form haze)}}{O_2(g)}$

$3CH_4(g) + 2O_3(g) \longrightarrow \underset{\substack{\text{Formaldehyde} \\ \text{(Unburnt hydrocarbon)}}}{3CH_2{=}O(g)}$

$+ \underset{\text{Acrolein}}{CH_2{=}CHCH{=}O} + H_2O$

18. (*a*) Thermal power plants emit oxides of nitrogen (NO_2) and sulphur (SO_2) in the atmosphere which are converted into HNO_3 and H_2SO_4 respectively in the pressure of rain water (H_2O).

$$4NO_2 + O_2 + 2H_2O \longrightarrow 4HNO_3$$

$$SO_2 + \frac{1}{2}O_2 + H_2O \longrightarrow H_2SO_4$$

Their presence in rain water becomes acidic (pH < 5.6) and it is called acid rain.

'Blue baby syndrome' is the condition due to poor oxygen transportation in the blood, resulting in blueness of the skin in babies.

Ozone layer depletion takes place due to the attack of chlorofluorocarbon (CFCs) to ozone molecules.

'Eutrophication' is associated with water pollution when huge quantities of phosphates and nitrates are released into aquatic ecosystem.

19. (*d*) BOD is defined as the amount of oxygen (ppm) required by bacteria to breakdown organic waste in certain volume of a water sample.

20. (*d*) According to W.H.O. and US environmental protection agency guidelines, maximum allowable concentration of metals in drinking water are as follows :

Metal	**Maximum concentration** (ppm or mg dm^{-3})
Cd	0.005
Mn	0.05 (option-c)
Al	0.2
Fe	0.2
Cu	3.0 (option-d)
Zn	5.0 (option-a)

24. (a) CH_4 is not present in the stratosphere and also it cannot diffuse or escape into the stratosphere like freon-12 (CF_2Cl_2) from the atmosphere. In the stratosphere, ozone layer depletion take place mainly by chlorofluorocarbons (CFCs) like CF_2Cl_2 and the mechanism of ozone layer depletion can be shown as:

(i) $CF_2Cl_2(g) \xrightarrow{h\nu} \dot{Cl}(g) + \dot{C}F_2Cl(g)$ [Option (d)]

(ii) $\dot{Cl}(g) + O_3(g) \longrightarrow ClO^{\bullet}(g) + O_2$

(iii) $ClO^{\bullet}(g) + O(g) \longrightarrow Cl^{\bullet}(g) + O_2(g)$ [Option (b)]

(iv) $\dot{Cl}(g) + \underset{\text{[Present in the stratosphere]}}{H_2O(g)} \longrightarrow HOCl(g) + H^{\bullet}(g)$

(v) $HOCl(g) \xrightarrow{h\nu} \dot{O}H(g) + Cl^{\bullet}(g)$ [Option (c)]

⇒ One $Cl^{\bullet}$ can destroy or deplete 10^5 O_3 molecules.

As (i) reaction is involved in the formation of photochemical smog, not in ozone layer depletion. So, option (a) is correct.

29. (*b*) Nuclear fusion is a reaction in which two or more atomic nuclei are combined to form one or more different atomic nuclei and subatomic particle.

31. (*c*) In air, nitrogen and oxygen occur naturally but they do not react to form oxides of nitrogen because the reaction is endothermic.

20

Practical Organic Chemistry

Objective Questions Type I [Only one correct option]

In each of the questions below, four choices are given of which only one is correct.

1. An organic compound gave positive iodoform and Tollen's tests. Functional group can be

(a) aldehyde (b) ketone
(c) enol (d) ester

2. Organic compound in (Q. 1) above is

(a) CH_3CH_2OH (b) CH_3CH_2CHO
(c) CH_3CHO (d) CH_3COCH_3

3. A compound liberates CO_2 with $NaHCO_3$ and also gives colour with neutral $FeCl_3$ solution. Compound can be

(a) 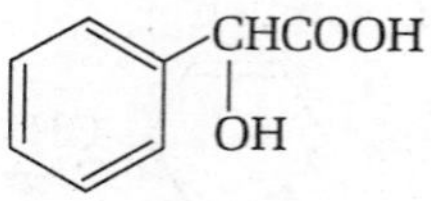

(b) 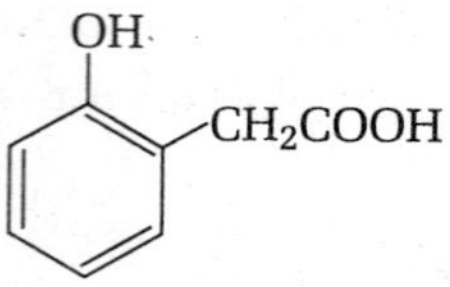

(c) 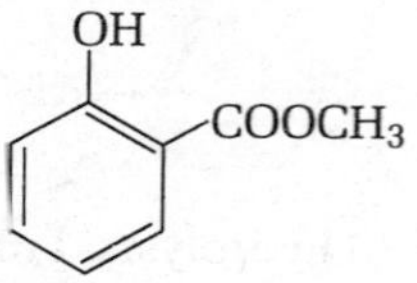

(d) 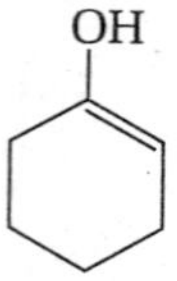

4. $RCOOH$ decomposes $NaHCO_3$ giving CO_2. Source of CO_2 is

(a) $RCOOH$ (b) $NaHCO_3$
(c) Both (a) and (b) (d) None of these

5. 3 moles of mixture of ethene and ethane are decolourised by 2 moles of Br_2. Percentage of ethene in the mixture is

(a) 50.00% (b) 66.66%
(c) 33.00% (d) 25.00%

6. A compound (X) on hydrolysis gave an acid and alcohol. Acid gave violet colour with neutral $FeCl_3$ while alcohol gave yellow precipitate on boiling with I_2 and NaOH. X can be

(a) 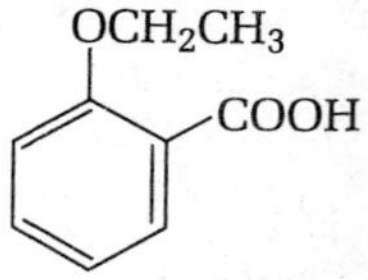

(b) 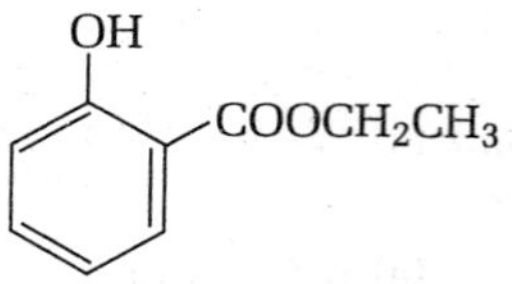

(c) 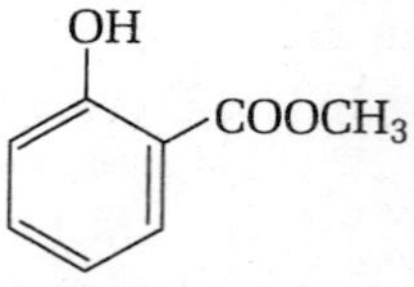

(d) 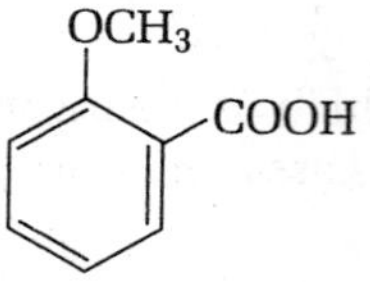

7. (X) and (Y) given below can be chemically distinguished using

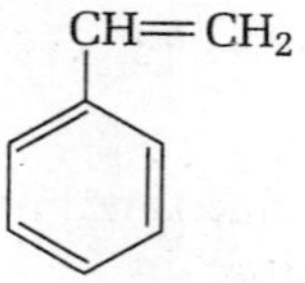

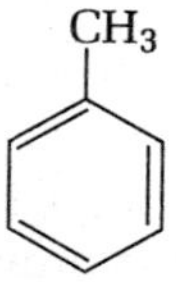

(a) Br_2 water (b) alkaline $KMnO_4$
(c) Both (a) and (b) (d) None of these

8. Consider following pairs of organic compounds

I. 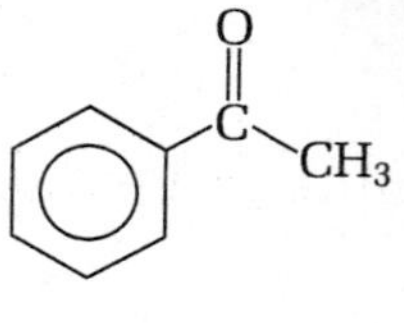

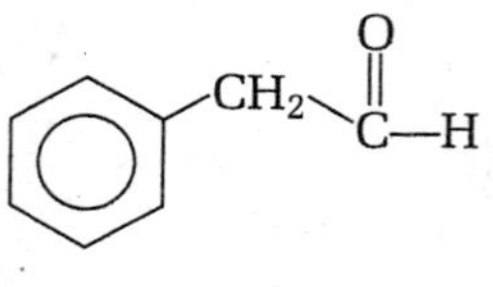

II. CH_3OH CH_3CH_2OH

III. $CH_3\overset{O}{\overset{\|}{C}}CH_3$ HCHO

A test that can make distinction between each pair is

(a) Lucas test (b) Silver-mirror test
(c) Victor Meyer's test (d) Iodoform test

9. Each pair has been matched with the suitable reagent used for making distinction. Which pair has been matched wrongly?

Pair	Reagent
(a) $CH_2{=}CH_2, CH_3{-}CH_3$	MnO_4^-/OH^-
(b) $CH_3CH_2C{\equiv}CH, CH_3C{\equiv}CCH_3$	Br_2 water
(c) $CH_3CH_2C{\equiv}CH, CH_3C{\equiv}CCH_3$	$AgNO_3/NH_4OH$
(d) 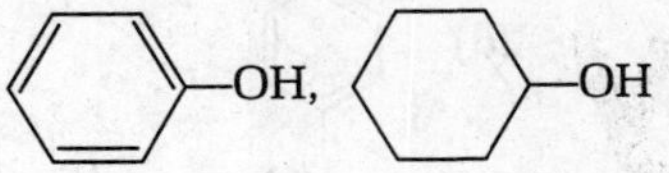	$FeCl_3$

10. Tollen's reagent can make distinction between
(a) glucose and fructose
(b) formaldehyde and formic acid
(c) glucose and benzaldehyde
(d) acetaldehyde and acetone

11. An organic compound X showing the following solubility profile is **[JEE Main 2019, April]**

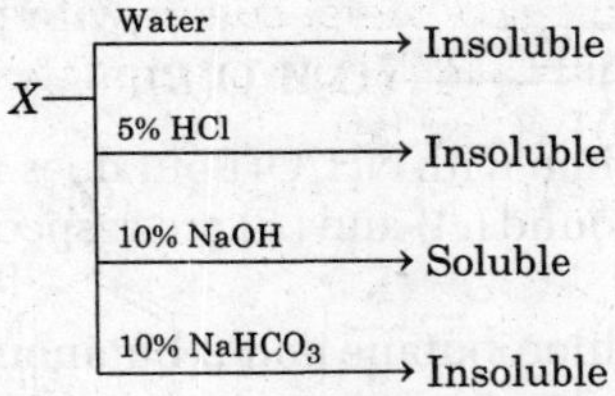

(a) *o*-toluidine (b) oleic acid
(c) *m*-cresol (d) benzamide

12. Which of the organic compounds will give red colour in Lassaigne test?

(a) NaCNS (b) $NH_2\overset{S}{\overset{\|}{C}}NH_2$

(c) $CH_2\overset{O}{\overset{\|}{C}}NH_2$ (d) 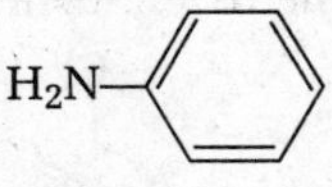

13. Detection of the chlorine is not possible without preparing sodium extract in

(a) 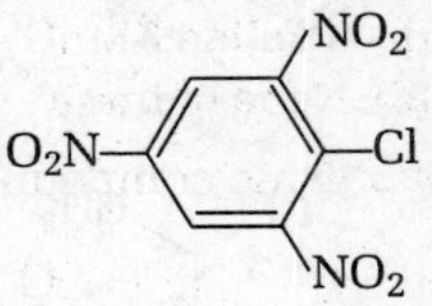 (b) $CHCl_3$

(c) 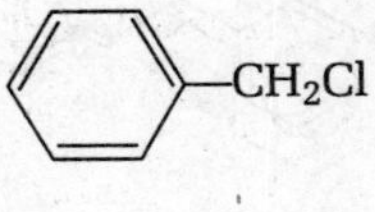 (d) $CH_2{=}CHCH_2Cl$

14. To sodium fusion extract Cl_2 water and CCl_4 were added and shaken well. There is violet colour in the lower part (organic layer) This indicates presence of
(a) bromine
(b) iodine and bromine
(c) chlorine
(d) iodine

15. Sulphur is converted into S^{2-} on fusion with sodium. Sulphide can be detected by
(a) lead acetate—when black precipitate is formed
(b) sodium nitroprusside when purple colour is formed
(c) Both (a) and (b)
(d) None of the above

16. The organic compound that gives following qualitative analysis is **[JEE Main 2019, April]**

Test	Inference
(i) Dil. HCl	Insoluble
(ii) NaOH solution	Soluble
(iii) Br_2/water	Decolourisation

(a) 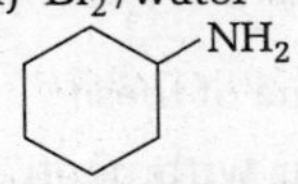 (b) 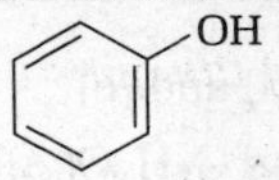

(c) 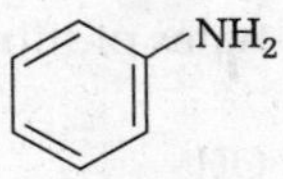 (d) 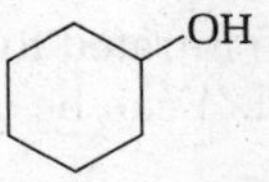

17. Which factor is most important in determining the chemistry of an organic molecule?
(a) The melting point
(b) The functional group
(c) The number of branches in the carbon chain
(d) The number of carbon-hydrogen bonds

18. Which of the following decolourises Br_2 water and also gives colour with $FeCl_3$ solution?

(a) $CH_3CH{=}CH_2$ (b) 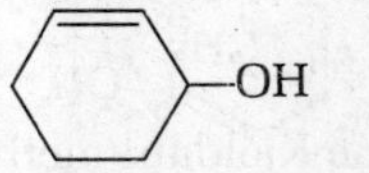

(c) 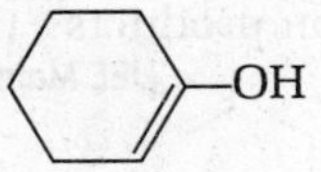 (d) 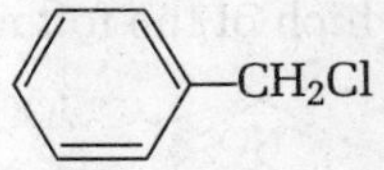

19. An ester group is subjected to hydrolysis. Products of hydrolysis will be tested for
(a) carboxylic and aldehydic groups
(b) carboxylic and ketonic groups
(c) aldehydic and ketonic groups
(d) carboxylic and alcoholic groups

20. Presence of unsaturation in organic compound is confirmed by
(a) bromine test (b) Baeyer's test
(c) Both (a) and (b) (d) None of these

21. Which of the following compounds can be confirmed by azo dye test?

(a) $CH_3CH{=}CH_2$

(b) 

(c) 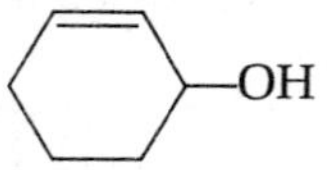

(d) 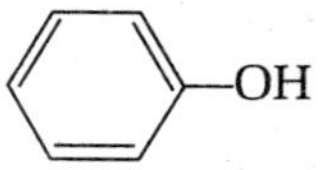

22. Test tube *A* contains CH_3COCH_3 and test tube *B* contains CH_3CHO. Only one test is allowed to make distinction between them. Best way is

(a) iodoform test (b) azo dye test

(c) CAN test (d) Tollen's test

23. Compound $C_7H_8O(A)$ gives colour with neutral $FeCl_3$. (*A*) can be

(a) 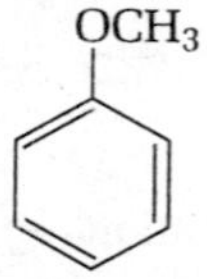

(b) 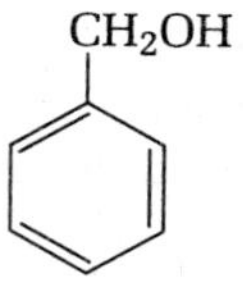

(c) Both (a) and (b) (d) None of these

24. Compound $C_7H_8O(A)$ gives colour with neutral $FeCl_3$ and can be nitrated to form three types of nitro compound. *A* can be

(a) 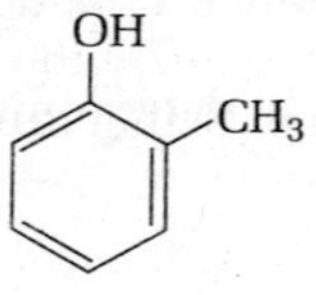

(b) 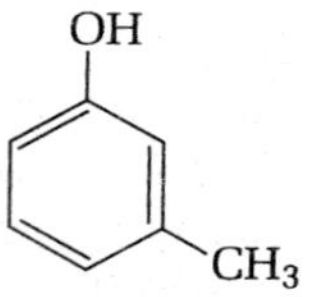

(c) 

(d) 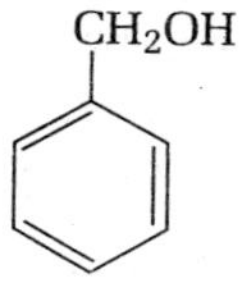

25. The Kjeldahl method of nitrogen estimation fails for which of the following reaction products? **[JEE Main 2020, Sep.]**

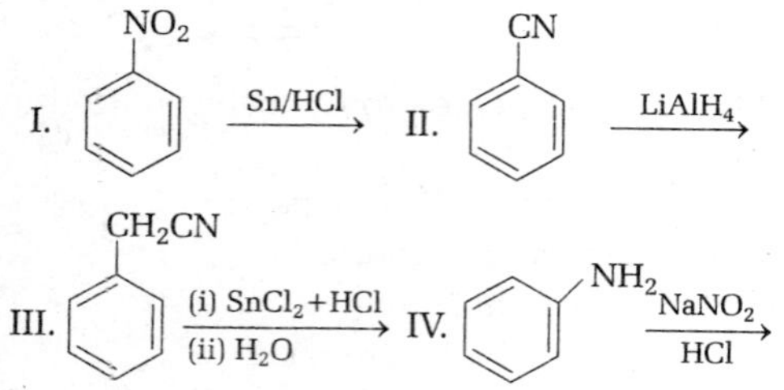

(a) III and IV (b) I and IV

(c) I, III and IV (d) II and III

26. 2-4 DNP test is given by **[JEE Main 2021, March]**

(a) aldehyde

(b) amine

(c) ester

(d) halogens

27. Nitrogen can be estimated by Kjeldhal's method for which of the following compound ? **[JEE Main 2021, March]**

(a) 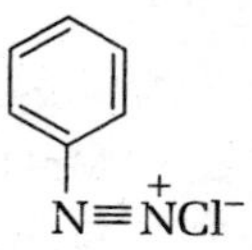

(b) 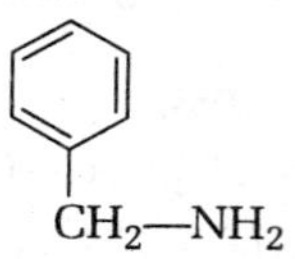

(c) 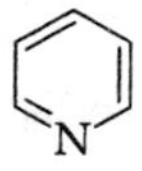

(d) 

28. An organic compound '*A*' on treatment with benzene sulphonyl chloride gives compound *B*. *B* is soluble in dil. NaOH solution. Compound *A* is **[JEE Main 2021, March]**

(a) $C_6H_5{-}N{-}(CH_3)_2$ (b) $C_6H_5{-}NHCH_2CH_3$

(c) $C_6H_5{-}CH_2NHCH_3$ (d) $C_6H_5{-}\underset{\displaystyle CH_3}{\underset{|}{C}H}{-}NH_2$

29. $C_4H_8Cl_2(A) \xrightarrow{\text{Hydrolysis}} C_4H_8O(B)$

B forms oxime with NH_2OH but does not give Tollen's test. Compound (*A*) and (*B*) are respectively **[JEE Main 2021, Feb.]**

(a) 2, 2-dichlorobutane and 2-butanone

(b) 2,2-dichlorobutane and 2-butanal

(c) 1,1-dichlorobutane and 2-butanal

(d) 1,2-dichlorobutane and 2-Butanone

30. Reaction of Grignard reagent, C_2H_5MgBr and C_8H_8O followed by hydrolysis gives compound '*A*' which reacts instantly with Lucas reagent to give compound *B*, $C_{10}H_{13}Cl$. The compound *B* is **[JEE Main 2021, March]**

(a) 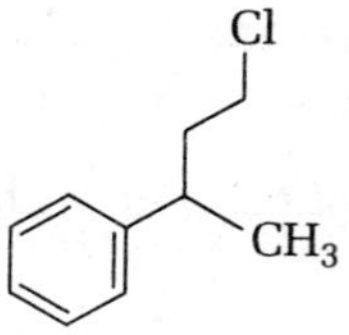

(b) 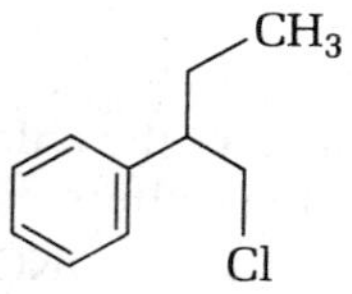

(c) 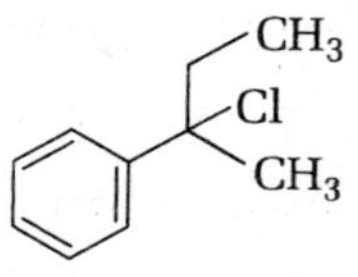

(d) 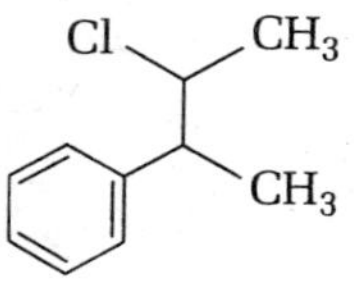

Objective Questions Type II [One or more than one correct option(s)]

In each of the questions below, four choices are given, of which one or more than one are correct.

1. $FeCl_3$ can be used as a reagent for testing

(a) 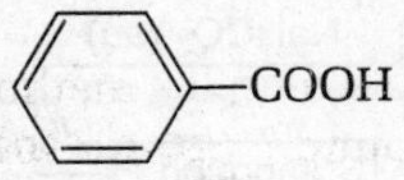

(b) CH_3COOH

(c) 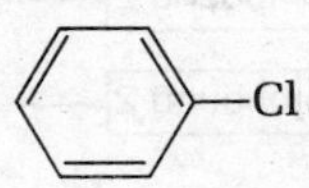

(d) $CH_3\underset{\displaystyle OH}{\underset{|}{C}}{=}CHCH_2CH_3$

2. Fehling solution can be used to make distinction between
(a) CH_3CHO and C_6H_5CHO
(b) CH_3COCH_3 and CH_3COCH_2OH
(c) HCOOH and HCHO
(d) HCOOH and CH_3COOH

3. Consider the following properties/tests,
I. Silver-mirror test
II. Liebermann's nitroso reaction
III. Fehling's test
IV. Baeyer's test
Sucrose does not give
(a) II, IV (b) I, III
(c) I, II, III (d) I to IV

4. Organic compound $A \xrightarrow{AgNO_3/HNO_3}$ white precipitate. Thus, A can be

(a) 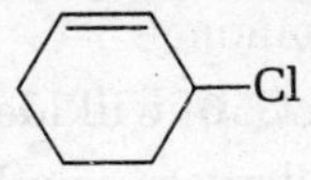

(b) $CH_2{=}CHCl$

(c) 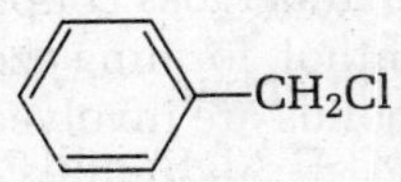

(d) 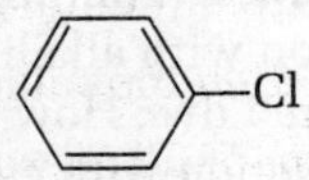

5. Sodium extract of thiourea will give .... colour in Lassaigne's test.
(a) blue (b) red (c) yellow (d) green

6. Sodium extract of urea gives blue/green colour due to the formation of Prussian blue which is
(a) $Fe^{III}[Fe^{II}(CN)_6]^-$ (b) $Fe^{II}[Fe^{III}(CN)_6]$
(c) $Fe^{III}[Fe^{III}(CN)_6]$ (d) $Fe^{II}[Fe^{II}(CN)_6]$

7. Reagent that can distinguish a set of benzaldehyde and formaldehyde is
(a) I_2/NaOH (b) Tollen's reagent
(c) Fehling's solution (d) Baeyer's reagent

8. Two test tubes contain succinic acid and acetic acid (but confirmed). Which will clearly distinguish the two?
(a) Neutral $FeCl_3$ (b) $NaHCO_3$
(c) Physical state (d) Smell

9. Glucose contains —CHO group and fructose contains $>C{=}O$ (keto group). Which can be used to distinguish the two?
(a) Fehling's solution
(b) Tollen's reagent
(c) Benedict's solution
(d) Optical rotation

10. The hydrolysis products of ethyl salicylate were separated into components. Which reagents can be used to distinguish them?
(a) Neutral $FeCl_3$
(b) Aqueous $NaHCO_3$
(c) I_2/NaOH, Δ
(d) Br_2 water

11. Carbylamine test can distinguish
(a) CH_3NH_2 and $C_6H_5NH_2$
(b) CH_3NH_2 and CH_3CONH_2
(c) CH_3NH_2 and $(CH_3)_2NH$
(d) NH_2CONH_2 and NH_2NH_2

12. A compound (X) of molecular formula C_3H_6O forms bisulphite complex, gives iodoform test but does not reduce Tollen's reagent. (X) on reaction with CH_3MgBr/H_3O^+ gives a compound (Y) that can
(a) give red colour with CAN
(b) give white turbidity immediately with Lucas reagent
(c) give iodoform test
(d) be dehydrated to alkene on reaction with heated Cu

13. Which of the following tests are correctly matched?

(a) Phenol	Phthalein test
(b) Benzyl amine	Azo dye test
(c) Phthalic acid	Fluorescence test
(d) CH_3CONH_2	Carbylamine test

14. C_7H_9N (amine) has five isomeric structures A, B, C, D and E (all aromatic class). How many isomers can give azo dye test?
(a) 2 (b) 3
(c) 4 (d) 5

15. Refer Q. 14 : Isomers giving azo-dye test $\xrightarrow{KMnO_4/OH^-} \xrightarrow[\Delta]{\text{Soda lime}} X$
X can
(a) give azo-dye test
(b) give carbylamine test
(c) be oxidised to benzoquinone on reaction with $K_2Cr_2O_7/H_2SO_4$
(d) be converted into benzyl alcohol or reaction with HNO_2

16. Positive Tollen's test is observed for [JEE Advance 2016]

(a) 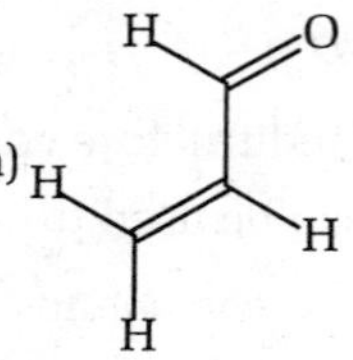

(b) 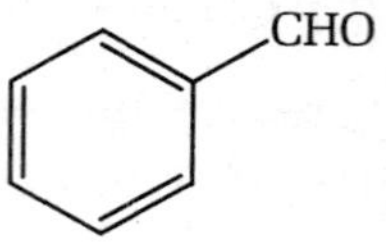

(c) 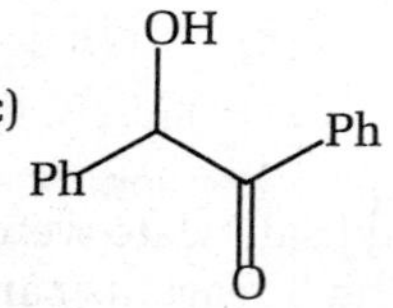

(d) 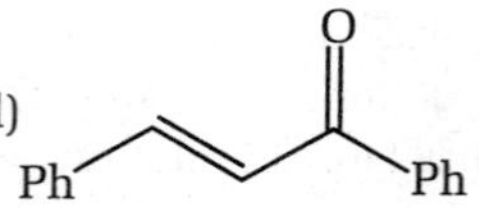

17. Identify the binary mixture(s) that can be separated into individual compounds, by differential extraction, as shown in the given scheme. [IIT JEE 2012]

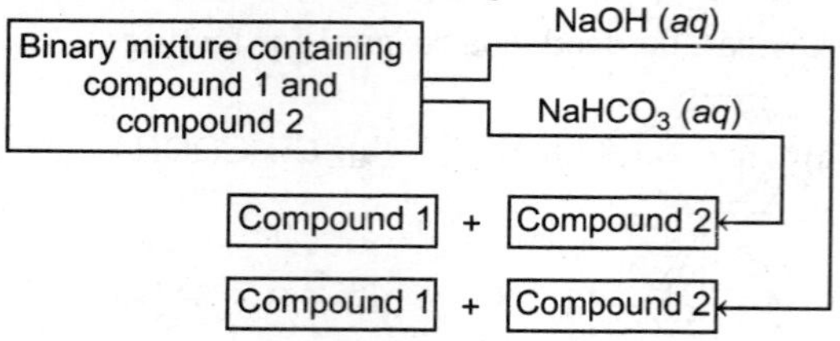

(a) C_6H_5OH and C_6H_5COOH
(b) C_6H_5COOH and $C_6H_5CH_2OH$
(c) $C_6H_5CH_2OH$ and C_6H_5OH
(d) $C_6H_5CH_2OH$ and $C_6H_5CH_2COOH$

Numerical Value Questions

All these questions have a Numerical value as their answer, solve the questions and write your answer.

1. How many of the isomeric carbonyl compounds $C_5H_{10}O$ will reduce Tollen's reagent?
2. How many of the isomeric $C_5H_{10}O$ will give iodoform test?
3. How many of the isomeric $C_5H_{10}O$ will form oximes?
4. How many of the following liberate CO_2 with $NaHCO_3$?

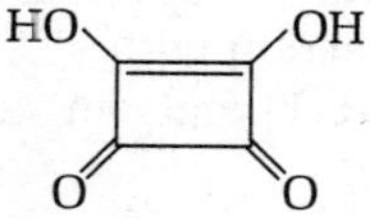

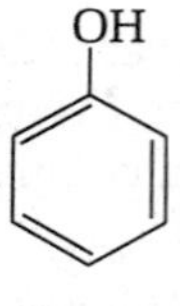

, 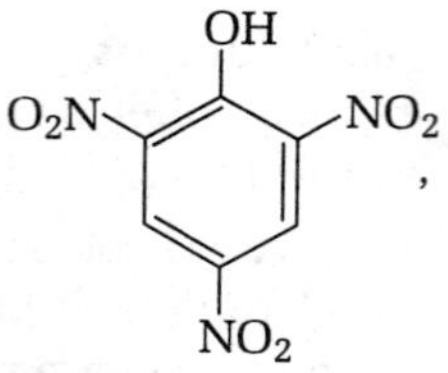

,

CH_3OH, CH_3CH_2OH,

5. How many of the following reagents can make distinction between phenol and ethanol?

$NaOH/I_2$, litmus, $FeCl_3$ CAN, 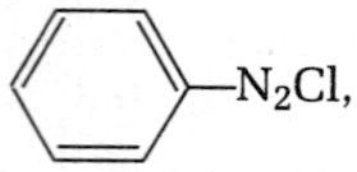

Na, Tollen's reagent, Fehling's solution?

6. In the following synthesis :

$$\underset{\underset{CH_3}{|}}{CH_3CH_2\,CH\,CH_2OH} \xrightarrow{\text{Conc. } H_2SO_4} \text{Major} \xrightarrow[H_2O_2,\,OH^-]{BH_3\cdot THF} A$$

How many of the following reagents will identify A? $NaOH/I_2$, Conc $HCl/ZnCl_2$, $K_2Cr_2O_7/H^+$, MnO_4^-/H^+, CAN, Cu, Fehling's solution, Tollen's reagent.

7. In the following synthesis,

$$\underset{\underset{CH_3}{|}}{CH_3CH_2\,CH\,CH_2OH} \xrightarrow{\text{Conc. } H_2SO_4} \text{Minor} \xrightarrow[H_2O_2,\,OH^-]{BH_3\cdot THF} B$$

How many of the reagents (as in Q. 6) will identify B?

8. Benzene diazonium chloride undergoes coupling reaction with alkaline β-naphthol, forming azo coloured dye. How many π bonds are involved in conjugation with each other?

Comprehension Based Questions

In these questions, a passage has been given followed by questions based on it. You have to answer the questions based on the passage given.

Passage 1 *Read the following experimental study and answer the questions at the end of it.*

A mixture of two aromatic compounds (A) and (B) was separated by dissolving in chloroform followed by extraction with aqueous KOH solution. The organic layer containing compound (A) when heated with alcoholic solution of KOH produced a compound (C), (C_7H_5N), associated with an unpleasant odour. The alkaline aqueous layer on the other hand, when heated with chloroform and then acidified gave a mixture of two isomeric compounds (D) and (E) of molecular formula $C_7H_6O_2$.

1. Compound (A) extracted into organic ($CHCl_3$) layer is

(a) 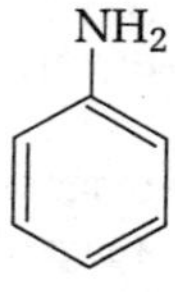

(b) 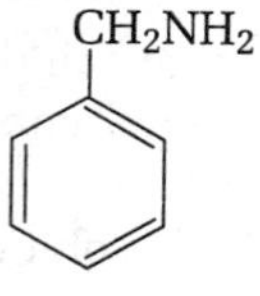

(c) 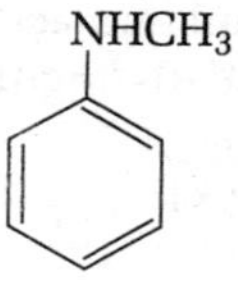

(d) 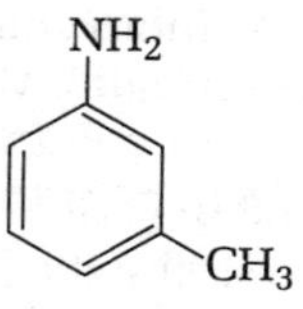

2. (*A*) has been tested above the unpleasant smell of the compound *C*. *C* is .... formed from *A* by .... reaction.

(a) 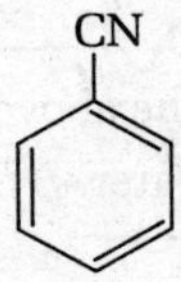 , Reimer-Tiemann

(b) 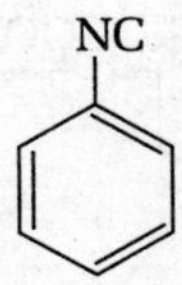 , Carbylamine

(c) 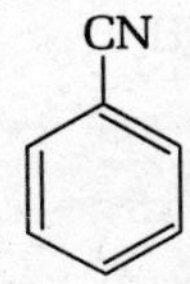 , Carbylamine

(d) 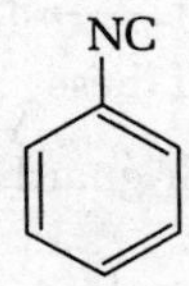 , Reimer-Tiemann

3. *D* and *E* are respectively

(a) 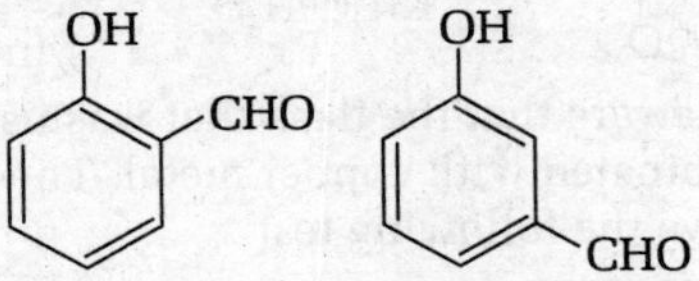

(b) 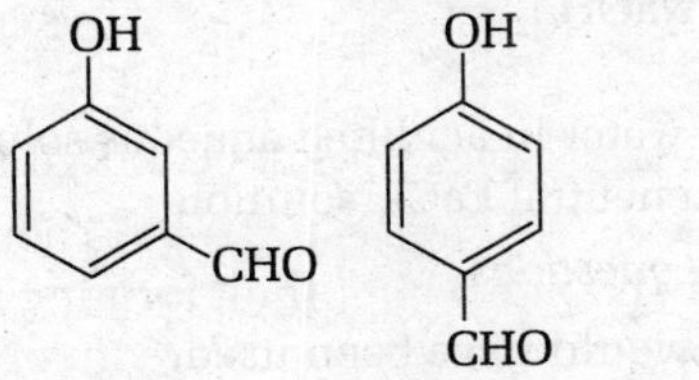

(c) 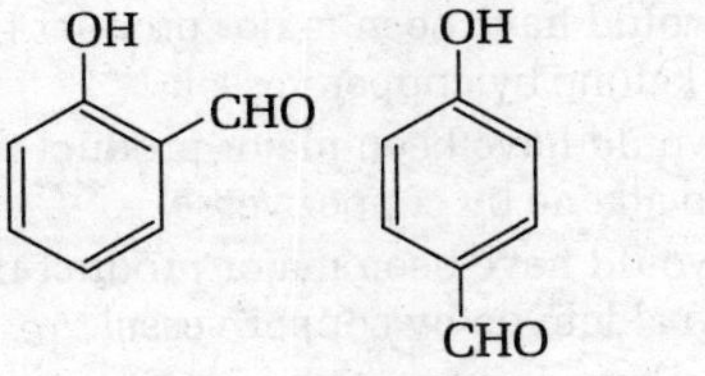

(d) 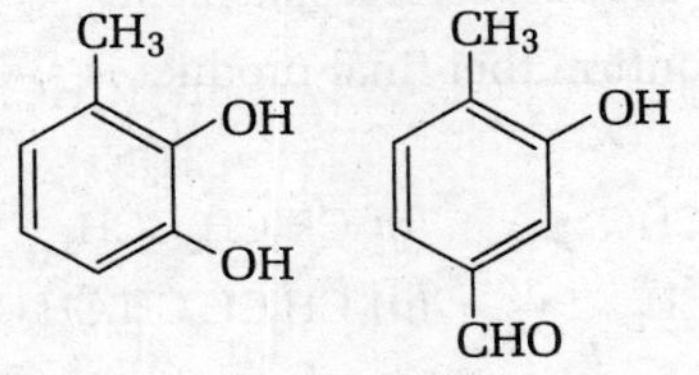

***Passage* 2** Mixture of organic compounds can be separated into individual components based on the solubility in different reagents. For Passage an acidic compound can be extracted into NaOH solution and a basic compound into HCl solution. Mixtures have been formed from the following compounds.

A. Naphthalene *B*. *p*-dichlorobenzene
C. Aniline *D*. Phenol
E. Benzoic acid *F*. CH_3OH
G. $CH_3CH_2CH_2NH_2$ *H*. $CH_3\underset{OH}{CH}CH_3$

Answer the questions based on the above compounds

1. HCl can be used to separate mixture of
(a) *A*, *B* (b) *C*, *D* (c) *C*, *G* (d) *G*, *H*

2. A mixture of two compounds (*X* and *Y*) in $CHCl_3$ was treated with NaOH and aqueous layer separated. $CHCl_3$ layer containing (*A*) on heating with KOH gives unpleasant smell of $Z(C_8H_7N)$. Compound in $CHCl_3$ layer is oxidised to the other components (*Y*) which on heating with sodalime forms hydrocarbon (*W*). Compound in NaOH layer on acidification followed by reaction with neutral $FeCl_3$ gives buff-coloured precipitate. *Y* is good food-preserver. Thus, compound (*X*) is

(a) 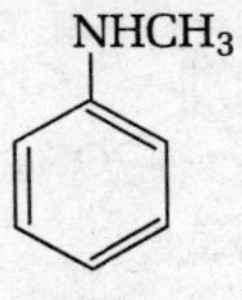 (b) 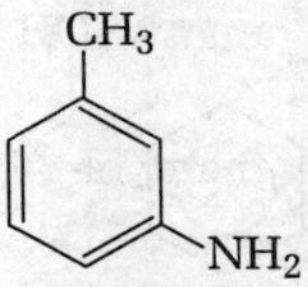

(c) 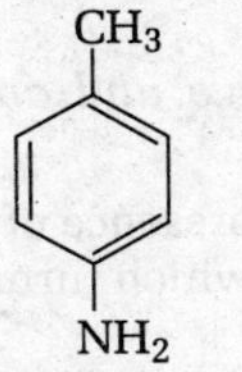 (d) 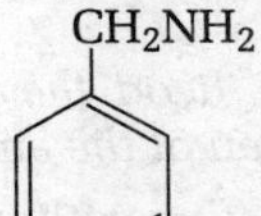

3. Distinction between F and H can be made by
(a) Iodoform test (b) Carbylamine test
(c) Phthalein test (d) Ceric ammonium nitrate

***Passage* 3** *Based on the following chemical reactions, answer the questions at the end.*

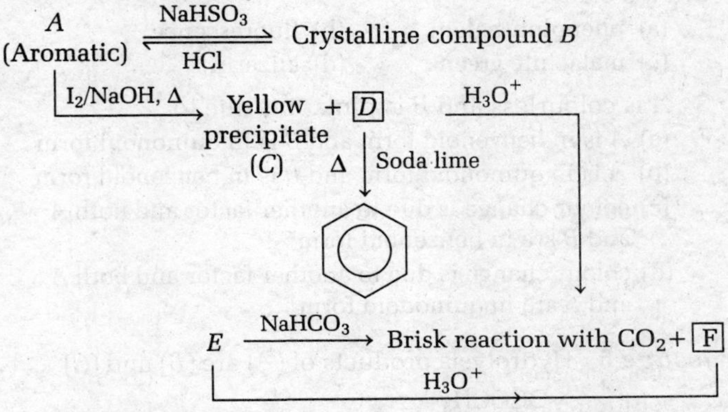

1. Suppose *A* and *E* are present in the mixture, then they can be separated using
(a) $NaHCO_3$ (b) $NaHSO_3$
(c) Both (a) and (b) (d) None of these

2. *E* can be confirmed by
(a) neutral $FeCl_3$ solution (b) $NaHCO_3$ solution
(c) Tollen's reagent (d) Benedict's solution

3. *A* and *E* are respectively

(a) 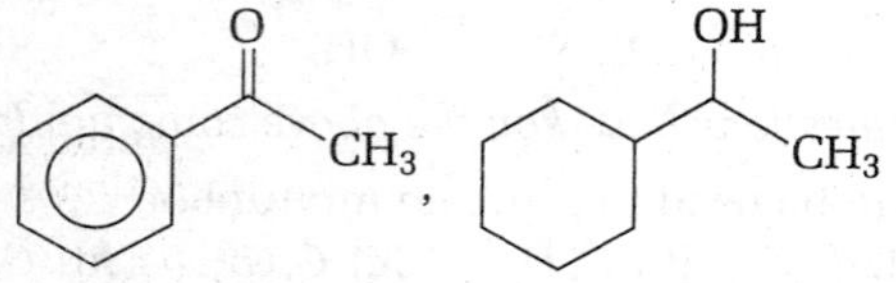

(b) 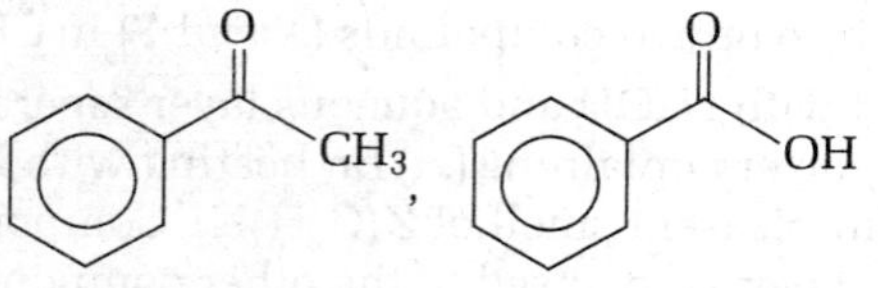

(c) 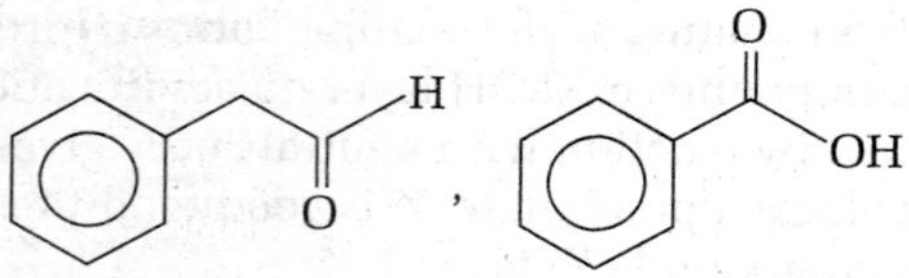

(d) 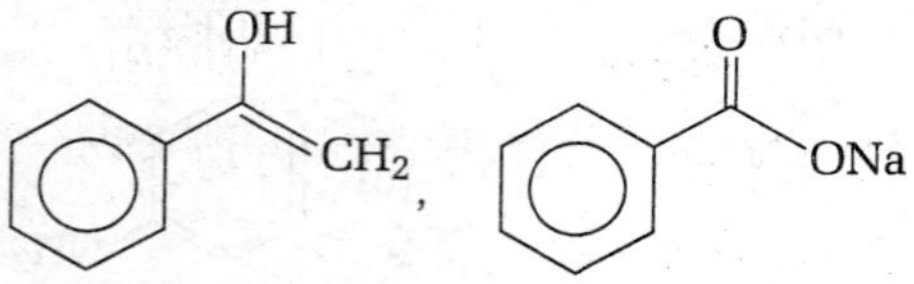

***Passage* 4** *Read the following passage and answer the questions given at the end :*

Phenol on heating with phthalic acid in presence of conc. H_2SO_4 forms a colourless compound (*A*) which turns to pink (*B*) on making it (*A*) alkaline.

1. This test is called
(a) fluorescence test
(b) phthalein test
(c) Liebermann's nitroso reaction
(d) azo-dye test

2. *A* is called
(a) phenolphthalein (b) fluorescence
(c) malachite green (d) alizarin

3. *A* is colourless and *B* is pink. It is due to
(a) *A* is in benzenoid form and *B* is in quinonoid form
(b) *A* is in quinonoid form and *B* is in benzenoid form
(c) colour change is due to another factor and both *A* and *B* are in benzenoid form
(d) colour change is due to another factor and both *A* and *B* are in quinonoid form

***Passage* 5** Hydrolysis products of (*A*) are (*B*) and (*C*)

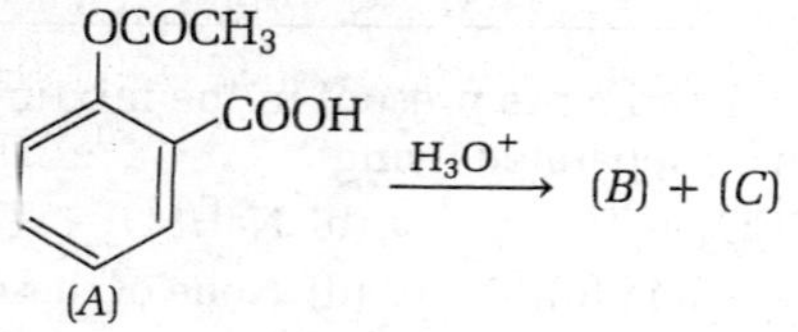

(*A*)

Answer the following questions.

1. Identify the common reagent that can identify distinguish by (*B*) and (*C*).
(a) Neutral $FeCl_3$ solution (b) $NaHCO_3$
(c) Litmus paper (d) All of the above

2. *B* gives yellow precipitate with Br_2 water. *B* can be

(a) CH_3COOH (b) 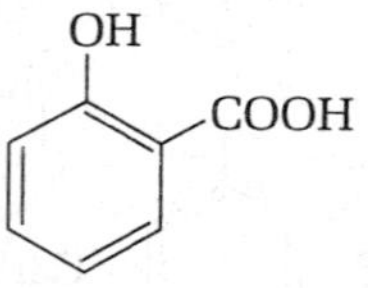

(c) 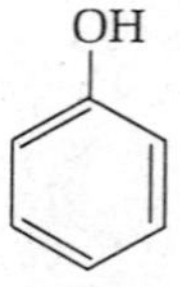 (d) HCOOH

3. How is (*A*) prepared?
(a) $(C) + PCl_5 \xrightarrow{B} (A)$ (b) $(B) + (C) \longrightarrow (A)$
(c) Both (a) and (b) (d) None of these

***Passage* 6** A graduate student ran the Grignard reagent shown in the following equation.

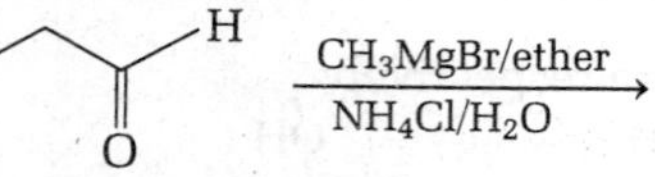

The student was unaware that the flask that was used for the reaction was contaminated with copper metal. The product was isolated and gave the following test

I. Yellow ppt with $NaOH/I_2$
II. forms oximes
III. decolourised Br_2 water in acidified aqueous solution
IV. gives colour with neutral $FeCl_3$ solution

Answer the following questions.

1. If glass vessel would have been used,
(a) 2° alcohol would have been major product that was oxidised to ketone by copper vessel.
(b) 3° alcohol would have been major product that was converted to alkene by copper vessel
(c) 1° alcohol would have been major product that was converted to aldehyde by copper vessel.
(d) None of the above is correct statement.

2. I and II tests confirm that final product is
(a) $CH_3CH_2CH_2CHO$ (b) $CH_3CH_2\overset{O}{\overset{\|}{C}}CH_3$
(c) $CH_3CH_2\underset{OH}{\underset{|}{C}}HCH_3$ (d) $CH_3CH_2CH_2CH_2OH$

3. III and IV test confirmed that under given condition product also changed to
(a) $CH_3CH_2\underset{OH}{\underset{|}{C}}{=}CH_2$ (b) $CH_3CH{=}\underset{OH}{\underset{|}{C}}CH_3$
(c) Both (a) and (b) (d) None of these

Matrix-Match Type

Given below are Matching Type Questions, with two columns (each having some items) each . Each item of Column I has to be matched with the items of Column II.

1. Match Column I (pair) with Column II (reagent) used for making distinction.

	Column I (Pair)		Column II (Reagent)
A.	$CH_3OH, (CH_3)_2CHOH$	1.	$NaOH/I_2$
B.	$CH_3CHO, HCHO$	2.	Br_2 water
C.	$CH_3C \equiv CH, CH_2=CH_2$	3.	$[Ag(NH_3)_2]^+$
D.	$CH_2=CH_2, CH_3-CH_3$	4.	Conc. $HCl/ZnCl_2$

2. Match Column I (compounds) with Column II (name).

	Column I		Column II
A.	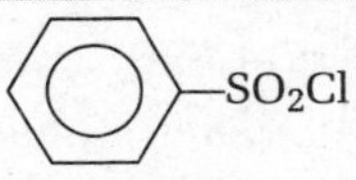	1.	Edman reagent
B.	MnO_4^-/OH^-	2.	Lucas' reagent
C.	$ZnCl_2/HCl$	3.	Hinsberg's reagent
D.	C_6H_5NCS	4.	Baeyer's reagent

3. Match the following.

	Column I (Compound)		Column II (Reagent for testing)
A.	HCHO	1.	Tollen's reagent
B.	CH_3CHO	2.	Fehling's solution
C.	CH_3COCH_3	3.	Iodoform test
D.	CH_3COCH_2OH	4.	Benedict's solution

4. Match the following.

	Column I (Compound)		Column II (Functional group)
A.	Resorcinol	1.	—OH (enol)
B.	Picric acid	2.	$-NO_2$
C.	Salol	3.	—COO*R*
D.	Ascorbic acid	4.	— OH (alcoholic)

5. Match the following.

	Column I (Functional group)		Column II (Reagent)
A.	—COOH	1.	$FeCl_3$
B.	$-CONH_2$	2.	NaOH
C.	$-NH_2$	3.	HNO_2
D.	—OH (enolic)	4.	$NaHCO_3$

6. The correct match between Column I and Column II is

	Column I (Drug)		Column II (Test)
A.	Chloroxylenol	1.	Carbylamine test
B.	Norethindrone	2.	Sodium hydrogen carbonate test
C.	Sulphapyridine	3.	Ferric chloride test
D.	Penicillin	4.	Bayer's test

[JEE Main 2019, Jan.]

Single Integer Answer Questions

Answer of these questions is a single digit lying between 0 to 9.

1. Alkaline $KMnO_4$ can oxidise benzyl alcohol to benzoic acid. The final state of oxidation number of reduced species is ....

2. Acidified $K_2Cr_2O_7$ oxidises alcohol to acid and a green-coloured salt is formed. Oxidation number of ion giving green colour is ....

3. In the detection of nitrogen in organic compound, a Prussian blue-coloured complex is formed. The sum of oxidation number of iron in this complex is ....

4. Tollen's reagent is reduced to silver-mirror by aldehydes. Oxidation state of silver is ....

5. Fehling's solution is reduced to red precipitate by aldehydes. Oxidation state of the reduced species is ....

6. Phenol form violet-coloured complex with $FeCl_3$. Coordination number of iron in the complex is ....

7. Benedict's solution contains citrate complexed to copper ion having coordination number ....

8. Resorcinol on heating with an organic acid in presence of conc. H_2SO_4 and on making the solution alkaline gives green fluorescence. This is a test of organic acids with basicity ....

9. In Tollen's test for aldehyde, the overall number of electron(s) transferred to the Tollen's reagent formula $[Ag(NH_3)_2]$ per aldehyde group to form silver mirror is ....

[JEE Main 2021, March]

Answers

Objective Questions Type I [Only one correct option]

1. (a)	2. (c)	3. (b)	4. (a)	5. (b)	6. (b)	7. (c)	8. (d)	9. (b)	10. (d)
11. (c)	12. (b)	13. (b)	14. (d)	15. (c)	16. (b)	17. (b)	18. (c)	19. (b)	20. (c)
21. (d)	22. (d)	23. (a)	24. (b)	25. (a)	26. (a)	27. (b)	28. (d)	29. (a)	30. (c)

Objective Questions Type II [One or more than one correct option(s)]

1. (a, b, c, d)	2. (a, b, d)	3. (a)	4. (a, c)	5. (b)
6. (a)	7. (c)	8. (a, c, d)	9. (a)	10. (a, b, c, d)
11. (b, c)	12. (b, d)	13. (a, c)	14. (b)	15. (a, b, c)
16. (a, b)	17. (d)			

Numerical Value Questions

1. (4)	2. (2)	3. (7)	4. (3)	5. (5)	6. (6)	7. (7)	8. (8)

Comprehension Type

Passage 1 – 1. (a) 2. (b) 3. (c)

Passage 2 – 1. (b) 2. (d) 3. (d)

Passage 3 – 1. (c) 2. (a) 3. (b)

Passage 4 – 1. (b) 2. (a) 3. (a)

Passage 5 – 1. (a) 2. (b) 3. (a)

Passage 6 – 1. (a) 2. (b) 3. (c)

Matrix-Match Type

1. A→(4); B→(1); C→(3); D→(2)
2. A→(3); B→(4); C→(2); D→(1)
3. A→(1,2,4); B→(2,3,4); C→(3); D→(1,2,3,4)
4. A→(1); B→(1,2); C→(1,3); D→(1,4)
5. A→(3); B→(4); C→(1); D→(1); E→(1)
6. A→(3); B→(4); C→(1); D→(2)

Single Integer Answer Questions

1. (4)	2. (3)	3. (5)	4. (0)	5. (1)	6. (6)	7. (4)	8. (2)	9. (2)

21. (*d*)

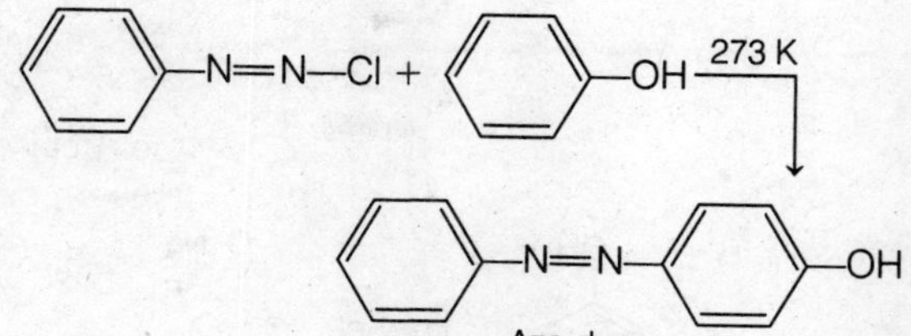

22. (*d*)

	CH_3COCH_3	CH_3CHO
(a)	✔	✔
(b)	✗	✗
(c)	✗	✗
(d)	✗	✔

24. (*b*) Given colour with $FeCl_3$ phenolic group.

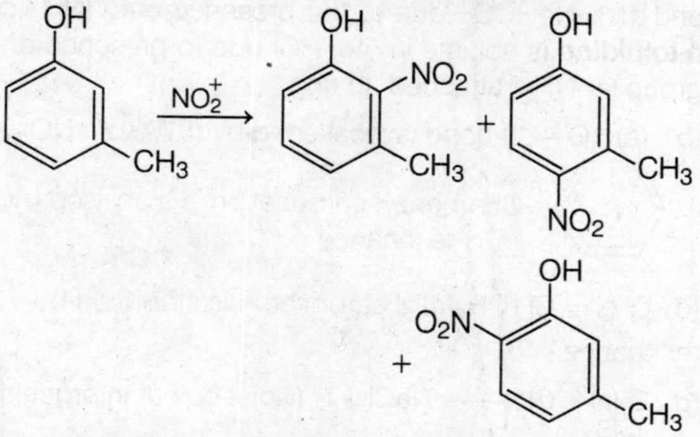

25. (*a*) Complete reactions I, II, III, IV are as follows :

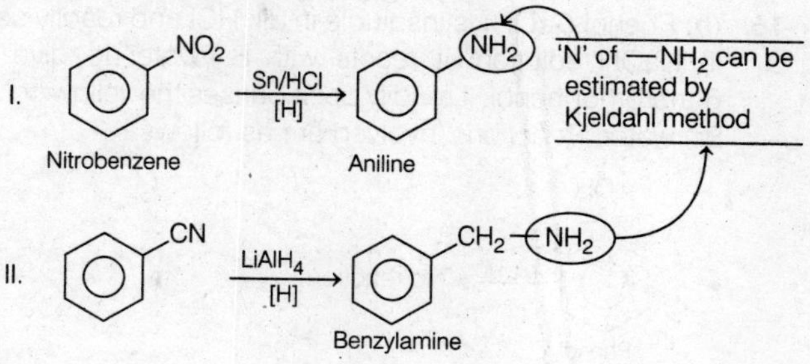

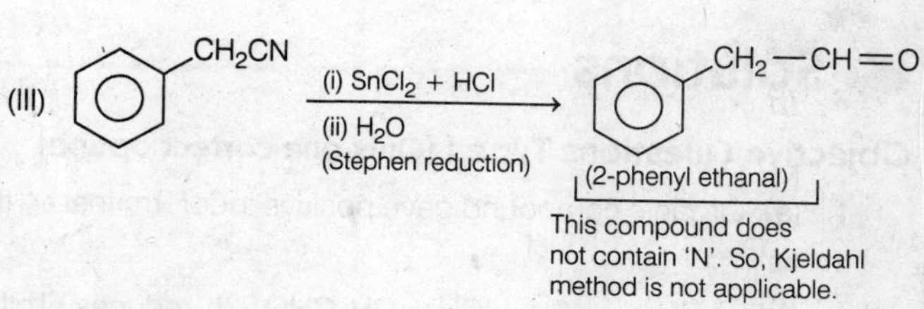

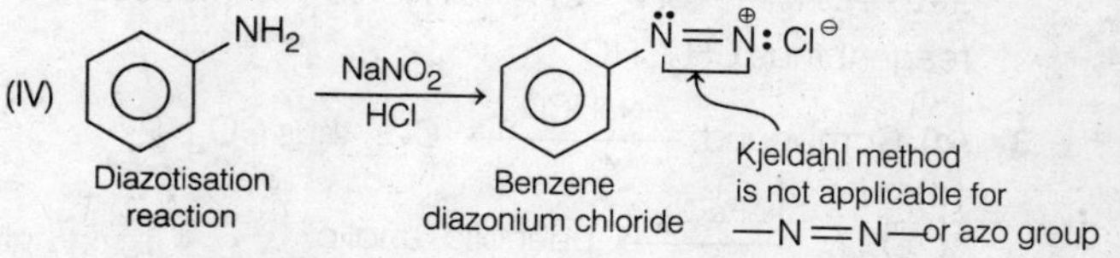

So, products of reactions (c) and (d) (option-a) fail to give Kjeldahl's method. So, option (a) is correct.

26. (*a*)

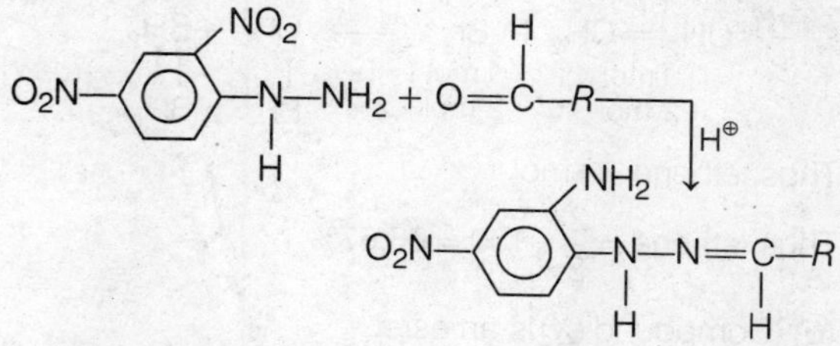

Both alkehyde and ketones gives the 2, 4 DNP test.

27. (*b*) Kjeldahl method is not applicable to compounds containing nitrogen in nitro group, azo groups and nitrogen present in the ring (e.g. pyridine) as nitrogen of these compounds does not change to ammonium sulphate under these conditions.

28. (*d*) Hinsberg reagent (benzene sulphonyl chloride) gives reaction product with 1° amine and it is soluble in dil. NaOH.

29. (*a*)

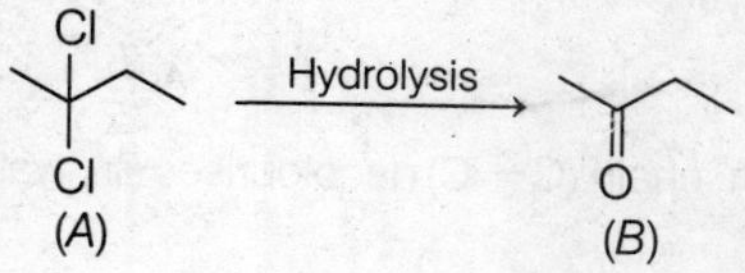

Solutions

Objective Questions Type I [Only one correct option]

1. (*a*) Organic compound gave positive iodoform test — thus, $-\overset{O}{\overset{||}{C}}-CH_3$, $-\overset{OH}{\overset{|}{C}H}-CH_3$, CH_3CHO. It reduces Tollen's reagent thus CH_3CHO

3. (*b*) Compound $\xrightarrow{NaHCO_3}$ CO_2 thus CO_2
   $\xrightarrow{FeCl_3}$ phenolic, enolic

4. (*b*) $\overset{*}{R}COOH + NaHCO_3 \longrightarrow \overset{*}{R}CO\overset{-}{O}\overset{+}{Na} + CO_2$

5. (*b*) Br_2 water is decolourised by ethene only

$$\underset{\substack{1\,mol\\2\,mol}}{CH_2{=}CH_2} + \underset{\substack{1\,mol\\2\,mol}}{Br_2} \longrightarrow \underset{Br}{\underset{|}{CH_2}}-\underset{Br}{\underset{|}{CH_2}}$$

Thus, ethene = 1 mol

Thus, ethene $= \frac{2}{3} \times 100 = 66.67\%$

6. (*b*) Compound (*X*) is an ester.

$$(X) \xrightarrow{H_3O^+} \text{alcohol} + \text{acid}$$

Alcohol gives iodoform test (yellow ppt. with $I_2/NaOH$)
Acid, gives violet colour with $FeCl_3$.
Thus, it is phenolic acid.

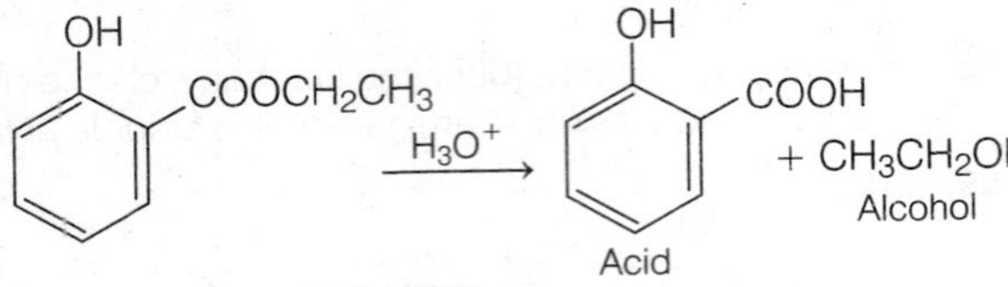

7. (*c*) Open chain (C=C) decolourises Br_2 water and alkaline $KMnO_4$.

	I	II	III
8. (*d*) **Lucas test**	No	No	No
Silver mirror test	Yes	No	Yes
Victor Meyer's Test	No	No	Yes
Iodoform test	Yes	Yes	Yes

11. (*c*) *m*-cresol is the organic compound that shows the following solubility profile.

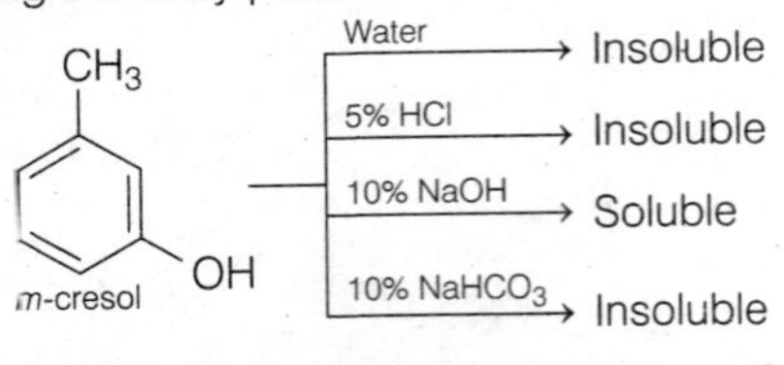

m-cresol on reaction with 10% NaOH forms 3-methyl sodiumphenoxide ion.

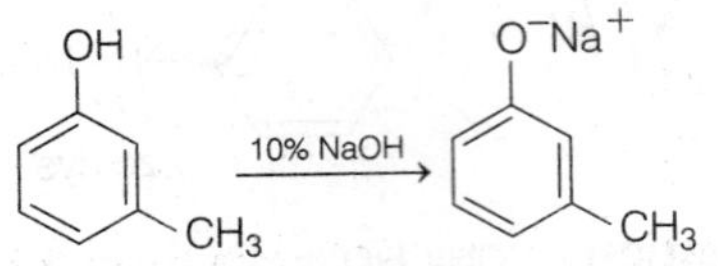

It does not react with H_2O, 5% HCl and 10% $NaHCO_3$.

Oleic acid ($C_{18}H_{34}O_2$) is soluble in 10% NaOH and 10% $NaHCO_3$ due to the presence of COOH group.

Benzamide ($C_6H_5\overset{O}{\overset{||}{C}}NH_2$) is insoluble in 5% HCl, 10% NaOH and 10% $NaHCO_3$ due to the presence $-CONH_2$ group. ***o*-toluidine** is soluble in 5%. HCl due to presence of basic group ($-NH_2$) attached to ring.

13. (*b*) (a) (C—Cl) bond is weakened by (EWG) $-NO_2$

(c) 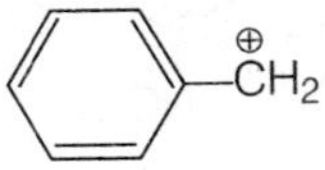 benzyl carbocation is stabilised by resonance

(d) $CH_2{=}CH\overset{\oplus}{C}H_2$ allyl carbocaton is stabilised by resonance.

14. (*d*) $\underset{(SE)}{2NaI + Cl_2} \longrightarrow NaCl + I_2$ (violet colour in organic layer)

16. (*b*) Phenol (ArOH) is insoluble in dil. HCl and readily soluble in NaOH solution. It reacts with Br_2/water to give 2, 4, 6-tribromophenol. It readily decolourises the yellow colour of Br_2 water. Reactions involved are as follows :

- 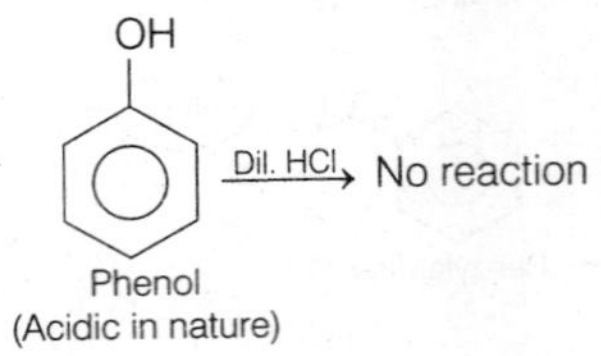

- 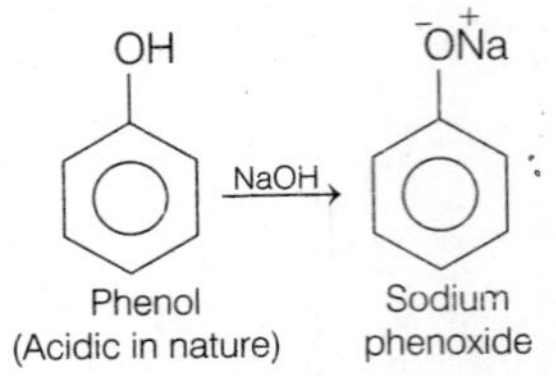

- 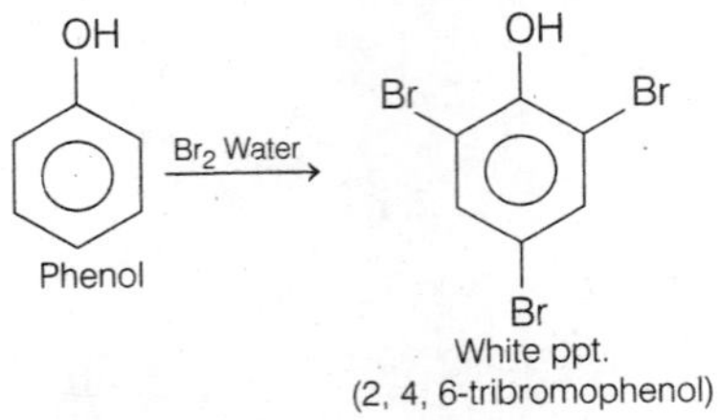